American Casebook Series
Hornbook Series and Basic Legal Texts
Nutshell Series

of

WEST PUBLISHING COMPANY

P.O. Box 43526
St. Paul, Minnesota 55164
January, 1984

ACCOUNTING

Faris' Law and Accounting in a Nutshell, approximately 392 pages, 1984 (Text)

Fiflis, Kripke and Foster's Teaching Materials on Accounting for Business Lawyers, 3rd Ed., approximately 784 pages, 1984 (Casebook)

Siegel and Siegel's Accounting and Financial Disclosure: A Guide to Basic Concepts, 259 pages, 1983 (Text)

ADMINISTRATIVE LAW

Davis' Cases, Text and Problems on Administrative Law, 6th Ed., 683 pages, 1977 (Casebook)

Davis' Basic Text on Administrative Law, 3rd Ed., 617 pages, 1972 (Text)

Davis' Police Discretion, 176 pages, 1975 (Text)

Gellhorn and Boyer's Administrative Law and Process in a Nutshell, 2nd Ed., 445 pages, 1981 (Text)

Mashaw and Merrill's Introduction to the American Public Law System, 1095 pages, 1975, with 1980 Supplement (Casebook)

Robinson, Gellhorn and Bruff's The Administrative Process, 2nd Ed., 959 pages, 1980, with 1983 Supplement (Casebook)

ADMIRALTY

Healy and Sharpe's Cases and Materials on Admiralty, 875 pages, 1974 (Casebook)

Maraist's Admiralty in a Nutshell, 400 pages, 1983 (Text)

Sohn and Gustafson's Law of the Sea in a Nutshell, approximately 250 pages, 1984 (Text)

AGENCY PARTNERSHIP

Fessler's Alternatives to Incorporation for Persons in Quest of Profit, 258 pages, 1980 (Casebook)

Henn's Cases and Materials on Agency, Partnership and Other Unincorporated Business Enterprises, 396 pages, 1972 (Casebook)

Reuschlein and Gregory's Hornbook on the Law of Agency and Partnership, 625 pages, 1979, with 1981 pocket part (Text)

Seavey's Hornbook on Agency, 329 pages, 1964 (Text)

Seavey and Hall's Cases on Agency, 431 pages, 1956 (Casebook)

Seavey, Reuschlein and Hall's Cases on Agency and Partnership, 599 pages, 1962 (Casebook)

Selected Corporation and Partnership Statutes and Forms, 556 pages, 1982

Steffen and Kerr's Cases and Materials on Agency-Partnership, 4th Ed., 859 pages, 1980 (Casebook)

Steffen's Agency-Partnership in a Nutshell, 364 pages, 1977 (Text)

AMERICAN INDIAN LAW

Canby's American Indian Law in a Nutshell, 288 pages, 1981 (Text)

Getches, Rosenfelt and Wilkinson's Cases on Federal Indian Law, 660 pages, 1979, with 1983 Supplement (Casebook)

ANTITRUST LAW

Gellhorn's Antitrust Law and Economics in a Nutshell, 2nd Ed., 425 pages, 1981 (Text)

Gifford and Raskind's Cases and Materials on Antitrust, 694 pages, 1983 (Casebook)

I

LAW SCHOOL PUBLICATIONS—Continued

ANTITRUST LAW—Continued

Oppenheim, Weston and McCarthy's Cases and Comments on Federal Antitrust Laws, 4th Ed., 1168 pages, 1981 (Casebook)

Posner and Easterbrook's Cases and Economic Notes on Antitrust, 2nd Ed., 1077 pages, 1981, with 1982–83 Supplement (Casebook)

Sullivan's Hornbook of the Law of Antitrust, 886 pages, 1977 (Text)

See also Regulated Industries, Trade Regulation

ART LAW

DuBoff's Art Law in a Nutshell, approximately 290 pages, 1984 (Text)

BANKING LAW

Lovett's Banking and Financial Institutions in a Nutshell, 409 pages, 1984 (Text)

White's Teaching Materials on Banking Law, 1058 pages, 1976, with Case and Statutory Supplement (Casebook)

BUSINESS PLANNING

Epstein and Scheinfeld's Teaching Materials on Business Reorganization Under the Bankruptcy Code, 216 pages, 1980 (Casebook)

Painter's Problems and Materials in Business Planning, 2nd Ed., approximately 1035 pages, 1984 (Casebook)

Selected Securities and Business Planning Statutes, Rules and Forms, 485 pages, 1982

CIVIL PROCEDURE

Casad's Res Judicata in a Nutshell, 310 pages, 1976 (text)

Cound, Friedenthal and Miller's Cases and Materials on Civil Procedure, 3rd Ed., 1147 pages, 1980 with 1984 Supplement (Casebook)

Ehrenzweig, Louisell and Hazard's Jurisdiction in a Nutshell, 4th Ed., 232 pages, 1980 (Text)

Federal Rules of Civil-Appellate-Criminal Procedure—West Law School Edition, 343 pages, 1983

Hodges, Jones and Elliott's Cases and Materials on Texas Trial and Appellate Procedure, 2nd Ed., 745 pages, 1974 (Casebook)

Hodges, Jones and Elliott's Cases and Materials on the Judicial Process Prior to Trial in Texas, 2nd Ed., 871 pages, 1977 (Casebook)

Kane's Civil Procedure in a Nutshell, 271 pages, 1979 (Text)

Karlen's Procedure Before Trial in a Nutshell, 258 pages, 1972 (Text)

Karlen, Meisenholder, Stevens and Vestal's Cases on Civil Procedure, 923 pages, 1975 (Casebook)

CIVIL PROCEDURE—Continued

Koffler and Reppy's Hornbook on Common Law Pleading, 663 pages, 1969 (Text)

McBaine's Cases on Introduction to Civil Procedure, 399 pages, 1950 (Casebook)

Park's Computer-Aided Exercises on Civil Procedure, 2nd Ed., 167 pages, 1983 (Coursebook)

Shipman's Hornbook on Common-Law Pleading, 3rd Ed., 644 pages, 1923 (Text)

Siegel's Hornbook on New York Practice, 1011 pages, 1978 with 1981–82 Pocket Part (Text)

See also Federal Jurisdiction and Procedure

CIVIL RIGHTS

Abernathy's Cases and Materials on Civil Rights, 660 pages, 1980 (Casebook)

Cohen's Cases on the Law of Deprivation of Liberty: A Study in Social Control, 755 pages, 1980 (Casebook)

Lockhart, Kamisar and Choper's Cases on Constitutional Rights and Liberties, 5th Ed., 1298 pages plus Appendix, 1981, with 1983 Supplement (Casebook)—reprint from Lockhart, et al. Cases on Constitutional Law, 5th Ed., 1980

Vieira's Civil Rights in a Nutshell, 279 pages, 1978 (Text)

COMMERCIAL LAW

Bailey's Secured Transactions in a Nutshell, 2nd Ed., 391 pages, 1981 (Text)

Epstein and Martin's Basic Uniform Commercial Code Teaching Materials, 2nd Ed., 667 pages, 1983 (Casebook)

Henson's Hornbook on Secured Transactions Under the U.C.C., 2nd Ed., 504 pages, 1979 with 1979 P.P. (Text)

Murray's Commercial Law, Problems and Materials, 366 pages, 1975 (Coursebook)

Nordstrom and Clovis' Problems and Materials on Commercial Paper, 458 pages, 1972 (Casebook)

Nordstrom and Lattin's Problems and Materials on Sales and Secured Transactions, 809 pages, 1968 (Casebook)

Nordstrom, Murray and Clovis' Problems and Materials on Sales, 515 pages, 1982 (Casebook)

Nordstrom's Hornbook on Sales, 600 pages, 1970 (Text)

Selected Commercial Statutes, 1379 pages, 1983

Speidel, Summers and White's Teaching Materials on Commercial and Consumer Law, 3rd Ed., 1490 pages, 1981 (Casebook)

Stockton's Sales in a Nutshell, 2nd Ed., 370 pages, 1981 (Text)

Stone's Uniform Commercial Code in a Nutshell, 507 pages, 1975 (Text)

Uniform Commercial Code, Official Text with Comments, 994 pages, 1978

LAW SCHOOL PUBLICATIONS—Continued

COMMERCIAL LAW—Continued

UCC Article 8, 1977 Amendments, 249 pages, 1978

UCC Article 9, Reprint from 1962 Code, 128 pages, 1976

UCC Article 9, 1972 Amendments, 304 pages, 1978

Weber and Speidel's Commercial Paper in a Nutshell, 3rd Ed., 404 pages, 1982 (Text)

White and Summers' Hornbook on the Uniform Commercial Code, 2nd Ed., 1250 pages, 1980 (Text)

COMMUNITY PROPERTY

Mennell's Community Property in a Nutshell, 447 pages, 1982 (Text)

Verrall and Bird's Cases and Materials on California Community Property, 4th Ed., 549 pages, 1983 (Casebook)

COMPARATIVE LAW

Barton, Gibbs, Li and Merryman's Law in Radically Different Cultures, 960 pages, 1983 (Casebook)

Glendon, Gordon, and Osakwe's Comparative Legal Traditions in a Nutshell, 402 pages, 1982 (Text)

Langbein's Comparative Criminal Procedure: Germany, 172 pages, 1977 (Casebook)

COMPUTERS AND LAW

Mason's An Introduction to the Use of Computers in Law, approximately 200 pages, 1984 (Text)

CONFLICT OF LAWS

Cramton, Currie and Kay's Cases-Comments-Questions on Conflict of Laws, 3rd Ed., 1026 pages, 1981 (Casebook)

Scoles and Hay's Hornbook on Conflict of Laws, Student Ed., 1085 pages, 1982 (Text)

Scoles and Weintraub's Cases and Materials on Conflict of Laws, 2nd Ed., 966 pages, 1972, with 1978 Supplement (Casebook)

Siegel's Conflicts in a Nutshell, 469 pages, 1982 (Text)

CONSTITUTIONAL LAW

Engdahl's Constitutional Power in a Nutshell: Federal and State, 411 pages, 1974 (Text)

Lockhart, Kamisar and Choper's Cases-Comments-Questions on Constitutional Law, 5th Ed., 1705 pages plus Appendix, 1980, with 1983 Supplement (Casebook)

Lockhart, Kamisar and Choper's Cases-Comments-Questions on the American Constitution, 5th Ed., 1185 pages plus Appendix, 1981, with 1983 Supplement (Casebook)—reprint from Lockhart, et al. Cases on Constitutional Law, 5th Ed., 1980

CONSTITUTIONAL LAW—Continued

Manning's The Law of Church-State Relations in a Nutshell, 305 pages, 1981 (Text)

Miller's Presidential Power in a Nutshell, 328 pages, 1977 (Text)

Nowak, Rotunda and Young's Hornbook on Constitutional Law, 2nd Ed., Student Ed., 1172 pages, 1983 (Text)

Rotunda's Modern Constitutional Law: Cases and Notes, 1034 pages, 1981, with 1983 Supplement (Casebook)

Williams' Constitutional Analysis in a Nutshell, 388 pages, 1979 (Text)

See also Civil Rights

CONSUMER LAW

Epstein and Nickles' Consumer Law in a Nutshell, 2nd Ed., 418 pages, 1981 (Text)

McCall's Consumer Protection, Cases, Notes and Materials, 594 pages, 1977, with 1977 Statutory Supplement (Casebook)

Selected Commercial Statutes, 1379 pages, 1983

Spanogle and Rohner's Cases and Materials on Consumer Law, 693 pages, 1979, with 1982 Supplement (Casebook)

See also Commercial Law

CONTRACTS

Calamari & Perillo's Cases and Problems on Contracts, 1061 pages, 1978 (Casebook)

Calamari and Perillo's Hornbook on Contracts, 2nd Ed., 878 pages, 1977 (Text)

Corbin's Text on Contracts, One Volume Student Edition, 1224 pages, 1952 (Text)

Fessler and Loiseaux's Cases and Materials on Contracts, 837 pages, 1982 (Casebook)

Freedman's Cases and Materials on Contracts, 658 pages, 1973 (Casebook)

Friedman's Contract Remedies in a Nutshell, 323 pages, 1981 (Text)

Fuller and Eisenberg's Cases on Basic Contract Law, 4th Ed., 1203 pages, 1981 (Casebook)

Hamilton, Rau and Weintraub's Cases and Materials on Contracts, approximately 950 pages, 1984 (Casebook)

Jackson and Bollinger's Cases on Contract Law in Modern Society, 2nd Ed., 1329 pages, 1980 (Casebook)

Keyes' Government Contracts in a Nutshell, 423 pages, 1979 (Text)

Reitz's Cases on Contracts as Basic Commercial Law, 763 pages, 1975 (Casebook)

Schaber and Rohwer's Contracts in a Nutshell, 2nd Ed., approximately 409 pages, 1984 (Text)

Simpson's Hornbook on Contracts, 2nd Ed., 510 pages, 1965 (Text)

COPYRIGHT

See Patent and Copyright Law

CORPORATIONS

Hamilton's Cases on Corporations—Including Partnerships and Limited Partnerships, 2nd Ed., 1108 pages, 1981, with 1981 Statutory Supplement and 1984 Supplement (Casebook)

Hamilton's Law of Corporations in a Nutshell, 379 pages, 1980 (Text)

Henn's Cases on Corporations, 1279 pages, 1974, with 1980 Supplement (Casebook)

Henn and Alexander's Hornbook on Corporations, 3rd Ed., Student Ed., 1371 pages, 1983 (Text)

Jennings and Buxbaum's Cases and Materials on Corporations, 5th Ed., 1180 pages, 1979 (Casebook)

Selected Corporation and Partnership Statutes, Regulations and Forms, 556 pages, 1982

Solomon, Stevenson and Schwartz' Materials and Problems on the Law and Policies on Corporations, 1172 pages, 1982 with 1983 Supplement (Casebook)

CORPORATE FINANCE

Hamilton's Cases and Materials on Corporate Finance, approximately 882 pages, 1984 (Casebook)

CORRECTIONS

Krantz's Cases and Materials on the Law of Corrections and Prisoners' Rights, 2nd Ed., 735 pages, 1981, with 1982 Supplement (Casebook)

Krantz's Law of Corrections and Prisoners' Rights in a Nutshell, 2nd Ed., 384 pages, 1983 (Text)

Popper's Post-Conviction Remedies in a Nutshell, 360 pages, 1978 (Text)

Robbins' Cases and Materials on Post Conviction Remedies, 506 pages, 1982 (Casebook)

Rubin's Law of Criminal Corrections, 2nd Ed., 873 pages, 1973, with 1978 Supplement (Text)

CREDITOR'S RIGHTS

Bankruptcy Code and Rules, Law School Ed., 438 pages, 1984

Epstein's Debtor-Creditor Law in a Nutshell, 2nd Ed., 324 pages, 1980 (Text)

Epstein and Landers' Debtors and Creditors: Cases and Materials, 2nd Ed., 689 pages, 1982 (Casebook)

Epstein and Sheinfeld's Teaching Materials on Business Reorganization Under the Bankruptcy Code, 216 pages, 1980 (Casebook)

Riesenfeld's Cases and Materials on Creditors' Remedies and Debtors' Protection, 3rd Ed., 810 pages, 1979 with 1979 Statutory Supplement and 1981 Case Supplement (Casebook)

CRIMINAL LAW AND CRIMINAL PROCEDURE

Cohen and Gobert's Problems in Criminal Law, 297 pages, 1976 (Problem book)

Davis' Police Discretion, 176 pages, 1975 (Text)

Dix and Sharlot's Cases and Materials on Criminal Law, 2nd Ed., 771 pages, 1979 (Casebook)

Federal Rules of Civil-Appellate-Criminal Procedure—West Law School Edition, 343 pages, 1983

Grano's Problems in Criminal Procedure, 2nd Ed., 176 pages, 1981 (Problem book)

Israel and LaFave's Criminal Procedure in a Nutshell, 3rd Ed., 438 pages, 1980 (Text)

Johnson's Cases, Materials and Text on Substantive Criminal Law in its Procedural Context, 2nd Ed., 956 pages, 1980 (Casebook)

Kamisar, LaFave and Israel's Cases, Comments and Questions on Modern Criminal Procedure, 5th ed., 1635 pages plus Appendix, 1980 with 1983 Supplement (Casebook)

Kamisar, LaFave and Israel's Cases, Comments and Questions on Basic Criminal Procedure, 5th Ed., 869 pages, 1980 with 1983 Supplement (Casebook)—reprint from Kamisar, et al. Modern Criminal Procedure, 5th ed., 1980

LaFave's Modern Criminal Law: Cases, Comments and Questions, 789 pages, 1978 (Casebook)

LaFave and Scott's Hornbook on Criminal Law, 763 pages, 1972 (Text)

Langbein's Comparative Criminal Procedure: Germany, 172 pages, 1977 (Casebook)

Loewy's Criminal Law in a Nutshell, 302 pages, 1975 (Text)

Saltzburg's American Criminal Procedure, Cases and Commentary, 2nd Ed., 1193 pages, 1984 (Casebook)

Uviller's The Processes of Criminal Justice: Investigation and Adjudication, 2nd Ed., 1384 pages, 1979 with 1979 Statutory Supplement and 1983 Update (Casebook)

Uviller's The Processes of Criminal Justice: Adjudication, 2nd Ed., 730 pages, 1979. Soft-cover reprint from Uviller's The Processes of Criminal Justice: Investigation and Adjudication, 2nd Ed. (Casebook)

Uviller's The Processes of Criminal Justice: Investigation, 2nd Ed., 655 pages, 1979. Soft-cover reprint from Uviller's The Processes of Criminal Justice: Investigation and Adjudication, 2nd Ed. (Casebook)

Vorenberg's Cases on Criminal Law and Procedure, 2nd Ed., 1088 pages, 1981 (Casebook)

LAW SCHOOL PUBLICATIONS—Continued

**CRIMINAL LAW AND CRIMINAL PRO-
CEDURE**—Continued

See also Corrections, Juvenile Justice

DECEDENTS ESTATES

See Trusts and Estates

DOMESTIC RELATIONS

Clark's Cases and Problems on Domestic
Relations, 3rd Ed., 1153 pages, 1980
(Casebook)

Clark's Hornbook on Domestic Relations,
754 pages, 1968 (Text)

Krause's Cases and Materials on Family
Law, 2nd Ed., 1221 pages, 1983 (Casebook)

Krause's Family Law in a Nutshell, 400
pages, 1977 (Text)

Krauskopf's Cases on Property Division at
Marriage Dissolution, 250 pages, 1984
(Casebook)

EDUCATION LAW

Alexander and Alexander's The Law of
Schools, Students and Teachers in a Nut-
shell, approximately 395 pages, 1984
(Text)

Morris' The Constitution and American Education, 2nd Ed., 992 pages, 1980 (Casebook)

EMPLOYMENT DISCRIMINATION

Player's Cases and Materials on Employment
Discrimination Law, 2nd Ed., approximately 675 pages, 1984 (Casebook)

Player's Federal Law of Employment Discrimination in a Nutshell, 2nd Ed., 402
pages, 1981 (Text)

See also Women and the Law

**ENERGY AND NATURAL RESOURCES
LAW**

Rodgers' Cases and Materials on Energy
and Natural Resources Law, 2nd Ed., 877
pages, 1983 (Casebook)

Selected Environmental Law Statutes, 768
pages, 1983

Tomain's Energy Law in a Nutshell, 338
pages, 1981 (Text)

See also Environmental Law, Oil and Gas,
Water Law

ENVIRONMENTAL LAW

Bonine and McGarity's Cases and Materials
on the Law of Environment and Pollution,
approximately 892 pages, 1984 (Casebook)

Findley and Farber's Cases and Materials on
Environmental Law, 738 pages, 1981,
with 1983 Supplement (Casebook)

Findley and Farber's Environmental Law in
a Nutshell, 343 pages, 1983 (Text)

ENVIROMENTAL LAW—Continued

Hanks, Tarlock and Hanks' Cases on Environmental Law and Policy, 1242 pages,
1974, with 1976 Supplement (Casebook)

Rodgers' Hornbook on Environmental Law,
956 pages, 1977 (Text)

Selected Environmental Law Statutes, 768
pages, 1983

See also Energy and Natural Resources Law,
Water Law

EQUITY

See Remedies

ESTATES

See Trusts and Estates

ESTATE PLANNING

Kurtz' Cases, Materials and Problems on
Family Estate Planning, 853 pages, 1983
(Casebook)

Lynn's Introduction to Estate Planning, in a
Nutshell, 3rd Ed., 370 pages, 1983 (Text)

See also Taxation

EVIDENCE

Broun and Meisenholder's Problems in Evidence, 2nd Ed., 304 pages, 1981 (Problem book)

Cleary and Strong's Cases, Materials and
Problems on Evidence, 3rd Ed., 1143
pages, 1981 (Casebook)

Federal Rules of Evidence for United States
Courts and Magistrates, 327 pages, 1983

Graham's Federal Rules of Evidence in a
Nutshell, 429 pages, 1981 (Text)

Kimball's Programmed Materials on Problems in Evidence, 380 pages, 1978 (Problem book)

Lempert and Saltzburg's A Modern Approach to Evidence: Text, Problems, Transcripts and Cases, 2nd Ed., 1296 pages,
1983 (Casebook)

Lilly's Introduction to the Law of Evidence,
486 pages, 1978 (Text)

McCormick, Elliott and Sutton's Cases and
Materials on Evidence, 5th Ed., 1212
pages, 1981 (Casebook)

McCormick's Hornbook on Evidence, 3rd
Ed., Student Ed., approximately 1006
pages, 1984 (Text)

Rothstein's Evidence, State and Federal
Rules in a Nutshell, 2nd Ed., 514 pages,
1981 (Text)

Saltzburg's Evidence Supplement: Rules,
Statutes, Commentary, 245 pages, 1980
(Casebook Supplement)

**FEDERAL JURISDICTION AND PROCE-
DURE**

Currie's Cases and Materials on Federal
Courts, 3rd Ed., 1042 pages, 1982 (Casebook)

LAW SCHOOL PUBLICATIONS—Continued

FEDERAL JURISDICTION AND PROCE-DURE—Continued

Currie's Federal Jurisdiction in a Nutshell, 2nd Ed., 258 pages, 1981 (Text)

Federal Rules of Civil-Appellate-Criminal Procedure—West Law School Edition, 343 pages, 1983

Forrester and Moye's Cases and Materials on Federal Jurisdiction and Procedure, 3rd Ed., 917 pages, 1977 with 1981 Supplement (Casebook)

Redish's Cases, Comments and Questions on Federal Courts, 878 pages, 1983 (Casebook)

Vetri and Merrill's Federal Courts, Problems and Materials, 2nd Ed., approximately 250 pages, 1984

Wright's Hornbook on Federal Courts, 4th Ed., Student Ed., 870 pages, 1983 (Text)

FUTURE INTERESTS

See Trusts and Estates

HOUSING AND URBAN DEVELOPMENT

Berger's Cases and Materials on Housing, 2nd Ed., 254 pages, 1973 (Casebook)—reprint from Cooper et al. Cases on Law and Poverty, 2nd Ed., 1973

See also Land Use

IMMIGRATION LAW

Weissbrodt's Immigration Law and Procedure in a Nutshell, approximately 337 pages, 1984 (Text)

INDIAN LAW

See American Indian Law

INSURANCE

Dobbyn's Insurance Law in a Nutshell, 281 pages, 1981 (Text)

Keeton's Cases on Basic Insurance Law, 2nd Ed., 1086 pages, 1977

Keeton's Basic Text on Insurance Law, 712 pages, 1971 (Text)

Keeton's Case Supplement to Keeton's Basic Text on Insurance Law, 334 pages, 1978 (Casebook)

Keeton's Programmed Problems in Insurance Law, 243 pages, 1972 (Text Supplement)

York and Whelan's Cases, Materials and Problems on Insurance Law, 715 pages, 1982 (Casebook)

INTERNATIONAL LAW

Henkin, Pugh, Schachter and Smit's Cases and Materials on International Law, 2nd Ed., 1152 pages, 1980, with Documents Supplement (Casebook)

INTERNATIONAL LAW—Continued

Jackson's Legal Problems of International Economic Relations, 1097 pages, 1977, with Documents Supplement (Casebook)

Kirgis' International Organizations in Their Legal Setting, 1016 pages, 1977, with 1981 Supplement (Casebook)

Weston, Falk and D'Amato's International Law and World Order—A Problem Oriented Coursebook, 1195 pages, 1980, with Documents Supplement (Casebook)

Wilson's International Business Transactions in a Nutshell, 2nd Ed., 476 pages, 1984 (Text)

INTERVIEWING AND COUNSELING

Binder and Price's Interviewing and Counseling, 232 pages, 1977 (Text)

Shaffer's Interviewing and Counseling in a Nutshell, 353 pages, 1976 (Text)

INTRODUCTION TO LAW

Dobbyn's So You Want to go to Law School, Revised First Edition, 206 pages, 1976 (Text)

Hegland's Introduction to the Study and Practice of Law in a Nutshell, 418 pages, 1983 (Text)

Kelso and Kelso's Studying Law: An Introduction, approximately 585 pages, 1984 (Coursebook)

Kinyon's Introduction to Law Study and Law Examinations in a Nutshell, 389 pages, 1971 (Text)

See also Legal Method and Legal System

JUDICIAL ADMINISTRATION

Carrington, Meador and Rosenberg's Justice on Appeal, 263 pages, 1976 (Casebook)

Nelson's Cases and Materials on Judicial Administration and the Administration of Justice, 1032 pages, 1974 (Casebook)

JURISPRUDENCE

Christie's Text and Readings on Jurisprudence—The Philosophy of Law, 1056 pages, 1973 (Casebook)

JUVENILE JUSTICE

Fox's Cases and Materials on Modern Juvenile Justice, 2nd Ed., 960 pages, 1981 (Casebook)

Fox's Juvenile Courts in a Nutshell, 3rd Ed., approximately 290 pages, 1984 (Text)

LABOR LAW

Gorman's Basic Text on Labor Law—Unionization and Collective Bargaining, 914 pages, 1976 (Text)

Leslie's Labor Law in a Nutshell, 403 pages, 1979 (Text)

Nolan's Labor Arbitration Law and Practice in a Nutshell, 358 pages, 1979 (Text)

LAW SCHOOL PUBLICATIONS—Continued

LABOR LAW—Continued

Oberer, Hanslowe and Andersen's Cases and Materials on Labor Law—Collective Bargaining in a Free Society, 2nd Ed., 1168 pages, 1979, with 1979 Statutory Supplement and 1982 Case Supplement (Casebook)

See also Employment Discrimination, Social Legislation

LAND FINANCE

See Real Estate Transactions

LAND USE

Hagman's Cases on Public Planning and Control of Urban and Land Development, 2nd Ed., 1301 pages, 1980 (Casebook)

Hagman's Hornbook on Urban Planning and Land Development Control Law, 706 pages, 1971 (Text)

Wright and Gitelman's Cases and Materials on Land Use, 3rd Ed., 1300 pages, 1982 (Casebook)

Wright and Webber's Land Use in a Nutshell, 316 pages, 1978 (Text)

See also Housing and Urban Development

LAW AND ECONOMICS

Goetz' Cases and Materials on Law and Economics, 547 pages, 1984 (Casebook)

Manne's The Economics of Legal Relationships—Readings in the Theory of Property Rights, 660 pages, 1975 (Text)

See also Antitrust, Regulated Industries

LAW AND MEDICINE—PSYCHIATRY

Cohen's Cases and Materials on the Law of Deprivation of Liberty: A Study in Social Control, 755 pages, 1980 (Casebook)

King's The Law of Medical Malpractice in a Nutshell, 340 pages, 1977 (Text)

Shapiro and Spece's Problems, Cases and Materials on Bioethics and Law, 892 pages, 1981 (Casebook)

Sharpe, Fiscina and Head's Cases on Law and Medicine, 882 pages, 1978 (Casebook)

LEGAL HISTORY

Presser and Zainaldin's Cases on Law and American History, 855 pages, 1980 (Casebook)

See also Legal Method and Legal System

LEGAL METHOD AND LEGAL SYSTEM

Aldisert's Readings, Materials and Cases in the Judicial Process, 948 pages, 1976 (Casebook)

LEGAL METHOD AND LEGAL SYSTEM—Continued

Bodenheimer, Oakley and Love's Readings and Cases on an Introduction to the Anglo-American Legal System, 161 pages, 1980 (Casebook)

Davies and Lawry's Institutions and Methods of the Law—Introductory Teaching Materials, 547 pages, 1982 (Casebook)

Dvorkin, Himmelstein and Lesnick's Becoming a Lawyer: A Humanistic Perspective on Legal Education and Professionalism, 211 pages, 1981 (Text)

Fryer and Orentlicher's Cases and Materials on Legal Method and Legal System, 1043 pages, 1967 (Casebook)

Greenberg's Judicial Process and Social Change, 666 pages, 1977 (Coursebook)

Kempin's Historical Introduction to Anglo-American Law in a Nutshell, 2nd Ed., 280 pages, 1973 (Text)

Kimball's Historical Introduction to the Legal System, 610 pages, 1966 (Casebook)

Mashaw and Merrill's Introduction to the American Public Law System, 1095 pages, 1975, with 1980 Supplement (Casebook)

Murphy's Cases and Materials on Introduction to Law—Legal Process and Procedure, 772 pages, 1977 (Casebook)

Reynolds' Judicial Process in a Nutshell, 292 pages, 1980 (Text)

See also Legal Research and Writing

LEGAL NEGOTIATION

Edwards and White's Problems, Readings and Materials on the Lawyer as a Negotiator, 484 pages, 1977 (Casebook)

Williams' Legal Negotiation and Settlement, 207 pages, 1983 (Coursebook)

LEGAL PROFESSION

Aronson's Problems in Professional Responsibility, 280 pages, 1978 (Problem book)

Aronson and Weckstein's Professional Responsibility in a Nutshell, 399 pages, 1980 (Text)

Mellinkoff's The Conscience of a Lawyer, 304 pages, 1973 (Text)

Mellinkoff's Lawyers and the System of Justice, 983 pages, 1976 (Casebook)

Pirsig and Kirwin's Cases and Materials on Professional Responsibility, 4th Ed., approximately 650 pages, 1984 (Casebook)

Schwartz and Wydick's Problems in Legal Ethics, 285 pages, 1983 (Casebook)

Selected Statutes, Rules and Standards on the Legal Profession, 249 pages, 1984

Smith's Preventing Legal Malpractice, 142 pages, 1981 (Text)

LEGAL RESEARCH AND WRITING

Cohen's Legal Research in a Nutshell, 3rd Ed., 415 pages, 1978 (Text)

LEGAL RESEARCH AND WRITING—
Continued

Cohen and Berring's How to Find the Law, 8th Ed., 790 pages, 1983. Problem book by Foster and Kelly available (Casebook)

Cohen and Berring's Finding the Law, 8th Ed., Abridged Ed., 556 pages, 1984 (Casebook)

Dickerson's Materials on Legal Drafting, 425 pages, 1981 (Casebook)

Felsenfeld and Siegel's Writing Contracts in Plain English, 290 pages, 1981 (Text)

Gopen's Writing From a Legal Perspective, 225 pages, 1981 (Text)

Mellinkoff's Legal Writing—Sense and Nonsense, 242 pages, 1982 (Text)

Rombauer's Legal Problem Solving—Analysis, Research and Writing, 4th Ed., 424 pages, 1983 (Coursebook)

Squires and Rombauer's Legal Writing in a Nutshell, 294 pages, 1982 (Text)

Statsky's Legal Research, Writing and Analysis, 2nd Ed., 167 pages, 1982 (Coursebook)

Statsky's Legislative Analysis: How to Use Statutes and Regulations, 2nd Ed., 217 pages, 1984 (Text)

Statsky and Wernet's Case Analysis and Fundamentals of Legal Writing, 2nd Ed., 441 pages, 1984 (Text)

Teply's Programmed Materials on Legal Research and Citation, 334 pages, 1982. Student Library Exercises available (Coursebook)

Weihofen's Legal Writing Style, 2nd Ed., 332 pages, 1980 (Text)

LEGISLATION

Davies' Legislative Law and Process in a Nutshell, 279 pages, 1975 (Text)

Nutting and Dickerson's Cases and Materials on Legislation, 5th Ed., 744 pages, 1978 (Casebook)

Statsky's Legislative Analysis: How to Use Statutes and Regulations, 2nd Ed., 217 pages, 1984 (Text)

LOCAL GOVERNMENT

McCarthy's Local Government Law in a Nutshell, 2nd Ed., 404 pages, 1983 (Text)

Michelman and Sandalow's Cases-Comments-Questions on Government in Urban Areas, 1216 pages, 1970, with 1972 Supplement (Casebook)

Reynolds' Hornbook on Local Government Law, 860 pages, 1982 (Text)

Stason and Kauper's Cases and Materials on Municipal Corporations, 3rd Ed., 692 pages, 1959 (Casebook)

Valente's Cases and Materials on Local Government Law, 2nd Ed., 980 pages, 1980 with 1982 Supplement (Casebook)

MASS COMMUNICATION LAW

Gillmor and Barron's Cases and Comment on Mass Communication Law, 4th Ed., approximately 1100 pages, 1984 (Casebook)

Ginsburg's Regulation of Broadcasting: Law and Policy Towards Radio, Television and Cable Communications, 741 pages, 1979, with 1983 Supplement (Casebook)

Zuckman and Gayne's Mass Communications Law in a Nutshell, 2nd Ed., 473 pages, 1983 (Text)

MILITARY LAW

Shanor and Terrell's Military Law in a Nutshell, 378 pages, 1980 (Text)

MORTGAGES

See Real Estate Transactions

NATURAL RESOURCES LAW

See Energy and Natural Resources Law, Environmental Law, Oil and Gas, Water Law

OFFICE PRACTICE

Hegland's Trial and Practice Skills in a Nutshell, 346 pages, 1978 (Text)

Strong and Clark's Law Office Management, 424 pages, 1974 (Casebook)

See also Legal Interviewing and Counseling, Legal Negotiation

OIL AND GAS

Hemingway's Hornbook on Oil and Gas, 2nd Ed., Student Ed., 543 pages, 1983 (Text)

Huie, Woodward and Smith's Cases and Materials on Oil and Gas, 2nd Ed., 955 pages, 1972 (Casebook)

Lowe's Oil and Gas Law in a Nutshell, 443 pages, 1983 (Text)

See also Energy and Natural Resources Law

PARTNERSHIP

See Agency—Partnership

PATENT AND COPYRIGHT LAW

Choate and Francis' Cases and Materials on Patent Law, 2nd Ed., 1110 pages, 1981 (Casebook)

Miller and Davis' Intellectual Property—Patents, Trademarks and Copyright in a Nutshell, 428 pages, 1983 (Text)

Nimmer's Cases on Copyright and Other Aspects of Law Pertaining to Literary, Musical and Artistic Works, 2nd Ed., 1023 pages, 1979 (Casebook)

POVERTY LAW

Brudno's Poverty, Inequality, and the Law: Cases-Commentary-Analysis, 934 pages, 1976 (Casebook)

LAW SCHOOL PUBLICATIONS—Continued

POVERTY LAW—Continued

LaFrance, Schroeder, Bennett and Boyd's Hornbook on Law of the Poor, 558 pages, 1973 (Text)

See also Social Legislation

PRODUCTS LIABILITY

Noel and Phillips' Cases on Products Liability, 2nd Ed., 821 pages, 1982 (Casebook)

Noel and Phillips' Products Liability in a Nutshell, 2nd Ed., 341 pages, 1981 (Text)

PROPERTY

Aigler, Smith and Tefft's Cases on Property, 2 volumes, 1339 pages, 1960 (Casebook)

Bernhardt's Real Property in a Nutshell, 2nd Ed., 448 pages, 1981 (Text)

Boyer's Survey of the Law of Property, 766 pages, 1981 (Text)

Browder, Cunningham and Smith's Cases on Basic Property Law, 4th Ed., approximately 1368 pages, 1984 (Casebook)

Bruce, Ely and Bostick's Cases and Materials on Modern Property Law, approximately 1000 pages, 1984 (Casebook)

Burby's Hornbook on Real Property, 3rd Ed., 490 pages, 1965 (Text)

Burke's Personal Property in a Nutshell, 322 pages, 1983 (Text)

Chused's A Modern Approach to Property: Cases-Notes-Materials, 1069 pages, 1978 with 1980 Supplement (Casebook)

Cohen's Materials for a Basic Course in Property, 526 pages, 1978 (Casebook)

Cunningham, Whitman and Stoebuck's Hornbook on the Law of Property, Student Ed., approximately 928 pages, 1984 (Text)

Donahue, Kauper and Martin's Cases on Property, 2nd Ed., 1362 pages, 1983 (Casebook)

Hill's Landlord and Tenant Law in a Nutshell, 319 pages, 1979 (Text)

Moynihan's Introduction to Real Property, 254 pages, 1962 (Text)

Phipps' Titles in a Nutshell, 277 pages, 1968 (Text)

Uniform Land Transactions Act, Uniform Simplification of Land Transfers Act, Uniform Condominium Act, 1977 Official Text with Comments, 462 pages, 1978

See also Housing and Urban Development, Real Estate Transactions, Land Use

REAL ESTATE TRANSACTIONS

Bruce's Real Estate Finance in a Nutshell, 292 pages, 1979 (Text)

Maxwell, Riesenfeld, Hetland and Warren's Cases on California Security Transactions in Land, 3rd Ed., approximately 710 pages, 1984 (Casebook)

REAL ESTATE TRANSACTIONS—Continued

Nelson and Whitman's Cases on Real Estate Transfer, Finance and Development, 2nd Ed., 1114 pages, 1981, with 1983 Supplement (Casebook)

Osborne's Cases and Materials on Secured Transactions, 559 pages, 1967 (Casebook)

Osborne, Nelson and Whitman's Hornbook on Real Estate Finance Law, 3rd Ed., 885 pages, 1979 (Text)

REGULATED INDUSTRIES

Gellhorn and Pierce's Regulated Industries in a Nutshell, 394 pages, 1982 (Text)

Morgan's Cases and Materials on Economic Regulation of Business, 830 pages, 1976, with 1978 Supplement (Casebook)

Pozen's Financial Institutions: Cases, Materials and Problems on Investment Management, 844 pages, 1978 (Casebook)

See also Mass Communication Law, Banking Law

REMEDIES

Dobbs' Hornbook on Remedies, 1067 pages, 1973 (Text)

Dobbs' Problems in Remedies, 137 pages, 1974 (Problem book)

Dobbyn's Injunctions in a Nutshell, 264 pages, 1974 (Text)

Friedman's Contract Remedies in a Nutshell, 323 pages, 1981 (Text)

Leavell, Love and Nelson's Cases and Materials on Equitable Remedies and Restitution, 3rd Ed., 704 pages, 1980 (Casebook)

McCormick's Hornbook on Damages, 811 pages, 1935 (Text)

O'Connell's Remedies in a Nutshell, 364 pages, 1977 (Text)

York and Bauman's Cases and Materials on Remedies, 3rd Ed., 1250 pages, 1979 (Casebook)

REVIEW MATERIALS

Ballantine's Problems

Black Letter Series

Smith's Review Series

West's Review Covering Multistate Subjects

SECURITIES REGULATION

Hazen's Hornbook on The Law of Securities Regulation, approximately 520 pages, 1984 (Text)

Ratner's Securities Regulation: Materials for a Basic Course, 2nd Ed., 1050 pages, 1980 with 1982 Supplement (Casebook)

Ratner's Securities Regulation in a Nutshell, 2nd Ed., 322 pages, 1982 (Text)

Selected Securities and Business Planning Statutes, Rules and Forms, 485 pages, 1982

LAW SCHOOL PUBLICATIONS—Continued

SOCIAL LEGISLATION

Brudno's Income Redistribution Theories and Programs: Cases-Commentary-Analyses, 480 pages, 1977 (Casebook)—reprint from Brudno's Poverty, Inequality and the Law, 1976

Hood and Hardy's Workers' Compensation and Employee Protection Laws in a Nutshell, 274 pages, 1984 (Text)

LaFrance's Welfare Law: Structure and Entitlement in a Nutshell, 455 pages, 1979 (Text)

Malone, Plant and Little's Cases on Workers' Compensation and Employment Rights, 2nd Ed., 951 pages, 1980 (Casebook)

See also Poverty Law

TAXATION

Dodge's Federal Taxation of Estates, Trusts and Gifts: Principles and Planning, 771 pages, 1981 with 1982 Supplement (Casebook)

Garbis and Struntz' Cases and Materials on Tax Procedure and Tax Fraud, 829 pages, 1982 with 1984 Supplement (Casebook)

Gunn's Cases and Materials on Federal Income Taxation of Individuals, 785 pages, 1981 with 1983 Supplement (Casebook)

Hellerstein and Hellerstein's Cases on State and Local Taxation, 4th Ed., 1041 pages, 1978 with 1982 Supplement (Casebook)

Kahn's Handbook on Basic Corporate Taxation, 3rd Ed., Student Ed., 614 pages, 1981 with 1983 Supplement (Text)

Kahn and Gann's Corporate Taxation and Taxation of Partnerships and Partners, 2nd Ed., approximately 1300 pages, 1984 (Casebook)

Kragen and McNulty's Cases and Materials on Federal Income Taxation, Vol. I: Taxation of Individuals, 3rd Ed., 1283 pages, 1979 with 1983 Supplement (Casebook)

Kragen and McNulty's Cases and Materials on Federal Income Taxation, Vol. II: Taxation of Corporations, Shareholders, Partnerships and Partners, 3rd Ed., 989 pages, 1981 with 1983 Supplement (Casebook)

McNulty's Federal Estate and Gift Taxation in a Nutshell, 3rd Ed., 509 pages, 1983 (Text)

McNulty's Federal Income Taxation of Individuals in a Nutshell, 3rd Ed., 487 pages, 1983 (Text)

Posin's Hornbook on Federal Income Taxation of Individuals, Student Ed., 491 pages, 1983 (Text)

Rice's Problems and Materials in Federal Estate and Gift Taxation, 3rd Ed., 474 pages, 1978 (Casebook)

Rice and Solomon's Problems and Materials in Federal Income Taxation, 3rd Ed., 670 pages, 1979 (Casebook)

TAXATION—Continued

Rose and Raskind's Advanced Federal Income Taxation: Corporate Transactions—Cases, Materials and Problems, 955 pages, 1978 (Casebook)

Selected Federal Taxation Statutes and Regulations, 1255 pages, 1983

Sobeloff and Weidenbruch's Federal Income Taxation of Corporations and Stockholders in a Nutshell, 362 pages, 1981 (Text)

TORTS

Christie's Cases and Materials on the Law of Torts, 1264 pages, 1983 (Casebook)

Green, Pedrick, Rahl, Thode, Hawkins, Smith and Treece's Cases and Materials on Torts, 2nd Ed., 1360 pages, 1977 (Casebook)

Green, Pedrick, Rahl, Thode, Hawkins, Smith, and Treece's Advanced Torts: Injuries to Business, Political and Family Interests, 2nd Ed., 544 pages, 1977 (Casebook)—reprint from Green, et al. Cases and Materials on Torts, 2nd Ed., 1977

Keeton, Keeton, Sargentich and Steiner's Cases and Materials on Torts, and Accident Law, 1360 pages, 1983 (Casebook)

Kionka's Torts in a Nutshell: Injuries to Persons and Property, 434 pages, 1977 (Text)

Malone's Torts in a Nutshell: Injuries to Family, Social and Trade Relations, 358 pages, 1979 (Text)

Prosser and Keeton's Hornbook on Torts, 5th Ed., Student Ed., approximately 1052 pages, 1984 (Text)

Shapo's Cases on Tort and Compensation Law, 1244 pages, 1976 (Casebook)

See also Products Liability

TRADE REGULATION

McManis' Unfair Trade Practices in a Nutshell, 444 pages, 1982 (Text)

Oppenheim, Weston, Maggs and Schechter's Cases and Materials on Unfair Trade Practices and Consumer Protection, 4th Ed., 1038 pages, 1983 (Casebook)

See also Antitrust, Regulated Industries

TRIAL AND APPELLATE ADVOCACY

Appellate Advocacy, Handbook of, 249 pages, 1980 (Text)

Bergman's Trial Advocacy in a Nutshell, 402 pages, 1979 (Text)

Binder and Bergman's Fact Investigation: From Hypothesis to Proof, approximately 350 pages, 1984 (Coursebook)

Goldberg's The First Trial (Where Do I Sit?) (What Do I Say?) in a Nutshell, 396 pages, 1982 (Text)

Hegland's Trial and Practice Skills in a Nutshell, 346 pages, 1978 (Text)

LAW SCHOOL PUBLICATIONS—Continued

TRIAL AND APPELLATE ADVOCACY—Continued

Hornstein's Appellate Advocacy in a Nutshell, approximately 270 pages, 1984 (Text)

Jeans' Handbook on Trial Advocacy, Student Ed., 473 pages, 1975 (Text)

McElhaney's Effective Litigation, 457 pages, 1974 (Casebook)

Nolan's Cases and Materials on Trial Practice, 518 pages, 1981 (Casebook)

Parnell and Shellhaas' Cases, Exercises and Problems for Trial Advocacy, 171 pages, 1982 (Coursebook)

Sonsteng, Haydock and Boyd's The Trialbook: A Total System for Preparation and Presentation of a Case, Student Ed., approximately 400 pages, 1984 (Coursebook)

TRUSTS AND ESTATES

Atkinson's Hornbook on Wills, 2nd Ed., 975 pages, 1953 (Text)

Averill's Uniform Probate Code in a Nutshell, 425 pages, 1978 (Text)

Bogert's Hornbook on Trusts, 5th Ed., 726 pages, 1973 (Text)

Clark, Lusky and Murphy's Cases and Materials on Gratuitous Transfers, 2nd Ed., 1102 pages, 1977 (Casebook)

Gulliver's Cases and Materials on Future Interests, 624 pages, 1959 (Casebook)

Gulliver's Introduction to the Law of Future Interests, 87 pages, 1959 (Casebook)—reprint from Gulliver's Cases and Materials on Future Interests, 1959

McGovern's Cases and Materials on Wills, Trusts and Future Interests: An Introduction to Estate Planning, 750 pages, 1983 (Casebook)

TRUSTS AND ESTATES—Continued

Mennell's Cases and Materials on California Decedent's Estates, 566 pages, 1973 (Casebook)

Mennell's Wills and Trusts in a Nutshell, 392 pages, 1979 (Text)

Powell's The Law of Future Interests in California, 91 pages, 1980 (Text)

Simes' Hornbook on Future Interests, 2nd Ed., 355 pages, 1966 (Text)

Turrentine's Cases and Text on Wills and Administration, 2nd Ed., 483 pages, 1962 (Casebook)

Uniform Probate Code, 5th Ed., Official Text With Comments, 384 pages, 1977

Waggoner's Future Interests in a Nutshell, 361 pages, 1981 (Text)

WATER LAW

Getches' Water Law in a Nutshell, approximately 400 pages, 1984 (Text)

Trelease's Cases and Materials on Water Law, 3rd Ed., 833 pages, 1979, with 1984 Supplement (Casebook)

See also Energy and Natural Resources Law, Environmental Law

WILLS

See Trusts and Estates

WOMEN AND THE LAW

Kay's Text, Cases and Materials on Sex-Based Discrimination, 2nd Ed., 1045 pages, 1981, with 1983 Supplement (Casebook)

Thomas' Sex Discrimination in a Nutshell, 399 pages, 1982 (Text)

See also Employment Discrimination

WORKERS' COMPENSATION

See Social Legislation

McCORMICK ON EVIDENCE
Third Edition

By

Edward W. Cleary,

General Editor

Professor of Law Emeritus, University of Illinois and Arizona State University

---

Contributing Authors

Kenneth S. Broun
Dean and Professor of Law, University of North Carolina

George E. Dix
Vinson & Elkins Professor of Law, The University of Texas

Ernest Gellhorn
Dean and Roush Professor of Law, Case Western Reserve University

D. H. Kaye
Professor of Law, Arizona State University

Robert Meisenholder
Professor of Law, University of Washington

E. F. Roberts
Edwin H. Woodruff Professor of Law, The Cornell Law School

John William Strong
Rosenstiel Professor of Law, University of Arizona

HORNBOOK SERIES
STUDENT EDITION

WEST PUBLISHING CO.
ST. PAUL, MINN., 1984

50 West Kellogg Boulevard
P.O. Box 43526
St. Paul, Minnesota 55164

Library of Congress Cataloging in Publication Data

McCormick, Charles Tilford, 1889–1963.
  McCormick on evidence.

  (Hornbook series student edition)
  Rev. ed. of: McCormick's handbook of the law of
evidence. 2nd ed. 1972.
  Includes index.
  1. Evidence (Law)—United States. I. Broun, Kenneth S.
II. McCormick, Charles Tilford, 1889–1963. McCormick's
handbook of the law of evidence. III. Title. IV. Series.
KF8935.M29 1984   347.73'6   83–26695
                      347.3076

ISBN 0–314–77625–7

Preface

In 1972, when the second edition of this work appeared, the proposed Federal Rules of Evidence had not yet become law, and there was no assurance that they ever would become law. As a result, references to them in the book were tentative and largely confined to footnotes. Yet the proposed rules were the wave of the future. Now in effect not only in the Federal system but also in more than half the States, and embodied in the revised Uniform Rules of Evidence (1974), largely without change of substance, they represent the present. They represent the present not only by virtue of legislative-type adoption but also through a multitude of instances of incorporation into local evidence law in the course of making law through judicial decision. And they represent the point of departure for the ongoing thinking that always characterizes the law of evidence.

The great by-product of the rules was the resurgence of interest in the law of evidence. During the protracted, sometimes tortuous, course from their inception to final enactment a vast amount of discussion and debate took place. Much of it was written, and a number of excellent books about the rules appeared. This momentum has by no means subsided, and interest in evidence and its underpinnings continues.

This book is not a book just about the Federal Rules, however. It is for jurisdictions that have the rules and for those that do not. It is a book about Evidence, what it is, where it came from, and its whys. It even speculates in some measure about the future. The rules are a milestone, not the end of the road.

Some concessions have necessarily been made as to style in order to retain the single volume format. The hyperextension of titles that has invaded the law reviews has suggested deletion of the titles of notes and comments when, as is almost always the case, the context indicates the subject. Omission of the year when the Supreme Court denied certiorari is the least concession that can be made to continuing assertions that denial lacks any significance at all. Citations, rather than being exhaustive, are selected with a view to informing, provoking, and suggesting avenues to further exploration when desired.

Producing a book for students, practitioners, judges, and scholars presents challenges and problems. Earlier editions have on occasion been criticized as too theoretical, but it is a criticism that is welcomed. For the common thread of theory should bind all classes of readers together. Any system of evidence not well founded in theory can be the basis only of rote learning and facile application, readily perverted and easily forgotten. An understanding of and frequent recurrence to basics leads to sound results as well as enhancing memory almost to the point of second nature.

With the passage of time, Dean McCormick's influence has grown, rather than diminished, and this volume is dedicated to his memory.

April, 1984
Tempe, Arizona

EDWARD W. CLEARY

WESTLAW Introduction

McCormick on Evidence offers a detailed and comprehensive treatment of the basic rules and principles of evidence law. However, law students and lawyers frequently need to find additional authority. In an effort to assist with comprehensive research of evidence law, preformulated WESTLAW references are included after each section of the text in this edition of the McCormick hornbook. The WESTLAW references are designed for use with the WESTLAW computer-assisted legal research service. By joining this publication with the extensive WESTLAW databases, the reader is able to move straight from the hornbook into WESTLAW with great speed and convenience.

Some readers may desire to use only the information supplied within the printed pages of this hornbook. Others, however, will encounter issues in evidence law that require further information. Accordingly, those who opt for additional material can rapidly and easily access WESTLAW, an electronic law library that possesses extraordinary currency and magnitude. Appendix A gives concise, step-by-step instruction on how to coordinate WESTLAW research with this hornbook.

Summary of Contents

Table of Contents

TITLE 1. INTRODUCTION

CHAPTER 1. PREPARING AND PRESENTING THE EVIDENCE

TITLE 2. EXAMINATION OF WITNESSES

CHAPTER 2. THE FORM OF QUESTIONS ON DIRECT: THE JUDGE'S WITNESSES: REFRESHING MEMORY

CHAPTER 3. THE REQUIREMENT OF FIRSTHAND KNOWLEDGE: THE OPINION RULE: EXPERT TESTIMONY

CHAPTER 4. CROSS–EXAMINATION AND SUBSEQUENT EXAMINATIONS

CHAPTER 5. IMPEACHMENT AND SUPPORT

TITLE 3. ADMISSION AND EXCLUSION

CHAPTER 6. THE PROCEDURE OF ADMITTING AND EXCLUDING EVIDENCE

TITLE 4. COMPETENCY

CHAPTER 7. THE COMPETENCY OF WITNESSES

TITLE 5. PRIVILEGE: COMMON LAW AND STATUTORY

CHAPTER 8. THE SCOPE AND EFFECT OF THE EVIDENTIARY PRIVILEGES

CHAPTER 9. THE PRIVILEGE FOR MARITAL COMMUNICATIONS

CHAPTER 10. THE CLIENT'S PRIVILEGE: COMMUNICATIONS BETWEEN CLIENT AND LAWYER

CHAPTER 11. THE PRIVILEGE FOR CONFIDENTIAL INFORMATION SECURED IN THE COURSE OF THE PHYSICIAN–PATIENT RELATIONSHIP

CHAPTER 12. PRIVILEGES FOR GOVERNMENTAL SECRETS

TITLE 6. PRIVILEGE: CONSTITUTIONAL

CHAPTER 13. THE PRIVILEGE AGAINST SELF–INCRIMINATION

CHAPTER 15. THE PRIVILEGE CONCERNING IMPROPERLY OBTAINED EVIDENCE

TITLE 7.   RELEVANCY AND ITS COUNTERWEIGHTS

CHAPTER 16.   RELEVANCE

CHAPTER 17.   CHARACTER AND HABIT

CHAPTER 18.   SIMILAR HAPPENINGS AND TRANSACTIONS

CHAPTER 19.   INSURANCE AGAINST LIABILITY

CHAPTER 20.   EXPERIMENTAL AND SCIENTIFIC EVIDENCE

TITLE 8.   DEMONSTRATIVE EVIDENCE

CHAPTER 21.   DEMONSTRATIVE EVIDENCE

TITLE 9.   WRITINGS

CHAPTER 22.   AUTHENTICATION

CHAPTER 23.   THE REQUIREMENT OF THE PRODUCTION OF THE ORIGINAL WRITING AS THE "BEST EVIDENCE"

TITLE 10. THE HEARSAY RULE AND ITS EXCEPTIONS

CHAPTER 24. THE HEARSAY RULE

CHAPTER 25. TESTIMONY TAKEN AT A FORMER HEARING OR IN ANOTHER ACTION

*

McCORMICK ON EVIDENCE
Third Edition

*

Title 1
INTRODUCTION
Chapter 1
PREPARING AND PRESENTING THE EVIDENCE

Table of Sections

---

§ 1. Planning and Preparation of Proof as Important as the Rules of Evidence

The law of Evidence is the system of rules and standards by which the admission of proof at the trial of a lawsuit is regulated. But it should be emphasized that this trial stage, when proof is offered and the rules of evidence come into play, is a late stage in a long process. Thus, every case which will be encountered, dealing with a dispute over a rule of evidence or its application, presents a situation in which the lawyers concerned have been required to shoulder many other tasks in the planning and production of testimony, and in anticipation of problems of presentation of proof at the trial under the law of evidence, long before any question of evidence law is presented to the court. As a reminder, some of these earlier stages in the problem of proof will be mentioned in this chapter.

WESTLAW REFERENCES

topic(307a) /p headnote(preparation production presentation /p proof evidence testimony /p trial* proceeding* hearing*)

---

§ 2. Preparation for Trial on the Facts, Without Resort to the Aid of the Court [1]

The client must be interviewed to ascertain the facts, and these interviews should

---

§ 2

1. There is much dross in the professional writing on this subject, but also much of value. See the various trial practice pamphlets of the Practising Law Institute; including Bodin, Marshalling the Evidence (1966); Frost & Ausubel, Preparation of a Negligence Case (1970); Kramer, Evidence in Negligence Cases (1981); Trial Evidence in Civil Cases (1969). For detailed practical suggestions in various volumes, see Belli, Modern Trials (2d ed.1982); Goldstein & Lake,

Trial Technique (2d ed.1969); Bailey & Rothblatt, Investigation and Preparation of Criminal Cases, Federal and State (1970); Keeton, Trial Tactics and Methods (2d ed.1973). Among the many articles concerning specific subjects, see Hornaday, Some Suggestions on the Investigation of Facts, 15 Ind.L.J. 499 (1940) (deals with interviewing of witnesses); Bowman, How to Make an Investigation, 21 Okl.B.A.J. 1346 (1950), 19 Ins.Counsel J. 23 (1952); Jeans, Evidentiary Effects and Tactical Options in the Use of Out of Court State-

include a tactful but searching cross-examination to overcome the client's natural tendency to confine the story to the facts favorable to himself. The witnesses who have firsthand knowledge of the transaction in controversy must likewise be interviewed, and where possible, their written statements taken.[2] Apart from the ordinary eyewitnesses, it is increasingly necessary to arrange for the employment of technical experts, such as physicians in personal injury cases, chemists and physicists in patent litigation, engineers and architects in controversies over construction contracts, psychiatrists in criminal cases, and handwriting experts in disputes over the genuineness of documents. To prepare himself to testify, and to give to counsel the information he will need to frame his questions at the trial, the expert must usually be furnished with a detailed request for an investigation and report upon specific questions.[3] Also, it will often be necessary to assemble available documentary evidence, such as contracts, letters, receipts, loose-leaf records, deeds, certified copies of conveyances, judgments, and decrees. Other physical evidence, such as the revolver of the attacker and the perforated coat of the victim in a murder case, or a sample of the goods in an action for breach of warranty, should be discovered and preserved for use at the trial. The lawyer, moreover, must be fertile in planning for the production of all those aids to the senses which quicken the jury's interest in and understanding of the testimony, such as photographs, motion picture films, X-ray photographs, plats, diagrams, and models. If pertinent, scientific evidence must be prepared. Where practicable, the task of proof should be lightened by securing written stipulations from opposing counsel of the existence of facts not in controversy, such as the execution of documents, or the ownership of

a vehicle, or of premises, involved in the suit. If it is anticipated that the terms of a document in the possession of the adversary will need to be proved by use of a copy, written notice to produce the original at the trial must be given to opposing counsel.

Manifestly, all of this preparation must be planned, and the plan will develop as new information is disclosed, but as the trial approaches, a definite program must be formulated. Each fact involved in the claim or defence should be listed, with the witnesses and documents by which it will be proved.[4] This may well be supplemented by a list of the witnesses in the order in which they will be called, including the subjects upon which they will be examined, and a separate list of exhibits, including witnesses who are to authenticate each exhibit. Finally, and most important, at the last minute before the witnesses are to go on the stand, the counsel who calls them must talk to each in order to ascertain what he is prepared to swear, to cause him to refresh his memory, if necessary, by reading his signed statement, and to warn him of the probable line of the adversary's cross-examination.

WESTLAW REFERENCES

chemist* physicist* /p expert* /p testi! witness** & topic(patents)

---

§ 3. Invoking the Aid of the Court in Preparing for Trial: Right to Interview Witnesses: Discovery and Depositions: Requests for Admission: Pretrial Conferences

From time to time the question arises whether counsel should have an unfettered opportunity to interview a witness. Resort to the court may be required to settle the matter. The question usually arises when opposing counsel has instructed a witness

---

ments (1978) (concerns use of the federal rules of evidence).

2. See § 3 infra concerning the right to interview witnesses.

3. See Carr, Pre-Trial Preparation of the Medical Evidence, 20 U.Kan.City L.Rev. 103 (1952); Investigat-

ing and Preparing the Medical Aspects of Personal Injury Actions, P.L.I. Forum Series (1957).

4. See Goldstein & Lake, Trial Technique §§ 2.48 (2d ed.1969) (questionnaire to witness), 3.17 (diagram of case), 5.03 (trial brief).

not to "talk" [1], or to "talk" only upon conditions,[2] or much less commonly when a court places limitations upon interviews.[3] Generally, it is said that a criminal defendant has the right to an opportunity to interview witnesses privately.[4] Apparently the prosecution in a criminal case has a similar right.[5]

§ 3

1. Vega v. Bloomsburgh, 427 F.Supp. 593 (D.Mass. 1977) (direction not to talk to opposing counsel without specific permission).

2. Gregory v. United States, 125 U.S.App.D.C. 140, 369 F.2d 185 (1966), cert. denied 396 U.S. 865 (". . . it was my advice that they not speak to anyone about the case unless I was present").

3. International Business Machines Corp. v. Edelstein, 526 F.2d 37 (2d Cir. 1975) (court ordered that if opposing counsel was not present stenographic report should be made for submission to the court).

4. Gregory v. United States, 125 U.S.App.D.C. 140, 369 F.2d 185 (1966), cert. denied 396 U.S. 865 (prosecutor stated, "it was my advice that they not speak to anyone about the case unless I was present"; failure of trial court to issue order to prosecutor that he permit the witnesses so advised to talk to defense counsel held error); Mota v. Buchanan, 26 Ariz.App. 246, 547 P.2d 517 (1976) (error to order that prosecutor be present at interview by defense counsel). See Annot. 14 A.L.R.3d 652; C.J.S. Criminal Law § 958; A.B.A. Standards Relating to the Administration of Justice, The Prosecution Function 3.1, and Discovery and Procedure Before Trial, 4.1.

The remedy is a court order to rescind any limitation or advice and instruct the witness that he may speak freely with opposing counsel if he wishes and that he is free to do as he pleases. Vega v. Bloomsburgh, 427 F.Supp. 593 (D.Mass.1977); United States v. Mirenda, 443 F.2d 1351 (9th Cir. 1971), cert. denied 404 U.S. 966.

In *Gregory* the court mentioned due process and elemental fairness, the right that the prosecutor not frustrate the defense, the necessity of the opportunity to interview in reaching the truth in the context of an adversary proceeding, the increasing trend to provide for discovery, and the duty to furnish witness lists.

In United States v. Mendez-Rodriguez, 450 F.2d 1 (9th Cir. 1971), it was held that the government could not remove aliens to Mexico, placing them beyond subpoena power, without first giving defendant's counsel an opportunity to interview them. The power to make a witness unavailable for subpoena is also involved in this sort of situation. See discussion in opinion in United States v. Ballesteros-Acuna, 527 F.2d 928 (9th Cir. 1975).

5. A.B.A. Standards Relating to The Administration of Criminal Justice, The Defense Function 4.3, and Discovery and Procedure Before Trial, 4.1; Hagan, Interviewing Witnesses in Criminal Cases, 28 Brooklyn L.Rev. 207 (1962). But it has been said that a witness has a right to have counsel present when interviewed by the prosecutor (to advise of constitutional rights).

There is an emerging similar right for both parties in civil cases.[6] Nevertheless, there are a few situations in which a court may refuse to interfere when witnesses are advised by counsel to limit interviews or refuse interviews.[7] The witness sought to be interviewed is free to refuse an interview.[8] De-

United States v. Standard Oil Co., 316 F.2d 884 (7th Cir. 1963).

6. International Business Machines Corp. v. Edelstein, 526 F.2d 37 (2d Cir. 1975) (reversing a trial court order that interviews with witnesses in the absence of opposing counsel must be had with stenographer present so that the interview could be made available to the court; interviews "may be conducted confidentially without the presence of opposing counsel or reporter, whenever the person interviewed is willing to proceed in this manner"). This case was cited in Vega v. Bloomsburgh, 427 F.Supp. 593 (D.Mass.1977).

7. Miscellaneous exceptional circumstances have been relied upon in a few cases to uphold denial of an interview. See Annot. 14 A.L.R.3d 652. A security problem may be crucial if the witness sought to be interviewed is an informer. United States v. Murray, 492 F.2d 178 (9th Cir. 1973), cert. denied 419 U.S. 942 (court refusal to order interview six months in advance of trial without prejudice to renew a motion for interview twenty-four hours before trial). In United States v. Cook, 608 F.2d 1175 (9th Cir. 1979), cert. denied 444 U.S. 1034, refusal of access to government witnesses who were in the Federal Witness Protection Program was upheld on the ground that in the particular circumstances the defendant was not thereby unfairly handicapped. But the court stated, "Our cases indicate that security concerns only justify a limitation upon the time and place of access."

In United States v. Leonard, 524 F.2d 1076 (2d Cir. 1975), cert. denied 425 U.S. 958, the court stated it need not decide how far discouraging IRS employees from submitting to interviews could go.

8. United States v. Mirenda, 443 F.2d 1351 (9th Cir. 1971), cert. denied 404 U.S. 966 (court order that the witness be instructed there was no restriction upon talking to defense counsel but that the matter was for the witness to decide).

There may be a factual question whether a refusal to interview or a limitation upon an interview by the witness was the result of the initiative of the witness or the result of advice and instruction to the witness. Byrnes v. United States, 327 F.2d 825 (9th Cir. 1964) (there was no limitation by party when party had first instructed persons to interview defendant's counsel only in the presence of other counsel, and then opposing party had revoked that instruction, and the judge had also told the persons that no one had any objection to their speaking freely with defendant's counsel); United States v. Dryden, 423 F.2d 1175 (5th Cir. 1970), cert. denied 398 U.S. 950 (the person to be interviewed was responsible for refusal to interview when he told a government agent to tell defense counsel he did not want to be interviewed and the agent related the message to

spite the existence of discovery devices, the right to an opportunity to interview is important in trial preparation.

The official discovery procedures in the various jurisdictions are treated at length in treatises and one-volume works concerning the subjects of civil and criminal procedure.[9] Consequently, only a very short and summary review of these procedures is included here.

In addition to preparation for trial without the use of any official pretrial procedures, adequate preparation requires the use of official procedures that are made available once a lawsuit has been commenced. Since the pleadings in civil cases may be fairly general and need not outline the opponent's factual case in any detail in many jurisdictions,[10] the rules for civil cases in many states provide for fairly thorough discovery processes by which each party may discover the facts and possible evidence in the case, and at least ascertain in part what detailed fact issues may arise for trial, as well as the opponent's positions concerning factual matters.[11]

One of the most important discovery procedures in civil cases is undoubtedly the procedure by which each party may orally examine the other under oath and may likewise examine any persons who may possibly have any knowledge of the subject matter of the lawsuit. Over half the states have substantially copied the federal rules for this procedure.[12] Although an order for a commission authorizing an officer to pre-

side at such an oral examination is still required in some states, the procedure for taking oral depositions more often specifies only a notice to the person to be examined and a subpoena requiring him to appear at a certain time and place for the examination before a notary public, plus a notice of the examination to the opposing party, if he is not the person to be examined.[13] In many jurisdictions, following the lead of the federal discovery process for civil cases, the examination upon oral deposition may seek information "reasonably calculated to lead to the discovery of admissible evidence" even if the information will not be admissible at the trial.[14] In these jurisdictions, effective employment of the taking of oral depositions will enable a party to discover the evidence both for and against his positions concerning the facts.

In civil cases, written interrogatories may also be directed to the opponent in many states, and he will be required to answer them.[15] Usually these interrogatories are used hand in hand with the procedure of taking oral depositions. Further a party is often permitted to secure an order requiring the adversary to permit him to examine all papers and things—even real property—relating to the subject matter of the suit.[16] At least in personal injury suits, and sometimes in other suits in which the physical or mental condition of a party is in issue, an order for examination of the condition of the party may be secured in over half the states.[17] Further, although not strictly speaking a discovery device, a party may in many states

---

counsel for defendant; also an instruction not to sign a statement was not an instruction to refuse an interview). See also, United States v. Matlock, 491 F.2d 504 (6th Cir. 1974), cert. denied 419 U.S. 864 (government attorney could tell witness he need not talk if he did not want to).

9. See Wright & Miller, Federal Practice and Procedure: Civil §§ 2001–2293. For procedures in criminal cases, see Wright, Federal Practice and Procedure: Criminal Rules 15, 16 (1982); 8 Moore's Federal Practice Rules 15, 16.

10. See Wright, Federal Courts § 68 (4th ed.1983); James & Hazard, Civil Procedure §§ 2.8, 2.11 (2d ed. 1977).

11. The discovery processes summarized in this section also afford means to preserve evidence for the trial.

12. Rules 26–37, Rules of Civil Procedure for the District Courts of the United States. At least 28 states have adopted the federal rules with variations.

13. Details in the Federal Rules of Civil Procedure are spelled out in Rule 30.

14. Fed.R.Civ.P. 26(b)(1). See detailed discussion in 4 Moore's Federal Practice ¶ 26.54.

15. Fed.R.Civ.P. 33. See general discussion in Wright, Federal Courts § 86 (4th ed.1983).

16. Fed.R.Civ.P. 34.

17. Fed.R.Civ.P. 35.

send requests for admissions to his opponent who must either admit or deny the detailed requests.[18]

Finally, the pretrial hearing or conference is authorized for civil cases in many jurisdictions, although it has not necessarily been frequently used in all of them.[19] When the case is approaching the time for trial, usually two or three weeks before the date set, the judge summons counsel for both sides, and sometimes the parties, and seeks to settle all preliminary questions of pleading, to ascertain the scope of the dispute, and to secure agreements as to the facts not really at issue. The original federal rule [20] mentions, as among the objects of the hearing:

"(1) The simplification of the issues;

. . .

"(3) The possibility of obtaining admissions of fact and of documents which will avoid unnecessary proof;

"(4) The limitation of the number of expert witnesses;

"(5) The advisability of a preliminary reference of issues to a master for findings to be used as evidence when the trial is to be by jury" . . . .

Pretrial conference can serve as a vehicle for reaching agreement upon various factual issues, although it will not necessarily have that result.[21]

A final step that should be mentioned before concluding this summary of ways in which the aid of the court is invoked in civil cases in the preparation for trial on the facts, is the procurement of the issuance and service of writs of subpoena for the witnesses who are to be used at the trial. In the case of a document or other physical evidence held by another, the party who desires its production at the trial may secure a subpoena duces tecum addressed to the possessor commanding him to attend the trial as a witness and to bring with him the document or other object.

It should be mentioned that the use of some of the above-described discovery devices may result in testimony and other evidence which may be introduced into evidence at the trial. The testimony upon the taking of oral or written depositions may be introduced under varying circumstances. Under rules similar to the federal rules, the deposition testimony of an opposing party may be introduced virtually without any conditions.[22] The most common conditions for the introduction of deposition testimony of persons other than witnesses are the requirements expressed in the federal rules of civil procedure.[23] Depositions are also admissible

---

18. This device is not usually available in states which have not adopted Rule 36, Federal Rules of Civil Procedure.

19. For general discussion of pretrial conferences, see Kincaid, A Judge's Handbook of Pre-Trial Procedure, 17 F.R.D. 437 (1955). Much useful information is contained in Manual for Complex Litigation, Part I (1981).

20. Fed.R.Civ.P. 16. The rule has been amended to state its purposes in more detail. The history of pretrial conference is outlined in Sunderland, The Theory and Practice of Pre-Trial Procedure, 36 Mich.L.Rev. 215 (1937).

21. See study of the pretrial conference in Rosenberg, The Pretrial Conference and Effective Justice 23–71 (1964).

22. Fed.R.Civ.P. 32(a)(2):

(2) The deposition of a party or of anyone who at the time of taking the deposition was an officer, director, or managing agent, or a person designated under Rule 30(b)(6) or 31(a) to testify on behalf of a public or private corporation, partnership or associa-

tion or governmental agency which is a party may be used by an adverse party for any purpose.

23. Rule 32(a)(1), (3) provides that depositions may be used at the trial in accordance with the following provisions:

(1) Any deposition may be used by any party for the purpose of contradicting or impeaching the testimony of deponent as a witness or for any other purpose permitted by the Federal Rules of Evidence.

. . .

(3) The deposition of a witness, whether or not a party, may be used by any party for any purpose if the court finds: (A) that the witness is dead; or (B) that the witness is at a greater distance than 100 miles from the place of trial or hearing, or is out of the United States, unless it appears that the absence of the witness was procured by the party offering the deposition; or (C) that the witness is unable to attend or testify because of age, illness, infirmity, or imprisonment; or (D) that the party offering the deposition has been unable to procure the attendance of the witness by subpoena; or (E) upon application and

under the terms of the federal rules of evidence.[24]

The proper use of all these pretrial devices for trial preparation is, of course, in and of itself an important art.

Discovery procedures available to a criminal defendant should also be mentioned. Only in somewhat recent times have rules or statutes been enacted to provide for any true discovery procedures for criminal defendants,[25] and these procedures are limited. The Crime Control Act of 1970 provides for taking depositions primarily for the preservation of the evidence of the witness (for future use as evidence) and not for the purpose of discovery of facts. For the first time depositions were authorized on motion of the government.[26] A broad discovery provision concerning discovery and examination by defendant of reports, tests, grand jury testimony, books, papers, documents, tangible objects, and places is provided for by Rule 16 of the federal criminal rules.[27] A more limited provision is made in the federal rules for discovery of matters of this kind by the government.[28]

In the various states, all manner of miscellaneous and limited provisions which might have some limited use for discovery of facts

exist, but no detailed review will be attempted here.[29]

 WESTLAW REFERENCES

headnote(right /s interview! /s witness**)

gregory /s "united states" u.s. & 369 /3 185

"international business" i.b.m. /s edelstein & 526 /3 37

"united states" u.s. /s mirenda & 443 /3 1331 & witness** /s refus! /s interview & court(dc)

deposition* /p notice* /p subpoena* /p appear!

reasonabl! /10 calculat! /10 discover! /10 admissible /10 evidence

pretrial /p conference* hearing* /p purpose* object! function* /p simplif! /p issue*

pretrial /p conference* hearing* /p purpose* object! function* /p unnecessary /2 proof

pretrial /p conference* hearing* /p purpose* object! function* /p limit! /p witness** expert*

pretrial /p conference* hearing* /p purpose* object! function* /p master /p finding* /p jur***

"duces tecum" /p tape* cassette* video

18 +s 3503 & deposition*

---

§ 4. The Order of Presenting Evidence at the Trial

Under the usual order of proceeding at the trial, including a trial under the Federal Rules of Evidence, the plaintiff, who has the burden of establishing his claim, will first introduce the evidence to prove the facts necessary to enable him to recover,[1] e.g., the

---

notice, that such exceptional circumstances exist as to make it desirable, in the interest of justice and with due regard to the importance of presenting the testimony of witnesses orally in open court, to allow the deposition to be used.

24. See § 254 infra.

25. See discussion and cited articles in Wright, Federal Practice and Procedure: Criminal § 251. See also § 97 infra.

26. 18 U.S.C.A. § 3503. See Wright, Federal Practice and Procedure: Criminal § 241.

27. Fed.R.Crim.P. 16.

28. Present Rule 16 conditions limited government discovery rights to situations in which defendant has sought discovery under the rule. See also Fed.R.Crim. P. 26.

29. See various state provisions cited in Advisory Committee Note for Rule 16, Preliminary Draft of Proposed Amendments to the Federal Rules of Criminal Procedure, January 31, 1970.

§ 4

1. This is the usual order, since the plaintiff has the "burden of proof," in the sense of the duty of first proceeding with evidence to establish the facts pleaded in the complaint. But this burden of opening the evidence usually carries with it the compensating advantage called the "right to open and close," that is, the privilege of having the first and the last word in the argument to the jury. To get this advantage, the defendant will occasionally admit the plaintiff's cause of action, and rest solely on some affirmative defense in the answer, and thus assume the burden of proceeding with the evidence first, along with the right to open and close the argument. The order of presenting evidence and the right to open and close are clearly described in Abbott, Civil Jury Trials chs. V and VI, (5th ed. 1935). See also 6 Wigmore, Evidence § 1866 (Chadbourn rev. 1976) (a helpful chart showing the stages in presenting evidence, and in examining the individual witness), § 1867 (discussing the power of the trial judge to permit variations from the usual order). As will appear in Chapter 36 herein, the sufficiency of the proof to meet the requirements of claim or defense is often a turning point in the case.

making of the contract sued on, its breach, and the amount of damages. At this stage the plaintiff will bring forward successively all the witnesses on whom he will rely to establish these facts, together with the documents pertinent for this purpose, which will be offered when they have been authenticated by the testimony of the witnesses. During this stage each witness of the plaintiff will first be questioned by the plaintiff's counsel, upon direct examination, then cross-examined by opposing counsel, and these examinations may be followed by re-direct and re-cross examinations. When all of the plaintiff's witnesses to his main case have been subjected, each in turn, to this process of questioning and cross-questioning, the plaintiff signifies the completion of his case in chief by announcing that he rests.

Then the defendant presents the witnesses (and also the documents and other tangible evidence) in support of his case. At this stage the defendant will produce evidence not only in denial of the plaintiff's claim, such as evidence that a contract sued on was never actually agreed on, or in a negligence case that some bodily injury was not permanent as claimed by the plaintiff, but also in support of any affirmative defenses which the defendant has pleaded, such as the defense of fraud in the procurement of a contract sued on, or the making of a release of a personal injury claim. Here again each witness's story on direct examination is subject to be tested by cross-examination and supplemented on re-direct, etc., before he leaves the stand. When the defendant has thus completed the presentation of his proof of affirmative defenses, if any, and his evidence in denial of the plaintiff's claims, the defendant announces that he rests.

The plaintiff is now entitled to another turn at bat. He may now present his case in rebuttal. The plaintiff is not entitled to present at this stage witnesses who merely support the allegations of the complaint, but

is confined to testimony which is directed to refuting the evidence of the defendant, unless the court in its discretion permits him to depart from the regular order of proof. The plaintiff's witnesses in rebuttal may be new ones, but he may often recall witnesses who testified for him on the case in chief, to answer some point first raised by the defendant's witnesses. In this, as in the other stages, the witness may not only be examined on direct, but cross-examined and re-examined. When the plaintiff's case in rebuttal is finished, he closes his case. If new points are brought out in the plaintiff's rebuttal evidence, the defendant may meet them by evidence in rejoinder, otherwise he closes his case at once. When both parties have announced that they have closed, the hearing on the facts comes to an end and the trial proceeds with the argument of counsel and the court's instructions to the jury.

To sum up: The stages of the hearing of the facts are

(1) the plaintiff's main case, or evidence in chief,

(2) the defendant's case or evidence in defense,

(3) the plaintiff's evidence in rebuttal, and

(4) the defendant's evidence in rejoinder.

In each of these stages, all of the witnesses to the facts appropriate at the particular period will be called by the party, and the examination of each witness may pass through these steps:

(1) the direct examination, conducted by the party who calls the witness,

(2) the cross-examination by the adversary,

(3) re-direct, and

(4) re-cross.[2]

Under Federal Rule of Evidence 611(a), the above-described order of a trial is ordinarily followed, but the court "shall exercise reasonable control over the mode and order

---

2. In general, the order of presentation of evidence is similar in a criminal case, with the prosecution taking the role of "plaintiff".

of interrogating witnesses and presenting evidence so as to (1) make the interrogation and presentation effective for the ascertainment of the truth, (2) avoid needless consumption of time, and (3) protect witnesses from harassment or undue embarrassment." The judge usually will not have sufficient reason to change the stages of the hearing as described above.[3] The primary focus of the rule is the control of the steps for examination of witnesses as described above and the nature of examination of witnesses.[4]

WESTLAW REFERENCES

right /10 open! /10 clos! /10 argument* /10
  jury
410k224
redirect /s examination* /s scope
recross /s examination* /s scope
611(a) /p witness** /p examination* interrogat!

---

3. Most often changes in the stages of a hearing that have been approved concern the permission to call and question a witness out of order or other matters concerning the questioning of a witness. See cases cited in Louisell & Mueller, Federal Evidence § 334 (1979). In Truman v. Wainwright, 514 F.2d 150 (5th Cir. 1975), the court approved the usual order as a constitutional matter by approving a ruling that defendant had no right to call a witness during the presentation of the state's case.

4. See cases cited in Weinstein & Berger, Evidence, ¶ 611. The Advisory Committee's Note, referring to clause (1) of Rule 611(a), quoted in the text, takes the position that the clause "relates in broad terms the power and obligation of the judge as developed under common law principles." See 6 Wigmore, Evidence §§ 1866, 1867 (Chadbourn rev. 1976).

Title 2

EXAMINATION OF WITNESSES

Chapter 2

THE FORM OF QUESTIONS ON DIRECT: THE JUDGE'S WITNESSES: REFRESHING MEMORY

Table of Sections

---

§ 5. The Form of Questions: (a) Questions Calling for a Free Narrative versus Specific Questions

The art of direct examination of your own witness, and of telling a composite story from the mouths of your own witnesses, is far more important, though perhaps less difficult, than the art of cross-examination.[1] One of the problems of tactics is whether the information which a particular witness will give can best be elicited by a succession of questions about specific facts and happenings or will be brought out more effectively by a general question. In the latter case, the attention of the witness will be directed to the incident in litigation by asking him whether he was on the scene at the time and then requesting him to tell what he saw and heard on that occasion. This latter method, narrative testimony, may often be more effective. The narrative does not seem to come from the counsel, as it might when specific interrogation is employed. If the witness has a good memory, a good personality, and some effectiveness in speaking, his spontaneous statement of his own story may well be more interesting and impressive. Scientific tests give some indication that spontaneous narrative is more accurate (because less influenced by suggestion) while the fully interrogated testimony is, naturally, more complete in its representa-

§ 5

1. See Wellman, Day in Court, Ch. 10 (1910), reprinted in Davenport, Voices in Court 86–98 (1958); Spellman, Direct Examination of Witnesses (1968).

tion of the facts.[2] Specific interrogation may be desirable to ensure the presentation of facts in proper order; to give the witness confidence in the courtroom; to supplement the testimony properly by visual aids, demonstrative evidence, and writings; to prevent dull testimony; and to accomplish a variety of other purposes.

If a witness is to be examined by the narrative method, counsel must plan to be ready to interrupt with specific questions, if necessary, or to supplement the narrative by specific questions which bring out omitted facts.

Under the prevailing view, there is no general rule of law requiring or preferring either form of questioning. Courts have emphasized the danger that when asked to tell his story the witness will include hearsay or other incompetent testimony,[3] but a proper caution by court or counsel, on the adversary's request, will usually prevent this. True, if the improper statement comes out in the story, there is only the remedy of striking out that part of the evidence. There is also a danger that counsel may waive an objection if he does not interrupt promptly and move to strike. But the need for eliciting what the witness knows in the most vivid and accurate way is an interest to be balanced against the need of the adversary for a fair opportunity to object. The guiding principle is that the trial judge has a discretion, not reviewable except for abuse,[4] to control the form of examination,[5] to the end that the facts may be clearly and expeditiously presented; hence he may permit either of the methods discussed.[6] It is believed, however, that whenever circumstances make narrative testimony feasible, its use is likely to be in the interest of the examining party and of the accurate disclosure of the truth, and that the use of this method will seldom be curbed by enlightened judges, except, perhaps, in criminal trials when it may entail the risk that testimony will be given concerning a matter which is not constitutionally admissible.

These principles are consistent with Federal and Revised Uniform Rule (1974) 611(a),[7] which provides:

> The court shall exercise reasonable control over the mode and order of interrogating witnesses and presenting evidence so as to (1) make the interrogation and presentation effective for the ascertainment of the truth, (2) avoid needless consumption of time, and (3) protect witnesses from harassment or undue embarrassment.

2. Gardner, The Perception and Memory of Witnesses, 18 Cornell L.Q. 391, 404 (1923), citing Marston, Studies in Testimony, 15 J.Crim.Law and Criminology, 1–31 (1924); Wigmore, The Science of Judicial Proof § 264 (3d ed., 1937).

But see Marshall, Marquis & Oskamp, Effects of Kind of Question and Atmosphere of Interrogation on Accuracy and Completeness of Testimony, 84 Harv.L. Rev. 1620 (1971).

3. State v. Allemand, 153 La. 741, 96 So. 552, 553 (1923) (better practice is to ask definite questions but here no prejudice); State v. Sullivan, 159 La. 589, 105 So. 631 (1925) (witness volunteered incompetent evidence in course of story which jury were instructed to disregard; no prejudice).

4. Pumphrey v. State, 84 Neb. 636, 122 N.W. 19, 21 (1909).

5. Ewing v. People, 87 Colo. 6, 284 P. 341 (1930); State v. Larsen, 42 Idaho 517, 246 P. 313, 314 (1926); Dec.Dig. Witnesses ⇐226; Model Code of Evidence Rule 105 (1942).

6. Northern Pacific Railway Co. v. Charless, 51 F. 562, 570 (9th Cir. 1892), reversed on other grounds 162 U.S. 359 (leading case permitting free narrative in court's discretion); Mobile, Jackson & Kansas City Railroad Co. v. Hawkins, 163 Ala. 565, 51 So. 37, 44 (1909); Temple v. State, 245 Ind. 21, 195 N.E.2d 850 (1964); People v. Belcher, 189 Cal.App. 404, 11 Cal. Rptr. 175 (1961); Kincaide v. Cavanagh, 198 Mass. 34, 84 N.E. 307 (1908) (within court's discretion to permit counsel to place statement of account before witness and ask her generally to explain each item); Hendricks v. St. Louis Transit Co., 124 Mo.App. 157, 101 S.W. 675, 676 (1907) (deposition); Pumphrey v. State, 84 Neb. 636, 122 N.W. 19, 21 (1909) (in court's discretion to require specific questions); Call v. Linn, 112 Or. 1, 228 P. 127, 130 (1924) (question should have been limited to time and place, but since answer so limited no harm); Deams v. State, 159 Tex.Cr.R. 496, 265 S.W.2d 96 (1954) (judge in discretion could require specific questions). See also Ward v. City of Pittsburgh, 353 Pa. 156, 44 A.2d 553 (1945), where it was held not improper for judge to permit witness, whose power of speech had been affected by a stroke, to give his testimony by a written statement, where he was present and could have been cross-examined.

7. The Advisory Committee's Note states that the federal rule restates common law principles in broad terms. See § 4 n. 4 supra.

WESTLAW REFERENCES

topic(witness**) /p headnote(specific /2 question*)
topic(witness**) /p headnote(general /2 question*
  narrative)

§ 6. The Form of Questions: (b) Leading Questions

In the preceding section, the method of soliciting the free and unguided narrative of the witness on direct examination is compared with the method of drawing out testimony by specific questions. A danger of the latter method is that the witness may acquiesce in a false suggestion. The suggestion itself may plant the belief in its truth. Some studies have confirmed the convictions of judges that this danger is greater than one who has had no experience with trials would suppose.[1] And, regardless of his beliefs, a friendly or pliant witness may follow suggestions on direct examination. On the other hand, it can be urged that there is little reason for barring suggestive questions.[2] In many instances, at least, the objection is trivial.

Nevertheless, subject to all of the conditions and limitations that are discussed in the remainder of this section, objections to leading questions have been preserved by the common law and by Rule 611(c) of the Federal and Revised Uniform Rules of Evidence.[3]

A leading question then is one that suggests to the witness the answer desired by the examiner. A question may be leading because of its form, but often the mere form of a question does not indicate whether it is leading. The question which contains a phrase like "did he not?" is obviously and invariably leading, but almost any other type of question may be leading or not, dependent upon the content and context. It is sometimes supposed that a question which can be answered yes or no is by that fact marked as leading, and the beginner may seek refuge in the form of a neutral alternative ("State whether or not . . .") to escape the charge of leading. But quite often the former kind of question will not be leading and equally often the latter kind will be.[4] The whole issue is whether an ordinary man would get the impression that the questioner desired one answer rather than another. The form of a question, or previous questioning, may indicate the desire, but the most important circumstance for consideration is the extent of the particularity of the question itself. If the question describes an incident in detail and asks if the incident happened, the natural inference is that the questioner expects an affirmative answer. Or if one alternative branch of a question is concrete and detailed and the other vague ("Was the sound like the scream of a woman in fear or was it otherwise?") the impression is that the first alternative is suggested. On the other hand, if a question is sufficiently neutral ("At what time did this occur?") or sufficiently balanced ("Was the water hot or cold?"), it is not leading.

As we have seen, the normal practice is for the careful lawyer to interview in ad-

§ 6

1. Gardner, The Perception and Memory of Witnesses, 18 Corn.L.Q. 391, 405 (1933), citing statements of psychologists and judges.

2. Cleary, Evidence as a Problem in Communicating, 5 Vand.L.Rev. 277, 287 (1952).

3. Fed.R.Evid. and Rev.Unif.R.Evid. (1974) 611(c) provide: "Leading questions should not be used on direct examination of a witness except as may be necessary to develop his testimony. Ordinarily leading questions should be permitted on cross-examination. When a party calls a hostile witness, an adverse party, or a witness identified with an adverse party, interrogation may be by leading questions."

As long as the traditional rule against leading questions is retained, the conditions of the application of the rule, as outlined in this section, are virtually a necessity.

4. A question which may be answered yes or no is not on that account leading unless it suggests the answer wanted. Harward v. Harward, 173 Md. 339, 196 A. 318 (1938); Implement Dealers Mutual Insurance Co. v. Castleberry, 368 S.W.2d 249 (Tex.Civ.App.1963). And it has been said that prefacing a question by "whether or not" seldom removes its leading character. State v. Murphy, 216 S.C. 44, 56 S.E.2d 736 (1949). For illustrative cases, see 3 Wigmore, Evidence §§ 769–772 (Chadbourn rev. 1970); Dec.Dig. Witnesses ☞240(3–5).

vance all witnesses whom he expects to call for direct examination to prove his own case. This practice is entirely proper, but it does create a probability that the lawyer and the witness will have reached an *entente* which will make the witness especially susceptible to suggestions from the lawyer. On the other hand, when counsel cross-examines a witness called by the adversary, he may have had no opportunity to talk to the witness previously, and in any event there is less likelihood of an understanding between them about the facts. Hence the practice: upon objection, the judge will ordinarily forbid leading questions on direct examination and will ordinarily permit them on cross-examination. But the entire matter of the allowability of leading questions is discretiona-

ry,[5] and the judge's action will not be reviewed unless it is charged that it amounted to, or contributed to, the denial of a fair trial.[6]

When the normal assumption about the relation between the witness and the examining counsel or his client appears unfounded, the usual practice is reversed. If, on direct, the witness appears hostile to the examiner, or reluctant, or unwilling; the danger of suggestion disappears, and the judge will permit leading questions,[7] and conversely, if on cross-examination the witness appears to be biased in favor of the cross-examining party, counsel may be prohibited from leading.[8]

In various other situations, leading questions are permitted. They may be used to

---

5. See, e.g., People v. Merritt, 367 Ill. 521, 12 N.E.2d 7 (1938); Commonwealth v. Sheppard, 313 Mass. 590, 48 N.E.2d 630 (1943); State v. Painter, 265 N.C. 277, 144 S.E.2d 6 (1965); Dec.Dig. Witnesses ⊛240(2). Under Fed.R.Evid. 611(c), the matter is also said to be primarily in the discretion of the trial judge. United States v. O'Brien, 618 F.2d 1234 (7th Cir. 1980), cert. denied 449 U.S. 858 (clause of Rule 611(c) that leading questions are permitted "when necessary to develop testimony" was mentioned); United States v. Brown, 603 F.2d 1022 (1st Cir. 1979) (witness described as "evasive", "adverse", confused, prolix, etc.).

6. The formula has been stated in various terms. In a leading case, United States v. Durham, 319 F.2d 590 (4th Cir. 1963) there was no abuse because there was no prejudice or clear injustice to a criminal defendant under described circumstances. The general notion has resulted in reversals through application of Rule 611(c) of the Federal Rules of Evidence. Leading questions which were prejudicial in substance were cause for reversal in United States v. Meeker, 558 F.2d 387 (7th Cir. 1977) (leading questions implied prior misconduct, guilt as charged in the suit, and irrelevant conduct). Exaggerated use of leading questions that warp a case may be abuse. Straub v. Reading Co., 220 F.2d 177 (3d Cir. 1955); United States v. Shoupe, 548 F.2d 636 (6th Cir. 1977) (extensive recitation in leading questions of unsworn and inadmissible statements of witness which inculpated defendant). See Dec.Dig. Appeal and Error ⊛971(5); Witnesses ⊛240(2).

Ordinarily, a successful objection to a leading question can be obviated by reframing the question even though theoretically prejudice might result because the suggestion has already been made. Allen v. Hartford Life Insurance Co., 72 Conn. 693, 45 A. 955, 956 (1900) (. . . "This result is an incident of that imperfection attaching to all that man does, and from which even judicial procedure cannot be kept free. The only remedy is a preventive one, and lies in the power of trial courts to regulate the conduct of counsel at the bar.").

While the judge has undoubted authority to foreclose the witness from answering at all on the matter inquired into by the leading question, 3 Wigmore, Evidence § 770, n. 4, (Chadbourn rev. 1970) and a fortiori to prevent counsel from returning to the matter except after an excursion into other matters sufficient to dissipate the effect of the leading question, the authority is seldom exercised.

7. People v. Gallery, 336 Ill. 580, 168 N.E. 650 (1929) (questions by prosecutor to unwilling state's witness; permissible to refresh memory, not to impeach); McNeill v. Fidelity & Casualty Co. of New York, 336 Mo. 1142, 82 S.W.2d 582 (1935) (plaintiff's examination of witness employed in agency of defendant insurance company); Dec.Dig. Witnesses ⊛244; Annot., 117 A.L.R. 328. In many jurisdictions, a rule or statute permits a party to call the adverse party and interrogate him by leading questions. Fed.R.Evid. 611(c) states broadly that leading questions may be used when "a party calls a hostile witness, an adverse party, or a witness identified with an adverse party." The hostility of the witness is for the judge to decide. United States v. Librach, 520 F.2d 550 (8th Cir. 1975), cert. denied 429 U.S. 939 (leading questions to evasive government witness, whose testimony surprised the prosecutor, were approved). The term "adverse party" causes few problems. A person "identified with a hostile party" is a broad clause that automatically includes various witnesses within its ambit. See dictum concerning an employee of opponent in Perkins v. Volkswagen of America, Inc., 596 F.2d 681 (5th Cir. 1979).

8. Moody v. Rowell, 34 Mass. (17 Pick.) 490, 498 (1835). "Ordinarily leading questions should be permitted on cross-examination." Fed.R.Evid. 611(c). The term "ordinarily" furnishes "a basis for denying the use of leading questions when the cross-examination is cross-examination in form only and not in fact, as for example the 'cross-examination' of a party by his own counsel after being called by his own opponent (savoring more of redirect) or of an insured defendant

bring out preliminary matters, such as the name and occupation of the witness; or to elicit matters not substantially in dispute.[9] They may be employed to suggest a subject or topic, as distinguished from an answer.[10] Additional relaxations are grounded in necessity. Thus, the judge, when need appears, will ordinarily permit leading questions to children, or to witnesses so ignorant, timid, weak-minded, or deficient in the English language, that they cannot otherwise be brought to understand what information is sought.[11] It is recognized, especially as to children,[12] that in these cases, the danger of false suggestion is at its highest, but it is better to face that danger than to abandon altogether the effort to bring out what the witness knows. Similarly, when a witness has been fully directed to the subject by non-leading questions without securing from him a complete account of what he is believed to know, his memory is said to be "exhausted" and the judge may permit the examiner to ask questions which by their particularity may revive his memory but which of necessity may thereby suggest the answer desired.[13]

In some jurisdictions, there is a long-standing practice that permits leading questions to a witness who, for impeachment purposes, is to testify to a statement of a previous witness that is inconsistent with the testimony of that witness.[14] Necessity again is said to be the basis of the practice. It might otherwise be impossible to call attention to the subject of the testimony.[15] It has been argued, however, that the practice should not be followed.[16]

WESTLAW REFERENCES

digest(leading /3 question* /p objection*)
611(c) & leading /3 question*
direct /2 examination* /p witness** /3 hostile reluctant unwilling evasive
direct /2 examination* /p witness** /p identifl /p adverse /p party parties
crossexamination* /p witness** /p bias! /p leading /3 question*

---

who proves to be friendly to the plaintiff." Advisory Committee's Note. However, the matter is in the trial court's discretion. Ardoin v. J. Ray McDermott & Co., Inc., 684 F.2d 335 (5th Cir. 1982) (on cross-examination of employee called by employer's opponent, trial court permitted leading questions by employer's counsel). See similar view in 3 Wigmore, Evidence § 773 (Chadbourn rev. 1970).

9. Southern Railway Co. v. Hall, 209 Ala. 237, 96 So. 73 (1923) (introductory questions identifying time and place of incident in suit). So also as to preliminary matters triable to the court in the absence of the jury. State v. Castelli, 92 Conn. 58, 101 A. 476, 479 (1917) (question whether threats were made or inducements given to secure confession); Dec.Dig. Witnesses ⇐241. The same view should be taken under Fed.R.Evid. 611(c). Louisell & Mueller, Federal Evidence § 339. See Advisory Committee's Note, Fed.R.Evid. 611(c).

10. Gerler v. Cooley, 41 Ill.App.2d 233, 190 N.E.2d 488 (1963); State v. Ward, 10 Utah 2d 34, 347 P.2d 865 (1958). The text should obviously apply under Fed.R. Evid. and Rev.Unif.R.Evid. (1974) 611(c).

11. United States v. Littlewind, 551 F.2d 244 (8th Cir. 1977) (leading questions to 13 and 14 year old prosecuting witnesses in rape cases were approved, citing Fed.R.Evid. 611(c)); Campion v. Lattimer, 70 Neb. 245, 97 N.W. 290 (1903) (ignorant, dull person); Preston v. Denkins, 94 Ariz. 214, 382 P.2d 686 (1963) (78 year old witness in poor health and with defective independent recall); Dec.Dig. Witnesses ⇐243.

12. See Coon v. People, 99 Ill. 368, 370 (1879).

McCormick et al. on Evid. 3rd Ed. H.B.—2

13. Gray v. Kelley, 190 Mass. 184, 76 N.E. 724 (1906); O'Hagan v. Dillon, 76 N.Y. 170, 173 (1879); People v. Jones, 221 Cal.App.2d 619, 34 Cal.Rptr. 618 (1963); 3 Wigmore, Evidence § 777 (Chadbourn rev. 1970); Dec.Dig. Witnesses ⇐242. This notion is included in Fed.R.Evid. 611(c) "to develop his testimony." Advisory Committee's Note. And where a hostile witness surprises the examiner by testimony contrary to his earlier statement before trial, the examiner may ask leading questions about the former statement, not to discredit but to refresh his recollection. People v. Gallery, 336 Ill. 580, 168 N.E. 650 (1929); People v. Jehl, 150 Cal.App.2d 665, 310 P.2d 495 (1957).

14. People v. Abair, 102 Cal.App.2d 765, 228 P.2d 336 (1951); Swanson v. McDonald, 58 S.D. 119, 235 N.W. 118 (1935) (citing authorities); Dec.Dig. Witnesses ⇐391.

15. 3 Wigmore, Evidence § 779 (Chadbourn rev. 1970). The practice is justified also as pinpointing the inquiry and thus avoiding the bringing out of incompetent matter which might result from general questions. Elgin, Joliet & Eastern Railway Co. v. Lawlor, 132 Ill. App. 280 (1907), affirmed 229 Ill. 621, 82 N.E. 407. It is justified under Fed.R.Evid. and Rev.Unif.R.Evid. (1974) 611(c). See n. 11 supra.

16. See Swoboda v. Union Pacific Railroad Co., 87 Neb. 200, 127 N.W. 215, 220, 221 (1910), and Norton v. Parsons, 67 Vt. 526, 32 A. 481, 482 (1895), which recognize, but deprecate, the practice.

§ 7. The Form of Questions: (c) Misleading and Argumentative Questions

The examiner may not ask a question that merely invokes the witness's assent to the questioner's inferences from or interpretations of the facts proved or assumed. This kind of question is subject to objection as "argumentative" [1] but the trial court has a wide range of discretion in enforcing the rule, particularly on cross-examination, the more frequent occasion for such questions. A still more common vice is for the examiner to couch the question so that it assumes as true matters to which the witness has not testified, and which are in dispute between the parties.[2] The danger here is two-fold. First, if the examiner is putting the question to a friendly witness, the recitation of the assumed fact may suggest the desired answer; and second, whether the witness is friendly or hostile, the answer is likely to be misleading. Oftentimes, the question will be so separate from the assumption that if the witness answers the question without men-

tioning the assumption, it is impossible to ascertain whether he ignored the assumption or affirmed it.

Occasionally questions are considered objectionable because they are too broad or too indefinite. Often this objection is in reality an objection of lack of relevancy.[3]

The principles mentioned in this section are not expressed specifically in the Federal or Revised Uniform Rules (1974), but they may be enforced by the trial court in its discretion under Rules 403 and 611(a).[4] As to Rule 403 see § 185 infra. For wording of Rule 611(a) see text supra at § 5 n. 7.

WESTLAW REFERENCES

misleading argumentative /3 question* /s witness**
broad indefinite /3 question* /s witness**

§ 8. The Judge May Examine [1] and Call [2] Witnesses

Under the Anglo-American adversary trial system, the parties and their counsel have

---

§ 7

1. Questions held argumentative: United States v. Cash, 499 F.2d 26 (9th Cir. 1974) ("As a matter of fact you drove the car that was parked outside the liquor store when he went in and stole some liquor, is not that a fact?", held argumentative but harmless error). Pettus v. Louisville & Nashville Railroad Co., 214 Ala. 187, 106 So. 807 (1926) ("If you had not been burning off the grass and weeds . . . on the right of way, it was still there?"); Johnson v. Wilmington City Railway Co., 23 Del. 5, 76 A. 961 (1905) ("Was there any other force of any kind, other than the suction created by the rapidly moving car, that would cause the rope to become entangled in the gearing?"); White v. State, 22 Okl.Cr. 131, 210 P. 313 (1922) (in mayhem prosecution, question, "Isn't it a fact that [defendant's] mouth is so small that he could not reach up and get it wide enough open to get [complainant's] ear in there?", argumentative where both mouth and ear were visible to jury); C.J.S. Witnesses § 328b(5); Goff, Argumentative Questions, 49 Calif.St.Bar J. 140 (1974).

2. Questions held objectionable: United States v. Medel, 592 F.2d 1305 (5th Cir. 1979), rehearing denied 597 F.2d 772 (question referring to specific facts not in evidence). Haithcock v. State, 23 Ala.App. 460, 126 So. 890 (1930) (questions on cross-examination of defendant's witness, as to how long defendant was making liquor); Price v. Rosenberg, 200 Mass. 36, 85 N.E. 887 (1908) (in action for price of goods, question to plaintiff as to how he knew that goods delivered were goods called for in contract, improper as assuming that the goods delivered were those called for); Reardon v. Bos-

ton Elevated Railway Co., 311 Mass. 228, 40 N.E.2d 865 (1942) (question as to how many years water used to come through walls, bad as assuming that it had come through it all in the past); Central Radiator Co. v. Niagara Fire Insurance Co., 109 N.J.L. 48, 160 A. 342 (1932) (questions as to what the custom is, without any previous testimony that any custom about the matter exists); Kirschman v. Pitt Publishing Co., 318 Pa. 570, 178 A. 828 (1935) (affirmative answer to question assuming disputed fact is no evidence of the fact assumed); Cherry v. Hill, 283 Ala. 74, 214 So.2d 427 (1968) (question as to how long witness had seen pedestrians use a roadway assumed pedestrians had been using roadway); Dec.Dig. Witnesses ☞237; 3 Wigmore, Evidence §§ 771, 780 (Chadbourn rev.1970).

But the questioner may properly assume the truth of a disputed fact previously testified to by the same witness. State v. Marshall, 105 Iowa 38, 74 N.W. 763 (1898); Graham v. McReynolds, 90 Tenn. 673, 18 S.W. 272 (1891) (question by court).

3. See for example, People v. Williams, 200 Cal. App.2d 838, 19 Cal.Rptr. 743 (1962); Dec.Dig. Witnesses ☞236.

4. See example cases cited in nn. 1 and 2, supra.

---

§ 8

1. 3 Wigmore, Evidence § 784 (Chadbourn rev.1970) 9 id. § 2484 (1981); Fed.R.Evid. and Rev.Unif.R.Evid.

---

2. See note 2 on page 15.

the primary responsibility for finding, selecting, and presenting the evidence.[3] However, our system of party-investigation and party-presentation has some limitations. It is a means to the end of disclosing truth and administering justice; and for reaching this end the judge may exercise various powers.

Prominent among these powers is his power to call and question witnesses.

Under the case law and the Federal Rules of Evidence the judge in his discretion may examine any witness to clarify testimony or to bring out needed facts which have not been elicited by the parties.[4] Also, it is sometimes said that the judge may have a duty to question witnesses, but the exercise of such a duty does not appear to have been enforced by any appellate court decisions.[5]

In those states—the great majority—in which the judge does not have power to comment on the weight of the evidence, the judge's questioning in jury cases must be cautiously guarded so as not to constitute an implied comment.[6] Thus, if the judge uses leading questions, suggesting the desired answer, the questions may strongly imply that the desired answer is the truth, and thus may offend the rule against comment.[7] Subject to the limitation that a leading question may constitute prohibited comment, it has been held that the policy against leading questions by counsel, namely, that of avoiding false testimony elicited by partisan suggestion,[8] has no application in general to judges,[9] whose office is to be impartial. This reasoning seems somewhat questiona-

(1974) 614, 706; C.J.S. Witnesses §§ 348–349; Annot., 84 A.L.R. 1172; Dec.Dig. Witnesses ☞246.

2. 9 Wigmore, Evidence § 2484 (Chadbourn rev. 1981); Fed.R.Evid. and Rev.Unif.R.Evid. (1974) 614, 706; C.J.S. Witnesses § 350; Annot., 67 A.L.R.2d 538; Annot., 95 A.L.R.2d 390; Dec.Dig. Witnesses ☞246(2).

3. The adversary system should be compared with the inquisitional system that prevails in some European countries where the judge has a wider responsibility for investigating the facts and presenting the proofs. See 9 Wigmore, Evidence § 2483 (Chadbourn rev.1981). In the adversary system, the judge cannot exclude a party from examining witnesses called by the party and proceed to conduct the direct examination himself. Dreyer v. Ershowsky, 156 App.Div. 27, 140 N.Y.S. 819 (1913).

4. State v. Kirby, 273 N.C. 306, 160 S.E.2d 24 (1968); Griffin v. United States, 83 U.S.App.D.C. 20, 164 F.2d 903 (1947); State v. Keehn, 85 Kan. 765, 118 P. 851 (1911); McLaughlin v. Municipal Court, 308 Mass. 397, 32 N.E.2d 266, 271 (1941); State v. Riley, 28 N.J. 188, 145 A.2d 601 (1958), cert. denied 359 U.S. 313; Fed.R.Evid. and Rev.Unif.R.Evid. (1974) 614(b).

Jurors, with the judge's leave, may question the witnesses. White v. Little, 131 Okl. 132, 268 P. 221 (1928); Stamp v. Commonwealth, 200 Ky. 133, 253 S.W. 242 (1923); C.J.S. Witnesses § 351; Annot., 31 A.L.R.3d 872. See O'Nellion v. Haynes, 122 Cal.App. 329, 9 P.2d 853 (1932), where a juror asked the defendant "You carry liability insurance, don't you?" and was answered, "Yes," before objection could be made. The privilege of permitting jurors to ask questions of witnesses should be granted only when in sound discretion of court it appears that it will aid a juror in understanding a material issue involved, and ordinarily when some juror has indicated that he wishes the point clarified. State v. Anderson, 108 Utah 130, 158 P.2d 127 (1945). A judge's invitation to jurors to interrogate witnesses was condemned in State v. Martinez, 7 Utah

2d 387, 326 P.2d 102 (1958). But opposing views have been taken. United States v. Callahan, 588 F.2d 1078 (5th Cir. 1979), cert. denied 444 U.S. 826 ("The proper handling of juror questions is a matter of procedure within the discretion of the trial judge.;" judge invited questions to be written down by the judge). If questions are allowed, a requirement that they be submitted to the judge in writing will facilitate consideration in the absence of the jury and avoid prejudice to an objecting party.

5. "He enjoys the prerogative, rising often to the standard of a duty, of eliciting those facts he deems necessary to the clear presentation of the issues. Pariser v. City of New York, 2 Cir., 146 F.2d 431." Clark, J., in United States v. Brandt, 196 F.2d 653, 655 (2d Cir. 1952); C.J.S. Witnesses § 348. See similar statements in federal opinions collected in Louisell & Mueller, Federal Evidence, § 365. All are dicta. Fed. R.Evid. 614(b) indicates the judge has discretion by stating the judge "may" interrogate witnesses. United States v. Trapnell, 512 F.2d 10 (9th Cir. 1975) (held that a trial judge did not have a duty to question although the defendant appeared pro se).

6. People v. De Lordo, 350 Ill. 148, 182 N.E. 726, 730, 731 (1932); Risley v. Moberg, 69 Wn.2d 560, 419 P.2d 151 (1966); Annot., 84 A.L.R. 1181.

7. People v. Bowers, 79 Cal. 415, 21 P. 752 (1889); Frangos v. Edmunds, 179 Or. 577, 173 P.2d 596 (1946); Anderson v. State, 83 Tex.Cr.R. 261, 202 S.W. 944 (1918); State v. Crotts, 22 Wash. 245, 60 P. 403 (1900).

8. See § 6 supra.

9. Commonwealth v. Galavan, 91 Mass. (9 Allen) 271 (1864); Connor v. Township of Brant, 31 Ont.L. Rep. 274 (1913). Instances wherein particular leading questions by the judge were held necessary and within his discretion: Stinson v. State, 125 Ark. 339, 189 S.W. 49 (1916) (carnal abuse, questions to victim); Driscoll v. People, 47 Mich. 413, 11 N.W. 221, 223 (1882); State v.

ble.[10] Also, questions which are aimed at discrediting or impeaching the witness, though allowable for counsel, when asked by the judge may often—not always—intimate the judge's belief that the witness has been lying, and thus be an implied comment on the weight of his testimony.[11]

In the federal courts and in the few states where the common law power to comment is retained, and in judge-tried cases in all jurisdictions, these restrictions on leading questions and impeaching questions are relaxed. Nevertheless, even then, the judge, though he has a wide power to examine witnesses, must avoid extreme exercises of the power to question, just as he must avoid extreme exercises of the power to comment. He must not assume the role of an advocate or of a prosecutor.[12] If his questions are too

partisan or even if they are too extensive, he faces the risk that the appellate court will find that he has crossed the line between judging and advocacy.[13] However, the mere number of questions put by the judge should not be a crucial factor. The nature of the questions is the most important matter.[14]

Not only may the judge examine witnesses called by the parties,[15] but in his discretion he may also, for the purpose of bringing out needed facts, call witnesses whom the parties might not have chosen to call.[16] The power to call witnesses has perhaps most often been exercised when the prosecution expects that a necessary witness will be hostile and desires to escape the necessity of calling him and being cumbered by the traditional rule against impeaching one's own witness. Under the Federal Rules of Evidence, although a party may impeach the

---

Riley, 28 N.J. 188, 145 A.2d 601 (1958), cert. denied 359 U.S. 313.

10. See remark in Commonwealth v. Berklowitz, 133 Pa.Super. 190, 2 A.2d 516 (1938).

11. State v. Drew, 213 S.W. 106 (Mo.1919) (questions indicating a purpose to discredit defendant and one of his witnesses). But it seems that not all questions bearing on credibility would show an adverse opinion, even though the answer might happen to be discrediting. Thus, neutral questions about knowledge or interest seemingly might be needed and desirable. See Madison v. State, 200 Md. 1, 87 A.2d 593 (1958) (murder; judge's questioning of accused held not erroneous: "A judge's right to ask questions is not confined to questions which have no possible bearing on credibility."). Accordingly, the view of the court in State v. Perry, 231 N.C. 467, 57 S.E.2d 774 (1950), that "it is improper for a trial judge to ask questions for the purpose of impeaching" may need qualification.

12. United States v. Lee, 107 F.2d 522, 529 (7th Cir. 1939); United States v. Welliver, 601 F.2d 203 (5th Cir. 1979); State v. Winchester, 166 Kan. 512, 203 P.2d 229, 233 (1949).

13. See United States v. Brandt, 196 F.2d 653 (2d Cir. 1952) (conviction set aside where judge asked more than 900 questions during eight-day trial and cross-examined accused and defense witnesses with apparent purpose of emphasizing inconsistencies in defense and discrediting defense witnesses; instructive opinion by Clark, J.); United States v. Fry, 304 F.2d 296 (7th Cir. 1962) (1,210 questions by judge); United States v. Hill, 332 F.2d 105 (7th Cir. 1964) (implication of incredulity by course of questioning); Taylor v. Taylor, 177 Minn. 428, 225 N.W. 287 (1929) (in judge-tried case judge by questioning took charge of party's case and became a partisan, but judgment not reversed).

14. Moore v. United States, 598 F.2d 439 (5th Cir. 1979) (the judge asked 105 questions compared to 41 by

defense counsel and 66 by the prosecutor, but the questions of the judge were "unbiased, patient, temperate, never argumentative or accusatory"). See discussion of pertinent factors concerning the nature of questions in Weinstein & Berger, Evidence ¶ 614[03], where it is also indicated that in the federal courts reversals for interrogation by the trial judge are rare. The use of leading questions may be a factor in ascertaining the existence of other pertinent factors in the judge's questioning which leads to reversal. Pollard v. Fennell, 400 F.2d 421 (4th Cir. 1968).

15. The previously-stated conditions apply.

16. Marin Water & Power Co. v. Railroad Commission, 171 Cal. 706, 154 P. 864, 867 (1916) (commission as a judicial tribunal may call witnesses); Merchants Bank v. Goodfellow, 44 Utah 349, 140 P. 759 (1914) (suit on bill of exchange, court called last endorser). See Annot., 67 A.L.R.2d 538; Annot., 95 A.L.R.2d 390; 51 Nw.U.L.Rev. 761 (1957); Fed.R.Evid. and Rev.Unif. R.Evid. (1974) 614(a), 706(a).

There has been a suggestion that in some cases, in the interest of justice, the judge may have the duty as well as the power to call witnesses and hence may be reversed for a failure to do so. See Moore v. Sykes' Estate, 167 Miss. 212, 149 So. 789 (1933); Frankfurter, J., dissenting, in Johnson v. United States, 333 U.S. 46, 55 (1948); 58 Yale L.J. 183 (1948). But efforts at reversal on this ground have been unavailing, e.g., Steinberg v. United States, 162 F.2d 120 (5th Cir. 1947); United States v. Lester, 248 F.2d 329 (2d Cir. 1957); State v. Hines, 270 Minn. 30, 133 N.W.2d 371 (1964); Halloran-Judge Trust Co. v. Carr, 62 Utah 10, 218 P. 138 (1923). And Wigmore denies the existence of a duty. 9 Wigmore, Evidence § 2484 (Chadbourn rev.1981). Fed.R.Evid. 614(a) states that the judge *may* call witnesses [emphasis added].

party's own witness, the prosecutor may not wish to call a witness and thereby be identified with the witness. The prosecutor may then invoke the judge's discretion to call the witness,[17] in which event either party may cross-examine and impeach him. Another use of the power, implemented by statute in some jurisdictions, is to mediate the battle of partisan expert witnesses employed by the parties, through the judge's resumption of his ancient power to call an expert of his own choosing, or one agreed upon by the parties, to give impartial testimony to aid him or the jury in resolving a scientific issue.[18] But the judge's power of calling witnesses in aid of justice is general and is not necessarily limited to meeting these particular needs.[19]

WESTLAW REFERENCES

410k246 /p judge* /3 examin! call*** question! interrogat! /3 witness**

---

17. See, e.g., Young v. United States, 107 F.2d 490 (5th Cir. 1939) (sole surviving eyewitness of homicide who had made inconsistent statements to prosecution); People v. Shelton, 388 Ill. 56, 57 N.E.2d 473 (1944) (rape of girl under age, court called joint indictee for whose integrity prosecution could not vouch); 3A Wigmore, Evidence § 918 (Chadbourn rev.1970); but the judge's discretion was limited to prosecution witnesses whose testimony relates directly to the issues upon a showing that the state was unable to vouch for credibility in People v. Moriarity, 33 Ill.2d 606, 213 N.E.2d 516 (1966).

Under Fed.R.Evid. 614(a), the matter is largely in the court's discretion. See United States v. Leslie, 542 F.2d 285 (5th Cir. 1976) (court approved the calling of three material witnesses by the trial court on government requests which were made on the ground that the witnesses were adverse and hostile and that prosecutor did not wish to adopt their testimony, even though he could use leading questions and impeach them if he called them. The appellate court also observed that the trial court "could properly protect the prosecution from whatever tendency the jury might have had to associate the witness with the calling party", citing Fed. R.Evid. 614). Compare United States v. Karnes, 531 F.2d 214 (4th Cir. 1976) (held error for court to call two witnesses when prosecutor would not call them and conceded he had no case without them). Calling witnesses at the request of the defense counsel has been assumed also to be in the discretion of the court. United States v. Herring, 602 F.2d 1220 (5th Cir. 1979), cert. denied 444 U.S. 1046.

In civil cases, the calling of witnesses by the judge for this purpose is said to be in his discretion. McBride v. Dexter, 250 Iowa 7, 92 N.W.2d 443 (1958); Fed.R.

§ 9. Refreshing Recollection:[1] Hypnosis

It is abundantly clear from everyday observation that the latent memory of an experience may be revived by an image seen, or a statement read or heard. This is a part of the group of phenomena which the classical psychologists have called the law of association. The recall of any part of a past experience tends to bring with it the other parts that were in the same field of awareness, and a new experience tends to stimulate the recall of other like experiences.[2] The effect of a reminder, encountered in reading a newspaper or in the conversation of a friend, which gives us the sensation of recognizing as familiar some happening which we had forgotten, and prompts our memory to bring back associated experiences, is a frequently encountered process.[3]

Evid. 614(a). But the case authority in civil cases is relatively sparse.

18. See, e.g., Citizens State Bank v. Castro, 105 Cal. App. 284, 287 P. 559 (1930) (handwriting expert, pursuant to statute); Polulich v. J.G. Schmidt Tool, etc. Co., 46 N.J.Super. 135, 134 A.2d 29 (1957) (workmen's compensation: deputy having power of judge may call impartial expert: extensive discussion); State v. Horne, 171 N.C. 787, 88 S.E. 433 (1916) (alienist in murder case: "expert witnesses . . . were originally regarded as amici curiae and were called generally by the court," citing 3 Chamberlayne, Evidence, §§ 2376, 2552); Scott v. Spanjer Brothers, 298 F.2d 928 (2d Cir. 1962); Annot., 95 A.L.R.2d 390; Fed.R.Evid. and Rev. Unif.R.Evid. (1974) 706.

See discussion in § 17 infra.

19. If there is no statutory or court rule authority, there may be practical problems concerning costs and pretrial services of the expert.

§ 9

1. 3 Wigmore, Evidence §§ 758–765 (Chadbourn rev. 1970); Maguire & Quick, Testimony, Memory and Memoranda, 3 How.L.J. 1 (1957); Fed.R.Evid. and Rev. Unif.R.Evid. (1974) 612; Weinstein & Berger, Evidence, ¶¶ 612[01]–[07]; Dec.Dig. Witnesses ⟨⟩253–260; Annots., 125 A.L.R. 19, 82 A.L.R.2d 473; Note, 3 U.C. L.A.L.Rev. 616 (1956); C.J.S. Witnesses § 357.

2. These are the principles of contiguity and similarity. See Gardner, The Perception and Memory of Witnesses, 18 Corn.L.Q. 390, 392 (1933); Hutchins &

---

3. See note 3 on page 18.

As we have seen,[4] the interviewing of witnesses by counsel who will examine them in court is a necessary step in preparing for trial. It is at this stage that the memory of the witness can best be refreshed about the facts of the case, by giving him the opportunity to read his own written statements previously made, or the letters, maps, or other documents in the case. It is only when this review of the data is insufficient to enable the witness to recall the facts while testifying that refreshing his memory on the stand is advisable. If it is matter which a jury would suppose he should remember unaided, the use of a crutch lessens their confidence in the testimony.

At trials, the practice has long been established that in interrogating a witness counsel may hand him a memorandum to inspect for the purpose of "refreshing his recollection," with the result that when he speaks from a memory thus revived, his testimony is what he says, not the writing.[5] This is the process of *refreshing recollection at the trial* in the strict and accurate sense.

But when this simple but helpful expedient had become established, it was natural for counsel to seek to carry it a step further. If the witness, being shown the writing, states that his memory is not revived thereby and that he cannot testify from a refreshed recollection, he may indicate on looking at the writing, that he recognizes it as a memorandum made by him when the facts were fresh in his mind, and *therefore*, though he has no present memory of the

transaction described, he is willing to testify that the facts were correctly recited in the memorandum. Thus the writing itself becomes the evidence. We now recognize this latter situation as quite a different process from the process of *refreshing recollection*. In the process of refreshing recollection, the witness testifies orally on his present refreshed memory; when his memory is not jogged, he merely relies upon his written recital of things remembered in the past as a basis for introducing the writing.[6]

The procedure of tendering a memorandum to the witness is followed in both cases but the underlying justification in the newer situation is quite different. It rests on the reliability of a writing which the witness swears is a *record of his past recollection*, and the writing is introduced into evidence. Appropriate safeguarding rules have been developed for this latter kind of memoranda, requiring that they must have been written by the witness or examined and found correct by him, and that they must have been prepared so promptly after the events recorded that the events must have been fresh in the mind of the witness when the record was made or examined and verified by him. In this volume these latter memoranda are considered separately, as a possible exception to the hearsay rule.[7]

Apparently, the earlier English cases of genuine refreshment of recollection imposed no restriction upon *the use of memoranda at the trial to refresh*.[8] The memoranda were not required to have been written by

Slesinger, Some Observations on the Law of Evidence—Memory, 41 Harv.L.Rev. 860 (1928); 2 Encyc. Brit. Association, Mental (1967), 15 id. Memory (1967).

3. "In permitting a witness to refresh his recollection by consulting a memorandum, the courts are in accord with present psychological knowledge. A distinction is drawn, in the analysis of the memory process, between *recall*, which is the reproduction of what has been learned, and *recognition*, which is recall with a time-factor added, or an awareness that the recall relates to past experience. It is with recognition that the law is principally concerned in permitting a witness to revive his recollection. The psychological evidence is clear that in thus allowing to be brought to mind what has been forgotten, the law is following sound psycho-

logical procedure." Cairn, Law and the Social Sciences 200 (1935).

4. See § 2 supra.

5. Henry v. Lee, 2 Chitty 124 (1810), cited 3 Wigmore, Evidence § 758 (Chadbourn rev. 1970).

6. See Jewett v. United States, 15 F.2d 955, 956 (9th Cir. 1926), and extended explanation in United States v. Riccardi, 174 F.2d 883 (3d Cir. 1949), cert. denied 337 U.S. 941.

7. See Ch. 30 infra. But if the memorandum was prepared by the witness it may be admissible as a nonhearsay statement. See § 251 infra.

8. Henry v. Lee, supra n. 5; Rex v. St. Martin's, 2 Ad. & El. 210, 111 Eng.Rep. 81 (K.B.1834).

the witness or under his direction, or to have been made near in time to the event. In the later-developed practice of introducing records of *past recollection*, restrictions of this kind were imposed with good reason. Since, however, the old name of "refreshing recollection" was given to both practices, it was natural that the restrictions developed for one kind of memoranda should be applied to the other.

Which is the wiser practice, the rule of the older cases, championed by Wigmore and by most present-day courts, to the effect that any memorandum, without restriction of authorship, time, or correctness, may be used when the purpose is to revive memory; or the rule requiring that the memorandum to refresh must meet the same tests as the record of past recollection? Even if the latter requirement is an historical or analytical blunder, it will be none the worse for that if it is a safeguard needed in the search for truth.

It is true that any kind of stimulus, "a song, or a face, or a newspaper item," [9] may produce the "flash" of recognition, the feeling that "it all comes back to me now." But

the genuineness of the feeling is no guaranty of the correctness of the image recalled. The danger that the mind will "remember" something that never happened is at least as great here as in the case of leading questions.[10] "Imagination and suggestion are twin artists ever ready to retouch the fading daguerrotype of memory." [11]

Thus, decisions which import into the realm of refreshing memory at the trial the requirements developed for memoranda of past recollection recorded, namely, the requirements that the witness must have made the writing or have recognized it as correct, and that the making or recognition must have occurred at the time of the event or while it was fresh in memory, [12] have a plausible basis in expediency.

Nevertheless, most courts today when faced with the clear distinction between the two uses of the memoranda, will adhere to the "classical" view that any memorandum or other object may be used as a stimulus to present memory, without restriction by rule as to authorship, guaranty of correctness, or time of making.[13] On balance, it would seem that this liberality of practice is the

---

9. See Jewett v. United States, supra, n. 6.

10. Hutchins and Slesinger, Some Observations on the Law of Evidence—Memory, 41 Harv.L.Rev. 860, 868, 869 (1928). See also the telling passage quoted from Bentham, 3 Wigmore, Evidence § 758 (Chadbourn rev. 1970).

11. Gardner, The Perception and Memory of Witnesses, 18 Corn.L.Q. 390, 401 (1933).

12. See, e.g., Putnam v. United States, 162 U.S. 687, 695 (1896) (transcript of prior testimony by witness not allowed to be used to refresh, because not contemporaneous with events testified about); State v. Patton, 255 Mo. 245, 164 S.W. 223 (1914) (similar to last; "the ease with which, as Prof. Muensterberg tells us, the human mind is influenced by suggestion would seem to form an insuperable psychological objection to the use of data for this purpose, of the correctness of which the witness is ignorant"); NLRB v. Hudson Pulp and Paper Corp., 273 F.2d 660 (5th Cir. 1960) (affidavit used was too remote in time; alternate ground of decision).

These requirements would create special difficulties in respect to the use of a transcript of the witness's own prior testimony. Hale, The Use by a Witness of His Own Prior Testimony for the Purpose of Refreshing His Recollection, 15 St. Louis L.Rev. 137, 146 (1930). However, most cases involving transcripts have not imposed the requirements. Annot., 82

A.L.R.2d 473, 597–602. See Ch. 25 infra, for introduction of the prior testimony itself into evidence.

13. For rule that witness need not have made the memorandum, see Henowitz v. Rockville Savings Bank, 118 Conn. 527, 173 A. 221, 222 (1934) (photograph of stairway excluded from evidence because not fairly representative, allowed to be used to refresh); People v. Griswold, 405 Ill. 533, 92 N.E.2d 91 (1950) (memorandum of conversation not made by witness); Commonwealth v. McDermott, 255 Mass. 575, 152 N.E. 704 (1926) (any paper though not made by witness); State v. Hale, 85 N.H. 403, 160 A. 95 (1932); Copeland Co. v. Davis, 125 S.C. 449, 119 S.E. 19 (1923); 3 Wigmore, Evidence § 759 (Chadbourn rev. 1970); Annot. 82 A.L.R.2d 473. Compare People v. Betts, 272 App.Div. 737, 74 N.Y.S.2d 791 (1947), 23 N.Y.U.L.Q. 529, 34 Va. L.Rev. 607. There the court held that a policeman who had destroyed the notes taken by him during a conversation with accused, and also his transcript from those notes, to avoid their use on cross-examination, was improperly allowed to refresh his memory from another version of his transcript embodied in the complaint. Also, compare Gardner v. Hobbs, 69 Idaho 288, 206 P.2d 539 (1949); State v. Peacock, 236 N.C. 137, 72 S.E.2d 612 (1952).

That a memorandum need not be made at or near the time of the event recorded, see Commonwealth v. McDermott, 255 Mass. 575, 152 N.E. 704 (1926); Sagers v.

wiser solution because there are other sufficient safeguards to protect against abuse. The first safeguard is the power of control by the trial judge. It is a preliminary question for his decision whether the memorandum actually does refresh, and from the nature of the memorandum and the witness's testimony he may find that it does not.[14] Moreover, in the exercise of his discretion to control the manner of the examination,[15] as in the case of leading questions, he may decline to permit the use of the aid to memory where he regards the danger of undue suggestion as outweighing the probable value.

The second safeguard is the rule which entitles the adverse party, when the witness seeks to resort to the memorandum, to inspect the memorandum so that he may object to its use if ground appears,[16] and to have the memorandum available for his reference in cross-examining the witness.[17] With the memorandum before him, the cross-examiner has a good opportunity to test the credibility of the witness's claim that his memory has been revived, and to search out any discrepancies between the writing and the testimony. This right to demand inspection has in the past usually been limited to writings used by the witness on the stand,[18] but the reasons seem in general equally applicable to writings used by the witness to refresh his memory before he tes-

---

International Smelting Co., 50 Utah 423, 168 P. 105 (1917); Smith v. Bergmann, 377 S.W.2d 519 (Mo.App. 1964) (memorandum prepared by witness the night before testifying).

That a witness need not vouch for the correctness of the memorandum is indicated by Williams v. Stroh Plumbing & Electric Inc., 250 Iowa 599, 94 N.W.2d 750 (1959); United States v. McKeever, 169 F.Supp. 426 (D.C.N.Y.1958). But some opinions contain a contrary implication. See, e.g., Tebeau v. Baden Equipment & Construction Co., 295 S.W.2d 184 (Mo.App.1956).

Fed.R.Evid. and Rev.Unif.R.Evid. (1974) 612 adopt the view stated in the text, although not by direct statement. See, e.g., United States v. Landof, 591 F.2d 36 (9th Cir. 1978) ("But, the law is clear that recollection can be refreshed from documents made by persons other than the witness.").

14. The statement of the witness is not conclusive when the circumstances show that his memory is in fact not revived. Weigel v. Powers Elevator Co., 49 N.D. 867, 194 N.W. 113, 120 (1923). Compare United States v. Riccardi, 174 F.2d 883 (3d Cir. 1949), in which it was held that the memory of witnesses who testified while consulting a lengthy list of articles was actually refreshed.

15. The element of discretion is recognized in United States v. Lonardo, 67 F.2d 883 (3d Cir. 1933); United States v. Boyd, 606 F.2d 792 (8th Cir. 1979) (the propriety of permitting use of a writing prepared by another); State v. Bradley, 361 Mo. 267, 234 S.W.2d 556 (1950); Myers v. Weger, 62 N.J.L. 432, 42 A. 280, 283 (1899); Dec.Dig. Witnesses ⟨key⟩255; C.J.S. Witnesses § 358; Under particular circumstances there could be clear abuse of discretion. United States v. Shoupe, 548 F.2d 636 (6th Cir. 1977).

16. Morris v. United States, 149 F. 123 (5th Cir. 1907); Shell Oil Co. v. Pou, 204 So.2d 155 (Miss.1967). See also State v. Gadwood, 342 Mo. 466, 116 S.W.2d 42, 51 (1938) (in trial judge's discretion whether inspection postponed to time of cross-examination); State v. Bean, 119 Vt. 184, 122 A.2d 744 (1956) (cites and applies State v. Gadwood).

Fed.R.Evid. 612 provides:

Except as otherwise provided in criminal proceedings by section 3500 of title 18, United States Code, if a witness uses a writing to refresh his memory for the purpose of testifying, either—

(1) while testifying, or

(2) before testifying, if the court in its discretion determines it is necessary in the interests of justice,

an adverse party is entitled to have the writing produced at the hearing, to inspect it, to cross-examine the witness thereon, and to introduce in evidence those portions which relate to the testimony of the witness. If it is claimed that the writing contains matters not related to the subject matter of the testimony the court shall examine the writing in camera, excise any portions not so related, and order delivery of the remainder to the party entitled thereto. Any portion withheld over objections shall be preserved and made available to the appellate court in the event of an appeal. If a writing is not produced or delivered pursuant to order under this rule, the court shall make any order justice requires, except that in criminal cases when the prosecution elects not to comply, the order shall be one striking the testimony or, if the court in its discretion determines that the interests of justice so require, declaring a mistrial.

Revised Uniform Rule (1974) 612 is to the same effect but with the two numbered subdivisions rearranged to avoid the possibility that a typesetter by running both together may expand the scope of the judge's discretion to apply to both.

---

17. Little v. United States, 93 F.2d 401 (8th Cir. 1937); People v. Gezzo, 307 N.Y. 385, 121 N.E.2d 380 (1954) (prejudicial error to refuse inspection); State v. Carter, 268 N.C. 648, 151 S.E.2d 602 (1966); Green v. State, 53 Tex.Cr.R. 490, 110 S.W. 920 (1908); Dec.Dig.

18. See note 18 on page 21.

tifies. The subject of inspection and use of writings to which the witness has referred prior to testifying at the trial is discussed at the end of the instant section.

Not only may the adversary inspect the memoranda used to refresh memory during the examination of a witness, but he may submit them to the jury for their examination.[19] On the other hand, the party offering the witness may not do so unless the memoranda constitute independent evidence and are not barred by the hearsay rule.[20] The cardinal rule is that unless they may be introduced under the hearsay rule or one of its exceptions, they are not evidence, but only aids in the giving of evidence. Consequently, a copy may be used without accounting for the original.[21]

The line between using the writing as an aid to memory and basing one's testimony upon it as a correct record of past memory is sometimes shadowy. Must it be shown that the witness has no present recollection of the matters embodied in the memorandum before he can use it as an aid to memory? It is sometimes said, even as a matter of case law under the Federal Rules of Evidence, that this must appear,[22] but it is be-

lieved that the requirement is unsound. The witness may believe that he remembers completely but on looking at the memorandum he would be caused to recall additional facts. As the Chinese proverb has it, "The palest ink is clearer than the best memory." On the other hand, there is here the ever-present danger that a suggestible witness may think that he remembers a fact because he reads it. It seems eminently a matter for discretion, rather than rule. Similarly, it would seem that a witness may recognize from present memory the correctness of successive facts set out in a memorandum, but that he may be unable, despite this recognition, to detail those facts from memory without continuing to consult the writing. Accordingly, the statement that a witness once refreshed must speak independently of the writing[23] seems too inflexible, and it is believed that the matter is discretionary and that the trial judge may properly permit the witness to consult the memorandum as he speaks, especially where it is so lengthy and detailed that even a fresh memory would be unable to recite all the items unaided.[24]

As mentioned previously in the instant section, various cases have refused to en-

Witnesses ⚬256; Annot., 125 A.L.R. 194; Annot., 82 A.L.R.2d 473, 557–562; 3 Wigmore, Evidence § 762 (Chadbourn rev. 1970).

See Rule 612, supra n. 16.

18. Star Manufacturing Co. v. Atlantic Coast Line Railroad Co., 222 N.C. 330, 23 S.E.2d 32 (1942) Annot., 125 A.L.R. 200; Annot., 82 A.L.R.2d 473, 562–569; C.J.S. Witnesses § 362.

19. See Annot., 125 A.L.R. 78. When so submitted by the adversary it would seem that he may place it in evidence, to let the jury compare it with the testimony. Riley v. Fletcher, 185 Ala. 570, 64 So. 85, 87 (1913); Annot., 82 A.L.R.2d 473, 518, 519; West's Ann.Cal.Evid. Code § 771; Fed.R.Evid. 612, supra n. 16. But see, contra, Jurgiewicz v. Adams, 71 R.I. 239, 43 A.2d 310 (1945).

20. Shear v. Rogoff, 288 Mass. 357, 193 N.E. 63 (1934); Miller v. Borough of Exeter, 366 Pa. 336, 77 A.2d 395 (1951); Dec.Dig. Witnesses ⚬257; Annot., 125 A.L.R. 65; Annot., 82 A.L.R.2d 473, 517, 518. The text is a proper interpretation of Fed.R.Evid. 612. See Weinstein & Berger, Evidence, ¶ 612[05].

21. Atlanta, & St. Andrews Bay Railway Co. v. Ewing, 112 Fla. 483, 150 So. 586 (1933); Commonwealth v. Levine, 280 Mass. 83, 181 N.E. 851 (1932); Dec.Dig. Witnesses ⚬255(5); Annot., 125 A.L.R. 50; Annot., 82

A.L.R.2d 473, 505, 506. The statement applies to Fed. R.Evid. 612. Weinstein & Berger, Evidence ¶ 612[01].

22. People v. Kraus, 377 Ill. 539, 37 N.E.2d 182 (1941); Battle Creek Food Co. v. Kirkland, 298 Mich. 515, 299 N.W. 167 (1941) (dictum); United States v. Morlang, 531 F.2d 183 (4th Cir. 1975) (case not decided under Fed.R.Evid.); Louisell & Mueller, Federal Evidence § 348; Dec.Dig. Witnesses ⚬254; C.J.S. Witnesses § 358; Annot., 125 A.L.R. 27; Annot., 82 A.L.R.2d 473.

In United States v. Jimenez, 613 F.2d 1373 (5th Cir. 1980) the court stated, referring to Fed.R.Evid. 612, that there would not need to be a showing of need for use of material that is covered by the so-called Jencks Act, 18 U.S.C.A. § 3500. But see discussion at n. 31, infra.

23. Roll v. Dockery, 219 Ala. 374, 122 So. 630 (1929) (dictum); C.J.S. Witnesses § 358.

24. United States v. Riccardi, 174 F.2d 883 (3d Cir. 1949) (list of articles); Ward v. Morr Transfer & Storage Co., 19 Mo.App. 83, 95 S.W. 964 (1906) (itemized list of goods lost); World Fire & Marine Insurance Co. v. Edmondson, 244 Ala. 224, 12 So.2d 754 (1924) (similar); People v. Allen, 47 Cal.App.2d 735, 118 P.2d 927 (1941) (aged witness' prior testimony read to her and she assented to its correctness).

force a demand for production at trial of matter reviewed by a witness to refresh memory prior to testifying.[25] However, there have been some decisions to the contrary.[26] The most important factor in this trend has been the adoption of Federal Rule of Evidence 612 with the provision that if a witness uses a writing to refresh his memory for the purpose of testifying, before testifying, an adverse party is entitled to have the writing produced at the hearing, to inspect it, to cross-examine the witness thereon, and to introduce into evidence those portions which relate to the testimony of the witness, although only if the court in its discretion determines such production is necessary in the interests of justice.[27]

A writing consulted to refresh memory may be a privileged one, e.g. a letter written by the client-witness to his attorney giving details of the case. In this event, the possibility of conflict arises between the disclosure requirement and the rule that confidential communications between attorney and client are privileged against disclosure. Should the act of consulting the writing be given the effect of a waiver of the privilege? Spelling out a waiver when the writing is consulted by the witness while testifying appears to present no problem; for a witness in effect to say that he can consult the writing while testifying in open court but refuse to allow the opposing party or his counsel to see what the writing is, would so undermine

credibility that the claim seems simply not to be made. In fact, usual practice is for examining counsel to establish the bona fides of what is going on by having the witness explain the nature of the document being consulted, and tendering it to opposing counsel. The problem area is when the writing is consulted in advance of trial as an aspect of preparation and in addition is privileged. Ordinarily the privilege involved will be either attorney-client [28] or the qualified privilege for "work product",[29] and the problem of waiver is discussed further in connection with those privileges.[30]

A further matter which must be considered in connection with Federal Rule of Evidence 612 is the relationship between that rule and Rule 26.2 of the Federal Rules of Criminal Procedure, which is the replacement for the so-called Jencks Act, 18 U.S.C.A. § 3500. It is discussed in a later section.[31]

The use of hypnosis as a technique for refreshing the recollection of witnesses is treated in the chapter on scientific and experimental evidence.[32]

 **WESTLAW REFERENCES**

refresh! /3 recollection memory /s writing* memorand!

refresh! /3 recollection memory /s newspaper* & court(md)

refresh! /3 recollection memory /s newspaper* & court(il)

record** /3 recollection

rule fed.r.evid! /3 612 & refresh! /3 recollection

But the witness must indicate that he is refreshed. Wolf v. Mallinckrodt Chemical Works, 336 Mo. 746, 81 S.W.2d 323 (1935); Freeland v. Peltier, 44 S.W.2d 404 (Tex.Civ.App.1931); Weinstein & Berger, Evidence ¶ 612[01]. And he cannot be allowed to read the writing in the guise of refreshment, as a cloak for getting in evidence an inadmissible document. Freeland v. Peltier, supra; S. W. Bridges & Co. v. Candland, 88 Utah 373, 54 P.2d 842, 846, 847 (1936). Of course when the writing is otherwise admissible as evidence in the case, it may be introduced and read by the witness. See Guiffre v. Carapezza, 298 Mass. 458, 11 N.E.2d 433 (1937).

25. See text at n. 18 supra. The text at nn. 16–19 supra is also applicable.

26. Early cases are primarily criminal cases. The Alpha, 44 F.Supp. 809, 815 (E.D.Pa.1942) (not a criminal case); State v. Deslovers, 40 R.I. 89, 100 A. 64, 69 (1917). If the memorandum is not in court or immedi-

ately available, the court should have a discretion whether to require its production. Commonwealth v. Lannan, 95 Mass. (13 Allen) 563, 569 (1866).

More recent cases usually involve a demand by defendant in a criminal case to examine documents used by government witnesses to refresh their memories. State v. Mucci, 25 N.J. 423, 136 A.2d 761 (1957) (noteworthy opinion by Heher, J.); People v. Scott, 29 Ill.2d 97, 193 N.E.2d 814 (1963); State v. Bradshaw, 101 R.I. 233, 221 A.2d 815 (1966).

27. For text of Fed.R.Evid. 612, see n. 16 supra.

28. See generally Ch. 10 infra.

29. See § 96 infra.

30. See § 93 infra.

31. § 97 infra.

32. § 206 infra at nn. 62–84.

Chapter 3

THE REQUIREMENT OF FIRSTHAND KNOWLEDGE: THE OPINION RULE: EXPERT TESTIMONY

Table of Sections

---

§ 10. The Requirement of Knowledge from Observation [1]

The common law system of proof is exacting in its insistence upon the most reliable sources of information. This policy is apparent in the Opinion rule, the Hearsay rule and the Documentary Originals rule. One of the earliest and most pervasive manifestations of this attitude is the rule requiring that a witness who testifies to a fact which can be perceived by the senses must have had an opportunity to observe, and must have actually observed the fact.[2] The same requirement, in general, is imposed upon declarations coming in under exceptions to the hearsay rule, that is, the declarant must so far as appears have had an opportunity to observe the fact declared.[3]

This requirement may easily be confused with the hearsay rule which bars the repeti-

§ 10

1. 2 Wigmore, Evidence §§ 650–670 (Chadbourn rev. 1979); Weinstein & Berger, Evidence ¶¶ 602, 701–706. C.J.S. Witnesses § 52; 81 Am.Jur.2d Witnesses §§ 75, 76; Dec.Dig. Witnesses ⚖37.

2. State v. Dixon, 420 S.W.2d 267 (Mo.1967); State v. Johnson, 92 Idaho 533, 447 P.2d 10 (1968).

Fed.R.Evid. and Rev.Unif.R.Evid. (1974) 602 provide: "A witness may not testify to a matter unless evidence is introduced sufficient to support a finding that he has personal knowledge of the matter. Evidence to prove personal knowledge may, but need not, consist of the testimony of the witness himself. This rule is subject to the provisions of Rule 703, relating to opinion testimony by expert witnesses."

3. 2 Wigmore, Evidence (Chadbourn rev. 1979) § 670; Adv.Com. Note, Fed.R.Evid. 803; and see the discussion herein of the various exceptions. There are some instances, however, in which the requirement is not applied, e.g., admissions of a party-opponent, see § 263 infra. And where reputation is used as hearsay evidence of a fact (see § 324), while the witness who testifies to the reputation must know the reputation, the community-talk itself need not be shown to be based on knowledge, though the reputation is limited to that in the locality where people would presumably know the reputed fact.

23

tion of out-of-court statements described as hearsay under that rule.[4] Technically, if the testimony of the witness on its face and in form purports to be testimony of observed facts, but the testimony is actually repetition of statements of others, the objection is that the witness lacks firsthand knowledge. If the form of the testimony indicates the witness is repeating out-of-court statements, the hearsay objection possibility is raised.[5] Often courts have disregarded this distinction.[6]

The burden of laying a foundation by showing that the witness had an adequate opportunity to observe is upon the party offering the testimony.[7] By failing to object the adversary waives the preliminary proof, but not the substance of the requirement, so that if it later appears that the witness lack-

ed opportunity, or did not actually observe the fact, his testimony will be stricken.[8] If under the circumstances proved, reasonable men could differ as to whether the witness did or did not have adequate opportunity to observe, then the testimony of the witness should come in, and the jury will appraise his opportunity to know in evaluating the testimony.[9]

In laying this foundation of knowledge, it is allowable for the examiner to elicit from the witness the particular circumstances which led him to notice or observe or remember the fact.[10]

While the law is exacting in demanding firsthand observation, it is not so impractical as to insist upon preciseness of attention by the witness in observing, or certainty of rec-

4. See § 247 infra.

5. Thus, the Advisory Committee's Note to Fed.R. Evid. 602 (see n. 2, supra) states, "This rule does not govern the situation of a witness who testifies to a hearsay statement as such, if he has personal knowledge of the making of the statement. Rules 801 to 805 would be applicable. This rule would, however, prevent him from testifying to the subject matter of the hearsay statement, as he has no personal knowledge of it."

See Fox v. Allstate Insurance Co., 22 Utah 2d 383, 453 P.2d 701 (1969) (court states counsel's hearsay objection should have been objection based upon lack of knowledge); Elizarraras v. Bank of El Paso, 631 F.2d 366 (5th Cir. 1980) (similar situation).

6. Citizens' Bank & Trust Co. v. Rudebeck, 90 Wash. 612, 156 P. 831 (1916). See United States v. Stout, 599 F.2d 866 (8th Cir. 1979), cert. denied 444 U.S. 877 (court upheld admission of testimony that was objected to as hearsay but a proper objection was arguably lack of personal knowledge).

7. State v. Prescott, 70 R.I. 403, 40 A.2d 721 (1944) (no error to exclude evidence where foundation not laid). This principle is adopted by Fed.R.Evid. and Rev.Unif.R.Evid. (1974) 602. See n. 2 supra. But the judge has discretion to admit the evidence, deferring the proof of knowledge to a later stage. Sofas v. McKee, 100 Conn. 541, 124 A. 380 (1924).

8. City National Bank v. Nelson, 218 Ala. 90, 117 So. 681, 61 A.L.R. 938, 944 (1928); State v. Dixon, supra, note 2; Jamestown Plumbing & Heating Co. v. City of Jamestown, 164 N.W.2d 355 (N.D.1969) (illustrates procedure). But it has been held that if there is no objection to the testimony of the witness on direct examination and no effort to show lack of knowledge in cross-examination, the presumption in the absence of anything to the contrary is that the witness is testifying of his own knowledge. Canal Insurance Co. v.

Winge Brothers, 97 Ga.App. 782, 104 S.E.2d 525 (1958). These concepts are consistent with, and should be followed under, Fed.R.Evid. and Rev.Unif.R.Evid. (1974) 602.

Although Fed.R.Evid. and Rev.Unif.R.Evid. (1974) 104(c) provide for a hearing on "preliminary matters" out of the hearing of the jury "when the interests of justice require", such hearings will often be unnecessary in applying Rule 602.

9. Senecal v. Drollette, 304 N.Y. 446, 108 N.E.2d 602 (1952) (error to exclude testimony of 12-year-old boys as to speed and make of automobile, based on brief glance). Many decisions apparently assume the principle stated in the text without discussion.

The text applies under Fed.R.Evid. 104(b), 602. Fed. R.Evid. 602, Advisory Committee's Note ("It will be observed that the rule is in fact a specialized application of the provisions of Rule 104(b) on conditional relevancy"). See also § 53 infra, for discussion related to Fed. R.Evid. 104(b).

10. Cole v. Lake Shore & Michigan Southern Railway Co., 105 Mich. 549, 63 N.W. 647 (1895) (witness could say that he remembered that the wind was so high because "we spoke about it"); Brown v. Chicago, Burlington & Quincy Railroad Co., 88 Neb. 604, 130 N.W. 265 (1911) (witness may state that his attention was called to approaching vehicle by remark of his little boy); People v. Neely, 163 Cal.App.2d 289, 329 P.2d 357 (1958) (witness may state reason he had occasion to recall a particular time, but erroneous exclusion cured by cross-examination).

The text is implied under Fed.R.Evid. 602. The Advisory Committee's Note for 602 states, "These foundation requirements [firsthand knowledge] may, of course, be furnished by the testimony of the witness himself; hence personal knowledge is not an absolute but may consist of what the witness thinks he knows from personal perception."

ollection in recounting the facts.[11] Accordingly, when a witness uses such expressions as "I think," "My impression is," or "In my opinion," this will be no ground of objection if it appears that he merely speaks from an inattentive observation, or an unsure memory,[12] though it will if the expressions are found to mean that he speaks from conjecture or from hearsay.[13]

One who has no knowledge of a fact except what another has told him cannot, of course, satisfy the present requirement of knowledge from observation. When the witness, however, bases his testimony partly upon firsthand knowledge and partly upon the accounts of others, the problem is one which calls for a practical compromise. Thus when he speaks of his own age,[14] or of his kinship with a relative,[15] the courts will allow the testimony. And when the witness testifies to facts that he knows partly at first hand and partly from reports, the judge, it seems, should admit or exclude according to the reasonable reliability of the evidence.[16]

 WESTLAW REFERENCES

witness** /s actually /s observe*

witness** /s firsthand /s knowledge

digest(witness** /s testif! requir! /s personal /s knowledge)

---

11. Ewing v. Russell, 81 S.D. 563, 137 N.W.2d 892 (1965) (testimony of condition of floor held admissible although witness also testified she "didn't pay any particular attention to the floor"); Eitel v. Times, Inc., 221 Or. 585, 352 P.2d 485 (1960) (alleged insufficient inspection of wire did not make testimony of its source inadmissible).

A similar viewpoint should be taken under Fed.R. Evid. 602. See United States v. Evans, 484 F.2d 1178 (2d Cir. 1973); Myrtle Beach Air Force Base Federal Credit Union v. Cumis Insurance Society, Inc., 681 F.2d 930 (4th Cir. 1982) (witness' knowledge need not be positive; court must find witness could not have actually perceived or observed). There still should be support for a "finding" of personal knowledge under the test stated in the text at n. 9 supra.

12. Auerbach v. United States, 136 F.2d 882 (6th Cir. 1943) (witness testified to identity of man he saw, "to the best of my belief" but acknowledging he might be mistaken, allowed); People v. Palmer, 351 Ill. 319, 184 N.E. 205 (1932) ("I believe"); E.F. Enoch Co. v. Johnson, 183 Md. 326, 37 A.2d 901 (1944) ("It looked like that truck . . . swung in"); Tews v. Bamrick, 148 Neb. 59, 26 N.W.2d 499 (1947) ("I guess," as to speed of car); Covey v. State, 232 Ark. 79, 334 S.W.2d 648 (1960) ("Seems like he said something like . . . "); 2 Wigmore, Evidence § 658 (Chadbourn rev. 1979).

13. United States v. Cox, 633 F.2d 871 (9th Cir. 1980), cert. denied 454 U.S. 844 (that witness had an impression of a matter); Lovejoy v. Howe, 55 Minn. 353, 57 N.W. 57 (1893) ("impression"); State v. Thorp, 72 N.C. 186 (1875) ("my best impression"); State v. Dixon, 420 S.W.2d 267 (Mo.1967) ("I think").

14. Antelope v. United States, 185 F.2d 174 (10th Cir. 1950) (statutory rape: victim may testify to her age and date of birth); State v. Olson, 260 Iowa 311, 149 N.W.2d 132 (1967) (extra-judicial statement of age).

So as to the age of a near relative. Hancock v. Supreme Council, 69 N.J.L. 308, 55 A. 246 (1903) (elder brother). See § 322 infra.

15. Brown v. Mitchell, 88 Tex. 350, 31 S.W. 621, 623 (1895) (witness testified that he was son of decedent, based on fact that she called him son and on other facts); State v. Schut, 71 Wn.2d 400, 429 P.2d 126 (1967) (parentage of witness). See § 322 infra.

16. The evidence was admitted in Hunt v. Stimson, 23 F.2d 447 (6th Cir. 1928) (sales manager of lumber yard testified to amount of lumber on hand, based on his estimates from inspection and tallies made by other employees); Schooler v. State, 175 S.W.2d 664 (Tex.Civ. App.1943) (geologist's testimony as to structure and oil prospects of land based on inspection and on reports of other geologists); Vogt v. Chicago, Milwaukee, St. Paul & Pacific Railroad Co., 35 Wis.2d 716, 151 N.W.2d 713 (1967) (wife permitted to testify to her husband's earnings although books were incomplete).

An example under Fed.R.Evid. 602 is United States v. Mandel, 591 F.2d 1347 (4th Cir. 1979), cert. denied 445 U.S. 959, 961 (senator's feelings and beliefs on governor's position on certain legislation held not admissible to the extent based upon hearsay; "The more difficult problem arises when the witness' belief is based in part on admissible testimony. We think this problem is one of degree. If the belief is primarily based upon hearsay, it is inadmissible. But if the belief is substantially based on admissible evidence, such as direct statements or acts by one of Governor Mandel's agents, then it should be admitted. The basis for the belief should be explored in each instance and a ruling on admissibility made when those facts are before the trial court.")

Fed.R.Evid. and Rev.Unif.R.Evid. (1974) 602 make clear that pursuant to Fed.R.Evid. and Rev.Unif.R. Evid. (1974) 703 an expert may testify without personal knowledge. See § 15 infra.

THE OPINION RULE [1]

§ 11. The Evolution of the Rule Against Opinions: Opinions of Laymen

The opinion rule, though it developed from practices and expressions of the English courts, was enforced more generally, and far more inflexibly, here than in the mother country.[2] In the first place a rule against "opinions" may have had a different meaning for the English judge. We are told that in English usage of the 1700's and earlier, "opinion" had the primary meaning of "notion" or "persuasion of the mind without proof or certain knowledge." [3] It carried an implication of lack of grounds, which is absent from our present-day meaning of the term "opinion" in this country. We use the word as denoting a belief, inference, or conclusion without suggesting that it is well- or ill-founded.

The requirement that witnesses must have personal knowledge, already discussed in the preceding section, was a very old rule, having its roots in medieval law,[4] which demanded that they speak only "what they see and hear." [5] The classic dictum of Coke in 1622, that "It is no satisfaction for a witness to say that he 'thinketh' or 'persuadeth himself' " [6] and Mansfield's statement in 1766, "It is mere opinion, which is not evidence" [7] are to be understood as condemning testimony when not based upon personal knowledge. Statements founded only on hearsay or conjecture would fall under this ban. But as Wigmore interprets the historical evidence, there was not until the 1800's any recognition of an opinion rule which would exclude inferences by witnesses possessing personal knowledge.[8]

By the middle of the 1800's [9] the disparagement of "mere opinion" in the sense of a notion or conjecture not rooted in observation had emerged into a much more questionable canon of exclusion. This was the doctrine that witnesses generally must give the "facts" and not their "inferences, conclusions, or opinions." [10]

§ 11

1. 7 Wigmore, Evidence §§ 1917–2028 (Chadbourn rev. 1978); Weinstein & Berger, Evidence ¶¶ 701[01]–[04]; Dec.Dig.Crim.Law ⟜448–494, Evidence ⟜470–574; 32 C.J.S. Evidence §§ 438–575; King & Pillinger, Opinion Evidence in Illinois (1942) (a work valuable in any jurisdiction for its original analysis and creative ideas).

2. See for example the brief treatment of opinion evidence in Phipson, Evidence ch. 36 (10th ed., 1963). See also Cowen & Carter, Essays on the Law of Evidence 163 (1956) ("In practice the English judges have paid little more than lip service to the rule.")

3. Samuel Johnson's Dictionary (1st ed., 1755) cited in King & Pillinger, op. cit. n. 1, at p. 8.

4. 9 Holdsworth, Hist.Eng.L. 211 (1926).

5. In 1349 it was held that witnesses were not challengeable "because the verdict will not be received from them, but from the jury; and the witnesses are to be sworn 'to say the truth,' without adding 'to the best of their knowledge,' for they should testify nothing but what they . . . know for certain, that is to say what they see and hear." Anon.Lib.Ass. 110, 11 (1349), quoted in Phipson supra § 11 n. 2, at p. 475.

6. Adams v. Canon, Dyer 53b, quoted 7 Wigmore, Evidence § 1917, p. 2 (Chadbourn rev.1979).

7. Carter v. Boehm, 3 Burr. 1905, 1918 (1766) quoted 7 Wigmore, Evidence § 1917, p. 7 (Chadbourn rev. 1978).

8. 7 Wigmore, Evidence § 1917 (Chadbourn rev. 1979). King and Pillinger, supra n. 1, at p. 7. The latter work cites Peake on Evidence, an English work published in 1801 as the source of the first statement that witnesses generally must state "facts" rather than "opinion."

9. See, e.g., Donnell v. Jones, 13 Ala. 490, 511 (1848) (opinion of one acquainted with business whether levy of attachment had destroyed credit and forced business into assignment, excluded. "The general rule requires, that witnesses should depose only to facts, and such facts too as come within their knowledge. The expression of opinions, the belief of the witness, or deductions from the facts, however honestly made, are not proper evidence as coming from the witness; and when such deductions are made by the witness, the prerogative of the jury is invaded.") It is notable, however, that even in the 1850's, the Illinois court states the matter thus hesitantly, "It is true, probably, that mere opinions, as opinions, when offered in evidence, should be confined to experts in the questions of skill or science as such, which are open to that kind of proof and for want of better." Butler v. Mehrling, 15 Ill. 488, 491 (1854). And Greenleaf in the 6th edition of his treatise, issued in 1852, when he deals with opinions in § 440 cites no cases for his statement that "the opinions of witnesses are in general not evidence" but devotes his numerous citations in the main to cases where opinions were received.

10. Among the leading cases which discussed the rule, in addition to the cases in the next preceding note,

This classic formula, based as it is on the assumption that "fact" and "opinion" stand in contrast and hence are readily distinguishable, proved to be the clumsiest of all the tools furnished the judge for regulating the examination of witnesses. It is clumsy because its basic assumption is an illusion. The words of the witness cannot "give" or recreate the "facts," that is, the objective situations or happenings about which the witness is testifying. Drawings, maps, photographs, even motion pictures, are only a remote and inaccurate portrayal of those "facts", and how much more distant approximations of reality are the word pictures of oral or written testimony. There is no conceivable statement however specific, detailed and "factual," that is not in some measure the product of inference and reflection as well as observation and memory. The difference between the statement, "He was driving on the left-hand side of the road" which would be classed as "fact" under the rule, and "He was driving carelessly" which would be called "opinion" is merely a difference between a more concrete and specific form of descriptive statement and a less specific and concrete form. The difference between so-called "fact," then, and "opinion," is not a difference between opposites or contrasting absolutes, but a mere difference in degree with no recognizable line to mark the boundary.[11]

If trial judges are given the task of distinguishing on the spur of the moment between "fact" and "opinion", no two judges, acting independently, can be expected to reach the same results on the same questions. Of course, it is true that many recurring questions have been used and hence have been customarily classified as calling for "fact" or "opinion", but in a changing world there will constantly be presented a myriad of new statements to which the judge must apply the distinction. Thus, good sense demands that the trial judge be accorded a wide range of discretion at least in classifying evidence as "fact" or "opinion," and probably in admitting evidence even where found to constitute opinion. Various courts have expressed this viewpoint.[12] It is incorporated in Federal Rule of Evidence and Revised Uniform Rule of Evidence (1974) 701.[13]

The recognition of the impossibility of administering the opinion standard as a mandatory rule, however, came but slowly. The alleviation of the strictness of the standard was at first limited to cases of strict necessity.[14] This rule as stated in the cited case, which in form of statement excludes

are Baltimore & Ohio Railroad Co. v. Schultz, 43 Ohio 270, 1 N.E. 324 (1885) (opinion of observer that fence not fit to keep stock off, excluded, see n. 14 infra); Graham v. Pennsylvania Co., 139 Pa. 149, 21 A. 151, 12 L.R.A. 293 (1891) (opinion of architect who had seen defendant's platform, for alighting passengers, that because of construction and lighting it was unsafe, excluded).

11. For a masterly exposition of this view, see 7 Wigmore, Evidence § 1919 (Chadbourn rev.1978). Another discussion, with vivid illustrative material, is King & Pillinger, Opinion Evidence in Illinois 1–6, 21–23 (1942).

12. Dersis v. Dersis, 210 Ala. 308, 311, 98 So. 27 (1923) ("A certain discretion is rightly vested in the trial courts in directing the search for the truth by this class of evidence, and their action should not be disturbed unless it is apparent some right of a party has been invaded or suppressed. We think a man sitting up all night with a sick man, or one grievously wounded in the head may form an opinion whether he is conscious or unconscious, which may be given to the jury for what it is worth"); Grismore v. Consolidated Products, 232 Iowa 328, 5 N.W.2d 646 (1942) ("The courts

and other authorities uniformly agree that the receipt of opinion evidence, whether lay or expert, and the extent to which it will be received in any particular case, are matters resting largely in the administrative discretion of the court."); Dowling v. L.H. Shattuck, Inc., 91 N.H. 234, 17 A.2d 529, 532 (1941); Wilson v. Pennsylvania Railroad Co., 421 Pa. 419, 219 A.2d 666 (1966); Osborn v. Lesser, 201 Kan. 45, 439 P.2d 395 (1968) interpreting K.S.A. 60–456(a), i.e., original Uniform Rule 56(1); and see other cases collected in C.J.S. Evidence § 449, p. 86.

13. United States v. Pierson, 164 U.S.App.D.C. 82, 503 F.2d 173 (1974).

14. See, e.g., the following passage from a former leading case: "A few general propositions are submitted, which, it is believed, fairly reflect the current of authority on the subject of the admissibility of the opinions of witnesses as evidence. (1) That witnesses shall testify to facts and not opinions is the general rule. (2) Exceptions to this rule have been found to be, in some cases, necessary to the due administration of justice. (3) Witnesses shown to be learned, skilled, or experienced in a particular art, science, trade, or business may, in a proper case, give their opinions upon a

opinion except in the circumstances listed, remains as the "orthodox" view in fewer and fewer state courts,[15] but in states which have not adopted the Federal Rules of Evidence (or a similar set of rules) the actual practice in the trial of cases is becoming, if indeed it has not always been, far more liberal than the older formulas, and might more accurately be reflected in a formula expressed by some courts that sanction the admission of opinions on grounds of "expediency" or "convenience" rather than "necessity." The so-called "short-hand rendition"

rule seems to incorporate this more liberal notion.[16] "Convenience" is a principle incorporated in Federal Rule of Evidence 701.[17]

It is believed that the standard actually applied by many of the trial judges of today includes the principle espoused by Wigmore, namely that opinions of laymen should be rejected only when they are superfluous in the sense that they will be of no value to the jury.[18] The value of opinions to the jury is the principal test of Federal Rule of Evidence and Revised Uniform Rule of Evidence (1974) 701.[19] It seems fair to observe that

---

given state of facts. This exception is limited to experts. (4) In matter more within the common observation and experience of men, non-experts may, in cases where it is not practicable to place before the jury all the primary facts upon which they are founded, state their opinions from such facts, where such opinions involve conclusions material to the subject of inquiry. (5) In such cases the witnesses are required, so far as may be, to state the primary facts which support their opinions." Baltimore & Ohio Railroad Co. v. Schultz, 43 Ohio 270, 1 N.E. 324, 331 (1885). This is no longer the law of Ohio, which has adopted Fed.R.Evid. 701.

15. See, Whitney v. Central Paper Stock Co., 446 S.W.2d 415 (Mo.App.1969) ("when it is impossible or extremely difficult for a witness to convey an actual and accurate meaning"; exclusion of opinion that wooden floor was "rotten" was held error); C.J.S. Evidence § 546(4), note 36. The standard is stated in varying terms. See, e.g., Beutenmuller v. Vess, 447 S.W.2d 519 (Mo.1969) (opinion may be stated when "facts and circumstances are such that they may not be readily and accurately described").

16. A long-established "exception" to the opinion-rule in some states is the practice of admitting "opinions" where they can be justified as "short-hand renditions" of a total situation, or as "statements of collective facts": Dulaney v. Burns, 218 Ala. 493, 513, 119 So. 21, 24 (1928) ("Did you ever say anything to influence him about not leaving anything to his kinfolks?"); Pollard v. Rogers, 234 Ala. 92, 173 So. 881 (1937) ("He looked like he was dying"; opinion has extensive discussion); City of Beaumont v. Kane, 33 S.W.2d 234, 241, 242 (Tex.Civ.App., 1930) ("The situation at the end of Pearl Street presented such an appearance that a stranger on a rainy night would be liable to drive off into the river."). State v. Morrow, 541 S.W.2d 738 (Mo. App.1976) ("When a witness has personally observed events, he may testify to his 'matter of fact' comprehension of what he has seen in a descriptive manner which is actually a conclusion, opinion, or inference, if the inference is common and accords with the experience of everyday life."). See cases cited in C.J.S. Evidence § 546(3).

17. For the text of Fed.R.Evid. 701, see n. 19 infra. See Kerry Coal Co. v. United Mine Workers, 637 F.2d 957 (3d Cir. 1981), cert. denied 454 U.S. 823 (that per-

sons were nervous and afraid was a shorthand rendition of observation of witness); United States v. Freeman, 514 F.2d 1184 (10th Cir. 1975) (speaking of certain testimony, the court stated, "He was merely giving a shorthand rendition of his knowledge of the total situation and the collective facts"). But Rule 701 does not limit lay opinion to statements which are permissible on the basis of "convenience." See n. 19, infra.

18. 7 Wigmore, Evidence § 1918 (Chadbourn rev. 1978). The test above is quoted in Allen v. Matson Navigation Co., 255 F.2d 273, 278 (9th Cir. 1958) (holding admissible testimony that floor was "slippery", a pre-Fed.R.Evid. decision).

19. Fed.R.Evid. and Rev.Unif.R.Evid. (1974) 701 incorporate the notion in the text in the form of an affirmative limitation "If the witness is not testifying as an expert, his testimony in the form of opinions or inferences is limited to those opinions of the witness which are (a) rationally based on the perception of the witness and (b) helpful to a clear understanding of his testimony or the determination of a fact in issue."

See illustrative cases, United States v. Mastberg, 503 F.2d 465 (9th Cir. 1974) (customs inspector could testify witness was nervous); United States v. Robinson, 544 F.2d 110 (2d Cir. 1976), cert. denied 434 U.S. 1050 (error to exclude testimony of resemblance of bank photograph to person absent from trial, even if not error to exclude similar testimony as to defendant because not helpful to jury and meaningless under Fed.R.Evid. 701); United States v. Calhoun, 544 F.2d 291 (6th Cir. 1976) (testimony of lay witness identifying subject of bank photograph); United States v. Smith, 550 F.2d 277 (5th Cir. 1977), cert. denied 434 U.S. 841 (not error to admit testimony of witness that another "understood the requirements" of a particular statute). Whether an inference is helpful or not is very much in the discretion of the court. On occasion even a general observation about another's specific state of mind will be helpful. See, e.g., Bohannon v. Pegelow, 652 F.2d 729 (7th Cir. 1981) (testimony that an arrest was motivated by racial prejudice).

The Advisory Committee's Note observes, "The rule assumes that the natural characteristics of the adversary system will generally lead to an acceptable result, since the detailed account carries more conviction than

the prevailing practice in respect to the admission of the opinions of non-expert witnesses may well be described, not as a rule excluding opinions, but as a rule of preference. The more concrete description is preferred to the more abstract. Moreover, it seems that the principal impact of the rule is upon the form of examination. The questions, while they cannot suggest the particular details desired, else they will be leading, should nevertheless call for the most specific account that the witness can give. For example, he must not be asked, "Did they agree?" but "What did they say?" When recognized as a matter of the form of the examination rather than the substance of the testimony—again, a difference of degree—the opinion rule, like other regulations of form, such as the control over leading questions and questions calling for a free narrative and over the order of proof is seen to fall naturally in the realm of discretion. Furthermore, it seems that this habit and tradition of Anglo-American lawyers to examine about specific details is a valuable heritage. The problem is to preserve this scientific habit of approach but yet to curb the time-wasting quibbling over trivial objections on the ground of "opinion" which may still be heard in those courts which attempt a literal application of the older formulas.

One solution is simply to eliminate the matter of lay opinion from the category of things governed by rules.[20] Supporters

would find a sufficient substitute in the natural desire of a lawyer to present a detailed case as being the most convincing technique and in the ability of the adversary on cross-examination to expose the non-existence or inconsistency of details not developed on direct. Of course, Federal Rule of Evidence and Revised Uniform Rule of Evidence 701 does not embody the above solution, but it does present a viable alternative solution. Under Rule 701 and Rule 602, the witness must have personal knowledge of matter that forms the basis of testimony of opinion;[21] the testimony must be based rationally upon the perception of the witness;[22] and of course, the opinion must be helpful to the jury (the principal test).[23] Contrary to some decisions under case law,[24] the witness need not relate the observed matters that are the basis of opinion,[25] although the judge should have discretion to require preliminary testimony of the facts observed. Finally, Rule 403 permits exclusion of inferences that are prejudicial, confusing, misleading or time-wasting.[26]

 **WESTLAW REFERENCES**

digest(witness** /s testif! testimony /s "opinion") % digest(expert)

headnote(rule* /10 evidence evid. /10 701)

digest(objection /s "opinion" /s evidence % expert)

---

the broad assertion, and a lawyer can be expected to display his witness to the best advantage. If he fails to do so, cross-examination and argument will point up the weakness. See Ladd, Expert Testimony, 5 Vand.L. Rev. 414, 415–417 (1952). If, despite these considerations, attempts are made to introduce meaningless assertions which amount to little more than choosing up sides, exclusion for lack of helpfulness is called for by the rule." See, e.g. United States v. Phillips, 600 F.2d 535 (5th Cir. 1979) (dictum that testimony of another's understanding was said to amount to little more than choosing up sides).

20. See 7 Wigmore, Evidence § 1929 (Chadbourn rev. 1978) (The Future of the Opinion Rule); Bozeman, Suggested Reforms of the Opinion Rule, 13 Temple U.L.Q. 296 (1939).

21. United States v. Jackson, 569 F.2d 1003 (7th Cir. 1978), cert. denied 437 U.S. 907 (requirement not met);

United States v. Oaxaca, 569 F.2d 518 (9th Cir. 1978), cert. denied 439 U.S. 926 (requirement met).

22. Fed.R.Evid. and Rev.Unif.R.Evid. (1974) 701, n. 19, supra. See, e.g., United States v. Cox, 633 F.2d 871 (9th Cir. 1980), cert. denied 454 U.S. 844 (impression voiced by witness did not rationally follow from facts she stated).

23. See n. 19 supra.

24. See cases cited at C.J.S. Evidence § 546(4).

25. Fed.R.Evid. and Rev.Unif.R.Evid. (1974) 701, n. 19 supra.

26. United States v. Calhoun, 544 F.2d 291 (6th Cir. 1976) (opinion of prosecution witness prejudicial because witness could not be fully subject to related cross-examination, citing Fed.R.Evid. 403). See § 185 infra.

§ 12. The Relativity of the Opinion Rule: Opinions on the Ultimate Issue

As pointed out in the next preceding section, the terms "fact" and "opinion" denote merely a difference of degree of concreteness of description or a difference in nearness or remoteness of inference. The opinion rule operates to prefer the more concrete description to the less concrete, the direct form of statement to the inferential. But there is still another variable in the equation. The purpose of the testimony has had an effect on the degree of concreteness required. In the outer circle of collateral facts, near the rim of relevancy, evidence in general terms will be received with relative freedom, but as we come closer to the hub of the issue, the courts have been more careful to call for details instead of inferences.[1]

The trial judge may well be more liberal in the use of his discretion to admit opinions and inferences as to collateral matters and less liberal in order to see that the concrete details are brought out as to more crucial matters. Is it expedient to go further and to tie his hands by a rule forbidding opinion-evidence as to these "ultimate" matters?

Undoubtedly there is a kind of statement by the witness which amounts to no more than an expression of his general belief as to how the case should be decided or as to the amount of unliquidated damages which should be given. It is believed all courts would exclude such extreme expressions.[2] There is no necessity for this kind of evidence; to receive it would tend to suggest that the judge and jury may shift responsibility for decision to the witnesses; and in any event it is wholly without value to the trier of fact in reaching a decision.

But until about 35 years ago, a very substantial number of courts had gone far beyond this commonsense reluctance to listen to the witness's views as to how the judge and jury should exercise their functions and had announced the general doctrine that witnesses would not be permitted to give their opinions or conclusions upon an ultimate fact in issue.[3]

The reason was sometimes given that such testimony "usurps the function"[4] or "invades the province"[5] of the jury. Obviously these expressions were not intended to be taken literally, but merely to suggest the danger that the jury might forego independent analysis of the facts and bow too readily to the opinion of an expert or otherwise influential witness.

Although the rule had been followed in many states prior to 1942,[6] a trend began to abandon or reject it[7] with the result that now in a majority of state courts an expert may state his opinion upon an ultimate fact, provided that all other requirements for admission of expert opinion are met.[8] The

§ 12

1. King & Pillinger, Opinion Evidence in Illinois 10 (1942).

2. See, e.g., Warren Petroleum Co. v. Thomasson, 268 F.2d 5 (5th Cir. 1959) (error to admit highway patrolman's statement after collision that owner of one of vehicles "should assume liability"; Duncan v. Mack, 59 Ariz. 36, 122 P.2d 215 (1942) (whether public convenience would be served by transfer of license); Grismore v. Consolidated Products, 232 Iowa 328, 5 N.W.2d 646 (1942) (opinions as to guilt, negligence, testamentary capacity, reasonable cause—dictum). Fed.R.Evid. 701, Advisory Committee's Note excerpt, § 11 n. 19 supra.

3. United States v. Spaulding, 293 U.S. 498, 506 (1935); State v. Carr, 196 N.C. 129, 144 S.E. 698 (1928) and earlier cases collected in Dec.Dig. Evidence ☞472 and 506, Criminal Law ☞450; and see 7 N.C.L.Rev. 320 (1928), 16 id. 180 (1938); 26 Ia.L.Rev. 819 (1941).

4. Chicago & Alton Railroad Co. v. Springfield & Northwestern Railroad Co., 67 Ill. 142 (1873).

5. De Groot v. Winter, 261 Mich. 660, 247 N.W. 69, 71 (1933). Michigan no longer follows the rule. See note 8 infra, and Federal Rule 704, text at n. 9 infra, which Michigan has adopted.

6. See sources cited in note 3 supra.

7. The trend appears to have begun with the leading case of Grismore v. Consolidated Products, 232 Ia. 328, 5 N.W.2d 646 (1942).

8. Cases included Rabata v. Dohner, 45 Wis.2d 111, 172 N.W.2d 409 (1969) (abandoning rule that expert opinions on ultimate facts must be based upon hypothetical questions); Redman v. Ford Motor Co., 253 S.C. 266, 170 S.E.2d 207 (1969) (stating that the matter is in the discretion of the trial judge); Groce v. Fidelity General Insurance Co., 252 Or. 296, 448 P.2d 554 (1968); Southern Pacific Co. v. Watkins, 83 Nev. 471, 435 P.2d 498 (1968); McKay Machine Co. v. Rodman,

trend culminated in the adoption of Federal Rule of Evidence 704:

> Testimony in the form of an opinion or inference otherwise admissible is not objectionable because it embraces an ultimate issue to be decided by the trier of fact.[9]

Some courts had already adopted the rule that opinions of laymen on ultimate facts were not precluded.[10] Other general rules of admissibility for such opinions may, however, preclude them in particular instances,[11] e.g., opinions as to how the case should be decided and the like. Under the most liberal rules those opinions would be excludable on the ground that their value is outweighed by "the danger of unfair prejudice, confusion of issues, or misleading the jury, or by considerations of undue delay, waste of time, or needless presentation of cumulative evidence." [12]

This change in viewpoint concerning "ultimate fact" opinion resulted from the fact that the rule excluding opinion on ultimate facts is unduly restrictive, with many possible close questions of application. The rule can often unfairly obstruct the presentation of a party's case, to say nothing of the illogic of the notion that opinions on ultimate facts usurp the function of the jury.[13] In jurisdictions in which the prohibitive rule is retained,[14] there must be difficult and confusing questions whether an opinion concerns an ultimate fact.[15]

Regardless of the rule concerning admissibility of opinion upon ultimate facts, courts do not permit opinion on a question of law,[16] unless the issue concerns a question of foreign law.[17] Nor do the Federal Rules of Evidence permit opinion on law except questions of foreign law.[18]

11 Ohio St.2d 77, 228 N.E.2d 304 (1967); In re Baxter's Estate, 16 Utah 2d 284, 399 P.2d 442 (1965); Commonwealth, Department of Highways v. Widner, 388 S.W.2d 583 (Ky.1965); Dudek v. Popp, 373 Mich. 300, 129 N.W.2d 393 (1964). See review of the cases in Stoebuck, Opinions on Ultimate Facts: Status, Trends, and a Note of Caution, 41 Denver L.C.J. 226 (1964); C.J.S. Evidence § 446(b). See also note 9, infra.

9. Revised Unif.R.Evid. (1974) 704 is identical.

10. Weber v. Chicago, Rock Island & Pacific Railway Co., 175 Iowa 358, 151 N.W. 852, 859, L.R.A. 1918A, 626 (1915) (lay opinion testimony as to whether spikes holding rails had been pulled with a crowbar, admissible) cited and discussed in Grismore v. Consolidated Products, 232 Iowa 328, 5 N.W.2d 646, 662 (1942); Model Code of Evidence Rule 401, adopted as case law, Church v. West, 75 Wn.2d 502, 452 P.2d 265 (1969). See also West's Ann.Cal.Evid.Code § 805, "Testimony in the form of an opinion that is otherwise admissible is not objectionable because it embraces the ultimate issue to be decided by the trier of fact."

11. See § 11 supra.

12. Fed.R.Evid. and Rev.Unif.R.Evid. (1974) 403; § 185 infra. United States v. Masson, 582 F.2d 961 (5th Cir. 1978) (distinguishes between questions of opinion of guilt of defendant and opinion on other possible matters of ultimate fact).

13. See the discussion in Grismore v. Consolidated Products, 232 Iowa 328, 5 N.W.2d 646 (1942); 7 Wigmore Evidence §§ 1920, 1921 (Chadbourn rev. 1978).

14. See, e.g., Hubbard v. Quality Oil Co. of Statesville, Inc., 268 N.C. 489, 151 S.E.2d 71 (1966); Redman v. Community Hotel Corp., 138 W.Va. 456, 76 S.E.2d 759 (1953).

15. Usually the process of breaking down general opinions concerning ultimate fact into more specific opinions is required to avoid opinions on ultimate facts. See, e.g., disagreement between court and counsel in Spiezio v. Commonwealth Edison Co., 91 Ill.App.2d 392, 235 N.E.2d 323 (1968). This process tends to result in inconsistent or unexplainable decisions. See, e.g., discussion of earlier Ohio cases, Note 20 U.Cin.L.Rev. 484 (1951). The prohibitive rule, involving the notion of invading the province of the jury, is easily confused with the notion that experts should not be heard on commonplace matters. See § 13 infra. In a very few decisions it has been intimated that the form of the testimony may be significant, in that a direct statement of fact in issue may be inadmissible, while a mere statement that it is the witness' opinion that the fact is so, or a statement in the subjunctive mood, would be allowable. Turnbow v. Hayes Freight Lines, Inc., 15 Ill. App.2d 57, 145 N.E.2d 377 (1957); Hubbard v. Quality Oil Co. of Statesville, Inc., 268 N.C. 489, 151 S.E.2d 71 (1966) (expert can testify what "would produce the result"). This has rightly been called a mere quibble. Annot., 78 A.L.R. 755, 758. The two forms are mere expressions of belief and should be treated alike.

16. The general rule is illustrated by Briney v. Tri-State Mutual Grain Dealers Fire Insurance Co., 254 Iowa 673, 117 N.W.2d 889 (1962) (testimony concerning legal effect of relationship between independent adjusters and fire insurance companies who hired them); Hawkins v. Chandler, 88 Idaho 20, 396 P.2d 123 (1964) (testimony that the law did not require the use of flares but error held not prejudicial); C.J.S. Evidence § 453.

17. See § 335 infra.

18. Marx & Co., Inc. v. The Diners' Club, Inc., 550 F.2d 505 (2d Cir. 1977), cert. denied 434 U.S. 861.

A court which does not ban opinion on the ultimate issue as such may nevertheless condemn a question phrased in terms of a legal criterion not adequately defined by the questioner so as to be correctly understood by laymen, the question being interpreted by the court as calling for a legal opinion. But it is often convenient or desirable to use questions that are not intended to call forth any legal conclusion but that are phrased in terms of some legal standard familiar to lawyers. There is thus a problem of interpretation of the questions.[19]

The problem has arisen often in relation to testimony on the issue of capacity to make a will. Thus, a court taking the view that there may be opinion upon an ultimate issue would approve a question, "Did X have mental capacity sufficient to understand the nature and effect of his will?" [20] but would frown on the question, "Did X have sufficient mental capacity to make a will?" [21] because the latter question may be incorrectly understood by the witness and the jury if they do not know the law's definition of "capacity to make a will." But a court which prohibits generally opinions on the ultimate issue might condemn both forms of questions,[22] or even one where the questioner breaks down "testamentary capacity" into its factual elements as legally defined.[23] Similar problems may arise in respect to such issues as undue influence, total and permanent disability, negligence, and the like.

On the whole, it is thought that the danger that these questions phrased in terms of "legal conclusions" will be understood as calling for a conclusion or opinion of law is very slight, since they will seldom be asked except when the popular meaning is approximately the same as the legal meaning. In a jurisdiction where there is no general rule against opinions on the ultimate issue, it seems that a request by the adversary that the questioner define his terms should be the only recourse.[24]

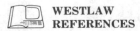

WESTLAW REFERENCES

synopsis,digest(witness /20 usurp! invad! /20 jury)

digest(expert /s witness /s "opinion" /s ultimate /s fact issue)

digest(ultimate +2 issue /p evidence /p admissib! inadmissib!)

---

19. McClellan v. French, 246 Ark. 728, 439 S.W.2d 813 (1969) (held that witness, in testifying a doctor was not guilty of malpractice, used the term in its connotation "standard medical procedure in the community"); Groce v. Fidelity General Insurance Co., 252 Or. 296, 448 P.2d 554 (1968) (no error in permitting witness to testify to "good faith" of insurer; (possibly dictum). But see Lindley v. Lindley, 384 S.W.2d 676 (Tex.1964) (doctor not permitted to testify that a person's belief was an "insane delusion" because his concept might be quite different from the legal concept).

20. See Scalf v. Collin County, 80 Tex. 514, 16 S.W. 314 (1891) (capacity to understand nature and effect of deed); McDaniel v. Willis, 157 S.W.2d 672 (Tex.Civ. App.1941, error ref'd) (opinion that testator mentally incapable of transacting business). See also, Slough, Testamentary Capacity: Evidentiary Aspects, 36 Texas L.Rev. 1, 5–16 (1957).

21. Brown v. Mitchell, 88 Tex. 350, 31 S.W. 621, 36 L.R.A. 64 (1895); Carr v. Radkey, 393 S.W.2d 806 (Tex. 1965). Speaking of Fed.R.Evid. 701 and 702, the Advisory Committee's Note states, "They also stand ready to exclude opinions phrased in terms of inadequately explored legal criteria. Thus the question, 'Did T have capacity to make a will?' would be excluded, while the question, 'Did T have sufficient mental capacity to know the nature and extent of his property and the natural objects of his bounty and to formulate a rational scheme of distribution?' would be allowed. McCormick § 12."

22. See Baker v. Baker, 202 Ill. 595, 67 N.E. 410 (1903) ("whether he was able understandingly to execute a will"); Schneider v. Manning, 121 Ill. 376, 12 N.E. 267 (1887) ("Had he mental capacity to dispose of his property by will or deed?") and see King & Pillinger, Opinion Evidence in Illinois 225–228 (1942).

23. Baddeley v. Watkins, 293 Ill. 394, 127 N.E. 725 (1920). But see Powell v. Weld, 410 Ill. 198, 101 N.E.2d 581 (1951).

24. This suggestion is cited in Groce v. Fidelity General Insurance Co., 252 Or. 296, 448 P.2d 554 (1968). It is in effect rejected in Carr v. Radkey, 393 S.W.2d 806 (Tex.1965). The text suggestion could be followed under Fed.R.Evid. and Rev.Unif.R.Evid. (1974) 701, 702, and 403, so long as the requirements of these rules are met.

§ 13. Expert Witnesses:[1] Subjects of Expert Testimony: Qualifications[2]

An observer is qualified to testify because he has firsthand knowledge of the situation or transaction at issue. The expert has something different to contribute. This is the power to draw inferences from the facts which a jury would not be competent to draw.[3] To warrant the use of expert testimony two general elements are required.

First, some courts state that the subject of inference must be so distinctively related to some science, profession, business or occupation as to be beyond the ken of laymen.[4] Some cases say that the judge has discretion in administering this rule.[5] Other cases will admit expert opinion concerning matters about which the jurors may have general knowledge if the expert opinion would still aid their understanding of the fact issue.[6] This latter standard is included within the terms of Federal Rule of Evidence and Revised Uniform Rule of Evidence 702.[7] In fact, Rule 702 should permit expert opinion even if the matter is within the competence of the jurors if specialized knowledge will be helpful, as it may be in particular situations.[8] Second, the witness must have sufficient skill, knowledge, or experience in or related to the pertinent field or calling as to make it appear that his opinion or inference will probably aid the trier in the search for truth.[9] The knowledge may be derived from

§ 13

1. See Ladd, Expert Testimony, 5 Vand.L.Rev. 414 (1952); Voorhis, Expert Opinion Evidence, 13 N.Y.L.F. 651, 657 (1967); Smith v. Hobart Manufacturing Co., 185 F.Supp. 751 (D.C.Pa.1960), for possibilities of abuse in using witnesses supposedly learned in one subject, or even in all subjects.

2. Dec.Dig.Crim.L. ☞477–481; Evidence ☞535–546; C.J.S. Evidence §§ 456–458; 7 Wigmore, Evidence §§ 1923, 1925 (Chadbourn rev. 1978); Weinstein & Berger, Evidence ¶¶ 702[01]–[07].

3. However, as the Advisory Committee's Note for Fed.R.Evid. 702 states in part, "Most of the literature assumes that experts testify only in the form of opinions. The assumption is logically unfounded. The rule [Rule 702] accordingly recognizes that an expert on the stand may give a dissertation or exposition of scientific or other principles relevant to the case, leaving the trier of fact to apply them to the facts."

4. Admissible: Hagler v. Gilliland, 292 Ala. 262, 292 So.2d 647 (1974) (manager of state employment service testifying concerning employability of plaintiff); Harp v. Illinois Central Railroad Co., 370 S.W.2d 387 (Mo. 1963) (opinion on causation seems clearly admissible). Inadmissible: Housman v. Fiddyment, 421 S.W.2d 284 (Mo.1967); Collins v. Zediker, 421 Pa. 52, 218 A.2d 776 (1966) (how fast does a person walk?); Hill v. Lee, 209 Va. 569, 166 S.E.2d 274 (1969) (whether automobile would make tracks in soil); Dec.Dig. ☞506.

5. Housman v. Fiddyment, n. 4 supra; see McCoid, Opinion Evidence and Expert Witnesses, 2 UCLA L.Rev. 356, 362–363 (1955).

6. Har-Pen Truck Lines, Inc. v. Mills, 378 F.2d 705 (5th Cir. 1967) (testimony of economics professor as to value of housewife's life); Currier v. Grossman's of New Hampshire, Inc., 107 N.H. 159, 219 A.2d 273 (1966) (opinion of cause of accident admissible when it "might aid the jury"); Miller v. Pillsbury Co., 33 Ill.2d 514, 211 N.E.2d 733 (1965) ("the trend is to permit expert testimony in matters which are complicated and admit expert opinion concerning matters about which the jurors may have general knowledge if the expert opinion would still aid their understanding of the fact issue.[6] This latter standard is included within the terms of Federal Rule of Evidence and Revised Uniform Rule of Evidence 702.[7] In fact, Rule 702 should permit expert opinion even if the matter is within the competence of the jurors if specialized knowledge will be helpful, as it may be in particular situations.[8] Second, the witness must have sufficient skill, knowledge, or experience in or related to the pertinent field or calling as to make it appear that his opinion or inference will probably aid the trier in the search for truth.[9] The knowledge may be derived from

outside the knowledge of the average person, and even as to matters of common knowledge and understanding where difficult of comprehension and explanation").

7. Fed.R.Evid. and Rev.Unif.R.Evid. (1974) 702 provide:

"If scientific, technical, or other specialized knowledge will assist the trier of fact to understand the evidence or to determine a fact in issue, a witness qualified as an expert by knowledge, skill, experience, training, or education, may testify thereto in the form of an opinion or otherwise."

8. Weinstein & Berger, Evidence ¶ 702[02]. See n. 9 infra.

9. Pennsylvania Threshermen, etc. Insurance Co. v. Messenger, 181 Md. 295, 29 A.2d 653 (1943) (professor of science may give computation of distances); Bebont v. Kurn, 348 Mo. 501, 154 S.W.2d 120 (1941) (one with long experience in railroad work as brakeman and otherwise could testify as to distance required for stopping train, though he had never been engineer); State v. Killeen, 79 N.H. 201, 107 A. 601 (1919) (experienced clerk who checks delivery orders may give opinion as to signatures). Aid to the trier of fact is the basic test for employment of expert opinion under Fed.R.Evid. and Rev.Unif.R.Evid. (1974) 702. The Advisory Committee's Note indicates the intention of the federal rule. It states, "Whether the situation is a proper one for the use of expert testimony is to be determined on the basis of assisting the trier. There is no more certain test for determining when experts may be used than the common sense inquiry whether the untrained layman would be qualified to determine intelligently and to the best possible degree the particular issue without enlightenment from those having a specialized understanding of the subject involved in the dispute.' Ladd, Expert Testimony, 5 Vand.L.Rev. 414, 418 (1952). When opinions are excluded, it is because they are unhelpful and therefore a waste of time. 7 Wigmore § 1918."

reading alone in some fields, from practice alone in some fields, or as is more commonly the case, from both.[10] While the court may rule that a certain subject of inquiry requires that a member of a given profession, as a doctor, an engineer, or a chemist be called; usually a specialist in a particular branch within a profession will not be required.[11] However, the practice in respect to experts' qualifications has not for the most part crystallized in specific rules, but is recognized as a matter for the trial judge's

discretion reviewable only for abuse.[12] Reversals for abuse are rare.

Finally, there is a question whether opinion evidence is admissible if the court believes that the state of the pertinent art or scientific knowledge does not permit a reasonable opinion to be asserted even by an expert.[13] Also, expert opinion need not be admitted if the court believes that an opinion based upon particular facts cannot be grounded upon those facts.[14]

10. Norfolk & Western Railway Co. v. Anderson, 207 Va. 567, 151 S.E.2d 628 (1966) (one expert qualified by experience and one by experience and study as to cause of tomato crop damage); Smith v. Cedar Rapids Country Club, 255 Iowa 1199, 124 N.W.2d 557 (1964) (wax salesman qualified by reading and experience as to qualities of wax); Central Illinois Light Co. v. Porter, 96 Ill.App.2d 338, 239 N.E.2d 298 (1968) (conservation officer and duck hunter qualified to give opinion as to effect of transmission lines on duck hunting); Grohusky v. Atlas Assurance Co., 195 Kan. 626, 408 P.2d 697 (1965) (one experienced in insurance business, but with little or no formal education, could testify as to practices and procedures in the insurance business).

"The rule [speaking of Fed.R.Evid. 702] is broadly phrased. The fields of knowledge which may be drawn upon are not limited merely to the 'scientific' and 'technical' but extend to all 'specialized' knowledge. Similarly, the expert is viewed, not in a narrow sense, but as a person qualified by 'knowledge, skill, experience, training or education.' Thus within the scope of the rule are not only experts in the strictest sense of the word, e.g. physicians, physicists, and architects, but also the large group sometimes called 'skilled' witnesses, such as bankers or landowners testifying to land values." Advisory Committee's Note, Fed.R.Evid. 702.

See also Kestenbaum v. Falstaff Brewing Corp., 514 F.2d 690 (5th Cir. 1975), cert. denied 424 U.S. 943 (opinion of landowner concerning value of his property admissible; a common result in many jurisdictions).

11. United States v. Viglia, 549 F.2d 335 (5th Cir. 1977), cert. denied 434 U.S. 834 (physician with no experience in treating for obesity could give opinion on use of controlled substance allegedly used for obesity); Parker v. Gunther, 122 Vt. 68, 164 A.2d 152 (1960) (general practitioner could testify as to brain damage); Seawell v. Brame, 258 N.C. 666, 129 S.E.2d 283 (1963) (general practitioner may testify injury caused or aggravated a neurosis, but testimony held inadmissible for other reasons); Wolfinger v. Frey, 223 Md. 184, 162 A.2d 745 (1960) (general practitioner may testify as to cause of kidney condition, citing many local cases); Dec.Dig. Evidence ⬡537.

12. United States v. Lopez, 543 F.2d 1156 (5th Cir. 1977), cert. denied 429 U.S. 1111 (trial court ruling that expert was not sufficiently qualified upheld; trial court would have been upheld had it ruled to the contrary);

McKiernan v. Caldor, Inc., 183 Conn. 164, 438 A.2d 865 (1981) (meteorologist's opinion on whether ground was frozen on a certain date); Moore, Kelly & Reddish, Inc. v. Shannondale, Inc., 152 W.Va. 549, 165 S.E.2d 113 (1968); Dec.Dig. Evidence ⬡546.

13. United States v. Watson, 587 F.2d 365 (7th Cir. 1978), cert. denied 439 U.S. 1132; Tonkovich v. Department of Labor and Industries, 31 Wn.2d 220, 195 P.2d 638 (1948). However, the principle in the text at least overlaps with the subject of the reliability of an expert opinion which depends upon the reliability of alleged scientific knowledge, principles or techniques, and may conflict with results in this latter area. See § 203 infra.

14. See, e.g., Huguley v. State, 39 Ala.App. 104, 96 So.2d 315 (1957), cert. denied 266 Ala. 697, 96 So.2d 319 (speed deduced from impact); Flores v. Barlow, 354 S.W.2d 173 (Tex.Civ.App.1962) (speed deduced from damaged condition of vehicles). For a variety of theories and results concerning the situation of opinions of speed based upon physical facts, see Annot. 29 A.L.R.3d 248.

Under Fed.R.Evid. 702, 703, and 705, the expert may testify only in terms of opinion subject to cross-examination and may base an opinion upon matters not of record—provisions which seem to indicate an overall intent that the questioning of the basis for an opinion should usually go to the weight and not the admissibility of the opinion. See, e.g., Singer Co. v. E.I. du Pont de Nemours & Co., 579 F.2d 433 (8th Cir. 1978). But if direct examination, cross-examination, and redirect examination reveal little or no factual basis for an opinion, it at least remains possible to have the opinion stricken. See reaction of the court in United States v. Hill, 481 F.Supp. 558 (D.C.Pa.1979) (no basis on which a psychologist could state an opinion concerning capacity of defendant to resist an entrapper) reversed on ground that expert had sufficient data not in evidence to testify to the susceptibility of defendant to entrapment to testify to the effect of particular informant's skill and cunning upon defendant's susceptibility, and on other grounds. 655 F.2d 512 (3d Cir. 1981), on remand 550 F.Supp. 983 (and see dissenting opinion). Or if the opponent is sufficiently and justifiably surprised by the calling of the expert to the stand and because of opposing counsel's failure to comply with discovery requirements, is not prepared, it is also possible the opinion may be inadmissible. Smith v. Ford Motor Co., 626

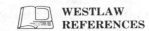

**WESTLAW
REFERENCES**

expert /s witness /p specialized /s knowledge

§ 14. Grounds for Expert Opinion: Hypothetical Questions [1]

The traditional view has been that an expert may state an opinion based on his firsthand knowledge of the facts, or based upon facts in the record at the time he states his opinion, or based partly on firsthand knowledge and partly on the facts of record.[2] If the opinion is to be based on the facts of record, such facts must be in the expert's possession by virtue of the expert having been present at the taking of the testimony of those facts,[3] or they may be furnished to the expert prior to testimony of any opinion by including them in a hypothetical question that asks the expert to assume their truth and state a requested opinion based upon them. However, these methods of eliciting expert opinion have been subject to much criticism; and in response, they are permitted but have been liberalized in the growing number of jurisdictions that have adopted the Federal and Revised Uniform Rules of Evidence, as well as in some other jurisdictions. Two major general changes have been made. First, on direct examination an expert may state an opinion without prior disclosure of the underlying data or facts, leaving the process of disclosure of such data to the opponent on cross-examination, if the opponent desires disclosure.[4] Second, specified types of facts and data which are not in the record and which are inadmissible are proper grounds for the expert's opinion.[5] At the same time, in these more liberal jurisdictions the traditional methods and procedures for eliciting expert opinion may still be employed.[6] The traditional views mentioned above are considered in this section, referring to their use when pertinent in the liberal jurisdictions, and the more recent liberal rules, mentioned above in general, are discussed in Sections 15 and 16.

If an expert witness has firsthand knowledge of material facts, he may describe what he has observed and give his inferences therefrom under both traditional views and the Federal Rules of Evidence.[7] When the expert has no firsthand knowledge of the sit-

---

F.2d 784 (10th Cir. 1980), cert. denied 450 U.S. 918. Considering Rule 403, expert opinion on marginally relevant subjects is less likely to be admissible when it might prejudice a criminal defendant. United States v. Green, 548 F.2d 1261 (6th Cir. 1977) (testimony as to effects of drug on users, in controlled substance prosecution).

§ 14

1. 2 Wigmore, Evidence §§ 672–686 (Chadbourn rev. 1979); Weinstein & Berger, Evidence ¶ 703[01]–[06]; C.J.S. §§ 549–560; Dec.Dig.Crim.Law ☞482–489, Evidence ☞547–557; McElhaney, Expert Witnesses and the Federal Rules of Evidence, 28 Mercer L.Rev. 463 (1977).

2. See n. 7 infra.

3. See n. 10 infra.

4. Fed.R.Evid. and Rev.Unif.R.Evid. (1974) 705 provide:

The expert may testify in terms of opinions or inference and give his reasons therefor without prior disclosure of the underlying facts or data, unless the court requires otherwise. The expert may in any event be required to disclose the underlying facts or data on cross-examination.

See also West's Ann.Cal.Evid.Code § 802; Kansas Stat.Ann., Code of C.P. §§ 60–456, 60–457; New Jersey Rules of Evid. 57, 58; McKinney's N.Y. CPLR 4515.

5. Fed.R.Evid. and Rev.Unif.R.Evid. (1974) 703 provide:

The facts or data in the particular case upon which an expert bases an opinion or inference may be those perceived by or made known to him at or before the hearing. If of a type reasonably relied upon by experts in the particular field in forming opinions or inferences upon the subject, the facts or data need not be admissible in evidence.

See also West's Ann.Cal.Evid.Code §§ 801(b), 804.

6. See nn. 4, 5 supra.

7. See Fed.R.Evid. 703, Advisory Committee's Note. The questions need not be couched in hypothetical form. Penn Fruit Co. v. Clark, 256 Md. 135, 259 A.2d 512 (1969); State v. Franks, 300 N.C. 1, 265 S.E.2d 177 (1980). Before the expert testifies to the inferences on this basis a few courts have required that the expert specify the basis of the opinion. See dictum in Cogdill v. North Carolina State Highway Commission, 279 N.C. 313, 182 S.E.2d 373 (1978). Substantial authority holds that data need not be stated before the statement of opinion. Fed.R.Evid. and Rev.Unif.R.Evid. (1974) 705; Commonwealth v. Johnson, 188 Mass. 382, 74 N.E. 939, 940 (1905) (dictum). The judge should have a broad

uation at issue, and has made no firsthand investigation of the facts, then traditionally the required method of securing the benefit of the expert's skill is by asking the expert to assume certain facts and then on these assumed facts to state opinions or inferences.[8] These questions are known as hypothetical questions, and the rules regulating their form and content have perhaps been developed more on the basis of theoretical logic than on the basis of practicalities. At the discretion of the judge hypothetical questions are permissible under the Federal Rules of Evidence and other liberal rules, but they are not usually required.[9]

In most jurisdictions with the more traditional views mentioned above it has been permissible to have an expert witness in court during the taking of testimony, and then when the expert is called as a witness to simplify a hypothetical question by merely asking the witness to assume the truth of the previous testimony heard by the witness, or some specified part of it, and to state an

opinion upon that assumption.[10] Again this practice is permissible in the discretion of the court under the Federal Rules of Evidence and other liberal rules.[11] The practice has some advantages and some limitations. Two obvious requirements are that the assumed facts must be clear to the jury and must not be conflicting. Otherwise the jury will not be given any aid. A question which asks the witness to assume the truth of one previous witness's testimony will usually meet these requirements,[12] but as the range of assumption is widened to cover the testimony of several witnesses,[13] or all the testimony for one side,[14] the risk of infraction of these requirements is increased; and when a hypothetical question covers all the testimony in the case, the question manifestly will be approved only when the testimony on the issue relating to the question is not conflicting and is brief and simple enough for the jury to recall its outlines without having them recited.[15]

discretion. Fed.R.Evid. and Rev.Unif.R.Evid. (1974) 703 (there need not be prior disclosure unless "the court requires otherwise"). See also, People v. Youngs, 151 N.Y. 210, 218, 45 N.E. 460, 462 (1896).

8. 2 Wigmore, Evidence § 676 (Chadbourn rev. 1979).

9. No authority requiring the use of a hypothetical question in any situation has been discovered. Depending upon the opportunity of a defendant in a criminal case to obtain adequate discovery, a hypothetical question of a prosecution expert might be required.

10. See 2 Wigmore, Evidence § 681 (Chadbourn rev. 1979); Annot., 82 A.L.R. 1460.

11. Fed.R.Evid. and Rev.Unif.R.Evid. (1974) 703. See n. 9 supra.

12. Bosse v. Ideco Division of Dresser Industries, Inc., 412 F.2d 567 (10th Cir. 1969).

It might be noted that Fed.R.Evid. and Rev.Unif.R. Evid. (1974) 701–705 do not specify requirements for hypothetical questions, but that the two requirements mentioned in the text follow from the requirement that opinions should be helpful to the trier of fact. See § 13 supra, at note 9.

13. Damm v. State, 128 Md. 665, 97 A. 645 (1916) (abortion: opinion of doctor based on evidence of attending and examining doctors, approved); Cornell v. State, 104 Wis. 527, 80 N.W. 745 (1899) (murder: defense, insanity: opinion of doctor based on 40 or 50 pages of testimony of other witnesses, approved on ground testimony not conflicting, and whether too vo-

luminous and complicated was in trial judge's discretion).

14. State v. Eggleston, 161 Wash. 486, 297 P. 162, 82 A.L.R. 1439, 1441 (1931) (murder: defense, insanity: "assuming all of the testimony given by the defendant's witnesses is true . . . what is your opinion as to whether the defendant was sane . . . ?" approved).

15. Rhea v. M–K Grocer Co., 236 Ark. 615, 370 S.W.2d 33 (1963); Shouse, Doolittle & Morelock v. Consolidated Flour Mills Co., 132 Kan. 108, 294 P. 657 (1931) (opinion as to value of legal services, from all the testimony, disapproved, testimony conflicting); State v. Reilly, 25 N.D. 339, 141 N.W. 720, 734 (1913) (discussing the practice). But compare State v. Carroll, 52 Wyo. 29, 69 P.2d 542, 550–552 (1937) where the court suggests that more consideration should be given to the fact that the cross-examiner has a complete opportunity to clear up any ambiguity in the hypothesis flowing from the conflict in the testimony.

A question based on prior testimony might include the inference of a prior expert witness. If it is apparent that the question only includes prior expert's descriptions and statements of facts and not their inference or conclusions, the question is not objectionable. Sepich v. Department of Labor and Industries, 75 Wn. 2d 312, 450 P.2d 940 (1969); Cody v. Toller Drug Co., 232 Iowa 475, 5 N.W.2d 824 (1942) (question which asked expert witness to assume truth of testimony of previous witness, a chemist, as to result of tests made by that witness, was proper). Also, whether opinion

The type of hypothetical questions just discussed, namely those based on other testimony in the case, satisfy the basic traditional requirement imposed on all hypothetical questions—that the facts assumed must be supported by evidence in the case.[16] This rule should not be a requirement for hypothetical questions in jurisdictions which follow the Federal Rules of Evidence.[17] Assuming a jurisdiction in which the requirement exists, the requirement is based on the notion that if the answering opinion is founded on premises of fact which the jury, for want of evidence, cannot find to be true, then they are equally disabled from using the answering opinion as the basis for a finding. Direct testimony supporting the fact assumed is not required. It is suffi-

cient if the fact is fairly inferable from the circumstances proved.[18] Moreover, the supporting evidence need not have been already adduced if the interrogating counsel gives assurance that it will be.[19] Further, it is no objection that the supporting evidence is controverted.[20] The opponent is entitled to put his side of the case to the witness for his opinion. However, it is thought there is a possible danger that, by omitting some of the facts, the proponent may present an unfair and inadequate picture to the expert and that the jury may give undue weight to the answer without considering its faulty basis. What safeguards have been supplied? Some decisions have required that all facts material to the question should be embraced in the hypothesis,[21] but this viewpoint seems

---

testimony is actually based upon other opinion testimony or other opinions may be a question. Dennis v. Prisock, 221 So.2d 706 (Miss.1969) ("she was being treated by doctors in Jackson and I had correspondence with doctors in Jackson" did not indicate the opinions of others). A question is raised because in some cases it has been held that in questions seeking an opinion it is improper to ask the witness to assume the truth of testimony which includes prior opinions. Annot., 98 A.L.R. 1109; C.J.S. Evidence § 356. The second opinion may be but an academic echo. At least the judge should have discretion to distinguish the shadowy line between "fact" and "opinion" in this area. However, under Fed.R.Evid. and Rev.Unif.R.Evid. (1974) 703, an expert may rely on facts or data reasonably relied upon by experts in the particular field, and under Rule 705 he need not even relate such matters before stating an opinion. By analogy, a persuasive conclusion is that the traditional rule barring opinion based upon opinion in hypothetical questions is inapplicable if the expert indicates that the pertinent opinion is of a type relied on in the particular field, even if there is no such indication until cross-examination.

16. Donaldson v. Buck, 333 So.2d 786 (Ala.1976); Barnett v. State Workmen's Compensation Commissioner, 153 W.Va. 796, 172 S.E.2d 698 (1970); Nisbet v. Medaglia, 356 Mass. 580, 254 N.E.2d 782 (1970); C.J.S. Evidence § 552, n. 33.

17. It should be concluded that material which may be relied upon by the expert under Fed.R.Evid. 703 should be includable in a hypothetical question if such material may be relied upon in an opinion without the use of a hypothetical question under Rule 705. Furthermore, it has been urged that because an expert may first merely state his opinion without answering a hypothetical question, requirements for hypothetical questions should be minimal. Apparently some judges have thought these notions to be impractical so long as a hypothetical question is used, because it has been indicated that such a question must be based on evidence

in the record. Logsdon v. Baker, 170 U.S.App.D.C. 360, 517 F.2d 174 (1975); Iconco v. Jensen Construction Co., 622 F.2d 1291 (8th Cir. 1980).

18. Farmer's Co-op Exchange of Weatherford v. Krewall, 450 P.2d 506 (Okl.1969); State ex rel. Richardson v. Edgeworth, 214 So.2d 579 (Miss.1968); Friedman v. General Motors Corp., 411 F.2d 533 (3d Cir. 1969); Dec.Dig. ☞553(3).

19. Gibson v. Healy Brothers & Co., 109 Ill.App.2d 342, 248 N.E.2d 771 (1969) (practice is to be discouraged but is within the sound discretion of the court). The rule was applied to cross-examination in Barretto v. Akau, 51 Hawaii 383, 463 P.2d 917 (1969) (cross-examination hypothetical to demonstrate alternative theories or contest a substantive element in the case).

It should be noted, however, that hypothetical questions may usually be put upon cross-examination to test the expert's knowledge and skill, even though the questions are not based upon evidence in the case. Randall v. Goodrich-Gamble Co., 244 Minn. 401, 70 N.W.2d 261 (1955); Seibert v. Ritchie, 173 Wash. 27, 21 P.2d 272 (1933); 2 Wigmore, Evidence § 684 (Chadbourn rev. 1979). This type of cross-examination should be permissible under the federal rules even though there is no compliance with Fed.R.Evid. 703.

20. Rasmussen v. Thilges, 174 N.W.2d 384 (Iowa 1970); Louisville & Nashville Railroad Co. v. Self, 45 Ala.App. 530, 233 So.2d 90 (1970); Kresha Construction Co. v. Kresha, 184 Neb. 188, 166 N.W.2d 589 (1969); Fidelity & Casualty Co. v. McKay, 73 F.2d 828 (5th Cir. 1934) (jury should be instructed to disregard answer if they find facts are not true); Martin v. Frear, 184 Neb. 266, 167 N.W.2d 69 (1969) (facts conforming to examiner's theory may be included even if they are controverted).

21. Stumpf v. State Farm Mutual Automobile Insurance Co., 252 Md. 696, 251 A.2d 362 (1969) (question should contain a fair summary of the material facts in evidence essential to the formulation of a rational opin-

undesirable because it is likely to multiply disputes as to the sufficiency of the hypothesis, and may tend to cause counsel, out of abundance of caution, to propound questions so lengthy as to be wearisome and almost meaningless to the jury.[22] The more expedient and more widely prevailing view is that there is no rule requiring that all material facts be included.[23] The safeguards are that the adversary may on cross-examination supply omitted facts and ask the expert if his opinion would be modified by them,[24] and further that the trial judge if he deems the original question unfair may in his discretion require that the hypothesis be reframed to supply an adequate basis for a helpful answer.[25]

As indicated in Section 16, infra, however, none of these traditional rules governing the requirements for hypothetical questions has furnished sufficient safeguards against evils arising from the use of these questions.

WESTLAW REFERENCES

digest(expert /s witness /s "opinion" /s
 hypothetical /s question* fact*)

---

ion concerning the matter to which it relates); Ames & Webb Inc. v. Commercial Laundry Co., Inc., 204 Va. 616, 133 S.E.2d 547 (1963) (question must embody all material facts which evidence tends to prove); Dec.Dig. Evidence ⚖553(2).

Various courts have also held that undisputed material facts should not be ignored. Jackson v. Nelson, 382 F.2d 1016 (10th Cir. 1967); Christianson v. City of Chicago Heights, 103 Ill.App.2d 315, 243 N.E.2d 677 (1968).

22. See, e.g., Treadwell v. Nickel, 194 Cal. 243, 228 P. 25, 35 (1924) where the court refers to a question "contained in some 83 pages of typewritten transcript, and an objection involved in 14 pages more of the record."

23. Napier v. Greenzweig, 256 F. 196 (2d Cir. 1919); Virginia Beach Bus Line v. Campbell, 73 F.2d 97 (3d Cir. 1934) (reviewing prior decisions); United States v. Aspinwall, 96 F.2d 867 (4th Cir. 1938); Dahlberg v. Ogle, 268 Ind. 30, 373 N.E.2d 159 (1978); Pickett v. Kyger, 151 Mont. 87, 439 P.2d 57 (1968); Gordon v. State Farm Life Insurance Co., 415 Pa. 256, 203 A.2d 320 (1964).

§ 15. Expert's Opinion Based on Reports of Others and Inadmissible or Unadmitted Data and Facts

A question calling for a direct opinion based upon firsthand knowledge of an expert is so direct, simple, and thus effective that a party may for similar reasons desire to obtain an opinion based upon reports of others. There formerly was a majority view, however, that a question is improper if it calls for the witness' opinion on the basis of reports that are not in evidence or are inadmissible in evidence under the hearsay rule (without reciting their contents as hypotheses, to be supported by other evidence as to their truth).[1] The essential reason in support of this view seemed to be that the jury was asked to accept as evidence the witness' inference, based upon someone's hearsay or upon other inadmissible facts which were presumably not supported by any evidence at the trial and which therefore the jury had no basis for finding to be true. Want of knowledge could also be asserted. This view was also taken when the witness was asked to give a similar direct (not hypothetical) opinion, not merely on the basis of reports, facts and data of this kind, but on these matters supplemented by the witness' own observation of the person or matter in

24. See authorities cited in n. 23 supra.

25. See authorities cited in n. 23 supra. Another view requires a question to adopt some reasonable or supportable factual theory based upon the facts of record. See Vermont Food Industries, Inc. v. Ralston Purina Co., 514 F.2d 456 (2d Cir. 1975) ("any combination of the facts within the tendency of the evidence"; not a decision under Fed.R.Evid.).

§ 15

1. Davies v. Carter Carburator, Division ACF Industries, Inc., 429 S.W.2d 738 (Mo.1968) (opinion based on history of patient stated to physician-expert); Kraner v. Coastal Tank Lines, Inc., 26 Ohio St.2d 59, 269 N.E.2d 43 (1971); Sykes v. Norfolk & Western Railway Co., 200 Va. 559, 106 S.E.2d 746 (1959) (excluding opinion based on a study of figures furnished by others and not under supervision of the expert or upon subject matter observed by the expert, a railroad crossing); Dec.Dig. Evidence ⚖555, Crim.Law ⚖486.

question.[2] However, in this latter situation there has been a strong case law trend toward a contrary view.[3] (There is also a suggested view that opinions based upon hearsay should be less objectionable if they are opinions upon subject matters that have an indirect relation to the fact issues in the case, rather than opinions directly concerning the facts in issue.)[4] The above trend was another trend in the area of evidence law which culminated in a broader view in Federal Rule of Evidence 703, which has been adopted in various state jurisdictions. Of course, under Rule 703 (and Rule 705) an expert may give a direct opinion upon facts and data, including reports, which are inadmissible or not introduced into evidence, provided the reports or other data are "of a type reasonably relied upon by experts in the particular field in forming opinions or in-

2. Wild v. Bass, 252 Miss. 615, 173 So.2d 647 (1965) (doctor may not base his opinion in part upon observation and in part upon history of patient related by patient's mother); Vick v. Cochran, 316 So.2d 242 (Miss. 1975); Dec.Dig. Evidence ⚖555, Crim.Law ⚖486.

The status of basis statements, relied upon for expert opinions, as hearsay exceptions under the Federal Rules is discussed in § 324.2 infra.

3. Schooler v. State, 175 S.W.2d 664 (Tex.Civ.App. 1943) (geologist testified to opinion as to prospects for oil in a certain region, based on his own inspection and upon geological reports); Sutherland v. McGregor, 383 S.W.2d 248 (Tex.Civ.App.1964) (opinion of petroleum engineer admissible though based partly on reports made by others); Trinity Universal Insurance Co. v. Town of Speedway, 137 Ind.App. 510, 210 N.E.2d 95 (1965) (estimate of cost of repair based in part upon reports of others; "an expert is competent to judge the reliability of statements made to him by other persons and taking these statements made to him by other persons together with his own first hand observations comprises a sufficient basis for a direct examination of his own professional opinion as to the cost of repairing the street"). See Moore v. Cataldo, 356 Mass. 325, 249 N.E.2d 578 (1969) (dictum taking view that under Finnegan v. Fall River Gas Works Co., 159 Mass. 311, 34 N.E. 523 (1893), opinion testimony might rest in part on hearsay). Other case law decisions have indicated a broader conclusion. Buckler v. Commonwealth, 541 S.W.2d 935 (Ky.1976) (an expert may properly express an opinion "based upon information supplied by third parties which is not in evidence, but upon which the expert customarily relies in the practice of his profession"). Actually, whether opinion can rest in part upon hearsay may well depend in case law in part upon the nature of the subject matter of the opinion and the nature of the hearsay involved. The question of whether opinion may be based in part upon information from others (that is not in evidence) has arisen most often in connection with the testimony of medical experts and property valuation experts. Most courts in which Fed. R.Evid. 703 has not been adopted will permit the opinion of the medical expert who has treated the patient whose condition is the subject of his opinion, although the opinion is based in part upon history given by the patient. See, Annot., 51 A.L.R.2d 1051, 1057. As to the admissibility of the history of the patient as substantive evidence, see §§ 292, 293 infra. Some courts also include within this rule information received from persons in the medical profession (or connected with it).

See Gray v. Bird, 380 S.W.2d 908 (Tex.Civ.App.1964) (psychiatrist's opinion). Some cases permit the treating medical expert to use in part a history furnished by a relative of the patient under particular circumstances. See Miller v. Watts, 436 S.W.2d 515 (Ky.1969) (history furnished by mother of infant patient). In some jurisdictions the above extensions have not been established. See, e.g., Seawell v. Brame, 258 N.C. 666, 129 S.E.2d 283 (1963).

On the other hand, some courts in which Fed.R. of Evid. 703 is not adopted have refused to permit opinion of so-called forensic medical experts, e.g., experts consulted only to prepare for trial, based in part on medical history related by the person examined or on information received from third persons. See Briney v. Williams, 143 Ind.App. 691, 242 N.E.2d 132 (1968) (opinion based on "subjective symptoms and statements of person who sought examination; otherwise patient's self-serving statements would be carried to jury and bolstered by the expert opinion); Goodrich v. Tinker, 437 S.W.2d 882 (Tex.Civ.App.1969) (statements and subjective symptoms of patient); Brown v. Blauvelt, 152 Conn. 272, 205 A.2d 773 (1964); Annot., 51 A.L.R.2d 1051, 1065. Whether a medical expert is one in this latter category is sometimes a difficult problem and may not depend entirely upon whether treatment was prescribed. See Goodrich v. Tinker, cited above. Some cases have attached weight to the time at which the expert was consulted. Annot., 51 A.L.R.2d 1051, 1078.

For the wide variety of former views upon all of the above and related matters see in general, Comment, 35 So.Calif.L.Rev. 193 (1962); Rheingold, The Basis of Medical Testimony, 15 Vand.L.Rev. 473 (1962). There is a pronounced trend in case law to permit opinion of valuation experts based in part upon personal knowledge and in part upon information received from others. See, Annot., 12 A.L.R.3d 1064. There is likewise a similar trend in case law concerning expert opinion of mental states based on reports of others. See Annot., 55 A.L.R.3d 551.

The above-mentioned trend also occurred in various states in which Fed.R.Evid. 703 has since been adopted. See the following text.

4. Town of Framingham v. Department of Public Utilities, 355 Mass. 138, 244 N.E.2d 281 (1969) (court approved expert's evaluation of studies on the effect of electromagnetic fields on human and animal systems).

ferences upon the subject." [5] This view is justified on the ground that an expert in a science is competent to judge the reliability of statements made to him by other investigators or technicians.[6] He is just as competent indeed to do this as a judge and jury are to pass upon the credibility of an ordinary witness on the stand. If the statements, then, are attested by the expert as the basis for a judgment upon which he would act in the practice of his profession, it seems that they should ordinarily be a sufficient basis even standing alone for his direct expression of professional opinion on the stand, and this argument is reinforced when the opinion is founded not only upon reports but also in part upon the expert's firsthand observation. The data of observation will usually enable the expert to evaluate the reliability of the statement.

The principal problem presented by Rule 703 is the interpretation of the language quoted above. The key language consists of the words, "reasonably relied upon" as further modified in the rule. A persuasive view is that the judge may rely on the expert's view in judging whether the standard of the rule is met at least in matters in which the judge is not equipped to "second guess" the expert.[7] However, the judge and attorneys may treat the matter in a hearing under Rule 104.[8] There are intimations of a restrictive view that if the data would have been or was excluded from the record as hearsay and can not meet a test of circumstantial trustworthiness for an exception to the hearsay rule, the standard of Rule 703 is not met.[9] In matters requiring any special knowledge for judgment, this latter view appears to depart from Rule 703 by imposing a separate hearsay exception requirement that Rule 703 seems to exclude. Another problem under Rule 703 in criminal cases is whether the defendant should or must have the opportunity of cross-examination of the persons who originated the data upon which an expert relies under the language of Rule 703. Rule 703 should probably be followed

---

5. Fed.R.Evid. and Rev.Unif.R.Evid. (1974) 703 provide:

"The facts or data in the particular case upon which an expert bases an opinion or inference may be those perceived by or made known to him at or before the hearing. If of a type reasonably relied upon by experts in the particular field in forming opinions or inferences upon the subject, the facts or data need not be admissible in evidence."

Thus opinion may be based on data presented to, or known by, the expert before trial, including data that is not introduced at the trial or data that is inadmissible and meets the standard of the second sentence of the rule. See United States v. Golden, 532 F.2d 1244 (9th Cir. 1976), cert. denied 429 U.S. 842 (testimony of market price of heroin based upon information from other agents); United States v. Sims, 514 F.2d 147 (9th Cir. 1975), cert. denied 423 U.S. 845 (opinion in part based upon inadmissible hearsay was held admissible, although Fed.R.Evid. 703 was not then effective); United States v. Morrison, 531 F.2d 1089 (1st Cir. 1976), cert. denied 429 U.S. 837 (analysis of betting slips and records based upon calculations and reports of others held admissible). Compare United States v. Brown, 548 F.2d 1194 (5th Cir. 1977) (court held a witness "was not in fact put on the stand as an expert" but was called to establish a [hearsay] fact, and on this basis her testimony was inadmissible hearsay).

See also West's Ann.Cal.Evid.Code §§ 801(b), 804.

6. The Advisory Committee's Note for Fed.R.Evid. 703 states in part: "The third source contemplated by the rule consists of presentation of data to the expert outside of court and other than by his own perception. In this respect the rule is designed to broaden the basis for expert opinions beyond that current in many jurisdictions and to bring the judicial practice into line with the practice of the experts themselves when not in court. Thus a physician in his own practice bases his diagnosis on information from numerous sources and of considerable variety, including statements by patients and relatives, reports and opinions from nurses, technicians and other doctors, hospital records, and X rays. Most of them are admissible in evidence, but only with the expenditure of substantial time in producing and examining various authenticating witnesses. The physician makes life-and-death decisions in reliance upon them. His validation, expertly performed and subject to cross-examination, ought to suffice for judicial purposes. Rheingold, supra, at 531 [Rheingold, The Basis of Medical Testimony, 15 Vand.L.Rev. 473 (1962), n. 9, supra]; McCormick § 15. A similar provision is California Evidence Code § 801(b)."

7. A possible example is United States v. Sims, 514 F.2d 147 (9th Cir. 1975), cert. denied 423 U.S. 485. See also Mannino v. International Manufacturing Co., 650 F.2d 846 (6th Cir. 1981).

8. If there is any issue on the matter, the judge must decide the issue.

9. See discussion of Zenith Radio Corp. v. Matsushita Electric Industrial Co., Limited, 505 F.Supp. 1313 (D.C.Pa.1981) in Weinstein & Berger, Evidence ¶ 703[03].

unless a government expert is in effect being used solely to bring before the jury otherwise inadmissible matter (particularly, inadmissible hearsay).[10]

Of course, almost all expert opinion embodies hearsay indirectly, a matter which the courts recognize and accept.[11]

 WESTLAW REFERENCES

expert /s witness /s "opinion" /s inadmissible unadmitted /s data facts

§ 16. Should the Hypothetical Question Be Retained?

The hypothetical question is an ingenious and logical device for enabling the jury to apply the expert's scientific knowledge to the facts of the case. Nevertheless, it has been largely a failure in practice and an obstruction to the administration of justice. If we require that it recite all the relevant facts, it becomes intolerably wordy. If we allow, as most courts do, the interrogating counsel to select such of the material facts as he sees fit,[1] we tempt him to shape a one-

sided hypothesis. Those expert witnesses who have given their views seem to agree that this partisan slanting of the hypothesis is the fatal weakness of the practice.[2] The legal writers who have studied the problem seem equally agreed in condemnation.[3]

What is the remedy? It seems hardly practicable to require the trial judge to undertake such a preliminary study of the case as would be necessary to enable him to make the selection of the significant facts to be included. It would be feasible for the questions to be framed by both counsel in conference with the judge, either at a pretrial hearing or during the trial, with the jury excluded.[4] But this is wasteful of time and effort. The only remaining expedient is the one generally advocated, namely, that of dispensing with the requirement that the question be accompanied by a recital of an hypothesis, unless the proponent elects to use the hypothetical form, or unless the trial judge in his discretion requires it. This is the procedure authorized by Federal and Revised Uniform Rule of Evidence (1974) 705 and a few other statutes and rules.[5] It is

---

10. See opinion in United States v. Lawson, 653 F.2d 299 (7th Cir. 1981), cert. denied 454 U.S. 1150 (when opinion is based entirely on reports, court says defendant must have had access to such reports and in this case had sufficient access).

11. Ryan v. Payne, 446 S.W.2d 273 (Ky.1969) (acceptable that expert consulted skidmark distance tables prior to taking stand); Thompson v. Underwood, 407 F.2d 994 (6th Cir. 1969) (acceptable for medical expert to testify to partial permanent disability of about 37 percent, the expert having used a manual published by the American Medical Association, but having also reached his own independent opinion); 2 Wigmore, Evidence § 665(b) (Chadbourn rev. 1979).

§ 16

1. See § 14 n. 23 supra.

2. See, e.g., White, Insanity and the Criminal Law 56 (1923) ("in a large experience, I have never known a hypothetical question, in a trial involving the mental condition of the defendant, which in my opinion offered a fair presentation of the case"); Hulbert, Psychiatric Testimony in Probate Proceedings, 2 Law & Contemp. Prob. 448, 455 (1935) ("But the present practice of misusing the hypothetical question as restatement of the case to re-impress the jury is bad strategy, though good tactics; bad strategy because it is so unfair, confusing and degrading that it does not clarify the issue nor help achieve justice"); Roberts, Some Observations

on the Problems of the Forensic Psychiatrist, 1965 Wis. L.Rev. 240, 258 (1965).

3. See, e.g., 2 Wigmore, Evidence § 686 (Chadbourn rev.1979) ("It is a strange irony that the hypothetical question, which is one of the truly scientific features of the rules of Evidence, should have become that feature which does most to disgust men of science with the law of Evidence."); Judge Learned Hand, New York Bar Association Lectures on Legal Topics, 1921–1922, ("the most horrific and grotesque wen on the fair face of justice"). See Rabata v. Dohner, 45 Wis.2d 111, 172 N.W.2d 409 (1969) stating in part, "moreover the members of this court, based upon their experience gleaned as practicing lawyers and trial judges, are satisfied that a mechanistic hypothetical question has the effect of boring and confusing the jury. Rather than inducing a clear expression of expert opinion and the basis for it, it inhibits the expert and forecloses him from explaining his reasoning in a manner that is intelligible to a jury."

4. See Hulbert, op. cit., n. 2, supra.

5. Fed.R.Evid. 705:

The expert may testify in terms of opinion or inference and give his reasons therefor without prior disclosure of the underlying facts or data, unless the court requires otherwise. The expert may in any event be required to disclose the underlying facts or data on cross-examination.

for the cross-examiner to bring out the basis for the expert's opinion if that is desired.[6] Manifestly, this does not lessen the partisanship of the question or the answer, but it does simplify the examination and removes the occasion for imperiling the judgment by mistakes in the form of hypothetical questions. Rule 705 does, however, give the judge discretion to require prior disclosure of basis facts, and it may be assumed that he will do so when there has not been adequate opportunity to discover them in advance, especially in criminal cases.

 **WESTLAW REFERENCES**

hypothetical /s question* /s prohibit!

§ 17. Proposals for Improvement of the Practice Relating to Expert Testimony.[1]

In common law countries we have the contentious, or adversary, system of trial, where the opposing parties, and not the judge as in other systems, have the responsibility and initiative in finding and presenting proof.[2] Advantageous as this system is in many respects, its present application in the procurement and presentation of expert testimony is widely considered a sore spot in judicial administration. There are two chief points of weakness in the use of experts. The first is the choice of experts by the party, who will naturally be interested in finding, not the best scientist, but the "best witness." As an English judge has said:

". . . the mode in which expert evidence is obtained is such as not to give the fair result of scientific opinion to the Court. A man may go, and does sometimes, to half-a-dozen experts . . . He takes their honest opinions, he finds three in his favor and three against him; he says to the three in his favor, 'will you be kind enough to give evidence?' and he pays the three against him their fees and leaves them alone; the other side does the same . . . I am sorry to say the result is that the Court does not get that assistance from the experts which, if they were unbiased and fairly chosen, it would have a right to expect."[3]

The second weakness is that the adversary method of eliciting scientific testimony, by direct and cross-examination in open court, frequently upon hypothetical questions based on a partisan choice of data, is ill-suited to the dispassionate presentation of technical data, and results too often in over-

---

See also West's Ann.Cal.Evid.Code § 802; Kan.Code Civ.Proc. K.S.A. 60–456–458; New Jersey Rules of Evid. 57, 58; McKinney's N.Y. CPLR 4515.

The expert may first merely be asked to state his pertinent opinion, but it is often necessary and desirable first to ask preliminary and explanatory foundation questions. Of course Fed.R.Evid. 705 allows the more traditional methods of examining experts to the extent indicated in § 14. For more detailed treatment of these matters see McElhaney, Expert Witnesses and the Federal Rules of Evidence, 28 Mercer L.Rev. 463 (1977).

6. The various methods for cross-examination and the usual restrictions under the Fed.R.Evid. apply to the cross-examination of the expert. Rules 403 and 611 may be applied to prevent irrelevant, confusing, or collateral matter. United States v. 10.48 Acres of Land, 621 F.2d 338 (9th Cir. 1980); United States v. Taylor, 510 F.2d 1283 (D.C.Cir. 1975), rehearing denied 516 F.2d 1243. Discretion generally should be exercised in favor of the cross-examiner.

In civil cases employment of Fed.R.Civ.P. 26(b)(4) and pretrial conferences will aid the conduct of the cross-examination. In criminal cases discovery will also be necessary to the extent available in order to cross-examine the expert effectively.

§ 17

1. Comprehensive discussions are to be found in 2 Wigmore, Evidence § 563 (Chadbourn rev. 1979); Second Annual Report, New York Law Revision Commission, 795–910 (1936); Expert Testimony (a series of several articles) 2 Law & Contemp.Prob. 401–527 (1935).

2. See Millar, Legal Procedure, 12 Encyc.Soc.Sc. 439, 450 (1934), and Millar, The Formative Principles of Primitive Procedure, 18 Ill.L.Rev. 1, 4 (1923), where the two principles of party-prosecution and judicial prosecution are contrasted, but it is pointed out that most systems of procedure make use of both principles in some degree.

3. Jessel, M. R., in Thorn v. Worthington Skating Rink Co., L.R. 6 Ch.D. 415, 416 (1876), note to Plimpton v. Spiller, 6 Ch.D. 412 (1877). See also similar criticisms by Grier, J., in Winans v. New York & Erie Railroad Co., 62 U.S. (21 How.) 88, 101 (1858); Henshaw, J., in In re Dolbeer's Estate, 149 Cal. 227, 243, 86 P. 695, 702 (1906) and Cartwright, C. J. in Opp v. Pryor, 294 Ill. 545, 128 N.E. 580 (1920).

emphasizing conflicts in scientific opinions which a jury is incapable of resolving.[4]

The remedy for the first weakness is not far to seek. It lies simply in using the trial judge's common law power to call experts. Cases are recorded as early as the 14th century—before witnesses were heard by juries—of the summoning of experts by the judges to aid them in determining scientific issues.[5] The existence of the judge's power to call witnesses generally and expert witnesses particularly seems well recognized in this country.[6] It has been declared by rules and statutes in a substantial number of states empowering the trial judge to summon expert witnesses of his own choosing.[7] Some of these provisions apply to scientific issues in any case, civil or criminal,[8] some

are limited to criminal cases [9] and some refer to issues of sanity in criminal cases.[10] The principle is implemented in the carefully drafted Model Expert Testimony Act approved in 1937 by the Commissioners on Uniform State Laws,[11] and embodied in abbreviated form in the former and present Uniform Rules of Evidence and Federal Rule of Evidence 706.[12] The substance of these proposals should be adopted in every state.[13]

The further mechanism of establishing panels of impartial experts designated by groups in the appropriate fields, from which panel court-appointed experts would be selected, should also be considered along with the above-mentioned systems of court-appointed expert witnesses.[14] An American Bar Association committee has approved in

---

4. See criticism cited in notes 1 and 2, supra.

5. Rosenthal, The Development of the Use of Expert Testimony, 2 Law & Contemp.Prob. 403, 406–411 (1935).

6. See § 8 supra; Notes, 51 Nw.U.L.Rev. 761 (1957), 12 Rutgers L.Rev. 375 (1957); Annot., 95 A.L.R.2d 390.

7. See collection of statutes in 2 Wigmore, Evidence § 563 (Chadbourn rev. 1979).

8. See, e.g., West's Ann.Cal.Evid.Code §§ 730–733; Rhode Island Gen.Laws 1956, § 9–17–19.

9. See, e.g., Florida R.Crim.P. 3.210; Wis.Stat.Ann. § 971.16.

10. See, e.g., Ohio R.C. § 2945.40.

11. The Act is set out in 1937 Handbook, Nat'l Conf.Com'rs on Unif.State Laws 339–348.

12. Fed.R.Evid. 706 provides:

(a) Appointment. The court may on its own motion or on the motion of any party enter an order to show cause why expert witnesses should not be appointed, and may request the parties to submit nominations. The court may appoint any expert witnesses agreed upon by the parties, and may appoint expert witnesses of its own selection. An expert witness shall not be appointed by the court unless he consents to act. A witness so appointed shall be informed of his duties by the court in writing, a copy of which shall be filed with the clerk, or at a conference in which the parties shall have opportunity to participate. A witness so appointed shall advise the parties of his findings, if any; his deposition may be taken by any party; and he may be called to testify by the court or any party. He shall be subject to cross-examination by each party, including a party calling him as a witness.

(b) Compensation. Expert witnesses so appointed are entitled to reasonable compensation in

whatever sum the court may allow. The compensation thus fixed is payable from funds which may be provided by law in criminal cases and civil actions and proceedings involving just compensation under the fifth amendment. In other civil actions and proceedings the compensation shall be paid by the parties in such proportion and at such time as the court directs, and thereafter charged in like manner as other costs.

(c) Disclosure of appointment. In the exercise of its discretion, the court may authorize disclosure to the jury of the fact that the court appointed the expert witness.

(d) Parties' experts of own selection. Nothing in this rule limits the parties in calling expert witnesses of their own selection.

See also § 8, supra, and Fed.R.Evid. 614. Insofar as Fed.R.Crim.P. 28 concerned appointment of experts, it has been replaced by Fed.R.Evid. 706.

Rev.Unif.R.Evid. (1974) 706 is the same as Fed.R. Evid. 706 except for minor stylistic difference.

13. The system of impartial court-appointed experts has not escaped attorneys' criticism or expert's criticism. See Levy, Impartial Medical Testimony—Revisited, 34 Temple L.Q. 416 (1961); Diamond, The Fallacy of the Impartial Expert, 3 Archives of Criminal Psychodynamics 221 (1959), excerpts reprinted in Allen, Furster and Rubin, Readings in Law and Psychiatry 145 (1968).

14. Review and discussion of various plans is found in Myers, "The Battle of the Experts": A New Approach to an Old Problem in Medical Testimony, 44 Neb.L.Rev. 539 (1965); Van Dusen, A United States District Judge's View of the Impartial Medical Expert System, 32 F.R.D. 498 (1963); Impartial Medical Testimony Plans, Alleghany County Medical Society Medico-Legal Committee (1961). See also, Botein, The New

principle this procedure for impartial medical expert witnesses.[15]

It is not only essential to reduce the partisan element in the selection of experts, but it is equally important that the contentious character of the presentation of the results of the expert's investigation be modified. Otherwise, the "battle of experts" might merely evolve into a battle of examiner and cross-examiner in the interrogation of the official expert at the trial. In some kinds of controversies a well-devised plan of scientific investigation and report may operate to reduce greatly the need for contested trials in court.[16] In the Uniform Act, it is provided that the court may require a conference of the experts, whether chosen by the court or the parties, so that they may as far as possible resolve together, in the light of the knowledge and observations of all of them, their differences of view and their difficulties in interpreting the data. As a result, there will be possibilities of a complete agreement which may practically settle the issue for the parties. If not, it will at least make clear the area of agreement and may narrow the controversy within manageable limits. Two or more experts, it is provided, may join in a single report. At the trial, moreover, the individual report of the expert witness, or a joint report, may be read to the court and jury as a part of his testimony, and he may be cross-examined thereon. (In

any event, each expert may be required to file a report which is subject to inspection.) The Act dispenses with the requirement of the use of the hypothetical question.[17]

There are other features of the common law procedure not dealt with in the former Uniform Act which greatly hamper the effectiveness of expert testimony. Among these are, first, the unsuitability of the jury, a body of laymen usually required to be unanimous, as a tribunal for appraising scientific evidence;[18] second, the rules of privilege, especially the physician-patient privilege and the privilege against self-crimination;[19] and third, the occasional employment by the courts of standards of liability, which do not accord with the scientific standards which the experts are accustomed to use as criteria, as in the case of the "understanding of right and wrong" test of responsibility of insane persons.[20]

Finally, it should be borne in mind that the need for better employment by the courts of the resources of technicians and scientists goes beyond the use of expert witnesses. A judge has said:

> "The methods of courts might well be supplemented by the use of well tested examples of administrative tribunals, of expert investigators acting for the court—engineers, scientists, physicians, economic and social investigators, as needed—in addition to, not in substitute for, similar experts acting for the parties . . .

York Medical Expert Testimony Project, 33 U.Det.L.J. 388 (1956).

A further, and perhaps more questionable suggestion is the plan for medical-malpractice panels, staffed by physicians and attorneys. A claim could be voluntarily submitted to the panel. If the panel found it meritorious, the panel would aid in securing medical testimony.

15. American Bar Association, Section of Judicial Administration, Committee on Impartial Medical Testimony, Report, 1956 (August); Handbook on the Improvement of the Administration of Justice, American Bar Association, 79–80 (5th ed. 1971).

16. In states where the statutes provide for the examination by psychiatrists of persons charged with serious crimes, the tendency has been for the prosecution, the defendant, and the court to acquiesce in the expert's conclusions in various situations. See Weihofen, An Alternative to the Battle of Experts: Hospital

Examination of Criminal Defendants Before Trial, 2 Law & Contemp.Prob. 419, 422 (1935); Overholser, The History and Operation of the Briggs Law of Massachusetts, 2 id. 436, 444.

17. See n. 1, supra.

18. Many related problems exist. For example, psychiatric expert testimony may well differ in that it may depend upon whether the expert is "dynamically" or "organically" or otherwise oriented. See Allen, Furster and Rubin, Readings in Law and Psychiatry 153 (1968).

19. See §§ 99 and 134 infra.

20. Weihofen, Insanity as a Defense in Criminal Law 64–68, 409–418 (1933). See also the body of literature which has grown up around Durham v. United States, 94 U.S.App.D.C. 228, 214 F.2d 862, 45 A.L.R.2d 1430 (1954).

"Why should not judge and jury in cases involving multitudinous scientific exhibits, or scientific questions, have the benefit of the assistance of those competent to organize such data and analyze such questions? Why should not courts have adequate fact finding facilities for all kinds of cases? Boards of directors do. Administrative tribunals do. The parties, and in a large sense the public, have an interest in the decision of cases on whole truth, not on partial understanding. The machinery and expert staffs developed by the interstate commerce commission, state public service commissions, and workmen's compensation boards have values for fact finding which may profitably be studied in reference to judicial reorganization . . . "[21]

The judicial tradition has known an abundance of procedures which are well adapted to the utilizing of the services and knowledge of experts. Perhaps pretrial conferences could be designed more specifically to deal with matters involving expert opinion. Most important is the power, often regulated by statute or rule, but in any event presumably one of the latent, "inherent" judicial powers,[22] of referring a question to a master, referee, auditor or similar officer, standing or special. The reference may contemplate merely an investigation and report, or a hearing followed by a report or a preliminary decision.[23] It has been urged that these traditional procedures be more widely used and more effectively prescribed by statute.[24] It is suggested likewise that the courts make wider use of the technical resources of the sister branch of the government, the administrative commissions.[25] It may be predicted that all of these opportunities of the courts for using expert knowledge less clumsily may eventually be employed more widely in the future. They would not merely be useful as aids to a more intelligent final trial of an issue in this context of employment of expert knowledge, but it is likely they would more and more often render trial unnecessary.

 WESTLAW REFERENCES

digest(rule* / 10   evidence evid. / 10   706)
"battle of experts"

§ 18. Application of the Opinion Rule to Out-of-Court Statements

Does the opinion rule apply to statements made out of court, and offered in court under some exception to the hearsay rule? If we accept the traditional view[1] that the opinion rule is a categorical rule of exclusion, rejecting a certain definable type of evidence, it is natural to assume that if this kind of evidence is excluded when elicited from a witness on the stand, it should also be rejected when offered in the form of the repetition in court of what some narrator has said out of court. Consequently, many decisions have simply discussed the admissibility of opinions contained in hearsay declarations as if they had been given by a witness on the stand, and have rejected or

---

21. Justice Harold M. Stephens, What Courts can Learn from Commissions, 21 A.B.A.J. 141, 142 (1933). Also, see generally, Ch. 37 infra.

22. See the opinion of Brandeis, J. in Ex parte Peterson, 253 U.S. 300, 312 (1919) (District Court may appoint auditor with provision that his report shall be used in evidence. "Courts have (at least in the absence of legislation to the contrary) inherent power to provide themselves with appropriate instruments required for the performance of their duties. Compare Stockbridge Iron Co. v. Cone Iron Works, 102 Mass. 80, 87–90 (1869). This power includes authority to appoint persons unconnected with the court to aid judges in the performance of specific judicial duties, as they may arise in the progress of a cause.")

A helpful discussion of the relative advantages and disadvantages of the use of adversary experts, masters, advisors, and court-appointed experts is found in Manual for Complex and Multidistrict Litigation, Appendix §§ 2.60, 3.40 (1982).

See Fed.R.Civ.P. 53.

23. Beuscher, The Use of Experts by the Courts, 54 Harv.L.Rev. 1105, 1111–1120 (1941).

24. Beuscher, op. cit., at p. 1126. There are, however, substantial general objections to the use of masters, and the like, even in a traditional way, in many types of cases.

25. Id. at 1123.

§ 18

1. See § 11 supra.

admitted them accordingly,[2] although common sense doubtless has an unspoken influence toward a more liberal treatment of the out-of-court opinions. If on the other hand we adopt the view to which the courts seem now to be tending namely, that the opinion rule is not an absolute rule of exclusion, but rather a relative rule for the examination of witnesses, preferring when it is feasible the more concrete form of examination to the more general and inferential,[3] then it becomes obvious that the opinion rule has no sensible application to statements made out of court. Sustaining an objection to counsel's question to a witness as calling for an "opinion" is usually not a serious matter since counsel can in most cases easily reframe the question to call for the more concrete statement. But to reject the statement of the out-of-court narrator of what he observed, as in a dying declaration, on the ground that the statement is too general in form to meet the courtroom rules of interrogation mistakes the function of the opinion rule and may shut out altogether a valuable item of proof. Many of the cases, and Wigmore, have taken this view as to admissions,[4] and it is believed that it is in the process of prevailing as to the other classes of declarations coming in under exceptions to the hearsay rule.[5]

Of course, the speciously similar question of the want of personal knowledge of the declarant should be distinguished. If it appears that the out-of-court declarant had not observed at first hand the fact declared, this goes not to form but to substance and is often fatal to admissibility if the statement is offered to prove the fact.[6]

 WESTLAW REFERENCES

expert /s extrajudicial

---

2. E.g., Philpot v. Commonwealth, 195 Ky. 555, 242 S.W. 839 (1922); Pendleton v. Commonwealth, 131 Va. 676, 109 S.E. 201 (1929) (dying declaration).

3. See §§ 11, 12 supra.

4. Swain v. Oregon Motor Stages, 160 Or. 1, 82 P.2d 1084 (1938) (statement by injured party after collision that he considered driver of other car to blame); Taylor v. Owen, 290 S.W.2d 771 (Tex.Civ.App.1956) (statement that other driver was not at fault); 4 Wigmore, Evidence § 1053(3) (Chadbourn rev. 1972); and see § 264

infra. Compare the similar problem presented in respect to evidence of inconsistent statements to impeach, § 35 infra. See treatment of each exception to the hearsay rule in Chapters 25–33 infra.

5. As to dying declarations see § 285 infra.

6. See §§ 285 and 300 infra. But the situation is to the contrary with respect to admissions, see § 264 infra and the entry of items in business records, see § 310 infra.

Chapter 4
CROSS–EXAMINATION AND SUBSEQUENT EXAMINATIONS

Table of Sections

---

§ 19. The Right of Cross-Examination:[1] Effect of Deprivation of Opportunity to Cross-Examine

For two centuries, common law judges and lawyers have regarded the opportunity of cross-examination as an essential safeguard of the accuracy and completeness of testimony,[2] and they have insisted that the opportunity is a right[3] and not a mere privilege.[4] This right is available, of course, at the taking of depositions, as well as on the

---

§ 19

1. As to cross-examination generally, see 5 Wigmore, Evidence §§ 1390–1394 (Chadbourn rev.1974), 6 id. §§ 1884–1894 (1976); Dec.Dig. Witnesses ☞266–284; C.J.S. Witnesses §§ 368–376; 81 Am.Jur. 2d Witnesses §§ 463–470, 515–517.

2. See 5 Wigmore, Evidence § 1367 (Chadbourn rev. 1974). See also Hungate v. Hudson, 353 Mo. 944, 185 S.W.2d 646, 157 A.L.R. 598 (1945).

3. Alford v. United States, 282 U.S. 687, 691 (1931). See also n. 9 infra.

4. Resurrection Gold Mining Co. v. Fortune Gold Mining Co., 129 F. 668, 674 (8th Cir. 1904).

examination of witnesses at the trial.[5] And the premise that the opportunity of cross-examination is an essential safeguard has been the principal justification for the exclusion generally of hearsay statements,[6] and for the admission as an exception to the hearsay rule of reported testimony taken at a former hearing when the present adversary was afforded the opportunity to cross-examine.[7] State constitutional provisions guaranteeing to the accused the right of confrontation have been interpreted as codifying this right of cross-examination,[8] and the right of confrontation required by the Sixth Amendment of the federal constitution in general guarantees the accused's right to the opportunity of cross-examination in criminal proceedings.[9]

What are the present consequences of a denial or failure of the right? There are several common situations.[10] First, a party testifying on his own behalf may unjustifiably refuse to answer questions necessary to a complete cross-examination. Here it is generally agreed that the adversary is entitled to have the direct testimony stricken out,[11] a result that seems warranted.

Second, a non-party witness may similarly refuse to be cross-examined, or to answer proper questions of the cross-examiner. Here the case is a little less clear, but the expressions of some judges and writers seem to sanction the same remedy of excluding the direct.[12] This minimizes the temptation for the party to procure the witness's refusal, a collusion which is often hard to prove and protects the right of cross-examination strictly. There is also some authority for the view that the matter should be left to the judge's discretion.[13] Finally, there is support for the notion that if the privilege against self-incrimination is invoked upon cross-examination to questions which go to the credibility of the witness and are otherwise collateral or immaterial, the testimony on direct examination should not be stricken, or at the least the judge should have an area

5. State ex rel. Bailes v. Guardian Realty Co., 237 Ala. 201, 186 So. 168 (1939). Fed.R.Civ.P. 30(c) and Fed.R.Crim.P. 15(b) recognize the right at the taking of depositions.

6. See § 245 infra.

7. See § 255 infra.

8. State v. Crooker, 123 Me. 310, 122 A. 865, 33 A.L.R. 821 (1923) (confrontation right does not mean merely that accused shall see the witness, but the right to cross-examine), and see § 252 infra.

9. Smith v. State of Illinois, 390 U.S. 129 (1968); Douglas v. Alabama, 380 U.S. 415 (1965); Pointer v. Texas, 380 U.S. 400 (1965); Barber v. Page, 390 U.S. 719 (1968); California v. Green, 399 U.S. 149 (1970); Chambers v. Mississippi, 410 U.S. 284 (1973); Davis v. Alaska, 415 U.S. 308 (1974).

10. See the analyses of these problems in 5 Wigmore, Evidence § 1390 (Chadbourn rev.1974), and in Degnan, Non-Rules Evidence Law: Cross-Examination, 6 Utah L.Rev. 323 (1959).

11. United States v. Panza, 612 F.2d 432 (9th Cir. 1979), cert. denied 447 U.S. 925 (defendant's refusal to answer prosecutor's questioning went to the core of the defense); People v. McGowan, 80 Cal.App. 293, 251 P. 643 (1926) (direct testimony of accused to an alibi stricken when on cross-examination he refused to answer question as to name of person who was with him at the time); Aluminum Industries, Inc. v. Egan, 61 Ohio App. 111, 22 N.E.2d 459 (1938) (direct testimony

of party-witness, refusing to answer pertinent cross-questions on unjustified ground of privilege). See also People v. Barthel, 231 Cal.App.2d 827, 42 Cal.Rptr. 290 (1965); In re Monaghan, 126 Vt. 53, 222 A.2d 665 (1966); C.J.S. Witnesses § 374; Dec.Dig. Witnesses ⊜284. Seemingly the cross-examiner could invoke the court's action to compel the witness to answer, if the privilege against self-incrimination has not been invoked or is not applicable, but is not required to do so.

12. Klein v. Harris, 667 F.2d 274 (2d Cir. 1981) (witness recalled and refused to answer questions relevant to previous testimony); United States v. Frank, 520 F.2d 1287 (2d Cir. 1975), cert. denied 423 U.S. 1087 (cross-examination went directly to the heart of the direct examination); State v. Davis, 236 Iowa 740, 19 N.W.2d 655 (1945) (but here held that full oportunity was later accorded); Hadra v. Utah National Bank, 9 Utah 412, 414, 35 P. 508 (1894) (deposition properly excluded for witness's refusal to answer material cross-question); 5 Wigmore, Evidence § 1391 (Chadbourn rev.1974); C.J.S. Witnesses § 374.

13. See Stephan v. United States, 133 F.2d 87 (6th Cir. 1943) (refusal to answer only a few of the cross-questions; judge in discretion properly refused to strike direct testimony); Moormeister v. Golding, 84 Utah 324, 27 P.2d 447 (1933) (whether deposition should be excluded for witness's failure to answer a question under notary's prompting, in judge's discretion). But in criminal cases, this rule raises constitutional questions. See text at n. 9 supra.

of discretion in making his ruling on that matter.[14]

Third, the witness may become, or purport to become, sick or otherwise physically or mentally incapacitated, before cross-examination is begun or completed. Many of such cases arouse suspicion of simulation, particularly when the witness is a party, and consequently the party's direct examination will often be excluded.[15] In the case of the non-party witness, the same result is usually reached,[16] but, at least in civil cases, it is arguable that this result should be qualified so that the judge is directed to exclude unless he is clearly convinced that the incapacity is genuine, in which event he should let the direct testimony stand. He should then be authorized to explain to the jury the weakness of such uncross-examined evidence.[17] Temporary incapacity may change this result, as indicated below.

The fourth situation is that of the death of the witness before the cross-examination. Here again it is usually said that the party thus deprived of cross-examination is entitled to have the direct testimony stricken,[18] unless, presumably, the death occurred during a postponement of the cross-examination consented to or procured by him.[19] In case of death there seems no adequate reason for excluding the direct testimony, except that exclusion may well be required if the witness is a state's witness in a criminal case. It has been suggested that exclusion of the direct should be discretionary[20] but no matter how valuable cross-examination may be, common sense tells us that the half-loaf of direct testimony is better than no bread at all.[21] To let the direct testimony stand was the accepted practice in equity.[22] It is submitted that except for the testimony of the state's witnesses in criminal cases the judge should let the direct testimony stand but

14. United States v. Cardillo, 316 F.2d 606 (2d Cir. 1963), cert. denied 375 U.S. 822, rehearing denied 375 U.S. 926; Coil v. United States, 343 F.2d 573 (8th Cir. 1965), cert. denied 382 U.S. 821; United States v. Smith, 342 F.2d 525 (4th Cir. 1965), cert. denied 381 U.S. 913 (repetitious cross-examination); United States v. Marcus, 401 F.2d 563 (2d Cir. 1968), cert. denied 393 U.S. 1023; Dunbar v. Harris, 612 F.2d 690 (2d Cir. 1979) (refusal to answer questions which went to credibility and were only collateral); United States v. Williams, 626 F.2d 697 (9th Cir. 1980), cert. denied 449 U.S. 1020 (judge could refuse to strike direct when cross-examination in which witness refused to answer went only to collateral matters); United States v. Seifert, 648 F.2d 557 (9th Cir. 1980) (judge had some discretion to decide when cross-examination went to direct or collateral matters); United States v. Stubbert, 655 F.2d 453 (1st Cir. 1981) (also distinguishing between cross-examination questions closely related to crime at issue and questions involving collateral or repetitious matter). But the thwarted cross-examination may be pertinent to material issues as well as to credibility as pointed out in Board of Trustees of Mt. San Antonio Jr. College District v. Hartman, 246 Cal.App.2d 726, 55 Cal.Rptr. 144 (1967) (but error held not prejudicial).

15. Louisville & Nashville Railroad Co. v. Gregory, 284 Ky. 297, 144 S.W.2d 519 (1940) (plaintiff suing for personal injuries testified from a cot and on cross-examination professed to be unable to proceed; judge refused to strike direct but offered to let defendant use cross-examination taken at former trial, which the defendant declined to do; held error to refuse to strike).

16. Wray v. State, 154 Ala. 36, 45 So. 697 (1908); People v. Cole, 43 N.Y. 508, 512 (1871). But where the importance of the direct has been unusually empha-

sized by the proponent, the failure of cross-examination may require a mistrial. United States v. Malinsky, 153 F.Supp. 321 (S.D.N.Y.1957).

17. This is suggested in Note, 27 Colum.L.Rev. 327 (1927). But it is doubtful that this procedure would be constitutional if the witness is one called by the prosecution in a criminal case. See n. 9 supra.

18. Kemble v. Lyons, 184 Iowa 804, 169 N.W. 117 (1918); Sperry v. Moore's Estate, 42 Mich. 353, 4 N.W. 13 (1880) (death during continuance procured by direct examiner); State v. Bigham, 133 S.C. 491, 131 S.E. 603 (1926); In re Sweeney's Estate, 248 Wis. 607, 22 N.W.2d 657 (1946) (right of cross-examination specially reserved by judge); C.J.S. Witnesses § 373.

19. See 5 Wigmore, Evidence § 1390, n. 6 (Chadbourn rev.1974). The cases cited there, however, are cases of disabilities other than death.

20. 5 Wigmore, Evidence § 1390, p. 135 (Chadbourn rev.1974) ("But the true solution would be to avoid any inflexible rule, and to leave it to the trial judge to admit the direct examination so far as the loss of cross-examination can be shown to him to be not in that instance a material loss") quoted approvingly in Kubin v. Chicago Title and Trust Co., 307 Ill.App. 12, 29 N.E.2d 859, 863 (1940) (ruling excluding direct examination affirmed in absence of showing of prejudice). See also, Treharne v. Callahan, 426 F.2d 58 (3d Cir. 1970).

21. See Note, 27 Colum.L.Rev. 327 (1927) which points out that the testimony is more trustworthy than evidence admitted under many of the established hearsay exceptions.

22. See Scott v. McCann, 76 Md. 47, 24 A. 536 (1892).

should be required on request to instruct the jury in weighing its value to consider the lack of opportunity to cross-examine.

The above results may be modified in certain situations. It has been held that where the incapacity is temporary the cross-examiner may not insist upon immediate exclusion of the direct testimony, but must be content with the offer of a later opportunity to cross-examine even when this makes it necessary for him to submit to a mistrial.[23]

It has been assumed in the preceding paragraphs that, though some cross-questions may have been answered, a failure to secure a complete cross-examination would be treated as if cross-examination had been wholly denied. It seems, however, that a cross-examination, though cut off before it is finished, may yet under the circumstances be found to have been so substantially complete as to satisfy the requirement of opportunity to cross-examine.[24] It also appears that cross-examination may be regarded in the particular situation as having been sufficient as to part of the direct testimony to allow that part to stand though the rest must be stricken.[25]

Finally, the infringement of the right of cross-examination may come, not from the refusal or inability of the witness, but from the action of the judge. The judge, as we shall see, has wide discretionary control over the *extent* of cross-examination upon particular topics, but the denial of cross-examinations altogether, or its arbitrary curtailment upon a proper subject of cross-examination will be ground for reversal.[26]

 WESTLAW REFERENCES

digest(depriv! /s opportunity /s crossexamin!)

impact effect consequences /s deny depriv! /s opportunity /s crossexamin!

---

§ 20. Form of Interrogation

In contrast with direct examination, cross-examination may usually be conducted by leading questions.[1] The cross-examiner's purpose in the main is to weaken the effect of the direct testimony, and furthermore, the witness is usually assumed to be a more or less uncooperative one. Consequently the danger of undue acquiescence in the examiner's suggestions is not ordinarily present. However, when it appears that the witness is biased in favor of the cross-examiner, and likely to be unduly yielding to the suggestions of leading questions the judge in many jurisdictions may restrain the asking of them,[2] and in those jurisdictions where the

---

23. Gale v. State, 135 Ga. 351, 69 S.E. 537 (1910) (where witness collapsed on defendant's cross-examination, no error in refusing to strike out the evidence when defendant declined to consent to mistrial).

24. Fuller v. Rice, 70 Mass. (4 Gray) 343 (1855).

25. United States v. Newman, 490 F.2d 139 (3d Cir. 1974) (the taking of the Fifth Amendment by a government witness to a question going to an important element should lead to the striking of the direct testimony going to that element (a partial striking of the direct)). See Curtice v. West, 50 Hun. 47, 48, 2 N.Y.S. 507 (1888) and compare In re Mezger's Estate, 154 Misc. 633, 278 N.Y.S. 669 (1935). See also Jaiser v. Milligan, 120 F.Supp. 599 (D.C.Neb.1954) (a cross-examination begun but unfinished through no fault of the witness or her attorney is said to suffice if its purposes have been substantially accomplished).

26. Alford v. United States, 282 U.S. 687 (1931) (refusal to permit cross-examination of government witness about his present residence, in custody of U.S. marshal, to show bias); Dixon v. United States, 333 F.2d 348 (5th Cir. 1964) (judge should not have refused cross-examination when judge questioned witness upon

return of jury to open court to ask a question of the judge; questioning enhanced credibility of an informer); Fahey v. Clark, 125 Conn. 44, 3 A.2d 313 (1938) (refusal to permit cross-examination of plaintiff about prior injury); People v. Crump, 5 Ill.2d 251, 125 N.E.2d 615 (1955) (refusal to permit cross-examination of accomplice witness to show that he was a drug addict or had used narcotics on day of crime).

In fact, the right of the criminal defendant in such a case in both state and federal courts is a federal constitutional right. See § 29, infra.

§ 20

1. Ewing v. United States, 135 F.2d 633 (D.C.Cir. 1943); In re Mitgang, 385 Ill. 311, 52 N.E.2d 807 (1944); 3 Wigmore, Evidence § 773 (Chadbourn rev.1970); Dec.Dig. Witnesses ⊕282.

Fed.R.Evid. and Rev.Unif.R.Evid. (1974) 611(c) provide: "Ordinarily leading questions should be permitted on cross-examination."

2. Moody v. Rowell, 34 Mass. 490, 498 (1835) ("So a judge may, in his discretion, prohibit certain leading questions from being put to an adversary's witness,

scope of cross-examination is limited, if the examiner goes beyond the proper field of cross-examination he may be required to refrain from leading the witness.[3] There are, on the other hand, a number of somewhat illogical decisions which permit leading questions on cross-examination even though the witness appears biased in favor of the cross-examiner.[4]

WESTLAW REFERENCES

digest(crossexamin! /20 leading /20 question!)

---

where the witness shows a strong interest or bias in favor of the cross-examining party, and needs only an intimation, to say whatever is most favorable to that party."); 3 Wigmore, Evidence § 773 (Chadbourn rev. 1970); Annot., 38 A.L.R.2d 952. See Tolomeo v. Harmony Short Line Motor Transport Co., 349 Pa. 420, 37 A.2d 511 (1944) (in collision case where plaintiff called defendant's bus driver to show defendant's ownership, court improperly permitted defendant to cross-examine driver by leading questions on negligence). But it is largely a matter of discretion. Lauchheimer & Sons v. Jacobs, 126 Ga. 261, 55 S.E. 55 (1906); Westland Housing Corp. v. Scott, 312 Mass. 375, 44 N.E.2d 959 (1942). Both are cases of a party called by his adversary and cross-examined by his own counsel.

The text is applicable under Fed.R.Evid. and Rev. Unif.R.Evid. (1974) 611(c) quoted in § 6, n. 3, supra. The Advisory Committee's Note states, "The purpose of the qualification 'ordinarily' is to furnish a basis for denying the use of leading questions when the cross-examination is cross-examination in form only and not in fact, as for example the 'cross-examination' of a party by his own counsel after being called by the opposing counsel (savoring more of re-direct) or of an insured defendant who proves to be friendly to the plaintiff."

3. People v. Melone, 71 Cal.App.2d 291, 162 P.2d 505 (1945).

The rule in the text is adopted by Fed.R.Evid. and Rev.Unif.R.Evid. (1974) 611(b), which reads,

Cross-examination should be limited to the subject matter of the direct examination and matters affecting the credibility of the witness. The court may, in the exercise of discretion, permit inquiry into additional matters as if on direct examination.

4. Martyn v. Donlin, 151 Conn. 402, 198 A.2d 700 (1964) (defense counsel permitted to use leading questions on cross-examination of defendant who had been

§ 21. Scope of Cross-Examination: Restriction to Matters Opened up on Direct: The Various Rules [1]

The practice varies widely in the different jurisdictions on the question whether the cross-examiner is confined in his questions to the subjects testified about in the direct examination, and if so to what extent.

The traditional rule of wide-open cross-examination. In England and some of the states, the simplest and freest practice prevails. In these jurisdictions, the cross-examiner is not limited to the topics which the direct examiner has chosen to open,[2] but is free to cross-examine about any subject relevant to any of the issues in the entire case, including facts relating solely to the cross-examiner's own case or affirmative defense.

---

called by plaintiff as an adverse witness); Wilcox v. Erwin, 49 S.W.2d 677 (Mo.App.1932) (similar case); Annot., 38 A.L.R.2d 952.

§ 21

1. See 6 Wigmore, Evidence §§ 1886–1891 (Chadbourn rev.1976); Weinstein & Berger, Evidence ¶ 611[02]; Dec.Dig. Witnesses ⟐269; C.J.S. Witnesses §§ 393–397; Notes, 37 Colum.L.Rev. 1373 (1937), 24 Iowa L.Rev. 564 (1939).

2. Mayor and Corporation of Berwick-on-Tweed, v. Murray, 19 L.J.Ch. 281, 286 (V.C., 1850); Morgan v. Brydges, 2 Stark, 314, 171 Eng.Rep. 657 (N.P.1818) (witness called by plaintiff for formal proof, may be cross-examined by defendant, his employer, on the whole case); Riddle v. Dorough, 279 Ala. 527, 187 So. 2d 568 (1966); Ariz.R.Evid. 611(b); ("Any witness may be cross-examined on any matter material to the case"); Ficken v. Atlanta, 14 Ga. 970, 41 S.E. 58 (1902); LSA–R.S. 15:280 (a witness who "has testified to any single fact . . . may be cross-examined upon the whole case"); King v. Atkins, 33 La.Ann. 1057, 1064 (1881); Me.R.Evid. 611(b) (court may limit cross-examination "in interests of justice"); Moody v. Rowell, 34 Mass. 490 (1835) (leading case, opinion by Shaw, C. J.); Mich.R.Evid. 611(b) (court "may limit" cross-examination); Mask v. State, 32 Miss. 405 (1856); Saxon v. Harvey, 190 So.2d 901 (Miss.1966); State v. West, 349 Mo. 221, 161 S.W.2d 966 (1942) (citing statutes permitting cross-examination "on the entire case" except in case of cross-examination of the accused, or the spouse of accused, in a criminal case); State v. Huskins, 209 N.C. 727, 184 S.E. 480 (1936); N.M.R.Evid. 611(b) (same as Maine rule); State v. Howard, 35 S.C. 197, 14 S.E. 481 (1892); Sands v. Southern Railway Co., 108 Tenn. 1, 64 S.W. 478 (1901); Pride v. Pride, 318 S.W.2d 715 (Tex. Civ.App.1958); Wentworth v. Crawford, 11 Tex. 127, 132 (1853); Wis.Stat.Ann. 906.11 (same as Maine rule); and cases cited C.J.S. Witnesses § 393, note 86.

The "restrictive" rule, in various forms, limiting cross-examination to the scope of the direct. The majority of the states have agreed in the view that the cross-examination must be limited to the matters testified to on the direct examination.[3] This general rule was adopted by the Federal Rules of Evidence.[4] This doctrine can be employed narrowly to restrict the cross-questions to those relating only to the same acts or facts,[5] and, perhaps, those occurring or appearing at the same time and place. The doctrine has often been formulated in a way to suggest this meaning. Thus, the cross-examination has been said to be limited to "the same points" brought out on direct,[6] to the "matters testified to," [7] to the "subjects mentioned," [8] and the like. Slightly more expansive is the extension to "facts and circumstances connected with" the matters stated on direct,[9] but this still suggests the requirement of identity of transaction, and proximity in time and space. Seemingly a much wider extension is accomplished by another variation of the formula. This is the statement that the cross-examination is limited to the matters opened in direct and to facts tending to explain, contradict, or discredit the testimony given in chief,[10] and even more widely, facts tending to rebut any "inference or deduction" from the matters testified on direct.[11] There is little consistency in the expression and the use of formulas, even in the same jurisdiction.[12] All express criteria are too vague to be employed with precision. Assuming that cross-examination is somehow to be limited to the subject matter of the direct examination, the subject matter of questions on direct examination can always be defined in particular instances with greater or lesser generality regardless of the general formulas.[13]

3. Among the leading cases which served to introduce this innovation upon common law practice were Ellmaker v. Buckley, 16 S. & R. 72, 77 (Pa.1827), People v. Horton, 4 Mich. 67, 82 (1856), and Philadelphia & Trenton Railroad Co. v. Stimpson, 39 U.S. (14 Pet.) 448, 461 (1840) by Story, J.

4. Fed. and Rev.Unif.R.Evid. (1974) 611(b) provide:

Cross examination should be limited to the subject matter of the direct examination and matters affecting the credibility of the witness. The court may, in the exercise of discretion, permit inquiry into additional matters as if on direct examination.

5. State v. Guilfoyle, 109 Conn. 124, 145 A. 761 (1929) (doctor testified to general description of wound, cross-examination as to opinion whether wound caused by near or far shot properly excluded); Wheeler & Wilson Manufacturing Co. v. Barrett, 172 Ill. 610, 50 N.E. 325 (1898) (plaintiff testified she bought and paid for sewing machine from defendant, cross-examination designed to show she took possession under written lease contract properly excluded); McNeely v. Conlon, 216 Iowa 796, 248 N.W. 17 (1933) (eye-witness described accident, prejudicial error to permit defendant on cross to elicit that witness just after and at scene said to defendant, "It was not your fault"); Nagel v. McDermott, 138 Wash. 536, 244 P. 977 (1926) (witness testified to location of bicycle in collision incident, but could not testify to speed of bicycle on cross-examination). But these cases are not necessarily consistent with others in the same jurisdictions. See, e.g., Iowa cases cited in n. 11 infra.

6. Carey v. City of Oakland, 44 Cal.App.2d 503, 112 P.2d 714 (1941).

7. McAden v. State, 155 Fla. 523, 21 So.2d 33 (1945); Nadeau v. Texas Co., 104 Mont. 558, 69 P.2d 586 (1937).

8. State v. Bagley, 339 Mo. 215, 96 S.W.2d 331 (1936) (the English rule not followed in criminal cases as to a defendant or his spouse; V.A.M.S. (Mo.) §§ 491.070, 546.260).

9. Story, J., in Philadelphia & Trenton Railroad Co. v. Stimpson, 39 U.S. (14 Pet.) 448, 461 (1840); Austin v. State, 14 Ark. 555, 563 (1854); Williams v. State, 32 Fla. 315, 317, 13 So. 834 (1893).

10. State v. Ragonesi, 112 R.I. 340, 309 A.2d 851 (1973) ("facts and matters brought out in direct examination"); Krametbauer v. McDonald, 44 N.M. 473, 104 P.2d 900 (1940); Lewis v. State, 458 P.2d 309 (Okl.Cr. 1969).

11. A case indicating this view is Conley v. Mervis, 324 Pa. 577, 188 A. 350, 108 A.L.R. 160 (1936) (suit for damages for injury caused by a truck; defendant denies ownership; plaintiff calls defendant as witness and proves on direct that defendant owned license plates on truck; held, error to refuse to permit defendant to be cross-examined by his own counsel to show the plates were taken from his place of business without his knowledge or consent; this was allowable to rebut the inference of ownership of the truck and agency of the driver which would be derived from ownership of the plates). See also Parente v. Dickinson, 391 Pa. 162, 137 A.2d 788 (1958); Crosby v. De Land District, 367 Ill. 462, 11 N.E.2d 937 (1937); State v. Harvey, 130 Iowa 394, 106 N.W. 938 (1906); Eno v. Adair County Mutual Insurance Association, 229 Iowa 249, 294 N.W. 323 (1940); and cases cited in Annot., 108 A.L.R. 167.

12. See Note, 37 Colum.L.Rev. 1373 (1937).

13. Two interesting theories, among others, are available for defining the scope of direct examination broadly. First, the scope of direct may be broadened and made to include the cross-examination by relating

In defining the subject matter of the direct examination Federal Rule of Evidence 611(b) should be interpreted to include the broader views expressed above, a viewpoint that is not inconsistent with the provision that the court may permit inquiry into additional matters as if on direct.[14]

All these limiting formulas have a common escape valve, namely, the notion that where part of a transaction, "res gestae," contract, or conversation has been revealed on direct, the remainder may be brought out on cross-examination.[15] The fact that this is substantially a mere statement of the converse of the limiting rule itself does not detract from its usefulness as an added tool for argument. This particular rule of completeness is unaffected by Federal Rule of Evidence 106, which does not apply to cross-examination after testimony upon direct.[16]

Another escape valve for appeal purposes is the notion that the trial judge has a certain amount of discretion in ruling upon the scope of cross-examination.

The half-open door: cross-examination extends to any matters except cross-examiner's affirmative case. A third view as to the scope of cross-examination would take a middle course between the two extremes. Under this view, now mostly obsolete, the cross-examiner could question the witness about any matters relevant to any issue in the action, except facts relating only to the cross-examiner's own affirmative case, such as defendant's affirmative defenses or cross-claims, or in case of a plaintiff, his new matter in reply.[17] This rather liberalized standard in some instances served as a half-way house, for a time, for courts which later turned to the "wide-open" practice.[18] It has

---

the direct and the cross to some issue of law in the case. See Graham v. Larimer, 83 Cal. 173, 23 P. 286 (1890) (in action on an illegal note the issue was whether a former holder was a holder in due course; on direct former stated only that he had bought the note for value and on cross was questioned whether he knew that the consideration was illegal). Second, all possibly related events in real life can be defined as within the scope of the direct or as the subject matter of direct, and the cross can be related to such events. See Security Benefit Association v. Small, 34 Ariz. 458, 272 P. 647 (1928) (issue in suit on life insurance policy was whether deceased was in good health when policy was taken out; deceased's mother stated on direct that she lived in California and that deceased's health was good when the policy was issued and on cross was asked why she returned with deceased to Arizona two months later).

14. The limit of cross-examination by leading questions to the subject matter of direct is subject to discretion of the trial judge. United States v. Gaston, 608 F.2d 607 (5th Cir. 1979).

15. Gilmer v. Higley, 110 U.S. 47 (1884) (transaction); Rosenberg v. Wittenborn, 178 Cal.App.2d 846, 3 Cal.Rptr. 459 (1960) (conversation); Ah Doon v. Smith, 25 Or. 89, 34 P. 1093 (1893) (transaction); Johnson v. Cunningham, 104 Ill.App.2d 406, 244 N.E.2d 205 (1969) (conversations); Glenn v. Philadelphia & W. C. Traction Co., 206 Pa. 135, 139, 55 A. 860 (1903) (conversation); Smith v. Philadelphia Traction Co., 202 Pa. 54, 51 A. 345 (1902) ("res gestae"); Vingi v. Trillo, 77 R.I. 55, 73 A.2d 43 (1950) (conversation); Dec.Dig. Witnesses ⟐268(3). But see In re Campbell's Will, 100 Vt. 395, 138 A. 725, 726 (1927) (will contest: proponents placed witness on stand who testified that Mrs. Campbell told her that instrument claimed to be a will was in trunk; contestants were allowed to bring out on cross-exami-

nation that Mrs. Campbell told her on same occasion that she wanted her husband to destroy the instrument; held, error, but harmless. "The fact that the proponents had, in effect, put in evidence a part of a statement of Mrs. Campbell, did not, of itself, entitle the contestants to put in all of that statement. The latter could give in evidence whatever Mrs. Campbell then said that tended to qualify, explain, or contradict what Mrs. Stevens had testified to, but no more."). See also § 56 infra.

16. See discussions in Weinstein & Berger, Evidence ¶ 106[01], [02]; Wright & Graham, Federal Practice and Procedure: Evidence § 5072.

17. Legg v. Drake, 1 Ohio St. 286, 290 (1853) (party may cross-examine "as to all matters pertinent to the issue on the trial; limited, however, by the rule that a party cannot, before the time of opening his own case introduce his distinct grounds of defense or avoidance" by cross-examination); Smith v. State, 125 Ohio St. 695 (1932); Dietsch v. Mayberry, 70 Ohio App. 527, 47 N.E.2d 404 (1942). See also, discussion of "Michigan rule" to date of the article, Comment, 36 U. of Det.L.J. 162 (1958).

The objection that the cross-examination elicits matter proper only to the cross-examiner's own case has often, in the past, been given as a ground of decision in states that follow the more restrictive practice limiting the cross to the scope of the direct. See n. 18 infra. But even under the more restrictive view, if the matter is opened in direct, it may be followed up in cross-examination, though this may happen to sustain the cross-examiner's affirmative claim or defense. Garlich v. Northern Pacific Railway Co., 131 F. 837 (8th Cir. 1904); and cases cited in C.J.S. Witnesses § 397.

18. See, e.g., Chandler v. Allison, 10 Mich. 460, 476 (1862) where this standard is perhaps first adumbrated,

the merit, as compared with the restrictive practice, of lessening dispute by widening the ambit of examination. Its present drawback is that it would often be difficult to determine, particularly under the liberal pleading rules of today, whether the matter inquired about does relate solely to the examiner's "distinct grounds of defense or avoidance."[19]

crossexamination /s limit*** /s scope /s direct

§ 22. Cross-Examination to Impeach Not Limited to the Scope of the Direct

One of the main functions of cross-examination is to afford an opportunity to elicit answers which will impeach the veracity, capacity to observe, impartiality, and consistency of the witness; and yet the direct can seldom be expected to touch explicitly on the points to which impeachment is directed. Accordingly, the rule prevails, even in jurisdictions adopting the most restrictive practice, that cross-examination to impeach is not, in general, limited to matters brought

when Campbell, J., in sustaining the propriety of cross-questions said, "They were designed to determine the real character of the transaction in issue. They did not relate to matter in avoidance of it. . . . " See also Rush v. French, 1 Ariz. 99, 139, 140, 25 P. 816, 828 (1874) (witness may be cross-examined "upon all matters pertinent to the case of the party calling him, except exclusively new matter; and nothing shall be deemed new matter except it be such as could not be given under a general denial"). Arizona now follows the "wide-open" practice, see note 2 supra. But see Silver v. London Assurance Corp., 61 Wash. 593, 112 P. 666 (1911) (apparently approving the "half-open door" rule). Washington now has adopted Fed.R.Evid. 611(b).

19. See discussion in Note, 37 Colum.L.Rev. 1373, 1382 (1937).

§ 22

1. Chicago City Railway Co. v. Carroll, 206 Ill. 318, 324, 68 N.E. 1087, 1089 (1903) (cross-question to doctor as to who paid him); Beck v. Hood, 185 Pa. 32, 38, 39 A. 842, 843 (1898) (that witness had talked at previous trial with foreman of jury); 6 Wigmore, Evidence § 1891 (Chadbourn rev. 1976); C.J.S. Witnesses §§ 484(2), 399a.

out in the direct examination.[1] This view is adopted in Federal Rule of Evidence 611(b).[2]

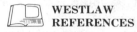

digest(purpose function +3 crossexamination)
crossexamination /s impeach! /s direct /s scope /s not

§ 23. Practical Consequences of the Restrictive Rules: Effect on Order of Proof: Side-Effects

It is sometimes asserted that the only "essential" difference between the "wide-open" and the restrictive rules as to scope of cross-examination is in the time or stage at which the witness may be called upon to testify to the facts inquired about.[1] Thus the difference between the rules would be primarily in their effect upon the order of proof.[2] Under the "wide-open" rule the witness may be questioned on the new matter on cross-examination, whereas under the restrictive rules the cross-examiner can merely postpone the questions until his own next stage[3] of putting on proof, and then call the witness and prove the same facts.[4] This difference is, of course, a substantial difference, but in many instances a mere postponement

2. Fed.R.Evid. and Rev.Unif.R.Evid. (1974) 611(b) permit cross-examination on "matters affecting the credibility of the witness".

§ 23

1. Valliant, J., in Ayers v. Wabash Railroad Co., 190 Mo. 228, 88 S.W. 608, 609 (1905); 6 Wigmore, Evidence § 1895 (Chadbourn rev. 1976).

2. H.R.Rep.No.93–650, 93d Cong., 2d Sess. remarks that the traditional rule [embodied in Fed.R.Evid. 611(b) at the instance of the House Committee on the Judiciary] "facilitates orderly presentation by each party at trial."

3. Grievance Committee of Bar of Fairfield Co. v. Dacey, 154 Conn. 129, 222 A.2d 339 (1966). As to the order of proof, by stages, of the respective parties, see § 4 supra.

4. If party avails himself of the opportunity to call the witness at a later stage, he cannot complain on appeal of a restriction on cross-examination. Clucas v. Bank of Montclair, 110 N.J.L. 394, 166 A. 311, 315, 88 A.L.R. 302 (1933); and see State v. Savage, 36 Or. 191, 61 P. 1128 (1900) (same questions asked on re-call).

of the questions will not necessarily be the result of a ruling excluding a cross-question as not in the scope of the direct. Unless the question is vital and he is fairly confident of a favorable answer, the cross-examiner will at the least take considerable risk if he calls the adversary's witness at a later stage as his own, and will often be motivated to abandon the inquiry. Getting concessions from the opponent's witness while his story is fresh is worth trying for. To call the perhaps unfriendly witness later when his first testimony is stale is usually a much less effective expedient. Also promotion of orderly presentation of proof, supposedly promoted by restrictive rules, may not be an effective reason in particular cases in which a party has injected an issue by one witness but not by a second witness who may not be cross-examined on the issue although he may have knowledge relevant to that issue.[5]

A ruling excluding questions as not within the scope of the direct is not the only consequence of the restrictive rule. There are many collateral effects. Thus the courts adopting the restrictive practice often say that if the cross-examiner, perhaps without objection, cross-examines on new matter he makes the witness his own.[6] This notion is stated in Federal Rule of Evidence 611(b).[7] This being so, he is normally forbidden to ask leading questions about the new matter,[8] and under the traditional rule against impeaching one's own witness[9] may be precluded from impeaching the witness as to those facts.[10] But because one may impeach one's own witness under Federal Rule of Evidence 607, one would not be precluded from impeaching the witness concerning the new matter brought out pursuant to Rule 611(b).[11] Furthermore, the application of the restrictive rule so as to exclude unfavorable testimony from the plaintiff's witness which could otherwise be elicited on cross-examination, may save the plaintiff from a directed verdict at the close of his case in chief.[12] This is usually a tactical advantage, affording the plaintiff a wider possibility for strengthening his case from his opponent's witnesses, even though the unfavorable testimony of the cross-examined witness may be later elicited by the defendant in the course of his own case in defense, and standing undisputed may thus ultimately result in a directed verdict, anyway. Finally, in one situation, the restrictive rule may become a rule of final exclusion, not a rule of postponement. This is the situation where the witness has a privilege not to be called as a witness by the cross-examiner. Thus, the privilege of the accused, and of the spouse of the accused, not to be called by the state in a criminal case may prevent the prosecutor from eliciting the new facts at a later stage, if he cannot draw them out on cross-examination.[13]

---

5. This suggestion is made in Weinstein, Mansfield, Abrams & Berger, Cases and Materials on Evidence 431 (7th ed. 1983). The authors raise the question whether the scope of cross-examination should be determined by the posture of the whole case rather than by the scope of the direct examination of the second witness mentioned in the text.

6. State v. Spurr, 100 W.Va. 121, 130 S.E. 81 (1925); 3A Wigmore, Evidence § 914 (Chadbourn rev. 1976) (critical of rule).

7. See § 21 n. 3, supra.

8. People v. Court of Oyer and Terminer, 83 N.Y. 436, 459 (1881). But this result rests upon an assumption of a hard-and-fast rule that leading questions are always permissible in the proper field of cross-examination and never in the proper area of direct. 3A Wigmore, Evidence § 915 (Chadbourn rev. 1970.) The criterion is whether the witness is probably willing or unwilling to yield to suggestion, and as to this there is usually no difference in the attitudes of the witness, when the question is, or is not, within the scope of the direct. See § 6 supra.

9. This rule, however, has now been much liberalized in many jurisdictions. See § 38 infra.

10. Pollard v. State, 201 Ind. 180, 166 N.E. 654 (1929); 3 Wigmore, Evidence § 914 (Chadbourn rev. 1970); Dec.Dig. Witnesses ⊙325.

11. See § 21 n. 4 supra.

12. Seemingly this was the result in the trial court of the judge's ruling limiting the cross-examination, in Conley v. Mervis, described in § 21, n. 11 supra. See also Ah Doon v. Smith, 25 Or. 89, 34 P. 1093 (1893) where the judge's ruling permitting the cross-examination as to alleged new matter exposed the plaintiff to a dismissal of the action at the close of his testimony.

13. See §§ 25, 26 infra.

WESTLAW REFERENCES

restrict! /15 crossexamination /30 scope order +3 proof /s crossexamin!

§ 24. The Scope of the Judge's Discretion Under the Wide-Open and Restrictive Rules

When Gibson, C. J.[1] and Story, J.[2] introduced the innovation upon the orthodox "wide-open" cross-examination, by suggesting that questioning about new matter was not proper at the stage of cross-examination, they thought of their admonitions as relating solely to the order of proof. Traditionally the order of proof[3] and the conduct and extent of cross-examination[4] have been said to be specially subject to discretionary control by the trial judge.

Accordingly, the earlier cases[5] and many of the more recent cases[6] in jurisdictions adopting the restrictive rule in any of its forms, emphasize the power of the trial

judge in his discretion to allow deviations. It has been said, indeed, that both the courts following the wide-open and those adopting the restrictive practice "recognize the discretionary power of the trial court to allow variations from the customary order and decline ordinarily to consider as an error any variation sanctioned by the trial court."[7] If this statement were fully true, the hazards of injustice at the trial, or of reversals on appeal, in the administration of either rule would not be substantial. But the statement probably paints too bright a picture.

In the states adopting "the scope of the direct" test, trial courts and lawyers tend to find it easier to administer the test as a rule than as a flexible standard of discretion. Also, appellate courts have reversed many cases for error in the application of the test, although there is a trend to give a greater scope of power to the trial judge.[8]

In jurisdictions following the traditional wide-open view, there seems to have been lit-

---

§ 24

1. In Ellmaker v. Buckley, 16 Sarg. & Rawles 72, 77 (Pa.1827).

2. In Philadelphia & Trenton Railroad Co. v. Stimpson, 39 U.S. (14 Pet.) 448, 461 (1840).

3. See 6 Wigmore, Evidence §§ 1867, 1885, 1886 (Chadbourn rev. 1976).

4. See 3A Wigmore, Evidence §§ 944, 983(2) (Chadbourn rev. 1970).

5. See, e.g., Chicago & Rock Island Railroad Co. v. Northern Illinois Coal & Iron Co., 36 Ill. 60 (1864); Glenn v. Gleason, 61 Iowa 28, 32, 15 N.W. 659, 661 (1883); Blake v. People, 73 N.Y. 586 (1878); Kaeppler v. Red River National Bank, 8 N.D. 406, 410, 79 N.W. 869 (1899); Schnable v. Doughty, 3 Pa.St. 392, 395 (1846); State v. Bunker, 7 S.D. 639, 642, 65 N.W. 33 (1895); Lueck v. Heisler, 87 Wis. 644, 58 N.W. 1101 (1894).

6. United States v. Diaz, 662 F.2d 713 (11th Cir. 1981) (extensive cross-examination permitted); United States v. Bright, 630 F.2d 804 (5th Cir. 1980); United States v. Gaston, 608 F.2d 607 (5th Cir. 1979) (many federal appellate opinions discuss specific reasons why it was proper to extend or to limit cross-examination); State v. Brathwaite, 164 Conn. 617, 325 A.2d 284 (1973); Goodbody v. Margiotti, 323 Pa. 529, 187 A. 425 (1936).

While in Federal Rule 611(b) the Congress substituted the more restrictive language set forth in § 21, n. 4 supra, in lieu of the rule adopted by the Supreme Court, the present phrasing is the mildly hortatory

"should," a guideline rather than the style of the Ten Commandments. Additionally, the Rule expressly confers on the judge discretion to allow inquiry into additional matters. The effect is to confine the matter largely to the trial level and to remove it from the area of profitable appellate review. See Adv.Com.Note to Rule 611(b), Preliminary Draft, 46 F.R.D. 161, 304. Similarly as to Rev.Unif.R.Evid. (1974) 611(b).

7. St. Louis, Iron Mountain & Southern Railway Co. v. Raines, 90 Ark. 398, 119 S.W. 665, 668 (1909).

8. See Note, 37 Colum.L.Rev. 1373, 1381 (1937) giving the results of a study of 810 decisions, indicating many reversals. More recent examples include Papa v. Youngstrom, 146 Conn. 37, 147 A.2d 494 (1958); Muscarello v. Peterson, 20 Ill.2d 548, 170 N.E.2d 564 (1960); State ex rel. Rich v. Bair, 83 Idaho 475, 365 P.2d 216 (1961); Shupe v. State, 238 Md. 307, 208 A.2d 590 (1965); Golden Gate Corp. v. Providence Redevelopment Agency, 106 R.I. 371, 260 A.2d 152 (1970).

For cases emphasizing the discretion of the court, see the cases in note 6, supra, and C.J.S. Witnesses § 396.

Where the adverse party is called as an adverse witness by his opponent, there seems to be a particularly strong tendency to emphasize on a practical level the judge's discretion in limiting cross-examination. See City of Kotzebue v. Ipalook, 462 P.2d 75 (Alaska 1969) (restriction of cross-examination was harmless error when witness could be called as an adverse witness); Kline v. Kachmar, 360 Pa. 396, 61 A.2d 825 (1948); Lindsay v. Teamster's Union Local No. 74, 97 N.W.2d 686 (N.D.1959).

tle tendency to apply the general notion that the order of proof is discretionary. The tradition has not been shaped in terms of order of proof, but in the language of a right to cross-examine upon the whole case.[9] The situation which puts the most strain upon the wide-open rule is the one where a party, usually the plaintiff, finds himself compelled at the outset to call from the adversary's camp either the party himself or some ally or employee to prove up a formal fact not substantially in dispute. Shall the adversary be allowed to disrupt the proponent's case at this stage by cross-examining the willing witness about matters of defense unrelated to the direct examination? This is an appealing situation for the exercise of a discretion to vary from the wide-open practice and to require the cross-examiner to call the witness for these new matters when he puts on his own case. So far, however, as the decisions examined reveal, the power is not emphasized in the "wide-open" jurisdictions.[10]

 **WESTLAW REFERENCES**

discretion /s "judge" /s scope extent /s crossexamination

discretion /s limit /s scope extent /s crossexamination

9. See Morgan v. Brydges, 2 Stark, 314, 171 Eng. Rep. 657 (N.P.1818) (witness called by plaintiff for formal proof, may be cross-examined by defendant, his employer, on the whole case); Cowart v. Strickland, 149 Ga. 397, 100 S.E. 447, 7 A.L.R. 1110, 1114 (1919) ("The rule in this state is that 'when a witness is called and examined, even to only a formal point, by one party, the other party has the right to cross-examine him as to all points.'")

However, the discretion of the court is emphasized in Boller v. Cofrances, 42 Wis.2d 170, 166 N.W.2d 129 (1969).

10. See § 25 infra.

§ 25

1. 6 Wigmore, Evidence § 1890 (Chadbourn rev. 1976); Weinstein & Berger, Evidence ¶ 611[02]; C.J.S. Witnesses §§ 399, 400; Dec.Dig. Witnesses ☞275(5), 275(8).

2. Roewe v. Lombardo, 76 Ill.App.2d 164, 221 N.E.2d 521 (1966); Ayres v. Keith, 355 S.W.2d 914 (Mo.

§ 25. Application of Wide-Open and Restrictive Rules to the Cross-Examination of Parties—(a) Civil Parties.[1]

In the cross-examination of party witnesses two situations are to be distinguished, namely, the hostile cross-examination by the adversary of a party who calls himself as a witness in his own behalf, and the friendly cross-examination by the counsel of a party who has been called as an adverse witness by his opponent. In the first situation, in jurisdictions following the restrictive rules it is sometimes held that while the range of discretion to permit the relaxation of the restrictive practice is wider,[2] the general limitation to the "scope of the direct," based on the maintenance of the normal order of proof is still applicable.[3] However, relaxation of the restrictive practice *only* for parties as mentioned above does not appear to be authorized by Federal Rule of Evidence 611(b).[4] A few cases, however, without much discussion of reasons have said that upon the hostile cross-examination of a party, the limitation to the scope of the direct will not be applied.[5] Of course, in the "wide-open" states the usual freedom from the restriction is accorded without question.

When a party calls the adverse party as a hostile witness, it is usually provided by

1962); Wagner v. Niven, 46 Tenn.App. 581, 332 S.W.2d 511 (1959).

3. Banks v. Bowman Dairy Co., 65 Ill.App.2d 113, 212 N.E.2d 4 (1965); Maul v. Filimon, 315 S.W.2d 859 (Mo.App.1958).

4. The last Advisory Committee's Note and the Congressional Committee Reports furnish no basis for reading the instant special relaxation into Rule 611(b), nor does the wording of the rule lead to such a result. Rather, the judge has general discretion as to all witnesses, particularly to extend the scope of cross-examination. See § 24, n. 6 supra. Some cases prior to the federal rules do indicate a special discretion as to parties. See, e.g., Rivers v. Union Carbide Corp., 426 F.2d 633 (3d Cir. 1970).

5. Felsenthal Co. v. Northern Assurance Co., 248 Ill. 343, 120 N.E. 268 (1918); Geelen v. Pennsylvania Railroad Co., 400 Pa. 240, 161 A.2d 595 (1960); Viens v. Lanctot, 120 Vt. 443, 144 A.2d 711 (1958); Ingles v. Stealey, 85 W.Va. 155, 158, 101 S.E. 167, 168 (1919).

statute or rule [6] that he may question him "as upon cross-examination," i.e., he may ask leading questions, and that he is not "bound" by the answers of the adverse witness, which means chiefly that he may impeach the testimony by showing inconsistent statements. When this examination, savoring so nearly of a cross-examination, is concluded, there is a view that gives no right to the party to be further examined immediately by his own counsel, but gives the judge a discretion to permit it or to require that his examination be deferred until the witness-party's own "case" is put on.[7] Most jurisdictions, however, permit the immediate further examination of the witness by his own counsel.[8] Presumably upon request the trial judge would forbid leading questions,[9] and there is no tendency here in the restrictive states to relax for this "cross-examination" of a friendly witness, the usual restrictions limiting the questions to the scope of the direct.[10]

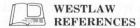 **WESTLAW REFERENCES**

digest(witness /s own /s behalf /p crossexamin!) & topic(110)

digest(crossexamin! /p hostile /p witness) % topic(110)

§ 26. Application of Wide-Open and Restrictive Rules to the Cross-Examination of Parties—(b) The Accused in a Criminal Case.[1]

As a means of implementing the prescribed order of producing evidence by the parties, the restrictive rules limiting cross-examination to the scope of the direct or to the proponent's case are arguably burdensome, but they are understandable. The cross-examiner who has been halted has at least a theoretical remedy. He may call the witness for questioning when he puts on his own next stage of evidence. However, when the restrictive practice is applied to the accused in a criminal case, as it is in jurisdiction that follow that practice generally,[2] the accused may carefully limit his direct examination to some single aspect of the case such as age, sanity, or alibi [3] and then invoke the

---

6. Fed.R.Evid. 611(c) provides in part, "When a party calls a hostile witness, an adverse party, or a witness identified with an adverse party, interrogation may be by leading questions." Under Fed.R.Evid. 607 a party may impeach a witness called by that party. Rev.Unif.R.Evid. (1974) 611(c) and 607 are identical or virtually so.

7. See, e.g., Davis v. Wright, 194 Ga. 1, 21 S.E.2d 88 (1942).

8. See, e.g., Peters v. Shear, 351 Pa. 521, 41 A.2d 556 (1945). Fed.R.Evid. and Rev.Unif.R.Evid. (1974) 611 seem to contemplate the immediate further examination. See n. 9 infra.

9. Fed.R.Evid. Rule 611(c) ("ordinarily leading questions should be permitted on cross-examination".) The Advisory Committee's Note explains: "The purpose of the qualification 'ordinarily' is to furnish a basis for denying the use of leading questions when the cross-examination is cross-examination in form only and not in fact, as for example the 'cross-examination' of a party by his own counsel after being called by the opponent (savoring more of redirect) or of an insured defendant who proves to be friendly to the plaintiff." Rev.Unif. R.Evid. (1974) is the same as the Federal Rule.

10. Grievance Committee of Bar of Fairfield Co. v. Dacey, 154 Conn. 129, 222 A.2d 339 (1966), appeal dismissed 386 U.S. 683, rehearing denied 387 U.S. 938.

§ 26

1. 6 Wigmore, Evidence § 1890 (Chadbourn rev. 1976) 8 id. §§ 2276(d), 2278 (McNaughton rev. 1961); Weinstein & Berger, Evidence ¶ 611[03]; Dec.Dig. Witnesses ⟊277(4); C.J.S. Witnesses § 400; Carlson, Cross-Examination of the Accused, 52 Cornell L.Q. 705 (1967).

2. Tucker v. United States, 5 F.2d 818 (8th Cir. 1925); Enriquez v. United States, 293 F.2d 788 (9th Cir. 1961); State v. Ragona, 232 Iowa 700, 5 N.W.2d 907, 909 (1942); Erving v. State, 174 Neb. 90, 116 N.W.2d 7 (1962), cert. denied 375 U.S. 876.

3. Except, of course, that cross-examination to impeach is not confined to the scope of the direct (see § 22 supra). State v. Shipman, 354 Mo. 265, 189 S.W.2d 273 (1945) (may be cross-examined about prior convictions); State v. Allnutt, 261 Iowa 897, 156 N.W.2d 266 (1968). And defendants are prone on direct to testify to their past records, which may open the door even wider to cross-examination on misconduct than the ordinary rule of impeachment would allow. See, e.g., Ivey v. State, 132 Fla. 36, 180 So. 368 (1938); State v. Hargraves, 62 Idaho 8, 107 P.2d 854 (1941); State v. McDaniel, 272 N.C. 556, 158 S.E.2d 874 (1968) vacated and remanded for consideration of other issues 392 U.S. 665, on remand 274 N.C. 574, 164 S.E.2d 469.

court's ruling that the cross-examination be limited to the matter thus opened. This restrictive practice has been criticized.[4] Of course, there is no problem of the accused escaping searching inquiry on the whole case if the scope of cross-examination is "wide-open."[5]

Regardless of whether the result under the restrictive rule may be desirable, it may be that the scope of cross-examination of the accused in a criminal case is not controlled solely by evidence case law, and statutes or rules governing the matter.[6] Federal Rule 611(b) is not intended to govern the extent to which an accused in a criminal case who testifies thereby waives the privilege against self-incrimination.[7] The outer limits of cross-examination may well be controlled, at least in the future, by constitutional doctrine concerning the extent to which the accused waives his privilege of self-incrimination by taking the stand and testifying.[8] Some judicial language suggests that under the Fifth Amendment of the United States Constitution the waiver should extend only to questioning concerning matters mentioned upon direct examination.[9] If this position ultimately prevails, state practice would be governed by the constitutional limits of waiver,[10] making "wide-open" cross-examination of criminal defendants, and perhaps even extremely liberal restrictive rules, unconstitutional.

 WESTLAW REFERENCES

digest(crossexamin! /p hostile /p witness) & topic(110)

digest(crossexamin! /s accused defendant /s scope /s discretion) & topic(110)

§ 27. Merits of the Systems of Wide-Open and Restricted Cross-Examination [1]

The principal virtue claimed for the restrictive rules is that they tend to require the parties to present their *facts* in due order, first the facts on which the plaintiff has the burden, then those which the defendant must prove, and so on, following the pre-

---

4. 6 Wigmore, Evidence § 1890, note 2 (Chadbourn rev. 1976).

5. Clarke v. State, 78 Ala. 474, 480, 56 Am.Rep. 45 (1885) ("cross-examination relating to any matter connected with the transaction, or pertinent to the issue, and impeachment . . . "); State v. McGee, 55 S.C. 247, 33 S.E. 353 (1899); Brown v. State, 38 Tex.Cr.R. 597, 44 S.W. 176 (1898). In Missouri, however, where the wide-open practice prevails in civil cases (see § 21, note 2, supra) the legislature has enacted that the accused and his spouse shall be shielded from cross-examination except upon matters referred to in the examination in chief. V.A.M.S. § 546.260, construed in State v. Davit, 343 Mo. 1151, 125 S.W.2d 47 (1939). See also, State v. Harvey, 449 S.W.2d 649 (Mo.1970).

6. See language in Tucker v. United States, 5 F.2d 818 (8th Cir. 1925); Fitzpatrick v. United States, 178 U.S. 304 (1900); Brown v. United States, 356 U.S. 148 (1958); United States ex rel. Irwin v. Pate, 357 F.2d 911 (7th Cir. 1966). But see Johnson v. United States, 318 U.S. 189 (1943).

See generally § 132 infra.

7. The Advisory Committee's Note states in part,

"The rule does not purport to determine the extent to which an accused who elects to testify thereby waives his privilege against self-incrimination . . . . In all events, the extent of the waiver of the privilege against self-incrimination ought not to be determined as a by-product of a rule on the scope of cross-examination."

The scope of waiver by a testifying defendant is discussed in § 132 infra.

8. See discussion in Carlson, Cross-Examination of the Accused, 52 Cornell L.Q. 705 (1967).

9. See cases cited in § 26, note 6, supra.

10. The privilege against self-incrimination under the Constitution of the United States was extended to the states in Malloy v. Hogan, 378 U.S. 1 (1964).

§ 27

1. See 6 Wigmore, Evidence §§ 1887, 1888 (Chadbourn rev. 1976) (marshaling arguments pro and con, including judicial views and favoring "wide-open" practice); Maguire, Evidence: Common Sense and Common Law, 45–49 (1947) (something for both sides); Weinstein & Berger, Evidence ¶ 611[02]. The compilers of the Model Code of Evidence made no clear choice. Rule 105(h) would leave to the judge's discretion "to what extent and in what circumstances a party cross-examining a witness may be forbidden to examine him concerning material matters not inquired about on a previous examination by the judge or by an adverse party".

The Proposed Federal Rules of Evidence, after initially favoring a restricted rule with discretion in the judge to depart from it, Fed.R.Evid. (P.D.1969) 611(b), later opted for a wide-open rule, also with discretion to depart from it. Fed.R.Evid. (R.D.1971) 611(b). The restricted rule was finally adopted by the Congress. Supra, § 20, n. 3.

scribed stages.[2] Avoided is the danger, mentioned in section 24 supra, that one party's plan of presenting *his* facts will be interrupted by the interjection on cross-examination of new and damaging matters which constitute his adversary's case. This interjection, if permitted, lessens the impact and persuasiveness of the proponent's facts. The nice case which he planned to lay out fact by fact has been muddled and complicated during its very presentation by new and doubt-raising facts drawn out in cross-examination of the proponent's own witnesses. The regular order of presenting the two parties' "cases" by separate stages is thus modified. The "case," formerly a single melody, becomes convertible to counterpoint.

It must be remembered, however, that like all rules of order, the common law order of proof by "cases" or stages, is to some extent arbitrary. Two witnesses cannot be allowed to speak at once, so some rules must be worked out as to who shall call the witnesses and in what order. A further rule, however, that a witness who knows many facts about the case shall be allowed to tell only certain ones at his first appearance, and as to others must be called later, seems even more artificial. The freer system under the wide-open practice by which on the direct examination the regular order of proof of the "cases" of the respective parties is maintained, but under which the adversary is free to draw out all the damaging facts on cross-examination, has a natural order of its own. The procedure by which each witness successively may be caused to tell all he knows about the case, is a system which would be followed spontaneously in any informal investigation untrammeled by rules. It serves the convenience of witnesses and may appear to the jury as a natural way of developing the facts. Moreover, to the objection that diversion into new paths upon cross-examination lessens the unity and persuasiveness of the direct examiner's presentation of his case, we may raise the doubt whether the direct examiner is in justice entitled to the psychological advantage of presenting his facts in this falsely simple and one-sided way.[3] Is he in justice entitled to this clear impact on the jury's mind, to this favorable first impression which, though to be answered later, may be hard to dislodge?

Another factor is the consideration of economy of time and energy. Obviously, the wide-open rule presents little or no opportunity for dispute in its application.[4] The restrictive practice in all its forms, on the other hand, can be productive in the courtroom of bickering over the choice of the numerous variations of the "scope of the direct" criterion, and of their application to particular cross-questions. These controversies are often reventilated on appeal, and there may be the possibility of reversal for error.[5] Observance of these vague and ambiguous restrictions is a matter of constant and hampering concern to the cross-examiner. If these efforts, delays and misprisions were the necessary incidents to the guarding of substantive rights or the fundamentals of fair trial, they might be worth the cost. As the price of the choice of an obviously debatable regulation of the order of evidence, the sacrifice seems misguided. The American Bar Association's Committee for the Improvement of the Law of Evidence for the year 1937–38 said this:

'The rule limiting cross-examination to the precise subject of the direct examination is probably the most frequent rule (except the Opinion rule) leading in trial practice today to refined and technical quibbles which obstruct the progress of the trial, confuse the jury, and give rise to appeal on technical grounds only. Some of the instances in which Supreme Courts have ordered new trials for the mere

---

2. See § 4 supra.

3. This query was first suggested by the late Professor Clarence Morris.

4. A glance at Dec.Dig. Witnesses ⊕269 demonstrates the almost entire absence of appellate dispute

over the application of the wide-open practice, and the large number of such questions from jurisdictions following the restrictive practice.

5. See § 24 n. 8 supra.

transgression of this rule about the order of evidence have been astounding.

'We recommend that the rule allowing questions upon any part of the issue known to the witness . . . be adopted. . . .'[6]

There are thus strong reasons for the "wide-open" rule.

WESTLAW REFERENCES

wideopen /s crossexamin!

policy policies consideration* /p scope extent /p crossexamin!

---

§ 28. Cross-Examination About Witness's Inconsistent Past Writings: Must Examiner Show the Writing to the Witness Before Questioning About Its Contents?

A fatal weakness of liars is letter writing. Betraying letters arc often inspired by mere boastfulness, sometimes by greed or other reasons. Properly used they have destroyed many a fraudulent witness.[1] An eminent trial lawyer makes these suggestions to the attacking cross-examiner:

. . . There is an art in introducing the letter contradicting the witness' testimony. The novice will rush in. He will obtain the false statement and then quickly hurl the letter in the face of the witness. The witness, faced with it, very likely will seek to retrace his steps, and sometimes do it skillfully, and the effect is lost.

The mature trial counsel will utilize the letter for all it is worth. Having obtained the denial which he wishes, he will, perhaps, pretend that he is disappointed. He will ask that same question a few moments later, and again and again get a denial. And he will then phrase— and this requires preparation—he will then phrase a whole series of questions not directed at that particular point, but in which is incorporated the very fact which he is ready to contradict—each time getting closer and closer to the language in the written document which he possesses, until he has induced the witness to assert not once, but many times, the very fact from which ordinarily he might withdraw by saying it was a slip of the tongue. Each time he draws closer to the precise language which will contradict the witness, without making the witness aware of it, until finally, when the letter is sprung, the effect as compared with the other method is that, let us say, of atomic energy against a firecracker.[2]

However, in some courts there may be an obstacle in the way of this effective method. This is the rule in *Queen Caroline's Case*, pronounced by English judges in an advisory opinion in 1820.[3] The significant part of the opinion for present purposes is the pronouncement that the cross-examiner cannot ask the witness about any statements made by the witness in writing, or ask whether the witness has ever written a letter of a given purport, without *first* producing the writing or letter and exhibiting it to the witness, and permitting the witness to read the writing or such part of it as the cross-examiner seeks to ask him about. Thus, in vain is the potential trap laid before the eyes of the bird. While reading the letter the witness will be warned by what he sees not to deny it and can quickly weave a new web of explanation.

---

6. See 6 Wigmore, Evidence § 1888, p. 711 (Chadbourn rev. 1976) where the relevant part of the Committee's report is set out in full.

§ 28

1. Probably the most famous instance is the demolition by Sir Charles Russell of the witness Richard Pigott before the Parnell Commission in 1888, described in ch. 20 of Wellman, The Art of Cross-Examination (4th ed. 1936), and set out in Busch, Law and Tactics in Jury Trials § 350 (1949). This and many other striking instances are detailed in 4 Wigmore, Evidence § 1260 (Chadbourn rev. 1972).

2. Nizer, The Art of Jury Trial, 32 Corn.L.Q. 59, 68 (1946). An instructive, similar suggestion as to the technique of "exposure by document" is found in Love,

Documentary Evidence, 38 Ill.Bar J. 426, 429–30 (1950). See also 4 Belli, Modern Trials § 63.30 (2d ed.1982).

3. 2 B. & B. 284, 286–90, 129 Eng.Rep. 976, 11 Eng. Rul.C. 183 (1820). (The House of Lords put the question to the judges: "First, whether, in the courts below, a party on cross-examination would be allowed to represent in the statement of a question the contents of a letter, and to ask the witness whether the witness wrote a letter to any person with such contents, or contents to the like effect, *without having first shown* to the witness the letter, and having asked that witness whether the witness wrote that letter and his admitting that he wrote such letter? . . . " Abbott, C. J., for the judges, answered the first question in the negative).

The rule that the writing must first be shown to the witness before he can be questioned about it was thought by the judges to be an application of the established practice requiring the production of the original document *when its contents are sought to be proved*.[4] This notion was a misconception in at least two respects. First, the cross-examiner is not seeking to prove *at this stage* the contents of the writing by the answers of the witness. On the contrary, his zealous hope is that the witness will deny the existence of the letter. Second, the original documents rule is a rule requiring the production of the document as proof of its contents to the judge and jury, not to the witness.[5] So obstructive did the powerful Victorian cross-examining barristers find the rule in the *Queen's Case* that they secured its abrogation by Parliament in 1854.[6]

When urged upon them, this practice requiring exhibition to the witness was usually accepted without question by American courts[7] and occasionally by legislators.[8] It is believed, however, that actual invocation of the rule in trials is relatively infrequent in most states in which the rule has not been changed, and that the generality of judges and practitioners in these jurisdictions are unaware of this possible hidden rock in the path of the cross-examiner.

So far, the rule has been discussed as it works in the situation where the cross-examiner is seeking to uncover in a dramatic and devastating fashion the perjury of a calculating witness. In this situation, the rule seems to blunt one of counsel's sharpest weapons of exposure. But the weapon may be misdirected. Innocent and well-meaning witnesses write letters and forget their contents and later testify mistakenly to facts inconsistent with the assertions in the letters. Their forgetfulness may need to be revealed, and their present testimony thus discredited to that extent. Arguably, however, they should not be invited by subtle questioning to widen the gap between their present statements and their past writings, and then be devastated by a dramatic exposure. Under this viewpoint, the judge should be vested with the discretion whether to permit the

---

4. This rule, also called the best evidence rule, is developed in Ch. 23 infra.

5. For these and other refutations of the theory of the *Queen's Case*, see the masterly discussion in 4 Wigmore Evidence § 1260 (Chadbourn rev. 1972).

6. St. 17 & 18 Vict. c. 125, § 24 ("A witness may be cross-examined as to previous statements made by him in writing or reduced into writing, relative to the subject-matter of the cause, without such writing being shown to him; but if it is intended to contradict such witness by the writing, his attention must, before such contradictory proof can be given, be called to those parts of the writing which are to be used for the purpose of so contradicting him; providing always that it shall be competent for the judge, at any time during the trial, to require the production of the writing for his inspection, and he may thereupon make such use of it for the purposes of the trial as he shall think fit").

7. See, e.g., Washington v. State, 269 Ala. 146, 112 So.2d 179 (1959) (cross-examination of accused as to statement signed by him; must be shown before questioning about contents); Glenn v. Gleason, 61 Iowa 28, 33, 15 N.W. 659, 661 (1883) (whole letter must be read, relying on 1 Greenleaf on Evidence § 463, which popularized the rule in this country before judges here became aware that it had been abrogated in England); McDonald v. Bayha, 93 Minn. 139, 100 N.W. 679 (1904); Price v. Grieger, 244 Minn. 466, 70 N.W.2d 421 (1955)

(cited with approval in Hillesheim v. Stippel, 283 Minn. 59, 166 N.W.2d 325 (1969); and cases collected 4 Wigmore, Evidence § 1263 (Chadbourn rev. 1972). Dec. Dig. Witnesses ⊙271(2), (4), 277(6); C.J.S. Witnesses § 391, notes 52, 53; 81 Am.Jur.2d Witnesses § 491.

The rule is often applied to cross-examination of parties about what they have written, see Washington v. State, supra, but if the original documents principle is the basis, it has no application, as a party's oral admission of what he has written is a recognized exception to that rule, see § 242 infra.

It is arguable that the rule is applicable to a signed deposition which may be looked on as a writing, and it is sometimes applied to them, though this seems an inconvenient practice. See 4 Wigmore, Evidence § 1262 (Chadbourn rev. 1972). But most courts have distinguished from depositions transcripts of oral testimony at a former trial, as to which the "show-me" rule is not applicable. Toohey v. Plummer, 69 Mich. 345, 349, 37 N.W. 297 (1888) (reporter's notes); Couch v. St. Louis Public Service Co., 173 S.W.2d 617, 622 (Mo.App.1943); Charles v. McPhee, 92 N.H. 111, 26 A.2d 30 (1942). Contra: Meadors v. Commonwealth, 281 Ky. 622, 136 S.W.2d 1066 (1940).

8. See, e.g., Georgia Code § 38–1803; Idaho Code § 9–1210. On the other hand, statutes and rules in various states have abrogated the rule. See n. 10 infra.

questioning about the writing without requiring its exhibition to the witness.[9]

In recognition of the disadvantages of the rule of *Queen Caroline's Case*, the Federal Rules of Evidence abolish the rule by permitting the cross-examination without prior showing of the writing to the witness, and substituting the requirement that the writing be shown or disclosed to opposing counsel on request as an assurance of good faith on the part of the cross-examiner.[10]

WESTLAW REFERENCES

inconsistent /s writing* letter /p crossexamin!

§ 29. The Standard of Relevancy as Applied on Cross-Examination:[1] Trial Judge's Discretion [2]

There are three main functions of cross-examination: (1) to shed light on the credibility of the direct testimony; (2) to bring out additional facts related to those elicited on direct,[3] and (3) in states following the "wide-open" rule,[4] to bring out additional facts which tend to elucidate any issue in the case. As to cross-examination designed to serve

the second or third of these functions, there seems to be no reason why the usual standard of relevancy as applied to testimony offered on direct examination should not equally be applied to facts sought to be elicited on cross-examination.[5]

As to the first function, that of evaluating the credibility of the evidence given on direct, the purpose is contrastingly different. Here the test of relevancy is not whether the answer sought will elucidate any of the main issues, but whether it will to a useful extent aid the court or jury in appraising the credibility of the witness and assessing the probative value of the direct testimony. There are many recognized lines of questioning for this purpose, none of which is commonly relevant to the main issues. In general the principles stated in this section are pertinent under Federal Rule of Evidence and Revised Uniform Rule of Evidence 611(b), which authorize cross-examination concerning "matters affecting the credibility of the witness." A familiar type is the question or series of questions, often used as preliminary questions on cross-examination, inquiring as to residence and occupation, designed to place the witness in his setting.[6]

---

9. Wash.R.Evid. 613(a) grants the judge discretion to require disclosure of the statement prior to cross-examination concerning the statement.

10. Fed. and Rev.Unif.R.Evid. (1974) 613(a) provide:

In examining a witness concerning a prior statement made by him, whether written or not, the statement need not be shown nor its contents disclosed to him at that time, but on request the same shall be shown or disclosed to opposing counsel.

The federal Advisory's Committee's Note observes:

The rule does not defeat the application of Rule 1002 relating to production of the original when the contents of a writing are sought to be proved. Nor does it defeat the application of Rule 26(b)(3) of the Rules of Civil Procedure, as revised, entitling a person on request to a copy of his own statement, though the operation of the latter may be suspended temporarily.

§ 29

1. Dec.Dig. Witnesses ☞270; 81 Am.Jur.2d Witnesses §§ 474–476, 520, 525, 529; C.J.S. Witnesses §§ 377, 386.

2. Dec.Dig. Witnesses ☞267; 81 Am.Jur.2d Witnesses §§ 474–476, 520, 525, 529; C.J.S. Witnesses §§ 386, 404.

3. See § 21 supra.

4. See § 21 supra.

5. See, e.g., Moulton v. State, 88 Ala. 116, 6 So. 758, 759 (1889) (cross-examination must relate to facts in issue, except that irrelevant questions which tend to test credibility may sometimes be asked); Marut v. Costello, 34 Ill.2d 125, 214 N.E.2d 768 (1966).

6. A leading case is Alford v. United States, 282 U.S. 687 (1931) (abuse of discretion for the judge to refuse to allow cross-examination of government's witness respecting his residence where the accused suspected that witness was detained in custody of federal authorities; "Cross-examination of a witness is a matter of right . . . . Its permissible purposes, among others, are that the witness may be identified with his community so that independent testimony may be sought and offered of his reputation for veracity in his own neighborhood . . . . that the jury may interpret his testimony in the light reflected upon it by knowledge of his environment . . . .".)

In Smith v. Illinois, 390 U.S. 129 (1968), the *Alford* case was carried further by holding that a criminal defendant was denied Sixth Amendment and Fourteenth Amendment rights under the United States Constitution when he was denied the right on cross-examination to ask the principal prosecution witness his correct

A further common question is, "Have you talked to anyone about this case?" [7] Another is the testing or exploratory type of question. In asking this kind of question, the cross-examiner (who it will be remembered may not have the advantage of having previously interviewed the witness) will ask disarming questions often remote from the main inquiry, which are designed to test by experiment the ability of the witness to remember detailed facts of the nature of those which he recited on direct, or his ability accurately to perceive such facts, or his willingness and capacity to tell the truth generally, without distortion or exaggeration.[8] This is part of the tradition and of the art of cross-examination and many of the famous instances of dramatically devastating cross-examinations are of this type.[9] The courts

recognize that a rule limiting questions to those relevant to the main issues would cripple the usefulness of this kind of examination.[10] A final instance of evaluative cross-examination is the direct attack by impeaching questions seeking to show such matters as bias, inconsistent statements, or conviction of crime.[11]

As to all the lines of inquiry mentioned in the next preceding paragraph, designed to shed light on the credibility of the witness and his direct testimony, the criteria of relevancy are vague, and the purpose of the cross-examiner is often experimental. Accordingly too tight a rein upon the cross-examiner may unduly curb the usefulness of the examination. On the other hand, dangers of undue prejudice [12] to the party or the witness and of waste of time from extended

name and address. The court quoted from Brookhart v. Janis, 384 U.S. 1, 3 (1966) to the effect that a denial of cross-examination "would be constitutional error of the first magnitude and no amount of showing of want of prejudice would cure it." However, the exact scope of the decision is not presently certain. Where defendant was permitted full examination on the place of the witness in life, including the fact that he was staying in a motel at government expense, the court's sustaining an objection to a question as to his "present" address was upheld in United States v. Teller, 412 F.2d 374 (7th Cir. 1969), cert. denied 402 U.S. 949. See also United States v. Lawler, 413 F.2d 622 (7th Cir. 1969), cert. denied 396 U.S. 1046 (inquiry barred as to where informer-witness was working at the time of trial); United States v. Lee, 413 F.2d 910 (7th Cir. 1969), cert. denied 396 U.S. 916 (cross-examination as to present address barred); United States v. Palermo, 410 F.2d 468 (7th Cir. 1969) (name and address need not be given if actual threat to life of witness is shown by prosecution to the judge in camera); United States v. Contreras, 602 F.2d 1237 (5th Cir. 1979), cert. denied 444 U.S. 971 (same).

7. The question is usually approved. See cases cited in Annot., 35 A.L.R.2d 1045. In various cases, exclusion of similar questions has been deemed error. See, e.g., United States v. Standard Oil Co., 316 F.2d 884 (7th Cir. 1963). But see State v. Yost, 241 Or. 362, 405 P.2d 851 (1965) (not error to exclude question asking witness with whom he had talked during recess when question did not shed some light on accuracy or credibility of the witness under all the circumstances).

8. Kervin v. State, 254 Ala. 449, 48 So.2d 204 (1950) (wide latitude to test recollection of witness is permitted subject to judge's discretion); People v. Sorge, 301 N.Y. 198, 93 N.E.2d 637 (1950) (proper for district attorney in cross-examining accused about other offenses, to persist after denial, "in the hope of inducing the witness to abandon his negative answers" and "on

the chance that he may change his testimony") but see § 42 infra. See also Alford v. United States, 282 U.S. 687, 692 (1931) ("Counsel often cannot know in advance what pertinent facts may be elicited on cross-examination. For that reason it is necessarily exploratory; and the rule that the examiner must indicate the purpose of his inquiry does not, in general, apply.") Enlightening discussion of the technique of the "testing" cross-examination, with examples, is found in Busch, Law and Tactics in Jury Trials § 303 (1949); Lake, How to Cross-Examine Witnesses Successfully 137–151 (1957).

9. For instructive examples, see Wellman, The Art of Cross-Examination ch. 26 (4th ed. 1936) (by Littleton); Reed, Conduct of Law Suits §§ 423–439 (2d ed. 1912); Kiendl, Some Aspects of Cross-Examination, 51 Case and Comment, No. 6, pp. 27–30 (1946); Busch, Law and Tactics in Jury Trials § 303 (1949); Belli, The Voice of Modern Trials Vol. III (long play recording); Heller, Do You Solemnly Swear? Part VI (1968).

10. Accordingly, some opinions point out that the rules of relevancy are not applied with the same strictness on cross-examination as on direct: State v. Smith, 140 Me. 255, 37 A.2d 246 (1944); O'Sullivan v. Simpson, 123 Mont. 314, 212 P.2d 435 (1949); Grocers Supply Co. v. Stuckey, 152 S.W.2d 911 (Tex.Civ.App.1941, error refused) (on cross-examination any fact bearing on credit of witness is relevant). Fed.R.Evid. and Rev.Unif.R. Evid. (1974) 611(b) permits cross-examination upon "matters affecting the credibility of the witness." Rule 611(a) clearly emphasizes the discretion of the trial court in these matters.

11. See Ch. 5 infra, dealing with impeachment of witnesses.

12. Lee Won Sing v. United States, 94 U.S.App.D.C. 310, 215 F.2d 680 (1954) (question on cross whether accused had paid his co-defendant $20,000 to plead guilty, asked without reasonable foundation, was improper and not adequately cured by instructions); State v.

exploration are apparent. Consequently, the trial judge has a recognized discretionary power to control the extent of examination.[13] This exercise of discretion will only be reviewed for abuse resulting in substantial harm to the complaining party.[14] An examination of a large number of these cases leaves the impression that in practice abuse is more often found when complaint is made that the judge has unduly curbed the examination than when undue extension of the discretion to permit the questioning is charged.[15]

WESTLAW REFERENCES

digest(crossexamin! /s relevan** irrelevan** /s discretion)

§ 30. The Cross-Examiner's Art

A cursory and general examination of the art of cross-examination, gleaned from the prolific writing on the subject,[1] may serve to aid the beginning advocate by bringing him some of the wisdom lawyers have learned from hard experience and may also serve to aid in considering the discussion in the next succeeding section, which attempts to appraise the significance of cross-examination.

Lampshire, 74 Wn.2d 888, 447 P.2d 727 (1969) (abuse of discretion to permit question in regard to large telephone bill incurred by defendant-witness). See Fed.R. Evid. and Rev.Unif.R.Evid. (1974) 403; § 185 supra.

13. Alford v. United States, 282 U.S. 687, 694 (1931) ("The extent of cross-examination with respect to an appropriate subject of inquiry is within the sound discretion of the trial court. It may exercise a reasonable judgment in determining when the subject is exhausted"; but here, excluding inquiry as to place of residence of witness held an abuse of discretion); Hider v. Gelbach, 135 F.2d 693 (4th Cir. 1943) (judge properly exercised discretion to curb repetitious cross-examination); Simpson v. State, 32 Wis.2d 195, 145 N.W.2d 206 (1966), cert. denied 386 U.S. 965 (objections to various questions to expert were sustained); Casey v. United States, 413 F.2d 1303 (5th Cir. 1969) (court excluded questions implying United States gave covert support to defendant's enterprise); State v. Cummings, 445 S.W.2d 639 (Mo.1969) (court could exclude question to prosecuting witness concerning an insurance requirement that he make a criminal charge); Dec.Dig. Witnesses ⬠267. Fed.R.Evid. 611(a) grants the trial court discretion concerning cross-examination on the type of irrelevant subjects mentioned in the text, but questions may be excluded also on the ground that they are prejudicial or otherwise violate Rule 403. United States v. Lustig, 555 F.2d 737 (9th Cir. 1977), cert. denied 434 U.S. 926.

14. Bates v. Chilton County, 244 Ala. 297, 13 So.2d 186 (1943); Commonwealth v. Greenberg, 339 Mass. 557, 160 N.E.2d 181 (1959).

15. For notable and instructive instances of holdings of abuse in curbing the cross-examination of government witnesses by the accused, see Alford v. United States, 282 U.S. 687 (1931); Davis v. Alaska, 415 U.S. 308 (1974); District of Columbia v. Clawans, 300 U.S. 617 (1937). Many kinds of rulings have been held an abuse of discretion. See, e.g., People v. Mason, 28 Ill. 2d 396, 192 N.E.2d 835 (1963) (limiting questions to show bias in an arguably close case on the question); United States v. Hogan, 232 F.2d 905 (3d Cir. 1956) (excluding cross-examination to the effect that witnesses

had their sentences postponed, etc., because they had agreed to testify for the government and hoped for preferential treatment). On the other hand, restrictions by federal trial judges have been upheld in particular circumstances on the ground that the cross-examination actually had was substantial and thorough and further examination would have been cumulative or repetitious. See, e.g., United States v. Headid, 565 F.2d 1029 (8th Cir. 1977).

§ 30

1. For a hundred years, lawyers have been fascinated with the topic and have developed practical maxims and gathered dramatic instances. Important is the section on the "Theory and Art" in 5 Wigmore, Evidence § 1368 (Chadbourn rev. 1974). Helpful and practical are the hints and examples in Busch, Law and Tactics in Jury Trials Ch. 15 (1949) and in Goldstein and Lane, Trial Technique Ch. 19 (1969). See also Reed, Conduct of Lawsuits (2d ed. 1912); Elliott, The Work of the Advocate (2d ed. 1912); Wellman, The Art of Cross-Examination (4th ed. 1936); Stryker, The Art of Advocacy Chs. 4, 5 (1954); Friedman, Essentials of Cross-Examination (1968); Mauet, The Fundamentals of Trial Techniques 237–294 (1980); Bodin, ed., Trial Techniques Library (1967); Harolds, Kelner and Fuchsberg, Examination of Witnesses (1965); Lake, How to Cross-Examine Witnesses Successfully (1957); Redfield, Cross-Examination and the Witness (1963); Wrottesley, The Examination of Witnesses in Court Ch. 3 (2d ed. 1926); and the ironic comments of Lord Darling in Scintillae Juris 61–70 (1914). Numerous readable articles include the following: Henderson, The High Art of Cross-Examination, 19 Case and Comment 594 (1913); Steeves, The Art of Cross-Examination, 38 Can.Law Times 97, quoted in The Dangers of Cross-Examination, 86 Cent.L.J. 206 (1918); Ramage, A Few Rules for Cross-Examination, 91 Cent.L.J. 354 (1920); Nizer, The Art of Jury Trial, 32 Corn.L.Q. 59 (1946); Comisky, Observations on the Preparation and Conduct of Cross-Examination, 2 Prac.Law. 24 (1956); Von Moschzisker, Some Maxims for Cross-Examination, 3 id. 78 (1957); Hilton, Cross-Examination of a Handwriting Expert by Test Problem, 13 Rutgers L.Rev. 306 (1958).

Preparation is the key. Certainly, some lawyers seem to have a native talent for conducting effective cross-examination. A great Victorian advocate, Montagu Williams, seemed to share this view when he said, "I am by trade a reader of faces and minds." [2] Today, however, the stress is upon thorough preparation, not upon sudden sallies of inspiration. [3] Improvisation is often necessary but its results are small compared to those from planned questions based on facts dug out before trial. The steps in preparation are explained in many of the works concerning the art of cross-examination. [4] Not all steps can be taken as to all adverse witnesses. Nor can every case bear the expense of thorough preparation. Nevertheless, preparation before trial is the only soil from which, in the day-to-day run of cases, successful cross-examination can grow. [5] At the trial, some lawyers recommend that notes in preparation for later questions should be made by an associate or by the client, rather than by the examiner. Oral suggestions to the examiner in court should be avoided. [6]

No cross-examination without a purpose. As we have seen, these purposes may be, first, to elicit new facts, qualifying the direct, or in some states bearing on any issue in the case; second, to test the story of the witness by exploring its details and implications, in the hope of disclosing inconsistencies or impossibilities; and third, to prove out of the mouth of the witness, impeaching

facts known to the cross-examiner such as prior contradictory statements, bias and conviction of crime. In considering any of these objectives, but particularly the latter two, the cross-examiner must be conscious that the odds are slanted against him. An unfavorable answer is more damaging when elicited on cross-examination. It is hard for a cross-examiner to win his case on cross-examination; it is easy for him to lose it. Accordingly, if the witness has done no harm on direct examination, a cross-examination for the second or third purpose is usually ill-advised. There remains the witness whose direct testimony has been damaging, or even threatens to be destructive of the cross-examiner's case if the jury believes it. Cross-examination will usually be needed, and whether the object shall be a skirting reconnaissance distant from the crucial issues, or a frontal attack on the story or the credit of the witness, will depend on the availability of impeaching material disclosed by preparation and on a judgment of the risks and advantages of the holding defence or the counter-attack. [7]

A question directed to a crucial or critical fact on which the outcome of the case depends should seldom be asked an adverse witness unless the cross-examiner is reasonably confident the answer will be favorable. Similarly, broad questions which open the door for an eager witness to reinforce his direct testimony with corroborating circum-

2. Quoted Elliott, op. cit. 231.

3. See especially the works of Busch and Goldstein, and the article of Nizer, cited above, n. 1. Nizer says at p. 68: "Most lawyers who will tell you of brilliant cross-examination will not confess this: We are entranced by a brilliant flash of insight which broke the witness, but the plain truth of the matter is, as brother to brother, that ninety-nine per cent of effective cross-examination is once more our old friend 'thorough preparation,' which places in your hands a written document with which to contradict the witness. That usually is the great gift of cross-examination."

4. See particularly, Busch, Law and Practice in Jury Trials §§ 286–290 (1949); Friedman, Essentials of Cross-Examinations 15–36 (1968).

5. That most of the famous, devastating cross-examinations were grounded in pre-trial preparation is illustrated by such celebrated instances as the cross-ex-

amination of Richard Pigott by Sir Charles Russell before the Parnell Commission, see Wigmore, op. cit. n. 18, supra, and Wellman, op. cit., ch. 22. It is even more clearly evident in that storehouse of great cross-examinations, Aron Steuer, Max D. Steuer, Trial Lawyer (1950), especially in the account of People v. Gardner in the second chapter.

6. Another phase of preparation that is often neglected is the cautioning of one's own witnesses about the probable line of cross-examinations, and especially warning them of such pitfall questions as "Whom have you talked to about this case?" and "When did you first know you would be called as a witness?" Goldstein and Lane, Trial Technique §§ 19.25, 19.30 (1969).

7. See the enlightening discussion in Kiendl, Some Aspects of Cross-Examination, 51 Case and Comment, No. 6, p. 25 (1946), and generally, Lake, How to Cross-Examine Witnesses Successfully (1957).

stances, e.g., "How do you explain?" or "How did it happen?" are usually ill-advised.[8] If a discrepant fact has been drawn out on cross-examination, it is often better to wait and stress the inconsistency in argument than to press the witness with it. It is the responsibility of the proponent's counsel to elicit an explanation, if any, on re-direct.

In conducting a testing or exploratory examination, for obvious reasons it is inadvisable to follow the order of the witness's direct testimony. "If the witness is falsifying, jump quickly with rapid-fire questions from one point of the narrative to the other, without time or opportunity for a connected narrative: backward, forward, forward, backward from the middle to the beginning, etc." [9]

Cross-examine for the jury, not for your client. It is often a temptation to the cross-examiner to display his wit and skill before his client, or to feed the vengeful feelings of the latter toward opposing witnesses by tripping and humiliating them upon cross-examination.[10] Frequently these small victories upon collateral inquiries are easy to secure. The odds between the experienced advocate and the witness, nervous in new surroundings, are not even. The cross-examiner needs constantly to remind himself that the jury is keenly aware of this inequality of position, and that each juror is prone to imagine himself in the shoes of the witness. Better results with the witness, and a better impression upon the jury will usually flow from tact and consideration than from bull-dozing and ridicule. The cloak falls more easily in the sunshine than in the hurricane. In the rare case when the cross-examiner is convinced that a crucial witness is dishonest and that he can demonstrate it, the attack must be pressed home to the jugular. But the cross-examiner should always be mindful of his duty to use his skills and weapons justly and fairly, and also of the need so to conduct himself that the jury, with its latent sympathy for witnesses, will be impressed with his fairness.[11]

Make one or two big points; end on a high note. When the cross-examiner has led up to and secured an important admission, he should not dull the edge of the effect by too many explanatory details, nor risk a recantation by calling for a repetition. He should pass on to another important point if he has one, and end the examination when his last big point is made. "When you have struck oil stop boring." [12]

While the above generalities are worthwhile general guideposts, the cross-examiner must adapt his techniques to the specific situation he faces. Of course, different experts might well use different techniques in cross-examining the same witness at a particular trial.[13]

 **WESTLAW REFERENCES**

art /5 crossexamin!
theory /5 crossexamin! % synopsis,digest(theory /s crossexamin!)

---

8. Goldstein and Lane, Trial Technique § 19.18 (1969).

9. Ramage, A Few Rules for the Cross-Examination of Witnesses, 91 Cent.L.J. 354 (1920). For illustrative instances see Reed, Conduct of Lawsuits 307–312 (2d ed. 1912).

10. "The object of cross-examination is not to produce startling effects, but to elicit facts which will support the theory intended to be put forward. Sir William Follett asked the fewest questions of any counsel I ever knew; and I have heard many cross-examinations from others listened to with rapture from an admiring client, each question of which has been destruction to his case." Sergeant Ballantine's Experiences, 1st Am. ed., 106, quoted in Reed, Conduct of Lawsuits 278 (2d ed. 1912).

11. These points are especiallly well made by Kiendl, op. cit., 51 Case & Comment, No. 6, pp. 24, 32 (1946). See also Goldstein and Lane, Trial Technique §§ 19.39–61 (1969).

12. Credited to Josh Billings in Steeves, The Dangers of Cross-Examination, 86 Cent.L.J. 206, 207 (1918). "If you have made a homerun do not run around the bases twice." Ramage, A Few Rules, 91 Cent.L.J. 354, 356 (1920). See also, Friedman, Essentials of Cross-Examination 119 (1968).

13. See, e.g., the cross-examination of the same witnesses by three different lawyers at a demonstration session in Examining the Medical Expert 143–148 (1969).

§ 31. Cross-Examination Revalued

Early Victorian writers on advocacy exaggerated the strategic significance of cross-examination as affecting the outcome of trials. One of them wrote, "There is never a cause contested, the result of which is not mainly dependent upon the skill with which the advocate conducts his cross-examination."[1] This stands in contrast with the view of Scarlett, a great "leader" of a later day, who said, "I learned by much experience that the most useful duty of an advocate is the examination of witnesses, and that much more mischief than benefit generally results from cross-examination. I therefore rarely allowed that duty to be performed by my colleagues. I cross-examined in general very little, and more with a view to enforce the facts I meant to rely upon than to affect the witness's credit,—for the most part a vain attempt."[2] Reed, who was one of our most sensible American writers on trial tactics, expresses the modern informed opinion when he says, "Sometimes a great speech bears down the adversary, and sometimes a searching cross-examination turns a witness inside out and shows him up to be a perjured villain. But ordinarily cases are not won by either speaking or cross-examining."[3] At the same time, most lawyers who write concerning the art of cross-examination still believe that failure to use this tool can lose a case.[4] To the advocate of today, it is often a means of gleaning additional facts but it is also still employed as a means of attack upon the credit of the direct testimony of the witness whenever possible.[5] Cross-examination of experts seems important in many instances. In fact, Federal Rule of Evidence 705 makes the opportunity to cross-examine particularly important if, as the rule permits, only an opinion in effect is elicited. Thus while cross-examination does not loom large as a determinant of victory in many cases, it still may be an important ingredient in other cases.

In the appraisal of policies upon which the modernizing of the existing system of evidence rules must be based, it seems that a similar evaluation of cross-examination as an engine for discovering truth is called for. The present assumption is that the statement of a declarant or witness, if opportunity for cross-examination is not afforded, is so fatally lacking in reliability that it is not even worth hearing in a court of justice, and that the opportunity for cross-examination is indispensable. Now obviously cross-examination is a useful device to secure greater accuracy and completeness for the witness's testimony as a whole, and in the hands of a skillful advocate will often—not always—expose fraud or honest error in the witness. But it has its own hazards of producing errors.[6] It is, in truth, quite doubtful whether

§ 31

1. Quoted from Cox, The Advocate 434, in Reed, Conduct of Lawsuits 277 (2d ed. 1912).

2. Memoir of Lord Abinger 75, quoted in Reed, op. cit. 278.

3. Reed, op. cit. 276.

4. "Failure to examine a witness's background, recollection, bias and knowledge of the subject still can and often does lose a case that should have been won." Friedman, Essentials of Cross-Examination 6 (1968).

5. "The type of cross-examination which is employed most frequently is that intended to discredit the direct testimony of the witness." Bodin, Principles of Cross-Examination, Trial Techniques Library 8 (1967).

6. For some accounts of staged experiments attempting to show some comparative results as to accuracy and completeness of free narrative, direct examination and cross-examination see Marston, Studies in Testimony, 15 J.Crim. Law & Criminology, 1 (1924); Cady, On the Psychology of Testimony, 35 Am.J.Psych. 10 (1924); Weld and Danzig, Study of Way in Which a Verdict is Reached by a Jury, 53 Am.J.Psych. 518 (1940) (effect of cross-examinations upon jurors during progress of simulated trial); Snee and Lush, Interaction of the Narrative and Interrogatory Methods of Obtaining Testimony, 11 Am.J.Psych. 229 (1941) and the conclusions thereon in Gardner, The Perception and Memory of Witnesses, 18 Corn.L.Q. 391, 404 (1933) and Burtt, Legal Psychology 147 (1931) ("It appears that when we really go after the observer in a rigorous fashion we tend to introduce some errors, perhaps through the mechanism of suggestion. . . .").

Some abuses of cross-examination are reflected in Erle Stanley Gardner, Confessions of a Cross-Examiner, 3 J.For.Sci. 374 (1958) (unfair questioning of a medical expert as to compensation). Hazards of inadequate mastery of the art of cross-examination which may add to production of error are pointed out in most of the references cited in § 30, note 1 supra.

it is not the honest but weak or timid witness, rather than the rogue, who most often goes down under the fire of a cross-examination.[7] Certainly every witness in judicial proceedings should in fairness be made available for cross-examination by the opponent wherever possible. But the premise that where cross-examination is not possible, as in the case of out-of-court statements, or as in the case of a witness who dies before cross-examination, the statement or testimony should generally be excluded for that reason alone, seems ill-founded. Cross-examination, it is submitted, should be considered as useful but not indispensable as an agency of discovering truth, and absence of opportunity to cross-examine should only be one factor to be weighed in determining whether the statement or testimony should be received. Such an approach to hearsay problems might lead us to conclude that when opportunity to cross-examine a witness is permanently cut off without fault of either party, the direct testimony should nevertheless be received as suggested in a previous section.[8] It might lead us to further conclude that hearsay statements should be admitted if the statement was made by the declarant on personal knowledge and reported by the witness at first hand, and if the declarant is now dead or unavailable for cross-examination or, on the other hand, if the declarant is alive and still available for cross-examination.[9] Perhaps written statements should be admitted wherever production for cross-examination can fairly be dispensed with.[10]

It should be noted, however, that although these modern viewpoints are supportable,

there remains a special problem concerning the criminal defendant's right of cross-examination under the Fifth, Sixth, and Fourteenth Amendments of the federal constitution and the scope of the right as it affects interrupted cross-examination and the scope of the hearsay rule.[11]

 WESTLAW REFERENCES

tactic** /10 crossexamin!

§ 32. Redirect and Subsequent Examinations [1]

One who calls a witness is normally required to elicit on his first examination, the direct, all that he wishes to prove by him. This norm of proving everything so far as feasible at the first opportunity is manifestly in the interest of fairness and expedition. Whether the cross-examiner is limited to answering the direct is, as we have seen, a matter as to which our jurisdictions are divided, with a much greater number favoring the restrictive rule.[2] As to the redirect, however, and all subsequent examinations, there is no such division and the practice is uniform that the party's examination is normally limited to answering any new matter drawn out in the next previous examination of the adversary. It is true that the judge under his general discretionary power to vary the normal order of proof may permit the party to bring out on redirect examination some matter which is relevant to his case or defense and which through oversight he has failed to elicit on direct.[3] Under Federal Rule of Evidence 611(a) the judge has broad discretion over the scope of redirect.[4]

---

7. Elliott, The Work of the Advocate 235 (2d ed. 1911).

8. Compare § 19, supra.

9. Compare Ch. 34, infra.

10. Compare Ch. 34, infra.

11. See § 19 supra, and § 252, infra.

§ 32

1. See 6 Wigmore, Evidence §§ 1896, 1897 (Chadbourn rev. 1976), Dec.Dig. Witnesses ⊶285–291; C.J.S. Witnesses §§ 417–429.

2. See § 21 supra.

3. State v. Conner, 97 N.J.L. 423, 118 A. 211 (1922); State v. Bennett, 158 Me. 109, 179 A.2d 812 (1962); Fisher Body Division, General Motors Corp. v. Alston, 252 Md. 51, 249 A.2d 130 (1969); C.J.S. Witnesses § 419.

4. The judge's discretion is emphasized in Fed. and Rev.Unif.R.Evid. (1974) 611(a) and 403. No fixed rules are spelled out. See United States v. Taylor, 599 F.2d 832 (8th Cir. 1979).

But the reply to new matter drawn out on cross-examination is the normal function of the redirect, and examination for this purpose is often a matter of right,[5] though its extent is subject to control in the judge's discretion.[6]

A skillful re-examiner may often draw the sting of a lethal cross-examination.[7] The reply on redirect may take the form of explanation, avoidance, or qualification of the new substantive facts or matters of impeachment elicited by the cross-examiner.[8] The direct approach, such as "What did you mean by"[9] or "What was your reason for"[10] a state-ment made by the witness on cross-examination, may often be proper, but a mere reiteration of assertions previously made on the direct or cross-examination is not usually sanctioned,[11] although the judge has an area of discretion in this matter.

The rule of completeness,[12] which permits proof of the remainder of a transaction, conversation, or writing when a part thereof has been proven by the adversary,[13] so far as the remainder relates to the same subject-matter,[14] is often invoked by the re-examiner. This principle is not abrogated by Feder-

Rule 611(a) provides for the judge's discretion as follows:

> The court shall exercise reasonable control over the mode and order of interrogating witnesses and presenting evidence so as to (1) make the interrogation and presentation effective for the ascertainment of the truth, (2) avoid needless consumption of time, and (3) protect witnesses from harassment or undue embarrassment.

5. United States v. Lopez, 575 F.2d 681 (9th Cir. 1978) (". . . redirect is normally limited to the scope of cross-examination . . . The judge, in his discretion, may allow a new line of questioning on redirect."; dictum). No authority pursuant to Fed.R.Evid. 611(a) has been discovered, but conceivably redirect could be so important that it would be required). Villeneuve v. Manchester Street Railway Co., 73 N.H. 250, 60 A. 748 (1905) (when inconsistent statement out of court proved on cross, witness and party have right that witness be permitted to explain on redirect); Gray v. Metropolitan Street-Railway Co., 165 N.Y. 457, 59 N.E. 262 (1901); Martin's Administrator v. Richmond Fredericksburg & Potomac Railroad Co., 101 Va. 406, 44 S.E. 695 (1903).

6. People v. Kynette, 15 Cal.2d 731, 104 P.2d 794 (1940); Commonwealth v. Galvin, 310 Mass. 733, 39 N.E.2d 656 (1942). For federal authority see n. 4 supra.

7. An interesting example is the examination by Sir Edward Carson quoted in 6 Wigmore, Evidence § 1896 (Chadbourn rev. 1976).

8. United States v. Peters, 610 F.2d 338 (5th Cir. 1980) (cross-examination by defense attorney brought out that no photographs or recordings were made of defendant's conversations with government agent; on redirect it was brought out that such actions were not normal procedure on a "hand-to-hand buy"); Johnson v. Minihan, 355 Mo. 1208, 200 S.W.2d 334 (1947) (collision case; plaintiff's witness, driver of car in which plaintiff was guest, admitted signing, without reading, damaging statements on cross-examination; abuse of discretion to deny redirect examination about fact that witness signed statement in order to secure settlement from defendant of witness's own claim); Long v. F.W.

Woolworth Co., 232 Mo.App. 417, 109 S.W.2d 85 (1937) (proper to allow plaintiff, asked on cross if she had consulted doctor, to explain on redirect that she had not, because she could not pay); Crowell v. State, 147 Tex. Cr.R. 299, 180 S.W.2d 343 (1944) (in prosecution for keeping bawdy house, where deputy sheriff on cross-examination admitted that he said he wanted to run defendant out of town, proper for him to explain on redirect that it was because of citizens' complaints against defendant); Hawkins v. United States, 417 F.2d 1271 (5th Cir. 1969) cert. denied 397 U.S. 914 (redirect concerning defendant's brutal treatment of witness was permitted to rebut attempted impeachment of witness on cross-examination, citing Beck v. United States, 317 F.2d 865 (5th Cir. 1963)); Abeyta v. People, 156 Colo. 440, 400 P.2d 431 (1965) (illustrating similar principle).

Whether a witness who admits a conviction on cross-examination is allowed on redirect to explain the circumstances of the conviction is the subject of conflicting decisions. See § 43 infra.

9. People v. Buchanan, 145 N.Y. 1, 39 N.E. 846, 853 (1895) (dictum); C.J.S. Witnesses § 421, note 61.

10. State v. Kaiser, 124 Mo. 651, 28 S.W. 182 (1894); C.J.S. Witnesses § 420, note 47.

11. Moore-Handley Hardware Co. v. Williams, 238 Ala. 189, 189 So. 757 (1939) (question calling for summation of witness's theory of accident as already given on direct and cross, properly excluded in judge's discretion); Clayton v. Bellatti, 70 Ill.App.2d 367, 216 N.E.2d 686 (1966); Forslund v. Chicago Transit Authority, 9 Ill.App.2d 290, 132 N.E.2d 801 (1956). But where witness on cross-examination was confronted with her written statement contradicting her story on direct, it was held proper to ask her on redirect whether her testimony on direct was true. Grayson v. United States, 107 F.2d 367 (8th Cir. 1939).

12. See § 56 infra.

13. State v. Kendrick, 173 N.W.2d 560 (Iowa 1970). See § 56 infra.

14. White v. Commonwealth, 292 Ky. 416, 166 S.W.2d 873 (1942); State v. Williams, 448 S.W.2d 865 (Mo. 1970).

al Rule of Evidence 106.[15] Moreover, the principle of curative admissibility,[16] under which evidence that is irrelevant or otherwise incompetent may sometimes be allowed to be answered by the adversary, is likewise frequently resorted to by the examiner on redirect.[17]

Recross-examination, following the rule of first opportunity mentioned above, is nor-

mally confined to questions directed to the explanation or avoidance of new matter brought out on redirect.[18]

 WESTLAW REFERENCES

digest(redirect /s examination /s scope)
digest(recrossexamination /p scope)

---

15. Fed.R.Evid. 106 concerns immediate introduction of part of a writing when another part is introduced.

16. See § 57 infra.

17. Barrett v. United States, 82 F.2d 528 (7th Cir. 1936); United States v. Maggio, 126 F.2d 155 (3d Cir. 1942); United States v. Maultasch, 596 F.2d 19 (2d Cir. 1979); Chamberlain v. State, 348 P.2d 280 (Wyo.1960). But the "open the gate" theory will not permit eliciting incompetent and prejudicial evidence on redirect, according to some cases. See, e.g., People v. Arends, 155 Cal.App.2d 496, 318 P.2d 532 (1958).

18. Where no new matter was opened on redirect the trial court's action in denying a recross was approved in Faulk v. State, 47 Ga.App. 804, 171 S.E. 570 (1933) and in Commonwealth v. Gordon, 598 Mass. 356,

254 N.E.2d 901 (1970); United States v. Fontenot, 628 F.2d 921 (5th Cir. 1980), cert. denied 452 U.S. 905 (trial judge properly restricted recross-examination when not sought to meet new matter on direct and was not necessary to a full and fair adjudication of the case). But a recross, though not in reply to new matter on redirect may be allowed in the court's discretion. Maryland Wrecking & Equipment Co. v. News Publishing Co., 148 Md. 560, 129 A. 836 (1925); Dege v. United States, 308 F.2d 534 (9th Cir. 1962) (matter referred to on cross-examination but not in redirect examination). Under Fed.R.Evid. 611(a) the judge has broad discretion. But there is also a limited right to recross-examination. United States v. Caudle, 606 F.2d 451 (4th Cir. 1979) (reversible error when defendant not permitted to recross-examine on redirect testimony in which additional details were recounted).

Chapter 5

IMPEACHMENT AND SUPPORT

Table of Sections

---

§ 33. Introductory: The Stages of Impeachment and the Lines of Attack

There are five main lines of attack upon the credibility of a witness.[1] The first, and probably the most effective and most frequently employed, is an attack by proof that the witness on a previous occasion has made statements <u>inconsistent</u> with his present testimony. The second is an attack by a showing that the witness is <u>biased</u> on account of emotional influences such as kinship for one party or hostility to another, or motives of pecuniary interest, whether legitimate or

---

§ 33

1. The components of credibility, i.e., the factors which determine whether testimony is believable, are the perception, memory, and narration of the witness. Morgan, Hearsay Dangers and the Application of the Hearsay Concept, 62 Harv.L.Rev. 177 (1948); Strahorn, A Reconsideration of the Hearsay Rule and Admissions, 85 U.Pa.L.Rev. 484, 485 (1937). See also the usual jury instructions on credibility. Sometimes

sincerity is also named, but in fact it seems to be but an aspect of the other three. While in theory the subject of impeachment might be organized according to these various "components," the rules have in fact grown up around particular techniques, without any particular consideration as to the particular component which may be under attack. As a result, the subject is here approached by examining the various techniques.

corrupt. The third is an attack upon the character of the witness. The fourth is an attack by showing a defect of capacity in the witness to observe, remember or recount the matters testified about. The fifth is proof by other witnesses that material facts are otherwise than as testified to by the witness under attack.[2] Finally, it might be observed that lack of religious belief is not available as a basis of attack on credibility. Some of these attacks are not specifically or completely treated by the Federal or Revised Uniform Rules of Evidence, but they are generally authorized by those rules.

The process of impeachment may be employed in two different stages. First, the facts discrediting the witness or his testimony may be elicited from the witness himself upon cross-examination. Certain kinds of attack are limited to this stage; it is said, "You must take his answer." Second, in some situations, the facts discrediting the witness are proved by extrinsic evidence, that is, the assailant waits until the time for putting on his own case in rebuttal, and then proves by a second witness or by documentary evidence, the facts discrediting the testimony of the witness attacked.

There is a cardinal rule of impeachment. Never launch an attack which implies that the witness has lied deliberately, unless you are convinced that the attack is justifiable, and is essential to your case. An assault which fails often produces in the jury's mind an indignant sympathy for the intended victim.

It is believed that, in general, there is less practical emphasis upon impeachment of witnesses than formerly, and that the elaborate system of rules regulating the practice and scope of impeachment which has been developed in the past is now applied with less strictness and is simplified by confiding the control less to rules and more to judicial discretion.

**WESTLAW
REFERENCES**

contradict! discredit!   /s   limit!   /s   crossexam!

---

§ 34. Prior Inconsistent Statements:[1] Degree of Inconsistency Required[2]

When a witness testifies to facts material in a case, the opponent may have available proof that the witness has previously made statements that are inconsistent with his present testimony. Under a modern view of the hearsay rule, these previous statements would be admissible as substantive evidence of the facts stated. This viewpoint is discussed in the chapter concerning hearsay.[3] However, under the more traditional views of hearsay these previous statements will often be inadmissible as evidence of what they state because they constitute hearsay and are not within any exceptions to the hearsay rule.[4] Even though inadmissible hearsay as evidence of the facts stated, they are nevertheless admissible for the limited purpose of impeaching the witness.[5] Subject to the extension that prior inconsistent statements are admissible as substantive ev-

---

2. Of course, credibility may also be attacked by eliciting on cross-examination statements from the witness contradictory to his own statements on direct or in other parts of the cross-examination. The practice of asking exploratory or testing questions designed to elicit self-contradictions is described in §§ 29, 30 supra.

§ 34

1. 3A Wigmore, Evidence §§ 1017–1046 (Chadbourn rev. 1970); Weinstein & Berger, Evidence ¶ 613[01]–[06], ¶ 607[06]; Hale, Prior Inconsistent Statements, 10 So.Cal.L.Rev. 135 (1937); Dec.Dig. Witnesses ⊕379–397; C.J.S. Witnesses §§ 573–628; 81 Am.Jur.2d Witnesses §§ 596–618.

2. 3A Wigmore, Evidence §§ 1040–1043 (Chadbourn rev. 1970); Weinstein & Berger, Evidence ¶ 607[06]; Dec.Dig. Witnesses ⊕386; C.J.S. Witnesses § 583.

3. See § 251 infra.

4. See generally Chapter 24 infra.

5. Any form of statement is acceptable. It may have been made orally, as testimony at another trial or by deposition, or in writing, as a letter, accident-report or witness-statement or affidavit, or in any other form. Conduct, likewise, evincing a belief inconsistent with the facts asserted on the stand is usable on the same principle. See, e.g., Missouri Pacific Transportation Co. v. Norwood, 192 Ark. 170, 90 S.W.2d 480 (1936) (assertion of negligence claim by witness admitted); State v. Fenix, 311 S.W.2d 61 (Mo.1958) (a purchase of prop-

idence because they are not hearsay if they were made under oath subject to the penalty of perjury at a trial, hearing or other proceeding, or in a deposition, the Federal and Revised Uniform Rules of Evidence preserve this traditional view.[6]

It is important to note that the treatment of inconsistent statements in this chapter is confined to the situation in which the statements are introduced for impeachment purposes but may not be used as substantive evidence (over proper objection of the opponent).[7] For this purpose, the making of the previous statements may be drawn out in cross-examination of the witness himself, or if on cross-examination the witness has denied making the statement, or has failed to remember it,[8] the making of the statement may be proved by another witness; but under the Federal and Revised Uniform Rules of Evidence the making of the statement may also be brought out by the second witness without prior inquiry of the witness who made it.[9] This form of impeachment is sometimes called "self-contradiction". It is to be distinguished from the mere production of other evidence as to material facts conflicting with the evidence of the assailed witness. The mere production of other evi-

dence that conflicts with the evidence of a witness is discussed in a later section.[10]

The theory of attack by prior inconsistent statements is not based on the assumption that the present testimony is false and the former statement true but rather upon the notion that talking one way on the stand and another way previously is blowing hot and cold, and raises a doubt as to the truthfulness of both statements.[11] More particularly the prior statement, assuming it is inadmissible as substantive evidence under the hearsay rule,[12] may be used in this context only as an aid in judging the credibility of the testimony with which the previous statement is inconsistent.[13] To create the abovementioned doubt by introduction of the previous statement of the witness, what degree of inconsistency between the testimony of the witness and his previous statement is required? The language of some of the cases seems overstrict in suggesting that a contradiction must be found,[14] and under the more widely accepted view any material variance between the testimony and the previous statement will suffice.[15] Accordingly, if the former statement fails to mention a material circumstance presently testified to, which it would have been natural to mention in the

---

erty for particular purpose held consistent and inadmissible); Dec.Dig. Witnesses ☞347. But settlements or offers to compromise are governed by other rules. See § 274 infra; Bratt v. Western Air Lines, 169 F.2d 214 (1948).

The use of unconstitutionally obtained evidence for purposes of impeachment is discussed in § 178 infra.

6. The limited extension admitting inconsistent statements as evidence, insofar as the hearsay rule is concerned is contained in Rule 801(d)(1). See § 251 infra. Rule 613 outlines the procedure to use inconsistent statements of the witness for impeachment purposes. For the text of Fed.R.Evid. and Rev.Unif.R. Evid. (1974) 613 see § 37, n. 12 infra.

7. The use of prior inconsistent statements as substantive evidence is discussed in § 251 infra.

8. See § 37 infra.

9. See § 37 infra.

10. See § 47 infra.

11. Compare the discussion in 3A Wigmore, Evidence § 1017 (Chadbourn rev. 1970).

12. See n. 4 supra.

13. See discussion in Chapter 24 infra.

14. See, e.g., Sanger v. Bacon, 180 Ind. 322, 328, 101 N.E. 1001, 1003 (1913) (must be contradictory construing the statement most favorably to the witness); State v. Bowen, 247 Mo. 584, 153 S.W. 1033, 1038 (1913) ("must be such as, either in their substance or their general drift, contradict"); and cases cited C.J.S. Witnesses § 583, n. 44.

15. United States v. Rogers, 549 F.2d 490 (8th Cir. 1976), cert. denied 431 U.S. 918 (when witness admitted making statement but testified he could not recollect it and when other circumstances indicated witness was fully aware of contents of statement, the statement was sufficiently inconsistent; the trial court should have considerable discretion with respect to evasive answers); Commonwealth v. West, 312 Mass. 438, 440, 45 N.E.2d 260, 262 (1942) ("And it is not necessary that there should be a contradiction in plain terms. It is enough if the proffered testimony, taken as a whole, either by what it says or by what it omits to say, affords some indication that the fact was different from the testimony of the witness whom it is sought to contradict."); O'Neill v. Minneapolis Street Railway Co., 213 Minn. 514, 7 N.W.2d 665, 669 (1942) ("Whether a prior statement does in fact impeach a witness does not depend upon the degree of inconsistency between his testimony and his prior statement. If there is any vari-

prior statement, the prior statement is sufficiently inconsistent.[16] Again, an earlier
statement by the witness that he had no
knowledge of facts now testified to, should
be provable.[17] Seemingly the test should be,
could the jury reasonably find that a witness
who believed the truth of the facts testified
to would have been unlikely to make a prior
statement of this tenor?[18] The Federal and
Revised Uniform Rules of Evidence do not
expressly indicate a test for inconsistency.
The liberal rules for inconsistency expressed
herein should govern.[19] Thus, if the previous statement is ambiguous and according
to one meaning would be inconsistent with
the testimony, it should be admitted for the
jury's consideration.[20] In applying the criterion of material inconsistency reasonable
judges will be likely to differ, and a fair
range of discretion should be accorded to the

trial judge. Moreover, it is to be hoped that
instead of restricting the use of prior statements by a mechanical use of the test of inconsistency, the courts will lean toward receiving such statements in case of doubt, to
aid in evaluating the testimony. The statements, indeed, having been made when
memory was more recent and when less
time for the play of influence has elapsed,
are often inherently more trustworthy than
the testimony itself.[21] A logical extension of
this reasoning justifies the admission of pri-
or testimony about an independent and unrelated event so similar to testimony now giv-
en as to arouse suspicion of fabrication.[22]

**WESTLAW
REFERENCES**

prior /s inconsisten! /p selfcontradict!

ance between them, the statement should be received
and its effect upon the credibility of the witness should
be left to the jury." Statement held not to meet the
test.); Morgan v. Washington Trust Co., 105 R.I. 13,
249 A.2d 48 (1969).

16. United States v. Standard Oil Co., 316 F.2d 884
(7th Cir. 1963) (prior statement omitted matters about
which witness seemingly testified at trial); Esderts v.
Chicago Rock Island & Pacific Co., 76 Ill.App.2d 210,
222 N.E.2d 117 (1966) cert. denied 386 U.S. 993 ("If a
witness fails to mention facts under circumstances
which make it reasonably probable he would mention
them if true, the omission may be shown as an indirect
inconsistency."); Erickson v. Erickson & Co., 212 Minn.
119, 2 N.W.2d 824 (1942) (workmen's compensation automobile accident claimant testified on stand that his
trip was for two purposes, one individual, the other for
the employer; held, his prior statements to adjuster
mentioning only the individual purpose admissible to
impeach). Contra: Hall v. Phillips Petroleum Co., 358
Mo. 313, 214 S.W.2d 438 (semble) (1948).

17. Hoagland v. Canfield, 160 F. 146, 171 (C.C.S.D.
N.Y.1908); In re Olson's Estate, 54 S.D. 184, 223 N.W.
41 (1929); C.J.S. Witnesses § 583, n. 52. Similarly, it
seems that a previous statement denying recollection
of facts testified to should be provable. But see Lewis
v. American Road Insurance Co., 199 Ga.App. 507, 167
S.E.2d 729 (1969) (witness refused to answer questions
on prior deposition; inadmissible); Grunewald v. United States, 353 U.S. 391 (1957) (defendant's refusal to
answer same questions before grand jury, on grounds
the answers would tend to incriminate him, was inadmissible because refusal was not inconsistent under
the circumstances). The text should be applicable under the federal rules.

18. Morgan v. Washington Trust Co., 105 R.I. 13,
249 A.2d 48 (1969). See United States v. Barrett, 539

F.2d 244 (1st Cir. 1976) ("It is enough if the proffered
testimony, taken as a whole, either by what it says or
by what it omits to say, affords some indication that
the fact was different from the testimony of the witness whom it is sought to contradict.").

19. The judge has discretion under Rule 403 to sustain objections if the risk that the jury will use an inconsistent statement in a particular instance as evidence (and not restrict the use to judging credibility) is
great.

20. State v. Kingsbury, 58 Me. 238, 242 (1870);
Town of Concord v. Concord Bank, 16 N.H. 26, 32
(1844); C.J.S. Witnesses § 583, n. 53, 54. But there
are contrary decisions. State v. Bush, 50 Idaho 166,
295 P. 432 (1930), and cases cited.

21. Commonwealth v. Jackson, 281 S.W.2d 891, 896
(Ky.1955). See the comment by Davis, J. for the court
in Judson v. Fielding, 227 App.Div. 430, 237 N.Y.S. 348,
352 (1929): "In considering the evidence so sharply in
dispute, the jury was entitled to know the contrary
views the witness had expressed when the incident was
fresh in his mind, uninfluenced by sympathy or other
cause. Very often by calm reflection a witness may
correct inaccurate observations or erroneous impressions hastily formed. But the jury should have all the
facts in making an appraisement of the value and
weight to be given the testimony."

See Ch. 24 infra.

22. People v. Rainford, 58 Ill.App.2d 312, 208
N.E.2d 314 (1965) (testimony of prosecuting witness in
prior rape case was exactly the same in unlikely details
as testimony of the witness in the instant prosecution
against the same defendants for assault with intent to
rape the witness in a different and independent incident).

§ 35. Prior Inconsistent Statements: Opinion in Form [1]

If a witness, such as an expert, testifies in terms of opinion, of course all courts will permit impeachment by showing a previous expression by the witness of an inconsistent opinion.[2] More troublesome is the question which arises when the witness testifies to specific facts and then is sought to be impeached by prior inconsistent expressions of opinion. For example, in a collision case the plaintiff's witness testifies to particular facts inculpating the driver of a bus involved in the accident. The opponent proposes to show that the witness said just after seeing the collision, "The bus was not to blame." [3]

Should the opinion rule be applied to exclude such an impeaching statement? The early American tradition of a strict rule against opinions has been much relaxed in recent trial administration.[4] What was once supposed to be a difference in kind between fact and opinion is now regarded as a difference in degree only.[5] Wigmore considers that the rule goes no further than to exclude opinion as superfluous when more concrete statements could be resorted to.[6] Thus, the principal practical value of the opinion rule is as a regulation of trial practice requiring the examining counsel to bring out his facts by more specific questions if practicable, before resorting to more general ones. For this reason, it is a mistake of policy to apply it to any out-of-court statements whatsoever, since no such controls are possible.[7] Moreover, when the out-of-court statement is not offered at all as evidence of the fact asserted, but only to show the asserter's inconsistency, the whole purpose of the opinion rule, to improve the objectivity and hence reliability of testimonial assertions, is quite inapplicable. Hence, though many earlier decisions, influenced perhaps by a statement in Greenleaf [8] and a casual English holding at *nisi prius*,[9] and some later opinions, exclude impeaching statements in opinion form,[10] the trend of holdings and the majority view is in accord with the commonsense notion that if a substantial inconsistency appears the form of the impeaching statement is immaterial.[11] This view is indirectly authorized by Federal and Revised Uniform Evidence Rule 701 because of the broad scope of that opinion rule.

§ 35

1. Dec.Dig. Witnesses ⊜384; C.J.S. Witnesses § 592. As noted in § 34, this section assumes that inconsistent statements are sought to be introduced only for impeachment purposes. 81 Am.Jur.2d Witnesses § 598; Annot., 66 A.L.R. 289, 158 A.L.R. 820.

2. Hutson v. State, 164 Tex.Civ.R. 24, 296 S.W.2d 245 (1956); McGrath v. Fash, 244 Mass. 327, 139 N.E. 303 (1923) (doctor who testified to moderate injuries, impeached by his statement after examining plaintiff that "this was the worst accident case he handled in the last ten years"); In re County Ditch, 150 Minn. 69, 184 N.W. 374 (1921) (value-witness impeached by his report on value as viewer); C.J.S. Witnesses § 581, n. 13.

3. Judson v. Fielding, 227 App.Div. 430, 237 N.Y.S. 348 (1929) (impeachment allowed).

4. See §§ 11, 12, 17 supra.

5. See §§ 11, 12 supra.

6. 7 Wigmore, Evidence § 1918 (Chadbourn rev. 1978).

7. See § 18 supra.

8. Greenleaf, Evidence § 449 (3d ed. 1846).

9. Elton v. Larkins, 5 Car. & P. 385, 172 Eng.Rep. 1020 (1832) (suit on marine policy; the broker who effected policy for the plaintiff, called as witness for defendants, testified to facts showing material concealment; plaintiff sought to show by extrinsic evidence after witness denied it, that witness had said that "the underwriters had not a leg to stand on," excluded by Tindal, C.J. as "only a contradiction on a matter of judgment").

10. See, e.g., City Bank v. Young, 43 N.H. 457, 460 (1862); Morton v. State, 43 Tex.Crim.R. 533, 67 S.W. 115 (1902), and see cases cited Annot., 158 A.L.R. 820, 821. See, also, Dorsten v. Lawrence, 20 Ohio App.2d 297, 253 N.E.2d 804 (1969); State v. Thompson, 71 S.D. 319, 24 N.W.2d 10 (1946); Hirsh v. Manley, 81 Ariz. 94, 300 P.2d 588 (1956) (rule applied where court thought the out-of-court opinion required expertise but witness had not been qualified as an expert); C.J.S. Witnesses § 592.

11. United States v. Barrett, 539 F.2d 244 (1st Cir. 1976), cert. denied 431 U.S. 918; Tigh v. College Park Realty Co., 149 Mont. 358, 427 P.2d 57 (1967); and see the description of the trend and the collections of cases in Annot., 158 A.L.R. 821–824, and in Grady, The Admissibility of a Prior Statement of Opinion for Purposes of Impeachment, 41 Cornell L.Q. 224 (1956). See also C.J.S. Witnesses § 592.

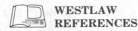

WESTLAW REFERENCES

digest(410 /p "opinion" /p inconsisten** /p impeach!)

§ 36. Prior Inconsistent Statements: Subject Matter

On cross-examination we have seen that strict rules of relevancy are relaxed,[1] and generally the trial judge in his discretion may permit the cross-examiner to inquire about any previous statements inconsistent with assertions, relevant or irrelevant, which the witness has testified to on direct or cross. At this stage, there is no strict requirement that the previous impeaching statements must not deal with "collateral" matters.[2] But as appears in the next paragraph, if the inquiry on cross-examination is as to inconsistent statements about "collat-

eral" matters, the cross-examiner must "take the answer"—he cannot bring on other witnesses to prove the making of the alleged statement.[3] Or if, as under the Federal and Revised Uniform Rules of Evidence, extrinsic evidence of inconsistent statements may be introduced before such cross-examination, the intrinsic evidence must not concern collateral matters.[4]

Extrinsic evidence, that is, the production of attacking witnesses, for impeachment by inconsistent statements, is sharply narrowed for obvious reasons of economy of time and attention. The tag, "You cannot contradict as to collateral matters," applies, and here the meaning is that to impeach by extrinsic proof of prior inconsistent statements, the statements must have as their subject (1) facts relevant to the issues in the cause, or (2) facts which are themselves provable by extrinsic evidence to discredit the witness.[5]

§ 36

1. See § 29 supra. The present section deals with self-contradiction as a technique of impeachment. Contradiction by other witnesses is considered in § 47, infra.

2. Howard v. City Fire Insurance Co., 4 Denio 502, 506 (S.Ct.N.Y.1847); Dane v. MacGregor, 94 N.H. 294, 52 A.2d 290 (1947); 3A Wigmore, Evidence § 1023 (Chadbourn rev. 1970).

Since the matter is within the discretion of the trial court, his ruling will usually be upheld upon appeal. See, e.g., Lenske v. Knutsen, 410 F.2d 583 (9th Cir. 1969); State v. Brewster, 75 Wn.2d 137, 449 P.2d 685 (1969) (trial judge permitted questions concerning collateral matter); Wiesemann v. Pavlat, 413 S.W.2d 23 (Mo.App.1967). Nevertheless, if the matter is clearly material it has been held that the cross-examination must be permitted. State v. Thompson, 280 S.W.2d 838 (Mo.1955); Healy v. City of Chicago, 109 Ill.App.2d 6, 248 N.E.2d 679 (1969). If the matter is immaterial and prejudicial, the trial judge may be reversed, at least if no appropriate requested instruction is given. Kantor v. Ash, 215 Md. 285, 137 A.2d 661 (1958).

It might be noted, however, that occasionally an opinion will contain a flat statement that cross-examination may not be had concerning an inconsistent statement on a matter that is collateral. Kantor v. Ash, supra; State v. Wilson, 158 Conn. 321, 260 A.2d 571 (1969).

3. That a denial on cross-examination of a statement relating to a "collateral" matter cannot be disputed by extrinsic evidence, see Montgomery v. Nance, 425 P.2d 470 (Okl.1967); State v. Mangrum, 98 Ariz. 279, 403 P.2d 925 (1965) (court states cross should have been permitted but the extrinsic evidence was inadmis-

sible); cases cited in Dec.Dig. Witnesses ⟨383; C.J.S. Witnesses § 611.

4. The prohibition against contradiction as to collateral matters is one of the number of assorted concepts collected together by Fed. and Rev.Unif.R.Evid. (1974) 403. Dolan, Rule 403: The Prejudice Rule in Evidence, 49 S.Cal.L.Rev. 220 (1976). See generally §§ 47 and 185 infra. See, e.g., United States v. Nace, 561 F.2d 763 (9th Cir. 1977).

5. The classic statement of the test of "collateralness" is in the opinions in Attorney-General v. Hitchcock, 1 Exch. 91, 99, 154 Eng.Rep. 38 (1847). That case was an information under the revenue laws. A witness for the plaintiff was asked on cross-examination if he had not said he had been offered 20 pounds to testify by officers of the Crown, which he denied. Held, the defendant could not call a witness to testify that the first witness had made the alleged statement. Pollock, C.B. said: "A distinction should be observed between those matters which may be given in evidence by way of contradiction as directly affecting the story of the witness touching the issue before the jury, and those matters which affect the motives, temper, and character of the witness, not with respect to his credit, but with reference to his feelings towards one party or the other. It is certainly allowable to ask a witness in what manner he stands affected toward the opposite party in the cause . . . and whether he has not used expressions importing that he would be revenged on some one or that he would give such evidence as might dispose of the cause in one way or the other. If he denies that, you may give evidence as to what he said,—not with the view of having a direct effect on the issue, but to show what is the state of mind of that witness in order that the jury may exercise their opinion as to how far he is to be believed." It should be

Facts showing bias or interest,[6] and presumably facts showing that the witness had no opportunity to know the material matters testified to,[7] would fall in the second class. This analysis of collateral matter should be followed generally under the Federal and Revised Uniform Rules of Evidence (in the introduction of inconsistent statements to impeach by extrinsic evidence).

A distinct but somewhat cognate notion is the view that if a party interrogates a witness about a fact which would be favorable to the examiner if true, and receives a reply which is merely negative in its effect on examiner's case, the examiner may not by extrinsic evidence prove that the first witness had earlier stated that the fact was true as desired by the inquirer.[8] An affirmative answer would have been material and subject to be impeached by an inconsistent statement, but a negative answer is not damaging to the examiner, but merely disappointing, and may not be thus impeached. In this situation the policy involved is not the saving of time and confusion, as before, but the protection of the other party against the hearsay use by the jury of the previous statement.[9]

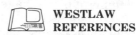 **WESTLAW REFERENCES**

410k383 /p contradict! /p collateral /p impeach!

§ 37. Prior Inconsistent Statements: Requirement of Preliminary Questions on Cross-Examination as "Foundation" for Proof by Extrinsic Evidence [1]

In 1820 in the answers of the judges in *Queen Caroline's Case*, it was announced: "If it be intended to bring the credit of a wit-

---

observed that the alleged statement was that the witness had been *offered* a bribe, not that he had accepted one. But query as to evidence of attempted bribery of a witness as an admission. See § 273 infra.

Another illuminating discussion is the opinion of Rutledge, J. in Ewing v. United States, 77 U.S.App.D.C. 14, 135 F.2d 633, 640–642 (1942). Here a witness for defendant accused of rape swore to facts which if believed made it impossible to believe complainant's story. Over the witness's denial, the government was (it was held) properly allowed to prove that the witness had said (1) I believe the defendant guilty but (2) he is facing the electric chair and I must be on his side. The court rejected the test of collateralness used in some cases (see, e.g., Butler v. State, 179 Miss. 865, 176 So. 589 (1937) whether the party would have been entitled to prove the matter "as part of his case," and appoved Wigmore's statement of the test as follows: "Could the fact as to which the prior self-contradiction is predicated have been shown in evidence for any purpose independently of the self-contradiction?" 3A Wigmore, Evidence § 1020 (Chadbourn rev. 1970). This seems to be equivalent to saying that the fact which is the subject of the previous statement must be (1) relevant to an issue, or (2) provable under impeachment practice by extrinsic evidence. Of course, the second previous statement in the *Ewing* case is not a prior inconsistent statement but is a direct expression of bias, and provable as such for impeachment regardless of self-contradiction. Somewhat similar is State v. Sandros, 186 Wash. 438, 58 P.2d 362 (1936), where, despite his denials, the state was allowed to prove that defense witness, claimed to be an accomplice with accused in forging a will, had (1) said that he had carried the will in his pocket for three weeks (which was material as tending to show it could not have been made at the time it was dated) and (2) made efforts to persuade a person to testify falsely to the genuineness of the signature. The court approved the Wigmore test, as given above.

6. See, e.g., *Ewing* and *Sandros* in the next preceding note.

7. See 3A Wigmore, Evidence § 1022 (Chadbourn rev. 1970).

8. Miller v. Comm., 241 Ky. 818, 45 S.W.2d 461 (1932) (witness for defense who denied she heard defendant say he was going to kill deceased, improperly allowed to be impeached by proof that she had said she had heard such threats); Woodroffe v. Jones, 83 Me. 21, 21 A. 177 (1890) (suit by wife for sprained ankle due to defective sidewalk; defense, plaintiff negligent in wearing high-heeled shoes; husband, as witness, denied on cross-examination that he had spoken to his wife about her high heels; held proof by another witness that he had said "that he told his wife about wearing such high heeled boots" improperly admitted to impeach his denial which was merely negative and without probative significance).

9. The pre-rules decision of United States v. Cunningham, 446 F.2d 194 (2d Cir. 1971), cert. denied 404 U.S. 950, reached this result with respect to a prior statement by the witness, otherwise inadmissible as hearsay. Of course, if the inconsistent statements of the witness are not hearsay, either under the more traditional rule, or modern rules such as Fed. and Rev. Unif.R.Evid. 801(d)(1), there would be no such hearsay use. See generally § 251 infra; § 34 supra.

§ 37

1. 3A Wigmore, Evidence §§ 1025–1039 (Chadbourn rev. 1970); Hale, Inconsistent Statements, 10 So.Cal. L.R. 135–147 (1937); Dec.Dig. Witnesses ☞388, 389; C.J.S. Witnesses §§ 598–612; 81 Am.Jur.2d Witnesses §§ 605–608.

ness into question by proof of anything he may have said or declared touching the cause, the witness is first asked, upon cross-examination, whether or not he has said or declared that which is intended to be proved." [2] Thus was crystallized a practice which was previously occasional and discretionary. Only later and gradually was it almost universally accepted in this country. [3] It came to be applied to both written and oral inconsistent statements. [4] The purposes of this traditional requirement are (1) to avoid unfair surprise to the adversary, (2) to save time, as an admission by the witness may make extrinsic proof unnecessary, and (3) to give the witness in fairness a chance to explain the discrepancy.

To satisfy the requirement in jurisdictions in which it still is enforced, the cross-examiner will ask the witness whether the witness made the alleged statement, giving its sub-

stance, and naming the time, the place, and the person to whom made. [5] The purpose of this particularity is, of course, to refresh the memory of the witness as to the supposed statement by reminding the witness of the accompanying circumstances. [6] If the witness denies the making of the statement, or fails to admit it, but says "I don't know" or "I don't remember" then the requirement of "laying the foundation" is satisfied and the cross-examiner, at the next stage of giving evidence, may prove the making of the alleged statement. [7] If, however, the witness unequivocally admits the making of the supposed statement, may the cross-examiner still choose to prove it again by another witness? Wigmore, with some support, suggests that the cross-examiner may, [8] but the prevailing view is to the contrary [9] and in the usual situation this seems the more expedient practice. [10]

2. 2 Brod. & Bing. 284, 313, 129 Eng.Rep. 976 (1820).

3. 3A Wigmore, Evidence § 1026 (Chadbourn rev. 1970). A foundation question has not been required in Massachusetts unless a party is attempting to impeach his own witness. Allin v. Whittemore, 171 Mass. 259, 50 N.E. 618 (1898) is a leading case. See also Thompson v. J.P. Morin & Co., 80 N.H. 144, 114 A. 274 (1921) (citing earlier cases). See n. 24 infra, concerning the rule that the matter should be in the discretion of the trial judge.

4. See § 28 supra.

5. This is the usual formula. See, e.g., Angus v. Smith, Moo. & M. 473, 474, 173 Eng.Rep. 1228 (1829) ("you must ask him as to time, place, and person . . . it is not enough to ask him the general question whether he has ever said so and so"); Peyton v. State, 40 Ala.App. 556, 120 So.2d 415 (1959), cert. denied 270 Ala. 740, 120 So.2d 429, cert. denied, 364 U.S. 870. The use of leading questions in examining the impeaching witness is discussed in § 6 at n. 14 supra.

6. Since the purpose of the foundation question is to warn the witness sufficiently of the out-of-court statement so that he may remember it, the usual formula may be relaxed under circumstances in which it is indicated that the witness was sufficiently warned although the foundation question was not completely specific under the formula. State v. Caldwell, 251 La. 780, 206 So.2d 492 (1968) (time not exactly specified); cases cited in C.J.S. Witnesses § 605.

7. People v. Perri, 381 Ill. 244, 44 N.E.2d 857 (1942) (denial); Ream's Administrator v. Greer, 314 S.W.2d 511 (Ky.1958) (witness stated he did not recall "Using those words"); Dec.Dig. Witnesses ⊜389; C.J.S. Witnesses §§ 610, 612.

8. 3A Evidence § 1037, note 4 (Chadbourn rev. 1970). A case supporting this view is People v. Schainuck, 286 N.Y. 161, 36 N.E.2d 94 (1941) (arson: prosecution witness admitted on cross-examination that in investigation-hearing by Fire Marshal he said he knew nothing about cause of fire; held, error to refuse request of defense counsel to inspect hearing-record with a view to proving statements of witness). Several cases in Illinois support the view that the inconsistent statement is admissible; others seem contrary. See discussion in People v. Knowles, 91 Ill.App.2d 109, 234 N.E.2d 149 (1968).

9. State v. Jackson, 248 La. 919, 183 So.2d 305 (1966) (writing; Art. 493 Code of Criminal Procedure applied); Alabama Electric Co-operative, Inc. v. Partridge, 284 Ala. 442, 225 So.2d 848 (1969) (writing); and decisions collected in C.J.S. Witnesses § 610.

10. It saves time and minimizes the calling of witnesses upon what is only a side issue; yet circumstances may be such, especially when the statement is in writing, that the judge's discretion to allow the impeachment to proceed should be recognized.

However, see suggestion in Gordon v. United States, 344 U.S. 414 (1953) (error to deny access to prior inconsistent written statements of government witness, despite his admission of inconsistency on cross-examination, since judge might nevertheless have admitted them "as a more reliable, complete and accurate source of information.").

Under Fed.R.Evid. 613, the judge may deny admission of extrinsic evidence of the inconsistent statement if the witness has already admitted making it. United States v. Jones, 578 F.2d 1332 (10th Cir. 1978), cert. denied 439 U.S. 913. However, the liberality of the rule in permitting extrinsic evidence of the prior inconsis-

The traditional requirement as explained above may well work unfairly for the impeacher, who may only learn of the inconsistent statement after the cross-examination of the witness has ended and the witness by leaving the court has made it impracticable to recall the witness for further cross-examination to lay a foundation belatedly. It is moreover a requirement which can serve as a trap since it must be done in advance before the final impeachment is attempted and is supremely easy to overlook. Based upon these and other considerations the Federal and Revised Uniform Rules of Evidence adopted a liberal view, abolishing the notion that the witness must on cross-examination be shown an inconsistent statement or be advised of its contents before being questioned about its substance in any way, and abandoning the requirement that the above-mentioned traditional foundation questions must be put to the witness on cross-examination before extrinsic evidence of the statement is introduced, i.e., before other witnesses testify to it or before an inconsistent writing is introduced.[11] Instead, under Federal and Revised Uniform Rule 613 the only requirements for introducing prior inconsistent written or oral statements of a witness are (1) that in questioning the witness concern-

ing written statements or the substance of the statements, they shall be shown or disclosed to the opposing counsel upon request, and (2) after introduction of the inconsistent statements by cross-examination of the witness or without prior warnings of any kind by extrinsic evidence, the witness shall be afforded the opportunity at a later appropriate stage of the proceedings to deny or explain them and opposing counsel shall have the opportunity to question the witness at an appropriate later time about them.[12] Even the opportunity of the witness to explain or deny later and the opportunity of the opposing counsel to question later can be ignored in the discretion of the judge "in the interests of justice." [13]

If the witness attacked is not on the stand but the testimony introduced was given in a deposition or at some other trial, most prior decisions otherwise applying the traditional requirements exclude the inconsistent statement unless the foundation question was asked at the prior hearing.[14] In this situation, at the discretion of the judge, the Federal and Revised Uniform Rule 613 should not require the opportunity of any denial or explanation by the witness or questioning by

tent statement before the attention of the witness is called to the statement should be extended so that in the discretion of the judge the extrinsic evidence can be introduced even if the witness has admitted the statement beforehand. See text of rule in n. 12 infra.

11. The Advisory Committee's Note describes the requirement that a cross-examiner must first show a prior statement of the witness to the witness before questioning the witness about it as a "useless impediment." It also states, "The traditional insistence that the attention of the witness be directed to the statement [the prior inconsistent statement] on cross-examination is relaxed in favor of simply providing the witness an opportunity to explain and the opposite party an opportunity to examine on the statement, with no specification of any particular time or sequence."

12. Fed.R.Evid. and Rev.Unif.R.Evid. (1974) 613 provides:

"(a) Examining witness concerning prior statement. In examining a witness concerning a prior statement made by him, whether written or not, the statement need not be shown nor its contents disclosed to him at that time, but on request the same shall be shown or disclosed to opposing counsel.

"(b) Extrinsic evidence of prior inconsistent statement of witness. Extrinsic evidence of a prior inconsistent statement by a witness is not admissible unless the witness is afforded an opportunity to explain or deny the same and the opposite party is afforded an opportunity to interrogate him thereon, or the interests of justice otherwise require. This provision does not apply to admissions of a party-opponent as defined in rule 801(d)(2)."

The Advisory Committee Note states:

"Under this procedure, several collusive witnesses can be examined before disclosure of a joint prior inconsistent statement."

See note 11 supra.

13. The Advisory Committee's Note states: "In order to allow for such eventualities as the witness becoming unavailable by the time the statement is discovered, a measure of discretion is conferred upon the judge. See Comment to California Evidence Code § 770 and New Jersey Evidence Rule 22(b)."

14. Doe v. Wilkinson, 35 Ala. 453 (1860); and cases cited 3A Wigmore, Evidence §§ 1031, 1032 (Chadbourn rev. 1970).

the opposing counsel.[15] When otherwise applicable, all of the above traditional requirements should be abandoned in the case of depositions based upon written interrogatories (which must be prepared in advance) or in the case of inconsistent statements made after the prior testimony was taken.[16]

If a party takes the stand as a witness, and the adversary desires to use a prior inconsistent statement of the witness, the statement is receivable in two aspects, first as the admission of the opposing party,[17] and second, as an inconsistent statement to impeach the witness. In the first aspect, it is relevant evidence upon the fact issues; in the second aspect, it is not.[18] In jurisdictions requiring traditional foundation questions for impeachment, the requirement is almost universally held inapplicable.[19] There is less danger of surprising a party than a witness, and the party will have ample opportunity for denial or explanation af-

ter the inconsistent statement is proved. In these jurisdictions the courts on occasion may inadvertently assume that the requirement applies to the party-witness.[20] Sometimes courts have imposed the requirement if the proponent offers the statement only for impeachment,[21] and one court held the judge has discretion to impose the requirement of a foundation question as prerequisite to proof of a party-witness admission.[22] These niggling qualifications seem hardly worth their salt and in jurisdictions which otherwise require the foundation question the sensible practice is the simple one of dispensing with the "foundation" entirely in respect to parties' admissions.

Federal and Revised Uniform Rule 613 have nothing to do with the introduction and admission into evidence of admissions of parties, even if the admissions have some effect on the credibility of the party as a witness.[23]

15. The judge is already given discretion "in the interests of justice" to dispense with the explanation or denial of the prior statement of the witness. See n. 12 supra.

16. People v. Collup, 27 Cal.2d 829, 167 P.2d 714, 718 (1946) (prosecution for rape: testimony of state's witness, at preliminary hearing read at trial; held, error to exclude evidence of subsequent inconsistent statements of witness, now absent from state; "the goal of all judicial proceedings is to bring before the trier of fact all pertinent evidence. Hence the rule allowing the use of former testimony is a salutary expedient . . . But it is equally clear that by reason of the same principle the impeaching evidence should be admitted for what it is worth"). See approving Note, 20 So.Calif.L.Rev. 102. See West's Ann.Cal.Evid.Code § 1202, providing that inconsistent statements of deponents in the same case may be introduced in effect without the use of a foundation question.

Similar questions arise with respect to impeachment by inconsistent statements of declarants whose hearsay declarations have been admitted under exceptions to the hearsay rule. Where foundation questions are otherwise required they are ignored in connection with the use of inconsistent statements. State v. Debnam, 222 N.C. 266, 22 S.E.2d 562 (1942) (dying declaration); 3A Wigmore, Evidence § 1033 (Chadbourn rev. 1970) (declarations against interest); Mobley v. Lyon, 134 Ga. 125, 67 S.E. 668 (1910) (attesting witnesses). Contra: Craig v. Wismar, 310 Ill. 262, 141 N.E. 766 (1923). But see People v. Hines, 284 N.Y. 93, 29 N.E. 2d 483 (1940). Fed.R.Evid. and Rev.Unif.R.Evid. (1976) 806 state the flat rule,

Evidence of a statement or conduct by the declarant at any time, inconsistent with his hearsay statement,

is not subject to any requirement that he may have been afforded an opportunity to deny or explain. If the party against whom a hearsay statement has been admitted calls the declarant as a witness, the party is entitled to examine him on the statement as if under cross-examination.

17. See ch. 26 infra.

18. See discussion in § 34 supra. But it should be noted that Fed.R.Evid. and Rev.Unif.R.Evid. (1974) 801(d)(1) provide that an inconsistent statement is not hearsay if given under oath and subject to the penalty of perjury at a trial, hearing, or other proceeding, or in a deposition. See § 251 infra.

19. State v. Hephner, 161 N.W.2d 714 (Iowa 1968); and cases cited 4 Wigmore, Evidence § 1051 (Chadbourn rev. 1972); Dec.Dig. Witnesses ⚖388(3); C.J.S. Witnesses § 604b.

20. See, e.g., Wiggins v. State, 27 Ala.App. 451, 173 So. 890 (1937); Finn v. Finn, 195 S.W.2d 679 (Tex.Civ. App.1946).

21. Washington & Old Dominion Railway Co. v. Smith, 53 App.D.C. 184, 289 F. 582 (1923); Industrial Farm Home Gas Co. v. McDonald, 234 Ark. 744, 355 S.W.2d 174 (1962); C.J.S. Witnesses § 604b.

22. Giles v. Valentic, 355 Pa. 108, 49 A.2d 384 (1946).

23. The last sentence of Fed.R.Evid. and Rev.Unif. R.Evid. (1974) 613(b) states:

"This provision does not apply to admissions of a party-opponent as defined in rule 801(d)(2)." See United States v. Cline, 570 F.2d 731 (8th Cir. 1978).

Again in jurisdictions in which a foundation question is required and it is overlooked, the judge should have discretion to consider such factors as the lack of knowledge of the inconsistent statement on the part of the impeacher when the witness was cross-examined, the importance or unimportance of the testimony under attack, and the practicability of recalling the witness for denial or explanation, and in the light of these circumstances to permit the impeachment without the foundation or to permit departure from the traditional time sequence if it seems fairer to do so.[24]

Some of the factors outlined just above should be taken into account by the judge in considering whether later denial or explanation by the witness or examination of the witness by the opponent may be abandoned "in the interests of justice" under Federal and Revised Uniform Rule of Evidence 613.[25]

 **WESTLAW
REFERENCES**

foundation   /s   "prior inconsistent statement*"

---

§ 38. Prior Inconsistent Statements: Rule Against Impeaching One's Own Witness [1]

The common law rule forbidding a party to impeach his own witness, which has been modified to an extent indicated later in this section or abandoned, is of obscure origin but probably is a late manifestation of the evolution of the common law trial procedure from an inquisitorial to a contentious or adversary system.[2] The prohibition was general, applying to all forms of impeachment. It applied not only to attack by inconsistent statements but to attack on character, or by a showing of bias, interest or corruption. It did not, however, forbid the party to introduce other evidence to dispute the facts testified to by his witness.[3]

Among the reasons, or rationalizations, found for the rule are, first, that the party by calling the witness to testify vouches for the trustworthiness of the witness, and second, that the power to impeach is the power to coerce the witness to testify as desired, under the implied threat of blasting the character of the witness if the witness does not. The answer to the first reason is that, except in a few instances such as character witnesses or expert witnesses, the party has little or no choice of witnesses. The party calls only those who happen to have observed the particular facts in controversy. The answers to the second reason are (a) that it applies only to two kinds of impeachment, the attack on character and the showing of corruption, and (b) that to forbid the

---

24. Model Code of Evidence Rule 106(2) leaves the enforcement of the requirement to the judge's discretion. West's Ann.Cal.Evid. Code § 770, and N.J.Evid. Rule 22(b) likewise give the judge discretion. Although there is no particular time sequence for explanation or denial by the witness of an inconsistent statement under Fed.R.Evid. and Rev.Unif.R.Evid. (1974) 613(b), the judge may dispense entirely with the requirement for denial or explanation "in the interests of justice." See n. 12 supra.

In a jurisdiction in which a foundation question is required it has been indicated that it may be error for the cross-examiner to fail to produce extrinsic evidence of the inconsistent statement. People v. Williams, 105 Ill. App.2d 25, 245 N.E.2d 17 (1969) (error not reversible under circumstances). Note that Fed.R.Evid. and Rev. Unif.R.Evid. (1974) 613(a) requires disclosure of the statement to the opposing counsel on request, as an assurance of good faith.

25. The Advisory Committees Note mentions discretion for eventualities such as the witness becoming unavailable by the time the statement is discovered.

§ 38

1. 3A Wigmore, Evidence §§ 896–918 (Chadbourn rev. 1970); Weinstein & Berger, Evidence ¶ 607[01]; Ladd, Impeachment of One's Own Witness—New Developments, 4 U.Chi.L.Rev. 69 (1936); Hauser, Impeaching One's Own Witness, 11 Oh.St.L.J. 364 (1950); Comment, 49 Va.L.Rev. 996 (1963); Dec.Dig. Witnesses ⇒320–325; C.J.S. Witnesses §§ 477, 578.

2. Ladd, supra n. 1, at p. 70.

3. Vondrashek v. Dignan, 200 Minn. 530, 274 N.W. 609 (1937) (principle recognized, but court refused to apply it to permit party to contradict by other witnesses his own testimony that he was not drunk—a picturesque case of behind the scenes conflict between the party and his insurer); Duffy v. National Janitorial Services, Inc., 429 Pa. 334, 240 A.2d 527 (1968); and cases cited in Dec.Dig. Witnesses ⇒320, 321, 400–402, and C.J.S. Witnesses § 630.

attack by the calling party leaves the party at the mercy of the witness and the adversary. If the truth lies on the side of the calling party, but the witness's character is bad, the witness may be attacked by the adversary if the witness tells the truth; but if the witness tells a lie, the adversary will not attack, and the calling party, under the rule, cannot. Certainly it seems that if the witness has been bribed to change the story, the calling party should be allowed to disclose this fact to the court.

The most important, because most effective, kind of impeachment, is by inconsistent statements and most of the cases that have applied the rule are of this type. It is difficult to see any justification for prohibiting this sort of showing as to the reliability of a witness who has testified contrary to a previous position. Perhaps there is a fear that the previous statement will be considered by the jury as substantive evidence of the facts asserted if, as in various jurisdictions, the statement for that purpose will be hearsay.[4] Except in those jurisdictions which have altogether abandoned it,[5] the common law rule against impeaching one's own witness persists for the most part with respect to attacks showing bias and attacks upon character.[6] On the other hand, it has been relaxed in a number of jurisdictions by statute or decision insofar as it prohibits impeachment by inconsistent statements. A provision in the draft of the Field Code of Civil Procedure in 1849 found fruit in the English Common Law Procedure Act of 1854, as follows (St.

17 & 18 Vict. c. 125, § 22): "[1] A party producing a witness shall not be allowed to impeach his credit by general evidence of bad character; [2] but he may, in case the witness shall in the opinion of the judge prove adverse, [3] contradict him by other evidence, [4] or by leave of the judge prove that he has made at other times a statement inconsistent with his present testimony." This statute was copied in a few states.[7] Other states, following the example of Massachusetts in 1869, have adopted the English statute except for omitting the troublesome condition that the witness must have proved "adverse." [8] Some courts have reached a similar result by decision.[9]

These statutes and similar decisions open the door to the most important type of impeachment of one's own witness, namely, prior inconsistent statements. But whether the extension is derived from statute or decision, two troublesome qualifications have been imposed on the reform by some courts. The first is that the party seeking to impeach must show that he is surprised at the testimony of the witness.[10] The second is that he cannot impeach unless the witness' testimony is positively harmful or adverse to his cause, reaching further than a mere failure ("I do not remember," "I do not know") to give expected favorable testimony.[11] These limitations are explainable only as attempts to safeguard the hearsay policy by preventing the party from proving the witness' prior statements in situations where it appears that its only value to the proponent

4. See § 251 infra.

5. See nn. 14, 15 infra.

6. See discussion in Comment, 49 Va.L.Rev. 996, 1009 (1963).

7. Va. Code 1950, § 8–292; 12 Vt.Stat.Ann. § 1642.

8. Ind.Burns' Ann.St. 34–1–14–15; Ky.R.Civ.P. 43.07; Texas, Vernon's Ann.C.C.P. art. 38.28; N.Y. CPL 60.35; N.Y. CPLR 4514 (limited to writings).

9. See, e.g., cases cited in n. 10 infra.

10. Cases cited C.J.S. Witnesses § 578c. Surprise is required at least by two statutes, D.C. Code § 14–104; Ga. Code § 38–1801 (if "entrapped"); and Ohio R.Evid. 607. The concept of "surprise," moreover, varies in the various jurisdictions. Sometimes "actual" or genuine surprise is required; in other decisions, it is not. See Comment, 49 Va.L.Rev. 996 (1963). A possible escape from the requirement can be had if the judge will "call" the witness as a court's witness. See § 8 supra.

11. Roe v. State, 152 Tex.Cr.R. 119, 210 S.W.2d 817 (1948); Virginia Electric & Power Co. v. Hall, 184 Va. 102, 34 S.E.2d 382 (1945); Wurm v. Pulice, 82 Idaho 359, 353 P.2d 1071 (1960) (statute permits impeachment by inconsistent statement); Commonwealth v. Strunk, 293 S.W.2d 629 (Ky.1956) (rule permits inconsistent statement; court states "where the witness testifies positively to the existence of a fact prejudicial to the party, or to a fact clearly favorable to the adverse party"); Ohio R.Evid. 607; cases cited in C.J.S. Witnesses § 578c; and see Comment, 49 Va.L.Rev. 996 (1963).

will be as substantive evidence of the facts asserted. The rule against such use of the statements, and the soundness of its policy, as well as growing authority to the contrary, is the theme of a subsequent section.[12]

The rule that prohibits or limits the impeachment of one's own witness is being abandoned in more and more jurisdictions.[13] Abandonment is accomplished by Federal and Revised Uniform Rule of Evidence (1974) 607.[14] The standard methods of impeachment are permitted under these rules.[15] There is some dispute whether and under what circumstances impeachment of one's own witness will be impermissible because of prejudice to the opposing party, particu-

larly in criminal cases.[16] It has been held that the prosecution may not call a witness in a criminal case to elicit testimony in order to introduce a favorable inconsistent statement of the witness under the guise of impeachment.[17] But it has also been suggested that if the testimony of the prosecution witness is of sufficient importance, the above holding should not be followed.[18] While the power to attack the character of one's own witness may often be of little value to the attacker, and is often of little moment to the administration of justice, a rule against the showing of prior inconsistent statements of one's own witness, to aid in evaluating the testimony of the witness, is

12. § 251 infra.

Two matters concerning the common law rule where it persists even in modified form should be mentioned. First, a principal means of escape from the prohibition, insofar as it prevents introduction of inconsistent statements, is by resort to questioning of the witness by the calling party about the previous statement not avowedly to discredit but to refresh the memory of the witness, or as it is sometimes more urgently phrased, "to awaken his conscience." People v. Michaels, 335 Ill. 590, 167 N.E. 857 (1929). Or "for the purpose of probing his recollection, recalling to his mind the statements he has previously made and drawing out an explanation of his apparent inconsistency." Bullard v. Pearsall, 53 N.Y. 230, 231 (1873); Hicks v. Coleman, 240 S.C. 227, 125 S.E.2d 473 (1962). Second, who is the party's own witness within the prohibitory rule? It is not the mere calling of the witness but the eliciting of the testimony of the witness that makes one the party's witness. Fall Brook Coal Co. v. Hewson, 158 N.Y. 150, 52 N.E. 1095 (1899). Moreover, in some jurisdictions restricting the cross-examination to the scope of the direct, if the cross-examiner elicits new matter the witness becomes the witness of the cross-examiner as to such testimony. 3A Wigmore, Evidence § 914 (Chadbourn rev. 1970); Dec.Dig. Witnesses ⬥325. In the case of deposition testimony it is the introduction of the deposition in evidence, not the taking of the deposition that constitutes the adoption of the witness as the party's own. Fed.R.Civ.P. 32(c); 3A Wigmore, Evidence §§ 912, 913 (Chadbourn rev. 1970). When a party calls an adverse party as a witness, the reasons for the prohibition, such as they are, seem inapplicable, and a few states expressly permit the calling party to impeach. See New Hamp. Rev.Stat.Ann. 516:24. In the absence of such a provision a few cases mechanically apply the prohibition. Price v. Cox, 242 Ala. 568, 7 So.2d 288 (1942) (can contradict but not impeach). See 3A Wigmore, Evidence § 916 (Chadbourn rev. 1970); C.J.S. Witnesses § 477d; Dec.Dig. Witnesses ⬥324. But see Wells v. Goforth, 443 S.W.2d 155 (Mo. 1969) (rejecting former rule that adverse party witness cannot be impeached by inconsistent statement al-

though statute permitted examination by cross-examination). When the same witness is called twice, first by A and then by B, some courts have been troubled. See decisions collected 3A Wigmore, Evidence § 913 (Chadbourn rev. 1970); C.J.S. Witnesses § 477e. The most practical solution would be to hold that the prohibitory rule does not apply at all, and both A and B may freely impeach. Next most sensible is to say, as some cases have indicated, that either A or B may impeach, at least by inconsistent statements, as to the testimony elicited by the other's call of the witness. See, e.g., People v. Van Dyke, 414 Ill. 251, 111 N.E.2d 165 (1953), cert. denied 345 U.S. 978, 1953 U.Ill.L.F. 296; Arnold v. Manzella, 186 S.W.2d 882 (Mo.App. 1945); Dec.Dig. Witnesses ⬥380(9). Another view that the witness is the witness of A, and A in any event is precluded, has less to commend it. Hanrahan v. New York Edison Co., 238 N.Y. 194, 144 N.E. 499 (1924); Dec.Dig. Witnesses ⬥380(9). Surely the worst solution is to hold that both parties have adopted the witness and neither may impeach. In re Campbell, 100 Vt. 395, 138 A. 725 (1927).

13. West's Ann.Cal.Evid. Code § 785; Kan.Stat. Ann. 60–420; Utah R.Evid. 20. But compare N.J.R. Evid. 20 which allows one generally to impeach one's own witness, but not by prior inconsistent statements except in the case of surprise.

14. Fed.R.Evid. and Rev.Unif.R.Evid. (1974) 607.

15. See United States v. Miller, 664 F.2d 94 (5th Cir. 1981), cert. denied 103 S.Ct. 121 (inconsistent statement); Beard v. Mitchell, 604 F.2d 485 (7th Cir. 1979) (bias; dictum).

16. See Weinstein & Berger, Evidence ¶ 607[01]. Citing authority, the authors suggest that the prejudicial effect of the impeachment should be considered under Rule 403, rather than the motive for impeachment pursuant to United States v. Morlang, note 17, infra.

17. United States v. Morlang, 531 F.2d 183 (4th Cir. 1975) (pre-rules).

18. United States v. DeLillo, 620 F.2d 939 (2d Cir. 1980), cert. denied 449 U.S. 835.

a serious obstruction to the ascertainment of truth, even in criminal cases. From the standpoint of a defendant in a criminal case, there is also a possibility of urging that forbidding a defendant from attacking a witness called by the defendant is unconstitutional in particular instances.[19]

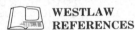

WESTLAW REFERENCES

synopsis,digest(impeach! /p "own witness" /p surprise)
headnote(rule* /10 evidence evid. /10 607)

§ 39. Previous Statements as Substantive Evidence of the Facts Stated

As previously indicated,[1] inconsistent statements of a witness are primarily treated in this chapter upon the assumption that they may be inadmissible as substantive evidence on the issues in the case under the traditional hearsay rule as administered in numerous states, and under the limited conditions in the Federal and Revised Uniform Rules of Evidence (1974) 801(d)(1). Of course, taking into account the limited federal exception in jurisdictions in which it is effective, and under the hearsay rule exceptions effective in the various jurisdictions, particular inconsistent prior statements of a witness may be admissible as substantive relevant evidence as well as for impeachment purposes. However, under another view, all prior inconsistent statements of a person who is available as a witness at the trial or testifies may be considered substan-

---

19. Chambers v. Mississippi, 410 U.S. 284 (1973).

§ 39

1. See § 34 supra.

§ 40

1. 3A Wigmore, Evidence §§ 943–969 (Chadbourn rev. 1970); Weinstein & Berger, Evidence ¶ 607[03]; Hale, Bias as Affecting Credibility, 1 Hastings L.J. 1 (1949); Dec.Dig. Witnesses ⊜363–378; C.J.S. Witnesses §§ 538–572; 81 Am.Jur.2d Witnesses §§ 547–562.

2. Since the definition of "relevance" in Rule 401 includes matters bearing on credibility, Rule 403 applies with similar breadth. Authority for extrinsic evidence of bias is also found in Rule 611(b), allowing cross-examination on "matters affecting the credibility of a wit-

tive evidence, not barred by the hearsay rule, and thus not restricted to the purpose of impeachment. This latter viewpoint is discussed in § 251.

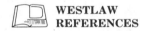

WESTLAW REFERENCES

jury /p charg! instruct! /p "prior inconsistent statement*" /p substanti** /5 evidence

§ 40. Bias[1]

Case law recognizes the slanting effect upon human testimony of the emotions or feelings of the witness toward the parties or the self-interest of the witness in the outcome of the case or in matters somehow related to the case. Partiality, or any acts, relationships or motives reasonably likely to produce it, may be proved to impeach credibility. While the Federal and Revised Uniform Rules of Evidence do not in terms refer to attacking the witness by showing bias, prejudice, or corruption, they clearly contemplate the use of the above-mentioned grounds of impeachment.[2] In fact, in criminal cases the defendant has a conditional constitutional right to so attack the credibility of government witnesses.[3] The power of the trial judge to impose limits on the above grounds for attacking a witness is mentioned later in this section.[4]

The kinds and sources of partiality are too infinitely varied to be reviewed exhaustively, but a few of the common instances may be mentioned. *Favor* or friendly feeling toward a party may be evidenced by family[5]

---

ness," and in Rule 607, allowing any party to attack credibility. See United States v. Smith, 550 F.2d 277 (5th Cir. 1977) (evidence that witness stated out of court that she had gone over her testimony with a defendant admissible to show bias, citing Rule 607); United States v. Hodnett, 537 F.2d 828 (5th Cir. 1976) (citing Rule 611(b)).

3. Davis v. Alaska, 415 U.S. 308 (1974); Greene v. Wainwright, 634 F.2d 272 (5th Cir. 1981).

4. See text following at nn. 24, 33–41 infra.

5. Christie v. Eager, 129 Conn. 62, 26 A.2d 352 (1942) (in suit by guest against motorist, duty of jury in weighing testimony of motorist and wife to consider fact the plaintiff is brother of motorist's wife, and that insurance company is the real defendant); Williams v.

or business relationship,[6] by employment by a party [7] or the party's insurer,[8] or by sexual relations,[9] or by particular conduct or expressions by the witness evincing such feeling.[10] It is commonly held in collision cases that when a witness appears for defendant the fact that he has made a claim against the defendant and has been paid a sum in settlement tends to show bias in favor of defendant.[11] Similarly, *hostility* toward a par-

ty may be shown by the fact that the witness has had a fight or quarrel with him,[12] or has a law-suit pending against him,[13] or has contributed to the defense [14] or employed special counsel to aid in prosecuting the party.[15] In criminal cases, the feeling of the witness toward the victim sheds light on his feeling toward the charge.[16] *Self-interest* of the witness is manifest when he is himself a party,[17] or a surety on the debt sued on.[18] It

State, 44 Ala.App. 503, 214 So.2d 712 (1968) (court should have permitted defendant to show that state's witness was "kin" to alleged victim of defendant); 3A Wigmore, Evidence § 949 (Chadbourn rev. 1970); C.J.S. Witnesses § 550.

6. Curry v. Fleer, 157 N.C. 16, 72 S.E. 626 (1911) (that witness for party had sold his land to him at big price, admissible); Aetna Insurance Co. v. Paddock, 301 F.2d 807 (5th Cir. 1962) (that witness had borrowed money from party); C.J.S. Witnesses § 551.

7. Arnall Mills v. Smallwood, 68 F.2d 57 (5th Cir. 1933) (witnesses' employment by defendant may be considered on credibility but is not, by itself, sufficient ground for disregarding their testimony); Dec.Dig. Witnesses ⚖369; C.J.S. Witnesses § 551.

8. It is usually held that the relevancy of the showing that the witness is an employee of defendant's liability insurer outweighs the danger of prejudice in disclosing the fact of insurance. Westgate Oil Co. v. McAbee, 181 Okl. 487, 74 P.2d 1150 (1937); Nunnellee v. Nunnellee, 415 S.W.2d 114 (Ky.1967); and see numerous decisions, pro and con, collected in Annot., 4 A.L.R.2d 779–781.

9. Parsley v. Commonwealth, 306 S.W.2d 284 (Ky. 1957) (rape; held evidence that defendant's fiancee who testified for him was pregnant by him was admissible to show her interest, as defendant's conviction would prevent his rendering aid and comfort to her); Annot., 25 A.L.R.3d 537; Dec.Dig. Witnesses ⚖370(4); C.J.S. Witnesses § 548.

10. United States v. Kerr, 464 F.2d 1367 (6th Cir. 1972) (witness paying certain bills of defendant's wife during defendant's imprisonment); State v. McKee, 131 Kan. 263, 291 P. 950 (1930) (witness for accused may be cross-examined as to furnishing appearance bond and advancing attorneys' fees for him); Junior Hall, Inc. v. Charm Fashion Center, Inc., 264 N.C. 81, 140 S.E.2d 772 (1965) (witness, a friend of plaintiff, could be asked whether she had appeared as witness for plaintiff in similar suit of plaintiff against a third person); 3A Wigmore, Evidence § 950 (Chadbourn rev. 1970).

11. See § 274 n. 24 infra.

12. United States v. Harvey, 547 F.2d 720 (2d Cir. (1976) (defendant was accused by government witness of being father of her child, refusing to support it, and beating the witness). Fields v. State, 46 Fla. 84, 35 So. 185, 186 (1903) (error to exclude cross-examination of state's witness as to "personal difficulty" with defen-

dant); 3A Wigmore, Evidence § 950 (Chadbourn rev. 1970).

In Jacek v. Bacote, 135 Conn. 702, 68 A.2d 144 (1949) a question asking whether witness was prejudiced against negroes, to which race defendant belonged, was held proper. See also United States v. Kartman, 417 F.2d 893 (9th Cir. 1969) (holding it was error to foreclose inquiry whether government witness had prejudice against persons who participated in anti-draft and anti-war demonstrations and hence against defendant); and cases cited in United States v. Kartman, supra.

13. State v. Michelski, 66 N.D. 760, 268 N.W. 713 (1936) (manslaughter by automobile; held defendant entitled to show that state's witnesses had civil actions against defendant arising from same collision, on far-fetched ground that conviction would be admissible to impeach defendant in civil actions); Blake v. State, 365 S.W.2d 795 (Tex.Cr.App.1963) (case involving embezzlement). But, on similar facts, the evidence was excluded in State v. Lawson, 128 W.Va. 136, 36 S.E.2d 26 (1945) and this was held a proper exercise of discretion. Cases are collected in 3A Wigmore, Evidence § 949, notes 5, 6 (Chadbourn rev. 1970); C.J.S. Witnesses § 546; Dec.Dig. Witnesses ⚖370(3).

A past unsuccessful prosecution of a defense witness may be shown. United States v. Senak, 527 F.2d 129 (7th Cir. 1975), cert. denied 425 U.S. 907.

14. State v. Cerar, 60 Utah 208, 207 P. 597 (1922).

15. Brogden v. State, 33 Ala.App. 132, 31 So.2d 144 (1947); State v. Wray, 217 N.C. 167, 7 S.E.2d 468 (1940) (court assumes fact relevant on bias, but upholds exclusion as being discretionary and not shown prejudicial).

16. Richardson v. State, 91 Tex.Cr. 318, 239 S.W. 218 (1922) (witness for defense said deceased "was dead in hell, where he ought to be").

17. Accordingly, it is held in some jurisdictions that the court, on request, must charge that the jury in weighing the party's testimony is to bear in mind his interest in the outcome. Denver City Tramway Co. v. Norton, 141 F. 599, 608 (8th Cir. 1905); C.J.S. Witnesses §§ 542, 543.

18. Southern Railway Co. v. Bunnell, 138 Ala. 247, 36 So. 380, 383 (1903) (question whether employee witness had given indemnity bond to employer defendant, proper).

may be shown likewise as reflecting on his interest that he is being paid by a party to give evidence, even though payment beyond regular witness fees may as in the case of an expert be entirely proper.[19] *Self-interest* may be shown also in a criminal case when the witness testifies for the state and it is shown that an indictment is pending against him,[20] or that he is an accomplice or co-indictee in the crime on trial.[21] Self-interest in an extreme form may be manifested in *corrupt* activity by the witness, such as seeking to bribe another witness,[22] or by taking or offering to take a bribe to testify falsely,[23] or by the making of other similar charges on other occasions without foundation.[24] The trial court has a great deal of discretion in deciding whether particular evidence indicates bias and prejudice. A large majority of appellate decisions examined approved the ruling of the trial judge on this score.

Preliminary question.[25] A majority of the courts impose the requirement of a foundation question as in the case of impeachment by prior inconsistent statements. Before the witness can be impeached by calling other witnesses to prove acts or declarations showing bias, the witness under attack must first have been asked about these facts on cross-examination.[26] There is federal case

19. Grutski v. Kline, 352 Pa. 401, 43 A.2d 142 (1945); 3A Wigmore, Evidence § 961, n. 2 (Chadbourn rev. 1970). A medical witness may be asked if the payment of his fee depends on the outcome of the case. Most cases hold that the judge in his discretion may permit the opponent to bring out the amount of extra compensation the expert witness has received or will receive or expects to receive. Current v. Columbia Gas of Kentucky, 383 S.W.2d 139 (Ky.1964) (judge limited attack to showing that witness was paid unspecified extra compensation; affirmed); cases cited in Annot., 33 A.L.R.2d 1170. In Reed v. Philadelphia Transportation Co., 171 Pa.Super. 60, 90 A.2d 371 (1952) the judge sustained objection to the question, "How much do you expect to get paid for testifying here today?"; the ruling was held reversible error. A witness as to value may be asked how much he has received from the defendant city for similar testimony in the past year. City of Chicago v. Van Schaack Brothers Chemical Works, 330 Ill. 264, 161 N.E. 486 (1928). See also Collins v. Wayne Corp., 621 F.2d 777 (5th Cir. 1980) (fees earned by expert in prior cases could be brought out).

20. United States v. Padgent, 432 F.2d 701 (2d Cir. 1970) (error to refuse to allow defense to bring out that government witness had jumped bail and was not being prosecuted for that offense); People v. Dillwood, 106 Cal. 129, 39 P. 438 (1895) (pendency of charges against witness as motive for testifying favorably to prosecution); State v. Ponthier, 136 Mont. 198, 346 P.2d 974 (1959) (same, citing many authorities); 3A Wigmore, Evidence § 967, n. 2 (Chadbourn rev. 1970).

The pressure to curry favor with the prosecutor is not present in a civil suit, and in a collision suit where plaintiff introduced as witness the driver of one of the cars, it was held error to permit the defendant to impeach him by showing that he had been indicted for driving while intoxicated on the occasion in question and that the indictment was pending because of its liability to misuse as evidence of his guilt. Holden v. Berberich, 351 Mo. 995, 174 S.W.2d 791, 149 A.L.R. 929 (1943), annotated on this point. But if it had appeared that plaintiff had instigated and was controlling the prosecution of the criminal case a different result might be warranted.

21. People v. Simard, 314 Mich. 624, 23 N.W.2d 106 (1946) (defendant should have been allowed to ask state's witness if she had not been arrested for participation in same crime); 3A Wigmore, Evidence § 967 (Chadbourn rev. 1970).

22. People v. Alcalde, 24 Cal.2d 177, 148 P.2d 627 (1944); 3A Wigmore, Evidence § 960 (Chadbourn rev. 1970). Or writing a letter designed to intimidate another witness into giving perjured testimony. State v. Moore, 180 Or. 502, 176 P.2d 631 (1947).

23. See Martin v. Barnes, 7 Wis. 239, 241, 242 (1858) (bargain between doctor-witness and plaintiff that she should pretend to be injured from fall, and they should share recovery); 3A Wigmore, Evidence § 961 (Chadbourn rev. 1970).

24. But the cases are conflicting. See 3A Wigmore, Evidence § 963, note 2 (Chadbourn rev. 1970); Annot., 69 A.L.R.2d 593, 602. Among those supporting this kind of impeachment is People v. Evans, 72 Mich. 367, 40 N.W. 473 (1888) (rape upon daughter: other false charges by daughter against other men, allowed). Such charges may also evidence mental abnormality, see § 45 infra. Compare cases involving the question whether a plaintiff may be cross-examined about the previous institution of other suits and claims to show "claim-mindedness." Mintz v. Premier Cab Association, Inc., 75 U.S.App.D.C. 389, 127 F.2d 744 (1942) (yes); Cammarata v. Payton, 316 S.W.2d 474 (Mo.1958) (no). See § 196 infra.

25. 3A Wigmore, Evidence § 964 (Chadbourn rev. 1970); Annot., 87 A.L.R.2d 407; Dec.Dig. Witnesses ⟨⟩373; C.J.S. Witnesses § 566.

26. People v. Payton, 72 Ill.App.2d 240, 218 N.E.2d 518 (1966); State v. Shaw, 93 Ariz. 40, 378 P.2d 487 (1963); Annot., 87 A.L.R.2d 407, 431.

As in the case of inconsistent statements, the preliminary question as to declarations showing bias should call attention to time, place, and persons involved. See Wright v. State, 133 Ark. 16, 201 S.W. 1107 (1918); State v. Harmon, 21 Wn.2d 581, 152 P.2d 314 (1944); cases cited in Annot., 87 A.L.R.2d 407, 431.

authority to this effect.[27] Fairness to the witness is most often given as the reason for the requirement, but the saving of time by making unnecessary the extrinsic evidence seems even more important. Some courts, adhering to the analogy of inconsistent statements, make a difference between declarations and conduct evidencing bias, requiring the preliminary question as to the former and not as to the latter.[28] But as suggested in a leading English case, words and conduct are usually intermingled in proof of bias, and "nice and subtle distinctions" should be avoided in shaping this rule of trial practice.[29] Better require a "foundation" as to both or neither. It seems that jurisdictions recognizing the requirement should recognize also a discretion in the judge to dispense with it when mere matters of indisputable relationship, such as kinship, are concerned, or where the foundation was overlooked and it is not feasible to recall the witness, or where other exceptional circumstances make it unfair to insist on the prerequisite.

A minority of holdings do not require any warning question on cross-examination of the principal witness as a preliminary to the introduction of extrinsic evidence of bias.[30] The Federal and Revised Uniform Rules (1974) are silent on the subject.[31] Since those rules have, with respect to prior inconsistent statements, shifted emphasis from preliminary foundation questioning to affording opportunity to explain or deny at some stage, with discretion in the judge to dispense with even that, a more exacting treatment of evidence of bias would scarcely be appropriate. The discretion granted the judge in Rule 611(a) [32] is adequate authority to follow the same pattern for bias as that laid out for prior inconsistent statements.

Cross-examination and extrinsic evidence; main circumstances. We have seen that in many states the impeacher must inquire as to the facts of bias on cross-examination as the first step in impeachment. It seems arguable that if the witness fully admits the facts claimed to show bias, the impeacher should not be allowed to repeat the same attack by calling other witnesses to the admitted facts.[33] And it is held that when the main circumstances from which the bias proceeds have been proven, the trial judge has a discretion to determine how far the details, whether on cross-examination or by other witness, may be allowed to be brought out.[34] After all, impeachment is not a central matter, and the trial judge, though he may not deny a reasonable opportunity at either stage to prove the bias of the witness, has a discretion to control the extent to

---

27. United States v. Marzano, 537 F.2d 257 (7th Cir. 1976), cert. denied 429 U.S. 1038 (reviewing prior federal cases); United States v. Harvey, 457 F.2d 720 (2d Cir. 1976) (foundation questions held sufficient).

28. Annot., 87 A.L.R.2d 407, 418–420, 423–426.

29. See the excerpt from the opinion of Abbott, C.J. in the Queen's Case, 2 Brod. & B. 284, 129 Eng.Rep. 976 (1820), quoted in Annot., 16 A.L.R. 989.

30. Kidd v. People, 97 Colo. 480, 51 P.2d 1020 (1935) (witness' threat to "pin something on" another witness unless he testified for the state); People v. Michalow, 229 N.Y. 325, 128 N.E. 228 (1920); Annot., 87 A.L.R.2d 407.

31. See § 37 n. 12 supra.

32. Fed.R.Evid. and Rev.Unif.R.Evid. (1974) 611(a) provide:

The court shall exercise reasonable control over the mode and order of interrogating witnesses and presenting evidence so as to (1) make the interrogation and presentation effective for the ascertainment

of the truth, (2) avoid needless consumption of time, and (3) protect witnesses from harassment or undue embarrassment.

33. This is the prevailing holding as to inconsistent statements, see § 37 supra, and similar reasons apply here, pro and con.

34. State v. Malmberg, 14 N.D. 523, 105 N.W. 614, 616 (1905) (village political rivalry; proof of main facts, matter of right; extent of proof of details, discretionary; here unduly curbed); Brink v. Stratton, 176 N.Y. 150, 68 N.E. 148 (1903) (similar); People v. Dye, 356 Mich. 271, 96 N.W.2d 788 (1959) (trial court permitted examination into details; approved); Dods v. Harrison, 51 Wn.2d 446, 319 P.2d 558 (1958) (trial court's refusal to permit examination as to details upheld); 3A Wigmore, Evidence § 951, note 2 (Chadbourn rev. 1970); C.J.S. Witnesses § 556. A few courts have held that if the witness admits bias in general terms this precludes further inquiry. See, e.g., Walker v. State, 74 Ga.App. 48, 39 S.E.2d 75, 77 (1946); 3A Wigmore, Evidence § 951, note 2 (Chadbourn rev. 1970).

which the proof may go.[35] He has the responsibility for seeing that the sideshow does not take over the circus. This result is indicated by decisions on the facts in several cases under the Federal Rules of Evidence.[36] It follows from the power of the trial judge to "exercise reasonable control" under the terms of Rule 611(a).[37] On the other hand, if the witness on cross-examination denies or does not fully admit the facts claimed to show bias, the attacker has the right to prove those facts by extrinsic evidence. In courtroom parlance, facts showing bias are not "collateral," [38] and the cross-examiner is not required to "take the answer" of the witness,[39] but may call other witnesses to prove them.[40] There are similar holdings under the Federal Rules of Evidence.[41]

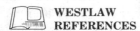 **WESTLAW REFERENCES**

impeachment /s foundation /s bias** influence*

§ 41. Character: In General

The character of a witness for truthfulness or mendacity is relevant circumstantial evidence on the question of the truth of particular testimony of the witness. The discussion of the rules which have developed as to character-impeachment will reveal certain general questions of balancing policies. Among them are these: How far in any particular situation does the danger of unfair prejudice against the witness and the party calling him from this type of impeachment outweigh the probable value of the light shed on credibility? Again, should the field of character-impeachment be limited so far as practicable to attack on the particular character-trait of truthfulness or should it extend to "general" character for its undoubted though more remote bearing upon truthfulness, on the notion that the greater includes the less? [1]

It seems probable, moreover, that the tendency is to use this form of attack more and more sparingly. It was part of the melodrama of the pioneer trial to find "the villain of the piece." It fits less comfortably into the more businesslike atmosphere of the present courtroom. Moreover, as a method of advocacy, the danger to the attacker is great if the attack fails of its mark, or if it is pressed too far. Finally, judges and lawyers are more and more conscious of their duty of fairness to witnesses. The Code of Profes-

---

35. Glass v. Bosworth, 113 Vt. 303, 34 A.2d 113 (1943) (wide scope on cross-examination, in court's discretion); People v. Lustig, 206 N.Y. 162, 99 N.E. 183, 186 (1912) (extent of testimony by other witnesses in court's discretion). See also Marcus v. City of Pittsburgh, 415 Pa. 252, 203 A.2d 317 (1964) (trial judge abused discretion by permitting examination which entered into prejudicial detail that was not impeaching).

36. United States v. Fitzgerald, 579 F.2d 1014 (7th Cir. 1978), cert. denied 439 U.S. 1002 ("But a trial court has wide discretion to limit cross-examination, particularly when further cross-examination into the witness' subjective thoughts would not be meaningful because of previous testimony revealing the witness' bias."); United States v. Diecidue, 603 F.2d 535 (5th Cir. 1979), cert. denied 445 U.S. 946 (probative value of additional evidence held very slight); United States v. Salsedo, 607 F.2d 318 (9th Cir. 1979) (defendant was denied inquiry into additional work of witness for Drug Enforcement Administration; test was whether jury already had sufficient information to appraise bias and motives of witness); United States v. Singh, 628 F.2d 758 (2d Cir. 1980), cert. denied 449 U.S. 1034 (similar test applied); United States v. Hawkins, 661 F.2d 436 (5th Cir. 1981), cert. denied 456 U.S. 991, (prosecution witnesses who were questioned about state of mind while in foreign jails did not have to be questioned

about further conditions in the jails because the jury was adequately informed about states of mind which were relevant to the issue of bias for the government).

37. See n. 32 supra.

38. State v. Day, 339 Mo. 74, 95 S.W.2d 1183, 1184 (1936); Smith v. Hockenberry, 146 Mich. 7, 109 N.W. 23, 24 (1906); C.J.S. Witnesses § 559.

39. Smith v. United States, 283 F.2d 16 (6th Cir. 1960), cert. denied 365 U.S. 847 (dictum); 3A Wigmore, Evidence § 1005(b), (c) (Chadbourn rev. 1970). See references to "taking the answer" in § 47 infra and § 36 supra.

40. Smith v. Hornkohl, 166 Neb. 702, 90 N.W.2d 347 (1958) (dictum); 3A Wigmore, Evidence § 943 (Chadbourn rev. 1970); C.J.S. Witnesses §§ 563, 565.

41. United States v. Harvey, 547 F.2d 720 (2d Cir. 1976); United States v. James, 609 F.2d 36 (2d Cir. 1979), cert. denied 445 U.S. 905; United States v. Frankethal, 582 F.2d 1102 (7th Cir. 1978).

§ 41

1. See the general discussion of relevancy and its counterweights in Ch. 16 infra, and of the relevancy of character evidence in various other situations in Ch. 17 infra.

sional Responsibility of the American Bar Association states the matter thus:

"In appearing in his professional capacity before a tribunal, a lawyer shall not:

. . .

(2) Ask any question that he has no reasonable basis to believe is relevant to the case and that is intended to degrade a witness or other person. . . ." [2]

WESTLAW REFERENCES

digest(character /s impeach! /s prejudic! relevan! irrelevan!)

§ 42. Character: Misconduct, for Which There Has Been No Criminal Conviction [1]

The English common law tradition of "cross-examination to credit" permits counsel to inquire into the associations and personal history of the witness, including any particular misconduct which would tend to

discredit his character, though it has not been the basis for conviction of crime. [2] (This is the kind of misconduct referred to in this section unless otherwise indicated.) Under the common law tradition the courts trusted the disciplined discretion of the bar to avoid abuses. [3] In this country, there is a confusing variety of decisions, occasionally even in the same jurisdiction. At present, however, it can be said generally that the majority of courts limit cross-examination concerning acts of misconduct as an attack upon character to acts which have some relation to the credibility of the witness. [4] This is the view adopted by Federal Rule of Evidence 608(b). [5] Some courts permit an attack upon character by fairly wide-open cross-examination upon acts of misconduct which show bad moral character and can have only an attenuated relation to credibility. [6] Finally, a number of courts prohibit altogether cross-examination as to acts of misconduct for impeachment purposes. [7] This latter

---

[2]. American Bar Association, Code of Professional Responsibility, Disciplinary Rule 7–106(C)(2), p. 88 (1969). Compare the phrasing of the duty in West's Ann.Cal.Bus. and Prof. Code § 6068: "To abstain from all offensive personality, and to advance no fact prejudicial to the honor or reputation of a party or witness, unless required by the justice of the cause with which he is charged."

§ 42

[1]. 3A Wigmore, Evidence §§ 981–987 (Chadbourn rev. 1970); Weinstein & Berger, Evidence ¶ 608[05]; Dec.Dig. Witnesses ⬚344, 349; C.J.S. Witnesses §§ 491–531.

[2]. 3A Wigmore, Evidence §§ 983–986 (Chadbourn rev. 1970); Phipson, Evidence §§ 541, 1551, 1552 (10th ed. 1963).

[3]. See quotations from Stephen and Birkenhead in 3A Wigmore, Evidence § 983 (Chadbourn rev. 1970); and 13 Halsbury's Laws of England, Evidence § 836 (2d ed. 1934) ("There are, also, certain limits, which must be determined by the discretion of the judge to the questions which may be asked affecting a witness's credit . . .").

[4]. Vogel v. Sylvester, 148 Conn. 666, 174 A.2d 122 (1961); Schreiberg v. Southern Coatings & Chemical Co., 231 S.C. 69, 97 S.E.2d 214 (1957); C.J.S. Witnesses §§ 502–506, 515.

[5]. Fed.R.Evid. and Rev.Unif.R.Evid. (1974) 608(b) provide:

Specific instances of the conduct of a witness, for the purpose of attacking or supporting his credibili-

ty, other than conviction of crime as provided in rule 609, may not be proved by extrinsic evidence. They may, however, in the discretion of the court, if probative of truthfulness or untruthfulness, be inquired into on cross-examination of the witness (1) concerning his character for truthfulness or untruthfulness, or (2) concerning the character for truthfulness or untruthfulness of another witness as to which character the witness being cross-examined has testified.

The giving of testimony, whether by an accused or by any other witness, does not operate as a waiver of his privilege against self-incrimination when examined with respect to matters which relate only to credibility.

See United States v. Cluck, 544 F.2d 195 (5th Cir. 1976) (extrinsic evidence of arrest and of crimes not admissible).

[6]. People v. Sorge, 301 N.Y. 198, 93 N.E.2d 637 (1950); State v. Jones, 215 Tenn. 206, 385 S.W.2d 80 (1964); C.J.S. Witnesses, § 515d. See Annot., 90 A.L.R. 870. The conduct need not be criminal. People v. Johnston, 228 N.Y. 332, 127 N.E. 186 (1920) (sending money to an accused prisoner for him to buy witnesses). The fact that the witness has been dishonorably discharged from the army was held so doubtful in its implications as to "moral character" as to warrant the judge, in discretion, to exclude the inquiry. Kelley v. State, 226 Ind. 148, 78 N.E.2d 547 (1948).

[7]. Christie v. Brewer, 374 S.W.2d 908 (Tex.Civ.App. 1964); Sparks v. State, 366 S.W.2d 591 (Tex.Cr.App. 1963); Commonwealth v. Schaffner, 146 Mass. 512, 16 N.E. 280 (1888) (but see Campbell v. Ashler, 320 Mass.

view is arguably the fairest and most expedient practice because of the dangers otherwise of prejudice (particularly if the witness
is a party), of distraction and confusion, of
abuse by the asking of unfounded questions,
and of the difficulties, as demonstrated in
the cases on appeal, of ascertaining whether
particular acts relate to character for truthfulness.[8]

The above-mentioned notions should be
distinguished from the showing of conduct
which indicates bias and prejudice, the showing of conduct as an admission, and the
showing of conduct for impeachment by contradiction.[9]

In this country, the danger of victimizing
witnesses and of undue prejudice to the parties has led most of our courts which permit
the showing of acts of misconduct under the
rules mentioned above, to recognize that
cross-examination concerning acts of misconduct is subject to a discretionary control by
the trial judge.[10] Some of the factors that

may, it seems sway discretion, are (1) whether the testimony of the witness under attack
is crucial or unimportant, (2) the relevancy
of the act of misconduct to truthfulness, depending upon the rule followed in the jurisdiction in that respect,[11] (3) the nearness or
remoteness of the misconduct to the time of
trial,[12] (4) whether the matter inquired into is
such as to lead to time-consuming and distracting explanations on cross-examination
or re-examination,[13] (5) whether there is undue humiliation of the witness and undue
prejudice.[14]

In the formative period of Evidence law,
there came to be recognized, as a sort of
vague corollary of the privilege against self-
incrimination, a privilege of a witness not to
answer questions calling for answers which
would degrade or disgrace him, provided
such questions were not material to the issues in the case.[15] The privilege, though
sporadically recognized from time to time

475, 70 N.E.2d 302 (1946) (mentioning discretion); Ber-
liner v. Schoenberg, 117 Pa.Super. 254, 178 A. 330
(1935); Commonwealth v. Ornato, 191 Pa.Super. 581,
159 A.2d 223 (1960), affirmed 400 Pa. 626, 163 A.2d 90,
cert. denied 364 U.S. 912; C.J.S. Witnesses § 515b.
Statutes prohibit the showing of acts of misconduct for
impeachment in some states. See, e.g., Idaho Code
§ 9–1302; West's Ann.Cal.Evid. Code § 787; N.J.Rule
of Evid. 22; Oregon Evid. Rule 608(1)(b).

8. Former Uniform Rule 22(d) provides that "evidence of specific instances of his conduct relevant only
as tending to prove a trait of his character, shall be
inadmissible." For the text of the Rev.Unif.R.Evid.
(1974) 608(b), see n. 5 supra. Another theory, akin to
but distinguishable from misconduct as showing character, is the theory that on cross-examination the examiner is entitled to place the witness in his setting by
showing his residence and occupation. See § 29, supra. As to whether this principle permits questions as
to a disreputable occupation, see cases pro and con collected in Dec.Dig. Witnesses ⬌344(4); Annot., 1
A.L.R. 1402.

9. See § 40 supra re bias, §§ 269–275 infra re admissions by conduct, and § 47 infra re impeachment by
contradiction. Inconsistent conduct is yet another subject. See § 37 supra. See United States v. Hodnett,
537 F.2d 828 (5th Cir. 1976) (certain misconduct admitted to show bias).

10. People v. Sorge, 301 N.Y. 198, 93 N.E.2d 637
(1950) (in abortion prosecution, accused properly cross-
examined as to previous abortions; manner and extent
in judge's discretion); State v. Neal, 222 N.C. 546, 23

S.E.2d 911 (1943) (accused in murder case properly
asked about previous cutting affrays, larceny, vagran-
cy, nuisance and violation of the prohibition law, in
judge's "sound discretion"); C.J.S. Witnesses § 515j.
Fed.R.Evid. and Rev.Unif.R.Evid. (1974) 608(b) specifically grant the judge discretion. Supra, n. 5. See,
e.g., United States v. Nogueira, 585 F.2d 23 (1st Cir.
1978). Rules 403, 608(b), and 611(a) should be taken
into account.

11. See nn. 4, 5, 6, supra. Illustrating Fed.R.Evid.
608(b), see United States v. Estell, 539 F.2d 697 (10th
Cir. 1976), cert. denied 429 U.S. 982 (court observes
that under the rule judge would have discretion to reject evidence that witness stole meat and passed worthless checks because such matters were not probative of
truthfulness); Tigges v. Cataldo, 611 F.2d 936 (1st Cir.
1979) (doubtful value of evidence in considering credibility of witness was one of factors considered).

12. United States v. Cox, 536 F.2d 65 (5th Cir.
1976); Shailer v. Bullock, 78 Conn. 65, 61 A. 65 (1905);
C.J.S. Witnesses § 515g.

13. See Robinson v. Atterbury, 135 Conn. 517, 66
A.2d 593 (1949).

These factors as well as the factor of undue
prejudice may be taken into account under Fed.R.Evid.
and Rev.Unif.R.Evid. (1974) 403.

14. See United States v. Kizer, 569 F.2d 504 (9th
Cir. 1978), cert. denied 435 U.S. 976. Fed.R.Evid. and
Rev.Unif.R.Evid. (1974) 403 and 611(a) are applicable.

15. See 3A Wigmore, Evidence §§ 984, 986(3)
(Chadbourn rev. 1970).

during the 1800s,[16] has in the present century been generally abandoned,[17] except as it is encysted in the Codes of a few states.[18] The practical protection to the witness is not so effective as that given by courts which prohibit such cross-examination altogether, since the prohibitory rule will be invoked by counsel or by the court of its own motion, whereas the privilege must be claimed by the witness, and such a claim is almost as degrading as an affirmative answer. Taking a somewhat intermediate position Federal and Revised Uniform Rule of Evidence (1974) 611(a) gives the court discretion to prevent harassment or embarrassment of witnesses when they are cross-examined pursuant to Rule 608(b) concerning acts of misconduct.[19]

In jurisdictions which permit character-impeachment by proof of misconduct for which no conviction has been had, an important curb is the accepted rule that proof is limited to what can be brought out on cross-examination. Thus, if the witness stands his ground and denies the alleged misconduct, the examiner must "take his answer," not

that he may not further cross-examine to extract an admission,[20] but in the sense that he may not call other witnesses to prove the discrediting acts.[21] This rule is adopted by Federal Rule of Evidence 608(b).[22]

A further important curb is the privilege against self-incrimination. While a witness who without objecting makes a partial disclosure of incriminating matter cannot then invoke the privilege when asked to make the disclosure complete,[23] it seems clear that the mere act of testifying cannot be regarded as a waiver of the privilege with respect to inquiry on cross-examination into criminal activities for the purpose of attacking his credibility.[24] While an accused, unlike an ordinary witness, has an option whether to testify at all, exacting such a waiver as the price of taking the stand leaves little of the right to testify in one's own behalf. Therefore Federal Rule of Evidence and Revised Uniform Rule of Evidence 608(b) provide that the giving of testimony by any witness, including an accused, does not waive the privilege as to matters relating only to credibility.[25]

---

16. See 3A Wigmore, Evidence §§ 986(3) note 13, 987 (Chadbourn rev. 1970).

17. Among decisions rejecting the privilege are Wallace v. State, 41 Fla. 547, 26 So. 713, 722 (1899); State v. Pfefferle, 36 Kan. 90, 92, 12 P. 406, 408 (1886) (degrading character of question factor for judge's discretion); Carroll v. State, 32 Tex.Cr.R. 431, 24 S.W. 100 (1893); State v. Carter, 1 Ariz.App. 57, 399 P.2d 191 (1965) (subject to discretion of the court).

18. Georgia Code, § 38–1205; Utah Code Ann.1953, 78–24–9.

19. United States v. Marchesani, 457 F.2d 1291 (6th Cir. 1972). Fed.R.Evid. and Rev.Unif.R.Evid. (1974) 611(a) provide, "The court shall exercise reasonable control over the mode and order of interrogating witnesses and presenting of evidence so as to . . . (3) protect witnesses from harassment or undue embarrassment."

20. People v. Sorge, 301 N.Y. 198, 93 N.E.2d 637 (1950) (when witness denies, examiner in good faith may question further in hope of inducing witness to change answer). But the judge has discretion to place limits on further exploration of a matter. United States v. Bright, 630 F.2d 804 (5th Cir. 1980).

21. State v. Bowman, 232 N.C. 374, 61 S.E.2d 107 (1950) (improper for state to attack credibility of defendant's witness by calling other witnesses to testify to

her acts of misconduct); C.J.S. Witnesses § 516; 3A Wigmore, Evidence § 979 (Chadbourn rev. 1970).

22. Fed.R.Evid. and Rev.Unif.R.Evid (1974) 608(b) provide that specific instances of misconduct may not be proved by extrinsic evidence. See United States v. Walton, 602 F.2d 1176 (4th Cir. 1979).

23. For more detailed discussion, see § 140 infra.

24. Coil v. United States, 343 F.2d 573 (8th Cir. 1965), cert. denied 382 U.S. 821.

Statements in such cases as People v. Sorge, 301 N.Y. 198, 93 N.E.2d 637 (1950), that a witness, including the defendant in criminal cases, may be asked on cross-examination "about any vicious or criminal act in his life that has a bearing on his credibility" must be read against an oversight of the constitutional limitation. When the question was raised in People v. Johnson, 228 N.Y. 332, 127 N.E. 186 (1920), the court conceded that the waiver resulting from an accused taking the stand did not extend to facts affecting credibility only.

25. Fed.R.Evid. and Rev.Unif.R.Evid. (1974) 608(b) supra n. 5. See Griffin v. California, 380 U.S. 609 (1965); Ferguson v. Georgia, 365 U.S. 570 (1961). Surely, today the right of the accused to testify in his own behalf must be of constitutional dimension. See Washington v. Texas, 388 U.S. 14 (1967).

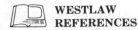

WESTLAW REFERENCES

digest(rule* +s 608(b) /p misconduct)

§ 43. Character: Conviction of Crime [1]

At common law the conviction of a person of treason or any felony, or of a misdemeanor involving dishonesty *(crimen falsi)*, or the obstruction of justice, rendered the convicted person altogether incompetent as a witness. These were said to be "infamous" crimes.[2] By statutes or rules which are virtually universal in the common law world, this primitive absolutism has been aban-

doned and the disqualification for conviction of crime has been abrogated, and by specific provision or by decision has been reduced to a mere ground of impeachment of credibility. Just as the common law definition of disqualifying crimes was not very precise, so also the abrogating statutes and rules are correspondingly indefinite,[3] and the resulting definitions of crimes for which a conviction[4] shall be ground of impeachment vary widely among the states that have not adopted Federal Rule of Evidence 609.[5]

A rule that would limit impeachment to conviction of crimes that involve dishonesty

§ 43

1. 3A Wigmore, Evidence §§ 980, 980a, 985–987 (Chadbourn rev. 1970); Weinstein & Berger, Evidence ¶ 609[01]–[11]; Ladd, Credibility Tests, 89 U.Pa.L.Rev. 166, 174 (1940); Dec.Dig. Witnesses ⬤345; 98 C.J.S. Witnesses §§ 507, 515i(3)(c), 534e; 58 Am.Jur. Witnesses §§ 734–753.

2. Greenleaf, Evidence § 373 (1842); 2 Wigmore, Evidence § 520 (Chadbourn rev. 1979).

3. See, e.g. Conn., C.G.S.A. § 52–145: "No person shall be disqualified as a witness in any action by reason of his interest in the event of the same as a party or otherwise, or of his belief in the existence of a Supreme Being, or of his conviction of crime; but such interest or conviction may be shown for the purpose of affecting his credit;" and other statutes and rules collected in 2 Wigmore, Evidence § 488 (Chadbourn rev. 1979).

4. Conviction, of course, is the present requirement, and though it was once thought otherwise, there cannot be inquiry about an accusation, though official, such as an arrest, indictment, or information. United States v. Dennis, 625 F.2d 782 (8th Cir. 1981); People v. Hardy, 70 Ill.App.3d 351, 26 Ill.Dec. 212, 387 N.E.2d 1042 (1979) (but questions as to pending charges which might show bias or interest are permissible); Commonwealth v. Ross, 434 Pa. 167, 252 A.2d 661 (1969) (arrest; opinion mentions exception as to indictment for same or closely related offense); Johnson v. State, 82 Nev. 338, 418 P.2d 495 (1966) (arrest; cross-examination at preliminary hearing); 3A Wigmore, Evidence § 980a (Chadbourn rev. 1970). Contra: People v. Brocato, 17 Mich.App. 277, 169 N.W.2d 483 (1969) (holding defendant as witness may not be so inquired into, but other witnesses of defendant may be in the discretion of the judge); Annot., 20 A.L.R.2d 1421. In collision cases, proof is often sought to be made, under guise of impeachment, that one of the drivers was arrested for negligent driving at the time of the collision. It may have a remote bearing upon bias, but its prejudicial use by the jury as hearsay evidence of guilt is an overweening danger, and the courts usually exclude it. See Holden v. Berberich, 351 Mo. 995, 174 S.W.2d 791 (1943) (cross-examination of driver as to indictment for

driving while intoxicated at time of collision); Annot., 149 A.L.R. 935.

5. A few jurisdictions have adhered to the loose common law definition, described above, of "infamous crimes." See, e.g., Md.Ann.C.J. 10–905. The California Code and some other codes specify only "felonies," a limitation which is at least simple to apply. West's Ann.Cal.Evid.Code § 788; Idaho Rules Civ.Proc., Rule 43(b)(6); Nev.Rev.Stat. 50.095. This is the construction some courts have placed upon statutes worded in terms of "crime" or "any crime." See, e.g., State v. Hurt, 49 N.J. 114, 228 A.2d 673 (1967). Some courts, unwilling to accept such simple tests, have read into general statutes that as to misdemeanors at least, the offense must be one involving "moral turpitude." Sims v. Callahan, 269 Ala. 216, 112 So.2d 776 (1959); Smith v. State, 346 S.W.2d 611 (Tex.Cr.App.1961) (conviction for selling and handling whiskey did not involve moral turpitude; Tasker v. Commonwealth, 202 Va. 1019, 121 S.E.2d 459 (1961) (misdemeanor did not involve moral turpitude); 12 Vermont Stat.Ann. § 1608; Annot., 97 A.L.R.3d 1150. Thus does the serpent of uncertainty crawl into the Eden of trial administration. Under a rule requiring moral turpitude it seems questionable whether the creation of a detailed catalog of crimes involving "moral turpitude" and its application at the trial and on appeal is not a waste of judicial energy in view of the size of the problem. Moreover, shifting the burden to the judge's discretion raises problems as to the adequacy of his information or basis upon which to exercise discretion. Still more uncertain is a rule that gives the judge discretion on the basis of whether the particular conviction substantially affects the credibility of the witness. See, e.g., Johnson v. State, 4 Md.App. 648, 244 A.2d 632 (1968).

The making of various minor changes and a few major changes in Fed.R.Evid. 609(a) in states which have adopted the federal rules indicates the tension between the considerations of simple administration and fairness to witnesses and parties.

In actions for injuries incurred in highway accidents, attempts are often made to cross-examine the participants about previous convictions for traffic offenses, but it is often held that these convictions do not show

or false statement would be fairly definite for administrative purposes but not an arbitrary criterion for fairness purposes.

The Federal Rule governing impeachment by proof of conviction of crime is the product of compromise.[6] Crimes of dishonesty or false statement, regardless of the punishment therefor, may be used against any witness, including an accused.[7] Other crimes punishable by less than imprisonment in ex-

cess of one year are never usable.[8] Against an accused who takes the stand or criminal defense witnesses, crimes punishable by death or imprisonment in excess of one year may be used, if the court determines that the probative value of the conviction outweighs its prejudicial effect on the defendant; but, in civil cases or against prosecution witnesses in criminal cases such crimes are usable without the weighing process.[9]

moral turpitude or affect veracity. Nesbit v. Cumberland Contracting Co., 196 Md. 36, 75 A.2d 339 (1950) (allowing plaintiff to be cross-examined about traffic offenses was improper, notwithstanding he had answered on cross-examination that he considered himself a good driver). Some cases do permit use of traffic offense convictions under various circumstances. Annot. 88 A.L.R.3d 74. Usually they would not be admissible under Fed.R.Evid. 609(a).

Convictions for violations of city ordinances cannot usually be used. Caldwell v. State, 282 Ala. 713, 213 So.2d 919 (1968); Massen v. State, 41 Wis.2d 245, 163 N.W.2d 616 (1969); Annot. 88 A.L.R.3d 74. Contra: Scott v. State, 445 P.2d 39 (Alaska 1968), cert. denied 393 U.S. 1082 (violation of city ordinance is a "crime" as that term is used in governing rule; the present Alaska rule permits showing of a crime if it involves dishonesty or false statement).

Thus the proposition that at least some crimes are relevant to credibility is generally accepted. The reasons for limiting inquiry into specific instances of misconduct which have not resulted in a conviction, discussed in the preceding section, tend to disappear: danger of self-incrimination is usually absent; risks of confusion and surprise are lessened; and risk of prejudice to a party from proof of conviction of an ordinary witness is so slight as scarcely to arouse comment.

The preliminary part of this present section is devoted to witnesses generally; the much more troublesome problems which arise when the witness is the accused in a criminal case are also the subject of special discussion in the text beginning at n. 44 infra.

6. Fed.R.Evid. 609(a) provides:

For the purpose of attacking the credibility of a witness, evidence that he has been convicted of a crime shall be admitted *if elicited from him or established by public record during cross-examination* but only if the crime (1) was punishable by death or imprisonment in excess of one year under the law under which he was convicted, and the court determines that the probative value of admitting this evidence outweighs its prejudicial effect to *the defendant*, or (2) involved dishonesty or false statement, regardless of the punishment. (Italics supplied.)

The revised Uniform Rule omits the first language in italics and substitutes "a party or the witness" for the second phrase in italics, but otherwise is identical with

the Federal Rule. These differences should be borne in mind in determining the applicability to the Uniform Rule of the following comments.

7. See n. 6 supra.

8. See n. 6 supra.

9. H.R.Rep.No. 93–1597, 93d Cong., 2d Sess. 9 (1974) (Conference Report). See explanation by Rep. Hungate, chairman of the House subcommittee, to the effect that the described convictions of prosecution witnesses in a criminal case may always be shown, but that the provision concerning the probative effect's outweighing prejudice to defendant applies to defense witnesses in criminal cases as well as to the defendant himself as a witness. 120 Cong.Rec., Pt. 30, 40891 (1974). See also United States v. Nevitt, 563 F.2d 406 (9th Cir. 1977), cert. denied 444 U.S. 847 (error to disallow impeachment of government witness by conviction of bomb threat; defense may always impeach prosecution witness by felony conviction, and judge has no discretion to weigh prejudicial effect). The burden of establishing that probative value outweighs prejudice to the defendant is on the prosecution. Compare Rule 403, where the burden of showing that prejudice outweighs probative value is on the objecting party. Trial judges are urged to make specific findings on prejudicial effect versus probative value. United States v. Mahone, 537 F.2d 922 (7th Cir. 1976), cert. denied 429 U.S. 1025.

The problems center on criminal defendants who elect to testify. Drawing on the *Luck* doctrine as developed in later cases (see note 46, infra), factors appropriate for consideration in the balancing process are (1) the nature of the crime, (2) recency of the prior conviction, (3) similarity between the crime for which there was prior conviction and the crime charged, (4) the importance of defendant's testimony, and (5) the centrality of the credibility issue. United States v. Hayes, 553 F.2d 824 (2d Cir. 1977), cert. denied 434 U.S. 867; United States v. Mahone, 537 F.2d 922 (7th Cir. 1976), cert. denied 429 U.S. 1025; Weinstein & Berger, Evidence ¶ 609[03]; Note, 71 Nw.U.L.Rev. 655 (1976).

(1) The nature of the crime is pertinent because some crimes not within clause (2) of Rule 609(a) are more "veracity-related" than others. United States v. Hayes, 553 F.2d 824 (2d Cir. 1977) (conviction for importation of heroin (smuggling) more closely related to veracity than conviction for possession of narcotics or a violent crime); United States v. Ortiz, 553 F.2d 782 (2d Cir. 1977), cert. denied 434 U.S. 897 (conviction for two

Crimes involving dishonesty or false statement, regardless of the punishment or against whom used, do not require balancing of probative value against prejudice.[10]

The use of any conviction is subject to time limits.[11]

Convictions in any state [12] or in federal court [13] are usable to impeach. Though a judgment against a lawyer of suspension or disbarment for criminal misconduct is not technically a conviction, it has been held to be provable to impeach.[14] In statutes relating to proceedings in juvenile courts it is frequently provided that an adjudication of delinquency shall not be used in evidence against the child in any other court and shall not be deemed a "conviction." These statutes are usually construed as precluding the finding from being used as a conviction to impeach credibility.[15] In various jurisdictions, as under the Federal Rules of Evidence, this matter is dealt with in detail by

separate heroin sales permits recognition "that a narcotics trafficker lives a life of secrecy and dissembling in the course of that activity, being prepared to say whatever is required by the demands of the moment, whether the truth or a lie"). (2) Recency of the conviction bears on the possibility of rehabilitation, which decreases with recency. Passage of time usually suggests some attenuation of the impact of the prior conviction. (3) Similarity of the subject of the prior conviction to the crime charged bears strongly on the possibility of prejudice, as inviting a direct inference of guilt rather than directing attention to credibility. See United States v. Hayes, 553 F.2d 824 (2d Cir. 1977), cert. denied 434 U.S. 867. Compare United States v. Hawley, 554 F.2d 50 (2d Cir. 1977). (4) Fear of opening up his record may deter a defendant from taking the stand, and thus warrant exclusion so that the jury may have the benefit of his testimony. See Judge Mansfield dissenting in United States v. Ortiz, 553 F.2d 782 (2d Cir. 1977), cert. denied 434 U.S. 897. This factor is closely related to the one which follows. (5) The factor of centrality of the credibility issue surfaces when the credibility of defendant is matched against that of his accuser, with the verdict depending on the result. See United States v. Ortiz, 553 F.2d 782 (2d Cir. 1977), cert. denied 434 U.S. 897; United States v. Fountain, 642 F.2d 1083 (7th Cir. 1981), cert. denied 451 U.S. 993 (excellent discussion affirming admission of conviction of premeditated murder conviction of defendant witness under particular circumstances).

In United States v. Lipscomb, 702 F.2d 1049 (D.C.Cir. 1983), the court held that the amount of background information as to the crime was within the discretion of the trial court; limiting to name of crime, date, and age, not an abuse of discretion.

The matter is highly appropriate as the subject of a defense motion in limine. See § 52 infra.

10. Supra, n. 6. Convictions for these crimes need not be punishable by imprisonment in excess of one year but may be misdemeanors. As to what crimes are included the congressional Conference Report, H.R. Rep.No. 1597, 93d Cong., 2d Sess. 9 (1974) cites as examples "crimes such as perjury or subornation of perjury, false statement, criminal fraud, embezzlement, or false pretense, or any other offense in the nature of crimen falsi, the commission of which involves some element of deceit, untruthfulness, or falsification bearing on the accused's propensity to testify truthfully." Under this view little meaning attaches to "dishonesty,"

save perhaps for embezzlement, and conflict among courts attempting to reconcile plain meaning with legislative history has resulted. See United States v. Smith, 179 U.S.App.D.C. 162, 551 F.2d 348 (1976) (attempted robbery conviction not admissible); United States v. Carden, 529 F.2d 443 (5th Cir. 1976), cert. denied 429 U.S. 848 (petty larceny conviction admissible).

If the conviction is for a crime of dishonesty or false statement, whether felony or misdemeanor, no balancing between prejudice and probative value is provided. United States v. Brashier, 548 F.2d 1315 (9th Cir. 1976), cert. denied 429 U.S. 1111.

For an extended discussion of Rule 609(a), see United States v. Smith, supra. See also United States v. Dixon, 547 F.2d 1079 (9th Cir. 1976); Annot., 39 A.L.R. Fed. 570.

11. See infra at nn. 21, 22.

12. City of Boston v. Santosuosso, 307 Mass. 302, 30 N.E.2d 278 (1940); State v. Velsir, 61 Wyo. 476, 159 P.2d 371 (1945).

13. See Burford v. Commonwealth, 179 Va. 752, 20 S.E.2d 509 (1942) where it was assumed that the federal conviction would be admissible if it met the Virginia standard of felony or misdemeanor affecting credibility. A state conviction may be proved in the federal court. Fed.R.Evid. 609(a), n. 6 supra, and Adv.Com. Note.

Convictions under the laws of another jurisdiction are treated by analogy to local crimes. People v. Kirkpatrick, 413 Ill. 595, 110 N.E.2d 519 (1953) (federal conviction of transporting stolen car in interstate commerce analogous to receiving stolen property, not infamous under state law and hence error to admit).

14. Lansing v. Michigan Central Railroad Co., 143 Mich. 48, 106 N.W. 692 (1906); State v. Pearson, 39 N.J.Super. 50, 120 A.2d 468 (1956) (and cases cited therein).

15. People v. Peele, 12 N.Y.2d 890, 237 N.Y.S.2d 999, 188 N.E.2d 265 (1963); State v. Coffman, 360 Mo. 782, 230 S.W.2d 761 (1950); Annot., 63 A.L.R.3d 1112; C.J.S. Witnesses § 510. But compare the views expressed in 3A Wigmore, Evidence §§ 924a, 980 (Chadbourn rev. 1970). He collects the statutes in § 196, note 5. In re Gault, 387 U.S. 1 (1967), fixing certain procedural requirements in juvenile cases, does not bear directly upon this subject.

general evidence rules or statutes.[16] Sometimes juvenile adjudications are admissible under such provisions.[17]

By case law a pardon does not prevent the use of the conviction to impeach.[18] The Federal Rules of Evidence adopt the same rule under stated conditions.[19] By the predominant view, including the Federal Rules of Evidence, the pendency of an appeal does

not preclude the use of the conviction for this purpose.[20] Most courts hold that lapse of time may prevent use of a conviction too remote in time if the judge in his discretion finds that under the circumstances it lacks probative value.[21] The Federal Rule of Evidence is more specific.[22] Case authority is divided respecting the use of a judgment based upon a plea of *nolo contendere*.[23]

16. Fed.R.Evid. 609(d) provides:

Evidence of juvenile adjudications is generally not admissible under this rule. The court may, however, in a criminal case allow evidence of a juvenile adjudication of a witness other than the accused if conviction of the offense would be admissible to attack the credibility of an adult and the court is satisfied that admission in evidence is necessary for a fair determination of the issue of guilt or innocence.

In the revised Uniform Rule, the phrase "Except as otherwise provided by statute" is inserted at the beginning of the second sentence; otherwise the rules are the same.

17. See n. 16 supra. A juvenile adjudication has been said to be admissible to impeach by contradiction when the subject of lack of convictions was "opened up" by the witness, United States v. Canniff, 521 F.2d 565 (2d Cir. 1975), cert. denied 423 U.S. 1059, and to impeach by showing bias under particular circumstances. Davis v. Alaska, 415 U.S. 308 (1974) (as a matter of constitutional right).

18. Richards v. United States, 89 U.S.App.D.C. 354, 192 F.2d 602 (1951) (one judge dissenting); Vedin v. McConnell, 22 F.2d 753 (9th Cir. 1927); C.J.S. Witnesses § 508; Annot., 30 A.L.R.2d 893. Contra: West's Ann.Cal.Evid.Code, § 788.

19. Fed.R.Evid. and Rev.Unif.R.Evid. (1974) 609(c) distinguish between pardons based upon findings of rehabilitation and subsequent good behavior or pardons based on findings of innocence, and other pardons. They provide:

Evidence of a conviction is not admissible under this rule if (1) the conviction has been the subject of a pardon, annulment, certificate of rehabilitation, or other equivalent procedure based on a finding of the rehabilitation of the person convicted, and that person has not been convicted of a subsequent crime which was punishable by death or imprisonment in excess of one year, or (2) the conviction has been the subject of a pardon, annulment, or other equivalent procedure based on a finding of innocence.

Compare United States v. Thorne, 547 F.2d 56 (8th Cir. 1976) (trial court could determine the witness had been rehabilitated on the basis of his activities and treatment and refuse to permit a showing of his prior conviction although the witness had no certificate of rehabilitation of any kind). See Annot., 42 A.L.R.Fed. 942.

20. People v. Bey, 42 Ill.2d 139, 246 N.E.2d 287 (1969); Suggs v. State, 6 Md.App. 231, 250 A.2d 670 (1969), and the many cases cited therein. Contra: cases cited in Suggs v. State, supra; C.J.S. Witnesses § 507f, and Annot., 16 A.L.R.3d 726.

Fed.R.Evid. and Rev.Unif.R.Evid. (1974) 609(e) provide: "The pendency of an appeal therefrom does not render evidence of a conviction inadmissible. Evidence of the pendency of an appeal is admissible."

21. Lanier v. State, 43 Ala.App. 38, 179 So.2d 167 (1965) (not abuse of discretion to admit conviction 30 years before trial). Decisions are collected in C.J.S. Witnesses § 507d, and Annot., 67 A.L.R.3d 824.

22. Fed.R.Evid. 609(b) provides:

Evidence of a conviction under this rule is not admissible if a period of more than ten years has elapsed since the date of the conviction or of the release of the witness from the confinement imposed for that conviction, whichever is the later date, unless the court determines, in the interests of justice, that the probative value of the conviction supported by specific facts and circumstances substantially outweighs its prejudicial effect. However, evidence of a conviction more than 10 years old as calculated herein, is not admissible unless the proponent gives to the adverse party sufficient advance written notice of intent to use such evidence to provide the adverse party with a fair opportunity to contest the use of such evidence.

The Revised Uniform Rule consists of the same language, omitting the word "unless" and all that follows it.

See remarks indicating that the degree by which probative value must outweigh prejudicial effects is even greater under the above rule than in the case of the same weighing process under the somewhat similar terms of Rule 609(a). United States v. Beahm, 664 F.2d 414 (4th Cir. 1981).

See Annot., 43 A.L.R.Fed. 398.

23. Commonwealth v. Snyder, 408 Pa. 253, 182 A.2d 495 (1962), cert. denied 371 U.S. 957 (admissible); Pfotzer v. Aqua Systems, Inc., 162 F.2d 779 (2d Cir. 1947) (admissible); Lacey v. People, 166 Colo. 152, 442 P.2d 402 (1968); West's Ann.Cal.Evid.Code, § 788. Contra: Clinkscales v. State, 104 Ga.App. 723, 123 S.E.2d 165 (1961), cert. denied 369 U.S. 888. See Annot., 146 A.L.R. 867. Many jurisdictions do not recognize the plea. Attitudes toward it are mixed.

The Federal Rule of Evidence should permit its use.[24]

The general rule in other situations is that proof of an official record must if feasible be made by the use of a certified or examined copy, in preference to oral testimony of its contents.[25] The rule was applied in England to proof of records of conviction, so as to preclude the cross-examiner from asking about convictions.[26] This practice still lingers in a few states,[27] but the inconvenience of the requirement, and the obvious reliability of the answer of a witness acknowledging his own conviction, have led most jurisdictions, by statute, rule, or decision, to permit the proof to be made either by production of the record or a copy, or by the oral statement of the convicted witness himself.[28] Here the cross-examiner need not "lay a foundation" for proof by copy or record,[29] nor is he bound to "take the answer" if the witness denies the conviction, but may prove it by the record.[30]

---

24. Rule 609(a), supra n. 6, is silent as to whether convictions based on pleas of nolo contendere may be used to impeach. However, Rule 410 renders a nolo plea inadmissible against the person making it, and Rule 803(22) recognizes a hearsay exception for felony convictions except on nolo pleas. While these two provisions might be thought to preclude the use of nolo convictions to impeach, convincing countervailing factors strongly indicate a contrary answer. If Rule 410 applies to convictions used to impeach, then a nolo conviction could be used to impeach any witness except a party. No reason for such a result is apparent. Rule 803(22) recognizes a hearsay exception for felony convictions, yet certain misdemeanors are usable for impeachment under Rule 609 which, if applicable, Rule 803(22) would exclude as hearsay. The conclusion must be that Rule 609 is a complete scheme; since it does not exclude nolo convictions, they are usable. This conclusion is reinforced by the history of the Federal Rule. In the Preliminary Draft of 1969, no mention of nolo convictions appeared. In the 1971 Draft they were expressly excluded. However, the reference to nolo convictions did not appear in the Rules adopted by the Supreme Court in 1972 or in the Rules as enacted by the Congress. Since to a large extent the Congress drew on the 1971 Draft in making changes in the Rules, it must be assumed that it was aware that at one stage convictions based on nolo pleas were expressly excluded from the Rule.

As an independent matter, it might be noted that it is unconstitutional to impeach a defendant by a prior conviction which was not constitutional because the accused had been denied counsel. Loper v. Beto, 405 U.S. 473 (1972).

25. See, e.g., Jones v. Melindy, 62 Ark. 203, 208, 36 S.W. 22, 23–24 (1896), and discussion § 240 infra, and 4 Wigmore, Evidence § 1269 (Chadbourn rev. 1972).

26. R. v. Castell Careinion, 8 East 77, 79, 103 Eng. Rep. 273 (K.B.1806).

27. People v. McCrimmon, 37 Ill.2d 40, 224 N.E.2d 822 (1967), cert. denied 389 U.S. 863 (to impeach defendant as a witness in a criminal case; dictum); Carrol v. Crawford, 218 Ga. 635, 129 S.E.2d 865 (1963); cases cited in C.J.S. Witnesses § 528b(3). Arguably the practice lessens the adverse impact of the evidence when the witness is the accused in a criminal case and affords some amelioration of his unfortunate predicament.

28. Gaskill v. Gahman, 255 Iowa 891, 124 N.W.2d 533 (1963); State v. Wolfe, 343 S.W.2d 10 (Mo.1961), cert. denied 366 U.S. 953. Authorities are collected in 4 Wigmore, Evidence § 1270, n. 5 (Chadbourn rev. 1972); C.J.S. Witnesses § 528b(3), n. 23, 24. A few courts have permitted impeachment by showing of a verdict of guilty without judgment and a few have rejected such proof. Annot., 14 A.L.R.3d 1272.

Fed.R.Evid. 609(a), supra n. 6, permits proof by questions on cross-examination or introduction of the record of the conviction on cross-examination. The cross-examination limitation does not appear in the revised Uniform Rule.

29. Moe v. Blue Springs Truck Lines, Inc., 426 S.W.2d 1 (Mo.1968).

Fed.R.Evid. 609(a) does not require any "foundation" question before the record is introduced. S.Rep.No. 93–1277 93d Cong., 2d Sess. 14 (1974) states: "It is to be understood however, that a court record of a prior conviction is admissible to prove that conviction if the witness has forgotten or denies its existence." This statement does not necessarily seem to require a "foundation" question as a matter of routine.

30. See n. 29, supra. A few cases have raised the question whether there is error if the prosecutor fails to introduce the record after the witness upon cross-examination denies the existence of a conviction. The decisions seem inconclusive. See Annot., 3 A.L.R.3d 965. A further question is whether the prosecutor must have at hand a properly authenticated record when there is first oral cross-examination pursuant to Fed.R.Evid. 609(a), or whether a "rap sheet" at hand is sufficient, or whether the prosecutor need have anything at hand. Compare United States v. Scott, 592 F.2d 1139 (10th Cir. 1979) (indicates "rap sheet" is sufficient); United States v. Cox, 536 F.2d 65 (5th Cir. 1976) (dictum; government should have certified copy of judgment available); United States v. Nevitt, 563 F.2d 406 (9th Cir. 1977), cert. denied 444 U.S. 847 (dictum; seems to indicate that defense need not have copy of record of conviction). A suggested approach is to require the cross-examiner to satisfy the judge in the latter's discretion, as to the existence of grounds for making the inquiry, particularly with respect to an accused-witness, by making a preliminary inquiry out of the presence of the jury, or by assurances of counsel. See Michelson v. United States, 335 U.S. 469 (1948).

How far may the cross-examiner go in his inquiries about convictions? He may ask about the name of the crime committed,[31] i.e. murder or embezzlement, and the punishment awarded.[32] It will certainly add to the pungency of the impeachment where the crime was an aggravated one if he may ask about the circumstances, for example, whether the murder victim was a baby, the niece of the witness.[33] And it has been suggested by a few courts that since proof by record is allowable, and the record might show some of these circumstances, the cross-examination should at least be permitted to touch all the facts that the record would.[34] On the whole, however, the more reasonable practice, minimizing prejudice

and distraction from the issues, is the generally prevailing one that beyond the name of the crime,[35] the time and place of conviction,[36] and the punishment;[37] further details such as the name of the victim [38] and the aggravating circumstances may not be inquired into.[39]

It may be thought that if the impeacher is precluded from showing details and circumstances of aggravation, the witness should similarly be cut off from explaining or extenuating the conviction or denying his guilt. Certainly it is impractical and forbidden to retry the case on which the conviction was based. And many cases forbid any explanation, extenuation or denial of guilt even by the witness himself on redirect.[40] This rule

31. United States v. Tumblin, 551 F.2d 1001 (5th Cir. 1977); State v. Phillips, 102 Ariz. 377, 430 P.2d 139 (1967); People v. Terry, 57 Cal.2d 538, 21 Cal.Rptr. 185, 370 P.2d 985 (1962), cert. denied 375 U.S. 960 (dictum); Barnett v. State, 240 Ind. 129, 161 N.E.2d 444 (1959); C.J.S. Witnesses § 515, p. 436.

32. United States v. Wolf, 561 F.2d 1376 (10th Cir. 1977) (dictum); Reid v. State, 100 Tex.Cr. 512, 271 S.W. 625 (1925) (payment of fine as prostitute); Finch v. State, 103 Tex.Cr. 212, 280 S.W. 597 (1926) (permissible to ask if he has not served a term in penitentiary). See Annots., 67 A.L.R.3d 761 and 775, indicating some contrary cases in certain instances.

33. Choice v. State, 54 Tex.Cr. 517, 521, 114 S.W. 132, 133 (1908) (properly excluded).

34. See State v. Lindsey, 27 Wn.2d 186, 177 P.2d 387 (1947) (court upheld cross-examination to show nature of offense and punishment "for the reason that these matters were set forth in the judgment of conviction"); see also State v. Rodia, 132 N.J.L. 199, 39 A.2d 484 (1944). ("Were you ever convicted of the crime of atrocious assault and battery by cutting," approved over objection that "by cutting" was improper, on ground that the charge of cutting would have been shown by the record of conviction); State v. Garvin, 44 N.J. 268, 208 A.2d 402 (1965) ("the statute has been consistently construed to authorize proof by cross-examination of what the record for conviction disclosed," citing cases). Very often, however, the "record" would be considered to include only the so-called Judgment of Conviction and Sentence which would show no more than the nature of a crime in terms of the governing criminal statute and no details of the punishment except the length of imprisonment, amount of fine, and probation, if any.

35. See n. 31, supra. Unfortunately, the name of a crime does not always indicate its nature, and when it is sought to classify a conviction as one involving dishonesty or false statement under Federal Rule 609(a), supra n. 6, either because it is a misdemeanor or in order to avoid balancing probative value against

prejudice, further inquiry may be required. United States v. Papia, 560 F.2d 827 (7th Cir. 1977) (original charge of forgery shown to have been bargained down to "some sort of false statement forgery in application for loan" from savings and loan association, with guilty plea to "some sort of theft under $100").

36. Hadley v. State, 25 Ariz. 23, 212 P. 458, 462 (1923) ("Were you ever convicted of a felony in Oklahoma," approved).

37. See n. 32 supra.

38. Stevens v. State, 138 Tex.Cr. 59, 134 S.W.2d 246 (1939).

39. United States v. Cox, 536 F.2d 65 (5th Cir. 1976) (reviews cases); State v. Norgaard, 272 Minn. 48, 136 N.W.2d 628 (1965) (age of girl involved in conviction for assault with intent to rape; but error not prejudicial in this instance); Powers v. State, 156 Miss. 316, 126 So. 12 (1930) ("You are under suspended sentence for beating your wife and son?", improper; approved in dictum in Emily v. State, 191 So.2d 925 (Miss.1966)); White v. State, 202 Miss. 246, 30 So.2d 894 (1947) (inquiry whether conviction for wilful trespass followed a withdrawn plea of guilty of burglary, improper); State v. Mount, 73 N.J.L. 582, 64 A. 124 (1906) (error to inquire of accused about particulars of prior assault for which he was convicted, such as size of the man assaulted and weapon used); C.J.S. Witnesses §§ 507, 515b(3)(c). But according to some courts, if the witness testifies to matters pertaining to a conviction on direct examination, he may "open the door" to some cross-examination of the circumstances. See, e.g., United States v. Wolf, 561 F.2d 1376 (10th Cir. 1977); State v. Rush, 248 Or. 568, 436 P.2d 266 (1968) (dictum); State v. Wilson, 26 Wn.2d 468, 174 P.2d 553 (1946).

40. State v. Gregg, 230 S.C. 222, 95 S.E.2d 255 (1956) (defendant-witness not permitted to state mitigating details on redirect examination); Mayo v. State, 32 Ala.App. 264, 24 So.2d 769 (1946) (accused-witness not allowed to show he was given probation for offence

is a logical consequence of the premise of conclusiveness of the judgment. It does not, however, satisfy our feeling that some reasonable outlet for the instinct of self-defense by one attacked should be conceded, if it can be done without too much damage to the business at hand. Accordingly a substantial number of courts, while not opening the door to a retrial of the conviction, do permit the witness himself to make a brief and general statement in explanation, mitigation, or denial of guilt,[41] or recognize a discretion in the trial judge to permit it.[42] Wigmore aptly terms it a "harmless charity to allow the witness to make such protestations on his own behalf as he may feel able to make with a due regard to the penalties of perjury."[43]

The sharpest and most prejudicial impact of the practice of impeachment by conviction (as is true also of cross-examination as to misconduct, see § 42, above) is upon one particular type of witness, namely, the accused in a criminal case who elects to take the stand. If the accused is forced to admit that he has a "record" of past convictions, particularly if the convictions are for crimes similar to the one on trial, there is an obvious danger that the jury, despite instructions, will give more heed to the past convictions as evidence that the accused is the kind of man who would commit the crime on charge, or even that he ought to be put away with-

out too much concern with present guilt, than they will to the legitimate bearing of the past convictions on credibility.[44] The accused, who has a "record" but who thinks he has a defense to the present charge, is thus placed in a grievous dilemma. If he stays off the stand, his silence alone will prompt the jury to believe him guilty. If he elects to testify, his "record" becomes provable to impeach him, and this again is likely to doom his defense. Where does the balance of justice lie? Most prosecutors would argue with much force that it would be misleading to permit the accused to appear as a witness of blameless life, and this argument has prevailed widely. An intermediate view, between permitting convictions generally to be introduced and excluding all convictions of the accused to impeach him as a witness, is a proposal that the convictions be restricted to those supposedly bearing directly upon character for truthfulness.[45] Another intermediate view, but with the disadvantage of uncertainty, was a rule which would permit the introduction of prior convictions of the defendant-witness in the discretion of the judge, who was to balance in each instance the possible prejudice against the probative value of the conviction as to credibility.[46] As already noted earlier in this section the Federal Rule of Evidence is a compromise that in effect combines the above two no-

---

for which convicted); Lamoureux v. New York, New Haven & Hartford Railroad Co., 169 Mass. 338, 47 N.E. 1009 (1897) (witness's extenuation properly excluded; leading opinion, by Holmes, J.); State v. Lapan, 101 Vt. 124, 141 A. 686 (1928) (extensive discussion, following preceding case).

41. 4 Wigmore, Evidence § 1117 note 3 (Chadbourn rev. 1972).

42. United States v. Bray, 445 F.2d 178 (5th Cir. 1971), cert. denied 404 U.S. 1002 (dictum; a pre-federal evidence rules case; but Fed.R.Evid. and Rev.Unif.R. Evid. (1974) 403 and 611(a) grant the judge discretion); Commonwealth v. Ford, 199 Pa.Super. 102, 184 A.2d 401 (1962) (approving judge's discretion in excluding reputation testimony but allowing introduction of pardon); Annot., 166 A.L.R. 211.

43. 4 Wigmore, Evidence § 1117, p. 251 (Chadbourn rev. 1972).

44. Griswold, The Long View, 51 A.B.A.J. 1017, 1021 (1965); Schaefer, Police Interrogation and the Privilege Against Self-Incrimination, 61 Nw.U.L.Rev.

506, 512 (1966); McGowan, Impeachment of Criminal Defendants by Prior Convictions, 1970 Ariz.St.L.J. 1. Statistical support is indicated in Kalven & Zeisel, The American Jury 124, 126–130, 144–146, 160–162 (1966).

45. Former Uniform Rule 21 limited provable convictions with respect to witnesses generally to those for crimes involving dishonesty or false statement.

46. In Luck v. United States, 121 U.S.App.D.C. 151, 348 F.2d 763 (1965), the court found authority for such an approach in the provision then in D.C. Code 1981, § 14–305 that conviction "may" be given in evidence to impeach. Brown v. United States, 125 U.S.App.D.C. 220, 370 F.2d 242 (1966) and Gordon v. United States, 127 U.S.App.D.C. 343, 383 F.2d 936 (1967), cert. denied 390 U.S. 1029, developed standards for the exercise of discretion, including the nature of the crime, nearness or remoteness in time, the subsequent career of the person, and whether the crime was similar to the one charged. Present D.C. Code 1981, § 14–305 contains provisions somewhat similar to those in Fed.R.Evid. 609 but with differences.

tions in a specific manner.[47] In Pennsylvania,[48] the accused who takes the stand is shielded, under certain circumstances, from cross-examination as to misconduct or conviction of crime when offered to impeach but not from proof of conviction by the record of conviction. Finally, the former Uniform Rule[49] provided that if the accused does not offer evidence supporting his own credibility the prosecution shall not be allowed, on cross-examination or otherwise, to prove for impeachment purposes his conviction of crime. The variety of solutions, both actual and proposed, indicate the stubborn and troublesome nature of the problem.

The suggestion has been made that impeachment of the accused by showing of prior convictions is an unconstitutional procedure, but at present, this result is not established.[50]

WESTLAW REFERENCES

digest(410k337 /p impeach! /p character /p arrest* indictment* accusation* investigation charge*)

impeach! /s "nolo contendere"

---

§ 44. Character: Impeachment by Proof of Opinion or Bad Reputation [1]

In most jurisdictions the impeacher may attack the character of a witness by using the following question formula with another witness:

"Do you know the general reputation at the present time of William Witness in the community in which he lives, for truth and veracity?"

"Yes."

"What is that reputation?"

"It is bad."

This routine is the distillation of traditions which became established in a majority of American courts. It was the result of choices between alternative solutions, some wise, some seemingly misguided.

Misguided it seems is the first choice of the doctrine that this attack on character for truth must be in the abstract, debilitated form of proof of reputation. By what is apparently a misreading of legal history,[2] the American courts have in the past generally prohibited proof of character by having a witness describe his belief or opinion of the character of the second witness under attack when the belief or opinion is based upon experience with the witness under attack and

---

47. See text at nn. 6–11 supra.

48. 42 P.S. § 5919.

In England the Criminal Evidence Act, 1898 (61 & 62 Vict. c. 36), subs. 1(f) provided: "A person charged and called as a witness in pursuance of this Act shall not be asked, and if asked shall not be required to answer, any question tending to show that he has committed or been convicted of or been charged with any offence other than that wherewith he is then charged, or is of bad character, unless—(i) the proof that he has committed or been convicted of such other offence is admissible evidence to show that he is guilty of the offence wherewith he is then charged; or (ii) he has personally or by his advocate asked questions of the witnesses for the prosecution with a view to establish his own good character, or has given evidence of his good character, or the nature or conduct of the defence is such as to involve imputations on the character of the prosecutor or the witnesses for the prosecution; or (iii) he has given evidence against any other person charged with the same offence." See analysis and discussion, 1 Wigmore, Evidence § 194a; Cross, Evidence ch. 15 (5th ed. 1979).

49. Former Uniform Rule 21: ". . . If the witness be the accused in a criminal proceeding, no evidence of his conviction of a crime shall be admissible for the sole purpose of impairing his credibility unless he has first introduced evidence admissible solely for the purpose of supporting his credibility."

50. See discussion in Note, 37 U.Cin.L.Rev. 168 (1968). Spencer v. Texas, 385 U.S. 554 (1967), sustaining the constitutionality of presenting evidence of prior convictions on an habitual criminal issue at the trial of the principal charge, may well be pertinent.

§ 44

1. See 3A Wigmore, Evidence §§ 920–930 (Chadbourn rev. 1970); Weinstein & Berger, Evidence ¶ 608[03], [04]. Ladd, Techniques of Character Testimony, 24 Iowa L.Rev. 498 (1939); Dec.Dig. Witnesses ⚖333–343, 356–358; C.J.S. Witnesses §§ 491–501; 81 Am.Jur.2d Witnesses §§ 563–568.

2. See 7 Wigmore, Evidence §§ 1981, 1982 (Chadbourn rev. 1978), and further discussion infra § 186.

upon observation of his conduct.[3] The limitation to reputation has been defended on the ground that to let in opinion from observation would provoke distracting side-issues over disputes about specific conduct of the witness attacked, since the impeaching witness may be cross-examined about the grounds of his opinion.[4] Furthermore, a difficult assessment of the impeaching witness might be necessary. These dangers undoubtedly exist, and the controversies would need to be held to reasonable limits by the judge. However, the question is whether the choice of reputation instead of experience and observation has not eliminated most of the objectivity from the attempt to appraise character, and has not encouraged the parties to select those who will give voice, under the guise of an estimate of reputation, to prejudice and ill-will. The hand is the hand of Esau, but the voice is the voice of Jacob. And, in addition, reputation in modern, impersonal urban centers is often evanescent, fragile, or actually non-existent.

Based upon reasons such as those stated above, the Federal Rules of Evidence and the Revised Uniform Rules of Evidence permit attack upon character by opinion, while at the same time retaining the traditional attack upon character by reputation.[5] Various aspects of this rule are considered throughout the remainder of this section.

The courts also have faced here a further choice—a recurrent one in various phases of character-impeachment—namely, shall the inquiry be as to "general character," or as to other specific types of bad traits such as sexual immorality, or shall it be directed solely and specifically to the trait of veracity? Surely it is clear that in this elusive realm of reputation as to character it is best to reach for the highest degree of relevancy that is attainable. Fortunately the great majority of our courts have taken this view and have limited the inquiry to "reputation for truth and veracity."[6] Opinion, as well as reputation, pursuant to Federal and Revised Uniform Rule of Evidence 608(a) is likewise

3. Gifford v. People, 148 Ill. 173, 176, 35 N.E. 754 (1893) (dictum); State v. Steen, 185 N.C. 768, 117 S.E. 793 (1923); State v. Polhamus, 65 N.J.L. 387, 47 A. 470 (1900). See also, cases in which direct opinion was sought in connection with attempts to obtain reputation testimony. Parasco v. State, 168 Tex.Cr.R. 89, 323 S.W.2d 257 (1959) ("In your opinion is the testimony of . . . under oath worthy of belief?"; held error); People v. Wendt, 104 Ill.App.2d 192, 244 N.E.2d 384 (1969).

Many courts, however, perhaps conscious of the weakness of evidence limited strictly to reputation, have compromised by permitting the injection of personal opinion by such questions as these (after proving bad reputation): "From that reputation, would you believe him on oath?" Burke v. Zwick, 299 Ill.App. 558, 20 N.E.2d 912 (1939). Or an even more curious straddle: "From your association with W. and from what you know about his reputation . . . do you believe him entitled to credit under oath?" See Bowles v. Katzman, 308 Ky. 490, 214 S.W.2d 1021 (1941). This general type of testimony added to the standard reputation testimony of a witness has been approved under Fed.R.Evid. 608(a). United States v. Davis, 639 F.2d 239 (5th Cir. 1981); Annot., 52 A.L.R.Fed. 440. However, the first type of question mentioned above which is asked upon the basis of the previous testimony of reputation by the witness may be doubtful as not being based upon the impeaching witness's rational perception of the witness attacked, a requirement under Fed. R.Evid. 701, i.e., as not being based upon first-hand

knowledge (see Fed.R.Evid. 602) upon which knowledge the opinion can be rationally based. See text of Rule 608(a) at n. 5 infra.

4. See People v. Van Gaasbeck, 189 N.Y. 408, 82 N.E. 718, 721 (1907) (discussing the analogous problem as to character-evidence offered by the accused on the issue of guilt). The contrary argument of policy is powerfully presented in 7 Wigmore, Evidence § 1986. The current trend in favor of allowing proof in the form of opinion is indicated in Fed.R.Evid. and Rev. Unif.R.Evid. (1974) 608(a), infra n. 5.

5. Fed.R.Evid. and Rev.Unif.R.Evid. (1974) 608(a) provide:

The credibility of a witness may be attacked or supported by evidence in the form of opinion or reputation, but subject to these limitations: (1) the evidence may refer only to character for truthfulness or untruthfulness, and (2) evidence of truthful character is admissible only after the character of the witness for truthfulness has been attacked by opinion or reputation evidence or otherwise.

It might be noted that presently at least four of the states which have generally adopted the federal rules have not permitted the use of opinion testimony to attack character.

6. McHargue v. Perkins, 295 S.W.2d 301 (Ky.1956); C.J.S. Witnesses § 497; 3A Wigmore, Evidence § 923 (Chadbourn rev. 1970); Dec.Dig. Witnesses ⌸342.

limited.[7] Only a few jurisdictions open the door, in addition, to reputation for "general character"[8] or "general moral character,"[9] and fewer still permit proof of reputation for specific traits other than veracity.[10]

The crucial time when the character of the witness under attack has its influence on his truth-telling is the time when he testifies.[11] But obviously reputation takes time to form and is the resultant of earlier conduct and demeanor, so that it does not precisely reflect character at a later date. The practical solution is to do what most courts actually do, that is, (1) to permit the reputation-witness to testify about the impeachee's "present" reputation as of the time of the trial, if he knows it,[12] and (2) to permit testimony as to reputation (which is usually a settled, continuing condition) as of any time before trial which the judge in his discretion finds is not too remote to be significant.[13] This practice should be permitted by Federal Rule of Evidence 608(a).[14] The opinion of the witness permitted by the federal rule should have a similar time relation to the trial.[15]

As to place of reputation,[16] the traditional inquiry is as to general reputation for veracity "in the community where he lives." The object of this limitation of place is obviously to restrict evidence of repute, to reputation among the people who know him best.[17] The limitation was appropriate for the situation in England (and less so in America) before the Industrial Revolution, when most

---

7. Fed.R.Evid and Rev.Unif.R.Evid. (1974) 608(a), supra n. 5 (character for "truthfulness or untruthfulness").

8. Grammer v. State, 239 Ala. 633, 196 So. 268, 272 (1940) (but reputation for specific traits of character is not permitted; see note 10 infra).

9. West's Ann.Ind. Code 34–1–14–13, 35–37–4–2; Iowa C.A. § 622.18; C.J.S. Witnesses § 498.

10. Among decisions excluding the evidence are Pugh v. State, 42 Ala.App. 499, 500, 169 So.2d 27, 28 (1964) (bad reputation for being a thief); State v. Mondrosch, 108 N.J.Super. 1, 259 A.2d 725 (1969) (reputation with regard to a propensity or an inclination to be accusatory in nature against others, applying Ev.Rules 22 and 47); State v. Albert, 241 Iowa 1000, 43 N.W.2d 703 (1950) (bad reputation for an honest, upright citizen and industrious man; dictum).

In cases of prosecutions for sexual offenses the reputation of the prosecutrix for lack of chastity is often excluded for the purpose of attacking credibility. Fed. R.Evid. 608(a) by its very terms should dictate that result. Fed.R.Evid. 412, the "rape shield" rule, specifically prohibits the use of reputation or opinion evidence of lack of chastity to attack the credibility of the prosecutrix. A complete summary of state "rape shield statutes" is contained in Tanford & Bocchino, Rape Victim Shield Laws and the Sixth Amendment, 128 U.Pa.L.Rev. 544, 591–602 (1980). Most of the cases that have admitted evidence of reputation for specific traits to attack credibility are cases of prosecutions for various sexual offenses in which reputation for lack of chastity is often the reputation introduced. Wheeler v. State, 148 Ga. 508, 97 S.E. 408 (1918); C.J.S. Witnesses § 504; Annot., 95 A.L.R.3d 1181, 1193 (forcible rape cases; Annot., 90 A.L.R.3d 1300 (statutory rape cases).

11. See United States v. Null, 415 F.2d 1178 (4th Cir. 1969) (when accused proves good character on issue of guilt, it is reputation at the time of act that counts, but if his credibility as a witness is in question, it is reputation at the time of trial that is proved).

Decisions as to time are collected in 3A Wigmore, Evidence § 928 (Chadbourn rev. 1970); Dec.Dig. Witnesses ☞343; C.J.S. Witnesses § 500.

12. Carter v. State, 226 Ala. 96, 145 So. 814 (1933) (time to which the character relates is "the time of trial and prior thereto"); Goehring v. Commonwealth, 370 S.W.2d 822 (Ky.1963) (time must be time of trial "and a reasonable period theretofore;" 9 months before trial was within a reasonable period). See also, Frith v. Commonwealth, 288 Ky. 188, 155 S.W.2d 851 (1941) (manslaughter: held impeachment by showing reputation for bad moral character as of time of trial ordinarily proper but error to admit where witness impeaching witness testifies bad reputation was due to the homicide).

13. Snow v. Grace, 29 Ark. 131, 136 (1874) (character seven years before properly received); Shuster v. State, 62 N.J.L. 521, 41 A. 701 (1898) (reputation 18 years before, properly excluded); State v. Thomas, 8 Wn.2d 573, 113 P.2d 73 (1941) (sodomy, evidence that prosecuting witness 13 years old had bad reputation for truth two years before trial, held, exclusion, in view of child's age, not abuse of discretion; careful opinion by Driver, J.).

14. United States v. Lewis, 482 F.2d 632, 641 (D.C. Cir.1973) (dictum; "at the time of trial and during a prior period not remote thereto").

15. The same results are dictated by relevancy principles.

16. See 3A Wigmore, Evidence § 930 (Chadbourn rev. 1970); Dec.Dig. Witnesses ☞343; C.J.S. Witnesses §§ 500, 520; Annot., 112 A.L.R. 1020.

17. See Brill v. Muller Brothers, Inc., 40 Misc.2d 683, 243 N.Y.S.2d 905 (1962), reversed because evidence rules inapplicable in arbitration proceeding 17 A.D.2d 804, 232 N.Y.S.2d 806, affirmed 13 N.Y.2d 776, 242 N.Y.S.2d 69, 192 N.E.2d 34 (1963), cert. denied 376 U.S. 927 (trial court stated that reputation testimony cannot come from a stranger sent out by the adverse party to investigate the reputation).

people lived either in small towns or in rural villages. But as an exclusive limitation it would not be appropriate in this country today, where a person may be little known in the suburb or city neighborhood where he lives, but well known in another locality where he spends his workdays or in several localities where he does business from time to time. Thus, today it is generally agreed that proof may be made not only of the reputation of the witness where he lives, but also of his repute, as long as it is "general" and established, in any substantial community of people among whom he is well known,[18] such as the group with whom he works,[19] does business [20] or goes to school.[21] These standards should apply under Federal Rule of Evidence 608(a).[22] The trial judge has a reasonable need of discretion to determine whether the reputation sought to be proved among the group in question meets these standards.[23]

Other problems arise when the attack on character is by opinion as authorized by Federal Rule of Evidence 608(a). Although it appears that an opinion of a lay person should be based on some firsthand knowledge pursuant to Rule 602 so that the opinion can be based on rational perception and be of aid to the jury as required by Rule 701, acts of misconduct cannot be brought out from the witness on direct examination because Rule 608(a) prohibits evidence of such acts by extrinsic evidence.[24] An adequate preliminary showing to meet the requirements of Rule 701 would be made by evidence of sufficient acquaintance with the witness to be attacked. Impeachment by experts is considered in the next section.

WESTLAW REFERENCES

digest(rule* ¦ o 608(a) /p reputation /p truth! veracity)

---

18. Craven v. State, 22 Ala.App. 39, 111 So. 767 (1927).

The question of place is often essentially a matter of the time when the reputation was acquired, discussed in the preceding paragraph. See, e.g., Lee v. State, 179 Miss. 122, 174 So. 85 (1937) (reputation in place where witness lived six months before trial, provable).

19. Hamilton v. State, 129 Fla. 219, 176 So. 89 (1937) (reputation could be proved by fellow-employees at hotel where accused worked); State v. Axilrod, 248 Minn. 204, 79 N.W.2d 677 (1956), cert. denied 353 U.S. 938 (not error to admit testimony confined primarily to community in which impeached witness worked).

20. Hubert v. Joslin, 285 Mich. 337, 280 N.W. 780 (1938) (reputation in locality 15 miles away from home, where he owned a farm, visited frequently and had many business dealings); State v. Henderson, 29 W.Va. 147, 1 S.E. 225, 240 (1886).

21. People v. Colantone, 243 N.Y. 134, 152 N.E. 700, 702 (1926) (error to exclude evidence of reputation of ex-soldier, by instructors at vocational school, members of his company in army, and member of disabled veterans' post of 250 men. "The determining factor is whether the community in which the defendant has lived his life is sufficiently large for the persons to become acquainted with his character and to form a general opinion of it. This we call general reputation. The cases are quite right which exclude evidence of reputation among such a small class of persons or business associates, as to make it, not a general reputation,

but rather the evidence of individual and independent dealings."). Compare Williams v. United States, 168 U.S. 382 (1897), (error to permit evidence of reputation of immigration inspector "in the custom house;" evidence as to his reputation "among the limited number of people in a particular public building" was inadmissible); State v. Swenson, 62 Wn.2d 259, 382 P.2d 614 (1963) (error to permit showing of reputation in the church of which impeached witness was a member or among people of that church).

22. See, e.g., United States v. Oliver, 492 F.2d 943 (8th Cir. 1974), cert. denied 424 U.S. 973 (error to exclude reputation testimony by former roommates who had known witness for seven weeks). See also remarks in United States v. Mandel, 591 F.2d 1347 (4th Cir. 1979), cert. denied 445 U.S. 961 (reputation in law office where witness worked).

23. Ulrich v. Chicago, Burlington & Quincy Railroad Co., 281 Mo. 697, 220 S.W. 682, 684 (1920) (judge did not abuse discretion in admitting evidence of plaintiff's reputation at time of trial in locality where he formerly lived and continued to do business); State v. McEachern, 283 N.C. 57, 194 S.E.2d 787 (1973) (extensive discussion, concluding that reputation from "any community or society in which the person has a well known or established reputation" qualifies).

Hearsay aspects of reputation evidence are discussed in §§ 248 and 324 infra.

24. See United States v. Hoskins, 628 F.2d 295 (5th Cir. 1980), cert. denied 449 U.S. 987.

§ 45. Defects of Capacity: Sensory or Mental [1]

Any deficiency of the senses, such as deafness, or color blindness or defect of other senses which would substantially lessen the ability to perceive the facts which the witness purports to have observed, should of course be provable to attack the credibility of the witness, either upon cross-examination or by producing other witnesses to prove the defect. Probably the limits and weaknesses of human powers of perception should be studied more widely by judges and lawyers in the interest of a more accurate and objective administration of justice.[2]

As to the mental qualities of intelligence and memory, a distinction must be made between attacks on competency [3] and attacks on credibility, the subject of this section. Sanity in any general sense is not the test of competency, and a so-called insane person is generally permitted to testify if he is able to

report correctly the matters to which he testifies and if he understands the duty to speak the truth.[4] Even more clearly, Federal Rule of Evidence 601, for use at least in federal question cases in federal courts, disassociates the subject of sanity or insanity from the subject of competency of witnesses to testify, although one could be sufficiently incompetent so that one's testimony would be barred if one did not have the capacity to recall or observe, understand the duty to tell the truth, or have the capacity to have personal knowledge.[5] Manifestly, however, the fact of mental "abnormality" either at the time of observing the facts or at the time of testifying will be provable, on cross or by extrinsic evidence, as bearing on credibility [6], often, as under the federal rules, in the discretion of the court.[7] The use of expert opinion as extrinsic evidence in this situation is discussed in the last part of this section.

What of defects of mind within the range of normality, such as a slower than average

§ 45

1. See 3A Wigmore, Evidence §§ 931–935, 989–995 (Chadbourn rev. 1970); Weinstein & Berger, Evidence ¶ 607[04]; C.J.S. Witnesses §§ 461, 470, 486, 487, 488; Annot., 20 A.L.R.3d 684.

2. See C.C. Moore, A Treatise on Facts (1908); Wigmore, Principles of Judicial Proof ch. 22 (3d ed. 1937); Sobel, Eye-Witness Identification: Legal and Practical Problems (1972); Gardner, The Perception and Memory of Witnesses, 18 Corn.L.Q. 391 (1933); E. Moore, Elements of Error in Testimony, 28 Or.L.Rev. 293 (1943).

3. See § 62 infra.

4. People v. Dixon, 81 Ill.App.2d 330, 225 N.E.2d 445 (1967); People v. Nash, 36 Ill.2d 275, 222 N.E.2d 473 (1966), cert. denied 389 U.S. 906; Dec.Dig. Witnesses ⊗41; and § 62, infra.

5. Excluding civil actions in which state law supplies the rule of decision as to an element of a claim or defense, Rule 601 provides, "Every person is competent to be a witness except as otherwise provided in these rules." The remaining rules do not mention defects of capacity.

However, in at least extreme cases of incompetency, one could be so incompetent as to make one's testimony irrelevant under Rules 401 and 402, or so incompetent that Rule 403 would bar testimony. Likewise a defect of capacity could be so great that one could not understand the concept of truth-telling duties under Rule 603 or would not be capable of having firsthand knowledge under Rule 602. For an example illustrating that mental incompetency is likely to go to credibility, see United States v. Lightly, 677 F.2d 1027 (4th Cir.

1982) (witness not held incompetent to be a witness because of a prior finding that he was criminally insane and incompetent to stand trial and also suffered from hallucinations).

6. State v. Vigliano, 50 N.J. 51, 232 A.2d 129 (1966) (error to sustain objection to cross-examination to show witness was committed to psychiatric ward during trial); State v. Miskell, 161 N.W.2d 732 (Iowa 1968) (permitting cross-examination showing witness had been adjudged senile); Commonwealth v. Towber, 190 Pa.Super. 93, 152 A.2d 917 (1959) (admission of hospital record showing commitment for mental treatment improperly refused). Cases are collected in 3A Wigmore, Evidence § 932, n. 1 (Chadbourn rev. 1970); Dec.Dig. Witnesses ⊗377; C.J.S. Witnesses § 461; Annot., 44 A.L.R.3d 1203. See also cases cited in n. 24, infra. But see, Adams v. Ford Motor Co., 103 Ill.App.2d 356, 243 N.E.2d 843 (1968) (sustaining rejection of offer of records of prior commitments of witness to mental institution).

7. "Interest in the outcome of litigation and mental capacity are, of course, highly relevant to credibility and require no special treatment to render them admissible along with other matters bearing upon the perception, memory, and narration of the witnesses." Fed.R. Evid. 601, Advisory Committee's Note. Extrinsic evidence of mental capacity would be permissible pursuant to the discretion of the judge under Rule 403. The court has similar discretion in controlling cross-examination. See, e.g., United States v. Lopez, 611 F.2d 44 (4th Cir. 1979) (judge upheld in refusing cross-examination concerning a psychiatric examination).

mind or a poorer than usual memory? These qualities reveal themselves in a testing cross-examination by a skilled questioner.[8] May they be proved by other witnesses? The decisions are divided.[9] It seems eminently a case for discretion.[10] The trial judge would determine whether the crucial character of the testimony attacked and the evaluative light shed by the impeaching evidence overbalance the time and distraction involved in opening this side-dispute. The development of standardized tests for intelligence and their widening use in business, government and the armed forces, suggest that they may eventually come to serve as useful aids in the evaluation of testimony.[11]

Abnormality, we have seen, is a horse of a different color. It is a standard ground of impeachment.[12] One form of abnormality exists when one is under the influence of drugs or drink. If the witness was under the influence at the time of the happenings which he reports in his testimony or is so at the time he testifies, this condition is provable, on cross or by extrinsic evidence, to impeach.[13] Habitual addiction stands differently. It is generally held that the mere fact of chronic alcoholism is not provable on credibility.[14] On the other hand, as to drug addiction to which more social odium has been attached, many decisions allow it to be shown to impeach, even without evidence that it did in the particular case affect truth-

8. That a cross-examination to test intelligence is usually allowable, see dicta in Blanchard v. People, 70 Colo. 555, 203 P. 662 (1922) and Henry v. State, 6 Okl. Cr. 430, 119 P. 278 (1911); Annot., 44 A.L.R.3d 1203.

9. Admissible: Isler v. Dewey, 75 N.C. 466 (1876) (evidence of impeaching witness that memory of impeached witness is weak); State v. Armstrong, 232 N.C. 727, 62 S.E.2d 50 (1950) (expert testimony that witness was a moron should not have been excluded). Excluded: Blanchard v. People, 70 Colo. 555, 203 P. 662 (1922) (forgery: witness for defendant testified that interlineation was made before instrument signed; held, error to permit witnesses to testify that he was of low intelligence); Fries v. Berberich, 177 S.W.2d 640 (Mo.App.1944) (expert testimony as to weak memory). Decisions are collected in 3A Wigmore, Evidence § 935, note 1 (Chadbourn rev. 1970); Annot., 20 A.L.R.3d 684, 696–697.

10. See, e.g., Mangrum v. State, 227 Ark. 381, 299 S.W.2d 80 (1957) (trial court rejection of testimony of counselor where witness had been a pupil, showing intelligence test score and conclusion of counselor, was properly within range of the trial court's discretion). See also, Polson v. State, 246 Ind. 674, 207 N.E.2d 638 (1965) (rejection of cross-examination question whether witness was "a little behind in school" was proper exercise of discretion). Fed. and Rev.Unif.R.Evid. (1974) 403 and 611 grant similar discretion.

11. See Hutchins & Slesinger, The Competency of Witnesses, 37 Yale L.J. 1017, 1019 (1928); Gardner, op. cit., 18 Corn.L.Q. 391, 409 (1933); Redmount, The Psychological Bases of Evidence Practices: Intelligence, 42 Minn.L.Rev. 559 (1958).

12. See note 7 supra.

13. Drink. Rheaume v. Patterson, 289 F.2d 611 (2d Cir. 1961) (dictum); Walker's Trial, 23 How.St.Tr. 1157 (1794) ("Do you know whether he had drunk any [liquor]?" "He had had a little; he knew what he was saying and doing." "Just as much as he knows now?" "He was not half so much in liquor then as he is now."); Olstad v. Fahse, 204 Minn. 118, 282 N.W. 694

(1938) (that the witness had been drinking beer at the time of the accident, and was under influence; extrinsic evidence allowable); 3A Wigmore, Evidence § 933 (Chadbourn rev. 1970); C.J.S. Witnesses § 461h. However, there is a variety of decisions whether or not particular evidence is admissible to prove intoxication at the time of the incident about which the witness testifies. See collection of Annot., 8 A.L.R.3d 749.

Drugs. Wilson v. United States, 232 U.S. 563 (1914) (witness having admitted addiction, and that she had taken a dose in the morning before testifying, was asked how often she used it and whether she had with her the "implements;" held, proper, to show whether at the moment of testifying she was under its influence); United States v. Hodges, 556 F.2d 366 (5th Cir. 1977), cert. denied 434 U.S. 1016 (witness admitted smoking marijuana cigarettes before a meeting; evidence of second witness excluded when no showing a second witness had expertise concerning effect of use of marijuana cigarettes); State v. Smith, 103 Wash. 267, 174 P. 9 (1918) (in prosecution for selling morphine without a physician's prescription where evidence showed that prosecuting witness was under the influence of morphine at the time of the alleged sale, expert testimony as to the effect of morphine upon the mind and memory of its user was admissible); Annot., 52 A.L.R. 848; Annot., 65 A.L.R.3d 705; C.J.S. Witnesses § 470.

14. Poppell v. United States, 418 F.2d 214 (5th Cir. 1969) (general reputation for intemperance could be excluded); Springer v. Reimers, 4 Cal.App.3d 325, 84 Cal. Rptr. 486 (1970) (must be shown that intoxication occurred contemporaneously with events about which witness testifies); Indemnity Insurance Co. v. Marshall, 308 S.W.2d 174 (Tex.Civ.App.1958) (similar case); C.J.S. § 461h; Annot., 8 A.L.R.3d 749. But it seems that where general moral character may be shown to impeach (see § 44 supra), habitual drunkenness is let in. Willis v. Wabash Railroad Co., 284 S.W.2d 503 (Mo. 1955) (permitted showing of incidents of drunkenness as immoral acts by cross-examination); Annot., 8 A.L.R.3d 749.

telling,[15] although more courts, absent a particular showing of effect on the witness's veracity, would exclude it.[16]   Most federal cases agree.[17]   In respect to both addictions the excluding courts seem to have the better of the arguments.   It can scarcely be contended that there is enough scientific agreement to warrant judicial notice that addiction in and of itself usually affects credibility.[18]   Certainly it is pregnant with prejudice. On the other hand, there is an increasing recognition among non-legal authorities that addiction may in various instances be linked with personality and other defects which do bear upon credibility.[19]

In recent decades with the growth in importance of psychiatry, the testimony of psychiatrists upon issues of sanity in cases of wills and crimes has become familiar to the legal profession.   Naturally, the use of expert psychiatric testimony as to mental disorders and defects suggests itself as a potential aid in determining the credibility of crucial witnesses in any kind of litigation. In one type of case, namely sex offenses, Wigmore and other commentators have urged the indispensable value of this kind of testimony, and in the past it has been approved by the courts.[20]   But Wigmore's positions that females who testify they have been sexually molested or attacked may often report such matters falsely, and that a judge should *always* be sure that the female victim—witness's social history and mental

15.   See, e.g., State v. Fong Loon, 29 Idaho 248, 158 P. 233 (1916); People v. Crump, 5 Ill.2d 251, 125 N.E.2d 615 (1955) (but in Illinois, cross-examiners must be prepared to make a showing concerning intended questions to bring out addiction; People v. Brown, 76 Ill. App.2d 362, 222 N.E.2d 227 (1966)); and see the valuable descriptions and analyses of the cases in Hale, Comment, 16 So.Calif.L.Rev. 333 (1943), and discussion and citations in 3A Wigmore, Evidence § 934 (Chadbourn rev. 1970); Annot., 52 A.L.R.2d 848; C.J.S. Witnesses § 470; Note, 1966 Utah L.Rev. 742.

16.   See e.g., Kelly v. Maryland Casualty Co., 45 F.2d 782 (W.D.Va.1929) (scholarly and comprehensive opinion by McDowell, J.), affirmed 45 F.2d 788 (4th Cir. 1930) without passing on this question, on the ground that the evidence offered did not show excessive use; People v. Smith, 4 Cal.App.3d 403, 84 Cal.Rptr. 412 (1970) (testimony as to narcotics addiction and its effects is not permitted unless it is followed by evidence that the witness attacked was under the influence at the trial, or at the time of the events to which he testifies, or that as a result his mental faculties were actually impaired); Annot., 65 A.L.R.3d 705; and see general references, next preceding note.

17.   See discussion in Weinstein & Berger, Evidence ¶ 607[04], suggesting counsel desiring to introduce drug use should first notify the court of all the details of usage and be ready to show its effect upon the credibility by expert testimony or recognized literature. The majority of federal cases have excluded evidence of general drug usage.   Compare United States v. Sampol, 636 F.2d 621 (D.C.Cir. 1980) (inquiry into general drug usage barred); United States v. Kizer, 569 F.2d 504 (9th Cir. 1978); cert. denied 435 U.S. 976, with United States v. Jackson, 576 F.2d 46 (5th Cir. 1978) (only general dictum that drug usage goes to credibility).

18.   In the *Kelly* case, supra n. 16, Judge McDowell marshals the medical opinions pro and con (45 F.2d 782, 784, 785). See also, the lengthy discussion in People v. Williams, cited below.

There is also disagreement whether expert opinion is admissible to show the effect of narcotic addiction upon credibility.   People v. Williams, 6 N.Y.2d 18, 187 N.Y.S.2d 750, 159 N.E.2d 549 (1959), cert. denied 361 U.S. 920, reviewing authorities at length.   See also Annot., 20 A.L.R.3d 684, 709.

19.   Comment 35 N.Y.U.L.Rev. 259 (1960); Mack, Forensic Psychiatry and the Witness—A Survey, 7 Clev.-Mar.L.Rev. 302, 311 (1958).

20.   See 3A Wigmore, Evidence §§ 934a, 924a, and 924b (Chadbourn rev. 1970), which substantially preserve the original Wigmore text.   The discussions are distinguished by headings related to impeachment by attack on moral character and by showing mental derangement or defects, but insofar as use of expert opinion on the "social history and mental makeup" of the complaining witness in cases charging sexual crimes is concerned, the sections are related.

Comments include the following: Machtinger, Psychiatric Impeachment in Sex Cases, 39 J.Crim.L. 750 (1949); Notes, 26 Ind.L.J. 98 (1950), 43 Iowa L.Rev. 650 (1958).

The following are pertinent cases: People v. Cowles, 246 Mich. 429, 224 N.W. 387 (1929) (evidence of doctors that the girl was a pathological liar and nymphomaniac received without objection); People v. Bastian, 330 Mich, 457, 47 N.W.2d 692 (1951); State v. Wesler, 137 N.J.L. 311, 59 A.2d 834 (1948) (testimony of doctors that girls are psychopaths and immoral and that psychopaths are prone to be untruthful did not require rejection of girls' stories); Miller v. State, 49 Okl.Cr. 133, 295 P. 403 (1930) (testimony of superintendent of insane hospital that girl, said to be nymphomaniac, was normal, admissible on credibility); Rice v. State, 195 Wis. 181, 217 N.W. 697 (1928) (indecent liberties with child; conviction set aside, relying on testimony of doctor that girl "had a mental condition calculated to induce unreal and phantom pictures in her mind").   The expert was not court-appointed in the above cases.

makeup are the subject of examination and testimony by a qualified physician, have been the subject of penetrating critical analysis of the basis for these views.[21] Most courts now hold that the matter of psychiatric testimony generally is one in the discretion of the trial judge, and many of these courts hold that the discretion to order an examination and permit such testimony should be exercised only for compelling reasons or in compelling circumstances.[22] Such circumstances are not at all clear; definite limiting conditions should at the least be de-

veloped; and in fact there is limited state authority that there should be no power at all to order a psychiatric examination and admit resulting testimony in trials for rape.[23]

Various courts have tended to take the position that there may be impeachment of principal witnesses in other cases by expert psychiatric opinion.[24] On the other hand, insofar as published opinions indicate, the federal courts have been disinclined to exercise their discretion to permit attacks by experts

---

21.　Bienen, A Question of Credibility: John Henry Wigmore's Use of Scientific Authority in Section 924a of the Treatise on Evidence, 19 Calif. Western L.Rev. 235 (1983).　Various other important articles are cited. The author emphasizes sex crimes in which young females are the victims.

22.　Among the cases indicating there should be compelling reasons for exercise of a judge's discretion to order an examination are Commonwealth v. Gibbons, 378 Mass. 766, 393 N.E.2d 400 (1979) (rape case; interpreting statute giving judge power to order an examination and considering various factors affecting that power); Washington v. State, 96 Nev. 305, 608 P.2d 1101 (1980) (implies lack of corroboration is a compelling reason); State v. Clasey, 252 Or. 22, 446 P.2d 116 (1968) (cites Ballard v. Superior Court, 64 Cal.2d 159, 49 Cal.Rptr. 302, 410 P.2d 838 (1966), as stating lack of corroboration or showing of some mental or emotional instability as compelling reason); Forbes v. State, 559 S.W.2d 318 (Tenn.1977).　See Annot. 18 A.L.R.2d 1433.

See also Government of Virgin Islands v. Scuito, 623 F.2d 869 (3d Cir. 1980) (alleged use of drugs causing some unusual behavior considered insufficient basis for examination in rape case; citing Benn below, countervailing considerations include infringement of right of privacy, trauma caused by order, possible harassment; embarrassment; deterrence of complaints by victims; see n. 23 infra); United States v. Benn, 476 F.2d 1127 (D.C.Cir. 1972) (corroborating circumstances justified failure to order examination; matter must be decided in the light of particular facts).

23.　See n. 22, supra.　Limiting conditions for an order of examination are advocated in O'Neale, Court Ordered Psychiatric Examination of a Rape Victim in a Criminal Rape Prosecution—Or How Many Times Must a Woman Be Raped? 18 Santa Clara L.Rev. 119 (1978). In State v. Clonz, 305 N.C. 116, 286 S.E.2d 793 (1982) the court in a second degree rape case held that absent statute the trial court does not have power to order a psychiatric examination of an unwilling witness, stating in part that such an order would be contrary to the public policy of a rape shield statute to prevent unnecessary intrusion into the privacy of sex crime victims.

See West's Ann.Cal. Penal Code § 1112:

"The trial court shall not order any prosecuting witness, complaining witness, or any other witness,

or victim in any sexual assault prosecution to submit to a psychiatric or psychological examination for the purpose of assessing his or her credibility."

Fed.R.Evid. 412 bars "opinion evidence of the past sexual behavior" of the victim of rape or an assault with intent to commit rape (as well as other evidence of past sexual behavior, under certain conditions).　It may be urged that such provisions bar psychiatric opinion based in any part upon "past sexual behavior," although legislative history does not specifically indicate such a conclusion.　For further material concerning Fed.R.Evid. 412, and rape shield statutes see § 44 n. 10 infra, § 193 infra.

In Scuito, supra n. 22, the appellate court mentioned that the trial judge's opinion "was not based on the letter but on the spirit of Rule 412," although it seems evident that the defense actually sought expert testimony of complainant's ability generally to perceive reality and to separate fact from fancy, rather than fantasizing about sex in particular.

24.　United States v. Hiss, 88 F.Supp. 559 (D.C.N.Y. 1950) (expert permitted to testify to diagnosis formed from courtroom observation that the star witness for the government was a psychopathic personality with "a tendency towards making false accusations"); Ingalls v. Ingalls, 257 Ala. 521, 59 So.2d 898 (1952) (doctor's opinion based upon a previous examination should have been admitted); Ellarson v. Ellarson, 198 App.Div. 103, 190 N.Y.S. 6 (1921) (doctor's opinion based upon a previous examination); State v. Burno, 200 N.C. 267, 156 S.E. 781 (1931) (opinion of an examining doctor as to mental state of prosecuting witness in prosecution for assault with intent to kill held properly admitted); Taborsky v. State, 142 Conn. 619, 116 A.2d 433 (1955) (opinion of psychiatrist in prosecution for murder, regarding hallucinations, delusions, etc. of prosecuting witness, would be admissible in a new trial); Annot., 20 A.L.R.3d 684.　However, a number of cases (primarily older cases) hold these opinions inadmissible.　See, e.g., n. 32, supra; Thompson v. Standard Wholesale Phosphate & Acid Works, 178 Md. 305, 13 A.2d 328 (1940); Mell v. State, 133 Ark. 197, 202 S.W. 33 (1918). See criticism of the earlier cases in Weihofen, Testimonial Competence and Credibility, 34 Geo.Wash.L.Rev. 53, 68 (1965).

on mental capacity affecting credibility.[25] If there is ground for believing that a principal witness is subject to some mental abnormality that may affect his credibility, a need for employment of the resources of psychiatry may exist.[26] Many courts today would accept the principle that psychiatric evidence should be received, at least in the judge's discretion, when its value outweighs the cost in time, distraction, and expense and other disadvantages.[27] The value seems to depend first upon the importance of the appraised witness's testimony, and second upon the opportunity of the expert to form a reliable opinion. This first factor, the importance of the testimony, is a relevant factor at least from the standpoint of policy considerations relating to the feasibility and desirability of subjecting witnesses (even party-witnesses) to an ordeal of psychiatric attack which may or may not be justified.[28] The above-mentioned second factor, opportunity to form a reliable opinion, raises difficulties. An opinion based solely upon a hypothetical question seems almost valueless here. Only

slightly more reliable is an opinion derived from the subject's demeanor and his testimony in the courtroom. Most psychiatrists would say that a satisfactory opinion can only be formed after the witness has been subjected to a clinical examination.[29] A discretionary power has been recognized in a few instances, granting the judge the power to order an examination of a prosecuting witness, but the conditions for exercising that discretion are unclear.[30] It seems the power to exercise discretion should exist in any type of case, to be exercised not only upon the bases of whether undue expenditure of time or expense and undue distraction will result, but also upon the bases of whether the witness is a key witness and whether there are substantial indications that the witness is suffering from mental abnormality at the time of trial or was so suffering at the time of the happening about which he testifies. Only if there is no power to order an examination should expert opinion on the bases of courtroom observation and reading

25. See, e.g., United States v. Demma, 523 F.2d 981 (9th Cir. 1975). See discussion in Weinstein & Berger, Evidence ¶ 607[04].

26. These are classified and described in comment, Psychiatric Evaluation of the Mentally Abnormal Witness, 59 Yale L.J. 1324, 1326 (1950); Weihofen, Testimonial Competence and Credibility, 34 Geo.Wash.L. Rev. 53 (1965). See suggestions for future studies in Juviler, Psychiatric Opinions as to Credibility of Witnesses: A Suggested Approach, 48 Calif.L.Rev. 648 (1960).

27. United States v. Butler, 156 U.S.App.D.C. 356, 481 F.2d 531 (1973). See discussion in People v. Williams, 6 N.Y.2d 18, 187 N.Y.S.2d 750, 159 N.E.2d 549 (1959) and Weihofen, Testimonial Competence and Credibility, 34 Geo.Wash.L.Rev. 53, 75–76 (1965). See also, Juviler, Psychiatric Opinions as to Credibility of Witnesses: A Suggested Approach, 48 Calif.L.Rev. 648 (1960). But see text at n. 25, supra.

28. Other factors should be pertinent. These include the invasion of the privacy of the witness, a showing that there is a relation between the asserted mental condition and the credibility of the witness, and the possibility of entering into collateral matter that is confusing to the jury. United States v. Lopez, 611 F.2d 44 (4th Cir. 1979) (but the court was dealing with cross-examination of the witness sought to be impeached).

29. Comment, 59 Yale L.J. 1324, at p. 1339 (1950); Note, 30 Neb.L.Rev. 513, 519 (1951); Weihofen, cited

supra, n. 26. A slashing cross-examination of the psychiatrist witness in United States v. Hiss, n. 24, supra, illustrates the difficulties of reliance upon observance of courtroom demeanor and upon a reading of the record.

30. Most of the cases seem to recognize the discretion although rejecting a contention that failure of the trial court to order an examination was an abuse of discretion. United States v. Riley, 657 F.2d l1377 (8th Cir. 1981), appeal after remand 684 F.2d 542, cert. denied 103 S.Ct. 742; United States v. Stout, 599 F.2d 866 (8th Cir. 1979), cert. denied 444 U.S. 877; United States v. Jackson, 576 F.2d 46 (5th Cir. 1978); Commonwealth v. Kosh, 305 Pa. 146, 157 A. 479 (1931); People v. Lewis, 25 Ill.2d 442, 185 N.E.2d 254 (1962); People v. Stice, 165 Cal.App.2d 287, 331 P.2d 468 (1958); State v. Cox, 352 S.W.2d 665 (Mo.1962); State v. Klueber, 81 S.D. 223, 132 N.W.2d 847 (1965); State v. Miller, 35 Wis.2d 454, 151 N.W.2d 157 (1967) (but court may not compel if witness refuses). In State v. Butler, 27 N.J. 560, 143 A.2d 530 (1958), the court stated that the state's witness should have been examined for competency and that evidence at the competency hearing would be admissible on the issue of credibility. On the other hand, for the view that the court has no power to order examination of witnesses, see State v. Walgraeve, 243 Or. 328, 412 P.2d 23 (1966), rehearing denied 243 Or. 328, 413 P.2d 609. See additional authority in Annot., 18 A.L.R.3d 1435.

of the record be considered.[31]   Even then, permitting opinion based upon such material seems very questionable.

Expert opinion on character for truthfulness or untruthfulness authorized by Federal and Revised Uniform Rule 608(a) should probably be distinguished from the subject discussed above, opinion of mental capacity to tell the truth.   Thus Rule 608(a) should not be considered direct authority for the type of opinion testimony discussed in this section.[32]

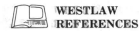

WESTLAW REFERENCES

410k327 /p drug* alcohol! addiction influence

---

§ 46. "Lie-Detectors" and "Truth Serums"

These devices offer interesting possibilities for the appraisal of the credibility of testimony—possibilities which have been realized to some extent in out-of-court investigations, and which may in the future be somehow directly utilized by the courts. They are discussed in the chapter on experimental and scientific evidence.[1]

§ 47. Impeachment by "Contradiction": Disproving the Facts Testified to by the First Witness [1]

"Contradiction" may be explained as follows.   Statements are elicited from Witness One, who has testified to a material story of an accident, crime, or other matters, to the effect that at the time he witnessed these matters the day was windy and cold and he, the witness, was wearing his green sweater. Let us suppose these latter statements about the day and the sweater to be "disproved."   This may happen in several ways. Witness One on direct or cross-examination may acknowledge that he was in error.   Or judicial notice may be taken that at the time and place it could not have been cold and windy, e.g., in Tucson in July.   But commonly disproof or "contradiction" is attempted by calling Witness Two to testify to the contrary, i.e., that the day was warm and Witness One was in his shirt-sleeves.   It is in this latter sense that the term "contradiction" is used in this section.[2]

What impeaching value does the contradiction have in the above situation?   It merely tends to show—for Witness One may be right and Witness Two may be mistaken— that Witness One has erred or falsified as to certain particular facts, and therefore is capable of error or lying, and this should be considered negatively in weighing his other

---

§ 47

---

31. See similar suggestion, Weihofen, Testimonial Competence and Credibility, 34 Geo.Wash.L.Rev. 53, 77–78 (1965).

32. It could be urged that the suggested distinction would often be merely verbal because an expert speaking in terms of opinion of "character" for truthfulness or untruthfulness would only be speaking of mental or emotional conditions associated with mental capacity for truth-telling but in a more direct way.   Whether there could be expertise on "character" for veracity might be questionable in many individual instances. Whether the jury would be aided by such claimed expertise might also be questionable in many instances. For a discussion of other difficulties in attempting to use expert opinion of character for truthfulness or untruthfulness, see Louisell & Mueller, Federal Evidence § 304.

§ 46

1. For discussion of detection of deception, see § 206 at nn. 18–61 infra.

1. 3A Wigmore, Evidence §§ 1000–1007 (Chadbourn rev. 1970); Weinstein & Berger, Evidence ¶ 607[05]; Dec.Dig. Witnesses ⚖➔398–409; C.J.S. Witnesses §§ 629–644.

The extent to which evidence obtained in violation of a constitutional right may be used to impeach is treated in § 178 infra.   The use of treatises to impeach experts is dealt with in § 321 infra.

2. In the courtroom and in the cases "contradiction" is loosely extended to include impeachment by proof of a prior inconsistent statement of the first witness ("self-contradiction").   See, e.g., Calley v. Boston & Maine Railroad Co., 92 N.H. 455, 33 A.2d 227 (1943). The proof by a second witness of the prior inconsistent statement usually entails a contradiction too, but it is the witness's inconsistency that is the heart of the attack.   See § 37 supra.

statements. But all human beings have this capacity and all testimony should be discounted to some extent for this weakness. It is true that the trial judge in his discretion may permit the cross-examiner to conduct a general test of the power of Witness One to observe, remember and recount facts unrelated to the case, to "test" or "explore" these capacities.[3] To permit a dispute, however, about such extraneous or "collateral" facts as the weather and the clothing of Witness One, that are material only for "testing" the witness, by allowing the attacker to call other witnesses to disprove them, is not practical. Dangers of surprise, of confusion of the jury's attention,[4] and of time-wasting[5] are apparent.

Therefore, many courts maintain the safeguarding rule that a witness may not be impeached by producing extrinsic evidence of "collateral" facts to "contradict" the first witness's assertions about those facts.[6] If the collateral fact sought to be contradicted is elicited on cross-examination, this safeguarding rule is often expressed by saying that the answer is conclusive or that the cross-examiner must "take the answer."[7] By the better view, if the "collateral" fact happens to have been drawn out on direct, the rule against contradiction should still be applied.[8] The danger of surprise is lessened, but waste of time and confusion of issues stand as objections.

What is to be regarded here as within this protean word of art, "collateral"? The inquiry is best answered by determining what facts are not within the term, and thus finding the escapes from the prohibition against contradicting upon collateral facts. The classical approach is that facts which would have been independently provable regardless of the contradiction are not "collateral."[9] This test has been recognized by some federal courts.[10]

Two general kinds of facts meet the test. The first kind are facts that are relevant to

---

3. See § 29 supra.

4. ". . . Witnesses are not expected to come prepared to sustain all the statements they have made upon subjects not involved in the controversy, and because its admission would involve the trial of too many issues as to the truth of the statements the determination of which would at last have little effect upon the decision of the cause." Williams, J., in Gulf, Colorado & Santa Fe Railway Co. v. Matthews, 100 Tex. 63, 93 S.W. 1068, 1070 (1906).

This is one of the very things that Fed. and Rev. Unif.R.Evid. (1974) 403 are designed to guard against. See also n. 27, infra.

5. "If we lived for a thousand years, instead of about sixty or seventy, and every case were of sufficient importance, it might be possible and perhaps proper to throw a light on matters in which every possible question might be suggested, for the purpose of seeing by such means whether the whole was unfounded, or what portion of it was not, and to raise every possible inquiry as to the truth of the statements made. But I do not see how that could be; in fact, mankind find it to be impossible. Therefore, some line must be drawn." Rolfe, B. in Attorney General v. Hitchcock, 1 Exch. 104, 154 Eng.Rep. 38 (1847). See n. 4, supra. See also n. 27, infra.

6. Klein v. Keresey, 307 Mass. 51, 29 N.E.2d 703 (1940); C.J.S. Witnesses § 633, note 87.

The prohibition against contradiction as to collateral matters is one of the concepts gathered together in Rule 403. Dolan, Rule 403: The Prejudice Rule in Evidence, 49 So.Cal.L.Rev. 220 (1976). See n. 27, infra.

The rule against impeaching on collateral matters may, however, on occasion yield to the theory that inadmissible evidence may be rebutted by evidence which otherwise would be inadmissible. See § 57 infra.

7. Howard v. State, 234 Md. 410, 199 A.2d 611 (1964); C.J.S. Witnesses § 633, note 88.

8. Lambert v. Hamlin, 73 N.H. 138, 59 A. 941 (1905); State v. Price, 92 W.Va. 542, 115 S.E. 393, 405 (1922); 3A Wigmore, Evidence § 1007 (Chadbourn rev. 1970). But many courts hold to the contrary. See, e.g., Howell v. State, 141 Ark. 487, 217 S.W. 457 (1920) (carnal knowledge; testimony of complainant on direct that she had never had intercourse with anyone but defendant should have been allowed to be contradicted, distinguishing situation where brought out on cross-examination) and cases cited Wigmore, ibid. and C.J.S. Witnesses § 633, n. 6. See § 57 infra.

9. State v. Kouzounas, 137 Me. 198, 17 A.2d 147 (1941); State v. Oswalt, 62 Wn.2d 118, 381 P.2d 617 (1963); 3A Wigmore, Evidence § 1003 (Chadbourn rev. 1970); C.J.S. Witnesses § 633b.

The same test of "collateralness" of subject matter is applied to impeachment by prior inconsistent statements. See § 36, supra; 3A Wigmore, Evidence § 1020 (Chadbourn rev. 1970).

10. See, e.g. United States v. Pisari, 636 F.2d 855 (1st Cir. 1981) (particular evidence said to be collateral). For suggested treatment under Fed.R.Evid. and Rev. Unif.R.Evid. (1974) see n. 27, infra.

the substantive issues in the case.[11] It may seem strained to label this proof of relevant facts with the terms, "contradiction" or "impeachment." But it does have the dual aspect of relevant proof and of reflecting on the credibility of contrary witnesses.[12] Here the "contradiction" theory has at least one practical consequence, namely, it permits contradicting proof, which without the contradiction would be confined to the case in chief, to be brought out in rebuttal.[13]

The second kind of facts meeting the above mentioned test for facts that are not collateral includes facts which would be independently provable by extrinsic evidence, apart from the contradiction, to impeach or disqualify the witness.[14] Among these are facts showing bias, interest,[15] conviction of

crime,[16] and want of capacity or opportunity for knowledge. This doctrine has been recognized in federal cases.[17] Facts showing misconduct of the witness (for which no conviction has been had) are not within this second kind of facts, but are collateral, and if denied on cross-examination cannot be proved to contradict.[18]

Finally, a third kind of fact must be considered. Suppose a witness has told a story of a transaction crucial to the controversy. To prove him wrong in some trivial detail of time, place or circumstance is "collateral." But to prove untrue some fact recited by the witness that if he were really there and saw what he claims to have seen, he could not have been mistaken about, is a convincing kind of impeachment that the courts must

11. Examples: Louisville Taxicab & Transfer Co. v. Tungent's Administrator, 313 Ky. 1, 229 S.W.2d 985 (1950) (in action for death of one riding in truck struck by defendant's taxicab at street intersection, testimony as to decedent's and truck driver's drunkenness at time of collision was admissible as bearing on questions of negligence and credibility of driver, who testified that neither she nor decedent drank any liquor during morning before collision); Thompson v. Walsh, 203 Okl. 453, 223 P.2d 357 (1950) (in action for injury to and death of cattle from drinking salt water negligently permitted to escape from defendants' oil lease testimony that salt water was seen running from defendants' wells into creek on day before trial was permissible to impeach the testimony of a defendant that salt water never escaped from the lease into the creek).

12. Thus, the case law limitation upon impeaching one's own witness does not prevent a party from contradicting his own witness by adducing contrary proof as to a material fact. Talley v. Richart, 353 Mo. 912, 185 S.W.2d 23 (1945); Dec.Dig. Witnesses ☞400, and see § 38, supra.

13. People v. Jeffrey, 233 Cal.App.2d 279, 43 Cal. Rptr. 524 (1965); Hensley v. Commonwealth, 264 Ky. 718, 95 S.W.2d 564 (1936) (wounding with intent to kill: where defendant said, on cross, that he did not remember whether he made a threat, evidence that he did threaten admissible, not only in chief, but in rebuttal, to contradict). See also United States v. Calvert, 523 F.2d 895 (8th Cir. 1975), cert. denied 424 U.S. 911 (dictum: but it is in trial court's discretion to exclude such evidence of the prosecution in rebuttal if the prosecution has been "lying in the weeds," waiting to contradict rather than presenting the evidence in the case in chief).

14. 3A Wigmore, Evidence § 1005 (Chadbourn rev. 1970). See n. 17 infra.

15. State v. Kouzounas, 137 Me. 198, 17 A.2d 147 (1941) (accused in arson prosecution, who had been

charged by witness with offering money to get him to change his testimony, denied on cross-examination that he visited lawyer with this witness; held, state may contradict this denial by evidence of lawyer that accused came to his office with witness). See § 40 supra.

16. Storer v. State, 84 Okl.Cr. 176, 180 P.2d 202 (1947). See § 43 supra.

17. See United States v. Robinson, 530 F.2d 1076 (D.C.Cir. 1976) (evidence showing bias); Annot., 60 A.L.R.Fed. 8. The Federal and Revised Uniform Rules of Evidence are not specific, but matters of this nature clearly fall within the definition of "relevancy" in Rule 401.

18. People v. Rosenthal, 289 N.Y. 482, 46 N.E.2d 895 (1943) (accused was asked on cross-examination about other like crimes, and denied them, held state cannot produce other witnesses to contradict); State v. Broom, 222 N.C. 324, 22 S.E.2d 926 (1942) (similar); Commonwealth v. Boggio, 204 Pa.Super. 434, 205 A.2d 694 (1964) (party cannot contradict answer to question whether witness ever had intercourse with another man). See § 42 supra.

Fed. and Rev.Unif.R.Evid. (1974) 608(b) contain the following provision:

Specific instances of the conduct of a witness, for the purpose of attacking or supporting his credibility, other than conviction of crime as provided in rule 609, may not be proved by extrinsic evidence. They may, however, in the discretion of the court, if probative of truthfulness or untruthfulness, be inquired into on cross-examination of the witness (1) concerning his character for truthfulness or untruthfulness, or (2) concerning the character for truthfulness or untruthfulness of another witness as to which character the witness being cross-examined has testified.

make place for, although the contradiction evidence is otherwise inadmissible because it is collateral under the tests mentioned above. To disprove such a fact is to pull out the linchpin of the story. So we may recognize this third type of allowable contradiction, namely, the contradiction of any part of the witness's account of the background and circumstances of a material transaction, which as a matter of human experience he would not have been mistaken about if his story were true.[19] This test is of necessity a vague one because it must meet an indefinite variety of situations, and consequently in its application a reasonable latitude of discretionary judgment must be accorded to the trial judge.[20] The Federal Rules of Evidence should permit such evidence in the discretion of the judge.[21]

Of course, the contradicting witness may simply state the facts as he asserts them, without reference to the prior testimony which is being contradicted. It seems, however, that where appropriate the contradiction may be more direct. Thus it would seem acceptable to recite in the question the pertinent part of the prior testimony of the first witness, and inquire, "What do you say as to the correctness of this statement?"[22]

The application of the standard theory of collateral contradiction discussed in this section has been criticized for use under the Federal Rules of Evidence on the ground that the result is a mechanically applied doctrine without consideration of properly pertinent matters. It is thus urged that the discretionary approach of Rule 403 should be substituted.[23] However, various federal

---

19. East Tennessee, Virginia & Georgia Railway Co. v. Daniel, 91 Ga. 768, 18 S.E. 22 (1893) (witness of alleged killing of mule at crossing accounted for his presence by saying he left home to get some tobacco, going to a certain store and getting the tobacco on credit, and on his way home he saw the accident; adversary offered evidence of store-keeper that witness did not buy tobacco at that time, held, erroneously excluded, "it was indirectly material because it contradicted the witness as to the train of events which led him to be present"); Stephens v. People, 19 N.Y. 549, 572 (1859) (murder by poisoning with arsenic; defendant's witnesses testified the arsenic was administered to rats in cellar where provisions kept; held proper for state to prove by another witness that no provisions were kept in cellar, "not strictly collateral"); Gulf, Colorado & Santa Fe Railway Co. v. Matthews, 100 Tex. 63, 93 S.W. 1068, 1070 (1906) (suit for death of M., run over by train; controverted issue was whether M. was sober and walking or drunk and lying on tracks; A., a hotel clerk, crucial witness for plaintiff, said M. left hotel early in morning, sober: foul play in the death of M. was publicly suspected; A. said on cross-examination that he had never mentioned M.'s presence and departure from hotel except a couple of times to one W.; defendant offered evidence that A. when he gave above testimony by deposition believed W. was dead, and produced W. and offered proof by him that A. had never told him about M.'s presence in the hotel; held exclusion of defendant's evidence was error. "Evidence therefore which bears upon the story of a witness with sufficient directness and force to give it appreciable value in determining whether or not that story is true cannot be said to be addressed to an irrelevant or collateral issue. . . . The effort of the defendant was . . . to maintain its contention that he had never told any one; and that fact being relevant, the defendant had the right, we think, to meet his apparent effort to break its force." Hartsfield v. Caroli-

na Casualty Insurance Co., 451 P.2d 576 (Alaska 1969) (on issue whether insurance cancellation notice was sent to defendant by insurer, defendant denied receipt and also receipt of notices of cancellations of the insurance from two other sources. Evidence of the mailing by the two latter sources was held not collateral.

20. The cases dealing with discretion in the field of contradiction seem to go further than the text. Some imply that the trial judge has a discretion to decide what is and is not "collateral." Radio Cab, Inc. v. Houser, 128 F.2d 604 (D.C.Cir. 1942). Others suggest that even if "collateral" the judge has a discretion to permit the contradiction. Salem News Co. v. Caliga, 144 F. 965 (1st Cir. 1906); Todd v. Bradley, 99 Conn. 307, 122 A. 68 (1923); Lizotte v. Warren, 302 Mass. 317, 19 N.E.2d 60 (1939) (self-contradiction by party). See cases collected in C.J.S. Witnesses § 633a, n. 1.

21. There appears to be no case explicitly discussing this test. But Fed. and Rev.Unif.R.Evid. (1974) 401 should permit it subject to the exercise of the trial court's discretion under Fed. and Rev.Unif.R.Evid. (1974) 403. In this situation the thrust of the inquiry, it should be noted, is directly whether the witness is telling the truth in this case, and not whether he has a character of being truthful, which is the kind of exploration contemplated by Rule 608(b).

22. See Uhlman v. Farm Stock & Home Co., 126 Minn. 239, 148 N.W. 102 (1914) and compare Scoggins v. Turner, 98 N.C. 135, 3 S.E. 719, 723 (1887). Cases are collected in C.J.S. Witnesses § 638.

23. Speaking of "Recasting the 'collateral matter' rule into a rule of discretion . . . ," Weinstein & Berger, Evidence ¶ 607[05] concludes, "The Federal Rules, while silent on the subject of impeachment by contradiction, should be used to reach results analogous to those reached under the [former] Uniform

opinions do mention "collateral" evidence.[24] Basically, Federal Rules of Evidence 401–403, which do govern impeachment by contradiction,[25] are entirely consistent with the "collateral" doctrine as discussed in this section, except that Rule 403 is explicit in the discretion granted the trial judge to admit or exclude contradictions found relevant under Rule 401.[26]

Of course, the label, "collateral" should not be used mechanically.[27]

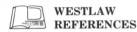

WESTLAW REFERENCES

impeach /s extrinsic /s collateral

Rules by substituting the discretion approach of Rule 403 for the collateral test advocated by case law."

24. See, e.g., United States v. Pisari, n. 10 supra.

25. Some opinions do mention the discretionary approach of applying Rule 403. See, e.g., Barrera v. E.I. Du Pont de Nemours and Co., Inc., 653 F.2d 915 (5th Cir. 1981), rehearing denied 661 F.2d 931.

26. See § 185, infra, for text of Fed.R.Evid. and Rev.Unif.R.Evid. (1974) 401–403.

27. An analysis of the language and of the Advisory Committee's Notes for Rules 401–403 indicates the intention that the discretion expressly granted by Rule 403 applies to evidence found relevant under Rule 401. See mention of the practical discretion of the judge under Rule 401 and the official discretion of the judge under Rule 403 in Wright & Graham, Federal Practice and Procedure: Evidence, § 5165. The use of the label, "collateral," in the context of the impeaching effect of contradictions, in effect merely adopts Rules 401 and 402, and it seems fairly obvious that Rule 403 is applicable as well. A position that Rule 403 is alone governing would thus not be compatible with the above view of Rules 401–403. Actually, as indicated in n. 20, discretion has played a part under the case law label, "collateral," and although that label in the past has sometimes been used without explanation and apparently mechanically, it cannot obscure the fact that the judge has the discretion granted by Rule 403 and the practical discretion existing under Rules 401 and 402.

§ 48

1. See 2 Wigmore, Evidence § 518 (Chadbourn rev. 1979) (competency), 3A id. § 936 (Chadbourn rev. 1970) (impeachment), 8 id. § 2213 (McNaughton rev. 1961) (privilege); Weinstein & Berger, Evidence ¶ 603[01] et seq., ¶ 610[01]; Comment by Chadbourn on State v. Beal, 199 N.C. 278, 154 S.E. 604, 1930, 9 N.C.L.Rev. 77 (1930); Annot., 95 A.L.R. 723; Swancara, Impeachment of Non-Religious Witnesses, 13 Rocky Mt.L.Rev. 336

§ 48. Beliefs Concerning Religion [1]

As indicated in a subsequent section,[2] the common law required as a qualification for taking the oath as a witness, the belief in a God who would punish untruth. This rule grew up in a climate of custom and assumptions which today seem primitive and archaic. It has quite generally been abandoned in most common law jurisdictions. General provisions like that in the Illinois constitution to the effect that "no person shall be denied any civil or political rights, privilege or capacity on account of his religious opinions"[3] have been construed in many states to abrogate the rule of incompetency to take the oath.[4] Nor is belief in God required by the Federal Rules of Evidence.[5]

(1941). Dec.Dig. Witnesses ⚓340(2); C.J.S. Witnesses § 511.

2. See § 63 infra.

3. Starks v. Schlensky, 128 Ill.App. 1, 4 (1906). Illinois constitutions have contained this provision since 1818.

4. See the constitutional and statutory provisions, and decisions interpreting them, from twenty-four states, compiled in 70 C.J. 98, 99, note 76, and see § 63 infra. A compilation of specific references to the articles and sections of the constitutions dealing with Witnesses appears in 3 Constitutions, 1813 (1938) published by N.Y. State Const. Committee. Forty jurisdictions are listed as having abolished by statute or constitutional provision the requirement for witnesses of religious belief. Torpey, Judicial Doctrines of Religious Rights 278 (1948).

5. Fed.R.Evid. 601 provides:

Every person is competent to be a witness except as otherwise provided in these rules. However, in civil actions and proceedings, with respect to an element of a claim or defense as to which State law supplies the rule of decision, the competency of a witness shall be determined in accordance with State law.

The corresponding revised Uniform Rule consists of only the first sentence.

Fed.R.Evid. and Rev.Unif.R.Evid. (1974) 603 provides,

Before testifying, every witness shall be required to declare that he will testify truthfully, by oath or affirmation administered in a form calculated to awaken his conscience and impress his mind with his duty to do so.

See Advisory Committee's Note.

Neither set of rules contains any competency requirement of religious belief.

The general tendency, as indicated in Sections 43 and 65, has been to convert the old grounds of incompetency to testify, such as interest and infamy, into grounds of impeaching credibility, and this principle of conversion has sometimes been expressly enacted in constitutional provisions and in statutes.[6] Should the principle be applied so as to permit the credibility of a witness to be attacked by showing that he is an atheist or an agnostic and does not believe in Divine punishment for perjury? The greater number of courts that answered the question at all said no, either by interpreting general provisions such as that quoted above from the Illinois constitution, or by mandate of specific constitutional, statutory, or rule language.[7] Thus many states recognize a privilege of the witness not to be examined about his own religious faith or beliefs, except so far as the judge in his discretion [8] finds that the relevance of the inquiry upon some substantive issue in the case outweighs the interest of privacy and the danger of prejudice.[9] A few, either reasoning from the conversion of grounds of incompetency into grounds for impeachment or following

specific provisions, may allow this ground of impeachment.[10] It is to be observed, however, that the common law analogy would not extend to permit inquiry into particular creeds, faiths or affiliations except as they shed light on the witness's belief in a God who will punish untruth.[11]

There is a strong reason why the legislatures and courts should, in addition to recognizing the privilege of a witness not to answer to his own religious beliefs, forbid the party to impeach by bringing other witnesses to attack the faith of the first one. This reason of course is that there is no basis for believing that the lack of faith in God's avenging wrath is today an indication of greater than average untruthfulness. Without that basis, the evidence of atheism is simply irrelevant upon the question of credibility.[12]

Federal and Revised Uniform Rule of Evidence (1974) 610 provides:

Evidence of the beliefs or opinions of a witness on matters of religion is not admissible for the purpose of showing that by reason of

6. Chadbourn, Comment, 9 N.C.L.Rev. 77, 78 n. 5 (1930).

7. Government of Virgin Islands v. Petersen, 553 F. 2d 324 (3d Cir. 1977); Annot., 76 A.L.R.3d 539.

8. Searcy v. Miller, 57 Iowa 613, 621, 10 N.W. 912, 916 (1881) ("He is not to be questioned as to his religious belief . . ."); Commonwealth v. Burke, 82 Mass. 33 (1860) (improper to question witness about his beliefs on voir dire or on cross-examination, despite statute permitting impeachment on this ground); Free v. Buckingham, 59 N.H. 219, 225 (1879) ("This is not because the inquiry might tend to disgrace him, but because it would be a personal scrutiny into the state of his faith and conscience, contrary to the spirit of our institutions"); 8 Wigmore, Evidence § 2213 (McNaughton rev. 1961).

9. Examples of situations where relevancy did outweigh: McKim v. Philadelphia Transportation Co., 364 Pa. 237, 72 A.2d 122 (1950) (under statute recognizing privilege judge properly permitted cross-examination of personal injury plaintiffs to show they were ministers in Jehovah's Witnesses sect and what their duties were, on issue of damages); Fort Worth & Denver City Railway Co. v. Travis, 45 Tex.Civ.App. 117, 99 S.W. 1141 (1907) (personal injury plaintiff could be cross-examined as to her beliefs as Christian Scientist, as to suffering, and as to whether her faith caused her not to take medicine prescribed). But compare cases

where inquiry into the plaintiff's faith as Christian Scientist was found not to be sufficiently relevant to the substantive issues. City of Montgomery v. Wyche, 169 Ala. 181, 53 So. 786 (1910); Adams v. Carlo, 101 S.W.2d 753 (Mo.App.1937).

10. Allen v. Guarante, 253 Mass. 152, 148 N.E. 461 (1925) and decisions cited from Georgia, Indiana, Iowa, and Massachusetts in Annot., 95 A.L.R. 726. Most of the cases, however, are obsolete.

11. "The credibility of witnesses can be affected only by evidence of their disbelief in the existence of God. . . . Adherence to any particular sect is no basis for argument in this respect." Allen v. Guarante, 253 Mass. 152, 148 N.E. 461, 462 (1925).

12. "Unorthodox religious convictions, even though they extend to the extremes of agnosticism and atheism, may quite often exist because of honest intellectual doubts. It is untenable to argue that there is a correlation between this kind of unorthodoxy and inveracity. That correlation which may exist between what Pope calls 'blind unbelief' and untruthfulness is so slight that the value of the evidence is outweighed by the possibilities for prejudice with which it is pregnant." Chadbourn, Comment, 9 N.C.L.Rev. 77, 81 (1930).

Fed.R.Evid. and Rev.Unif.R.Evid. (1974) 610, n. 7 supra.

their nature his credibility is impaired or en-hanced.[13]

**WESTLAW
REFERENCES**

credibility impeach!   /p   religi! atheis* agnostic!

§ 49. Supporting the Witness

Impeachment is not a dispassionate study of the capacities and character of the witness, but is regarded in our tradition as an *attack* upon his credibility. Under our ad-

versary system of trials the opponent must be given an opportunity to meet this attack by evidence sustaining or rehabilitating the witness. One general principle, operative under both case law and the Federal Rules of Evidence, is that in the absence of an attack upon credibility no sustaining evidence is allowed.[1] A second truism is that when there has been evidence of impeaching facts the proponent may bring contradictory evidence asserting the untruth of the alleged impeaching facts. Such a denial is always relevant and generally allowable.[2]

13. The Advisory Committee's Note to the Federal Rule points out that the rule does not bar disclosure of affiliation with a church which is a party to the litigation for the purpose of showing interest or bias.

§ 49

1. United States v. Jackson, 588 F.2d 1046 (5th Cir. 1979), rehearing denied 591 F.2d 1343, cert. denied 442 U.S. 941 (reputation for truthfulness; see Fed.R.Evid. and Rev.Unif.R.Evid. (1974) 608(a), which provides in part, ". . . (2) evidence of truthful character is admissible only after the character of the witness for truthfulness has been attacked by opinion or reputation evidence or otherwise."); United States v. Awkard, 597 F.2d 667 (9th Cir. 1979), cert. denied 444 U.S. 885 (bolstering of witness by calling expert on hypnosis); State v. Harmon, 278 S.W. 733 (Mo.1925) (testimony offered to support unimpeached character for truth of accused as witness, properly excluded); McPherson v. State, 271 Ala. 533, 125 So.2d 709 (1960) (defendant properly refused permission to show good reputation of a defense witness for truth and veracity); State v. Parsons, 83 N.J.Super. 430, 200 A.2d 340 (1964) (state properly refused permission to support state's witness by showing he changed his story after being shown results of a polygraph test, thus anticipating an attack on the credibility of the state's witness); Martin v. Crow, 372 S.W.2d 724 (Tex.Civ.App.1963) (not error to refuse to permit plaintiff's witness to testify that he had no interest in the suit); Annot., 15 A.L.R. 1065, 33 id. 1220; Annot., 55 A.L.R.Fed. 440; C.J.S. Witnesses § 471.

The exclusion of character-support, in the absence of attack, is frequently explained as the corollary of a presumption that the character of the witness is good. See, e.g., Johnson v. State, 129 Wis. 146, 108 N.W. 55, 58 (1906). 4 Wigmore, Evidence § 1104 n. 1 (Chadbourn rev. 1972), says that the character is simply unknown.

It has been held that an act done by the witness which is consistent with his testimony about the main fact is admissible, even in the absence of attack, as corroborating the testimony. State v. Slocinski, 89 N.H. 262, 197 A. 560 (1938) (witness to arson threat, allowed to testify that he reported the threat to the police and to his own lawyer, at the time it was made). Such evidence may often be justified as furnishing relevant cor-

roboratory evidence. Mahoney v. Minsky, 39 N.J. 208, 188 A.2d 161 (1963) (testimony by witness that he made a cash payment of $2500 and cashed a check to obtain the cash amount; error to refuse admission of the check).

Nor can the party, per se, bolster his witness by proof, in the case in chief, that the witness has previously told the same story that he tells on the stand. Newton v. State, 147 Tex.Cr.R. 400, 180 S.W.2d 946 (1944) (prosecuting witness in attempted murder, where issue is identity of assailant, allowed to recite his report to guests of identity of telephone caller on night of attack, held error); State v. Herrera, 236 Or. 1, 386 P.2d 448 (1963) (prosecution witness' prior consistent statement was admitted; error, however, was not reversible error because defendant later impeached the witness); 4 Wigmore, Evidence § 1124 (Chadbourn rev. 1972). This can be justified on grounds of saving of time, by avoiding a defense of the witness before a need for one appears. In addition, the prior statement may be inadmissible as proof on the issues because it is hearsay for that purpose. However, if the statement is offered to meet an express or implied charge of recent fabrication or improper influence or motive, Fed. R.Evid. and Rev.Unif.R.Evid. (1974) 801(d)(1)(B) provide that the statement is not hearsay. See § 251 infra. But when the principal fact to which this "bolstering" evidence is addressed is later denied by the adversary's witness (as in the *Newton* case cited above), does this furnish the "attack" and convert the present point into one of mere order of proof? Usually mere contradiction in relevant testimony is not an attack. See text at n. 12, infra.

2. Thus, evidence of bad character to impeach may be rebutted by evidence of good character. See Fed.R. Evid. and Rev.Unif.R.Evid. (1974) 608(a) quoted in part in n. 1 supra; Prentiss v. Roberts, 49 Me. 127, 137 (1860); 4 Wigmore, Evidence § 1105 (Chadbourn rev. 1972); C.J.S. Witnesses § 534. Some courts at least permit a summary denial or explanation by the witness of guilt where he has been impeached by conviction. See § 43 notes 41, 42 supra; C.J.S. Witnesses § 534. Facts showing bias may of course be denied, 4 Wigmore, Evidence § 1119 (Chadbourn rev. 1972), or explained, United States v. Mitchell, 556 F.2d 371 (6th Cir. 1977), cert. denied 434 U.S. 925; People v. Burke, 52 Ill.App.2d 159, 201 N.E.2d 636 (1964). See also,

A discussion of rehabilitation and support of witnesses is more readily organized around the techniques employed than in terms of principle, just as was seen to be the case with respect to impeachment. The two most common specific methods that are attempted are (1) introduction of supportive evidence of good character of the witness attacked, and (2) introduction of consistent statements of the witness who has been attacked. The most common rehabilitation problem is whether these two types of rehabilitation evidence may be introduced in connection with the various methods of impeachment that have been attempted, as outlined in the previous sections of this chapter. The general test for solution is whether evidence of the good character of the witness or of his consistent statements is

logically relevant to explain the impeaching fact. The rehabilitating facts must meet a particular method of impeachment with relative directness. The wall, attacked at one point, may not be fortified at another and distinct point.[3] Credibility is a side issue and the circle of relevancy in this context may well be drawn narrowly. How narrowly is a question of degree as to which reasonable courts differ.

When may the party supporting the witness, who has been attacked by one of the impeachment methods discussed in this chapter, offer evidence of good character of the witness for truth? Certainly attacks by evidence of bad reputation,[4] bad opinion of character for truthfulness,[5] conviction of crime,[6] or eliciting from the witness on

United States v. Brown, 547 F.2d 438 (8th Cir. 1977), cert. denied 430 U.S. 937 (proper to admit extrinsic evidence to rebut incident relied upon to show bias (cf. United States v. Scholle, 553 F.2d 1109 (8th Cir. 1977)), (cert. denied 434 U.S. 940); Ryan v. Dwyer, 33 A.D.2d 878, 307 N.Y.S.2d 565 (1969) (party calling witness may prove any fact tending to show absence of interest or bias of witness; here after a showing that witness settled a claim with plaintiff, arising out of the accident, a similar settlement with defendant may be proved). The making of an inconsistent statement may also be denied or explained. Tri-State Transfer Co. v. Nowotny, 198 Minn. 537, 270 N.W. 684 (1936) (rebutting witness may testify that complaint introduced as inconsistent statement of former witness, was not drawn by him but by attorney); Ryan v. Dwyer, cited supra (witness may explain inconsistent statement; dictum that he may deny making it). See also, United States v. Holland, 526 F.2d 284 (5th Cir. 1976), on rehearing 537 F.2d 821, rehearing denied 541 F.2d 281 (later correction of misstatement before grand jury).

The general statement in the text finds support under the Federal and Revised Uniform Rules in the fact that such evidence undoubtedly falls within the definition of "relevant evidence" in Rule 401.

It seems clear from the context of Rule 608(b) and from the tenor of the federal Advisory Committee's Note, that the limitations on the use of specific instances of conduct therein are intended to apply only with respect to character for truthfulness, not with respect to other kinds of attacks on credibility, such as bias or motive to falsify. For text of Rule 608(b) see § 42, n. 5 supra. Compare United States v. Scholle, supra.

3. See Holmes, J., in Gertz v. Fitchburg Railroad Co., 137 Mass. 77, 78 (1884). In holding that the plaintiff, impeached as a witness by conviction of crime, could give evidence of his good reputation for truth, he said: "We think that the evidence of his reputation for

truth should have been admitted, and that the exception must be sustained. There is a clear distinction between this case and those in which such evidence has been held inadmissible, for instance, to rebut evidence of contradictory statements; Russell v. Coffin, 8 Pick. 143; Brown v. Mooers, 6 Gray 451; or where the witness is directly contradicted as to the principal fact by other witnesses. Atwood v. Dearborn, 1 Allen, 483.

"In such cases, it is true that the result sought to be reached is the same as in the present,—to induce the jury to disbelieve the witness. But the mode of reaching the result is different. For, while contradiction or proof of contradictory statements may very well have the incidental effect of impeaching the character for truth of the contradicted witness in the minds of the jury, the proof is not directed to that point. The purpose and only direct effect of the evidence are to show that the witness is not to be believed in this instance. But the reason why he is not to be believed is left untouched. That may be found in forgetfulness on the part of the witness, or in his having been deceived, or in any other possible cause. The disbelief sought to be produced is perfectly consistent with an admission of his general good character for truth, as well as for the other virtues; and until the character of a witness is assailed, it cannot be fortified by evidence."

4. See n. 2 supra and Fed.R.Evid. 608(a), Advisory Committee's Note.

5. Fed.R.Evid. 608(a) and Advisory Committee's Note.

6. See n. 3, supra; Fed.R.Evid. 608(a), Advisory Committee's Note. See likewise Derrick v. Wallace, 217 N.Y. 520, 112 N.E. 440 (1916); C.J.S. Witnesses § 534; 4 Wigmore, Evidence § 1106 (Chadbourn rev. 1972). But see Commonwealth v. Ford, 199 Pa.Super. 102, 184 A.2d 401 (1962) (affirming rejection of reputation evidence and stating matter was within the discretion of the trial judge).

cross-examination acknowledgment of misconduct which has not resulted in conviction,[7] will all open the door to character support. The evidence of good character for truth is logically relevant to meet these kinds of impeachment. Moreover, a slashing cross-examination may carry strong accusations of misconduct and bad character, which the witness's denial will not remove from the jury's mind. If the judge considers that fairness requires it, he may permit evidence of good character, a mild palliative for the rankle of insinuation by such cross-examination.[8]

Corrupt conduct of a witness of a sort to show bias should also seemingly be regarded as including an attack on veracity-character and thus warranting character support,[9] but impeachment for bias or interest by

facts not involving corruption, such as proof of family relationship,[10] may not be met by proof of good character for truth.

Attempts to support the witness by showing his good character for truth have resulted in contradictory conclusions when the witness has been impeached by evidence of an inconsistent statement, or has been met by the adversary's evidence denying the facts to which the witness has so testified. If the witness has been impeached by the introduction of an inconsistent statement, the greater number of courts permit a showing of his good character for truth,[11] but if the adversary has merely introduced evidence denying the facts to which the witness testified, the greater number of cases will not permit a showing of the witness's good character for truth.[12] Convenient as automatic

---

7. Fed.R.Evid. 608(a), Advisory Committee's Note; First National Bank v. Blakeman, 19 Okl. 106, 91 P. 868 (1907) ("when the witness has been impeached by evidence of particular acts of criminal or moral misconduct, either on cross-examination or by record of conviction," citing cases); 4 Wigmore, Evidence § 1106 (Chadbourn rev. 1972).

8. United States v. Scholle, 553 F.2d 1109 (8th Cir. 1977), cert. denied 434 U.S. 940 (dictum); Harris v. State, 49 Tex.Cr.R. 338, 94 S.W. 227 (1906) (most rigid cross-examination, in a manner tending to bring witness into disrepute before jury and indirectly attack his testimony). See also Commonwealth v. Ingraham, 73 Mass. (7 Gray) 46, 49 (1856) which sanctions proof of good character after a mere abortive attempt to prove the witness's bad character; C.J.S. Witnesses § 532. Mere inconsistencies in the testimony of the witness, exposed by cross-examination, were held insufficient to justify good character reputation evidence in Royal v. Cameron, 382 S.W.2d 335 (Tex.Civ.App.1964).

9. Fed.R.Evid. 608(a), Advisory Committee's Note; People v. Ah Fat, 48 Cal. 61, 64 (1874) (evidence that state's witness had offered to identify killer "if there was any coin in it"). See also, Rodriguez v. State, 165 Tex.Cr.R. 179, 305 S.W.2d 350 (1957) (where attempt has been made to show corrupt motives of witness).

10. Fed.R.Evid. 608(a), Advisory Committee's Note; Lassiter v. State, 35 Ala.App. 323, 47 So.2d 230 (1950), Note, 3 Ala.L.Rev. 206 (1950).

11. Dickson v. Dinsmore, 219 Ala. 353, 122 So. 437 (1929); Turner v. State, 112 Tex.Cr.R. 245, 16 S.W.2d 127 (1929). Contra: State v. Hoffman, 134 Iowa 587, 112 N.W. 103 (1907). See 4 Wigmore, Evidence § 1108 (Chadbourn rev. 1972); C.J.S. Witnesses § 623; Annot., 6 A.L.R. 862. But the preferable approach, at least under the Fed.R.Evid., is to place this matter in the discretion of the judge who can consider the circumstances under which each inconsistent statement was

made. See Outlaw v. United States, 81 F.2d 805 (5th Cir. 1936), cert. denied 298 U.S. 665; Beard v. Mitchell, 604 F.2d 485 (7th Cir. 1979).

12. Louisville & Nashville Railroad Co. v. McClish, 115 F. 268 (C.C.A.Tenn.1902, opinion by Day, J.) (witness who testified he saw decedent pass along railway track shortly before train passed, contradicted by witness who testified first witness was not at the scene but was in opera house at the time; held error to admit character-support, though contradiction "admits of no reconciliation . . . upon any theory of honest mistake or failure of memory"); Whaley v. State, 157 Fla. 593, 26 So.2d 656 (1946) (murder: material conflict between testimony of accused and of officers as to terms of alleged oral confession, does not warrant admission of defendant's good reputation for truth). Contra: Redd v. Ingram, 207 Va. 939, 154 S.E.2d 149 (1967). See 4 Wigmore, Evidence § 1109 (Chadbourn rev. 1972); C.J.S. Witnesses § 643.

Again, the Fed.R.Evid. should permit the matter to be in the judge's discretion. See Rule 608(a), Advisory Committee's Note, which states in part: "Whether evidence in the form of contradiction is an attack upon the character of the witness must depend in part upon the circumstances." See also discussion in the opinion in United States v. Medical Therapy Sciences, Inc., 583 F.2d 36 (2d Cir. 1978), cert. denied 439 U.S. 1130. But compare United States v. Jackson, 588 F.2d 1046 (5th Cir. 1979), cert. denied 442 U.S. 941.

Wigmore, supra, suggests that the argument for supporting character here is weaker than in the case of impeachment for inconsistency. This may be so when viewed from the requirement of an attack on character, but from the view of the administration of justice can one imagine a greater need for the jury to know "what manner of man" the witness is than in these cases of irreconcilable conflicts? It is only a pity that the minority who admit character support, have nothing bet-

answers to these seemingly minor trial questions may be, surely it is unrealistic to handle them in a mechanical fashion. A more sensible view is the notion that the judge should consider in each case whether a particular impeachment for inconsistency or a conflict in testimony,[13] or either of them, amounts in net effect to an attack on character for truth and should exercise his discretion accordingly to admit or exclude the character-support.[14] It has been suggested this view is embodied in the Federal Rules of Evidence.[15]

Turning to the attempts to rehabilitate or support a witness by introduction of a prior statement consistent with his present testimony after the credibility of the witness has been attacked in some way, a similar question arises. What kind of attack upon the witness opens the door to evidence of prior statements by the witness consistent with his present story [16] on the stand? When the attack takes the form of impeachment of character, by showing misconduct, convictions or bad reputation, it is generally agreed that there is no color for sustaining by consistent statements.[17] The defense does not meet the assault. Further, if the attacker has charged bias, interest, corrupt influence, contrivance to falsify, or want of capacity to observe or remember, the applicable principle is that the prior consistent statement has no relevancy to refute the charge unless the consistent statement was made before the source of the bias, interest, influence or incapacity originated.[18] The

---

ter to avail themselves of than the feeble aid of "reputation for truth." Surely it is here that progress is needed so that courts may use an observer's opinion from observation of the witness's character, see § 41 supra; results of deception-tests, see § 46 supra; and results of tests for capacity to perceive and remember, see § 45 supra.

13. In many cases of inconsistent statements there will be both an inconsistency and a conflict of evidence in the sense that the witness denies the making of the inconsistent statement and also in the sense that the substantive story of the witness is contradicted.

14. See the stress placed upon discretion in Outlaw v. United States, 81 F.2d 805, 808 (5th Cir. 1936) and in First National Bank v. Blakeman, 19 Okl. 106, 91 P. 868, 871 (1907).

15. See mention of Fed.R.Evid. in nn. 11, 12, supra.

16. It should first be noted that in various states the rule has been and still is that consistent statements of a witness can not be introduced as "substantive evidence" but must be confined to the purpose of "rehabilitating" a witness. In other words such evidence is regarded by these courts as inadmissible hearsay if within the definition of hearsay and not within any exception to the hearsay rule. See § 251 infra. On the other hand, Fed.R.Evid. and Rev.Unif.R.Evid. (1974) 801(d)(1)(B) provide that a prior statement of a witness, who testifies at a trial or hearing and is subject to cross-examination concerning the statement, is not hearsay if the statement is "(B) consistent with his testimony and is offered to rebut an express or implied charge against him of recent fabrication or improper influence or motive."

There is an important substantial question under the Federal and Uniform Rules whether the above conditions for the use of consistent statements as non-hearsay substantive evidence govern the use of consistent statements merely to support the credibility of a witness whose credibility has been attacked. There is at

present federal authority that Rule 801(d)(1)(B) governs the conditions under which consistent statements can be used merely to bolster the credibility of the attacked witness. See United States v. Quinto, 582 F.2d 224 (2d Cir. 1978) and discussions in opinions in United States v. Rubin, 609 F.2d 51 (2d Cir. 1979), affirmed on other grounds 449 U.S. 424. See also Annot., 47 A.L.R.Fed. 639 for cases which seem to assume this conclusion. The opposing viewpoint is that the question of admission of consistent statements merely for rehabilitation purposes is a matter of discretion of the trial judge, who, as a matter of relevancy under Rule 401, should decide whether a consistent statement will tend to meet the particular attack(s) on the credibility. A similar theory regarding the admission of consistent statements when an attack has been made by inconsistent statements is discussed in Weinstein & Berger, Evidence ¶ 607[08].

No matter which of the above theories in applying the Fed.R.Evid. is followed, the conclusions stated in the instant text paragraph should be correct under the federal rules. See, for example, United States v. Williams, 573 F.2d 284 (5th Cir. 1979) (attack by showing of bias by suggestion that testimony had been influenced by government actions permitted showing of consistent statement of witness). This latter case can be interpreted to mean, contrary to other cases indicated above, that Rule 801(d)(1)(B) itself does not necessarily require that the consistent statement or motives mentioned in the rule exist *before* the inconsistent statement. See also Annot., 47 A.L.R.Fed. 639.

17. Stanford v. State, 34 Tex.Cr.R. 89, 29 S.W. 271 (1895) (bad reputation); 4 Wigmore, Evidence § 1125 (Chadbourn rev. 1972); Annot., 75 A.L.R.2d 909, 927.

18. Excluded on this ground: Abernathy v. Emporia Manufacturing Co., 122 Va. 406, 95 S.E. 418 (1918) (corrupt offer by witness to sell testimony; consistent statement not shown to have been before the corrupt intent arose, improperly received); Sesterhenn v. Saxe,

above results should ordinarily be reached under the Federal Rules of Evidence.[19]

There is much division of opinion on the question whether impeachment by inconsistent statements opens the door to support by proving consistent statements.[20] A few courts hold generally that the support is permissible.[21] This rule has the merit of easy application in the court room. Some courts, since the inconsistency remains despite all consistent statements, hold generally that it does not.[22] But certain modifications or even a complete departure from these general rules should be recognized. If the at-

tacked witness denies the making of the inconsistent statement then some courts consider that the evidence of consistent statements near the time of the alleged inconsistent one, is relevant to fortify his denial.[23] Again, if in the particular situation, the attack by inconsistent statement is accompanied by, or interpretable as, a charge of a plan or contrivance to give false testimony, then proof of a prior consistent statement *before* the plan or contrivance was formed, tends strongly to disprove that the testimony was the result of contrivance. Here all courts agree.[24] It is for the judge to decide

88 Ill.App.2d 2, 232 N.E.2d 277 (1967) (consistent statement held inadmissible when impeachment attempt went to showing bias and not a recent fabrication); People v. Gardineer, 2 Mich.App. 337, 139 N.W.2d 890 (1966) (statement after alleged bias held inadmissible). Admitted where statement was made before the alleged influence arose: People v. Kynette, 15 Cal.2d 731, 104 P.2d 794 (1940); Burns v. Clayton, 237 S.C. 316, 117 S.E.2d 300 (1960) (consistent statement made by witness "prior to the existence of his relation to cause"; impeachment suggesting witness had been paid to testify falsely). See Annot., 140 A.L.R. 21, 80, 117–128; Annot., 75 A.L.R.2d 909, 937.

If the witness's accuracy of memory is challenged, it seems clear common sense that a consistent statement made shortly after the event and before he had time to forget, should be received in support. ". . . The accuracy of memory is supported by proof that at or near the time when the facts deposed to have transpired, and were fresh in the mind of the witness, he gave the same version of them that he testified to on the trial." Smith, C.J. in Jones v. Jones, 80 N.C. 246, 250 (1879). Relying upon particular circumstances, the judge should use this theory in applying Fed.R.Evid. and Rev.Unif.R.Evid. (1974). See also Cross v. State, 118 Md. 660, 86 A. 223, 227 (1912). But some courts seem to reject this view. Annot., 140 A.L.R. 21, 48; Annot., 75 A.L.R.2d 909, 929.

19. See n. 16, supra.

20. See decisions collected in 4 Wigmore, Evidence § 1126 (Chadbourn rev. 1972); Weinstein & Berger, Evidence ¶ 607[08]; Annot., 140 A.L.R. 21, 49–77; Annot., 75 A.L.R.2d 909, 930–935; Dec.Dig. Witnesses ⚖395, 414(2).

21. See, e.g., Cross v. State, 118 Md. 660, 86 A. 223 (1912); Stafford v. Lyon, 413 S.W.2d 495 (Mo.1967); State v. Bethea, 186 N.C. 22, 118 S.E. 800 (1923) (allowable after any form of impeachment); Annot., 140 A.L.R. 21, 59; Annot., 75 A.L.R.2d 909, 933.

22. See, e.g., Commonwealth v. Jenkins, 76 Mass. (10 Gray) 485, 488 (1858).

23. Parker v. State, 183 Ind. 130, 108 N.E. 517 (1915) (rule recognized); Twardosky v. New England Telephone & Telegraph Co., 95 N.H. 279, 62 A.2d 723

(1948); Donovan v. Moore McCormack Lines, 266 App. Div. 406, 42 N.Y.S.2d 441 (1943); Annot., 140 A.L.R. 21, 68; Annot., 75 A.L.R.2d 909, 938. Contra: Burks v. State, 78 Ark. 271, 93 S.W. 983 (1906). See also Commonwealth v. White, 340 Pa. 139, 16 A.2d 407 (1940), which suggests that where the witness denies the inconsistent statement the admission of the supporting statement is in the judge's discretion.

There seems to be no direct authority under the Fed.R.Evid., but the matter should be treated as one of relevancy under Rule 401, subject to the limitations of Rule 403.

24. State v. Galloway, 247 A.2d 104 (Me.1968); People v. Mirenda, 23 N.Y.2d 439, 297 N.Y.S.2d 532, 245 N.E.2d 194 (1969) (witness himself testified to consistent statement on redirect); People v. Singer, 300 N.Y. 120, 89 N.E.2d 710 (1949), noted 35 Cornell L.Q. 867. In the last case the court points out that though the common phrase is "recent" fabrication or contrivance, the "recent" is misleading. It is not required to be recent as regards the trial, but only that the contrivance be more recent than the consistent statement. See cases collected 4 Wigmore, Evidence § 1129 (Chadbourn rev. 1972); C.J.S. Witnesses § 624; Annot., 140 A.L.R. 21, 93–128; Annot., 75 A.L.R.2d 909, 939–946. Some decisions also mention that the consistent statement should have been made before the witness would foresee its effect upon the fact issue, see Annot., 75 A.L.R.2d 909, 946, or before motive to falsify even if made before an inconsistent statement, Giordano v. Eastern Utilities, Inc., 9 A.D.2d 947, 195 N.Y.S.2d 753 (1959).

Clearly, when made before the occurrence of the matters mentioned in the text, consistent statements are admissible under Fed.R.Evid. and Rev.Unif.R.Evid 801(d)(1)(B), quoted in n. 16, supra. If admissible as substantive evidence under that rule such statements must be admissible simply for rehabilitation purposes as well. However, the judge will have a certain amount of practical discretion because the authority for admissibility is Rule 401. See n. 27, infra.

Also, there is authority that if the inconsistent statement used to impeach is part of a statement, the remainder may be introduced to explain or negative the

whether the impeachment amounts to a charge of contrivance, and ordinarily this is the most obvious implication. If it does not, then it may often amount to an imputation of inaccurate memory. If so the consistent statement made when the event was recent and memory fresh should be received in support.[25] Recognition of these modifications would leave it still open to these courts to exclude various statements procured after the inconsistent statement, and thus to discourage pressure on witnesses to furnish successive counter-statements.[26]

The above modifications could be the governing rules in the interpretation of the Federal Rules of Evidence.[27] Under a broader viewpoint the judge has at least practical discretion under Rule 401 to determine whether any particular circumstances justify admission of consistent statements to rehabilitate the witness. This interpretation is a basically different approach.[28] Yet it would

permit judges to discourage pressure for successive counter statements of witnesses.

The fact of a complaint of rape and in some instances the details of the complaint have been held admissible. Both the fact of complaint and, where allowed, the details of the complaint may be admissible on the theory of rehabilitating or bolstering the complaining witness,[29] but since this evidence may also come in as substantive evidence under some theories, the matter is dealt with later.[30] Likewise, prior consistent statements of identification may be admissible substantively or to rehabilitate, but because prior identifications may be admissible as substantive evidence and also involve constitutional requirements, the subject is also discussed elsewhere.[31]

WESTLAW REFERENCES

digest(impeach! /s rehabilitat! accredit! /s witness)

---

inconsistent part. Affronti v. United States, 145 F.2d 3 (8th Cir. 1944); C.J.S. Witnesses § 622. Fed.R.Evid. 106 is a related principle.

See § 56 infra for a further related principle.

25. See n. 18 supra.

26. These after-statements have often been excluded. See, e.g., Weiler v. Weiler, 336 S.W.2d 454 (Tex. Civ.App.1960); United States v. Sherman, 171 F.2d 619 (2d Cir. 1948, opinion by L. Hand, J.); Crawford v. Nilan, 289 N.Y. 444, 46 N.E.2d 512 (1943) (consistent statement procured from witness on morning of trial, held improperly admitted); Sweazey v. Valley Transport, 6 Wn.2d 324, 107 P.2d 567 (1940). The last two cases exemplify the stresses of the race for statements in accident controversies. See Maguire, Evidence: Common Sense and Common Law 63 (1947). Pressures by investigators of defendants and insurance companies often secure from witnesses one-sided statements in defendants' favor, and if the witness's testimony diverges in plaintiff's favor, these come in as inconsistent statements. The obviously needed opportunity to counter these statements comes in the witness's opportunity to deny or explain on cross-examination and re-direct. In a New York case where the plaintiff raised doubts as to the accuracy of his signed inconsistent statement written by defendant's investigator and said that he "talked him into giving it," the court admitted the plaintiff's consistent statement made five days later to plaintiff's employer and not for the purpose of the action, as bearing on the issue as to the accuracy of the inconsistent statement. One judge dissented in a vigorous opinion. Donovan v. Moore McCormack Lines, 266 App.Div. 406, 42 N.Y.S.2d 441 (1943). But see n. 28 infra.

27. For example, see United States v. Quinto, 582 F.2d 224 (2d Cir. 1978) (opinion states consistent statement must meet the requirements listed in Rule 801(d)(1)(B) and that consistent statement must be made before motive to fabricate). The text statement assumes that Rule 801(d)(1)(B) states the conditions for use of inconsistent statements to rehabilitate a witness as well as the conditions under which such statements may be considered substantive evidence, i.e., non-hearsay. Even under this motion, the judge should have discretion. See discussion in n. 16 supra.

28. Inherent in this view is the notion that Rule 801(d)(1)(B) does not state the conditions under which consistent statements may be used to rehabilitate a witness. See n. 16. Rule 401 would be applied to the circumstances in each individual situation. For example, an inconsistent statement alone might constitute sufficient reason to introduce a consistent statement. (But see United States v. Quinto, n. 27 supra, which apparently does not state the instant theory.) The consistent statement could be one made after the contrivance or occurrence of improper influence or motive to testify. See Hanger v. United States, 398 F.2d 91 (8th Cir. 1968), cert. denied 393 U.S. 1119, rehearing denied 395 U.S. 971, discussed in Weinstein & Berger, Evidence, ¶ 607[08].

29. See 4 Wigmore, Evidence §§ 1134–1140 (Chadbourn rev. 1972), 6 id. §§ 1760, 1761 (Chadbourn rev. 1976); Dec.Dig. Rape ⊱48; C.J.S. Rape § 53.

30. See § 297.

31. See §§ 173, 174, 251, infra.

§ 50. Proposed Changes in Existing Law

One who has read the description of the present practice of impeachment and support, in the preceding sections, will have marveled at the archaic and seemingly, arbitrary character of various rules. He will also have observed with regret the laggard pace of the law in taking advantage of the techniques and knowledge which are afforded by the modern sciences of physiology and psychology in appraising the perception, memory, and veracity of witnesses. Two principal retarding influences are apparent, namely, an undue distrust by the judges of the capacity of jurors, and an over-emphasis upon the adversary or contentious aspect of our trial tradition.

As indicated throughout this chapter, the Federal and revised Uniform Rules of Evidence have made various improvements in the impeachment and support areas. Further improvements may still be made. Classifying inconsistent statements as simply non-hearsay would simplify the use of such statements.[1] It would appear worthwhile to re-examine the former Uniform Rule to the effect that the accused in a criminal case who elects to testify in his defense is shielded from impeachment by evidence of other crime unless he has offered evidence in support of his credibility.[2] Such a change could lead to the re-consideration of further limitations on the use of convictions to impeach other witnesses. It would be desirable to develop a statute or court rule concerning the use at the trial of polygraph tests, truth serum tests, voice analysis lie detection tests, and other supposed scientific means of testing credibility. Likewise refreshing memory by means of hypnosis should be accepted or rejected or conditioned by direct rule rather than by case law.

§ 50

1. The present limitations in Fed.R.Evid 801(d)(1)(A), added by the Congress, should be eliminated.

2. Rule 21, original Uniform Rules of Evidence (1953).

Title 3

ADMISSION AND EXCLUSION

Chapter 6

THE PROCEDURE OF ADMITTING AND EXCLUDING EVIDENCE

Table of Sections

§ 51. Presentation of Evidence: Offer of Proof

At the outset, it should be noted that our adversary system imposes on the parties the burden of presenting evidence at the trial pursuant to rules and practices that make it clear when proof has been presented so that it is officially introduced and thereupon can be considered by the trier of fact in the resolution of fact issues.[1] The rules of practice concerning presentation of evidence, offers of proof, and the taking of objections are thus slanted to secure this result.

The presentation of things such as writings, photographs, knives, guns, and all kinds of tangible things often proves troublesome to neophytes.[2] There are variations in local procedures, but the process may be shortly and generally described here.[3] The

---

§ 51

1. The fact issues at the trial should be decided upon the facts "in the record", i.e., facts officially introduced in accordance with the rules of practice, and facts which the court may judicially notice. See Ch. 35 infra.

2. Introduction of depositions does not require the procedures described in the subsequent text.

3. The techniques for introducing things in evidence as exhibits are described and illustrated in detail in Goldstein & Lane, Trial Technique §§ 12.01–12.58 (2d ed. 1969); Keeton Trial Tactics and Methods 63–70 (1973); Virgie v. Stetson, 73 Me. 452, 461 (1882); C.J.S. Trial §§ 61–84.

party wishing to introduce any sort of evidence of this type should first have the thing marked by the clerk for identification as an exhibit for the party.[4] Having had the thing marked by the clerk for identification as an exhibit, the proponent should "lay the foundation" for its introduction as an exhibit by having it appropriately identified or authenticated by the testimony of a witness who is qualified to identify or authenticate it.[5]

Next, the proposed exhibit should be submitted to the opposing attorney for his inspection, at least upon his request, and then the proponent should present it to the judge, stating, e.g., "Plaintiff offers this (document or object, describing it), marked, 'Plaintiff's Exhibit No. 2' for identification, as Plaintiff's Exhibit No. 2." At this point, the opponent may make his objection to its receipt in evidence, and the judge will make his ruling upon the objection. Assuming the judge rules that the thing will be accepted in evidence, if it is a writing, it may be read to the jury by the counsel offering it or by the witness, or if it is a thing it may be shown, or passed, to the jury, in the discretion of the

judge or in accordance with local custom or rules, for inspection by the jury.

Of course, the usual way of presenting oral testimony is to call the witness to the stand and ask him questions. Normally, (but not always) the opponent is required to object to testimony by objections to the questions of the examiner before the witness answers the questions.[6] Ordinarily, the admissibility of testimony is thus decided by the judge's sustaining or overruling objections to questions. If the court sustains an objection to a question, the witness is prevented from answering the question and from testifying to that extent.

In such case, for two reasons, the proponent of the question should ordinarily make "an offer of proof." The usual practice is for the proponent to state to the judge what the witness would say if he were permitted to answer the question and what he expects to prove by the answer to the question.[7] While a secondary reason for an offer of proof is that it permits the judge to consider further the claim for admissibility, the primary reason is to include the proposed an-

---

4. The usual purpose of having the clerk mark proposed exhibits for identification is to make them part of the record in case they are refused as exhibits. See Duncan v. McTiernan, 151 Conn. 469, 199 A.2d 332 (1964) (stating that it is error for the trial court to refuse to permit a proposed exhibit to be marked for identification). Tags may be used for marking, if needed.

5. Certain items are "self-authenticating". See generally Authentication, Ch. 22 infra.

6. See § 52 infra.

7. Fed. and Rev.Unif.R.Evid. (1974) 103:

(a) **Effect of Erroneous Ruling.** Error may not be predicated upon a ruling which admits or excludes evidence unless a substantial right of the party is affected, and

. . .

(2) **Offer of Proof.** In case the ruling is one excluding evidence, the substance of the evidence was made known to the court by offer or was apparent from the context within such questions were asked.

(b) **Record of Offer and Ruling.** The court may add any other or further statement which shows the character of the evidence, the form in which it was offered, the objection made, and the ruling thereon. He may direct the making of an offer in question and answer form.

(c) **Hearing of Jury.** In jury cases, proceedings shall be conducted, to the extent practicable, so as to prevent inadmissible evidence from being suggested to the jury by any means, such as making statements or offers of proof or asking questions in the hearing of the jury.

The term "proffer" is sometimes used to describe an offer of proof.

For cases stating the requirement of an offer of proof, see Philadelphia Record Co. v. Sweet, 124 Pa. Super. 414, 188 A. 631 (1936) (reversible error to refuse counsel opportunity of making offer); D'Acchioli v. Cairo, 87 R.I. 345, 141 A.2d 269 (1958) (rule applied to trial without a jury). See generally, Weinstein & Berger, Evidence ¶ 103[03]; Dec.Dig. ☜44–49; C.J.S. Trial §§ 73–84; Annot., 89 A.L.R.2d 279. See also, n. 16, infra.

When an offer of proof is proper, the trial court must permit it to be made. See C.J.S. Trial § 73; Annot., 89 A.L.R.2d 279, 286–287.

On occasion, under Fed.R.Evid. 103(b), circumstances may call for the judge to direct that the offer be made by questions and answers of the witness (out of the hearing of the jury). Doubts as to what the witness might say are settled. This method deals with questionable offers. On the other hand, the questioner should seek to make offers by questions and answers if accuracy in the record may become important.

swer and expected proof in the official record of the trial, so that in case of appeal upon the judge's ruling, the appellate court may understand the scope and effect of the question and proposed answer in considering whether the judge's ruling sustaining an objection was proper. The trial court must usually require this offer of proof to be made out of the hearing of the jury. Federal Rule of Evidence 103(c) requires this be done to the extent practicable.[8] It is also important to note that upon cross-examination the requirement can be relaxed.[9]

For the purpose of appeal, a question, in the context of the record, may itself so specifically indicate the purport of the expected answer that the appeal court will consider the propriety of the ruling upon the question without an offer of proof.[10] But when, as is more usual, an offer of proof is required before the appellate court will consider a ruling sustaining an objection to a question, the statement constituting the offer of proof must be reasonably specific[11] and must state the purpose of the proof offered unless

---

8. Fed.R.Evid. and Rev.Unif.R.Evid. (1974) 103(c), supra n. 7. In fact, delay of an offer of proof until the day after exclusion of testimony has been held justified on the ground that counsel did not wish to make the offer of proof in the hearing of the jury. United States v. Robinson, 544 F.2d 110 (2d Cir. 1976). Usually the offer of proof can be made immediately after the ruling by requiring counsel to approach the bench so the jury cannot hear or by recessing the jury. For case law see C.J.S. Trial § 84.

While so-called motions in limine and related procedures are most commonly employed to obtain an advance ruling excluding evidence, see § 52 infra, text at notes 12–20, nothing in their nature precludes resort to them as a means of obtaining an advance ruling in favor of the proponent of evidence.

9. On cross-examination, the examining counsel is ordinarily assumed not to have had an advance opportunity to know what the witness will answer, and the requirement of an offer will not usually be applied. Cohen v. Cohen, 196 Ga. 562, 27 S.E.2d 28, 30 (1943); Higgins v. Pratt, 316 Mass. 700, 56 N.E.2d 595 (1944); Calci v. Brown, 95 R.I. 216, 186 A.2d 234 (1962) (dictum). This should often be a proper viewpoint under Fed.R.Evid 103(a)(2), n. 7 supra, although the rule should not be interpreted to make a flat exception. See statement in Saltzman v. Fullerton Metals Co., 661 F.2d 647 (7th Cir. 1981) not making any exception. But even on cross-examination the court in its discretion may require counsel to hint his purpose far enough to show the materiality of the answer hoped for, or enough must be made to appear so that error will be indicated upon appeal. Fahey v. Clark, 125 Conn. 44, 3 A.2d 313 (1938) (court here required too strong an assurance); Lavieri v. Ulysses, 149 Conn. 396, 180 A.2d 632 (1962) (insufficient hint); Perry v. Carter, 332 Mass. 508, 125 N.E.2d 780 (1955) (error in exclusion of questions did not appear from questioning). This discretion probably exists under Fed.R.Evid 103(a)(2) n. 7 supra. A possible example is United States v. Medel, 592 F.2d 1305 (5th Cir. 1979), rehearing denied 597 F.2d 772. If an objection is sustained, and the cross-examiner believes the matter is of sufficient importance in making a record or persuading the judge to change the ruling, the cross-examiner should not take the risk of continuing the cross-examination without making an offer of proof or indicating the general purpose of the questioning. There is a practical difficulty. If it is im-

portant not to warn the witness concerning answers desired, an attempt should be made to make the offer of proof out of the hearing of the witness. The judge should not exercise the power under Rule 103(b) to require the question(s) and answer(s) of the witness. And it has been held that the cross-examiner may make an offer of proof if he desires to do so. Abbadessa v. Tegu, 122 Vt. 338, 173 A.2d 153 (1961). This should be the federal rule as well.

10. Fed.R.Evid. 103(a)(2), n. 7 supra; Hartnett v. Boston Store, 265 Ill. 331, 106 N.E. 837 (1914); Marshall v. Marshall, 71 Kan. 313, 80 P. 629, 630 (1905) (". . . the question itself may be, and often is, of such character that, in connection with the other proceedings, it clearly indicates the materiality of the answer sought, and renders superfluous any statement as to what it is expected to be," a dictum); Hartwig v. Olson, 261 Iowa 1265, 158 N.W.2d 81 (1968) (dictum); Manning v. Redevelopment Agency of Newport, 103 R.I. 371, 238 A.2d 378 (1968) (court held answer to particular question was not apparent in part).

Obviously, the skillful trial lawyer will make an offer rather than gambling on a successful invocation of this approach, which is often the resort of those who forgot.

11. United States v. Winkle, 587 F.2d 705 (5th Cir. 1979), cert. denied 440 U.S. 827; Kane v. Carper-Dover Mercantile Co., 206 Ark. 674, 177 S.W.2d 41 (1944) ("we offer to prove . . . that C.D. is not the proper plaintiff for recovery or damage:" too indefinite; must be so specific as to give the opportunity to court to rule on particular testimony); Ostmo v. Tennyson, 70 N.D. 558, 296 N.W. 541 (1941) (must show what facts are sought to be introduced, so that court may see whether they have any bearing); Shoemaker v. Selnes, 220 Or. 573, 349 P.2d 473 (1960) (one offer so vague it could not be understood; second offer stated counsel "believed" witness would testify as specified).

Compare Moran v. Levin, 318 Mass. 770, 64 N.E.2d 360 (1945) (deceit for sale of dairy cows, one of which was alleged not to produce milk because diseased, plaintiff's offer to show by plaintiff and wife "certain representations made by defendant with reference to the condition, the health of these cows, as to whether they were milk producers" held, sufficient though a "summary" or "abstract" of the proposed evidence).

the purpose is apparent.[12] Where the offered testimony suggests a question as to its materiality or competency, the offer of proof must indicate the facts on which relevancy [13] or admissibility of the testimony depends.[14] As indicated in the footnotes, these matters apply to Federal Rule of Evidence 103.[15]

If counsel specifies a purpose for which the proposed evidence is inadmissible and the judge excludes, counsel cannot complain of the ruling on appeal though it could have been rightly admitted for another purpose.[16]

If part of the evidence offered, as in the case of a deposition, a letter, or a conversation, is admissible and a part is not, it is incumbent on the offeror, not the judge, to select the admissible part. If counsel offers both good and bad together and the judge rejects the entire offer, the offeror may not complain on appeal.[17]

The method of offer of proof described above assumes there is a witness upon the stand who is being questioned.[18] Suppose, however, that there are several witnesses who are available, but not in court, to prove

12. Holman v. Kemp, 70 Minn. 422, 73 N.W. 186, 188 (1897) (counsel asked plaintiff if he did not drink a good deal before the accident, excluded; appellant claimed this was relevant to explain plaintiff's physical condition at time of trial; held, insufficient offer. "If such was the real purpose of the evidence, it was not apparent upon the record, and the trial court's attention should have been specifically called to the object of the evidence."); Davey Brothers, Inc. v. Stop & Shop, Inc., 351 Mass. 59, 217 N.E.2d 751 (1966) (offer of proof failed to indicate purpose for which testimony would be relevant); and cases cited C.J.S. Trial § 76.

Fed.R.Evid. 103(a)(2), n. 7 supra, speaks of a showing of "the substance of the evidence." Nevertheless, to make sure error is shown, where appropriate, the purpose and theory of the evidence should also be stated. Fed.R.Civ.P. 46 requires that the party make known to the court "the action which he desires the court to take or his objection to the action of the court *and his grounds therefor* . . . ." (Italics supplied.) Fed.R. Crim.P. 51 contains the same language. Both rules, of course, apply to evidentiary as well as other matters.

13. Braman v. Wiley, 119 F.2d 991 (7th Cir. 1941) (collision; there was evidence that defendant was drunk; defendant offered a witness to testify to a conversation with defendant soon after; on appeal defendant contended this was material to negative drunkenness; held, not relevant to the purpose stated); Ex parte Taylor, 322 S.W.2d 309 (Tex.Civ.App.1959) (statement that "the whole matter is relevant to this matter" held insufficient when judge inquired as to purpose of question); Fuchs v. Kupper, 22 Wis.2d 107, 125 N.W.2d 360 (1963) (question immaterial in absence of offer of proof of additional facts). Unless relevancy must have been apparent: Joslin v. Idaho Times Publishing Co., 60 Idaho 235, 91 P.2d 386 (1939); Creighton v. Elgin, 387 Ill. 592, 56 N.E.2d 825 (1944) (question itself showed purposes and materiality).

14. Deaton & Son v. Miller Well Servicing Co., 231 S.W.2d 944 (Tex.Civ.App.1950) (party offering evidence which would ordinarily be hearsay—here declarations of an agent—must show facts bringing it under some exception); Clements v. Jungert, 90 Idaho 143, 408 P.2d 810 (1965) (party offering evidence excluded as hearsay was required to show authority of declarer).

15. See nn. 10–12 supra.

16. Huff v. White Motor Corp., 609 F.2d 286 (7th Cir. 1979); United States v. Grapp, 653 F.2d 189 (5th Cir. 1981). Fed.R.Evid. 103(a)(2) does not mention the principle in the text, but the notion of waiver is easily distilled out of Fed.R.Civ.P. 46 and Fed.R.Crim.P. 51. Other authority includes Dietrich v. Kettering, 212 Pa. 356, 61 A. 927 (1905); Davey Brothers, Inc., v. Stop and Shop, Inc., n. 12 supra. Likewise, if a specific ground for admission is claimed in the offer of proof but is not applicable and the judge excludes the evidence, the proponent cannot complain if there was another ground for admission. United States v. Anderson, 618 F.2d 487 (8th Cir. 1980); United States v. Sims, 617 F.2d 1371 (9th Cir. 1980); Johnson v. Rockaway Bus Corp., 145 Conn. 204, 140 A.2d 708 (1958) (claim of admissibility as a declaration against interest precluded consideration on appeal of admissibility as an admission of a party); Watkins v. Watkins, 397 S.W.2d 603 (Mo.1966) (on cross-examination examiner made an offer of proof apparently on basis matter was relevant to issues; bearing on credibility not considered on appeal); C.J.S. Trial § 82; Annot., 89 A.L.R.2d 279, 306.

17. For federal rule purposes see comment in n. 16 supra. Other cases include Sooner Pipe & Supply Corp. v. Rehm, 447 P.2d 758 (Okl.1968) (offer of incompetent evidence included); Morris v. E.I. DuPont de Nemours & Co., 346 Mo. 126, 139 S.W.2d 984 (1940) (motion picture, in part irrelevant); Williams v. Rhode Island Hospital Trust Co., 88 R.I. 23, 143 A.2d 324 (1958); C.J.S. Trial § 82; Annot., 89 A.L.R.2d 279, 306.

18. In the case of a single witness, an offer of proof is usually held ineffective when made before putting a question to the witness (to which objection may be taken) and some cases hold that a witness must ordinarily be placed on the stand and questioned in connection with the making of an offer of proof. See other cases cited in Annot., 89 A.L.R.2d 279, 283–286. However, Fed. and Rev.Unif.R.Evid. (1974) 103(c), n. 7, supra, contemplate that questions in a line of questioning need not be asked before the jury when beginning questions have not been permitted. Rather, the federal Advisory Committee's Note states: "The judge can foreclose a particular line of testimony and counsel can protect the record without a series of questions before the jury, designed at best to waste time and at worst 'to waft into the jury box' the very matter sought to be excluded." For other supporting cases involving one

a line of facts, and the judge's rulings on the law have indicated that he will probably exclude this line of testimony, or the judge rules in advance that the line of testimony is inadmissible. Must the party produce each of these witnesses, question them, and on exclusion, state the purport of each expected answer? A few decisions have said that this procedure must be followed before an effective ruling can be secured.[19] Obviously it would often be a wasteful performance which witnesses, counsel, and judge would desire to avoid. The better view is that it is not invariably essential, but that a sufficient offer of proof may be made without producing the witnesses, if it is sufficiently specific [20] and if there is nothing in the record to indicate a want of good faith or inability to produce the proof.[21]

WESTLAW REFERENCES

offer /3 proof /s hearing /3 jury
offer /3 proof /s requir! /s specific purpose %
    358k133

witness, see Missouri Pacific Railway Co. v. Castle, 172 F. 841 (8th Cir. 1909); Garvey v. Chicago Railways Co., 339 Ill. 276, 171 N.E. 271, 274, 275 (1930) (offer of evidence on motion for new trial without producing witness held sufficient, distinguishing Chicago City Railway Co. v. Carroll, 206 Ill. 318, 68 N.E. 1087 (1903)).

19. Chicago City Railway Co. v. Carroll, 206 Ill. 318, 68 N.E. 1087 (1903); Eschbach v. Hurtt, 47 Md. 61, 66 (1877) ("If the defendant had at the trial witnesses who could have proved . . . it was his duty to have called them or one of them to the stand and propounded appropriate questions. . . ."). Fed. and Rev. Unif.R.Evid. (1974) 103(b) and 611(a) may permit a judge to require this procedure but he should in his discretion not often do so. See n. 21 infra.

20. It would seem wise to name the witness or witnesses and to indicate the particulars that each would prove.

21. See comment concerning the federal rules in n. 18 supra. Scotland County v. Hill, 112 U.S. 183, 186 (1884) ("If the trial court has doubts about the good faith of an offer of testimony, it can insist on the production of the witness, and upon some attempt to make the proof, before it rejects the offer; but if it does reject it, and allows a bill of exceptions which shows that the offer was actually made and refused, and there is nothing else in the record to indicate bad faith, an appellate court must assume that the proof could have been made. . . ." [of course bills of exception are mostly obsolete; see § 52, infra]); Witt v. Voigt, 162 Wis. 568, 156 N.W. 954 (1916) (counsel said he had wit-

§ 52. Objections [1]

If the administration of the exclusionary rules of evidence is to be fair and workable the judge must be informed promptly of contentions that evidence should be rejected, and the reasons therefor. The initiative is placed on the party, not on the judge. The general approach, accordingly, is that a failure to object to an offer of evidence at the time the offer is made, assigning the grounds, is a waiver upon appeal of any ground of complaint against its admission. It is important to note, however, that this usual approach is modified by the doctrine of plain error, which is discussed at the end of this section.

Time of Making: Motions to Strike. Consistently with the above approach, counsel is not allowed to gamble upon the possibility of a favorable answer,[2] but must object to the admission of evidence as soon as the ground for objection becomes apparent.[3] Usually, in the taking of testimony of a witness an objection is apparent as soon as the

nesses in court who would testify to certain facts, whereon court said such evidence would not be received, held a sufficient offer).

§ 52

1. 1 Wigmore, Evidence § 18 (3d ed. 1940); Weinstein & Berger, Evidence ¶ 103[02]; Dec.Dig. Trial ⊕73–97; C.J.S. Trial §§ 113–132; 75 Am.Jur.2d Trial §§ 162–188.

2. Fed.R.Evid. and Rev.Unif.R.Evid. (1974) 103(a)(1) embody the principles set forth in this paragraph of the text:

(a) **Effect of Erroneous Ruling.** Error may not be predicated upon a ruling which admits or excludes evidence unless a substantial right of the party is affected, and

(1) **Objection.** In case the ruling is one admitting evidence, a timely objection or motion to strike appears of record, stating the specific ground of objection, if the specific ground was not apparent from the context; . . . .

[See opinions in Reagan v. Brock, 628 F.2d 721 (1st Cir. 1980); United States v. Armedo-Sarmiento, 545 F.2d 785 (2d Cir. 1976), cert. denied 430 U.S. 917. See also Hastings v. Serleto, 61 Cal.App.2d 672, 143 P.2d 956 (1943); Kuiken v. Garrett, 243 Iowa 785, 51 N.W.2d 149 (1952)].

3. See n. 2 supra. See also Cheffer v. Eagle Discount Stamp Co., 348 Mo. 1023, 156 S.W.2d 591 (1941).

question is asked, since the question is likely to indicate that it calls for inadmissible evidence. Then counsel must, if opportunity affords, state his objection before the witness answers.[4] But sometimes an objection before an answer to a question is not feasible. A forward witness may answer before counsel has a chance to object.[5] A question which is not objectionable may be followed by an objectionable unresponsive answer.[6] Or, after the evidence is received, a ground of objection to the evidence may be disclosed for the first time in the later course of the trial.[7] In all these cases, an "after-objection" may be stated as soon as the ground appears. The proper technique, for such an objection is to phrase a motion to strike out the objectionable evidence, and to request an instruction to the jury to disregard the evidence. Counsel should use the term "motion to strike," as just indicated, but it seems that any phraseology which directs the judge's attention to the grounds as soon as they appear, and asserts the objection, should be sufficient.[8]

In the taking and subsequent use at the trial of depositions on oral or written questions, the time when objections must be made to the questions and answers is a matter variously regulated by rules and statutes in the different jurisdictions.[9] Usually objections going to the "manner and form" of the questions or answers, such as objections to leading questions or disclaimers of unresponsive answers—sometimes opinions and secondary evidence are put in this class—, must be made at the time of taking the deposition and disposed of upon motion before the trial.[10] Objections going to the "substance," such as relevancy and hearsay, may usually be urged for the first time when the deposition is offered in evidence at the trial.[11]

If evidence was introduced at the first trial of a case, and an available objection was not made at the first trial, may the same evidence when tendered at a second trial of the same case be effectively objected to at the second trial for the first time? See § 259, infra.

4. See federal cases cited in n. 2, supra. See also Stark's Administratrix v. Herndon's Administrator, 292 Ky. 469, 166 S.W.2d 828 (1942) (question asked by juror); Lineberry v. Robinett, 446 S.W.2d 481 (Mo.App. 1969).

5. A motion to strike should then be made. Wightman v. Campbell, 217 N.Y. 479, 112 N.E. 184 (1916) (but in the particular situation an objection sufficed); Sorenson v. Smith, 65 Or. 78, 129 P. 757, 131 P. 1022 (1913). These rules are undoubtedly effective under Fed.R.Evid. 103(a)(1), n. 2 supra.

6. Wallace v. American Toll Bridge Co., 124 Or. 179, 264 P. 351 (1928) (proper question, improper answer, approved practice is motion to strike); Brown v. Parker, 375 S.W.2d 594 (Mo.App.1964) (dictum).

The mere fact that the answer is unresponsive is not an objection available to the opponent. Hester v. Goldsbury, 64 Ill.App.2d 66, 212 N.E.2d 316 (1965) and cases cited therein; Isham v. Birkel, 184 Neb. 800, 172 N.W.2d 92 (1969) (exclusion by trial judge on objection of opponent held reversible error under particular circumstances). The objection is only available to the questioner, who may move to strike. Davidson v. State, 211 Ala. 471, 100 So. 641 (1924).

Again, these principles are applicable under Fed.R. Evid. 103(a)(1), n. 2 supra.

7. See Young v. Dueringer, 401 S.W.2d 165 (Mo. App.1966).

8. Mere labels should not make a difference under Fed.R.Evid 103(a)(1). See also Hackenson v. City of Waterbury, 124 Conn. 679, 2 A.2d 215 (1938) (where plaintiff-witness "jumped the gun" and answered a question before defendant objected, and court sustained the objection; held, sufficient to eliminate evidence from jury's consideration, though there was no motion to strike); Wightman v. Campbell, 217 N.Y. 479, 112 N.E. 184 (1916) (where first question in series in proving the making by witness of a survey of land was answered before objection, and objection then made "to all that proof," and overruled; held, objector has benefit of his exception without motion to strike).

As to the adequacy of instructions to disregard, see § 58 n. 17, and § 59 infra.

9. Decisions are collected in Dec.Dig. Depositions ⬡105–111, and C.J.S. Depositions §§ 101–105. See Fed.R.Civ.P. 32(b) and (d), adopted in many states and Fed.R.Crim.P. 15 and 16.

10. Fed.R.Civ.P. 32(b) and (d); 1 Wigmore, Evidence § 18, notes 7–14 (3d ed. 1940); C.J.S. Depositions § 101.

A fair rule of thumb is to include in this category objections which probably could have been obviated by the examiner if raised at the time.

But see Fed.R.Crim.P. 16.

11. See references n. 9 supra.

Motions in Limine. A motion for an advance ruling on the admissibility of evidence is a relatively modern device for obtaining rulings on evidence before the evidence is sought to be introduced.[12] The purpose of such motions may be "to insulate the jury from exposure to harmful inadmissible evidence" or to afford a basis for strategic decisions.[13] Advance rulings upon objections may be sought prior to trial or at the trial in advance of the presentation of evidence.[14] The usual rule is that the judge has a wide discretion to make or refuse to make advance rulings,[15] although it has been held that such advance rulings may not be had.[16] Unless the decision of a motion first requires a factual background of the evidence as it develops at the trial, and as long as the matter is left primarily within the discretion of the trial judge, the use of a motion in limine to make advance objections for the purposes mentioned above should be encouraged.[17] In view of some case disagreement, it has been recommended that objections that have been overruled at a hearing on a motion in limine should be repeated at the trial to make sure that appeal rights are preserved.[18] If motions in limine are to be permitted as a means of advance objection, there are also instances when it would be desirable to permit such motions by the future proponent of evidence.

The instant type of motion should be distinguished from motions for suppression of evidence which may be required,[19] as well as from hearings on preliminary fact questions at the trial.[20]

General and Specific Objections.[21] The precept constantly urged is that objections must be accompanied by a reasonably definite statement of the grounds,[22] that is to say, that objections must reasonably indicate the appropriate rules of evidence as reasons for the objections made. These objections are labeled specific objections in contrast to so-called general objections which assign no such grounds for the objection. One purpose of the requirement is that the judge may understand the question raised and that the adversary may have an opportunity to

---

12. Gamble, The Motion *In Limine*: A Pretrial Procedure That Has Come of Age, 33 Ala.L.Rev. 1 (1981). Rothblatt & Leroy, The Motion in Limine in Criminal Trials, 60 Ky.L.J. 611 (1972); Comments, 29 Ark.L.Rev. 247 (1975), 27 U.Fla.L.Rev. 531 (1975), 9 Gonzaga L.Rev. 780 (1974), 35 Mont.L.Rev. 362 (1974); Annot. 63 A.L.R.3d 311.

13. Cleary & Strong, Cases, Evidence 32, n. 5 (3d ed. 1981).

14. Motions at the trial may be untimely if an intolerable, extensive interruption at the trial is required. United States v. Murray, 492 F.2d 178 (9th Cir. 1973), cert. denied 419 U.S. 942.

15. United States v. Kahn, 472 F.2d 272 (2d Cir. 1973), cert. denied 411 U.S. 982; United States v. Evanchik, 413 F.2d 950 (2d Cir. 1969); United States v. Oakes, 565 F.2d 170 (1st Cir. 1977). These cases and others involve a motion in advance to exclude alleged prejudicial and inadmissible evidence on cross-examination of a defendant if he takes the stand. See also, United States v. Palumbo, 401 F.2d 270 (2d Cir. 1968), cert. denied 394 U.S. 947. However, it has been said that in the instant situation a refusal to exclude may not be challenged on appeal if the defendant does not take the stand. United States v. Fulton, 549 F.2d 1325 (9th Cir. 1977).

Authority under the Federal and Revised Uniform Rules Evid. may be found in Rules 103(c), 104(c), and 611(a), in rules on pretrial conference and other pretrial

proceedings, and in the general power of courts to control proceedings before them.

Like other interlocutory orders and rulings, rulings on these matters would ordinarily remain subject to reconsideration by the judge at any time during the trial. However, when strategy has been developed in reliance on the ruling, as when an accused takes the stand in reliance on a ruling excluding impeachment by prior convictions, a subsequent reversal of his ruling by the trial judge may well be an abuse of discretion.

16. See, e.g., State v. Flett, 234 Or. 124, 380 P.2d 634 (1963); 63 A.L.R.3d 311.

17. United States v. Oakes, 565 F.2d 170 (1st Cir. 1977) (whether to make advance ruling on admissibility of prior convictions to impeach accused if he takes the stand within discretion of trial judge, but practice strongly encouraged).

18. Weinstein & Berger, Evidence, ¶ 103[02].

19. See § 180 infra.

20. See § 53 infra.

21. 1 Wigmore, Evidence § 18(c)(1) (2) (3d ed. 1940); Weinstein & Berger, Evidence ¶ 103[02]; Dec.Dig. Trial ⚖81–84; C.J.S. Trial §§ 123–132; C.J.S. Criminal Law § 1036.

22. See Fed. and Rev.Unif.R.Evid (1974) 103(a)(1), n. 2 supra. See also, e.g. Craig v. Citizens Trust Co., 217 Ind. 434, 26 N.E.2d 1006 (1940).

remedy the defect, if possible.[23] This precept does not *per se* ban the use of general objections (objections which state no grounds) at the trial,[24] but rather it is one that is enforced to a certain extent on appeal. Thus the second purpose of the requirement is to make a proper record for the reviewing court in the event of an appeal. If the judge *overrules* a general objection, the objecting party may not ordinarily complain of the ruling on appeal by urging a valid ground not mentioned when the objection was made.[25] However, there are three exceptional situations in which this rule on appeal may not be followed—in which the appeal court will consider whether a valid ground of objection resulted in an erroneous overruling although it was, of course, not stated by the general objection made to the trial judge. The first is that, if the ground for exclusion should have been obvious to judge and opposing counsel without stating it, the want of specification of the ground is immaterial for purposes of complaining on appeal of the judge's action in overruling the general objection.[26] This exception is clear good sense. Second, it has also been said that if the evidence is not admissible for any purpose, the general objection may be sufficient to secure on appeal a review of the judge's action in overruling the objection.[27]

This exception is not effective under Federal Rule of Evidence 103(a)(1)[28] and does not make sense for if the ground is not apparent, it seems there is still need for specification, for appeal purposes. Third, it has been suggested that if the omitted ground was one that could not have been obviated, the general objection may serve to secure consideration on appeal of an unstated specific ground for objection.[29] It is believed that this exception overlooks the consideration that though the objection to the particular evidence could not have been obviated, yet if the ground of objection had been stated the judge and adverse counsel might have appreciated its force, and the offer might have been excluded or withdrawn, and the adversary might have introduced other evidence to fill the gap.[30] Thus this third exception is not authorized under Federal Rule Evid. 103(a)(1).[31]

As a result of the above-mentioned rules, a trial judge's action in overruling a general objection will usually be supported on appeal. And if the trial judge *sustains* a general objection, the upper court is again charitable toward his ruling. "When evidence is *excluded* upon a mere general objection, the ruling will be upheld, if any ground in fact existed for the exclusion. It will be assumed, in the absence of any request by the

---

23. City of Yuma v. Evans, 85 Ariz. 229, 336 P.2d 135 (1959).

24. Fed.R.Evid. 103(a)(1), n. 2 supra, does not ban the use of general objections at the trial because the rule governs treatment of rulings on appeal and motions for new trial.

25. Fed.R.Evid. 103(a)(1), n. 2 supra, embodies this general rule. For case law see, e.g., Reed v. Trainor, 142 Ind.App. 192, 233 N.E.2d 685 (1968); C.J.S. Appeal and Error §§ 247, 253; C.J.S. Trial § 124.

26. Fed. and Rev.Unif.R.Evid. (1974) 103(a)(1) (error may not be predicated upon a ruling admitting evidence unless a timely specific objection was made "if the specific ground was not apparent from the context"). Case law is similar. Styblo v. McNeil, 217 Ill. App. 316, 45 N.E.2d 1011 (1943) ("An objection, except where it is obvious, should be stated in such a manner as to inform the court of the point being urged"); Johnson v. Jackson, 43 Ill.App.2d 251, 193 N.E.2d 485 (1963) ("it is difficult to show that a particular defect cannot be cured or that the ground for objection is obvious;" held not obvious in this case); Floy v. Hibbard,

227 Iowa 149, 287 N.W. 829 (1939) (general objection sufficient, "where the grounds of the objection are discernible").

On appeal, however, reliance on this doctrine may indicate oversight in failing to "protect the record" or lack of knowledge of a supposedly apparent specific objection.

27. Granberry v. Gilbert, 276 Ala. 486, 163 So.2d 641 (1964) (if illegal for any purpose, and incurable by other evidence or by reframing question); Scally v. Flannery, 292 Ill.App. 349, 11 N.E.2d 123 (1937); State v. Rauscher Chevrolet Co., 291 S.W.2d 89 (Mo.1956).

28. Fed.R.Evid. and Rev.Unif.R.Evid. (1974) 103(a) (1), n. 2 supra.

29. Floy v. Hibbard, 227 Iowa 149, 287 N.W. 829 (1939); Smith v. Fine, 351 Mo. 1179, 175 S.W.2d 761 (1943).

30. See Campbell v. Paschall, 132 Tex. 226, 121 S.W.2d 593 (1938).

31. Fed. and Rev.Unif.R.Evid. (1974) 103(a)(1), n. 2 supra.

opposing party or the court to make the objection definite, that it was understood, and that the ruling was placed upon the right ground."[32]

Examples of general objections are "I object;"[33] or objections on the ground that the evidence is "inadmissible,"[34] "illegal,"[35] or "incompetent,"[36] or is not proper testimony for the jury;[37] or an objection "on all the grounds ever known or heard of".[38] One of the most overworked forms is an objection on the ground that the evidence is "incompetent, irrelevant and immaterial." Its rhythm and alliteration have seduced some lawyers to employ it as a routine and meaningless ritual, a "vain repetition." Thus, courts frequently treat this form as equivalent merely to the general objection,[39] "I object." The word "incompetent" as applied to evidence means no more than inadmissible, and thus cannot be said to state a ground of objection. However, the terms, "irrelevant and immaterial," do state, though general in terms, a distinct and substantial ground for exclu-

sion.[40] A requirement that the objector state specifically wherein the evidence, as applied to the particular issues, is irrelevant or immaterial, as some courts seem to demand, seems in many situations unduly burdensome as involving the difficulties usually associated with proving a negative. It would be far more practical to consider the irrelevancy objection in this general form as the equivalent of a specific objection with the qualification that if the judge has any doubt of relevancy, he may call upon the proponent to explain the purpose of the proof.[41]

While an objection of irrelevancy in general form has on occasion been held sufficient to raise a claim of prejudice in the sense of arousing personal animus against the party,[42] it would seem in principle that such an objection should not carry with it the matters listed in Rule 403, under the Federal Rules.[43] These matters can readily be raised specifically and do not entail the burden of establishing a negative mentioned above.[44]

---

32. Tooley v. Bacon, 70 N.Y. 34, 37 (1877). See also 1 Wigmore, Evidence § 18; C.J.S. Trial § 124b. If the offering counsel requests a statement of the specific grounds for excluding the evidence, the trial judge is obligated either to furnish it himself or to require objecting counsel to furnish it. Colburn v. Chicago, St. P., M. & O. Ry. Co., 109 Wis. 377, 85 N.W. 354 (1901); United States v. Hibler, 463 F.2d 455 (9th Cir. 1972); United States v. Dwyer, 539 F.2d 924 (2d Cir. 1976). If in doubt, offering counsel should follow this procedure. While in terms, Federal Rule 103(a) strictly applies only to saving error for review, its principal purpose and thrust is to promote precision and clarity of evidence rulings at trial, Saltzburg & Redden, Federal Rules of Evidence Manual, Rule 103 (2d ed., 1981 Supp.), and the suggested procedure is available under the Federal Rules.

Once the general objection has been converted into a specific one, further developments will follow the course prescribed for specific objections. See text at nn. 50–53 infra.

33. See language in United States v. Hutcher, 622 F.2d 1083 (2d Cir. 1980), cert. denied 449 U.S. 875. The forms at nn. 33–39 are clearly not specific objections for the purposes of Fed.R.Evid. 103(a)(1), n. 2 supra. See also nn. 30, 31 supra. Gerald v. Caterers, Inc., 382 S.W.2d 740 (Mo.App.1964); C.J.S. Trial § 124c.

34. Fowler v. Wallace, 131 Ind. 347, 31 N.E. 53 (1892).

35. Johnston v. Johnston, 174 Ala. 220, 57 So. 450 (1912).

36. Minchen v. Hart, 72 F. 294 (8th Cir. 1896); C.J.S. Trial § 124c.

37. Itasca Lumber Co. v. Martin, 230 F. 584 (8th Cir. 1916).

38. Johnston v. Clements, 25 Kan. 376 (1881) (possibly a world's record). For additional examples of general objections, see C.J.S. Trial § 124.

39. Vogel v. Sylvester, 148 Conn. 666, 174 A.2d 122 (1961) (objection on basis of irrelevancy); Goldfoot v. Lofgren, 135 Or. 533, 296 P. 843 (1931); Dec.Dig. Trial ⟨=83(2); C.J.S. Trial § 124c.

40. See M. Graham, Handbook of Federal Evidence 13 n. 26 (1981). As to relevancy and materiality generally, see ch. 16 infra.

41. Ample authority for this approach is found in Fed.R.Civ.P. 46 and Fed.R.Crim.P. 51, supra § 51, n. 12. At this stage, each party desires the court to take action in his favor and is obliged to state his grounds.

42. See, e.g., Hungate v. Hudson, 353 Mo. 944, 185 S.W.2d 646 (1945).

43. Objections available under Rule 403 include "unfair prejudice, confusion of the issues, or misleading the jury . . . undue delay, waste of time, or needless presentation of cumulative evidence." See § 185 infra.

44. Of the objections listed in Rule 403, n. 43 supra, only the first three are likely candidates for success on review.

Objections should be specific not only with respect to the statement of grounds, but also with respect to a particular part of an offer, in view of another rule as to saving error for appeal. If evidence sought to be introduced consists of several statements or items tendered as a unit, e.g., a deposition, a letter, a conversation, a transcript of testimony or the like, and if the objection is to the whole of the evidence when parts are subject to the objection made and parts are not, the judge will not be put in error for overruling the objection.[45] It is not the judge's duty to sever the bad parts if some are good.[46] Obviously such a rule should not be administered rigidly by the appellate courts but with due concession, if need be, to the realities of the particular trial situation.

Even more clearly, if evidence offered is properly admissible on a particular issue, but not upon some other issue, or is admissible against one party but not against another,[47] an objector who asks that this evidence be excluded altogether, though he assigns grounds, cannot complain on appeal if his objection is overruled. He should have asked that the admission of the evidence be limited to the particular purpose or party.[48]

On appeal, the *overruling* of an untenable specific objection will not be overturned because there was a tenable ground for exclusion which was not urged in the trial court.[49]

If an untenable specific objection is *sustained*, there is authority that the appellate court will uphold the ruling if there is any other ground for doing so, even though not urged below.[50] There is no point in ordering a retrial if the evidence would then be excluded on the proper ground. However, some qualifications must be made. If the correct objection, had it been made, could have been obviated,[51] or admissible evidence could have been substituted, then a retrial seems appropriate. If a ruling upon the proper objection at the second trial would involve the judge's discretion, a new trial would be appropriate unless the judge on remand determines that his discretion would be exercised in favor of exclusion.[52] A similar result should follow where findings of fact are required as a preliminary to determining admissibility.[53]

Repetition of Objections. A offers testimony by one witness which his adversary, B, thinks is incompetent. He objects, and the objection is *sustained*. In such event, if A

45. United States v. McGrath, 622 F.2d 36 (2d Cir. 1980); Clayton v. Prudential Insurance Co. of America, 4 N.C.App. 43, 165 S.E.2d 763 (1969) (objection to letter as a whole was insufficient although part was inadmissible because hearsay and opinion); Jacobson v. Bryan, 244 Wis. 359, 12 N.W.2d 789 (1944) (traffic officer's report of accident partly based on personal knowledge, partly not; objection to whole report, insufficient); Dec.Dig. Trial ⊜85; C.J.S. Trial § 130.

46. An objection which fails to separate out the objectionable part as the subject of the objection lacks the specificity mandated by Rule 103(a)(1), supra n. 2. See United States v. McGrath, n. 45 supra; Wright & Graham, Federal Practice and Procedure: Evidence § 5036. See also Mucci v. LeMonte, 157 Conn. 566, 254 A.2d 879 (1969). And the judge may sustain the objection without error, since he has no duty to separate the good from the bad. See § 51 supra.

47. *Issues.* Finley v. Smith, 240 Ark. 323, 399 S.W.2d 271 (1966); Curtin v. Benjamin, 305 Mass. 489, 26 N.E.2d 354 (1940); Dec.Dig. Trial ⊜86.

Parties. Solomon v. Dabrowski, 295 Mass. 358, 3 N.E.2d 744 (1936); Dec.Dig. Trial ⊜87.

If such a limitation is not requested, the objection lacks the specificity mandated by Rule 103(a)(1), supra n. 2.

48. Finley v. Smith, n. 47, supra; Walls v. Clark, 252 Or. 421, 449 P.2d 141 (1969) (parties).

49. This is the result both at common law and under Fed. and Rev.Unif.R.Evid. (1974) 103(a)(1). An untenable specific objection is the same as no objection at all. United States v. Ruffin, 575 F.2d 346, 355 (2d Cir. 1978) (objection below of irrelevancy did not support appeal claim of hearsay); Gray v. Lucas, 677 F.2d 1086, 1099 n. 13 (5th Cir. 1982), rehearing denied 685 F.2d 139, cert. denied 103 S.Ct. 1886, (hearsay claim not considered on appeal because not raised below); United States v. Brady, 595 F.2d 359 (6th Cir. 1979), cert. denied 444 U.S. 862; Kroger Grocery & Baking Co. v. Harpole, 175 Miss. 227, 166 So. 335 (1936); People ex rel. Blackmon v. Brent, 97 Ill.App.2d 438, 240 N.E.2d 255 (1968); State v. Dietz, 115 N.W.2d 1 (N.D.1962).

50. See 1 Wigmore, Evidence § 18 at 345 (3d ed. 1940).

51. See discussion in Morgan, Basic Problems in Evidence 54 (1962).

52. See Saltzburg, Another Ground for Decision—Harmless Trial Court Errors, 47 Temple L.Q. 193 (1974).

53. Id.

offers similar testimony by the same or another witness, B must of course repeat his objection if he is to complain of the later evidence.[54] Suppose, however, the first objection is *overruled*. Must B then repeat his objection when other like evidence similarly objectionable is offered? A few decisions intimate that he must,[55] a practice which places B in the invidious semblance of a contentious obstructor, and conduces to waste of time and fraying of patience. Most courts, however, hold that B is entitled to assume that the judge will continue to make the same ruling and that he need not repeat the objection.[56] It seems that the consequence of this view should be, that the first objection remains good and is not waived, and that in addition, the reach of this objection extends to all similar evidence subject to

the same objection. It seems that in any jurisdiction where the practice in this respect is at all doubtful, it is a wise precaution for objecting counsel to ask the judge to have the record show that it is understood that the objection goes to all other like evidence, and when later evidence is offered, to have it noted that the earlier objection applies.

The Exception.[57] Closely associated with the objection but distinct from it in the classic common law practice was the exception.[58] The Federal rules and the practice in many states have dispensed with exceptions, and have provided that for all purposes formerly served thereby, "it is sufficient that a party, at the time the ruling or order of the court is made or sought, makes known to the court the action which he desires the court to take or his objection . . . and his grounds

54. Wagner v. Jones, 77 N.Y. 590 (semble) (1879); Frost v. Goddard, 25 Me. 414 (1845). The instant rule is embodied in Fed. and Rev.Unif.R.Evid. (1974) 103(a)(1), n. 2 supra.

55. Shelton v. Southern Railway Co., 193 N.C. 670, 139 S.E. 232 (1927).

56. Tucker v. Reil, 51 Ariz. 357, 77 P.2d 203 (1938); Louisville & Nashville Railroad Co. v. Rowland's Administrator, 215 Ky. 663, 286 S.W. 929 (1926); West-Nesbitt, Inc. v. Randall, 126 Vt. 481, 236 A.2d 676 (1967); Dec.Dig. Trial ⟜79; C.J.S. Trial § 122; 53 Am. Jur. Trial § 146, and see Ladd, Common Mistakes in the Technique of Trial, 22 Iowa L.Rev. 609, 612–617 (1937).

The "continuing objection" is not specifically mentioned by Fed. and Rev.Unif.R.Evid. (1974) 103(a)(1), n. 2 supra. The federal Advisory Committee's Note indicates it is authorized by its reference to California Code § 353. See Wright & Graham, Federal Practice and Procedure: Evidence § 5037.

57. 1 Wigmore, Evidence § 20 (3d ed. 1940); Dec. Dig. Trial ⟜99–105; C.J.S. Trial § 146; 75 Am.Jur.2d Trial §§ 185–188.

58. The function and procedure of bills of exception are described in Green, Basic Civil Procedure 254–255 (2d ed. 1979):

. . . [T]he only function of the appellate court was to review alleged errors of law, and in so doing it was confined to the common law record which consisted of the writ (summons), the return, pleadings, verdict and judgment. The court could not review the facts since they were the sole province of the jury, and furthermore no record of the testimony was kept. Consequently the scope of review was very narrow, at least until the year 1285 when Parliament passed the famous Statute of Westminster II which, among other things, provided for Bills of Exceptions.

The purpose of a Bill of Exceptions was to bring before the appellate court for review matters which otherwise would not appear on the common law record due to the fact that there were no court reporters to record the testimony and the proceedings at the trial. This was before the days of shorthand and recording devices. After the Statute of Westminster II if a litigant believed the court had erred in a ruling, he could make it a matter of record by "saving his exception." For example, if counsel had objected to a question asked of a witness and the court had overruled the objection and counsel thought the ruling was erroneous, he could say, "If the court please, I desire to save an exception to your honor's ruling." The judge was then obliged to stop the trial and call the scrivener who, with his quill pen, would make a record on parchment which would read something like the following: (after giving the caption of the case) "Elmer Zilch, a witness sworn in the above entitled case, was asked the following question, 'Have you stopped beating your wife?' to which counsel for the defendant objected on the ground the question was improper because an answer either way would incriminate him; whereupon, after argument the court overruled the objection, to which ruling the defendant duly saved his exception." When this document was completed, it would be signed by the judge. During the course of the trial numerous exceptions might be "saved." At the conclusion of the trial they would be bound together and certified by the trial judge as the Bill of Exceptions in the case, and they would be attached to and become a part of the record on appeal. Today, with modern methods of court reporting, this antiquated method of preserving a record has become obsolete and court rules make "exceptions" unnecessary. (Footnotes omitted.)

therefor." [59] Nevertheless, for reasons such as an attempt to impress a jury, some attorneys persist in making statements that they except to a ruling in jury cases in jurisdictions in which exceptions are unnecessary.

The Tactics of Objecting. Jurors want to know the facts and they may well look upon objections as attempts to hide the facts, and upon successful objections as the actual suppression of facts.[60] If this description of the jury's attitude is sound, certain consequences as to desirable tactics seem to follow.

No objections should be made unless there is reason to believe that the making of the objection will do more good than harm. If an objection has little chance of being sustained, at the trial or on appeal, it should usually not be made. It has also been pointed out that objections to leading questions, or to opinion evidence, frequently result in strengthening the examiner's case by requiring him to elicit his testimony in more concrete and convincing form.[61] In general, objections should be few and should be directed only to evidence which if admitted will be substantially harmful, and then only if the objector believes he can obtain a favorable ruling at the trial or upon appeal.[62]

Finally, since objections are usually made in the jury's presence, the manner of the objector and the terms of the objection are important. An objection should be stated so that it does not appear to rest merely upon some technical rule.[63] Thus, an objection to

a copy under the best evidence rule should not be stated solely in terms of "secondary evidence" but should also be grounded upon the safer reliability of the original writing. The objection of "hearsay," for example, should be expanded by an explanation of the need, in justice and fairness, for producing the original informant so that the jury may see him, and his sources of knowledge may be explored.

Withdrawal of Evidence. The Federal and revised Uniform Rules of Evidence (1974) do not in terms deal with the subject of withdrawal of evidence. A reasonable interpretation of Rule 611(a), however, would include permitting withdrawal as an aspect of the court's discretionary control over the presentation of evidence. Such discretion could be exercised in accordance with the following acceptable case law principles. If a party has introduced evidence which is not objected to and which turns out to be favorable to the adversary, it has sometimes been intimated that the offering party may withdraw the evidence as of right.[64] The accepted rule seems to be, however, that such a withdrawal is not of right. Rather, the adversary is entitled to have the benefit of the testimony as it bears in his favor,[65] unless the special situation makes it fair for the judge in his discretion to permit the withdrawal.[66] On the other hand, if the evidence is admitted over the adversary's objection, and the proponent later decides to yield to the objection, and asks to withdraw the evi-

59. Fed.R.Civ.P. 46; Fed.R.Crim.P. 51.

60. See general discussion in Keeton, Trial Tactics and Methods, 2d ed. 166–190 (1973).

61. Ladd, Common Mistakes in the Technique of Trial, 22 Iowa L.Rev. 609, 617 (1937).

62. Goldstein & Lane, Trial Technique § 13.01 (2d ed. 1969).

63. See examples of objections in Busch, Law and Tactics in Jury Trials §§ 488, 492 (1949); Goldstein & Lane, Trial Technique ch. 13 (2d ed. 1969); Keeton, Trial Tactics and Methods, 2d ed. 210– 215 (1973).

64. See Young v. United States, 97 F.2d 200, 205 (5th Cir. 1938), and Note, 17 Tex.L.Rev. 373, 374 (1939).

65. Alabama Great Southern Railroad Co. v. Hardy, 131 Ga. 238, 62 S.E. 71 (1908) (enlightening discussion); Page v. Payne, 293 Mo. 600, 240 S.W. 156 (1922) (defendant had no right to withdraw parts of documents introduced by him); Looman Realty Corp. v. Broad Street National Bank, 74 N.J.Super. 71, 180 A.2d 524 (1962) (no withdrawal unless evidence irrelevant or immaterial); 1 Wigmore, Evidence § 17c, (3d ed. 1940); Dec.Dig. Trial ⚖58; C.J.S. Trial § 93.

66. Maas v. Laursen, 219 Minn. 461, 18 N.W.2d 233, 235 (1945) (discretionary, may be allowed if evidence irrelevant, or if favorable only to withdrawing party; court here did not err in denying withdrawal).

dence, the court may revoke its ruling and permit the withdrawal.[67]

Plain Error Rule. Many of the criteria for the so-called "harmless error" rule and the "plain error" rule are similar, but the two concepts so labeled should be distinguished. Federal and Revised Uniform Rule of Evidence (1974) 103 defines "harmless error" generally by its opening statement, "Error may not be predicated upon a ruling which admits or excludes evidence unless a substantial right of a party is affected . . . ." Plain error is defined in Rule 103(d) as follows, "Nothing in this rule precludes taking notice of plain errors affecting substantial rights although they were not brought to the attention of the court." Thus harmless error denotes error in rulings which is not cause for reversal; plain error denotes error sufficiently serious to justify considering it on appeal despite a failure to observe the usual procedural requirements for saving error for review. This subsection is confined to plain error.[68] It has been observed that for harmless error the courts speak as though the error must be prejudicial to the appellant, but for plain error the error must have very prejudicial effects, yet little difference can be found in the ways these concepts are applied in actual cases.[69]

For many reasons, including the hesitation of appellate courts to interfere with lower court trial responsibilities,[70] lack of details on appeal that relate to the question of whether there was error or substantial error,[71] and the possible questionable effect of claimed plain error on trials and their results, there appears to be a tendency to avoid a holding that plain error occurred even in criminal cases.[72] A holding of plain error is more likely to be the cause for reversal in errors involving the constitutional rights of criminal defendants.[73] Reversals on the basis of plain error are much less common in civil cases than in criminal cases, perhaps in part because liberty and life are not involved as a motive to apply the doctrine and thus interfere with the usual adversary trial system.[74]

The application of the doctrine depends upon a case to case analysis. General factors are considered elsewhere.[75]

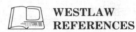 **WESTLAW REFERENCES**

Time of Making: Motions to Strike
motion /3 strike /s objection /s soon prompt! time! immediate!

Motions in Limine
digest(limine /p review!)

General and Specific Objections
digest(fail! /s object! /s specific! definite)

Repetition of Objections
30k233(2)

Tactics of Objecting
digest(objection! /s hearing /3 jury)

---

67. Alabama Great Southern Railroad Co. v. Hardy, 131 Ga. 238, 62 S.E. 71, 72 (1908); McCarty v. Bishop, 231 Mo.App. 604, 102 S.W.2d 126 (1937) (may be withdrawn in court's discretion, despite objection of opposing party).

68. See Weinstein & Berger, Evidence ¶ 103[07] (also mentions that exclusion without a proper offer of proof may be plain error); C.J.S. Appeal and Error § 245; C.J.S. Criminal Law § 1669, 1772; Adv.Com. Note, Fed.R.Evid. 103(d).

69. Weinstein & Berger, Evidence ¶ 103[07], quoting 8A Moore's Federal Practice ¶ 52.02.

70. Of course, the trial judge may object or suggest objections to the attorney. See § 55 infra.

71. Weinstein & Berger, Evidence, ¶ 103[07], quoting Sykes v. United States, 373 F.2d 607 (5th Cir. 1966), cert. denied 386 U.S. 977.

72. See cases cited in Wright & Graham, Federal Practice and Procedure: Evidence § 5036. But there are many cases in which plain error was cause for reversal. See sources cited in n. 68 supra.

73. Chapman v. California, 386 U.S. 18 (1967) indicates, "before a federal constitutional error can be harmless, the court must be able to declare a belief that it was harmless beyond a reasonable doubt . . . ." But see discussion of an "overwhelming evidence" standard in § 183, infra. Some errors may be so basic that reversal will be automatic.

74. In civil cases reversal for plain error has been termed rare. Louisell & Mueller, Federal Evidence, § 22. The Federal Rules of Criminal Procedure contain a plain error rule, Fed.R.Crim.P. 52(b), but the Federal Rules of Civil Procedure do not.

75. See, e.g., Weinstein & Berger, Evidence ¶ 103[07], [08].

Withdrawal of Evidence

110k677

Plain Error Rule

"plain error"   /s   harmless

§ 53. Preliminary Questions of Fact Arising on Objections [1]

The great body of the law of evidence consists of rules that operate to exclude relevant evidence.[2] Examples are the hearsay rule, the rule preferring original writings, and the various rules of privilege for confidential communications. These exclusionary rules are all "technical" in the sense that they have been developed by a special professional group, namely judges and lawyers, and in the further sense that for long-term ends they sometimes obstruct the ascertainment of truth in the particular case. Many if not most of these technical exclusionary rules, and the exceptions thereto, are in terms conditioned upon the existence of certain facts. Thus a copy of a writing will not be received unless the original is lost, destroyed, or otherwise unavailable.[3] Suppose a copy is offered and there is conflicting evidence as to whether the original is destroyed or intact. The judge of course ascertains and announces the rule of evidence law setting up the criterion of admission or exclusion, but who is to decide whether the original is lost, destroyed or unavailable—the preliminary question of fact upon which hinges the *application* of the rule of evidence law?

Issues of fact are usually left to the jury, but there are strong reasons here for not doing so. If the special question of fact were submitted to the jury when objection was made, cumbersome and awkward problems about unanimity would be raised. If the judge admitted the evidence (the copy as above) to the jury and directed them to disregard it unless they found that the disputed fact existed, the aim of the exclusionary rule would likely be frustrated, for two reasons. First, the jury would often not be able to erase the evidence from their minds, if they found that the conditioning fact did not exist. They could not if they would. Second, the average jury would not be interested in performing this intellectual gymnastic of "disregarding" the evidence. They are intent mainly on reaching their verdict in a case in accord with what they believe to be true, rather than in enforcing the long-term policies of evidence law.

Accordingly, under the traditional view and the generally accepted principle the trial judge decides with finality those preliminary questions of fact upon which depends the admissibility of an item of evidence that is objected to under an exclusionary rule of evidence.[4] This principle is incorporated in

§ 53

1. 9 Wigmore, Evidence § 2550 (Chadbourn rev. 1981); Weinstein & Berger, Evidence ¶¶ 104[01]–[12]; Maguire, Evidence: Common Sense and Common Law 211–230 (1947); Maguire and Epstein, Preliminary Questions of Fact, 40 Harv.L.Rev. 392 (1927); Morgan, Functions of Judge and Jury in Preliminary Questions 43 Harv.L.Rev. 165 (1929); Dec.Dig. Trial ⬤138; Dec. Dig. Criminal Law ⬤736; C.J.S. Trial § 207.

2. "And chiefly it [the law of evidence] determines as among probative matters . . . what classes of things shall not be received. This excluding function is the characteristic one in our law of evidence." Thayer, Preliminary Treatise on Evidence 264 (1898).

3. See § 230 infra.

4. The following situations are illustrative. Bartlett v. Smith, 11 M. & W. 483, 152 Eng.Rep. 895 (Exch., 1843) (question whether bill drawn in London or Dublin, on which depended its admissibility under the Stamp Act, should have been decided by judge instead of leaving to jury); Sylvania Electric Products, Inc. v. Flanagan, 352 F.2d 1005 (1st Cir. 1965) (under the best evidence rule the judge must decide that the original has become unavailable); W. A. Manda, Inc. v. City of Orange, 82 N.J.L. 686, 82 A. 869 (1912) (eminent domain: evidence of prices paid for other properties, admissible if substantially similar property, which is to be decided by judge); State v. Maynard, 184 N.C. 653, 113 S.E. 682 (1922) (admissibility in criminal case of former testimony of witness, held judge properly decided and refused to submit to jury, preliminary question whether witness absent by defendant's procurement); Potter v. Baker, 162 Ohio St. 488, 124 N.E.2d 140 (1955) (accuracy of words testified to, nature of occurrence, etc., are preliminary questions for judge in decision concerning admissibility of spontaneous exclamations as exceptions to the hearsay rule).

If reasonably supported by the evidence, his decision will not be reversed. Smith v. United States, 106 F.2d 726 (4th Cir. 1939) (sufficiency of showing of unavailability, where witness temporarily ill); People v. Cen-

Federal and Revised Uniform Rule of Evidence (1974) 104(a).[5] The same practice extends to the determination of preliminary facts conditioning the application of the rules as to competency [6] and privileges [7] of

witnesses. On all these preliminary questions the judge, on request, will hold a hearing in which each side may produce evidence.[8]

---

ters, 56 Cal.App.2d 631, 133 P.2d 29 (1943) (sufficiency of showing of diligence in search for absent witness).

See § 161 infra, for rules concerning the admission of confessions of a criminal defendant.

5. Fed. and Rev.Unif.R.Evid. (1974) 104(a) provides:

Preliminary questions concerning the qualification of a person to be a witness, the existence of a privilege, or the admissibility of evidence shall be determined by the court, subject to the provisions of subdivision (b). In making its determination it is not bound by the rules of evidence except those with respect to privileges.

Subdivision (b), to which reference is made, states a special rule for so-called "conditionally relevant" evidence. See text at n. 10, infra.

6. Bell v. State, 164 Ga. 292, 138 S.E. 238 (1927) (competency of nine-year-old boy as witness, for judge, error to submit to jury); Moosbrugger v. Swick, 86 N.J.L. 419, 92 A. 269 (1914) (whether assignor of claim sued on had assigned in good faith and hence escaped incompetency under Dead Man's Act, for judge).

Unless the competency of a witness is determined under state law in connection with testimony that relates to an element of a claim or defense as to which state law supplies the rule of decision, Fed.R.Evid. 601 will rarely raise a matter of competency. However, the qualification of an expert to testify pursuant to Fed.R.Evid. 702 is a matter to be decided by the judge. See, e.g., United States v. Haro-Espinosa, 619 F.2d 789 (9th Cir. 1979).

7. Robinson v. United States, 144 F.2d 392 (6th Cir. 1944) (attorney-client communications); Phelps Dodge Corp. v. Guerrero, 273 Fed. 415 (9th Cir. 1921) (physician-patient privilege). The last case holds that the burden of proof of the facts of privilege is on the asserter of the privilege.

Whether common law principles or state law govern privileges under Fed.R.Evid. 501, Rule 104(a) assures the result in the text.

8. Should the exclusionary law of evidence, "the child of the jury system" in Thayer's phrase, be applied to this hearing before the judge? Sound sense backs the view that it should not, and that the judge should be empowered to hear any relevant evidence, including affidavits or other hearsay. Judicial expressions both for and against this view are found. Cases for include Schwimmer v. United States, 232 F.2d 855, 863 (8th Cir. 1956), cert. denied 352 U.S. 833 (court not bound by technical rules of evidence in passing on question of waiver of privilege); Healy v. Rennert, 9 N.Y.2d 202, 213 N.Y.S.2d 44, 173 N.E.2d 777 (1961) (letter admissible to establish unavailability of witness to allow use of prior testimony). Contra, holding affidavits inadmissible, Becker v. Quigg, 54 Ill. 390 (1870); Poignand v. Smith, 25 Mass. 272, 277 (1829). Fed. and Rev.Unif.R.

Evid. (1974) 104(a) provides that in making preliminary determinations of admissibility of evidence the court "is not bound to by the rules of evidence except those with respect to privileges." Rule 1101(d)(1) lists as one of the situations where the rules (except with respect to privileges) do not apply: "The determination of questions of fact preliminary to admissibility of evidence when the issue is to be determined by the court under rule 104." The slight difference in language between the quoted second sentence of Rule 104(a) and Rule 1101(d)(1) is without significance, the latter being merely a restatement of the former, as pointed out in the Advisory Committee's Note to the latter. In United States v. Matlock, 415 U.S. 164 (1974), the Court had before it the question of the correctness of the trial court's exclusion, at a suppression hearing, of hearsay statements by defendant's alleged cohabitant relied upon by the government to establish her standing to consent to the search and seizure in question. The Court referred to the two rules cited above as being in essentially the same language and reflecting the general views of various authorities, and held that the court should have considered the excluded hearsay. While the rules were at the time before the Congress and in a state of suspense, it is obvious that the result would be the same under the rules.

What should be the burden of proof, i.e. required measure of persuasion, at the hearing? The Federal and Revised Uniform Rules (1974) are silent. The most commonly accepted standard is the preponderance of the evidence test. United States v. Enright, 579 F.2d 980 (6th Cir. 1978) (introduction of statement of co-conspirator); Annot., 44 A.L.R.Fed. 627. The Supreme Court held in Lego v. Twomey, 404 U.S. 477 (1972), that the voluntariness of a confession as a constitutional matter need only be established by a preponderance of the evidence. In view of the strict precautions surrounding the admission of confessions, it is highly unlikely that a higher standard would be required in other situations. It is, however, open to the States to fix higher standards. The argument has been made that the standard should depend in all situations, as well as in those involving constitutional issues, upon the type of case, the purpose of the rule giving rise to the preliminary fact question, and whether the rule relates to the reliability of the evidence. Saltzburg, Standards of Proof and Preliminary Questions of Fact, 27 Stan.L.Rev. 271 (1975). No substantial disposition to follow this pattern is apparent.

It is usually assumed as a general proposition that the proponent of the evidence has the burden of establishing the preliminary facts, but that the opposing party has the burden of producing evidence to show the existence of grounds for objection otherwise. Wright & Graham, Federal Practice and Procedure § 5053. The allocation of burdens on constitutional issues is discussed in § 180 at nn. 19–28 infra.

The foregoing discussion involves situations where the competency of evidence is attacked, and it is sought to be excluded under a "technical" exclusionary rule. Those situations are to be distinguished from another type of situation, namely those in which the relevancy, i.e. probative value, of a fact offered in evidence depends on the existence of another, and preliminary, fact. As the Advisory Committee's Note to Federal Rule of Evidence 104(b) observes:

> Thus when a spoken statement is relied upon to prove notice to X, it is without probative value unless X heard it. Or if a letter purporting to be from Y is relied upon to establish an admission by him, it has no probative value unless Y wrote or authorized it. Relevance in this sense has been labelled "conditional relevancy." Morgan, Basic Problems of Evidence 45–56 (1962).[9]

These factual questions of conditional relevancy are to be distinguished from questions whether particular evidence is relevant as a matter of law, such as whether evidence that accused purchased on the day before a murder a weapon of the type used in the killing is relevant. Questions of the latter nature are, of course, for the judge, as are matters of law generally.

The factual questions of conditional relevancy are well within the competency of juries and involve the kind of questions with which we are accustomed to see juries deal. Did A say such-and-such? Did B hear him? Did C sign the letter offered in evidence? And so on. Jury trials would be curtailed greatly if judges gave the final decisions on these questions. The judge is not, however, eliminated from the picture but divides his responsibility with the jury in the following manner. The judge requires the proponent to bring forward evidence from which the jury could find the existence of the preliminary fact. The opposing party may then bring in disputing evidence. If on all the evidence the judge determines that the jury could not find the existence of the preliminary fact, he excludes the evidence. Otherwise, the question is for the jury.

The procedure described above was and is followed at common law [10] and is embodied

As to keeping preliminary fact matter from coming to the attention of the jury, Fed. and Rev.Unif.R.Evid. (1974) 104(c) provide:

> Hearings on the admissibility of confessions shall in all cases be conducted out of the hearing of the jury. Hearings on other preliminary matters shall be so conducted when the interests of justice so require or, when an accused is a witness, if he so requests.

As the federal Advisory Committee's Note to Rule 104(c) observes with respect to preliminary matters other than confessions and testimony by an accused person:

> Otherwise, detailed treatment of when preliminary matters should be heard outside the hearing of the jury is not feasible. The procedure is time consuming. Not infrequently the same evidence which is relevant to the issue of establishment of a condition precedent to admissibility is also relevant to weight or credibility, and time is saved by taking foundation proof in the presence of the jury. Much evidence on preliminary questions, though not relevant to jury issues, may be heard by the jury with no adverse effect. A great deal must be left to the discretion of the judge who will act as the interests of justice require.

9. Adv.Com.Note, Fed.R.Evid. 104(b). See also Morgan, Functions of Judge and Jury in Preliminary Questions of Fact, 43 Harv.L.Rev. 164, 164–175 (1929).

See the general treatment of authentication as an aspect of conditional relevancy, Ch. 22 infra.

10. Patton v. Bank of Lafayette, 124 Ga. 965, 53 S.E. 664 (1906) (suit on note, execution denied; held, note admissible when evidence offered from which it could be found to be genuine); Coleman v. McIntosh, 184 Ky. 370, 211 S.W. 872 (1919) (breach of promise; defendant offered in evidence a purported letter from plaintiff to another man; plaintiff denied she wrote it and judge excluded; held, error, there being some evidence of genuineness, letter should have been admitted and authenticity left to jury); Winslow v. Bailey, 16 Me. 319 (1839) (defense to note on ground of fraudulent misrepresentation; defendant offered as evidence of the false statement, a certificate of a third person as to the amount of timber on a tract; held, judge properly ruled that he should not determine whether the certificate was used as an inducement to plaintiff, but should only require prima facie evidence of this, before admitting the certificate); Coghlan v. White, 236 Mass. 165, 128 N.E. 33 (1920) (whether required statutory written notice was delivered to defendant was not for judge as fact preliminary to admitting notice in evidence, but for jury on conflicting testimony). But the distinction is one over which the courts occasionally stumble. Gila Valley, Globe & Northern Railway v. Hall, 232 U.S. 94 (1914) (there was issue whether plaintiff knew of defect in appliance; defendant offered evidence of remark about defect made when plaintiff less than 20 yards away: on objection judge excluded on

in Federal and Revised Uniform Rule of Evidence (1974) 104(b), which reads:

> When the relevancy of evidence depends on the fulfillment of a condition of fact, the court shall admit it upon, or subject to, the introduction of evidence sufficient to support a finding of the fulfillment of the condition.

Some situations have not readily lent themselves to treatment as a member of either of the two groupings discussed above and accordingly require further discussion.

First, confessions are subject to their own special rules, which are treated elsewhere.[11]

Second, in cases involving offers of dying declarations some courts have given the jury a share in deciding the preliminary question whether declarant had the settled, hopeless expectation of death required for that exception to the hearsay rule.[12] This pattern is not followed by Federal and Revised Uniform Rule of Evidence (1974) 104.[13]

Third, in a troublesome group of cases the preliminary fact question coincides with one of the ultimate disputed fact-issues that the jury will normally decide. Several examples may be given. (1) In a bigamy prosecution where the first marriage is disputed, the second wife is offered as a state's witness, and defendant objects under a statute disqualifying the wife to testify against her husband. (2) Plaintiff sues on a lost writing, and defendant contends that it was not lost because it never existed. (3) In a prosecution for conspiracy, the state offers an alleged declaration by a co-conspirator made during the course of and in furtherance of the conspiracy. Defendants deny that the conspiracy ever existed. The results that have been reached lack much in the way of consistency.

In Example (1) the preliminary question involves the competency of the witness, a question for the judge at common law or under Rule 104(a) if it were not for the overlap with the jury issue whether she was the wife. To allow the judge to decide her competency seems not to embarrass the jury trial in any way; his decision need not be communicated to the jury; and additional useful evidence may be made available. Accordingly the cases have tended to leave the decision to the judge.[14] In Example (2) the preliminary question whether a writing was

---

ground not proved to have been heard by plaintiff: held, no error, preliminary question for judge); Dexter v. Thayer, 189 Mass. 114, 75 N.E. 223 (1905) (whether agreement between parties alleged to have been made for one by purported agent, was authorized, preliminary fact for judge). See also, West's Ann.Cal.Evid. Code, § 403; N.J.R.Ev. 8(2).

11. Infra § 161.

12. The nature of the requirement is discussed in § 282 infra. Some decisions have admitted dying declarations if reasonable persons could differ as to whether declarant was conscious of impending death. Emmett v. State, 195 Ga. 517, 25 S.E.2d 9, 19 (1943); People v. Denton, 312 Mich. 32, 19 N.W.2d 476 (1945). Sometimes the practice has been for the judge to determine the preliminary question, but requires him, if he admits, to instruct the jury to disregard if they find no consciousness. State v. Garver, 190 Or. 291, 225 P.2d 771, 780 (1950).

A majority, however, have followed the practice that fact questions with respect to this requirement are preliminary fact questions for the judge. Comer v. State, 212 Ark. 66, 204 S.W.2d 875 (1947); Tillman v. State, 44 So.2d 644 (Fla.1950); People v. Hubbs, 401 Ill. 613, 83 N.E.2d 289, 297 (1949) (admissibility for court, weight for jury); State v. Rich, 231 N.C. 696, 58 S.E.2d 720 (1950); West's Ann.Cal.Evid.Code, § 405. But if the judge admits the declaration the jury in appraising its weight may consider, among other factors of credibility, whether they believe that the declaration was made under a sense of impending death. Comm. v. Knable, 369 Pa. 171, 85 A.2d 114 (1952). Hence they are entitled to hear the evidence as to the circumstances of the making of the declaration. Conway v. State, 177 Miss. 461, 171 So. 16 (1936); State v. Dotson, 96 W.Va. 596, 123 S.E. 463, 464 (1924).

Cases pro and con are collected in 5 Wigmore, Evidence § 1451 (Chadbourn rev. 1974), and in Dec.Dig., Homicide ⊂⇒218.

13. No provision excludes the dying declaration hearsay exception from the operation of Fed. and Rev. Unif.R.Evid. (1974) 104(a), for determination by the judge. It should, however, be noted that Rule 104(e) provides:

> This rule does not limit the right of a party to introduce before the jury evidence relevant to weight or credibility.

The rule thus follows the majority view described in n. 12 supra.

14. Matz v. United States, 81 U.S.App.D.C. 326, 158 F.2d 190 (1946). See also State v. Lee, 127 La. 1077, 54 So. 356 (1911) (murder by Mack Lee conceded, but defendant claims he is not Mack Lee; defense offers as a witness the wife of Mack Lee, who presumably would have testified defendant was not her husband; trial

lost is for the judge at common law or under Rule 104(a), but evidently it cannot have been lost if it never existed. Aside from the question of loss, the execution of the document would be a jury question, with the preliminary question of authentication for admissibility purposes one for the jury at common law or under Rule 104(b). The basic issue in the case quite clearly is whether the original writing ever existed; the question whether it has been lost is subsidiary. Sound judgment appears to call for decision of the basic question by the jury, rather than having it subsumed into the judge's question. This is the result, both by decision [15] and under Rule 1008,[16] for if the judge decided that the writing never existed and excludes the secondary evidence, the case is ended without ever going to the jury on the central issue.[17] In Example (3), at common law the cases were divided as to whether the judge should make the preliminary determination whether a conspiracy existed and defendant and declarant were members of it, or the judge should admit the evidence upon a prima facie showing, instructing the jury to disregard it if they found these matters not proved.[18] Supporting the first position is the view that, by rather casual analysis, the judge is dealing with the applicability of a supposed hearsay

exception for declarations by a co-conspirator, with the preliminary question to be decided by the judge. This reasoning leads to application of Rule 104(a) under the Federal and Revised Uniform Rules. Under a proper analysis, however, virtually all declarations by co-conspirators will be found to qualify as "verbal acts," [19] and hence not hearsay in the first place, by analysis or rules definition.[20] This reasoning would lead to the jury's making the preliminary determination, after screening by the judge, as a question of conditional relevancy, whether at common law or under Rule 104(b). Whatever the merits of these positions, the fact is that the holdings under the Federal Rules have allocated the preliminary determination to the judge, excluding jury participation except with respect to the ultimate issue.[21] This result is probably the result of two considerations: the difficulty, and to some extent unreality, of submitting the preliminary question to the jury, and the understandable wish to extend judicial control over the use of conspiracy charges by prosecutors.

WESTLAW REFERENCES

digest(relevan! probative /s fact /p objection*)

---

judge, after preliminary hearing rejected witness under statute forbidding wife to testify for husband, on the ground that he was satisfied that the accused was Mack Lee; held, no error, general rule applies).

15. Stowe v. Querner, L.R. 5 Exch. 155 (1870); St. Croix v. Seacoast Canning Co., 114 Me. 521, 96 A. 1059 (1916); Fauci v. Mulready, 337 Mass. 532, 150 N.E.2d 286 (1958). See Maguire & Epstein, Preliminary Questions, 40 Harv.L.Rev. 392, 415–420 (1927).

16. Fed. and Rev.Unif.R.Evid. (1974) 1008 provide:

When the admissibility of other evidence of contents of writings, recordings, or photographs under these rules depends upon the fulfillment of a condition of fact, the question whether the condition has been fulfilled is ordinarily for the court to determine in accordance with the provisions of rule 104. However, when an issue is raised (a) whether the asserted writing ever existed, or (b) whether another writing, recording, or photograph produced at the trial is the original, or (c) whether other evidence of contents correctly reflects the contents, the issue is for the trier of fact to determine as in the case of other issues of fact.

In United States v. Gerhart, 538 F.2d 807 (8th Cir. 1976), the court extended the rule to include the question whether an original is lost.

The finding of personal knowledge under Rule 602 and of authenticity under Rule 901 are both to be decided under Rule 104(b), rather than solely by the judge under Rule 104(a). Adv.Com.Notes, Fed.R.Evid. 602, 901.

17. Levin, Authentication and Content of Writings, 10 Rutgers L.Rev. 632, 644 (1956).

18. Weinstein & Berger, Evidence ¶ 104[05].

19. Infra § 267 n. 39.

20. Under Fed. and Rev.Unif.R.Evid. 801(d)(2)(E) a statement is not hearsay if it is offered against a party and is

a statement by a co-conspirator of a party during the course and in furtherance of the conspiracy.

21. See, e.g. United States v. James, 590 F.2d 575 (5th Cir. 1978), cert. denied 442 U.S. 917; United States v. Jackson, 627 F.2d 1198 (D.C.Cir. 1980). Additional decisions are listed in Weinstein & Berger ¶ 104[05].

§ 54. Availability as Proof of Evidence Admitted Without Objection

As indicated in section 52, a failure to make a sufficient objection to evidence which is incompetent waives any ground of complaint as to the admission of the evidence.[1] But it has another effect, equally important. If the evidence is received without objection, it becomes part of the evidence in the case, and is usable as proof to the extent of the rational persuasive power it may have.[2] The fact that it was inadmissible does not prevent its use as proof so far as it has probative value. The incompetent evidence, unobjected to, may be relied on in argument,[3] and alone or in part may support a verdict or finding.[4] This principle is almost universally accepted.[5] The Federal and Revised Uniform Rules of Evidence are silent on this subject but raise no doubt as to the continued applicability of the rules in this section. The principle applies to any ground of incompetency under the exclusionary rules. It is most often invoked in respect to hearsay,[6] but it has been applied to evidence vulnerable as secondary evidence of writings,[7] opinions,[8] evidence elicited from incompetent witnesses [9] or subject to a privilege,[10] or subject to objection because of the want of authentication of a writing,[11] of the lack-of-knowledge qualification of a witness,[12] or of the expertness qualification.[13]

§ 54

1. This statement is subject to the "plain error" rule. See § 52 supra.

2. McWilliams v. R & T Transport, Inc., 245 Ark. 882, 435 S.W.2d 98 (1968) (hearsay); Old v. Cooney Detective Agency, 215 Md. 517, 138 A.2d 889 (1958). Again the text is subject to the "plain error" rule. See § 52 supra.

3. Birmingham Electric Co. v. Wildman, 119 Ala. 547, 24 So. 548 (1898); Chicago & Eastern Illinois Railroad Co. v. Mochell, 193 Ill. 208, 61 N.E. 1028 (1901).

4. Indianapolis Blue Print & Manufacturing Co. v. Kennedy, 215 Ind. 409, 19 N.E.2d 554 (1939); Department of Emp. Sec. v. Minnesota Drug Products, 258 Minn. 133, 104 N.W.2d 640 (1960) (dictum); Gregoire v. Insurance Co. of North America, 128 Vt. 255, 261 A.2d 25 (1969); Dafoe v. Grantski, 143 Neb. 344, 9 N.W.2d 488 (1943) (hearsay standing alone may sustain a finding), and see decisions collected in Dec.Dig. ⊗105; C.J.S. Trial §§ 150–156.

But see Pearson v. Stevens, 446 S.W.2d 381 (Tex.Civ. App.1969) (contra as to hearsay forming basis of finding of fact or judgment). See n. 5 infra.

5. See references in next preceding note. However, in Texas and Georgia, hearsay admitted without objection is said to have no probative force. See extensive discussion in Annot., 79 A.L.R.2d 890. This notion is also expressed in Wheelock Brothers, Inc. v. Lindner Packing & Provision Co., 130 Colo. 122, 273 P.2d 730 (1954) (hearsay insufficient in determining whether plaintiff made a prima facie case).

6. Ventromile v. Malden Electric Co., 317 Mass. 132, 57 N.E.2d 209 (1944) (statement of plaintiff after accident made in presence of defendant's employee); De Moulin v. Rotheli, 354 Mo. 425, 189 S.W.2d 562 (1945) (statement by manager of defendant's grocery store after plaintiff's fall); People v. McCoy, 101 Ill.App.2d 69, 242 N.E.2d 4 (1968) (unusual case in which prosecuting attorney took stand and presented state's case). See n. 5, supra, for contrary view. Annot., 79 A.L.R.2d 890, collects numerous cases.

7. Elster's Sales v. Longo, 4 Cal.App.3d 216, 84 Cal. Rptr. 83 (1970); Carter v. Commonwealth, 450 S.W.2d 257 (Ky.1970); Glover v. Mitchell, 319 Mass. 1, 64 N.E.2d 648 (1946) (federal price regulations); Dec.Dig. Trial ⊗105(5).

8. Curtin v. Franchetti, 156 Conn. 387, 242 A.2d 725 (1968) (opinion as to ownership of property); Word v. City of St. Louis, 617 S.W.2d 479 (Mo.App.1981) (that plaintiff knew a hole had been there for a long time because of presence of cracks in the asphalt); Dieter v. Scott, 110 Vt. 376, 9 A.2d 95 (1939) (testimony of defendant that he acted as agent of lessee is a conclusion, but not objected to, it is entitled to consideration if not in conflict with underlying facts regarding the relationship); Dec.Dig. Trial ⊗105(3). But the Georgia court did weaken when the opinion was on the ultimate issue. Morgan v. Bell, 189 Ga. 432, 5 S.E.2d 897 (1940) (mental capacity to make will).

9. Walker v. Fields, 247 S.W. 272 (Tex.Com.App. 1923) (testimony of interested survivor, not objected to, "not without probative force"); Estate of Berg, 34 Ill. App.3d 379, 340 N.E.2d 51 (1975). Contra: Brittain v. McKim, 204 Ark. 647, 164 S.W.2d 435 (1942) (result based on fact that incompetency rule was contained in the constitution), but disapproved in Starbird v. Cheatham, 243 Ark. 181, 419 S.W.2d 114 (1967).

10. Gruner v. Gruner, 165 S.W. 865 (Mo.App.1914) (marital communications).

11. Collins v. Streitz, 95 F.2d 430 (9th Cir. 1938); Elswick v. Charleston Transit Co., 128 W.Va. 241, 36 S.E.2d 419 (1946) (city ordinance: failure to object waives proof of existence and authenticity); Dec.Dig. Trial ⊗105(4).

12. See Winsor v. Hawkins, 130 Conn. 669, 37 A.2d 222 (1944) (plaintiff's testimony, received without objection, that she had neuritis and water on the knee, though she probably had it secondhand from doctor, could be given such weight as it deserved).

13. McGuire v. Baird, 9 Cal.2d 353, 70 P.2d 915 (1937) (malpractice: defendant by not objecting admitted qualifications of plaintiff's doctor to testify to skill

Relevancy and probative worth, however, stand on a different footing. If the evidence has no probative force, or insufficient probative value to sustain the proposition for which it is offered, the want of objection adds nothing to its worth [14] and it will not support a finding. It is still irrelevant or insufficient. However, the failure to object to evidence related to the controversy but not covered by the pleadings, may amount to the informal framing of new issues.[15] When this is held to have been the result, the failure to object on the ground that the evidence is not material to any issue raised by the pleadings is waived,[16] and the evidence will support the proponent's side of the new informal issue.[17]

 WESTLAW REFERENCES

digest(incompetent inadmiss! /2 evidence /3 admit!)

---

ordinarily exercised in that community); Woods v. Siegrist, 112 Colo. 257, 149 P.2d 241 (1944) (evidence of chiropractor-witness, whose qualifications were not objected to, sustains findings though contradicted by qualified neurologists); Jones v. Treegoob, 433 Pa. 225, 249 A.2d 352 (1969); Dec.Dig. Trial ⟨⟨105(3).

14. Danany v. Cuneo, 130 Conn. 213, 33 A.2d 132 (1943); Marshall v. Kleinman, 186 Conn. 67, 438 A.2d 1199 (1982); Craig v. Citizens' Trust Co., 217 Ind. 434, 26 N.E.2d 1006 (1940); DeLong v. Iowa State Highway Commission, 229 Iowa 700, 295 N.W. 91, 97 (1941) (but here the court goes on to adopt the untenable view that inadmissible hearsay, standing alone, can never have sufficient probative worth to support a finding).

15. Many jurisdictions have adopted Rule 15(b) of the Federal Rules of Civil Procedure. Pursuant to this rule pleadings are deemed amended when issues not raised by the pleadings are "tried by the express or implied consent of the parties" at the trial. Under this wording evidence not objected to can raise new issues not within the pleadings. E.g., Niedland v. United States, 338 F.2d 254 (3d Cir. 1964). See Wright & Miller, Federal Practice and Procedure: Civil § 1493. Cases not governed by the rule have reached a similar result. Phillips v. New Amsterdam Casualty Co., 193 La. 314, 190 So. 565 (1939). Under the federal rule, however, even if the evidence not within the issues is not objected to, there is no implied consent to the new issue raised if the opposing party was not and should not have been aware that a new issue was being raised by the evidence to which no objection was made. This situation is most likely to occur when the evidence in question relates to an issue already raised by the pleadings and also a new issue. See Otness v. United States, 23 F.R.D. 279 (D.C.Alaska, 1959).

§ 55. Waiver of Objection

A failure to assert an objection promptly and specifically is a waiver.[1] What other conduct is a waiver?

Demand for inspection of a writing. One party, D, gives notice to his opponent, O, to produce a document, and O does produce it at the trial. Thereupon in open court D asks to inspect it, and is allowed to do so. The document if offered by O would be inadmissible, except for the notice, production, and inspection. Do these facts preclude D from objecting when the document is offered by O? England, Massachusetts, and a few other states have said yes, D is precluded from objecting.[2] This result was based at first upon the notion that it would be unconscionable to permit the demanding party to examine the private papers of the producing party without being subjected to some corre-

16. See n. 15 supra. This result was reached absent Rule 15(b) of Fed.R.Civ.P. in Atlanta Enterprises v. James, 68 Ga. 773, 24 S.E.2d 130 (1943).

17. See n. 15 supra. Again this result is reached absent Rule 15(b), Fed.R.Civ.P. in Wood v. Claxton, 199 Ga. 809, 35 S.E.2d 455 (1945).

§ 55

1. See § 52 supra. The use of a term, or a concept labeled, "waiver" in the situations discussed generally in this section has been strongly criticized. Wright & Graham, Federal Practice and Procedure: Evidence § 5039. It appears that many courts have not used the term in its strictly technical sense, but as a label of convenience for doctrines stated in the original text. Many of the original case citations in the instant section indicate no confusion with the strictly orthodox terms, "waiver" and "estoppel," as used in other areas of the law.

See further § 136 n. 6 infra.

2. Wharem v. Routledge, 5 Esp. 235, 170 Eng.Rep. 797 (Nisi Prius, 1805, Lord Ellenborough); Calvert v. Flower, 7 Car. & P. 386, 173 Eng.Rep. 172 (1836); United States Fidelity & Guaranty Co. v. Continental Baking Co., 172 Md. 24, 190 A. 768 (1937) (witness statement, but when admitted it only bears on credibility and does not "prove the fact"); Clark v. Fletcher, 83 Mass. (1 Allen) 53 (1861) (leading case); Leonard v. Taylor, 315 Mass. 580, 53 N.E.2d 705 (1944); Decker v. George W. Smith & Co., 88 N.J.L. 630, 96 A. 915 (1916), and cases cited in Annot., 151 A.L.R. 1006, 1012. However, as remarked in Zimmerman v. Zimmerman, 12 N.J.Super. 61, 79 A.2d 59 (1950), the spirit of the federal discovery rules adopted in New Jersey "seems to run counter" to the old practice as indicated in Decker v. George W. Smith & Co., supra. This *Zimmerman*

sponding risk on his own part.[3] A later case, however, has justified the result on the ground that the party who is called on in open court before a jury to produce a writing for inspection may be suspected of evasion or concealment unless he is given the privilege of introducing the writing.[4] Cases from other states recognize that the older policy against compelled disclosure to his adversary of relevant writings in possession of a party is now outmoded[5] and that the prevailing policy is just the opposite, namely, that of exerting pressure for full disclosure except for privileged matter. Accordingly, these states reject the rule,[6] and permit him to assert any pertinent objection if the producing party offers the writing. This rule is consistent with Federal and Revised Uniform Rule of Evidence (1974) 103(a)(1). It

should be emphasized that the older policy is inconsistent with the pretrial discovery policy of the federal civil discovery rules, which have been adopted in many states.[7]

Failure to object to earlier like evidence. A party has introduced evidence of particular facts without objection. Later he offers additional evidence, perhaps by other witnesses or writings, of the same facts or a part thereof. May the adversary now object, or has he waived his right by his earlier quiescence? It is often summarily stated in the opinions that he is precluded from objecting.[8] But in opinions where the question is carefully discussed it is usually concluded that the mere failure to object to other like evidence is not a waiver of objection to new incompetent evidence.[9] This concept should be applied under the Federal and Revised

viewpoint should apply in states which have adopted in substance the federal discovery rules. See also Dec. Dig. Evidence ⧄368(14).

But the rule does not apply in any event when the writing is used by one party to refresh the memory of his witness: the other party is entitled to inspect the writing without being penalized by being required to permit its introduction in evidence. Clearly the supposed reason of the rule does not apply. Nussenbaum v. Chambers & Chambers, 322 Mass. 419, 77 N.E.2d 780 (1948). See § 9, n. 35 supra.

3. Clark v. Fletcher, next preceding note, at p. 57, quoted 151 A.L.R. 1013.

4. Leonard v. Taylor, note 2 supra. This shifting of ground, however tenuous the new justification may seem, at least implies that the rule should be restricted to the limits of the new reason, namely, to jury trials where request for inspection is made in the jury's presence.

5. See the vigorous criticism of the rule in 7 Wigmore, Evidence § 2125 (Chadbourn rev. 1978).

6. Scully v. Morrison Hotel Corp., 118 Ill.App.2d 254, 254 N.E.2d 852 (1969) (rejecting "English" rule in Illinois); Morgan v. Paine, 312 A.2d 178 (Me.1973) (overruling prior cases); Merlino v. Mutual Service Casualty Insurance Co., 23 Wis.2d 571, 127 N.W.2d 741 (1964); Kane v. New Idea Realty Co., 104 Conn. 508, 133 A. 686 (1926) (party called on to produce may not require that demanding party promise to put writing in evidence, before surrendering it for inspection); Smith v. Rentz, 131 N.Y. 169, 30 N.E. 54, 56 (1892) ("The party who has in his possession books or papers which may be material to the case of his opponent has no moral right to conceal them from his adversary. . . . The party calling for books and papers would be subjected to great hazard if an inspection merely, without more, would make them evidence in the case. That rule tends rather to the suppression than the as-

certainment of truth, and the opposite rule is, as it seems to us, better calculated to promote the ends of justice."); Summers v. McKim, 12 Serg. & R. (Pa.) 405, 411 (1825); Ellis v. Randle, 24 Tex.Civ.App. 475, 60 S.W. 462, 465 (1900).

7. See Zimmerman v. Zimmerman, n. 2 supra.

8. Star Realty v. Strahl, 261 Iowa 362, 154 N.W.2d 143 (1967); Rash v. Waterhouse, 124 Vt. 476, 207 A.2d 130 (1965); State v. Tranchell, 243 Or. 215, 412 P.2d 520 (1966) (matter is in discretion of the court); Shelton v. Southern Railway Co., 193 N.C. 670, 139 S.E. 232 (1927) (benefit of exception ordinarily lost if same evidence admitted earlier or later without objection—an arguendo statement); C.J.S. Trial § 115.

But no court would hold that because earlier evidence was subject to an objection under a particular exclusionary rule, e.g., hearsay, and was received without objection, that this would preclude the adversary to assert this ground of objection against new evidence. See, e.g., New York Life Insurance Co. v. Neasham, 250 F. 787 (9th Cir. 1918) (consent to use transcript of testimony of one witness at coroner's hearing, not waiver of right to object to transcript of testimony of another witness at same hearing).

9. Lowery v. Jones, 219 Ala. 201, 121 So. 704, 64 A.L.R. 553 (1929) ("If these [later] objections had been sustained, the force of the former testimony would probably have been weakened in the mind of the jury"); Slocinski v. Radwan, 83 N.H. 501, 144 A. 787 (1929); Bobereski v. Insurance Co. of Pa., 105 Pa.Super. 585, 161 A. 412, 415 (1932) (". . . the fact that incompetent, irrelevant, and immaterial evidence may be introduced on a trial by one party, without objection from the other party, because he may deem it of no importance and harmless, does not prevent the latter from objecting to the further introduction and elaboration of such evidence when he is of opinion that it is both important and harmful. The principle of estoppel does

Uniform Rules of Evidence.[10] Of course, an overruling of this new objection will frequently not be prejudicial, but that is a different question.[11] The practice of the best advocates of withholding objection unless it is clear that the evidence would be damaging is in the interest of dispatch of business and would be encouraged by the nonwaiver rule. On the other hand, when the evidence of the fact, admitted without objection, is extensive,[12] and the fact though incompetent has some probative value, the trial judge should be conceded a discretion to find that the objector's conduct has amounted to a waiver. Again, this condition upon the previously stated rule should be followed under the Federal and Revised Uniform Rules of Evidence.

The Offering of Like Evidence by the Objector. If it happens that a party who has objected to evidence of a certain fact himself produces evidence from his own witness of the same fact, he has waived his objection.[13] This result should be reached under the Federal and Revised Uniform Rules of Evidence.[14] However, when his objection is made and overruled he is required and entitled to treat this ruling as the "law of the trial" and to explain or rebut, if he can, the evidence which has come in over his protest. Consequently, it will not be a waiver if he cross-examines the adversary's witness about the matter,[15] even though the cross-examination entails a repetition of the fact,[16] or if he meets the testimony with other evidence which under the theory of the objection would be incompetent.[17] The Federal and Revised Uniform Rules of Evidence should not change the above results.[18] The closely related question of whether he may so meet the testimony by extrinsic evidence at all is considered in Section 57. Generally, he may do so.

Exclusion by Judge in Absence of Objection. A party's failure to object usually waives the objection and precludes the party from complaining if the evidence is let in.[19] But the failure by the party does not of it-

not apply in such case."); McLane v. Paschal, 74 Tex. 27, 11 S.W. 837, 889 (1889).

10. This position is also taken in Wright & Graham, Federal Practice and Procedure: Evidence § 5039.

11. As pointed out by Phillips, C.J. in Slayden v. Palmo, 103 Tex. 413, 194 S.W. 1103, 1104 (1917).

12. Of course, evidence and counterevidence may make the fact material, though not pleaded. See, e.g., Sweazey v. Valley Transport, 6 Wn.2d 324, 107 P.2d 567 (1940), and see § 54 n. 3 supra.

13. Trouser Corp. v. Goodman & Theise, 153 F.2d 284 (3d Cir. 1946) (recognizing principle: but not clear here whether elicited in effort to rebut); Inter-City Trucking Co. v. Mason & Dixon Lines, 38 Tenn.App. 450, 276 S.W.2d 488 (1955); City of Houston v. McFadden, 420 S.W.2d 811 (Tex.Civ.App.1967); Ryder v. Board of Health, 273 Mass. 177, 173 N.E. 580 (1930); In re Forsythe's Estate, 221 Minn. 303, 22 N.W.2d 19 (1946) (other letter from same person giving similar but more prejudicial facts, a waiver); and cases in 1 Wigmore, Evidence § 18, note 35 (3d ed. 1940); C.J.S. Trial §§ 116, 661. See also, Russian v. Lipet, 103 R.I. 461, 238 A.2d 369 (1968) (elicited same testimony from same witness).

14. The party should not be permitted "to blow hot and cold" in this way. Perhaps the overall result can be viewed as a simple lack of objection under F.Evid.R. 103(a).

15. Chester v. Shockley, 304 S.W.2d 831 (Mo.1957); Sayner v. Sholer, 77 N.M. 579, 425 P.2d 743 (1967); Haase v. Ryan, 100 Ohio App. 285, 136 N.E.2d 406, 410

(1955); Cathey v. Missouri, Kansas & Texas Railway Co. of Texas, 104 Tex. 39, 133 S.W. 417 (1911). There are some holdings to the contrary, see, e.g., Grain Dealers Mutual Insurance Co. v. Julian, 247 S.C. 89, 145 S.E.2d 685 (1965) (previous objection must be reserved).

Similarly, when the evidence objected to is elicited on cross-examination, the objector may seek to explain or refute on redirect without a waiver. Tucker v. Reil, 51 Ariz. 357, 369, 77 P.2d 203 (1938).

16. See, e.g., *Cathey* in next preceding note. While calling for a repetition is a permissible part of a testing or exploratory cross-examination, as a tactical matter such repetition should be held to a minimum.

17. State v. Tiedemann, 139 Mont. 237, 362 P.2d 529 (1961); Glennon v. Great Atlantic & Pacific Tea Co., 87 R.I. 454, 143 A.2d 282 (1958); Salt Lake City v. Smith, 104 F. 457, 470 (8th Cir. 1900); State v. Beckner, 194 Mo. 281, 91 S.W. 892, 896 (1906) (accused did not waive objection to evidence of his bad character by meeting it with evidence of good character).

18. See general agreement in Wright & Graham, Federal Practice and Procedure: Evidence § 5039; Louisell & Mueller, Evidence § 11, citing, among other cases, United States v. De Carlo, 458 F.2d 358, 372, n. 1 (3d Cir. 1972), cert. denied 409 U.S. 843; United States v. Rios, 611 F.2d 1335, 1339, n. 4 (10th Cir. 1979), appeal after remand 637 F.2d 728, cert. denied 452 U.S. 918.

19. See § 52 supra.

self preclude the trial judge from excluding the evidence on his own motion if the witness is disqualified for want of capacity or the evidence is incompetent, and he considers that the interests of justice require the exclusion of the testimony.[20] The Federal and Revised Uniform Rules of Evidence grant the judge sufficiently broad powers to follow the principles outlined in this paragraph.[21] There is much evidence, however, such as reliable affidavits or copies of writings, which though incompetent under the technical exclusionary rules, may be valuable in the particular situation and which the trial judge in the absence of objection would not be justified in excluding. It is only when the evidence is irrelevant, unreliable, misleading, or prejudicial, as well as incompetent, that the judge should exercise his discretionary power to intervene. Privileged evidence, such as confidential communications between husband and wife, should be treated differently. The privileges protect the outside interests of the holders, not the interest of the parties in securing justice in the present litigation. Accordingly, in case privileged matter is called for, and the holder is present, the judge may if necessary explain the privilege to the holder, but will not assert it of his own motion; but if the holder is absent the judge, in some jurisdictions, has a discretionary power to assert it in his behalf.[22]

WESTLAW REFERENCES

Demand for Inspection of a Writing
"implied consent" /s object! /s new

Failure to Object to Earlier Like Evidence
like same /2 evidence fact /10 object!

The Offering of Like Evidence by the Objector
waive* /3 object! /s same /2 testimony witness

Exclusion by Judge in Absence of Objection
digest(evidence /p "judge" /s "own motion")

---

20. Barber v. State Highway Commission, 80 Wyo. 340, 342 P.2d 723 (1959); Bodholdt v. Garrett, 122 Cal. App. 566, 10 P.2d 533 (1932) (truck driver's unexcited statement that broken spring was cause of collision, excluded by judge: held, no error. "The court on its own motion in the interest of justice may exclude. . . . " Query, whether the ruling was in the interest of justice); South Atlantic S.S. Co. v. Munkacsy, 37 Del. 580, 187 A. 600 (1936) (suit by seaman for injury: opinion of boatswain as to safe character of work, excluded by judge; held, no error; "the trial judge is something more than a mere umpire;" careful exposition of judge's authority); City of Detroit v. Porath, 271 Mich. 42, 260 N.W. 114 (1935) (irrelevant picture); Electric Park Amusement Co. v. Psichos, 83 N.J.L. 262, 83 A. 766 (1912) (judge upheld in excluding opinion of expert of inadequate qualification, distinguishing case of disqualification for interest which parties may effectively waive; Wisniewski v. Weinstock, 130 N.J.L. 58, 31 A.2d 401 (1943) (truck driver's testimony as to speed from tire-tracks excluded for lack of qualification); Best v. Tavenner, 189 Or. 46, 218 P.2d 471 (1950) (where witness died from stroke after direct testimony partly completed, judge had discretion to withdraw testimony from jury on own motion, or declare mistrial); King v. Baker, 109 Ga.App. 235, 136 S.E.2d 8 (1964) (judge excluded answer which was not responsive but was otherwise admissible). Cases are collected in Dec. Dig. Trial ⚷105(6) and in C.J.S. Trial § 156.

It is even sometimes said that the judge at the close of the case may of his own motion withdraw incompetent evidence from the jury though not objected to when received. See, e.g., American Workmen v. Ledden, 196 Ark. 902, 120 S.W.2d 346 (1938). But an opposite result is advocated "to prevent unfairness, in that, if the counsel offering the testimony were made aware of the objection to the testimony at the time, he would have had an opportunity to cure it." Electric Park Amusement Co. v. Psichos, supra, 83 A. 766, 768.

21. The broad power of the judge to control the presentation of evidence so as to "make the interrogation and presentation effective for the ascertainment of the truth," under Fed. and Rev.Unif.R.Evid. (1974) 611(a), coupled with the plain error provisions of Rule 103(d), afford a base for the principle in the text. See United States v. Wright, 542 F.2d 975 (7th Cir. 1976), cert. denied 429 U.S. 1073 (trial judge could on own initiative bar line of questioning as irrelevant).

22. People v. Atkinson, 40 Cal. 284 (1870) (where witness, an attorney, on examination was unable to say whether communications from client were public or private, judge, over defendant-client's objection admitted the evidence, held error, and by way of dictum that the court should have excluded on its own motion); Hodges v. Millikin, 1 Bland Ch. (Md.) 503, 509 (1828) ("and if the client be no party . . . the lips of his attorney must remain closed and the Court cannot allow him to speak. . . . "). West's Ann.Cal.Evid.Code § 916 requires the judge to exclude privileged information if no person authorized to claim the privilege is present.

§ 56. The Effect of the Introduction of Part of a Writing or Conversation [1]

Two important considerations come into play when a party offers in evidence a portion only of a writing, or of an oral statement or conversation. The first is the danger of admitting the portion only, thereby wresting a part of such a body of expressions out of its context. "The fool hath said in his heart, there is no God," [2] where the last phrase only is quoted, is an example of the possibilities of distortion.[3] This danger, moreover, is not completely averted by a later, separate, supplying of the relevant omitted parts. The distorted impression may sometimes linger, and work its influence at the subconscious level. Second is the opposing danger of requiring that the whole be offered, thereby wasting time and attention by cumbering the trial and the record, in the name of completeness, with passages and statements which have no bearing on the present controversy.

In the light of these alternatives, is a party who seeks to give in evidence part of a writing or statement required to offer it in entirety, or at least all of it that is relevant to the facts sought to be proved? The prevailing practice seems to permit the proponent to prove only such part as he desires.[4] However, to guard against the danger of an ineradicable false first impression, the adversary should and now often can be permitted, within the court's discretion, to require the proponent to prove so much as pertains to the fact sought to be proved, that is, all that explains or is useful in interpreting the part proved.[5] Federal and Revised Uniform Rule of Evidence (1974) 106 specifies this rule for writings or recorded statements, whether or not the remainder required to be introduced is otherwise admissible.[6] The trial judge appears to have the same power to require the introduction of remainder of conversations under Rule 611(a), but the remainder must be otherwise admissible evidence.[7]

<hr/>

§ 56

1. 7 Wigmore, Evidence §§ 2094–2125 (Chadbourn rev. 1978) Dec.Dig. Evidence ⊕155(8, 10); C.J.S. Evidence §§ 190, 774.

2. The oft-repeated classic illustration, see 7 Wigmore, Evidence § 2094 (Chadbourn rev. 1978).

3. "The setting of a word or words gives character to them, and may wholly change their apparent meaning. A notable instance of such practice is that of the minister, displeased with the manner of hairdressing used by the women of his congregation, who preached from the text, 'Topknot come down!' which was found to be the latter part of the scriptural injunction, 'Let them that be upon the housetop not come down.'" Lattimore, J., in Weathered v. State, 129 Tex.Cr. 514, 89 S.W.2d 212, 214 (1935).

4. See, e.g., Melnick v. Melnick, 154 Pa.Super. 481, 36 A.2d 235 (1944) (plaintiff could offer a part of the petition and admission in corresponding paragraph of answer without including other matters in that paragraph by way of avoidance or defense); and see State Highway Department v. Thomas, 115 Ga.App. 372, 154 S.E.2d 812 (1967) (attorney could introduce part of a lease contract).

But see Flood v. Mitchell, 68 N.Y. 507, 511 (1877) (whole of instrument creating or transferring rights should be introduced). See also 7 Wigmore, Evidence § 2099 (Chadbourn rev. 1978). With respect to testimony given at a former trial, it is fairly common to require that the substance of all the testimony of the witness on the particular subject be given, though there

are holdings to the contrary. 7 Wigmore, Evidence § 2098, n. 4, § 2099(4) (Chadbourn rev. 1978).

5. See nn. 6, 7, infra. F.R.Civ.P. 32(a)(4) contains the following practical and flexible rule for depositions: "If only part of a deposition is offered in evidence by a party, an adverse party may require him to introduce any other part which ought in fairness to be considered with the part introduced, and any party may introduce any other parts." The fairness concept originated in Ill.Sup.Ct.R. 212(c).

6. Fed.R.Evid. 106 provides:

When a writing or recorded statement or part thereof is introduced by a party, an adverse party may require him at that time to introduce any other part or any other writing or recorded statement which ought in fairness to be considered contemporaneously with it.

The Revised Uniform Rule (1974) substitutes "Whenever;" otherwise it is identical.

See, e.g., United States v. Rubin, 609 F.2d 51 (2d Cir. 1979), affirmed 449 U.S. 424 (to avoid a confusing or misleading impression of parts of notes of interview).

It has been properly assumed that a "recorded" statement applies to a tape recording. United States v. Salsedo, 607 F.2d 318 (9th Cir.1979); Re Air Crash Disaster at John F. Kennedy International Airport, 635 F.2d 67 (2d Cir.1980).

7. The Advisory Committee's Note for Rule 106 states, "For practical reasons, the rule is limited to writings and recorded statements and does not apply to

As to the adversary's other alternative the cases are much clearer and more consistent. He may wait until his own next stage of presenting proof, and then merely by reason of the fact that the first party has introduced a part, he has the right to introduce the remainder of the writing, statement, correspondence, former testimony, or conversation so far as it relates to the same subject matter and hence tends to explain and shed light on the meaning of the part already received.[8] This right is subject to the qualification that where the remainder is incompetent, not merely as to form as in the case of secondary evidence or hearsay, but because of its prejudicial character then the trial judge should exclude if he finds that the

danger of prejudice outweighs the explanatory value.[9]

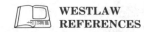

157k155(8)

§ 57. Fighting Fire with Fire: Inadmissible Evidence as Opening the Door.[1]

One party offers evidence which is inadmissible. Because the adversary fails to object, or because he has no opportunity to do so, or because the judge erroneously overrules an objection, the incompetent evidence comes in. Is the adversary entitled to answer this evidence, by testimony in denial or

---

conversations." Because, as indicated in the text, the judge's power under Rule 611 does not include the authority to require the proponent to include an omitted part of a conversation that is otherwise inadmissible, this power does not strictly overlap the provisions of Rule 106 concerning writings and recorded statements. Thus rule 106 should not be read to exclude the power of the judge under Rule 611 as stated in the text.

8. Fed.R.Evid. 106, Advisory Committee's Note states, "The rule does not in any way circumscribe the right of the adversary to develop the matter on cross-examination or as part of his own case."

The rule does not apply to conversations, but it should not affect the application of the rules in the text to writings, recorded statements, or conversations.

West's Ann.Cal.Evid.Code, § 356 provides,

Where part of an act, declaration, conversation, or writing is given in evidence by one party, the whole on the same subject may be inquired into by an adverse party; when a letter is read, the answer may be given; and when a detached act, declaration, conversation or writing is given in evidence, any other act, declaration, conversation, or writing which is necessary to make it understood may also be given in evidence.

The results indicated by this statute have been dictated by various similar statutes and by case law without benefit of statutes. See, e.g., Dispenza v. Picha, 98 Ill.App.2d 110, 240 N.E.2d 325 (1968) (conversation); Stewart v. Sioux City & New Orleans Barge Lines, Inc., 431 S.W.2d 205 (Mo.1968) (plaintiff introduced hospital record insofar as it recorded various matters, some inadmissible; defendant could then introduce remainder containing diagnosis based on such matters). But the remaining portion sought to be introduced must be related to the use of the part initially introduced, if that use was a limited one. Rosener v. Larson, 255 Cal.App.2d 871, 63 Cal.Rptr. 782 (1968) (a limited use of a doctor's report not as evidence but as basis for an expert's opinion did not authorize introduction of another inadmissible portion containing conclu-

sions); Camps v. New York City Transit Authority, 261 F.2d 320 (2d Cir.1958) (use of initial part for impeachment).

It has sometimes been said that this type of "remainder" evidence is a mere aid in interpreting the evidence already received or in appraising credibility, and is not itself substantive evidence. People v. Schlessel, 196 N.Y. 476, 90 N.E. 44 (1909); 7 Wigmore, Evidence § 2113 (Chadbourn rev. 1978). But in another place, Wigmore has properly termed this "an artificial doctrine tending to a quibble." Student Textbook on Evidence 322 (1935). It is not the more usual rule. Statutes and cases permitting the remainder to be introduced to make the part already introduced "fully understood, to explain the same" are not usually to be understood in the above-mentioned limited sense.

9. Fed. and Rev.Unif.R.Evid. (1974) 403 dictates this result. See also Socony Vacuum Oil Co. v. Marvin, 313 Mich. 528, 21 N.W.2d 841 (1946) (when part of transcribed interview between plaintiff's investigator and defendant was introduced by plaintiff, defendant not entitled to offer remaining part stating his poor financial condition and that he was not insured); Jeddeloh v. Hockenhull, 219 Minn. 541, 18 N.W.2d 582 (1945) (where part of conversation after accident proved, door not opened to proof of part showing defendant insured); State v. Skaug, 63 Nev. 59, 161 P.2d 708 (1945) (separable part of confession showing commission of other unconnected crimes should have been excluded).

§ 57

1. See 1 Wigmore, Evidence § 15 ("Curative Admissibility") (3d ed. 1940); Weinstein & Berger, Evidence ¶ 103[2]; Note, 35 Mich.L.Rev. 636 (1937); Dec.Dig. Evidence ⊕155(5); C.J.S. Evidence § 190a; 29 Am.Jur.2d Evidence § 267.

The kinship between the subject matter of the present section and waiver of objections, § 55 supra, is apparent, but cognizance must be taken of differences noted in the text.

explanation of the facts so proved? It has been stated that in some jurisdictions the adversary is not entitled to so meet the evidence, in others he may do so, and finally in some he may do so if he would be prejudiced by rejection of efforts to meet the evidence; but that in reaching these results many of the decisions seem merely to affirm the action of the trial court.[2] However, most of the courts seem to say generally that "one who induces a trial court to let down the bars to a field of inquiry that is not competent or relevant to the issues cannot complain if his adversary is also allowed to avail himself of the opening."[3] Federal cases have applied this general notion in various situations.[4]

Many of these pronouncements do not settle the questions as to how the trial judge should deal with the problem, or as to whether the adversary is entitled as of right to introduce the answering evidence. Because of the many variable factors affecting the solution in particular cases the decisions do not lend themselves easily to generalizations, but the following conclusions, having some support in the decisions, are submitted as reasonable:

(1) If the incompetent evidence sought to be answered is immaterial and not prejudice-arousing, the judge, to save time and to avoid distraction of attention from the issues, should refuse to hear answering evidence; but if he does hear it, under the prevailing view, the party opening the door has no standing to complain.[5]

(2) If the evidence, though inadmissible, is relevant to the issues and hence probably

---

2. 1 Wigmore, Evidence § 15 (3d ed. 1940).

3. St. Clair County v. Bukacek, 272 Ala. 323, 131 So.2d 683 (1961) (irrelevant evidence; "rule is that irrelevant, incompetent or illegal evidence may be admitted to rebut evidence of like character"); Hartman v. Maryland Casualty Co., 417 S.W.2d 640 (Tex.Civ.App. 1967); Mobile & Birmingham Railroad Co. v. Ladd, 92 Ala. 287, 9 So. 169 (1891) (meeting immaterial evidence that night was dark by evidence that moon was shining); Perkins v. Hayward, 124 Ind. 445, 24 N.E. 1033, 1034 (1890); Sisler v. Shafer, 43 W.Va. 769, 28 S.E. 721 (1897) ("strange cattle having wandered through a gap made by himself, he cannot complain"); Corley v. Andrews, 349 S.W.2d 395 (Mo.App.1961) (counter evidence was hearsay; "should have been allowed").

Some courts, however, have, at least occasionally, expressed the view that admission of incompetent evidence does "not open the door" to answering inadmissible evidence. People v. McDaniel, 59 Cal.App.2d 672, 140 P.2d 88 (1943); Savannah News-Press, Inc. v. Hartridge, 110 Ga.App. 203, 138 S.E.2d 173 (1964) (immaterial evidence; introduction did not entitle opponent to rebuttal evidence; "there can be no equation of errors in the trial of a case").

Other courts have stated that the admission of incompetent evidence "opens the door" only if the opponent is prejudiced unless he can meet the evidence. Thurman v. Pepsi-Cola Bottling Co., 289 N.W.2d 141 (Minn.1980) (if evidence is inadmissible and non-prejudicial, rebutting evidence is not admissible); United States v. Nardi, 633 F.2d 972 (1st Cir. 1980) ("no prejudice to be rebutted"); 1 Wigmore, Evidence § 15 (3d ed. 1940).

4. CCMS Publishing Co. v. Dooley-Maloof, Inc., 645 F.2d 33 (10th Cir.1980) (appellant introduced evidence of compromise on cross-examination of opponent; opponent "was entitled to rebut"); United States v. Doran, 564 F.2d 1176 (5th Cir.1977), cert. denied 435 U.S.

928 (defendant testified he refused plea bargaining deal; on cross-examination government could ask him about otherwise inadmissible counter-offer); United States v. James, 555 F.2d 992 (D.C.Cir.1977) ("ordinarily evidence inadmissible to prove the case-in-chief is rendered admissible only if the defendant himself introduces the evidence or is in some manner estopped from objecting to its use;" but principle held inapplicable on the facts at hand); In re Aircrash in Bali, Indonesia on April 22, 1974, 684 F.2d 1301 (9th Cir.1982) (alternate reason for admission of incompetency of pilot was opponent's evidence that pilot was competent); United States v. Giese, 597 F.2d 1170 (9th Cir.1979), cert. denied 444 U.S. 979 (defendant introduced the acts of selling, owning, and reading various books to show peaceable character opening door to cross-examination as to contents of a particular book); Croce v. Bromley Corp., 623 F.2d 1084 (5th Cir.1980), cert. denied 450 U.S. 981 (approval of trial court's decision in admitting past conduct of a pilot to rebut previous evidence to the contrary; all such evidence went to inadmissible purpose of showing pilot's reputation. The rule was applied to justify government evidence to contradict statement of defendant for impeachment purposes although the government evidence was introduced first in time. United States v. Benedetto, 571 F.2d 1246 (2d Cir.1978).

5. If the evidence sought to be answered is immaterial, the rule against contradicting on a collateral issue would generally indicate exclusion of evidence in answer to it. See § 47 supra. If, however, the opening-the-door theory prevails, then attention ought to be given to the nature of the original and rebutting evidence. Ordinarily no more of a problem may be presented than a possible harmless excursion into immateriality, as suggested in note 3, supra, but on occasion a relatively slight breach of materiality may be used as an excuse to violate fundamental exclusionary principles. Illustrative are the cases where an accused takes

damaging to the adversary's case, or though irrelevant is prejudice-arousing to a material degree, and if the adversary has seasonably objected or moved to strike, then the adversary should be entitled to give answering evidence as of right.[6] By objecting he has done his best to save the court from mistake, but his remedy by assigning error to the ruling is not an adequate one.[7] He needs a fair opportunity to win his case at the trial by refuting the damaging evidence. This situation should be distinguished from the question, considered in section 55, whether the prior objection is waived if the answering evidence is permitted.

(3) If again the first incompetent evidence is relevant, or though irrelevant is prejudice-arousing, but the adversary has failed to object or to move to strike out, where such an objection might apparently have avoided the harm, then the allowance of answering evidence should rest in the judge's discretion.[8] He should weigh the probable influence of the first evidence, the time and distraction incident to answering it, and the possibility and effectiveness of an instruction to the jury to disregard it. However, here various courts have indicated that introduction of the answering evidence is a matter of right.[9]

(4) In any event, if the incompetent evidence, or even the inquiry eliciting it, is so prejudice-arousing that an objection or motion to strike cannot have erased the harm, then it seems that the adversary should be entitled to answer it as of right.[10]

It will be noted that the question discussed in this section as to rebutting incompetent evidence, is a different one from whether a party's introduction of evidence incompetent under some exclusionary rule (such as hearsay or secondary evidence of writings) gives license to the adversary to in-

---

the stand and makes an overly-broad denial of guilt ("I never"). Numerous decisions allow the prosecutor to rebut by evidence of otherwise inadmissible other offenses. People v. Westek, 31 Cal.2d 469, 190 P.2d 9 (1948); State v. Barnett, 156 Kan. 746, 137 P.2d 133 (1943). In Walder v. United States, 347 U.S. 62 (1954) this principle was carried to the extreme of allowing the results of an unconstitutional search and seizure to be introduced. See § 178 infra. If the statement is elicited on cross-examination, much authority refuses to allow it to be used as a door opener. State v. Goldsmith, 104 Ariz. 226, 450 P.2d 684 (1969); Dalton v. People, 224 Ill. 333, 79 N.E. 669 (1906); and Agnello v. United States, 269 U.S. 20 (1925) disallowed use of the results of an unconstitutional search and seizure under these circumstances. The preferable result would be disallowance of prejudicial answering evidence without regard to whether elicited on direct or cross. State v. Johnson, 94 Ariz. 303, 383 P.2d 862 (1963). Objection to the original immaterial evidence or an instruction to disregard it should protect the interests of the prosecution adequately.

6. Budd v. Meriden Electric Co., 69 Conn. 272, 37 A. 683 (1897); Bremhorst v. Phillips Coal Co., 202 Iowa 1251, 211 N.W. 898, 904 (1927) ("It was the duty of the court to give both parties the benefit of the same rules of evidence."); Lake Roland Elevated Railway Co. v. Weir, 86 Md. 273, 37 A. 714, 715 (1897) (a considered dictum); Mattechek v. Pugh, 153 Or. 1, 55 P.2d 730, 168 A.L.R. 725 (1936). Contra: Buck v. St. Louis Union Trust Co., 267 Mo. 644, 185 S.W. 208, 213 (1916) (". . . his objection will save him on appeal and he needs no other protection.") See Note, 35 Mich.L.Rev. 636, 637 (1937).

7. Note, 35 Mich.L.Rev. 636, 637 (1937). Wigmore takes the opposite view. 1 Evidence § 15 (3d ed. 1940).

8. Grist v. Upjohn Co., 16 Mich.App. 452, 168 N.W.2d 389 (1969) (permitting introduction of hearsay concerning same conversation was within the court's discretion; Crosby v. Keen, 200 Miss. 590, 28 So.2d 322 (1946); Biener v. St. Louis Public Service Co., 160 S.W.2d 780 (Mo.App.1942) (semble); Franklin Fire Insurance Co. v. Coleman, 87 S.W.2d 537 (Tex.Civ.App. 1935) (suit on fire policy, defense, arson; defendant's witness volunteered statement that he arrested plaintiff after the fire; held, permitting defendant to show that complaint on which he was arrested was dismissed was discretionary).

9. Moschetti v. City of Tucson, 9 Ariz.App. 108, 449 P.2d 945 (1969); London v. Standard Oil Co. of California, 417 F.2d 820 (9th Cir.1969); Sprenger v. Sprenger, 146 N.W.2d 36 (N.D.1966) (counter evidence objectionable under the best evidence rule); Shoup v. Mannino, 188 Pa.Super. 457, 149 A.2d 678 (1959); Commonwealth v. Wakelin, 230 Mass. 567, 575, 576, 120 N.E. 209, 212, 213 (1918).

10. Thus, in State v. Witham, 72 Me. 531, 535 (1881) the birth of a child to an unmarried woman was improperly admitted as evidence of defendant's adultery, and counterevidence of other men's intercourse was received to rebut it. The court said: "The introduction of immaterial testimony to meet immaterial testimony on the other side is generally within the discretion of the presiding judge. But if one side introduces evidence irrelevant to the issue, which is prejudicial and harmful to the other party, then, although it comes in without objection, the other party is entitled to introduce evidence which will directly and strictly contradict it.

troduce other evidence which is incompetent under the same exclusionary rule but which bears on some different issue or is not relevant to the original incompetent evidence.[11] The doctrine of "opening the door" has not been extended to that extent.

**WESTLAW
REFERENCES**

"answering evidence"

§ 58. Admissibility of Evidence Dependent on Proof of Other Facts: "Connecting Up"[1]

Very often the relevancy or admissibility of evidence of a particular fact hinges upon the proof of other facts. Thus, proof that a swaying automobile passed a given spot at a certain time,[2] or that a conversation was had by the witness at a given time and place with an unidentified stranger,[3] will become relevant and significant only when the automobile is identified as the defendant's, or the stranger is shown to be the deceased for whose death the plaintiff is suing. So evidence of acts and declarations may not become material or admissible until shown to be those of an agent of the other party,[4] and a copy of a writing may not become compe-

tent evidence until the original is proven to be lost or destroyed.[5] Some of these missing facts may be thought of, in terms of the logic of pleading or argument, as preliminary to the fact offered, some as co-ordinate with it. It matters not. In either event, often only one fact can be proven at a time or by a given witness, and the order of convenience in calling witnesses or of clear presentation may not in a particular case be the order of logical statement.[6]

Who decides the order of facts? In the first instance, the offering counsel does so by making his offer. The court in its general discretionary supervision of the order of proof,[7] may, to avoid a danger of prejudice or confusion, require that the missing fact be proved first.[8] But it seldom does, and the everyday method of handling the situation when the adversary objects to the relevancy or the competency of the offered fact is to permit it to come in conditionally, upon the assurance, express or implied, of the offering counsel that he will "connect up" the tendered evidence by proving, in the later progress of his case, the missing facts.[9] Federal and Revised Uniform Rules of Evidence 104(b) and 611(a) give the court this same authority.[10]

---

11. The distinction is acutely discussed in Longmire v. Diagraph-Bradley Corp., 237 Mo.App. 553, 176 S.W.2d 635, 646 (1944), and applied in Daniels v. Dillinger, 445 S.W.2d 410 (Mo.App.1969).

§ 58

1. 1 Wigmore, Evidence § 14 (3d ed. 1940), 6 id. § 1871 (Chadbourn rev. 1976); Note, 32 Ill.L.Rev. 882 (1938); Annot., 88 A.L.R.2d 12; Dec.Dig. Trial ⚖=51, 79, 90; C.J.S. Trial § 85.

2. State v. Freeman, 93 Utah 125, 71 P.2d 196 (1937).

3. Atlanta & Western Point Railroad Co. v. Truitt, 65 Ga.App. 320, 16 S.E.2d 273 (1941).

4. Smith v. Ohio Millers' Mutual Fire Insurance Co., 320 Mo. 146, 6 S.W.2d 920 (1928).

5. See Ch. 23 infra.

6. See the remarks of Miller, J. in a conspiracy case: "The logical sequence of events—from agreement in a common purpose to perpetration of an act designed to carry it out—does not require that introduction of the evidence must follow that same rigorous sequence." McDonald v. United States, 77 U.S.App. D.C. 33, 133 F.2d 23 (1942).

7. Fed. and Rev.Unif.R.Evid. (1974) 103; Matz v. United States, 81 U.S.App.D.C. 326, 158 F.2d 190 (1946) (order of prosecution's evidence in a bigamy case); and see 6 Wigmore, Evidence §§ 1867, 1871 (Chadbourn rev. 1976).

8. Gerber v. Columbia Palace Corp., 183 A.2d 398 (D.C.Mun.App.1962) (judge ruled evidence inadmissible without proof of other facts).

9. For decisions approving the practice see, e.g., Wickman v. Bohle, 173 Md. 694, 196 A. 326 (1938); Innes v. Beauchene, 370 P.2d 174 (Alaska 1962); Brown v. Neal, 283 N.C. 604, 197 S.E.2d 505 (1973).

10. Rule 104(b) provides that when relevancy depends upon a condition of fact, the court may admit the evidence "subject to" the introduction of evidence to support a finding of fulfillment of the condition. See the rule at § 53, n. 15. Rule 611(a) recognizes the authority of the judge to control the mode and order of interrogating witnesses and presenting evidence. See United States v. Kenny, 645 F.2d 1323 (9th Cir.1980, cert. denied 454 U.S. 828 (court in its discretion could permit additional proof of defendant's participation in conspiracy before introducing of evidence of existence of conspiracy; but court may require the latter evidence to be introduced first, particularly if it has

In a long trial, however, where the witnesses are many and the facts complex, it is easy for the offering counsel to forget the need for making the required "connecting" proof, and for the judge and the adversary to fail to observe this gap in the evidence. Who invokes the condition subsequent, upon such a breach? The burden is placed upon the objecting party to renew the objection and invoke the condition.[11] By the majority view this is to be done by a motion to strike out the evidence conditionally received,[12] when the failure of condition becomes apparent. It seems that it does become apparent when the offering party completes the particular stage of his case in which the evidence was offered,[13] and that when he "rests" without making the missing proof, the adversary should then move to strike, failing which, he cannot later claim as of right to invoke the condition. Some weight should be given, however, to the duty assumed by the offering party in promising to furnish the connecting proof, and recognition of this can best be given by according the trial judge a discretion to allow the adversary to invoke the condition, if the continuing availability of the missing proof makes

it fair to do so, at any time before the case is submitted to the jury or before final judgment in a judge-tried case.[14] Though some courts have considered the difference in form material, it seems that a motion to strike, a motion to withdraw the fact from the jury, or a request that the jury be instructed to disregard the evidence should each be regarded as a sufficient invocation of the condition. The discussion in this paragraph is compatible with Federal and Revised Uniform Rules of Evidence 104(b) and 611(a).

To be distinguished from the practice described above of conditional admission pending further proof, is the practice of admitting evidence provisionally where objection is made, subject to a later ruling on the objection in the light of further consideration when the case has been more amply developed. Here again the objecting counsel, to preserve the objection, must renew the objection before the case is concluded.[15] The practice occasionally seems appropriate enough in a judge-tried case [16] but where the trial is with a jury there is danger that letting the evidence in, even provisionally, may make an impression that a later ruling of ex-

doubts as to the ability to prove existence of conspiracy).

11. Webb v. Biggers, 71 Ga.App. 90, 30 S.E.2d 59 (1944); Annot., 88 A.L.R.2d 12, 23–31; Dec.Dig. Trial ☞79.

12. Little Klamath Water Ditch Co. v. Ream, 27 Or. 129, 39 P. 998 (1895); State v. Freeman, 93 Utah 125, 71 P.2d 196 (1937) (motion to strike necessary; request for instruction to disregard, at close of case, insufficient: full discussion, one judge dissenting); Arnold v. Ellis, 5 Mich.App. 101, 145 N.W.2d 822 (1966) (in judge-tried case, judge could consider evidence when no motion to strike was made). But it has been said in one decision that in a jury case a motion for an instruction to disregard the evidence is the proper recourse. Kolka v. Jones, 6 N.D. 461, 71 N.W. 558, 564 (1897). See also, Caley v. Manicke, 29 Ill.App.2d 323, 173 N.E.2d 209 (1961) rev'd 24 Ill.2d 390, 182 N.E.2d 206 (dictum that failure to connect "at the very least would occasion an instruction to disregard"). As a practical matter, both a motion to strike and a request for an instruction should be made. Decisions are collected in 6 Wigmore, Evidence § 1871, note 6 (Chadbourn rev. 1976); Annot., 88 A.L.R.2d 12, 102.

Normally, it is assumed when evidence is improperly received or is not "connected up," an instruction to dis-

regard is a sufficient corrective. But the evidence may be so prejudicial that an instruction does not cure the harm. National Cash Register Co. v. Kay, 119 S.W.2d 437 (Mo.App.1938). "Human nature does not change merely because it is found in the jury box. The human mind is not a slate, from which can be wiped out, at the will and instruction of another, ideas and thoughts written thereon." People v. Deal, 357 Ill. 634, 192 N.E. 649, 652 (1934). Fed. and Rev.Unif.R.Evid. (1974) 403 authorizes the court to weigh the prejudice and the efficacy of an instruction. See the discussion of the adequacy of curative and limiting instructions in § 59 infra.

13. In Keber v. American Stores Co., 116 N.J.L. 437, 184 A. 795 (1936) this was said to be the proper time and that an earlier motion was premature. See also Note, 32 Ill.L.Rev. 882, 883 (1938); Annot., 88 A.L.R.2d 12, 107.

14. Note, 32 Ill.L.Rev. 882, 884 (1938).

15. McGee v. Maryland Casualty Co., 240 Miss. 447, 127 So.2d 656 (1961) (jury case). See cases collected in Annot., 88 A.L.R.2d 12, 109 et seq.

16. Its advantages are pointed out by Sanborn, Cir. J., in Builders' Steel Co. v. Commissioner, 179 F.2d 377, 379 (8th Cir.1950).

clusion may not erase [17]—a danger that here seems unnecessary to incur. Accordingly this practice, though doubtless in the realm of discretion, has been criticised.[18] It should be avoided.

 WESTLAW REFERENCES

digest(connecting /2 up proof facts)

§ 59. Evidence Admissible for One Purpose, Inadmissible for Another: "Limited Admissibility"[1]

An item of evidence may be logically relevant in several aspects, as leading to distinct inferences or as bearing upon different issues. For one of these purposes it may be competent but for another incompetent. In this frequently arising situation, subject to the limitations outlined below, the normal practice in case law and under the Federal and Revised Uniform Rules of Evidence (1974) is to admit the evidence.[2] The interest of the adversary is to be protected, not by an objection to its admission,[3] but by a request at the time of the offer for an instruction that the jury is to consider the evidence only for the allowable purpose.[4] Such an instruction may not always be effective, but admission of the evidence with the limiting instruction is normally the best available

---

17. McKee v. Bassick Mining Co., 8 Colo. 392, 8 P. 561 (1885). But though sometimes criticized this practice has been used in jury cases. See cases in Annot., 88 A.L.R.2d 12, 108–122; Dec.Dig. Trial ☞51. It is forbidden by statute in Connecticut even in judge-tried cases. Conn.Gen.St.Ann. § 52–208, construed in Kovacs v. Szentes, 130 Conn. 229, 33 A.2d 124 (1943). See n. 12, supra, as to the effectiveness of instructions to disregard.

18. See, e.g., Missouri Pacific Transportation Co. v. Beard, 179 Miss. 764, 176 So. 156 (1937); Dec.Dig. Trial ☞51; Annot., 88 A.L.R.2d 12, 121–122.

§ 59

1. 1 Wigmore, Evidence § 13 (3d ed. 1940); Weinstein & Berger, Evidence ¶ 105 [01]–[07]; Dec.Dig. Trial ☞48; C.J.S. Trial §§ 87, 88.

2. Lubbock Feed Lots v. Iowa Beef Processors Inc., 630 F.2d 250 (5th Cir.1980), rehearing denied 634 F.2d 1355 (evidence constituting inadmissible hearsay to show agency was admissible for impeachment by contradiction); Sprinkle v. Davis, 111 F.2d 925 (4th Cir.1940) (suit for injury to highway workman, plaintiff, by defendant's automobile: court erred in excluding defendant's evidence that plaintiff had been compensated by Highway Department; not admissible on issue of liability or damages but admissible to show bias of witnesses who were highway employees); Williams v. Milner Hotels Co., 130 Conn. 507, 36 A.2d 20 (1944) (guest, suing hotel for having been bitten by rat while lying in bed, could prove that rat-holes in room were later closed by tin patches; inadmissible as admission of fault, admissible to show control, existence of rat-holes, and to corroborate guest's evidence); Low v. Honolulu Rapid Transit Co., 50 Hawaii 582, 445 P.2d 372 (1968); Stoeppelman v. Hays-Fendler Const. Co., 437 S.W.2d 143 (Mo.App.1969) (evidence showing insurance existed properly admissible to show control exercised over property).

See the qualifications in the text in this section. Fed. and Rev.Unif.R.Evid. (1974) 105 assume the practice. See Rule in n. 4 infra.

It seems, however, that the proponent, to complain of the judge's exclusion of evidence inadmissible in one aspect, must have stated the purpose for which it is competent, Archer v. Sibley, 201 Ala. 495, 78 So. 849 (1918), unless the admissible purpose is plainly apparent. Kansas City Southern Ry. Co. v. Jones, 241 U.S. 181 (1916). The rule was applied where an admissible purpose and an inadmissible purpose were stated, in Richter's Bakery, Inc. v. Verden, 394 S.W.2d 230 (Tex. Civ.App.1965). See C.J.S. Trial § 87. These rules merely apply the normal requirements for making an operative offer of proof in other situations in which an objection is sustained. See analogous rules at § 51 nn. 16, 17 supra.

3. Scott v. Missouri Insurance Co., 361 Mo. 51, 233 S.W.2d 660 (1950) (action on life policy; defendant offered report of its investigators on the death; plaintiff objected as hearsay, and judge excluded; held error to exclude, should have admitted to show good faith in denying liability with limiting instruction, if requested); Bialek v. Pittsburgh Brewing Co., 430 Pa. 176, 242 A.2d 231 (1968) (proper to admit evidence to show article was not defective with instruction indicating evidence should not be used for improper purpose of showing due care, which was not in issue).

4. Fed. and Rev.Unif.R.Evid. (1974) 105 provide:

When evidence which is admissible as to one party or for one purpose but not admissible as to another party or for another purpose is admitted, the court, upon request, shall restrict the evidence to its proper scope and instruct the jury accordingly.

It will be observed that the rule does not purport to determine when such evidence should be admitted but assumes that a ruling has been made in favor of admissibility. See n. 5, infra, as to admissibility. Under the federal rule, the judge may give an instruction on his own initiative without any request. See discussion in Weinstein & Berger, Evidence ¶ 105[05]. This source also discusses whether omission of an instruction might be plain error.

Pertinent cases include United States v. Vitale, 596 F.2d 688 (5th Cir.1979), cert. denied 444 U.S. 868:

reconciliation of the respective interests. It seems, however, that in situations, where the danger of the jury's misuse of the evidence for the incompetent purpose is great, and its value for the legitimate purpose is slight or the point for which it is competent can readily be proved by other evidence, the judge's power to exclude the evidence altogether is clear in case law and under the Federal and Revised Uniform Rules of Evidence.[5]

Similarly, subject to the restrictions stated in the above and following paragraphs, evidence may frequently be competent as against one party, but not as against another, in which event the practice is to admit the evidence, with an instruction, if request-

ed, that the jury are to consider it only as to the party against whom it is competent.[6]

However, limiting instructions are not sufficient to insure against misuse by the jury of the confessions or admissions of a codefendant who does not take the stand when the confessions or admissions implicate the defendant. A violation of the Sixth Amendment right to confront witnesses results.[7] This rule is applicable in state courts.[8] However if the case against the defendant was so overwhelming, apart from a confession or an admission of a codefendant, that its admission into evidence was harmless beyond a reasonable doubt, the Supreme Court will not require reversal.[9] It can not be concluded generally that if one purpose of two or more uses of evidence against a criminal

Hatfield v. Levy Bros., 18 Cal.2d 798, 117 P.2d 841 (1941) (opponent, not having requested instruction, waived right thereto); Bouchard v. Bouchard, 313 Mass. 531, 48 N.E.2d 161 (1943); Rynar v. Lincoln Transit Co., 129 N.J.L. 525, 30 A.2d 406, 409 (1943) (". . . The party . . . may summon the court's assistance by request for charge or other appropriate means.") Sims v. Struthers, 267 Ala. 80, 100 So.2d 23 (1958) (admission not error when instruction was not requested on ground that the remedy was a request for an instruction); State ex rel. State Highway Comm'n v. Yackel, 445 S.W.2d 389 (Mo.App.1969) (if party feared improper use of the evidence, he should have requested an instruction).

5. Fed. and Rev.Unif.R.Evid. (1974) 403 clearly authorizes the court to consider the overall prejudicial effect of the evidence and whether an instruction would be sufficient to avoid such an effect. Such an effect is particularly important in criminal cases, especially when the prosecution attempts to show other crimes of the defendant under Fed. and Rev.Unif.R.Evid. (1974) 404(b) as evidence of motive, intent, etc. under the terms of that rule. See § 190, infra. In distinguishing Fed.R.Evid. 105 from other rules, the Advisory Committee's Note states, "The wording of the present rule . . . [repels] any implication that limiting or curative instructions are sufficient for all situations." See also n. 4 supra.

Case law is to the same effect. Adkins v. Brett, 184 Cal. 252, 193 P. 251, 254 (1920) (in husband's action for alienation, evidence of wife's statement as to parties with and gifts from defendant, though would ordinarily be competent to show wife's feelings, might be excluded if danger great that jury would use it as evidence of defendant's conduct). See also Shepard v. United States, 290 U.S. 96, 103 (1933); State v. Goebel, 40 Wn. 2d 18, 240 P.2d 251 (1952) (evidence of other crimes admissible for specific purpose should be excluded in discretion of the court if unduly prejudicial).

6. Grimm v. Gargis, 303 S.W.2d 43 (Mo.1957) (evidence properly admissible against one party with proper instruction); Chesapeake & Ohio Railway Co. v. Boyd's Administrator, 290 Ky. 9, 160 S.W.2d 342 (1942) (statement of engineer, codefendant, admissible against him, if not against railway; general objection without request to limit the evidence ineffective); Ft. Worth Hotel Co. v. Waggoman, 126 S.W.2d 578 (Tex. Civ.App.1939) (evidence admissible against one of defendants, joint tortfeasors, not subject to objection by other defendant; his only relief is a request to have it limited).

But if the evidence is offered generally and excluded there is no error. Hudson v. Smith, 391 S.W.2d 441 (Tex.Civ.App.1965), unless of course, undue prejudice results or a constitutional rule is involved. See n. 7, infra. With the same limitations, if there is only an objection and no request for instruction or actual instruction, there is no error. American Medical Association v. United States, 130 F.2d 233 (D.C.Cir.1942) affirmed 317 U.S. 519. See n. 5 supra.

7. Bruton v. United States, 391 U.S. 123 (1968). See The Supreme Court, 1967 Term, 82 Harv.L.Rev. 95, 231–238 (1968). The decision was held to have retroactive effect in Roberts v. Russell, 392 U.S. 293 (1968), reh. denied 393 U.S. 899.

So-called "interlocking confessions" (when defendant's own confession is also before the jury) are at least usually harmless. Parker v. Randolph, 442 U.S. 62 (1979). When the co-defendant takes the stand subject to cross-examination, and his testimony exculpates the defendant, his confession may be used. Nelson v. O'Neill, 402 U.S. 622 (1971).

See § 279 infra.

8. Harrington v. California, 395 U.S. 250 (1969).

9. Harrington v. California, 395 U.S. 250 (1969); Chapman v. California, 386 U.S. 18, Comment, 83 Harv. L.Rev. 814 (1970). See § 182 infra.

defendant violates constitutional rights of the defendant, the evidence is completely inadmissible.[10]

WESTLAW REFERENCES

limit! /2 admissibility

§ 60. Admission and Exclusion of Evidence in Trials Without a Jury

Thayer considers that our law of evidence is a "product of the jury system . . . where ordinary untrained citizens are acting as judges of fact." [1] It might have been more expedient if these rules had been at least in the main, discarded in trials before judges.[2] Their professional experience in valuing evidence greatly lessens the need for exclusionary rules. But the traditional starting point is that in general the jury-trial system of evidence governs in trials before the judge as well.[3] Nevertheless, the feeling of the inexpediency of these restrictions as applied to judges has caused courts to say that the same strictness will not be observed in applying the rules of evidence in judge-trials as in trials before a jury, and it is difficult to avoid reaching the same result under the Federal and Revised Uniform Rules of Evidence (1974).[4]

The most important influence in encouraging trial judges to take this attitude toward evidence rules in nonjury cases is a rule obtaining in most appellate courts. These courts have said that in reviewing a case tried without a jury the admission of incompetent evidence over objection will not ordinarily be a ground of reversal if there was competent evidence received sufficient to support the findings. The judge will be presumed to have disregarded the inadmissible and relied on the competent evidence.[5] If he errs, however, in the opposite direction, by excluding evidence which he ought to have received, his ruling will of course be subject to reversal [6] if it is substantially harmful to the losing party.

These contrasting attitudes of the appellate courts toward errors in receiving and those in excluding evidence seem to support

---

10. See, e.g., United States v. Havens, 446 U.S. 620 (1980) on remand 625 F.2d 1311 (5th Cir.), rehearing denied 448 U.S. 911, cert. denied 450 U.S. 995 (evidence illegally obtained and inadmissible as proof of government case held admissible to impeach defendant by contradiction under certain circumstances); Harris v. New York, 401 U.S. 222 (1971) (statements not admissible under Miranda v. Arizona, 384 U.S. 436 (1966), rehearing denied 385 U.S. 890, could be used to impeach by inconsistent statement technique).

§ 60

1. Preliminary Treatise on Evidence 509 (1898).

2. See argument for special rules in judge-tried cases, Davis, An Approach to Rules of Evidence for Nonjury Cases, 50 A.B.A.J. 723 (1964), Hearsay in Nonjury Cases 83 Harv.L.Rev. 1362 (1970).

3. See, e.g., Stewart v. Prudential Insurance Co., 147 Pa.Super. 296, 24 A.2d 83 (1942).

4. See e.g., Clark v. United States, 61 F.2d 695 (8th Cir.1933), affirmed 289 U.S. 1; Weisenborn v. Rutledge, 233 Mo.App. 464, 121 S.W.2d 309, 313 (1938); and numerous cases collected in Dec.Dig. Trial ⬡377(1); C.J.S. Trial § 589.

The rules contain no specific provision governing judge-tried cases. However, Rules 102 (statement of purpose), 103 (error in admitting or excluding must affect substantial right), and 611 (broad powers to control trial), all lead to the conclusion that failure to fol-

low the lead of the case law would violate the spirit and to a large degree the letter of the Rules.

5. Clark v. United States, 61 F.2d 695 (8th Cir.1932), affirmed 289 U.S. 1; General Metals, Inc. v. Truitt Manufacturing Co., 259 N.C. 709, 131 S.E.2d 360 (1963); Lenahan v. Leach, 245 Or. 496, 422 P.2d 683 (1967); Gray v. Grayson, 76 N.M. 255, 414 P.2d 228 (1966) (but findings indicated evidence erroneously admitted did affect trial judge's decision; reversed); Dec.Dig. Appeal & Error ⬡931(6); C.J.S. Appeal and Error § 1564e; Maguire & Epstein, Preliminary Questions of Fact, 36 Yale L.J. 1100, 1115 (1927). See explanation of harmless error in § 52, at n. 68, supra.

Occasional decisions decline to apply the presumption when the evidence was objected to and the objection overruled. Farish v. Hawk, 241 Ala. 352, 2 So.2d 407 (1941) (equity case); (but cf. Bessemer Theatres v. City of Bessemer, 261 Ala. 632, 75 So.2d 651 (1954) nonjury law case); Bellew v. Iowa State Highway Comm'n, 171 N.W.2d 284 (Iowa 1969) (prejudice presumed unless record affirmatively shows evidence was later discarded; record so indicated).

6. Examples of reversals where the exclusion was found prejudicial: Kelly v. Wasserman, 5 N.Y.2d 425, 158 N.E.2d 241, 185 N.Y.S.2d 538 (1959) (tried before referee); McCloskey v. Charleroi Mountain Club, 390 Pa. 212, 134 A.2d 873 (1957). See Dec.Dig. Appeal & Error ⬡1056(5); C.J.S. Appeal and Error § 1746, notes 13, 14.

the wisdom of the practice adopted by many experienced trial judges in nonjury cases of provisionally admitting all evidence which is objected to if he thinks its admissibility is debatable,[7] with the announcement that all questions of admissibility will be reserved until the evidence is all in. In considering the objections if renewed by motion to strike at the end of the case, he will lean toward admission rather than exclusion[8] and at the end will seek to find clearly admissible testimony on which to base his findings.[9] This practice will lessen the time spent in arguing objections and will ensure that appellate courts will have in the record the evidence that was rejected as well as that which was received. This will often help them to make an end of the case.[10] It will readily be seen, however, that this practice of hearing everything first and deciding upon its competency later creates an atmosphere which muffles the impact and de-emphasizes the importance of the exclusionary rules of evidence.

 WESTLAW REFERENCES

30k931(6)

---

7.   Builders Steel Co. v. Commissioner, 179 F.2d 377, 379 (8th Cir.1950) (valuable discussion); Powell v. Adams, 98 Mo. 598, 12 S.W. 295, 297 (1889); Degginger v. Martin, 48 Wash. 1, 92 P. 674 (1907); Simpson v. Vineyard, 324 S.W.2d 276 (Tex.Civ.App.1959); Holendyke v. Newton, 50 Wis. 635, 638, 7 N.W. 558 (1880) (referee or judge should be very careful in rejecting evidence, and where there is reasonable doubt, though he thinks it inadmissible, should receive it subject to objections); C.J.S. Trial § 589.

But occasionally appellate courts disapprove. See Kovacs v. Szentes, 130 Conn. 229, 33 A.2d 124 (1943) (based on Conn.Gen.St.Ann. § 52–208 forbidding court to admit evidence subject to objection unless parties agree; "A judge has not such control over his mental faculties that he can definitely determine whether or not inadmissible evidence he has heard will affect his mind . . . "); Havas v. 105 Casino Corp., 82 Nev. 282, 417 P.2d 239 (1966) ("We disapprove the practice of trial courts holding in abeyance rulings on evidence. It precipitates all manners of difficulty."); Holcombe v. Hopkins, 314 Mass. 113, 49 N.E.2d 722 (1943) (semble); Dec.Dig. Trial ☞51, 379.

8.   See *Powell, Degginger* and *Holendyke* in next preceding note.

9.   As in Hatch v. Calkins, 21 Cal.App.2d 364, 122 P.2d 126 (1942) where the judge in his memorandum decision recited that his decision was based on the competent portion of certain affidavits.

10.   As pointed out in the decisions cited in the first paragraph of note 7, supra. See also the discussion of offers of proof, supra § 51.

Title 4
COMPETENCY
Chapter 7
THE COMPETENCY OF WITNESSES

Table of Sections

---

§ 61. In General [1]

The common law rules of incompetency have been undergoing a process of piecemeal revision by statutes for over a century, so that today most of the former grounds for excluding a witness altogether have been converted into mere grounds of impeaching his credibility.

Since the disqualification of witnesses for incompetency is thus dwindling in importance, and since the statutory modifications and the modifications in states which have adopted the Federal Rules of Evidence or the Revised Uniform Rules of Evidence, vary from state to state, a development here of the law in the different jurisdictions is not justified. The common law grounds of incompetency and the general lines of statutory and rule change are summarized in the following sections.

 WESTLAW REFERENCES

competen** incompeten** /s witness** /s disqualif!

---

§ 61

1. 2 and 3 Wigmore, Evidence §§ 483–721 (Chadbourn rev. 1979); Weinstein & Berger, Evidence ¶¶ 601[01]–[07]. The history of the subject is fully treated in 9 Holdsworth Hist.Eng.Law 177–197 (1926) and briefly in Rowley, The Competency of Witnesses, 24 Iowa L.Rev. 482 (1939). A valuable summary is Fryer, Note on Disqualification of Witnesses, Selected Writings on Evidence and Trial 345 (1957).

§ 62. Mental Incapacity [1] and Immaturity [2]

There is no rule which excludes an insane person as such,[3] or a child of any specified age, from testifying,[4] but in each case the traditional test is whether the witness has intelligence enough to make it worthwhile to hear him at all and whether he feels a duty to tell the truth.[5] Is his capacity to observe, remember, and recount, such that he can probably bring added knowledge of the facts?[6] The major reason for disqualification of the persons mentioned in this section to take the stand is the judges' distrust of a jury's ability to assay the words of a small child or of a deranged person. Conceding the jury's deficiencies, the remedy of excluding such a witness, who may be the only person available who knows the facts, seems inept and primitive. Though the tribunal is unskilled, and the testimony difficult to weigh, it is still better to let the evidence come in for what it is worth, with cautionary instructions. Revised Uniform Rule of Evidence 601 and the first sentence of Federal Rule of Evidence 601 reflect the above and additional reasoning by providing every person is competent to be a witness unless otherwise provided in the rules.[7] No exception

§ 62

1. 2 Wigmore, Evidence §§ 492–501 (Chadbourn rev. 1979); Weinstein & Berger, Evidence ¶ 601[03]; C.J.S. Witnesses § 57; Annot., 26 A.L.R. 1491, 148 A.L.R. 1140; Dec.Dig. Witnesses ⟨⟩39–41; Weihofen, Testimonial Competence and Credibility, 34 Geo.Wash. L.Rev. 53 (1965).

2. 2 Wigmore, Evidence §§ 505–509 (Chadbourn rev. 1979); Weinstein & Berger, Evidence ¶ 601[03]; C.J.S. Witnesses § 58; Annot., 81 A.L.R.2d 386; Dec. Dig. Witnesses ⟨⟩40, 45.

3. People v. McCaughan, 49 Cal.2d 409, 317 P.2d 974 (1957); Truttmann v. Truttmann, 328 Ill. 338, 159 N.E. 775 (1927) (mental defective competent); People v. Lambersky, 410 Ill. 451, 102 N.E.2d 326 (1951); State v. Wildman, 145 Ohio St. 379, 61 N.E.2d 790 (1945) (imbecile girl competent).

4. Radiant Oil Co. v. Herring, 146 Fla. 154, 200 So. 376, 377 (1941) ("not an arbitrary age but the degree of intelligence . . . is the test . . ."); Rueger v. Hawks, 150 Neb. 834, 36 N.W.2d 236, 244 (1949) ("There is no precise age which determines the question of a child's competency"); Litzkuhn v. Clark, 85 Ariz. 355, 339 P.2d 389 (1959); Artesani v. Gritton, 252 N.C. 463, 113 S.E.2d 895 (1960) (error to exclude seven-year old child as witness solely "by reason of age"). The statutes that refer to "children under ten years of age who appear incapable of receiving just impressions of the facts respecting which they are examined, or of relating them truly," do not change the rule stated in the text. See, e.g., Litzkuhn v. Clark, supra.

5. State v. Segerberg, 131 Conn. 546, 41 A.2d 101, 102 (1945) ("The principle . . . is that the child shall be sufficiently mature to receive correct impressions by her senses, to recollect and narrate intelligently and to appreciate the moral duty to tell the truth"); Burman v. Chicago Great Western Railway Co., 340 Mo. 25, 100 S.W.2d 858 (1936) (child, 5 at time of injury, 8 at time of trial, competent though had been held incompetent at earlier trial); State v. Smith, 16 Utah 2d 374, 401 P.2d 445 (1965).

The judge will ordinarily conduct an interrogation of the witness to ascertain and test his capacity if the question is raised. Commonwealth v. Tatisos, 238 Mass. 322, 130 N.E. 495 (1921).

6. The test has sometimes been phrased in language as a requirement that the witness must have intelligence enough to "understand the nature and obligation of an oath." This requirement is manifestly inappropriate. It confounds a religious standard with a mental standard, and if literally applied the most intelligent witness could hardly meet the standard, much less a child or an insane person. Examples of decisions in which the court recites this as one of the tests are Bielecki v. State, 140 Tex.Cr.R. 355, 145 S.W.2d 189 (1945), and Mullins v. Commonwealth, 174 Va. 472, 5 S.E.2d 499 (1939). See C.J.S. Witnesses § 63.

7. Rev.Unif.R.Evid. (1974) 601 adopts the first sentence of Fed.R.Evid. 601: "Every person is competent to be a witness except as otherwise provided in these rules." As in Fed.R.Evid. only judges (Rule 605) and jurors (Rule 606) are made incompetent to be witnesses in the trials in which they act as such. See § 68, infra. Also see below for modification of the federal rule by a second sentence for use in diversity cases. Further, under Fed.R.Evid. and Rev.Unif.R.Evid. (1974) 603 a witness must somehow indicate that he will tell the truth.

The Advisory Committee's Note to Fed.R.Evid. 601 states

No mental or moral qualifications for testifying as a witness are specified. Standards of mental capacity have proved elusive in actual application. A leading commentator observes that few witnesses are disqualified on that ground. Weihofen, Testimonial Competence and Credibility, 34 Geo.Wash.L.Rev. 53 (1965). Discretion is regularly exercised in favor of allowing the testimony. A witness wholly without capacity is difficult to imagine. The question is one particularly suited to the jury as one of weight and credibility, subject to judicial authority to review the sufficiency of the evidence. 2 Wigmore §§ 501, 509. Standards of moral qualification in practice consist essentially of evaluating a person's truthfulness in terms of his own answers about it. Their principal utility is in affording an opportunity on voir dire examination to impress upon the witness his moral du-

is made for mental incapacity or immaturity.[8] As already indicated,[9] mental derangement, where it affects the ability of the witness to observe, remember, and recount, may always be proved to attack credibility.

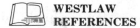

**WESTLAW
REFERENCES**

child! /s witness** testi! /s duty obligation /s truth

digest(child! /s witness** /s capacit! incapacit!)

---

ty. This result may, however, be accomplished more directly, and without haggling in terms of legal standards, by the manner of administering the oath or affirmation under Rule 603.

See United States v. Roach, 590 F.2d 181 (5th Cir.1979).

In the federal courts in civil cases Fed.R.Evid. 601 presents a problem because of its second sentence, which reads, "However, in civil actions and proceedings, with respect to an element of a claim or defense as to which State law supplies the rule of decision, the competency of a witness shall be determined in accordance with state law."

The provision for applying state law to the competency of witnesses is not absolutely clear. The congressional Conference Report on the Federal Rules states: "If an item of proof tends to support or defeat a claim or defense, or an element of a claim or defense, and if state law supplies the rule of decision for that claim or defense, then state competency law applies to that item of proof. For reasons similar to those underlying its action on Rule 501, the Conference adopts the House provision." The Conference Report for Fed.R.Evid. 501 takes the position, under a similar provision in that rule, that in "nondiversity jurisdiction civil cases, federal privilege law will generally apply . . . . When a federal court chooses to absorb state law, it is applying the state law as a matter of federal common law." H.R., Fed. Rules of Evidence, Conf.Rep. No. 1597, 93d Cong., 2d Sess. On the other hand, in diversity cases the same Conference Report pointed out that, if in diversity cases a claim or defense is based upon federal law, federal privilege law and not state privilege law would apply to such claims or defenses in diversity cases. Assuming the above statements represent the intention of Congress and the meaning of Rule 601, Congress probably has the power to enact such a statute, limiting reference to state law as to competency to diversity cases under the terms of the rule. See cases cited in the Conference Report. But see Wright, Federal Courts § 60 (4th ed. 1983).

Thus the apparent intent stated above is that application of state competency rules in diversity cases depends upon whether such issues are governed by state law. Under this view state competency law governs

§ 63. Religious Belief [1]

Belief in a divine being who, in this life or hereafter, will punish false swearing was a prerequisite at common law to the capacity to take the oath.[2] Members of many major religions could meet the test, but members of other religions, as well as atheists and agnostics, could not. This ground of incapacity has fortunately been abandoned in most state jurisdictions,[3] either by explicit state constitutional or statutory provisions,[4] or by expansive interpretation of state provisions forbidding deprivation of rights for religious beliefs,[5] or by changing the common

when the witness testifies on any issues governed by state law. This view should be followed because it is relatively straightforward in theory and should afford few problems in most diversity cases (which do not involve issues dependent upon federal law). In diversity cases, the testimony of witnesses who are incompetent under state law could be limited to testimony on federal issues. If the same testimony of such a witness were relevant upon both state and federal issues, the matter could be handled by proper instructions to the jury in a jury-tried case.

8. See n. 7 supra. By general language or specific language a few states that have adopted the Fed.R. Evid. retain mental incapacity and immaturity as a possible basis for competency. See, e.g. Alaska R.Evid. 601; Ohio R.Evid. 601.

9. See § 45 supra.

§ 63

1. 2 Wigmore, Evidence § 518 (Chadbourn rev. 1979), 6 id. §§ 1816–1829 (Chadbourn rev. 1976); Weinstein & Berger, Evidence ¶ 601[03]; C.J.S. Witnesses § 62; Dec.Dig. Witnesses ⊙⇒44, 227.

2. Attorney-General v. Bradlaugh, [1885], L.R. 2 Q.B.D. 697; 6 Wigmore, Evidence § 1817 (Chadbourn rev. 1976).

3. See the constitutional and statutory provisions listed and described in 6 Wigmore, Evidence § 1828, note 1 (Chadbourn rev. 1976).

4. E.g., Calif.Const.1879, art. I, § 4 ("No person shall be rendered incompetent to be a witness or juror on account of his opinions on matters of religious belief"); New York Const.1895, Art. I, § 3 (similar to last, as to witnesses); Texas Const.1876, Art. I, § 5 ("No person shall be disqualified to give evidence in any of the courts of this state on account of his religious opinions or for want of any religious belief . . . "); Penn., 28 P.S. § 312 ("The capacity of any person who shall testify in any judicial proceeding shall be in no wise affected by his opinions on matters of religion.")

5. E.g., Hroneck v. People, 134 Ill. 139, 152, 24 N.E. 861, 865 (1890) (under constitution which provided that

law "in the light of reason and experience," [6] or because such a requirement would be inconsistent with our law and with the spirit of our institutions,[7] or by adoption of the Federal Rules of Evidence or the Revised Uniform Rules of Evidence 601 and 603 [8]. In any event, this rule of incapacity appears to be prohibited in any state or federal court by the first and fourteenth amendments of the federal constitution.[9] A witness can object to an oath directly or inferentially stating his belief in God, but it has been held that routinely swearing witnesses to tell the truth using the phrase, "so help me God," does not vitiate a trial, when the witnesses have not objected.[10] Probably the loser has no standing to object on appeal in such a case, but it is conceivable that in some circumstances he could make a strained argument that he has an interest and is affected. Inquiry into the religious opinions of the witness for impeachment purposes is discussed in another section.[11]

"no person shall be denied any civil or political right, privilege or capacity on account of his religious opinions" a witness is qualified though he lacked the religious belief required at common law; see Const.1970, Art. I, § 3); and see State v. Levine, 109 N.J.L. 503, 162 A. 909 (1932), 33 Col.L.Rev. 539 (under Art. 1, § 4, N.J.Const., which provided that no person shall be denied enjoyment of civil rights because of religious principles, it was error to deny accused privilege of affirming as a witness on account of his want of religious belief, even though he was allowed to tell his story to the jury.)

6. See Gillars v. United States, 87 U.S.App.D.C. 16, 182 F.2d 962, 969, 970 (1950) (proper to allow a witness to "affirm" and testify though he did not believe in divine punishment for perjury and though D.C.Code, Title 14, § 101 provided that "all evidence shall be given under oath according to the forms of the common law," except that a witness with conscientious scruples against an oath may affirm).

See also Flores v. State, 443 P.2d 73 (Alaska 1968) (witness who was sworn under the usual oath competent although in cross-examination he stated he did not believe in God).

7. See n. 5 supra.

8. See Fed.R.Evid. (1st sentence) and Rev.Unif.R. Evid. (1974) 601, § 62 n. 7 supra. And Fed.R.Evid. and Rev.Unif.R.Evid. (1974) 603 confirms the text. It provides: "Before testifying, every witness shall be required to declare that he will testify truthfully, by oath or affirmation in a form calculated to awaken his conscience and impress his mind with his duty to do so."

WESTLAW REFERENCES

religio! atheis! agnostic! /s witness** testi! /s competen** incompeten**

---

§ 64. Conviction of Crime [1]

The common law disqualified altogether the witness who had been convicted of treason, felony, or a crime involving fraud or deceit.[2] In England and in most of the states during the last hundred years this disqualification has been swept away by legislation.[3] In 1917, the Supreme Court of the United States determined that "the dead hand of the common law rule" of disqualification should no longer be applied in criminal cases in the federal courts.[4] The disqualification is not recognized in Federal Rule of Evidence and Revised Uniform Rule of Evidence (1974) 601.[5] In a few states, however, it has been retained for conviction of perjury and subornation thereof.[6] These statutes are now of questionable validity under a

---

Gantz v. State, 18 Ga.App. 154, 88 S.E. 993, (1916) (cited in Pitts v. State, 219 Ga. 222, 132 S.E.2d 649 (1963)).

9. The textual statement may be inferred from Torcaso v. Watkins, 367 U.S. 488 (1961) (belief in God, as a Maryland constitutional test for public office, was held unconstitutional under the First and Fourteenth Amendments of the federal constitution).

10. State v. Albe, 10 Ariz.App. 545, 460 P.2d 651 (1969).

11. See § 48 supra.

§ 64

1. 2 Wigmore, Evidence §§ 488, 519–524 (Chadbourn rev. 1979); Weinstein & Berger, Evidence ¶ 601[03]; C.J.S. Witnesses §§ 65–67; Dec.Dig. Witnesses ⊗48, 49.

2. Wigmore, Evidence §§ 519, 520 (Chadbourn rev. 1979).

3. See the statutes collected in 2 Wigmore, Evidence § 488 (Chadbourn rev. 1979). Some of the cited statutes that retain vestiges of the common law rule have been amended since the collection was compiled.

4. Rosen v. United States, 245 U.S. 467 (1917).

5. See § 62 n. 7 supra.

6. The majority of courts have denied disqualification by reason of a conviction in another state, although conviction in the forum would have resulted in disqualification. See Annot., 2 A.L.R.2d 579. Any of these statutes still remaining would be abrogated by Rev.Unif.R.Evid. (1974) 601, supra § 62 n. 7.

holding of the Supreme Court of the United States that declared unconstitutional Texas statutes which barred the persons charged or convicted as co-participants in the same crime from testifying for each other.[7]

 WESTLAW REFERENCES

convict! /s crime criminal /s disqualif! /s witness** testi!
rosen /15 245 /5 467

---

§ 65. Parties and Persons Interested: The Dead Man Statutes [1]

By far the most drastic of the common law rules of incompetency was the rule that excluded the testimony of the parties to the lawsuit and of all persons having a direct pecuniary or proprietary interest in the outcome. In effect, this rule imposed a disability upon the party to testify in his own behalf and conferred upon him a privilege not to be used as a witness against himself by the adversary. The disability had the specious justification of preventing self-interested perjury; the privilege had not even a specious excuse. It is almost unbelievable that the rule could have continued in force in England until the middle of the 19th century, and in this country for a few decades longer. In England, the reform was sweeping, and no shred of disqualification in civil cases remains.

In this country, however, a compromise was forced upon the reformers. The objection was raised that in controversies over contracts or other transactions where one party to the transaction had died and the other survived, hardship and fraud would re-sult if the surviving parties or interested persons were permitted to testify to the transactions. The survivor could testify though the adverse party's lips would be sealed in death. This is a seductive argument. It was accepted in nearly all the early statutes, at a time when the real dispute was whether the general disqualification should be abolished or retained, and the concession for survivors' cases undoubtedly seemed a minor one. But the concession where it still exists has now become so ingrained a part of judicial and professional habits of thinking that it is hard to dislodge by argument.

Accordingly, statutes in many states provide that the common law disqualification of parties and interested persons is abolished, except that they remain disqualified to testify concerning a transaction or communication with a person since deceased in a suit prosecuted or defended by the executor or administrator of the decedent.[2] However, it is often provided by the statute or by case law that the surviving party or interested person may testify if called by the adversary, i.e., by the executor or administrator, thus abrogating the privilege feature of the common law rule. The practical consequence of these statutes is that if a survivor has rendered services, furnished goods or lent money to a man whom he trusted, without an outside witness or admissible written evidence, he is helpless if the other dies and the representative of his estate declines to pay. The survivor's mouth may even be closed in an action arising from a fatal automobile collision,[3] or in a suit upon a note or

---

7. Washington v. Texas, 388 U.S. 14 (1967).

§ 65

1. 2 Wigmore, Evidence §§ 575–580 (Chadbourn rev. 1979); Weinstein & Berger, Evidence ¶ 601[03]; C.J.S. Witnesses §§ 132–251; Dec.Dig. Witnesses ⊂⇒80–183½; Ray, Dead Man's Statutes, 24 Ohio St.L.J. 89 (1963).

2. This is the most common general form, but the variants are so numerous that no statute seems entirely typical. The cases interpreting one statute must be treated with great caution in the interpretation of an-

other statute, and a great deal of confusing and conflicting interpretive case law exists. Some statutes apply to suits by or against other persons deriving interests from a deceased person, as well as to suits by or against guardians of incompetents. The variations in the statutes were summarized and graphically charted in Vanderbilt, Minimum Standards of Judicial Administration 334–341 (1949).

3. Annot., 80 A.L.R.2d 1296; Dec.Dig. Witnesses ⊂⇒159(3); Stout, Should the Dead Man's Statute Apply to Automobile Collisions, 38 Texas L.Rev. 14 (1959).

an account which the survivor paid in cash without taking a receipt.

Most commentators agree that the expedient of refusing to listen to the survivor is, in the words of Bentham, a "blind and brainless" technique. In seeking to avoid injustice to one side, the statute-makers ignored the equal possibility of creating injustice to the other. The temptation to the survivor to fabricate a claim or defense is obvious enough, so obvious indeed that any jury will realize that his story must be cautiously heard. A searching cross-examination will usually, in case of fraud, reveal discrepancies inherent in the "tangled web" of deception. In any event, the survivor's disqualification is more likely to balk the honest than the dishonest survivor. One who would not balk at perjury will hardly hestitate at suborning a third person, who would not be disqualified, to swear to the false story.

The lawmakers and courts are being brought to see the blindness of the traditional survivors' evidence acts, and liberalizing changes are being adopted. A few states have provided that the survivor may testify, but his testimony will not support a judgment unless corroborated by other evidence.[4]

Others authorize the trial judge to permit the survivor to testify when it appears that his testimony is necessary to prevent injustice.[5] Both of these solutions have reasonably apparent drawbacks [6] which are avoided by a third type of statute that sweeps away the disqualification entirely and permits the survivor to testify without restriction, but seeks to minimize the danger of injustice to the decedent's estate by admitting any writings of the deceased or evidence of oral statements made by him, bearing on the controversy, both of which would ordinarily be excluded as hearsay.[7]

Federal Rule of Evidence (except in diversity cases) and Revised Uniform Rule of Evidence (1974) 601 abandon the instant disqualification altogether.[8] Not all states which have copied the Federal Rules have done so.[9]

Interest, then, as a disqualification in civil cases has been discarded, except for the fragmentary relic retained in the survivors' evidence statutes. The disqualification of parties defendant in criminal cases which at common law prevented the accused from being called as a witness by either side has been abrogated in England and in this coun-

4. Statutes and cases are collected in Annot., 21 A.L.R.2d 1013.

These statutes do not concern the competency of the witness to testify but only the effect of his testimony. Therefore, Fed.R.Evid. 601 should not apply insofar as it refers to state law issues in diversity cases. Whether such statutes would be per se applicable on state issues in federal court under the *Erie* doctrine is a different question. Arguably they would not be. See Byrd v. Blue Ridge Electric Co-op Inc., 356 U.S. 525 (1958). An analogy might be made to diversity cases concerning sufficiency of evidence, in which more often than not a federal test (and not a state test) is said to be governing. Wright & Miller, Federal Practice and Procedure: Civil § 2525. A contrary view is apparently implied in Weinstein & Berger, Evidence ¶ 601[03]. See n. 7 infra.

5. See Ariz.Rev.Stat. § 12–2251.

Since this statute affects the competency of witnesses to testify, Fed.R.Evid. 601, insofar as it speaks of state issues, should govern. See § 62 n. 7 supra.

6. Ray, Dead Man's Statutes, 24 Ohio St.L.J. 89 (1963).

7. This solution was recommended by the American Bar Association in 1938, as follows: "That the rule ex-

cluding testimony of an interested party as to transactions with deceased persons, should be abrogated by the adoption of a statute like that of Connecticut, which removes the disqualification of the party as a witness and permits the introduction of declarations of the decedent, on a finding by the trial judge that they were made in good faith and on decedent's personal knowledge." As of 1949, six states, Connecticut, Louisiana, Massachusetts, Oregon, Rhode Island and South Dakota, had such statutes. Vanderbilt, 334, 338, supra, n. 27. New Hampshire also adopted the provision. For discussion of the entire problem and the alternative solutions, see 2 Wigmore, Evidence § 578 (Chadbourn rev. 1979); Morgan and others, The Law of Evidence, Some Proposals for Its Reform, Ch. III (1927); Ladd, The Dead Man Statute, 26 Iowa L.Rev. 201 (1941); Ray, Dead Man's Statutes, 24 Ohio St.L.J. 89 (1963).

The comment in n. 4 supra, is applicable except that "sufficiency of evidence cases" are not applicable.

8. See § 62 n. 7 supra.

9. At least four retained a dead man's statute in some form. The majority did not do so.

try to the extent it disabled the defendant to testify in his own behalf, but it survives to the extent that the prosecution cannot call him.   In this form, it is a rule of privilege, and constitutes one aspect of the privilege against self-incrimination, treated in a later section.[10]

While the disqualification of parties and persons interested in the result of the lawsuit has thus been almost entirely swept away, the fact of interest of the witness, whether as a party or otherwise, is by no means disregarded.   It may be proved to impeach credibility,[11] and in most jurisdictions the court will instruct that a party's testimony may be weighed in the light of his interest.[12]

 **WESTLAW REFERENCES**

dead /2 man /2 statute* act*

§ 66.   Husbands and Wives of Parties [1]

Closely allied to the disqualification of parties, and even more arbitrary and misguided, was the early common law disqualification of the husband or wife of the party. This disqualification prevented the party's

husband or wife from testifying either for or against the party in any case, civil or criminal.[2] Doubtless we should classify the disability of the husband or wife as a witness to testify *for* the party-spouse as a disqualification, based upon the supposed infirmity of interest, and the rule enabling the party-spouse to prevent the husband or wife from testifying *against* the party as a privilege.[3]

Of course, the common law rule has been modified.   In the majority of jurisdictions statutes have made the husband or wife fully competent to testify for or against the party-spouse in civil cases.[4]   In criminal cases, the disqualification of the husband or wife to testify for the accused spouse has been removed, but it is sometimes provided that the prosecution may not call the spouse, without the consent of the accused spouse, thus preserving for criminal cases the privilege of the accused to keep the spouse off the stand altogether.[5]   In some jurisdictions either spouse may claim the privilege.[6]   In federal criminal cases only the spouse who is to be called by the prosecution as a witness may claim the privilege.[7]   Federal Rule of Evidence 501 presents an unusual situation in the federal rule system.[8]   In other juris-

---

10.   See §§ 116, 130, infra.

11.   See § 40 supra.

12.   Hancheft v. Haas, 219 Ill. 546, 76 N.E. 845 (1906); Lovely v. Grand Rapids & Indiana Railway Co., 137 Mich. 653, 100 N.W. 894 (1904); State v. Turner, 320 S.W.2d 579 (Mo.1959); C.J.S. Trial § 276.

§ 66

1.   2 Wigmore, Evidence §§ 488 (statutes), 600–620, (Chadbourn rev. 1979) (marital disqualification to testify for the spouse),   8 id. §§ 2227–2245 (privilege of party-spouse to prevent other spouse from testifying against the party) (McNaughton rev. 1961); Weinstein & Berger, Evidence ¶¶ 501[03], 601[03]; C.J.S. Witnesses §§ 75–104; Dec.Dig. Witnesses ☞51–65; Hutchins & Slesinger, Some Observations on the Law of Evidence: Family Relations, 13 Minn.L.Rev. 675 (1929); Note, 56 Nw.L.Rev. 208 (1961).

2.   See authorities in next preceding note.   See also survey of the law in the various American jurisdictions in Note, 38 Va.L.Rev. 359 (1952).

3.   28 Wigmore, Evidence § 2227 (McNaughton rev. 1961).

4.   See statutes collected in 2 Wigmore, Evidence § 488 (Chadbourn rev. 1979), 8 id. § 2245 (McNaughton

rev. 1961), and summary of statutes in Note, 38 Va.L. Rev. 359 (1952).

5.   See tabulation in n. 9 in the opinion in Trammel v. United States, 445 U.S. 40 (1980).   See also sources cited in n. 4, supra.   State v. Dunbar, 360 Mo. 788, 230 S.W.2d 845, 849 (1950) (prosecution of husband for shooting wife in arm, so that it had to be amputated; held under statute that wife though competent was not compellable to testify, reversing defendant's conviction because she was required to testify; this ignores the principle that a party cannot complain of the infringement of a witness's privilege, see § 73 infra).

6.   See sources cited in n. 5 supra.

7.   Trammel v. United States, 445 U.S. 40 (1980). The result stated in this opinion is contrary to Rule 505 as promulgated by the Supreme Court but deleted by Congress.   See also n. 8 infra.

8.   Fed.R.Evid. 601 should govern the subject of whether one spouse may testify *for* the other.   See text at n. 3, supra.

Fed.R.Evid. 501 governs the possible disqualification of one spouse to testify *against* the other.   Fed.R. Evid. 501 states:

Except as otherwise required by the Constitution of the United States or provided by Act of Congress

dictions spouses may be called to the stand to testify just as any other witnesses.[9]

Even at common law the instant privilege was withheld from the husband in criminal prosecutions against him for wrongs directly against the person of the wife.[10] The statutes which retain the instant privilege usually broaden this exception to include prosecution of any "crime committed by one against the other" and various other miscellaneous exceptions.[11] There is some disagreement concerning the time in which the instant privilege exists, but most courts regard the initial time at which it comes into being as the date of the creation of the marriage and the terminal date as the date of termination of marriage, as by divorce.[12]

Several procedural questions may arise. The holder of the privilege must be ascertained.[13] There is disagreement whether it is error for the prosecution to call the spouse to the stand in a criminal case thereby forcing the accused spouse or the witness' spouse to object in the presence of the jury.[14] Most courts protect the privilege by denying the right to comment upon its exercise.[15]

The privilege is sometimes applied to extra-judicial statements of the spouse.[16]

The privilege has sometimes been defended on the ground that it protects family harmony. But family harmony is nearly always past saving when the spouse is willing to aid the prosecution. The privilege is an archaic

or in rules prescribed by the Supreme Court pursuant to statutory authority, the privilege of a witness, person, government, State or political subdivision thereof shall be governed by the principles of the common law as they may be interpreted by the courts of the United States in the light of reason and experience. However, in civil actions and proceedings, with respect to an element of a claim or defense as to which State law supplies the rule of decision, the privilege of a witness, person, government, State, or political subdivision thereof shall be determined in accordance with State law.

Trammel v. United States, 445 U.S. 40 (1980) confirms the legislative history which indicated that Fed. R.Evid. 501 governed the instant privilege relating to the calling of a spouse to the stand. It also held as indicated in n. 7 supra. There is no indication that the instant privilege will be applied in federal question civil cases.

Of course in diversity cases the standard for application of the instant privilege is state law as described in the rule. When a diversity case subject matter relates to a state other than the state in which the district court sits and the nature and scope of the privilege differs in the two states, a choice of law problem may arise. The present most favored solution is for the federal district court to follow the current conflict of law doctrine of the state in which the district court sits, in accordance with the general doctrine in Klaxon v. Stentor Electric Manufacturing Co., 313 U.S. 487 (1941). Various views are discussed in Wright & Graham, Federal Practice and Procedure: Evidence § 5435.

Pre-*Trammel* federal cases on various aspects of the federal privilege are collected in 45 A.L.R.Fed. 735.

9. See sources cited in n. 5 supra.

10. 1 Blackstone, Commentaries 443 (1765); 8 Wigmore, Evidence § 2239 (McNaughton rev. 1961).

11. 2 Wigmore, Evidence § 488 (Chadbourn rev. 1979) 8 id. §§ 2239, 2240 (McNaughton rev. 1961). And the statutes frequently go further and expressly

except particular crimes (aside from crimes against the person or property of the spouse) such as bigamy, adultery, rape, crimes against the children of either or both, and abandonment and support proceedings. Note 38 Va.L.Rev. 359, 364, 365 (1952); 8 Wigmore, Evidence § 2240 (McNaughton rev. 1961); Annot., 93 A.L.R.3d 1018 (offense against child), 36 A.L.R.3d 820 (offense against spouse and another). Occasionally similar results are reached in the absence of express exceptions in the disqualifying statute. State v. Kollenborn, 304 S.W.2d 855 (Mo.1957) (in prosecution of husband for assault on their minor child, wife could testify for state). See also Wyatt v. United States, 362 U.S. 525 (1960) (transportation of wife for purpose of prostitution, in violation of Mann Act is crime against her and she can be compelled to testify).

12. 8 Wigmore, Evidence § 2237 (McNaughton rev. 1961). See dictum in Pereira v. United States, 347 U.S. 1 (1953). In pre-*Trammel* decisions it has been held that defendant who left wife could not claim privilege under the particular circumstances. United States v. Cameron, 556 F.2d 752 (5th Cir.1977); United States v. Brown, 605 F.2d 389 (8th Cir.1979), cert. denied 444 U.S. 972.

13. See sources cited in n. 5 supra; also § 73 infra.

14. State v. Tanner, 54 Wn.2d 535, 341 P.2d 869 (1959) (improper to force objection before jury, but case may be restricted to its facts); Hignett v. State, 168 Tex.Cr.R. 380, 328 S.W.2d 300 (1959) (requiring defendant to object in presence of jury is error); State v. Hixson, 237 Or. 402, 391 P.2d 388 (1964) (contra; not error to call spouse to stand and request defendant's permission to examine her); Annot., 76 A.L.R.2d 920.

15. See cases cited at 8 Wigmore, Evidence § 2243 (McNaughton rev. 1961).

16. See cases cited in 8 Wigmore, Evidence § 2232 (McNaughton rev. 1961), but vicarious admissions and a few other exceptions are noted. A contrary decision is Eubanks v. State, 242 Miss. 372, 135 So.2d 183 (1961) (extra-judicial statement of wife admitted as part of the res gestae).

survival of a mystical religious dogma [17] and of a way of thinking about the marital relation that is today outmoded.[18]

Both the instant privilege, and the ancient disqualification, must be clearly distinguished from another privilege—the privilege against disclosure of confidential communications between husband and wife. It is discussed in another place.[19]

 WESTLAW REFERENCES

digest(husband* wi*e* spous** /3 privilege)
trammel /15 445 /5 40
headnote(rule* /10 evidence evid. /10 501 /30 husband* wi*e* spous**)
opinion(fed.r.evid! rule /3 501 /p husband* wi*e* spous**)

§ 67. Incompetency of Husband and Wife to Give Testimony on Non-Access [1]

In 1777, in an ejectment case where the issue of the legitimacy of the claimant was raised, Lord Mansfield delivered a pronouncement which apparently was new-minted doctrine, "that the declarations of a father or mother cannot be admitted to bastardize the issue born after marriage . . . it is a rule founded in decency, morality and policy, that they shall not be permitted to say after marriage that they have had no connection and therefore that the offspring is spurious. . . . " [2] This invention of the great jurist though justly criticised by Wigmore as inconsistent, obstructive and pharisaical,[3] was followed by later English decisions [4] until abrogated by statute,[5] and has been accepted by some courts in this country.[6] A few courts have wisely rejected it by construing the general statutes abolishing the incompetency of parties and of spouses as abolishing this eccentric incompetency also,[7] but other courts have not yielded to this argument.[8] The points of controversy in the application of the rule are (a) whether it is limited strictly to evidence of non-access,[9] or whether it extends to other

17. Coke, Commentary on Littleton 6b (1628), ". . . a wife cannot be produced either for or against her husband, *"quia sunt duae animae in carne una"* ("for they are two souls in one flesh").

18. See Hutchins & Slesinger, Some Observations on the Law of Evidence: Family Relations, 13 Minn.L. Rev. 675, 678 (1929), but compare Note, 17 U.Chi.L. Rev. 525, 530 (1950) and § 86 infra. See also the criticisms of the privilege collected in 8 Wigmore, Evidence § 2228, (McNaughton rev. 1961), ranging from the philippic by Jeremy Bentham in 1827 to the recommendation for its abolition by the Committee on the Improvement of the Law of Evidence of the American Bar Association in 1937.

19. See Ch. 9 infra.

§ 67

1. 7 Wigmore, Evidence §§ 2063, 2064 (Chadbourn rev. 1978); C.J.S. Witnesses § 90; Dec.Dig. Witnesses ⬅57; Annot., 49 A.L.R.3d 212.

2. Goodright v. Moss, 2 Cowp. 291, 98 Eng.Rep. 1257 (1777).

3. 7 Wigmore, Evidence § 2064 (Chadbourn rev. 1978). See also § 205 at nn. 36–39 as to conclusive effect of negative results of scientific tests for paternity.

4. See, e.g., Russell v. Russell, [1924] App.C. 687 (H.L.)

5. St.1949, 12, 13, and 14 Geo. 6, ch. 100, Law Reform (Miscellaneous Provisions) Act, 1949, § 7 ("evidence of a husband or wife shall be admissible in any proceedings to prove that marital intercourse did or did not take place between them during any period . . .

husband or wife shall not be compellable in any proceeding to give evidence of the matters aforesaid"). Similar provisions are contained in St.1950, 14 Geo. 6, ch. 25, Matrimonial Causes Act, 1950, § 32.

6. See authorities cited in n. 1 above. The realistic opinion of Smith, C.J., writing for the court in Moore v. Smith, 178 Miss. 383, 172 So. 317 (1937), rejects outright the reasoning in Goodright v. Moss, supra, n. 2. The principle is not accepted by the Fed.R.Evid. or the Unif.R.Evid.

7. In re McNamara's Estate, 181 Cal. 82, 183 Pac. 552, 7 A.L.R. 313, 325 (1919); State v. Soyka, 181 Minn. 533, 233 N.W. 300 (1930); Loudon v. Loudon, 114 N.J. Eq. 242, 168 A. 840, 89 A.L.R. 904 (Ct.Errors & App. 1933) (extensive discussion by Perskie, J.); State v. Schimschal, 73 Wash.2d 141, 437 P.2d 169 (1968); Ventresco v. Bushey, 159 Me. 241, 191 A.2d 104 (1963) (overruling Hubert v. Cloutier, 135 Me. 230, 194 A. 303 (1937) and citing additional cases).

8. See, e.g., State v. Wade, 264 N.C. 144, 141 S.E.2d 34 (1965); State ex rel. Worley v. Lavender, 147 W.Va. 803, 131 S.E.2d 752 (1963).

Specific statutes, however, often limit or abrogate the rule in particular proceedings. See, e.g., the statutes described in Sayles v. Sayles, 323 Mass. 66, 80 N.E.2d 21, 22 (1948) (statutes permitting spouses testimony to non-access in prosecutions for non-support and in illegitimacy proceedings).

9. As held in Hall v. State, 176 Md. 488, 5 A.2d 916 (1939) but possibly the Lord Mansfield rule, abolished in part by the legislature, should be considered ineffective, Shelly v. Smith, 249 Md. 619, 241 A.2d 682 (1968);

types of evidence showing that some one other than the husband is the father,[10] (b) whether the rule is limited to proceedings wherein legitimacy is in issue[11] or extends to suits for divorce where the question is adultery rather than the legitimacy of the child,[12] and (c) whether it is confined to prohibiting the testimony of husband and wife on the stand,[13] or extends to excluding evidence of the previous admissions or declarations of the spouse.[14] In view of the impolicy of the rule it is believed that in all these instances the more restrictive application is to be preferred.

 **WESTLAW
REFERENCES**

husband* wi*e* spous** /3 disqualif! competen** incompeten** /s nonaccess

---

Commonwealth v. Gantz, 128 Pa.Super. 97, 193 A. 72 (1937); Commonwealth v. Ludlow, 206 Pa.Super. 464, 214 A.2d 282 (1966).

10. As in Grates v. Garcia, 20 N.M. 158, 148 P. 493 (1915); Esparza v. Esparza, 382 S.W.2d 162 (Tex.Civ. App.1964).

11. The reasoning, if not the holding, in Sayles v. Sayles, 323 Mass. 66, 80 N.E.2d 21 (1948), supports the view that a suit for divorce for adultery is not within the rule. Biggs v. Biggs, 253 N.C. 10, 116 S.E.2d 178 (1960), seems a holding to that effect.

12. As in Gonzalez v. Gonzalez, 177 S.W.2d 328 (Tex.Civ.App.1943).

13. As held in Sayles v. Sayles, 323 Mass. 66, 80 N.E.2d 21 (1948).

14. As Zakrzewski v. Zakrzewski, 237 Mich. 459, 212 N.W. 80 (1927) (wife's admission that child not her husband's excluded under the rule); Schmidt v. State, 110 Neb. 504, 194 N.W. 679, 681 (1923) (wife's declarations); West v. Redmond, 171 N.C. 742, 88 S.E. 341 (1916). See Annot., 31 A.L.R.2d 989, 1024; Annot., 49 A.L.R.3d 212, 239.

§ 68

1. 6 Wigmore, Evidence § 1909 (Chadbourn rev. 1976); Weinstein & Berger, Evidence ¶ 605[01]–[04]; C.J.S. Witnesses § 105; 81 Am.Jur.2d Witnesses § 101; Dec.Dig. Witnesses ⊂=68–70; Annot., 157 A.L.R. 315.

2. 6 Wigmore, Evidence § 1910 (Chadbourn rev. 1976), 8 id. §§ 2345–2356 (McNaughton rev. 1961); Weinstein & Berger, Evidence ¶ 606[01]–[07]; C.J.S. Witnesses § 108; C.J.S. New Trial § 169; 81 Am.Jur. 2d Witnesses § 102; Dec.Dig. Witnesses ⊂=73, New Trial ⊂=141–143.

3. Thus, it is not uncommon for judges to testify about matters occurring in former trials in which they presided. Woodward v. City of Waterbury, 113 Conn. 457, 155 A. 825 (1931); State v. Hindman, 159 Ind. 586, 65 N.E. 911 (1903). They should be competent witness-

§ 68. Judges [1] and Jurors [2]

A judicial officer called to the stand in a case in which he is not sitting as a judge is not disqualified by his office from testifying.[3] But when a judge is called as a witness in a trial before him, his role as witness is manifestly inconsistent with his customary role of impartiality in the adversary system of trial.[4] Nevertheless, under the older view he was in general regarded as a competent witness,[5] though he might have a discretion to decline to testify.[6] This view is preserved in some state statutes[7] but is subject to criticism.[8] A second view is that the judge is disqualified from testifying to material, disputed facts, but may testify to matters merely formal and undisputed.[9] This distinction is not easy to draw, and formal

es in subsequent habeas corpus proceedings. See Leighton v. Henderson, 220 Tenn. 91, 414 S.W.2d 419 (1967); Annot., 86 A.L.R.3d 633; Report of the Special Committee on the Propriety of Judges Appearing as Witnesses, 36 A.B.A.J. 630 (1950).

4. "The two characters are inconsistent with each other and their being united in one person is incompatible with the fair and safe administration of justice." Parker, J., in Morss v. Morss, 11 Barb. (N.Y.) 510, 511 (1851).

5. See examples in the English practice in the 1600s and 1700s, described in 6 Wigmore, Evidence § 1909, note 1 (Chadbourn rev. 1976).

6. See O'Neill & Hearne v. Bray's Administratrix, 262 Ky. 377, 90 S.W.2d 353 (1936); O'Neal v. State, 106 Tex.Cr. 158, 291 S.W. 892 (1927).

7. See similar statutes described in 6 Wigmore, Evidence § 1909 (Chadbourn rev. 1976). The Tennessee statute is applied in State ex rel. Phillips v. Henderson, 220 Tenn. 701, 423 S.W.2d 489 (1968).

Under the view that a judge is competent as a witness, he should give his evidence under the procedures which apply to other witnesses. Great Liberty Life Insurance Co. v. Flint, 336 S.W.2d 434 (Tex.Civ.App. 1960).

8. The Advisory Committee's Note for Fed.R.Evid. 605 states in part concerning the presiding judge as a witness:

> Who rules on objections? Who compels him to answer? Can he rule impartially on the weight and admissibility of his own testimony? Can he be impeached or cross-examined effectively? Can he, in a jury trial, avoid conferring his seal of approval on one side in the eyes of the jury? Can he, in a bench trial, avoid an involvement destructive of impartiality?

9. Wingate v. Mach, 117 Fla. 104, 157 So. 421 (1934) (testimony as to formal matter did not constitute the

matters nearly always can be proved by other witnesses. Accordingly the third view, for which support is growing, that a judge is incompetent to testify in a case which he is trying,[10] seems the most expedient one. It is embodied in Federal and Revised Uniform Rule of Evidence 605.[11] This rule provides for an "automatic" objection.[12]

A somewhat similar danger to the impartial position of the tribunal is present when a juror sitting in a case is called as a witness. Thus Federal and Revised Uniform Rule of Evidence (1974) 606(a) provides that the juror is incompetent as a witness.[13] By adoption of this rule in state jurisdictions, substantial inroads have been made on the traditional common law and the statutes to the contrary.[14]

There is a separate traditional doctrine that a juror is incompetent to testify in impeachment of the juror's verdict.[15] This doctrine has been much criticized, but retains currency in the decisions.[16] Though arbitrary in its limits in that it disqualifies jurors

---

judge a "material" witness under disqualifying statute); State ex rel. Smith v. Wilcoxen, 312 P.2d 187 (Okl.Cr.1957) (judge not competent to testify to material facts and if he is to be called he should disqualify himself). This view seems to be advocated by Wigmore. See 6 Evidence § 1909 (Chadbourn rev. 1976).

10. See the general statements of the rule of disqualification, or of the impropriety of testimony by the judge, in State v. Sandquist, 146 Minn. 322, 178 N.W. 883, 885 (1920); Brashier v. State, 197 Miss. 237, 20 So. 2d 65, 157 A.L.R. 311, 313 (1944); Maitland v. Zanga, 14 Wash. 92, 44 P. 117 (1896); State v. Eubanks, 232 La. 289, 94 So.2d 262 (1957) reversed on other grounds 356 U.S. 584. See Report of the Special Committee on the Propriety of Judges Appearing as Witnesses, 36 A.B.A.J. 630, 633 (1950) ("The modern rule is that a judge is not a competent witness in a case in which he is presiding, unless there is a statute permitting it.").

Nevertheless, even though the judge may be incompetent, his testimony, if not harmful, may not be ground for reversal. See, e.g., McCaffrey v. State, 105 Ohio St. 508, 138 N.E. 61, 63 (1922), and cases cited in Annot., 157 A.L.R. 315, 319, 320.

11. Fed. and Rev.Unif.R.Evid. (1974) 605 provides:

The judge presiding at the trial may not testify in that trial as a witness. No objection need be made in order to preserve the point.

See Kennedy v. Great Atlantic & Pacific Tea Co., 551 F.2d 593 (5th Cir.1977) (error to allow judge's law clerk to testify as to private view of premises where accident occurred, citing Rule 605).

12. The Advisory Committee's Note explains:

To require an actual objection would confront the opponent with a choice between not objecting, with the result of allowing the testimony, and objecting, with the probable result of excluding the testimony but at the price of continuing the trial before a judge likely to feel that his integrity had been attacked by the objector.

13. Rule 606(a) provides:

A member of the jury may not testify as a witness before that jury in the trial of the case in which he is sitting as a juror. If he is called so to testify, the opposing party shall be afforded an opportunity to object out of the presence of the jury.

See also West's Ann.Cal.Evid.Code, § 704.

14. Statutes have frequently provided to the contrary. See, e.g., State v. Cavanaugh, 98 Iowa 688, 68 N.W. 452 (1896) (juror may testify, under I.C.A. § 780.17; but I.C.A. 813.2, Rule 18 now provides to the contrary). Of course instances in which jurors will be called as ordinary witnesses are rare because of the procedures for selection of the jurors.

15. Like the rule forbidding parents to bastardize their issue, see § 67, supra, this dogma was an innovation introduced by Lord Mansfield. The parent case was Vaise v. Delaval, 1 T.R. 11, 99 Eng.Rep. 944 (K.B. 1785). There affidavits of jurymen that their verdict was based on chance was rejected and Lord Mansfield said: "The Court cannot receive such an affidavit from any of the jurymen themselves, in all of whom such conduct is a very high misdemeanor; but in every such case the Court must derive their knowledge from some other source, such as some person having seen the transaction through a window or by some such other means". The weaknesses of this position are pointed out in 8 Wigmore, Evidence §§ 2352, 2353 (McNaughton rev. 1961).

16. See, e.g., Hoffman v. City of St. Paul, 187 Minn. 320, 245 N.W. 373 (1932) (affidavits as to quotient verdict excluded) and cases collected in 8 Wigmore, Evidence § 2354 (McNaughton rev. 1961) and in Dec.Dig. New Trial ⬥142, 143.

The various problems are analyzed and the lines of decision indicated in an extensive comment, Impeachment of Jury Verdicts, 25 U.Chi.L.Rev. 360 (1958).

Some courts which have followed the dogma of the juror's incompetency to impeach his verdict have limited the disqualification to testimony about matters occurring within the jury room, and allowed the juror to testify to irregularities occurring outside. Pierce v. Brennan, 83 Minn. 422, 86 N.W. 417 (1901) (jurors' affidavits as to their privately viewing the scene); and see Welshire v. Bruaw, 331 Pa. 392, 200 Atl. 67 (1938) (while jurors cannot testify to misconduct among themselves in jury room, can testify as to misconduct there of outsiders—here a drunken tipstaff puts pressure on them for a verdict by remarks in jury room). The disqualification to "impeach" the verdict does not preclude the juror from testifying in support of the ver-

but not officers and eavesdroppers who may gain knowledge of misconduct,[17] it does serve to protect in some measure the finality of verdicts, and it is this policy that has doubtless led to its survival. Other courts would abandon the rule of disqualification, and would permit jurors to testify to misconduct and irregularities which are ground for new trial.[18] For protection of finality they would trust to a doctrine which excludes, as immaterial, evidence as to the expressions and arguments of the jurors in their deliberations and evidence as to their own motives,

dict, when it is attacked by testimony of outsiders. Morakes v. State, 201 Ga. 425, 40 S.E.2d 120, 127 (1946); Iverson v. Prudential Insurance Co., 126 N.J.L. 280, 19 A.2d 214 (Ct.E. & A.1941).

17. Reich v. Thompson, 346 Mo. 577, 142 S.W.2d 486, 129 A.L.R. 795, 802, 803 (1940), annotated on this point. In the cited case testimony of the clerk, who overheard from adjoining room statements made in the jury room, was held admissible.

18. Some leading opinions favoring this view: Whyte, J., in Crawford v. State, 10 Tenn. (2 Yerg.) 60, 67 (1821); Cole, J., in Wright v. Illinois & Miss. Telegraph Co., 20 Iowa 195, 210 (1866). For other decisions and statutes in the various jurisdictions see 8 Wigmore, Evidence § 2354 notes 1, 2; (McNaughton rev. 1961); Annot., 48 A.L.R.2d 971.

19. Davis v. United States, 47 F.2d 1071 (5th Cir. 1931) (testimony of some jurors that defendant's failure to take stand was discussed as indicating guilt and that this was given weight, excluded); Caldwell v. E.F. Spears & Sons, 186 Ky. 64, 216 S.W. 83 (1919) (that jury misunderstood instructions); Collings v. Northwestern Hospital, 202 Minn. 139, 277 N.W. 910 (1938) (same as last); State v. Best, 111 N.C. 638, 15 S.E. 930 (1892) (affidavit of five jurors that they assented to verdict of guilty on belief that recommendation to mercy would save accused from death penalty). Such matters are said to "inhere in the verdict." Decisions are collected in 8 Wigmore, Evidence § 2349 (McNaughton rev. 1961); Dec.Dig. New Trial ⟻143(4, 5).

While these expressions and mental operations are thus no ground of attack upon the verdict, it seems that when an allowable attack is made for misconduct, such as an unauthorized view, evidence of the jurors as to whether the misconduct actually influenced their finding (and this evidence would usually support the verdict) might be received. Caldwell v. Yeatman, 91 N.H. 150, 15 A.2d 252 (1940) (semble). But some decisions are to the contrary. People v. Stokes, 103 Cal. 193, 37 Pac. 207, 209 (1894) (dictum); City of Houston v. Quinones, 142 Tex. 282, 177 S.W.2d 259 (1944). See Annot., 58 A.L.R.2d 556. But as to the influence on the jurors of erroneous instructions, improper arguments of counsel, etc., as distinguished from misconduct of the jurors, the considerations may well be different and the test may be, not were the jurors

beliefs, mistakes and mental operations generally, in arriving at their verdict.[19] Federal and Revised Uniform Rule of Evidence (1974) 606(b) take a more conservative tack based upon prior federal case law.[20] First these rules do not equate with, or govern, grounds for a new trial, but merely govern the competency of jurors to testify concerning the jury process.[21] Second, in addition to jurors' thought processes, discussions, motives, beliefs, and mistakes, they exclude irregular juror conduct in the jury room.[22] Third, they do not exclude juror testimony of

influenced, but was the instruction or the argument calculated to mislead. See, e.g., People v. Duzan, 272 Ill. 478, 112 N.E. 315 (1916) (error in refusing instruction, jurors' evidence that they did not notice that instruction was marked refused, rejected); 8 Wigmore, Evidence § 2349 (McNaughton rev. 1961).

20. Fed.R.Evid. 606(b) provides:

Upon an inquiry into the validity of a verdict or indictment, a juror may not testify as to any matter or statement occurring during the course of the jury's deliberations or to the effect of anything upon his or any other juror's mind or emotions as influencing him to assent to or dissent from the verdict or indictment or concerning his mental processes in connection therewith, except that a juror may testify on the question whether extraneous prejudicial information was improperly brought to the jury's attention or whether any outside influence was improperly brought to bear upon any juror. Nor may his affidavit or evidence of any statement by him concerning a matter about which he would be precluded from testifying be received for these purposes.

Revised Unif.R.Evid. 606(b) is substantially the same.

21. The Advisory Committee's Note states,

This rule does not purport to specify the substantive grounds for setting aside verdicts for irregularity; it deals only with the competency of jurors to testify concerning those grounds.

22. The federal Advisory Committee's Note states concrete instances that illustrate the operation of Rule 606(b) as follows:

Under the federal decisions the central focus has been upon insulation of the manner in which the jury reached its verdict, and this protection extends to each of the components of deliberation, including arguments, statements, discussions, mental and emotional reactions, votes, and any other feature of the process. Thus testimony or affidavits of jurors have been held incompetent to show a compromise verdict, Hyde v. United States, 225 U.S. 347, 382 (1912); a quotient verdict, McDonald v. Pless, 238 U.S. 264 (1915); speculation as to insurance coverage, Holden v. Porter, 405 F.2d 878 (10th Cir.1969), Farmers Coop. Elev. Ass'n v. Strand, 382 F.2d 224, 230 (8th Cir.

extraneous prejudicial influences.[23] Fourth, they do not preclude testimony of others about their knowledge of jury misconduct.[24]

To be distinguished from these rules of incompetency and exclusion, is the doctrine which has the support of Wigmore [25] and of some judicial expressions,[26] to the effect that each juror has a privilege against the disclosure in court of his communications to the other jurors during their retirement.

WESTLAW REFERENCES

digest(judge* judicial /s disqualif! competen** incompeten** /s witness** testi!)

§ 69. Firsthand Knowledge and Expertness

Two other rules, already considered, may be related to the subject of competency of witnesses. These rules are the requirement that a witness testifying to objective facts must have had means of knowing them from observation,[1] and the rule that one who

would testify to his inference or opinion in matters requiring special training or experience to understand, must be qualified as an expert in the field.[2] It should be noted that unlike most of the other rules of competency, which go to the capacity of the witness to speak at all, these last are directed to his capacity to speak to a particular matter.

WESTLAW REFERENCES

witness** testi! expert /s qualif! /s training experience education

§ 70. The Procedure of Disqualification [1]

Under the earlier common law practice, the witness was not sworn until he was placed upon the stand to begin his testimony. Before the oath was administered the adversary had an opportunity to object to his competency and the judge or counsel would then examine the witness touching upon his qualifications, before he was sworn as a wit-

---

1967), cert. denied 389 U.S. 1014; misinterpretation of instructions, Farmers Coop. Elev. Ass'n v. Strand, supra; mistake in returning verdict, United States v. Chereton, 309 F.2d 197 (6th Cir.1962); interpretation of guilty plea by one defendant as implicating others, United States v. Crosby, 294 F.2d 928, 949 (2d Cir. 1961). The policy does not, however, foreclose testimony by jurors as to prejudicial extraneous information or influences injected into or brought to bear upon the deliberative process. Thus a juror is recognized as competent to testify to statements by the bailiff or the introduction of a prejudicial newspaper account into the jury room, Mattox v. United States, 146 U.S. 140 (1892). See also Parker v. Gladden, 385 U.S. 363 (1966).

Various other illustrations of matters to which the jurors may testify are related in Weinstein & Berger, Evidence ¶ 606[04].

23. See n. 22 supra.

24. See federal Advisory Committee's Note to Rule 606(b). The rule does not relate to secrecy or disclosure but only to the competency of jurors as witnesses and certain evidence given by jurors.

25. 8 Evidence § 2346 (McNaughton rev. 1961).

26. In Clark v. United States, 289 U.S. 1 (1933), on appeal from a conviction of a juror for contempt in giving false answers, Cardozo, J., for the court said: "The books suggest a doctrine that the arguments and votes of jurors, the media concludendi, are secrets, protected from disclosure unless the privilege is waived. . . . Freedom of debate might be stifled and independence

of thought checked if jurors were made to feel that their arguments and ballots were to be freely published to the world. The force of these considerations is not to be gainsaid. . . . Assuming that there is a privilege which protects from impertinent exposure the arguments and ballots of a juror while considering his verdict, we think the privilege does not apply where the relation giving birth to it has been fraudulently begun or fraudulently continued." The privilege was held inapplicable because of such fraudulent conduct.

§ 69

1. See § 10 supra. The requirement of firsthand knowledge on the part of witnesses not testifying as experts is not a question of competency in the traditional sense. Thus Fed.R.Evid. 104(a), which states that qualification of a person to be a witness is a question for the court, is not applicable to questions of firsthand knowledge. Rather these are questions of conditional relevancy, with the judge presiding at the threshold and the jury making the final determination, as pointed out in the Advisory Committee's Note to Rule 602. See Joy Manufacturing Co. v. Sola Basic Industries, Inc., 697 F.2d 104 (3d Cir.1982); see § 53 supra as to conditional relevancy generally.

2. See § 13 supra.

§ 70

1. 2 Wigmore, Evidence §§ 483–487 (Chadbourn rev. 1979), Weinstein & Berger, Evidence, ¶ 601[03]–[04]; C.J.S. Witnesses §§ 115–119; Dec.Dig. Witnesses ⊜76–79, 121–124, 180–183.

ness. This was known as a voir dire examination. Traditionally when the witness is first called to the stand to testify, the opponent has been required to challenge his competency, if grounds of challenge are then known to him.[2]

Except possibly for diversity cases, the situation described above is quite different from that prescribed by Federal Rule of Evidence 601 in the federal courts, because of the limited scope of the subject of competency of witnesses.[3] The situation is also different under the Revised Uniform Rule of Evidence 601.[4] In effect the procedure for challenging judges and jurors as witnesses is prescribed by Rules 605 and 606.[5] In federal criminal cases the privilege of the spouse witnesses to object to being called by the prosecution may probably be exercised before the spouse witness takes the stand. Since the objections of incapacity and immaturity do not bear upon competency but rather upon credibility, these matters need not be raised before the witness begins to testify.[6] Even in diversity cases in federal court, the federal court should not be bound by the exact procedures of objection followed in any particular state.

Finally, under both case law and the Federal and Revised Uniform Rules of Evidence, the offering party must first show knowledge or expertness of the witness, usually by questioning the witness to show the witness is qualified.[7]

If a question of fact is disputed or doubtful on the evidence, the trial judge sitting with a jury does not submit this question of fact to the jury, except questions whether the witness has firsthand knowledge.[8] As with all similar issues of fact arising in the determination of the admissibility of evidence [9] the judge himself decides the preliminary issue and sustains or rejects accordingly the challenge to the witness or the objection to evidence.[10]

 **WESTLAW REFERENCES**

"voir dire" /25 witness** /25 qualif! disqualif!

§ 71. Probable Future of the Rules of Competency

The rules which disqualify witnesses who have knowledge of relevant facts and mental capacity to convey that knowledge are serious obstructions to the ascertainment of truth. For a century the course of legal evolution has been in the direction of sweeping away these obstructions. To that end Federal Rules of Evidence 601 through 606 (deleting the second sentence of Rule 601), or the similar rules of the Revised Uniform Rules of Evidence should be adopted in more

---

2. 2 Wigmore, Evidence § 586 (Chadbourn rev. 1979). If it is error for the accused to call a spouse to the stand and require the accused spouse to object before the jury, as it is in some courts, see § 66, supra, § 76, infra, prior voir dire examination without the presence of the jury is required. In some courts, voir dire examination may also be required of proposed infant witnesses and in some circumstances of proposed witnesses who are allegedly incompetent. Saucier v. State, 156 Tex.Cr.R. 301, 235 S.W.2d 903 (1951), cert. denied 341 U.S. 949, rehearing denied 342 U.S. 843 (challenge to mental competency of witness). It often seems assumed that the examination should be held in the presence of the jury presumably because it can affect credibility in any event. If the grounds of incompetency are not known when the witness takes the stand but are disclosed in the testimony, the challenge may then be made. Nunn v. Slemmons' Administrator, 298 Ky. 315, 182 S.W.2d 888 (1944). If the challenge goes to incompetency generally, as for mental incompetency, the burden rests on the objector to show by examination of the challenged witness, or by other evi-

dence, that the disqualification exists. State v. Barker, 294 Mo. 303, 242 S.W. 405 (1922); Batterton v. State, 52 Tex.Cr.R. 381, 107 S.W. 826 (1908); 2 Wigmore, Evidence §§ 484, 497 (Chadbourn rev. 1979).

3. See the prior sections in this chapter.

4. See the rule at § 62, n. 6 supra.

5. See § 68 supra.

6. See § 62 n. 6.

7. See §§ 10, 13 supra.

8. See § 69, n. 1 supra.

9. See § 53 supra. Fed. and Rev.Unif.R.Evid. (1974) 104(a) provide:

Preliminary questions concerning the qualification of a person to be a witness . . . shall be determined by the court . . . .

10. De Silvey v. State, 245 Ala. 163, 16 So.2d 183 (1944); State v. Teager, 222 Iowa 391, 269 N.W. 348 (1936); 2 Wigmore, Evidence § 487 (Chadbourn rev. 1979); Dec.Dig. Witnesses ⟐79(1).

state jurisdictions. Congress should exercise the power to adopt these rules without qualification for diversity cases.[1]

§ 71

1. The second sentence of Fed.R.Evid. 601 was added by the Congress. It was pointed out that the original Rule's making so-called Dead Man's Statutes of the

 **WESTLAW REFERENCES**

uniform /3 rule* /3 evidence

states inapplicable in federal courts was a center of controversy. House Comm. on Judiciary, Fed. Rules of Evidence, H.R.Rep. No. 650, 93d Cong., 1st Sess., p. 9 (1973).

Title 5

PRIVILEGE: COMMON LAW AND STATUTORY

Chapter 8

THE SCOPE AND EFFECT OF THE EVIDENTIARY PRIVILEGES

Table of Sections

§ 72. The Purposes of Rules of Privilege:[1] (a) Other Rules of Evidence Distinguished

The overwhelming majority of all rules of evidence have as their ultimate justification some tendency to promote the objectives set forward by the conventional witness' oath, the presentation of "the truth, the whole truth, and nothing but the truth." Thus such prominent exclusionary rules as the

§ 72

1. As to the basis of privileges generally, see 8 Wigmore, Evidence §§ 2192, 2197, 2285 (McNaughton rev. 1961) and the opinion of Learned Hand, Circuit Judge, in McMann v. Securities and Exchange Commission, 87 F.2d 377, 378 (2d Cir. 1937), cert. denied 301 U.S. 684 (denying the claim of a customer to a privilege against the disclosure of his broker's records relating to his trading account) ("The suppression of truth is a grievous necessity at best, more especially when as here its inquiry concerns the public interest; it can be justified at all only when the opposed private interest is supreme." See also, Barnhart, Theory of Testimonial Competency and Privilege, 4 Ark.L.Rev. 377 (1950); Donnelly, The Law of Evidence: Privacy and Disclosure, 14 La.L.Rev. 361 (1954); Falknor, Extrinsic Policies Affecting Admissibility, 10 Rutgers L.Rev. 574 (1956); Katz, Privileged Communications: A Proposal for Reform, 1 Dalhousie L.J. 597 (1974); Ladd, Privileges, 1969 L. & Soc. Order 555; Louisell, Confidentiality, Conformity, and Confusion: Privileges in Federal Court Today, 31 Tul.L.Rev. 101 (1956); Tacon, A Ques-

hearsay rule, the opinion rule, the rule excluding bad character as evidence of crime, and the original documents (or "Best Evidence") rule, have as their common purpose the elucidation of the truth, a purpose which these rules seek to effect by operating to exclude evidence which is unreliable or which is calculated to prejudice or mislead.

By contrast the rules of privilege, of which the most familiar are the rule protecting against self-incrimination and those shielding the confidentiality of communications between husband and wife, attorney and client, and physician and patient, are not designed or intended to facilitate the fact-finding process or to safeguard its integrity. Their effect instead is clearly inhibitive; rather than facilitating the illumination of truth, they shut out the light.[2]

Rules which serve to render accurate ascertainment of the truth more difficult, or in some instances impossible, may seem anomalous in a rational system of fact-finding.[3] Nevertheless, rules of privilege are not without a rationale. Their warrant is the protection of interests and relationships which, rightly or wrongly, are regarded as of sufficient social importance to justify some sacri-

fice of availability of evidence relevant to the administration of justice.[4]

The interests allegedly served by privileges, as might be expected, are varied. The great constitutional protections which have evolved around self-incrimination, confessions, and unlawfully obtained evidence are considered elsewhere.[5] They are commonly classed as privileges.

Of the rules treated here, a substantial number operate to protect communications made within the context of various professional relationships, e.g., attorney and client, physician and patient, clergyman and penitent. The rationale traditionally advanced for these privileges is that public policy requires the encouragement of the communications without which these relationships cannot be effective. This rationale, today sometimes referred to as the utilitarian justification for privilege, found perhaps its strongest supporter in Dean Wigmore who seems to have viewed it as the chief, if not the exclusive, basis for privilege.[6] Wigmore's views have been widely accepted by the courts, and have largely conditioned the development of thinking about privilege.[7]

tion of Privilege: Valid Protection or Obstruction of Justice, 17 Osgoode Hall L.J. 335 (1979). For discussions of privilege under modern codifications, including the Federal Rules of Evidence, see § 76 infra.

2. State v. 62.96247 Acres of Land in New Castle County, 193 A.2d 799 (Del.Super.1963) (Lynch, J.: "There are many exclusionary rules of evidence that are intended to withhold evidence which is regarded as unreliable or regarded as prejudicial or misleading, but rules of privileged communications have no such purpose. Such rules of privilege preclude the consideration of competent evidence which could aid in determining the outcome of a case, and privilege in no way can be justified as a means of promoting a fair settlement of disputes.")

3. See Elkins v. United States, 364 U.S. 206, 234 (1960) (Frankfurter, J., dissenting: privileges justified "only to the very limited extent that permitting a refusal to testify or excluding relevant evidence has a public good transcending the normally predominant principle of utilizing all rational means for ascertaining truth.")

4. See State v. 62.96247 Acres of Land in New Castle County, 193 A.2d 799 (Del.Super.1963) (Lynch, J.: "Thus, the duty of the confidant of nondisclosure of confidential communications is imposed to protect the

reliance interest of the communicant, with an assent of the community. This reliance interest is protected because such protection will encourage certain communications. Encouraging these communications is desirable because the communications are necessary for the maintenance of certain relationships. It is socially desirable to foster the protected relationships because other beneficial results are achieved, such as the promotion of justice, public health and social stability. These goals are promoted in furtherance of a well-organized, peaceful society, which in turn is considered necessary for human survival.")

5. See Chs. 13, 14, and 15 infra.

6. See Louisell, Confidentiality, Conformity, and Confusion: Privileges in Federal Court Today, 31 Tul. L.Rev. 101, 111 (1956).

7. Particularly influential have been Wigmore's stated four essential conditions for the establishment of a privilege. See 8 Wigmore, Evidence § 2285 (McNaughton rev. 1961):

(1) The communications must originate in a confidence that they will not be disclosed;

(2) This element of confidentiality must be essential to the full and satisfactory maintenance of the relation between the parties;

More recently another, and analytically distinct, rationale for privilege has been advanced. According to this theory certain privacy interests in the society are deserving of protection by privilege irrespective of whether the existence of such privileges actually operates substantially to affect conduct within the protected relationships.[8] Thus, while it has been suggested that communications between husband and wife and physician and patient do not have their genesis in the inducement of the privileges accorded them, some form of these privileges is nevertheless seen as justified on the alternative basis that they serve to protect the essential privacy of certain significant human relationships.[9] Given its comparatively recent origin, this latter rationale probably has not operated as a conscious basis for either the judicial or legislative creation of existing privileges. Today's judicial tendency to pour new wine into old bottles, however, may serve to make the nonutilitarian theory a factor in the subsequent development of thinking about privilege.[10]

It is open to doubt whether all of the interests and relationships which have sometimes been urged as sufficiently important to justify the creation of privileges really merit this sort of protection bought at such a price. Moreover, even if the importance of given interests and relationships be conceded, there remain questions as to whether evidentiary privileges are appropriate, much less sufficient, mechanisms for accomplishing the desired objectives. In any event, it is clear that in drawing their justifications from considerations unrelated to the integri-

ty of the adjudication process, rules of privilege are of a different order than the great bulk of evidentiary rules.

WESTLAW REFERENCES

rule* /3 privilege* /p protect! /p communication*

§ 72.1 The Purposes of Rules of Privilege: (b) Certain Rules of Exclusion Distinguished

As developed in a subsequent section,[1] true rules of privilege may be enforced to prevent the introduction of evidence even though the privilege is that of a person who is not a party to the proceeding in which the privilege is involved. This characteristic serves to distinguish certain other rules which, like privileges, are intended to encourage or discourage certain kinds of conduct. Among these latter rules may be included those excluding offers of compromise[2] and subsequent remedial measures following an injury.[3]

Functionally, the policies toward which these latter rules are directed may be fully realized by implementing the rules only in litigation to which the person sought to be actuated by the rule is a party. For example, the rule excluding evidence of offers of compromise is designed to encourage compromise; admitting the evidence in a case to which the offeror is not a party will in no wise operate to discourage compromises. Accordingly, such rules may be asserted only by a party. This consideration, in addition to the fact that these rules are also jus-

(3) The relation must be one which in the opinion of the community ought to be sedulously fostered; and

(4) The injury that would inure to the relation by the disclosure of the communications must be greater than the benefit thereby gained for the correct disposal of litigation.

8. See Black, The Marital and Physician Privileges—Reprint of a Letter to a Congressman, 1975 Duke L.J. 45; Note, 56 Ind.L.J. 121 (1980).

9. Austin, The Use of Privileged Communications for Impeachment Purposes, 49 N.Y.S.B.J. 564 (1977); Saltzburg, Privileges and Professionals: Lawyers and

Psychiatrists, 66 Va.L.Rev. 597 (1980); Comment, 9 U.C.D.L.Rev. 477 (1976).

10. See, Roberts v. Superior Court, 9 Cal.3d 330, 107 Cal.Rptr. 309, 508 P.2d 309 (1973) ("Potential encroachment upon constitutionally protected rights of privacy" required liberal construction of California psychotherapist-patient privilege.).

§ 72.1

1. § 73 infra.

2. See § 274 infra.

3. See § 275 infra.

tified in part by considerations relating to relevancy, makes classification as rules of privilege analytically imprecise.

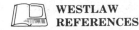

WESTLAW REFERENCES

offer* /3 compromise settlement /s exclu! /s evidence

subsequent /3 remedial /3 measure*

---

§ 73. Procedural Recognition of Rules of Privilege

In one important procedural respect, rules of privilege are similar to other evidentiary rules. The fact that most exclusionary rules are intended to protect the integrity of the fact-finding process while rules of privilege look toward the preservation of confidences might lead the casual reflector to conclude that the former will operate inexorably to exclude untrustworthy evidence while the latter will only be enforced at the option of the holder of the privilege. Such, we know, is not the case. Neither set of rules is self-executing:[1] rules of exclusion, no less than rules of privilege, must be asserted to be effective, and if not asserted promptly will ordinarily be waived.[2] Instead, the distinction in purpose between the two types of rules is reflected by a difference in the persons who may claim their benefit and, perhaps today, in what forum.

§ 73

1. Morgan, Some Problems of Proof 100–101 (1956).

2. Diaz v. United States, 223 U.S. 442 (1911) (hearsay); Halley v. Brown, 92 N.H. 1, 24 A.2d 267 (1942) (same); Southland Equipment Co. v. Hooks, 8 N.C.App. 98, 173 S.E.2d 641 (1970); 1 Wigmore, Evidence, § 18 n. 1 (3d ed. 1940); Fed.R.Evid. 103(a)(1). And see §§ 52, 55 supra.

§ 73.1

1. See Notes, 34 Ky.L.J. 213 (1946), 20 U.Cin.L.Rev. 76 (1951); Annot., 2 A.L.R.2d 645; 58 Am.Jur. Witnesses § 368; Dec.Dig. Witnesses ☜217.

2. Henard v. Superior Court, 26 Cal.App.3d 129, 102 Cal.Rptr. 721 (1972) (party opponent not entitled to claim physician-patient privilege of others); Commonwealth v. McKenna, 206 Pa.Super. 317, 213 A.2d 223

WESTLAW REFERENCES

diaz /s "united states" u.s. & 223 +s 442 rule fed.r.evid! /3 103(a)(1)

§ 73.1 Procedural Recognition of Rules of Privilege: (a) Who May Assert?[1]

This difference in foundation between the two groups of rules manifests itself in another line of cleavage. The rule of exclusion or preference, being designed to make the trial more efficient as a vehicle of fact disclosure, may be invoked as of right only by the person whose interest in having the verdict follow the facts is at stake in the trial. Thus, when evidence condemned by one of these rules is offered, only the adverse party may object, unless the judge elects to interpose. But by contrast, if the evidence is privileged, the right to object does not attach to the opposing party as such, but to the person vested with the outside interest or relationship fostered by the particular privilege.[2] True, other persons present at the trial, including the adverse party,[3] may call to the court's attention the existence of the privilege, or the judge may choose to intervene of his own accord to protect it, but this is regarded as having been done on behalf of the owner of the privilege.[4]

The right to complain on appeal is a more crucial test. If the court erroneously recognizes an asserted privilege and excludes proffered testimony on this ground, of

(1965) (defendant not entitled to assert co-defendant's attorney-client privilege); 8 Wigmore, Evidence § 2196 (McNaughton rev. 1961).

3. People v. Vargas, 53 Cal.App.3d 516, 126 Cal. Rptr. 88 (1975) (in absence of defendant privilege holder his attorney, or court, had duty to raise privilege); Mayer v. Albany Medical Center Hospital, 56 Misc.2d 239, 288 N.Y.S.2d 771 (1968) (privilege of non-party may be raised by any party); Comment, 30 Colum.L. Rev. 686, 690 (1930).

4. Touma v. Touma, 140 N.J.Super. 544, 357 A.2d 25 (1976) (marriage counselor not entitled to assert privilege waived by both spouses); Commonwealth ex rel. Romanowicz v. Romanowicz, 213 Pa.Super. 382, 248 A.2d 238 (1968) (physician-patient privilege not assertable by physician over patient's wishes).

course the tendering party has been injured in his capacity as litigant and may complain on appeal. But if a claim of privilege is wrongly denied, and the privileged testimony erroneously let in, the distinction which we have suggested between privilege and a rule of exclusion would seem to be material. If the adverse party to the suit is likewise the owner of the privilege, then, while it may be argued that the party's interest *as a litigant* has not been infringed,[5] most courts decline to draw so sharp a line, and permit him to complain of the error.[6]

Where, however, the owner of the privilege is not a party to the suit, it is somewhat difficult to see why this invasion of a third person's interest should be ground of complaint for the objecting party, whose only grievance can be that the overriding of the outsider's rights has resulted in a fuller fact-disclosure than the party desires. It has not been thought necessary to afford this extreme sanction in order to prevent a breakdown in the protection of privilege.[7] In at least two classes of privileges, the privileges against self-incrimination[8] and against the use of evidence secured by unlawful search or seizure,[9] this distinction has been clearly perceived and the party is quite consistently denied any ground for reversal, despite the

constitutional bases of the two privileges. The results in cases of erroneous denials of other privileges are more checkered; a considerable number of the older cases seem to allow the party to take advantage of the error on appeal.[10]

The California Code of Evidence, one of the few modern codifications to address the question, is clear-cut. It provides: "A party may predicate error on a ruling disallowing a claim of privilege only if he is the holder of the privilege, except that a party may predicate error on a ruling disallowing a claim of privilege by his spouse . . . "[11]

 **WESTLAW REFERENCES**

object! assert! claim! invok! /s attorney-client /s privilege*

object! assert! claim! invok! /s physician-patient /s privilege*

object! assert! claim! invok! /s husband-wife marital /s privilege*

---

§ 73.2 Procedural Recognition of Rules of Privilege: (b) Where May Privilege Be Asserted?—Rules of Privilege in Conflict of Laws.[1]

Under traditional choice of law doctrine all rules of evidence, including those of privi-

---

5. Wigmore, Evidence § 2196 (McNaughton rev. 1961).

6. People v. Werner, 225 Mich. 18, 195 N.W. 697 (1923) (privilege not to have husband testify); Garrett v. State, 118 Neb. 373, 224 N.W. 860 (1929) (same); People v. Brown, 72 N.Y. 571, 28 Am.Rep. 183 (1878) (self-disgracing testimony); Ex parte Lipscomb, 111 Tex. 409, 239 S.W. 1101 (1922) (where attorney refuses to testify as to communications with client, in a suit to which the client is a party, the attorney when committed for contempt cannot test by habeas corpus the propriety of the denial of the privilege; appeal by the client is the proper remedy); Comment, 30 Colum.L.Rev. 686, 693, n. 41 (1930).

7. But see the vigorous expression of an opposing view by the dissenting judges in State v. Snook, 94 N.J. Law 271, 109 Atl. 289, 290 (1920).

8. See § 120 infra.

9. See § 179 infra.

10. Many of the cases are explainable by the fact that the question of the party's standing to raise the point was not noticed, e.g., Bell v. State, 88 Tex.Cr.R. 64, 224 S.W. 1108 (1920) (marital communications; wit-

ness' privilege denied; defendant allowed to assign as ground of error on appeal). In other cases the court assumes that the evidence usually classified as privileged is "unlawful" or incompetent, e.g., Kaye v. Newhall, 356 Mass. 300, 249 N.E.2d 583 (1969).

A few opinions in cases permitting the party to complain place it expressly on ground of public policy. State v. Barrows, 52 Conn. 323 (1884) (client's privilege); Bacon v. Frisbie, 80 N.Y. 394, 36 Am.Rep. 627 (1880) (client's privilege). The more recent cases where the point is considered seem to be gravitating, under the influence of the Wigmore treatise (n. 5 supra), to the contrary holding. Matthews v. McNeill, 98 Kan. 5, 157 P. 387 (1916); Martin v. State, 203 Miss. 187, 33 So.2d 825 (1948). But a few contrary decisions continue to appear. Stauffer v. Karabin, 30 Colo.App. 357, 492 P.2d 862 (1971). See also Comment, 30 Colum. L.Rev. 686, 694 (1930); Annot., 2 A.L.R.2d 645.

11. West's Ann.Cal.Evid.Code § 918.

§ 73.2

1. See generally, Dunham, Testimonial Privileges in State and Federal Courts: A Suggested Approach, 9 Willamette L.J. 26 (1973); Reece & Leiwant, Testimoni-

lege, were viewed as procedural and thus appropriately supplied by the law of the forum.[2] This approach naturally tended to suppress any consideration of the differences in purpose clearly existing between rules of exclusion and preference on the one hand, and rules of privilege on the other.

Modern conflict of laws analysis, by contrast, inclines toward resolution of choice of law questions through evaluation of the policy interests of the respective jurisdictions which have some connection with the transaction in litigation. Under this approach, the forum will almost invariably possess a strong interest in a correct determination of the facts in dispute before its courts, and therefore a strong interest in the application of its rules of exclusion and preference. By contrast, the forum may have virtually no interest in applying its rules of privilege in a case where the relationship or interest sought to be promoted or protected by the privilege had its contacts exclusively with another jurisdiction.[3]

Thus, for example, if a given professional relationship is carried out exclusively in State X which itself does not extend a privilege to protect that relationship, there would seem to be no compelling reason for the forum, State Y, to apply its own rules of privilege, thus denying its court the benefit of

helpful evidence. No interest either of the forum or of State X argues for recognition of the forum's privilege in such a case.[4]

In short, though case law to date is somewhat sparse, the basic difference in purpose between rules of privilege and other rules of evidence should prove of increasing significance in the resolution of choice of law problems.

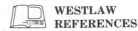

WESTLAW REFERENCES

privilege* /p choice conflict /3 law*

---

§ 74. Limitations on the Effectiveness of Privileges—(a) Risk of Eavesdropping and Interception of Letters

Since privileges operate to deny litigants access to every man's evidence, the courts have generally construed them no more broadly than necessary to accomplish their basic purposes. One manifestation of this tendency is to be seen in the general rule that a privilege operates only to preclude testimony by parties to the confidential relationship. Accordingly, a number of older decisions held that an eavesdropper may testify to confidential communications,[1] and that a letter, otherwise confidential and privileged, is not protected if it is purloined or otherwise intercepted by a third person.[2]

---

al Privileges and Conflict of Laws, 41 Law & C. P. 85 (1977); Sterk, Testimonial Privileges: An Analysis of Horizontal Choice of Law Problems, 61 Minn.L.Rev. 461 (1977); Weinstein, Recognition in the United States of Privileges of Another Jurisdiction, 56 Colum.L.Rev. 537 (1956).

Choice of law questions arising in federal courts are further treated infra at § 76.1.

2. Restatement (First) of Conflict of Laws § 597 (1934). Metropolitan Life Insurance Co. v. McSwain, 149 Miss. 455, 115 So. 555 (1928).

3. Authorities cited supra n. 1.

4. See Restatement (Second) of Conflict of Laws § 139(1) (1971): "Evidence that is not privileged under the local law of the state having the most significant relationship with the communication will be admitted, even though it would be privileged under the local law of the forum, unless the admission of such evidence would be contrary to the strong public policy of the forum." But see Hare v. Family Publications Service, Inc., 334 F.Supp. 953 (D.Md.1971) (holding Maryland

accountant-client privilege applicable to protect communications made in New York which recognized no privilege.)

§ 74

1. This seems to have been the holding even when the overhearing was not due to carelessness on the part of the confidants. Commonwealth v. Griffin, 110 Mass. 181 (1872) (conversation in jail of husband and wife, overheard by officers in concealment); Commonwealth v. Wakelin, 230 Mass. 567, 120 N.E. 209 (1918) (dictograph hidden in cell of husband and wife); Clark v. State, 159 Tex.Cr.R. 187, 261 S.W.2d 339 (1953) (conversation of accused with attorney over long distance telephone reported by operator who eavesdropped in violation of company rule); Annot., 33 L.R.A.,N.S., 477, 485, 63 A.L.R. 107; 58 Am.Jur.2d Witnesses §§ 155, 187; Dec.Dig. Witnesses ⏀206.

2. Intercepted letters, admitted: Hammons v. State, 73 Ark. 495, 84 S.W. 718, 68 L.R.A. 234 (1905); People v. Dunnigan, 163 Mich. 349, 128 N.W. 180, 31 L.R.A.,N.S., 940 (1910); Commonwealth v. Smith, 270

This principle, however, has only infrequently been carried to the extent of allowing a privilege to be breached if the interception is made possible by the connivance of a party to the confidential relationship.[3]

Though the same general rule is still sometimes applied,[4] most modern decisions do no more than hold that a privilege will not protect communications made under circumstances in which interception was reasonably to be anticipated.[5] Certainly, a qualification of the traditional rule in terms of the reasonable expectations of the privileged communicator may provide a desirable common law readjustment to cope with the alarming potential of the modern eavesdropper. While in earlier times the confidentiality of privileged communications could gener-

ally be preserved by a modest attention to security,[6] homespun measures will hardly suffice against the modern panoply of electronic paraphernalia.[7]

The vastly enhanced technology of eavesdropping has drawn a variety of legislative reactions more directly responsive to the problem. These have included state statutes prohibiting wiretapping and electronic surveillance and denying admissibility to evidence obtained in violation.[8] Such provisions are of course in addition to that protection which may rest on constitutional grounds. Moreover, statutes and rules defining the privileges have begun to include provisions entitling the holder to prevent anyone from disclosing a privileged communication.[9]

Pa. 583, 113 Atl. 844 (1921). Testimony of person who saw letters without recipient's connivance, admitted: Harris v. State, 72 Tex.Cr.R. 117, 161 S.W. 125 (1913). But a conflicting view excludes the letters, whether secured with or without the addressee's consent. McKie v. State, 165 Ga. 210, 140 S.E. 625 (1927) (letters of wife to husband, produced at trial of wife for husband's murder, by temporary administrator appointed during trial to secure the letter from husband's deposit box offered by state, held inadmissible.) See also 8 Wigmore, Evidence §§ 2325, 2326, 2329 (McNaughton rev. 1961); 58 Am.Jur.2d, Witnesses § 143.

3. See, e.g., State v. Sysinga, 25 S.D. 110, 125 N.W. 879 (1910). The majority rule declines to allow privilege to be vitiated through connivance; United States v. Neal, 532 F.Supp. 942 (D.Colo.1982) (collecting cases and citing majority rule); People v. Dubanowski, 75 Ill. App.3d 809, 31 Ill.Dec. 403, 394 N.E.2d 605 (1979); Hunter v. Hunter, 169 Pa.Super. 498, 82 A.2d 401 (1951).

4. Howton v. State, 391 So.2d 147 (Ala.Crim.App. 1980) (jailhouse letter read by officer; old rule applied despite availability of basis that no confidentiality could be expected); Erlich v. Erlich, 278 App.Div. 244, 104 N.Y.S.2d 531 (1951) (wiretaps of attorney-client communications held admissible); State v. Slater, 36 Wn.2d 357, 218 P.2d 329 (1950) (testimony of officer overhearing husband-wife communication from adjacent hotel room).

5. A number of cases upholding admissibility on the facts before them state or imply that a reasonable expectation of privacy will bar the eavesdropper's testimony. Narten v. Eyman, 460 F.2d 184 (9th Cir. 1969) (court notes lack of evidence that eavesdropping was surreptitious); Proffitt v. State, 315 So.2d 461, 464 (Fla.1975), rehearing denied 429 U.S. 875 (court characterizes issue as whether "appellant and his wife knew or should have known that their privileged communica-

tion was being overheard."), 4 Fla.St.L.Rev. 553 (1976). See also 2 Weinstein & Berger, Evidence ¶ 503(b)[02] (1977) (noting trend away from traditional rule and toward honoring of privilege where reasonable precautions taken).

6. See Wolfle v. United States, 291 U.S. 7 (1934) (noting that husband-wife communications may generally easily be kept confidential; testimony of public stenographer to whom husband dictated letter, not barred by privilege).

7. Lanza v. New York State Legislative Committee, 3 N.Y.S.2d 92, 164 N.Y.S.2d 9, 143 N.E.2d 772 (1957), cert. denied 355 U.S. 856 ("who could forsee the development of electronic devices making useless the most elaborate precautions to safeguard the confidences of attorney and client") reversed 3 N.Y.S.2d 877, 166 N.Y.S.2d 500, 145 N.E.2d 178 (1957) (statute codifying attorney-client privilege not applicable to prevent nontestimonial disclosure of communication by third person; injunction denied); 42 Minn.L.Rev. 664, 37 Neb.L. Rev. 472, 106 Pa.L.Rev. 307, 36 Texas L.Rev. 505, 32 N.Y.U.L.Rev. 1309. See also State v. Cory, 62 Wn.2d 371, 382 P.2d 1019 (1963) (holding "odious practice of eavesdroping on privileged communications between attorney and client" violated privilege as well as constitutional right to counsel; prosecution dismissed).

8. West's Ann.Cal.Penal Code §§ 631(c), 632(d); Ill. Rev.Stat. c. 38, ¶ 14–5 (1981). So strictly drawn is the Illinois statute that a specific exemption was included in order to allow the hard-of-hearing to wear hearing aids.

See the discussion of proceedings to which the Fourth Amendment applies in § 167 infra, and of eavesdropping in § 169 infra.

9. With respect to the attorney-client privilege, West's Ann.Cal.Evid.Code, § 954.

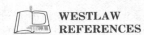

**WESTLAW
REFERENCES**

eavesdropp! intercept! wiretap! surveillance   /p   privilege*
  nonprivilege*

---

§ 74.1   Limitations on the Effectiveness of Privileges: (b) Adverse Arguments and Inferences From Claims of Privilege

The underlying conflict comes most clearly in view in the decisions relating to the allowability of an adverse inference from the assertion of privilege. Plainly, the inference may not ordinarily be made against a party when a witness for that party claims a privilege personal to the witness, for this is not a matter under the party's control.[1] But where the party himself suppresses evidence by invoking a privilege given to him by the law, should an adverse inference be sanctioned? The question may arise in various forms, for example, whether an inquiry of the witness, or of the party, calling for information obviously privileged, may be pressed for the pointed purpose of forcing the party to make an explicit claim of the privilege in the jury's hearing, or again, whether the inference may be drawn in argument, and finally, whether the judge in the instructions may mention the inference as a permissible one.

Under familiar principles an unfavorable inference may be drawn against a party not only for destroying evidence, but for the mere failure to produce witnesses or documents within his control.[2] No showing of wrong or fraud seems to be required as a foundation for the inference that the evidence if produced would have been unfavorable. Why should not this same conclusion be drawn from the party's active interposing of a privilege to keep out the evidence? A

leading case for the affirmative is Phillips v. Chase,[3] where the court said:

> "It is a rule of law that the objection of a party to evidence as incompetent and immaterial, and insistence upon his right to have his case tried according to the rules of law, cannot be made a subject of comment in argument.[4] . . . On the other hand, if evidence is material and competent except for a personal privilege of one of the parties to have it excluded under the law, his claim of the privilege may be referred to in argument and considered by the jury, as indicating his opinion that the evidence, if received, would be prejudicial to him."

An oft-quoted statement by Lord Chelmsford gives the contrary view:

> "The exclusion of such evidence is for the general interest of the community, and therefore to say that when a party refuses to permit professional confidence to be broken, everything must be taken most strongly against him, what is it but to deny him the protection which, for public purposes, the law affords him, and utterly to take away a privilege which can thus only be asserted to his prejudice?"[5]

The first of these arguments is based upon an unfounded distinction between incompetent and privileged evidence, namely, a supposition that the privilege can be waived and the incompetency cannot.[6] As we have seen, both may be waived with equal facility. As to the second, it may be an overstatement to say that permitting the inference "utterly takes away" the privilege. A privilege has its most substantial practical benefit when it enables a party to exclude from the record a witness, document, or line of proof which is essential to the adversary's case, lacking which he cannot get to the jury at all on a vital issue. The inference does not supply the lack of proof.[7] In other situations, the benefit accruing from a successful

---

§ 74.1

1. See § 73 supra, and more particularly as to self-incrimination § 120 infra.

2. See § 272 infra.

3. 201 Mass. 444, 480, 87 N.E. 755, 758 (1909), writ of error dismissed 216 U.S. 616 (1910).

4. See also 5 Busch, Law and Tactics in Jury Trials § 658 (1963).

5. Wentworth v. Lloyd, 10 H.L.Cas. 589, 591 (1864).

6. See § 73 supra. In fact both can be waived, and if the ability of the opponent to waive is the basis for allowing the argument, then the text statement at note 4 would be incorrect (which it is not).

7. See § 272 infra.

claim of privilege will depend upon circumstances. It is evident, however, that in a case which does survive a motion for a directed verdict or its equivalent, allowing comment upon the exercise of a privilege or requiring it to be claimed in the presence of the jury tends greatly to diminish its value. In Griffin v. California [8] the Supreme Court held that allowing comment [9] upon the failure of an accused to take the stand violated his privilege against self-incrimination "by making its assertion costly." Whether one is prepared to extend this protection to all privileges probably depends upon his attitude towards privileges in general and towards the particular privilege involved. The cases, rather naturally, are in dispute.[10] It is submitted that the best solution is to recognize only privileges which are soundly based in policy and to accord those privileges the fullest protection. Thus comment, whether by judge or by counsel, or its equivalent of requiring the claim to be made in the presence of the jury, and the drawing of inferences from the claim, all would be foreclosed.[11]

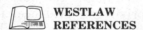

WESTLAW
REFERENCES

infer! argument* /s advers! prejudic! unfavorable /p privilege*

§ 74.2   Limitations on the Effectiveness of Privileges: (c) Constitutional Limitations on Privilege

A hitherto unrecognized source of limitations on privilege in criminal cases has in recent years emerged as a result of decisions of the Supreme Court dealing with the com-

pulsory process and confrontation clauses of the Constitution of the United States.

The three cases which have figured in this development are Washington v. Texas,[1] Davis v. Alaska,[2] and Nixon v. United States.[3] In Washington v. Texas, the Court held the provisions of the compulsory process clause binding upon states as a component of due process, and struck down a Texas statute which rendered persons charged or convicted as co-participants in the same crime incompetent to testify for one another. The Court's decision stressed the "absurdity" of the statute and specifically held only that the constitutional provision is violated by "arbitrary rules that prevent whole categories of defense witnesses from testifying . . . . " [4] The Court expressly disclaimed any implied disapproval of testimonial privileges which it noted are based upon quite different considerations.

In Davis v. Alaska, the Court held that the confrontation clause was violated by application of a state statute privileging juvenile records where the result was to deny the defendant the opportunity to elicit on cross-examination the probationary status of a critical witness against him. Recognizing the strength of the state policy in favor of preserving the confidentiality of juveniles' records, the Court nevertheless held that this policy must yield to the superior interest of the defendant in effective confrontation. Significantly, the Court's decision did not compel disclosure of the juvenile record, but only remanded the case for further proceedings not inconsistent with the Court's opinion.

---

8.   380 U.S. 609 (1965).

9.   The comment assumed the form both of a jury instruction and argument by the prosecutor, but the Court indicated that either alone would be a violation.

10.   For cases see Annots., 144 A.L.R. 1007 (requiring claim to be made or asking party if he will waive, in presence of jury), 76 A.L.R.2d 920 (calling of spouse of accused by prosecution), 32 A.L.R.3d 906 (comment in argument on exercise of privilege), 34 A.L.R.3d 775 (comment by judge in summing up or instructing).

11.   See West's Ann.Cal.Evid. Code, § 913; N.J.Ev. Rule 39; Proposed Fed.R.Evid. 513, 56 F.R.D. 260, not enacted by the Congress.

§ 74.2

1.   388 U.S. 14 (1967), on remand 417 S.W.2d 278 (Tex.Cr.App.).

2.   415 U.S. 308 (1974).

3.   418 U.S. 683 (1974).

4.   Washington v. Texas, 388 U.S. 14, 22 (1967), on remand 417 S.W.2d 278 (Tex.Cr.App.).

Finally, in Nixon v. United States, the Court held that a claim of absolute privilege of confidentiality for general presidential communications in the performance of the office would not prevail "over the fundamental demands of due process of law in the fair administration of criminal justice. The generalized assertion of privilege must yield to the demonstrated, specific need for evidence in a pending criminal trial."[5]

Taken together, and despite the somewhat distinctive fact situations involved, these cases fairly raise the question as to the viability of a claim of privilege when a criminal defendant asserts: (1) a need to introduce the privileged matter as exculpatory, or (2) a need to use the privileged matter to impeach testimony introduced against him.[6] The question is of course not altogether a novel one. Privileges running in favor of the government, such as the informer's privilege, have long been qualified to accommodate the defendant's rights of confrontation.[7] Similarly, the state has frequently been precluded from relying upon the testimony of a witness whose claim of privilege on self-incrimination grounds prevents effective cross-examination.[8]

A number of State decisions, purporting to give effect to the constitutional holdings of Davis and Nixon, have resolved conflicts between the rights of a defendant on the one hand and claims of private privilege on the other by overriding the latter and forcing (or attempting to force) the testimony of the privilege holder.[9]

These results might suggest that the doctrines of Davis and Nixon, especially when construed by courts long impatient with the inhibiting effects of privilege, will serve to negate any claim of private privilege challenged by a criminal defendant. Two considerations, however, would indicate that such a conclusion is broader than that required by the constitutional decisions of the Supreme Court.

In the first instance, it is probable that the defendant's ability to challenge claims of privilege as impairing his "right to present a defense" will to some extent be dependent upon the criticality to that defense of the matter protected by the privilege.[10] In Davis, the privileged matter in effect represented a significant and irreplaceable means of impeaching the chief prosecution witness. By contrast, where the privileged matter desired is of significantly lesser probative force or simply cumulative, its denial to the defendant has been held not to violate the constitutional guarantees.[11]

Again, in cases where assertion of the privilege does substantially conflict with the defendant's right to defend, there is no constitutional necessity that the conflict be resolved by violation of the privilege as opposed to dismissal of the prosecution. Thus, in Davis, the Supreme Court did not mandate breach of the privilege, but remanded for proceedings not inconsistent with the Court's opinion. The problem in these cases therefore frequently should be viewed as one of statutory construction, since it is conceivable that a legislature, forced to the

5. Nixon v. United States, 418 U.S. 683, 713 (1974).

6. See generally, Clinton, The Right to Present a Defense: An Emergent Constitutional Guarantee in Criminal Trials, 9 Ind.L.Rev. 713 (1976); Westen, The Compulsory Process Clause, 73 Mich.L.Rev. 71 (1974); Notes, 73 Mich.L.Rev. 1465 (1975), 30 Stan.L.Rev. 935 (1978).

7. Roviaro v. United States, 353 U.S. 53 (1957).

8. See § 19 supra.

9. Salazar v. State, 559 P.2d 66 (Alaska 1976); Hammarley v. Superior Court, 89 Cal.App.3d 388, 153 Cal.Rptr. 608 (1979); People v. Pate, 625 P.2d 369 (Colo.1981); State v. Hembd, 305 Minn. 120, 232 N.W.2d 872 (1975); In re Farber, 78 N.J. 259, 394 A.2d

330 (1978), cert. denied 439 U.S. 997. See also M. v. K., 186 N.J.Super. 363, 452 A.2d 704 (1982) (statutory privilege for communications between marriage counselor and persons counseled denies child's due process rights to all material evidence in custody proceeding; Davis not cited).

10. See, as supporting such a limitation, Hill, Testimonial Privilege and Fair Trial, 80 Colum.L.Rev. 1173 (1980); Note, 30 Stan.L.Rev. 935, 964 (1978). But see Westen, Compulsory Process II, 74 Mich.L.Rev. 191, 211 (1975).

11. United States v. Brown, 634 F.2d 819 (5th Cir. 1981), rehearing denied 640 F.2d 385.

choice, might elect to prefer the values protected by some privileges even above the interest of effective prosecution of the criminal laws.[12] Though the decisions to date have largely ignored this possible interpretation of privilege statutes, articulation of such an intent is perhaps not beyond the reach of informed draftsmanship. A welcome by-product of this conflict may be more considered legislative judgments both concerning the creation of privileges and the ultimate price which society is willing to pay for the protection which they afford.

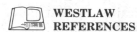

WESTLAW REFERENCES

compulsory /2 process /p privilege* nonprivilege* /p testi!

confrontation /3 right* clause* /p privilege* nonprivilege*

§ 75. The Sources of Privilege

The earliest recognized privileges were judicially created, the origin of both the husband-wife and attorney-client privileges being traceable to the received common law.[1] The development of judge-made privileges, however, virtually halted over a century ago.[2] Though it is impossible definitely to ascribe a reason for this cessation, a contributing factor was undoubtedly a judicial tendency to view privileges from the standpoint of their hindrance to litigation. Certainly the vantage point of the legal profession in

general, and of the judiciary in particular, is such as to force into prominence the more deleterious aspects of privilege as impediments to the fact-finding process. By contrast, many of the beneficial consequences claimed for privilege can be expected to be observable only outside the courtroom, and even then are often difficult of empirical demonstration.[3]

Perhaps as a consequence, during the 19th century the source of newly created privileges shifted decisively from the courts to the legislatures. New York enacted the first physician-patient privilege in 1828,[4] and the vast majority of new privileges created since that time have been of legislative origin. The trend extended to codification even of the preexisting common law privileges, and today the husband-wife and attorney-client privileges are statutorily controlled in most states.[5]

It may be argued that legitimate claims to confidentiality are more equitably received by a branch of government not preeminently concerned with the factual results obtained in litigation, and that the legislatures provide an appropriate forum for the balancing of the competing social values necessary to sound decisions concerning privilege. At the same time, while there is no doubt that some of the statutorily created privileges are soundly based, legislatures have on occasion been unduly influenced by powerful groups seeking the prestige and convenience

---

12. See Hill, supra n. 10; Westen, Reflections on Alfred Hill's "Testimonial Privilege and Fair Trial," 14 U.Mich.J.L.Ref. 371 (1981).

§ 75

1. See §§ 78 and 87 infra.

2. Exceptions are noteworthy. See Mullen v. United States, 105 U.S.App.D.C. 25, 263 F.2d 275 (1958) (privilege recognized for confessional-type statement to clergyman without assistance of statute); State v. Sandstrom, 224 Kan. 573, 581 P.2d 812 (1978), cert. denied 440 U.S. 929 (recognizing limited newsperson's privilege "although such does not exist by statute or common law"); Opinion of the Justices, 117 N.H. 390, 373 A.2d 644 (1977) (semble). Most proposals for new privileges, not surprisingly, look toward legislative action. See, e.g., Coburn, Child-Parent Communications: Spare the Privilege and Spoil the Child, 74 Dick.L.Rev. 599 (1970).

Significantly, however, Fed.R.Evid. 501 will allow the judicial creation of new privileges. See In re Dinnan, 661 F.2d 426 (5th Cir. 1981), rehearing denied 666 F.2d 592.

3. See Saltzburg, Privileges and Professionals: Lawyers and Psychiatrists, 66 Va.L.Rev. 597, 599–600 (1980). See also Rosenburg, The New Tools in Law, 52 Marq.L.Rev. 539 (1969) (urging greater use of social science research techniques to validate assumptions underlying privilege.) For an effort to secure this type of data, see Blasi, The Newsman's Privilege: An Empirical Study, 70 Mich.L.Rev. 229 (1971).

4. N.Y.Rev.Stats.1829, Vol. II, Part III, c–7, Tit. 3, art. eight, § 73.

5. The statutes are collected in 8 Wigmore, Evidence §§ 488, 2292 (McNaughton rev. 1961).

of a professionally based privilege.[6] One result of the process has been that the various states differ substantially in the numbers and varieties of privilege which they recognize.

Until very recently, the heavy consensus of opinion among commentators has favored the narrowing the field of privilege,[7] and attempts have been made, largely without success, to incorporate this view into the several 20th century efforts to codify the law of evidence. The draftsmen of both the Model Code of Evidence [8] and the 1953 Uniform Rules of Evidence [9] favored limitations on the number and scope of privileges. The final versions of both of these codifications, however, contained the generally recognized common law and statutory privileges substantially unimpaired.[10]

The Federal Rules of Evidence as proposed by the Advisory Committee and approved by the Supreme Court contained provisions recognizing and defining nine non-constitutional privileges: required reports,[11] attorney-client,[12] psychotherapist-patient,[13]

husband-wife,[14] clergyman-communicant,[15] political vote,[16] trade secrets,[17] secrets of state and other official information,[18] and identity of informer.[19] In addition, proposed Rule 501 specifically limited the privileges to be recognized in the federal courts to those provided for by the Rules or enacted by the Congress.[20] When the Rules were submitted to the Congress the privilege provisions excited particular controversy,[21] with the result that all of the specific rules of privilege were excised from the finally enacted version of the Rules.[22]

The failure of Congress to enact specific rules of privilege left the Federal Rules of Evidence with a large gap when viewed as a potential model code for possible adoption by the states. Therefore, in promulgating the Revised Uniform Rules of Evidence (1974), based almost entirely on the Federal Rules, the National Conference of Commissioners on Uniform State Laws included specific rules of privilege.[23] These are substantially the version of the Federal Rules submitted to Congress, but contain some notable

---

6. See 8 Wigmore, Evidence § 2286 at 532 (McNaughton rev. 1961).

7. Maguire, Common Sense and Common Law 99–101 (1947); 8 Wigmore, Evidence §§ 2285–86 (McNaughton rev. 1961); Chafee, Privileged Communications: Is Justice Served By Closing the Doctor's Mouth on the Witness Stand? 52 Yale L.J. 607 (1943); McCormick, The Scope of Privilege in the Law of Evidence, 16 Tex.L.Rev. 447 (1938); Radin, "The Privilege of Confidential Communication Between Lawyer and Client, 16 Calif.L.Rev. 487 (1928). And see 5 Bentham, Rationale of Judicial Evidence 302 (J.S. Mill ed. 1827).

8. American Law Institute Proceedings 187 (1941–1942).

9. See Uniform Rules of Evidence, Prefatory Note (1953).

10. Model Code of Evidence, Foreword, 17 (1942); Uniform Rules of Evidence, Rules 23 to 39 and Comments (1953).

11. Deleted Rule 502, 56 F.R.D. 234.

12. Deleted Rule 503, 56 F.R.D. 235.

13. Deleted Rule 504, 56 F.R.D. 240.

14. Deleted Rule 505, 56 F.R.D. 244.

15. Deleted Rule 506, 56 F.R.D. 247.

16. Deleted Rule 507, 56 F.R.D. 249.

17. Deleted Rule 508, 56 F.R.D. 249.

18. Deleted Rule 509, 56 F.R.D. 251.

19. Deleted Rule 510, 56 F.R.D. 255.

20. Deleted Federal Rule 501, 56 F.R.D. 230, reads:

Except as otherwise required by the Constitution of the United States or provided by Act of Congress, and except as provided in these rules or in other rules adopted by the Supreme Court, no person has a privilege to:

(1) Refuse to be a witness; or

(2) Refuse to disclose any matter; or

(3) Refuse to produce any object or writing; or

(4) Prevent another from being a witness or disclosing any matter or producing any object or writing.

With some slight modification to adapt it to State use, this is now Revised Uniform Rule Evid. (1974) 501.

21. Summaries of major points in the controversy may be found in Krattenmaker, Interspousal Testimonial Privileges Under the Federal Rules of Evidence: A Suggested Approach, 64 Geo.L.J. 613 (1976) and 2 Weinstein and Berger, Evidence ¶ 501[01] (1981).

22. For the text of Fed.R.Evid. 501 as adopted by the Congress, see § 76 infra.

23. See Revised Uniform Rules of Evidence (1974) 502–509.

changes.[24] Some states adopting rules or codes based upon the Federal Rules have adopted the proposed Federal Rules concerning privilege, others have adopted the Uniform Rules on this subject, and some have retained their antecedent rules of privilege.[25]

WESTLAW REFERENCES

histor! origin* "common law" /3 privilege* /p
   husband-wife marital
histor! origin* "common law" /3 privilege* /p
   attorney-client

§ 76. The Current Pattern of Privilege

The failure of Congress to enact specific rules of privilege for the federal courts effectively precluded any immediate prospect of substantial national uniformity in this area. It is arguable that, in light of the strength and contrariety of views which the subject generates, hope for such a consensus was never realistic.[1] In any event, the present form of Federal Rule of Evidence 501 perpetuates a fluid situation in the federal law of privilege and affords the states little inducement to adopt identical or similar schemes of privilege. The variegated pattern of privilege in both federal and state courts, described below, thus seems likely to remain the case for the foreseeable future.

WESTLAW REFERENCES

rule fed.r.evid! /3 501 /p privilege*

---

24. The changes are presented in detail in 2 Weinstein and Berger, Evidence ¶¶ 502–510 (1981).

25. Ibid.

§ 76

1. It is noteworthy that even Nevada, a state so enthusiastic over the prospects afforded by the project that it adopted the rules embodied in the Preliminary Draft of Federal Rules of Evidence for United States District Courts and Magistrates (1969), substituted its own preexisting rules of privilege.

76.1

1. The text of deleted Fed.R.Evid. 501 appears supra § 75 n. 20.

§ 76.1 The Current Pattern of Privilege: (a) Privilege in Federal Courts

The Proposed Federal Rules of Evidence recognized only privileges emanating from federal sources and their enactment would have created a unitary scheme of privilege applicable to all cases regardless of jurisdictional ground.[1] The congressionally enacted rules, however, establish a bifurcated system of privilege rules. Federal Rule Evid. 501 provides:

> Except as otherwise required by the Constitution of the United States or provided by Act of Congress or in rules prescribed by the Supreme Court pursuant to statutory authority, the privilege of a witness, person, government, State, or political subdivision thereof shall be governed by the principles of the common law as they may be interpreted by the courts of the United States in the light of reason and experience. However, in civil actions and proceedings, with respect to an element of a claim or defense as to which State law supplies the rule of decision, the privilege of a witness, person, government, State, or political subdivision thereof shall be determined in accordance with State law.

Under Rule 501, then, common law, "as interpreted . . . in the light of reason and experience," will determine the privileges applicable in federal question and criminal cases, while privileges in diversity actions will derive from state law. In the former types of cases, it seems likely that the rules promulgated by the Supreme Court will prove influential as indicators of "reason and experience."[2] But it is also apparent

---

2. See the statement of Weinstein, J., in United States v. Mackey, 405 F.Supp. 854, 857 (E.D.N.Y.1975):

> Despite their deletion by Congress, the privilege rules promulgated by the Supreme Court remain of considerable utility as standards. Congress expressed no disagreement with their substance; it eliminated them primarily because they were considered substantive in nature and not a fit subject for rule making.
>
> The specific rules on privilege promulgated by the Supreme Court are reflective of "reason and experience." They are the culmination of three drafts prepared by an Advisory Committee consisting of judges, practicing lawyers and academicians. In its many years of work, the Committee considered hun-

that the intent of Rule 501 is not to limit the number and type of privileges recognized to those included in the proposed rules.[3] A significant question exists whether this freedom should be used to recognize and apply state privileges in cases where Rule 501 does not require such to be done.[4]

The situation with respect to cases in which state law provides the rule of decision, primarily diversity cases, is somewhat clearer. Presumably a federal court today would not, as was sometimes done prior to the enactment of Rule 501, enforce a privilege in a diversity case which is not recognized by applicable state law. A major question remains, however, as to the process by which the existence or absence of an "applicable" state privilege will be determined in conflict of law situations.

It has been argued that, given the status of Rule 501 as an Act of Congress, the federal courts, in determining the applicable state law of privilege are not constrained to accept state conflict of laws principles. Though this position has been supported by a number of commentators,[5] a majority of the cases decided since enactment of the Federal Rules have continued to follow the doctrine of Klaxon v. Stentor Electric Manufacturing Co.[6] and thus to look to state choice of law rules in determining what state's privilege should be applied.[7]

 WESTLAW REFERENCES

light /5 reason /5 experience & rule fed.r.evid! /3 501

---

§ 76.2 The Current Pattern of Privilege: (b) State Patterns of Privilege

State patterns in the recognition of privileges vary greatly. As developed in succeeding chapters, all states possess some form of husband-wife,[1] and attorney-client privilege.[2] All afford some protection to

dreds of suggestions received in response to the circulation of the drafts throughout the legal community. Finally, they were adopted by the Supreme Court by an eight to one vote. The rule against advisory opinions is only slightly more violated by giving weight to this vote than it would have been had Congress not vetoed these provisions, and had they become "Rules," rather than "standards."

As its commentary indicates, the Advisory Committee in drafting the privilege rules was for the most part restating the law applied in the federal courts. These rules or standards, therefore, are a convenient comprehensive guide to the federal law of privileges as it now stands, subject of course to a considerable flexibility of construction.

See also Schwartz, Privileges Under The Federal Rules of Evidence—A Step Forward?, 38 U.Pitt.L.Rev. 79 (1976); Krattenmaker, Interpersonal Testimonial Privilege—A Suggested Approach to the Federal Rules, 64 Geo.L.J. 613 (1976); Federal Rules of Evidence Symposium, 49 Temp.L.Q. 860 (1976).

3. Trammel v. United States, 445 U.S. 40 (1980) ("In rejecting the proposed rules and enacting Rule 501, Congress manifested an affirmative intention not to freeze the law of privilege. Its purpose rather was to 'provide the courts with the flexibility to develop rules of privilege on a case-by-case basis' . . . .").

4. It has been argued that Rule 501 envisions that even in federal question cases federal courts should defer to state privilege law absent overriding federal policy to the contrary. Kaminsky, State Evidentiary Privileges for Federal Civil Litigation, 43 Ford.L.Rev. 923

(1975). The concept that state privileges should be considered in this context has received some judicial support. Lora v. Board of Education, 74 F.R.D. 565 (E.D.N.Y.1977) (Weinstein, J. "If the state holds out the expectation of protection to its citizens they should not be disappointed by a mechanical or unnecessary application of the federal rule;" but privilege denied). See, however, American Civil Liberties Union of Mississippi, Inc. v. Finch, 638 F.2d 1336, 1343 (5th Cir. 1981) ("That the courts of a particular state would recognize a given privilege will not often of itself justify a federal court in applying that privilege.")

5. Berger, Privileges, Presumptions, and Competency of Witnesses in the Federal Court: A Federal Choice of Law Rule, 42 Brooklyn L.Rev. 417 (1976). Also supporting a federal choice of law rule, see Dunham, Testimonial Privileges in State and Federal Courts: A Suggested Approach, 9 Willamette L.J. 26 (1973). A contrary view is Wellborn, The Federal Rules of Evidence and the Application of State Law in the Federal Courts, 55 Tex.L.Rev. 371 (1977).

6. 313 U.S. 487 (1941).

7. See, e.g., Samuelson v. Susen, 576 F.2d 546 (3d Cir. 1978); Union Planters National Bank v. ABC Records, Inc., 82 F.R.D. 472 (W.D.Tenn.1979). But see, Mitsui & Co. (U.S.A.) Inc. v. Puerto Rico Water Resources Authority, 79 F.R.D. 72 (D.P.R.1978).

§ 76.2

1. See Ch. 9 infra.

2. See Ch. 10 infra.

certain government information.[3] Most, though not all, allow at least a limited privilege to communications between physician and patient.[4] In addition several other privileges are worthy of specific mention.

Though probably not recognized at common law, one of the most widely adopted privileges among American states is that protecting confidential communications between clergymen and penitents.[5] Wigmore's seemingly grudging acceptance of the privilege perhaps reflects the difficulty of justifying its existence on exclusively utilitarian grounds,[6] since at least where penitential communications are required or encouraged by religious tenets, they are likely to continue to be made irrespective of the presence or absence of evidentiary privilege. A firmer ground appears available in the inherent offensiveness of the secular power attempting to coerce an act violative of religious conscience.[7] Implementing a decent regard for religious convictions while at the same time avoiding making individual conscience the ultimate measure of testimonial obligation has proved to be attended by some difficulties. Early statutory forms of the privilege undertook to privilege only penitential communications "in the course of

discipline enjoined by the church" to which the communicant belongs.[8] This limitation, however, has been urged to be unduly, perhaps unconstitutionally, preferential to the Roman Catholic and a few other churches.[9] The statutes have, accordingly, generally been broadened. Revised Uniform Rule of Evidence (1974) 505 is typical in extending the privilege generally to "confidential communication[s] by a person to a clergyman in his professional character as spiritual advisor."[10] It remains an open question whether even such an ecumenical privilege can withstand an appropriate challenge based upon the establishment clause of the First Amendment.[11]

One of the most persistently advocated privileges for many years, but particularly during the past decade, has been one shielding journalists from being testimonially required to divulge the identities of news sources.[12] The rationale asserted for this privilege is analogous to that underlying the long-standing governmental informers privilege and is exclusively utilitarian in character.[13] Thus, it is contended that the news sources essential to supply the public's need for information will be "dried up" if their identities are subject to compelled disclo-

---

3. See Ch. 12 infra.

4. See Ch. 11 infra.

5. All but three states, Alabama, Connecticut, and Mississippi, appear to recognize the privilege. Statutes are collected in 8 Wigmore, Evidence § 2395 (McNaughton rev.).

Concerning the privilege generally, see Callahan, Historical Inquiry into the Priest-Penitent Privilege, 36 Jurist 328 (1976); Hogan, A Modern Problem on the Privilege of the Confessional, 6 Loy.L.Rev. 1 (1951); Kuhlman, Communications to Clergymen—When are They Privileged?, 2 Val.U.L.Rev. 265 (1968); Reece, Confidential Communications to the Clergy, 24 Ohio St. L.J. 55 (1963); Shetreet, Exemptions and Privileges on the Grounds of Religion and Conscience, 62 Ky.L.J. 377 (1974); Annots., 49 A.L.R.3d 1205; 71 A.L.R.3d 794.

6. 8 Wigmore, Evidence § 2396 (McNaughton rev. 1961).

7. See 4 Bentham, Rationale of Judicial Evidence 588 (J.S. Mill ed. 1827) ("But with any toleration, a coercion of this nature is altogether inconsistent and incompatable").

8. The privilege still appears in this form in some statute books. See, e.g., Ariz.Rev.Stat.Ann. § 12–2233 (1982).

9. See Kuhlman, supra n. 5.

10. Revised Uniform Rule of Evidence 505 (1974).

11. See Stoyles, supra, n. 5. This contention was advanced in In re Lifschutz, 2 Cal.3d 415, 85 Cal.Rptr. 829, 467 P.2d 557 (1970). The court avoided what it characterized as a "potentially difficult constitutional question," by holding that only one seeking material protected by the privilege has standing to raise the constitutional issue.

12. Cases and statutes are collected in 8 Wigmore, Evidence § 2286, nn. 9, 21 (McNaughton rev. 1961). The innumerable recent treatments include: Blasi, The Newsman's Privilege: An Empirical Study, 70 Mich.L. Rev. 229 (1971); Eckhardt & McKey, Reporter's Privilege: An Update, 12 Conn.L.Rev. 434 (1980); Note, 80 Yale L.J. 336 (1970).

13. The nature of the objective professed would appear to necessitate an absolute, or almost absolute privilege. See Note, 80 Yale L.J. 336 (1970). But see text accompanying n. 18 infra.

sure.[14] Numerous attempts to have the privilege enacted by federal statute have failed, and it is not one of those privileges incorporated into the Revised Uniform Rules of Evidence (1974).[15] Moreover, the argument that a journalist's privilege is constitutionally to be implied from the First Amendment guarantee of a free press was rejected by the Supreme Court in Branzburg v. Hayes.[16] However, taking note that this rejection did not command an absolute majority of the Court,[17] a substantial number of lower federal courts have undertaken to recognize a qualified journalist's privilege[18] which may be penetrated by appropriate showings on the part of the party desiring the privileged information.[19] Though occasionally referred to as a common law creation, the privilege has generally been said to derive from the First Amendment.[20] Some form of privilege for journalists has been

created by statute,[21] or in a few cases by judicial decision,[22] in a substantial number of states. Unlike other professional privileges, it is generally conceived as belonging to the journalist, to be claimed or waived irrespective of the wishes of the news source.

Communications to accountants are privileged in perhaps a third of the states.[23] This privilege is most closely analogous to that for attorney-client,[24] though the social objective to be furthered is arguably a distinguishable and lesser one.

There is occasional recognition of privilege for communications to confidential clerks, stenographers and other "employees" generally, school teachers, school counselors, participants in group psychotherapy, nurses, marriage counselors, private detectives, and social workers.[25] A privilege for parent-minor child communications has been recom-

---

14. For an extended articulation of the asserted justification for the privilege, see United States v. Criden, 633 F.2d 346, 335–6 (3d Cir. 1980), cert. denied 449 U.S. 1113.

15. No journalist privilege is included in the revised Uniform Rules, just as none was included in the Supreme Court's version of the Federal Rules. Federal statutes do not deal with the subject, though numerous bills have been introduced. For a compilation of state statutes, see Caldero v. Tribune Publishing Co., 98 Idaho 288, 562 P.2d 791, 794, n. 1 (1977) cert. denied 434 U.S. 930. See also Shield Laws, Council of State Governments (1973).

16. 408 U.S. 665 (1972). See also Herbert v. Lando, 441 U.S. 153 (1979) (rejecting First Amendment "editorial process" privilege.)

17. Mr. Justice Powell, who cast the deciding vote in *Branzburg*, authored a concurring opinion favoring a "balancing test," i.e., a qualified privilege. This fact has not been lost upon the lower federal courts. See Riley v. City of Chester, 612 F.2d 708 (3d Cir. 1979) (adopting Powell formulation).

18. Baker v. F & F Investment, 470 F.2d 778 (2d Cir. 1972), cert. denied 411 U.S. 966 (1973); United States v. Burke, 700 F.2d 70 (2d Cir. 1983); Riley v. City of Chester, supra n. 17; Cervantes v. Time, Inc., 464 F.2d 986 (8th Cir. 1972), cert. denied 409 U.S. 1125; Silkwood v. Kerr-McGee Corp., 563 F.2d 433 (10th Cir. 1978); Zerilli v. Smith, 656 F.2d 705, 712 (D.C.Cir. 1981) (stating "in the ordinary case the civil litigant's interest in disclosure should yield to the journalist's privilege.") But compare In the Matter of Myron Farber, 78 N.J. 259, 394 A.2d 330 (1978), cert. denied 439 U.S. 997.

19. In the Third Circuit the requirements for overcoming the privilege are said to be three:

"First, the movant must demonstrate that he has made an effort to obtain the information from other sources. Second, he must demonstrate that the only access to the information sought is through the journalist and her sources. Finally, the movant must persuade the Court that the information sought is crucial to the claim." United States v. Cuthbertson, 651 F.2d 189, 195–6 (3d Cir. 1981), cert. denied 454 U.S. 1056.

20. See cases cited, supra n. 18 The source of the privilege has obvious implications for its potential applicability to diversity and state litigation. See Miller v. Transamerican Press, Inc., 621 F.2d 721 (5th Cir. 1980), supplemented, rehearing denied 628 F.2d 932, cert. denied 450 U.S. 1041 (stating First Amendment privilege available in diversity case but holding discovery permissible on facts).

21. See n. 15 supra.

22. See, e.g., Opinion of the Justices, 117 N.H. 390, 373 A.2d 644 (1977).

23. Statutes are cited and summarized in 8 Wigmore, Evidence § 2286 n. 22 (McNaughton rev. 1961). See Notes, 28 Okla.L.Rev. 637 (1975), 46 N.C.L.Rev. 419 (1968). And see United States v. Kovel, 296 F.2d 918 (2d Cir. 1961) (accountant as attorney's agent; disclosures privileged).

24. See United States v. Arthur Young & Co., 677 F.2d 211 (2d Cir. 1982) (recognizing an accountant's "work product" privilege).

25. See 8 Wigmore, Evidence § 2286 (McNaughton rev. 1961).

mended [26] and has received some scanty judicial approval,[27] as has a privilege for scientific researcher-subject.[28] The best which may be said for most of these "novelty" privileges is that few occasions are likely to arise affording the opportunity to invoke them.

 WESTLAW REFERENCES

clergy! priest* /5 privilege*
accountant* /5 privilege*
psychotherap! /5 privilege*
journalist* /5 privilege*
"social worker*" /5 privilege*

§ 77. The Future of Privilege

Despite the rejection by the Congress of the Proposed Federal Rules of Evidence relating to privilege and the resultant failure to effect substantive changes in this area, several concurrent developments may portend certain new directions in the development of the law of privilege.

The vehemence of the attacks leveled at certain of the proposed Federal Rules on privilege suggests that the basic concept of evidentiary privilege, despite its deleterious consequences for the administration of justice, will not down in the foreseeable future. Many of these attacks, predictably, came from groups specifically interested in the preservation or creation of particular privileges.[1] Much more significantly, the cause

of privilege was also espoused by an unprecedentedly large segment of the academic community.[2] The latter response was in large part precipitated by a generalized concern over the increasing intrusiveness of modern society into human privacy, a concern reflected in several Supreme Court decisions conferring constitutional status upon certain aspects of privacy.[3]

While the ultimate strategic significance of evidentiary privilege as a bastion for defending privacy values may be doubted, the focus on privacy as an operative basis for the recognition of some privileges is believed to be a healthy and overdue development. At the optimum, it may offer a theoretical basis for a more satisfactory accommodation than has heretofore been achieved between the legitimate demands for freedom against unwarranted intrusion on the one hand and the basic requirements of the judicial system on the other.

The traditionally felt need, stemming largely from Wigmore's dictum, to justify all privileges in terms of their utilitarian value leads not only to the assertion of highly questionable sociological premises, but also, affords little prospect for meaningful reconciliation of values in this area. Traditional evidentiary privilege necessarily paints with a broad brush since the achievement of utilitarian objectives requires privileges which are essentially absolute in character.[4] But if it is recognized that not all privileges are

26. Bauer, Recognition of a Parent-Child Testimonial Privilege, 23 St.L.U.L.J. 676 (1979); Coburn, Child-Parent Communications; Spare the Privilege and Spoil the Child, 74 Dick.L.Rev. 599 (1970); Stanton, Child-Parent Privilege for Confidential Communications: An Examination and Proposal, 16 Family L.Q. 1 (1982); Note, 16 San Diego L.Rev. 811 (1978).

27. People v. Doe, 61 A.D.2d 426, 403 N.Y.S.2d 375 (1978).

28. Richards of Rockford, Inc. v. Pacific Gas & Electric Co., 71 F.R.D. 388 (N.D.Cal.1976). And see Delgado & Millen, God, Galileo, and Government: Toward Constitutional Protection for Scientific Inquiry, 53 Wash.L.Rev. 349 (1978); Nejelski and Lerman, A Researcher-Subject Testimonial Privilege, 1971 Wis.L. Rev. 1085.

§ 77

1. See generally Hearings Before the Special Subcommittee on Reform of Federal Criminal Laws of the House Committee on the Judiciary on Proposed Rules of Evidence, 93d Cong., 1st Sess., ser. 2 (1973).

2. This reaction was expressed not only in communications to Congress, id. at 195, 240, but in a variety of publications. See, e.g., Black, The Marital and Physician Privileges—Reprint of a Letter to a Congressman, 1975 Duke L.J. 45; Krattenmaker, Testimonial Privilege in Federal Courts: An Alternative to the Federal Rules of Evidence, 62 Geo.L.J. 61 (1973).

3. E.g., Griswold v. Connecticut, 381 U.S. 479 (1965); Roe v. Wade, 410 U.S. 113 (1973), rehearing denied 410 U.S. 959.

4. See Note, 91 Harv.L.Rev. 464, 468 (1977) (excellent though critical statement of the rationale of absolute privilege).

based on identical considerations or will have identical effects if allowed in litigation, it will be seen that not all privileges need make such large demands.[5] If the object aimed at is not the inducement of conduct in certain relationships but the protection of individual privacy from unnecessary or trivial intrusions, the implementation of the privilege is amenable to the finer touch of the specific solution. Thus, a decision in the particular case that sufficiently grave considerations demand disclosure will, to be sure, impact adversely on the privilege holder, but no more extended societal interest will be impaired.

Another factor may also contribute to a greater use of qualified or conditional privileges which are subject to suspension on ad hoc determination of particular need for evidence in a given case. It is already clear that the law of privilege must to some extent accommodate to the developing rights of criminal defendants under the confrontation and compulsory process clauses.[6] At the same time it is desirable, whenever possible, to avoid a choice between the automat-

ic and total override of privilege whenever a criminal defendant asserts a need for privileged matter, and the dismissal of the charges if the privilege is to be sustained. At least in those instances where accomplishment of the privilege objective does not necessitate absolute protection, an in camera weighing of the potential significance of the matter sought as against the considerations of privacy underlying the privilege may represent a desirable compromise.

Though necessarily entailing a certain amount of procedural inconvenience and a considerable amount of judicial discretion, this solution has recommended itself to a number of commentators and courts. It is perhaps reasonable to predict that an increased involvement of judges in the general area of privacy and confidentiality may be in the making.

 **WESTLAW REFERENCES**

privilege* /p societ** social** privacy /2 polic*** interest*

---

5. See Saltzberg, Privileges and Professionals: Lawyers and Psychiatrists, 66 Va.L.Rev. 597, 622 (1980) ("Privileges are not all equally important; they

vary with the interests they protect and the policies they promote.")

6. See § 74, supra, text beginning at n. 1.

Chapter 9

THE PRIVILEGE FOR MARITAL COMMUNICATIONS [1]

Table of Sections

§ 78. History and Background and Kindred Rules [2]

We are dealing here with a late offshoot of an ancient tree. The older branches are discussed in another chapter.[3] Those earlier rules, to be sharply distinguished from the present doctrine, are first, the rule that the spouse of a party or person interested is disqualified from testifying for the other spouse, and second, the privilege of a party against having the party's husband or wife called as an adverse witness. These two earlier rules forbid the calling of the spouse as a witness at all, for or against the party, regardless of the actual testimony to be elicited, whereas the privilege presently discussed is limited to a certain class of testimony, namely communications between the spouses or more broadly in some states, information gained on account of the marital relation.

The movement for procedural reform in England in the first half of the 1800s found expression in the evidence field in agitation for the break up of the system of disqualification of parties and spouses. One of the auxiliary reasons which had been given to justify the disqualification of spouses was that of preserving marital confidences.[4] As to the disqualification of spouses the reform was largely accomplished by the Evidence Amendment Act, 1853. On the eve of this legislation, Greenleaf writing in this country

---

1. 8 Wigmore, Evidence §§ 2332–2341 (McNaughton rev. 1961); Dec.Dig. Witnesses ⇐187–195; C.J.S. Witnesses §§ 266–275; 58 Am.Jur. 2d Witnesses §§ 148–171.

§ 78

2. 8 Wigmore, Evidence §§ 2332–2334 (McNaughton rev. 1961).

3. See § 66, supra.

4. See 8 Wigmore, Evidence § 2333 (McNaughton rev. 1961); Taylor, Evidence, 899 (1848) (recounting this as a reason given but rejecting it as "too large"), quoted Shenton v. Tyler, L.R.1939 Ch.D. 620, 634.

in 1842, clearly announced the existence of a distinct privilege for marital communications, and this pronouncement was echoed in England by Best in 1849,[5] though seemingly there was little or no support for such a view in the English decisions.[6] Moreover, the Second Report of 1853 of the Commissioners on Common Law Procedure, after rejecting the arguments for the outmoded rules of disqualification, calls attention to the special danger of "alarm and unhappiness occasioned to society by . . . compelling the public disclosure of confidential communications between husband and wife . . ." and declares that "[a]ll communications between them should be held to be privileged."[7]

However, though the policy supporting a privilege for marital communications had thus been distinctly pointed out, there had

been little occasion for its judicial recogniztion, since the wider disqualifications of the spouses of parties left small possibility for the question of the existence of such a privilege to arise.[8]

Nevertheless, the English Act of 1853, mentioned above, after it abolished the disqualification of husbands and wives of the parties, enacted that "no husband shall be compellable to disclose any communication made to him by his wife during the marriage, and no wife shall be compellable to disclose any communication made to her by her husband during the marriage."[9] Moreover, nearly all the states in this country, while making spouses competent to testify, have included provisions disabling them from testifying to communications between them.[10]

5.   See the citations to these early editions of Greenleaf and Best in Shenton v. Tyler, L.R. 1939 Ch.D. 620, 633, 634.

6.   The English decisions before 1853 are carefully dissected in the opinion of Greene, M.R. in Shenton v. Tyler, supra n. 5.

7.   See quotation from this report, 8 Wigmore, Evidence § 2332 (McNaughton rev. 1961).

8.   See 8 Wigmore, Evidence § 2333 (McNaughton rev. 1961).

9.   St. 16 & 17 Vict. c. 83, § 3.

10.   See, for example:

West's Ann.Cal.Evid.Code Art. 5.

§ 980.   **Privilege for confidential marital communications.** Subject to Section 912 [waiver] and except as otherwise provided in this article, a spouse (or his guardian or conservator when he has a guardian or conservator), whether or not a party, has a privilege during the marital relationship and afterwards to refuse to disclose, and to prevent another from disclosing, a communication if he claims the privilege and the communication was made in confidence between him and the other spouse while they were husband and wife.

§ 981.   **Exception: Crime or fraud.** There is no privilege under this article if the communication was made, in whole or in part, to enable or aid anyone to commit or plan to commit a crime or a fraud.

§ 982.   **Exception: Commitment or similar proceeding.** There is no privilege under this article in a proceeding to commit either spouse or otherwise place him or his property, or both, under the control of another because of his alleged mental or physical condition.

§ 983.   **Exception: Proceeding to establish competence.** There is no privilege under this article in a proceeding brought by or on behalf of either spouse to establish his competence.

§ 984.   **Exception: Proceeding between spouses.** There is no privilege under this article in:

(a) A proceeding brought by or on behalf of one spouse against the other spouse.

(b) A proceeding between a surviving spouse and a person who claims through the deceased spouse, regardless of whether such claim is by testate or intestate succession or by inter vivos transaction.

§ 985.   **Exception: Certain criminal proceedings.** There is no privilege under this article in a criminal proceeding in which one spouse is charged with:

(a) A crime committed at any time against the person or property of the other spouse or of a child of either.

(b) A crime committed at any time against the person or property of a third person committed in the course of committing a crime against the person or property of the other spouse.

(c) Bigamy.

(d) A crime defined by Section 270 or 270a of the Penal Code. [Nonsupport of child or wife.]

§ 986.   **Exception: Juvenile court proceeding.** There is no privilege under this article in a proceeding under the Juvenile Court Law. . . .

§ 987.   **Exception: Communication offered by spouse who is criminal defendant.** There is no privilege under this article in a criminal proceeding in which the communication is offered in evidence by

In the light of this history the Court of Appeal in England has denied that there was any common law privilege for marital communications.[11] In this country, however, the courts have frequently said that the statutes protecting marital communications from disclosure are declaratory of the common law.[12] Moreover, some courts have even held the "common law" rule to be in effect without benefit of statute,[13] at least until legislatively abrogated.[14]

In addition to the vitality which it has displayed in the courts, the rule discussed here has been viewed by some legal commentators as the most defensible of the various forms of marital privilege. However, Federal Rule of Evid. 505 as approved by the Supreme Court but deleted by the Congress, recognized no privilege for confidential communications between spouses, limiting the privilege to that of an accused in a criminal proceeding to prevent his spouse from testifying against him.[15] The Revised Uniform Rules narrowed the wording to make the privilege one for confidential communications, still restricting the privilege to an accused in a criminal proceeding.[16] Some states adopting a version of the Federal or of the Revised Uniform Rules extend the

---

a defendant who is one of the spouses between whom the communication was made.

N.Y. CPLR § 4502.

(b) Confidential communication privileged. A husband or wife shall not be required, or, without consent of the other if living, allowed, to disclose a confidential communication made by one to the other during marriage.

Statutes on this topic are compiled in 2 Wigmore, Evidence § 488 (Chadbourn rev. 1979). See generally, Comment, 56 Nw.U.L.Rev. 208, 216 (1961).

11. Shenton v. Tyler, L.R. 1939 Ch.D. 620, and see Notes, 55 Law Q.Rev. 329, Holdsworth, 56 id. 137. In this case the court held that the English statute, quoted at note 9, supra, providing that "husbands" and "wives" shall not be compellable to testify to communication, did not apply to exempt a surviving widow from interrogation as to conversations with her husband claimed to have created a secret trust in favor of the plaintiff, a third person.

12. Hopkins v. Grimshaw, 165 U.S. 342 (1897); Hagerman v. Wigent, 108 Mich. 192, 194, 65 N.W. 756 (1896); Gjesdahl v. Harmon, 175 Minn. 414, 221 N.W. 639, 641 (1928); 70 C.J. 379, note 90(b); C.J.S. Witnesses § 266.

13. Arnold v. State, 353 So.2d 524 (Ala.1977), on remand 353 So.2d 527 (common law marital communications privilege recognized in presence of statute codifying marital privilege but containing no communications privilege).

14. See State v. Angell, ___ R.I. ___, 405 A.2d 10 (1979) (holding common law privilege impliedly repealed in criminal cases; statute relating to competency of spouses in civil cases contained communications provision, while similar statute for criminal cases did not). But compare Burton v. State, 501 S.W.2d 814 (Tenn.Cr.App.1973) (retaining communications privilege under similar statutory configuration).

15. Deleted Rule 505, 56 F.R.D. 244, read:

(a) General Rule of Privilege. An accused in a criminal proceeding has a privilege to prevent his spouse from testifying against him.

(b) Who May Claim the Privilege. The privilege may be claimed by the accused or by the spouse on his behalf. The authority of the spouse to do so is presumed in the absence of evidence to the contrary.

(c) Exceptions. There is no privilege under this rule (1) in proceedings in which one spouse is charged with a crime against the person or property of the other or of a child of either, or with a crime against the person or property of a third person committed in the course of committing a crime against the other, or (2) as to matters occurring prior to the marriage, or (3) in proceedings in which a spouse is charged with importing an alien for prostitution or other immoral purpose in violation of 8 U.S.C. § 1328, with transporting a female in interstate commerce for immoral purposes or other offense in violation of 18 U.S.C. §§ 2421–2424, or with violation of other similar statutes.

16. Unif.R.Evid. (1974) 504 reads:

(a) Definition. A communication is confidential if it is made privately by any person to his or her spouse and is not intended for disclosure to any other person.

(b) General Rule of Privilege. An accused in a criminal proceeding has a privilege to prevent his spouse from testifying as to any confidential communication between the accused and the spouse.

(c) Who May Claim the Privilege. The privilege may be claimed by the accused or by the spouse on behalf of the accused. The authority of the spouse to do so is presumed.

(d) Exceptions. There is no privilege under this rule in a proceeding in which one spouse is charged with a crime against the person or property of (1) the other, (2) a child of either, (3) a person residing in the household of either, or (4) a third person committed

privilege to both civil and criminal cases.[17] Under Federal Rule of Evidence 501, as adopted by Congress, the federal courts have continued to recognize a marital communications privilege as effective by common law.[18]

 WESTLAW REFERENCES

histor! "common law" /p marital husband-wife /p privilege*

rule evidence fed.r.evid! unif.r.evid! /3 504 /p confiden!

"common law" & rule fed.r.evid! evidence /3 501 /30 marital husband-wife /5 privilege* & court(ca9)

§ 79. What is Privileged: Communications Only, or Acts and Facts?[1]

Greenleaf, arguing in 1842 for a privilege distinct from marital incompetency, and furnishing the inspiration for the later statutes by which the privilege was formally enacted, spoke only of "communications" and "conversations."[2] Those later statutes them-

selves (except one or two[3]) sanctioned the privilege for "communications" and for nothing beyond.[4] Accordingly it would seem that the privilege should be limited to *expressions* intended by one spouse to convey a meaning or message to the other. These expressions may be by words, oral, written or in sign-language, or by expressive acts, as where the husband opens a trunk before his wife and points out objects therein to her.[5] Moreover, the protection of the privilege will shield against indirect disclosure of the communication,[6] as where a husband is asked for his wife's whereabouts which he learned only from her secret communication.[7] It seems, nevertheless, that logic and policy should cause the courts to halt with communications as the furthest boundary of the privilege, and a substantial number have held steadfast at this line.[8]

An equal or greater number of courts, however, have construed their statutes which say "communications" to extend the privilege to acts, facts, conditions, and trans-

---

in the course of committing a crime against any of them.

17. E.g. Maine R.Evid. 504; Wis.Stats.Ann. 905.05.

18. Cases are collected in Annot., 46 A.L.R.Fed. 735.

§ 79

1. 8 Wigmore, Evidence § 2337 (McNaughton rev. 1961); Annot., 10 A.L.R.2d 1389; Notes, 35 Corn.L.Q. 187 (1949), 57 J.Crim.L. & Cr. 205 (1956), 34 Minn.L. Rev. 257 (1950), 3 Vand.L.Rev. 656 (1950), 35 Va.L.Rev. 1111 (1949).

2. See § 78 supra.

3. Ohio R.C. § 2317.02 ("communication made by one to the other, or an act done by either in the presence of the other, during coverture unless . . . in the known presence or hearing of a third person competent to be a witness"); Tenn. Code Ann. § 24–1–201 (". . . neither husband nor wife shall testify to any matter that occurred between them by virtue of or in consequence of the marital relation").

4. See the statutes compiled in 2 Wigmore, Evidence § 488 (Chadbourn rev. 1979); also those quoted in § 78 n. 10 supra.

5. See State v. Smith, 384 A.2d 687 (Me.1978) (husband's display of items to wife was, under circumstances, said by court to be equivalent to assertion, "I have stolen a gun and a camera").

6. See by analogy Quarfot v. Security National Bank & Trust Co., 189 Minn. 451, 453, 249 N.W. 668

(1933) (in action against executor to recover note alleged to constitute gift, plaintiff's testimony stating reason why he left note in decedent's possession held inadmissible as conclusion and as concerning conversation with deceased).

7. Blau v. United States, 340 U.S. 332 (1951) (witness's wife was hiding out to avoid service of subpoena in connection with Communist investigation; held, since witness got his knowledge of his wife's whereabouts from what she "secretly told" him, he could refuse to disclose); Hipes v. United States, 603 F.2d 786 (9th Cir. 1979) (witness asked nature of husband's duties; government made no showing that knowledge came other than from husband).

8. Pereira v. United States, 347 U.S. 1 (1954); United States v. Smith, 533 F.2d 1077 (8th Cir. 1976) (testimony of wife that husband placed package of heroin in her underclothing did not violate communications privilege; while acts may constitute communications, for privilege to apply some message must be conveyed); State v. Drury, 110 Ariz. 447, 520 P.2d 495 (1974) (defendant urged expansion of privilege to cover acts as well as communications; extension denied, as "the privilege serves no real function in the reality of married life"); Tanzola v. DeRita, 45 Cal.2d 1, 285 P.2d 897 (1955) (where husband placed check on desk of wife who was his office assistant and who deposited check in his personal account according to custom, the husband's act was not "communicative"); Notes, 35 Corn. L.Q. 187 (1949), 34 Tex.L.Rev. 474 (1951).

actions not amounting to communications at all. One group seems to announce the principle that acts done privately in the wife's presence amount to "communications."[9] Another would go even further and say that any information secured by the wife as a result of the marital relation and which would not have been known in the absence of such relation is protected.[10] Some at least of this latter group would hold that information secured by one spouse through observation during the marriage as to the health,[11] or intoxication, habitual or at a particular time,[12] or the mental condition[13] of the other spouse, would be protected by the privilege.

All extensions beyond communications seem unjustified by the theory of this privilege. The attitude of the courts in these cases seems to reflect a confusion with the quite distinguishable purpose of preserving family harmony by disqualifying one spouse from giving any testimony whatsoever against the other.[14] Whatever the merits of the latter principle, its attempted implementation under the guise of a communications privilege can only lead to anomalous results, for the bulk of the cases involve factual situations in which the marriage has already been destroyed. It is believed a different attitude would be wiser, namely that of accepting the view that privileges in general, and this privilege for marital confidences in particular, are inept and clumsy devices for promoting the policies they profess to serve, but are extremely effective as stumbling blocks to obstruct the attainment of justice. Accordingly, at the very least, the movement should be toward restriction of these devices rather than their expansion through theoretically dubious applications.

A specific instance of development in the proper direction has recently been evident in statutes and cases which exclude from the protection of the privilege communications in furtherance of crime or fraud.[15] This exception, long recognized to restrict the cog-

---

9. Smith v. State, 344 So.2d 915 (Fla.1977), cert. denied 353 So.2d 679 (wide variety of acts and comments incident to an elaborate attempt to dispose of body of husband's murder victim held to be communications); Shepherd v. State, 257 Ind. 229, 277 N.E.2d 165 (1971) (husband's testimony against former wife to the effect that she had driven car for him during burglary held improperly admitted; participation in crime was a matter of confidence); People v. Daghita, 299 N.Y. 194, 86 N.E.2d 172, 10 A.L.R.2d 1385 (1949) (husband charged with theft, wife's testimony as to the husband's acts in her presence of bringing in the loot and hiding it under the bed and in the basement held violation of statutory privilege for "confidential communication"); Menefee v. Commission, 189 Va. 900, 55 S.E.2d 9 (1949), 34 Minn.L.Rev. 257 (1950) (wife's testimony as to husband's leaving home before robbery, as to time of returning, as to his placing pistol on mantel-piece, and as to her driving with him near where stolen safe was hid, held privileged as "communication privately made"). Perhaps the reductio ad absurdum of the "acts" cases is State v. Robbins, 35 Wn.2d 389, 213 P.2d 310 (1950). There the husband was charged with automobile theft, and evidence of his former wife that when she was presenting application for license for the stolen car at the office her husband was waiting outside in an automobile was a "communication" and privileged. The court said, "It is obvious that he would not have waited in the automobile had he not relied on the confidence between them by reason of the marital relation."

In People v. Melski, 10 N.Y.2d 78, 217 N.Y.S.2d 65, 176 N.E.2d 81 (1961) the New York Court of Appeals held by a four to three decision that there was no privilege for the wife's observation of her husband, the de-

fendant, and several of his friends in defendant's kitchen with stolen guns. The dissent asserted that the presence of the third persons did not destroy confidentiality but was "part of the very fact confidentially communicated."

10. Prudential Insurance Co. v. Pierce's Administratrix, 270 Ky. 216, 109 S.W.2d 616 (1917) (formula held to apply to knowledge gleaned by the wife from the entry of husband's birth in his family Bible).

11. Griffith v. Griffith, 162 Ill. 368, 44 N.E. 820 (1896) (impotence); Willey v. Howell, 168 Ky. 466, 182 S.W. 619 (1916) (venereal disease). But it has been held that testimony as to the general condition of health, accessible to other persons, would not be privileged. Supreme Lodge v. Jones, 113 Ill.App. 241 (1903), and see Annot., 10 A.L.R.2d 1397–1400.

12. Monaghan v. Green, 265 Ill. 233, 106 N.E. 792 (1914). Contra: In re Van Alstine's Estate, 26 Utah 193, 72 P. 942 (1903) (privilege does not cover testimony as to facts learned from observation). See Annot., 10 A.L.R.2d 1389, 1400.

13. McFadden v. Welch, 177 Miss. 451, 170 So. 903 (1936). Contra: Lanham v. Lanham, 62 Tex.Civ.App. 431, 146 S.W. 635 (1912) (husband's demeanor in wife's presence on train); Annot., 10 A.L.R.2d 1389, 1401.

14. See § 66 supra.

15. A few states have recognized this exception by statute. See e.g., West's Ann.Cal.Evid. Code § 981, quoted supra § 78, n. 10; Kan.Stat.Ann. 60–437(b)(5). Several federal circuits and some states have adopted the exception by judicial decision. See United States v. Mendoza, 574 F.2d 1373 (5th Cir. 1978), rehearing de-

nate privilege for attorney-client communications, seems amply justified in the present context as well.

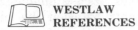
WESTLAW REFERENCES

wigmore /3 2337 & court(wa)
headnote(act* /s marital husband-wife /s privilege*)
2317.02 & court(oh)
60–437 & court(ks)

§ 80. The Communication Must Be Confidential [1]

Most statutes expressly limit the privilege to "confidential communications."[2] However, even where the words used are "any communication" or simply "communications," the notion that the privilege is born

of the "common law" and the fact that the pre-statutory descriptions of the privilege had clearly based it upon the policy of protecting confidences,[3] have actuated most courts to read into such statutes the requirement of confidentiality.[4] Communications in private between husband and wife are assumed to be confidential [5], though of course this assumption will be strengthened if confidentiality is expressly affirmed, or if the subject is such that the communicating spouse would probably desire that the matter be kept secret, either because its disclosure would be embarrassing or for some other reason. However, a variety of factors, including the nature of the message or the circumstances under which it was delivered, may serve to rebut a claim that confidentiality was intended.[6] In particular, if a third

nied 579 F.2d 644 (adopting rule that interspousal communications about crimes in which spouses are jointly participating do not come within the privilege); United States v. Kahn, 471 F.2d 191 (7th Cir. 1972), reversed on other grounds 415 U.S. 143 (1973) (tapped phone conversations concerning illegal betting activity "had to do with the commission of a crime and not with the privacy of the . . . marriage"; privilege inapplicable): State v. Smith, 384 A.2d 687, 693 (Me.1978) ("We do not believe that the purpose behind the marital privilege is served by permitting spouses engaged in criminal activity to raise a cloud of secrecy around their communications regarding that activity. Such communications do not foster the type of honesty and mutual trust upon which fulfilling marital relations ought to be predicated.") But compare Smith v. State, 344 So. 2d 915 (Fla.App.1977), cert. denied 353 So.2d 679 (rejecting furtherance of crime exception on ground of harm it would inflict on policy of privilege).

Of course even where recognized the exception does not render admissible confessions of crime by one spouse to a nonparticipating spouse. See State v. Holt, 223 Kan. 34, 574 P.2d 152 (1977) (Kansas statute cited above did not remove privilege with respect to note confessing completed crime left by defendant for wife; but admission harmless error).

§ 80

1. 8 Wigmore, Evidence § 2336 (McNaughton rev. 1961); Dec.Dig. Witnesses ⟐192, 193; C.J.S. Witnesses § 268.

2. See statutes compiled in 2 Wigmore, Evidence § 488 (Chadbourn rev. 1979). See also California and New York provisions, supra § 78 n. 10.

3. See § 78 supra.

4. New York Life Insurance Co. v. Mason, 272 F. 28 (10th Cir. 1921) ("any communications" in R.C.M.1947, § 93–701–3 should be interpreted as limited to confi-

dential statements); Shepherd v. Pacific Mutual Life Insurance Co., 230 Iowa 1304, 300 N.W. 556 (1941); Thayer v. Thayer, 188 Mich. 261, 154 N.W. 32, 35 (1915). Contra: Pugsley v. Smyth, 98 Or. 448, 194 P. 686 (1921) (reviewing statutes and decisions in various states). See generally C.J.S. Witnesses § 268.

5. Blau v. United States, 340 U.S. 332 (1951); Hipes v. United States, 603 F.2d 786 (9th Cir. 1979); West's Ann.Cal.Evid. Code § 917. But compare People v. Burton, 6 Ill.App.3d 879, 286 N.E.2d 792 (1972), cert. denied 411 U.S. 937 ("presumption" of confidentiality for statements does not attach to acts even where communicative).

6. For general discussions, see Parkhurst v. Berdell, 110 N.Y. 386, 393, 18 N.E. 123, 127 (1888) ("such communications as are expressly made confidential, or such as are of a confidential nature, or induced by the marital relation"); Mitchell v. Mitchell, 80 Tex. 101, 15 S.W. 705 (1891) ("determined by the subject-matter of the communication or the circumstances under which it was made or both").

See Yoder v. United States, 80 F.2d 665 (10th Cir. 1935) (husband left note for wife at their home written on large cardboard; held not privileged); Resnover v. State, 267 Ind. 597, 372 N.E.2d 457 (1978) (husband's communication to wife of jailbreak plan held not confidential where plan was to be communicated to additional participants); Guyette v. State, 84 Nev. 160, 438 P.2d 244 (1968) (letters written by husband in jail awaiting trial handed to sheriff for delivery to wife and not folded, sealed, or otherwise arranged to suggest confidentiality held not privileged); State v. Fiddler, 57 Wn.2d 815, 360 P.2d 155 (1961) (husband sent letters to illiterate wife knowing someone would have to read them to her).

In People v. Dudley, 24 N.Y.2d 410, 301 N.Y.S.2d 9, 248 N.E.2d 860 (1969) the court held that husband's acts and statements concerning murder committed by

person (other than a child of the family) is present to the knowledge of the communicating spouse, this stretches the web of confidence beyond the marital pair, and the communication is unprivileged.[7] If children of the family are present this likewise deprives the conversation of protection unless the children are too young to understand

him were not privileged where husband's threats to kill wife if she disclosed information indicated that husband did not rely upon the confidentiality of the relationship.

Threats of bodily harm, though in secret, being a violation of marital duty, should not, it seems, be privileged. People v. Zabijak, 285 Mich. 164, 280 N.W. 149 (1938). Contra: O'Neil v. O'Neil, 264 S.W. 61 (Mo.App. 1924) (private threats privileged, unless accompanied by violence). In a New York suit for separation, the husband defended on grounds of cruelty and testified that the wife said she had committed adultery with another man and they were going away. Two judges thought the communication not privileged because not prompted by confidentiality of marriage relation; three judges concurred in result but on grounds of an exception for wrongs by one spouse against the other; two dissented. Poppe v. Poppe, 3 N.Y.2d 312, 165 N.Y.S.2d 99, 144 N.E.2d 72 (1957), 58 Colum.L.Rev. 126 (1958), § 84 n. 8 infra.

7. Pereira v. United States, 347 U.S. 1 (1954) ("The presence of a third party negatives the presumption of privacy."); United States v. Mitchell, 137 F.2d 1006 (1943) (threats against wife in presence of others); Shepherd v. Pacific Mutual Life Insurance Co., 230 Iowa 1304, 300 N.W. 556 (1941) (negotiations between husband, wife, and her father); Gutridge v. State, 236 Md. 514, 204 A.2d 557 (1964) (defendant in jail sent oral message to wife by a trusty); People v. Ressler, 17 N.Y.2d 174, 269 N.Y.S.2d 414, 216 N.E.2d 582 (1966) (conversation between husband and wife in presence of victim of homicide before he was slain by husband); Dec.Dig. Witnesses ⊕193; C.J.S. Witnesses § 271.

A letter from a husband to his wife, dictated by him to a stenographer, has been held not privileged. "Normally husband and wife may conveniently communicate without stenographic aid, and the privilege of holding their confidences immune from proof in court may be reasonably enjoyed and preserved without embracing within it the testimony of third persons to whom such communications have been voluntarily revealed. . . . The privilege suppresses relevant testimony, and should be allowed only when it is plain that marital confidence cannot otherwise reasonably be preserved. Nothing in this case suggests any such necessity." Wolfle v. United States, 291 U.S. 7, 16, 17 (1934) (Stone, J.)

In Breimon v. General Motors Corp., 8 Wn.App. 747, 509 P.2d 398 (1973), it was held that the presence of a third person cannot be established, and the privilege thus destroyed, by the unsupported testimony of the spouse receiving the communication.

what is said.[8] The fact that the communication relates to business transactions may show that it was not intended as confidential.[9] Examples are statements about business agreements between the spouses,[10] or about business matters transacted by one spouse as agent for the other,[11] or about

8. Freeman v. Freeman, 238 Mass. 150, 130 N.E. 220 (1921) (in presence of children, the oldest nine years old, held, for the judge to determine whether old enough to pay attention and understand); Hicks v. Hicks, 271 N.C. 204, 155 S.E.2d 799 (1967) (presence of 8 year old daughter did not destroy privilege); Fuller v. Fuller, 100 W.Va. 309, 130 S.E. 270 (1925) (in presence of 13 year old daughter, not privileged); C.J.S. Witnesses § 271.

9. "So, too, it cannot be that the rule of privilege must be held to extend so far as to exclude all communications between husband and wife having reference to business relations existing either as between them directly, or as between them—one or both—and others. Certainly as to business relations existing between husband and wife directly, there can be no adverse consideration of public policy. Quite to the contrary, public policy, as reflected by statute and by our decisions, permits of such relations to the fullest extent. And it would be shocking to say that a contract thus made, or rights or liabilities thus accruing, could not be enforced because, forsooth, a communication between the parties having relation thereto, and essential to proof, was privileged. The cases are almost unanimously against such a conclusion." Bishop, J. in Sexton v. Sexton, 129 Iowa 487, 105 N.W. 314, 316 (1905). See C.J.S. Witnesses § 269d, p. 772; Annot., 4 A.L.R.2d 835.

10. Appeal of Spitz, 56 Conn. 184, 14 A. 776 (1887) (claim of wife against insolvent estate of husband: held, wife's testimony as to husband's promises and representations which induced her to advance money, not privileged; "they were no more privileged than a promissory note would have been if he had made his contract in that form"); Brooks v. Brooks, 357 Mo. 343, 208 S.W.2d 279, 4 A.L.R.2d 826, 832 (1948) (wife sues husband for proceeds of joint adventure. "In actions between a husband and wife involving property rights the rule excluding relevant conversations . . . yields to the necessity of the situation for the prevention of injustice. . . ."); Bietman v. Hopkins, 109 Ind. 177, 9 N.E. 720 (1887) (in suit by husband's creditor to set aside husband's deed to wife, plaintiff objects to wife's testimony that deed given to repay advances—seemingly could be based on ground that the plaintiff is not the holder of the privilege); Ward v. Oliver, 129 Mich. 300, 88 N.W. 631 (1902) (similar to last).

11. Schmied v. Frank, 86 Ind. 250, 257 (1882) (wife's testimony that she authorized husband to buy note as her agent, not privileged: such authority "is intended to be known and would be worthless unless known"); Lurty's Curator v. Lurty, 107 Va. 466, 59 S.E. 405 (1907) (husband's account of money due wife on sale of their joint property not privileged).

property [12] or conveyances. [13] Usually such statements relate to facts which are intended later to become publicly known. To cloak them with privilege when the transactions come into litigation would be productive of special inconvenience and injustice.

WESTLAW REFERENCES

410k192
410k193
marital husband* wi*e* spous** /p communicat! /p assume* presum! /p confidential private

---

§ 81. The Time of Making the Communication:[1] Marital Status

The privilege is created to encourage marital confidences and is limited to them. Consequently, communications between the husband and wife before they were married,[2] or after their divorce [3] are not privileged. And attempts to assert the privilege by participants in "modern" living arrangements argued to be the functional equivalents of marriage have to date uniformly been rejected by the courts.[4] The requirement of a valid marriage may be satisfied by a valid common law marriage,[5] if it can be proved, but a bigamous marriage will not suffice.[6] This latter holding should, by analogy to other privileges, be relaxed where the party seeking the benefit of the privilege was ignorant of the status of the other purported spouse.[7] It is suggested that there is no meaningful distinction to be drawn between this latter situation and that in which a communication made during a purported marriage, later annulled for fraud by the victim of the fraud, has been held privileged.[8]

What of a husband and wife living apart? It has been said that the privilege "should not apply when the parties are living in separation and especially, as in this case, so living under articles of separation, and the one making the communication is actively hostile to the other."[9] Against the view, however, may be urged the consideration that communication in this context is far more likely to be related to preservation of the marriage [10] than are the vast bulk of admittedly privi-

12. Hagerman v. Wigent, 108 Mich. 192, 65 N.W. 756 (1896) (wife's delivery of mortgage to husband with instructions to give to plaintiff after wife's death, not privileged, as it was expected to be disclosed); Parkhurst v. Berdell, 110 N.Y. 386, 18 N.E. 123 (1888) (husband's conversation with wife as to securities in his hands belonging to third person, not privileged; "they were ordinary conversations, relating to matters of business, which there is no reason to suppose he would have been unwilling to hold in the presence of any person").

13. Eddy v. Bosley, 34 Tex.Civ.App. 116, 78 S.W. 565 (1903) (communication by husband to second wife preceding his deed to her advising her of the interest of his children in the property will be received to show notice to her; claim of privilege overruled on ground that the conveyance "if accomplished would operate as a fraud" upon the children).

§ 81

1. C.J.S. Witnesses § 267.

2. United States v. Pensinger, 549 F.2d 1150 (8th Cir. 1977); Forshay v. Johnston, 144 Neb. 525, 13 N.W.2d 873 (1944) (agreement establishing a common law marriage not a "communication between husband and wife"); Dec.Dig. Witnesses ☞194.

3. Yoder v. United States, 80 F.2d 665 (10th Cir. 1935).

4. See, People v. Delph, 94 Cal.App.3d 411, 156 Cal. Rptr. 422 (1979); State v. Lard, 86 N.M. 71, 519 P.2d

307 (1976); Annot., 4 A.L.R.4th 422. See also Comment, 1977 Ariz.St.L.J. 411 (advocating continued denial of the privilege).

5. See, United States v. Boatwright, 446 F.2d 913 (5th Cir. 1970) (claimant failed to establish valid common law marriage); State v. Alford, 298 N.C. 465, 259 S.E.2d 242 (1979) (semble).

6. United States v. Neeley, 475 F.2d 1136 (4th Cir. 1973) (marriage claimed to support communications privilege not only bigamous but probably known to be so by both "spouses"); People v. Mabry, 71 Cal.2d 430, 78 Cal.Rptr. 655, 455 P.2d 759 (1969) (distinguishing People v. Godines, infra n. 8, on ground that bigamous marriage is void rather than voidable).

7. For a criticism of the holding of People v. Mabry, supra n. 6, on this ground, see Comment, 9 U.C.D.L. Rev. 569, 600 (1976).

8. People v. Godines, 17 Cal.App.2d 721, 62 P.2d 787 (1936) 25 Calif.L.Rev. 619 (1937).

9. Holyoke v. Holyoke's Estate, 110 Me. 469, 87 Atl. 40 (1913). See also McEntire v. McEntire, 107 Ohio St. 510, 140 N.E. 328 (1923) (communications about property settlement between spouses who had been separated under oral agreement for several months), and cases cited C.J.S. Witnesses § 267.

10. This seems to be assumed without discussion in McCoy v. Justice, 199 N.C. 637, 155 S.E. 452 (1930).

leged communications. This fact, coupled with the pragmatic difficulty involved in determining when hostility between the spouses has become implacable, argues for the more easily administered approach of terminating the privilege only upon a decree of divorce. In any event, this latter view is generally adopted.[11]

 WESTLAW REFERENCES

marri! /3 time exist! /s privilege*

§ 82. Hazards of Disclosure to Third Persons Against the Will of the Communicating Spouse [1]

The weight of decision seems to support the view that the privilege does not protect against the testimony of third persons who have overheard (either accidentally or by eavesdropping) an oral communication between husband and wife,[2] or who have secured possession or learned the contents of a

letter from one spouse to another by interception,[3] or through loss or misdelivery by the custodian.[4] There is one important qualification which many if not most of the cases announce, namely that the privilege will not be lost if the eavesdropping,[5] or the delivery or disclosure of the letter [6] be due to the betrayal or connivance of the spouse to whom the message is directed. Just as that spouse would not be permitted, against the will of the communicating spouse, to betray the confidence by testifying in court to the message, so he or she may not effectively destroy the privilege by out-of-court betrayal.

The first-mentioned doctrine, that the eavesdropper or the interceptor of the letter may testify to the confidential message, is sometimes supported on the ground that the particular statute is phrased in terms of incompetency of the spouses to testify to the communication, and should not be extended to disqualify third persons.[7] Perhaps it may better be sustained on the more general

---

11. See Coleman v. State, 281 Md. 538, 380 A.2d 49 (1977) (holding privilege applicable to communication made after husband had been served in divorce proceeding); People v. Fields, 38 A.D.2d 231, 328 N.Y.S.2d 542 (1972), order affirmed 31 N.Y.2d 713, 337 N.Y.S.2d 517, 289 N.E.2d 557 (citing practical difficulty of ascertaining "genuine" existence of marriage); Muetze v. State, 73 Wis.2d 117, 243 N.W.2d 393 (1976) (impending dissolution of marriage has no effect on communications privilege). See also Annot., 98 A.L.R.2d 1285.

§ 82

1. 8 Wigmore, Evidence § 2339 (McNaughton rev. 1961); Annot., 63 A.L.R. 107; C.J.S. Witnesses §§ 270, 271.

2. State v. Slater, 36 Wn.2d 357, 218 P.2d 329 (1950) (eavesdropper); Nash v. Fidelity Phenix Fire Insurance Co., 106 W.Va. 672, 146 S.E. 726, 63 A.L.R. 101, 104 (1929) (same). But see notes 12 and 13 infra.

3. Howton v. State, 391 So.2d 147 (Ala.Crim.App. 1980) (jailhouse letter read by officer); Batchelor v. State, 217 Ark. 340, 230 S.W.2d 23 (1950) (letter to wife intercepted by jailer); People v. Dunnigan, 163 Mich. 349, 128 N.W. 180 (1910) (spy entering prisoner's cell ostensibly to cut his hair promises to take letter to wife but gives it to sheriff).

4. Hammons v. State, 73 Ark. 495, 84 S.W. 718 (1905) (letter to wife from defendant in jail delivered by messenger to wife's father: two judges dissenting); O'Toole v. Ohio German Fire Insurance Co., 159 Mich. 187, 123 N.W. 795 (1909) (letter from wife to husband, dropped and lost by husband).

5. Hunter v. Hunter, 169 Pa.Super. 498, 83 A.2d 401 (1951) (husband suing wife for divorce offers wire-recordings of their conversation in bed: the wire-recorder having been set up by plaintiff's son, with plaintiff's connivance without wife's knowledge, held privileged), 1 Buff.L.Rev. 314 (1952) 50 Mich.L.Rev. 933 (1952).

6. United States v. Neal, 532 F.Supp. 942 (D.C.Colo. 1982) (collecting cases and following majority rule); People v. Dubanowski, 75 Ill.App.3d 809, 31 Ill.Dec. 403, 394 N.E.2d 605 (1979). See also, Annot. 3 A.L.R.4th 1104; McCoy v. Justice, 199 N.C. 637, 155 S.E. 452 (1930) (husband's letters disclosed by wife to third persons). Nevertheless, there are a number of cases which disregard this element of betrayal and hold the privilege not applicable. State v. Sysinger, 25 S.D. 110, 125 N.W. 879 (1910) (prisoner's letter to wife, delivered by her to State's attorney); Annot., 63 A.L.R. 107, 124.

7. Commonwealth v. Wakelin, 230 Mass. 567, 120 N.E. 209, 212 (1918); Connella v. Terr., 16 Okl. 365, 86 P. 72, 75 (1906). In Rumping v. Director of Public Prosecutions, H.L. (1962) 3 All E.R. 256 (1962) the accused, a mate on a Dutch ship, wrote a letter to his wife amounting to a confession of murder, handed the letter in a sealed envelope to a member of the ship's crew to post when the ship reached a port outside England. When the accused was arrested the man gave the letter to the captain who turned it over to the police. The House of Lords held the letter admissible on the ground that the Criminal Evidence Act, 1898, does not recognize a privilege for confidential communications in providing that: "No husband shall be compellable to disclose any communication made to him by his

view that since the privilege has as its only effect the suppression of relevant evidence, its scope should be confined as narrowly as is consistent with reasonable protection of marital communications.

In this latter view, it seems, since the communicating spouse can ordinarily take effective precautions against overhearing, he should bear the risk of a failure to use such precautions.[8] Moreover, if he sends a messenger with a letter, he should ordinarily assume the risk that the chosen emissary may lose or misdeliver the message.[9] The rationale that the spouses may ordinarily take effective measures to communicate confidentially tends to break down where one or both are incarcerated.[10] However, communications in the jailhouse are frequently held not privileged, often on the theory that no confidentiality was or could have been expected.[11]

As has been observed elsewhere, the development of sophisticated eavesdropping techniques has led to curbs upon their use and upon the admissibility of evidence obtained thereby.[12] It has also led to including in rules governing privileged communications provisions against disclosure by third persons.[13]

If the spouse to whom the letter is addressed dies and it is found among the effects of the deceased, may the personal representative be required or permitted to produce it in court? Here is no connivance or betrayal by the deceased spouse, and on the other hand this is not a disclosure against which the sender could effectively guard. If the privilege is to be held, as most courts do,[14] to survive the death of one of the spouses, it seems that only a court which strictly limits the effect of the statute to restraining the spouses themselves from testifying, could justify a denial of the privilege in this situation.[15]

 **WESTLAW REFERENCES**

intercept! eavesdropp! surveill! wiretap! /s marital
husband* wife wives spous**

§ 83. Who Is the Holder of the Privilege? Enforcement and Waiver

Greenleaf in 1842, in foreshadowing the protection of marital communications, wrote of the projected rule as a "privilege" based on "public policy." Many legislatures, however, when they came to write the privilege into law phrased the rule simply as a survival in this special case of the ancient incompetency of the spouses, which the same statutes undertook to abolish or restrict. So it is often provided that the spouses are "incompetent" to testify to marital communications. Consequently, the courts frequently

---

wife during the marriage, and no wife shall be compellable to disclose any communication made to her by her husband during the marriage."

8. Commonwealth v. Everson, 123 Ky. 330, 96 S.W. 460, 461 (1906) (likened to attorney-client privilege as to which "it has been said that if persons wish the communications they have with their attorneys to be kept secret, they should be careful not to talk in the hearing of others"); 8 Wigmore, Evidence §§ 2339(1), 2326 (McNaughton rev. 1961).

9. See *Hammons* and *O'Toole* cases, supra note 4.

10. Commonwealth v. Wakelin, 230 Mass. 567, 120 N.E. 209 (1918) (dictograph planted in cell where husband and wife were held).

11. People v. Santos, 26 Cal.App.3d 397, 102 Cal. Rptr. 678 (2nd Dist. 1972); State v. Smyth, 7 Wn.App. 50, 499 P.2d 63 (1972). But compare Ward v. State, 70 Ark. 204, 66 S.W. 926 (1902) (letter to wife and enclosure to third person given by husband in jail to wife and seized from her by officers, held, the former privileged, the latter not); North v. Superior Court, 8 Cal.3d 301, 104 Cal.Rptr. 833, 502 P.2d 1305 (1972) (privilege upheld where detective induced belief that conversation would be private), 61 Cal.L.Rev. 457 (1973).

12. See § 74 supra, and §§ 169, 176 infra.

13. West's Ann.Cal.Evid.Code § 980, quoted § 78 n. 10 supra.

14. See § 85 infra.

15. Privilege applied: Bowman v. Patrick, 32 Fed. 368 (C.C.Mo.1887); McKie v. State, 165 Ga. 210, 140 S.E. 625 (1927) (trial of wife for murder of husband; wife's letter to husband, produced by his temporary administrator, held improperly admitted, two judges dissenting), noted critically, 37 Yale L.J. 669. Privilege denied: Dickerson v. United States, 65 F.2d 824 (1st Cir. 1933) (trial of husband for murder of wife; letter to wife found by third person among her effects, held admissible).

overlook this "common law" background [1] of privilege, and permit any party to the action to claim the benefit of the rule by objection. Doubtless counsel often fail to point out that privilege, not incompetency, is the proper classification, and that the distinctive feature of privilege is that it can only be claimed by the holder or beneficiary of the privilege, not by a party as such.[2] The latter principle is clearly correct.[3]

Who is the holder? Wigmore's argument, that the policy of encouraging freedom of communication points to the communicating spouse as the holder,[4] seems convincing. Under this view, in the case of a unilateral oral message or statement, of a husband to his wife, only the husband could assert the privilege, where the sole purpose is to show the expressions and attitude of the husband. If the object, however, were to show the wife's adoption of the husband's statement by her silence, then the husband's statement and her conduct both become her communication and she can claim the privilege. Similarly, if a conversation or an exchange of correspondence between them is offered to show the collective expressions of them

both, either it seems could claim privilege as to the entire exchange.

A failure by the holder to assert the privilege by objection, or a voluntary revelation by the holder of the communication,[5] or of a material part, is a waiver. The judge, however, may in some jurisdictions in his discretion protect the privilege [6] if the holder is not present to assert it, and objection by a party not the holder may serve the purpose of invoking this discretion, though the party may not complain [7] if the judge fails to protect this privilege belonging to the absent spouse.

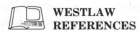

WESTLAW REFERENCES

waiv! /5 marital husband* wi*e* spous** /5 privilege*

§ 84. Controversies in Which the Privilege Is Inapplicable [1]

The common law privilege against adverse testimony of a spouse was subject to an exception in cases of prosecution of the husband for offenses against the wife, at least those of violence.[2] When nineteenth century

§ 83

1. See § 78 supra.

2. See § 73 supra.

3. Luick v. Arends, 21 N.D. 614, 132 N.W. 353, 362, 363 (1911) (statutory phrase, "nor can either be . . . without consent of the other examined as to any communication" creates a privilege, not a disqualification, which only a spouse can assert, and the defendant, in the alienation suit here, cannot assert the privilege or complain on appeal of its denial); Coles v. Harsch, 129 Or. 11, 276 P. 248, 253–255 (1929) (alienation action, plaintiff's wife having later married defendant; defendant, not being the holder of the privilege, could not object at the trial or on appeal to plaintiff's disclosure of marital communications); Patterson v. Skoglund, 181 Or. 167, 180 P.2d 108 (1947) (only husband or wife, not the defendant, can assert the privilege).

4. 8 Wigmore, Evidence § 2340(1) (McNaughton rev. 1961). This view seems to be that most widely followed. See United States v. Figueroa-Paz, 468 F.2d 1055 (9th Cir. 1972). But virtually every other possibility may be found applied. Thus, Rev. Uniform Evid. Rule 504 (1974) restricts the privilege to criminal cases and confers it only on the accused. West's Ann.Cal. Evid. Code § 980 makes both spouses holders. And N.M.S.A.1975 § 20–1–12 places the privilege in the witness spouse.

5. United States v. Figueroa-Paz, 468 F.2d 1055 (9th Cir. 1972) (communications privilege must be continuously asserted or it will be waived); Pendleton v. Pendleton, 103 Ohio App. 345, 145 N.E.2d 485 (1957) (privilege may be waived, and once waived may not later be asserted in the same cause); West's Ann.Cal.Evid.Code § 912(a). It is suggested in Fraser v. United States, 145 F.2d 139, 144 (6th Cir. 1945) cert. denied 324 U.S. 849, that when the husband claims the privilege on the stand, but answers when ordered by the court to do so, this is a waiver, but this conclusion seems questionable.

See, e.g., United States v. Lilley, 581 F.2d 182 (8th Cir. 1978) (disclosure by holder spouse waives privilege); People v. Worthington, 38 Cal.App.3d 359, 113 Cal.Rptr. 322 (1974)

6. Coles v. Harsch, 129 Or. 11, 276 P. 248, 255 (1929); Model Code of Evidence Rule 105(e).

7. See decisions cited note 3 supra.

§ 84

1. 8 Wigmore, Evidence § 2338 (McNaughton rev. 1961); C.J.S. Witnesses § 273; 58 Am.Jur.2d Witnesses §§ 151, 169; Model Code of Evidence Rule 216.

2. See § 66, supra, and 8 Wigmore, Evidence § 2239 (McNaughton Rev. 1961).

statutes in this country limited and regulated this privilege and the incompetency of spouses as witnesses and defined the new statutory privilege for confidential communications the common law exception above mentioned was usually incorporated and extended, and frequently other exceptions were added. Under these statues [3] it is not always clear how far the exceptions are intended to apply only to the provisions limiting the competency of the spouses as witnesses, or whether they apply also to the privilege for confidential communications. Frequently, however, in the absence of a contrary decision, it is at least arguable that the exception does have this latter application, and in some instances this intent is clearly expressed. Any other result would, in principle, indeed be difficult to justify.

The types of controversies in which the marital communication privilege is made inapplicable vary, of course, from state to state. They may be derived from express provision, from statutory implication, or from decisions based upon common law doctrine.[1] They may be grouped as follows:[5]

1. Prosecutions for crimes committed by one spouse against the other or against the children of either. Besides statutes in general terms, particular crimes, most frequently family desertion and pandering, are often specified, and as to these latter the withdrawal of the privilege for communications is usually explicit.

2. Actions by one of the spouses against an outsider for an intentional injury to the marital relation. Thus far this exception has been applied, sometimes under statutes, sometimes as a continuation of common law tradition, chiefly in actions for alienation of affection or for criminal conversation.[6] It is usually applied to admit declarations expressive of the state of affection of the alienated spouse.[7]

3. Actions by one spouse against the other. Some of the statutes are in this broader form. Some apply only to particular kinds of actions between them, of which divorce suits are most often specified. This exception for controversies between the spouses,[8] which should extend to controversies between the representatives of the spouses, seems worthy of universal acceptance. In the analogous case of clients who jointly consult an attorney, the clients are held to have no privilege for such consultation in controversies between themselves.[9] So here it seems that husband and wife, while they would desire that their confidences be shielded from the outside world, would ordinarily anticipate that if a controversy between themselves should arise in which their

---

3. See the compilation of statutes in 2 Wigmore, Evidence § 488 (Chadbourn rev. 1979).

4. See e.g., United States v. Walker, 176 F.2d 564, 568 (2d Cir. 1949) (L. Hand, C. J.: "We do not forget that a wife from the earliest times was competent to testify against her husand, when the crime was an offense against her person. . . . The same exception probably extends to the privilege against the admission of confidential communications"); People v. McCormack, 278 App.Div. 191, 104 N.Y.S.2d 139, 143 (1951) (common law exception for testimony as to assaults on wife is to be read into statute creating privilege, though exception not mentioned).

5. Compare West's Ann.Cal.Evid.Code § 972, supra § 78 n. 10.
See the exceptions in the California statute quoted § 78 n. 10 supra.
Cases involving crimes by one spouse against the other are collected, Annot., 11 A.L.R.2d 646; For cases involving crimes against the child of one spouse, see Annot., 93 A.L.R.3d 1018.

6. Stocker v. Stocker, 112 Neb. 565, 199 N.W. 849, 36 A.L.R. 1063 (1924); Hafer v. Lemon, 192 Okl. 578, 79 P.2d 216 (1938). Contra: Gjesdal v. Harmon, 175 Minn. 414, 221 N.W. 639 (1928); McKinnon v. Chenoweth, 176 Or. 74, 155 P.2d 944 (1945). Cases are collected in Annot., 36 A.L.R. 1068.

7. Annot., 36 A.L.R. 1068, 1070.

8. See statutes in 2 Wigmore, Evidence § 488 (Chadbourn rev. 1979). And see Poppe v. Poppe, 3 N.Y.2d 312, 165 N.Y.S.2d 99, 144 N.E.2d 72, 76 (1957), 58 Colum.L.Rev. 126 (1958), where, absent an explicit statutory exception, an exception was recognized in a separation suit for the wife's declaration that she had committed adultery and "they thought they would go away together," which was relied on as an act of cruelty by the defending husband. See also the reference to this case in § 80 n. 6 supra. Compare Oliver v. Oliver, 325 S.W.2d 33 (Mo.App.1959) (divorce action; communications held privileged).

9. See § 91 infra.

mutual conversations would shed light on the merits, the interests of both would be served by full disclosure.[10]

4. A criminal prosecution against one of the spouses in which a declaration of the other spouse made confidentially to the accused would tend to justify or reduce the grade of the offense.[11]

WESTLAW REFERENCES

marital husband* wi*e* /s privilege* /s inapplicab! unavailab!

§ 85. If the Communication Was Made During the Marriage, Does Death or Divorce End the Privilege? [1]

The incompetency of husband or wife to testify for the other, and the privilege of each spouse against adverse testimony are terminated when the marriage ends by death or divorce.[2] The privilege for confidential communications of the spouses, however, was based, in the mind of its chief sponsor, Greenleaf, upon the policy of encouraging confidences, and its sponsor thought that encouragement required not merely temporary

---

but permanent secrecy.[3] The courts in this country have accepted this need for permanent protection [4]—though it may be an unrealistic assumption—and about one-half of our statutes codifying the privilege explicitly provide that it continues after death or divorce.[5] In fact, this characteristic accounts for a large proportion of the attempted invocations of the communications privilege, since if the marriage has not been terminated one of the other, more embrasive marital privileges will frequently apply. But it is probably in these cases where the marital tie has been severed that the supposed policy of the privilege has the most remote and tenuous relevance, and the possibilities of injustice in its application are most apparent. Wigmore points out that in this area, "there must arise occasional instances of hardship where ample flexibility should be allowed in the relaxation of the rule."[6]

In the famous English case of Shenton v. Tyler,[7] the court was faced with one of those instances of hardship. The plaintiff sued a widow and alleged that her deceased husband had made an oral secret trust, known to the widow, for the benefit of plaintiff, and

---

10. However, in *Poppe*, supra n. 8, the dissenting judges thought this the kind of free communication encouraged by the law.

11. Texas Vernon's Ann.C.C.P. art. 38.11 recognizes an exception, "where one or the other is on trial for an offense and a declaration or communication made by the wife to the husband or by the husband to the wife goes to extenuate or justify the offense." Wigmore argues for such an exception. Wigmore, Evidence § 2338(4) (McNaughton rev. 1961). And he calls attention to the "cruel absurdity" of excluding the communication in these circumstances in Steeley v. State, 17 Okl.Cr. 252, 187 P. 820 (1920) (defendant charged with murder of wife's paramour could not testify to wife's communications to him disclosing deceased's conduct in debauching her) and other cases cited. This view is adopted in Model Code of Evidence Rule 216(d) and Comment.

§ 85

1. 8 Wigmore, Evidence § 2341 (McNaughton rev. 1961); C.J.S. Witnesses § 275; 58 Am.Jur.2d Witnesses § 153; Dec.Dig. Witnesses ⊚195.

2. See § 66 supra.

3. "The happiness of the married state requires that there should be the most unlimited confidence between husband and wife; and this confidence the law

---

secures by providing that it shall be kept forever inviolable; that nothing shall be extracted from the bosom of the wife which was confided there by the husband. Therefore, after the parties are separated, whether it be by divorce or by the death of the husband, the wife is still precluded from disclosing any conversations with him . . . ." 1 Greenleaf, Evidence 296 (13th ed. 1876).

4. See, e.g., United States v. Pensinger, 549 F.2d 1150 (8th Cir. 1977) (divorce does not terminate privilege, but communications not protected because in presence of third persons); Shepherd v. State, 257 Ind. 229, 277 N.E.2d 165 (1971) (divorced wife barred by privilege from testifying about acts which were matter of confidence); Breimon v. General Motors Corp., 8 Wn.App. 747, 509 P.2d 398 (1973) (divorced wife precluded from testifying concerning admission made by former husband; "A spouse should not be placed in fear that a future change in marital status would find his innermost secrets broadcast.")

5. See the compilation of statutes in 2 Wigmore. Evidence § 488 (Chadbourn rev. 1961).

6. 8 Wigmore, Evidence § 2341 (McNaughton rev. 1961).

7. L.R. [1939] Ch.Div. 620 (C.A.).

sought to interrogate the widow. The widow relied on sec. 3 of the Evidence Amendment Act, 1853, as follows: ". . . no wife shall be compellable to disclose any communication made to her during the marriage." The court rejected the Greenleaf theory of a common law privilege for communications surviving the end of the marriage, and was "unable to find any warrant for extending the words of the section by construction so as to include widowers and widows and divorced persons."[8] However debatable may be the court's position that there was no common law privilege for marital communications,[9] it seems clear that the actual holding that the privilege for communications ends when the marriage ends is preferable in policy to the contrary result reached under American statutes and decisions.

 **WESTLAW
REFERENCES**

marital husband* wi*e* spous** /s privilege* /s
divorce* /s terminat!

§ 86. Policy and Future of the Privilege [1]

The argument traditionally advanced in support of the marital communications privilege is that the privilege is needed to encourage marital confidences, which confidences in turn promote harmony between husband and wife. This argument, now reit-

erated for almost a century and a half, obviously rests upon certain assumptions concerning the knowledge and psychology of married persons. Thus it must be assumed that spouses will know of the privilege and take its protection into account in determining to make marital confidences, or at least, which is not the same thing, that they would come to know of the absence of the privilege if it were withdrawn and be, as a result, less confiding than at present.

In the absence of any empirical validation, these propositions have appeared highly suspect to many,[2] though not all,[3] commentators. Thus the most convincing answer to the argument of policy appears to be that the contingency of courtroom disclosure would almost never (even if the privilege did not exist) be in the minds of the parties in considering how far they should go in their secret conversations. What encourages them to fullest frankness is not the assurance of courtroom privilege, but the trust they place in the loyalty and discretion of each other. If the secrets are not told outside the courtroom there will be little danger of their being elicited in court. In the lives of most people appearance in court as a party or a witness is an exceedingly rare and unusual event, and the anticipation of it is not one of those factors which materially influence in daily life the degree of fullness of marital disclosures.[4] According-

---

8. L.R. [1939] Ch.Div. 620, 652 (by Luxmoore, L.J.).

9. See § 78 supra.

§ 86

1. 8 Wigmore, Evidence § 2332 (McNaughton rev. 1961); C.J.S. Witnesses § 266; 58 Am.Jur.2d Witnesses § 148; Dec.Dig., Witnesses ⊶188(1). The foregoing give the supporting arguments of policy.

2. Hutchins & Slesinger, Some Observations on the Law of Evidence: Family Relations, 13 Minn.L.Rev. 675, 682 (1929); Hines, Privileged Testimony of Husband and Wife in California, 19 Calif.L.Rev. 390, 410–414 (1931). Comment, 7 Cumb.L.Rev. 307, 319 (1976) (". . . it could not be said that the parties normally would have anticipated such an event as being forced to testify when they made the communication."); Note, 86 Dick.L.Rev. 491 (1982).

3. Krattenmaker, Interspousal Testimonial Privileges Under the Federal Rules of Evidence: A Suggested Approach, 64 Geo.L.J. 613 (1976); Reutlinger,

Policy, Privacy, and Prerogatives: A Critical Examination of the Proposed Federal Rules of Evidence as They Affect Marital Privilege, 61 Calif.L.Rev. 1353 (1973).

4. ". . . Very few people ever get into court, and practically no one outside the legal profession knows anything about the rules regarding privileged communications between spouses. As far as the writers are aware (though research might lead to another conclusion) marital harmony among lawyers who know about privileged communications is not vastly superior to that of other professional groups." Hutchins & Slesinger, supra n. 101 at p. 682.

Proposed Fed.R.Evid. (1971) 505, did not include a privilege for confidential communications. The Advisory Committee's Note to this proposed rule states with respect to the privilege:

"The rule recognizes no privilege for confidential communications. The traditional justifications for privileges not to testify against a spouse and not to

ly, we must conclude that, while the danger of injustice from suppression of relevant proof is clear and certain,[5] the probable benefits of the rule of privilege in encouraging marital confidences and wedded harmony is at best doubtful and marginal.

Probably the policy of encouraging confidences is not the prime influence in creating and maintaining the privilege. It is really a much more natural and less devious matter. It is a matter of emotion and sentiment. All of us have a feeling of indelicacy and want of decorum in prying into the secrets of husband and wife.

As pointed out in an earlier section,[6] this "privacy" rationale, particularly in the case of marital privilege, has been widely advanced in recent years. It may be hoped that increasing recognition of the true operative basis for affording privilege to the marital partners will in turn draw with it acceptance of the logical implications of that rationale, and that the privilege can accordingly be reshaped into a less anomalous form.

A desirable first step is to recognize that delicacy and decorum, while worthy and deserving of protection, will not stand in the

balance where there is a need for otherwise unobtainable evidence critical to the ascertainment of significant legal rights. This disproportion, together with the consideration that maintenance of privacy as a general objective is not critically impaired by its sacrifice in cases of particular need, argues for treating this privilege as a qualified one.[7] This view, in turn, would remove much of the felt need to hedge the privilege narrowly about with not completely logical exceptions and qualifications, perhaps largely out of the fear that a more liberal ambit of the privilege will inexorably lead to loss of critical evidence in future cases.

Again, a particularly anomalous characteristic of the present privilege, if protection of marital privacy be accepted as its justification, is its extension to testimony sought after the termination of the marriage by death or divorce.[8] This extension, which accounts for the majority of seriously deleterious consequences of the privilege, arguably serves, at most, the quite inferior privacy interest in the confidences of past marriages. The practical consequences of eliminating this feature would differ little from those occasioned by placing the privilege, as is some-

be testified against by one's spouse have been the prevention of marital dissension and the repugnancy of requiring a person to condemn or be condemned by his spouse. 8 Wigmore §§ 2228, 2241 (McNaughton rev. 1961). These considerations bear no relevancy to marital communications. Nor can it be assumed that marital conduct will be affected by a privilege for confidential communications of whose existence the parties in all likelihood are unaware. The other communication privileges, by way of contrast, have as one party a professional person who can be expected to inform the other of the existence of the privilege. Moreover, the relationships from which those privileges arise are essentially and almost exclusively verbal in nature, quite unlike marriage. See Hutchins & Slesinger, Some Observations on the Law of Evidence: Family Relations, 13 Minn.L.Rev. 675 (1929). Cf. McCormick § 90; 8 Wigmore § 2337 (McNaughton rev. 1961)."

5. Examples of cases where the possibilities of injustice seem conspicuous are In re DeNeef, 42 Cal.App. 2d 691, 109 P.2d 741 (1941) (wife sues on life insurance policy taken out in her favor by deceased husband. Defense: fraudulent representations by husband as to his health. Held, wife cannot be interrogated as husband's statements to her as to his physical condition.

"We are not concerned with the reason for the rule or its effect on the administration of justice"); McKie v. State, 165 Ga. 210, 140 S.E. 625 (1927) (wife's conviction for murder of husband because of admission of wife's letters to husband, found in his effects after he was killed); Todd v. Barbee, 271 Ky. 381, 111 S.W.2d 1041 (1938) (excluding husband's testimony that he gave wife money to pay rent) and People v. Daghita, 299 N.Y. 194, 86 N.E.2d 172 (1949) (error to allow wife to testify in prosecution of husband for grand larceny, that she saw him bringing stolen property into their home and hiding it under his bed).

6. See § 72 supra. See also, Borden, In Defense of the Privilege for Confidential Marital Communications, 39 Ala.Law. 575, 581 (1978) (". . . the benefit of the privilege derives not from its encouragement of confidence, but from the recognition that the confidence once having existed, deserves protection").

7. See § 78 supra, concerning the expanded use of qualified or conditional privilege.

8. Elimination of this feature has previously been advocated. See, e.g., original Uniform Rule 28 (1953), which would have terminated the privilege upon death or divorce.

times done today,[9] in the hands of the testifying spouse or former spouse.[10] However, the expedient suggested here is thought more compatable with the evolving theory of the privilege.[11]

Finally, though the time is yet far removed, it may someday be recognized that a communications privilege, however appropriate to professional relationships, is highly unsuited to the marital context,[12] being at some points too broad [13] and at others too narrow [14] appropriately to protect the essential private aspects of marriage.

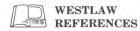

WESTLAW REFERENCES

marital husband* wi*e* spous**   /s   privilege*   /s
encourage! promot! protect!   /s   confiden!   /s   policy
policies

---

9. See § 83 supra at n. 4. See also Note, 86 Dick.L. Rev. 491 (1982) (advocating this modification).

10. Review of the cases involving post-dissolution claims of the privilege will reveal that in virtually every instance the offered testimony of the witness spouse appears to have been voluntary. See § 85, supra at n. 4.

11. The termination of the privilege upon death or divorce has no effect upon pre-dissolution admissibility. By contrast, placement of the privilege in the hands of the witness spouse can affect these situations.

12. The Advisory Committee on the Federal Rules of Evidence observed in its note on proposed Rule 505 (marital privilege): "[T]he relationships from which those/professional/privileges arise are essentially and almost exclusively verbal in nature, quite unlike marriage." This comment has been widely criticized, not on grounds that it is inaccurate, but apparently in the mistaken belief that it implied some inferiority of the marital to the professional relationship, thus paving the way for abolition of privilege for the former. Black, The Marital and Physician Privileges—Reprint of a Letter to A Congressman, 1975 Duke L.J. 45. The logical thrust of the comment, however, is that given the nature of the marital relationship, a *communications* privilege is inappropriate to it.

13. The overbreadth of the privilege is reflected in the recurrent necessity of excepting from its operation communications relating to obviously non-intimate subjects such as business and property. See § 80 nn. 10–13 supra. See also, Comment, 56 Ind.L.J. 121 (1981) (arguing from the fact that most marital communications have no confidential or private aspect that the privilege should be limited to communications concerning "sexual and affectional" matters).

14. The deficiencies of a communications privilege in the marital context are reflected in the tortured and distorted definitions by which a number of courts have expanded the privilege to cover acts. These deficiencies are also dramatically illustrated by Chamberlin v. Chamberlin, 230 S.W.2d 184 (Mo.App.1950) in which wife's testimony that husband made "unnatural sexual demands" of her was not privileged because such demands were not shown to have been made verbally.

Chapter 10

THE CLIENT'S PRIVILEGE: COMMUNICATIONS
BETWEEN CLIENT AND LAWYER

Table of Sections

§ 87. Background and Policy of the Privilege

The notion that the loyalty owed by the lawyer to his client disables him from being a witness in his client's case is deep-rooted in Roman law.[1] This Roman tradition may or may not have been influential in shaping the early English doctrine of which we find the first traces in Elizabeth's time, that the oath and honor of the barrister and the attorney protect them from being required to disclose, upon examination in court, the secrets of the client.[2] But by the eighteenth century in England the emphasis upon the code of honor had lessened and the need of the ascertainment of truth for the ends of justice loomed larger than the pledge of secrecy. So a new justification for the lawyer's exemption from disclosing his client's secrets was found. This was the theory that claims

---

§ 87

1. See Radin, The Privilege of Confidential Communication between Lawyer and Client, 16 Calif.L.Rev. 487, 488 (1928). As to the history and foundations of the privilege generally, see also Cain, The Attorney's Obligation of Confidentiality—Its Effect on the Ascertainment of Truth in an Adversary System of Justice, 3 Glendale L.Rev. 81 (1978); Fried, The Lawyer as Friend: The Moral Foundations of the Attorney-Client Relation, 85 Yale L.J. 1060 (1976); Hazard, An Historical Perspective on the Attorney-Client Privilege, 66 Calif.L.Rev. 1061 (1978); Note, 91 Harv.L.Rev. 464 (1977).

2. 8 Wigmore, Evidence § 2290 (McNaughton rev. 1961) (history of the privilege).

and disputes which may lead to litigation can most justly and expeditiously be handled by practised experts, namely lawyers, and that these experts can act effectively only if they are fully advised of the facts by the parties whom they represent.[3] Full disclosure will be promoted if the client knows that what he tells his lawyer cannot, over his objection, be extorted in court from the lawyer's lips.

The proposition is that the detriment to justice from a power to shut off inquiry into pertinent facts in court will be outweighed by the benefits to justice (not to the client) from a franker disclosure in the lawyer's office. Wigmore, who supports the privilege, acknowledges that "Its benefits are all indirect and speculative; its obstruction is plain and concrete."[4]

The tendency of the client in giving his story to his counsel to omit all that he suspects will make against him is a matter of everyday professional observation. It makes it necessary for the prudent lawyer to cross-examine his client searchingly about possible unfavorable facts. Perhaps in criminal cases the accused if he knew the lawyer could be compelled to repeat the facts disclosed might be induced by fear of this to withhold an acknowledgement of guilt. He knows that the prosecution cannot compel him, the accused, to testify. And in civil cases, before the mid-nineteenth century statutes making parties compellable to testify, the party might have feared to give damaging facts to his counsel if the latter could have been called to disclose these admissions in court. Now, however, when the civil par-

ty knows that he himself can be called as a witness by the adversary, the danger from disclosure to counsel is less important.

Perhaps we need not yield fully to the force of Bentham's slashing argument that the privilege is not needed by the innocent party with a righteous cause or defense, and that the guilty should not be given its aid in concerting a false one.[5] Wigmore in answer points out that in lawsuits all is not black and white but a client's case may be one where there is no clear preponderance of morals and justice on either side, and he may mistakenly think a fact fatal to his cause when it is not, and thus be impelled, if there were no privilege, to forego resort to counsel for advice in a fair claim.[6] Yet it must be acknowledged that the existence of the privilege may often instead of avoiding litigation upon unfounded claims, actually encourage such litigation. A rascally client consults one lawyer who tells him that certain facts disclosed are fatal to his case. The client then goes to another attorney and tells the story differently, so that a claim may be supported—a course which in the absence of the privilege would be much more dangerous.[7]

If one were legislating for a new commonwealth, without history or customs, it might be hard to maintain that a privilege for lawyer-client communications would facilitate more than it would obstruct the administration of justice. But we are not writing on a blank slate. Our adversary system of litigation casts the lawyer in the role of fighter for the party whom he represents. A strong

3. ". . . An increase of legal business, and the inabilities of parties to transact that business themselves, made it necessary for them to employ . . . other persons who might transact that business for them; that this necessity introduced with it the necessity of what the law hath very justly established, an inviolable secrecy to be observed by attornies, in order to render it safe for clients to communicate to their attornies all proper instructions. . . ." Mounteney, B. in Annesley v. Earl of Anglesea, 17 How.St.Tr. 1225 (1743) quoted in 8 Wigmore, Evidence § 2291 (McNaugton rev. 1961) (policy of the privilege).

4. 8 Wigmore, Evidence § 2291, p. 554 (McNaughton rev. 1961). For an opposing view see Barnhart,

Privilege in the Uniform Rules of Evidence, 24 Ohio St. L.J. 131 (1963).

5. See Bentham, Rationale of Judicial Evidence (1827), 7 The Works of Jeremy Bentham 473, 474, 475, 477, 479 (Bowring ed. 1842), passages quoted Wigmore, op. cit., § 2291.

6. 8 Wigmore, Evidence § 2291, p. 552 (McNaughton rev. 1961).

7. Radin, op. cit., 16 Calif.L.Rev. at 490. See also Morgan, Foreword, Model Code of Evidence 26, 27 (1942).

sentiment of loyalty attaches to the relationship, and this sentiment would be outraged by an attempt to change our customs so as to make the lawyer amenable to routine examination upon the client's confidential disclosures regarding professional business. Loyalty and sentiment are silken threads, but they are hard to break. Accordingly, confined as we are by this "cake of custom," it is unlikely that enough energy could now be generated to abolish the privilege, particularly since its obstructive effect has been substantially lessened by the development of liberal doctrines as to waiver and as to denial of the privilege in case of consultation for unlawful ends. Nevertheless, some progress toward liberalization of the practice, some better reconciliation of the conflicting pulls of sentiment and delicacy on the one hand and of the need, on the other, for full ascertainment of the crucial facts by a tribunal of justice, seems possible. It has been suggested that:

1. The lawyer's duty to maintain out of court the secrecy of his client's confidential disclosures be retained intact. This assurance furnishes to most clients having a good faith claim or defense all the security (and hence encouragement to full disclosure) for which they would feel any need.[8]

2. The present privilege against disclosure of such communications in judicial proceedings, should be made subject to the exception that the trial judge may require a particular disclosure if he finds that it is necessary in the administration of justice.[9] Notwithstanding such a change, the present reluctance of lawyers to call an opposing counsel for routine examination on his client's case would continue as a restraining influence. The duty to the client of secrecy would still be recognized and protected in the ordinary course, but the lawyer's duty as an officer of the court to lend his aid in the last resort to prevent a miscarriage of justice would be given the primacy which a true balancing of the two interests would seem to demand.

A clear statement of the scope of the privilege as now generally accepted is embodied in the Revised Uniform Evid. Rules (1974).[10]

The application of the privilege for the benefit of a corporate client, as distin-

---

8. American Bar Association Code of Professional Responsibility, Disciplinary Rule 4–101:

Preservation of Confidences and Secrets of a Client.

(A) "Confidence" refers to information protected by the attorney-client privilege under applicable law, and "secret" refers to other information gained in the professional relationship that the client has requested be held inviolate or the disclosure of which would be embarrassing or would be likely to be detrimental to the client.

(B) Except when permitted under DR 4–101(C), a lawyer shall not knowingly:

(1) Reveal a confidence or secret of his client.

(2) Use a confidence or secret of his client to the disadvantage of the client.

(3) Use a confidence or secret of his client for the advantage of himself or of a third person, unless the client consents after full disclosure.

(C) A lawyer may reveal:

(1) Confidences or secrets with the consent of the client or clients affected, but only after a full disclosure to them.

(2) Confidences or secrets when permitted under Disciplinary Rules or required by law or court order.

(3) The intention of his client to commit a crime and the information necessary to prevent the crime.

(4) Confidences or secrets necessary to establish or collect his fee or to defend himself or his employees or associates against an accusation of wrongful conduct.

(D) A lawyer shall exercise reasonable care to prevent his employees, associates, and others whose services are utilized by him from disclosing or using confidences or secrets of a client, except that a lawyer may reveal the information allowed by DR 4–101 (C) through an employee.

9. See § 77 supra.

10. Revised Uniform Rule of Evidence (1974) 502:

(a) **Definitions**. As used in this rule:

(1) A "client" is a person, public officer, or corporation, association, or other organization or entity, either public or private, who is rendered professional legal services by a lawyer, or who consults a lawyer with a view to obtaining professional legal services from him.

(2) A representative of the client is one having authority to obtain professional legal services, or to act on advice rendered pursuant thereto, on behalf of the client.

guished from a natural person, was never questioned until a federal district court in 1962 held that a corporation is not entitled to claim the privilege.[11] The decision attracted wide attention and much comment, most of which was adverse, until reversed on appeal.[12] There seems to be little reason to believe that the issue will arise soon again.[13]

(3) A "lawyer" is a person authorized, or reasonably believed by the client to be authorized, to engage in the practice of law in any state or nation.

(4) A "representative of the lawyer" is one employed by the lawyer to assist the lawyer in the rendition of professional legal services.

(5) A communication is "confidential" if not intended to be disclosed to third persons other than those to whom disclosure is made in furtherance of the rendition of professional legal services to the client or those reasonably necessary for the transmission of the communication.

(b) **General Rule of Privilege.** A client has a privilege to refuse to disclose and to prevent any other person from disclosing confidential communications made for the purpose of facilitating the rendition of professional legal services to the client (1) between himself or his representative and his lawyer or his lawyer's representative, (2) between his lawyer and the lawyer's representative, (3) by him or his representative or his lawyer or a representative of the lawyer to a lawyer or a representative of a lawyer representing another party in a pending action and concerning a matter of common interest therein, (4) between representatives of the client or between the client and a representative of the client, or (5) among lawyers and their representatives representing the same client.

(c) **Who May Claim the Privilege.** The privilege may be claimed by the client, his guardian or conservator, the personal representative of a deceased client, or the successor, trustee, or similar representative of a corporation, association, or other organization, whether or not in existence. The person who was the lawyer or the lawyer's representative at the time of the communication is presumed to have authority to claim the privilege but only on behalf of the client.

(d) **Exceptions.** There is no privilege under this rule:

(1) *Furtherance of Crime or Fraud.* If the services of the lawyer were sought or obtained to enable or aid anyone to commit or plan to commit what the client knew or reasonably should have known to be a crime or fraud;

(2) *Claimants Through Same Deceased Client.* As to a communication relevant to an issue between parties who claim through the same deceased client, regardless of whether the claims are by testate or intestate succession or by inter vivos transaction;

The scope of the privilege in the corporate context, however, has presented an exceptionally troublesome question which is even yet not fully resolved. The difficulty is basically one of extrapolating the essential operating conditions of the privilege from the paradigm case of the traditional individual client who both supplies information to, and receives counsel from, the attorney. Are

(3) *Breach of Duty by a Lawyer or Client.* As to a communication relevant to an issue of breach of duty by the lawyer to his client or by the client to his lawyer;

(4) *Document Attested by a Lawyer.* As to a communication relevant to an issue concerning an attested document to which the lawyer is an attesting witness;

(5) *Joint Clients.* As to a communication relevant to a matter of common interest between or among two or more clients if the communication was made by any of them to a lawyer retained or consulted in common, when offered in an action between or among any of the clients; or

(6) *Public Officer or Agency.* As to a communication between a public officer or agency and its lawyers unless the communication concerns a pending investigation, claim, or action and the court determines that disclosure will seriously impair the ability of the public officer or agency to process the claim or conduct a pending investigation, litigation, or proceeding in the public interest.

Except that deleted Federal Rule Evid. 503 did not contain provisions (a)(2) and (d)(6) of the Revised Uniform Rule and except for insignificant stylistic differences, the rules are the same.

11. Radiant Burners, Inc. v. American Gas Association, 207 F.Supp. 771 (N.D.Ill.1962).

12. Radiant Burners, Inc. v. American Gas Association, 320 F.2d 314, 98 A.L.R.2d 228, and note, (7th Cir. 1963) cert. denied 375 U.S. 921. The case is remarkable for the number of amici curiae briefs urging reversal including briefs from the Chicago Bar Ass'n., the Illinois State Bar Ass'n., and the American Bar Ass'n.

For comment on the District Court decision, see 76 Harvard L.Rev. 655 (1963), 52 Ill.B.J. 666 (1963), 61 Mich.L.Rev. 603 (1963), 57 Nw.U.L.Rev. 596 (1962).

On the privilege as applied to corporations generally, see Simon, The Attorney-Client Privilege as Applied to Corporations, 65 Yale L.J. 953 (1956).

13. Revised Uniform Rule of Evidence (1974) 502(a) defines a client within the lawyer-client privilege as follows:

(1) A "client" is a person, public officer, or corporation, association, or other organization or entity, either public or private, who is rendered professional legal services by a lawyer, or who consults a lawyer with a view to obtaining professional legal services from him.

both of these aspects of the relationship to be protected in the corporate setting, in which the corporate agents in a position to furnish the pertinent facts are not necessarily those empowered to take action responsive to legal advice based upon those facts? Early decisions focused upon the first half of this dichotomy, and extended the privilege expansively to communications from any "officer or employee" of the client corporation.[14] This emphasis was dramatically reversed by the case of City of Philadelphia v. Westinghouse Electric Corp.,[15] which propounded a "control group" test under which the privilege was restricted to communications made by those corporate functionaries "in a position to control or even to take a substantial part in a decision about any action which the corporation may take upon the advice of the attorney."[16]

The "control group" theory was widely,[17] though not universally,[18] followed by the courts until the 1981 decision of the Supreme Court in Upjohn Co. v. United States.[19] While the Court specifically declined in Upjohn to attempt the formulation of a definitive rule,[20] it did specifically reject the control group principle as one which "cannot . . . govern the development of the law in this area."[21] The principal defi-

ciency which the Court noted as inherent in the control group test is its failure to recognize the function of the privilege as protecting the flow of information to the advising attorney.[22] The opinion does suggest limitations however, in that such information will be privileged only if: (1) it is communicated for the express purpose of securing legal advice for the corporation; (2) it relates to the specific corporate duties of the communicating employee; and (3) it is treated as confidential within the corporation itself.[23]

 **WESTLAW REFERENCES**

policy policies   /s   attorney-client   /s   privilege*

§ 88. The Professional Relationship

The privilege for communications of a client with his lawyer hinges upon the client's belief that he is consulting a lawyer in that capacity and his manifested intention to seek professional legal advice.[1] It is sufficient if he reasonably believes that the person consulted is a lawyer, though in fact he is not.[2] Communications in the course of preliminary discussion with a view to employing the lawyer are privileged though the employment is in the upshot not accepted.[3] The burden of

---

14. United States v. United Shoe Machinery Corp., 89 F.Supp. 357 (D.C.Mass.1950); Zenith Radio Corp. v. Radio Corp. of America, 121 F.Supp. 792 (D.C.Del. 1954); United States v. Aluminum Co. of America, 193 F.Supp. 251 (N.D.N.Y.1960).

15. 210 F.Supp. 483 (E.D.Pa.1962), mandamus and prohibition denied sub nom. General Electric Co. v. Kirkpatrick, 312 F.2d 742 (3d Cir. 1962), cert. denied 372 U.S. 943.

16. 210 F.Supp. at 485.

17. In re Grand Jury Investigation (Sun Co.), 599 F.2d 1224 (3d Cir. 1979); Virginia Electric & Power Co. v. Sun Shipbuilding and Dry Dock Co., 68 F.R.D. 397 (E.D.Va.1975); Garrison v. General Motors Corp., 213 F.Supp. 515 (S.D.Cal.1963).

18. See Harper and Row Publishers, Inc. v. Decker, 423 F.2d 487 (7th Cir. 1970), affirmed by an equally divided Court 400 U.S. 348.

19. 449 U.S. 383 (1981).

20. 449 U.S. at 386, 396. This failure was strenuously criticized by Chief Justice Burger in a concurring opinion. 449 U.S. at 402 (". . . I believe that we should articulate a standard that will govern similar

cases and afford guidance to corporations, counsel advising them, and federal courts." Burger, C.J., concurring in part and concurring in the judgment).

21. 449 U.S. at 402.

22. Id. at 390.

23. Id. at 394.

§ 88

1. See Note, 24 Iowa L.Rev. 538 (1939).

2. People v. Barker, 60 Mich. 277, 27 N.W. 539 (1886) (confession to detective pretending to be an attorney); Rev.Unif.R.Evid. (1974) 502(a)(3) supra § 87, n. 10.

3. In re Dupont's Estate, 60 Cal.App.2d 276, 140 P.2d 866 (1943) (preliminary negotiations fell within language of Code Civ.Proc. § 1881, subd. 2 conferring privilege to communications, "in the course of professional employment," "no person could ever safely consult an attorney for the first time . . . if the privilege depended on the chance of whether the attorney after hearing the statement of the facts decided to accept the employment or decline it"); Denver Tramway Co. v. Owens, 20 Colo. 107, 36 P. 848 (1894); Keir v.

proof (presumably in both senses) rests on the person asserting the privilege to show that the consultation was a professional one.[4] Payment or agreement to pay a fee, however, is not essential.[5] But where one consults an attorney not as a lawyer but as

a friend[6] or as a business adviser[7] or banker,[8] or negotiator,[9] or as an accountant,[10] or where the communication is to the attorney acting as a "mere scrivener"[11] or as an attesting witness to a will or deed,[12] or as an executor[13] or as agent,[14] the consultation is

State, 152 Fla. 389, 11 So.2d 886 (1943) (letters); Taylor v. Sheldon, 172 Ohio St. 118, 173 N.E.2d 892 (1961); In re Graf's Estate, 119 N.W.2d 478 (N.D.1963); Of course, statements made after the employment is declined are not privileged. McGrede v. Rembert National Bank, 147 S.W.2d 580 (Tex.Civ.App.1941).

Rev.Unif.R.Evid. (1974) 502(b) covers the matter by extending the privilege to communications "for the purpose of facilitating the rendition" of legal services.

4. United States v. Landorf, 591 F.2d 36 (9th Cir. 1978); McGrede v. Rembert National Bank, 147 S.W.2d 580 (Tex.Civ.App.1941); McKnew v. Superior Court, 23 Cal.2d 58, 142 P.2d 1 (1943).

5. United States v. Costanzo, 625 F.2d 465 (3d Cir. 1980); Matters v. State, 120 Neb. 404, 232 N.W. 781 (1930); Hodge v. Garten, 116 W.Va. 564, 182 S.E. 582 (1935); C.J.S. Witnesses § 277, n. 41.

6. Modern Woodmen v. Watkins, 132 F.2d 352 (5th Cir. 1942) (disclosure of suicidal intent); Solon v. Lichtenstein, 39 Cal.2d 75, 244 P.2d 907 (1952); Lifsey v. Mims, 193 Ga. 780, 20 S.E.2d 32 (1942) (lawyer drawing deed as a "friendly act"); In re Conner's Estate, 33 N.W.2d 866 (1948) (modified on other grounds, 240 Iowa 479, 36 N.W.2d 833 (1949) (divulging grandson's illegitimacy, to secure friend's help in telling boy).

7. United States v. Davis, 636 F.2d 1028 (5th Cir. 1981); United States v. United Shoe Machinery Corp., 89 F.Supp. 357 (D.Mass.1950) (a communication soliciting business advice, not privileged, and attorney-client privilege does not extend to attorneys employed in a department of corporation which functions as a business branch, but does exist between corporation and attorneys in its legal department who perform substantially the same service as outside counsel); United States v. Vehicular Parking, 52 F.Supp. 751 (D.Del. 1943) (business advice and directions by attorney who was promoter, director and manager of corporation concerned); Clayton v. Canida, 223 S.W.2d 264 (Tex. Civ.App.1949) (attorney acting as accountant, income tax return). However, where business and legal advice are intertwined and the legal component predominates, the privilege has been held to apply. Sedco International, S.A. v. Cory, 683 F.2d 1201 (8th Cir. 1982), cert. denied 103 S.Ct. 379. As to the position of "house counsel" in respect to the privilege, see Simon, The Attorney Client Privilege as Applied to Corporations, 65 Yale L.J. 953, 969–978 (1956).

8. Belcher v. Somerville, 413 S.W.2d 620 (Ky.1967).

9. Myles v. Rieser Co. Inc. v. Loew's Inc., 194 Misc. 119, 81 N.Y.S.2d 861 (1948) (attorneys acting both as lawyers and as negotiators; communications in latter capacity not privileged); Henson v. State, 97 Okl.Cr. 240, 261 P.2d 916 (1953) (communication between defendant and attorney sharing office and secretary with defendant's attorney, not privileged and no attorney-

client relationship existed where defendant knew attorney represented another and attorney tried to settle differences between his client and defendant).

10. Olender v. United States, 210 F.2d 795 (9th Cir. 1954) (attorney engaged as an accountant to prepare financial statement and income tax returns).

See further n. 16 infra.

11. The phrase is often used as a justification for denying the privilege, see e.g., Benson v. Custer, 236 Iowa 345, 17 N.W.2d 889 (1945); Sparks v. Sparks, 51 Kan. 195, 201, 32 P. 892 (1893). The distinction is usually drawn between instances where the lawyer is employed merely to draft the document and cases where his advice is sought as to terms and effect. Mueller v. Batcheler, 131 Iowa 650, 652, 109 N.W. 186, 187 (1906) (conveyances); Dickerson v. Dickerson, 322 Ill. 492, 153 N.E. 740 (1926) (deed); Cranston v. Stewart, 184 Kan. 99, 334 P.2d 337 (1959); Wilcox v. Coons, 359 Mo. 52, 220 S.W.2d 15 (1949); Shelley v. Landry, 97 N.H. 27, 79 A.2d 626 (1951). Bolyea v. First Presbyterian Church of Wilton, 196 N.W.2d 149 (N.D.1972) (privilege held inapplicable where attorney employed as scrivener offered legal advice which was rejected by client). Usually it will be found that an attorney asked to draw a will, is not a mere scrivener, but is acting professionally. Booher v. Brown, 173 Or. 464, 146 P.2d 71 (1944). And the strict view of privilege in respect to the employment of lawyers as conveyancers seems somewhat inconsistent with the bar's present-day emphasis upon the importance of this as a lawyer's function. See Houck, Real Estate Instruments and the Bar, 5 Law & Contemp.Prob. 66 (1938).

12. Smith v. Smith, 222 Ga. 694, 152 S.E.2d 560 (1966) (lawyer may testify as to client's mental condition, his knowledge of the contents and other pertinent facts attending execution of contract, prepared and attested to by him); In re Heiler's Estate, 288 Mich. 49, 284 N.W. 641 (1939) (lawyer attesting will could testify to what he learned in his capacity as witness); Larson v. Dahlstrom, 214 Minn. 304, 8 N.W.2d 48 (1943) (lawyer attesting deed could testify to statements made by client at time of execution as bearing on mental condition); Anderson v. Thomas, 108 Utah 252, 159 P.2d 142 (1945) (deed; attesting lawyer may testify to conversations at time of execution).

13. Peyton v. Werhane, 126 Conn. 382, 11 A.2d 800 (1940).

14. United States v. Bartone, 400 F.2d 459 (6th Cir. 1969), cert. denied 393 U.S. 1027 (services consisted of tracing funds); Banks v. United States, 204 F.2d 666 (8th Cir. 1953) (attorney acting also in capacity of agent in negotiations with Internal Revenue Officer); Pollock v. United States, 202 F.2d 281 (5th Cir. 1953) (money deposited with attorney to be applied on purchase of real estate); Hansen v. Janitschek, 31 N.J.

not professional nor the statement privileged. There is some conflict in the decisions as to whether the privilege is available for communications to an administrative practitioner who is not a lawyer.[15] However, the privilege will generally be applicable even where the services performed by a lawyer are not necessarily available only from members of the legal profession.[16]

Ordinarily an attorney can lawfully hold himself out as qualified to practice only in the state in which he is licensed, and consultation elsewhere on a continuing basis would traditionally not be privileged,[17] but excep-

tionally by custom he might lawfully be consulted elsewhere in respect to isolated transactions, and Revised Uniform Evidence Rule (1974) 502(a)(3) requires only that he be authorized or reasonably be believed to be authorized "in any state or nation."[18]

Traditionally, the relationship sought to be fostered by the privilege has been that between the lawyer and a private client, but more recently the privilege has been held to extend to communications to an attorney representing the state.[19] However, disclosures to the public prosecuting attorney by an informer are not within the attorney-cli-

545, 158 A.2d 329 (1960) (attorney-client relationship held not to exist where attorney employed solely to assist in obtaining loan). See also Zenith Radio Corp. v. Radio Corp. of America, 121 F.Supp. 792 (D.Del.1954) critically noted 23 Geo.Wash.L.Rev. 786 (1955) (attorney-employee of corporate patent department would be regarded as "acting as a lawyer" within discovery rule when preponderantly engaged in giving legal advice but not when largely concerned with technical aspects of a business or engineering character). In Sperti Products, Inc. v. Coca-Cola Co., 262 F.Supp. 148 (D.Del. 1966) the same court held that the rule of *Zenith* did not extend to take communications between clients and outside attorneys who represent them before the Patent Office outside the privilege. The Court cited Chore-Time Equipment, Inc. v. Big Dutchman, Inc., 255 F.Supp. 1020 (W.D.Mich.1966) (communications between outside patent attorney and client privileged).

For cases on the above as well as related categories, see C.J.S. Witnesses § 280.

15.   Decisions denying the privilege to administrative practitioners include: United States v. Zakutansky, 401 F.2d 68 (7th Cir. 1968), cert. denied 393 U.S. 1021 (work papers used by accountant in preparing tax return); Falsone v. United States, 205 F.2d 734 (5th Cir. 1953) (certified public accountant having the same rights as an enrolled attorney under Treasury Department regulations); United States v. United Shoe Machinery Corp., 89 F.Supp. 357 (1950) (patent solicitors not members of bar employed in corporation's patent department); Kent Jewelry Corp. v. Kiefer, 113 N.Y.S.2d 12 (Sup.1952) (patent agent authorized to practice before the United States Patent Office). But compare In re Ampicillin Antitrust Litigation, 81 F.R.D. 377 (D.D.C.1978) (privilege applicable to communications to patent agents registered with the U.S. Patent Office; collecting authorities to the same effect).

16.   United States v. Summe, 208 F.Supp. 925 (D.C. Ky.1962) (lawyer employed to fill out tax return); Ellis-Foster Co. v. Union Carbide & Carbon Corp., 159 F.Supp. 917 (D.C.N.J.1958), reversed on other grounds in 284 F.2d 917 (3d Cir. 1962) (patent office proceedings conducted by lawyer). Compare United States v. Mer-

rell, 303 F.Supp. 490 (N.D.N.Y.1969) (schedule of income and expenses furnished by client, and attorney's working papers, intended to be disclosed in returns and not confidential). See generally Petersen, Attorney-Client Privilege in Internal Revenue Service Investigations, 54 Minn.L.Rev. 67 (1969), Annot., 15 A.L.R.Fed. 771.

17.   United States v. United Shoe Machinery Corp., 89 F.Supp. 357 (D.Mass.1950).

18.   Zenith Radio Corp. v. Radio Corp. of America, 121 F.Supp. 792, 794 (D.Del.1954) ("Bar membership should properly be of the court for the area wherein the services are rendered, but this is not a sine qua non, e.g., visiting counsel, long distance services by correspondence, pro hac vice services, 'house counsel' who practice law only for the corporate client and its affiliates and not for the public generally, for which local authorities do not insist on admission to the local bar."); Georgia Pacific Plywood Co. v. United States Plywood Corp., 18 F.R.D. 463 (S.D.N.Y.1956) (where house counsel of corporation not licensed in state where suit pending was actively engaged in legal service to corporation in multi-state litigation communications with him relating to legal service were privileged); Paper Converting Machine Co. v. FMC Corp., 215 F.Supp. 249 (E.D.Wis.1963) (patent counsel member of Ohio bar but not of California bar where employed, communications held privileged). In theory, making existence of the privilege dependent upon the technicalities of the attorney's admission status appears dubious. Absent such a limitation, the client is afforded more protection when consulting an imposter than when consulting an attorney unlicensed in the jurisdiction. See § 87, n. 10 supra for text of Uniform Rule.

19.   People v. Glen Arms Estate, Inc., 41 Cal.Rptr. 303, 230 Cal.App.2d 841 (1965); Hartford Accident & Indemnity Co. v. Cutter, 108 N.H. 112, 229 A.2d 173 (1967); Riddle Spring Realty Co. v. State, 107 N.H. 271, 220 A.2d 751 (1966) (appraisals and reports confidentially made at request of attorney for state held privileged. See Rev.Unif.R.Evid. (1974) 502(a)(1), supra § 87, n. 10.

ent privilege,[20] but an analogous policy of protecting the giving of such information has led to the recognition of a privilege against the disclosure of the identity of the informer, unless the trial judge finds that such disclosure is necessary in the interests of justice.[21] Communications to an attorney appointed by the court to serve the interest of a party are of course within the privilege.[22] A communication by a lawyer to a member of the Board of Governors of the state bar association, revealing a fraudulent conspiracy in which he had been engaged and expressing his desire to resign from the practice of law was held not privileged.[23]

Wigmore argued for a privilege analogous to the lawyer-client privilege for "confessions or similar confidences" made privately by persons implicated in a wrong or crime to the judge of a court.[24] As to judges generally there seems little justification for such a privilege if the policy-motive is the furtherance of the administration of justice by encouraging a full disclosure.[25] Unlike the lawyer the judge needs no private disclosures in advance of trial to enable him to perform his functions. In fact such revelations would ordinarily embarrass rather than aid him in carrying out his duties as a

trial judge.[26] The famous case of Lindsey v. People,[27] however, raised the question whether the judge of a juvenile court does not stand in a special position with regard to confidential disclosures by children who come before him. The majority of the court held that when a boy under promise of secrecy confessed to the judge that he had fired the shot that killed his father the judge was compellable, on the trial of the boy's mother for murder, to divulge the confession. The court pointed out that a parent who had received such a confidence would be compellable to disclose.[28] In the case of this particular court the need for encouraging confidences is clear, but in most cases the most effective encouragement will come from the confidence-inspiring personality of the judge, even without the aid of assurances of secrecy.[29] The court's conclusion that the need for secrecy for this type of disclosure does not outweigh the sacrifice to the administration of justice from the suppression of the evidence seems justifiable.

 WESTLAW REFERENCES

sh 27 nw 539

uniform /s evidence /s 502(b) & court(ar)

---

20. Fite v. Bennett, 142 Ga. 660, 83 S.E. 515 (1914); Cole v. Andrews, 74 Minn. 93, 76 N.W. 962 (1898); Application of Heller, 184 Misc. 75, 53 N.Y.S.2d 86 (1945).

21. Wilson v. United States, 59 F.2d 390 (3d Cir. 1932); 8 Wigmore, Evidence §§ 2374, 2375 (McNaughton rev. 1961). See § 111 infra.

22. Jayne v. Bateman, 191 Okl. 272, 129 P.2d 188 (1942) (lawyer appointed as guardian ad litem of incompetent party apparently expected to act as attorney also).

23. Steiner v. United States, 134 F.2d 931 (5th Cir. 1943).

24. 8 Wigmore, Evidence § 2376 (McNaughton rev. 1961).

25. Authority is scanty. People v. Pratt, 133 Mich. 125, 94 N.W. 752, 67 L.R.A. 923 (1903) tends to support the privilege. Of opposite tendency are People v. Sharac, 209 Mich. 249, 176 N.W. 431 (1920); Agnew v. Agnew, 52 S.D. 472, 218 N.W. 633 (1928), and Lindsey v. People, cited in n. 27, infra.

26. Prichard v. United States, 181 F.2d 326 (6th Cir. 1950), affirmed 339 U.S. 974 (communications between

judge and attorney seeking legal advice concerning his conduct which was to be investigated by a grand jury called by the judge to investigate election frauds, not privileged and attorney-client relationship did not arise).

27. 66 Colo. 343, 181 P. 531, 16 A.L.R. 768 (1919) (three judges dissenting), 33 Harv.L.Rev. 88, 35 id. 693, 29 Yale L.J. 356, 4 Minn.L.Rev. 227; State v. Bixby, 27 Wn.2d 144, 177 P.2d 689 (1947).

28. The continuing strength of the court's argument by analogy will, of course depend on the future of the parent-child privilege. See supra § 76.

29. The special nature of juvenile court proceedings with respect to the need for confidentiality of reports and records is recognized by modern juvenile court statutes. See statutes set out in 8 Wigmore, Evidence § 2376 n. 3 (McNaughton rev. 1961).

Cases recognizing the application of the informer's privilege for information given to judges (see cases pro and con collected in Annot., 59 A.L.R. 1555) are to be distinguished.

§ 89. Subject-Matter of the Privilege—
(a) Communications

The modern justification of the privilege, namely, that of encouraging full disclosure by the client for the furtherance of the administration of justice,[1] might suggest that the privilege is only a one-way one, operating to protect communications of the client or his agents [2] to the lawyer or his clerk [3] but not vice versa. However, it is generally held that the privilege will protect at least those attorney to client communications which would have a tendency to reveal the confidences of the client.[4] In fact, only rarely will the attorney's words be relevant for any purpose other than to show the client's communications circumstantially, or to establish an admission by the client by his fail-

ure to object.[5] Accordingly, the simpler and preferable rule, adopted by a number of statutes and the Revised Uniform Evidence Rules (1974)[6] and by the better reasoned cases,[7] extends the protection of the privilege also to communications by the lawyer to the client.

An even more embracive view, adopted by statute in a few states,[8] would protect against disclosure by the attorney of any knowledge he has gained while acting as such, even information obtained from sources other than the client. Such an extension finds no justification in modern day policy, and perhaps is a carry-over from the days when the privilege was thought of as primarily for the protection of the honor of the profession. In any event, the more widely prevailing rule does not bar divul-

§ 89

1. See § 87 supra.

2. Anderson v. Bank of British Columbia [1876] L.R. 2, Ch.D. 644 (Ct.App.); Wheeler v. Le Marchant [1881] L.R. 17, Ch.D. 675 (Ct.App.); State v. 62.96247 Acres of Land in New Castle County, 193 A.2d 799 (Del.Super.1963) (expert appraiser employed by client who aided attorney in preparation of case barred by privilege from testifying for opponents); Annot., 139 A.L.R. 1250; Note, 1943 Wis.L.Rev. 424.

3. United States v. Kovel, 296 F.2d 918 (2d Cir. 1961) (statements to accountant in employ of attorney); State v. Krich, 123 N.J.L. 519, 9 A.2d 803 (1939) (communication to attorney's secretary); Wigmore, Evidence § 2301 (McNaughton rev. 1961); Annot., 53 A.L.R. 369.

4. Matter of Fischel, 557 F.2d 209 (9th Cir. 1977).

5. A defamatory statement made by the lawyer in declining employment and sought to be proved solely as a basis for an action against the lawyer for slander was held privileged in Minter v. Priest, [1929] 1 K.B. 655. It is criticized as unwarranted by the policy of the privilege in a Note, 43 Harv.L.Rev. 134.

Communications upon their respective clients' business between counsel defending them against a common charge have been said to be within the privilege. Continental Oil Co. v. United States, 330 F.2d 347, 9 A.L.R.3d 1413 (9th Cir. 1964) (exchange of confidential memoranda between counsel for several clients summoned before grand jury investigating antitrust violations); In re Felton, 60 Idaho 540, 94 P.2d 166 (1939); C.J.S. Witnesses § 276e; Annot., 9 A.L.R.3d 1420.

Rev.Unif.R.Evid. (1974) 502(b)(3), dealing with "pooled information" cases, is set forth in note 6 infra.

See also Missouri, Kansas & Texas Railway Co. v. Williams, 43 Tex.Civ.App. 549, 96 S.W. 1087 (1906) (general counsel of railway writes to local attorney).

United States v. United Shoe Machinery Corp., 89 F.Supp. 357 (privilege extends to communications to and from corporation's outside counsel or general counsel and staff and employees in its patent department); General Accident Fire & Life Assurance Corp. v. Mitchell, 128 Colo. 11, 259 P.2d 862 (1953) (order for production of all correspondence between home office and local counsel and local agents and all telegrams and written memoranda between home office, its attorneys and agents and insured, should have been denied on ground of privilege).

6. See, statutes set out in 8 Wigmore, Evidence § 2292 n. 2 (McNaughton rev. 1961.)

Rev.Unif.R.Evid. (1974) 502:

(b) General Rule of Privilege. A client has a privilege to refuse to disclose and to prevent any other person from disclosing confidential communications made for the purpose of facilitating the rendition of professional legal services to the client, (1) between himself and his representative and his lawyer or his lawyer's representative, or (2) between his lawyer and the lawyer's representative, or (3) by him or his lawyer to a lawyer representing another in a matter of common interest, or (4) between representatives of the client or between the client and a representative of the client.

7. United States v. Amerada Hess Corp., 619 F.2d 980 (3d Cir. 1980); In re LTV Securities Litigation, 89 F.R.D. 595 (N.D.Tex.1981) (strongly criticizing rule that attorney-client communications are protected only where revelatory of client confidence on grounds that all attorney advice tends to reveal client communications, that rule does not recognize fact-gathering role of attorney, and that narrower rule makes scope of privilege uncertain); In re Navarro, 93 Cal.App.3d 325, 155 Cal.Rptr. 522 (1979) (applying California statute).

8. See statutes quoted in 8 Wigmore, Evidence § 2292, n. 2 (McNaughton rev. 1961).

gence by the attorney of information communicated to him or his agents by third persons.[9] Nor does information so obtained become privileged by being in turn related by the attorney to the client in the form of advice.[10]

The commonly imposed limitation of protection to communications passing between client and attorney, while logically derived from the policy rationale of the privilege, does raise certain problems of construction where the information acquired by the attorney does not come in the conventional form of oral or written assertions by the client. Initially it is fairly easy to conclude, as most authority holds, that observations by the lawyer which might be made by anyone, and which involve no communicative intent by the client, are not protected.[11] Conversely, testimony relating intentionally communicative acts of the client, as where he rolls up his sleeve to reveal a hidden scar or opens the drawer of his desk to display a revolver, would as clearly be precluded as would the recounting of statements conveying the same information. Much more problematic are cases in which the client delivers tangi-

ble evidence such as stolen property to the attorney, or confides facts enabling the attorney to come into the possession of such evidence. Here the decisions are somewhat conflicting,[12] reflecting the virtual impossibility of separating the act of confidence which may legitimately be within the privilege from the preexisting evidentiary fact which may not. To resolve the dilemma, one carefully reasoned argument is that the privilege should not operate to bar the attorney's disclosure of the circumstances of acquisition,[13] since to preclude the attorney's testimony would offer the client a uniquely safe opportunity to divest himself of incriminating evidence without leaving an evidentiary trail.[14]

Difficulties also arise in applying the communications-only theory when one assisting the lawyer, e.g., an examining physician, learns and communicates to the lawyer matters not known to the client. The privilege seems to apply with respect to the communication itself. If the physician is considered as aligned with the client, his knowledge would be that of the client and not privileged; but if aligned with the lawyer, the

9. Matter of Walsh, 623 F.2d 489 (7th Cir. 1980), cert. denied 449 U.S. 994; Morrell v. State, 575 P.2d 1200 (Alaska 1978).

10. Giordani v. Hoffmann, 278 F.Supp. 886 (E.D.Pa. 1968).

11. United States v. Pipkins, 528 F.2d 559 (5th Cir. 1976), cert. denied 426 U.S. 952 (identification of physical characteristics readily observable by anyone not within privilege); Clark v. Skinner, 334 Mo. 1190, 70 S.W.2d 1094 (1934) (attorney's knowledge of client's mental capacity and of want of any undue influence and that deeds were delivered, not privileged); State v. Fitzgerald, 68 Vt. 125, 34 A. 429 (1896) (attorney's testimony to client's intoxication, observable by all, not privileged); 8 Wigmore, Evidence § 2306 (McNaughton rev. 1961).

12. The privilege is not generally viewed as affording the attorney license to withhold evidence from the judicial system. See In re January 1976 Grand Jury, 534 F.2d 719 (7th Cir. 1976) (privilege not applicable to resist subpoena for money, turned over to attorney by clients suspected of bank robbery); In re Ryder, 263 F.Supp. 360 (E.D.Va.1967), affirmed 381 F.2d 713 (4th Cir.) (attorney suspended from practice for taking possession of gun and money and secreting them in safe deposit box pending termination of trial); State ex rel. Sowers v. Olwell, 64 Wn.2d 828, 394 P.2d 681 (1964).

As to the question whether the attorney must divulge his source, compare State v. Douglass, 20 W.Va. 770 (1882) (counsel's testimony that he received pistol from client, privileged) and Anderson v. State, 297 So.2d 871 (Fla.App.1974) (delivery of stolen merchandise to attorney's receptionist by defendant was privileged communication) with Hughes v. Meade, 453 S.W.2d 538 (Ky.1970) (lawyer required to divulge identity of person delivering stolen property to him). And see People v. Meredith, 29 Cal.3d 682, 175 Cal.Rptr. 612 (1981) in which defendant told attorney that he had burned murder victim's wallet and placed it in a trash can, and attorney sent investigator to retrieve wallet. The court held that while the initial communication was within the privilege, once the attorney sent the investigator to retrieve the property the testimony of the latter concerning the location and condition of the property was unprotected. Noted critically in 70 Calif.L.Rev. 1048 (1982).

13. Saltzburg, Communications Falling Within the Attorney-Client Privilege, 66 Iowa L.Rev. 811 (1981)

14. Id. at 838. "Only by having the lawyer transfer the evidence to the government for her is the client able to 'launder' the evidence—that is, remove it from her possession and place it in the hands of the government without having the government connect it up with its source."

privilege seems to apply, as held in the leading case.[15]

The application of the privilege to writings presents practical problems requiring discriminating analysis. A professional communication in writing, as a letter from client to lawyer for example, will of course be privileged.[16] These written privileged communications are steadily to be distinguished from preexisting documents or writings, such as deeds, wills, and warehouse receipts, not in themselves constituting communications between client and lawyer. As to these preexisting documents two notions come into play. First, the client may make communications about the document by words or by acts, such as sending the document to the lawyer for perusal or handing it to him and calling attention to its terms. These communications, and the knowledge of the terms and appearance of the documents which the lawyer gains thereby are privileged from disclosure by testimony in court.[17] Second, on a different footing entirely stands the question, shall a lawyer who has been entrusted with the possession of a document by his client be subject to an order of court requiring him to produce the document at the trial or in pretrial discovery proceedings whether for inspection or for use in evidence? The policy of encouraging full disclosure does of course apply to encouraging the client to apprise his lawyer of the terms of all relevant documents, and the disclosure itself and the lawyer's knowledge gained thereby as we have seen are privileged. It is true also that placing the documents in the lawyer's hands is the most convenient means of disclosure. But the next step, that of adding to the privilege for communications a privilege against production of the preexisting documents themselves, when they would be subject to production if still in the possession of the client, would be an intolerable obstruction to justice. To prevent the court's gaining access to a relevant document a party would only have to send it to his lawyer. So here this principle is controlling: if a document would be subject to an order for production if it were in the hands of the client it will be equally subject to such an order if it is in the hands of his attorney.[18] An opposite conclusion would serve the policy of encouraging the client to make full disclosure to his lawyer right enough, but reasonable encouragement is given by the privilege for communications *about* documents, and the price of an additional privilege would be intolerably high. There are other doctrines which may impel a court to recognize a privilege against production of a

15. City and County of San Francisco v. Superior Court, 37 Cal.2d 227, 231 P.2d 26 (1951). Unless this is regarded as privileged, Fed.R.Civ.P. 26(b)(4)(B) seems to permit discovery in such case if hardship is shown. Distinguish the situation of the expert who examines for the purpose of testifying, thus contemplating disclosure and eliminating the privilege. See § 91, n. 6 infra.

16. Peyton v. Werhane, 126 Conn. 382, 11 A.2d 800 (1940).

An interesting case presented the question whether confidential letters of the client were usable, not as evidence of their contents but as specimens for comparison by expert witnesses with an anonymous letter charged to have been written by the client. People v. Smith, 318 Ill. 114, 149 N.E. 3 (1925) (not privileged against use for this purpose).

17. Wheatley v. Williams, 1 M. & W. 533, 150 Eng. Rep. 546 (Exch.1836) (attorney not required to testify whether paper shown him by client bore a stamp); United States v. Hankins, 631 F.2d 360 (5th Cir. 1980)

(tax counsel not required to reveal which books of client's he had examined).

But the act of the execution of a document by the client in the lawyer's presence is not ordinarily intended as a confidential communication and thus is usually not privileged. Chapman v. Peebles, 84 Ala. 283, 4 So. 273 (1888). *A fortiori*, when the attorney signs as a witness and takes the acknowledgment of the client as a notary. McCaw v. Hartman, 190 Okl. 264, 122 P.2d 999 (1942).

18. Fisher v. United States, 425 U.S. 391 (1976); Sovereign Camp v. Reed, 208 Ala. 457, 94 So. 910 (1922); Andrews v. Railway Co., 14 Ind. 169, 174 (1860); Palatini v. Sarian, 15 N.J.Super. 34, 83 A.2d 24 (1951); Pearson v. Yoder, 39 Okl. 105, 134 Pac. 421, 48 L.R.A.,N.S., 334 (1913); 8 Wigmore, Evidence § 2307 (McNaughton rev. 1961).

And as a necessary incident the attorney may be required to testify whether he has possession of such a document of the client. Guiterman, Rosenfield & Co. v. Culbreth, 219 Ala. 382, 122 So. 619 (1929).

preexisting document,[19] but not the doctrine of privilege for lawyer-client communications.

WESTLAW REFERENCES

privilege* /p attorney lawyer client /p produc! /p document* /p preexist!

---

§ 90. Subject-Matter of the Privilege— (b) Fact of Employment and Identity of the Client

When a client consults an attorney for a legitimate purpose, he will seldom, but may occasionally, desire to keep secret the very fact of consultation or employment of the lawyer. Nevertheless, consultation and employment are something more than a mere private or personal engagement. They are

19. See § 96 infra.

§ 90

1. Behrens v. Hironimus, 170 F.2d 627 (4th Cir. 1948). See authorities collected in 8 Wigmore, Evidence § 2313 (McNaughton rev. 1961); C.J.S. Witnesses § 283e; Annot., 16 A.L.R.3d 1047.

2. Behrens v. Hironimus, 170 F.2d 627 (4th Cir. 1948); Tomlinson v. United States, 68 App.D.C. 106, 93 F.2d 652, 114 A.L.R. 1315 (1937) (robbery: one of the defendants, a lawyer, testified on direct, that a codefendant was brought into his office by "a client," held, he was properly required on cross-examination to identify the client); United States v. Pape, 144 F.2d 778 (2d Cir. 1944) (prosecution for violation of Mann Act; lawyer-witness properly allowed to be asked by prosecution whether accused employed him to represent the woman whom he was charged with transporting and himself; Learned Hand, Cir. J., dissenting); In re Richardson, 31 N.J. 391, 157 A.2d 695 (1960) (attorney-client relation does not privilege lawyer from disclosing the identity of the person who retained him, or of the person who paid his fee); People ex rel. Vogelstein v. Warden of County Jail, 150 Misc. 714, 270 N.Y.S. 362 (S.Ct. Sp.T.1934, affirmed without opinion, 242 App.Div. 611, 271 N.Y.S. 1059) (attorney who entered appearance for fifteen defendants charged with violation of gambling laws, required in grand jury investigation to testify as to whether one person, the man behind the scene, had not employed him to act for all these defendants; opinion by Shientag, J., is the best on the question); Priest v. Hennessy, 51 N.Y.2d 62, 431 N.Y.S.2d 511, 409 N.E.2d 110 (1980) (privilege inapplicable to prevent disclosure of identity of person paying attorney to represent prostitutes; strong dissent); In re Illidge, 162 Or. 303, 91 P.2d 1100 (1939) (attorney accused in disbarment proceedings properly compelled to testify as to identity and residence of client for whom he had entered appearance as counsel in a lawsuit).

the calling into play of the services of an officer licensed by the state to act in certain ways in furtherance of the administration of justice, and vested with powers of giving advice on the law, of drafting documents, and of filing pleadings and motions and appearing in court for his client, which are limited to this class of officers.

Does the privilege for confidential communications extend to the fact of consulting or employing such an officer, when intended to be confidential? The traditional and still generally applicable rule denies the privilege for the fact of consultation or employment,[1] including the component facts of the identity of the client,[2] such identifying facts about him as his address and occupation,[3] the identity of the lawyer,[4] and the scope or object [5] of the employment.[6]

3. United States v. Lee, 107 F. 702 (E.D.N.Y.1901); Falkenhainer v. Falkenhainer, 198 Misc. 29, 97 N.Y.S.2d 467 (1950); Dike v. Dike, 75 Wn.2d 1, 448 P.2d 490 (1968) (whereabouts of client who had possession of child in violation of custody order); Annot., 114 A.L.R. 1328.

4. Tomlinson v. United States, supra n. 2.

5. Howell v. Jones, 516 F.2d 53 (5th Cir. 1975), rehearing denied 521 F.2d 815, cert. denied 424 U.S. 916, rehearing denied 425 U.S. 945; Goddard v. United States, 131 F.2d 220 (5th Cir. 1942).

6. Upon an issue as to whether some act done by the attorney was authorized, the attorney may testify as to the terms of employment. In re Michaelson, 511 F.2d 882 (9th Cir. 1976) (attorney's authority to file public document; no privilege); Pacific Telephone & Telegraph Co. v. Fink, 141 Cal.App.2d 332, 296 P.2d 843 (1956) (authority to enter into stipulation under which default judgment was taken); Sachs v. Title Insurance & Trust Co., 305 Ky. 153, 202 S.W.2d 384 (1947) (on question whether defendant in prior judgment was before court, attorney who appeared for her can testify to employment to defend suit); Kentucky-Virginia Stages v. Tackett, 298 Ky. 78, 182 S.W.2d 226 (1944) (whether one of attorneys in instant case was authorized to file motion for new trial); Coley v. Hall, 206 Ark. 419, 175 S.W.2d 979 (1943) (client claimed attorney who filed suit was unauthorized); Falkenhainer v. Falkenhainer, 198 Misc. 29, 97 N.Y.S.2d 467 (1950).

It may be, however, that when the object of the employment is not directly in issue but only circumstantially relevant, the testimony would be limited to a more general statement of purpose. See Chirac v. Reinicker, 11 Wheat. (U.S.) 280 (1826) (in action for mesne profits, court intimated that attorneys·could be asked whether they appeared in former ejectment suit for one of present defendants, but questioned whether they could be asked if they were employed by him to

Several reasons have been advanced as a basis for denying protection to the client's identity, most notably that "the mere fact of the engagement of counsel is out of the rule [of privilege] because the privilege and duty of silence do not arise until the fact is ascertained."[7] Additionally, it is said that a party to legal proceedings is entitled to know the identity of the adversary who is putting in motion or staying the machinery of the court.[8] Such propositions, however, shed little light on the real issue, i.e., whether client anonymity is in some cases essential to obtaining the proper objectives of the privilege.

In recent years many courts, largely influenced by the leading decision in Baird v. Koerner[9] have recognized that the rule excluding client identity from the protection of the privilege is not an inflexible one. Thus exceptions to the general rule have been made[10] where disclosure would "provide a link in an existing chain of inculpatory events or would implicate the client in the very criminal activity for which legal advice was sought, or [where] so much of the actu-

al communication has already been disclosed that identification of the client would amount to a disclosure of a confidential communication."[11] Similarly, some courts have under certain circumstances been willing to accord protection to other client facts such as location and occupation.[12]

It is arguable that the decisions following Baird, though introducing a wholesome flexibility into the general rule, have nevertheless blazed a false trail in making the exceptions to the rule turn largely upon the severity of potential harm to the client[13] rather than upon the question whether the protection afforded works in aid of a legitimate function of the attorney in his professional role.[14] Thus it has been suggested that the agencies performed by attorneys in some of the cases presenting the issue were neither part of the attorney's unique role nor appropriate for immunization from public disclosure and scrutiny. One who reviews the cases in this area will be struck by the prevailing flavor of chicanery and sharp practice pervading most of the attempts to suppress proof of professional employment,

conduct the suit for him as landlord of the premises); Stephens v. Mattox, 37 Ga. 289 (1867) (similar; whether employed by plaintiff to sue for him individually or in his right as administrator).

7. Shientag, J. in People v. Warden, 270 N.Y.S. at 369 cited n. 2, supra. But the party propounding the question as to the identity of the client may state and assume that the relationship exists, so that there is no need to establish it. In re Shawmut Mining Co., 94 App.Div. 156, 87 N.Y.S. 1059, 1062 (1904).

8. "Every litigant is in justice entitled to know the identity of his opponents." 8 Wigmore, Evidence § 2313 (McNaughton rev. 1961).

9. 279 F.2d 623 (9th Cir. 1960). The Baird decision upheld a claim of privilege by an attorney who had mailed a check for back taxes to the IRS on behalf of an anonymous client. The case is noted in 49 Calif.L. Rev. 382 (1961); 39 Tex.L.Rev. 512 (1961); 47 Va.L. Rev. 126 (1961).

10. NLRB v. Harvey, 264 F.Supp. 770 (W.D.Va. 1966) on remand from 349 F.2d 990 (4th Cir. 1965) (identity of client held within privilege in National Labor Relations Board proceedings where an attorney not connected with the case under investigation employed a private investigator to keep a union organizer under surveillance at request of a client who was a business competitor of the employer in the NLRB proceeding); In re Grand Jury Proceedings, 517 F.2d 666 (5th Cir.

1975), rehearing denied 521 F.2d 815 (privilege allowed to prevent disclosure of persons who had retained attorneys to represent defendants at trial where probable consequence of disclosure would have been that fees paid exceeded reported incomes of payors); Tillotson v. Boughner, 350 F.2d 663 (7th Cir. 1965) (similar to Baird).

11. Larkin, Federal Testimonial Privileges 2–25 (1982).

12. In re Stoler, 397 F.Supp. 520 (S.D.N.Y.1975); Brennan v. Brennan, 281 Pa.Super. 362, 422 A.2d 510 (1980).

13. See State v. Bean, 239 N.W.2d 556 (Iowa 1976) (identity of client privileged in exceptional cases where disclosure could harm client).

14. Saltzburg, Communications Falling Within the Attorney-Client Privilege, 66 Iowa L.Rev. 811, 823 (1981) ("It is a different matter . . . when the client seeks to have the lawyer perform an act as the client's agent that would be subject to scrutiny by courts if performed by other agents—for example, transmitting money from the client to someone else—without the lawyer having to reveal the identity of the principal. In this type of case, the concealment of identity would tend to allow persons to engage in activities that ordinarily would be subject to inquiry and to insulate themselves from otherwise proper scrutiny.").

and general application of a rule of disclosure seems the approach most consonant with the preservation of the repute of the lawyer's high calling.[15] At the same time, much should depend upon the client's objective in seeking preservation of anonymity, and cases will arise in which protection of the client's identity is both proper and in the public interest.[16]

 WESTLAW REFERENCES

baird koerner   /15 279 /5 623

---

§ 91. The Confidential Character of the Communications: Presence of Third Persons and Agents: Joint Consultations and Employments: Controversies Between Client and Attorney

It is of the essence of the privilege that it is limited to those communications which the client either expressly made confidential or which he could reasonably assume under the circumstances would be understood by the attorney as so intended. This common law requirement seems to be read into those statutes which codify the privilege without mentioning the confidentiality requirement.[1] A mere showing that the communication was from client to attorney does not suffice, but the circumstances indicating the intention of secrecy must appear.[2] Wherever the matters communicated to the attorney are intended by the client to be made public or revealed to third persons, obviously the element of confidentiality is wanting.[3] Similarly, if the same statements have been made by the client to third persons on other occasions this is persuasive that like communications to the lawyer were not intended as confidential.[4]

Questions as to the effect of the presence of persons other than the client and the lawyer often arise. At the extremes answers would be clear. Presumably the presence of a casual disinterested third person within

---

15. "The conclusion reached would seem to be inevitable, if we are to maintain the honor of the profession, and make an officer of the court an agency to advance the ends of justice, rather than to be used as an instrument to subvert them. The identity of an employer or client who retains a lawyer to act for him or for others in a civil or criminal proceeding should not be veiled in mystery. The dangers of disclosure are shadowy and remote; the evils of concealment are patent and overwhelming. As between the two social policies competing for supremacy, the choice is clear. Disclosure should be made if we are to maintain confidence in the bar and in the administration of justice." Shientag, J. in People v. Warden, supra n. 2, 270 N.Y.S. at p. 371.

16. In re Kaplan, 8 N.Y.2d 214, 168 N.E.2d 660, 203 N.Y.S.2d 836 (1960) (client's communication to attorney for purpose of disclosing wrongdoing by others communicated by attorney to public officials held to justify protection of identity of client), 10 Buffalo L.Rev. 364 (1961), 46 Iowa L.Rev. 904 (1961), 59 Mich.L.Rev. 791 (1961), 12 Syracuse L.Rev. 408 (1961).

§ 91

1. See statutes, privileging "communications" generally, quoted in 8 Wigmore, Evidence § 2292, note 2 (McNaughton rev. 1961).

2. Gardner v. Irvin, L.R.Exch.Div. 49, 53 (1878); Hiltpold v. Stern, 82 A.2d 123, 26 A.L.R.2d 852 (D.C. Mun.App.1951).

3. United States v. Tellier, 255 F.2d 441 (2d Cir. 1958), 37 Texas L.Rev. 337 (attorney's advice to client where client expected attorney to prepare letter to third person setting forth his objections); Wilcoxon v. United States, 231 F.2d 384 (10th Cir. 1956), cert. denied 851 U.S. 943 (private directions by client to attorney on preliminary hearing that he should propound certain questions to witness, not privileged); Himmelfarb v. United States, 175 F.2d 924 (9th Cir. 1949), cert. denied 338 U.S. 860 (disclosures to accountant by attorney, impliedly authorized by client under special circumstances of previous meetings with accountant concerning income taxes and client's knowledge of accountant's employment with attorney); Hill v. Hill, 106 Colo. 492, 107 P.2d 597 (1940) (letters by wife to attorney giving data on alimony in arrears, with intention that he should present the information to delinquent husband); Spencer v. Burns, 413 Ill. 420, 108 N.E.2d 413 (1952) (statement of true marital status made by client for purpose of transmission to seller and examiner of title to property client wished to purchase); People v. Doe, 59 Ill.App.3d 627, 16 Ill.Dec. 868, 375 N.E.2d 975 (1978) (suicide note found and delivered to attorney by relatives not intended to be confidential); Clayton v. Canida, 223 S.W.2d 264 (Tex. Civ.App.1949) (information given to attorney for use in preparing income tax return for transmittal to Internal Revenue Department); Anderson v. Thomas, 108 Utah 252, 159 P.2d 142 (1945) (suit to cancel deed of deceased for mental incapacity, testimony of attorney that deceased asked him to arrange for bank not to cash his checks without attorney's approval, not privileged).

4. Solon v. Lichtenstein, 39 Cal.2d 75, 244 P.2d 907 (1952); Bryan v. Barnett, 205 Ga. 94, 52 S.E.2d 613 (1949); Travelers Indemnity Co. v. Cochrane, 155 Ohio St. 305, 98 N.E.2d 840 (1951).

hearing to the client's knowledge would demonstrate that the communication was not intended to be confidential.[5] On the other hand if the help of an interpreter is necessary to enable the client to consult the lawyer his presence would not deprive the communication of its confidential and privileged character.[6] Moreover, in cases where the client has one of his agents attend the conference,[7] or the lawyer calls in his clerk [8] or confidential secretary,[9] the presence of these intermediaries will be assumed not to militate against the confidential nature of the consultation, and presumably this would not be made to depend upon whether the presence of the agent, clerk or secretary was in the particular instance reasonably necessary to the matter in hand.[10] It is the way business is generally done and that is enough. As to relatives and friends of the client, the results of the cases are not consistent,[11] but it seems that here not only might

5. Mason v. Mason, 231 S.W. 971 (Mo.1921); Re Quick's Estate, 161 Wash. 537, 297 P. 198 (1931), and cases collected in 8 Wigmore, Evidence § 2311, note 6 (McNaughton rev. 1961); C.J.S. Witnesses § 290; Note, 36 Mich.L.Rev. 641 (1938); Annot., 96 A.L.R.2d 125.

In the case of persons overhearing without the knowledge of the client, it seems that the more reasonable view if there is to be any privilege at all, would protect the client against disclosure, unless he has failed to use ordinary precautions against overhearing, but the cases permit the eavesdropper to speak. Van Horn v. Commonwealth, 239 Ky. 833, 40 S.W.2d 372 (1931), and see Perry v. State, 4 Idaho 224, 38 P. 655 (1894) (court mentions want of precaution); Schwartz v. Wenger, 267 Minn. 40, 124 N.W.2d 489 (1963) (conversation between client and attorney in public corridor of courthouse overheard by third person, held not privileged). But Rev.Unif.R.Evid. 502(b) allows the client to prevent disclosure by third persons who overhear communications intended to be confidential. See n. 10 supra.

6. Du Barre v. Linette, Peake 108, 170 Eng.Rep. 96 (N.P.1791); State v. Loponio, 85 N.J.L. 357, 88 A. 1045 (1913).

In United States v. Kovel, 296 F.2d 918 (2d Cir. 1961), the court relied upon the analogy of an interpreter, in applying the privilege to an accountant employed by the lawyer to assist in the litigation.

7. In re Busse's Estate, 332 Ill.App. 258, 75 N.E. 36, 38 (1947) (client's agent who was nurse and business caretaker present at conference with attorney); Foley v. Poschke, 137 Ohio St. 593, 31 N.E.2d 845 (1941) (detective employed by divorce plaintiff to investigate husband's conduct present at conference with lawyer).

Of course, the presence of additional counsel to participate in the consultation does not detract from confidentiality. Dickerson v. Dickerson, 322 Ill. 492, 153 N.E. 740 (1926).

8. Sibley v. Wopple, 16 N.Y. 180 (1857); Hunt v. Taylor, 22 Vt. 556 (1850); Annot., 96 A.L.R.2d 125, 133.

A substantial number of state statutes provide that communications to the employees of the attorney are privileged. See statutes collected and quoted, 8 Wigmore, Evidence § 2292, note 2 (McNaughton rev. 1961). And disclosures to a physician employed by the client's attorney to examine the client have been held subject to the attorney-client privilege. City & County of San Francisco v. Superior Court, 37 Cal.2d 227, 231 P.2d 26 (1951); Annot., 96 A.L.R.2d 159, 160.

A law student in the office is not within the rule, unless he acts as clerk. Wartell v. Navograd, 48 R.I. 296, 137 A. 776, 53 A.L.R. 365 (1927).

9. Taylor v. Taylor, 179 Ga. 691, 693, 177 S.E. 582 (1934) ("Under modern practice of law the business of an attorney in most offices cannot be conducted without such an assistant;" Ga.Code, § 38–419, however, expressly extended privilege to communications to attorney "or his clerk"). A Texas case would seemingly give the privilege only when the secretary or stenographer is the medium of communication. Otherwise, the court suggests "it could as well be claimed that the rule would extend to the employee, who swept the attorney's floor." Morton v. Smith, 44 S.W. 683, 684 (Tex.Civ.App.1898) (stenographer allowed to testify to statements made by client to attorney).

10. But see Morton v. Smith, supra, and Himmelfarb v. United States, 175 F.2d 924 (9th Cir. 1949) (testimony of accountant employed as attorney's agent, not privileged where his presence at conference with client was not indispensably necessary to communication between attorney and client). Compare United States v. Kovel, n. 6 supra.

Under Rev.Unif.R.Evid. (1974) 502(a)(5) a communication is confidential "if not intended to be disclosed to third persons other than those to whose disclosure is made in furtherance of the rendition of professional legal services to the client or those reasonably necessary for the transmission of the communication." See Adv. Comm. Note to proposed Fed.Rule Evid. 503 (not enacted), 56 F.R.D. 237.

11. United States v. Bigos, 459 F.2d 639 (1st Cir. 1972), cert. denied 409 U.S. 847 (privilege upheld for communication in presence of client's father; presence of 3rd persons only indicative of non-confidentiality, not determinative); Cafritz v. Koslow, 167 F.2d 749 (D.C.Cir. 1948) (sister accompanies brother, client, to attorney's office; "There was no identity of interest between [brother and sister] nor can it be said that [sister] stood in relation of agent to [brother]"); Baldwin v. Commissioner of Internal Revenue, 125 F.2d 812, (9th Cir. 1942) (son accompanied mother to conferences with her attorney over proposed transfer of some of her property to son, held presence of son did not destroy privilege but chiefly on ground that it was joint consultation in which son was interested); Smith v. State, 204 Ga. 184, 47 S.E. 579 (1948) (murder prosecu-

it be asked whether the client reasonably understood the conference to be confidential but also whether the presence of the relative or friend was reasonably necessary for the protection of the client's interests in the particular circumstances.[12]

When two or more persons, each having an interest in some problem, or situation, jointly consult an attorney, their confidential communications with the attorney, though known to each other, will of course be privileged in a controversy of either or both of the clients with the outside world, that is, with parties claiming adversely to both or either of those within the original charmed circle.[13] But it will often happen that the two original clients will fall out between themselves and become engaged in a controversy in which the communications at their joint consultation with the lawyer may be vitally material. In such a controversy it is clear that the privilege is inapplicable. In the first place the policy of encouraging disclo-

sure by holding out the promise of protection seems inapposite, since as between themselves neither would know whether he would be more helped or handicapped, if in any dispute between them, both could invoke the shield of secrecy. And secondly, it is said that they had obviously no intention of keeping these secrets from each other, and hence as between themselves it was not intended to be confidential. In any event, it is a qualification of frequent application[14] and of even wider potentiality, not always recognized. Thus, in the situation mentioned in the previous paragraph where a client calls into the conference with the attorney one of the client's agents, and matters are discussed which bear on the agent's rights against the client, it would seem that in a subsequent controversy between client and agent, the limitation on the privilege accepted in the joint consultation cases should furnish a controlling analogy.[15]

---

tion, evidence of what was said in conference with attorney by wife of defendant, when deceased was present, held privileged, without discussion); Bowers v. State, 29 Ohio St. 542, 546 (1876) (prosecution for seduction of girl under eighteen; girl's statements at conference with attorney consulted about bastardy proceedings against defendant held privileged despite presence of girl's mother).

12. Compare the remarks of the court in Bowers v. State, in the preceding note: "We think it is only a dictate of decency and propriety to regard the mother in such a case as being present and acting in the character of confidential agent of her daugher. The daughter's youth and supposed modesty would render the participation of her mother appropriate and necessary." 29 Ohio St. at 546.

13. People v. Abair, 102 Cal.App.2d 765, 228 P.2d 336 (1951); In re Selser, 27 N.J.Super. 259, 99 A.2d 313 (1953); State v. Archuleta, 29 N.M. 25, 217 P. 619 (1923) and cases cited in Annot., 141 A.L.R. 562 (communication privileged as against the state in a criminal case, although parties fell out and one acts as witness against others); Minard v. Stillman, 31 Or. 164, 49 P. 976 (1897); Vance v. State, 190 Tenn. 521, 230 S.W.2d 987, cert. den. 339 U.S. 988 (communications at conference between codefendants and their separate counsel in preparation of joint defense, privileged as against the state in a criminal case, but not privileged where one defendant makes no defense).

14. Grand Trunk Western Railroad Co. v. H. W. Nelson Co., 116 F.2d 823, rehearing denied 118 F.2d 252 (6th Cir. 1941); Re Bauer, 79 Cal. 304, 21 P. 759 (1889); Luthy v. Seaburn, 242 Iowa 184, 46 N.W.2d 44

(1951); Thompson v. Cashman, 181 Mass. 36, 62 N.E. 976 (1902); Wahl v. Cunningham, 320 Mo. 57, 6 S.W.2d 576, 67 A.L.R. 489 (1928); Jenkins v. Jenkins, 151 Neb. 113, 36 N.W.2d 635 (1949); Hurlburt v. Hurlburt, 128 N.Y. 420, 28 N.E. 651, 26 Am.St.Rep. 482 (1891); Emley v. Selepchak, 76 Ohio App. 257, 63 N.E.2d 919 (1945); and cases cited in 8 Wigmore, Evidence § 2312 (McNaughton rev. 1961); Annot., 141 A.L.R. 553.

It has been held that the beneficiary of a contract made by the jointly consulting clients at the conference or discusssed thereat, stands in the shoes of the parties and is entitled to disclosure. Allen v. Ross, 199 Wis. 162, 225 N.W. 831, 64 A.L.R. 180 (1929). So also as to personal representatives and others in privity. Hurlburt v. Hurlburt, supra (action by administrator of one client against administratrix of the other). Query as to judgment creditors, but seemingly they should be in like case. Annot., 141 A.L.R. 558.

The analogy to two persons consulting the same lawyer on a common matter has been invoked to deny a claim of privilege by management in stockholder's derivative suits with respect to communications between management and corporate counsel prior to the litigation. Garner v. Wolfinbarger, 430 F.2d 1093 (5th Cir. 1970); Pattie Lea, Inc. v. District Court, 161 Colo. 493, 423 P.2d 27 (1967) (accountant privilege). But see Note, 69 Colum.L.Rev. 309 (1969).

15. But in the only cases encountered in which this situation was presented the analogy was not discussed and the privilege was sustained against the agent. In re Busse's Estate and Foley v. Poschke, cited and described in note 7, supra. The Busse case is criticized

One step beyond the joint consultation where communications by two clients are made directly in each other's hearing is the situation where two parties separately interested in some contract or undertaking, as in the case of borrower and lender or insurer and insured, engage the same attorney to represent their respective interests, and each communicates separately with the attorney about some phase of the common transaction. Here again it seems that the communicating client, knowing that the attorney represents the other party also, would not ordinarily intend that the facts communicated should be kept secret from him.[16] Accordingly, the doctrine of limited confidentiality has been applied to communications by the insured under a liability insurance policy to the attorney employed by the insurance company to represent both the

company and the insured. A confidential statement made by the insured to the attorney, or to the insurer for the use of the attorney, would thus be privileged if sought to be introduced at the trial of the injured person's action against the insured,[17] but not in a controversy between the insured, or one claiming under him, and the company itself over the company's liability under the policy.[18]

The weight of authority seems to support the view that when client and attorney become embroiled in a controversy between themselves, as in an action by the attorney for compensation or by the client for damages for the attorney's negligence, the seal is removed from the attorney's lips.[19] Though sometimes rested upon other grounds [20] it seems that here again the notion that as between the participants in the

on this point in Note, 61 Harv.L.Rev. 717, and on another point in Note, 15 U.Chi.L.Rev. 989.

16. See, e.g., Gottwald v. Mettinger, 257 App.Div. 107, 12 N.Y.2d 241 (1939) (in suit on bond where attorney originally represented borrower and lender in arranging loan, statement of borrower to attorney of amount owed, not privileged.)

17. Vann v. State, 85 So.2d 133, (Fla.1956) (where policy required insurer to defend insured through its attorney, communications between the insured and insurer intended for the use of attorney, are privileged; Asbury v. Beerbower, 589 S.W.2d 216 (Ky.1979); State v. Pratt, 284 Md. 516, 398 A.2d 421 (1979); In re Klemann, 132 Ohio St. 187, 5 N.E.2d 492 (1936) (in suit of injured person, written statement made by insured to insurance company for transmittal to attorney held privileged).

But see Jacobi v. Podevels, 23 Wis.2d 152, 127 N.W. 2d 73 (1964) (statement by insured to adjuster for his insurer before commencement of action, not privileged).

18. Henke v. Iowa Home Mutual Casualty Co., 249 Iowa 614, 87 N.W.2d 920 (1958), 44 Iowa L.Rev. 215 (action by insured against insurer for negligent failure to settle claims against insured); Klefbeck v. Dous, 302 Mass. 383, 19 N.E.2d 308 (1939) (suit by injured party after judgment to subject policy to payment of judgment, defended by insurer on ground automobile not legally registered in state of issuance; held, plaintiff, claiming under insured, entitled to use letter of attorney, acting for both, to insurer); Travelers Indemnity Co. v. Cochrane, 155 Ohio St. 305, 98 N.E.2d 840 (1951); Shafer v. Utica Mutual Insurance Co., 248 App.Div. 279, 289 N.Y.S. 577 (1936) (action by injured party after judgment to subject policy to payment of judgment contested by company on ground of failure of insured to cooperate; held, company entitled to prove state-

ments of insured to joint attorney); Liberty Mutual Insurance Co. v. Engels, 41 Misc.2d 49, 244 N.Y.S.2d 983 (1963); Hoffman v. Labutzke, 233 Wis. 365, 289 N.W. 652 (1940) (on motion to set aside verdict against automobile liability insurer for damages to injured party, on ground of non-cooperation by insured, statement of insured to joint attorney not privileged); Annot., 22 A.L.R.2d 659, 662.

19. Sokol v. Mortimer, 81 Ill.App.2d 55, 225 N.E.2d 496 (1967) (attorney's suit for fee); Mave v. Baird, 12 Ind. 318 (1859) (suit by client for negligence); Weinshenk v. Sullivan, 100 S.W.2d 66 (Mo.App.1937) (attorney's suit for compensation); Stern v. Daniel, 47 Wash. 96, 91 P. 552 (1907) (lawyer's suit for fee; client's letters to lawyer not privileged though it discloses client's improper conduct. "They would have been privileged, no doubt as between either of the parties to this suit and third parties; but as between the attorney and client the rule of privilege will not be enforced where the client charges mismanagement of his cause by the attorney, as was the case here, and where it would be a manifest injustice to allow the client to take advantage of the rule of privilege to the prejudice of the attorney, or when it would be carried to the extent of depriving the attorney of the means of obtaining or defending his own rights."); State v. Markey, 259 Wis. 527, 49 N.W.2d 437 (1951).

Under Rev.Unif.R.Evid. (1974) 502(d)(3) there is no privilege as to "a communication relevant to a breach of duty by the lawyer to his client or by the client to his lawyer."

20. As that a contract for compensation is not a communication from the client, and is "collateral" to the professional relation. Strickland v. Capital City Mills, 74 S.C. 16, 54 S.E. 220, 7 L.R.A.,N.S., 426 (1906); Baskerville v. Baskerville, 246 Minn. 496, 75 N.W.2d 762 (1956).

conference the intention was to disclose and not to withhold the matters communicated offers a plausible reason.[21] As to what is a controversy between lawyer and client the decisions do not limit their holdings to litigations between them, but have said that whenever the client, even in litigation between third persons, makes an imputation against the good faith of his attorney in respect to his professional services, the curtain of privilege drops so far as necessary to enable the lawyer to defend his conduct.[22] Perhaps the whole doctrine, that in controversies between attorney and client the privilege is relaxed, may best be based upon the ground of practical necessity that if effective legal service is to be encouraged the privilege must not stand in the way of the lawyer's just enforcement of his rights to be paid a fee and to protect his reputation. The only question about such a principle is whether in all cases the privilege ought not to be subject to the same qualification, that it should yield when the evidence sought is necessary to the attainment of justice.

WESTLAW REFERENCES

attorney lawyer client /p communication* /p privilege* /p third-part*** secretary clerk paralegal assistant stenographer

When the client claims that the attorney has given incompetent advice the lawyer may testify as to the advice given. Leverich v. Leverich, 340 Mich. 133, 64 N.W.2d 567 (1954); Chase v. Chase, 78 R.I. 278, 81 A.2d 686 (1951).

21. Minard v. Stillman, 31 Or. 164, 49 P. 976 (1897); see 8 Wigmore, Evidence § 2312(2) (McNaughton rev. 1961).

22. Meyerhofer v. Empire Fire & Marine Insurance Co., 497 F.2d 1190 (2d Cir. 1974); Pierce v. Norton, 82 Conn. 441, 74 Atl. 686 (1909); Hyde v. State, 70 Ga. App. 823, 29 S.E.2d 820 (1944); Moore v. State, 231 Ind. 690, 111 N.E.2d 47 (1953); State v. Journey, 207 Neb. 717, 301 N.W.2d 82 (1981); Doll v. Loesel, 288 Pa. 527, 136 Atl. 796 (1927); Chase v. Chase, 78 R.I. 278, 81 A.2d 686 (1951).

§ 92. The Client as the Holder of the Privilege: Who May Assert, and Who Complain on Appeal of Its Denial?[1]

A rule regulating the *competency* of evidence or of witnesses—a so-called "exclusionary" rule—is normally founded on the policy of safeguarding the fact-finding process against error, and it is assertable by the party against whom the evidence is offered. The earmarks of a *privilege*, as we have seen, are first, that it is not designed to protect the fact-finding process but is intended to protect some "outside" interest, other than the ascertainment of truth at the trial, and second, that it cannot be asserted by the adverse party as such, but only by the person whose interest the particular rule of privilege is intended to safeguard.[2] While once it was conceived that the privilege was set up to protect the lawyer's honor, we know that today it is agreed that the basic policy of the rule is that of encouraging clients to lay the facts fully before their counsel. They will be encouraged by a privilege which they themselves have the power to invoke. To extend any benefit or advantage to someone as attorney, or as party to a suit, or to people generally, will be to suppress relevant evidence without promoting the purpose of the privilege.

Accordingly it is now generally agreed that the privilege is the client's and his alone, and Revised Uniform Rule (1974) 502(b) vests the privilege in the client.[3] It is thought that this would be recognized even

§ 92

1. See 8 Wigmore, Evidence § 232 (McNaughton rev. 1961); Note, 30 Colum.L.Rev. 686 (1930); 81 Am. Jur.2d Witnesses §§ 219, 220.

2. See the discussion in § 72, supra of the distinction between competency and privilege.

Of course, a party may be the holder of a privilege.

3. Among the many cases where this is recognized are Minter v. Priest, [1930] A.C. 558, 579 (By Lord Atkin: "That the right to have such communications so protected is the right of the client only. In this sense it is a 'privilege,' the privilege of the client"); Abbott v. Superior Court, 78 Cal.App.2d 19, 177 P.2d 317 (1947) (where client has no privilege because of his illegal purpose, attorney has none); Foster v. Hall, 12 Pick. (Mass.) 89 (1931); Russell v. Second National Bank, 136

in those states which, before modern notions of privilege and policy were adequately worked out, codified the rule in terms of inadmissibility of evidence of communications, or of incompetency of the attorney to testify thereto.[4] These statutes are generally held not to be intended to modify the common law doctrines.[5]

It is not surprising that the courts, often faced with statutes drafted in terms of obsolete theories, and reaching these points rarely and usually incidentally, have not worked out a consistent pattern of consequences of this accepted view that the rule is one of privilege and that the privilege is the client's. It is believed that the applications suggested below are well grounded in reason and are supported by some authority, whether of text or decision.

First, it is clear that the client may assert the privilege even though he is not a party to the cause wherein the privileged testimony is sought to be elicited.[6] Second, if he is present at the hearing whether as party, witness, or bystander he must assert the privilege personally or by attorney, or it will be waived.[7] Third, in some jurisdictions, if he is not present at the taking of testimony, nor a party to the proceedings, the privilege may be called to the court's attention by anyone present, such as the attorney[8] for the absent client, or a party in the case,[9] or the court of its own motion may protect the privilege.[10] Fourth: While if an asserted privilege is erroneously sustained, the aggrieved party may of course complain on appeal of the exclusion of the testimony, the erroneous denial of the privilege can only be complained of by the client whose privilege has been infringed. This opens the door to appellate review by the client if he is also a party and suffers adverse judgment.[11] If he

N.J.L. 270, 55 A.2d 211 (1947); Ex parte Lipscomb, 111 Tex. 409, 239 S.W. 1101 (1922).

Who may claim the privilege on behalf of the client is covered by Rev.Unif.R.Evid. (1974) 502(c). For text see supra § 87, n. 10.

4. See the statutes collected and quoted in 8 Wigmore, Evidence § 2292, n. 2 (McNaughton rev. 1961).

5. See e.g. In re Young's Estate, 33 Utah 382, 94 P. 731, 732 (1908) where the court said: "Subdivision 2 of section 3414, Rev.St.1898, so far as material to the present inquiry, provides as follows: 'An attorney cannot, without the consent of his client, be examined as to any communication made by the client to him, or his advice given therein in the course of professional employment.' It will be observed that, under the foregoing provision, the privilege therein given, as at common law, is purely personal, and belongs to the client. If the client waives the privilege, neither the attorney nor any one else may invoke it. It is likewise apparent that the privilege given by the statute is simply declaratory of that existing at common law. Without this statute, therefore, in view of section 2488, Rev.St.1898, in which the common law of England is adopted, the privilege would exist and be in force in this state. The mere fact that the common-law privilege is declared in statutory form does not extend the scope of its operation."

6. See Ex parte Martin, 141 Ohio St. 87, 47 N.E.2d 388 (1943) (client who was a witness whose testimony by deposition was sought, allowed to test question of privilege).

7. Steen v. First National Bank, 298 F. 36 (8th Cir. 1924) (client's testimony on preliminary hearing to conversation with lawyer, a waiver); Hill v. Hill, 106 Colo. 492, 107 P.2d 597 (1940) (client as witness asked for

production of documents to refresh her memory, waiver of privilege, if any, for documents). See § 93 infra.

8. Republic Gear Co. v. Borg-Warner Corp., 381 F.2d 551 (2d Cir.1967), "Not only may an attorney invoke the privilege in his client's behalf when the client is not a party to the proceeding in which disclosure is sought, (citations omitted) but he should do so, for he is 'duty-bound to raise the claim in any proceeding in order to procommunications made in confidence.' . . . ."); Chicago Great Western Railway Co. v. McCaffrey, 178 Iowa 1147, 160 N.W. 818 (1917) (attorney for railway, party to present suit, asked to produce correspondence with client properly claimed privilege).

Rev.Unif.R.Evid. (1974) 502(c) provides: "The person who was the lawyer at the time of the communication may claim the privilege but only on behalf of the client. His authority to do so is presumed in the absence of evidence to the contrary." West's Ann.Cal.Evid.Code, §§ 954, 956 require the lawyer to claim the privilege unless instructed otherwise by the holder.

9. O'Brien v. New England Mutual Life Insurance Co., 109 Kan. 138, 197 P. 1100 (1921) (absent client's privilege asserted, apparently by lawyer-witness or by party).

10. Tingley v. State, 16 Okl.Cr. 639, 184 P. 599 (1919). And the judge may advise the witness of the privilege. See State v. Madden, 161 Minn. 132, 134, 201 N.W. 297, 298 (1924).

See also § 73 supra.

11. Ex parte Lipscomb, 111 Tex. 409, 239 S.W. 1101, 1105 (1922) (attorney for one of the parties when required by judge to testify to transaction with client, refused and sought to raise question of privilege on

is not a party, the losing party in the cause, by the better view is without recourse.[12] Relevant, competent testimony has come in, and the privilege was not created for his benefit. But the witness, whether he is the client or his attorney, may refuse to answer and suffer an adjudication of contempt and may, in some jurisdictions at least, secure review on habeas corpus if the privilege was erroneously denied.[13] This remedy, however, is calculated to interrupt and often disrupt progess of the cause on trial. Does a lawyer on the witness stand who is asked to make disclosures which he thinks may constitute an infringement of his client's privilege, owe a duty to refuse to answer and if necessary to test the judge's ruling on habeas corpus or appeal from a judgment of contempt? It seems clear that, unless in a case of flagrant disregard of the law by the judge, the lawyer's duty is merely to present his view that the testimony is privileged, and

if the judge rules otherwise, to submit to his decision.[14]

 WESTLAW REFERENCES

object! assert! claim! /s privilege* /s attorney lawyer client

§ 93. Waiver [1]

Since as we have seen, it is the client who is the holder of the privilege, the power to waive it is his, and he alone, or his attorney or agent acting with his authority, or his representative may [2] exercise this power. Waiver includes, as Wigmore points out, not merely words or conduct expressing an intention to relinquish a known right, but conduct, such as a partial disclosure, which would make it unfair for the client to insist on the privilege thereafter.[3]

Of course, if the holder of the privilege fails to claim his privilege by objecting to disclosure by himself or another witness

---

habeas corpus; held, writ denied because of client's adequate remedy by appeal).

12. Schaibly v. Vinton, 338 Mich. 191, 61 N.W.2d 122 (1953); Dowie's Estate, 135 Pa. 210, 19 A. 936 (1890).

13. Ex parte Martin, 141 Ohio St. 87, 47 N.E.2d 388 (1943); Elliott v. United States, 23 App.D.C. 456 (1904); C.J.S. Habeas Corpus § 37, note 77. But not if the client is a party and so has an adequate remedy by appeal. Ex parte Lipscomb, note 11 supra.

Appeal from the judgment of contempt is ordinarily available as a means of reviewing the ruling, and enforcement of the judgment will be stayed pending review. But see Dike v. Dike, 75 Wn.2d 1, 448 P.2d 490 (1968), 45 Wash.Law Rev. 181 (1970) in which the trial judge had the lawyer handcuffed, removed to the county jail, fingerprinted, "mugged," and held until released on $5,000 bail. The court on appeal vacated the contempt order, while ruling at the same time that the order to disclose was not erroneous.

See also Note, 1968 Wis.Law Rev. 1193.

14. Compare the remarks of Shaw, C.J., in Foster v. Hall, 12 Pick. (Mass.) 89, (1831): "Mr. Robinson [an attorney-witness] very properly submitted it to the court to determine, on the facts disclosed, whether he should answer, or not, having no wish either to volunteer or withhold his testimony. The rule in such case is, that the privilege of confidence is the privilege of the client, and not of the attorney, and, therefore, whether the facts shall be disclosed or not, must depend on the just application of the rule of law, and not upon the will of the witness."

A.B.A. Code of Professional Responsibility, Disciplinary Rule 4-101(C): "A lawyer may reveal . . . (2) Confidences or secrets when . . . required by law or court order."

§ 93

1. See 8 Wigmore, Evidence §§ 2327-2329 (McNaughton rev. 1961); Note, 16 Minn.L.Rev. 818 (1932); Dec.Dig. Witnesses ⚖219(3); 81 Am.Jur.2d Witnesses §§ 189, 223-229.

2. Lietz v. Primock, 84 Ariz. 273, 327 P.2d 288, 67 A.L.R.2d 1262 (1958) (guardian ad litem, in controversy with attorney); Wilcox v. Coons, 359 Mo. 52, 220 S.W. 2d 15 (1949) (either personal representative or devisee of deceased may waive); In re Selser, 27 N.J.Super. 257, 99 A.2d 313 (1951) (personal representative of deceased client); Yancy v. Erman, 99 N.E.2d 524 (Ohio App.1951) (guardian of an incompetent client may waive his privilege), 36 Minn.L.Rev. 408 (1952); Annot., 67 A.L.R.2d 1268. And see Rev.Unif.R.Evid. (1974) 502(c), supra n. 10 § 87.

3. 8 Wigmore, Evidence § 2327 (McNaughton rev. 1961).

Traditionally, waiver is described as intentional relinquishment of a known right. Johnson v. Zerbst, 304 U.S. 458, 464 (1938). However, voluntary disclosure, regardless of knowledge of the existence of the privilege, deprives a subsequent claim of privilege based on confidentiality of any significance.

when he has an opportunity to do so, he waives his privilege as to the communications so disclosed.[4]

By the prevailing view, which seems correct, the mere voluntary taking the stand by the client as a witness in a suit to which he is party and testifying to facts which were the subject of consultation with his counsel is no waiver of the privilege for secrecy of the communications to his lawyer.[5] It is the communication which is privileged, not the facts. If on direct examination, however, he testifies to the privileged communications, in part, this is a waiver as to the remainder of the privileged consultation or consultations about the same subject.[6]

What if the client is asked on cross-examination about the communications with his lawyer, and he responds without asserting his claim of privilege? Is this a waiver? Unless there are some circumstances which show that the client was surprised or misled, it seems that the usual rule that the client's failure to claim the privilege when to his knowledge testimony infringing it is offered,[7] would apply here,[8] and that the decisions treating such testimony on cross-examination as being involuntary and not constituting a waiver [9] are hardly supportable.

How far does the client waive by calling the attorney as a witness? If the client elic-

---

4. Steen v. First National Bank, 298 F. 36 (6th Cir. 1924); Hurley v. McMillan, 268 S.W.2d 229 (Tex.Civ. App.1954); C.J.S. Witnesses, § 310, note 76. But see People v. Kor, 129 Cal.App.2d 436, 277 P.2d 94 (1955) (failure of one of defendants, who jointly consulted a lawyer, to claim his privilege when examined about disclosures to attorney, does not waive his right to claim privilege against examination of attorney about the same disclosures). The decision is criticized, it seems soundly, in Note 2 UCLA L.Rev. 573.

5. Magida v. Continental Can Co., 12 F.R.D. 74 (1951); Bigler v. Reyher, 43 Ind. 112 (1873); Barker v. Kuhn, 38 Iowa 392 (1874); State v. White, 19 Kan. 445, 27 Am.Rep. 137 (1877); Shelly v. Landry, 97 N.H. 27, 79 A.2d 626 (1951). An early Massachusetts decision is to the contrary. Woburn v. Henshaw, 101 Mass. 193, 200 (1869). But there is some inconsistency in later opinions, see Spalding, The Uncertain State of the Law as to Waiver of Professional Confidences, 20 Mass.L.Q. 16 (May, 1935). So also decisions under statutes, in Ohio and Oregon. Spitzer v. Stillings, 109 Ohio 297, 142 N.E. 365 (1924) (in civil cases, under R.C. § 2317.02; Sitton v. Peyree, 117 Or. 107, 241 P. 62 (1925) (under ORS 44–040); Note, 33 Yale Law J. 782; Annot., 51 A.L.R.2d 521.

The accused in a criminal case by taking the stand waives his privilege against self-incrimination, at least pro tanto, see § 132, infra, but not his privilege for communications with his attorney, unless he voluntarily gives evidence respecting the privileged matter. People v. Shapiro, 308 N.Y. 453, 126 N.E.2d 559, 51 A.L.R.2d 515 (1955); Jones v. Jones, 208 Misc. 721, 144 N.Y.S.2d 820 (1955); Note, 41 Iowa L.Rev. 457.

6. United States v. McCambridge, 551 F.2d 865 (1st Cir.1977); Howell v. United States, 442 F.2d 265 (7th Cir.1971); United States v. Pauldino, 487 F.2d 127 (10th Cir.1973); Kelly v. Cummens, 143 Iowa 148, 121 N.W. 540, 20 Ann.Cas. 1283 (1909); Chase v. Chase, 78 R.I. 278, 81 A.2d 686 (1951); Rodriguez v. State, 130 Tex. Cr.R. 438, 94 S.W.2d 476 (1936). Similarly, if the party-client introduces part of his correspondence with his attorney, the production of all the correspondence

could be demanded. Kunglig Jarnvagsstyrelson v. Dexter & Carpenter, 32 F.2d 195 (2d Cir.1929). Under exceptional circumstances, however, the waiver has sometimes been restricted to the matter actually disclosed. Weil v. Investment/Indicators, Research and Management, Inc., 647 F.2d 18 (9th Cir.1981) (disclosure to opposing counsel, not court; no harm to opposing party); Champion International Corp. v. International Paper Co., 486 F.Supp. 1328 (N.D.Ga.1980) (inadvertent disclosure during discovery). Testimony by the client in a prior suit may constitute a waiver of the privilege. Agnew v. Superior Court, 156 Cal.App. 2d 838, 841, 320 P.2d 158 (1958). See also the decisions cited in note 6 § 92 supra.

7. See, e.g, Rock v. Keller, 312 Mo. 458, 278 S.W. 759 (1926); Weisser v. Preszler, 62 N.D. 75, 241 N.W. 505 (1932).

8. General Accident, Fire & Life Assurance Corp. v. Savage, 35 F.2d 587, 592 (8th Cir.1929); Steen v. First National Bank, 298 F. 36, 43 (6th Cir.1924); Raleigh & Charleston Railroad Co. v. Jones, 104 S.C. 332, 88 S.E. 896, 898 (1916) (failure to object on cross-examination entitles other party to call attorney); Pinson v. Campbell, 124 Mo.App. 260, 101 S.W. 621 (1907) (similar). It is clear, of course, that the party-witness may claim the privilege during the cross-examination. Ex parte Bryant, 106 Or. 359, 210 P. 454 (1922).

9. Seaboard Air Line Railway Co. v. Parker, 65 Fla. 543, 62 So. 589 (1913); Lauer v. Banning, 140 Iowa 319, 118 N.W. 446, 450 (1908), on later appeal, 152 Iowa 99, 131 N.W. 783 (1911); Foley v. Poschke, 66 Ohio App. 227, 32 N.E.2d 858, 861 (1940), affirmed 137 Ohio St. 593, 31 N.E.2d 845 (1941); State v. James, 34 S.C. 49, 12 S.E. 657 (1891). In none of these opinions is there any discussion of why the usual rule of waiver from failure to object does not apply. In most of them, however, the testimony on cross-examination consisted of a denial of having made to the attorney the statement inquired about, and it is arguable that a layman might not realize when he anticipated making such an answer, that there was any occasion to claim privilege.

its testimony from the lawyer-witness as to privileged communications this obviously would waive as to all consultations relating to the same subject,[10] just as the client's own testimony would.[11] It would seem also that by calling the lawyer as a witness he opens the door for the adversary to impeach him by showing his interest.[12] And it seems reasonable to contend as Wigmore does [13] that if the client uses the lawyer to prove matter which he would only have learned in the course of his employment this again should be considered a waiver as to related privileged communications.[14] But merely to call

10. Brooks v. Holden, 175 Mass. 137, 55 N.E. 802 (1900); 8 Wigmore, Evidence § 2327 (McNaughton rev. 1961).

11. See cases cited note 6, supra.

12. Conyer v. Burckhalter, 275 S.W. 606 (Tex.Civ. App., 1925) (error to exclude cross-examination as to attorney's fee interest in outcome of suit); Moats v. Rymer, 18 W.Va. 642, 41 Am.Rep. 703 (1881).

13. See reference, n. 10 supra.

14. This view seems supported by the result in Jones v. Marble Co., 137 N.C. 237, 49 S.E. 94 (1904) (action for attorney's fees; defendant called attorney formerly associated with plaintiff in employment for which fee is claimed, to testify that fee claimed is excessive; held, this waived defendant's right to object to plaintiff's introducing letter from witness during pendency of employment which would otherwise have been privileged).

But there is authority for the view that if the lawyer's testimony does not relate to the privileged communications themselves, there is no waiver. Drayton v. Industrial Life & Health Insurance Co., 205 S.C. 98, 31 S.E.2d 148 (1944).

15. See 8 Wigmore, Evidence § 2327 (McNaughton rev. 1961); Note, 16 Minn.L.Rev. 818, 827 (1932). But see Martin v. Shaen, 22 Wn.2d 508, 156 P.2d 681, 685 (1945) (where attorney-executor testified that he received a certain deed from the deceased client, and the court said that when he "voluntarily took the stand and testified upon a vital issue in the case, he waived the privilege of withholding his testimony as to all matters relevant to that issue" including communications between lawyer and client at the time the deed was placed in the lawyer's hands.)

16. A.B.A.Code of Professional Responsibility:

DISCIPLINARY RULES

DR 5-101 Refusing Employment When the Interests of the Lawyer May Impair His Independent Professional Judgment.

. . .

(B) A lawyer shall not accept employment in contemplated or pending litigation if he knows or it is

the lawyer to testify to facts known by him apart from his employment should not be deemed a waiver of the privilege. That would attach too harsh a condition on the exercise of the privilege.[15] Unless the lawyer-witness is acting as counsel in the case on trial, there is no violation of the Code of Professional Responsibility,[16] and if he is, it recognizes that his testifying may be essential to the ends of justice. Moreover, these are matters usually governed not by the client but by the lawyer, to whom the ethical mandate is addressed.

obvious that he or a lawyer in his firm ought to be called as a witness, except that he may undertake the employment and he or a lawyer in his firm may testify:

(1) If the testimony will relate solely to an uncontested matter.

(2) If the testimony will relate solely to a matter of formality and there is no reason to believe that substantial evidence will be offered in opposition to the testimony.

(3) If the testimony will relate solely to the nature and value of legal services rendered in the case by the lawyer or his firm to the client.

(4) As to any matter, if refusal would work a substantial hardship on the client because of the distinctive value of the lawyer or his firm as counsel in the particular case.

DR 5-102 Withdrawal as Counsel When the Lawyer Becomes a Witness.

(A) If, after undertaking employment in contemplated or pending litigation, a lawyer learns or it is obvious that he or a lawyer in his firm ought to be called as a witness on behalf of his client, he shall withdraw from the conduct of the trial and his firm, if any, shall not continue representation in the trial, except that he may continue the representation and he or a lawyer in his firm may testify in the circumstances enumerated in DR 5-101(B)(1) through (4).

(B) If, after undertaking employment in contemplated or pending litigation, a lawyer learns or it is obvious that he or a lawyer in his firm may be called as a witness other than on behalf of his client, he may continue the representation until it is apparent that his testimony is or may be prejudicial to his client.

In an earlier section [17] discussing a witness' use of a writing to refresh his recollection for purposes of testifying, it was pointed out that, under both common law and Federal Evidence Rule 612, if a witness consulted a writing to refresh his recollection while testifying, opposing counsel is entitled to inspect it, to cross-examine the witness upon it, and to introduce in evidence portions that relate to the testimony of the witness. It was further pointed out that if the document were privileged, e.g. an attorney-client communication, such act of consultation would effect a waiver of the privilege.[18] And finally, the problem area was said to be when the privileged writing was consulted by the witness prior to testifying. At common law authority generally was against requiring disclosure of writings consulted prior to testifying, and under that view the problem of waiver of privilege does not arise. However, an increasing number of cases have allowed disclosure, and Federal Evidence Rule 612 gives the trial judge discretion to order disclosure.[19] Should this discretionary power of the judge extend also to deciding whether a waiver of privilege has occurred? Or should it be said that on the one hand waiver never occurs, or on the other that it always occurs? The Report of the House Committee on the Judiciary took a strict no-waiver position,[20] but no language to that effect was incorporated in Rule 612.

Nor was there included any specific provision that privilege should always be waived. The discretionary provision was inserted almost as a matter of necessity to limit disclosure of the potentially vast volume and variety of documents that might be consulted before testifying to those truly bearing on the testimony of the witness, and similar considerations are pertinent to the waiver question. While the cases are mixed, the preferred view seems to be that the judge's discretion extends not only to the threshold question whether connection with the testimony is sufficient to warrant disclosure but also to the question whether its importance is sufficient to override the privilege, given all the circumstances.[21]

When at an earlier trial or stage of the case the privilege has been waived and testimony as to the privileged communications elicited without objection, the prevailing view is that this is a waiver also for any subsequent hearing of the same case.[22] In the words of Holmes, J., "the privacy for the sake of which the privilege was created was gone by the appellant's own consent, and the privilege does not remain in such circumstances for the mere sake of giving the client an additional weapon to use or not at his choice."[23] The same reasons seem to apply where the waiver was thus publicly made upon the trial of one case, and the privilege later sought to be asserted on the hearing of

17.   See § 9 supra, at nn. 14–21.

18.   See § 9 supra, at n. 28.

19.   Fed.R.Evid. 612, Adv.Comm.Note. For text of Rule 612 see § 9 n. 16.

20.   "The Committee intends that nothing in the Rule be construed as barring the assertion of a privilege with respect to writings used by a witness to refresh his memory." House Comm. on Judiciary, Fed. Rules of Evidence, H.R.Rep. No. 650, 93d Cong., 1st Sess., p. 13 (1973).

21.   Wheeling-Pittsburgh Steel Corp. v. Underwriters Laboratories, Inc., 81 F.R.D. 8 (N.D.Ill.1978) (employee-witness reviewed file "Communications with Counsel" prior to testifying; held, attorney-client privilege waived); Marshall v. United States Postal Service, 88 F.R.D. 348 (D.C.D.C.1980) (waiver of attorney-client privilege extends only to documents consulted, not to genesis of those documents); Joseph Schlitz Brewing Co. v. Muller & Phipps, Limited, 85 F.R.D. 118 (W.D.

Mo.1980) (entire file not opened up by merely "looking at it;" must show documents were actually examined; privileged documents should have "special discretionary safeguards against disclosure). See United States v. American Telephone & Telegraph Co., 642 F.2d 1285 (D.C.Cir.1980), suggesting a stricter standard of waiver for work product than for attorney-client in inter-party disclosure situations. See Weinstein & Berger, Evidence ¶ 612[04].

22.   Green v. Crapo, 181 Mass. 55, 62 N.E. 956, 959 (1902) (waiver at probate court hearing, effective at subsequent hearing on appeal); In re Whiting, 110 Me. 232, 85 A. 79 (1913) (similar); 8 Wigmore, Evidence § 2328 (McNaughton rev. 1961); Note, 16 Minn.L.Rev. 818, 829 (1932). See also discussions of the question as applied to waiver of objections generally by waiver at an earlier trial: 81 Am.Jur.2d Witnesses § 147; Annot. 79 A.L.R. 176.

23.   Green v. Crapo, supra, n. 22, 62 N.E. 956, 959.

another cause.[24] How far does this argument of once published, permanently waived, apply to out-of-court disclosures made by the client or with his consent? Authority is scanty, but it seems that if the client makes public disclosure, this should clearly be a waiver,[25] and even where privately revealed to a third person,[26] or authorized to be revealed.[27] It should have the same effect, by analogy to the cases which deny privilege when a third person is present at the consultation.[28]

The question as to who may waive the privilege after the death of the client will be considered in the next section.

WESTLAW
REFERENCES

attorney lawyer client /s waiv** /s privilege*
rule fed.r.evid! evidence /5 612 /p disclosure & court(ca5)

---

24. Thus in Steen v. First National Bank, 298 F. 36 (6th Cir.1924) it was held that a failure to object to questions to the client's representative about privileged matter at the preliminary hearing in a criminal prosecution, prevented assertion of the privilege at the trial of an action for malicious prosecution. Compare Alden v. Stromsem, 347 Ill.App. 439, 106 N.E.2d 837 (1952) (in suit for engineering fees, communications disclosed by both parties at previous trial for attorney fees, not privileged). But see Matison v. Matison, 95 N.Y.S.2d 837, affirmed on appeal 97 N.Y.S.2d 550 (1950) (in action by third party, communications between attorney and client were privileged, though attorney had testified thereto in previous action by him for attorney fees).

25. In re Burnette, 73 Kan. 609, 85 P. 575, 583 (1906) (procured stranger to read, published contents in newspaper interview, and spread substance on record of a court in a pleading).

26. Holland v. State, 17 Ala.App. 503, 86 So. 118 (1920) (oral disclosure by defendant to witness of advice given him by lawyers); and see Seeger v. Odell, 64 Cal.App.2d 397, 148 P.2d 901, 906 (1944).

In Diversified Industries, Inc. v. Meredith, 572 F.2d 596 (7th Cir.1977) (en banc), the court declined to apply the rule cited where disclosure of privileged information had been made voluntarily to the SEC in a separate investigation. See also, Byrnes v. IDS Realty Trust, 85 F.R.D. 679 (S.D.N.Y.1980) (semble). However, in Permian Corp. v. United States, 665 F.2d 1214 (D.C.Cir.1981), the court found this "limited waiver" theory "wholly unpersuasive."

27. Phillips v. Chase, 201 Mass. 444, 87 N.E. 755, 131 Am.St.Rep. 406 (1909) (deceased client had requested attorney to communicate facts disclosed to him, to her brothers after her death); Halloran v. Tousignant,

§ 94. The Effect of the Death of the Client [1]

The accepted theory is that the protection afforded by the privilege will in general survive the death of the client.[2] But under various qualifying theories the operation of the privilege has in effect been nullified in the class of cases where it would most often be asserted after death, namely, cases involving the validity or interpretation of a will, or other dispute between parties claiming by succession from the testator at his death. This result has been reached by different routes. Sometimes the testator will be found to have waived the privilege in his lifetime, as by directing the attorney to act as an attesting witness.[3] Wigmore argues, as to the will contests, that communications of the client with his lawyer as to the making of a will are intended to be confidential

---

230 Minn. 399, 41 N.W.2d 874 (1950) (arrangement of insurance carriers to exchange statements of their insured, as waiver of privilege). As to latter case, however, compare nn. 17 and 18, § 91 supra.

28. Revised Uniform Rule of Evidence 510 (1974) takes this position with respect to all privileges. The rule provides:

A person upon whom these rules confer a privilege against disclosure waives the privilege if he or his predecessor while holder of the privilege voluntarily discloses or consents to disclosure of any significant part of the privileged matter. This rule does not apply if the disclosure itself is privileged.

But see United States v. American Telephone & Telegraph Co., supra n. 21.

§ 94

1. See 8 Wigmore, Evidence §§ 2314, 2329 (McNaughton rev. 1961); Model Code of Evidence Rule 213(2); Annot., 64 A.L.R. 184, 66 A.L.R.2d 1302; 81 Am.Jur.2d Witnesses § 201.

2. State v. Macumber, 112 Ariz. 569, 544 P.2d 1084 (1976), appeal after remand 119 Ariz. 516, 582 P.2d 162, cert. denied 439 U.S. 1006; In re Busse's Estate, 332 Ill.App. 258, 75 N.E.2d 36 (1947); Martin v. Shaen, 22 Wn.2d 505, 156 P.2d 681 (1945); 8 Wigmore, Evidence § 2323 (McNaughton rev. 1961). Rev.Unif.R.Evid. (1974) 502(c) allows the personal representative of a deceased client to claim the privilege, but is subject to 503(d)(2) as between persons who claim through the same deceased client. See n. 6, infra.

3. In re Landauer's Estate, 261 Wis. 314, 52 N.W.2d 890, rehearing denied 53 N.W.2d 627 (1952); Annot., 64 A.L.R. 192, 66 A.L.R.2d 1310. See § 91, n. 3, supra.

in his lifetime but that this is a "temporary confidentiality" not intended to require secrecy after his death [4] and this view finds approval in some decisions.[5] Other courts say simply that where all the parties claim under the client the privilege does not apply.[6] The distinction is taken that when the contest is between a "stranger" and the heirs or personal representatives of the deceased client, the heirs or representatives can claim privilege,[7] and they can waive it.[8] Even if the privilege were assumed to be applicable in will contests, it could perhaps be argued that since those claiming under the will and those claiming by intestate succession both equally claim under the client, each should have the power to waive.[9]

This doctrine that the privilege is ineffective, on whatever ground, when both litigants claim under the deceased client has been applied to suits by the heirs or representatives to set aside a conveyance by the deceased for mental incapacity [10] and to suits for the enforcement of a contract made by the deceased to make a will in favor of plaintiff.[11] The cases encountered where the party is held to be a "stranger" and hence not entitled to invoke this doctrine are cases where the party asserts against the estate a claim of a promise by the deceased to pay, or make provision in his will for payment, for services rendered.[12] It may well be questioned whether the deceased would have been more likely to desire that his attorney's lips be sealed after his death in the determination of such claims than in the case of a controversy over the validity of the will. The attorney's offered testimony would seem to be of more than average reliability.

4. 8 Wigmore, Evidence § 2314 (McNaughton rev. 1961).

5. See, e.g., Dickerson v. Dickerson, 322 Ill. 492, 153 N.E. 740 (1926) (communications between client and attorneys concerning deed, intended to be confidential during client's lifetime only); Hecht's Admr. v. Hecht, 272 Ky. 400, 114 S.W.2d 499 (1938) (death removes the pledge of secrecy); Snow v. Gould, 74 Me. 540, 543 (1883); In re Graf's Estate, 119 N.W.2d 478 (N.D.1963).

6. Russell v. Jackson, 9 Hare 387, 392, 68 Eng.Rep. 558, 560 (V.C.1851) ("The disclosure in [testamentary] cases can affect no right or interest of the client. The apprehension of it can present no impediment to the full statement of his case to his solicitor. . . . In the cases of testamentary dispositions the very foundation on which the rule proceeds seems to be wanting . . . ."); Glover v. Patten, 165 U.S. 394, 406 (1897) (bill by devisees to construe will and to charge estate with claims); Clark v. Turner, 183 F.2d 141 (D.C.Cir. 150) (in suit to establish lost will, testimony as to existence of will); Olsson v. Pierson, 237 Iowa 1342, 25 N.W.2d 357 (1946) (suit to set aside conveyance of deceased for constructive fraud and mental incapacity); Stevens v. Thurston, 289 A.2d 398 (N.H.1972); In Re Kemp's Will, 236 N.C. 680, 73 S.E.2d 906 (1953) (will contest—mental capacity); Mekus v. Thompson, 266 N.W.2d 920 (N.D.1978); Gaines v. Gaines, 207 Okl. 619, 251 P.2d 1044 (1953) (in action to construe written assignment of deceased, testimony of attorney and his stenographer as to statements of deceased concerning his intentions); Pierce v. Farrar, 60 Tex.Civ.App. 12, 126 S.W. 932 (1910) (will contest, undue influence); In re Young's Estate, 33 Utah 382, 94 P. 731, 17 L.R.A.,N.S., 108 (1908) (will contest, undue influence); Re Healy, 94 Vt. 128, 109 Atl. 19 (1920) (will contest, mental capacity); Rev.Unif.R.Evid. (1974) 502(d)(2), supra § 87 n. 10; Annot., 64 A.L.R. 185–189, 66 A.L.R.2d

1395, 1396. Contra: In re Coon's Estate, 154 Neb. 690, 48 N.W.2d 778 (1951).

7. Doyle v. Reeves, 112 Conn. 521, 152 A. 882 (1931) (claim of servant against estate for value of services to deceased); In re Busse's Estate, 332 Ill.App. 258, 75 N.E.2d 36 (1947) (similar); McCaffrey v. Estate of Brennan, 533 S.W.2d 264 (Mo.App.1976); In re Smith's Estate, 263 Wis. 441, 57 N.W.2d 727 (1953); Annot., 64 A.L.R. 191, 66 A.L.R.2d 1307. In Doyle v. Reeves, supra, the plaintiff seems to have relied on a promise by decedent to make provision in his will for payment for the services.

8. Phillips v. Chase, 201 Mass. 444, 87 N.E. 755 (1909) (in controversy with stranger, either personal representative or heir may waive—dictum).

9. See Wilcox v. Coons, 359 Mo. 52, 220 S.W.2d 15 (1949) (privilege of deceased client accrues to his personal representatives and may be waived either by his grantees under deed or his devisees under will.) See also Walton v. Van Camp, 283 S.W.2d 493 (Mo.1955).

10. Olsson v. Pierson, 237 Iowa 1342, 25 N.W.2d 357 (1946).

11. Eicholtz v. Grunewald, 313 Mich. 666, 21 N.W.2d 914 (1946) (suit by children to enforce contract of parents to make mutual wills and to set aside conveyance by father); Cummings v. Sherman, 16 Wn.2d 88, 132 P.2d 998 (1943) (similar); Allen v. Ross, 199 Wis. 162, 225 N.W. 831, 64 A.L.R. 180 (1929) (similar). But see, In re Smith's Estate, McGlone v. Fairchild, 263 Wis. 441, 57 N.W.2d 727 (1953) (in suit against estate based upon breach of contract by testatrix in making her last will, attorney's testimony privileged on ground that claimants were not claiming through testatrix but asserting adverse claim against the estate).

12. See the cases cited in n. 7, supra.

If such testimony supporting the claim is true, presumably the deceased would have wanted to promote, rather than obstruct, the success of the claim. It would be only a short step forward for the courts to apply here the notion that the privilege is "personal" to client, and to hold that in all cases death terminates the privilege. This could not to any substantial degree lessen the encouragement for free disclosure which is the purpose of the privilege.

WESTLAW REFERENCES

digest(attorney lawyer client /s privilege* /s death die* dying)

§ 95

1. 8 Wigmore, Evidence §§ 2298, 2299 (McNaughton rev. 1961); Gardner, The Crime or Fraud Exception to the Attorney-Client Privilege, 47 A.B.A.J. 708 (1961); Dec.Dig. Witnesses ⊶201(2); C.J.S. Witnesses § 285; 81 Am.Jur.2d Witnesses §§ 208–210; Annot., 125 A.L.R. 508.

2. Queen v. Cox, 14 Q.B.D. 153 (C.C.R.1884) (prosecution for conspiracy to defraud judgment creditor by transfer of debtor's property; communications between debtor and solicitor in respect to preventing collection of judgment by transfer of assets, not privileged); Matter of Doe, 551 F.2d 899 (2d Cir.1977) (conversation disclosing client's plan to bribe juror); Fidelity-Phenix Fire Insurance Co. of New York v. Hamilton, 340 S.W.2d 218 (Ky.1960) (conversation tending to show fraudulent claim under fire insurance policy), 21 Md.L.Rev. 270 (1960); Standard Fire Insurance Co. v. Smithhart, 183 Ky. 679, 211 S.W. 441, 5 A.L.R. 972 (1919) (communications by insured in fire policy tending to show arson and fraudulent claim); Gebhardt v. United Railways Co. 220 S.W. 677, 679, 9 A.L.R. 1076 (Mo.1920) (client asserting personal injury on street car, discloses to attorney that she was not on car; "The law does not make a law office a nest of vipers in which to hatch out frauds and perjuries"); Ott v. State, 87 Tex.Cr. 382, 222 S.W. 261 (1920) (husband consults attorney as to what punishment would probably be incurred if he killed his wife); Annot., 2 A.L.R.3d 861. And see Callan & David, Professional Responsibility and the Duty of Confidentiality: Disclosure of Client Misconduct in an Adversary System, 29 Rutgers L.Rev. 332 (1976).

A leading case recognizes the rule, but places a seemingly unjustifiable restriction upon it in holding that the client may assert the privilege when he is sued or prosecuted for a different crime from the one in-

§ 95. Consultation in Furtherance of Crime or Fraud[1]

Since the policy of the privilege is that of promoting the administration of justice, it would be a perversion of the privilege to extend it to the client who seeks advice to aid him in carrying out an illegal or fraudulent scheme. Advice given for those purposes would not be a professional service but participation in a conspiracy. Accordingly, it is settled under modern authority that the privilege does not extend to communications between attorney and client where the client's purpose is the furtherance of a future intended crime or fraud.[2] Advice secured in aid of a legitimate defense by the client against a charge of past crimes or past misconduct, even though he is guilty, stands on a different footing and such consultations are privileged.[3] If the privilege is to be de-

volved in the consultation. Alexander v. United States, 138 U.S. 353 (1891) (client on trial for murder of his partner; error to admit communications to lawyer asserted to show plan to convert murder-victim's property). This restriction was called a "dictum" and rejected in In re Sawyer's Petition, 229 F.2d 805 (7th Cir. 1956), 45 Calif.L.Rev. 75.

If the client consults the lawyer about a proposed course of action, about the legality of which he is doubtful and is advised that it would be unlawful and then desists, it can not be said that the consultation was in furtherance of wrong. Cummings v. Commonwealth, 221 Ky. 301, 298 S.W. 943 (1927). But a case which on this ground holds privileged a consultation about the effect of altering a deed in the client's favor, where the deed was later actually altered by someone, seems a misapplication. Williams v. Williams, 108 S.W.2d 297 (Tex.Civ.App.1937). The client could hardly have supposed that such an alteration could be innocent and the inquiry is itself strong circumstantial evidence that the client participated in the alteration.

In order to protect the client who acts upon professional advice in committing what later is ruled to be a crime or fraud, Rev.Unif.R.Evid. (1974) 502(d)(1) applies the furtherance of crime or fraud exception only when the client knew or reasonably should have known the act to be a crime or fraud.

To the same effect is State ex rel. North Pacific Lumber Co. v. Unis, 282 Or. 457, 579 P.2d 1291 (1978). Conversely, the attorney's misuse of confidential information to defraud will not defeat the privilege. Glade v. Superior Court, 76 Cal.App.3d 738, 143 Cal.Rptr. 119 (1978).

3. "The privileged communications may be a shield of defense as to crimes already committed, but it cannot be used as a sword or weapon of offense to enable

nied on the ground of unlawful purpose, the client's guilty intention is controlling, though the attorney may have acted innocently and in good faith.[4]

Must the judge, before denying the claim of privilege on this ground find as a fact, after a preliminary hearing if contested, that the consultation was in furtherance of crime or fraud? This would be the normal procedure in passing on a preliminary fact on which the admissibility of evidence depends, but here this procedure would facilitate too far the use of the privilege as a cloak for crime. As a solution, some courts have cast the balance in favor of disclosure by requiring only that the one who seeks to avoid the privilege bring forward evidence from which the existence of an unlawful purpose could reasonably be found.[5] Even this limitation seems needless when, as is commonly the

case, the examining counsel has sufficient information to focus the inquiry by specific questions, thus avoiding any broad exploration of what transpired between attorney and client.[6]

Questions arise fairly frequently under this limitation upon the privilege in the situation where a client has first consulted one attorney about a claim, and then employs other counsel and brings suit. At the trial the defense seeks to have the first attorney testify to disclosures by the client which reveal that the claim was fabricated or fraudulent. This of course may be done,[7] but if the statements to the first attorney would merely reveal variances from the client's later statements or testimony, not sufficient to evidence fraud or perjury, the privilege would stand.[8]

persons to carry out contemplated crimes against society." Gebhardt v. United Railways Co., 220 S.W. 677, 699, 9 A.L.R. 1076 (Mo.1920). Clark v. State, 261 S.W.2d 339 (Tex.Cr.1953), cert. denied 346 U.S. 855; State ex rel. Sowers v. Olwell, 64 Wn.2d 828, 394 P.2d 681, 16 A.L.R.3d 1021 (1964) (knife obtained by attorney as result of confidential communication from client held not privileged from production but prosecution barred from disclosing source); Annot., 16 A.L.R.3d 1029. And see § 89 nn. 12–14 supra.

4. Queen v. Cox, 14 Q.B.D. 153 (C.C.R.1884); United States v. Hodge, 548 F.2d 1347 (9th Cir.1977); In re Selser, 15 N.J. 393, 105 A.2d 395 (1954); 24 Fordham L.Rev. 290 (1955), 30 N.Y.U.L.Rev. 1251 (1955); Orman v. State, 22 Tex.App. 604, 3 S.W. 468 (1886); Annot., 125 A.L.R. at 520. A converse question is raised in Clark v. State, next preceding note. The accused called his lawyer and told him that he had just killed his former wife. Though seemingly the call was for counsel in his defence, the lawyer volunteered advice that he should get rid of the fatal weapon. Apparently this advice was taken, as the weapon was not found. The court held that "the conversation was admissible as not within the realm of legitimate professional counsel and employment" (p. 347).

5. O'Rourke v. Darbishire, [1920] App.C. 581, 604, 614, 622 (H.L.) (evidence and not mere pleading of fraud required); Clark v. United States, 289 U.S. 1 (1933) ("There must be a showing of a prima facie case sufficient to satisfy the judge that the light should be let in"); United States v. Calvert, 523 F.2d 895 (8th Cir. 1975), cert denied 424 U.S. 911 (1976); In re Berkeley & Co., Inc., 629 F.2d 548 (8th Cir.1980); United States v. Bob, 106 F.2d 37, 125 A.L.R. 502, 506 (2d Cir.1939), cert. denied 308 U.S. 589; Pollock v. United States, 202 F.2d 281 (5th Cir.1953), cert. denied 345 U.S. 993 (communication not privileged, where communication was

made in furtherance of crime of which client was charged and evidence had been introduced giving color to the charge); United States v. Weinberg, 226 F.2d 161 (3d Cir.1955); United Services Automobile Association v. Werley, 526 P.2d 28 (Alaska 1974); In re Selser, 15 N.J. 393, 105 A.2d 395 (1954), noted 24 Fordham L.Rev. 290 (1955), 30 N.Y.U.L.Rev. 1251 (1955).

The case most often relied upon to support the requirement of a preliminary prima facie showing, Clark v. United States, supra, actually involved the privilege of a petit juror, not that of attorney-client.

Of course, the inference of the client's wrongful intent will often be a circumstantial one. See, e.g., Sawyer v. Stanley, 241 Ala. 39, 1 So.2d 21 (1941) where a will was contested for forgery and evidence of an attorney was admitted that the purported beneficiary asked him whether decedent had left a will, without disclosing existence of purported will.

6. Thus in cases of fraudulent suits, where successive attorneys have been consulted, it seems common for the first attorney to furnish complete information to the defense. See cases cited n. 7 infra and A.B.A. Code of Professional Responsibility, Disciplinary Rule 4–101(C)(3).

7. In re Koellen's Estate, Willie v. Lampe, 167 Kan. 676, 208 P.2d 595 (1949) (client admitted to first lawyer that he had forged will which he later sought to probate, not privileged); Standard Fire Ins. Co. v. Smithhart, 183 Ky. 679, 211 S.W. 441, 5 A.L.R. 972 (1919) (client sought first lawyer to sue on fire policy, disclosing that she had connived in burning her house; not privileged); Gebhardt v. United Railways Co., 220 S.W. 677, 9 A.L.R. 1076 (Mo.1920) (fabricated personal injury claim: no privilege).

8. Nadler v. Warner Co., 321 Pa. 139, 184 A. 3 (1936); (offer to show statement of personal injury

It has been questioned whether the traditional statement of the area of the limitation, that is in cases of communications in aid of crime or fraud, is not itself too limited. Wigmore argues that the privilege should not be accorded to communications in furtherance of any deliberate scheme to deprive another of his rights by tortious or unlawful conduct.[9] Stricter requirements such as that the intended crime be *malum in se* or that it involve "moral turpitude," suggested in some of the older decisions,[10] seem out of place here where the only sanction proposed is that of opening the door to evidence concededly relevant upon the issue on trial.

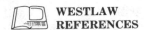

WESTLAW REFERENCES

further! propose* inten! future /3 crime criminal fraud / s attorney lawyer client /3 privilege*

---

§ 96. Protective Rules Relating to Materials Collected for Use of Counsel in Preparation for Trial: Reports of Employees, Witness-Statements, Experts' Reports, and the Like

A heavy emphasis on the responsibility of counsel for the management of the client's litigation is a characteristic feature of the adversary or contentious system of procedure of the Anglo-American tradition. The privilege against disclosure in court of confidential communications between lawyer and client as we have seen, is supported in modern times upon the policy of encouraging free disclosure by the client in the attorney's office to enable the lawyer to discharge that responsibility.[1] The need for this encouragement is understood by lawyers because the problem of the guarded half-truths of the reticent client is familiar to them in their day-to-day work.

Closely allied to this felt need of promoting a policy of free disclosure by the client to enable the lawyer to do the work of managing his affairs most effectively in the interests of justice, is a feeling by lawyers of a need for privacy in their work and for freedom from interference in the task of preparing the client's case for trial. Certainly if the adversary were free at any time to inspect all of the correspondence, memoranda, reports, exhibits, trial briefs, drafts of proposed pleadings, and plans for presentation of proofs, which constitute the lawyer's file in the case, the attorney's present freedom to collect for study all the data, favorable and unfavorable, and to record his tentative impressions before maturing his conclusions, would be cramped and hindered.

The natural jealousy of the lawyer for the privacy of his file, and the court's desire to protect the effectiveness of the lawyer's work as the manager of litigation, have found expression, not only as we have seen in the evidential privilege for confidential lawyer-client communications, but in rules and practices about the various forms of pretrial discovery.[2] Thus, under the old chancery practice of discovery, the adversary was not required to disclose, apart from his own testimony, the evidence which he would use, or the names of the witnesses he would call in support of his own case.[3] The same restriction has often been embodied in,

---

claimant, merely inconsistent with present position but not claimed to show fraud, rejected); Thomas v. Jones, 105 W.Va. 46, 141 S.E. 434 (1928) (inconsistency not such as to show fraud).

9. 8 Wigmore, Evidence § 2298, p. 577 (McNaughton rev. 1961).

West's Ann.Cal.Evid.Code § 956 and Rev.Unif.R. Evid. (1974) 502(d)(1), however, say "fraud" in lieu of "tort," in view of the technical nature of many torts.

10. Bank of Utica v. Mersereau, 3 Barb.Ch. 528, 598 (1848) (limited to felony or malum in se); Hughes v. Boone, 102 N.C. 137, 9 S.E. 286, 292 (1889) (similar dictum).

§ 96

1. See § 87 supra.

2. General discussions of discovery will be found in James & Hazard, Civil Procedure Ch. 6 (2d ed. 1976); Wright, Law of Federal Courts §§ 81–90 (4th ed. 1983); Developments in the Law—Discovery, 74 Harv.L.Rev. 940 (1961).

3. Ragland, Discovery Before Trial Ch. 15 (1932); 6 Wigmore, Evidence § 1856 (Chadbourn rev. 1976); Sunderland, Scope and Method of Discovery Before Trial, 42 Yale L.J. 862, 866 (1933); Dec.Dig. Discovery ⊙8.

or read into, the statutory discovery systems.[4]

Counterbalancing this need for privacy in preparation, of course, is the very need from which the discovery devices spring, namely, the need to make available to each party the widest possible sources of proof as early as may be so as to avoid surprise and facilitate preparation.[5] The trend has been in the direction of wider recognition of this latter need, and the taboo against the "fishing expedition"[6] has yielded increasingly to the proposition that the ends of justice require a wider availability of discovery than in the past. Accordingly there has developed an impressive arsenal of instruments of discovery, including interrogatories to the adverse party, demands for admissions, oral and written depositions of parties and witnesses, production of documents or things, entry upon land, and physical and mental examinations.[7] In recent years some disenchantment with discovery has surfaced with claims that it was used as an instrument of harassment, was unduly time-consuming, and was excessively costly.[8] Some amendments to the Federal Rules of Civil Procedure are presently under way[9] dealing largely with increased involvement of trial judges and are not likely to have a substantial direct impact upon the matters here under discussion. We turn then to examine the extent to which the increase in the scope of discovery has served to diminish privacy of preparation.

Attorney-Client privilege. In the first place, of course, it is recognized that if the traditional privilege for attorney-client communications applies to a particular writing which may be found in a lawyer's file, the privilege exempts it from pretrial discovery proceedings,[10] such as orders for production or questioning about its contents in the taking of depositions. On the other hand, if the writing has been in the possession of the client or his agents and was there subject to discovery, it seems axiomatic that the client cannot secure any exemption for the document by sending it to an attorney to be placed in his files.[11]

How do these distinctions apply to a report made by an agent to the client of the results of investigation by himself or another agent of facts pertinent to some matter which later becomes the subject of litigation,[12] such as a business dispute or a personal injury. It has usually been held that an agent's report to his principal though made in confidence is not privileged as such,[13] and looked on as a mere preexisting document it would not become privileged when sent by the client-principal to his lawyer for his information when suit is brought or threatened.[14] The problem frequently arises in connection with proceedings for discovery of accident reports by employees, with lists of eyewitnesses, and in connection with signed statements of witnesses attached to such reports or secured separately by investigators employed in the client's claim department or by an insurance company with whom the client carries insurance

---

4. Ragland, supra n. 3; 6 Wigmore, Evidence §§ 1856a, 1856b (Chadbourn rev. 1976).

5. 4 Moore, Federal Practice ¶ 26.02 (1983); Wright, supra n. 2, § 81; Goodrich, J., in Hickman v. Taylor, 153 F.2d 212, 217 (3d Cir.1945), affirmed 329 U.S. 495.

6. Hickman v. Taylor, 329 U.S. 495, 507 (1947).

7. See Federal Rules of Civil Procedure 26–37. Many states have followed the lead of these highly influential rules.

8. Wright, supra n. 2, § 81 at p. 542.

9. Id.

10. Upjohn Co. v. United States, 449 U.S. 383 (1981) (IRS summons). Fed.R.Civ.P. 26(b)(1) specifically ex-

cludes privileged matter from the reach of discovery. Dec.Dig. Discovery Key 90.

11. Supra § 89 nn. 16–19.

12. See Simon, Attorney-Client Privilege as Applied to Corporations, 65 Yale L.J. 953 (1956).

13. Southwark & V. Water Co. v. Quick, 3 Q.B.D. 315, 9 Eng.Rul.Cas. 587 (C.A.1878); Schmitt v. Emery, 211 Minn. 547, 2 N.W.2d 413, 416, 139 A.L.R. 1242 (1942); Annot., 146 A.L.R. 977, 978.

It should be borne in mind that the problem here is one of privilege, not of admissibility in evidence. As to the latter, see § 267 infra.

14. See § 89 supra.

against liability.[15] Revised Uniform Evidence Rule (1974) 502(b) extends the privilege to confidential communications for the purpose of facilitating the rendition of legal services to the client to communications "(4) between representatives of the client or between the client and representatives of the client . . . . ." The import of this provision remains largely unexplored.

Whether a communication by the client's agent, on behalf of the client, to the latter's attorney would be privileged, has been discussed elsewhere.[16] Under the recent Supreme Court decision in Upjohn v. United States [17] the attorney-client privilege will protect intra-corporate communications made for the purpose of securing legal advice if, additionally, the communication relates to the communicating employee's [18] assigned duties and is treated as confidential by the corporation. The communications in question were made by the employees directly to General Counsel and other lawyers representing the corporation in the investigation. An analogous rule would seem appropriate for application to agency situations not involving corporations.

By contrast, routine reports of agents made in the regular course of business, before suit is brought or threatened, have usually, though not always, been treated as pre-existing documents which not being privileged in the client's hands do not become so when delivered into the possession of his attorney.[19] It is clear, however, that these classifications are not quite mutually exclusive and that some cases will fall in a doubtful borderland.[20] And the law is in the making on the question whether a report of accident or other casualty, by a policy-holder or his agents to a company insuring the policy-holder against liability, is to be treated as privileged when the insurance company passes it on to the attorney who will represent both the company and the insured.[21] Reasonably the insurance company may be

---

15. Cases involving the claim of privilege for such reports and statements are collected in Note 26 Minn. L.Rev. 744 (1942); Annot., 22 A.L.R.2d 659.

16. See § 87.

17. 449 U.S. 383 (1981).

18. See § 87 supra, at n. 23.

19. Woolley v. North London R. Co., L.R 4 C.P. 602 (1869) (court allowed inspection of reports of accident by guard of train, an inspector, and the locomotive superintendent to the general manager; significant question was not time of reports nor whether confidential, but whether made in ordinary course of duty); Anderson v. Bank of British Columbia, L.R. 2 Ch.Div. 644 (C.A.1876) (letter from manager of branch bank to head office in response to telegram, reporting on transfer of funds from one account to another, written before suit filed though litigation then probable, not privileged against production, since there was no suggestion in the telegram that the report was for submission to counsel); Hurley v. Connecticut Co., 118 Conn. 276, 172 A. 86 (1934) (motorman's report of accident subject to inspection; mere fact that it was made for preparation against possibility of litigation not sufficient for privilege); Wise v. Western Union Telegraph Co., 178 A. 640 (Del.Super.1935) (report from one branch office to another, at latter's request, upon complaint of patron that forged telegram transmitted in his name; held not privileged from discovery in absence of clear showing that document was prepared with bona fide intention of laying before attorney); Linton v. Lehigh Valley Railroad Co., 25 A.D.2d 334, 269 N.Y.S.2d 490 (1966) (reports of members of train crew discoverable); Robertson v. Commonwealth, 181 Va. 520, 25

S.E.2d 352, 146 A.L.R. 966 (1943) (motorman's report of accident made in course of ordinary duty before suit brought or threatened required to be produced at trial by counsel from his files); 8 Wigmore, Evidence § 2318 (McNaughton rev. 1961); Annot., 146 A.L.R. 977, 980.

20. See, e.g., The Hopper No. 13, [1925] Prob. 52 (shipmaster's report required by general rule, of a collision, on a printed form headed "confidential report . . . in view of anticipated litigation," sent to solicitors; held, privileged); Jessup v. Superior Court, 151 Cal.App.2d 102, 311 P.2d 177 (1957) (father of boy drowned in municipal pool not entitled to inspect report of investigation made for use of city attorney for defense purposes, where that was dominant purpose though it might also be used for study in accident prevention). Note, 88 U.Pa.L.Rev. 467, 469 (1940).

Resolving the question according to the dominant purpose of the report, as in Holm v. Superior Court, 42 Cal.2d 500, 267 P.2d 1025, 268 P.2d 722 (1954), will often pose difficulties of practical application. A suggested solution is to apply the privilege only to reports having no purpose except use in litigation. Note, 21, U.Chi.L.Rev. 752 (1954).

21. Privilege denied: Virginia-Carolina Chemical Co. v. Knight, 106 Va. 674, 680, 56 S.E. 725, 727 (1907); Brown v. Meyer, 137 Kan. 553, 21 P.2d 368 (1933). Privilege accorded: People v. Ryan, 30 Ill.2d 456, 197 N.E.2d 15 (1964); Brakhage v. Graff, 190 Neb. 53, 206 N.W.2d 45 (1973); In re Klemann, 132 Ohio St. 187, 5 N.E.2d 492, 108 A.L.R. 505 (1936); New York Casualty Co. v. Superior Court, 30 Cal.App.2d 130, 85 P.2d 965 (1938). Notes, 48 Mich.L.Rev. 364 (1950), 26 Minn.L.

treated as an intermediary to secure legal representation for the insured, by whom the confidential communications can be transmitted as through a trusted agent. A report to a liability insurer can have no purpose other than use in potential litigation.[22]

Work product. The discussion thus far has centered upon the extent to which the attorney-client privilege, just as any other privilege, can be invoked as a bar to discovery. Another, and much more frequently encountered limitation upon discovery of materials contained in the files of counsel, is furnished by the so-called "work product" doctrine, exempting trial preparations, in varying degrees, from discovery.[23]

On June 14, 1946, the Advisory Committee on Federal Rules of Civil Procedure recommended the following amendment to Federal Rule 30(b):

The court shall not order the production or inspection of any writing obtained or prepared by the adverse party, his attorney, surety, indemnitor, or agent in anticipation of litigation or in preparation for trial unless satisfied that denial of production or inspection will unfairly prejudice the party seeking the production or inspection in preparing his claim or defense or will cause him undue hardship or injustice. The court shall not order the production or inspection of any part of the writing that reflects an attorney's mental impressions, conclusions, opinions, or legal theories, or, except as provided in Rule 35, the conclusions of an expert.

The Supreme Court took no action on the proposed amendment but on January 3, 1947, handed down the decision in Hickman v. Taylor,[24] which is summarized below.

A tugboat, while helping tow a B. & O. Railroad carfloat, sank in the Delaware river, drowning five of the crew. Three days later, the two partner-owners of the tug and their underwriters hired Fortenbaugh's law firm to defend them against potential litigation arising from the drownings and to sue the railroad for damage to the tug. After a public Steamboat Inspectors' hearing, at which the four survivors testified, Fortenbaugh obtained signed statements from them. He also interviewed other persons, in some instances making memoranda. One action for death under the Jones Act was filed, the other death claims being settled. Plaintiff's Interrogatory 38 asked whether statements of witnesses were obtained; if written, copies were to be furnished; if oral, the exact provisions were to be set forth in detail. Upon refusal to comply, the two owners and Fortenbaugh were

---

Rev. 744, 745 (1941), 88 U.Pa.L.Rev. 467, 470 (1940); Annot., 22 A.L.R.2d 659.

22. The case for applying the privilege is particularly appealing when the report contains incriminating statements, as in People v. Ryan, supra n. 21. If the attorney-client privilege is denied, the insured is confronted with an unhappy choice between breaching the clause of his policy requiring him to co-operate in the defense of claims and waiving his privilege against self-incrimination.

23. The general provisions governing discovery under the Federal Rules of Civil Procedure are set out in Rule 26. The methods and general scope of discovery are as follows:

(a) **Discovery Methods.** Parties may obtain discovery by one or more of the following methods: depositions upon oral examination or written questions; written interrogatories; production of documents or things or permission to enter upon land or other property, for inspection and other purposes; physical and mental examinations; and requests for admission. . . .

(b) **Scope of Discovery.** Unless otherwise limited by order of the court in accordance with these rules, the scope of discovery is as follows:

(1) *In General.* Parties may obtain discovery regarding any matter, not privileged, which is relevant to the subject matter involved in the pending action, whether it relates to the claim or defense of the party seeking discovery or to the claim or defense of any other party, including the existence, description, nature, custody, condition and location of any books, documents, or other tangible things and the identity and location of persons having knowledge of any discoverable matter. It is not ground for objection that the information sought will be inadmissible at the trial if the information sought appears reasonably calculated to lead to the discovery of admissible evidence.

Rule 26(c) provides that upon proper showing the court may make any order which justice requires to protect a party or person from "annoyance, embarrassment, oppression, or undue burden or expense."

24. 329 U.S. 495 (1947).

adjudged in contempt.[25] The Third Circuit Court of Appeals reversed, and the Supreme Court granted certiorari.

During oral argument, the following exchange occurred:

Mr. Justice Jackson: What would be the practical effect in the daily functioning of our judicial system if we order counsel to produce as requested in Interrogatory 38?

Mr. Fortenbaugh: In my judgment, interviews will go unrecorded, unpleasant sources will not be pursued, and counsel will be tempted to keep files under his bed at home.

The Supreme Court affirmed the judgment of the Court of Appeals. The problem, said the Court, was to balance the interest in privacy of a lawyer's work against the interest supporting reasonable and necessary inquiries. Proper preparation of a client's case demands that information be assembled and sifted, legal theories be prepared, and strategy be planned "without undue and needless interference."[26] If the product of this work (interviews, statements, memoranda, etc.) were available merely on demand, the effect on the legal profession would be demoralizing. Discovery may be had where relevant and non-privileged facts, necessary for preparation of the opposing party's case, remain hidden, or the witness unavailable. The burden is on the party seeking to invade the privacy of the lawyer to show justifica-

tion; this is "implicit in the rules as now [in 1947] constituted."[27] Rule 34 requires a showing of good cause for an order to produce documents, and Rule 30(b) gives the judge authority to limit examination upon the taking of a deposition when it appears that the examination is being conducted in bad faith or so as to annoy, embarrass, or oppress. Here no attempt was made to show need for the written statements. And as for the oral statements, to require Fortenbaugh to reproduce them would have a highly adverse effect upon the legal profession, making the lawyer more an ordinary witness than an officer of the court. Under the circumstances of this case, no showing could be made that would justify requiring disclosure of the mental impressions of counsel as to what the witnesses told him.

Considerable disagreement in the lower courts as to the meaning of Hickman v. Taylor followed that decision, no doubt resulting at least in part from the labored path followed by the Court to the conclusion that the matter of a qualified work product privilege was in fact covered by its own rules as then written. Finally after more than 20 years, the Court in 1970 adopted an amended Rule 26(b), with subdivision (3) directed in specific terms to the scope of the qualified work product privilege.[28] Nonetheless, Hickman v. Taylor remains a "brooding

---

25. The reports of the decisions as the case progressed through the courts convey the impression that Mr. Fortenbaugh and his clients were jailed for contempt, but that was not the case. Enforcement of the contempt judgment was stayed from the time of its entry until the ultimate disposition of the proceeding. Fortenbaugh, Hickman versus Taylor Revisited, 13 Defense L.J. 1, 13 (1964).

26. 329 U.S. at 511.

27. 329 U.S. at 512.

28. Fed.R.Civ.P. 26(b)(3):

(3) *Trial Preparation: Materials.* Subject to the provisions of subdivision (b)(4) of this rule, a party may obtain discovery of documents and tangible things otherwise discoverable under subdivision (b)(1) of this rule and prepared in anticipation of litigation or for trial by or for another party or by or for that other party's representative (including his attorney, consultant, surety, indemnitor, insurer, or agent) only upon a showing that the party seeking

discovery has substantial need of the materials in the preparation of his case and that he is unable without undue hardship to obtain the substantial equivalent of the materials by other means. In ordering discovery of such materials when the required showing has been made, the court shall protect against disclosure of the mental impressions, conclusions, opinions, or legal theories of an attorney or other representative of a party concerning the litigation.

A party may obtain without the required showing a statement concerning the action or its subject matter previously made by that party. Upon request, a person not a party may obtain without the required showing a statement concerning the action or its subject matter previously made by that person. . . .

Fed.R.Civ.P. 26(b)(4) contains provisions relating to discovery of facts known and opinions held by experts.

The requirement of a showing of good cause has been eliminated from Rule 34 in favor of a provision substituting the need requirement of Rule 26(b).

omnipresence," much cited and quoted by the courts, and in fact still governs an important area of the qualified work product privilege.[29]

These salient provisions of Rule 26(b)(3) should be noted:[30]

(1) In terms its work product immunity extends only to "documents and tangible things.[31]" yet discovery of documents constituted only one-half the subject of Hickman v. Taylor. The other half, i.e. mental impressions and the like, receives only pendant mention in the second sentence of Rule 26(b)(3), discussed in paragraph (5) below.

(2) The document or thing must have been "prepared in anticipation of litigation or for trial." If this scope seems unduly limited, it must be remembered that litigation is the frame of reference for work product. When the lawyer is engaged in rendering other services, e.g. the drafting of a contract, information which he needs will most likely be communicated by the client, falling within the attorney-client privilege. Information from outside sources is peculiarly a characteristic of the litigation situation.[32]

(3) Hickman v. Taylor on its facts dealt only with work produced by an attorney, leaving open a troublesome question as to the status of the product of claim adjusters, investigators, and the like. The rule, however, is specific, speaking of documents prepared "by or for another party or by or for that other party's representative (including his attorney, consultant, surety, indemnitor, insurer, or agent)."

(4) The requirement of need is spelled out "only upon a showing that the party seeking discovery has substantial need of the materials in the preparation of his case and that he is unable without undue hardship to obtain the substantial equivalent of the materials by other means."[33]

(5) The judge in ordering discovery of covered materials is directed to "protect against disclosure of the mental impressions, conclusions, opinions, or legal theories of an attorney or other representative of a party concerning the litigation." Literally read, the rule appears to protect mental impressions and the like of the lawyer only against disclosure that would be incidental to disclosure of documents and tangible things, in

---

29. See Upjohn Co. v. United States, 449 U.S. 383, 397–402 (1981).

30. For more extended coverage, see Wright, Law of Federal Courts § 82 (4th ed. 1983).

31. See n. 36 infra.

32. See, e.g., Upjohn Co. v. United States, supra n. 29, at 397.

33. Among the many cases construing the "substantial need" requirement, the following may be noted: United States v. American Telephone & Telegraph Co., 642 F.2d 1285 (D.C.Cir.1980) (showing of substantial need inadequate); In re LTV Securities Litigation, 89 F.R.D. 595 (N.D.Tex.1981) (same); Jarvis, Inc. v. American Telephone & Telegraph Co., 84 F.R.D. 286 (D.Colo.1979) (substantial need present where materials relevant and not otherwise available to requesting party); American Standard, Inc., v. Bendix Corp., 80 F.R.D. 706 (W.D.Mo.1978). Substantial need, however, does not vary, as noted, from the earlier required "good cause" of then Rule 34, and the decisions applying that earlier standard remain in point. See, e.g., Martin v. Capital Transit Co., 170 F.2d 811 (D.C.Cir. 1948) (employee's report of accident, motion for discovery denied; movant must show in motion and affidavit grounds of "good cause"); Newell v. Capital Transit Co., 7 F.R.D. 732, 11 Fed.Rules Serv. 34.411 Case 2 (D.C.1948) (plaintiff's motion for discovery of witness-statements taken by defendant's investigators; fact

that plaintiff unconscious after accident and his lawyers unable to locate witnesses is good cause); Lauritzen v. Atlantic Greyhound Corp., 8 F.R.D. 237, 11 Fed. Rules Serv. 34.411 case 6 (E.D.Tenn.1948) (plaintiffs sue for death of son in bus accident and seek discovery, list of witnesses and statements, sufficient); Lindsay v. Prince, 8 F.R.D. 233, 11 Fed.Rules Serv. 34.411 case 5 (N.D.Ohio 1948) (defendant in personal injury, sued belatedly after plaintiff had sued other person, was not present at accident and made no investigation, sufficient); Haase v. Chapman, 308 F.Supp. 399 (W.D. Mo.1969) (where judgment debtor might have been engaged in fraudulent transactions involving corporation, calculated to conceal assets subject to execution good cause existed for broad discovery of records of corporation by judgment creditor); Merrin Jewelry Co. v. St. Paul Fire & Marine Insurance Co., 49 F.R.D. 54 (1969) (uniqueness of documents established the required good cause for discoverability); Talbott Construction Co. v. United States, 49 F.R.D. 68 (1969) (good cause as required by the rule for production of documents implies greater showing of need than relevance and materiality); Shultz v. Midtown, 49 F.R.D. 94 (1969) (before a court may grant an order requiring production of documents, it must be satisfied not only as to presence of relevancy and absence of privilege, the normal requisite for discovery, but also to presence of good cause for moving party's request).

this regard being absolute in terms. If, however, counsel had not reduced a witness' statement to writing and counsel's deposition were taken in an effort to discover what the witness had said,[34] Rule 26(b)(3) literally would not apply. Under these circumstances, however, it seems inconceivable that courts would not fall back upon Hickman v. Taylor and require an extraordinarily strong showing of need, as has indeed been the case.[35]

(6) A person, whether a party or a witness, is entitled to a copy of his own statement merely by requesting it; no showing of need is required.

The rule, it should be observed, does not immunize facts, or the identities of persons having knowledge of facts, or the existence of documents as contrasted with the documents themselves.[36] Nor does the rule spell

out the breadth of application or the duration of the qualified privilege that it recognizes. Does it apply at trial?[37] Can it be invoked in other proceedings?[38] Case law is meagre.

A further provision of revised Rule 26(b)(4) permits, in proper circumstances, discovery of facts and opinions of experts whom the party expects to call as witnesses at trial or who have been retained but are not expected to testify.[39]

 WESTLAW REFERENCES

Attorney-Client Privilege

witness** /3 record* statement* /s attorney lawyer client /3 privilege*

Work Product

"work product" /s attorney lawyer client /3 privilege* hickman taylor /15 329 /5 495 & "work product"

---

34. Hickman v. Taylor, 329 U.S. 495, 504 (1947) indicated that deposing counsel is the proper procedure for attempting to force disclosure.

35. Upjohn v. United States, 449 U.S. 383, 507–508 (1981).

36. Hickman v. Taylor, supra n. 34, at 507–508.

37. United States v. Nobles, 422 U.S. 225, 239 (1975) suggests that the qualified privilege may be invoked at trial.

38. Duplan Corp. v. Moulinage et Retorderie de Chavanoz, 487 F.2d 480 (4th Cir.1973) recognized the qualified privilege in another unrelated case. On further appeal, 509 F.2d 730 (1974), cert. denied 420 U.S. 997. See Wright & Miller, Federal Practice and Procedure § 2024, pp. 200–02.

39. Fed.R.Civ.P. 26(b)(4) provides:

(4) *Trial Preparation: Experts.* Discovery of facts known and opinions held by experts, otherwise discoverable under the provisions of subdivision (b) (1) of this rule and acquired or developed in anticipation of litigation or for trial, may be obtained only as follows:

(A)(i) A party may through interrogatories require any other party to identify each person whom the other party expects to call as an expert witness at trial, to state the subject matter on which the expert is expected to testify, and to state the substance of the facts and opinions to which the expert is expected to testify and a summary of the grounds for each opinion. (ii) Upon motion, the court may order further discovery by other means, subject to such restrictions as to scope and such provisions, pursuant to subdivision (b)(4)(C) of this rule, concerning fees and expenses as the court may deem appropriate.

(B) A party may discover facts known or opinions held by an expert who has been retained or specially employed by another party in anticipation of litigation or preparation for trial and who is not expected to be called as a witness at trial, only as provided in Rule 35(b) or upon a showing of exceptional circumstances under which it is impracticable for the party seeking discovery to obtain facts or opinions on the same subject by other means.

. . .

See Advisory Committee's Note, 48 F.R.D. 487, 503–505. An extensive recent decision reviewing the requirements of the rule and the decisions construing it is Ager v. Jane C. Stormont Hospital, 622 F.2d 496 (10th Cir.1980) noted 60 N.C.L.Rev. 695 (1980). See also, Connors, A New Look At An Old Concern—Protecting Expert Information From Discovery Under the Federal Rules, 18 Duquesne L.Rev. 271 (1978); Friedenthal, Discovery and Use of an Adverse Party's Expert Information, 14 Stan.L.Rev. 455 (1962); Graham, Discovery of Experts Under Rule 26(b)(4) of the Federal Rules of Civil Procedure, 1976 U.Ill.L.F. 895, 1977 id. 169; Long, Discovery and Experts Under the Federal Rules of Civil Procedure 38 F.R.D. 111 (1965); Note, Protection of Opinion Work Product Under the Federal Rules of Civil Procedure, 64 Va.L.Rev. 333 (1978); Annot. 33 A.L.R.Fed. 403.

Under some circumstances, where the expert is retained, not to testify but to assist in the management of the litigation as "associate counsel," the attorney-client privilege may be applicable. See § 89, n. 16. To that extent, the privilege may operate as a limitation upon the discovery provided in Rule 26(b)(4).

§ 97. Discovery in Criminal Cases: Statements by Witnesses

The development of discovery in criminal cases has, for a variety of reasons, lagged far behind that available in the civil area.[1] The pros and cons of the continuing debate on the subject are outside the scope of the present treatment, though it is pertinent to

§ 97

1. Generally, see Brennan, The Criminal Prosecution: Sporting Event or Quest for Truth? 1963 Wash. U.L.Q. 279; Flannery, The Prosecutor's Case Against Liberal Discovery, 33 F.R.D. 74 (1963); Fletcher, Pretrial Discovery in State Criminal Cases, 12 Stan.L.Rev. 293 (1960); Goldstein, The State and the Accused: Balance of Advantage in Criminal Procedure, 69 Yale L.J. 1149 (1960); Kaufman, Discovery in Criminal Cases, 44 F.R.D. 481 (1968); Louisell, Criminal Discovery: Dilemma Real or Apparent? 49 Calif.L.Rev. 56 (1961); Nakell, Criminal Discovery for the Defense and the Prosecution—The Developing Constitutional Considerations, 50 N.C.L.Rev. 437 (1972); Traynor, Ground Lost and Found in Criminal Discovery, 39 N.Y.U.L.Rev. 228 (1964); Notes, 1955 U.Ill.L.F. 158, 59 W.Va.L.Rev. 221 (1957), 60 Yale L.J. 626 (1951); 6 Wigmore, Evidence §§ 1850–1855b, 1859g, 1863 (Chadbourn rev. 1976); Dec.Dig. Criminal Law ⟝627½.

2. See Wright, Federal Practice and Procedure § 252: ". . . those who favor broad discovery are plainly winning the fight . . . ."

3. Fed.R.Crim.P. 16 contains the following provisions. It will be noted that subdivisions (a)(2) and (b)(2) deal specifically with work product protection; also that reference to 18 U.S.C.A. 3500 remains in (a)(2) although that act has been superseded by Criminal Rule 26.2, see n. 9 infra.

Rule 16.

DISCOVERY AND INSPECTION

(a) Disclosure of evidence by the government.

(1) Information subject to disclosure.

(A) Statement of defendant. Upon request of a defendant the government shall permit the defendant to inspect and copy or photograph: any relevant written or recorded statements made by the defendant, or copies thereof, within the possession, custody or control of the government, the existence of which is known, or by the exercise of due diligence may become known, to the attorney for the government; the substance of any oral statement which the government intends to offer in evidence at the trial made by the defendant whether before or after arrest in response to interrogation by any person then known to the defendant to be a government agent; and recorded testimony of the defendant before a grand jury which relates to the offense charged.

. . . .

(C) Documents and tangible objects. Upon request of the defendant the government shall permit

observe that the trend seems clearly in the direction of more liberal discovery in the criminal area.[2] This expansion of criminal discovery, like its earlier civil analogue, has raised the question whether "work product" should be afforded protection, and even the more advanced rules and proposals on the subject do undertake to provide such protection.[3]

the defendant to inspect and copy or photograph books, papers, documents, photographs, tangible objects, buildings or places, or copies or portions thereof, which are within the possession, custody or control of the government, and which are material to the preparation of his defense or are intended for use by the government as evidence in chief at the trial, or were obtained from or belong to the defendant.

(D) Reports of examinations and tests. Upon request of a defendant the government shall permit the defendant to inspect and copy or photograph any results or reports of physical or mental examinations, and of scientific tests or experiments, or copies thereof, which are within the possession, custody, or control of the government, the existence of which is known, or by the exercise of due diligence may become known, to the attorney for the government, and which are material to the preparation of the defense or are intended for use by the government as evidence in chief at the trial.

(2) Information not subject to disclosure. Except as provided in paragraphs (A), (B), and (D) of subdivision (a)(1), this rule does not authorize the discovery or inspection of reports, memoranda, or other internal government documents made by the attorney for the government or other government agents in connection with the investigation or prosecution of the case, or of statements made by government witnesses or prospective government witnesses except as provided in 18 U.S.C. § 3500.

(3) Grand jury transcripts. Except as provided in Rule 6 and subdivision (a)(1)(A) of this rule, these rules do not relate to discovery or inspection of recorded proceedings of a grand jury.

(b) Disclosure of evidence by the defendant.

(1) Information subject to disclosure.

(A) Documents and tangible objects. If the defendant requests disclosure under subdivision (a)(1) (C) or (D) of this rule, upon compliance with such request by the government, the defendant, on request of the government, shall permit the government to inspect and copy or photograph books, papers, documents, photographs, tangible objects, or copies or portions thereof, which are within the possession, custody, or control of the defendant and which the defendant intends to introduce as evidence in chief at the trial.

(B) Reports of examinations and tests. If the defendant requests disclosure under subdivision (a) (1)(C) or (D) of this rule, upon compliance with such

A distinguishable question which has drawn considerable attention is whether disclosure should be granted of material at, as opposed to before, trial. At a fairly early date, both federal and state decisions [4] had espoused the view that when the statements of prosecution witnesses contradicting their trial testimony are shown to be in the hands of the government the defendant is entitled to demand their production at the trial. But despite this background, the famous *Jencks* [5] case was widely viewed as a startling incursion into new territory. The Supreme Court held in that case that the trial court had erroneously denied defense requests to inspect reports of two undercover agents who were government witnesses. It was not required, said the Court, that defendant show that the reports were inconsistent

with the witnesses' testimony; if they related to the same subject, defendant was entitled to make the decision whether they were useful to the defense. The dissent condemned the holding as affording the criminal "a Roman holiday for rummaging through confidential information [in government files] as well as vital national secrets." [6] This view was echoed in widespread protests by the press, by the Department of Justice, and in the halls of Congress where the so-called Jencks Act of 1959 [7] was hastily enacted.[8] Despite this background, the Act was for the most part a codification of the decision which had been so vehemently attacked. The Act has now been superseded [9] by Rule 26.2 of the Federal Rules of Criminal Procedure.[10] However, the terms of the Act must be considered in examining

request by the government, the defendant, on request of the government, shall permit the government to inspect and copy or photograph any results or reports of physical or mental examinations and of scientific tests or experiments made in connection with the particular case, or copies thereof, within the possession or control of the defendant, which the defendant intends to introduce as evidence in chief at the trial or which were prepared by a witness whom the defendant intends to call at the trial when the results or reports relate to his testimony.

(2) **Information not subject to disclosure.** Except as to scientific or medical reports, this subdivision does not authorize the discovery or inspection of reports, memoranda, or other internal defense documents made by the defendant, or his attorneys or agents in connection with the investigation or defense of the case, or of statements made by the defendant, or by government or defense witnesses, or by prospective government or defense witnesses, to the defendant, his agents or attorneys.

See also ABA Standards for Criminal Justice, Discovery and Procedure Before Trial, Parts II and III.

4. Gordon v. United States, 344 U.S. 414 (1953); People v. Riser, 47 Cal.2d 566, 305 P.2d 1, 13 (1957), cert. denied 353 U.S. 930.

5. Jencks v. United States, 353 U.S. 657 (1957) (prosecution of labor union official for filing false non-Communist affidavit with NLRB).

6. 353 U.S. at 681–682.

7. 18 U.S.C.A. § 3500.

8. The history of the legislation is graphically recounted in Keeffe, Jinks and Jencks, 7 Cath.U.L.Rev. 91 (1958).

9. The Act has not formally been repealed, apparently awaiting the long pending revision of Title 18. However, Rule 26.2 of the Federal Rules of Criminal

Procedure, covering the same subject matter, was promulgated by the Supreme Court and transmitted to the Congress, where its effective date was postponed to December 1, 1980 unless other action was taken. Efforts to defeat the rule failing, it took effect December 1, 1980. This history warrants the conclusion that the rule has replaced the Act.

10. Fed.R.Crim.P. 26.2 provides:

PRODUCTION OF STATEMENTS OF WITNESSES

(a) **Motion for Production.** After a witness other than the defendant has testified on direct examination, the court, on motion of a party who did not call the witness, shall order the attorney for the government or the defendant and his attorney, as the case may be, to produce, for the examination and use of the moving party any statement of the witness that is in their possession and that relates to the subject matter concerning which the witness has testified.

(b) **Production of Entire Statement.** If the entire contents of the statement relate to the subject matter concerning which the witness has testified, the court shall order that the statement be delivered to the moving party.

(c) **Production of Excised Statement.** If the other party claims that the statement contains matter that does not relate to the subject matter concerning which the witness has testified, the court shall order that it be delivered to the court in camera. Upon inspection, the court shall excise the portions of the statement that do not relate to the subject matter concerning which the witness has testified, and shall order that the statement, with such material excised, be delivered to the moving party. Any portion of the statement that is withheld from the defendant over his objection shall be preserved by the attorney for the government, and, in the event of a conviction and

the effect of Rule 26.2, as will appear from the subsequent discussion.

Subsection (a) of the Act as amended provided that no statement by a government witness or prospective witness should be the subject of subpoena, discovery, or inspection until the witness has testified on direct examination in the trial. Subsection (b) provided that after a witness called by the government has testified on direct the court should, on motion of defendant, order the government to produce any statement (as later defined) relating to the subject matter of his testimony. Under subsection (c) the court will in case of question examine the statement and excise portions not related to the testimony. If, under subsection (d), the government elects not to comply with the order to produce, the testimony is to be stricken or, if justice requires, a mistrial is to be declared. In subsection (e), "statement" as used in subsections (b), (c), and (d) is defined; the definition is very precise and narrow, designed to include only statements that beyond any reasonable question represent with a very high precision the words used by the witness. It will be observed that subsection (a) was designed to bar disclosure of any statement of a witness, regardless of how

precise or imprecise a rendition it might be, unless and until the witness had testified for the government. After that testimony had been given, then disclosure was allowed and required but only as to highly precise statements, as defined in (e). If a writing were not a statement at all, in the broad sense of (a), the Act did not affect it.[11] Writings which were statements in the broad sense of (a), but not within the strict definition of (e), or within (e) but whose maker did not testify, remained locked away,[12] except as they might be obtainable under Brady v. Maryland,[13] or under Evidence Rule 612 discussed below.

For the most part Rule 26.2 transposed the Act into the Federal Rules of Criminal Procedure.[14] Some changes must, however, be noted. Rule 26.2 does not contain the prohibition of subsection (a) of the Act against compelling disclosure of a statement, in the broad sense, unless and until the witness has testified on direct. Thus Rule 26.2 deals only with compelling production of statements within the strict definition of subsection (e) of the Act, which is retained as subdivision (F) of the Rule. But as a companion to Rule 26.2, there was at the same time added to Rule 17 of the Criminal

an appeal by the defendant, shall be made available to the appellate court for the purpose of determining the correctness of the decision to excise the portion of the statement.

(d) Recess for Examination of Statement. Upon delivery of the statement to the moving party the court, upon application of that party may recess proceedings in the trial for the examination of such statement and for preparation for its use in the trial.

(e) Sanction for Failure to Produce Statement. If the other party elects not to comply with an order to deliver a statement to the moving party, the court shall order that the testimony of the witness be stricken from the record and that the trial proceed, or, if it is the attorney for the government who elects not to comply, shall declare a mistrial if required by the interest of justice.

(f) Definition. As used in this rule, a "statement" of a witness means:

(1) a written statement made by the witness that is signed or otherwise adopted or approved by him;

(2) a substantially verbatim recital of an oral statement made by the witness that is recorded

contemporaneously with the making of the oral statement and that is contained in a stenographic, mechanical, electrical, or other recording or a transcription thereof; or

(3) a statement, however taken or recorded, or a transcription thereof, made by the witness to a grand jury.

11. Simmons v. United States, 390 U.S. 377 (1967) (photograph not attached to a statement); Communist Party v. Subversive Activities Control Board, 254 F.2d 314 (D.C.Cir.1958) (Department of Justice records of payments made to informant-witness).

12. Palermo v. United States, 360 U.S. 343, 351 (1959) (government agent's summary of interview with witness not a "statement" within subsection (e) of Act and production not required). Although agreeing with the result, four members of the Court disagreed with the ruling of exclusivity.

Note also the work product protections of Fed.R. Crim.P. 16(a)(2) and (b)(2), supra n. 2.

13. 373 U.S. 83 (1963). See § 252 n. 10 infra.

14. For text of rule see n. 10 supra.

Rules, which deals with subpoenas, a new subdivision (h):

> Statements made by witnesses or prospective witnesses may not be subpoenaed from the government or the defendant under this rule, but shall be subject to production only in accordance with the provisions of Rule 26.2.[15]

While superficially this may appear to constitute no more than a relocation of subsection (a) of the Act, in fact the separation undermines the force of any argument that Rule 26.2 controls all statements of witnesses and prospective witnesses, in the broad sense, and leaves it effective only with regard to statements as narrowly defined in subdivision (F) of Rule 26.2. This is important in connection with the relationship between Rule 26.2 and Evidence Rule 612, discussed below.

A further highly significant change effected by Rule 26.2 was the expansion of coverage to include statements by defense witnesses and prospective witnesses as well as those for the government.[16] This change was stimulated by the Supreme Court's decision in United States v. Nobles.[17] As under the Act, the penalty for refusal is striking of the testimony, with the further provision that if the refusing party is the government a mistrial may be declared if justice requires.[18] A defendant cannot, of course, be allowed to abort a trial by refusing to deliver a statement.

In an earlier section[19] attention was directed to the need to examine the relationship between Criminal Rule 26.2 and Evidence Rule 612. That section pointed out

that when a witness while testifying refers to a writing to refresh his memory, an opposing party is entitled to inspect it, to cross-examine upon it, and to introduce in evidence portions related to the testimony of the witness; if the reference for refreshing was prior to testifying, access to and use of the writing is subject to the court's discretion.[20] If the writing consulted for refreshment is the statement of a witness or prospective witness, the potential for conflict between Criminal Rule 26.2 and Evidence Rule 612 is seen. If the writing is a statement within the strict definition of Rule 26.2(F), the conflict is in reality no more than an overlap, as under either rule disclosure is required once the witness has testified on direct. But when the statement is a statement in the broad sense, as under subsection (a) of the Act, but not within the strict definition of subsection (e) of the Act, the construction in *Palermo*[21] as previously observed, was that no disclosure was available. The confusion is compounded by the fact that Rule 612 opens with the phrase, "Except as otherwise provided in criminal proceedings by section 3500 of title 18, United States Code . . . " and has not been amended. What is the effect of the exception? Does subsection (a) of the Act continue with its former effect? Did *Palermo* survive, pro tanto, the subsequent enactment of Rule 612? A satisfactory resolution probably lies only in the legislative sphere. Meanwhile a look at fundamentals may suggest a satisfactory construction. Both the Act (and Rule 26.2) and Rule 612 are direct-

---

15. Fed.R.Crim.P. 17(h), effective Dec. 1, 1980.

16. Fed.R.Crim.P. 26.2(a), supra n. 10.

17. 422 U.S. 255 (1975). A defense investigator had interviewed government identification witnesses before trial, and the defense proposed to call him to impeach them. The judge ruled that this would be allowed only if his interview report was given to the government. The defense refused, and the testimony was excluded. The Supreme Court ruled that the work product protection was waived as to the subject matter of the testimony by the "testimonial" use of the report in cross-examination of the identification witnesses and attempting to refresh the recollection of one of them.

As to the inclusion of statements by defense witness in Rule 26.2, see Pulaski, Extending the Disclosure Requirements of the Jencks Act to Defendants: Constitutional and Nonconstitutional Considerations, 64 Iowa L.Rev. 1 (1978), Federal Rule 26.2 and the New Mutuality of Discovery: Constitutional Objections and Tactical Suggestions, 17 Crim.L.Bull. 285 (1981). See also § 133 at n. 7 infra.

18. Fed.R.Crim.P. 26.2(E) supra n. 10.

19. See § 9 supra.

20. Fed.R.Evid. 612.

21. Supra n. 12.

ed to testing the credibility of witnesses.[22] One pursues that end by giving access to statements which, if inconsistent, undoubtedly qualify for impeachment by that route. The other pursues the same end by giving access to materials generally, whether statements or not, which may have influenced the memory and narrative of the witness. Both can operate side by side without real conflict. The tangle is one of language, not of goals. This result is fairly reachable within the present language in view of the disappearance of subsection (a) of the Act, as noted above.[23]

WESTLAW REFERENCES

jenck* /2 act*

---

22. Fed.R.Evid. 612, Adv.Comm.Note.

23. Supra at n. 15. For a canvass and evaluation of possible solutions, see Foster, The Jencks Act—Rule 26.2—Rule 612 Interface—"Confusion Worse Confounded," 34 Okla.L.Rev. 679 (1981). The same result as in the text is reached by Weinstein & Berger, Evidence § 612 [02]–[04], but by a different route. Contra, Louisell & Mueller, Federal Evidence § 349 (1979), prior to effective date of Criminal Rules 17(h) and 26.2.

Although the Supreme Court disclaimed a constitutional base for *Jencks*, United States v. Augenblick, 393 U.S. 348 (1969), one cannot be unmindful of the constitutional support that has been given to the defense right to attack the credibility of prosecution witnesses, whether by cross-examination, Alford v. United States, 282 U.S. 687 (1931), or testimony of impeaching witnesses, Davis v. Alaska, 415 U.S. 308 (1974).

Chapter 11

THE PRIVILEGE FOR CONFIDENTIAL INFORMATION SECURED IN THE COURSE OF THE PHYSICIAN–PATIENT RELATIONSHIP

Table of Sections

---

§ 98. The Statement of the Rule and Its Purpose

The common law knew no privilege for confidential information imparted to a physician. When a physician raised the question before Lord Mansfield whether he was required to disclose professional confidences, the great Chief Justice drew the line clear. "If a surgeon was voluntarily to reveal these secrets, to be sure, he would be guilty of a breach of honor and of great indiscretion; but to give that information in a court of justice, which by the law of the land he is bound to do, will never be imputed to him as any indiscretion whatever." [1]

The pioneer departure from the common law rule was the New York statute of 1828 which in its original form was as follows: "No person authorized to practice physic or surgery shall be allowed to disclose any information which he may have acquired in attending any patient, in a professional character, and which information was necessary to

---

§ 98

1. The Duchess of Kingston's Trial, 20 How.St.Trials 573 (1776). See, in general, the able treatise, De Witt, Privileged Communications Between Physician and Patient (1958); 8 Wigmore, Evidence §§ 2380–2391 (McNaughton rev. 1961); Model Code of Evidence Rules 220–223 and commentary; C.J.S. Witnesses §§ 293–301; Dec.Dig. Witnesses ⊙208–214, 217, 219(4–6), 220–223. See also Hammelmann, Professional Privilege: A Comparative Study, 28 Can.Bar Rev. 750 (1950); Freedman, Medical Privilege, 32 id. 1 (1954); Comments, 33 U.Fla.L.Rev. 394 (1981), 58 W.Va.L.Rev. 76 (1955).

Helpful local treatments include, Olson, A Look at West's Ann. Indiana Code 34–1–14–5: Indiana's Physician Privilege, 8 Val.U.L.Rev. 38 (1973); Notes, 55 Or. L.Rev. 459 (1976), 7 Tulsa L.Rev. 157 (1971).

enable him to prescribe for such patient as a physician, or to do any act for him as a surgeon." [2]

Another early act which has been widely copied is the provision of the California Code of Civil Procedure of 1872, § 1881, par. 4, "A licensed physician or surgeon cannot, without the consent of his patient, be examined in a civil action as to any information acquired in attending the patient which was necessary to enable him to prescribe or act for the patient."

The rationale traditionally asserted to justify suppression in litigation of material facts learned by a physician is the encouragement thereby given to the patient freely to disclose all matter which may aid in the diagnosis and treatment of disease and injury. To obtain this end, so the argument runs, it is necessary to secure the patient from disclosure in court of potentially embarrassing private details concerning health and bodily condition.[3] The validity of this utilitarian justification of the privilege has been questioned by many on the ground that the average patient, in consulting a physician, will have his thoughts centered upon his illness or injury and the prospects for betterment or cure, and will spare little thought for the remote possibility of some eventual disclosure of his condition in court.[4] Accordingly, if an assurance of confidentiality has little importance in the play of forces

upon the patient, it might well be concluded that the privilege is largely ineffective in attaining its avowed objective. Despite these arguments, however, the number of states adhering to the common law and refusing any general physician-patient privilege has slowly but steadily dwindled.[5]

Over the same period, there has been a strong trend toward the recognition of two related but distinguishable privileges protecting, respectively, communications between psychiatrist and patient and psychologist and patient. Though the former profession, being medically trained, has always come within the ambit of the older physician-patient privilege where that privilege is recognized, it has been cogently argued that accepted practice in the treatment of mental illness involves considerations not encountered in other medical contexts. The following statement is frequently quoted in this regard.

> Among physicians, the psychiatrist has a special need to maintain confidentiality. His capacity to help his patients is completely dependent upon their willingness and ability to talk freely. This makes it difficult if not impossible for him to function without being able to assure his patients of confidentiality and, indeed, privileged communication . . . A threat to secrecy blocks successful treatment.[6]

The uniqueness of the psychiatrist-patient relationship led to the inclusion in the pro-

2. N.Y.Rev.Stats.1829, vol. II, Part III, c. 7, Tit. 3, art. eight, § 73.

3. This is stated as the aim of the privilege in Falkinburg v. Prudential Insurance Co., 132 Neb. 831, 273 N.W. 478 (1937) (to enable patient to secure medical service without fear of betrayal); Woernle v. Electromatic Typewriters, 271 N.Y. 228, 2 N.E.2d 638 (1936) (to prevent physician from disclosing matters which might humiliate the patient).

4. Morgan, Foreward to Model Code of Evidence 28 (1942) ("The ordinary citizen who contemplates consulting a physician not only has no thought of a lawsuit, but he is entirely ignorant of the rules of evidence. He has no idea whether a communication to a physician is or is not privileged. If he thinks at all about the matter, he will have no hesitation about permitting the disclosure of his ailments except in case of a disease which he considers disgraceful."); Lora v. Board of Education, 74 F.R.D. 565, 574 (E.D.N.Y.1977) (privilege has "been object of nearly unanimous scholarly criti-

cism"). Nor, in the view of at least some physicians, will absence of privilege work any effect on the doctor. Comment, Privileged Communications, 197 J.A.M.A. 257, 258 (1966) ("[T]he physician being called upon with comparative infrequency to make disclosures, would not be consciously affected in his relation with the patient.")

5. In 1943, 17 states were without the privilege. Chafee, Is Justice Served by Closing the Doctor's Mouth? 52 Yale L.J. 607 (1943). This number has now dwindled to less than 10. See 8 Wigmore, Evidence § 2380 (McNaughton rev. 1961).

6. Report No. 45, Group for the Advancement of Psychiatry 92 (1960). See also Taylor v. United States, 222 F.2d 398, 401 (D.C.Cir.1955); Slovenko, Psychiatry and a Second Look at the Medical Privilege, 6 Wayne L.Rev. 175 (1960); Slovenko, Psychotherapy and Confidentiality, 24 Clev.St.L.Rev. 375 (1975); Note, 47 Nw.L. Rev. 384 (1952).

posed Federal Rules of Evidence of a psychotherapist-patient privilege even though no general physician-patient privilege was suggested.[7] The Revised Uniform Rules (1974) retained this privilege, but make the rule optionally one extending to confidential communication to a physician as well as to a psychotherapist.[8] In the same vein, several of the states which continue to reject a general physician-patient privilege have enacted privileges applicable to the more limited psychotherapeutic context.[9] And, recognizing that the treatment of mental illness is carried out by clinical psychologists as well as by psychiatrists, several states have enacted psychologist-patient privileges.[10]

Even in the absence of statute, some privilege-like protection of certain aspects of the physician-patient relationship appears to be emerging as a function of federal constitutional guarantees of the right of privacy. In Whalen v. Doe,[11] the constitutionality of a New York statute creating a state data bank of the names and addresses of persons obtaining certain drugs by medical prescription was challenged, *inter alia*, on the ground that patients would be deterred from obtaining appropriate medication by the apprehension that disclosure of their names would stigmatize them as drug addicts. Though garbed in constitutional vestments as an impairment of the right to make personal deci-

7. Deleted Federal Rule of Evidence 504, 56 F.R.D. 240.

8. Rev.Unif.R.Evid. (1974) 503 reads:

(a) **Definitions.** As used in this rule:

(1) A "patient" is a person who consults or is examined or interviewed by a [physician or] psychotherapist.

[(2) A "physician" is a person authorized to practice medicine in any state or nation, or reasonably believed by the patient so to be.]

(3) A "psychotherapist" is (i) a person authorized to practice medicine in any state or nation, or reasonably believed by the patient so to be, while engaged in the diagnosis or treatment of a mental or emotional condition, including alcohol or drug addiction, or, (ii) a person licensed or certified as a psychologist under the laws of any state or nation, while similarly engaged.

(4) A communication is "confidential" if not intended to be disclosed to third persons, except persons present to further the interest of the patient in the consultation, examination, or interview, persons reasonably necessary for the transmission of the communication, or persons who are participating in the diagnosis and treatment under the direction of the [physician or] psychotherapist, including members of the patient's family.

(b) **General Rule of Privilege.** A patient has a privilege to refuse to disclose and to prevent any other person from disclosing confidential communications made for the purpose of diagnosis or treatment of his [physical,] mental or emotional condition, including alcohol or drug addiction, among himself, his [physician or] psychotherapist, and persons who are participating in the diagnosis or treatment under the direction of the [physician or] psychotherapist, including members of the patient's family.

(c) **Who May Claim the Privilege.** The privilege may be claimed by the patient, his guardian or conservator, or the personal representative of a deceased patient. The person who was the [physician or] psychotherapist at the time of the communication is presumed to have authority to claim the privilege but only on behalf of the patient.

(d) **Exceptions.**

(1) *Proceedings for Hospitalization.* There is no privilege under this rule for communications relevant to an issue in proceedings to hospitalize the patient for mental illness, if the psychotherapist in the course of diagnosis or treatment has determined that the patient is in need of hospitalization.

(2) *Examination by Order of Court.* If the court orders an examination of the [physical,] mental, or emotional condition of a patient, whether a party or a witness, communications made in the course thereof are not privileged under this rule with respect to the particular purpose for which the examination is ordered unless the court orders otherwise.

(3) *Condition an Element of Claim or Defense.* There is no privilege under this rule as to a communication relevant to an issue of the [physical,] mental, or emotional condition of the patient in any proceeding in which he relies upon the condition as an element of his claim or defense or, after the patient's death, in any proceeding in which any party relies upon the condition as an element of his claim or defense.

9. See, e.g., Fla.Evid.Code § 90.503.

10. See 8 Wigmore, Evidence § 2286, n. 22b (Supp. 1981) (McNaughton rev. 1961). Such statutes do not by their literal terms apply to psychiatrists. Where the enacting jurisdiction limits the ambit of its physician-patient privilege (applicable to psychiatrists) the result may be the anomalous conference of greater protection upon the psychologist's patient than the psychiatrist's. Miller v. Colonial Refrigerated Transportation, 81 F.R.D. 741 (M.D.Pa.1979) (noting this situation in Pennsylvania); Slovenko, Psychiatry and a Second Look at the Medical Privilege, supra note 6.

11. 429 U.S. 589 (1977).

sions, this argument bears a striking resemblance to the traditional rationale of privilege.

While upholding the statute in *Whalen,* the Supreme Court did so on the basis of reasoning which strongly suggests the existence of some constitutional right on the part of patients to preserve confidentiality with respect to medical treatment. Though this right has been characterized as yet unclear and undefined [12] its existence has been acknowledged by a number of lower federal and state courts.[13]

12. Lora v. Board of Education, 74 F.R.D. 565 (E.D. N.Y.1977).

13. Caesar v. Mountanos, 542 F.2d 1064 (9th Cir. 1976) (recognizing constitutional protection for qualified psychotherapist-patient confidentiality, but upholding contempt citation of psychiatrist); Hawaii Psychiatric Society v. Ariyoshi, 481 F.Supp. 1028 (D. Hawaii 1979); United States ex rel. Edney v. Smith, 425 F.Supp. 1038 (E.D.N.Y.1976) (discussing and implicitly accepting constitutional status of psychotherapist-patient privilege but finding no violation on facts), affirmed sub nom. Edney v. Smith, 556 F.2d 556; In re Lifschutz, 2 Cal.3d 415, 85 Cal.Rptr. 829, 467 P.2d 557 (1970) (confidentiality of psychotherapeutic session falls within constitutionally protected "zone of privacy," but protection not absolute; contempt citation of psychiatrist affirmed); In re "B," 482 Pa. 471, 394 A.2d 419 (1978) (plurality opinion). Contra: Felber v. Foote, 321 F.Supp. 85 (D.Conn.1970); Bremer v. State, 18 Md. App. 291, 307 A.2d 503 (1973), cert. denied 415 U.S. 930.

§ 99

1. The statutes usually specify "physician" or "physician and surgeon," and sometimes require that they be "licensed" or "authorized." Accordingly, the decisions usually deny the privilege for communications to other practitioners, such as dentists, Belichick v. Belichick, 37 Ohio App.2d 95, 307 N.E.2d 270 (1973); optometrists, People v. Baker, 94 Mich.App. 365, 288 N.W.2d 430 (1979); druggists, Green v. Superior Court In and For San Joaquin County, 220 Cal.App.2d 121, 33 Cal.Rptr. 604 (1963); social workers, Fitzgerald v. A.L. Burbank & Co., 451 F.2d 670 (2d Cir.1971); chiropractors, S.H. Kress & Co. v. Sharp, 156 Miss. 693, 126 So. 650 (1930) (dictum). Contra, Collins v. Bair, 256 Ind. 230, 268 N.E.2d 95 (1971) (chiropractor). See also Annot. 68 A.L.R. 176; Dec.Dig. ☞208(3). An intern may be a "physician" though not yet licensed to practice. Franklin Life Insurance Co. v. William J. Champion & Co., 353 F.2d 919 (6th Cir.1965), cert. denied 384 U.S. 928.

WESTLAW REFERENCES

physician* psych! /p patient* /p privilege* secre** confidential! /p name ident!

child children boy* girl* /s molest! abus! fondl! indecent /p physician* psych /p patient* /p privilege* secre** confidential!

physician* psych! /s patient* /s privilege* secre** confidential! /p unconstitutional constitution!

---

§ 99. Relation of Physician and Patient

The first requisite for the privilege is that the patient must have consulted the physician [1] for treatment or for diagnosis looking toward treatment.[2] If consulted for treatment it is immaterial by whom the doctor is employed.[3] Usually, however, when the doc-

Where a distinct privilege is granted to a related profession, the same principle is usually applied. State v. Gotfrey, 598 P.2d 1325 (Utah 1979) (psychologist-patient privilege unavailable because psychologist not licensed as required by statute).

As to nurses, assistants, and technicians, see § 101 infra. For privileged aspects of hospital records, see § 313 infra.

A patient's reasonable belief that he was consulting a licensed medical practitioner is sufficient to create privilege under some statutes. West's Ann.Cal.Evid. Code § 1010; Ill.Rev.Stat. ch. 51, ¶ 5.2. See Comment, 61 Calif.L.Rev. 1050 (1973).

2. City and County of San Francisco v. Superior Court, 37 Cal.2d 227, 231 P.2d 26 (1951); Osborn v. Fabatz, 105 Mich.App. 450, 306 N.W.2d 319 (1981). Dec.Dig. Witnesses ☞210. The consultation contemplated remedial measures if possible in Bassil v. Ford Motor Co., 278 Mich. 173, 270 N.W. 258 (1936) (husband and wife consult doctor to ascertain why child not born of their union). And compare Vaughan v. Martin, 145 Ind.App. 455, 251 N.E.2d 444 (1969) (Christian Scientist examined by physician to obtain certificate to enter nursing home; privilege held created under local statute). If treatment was the object of the communication, the fact that treatment did not occur will not destroy privilege. Triplett v. Board of Social Protection, 19 Or.App. 408, 528 P.2d 563 (1974). However, information gained by the physician before subject became a patient is not privileged. Ranger, Inc. v. Equitable Life Assurance Society, 196 F.2d 968 (6th Cir.1952).

3. Russell v. Penn Mutual Life Insurance Co., 70 Ohio App. 113, 41 N.E.2d 251 (1941) (doctors who attended insured, apparently employed by life insurance company). See also Malone v. Industrial Commission, 140 Ohio St. 292, 43 N.E.2d 266 (1942) (privilege for communications to plant physician to whom employee was taken while in semi-conscious condition for examination and treatment). And when a patient goes, or is taken unconscious, to a hospital for care or treatment, the hospital doctors who are charged with the duties of

tor is employed by one other than the patient, treatment will not be the purpose and the privilege will not attach. Thus, when a driver at the request of a public officer is subjected to a blood test for intoxication,[4] or when a doctor is appointed by the court [5] or the prosecutor [6] to make a physical or mental [7] examination, or is employed for this purpose by the opposing party,[8] or is selected by a life insurance company to make an examination of an applicant for a policy [9] or even when the doctor is employed by plaintiff's own lawyers in a personal injury case to examine plaintiff solely to aid in preparation for trial,[10] the information secured is not within the present privilege. But when the patient's doctor calls in a consultant physi-

examination, diagnosis, care or treatment are within the purview of the privilege statute. State v. Staat, 291 Minn. 394, 192 N.W.2d 192 (1971); Branch v. Wilkinson, 198 Neb. 649, 256 N.W.2d 307 (1977). Annot., 22 A.L.R. 1217. Where the defendant, after being involved in a fatal automobile accident was taken to the county hospital by police after his arrest for examination, statements given by him to hospital physician as to his medical history of epilepsy were, under the circumstances, communications for the purpose of treatment and were privileged. People v. Decina, 2 N.Y.2d 133, 157 N.Y.S.2d 558, 138 N.E.2d 799 (1956), 43 Cornell L.Q. 295. So also if the doctor, though employed by the defendant, examines the plaintiff in the hospital under circumstances causing the patient to believe that the examination is part of the hospital's care. Ballard v. Yellow Cab Co., 20 Wn.2d 67, 145 P.2d 1019 (1944).

4. The decisions are somewhat conflicting, but may generally be reconciled on the ground that tests run for medical reasons are privileged while those without medical purpose at request of police are not. See Ragsdale v. State, 245 Ark. 296, 432 S.W.2d 11 (1968) (blood test for purposes of treatment not admissible); Branch v. Wilkinson, 198 Neb. 649, 256 N.W.2d 307 (1977) (physician testified test run as part of standard diagnostic battery; privilege upheld); State in Interest of M.P.C., 165 N.J.Super. 131, 397 A.2d 1092 (1969) (results of tests requested by police not within privilege). If the test is made pursuant to an implied consent statute the privilege generally will not attach. State v. Erickson, 241 N.W.2d 854 (N.D.1976). See also, De Witt, Privileged Communications Between Physician and Patient 114 (1958).

5. State v. Cole, 295 N.W.2d 29 (Iowa 1980) (where court order for examination clearly specified limited purpose, physician precluded from establishing confidential relationship); State v. Campbell, 210 Kan. 265, 500 P.2d 21 (1972) (commissioner appointed by court to examine defendant; no privilege available) (alternative holding).

6. State v. Steelman, 120 Ariz. 301, 585 P.2d 1213 (1978) (defendant's claim that he expected examining physicians to help him with drug withdrawal symptoms held question of fact within discretion of trial court; denial of privilege upheld); People v. Henderson, 19 Cal.3d 86, 137 Cal.Rptr. 1, 560 P.2d 1180 (1977) (psychiatrist interviewing on instruction of prosecutor clearly indicated status; no privilege). But see State v. Toste, 178 Conn. 626, 424 A.2d 293 (1979) (privilege available where psychiatrist examined at request of state but not pursuant to court order as required by local statute).

7. When the purpose of the examination is solely to ascertain the person's mental condition, the physician-patient relationship is not created, and there is no privilege on that score for the person's disclosures. Williamson v. State, 330 So.2d 272 (Miss.1976); State v. Fouquette, 67 Nev. 505, 221 P.2d 404 (1950); State v. Riggle, 76 Wyo. 1, 298 P.2d 349 (1956); Simecek v. State, 243 Wis. 439, 10 N.W.2d 161 (1943); Dec.Dig. Witnesses ⊕209. But where the purpose of the committal to the hospital includes treatment as well as diagnosis, the disclosures will be protected. Taylor v. United States, 95 U.S.App.D.C. 373, 222 F.2d 398, 401, 402 (1955); State v. O'Neill, 274 Or. 59, 545 P.2d 97 (1976) (privilege available to patient involuntarily committed under dangerous person statute). Notes, 54 Mich.L.Rev. 423, 40 Minn.L.Rev. 621, 1955 Wash.U.L. Q. 405, Selected Writings on Evidence and Trial 258 (Fryer ed. 1957). And where the appointed panel includes the defendant's own psychiatrist who shared with the others his information gained in previous treatment, their testimony as to their findings is privileged. People v. Wasker, 353 Mich. 447, 91 N.W.2d 866 (1958).

As to whether an order for mental examination of an accused violates the privilege against self-incrimination, see § 134 infra.

8. Heath v. Broadway & Seventh Avenue Railroad Co., 8 N.Y.S. 863 (Super.Ct.Gen.T., 1890). But when the patient supposes that the doctor is a hospital specialist acting on his behalf, the privilege has been held to apply. Arizona & New Mexico Railway Co. v. Clark, 207 F. 817 (9th Cir.1913).

9. McGinty v. Brotherhood of Railway Trainmen, 166 Wis. 83, 164 N.W. 249 (1917); 70 C.J. 441, n. 94. And so of an examination by employer's physician of an applicant for employment. Montzoukos v. Mutual Beneficial Health & Accident Insurance Co., 69 Utah 309, 254 P. 1005 (1927). Similarly examination of a juvenile directed by subject's probation officer was held not privileged in Rusecki v. State, 56 Wis.2d 299, 201 N.W.2d 832 (1972).

10. City and County of San Francisco v. Superior Court, 37 Cal.2d 227, 231 P.2d 26 (1951) (but held that the communications were privileged under the attorney-client privilege), 25 So.Cal.L.Rev. 237, 13 U.Pitt.L. Rev. 428; State v. Pratt, 284 Md. 516, 398 A.2d 421 (1979) (semble); Lindsay v. Lipson, 367 Mich. 1, 116 N.W.2d 60 (1962).

cian to aid in diagnosis or treatment, the disclosures are privileged.[11]

If the patient's purpose in the consultation is an unlawful one, as to obtain narcotics in violation of law,[12] or as, by some authority, a fugitive from justice to have his appearance disguised by plastic surgery,[13] the law withholds the shield of privilege.

It has been held that where a doctor has attended a mother in her confinement and the newborn child, the child is a patient and can claim privilege against the doctor's disclosure of facts as to the apparent maturity of the child at birth.[14]

After the death of the patient the relation is ended and the object of the privilege can no longer be furthered. Accordingly, it seems the better view that facts discovered in an autopsy examination are not privileged.[15]

11. Leonczak v. Minneapolis, St. Paul & Sault Ste. Marie Railway Co., 161 Minn. 304, 201 N.W. 551 (1924); C.J.S. Witnesses § 294, n. 34.

12. The rule is codified in Uniform Narcotic Drug Act (1932, as amended 1958), § 17, par. 2, which provides that information given to a doctor "in an effort unlawfully to procure a narcotic drug, or unlawfully to procure the administration of any such drug" shall not be privileged. The Act has largely been replaced by the Uniform Controlled Substances Act (1970), which is silent on the subject. Such a provision scarcely seems necessary as no treatment is involved.

13. See Model Code of Evidence Rule 222: "No person has a privilege under Rule 221 if the judge finds that sufficient evidence, aside from the communication, has been introduced to warrant a finding that the services of the physician were sought or obtained to enable or aid anyone to commit or to plan to commit a crime or a tort, or to escape detection or apprehension after the commission of a crime or a tort."

14. Jones v. Jones, 208 Misc. 721, 144 N.Y.S.2d 820 (S.Ct.Sp.T.1955); Notes, 28 Rocky Mt.L.Rev. 425, 7 Syracuse L.Rev. 347.

15. Eureka-Maryland Assurance Co. v. Gray, 74 U.S.App.D.C. 191, 121 F.2d 104 (1941); Ferguson v. Quaker City Life Insurance Co., 146 A.2d 580 (D.C. Mun.App.1958); Cross v. Equitable Life Assurance Society, 228 Iowa 800, 293 N.W. 464 (1940). Decisions pro and con are cited in 8 Wigmore, Evidence § 2382 n. 11 (McNaughton rev. 1961) and Note, 12 Minn.L.Rev. 390 (1928). The point should not be confused with the distinct question of the preservation of inter vivos confidences after the patient's death. See § 102, infra.

§ 100

1. See § 98 supra.

WESTLAW
REFERENCES

synopsis,digest(plant company employe** /p doctor* physician* /p patient* /p privilege* secre** confidential!

§ 100. Subject Matter of the Privilege: Information Acquired in Attending the Patient and Necessary for Prescribing

Although a considerable number of the statutes speak of "communications," most of them follow the lead of the pioneer New York and California provisions [1] in extending the privilege to all "information," secured by the doctor through his observation or examination [2] or by explicit communication from the patient, so far as "necessary to enable him to prescribe or act for the patient." [3]

While the information secured by the physician may be privileged, the fact that he has

2. This result is reached in many states which have "communication" statutes, e.g., Heuston v. Simpson, 115 Ind. 62, 17 N.E. 261 (1888) (knowledge gained from words or by observation); Burns v. Waterloo, 187 Iowa 922, 173 N.W. 16 (1919) (intoxication, observed by doctor); McKee v. New Idea, 44 N.E.2d 697 (Ohio App. 1942) (submission to examination is "communication"). But compare, e.g., Commonwealth ex rel. Platt v. Platt, 266 Pa.Super. 276, 404 A.2d 410 (1979) (privilege not applicable to observations as opposed to communications). And of course is also reached in the states having "information" statutes. Smoot v. Kansas City, 194 Mo. 513, 92 S.W. 363, 367 (1906) (information acquired from inspection, examination or observation, after the patient has submitted to examination); Hansen v. Sandvik, 128 Wash. 60, 222 P. 205 (X-ray photograph taken by attending doctor, privileged). Probably information which is apparent to everyone should not be regarded as privileged. People v. De France, 104 Mich. 563, 570, 62 N.W. 709, 711 (1895).

Cases involving discovery by medical personnel of physical objects on patient's person have failed to develop a satisfactory rationale. State v. Staat, 291 Minn. 394, 192 N.W.2d 192 (1971) (bottles of narcotics discovered by hospital orderly; privilege held not available on ground orderly not shown conclusively to be acting as physician's agent); State v. McCoy, 70 Wn.2d 964, 425 P.2d 874 (1967), cert denied 389 U.S. 873 (bag of marijuana found in patient's sock by nurses in emergency room; privilege not available because discovery occurred before arrival of physician). See § 101 infra.

3. Instances of disclosures not necessary for treatment: Cook v. People, 60 Colo. 263, 153 P. 214 (1915) (defendant refused to allow physician to remove bullet from wound or tell how it was received); Meyers v. State, 192 Ind. 592, 137 N.E. 547, 24 A.L.R. 1196 (1922) (patient's threats, overheard by doctor, to kill his wife);

been consulted by the patient and has treated him,[4] and the number and dates of his visits,[5] are not within the shelter of the privilege.

The extent to which the privilege attaches to the information embodied in hospital records is discussed in the chapter on Business Records.[6]

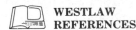

WESTLAW REFERENCES

necessary unnecessary /s treat! diagnos! /p doctor* psych! physician* /p patient* /p privilege* secre** confidential!

synopsis,digest("income tax**" "internal revenue" & doctor* hospital* physician* /s patient* /s privilege* secre** confidential! & court(ca2)

---

§ 101. The Confidential Character of the Disclosure: Presence of Third Persons and Members of Family: Information Revealed to Nurses and Attendants: Public Records

We have seen that the statutes existing in many states codifying the privileges for

Griffith v. Continental Casualty Co., 299 Mo. 426, 253 S.W. 1043 (1923) (patient's statement that life not worth living, might as well jump in river); see C.J.S. Witnesses § 295. It may well be debatable in a particular case whether the patient's statement as to how an accident happened, for which he is being treated, is information necessary for the treatment. See Raymond v. Burlington, Cedar Rapids & Northern Railway Co., 65 Iowa 152, 21 N.W. 495 (1884) (privileged); Green v. Metropolitan Street Railway Co., 171 N.Y. 201, 63 N.E. 958 (1902) (not privileged: three judges dissenting). And whether the privilege attaches to the doctor's observation, when called to treat one injured by a collision or assault, that the patient shows signs of liquor, has been made to turn on this question. State v. Aguirre, 167 Kan. 266, 206 P.2d 118 (1949) (not privileged); Perry v. Hannagan, 257 Mich. 120, 241 N.W. 232, 79 A.L.R. 1127 (1932) (same: two judges dissenting). But other decisions sustaining the privilege without discussing the question of "necessity" are cited in Annot., 79 A.L.R. 1131.

4. In re Albert Lindley Lee Memorial Hospital, 209 F.2d 122 (2d Cir.1953), cert. denied 347 U.S. 960 (names of patients not privileged in investigation of doctor's income tax liability), 67 Harv.L.Rev. 1272; Cranford v. Cranford, 120 Ga.App. 470, 170 S.E.2d 844 (1969) (records incidentally revealing patient's names sought to determine husband's income in divorce action). See also De Witt, Privileged Communications Between Physician and Patient § 47 (1958).

Here again, however, a distinction may be supported between the general physician-patient relationship and

marital communications and those between attorney and client usually omitted the requirement that to be privileged such communications must have been made in confidence. Nevertheless, the courts have read this limitation into these statutes, assuming that the legislatures must have intended this common law requirement to continue.[1] The statutes giving the patient's privilege for information gained in professional consultations again omit the adjective "confidential." [2] Should it nonetheless be read in, not as a continuation of a common law requirement, but as an interpretative gloss, spelled out from policy and analogy? Certainly the policy arguments are strong. First is the policy of holding all privileges within reasonable bounds since they cut off access to sources of truth. Second, the argument that the purpose of encouraging those who would otherwise be reluctant, to disclose necessary facts to their doctors, will be adequately served by extending a privilege for only

that of psychotherapist-patient. Revelation of the patient's identity in the latter context necessarily exposes something concerning the nature of the condition and treatment, and some statutes have therefore undertaken to privilege the patient's identity in this context. See, e.g., Vernon's Ann. Texas Civ.St. art. 5561h, construed in Ex parte Abell, 613 S.W.2d 255 (Tex.1981), to apply retroactively to preclude discovery of names of other patients of psychiatrist in suit by two patients alleging psychiatrist induced them to engage in sexual relations with him. And see Rudnick v. Superior Court of Kern County, 11 Cal.3d 924, 114 Cal.Rptr. 603, 523 P.2d 643 (1974) (patient's identity privileged only if context will reveal nature of illness).

5. Padovani v. Liggett & Myers Tobacco Co., 23 F.R.D. 255 (E.D.N.Y.1959) ("The mere *facts* that on certain occasions the plaintiff submitted himself for diagnosis and treatment, as well as the dates of same, the names and addresses of the physicians, whether or not diagnoses were reduced to writing, and related matters, are subject to disclosure so long as the subject communicated is not stated."); Polish Roman Catholic Union v. Palen, 302 Mich. 557, 5 N.W.2d 463 (1942); Jenkins v. Metropolitan Life Insurance Co., 171 Ohio St. 557, 173 N.E.2d 122 (1961); In re Judicial Inquiry, 8 A.D.2d 842, 190 N.Y.S.2d 406 (1959).

6. See § 313 infra.

§ 101

1. See §§ 80, 91 supra,

2. See § 98 supra.

such disclosures as the patient wishes to keep secret.

This principle of confidentiality [3] is supported by those decisions which hold that if a casual third person is present with the acquiescence of the patient at the consultation, the disclosures made in his presence are not privileged,[4] and thus the stranger, the patient and the doctor may be required to divulge them in court.

Under this view, however, if the third person is present as a needed and customary participant in the consultation, the circle of confidence may be reasonably extended to include him and the privilege will be maintained. Thus the presence of one sustaining a close family relationship to the patient should not curtail the privilege.[5] And the nurse present as the doctor's assistant during the consultation or examination, or the technician who makes tests or X-ray photographs under the doctor's direction, will be looked on as the doctor's agent in whose keeping the information will remain privileged.[6] But the application of strict agency principles in this context would seem inconsistent with the realities of modern medical practice,[7] and the preferable view is that of the courts which have based their decisions upon whether the communication was functionally related to diagnosis and treatment.[8]

3. See 8 Wigmore, Evidence § 2381 (McNaughton rev. 1961); C.J.S. Witnesses § 296; Dec.Dig. Witnesses ⊗213.

4. Horowitz v. Sacks, 89 Cal.App. 336, 265 P. 281 (1928) (several members of family present); In re Swartz, 79 Okl. 191, 192 P. 203, 16 A.L.R. 450, 453 (1920) (citing authorities); Note, 16 Neb.L.Bull. 206 (1937); Annot., 96 A.L.R. 1419; C.J.S. Witnesses § 299.

5. Grosslight v. Superior Court, 72 Cal.App.3d 502, 140 Cal.Rptr. 278 (1977) (privilege covers confidential communications to psychiatric personnel by intimate family members); Bassil v. Ford Motor Co., 278 Mich. 173, 270 N.W. 258, 107 A.L.R. 1491, 1493 (1936) (husband and wife consult doctor about their childlessness: but the principle of joint consultation could have been relied on); Denaro v. Prudential Insurance Co., 154 App.Div. 840, 139 N.Y.S. 758, 761 (1913) ("when a physician enters a house for the purpose of attending a patient, he is called upon to make inquiries, not alone of the sick person, but of those who are about him and who are familiar with the facts, and communications necessary for the proper performance of the duties of a physician are not public, because made in the presence of his immediate family or those who are present because of the illness of the person").

6. Schultz v. State, 417 N.E.2d 1127 (Ind.App.1981), rehearing denied __ Ind.App. __, 421 N.E.2d 22 (technician who drew blood for testing under direction of physician covered by privilege, though privilege waived): Ostrowski v. Mockridge, 242 Minn. 265, 65 N.W.2d 185 (1954) (nurse assisting doctor at examination; decisions cited and analyzed); Mississippi Power & Light Co. v. Jordan, 164 Miss. 174, 143 So. 483 (1932) (knowledge gained by nurse in assisting doctor to treat patient privileged); Culver v. Union Pacific Railway Co., 112 Neb. 441, 199 N.W. 794, 797 (1924) (question to nurse as to doctor's taking blood specimen from patient in her presence and directing her to send the specimen for a test, and the results thereof privileged, as she acted as agent of doctor); State v. Bryant, 5 N.C. App. 21, 167 S.E.2d 841 (1969); and cases cited in Note, 22 Marq.L.Rev. 22 (1938), Annot., 47 A.L.R.2d 742.

A few courts will deny the privilege even when the nurse is acting as the doctor's assistant, see, e.g., Weis v. Weis, 147 Ohio St. 416, 72 N.E.2d 245, 169 A.L.R. 668 (1947). On the topic generally see Dec.Dig. Witnesses ⊗209; Annot., 47 A.L.R.2d 742.

The patient-privilege statute occasionally specifically includes information given to nurses within the scope of the privilege. NYCPLR § 4504. See 8 Wigmore, Evidence § 2380, note 5 (McNaughton rev. 1961).

For privileged aspects of hospital records, see § 313 infra.

If the statement is not one looking toward diagnosis or treatment or is made to one not concerned with the patient's medical care, then the privilege should not apply. State v. Tornquist, 254 Iowa 1135, 120 N.W.2d 483 (1963) (statement overheard by nursing director not concerned with treatment) (alternative holding); State v. Anderson, 247 Minn. 469, 78 N.W.2d 320 (1956) (statement to nurse as to identity of driver of car).

7. Thus cases suggesting that the privilege does not attach until such time as a physician arrives, e.g., Ramon v. State, 387 So.2d 745 (Miss.1980) (nurse in emergency room not agent of physician); State v. Burchett, 302 S.W.2d 9 (Mo.1957) (nurse's observations of defendant before arrival of physician not privileged) (alternative holding); State v. McCoy, 70 Wn.2d 964, 425 P.2d 874 (1967), cert. denied 389 U.S. 873 (nurses undressing patient in emergency room not subject to physician's direction), or that the actions of medical personnel must be specifically directed by a physician, e.g., Block v. People, 125 Colo. 36, 240 P.2d 512 (1952), cert. denied 343 U.S. 978, rehearing denied 344 U.S. 848 (blood test taken by technician); State v. Staat, 291 Minn. 394, 192 N.W.2d 192 (1971), would seem at odds with modern emergency room procedure. In virtually all of the cases applying this rationale, better alternative grounds of admissibility were available, generally that the statement or communication did not relate to diagnosis or treatment.

8. Franklin Life Insurance Co. v. William J. Champion & Co., 350 F.2d 115 (6th Cir.1965), rehearing denied 353 F.2d 919, cert. denied 384 U.S. 928 (revelation

What if the patient is taken in custody by an officer to the hospital, where he is examined and treated by a doctor and makes disclosures, willy nilly in the hearing range of the officer. Are these disclosures "confidential?" [9]

Many courts on the other hand do not analyze the problems in terms of whether the communications or disclosures were confidential and professional, but rather in terms of what persons are intended to be silenced as witnesses. This seems to be sticking in the bark of the statute, rather than looking at its purpose. Thus these courts, if casual third persons were present at the consultation, will still close the mouth of the doctor but allow the visitor to speak.[10] And if nurses or other attendants or technicians gain information necessary to treatment they will be allowed by these courts to speak (unless the privilege statute specifically names them) but the physician may not.[11]

When the attending physician is required by law to make a certificate of death to the public authority, giving his opinion as to the cause, the certificate should be provable as a public record, despite the privilege. The duty to make a public report overrides the general duty of secrecy, and in view of the availability of the record to the public, the protection of the information from general knowledge, as contemplated by the privilege, cannot be attained. Accordingly, under the prevailing view, the privilege does not attach.[12]

Today, state and local laws increasingly impose upon physicians requirements to report various types of patient information related to the public health and safety, e.g., the treatment of gunshot wounds, venereal disease, mental illness, and the occurrence of fetal death.[13] Generally, state schemes for the collection and preservation of such data and its use by appropriate authorities have been upheld as against challenges based either upon a constitutional right of privacy or the professional privilege.[14] In some instances, e.g., the reporting of gun-

of statement of medical history to intern on hospital admission held just as contrary to policy of statute as statement to physician); Blue Cross of Northern California v. Superior Court of Yolo County, 61 Cal.App.3d 798, 132 Cal.Rptr. 635 (1976) (claims filed with health insurer to obtain payment for medical services held "reasonably necessary" to obtain diagnosis and treatment).

9. A leading New York decision holds that despite the presence of a police guard, the question is whether under all the circumstances the disclosures were intended to be confidential. People v. Decina, 2 N.Y.2d 133, 157 N.Y.S.2d 558, 138 N.E.2d 799 (1956). But another court assumed that the presence of officers who had custody of the patient would like the presence of casual third persons render the disclosure nonconfidential. State v. Thomas, 78 Ariz. 52, 275 P.2d 408 (1954).

10. Iwerks v. People, 108 Colo. 556, 120 P.2d 961 (1942) (deputy sheriff present at doctor's examination of injured prisoner may testify as to what examination disclosed and prisoner's statements to doctor); Springer v. Byram, 137 Ind. 15, 36 N.E. 361, 363 (1894) (ambulance drivers could testify to accident victim's statements to doctor); Indiana Union Traction Co. v. Thomas, 44 Ind.App. 468, 88 N.E. 356, 359 (1909) (patient privileged not to disclose communications with doctor, though in presence of daughter and friend); Leeds v. Prudential Insurance Co., 128 Neb. 395, 258 N.W. 672, 96 A.L.R. 1414, 1418 (1935) (bringing friend to consultation does not waive privilege); Annot., 96 A.L.R. 1419; C.J.S. Witnesses § 299.

And, as in the case of the other privileges for confidential communications, the eavesdropper is permitted to testify to what he overhears. Ryan v. Industrial Commission, 72 N.E.2d 907 (Ohio App.1946) (dictum).

11. Collins v. Howard, 156 F.Supp. 322 (S.D.Ga. 1957); First Trust Co. v. Kansas City Life Insurance Co., 79 F.2d 48, 52 (8th Cir.1935) (nurse and dietician could testify as to information gained in carrying out doctors' instructions for care of patient); Weis v. Weis, 147 Ohio St. 416, 72 N.E.2d 245, 169 A.L.R. 668 (1947) (similar to last); Prudential Insurance Co. v. Kozlowski, 226 Wis. 641, 276 N.W. 300 (1937) (testimony of nurse and X-ray operator received); Note, 22 Marq.L. Rev. 211 (1938); Annot., 47 A.L.R.2d 742.

12. Polish Roman Catholic Union v. Palen, 302 Mich. 557, 5 N.W.2d 463 (1942); Engel v. Starry, 268 Minn. 252, 128 N.W.2d 874 (1964); Randolph v. Supreme Liberty Life Insurance Co., 359 Mo. 251, 221 S.W.2d 155 (1949); Perry v. Industrial Commission, 160 Ohio St. 520, 117 N.E.2d 34 (1954); and cases cited 8 Wigmore, Evidence § 2385a (McNaughton rev. 1961). Contra: Davis v. Supreme Lodge, 165 N.Y. 159, 58 N.E. 891 (1900) (two judges dissenting). Compare the similar question about the records of public hospitals, discussed in 8 Wigmore, Evidence § 2382(3) (McNaughton rev. 1961), and see § 313 infra.

13. Compare the list of types of required reports noted by the United States Supreme Court in Whalen v. Roe, 429 U.S. 589, 602 (1976).

14. Whalen v. Roe, 429 U.S. 589 (1976) (upholding constitutionality of New York statute requiring recor-

shot wounds, the privilege has been held to be qualified to the extent of the reporting requirement, with the result that the physician may testify to any fact included within the report.[15] Many of the reporting systems, however, obviously do not envision general disclosure of the data collected, and maintenance of some degree of confidentiality may in fact be indispensable to constitutionality.[16]

WESTLAW REFERENCES

synopsis,digest(employee* nurse* technician* assistant* agent* /p doctor* hospital* psych! physician* /p patient* /p privilege* secre** confidential!

venereal abortion abus! public /s record* report! /p doctor* hospital* psych! physician* /s patient* /s privilege* secre** confidential!

§ 102. Rule of Privilege, Not Incompetency: Privilege Belongs to the Patient, Not to an Objecting Party as Such: Effect of the Patient's Death

As has been pointed out in the discussion of privileges generally,[1] the rule which excludes disclosures to physicians is not a rule of incompetency of evidence serving the end of protecting the adverse party against unreliable or prejudicial testimony. It is a rule of privilege protecting the extrinsic interest of the patient and designed to promote health, not truth. It encourages free disclosure in the sickroom by preventing disclosure in the courtroom. The patient is the person to be encouraged and he is the holder of the privilege.[2]

Consequently, he alone during his lifetime has the right to claim or to waive the privilege. If he is in a position to claim it and does not, it is waived [3] and no one else may assert it.[4] If he is not present and so far as known is unaware of the proposed disclosure, the judge in his discretion according to some authority may enforce the privilege of his own motion.[5] Accordingly, if the judge at the suggestion of a party or counsel or the physician-witness, enforces the privilege, this is not to be understood as the assertion of a right by the party or counsel or witness but as an informal invocation of discretion. The adverse party as such has no interest to

---

dation of names and addresses of all persons obtaining certain drugs by prescription); Planned Parenthood of Central Missouri v. Danforth, 428 U.S. 52 (1975) (semble; abortions); Gabor v. Hyland, 166 N.J.Super. 275, 399 A.2d 993 (1979) (injunctive relief denied where sought to eliminate clause in Medicaid benefit form authorizing release of all medical information by providers of reimbursable services); Volkman v. Miller, 52 A.D.2d 146, 383 N.Y.S.2d 95 (1976), affirmed 41 N.Y.2d 946, 394 N.Y.S.2d 631, 363 N.E.2d 355. But see, Hawaii Psychiatric Society v. Ariyoshi, 481 F.Supp. 1028 (D. Hawaii 1979).

15. Freeman v. State, 258 Ark. 617, 527 S.W.2d 909 (1975); People v. Lay, 254 App.Div. 372, 5 N.Y.S.2d 325 (1938), affirmed 279 N.Y. 737, 18 N.E.2d 686; State v. Antill, 176 Ohio St. 61, 197 N.E.2d 548 (1964). See also, N.J.Stat.Ann. 2A:84A–22.2 (privilege does not extend to reports required to be filed by physician or patient).

16. In Whalen v. Roe, supra n. 14, the Supreme Court, in upholding the New York statute, placed considerable emphasis on the restricted number of persons who would have access to the reported information. Compare, however, Carr v. Schmid, 105 Misc.2d 645, 432 N.Y.S.2d 807 (1980) (allowing discovery of record of plaintiff's venereal disease from public agency on basis of litigant-patient exception).

§ 102

1. See § 72 supra.

2. Metropolitan Life Insurance Co. v. Kaufman, 104 Colo. 13, 87 P.2d 758 (1939) (physician compelled to give testimony where privilege had been waived by patient. "Privileged communications are personal to the patient only."); Maas v. Laursen, 219 Minn. 461, 18 N.W.2d 233, 158 A.L.R. 213 (1945) (dictum, privilege belongs to patient and can be waived only by him); 8 Wigmore, Evidence § 2386 (McNaughton rev. 1961); Dec.Dig. Witnesses ⟨⤺217.

3. People v. Bloom, 193 N.Y. 1, 85 N.E. 824 (1908) (patient who fails to claim privilege against testimony of his physicians, at first trial, a civil case, waives permanently and cannot object to similar testimony at his later trial for perjury).

4. See State v. Thomas, 1 Wn.2d 298, 95 P.2d 1036 (1939) (defendant charged with carnal knowledge of child, could not object to physician's testimony where child and mother did not; but here physician made examination at instance of county and doctor-patient relation probably did not exist). A similar holding on similar facts is State v. Fackrell, 44 Wn.2d 874, 271 P.2d 679, 681 (1954).

5. Model Code of Evidence Rule 105, "The judge . . . in his discretion determines . . . (e) whether to exclude, of his own motion, evidence which would violate a privilege of a person who is neither a party nor the witness from whom the evidence is sought if the privilege has not been waived or otherwise terminated. . . ."

protect if he is not the patient, and thus cannot object as of right,[6] and should have no right to complain on appeal if the patient's privilege is erroneously denied.[7]

The whole supposition of the patient-privilege legislation, that the patient's fear of revelation in court of the information he gives the doctor will be such as to discourage free disclosure, is highly speculative. To think that he is likely to be influenced by fear that such revelations may occur after his death seems particularly fanciful. A rule that the privilege terminated with the patient's death would have reached a common-sense result which would have substantially lessened the obstructive effect of the privilege. The courts, however have not taken this tack but hold that the privilege continues after death.[8] Nevertheless, in contests of the survivors in interest with third parties, e.g., actions to recover property claimed to belong to the deceased, actions for the death of the deceased, or actions upon life insurance policies, the personal representative, heir or next of kin, or the beneficiary in the policy may waive the privilege,[9] and, by the same token, the adverse party may not effectively assert the privilege.[10] In contests over the validity of a will, where both sides—the executor on the one hand and the heirs or next of kin on the other—claim under and not adversely to the decedent, the assumption should prevail that the decedent would desire that the validity of his will should be determined in the fullest light of the facts.[11] Accordingly in this situation either the executor or the contestants may effectively waive the privilege without the concurrence of the other.[12]

West's Ann.Cal.Evid.Code §§ 994, 995 require the physician to claim the privilege unless otherwise instructed by the patient. And see, Osterman v. Ehrenworth, 106 N.J.Super. 515, 256 A.2d 123 (1969) (privilege held applicable to prevent disclosure by interrogatory names of non-party patients of defendant).

6. Thus, after the death of the patient, in a suit on an insurance policy, the insurer cannot assert the privilege. Olson v. Court of Honor, 100 Minn. 117, 110 N.W. 374, 377 (1907); Hier v. Farmers Mutual Fire Insurance Co., 104 Mont. 471, 67 P.2d 831, 110 A.L.R. 1051 (1937). Contra: Westover v. Aetna Life Insurance Co., 99 N.Y. 56, 1 N.E. 104 (1885). See Annot., 2 A.L.R.2d 645, 658.

7. See Vance v. State, 143 Miss. 121, 108 So. 433, 45 A.L.R. 1348 (1926). In that case the defendant charged with murder objected to the testimony of the physician who examined the victim, and this was overruled. Ethridge, J. held that "if it was error to admit the evidence it is error of which he [the accused] cannot complain." Two judges concurred in affirmance on another ground. Three judges dissented.

8. Bassil v. Ford Motor Co., 278 Mich. 173, 270 N.W. 258, 107 A.L.R. 1491 (1936). Acc. West's Ann. Cal.Evid.Code § 993.

9. Emmett v. Eastern Dispensary and Casualty Hospital, 396 F.2d 931 (D.C.Cir.1967) (next of kin had right to waive privilege and obtain medical records of deceased in support of possible malpractice action); Harvey v. Silber, 300 Mich. 510, 2 N.W.2d 483 (1942) (administrator suing for death due to defendants' alleged malpractice); Colwell v. Dwyer, 35 N.E.2d 789 (Ohio App.1941) (administrator plaintiff in death action); State ex rel. Calley v. Olsen, 271 Or. 369, 532 P.2d 230 (1975) (beneficiary under life policy allowed to waive over opposition of personal representative). In Fleet Messenger Service, Inc. v. Life Insurance Co. of North America, 205 F.Supp. 585 (S.D.N.Y.1962), affirmed 315 F.2d 593 (2d Cir.1963), an action to recover the proceeds of a life policy, the claim of privilege by the widow and the personal representative, neither of whom was a beneficiary, was rejected on ground that only parties may claim the privilege. But the result here would better have been justified as a waiver by the beneficiary.

10. Wimberley v. State, 217 Ark. 130, 228 S.W.2d 991 (1950); Jasper v. State, 269 P.2d 375 (Okl.Cr.1954); Dec.Dig. Witnesses ☞217, and see cases cited note 6, supra. An early New York case, however, holds that any party may raise the objection, and it remains for the patient to waive. Westover v. Aetna Life Insurance Co., 99 N.Y. 56, 1 N.E. 104, 105, 106 (1885). This position seems insupportable.

11. "If he did not have testamentary capacity, then the paper was not his will, and it is not the policy of the law to maintain such an instrument. It is undoubtedly the policy of the law to uphold the testamentary disposition of property, but not until it is ascertained whether such a disposition has been made. . . . And no one can be said to represent the deceased in that contest, for he could only be interested in having the truth ascertained, and his estate can only be protected by establishing or defeating the instrument as the truth so ascertained may require. The testimony of the attending physician is usually reliable, and often controlling, and to place it at the disposal of one party to such a proceeding and withhold it from the other would be manifestly partial and unjust." Ladd, J., in Winters v. Winters, 102 Iowa 53, 71 N.W. 184, 185 (1897).

12. Hyatt v. Wroten, 184 Ark. 847, 43 S.W.2d 726 (1931) (heirs); Gorman v. Hickey, 145 Kan. 54, 64 P.2d 587 (1937) (heir contesting will could waive though executor opposed waiver); Lembke v. Unke, 171 N.W.2d 837 (N.D.1969) (heirs entitled to waive in will contest;

WESTLAW
REFERENCES

death deceased decedent /p executor* executrix "personal representative*" heir* & doctor* hospital* physician* /s patient* /s privilege* secre** confidential!

---

§ 103. What Constitutes a Waiver of the Privilege?

The physician-patient statutes, though commonly phrased in terms of incompetency, are nevertheless held to create merely a privilege for the benefit of the patient, which he may waive.[1]

Generally [2] it is agreed that a contractual stipulation waiving the privilege, such as is frequently included in applications for life or health insurance, or in the policies themselves, is valid and effectual.[3]

How far does the patient's testifying waive the privilege? Doubtless, if the patient on direct examination testifies to,[4] or adduces other evidence of,[5] the communications exchanged or the information furnished to the doctor consulted this would waive in respect to such consultations. When, however, the patient in his direct testimony does not reveal any privileged matter respecting the consultation, but testifies only to his physical or mental condition, existing at the time of such consultation, then one view is that, "where the patient tenders to the jury the issue as to his physical condition, it must in fairness and justice be held that he has himself waived the obligation of secrecy." [6] This view has the great merit of curtailing the scope of an obstructive privilege, but there are a number of courts which

overruling prior decision denying waiver after patient's death); Haverstick v. Banet, 267 Ind. 351, 370 N.E.2d 341 (1977) (semble); Annot., 97 A.L.R. 393. And see Note, 39 Minn.L.Rev. 800 (1955).

Suits attacking conveyances by the deceased are generally held to be governed by the same principle. Calhoun v. Jacobs, 141 F.2d 729 (D.C.Cir.1944); McDonald v. McDonald, 53 Wis.2d 371, 192 N.W.2d 903 (1972).

An alternative approach in will contest cases is suggested in *Winters*, supra n. 11, namely that neither side may assert the privilege since the determination of who steps into the shoes of the decedent must await the outcome of the suit. See also § 95 supra, where the attorney-client privilege is involved.

§ 103

1. Stayner v. Nye, 227 Ind. 231, 85 N.E.2d 496 (1949).

2. In Michigan such an agreement to waive has been held invalid as against public policy. Gilchrist v. Mystic Workers of the World, 196 Mich. 247, 248, 163 N.W. 10, 11 (1917). A New York statute which provided that a waiver "must be made in open court, on the trial of the action or proceeding, and a paper executed by a party prior to the trial . . . shall be insufficient," is no longer in effect. N.Y.C.P.L.R. 4504.

3. Jones v. Prudential Life Insurance Co., 388 A.2d 476 (D.C.App.1978); Murphy v. Mutual Life Insurance Co., 62 Idaho 362, 112 P.2d 993, 994 (1941); Templeton v. Mutual Insurance Co., 177 Okl. 94, 57 P.2d 841 (1936); 1 Wigmore, Evidence § 7a (3d ed. 1940); Note, 16 N.C.L.Rev. 53 (1938); Annot., 54 A.L.R. 412; Dec. Dig. Witnesses ⏤219(6). But occasionally a court by an eccentric interpretation may emasculate the waiver. Noble v. United Beneficial Life Insurance Co., 230 Iowa 471, 297 N.W. 881 (1941) (consent to doctor's furnishing to insurer information gained in attending pa-

tient is not waiver of privilege as to doctor's testimony in court.)

4. Mauro v. Tracy, 152 Colo. 106, 350 P.2d 570 (1963) (plaintiff's testimony concerning treatment waived privilege in personal injury case); Dennis v. Prisock, 254 Miss. 574, 181 So.2d 125 (1965), appeal after remand 221 So.2d 706 (privilege waived where patient testifies in detail about nature of injuries and consultations with physician). Epstein v. Pennsylvania Railroad Co., 250 Mo. 1, 156 S.W. 699 (1913) (". . . since plaintiff had himself voluntarily gone upon the stand, and in his case in chief, as a witness for himself, laid bare for lucre's sake all of the secrets of his sickroom, since he had told and retold what Dr. Elston, his physician, said to him, and what he said to Elston, since he had told the precise nature of his alleged hurts as he said Elston found them, and since he had also voluntarily related the treatment professionally given to him by Elston, he waived the competency of other physicians, also there present, having knowledge of the identical facts."); Annot., 114 A.L.R. 798, 802. The principle is applicable irrespective of whether the witness is a party. See People v. Lowe, 96 Misc.2d 33, 408 N.Y.S.2d 873 (1978) (defendant in criminal prosecution allowed to obtain victim's records of mental treatment; victim's testimony that he suffered brain injury during WWII held to constitute waiver). But the court's readiness to find waiver in this case may have been increased by a desire to avoid conflict between the privilege and defendant's constitutional rights.

5. Buckminster's Estate v. Commissioner of Internal Revenue, 147 F.2d 331 (2d Cir.1944) (executrix introducing statements and diagnosis of physician who attended decedent waived privilege).

6. Andrews, J. in Hethier v. Johns, 233 N.Y. 370, 135 N.E. 603 (1922); 8 Wigmore, Evidence § 2389(2) (McNaughton rev. 1961).

hold that the patient's testimony as to his condition without disclosure of privileged matter is not a waiver.[7] If the patient reveals privileged matter on cross-examination, without claiming the privilege, this is usually held not to be a waiver of the privilege enabling the adversary to make further inquiry of the doctors, on the ground that such revelations were not "voluntary."[8] The counter-argument, that the failure to assert the privilege should be a complete waiver, seems persuasive.

If the patient examines a physician as to matters disclosed in a consultation, or course of treatment, of course this is a waiver and opens the door to the opponent to examine him about any other matters then disclosed.[9] And if several doctors participated jointly in the same consultation or course of treatment the calling of one to disclose part of the shared information waives objection to the adversary's calling any other of the joint consultants to testify about the consultation, treatment or the results thereof.[10] Liberal courts go further and hold that calling by the patient of one doctor and eliciting privileged matter from him opens the door to the opponent's calling other doctors consulted by the patient at other times to bring out any facts relevant to the issue on which the privileged proof was adduced.[11] It is not consonant with justice and fairness to per-

7. Arizona & New Mexico Railway Co. v. Clark, 235 U.S. 669 (1915) (plaintiff testified as to his injury and called nurse as witness, held no waiver under Arizona statute which provides that it is waiver if patient testifies as "to such communications," Hughes and Day, JJ., dissenting); Bryan Brothers Packing Co. v. Grubbs, 251 Miss. 52, 168 So.2d 289 (1964) (no waiver arising from plaintiff's testimony in personal injury case that she had been treated by a particular doctor); Harpman v. Devine, 133 Ohio St. 1, 10 N.E.2d 776, 114 A.L.R. 789 (1937) (two judges dissenting), critically noted 51 Harv.L.Rev. 931; Hudson v. Blanchard, 294 P.2d 554 (Okl.1956), critically noted 11 Okla.L.Rev. 450; Schaffer v. Spicer, 88 S.D. 36, 215 N.W.2d 134 (1974) (child custody; no waiver from wife's testimony that particular psychiatrist had treated her); Clawson v. Walgreen Drug Co., 108 Utah 577, 162 P.2d 759 (1945) (no waiver when patient testified concerning nature and extent of injury, but did not give evidence of what doctors told him nor of details of treatment); Noelle v. Hoquiam Lumber & Shingle Co., 47 Wash. 519, 92 P. 372 (1907) (forceful dissent by Root, J., joined by Hadley, C.J.); Green v. Nebagamain, 113 Wis. 508, 89 N.W. 520 (1902), and cases cited in Annot., 114 A.L.R. 798; Dec.Dig. Witnesses ⟜219(5).

See Bond v. Independent Order of Foresters, 69 Wn. 2d 879, 421 P.2d 351 (1966) (holding that pretrial deposition given by plaintiff testifying as to the nature and extent of her injuries did not constitute a waiver of the privilege).

8. Johnson v. Kinney, 232 Iowa 1016, 7 N.W.2d 188, 144 A.L.R. 997 (1943); Hemminghaus v. Ferguson, 358 Mo. 476, 215 S.W.2d 481 (1948) overruled on another aspect of waiver of the privilege in State ex rel. McNutt v. Keet, 432 S.W.2d 597 (Mo.1968) (deposition of adverse party taken under the rules for cross-examination). Harpman v. Devine, 133 Ohio St. 1, 10 N.E.2d 776, 114 A.L.R. 789 (1937) and cases cited in Annot., 114 A.L.R. 798, 806.

9. Maas v. Laursen, 219 Minn. 461, 18 N.W.2d 233, 158 A.L.R. 215 (1945); Demonbrunn v. McHaffie, 348 Mo. 1120, 156 S.W.2d 923 (1942); Unick v. Kessler Me-

morial Hospital, 107 N.J.Super. 121, 257 A.2d 134 (1969).

10. Doll v. Scandrett, 201 Minn. 319, 276 N.W. 281 (1937) (three judges dissenting), 22 Minn.L.Rev. 580; Morris v. New York, Ontario & Western Railway Co., 148 N.Y. 88, 42 N.E. 410 (1895). Contra: Jones v. Caldwell, 20 Idaho 5, 116 P. 110 (1911). See Annot., 5 A.L.R.3d 1244.

11. DeGroff v. Clark, 358 Mich. 274, 100 N.W.2d 214 (1960) (waiver in such circumstances provided for by local statute); Weissman v. Wells, 306 Mo. 82, 267 S.W. 400 (1924) (personal injury plaintiff who claimed nervous state due to injury, by calling doctor to testify to her condition after injury waived objection to defendant's proving by other doctor her same condition before injury); Steinberg v. New York Life Insurance Co., 263 N.Y. 45, 188 N.E. 152 (1933), cert. denied 293 U.S. 616 (plaintiff suing on disability policy puts doctor on stand to prove that he has had disability from tuberculosis since time of claim; held this warrants defendant in proving by another doctor that plaintiff had same disease several years before, in support of its plea of misrepresentation); Robinson v. Lane, 480 P.2d 620 (Okl.1971) (plaintiff's testimony concerning injuries waived privilege with respect to physicians other than those called by him; earlier precedent to the contrary overruled), 24 Okla.L.Rev. 380 (1971); McUne v. Fuqua, 42 Wn.2d 65, 253 P.2d 632 (1953) (lucid discussion by Hamley, J.); and cases cited in Annot., 5 A.L.R.3d 1244. See also, Hogan, Waiver of the Physician-Patient Privilege in Personal Injury Litigation, 52 Marq. L.Rev. 75 (1968).

Compare the provision in Rule 35(b)(2) of the Federal Rules of Civil Procedure to the effect that if a person who has been examined by a physician under order of court, requests and obtains a copy of the doctor's report, he "waives any privilege he may have . . . regarding the testimony of every other person who has examined him or may thereafter examine him in respect of the same mental or physical condition." The physician-patient privilege and Rule 35 are acutely discussed in

mit the patient to reveal his secrets to several doctors and then when his condition comes in issue to limit the witnesses to the consultants favorable to his claims.[12] But a substantial number of courts balk at this step.[13]

A failure by a patient to object to the testimony of one of his physicians called by the adversary seems generally to be given the same effect, in respect to waiver, that the particular court would give to the patient's calling and examination of the doctor as his own witness.[14]

A shrinking from the embarrassment which comes from exposure of bodily disease or abnormality is human and natural. It is arguable that legal protection from exposure is justified to encourage frankness in consulting physicians. But it is not human, natural, or understandable to claim protection from exposure by asserting a privilege for communications to doctors, at the very same time when the patient is parading before the public the mental or physical condition as to which he consulted the doctor by

bringing an action for damages arising from that same condition.[15] This in the oft-repeated phrase is to make the privilege not a shield only, but a sword. Consequently, the California statute provides that there is no physician patient-privilege "as to a communication relevant to an issue concerning the condition of the patient" if the issue has been tendered by the patient or any party claiming through or under him or for his wrongful death.[16] Unfortunately, not all local statutes are as wisely drawn.[17] For this and other reasons, a substantial number of courts have refused to find that the commencement of an action involving the physical or mental condition of the plaintiff operates as a waiver of the privilege.[18] Such a position effectively negates the possibility of discovery on a central issue of these cases. To alleviate this difficulty some courts hold that where the trial cannot proceed without waiver of the privilege by the plaintiff, the action will be stayed until such time as the plaintiff will permit pretrial examination of the doctor.[19] Another method of attempting

---

Hardy v. Riser, 309 F.Supp. 1234 (N.D.Miss.1970). See also, Note, 17 S.D.L.Rev. 188 (1972).

12. "A litigant should not be allowed to pick and choose in binding and loosing; he may bind or he may loose. . . . He may choose a serviceable and mellow one out of a number of physicians to fasten liability upon the defendant, and then, presto! change! exclude the testimony of those not so mellow and serviceable, to whom he has voluntarily given the same information and the same means of getting at a conclusion on the matter already uncovered by professional testimony to the jury. There is no reason in such condition of things, and where reason ends the law ends." Lamm, J. in Smart v. Kansas City, 208 Mo. 162, 105 S.W. 709, 722 (1907).

13. No waiver as to doctors consulted separately. Mays v. New Amsterdam Casualty Co., 40 U.S.App. D.C. 249, 46 L.R.A.,N.S., 1108, 1112 (1913); Acme-Evans Co. v. Schnepf, 214 Ind. 394, 14 N.E.2d 561 (1938); Brown v. Guiter, 256 Iowa 671, 128 N.W.2d 896 (1964) and cases cited in Annot., 5 A.L.R.3d 1244; 58 Am.Jur. Witnesses § 458; Dec.Dig. Witnesses ⟐219(5).

14. Captron v. Douglass, 193 N.Y. 11, 85 N.E. 827 (1908) (malpractice; failure of plaintiff to object to testimony of one of two doctors who treated him after defendant did, was waiver as to other also).

15. "The patient-litigant exception precludes one who has placed in issue his physical condition from invoking the privilege on the ground that disclosure of his condition would cause him humiliation. He cannot

have his cake and eat it too." City and County of San Francisco v. Superior Court, 37 Cal.2d 227, 231 P.2d 26, 28, 25 A.L.R.2d 1418 (1951) (by Traynor, J.).

16. West's Ann.Cal.Evid.Code § 996. Rev.Unif.R. Evid. (1974) 503(d)(3) provides:

There is no privilege under this rule as to a communication relevant to an issue of the [physical,] mental, or emotional condition of the patient in any proceeding in which he relies upon the condition as an element of his claim or defense or, after the patient's death, in any proceeding in which any party relies upon the condition as an element of his claim or defense.

17. A number of older statutes provide in terms that waiver will occur "if the patient testifies in his own behalf." If strictly construed, this language of course precludes pre-trial waiver by filing. See Woosley v. Dunning, 268 Or. 233, 520 P.2d 340 (1974). The problems raised by such statutes are discussed in Note, 17 S.D.L.Rev. 188 (1972).

18. Federal Mining & Smelting Co. v. Dalo, 252 F. 356 (10th Cir.1918); State ex rel. Floyd v. Court of Common Pleas, 55 Ohio St.2d 27, 377 N.E.2d 794 (1978); Avery v. Nelson, 455 P.2d 75 (Okl.1969) noted critically in 23 Okla.L.Rev. 115; Woosley v. Dunning, supra n. 17; Bond v. Independent Order of Foresters, 69 Wn.2d 879, 421 P.2d 351 (1966).

19. Mariner v. Great Lakes Dredge & Dock Co., 202 F.Supp. 430 (N.D.Ohio 1962); Awtry v. United States,

to accommodate the outmoded rule to modern discovery processes is found in the holding that commencement of the action effects a qualified waiver of the privilege for discovery purposes, leaving the ultimate scope of waiver to be determined by the nature of plaintiff's evidence at trial.[20] Though such temporizations are salutary modifications of the strict rule of non-waiver by filing, the clearly preferable position is that waiver of the privilege occurs upon commencement of the action, and an increasing number of jurisdictions appears to be subscribing to this latter rule.[21] As Chief Justice Lamm said in respect to another phase of waiver of the patient's privilege, "The scandals in beating down the truth arising from a too harsh and literal interpretation of this law (if unaided and unrelieved by waiver) every one of us knows by experience and observation in the courtroom."[22]

If a testator by his request procures an attending doctor to subscribe his will as an attesting witness this is a waiver of the privilege as to all facts affecting the validity of the will.[23]

WESTLAW REFERENCES

synopsis,digest(crossexamin! /p waive* nonwaiver & doctor* hospital* physician* /p patient* /p privilege* secre** confidential!)

synopsis,digest(volunt! involuntar! /p waive* nonwaiver & doctor* hospital* physician* /p patient* /p privilege* secre** confidential!)

---

§ 104. Kinds of Proceedings Exempted From the Application of the Privilege [1]

Unless the statute creating the privilege limits its application the privilege generally applies to criminal as well as civil proceedings.[2] However, criminal prosecutions generally [3] and workmen's compensation proceedings [4] are frequently withdrawn by statute from the operation of the privilege. Other types of controversies in which the privilege is occasionally withheld or curtailed

---

27 F.R.D. 399 (S.D.N.Y.1961); Kriger v. Holland Furnace Co., 12 A.D.2d 44, 208 N.Y.S.2d 285 (1960).

20. This rule was instituted in Michigan by Eberle v. Savon Food Stores, Inc., 30 Mich.App. 496, 186 N.W.2d 837 (1971).

21. Petition of Trinidad Corp., 238 F.Supp. 928 (E.D. Va.1965); Mathis v. Hilderbrand, 416 P.2d 8 (Alaska 1968) (holding that the plaintiff by bringing a personal injury suit waived the privilege to the extent that the attending physicians could be required to testify on pretrial depositions with respect to the injuries sued upon); Collins v. Bair, 256 Ind. 230, 268 N.E.2d 95 (1971) (privilege waived as to all matters patient has voluntarily put in issue by way of claim, counterclaim, or affirmative defense); Glenn v. Kerlin, 248 So.2d 834 (La.App.1971) (construing statute requiring same result); State ex rel. McNutt v. Keet, 432 S.W.2d 597 (Mo.1968) (privilege waived once plaintiff's physical condition at issue under pleadings); Mattison v. Poulen, 134 Vt. 158, 353 A.2d 327 (1976) (privilege waived by commencement of action). See also Annot., 21 A.L.R.3d 912.

It would appear, however, that waiver will not occur if the patient is not the party responsible for placing physical or mental condition in issue. See, e.g., Mohammad v. Mohammad, 358 So.2d 610 (Fla.Dist.Ct.App. 1978), appeal after remand 371 So.2d 1070 (wife in custody case did not waive privilege by denying husband's allegations as to her mental condition).

22. Epstein v. Pennsylvania Railroad Co., 250 Mo. 1, 156 S.W. 699, 711 (1913).

23. In re Mullin's Estate, 110 Cal. 252, 42 P. 645 (1895); Stormon v. Weiss, 65 N.W.2d 475, 512

(N.D.1954); 8 Wigmore, Evidence § 2390(1) (McNaughton rev. 1961).

§ 104

1. C.J.S. Witnesses § 301; 58 Am.Jur.2d Witnesses § 246; Dec.Dig. Witnesses ⟷208(2).

2. 8 Wigmore, Evidence § 2385 (McNaughton rev. 1961); C.J.S. Witnesses § 301; Annot., 7 A.L.R.3d 1458. But see Moosa v. Abdalla, 248 La. 344, 178 So. 2d 273 (1965) holding that under the Louisiana statute, Annotated R.S. 15:476, the privilege applies in criminal but not in civil cases.

3. The original California Code provision, C.C.P. § 1881, par. 4, was limited to "a civil action," and this limitation was followed by many states which took over that code, e.g., Idaho, Oregon, South Dakota and Washington. But Washington extends the privilege to criminal proceedings despite the limitation of the statute. State v. Broussard, 12 Wn.App. 355, 529 P.2d 1128 (1974). The present California Code provides there is no physician-patient privilege in a criminal proceeding. West's Ann.Cal.Evid.Code § 998. See the statutes as compiled in 8 Wigmore, Evidence § 2380, note 5 (McNaughton rev. 1961). Most states apart from specific provision seem to deny the accused the power to assert the privilege as to information given by the victim of a crime to a physician. Annot., 2 A.L.R.2d 645.

4. More than half the states which have the privilege provide that it shall not apply in Workmen's Compensation proceedings. See the statutes compiled in 8 Wigmore, Evidence § 2380, note 6 (McNaughton rev. 1961).

in the statutes are actions for malpractice,[5] prosecutions for homicide,[6] lunacy proceedings [7] and will contests.[8] Whenever the issue turns upon the diagnosis and treatment of attending physicians and their assistants, then the application of the privilege closes the main source of knowledge and can end only in frustration and injustice. Thus, in New York City the City Council under statutory authority provided for a Committee with subpoena powers to investigate charges of maladministration of Lincoln Hospital. The Committee called upon the Commissioner of Hospitals to produce the records of treatment of certain patients. It was held, however, that the privilege forbade such production.[9] Here it seems strongly arguable that the very policy of promoting better medical care, which is the purpose of the privilege, should lead the court to open the door for this investigation.[10]

WESTLAW REFERENCES

child children boy* girl* /s molest! abus! fondl! indecent /p physician* doctor* hospital* /p patient* /p privilege* secre** confidential!

psych! physician* doctor* hospital* /p patient* /p privilege* secre** confidential!

workm*n worker* /2 compensation /p psych! physician* doctor* hospital* /p patient* /p privilege* secre** confidential!

---

5. As in West's Ann.Cal.Evid.Code, § 1001. See 8 Wigmore, Evidence § 2380, note 5 (McNaughton rev. 1961). And even in the absence of specific provision, it is sometimes held that in such a suit the defendant, despite the privilege, must be permitted to testify to the facts necessary to his defence. Otto v. Miami Valley Hospital Society of Dayton, Ohio, Inc., 26 Ohio Misc. 72, 266 N.E.2d 270 (Ohio C.P.1971). See also Havener, Malpractice Medical Discovery v. Physician-Patient Privilege—Something's Got to Give, 35 Ins.Coun.J. 40 (1968).

6. As in the District of Columbia and in Wisconsin. See statutes compiled in 8 Wigmore, Evidence § 2380, note 5 (McNaughton rev. 1961).

7. As in West's Ann.Cal.Evid.Code § 1004.

8. As in West's Ann.Cal.Evid.Code §§ 1000, 1003. And see § 102 supra.

9. New York City Council v. Goldwater, 284 N.Y. 296, 31 N.E.2d 31, 133 A.L.R. 728 (1940) (two judges dissenting).

10. See Note, 26 Corn.L.Q. 482, 484. For other notes, see 4 U.Detroit L.J. 173, 54 Harv.L.Rev. 705, 16

§ 105. The Policy and Future of the Privilege [1]

Some statements of Buller, J., in 1792 in a case involving the application of the attorney-client privilege seem to have furnished the inspiration for the pioneer New York statute of 1828 on the doctor-patient privilege. He said: "The privilege is confined to the cases of counsel, solicitor, and attorney. . . . It is indeed hard in many cases to compel a friend to disclose a confidential conversation; and I should be glad if by law such evidence could be excluded. It is a subject of just indignation where persons are anxious to reveal what has been communicated to them in a confidential manner. . . . There are cases to which it is much to be lamented that the law of privilege is not extended; those in which medical persons are obliged to disclose the information which they acquire by attending in their professional characters." [2]

These comments reveal attitudes which have been influential ever since in the spread of statutes enacting the doctor-patient privilege. One attitude is the shrinking from forcing anyone to tell in court what he has learned in confidence. It is well understood today, however, that no such sweeping curtain for disclosure of confidences in the

---

Ind.L.J. 592, 39 Mich.L.Rev. 1258, 89 U.Pa.L.Rev. 961. See also Annot., 133 A.L.R. 732.

§ 105

1. There is a wealth of cogent discussion of the policy of the privilege. Most of the older treatments are adverse. Wigmore's scalpel cuts deepest. 8 Evidence § 2380a (McNaughton rev. 1961). Other excellent discussions: De Witt, Privileged Communications Between Physician and Patient, Ch. IV (1958); Chafee, Is Justice Served by Closing the Doctor's Mouth?, 52 Yale L.J. 607 (1943); Purrington, An Abused Privilege, 6 Colum.L.Rev. 388 (1906) (historical, comparative, critical); Notes, 33 Ill.L.Rev. 483 (1939), 12 Minn.L.Rev. 390 (1928). See also for worthwhile treatments: Welch, Another Anomaly—the Patient's Privilege, 13 Miss.L.J. 137 (1941) (emphasis on local decisions); Curd, Privileged Communications between Doctor and Patient—an Anomaly, 44 W.Va.L.Q. 165 (1938); Long, Physician-Patient Privilege Obstructs Justice, 25 Ins. Counsel J. 224 (1958). But compare the commentaries cited infra at n. 4.

2. Wilson v. Rastall, 4 Term, Rep. 753, 759, 100 Eng.Rep. 1287 (K.B.1792).

courtroom could be justified. Another is the complete failure to consider the other side of the shield, namely, the loss which comes from depriving the courts of any reliable source of facts necessary for the right decision of cases.

Perhaps the main burden of Justice Buller's remarks, however, is the suggestion that since the client's disclosures to the lawyer are privileged, the patient's disclosures to the doctor should have the same protection. This analogy has probably been more potent than any other argument, particularly with the lawyers in the legislatures. They would be reluctant to deny to the medical profession a recognition which the courts have themselves provided for the legal profession. Manifestly, however, the soundness of the privilege may not be judged as a matter of rivalry of professions, but by the criterion of the public interest.

Some of the analytical weaknesses of the utilitarian rationale of the privilege, except in the psychotherapeutic context, have been noted earlier.[3] To these must be added the perplexities and confusions arising from judicial and legislative attempts to render tolerable a rule which essentially runs against

the grain of justice, truth, and fair dealing. The uncertainties of application of a privilege so extensively and variously qualified and restricted should suffice conclusively to rebut any continuing effort to justify it on utilitarian grounds, for no one familiar with the vagaries of its operation will be disposed to repose confidence in its protection. Those not so knowledgeable will often find it a snare and a delusion.

A more tenable argument, however, has been increasingly advanced in recent years. This view holds that the privilege should not be viewed as operating to inspire the making of medical confidences but rather as protecting such confidences once made.[4] In support of this position it is contended that the legitimate interest in the privacy of the physician-patient relationship should not be subject to casual breach by every litigant in single-minded pursuit of the last scrap of evidence which may marginally contribute to victory in litigation. While it is true that the privilege will occasionally be seen operating to prevent such unwarranted intrusions,[5] it is debatable whether the value of such protection is sufficiently great to justify both the suppression of critical evidence in other

The Revisers who drafted the New York statute, supported it in their report as follows: "In 4 Term, Rep. 580, Buller, J. (to whom no one will attribute a disposition to relax the rules of evidence), said it was 'much to be lamented' that the information specified in this section was not privileged. Mr. Phillips expresses the same sentiment in his treatise on evidence, p. 104. The ground on which communications to counsel are privileged, is the supposed necessity of a full knowledge of the facts, to advise correctly, and to prepare for the proper defense for prosecution of a suit. But surely the necessity of consulting a medical adviser, when life itself may be in jeopardy, is still stronger. And unless such consultations are privileged, men will be incidentally punished by being obliged to suffer the consequences of injuries without relief from the medical art and without conviction of any offense. Besides, in such cases, during the struggle between legal duty on the one hand, and professional honor on the other, the latter, aided by a strong sense of the injustice and inhumanity of the rule, will in most cases furnish a temptation to the perversion or concealment of truth, too strong for human resistance. In every view that can be taken of the policy, justice or humanity of the rule, as it exists, its relaxation seems highly expedient. It is believed that the proposition in the section is so guarded, that it cannot be abused by applying it to

cases not intended to be privileged." Original Reports of Revisers, vol. 5, p. 34, quoted Purrington, op. cit., 6 Colum.L.Rev. 392, 393 (1906).

3. See § 98 supra.

4. Black, Marital and Physician Privileges—A Reprint of a Letter to a Congressman, 1975 Duke L.J. 45, 50 ("But evaluation of a rule like this [privilege] entails not only a guess as to what conduct it will motivate, but also an estimate of its intrinsic decency . . . Why does this judgment of decency altogether vanish, sink to absolute zero, as soon as somebody files any kind of non-demurrable complaint . . . "); Krattenmaker, Testimonial Privileges in Federal Courts: An Alternative to the Proposed Federal Rules of Evidence, 62 Geo.L.J. 61, 92 (1973) ("Proponents of testimonial privileges need not carry the burden of proving what factors influence behavior. Privileges are important for other reasons as well . . . Most important . . . is the simple fact that when a particular confident's claim of privilege is upheld, so is his very right of privacy.").

5. See Grey v. Los Angeles Superior Court, 62 Cal. App.3d 698, 133 Cal.Rptr. 318 (1976) (insurer presented with claim under accidental death policy sought to depose psychiatrist on "surmise" that result might be evidence of suicide).

cases and the costs of administering a highly complex rule.

Complete abolition of the privilege, however, appears a utopian hope given current political realities. Perhaps the happiest realizeable alternative is that long followed by the state of North Carolina, which qualifies its statutory privilege with the provision that "the court, either at trial or prior thereto . . . may compel such disclosure when, in his opinion, the same is necessary to a proper administration of justice." [6]

6. N.C.G.S. § 8–53 (1981). Such a proviso was recommended for enactment by other states by Committee on the Improvement of the Law of Evidence of the American Bar Association for 1937–38. 8 Wigmore, Evidence § 2380a, n. 4 (McNaughton rev. 1961).

See Sims v. Charlotte Liberty Mutual Insurance Co., 257 N.C. 32, 125 S.E.2d 326 (1962) where Moore, J., in a perceptive opinion observed with respect to the application of G.S. § 8–53, "It seems to us that the privilege statute, when strictly applied without the exercise of discretion on the part of the judge, is more often unjust than just . . . Our Legislature intended the

Such a statute, perceptively and sensitively applied, would not only allow protection of privacy against trivial intrusion but would draw from the privilege the threat of injustice which it has long carried.

 WESTLAW REFERENCES

physician* doctor* hospital* /p patient* /p privilege* secre** confidential & court(wa)

policy policies /p physician* doctor* hospital* /p patient* /p privilege* secre** confidential!

statute to be a shield and not a sword. It was careful to make provision to avoid injustice and suppression of truth by putting it in the power of the trial judge to compel disclosure. Judges should not hesitate to require the disclosure where it appears to them to be necessary in order that the truth be known and justice be done. The Supreme Court cannot exercise such authority and discretion, nor can it repeal or amend the statute by judicial decree. If the spirit and purpose of the law is to be carried out, it must be at the superior court level."

The *Sims* case is noted in 41 N.C.L.Rev. 621 (1963).

Chapter 12

PRIVILEGES FOR GOVERNMENTAL SECRETS

Table of Sections

---

§ 106. Other Principles Distinguished

In discussing the evidential privileges and rules of exclusion in respect to the production and admission of writings and information in the possession of government officers, it is well to mark off at the outset some other principles which may hinder the litigant seeking facts from the government, but which are beyond our present inquiry. Among them are these: (a) questions of substantive privilege of government officers from liability for their acts and words,[1] (b) questions as to the general exemption of the chief executive and other high officers from judicial process to enforce their appearance or attendance or to compel them to give evidence,[2] and (c) questions as to the irremovability of official records.[3]

WESTLAW REFERENCES

spalding /5 161 /5 483
sh 161 u.s. 483

---

§ 106

1. See, e.g., Spalding v. Vilas, 161 U.S. 483 (1896) (exemption of Postmaster General from civil liability for official statement); Prosser, Torts § 132 (4th ed.); 8 Wigmore, Evidence § 2368 (McNaughton rev. 1961).

2. See 8 Wigmore, Evidence §§ 2360–2371 (McNaughton rev. 1961); Bishop, The Executive's Right of Privacy: An Unresolved Constitutional Question, 66 Yale L.J. 477 (1957); Hardin, Executive Privilege in the Federal Courts, 71 Yale L.J. 879 (1962); Hennings et al., Symposium, 19 Fed.Bar J. 1 (1959); Taubeneck and Sexton, Executive Privilege and the Court's Right to Know, 48 Geo.L.J. 486 (1960).

3. See, e.g., Dunham v. Chicago, 55 Ill. 357 (1870) (court will not order removal where certified copies will serve as well); 8 Wigmore, Evidence § 2373 (McNaughton rev. 1961).

§ 107. The Common Law Privileges for Military or Diplomatic Secrets and Other Facts the Disclosure of Which Would be Contrary to the Public Interest [1]

Since the turn of the century the activities of government have multiplied in number and widened in scope, and the need of litigants for the disclosure and proof of documents and other information in the possession of government officials has correspondingly increased. When this need is asserted and opposed, the resultant question requires a delicate and judicious balancing of the public interest in the secrecy of "classified" official information against the public interest in the protection of the claim of the individual to due process of law in the redress of grievances.[2]

It is generally conceded that a privilege and a rule of exclusion should apply in the case of writings and information constituting military or diplomatic secrets of state.[3]

§ 107

1. 8 Wigmore, Evidence §§ 2378, 2378a, 2379 (McNaughton rev. 1961); 4 Moore's Federal Practice ¶ 26.61 (1970); Sanford, Evidentiary Privileges Against the Production of Data within the Control of Executive Departments, 3 Vand.L.Rev. 73 (1949); Berger & Krash, Government Immunity from Discovery, 59 Yale L.J. 1451 (1950); Bishop, The Executive's Right of Privacy: An Unresolved Constitutional Question, 66 Yale L.J. 477 (1957); Carrow, Governmental Nondisclosure in Judicial Proceedings, 107 U.Pa.L.Rev. 166 (1958); Cox, Executive Privilege, 122 U.Pa.L.Rev. 1383 (1974); Hardin, Executive Privilege in the Federal Courts, 71 Yale L.J. 879 (1962); Gromley, Discovery Against the Government of Military and Other Confidential Matters, 43 Ky.L.J. 343 (1955); Hennings et al., Symposium, 19 Fed.Bar J. 1 (1959); Mitchell, Governmental Secrecy in Theory and Practice, 58 Colum.L.Rev. 199 (1958); Rogers, Constitutional Law: The Papers of the Executive Branch, 44 A.B.A.J. 941 (1958); Taubeneck and Sexton, Executive Privilege and the Court's Right to Know, 48 Geo.L.J. 486 (1960); Zagel, State Secrets Privilege, 50 Minn.L.Rev. 875 (1966); Comment, 1974 U.Ill.L.F. 631.

2. "Besides, the public good is in nothing more essentially interested, than in the protection of every individual's private rights, as modelled by the municipal law." 1 Blackstone, Commentaries *139 (1765), referred to in Pound, Administrative Discretion and Civil Liberties in England, 56 Harv.L.Rev. 806, 814 (1943).

3. 8 Wigmore, Evidence § 2378(2) (McNaughton rev. 1961). Examples of decisions in which the existence of a privilege for military or diplomatic secrets was affirmed or assumed: Aaron Burr's Trial, Robertson's Rep. I, 121, 127, 186, 255, II, 536 (1807) described and quoted from in 8 Wigmore, Evidence (3d ed. 1940) § 2379, p. 799 (subpena duces tecum issued by Marshall, C.J., to President Jefferson to produce correspondence with General Wilkinson, over objection of government that it involved relations with France and Spain; Marshall, C.J.: "There is certainly nothing before the Court which shows that the letter in question contains any matter the disclosure of which would endanger the public safety; . . . if it does contain any matter which it would be imprudent to disclose, which it is not the wish of the Executive to disclose, such matter, if it be not immediately and essentially applicable to the point, will of course be suppressed. . . ."); Totten v. United States, 92 U.S. 105 (1875) (action by former spy, after Civil War, for services during war under contract with President; held, action denied since its maintenance will endanger secrecy of such employments); Firth Sterling Steel Co. v. Bethlehem Steel Co., 199 F. 353 (E.D.Pa.1912) (copies of drawings of armor-piercing projectiles made by Navy and classed as secret, excluded by court on objection, though witness did not claim privilege, recognizing "rule of public policy forbidding the disclosure of military secrets.")

In United States v. Reynolds, 345 U.S. 1 (1953), Vinson, C.J., for the court, after referring to "the privilege against revealing military secrets, a privilege which is well established in the law of evidence," said: "Judicial experience with the privilege which protects military and state secrets has been limited in this country. English experience has been more extensive, but still relatively slight compared with other evidentiary privileges. Nevertheless, the principles which control the application of the privilege emerge quite clearly from the available precedents. The privilege belongs to the Government and must be asserted by it; it can neither be claimed nor waived by a private party. It is not to be lightly invoked. There must be a formal claim of privilege, lodged by the head of the department which has control over the matter, after actual personal consideration by that officer."

See also Machin v. Zuckert, 114 U.S.App.D.C. 335, 316 F.2d 336 (1963), cert. denied 375 U.S. 896 (investigative reports of Department of Air Force concerning aircraft accident held privileged in suit between private litigants where disclosure would hamper efficient operation of important program and perhaps impair national security by weakening a branch of the military).

Deleted Fed.R.Evid. 509, Military and State Secrets:

(a) General Rule of Privilege. The government has a privilege to refuse to give evidence and to prevent any person from giving evidence upon a showing of reasonable likelihood of danger that disclosure of the evidence will be detrimental or injurious to the national defense or the international relations of the United States.

(b) Procedure. The privilege may be claimed only by the chief officer of the department of government administering the subject matter which the evidence concerns. The required showing may be made in whole or in part in the form of a written statement. The judge may hear the matter in chambers, but all

Wigmore seems to regard it as doubtful whether the denial of disclosure should go further than this,[4] but state statutes in this country sometimes state the privilege in broader terms,[5] and the English decisions seem to have accepted the wide generalization that official documents and facts will be privileged whenever their disclosure would be injurious to the public interest.[6] Whether this wider principle is justified in point of policy is open to serious question.

 WESTLAW REFERENCES

privilege* exclusion* /p writing* inform! /p military diplomatic /p secret*

---

§ 108. Qualified Privileges for Government Information: The Constitutional Presidential Privilege: Common Law Privileges for Agency Deliberations and Law Enforcement Investigational Files

The case of United States v. Nixon [1] brought into sharp focus both the limits of the long-standing executive privilege protecting diplomatic and military secrets and the distinguishable question as to whether some broader privilege protects confidential communications between the President and his or her immediate advisors. The decision of the Supreme Court in that case, while apparently recognizing a constitutionally based privilege of this nature, nevertheless held that the privilege is a qualified one and subject to invasion upon a showing of demonstrable need for evidence relevant to a criminal proceeding. The presidential privilege has occasioned considerable discussion by

---

counsel are entitled to inspect the claim and showing and to be heard thereon. The judge may take any protective measure which the interests of the government and the furtherance of justice may require.

(c) Notice to Government. If the circumstances of the case indicate a substantial possibility that a claim of privilege would be appropriate but has not been made because of oversight or lack of knowledge, the judge shall give or cause notice to be given to the officer entitled to claim the privilege and shall stay further proceedings a reasonable time to afford opportunity to assert a claim of privilege.

(d) Effect of Sustaining Claim. If a claim of privilege is sustained in a proceeding to which the government is a party and it appears that another party is thereby deprived of material evidence, the judge shall make any further orders which the interests of justice require, including striking the testimony of a witness, declaring a mistrial, finding against the government upon an issue as to which the evidence is relevant, or dismissing the action.

Rev.Unif.R.Evid. 508 provides in part:

(a) If the law of the United States creates a governmental privilege that the courts of this State must recognize under the Constitution of the United States, the privilege may be claimed as provided by the law of the United States.

(b) No other governmental privilege is recognized except as created by the Constitution or statutes of this State.

4. See 8 Wigmore, Evidence § 2378, n. 7 (McNaughton rev. 1961).

5. West's Ann.Cal.Evid.Code § 1040:

Privilege for official information. (a) As used in this section, "official information" means information acquired in confidence by a public employee in the course of his duty and not open, or officially disclosed, to the public prior to the time the claim of privilege is made.

(b) A public entity has a privilege to refuse to disclose official information, and to prevent another from disclosing such information, if the privilege is claimed by a person authorized by the public entity to do so and:

(1) Disclosure is forbidden by an act of the Congress of the United States or a statute of this state; or

(2) Disclosure of the information is against the public interest because there is a necessity for preserving the confidentiality of the information that outweighs the necessity for disclosure in the interest of justice; but no privilege may be claimed under this paragraph if any person authorized to do so has consented that the information be disclosed in the proceeding. In determining whether disclosure of the information is against the public interest, the interest of the public entity as a party in the outcome of the proceeding may not be considered.

For additional statutes, see 8 Wigmore, Evidence § 2378, n. 9 (McNaughton rev. 1961). See also Dec. Dig. Witnesses ⟳216; Annot., 165 A.L.R. 1302, 1311. The Revised Uniform Evid.Rules (1974) contain no provision of this nature.

6. The opinion of Viscount Simon, L.Ch., for the House of Lords in Duncan v. Cammell, Laird & Co., [1942] App.C. 624 accepts this principle and reviews the supporting precedents.

§ 108

1. 418 U.S. 683 (1974).

constitutional scholars,[2] but will, for all of its importance to our system of government, rarely be encountered.

Of much greater everyday significance is the enormous quantity of information produced, collected, and compiled by the governmental agencies which have proliferated since the end of World War II. Only an infinitesimal amount of this governmental information will fall within the previously discussed privilege protecting military and diplomatic secrets. What then of the vast remainder?

Until fairly recently, this great store of information, though not within the ambit of any well-defined evidentiary privilege, was as a practical matter extremely difficult or impossible to obtain. Prior to its amendment in 1958, the so-called Federal Housekeeping Act[3] was assumed by administrators to authorize the issuance of regulations requiring governmental personnel in the ac-

tual possession of governmental documents and records to decline to produce them even when served with a subpoena issued by a court. The validity of these regulations was consistently upheld by the Supreme Court,[4] and though the cases never went to the extent of holding that the Act created a statutory privilege the practical effect was that private litigants were unable to obtain needed information.

The overall accessibility of governmental information has more recently been dramatically increased by new legislation. In 1958, the Federal Housekeeping Act was amended by the Congress to include a provision removing any possible implication that the Act was intended to create a statutory privilege,[5] and the intent of this amendment has been observed in subsequent court decisions.[6] Access to governmental information has been even more substantially increased with

---

2. Cox, Executive Privilege, 122 U.Pa.L.Rev. 1383 (1974); Nathanson, From Watergate to Marbury v. Madison: Some Reflections on Presidential Privilege in Current Historical Perspective, 16 Ariz.L.Rev. 59 (1974); The Supreme Court, 1973 Term, Freund, Foreward: On Presidential Privilege, 88 Harv.L.Rev. 13 (1974); Symposium, 22 U.C.L.A.L.Rev. 1 (1974); Symposium, 9 Loy.–L.A.L.Rev. (1976). Berger, How the Privilege for Governmental Information Met Its Watergate, 25 Case W.Res.L.Rev. 747 (1975), traces the history of deleted Federal Rule 509 in the Congress and suggests that, had it been in effect when *Nixon* was decided, a more acceptable basis for decision would have been at hand.

3. 5 U.S.C.A. § 822, R.S. § 161 (1875) provided as follows: "The head of each department is authorized to prescribe regulations, not inconsistent with law, for the government of his department, the conduct of its officers and clerks, the distribution and performance of its business, and the custody, use, and preservation of the records, papers, and property appertaining to it."

4. Boske v. Comingore, 177 U.S. 459 (1900) (statute conferring rulemaking power on heads of departments valid under the "necessary and proper" clause and Treasury regulation prohibiting production of records by collector of internal revenue valid; collector punished for contempt by state court for nonproduction discharged on habeas corpus); United States v. Ragen, 340 U.S. 462 (1951) (similar regulations of Attorney General approved, following above decision, in its application to subordinate officers; "When one considers the variety of information contained in the files of any government department and the possibilities of harm from unrestricted disclosure in court, the usefulness,

indeed the necessity, of centralizing determination as to whether subpoenas duces tecum will be willingly obeyed or challenged is obvious.").

5. P.L. 85–619, 72 Stat. 547 (1958). The Act in its present form reads: "The head of an Executive department or military department may prescribe regulations for the government of his department, the conduct of its employees, the distribution and performance of its business, and the custody, use, and preservation of its records, papers, and property. This section does not authorize withholding information from the public or limiting the availability of records to the public." 5 U.S.C.A. § 301.

See Note, 69 Yale L.J. 452 (1960).

6. Olson Rug Co. v. N.L.R.B., 291 F.2d 655 (7th Cir. 1961); Sperandeo v. Milk Drivers and Dairy Employees Local Union, 334 F.2d 381 (10th Cir.1964); Rosee v. Board of Trade of the City of Chicago, 35 F.R.D. 512 (N.D.Ill.1964) (reports of commodity transactions held not privileged from disclosure under Commodity Exchange Act authorizing the Secretary of Agriculture to make investigations and to "publish from time to time, in his discretion, the result of such investigation and such statistical information gathered therefrom as he may deem of interest to the public, except data and information which would separately disclose the business transactions of any person and trade secrets or names of customers . . . ." The Court pointed out that where Congress has intended to prohibit the use of government-held data in judicial proceedings it has not talked in terms of "publish" or "publication" but has expressed the prohibition explicitly, citing examples of such statutes).

the enactment by the Congress,[7] and by many state legislatures, of Freedom of Information legislation. While these statutes are directed toward availability of information for the public in general and the news media in particular their importance in clearing the way for discovery in litigation will be readily apparent. To proceed under the federal Freedom of Information Act no standing or particularized need for the desired information need be shown, and any person is eligible to proceed under the provisions of the statute. Not all governmental information may, however, be obtained through suit under FOIA. The statute contains a number of exceptions which have an indirect but substantial effect upon certain questions of privilege.[8]

Turning to the question of newly emergent privileges protecting governmental information, the general erosion of governmental secrecy has forced into prominence the fact that some types of governmental information are more sensitive than others and may warrant at least qualified protection from public disclosure. This recognition has in turn led to the emergence of two qualified common law privileges unknown to earlier law, one protecting certain aspects of governmental agency policy deliberations,[9] and another shielding law enforcement investigational files.[10]

---

7. 5 U.S.C.A. § 552. The Act reads:

(a)(3) . . . [E]ach agency, on request for identifiable records made in accordance with published rules stating the time, place, fees to the extent authorized by statute, and procedure to be followed, shall make the records promptly available to any person. On complaint, the district court of the United States in the district in which the complainant resides, or has his principal place of business, or in which the agency records are situated, has jurisdiction to enjoin the agency from withholding agency records and to order the production of any agency records improperly withheld from the complainant. In such a case the court shall determine the matter de novo and the burden is on the agency to sustain its action. In the event of noncompliance with the order of the court, the district court may punish for contempt the responsible employee, and in the case of a uniformed service, the responsible member. Except as to causes the court considers of greater importance, proceedings before the district court, as authorized by this paragraph, take precedence on the docket over all other causes and shall be assigned for hearing and trial at the earliest practicable date and expedited in every way.

. . .

(b) This section does not apply to matters that are—

(1) specifically required by Executive order to be kept secret in the interest of the national defense or foreign policy;

(2) related solely to the internal personnel rules and practices of an agency;

(3) specifically exempted from disclosure by statute;

(4) trade secrets and commercial or financial information obtained from a person and privileged or confidential;

(5) inter-agency or intra-agency memorandums or letters which would not be available by law to a party other than an agency in litigation with the agency;

(6) personnel and medical files and similar files the disclosure of which would constitute a clearly unwarranted invasion of personal privacy;

(7) investigatory files compiled for law enforcement purposes except to the extent available by law to a party other than an agency;

(8) contained in or related to examination, operating, or condition reports prepared by, on behalf of, or for the use of an agency responsible for the regulation or supervision of financial institutions; or

(9) geological and geophysical information and data, including maps, concerning wells.

(c) This section does not authorize withholding of information or limit the availability of records to the public, except as specifically stated in this section. This section is not authority to withhold information from Congress.

The legislative history of this act appears in House Report No. 1497, U.S.Code Congressional and Administrative News, 89th Congress—Second Session, Vol. 2, p. 2418.

8. For the text of the act, see n. 7 supra.

9. E.P.A. v. Mink, 410 U.S. 73 (1973); Pacific Molasses Co. v. N.L.R.B., 577 F.2d 1172 (5th Cir.1978); National Courier Association v. Board of Governors of the Federal Reserve System, 516 F.2d 1229 (D.C.Cir.1975).

10. Black v. Sheraton Corp. of America, 564 F.2d 531 (D.C.Cir.1977); Stephens Produce Co., Inc. v. N.L.R.B., 515 F.2d 1373 (8th Cir.1975).

While the two qualified privileges noted have been judicially created through the common law process,[11] their relationship to two exception provisions of the FOIA [12] which deal with the same generic matter cannot be overlooked. In fact, it may be said that the FOIA exceptions preserve conditions under which the evidentiary privileges may exist and in effect define their maximum spheres of operation. For while the FOIA does not address itself to questions of evidentiary admissibility,[13] it would be anomalous in the extreme to forbid by evidentiary privilege the disclosure in litigation of information accessible to any citizen under FOIA.[14] A moment's reflection, however, will suggest that the converse does not hold, and that the evidentiary privileges might meaningfully and reasonably be viewed as protecting *less* than the total sum of information denied the general public under the FOIA exceptions. Such a differentiation is justifiable on the ground that the litigant's interest in access to evidence will sometimes be stronger than the ordinary citizen's interest in merely obtaining information.[15] It has accordingly been held that not all information exempt from disclosure under the exceptions to FOIA will necessarily be protected by privilege if sought by discovery processes for purposes of litigation.[16] The foregoing synopsis will suggest that the

multitudinous decisions construing the exception provisions of FOIA will be of varying precedential value concerning the scope of the privileges discussed below.

(a) The Agency Policy Deliberations Privilege.[17]

This privilege protects communications made between governmental personnel, or between governmental personnel and outside consultants, which consist of advisory opinions and recommendations preliminary to the formulation of agency policy.[18] Like other communications privileges, that protecting governmental agency deliberations seeks to encourage a free flow of communication in the interest of some larger end, in this instance the objective of establishing agency policy only after consideration of the full array of contrasting views on the subject.[19] Here, as elsewhere, it is assumed that total candor will be enhanced, and the quality of governmental decision-making correspondingly improved, by an assurance of at least qualified confidentiality.

Other contributory policies supporting the recognition of this privilege have been said to be that it avoids premature and potentially misleading public disclosure of possible agency action, and assures that governmental decision-makers will be judged solely upon the quality of their decisions without re-

---

11. E.P.A. v. Mink, 410 U.S. 73 (1973). See also Larkin, Federal Testimonial Privileges § 5.01 (1982).

12. 5 U.S.C.A. § 552(b)(5) and (7). For the text of these subsections, see n. 7 supra.

13. N.L.R.B. v. Sears, Roebuck & Co., 421 U.S. 132, 143 (1975) (FOIA "is fundamentally designed to inform the public about agency action and not to benefit private litigants.").

14. Larkin, Federal Evidentiary Privilege § 5.01 (1982) at n. 17 ("The FOIA sets a floor for the claim of executive privilege in this area. Availability under the FOIA should always defeat a claim of privilege.").

15. "The problems of what a citizen should be able to get from a Government agency when he has simply the general interest of the citizen in finding out what is going on and the problems of the litigant who has a particular need are obviously very different and almost by hypothesis what is the right solution for the first cannot be the right solution for the second." Testimony of Friendly, J., Hearings on Proposed Federal Rules

of Evidence, Subcommittee on Reform of Federal Criminal Laws of the Committee on the Judiciary, House of Representatives, 93rd Congress, 1st Session, Sec. 2, p. 274 (1973).

Proposed Fed.R.Evid. 509, if it had been enacted, would have created at least qualified evidentiary privilege for matter covered by any of the exceptions of the FOIA. See text of rule 509, supra n. 3.

16. N.L.R.B. v. Sears, Roebuck & Co., 421 U.S. 132 (1975).

17. See generally, Cox, Executive Privilege, 122 U.Pa.L.Rev. 1383 (1974); Berger, The Incarnation of Executive Privilege, 22 U.C.L.A.L.Rev. 4 (1974).

18. Murphy v. Department of Army, 613 F.2d 1151 (D.C.Cir.1979); Sterling Drug, Inc. v. Harris, 488 F.Supp. 1019 (S.D.N.Y.1980).

19. In re Franklin National Bank Securities Litigation, 478 F.Supp. 577 (E.D.N.Y.1979) (privilege protects candid policy discussion).

gard to the quality of other options considered and discarded.[20]

To come within the rationale of the privilege, the matter sought to be kept confidential must have been communicated prior to the finalization of the policy at which it was directed, and must have constituted opinion or evaluation as opposed to the mere reporting of objective facts.[21] It is not, however, material whether the communication reflected the view which ultimately became embodied in agency policy, or even whether the communication was considered or totally ignored by the decision-maker.[22] The privilege is that of the government, and would appear to be claimable indefinitely since it is terminated neither by the adoption of the policy concerned nor by the death of the author of the privileged matter.[23] As further discussed below, the privilege is a conditional one only, and is therefore subject to invasion upon a sufficient showing of necessity.[24]

(b) The Privilege for Investigative Files Relating to Law Enforcement.

The purpose of the qualified protection afforded to the files and reports of investigations directed toward enforcement of the law may readily be deduced from the nature of the subject matter protected. Public disclosure of the files of such investigations may frequently have untoward results from the standpoint of effective law enforcement. These may include compromising the identity of confidential sources of information, disclosing the targets of the investigation or

the techniques being used to pursue it,[25] or revealing the nature of the case being prepared, thus facilitating the preparation of defenses.[26] An additional non-governmental interest supporting recognition of the privilege exists in that its application will prevent the casting of unnecessary suspicion upon persons ultimately exonerated by the investigative process.[27]

To come within the ambit of the privilege, the investigation must be one directed at the enforcement of the law, criminal or civil, and must be conducted by an agency charged by law with law enforcement functions.[28] Unlike the privilege for agency deliberations, the present privilege is commonly held to expire with the termination of the specific governmental undertaking to which the privileged matter relates.[29] This privilege, too, is conditional, but in the unusual sense that it will not attach at all failing an initial government demonstration that some specific detriment of the types sought to be avoided will ensue from disclosure of the matter sought to be protected.[30]

 WESTLAW REFERENCES

nixon /15 418 /5 683 & executive president! /p privilege* /p qualified
5 +2 552 & "freedom of information" FOIA & exception*

The Agency Policy Deliberations Privilege
5 +2 552(b)(5) & policy policies /s deliberation*

The Privilege for Investment Files Relating to Law Enforcement
5 +2 552(b)(7) & investigat! /s file* record* document*

20. Jordan v. United States Department of Justice, 591 F.2d 753 (D.C.Cir.1978).

21. Jupiter Painting Contracting Co. v. United States, 87 F.R.D. 593 (E.D.Pa.1980).

22. Lead Industrial Association, Inc. v. OSHA, 610 F.2d 70 (2d Cir.1980).

23. Kaiser Aluminum & Chemical Corp. v. United States, 141 Ct.Cl. 38, 157 F.Supp. 939 (1958).

24. Kerr v. United States District Court, 426 U.S. 394 (1976); Machin v. Zuchert, 316 F.2d 336 (D.C.Cir. 1963), cert. denied 375 U.S. 896, appeal after remand 336 F.2d 914 (D.C.Cir.).

25. Ferri v. Bell, 645 F.2d 1213 (3d Cir.1981), modified 671 F.2d 769.

26. Murphy v. F.B.I., 490 F.Supp. 1138 (D.D.C.1980).

27. Dorsen & Shattuck, Executive Privilege, the Congress, and the Courts, 35 Ohio St.L.J. 1 (1974).

28. Lamont v. Department of Justice, 475 F.Supp. 761 (S.D.N.Y.1979).

29. Frankenhauser v. Rizzo, 59 F.R.D. 339 (E.D.Pa. 1973).

30. The showing, however, need not be specific to the case at hand, but may be based on the likelihood of the apprehended interference as indicated by experience. Kanter v. I.R.S., 478 F.Supp. 552 (N.D.Ill.1979).

sh 87 frd 593
sh 475 f.s. 761

§ 109. Effect of the Presence of the Government as a Litigant

To the extent that the Freedom of Information Act is available as a means for obtaining government records and information for use in evidence, as discussed in the preceding section, no distinction is made between situations where the litigation is between parties other than the government and those where the government is a party. However, when procedures other than under the Act are resorted to, the difference may be substantial.

When the government is not a party and successfully resists disclosure sought by a party, the result is simply that the evidence is unavailable, as though a witness had died, and the case will proceed accordingly, with no consequences save those resulting from the loss of the evidence. But when the government is a party, whether by resorting to the courts as plaintiff in civil or criminal proceedings or by virtue of consenting to be sued as defendant,[1] it is in court as a litigant, with important consequences. By invoking the court's aid by bringing suit, the government seems clearly to waive any claim of executive immunity in that the court can deny use of its facilities unless the government submits to making disclosure.[2] Accordingly, in a criminal prosecution the court may give the government the choice of making disclosure of matters of significance to the defense or suffering dismissal of the proceeding; any executive immunity is waived, and the government cannot as litigant invoke an evidentiary privilege, e.g., for military secrets, while at the same time seeking to proceed affirmatively with respect to its subject matter.[3] Nor may the government as plaintiff in a civil action proceed affirmatively against a defendant while at the same time seeking under the guise of privilege to deprive the defendant of evidence useful to the defense of the action.[4] On the other hand, when the government is defendant, as under the Tort Claims Act, an adverse finding cannot be rendered against it as the price of asserting an evidentiary privilege. This is not one of the terms upon which Congress has consented that the United States be subjected to liability.[5]

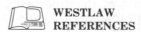 **WESTLAW REFERENCES**

reynolds /155 345 /5 1 /p government! /p privilege* /p depriv!

§ 109

1. E.g., under the Tort Claims Act, 28 U.S.C.A. § 2674.

2. Thus it may fairly be said, "The Government as a litigant is, of course, subject to the rules of discovery." United States v. Procter & Gamble Co., 356 U.S. 677, 681 (1958). See also Bank Line, Ltd. v. United States, 163 F.2d 133 (2d Cir.1947). The fact that enforcement measures may be designed to avoid confronting the embarrassing question whether a cabinet member may be committed for contempt makes them no less enforcement measures.

3. United States v. Andolschek, 142 F.2d 503, 506 (2d Cir.1944) (in prosecution of inspectors of Alcohol Tax Unit for illegal dealings with permittees, error to sustain government's claim of privilege for reports of inspectors to their superiors as to these dealings; L. Hand, J.: "While we must accept it as lawful for a department of the government to suppress documents, even when they will help determine controversies between third persons, we cannot agree that this should include their suppression in a criminal prosecution, founded upon those very dealings to which the documents relate, and whose criminality they will, or may, tend to exculpate."); United State v. Grayson, 166 F.2d 863, 870 (2d Cir.1948) (prosecution for fraudulent use of mails and violation of Securities Act, held error to exclude as confidential pertinent documents in possession of Securities and Exchange Commission). See also Reynolds v. United States, 345 U.S. 1, 12 (1953).

4. In United States v. Cotton Valley Operators Committee, 9 F.R.D. 719 (W.D.La.1949), a civil antitrust action, the Government failed to comply with the order to produce certain reports and correspondence and the action was dismissed. The judgment was affirmed by an equally divided court in 339 U.S. 940. See also United States v. Procter & Gamble Co., supra n. 2.

5. If the matter arises in connection with efforts to obtain discovery, as in United States v. Reynolds, 345 U.S. 1 (1953), then it is significant that Fed.R.Civ.P. 26(b)(1) exempts from discovery matters which are privileged under the rules of evidence. The drawing of an adverse inference from a claim of privilege generally is discussed in § 74 supra.

§ 110. The Scope of the Judge's Function in Determining the Validity of the Claim of Privilege [1]

When the head of department has made a claim of privilege for documents or information under his control as being military or diplomatic secrets is this claim conclusive upon the judge? Is the judge entitled to ascertain the content of the information withheld, and to apply for himself the standard of danger to the public interest? A decision of the House of Lords in 1942 limits the judge's function to ascertaining whether the claim is made by the proper officer in proper form. If he decides that it is, the claim is conclusive.[2] This view, though criticized by some commentators as unnecessarily inflexible,[3] has been followed by the great majority of American decisions.[4] Understandably, the courts are reluctant to view even the most pressing need of a private litigant for evidence as justification for jeopardizing, however slightly, a national interest asserted to be vital by a senior official of the executive branch.[5]

Once we leave the restricted area of military and diplomatic secrets, however, a greater role for the judiciary in the determination of governmental claims of privilege becomes not only desirable but necessary. The head of an executive department can appraise the public interest of secrecy as well (or perhaps in some cases better) than the judge, but his official habit and leaning tend to sway him toward a minimizing of the interest of the individual. Under the normal administrative routine the question will come to him with recommendations from cautious subordinates against disclosure and in the press of business the chief is likely to approve the recommendation about such a seemingly minor matter without much independent consideration.[6] The determination of questions of fact and the applications of legal standards thereto in passing upon the admissibility of evidence and the validity of claims of evidential privilege are traditionally the responsibility of the judge. As a public functionary he has respect for the executive's scruples against disclosure and at the same time his duties require him constantly to appraise private interests and to reconcile them with conflicting public policies; he may thus seem better qualified than the executive to weigh both interests understandingly and to strike a wise balance.

The foregoing considerations largely explain the fact that privileges running in

§ 110

1. 8 Wigmore, Evidence §§ 2378, 2379 (McNaughton rev. 1961); Notes, 18 U.Chi.L.Rev. 122 (1950), 41 J.Crim.L. 330 (1950), 47 Nw.U.L.Rev. 259, 268 (1952), 47 Nw.U.L.Rev. 519, 527 (1952), 29 N.Y.U.L.Rev. 194 (1954).

2. Duncan v. Cammel, Laird & Co., [1942] App.C. 624. The holding is vigorously criticized in Note, 69 L.Q.Rev. 449 (1953).

3. Berger, The Incarnation of Executive Privilege, 22 UCLAL.Rev. 4 (1974).

4. Halkin v. Helms, 598 F.2d 1 (D.C.Cir. 1978); Swanner v. United States, 406 F.2d 716 (5th Cir. 1969), on remand 309 F.Supp. 1183 (D.C.Ala.).

5. Zagel, The State Secrets Privilege, 50 Minn.L. Rev. 875, 910 (1966) ("There is no greater reason for secrecy than protecting the military and diplomatic welfare of the nation").

6. See the graphic comments of Wigmore to like effect. 8 Evidence § 2378 n. 7 (McNaughton rev. 1961).

In speaking of the grounds which should influence the executive, Simons, L. Ch., said in Duncan v. Cammel, Laird & Co., [1942] App.C. 624, 642: "It would not be a good ground that, if they were produced, the consequences might involve the department or the government in parliamentary discussion or in public criticism, or might necessitate the attendance as witnesses or otherwise of officials who have pressing duties elsewhere. Neither would it be a good ground that production might tend to expose a want of efficiency in the administration or tend to lay the department open to claims for compensation. In a word, it is not enough that the minister of the department does not want to have the documents produced. The minister, in deciding whether it is his duty to object, should bear these considerations in mind, for he ought not to take the responsibility of withholding production except in cases where the public interest would otherwise be damnified, for example, where disclosure would be injurious to national defence, or to good diplomatic relations, or where the practice of keeping a class of documents secret is necessary for the proper functioning of the public service." And in Robinson v. State of South Australia, [1931] App.C. 704, 715, the court declared that "the fact that production of the documents might in the particular litigation prejudice the Crown's own case" is not a legitimate reason for claiming privilege.

favor of government, other than that for military and diplomatic secrets, are uniformly held to be qualified ones only.[7] Thus, where these privileges are claimed, it is for the judge to determine whether the interest in governmental secrecy is outweighed in the particular case by the litigant's interest in obtaining the evidence sought. A satisfactory striking of this balance will, on the one hand, require consideration of the interests giving rise to the privilege and an assessment of the extent to which disclosure will realistically impair those interests. On the other hand, factors which will affect the litigant's need will include the significance of the evidence sought for the case, the availability of the desired information from other sources, and in some instances the nature of the right being asserted in the litigation. Here, as with other qualified privileges, the possibility of in camera inspection by the court offers a practical expedient for

testing the claim of privilege without, by that testing process, destroying irretrievably the secrecy which the privilege is designed to preserve.

WESTLAW REFERENCES

judicia! /p camera

§ 111. The Privilege Against the Disclosure of the Identity of an Informer [1]

Informers are shy and timorous folk, whether they are undercover agents of the police or merely citizens stepping forward with information about violations of law, and if their names were subject to be readily revealed, this enormously important aid to law enforcement would be almost cut off. On this ground of policy, a privilege is recognized in respect to disclosure of the identity of an informer,[2] who has given information

---

7. Larkin, Federal Testimonial Privileges, § 5.03(2) (1982) ("Executive privileges other than those that cover state secrets are not absolute"). See also, Dorsen & Shattuck, Executive Privilege, The Congress, and the Courts, 35 Ohio St.L.J. 1 (1974).

§ 111

1. 8 Wigmore, Evidence § 2374 (McNaughton rev. 1961); Annot., 76 A.L.R.2d 262 (1961); 1 L.Ed.2d 1998; 21 Am.Jur.2d Criminal Law § 332; 81 Am.Jur.2d Witnesses § 294; C.J.S. Witnesses § 264, p. 751; Dec.Dig. Witnesses ⊂⊃216. See also Katz, The Paradoxical Role of Informers within the Criminal Justice System: A Unique Perspective, 7 U.Dayton L.Rev. 51 (1981), and Comments, 63 Yale L.J. 206 (1953) 29 N.Y.U.L.Rev. 194, 200 (1954). The policy of the privilege seems drawn in question by the vigorous language of Mr. Justice Douglas's dissent in United States v. Nugent, 346 U.S. 1, 13 (1953) where the court held that one who claimed draft exemption was not entitled, in an advisory hearing in the Department of Justice, to see the F.B.I. reports containing information received from informers.

See also Fed.R.Evid. (R.D.1971) 510.

2. Marks v. Beyfus, 25 Q.B.D. 494 (Ct.App.1890) (action for malicious prosecution; plaintiff sought to elicit from Director of Public Prosecutions, the name and statement of informers—who were presumably the present defendants—but the witness declined unless the judge was of opinion that he should disclose, but the judge declined to order him to answer; on plaintiff's appeal, held, no error—not a matter of discretion, but judge should exclude under the rule of policy, except where the evidence is needed to establish the innocence of an accused); Worthington v. Scribner, 109

Mass. 487, 12 Am.Rep. 736 (1872) (action for false charges made to U.S. Treasury that plaintiff was an imposter; interrogatories to the defendant as to his giving this information; held defendant privileged not to answer); Dellastatious v. Boyce, 152 Va. 368, 147 S.E. 267 (1929) (action for damages for trespass on premises and false arrest against prohibition inspector and special deputies in execution of warrant; error in requiring officer to disclose from whom he secured information on which warrant was issued).

Rev.Unif.R.Evid. (1974) 509 reads:

(a) Rule of Privilege. The United States or a state or subdivision thereof has a privilege to refuse to disclose the identity of a person who has furnished information relating to or assisting in an investigation of a possible violation of a law to a law enforcement officer or member of a legislative committee or its staff conducting an investigation.

(b) Who May Claim. The privilege may be claimed by an appropriate representative of the public entity to which the information was furnished.

(c) Exceptions:

(1) *Voluntary Disclosure; Informer a Witness.* No privilege exists under this rule if the identity of the informer or his interest in the subject matter of his communication has been disclosed to those who would have cause to resent the communication by a holder of the privilege or by the informer's own action, or if the informer appears as a witness for the government.

(2) *Testimony on Relevant Issue.* If it appears in the case that an informer may be able to give testimony relevant to any issue in a criminal case

about supposed crimes to a prosecuting or investigating officer or to someone for the purpose of its being relayed to such an officer.[3] The privilege runs to the government or state, and may be invoked by its officers who as witnesses or otherwise are called on

> or to a fair determination of a material issue on the merits in a civil case to which a public entity is a party, and the informed public entity invokes the privilege, the court shall give the public entity an opportunity to show *in camera* facts relevant to determining whether the informer can, in fact, supply that testimony. The showing will ordinarily be in the form of affidavits, but the court may direct that testimony be taken if it finds that the matter cannot be resolved satisfactorily upon affidavit. If the court finds there is a reasonable probability that the informer can give the testimony, and the public entity elects not to disclose his identity, in criminal cases the court on motion of the defendant or on its own motion shall grant appropriate relief, which may include one or more of the following: requiring the prosecuting attorney to comply, granting the defendant additional time or a continuance, relieving the defendant from making disclosures otherwise required of him, prohibiting the prosecuting attorney from introducing specified evidence, and dismissing charges. In civil cases, the court may make any order the interests of justice require. Evidence submitted to the court shall be sealed and preserved to be made available to the appellate court in the event of an appeal, and the contents shall not otherwise be revealed without consent of the informed public entity. All counsel and parties are permitted to be present at every stage of proceedings under this subdivision except a showing *in camera* at which no counsel or party shall be permitted to be present.

Deleted Federal Rule 510, which the revised Uniform Rule otherwise follows, contained an additional exception:

> (3) *Legality of Obtaining Evidence.* If information from an informer is relied upon to establish the legality of the means by which evidence was obtained and the judge is not satisfied that the information was received from an informer reasonably believed to be reliable or credible, he may require the identity of the informer to be disclosed. The judge shall, on request of the government, direct that the disclosure be made *in camera*. All counsel and parties concerned with the issue of legality shall be permitted to be present at every stage of proceedings under this subdivision except a disclosure *in camera*, at which no counsel or party shall be permitted to be present. If disclosure of the identity of the informer is made *in camera*, the record thereof shall be sealed and preserved to be made available to the appellate court in the event of an appeal, and the contents shall not otherwise be revealed without consent of the government.

for the information,[4] and runs also, according to some authority, to one charged with being an informer,[5] and when neither the government nor the informer is represented at the trial, in some jurisdictions the judge as in other cases of privilege [6] may invoke it

The Advisory Committee's Note states that the procedure is consistent with McCray v. Illinois, 386 U.S. 300 (1967), rehearing denied 386 U.S. 1042, and cases there discussed.

3. See Hardy's Trial, 24 How.St.Tr. 99 (1794), quoted 8 Wigmore, Evidence (3d ed. 1940) § 2374, p. 751 (Erie, L.C.J.: "I cannot satisfy myself that there is any substantial difference between the case of this man's going to a justice of the peace . . . or to some other person who communicated with a justice. . . . ").

While traditionally thought of in respect to information about crimes, an increasing body of authority recognizes that similar considerations may be present in cases of informing of other kinds of law violation and that the privilege should prevail there also. Mitchell v. Roma, 265 F.2d 633 (3d Cir. 1959) (violations of Fair Labor Standards Act); Brennan v. Engineered Products, Inc., 506 F.2d 299 (8th Cir. 1974) (semble).

The revised Uniform Rule (1974), supra n. 2, is not limited to criminal violations.

4. This is probably the most frequent source of objection, see e.g., Marks v. Beyfus, note 2, above; Wilson v. United States, 59 F.2d 390 (3d Cir. 1932) (on petition to suppress evidence secured on liquor raid; deputy prohibition commissioner refused to answer question as to source of information on raid and was committed for contempt; held, the court should have sustained his claim of privilege); Bocchicchio v. Curtis Publishing Co., 203 F.Supp. 403 (E.D.Pa.1962) (local police officer not represented by counsel successful in claiming the privilege when called as witness in civil libel action).

5. Worthington v. Scribner, note 2, supra; Wells v. Toogood, 165 Mich. 677, 131 N.W. 124 (1911) (action for slander against alleged informer; when officer was asked as to complaint of theft made to him by defendant, defendant's counsel objected).

Compare: "What is usually referred to as the informer's privilege is in reality the Government's privilege to withhold from disclosure the identity of persons who furnish information of violations of law to officers charged with enforcement of that law. [Citations omitted.] The purpose of the privilege is the furtherance and protection of the public interest in effective law enforcement. The privilege recognizes the obligation of citizens to communicate their knowledge of the commission of crimes to law-enforcement officials and, by preserving their anonymity, encourages them to perform that obligation." Burton, J., in Roviaro v. United States, 353 U.S. 53, 59 (1957). The revised Uniform Rule, supra n. 53, allows the privilege to be claimed only by public entities.

6. See § 73 supra.

for the absent holder.[7] It is disputed whether the privilege is confined to disclosure of identity [8] or extends also to the contents of the communication.[9] Seldom will the contents of the statement be competent if the name is undisclosed, but it is believed that the policy of the privilege does not apply to shielding the purport of the communication from disclosure. Of course, if revealing the contents will in the circumstances probably reveal the identity of the informer, the privilege should attach.

The privilege has two important qualifications, one obvious and the other not so obvious but just. The first is that when the identity has already become known to "those who would have cause to resent the communication," the privilege ceases.[10] The second is that when the privilege is asserted by the state in a criminal prosecution, and the evidence of the identity of the informer becomes important to the establishment of the defence, the court will require the disclosure,[11] and if it is still withheld, that the prosecution be dismissed.[12] While the inher-

7. See the statement of Bowen, L.J., in Marks v. Beyfus, described note 2, supra: ". . . the privilege does not depend upon the witness claiming it when asked the question; but the judge should refuse to allow the question as soon as it is asked." (p. 500).

8. This is the view of 8 Wigmore, Evidence § 2374, p. 765 (McNaughton rev. 1961) and the form in which the doctrine is stated in many of the leading opinions, see, e.g., Marks v. Beyfus, Worthington v. Scribner, both cited in note 2, above, and Scher v. United States, 305 U.S. 251, 254 (1938) (". . . public policy forbids disclosure of an informer's identity"). See also Bowman Dairy Co. v. United States, 341 U.S. 214, 221 (1951), where in an antitrust prosecution it was held that the government could be required to produce complaints and statements received from third persons, but that the court must be "solicitous to protect against disclosures of the identity of informants. . . . "

9. Numerous opinions state the doctrine as including the contents of the statement but usually in situations where the wider coverage is not material. See, e.g., Michael v. Matson, 81 Kan. 360, 105 P. 537 (1909) and Wells v. Toogood, note 5, supra.

10. The quoted language is from Roviaro v. United States, 353 U.S. 53, 60 (1957). The limitation is appropriate since many disclosures, e.g. to other law enforcing agencies, obviously should not effect a waiver. Compare United States v. Long, 533 F.2d 505 (9th Cir. 1976), cert. denied 429 U.S. 829 (holding privilege still effective after disclosure of informer's name to defense by government; others in community likely to resent informer's conduct).

In Westinghouse Electric Corp v. City of Burlington, 122 U.S.App.D.C. 65, 351 F.2d 762 (1965) the filing of a civil antitrust action was held to have eliminated any privilege with respect to complaints by plaintiffs to the Attorney General. The complaints were material to a defense of statute of limitations. See also, on remand, City of Burlington v. Westinghouse Electric Co., 246 F.Supp. 839 (D.D.C.1965).

11. In Roviaro v. United States, 353 U.S. 53 (1957), a narcotics conviction was reversed for refusal to require disclosure of an informer's identity. The informer was in fact far more than an informer; he was present at the transportation and participated in the sale, on both of which counts accused was charged. The

Court pointed out that the "informer" might have testified to an entrapment, thrown doubt on the identity of the accused or the package, testified as to accused's lack of knowledge of the contents, or contradicted the government's version of an important conversation. Merely being an informer does not insulate against disclosure when the informer's activities go beyond informing. This sort of going-beyond seems more likely to occur when the offense is of a continuing type, e.g., narcotics sales, rather than a single nonrepetitive crime such as murder.

The much litigated question whether the prosecution must disclose his identity when information from an informer has been relied upon to establish probable cause, and the lawfulness of a search and seizure is in question, was answered in the negative in McCray v. Illinois, 386 U.S. 300 (1967). Neither due process nor right of confrontation was violated, said the Court. Justice Douglas, in dissent, suggested that the result was to entrust the Fourth Amendment exclusively to the police. See LaFave, Probable Cause from Informants: The Effects of Murphy's Law on Fourth Amendment Adjudication, 1977 U.Ill.L.F. 1.

When the informer testifies, should disclosure of his status be required as a possible indication of bias? A negative answer was given in Attorney General v. Briant, 15 M. & W. 159, 153 Eng.Rep. 808 (Exch.1846). The result is difficult to defend. Compare Harris v. United States, 371 F.2d 365 (9th Cir. 1967) (trial judge allowed protracted inquiry).

12. "It is a sound rule to keep secret information furnished to the state of violations of its laws, but this commendable public policy must yield to a higher, or at least an equal, right accorded to an accused to have a court investigate the facts material to his offense in a criminal prosecution, and sometimes the departments of government will be put to a choice of either foregoing a criminal prosecution or disclosing the source of material information necessary to the conduct of orderly judicial procedure." United States v. Keown, 19 F.Supp. 639, 646 (W.D.Ky.1937).

A related duty has been seen to devolve upon the prosecution as a corollary of Roviaro v. United States. Thus, the government must not only reveal the identity of an informer in appropriate cases, but must exercise reasonable diligence toward the end that information

ent fairness of this second exception is apparent, it poses difficulties of implementation if the privilege is not to be rendered meaningless by automatic defense allegations of the informer's potential value as a witness. To avoid this result the expedient widely used, and sometimes seemingly required, is an in camera hearing on the nature of the informer's probable testimony.[13] The trial court may then assess the balance between the value of that testimony to the defense and the significance of the considerations underlying the privilege in the particular case.

In recent years, factors closely analogous to those giving rise to the informer's privilege have led to extensive recognition of a similar privilege protecting the confidentiality of police surveillance locations.[14]

WESTLAW REFERENCES

fed.r.evid! rule* /3 510 509 & privilege* /p disclos! /p informant*
110k627.10(1)
roviaro /15 353 /5 53
110k627.10(1) /p establish! /p defen*e*
roviaro /s hearing
privilege* /p police! /p surveillance /p location*

---

as to the informer's whereabouts can be supplied to the defendant. United States v. Williams, 496 F.2d 378 (1st Cir. 1974). But breach of this latter duty will generally lead to a new trial rather than dismissal of the charges. Velarde-Villarreal v. United States, 354 F.2d 9 (9th Cir. 1965).

13. In camera proceedings for this purpose are commonly referred to in the cases as *Roviaro* hearings. For a helpful discrimination between those cases in which such a hearing is and is not required, see Suarez v. United States, 582 F.2d 1007 (5th Cir. 1978). As to the factors to be considered by the trial court in such a hearing, see United States v. Gonzales, 606 F.2d 70 (5th Cir. 1979).

14. See, e.g., United States v. Green, 670 F.2d 1148 (D.C.Cir.1981).

§ 112

1. 8 Wigmore, Evidence § 2377 (McNaughton rev. 1961); Annot., 165 A.L.R. 1302; Note, The Required Report Privileges, 56 Nw.U.L.Rev. 283 (1961); 81 Am. Jur.2d §§ 287–293; Dec.Dig. Witnesses ⊂⇒216.

2. Peden v. Peden's Administrator, 121 Va. 147, 92 S.E. 984, 2 A.L.R. 1414 (1917) (report of property for taxation); Panik v. Didra, 370 Pa. 488, 88 A.2d 730

§ 112. Statutory Privileges for Certain Reports of Individuals to Government Agencies: Accident Reports, Tax Returns, etc.[1]

A policy faintly similar to that which has prompted the common law privilege for the identity of informers may be thought to have some application to all reports required by law to be made by individuals to government agencies, giving information needed in the administration of their public functions. If the statements may be used against the reporters, they may in some degree be discouraged from making full and true reports. On the other hand, these reports often deal with facts highly material in litigation, and an early report to government may be reliable and pressingly needed for ascertainment of the facts. The latter interest has prevailed with the courts, and in the absence of a statutory provision creating the privilege there is no privilege for these reports.[2] In the legislative halls, however, when bills requiring such reports are proposed, the supposed need for encouraging frank and full reports frequently looms large to the proponents of the measures, and statutory privileges for reports of highway [3] and industrial

---

(1952) (report of accident required by city ordinance not privileged in absence of provision for privilege). Compare, however, Gerry v. Worcester Consolidated Street Railway Co., described in note 4, infra.

3. An extensive opinion discussing some of the problems arising under the statutory privilege for highway accident reports, quoting from the statutes and citing cases from various states, is that of Knutson, J., in Rockwood v. Pierce, 235 Minn. 519, 51 N.W.2d 670 (1952) (oral admissions made by defendant to highway patrolman as basis for latter's official report, which would be privileged under M.S.A. § 169.09, subd. 13, are not privileged). The case is noted in 36 Minn.L.Rev. 540. See also Notes, 44 Iowa L.Rev. 210 (1958), 11 Wyo.L.J. 99 (1957). To the same effect is Grocers Wholesale Co-operative, Inc. v. Nussberger Trucking Co., 192 N.W.2d 753 (Iowa 1971), noted 22 Drake L.Rev. 415 (1972). The statutes and cases are collected in Annot., 165 A.L.R. 1302, 1315, and in 8 Wigmore, Evidence § 2377, note 8 (McNaughton rev. 1961). See also Annot., 12 A.L.R.Fed. 941 (collecting cases involving reports of motor carriers to the I.C.C. privileged under the Interstate Commerce Act, 49 U.S. C.A. § 320(f)).

accidents [4] and returns of property [5] and income [6] for taxation are common. The soundness of a policy extending greater protection to these reports than is required by constitutional guarantees [7] is dubious, and in some instances seems to imply a greater need for accuracy in governmental statistic gathering than in judicial fact-finding. But where the policy is effectively adopted by statute, its unwisdom is submitted not to justify judicial incursions upon the protection ostensibly afforded.[8]

WESTLAW REFERENCES

digest(privilege* /p require* /p report*)

§ 113. The Secrecy of Grand Jury Proceedings: (a) Votes and Expressions of Grand Jurors: (b) Testimony of Witnesses

The taking of evidence by grand jurors and their deliberations have traditionally been shrouded in secrecy.[1] The ancient oath administered to the grand jurors bound them to keep secret "the King's counsel, your fellows' and your own." [2]

---

4. Louisville & Nashville Railroad Co. v. Stephens, 298 Ky. 328, 182 S.W.2d 447 (1944) (action for death: error to admit reports made by railway to Interstate Commerce Commission, which are privileged under provisions of Boiler Inspection Act, 45 U.S.C.A. §§ 33, 41); Gerry v. Worcester Consolidated Street Railway Co., 248 Mass. 559, 143 N.E. 694, 697 (1924) (death injury; report of injury erroneously received as admission in view of St.1913, c. 746, providing that reports to Industrial Accident Board "shall be kept available by the said Board, and shall be furnished in request to the State Board of Labor and Industries for its own use:" "In giving this information to the Industrial Accident Board, the defendant's report was in the nature of a privileged communication; and although not expressly privileged by the words of the statute, it was not intended that these reports should be availed of in an action at law arising out of the subject-matter of the suit.").

5. Brackett v. Commission, 223 Mass. 119, 111 N.E. 1036 (1916) (corporation tax return); Williams v. Brown, 137 Mich. 569, 100 N.W. 786 (1904) (error to permit discrediting plaintiff, who had testified to value of property, by producing his statements while listing property for taxes, in view of statute limiting use of such statements); Re Manufacturers Trust Co., 269 App.Div. 108, 53 N.Y.S.2d 923 (1945) (corporation's franchise tax return; interpreting statute forbidding divulging of tax information).

6. Provisions for secrecy of state income tax returns are construed in Webb v. Standard Oil Co., 49 Cal.2d 509, 513, 319 P.2d 621, 624 (1957) (a major "purpose of . . . statutory provisions prohibiting disclosure is to facilitate tax enforcement by encouraging a taxpayer to make full and truthful declarations in his return, without fear that these statements will be revealed or used against him for other purposes"); New York State Department of Taxation and Finance v. New York State Department of Law, 44 N.Y.2d 575, 406 N.Y.S.2d 747, 378 N.E.2d 110 (1978) (thorough discussion of justifications underlying privilege).

7. Required reports may, of course, raise problems of self-incrimination. See § 142 infra. The privileges discussed in the present section may to some degree represent an effort to meet that problem.

8. Hickok v. Margolis, 221 Minn. 480, 22 N.W.2d 850 (1946).

Deleted Federal Rule 502, 56 F.R.D. 234, provides:

A person, corporation, association, or other organization or entity, either public or private, making a return or report required by law to be made has a privilege to refuse to disclose and to prevent any other person from disclosing the return or report, if the law requiring it to be made so provides. A public officer or agency to whom a return or report is required by law to be made has a privilege to refuse to disclose the return or report if the law requiring it to be made so provides. No privilege exists under this rule in actions involving perjury, false statements, fraud in the return or report, or other failure to comply with the law in question.

The purpose of the rule was to give limited recognition to state statutory privileges in federal courts. The revised Uniform Rules (1974) omit the provision.

For the type of situation resulting from the absence of a rule similar to deleted Fed.R.Evid. 502, see In the Matter of Grand Jury Impaneled January 21, 1975, 541 F.2d 373 (3d Cir. 1976) (federal court not obliged to honor privilege for report created by state court rule).

§ 113

1. Calkins, Grand Jury Secrecy, 63 Mich.L.Rev. 455 (1965); Comment, 38 Fordham L.Rev. 307 (1969); 8 Wigmore, Evidence § 2360 (McNaughton rev. 1961); C.J.S. Grand Juries § 43; 38 Am.Jur.2d Grand Jury §§ 39–41; Dec.Dig. Grand Jury ⊕41; Annot., 127 A.L.R. 272.

2. For a modern counterpart, see Fed.R.Crim.P. 6(e):

(e) Secrecy of Proceedings and Disclosure.—

. . .

(2) General Rule of Secrecy. A grand juror, an interpreter, a stenographer, an operator of a recording device, a typist who transcribes recorded testimony, an attorney for the Government, or any person to whom disclosure is made under paragraph (3)(a)(ii) of this subdivision shall not disclose matters occurring before the grand jury, except as otherwise provided for in these rules. No obligation of secrecy may be

Several objectives are commonly suggested as being promoted by the policy of secrecy: to guard the independence of action and freedom of deliberation of the accusatory body, to protect the reputations of those investigated but not indicted, to prevent the forewarning and flight of those accused before publication of the indictment, and to encourage free disclosure by witnesses.[3] The procedure for attaining them assumes two forms, somewhat loosely described as "privilege." The first is a privilege against disclosure of the grand jurors' communications to each other during their deliberations and of their individual votes.[4] The propriety of such a measure as an assurance of free and independent deliberation can scarcely be doubted, though it may be of slight practical importance in view of the infrequency with which these communications and votes will be relevant to any material inquiry.[5] The second of these privileges involves disclosure of the testimony given by witnesses before the grand jury, and as an area of substantial controversy deserves thoughtful scrutiny.

While the grand jury in its origins may in considerable measure have been an instrument of and subservient to the crown, its position as an important bulwark of the rights of English citizens was established by the end of the 17th century.[6] This latter aspect is evident in the provision of the Fifth Amendment of the Constitution of the United States requiring presentment or indictment as a precondition of prosecution for a capital or infamous crime. During this period the grand jury's independence of incursion by both prosecution and defense appears to have been well recognized, and prosecutors were admitted to its councils only by suffrance.[7] However, the decline in the feeling of need for the grand jury as a protector of individual liberties which caused

---

imposed on any person except in accordance with this rule. A knowing violation of Rule 6 may be punished as a contempt of court.

(3) Exceptions.

(A) Disclosure otherwise prohibited by this rule of matters occurring before the grand jury, other than its deliberations and the vote of any grand juror, may be made to—

(i) an attorney for the government for use in the performance of such attorney's duty; and

(ii) such government personnel as are deemed necessary by an attorney for the government to assist an attorney for the government in the performance of such attorney's duty to enforce federal criminal law.

(B) Any person to whom matters are disclosed under subparagraph (A)(ii) of this paragraph shall not utilize that grand jury material for any purpose other than assisting the attorney for the government in the performance of such attorney's duty to enforce federal criminal law. An attorney for the government shall promptly provide the district court, before which was impaneled the grand jury whose material has been so disclosed, with the names of the persons to whom such disclosure has been made.

(C) Disclosure otherwise prohibited by this rule of matters occurring before the grand jury may also be made—

(i) when so directed by a court preliminarily to or in connection with a judicial proceeding; or

(ii) when permitted by a court at the request of the defendant, upon a showing that grounds may exist for a motion to dismiss the indictment because of matters occurring before the grand jury. . . .

3. The classical justifications for grand jury secrecy are set forth in United States v. Rose, 215 F.2d 617, 628–629 (3d Cir. 1954).

4. Wm. J. Burns Int'l Detective Agency v. Holt, 138 Minn. 165, 164 N.W. 590 (1917) (action to recover for detective services allegedly rendered at request of grand jurors; conversations among members, during deliberations, about employing detectives, excluded); Opinion of the Justices, 96 N.H. 530, 73 A.2d 433 (1950) (power of legislative investigating committee does not extend to inquiring into grand jurors' votes and opinions); Fed.R.Crim.P. 6(e), supra, n. 2; 8 Wigmore, Evidence § 2361 (McNaughton rev. 1961). But the privilege does not extend to deliberations in the course of preparing a report which was outside the lawful functions of the grand jury. Bennett v. Stockwell, 197 Mich. 50, 163 N.W. 482 (1917).

5. 8 Wigmore, Evidence §§ 2361, 2364 (McNaughton rev. 1961). But see Wm. J. Burns Int'l Detective Agency v. Holt, supra n. 4.

6. 1 Holdsworth, A History of English Law 321–323 (7th ed. 1956); Younger, The People's Panel (1963); Goldstein, The State and the Accused: Balance of Advantage in Criminal Procedure, 69 Yale L.J. 1149, 1170 (1960). The key case, Earl of Shaftesbury's Trial, 8 How.St.Tr. 759 (1681), is quoted in 8 Wigmore, Evidence § 2360, p. 729 (McNaughton rev. 1961).

7. Younger, op.cit., supra n. 6, p. 77; People v. Klaw, 53 Misc. 158, 104 N.Y.S. 482 (1907).

its abolition in England [8] seems in this country to have led to a return of the grand jury, in its accusatorial capacity, to the role of subordinate arm of the prosecution, operating to a degree as rubber stamp but on occasion as a powerful instrumentality of discovery. Thus we find statutes and rules providing for the presence of prosecuting attorneys and stenographers except when the grand jury is deliberating or voting.[9] Although prosecutors typically enjoy access to grand jury material,[10] there is in the federal system a strong principle that the grand jury is "fundamentally an arm of the judiciary,"[11] and that as a result the disclosure and use of grand jury records are within judicial rather than prosecutorial control.[12]

Among others having a potential need for access to transcripts of testimony before a grand jury, perhaps the strongest case may be made for the criminal defendant. The right of an accused to a copy of his own recorded grand jury testimony is today recognized by statute or rule in a number of states [13] and in the federal courts.[14] Considerations of basic fairness (and the inapplicability of the justifications for grand jury secrecy in this context) argue strongly for this access. The question of defense access to the testimony of other grand jury witnesses earlier drew what has been characterized as a "curiously ambivalent" [15] response from the Supreme Court. This question has now largely been resolved in the defendant's favor by an amendment to the Jencks Act [16] which confers a right to such material with respect to government witnesses once they have testified on direct. No infringement of the objectives of secrecy mentioned at the beginning of this section can result from this measure of disclosure, and it would seem to constitute the least acceptable minimum for state [17] as well as federal courts.

---

8. Administration of Justice Act of 1933, 23 & 24 Geo. 5, c. 36.

9. E.g., F.R.Crim.P. 6(d): "Attorneys for the government, the witness under examination, interpreters when needed and, for the purpose of taking the evidence, a stenographer or operator of a recording device may be present while the grand jury is in session, but no person other than the jurors may be present while the grand jury is deliberating or voting."

10. See, e.g., Fed.R.Crim.P. 6(e), supra, n. 2.

Illustrative instances of prosecution use of transcript or testimony of grand jurors themselves are: People v. Goldberg, 302 Ill. 559, 135 N.E. 84 (1922) (impeachment of defense witness); United States v. Socony-Vacuum Oil Co., 310 U.S. 150, 233 (1940) (refreshing recollection of government witness); Izer v. State, 77 Md. 110, 26 A. 282 (1893) (proving perjury before grand jury).

11. In re Grand Jury Investigation of Cuisinarts, Inc., 665 F.2d 24, 31 (2d Cir. 1981). See also United States v. Procter & Gamble Co., 356 U.S. 677, 684–685 (1958) ("Grand jury minutes and transcripts are not the property of the Government's attorneys, agents, or investigators . . . Instead, those documents are records of the court").

12. See, e.g., In re Special February 1975 Grand Jury, 662 F.2d 1232 (7th Cir. 1981) (U.S. Attorney's request to supply grand jury material to I.R.S. denied); United States v. Malatesta, 583 F.2d 748 (5th Cir. 1978), on rehearing 590 F.2d 1379, cert. denied 440 U.S. 962, cert. denied 444 U.S. 846 (Fed.R.Crim.P. 6(e) did not permit prosecutor to read grand jury testimony to another grand jury without court order; but violation of rule held not per se to invalidate indictment).

13. See, e.g., Iowa Code Ann. § 813.2, Rule 13; Ky. R.Crim.P. 5.16.

14. Fed.R.Crim.P. 16(a)(1)(A). Rule 6 (e)(1) requires the recording of all grand jury proceedings except when deliberating or voting.

15. Sherry, Grand Jury Minutes: The Unreasonable Rule of Secrecy, 48 Va.L.Rev. 668, 670 (1962). Federal cases are collected in Annot., 3 A.L.R.Fed. 29.

Pittsburgh Plate Glass Co. v. United States, 360 U.S. 395 (1959), rehearing denied 361 U.S. 855 (trial judge did not err in denying production of minutes of grand jury in absence of a showing of "a particularized need" which outweighed the policy of secrecy. The Court held that disclosure on cross-examination that a trial witness had testified on the same general subject matter before the grand jury "—and nothing more—" did not entitle the defense to production of the grand jury minutes as a matter of absolute right). But compare Dennis v. United States, 384 U.S. 855 (1966).

16. 18 U.S.C.A. § 3500; Fed.R.Crim. P. 26.2.

17. A.B.A. Project on Minimum Standards for Criminal Justice, Standards Relating to Discovery and Procedure Before Trial 52, 64–66, and Supp. 2 (1970), sensibly suggests that these items be furnished in advance, in order to expedite the trial. Accord, Harris v. United States, 433 F.2d 1127, 1129 (D.C.Cir.1970) ("We note with particular approval the Government's current practice of making the grand jury testimony of its prospective witnesses available to defence counsel at the commencement of the trial . . . .").

Civil litigants who today seek to penetrate the veil of grand jury secrecy in federal courts continue to face the necessity of demonstrating, as earlier required more generally in United States v. Procter & Gamble Co.,[18] a "particularized need" for the material. This requirement, though frequently condemned by commentators,[19] has recently been reasserted by the Supreme Court.[20] It therefore seems clear that federal grand jury secrecy will continue to enjoy substantial protection for the foreseeable future.

Despite the stringent language of the federal rule imposing secrecy on grand jury proceedings,[21] witnesses are pointedly omitted from the enumeration of persons bound by its provisions,[22] and the rule seems to place no obstacle in the way of the practice of "debriefing" witnesses after they have given testimony.[23] That the judge has authority to administer an oath of secrecy to witnesses seems no longer to remain a possibility.[24]

In striking contrast to the secrecy surrounding federal grand jury proceedings are state statutes requiring that a complete transcript be furnished each defendant shortly after his indictment.[25]

 WESTLAW REFERENCES

193k41 /p vot*** deliberat! communicat!
193k41 /p testi! /p witness**
cr.proc! f.r.cr.p. "criminal procedure" /5 6(d)
headnote(18 +5 3500) & date(after 1984)

---

18. 356 U.S. 677 (1958).

19. See, e.g., Knudsen, Pretrial Disclosure of Grand Jury Testimony, 48 Wash.L.Rev. 423 (1973) (advocating doing away with secrecy except where government shows good cause); Comment, 58 Tex.L.Rev. 623 (1980).

20. Douglas Oil Co. v. Petrol Stops Northwest, 441 U.S. 211 (1979), on remand 605 F.2d 494 (9th Cir.), appeal after remand 647 F.2d 1005 ("It is clear from *Procter & Gamble* and *Dennis* that disclosure is appropriate only in those cases where the need for it outweighs the public interest in secrecy, and that the burden of demonstrating this balance rests upon the private party seeking disclosure. It is equally clear that as the considerations justifying secrecy become less relevant, a party asserting a need for grand jury transcripts will have a lesser burden in showing justification").

21. Fed.R.Crim.P. 6(e), quoted supra n. 2.

22. Original Committee Note to F.R.Crim.P. 6(e) par. 2.

23. 8 Moore's Federal Practice ¶ 6.05 (Cipes ed. 1970); Wright, Federal Practice and Procedure: Criminal § 106 (2d ed.). Local statutes should be checked with respect to state practice.

24. See cases cited in 38 Am.Jur.2d Grand Jury § 40, and C.J.S. Grand Juries § 43(a). Goodman v. United States, 108 F.2d 516, 127 A.L.R. 265 (9th Cir. 1939), in which a witness before a grand jury was held properly required to take an oath of secrecy, was decided prior to the adoption of the Federal Rules of Criminal Procedure. Compare United States v. Radetsky, 535 F.2d 556, 569 (10th Cir. 1976), cert. denied 429 U.S. 820 (judge's admonition of secrecy to witness unauthorized under Fed.R.Crim.P. 6(e), but harmless); In re Grand Jury Investigation (Lance), 610 F.2d 202, 217 (5th Cir. 1980).

25. Ariz.Rev.Stat. § 21–411; West's Ann.Cal.Penal Code § 938.1; Minn.R.Crim.P., Rule 18.05; 22 Okl.St. Ann. § 340.

Title 6
PRIVILEGE: CONSTITUTIONAL
Chapter 13
THE PRIVILEGE AGAINST SELF–INCRIMINATION

Table of Sections

§ 114. The History of the Privilege: (a) Origin of the Common Law Privilege [1]

Because of relatively widespread doubt as to the wisdom of the privilege against self-incrimination,[2] the origin and development of the rule have been of special interest to legal scholars. Unfortunately important aspects of the matter are still clouded with doubt. What is known suggests that the privilege had its roots in opposition to the use of the *ex officio* oath by the English ecclesiastical courts and that its development was intimately intertwined with the political and religious disputes of early England. The most significant ambiguity is whether the privilege as finally applied in the common law courts after 1700 represented a logical extension of principle underlying earlier opposition to the procedures of ecclesiastical courts, or rather, whether it represented condemnation by association of a procedure not inherently inconsistent with prevailing values.

Prior to the early 1200's, trials in the ecclesiastical courts had been by ordeal or compurgation oath, the formal swearing by the party and his oath helpers. Under the influence of Pope Innocent III, however, there was introduced into the ecclesiastical courts the "jusjurandum de veritate dicenda" or inquisitorial oath.[3] Unlike the procedure used in the administration of the compurgation oath, the inquisitorial oath involved active interrogation of the accused by the judge in addition to the accused's uncomfortable consciousness of his oath to reveal the entire truth of the matter under inquiry. There was some formal limitation upon the power of the ecclesiastical courts to use this new device. An accused could not be put to his oath in the absence of some presentation, which could take the form of formal accusation by one who thereby became a party to the resulting proceeding, denunciation to the court by one unwilling to become a party, or the accused's "popular reputation" as guilty of the subject of the inquiry.[4] The extent to which these restrictions were observed in practice is open to doubt. Mary Hume Maguire asserts that "in England *ex officio* procedure as practiced recognized little necessity of presentment by 'common report' or 'violent suspicion.' The judge *ex officio*, i.e., by virtue of his office as judge, summoned the party into court, and instituted action."[5] In practice then, an individual could be called before the court and made to respond to a broad inquiry into his affairs without regard to the nature or strength of the accusations against him.

The precise nature of the early opposition to the practices of the ecclesiastical courts is in dispute. Wigmore argues that the first three centuries of opposition were based solely upon a desire to limit the potentially expansive jurisdiction of the ecclesiastical courts.[6] Maguire, on the other hand, asserts that in addition to the jealousy of jurisdic-

---

§ 114

1. See generally 8 Wigmore, Evidence § 2250 (McNaughton rev. 1961); Levy, Origins of the Fifth Amendment (1968); M. Maguire, Attack of the Common Lawyers on the Oath Ex Officio, in Essays in History and Political Theory in Honor of Charles H. McIlwain (1936); Corwin, The Supreme Court's Construction of the Self-Incrimination Clause, 29 Mich. L.Rev. 1 (1930); Morgan, The Privilege Against Self-Incrimination, 34 Minn.L.Rev. 1 (1949); Pittman, The Colonial and Constitutional History of the Privilege Against Self-Incrimination in America, 21 Va.L.Rev. 763 (1935); Riesenfeld, Law-Making and Legislative Precedent in American Legal History, 33 Minn.L.Rev. 103 (1949).

2. Riesenfeld asserts that the maxim, *No man shall be compelled to accuse himself,* can be traced to a statement of St. Chrysostomous in his commentary to St. Paul's Epistle to the Hebrews. The statement translates as "I don't tell you to display that [your sin] before the public like a decoration, nor to accuse yourself in front of others." The maxim also appeared in early canonist writings and was incorporated into Gratian's Decretum, a restatement of earlier canon law, as "I do not tell you to incriminate yourself publicly or to accuse yourself in front of others." Riesenfeld, supra note 1, at 118. But see Corwin, supra note 1, at 3, who challenges the assertion that the maxim was derived from canon law.

3. 8 Wigmore, Evidence § 2250 (McNaughton rev. 1961) p. 273.

4. Maguire, supra note 1, at 203.

5. Id. at 203.

6. 8 Wigmore, Evidence § 2250 (McNaughton rev. 1961), p. 278.

tion there was "steady and growing opposition to the administration of the oath itself as 'repugnant to the ancient customs of our Realm' and contrary to the spirit of the common law." [7]

In any case, opposition to the oath became much greater when the procedure was adopted by two new courts and used for essentially political purposes.[8] In 1487 the Court of the Star Chamber was authorized to pursue its broad political mandate by means of the oath.[9] The Star Chamber was not even subjected to the requirement of presentation that theoretically provided protection from broad "fishing inquisitions" by the ecclesiastical courts. About one hundred years later the same procedure was authorized for the Court of the High Commission in Causes Ecclesiastical, established to maintain conformity to the recently established church.[10] The freewheeling methods of these politically-minded courts—including the use of torture [11]—undoubtedly stimulated a great deal of additional opposition to the oath procedures.

Required self-incrimination and the use of the oath were not confined to the ecclesiastical courts and the courts of High Commission and Star Chamber. In criminal trials the accused was expected to take an active part in the proceedings, often to his own detriment.[12] He was examined before trial by justices of the peace, and the results of this examination were preserved for use by the judge at trial. Only in limited classes of

cases was the examination under oath. This was not out of tenderness for the accused, but rather because it was believed that administering an oath would unwisely permit the accused to place before the jury an influential denial of guilt made under oath.[13] When formally accused, the defendant was required to plead and submit to trial; failure to do so sometimes resulted in extreme forms of torture. Once trial had begun, the accused was subject to vigorous interrogation.[14] He again was not placed under oath, but this again was because permitting him to take the oath would make available too easy a means of avoiding liability. Responding to Wigmore's suggestion that there was no opposition to inquisitorial procedures in the common law courts,[15] Maguire cites a series of petitions sent to the Crown in the mid 1300's from Commons, urging the king to prohibit in the King's Council the use of the oath procedure found objectionable in the ecclesiastical courts.[16] It is not clear, however, whether the basis for this complaint was the use of the oath procedure itself or the abuse of it by putting individuals to their oaths in the absence of a presentation.

Whatever its nature, opposition to the procedures of the High Commission and the Star Chamber was greatly stimulated by the efforts of John ("Freeborn John") Lilburn,[17] a vocal opponent of the Stuarts (although he later collided with the Parliament's government). Arrested upon a charge before the Star Chamber involving the printing or importing of heretical and seditious books,

7. Maguire, supra note 1, at 205.

8. The power of the ecclesiastical courts to use the *ex officio* oath was severely limited in the early 1600's due in large part to the efforts of Sir Edward Coke who became Chief Justice of the Common Pleas in 1606. As early as 1607 Coke held that the ecclesiastical courts had the power to administer the *ex officio* oath to laymen only in cases relating to wills or marriages (causes testamentary or matrimonial) and to ecclesiastics only in regard to matters not punishable at common law. Corwin, supra note 1, at 6–8; 8 Wigmore, Evidence § 2250 (McNaughton rev. 1961), p. 280.

9. 3 Hen. VII c. 1; 8 Wigmore, Evidence § 2250 (McNaughton rev. 1961), p. 278.

10. 1 Eliz. I, ch. 1; Maguire, supra note 1, at 213–16.

11. Pittman, supra note 1, at 773, citing Jardine, Use of Criminal Torture in Criminal Law of England 13 (1837).

12. Morgan, supra note 1, at 12–23; 8 Wigmore, Evidence § 2250 (McNaughton rev. 1961), p. 285–86.

13. 8 Wigmore, Evidence § 2250 (McNaughton rev. 1961), p. 285.

14. Stephen, I History of the Criminal Law of England 325–26 (1883).

15. 8 Wigmore, Evidence § 2250 (McNaughton rev. 1961), p. 285.

16. Maguire, supra n. 1, at 207–08.

17. 8 Wigmore, Evidence § 2250 (McNaughton rev. 1961), p. 282–83 summarizes the trial, which is reported at 3 How.St.Tr. 1315 (1637).

Lilburn denied these charges under the Attorney-General's interrogation. When asked about other matters, however, he refused to respond. For his failure to take a legal oath, he was whipped and pilloried. Undaunted, Lilburn applied to Parliament. In 1641 Commons voted that the sentence was illegal and voted reparation; in 1645, the House of Lords concurred that the sentence was illegal and must be vacated. Broader legislative relief preceded Lilburn's, when in 1641 the Long Parliament passed a bill to abolish the Courts of High Commission and Star Chamber and to prohibit the administration of an *ex officio* oath requiring an answer to "things penal." [18] It is possible, however, that this did not prevent the ecclesiastical courts from using the oath procedure upon proper presentment or in penal matters lying within the ecclesiastical jurisdiction. [19]

After 1641, the common law courts began to apply to their own procedure some of the restrictions that had been urged for their ecclesiastical counterparts. The reform, however, affected only the trial procedure; the practice of pre-trial examination (and use of the results at trial) remained unmodified until 1848. But there is general agreement that by 1700 extraction of an answer in any procedure in matters of criminality or forfeiture was improper. [20]

It is difficult to draw many helpful conclusions from the historical origin of the privilege. Wigmore accepts Bentham's suggestion that the privilege as ultimately applied in the common law courts was essentially a matter of overkill. [21] After early opposition to the scope of the jurisdiction of the ecclesiastical courts, Bentham asserts, attention was turned to their abuse of the oath whereby an individual was put to his oath without proper presentment. This procedure, pursuant to which an individual was required to

respond accurately and fully to broad questions concerning his activities, was sometimes accompanied by torture and became the vehicle for effectuating the policies of foreign popes, bigoted prelates suppressing religious diversity, and dictatorial kings. Because of strong emotional feeling against the abuse of the procedure, the common law courts unnecessarily and illogically (according to Bentham) accepted the proposition that not only was it improper to compel an individual to respond to interrogation when no charge had been made against him, but also that it was inherently improper to compel him to respond at all. Wigmore and Bentham find no basis for the latter proposition in the history of opposition to the oath procedure. But perhaps this is too narrow a reading of the historical material. Even if the initial objection was only to the impropriety of putting individuals to their oath without presentation, this policy suggests at least limited objection to the use of information extracted from the mouth of the accused as the basis for a criminal prosecution. This early suspicion of compulsory self-incrimination—even if it extended only to situations where compulsion was exerted before an accusation had been made by some other method—is in no way inconsistent with later condemnation of the practice in broader circumstances. In fact both seem to be based upon a feeling that compelling an individual to provide the basis for his own penal liability should be limited because the position in which it places the individual—making a choice between violating a solemn oath and incurring penal liability—weighs against important policies of individual freedom and dignity. At first, there may have been agreement that the need to secure sufficient evidence for conviction from one whom there was significant reason to believe was guilty outweighed the invasion of personal dignity. But the decision of the common law courts

18. 8 Wigmore, Evidence § 2250 (McNaughton rev. 1961), pp. 282–84.

19. Id. at 284.

20. Id. at 290–91.

21. Id., at 292, citing J. Bentham, Rationale of Judicial Evidence, in 7 The Works of Jeremy Bentham 456, 462 (Bowring ed. 1843). This view was also accepted in the first edition of this text. McCormick, Evidence 255 (1954).

in the later 1600's that even this did not outweigh the policy can certainly be viewed as consistent with and a logical extension of the opposition to the procedures of the ecclesiastical courts and the courts of Star Chamber and High Commission.

 WESTLAW REFERENCES

di self-incrimination
wigmore /s evidence /s 2250
"star chamber"
opinion(lilburn & "star chamber")

---

§ 115. The History of the Privilege: (b) Development of the Privilege in America [1]

There is also significant disagreement over the development of the privilege in America. Wigmore asserts that the privilege "remained an unknown doctrine" in the colony of Massachusetts for a generation after 1641.[2] Pittman, however, concludes that significant post-1640 opposition to testimonial compulsion developed in the New England colonies as well as in England and for largely the same reasons.[3] According to him, the New England magistrates, claiming divine authority, were opposed by the Puritans, who sought removal of the right to compel self-incriminating testimony because they saw it as a means of enforcing compliance with an established church.

There is some evidence of the privilege in early colonial America.[4] Pittman concludes that the privilege in regard to an accused was fairly well established in the New England colonies before 1650 and in Virginia soon after.[5] In any case, it was inserted in the constitutions or bills of rights of seven American states before 1789,[6] and has since spread to all state constitutions except those of Iowa and New Jersey. In both of the latter states, however, it was accepted as a matter of nonconstitutional law.[7]

There is also dispute over the source of the provision in the Fifth Amendment to the federal constitution.[8] The first two editions of Wigmore's treatise argued that "the real explanation of the colonial convention's insistence upon it would seem to be found in the agitation then going on in France against the inquisitorial feature of the Ordinance of 1670."[9] Pittman, however, argued that the stream of influence was in fact running towards France from the American colonies at this time and that the colonies' own experience with high-handed prerogative courts provided the incentive for the drive to insert the privilege into the Bill of Rights.[10] Wigmore's treatise now agrees.[11] In addition, Pittman suggests, American statesmen recognized that in the new nation there existed conflicts of interest and authority much the same as underlay the conflict between the Church and the Crown in England. The Fifth Amendment privilege, he concluded, not only was an answer to numerous instances of colonial misrule but was a shield

---

§ 115

1. See generally 8 Wigmore, Evidence § 2250(4) (McNaughton rev. 1961), Levy, Origins of the Fifth Amendment 333–404 (1968).

2. 8 Wigmore, Evidence § 2250 (McNaughton rev. 1961), p. 293.

3. Pittman, The Colonial and Constitutional History of the Privilege Against Self-Incrimination in America, 21 Va.L.Rev. 763, 775 (1935).

4. Id. at 776–79.

5. Id. at 781.

6. Virginia (1776), Pennsylvania (1776), Maryland (1776), North Carolina (1776), Vermont (1777), Massachusetts (1780), and New Hampshire (1784). Pittman, supra n. 3, at 765.

7. See State v. Height, 117 Iowa 650, 91 N.W. 935 (1902) (state constitutional guarantee of due process in-

cludes protection from compelled self-incrimination); State v. White, 27 N.J. 158, 142 A.2d 65 (1958) (no state constitutional prohibition against compelled self-incrimination but statutory provisions are "no less urgent and protective"). See generally, Pittman, supra note 3, at 763 n. 1.

8. See generally Levy, Origins of the Fifth Amendment 405–432 (1968); Mayers, The Federal Witness' Privilege Against Self-Incrimination: Constitutional or Common Law? 4 Am.J. Legal History 107, 108–20 (1960).

9. See 8 Wigmore, Evidence § 2250 (McNaughton rev. 1961), p. 261, n. 1(4).

10. Pittman, supra n. 3, at 765.

11. 8 Wigmore, Evidence § 2250 (McNaughton rev. 1961), p. 294.

against "the evils that lurk[ed] in the shadows of a new and untried sovereignty." [12]

There is some variation in the phraseology of the privilege as embodied in various constitutions.[13] The Fifth Amendment to the United States Constitution provides that "No person shall be . . . compelled in any criminal case to be a witness against himself . . ." and some state constitutional provisions use virtually identical language. Some state provisions prohibit compelling a person to "testify" against himself; it is doubtful that there is any difference of importance between these provisions and those using the language of the Fifth Amendment. But other state constitutions prohibit a person from being compelled to "give evidence" against himself. These may provide the holders of the privilege thereby created with broader protection than is available under other formulations.[14]

 WESTLAW REFERENCES

digest(constitutional /p selfincrimin! /s compulsory compel!)

---

§ 116. The History of the Privilege: (c) Development of the Two Branches of the Privilege—The Privilege of an Accused in a Criminal Proceeding and the Privilege of a Witness

Historically, the privilege developed from objections to the procedure whereby the ecclesiastical courts were able to compel one against whom no charge had been made to respond in incriminating fashion to broad questions posed to him. Nevertheless, when the common law courts began to apply the privilege in their own proceedings, it soon became clear that the privilege could be invoked not only by a defendant in a criminal prosecution but also by a witness whose conviction could not procedurally be a consequence of the proceeding.[1] There is no historical indiction that this was recognized as an important step in the growth of the privilege. Whatever the rationale of the English courts for refusing to restrict the privilege to one himself on trial for a criminal offense, it was not discussed in the written decisions.

The early state constitutional provisions as well as the Fifth Amendment language permit a construction that prohibits only compulsion to cause an individual to give oral testimony in a criminal proceeding in which he is a defendant. Several authorities have argued that this was their original meaning.[2] This position is strengthened by the fact that early American cases upholding a witness's refusal to answer relied not on existing state constitutional provisions but rather on the existence of the common law privilege which clearly encompassed a witness in a criminal or civil proceeding.[3]

In any case, the Fifth Amendment privilege was not formally broadened beyond the apparent initial intent of the state provisions until a century after its adoption. In Counselman v. Hitchcock,[4] decided in 1892, the Supreme Court rejected the government's contention that the constitutional privilege extended a narrower privilege than the common law and that under the Fifth Amendment a witness could invoke the protection

---

12. Pittman, supra n. 3, at 789.

13. See generally, Hansen v. Owens, 619 P.2d 315, 318–319 (Utah 1980) (Stewart, J., dissenting); 21A Am. Jur.2d Criminal Law § 936.

14. Utah Const. Art. I, Sec. 12 ("The accused shall not be compelled to give evidence against himself . . . ."). Ga.Const. Art. 1, § 1, Par. 13 provides that, "No person shall be compelled to give testimony tending in any manner to criminate himself." But Ga. Code § 38–415(a) provides that, "No person . . . shall be compellable to give evidence for or against himself." The effect of this language is discussed in Section 124 infra.

§ 116

1. 8 Wigmore, Evidence § 2250 (McNaughton rev. 1961), p. 290. Levy, Origins of the Fifth Amendment 313 (1968) reported that the privilege had been extended to witnesses in the trial of King Charles in 1649.

2. Corwin, The Supreme Court's Interpretation of the Self-Incrimination Clause, 29 Mich.L.Rev. 1, 2 (1930); Mayers, The Federal Witness' Privilege Against Self-Incrimination: Constitutional or Common-Law, 4 Am.J. Legal History 107 (1960).

3. Mayers, supra n. 2, at 124.

4. 142 U.S. 547 (1892).

only when called upon to testify in a criminal case in which he was the accused. The precise holding was relatively narrow—that one called before a grand jury could invoke the privilege because the grand jury proceeding was a "criminal case" within the meaning of the amendment—but the language portended a broader expansion of the privilege.[5] Thirty years later, in holding the privilege available to a bankrupt sought to be examined concerning his estate, the Court could say with confidence:

> "The Government insists, broadly, that the constitutional privilege against self-incrimination does not apply in any civil proceeding. The contrary must be accepted as settled. The privilege is not ordinarily dependent upon the nature of the proceeding in which the testimony is sought or is to be used. It applies alike to civil and criminal proceedings, wherever the answer might tend to subject to criminal responsibility him who gives it. The privilege protects a mere witness as fully as it does one who is also a party defendant." [6]

It is now generally accepted that the state constitutional provisions as well as that of the Fifth Amendment may be invoked by one whose testimony is sought in a proceeding other than a criminal prosecution in which he is the defendant.[7] In view of the application of the federal privilege to the states,[8] however, it is now the scope of the federal privilege which is of primary importance. It is also clear that the right of one not a defendant in a criminal case to decline to provide information tending to show that he has committed a criminal offense is merely one aspect of the broad privilege against self-incrimination. But there are significantly different problems raised when the privilege is invoked by one not a defendant in a criminal prosecution. There is, therefore, analytical value in considering separately the two aspects or "branches" of the privilege: the privilege of the accused in a criminal proceeding, and the privilege of one not an accused (usually referred to as the privilege of a witness).

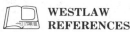 **WESTLAW REFERENCES**

110k417(15)

topic(410) & selfincrimin! /s testimon!

accused defendant* /s selfincrimin! /p testi! & topic(110)

digest("criminal law" /p accused defendant* /p selfincrimin! /p testi!

§ 117. The History of the Privilege: (d) Application of the Fifth Amendment Privilege to the States

In a long series of early decisions the United States Supreme Court made clear that it did not regard the Fifth Amendment's privilege against compulsory self-incrimination as binding on the states by reason of the due process clause of the Fourteenth Amendment.[1] Malloy v. Hogan,[2] decided in 1964, reversed this line of cases, thereby shifting the emphasis of any examination of the privilege from the state rules to the federal constitution.

Mr. Justice Brennan, speaking for the Court, justified the shift with two basic arguments. First, he relied heavily upon the line of Supreme Court decisions holding use of coerced confessions in state criminal prosecutions a denial of due process of law.[3] Despite the Court's initial position that the coerced confession rule did not rest upon the

---

5. "It is impossible that the meaning of the constitutional provision can only be, that a person shall not be compelled to be a witness against himself. It would doubtless cover such cases; but it is not limited to them. The object was to insure that a person should not be compelled, when acting as a witness to any investigation, to give testimony which might tend to show that he himself had committed a crime. The privilege is limited to criminal matters, but it is as broad as the mischief against which it seeks to guard." Id. at 562.

6. McCarthy v. Arndstein, 266 U.S. 34, 40 (1924).

7. 8 Wigmore, Evidence § 2252 (McNaughton rev. 1961), pp. 326–27.

8. See § 117 infra.

§ 117

1. Twining v. New Jersey, 211 U.S. 78, 113 (1908); Cohen v. Hurley, 366 U.S. 117 (1961); Snyder v. Massachusetts, 291 U.S. 97 (1934).

2. 378 U.S. 1 (1964), noted in The Supreme Court, 1963 Term. 78 Harv.L.Rev. 223 (1964).

3. Malloy v. Hogan, 378 U.S. 1, 6–8 (1964).

Fifth Amendment privilege,[4] the line of cases, as the Court read them in *Malloy*, soon abandoned that position and came to accept fully the underlying federal standard governing admissibility which in turn was based upon the Fifth Amendment privilege. Speaking of this shift in the coerced confession cases, Mr. Justice Brennan concluded:

"The shift reflects recognition that the American system of criminal prosecution is accusatorial, not inquisitorial, and that the Fifth Amendment privilege is its essential mainstay. . . . Governments, state and federal, are thus constitutionally compelled to establish guilt by evidence independently and freely secured, and may not by coercion prove a charge against an accused out of his own mouth. Since the Fourteenth Amendment prohibits the states from inducing a person to confess through 'sympathy falsely aroused' . . . or other like inducement far short of 'compulsion by torture' . . . it follows *a fortiori* that it also forbids the States to resort to imprisonment, as here, to compel him to answer questions that might incriminate him. The Fourteenth Amendment secures against state invasion the same privilege that the Fifth Amendment guarantees against federal infringement—the right of a person to remain silent unless he chooses to speak in the unfettered exercise of his own will, and to suffer no penalty . . . for such silence."[5]

The Court also relied upon Mapp v. Ohio,[6] holding that the Fourteenth Amendment required that states in a criminal prosecution exclude evidence obtained by means of a search and seizure unreasonable within the meaning of the Fourth Amendment. The exclusionary rule applied to the states in *Mapp*, Mr. Justice Brennan declared, rested on the Fifth Amendment privilege against self-incrimination as well as the Fourth Amendment right to be free from unreasonable searches and seizures.[7] *Mapp*, then, to a limited extent had already applied the Fifth Amendment privilege to the states.

Not only is the Fifth Amendment privilege binding upon the states under *Malloy*, but the Court also made clear that its application in state courts must be consistent with federal constitutional standards. Rejecting the contention that the availability of the federal privilege to a witness in a state proceeding should be determined according to a less stringent standard than is applicable in a federal proceeding, the Court responded, "It would be incongruous to have different standards determine the validity of a claim of privilege based on the same feared prosecution, depending on whether the claim was asserted in a state or federal court. Therefore, the same standards must determine whether an accused's silence in either a federal or state proceeding is justified."[8]

As a result of *Malloy*, any examination of the current scope of the privilege against compulsory self-incrimination must emphasize the federal decisions in the area. *Malloy* makes clear not only that the states are bound by the privilege as embodied in the Fifth Amendment and federal decisions developing the "federal standard" for its application, but in addition that the federal courts will not be reluctant to examine thoroughly and review the application of the privilege and the federal standards to specific factual situations by the states.

4. Brown v. Mississippi, 297 U.S. 278, 285 (1936). See the discussion of the relationship of the privilege to the rule prohibiting use of coerced confessions in § 144, infra.

5. Malloy v. Hogan, 378 U.S. 1, 7–8 (1964).

6. 367 U.S. 643 (1961).

7. Malloy v. Hogan, 378 U.S. 1, 8–9 (1964). Heavy reliance was placed upon the analysis in Boyd v. United States, 116 U.S. 616 (1886); see § 126 infra.

8. Malloy v. Hogan, 378 U.S. 1, 9–14 (1964). Mr. Justice White, joined by Mr. Justice Stewart, dissented on the ground that even applying the federal standard, Malloy had not properly invoked the privilege. Mr. Justice Harlan, joined by Mr. Justice Clark, agreed with Mr. Justice Stewart: "The Court's reference to a federal standard is, to put it bluntly, simply an excuse for the Court to substitute its own superficial assessment of the facts and state law for the careful and better informed conclusions of the state courts." Id. at 33 (Mr. Justice Harlan, dissenting).

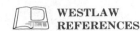

§ 118. The Policy Foundations of the Modern Privilege [1]

It has been argued that whatever its propriety in the days of the Court of the Star Chamber, the privilege against compulsory self-incrimination is no longer a justifiable limitation upon the right of the state to demand cooperation in its investigation.[2] Opponents of the privilege make several points. First, dangers of the nature and scope of those against which the privilege historically protected—physical torture as a means of compelling responses to general inquiries—no longer exist.[3] Second, the privilege deprives the state of access to a valuable source of reliable information, the subject of the investigation himself, and therefore purchases whatever values it attains at too great a cost to the inquiry for truth. The subject is an especially valuable source of information when the alleged crime is one of the sophisticated "white collar" offenses, and in such situations the privilege may deny the prosecution access to the *only* available information.[4] Third, the privilege may as a practical matter be impossible to implement effectively. Although the law may extend the theoretical right to remain silent at

no or minimal cost, in fact it is inevitable that inferences will be drawn from silence and that the inferences will be acted upon. Since these inferences are drawn from inherently ambiguous silence, they are less reliable than inferences from other sources, including compelled self-incriminatory testimony. The result is that one who chooses to invoke the privilege is not protected, but rather is subjected to potential prejudice in a manner ill designed to promote his own best interests.

Proponents of the privilege argue that the historical danger underlying the privilege still exists; the use of physical torture to compel incriminating admissions is not unknown today.[5] But in any case, the increased sensitivity of society might well find incarceration for contempt for refusal to testify as abhorrent as physical torture was regarded in the fifteenth century. Thus the historical basis for the privilege—or its modern equivalent—still provides a justification for its continued existence.

In addition, however, the privilege has come to serve functions other than its historical function of preventing the application of physical force to extract admissions of guilt of otherwise unprovable offenses.[6] These functions may justify its present existence without regard to its effectiveness in fulfilling its traditional role. In several ways, for example, the privilege serves the function of protecting the innocent from unjustified con-

§ 118

1. See generally 8 Wigmore, Evidence § 2251 (McNaughton rev. 1961); Greenawalt, Silence as a Moral and Constitutional Right, 23 William & Mary L.Rev. 15 (1981); O'Brien, The Fifth Amendment: Fox Hunters, Old Women, Hermits, and the Burger Court, 54 Notre Dame Law. 26, 35–54 (1978); Clapp, Privilege Against Self-Incrimination, 10 Rutgers L.Rev. 541 (1956).

2. Carman, A Plea for Withdrawal of Constitutional Privilege from the Criminal, 22 Minn.L.Rev. 200 (1937); Pound, Legal Interrogation of Persons Accused or Suspected of Crime, 24 J.Crim.L., C. & P.S. 1014 (1934); Terry, Constitutional Provisions Against Forcing Self-Incrimination, 15 Yale L.J. 127 (1905); Wigmore, Nemo Tenetur Seipsum Prodere, 5 Harv.L.Rev. 71, 85–87 (1891).

3. Critics have been especially eager to point out that there is little danger of physical abuse in the course of the formal trial, during which the privilege clearly applies, and that the privilege traditionally extended little aid to those in police custody, where the danger of physical abuse is much greater. E.g., American Law Institute, Model Code of Evidence, Comment on Rule 201(1) (1942). This argument is of somewhat less weight now that the privilege is applicable to police interrogation. See § 125 infra.

4. See Terry, supra note 2.

5. E.g., Beecher v. Alabama, 389 U.S. 35 (1967) (defendant threatened by police with firearms in effort to secure confession).

6. See Murphy v. Waterfront Commission, 378 U.S. 52, 55 (1964).

viction.[7] One who is under the strain of actual or potential accusation, although innocent, may be unduly prejudiced by his own testimony for reasons unrelated to its accuracy. For example, he may have physical traits or mannerisms that would cause an adverse reaction from the trier of fact. Or, he might, under the strain of interrogation, become confused and thereby give an erroneous impression of guilt. Thus the privilege affords such an individual the opportunity to avoid discussing an incriminating situation and the danger of creating an unreliable but prejudicial impression of guilt.[8] In addition, the privilege is one part—but an important part—of our accusatorial system which requires that no criminal punishment be imposed unless guilt is established by a large quantum of especially reliable evidence. By denying the prosecution access to what is regarded as an inherently suspect type of proof—the self-incriminating admissions of the accused—the privilege forces the prosecution to establish its case on the basis of more reliable evidence,[9] thus creating an additional assurance that every person convicted is in fact guilty as charged.

The privilege also, and perhaps most importantly, serves the function of assuring that even guilty individuals are treated in a manner consistent with basic respect for human dignity. Wholly apart from its function in assuring the accuracy of the guilt-determining process, the privilege demands that even those guilty of an offense not be compelled beyond a certain extent to participate in the establishment of their own guilt.[10] This is based upon the feeling that to require participation would be simply too great a violation of the dignity of the individual, whether or not he is guilty of a criminal offense. In part, this seems to be based upon the conclusion that compulsory incrimination faces a guilty person with a dilemma too cruel to be justifiable. To place an individual in a position in which his natural instincts and personal interests dictate that he should lie and then to punish him for lying, or for refusing to lie or violate his natural instincts, is an intolerable invasion of his personal dignity. In many cases, Judge Frank has argued, "the state would be forcing him to commit a crime and then punishing him for it." [11]

Apart from its value to individuals, whether innocent or guilty, the privilege also serves broader functions. It encourages respect for and protects the dignity of the judicial system. By removing a significant incentive for perjury, encouraging witnesses to come forward by removing the danger that they will be compelled to incriminate themselves, and forcing prosecutors to rely upon evidence more reliable than incriminating admissions of the accused, the privilege enhances the judicial process's access to reli-

7. Griswold, The Fifth Amendment Today 20–21 (1955). Dean Griswold later, however, suggested that it had been a mistake to defend the privilege on the ground that it is "basically designed to protect those innocent of crime, at least in any numerical sense." Griswold, The Right to be Let Alone, 55 Nw.U.L.Rev. 216, 223 (1960).

8. See Wilson v. United States, 149 U.S. 60, 66 (1893).

9. The classic statement of this position was reported by Sir James FitzJames Stephen and attributed by him to an experienced Indian civil officer. Explaining why prisoners were sometimes tortured, the officer stated:

"There is a great deal of laziness in it. It is far pleasanter to sit comfortably in the shade rubbing red pepper into a poor devil's eyes than to go about in the hot sun hunting up evidence." Stephen, A History of the Criminal Law of England 442 n. 1 (1883).

10. "[W]e do not make even the most hardened criminal sign his own death warrant, or dig his grave, or pull the lever that springs the trap on which he stands. We have through the course of history developed a considerable feeling of the dignity and intrinsic importance of the individual man. Even the evil man is a human being." Griswold, The Fifth Amendment Today 7 (1955).

11. United States v. Grunewald, 233 F.2d 556, 591 (2d Cir. 1956) (Frank J. dissenting), reversed 353 U.S. 391 (1957). Gerstein, The Demise of Boyd: Self-Incrimination and Private Papers in the Burger Court, 27 UCLA L.Rev. 343, 347 (1979) argues a variation on this theme. Each person should be free to come to terms in his own conscience with accusations of guilt of wrongdoing. Compelled self-incrimination interferes with this by requiring a public display of self-accusation and thus self-condemnation, which in turn impinges upon the individual's ability to decide freely how to come to terms with the accusation.

able information on which to make its decisions.[12] By tending to equalize the position of the lone suspect who is confronted with the huge investigatory and prosecutorial apparatus of the state, the privilege helps to make the criminal trial more nearly a contest between equals, thereby maximizing the opportunity for full development of the facts and an accurate resolution of the cases within the framework of the adversary system. By preventing the prosecution from degenerating into scenes which much of the population would find offensive, the privilege maintains public respect for the entire judicial process.[13]

Finally, the privilege deprives the state of a weapon which is particularly subject to abuse in especially sensitive areas.[14] Compelled self-incrimination, as history demonstrates, can serve as a valuable tool for suppressing dissent, opposition to the existing political authorities, and freedom of thought and opinion. In view of the difficulty—and perhaps impossibility—of making the right to compel incriminating answers available only in those situations in which no danger is posed to these areas of broad social concern, denying this right to the state in all situations is justified.

The privilege obviously reflects a large number of values, and consequently it is reasonable that its effect differs with the extent to which various values are affected by specific situations. This is most apparent in the difference between the privilege of an accused and that of one not an accused. Although many of the values served by the privilege are furthered by extending it to one who is not, when called upon to testify, himself on trial, the fact that the state's objective is not to secure this individual's conviction somewhat reduces the incentive for abuse of the interrogative process as applied to him. It is therefore appropriate to limit somewhat the impact of the privilege in this situation. This is accomplished by requiring one not an accused to submit to interrogation and to assert the privilege only in response to specific questions. The development of the privilege in other aspects is showing the same flexibility. For example, the privilege has been extended to one under police interrogation despite ambiguity as to the extent to which police agencies may require or encourage an incriminating response. Moreover, the subject of interrogation is protected by other factors, such as the right to counsel and the rule requiring the exclusion of nonvoluntary statements he may make. In this context the privilege apparently does not always shield the accused from all interrogation, although it requires that any questioning be conducted under circumstances designed to assure an effective right to assert the privilege in response to specific questions should the subject choose to do so.

The continued vitality and general acceptance of the privilege depend upon the maintenance of sufficient flexibility to adjust the privilege to different times and different contexts. The privilege as it exists today is a far different rule from that imposed upon the ecclesiastical courts in the seventeenth century, and it serves significantly different functions. Even today, the privilege of a member of a partnership engaging in a regulated business activity is far different from the privilege of a defendant on trial for robbery, and far different policy factors are involved in the two situations. If the privilege is to remain viable it must retain such flexibility, and it must reflect an appropriate balance among the wide variety of policy factors as they are affected by the specific context in which it is invoked.

12. Meltzer, Required Records, the McCarran Act, and the Privilege Against Self-Incrimination, 18 U.Chi. L.Rev. 687, 701 (1951) suggests that reliable self-incriminating testimony cannot be compelled, so that "unwillingness to command the impossible" is the most intelligible basis for the privilege in most situations.

13. Stephen, 1 A History of the Criminal Law of England 441 (1883).

14. Griswold, The Right to be Let Alone, 55 Nw. U.L.Rev. 216, 223 (1960).

**WESTLAW
REFERENCES**

selfincrimin! /s contempt /s privilege

murphy /15 378 /5 52

synopsis,judge(frank) & selfincrimin! /s compel!
compulsory

synopsis,digest(selfincrimin! /p police sheriff* constable*
officer* /p interrog!)

---

§ 119. The Procedural Manner of Effectuating the Privilege

The privilege against self-incrimination may be asserted in a variety of ways. The first, of course, is a blanket refusal to submit to interrogation which might lead to incrimination, as in the case of an accused in a criminal proceeding who is entitled to decline to take the witness stand at all. Second, an individual who is faced with a specific inquiry may decline to respond. Thus a witness who has taken the stand may decline to respond to specific questions on the basis that to do so would constitute self-incrimination. Third, one who has been subjected to what he views as a violation of his privilege may question the propriety of official use of the result of that activity. Thus a criminal defendant, to put the most obvious case, may object to the introduction in evidence against him of his testimony in a prior proceeding given in response to judicial compulsion. Finally, the privilege may be asserted as a substantive defense to a criminal charge on the basis that compliance with the requirements of the law would have consti-

tuted self-incrimination. Thus the privilege may be raised as a defense in a prosecution for failure to obtain a gambling stamp on the grounds that compliance with the stamp requirement would have required that the defendant incriminate himself.

These various aspects are discussed in the sections which follow.

§ 120. The Personal Nature of the Privilege [1]

The case law makes frequent reference to the personal nature of the privilege, but these often offhand comments are somewhat misleading. It is clear that a criminal defendant cannot invoke the privilege of witnesses,[2] codefendants, or even co-conspirators.[3] Nor can he successfully complain that their privilege was violated. It is also clear that an attorney cannot invoke the privilege of his client for his own protection.[4] For example, an attorney called as a witness before a grand jury cannot refuse to respond to a question on the ground that the answer would incriminate his client.[5] He can, however, as agent for his client invoke the privilege of his client for the protection of the client.[6] Thus an attorney who appears before a court as counsel for his client may at that time object to a proposed order on the basis that it would compel his client to incriminate himself (or, alternatively, he may waive his client's privilege).[7]

---

§ 120

1. See generally 8 Wigmore, Evidence § 2270(1) (McNaughton rev. 1961); 81 Am.Jur.2d Witnesses § 33; C.J.S. Witnesses § 451 (1957); Dec.Dig. Witnesses ⟦306. See also Annot., 37 A.L.R.3d 1373.

2. State v. Dickens, 66 Wn.2d 58, 401 P.2d 321 (1965).

3. Poole v. United States, 329 F.2d 720 (9th Cir. 1964).

4. United States v. Goldfarb, 328 F.2d 280 (6th Cir. 1964).

5. Id. at 282.

6. Farmer v. State, 5 Md.App. 546, 248 A.2d 809 (1968); People v. Myers, 35 Ill.2d 311, 220 N.E.2d 297 (1966) (attorney in possession of client's letters could

invoke client's privilege in response to subpoena duces tecum). Contra, Sears, Roebuck & Co. v. American Plumbing & Supply Co. 19 F.R.D. 334, 341 (E.D.Wis. 1956) (dictum); State v. Manning, 134 N.W.2d 91 (N.D.1965) (trial court properly overruled objection by defendant's counsel that question asked of defendant during cross-examination might tend to convict of a collateral crime; waiver also used as alternative basis of holding). Defendant's counsel, of course, cannot invoke the privilege for a witness. State v. Evans, 249 La. 861, 192 So.2d 103 (1966). See the discussions in Brody v. United States, 243 F.2d 378, 387 n. 5 (1st Cir. 1957); United States v. Judson, 322 F.2d 460, 463–68 (9th Cir. 1963).

7. Brody v. United States, 243 F.2d 378, 387 (1st Cir. 1957).

§ 121. General Scope of the Privilege: (a) What Is Protected Against [1]

The danger against which the privilege expressly protects its holders is that of incrimination. Despite vigorous objection, it has uniformly been held that the privilege does not protect against the disgrace and practical excommunication from society resulting from disclosure of matters which, under the circumstances, could not give rise to criminal liability.[2] It is only the danger of formal imposition of *legal criminal liability* against which the privilege protects. It is not clear, however, which incidents of a criminal proceeding constitute "incrimination" within the meaning of the privilege. No serious question exists as to one who has not yet been tried; the danger of trial, conviction, and imprisonment is clearly within the scope of the privilege. Nor is there any doubt that when the danger of such proceedings has been removed by passage of the period of limitations,[3] pardon,[4] prior conviction or acquittal,[5] or a grant of immunity[6] no danger within the scope of the privilege exists.

An accused person who has been convicted in the technical sense may, of course, harbor hopes of that conviction being invalidated and may also fear that compelled disclosures might consequently incriminate him in a reprosecution following invalidation of his present conviction. Where appeal as of right is pending or is still available, the courts have lent a sympathetic ear to this argument. In such situations, the mere fact of conviction does not remove the danger of incrimination.[7] Where only discretionary appellate review and collateral attack are available, however, the matter is more problematic. Since the time during which discretionary review is available will ordinarily be quite short, little would be lost by permitting a convicted defendant who has such review available to retain the privilege.[8] But different considerations might well govern the effect of possible collateral attack, since this is ordinarily available without regard to limited time periods. The best solution would seem

---

§ 121

1. See generally 8 Wigmore, Evidence §§ 2254, 2255, 2256, 2257 (McNaughton rev. 1961); 81 Am.Jur. 2d Witnesses §§ 38, 41; C.J.S. Witnesses §§ 437, 438, 439, 444, 445, 446.

2. See the dissent of Justice Douglas in Ullmann v. United States, 350 U.S. 422, 440 (1956), arguing on historical grounds that the privilege was intended to protect against infamy which "was historically considered to be punishment as effective as fine and imprisonment." Id. at 451. Reasoning that the essence of infamy was the impact of public opinion, he concludes that the privilege should protect against the impact of public opinion even in the absence of any governmental action. Id. at 451–454. See also Brown v. Walker, 161 U.S. 591, 628 (1896) (Field, J., dissenting).

3. Markey v. Lee, 224 So.2d 789 (Fla.App.1969). But see Commonwealth v. Lenart, 430 Pa. 144, 242 A.2d 259 (1968) (running of the period of limitations would not justify contempt citation for refusal to testify because it constituted only a bar to conviction rather than prosecution and the interrogation might reveal crimes not barred by statute of limitation).

4. Moore v. Backus, 78 F.2d 571 (7th Cir. 1935), cert. denied 296 U.S. 640.

5. Ex parte Critchlow, 11 Cal.2d 751, 81 P.2d 966 (1938); People ex rel. Gross v. Sheriff, 277 App.Div. 546, 101 N.Y.S.2d 271 (1950), affirmed 302 N.Y. 173, 96 N.E.2d 763.

6. See § 143 infra.

7. See, e.g., State v. Gretzler, 126 Ariz. 60, 88, 612 P.2d 1023, 1051 (1980), appeal after remand 128 Ariz. 583, 627 P.2d 1081; State v. Johnson, 77 Idaho 1, 287 P.2d 425 (1955), cert. denied 350 U.S. 1007; State v. Darby, 403 So.2d 44, 48 (La.1981), cert. denied 454 U.S. 1152; State v. Sutterfield, 45 Or.App. 145, 607 P.2d 789 (1980); People v. Giacalone, 399 Mich. 642, 250 N.W.2d 492 (1977). United States v. Gernie, 252 F.2d 664 (2d Cir. 1958), cert. denied 356 U.S. 968, rehearing denied 357 U.S. 944, often cited for the proposition that conviction renders the privilege inapplicable, did not consider the effect of the availability of appeal. See also, State v. Grimmer, __ W.Va. __, 251 S.E.2d 780 (1979) (witness who had pleaded guilty but also announced intent to appeal properly permitted to invoke privilege even though appeal was not "pending"). But after sentencing has been completed and the time for appeal has expired (or appeal has been unsuccessfully taken), a convicted defendant may be compelled to testify unless the possibility of collateral attack dictates otherwise. See State v. Verdugo, 124 Ariz. 91, 93, 602 P.2d 472, 474 (1979).

8. Compare In re Bando, 20 F.R.D. 610 (D.N.Y. 1957), reversed on other grounds sub nom. United States v. Miranti, 253 F.2d 135 (2d Cir. 1958) (pendency of application for certiorari to Supreme Court of United States to review conviction did not provide a basis for invoking the privilege).

to be to treat the possibility of successful collateral attack and retrial as raising the question of whether the facts raise a "real and appreciable" danger of incrimination.[9] In the absence of some specific showing that collateral attack is likely to be successful, the availability of such attack is unlikely to mean that despite the conviction the accused is still subject to a "real and appreciable" danger of incrimination.

A very different issue is presented when an accused person claims the privilege not in regard to conviction but in order to avoid testimonial disclosures that might subject him to a more severe penalty. In such situations, the question becomes whether an increase in the severity of the penalty is, or should be, "incrimination" within the meaning of the privilege. In Estelle v. Smith,[10] the Supreme Court held that the Fifth Amendment privilege protected a convicted accused person from the additional danger of being sentenced to death rather than life imprisonment. It is difficult to discern an acceptable basis for regarding the life-death sentencing decision as involving incrimination for purpose of the privilege but other sentencing decisions as not invoking the right to be free from compelled self-incrimination. *Smith*, then, probably establishes that the privilege protects an accused person against compelled testimonial activity that would tend to increase the penalty to which

he would be subject upon conviction.[11] This is consistent with the general approach of the lower courts to the original sentencing matter.[12] In interesting contrast, several cases have held that the privilege does not protect a convicted person against revocation of probation and imposition of a prison sentence.[13] This is a difficult distinction to defend, but perhaps an acceptable rationale is that a defendant may, as condition of receiving probation, be required to waive or surrender the privilege concerning his compliance with the conditions of that probation.[14]

A related but distinguishable question is the extent to which the privilege extends protection against compelled testimonial participation in collateral aspects of prosecution that are not literally incriminating but may affect the litigation process. Under due process standards, for example, an accused person who is incompetent to stand trial cannot be tried [15] and obviously cannot be convicted. But in Estelle v. Smith,[16] the Court in dictum suggested that the Fifth Amendment privilege did not protect accused persons against being compelled to provide testimonial information that would tend to result in their being found competent. It is unclear whether this signals a general rule that the privilege will not be construed as protecting against procedural "disadvantages" during criminal litigation that are not directly related to the

---

9. See § 123 infra. Several courts have taken this approach. See State v. Verdugo, 124 Ariz. 91, 602 P.2d 472 (1979); Commonwealth v. Rodgers, 472 Pa. 435, 372 A.2d 771 (1977). In *Verdugo*, the court found insufficient danger of incrimination where the conviction had been affirmed on direct appeal four years earlier, no post-conviction attack had been filed, and the defense testimony was that the estimated likelihood of success on collateral attack was between 15 and 30%.

10. 451 U.S. 454 (1981).

11. Some of the language used by the Court was quite narrow, as when it spoke of "execution." Id., at 462. But other language is broader. Thus the Court described the basic constitutional principle at issue as the requirement that the State produce evidence by its own labors when it "proposes to convict *and punish* an individual . . . " Id. (emphasis by the Court).

12. Meehan v. State, 397 So.2d 1214 (Fla.App.1981) (defendant could not be called as witness by state to

admit prior convictions alleged to bring habitual criminal sentencing provisions into operation); Smith v. State, 283 Md. 187, 388 A.2d 539 (1978), cert. denied 439 U.S. 1130.

13. Wilson v. State, 621 P.2d 1173 (Okl.Cr.App. 1980); State v. Heath, 343 So.2d 13 (Fla.1977), cert. denied 434 U.S. 893.

14. See State v. Heath, 343 So.2d 13 (Fla.1977), cert. denied 434 U.S. 893.

15. See generally Pate v. Robinson, 383 U.S. 375 (1966).

16. 451 U.S. 454 (1981). In *Smith*, a psychiatrist had examined the accused without warning him of his right to remain silent. Had the testimony arising from this examination been used only to assure that Smith was competent to stand trial, the Court commented, "no Fifth Amendment issue would have arisen." Id., at 465.

finding of guilt or, perhaps, the harshness of the penalty to be imposed. It may be that the privilege will not protect an accused person against being compelled to disclose information that may tend to result in pretrial release being denied [17] or challenged evidence being held admissible. Perhaps *Smith* can best be regarded as resting upon the unique nature of the competency inquiry, which arguably can often be resolved adequately only if the accused is compelled to submit to a psychiatric examination. In other situations, an accused person should be protected against being compelled to disclose information that would put him at a procedural disadvantage in the prosecution, at least in the absence of countervailing considerations as compelling as those in the competency area. This would be most consistent with the values underlying the privilege.

The privilege by its terms protects against only those disclosures or the use of disclosures which lead to, or perhaps are related to, litigation that can result in "incrimination" or criminal conviction. But the courts have been unwilling to limit application of the privilege to those forms of legal liability that are labeled criminal. What forms of noncriminal legal liability invoke the privilege, however, remains a difficult question. In Boyd v. United States,[18] the Supreme Court held that "proceedings instituted for the purpose of declaring the forfeiture of a man's property by reason of offenses committed by him, though they may be civil in form, are in their nature criminal." Thus the privilege protects against forfeiture, at least where such action is based on conduct that could also serve as the basis for a criminal prosecution. In In re Gault [19] the Court held that the privilege protected against being found a delinquent child. This determination apparently rested largely upon the fact that a determination of delinquency could lead to a loss of liberty which the Court was unable or unwilling to distinguish from the imprisonment that sometimes follows criminal conviction. But in Baxter v. Palmigiano,[20] the Court almost offhandedly held that disciplinary penalties imposed upon a convicted prison inmate were not "incrimination" and did not themselves invoke the privilege.

The lower courts have tended to find that the privilege does protect against being found in contempt of court, at least where the contempt is criminal rather than civil,[21] but does not protect members of the bar against imposition of disciplinary sanctions.[22] Despite the emphasis in *Gault* upon the effect of loss of liberty, the lower courts have split on whether the privilege protects against compulsory hospitalization or treatment for mental abnormality.[23] There are, of course, numerous other types of liability

---

17. See Ex parte Davis, 542 S.W.2d 192, 198 (Tex. Cr.App.1976), holding that the trial judge did not infringe the privilege in requiring a capital murder defendant to submit to a psychological analysis for purposes of determining whether to admit him to bail. The resulting information, concluded the court, was not used to "incriminate" the defendant even though it apparently was considered in denying pretrial release.

18. 116 U.S. 616 (1886).

19. 387 U.S. 1 (1967). See Annot., 43 A.L.R.3d 1128, 1133.

20. 425 U.S. 308, 316 (1978).

21. In re Marriage of Walden, 93 Ill.App.3d 699, 49 Ill.Dec. 25, 417 N.E.2d 715 (1981) (violation of privilege to call as a witness the respondent in criminal contempt proceedings for violation of order entered in dissolution of marriage proceedings); Katz v. Commonwealth, 379 Mass. 305, 399 N.E.2d 1055 (1979); Town of Nottingham v. Cedar Waters, Inc., 118 N.H. 282, 385 A.2d 851

(1978); Ex parte Roper, 592 S.W.2d 433 (Tex.Civ. App.—Fort Worth 1979).

22. E.g., In re March, 71 Ill.2d 382, 17 Ill.Dec. 214, 376 N.E.2d 213 (1978); Mississippi State Bar v. Attorney-Respondent, 367 So.2d 179 (Miss.1979). Both cases discussed the need to distinguish from the issue presented for decision in Spevack v. Klein, 385 U.S. 511 (1967), and the propriety of imposing a burden upon a proper invocation of the privilege.

23. The majority of decisions hold the privilege inapplicable. E.g., Cramer v. Tyars, 23 Cal.3d 131, 151 Cal.Rptr. 653, 588 P.2d 793 (1979); People ex rel. Keith v. Keith, 38 Ill.2d 405, 231 N.E.2d 387 (1967); State ex rel. Kiritsis v. Marion Probate Court, 269 Ind. 550, 381 N.E.2d 1245 (1978); In re Field, 120 N.H. 206, 412 A.2d 1032 (1980). Contra, Lessard v. Schmidt, 349 F.Supp. 1078 (E.D.Wis.1972), vacated and remanded 414 U.S. 473, on remand 379 F.Supp. 1376 (E.D.Wis.), vacated and remanded 421 U.S. 957, on remand 413 F.Supp. 1318 (E.D.Wis.). Perhaps the matter is resolved. The

that might arguably be regarded as involving "incrimination." Several courts [24] have used a multi-criteria approach to determining whether such liability invokes the privilege. Under this approach, liability is more likely to be regarded as "incriminating" and as invoking the privilege if:

(1) it is based on conduct that is traditionally or by its nature criminal;

(2) the penalty is one traditionally criminal in nature (such as a "fine") or severe;

(3) there are collateral consequences to being found liable and these appear punitive rather than "regulatory;"

(4) the motive in imposing liability or the effect of being found liable are punitive, condemnatory, or stigmatizing; and

(5) pretrial procedures familiar to criminal litigation (such as arrest and detention) are utilized in the process of imposing liability.

Applying this approach, the Wyoming Supreme Court held that a "penalty" of up to $10,000 per day for violation of provisions of the state's Environmental Quality Act governing public water supplies, recoverable in an action by private persons and labeled "civil," was not criminal in nature and the defendants in such actions could be compelled to testify as witnesses.[25] While this approach seems largely satisfactory, it

might well be desirable to add consideration of whether the extension of the privilege to the type of liability at issue would have the practical effect of frustrating an important public interest best effectuated through the liability. In holding that the privilege did not protect against loss of parental rights, for example, the New Hampshire Supreme Court [26] relied heavily upon its conclusion that applying the privilege and permitting parents to prevent psychiatric examinations would frustrate the procedure for protecting young children from dangerously abnormal parents.

Three matters must be distinguished from the issue as to the dangers against which the privilege protects. First is the ancient privilege against compelled answers to matters not material to the issues which would disgrace or degrade (although not incriminate) the witness.[27] This privilege has been abandoned in England [28] and in most American states, except in a few where it is embodied in statute.[29] The policy underlying this privilege is probably better served by the rules relating to the permissible scope of cross-examination as to collateral misconduct of a witness and extrinsic proof of such misconduct.[30]

privilege was held inapplicable in French v. Blackburn, 428 F.Supp. 1351 (M.D.N.C.1977). The judgment of the District Court was summarily affirmed on appeal as of right. 443 U.S. 901 (1979). See generally Wesson, The Privilege Against Self-Incrimination in Civil Commitment Proceedings, 1980 Wis.L.Rev. 697.

24. Brown v. Multnomah County District Court, 280 Or. 95, 570 P.2d 52 (1977); Nickelson v. People, 607 P.2d 904 (Wyo.1980).

25. Nickelson v. People, 607 P.2d 904, 909–910 (Wyo.1980). See also, Amato v. Porter, 157 F.2d 719 (10th Cir. 1946), cert. denied 329 U.S. 812 (privilege does not protect against triple damage recovery for violation of price fixing statute); Childs v. McCord, 420 F.Supp. 428, 432 (D.Md.1976), affirmed 556 F.2d 1178 (4th Cir.) (no protection against revocation of license to operate as professional engineer); In re Colacasides, 6 Mich.App. 298, 148 N.W.2d 898 (1967), affirmed 379 Mich. 69, 150 N.W.2d 1 (no protection against revocation of license to run restaurant and dispense alcoholic beverages).

26. In re Fay G., 120 N.H. 153, 156, 412 A.2d 1012, 1015 (1980).

27. 3A Wigmore, Evidence § 984 (Chadbourn rev. 1970); C.J.S. Witnesses § 445; Dec.Dig. Witnesses ⟜296.

28. 3A Wigmore, Evidence § 984 (Chadbourn rev. 1970).

29. E.g., Utah Code Ann. 1953, 78–24–9:

"A witness . . . need not . . . give an answer which will have a direct tendency to degrade his character, unless it is to the very fact in issue or to a fact from which the fact in issue would be presumed. But a witness must answer as to the fact of his previous conviction of felony."

See In re Peterson, 15 Utah 2d 27, 386 P.2d 726 (1963) (witness need not answer whether he and defendant in homicide prosecution had homosexual relations; although the answer might tend to establish a motive, such motive would not be a "fact in issue" or "a fact from which the fact in issue would be presumed").

30. See § 42 supra.

The second matter is the extent to which substantive disadvantages may be imposed upon an individual because of his invocation of the privilege.[31] In a series of decisions, the United States Supreme Court has held that a teacher may not be discharged solely because he invoked the privilege before a congressional committee,[32] that an attorney could not be disbarred because he refused, in reliance on the privilege, to produce documents during a judicial investigation into his alleged professional misconduct,[33] that a police officer could not be dismissed for refusing to sign a general waiver of immunity during an investigation regarding the "fixing" of traffic tickets,[34] that a person who refuses to waive his privilege when called before a grand jury investigating public contracts cannot be barred from state public contracting for five years,[35] and that an officer of a political party cannot be barred from party or public office for five years because he refuses to testify or waive immunity when called before a grand jury to testify concerning the conduct of his office.[36] In each case the question was not whether the individual would be subjected to incrimination in violation of the privilege, but rather whether, as a consequence of his invoking the privilege, the state could act against him in other ways. The opinions' discussion makes clear that the Court distinguishes between potential incrimination as that term was defined above and collateral results of invoking the privilege. If the individual might be subjected to incrimination, there is no room for flexibility; the privilege requires that he be extended the right to remain silent or, if compelled to speak, to complete immunity from the incrimination. On the other hand, if as a result of availing himself of this right certain nonincriminating consequences might result, the danger posed

to the privilege by these consequences must be balanced against the governmental interest in both compelling the testimony and imposing the consequences. Thus the police officer could have been discharged if "he had refused to answer questions specifically, directly and narrowly related to the performance of his official duties, without being required to waive his immunity with respect to the use of his answers or the fruits thereof in a criminal prosecution of himself."[37] In this situation, the danger posed to the interests protected by the privilege would be outweighed by the governmental interest in maintaining the integrity of its police forces. But where the government had broadened its inquiry far beyond the scope necessary to effectuate this interest, the increased danger to the privilege tipped the balance the other way.

The previous trend towards prohibiting burdens upon an exercise of the privilege was ended in 1976 with Baxter v. Palmigiano.[38] A prison inmate who was the subject of disciplinary proceedings, the Court held, could invoke his privilege on the ground that the conduct he would have to admit might also subject him to criminal prosecution. But, it continued, the privilege was not violated if disciplinary authorities were permitted to consider his invocation of the privilege as tending to show his guilt of the disciplinary charge. The Court apparently considered important state interests in preserving order in correctional facilities and the need for inmate testimony in accomplishing this. Further, it emphasized that unlike the situation in previous cases, the penalty here—the finding of "guilt" in the disciplinary proceeding—could not be based entirely upon the inmate's action in invoking the privilege.

31. 8 Wigmore, Evidence § 2272(2) (McNaughton rev. 1961).

32. Slochower v. Board of Higher Education, 350 U.S. 551 (1956).

33. Spevack v. Klein, 385 U.S. 511 (1967). For a critical appraisal of the decision, see Cole, Bar Discipline and Spevack v. Klein, 53 A.B.A.J. 819 (1967).

34. Gardner v. Broderick, 392 U.S. 273 (1968).

35. Lefkowitz v. Turley, 414 U.S. 70 (1973).

36. Lefkowitz v. Cunningham, 431 U.S. 801 (1977).

37. 392 U.S. at 278.

38. 425 U.S. 308 (1976).

Baxter cited [39] and apparently approved the "prevailing rule," long applied by the lower courts,[40] that the Fifth Amendment does not forbid the drawing of adverse inferences against parties to civil actions when they invoke the privilege during testimony relevant to the litigation. As one court has suggested, an inference may be drawn that the party's testimony "would have been incriminating in all ways suggested by any other evidence." [41] This rule, as contrasted with the prohibition against an adverse inference from an accused's failure to testify at his own trial,[42] has been explained on the ground that in civil litigation the parties are on equal footing.[43] Consequently, there is no need for an anti-inference rule to protect the party invoking the privilege from oppression by the State exercising its "awesome powers of investigation."

What the courts have traditionally regarded as a distinguishable matter arises when the plaintiff in civil litigation invokes the privilege during discovery proceedings.[44] Generally, this has been regarded as justification for dismissal of the claim.[45] But automatic dismissal seems inappropriate, especially since a plaintiff who invokes the privilege during actual testimony may suffer

no more than an adverse inference. Moreover, such action may well constitute an excessive burden on the plaintiff's invocation of the privilege. Even *Baxter* strongly suggested that the Fifth Amendment would be violated if the invocation of the privilege were made determinative of the outcome of the litigation. Increasing sensitivity to these considerations has led some courts to abandon the automatic dismissal rule. *Wehling v. Columbia Broadcasting System*,[46] probably the leading case, directs trial judges faced with such situations to measure the competing interests of the parties with a view towards accommodating those interests if possible. Dismissal is to be ordered only if other and less burdensome remedies— such as delaying some or all discovery until expiration of the period of limitations (or presumably completion of criminal proceedings)—would be ineffective or unfair. In determining the fairness of such delay, the court stressed, it is necessary to consider the extent to which delay might deprive the defendant of access to or the ability to use information or evidence. Under this approach, dismissal may still be appropriate, but only if the defendant establishes that delay would unfairly affect the defendant's

---

39. Id. at 318.

40. Arthurs v. Stern, 560 F.2d 477 (1st Cir. 1977), cert. denied 434 U.S. 1034 (adverse inference in disciplinary proceeding against physician); Olin Corp. v. Castells, 180 Conn. 49, 428 A.2d 319 (1980); Marine Midland Bank v. John E. Russo Produce Co., 50 N.Y.2d 31, 427 N.Y.S.2d 961, 405 N.E.2d 205 (1980) (jury in conventional civil litigation can be told to consider party's invocation of privilege). Federal Rule Evid. 513(a) as adopted by the Supreme Court provided with respect to privileges generally:

Comment or Inference Not Permitted. The claim of a privilege, whether in the present proceeding or upon a prior occasion, is not a proper subject of comment by judge or counsel. No inference may be drawn therefrom.

This provision was not included in the rules enacted by Congress. It is found, however, in revised Uniform Rule (1974) 512(a).

Some lower courts have also read *Baxter* as approving penalties following invocation of the privilege if other evidence is also required. See Giampa v. Illinois Civil Service Commission, 89 Ill.App.3d 606, 44 Ill.Dec. 744, 411 N.E.2d 1110 (1980) (public employee can be

discharged in proceeding in which invocation of privilege is considered along with other evidence, citing *Baxter*); Wilson v. Commonwealth, Department of Education, 63 Pa.Cmwlth. 275, 437 A.2d 1286 (1981) (police officer could be dismissed where evidence included but was not limited to his refusal to testify concerning charges).

See generally, Annot., 4 A.L.R.3d 545 (penalties in civil action for asserting privilege); § 76 supra.

41. Winterland Concessions Co. v. Sileo, 528 F.Supp. 1201, 1215 (N.D.Ill.1981).

42. See § 131 infra.

43. Marine Midland Bank v. John E. Russo Produce Co., 50 N.Y.2d 31, 42, 427 N.Y.S.2d 961, 967, 405 N.E.2d 205, 211 (1980).

44. See generally Note, 66 Iowa L.Rev. 575 (1981); Comment, 48 Univ.Chi.L.Rev. 158 (1981).

45. See, e.g., Lyons v. Johnson, 415 F.2d 540 (9th Cir. 1969), cert. denied 397 U.S. 1027; Independent Productions Corp. v. Loew's, Inc., 22 F.R.D. 266 (S.D.N.Y. 1958).

46. 608 F.2d 1084 (5th Cir. 1979), rehearing denied 611 F.2d 1026.

ability effectively to defend against the claim.[47]

The third matter to be distinguished from the dangers against which the privilege protects is the effect upon a criminal defendant when the prosecution calls a witness who then, before the jury, invokes his own privilege against compelled self-incrimination.[48] In Namet v. United States,[49] the Supreme Court suggested that such action might be reversible error if it constitutes a "conscious and flagrant" effort to build a case from inferences drawn from use of the privilege or if the facts of a particular case strongly suggested that inferences from a witness' refusal to answer "added critical weight to the prosecution's case," in a manner not subject to cross-examination because of the witness' refusal to respond to questions. At least the second possibility appears to have been given constitutional status in Douglas v. Alabama,[50] holding that the state defendant's sixth and fourteenth amendments' right to confrontation was violated by the prosecutor's action in extensively questioning a witness regarding a purported pretrial statement of the witness implicating the defendant, where the witness invoked the privilege and declined to respond to any questions concerning the matter. Both state and federal lower courts have held that questioning and perhaps even merely calling a prosecution witness who invokes the privilege before the jury will sometimes constitute reversible error.[51] But this is not because of any intrusion upon the defendant's interests under the privilege. Rather, it is because—as Namet suggests—such action sometimes creates an unacceptable risk that the jury will draw an inference adverse to the defendant from the witness' use of the privilege, an inference which the defendant cannot subject to critical scrutiny because the witness' action precludes effective or perhaps any cross-examination.

Although Namet suggests that a prosecutor's bad faith might alone render such action a violation of a defendant's rights, the courts have tended to use a multi-factor analysis in determining whether, on the facts of a particular case, calling or questioning a witness who invokes the privilege invalidates a conviction.[52] One court recently listed the following considerations: "the prosecutor's intent in calling the witness; the number of questions which elicit an assertion of the Fifth Amendment privilege; whether defense counsel objects to the prosecutor's conduct; whether the prosecutor attempts to draw adverse inferences in closing argument from the witness' refusal to testify; whether defense counsel himself attempts to rely upon the assertion of a privilege or other aspects of the witness' testimony; whether the allegedly adverse inferences drawn from an assertion of the tes-

47. See also, Baker v. Limber, 647 F.2d 912 (9th Cir. 1981); Black Panther Party v. Smith, 661 F.2d 1243, 1270–1274 (D.C.Cir.1981), vacated and remanded with instruction to dismiss complaint with prejudice 102 S.Ct. 3505; Backos v. United States, 82 F.R.D. 743 (E.D.Mich.1979).

48. See generally Annot., 86 A.L.R.2d 1443; Dec. Dig. Criminal Law ☞706(7).

49. 373 U.S. 179 (1963).

50. 380 U.S. 415 (1965).

51. Higgs v. Commonwealth, 554 S.W.2d 74 (Ky. 1977) (co-indictee called despite prosecutor's awareness that she would invoke the privilege and was asked whether defendant had admitted the crime to her). See also, Shockley v. State, 335 So.2d 659 (Ala.Cr.App. 1976), affirmed 335 So.2d 663 (Ala.); Richardson v. State, 246 So.2d 771 (Fla.1971); People v. Giacalone, 399 Mich. 642, 250 N.W.2d 492 (1977). Most courts appear to regard Douglas as giving constitutional status

to at least parts of the Namet analysis. Zeigler v. Callahan, 659 F.2d 254, 272 n. 12 (1st Cir. 1981); Rado v. Connecticut, 607 F.2d 572, 581 (2d Cir. 1979), cert. denied 447 U.S. 920. Compare Burkley v. United States, 373 A.2d 878, 881 (D.C.App.1977) (persistant questioning of witness who invoked privilege did not present constitutional issue, citing Namet).

52. See State v. Blankinship, 127 Ariz. 507, 622 P.2d 66 (App.1980) (no reversible error, emphasizing lack of bad faith); Commonwealth v. Martin, 372 Mass. 412, 362 N.E.2d 507 (1977) (no reversible error because no bad faith, legitimate doubt as to whether witness would invoke privilege if called, questions asked were not "fact laden," other evidence constituted "strong case" for guilt, and trial judge instructed that no inference was to be drawn); State v. Black, 291 N.W.2d 208 (Minn.1980) (no reversible error, in light of witness' conflicting indications as to whether privilege would be invoked, absence of any basis for invoking privilege, short nature of questions asked).

timonial privilege relate to central issues in the case or collateral matters; and whether the inference is the only evidence bearing upon the issue or is cumulative of other evidence." [53] In addition, careful instructions by the trial judge that no inference may be drawn from the witness' action will sometimes cure what would otherwise be a reversible error.[54]

The *Namet*-type situation must be distinguished from another problem: May a defendant who professes a need for a witness' testimony that is unavailable because of the witness' use of the privilege nevertheless call the witness and compel him to invoke his privilege before the jury? [55] This, of course, creates no danger to the defendant's right of confrontation and cross-examination. But it does infringe upon whatever similar interests are held by the prosecution. It also, on the other hand, may involve defendants' interest in having maximum possible opportunity to use available witnesses, an interest to some extent embodied in their right of compulsory process. In general, courts have been hostile to efforts of this sort. As the court explained in United States v. Lacouture,[56] a witness' invocation of the privilege often suggests two possible infer-

ences: (a) the witness was involved in the offense along with the defendant; and (b) the witness committed the offense in a manner tending to exonerate the defendant. In many or most cases, the jury would be left to speculate as to which is more likely, and the need to avoid such speculation justifies hostility to the tactic at issue. Some courts apply an absolute prohibition against defense efforts to compel witnesses to invoke their privilege before the jury.[57] Others recognize discretion in the trial court judge, apparently intending this to be exercised by determining whether, on the facts of the case, the inference urged by the defense is strong enough to justify permitting the witness to be called.[58] Refusing a defense request of this sort creates special problems where the defensive theory or case is such that the jury might draw an inference adverse to the defense from a failure to call the witness. In such situations, several courts [59] have encouraged the giving of so-called neutralizing instructions. These instructions tell the jurors that for reasons developed out of their presence, the witness is not available to either side and they should draw no inference from the witness' nonappearance. This entire matter, however, is totally unrelated to

---

53. Zeigler v. Callahan, 659 F.2d 254, 272 (1st Cir. 1981).

54. Id., at 273. The Sixth Circuit has held that the government may call a witness and intentionally have that witness invoke the privilege before the jury where the government's case would be "seriously prejudiced" by a failure to pursue this course. United States v. Kilpatrick, 477 F.2d 357 (6th Cir. 1973); United States v. Compton, 365 F.2d 1 (6th Cir. 1966), cert. denied 385 U.S. 956. But see, United States v. Vandetti, 623 F.2d 1144, 1147 (6th Cir. 1980) (practice permitted by prior cases is imbued with potential for unfair prejudice and trial judge should closely scrutinize any effort to use it).

55. See generally Dec.Digest Criminal Law ⟨key⟩707.

56. 495 F.2d 1237, 1240 (5th Cir. 1974), cert. denied 419 U.S. 1053.

57. People v. Dikeman, 192 Colo. 1, 555 P.2d 519 (1976), overruling O'Chiato v. People, 73 Colo. 192, 214 P. 404 (1923); State v. Berry, 324 So.2d 822, 830 (La. 1975), cert. denied 425 U.S. 954; Commonwealth v. Greene, 445 Pa. 228, 285 A.2d 865 (1971). These cases generally note the prohibition against the prosecution compelling a witness to invoke the privilege before the

jury and find no basis for applying a different rule to the defense.

58. United States v. Bowman, 636 F.2d 1003, 1013–1014 (5th Cir. 1981); United States v. Johnson, 488 F.2d 1206, 1211 (1st Cir. 1973); People v. Thomas, 51 N.Y.2d 466, 434 N.Y.S.2d 941, 415 N.E.2d 931 (1980). Despite this recognition, the appellate cases generally affirm refusals to permit the defense to call the witness as involving no abuse of discretion. But see People v. Johnson, 86 Mich.App. 430, 272 N.W.2d 672 (1979), in which the state proved that marijuana was found in the defendants' house trailer, a number of people were present, and no one was in obvious control of the marijuana. The state failed to produce one "res gestae" witness who had been present and in whose car a baggie of a brownish-green substance had been found. Finding that the failure to produce this witness required a new trial despite evidence that the witness would have invoked his privilege against self-incrimination if called, the court appears to have assumed that on the facts the defense was entitled to have this witness invoke his privilege before the jury.

59. United States v. Martin, 526 F.2d 485, 486–487 (10th Cir. 1975); Commonwealth v. Greene, 445 Pa. 228, 285 A.2d 865 (1971).

the self-incrimination rights of defendants and witnesses but rather involves considerations of probative value, jury speculation, and perhaps of defendants' rights of compulsory process.[60]

WESTLAW REFERENCES

410k297(13)

digest(convict! /p appeal! /p selfincrimin!)

compel! compulsory /s testimon! testif! disclos! /s accused defendant! /p senten! probation*

93k3 93k4 /p incrimin!

criter! reason! rational! /s invok! initiat! hold! /s privilege /p selfincrimin! incrimin!

witness! appellant* defendant* /s answer! testi! /p degrad! disgrac!

synopsis,digest(silen! /p privilege /p selfincrim! incrimin! /p infer!)

title(wehling) & court(ca5)

sh 608 f2d 1084

"reversible error" /p infer! /p silen! /p testif! testimon!

"judge" /s instruct! /p infer! /s witness**

digest(jury juries /p speculat! infer! /p testif! testimon! /p witness!)

---

60. In de Luna v. United States, 308 F.2d 140 (5th Cir. 1962), rehearing denied 324 F.2d 375, the court suggested that codefendants with strongly inconsistent defense theories were entitled to separate trials if one intended to testify and sought to comment upon the failure to his codefendant to present his defensive theory by personal testimony. See § 131 n. 23 infra. It might follow from this that at such a separate trial the testifying defendant has the right to call the other defendant and require him to invoke his privilege before the jury as a foundation for the comment that *de Luna* suggests he is entitled to make as a matter of confrontational right. The Fifth Circuit, in adopting a discretionary rule in *Lacouture,* simply noted without discussion that the witness whose testimony was at issue was not a codefendant. 495 F.2d at 1238 n. 1. Other courts have rejected the notion that a witness' codefendant status requires any separate consideration. Commonwealth v. Greene, 445 Pa. 228, 285 A.2d 865 (1971) (no right to call coindictee to be tried separately); State v. Smith, 74 Wn.2d 744, 446 P.2d 571, 580–581 (1969), vacated and remanded on death penalty issue 408 U.S. 934 (testifying defendant's desire to call nontestifying codefendant did not require severance of trials and no error in refusing to permit codefendant to be called, rejecting compulsory process argument); State v. Travis, 541 P.2d 797 (Utah 1975) (defendant had no right to call codefendant, after severance, and require him to invoke privilege before jury).

---

§ 122

1. See generally 8 Wigmore, Evidence § 2258 (McNaughton rev. 1961); 81 Am.Jur.2d Witnesses § 43;

---

§ 122. General Scope of the Privilege: (b) Incrimination Under the Laws of Another Sovereign [1]

The situations in which the danger of incrimination under the laws of another sovereign may be presented can be divided as follows: (a) a witness in either state or federal court claims danger of incrimination under the laws of a foreign country;[2] (b) a witness in a state court claims danger of incrimination under the laws of another state;[3] (c) a witness in a state court claims danger of incrimination under the federal laws;[4] (d) a witness in a federal court claims danger of incrimination under state laws.[5] Traditionally, most courts took the position that the privilege protected against only incrimination under the laws of the sovereign which was attempting to compel the incriminating information.[6] In part, the basis for this conclusion seems to have been that courts regarded the danger of prosecution by another sovereignty as so unlikely as to not deserve

---

Annot., 59 A.L.R. 895; Annot., 82 A.L.R. 1380; Dec. Dig. Witnesses ☞297(14).

2. In re Parker, 411 F.2d 1067 (10th Cir. 1969), vacated as moot 397 U.S. 96; Republic of Greece v. Koukouras, 264 Mass. 318, 162 N.E. 345 (1928).

3. State ex rel. Doran v. Doran, 215 La. 151, 39 So. 2d 894 (1949) (claim of privilege sustained because prosecution in another state "is not only impending but an actual fact"); State v. Wood, 99 Vt. 490, 134 A. 697 (1926) ("the only danger to be considered is such as arose within this jurisdiction"); In re Werner, 167 App. Div. 384, 152 N.Y.S. 862 (1915) (witness failed to show any real and substantial danger of use in prosecution under laws of another state).

4. Jack v. Kansas, 199 U.S. 372 (1905) (no "real danger" of federal prosecution or use of evidence by federal authorities, so action by state in compelling testimony not violation of due process clause of Fourteenth Amendment); Commonwealth v. Rhine, 303 S.W.2d 301 (Ky.1957) (state constitutional privilege protects against incrimination under federal as well as state law); People v. Den Uyl, 318 Mich. 645, 29 N.W.2d 284 (1947) (state constitutional privilege, to be effective, must prohibit the compulsion of testimony which might be used in pending federal prosecution); Ex parte Copeland, 91 Tex.Cr.R. 549, 240 S.W. 314 (1922) (no real danger of use).

5. Brown v. Walker, 161 U.S. 591 (1896); Hale v. Henkel, 201 U.S. 43 (1906).

6. See cases cited in notes 3, 4, and 5 supra.

protection under the privilege.[7] It has also been argued, however, that the purpose of the privilege is to prevent a sovereign from enlisting an accused's aid in achieving his own conviction and that this is not violated if the revelations compelled are of interest only to another sovereign. Thus the motive of the inquiring sovereign to inflict brutality is absent, and the dangers which the privileges guards against are not present.[8]

This position was undermined, however, by the Supreme Court of the United States in Murphy v. Waterfront Commission.[9] Murphy and several others had been subpoenaed to testify before the Waterfront Commission regarding a work stoppage at certain New Jersey piers. Despite a grant of immunity to prosecution under New Jersey and New York law, they refused to testify on the ground that their responses might tend to incriminate them under federal law. Reversing the New Jersey Supreme Court, the United States Supreme Court held that the federal constitutional privilege protects a state witness from prosecution under federal as well as state law.[10] Emphasis was placed on the practical dangers in a time of "cooperative federalism" of actual use of testimony procured by a state in federal prosecutions.[11] The argument that a sovereign's grant of immunity removed the motive for it to engage in brutality was rejected as resting on too narrow a view of the interests the privilege is designed to protect.[12] As a means of effectuating the holding, the Court continued, it would direct as an exercise of its supervisory powers over lower federal courts that evidence obtained as the result of revelations compelled by a

state under a grant of immunity from its own prosecutions would be inadmissible in federal trial.[13] Moreover, a defendant need only show initially that he has testified to matters related to the federal prosecution; the burden then shifts to the federal prosecution to establish an independent source for the offered proof and therefore that it was not tainted by the state action.[14] In dictum, the Court also indicated that the privilege would protect a federal witness against incrimination under state as well as federal law.[15]

Murphy does not necessarily resolve the problems raised in situations (a) and (b) at the beginning of this section. But the decision has destroyed the conceptual basis, weak as it was, for the traditional view that in those situations the privilege was inapplicable. It seems clear that the Court will regard the danger of incrimination under the law of another state as invoking the privilege.[16] When the danger is of incrimination under the law of a foreign sovereign, the matter is more difficult. Compelling testimony that is incriminating in this fashion, especially given *Murphy*, seems as offensive to the policies on which the privilege rests as is compelling testimony in other situations clearly covered by the privilege. But American jurisdictions lack any apparent ability to prevent the use of compelled testimony or evidence derived from it in foreign jurisdictions. Thus testimony of this sort might well be ruled unavailable even pursuant to a grant of immunity. In deciding whether the privilege applies, it is necessary to weigh the policies underlying the privilege against the risk that applying the privilege to incrimina-

7. Brown v. Walker, 161 U.S. 591, 608 (1896); In re Werner, 167 App.Div. 384, 152 N.Y.S. 862 (1915).

8. 8 Wigmore, Evidence § 2258, at 345 (McNaughton rev. 1961); McNaughton, Self-Incrimination Under Foreign Law, 45 Va.L.Rev. 1299 (1959). Compare Grant, Federalism and Self-Incrimination, 4 UCLA L.Rev. 549 (1957).

9. 378 U.S. 52 (1964), noted in The Supreme Court, 1963 Term, 78 Harv.L.Rev. 143, 227 (1964), 31 Brooklyn L.Rev. 157 (1964), 10 N.Y.L. Forum 627 (1964).

10. Murphy v. Waterfront Commission, 378 U.S. 52, 77–78 (1969).

11. Id. at 55–56.

12. Id. at 56 n. 5.

13. Id. at 79.

14. Id. at 79 n. 18.

15. Id. at 78.

16. See United States v. Metz, 608 F.2d 147, 156 (5th Cir. 1979), cert. denied 449 U.S. 821 (danger of incrimination under state law provided basis for witness invoking privilege despite guilty plea and conviction in federal prosecution).

tion under the laws of a foreign sovereign would render the testimony totally unavailable, a cost not involved in the other situations posited at the beginning of this section. The Supreme Court has acknowledged the issue but has not found occasion to resolve it;[17] the lower courts are split.[18]

The expansion of protection to incrimination under the laws of other sovereigns has created some difficulty in regard to various jurisdictions' ability to compel testimony by granting immunity. One court held that a state grant of immunity was ineffective to remove the protection of the privilege in regard to testimony potentially incriminating under federal law because no immunity from federal prosecution or use of the testimony had been obtained from federal authorities and the state authorities lacked authority to grant such immunity.[19] But this seems to ignore the holding in *Murphy* that the compulsion of testimony under a state grant of immunity would—apparently automatically—create use immunity from any potentially incriminating use of the testimony under federal law.[20] If a state were to grant transactional immunity, however, it seems that the protection in the federal forum would again be only from use of the compelled testimony and other evidence derived from it.[21] *Murphy* does not suggest that a state's decision to grant transactional rather than use immunity obligates the fed-

eral courts to refuse to entertain a prosecution.

Situation (b) presents a different problem. *Murphy* was an exercise of the Supreme Court's supervisory power and thus is clearly not binding on the states; *Murphy*, then, does not control the inadmissibility of testimony compelled by one state under a grant of immunity when offered in a prosecution by another state. But the Court has, in another context, made clear that testimony compelled under a grant of immunity and the threat of contempt is the "essence" of coerced testimony and thus inadmissible under due process even for impeachment purposes.[22] It seems to follow clearly that when a defendant is granted immunity in one state and the resulting testimony is later offered against him in another state, the due process prohibition against the use of coerced and thus involuntary "confessions" bars its admissibility. Whether a defendant can resist testifying in one state on the basis that his testimony would be incriminating under the law of another state and that his right to be free from the use of his immunized testimony in the second state is insufficiently well established[23] is more problematic. But on balance, the due process prohibition against compelled incriminating admissions seems so clearly applicable that such a witness can be compelled to respond.[24]

17. See Zicarelli v. New Jersey State Commission of Investigation, 406 U.S. 472, 478–481 (1972) (no danger of incrimination under laws of foreign nation, so no need to address effect of such danger).

18. See In re Baird, 668 F.2d 432, 434 n. 7 (8th Cir. 1982), cert. denied 456 U.S. 982. Compare Mishima v. United States, 507 F.Supp. 131 (D.Alaska 1981) (rationale of *Murphy* requires extending protection to incrimination under laws of foreign sovereign); United States v. Trucis, 89 F.R.D. 671 (E.D.Pa.1981); and In re Letters Rogatory From 9th Criminal Division, 448 F.Supp. 786 (S.D.Fla.1978) with In re Campbell, 628 F.2d 1260 (9th Cir. 1980) (Ninth Circuit's cases establish that privilege does not protect against incrimination under laws of foreign sovereign).

19. State v. Urioste, 95 N.M. 712, 625 P.2d 1229 (App.1980).

20. See Agrella v. Rivkind, 404 So.2d 1113 (Fla.App. 1981).

21. See Surina v. Buckalew, 629 P.2d 969, 980 (Alaska 1981) (state grant of transactional immunity will bar federal prosecution only if "endorsed" by federal authorities).

22. New Jersey v. Portash, 440 U.S. 450 (1979). In Zicarelli v. New Jersey State Commission of Investigation, 406 U.S. 472, 475–476 (1972) the Court appeared to assume, without discussion, that a witness granted immunity by a state would be free from the use of that testimony and derivative evidence in a prosecution by another state.

23. See § 143 infra.

24. State v. Talsma, 2 Kan.App.2d 551, 584 P.2d 145 (1978) (grant of immunity under Kansas statute will prohibit use of testimony or derivative evidence in prosecutions in other states).

WESTLAW REFERENCES

incrimin! /p foreign /s countr! sovereign & court (ca9 ca10)

murphy /15 378 /5 52

protect! /p incrimin! /p foreign /p sovereign countr! & court(ca2 ca5 ca9)

"transactional immunity"

immuni! /p prohibit! inadmiss! /p testimon!

---

§ 123. General Scope of the Privilege: (c) Danger of Incrimination Must Be "Real and Appreciable"[1]

Early in the development of the federal constitutional privilege it was established that the danger of incrimination must be "real and appreciable." A danger "imaginary and unsubstantial" would not be sufficient.[2] This is apparently still the formal requirement.[3] Much reliance in the cases has been placed on the English decision in Queen v. Boyes.[4] A witness asserted the danger of parliamentary impeachment as a basis for invoking the privilege. Rejecting this, the court held:

> "[T]he danger to be apprehended must be real and appreciable, with reference to the ordinary operation of the law in the ordinary course of things—not a danger of an imaginary and unsubstantial character, having reference to some extraordinary and barely possible contingency, so improbable that no reasonable man would suffer it to influence his conduct."[5]

§ 123

1. See generally 81 Am.Jur.2d Witnesses § 39; Comment, 72 J.Crim.L. & C. 671 (1981); Dec.Dig. Witnesses ☞297.

2. Brown v. Walker, 161 U.S. 591 (1896).

3. Marchetti v. United States, 390 U.S. 39, 48 (1968).

4. 1 B. & S. 311, 121 Eng.Rep. 730 (K.B.1861).

5. Id. at 330, 121 Eng.Rep. at 738.

6. Brown v. Walker, 161 U.S. 591 (1896) (possibility of conviction under laws of another sovereign a danger of an imaginary and unsubstantial character); Rogers v. United States, 340 U.S. 367, 374–75 (1951) (after witness had admitted holding office of treasurer of Communist Party, disclosure of acquaintance with her successor presents no more than a mere imaginary possibility of increasing the danger of prosecution).

7. Commonwealth v. Carrera, 424 Pa. 551, 227 A.2d 627 (1967).

This formula was invoked by the United States Supreme Court in several early cases as a basis for holding the privilege inapplicable.[6] A Pennsylvania case,[7] however, is illustrative of the now prevailing general judicial attitude that almost any conceivable danger is "real and appreciable". The defendant, an unmarried woman, refused to testify before a grand jury concerning an abortion allegedly performed upon her, asserting the danger of criminal prosecution on the basis of the sexual intercourse giving rise to the child. Upholding her claim, the Pennsylvania Supreme Court commented:

> "[U]nless unusual circumstances exist as e.g., rape, common sense dictates that an unmarried female who admits an abortion has been performed upon her acknowledges and admits she has committed fornication. This, in itself, was sufficiently reasonable cause to give the appellant apprehension of the danger of prosecution. Remote though it may be, it still existed."[8]

WESTLAW REFERENCES

incrimin! /p real /2 appreciable

---

§ 124. General Scope of the Privilege: (d) Activity Sought to Be Compelled Must Be "Testimonial"[1]

It is arguable from the policies underlying the privilege that it ought to protect against any compelled cooperation of an accused in

8. Id. at 554, 227 A.2d at 629. See also, Vail v. Vail, 360 So.2d 985 (Ala.Civ.App.1977), reversed on other grounds 360 So.2d 992 (Ala.) (prosecution for adultery "unlikely" but "a possibility," so testimony concerning adulterous activity could not be compelled); Matter of Grant, 83 Wis.2d 77, 264 N.W.2d 587 (1978) (likelihood of information regarding sexual activity being used to prosecute not sufficiently low to permit compelled testimony concerning such activity).

§ 124

1. See generally 8 Wigmore, Evidence §§ 2263–2265 (McNaughton rev. 1961); Maguire, Evidence of Guilt § 2.04 (1959); Arenella, *Schmerber* and the Privilege Against Self-Incrimination: A Reappraisal, 20 Am. Crim.L.Rev. 31 (1982); Dann, The Fifth Amendment Privilege Against Self-Incrimination: Extorting Physical Evidence From A Suspect, 43 So.Cal.L.Rev. 597 (1970); 21A Am.Jur.2d Criminal Law §§ 798–803, 945–949; 81 Am.Jur.2d Witnesses § 40; C.J.S. Wit-

the procedure invoked by the state to punish him. Insofar as the privilege rests upon the inviolability of certain aspects of the human personality, it would be entirely consistent to hold that the privilege protects against any infringements of those aspects. The Supreme Court of the United States has, however, made clear that the scope of the Fifth Amendment privilege does not coincide with the "complex of values it helps to protect." [2] As early as 1910, the Court held that accused's privilege was not violated when he was compelled to put on a blouse for purposes of determining whether it fitted him.[3] "[T]he prohibition . . . ," declared the Court, "is a prohibition of the use of physical or moral compulsion to exact communications from him . . . " [4] Assuming that the privilege does not prevent compelling the accused's active cooperation in noncommunicative activity, however, the scope of the protection afforded is still not clear.

There are three potential formulations of the criterion to be used to determine whether a given activity is "communicative" and therefore within the scope of the protection of the privilege. First, the term might be limited to words spoken by the subject. This is the position urged by Wigmore.[5] Second, the test might readily be expanded to cover any activity performed for the purpose of communicating. In addition to spoken words, then, the privilege would cover gestures and other activities intended by the actor to communicate thoughts to another. Finally, the privilege's protection might be expanded to cover any activities of the subject which, if used to prove guilt, require reliance upon the accuracy of the accused's participation.[6] For example, taking the accused's fingerprints and relying on them in court would involve no such element. But in-court identification based upon the witness's hearing the accused speak during a police lineup would involve this element, as the reliability of the identification is dependent upon the accused having spoken during the lineup in a normal way or in the way in which he spoke at the time he was initially observed (or in which he would have spoken had he been the one observed) by the witness.[7]

The leading case on the nature of the activity protected by the Fifth Amendment privilege is Schmerber v. California.[8] Explaining that the privilege "protects an accused only from being compelled to testify against himself, or otherwise provide the state with evidence of a testimonial or communicative nature," [9] the Court held that blood extracted from a non-consenting suspect, "although an incriminating product of compulsion, was neither [his] testimony nor evidence relating to some communicative act or writing by [him. Thus] it was not inadmissible on privilege grounds." [10] Although it did not define precisely what was meant by evidence of a "testimonial or communicative nature", the Court expressly disclaimed adopting Wigmore's view as to the scope of the privilege.[11]

---

nesses § 447; Dec.Dig. Criminal Law ☞393(1), 393(3), 393(4), Witnesses ☞298½.

2. Schmerber v. California, 384 U.S. 757, 762 (1966).

3. Holt v. United States, 218 U.S. 245 (1910).

4. Id. at 252–253.

5. 8 Wigmore, Evidence § 2263, pp. 378–79 (McNaughton rev. 1961). See the plurality opinion in California v. Byers, 402 U.S. 424 (1971) (joined in by four justices), upholding a statute requiring the driver of a motor vehicle involved in an accident to stop and furnish his name and address. "The act of stopping," Chief Justice Burger declared, "is no more testimonial—indeed less so in some respects—than requiring a person in custody to stand or walk in a police lineup, to speak prescribed words, to give samples of handwrit-

ing, fingerprints or blood." A majority of the Court, however, agreed that this action was "testimonial" within Fifth Amendment meaning.

6. See Maguire, Evidence of Guilt 31 (1959).

7. Cf. State v. Jones, 188 Wash. 275, 62 P.2d 44 (1936) (defendant required to pronounce certain words for purposes of proving that his pronunciation of them at an earlier time was caused by intoxication rather than a speech defect or characteristic).

8. 384 U.S. 757 (1966).

9. Id. at 761.

10. Id. at 765.

11. Id. at 763, n. 7.

Subsequent cases from both the Supreme Court and lower tribunals suggest that the middle alternative has found widest acceptance. The tendency has been to uphold any requirement that the accused engage in non-verbal activity. Among those activities that have been held beyond the protection of the privilege have been participation in a lineup,[12] seizure of marked money or other physical evidence from an accused,[13] fingerprints taken from the accused,[14] photographs taken of the accused while in custody,[15] and requiring the accused to remove clothing[16] or a toupee[17] for identification purposes. Further, it is no violation of the privilege to compel the suspect to speak[18] or to write,[19] if this is done only to determine the physical characteristics of the suspect's voice or handwriting rather than the substance of what the suspect says or writes.[20]

Several state courts have construed state constitutional privileges as not requiring that the compelled activity have any testimonial aspects. Heavy reliance appears to be placed on the use of language in the state provisions prohibiting persons from compulsion to "give evidence" against themselves.[21] But these courts have read their state privileges as barring only compelled affirmative activity on the part of the suspect. While it is a violation of these provisions to compel a suspect to produce a handwriting exemplar,[22] the privilege imposes no barrier to surgical removal of a bullet,[23] the taking of hair samples,[24] or securing fingerprints from

12. United States v. Wade, 388 U.S. 218, 221–23 (1967).

13. United States v. Vickers, 387 F.2d 703 (4th Cir. 1967), cert. denied 392 U.S. 912.

14. State v. Stuard, 104 Ariz. 305, 452 P.2d 98 (1969) (permissible to take defendant's fingerprints in open court and compare them with those of a prior offender); Washington v. State, 434 S.W.2d 138 (Tex.Cr. App.1968).

15. State v. Strickland, 5 N.C.App. 338, 168 S.E.2d 697 (1969), reversed on other grounds 276 N.C. 253, 173 S.E.2d 129 (motion picture of accused after arrest properly admitted to illustrate police officer's testimony that accused was intoxicated).

16. Vincent v. State, 256 A.2d 268 (Del.1969) (proper to require accused to remove shirt to permit inspection of scratches).

17. People v. Collins, 16 Mich.App. 667, 168 N.W.2d 624 (1969) (accused properly required to remove toupee at preliminary hearing).

18. United States v. Dionisio, 410 U.S. 1 (1973) (grand jury subpoena properly required witness to appear at office of U.S. Attorney and read transcript of conversation so witness' voice could be compared with an intercepted conversation to determine if witness had been a party to that conversation).

19. Gilbert v. California, 388 U.S. 263, 266 (1967) (accused may be compelled to furnish handwriting exemplars).

20. In South Dakota v. Neville, 103 S.Ct. 916 (1983), the Court considered the potential testimonial aspects of a driver's refusal to submit to a chemical test to determine the alcohol content of his blood. Under the state statute at issue, a driver's refusal to submit to such a test may be used against the defendant at trial. S.D. Codified Laws 32–23–10.1, 19–14–28.1. The state court had held that a driver's refusal to submit to a blood alcohol test, unlike the products of the test, constitutes "a tacit or overt expression and communication" of the driver's thoughts and thus may not be compelled under the Fifth Amendment. State v. Neville, 312 N.W.2d 723, 726 (S.D.1981). The Supreme Court commented that it found "considerable force" in the suggestion that refusal to submit to the test, like flight and suppression of evidence, is merely circumstantial evidence of consciousness of guilt and not a testimonial communication within the protection of the privilege. 103 S.Ct. at 921. But, it continued, the line between such nontestimonial conduct and communications and testimony cannot be "readily drawn" in many situations arising after officers have sought submission to the test:

> The situations arising from a refusal present a difficult gradation from a person who indicates refusal by complete inaction, to one who nods his head negatively, to one who states, "I refuse to take the test," to the respondent here, who stated, "I'm too drunk, I won't pass the test."

Id., U.S. at 922. Apparently to avoid extensive future litigation over whether such situations involve testimonial evidence, the Court declined to rest its decision on the potentially noncommunicative nature of the refusal at issue. Instead, it concluded that the privilege was not infringed because there was no impermissible compulsion. See § 125, infra.

21. See Hansen v. Owens, 619 P.2d 315 (Utah 1980), suggesting that language embodied in constitutional provisions is likely to have been chosen with special care.

22. State v. Armstead, 152 Ga.App. 56, 262 S.E.2d 233 (1979); Hansen v. Owens, 619 P.2d 315 (Utah 1980).

23. Creamer v. State, 229 Ga. 511, 192 S.E.2d 350 (1972), cert. dismissed 410 U.S. 975.

24. State v. McCumber, 622 P.2d 353 (Utah 1980); State v. Van Dam, 554 P.2d 1324 (Utah 1976).

a suspect [25] because none of these procedures involves compelling the suspect to act affirmatively in a manner that results in evidence being developed. These courts appear to have adopted the third formulation of this aspect of the privilege discussed earlier.

Despite the widespread acceptance of the requirement that compelled activity be testimonial in order to invoke the privilege, there has been little development of the rationale for the requirement. The need for testimonial aspects renders available a great deal of information useful in apprehending and convicting offenders that other formulations of the privilege would place beyond reach. But is the line so drawn related in a reasonable way to the policies served by the privilege? To the extent that the privilege is based upon general notions of human dignity, probably not. Compelling an accused to appear and speak in a lineup is unlikely to be less intrusive upon dignity notions than compelling the same suspect to acknowledge his whereabouts on the day of the offense. But the testimonial requirement may serve other functions more directly related to the purpose of the privilege. To some extent, the results of testimonial activity are more within the volitional control of the suspect than other forms of compelled participation in the investigatory and prosecution process. Thus if the government is permitted to use compulsion to cause an accused to engage in testimonial activity, it may have a greater incentive to use excessive force to compel the results desired by the government, that is, a communication of the substance which the government wants. A suspect who responds to such compulsion may, of course, respond inaccurately to avoid the coercion.

Limiting the privilege to testimonial activity, then, may serve to apply it to those situations where the compulsion is most likely to be excessive or abused and where it is most likely to result in obtaining unreliable evidence.[26]

 WESTLAW REFERENCES

digest,synopsis(testimonial /s evidence /s commun!)
testimonial /p compel! compul! /s activit!

§ 125. General Scope of the Privilege: Compulsion [1]

The additional and independent requirement of compulsion has served to expand and, more recently, to contract the coverage of the privilege. Traditionally, the privilege was regarded as applicable only where the compulsion exerted upon the holder was "legal compulsion," that is, compulsion authorized by law to compel answers to questions.[2] The Supreme Court has recently observed that testimony given under the threat of contempt citation is the essence of the sort of coerced testimony to which the Fifth Amendment privilege is applicable.[3] In Miranda v. Arizona,[4] however, the Court held that despite the lack of "legal" authority for police to compel answers to their questions, custodial police interrogation did invoke the protection of the privilege. Reasoning that to permit compelled pretrial elicitation of self-incriminating statements would render the privilege at trial an empty formality, the Court held that the privilege is available outside of the judicial context, and protects persons "in all settings . . . from being compelled to incriminate themselves." [5]

---

25. Weaver v. State, 161 Ga.App. 421, 288 S.E.2d 687 (1982).

26. Some characteristics of some nontestimonial conduct are, of course, within the volitional control of the actor. One has some control over the physical characteristics of one's voice and handwriting. It is arguable, therefore, that the testimonial requirement does exclude from the coverage of the privilege some compelled activity that raises the same dangers to the policies protected by the privilege as are posed by compelled testimonial activities.

§ 125

1. See generally, 8 Wigmore, Evidence § 2252, pp. 327–29 (McNaughton rev. 1961); Ritchie, Compulsion that Violates the Fifth Amendment: The Burger Court's Definition, 61 Minn.L.Rev. 383 (1977).

2. See generally, Note 5 Stan.L.Rev. 459 (1953).

3. New Jersey v. Portash, 440 U.S. 450, 459 (1979).

4. 384 U.S. 436 (1966), rehearing denied 385 U.S. 890.

5. Id., at 467.

More recently, in contrast, the requirement of compulsion has served to limit the reach of the privilege. In Garner v. United State,[6] the Court held that one who fails to assert the privilege prior to disclosing incriminating information in an income tax return cannot be said to have disclosed that information in response to compulsion and thus had experienced no deprivation of the privilege. Thus the requirement of compulsion serves as the conceptual basis for many of the procedural requirements imposed upon one who seeks the protection of the privilege.[7]

In addition, the requirement of compulsion and that the compulsion elicit the testimonial activity invoking the privilege has greatly limited the effect of the privilege upon compelled production and seizures of documents. The act of placing information in written form is probably testimonial within the meaning of the privilege; a witness could not be compelled to write out rather than orally articulate self-incriminating information.[8] But once information is voluntarily placed in written form, the privilege provides no protection against the use of compulsion by the government to obtain access to the document and its informational contents. While there is compulsion exerted and an increased risk of incrimination, the compulsion has not been imposed to coerce the *testimonial* activity which is protected by the privilege. If a person commits incriminating information to writing, therefore, the Fifth Amendment provides no protection against that writing being seized in an otherwise valid search[9] or even against the person himself being compelled to produce upon demand the document containing that information,[10] unless the compelled production of the document otherwise intrudes upon the privilege.[11]

Whether this last limitation is desirable is subject to some dispute. Using a defendant's voluntarily-written admissions to convict him may violate the sense that the government should be required to prove guilt without the assistance of the defendant; the defendant's interest in being free from providing such compelled assistance may be infringed in an especially significant manner when he is compelled actively to produce the documents containing the admission. Yet the limitation of the privilege to compelled *testimonial* activities reflects a policy judgment that the government should not be barred from compelling all defendant assistance or exploiting earlier decisions by a defendant that now render incriminating evidence available to the government. If the rationale for requiring that the compelled activity be testimonial is that compelling testimonial activity creates the greatest danger of abuse, that rationale indicates that privilege should be inapplicable here. If the government is seeking, or seeking to use, an already completed self-incriminatory document, there is unlikely to be any opportunity for or incentive to use excessive or offensive coercion to persuade the subject to change that document. If the limitation of the privilege to compelled testimonial conduct is sound, the failure to construe the privilege to protect against the use of or quest for previously-made documentary admissions is also sound.

Further, the compulsion must be "impermissible." In South Dakota v. Neville,[12] the Supreme Court considered the admissibility under the Fifth Amendment privilege of a driver's refusal to submit to a blood alcohol test, offered by the prosecution as evidence of the driver's intoxication. The driver himself had embellished his refusal by telling the officers, "I'm too drunk, I won't pass the

---

6.   424 U.S. 648 (1976).

7.   See § 136 infra.

8.   See Fisher v. United States, 425 U.S. 391, 410 n. 11 (1976) (in subpoena context, fact that person subpoenaed has written subpoenaed document is not controlling "unless the Government has compelled the subpoenaed person to write the document . . . .").

9.   Andresen v. Maryland, 427 U.S. 463 (1976).

10.   Fisher v. United States, 425 U.S. 391 (1976).

11.   See § 126 infra.

12.   103 S.Ct. 916 (1983). The Court's discussion of the arguably testimonial aspects of the refusal is considered in § 124 n. 20 supra.

test." There was no "direct coercion" to take the test, the Court noted, since the driver was given the choice of submitting to it. But the indirect pressure exerted by the need to make this choice did not render the resulting choice "compelled" within the meaning of the privilege. The criminal process often requires suspects and defendants to make choices and the Fifth Amendment does not necessarily preclude this:

> [T]he values behind the Fifth Amendment are not hindered when the state offers a suspect the choice of submitting to the blood-alcohol test or having his refusal used against him. . . . [T]he state could legitimately compel the suspect, against his will, to accede to the test. Given, then, that the offer of taking a blood-alcohol test is clearly legitimate, the action becomes no *less* legitimate when the State offers a second option of refusing the test, with the attendant penalties for making that choice.[13] (Emphasis in original.)

The refusal, therefore, is not an act coerced by the officer and is not protected by the privilege.

WESTLAW REFERENCES

"legal compulsion" & privilege /p incrimin!

garner /15 424 /4 648

compel! compul! /s document* /s production seiz! /p privilege

neville /15 103 /5 916

§ 126. The Privilege as Related to Documents and Tangible Items: (a) Compulsory Production [1]

The subpoena power has traditionally included the ability to compel the person to whom the subpoena is directed to produce papers, documents, and other physical items. A subpoena which so directs the production of items is generally called a subpoena *duces tecum.*[2] The Fifth Amendment privilege against compelled self-incrimination places some limits upon the use of the subpoena to compel the productions of physical items, although it is now clear that these limits are fewer than has traditionally been assumed. In Boyd v. United States,[3] the Court indicated that the Fourth and Fifth Amendments prohibited compelling a person to produce personal and business documents and perhaps other tangible items as well. But such a broad reading of *Boyd* is no longer permissible.

It is clear that the Fifth Amendment provides no protection concerning the contents of subpoenaed documents.[4] Even if the documents contain information personally placed into them by the person to whom the subpoena is directed, the subpoena does not purport to compel that process of "communicating" the information to written form. Any testimonial aspect of this communication is not compelled and therefore is not within the protection of the privilege. This means, then, that for purposes of Fifth Amendment analysis a subpoena for docu-

13. 103 S.Ct. at 923. The Court also noted that the State generally desires that the driver take the test, because a positive blood-alcohol test is usually more persuasive evidence of intoxication than is a driver's refusal to submit to the test. The situation is not, it noted, one in which the State "has subtly coerced respondent into choosing an option it had no right to compel, rather than offering a true choice." Id. Presumably, such a subterfuge would encounter at least serious difficulties under the privilege.

§ 126

1. See generally, 8 Wigmore, Evidence § 2294 (McNaughton rev. 1961); Note, 95 Harv.L.Rev. 683 (1982); 21A Am.Jur.2d Criminal Law §§ 704, 739; 81 Am.Jur. 2d Witnesses §§ 44–48; C.J.S. Witnesses § 448; Annot., 48 L.Ed.2d 884; Dec.Dig. Witnesses 🔑298.

2. See State ex rel. Pollard v. Criminal Court, 263 Ind. 236, 329 N.E.2d 573 (1975).

3. 116 U.S. 616 (1886).

4. Fisher v. United States, 425 U.S. 391, 409 (1976). See also, Andresen v. Maryland, 427 U.S. 463 (1976) (Fifth Amendment imposed no bar to state's use of records obtained from Andresen by a reasonable search, although the contents were incriminating and contained some statements made by Andresen himself). See generally, McKenna, The Constitutional Protection of Private Papers: The Role of a Hierarchical Fourth Amendment, 53 Ind.L.J. 55 (1977–78) (*Fisher* and *Andresen* mean that sole source of constitutional protection for private papers is in the Fourth rather than Fifth Amendment).

ments or papers should be treated no differently than a subpoena for physical items.

Compliance with a subpoena does, however, involve certain implicit testimonial communications by the person. By producing certain items, the respondent communicates at least the following information: (a) the items produced exist; (b) the items were within the possession or control of the respondent; and (c) the respondent believes or has some reason to believe that the items produced are those described in the subpoena. This information may be incriminating in any of several ways. It may be admissible evidence concerning an element of an offense; if the item produced is contraband, for example, the respondent's production of it may constitute an acknowledgement of illegal possession. Or, the information may be of value in ongoing investigation into possible criminal activity by the respondent. Further, if the item is offered at trial, the respondent's conduct in producing it may constitute admissible evidence tending to meet authentication requirements; thus compliance may involve what is often called "implicit authentication" of the items. Until 1976, it was widely assumed that these dangers, and particularly the risk of "implicit authentication," barred the compulsory production of documents and items which could incriminate the respondent, even though these items might be seized in an otherwise reasonable search and then used to incriminate the respondent.[5]

In Fisher v. United States,[6] the Supreme Court held that the Fifth Amendment imposed no barrier to subpoenaing from certain taxpayers or their lawyers certain documents prepared by the taxpayers' accountants which contained information potentially incriminating under federal tax laws. After noting that the "implicit authentication"

danger was the "prevailing justification" for a general self-incrimination bar to compulsory production of incriminating documents or items, the Court found the rationale for a bar inapplicable to the cases. Since the respondents had not prepared the documents sought, they lacked personal knowledge as to the nature of the documents and thus any implied assertions contained in their compliance would not be admissible to authenticate the documents were they ever to be offered against the respondents at a criminal trial.[7] In regard to other admissions that might be made by the act of complying—specifically, the acknowledgement that the respondents had certain papers given them by their accountants and that the respondents believed these papers to be those called for by the subpoena—the Court held that an insufficient risk of incrimination had been established. The facts made clear that the government was aware before the subpoena issued that such documents existed and were in the possession of the respondents; any admissions concerning these matters, then, added "little or nothing" to the information available to the government.[8] Further, to the extent that compliance provided the government with information, the respondents had not made an adequate showing that it was incriminating within the meaning of the privilege. Consulting an accountant concerning tax liability and accepting papers concerning the accountant's work is not itself illegal and the respondents had failed to establish or point out how providing the government with information that they had engaged in such conduct would be incriminating within the meaning of the privilege.[9]

Fisher makes clear that there is no blanket Fifth Amendment prohibition against compulsory production of items, whether

---

5. E.g., People v. Defore, 242 N.Y. 13, 27, 150 N.E. 585, 590 (1926), cert. denied 270 U.S. 657 (Cardozo, J.): "A defendant is 'protected from producing his documents in response to a subpoena duces tecum, for his production of them in court would be his voucher of their genuineness.' There would then be 'testimonial compulsion.'"

6. 425 U.S. 391 (1976).

7. Id. at 412–13.

8. Id. at 411 (existence and location of the documents was "a foregone conclusion" on facts of case).

9. Id. at 411–412.

documents or not, that may be incriminating to the person from whom they are demanded. It also confirms that in some situations, compelled production is barred by the Fifth Amendment. Beyond this, the significance of the decision is uncertain. If the items called for are ones of which the respondent has personal knowledge, so the respondent's act of complying would be admissible to authenticate the items if offered by the prosecution, is the risk of "implicit authentication" always or usually sufficient to bar compelled production? Should it make any difference if the prosecution establishes that it would be able at any subsequent trial to produce other authenticating testimony and represents that it will not make use of the respondent's conduct to authenticate the item?

The First Circuit [10] has reasoned that where it appears that the respondent's act of production would be sufficient to authenticate the item, compelled production is barred even if other sufficient authenticating testimony is available to the prosecution. Consequently, a subpoena calling for the compelled production of such an item is unenforceable unless accompanied by a grant of immunity from the use of the respondent's conduct and derivative evidence.[11] The immunity need not, however, include protection from use of the item itself or, in the case of a document, from use of the con-

tents of the document.[12] Other courts, apparently relying on the emphasis in *Fisher* upon the facts of the cases before the Court, have held that one resisting a subpoena has the burden of moving forward to show that compliance would create a real and appreciable danger of incrimination, whether by means of "implicit authentication" or otherwise.[13] So read, *Fisher* merely reflects an application to the compelled production situation of the general requirement.[14] On the facts of particular cases, under this approach, a sufficient risk of incrimination might be found from the risk of providing the government with evidence usable for authentication purposes and also in the admission of the possession [15] or even the existence of the items sought.[16]

On balance, the broad approach of the First Circuit seems preferable. Enforcement of a subpoena, then, should be barred if either it reasonably appears from the face of the situation that the respondent's act of compliance would be admissible for authentication purposes or would provide the government with information meeting Fifth Amendment incrimination requirements in other ways. To require scrutiny of each case for other possibly authenticating evidence, the adequacy of that evidence, and the prosecution's willingness to rely exclusively upon other evidence would be disruptive and, in many cases, too difficult an un-

---

10. In re Grand Jury Proceedings United States, 626 F.2d 1051 (1st Cir. 1980).

11. See § 143 infra.

12. 626 F.2d at 1058. See also In re Grand Jury Subpoena, 646 F.2d 963 (5th Cir. 1981) (subpoena not enforceable despite government's assertion that it could authenticate records with other testimony and would not disclose respondent's "implicit authentication" to jury); United States v. Beattie, 541 F.2d 329 (2d Cir. 1976) (fact that respondent wrote letters demanded by subpoena was sufficient to bar compelled production); State ex rel. Hyder v. Superior Court, 128 Ariz. 253, 625 P.2d 316 (1981) (subpoena for letters allegedly written by father to daughter discussing illegal sexual activity with her cannot be compelled because production would be acknowledgement of authorship).

13. Matter of Grand Jury Empanelled February 14, 1978, 603 F.2d 469, 477 (3d Cir. 1979). See also, State Department of Revenue v. Oliver, 636 P.2d 1156, 1163 n. 11 (Alaska 1981) ("blanket refusal" to produce not

sufficient to invoke privilege; *Fisher* requires a showing of a substantial and real hazard from production).

14. See § 125 supra.

15. See State v. Alexander, 281 N.W.2d 349 (Minn. 1979) (subpoena to produce film for showing to determine whether it was obscene, in absence of grant of immunity, not enforceable, because it would constitute an admission of custody or control of film).

16. In Matter of Grand Jury Subpoena Duces Tecum, 466 F.Supp. 325 (S.D.N.Y.1979) the subpoena called for records concerning money transferred to or from named other persons. At a hearing held on the respondent's objection to the subpoena, the government's responses to the judge's questions convinced the judge that the government was uncertain as to whether any such records existed. Quashing the subpoena, the court relied upon the tacit acknowledgement concerning the existence of the records that would be made by compliance and the danger of incrimination in such an acknowledgement.

dertaking. In other situations where the risk of "implicit authentication" does not invoke the privilege, there seems to be no reasonable alternative but to apply standard Fifth Amendment analysis and to examine whether a sufficient risk of incrimination exists given the testimonial contents of the respondent's act of complying under the circumstances. Availability to the government of use immunity as a means of avoiding any bars placed on compelled production, of course, mitigates the harshness of such an approach upon the government. Granting such immunity may create a burden of establishing the independent source of other evidence at trial, but given the risks posed by compelled production to the values protected by the privilege this burden is justified.

 WESTLAW REFERENCES

410k298

"duces tecum" /p privilege /p incrimin!

subpoen! /s document* "duces tecum" /p tax taxes taxpayer* /p incrimin!

document* "duces tecum" /p subpoen! /p authent! /p defendant* accused respondent* witness!

fisher /15 425 /5 391

di authentication

§ 127

1. See generally Bradley, Constitutional Protection for Private Papers, 16 Harv.C.R.–C.L.L.Rev. 461 (1981); Gerstein, The Demise of *Boyd*: Self-Incrimination and Private Papers in the Burger Court, 27 UCLA L.Rev. 343 (1979); McKenna, The Constitutional Protection of Private Papers: The Role of a Hierarchical Fourth Amendment, 53 Ind.L.J. 55 (1977–78).

2. E.g., Frankfurter, J., in Davis v. United States, 328 U.S. 582, 595 (1946), observed that "private papers of an accused cannot be seized even through legal process because their use would violate the prohibition of the Fifth Amendment against self-incrimination." See also Brock v. United States, 223 F.2d 681, 686 (5th Cir. 1955) ("Private papers of evidentiary value alone are not admissible in evidence as against the Fifth Amendment, even where the Fourth Amendment has not been violated."); Westside Ford v. United States, 206 F.2d 627, 633, n. 3 (9th Cir. 1953) ("where the documents are relevant to an inquiry conducted for a lawfully authorized purpose . . . the Fourth Amendment is no bar to their inspection, whether they be of a quasi-public character or purely private. In such a case, the only valid ground of objection is the self-incrimination privilege . . . "); People v. Ellis, 65 Cal.2d 529, 535, 55 Cal.Rptr. 385, 388, 421 P.2d 393, 396 (1966) ("A related

§ 127. The Privilege as Related to Documents and Tangible Items: (b) Limits on Seizure and Use of "Private Papers": "Mere Evidence"[1]

Support has been advanced in the cases for the view that some limitation upon the right of the state to seize and use private documents of an accused arises from the privilege against self-incrimination, taken either alone [2] or in conjunction with other constitutional provisions.[3] This view was generally expressed in connection with discussion of the "mere evidence" rule, to the effect that items solely of "evidential" value were exempt from seizure and use in evidence.[4] The exemption did not extend to the instrumentalities or the fruits of the crime, nor did it extend to contraband. Enforcement of the rule was most enthusiastic when the item involved was a personal document, such as a diary.[5] Beyond that, application became uncertain and difficult.[6] For example, what might be mere evidence in one situation could be an instrumentality in another.[7] The most important objection to

view of the individual interests protected by the privilege focuses on the right of privacy . . . . The Fifth Amendment right of privacy protects at least uncommunicated thoughts and has been extended to preclude compelled production of private papers and documents.").

3. Usually the Fourth Amendment is the other provision invoked. Boyd v. United States, 116 U.S. 616 (1886); Gouled v. United States, 255 U.S. 298, 309 (1921).

4. See generally Shellow, The Continued Vitality of the Gouled Rule: The Search For and Seizure of Evidence, 48 Marq.L.Rev. 172 (1964); Note, 54 Geo.L.J. 593 (1966); Comment, 20 U.Chi.L.Rev. 319 (1953).

5. See, e.g., United States v. Stern, 225 F.Supp. 187 (S.D.N.Y.1964) (personal diary improperly seized).

6. Shellow, supra note 4, at 179, suggests that "while the courts speak in broad terms of evidentiary materials being immune from seizure, the rule is applied only to private documents."

7. Compare Matthews v. Correa, 135 F.2d 534 (2d Cir. 1943) (address book a fruit of the crime of concealing certain property from the trustee in bankruptcy) with United States v. Lerner, 100 F.Supp. 765 (N.D.Cal. 1951) (address book merely evidence of crime of har-

the "mere evidence" rule, however, was the inappropriateness of its reliance on the Fifth Amendment. Since, as pointed out elsewhere,[8] the Fifth Amendment applies only in those situations in which coercion might be applied for the purpose of compelling the subject to do something in response, the values here—and which the privilege resolves, rightly or wrongly—are significantly different from the values involved in determining whether once an individual has done something, such as transcribing his thoughts on paper, he should be entitled to preserve that past act free from official scrutiny. His initial activity may or may not have been testimonial, depending upon whether he intended that the transcription serve the function of communicating his thoughts to another individual, but in any event authorizing the use of such transcriptions would not encourage police to exert the types of coercion that the privilege historically protected against, because by definition these transcriptions would have been made before the opportunity for coercion existed.

In Warden, Maryland Penitentiary v. Hayden,[9] the Supreme Court announced its abandonment of the mere evidence rule. The language of the Court, however, left open the question "whether there are items of evidential value whose very nature precludes them from being the object of a reasonable search and seizure."[10] The rationale for the Court's recent holdings that the Fifth Amendment provide no protection against

the use of properly obtained self-incriminating business records[11] also suggests that the private nature of documents obtained and used in ways otherwise not violating the privilege is of no significance. Yet in both major cases the Court appeared careful to limit its discussion to *business* papers.[12] One court[13] has recently held that the privacy interests recognized in early Fifth Amendment discussions are still protected by the privilege and therefore pocket-sized appointment books, generally carried by the subject on his person, and containing entries made by the subject and apparently not disclosed to others, were protected by still-viable privacy aspects of the Fifth Amendment. A subpoena for the books therefore could not be enforced.

On balance, the privilege against compelled self-incrimination is a poor vehicle for extending to private papers any protection they might deserve. Given recent developments concerning the privilege, especially the reduced protection against compelled production of business documents, the privilege contains little of value in determining what documents to protect and how to protect them. Further, even if some such documents should be protected, it may well be that the protection should not be absolute, that is, there should not be a total bar to access to them. If special protection is to be afforded such papers but the government is to be permitted access to them under what are perhaps especially important circum-

boring a fugitive). The underlying problem was the absence of clear definitions of the various categories, i.e., contraband, fruits, and instrumentalities. See Note, supra, n. 4, at 606–621; Comment, supra n. 4, at 320–22.

8. See § 125 supra.

9. 387 U.S. 294 (1967).

10. Id. at 303.

11. See § 126 supra.

12. Andresen v. Maryland, 427 U.S. 463, 472 (1976) ("We do not agree . . . that [the] broad statements [in earlier cases] compel suppression of this petitioner's *business* records as a violation of the Fifth Amendment."); Fisher v. United States, 425 U.S. 391, 414 (1976) ("Whether the Fifth Amendment would shield the taxpayer from producing his own tax records in his

possession is a question not involved here; for the papers demanded here are not his '*private papers*,' . . . .") (emphasis supplied).

13. In re Grand Jury Proceedings, 632 F.2d 1033 (3d Cir. 1980). The court acknowledged the belief by others that the privacy aspects of the Fifth Amendment are in demise, but explicitly rejected this approach. Id., at 1044 n. 23. In Matter of Grand Jury Empaneled March 19, 1980, 680 F.2d 327, 334 (3d Cir. 1982), cert. granted 103 S.Ct. 1890, the court held that the Fifth Amendment's protection of personal records also extended to records used in a business operated as a sole proprietorship. See also, United States v. Miller, 660 F.2d 563, 567 (5th Cir. 1981), modified 675 F.2d 711 (5th Cir.), vacated as moot 685 F.2d 123 (despite *Fisher, Boyd* is alive).

stances, the Fourth Amendment's requirement that searches for and of papers and seizures of them be "reasonable" would be a more appropriate vehicle for the development of protection.

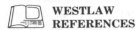

**WESTLAW
REFERENCES**

record* document* paper* /s private personal /p
   incrimin! /p seiz!
hayden /15 387 /5 294 & date(after 1979)
business! /s record* paper* file* document* /p seiz!
   /p incrimin!

§ 128. The Privilege as Related to Corporations, Associations, and Their Agents: (a) The Privilege of the Organization [1]

Although at common law only a natural person could be convicted of a crime, it is now clear that corporations and sometimes even unincorporated entities can be criminally liable by virtue of acts performed by an agent of the organization.[2] It has also been held that a subpoena *duces tecum* may be directed to a corporation itself rather than to the officers or agents of the organization,[3] although it is obvious that compliance will have to be accomplished through the actions of the organization's agents. May an organization, or the organization's agents on its behalf, decline to "testify" or to produce items because of the danger that such action will incriminate the organization?

The proposition that a corporation was protected against self-incrimination was rejected by the Supreme Court in Hale v. Henkel.[4] To some extent, this result seems to have been reached in reliance upon the perceived personal nature of the privilege and the inability of any person, even an officer

or agent of the corporation, to invoke any such privilege the organization may have.[5] But more substantively the Court reasoned that a corporation, as a creature of the state, has only those rights and privileges conferred by law. Generally, a state in authorizing a corporation to be formed reserves the right of visitation, that is, the right to inspect the corporation's books and records, to assure that the entity is not abusing its powers.[6] The rights of a corporation, then, virtually by definition do not include the right to avoid compulsory self-incrimination. It has been assumed that if a corporation has no privilege, other organizations do not as well.[7] As Justice Marshall commented in Bellis v. United States, "no artificial organization may utilize the personal privilege against compulsory self-incrimination."[8]

This result seems generally consistent with the policies on which the privilege is based. To the extent that the privilege rests upon the need to avoid depreciating and intrusive pressures to engage in conduct inconsistent with one's dignity as a human being, of course, a nonhuman entity cannot suffer the harm against which the privilege is designed to protect. Moreover, as the Court emphasized in Hale v. Henkel, corporations (and other organizations) wield a great deal of power in society. Permitting these units to resist inquiry by affording them the same privilege as a natural person would greatly frustrate government's ability to carry out many legitimate and important tasks.[9] To the extent that the policies supporting the privilege suggest its application to associations, there are probably more weighty countervailing considerations.

---

§ 128

1. See generally, 8 Wigmore, Evidence §§ 2259a, 2259b (McNaughton rev. 1961); Note 112 Pa.L.Rev. 394 (1964); 81 Am.Jur.2d Witnesses § 33; C.J.S. Witnesses § 431; Dec.Digest Witnesses ⊕306.

2. LaFave & Scott, Criminal Law § 33 (1972).

3. Wilson v. United States, 221 U.S. 361, 374–375 (1911).

4. 201 U.S. 43 (1906).

5. Id. at 69–70.

6. Id. at 74–75.

7. United States v. White, 322 U.S. 694 (1944) (assuming that labor union had no privilege which agent of union could assert).

8. Bellis v. United States, 417 U.S. 85, 90 (1974) (small law partnership). See text infra at § 129, n. 10.

9. Hale v. Henkel, 201 U.S. 43, 74 (1906). See also Bellis v. United States, 417 U.S. 85, 90 (1974); United States v. White, 322 U.S. 694, 700 (1944).

WESTLAW REFERENCES

§ 129. The Privilege as Related to Corporations, Associations, and Their Agents: (b) Availability of the Privilege to Agents [1]

If a witness who is an agent of an organization may not refuse to testify or produce items on the ground that to do so would incriminate the organization, may a refusal be based upon his perceived risk of his own incrimination? May, for example, an officer of a corporation decline to produce the corporation's documents in response to a subpoena *duces tecum* on the ground that the documents or their production will tend to incriminate him personally?[2] This was answered in the negative by the Supreme Court in Wilson v. United States.[3] Corporate records, the Court reasoned, are analogous to public records and maintained subject to the right of the state to inspect them. A corporate agent, then, by voluntarily accepting custody of the corporation's records will be held also to have accepted the obligation to produce them upon demand. This holds true even if the officer's production results in increasing the risk of personal incrimination. To this extent, the agent of an organization loses the protection that the privilege would otherwise afford him personally. This holding rests not upon a conscious and intentional waiver of the privilege

by the corporate officer but rather upon the policy decision that the privilege must be regarded as inapplicable in this situation, without regard to the intent of the officer. The duty to produce an organization's records may outlive the organization. Thus one who was the agent of a now-defunct organization but still retains the organization's records must produce them regardless of the self-incriminatory effects of such action.[4]

The extent to which an agent of an association may be required to do more than physically produce records of the association is unclear. In Wilson v. United States the Court commented that such agents "may decline to utter upon the witness stand a single self-incriminating word."[5] But a line of lower court cases stands for the proposition that a corporate officer who can be compelled to produce corporate documents may also be required, by oral testimony, to identify them even if this increases the risk of his personal criminal liability.[6] In Curcio v. United States[7] the Supreme Court, without specifically passing on the issue, indicated that this testimony may merely make explicit what is implicit in the production of the documents themselves and therefore subject the officer "to little, if any, further danger of incrimination." Though such testimony may be compelled, little more can be demanded. In *Curcio*, the witness, an agent of a labor union, was subpoenaed to produce certain union records. He testified that the records had been prepared but that they were not then in his possession. When asked about the whereabouts or possession of the records, he invoked his privilege.

§ 129

1. See generally, 8 Wigmore, Evidence (McNaughton rev.), § 2259b; 8 Am.Jur.2d Witnesses §§ 47–48.

2. Given the recent restriction of the privilege in regard to the compulsory production of documents, see § 126 supra, the danger that the documents or their production will create a significant risk of testimonial incrimination may often be absent.

3. 221 U.S. 361 (1911). See also Essgee Co. v. United States, 262 U.S. 151 (1923).

4. Wheeler v. United States, 226 U.S. 478 (1913); Grant v. United States, 227 U.S. 74 (1913).

5. 221 U.S. at 385.

6. The leading case is United States v. Austin-Bagley Corp., 31 F.2d 229 (2d Cir. 1929), cert. denied 279 U.S. 863. For other cases, see Curcio v. United States, 354 U.S. 118, 125 n. 3 (1957). *Austin-Bagley Corp.* has been held to have current vitality. Apache Corp. v. McKeen, 529 F.Supp. 459, 462 (W.D.N.Y., 1982); In re Agan, 498 F.Supp. 493, 495–496 (N.D.Ga.1980).

7. 354 U.S. 118 (1957).

Holding that the witness could not be compelled to answer these questions, the Court rejected the Government's argument that an agent of an organization has no privilege concerning the whereabouts of the organization's books and records. Unlike questions asking only for an identification of documents already produced by the witness, questions of the sort at issue pose a significant risk of personal incrimination. Nothing in the witness' action in becoming an agent of the organization requires that he be deprived of this aspect of Fifth Amendment protection.

It is clear from the early cases, then, that by associating with a corporation and assuming control over the corporation's documents, a person loses the right to invoke the privilege in regard to the production of those documents. It is also clear that one doing business as a sole proprietorship retains the protection he would otherwise have. If he is entitled as a private person to resist production of documents on the basis of his privilege, he may continue to do so despite the fact that the documents sought concern his business endeavors.[8]

To what extent, however, does one lose the protection of the privilege by joining a nonincorporated association and accepting possession of documents or records related to the business of that association?

In United States v. White [9] the Supreme Court made clear that the rule extended beyond corporations and held that one who had accepted the records of a labor union as an agent of that union had no right under the privilege to resist a demand for the production of the union's records. The same rule was applied to one of three partners in a law firm by Bellis v. United States.[10] *Bellis* also attempted to clarify the standard for determining what nonincorporated associations, if joined by an individual, might lead to loss of the individual's protection of the privilege. One who holds organizational records as the representative of an unincorporated association, the Court reasoned, loses the privilege in regard to the production of those records if the organization

"is recognized as an independent entity apart from its individual members. The group must be relatively well organized and structured, and not merely a loose, informal association of individuals. It must maintain a distinct set of organizational records, and recognize rights in its members of control and access to them. . . . In other words, it must be fair to say that the records demanded are the records of the organization rather than those of the individual . . . ." [11]

---

8. See I.C.C. v. Gould, 629 F.2d 847 (3d Cir. 1980). In Matter of Grand Jury Empanelled March 19, 1980, 680 F.2d 327, 330 (3d Cir. 1982), cert. granted 103 S.Ct. 1890, the Government argued that it is anomalous that a corporation or partnership, no matter how small or personal, enjoys no Fifth Amendment rights, while a sole proprietorship, no matter how large and impersonal, is shielded by the privilege of the proprietor. While characterizing the argument as having "considerable analytic appeal," the court found it contrary to current law.

The extent to which the privilege permits a private person to resist production of documents remains somewhat unclear; see §§ 126–127 supra. To the extent that the cases discussed in § 126 have reduced the protection provided by the privilege against compelled production of documents, this reduction in coverage obviously applies to situations in which the person holds the documents as a sole proprietor of a business endeavor. Where the documents are used for business purposes, of course, the argument that their "personal" nature protects the person from compelled disclosure, see § 127 supra, is quite weak, even if the privi-

lege does protect against compelled production of some purely personal documents. If the documents are used for purposes of a highly regulated business endeavor, compelled production may be permissible under the "required records" doctrine; see § 142 infra.

Given the informality of many small business ventures, the capacity in which a person holds documents may present a complicated factual question. In In re Oswalt, 607 F.2d 645 (5th Cir. 1979), for example, the court concluded that "Wm. Maxwell Construction Company" involved both a corporation and sole proprietorship and that the two were separate entities. Further, the sole activity of the corporation had been to borrow money for use by the sole proprietorship. Consequently, records relating to the construction business were determined to have been held by the witness in his capacity as a sole proprietor rather than as an agent of the corporation and he could invoke his privilege in response to a demand that he produce them.

9.   322 U.S. 694 (1944).

10.   417 U.S. 85 (1974).

11.   Id. at 92–93.

The partnership in *Bellis* had three partners and six employees. Despite its "modest size," the Court concluded it met the standard. It was not merely temporary, but in fact had lasted fifteen years. While it may not have had a formal constitution or by-laws, state partnership law imposed a certain organizational structure on the firm and permitted it to be sued and to hold title to property. The firm maintained a bank account in the firm name, filed partnership tax returns and "in general, held itself out to third parties as an entity with an independent institutional identity." Consequently, the subpoenaed partner had no right under the privilege, despite the risk of personal incrimination, to refuse production of partnership records. The Court observed, however, that a different result might have been reached if the case had involved "a small family partnership" or there had been some relationship of confidentiality among the partners existing before formation of the association.[12]

Following *Bellis*, the lower courts have tended to find most business organizations sufficient to destroy the privilege in regard to those who retain access to the organizations' records. Thus the risk of personal incrimination has been held no bar to the compelled production of records of a small family trust from the trustee[13] and of the records of a business formed by the tenants in common of certain realty for purposes of conducting business related to that realty.[14] The records of professional corporations have been held subject to compelled production, even where these corporations are not

given all of the characteristics of a corporation by state law and where state law purports to preserve the professional relationship between the "employees" of the professional corporation and their clients or patients.[15] In one unusual case, a lawyer was permitted to assert his personal privilege in regard to records relating to his law practice, despite evidence that the lawyer and his brother had held themselves out to clients and the public as a partnership for nine years. The court stressed, however, that no partnership tax return had been filed, there were no jointly-held property or records, no profit-sharing arrangements had been made, the two lawyers kept separate bank accounts, and the office space had been rented by the lawyer in his apparently individual capacity.[16]

Even if the organization is an "independent entity" within the meaning of that term in *Bellis*, an agent of the organization loses his privilege only in regard to those records which he holds in a representative capacity.[17] Put another way, it is clear that one who acts as an agent of an organization retains his privilege in regard to personal records or documents. Whether particular documents or records are personal or are rather organizational records held in a representative capacity can present a difficult problem. In *Bellis*, the Court concluded that the records sought in that case, financial books and records of the law firm, were partnership documents held by the witness in a representative capacity. Among the relevant considerations were the extent to which the records dealt with organizational as opposed

12. Id. at 101.

13. United States v. Harrison, 653 F.2d 359 (8th Cir. 1981). The court noted that the trust filed income tax returns and was a legal entity under state law.

14. In re Grand Jury Proceedings, 576 F.2d 703 (6th Cir. 1978), cert. denied 439 U.S. 830. Although it emphasized that the organization was not a partnership under the state law, the court further concluded that the activities of the organization—titled, "G & S Investments"—were not wholly those of the subpoenaed tenant himself.

15. E.g., United States v. Radetsky, 535 F.2d 556, 568–569 (10th Cir. 1976), cert. denied 429 U.S. 820;

Reamer v. Beall, 506 F.2d 1345 (4th Cir. 1974), cert. denied 420 U.S. 955 (physician-witness was sole stockholder and sole professional employee of corporation); In re Jellen, 521 F.Supp. 251 (N.D.W.Va.1981); In re Zisook, 88 Ill.2d 321, 58 Ill.Dec. 786, 430 N.E.2d 1037 (1981) (attorney practicing as a professional corporation).

16. Matter of Special Grand Jury No. 1, 465 F.Supp. 800 (D.Md.1978).

17. Bellis v. United States, 417 U.S. 85, 98–100 (1974).

to personal matters, the nature of the witness' ownership interests in the records, the extent to which other members of the organization had actual access or the right of access to the records, and any right the witness had to use the records for personal, i.e., nonorganizational, purposes. The records sought in *Bellis* dealt exclusively with firm business, the witness' sole ownership interest was created by his status as a partner in the organization, other members of the firm had a legal right of access to the records and had previously had actual custody of some of them, and the witness had no right to use them for nonpartnership purposes. Other situations may be more problematic. In one recent case, a grand jury subpoena sought to compel the witness, an assistant treasurer for a corporation, to produce a desk calendar and a pocket calendar. Both contained entries relating to corporation business matters; the pocket calendar was also used by the witness for notes concerning personal matters such as physicians' appointments. Reasoning in part that the corporation provided the desk unit but not the pocket calendar and that another corporation employee, the witness' secretary, had access to the desk calendar but not the pocket calendar, the court held that the pocket calendar was possessed by the witness in a personal capacity while the desk unit was possessed by him in his capacity as a corporate agent. He could assert his personal privilege, then, to bar compelled production of only the pocket calendar.[18]

WESTLAW REFERENCES

410K298

witness! /p officer* agent* represent! /s organization* corporation* association* compan! /p testif! testimon! document* record* file* paper* "duces tecum" item* / p incrimin!

control! posses! /s record* paper* document* file* /s compan! corporation* organization* association* /p incrimin!

white /15 322 /5 694

bellis /15 417 /5 85

§ 130. The Privilege of an Accused in a Criminal Proceeding: (a) Definition of an Accused in a Criminal Proceeding [1]

The privilege confers a significantly different right upon one who is the accused in a criminal proceeding as compared to one who is simply a witness in a criminal or other proceeding. Basically, the right of an accused is the right not only to avoid giving incriminating responses to inquiries put to him but also to be free from the inquiries themselves. Thus the privilege of an accused allows him not only to refuse to respond to questions directed at his alleged participation in the offense but also entitles him not even to be called as a witness at his own trial.[2] Because of this significant difference in the application of the privilege to the two situations, it becomes important to define an accused in a criminal proceeding.

The traditional view has been that an individual does not become an accused until the criminal process has been formally brought to bear upon him. Thus at such proceedings as a grand jury investigation,[3] a coroner's in-

---

18. The trial judge had first overruled the witness' claim of the privilege in regard to both items and on appeal this determination was remanded for further consideration. Grand Jury Subpoena Duces Tecum v. United States, 657 F.2d 5 (2d Cir. 1981). In a nonexhaustive list of factors it regarded as relevant to the determination, the appellate court listed: "who prepared the document, the nature of its contents, its purpose or use, who maintained possession and who had access to it, whether the corporation required its preparation, and whether its existence was necessary to the conduct of the corporation's business." Id. at 8. On remand, the witness' claim of the privilege was sustained insofar as it related to the pocket calendar. 522 F.Supp. 977 (S.D.N.Y.1981).

§ 130

1. See generally C.J.S. Witnesses § 441.

2. United States v. Echeles, 352 F.2d 892 (7th Cir. 1965), cert. denied 382 U.S. 955 (one defendant may not call another defendant to stand); United States v. Housing Foundation of America, Inc., 176 F.2d 665 (3d Cir. 1949); 8 Wigmore, Evidence § 2268 (McNaughton rev. 1961).

3. See United States v. Winter, 348 F.2d 204, 207–208 (2d Cir. 1965) (and cases cited therein); United States v. Cleary, 265 F.2d 459 (2d Cir. 1959); United States v. Price, 163 F. 904 (S.D.N.Y.1908), affirmed 216 U.S. 488; Ex parte Barnes, 73 Tex.Cr.R. 583, 166 S.W. 728 (1914); In re Lemon, 15 Cal.App.2d 82, 59 P.2d 213 (1936). New York, however, has held that under the

quest,[4] and a preliminary hearing,[5] all theoretically designed to determine whether formal criminal processes should be invoked, no one has a right to refuse all cooperation in the inquiry.[6] The matter is often intertwined with related but separable questions, such as whether a witness in such a situation has been adequately informed of his right to decline to answer if that answer would tend to incriminate [7] and whether he has a right to counsel under the circumstances.[8]

The basis for the traditional position was somewhat shaken by the Supreme Court's decisions culminating in Miranda v. Arizona.[9] Under the rules announced in *Miranda*, if the subject of custodial interrogation indicates "in any manner" that he wishes to remain silent, the interrogation must cease.[10] If the subject's attorney is present, however, the Court noted that "there may be some circumstances in which further questioning would be permissible," apparently those in

which it could be ascertained that any incriminating responses elicited were free of any compulsion and constituted a free and voluntary waiver of the privilege.[11] Thus a suspect has at least a limited right to be free from interrogation even before the formal criminal process has been put into operation.

The extent to which a person who is the subject of investigatory procedures—most importantly the grand jury—is to be accorded the privilege of an accused depends in large part upon which function of the privilege of an accused is emphasized. In part, an accused is spared the necessity of having to submit at trial to questions and to invoke the privilege in regard to each in order to avoid emphasizing to the trier of fact the invocation of the privilege. This minimizes the possibility that an adverse inference will be drawn from the invocation of the privilege. If this function is emphasized, the privilege should not apply to grand jury and similar proceedings. Since guilt is not at is-

state constitutional privilege a prospective defendant or one who is "a target of an investigation" has a right not to be examined before a grand jury. If he is called before the grand jury, he is entitled to the dismissal of any resulting indictment. People v. Laino, 10 N.Y.2d 161, 218 N.Y.S.2d 647, 176 N.E.2d 571 (1961), appeal dismissed and cert. denied 374 U.S. 104; People v. Steuding, 6 N.Y.2d 214, 189 N.Y.S.2d 166, 160 N.E.2d 468 (1959).

4. In Dykes v. State, 232 Miss. 379, 99 So.2d 602 (1957), the accused had testified before a coroner's inquest. The trial court did not admit this testimony at trial but also denied the defendant's plea of complete immunity. The Mississippi Supreme Court held that the testimony before the inquest was voluntary and that the accused had apparently waived his limited right to decline to answer specific questions.

5. The constitutional position of a prisoner at a preliminary hearing is not clear. Most states specifically confer at least a limited right not to be called, either by statute or practice. E.g., West's Ann.Cal.Penal Code § 866.5 (1970) ("The defendant may not be examined at the examination, unless he is represented by counsel, or unless he waives his right to counsel after being advised at such examination of his right to aid counsel.") See generally Kauper, Judicial Examination of the Accused—A Remedy for the Third Degree, 30 Mich.L. Rev. 1224, 1236–38 (1931). There is a lack of case law on the role played by the privilege in this situation. See Wood v. United States, 75 U.S.App.D.C. 274, 128 F.2d 265, 270–271 (1942) ("The court has the power to examine the accused and others. . . . It cannot be . . . that the court's power to examine the accused,

though conferred by statute, means authority to compel him to answer . . . "); State v. Zappia, 8 Ariz. App. 549, 448 P.2d 119 (1968) (right at preliminary to decline to take stand one of statutory origin). See generally Annot., 38 A.L.R.2d 225, 237; People v. Jackson, 23 Ill.2d 263, 178 N.E.2d 310 (1961) (apparently approving of calling the accused to the stand at the preliminary hearing but insisting that he be adequately informed of his right to refuse to respond to incriminating questions).

6. This was the view taken in the first edition of this text. McCormick, Evidence § 122, pp. 258–59 n. 67 (1954). Cf. Annot., 5 A.L.R.2d 1404, 1425 (admissibility of statement or testimony of accused at preliminary hearing).

In Garner v. United States, 424 U.S. 648 (1976), the Supreme Court used the term "witness" in the self-incrimination context and defined it as meaning "one who, at the time disclosures are sought from him, is not a defendant in a criminal proceeding." As examples, the Court mentioned persons called to testify in civil or criminal litigation or before a legislative or administrative body possessing subpoena power, persons filing tax returns required by law, and individuals giving testimony before a grand jury. 424 U.S. at 652 n. 7.

7. See §§ 137, 153 infra.

8. Id.

9. 384 U.S. 436 (1966).

10. Id. at 444–445.

11. Id. at 474 n. 44.

sue, there is no danger that requiring the subject specifically to invoke the privilege in response to particular questions will lead to inferring guilt from his invocation of the privilege. But, on the other hand, an accused is undoubtedly also accorded the prerogative of declining to submit to interrogation to remove any vestiges of—and any incentive for—the abuses of interrogation against which the privilege has historically protected those who invoke it. The opportunity to interrogate, of course, also creates an incentive to make maximum use of that opportunity by techniques which may approach coercion or trickery. An accused subjected to such interrogation may well lose the ability intelligently to invoke the privilege that is essential to its effective operation. If this function of the privilege is emphasized, the privilege of an accused should be extended to the subject of grand jury and similar investigatory proceedings.[12]

Against these dangers to the interests protected by the privilege must be weighed the interests of the public in the efficient conduct of investigations. To extend the privilege of an accused to the subjects of the proceedings preliminary to formal trial may severely limit the effectiveness of these proceedings in accomplishing their investigatory and screening functions. Moreover, it may not be necessary to expand the privilege to this extent to achieve the desired objectives. It is arguable that if the right to counsel was clearly extended to those appearing in investigatory procedures and the subjects' right to be fully apprised of their rights and the factual situation was made clear, their rights would be sufficiently protected without undue infringement upon

public interests by extending to them only the privilege of a witness.

A distinction can probably be drawn between those situations in which the objective is a general investigatory one and those in which it is merely the accumulation of evidence to convict one whose prosecution has already been decided upon. In regard to the former, reliance upon the right of counsel and the privilege as accorded a witness represents the most appropriate balance of the conflicting values. As to the latter, the situation seems sufficiently akin to the formal trial itself to require that the subject be accorded the privilege of an accused, that is, the right to decline to be subjected to formal interrogation at all. Under some circumstances, coroner's inquests, police investigations, and grand jury proceedings would come within the former. Under other circumstances —when the decision to prosecute had already been made, for example—these same proceedings would come within the latter category. The preliminary examination, however, would almost inevitably come within the latter, and in these proceedings the subject should therefore be extended the accused's privilege to decline to be subjected to formal questioning.

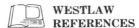

WESTLAW REFERENCES

synopsis,digest(preliminar! /s proceeding* hearing* inquest* /p accused defendant* /p incrimin!)

110k366(4)

digest,synopsis(interrog! /p silen! /p incrimin!)

miranda /15 384 /5 436 & date(after 6/1/83)

---

12. People v. Laino, 10 N.Y.2d 161, 218 N.Y.S.2d 647, 176 N.E.2d 571 (1961), appeal dismissed and cert. denied 374 U.S. 104, provides a concrete example of the dangers involved in refusing to permit a witness called by the grand jury to decline to submit to interrogation. Laino had been called before a grand jury investigating official misconduct in the purchase by the city of supplies from him. At the outset, Laino made clear that

§ 131. The Privilege of an Accused in a Criminal Proceeding: (b) Comment on

he desired to invoke the privilege; it later became clear that his records and transactions revealed failure accurately to report earnings for tax purposes. Despite his obvious desire to invoke the privilege, however, he failed to do so for reasons not entirely clear; probably either he erroneously felt that he had been granted immunity, or he felt that he had already sufficiently invoked it.

Failure to Testify and Other Forms of "Coercion" [1]

Because the scope of the privilege is, once the subject is identified as an accused, apparently so clear, it might be anticipated that what constitutes coercion would not constitute a troublesome question. Yet this has not been the case. In Griffin v. California,[2] the Supreme Court held that the federal constitutional privilege was violated by a prosecutor's argument which urged and a jury instruction which authorized the jury to draw an inference of guilt from a defendant's failure to testify when his testimony could have reasonably been expected to deny or explain matters proved by the prosecution. This, the Court concluded, constituted a penalty for exercising the privilege and a remnant of the inquisitorial system of criminal justice which the privilege prohibits.[3] "What the jury may infer given no help from the court is one thing," noted the Court. "What they may infer when the court solemnizes the silence of the accused into evidence against him is quite another." [4]

Development of the *Griffin* holding that a criminal defendant may not be penalized for invoking the privilege has given rise to matters that can be divided into several categories: (a) a defendant's ability to attack a conviction on the ground that it is based in part at least upon his failure to testify; (b) the validity of procedural rules that place a defendant at a disadvantage because he has invoked his privilege and refused to testify; (c) the validity of presumptions that arguably burden the privilege; (d) instructions that must or should be given to juries concerning a defendant's right not to testify; and (e) comments or arguments by participants in the trial that serve to call attention to or burden a defendant's failure to testify in his own behalf.

Cases dealing with the category (a) affirm that the trier of fact must not draw an inference of guilt from the defendant's failure to testify. But no significant scrutiny of the trier of fact's decision-making process is available. In jury convictions, the rule that jurors may not impeach their own verdict by testifying to the mental processes by which they arrived at their verdict generally precludes inquiry into the matter.[5] In cases of conviction by the judge, the few cases find in the judge's offhand comments insufficient evidence that the judge attached enough weight to the defendant's failure to testify to warrant reversal.[6] The unwillingness of reviewing courts to scrutinize the mental processes of the trier of fact is probably justified as a general rule. But this refusal to permit defendants to inquire into possible

§ 131

1. See generally 8 Wigmore, Evidence § 2272 (McNaughton rev. 1961); Ayer, The Fifth Amendment and the Inference of Guilt from Silence: Griffin v. California After Fifteen Years, 78 Mich.L.Rev. 841 (1980); 21 Am.Jur.2d Criminal Law § 705; 21A Am.Jur.2d Criminal Law §§ 944–950; 81 Am.Jur.2d Witnesses § 37; C.J.S. Criminal Law § 993(c); Dec.Dig. Criminal Law ⚖656(7).

2. 380 U.S. 609 (1965). The decision invalidated a provision of the California constitution allowing comment. The great weight of authority in the states, by statute or decision, was already opposed to allowing comment. Id. at 611 n. 3.

3. Id. at 614.

4. Id. The Court had held in Wilson v. United States, 149 U.S. 60 (1893), that comment was improper in a federal trial, although the stated basis of the decision was statutory rather than constitutional.

5. See Cunningham v. United States, 356 F.2d 454 (5th Cir. 1966), cert. denied 384 U.S. 952 (trial court did not err in refusing to permit defense counsel to examine jurors on whether they considered defendant's failure to testify, because jurors will not be heard to impeach their own verdict). See § 68 supra. But see, Smith v. State, 530 S.W.2d 827, 829–830 (Tex.Cr.App. 1975) (evidence that jurors discussed and considered defendant's failure to testify established juror misconduct that required new trial).

6. In People v. Padilla, 240 Cal.App.2d 114, 49 Cal. Rptr. 340, 342 (1966), the trial judge commented, "There are five different factors that persuade me that the defendant should be found guilty. . . . In addition to all this, which is most convincing, I am impressed by the defendant not taking the stand and indicating that the matter [narcotics] is not his." See also Bowen v. State, 5 Md.App. 713, 249 A.2d 499, 502 (1969) (trial judge commented that had defendant taken the stand, "I might have been able to have elicited some information from you that might have persuaded me to have acquitted. . . . ").

consideration of the defendant's failure to testify is in contrast to the courts' frequent speculation as to the possible effects of comments by the trial judge and prosecutor upon the jury's consideration of the defendant's failure to testify in his defense.

Issues in category (b) relate to situations in which procedural rules arguably impose a disadvantage upon a defendant who exercises his Fifth Amendment privilege. In Simmons v. United States,[7] the Supreme Court held that testimony given by a defendant at a hearing on a motion to suppress evidence made on Fourth Amendment grounds could not be used against the defendant at trial. In part, the Court reasoned that permitting the use of the evidence would mean that a defendant who invoked his right to remain silent must thereby lose an important advantage in implementing his Fourth Amendment rights, that is, he would be unable to offer his own testimony in support of his Fourth Amendment claims. *Simmons* can be read, therefore, as invalidating at least some procedural rules that disadvantage one who invokes the privilege. But in McGautha v. California,[8] the Court rejected a similar argument directed against a unitary trial procedure in which a jury in a capital case considered both guilt or innocence and penalty at the same time. It was urged that *Simmons* invalidated such a procedure, because a defendant who invoked his right to silence on guilt-innocence thereby lost his right to testify personally on the important issue of penalty. In rejecting the proposition that this was an intolerable burden on

the exercise of the privilege, the Court construed *Simmons* as resting primarily upon defendants' Fourth Amendment interests. The "purely Fifth Amendment interests" involved, the Court concluded, were insubstantial.[9] As so limited, *Simmons* has little current significance as a Fifth Amendment case.

Category (c) of issues is raised by presumptions that arguably place an excessive burden upon the failure of the defendant to testify or at least call the attention of the jury to the defendant's decision. It seems clear, however, that if the inference is otherwise appropriate, instructing the jury concerning it will not violate the privilege. The Supreme Court found no impermissible pressure upon a defendant to testify in an instruction telling the jury it was permitted to infer knowledge that heroin was smuggled from the fact of possession of such heroin.[10] Later, in Barnes v. United States,[11] no Fifth Amendment defect was found in an instruction permitting the jury to infer knowledge that property was stolen from proof of possession of recently stolen property, not satisfactorily explained. This, like any evidence of guilt, increases the pressure upon the defendant to testify, the Court reasoned, but this is not impermissible. "The mere massing of evidence against a defendant cannot be regarded as a violation of his privilege against self-incrimination." [12]

Category (d) of issues concerns instructions that should or must be given in jury trials to implement the defendant's privilege.

---

7. 390 U.S. 377 (1968), on remand 395 F.2d 769 (7th Cir.), appeal after remand 424 F.2d 1235.

8. 402 U.S. 183 (1971), rehearing denied 406 U.S. 978.

9. Id. at 212. Without questioning the propriety of *Simmons'* result, the *McGautha* Court characterized the reasoning of *Simmons*, insofar as it involved both the Fifth and Fourth Amendments, as "open to question." Id.

10. Turner v. United States, 396 U.S. 398 (1970), rehearing denied 397 U.S. 958.

11. 412 U.S. 837 (1973).

12. Id., at 847. Reliance was placed on Yee Hem v. United States, 268 U.S. 178 (1925), upholding a statute

prohibiting concealment of opium imported after a specified date and, by means of a presumption, placing upon a defendant the burden of proving that opium was imported prior to that date. Rejecting the argument that this compelled defendants to testify, the Court emphasized that the statute did not require that proof be by the defendant's personal testimony. "If the accused happens to be the only repository of the facts necessary to negate the presumption arising from his possession, that is a misfortune which the statute under review does not create but which is inherent in the case." Id., at 185. For discussion of constitutionality of presumptions in criminal cases generally, see § 347 infra.

Griffin itself made clear, of course, that the jurors may not be told that they may draw from the defendant's failure to testify an inference of guilt. In Carter v. Kentucky,[13] the Court held that upon request the Fifth Amendment requires trial judges to instruct the jury that no inference may be drawn from a defendant's failure to testify. "No judge can prevent jurors from speculating about why a defendant stands mute in the face of a criminal accusation," the Court reasoned, "but a judge can, and must, if requested to do so, use the unique power of the jury instruction to reduce that speculation to a minimum." But in Lakeside v. Oregon,[14] the Court found no Fifth Amendment violation in a trial judge's giving such an instruction over the defendant's objection. *Griffin*, the Court reasoned, was concerned only with adverse comment. It rejected as "speculative" Lakeside's argument that the jurors might, in the absence of instructions, take no notice of his failure to testify, and if given cautionary instructions, might totally disregard those directives and draw an inference from the failure to testify. Sound policy may direct that a trial judge respect a defendant's desire that cautionary instructions not be given, the Court commented, and states remain free to prohibit cautionary instructions over defendants' objections as a matter of state law. This seems clearly desirable. How jurors respond to defendants' failure to testify and various instructions related to this remains a matter of speculation. Given that the decision must be based upon

speculation, it seems that defendants and their lawyers are entitled to have their own speculation determinative as to whether cautionary instructions are given.

The final category of issues presents the greatest difficulty. During the course of proceedings before a jury, the presiding judge and the lawyers sometimes make statements or arguments that, especially when considered with leisurely care, might be construed as relating to the defendant's failure to testify. When such comments or arguments violate *Griffin* is unclear. As a general matter, many courts take the position that a statement violates *Griffin* only if it was manifestly intended as a comment on the defendant's failure to testify or was such that the jury would naturally and necessarily take it as such a comment.[15] Others articulate what appears to be a broader criterion, under which a Fifth Amendment violation occurs if a comment is made that is "fairly susceptible" of being construed by the jury as referring to the defendant's failure to testify.[16] Whatever the general standard, violations have been found where the prosecutor gestured towards the defendant during final argument and asked, "Who else could have testified in this case?"[17] and where, again during final argument, the prosecutor stated he was leaving the jury with one question, the location of the defendant on the night of the offense, and further, "that question was the question that was never answered by the defendant."[18] On the other hand, there is widespread

---

13. 450 U.S. 288 (1981).

14. 435 U.S. 333 (1978).

15. United States v. Haynes, 573 F.2d 236, 239 (5th Cir. 1978), cert. denied 439 U.S. 850; Brown v. United States, 383 A.2d 1082, 1085 (D.C.App.1978). Some courts use only one prong of this test, apparently focusing upon the likely effect of the comment rather than upon the intent with which it was made. E.g., Deutscher v. State, 95 Nev. 669, 601 P.2d 407, 416 (1979).

16. David v. State, 369 So.2d 943, 944 (Fla.1979). Cf. Commonwealth v. Goulet, 374 Mass. 404, 372 N.E.2d 1288 (1978) (violation occurs if remark can be "fairly understood" as permitting jury to draw adverse inference from the defendant's failure to testify).

17. Eberhardt v. Bordenkircher, 605 F.2d 275, 278 (6th Cir. 1979).

18. State v. Cannon, 118 Ariz. 273, 576 P.2d 132 (1978). See also, United States v. Parker, 549 F.2d 1217 (9th Cir. 1977), cert. denied 430 U.S. 971 (after defendant exhibited capped tooth to jury and government witnesses acknowledged they did not observe the perpetrators of the robbery at issue with such a tooth, prosecutor improperly argued to jury that defendant "didn't tell us" whether tooth had been capped before or after date of robbery); Adams v. State, 263 Ark. 536, 566 S.W.2d 387 (1978) (prosecutor improperly argued to jury, "How many witnesses did the defense put on for your consideration?"); State v. Libby, 410 A.2d 562 (Me.1980), appeal after remand 435 A.2d 1075 (after reminding jury of state's evidence that gun

agreement that the prosecution can comment on the failure of the defense to produce any evidence without violating *Griffin*.[19] Moreover, it is permissible as a general matter for the prosecution to argue that particular evidence is uncontradicted, although *Griffin* may be violated by such an argument if it appears that the jury would most likely conclude that the natural source of contradictory evidence would have been the defendant's personal testimony.[20]

It has been suggested reasonably that comments by the judge are more likely to influence the jury than comments and argument by the prosecutor and therefore require greater scrutiny under *Griffin*.[21] But offhand references, even by the judge, to the defendant's failure to testify made in the

course of rulings and discussion may well not violate the privilege. Thus when a trial judge, while ruling on questions raised during defense counsel's cross-examination of a government witness, commented, "If you want to put [the defendant] on the stand, that is a different matter," and upon request instructed the jury to disregard the remark, no violation was found.[22] As this case indicated, instructions to disregard the remark and to give no consideration to the defendant's failure to testify may cure at least nonegregious improper comments. Further, in some circumstances and especially where the evidence of guilt is overwhelming and uncontradicted, even a clearly improper comment can be harmless error.[23]

owned by defendant Libby was found at scene of crime prosecutor improperly argued, "I think you are entitled to hear from [the defendants], or at least Mr. Libby's counsel, how that could occur."); State v. Eaton, 569 P.2d 1114 (Utah 1977) (in drug sale case, prosecutor improperly argued that only the state witness who allegedly purchased drugs and the defendant knew what took place and asked, "What does the defendant tell us?").

19. United States v. Bright, 630 F.2d 804, 825 (5th Cir. 1980) (emphasizing the need to put argument in terms of the *defense*—as opposed to the *defendant*—failing to produce evidence); State v. Stanfield, 292 N.C. 357, 233 S.E.2d 574, 581 (1977); State v. Livingston, 607 S.W.2d 489, 492 (Tenn.Cr.App.1980). In United States v. Gainey, 380 U.S. 63 (1965), the jury was told that proof of the defendant's presence at the site of an illegal still could be sufficient to prove guilt of illegal possession of a still and of carrying on illegal business of a distillery, "unless the defendant by the evidence in the case and by proven facts and circumstances explains such presence to the satisfaction of the jury." This was held—before *Griffin*—not to constitute a comment on the defendant's failure to testify. Id., at 70–71.

20. United States v. Sorzano, 602 F.2d 1201, 1202 (5th Cir. 1979), cert. denied 444 U.S. 1018; White v. State, 377 So.2d 1149, 1150 (Fla.1979), cert. denied 449 U.S. 845. See Todd v. State, 598 S.W.2d 286, 294–295 (Tex.Cr.App.1980), reviewing cases from that jurisdiction finding that in the context the comments too directly referred to the defendant's failure to contradict the state's evidence by personal testimony. Robinson v. State, 352 So.2d 11 (Ala.Cr.App.), cert. denied 352 So. 2d 15 (Ala.) illustrate an improper comment. The state had called two witnesses who testified that the defendant had driven—alone—up and down a road near the location of the offense. The prosecutor's comment that the defense had produced no evidence as to why he had so driven was held improper given that the de-

fendant himself was apparently the only person who could have given such an explanation. There is some variation among the lower courts as to permissibility of comments of this sort. Compare People v. Garcia, 95 Ill.App.3d 792, 51 Ill.Dec. 68, 420 N.E.2d 482 (1981) (comment is permissible even where defendant is only person who could refute state's evidence, if comment is not intended or calculated to direct jury's attention to defendant's failure to testify) with Dooley v. State, 271 Ind. 404, 393 N.E.2d 154, 155 (1979) (comment on absence of testimony that defendant is innocent is error unless it affirmatively appears that there are witnesses other than the defendant who could have testified to his innocence). See generally, United States v. Sanders, 547 F.2d 1037, 1041–1043 (8th Cir. 1976), cert. denied 431 U.S. 956, cautioning against argument that government's evidence is "undenied" and indicating that such arguments are risky and call into play "more searching review" than other arguments. In Lockett v. Ohio, 438 U.S. 586 (1978), no *Griffin* violation was found in the prosecutor's reference to the state's evidence as "unrefuted" and "uncontradicted," where defense counsel had outlined an anticipated defense and had expressed before the jury the anticipation that the defendant would testify. Id. at 595.

21. Commonwealth v. Goulet, 374 Mass. 404, 372 N.E.2d 1288 (1978).

22. United States v. Haynes, 573 F.2d 236 (5th Cir. 1978), cert. denied 439 U.S. 850.

23. Brown v. United States, 383 A.2d 1082, 1085 (D.C.App.1978); Deutscher v. State, 95 Nev. 669, 601 P.2d 407, 416 (1979).

Special comment problems are sometimes created when fewer than all defendants being jointly tried waive the privilege and testify. May counsel for a testifying defendant during argument call the jury's attention to the failure of another defendant to testify and perhaps contrast this with his own client's willingness to take the witness stand? de Luna v. United

---

§ 132. The Privilege of an Accused in a Criminal Proceeding: (c) Waiver of the Privilege by Voluntary Testimony [1]

Probably because of the absolute nature of the privilege of an accused, courts have been willing to find broad waivers of the privilege in the decisions of accused persons to testify in their own behalf. The Supreme Court has rejected the argument that an accused should, like an ordinary witness, be held to have waived the privilege only when testimony which was itself incriminating was given:

> "[The accused] has the choice, after weighing the advantages of the privilege against self-incrimination against the advantages of putting forward his version of the facts and his reliability as a witness, not to testify at all. He cannot reasonably claim that the Fifth Amendment gives him not only this choice but, if he elects to testify, an immunity from cross-examination on the matters he has himself put in dispute. It would make of the Fifth Amendment not only a humane safeguard against judicially coerced self-disclosure but a positive invitation to mutilate the truth a party offers to tell.[2] "

Although a few problems have arisen in defining the "testimony" of an accused that constitutes the waiver,[3] the major difficulties in applying this rule have involved defining the scope of the waiver resulting from testimony. Traditionally, many courts have taken the position that a defendant who

---

States, 308 F.2d 140 (5th Cir. 1962), rehearing denied 324 F.2d 375, held that on the facts of the case the tension between the right of the testifying defendant to all rational inferences from his co-defendant's failure to testify and the nontestifying defendant's right to avoid comment on his use of the privilege required separate trials. Id. at 155. Dictum suggests that the court regarded the comment made by counsel for the testifying defendant as an exercise of his client's right of confrontation. Id. at 143. *de Luna* has been held to have no application where counsel for the testifying defendant does not refer to the nontestifying defendant but merely emphasizes the significance the jury might give his client's willingness to testify. United States v. Berkowitz, 662 F.2d 1127, 1136–1137 (5th Cir. 1981). See also United States v. Anderson, 498 F.2d 1038, 1046 (D.C.Cir.1974), affirmed 422 U.S. 171. Several courts have limited *de Luna* to situations presenting extreme inconsistency between the defensive positions of the testifying and nontestifying defendants. Only where those positions are "truly antagonistic" does counsel for the testifying defendant have a "duty" to comment on the discrepancies between the defendants' approaches to invoking the privilege. Where no such "duty" to comment exists, the defendants can be tried jointly and counsel for the testifying defendant can be barred from commenting on the failure of the nontestifying defendant to waive the privilege. See United States v. Lemonakis, 485 F.2d 941, 952 (D.C.Cir. 1973), cert. denied 415 U.S. 989; State v. Gibbons, R.I. 418 A.2d 830 (1980).

§ 132

1. See generally 8 Wigmore, Evidence §§ 2276(b), 2277 (McNaughton rev. 1961); Carlson, Cross-Examina-

tion of the Accused, 52 Cornell L.Q. 705 (1967); 21 Am. Jur.2d Criminal Law § 710; 21A Am.Jur.2d Criminal Law §§ 941–42; C.J.S. Witnesses §§ 888, 889; Dec. Dig. Witnesses ⊶301, 305(2).

2. Brown v. United States, 356 U.S. 148, 155–56 (1958).

3. In *Brown*, the Court was careful to state that it was the testimony and not the action in taking the stand that constituted the waiver. Id. at 156–157. There is, however, some question as to what constitutes "testimony." In State v. Norris, 577 S.W.2d 941 (Mo.App.1979), defendant sought to try on a shoe which the prosecution's evidence showed had been found near the premises which the defendant was charged with burglarizing. He did not, however, want to become a witness. On appeal, the trial court's refusal to permit the defendant to try on the shoe without becoming a witness was held in error. After reviewing the sometimes conflicting cases, the court concluded that since the action in trying on the shoe would not be "testimonial," and since the prosecution could compel the defendant to do it without infringing the privilege, the defendant was entitled to do it himself without loss of the right to claim the privilege. See also, United States ex rel. Mitchell v. Pinto, 438 F.2d 814 (3d Cir. 1971), cert. denied 402 U.S. 961 (action of defendant in rising from his seat and standing next to a witness to demonstrate a resemblance was not "testimony"). The making of an unsworn statement by the accused before the jury, as allowed in some jurisdictions, does not justify cross-examination without his consent. Shoffeitt v. State, 107 Ga.App. 217, 129 S.E.2d 572 (1963).

chooses to testify becomes subject to cross-examination under the jurisdiction's applicable rules and waives the privilege to the extent necessary to permit such cross-examination.[4] Under this approach, a testifying defendant may not only be questioned concerning matters testified to on direct examination but in addition he may be subject to searching cross-examination for impeachment purposes.[5] Except with respect to impeachment, it is not a basis for restricting cross-examination that the response may be incriminating in regard to an offense other than the one for which the accused is presently being tried.[6] He may not only be compelled to respond to questions but he may also be forced to produce demonstrative evidence or documents.[7]

This approach, which defines the scope of waiver by the jurisdiction's rules concerning permissible cross-examination, is unfortunate. Some jurisdictions restrict cross-examination to matters testified to on direct examination, while a number of states apply the "Massachusetts" or "English" rule which permits cross-examination on all phases of the case.[8] There is no reason why the scope of a federal constitutional right should vary depending upon the jurisdiction's choice of a cross-examination rule. More important, the two matters—defining the scope of a waiver of self-incrimination by testifying and defining the scope of cross-examination—are not identical, and fundamentally different factors are involved in resolving each. The scope of cross-examination is essentially a matter of control over the order of production of evidence; the primary policy being served by limiting scope is the orderly conduct of the trial. The waiver issue, however, involves the "fairness" of requir-

---

4. Gandy v. United States, 386 F.2d 516 (5th Cir. 1967), cert. denied 390 U.S. 1004; Booker v. State, 397 So.2d 910, 914 (Fla.1981), cert. denied 102 S.Ct. 493 ("A defendant who takes the stand as a witness in his own behalf occupies the same status as any other witness, and all the rules applicable to other witnesses are likewise applicable to him."); People v. Williams, 66 Ill.2d 478, 363 N.E.2d 801 (1977), appeal after remand 82 Ill. App.3d 490, 37 Ill.Dec. 547, 402 N.E.2d 437. This position finds support in the *Brown* language: "[T]he breadth of [an accused's] waiver is determined by the scope of relevant cross-examination." 356 U.S. at 154–155. See also, Johnson v. United States, 318 U.S. 189 (1943), rehearing denied 318 U.S. 801; Raffel v. United States, 271 U.S. 494, 497 (1926); Fitzpatrick v. United States, 178 U.S. 304, 315 (1900). Of course, no waiver can be found if the accused was unaware of the privilege. Cf. Annot., 79 A.L.R.2d 643 (duty of court to inform unrepresented defendant of privilege).

5. United States v. Greenberg, 268 F.2d 120 (2d Cir. 1959); Reilly v. State, 212 So.2d 796 (Fla.App.1968); Dorroh v. State, 229 Miss. 315, 90 So.2d 653 (1956); State v. Dean, 400 S.W.2d 413 (Mo.1966). For a discussion of the general scope of cross-examination, see §§ 21, 22, supra. There are few cases finding error in the scope of the prosecution's examination of the accused. Tucker v. United States, 5 F.2d 818 (8th Cir. 1925), enforced the federal rule on cross-examination as applied to an accused. The accused, charged with use of the mails to defraud, took the stand and testified as to the details of his promotional scheme, obviously for the purposes of refuting the allegation of a fraudulent intent. On cross-examination the prosecution elicited from the accused testimony concerning his participation in placing a newspaper advertisement, which had been alleged to establish use of the mails. On appeal it was held that the testimony as to the

scheme did not waive the privilege in regard to the placing of the advertisement, which was characterized as relating to a different element of the offense. Other cases reversing seem to be based upon a rule of evidence rather than upon a careful definition of the privilege itself. United States v. Green, 648 F.2d 587 (9th Cir. 1981) (cross-examination of defendant concerning prior drug related activities); State v. Frese, 256 Iowa 289, 127 N.W.2d 83 (1964) (defendant, taking the stand in trial for rape, asked about the whereabouts of his three alleged companions, who were imprisoned); State v. Leuty, 247 Iowa 251, 73 N.W.2d 64 (1955) (defendant, in trial for incest, asked about illicit relationship with another woman). See also People v. Butler, 65 Cal.2d 569, 55 Cal.Rptr. 511, 421 P.2d 703 (1967) (dictum) (at trial on guilt, accused may not be cross-examined concerning circumstances of prior offenses, punishment imposed, or conduct during incarceration, although these would be properly subjects of inquiry at the penalty trial). Cf. State v. Hines, 270 Minn. 30, 133 N.W.2d 371 (1964).

6. Johnson v. United States, 318 U.S. 189 (1943); Carpenter v. United States, 264 F.2d 565, 569–70 (4th Cir. 1959); People v. De Georgio, 185 Cal.App.2d 413, 8 Cal.Rptr. 295 (1960); State v. Manning, 134 N.W.2d 91 (N.D.1965). See § 42 supra as to claiming the privilege on cross-examination directed to impeachment. See § 140 infra with respect to waiver by witnesses generally through disclosure of incriminating matters without claiming the privilege.

7. State v. Taylor, 99 Ariz. 85, 407 P.2d 59 (1965), cert. denied 384 U.S. 979, discusses and cites the cases and adopts the view of the "numerical majority and better reasoned cases" that physical acts or exhibitions may be required.

8. See § 21 supra.

ing a defendant to forfeit the protection of the privilege in order to place his own version of the facts before the trier of fact. An ordinary witness usually has no interest which deserves legal protection in restricting cross-examination; the accused, however, has the interests recognized by the privilege. The balance in regard to the scope of waiver should be struck independently of the scope of cross-examination of the ordinary witness.[9]

Several alternatives exist to the traditional approach that ties the scope of waiver to scope of permissible cross-examination of a regular witness. One of them would regard the accused as having waived the privilege as to all aspects of the offense as to which he has testified.[10] It has the advantage of simplicity and ease of application, but it may run counter to the basic purpose of the privilege. The privilege is not merely against taking the stand and hence readily said to be waived *in toto* by such action, but against self-incrimination. A rule of blanket waiver would not only discourage accused persons from testifying at all but would in effect

make them prosecution witnesses, confronting them with the "cruel trilemma of self-accusation, perjury, or contempt."[11]

A number of courts have drawn upon language from McGautha v. California[12] and now state that the decision of an accused to testify in his own behalf means that as a result of that decision the accused cannot later claim the privilege on matters "reasonably related to the subject matter of his direct examination."[13] The tendency, however, has been to construe broadly "matters of . . . direct examination" and the necessary relationship between those and the questions asked on cross-examination.[14] It is doubtful that this articulation of the waiver criterion, which is clearly the increasing trend, has resulted in different results in many cases.

It is arguable that both approaches result in rendering the privilege unavailable in situations where that result cannot be justified in terms of the rationale for the waiver rule. In several types of situations, a defendant may seek to testify but also to avoid having to address some matters that have developed. For example, as in People v. Perez,[15]

---

9. This was expressly recognized in Neely v. State, 97 Wis.2d 38, 292 N.W.2d 859 (1980). The draftsmen of the Federal Rules of Evidence expressly disclaimed any intent to affect the scope of waiver of the privilege by defining the scope of cross-examination of a witness. Fed.R.Evid. 611(b), Advisory Committee's Note. See United States v. Beechum, 582 F.2d 898, 907 (5th Cir. 1978), cert. denied 440 U.S. 920 (en banc).

10. See 8 Wigmore, Evidence § 2276 (McNaughton rev. 1961).

11. The quotation is from Murphy v. Waterfront Commission, 378 U.S. 52, 55 (1964). The analysis is found in People v. Schader, 71 Cal.2d 761, 80 Cal.Rptr. 1, 457 P.2d 841 (1969), oddly enough by the same court which decided People v. Perez, infra n. 15.

12. 402 U.S. 183 (1971), rehearing denied 406 U.S. 978.

13. Id., at 215, citing Brown v. United States, see text at note 2 supra, as well as other cases.

14. United States v. Beechum, 582 F.2d 898 (5th Cir. 1978), cert. denied 440 U.S. 920 (discussed in the text at note 16 infra). United States v. Hearst, 563 F.2d 1331 (9th Cir. 1977), cert. denied 435 U.S. 1000, involved a prosecution for robbery that occurred in April, 1974. The defendant took the stand and testified to her abduction in February, 1974 and to abuse by her captors until their arrival in Las Vegas in September, 1974; she also testified to the events of her arrest

in San Francisco in September, 1975. Holding that the defendant waived the privilege in regard to events occurring from September, 1974 to September, 1975, the court reasoned that the natural inference of her testimony was that she acted under the influence of her captors during the entire period from February, 1974 until September, 1975. Questions concerning the year prior to her arrest were therefore reasonably related to the subject matter of her direct examination. Id., at 1340–41. See also Neely v. State, 97 Wis.2d 38, 292 N.W.2d 859 (1980) (defendant who testified that he was not a participant in killing of victim could be cross-examined concerning incidents several days before killing in which he and others sought victim for purposes of killing him).

15. 65 Cal.2d 615, 55 Cal.Rptr. 909, 422 P.2d 597 (1967), cert. dismissed 395 U.S. 208. See Comment, 41 Temp.L.Q. 458 (1968).

The problem could be avoided, of course, by severing the charges. But if the charges were properly joined, an accused's expression of desire to testify as to less than all of them may not give rise to a right to severance. At best, such a motion may be directed to the trial court's discretion. See United States v. Forrest, 623 F.2d 1107, 1115 (5th Cir. 1980), cert. denied 449 U.S. 924 (defendant failed to show that he had important testimony to give on one count and a "strong need" to refrain from testifying on the other); State v. Hall, 103 Wis.2d 125, 307 N.W.2d 289 (1981). See gen-

a defendant may seek to testify concerning fewer than all of several different charges on which he is being tried. United States v. Beechum [16] presented a more complicated problem. Beechum, a part-time mailman, was charged with possession of a silver dollar, knowing it to have been stolen from the mails. The government's evidence included proof that at the time of his arrest he had also been found in possession of credit cards that had been mailed to persons on his mail route some ten months before the arrest. At trial, he wished to take the stand and testify that he had taken possession of the silver dollar intending to turn it in to his superiors. He also sought, however, to avoid addressing possession of the credit cards on either direct or cross-examination. In neither case was the defendant successful. The Perez court justified its result in terms of the jurisdiction's broad rule defining the scope of cross-examination. In Beechum, the court applied the criterion requiring relevance to matters raised on direct examination; after observing that the accused's proposed testimony would address intent, the court concluded that the possession of the credit cards also bore on intent and therefore his direct testimony would waive his privilege concerning that matter.

The rationale for requiring a defendant to submit to cross-examination as a condition of permitting him to testify in his own behalf is primarily if not exclusively to provide reasonable assurance that his testimony, like any other, is subjected to procedures believed to provide assurance of accuracy. A defendant should neither be invited nor permitted, in the Supreme Court's own words, "to mutilate the truth [he] offers to tell." [17] But would permitting Perez to avoid cross-examination concerning some of the offenses charged or permitting Beechum to avoid questioning regarding his possession of the credit cards constitute authorization

to so mutilate the truth concerning those matters the defendants wished to address?

Perez is the easier of the cases. Although the charges have been joined for trial, they are independent. If Perez is permitted to avoid cross-examination concerning one offense, this does not affect the prosecution's ability to subject his testimony concerning the other offense to normal credibility attack. Beechum is more difficult. His direct testimony would, of course, challenge the adequacy of the government's case on motive. The possession of the credit cards also bears on motive. But if Beechum is not required to undergo cross-examination concerning his possession of the cards, this in no way reduces the strength of the inference which the trier of fact may draw from the government's evidence of his possession. It is arguable, in other words, that in Beechum the government's ability to obtain advantage from its evidence that Beechum possessed stolen credit cards for a prolonged period was in no direct and important way affected by Beechum's testimony that he did not intend "improper" possession of the silver dollar. If this is correct, the rationale for finding any waiver of the privilege as a result of an accused testifying suggests that this waiver not extend so as to require that the accused submit to cross-examination concerning the matter not addressed on direct.

If this result is desirable, it suggests, of course, the impropriety of the "scope of cross-examination" and "all aspects of the offense" criteria for defining the scope of waiver. But even the "relationship to subject matter addressed on direct" standard that is being increasingly accepted is often applied so as to find waivers in situations similar to Beechum. [18] A preferable standard would focus directly upon the scope of waiver needed to subject the accused's testimony on direct examination to scrutiny regarding its truth. The question would not

---

erally State v. Perry, 116 Ariz. 40, 567 P.2d 786, 795–797 (App.1977).

16. 582 F.2d 898 (5th Cir. 1978), cert. denied 440 U.S. 920.

17. See text at note 2 supra, quoting from Brown.

18. See note 14 supra.

be simply whether the proposed (and further incriminating) cross-examination involved a matter related to the direct examination. Rather, cross-examination of a testifying accused would be permissible only if it appeared necessary to avoid depriving the prosecution of a reasonable opportunity to test those assertions made by the defendant during direct testimony. A conclusory denial concerning a broad matter (such as motive in *Beechum*) should not be enough, without more, to subject a testifying defendant to cross-examination concerning incriminating details which the prosecution has been permitted to prove but which the accused did not address in his direct examination.[19]

The waiver has traditionally been regarded as effective throughout the proceeding in which the accused testifies. During that proceeding the privilege does not reattach if the accused physically leaves the witness stand, and he can be recalled and required to testify again if this is otherwise procedurally proper.[20] On the other hand, testifying in one proceeding does not affect the right to invoke the privilege in a separate and independent proceeding. It may, however, be permissible to cross-examine an accused who testifies at trial concerning his failure to testify in previous proceedings.[21] Nor is an accused who testifies at one trial precluded from invoking the privilege during a second trial of the same charge.[22] Unlike the privilege of the witness, the privilege of the accused has not given rise to many questions concerning the prospective scope of a waiver.[23] Thus, although there may be some question concerning the position of a witness,[24] it is unlikely that an accused waives his right to invoke the privilege at trial by voluntarily testifying before a grand jury. Such a distinction between the accused and a witness is difficult to justify on theoretical grounds and, if made, must rest primarily on the proposition that the interests protected by the privilege are placed in greater danger when the holder is himself on trial and so the waiver doctrine will be correspondingly restricted in its application to this situation.

 **WESTLAW REFERENCES**

waiv! /6 testif! testimon! /p crossexamin! /p
incrimin! impeach! privilege

di testimony

410k305(2)

massachusett* english /2 rule* /s crossexamin!

---

19. A right to make a "limited waiver" was recognized in Calloway v. Wainwright, 409 F.2d 59 (5th Cir. 1969), cert. denied 395 U.S. 909. Since state law gave a defendant a right to have the jury consider the voluntariness of a confession already held admissible by the trial judge, a defendant who wishes to utilize this opportunity was held to have the right to testify before the jury on only the voluntariness of his confession. There has been a marked unwillingness, however, to find that a defendant's testimony was sufficiently limited to matters adequately collateral to invoke this rule. See McGahee v. Massey, 667 F.2d 1357 (11th Cir. 1982), cert. denied 103 S.Ct. 255 (defendant's testimony concerning his whereabouts on date when state witness testified he had been at location where crime was later committed constituted testimony on identity and *Calloway* inapplicable); United States v. Hearst, 563 F.2d 1331, 1339–1340 (9th Cir. 1977), cert. denied 435 U.S. 1000 (testimony of defendant concerning coercion went to intent as well as to voluntariness of confession and *Calloway* inapplicable); State v. Bonet, 132 N.J. Super. 186, 333 A.2d 267 (1975). *Calloway* has been

distinguished as involving a right under state law to testify only as to voluntariness of a confession. See State v. Day, 391 So.2d 1147 (La.1980) (upholding state statute providing that waiver by taking the stand is waiver for all purposes).

Compare the discussion of the effect of an overly broad assertion of innocence by the accused in his testimony as opening the door to otherwise inadmissible evidence of other crimes in § 57 n. 10 supra.

20. State v. Coty, 229 A.2d 205 (Me.1967); People v. Barboza, 213 Cal.App.2d 441, 28 Cal.Rptr. 805 (1963).

21. See § 160 infra.

22. Cf. United States v. Miranti, 253 F.2d 135 (2d Cir. 1958).

23. State v. Grady, 153 Conn. 26, 211 A.2d 674 (1965) (defendant who took stand during trial of first part of indictment did not waive privilege with regard to trial on second portion of indictment charging habitual criminality).

24. See § 140 infra.

§ 133. Special Problems: (a) Limits on Pretrial Discovery by the Prosecution Imposed by the Privilege [1]

The increasing liberality with which discovery is granted to defendants in criminal litigation [2] has brought a demand that discovery be made a "two-way" street, and both legislation and judicial decisions have increasingly found certain duties on the part of the defense to make disclosure to the prosecution. This may involve only notice of intention to rely upon a certain theory or "defense"—such as alibi or insanity—at trial. Again, it may require further disclosure concerning such matters, as, for example, by requiring in the case of alibi that the defense disclose where it will attempt to establish that the defendant was at the time of the offense or the names, addresses, and perhaps prior statements of defense witnesses. Finally, the defense may be required to disclose information that it would not ultimately disclose at trial. In one case the defense was ordered to disclose evidence that the victim had at the request of a defense investigator identified a photograph of the defendant as that of the perpetrator of the offense.[3] Disclosure by the defense may raise a number of important matters, including possible infringements upon the defendant's right to the effective assistance of counsel.[4] This section considers only the possibility that compelled disclosure violates the defendant's privilege against self-incrimination.

In two major decisions the Supreme Court has greatly limited the potential effect of the Fifth Amendment privilege upon defendant disclosure requirements. In Williams v. Florida,[5] the Court found no Fifth Amendment violation in a requirement that the defense provide pretrial notice of intent to claim alibi and disclosure to the prosecution of the place where the defense evidence would tend to show the defendant was, as well as the names and addresses of witnesses the defense intends to call to support the claim of alibi. Reasoning that the requirement did nothing more than accelerate disclosure which the defense would otherwise make at trial, the Court reasoned that "[n]othing in the Fifth Amendment privilege entitles a defendant as a matter of constitutional right to await the end of the State's case before announcing the nature of his defense . . . ."[6] This rationale, if applied to defense disclosure generally, would, of course, permit pretrial disclosure of any information which would be disclosed during trial. It would not, however, deny Fifth Amendment protection to potentially incriminating information which—because of its incriminating nature, perhaps—the defense does not intend to use at trial.

The scope of Fifth Amendment protection was further limited and a potentially broader rationale for such limitation was ap-

§ 133

1. See generally, Allis, Limitations on Prosecutorial Discovery of the Defense Case in Federal Courts: The Shield of Confidentiality, 50 So.Cal.L.Rev. 461, 488–99 (1977); Deitzler, Klimas & Auvil, Prosecutorial Discovery: An Overview, 83 W.Va.L.Rev. 187 (1980); Nakell, Criminal Discovery for the Defense and the Prosecution—The Developing Constitutional Considerations, 50 N.C.L.Rev. 437 (1972); Smith and McCollom, Counter-Discovery in Criminal Cases: Fifth Amendment Privilege Abridged, 54 A.B.A.J. 256 (1968); Wilder, Prosecution Discovery and the Privilege Against Self-Incrimination, 6 Am.Crim.L.Q. 3 (1967); Louisell, Criminal Discovery and Self-Incrimination: Roger Traynor Confronts the Dilemma, 53 Cal.L.Rev. 89 (1965); Van Kessel, Prosecutorial Discovery and the Privilege Against Self-Incrimination: Accommodation or Capitulation, 4 Hastings Const.L.Q. 855 (1977); Comment, 35 Fordham

L.Rev. 315 (1966); 21 Am.Jur.2d Criminal Law § 707; Dec.Dig. Criminal Law ☞627.5(3).

2. See generally, Traynor, Ground Lost and Found in Criminal Discovery, 39 N.Y.U.L.Rev. 228 (1964).

3. State v. Williams, 80 N.J. 472, 404 A.2d 34 (1979).

4. See State v. Williams, note 3 supra, holding that the disclosure required by the trial court denied Williams his right to effective assistance of counsel.

5. 399 U.S. 78 (1970).

6. Id. at 85. The Court has found a due process requirement that any notice of alibi disclosure requirement imposed be reciprocal. See Wardius v. Oregon, 412 U.S. 470 (1973). This apparently means that the prosecution must, after receiving the information from the defense, be required to notify the defense of any witnesses it intends to offer to rebut the alibi.

parently accepted in United States v. Nobles.[7] The trial court had ordered the defense to disclose to the prosecution portions of the report of a defense investigator concerning prior statements purportedly made to the investigator by prosecution witnesses. These statements were inconsistent with those witnesses' trial testimony. When the defense declined to make the disclosure, the trial judge refused to permit the defense investigator to testify concerning the statements. Reasoning that the Fifth Amendment protects a defendant only against being personally compelled to make testimonial disclosures, the Court found no constitutional defect in the trial court's action. The investigator's report contained only testimonial disclosures made to the investigator by persons other than the defendant, reasoned the majority, so disclosure under compulsion would involve no compelled testimonial activity by the defendant. Thus no value protected by the Fifth Amendment was infringed by the order of disclosure.[8] The rationale for the *Nobles* result, if taken beyond the case, would find no Fifth Amendment limit on defense disclosure—even if the defense did not intend to disclose the information later at trial—as long as the information disclosed had a source other than the defendant himself.

Given the inconsistency between the rationales used in *Williams* and *Nobles,* as well as the limited scope given the Fifth Amendment by these cases, it is arguable that a more careful examination of the desirable role of the amendment in this area is in order. It might be most useful to consider the ways in which defense disclosure might infringe upon the values protected by the privilege and then to evaluate whether this danger of infringement justifies a construction of the amendment as a bar to defense disclo-

sure. Initially, of course, it can be urged that any compelled participation by the defendant or his agents in the process of securing conviction is inconsistent with the underlying notion of the amendment. But this has been rejected through the requirement of "testimonial" compulsion [9] and the general recognition that the protection of the privilege is not as broad as the principles underlying it.[10]

It is also clear that defense compliance with demands for disclosure involves some of the same tacit admissions as are involved in compelled disclosure of documents and other items in response to a subpoena. But it is now clear that this theoretical possibility of testimonial incrimination is not alone enough to invoke the privilege in the subpoena situation [11] and, as the New York Court of Appeals recently recognized, ought not to be sufficient to bar compelled disclosure here.[12] If, however, compelled disclosure in a particular case presents the sorts of dangers that invoke the privilege in the subpoena context, it seems clear that the privilege should also bar compelled compliance with a discovery requirement.

It is also possible that disclosure may provide information tending to incriminate the defendant in regard to offenses other than that with which he is presently charged. The likelihood of this seems insufficient, however, to invoke the privilege in all such situations. If a defendant's claim of the privilege in this regard meets general requirements for establishing a sufficient danger of such incrimination [13] on the facts of any particular case, however, it seems clear that compliance with disclosure requirements should not be compelled.

In *Williams,* the Court held that the Fifth Amendment does not protect the timing of disclosure, without fully exploring the inter-

---

7.   422 U.S. 225 (1975), on remand 522 F.2d 1274 (9th Cir.). See also § 97 at n. 17 supra.

8.   Id. at 233–234.

9.   See § 124 supra.

10.   See § 124, at n. 2 supra, quoting Schmerber v. California, 384 U.S. 757, 762 (1966).

11.   See § 126 supra.

12.   People v. Copicotto, 50 N.Y.2d 222, 229, 428 N.Y.S.2d 649, 654, 406 N.E.2d 465, 470 (1980).

13.   See § 124 supra.

ests that might be involved in the timing problem. To the extent that a defendant's interest in control over timing is based upon his interest in the tactical advantage of shock and surprise, perhaps there can be no question that it ought not to come within the protection of the privilege. But it can also be argued that often a defense decision as to whether to produce evidence cannot be made intelligently until the prosecution's case is closed. Only then can the defense adequately consider the advantages of producing evidence as compared with reliance upon inadequacies of the prosecution's case. If pretrial disclosure is required on the basis that the defense may want, at trial, to disclose the evidence, it can be argued that the defense's ability to make this choice at trial has been hampered in a manner that infringes upon the values protected by the privilege.[14] While it can be urged that the prosecution can be barred from making any use of information derived from defense disclosure until and if the defense actually uses at trial the information disclosed earlier, this may prove impossible to accomplish in practice.

Finally, it may be urged that a defendant's interest in avoiding pretrial disclosure rests upon the practical danger that pretrial disclosure more than trial disclosure creates the risk that the prosecution will be able to exploit the information by using it to develop further evidence tending to show the defendant's guilt of the offense charged. Some of this evidence may be accurately characterized as rebuttal evidence; thus disclosure concerning alibi claims may permit the prosecution to develop information challenging the credibility of a defendant's particular alibi witnesses.[15] In addition, however, interviews with persons such as defense alibi witnesses may also provide leads to evidence that tends to show guilt in a manner other than by challenging the credibility of these witnesses.[16] A defendant may have an interest in minimizing the prosecution's ability to use disclosure to develop evidence of either sort. *Williams* assumed that defendants' have no interest protected by the Fifth Amendment in retaining control over timing so as to reduce the prosecution's ability to develop rebuttal evidence.[17] But it is arguable that the Court did not adequately consider defendants' interest in reducing the prosecution's ability to use defense disclosures to develop non-rebuttal evidence of guilt. On the other hand, this danger may be so remote or infrequently encountered that it should be regarded as significant only where a defendant, on the facts of a particular case, establishes the existence of sufficient danger of this sort of prejudice to bring the privilege into play.

The lower courts have generally found no self-incrimination limits upon the developing requirements of defense disclosure.[18] Most have considered, however, only requirements of pretrial disclosure of matters it is assumed will be disclosed by the defense during trial. Several state courts, on the

---

14. In *Williams*, the Court concluded that the required disclosure did not impede the defense's ability to make a free choice at trial as to whether to present the alibi evidence or not. 399 U.S. at 85–86. Compare Brooks v. Tennessee, 406 U.S. 605 (1972), holding that a statute requiring that a defendant desiring to testify do so before presenting other testimony violated the Fifth Amendment.

15. See Scott v. State, 519 P.2d 774, 787 (Alaska 1974) ("[Disclosure of alibi information] could be particularly incriminating if the state were able to demonstrate that no one else in [the alibi] location had seen the accused during the relevant time period.").

16. See Scott v. State, supra n. 15 (disclosure of place where defendant will claim to have been in course of alibi "defense" may be incriminating because persons police may locate at the premises "may be able to provide the police with information probative of the defendant's guilt—information the police might never have found but for the compelled disclosure").

17. 399 U.S. at 85.

18. State ex rel. Keller v. Criminal Court, 262 Ind. 420, 317 N.E.2d 433 (1974) (no self-incrimination defect in broad disclosure requirements requiring notice of defenses, witnesses who will be called, and statements of these witnesses); Commonwealth v. Donovan, 610 S.W.2d 601 (Ky.1980) (although compelled production of names and addresses of defense witnesses was not authorized by state statute, such disclosure did not violate defendant's self-incrimination rights); People v. Copicotto, 50 N.Y.2d 222, 428 N.Y.S.2d 649, 406 N.E.2d 465 (1980). Fed.R.Crim.P. 16(b) was upheld in United States v. Bump, 605 F.2d 548 (10th Cir. 1979).

other hand, have held that state self-incrimination privileges impose a more significant limitation upon compelled defense disclosure than, after *Williams* and *Nobles*, is imposed as a matter of Fifth Amendment law.[19] In evaluating the efforts to delineate a satisfactory scope of self-incrimination protection in this area, it might be well to consider whether some of the interests involved might be better protected under other doctrines. To the extent that what is really at issue is the integrity of information developed during the defense preparation, perhaps a more effective vehicle for developing the limits of confidentiality would be the right to effective assistance of counsel, as embodied in the Sixth and Fourteenth Amendments.

**WESTLAW
REFERENCES**

307ak183

synopsis,digest(pretrial /3 discovery /p incrimin!)

williams /3 florida /15 399 /5 78

synopsis,digest(prosecut! /5 notif! disclos! /5 defense
　defendant* accused /20 witness!)

nobles /15 422 /5 225

digest,synopsis(alibi* /p disclos! notif! /p prosecut!
　/p witness!)

---

§ 134.　Special Problems: (b) Psychiatric Examinations and the Privilege of the Accused [1]

A psychiatric [2] evaluation of a criminal defendant may be made for any of numerous

purposes. It may be intended to determine whether the defendant presents a risk of suicide while in pretrial detention. Or, it may be intended to gather information for use in deciding whether or under what circumstances to release the defendant pending trial, whether the defendant is competent to stand trial,[3] whether the defendant is insane or was otherwise afflicted with an abnormality at the time of the offense that affects his responsibility, or in making an appropriate sentencing disposition. A psychiatrist who examines a defendant for one purpose may, of course, later be called upon to express an opinion on some other aspect of the case. This variety of procedural aspects of psychiatric examinations complicates the task of evaluating the relevance of the privilege against self-incrimination to such examinations.

The initial question, of course, is whether the privilege applies at all. Some courts have regarded such examinations as involving no compelled *testimonial* activity by the accused; even responses to questions, these courts reason, are not considered for the truth of any assertions in those responses but for what the characteristics of the response suggest to the expert about the accused's mental condition.[4] While it is possible that some psychiatric evaluations might be limited to efforts to elicit nontestimonial information, most are almost certainly in-

---

19. The leading cases are Scott v. State, 519 P.2d 774 (Alaska 1974) and Prudhomme v. Superior Court, 2 Cal.3d 320, 85 Cal.Rptr. 129, 466 P.2d 673 (1970). *Prudhomme* was based on federal constitutional grounds but its result has been reaffirmed on state grounds. Allen v. Superior Court, 18 Cal.3d 520, 525, 134 Cal.Rptr. 774, 776, 557 P.2d 65, 67 (1976). See also, Richardson v. District Court, 632 P.2d 595 (Colo. 1981) (no self-incrimination violation in requirement for disclosure of nature of any defense and names and addresses of witnesses, but disclosure of prior statements of defense witnesses would present possible self-incrimination problems).

§ 134

1. See generally Berry, Self-Incrimination and the Compulsory Mental Examination: A Proposal, 15 Ariz. L.Rev. 919 (1973); Danforth, Death Knell for Pre-Trial Mental Examination? Privilege Against Self-Incrimination, 19 Rutgers L.Rev. 489 (1965); Comment, *Mi-*

randa on the Couch: An Approach to Problems of Self-Incrimination, Right to Counsel, and *Miranda* Warnings in Pre-Trial Psychiatric Examinations of Criminal Defendants, 11 Colum.J.L. & Soc.Prob. 403 (1975); Note, 50 Geo.Wash.L.Rev. 275 (1982); 21 Am. Jur.2d Criminal Law § 714; 21A Am.Jur.2d Criminal Law § 949; Annot., 32 A.L.R.2d 434.

2. While this discussion refers for convenience to "psychiatric" interviews, the discussion applies equally to examinations by other mental health professionals, such as clinical psychologists.

3. It is clear that due process prohibits the trial of an incompetent defendant. Pate v. Robinson, 383 U.S. 375 (1966).

4. See Loveless v. State, 592 P.2d 1206 (Alaska 1979), appeal after remand 634 P.2d 941 (although examination involved a "verbal exchange," most responses were to test questions and all responses were important not for their content but as a means of as-

tended to elicit at least some testimonial responses. In Estelle v. Smith,[5] the Supreme Court rejected the argument that the examination at issue involved only nontestimonial communications from the accused. The record showed that the examiner relied upon the accused's account of the offense given during the interview and the accused's failure to express remorse. Since the psychiatric testimony was based upon the substance of disclosures made during the examination, the Fifth Amendment privilege was held "directly involved." [6]

It is also possible that at least some examinations do not "compel" responses within the meaning of the privilege, because the accused is not compelled to respond to particular questions.[7] This presents an issue similar to that raised by custodial police interrogation [8] and should probably be resolved similarly. Where the accused is compelled by court order to submit to the examination or where the accused is in custody and that opportunity is utilized to conduct an examination, there is significant practical pressure on the defendant to respond to particular questions. In the absence of safeguards sufficient to assure that the accused is aware of and able effectively to utilize any right that exists not to respond to particular questions, the testimonial responses to questions posed during a court-ordered or custodial examination should be regarded as compelled within the meaning of the privilege.[9]

The most troublesome issue is whether, and when, the compelled testimonial responses are incriminating. It now seems reasonably clear that this will depend upon which of the various possible uses are made of the results of the examination. In Estelle v. Smith,[10] the Supreme Court commented that if the results of a court-ordered examination were confined to determining the accused's competency to stand trial, "no Fifth Amendment issue would have arisen." [11] This is apparently because a finding of competency simply removes a potential bar to trial of the accused and thus does not constitute "incrimination" within the meaning of the privilege. In *Smith*, however, the results of the examination were used in an effort to secure the death penalty. This was held to constitute use for incriminatory purposes and to invoke the federal constitutional privilege. Whether use of the information in noncapital sentencing proceedings would constitute incrimination is an uncertain matter previously discussed.[12] While not entirely clear, it is likely that the use of interview results for making pretrial release decisions would similarly not constitute incriminatory use and thus would not invoke the Fifth Amendment.

The major issue arises when the results of an examination are used by the prosecution on issues related to criminal responsibility. This is generally in response to an accused's claim of insanity, but the same problem is arguably posed when the results are used on such matters as diminished capacity and in-

---

certaining the defendant's mental state). See generally, Judge Bazelon's dissent in United States v. Byers, No. 78–1451 (D.C.Cir.1980), excerpted in 5 Mental Disability L.Rep. 267, 269 (1981) (psychiatric examinations involve different techniques, some of which result in testimonial responses and some of which do not).

5.   451 U.S. 454 (1981).

6.   Id. at 464–65.

7.   See Commonwealth v. Kampo, 480 Pa. 516, 391 A.2d 1005 (1978); Commonwealth v. Glenn, 459 Pa. 545, 330 A.2d 535 (1974) (error for psychiatrist to testify that accused invoked right of silence during exam). See also State v. Corbin, 15 Or.App. 536, 516 P.2d 1314 (1973), appeal after remand 22 Or.App. 505, 539 P.2d 1113.

8.   See § 125 supra.

9.   The Supreme Court appeared to recognize this in Estelle v. Smith supra, when it equated a court-ordered psychiatric examination with custodial police interrogation for purposes of considering whether a warning was required. 451 U.S. at 467. Although the court order was apparently addressed only to the psychiatrist and did not by its terms purport to direct the accused to respond to the question, the Court did not pause to consider the possibility that the accused's responses might not be regarded as "compelled" for this reason.

10.   451 U.S. 454 (1981).

11.   Id. at 465.

12.   See § 121 infra.

toxication. Some courts take the position that such use does not amount to incriminating use, as long as the testimony does not result in specific factual admissions made by the accused during the examination being used to establish that the accused did in fact engage in the conduct constituting the crime charged.[13] Under this approach, it may be permissible for a psychiatrist to recount such admissions during testimony if the jury is instructed to consider them only as bearing upon the weight to be given the witness' conclusions.[14] It has been suggested that the use of the products of an examination would be incriminating use if, under the applicable substantive criminal law, the testimony went to a matter which was an element of the crime charged rather than a "defense," or in any case went to a matter on which the prosecution had the burden of proof.[15] This entire approach seems artificial and unacceptable. Responsibility issues—whether denominated insanity, diminished capacity, state of mind, or intoxication—all bear upon the accused's guilt or innocence. How a jurisdiction decides to allocate the burdens of pleading, going forward with evidence, and persuasion should not be determinative of the privilege's applicability, because they turn on considerations other than those related directly to liability. When the products of an

examination are offered by the prosecution on a responsibility issue, the use should be regarded as an incriminating use under *Smith*, and the privilege should be regarded as invoked.

It should also be clear, however, that there is substantial unfairness in permitting an accused to secure and use expert testimony based upon clinical examination of the accused while denying the prosecution access to the only reasonable source of potential rebuttal testimony, the accused himself. Virtually every court that has considered the issue has concluded that the prosecution has some right of access to the accused in such circumstances.[16] Some reason that this use of an examination's results is not incriminating,[17] which appears to be simply incorrect. A more satisfactory rationale for the result is waiver: by certain action, the defendant loses the right to rely on the privilege in certain circumstances.[18] As the Massachusetts Court has recognized,[19] the privilege should be rendered unavailable only if the defense offers expert testimony based upon clinical examination of the accused himself. Further, the trial court might reasonably be given the authority to demand advance notice of intent to offer such testimony. But efforts to raise responsibility issues with other sorts of evidence, such as lay testimony, do

---

13. United States v. Jines, 536 F.2d 1255 (8th Cir. 1976), cert. denied 429 U.S. 942; Presnell v. State, 241 Ga. 49, 243 S.E.2d 496 (1978), reversed on other grounds 439 U.S. 14, on remand 243 Ga. 131, 252 S.E.2d 625, cert. denied 444 U.S. 885.

14. See, e.g., United States v. Whitlock, 663 F.2d 1094, 1107 (D.C.Cir.1980); Scott v. Oliver, 552 F.2d 20 (1st Cir. 1977). The *Whitlock* court commented that "grave concerns" would have been generated had the psychiatric testimony been used to prove "guilt." See McKenna v. State, ___ Nev. ___, 639 P.2d 557 (1982) (violation of due process to use admissions made during sanity examination to establish guilt and this result is consistent with Estelle v. Smith. See also, People v. Rosenthal, 617 P.2d 551 (Colo.1980) (state and federal self-incrimination clauses would be violated by state's use on guilt of testimony of privately-retained psychiatrist who interviewed accused on behalf of defense).

15. Battie v. Estelle, 655 F.2d 692, 701 n. 21 (5th Cir. 1981).

16. Id. at 702.

17. United States v. Hinckley, 525 F.Supp. 1342, 1349 (D.D.C.1981), affirmed 672 F.2d 115 (D.C.Cir.) (Estelle v. Smith did not change circuit's rule that use of products of competency examination to rebut insanity evidence is not incriminating).

18. Battie v. Estelle, 655 F.2d 692, 701 (5th Cir. 1981); State v. Jones, 359 So.2d 95 (La.1978), cert. denied 439 U.S. 1049; Blaisdell v. Commonwealth, 372 Mass. 753, 364 N.E.2d 191, 200 (1977).

19. Blaisdell v. Commonwealth, 372 Mass. 753, 766–68, 364 N.E.2d 191, 200–201 (1977). See also Battie v. Estelle, 655 F.2d 692 (5th Cir. 1981) (merely requesting or submitting to psychiatric evaluation is not waiver). Courts seem generally to have assumed that a waiver of this sort is in a sense retroactive in that it permits the use of testimony based on a previously-conducted examination that would otherwise have been regarded as violative of the accused's self-incrimination rights. The issue as to whether the waiver must occur before the examination is conducted was noted but not addressed in Spivey v. Zant, 661 F.2d 464, 475 n. 18 (5th Cir. 1981), cert. denied 102 S.Ct. 3495.

not place the prosecution at a competitive disadvantage and should not be regarded as rendering the privilege inapplicable.

Once the scope of the privilege's applicability in this context is discerned, it is necessary to determine its content where it applies. In Estelle v. Smith, the Supreme Court held that where the results of an examination were offered to support the prosecution's contention that the death penalty should be imposed, the testimony would be admissible under Fifth Amendment standards only if the prosecution proved that the accused had been informed of this possible use of the results of the interview and of his right to remain silent and that the accused after such a warning voluntarily consented to the examination.[20] The Court did not consider whether the psychiatric interview, like custodial police interrogation, also gave rise to a right to the presence of counsel and to appointment of counsel for indigent accused persons. Its comments, however, suggest sympathy with the general hostility of lower courts to arguments for such additional protections from the privilege.[21] This hostility rests in part upon the perception that abuse of the opportunity to question is less likely in psychiatric interview than during custodial police interrogation. It also, however, is based to a large extent upon the perceptions that the social need for such interviews is great and the presence of an attorney during them would greatly reduce their effectiveness and the value of the resulting expert testimony.

The waiver theory is well-established in regard to the use of examinations for responsibility issues. It may, however, also be extended to other situations in which use of the testimony is for an "incriminating" purpose. In Smith, for example, the Court clearly left open the possibility that if the accused had introduced psychiatric testimony at the capital sentencing hearing or indicated an intention to do so, the privilege might not bar the prosecution's use of testimony based on an interview conducted without securing the informed waiver required on the facts before it.[22]

When the examination is sought later during criminal proceedings, the significance of the Fifth Amendment privilege against self-incrimination may be less than the impact of the Sixth Amendment. In *Smith*, the Court held that an accused person's Sixth Amendment right to the assistance of counsel applies to a psychiatric examination conducted at or after the time that "adversary judicial proceedings" have been initiated against him. This right apparently requires that counsel be provided, that counsel be notified in advance concerning the examination and the purpose of the inquiry, and an opportunity to be adequately advised by counsel concerning the desirability of submitting to the examination.[23] The Court disclaimed holding that this Sixth Amendment right was unwaivable but found no occasion on the facts before it to consider what would be necessary to establish the voluntary, knowing, and intelligent waiver of a known right that would be required for any such waiver.[24] While this is not entirely clear, it appears that the prosecution's burden of establishing an effective waiver of the Sixth Amendment right to counsel, where it has attached, is substantially greater than that of establishing an effective waiver of the privilege against compulsory self-incrimination.

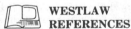 **WESTLAW REFERENCES**

synopsis,digest(psychiatr! /p exam! evaluat! /p accused defendant* /p incrimin!)

synopsis,digest(psychiat! mental* /5 examin! evaluat! /p pretrial)

psychiatr! /6 testif! testimon! /p accused defendant* /p incrimin!

20.   451 U.S. at 468.

21.   Id. at 470 n. 14.

22.   Id. at 465-466.

23.   Id. at 469–71. See also Spivey v. Zant, 661 F.2d 464 (5th Cir. 1981), cert. denied 102 S.Ct. 3495 (Sixth

Amendment would be violated by state's use of products of post-indictment interview conducted when defendant was unrepresented, although defense had produced evidence tending to show insanity).

24.   Id. at 471 n. 16.

estelle /15 451 /5 454
compel! compulsor! /3 testimon! exam! evaluat! testif!
/p psychiatr! mental insan! sane sanity /p incrimin!

---

§ 135. The Privilege of a Witness: (a) Proceedings in Which the Privilege May Be Invoked.[1]

The privilege of one not an accused is a privilege to be free from legal coercion imposed to compel an incriminating response to questions which may be put to the individual. Thus it is clear that the privilege extends to a party or witness in civil litigation,[2] not only during trial but in pretrial discovery proceedings,[3] a witness in a criminal proceeding,[4] a witness in a grand jury proceeding[5] or a legislative investigation,[6] and one who is subjected to police interrogation[7] or questioning by an administrative official or board.[8] When the coercion applied to compel a response is not sanctioned by law, the privilege—which is a legal rule—is probably not applicable. The matter is relatively academic, as when the coercion being applied is extra-legal the availability or nonavailability of a legal privilege is unlikely to affect the subject of the coercion. But from an analytic sense, it is more appropriate to deal with

these situations as questions of admissibility under the "voluntariness" rule.[9]

 WESTLAW REFERENCES

miranda /15 384 /5 436 & date(1983)
mccarthy /15 266 /5 34
410k304(4)

---

§ 136. The Privilege of a Witness: (b) Manner of Invoking the Privilege[1]

The privilege of one not an accused is a privilege to decline to respond to inquiries, not a prohibition against inquiries designed to elicit responses incriminating in nature. Because of this difference in the nature of the privilege of one not an accused, the manner of invoking it correspondingly differs from the manner of invoking the privilege of an accused. Thus by universal holding, one not an accused must submit to inquiry (including being sworn, if the inquiry is one conducted under oath) and may invoke the privilege only after the potentially incriminating question has been put. Moreover, invoking the privilege does not end the inquiry and the subject may be required to invoke it

§ 135

1. See generally, 8 Wigmore, Evidence § 2252 (McNaughton rev.1961); 81 Am.Jur.2d Witnesses § 32; C.J.S. Witnesses § 433; Dec.Dig. Witnesses ⟳293, 293½.

2. McCarthy v. Arndstein, 266 U.S. 34 (1924) (bankruptcy); Kendall v. Gore Properties, 98 U.S.App.D.C. 378, 236 F.2d 673 (1956); In re Sterling-Harris Ford, Inc., 315 F.2d 277 (7th Cir. 1963); Application of Leavitt, 174 Cal.App.2d 535, 345 P.2d 75 (1959); Heidt, The Conjurer's Circle: The Fifth Amendment Privilege in Civil Cases, 91 Yale L.J. 1062 (1982).

3. Bradley v. O'Hare, 2 A.D.2d 436, 156 N.Y.S.2d 533 (1956) (refusal to respond to pre-trial order regarding production of books); Allred v. Graves, 261 N.C. 31, 134 S.E.2d 186 (1964).

4. See § 116 supra.

5. United States v. Pile, 256 F.2d 954 (7th Cir. 1958); Commonwealth v. Rhine, 303 S.W.2d 301 (Ky.1957). See generally Annot., 38 A.L.R.2d 225.

6. Quinn v. United States, 349 U.S. 155 (1955) (privilege invoked before subcommittee of House of Representatives Committee on Unamerican Activities); Unit-

ed States v. Di Carlo, 102 F.Supp. 597 (N.D.Ohio, 1952); State v. Spindel, 24 N.J. 395, 132 A.2d 291 (1957) (answer elicited by Joint Legislative Committee to Study Wiretapping and the Unauthorized Recording of Speech not admissible in criminal proceeding). See Note 49 Colum.L.Rev. 87 (1949); Dec.Dig. Witnesses ⟳297(7).

7. Miranda v. Arizona, 384 U.S. 436 (1966).

8. In re Groban's Petition, 352 U.S. 330 (1957) (state fire marshal's investigation); Smith v. United States, 337 U.S. 137 (1949) (testimony given before an examiner of the Office of Price Administration under subpoena); Chapman v. Division of Employment Security of Department of Labor, 104 So.2d 201 (La.App.1958) (proceeding for unemployment compensation); Oleshko v. New York State Liquor Authority, 29 A.D.2d 84, 285 N.Y.S.2d 696 (1967), affirmed 21 N.Y.2d 788, 288 N.Y.S.2d 474, 235 N.E.2d 447 (1968).

9. See § 147 infra.

§ 136

1. See generally 8 Wigmore, Evidence § 2268 (McNaughton rev.1961); 81 Am.Jur.2d Witnesses § 36; C.J.S. Witnesses § 452; Dec.Dig. Witnesses ⟳307.

as to any or all of an extended line of questions.[2]

The rationale for requiring a witness to submit to questioning and to assert the privilege if he desires to invoke it is that the nature of the privilege so requires. Since the privilege is applicable only if the specific response would come within the scope of protection and the witness is not the ultimate arbiter of whether this is the situation,[3] a decision on the propriety of invoking it cannot be made unless the question has been put and the witness has asserted his basis for refusal to answer. Of course, this procedure endangers to some extent the values which the privilege is designed to protect. Subjecting a witness to a series of questions to which he must respond by invoking the privilege is somewhat akin to the interrogation which the privilege has historically sought to protect against. Requiring that the witness make a question-by-question judgment on the legal necessity of responding creates a danger that the privilege will not be invoked because of confusion or physical exhaustion rather than the knowing and intentional decision not to invoke it required for a waiver of a constitutional right. Against these dangers, however, must be weighed the public interest in obtaining as much information as possible without directly infringing on the witness's protected rights. Moreover, where the purpose of the inquiry is not the taking of action against the subject of the inquiry, the danger of improper use of the inquiry is reduced. On balance, therefore, the

policy factors support the imposition of a more stringent and complex procedure upon one not an accused who wishes to invoke the privilege.

A witness who fails to invoke the privilege in this manner and makes incriminating admissions has lost the privilege in the sense that these admissions may be used against the witness in later criminal prosecutions against him. Thus in Garner v. United States [4] Garner filed federal income tax returns reporting certain income from "gambling" and "wagering." These returns were held properly admitted against him in his later prosecution for conspiracy to use interstate facilities to transmit information relating to gambling.

Situations such as those in *Garner* might be approached as raising issues of waiver. Under such an approach, the standard criterion for evaluating the effectiveness of a purported waiver of most federal constitutional rights might be applied; this would require that the witness' conduct be a voluntary relinquishment of a known right.[5] Under this approach, however, effective waivers would often be found wanting. Garner, for example, most likely did not regard his action in filing the returns as a voluntary relinquishment of what he understood was his privilege to decline to provide the government with the information contained in the returns.

In *Garner*, the Supreme Court chose to approach these situations not as involving waiver issues [6] but rather as raising the

---

2. United States v. Luxenberg, 374 F.2d 241 (6th Cir. 1967); United States v. Harmon, 339 F.2d 354 (6th Cir. 1964), cert. denied 380 U.S. 944; People v. Austin, 159 Colo. 445, 412 P.2d 425 (1966); Shifflett v. State, 245 Md. 169, 225 A.2d 440 (1967); Royal v. State, 236 Md. 443, 204 A.2d 500 (1964); Hinds v. John Hancock Mutual Life Insurance Co., 155 Me. 349, 155 A.2d 721 (1959).

3. See § 139 infra.

4. 424 U.S. 648 (1976).

5. See Johnson v. Zerbst, 304 U.S. 458 (1938).

6. The majority acknowledged that some cases have used waiver terminology. This usage is not "analytically sound," the Court concluded, and it commented that the term "waiver" is best reserved "for the pro-

cess by which one affirmatively renounces the protection of the privilege." 424 U.S. at 654 n. 9. The rationale for this was not developed. Citing Schneckloth v. Bustamonte, 412 U.S. 218 (1973), on remand 479 F.2d 1047 (9th Cir.), the Court commented that "we have recently made clear that an individual may lose the benefit of the privilege [against compelled self-incrimination] without making a knowing and intelligent waiver." 424 U.S. at 654 n. 9. But *Bustamonte* involved on its facts the Fourth Amendment right to be free from unreasonable searches and seizures. In the course of the *Bustamonte* discussion, the Court commented that the requirement of a knowing and intelligent waiver has been applied to those rights guaranteed to a criminal defendant in order to preserve a "fair" trial, apparently using "fair" in the sense of ac-

question of whether the witness' disclosures were "compelled" within the meaning of the privilege. In ordinary cases, the Court concluded, a witness—even if under compulsion to testify or otherwise make disclosures—who makes incriminating disclosures rather than invoking the privilege has not been compelled to incriminate himself within the meaning of the Fifth Amendment.[7]

The Court's choice of analysis is important, because it dispenses with the need that would arise under a waiver approach to find, on the facts of each case, an understanding of the effects of disclosure and a "voluntary" decision to accept those effects. Like other nonwaiver rules of preclusion or forfeiture,[8] the *Garner* rule rests on policy concerns other than the witness' conscious decision to forego exercise of the right that the rule ultimately renders unavailable. The Government undoubtedly has a legitimate and important interest in compelling testimony and other disclosure in pursuit of legitimate governmental objectives. Often, and perhaps usually, pursuit of this interest does not involve or endanger anyone's interest in avoiding compelled self-incrimination. Compelling the government to anticipate when its inquiries will involve subjects' self-incriminating interests and then to raise these matters on its own initiative would impose an unreasonable and disruptive burden upon the government's pursuit of its legitimate functions. Subjects of such inquiries, on the other hand, can generally be assumed to

know when governmental inquiries endanger their self-incrimination interests and to have sufficient incentive to raise the matter when such danger is involved.[9] Requiring that the witness invoke the privilege is a reasonable allocation of responsibility for interjecting self-incrimination considerations into a government inquiry and avoids imposing upon the government a duty to anticipate self-incriminating issues.

In *Garner* the Supreme Court also addressed the right of a witness to a judicial determination of the propriety of a claim of the privilege before he is required to assert the claim in a context penalizing an improper claim of the privilege. In most situations, such as in-court testimony, a witness who asserts the privilege is afforded a ruling by the trial court on the validity of the assertion. If the trial court rules that the claim is not a valid one, the witness is generally as a matter of practice if not of absolute right given the opportunity to testify before contempt penalties are assessed.[10] Garner, however, urged that if he asserted his privilege by failing to respond to certain questions on his tax return and if this assertion was ultimately determined to be without merit, he could nevertheless be prosecuted for failing to make a return without an opportunity to comply. A preliminary-ruling procedure for testing the validity of assertions of the privilege, the Court commented, might well serve the best interest of the Government as well as of the taxpayer. But

---

ceptably accurate. 412 U.S. at 237. It further observed that purported "waivers" of the privilege against self-incrimination made before administrative agencies and congressional committees have been evaluated under the "knowing and intelligent" waiver standard. Id., at 238. But it noted Marchetti v. United States, 390 U.S. 39 (1968) as an "apparent exception" not subjected to the requirement of a knowing and intelligent waiver. Id., at 237 n. 18. *Garner's* apparent holding that the privilege against compelled self-incrimination can—sometimes at least—be lost by decisions that are not effective waivers under the Johnson v. Zerbst criterion is not well defended in the opinion.

See further § 55 n. 1 supra.

7. 424 U.S. at 665.

8. See generally, Dix, Waiver in Criminal Procedure: A Brief for More Careful Analysis, 55 Tex.L.

Rev. 193 (1977); Spritzer, Criminal Waiver, Procedural Default and the Burger Court, 126 U.Pa.L.Rev. 473 (1978); Westen, Away from Waiver: A Rationale for the Forfeiture of Constitutional Rights in Criminal Procedure, 75 Mich.L.Rev. 1214 (1977). See also, Dix, Waiver as an Independent Aspect of Criminal Procedure: Some Comments on Professor Westen's Suggestion, 1979 Ariz.St.L.J. 67.

9. Cf. Garner v. United States, 424 U.S. 648, 655 (1976): "Unless a witness objects, a government ordinarily may assume that its compulsory processes are not eliciting testimony that [the subject] deems to be incriminating. Only the witness knows whether the apparently innocent disclosure sought may incriminate him, and the burden appropriately lies with him to make a timely assertion of the privilege."

10. 424 U.S. at 663.

the majority concluded that no such procedure is constitutionally mandated.[11] Justice Marshall, joined by Justice Brennan, disagreed that a witness such as Garner could be compelled to test the validity of an assertion of the privilege at the risk of criminal liability. One such as Garner, he urged, must be given either a preliminary judicial ruling on his claim of the privilege or, in later criminal proceedings, afforded a defense of good-faith reliance upon a claim of the privilege. If neither is provided, Justice Marshall concluded, the witness has been denied the free choice to claim the privilege and any disclosures made must be regarded as "compelled" within the meaning of the privilege.[12]

 WESTLAW REFERENCES

garner /15 424 /5 648

digest,synopsis(disclos! volunt! /4 testif! tootimonl document* paper* file* record* /p incrimin! "fifth amendment" /p witness!)

privilege "fifth amendment" /s defense /p liabl! incrimin!

digest,synopsis(den*** /s privilege "fifth amendment" /p contempt)

---

§ 137. The Privilege of a Witness: (c) Right to Counsel and to Be Informed Regarding the Privilege [1]

Since one who is not the accused in a criminal proceeding is not entitled to be free from potentially self-incriminating interrogation, it might be expected that safeguards would be erected to assure that during such interrogation the privilege was not endangered.

When the litigation in which the witness testifies is in no way directed against the witness, as in civil litigation and a criminal trial of someone other than the witness, the courts repeatedly say that the court, on its own motion or at the suggestion of one of the parties, has the discretion but not a duty to take reasonable steps to safeguard the self-incrimination interests of a witness.[2] These steps may consist of warning the witness concerning the danger of self-incrimination and providing the witness with a clear opportunity to decline to answer. Or, they may be more dramatic, such as advising the witness to consult an attorney or even appointing an attorney to advise the witness, and perhaps also continuing the proceeding to permit the witness to seek advice and decide how to respond. Some cases do speak of a "duty" on the part of the trial judge to take such steps.[3] But the discussions are confused by the posture of most of the cases. Because of the personal nature of the privilege, it is generally clear that the parties have no standing to complain of the trial judge's possible failure adequately to safeguard the self-incrimination privilege of a witness. Thus any duty that exists is not

---

11. Id. at 664.

12. Id. at 667–668 (Marshall, J., concurring in the judgment). The majority concluded that good faith reliance on the privilege would be a defense under the statute defining the offense with which Garner was charged. Id. at 663 n. 18. Whether the majority would regard such a defense as constitutionally necessary is unclear. The Court commented only that, "The Fifth Amendment itself guarantees the taxpayer's insulation against liability imposed on the basis of a valid and timely claim of privilege . . . ." (emphasis supplied). Id. at 662–663.

§ 137

1. See generally 8 Wigmore, Evidence § 2269 (McNaughton rev.1961); 81 Am.Jur.2d Witnesses § 50; C.J.S. Witnesses § 449; Dec.Dig. Witnesses ☞302.

2. United States v. Morrison, 535 F.2d 223, 228 (3d Cir. 1976); United States ex rel. Robinson v. Zelker, 468 F.2d 159, 162 n. 5 (2d Cir. 1972), cert. denied 411

U.S. 939 (proper for judge sua sponte to advise witnesses of danger that answer might tend to incriminate as accomplices and advise them to consult lawyer); People v. Pantoja, 35 Ill.App.3d 375, 342 N.E.2d 110 (1976); State v. Mattatall, 114 R.I. 568, 337 A.2d 229 (1975). See also Frase v. Johnson, 9 Wn.App. 634, 513 P.2d 857 (1973) (rights of party to civil action not abridged when court and counsel for other side advised witness of right not to respond, given that elicited testimony would amount to admission of perjury at prior trial).

3. Pugh v. State, 376 So.2d 1135, 1144 (Ala.Cr.App. 1979), cert. denied 376 So.2d 1145 (Ala.) (when trial court was informed by prosecutor that defense witness might incriminate himself, trial court had duty and no other choice but to inform witness of right to silence and provide him with representation); State v. Schaub, 46 Ohio St.2d 25, 346 N.E.2d 295 (1976) (trial court has duty to protect rights of witnesses).

one enforceable by the parties to the litigation.[4]

A special problem is created, however, when—perhaps at the prosecution's request—a defense witness in a criminal trial is cautioned concerning the privilege. Here, the defendant clearly has a legitimate and enforceable interest, protected by the Sixth Amendment, in securing the witness' testimony. The trial judge has an unquestionable duty to accommodate carefully both the witness' interest in avoiding compelled self-incrimination and the defendant's interest in having all available evidence not barred by other legal doctrines. Generally, precautionary efforts by the court designed to assure respect for the witness' rights will not infringe upon the defendant's Sixth Amendment right to compel testimony.[5] But in extreme cases, a trial judge's admonishments or other responses might be so vigorous or out of proportion to the danger involved as to constitute a violation of the Sixth Amendment. This danger is especially great if the trial judge permits the prosecutor to perform or participate in the process of warning or advising the defense witness.[6]

The situation is significantly different where the proceeding in which the witness testifies is one that may result in the development of evidence tending to implicate the witness in a criminal offense or even the return of formal, criminal charges against him. The issue is raised most pointedly by the status of a grand jury witness, especially one who is or may be the subject or target of the grand jury's investigation or pending charges. It is reasonably clear that even one who is the target of a grand jury investigation does not have the privilege of a criminal defendant in that investigation and therefore may be compelled to appear and respond to questions.[7] It is equally clear that such a witness may, in response to particular questions, decline to answer responsively in reliance upon his privilege.[8] The major question is the need for additional protection for the privilege in this context.

Much of the discussion has centered around the applicability in this context of the protections afforded by Miranda v. Arizona[9] to one who is subjected to custodial interrogation, the right to an appointed attorney for one unable to afford retained counsel, and the right to be warned concerning the right to remain silent and to have counsel. The Supreme Court has firmly resolved very few issues in this area. In general, however, the Court has been quite hostile to efforts to persuade it to expand protections for witnesses in the grand jury context. This seems to be based on two grounds. First, the Court perceives the grand jury as unlikely to place improper pressure upon witnesses, because of the citizen composition of the bodies and judicial supervision of them.[10] Second, the Court appears to regard the flexibility of grand jury internal proce-

---

4. Bailey v. State, 398 So.2d 406 (Ala.Cr.App.1981) (defendant cannot complain on appeal of failure of trial court to warn state witnesses as to danger of self-incrimination). Informing the witness of his rights in the presence of the jury, of course, creates a danger that the jury will impermissibly infer from the situation that the testimony not given would have been unfavorable to one party to the litigation. See § 120 supra.

5. State v. Schaub, 46 Ohio St.2d 25, 346 N.E.2d 295 (1976).

6. People v. Shapiro, 50 N.Y.2d 747, 431 N.Y.S.2d 422, 409 N.E.2d 897 (1980) (prosecutor's threats to pursue perjury prosecution of defense witness if witness testified in a manner inconsistent with prior testimony violation of due process; on retrial, witnesses must be granted immunity). See also, Webb v. Texas, 409 U.S. 95 (1972) (trial judge violated defendant's Sixth and

Fourteenth Amendment rights by gratuitously singling out one defense witness, administering lengthy lecture on perjury, implying that he expected witness to lie, and assuring witness that if he lied he would be prosecuted, probably convicted, given sentence consecutive to one he was already serving, and stating that parole opportunities would be impaired).

7. See § 130 supra.

8. See United States v. Mandujano, 424 U.S. 564, 572 (1976), on remand 539 F.2d 106 (5th Cir.).

9. 384 U.S. 436 (1966), rehearing denied 385 U.S. 890. See § 150 infra.

10. See United States v. Mandujano, 425 U.S. 564, 580 (1976), on remand 539 F.2d 106 (5th Cir.), emphasizing minimal likelihood of abuse and supervision of judge as basis for regarding grand jury as "a setting wholly different" from custodial police interrogation.

dures as important to their ability to perform their tasks. Expansion of witnesses' rights, and particularly the involvement of lawyers in the process, is, under this view, likely to impede the effectiveness of the grand jury's proceedings.[11]

In United States v. Mandujano,[12] the prosecutor had informed the grand jury witness that despite his indigency he was entitled to representation but the lawyer would have to remain outside the grand jury room although he would be available for consultation. The Court characterized this as "plainly a correct recital of the law" and noted that under "settled principles" a grand jury witness is not entitled to have "his attorney" in the grand jury room.[13] While the Court thus seems to have approved the traditional rule that a grand jury witness is entitled to consult with an attorney before responding to particular questions, it is by no means clear that it has approved the prosecutor's apparent representation in *Mandujano* that an indigent witness who wanted representation of this sort was entitled to a lawyer at public expense. Some states do, by statute, permit at least "target witnesses" to have counsel in the grand jury room. Efforts to avoid disruption by so extending the right to counsel have been made by provisions that counsel may only advise the witness and that no witness may decline to appear because of his lawyer's unavailability.[14]

The Court has specifically declined to decide whether a grand jury witness is entitled to any warnings at all concerning the right to decline self-incriminating answers to questions asked during testimony.[15] Certainly, the *Miranda* warning that complete right to silence exists is not required, as the witness does have the legal duty to respond to nonincriminating questions. In United States v. Washington,[16] the Court made clear that a simple and comprehensive statement by the prosecutor as to witness' right to decline answers would meet any possible right to warnings. More important, the Court has found no need to decide whether a witness who is a target of a grand jury investigation is entitled, upon being compelled to appear and testify, to be warned of that fact. In *Washington* the Court's dictum reflects clear hostility towards a requirement of such warnings. Both target and nontarget witnesses, the Court reasoned, have the same right against compelled self-incrimination during a grand jury appearance. Since target witness status does not affect the scope of constitutional protection, the majority indicated that it saw a warning of such status as adding nothing of value of protection of Fifth Amendment rights in this area.[17] While such warnings are required by state law in some jurisdictions,[18] it appears quite unlikely that the Court will construe the Fifth Amendment privilege as requiring them.

On balance, the Court's approach seems artificial. While target-witness status may not affect a witness' formal legal rights, it may well mean that a witness is better advised to secure legal advice and to exercise caution than is otherwise necessary. Requiring that a person who is already known

---

11. Cf. United States v. Dionisio, 410 U.S. 1, 17 (1973) (to saddle grand juries with "minitrials" and "preliminary showings" would impede investigations and frustrate administration of criminal laws).

12. 425 U.S. 564 (1976), on remand 539 F.2d 106 (5th Cir.).

13. Id. at 581. See also, In re Groban, 352 U.S. 330 (1957) (witnesses summoned to appear and testify in fire marshall's investigation into burning of their structures were not entitled to be represented by counsel at that proceeding).

14. See Colo.Rev.Stat.1973, 16–5–204(4)(d) (any witness summoned is entitled to have counsel present, but "counsel for the witness shall be permitted only to counsel the witness and shall not make objections, arguments, or address the grand jury"). Ariz.Rules Crim.Proc., Rule 12.6 and N.M.Stat.Ann.1978, § 31–6–4(B), (C) are limited to target witnesses. Mass. Gen.Laws Ann. c. 277, § 14A provides that "[n]o witness may refuse to appear for reason of unavailability of counsel for that witness."

15. United States v. Washington, 431 U.S. 181, 190 (1977).

16. 431 U.S. 181 (1977).

17. Id. at 189.

18. See the statutes cited in note 14, supra.

to be a target witness be informed of that fact before testimony is begun would impose little burden on the grand jury process and might well serve significant Fifth Amendment functions. Whether the privilege should be regarded as conferring a right to have counsel present in the grand jury chamber is more problematic. Given the danger of confusion on the part of a witness, however, and the minimal danger of disruption if counsel's permissible role is carefully defined in advance, on balance the privilege would be best served by permitting witnesses to be accompanied by counsel and, at least in the case of target witnesses, of requiring that witnesses unable to secure their own representation be provided legal representation at public expense.

If the privilege of a witness has been violated in the course of litigation, the only available remedy appears to be the exclusion of the testimony elicited and any other evidence derived from it when and if that evidence is offered in later criminal litigation. A witness who is improperly interrogated before a grand jury is almost certainly entitled to only this remedy and not to have any resulting indictment dismissed.[19] Where the witness responds to the situation by committing perjury, however, it is likely that no remedy at all is available. In United States v. Wong,[20] a witness in a grand jury proceeding was warned of her privilege; she then denied certain criminal activity. When prosecuted for perjury, she established that because of her limited command of English, she had not understood the warnings. The Supreme Court nevertheless held that her testimony, given with apparent ignorance of

a right to refuse to respond, could be used in a perjury prosecution. Perjury, the Court concluded, is not an acceptable response to an interrogation conducted in violation of the witness' Fifth Amendment privilege.

 WESTLAW REFERENCES

410k302
advis! warn! instruct! /4 witness! /s incrimin!
digest,synopsis("grand jury" "custodial interrog!" /p entitle* right provid! /2 counsel! lawyer* attorney*)
mandyjano /15 425 /5 564
improper! violat! /6 interrog! question! /10 "grand jury"

---

§ 138. The Privilege of a Witness: (d) Definition of Incriminatory Response [1]

The requirement that a demanded response be "incriminatory" has not been construed strictly by the courts. The statements demanded, for example, need not be such as would themselves support a criminal conviction, and it is sufficient if they would furnish a link in the chain of circumstantial evidence necessary for conviction.[2] Moreover, it is not necessary that the witness anticipate that the responses themselves be used as evidence even in this limited fashion. It is enough if the responses would provide a lead to a source of evidence which might be used.[3] This attitude, of course, is consistent with the proposition that the answer need only have a *tendency* to incriminate. It is also sufficient, though the response itself creates no significant danger of incrimination, that it may operate as a waiver of the privilege in regard to further questions which may create such a danger;[4] the questions asked cannot be considered in isolation

---

19. See United States v. Blue, 384 U.S. 251 (1966) (if government acquired evidence in violation of Fifth Amendment, defendant was not entitled to dismissal of indictment but must challenge admissibility of evidence when case progresses to trial).

20. 431 U.S. 174 (1977).

§ 138

1. See generally 8 Wigmore, Evidence § 2260 (McNaughton rev.1961); 81 Am.Jur.2d Witnesses § 38; C.J.S. Witnesses § 436; Dec.Dig. Witnesses ⊕297(1), (2).

2. Blau v. United States, 340 U.S. 159, 161 (1950).

3. Counselman v. Hitchcock, 142 U.S. 547, 564 (1892) (the defect in the immunity statute at issue was that "it could not, and would not, prevent the use of his testimony to search out other testimony to be used in evidence . . . "); Hashagen v. United States, 283 F.2d 345, 348 (9th Cir. 1960); In re Levinson, 219 F.Supp. 589 (S.D.Cal.1963).

4. Malloy v. Hogan, 378 U.S. 1, 14 (1964).

and must be viewed together with other aspects of the inquiry.[5]

The scope of what is incriminating as thus evolved is illustrated by Malloy v. Hogan.[6] Malloy, convicted in 1959 of a gambling charge, was required to appear before a grand jury investigating gambling activities. When asked about the activities out of which his prior conviction had grown, he claimed his privilege. The Connecticut state courts overruled this claim on the ground that he was adequately protected by the double jeopardy rule and a one-year statute of limitations. The Supreme Court reversed on the ground that the prosecution desired ultimately to elicit from Malloy the names of those engaged with him in the illegal venture which formed the basis for the 1959 conviction. Under these circumstances, the court held, Malloy might fear that if these individuals were still engaged in illegal activities, the disclosures called for by the questions might furnish a link in a chain of evidence connecting him with more recent crimes for which he still might be prosecuted.[7]

 **WESTLAW
REFERENCES**

di incriminatory statement
malloy /15 375 /5 1

---

§ 139. The Privilege of a Witness: (e) Determination Whether a Specific Response Would Be Incriminatory [1]

Determining whether a specific demanded response would be incriminatory and thus within the protection of the privilege presents a more difficult problem than the general definition of incriminating responses. In some cases, of course, the matter is clear, as the question on its face calls for an incriminating response.[2] The difficulty centers around questions which are on their face innocent, as, for example, the question, "Do you know John Bergoti?" [3] When a witness invokes the privilege in response to such a question, these questions are raised: (a) who decides whether the response is incriminatory; (b) by what criterion is the propriety of the witness's invocation of the privilege determined; and (c) procedurally, who bears the burden of proof and the burden of making a factual record on which the issue is determined?

As to (a), the cases accept the proposition that the witness himself is not the final arbiter of whether his invocation is proper. Rather, the court itself has the obligation to determine whether the refusal to answer is in fact justifiable under the privilege.[4] Indeed, a contrary view would subordinate the effective operation of the judicial system to the desires of witnesses. The significance of this position, however, is clearly related to the other issues, as the effectiveness of granting the court authority to decide the matter depends in practice upon the criterion by which it decides the matter and the extent to which it can obtain a factual basis on which to make the decision.

As to the question (b), the traditional statement of the criterion has been that "the Court must see, from the circumstances of the case, and the nature of the evidence which the witness is called to give, that

---

5. United States v. Gordon, 236 F.2d 916 (2d Cir. 1956).

6. 378 U.S. 1 (1964).

7. Id. at 13.

§ 139

1. See generally 8 Wigmore, Evidence § 2260 (McNaughton rev. 1961); 81 Am.Jur.2d Witnesses §§ 49–53; C.J.S. Witnesses §§ 453, 454; Annot., 88 A.L.R.2d 463, 51 A.L.R.2d 1178. Cf. Annot., 19 A.L.R.2d 388 (right to invoke privilege in regard to relationship to organization); Dec.Dig. Witnesses ☞297(10), 307, 308.

2. "Did you bribe Officer Smith?" would be such a question. In re Boiardo, 34 N.J. 599, 170 A.2d 816 (1961).

3. See Malloy v. Hogan, 378 U.S. 1, 11–14 (1964), supra n. 6, § 138.

4. Hoffman v. United States, 341 U.S. 479, 486 (1951); Hashagen v. United States, 283 F.2d 345 (9th Cir. 1960); In re Newton, 12 Ohio App.2d 191, 231 N.E.2d 880 (1967); In re Petty, 18 Utah 2d 320, 422 P.2d 659 (1967).

there is reasonable ground to apprehend danger to the witness from his being compelled to answer." [5] Under this test, it seems that the court must find reasonable ground to believe that the witness is criminally liable and reasonable ground to believe that the response would at least lead to a link in the chain of evidence necessary for conviction. Thus a finding that the danger of a criminal prosecution is not "real and appreciable" requires the conclusion that invoking the privilege to protect against the danger is improper. Moreover, a trial judge is not limited to the record in the case in which the privilege is invoked, but may consider newspaper reports,[6] other proceedings [7] and general knowledge concerning the activities of human beings.[8]

On question (c), the traditional view has been that the witness, in order to avoid liability for contempt on the basis of his refusal to answer, may be required to provide sufficient information on which the court may find that a real danger of incrimination exists.[9] This limited requirement of disclosure as a condition of invoking the privilege clearly poses some danger to the interests the privilege is designed to protect. The classic defense of it was stated by Judge Learned Hand: "The . . . questions were on their face innocent, and it lay upon the defendant to show that the answers might criminate him. . . . Obviously a witness may not be compelled to do more than show that the answer is likely to be dangerous to

him, else he would be forced to disclose those very facts which the privilege protects. Logically, indeed, he is boxed in a paradox, for he must prove the criminatory character of what it is his privilege to protect because it is criminatory. The only practicable solution is to be content with the door's being set a little ajar, and while at times this no doubt partially destroys the privilege . . . nothing better is available." [10] Unless a minimum disclosure of the circumstances is compelled, the argument is, the court cannot exercise its function of determining the appropriateness of the witness's invocation of the privilege. For example, a witness subpoenaed to produce certain records of a travel agency can be required to testify as to whether the agency is a partnership because this information is essential to determining the propriety of the attempt to invoke the privilege.[11] The dilemma of a witness is best illustrated by those cases in which a witness believes that an accurate response would be inconsistent with earlier testimony and tend to bring about a perjury prosecution based upon the earlier statement. To require any explanation, of course, would alert authorities to the possibility of perjury and perhaps stimulate an investigation that would lead to prosecution and conviction.

These traditional formulations of answers to questions (b) and (c) respecting the determination of the propriety of a witness's invocation of the privilege have been severely

---

5. Mason v. United States, 244 U.S. 362, 365 (1917). The phrase was initially used by Cockburn, C.J. in The Queen v. Boyes, 1 B. & S. 311, 330, 121 Eng.Rep. 730, 738 (Q.B.1861).

6. Hoffman v. United States, 341 U.S. 479 (1951); In re Portell, 245 F.2d 183 (7th Cir. 1957).

7. In Young v. Knight, 329 S.W.2d 195 (Ky.1959) the court relied upon the witness's earlier statement before a grand jury to hold that her testimony would show only presence at the scene of the crime, a circumstance that would not give rise to criminal liability. See also Hoffman v. United States, 341 U.S. 479 (1951) (judge who had impaneled grand jury should have considered the grand jury's purpose as set out in his charge to them.)

8. Hoffman v. United States, 341 U.S. 479 (1951) (judge should have considered that the chief occupation of some individuals involves evasion of federal laws).

9. Presta v. Owsley, 345 S.W.2d 649 (Mo.App.1961) (witness has burden of proof of issue of incriminatory nature of answer); In re Boyd, 36 N.J. 285, 176 A.2d 793 (1963) ("naked assertion of possible incrimination by a mere statement of the abstract proposition" did not prevent contempt citation); In re Boiardo, 34 N.J. 599, 170 A.2d 816 (1961) ("except where the question itself contains the threat . . . a refusal to answer must be supplemented by a statement of the area of nature of the criminal exposure which is feared").

10. United States v. Weisman, 111 F.2d 260, 261–262 (2d Cir. 1940) (Hand, J.).

11. Nitti v. United States, 336 F.2d 576 (10th Cir. 1964).

shaken, however, and it is doubtful whether they accurately state existing law. The leading case is Hoffman v. United States,[12] in which the petitioner, subpoenaed before a federal grand jury, declined to answer any questions regarding recent contacts with one Weisberg, a witness who had not responded to a subpoena issued by the grand jury. The Court of Appeals held that there had been an insufficient showing of the relationship between possible responses and criminal liability; the Supreme Court reversed. "To sustain the privilege," the Court stated, "it need only be evident from the implications of the question, in the setting in which it was asked, that a responsive answer to the question or an explanation of why it cannot be answered might be dangerous because injurious disclosure could result." [13] After examining the circumstances which the trial judge should have considered—including the purpose of the grand jury investigation, Hoffman's admitted long acquaintance with Weisberg, general knowledge that the chief occupation of some individuals is criminal activity and that one person with a criminal record (which Hoffman had) called before a grand jury might be hid-

ing another person also called—the Court concluded that "in this setting it was not '*perfectly clear*, from a careful consideration of all the circumstances in the case, that the witness is mistaken, and that the answer[s] *cannot possibly* have such tendency' to incriminate." [14] The Court's first statement seems consistent with traditional doctrine—unless the court can conclude that further inquiry would create a danger of injurious disclosure it cannot sustain the claim of privilege, and if this conclusion cannot be drawn from circumstances already available for scrutiny the witness has the obligation to bring the necessary circumstances to the attention of the court. The second statement, on the other hand, indicates that the court may not refuse to sustain the privilege unless it can conclude that the witness's invocation is improper; this, of course, reallocates the burden and suggests that, in the absence of a sufficient factual basis for the conclusion, the claim of privilege must be allowed.

A number of courts have adopted the approach suggested by the second statement in *Hoffman*.[15] But some of these have further concluded that it is nevertheless imper-

---

12. 341 U.S. 479 (1951). The suggestion that *Hoffman* indicated a liberalization of the definition of incriminating response is strengthened by the Court's subsequent per curiam reversals of several other decisions of the courts of appeal. Simpson v. United States, 355 U.S. 7 (1957), reversing Wollam v. United States, 244 F.2d 212 (9th Cir. 1957), MacKenzie v. United States, 244 F.2d 712 (9th Cir. 1957), and Simpson v. United States, 241 F.2d 222 (9th Cir. 1957); Singleton v. United States, 343 U.S. 944, reversing 193 F.2d 464 (3d Cir. 1952). See the discussion in Shendal v. United States, 312 F.2d 564 (9th Cir. 1963).

13. Hoffman v. United States, 341 U.S. 479, 486–487 (1951).

14. Id. at 488. The phrase was taken from the following passage in Temple v. Commonwealth, 75 Va. 892, 898 (1881):

"[W]here the witness on oath declares his belief that the answer to the question would criminate, or tend to criminate him, the court cannot compel him to answer, unless it is *perfectly clear*, from a careful consideration of all the circumstances in the case, that the witness is mistaken, and that the answer *cannot possibly* have such tendency."

15. In re U.S. Hoffman Can Corp., 373 F.2d 622 (3d Cir. 1967); United States v. Chandler, 380 F.2d 993 (2d

Cir. 1967); American Cyanamid Co. v. Sharff, 309 F.2d 790, 794 (3d Cir. 1962); United States v. Gordon, 236 F.2d 916 (2d Cir. 1956); Application of Leavitt, 174 Cal. App.2d 535, 345 P.2d 75 (1959); Reynolds v. Pope, 28 Conn.Sup. 59, 249 A.2d 260 (1968); Richardson v. State, 285 Md. 261, 401 A.2d 1021, 1025 (1979); People v. Joseph, 14 Mich.App. 494, 165 N.W.2d 633 (1968), affirmed in part, reversed in part 384 Mich. 24, 179 N.W.2d 383 ("it must be perfectly clear that the questions asked could not possibly have elicited testimony incriminating to the witness"); Murphy v. Commonwealth, 354 Mass. 81, 235 N.E.2d 552 (1968) (record inadequate to support conclusion that answers could not possibly lead to injurious disclosures); Commonwealth v. Baker, 348 Mass. 60, 201 N.E.2d 829 (1964), overruling Sandrelli v. Commonwealth, 342 Mass. 129, 172 N.E.2d 449 (1961) to the extent that it might require a lesser proof; State ex rel. Harry Shapiro, Jr., Realty & Investment Co. v. Cloyd, 615 S.W.2d 41 (Mo.1981); Layman v. Webb, 350 P.2d 323 (Okl.Cr.1960); Commonwealth v. Rolon, 486 Pa. 573, 406 A.2d 1039 (1979); Commonwealth v. Hawthorne, 428 Pa. 260, 236 A.2d 519 (1968); Hummell v. Superior Court, 100 R.I. 54, 211 A.2d 272 (1965) ("In our opinion [*Hoffman*] makes clear the duty of the court to refrain from placing upon the witness the burden of establishing the incriminating nature of responses to the questions by making dis-

missible to sustain a witness' claim of the privilege on the basis of the claim alone.[16] The question is to some degree academic. There are few situations in which no circumstances are presented from which the court can draw its conclusions, so the burden of producing a minimal factual showing may often be unimportant. Many witnesses who claim the privilege, moreover, may be unrepresented by counsel and will—whether required to or not—disclose information sufficient to establish a basis for fear of incrimination. Nevertheless, there remains uncertainty as to the propriety of sustaining a claim of the privilege if, because of the refusal of the witness to respond further or the failure of the judge to make inquiry, the record shows no more than a claim of the right to decline to respond.

A literal application of the second *Hoffman* statement would seem to require that in such situations the claim be sustained. This, however, is arguably inconsistent with the universally-accepted proposition, discussed above,[17] that the court rather than the witness must determine the propriety of the claim to the privilege. Some discussions tend to obscure the issue with general references to the need to decide each case on its own facts [18] and to the existence of substan-

tial discretion in the trial judge.[19] Several courts have recognized that *Hoffman* precludes placing any ordinary burden of proof on the witness but have attempted to substitute what is basically a requirement of argument. Under this approach, a witness has in situations apparently devoid of any risk of incrimination the burden of "showing" by argument how the answer to the question asked might link the witness to criminal liability and of convincing the trial judge that this "course and scheme of linkage" is not incredible under the circumstances.[20] This might mean, for example, that an unsworn argument by counsel that a response would tend to disclose perjury on the part of the witness would be enough.[21] No sworn acknowledgement of such perjury would be required of the witness. Yet this might defeat the privilege. The unsworn assertion might be fully effective in alerting prosecution authorities to the need to further scrutinize prior testimony of the witness and thus be fully as "incriminating" as compelled sworn testimony to that effect.

Because of this risk, some courts have apparently adopted a literal reading of the second statement by the Court in *Hoffman*. The Missouri Supreme Court,[22] for example, rejected the position taken by a lower Mis-

---

closures that in themselves would be incriminating"). Compare Gambale v. Commonwealth, 355 Mass. 394, 245 N.E.2d 246 (1969), cert. denied 396 U.S. 881 (employee of club who was present at stabbing and admitted striking victim could be compelled to testify to what he observed at the scene of the stabbing, because "the questions . . . were not accusatory and did not implicate him as a participant" and "mere presence at [the scene of the crime] . . . is not enough to allow a claim of privilege."). In regard to a subpoena *duces tecum*, see United States v. Cogan, 257 F.Supp. 170 (S.D.N.Y.1966).

Other courts, however, have relied upon the Court's first statement in *Hoffman* and have taken an approach more consistent with the traditional analysis. Thus in Johnson County National Bank v. Grainger, 42 N.C.App. 337, 256 S.E.2d 500 (1979), cert. denied 298 N.C. 304, 259 S.E.2d 300, the court held that where it is not immediately apparent to the trial judge that a witness' answer would tend to incriminate, the judge should inquire further. If on appeal the record fails to show some rational grounds for believing a real danger of self-incrimination exists, a trial judge's denial of the claim will not be reversed. See also, Brunswick Corp.

v. Doff, 638 F.2d 108, 110 (9th Cir. 1981), cert. denied 454 U.S. 862.

16. E.g., Commonwealth v. Rolon, 486 Pa. 573, 406 A.2d 1039 (1979); State v. Pari, ___ R.I. ___, 430 A.2d 429 (1981).

17. See text at note 4 supra.

18. E.g., Dorgan v. Kouba, 274 N.W.2d 167 (N.D. 1978).

19. Rey v. Means, 575 P.2d 116 (Okl.1978).

20. United States v. Coffey, 198 F.2d 438, 440 (3d Cir. 1952); North American Mortgage Investors v. Pomponio, 219 Va. 914, 919, 252 S.E.2d 345, 348–349 (1979).

21. See State v. Zamora, 84 N.M. 245, 501 P.2d 689 (App.1972), in which an unsworn claim by counsel that perjury would be disclosed was held sufficient. Compare People v. Borjas, 191 Colo. 218, 552 P.2d 26 (1976), relying upon a "statement" that a false report had been previously given.

22. State ex rel. Harry Shapiro, Jr., Realty & Investment Co. v. Cloyd, 615 S.W.2d 41 (Mo.1981).

souri appellate tribunal requiring the witness or his counsel to make a statement "in general terms" of a "rational basis" upon which the answers to the question asked could conceivably incriminate the witness.[23] Relying heavily upon *Hoffman*, the court held that "once a witness claims the privilege . . . *a rebuttable presumption arises that the witness' answer might tend to incriminate him,* a presumption that can be rebutted by a demonstration by the party seeking the answer that such answer 'cannot possibly' have such tendency to incriminate." [24] This, the court reasoned, is consistent with the proposition that the court rather than the witness is to decide whether the privilege has been properly invoked, because the court must determine whether the presumption has been rebutted.

 WESTLAW REFERENCES

hoffman /15 341 /5 479
410k308

---

§ 140. The Privilege of a Witness: (f) "Waiver" by Disclosure of Incriminating Facts [1]

The accused in a criminal proceeding by the mere act of testifying forfeits his privilege to a significant extent.[2] This rule obviously cannot hold true in regard to one not an accused, as such a person has no privilege to decline to testify and therefore would be in effect precluded from ever invoking the privilege. On the other hand, after a witness has revealed a certain amount of information, requiring him to make further disclosure may not significantly endanger the interests which the privilege pro-

tects. When, however, does the witness reach the point at which he may no longer invoke the privilege?

The leading case is Rogers v. United States [3] in which petitioner had testified before a grand jury to having held the office of Treasurer of the Communist Party and to having had possession of its membership lists and books until January of 1948, at which time she turned them over to another. When asked the identity of the person to whom she turned them over, she declined to answer. Affirming a sentence for contempt, the Supreme Court found that in view of her prior testimony, petitioner was not justified in declining to reveal the name of the person to whom the documents had been given, relying upon the well-accepted rule that where incriminating facts have been revealed without claiming the privilege, the privilege cannot be invoked to avoid disclosure of the details.

There are several aspects of uncertainty regarding the rationale for the *Rogers* result and, correspondingly, for determining whether in particular cases a witness has lost the right to rely upon the privilege. First, it is uncertain whether the prior testimony purportedly resulting in loss of the privilege must constitute a knowing and intelligent waiver as is often required for loss of an important constitutional right. While the *Rogers* opinion is not entirely clear on this, it appears that the witness' loss of the ability to rely on the privilege under *Rogers* is not based on waiver principles.[4] Consequently, the initial testimony need not meet the traditional "knowing and intelligent" test before the witness may be compelled to testify further.[5]

---

23. See Cantor v. Saitz, 562 S.W.2d 774 (Mo.App. 1978).

24. 615 S.W.2d at 46.

§ 140

1. See generally 8 Wigmore, Evidence § 2276(b)(1) (McNaughton rev.1961); Note, 14 Stan.L.Rev. 811 (1962); 81 Am.Jur.2d Witnesses §§ 62–68 (1976); C.J.S. Witnesses § 456; Dec.Dig. Witnesses ⊕305(1).

2. See § 132 supra.

3. 340 U.S. 367 (1951).

4. "Requiring full disclosure of details after a witness freely testifies as to a criminating fact does not rest upon a further 'waiver' of the privilege against self-incrimination." 340 U.S. at 374.

5. Taylor v. Commonwealth, 369 Mass. 183, 189–190, 338 N.E.2d 823, 827–828 (1975). See also, State v. Ahmadjian, ___ R.I. ___, 438 A.2d 1070, 1076 (1981) (under *Brown*, ability to rely on privilege can be lost by either intentional relinquishment or abandon-

Second, it is somewhat unclear the extent to which the *Rogers* result is based upon the need to avoid distortion of evidence. In *Rogers*, the Court noted that to permit a claim of the privilege "would open the way to distortion of facts by permitting a witness to select any stopping place in the testimony." [6] It is possible, of course, to read *Rogers* as concluding that whatever remaining interest the witness has in being able to invoke the privilege, this interest is outweighed by the general need to avoid triers of fact having to resolve cases on the basis of evidence distorted by witnesses' arbitrary decisions to invoke the privilege and thus preclude further inquiry into matters concerning which they have testified.[7] In Klein v. Harris,[8] the Second Circuit found this consideration so important as to require, before a witness is found to have lost the ability to claim the privilege, a determination that "the witness' prior statements have created a significant likelihood that the finder of fact will be left with and prone to rely on a distorted view of the truth." [9] Most courts, however, seem convinced that while the need to avoid distortion may be a consideration supporting the *Rogers* result, it is not so central a rationale as to warrant incorporation into the criteria for determining whether *Rogers* controls particular fact situations.

Third, it is uncertain the extent to which *Rogers* is merely an application of the general requirement that a demanded answer be incriminating.[10] The Court observed that in regard to each question as to which Rogers invoked her privilege, the court must consider her prior testimony and determine "whether the answer to that particular question would subject the witness to a 'real danger' of further crimination." [11] Rogers' contempt commitment was upheld because the Court found the question at issue would not increase her danger of prosecution and conviction.[12] This, of course, provides a satisfactory rationale for the *Rogers* result that requires recourse to neither waiver considerations nor the danger of distortion presented by any particular facts. It further provides the basis for a criterion for applying *Rogers* to additional situations. Most courts appear to have relied exclusively on this rationale and have asked in such situations whether responding to the question asked would, given the witness' prior testimony, increase the risk of incrimination. Only if the answer is negative has the witness lost the right to claim the privilege.[13]

Following this view of *Rogers* and the generally liberalized approach of the Supreme Court towards the privilege, lower courts have found relatively few situations

ment of the privilege or by disclosure). But some courts have applied a waiver requirement. United States v. Lyon, 397 F.2d 505 (7th Cir. 1968), cert. denied 393 U.S. 846 (testimony given under mistaken impression that immunity was granted not "waiver" and would not result in loss of ability subsequently to invoke privilege); State ex rel. Newman v. Anderson, 607 S.W.2d 445, 451 (Mo.App.1980) (answer to vague question failing effectively to disclose nature of inquiry was not knowing and intelligent waiver and did not require response to further questions). The Court's apparent conclusion, see § 136 supra, that the privilege may be lost by a failure to invoke it that does not constitute a waiver, of course, suggests that waiver standards need not be met here.

6. 340 U.S. at 371.

7. See Taylor v. Commonwealth, 369 Mass. 183, 190, 338 N.E.2d 823, 828 (1975).

8. 667 F.2d 274 (2d Cir. 1981).

9. Id. at 287.

10. See § 123 supra.

11. 340 U.S. at 374.

12. Id. at 374–375.

13. United States v. Haro, 573 F.2d 661, 669 (10th Cir. 1978), cert. denied 439 U.S. 851 (testimony by witness that he had "observed" burglary did not require that he answer whether he had participated in it); United States v. Colyer, 571 F.2d 941, 944 n. 3 (5th Cir. 1978), cert. denied 439 U.S. 933 (testimony by witness that he had gone to bar frequented by gays and invited a man to come home with him did not require that he respond to question as to whether he was a homosexual); Commonwealth v. Funches, 379 Mass. 283, 397 N.E.2d 1097 (1979) (testimony by witness that subjects told him they were at location to buy heroin did not require that witness respond to question concerning whether he talked with subjects about price). Compare Draper v. State, 596 S.W.2d 855, 857 (Tex.Cr.App. 1980) (witness who testified that he had phoned defendant and had arranged to meet with defendant at time and place of defendant's arrest should have been compelled to disclose the purpose of the meeting over a claim of the privilege).

in which a witness may be compelled to continue with his testimony. This trend has been reinforced by holdings that a person who testifies does not subject himself to a duty to respond to questions as to separate crimes unrelated to his direct testimony, sought only for purposes of impeachment.[14]

A special problem arises when a witness whose testimony is potentially damaging to a criminal defendant invokes the privilege on cross-examination. In such a situation, severe danger is posed to the defendant's Sixth Amendment right to effective confrontation of witnesses presented against him.[15] The defendant's remedy depends upon the extent to which the inability to test the witness's testimony is affected.[16]

The case law generally distinguishes between a witness' invoking the privilege in regard to matters collateral to the direct examination, which does not require striking of the witness' direct testimony, and invoking the privilege in regard to matters directly re-

lated to the direct examination, which entitles the defendant to have the direct testimony striken.[17] These terms, given their uncertainty in application, can be no more than guidelines, however, and the ultimate question must be whether the defendant's inability to test the accuracy of the witness' direct examination has been such as to create a substantial risk of prejudice.[18] Where no such risk has been created, the direct examination need not be stricken, although the jury might be instructed to evaluate it in light of the defendant's inability to secure answers to all of the questions the defense was entitled to ask.[19]

Waiver of the privilege by one not an accused, as the waiver of the privilege of an accused, is effective throughout but not beyond the "proceeding" in which it is made.[20] Thus it applies to additional appearances during the same proceeding but not to appearances in separate and independent proceedings. In regard to the privilege of a

14. See § 42 at nn. 23–25 supra.

15. Pointer v. Texas, 380 U.S. 400 (1965) (admission into evidence at trial of transcript of testimony taken at a preliminary hearing at which the accused lacked counsel and therefore was unable effectively to cross-examine constituted a denial of right to confrontation).

Other aspects of claims of the privilege by witnesses are discussed in § 120, supra. See generally Annot., 19 A.L.R.4th 368 (effect of prosecution calling witness to extract claim of self-incrimination).

16. For full discussions of this matter, see Coil v. United States, 343 F.2d 573 (8th Cir. 1965), cert. denied 382 U.S. 821; United States v. Cardillo, 316 F.2d 606 (2d Cir. 1963), cert. denied 375 U.S. 822.

17. United States v. Martino, 648 F.2d 367 (5th Cir. 1981), cert. denied 102 S.Ct. 2006; United States v. Diecidue, 603 F.2d 535 (5th Cir. 1979), cert. denied 445 U.S. 946; United States v. Seifert, 648 F.2d 557 (9th Cir. 1980); United States v. Brierly, 501 F.2d 1024 (8th Cir. 1974), cert. denied 419 U.S. 1052. Trial judges have wide discretion as to whether the witness' direct testimony must be stricken, United States v. Seifert, supra, and appellate review may be limited to abuse of discretion. United States v. Brierly, supra. See also § 19 supra.

18. See United States v. Seifert, 648 F.2d 557, 561–562 (9th Cir. 1980). In Dunbar v. Harris, 612 F.2d 690 (2d Cir. 1979), the witness, who had "set up" the three drug transactions for which the defendant had been prosecuted and who had observed one, invoked the privilege when asked on cross-examination about prior drug transactions. No constitutional error was

found in the trial court's failure to strike the witness' direct testimony, because the question went only to general credibility and thus involved a "collateral" matter. Striking the testimony would have been mandatory, the court commented, if the questions had gone to the truthfulness of the witness' testimony concerning specific events related to the crimes charged, such as the identity of the defendant as the seller.

19. In United States v. Seifert, 648 F.2d 557, 560–561 (9th Cir. 1980) the court held that the defendant was entitled to have the witness invoke the privilege before the jury. Unlike the situation presented when a witness refuses to give any testimony in reliance upon the privilege, the court concluded, the jury will be unlikely to give undue weight to the witness' action in regard to only a few questions.

20. Ottomano v. United States, 468 F.2d 269, 273 (1st Cir. 1972), cert. denied 409 U.S. 1128 (testimony at his own previous trial did not constitute waiver of privilege when witness was called to testify at trial of alleged co-conspirator); United States v. Miranti, 253 F.2d 135 (2d Cir. 1958) (witness' second appearance before same grand jury was not in "same proceeding" as first appearance and privilege could be invoked, where the appearances were a year apart and the witness had, in the interim, been convicted for offenses relating to the first appearance). The tendency to give limited effect to such "waivers" is well illlustrated by State v. Adams, 277 S.C. 115, 283 S.E.2d 582, 585 (1981), holding that a defendant's testimony at the guilt-innocence stage of his capital murder trial was not a waiver of the privilege in regard to the post-conviction penalty hearing.

witness, however, there has been more dispute as to what constitutes a separate and independent proceeding. Most litigation has concerned the effect of disclosure during initial stages of a criminal prosecution upon the person's ability to invoke the privilege at trial, and, specifically, upon the ability of a witness who has answered questions during a grand jury proceeding to invoke the privilege in regard to those same questions at the trial of the case. The overwhelming weight of authority holds that grand jury proceedings and other early stages of a prosecution are separate and independent of the trial of the case, and a waiver at these early stages does not preclude a witness from invoking the privilege at trial.[21] A contrary result concerning the effect of testimony before a grand jury was reached in Ellis v. United States,[22] relying primarily upon what the court perceived as the absence of any increased risk of incrimination created by compelling the witness to repeat previously-made disclosures at trial. This result seems inappropriate. In theory, a witness may be subject to no additional legal detriment by being required to repeat testimony. The fact of having testified in a self-incriminating manner on two occasions, however, may encourage prosecution or increase the credibility of those admissions if offered at trial. Moreover, there is a reasonable possi-

bility that in the excitement and confusion generated by rigorous examination and cross-examination the witness will, at trial, make admissions beyond those previously made.[23] The traditional rule is most consistent with the spirit of the privilege.

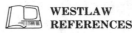

WESTLAW REFERENCES

410k305(1)
410k305(2)
rogers /15 340 /5 367

§ 141. Agreement to Waive the Privilege[1]

It is clear from the previous discussion that an accused person forfeits his privilege to a significant extent by testifying in his own behalf[2] and that one not an accused by testifying to incriminating matters loses the right under certain circumstances to decline to elaborate on those or related matters.[3] But may one agree in advance to forego the protection of the privilege and later be held to that promise? Few discussions of the matter are satisfactorily conclusive, but the Supreme Court has recently drastically reduced the potential effectiveness of any such contractual commitment.

Wigmore[4] takes the position that a contract, either expressed or implied, to waive the privilege is if otherwise enforcible bind-

---

21. The leading case is In re Neff, 206 F.2d 149 (3d Cir. 1953). See also, United States v. James, 609 F.2d 36, 45 (2d Cir. 1979), cert. denied 445 U.S. 905; United States v. Licavoli, 604 F.2d 613, 623 (9th Cir. 1979), cert. denied 446 U.S. 935 (refusing to follow *Ellis*, discussed in the text at note 22, infra). See also, Commonwealth v. Rodgers, 472 Pa. 435, 372 A.2d 771 (1976) (testimony at preliminary hearing is not bar to claim of privilege by witness at trial).

22. 416 F.2d 791 (D.C.Cir.1969).

23. See Instituto Nacional De Comercialization Agricola (Indeca) v. Continental Illinois National Bank, 530 F.Supp. 276, 278 (N.D.Ill.1981). The *Ellis* court attempted to meet this concern by making clear that the witness retained the right to invoke the privilege in regard to questions that called for answers going beyond the previous disclosure. 416 F.2d at 803. Further, it held that to protect this right a witness is entitled to representation by counsel, provided at state expense if necessary. Id. at 805. The court's willingness to find a waiver was clearly influenced by what it perceived as

the considerable public need for trial testimony in cases of the sort before it. Id. at 801–802. To the extent that *Ellis* rests upon this sort of consideration rather than the absence of a danger of further incrimination, of course, it has no applicability to situations not involving the criminal trial of a defendant. See Instituto Nacional v. Continental Illinois National Bank, supra (*Ellis* rationale not applicable where witness who testified before grand jury seeks to invoke privilege in deposition related to civil litigation).

§ 141

1. See generally 8 Wigmore, Evidence § 2275(a) (McNaughton rev.1961); Boudin, The Constitutional Privilege in Operation, 12 Lawyers Guild Rev. 128, 139–40 (1952).

2. § 132 supra.

3. § 140 supra.

4. 8 Wigmore, Evidence § 2275(a) (McNaughton rev.1961).

ing upon the party who agrees to waive his privilege. While the contract will not be specifically enforced (i.e., the party will not be held in contempt for refusal to testify) unless there is also a fiduciary duty or some other important public policy involved,[5] it will be given effect in determining rights between the parties to the agreement.[6] Little authority is cited, although Wigmore's position is more lenient than that of the original Uniform Rules (1953), which stated that one who would otherwise have a privilege "has no such privilege" if he has contracted with anyone not to claim it.[7]

The effectiveness of any agreement of this nature respecting a constitutional privilege was minimized by the Supreme Court in Stevens v. Marks.[8] Petitioner, a New York police officer, had, under threat of discharge from his employment, signed a waiver which the Court interpreted as purporting to have the effect of depriving him of his privilege as well as any immunity to which he might be entitled under New York law.[9] Reversing petitioner's contempt conviction for refusal to testify, the Court assumed the waiver valid but held that no justification appeared for denying the petitioner the right

to withdraw it. Therefore, his effort to withdraw it [10] and rely on his privilege was effective. After *Stevens*, the value of a contract analysis in this context seems minimal. *Stevens* makes clear that even if valid the agreement can generally be revoked and thus it is not necessary to reach the question of specific enforceability. Insofar as the impact of such an agreement would be to place the waiving party at some other disadvantage vis-à-vis the state, the matter would seem to be more appropriately handled as raising the issue whether an impermissible burden had been imposed on the exercise of the privilege.[11]

Insofar as the exercise of the privilege constitutes a breach of an agreement between two (or more) entirely private parties, the matter would seem to remain essentially private and any burden imposed on the party waiving the privilege would not be a state-imposed disadvantage.[12] It would, therefore, be beyond the scope of the protection afforded by the privilege.

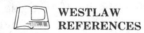 **WESTLAW REFERENCES**

410k219(6)

---

5. Probably the leading case for this proposition is United States v. Field, 193 F.2d 92 (2d Cir. 1952), cert. dismissed 342 U.S. 908. Appellants were trustees of a bail fund which had furnished bail for the unsuccessful petitioners in Dennis v. United States, 341 U.S. 494 (1950). When four of the petitioners did not appear to commence service of their sentence, their bail was declared forfeited, and the trustees were examined by the court and by a grand jury, during which they invoked their privilege in response to questions relevant to the whereabouts of the fugitives. In affirming contempt convictions, the Second Circuit reasoned that by assuming the position of bondsmen, the trustees had lost the right to invoke the privilege in regard to these matters. The court seemed to find an implied term of the bail contract with this effect. Boudin, supra n. 61, severely criticizes the holding.

6. Hickman v. London Assurance Corp., 184 Cal. 524, 195 P. 45 (1920) (judgment ordered for insurer in action on a contract of insurance which provided for the insured to submit to examination under oath, on the ground that the privilege did not prevent the enforcement of the insured's contract).

7. Original Uniform Rule 37 (1953). No corresponding provision appears in the Revised Uniform Evid. Rules (1974).

8. 383 U.S. 234 (1966).

9. Mr. Justice Harlan argued in dissent that the waiver signed by the petitioner was only a waiver of immunity rights under New York law and did not purport to deprive him of his federal constitutional privilege. Id. at 247 (Mr. Justice Harlan, dissenting). If this is an accurate characterization petitioner's privilege was legally intact but he could not testify (to save his employment) and escape prosecution by virtue of the state immunity statutes. The majority, however, cites convincingly from the record as proof that all concerned considered the effect of the document as a forfeiture of the privilege. Id. at 237–238.

10. The Court left open the possibility that withdrawal of a waiver might in some circumstances cause sufficient administrative inconvenience as to constitute "justification." Id. at 244 n. 10.

11. See § 121 supra.

12. Conceivably a private agreement could impose a disadvantage of such a significant nature that judicial enforcement of it would be state action. Cf. Shelley v. Kraemer, 334 U.S. 1 (1948).

§ 142. The "Required Records" Exception [1]

Access to carefully compiled records of regulated businesses and individuals is important to the success of many governmental regulatory schemes, schemes which are enforced in part at least by criminal sanctions imposed upon those who fail to comply. This need raises problems under the privilege. First, if a person is required to transcribe or otherwise maintain records which might subsequently be used to incriminate him, the requirement that the records be kept is quite arguably a compelling of testimonial activity in violation of the privilege.[2] Second, insofar as the government may compel one who has such records to produce them, the implied representations of the act of production may constitute a representation that the records produced are those demanded and thus may come within the privilege.[3] The required records exception to the privilege addresses itself to these issues: to what extent may the government require one to compile, maintain, and produce or permit inspection of records regarding one's activities, and then use these records, or information obtained by their use, in a criminal prosecution?

The leading case for the government's right to require, compel production of, and use records of this description in criminal prosecutions is Shapiro v. United States.[4]

Petitioner, a wholesale fresh produce dealer, was subject to the wartime Emergency Price Control Act of 1942.[5] Regulations promulgated under the Act required that anyone subject to the Act "preserve for examination by the Office of Price Administration all his records, including invoices, sales tickets, cash receipts, or other written evidences of sale or delivery . . . " and that he keep records of the kind he customarily had kept. In response to a subpoena *duces tecum*, petitioner produced the materials required by the Act. When he was subsequently prosecuted for violation of the Act he asserted as a plea in bar that the compulsory production of the materials had given him immunity, or, if no such immunity had been granted, that the statute under which he was prosecuted was unconstitutional. In rejecting his argument, the Court held that production of the material in issue could constitutionally be required of petitioner by the government without granting him immunity from prosecution or from its use. Although acknowledging limits on the government's right to require the keeping of records which must be made available to government investigators, the Court declared that "no serious misgivings that those bounds have been overstepped would appear to be evoked when there is a sufficient relationship between the activity sought to be regulated and the public concern. . . . " [6]

The bounds of this right remained substantially unexplored [7] until 1965 when the Court held in Albertson v. Subversive Activi-

---

§ 142

1. See generally 8 Wigmore, Evidence §§ 2259c, 2259d (McNaughton rev.1961); Meltzer, Required Records, the McCarran Act and the Privilege Against Self-Incrimination, 18 U.Chi.L.Rev. 687, 708 (1951); Comment, 65 Colum.L.Rev. 681 (1965); 81 Am.Jur.2d Witnesses § 45 (1976); C.J.S. Witnesses § 448, p. 282; Dec.Dig. Criminal Law ⚖=393(1).

2. See § 124 supra.

3. See § 126 supra. To the extent, of course, that the cases discussed in § 126 have reduced the limits placed by the privilege upon compelled production of documents, no exception to the privilege is necessary to compel their production. Even if compelled production of such records does not constitute compelled testimonial self-incrimination, however, the requirement

that the records be maintained, see text at n. 2 supra, will still invoke the protection of the privilege and necessitate the exploration of a possible exception to that protection for required records.

4. 335 U.S. 1 (1948).

5. Ch. 26, 56 Stat. 23.

6. Shapiro v. United States, 335 U.S. 1, 32 (1948).

7. In United States v. Sullivan, 274 U.S. 259 (1927), the Court had held that the privilege did not entitle the petitioner to decline to file an income tax return, although it suggested that the privilege might have been invoked to sustain a refusal to respond to specific portions of the return. In United States v. Kahriger, 345 U.S. 22 (1953), the Court had held the federal wagering tax provisions valid under constitutional attack on the

ties Control Board [8] that officers of the Communist Party could not be required to file a registration statement for the party as required by the Subversive Activities Control Act of 1950. Three years later, in a trilogy of cases—Marchetti v. United States,[9] Grosso v. United States,[10] and Haynes v. United States [11]—the Court held that individuals could not be required to register or to pay the occupational tax as required by the federal wagering tax statutes [12] nor could they be required to register a regulated firearm as required by federal statute.[13] In distinguishing the required record doctrine and *Shapiro* the Court outlined the limits of the required records rule as follows:

"The premises of the doctrine, as it is described in *Shapiro*, are evidently three: first, the purposes of the United States' inquiry must be essentially regulatory; second, information is to be obtained by requiring the preservation of records of a kind which the regulated party has customarily kept; and third, the records themselves must have assumed 'public aspects' which render them at least analogous to public documents." [14]

The federal wagering tax provisions and the firearm registration requirements, like the registration requirements in *Albertson*, were not essentially regulatory but rather concerned an area "permeated with criminal statutes" and were directed at "a highly selective group inherently suspect of criminal

activities." [15] The records concerned in the wagering tax provisions, moreover, lacked any aspects making them analogous to public documents, and the information which the statute required be provided was unrelated to any records of the kind the individual customarily kept; thus the second and third requirement were also not met.[16]

An amended version of the National Firearms Act was, however, upheld in United States v. Freed.[17] Under the amended version, all possessors of firearms rather than principally those engaged in unlawful activities were required to comply. In addition, only one who lawfully made, manufactured, or imported firearms was required to register them prior to their transfer; the transferee had no such obligation, although the application for registration was required to include the transferee's photograph and fingerprints. (The statute also prohibited the receipt or possession of a firearm by one to whom the firearm was not registered under the act.) Finally, the federal statute specifically prohibited direct or indirect use of information or evidence provided in compliance with the act in any criminal prosecution involving a violation of the law occurring prior to or concurrently with the filing of the information or the compiling of the records containing such information. The Solicitor General of the United States represented to

basis that they required only disclosure of future criminal activities and that the privilege provided no protection against compelled disclosures relating to future acts. This rationale was also used in Lewis v. United States, 348 U.S. 419 (1955). In Marchetti v. United States, 390 U.S. 39, 52–53 (1968), the Court commented that this analysis had overlooked significant hazards of incrimination as to past acts and, in any case, had hinged upon an "excessively narrow view of the scope of the constitutional privilege."

8.   382 U.S. 70 (1965).

9.   390 U.S. 39 (1968).

10.   390 U.S. 62 (1968).

11.   390 U.S. 85 (1968).

12.   Marchetti v. United States, 390 U.S. 39 (1968); Grosso v. United States, 390 U.S. 62 (1968).

13.   Haynes v. United States, 390 U.S. 85 (1968).

14.   Grosso v. United States, 390 U.S. 62, 67–68 (1968).

15.   The federal wagering tax provisions were subsequently amended so as to permit use of information obtained from the required records to be used only for civil or criminal enforcement of the wagering tax statute. 26 U.S.C.A. § 4424. This increased "regulatory" flavor has enabled the amended provisions to withstand attack. See United States v. Haydel, 649 F.2d 1152 (5th Cir. 1981), cert. denied 455 U.S. 1022 (Fifth Amendment not violated by statute's requirements that records be kept). But the Fifth Circuit has reserved decision on whether the Fifth Amendment would permit use of information derived from such records in prosecution for gambling offenses as opposed to prosecutions for failing to pay the wagering tax which is the primary regulatory objective of the statutory scheme. Id. at 1159 n. 15.

16.   In Leary v. United States, 395 U.S. 6 (1969), the Court held invalid the transfer tax provisions of the Marijuana Tax Act on the same grounds.

17.   401 U.S. 601 (1971).

the Supreme Court of the United States that as a matter of practice no information filed was disclosed to any law enforcement agency except as necessary to an investigation or prosecution under the act. Responding to the argument that the transferee's required cooperation in providing a photograph and fingerprints to be included in the application for registration would be compelled self-incrimination, the Court responded that in light of the prohibition against use of the information and the administrative practice of non-disclosure, the danger of incrimination was merely "trifling or imaginary." [18] Moreover, commented Mr. Justice Douglas for the Court, the self-incrimination clause could not be given as expansive an interpretation as would be required to establish a periphery which protects a person against not only past or present transgressions but also a career of crime about to be launched.[19]

A variety of rationales have been suggested for the "required records" exception, but none provides a satisfactory method of measuring its scope. Relying on the rule that a document, entry, or writing which is part of the state's official records is available for inspection and use without regard to tendency to incriminate its custodian,[20] it has been suggested that a public property right attaches to records which are part of a regulatory scheme and that this property right in the public creates the public right to access and use.[21] This reasoning, however, begs the question—to what extent may and should the law attach such a property right? Another analysis suggests that since the

state may prohibit the regulated activity it has the power to condition its performance upon forfeiture or "implied waiver" of the privilege.[22] This analysis, rejected in *Marchetti*,[23] does not explain application of the exception to businesses whose prohibition might well be beyond the legislative power in any reasonably conceivable situation and, like the "property right" analysis, begs the underlying question. The best approach seems simply in recognizing the doctrine as a limitation on the privilege based upon the public need for information in limited circumstances to make effective public regulation of certain activities. Thus in a specific case the question becomes whether there is a sufficient public interest to outweigh the strong policy in favor of maintaining the protection of the privilege. Following the Court's analysis of *Shapiro*, this should include: (a) a consideration of the importance of effective regulation of the underlying activity; (b) the availability of methods other than compulsory self-incrimination as a means of making this regulation effective; (c) the burden placed on the person by the requirement, as, for example, whether he is required to perform extensive activities to collect the information that he would not otherwise perform, or whether the requirement is simply that he grant access to information that he would otherwise keep for his own use; (d) the extent to which the records are simply a convenient method of collecting essentially public information (such as the sales of a business) as opposed to requiring that the individual record and

18. Id. at 606.

19. Id. at 606–607.

20. 8 Wigmore, Evidence § 2259(1) (McNaughton rev.1961).

21. Comment, 65 Colum.L.Rev. 681, 685–86 (1968), reading *Shapiro* as suggesting this analysis and citing Boyd v. United States, 116 U.S. 616 (1886), as precedent.

22. McCormick, Evidence § 134, pp. 282–283 (1954); Lewis v. United States, 348 U.S. 419 (1955).

23. Marchetti v. United States, 390 U.S. 39, 51–52 (1968). The argument was made in *Lewis* that since the petitioner had no constitutional right to gamble he had no right to gamble free of the duty to incriminate

himself for doing so. He was put to the choice of either not gambling or gambling and forfeiting the privilege. The Court in *Marchetti* responded:

"We find this reasoning no longer persuasive. The question is not whether petitioner has a 'right' to violate state law, but whether, having done so, he may be compelled to give evidence against himself. The constitutional privilege was intended to shield the guilty and imprudent as well as the innocent and foresighted; if such an inference of antecedent choice were alone enough to abrogate the privilege's protection, it would be excluded from the situations in which it has historically been guaranteed, and withheld from those who most require it." Id. at 51.

submit to public authorities information of a personal nature that would not otherwise be disclosed; (e) the extent to which the information revealed would be of value to the government for purposes other than the criminal prosecution of the individual to reveal it; and (f) the existence and effectiveness of any limitations upon the access of prosecuting agencies to the information.[24]

Lower court litigation has often centered on whether particular records have sufficient "public aspects" to bring them within the required records doctrine. Generally, the courts have been willing to find adequate public aspects. Thus the courts have found within the exception records of a customhouse brokerage service, kept pursuant to regulations of the United States Custom Service,[25] records concerning funds entrusted to lawyers by their clients,[26] escrow accounts of real estate brokers,[27] and records of a pharmacy concerning various customers

and the prices charged them maintained pursuant to federal regulations and a medicaid provider program agreement.[28]

If the requirement that records be kept does not violate the Fifth Amendment, it seems to follow that the records may be seized in an otherwise permissible search and used in evidence in a criminal prosecution.[29] Further, those required to maintain the records may, in response to an otherwise valid subpoena or other demand, be required to surrender the records. The exception for required records also removes the Fifth Amendment's protection for any direct or implied testimonial authentication or other disclosure involved in such production.[30]

WESTLAW REFERENCES

synopsis,digest("required record*" /s except! exempt!)
shapiro /15 335 /5 1

---

24. In California v. Byers, 402 U.S. 424 (1971), the Supreme Court upheld the constitutionality of a statute requiring drivers of vehicles involved in accidents to stop and leave their names and addresses. The plurality opinion, joined in by four justices, held that in view of the nature of the group at which the requirement was aimed (not one composed of those "inherently suspect of criminal activities"), there was no substantial danger of incrimination. In the alternative, the opinion suggested that the activity involved was not "testimonial". Mr. Justice Harlan, whose concurrence established a majority, disagreed with the grounds relied upon by the plurality. Where self-reporting is used as a means of achieving regulatory goals, he concluded, "we must deal in degrees." "Considering the noncriminal governmental purpose in securing the information, the necessity for self-reporting as a means of securing the information, and the nature of the disclosures involved," the privilege against self-incrimination was not infringed and no immunity need be afforded the driver who complies with the statutory requirement. In view of the strong arguments that can be made against the reasoning of the plurality opinion (see Mr. Justice Brennan's dissent), Mr. Justice Harlan's analysis seems more satisfactory and consistent with Fifth Amendment policies.

25. In re Grand Jury Proceedings, 601 F.2d 162 (5th Cir. 1979). The fact that the requirement that the records be kept was established by administrative regulations rather than actual specific provision of legisla-

tion was held of no significance. Id., at 168. See also Matter of Morris Thrift Pharmacy, 397 So.2d 1301, 1304 n. 9 (La.1981). But in the absence of a requirement that the records be kept in either the legislation or administrative regulations authorized by the legislation, the records will not come within the exception. In People v. Mileris, 103 Ill.App.3d 589, 59 Ill.Dec. 307, 431 N.E.2d 1064 (1981), the state's Workmen's Compensation Act required a physician who made a report of an examination under the Act to give a copy of that report to the employee. It also authorized the Commission to obtain the physician's records by subpoena. But since the statute did not affirmatively require that any records be kept, records nevertheless maintained by a physician were held to not be within the required records exception.

26. In re Kennedy, 442 A.2d 79 (Del.1982) (dictum); Andresen v. Bar Association of Montgomery County, 269 Md. 313, 305 A.2d 845 (1973), cert. denied 414 U.S. 1065.

27. State Real Estate Commission v. Roberts, 441 Pa. 159, 271 A.2d 246 (1970), cert. denied 402 U.S. 905.

28. Matter of Morris Thrift Pharmacy, 397 So.2d 1301 (La.1981).

29. United States v. Haydel, 649 F.2d 1152, 1159 (5th Cir. 1981), cert. denied 455 U.S. 1022.

30. See In re Grand Jury Proceedings, 601 F.2d 162, 171 (5th Cir. 1979).

§ 143. Removing the Danger of Incrimination: Immunity and Immunity Statutes [1]

Since criminal liability for an act is a matter of legal mandate rather than an inherent characteristic of the act itself, it follows that the liability may also be removed by legal action. Removing liability removes the danger against which the privilege protects and makes the privilege unavailable. Thus if no conviction is possible because of a prior conviction [2] or acquittal,[3] passage of the period of limitations,[4] or executive pardon,[5] the privilege cannot be invoked. The same holds true if the one from whom testimony is sought is effectively granted legal immunity from any danger arising from his testimony which is within the protection of the privilege.[6]

Although in some jurisdictions prosecuting attorneys have been found to have inherent power to confer immunity,[7] in most jurisdictions their ability to do so depends upon specific legislative authorization.[8] Legislative activity in this area, however, has been piecemeal and the statutory provisions for conferring immunity are consequently varied and often confusing. Most jurisdictions have a number of different provisions each relating to a single crime or a limited category of crimes difficult to prove unless a participant "turns State's evidence;" these provisions often differ in phraseology and substance within a jurisdiction.[9] Some states and the United States, however, have enacted general immunity statutes [10] and Rule 732 of the Uniform Rules of Criminal

§ 143

1. See generally 8 Wigmore, Evidence §§ 2281–84 (McNaughton rev.1961); Mykkeltvedt, To Supplant the Fifth Amendment's Right against Compulsory Self-Incrimination: The Supreme Court and Federal Grants of Witness Immunity, 30 Mercer L.Rev. 633 (1979); Comment, 19 Vill.L.Rev. 470 (1974); Comment, 72 Yale L.J. 1568 (1963); 81 Am.Jur.2d Witnesses §§ 54–61 (1976); Annot., 13 A.L.R.2d 1439; C.J.S. Witnesses § 439; Dec.Dig. Witnesses ⚬⇒303, 304.

2. Rhea v. State, 226 Ark. 581, 291 S.W.2d 505 (1956).

3. See § 121 supra at n. 5.

4. Id. at n. 3.

5. Id. at n. 4.

6. It has been argued that immunity statutes cannot confer adequate immunity because the witness may despite the immunity be subjected to prosecution and required to assert a plea in bar or obtain a favorable ruling on a motion to quash. Brown v. Walker, 161 U.S. 591, 621–22 (1896) (Mr. Justice Shiras, dissenting). This view has found little support.

7. The Texas courts have found inherent power. Ex parte Copeland, 91 Tex.Cr.R. 549, 240 S.W. 314 (1922); Ex parte Muncy, 72 Tex.Cr.R. 541, 163 S.W. 29 (1914). See also, Surina v. Buckalew, 629 P.2d 969 (Alaska 1981) (prosecutor has inherent power to grant transactional or use immunity). Other courts have found less formal ways of avoiding the undesirable consequences which might flow from a promise of immunity without legislative authorization. Lowe v. State, 111 Md. 1, 73 A. 637 (1909), suggested that although an unauthorized promise of immunity from a prosecutor could not be pleaded in bar, the trial court should upon a showing of the promise continue the case to give the prosecutor an opportunity to file a *nolle prosequi* or to give the defendant an opportunity

to apply for a pardon. The Illinois Supreme Court arrived at an interesting compromise. A defendant who testified pursuant to an unauthorized promise of immunity from the prosecutor was held entitled to a discharge in a subsequent prosecution brought in violation of the promise. People v. Bogolowski, 326 Ill. 253, 157 N.E. 181 (1927). But the court refused to give such a promise full logical effect, and a witness who refused to testify after receiving a prosecutor's promise of immunity could not be held in contempt. People v. Rockola, 339 Ill. 474, 171 N.E. 559 (1930). The actual reason underlying the decision probably was a reluctance in effect to confer a pardoning power upon prosecutors without judicial supervision.

8. Governmental Ethics Commission v. Cahill, 225 Kan. 772, 594 P.2d 1103 (1979), cert. denied 444 U.S. 1007; Commonwealth v. Brown, 619 S.W.2d 699, 702 (Ky.1981). See generally Annot., 13 A.L.R.2d 1439. Where limited statutory authority to grant immunity exists and the courts recognize no inherent authority in prosecutors to grant immunity, informal efforts to confer immunity or purported grants of immunity beyond the scope of the statutes have not been favored. E.g., Ex parte Johnsey, 384 So.2d 1189 (Ala.Cr.App.1980), cert. denied 384 So.2d 1191 (Ala.) (order broader than statute invalid); Campos v. State, 91 N.M. 745, 580 P.2d 966 (1978) (in light of statute structuring immunity process, informal agreement not complying with statute is not effective).

9. Statutes are collected in 8 Wigmore, Evidence § 2281 n. 11 (McNaughton rev.1961).

10. West's Ann.Cal.Penal Code §§ 1324, 1324.1; N.Y.Crim.Pro.Law §§ 50.10, 50.20.

Title II of the Organized Crime Control Act of 1970 repealed more than fifty specific federal immunity statutes and substituted a general immunity statute 18 U.S.C.A. §§ 6001–6005. See McClellan, The Organized Crime Control Act (S. 30) or Its Critics: Which Threat-

Procedure (1974) [11] is also available as a guide. It will be observed that the Uniform Rule provides for transactional immunity, a choice which was made with great care.[12]

The major question in regard to immunity has been the scope of immunity that is necessary or desirable in order to render the privilege inapplicable. In 1892, the Supreme Court held that an immunity statute which conferred limited "use immunity"—that is, protection from the subsequent use of the witness' immunized testimony against the witness in a criminal prosecution—was inadequate where it did not protect the witness from the use of evidence obtained by using immunized testimony—that is, derivative evidence—as well as the testimony itself.[13] Dictum in the Court's opinion was widely regarded as committing the Court to the position that "transactional immunity"—that is, immunity from prosecution for those transactions about which the witness testified under immunity—is necessary to render the privilege effectively unavailable to a witness.

The major concern regarding immunity from the use of testimony and other evidence derived from that testimony is that it may be ineffective in practice. The prosecution may in fact be able to exploit a person's immunized testimony to his disadvantage in later prosecutions because of the person's inability to convince the courts that evidence offered by the prosecution was in fact obtained by exploiting the person's earlier immunized testimony. The matter was finally addressed in Kastigar v. United States,[14] in which the Court held that the Fifth Amendment does not require a grant of transactional immunity before a witness may be compelled to testify. The sole concern of the privilege, reasoned the majority, is the prevention of compulsion to give testimony that leads to the infliction of penalties affixed to criminal acts. "Immunity from the use of compelled testimony, as well as evidence derived directly and indirectly therefrom, affords this protection." [15] Turning to the long-standing concerns regarding the implementation of such grants of use immunity, the Court indicated that once a defendant establishes that he has previously testified under a grant of immunity concerning matters relating to the prosecution, the prosecution—upon defense objection—must affirmatively prove that the evidence it offers against the defendant is derived from a le-

---

ens Civil Liberties? 46 Notre Dame Law. 55, 82–86 (1970).

11. The text of Rule 732 of the Uniform Rules of Criminal Procedure is as follows:

(a) **Compelling production of information despite assertion of privilege.** In any proceeding under these Rules, if a witness refuses to answer or produce information on the basis of his privilege against self-incrimination, the [district] court, unless it finds that to do so would not further the administration of justice, shall compel him to answer or produce information if:

(1) The prosecuting attorney makes a written request to the [district] court to order the witness to answer or produce information, notwithstanding his claim of privilege; and

(2) The [district] court informs the witness that by so doing he will receive immunity under subdivision (b).

(b) **Nature and scope of immunity.** If, but for this Rule, the witness would have been privileged to withhold the answer or information given, and he complies with an order under subdivision (a) compelling him to answer or produce information, he may not be prosecuted or subjected to criminal penalty in the courts of this State for or on account of any transaction or matter concerning which, in compliance with the order, he gave answer or produced information.

(c) **Exception for perjury and contempt.** A witness granted immunity under this Rule may nevertheless be subjected to criminal penalty for any perjury, false swearing, or contempt committed in answering, failing to answer, or failing to produce information in compliance with the order.

12. See Comment, Rule 32, Uniform Rules of Criminal Procedure (1974).

13. Counselman v. Hitchcock, 142 U.S. 547, 585 (1892) ("We are clearly of opinion that no statute which leaves the party or witness subject to prosecution after he answers the criminating question put to him, can have the effect of supplanting the privilege conferred by the Constitution of the United States.").

14. 406 U.S. 441 (1972), rehearing denied 408 U.S. 931. See also, Zicarelli v. New Jersey State Commission of Investigation, 406 U.S. 472 (1972), a companion case to *Kastigar*, upholding a state immunity statute providing for use immunity. See generally Annot., 53 A.L.R.2d 1030.

15. Id. at 453.

gitimate source wholly independent of the previously compelled testimony.[16]

Kastigar has rendered a substantial amount of immunity legislation unnecessarily (although perhaps not undesirably) broad. Courts have quite properly regarded the Fifth Amendment as requiring no more than use immunity, although a statute which fails clearly to protect the witness from the use of derivative evidence is insufficient foundation for a grant of immunity that removes the privilege.[17] As a matter of state constitutional law or legislative policy, however, it may still be appropriate to rely upon the concern expressed in Justice Marshall's *Kasti-*

gar dissent: the "inevitable uncertainties of the fact-finding process" mean that even compelling the prosecution to establish an independent source for its evidence cannot adequately assure that one prosecuted for a matter concerning which he has previously been compelled to testify under immunity is actually in the exact same position as if he had not so testified.[18] Under this view, of course, transactional immunity may still be required as a matter of policy or of state constitutional construction.[19]

Although procedures for bringing immunity into effect depend upon the specific statute involved, the better drafted statutes

---

16. Id. at 460–461.

Use rather than transactional immunity will present more issues concerning the scope of immunity granted and the authority to determine that scope. In Pillsbury Co. v. Conboy, 103 S.Ct. 608 (1983), for example, a witness had been granted use immunity and had testified before a grand jury. Subsequently, the plaintiff in a civil suit sought to take his deposition and asked, on the basis of his grand jury testimony, whether he had "so testified" on that occasion. Conboy refused to answer in reliance upon his privilege against compelled self-incrimination. The trial court held him in contempt, apparently on the ground that the earlier grant of immunity also required him to respond to the same questions he answered in the grand jury context when those were asked in the civil litigation context. But the Supreme Court held that Conboy's refusal to answer was supported by his privilege. If the original grant of immunity was construed so as to require testimony in proceedings other than the grand jury, the Court reasoned, the parties to those other proceedings might be empowered to elicit information beyond that elicited by the Government before the grand jury. This information, of course, could not then be used by the Government in any criminal prosecution of Conboy. Use immunity is intended to give the Government control over the extent to which it sacrifices available evidence in order to obtain compelled testimony. To construe the grant of immunity in such a manner as to permit the parties to private litigation to affect the consequences of the grant would be inconsistent with this purpose. The Court noted but did not reach the question whether, if Conboy had chosen to answer, his answers would have been the "fruit" of his earlier compelled testimony before the grand jury and thus unavailable to the Government under the terms of the grant of immunity. 103 S.Ct. at 614, n. 13.

17. People ex rel. MacFarlane v. Sari, 196 Colo. 235, 585 P.2d 591 (1978); Commission on Special Revenue v. Ziskis, 35 Conn.Sup. 105, 398 A.2d 315 (1978); Eastham v. Arndt, 28 Wn.App. 524, 624 P.2d 1159 (1981).

18. 406 U.S. at 468–469 (Marshall, J., dissenting). Justice Marshall urged that the information necessary

to determine whether evidence was obtained by exploiting immunized testimony is uniquely within the access of the prosecution. Generally, the prosecution's "mere assertion" that evidence has an independent source will suffice to meet its burden and defendants will not have access to the information necessary to determine the validity of that claim. In addition, investigations will often involve numerous steps and different government agencies. As a result, even a prosecutor's good faith belief that evidence offered was not derived from immunized testimony cannot be relied upon because prosecutors will often be unaware of the ultimate source of the evidence.

19. Interjurisdictional problems, of course, complicate the matter. Might one jurisdiction's decision that transactional immunity is desirable as a matter of policy impose an unfair obstruction upon the ability of other jurisdictions that are concerned in the matter to pursue their own objectives? See Kastigar v. United States, 406 U.S. 441, 463–466 (1972), rehearing denied 408 U.S. 931 (Douglas, J., dissenting). A jurisdiction probably, however, lacks the ability to compel other jurisdictions to forego criminal prosecution. If state A grants a witness transactional immunity and then compels testimony concerning a matter that is also incriminating under the laws of state B, it seems likely that state B may still prosecute the witness. State B would, however, be unable to use the testimony compelled by state A or evidence derived therefrom. See Agrella v. Rivkind, 404 So.2d 1113 (Fla.App.1981) (state grant of transactional immunity results only in protection against use of evidence in federal prosecution but this is sufficient to render privilege unavailable to witness); In re Birdsong, 216 Kan. 297, 532 P.2d 1301 (1975). This seems a reasonable compromise between each jurisdiction's interest in making for internal purposes the choice between use and transactional immunity and each jurisdiction's interest in being free from having that decision made for it in particular cases by the legislature, courts, or prosecutors of other jurisdictions.

have in common several important requirements that must be complied with in order to divest the witness of his privilege: [20]

(1) The witness must be faced with an attempt by the state to use its power of testimonial inquiry. Thus the witness's position must be such that if he wrongfully refused to answer he would be subject to legal sanctions.

(2) The witness must invoke the privilege.[21] If the witness is willing to testify without the grant of immunity, there would be little reason for the state to grant immunity and much reason not to do so. It is often required, therefore, that before immunity can be conferred the questions must be put to the witness and he must decline to answer them, relying on his privilege.

(3) The application for immunity must be made by the prosecution authorities. The decision to seek immunity in return for testimony involves a determination that the value of the testimony would ultimately be greater than the value of the right to prosecute the witness or to use any testimony that he might be persuaded to give without the immunity. This is essentially a matter within the province of prosecution authorities, and many statutes make explicit their option

to decide whether to attempt to forfeit possible actions against the witness.

(4) The grant must be approved by the court, which under the Uniform Rule and some statutes may decline to approve it if to do so would be clearly to the contrary of the public interest. This requirement serves the purpose of formalizing the "agreement" and making it a matter of formal court record. It also provides the witness with notice that immunity has been granted and that he may no longer rely on the privilege. In addition, however, many statutes appear to be based on the policy that there should be some check on the prosecutor's power to forfeit the state's right to proceed against individuals who may well be guilty of criminal offenses.

No such carefully defined procedure is defined in many of the statutes, especially the so-called "automatic" immunity statutes which by their terms provide only that in a given situation a witness shall not be excused from testifying and then direct that the witness is to be protected from prosecution or the use of his testimony.[22] Nevertheless, a witness may not be held in contempt for failure to testify under even these automatic statutes unless "it has been demonstrated to him that an immunity, as broad in scope as the privilege it replaces, is available

---

20. See generally 8 Wigmore, Evidence § 2282 (McNaughton rev. 1961). In the Uniform Rule, n. 11 supra, and some statutes the procedure is carefully defined. E.g., West's Ann.Cal.Penal Code, § 1324. In others, all or some of these requirements may be read in. Special difficulties are raised by the "automatic" immunity statutes; see note 22 infra.

21. See Annot., 145 A.L.R. 1416. But see United States v. Monia, 317 U.S. 424 (1943) (since statute would appear to layman to grant immunity to one who simply testifies on request, there is no need for witness specifically to claim privilege).

22. See Marcus v. United States, 310 F.2d 143 (3d Cir. 1962) ("The immunity conferred by [47 U.S.C.A. § 409(1)] is the automatic statutory consequence of compulsory testimony."). The immunity conferred under these statutes has been held to extend only to matters which the testimony concerned "in a substantial way." Heike v. United States, 227 U.S. 131 (1913). The danger of the automatic immunity acts is that a government official may find after an investigation

that by calling witnesses he has unintentionally conferred immunity upon them. United States v. Weber, 255 F.Supp. 40 (D.N.J.1965), affirmed sub nom. United States v. Fisher, 384 U.S. 212 (1966); United States v. Niarchos, 125 F.Supp. 214 (D.D.C.1954) (immunity conferred without regard to prosecutor's intent to confer immunity when subject matter of inquiry was "substantially related" to offenses); State ex rel. Lurie v. Rosier, 226 So.2d 825 (Fla.App.1969). See generally Wexler, Automatic Witness Immunity Statutes and the Inadvertent Frustration of Criminal Prosecutions: A Call for Congressional Action, 55 Geo.L.J. 656 (1967), urging that the statutes be amended so that no immunity is conferred unless the witness specifically claims immunity and is nevertheless required to answer. The new general federal immunity provision (see n. 10, supra) provides for immunity only when "a witness refuses, on the basis of his privilege against self-incrimination, to testify or provide other information" and an order is communicated to him ordering him to testify or to provide such information. 18 U.S.C.A. § 6002.

and applicable to him." [23]   It is reasonable that this demonstration must include a representation by the court that in fact the statutory requirements have been complied with and the immunity has been validly conferred.

It is generally held that immunity does not protect the witness from prosecution for perjury committed in the giving of the immunized testimony. Thus a witness granted either transactional or use immunity may be prosecuted for perjury committed during the testimony and the testimony may be admitted as evidence during that prosecution.[24] Further, in United States v. Apfelbaum,[25] the Supreme Court held that neither the Fifth Amendment nor the federal immunity statute limited the government to using, in a perjury prosecution, the immunized testimony alleged to be the "corpus delicti" or "core" of the offense. Other immunized testimony could be used against the witness if it was relevant to the charge of perjury.

Special problems remain, however, when immunized testimony tends to prove that the witness committed perjury during other testimony, either before or after the immunized testimony. The majority's language in *Apfelbaum* suggests that the Fifth Amendment imposes no barrier to the use of immunized testimony in either situation: "[N]either the [federal] immunity statute nor the Fifth Amendment precludes the use of [a witness'] immunized testimony at a subsequent prosecution for making false statements, so long as that testimony conforms to otherwise applicable rules of evidence." [26]   Three members of the Court expressed reservations concerning this broad dictum.[27]   There is lower court authority for the proposition that a grant of immunity must protect the witness against the use of immunized testimony in a prosecution for perjury committed at a previous time.[28]   It may follow that full protection also requires that a prosecution for prior perjury be barred if the entire matter was disclosed and

23. Stevens v. Marks, 383 U.S. 234, 246 (1966), relying on Raley v. Ohio, 360 U.S. 423 (1959). In *Raley* petitioners had been called to testify before a state commission. They had been expressly told that the privilege applied, and had declined to answer questions. Later, they were prosecuted under a statute making it a criminal offense to refuse to testify "when lawfully required" to do so; an automatic immunity statute, the state argued, made their reliance on the privilege improper. In view of commands that were not only vague and contradictory but "actively misleading," the Court held, the convictions could not be sustained. Cf. United States v. Monia, 317 U.S. 424 (1943) (in view of statutory language, a witness need not specifically assert the privilege when subpoenaed to testify in order to obtain immunity granted under statute). It follows that while a court may save a statute which compels self-incrimination by judicially creating a grant of immunity, Murphy v. Waterfront Commission of New York Harbor, 378 U.S. 52 (1964) (right to have compelled testimony and fruits excluded in federal courts saves state immunity legislation); Byers v. Justice Court of Mendocino County, 71 Cal.2d 1039, 80 Cal. Rptr. 553, 458 P.2d 465 (1969), a witness cannot be punished for failure to comply with the compulsion unless he is made aware of the immunity and given a chance to answer. Murphy v. Waterfront Commission of New York Harbor, supra, at 79–80.

24. Glickstein v. United States, 222 U.S. 139 (1911) (witness may be prosecuted for perjury committed while testifying pursuant to statute directing that "no testimony given [under immunity] . . . shall be offered in evidence against him in any criminal proceed-

ing", and the witness's allegedly perjurious testimony may be admitted in evidence in the perjury prosecution); Washburn v. State, 167 Tex.Cr.R. 125, 318 S.W.2d 627 (1959), cert. denied 359 U.S. 965 (witness granted immunity was nevertheless subject to penalties for perjury and therefore competent).

Whether a grant of immunity is "voided" or otherwise rendered ineffective by perjury during the immunized testimony is uncertain. But see United States v. Kurzer, 534 F.2d 511, 518 (2d Cir. 1976), opinion after remand 422 F.Supp. 487 (D.C.N.Y.) (ordinarily the government should respond to a belief that an immunized witness lied during testimony by pursuing perjury or contempt charges rather than by attempting to abrogate the previous grant of immunity). See also Corson v. Hames, 239 Ga. 534, 238 S.E.2d 75 (1977) (immunity cannot be conditioned upon the testimony being full, complete, and truthful in every particular).

25. 445 U.S. 115 (1980), on remand 621 F.2d 62 (3rd Cir.).

26. Id. at 131.

27. Id. at 132–33 (Brennan, J., concurring in the judgment); id. at 133 (Blackmun, J., joined by Marshall, J., concurring in the judgment).

28. In re Grand Jury Proceedings, 644 F.2d 348 (5th Cir. 1981). See also, People v. Walker, 28 Ill.2d 585, 192 N.E.2d 819 (1963); State v. Paquette, 117 R.I. 638, 369 A.2d 1096 (1977) (transactional grant of immunity precludes prosecution for perjury during earlier testimony inconsistent with immunized testimony).

stimulated only by the witness' immunized testimony. Further, it has been urged that a witness must also be protected against the use of prior testimony to prove perjury during immunized testimony,[29] apparently on the rationale that the incriminating significance of the prior testimony was discovered by exploiting the witness' immunized testimony. It seems quite unlikely that the Fifth Amendment will be held to bar the use of admitted accurate immunized testimony to prove subsequent perjury. Just as there is no doctrine of "anticipatory contempt" in this area,[30] there is probably no "anticipatory perjury" doctrine that permits a person to gain immunity from later perjury by submitting to a demand for immunized testimony. Nor does the need for immunity to correspond to the protection it replaces demand any such doctrine.

If after giving immunized testimony, a witness is later prosecuted and testifies in his own defense, the immunized testimony may not be used for impeachment purposes.[31] Even if the immunized testimony tends reliably to suggest that the witness-defendant is committing perjury and thus should not be believed, the Supreme Court has made clear, this use of the testimony is not permissible. Immunized testimony is "the essence of coerced testimony" and thus inadmissible in light of the Fifth and Fourteenth Amendments' bar upon the use of compelled self-incrimination.

A special problem arises if a witness is granted transactional immunity on the assumption that the testimony will be incriminating but the testimony given turns out not to incriminate the witness. It has been suggested, on the basis of scant authority,[32] that legislatures do not intend to confer immunity in such situations without obtaining a benefit in return and therefore the transactional immunity becomes ineffective if the testimony is not incriminating.

Immunity is generally granted at the instance of the prosecution and for the purpose of obtaining information or testimony for the government's purposes. Often, the government's purpose is to make testimony available that incriminates someone other than the witness. Criminal defendants are urging with increasing frequency, however, that in at least some situations defendants are or should be entitled to have immunity granted to witnesses whose testimony would be favorable to the defense. Failing to grant such immunity sometimes, it is argued, violates defendants' Sixth Amendment right to compel testimony for defensive purposes.[33] Certain procedural difficulties are created by such claims, as immunity statutes often provide for grants of immunity only upon motion of the prosecution; thus the defense may lack statutory authority for a motion to have witnesses granted immunity. In Gov't of Virgin Islands v. Smith,[34] however, the court held that at least where the government's refusal to grant immunity to a defense witness is made with the deliberate intent of distorting judicial factfinding procedures, the trial court should dismiss the prosecution unless the government pursues its statutory right to request immunity for the defense witness. Further, the court held that the trial court should exercise inherent authority to grant judicial immunity to defense witnesses where it is shown that

---

29. In re Grand Jury Proceedings, 644 F.2d 348 (5th Cir. 1981).

30. See United States v. Bryan, 339 U.S. 323, 342 (1950), rehearing denied 339 U.S. 991 (testimony of witness who testified but refused to produce documents could be used in prosecution for "wilful default" despite automatic immunity statute).

31. New Jersey v. Portash, 440 U.S. 450 (1979).

32. 8 Wigmore, Evidence § 2282, pp. 512–13 (McNaughton rev.1961), relying on Carchidi v. State, 187 Wis. 438, 204 N.W. 473 (1925).

33. See generally Washington v. Texas, 388 U.S. 14 (1967), on remand 417 S.W.2d 278 (Tex.Cr.App.)

34. 615 F.2d 964 (3d Cir. 1980). See also People v. Shapiro, 50 N.Y.2d 747, 431 N.Y.S.2d 422, 409 N.E.2d 897 (1980) (prosecutor's threats of perjury to defense witness violated due process; inability to erase effect of this from witness' mind means immunity must be granted).

their testimony would be both exculpatory and "essential" to the defense and that there is no strong governmental interest militating against the grant of immunity. Other courts have refused to follow *Smith*, however, and the overwhelming tendency has been to find that the Sixth Amendment creates no general right in defendants to have their witnesses granted immunity to secure testimony.[35]

35.   United States v. Hunter, 672 F.2d 815 (10th Cir. 1982); United States v. Herbst, 641 F.2d 1161 (5th Cir. 1981), cert. denied 454 U.S. 851. A number of courts, however, have left open the possibility that under certain circumstances a defense witness might have to be granted immunity.   United States v. Praetorius, 622 F.2d 1054, 1064 (2d Cir. 1979), cert. denied 449 U.S. 860; Earl v. United States, 361 F.2d 531 (D.C.Cir.1966), cert. denied 388 U.S. 921 (stronger case for immunizing defense witnesses would be made if government had made its case based on witnesses granted immunity); People v. Sapia, 41 N.Y.2d 160, 391 N.Y.S.2d 93, 359

110k706(7)
410k304(4)
kastiger /15   406   /5   441
synopsis,digest("transactional immunity")

N.E.2d 688 (1976), cert. denied 434 U.S. 823 (immunity might be necessary if witness was, as agent of the state, an active participant in the criminal transaction).

Wigmore argues that making immunity available to defense witnesses would permit an offender to secure immunity by contriving with a defendant to be called as a witness. 8 Wigmore, Evidence § 2282, p. 519 (McNaughton rev.1961).   But if the grant of immunity required court approval, this danger would be greatly minimized.

Chapter 14

CONFESSIONS

Table of Sections

§ 144. "Confessions" and Admissibility

In criminal prosecutions, among the most frequently-raised evidentiary issues are those relating to the admissibility of self-incriminating statements or admissions by the defendant. These issues are the subject of the present Chapter.

Definition of "Confession." Traditional analysis sometimes requires inquiry into whether a self-incriminating statement by a defendant is a "confession" within a rather specialized meaning of that term. Some of the limitations or ancilliary requirements placed upon the admissibility of "confessions" are not applied when the self-incriminating statement is not a "confession." [1]

§ 144

1. Commonwealth v. Palmer, 265 Pa.Super. 462, 402 A.2d 530 (1979) (rule that corpus delicti must be established before confessions is admitted does not apply when admission is offered by state); People v. Stanton, 16 Ill.2d 459, 158 N.E.2d 47 (1959) (statute requiring copy of confession and list of witnesses be given to defense did not apply when only a statement not amounting to confession was used); People v. Williams, 71 Cal.2d 614, 79 Cal.Rptr. 65, 456 P.2d 633 (1969) (erroneous introduction of confession always requires reversal but erroneous admission of admission requires reversal

Where such a distinction is necessary, a "confession" is generally defined as a statement admitting or acknowledging all facts necessary for conviction of the crime at issue.[2] An "admission," on the other hand, consists of an admission or acknowledgment of a fact or facts tending to prove guilt but falling short of an admission to all essential elements of the crime.[3]

Both "confessions" and "admissions" are sometimes distinguished from so-called "exculpatory statements." The latter are defined as assertions by the accused intended at the time to show him guiltless but which, by the time of trial, tend to incriminate him.[4] A frequent use of exculpatory statements by the prosecution in criminal litigation is to introduce them together with evidence tending to establish their falsity. The jury is then asked to infer from the fact that the defendant offered a false exculpatory statement that he was conscious of his own guilt and, ultimately, was in fact guilty.[5] Exculpatory statements and admissions may also, of course, be used to prove guilt in circumstan-

tial ways other than this "consciousness of guilt" route.

In general, it is unlikely that these traditional distinctions have much current validity, at least in regard to the major issues in confession law. Miranda v. Arizona,[6] for example, clearly rejected the distinction insofar as its holding was concerned. Thus *Miranda's* requirements must be complied with to establish the admissibility of any self-incriminating statement resulting from custodial interrogation, whether that statement would, in traditional terms, be labeled a confession, an admission, or an exculpatory statement. It remains possible, however, that some legal requirements might apply to less than all self-incriminating statements of the defendant offered by the prosecution, most likely only to what would traditionally be regarded as confessions.[7]

This chapter, however, will assume unless a particular discussion requires otherwise that no distinction is appropriately drawn among self-incriminating admissions. Thus confession, admission, and statement are

only when error was prejudicial); State v. Hallam, 175 Mont. 492, 575 P.2d 55 (1977) (state's proof of a confession, but not an admission, is direct evidence of guilt and eliminates need for circumstantial evidence instruction).

2. Gladden v. Unsworth, 396 F.2d 373, 375 n. 2 (9th Cir. 1968); People v. Fitzgerald, 56 Cal.2d 855, 861, 17 Cal.Rptr. 129, 132, 366 P.2d 481, 484 (1961). Some definitions put the matter in somewhat more concise terms. See State v. Hallam, 175 Mont. 492, 503, 575 P.2d 55, 62 (1977) ("A 'confession' is an admission of crime itself"); State v. Schomaker, 303 N.W.2d 129, 130 (Iowa 1981) (confession is "an acknowledgment in express terms by a party in a criminal case of his guilt of the crime charged"). The statement does not, of course, have to include an express recitation of the elements of the offense. In State v. Hallam, supra, the defendant engaged in a conversation with a fireman concerning whether or not investigating authorities thought a particular fire was arson. At one point, the defendant explained, "[T]he reason that I am really worried is because I did do it." This was held to constitute a confession to arson.

3. State v. Hallam, 175 Mont. 492, 503, 575 P.2d 55, 62 (1977) ("an 'admission' concerns only some specific fact which, in turn, tends to establish guilt or some element of the offense").

4. United States v. Riley, 657 F.2d 1377, 1381 n. 5 (8th Cir. 1981) (exculpatory statements are "declara-

tions against the declarant's interest which indicate that the declarant is not responsible for the crime charged"); State v. Cobb, 2 Ariz.App. 71, 73, 406 P.2d 421, 423 (1965) (exculpatory statement is "a statement which tends to justify, excuse or clear the defendant from alleged fault or guilt"). See also, Opper v. United States, 348 U.S. 84, 91 (1954) (exculpatory statements "explain actions rather than admit guilt"). Confessions, admissions, and exculpatory statements are distinguished in State v. Cobbs, supra, and People v. Utley, 77 Misc.2d 86, 92, 353 N.Y.S.2d 301, 311 (1974).

5. United States v. Perry, 643 F.2d 38, 52 (2d Cir. 1981), cert. denied sub nom. Patterson v. United States, 454 U.S. 835 (defendant's false statement that boxes contained popcorn admissible as false exculpatory statement upon proof that boxes contained mannite); State v. Kasper, 137 Vt. 184, 404 A.2d 85 (1979) (false alibi admissible to prove guilt). See also, United States v. Green, 594 F.2d 1227, 1229 n. 1 (9th Cir. 1979), cert. denied 444 U.S. 583; People v. Cramer, 67 Cal.2d 127, 60 Cal.Rptr. 230, 429 P.2d 582 (1967); Fox v. United States, 421 A.2d 9, 13–14 (D.C.App.1980); Russell v. State, 583 P.2d 690, 699 (Wyo.1978). See generally, Dec.Digest Criminal Law ⊕351(10).

6. 384 U.S. 436 (1966). This was reaffirmed in Rhode Island v. Innis, 446 U.S. 291, 301 n. 5 (1980). See generally, §§ 150–153 infra.

7. Cases cited in n. 1 supra.

generally used interchangably in the discussion.

Manner of Proving Confession. A confession may, of course, consist of an oral admission by the defendant and the state may prove such an oral statement; the absence of a written embodiment does not preclude admissibility of the oral confession.[8] When there is a written document purporting to embody the defendant's out-of-court admissions, however the matter becomes somewhat more complicated. A written confession, like any other proffered documentary evidence, requires authentication. But there is no requirement that the defendant have signed the confession.[9] It is sufficient that the defendant has otherwise adopted the substance of the written document, as where there is proof that it was read to him and he orally acknowledged that it accurately reflected his earlier oral statement.[10] Even where there is no evidence of such adoption by the defendant, a written or typed document is admissible if there is other testimo-

ny that it accurately reflects what the defendant orally said at the relevant time.[11]

Theory of Admissibility. Confessions and admissions, as defined above, are out-of-court statements quite frequently offered to prove the truth of matters asserted therein and thus potentially subject to exclusion under the prohibition against hearsay. Nevertheless, there is general agreement that the prosecution is entitled to introduce confessions. The conceptual basis for this position is, however, unclear. If the justification for the admissibility of confessions turns upon whether confessions are within the rationale of one or more of the traditional exceptions to the prohibition against hearsay, certain difficulties arise.

Wigmore and Morgan[12] group together in one exception to the hearsay rule statements made by criminal defendants and those made by parties to civil litigation. This exception is based, in their view, upon the assumption that the major justification for excluding hearsay is the unavailability of the declarant for cross-examination. Since both

8. United States v. Dodier, 630 F.2d 232, 236 (4th Cir. 1980); United States v. Morris, 491 F.Supp. 226, 230 (S.D.Ga.1980); Hayes v. State, 152 Ga.App. 858, 859, 264 S.E.2d 307, 309 (1980). Contra, Vernon's Ann. Tex.Code Crim.Pro. art. 38.22, § 3(a) (general rule, subject to exceptions set out in statute, is that oral confession is inadmissible). See generally Annot., 23 A.L.R.2d 919; Dec.Dig. Criminal Law ⊸530.

9. State v. Shaffer, 229 Kan. 310, 624 P.2d 440 (1981); Commonwealth v. Harper, 485 Pa. 572, 403 A.2d 536 (1979). Contra, Vernon's Ann.Tex.Code Crim. Pro. art. 38.22, § 1 (admissible written statement defined as one signed by accused or made in accused's own handwriting). There is some suggestion that the written document may not be admissible but its admission is not prejudicial if there has been testimony that the defendant orally made the admissions contained in the document. See McBryar v. State, 368 So.2d 568, 573 (Ala.Crim.App.1979), cert. denied 368 So.2d 575 (Ala.).

10. See Commonwealth v. Harper, 485 Pa. 572, 403 A.2d 536 (1979), where the written confession of a defendant who could not read or write was held admissible upon a showing that the officers had read it to him and he "adopted" it.

11. State v. Shaffer, 229 Kan. 310, 624 P.2d 440 (1981) (transcript of notes of shorthand reporter properly read into evidence on testimony by reporter that transcript accurately reflected what defendant said). Compare State v. Rosa, 170 Conn. 417, 365 A.2d 1135

(1976), cert. denied 429 U.S. 845, in which the trial court was held properly to have excluded a written statement typed by a police stenographer who did not speak Spanish; the defendant, who did not speak English, had orally confessed in Spanish which was translated for the stenographer by a bilingual officer. The stenographer, of course, could not testify as to the accuracy of the statement because of the language barrier. The court indicated, however, that the statement would have been admissible if the stenographer had understood both languages and had testified that the statement, in English, accurately reflected what the defendant had said in Spanish, or if the interpreter who had translated at the station had testified at trial as to the accuracy of the statement. 170 Conn. at 427 n. 6, 365 A.2d at 1141 n. 6. See the hearsay exception for recorded recollection, Ch. 30 infra.

12. 3 Wigmore, Evidence § 816 (Chadbourn rev. 1970): "[T]he ground for receiving admissions in general . . . suffices also for confessions." Morgan, Admissions as an Exception to the Hearsay Rule, 30 Yale L.J. 355 (1921). See also Maguire, Evidence of Guilt, § 1.02 (1959) (confessions "a specialized sort of admission"); Green v. Georgia, 442 U.S. 95, 97 n. 3 (1979), on remand 244 Ga. 27, 257 S.E.2d 543, appeal after remand 246 Ga. 598, 272 S.E.2d 475, cert. denied 450 U.S. 936, rehearing denied 451 U.S. 933 (confession to crime under Georgia law is not considered hearsay when offered against the declarant).

criminal defendants and parties to civil litigation are available for examination during trial, the argument goes, the rationale for the hearsay rule does not apply.

There are weaknesses in this explanation. First, historically out-of-court statements of defendants were admissible before a party to a civil suit or an accused in a criminal proceeding became a competent witness.[13] Thus under this explanation the exception would have preceded its justification. Second, it is clear that the Fifth Amendment privilege against compulsory self-incrimination recognizes a right on the part of a criminal defendant to decline to submit to either direct or cross-examination at trial. Justification of a confession exception to the hearsay rule on the availability of the opportunity to waive this right may be inconsistent with the solicitude with which the privilege has recently been treated.[14]

The hearsay exception for declarations against interest has also been offered as a basis for the rule regarding out-of-court statements of an accused.[15] This, too, is subject to question. That a declaration was, at the time made, against the penal interests of the declarant was not traditionally considered sufficient to bring it within this exception.[16] Moreover, the confession rule includes statements—especially admissions and exculpatory statements—which were not against even the penal interests of the declarant at the time they were made and

thus would not today come within this version of the exception.

These possible difficulties of theory are simply bypassed by the Federal Rules of Evidence and substantial other modern thought which do not class admissions of party-opponents, including confessions, as hearsay at all.[17] Thus the admissibility of self-incriminating statements need not be evaluated in terms of compliance with any other traditional exception to the prohibition against hearsay but is left free to be considered *de novo*. A confession, especially one that survives the multiple attacks that can be made upon its admissibility, has traditionally been regarded as extraordinarily reliable evidence of the defendant's guilt.[18] While a defendant can attack a confession via personal trial testimony only by surrendering important procedural advantages, nevertheless this opportunity is available. On balance, the generally high probative value of this kind of evidence and the availability of means to address any doubts concerning reliability that might arise in particular cases support admission in evidence. It is useful, however, to approach the entire area of confession law with recognition that such evidence has been exempted from a general prohibition against the use of out-of-court statements.

Exclusionary Rules in Confession Law. Given the general principle that defendants' confessions are admissible to prove guilt, confession law becomes primarily an explo-

---

13. Wigmore points out that extra-judicial confessions were received (without any voluntariness consideration) during 1500's and 1600's. 3 Wigmore, Evidence § 818 (Chadbourn rev.1970). The rule that parties to a criminal or civil case were incompetent as witnesses, however, survived until mid-19th century. § 65 infra.

14. See § 131 supra.

15. Developments in the Law—Confessions, 79 Harv.L.Rev. 935, 953 (1966). See Opper v. United States, 348 U.S. 84, 90 (1954) (admissions by defendant "are competent as an admission against interest"). The phrase "admission against interest" involves a confusing commingling of two concepts, i.e. admissions of a party-opponent and declarations against interest. See § 276 infra.

16. See § 278 infra. The current trend is to consider a penal interest sufficient to satisfy the exception. Id.

17. See § 262 infra.

18. The classic statement of this position is that of Justice Harlan in Hopt v. Utah, 110 U.S. 574, 584–585 (1884):

A confession if freely and voluntarily made, is evidence of the most satisfactory character. Such a confession, said Eyre, C.B., 1 Leach 263, "is deserving of the highest credit, because it is presumed to flow from the strongest sense of guilt, and, therefore, it is admitted as proof of the crime to which it refers." . . . [T]he presumption upon which weight is given to such evidence [is] . . . that one who is innocent will not imperil his safety or prejudice his interests by an untrue statement . . . .

ration of rules that prevent the use of particular categories of confessions. These rules are of several different sorts. To a large extent, many confession rules are merely examples of the sort of exclusionary sanctions discussed in Chapter 15. That is, exclusion of the confession is mandated by a perceived need to implement policies other than the accurate ascertainment of the "truth." For example, the requirements that confessions be excluded if they are shown to be sufficiently related to an unlawful arrest [19] and—perhaps—to a delay in presenting the defendant before a judicial officer following arrest [20] are designed to implement the rules relating to the validity of arrests and prompt presentation. The *Miranda* requirements [21] pose a somewhat different issue. While to some extent the *Miranda* rules are designed to implement requirements seen as serving the purpose of preventing suspects from making inaccurate confessions, there may be little reason to believe that violation of those rules in a particular case suggests any significant doubt concerning the accuracy of the confession at issue.

The traditional voluntariness requirement,[22] on the other hand, is distinguishable from these other rules. Historically, the requirement appears to have developed as a means of assuring the accuracy of confessions,[23] and to some extent it still serves that purpose. Thus the voluntariness rule can be regarded as analogous to the due process prohibition against the use of eyewitness testimony after the witness has been exposed to an extraordinarily suggestive identification procedure;[24] both rules facilitate the accurate ascertainment of facts by safe-

guarding against unreliable evidence. But it is equally clear that as the voluntariness requirement has developed,[25] it has come to serve other functions as well. Among these are the prevention of certain types of law enforcement conduct, some of which are offensive because of the risk of unreliable resulting confessions and some of which are offensive for other reasons unrelated to the accuracy of the statements obtained.

 WESTLAW REFERENCES

Definition of Confession
digest(confession* /p defin!)

Manner of Proving Confession
topic(admission* confess! statement*) /p oral /p proof prove* proving

synopsis,digest(admission* confess! statement* /p illitera!)

synopsis,digest(admission* confess! statement* /p bilingual translat! spanish foreign native)

Theory of Admissibility
wigmore /4 evidence /4 816 & court(pa)

Exclusionary Rules in Confession Law
digest(hearsay /p exception* /p confess!)

§ 145. Corroboration and Independent Proof of the *Corpus Delicti* [1]

Early reservations as to the probative value of at least some confessions gave rise to a common law requirement that in order for a conviction based upon a confession to be sustained, the confession must have been corroborated by other evidence introduced at trial.[2] This requirement is widely if not universally recognized in modern law and is quite frequently embodied in statutes. [3] Despite its initial development in cases involv-

---

19. See § 157 infra.

20. See § 156 infra.

21. See §§ 150–153 infra.

22. See §§ 146–149 infra.

23. See §§ 146–147 infra.

24. See § 174 infra.

25. See § 147 infra.

§ 145

1. See generally 7 Wigmore, Evidence §§ 2070–2075 (Chadbourn rev.1978); Margolis, Corpus Delicti: State

of the Disunion, 2 Suffolk U.L.Rev. 44 (1966); Comment, 20 U.C.L.A.L.Rev. 1055 (1973); Developments in the Law—Confessions, 79 Harv.L.Rev. 938, 1072–84 (1966); Notes, 46 Fordham L.Rev. 1205 (1978), 103 U.Pa.L.Rev. 638 (1955); 30 Am.Jur.2d Evidence §§ 1136–1139; Annot., 45 A.L.R.2d 1316; C.J.S. Criminal Law § 839; Dec.Dig. Criminal Law ⬤533–35.

2. 7 Wigmore, Evidence §§ 2070–71 (Chadbourn rev.1978), discusses the historical background.

3. For statutory formulations, see Ga.Code, § 38–420 ("A confession alone, uncorroborated by any other evidence, shall not justify a conviction."); Iowa

ing violent crimes, the requirement is now applicable in all criminal cases. In the federal courts, at least, it applies not only to "confessions" in the traditional sense of the word [4] but also to admissions and exculpatory statements.[5] On the other hand, there is authority for the proposition that the corroboration requirement does not apply to judicial confessions.[6] In Warszower v. United States,[7] the Supreme Court found no need to corroborate a statement by the defendant, made *prior* to the allegedly false statement involved in the offense for which the defendant was being tried, where that earlier statement was used by the Government to prove the inaccuracy of the later statement.

Much confusion has been caused by failure to distinguish between two different formulations of the requirement. One requires only that in addition to the confession the record contain evidence tending to establish the reliability of the confession. The other—a requirement of independent proof of the *corpus delicti*—requires that the corroborating evidence tend to prove the commission of the crime at issue.

The second formulation of the requirement is sometimes phrased as a prerequisite for admissibility of a confession. Thus, it is said that the prosecution must introduce independent proof of the *corpus delicti* before the defendant's confession is admissible.[8] But trial courts are recognized as having broad discretion concerning the order of proof. Even under this statement of the requirement reversible error is not committed when a confession is accepted before such corroborating evidence is produced if, before the evidence closes, independent proof of the *corpus delicti* is placed in the record.[9]

Independent Proof of the Corpus Delicti. The vast majority of American jurisdictions have adopted the second of the two approaches distinguished above and require that the evidence contain independent proof of the *corpus delicti*. This, of course, requires that *corpus delicti* be defined. Literally, the phrase means the "body of the crime." To establish guilt in a criminal case, the prosecution must ordinarily show that (a) the injury or harm constituting the crime occurred; (b) this injury or harm was caused

R.Crim.Pro. 20(4) ("Out-of-court confessions cannot support a conviction unless corroborated by other evidence."); N.Y.—McKinney's Crim.Proc.L. § 60.50 (conviction not permitted "solely upon evidence of a confession or admission made by [the defendant] without additional proof that the offense charged has been committed"); Or.Rev.Stat. § 136.425(1) ("a confession only [is not] sufficient to warrant . . . conviction without some other proof that the crime has been committed").

The Massachusetts court rejected a corroboration requirement as too rigid in Commonwealth v. Kimball, 321 Mass. 290, 73 N.E.2d 468 (1947). See also Commonwealth v. Fiore, 364 Mass. 819, 288, 308 N.E.2d 902, 906 (1974).

The corroboration requirement must be distinguished from the common law rule that a murder conviction required direct proof of death of the victim or of the act of the defendant alleged to have caused the death of the victim. This rule required proof that the body of a homicide victim was found, although there were numerous exceptions. See generally, People v. Lipsky, 57 N.Y.2d 560, 457 N.Y.S.2d 451, 443 N.E.2d 925 (1982).

4. See generally § 144 supra.

5. See text at note 28 infra.

6. State v. Schomaker, 303 N.W.2d 129 (Iowa 1981), reasoning that the circumstances casting doubt upon the reliability of out-of-court confessions and state-

ments are generally not presented when the state offers a statement made in open court. Thus the rationale for requiring corroboration does not apply. 303 N.W.2d at 130.

7. 312 U.S. 342 (1941).

8. State v. Weis, 92 Ariz. 254, 260, 375 P.2d 735, 739 (1962) cert. denied 389 U.S. 899.

9. Tice v. State, 386 So.2d 1180, 1186 (Ala.Crim. App.1980), writ denied 386 So.2d 1187; State v. Romero, 369 So.2d 1342, 1343 (La.1979). See also, Pawlowski v. State, 269 Ind. 350, 380 N.E.2d 1230 (1978), in which no abuse of discretion was found in permitting the prosecution to reopen the taking of evidence to prove the *corpus delicti*.

In at least some jurisdictions the adequacy of corroboration is a jury issue and the defendant is entitled to have the jury properly instructed on the need for corroboration. See People v. Eaton, 25 A.D.2d 692, 268 N.Y.S.2d 255 (1966) (error, despite absence of request, to fail to charge jury on need to prove dehors the defendant's confession the causing of homicide victim's death by criminal act). But even in those jurisdictions, no error is committed by failing to instruct the jury on corroboration if it is clear on appeal that adequate corroboration existed. State v. Snedecor, 294 So.2d 207 (La.1974); Aranda v. State, 506 S.W.2d 221 (Tex.Cr. App.1974).

by someone's criminal activity; and (c) the defendant was the guilty party. It is widely accepted that the corpus delicti consists only of (a) and (b).[10] The corroborating evidence need not tend to establish that the defendant was the guilty party.[11] Nor is it necessary that the corroborating evidence tend to disprove any defensive claim urged by the defendant.[12]

Even as so defined, however, the concept of *corpus delicti* is not entirely clear. There is some authority for the proposition that injury or harm within the meaning of this definition means all elements of the crime charged other than the defendant's identity as the perpetrator.[13] Thus it may be necessary to identify carefully all elements of the prosecution's case and to inquire whether evidence other than the defendant's confession tends to prove each. On the other hand, injury or harm may not be so broadly defined. Thus it may be sufficient that the corroborating evidence tends to establish the major or essential harm or perhaps the prohibited conduct. Under this approach, it would not be controlling if some

elements of the crime—such as certain circumstances that must, under the definition of the offense, exist for the conduct to be criminal—are proved only by the defendant's confession.[14] Which approach is required has become increasingly important as modern penal codes define offenses more carefully and in increasingly complex fashion.

A special problem arises in felony murder prosecutions where the corroborating evidence tends to show the criminal causing of the victim's death but not the commission of the felony necessary to make the killing felony murder. Does the *corpus delicti* of felony murder include the commission of the felony? The California Court[15] has answered negatively, thereby rejecting the proposition that the *corpus delicti* includes all matters (other than the perpetrator's identity) which the state must show for conviction. The Michigan Court, however, has held that the corroboration must tend to prove the felony.[16] It adopted the dissenting opinion of the court below, which argued that given the significance of the underlying felony in a felony murder prosecution, the

10. Thomas v. State, 393 So.2d 504 (Ala.Crim.App. 1981); People v. Towler, 31 Cal.3d 105, 181 Cal.Rptr. 391, 641 P.2d 1253 (1982); State v. Carson, 336 So.2d 844 (La.1976), appeal after remand 367 So.2d 859; State v. Halstead, ___ R.I. ___, 414 A.2d 1138 (1980).

11. Mosley v. State, 246 Ark. 358, 438 S.W.2d 311 (1969); Self v. State, 513 S.W.2d 832 (Tex.Cr.App.1974).

12. People v. Murray, 40 N.Y.2d 327, 331, 386 N.Y.S.2d 691, 694, 353 N.E.2d 605, 608 (1976), cert. denied 430 U.S. 948 (no requirement in homicide case to negate self-defense).

13. Ruiz v. State, 388 So.2d 610 (Fla.App.1980), review denied 392 So.2d 1380 (1981), defining the *corpus delicti* as including all elements of the crime. In *Ruiz*, the offense at issue was accessory after the fact to a felony; while the court found an absence of independent evidence that the felon was in fact aided, it also relied upon the absence of such evidence other than the defendant's confession to show other elements of the offense, including the defendant's awareness that the person aided had committed a felony and the absence of a familial relationship between the defendant and the person aided. See also, Forte v. United States, 94 F.2d 236 (D.C.Cir.1937) (*corpus delicti* of transporting motor vehicle in interstate commerce knowing it to have been stolen included awareness that the vehicle was stolen); People v. Dalton, 93 Ill.App.3d 264, 48 Ill. Dec. 795, 417 N.E.2d 197 (1981) (*corpus delicti* of indecent liberties with a minor included age of victim).

14. State v. Cook, 26 Ariz.App. 198, 547 P.2d 50 (1976), affirmed on this ground but reversed in part on other grounds 115 Ariz. 188, 564 P.2d 877 (1977), concluding that in a first degree burglary prosecution the occurrence of the entry in the nighttime was not part of the *corpus delicti* where proof of this fact did not render otherwise noncriminal conduct criminal but merely increased the degree of the offense. Cf. Isaacs v. United States, 159 U.S. 487 (1895), a pre-*Opper* case, see text at n. 28 infra, in which the Court appeared to apply the *corpus delicti* rule but found, in a prosecution of an Indian for killing a white person in Indian country, that proof that the victim was a white person "had no bearing upon the question of the *corpus delicti* . . . and bore only upon the jurisdiction of the court." 159 U.S. at 490. Those felony murder cases finding no need for corroboration regarding the underlying felony, discussed in the text at n. 15 infra, also support this position.

15. People v. Cantrell, 8 Cal.3d 672, 105 Cal.Rptr. 792, 504 P.2d 1256 (1973). Accord, Harrison v. State, 269 Ind. 677, 382 N.E.2d 920 (1978), cert. denied 441 U.S. 912 (1979); Gentry v. State, 416 So.2d 650 (Miss. 1982).

16. People v. Allen, 390 Mich. 383, 212 N.W.2d 21 (1973).

policy of the *corpus delicti* rule dictated that the corroborating evidence tend to prove this important element of the prosecution's case.[17] The New York Court split evenly on the issue,[18] and then adopted the approach of the California court.[19]

In regard to the quantum of evidence necessary, there is widespread but apparently not universal [20] agreement that the corroborating evidence need not establish the *corpus delicti* beyond a reasonable doubt. Wide variation exists in the statement of the standard for determining the sufficiency of the evidence.[21] If this is met, however, it is quite clear that this evidence and the defendant's confession can be considered together in determining whether the prosecution has proved those matters constituting the *corpus delicti* beyond a reasonable doubt.[22] The corroborating evidence need not necessarily be direct evidence; circumstantial proof will do.[23] On the other hand, another uncorroborated statement of the defendant cannot be used to meet the requirement; a conviction will not, in other words, be upheld upon proof of two or more otherwise uncorroborated confessions.[24]

The application of the *corpus delicti* rule is perhaps best illustrated by the arson cases. In Adrian v. State,[25] the state proved

that the defendant confessed to setting a fire intentionally that damaged a house-trailer; he described in his confession starting the fire in the garage below the trailer. A number of witnesses testified to various details of the fire, including that it appeared to have started in the garage below the trailer. On appeal, the conviction was reversed. While the evidence left no doubt that a fire had occurred, there was no evidence apart from the confession that the fire was the result of criminal agency, i.e., that it was intentionally set. But where an effort is made to meet this, the requirement has substantial flexibility. Thus in State v. Zuercher,[26] evidence that the defendant harbored ill will towards the owner of the damaged structure and had been in the area shortly before the fire was discovered was held sufficient.

Evidence Tending to Establish the Trustworthiness of Confession. In Warszower v. United States,[27] the Supreme Court discussed but found no occasion to reach the defendant's contention that as a matter of federal law a conviction in federal court could not rest upon an uncorroborated confession and, further, that the corroboration "must reach to each element of the *corpus delicti.*" A requirement of corroboration was adopted, however in Opper v. United

17. People v. Allen, 39 Mich.App. 483, 496, 197 N.W.2d 874, 880 (1972) (Levin, J., dissenting), reversed 390 Mich. 383, 212 N.W.2d 21.

18. People v. Murray, 40 N.Y.2d 327, 386 N.Y.S.2d 691, 353 N.E.2d 605 (1976), cert. denied 430 U.S. 948.

19. People v. Daley, 47 N.Y.2d 916, 419 N.Y.S.2d 485, 393 N.E.2d 479 (1979); People v. Davis, 46 N.Y.2d 780, 413 N.Y.S.2d 911, 386 N.E.2d 823 (1978).

20. The Louisiana Court has held that the *corpus delicti* must be established by evidence "which the jury may accept as establishing that fact beyond a reasonable doubt." State v. Carson, 336 So.2d 844, 847 (La. 1976), appeal after remand 367 So.2d 859.

21. Cole v. State, 352 So.2d 17 (Ala.Crim.App.1977), cert. denied 352 So.2d 20 ("testimony sufficient to make it appear prima facie that a crime has been committed"); State v. Janise, 116 Ariz. 557, 570 P.2d 499 (1977) (only "a reasonable inference of the corpus delicti must exist"); People v. Towler, 31 Cal.3d 105, 181 Cal.Rptr. 391, 641 P.2d 1253 (1982) ("slight or prima facie proof is sufficient"); State v. Allen, 335 So.2d 823 (Fla.1976) ("substantial evidence tending to show commission of the charged crime"); State v. Snow, 438

A.2d 485 (Me.1981) ("less than a 'fair preponderance of the evidence' "); Commonwealth v. Byrd, 490 Pa. 544, 417 A.2d 173 (1980) (corroborative evidence is insufficient if it is merely equally as consistent with accident as with crime").

22. People v. Willingham, 89 Ill.2d 352, 59 Ill.Dec. 917, 432 N.E.2d 861 (1982); State v. Hankins, 599 S.W.2d 950 (Mo.App.1980).

23. State v. Grant, 177 Conn. 140, 411 A.2d 917 (1978); Anthony v. State, ___ Ind. ___, 409 N.E.2d 632, 635 (1980) (reasoning that *corpus delicti* need not be proved beyond a reasonable doubt by corroborating evidence); White v. State, 591 S.W.2d 851, 864 (Tex.Cr. App.1979).

24. E.g., Ross v. State, 268 Ind. 471, 376 N.E.2d 1117 (1978), cert. denied 439 U.S. 1080; State v. Charity, 587 S.W.2d 350, 354 (Mo.App.1979) ("An extrajudicial confession or admission cannot be used to corroborate another extrajudicial confession or admission.").

25. 587 S.W.2d 733 (Tex.Cr.App.1979).

26. 11 Wn.App. 91, 521 P.2d 1184 (1974).

27. 312 U.S. 342 (1941).

States [28] and the Court held that the possibilities of error that justified the requirement in regard to confessions also demanded that it be applied to admissions and exculpatory statements.[29] Turning to the standard for determining whether corroborating evidence is sufficient, the Court rejected the proposition that the corroborating evidence must tend to establish "the whole of the *corpus delicti*." Instead, it opted to require only "substantial independent evidence which would tend to establish the trustworthiness of the statement." [30]

The facts of *Opper* indicate the significance of the difference in approach. Opper was charged with inducing a federal employee to accept compensation for services, by making a payment of money to him, where these services were to be rendered in a matter before a federal agency in which the United States was a party. The Government introduced a statement of Opper in which he admitted giving the employee money when the employee appeared at Opper's Chicago office on a specified date. Other evidence was introduced tending to show that the employee did fly to Chicago on the specified date and confirming details of Opper's explanation as to how he obtained the money he gave to the employee. The Court

noted that the corroborating evidence tended to establish only the payment of the money. If the *corpus delicti* of the offense consisted of all elements of the crime, it included the rendering of services by the employee in return for the money. Consequently, the corroborating evidence failed to address all elements of the *corpus delicti* thus construed. It did, however, tend to confirm the truthfulness of those relevant facts admitted in Opper's statement. This, the Court held, was sufficient.

Perhaps the Court's approach can be supported by its conclusion in *Opper* that the corroboration requirement should apply to statements other than confessions. The function of the corroboration requirement, the Court suggested in *Opper*, is to provide reasonable assurance as to the accuracy of the facts admitted in the statement.[31] Where the statement to be corroborated consists of an admission of some relevant facts but not all facts necessary to prove guilt, therefore, the rationale for the corroboration requirement suggests that it ought not to demand that the corroborating evidence address those parts of the *corpus delicti* which the Government has not attempted to establish by the defendant's statement. The corroboration requirement, in other words,

---

28. 348 U.S. 84 (1954).

29. 348 U.S. at 90–92. The Court emphasized that such evidence has "the same possibilities for error as confessions," and therefore the corroboration requirement should be applied. In regard to exculpatory statements, the Court without full discussion rejected the Government's argument that the risks of unreliability were not present because such statements are unlikely to be the result of coercion or inducements. Id. at 92. This appears to be based on the Court's perception that the risk of unreliability is not—or at least is not *exclusively*—that of a defendant inaccurately making a statement but rather that of a witness inaccurately recounting in court what the defendant said on a prior occasion. When admissions and exculpatory statements are offered by the prosecution at trial, there may be inducements to a prosecution witness to "recall" a version favorable to the prosecution; thus the same risk—or at least a sufficient risk of the same sort—arguably is presented.

30. Id. at 93. The requirement was applied in Wong Sun v. United States, 371 U.S. 471 (1963).

As to the quantum of proof necessary, the Court in Smith v. United States, 348 U.S. 147, 156 (1954), noted

that there was agreement that the corroborating evidence did not have to establish the offense beyond a reasonable doubt or even by a preponderance of the evidence. Apparently the requirement is that there be "substantial" evidence independent of the self-incriminating statement of the defendant and the combination of the two types of evidence must prove the offense beyond a reasonable doubt. Id.

The *Opper* approach has been followed by Alaska. Jacinth v. State, 593 P.2d 263, 266 (Alaska 1979); Armstrong v. State, 502 P.2d 440, 447 (Alaska 1972). Wisconsin has not expressly adopted the federal approach but in rejecting the *corpus delicti* formulation appears to have accepted a very similar criterion. See Larson v. State, 86 Wis.2d 187, 198, 271 N.W.2d 647, 651–52 (1978) ("A conviction may rest on a defendant's confession where any significant fact is corroborated."); Holt v. State, 17 Wis.2d 468, 117 N.W.2d 626 (1962); Potman v. State, 259 Wis. 234, 47 N.W.2d 884 (1951).

31. 348 U.S. at 93: "It is sufficient if the corroboration supports the essential facts admitted sufficiently to justify a jury inference of their truth."

should apply only to those matters which the prosecution attempts to prove in part at least by the accused's self-incriminating statement.[32] On the other hand, as the Court announced in Smith v. United States,[33] the requirement means that there must be corroboration in regard to all elements of the offense which the Government seeks to establish by admissions alone.[34]

It would follow from this that if the Government relies on a confession in the traditional sense, that is, an admission of all facts necessary to prove guilt, the rationale of the federal corroboration rule would demand that the corroborating evidence tend to establish all elements of the *corpus delicti*. The difference between the two approaches, then, would be significant only where the requirement was applied to a statement of the accused amounting to less than a confession under the traditional distinctions.

In practice, however, this does not seem to have been followed by the lower federal courts, which have imposed only a general requirement of corroborating evidence tending to establish the trustworthiness of the confession.[35] Without regard to any re-

quirement of corroboration, of course, the evidence must be sufficient to establish all elements of the crime charged beyond a reasonable doubt. Therefore, if the Government relies in part at least upon proof that the defendant has admitted some but not all of the elements of the crime—as in *Opper*— the evidence taken as a whole must amount to proof beyond a reasonable doubt as to those unadmitted elements. In many and perhaps most cases, the evidence necessary to meet this requirement would also serve to provide corroboration in regard to the remaining elements of the *corpus delicti*. In a few cases, however, evidence sufficient to meet the general requirement of proof beyond a reasonable doubt may be insufficient to comply with a requirement that all elements of the *corpus delicti* be established by the perhaps more direct evidence requirement of the corroboration rule.

Continued Justification for Corroboration Requirement. There is increasing reason to believe that the corroboration requirement, however stated, may have outlived its usefulness.[36] Among recent developments have been those relating to confessions dis-

32. In United States v. Calderon, 348 U.S. 160 (1954), an appeal from a conviction for income tax evasion, the Court held that when a defendant introduces evidence in his own behalf after a defense motion for acquittal has been made and overruled, corroboration can be found in the evidence introduced by either the prosecution or the defense. 348 U.S. at 164.

33. 348 U.S. 147, 156 (1954).

34. In Smith v. United States, 348 U.S. 147 (1954), the offense was tax evasion, which the Court characterized as involving no tangible injury which could be isolated as a *corpus delicti*. As a result, it reasoned, applying the corroboration requirement would necessarily involve placing a duty on the Government to prove by independent evidence the identity of the defendant as the perpetrator. Rather than reject the corroboration requirement, the Court chose to impose such a requirement. 348 U.S. at 153–54. Thus in regard to certain offenses the corroborating evidence will necessarily include proof of the identity of the perpetrator. See Wong Sun v. United States, 371 U.S. 471, 489 n. 15 (1963). Compare, United States v. Johnson, 589 F.2d 716 (D.C.Cir.1978) (in robbery prosecution no need for corroborating evidence to link defendant with robbery); United States v. Vega-Limon, 548 F.2d 1390 (9th Cir. 1977) (conspiracy, since it required proof of an agreement and an overt act, was not an intangible of-

fense and therefore corroborating evidence did not have to implicate defendant in the crime).

Further, in United States v. Calderon, 348 U.S. 160, 165 (1954) the Court held that one self-incriminating statement obtained from the defendant "standing uncorroborated, cannot serve to corroborate [the defendant's] other admissions." Thus ordinarily confessions or admissions cannot corroborate each other. But compare, United States v. Johnson, supra, at 720 (independently corroborated statements can be used to corroborate other statements).

35. United States v. Kampiles, 609 F.2d 1233 (7th Cir. 1979), cert. denied 446 U.S. 954 (1980) (sufficient if evidence establishing reliability of confession is introduced even if this fails to establish the *corpus delicti*; if this is done, "the confession itself may supply whatever elements of the offense are not proved by independent evidence"); United States v. Gresham, 585 F.2d 103 (5th Cir. 1978) (where adequate corroboration presented, not necessary for all parts of the confession to be bolstered).

36. Comment, 20 U.C.L.A.L.Rev. 1055 (1973) (rule is ineffective in preventing convictions on false testimony and "pragmatic scrutiny" indicates it should be abolished); Development in the Law—Confessions, 79 Harv.L.Rev. 938, 1084 (1966) ("serious consideration should be given to elimination of the *corpus delicti* re-

cussed in this chapter as well as the federal "constitutionalization" of the requirement that criminal convictions rest on evidence proving guilt beyond a reasonable doubt.[37] These are designed to protect against convictions based on insufficient evidence in general and, in particular, to safeguard defendants from the use of unreliable confessions to prove their guilt. Whether in light of these developments the corroboration requirement remains justified is problematic.

If conscientiously applied, the requirement—especially the *corpus delicti* formulation—contains fertile ground for numerous arguments and complexities of application. Definition of the *corpus delicti* may have been a relatively simple task when crimes were few and concisely defined. But increased use of the criminal sanction has greatly increased the number of criminal offenses. Further, modern statutes tend to define offenses more precisely and in greater detail than traditional case law. Defining the *corpus delicti* has thus become more complex. Comprehensive definitions of the *corpus delicti*, if incorporated into the corroboration requirement, may impose an unrealistic or at least unnecessary burden upon the prosecution.

Some results under the requirement may be indefensible. If, for example, the prosecution relies in part upon a defendant's out-of-court admission to one of numerous facts necessary to prove guilt, there would seem to be no justification for an application of the *corpus delicti* formulation of the requirement in a fashion that would increase the prosecution's burden in regard to those elements not addressed by the admission. On the other hand, if the prosecution's case consists primarily of the defendant's out-of-court acknowledgment of the accuracy of all or most of the prosecution's allegations, it is

arguable that despite the developments described above there remains a special need for caution.

The traditional requirement of independent proof of the *corpus delicti* seems fraught with opportunity for needless dispute. The best approach would seem to be that adopted in *Opper* and *Smith:* insofar as the prosecution relies upon the defendant's out-of-court statement to prove one or more facts at trial, the record must contain reasonable evidence other than the statement tending to prove that fact. But no more should be required. Specifically, the prosecution's use of a defendant's self-incriminating out-of-court statement, no matter how narrowly incriminating, should quite clearly not give rise to any broad duty such as that to establish by some sort of independent evidence all elements of the *corpus delicti*.

 WESTLAW REFERENCES

synopsis,digest(confess! exculpatory admission* /p uncorroborat! corroborat! /p probative)

Independent Proof of the Corpus Delicti

synopsis,digest("corpus delicti" /p defin! mean! term* phrase element* /p confess! admission* statement*)

synopsis,digest("corpus delicti" /p corroborat! uncorroborat! /p confess! admission* statement*)

Evidence Tending to Establish the Trustworthiness of the Confession

synopsis,digest("corpus delicti" /p corroborat! uncorroborat! independent! /p sufficien! insufficien! /p confess! admission* statement*)

"corpus delicti" /p corroborat! uncorroborat! independent! /p trustworth! veracity verif! truth! accura! /p confess! admission* statement*

synopsis,digest("corpus delicti" /p independent! corroborat! uncorroborat! /p "reasonable doubt" /p confess! admission* statement*)

Continued Justification for Corroboration Requirement

sh 348 us 84
sh 75 sct 158
sh 348 us 147

---

quirement"); Note, 46 Fordham L.Rev. 1205, 1235 (1978) (rule is duplicative of other confession doctrines).

37. See Jackson v. Virginia, 443 U.S. 307 (1979), rehearing denied 444 U.S. 890, holding that a defendant convicted in state court is entitled to federal habeas

corpus relief if in federal proceedings it is determined that no rational trier of fact could have found the essential elements of the crime beyond a reasonable doubt on the evidence produced by the state. 443 U.S. at 319.

sh 75 sct 194

§ 146. Voluntariness: (a) The Common Law Rule

Before the mid-1700s, out-of-court statements of an accused person were admissible against him at his trial without regard to the manner in which they had been obtained.[1] A plea of guilty on arraignment, however, was required not to "proceed from fear, menace, or duress."[2] The distinction, according to Wigmore, was justified on the ground that the plea was a conviction in itself and properly subject to extraordinary scrutiny, an inquiry not justified when what was involved was only one piece of the evidence on which a verdict would be returned.[3] There is little evidence of the manner in which the voluntariness requirement was extended from pleas to extrajudicial statements of the accused. But in 1775, Lord Mansfield commented offhandedly that "[t]he instance has frequently happened, of persons having made confessions under threats or promises: the consequence as frequently has been, that such examinations and confessions have not been made use of against them on their trial."[4] The early discussions make quite clear that the rationale for the rule was the purported lack of reliability of statements motivated not by guilt but by a desire to avoid discomfort or to secure some favor.[5]

In its first confession case, Hopt v. Utah,[6] the Supreme Court of the United States accepted—apparently as a matter of federal evidence law governing the conduct of criminal trials in federal court—the well-developed common law requirement of voluntariness. That requirement, the Court explained, commands that a confession be held inadmissible

> when the confession appears to have made either in consequence of inducements of a temporal nature, held out by one in authority, touching the charge preferred, or because of a threat or promise by or in the presence of such person, which, operating upon the fears or hopes of the accused, in reference to the charge, deprives him of that freedom of will or self-control essential to make his confession voluntary within the meaning of the law.[7]

In most if not all jurisdictions the requirement of voluntariness became and probably remains a mandate of nonconstitutional evidence law. But the federal "constitutionalization" of the voluntariness requirement[8] has detracted from any state law basis it may have. The prevailing tendency is to assume uncritically the existence of a single voluntariness requirement mandated by federal constitutional considerations.

WESTLAW REFERENCES

"common law" /p volunt! involuntar! "free will" /p confess! statement* admission* % "common law" /2   marriage husband wife

§ 147. Voluntariness: (b) The Federal Constitutional Standard[1]

The federal constitutionalization of the voluntariness standard, or at least of part of that standard, has a rather convoluted histo-

---

§ 146

1. 3 Wigmore, Evidence § 818 (Chadbourn rev. 1970).

2. Id.

3. Id.

4. Rudd's Case, 1 Leach Cr.C. 115, 118, 168 Eng. Rep. 160, 161 (1775). See generally 3 Wigmore, Evidence § 819 (Chadbourn rev.1970).

5. The King v. Warickshall, 168 Eng.Rep. 234, 134–35, 1 Leach Cr.C. 263, 263–64 (K.B.1783):

> Confessions are received in evidence, or rejected as inadmissible, under a consideration whether they are or are not entitled to credit. . . . [A] confession

forced from the mind by the flattery of hope, or by the torture of fear, comes in so questionable a shape when it is to be considered as the evidence of guilt, that no credit ought to be given to it . . . ."

See generally 3 Wigmore, Evidence § 822 (Chadbourn rev.1970).

6. 110 U.S. 574 (1884).

7. 110 U.S. at 585.

8. See § 147 infra.

§ 147

1. See generally 3 Wigmore, Evidence §§ 824–855a (Chadbourn rev.1970); Gangi, A Critical View of the

ry. Only thirteen years after *Hopt*, the Court—in Bram v. United States [2]—commented that whenever in federal criminal trials an issue arises as to the voluntariness of a confession, "the issue is controlled by that portion of the Fifth Amendment to the Constitution of the United States, commanding that no person 'shall be compelled in any criminal case to be a witness against himself.' " [3] The Amendment, continued the Court, embodied the common law rule of voluntariness. [4]

Because the Fifth Amendment was not held binding on the states until 1964, [5] the *Bram* approach did not result in imposing the voluntariness rule upon the states as a matter of federal constitutional law. In Brown v. Mississippi, [6] decided in 1936, however, the Court held that a state court conviction resting upon a confession extorted by brutality and violence violated the accused's general right to due process guaranteed by the Fourteenth Amendment. Subsequent cases made clear that any use in a state criminal prosecution of a coerced confession violated the federal standard. [7]

In 1966, after the Fifth Amendment was held binding on the States, the Court characterized the due process standard developed in *Brown* and its progeny as "the same general standard which [is] applied in federal prosecutions—a standard grounded in the policies of the privilege against self-incrimination." [8] This is probably an oversimplification. In Blackburn v. Alabama, [9] the Court stated that "a complex of values underlies the stricture against use by the state of confessions which, by way of convenient shorthand, this Court terms involuntary." [10] Included in this "complex of values" are almost certainly the following:

(1) Protection of particular defendants against use of inaccurate confessions. In part, the voluntariness requirement still reflects concern regarding the reliability of involuntary confessions. This, however, has most likely become a relatively minor consideration supporting the requirement.

(2) Discouragement of police practices that are likely, as a general matter, to result in unreliable confessions. On a different level of generality, the voluntariness requirement undoubtedly reflects a general concern that certain police practices create a risk of inaccurate or at least misleading self-incriminating statements. Thus the rule serves to discourage these practices by excluding involuntary confessions, without regard to whether on the facts of each particular case the risk of an inaccurate confession resulting was an importantly high one. [11]

(3) Discouragement of police practices which are unacceptable or undesirable on other grounds. It seems clear that in part the voluntariness rule came to serve as a vehicle for discouraging police practices that were regarded as undesirable for reasons other than any tendency to elicit unreliable

Modern Confession Rule: Some Observations on Key Confession Cases, 28 Ark.L.Rev. 1 (1974); Grano, Voluntariness, Free Will, and the Law of Confessions, 65 Va.L.Rev. 859 (1979); Kamisar, What is an "Involuntary" Confession? Some Comments on Inbau and Reid's Criminal Interrogation and Confessions, 17 Rutgers L.Rev. 728 (1963); King, Developing a Future Constitutional Standard for Confessions, 8 Wayne L.Rev. 481 (1962); Schulhofer, Confessions and the Court, 79 Mich.L.Rev. 865, 867–878 (1981); Comment, 31 U.Chi.L. Rev. 313 (1964); 29 Am.Jur.2d Evidence §§ 529, 543–54 (1967); C.J.S. Criminal Law §§ 817(2)–29; Dec.Digest Criminal Law ⚖406(3), 412.1(1)–(4).

2. 168 U.S. 532 (1897).

3. 168 U.S. at 542.

4. Id. at 548.

5. See § 117 supra.

6. 297 U.S. 278 (1936). See generally Ritz, Twenty-five Years of State Criminal Confession Cases in the U.S. Supreme Court, 19 Wash. & Lee L.Rev. 35 (1962); Way, The Supreme Court and State Coerced Confessions, 12 J.Public Law 53 (1963).

7. See Lynumn v. Illinois, 372 U.S. 528 (1963); Payne v. Arkansas, 356 U.S. 560 (1958). For a discussion of whether improper admission of an involuntary confession can ever be harmless error, see § 182 infra.

8. Davis v. North Carolina, 384 U.S. 737, 740 (1966).

9. 361 U.S. 199 (1960).

10. 361 U.S. at 207.

11. Cf. Kamisar, What is an "Involuntary" Confession? Some Comments on Inbau and Reid's Criminal Interrogation and Confessions, 17 Rutgers L.Rev. 728, 753–759 (1963).

confessions. This, of course, is closely related to self-incrimination concerns.[12] Physical abuse, for example, is most likely inconsistent with the manner in which modern society demands that even guilty persons be treated, without regard to the risk—if any— that such abuse will result in unreliable evidence being obtained and used to convict.

(4) Preservation of the trial rights of an accused.[13] Because of the heavy weight which a trier of fact is likely to give a self-incriminatory statement of a defendant, the introduction of a confession may well make other aspects of a criminal trial mere window dressing. Yet there is some reason to believe that compelling the prosecution to produce substantial evidence of defendants' guilt serves important social purposes, including the minimization of the risk that the criminal process will be usable for political or other irregular purposes. In part, the voluntariness requirement appears to reflect a view that use of confessions ought to be limited so that in many or most cases the prosecution will still be required to shoulder its heavy trial burden of producing evidence and that the trial process will maintain its importance.

As the rationale for the voluntariness requirement and its entrenchment in federal constitutional law has developed, the application of the requirement has also changed. The impact of promises [14] or deception [15] during interrogation present special problems that are best discussed separately. In re-

gard to general situations, however, increasing emphasis has been placed on the "psychological" rather than the physical impact of circumstances and techniques of interrogation.[16] The ultimate inquiry has become whether, given the totality of the circumstances under which the decision to confess was made, the defendant's will to resist confessing was overborne. In 1961 Justice Frankfurter effectively stated the inquiry as follows:

> The ultimate test . . . [is] voluntariness. Is the confession the product of an essentially free and unconstrained choice by its maker? If it is, if he has willed to confess, it may be used against him. If it is not, if his will has been overborne and his capacity for self-determination critically impaired, the use of his confession offends due process.[17]

In making the necessary inquiry, the Court has looked at various aspects of the circumstances surrounding the decision to confess. These have included the time of day or night,[18] the existence or length of interrogation that preceded the decision,[19] the quality of the physical circumstances in which the accused was detained or located during the pre-confession period,[20] and similar matters. These, on the other hand, have been evaluated in light of various characteristics of the accused relevant to the impact of these circumstances. Among the factors that have been considered as tending to show involuntariness have been youth,[21] female sex,[22] minority racial status,[23] physical

---

12. See § 118 supra.

13. See generally Comment, 31 U.Chi.L.Rev. 313, 320–27 (1964); Lisenba v. California, 314 U.S. 219 (1941), rehearing denied 315 U.S. 826.

14. See § 148 infra.

15. See § 149 infra.

16. See Ashcraft v. Tennessee, 322 U.S. 143 (1944).

17. Culombe v. Connecticut, 367 U.S. 568, 602 (1961).

18. Cf. Greenwald v. Wisconsin, 390 U.S. 519 (1968), conformed to 38 Wis.2d 647, 158 N.W.2d 293 (arrest at 10:45 p.m. and interrogation from then until midnight).

19. Watts v. Indiana, 338 U.S. 49 (1949) (5 days of interrogation); Turner v. Pennsylvania, 338 U.S. 62 (1949), mandate conformed to 67 A.2d 441.

20. Greenwald v. Wisconsin, 390 U.S. 519 (1968), conformed to 38 Wis.2d 647, 158 N.W.2d 293 (defendant spent overnight in jail cell with plank as bed and claimed inability to sleep); Brooks v. Florida, 389 U.S. 413 (1967) (subject confined for 14 days in "punishment cell," with no external windows and no bed or furnishings except a hole flush with the floor that served as a commode).

21. Gallegos v. Colorado, 370 U.S. 49 (1962), rehearing denied 370 U.S. 965 (14-year-old youth "cannot be compared with an adult in full possession of his senses and knowledgeable of the consequences of his admissions").

22. Lynumn v. Illinois, 372 U.S. 528 (1963).

23. Beecher v. Alabama, 389 U.S. 35 (1967) (black defendant accused of raping white woman).

illness, injury, or infirmity,[24] psychological abnormality,[25] low educational level,[26] and little or no prior experience with law enforcement practices and techniques.[27] The extent to which officers informed the accused of his legal rights—and especially his right not to give a self-incriminating statement—or the extent to which the accused was actually aware of those rights—is also of significance.[28]

While there is widespread agreement that evidence that the accused was intoxicated at the time of a confession is relevant,[29] there is also an apparent reluctance to give this actual controlling significance. Traditionally, a number of courts have applied what appears to be a special criterion that requires that intoxication have reached the undefined point of "mania" or at least have rendered the accused unable to understand the meaning of his statements before it would render those statements involuntary.[30] Some courts appear still to adhere to this approach,[31] although others purport to give evidence of intoxication as much weight as it is objectively entitled to have in the due process inquiry.[32] There appears to be no justification for giving evidence of intoxication any less than the full weight to which it is logically entitled, insofar as it tends to show that a confession was given under circumstances rendering it involuntary under the general standard.

The increasing significance of supporting considerations other than reliability for the voluntariness requirement is evidenced by the Supreme Court's insistence that the voluntariness of a confession be determined without regard to the reliability of the confession at issue.[33] To some extent, of course, this undoubtedly reflects a desire to exclude confessions that are reliable as a

---

24. Mincey v. Arizona, 437 U.S. 385 (1978) (suspect wounded by gunshot and undergoing medical treatment at time of interrogation); Greenwald v. Wisconsin, 390 U.S. 519 (1968), conformed to 38 Wis.2d 647, 158 N.W.2d 293 (suspect had high blood pressure and was without medicine); Beecher v. Alabama, 389 U.S. 35 (1967) (gunshot wound in leg).

25. Culombe v. Connecticut, 367 U.S. 568 (1961) (accused was mental defective of moron class); Fikes v. Alabama, 352 U.S. 191 (1957), rehearing denied 352 U.S. 1019 (evidence that defendant was "a schizophrenic and highly suggestible").

26. Greenwald v. Wisconsin, 390 U.S. 519 (1968), conformed to 38 Wis.2d 647, 158 N.W.2d 293 (defendant had only ninth grade education). Compare, Crooker v. California, 357 U.S. 433 (1958) (evidence that suspect was a college graduate who had attended one year of law school considered in holding confession voluntary).

27. Lynumn v. Illinois, 372 U.S. 528 (1963) (suspect had no prior experience with criminal law).

28. Greenwald v. Wisconsin, 390 U.S. 519 (1968), conformed to 38 Wis.2d 647, 158 N.W.2d 293 (no advice of constitutional right). Compare the significance given in Frazier v. Cupp, 394 U.S. 731 (1969) to a showing that officers had advised the suspect of his rights.

29. See generally Annot., 69 A.L.R.2d 362 (1960); Dec.Dig. Criminal Law ⟐526.

30. See State v. Smith, 342 S.W.2d 940 (Mo.1961); State v. Logner, 266 N.C. 238, 145 S.E.2d 867 (1966), cert. denied 384 U.S. 1013.

31. See Hollis v. State, 399 So.2d 935, 938–939 (Ala. Crim.App.1981); State v. Gullett, 606 S.W.2d 796, 807 (Mo.App.1980).

A number of courts articulate criteria that suggest they are giving evidence of intoxication somewhat limited significance but perhaps more than the "mania" standard provides. See State v. Robinson, 384 So.2d 332, 335 (La.1980) (intoxication will render a confession inadmissible only if it negated the defendant's comprehension and rendered him unconscious of the consequences of what he was saying); State v. Green, 613 S.W.2d 229, 233 (Tenn.Cr.App.1980) (intoxication will not render confession inadmissible if the defendant, despite the intoxication, was capable of making a narrative of past events and of stating his own participation in the offense). These standards appear, however, to emphasize any impact the intoxication may have had upon the defendant's ability intellectually to understand his situation. Thus they may detract from any effect the intoxication may have had upon his ability to respond "voluntarily" to circumstances which he adequately understood. Compare State v. Garner, 294 N.W.2d 725 (Minn.1980) (intoxication increased defendant's susceptibility to stressing techniques and therefore contributed to the involuntariness of his confession).

32. McCorquodale v. Balkcom, 525 F.Supp. 408, 420–421 (N.D.Ga.1981); United States v. Babb, 448 F.Supp. 794 (D.S.C.1978) (intoxication goes to whether prosecution has shown that confession was product of rational intellect and free will); Smith v. State, 141 Ga. App. 720, 234 S.E.2d 385 (1977) (confession admissible despite intoxication where defendant's condition was "not inconsistent with the ability to freely and voluntarily waive rights for the purposes of making a confession").

33. Haynes v. Washington, 373 U.S. 503 (1963) (error to suggest to jury that if confession was involuntary it might nevertheless be considered if corroborated

means of discouraging police practices that are viewed, in general terms, as creating a risk of stimulating inaccurate confessions. But it almost certainly also reflects a strongly-held perception by the Court that the voluntariness rule should serve functions other than that of promoting the reliable ascertainment of guilt at trial.

The Supreme Court's decision in 1966 to abandon almost exclusive reliance upon voluntariness as the federal constitutional vehicle for dealing with the admissibility of confessions [34] has left the current significance of the traditional voluntariness doctrine in some doubt. Nevertheless, it appears that the doctrine continues to have substantial current vitality. In those situations not involving both "custody" and "interrogation," [35] the *Miranda* requirements do not apply and voluntariness remains the major federal constitutional requirement bearing upon admissibility. When a confession obtained during custodial interrogation in violation of the *Miranda* requirements is offered to impeach a defendant who testifies at trial, the voluntariness of that confession appears to play a significant if not controlling role in determining its admissibility for that limited purpose.[36] But perhaps most important, even where *Miranda* applies and no violation of its *per se* requirements exists, the prosecution must show effective waiver of the right to remain silent and, in most situations, of the right to the presence of an attorney during the interrogation. Whether the effectiveness of these waivers

is to be determined by applying the traditional voluntariness criteria is not entirely clear, but there is little doubt that traditional voluntariness law will, at a minimum, be influential in resolving those questions.[37]

 WESTLAW REFERENCES

synopsis,digest(volunt! involuntar! "free will" /p confess! statement* admission* /p fifth 5th constitution! unconstitutional /p promise* induce! lenien! plea)

synopsis,digest(volunt! involuntar! "free will" /p confess! statement* admission* /p custod! holdover incarcerat! /p miranda)

volunt! involuntar! "free will" /p confess! statement* admission* /p custod! holdover incarcerat! /p miranda /p impeach!

---

§ 148. Voluntariness: (c) Promises of Benefits [1]

In contrast to the general flexibility of the voluntariness requirement, the aspect of the voluntariness standard relating to "promises of benefits" has traditionally been regarded as imposing a somewhat rigid prohibition against affirmative inducements to an accused made in an effort to secure a confession. *Hopt's* statement of the common law rule included a requirement that a confession be held inadmissible if made "in consequence of inducements of a temporal nature, held out by one in authority, touching the charge preferred, or because of a . . . promise by or in the presence of such person . . . in reference to the charge . . . ." [2] *Bram's* summary of the "legal principle" embodied in the Fifth Amendment

by other evidence); Rogers v. Richmond, 365 U.S. 534, 543 (1961) (question of admissibility of confession impermissibly "was answered by reference to a legal standard which took into account the circumstance of probable truth or falsity").

34. See, e.g., United States v. Wertz, 625 F.2d 1128 (4th Cir. 1980), cert. denied 449 U.S. 904; United States v. Mullens, 536 F.2d 997 (2d Cir. 1976). For a discussion of the requirements of "custody" and "interrogation," see § 150 infra.

There is also authority for the proposition that when a confession obtained in a foreign jurisdiction by foreign officials is offered in an American criminal trial, *Miranda* does not apply because its application would not serve the intended function of limiting domestic law enforcement conduct. In such cases, voluntariness

determines admissibility of the statement. See United States v. Nolan, 551 F.2d 266 (10th Cir. 1977), cert. denied 434 U.S. 904; United States v. Mundt, 508 F.2d 904 (10th Cir. 1974), cert. denied 421 U.S. 949.

35. See § 151 infra.

36. See § 162 infra.

37. See § 153 infra.

§ 148

1. See generally Dix, Mistake, Ignorance, Expectation of Benefit, and the Modern Law of Confessions, 1975 Wash.U.L.Q. 275; 29 Am.Jur.2d Evidence §§ 558–565; 23 C.J.S. Criminal Law § 825; Dec.Dig. Criminal Law ⊨520(1)–(8).

2. See § 146 n. 7 supra.

included the demand that a confession "must not be . . . obtained by any direct or implied promises, however slight . . .."[3] In *Bram* itself, the confession had been given after a law enforcement officer had told the accused, "If you had an accomplice, you should say so, and not have the blame of this horrible crime on your own shoulders." This, the Court concluded, might well have been understood by Bram as holding out an encouragement that by disclosing his accomplice he might at least obtain mitigation of the punishment which would be imposed for the offense and therefore was among the grounds on which the confession at issue was inadmissible.[4]

In Brady v. United States[5] the Court explained the rationale for the promise rule that it has apparently incorporated into the federal constitutional voluntariness standard:

> *Bram* dealt with a confession given by a defendant in custody, alone and unrepresented by counsel. In such circumstances, even a mild promise of leniency was deemed sufficient to bar the confession, not because the promise was an illegal act as such, but because defendants at such times are too sensitive to inducement and the possible impact on them too great to ignore and too difficult to assess.[6]

This rationale, the Court further explained, justified its refusal to extend the promise prohibition to guilty pleas; since defendants entering guilty pleas are represented by counsel and have adequate opportunity to assess the wisdom of accepting a promise of leniency in return for a plea, a promise of such leniency would not, as a matter of federal constitutional law, render the plea of guilty involuntary.[7]

Brady, however, highlights what is perhaps the major difficulty in applying the traditional promise rule in the contemporary criminal procedure context. Properly or not, plea bargaining has become an accepted and

legally permissible aspect of the processing of criminal cases. Guilty pleas may be encouraged by promises of lenient dispositions in return for such pleas. Not unexpectedly, both law enforcement officers and suspects sometimes seek to begin and perhaps conclude such bargaining during the police investigatory stage. If the process is concluded at that stage, the suspect's agreement will most likely be embodied in a confession. Application of the traditional confession rule, however, would render these confessions inadmissible. This, of course, would preclude or at least tend to discourage such early efforts to arrive at a negotiated settlement.

It may be that this effect of applying the traditional confession promise rule is desirable. Plea bargaining may be acceptable when carried on later in the process, because defendants are likely at that time to decide how to respond to the promises of leniency with the advice of counsel and after some comparative leisure for consideration. But defendants' responses to similar promises during the early investigatory stages may create too high a risk of unacceptable responses. If continued adherence to the confession rule has the effect of relegating plea negotiation to later stages in the processing of criminal cases, it may be desirable and perhaps constitutionally essential. On the other hand, strong pressure to permit negotiation and settlement earlier in the process may lead to circumvention and dilution of the confession rule to the point where it becomes useless. Acceptance of plea bargaining and its possible inevitable involvement in law enforcement interrogation, then, may have rendered the traditional promise rule obsolete or at least unrealistic.

The voluntariness requirement as applied to out-of-court confessions, however, is still generally regarded as embodying a prohibi-

---

3. Bram v. United States, 168 U.S. 532, 542–43 (1897). See § 147 at n. 4 supra.

4. 168 U.S. at 564–565.

5. 397 U.S. 742 (1970).

6. 397 U.S. at 754.

7. Id. at 754–755. See also Bordenkircher v. Hayes, 434 U.S. 357 (1978), rehearing denied 435 U.S. 918.

tion against promises.[8] But the apparent rigidity of this approach suggested by some of the language used has been greatly modified by a number of developments related to the promise rule.

As a preliminary matter, however, it is useful to note that in the context of law enforcement interrogations "promises" are not easy to define or identify.[9] In many situations, discussions lend themselves to characterization either as a representation that something undesired will occur if a confession is not given or that something desired will occur if the statement is forthcoming. Whether an interrogator's language will be construed as promising a benefit or as threatening a detriment in such situations is a matter of very subjective choice. But insofar as promises invoke a more rigid rule

Specificity of Promise. Perhaps the most dramatic limitation of the promise rule has been the increasing insistence of courts that the promise be shown to be a specific and perhaps even an unqualified one. A mere general exhortation to tell the truth, of course, is not such a specific promise.[10] But the clear trend is towards also regarding as insufficient a representation that a confession might or even is likely to result in some advantage, such as a less severe penalty, as long as the "promisor" caveats this with a disclaimer that he is unable to make any absolute commitment.[11] To some extent, this is supported on what is almost a "harmless

than threats (which may merely go to whether the suspect's will was overborne), the results of this subjective labeling process may be quite important.

---

8. People v. Jimenez, 21 Cal.3d 595, 147 Cal.Rptr. 172, 580 P.2d 672 (1978) (confession rendered inadmissible by officer's statement to defendant that if he talked about the case the officer would tell the jury and they would go lighter on him); Foreman v. State, 400 So.2d 1047 (Fla.App.1981) (confession rendered inadmissible where officer told suspect that if property taken in burglary was returned, victim would not be inclined to prosecute); State v. Tardiff, 374 A.2d 598 (Me.1977) (confession inadmissible because officer told suspect he "felt sure" captain would agree to charge defendant with only one burglary if defendant was willing "to clear up all the matters he had pending"); Vanderbilt v. State, 563 S.W.2d 590 (Tex.Cr.App.1978) (promise not to seek death penalty rendered confession involuntary).

The rule, or some version of it, has sometimes been embodied in statutory form. See Ga.Code, § 38–411 (for confession to be voluntary and admissible, it must not have been induced "by the slightest hope of benefit"). See also, Kan.Stat.Ann. 60–460(f), providing that a statement by the accused is admissible only if the judge finds, among other matters, that the accused was not induced to make the statement:

by threats or promises concerning action to be taken by a public official with reference to the crime, likely to cause the accused to make such a statement falsely, and made by a person whom the accused reasonably believed to have the power or authority to execute the same.

It is also, of course, necessary that the promise have induced the confession. A promise not communicated to the defendant before the confession is made will not invalidate the confession. State v. Broome, 268 S.C. 99, 232 S.E.2d 324 (1977). If the promise is revoked before the confession is given, it is unlikely to be found to have stimulated the confession. State v. Watts, 639 P.2d 158 (Utah 1981) (offer to "forget" shoplifting

withdrawn by calling authorities). Events intervening between the promise and the confession may establish that the promise did not motivate the confession. See Nettless v. State, 409 So.2d 85 (Fla.App.1982), review denied 418 So.2d 1280 (Fla.) (discussion with other officers and father and further warnings after promise "attenuated" effect of promise).

9. See Holt v. State, 372 So.2d 370, 374 (Ala.1978), on remand 372 So.2d 375 (Ala.Crim.App.), writ denied 372 So.2d 377.

10. Fowler v. State, 246 Ga. 256, 271 S.E.2d 168 (1980) (confession admissible despite officer's testimony that he told defendant that "it looked like he's in a heap of trouble and it would behoove him if he shot straight at us"); People v. Wipfler, 68 Ill.2d 158, 11 Ill. Dec. 262, 368 N.E.2d 870 (1977) (officer's statement to accused, "if someone did something wrong he should be a man and admit it," was only an exhortation to tell the truth and would be considered as one of the totality of the circumstances bearing on voluntariness).

11. State v. McVay, 127 Ariz. 18, 617 P.2d 1134 (1980) (prison guard's representation that confession would be mentioned to warden and warden would decide whether prisoner would be removed from isolation cell was only expression of a "possibility," not a promise); Smith v. State, ___ Ind. ___, 432 N.E.2d 1363 (1982) (statement that confession would be to defendant's advantage and court would probably take it into consideration too vague and indefinite to be promise); State v. Harwick, 220 Kan. 572, 552 P.2d 987 (1976) (detective's statement that he could make no promises but he would talk to prosecutor and more than likely defendant would not be charged with more crimes and "maybe" prosecutor's office would be of help on sentencing was not a promise); State v. Orscanin, 283 N.W.2d 897 (Minn.1979), cert. denied 444 U.S. 970 (parole officer's representation that cooperation and confession would cause things to "work out better" was

error" rationale; such inducements most likely do not inform suspects of anything that the suspects would not guess for themselves. Therefore, the inducements are unlikely to have influenced the suspects' decisions.[12]

It is at least arguable that as modified by a requirement that the promises be "specific," the promise rule has lost most of its meaning. As so qualified, the rule can be met by officers' disclaimers of an ability to "promise" or "guarantee" certain results. Yet suspects are quite unlikely to give such verbal boilerplate any significance in deciding how to respond. If the effect of the promise rule is merely to require that persons in authority add such disclaimers to their promises, it probably accomplishes little.

Promises Solicited by Suspect. A number of courts have held that promises that would otherwise render a confession involuntary will not be given that effect if the promises were solicited by the suspect. This has meant that if, during the conversation leading to the confession, the evidence shows that it was the suspect rather than the authorities who first raised the possibility of a benefit to be obtained from the giving of a confession, a subsequent promise of such a benefit will not invalidate the confession.[13] To some extent, this approach may rest upon a notion that a defendant who seeks a promise is somehow "estopped" from later complaining that it was made. But more important, it represents an effort to accommodate what are perceived as the realities of plea negotiation without totally

abandoning the promise rule. Perhaps the approach has merit. Suspects who affirmatively seek to begin what is functionally the process of plea bargaining at this stage may neither require nor deserve the protection that would be afforded by a relatively inflexible confession promise rule that would render any resulting confessions unavailable to prosecuting authorities. On the other hand, given the widespread awareness of plea bargaining, it seems more likely that there is little significance in which party first raises the matter. If there is something offensive in giving effect to a suspect's decision to confess made in return for a promise of leniency, this offensiveness is not greatly reduced by a showing that the suspect first articulated an interest in having such a promise made.

Requirement of Person in Authority. The prohibition as stated in *Hopt* and subsequently is against promises or inducements by a person in a position of authority. In *Bram*, the Court noted this requirement in the English formulation of the rule and some split in American authority as to its applicability; whether it should be regarded as a limitation upon the Fifth Amendment requirement was not before the Court and thus not considered.[14] It is, however, generally accepted. Some doubt has arisen as to what constitutes sufficient actual or perhaps "apparent" authority. In Johnson v. State,[15] the Alabama Court of Criminal Appeals noted that there is no absolute requirement that the promisor be a law enforcement officer. But, it continued, "before a promise of benefit from a non-law enforcement officer will

common sense advice and not promise). There is widespread agreement that merely telling a defendant that his cooperation will be made known to prosecution authorities is not a promise. United States v. Curtis, 562 F.2d 1153 (9th Cir. 1977), cert. denied 439 U.S. 910; Moss v. State, 347 So.2d 569 (Ala.Crim.App.1977). Contra, Fillinger v. State, 349 So.2d 714 (Fla.App.1977), cert. denied 374 So.2d 101 (Fla.1979).

12. See State v. Petterway, 403 So.2d 1157 (La. 1981) (deputy's statement to defendant that things would go easier for him if he confessed were only musings not much beyond which defendant might well have concluded for himself).

13. Eakes v. State, 387 So.2d 855, 860 (Ala.Crim. App.1978) ("a confession is not rendered involuntary by a promise of benefit that was solicited freely and voluntarily by the accused"); State v. Torres, 121 Ariz. 110, 588 P.2d 852 (App.1978); State v. Harwick, 220 Kan. 572, 552 P.2d 987 (1976).

14. Bram v. United States, 168 U.S. 532, 559 (1897).

15. 378 So.2d 1164 (Ala.Crim.App.1979), writ quashed 378 So.2d 1173 (Ala.).

render a confession . . . involuntary, the circumstances must be such that the defendant fairly supposed that the promisor had the power to secure the promised benefit for the accused." [16] Under this standard, a promise made by a jail trusty was held not to invoke the rule. It is widely and uncritically—but not universally—accepted that the complaining witness or victim of the offense is a person in a position of sufficient authority.[17] This is apparently in recognition of the widespread practice of abandoning prosecution if such a person seeks that course of action, even though the victim of the offense has no official power to control whether charges will be pursued.

Promises of "Collateral" Benefits. The *Hopt* statement of the common law rule qualified "inducements" with a requirement that the inducements be ones "touching the charge preferred." [18] Some courts continue to apply this qualification, thus limiting the rule to promises of some specific advantage in the processing of the criminal charges that are under investigation. Pursuing this approach, for example, the South Carolina Supreme Court in State v. Rook [19] held that any promises made to the defendant that he would, in return for confessing, receive help for his drinking and family problems did not affect the admissibility of his confession. Such promises, reasoned the court, did not relate to the processing of the murder, rape,

and kidnapping charges under investigation and therefore concerned a collateral matter; they consequently did not bring the promise rule into play.

The difficulty of justifying a dramatic distinction between the effects given promises of collateral benefits and other promises of direct advantages has caused a number of courts to discard or modify it. The Alabama Court, for example, read Supreme Court voluntariness cases as implicitly giving effect to promises concerning collateral benefits and therefore rejected the distinction.[20] Other courts have treated promises of collateral benefits as rendering confessions involuntary if, but only if, those promises were, on the facts, likely to produce a false confession.[21] The Missouri Court, in State v. Harvey,[22] noted the lack of definitive authority on the matter. It concluded that the reduced danger posed by such promises justified abandoning any *per se* rule and instead concluded that such promises are to be considered in determining whether, given the totality of the circumstances, the accused's will was overborne.[23]

Continued Vitality of "Rigid" Rule. A variety of considerations arguably militate against continued adherence to a voluntariness standard that applies a rather rigid set of special rules when a confession is shown to have been given after a "promise." One,

---

16. Id. at 1169.

17. Fisher v. State, 379 S.W.2d 900 (Tex.Cr.App. 1964). Contra, State v. Watts, 639 P.2d 158 (Utah 1981) (store manager who apprehended defendant for shoplifting not person in authority).

Compare Weatherly v. State, 477 S.W.2d 572 (Tex.Cr. App.1972), refusing to hold a confession inadmissible because of defense counsel's advice to defendant that making a statement would facilitate defendant's release on bail. Defense counsel, the court reasoned, is not a person "in authority" within the meaning of the promise rule.

18. See § 146 at n. 7 supra.

19. 304 N.C. 201, 283 S.E.2d 732 (1981), cert. denied 455 U.S. 1038.

20. Holt v. State, 372 So.2d 370 (Ala.1978), reversing 372 So.2d 364 (Ala.Crim.App.1977).

21. State v. Kanive, 221 Kan. 34, 558 P.2d 1075 (1976) (any promise by officer to discontinue investiga-

tion of rape of defendant's grandmother was not likely to have caused defendant falsely to admit guilt of unrelated murder and robbery); State v. Aguirre, 91 N.M. 672, 579 P.2d 798 (App.1978), cert. denied 91 N.M. 751, 580 P.2d 972 (promise that defendant would not be charged with other burglaries not such under standard as to render his confession to first burglary inadmissible).

22. 609 S.W.2d 419 (Mo.1980).

23. In *Harvey,* supra n. 22, officers had told the defendant that if he revealed where a stolen weapon was located, he would not be prosecuted for stealing the weapon. He did so. His admission was then used in a prosecution for a homicide committed with the gun. Since the prosecution was for homicide, the promise concerning prosecution for theft concerned a collateral matter; on the totality of the circumstances, the court found the confession voluntary.

of course, is the difficulty of meaningfully defining promises and distinguishing them from other statements made during pre-confession interrogation. Another is the absence of any defensible basis for distinguishing, in terms of likely impact, between promises and other statements made to suspects. Finally, any acceptable rule seems to require so many qualifications and limitations that it is arguable that efforts to continue to apply a special promise rule, more stringent than the criteria applied to other factors, are likely to prove ineffective in application.

Some courts have abandoned the traditional prohibition against promises by construing the promise rule as applicable only to those promises likely to induce a suspect to confess without regard to his actual guilt or innocence.[24] As in the case of deception,[25] this approach is open to question. Whether federal constitutional considerations permit this consideration of reliability is unclear.[26] Further, it is arguable that such an approach fails to address the major reasons why promises might require separate treatment. The Supreme Court's *Brady* defense of the promise rule was not based on the risk that suspects will respond to promises by inaccurately confessing. Rather, it emphasized the danger that at this preliminary stage of the matter defendants are not adequately equipped to make a decision "fairly" that may have the practical effect of rendering the entire opportunity for trial much less meaningful. Promises of benefits, it might be argued, more than other factors are likely to stimulate defendants into making premature and thus insufficiently informed and considered decisions to confess. If the con-

fession rule rests upon this perceived need to protect suspects from insufficiently considered and thus "unfair" decisions to confess, emphasis upon those promises exceptionally likely to stimulate inaccurate confessions is, of course, inappropriate.

Some courts have concluded that contemporary circumstances and other considerations have destroyed the justification for any special treatment of confessions in the formulation and application of the voluntariness rule. Under this approach, any showing that the suspect was promised advantages in return for a confession is to be considered, along with the remainder of the "totality of the circumstances," in addressing the ultimate voluntariness question: was the defendant's will overborne at the time he confessed?[27] If not, the fact that the pre-confession exchange between the defendant and law enforcement officers involved some statements by the latter that can be characterized as "promises" is of no significance.

As in the case of deception, it is at least arguable that the major current issue should be framed in terms of the extent to which promises will render ineffective a waiver of a suspect's Fifth Amendment rights as defined in *Miranda;* this is discussed below.[28]

 **WESTLAW REFERENCES**

volunt! involuntar! "free will" /p confess! statement* admission* /p promise* induce! reduc! benefit* lenien! plea lesser /p estop! solicit!

Requirement of Person in Authority

volunt! involuntar! "free will" /p confess! statement* admission* /p promise* induce***** reduc! benefit* lenien** plea lesser /p authori******

24. Frazier v. State, 107 So.2d 16 (Fla.1958); Robinson v. State, 247 Miss. 609, 157 So.2d 49 (1963); Fisher v. State, 379 S.W.2d 900 (Tex.Cr.App.1964). Generally, application of this standard results in a confession being found admissible. Dix, supra n. 1, at 306. But see Walker v. State, 626 S.W.2d 777 (Tex.Cr.App.1982) (promise to defendant that if he "cleared up" all his burglaries and signed a confession, he would receive a maximum prison term of ten years was of "such character as would be likely to influence a defendant to speak untruthfully").

25. See § 149 infra.

26. See § 149 infra, discussing the issue in the context of deception.

27. Stobaugh v. State, 614 P.2d 767 (Alaska 1980); State v. Alger, 100 Idaho 675, 603 P.2d 1009 (1979); State v. Edwards, 49 Ohio St.2d 31, 358 N.E.2d 1051 (1976), vacated and remanded on other grounds 438 U.S. 911.

28. See § 153 infra.

§ 149. Voluntariness: (d) Deception [1]

Although there was apparently little case law, the common law voluntariness standard—as far as can be determined—appears to have made any showing that a confession was obtained in response to deception largely if not entirely irrelevant to the voluntariness of a challenged confession.[2] The matter was not addressed in the federal constitutional context by the United States Supreme Court until *Frazier v. Cupp*[3] in 1969. During interrogation concerning a homicide, Frazier informed officers that he had been with his cousin Rawls at the time of the offense. The officers then falsely told Frazier that Rawls had been taken into custody and had confessed. Frazier subsequently made a confession later used against him in his state criminal prosecution. Responding almost offhandedly to the claim

that this deception rendered the confession involuntary, the Court—without citing any authority or offering any rationale—stated, "The fact that the police misrepresented the statements that Rawls had made is, while relevant, insufficient in our view to make this otherwise voluntary confession inadmissible." [4]

Following the Supreme Court's lead in *Frazier*, the lower courts have considered deception in determining the voluntariness of a confession but have seldom regarded it as determinative.[5] Some case law suggests that deception during interrogation may in itself render a resulting confession involuntary, but only if the deception is "calculated" or likely to produce an inaccurate confession.[6] Whether this approach is constitutionally permissible is unclear. It is arguably inconsistent with the Supreme Court's insistence that voluntariness be determined without regard to the reliability or accuracy of particular challenged confessions.[7] On the other hand, perhaps this due process requirement does not bar the formulation of subrules that address the likelihood of particular *types* of interrogation tactics producing unreliable confessions; administration of such subrules, of course, could proceed without direct inquiry into the accuracy of particular confessions. Moreover, the bar against inquiry into reliability may apply only to confessions challenged on

---

§ 149

1. See generally, Dix, Mistake, Ignorance, Expectation of Benefit, and the Modern Law of Confessions, 1975 Wash.U.L.Q. 275; White, Police Trickery in Inducing Confessions, 127 U.Pa.L.Rev. 581 (1979); Notes, 10 Rutgers-Camden L.J. 109 (1978), 32 Vand.L.Rev. 1167 (1979); 29 Am.Jur.2d Evidence §§ 571–72; C.J.S. Criminal Law § 827; Dec.Dig. Criminal Law ⟹523.

2. See Dix, supra n. 1, at 282.

3. 394 U.S. 731 (1969).

4. 394 U.S. at 739.

5. United States ex rel. Hall v. Director, 578 F.2d 194 (7th Cir. 1978), cert. denied 439 U.S. 958 (officers' intentional misrepresentation that accomplices in robbery had said that defendant originated idea and that one had put the blame on defendant did not, considering the totality of the circumstances, render the confession involuntary); State v. Stevenson, 200 Neb. 624, 264 N.W.2d 848 (1978). Compare, Schmidt v. Hewitt,

573 F.2d 794 (3d Cir. 1978) (state court's apparent disregard of evidence that officers misrepresented that accomplices had confessed as well as other evidence suggesting involuntariness rendered state court's determination of confession's admissibility defective; federal habeas corpus court should have held hearing on voluntariness).

6. Sovalik v. State, 612 P.2d 1003, 1007 n. 4 (Alaska 1980). Generally, however, law enforcement misrepresentations as to the strength of the case against the suspect are not regarded as sufficiently likely to produce a false statement to invoke the rule. Matter of D.A.S., 391 A.2d 255 (D.C.App.1978). See, State v. Churchill, 231 Kan. 408, 646 P.2d 1049 (1982), holding that a false statement to the defendant that he had not "passed" a polygraph test was not calculated to produce a confession irrespective of its truth or falsity and therefore did not render the resulting confession inadmissible.

7. See § 147 supra.

what might be called "core involuntariness" grounds, that is, claims of coercion or overbearing of the will. Thus the due process standard may contain the flexibility necessary, when other matters are raised, to permit reliability to be addressed.

In general, however, the lower courts have utilized the flexibility of the voluntariness rule to hold confessions admissible despite evidence that deception was used in their elicitation. Where there is substantial other evidence tending to show involuntariness, however, proof that the officers used deception may be given significant and perhaps controlling weight. It is clear, at least, that trial judges have the discretion so to regard evidence of deception. This approach is illustrated by Gaspard v. State.[8] During Gaspard's interrogation concerning the abduction of a young woman, he was given a polygraph test. During that test, he was falsely told that the young woman had been found dead and that the polygraph indicated that he lied when he claimed that the woman had been alive when he had last seen her. Approving the trial judge's holding that his subsequent confession to the abduction was involuntary, the appellate tribunal stressed Gaspard's prolonged interrogation and his exhausted condition in addition to the officers' blatant deception during the questioning.[9]

It is arguable that the deception cases highlight the deficiencies of the voluntariness standard. The case law evidences a strong distaste for and disapproval of deception but also a stronger reluctance to regard

it as controlling on the issue of admissibility. As a result, the case law contains no useful guidelines concerning the use that can be made of what is clearly a frequently-invoked interrogation device. Moreover, trial judges are given little if any guidance concerning the significance to give to evidence of deception and the method to be used to weigh such evidence against other considerations relevant to the voluntariness inquiry. This lack, however, most likely reflects a general inability—or unwillingness—to come to grips with the underlying question of the acceptability of deception as an interrogation technique. The widespread distaste for deception appears to be tempered with a rather ill-defined perception that the practicalities of law enforcement demand that it be somewhat available. Yet the task of defining what kind of deception is acceptable and under what circumstances it is or should be permissible is so difficult that linedrawing has seldom been attempted.[10] The "totality of the circumstances" analysis required by the voluntariness rule not only permits but arguably encourages avoidance of the issue; cases can readily be disposed of by merely adding deception to the other circumstances to be considered. Whether certain types of deception are, at least under certain circumstances, so offensive to notions of fairness as to be unacceptable as a matter of due process deserves to be addressed directly and thoroughly. Law enforcement personnel deserve more specific guidance than they can obtain from present case law. The cursory disposition of the issue in *Frazier* fails to

---

8. 387 So.2d 1016 (Fla.App.1980).

9. See also State v. Garner, 294 N.W.2d 725 (Minn. 1980) (confession held involuntary in light of evidence that officer told defendant, intending to deceive him, that defendant's possession of firearm was unlawful, that officer threatened to charge other offenses if confession not given, and that officer approached defendant during interrogation "in an intimidating way"); State v. Burdick, 57 Or.App. 601, 646 P.2d 91 (1982) (trial court properly held confession involuntary, given evidence of prolonged interrogation, defendant's condition, and evidence that officers misrepresented to defendant that they had witnesses who would testify that defendant admitted offense and was seen at homicide scene).

10. The American Law Institute's Model Code of Pre-arraignment Procedure would specifically bar officers from misrepresenting to a suspect during interrogation that the suspect is legally obligated to make a statement. Model Code of Pre-Arraignment Procedure § 140.2 (Official Draft, 1975). But no effort was made to promulgate rules for other types of deception. Instead, the drafters suggested that the matter be left for judicial development under a broad prohibition against any "unfair undermining of the suspect's ability to make a choice". Id., Commentary to § 140.4, p. 356, referring to § 140.4(b).

meet or even acknowledge the arguments that might be made for certain *per se* rules prohibiting at least certain forms of deception during interrogation.

Since 1966 and the development of the *Miranda* requirements, many cases present the arguably distinguishable question of whether deception renders ineffective a suspect's waivers of the *Miranda* rights. This is discussed below.[11]

 WESTLAW REFERENCES

synopsis,digest(volunt! involuntar! "free will" /p confess! statement* admission* /p deception deceiv! false trick!)
sh 646 p2d 1049
sh 887 so2d 1016

§ 150. Fifth Amendment Self-Incrimination: (a) Evolution of *Miranda* [1]

During the years preceding 1966, the Supreme Court apparently became increasingly disenchanted with the federal constitutional requirement of voluntariness as a means of dealing with what the Court perceived as the problems related to confessions.[2] This disenchantment appears to have been based in part upon the Court's conclusion that its decisions applying the voluntariness standard did not provide clear enough guidelines for law enforcement conduct during interrogation. This is perhaps inherent in the implementation of a standard under which few if any of the "totality of the circumstances" are controlling in any cases. Seldom is a reviewing court called upon to rule specifically upon the effect of particular types of con-

duct. In any case, the years of effort with the voluntariness test left both law enforcement officers and lower courts with few concrete rules that could objectively be applied to determine the propriety of interrogation methods and the admissibility of resulting statements.

In addition, however, the Court appears to have concluded that the voluntariness test was inadequate to deal with some considerations that the Court's increased sensitivity had led it to conclude posed important dangers to constitutional interests.[3] These considerations involved such matters as deception during interrogation, exploiting the ignorance of suspects concerning legal or factual matters, and interrogation techniques that consisted of manipulating an accused's emotional response to a situation so as to increase the likelihood of a confession. The voluntariness test may have provided an adequate vehicle for condemnation of overt brutality and perhaps even "psychological coercion." But it did not, the Court concluded, constitute an appropriate means of dealing with the wide variety of practices or tactics that might not properly be subjected to total condemnation but which gave rise to concern.

Part of the reason why the voluntariness test did not offer an adequate vehicle for addressing more subtle problems was that in application the standard required extensive inquiry into complex factual matters. Often these inquiries developed into swearing matches between accused persons and law enforcement officers. The Court appears to have become convinced that too often defen-

---

11. See § 153 infra.

§ 150

1. See generally Gangi, A Critical View of the Modern Confession Rule: Some Observations of Key Confession Cases, 28 Ark.L.Rev. 1 (1974); Keefe, Confessions, Admissions and the Recent Curtailment of the Fifth Amendment Protection, 51 Conn.B.J. 266 (1977); Schulhofer, Confessions and the Court, 79 Mich.L.Rev. 865 (1981).

2. For a full discussion of these matters, see Schulhofer, Confessions and the Court, 79 Mich.L.Rev. 865, 867–878 (1981).

3. In *Miranda* itself, the Court discussed at great length interrogation tactics which it clearly regarded as dangerous to interests protected by the Fifth Amendment. 384 U.S. at 448–455. The cases before it, the Court noted, might not have been found to have resulted in statements involuntary in "traditional terms." Id. at 457. Nevertheless, the Court clearly saw the defendants' Fifth Amendment interests as significantly endangered by the manner in which the statements at issue were elicited.

dants lost these contests and thus were deprived of any practical advantages of the voluntariness requirement.[4] Further, if the voluntariness test were expanded in an effort to address more subtle law enforcement practices, these difficulties could be expected to increase. Defendants who had been subjected to these subtle practices would have more difficulty in establishing, as a matter of fact, that the practices had taken place than they would have in establishing the occurrence of overt brutality.

Finally, the Court was apparently frustrated with the continuing and burdensome need to review lower court decisions applying the voluntariness standard. Despite numerous indications that the Court intended the voluntariness standard to be applied with increased sensitivity to the problems it perceived, lower courts continued to apply it in a manner requiring continual monitoring of the results by the Court. This monitoring process added both to the Court's workload and to the overall cost of administration of the voluntariness rule. Adequate application of the voluntariness test and its totality of the circumstances approach required extensive time and resources, at the trial court level, on first-level appeal, and in the Supreme Court itself. Yet despite the extensive judicial time spent on this task, the return was arguably low. Few concrete standards for law enforcement conduct had developed, the subtle problems had not been addressed, and recurring instances of clearly impermissible interrogation practices revealed that even coercion and psychological brutality were not being prevented.[5]

In 1964, however, the Court gave a preliminary hint that the right to representation by counsel might be called into play to address these problems.[6] Later the same year, in Escobedo v. Illinois,[7] the Court found a violation of the Sixth Amendment right to the assistance of counsel where the suspect had been taken into custody, the investigation had focused upon that suspect, the suspect had requested and been denied an opportunity to consult with an attorney he had retained, and the police had not effectively warned him of his absolute right to remain silent. A confession obtained as a result of this Sixth Amendment violation, the Court further held, could not be used to prove the suspect's guilt in a state criminal prosecution.

In 1966, lightning struck.[8] In an opinion actually disposing of four cases but known generally as Miranda v. Arizona,[9] the Court adopted a right to representation as a comprehensive new federal constitutional approach to problems of police custodial interrogation. The resulting *"Miranda requirements"* and their continued desirability and justification present the most important and pervasive issue in contemporary confession law.

From a doctrinal perspective, the major development in *Miranda* was the Court's conclusion that custodial law enforcement interrogation implicated the Fifth Amendment's privilege against compelled self-incrimination, which had been held binding on the states two years earlier.[10] Prior to *Miranda*, the privilege had been limited to those situations in which the questioner had the legal right to compel answers. Since

---

4. See Schulhofer, supra n. 1, at 870–871.

5. 384 U.S. at 445–447 (examples of brutality undoubtedly "the exception" but nevertheless "sufficiently widespread to be the object of concern").

6. Massiah v. United States, 377 U.S. 201 (1964) (Sixth Amendment right to counsel violated by post-indictment elicitation of self-incriminating statement by officer). This right to counsel is developed in § 155 infra.

7. 378 U.S. 478 (1964).

8. The phrase "Lighting strikes" was used in Kamisar, Equal Justice in the Gatehouses and Mansions of American Criminal Procedure, in Criminal Justice in Our Time 50 (Howard ed. 1965) to describe the impact of *Escobedo*. Professor Kamisar accommodated the uncertainty as to the significance of *Escobedo* by adding, "—or Does it?" As applied to *Miranda*, however, no such caveat seems appropriate.

9. 384 U.S. 436 (1966), rehearing denied 385 U.S. 890.

10. Malloy v. Hogan, 378 U.S. 1 (1964).

law enforcement officers had no legal authority to penalize refusals to answer their questions, the traditional view had been that questioning by the officers did not implicate the privilege.[11] Rejecting this distinction, the Court reasoned that "as a practical matter, the compulsion to speak in the isolated setting of the police station may well be greater than in courts or other official investigations [where the legal power to compel answers may be exercised]." [12]

Turning to the question of the implementation of the privilege in this context, the Court concluded that—"until we are shown other procedures which are at least as effective in apprising accused persons of their right of silence and in assuring a continuous opportunity to exercise it" [13]—several requirements are imposed by the Fifth Amendment. First, the suspect is entitled to the presence of counsel during custodial interrogation. Because no defensible line can be drawn between affluent and less solvent defendants, an indigent suspect must be afforded the right of representation by appointed counsel. Second, the suspect is entitled to be informed of his rights, including the right to silence and the attendant right to representation. Third, the suspect is entitled, under certain circumstances, to avoid interrogation by asserting his rights. Finally, before the prosecution may utilize against a defendant a self-incriminating statement obtained during custodial interrogation it must carry the "heavy burden" of establishing an effective waiver of the right to remain silent and, if no lawyer was present during the interrogation, an effective waiver of the right to counsel.

It is clear, however, that the Court was not attempting to address the entire range of problems posed by eliciting or accepting self-incriminating admissions from persons suspected of crimes and later use of those statements to prove defendants' guilt. Instead, the Court carved out the process of eliciting self-incriminating statements from suspects during law enforcement custody as a problem of special importance and undertook to address it comprehensively.

The next three sections consider the details of the *Miranda* holding. Section 151 addresses the applicability of the requirements and the threshold inquiries as to the existence of custody and interrogation. Section 152 discusses compliance with the so-called *per se* requirements of *Miranda*. Finally, Section 153 addresses the task of establishing waiver of the *Miranda* rights and the effectiveness of those waivers that are proved to have been made.

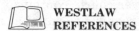 **WESTLAW REFERENCES**

synopsis,digest(volunt! involuntar! "free will" /p confess! statement* admission* & custod! holdover incarcerat! /p miranda)

§ 151. Fifth Amendment Self-Incrimination: (b) Applicability of *Miranda* [1]

Miranda clearly applies only if two threshold conditions are established: the defendant must have been in "custody" and the officers must have engaged in "interrogation."

Custody. The rigorous measures taken in *Miranda* to protect the privilege against compelled self-incrimination were justified, the Court reasoned, because of the inherent pressures generated by the fact of custody. In several subsequent cases, the Court has made clear that custody remains a firm requirement for application of those measures.

---

11. See generally, 8 Wigmore, Evidence § 2252, pp. 327–29 (McNaughton rev. 1961).

12. 384 U.S. at 461.

13. Id. at 467.

§ 151

1. See generally, Graham, What is "Custodial Interrogation?" California's Anticipatory Application of Miranda v. Arizona, 14 U.C.L.A.L.Rev. 59 (1966); Smith, The Threshold Question in Applying Miranda: What Constitutes Custodial Interrogation? 25 S.C.L.Rev. 699 (1974); Annot., 31 A.L.R.3d 565.

In Orozco v. Texas,[2] officers entered the defendant's bedroom, surrounded his bed, and began to question him. The state apparently urged that *Miranda* be limited to those situations giving rise to what the Court had perceived to be the underlying problem, that is, custodial interrogation in a law enforcement environment. Thus, it urged, interrogation in a suspect's own home (or presumably other "familiar surroundings") should not invoke the *Miranda* requirements. Rejecting this, the Court simply noted that it had, after careful consideration, concluded in *Miranda* itself that the requirements applied while a suspect was being interrogated while "in custody at the station or otherwise deprived of his freedom of action in any significant way."[3] In Mathis v. United States,[4] the interrogation took place while the defendant was in custody for an offense unrelated to that involved in the interrogation. Finding *Miranda* applicable, the Court quite summarily rejected the suggestion that it be limited to situations in which the suspect was "in custody" in connection with the offense for which he was being questioned.

The requirement of custody was reaffirmed in Oregon v. Mathiason,[5] involving a parolee interviewed by a police officer at the state patrol office. Mathiason came pursuant to a message from the officer that he would "like to discuss something." At the meeting the officer told Mathiason that he was not under arrest. During the discussion Mathiason acknowledged commission of a theft and burglary. The state court had found *Miranda* applicable on the basis of its conclusion that the interrogation took place in a "coercive environment." The Supreme Court first rejected the suggestion that *Miranda* applies where the suspect is not in custody but where the atmosphere is nevertheless "coercive." "It was [the 'in custody'] coercive environment to which *Miranda* by its terms was made applicable, and as to which it is limited."[6] Then it addressed the facts before it and found that they clearly showed that Mathiason had not been in custody within the meaning of *Miranda*.[7]

The primary issue left unsettled by these cases is the extent to which it is the subject's perception or the officer's actions that determine custody. In *Mathiason*, the Court stated, "*Miranda* warnings are required only where there has been . . . a restriction on a person's freedom as to render him 'in custody.'"[8] This might be read as requiring that the officer have actually acted so as to restrict liberty. Thus a suspect who reasonably—and accurately—perceived that any effort on his part to leave the confrontation would be met by restraint would not be "in custody," where the officer had no occasion to impose such restraint. *Mathiason*, however, was a *per curiam* decision made without full argument, and it is unlikely that the Court intended it to have this effect. Given the emphasis in *Miranda* itself upon the subject's perception, this perception should be the controlling consideration. Whether custody exists, then, where no actual restraint has been imposed should depend upon whether the suspect both actually and reasonably perceived that if he attempted to break off the confrontation with the officers this would be prevented. This has, in general, been the approach of the lower courts.[9]

---

2. 394 U.S. 324 (1969).

3. 394 U.S. at 327.

4. 391 U.S. 1 (1968).

5. 429 U.S. 492 (1977) (per curiam).

6. 429 U.S. at 495.

7. Justice Stevens, dissenting, characterized the issues presented by the case as "too important to be decided summarily" and indicated that they should not be resolved without the benefit of full argument and plenary consideration. Id. at 500.

See also, California v. Beheler, 103 S.Ct. 3517 (1983) (compliance with *Miranda* not necessary where suspect voluntarily comes to station, a "brief interview" occurs, and suspect is permitted to leave unhindered)

8. Oregon v. Mathiason, 429 U.S. 492, 495 (1977).

9. See United States v. Kennedy, 573 F.2d 657, 660 (9th Cir. 1978) (could defendant have reasonably believed she could not leave freely); United States v. Jones, 630 F.2d 613, 616 (8th Cir. 1980) (no custody because suspect could not have reasonably believed she was in custody).

Interrogation. The requirement of interrogation has given rise to less Supreme Court litigation than that of custody and remained virtually unaddressed until Rhode Island v. Innis.[10] In *Innis*, however, the Court rejected the argument that *Miranda* is limited to what might be called, "express interrogation:"

> [T]he term "interrogation" under *Miranda* refers not only to express questioning, but also to any words or actions on the part of the police (other than those normally attendant to arrest and custody) that the police should know are reasonably likely to elicit an incriminating response from the suspect.[11]

Application of the test to determine whether law enforcement conduct was the "functional equivalent" of express interrogation focuses primarily upon the perception of the suspect. Evidence that words or conduct were intended by the officer to elicit a self-incriminating admission from the suspect does not itself establish that interrogation took place; it may, however, strongly tend to show that the officer knew or should have known his words or conduct were sufficiently likely to elicit the desired response.[12]

Applying this standard to the facts before it, the Court evidenced a marked reluctance to find interrogation. Innis had been apprehended in an area where he was thought to have concealed a firearm used in a murder. Three officers accompanied him in a police vehicle to headquarters. During the trip, one officer observed to another that many handicapped children from a local school for the impaired were in the area, and "God forbid one of them might find a weapon . . . and . . . hurt themselves." Innis then interrupted with an offer to show the of-

ficers where a weapon (which turned out to be the murder weapon) was located. The Court characterized the officers' conversation as "no more than a few off-hand remarks." No indication was found that the officers intended their remarks to elicit a response from Innis, the Court continued. Further, in the absence of more—such as awareness that Innis was particularly sensitive to appeals concerning handicapped children—the officers should not have been aware that their comments would move Innis to make a self-incriminating admission of the location of the weapon. On balance, this seems to do inadequate credit to the imagination and sensitivity of the officers. The Court's relatively broad definition of interrogation appears to be offset by a marked reluctance to apply it realistically.

A curious twist on the issue was presented in South Dakota v. Neville.[13] State law required a person under certain circumstances to submit to a blood alcohol test; a refusal to comply with a proper demand for such submission could be used as evidence that the subject was intoxicated. Rejecting the argument that admission of a subject's refusal was permissible only if the demand was preceded by compliance with *Miranda*, the Court explained:

> In the context of an arrest for driving while intoxicated, a police inquiry of whether a suspect will take a blood-alcohol test is not an interrogation within the meaning of *Miranda*. . . . [P]olice words or actions "normally attendant to arrest and custody" do not constitute interrogation. The police inquiry here is highly regulated by state law, and is presented in virtually the same words to all suspects. It is similar to a police request to submit to fingerprinting or photography.[14]

10. 446 U.S. 291 (1980). The case is discussed in Grano, Rhode Island v. Innis: A Need to Reconsider the Constitutional Premises Underlying the Law of Confessions, 17 Am.Crim.L.Rev. 1 (1979); White, Rhode Island v. Innis: The Significance of a Suspect's Assertion of His Right to Counsel, 17 Am.Crim.L.Rev. 53 (1979) (both discussing lower court decision); White, Interrogation Without Questions: Rhode Island v. Innis and United States v. Henry, 78 Mich.L.Rev. 1209 (1980).

11. 446 U.S. at 301.

12. Id. at 301 n. 7.

13. 103 S.Ct. 916 (1983).

14. 103 S.Ct. at 923. Traditionally, lower courts have held that compliance with *Miranda* is not necessary during the booking process, despite the fact that the questions asked during this process literally come within the *Miranda* requirements. This is apparently on the assumption that such questioning is so unlikely to elicit incriminating information that the questioning is not "incriminating." See People v. Weathington, 76

Questioning During Field Stops. A special problem is posed by field stops for investigation, permitted under the Fourth Amendment upon "reasonable suspicion" that the suspect is involved in—or perhaps has information related to—criminal activity.[15] To what, if any, extent must questioning in this context comply with the *Miranda* requirements? Literally, of course, the threshold requirements are almost always met; the suspect has been deprived of liberty by the stop and the officer generally is engaging in express questioning.

In *Miranda* itself, the Court commented that "general on-the-scene questioning as to facts surrounding a crime or other general questioning of citizens in the factfinding process is not affected by our holding."[16] It seems clear that if an officer arrives at a scene and must, as a matter of clear necessity, decide how to respond, some questioning is essential. Wounded persons may need attention. It may be almost equally important to know whether some other persons not present should be sought and apprehended. To require compliance with *Miranda* before asking questions addressing these matters would be unrealistic. The *Miranda* Court's language seems intended to exempt such situations from the decision's requirements.

On the other hand, it is clear that in many such situations the officer's inquiries progress from such general inquiries to questions that can serve little purpose other than the development of evidence to convict the suspect. Where inquiry is not necessary to make emergency field decisions, the rationale for regarding *Miranda* as inapplicable arguably disappears. It may, however, be unrealistic to expect officers, in such situations, to make careful distinctions and to remain attentive to the need to identify the point at which compliance with *Miranda* becomes necessary. For whatever reason, the lower courts have tended quite uncritically to regard *Miranda* as inapplicable to these situations without regard to whether the inquiries have progressed beyond the emergency point.[17]

If a person questioned during such an encounter were to invoke the right to counsel, there would almost always be no way to comply and therefore the functional effect would be to preclude questioning. Postponing the questions until provision of a lawyer was possible would frequently result in prolonging and shifting the site of the detention beyond what is normally permissible upon less than probable cause.[18] It can be argued that to require a suspect to endure longer

---

Ill.App.3d 173, 31 Ill.Dec. 741, 394 N.E.2d 1059 (1979), affirmed 82 Ill.2d 183, 44 Ill.Dec. 496, 411 N.E.2d 862 (1980). The discussion in *Neville*, of course, tends to affirm the accuracy of this approach. But several cases have cast doubt on this assumption. In People v. Rucker, 26 Cal.3d 368, 162 Cal.Rptr. 13, 605 P.2d 843 (1980), the court held that while *Miranda* need not be complied with during the booking process, any responses given by the defendant that later turn out to be incriminating may not be used if there has not been compliance. See also, Cavaness v. State, 581 P.2d 475, 480 (Okl.Cr.App.1978), cert. denied 439 U.S. 1117 (error to admit against defendant in prosecution for possession of marijuana his acknowledgment, made during booking, that premises were his residence, where compliance with *Miranda* not shown).

15. See generally, § 172 infra.

16. Miranda v. Arizona, 384 U.S. 436, 477 (1966).

17. State v. Dickey, 125 Ariz. 163, 608 P.2d 302 (1980). Contra, Whitfield v. State, 287 Md. 124, 411 A.2d 415 (1980), cert. dismissed 446 U.S. 993 (if suspect is in custody, situation is not one involving only "on the scene" investigations to which *Miranda* does not apply). In Bailey v. State, 153 Ga.App. 178, 264 S.E.2d

710 (1980) the court considered the admissibility of the defendant's responses to the questions asked by an officer arriving at the scene of a reported shooting. The officer's initial questions were not subject to *Miranda*, the court held, under the on-the-scene exception. But once the officer had developed information indicating that the suspect had shot the victim in a manner involving potential criminal liability, the exception ceased to apply and a failure to comply with *Miranda* required exclusion of answers to subsequent questions.

18. See generally § 172 infra. The American Law Institute's Model Code of Pre-Arraignment Procedure suggests a warning that the detainee is not required to say anything and that anything said may be used in evidence. Model Code of Pre-Arraignment Procedure § 110.1(5)(1)(i) (Official Draft, 1975). The Commentary suggests doubt as to whether this is sufficient (citing *Orozco*) and the Code offers the following as a possible supplement to the warning in this context:

that he will not be questioned unless he wishes, and that if he wishes to consult a lawyer or have a lawyer present during questioning, he will not be questioned at this time, and that after being taken to the

detention than is otherwise permissible as a condition of asserting the right to counsel is an unreasonable burden upon that right. Perhaps in nonarrest field stop situations, the right to counsel should be regarded as inapplicable. An officer making such a stop, then, would be required to give no warnings before asking "emergency" questions and to advise the suspect only of his right to silence before making further inquiries.[19]

Custodial Interrogation by Private Persons. In *Miranda*, the Court defined custodial interrogation in language suggesting that it was limited to such activity by law enforcement officers.[20] Lower courts have followed this suggestion and have held the *Miranda* requirements inapplicable to custodial interrogation by private persons.[21] The rationale for this position was recently developed by the California Supreme Court:

> Unless [private persons] represent themselves as police they do not enjoy the psychological advantage of official authority, a major tool of coercion. Moreover, there appears little evidence of abusive techniques by [private per-

sons] similar to those that *Miranda* charged against the police.[22]

On the other hand, there has been acknowledgment that involvement by law enforcement officers in action directly undertaken by private persons can be such as to bring *Miranda* into play; this is generally stated as requiring that the private persons be shown to be acting as "agents" of law enforcement officers, a showing difficult for defendants to make.[23] The major area of controversy has been in regard to private security personnel. It is at least arguable that the rationale expressed by the California court for regarding *Miranda* inapplicable to private party activity does not apply when the private persons represent themselves to have some special status by wearing uniforms clearly resembling those of law enforcement personnel and behave in a fashion that arguably distinguishes them from persons on the street. Nevertheless, the lower courts have reasoned that such security personnel have in fact no more power than other private persons and generally are not subject to *Miranda*.[24] There is, howev-

---

stationhouse a lawyer will be furnished him prior to questioning if he is unable to obtain one.
Id. § 110.2(5)(a)(iv).

19. The Court has acknowledged that some custodial questioning might be exempted from *Miranda*. In Estelle v. Smith, 451 U.S. 454 (1981), addressing the applicability of *Miranda* to a psychiatric interview, the State urged that the privilege was inapplicable because the interviewer did not seek answers to be used for the testimonial content of what was said. Apparently leaving open the possibility that some interviews might be so characterized and thus perhaps be said not to involve "interrogation", the Court concluded that the record in the case before it established that the interviewer used the testimonial contents of the defendant's answers and thus the privilege applied.

20. Miranda v. Arizona, 384 U.S. 436, 444 (1966) ("By custodial interrogation, we mean questioning initiated *by law enforcement officers* after a person has been taken into custody or otherwise deprived of his freedom of action in any significant way.") (emphasis supplied).

21. People v. Farmer, 91 Ill.App.3d 262, 46 Ill.Dec. 726, 414 N.E.2d 779 (1980) (defendant's brother, an alderman and "special patrolman" authorized to act as peace officer at request of Chief of Police, was not required to comply with *Miranda*); Worthington v. State, ___ Ind. ___, 405 N.E.2d 913 (1980), cert. denied 451 U.S. 915 (fellow jail inmate not required to observe

Miranda); State v. Hallam, 175 Mont. 492, 575 P.2d 55 (1978) (fireman not law enforcement officer); State v. Zeko, 176 Conn. 421, 407 A.2d 1022 (1979) (bailbondsman not law enforcement officer required to comply with *Miranda*).

22. In re Deborah C., 30 Cal.3d 125, 133, 177 Cal. Rptr. 852, 855–56, 635 P.2d 446, 449 (1980).

23. See Terry v. State, 397 So.2d 217 (Ala.Crim.App. 1981), cert. denied 397 So.2d 223 (Ala.). The reluctance of the lower courts to find the required relationship to bring *Miranda* into play is illustrated by West v. State, 178 Ind.App. 522, 383 N.E.2d 398 (1978). When officers responding to a burglary alarm found the store secured, one Allen Buckshot, an assistant manager was called. Buckshot let the officers in and accompanied them while they located and apprehended the defendant. When the officers looked for anyone else, Buckshot had a "conversation" with the defendant concerning his entry into the store. *Miranda* was held inapplicable, because Buckshot was not acting as a law enforcement officer.

24. Matter of Victor F., 112 Cal.App.3d 673, 169 Cal.Rptr. 455 (1980). See also, Terry v. State, 397 So. 2d 217 (Ala.Crim.App.1981), cert. denied 397 So.2d 223 (Ala.); In re Deborah C., 30 Cal.3d 125, 177 Cal.Rptr. 852, 635 P.2d 446 (1980); People v. Johnson, 101 Misc. 2d 833, 422 N.Y.S.2d 296 (1979); State v. Pickett, 37 Or.App. 239, 586 P.2d 824 (1978).

er, some indication that on the facts of particular cases a sufficiently close relationship may exist between private security persons and law enforcement so that, for *Miranda* purposes, the private security personnel become subject to the *Miranda* requirements.[25]

 WESTLAW REFERENCES

Custody

synopsis,digest(volunt! involuntar! "free will" /p confess! statement* admission* & custod! holdover incarcerat! /p miranda)

synopsis,digest(volunt! involuntar! "free will" /p confess! statement* admission* & custod! holdover incarcerat! /p miranda & custod! /p defin! mean!)

synopsis,digest(volunt! involuntar! "free will" /p confess! statement* admission*) & custod! /p coercive depriv! restrict! /s environment atmosphere liberty freedom

Interrogation

synopsis,digest(volunt! involuntar! "free will" /p confess! statement* admission* & interrogat! /10 defin! mean!)

Field stops

synopsis,digest(volunt! involuntar! "free will" /p confess! statement* admission*) & interrogate* interrogation* question! /p roadblock* field scene

Custodial Interrogation by Private Persons

interrogation* question! /p "private person*""concerned citizen*" vigilante! & synopsis,digest(confess! statement* admission* & volunt! involunt! "free will")

---

§ 152. Fifth Amendment Self-Incrimination: (c) Compliance With *Miranda*

Consideration of the requirements of *Miranda* and of methods of compliance with

those requirements is facilitated by distinguishing between two types of requirements imposed by the decision. The first consists of what might be called *per se* requirements. Violation of these requirements renders a resulting confession inadmissible without regard to any further inquiry into the impact of that violation upon the defendant's decisionmaking process. The second category consists of requirements relating to the defendant's decisionmaking process. Virtually all of these requirements relate to an effective waiver of the *Miranda* rights to silence and to the presence of counsel during custodial interrogation. This section addresses the *per se* requirements; the waiver questions are addressed in the next section.

Warnings. Perhaps the most widely-recognized of the *Miranda* requirements is the requirement of certain warnings. In the Court's own words,[1] the warning must include the following:

1. "[You have] the right to remain silent;"[2]

2. "[A]nything [you say] can and will be used against [you] in court;"[3]

3. "[You] have the right to consult with a lawyer and to have the lawyer with [you] during interrogation;"[4] and

4. "[I]f [you] cannot afford an attorney one will be appointed for [you] prior to any questioning if [you] so [desire]."[5]

The first three elements are "absolute prerequisite[s]" to proper custodial interrogation. Failure to give them cannot be "cured" by evidence that the suspect was al-

25. See People v. Glenn, 106 Misc.2d 806, 435 N.Y.S.2d 516 (1981), in which the court was convinced that the store at issue followed a policy of having a store detective question shoplifting suspects without complying with *Miranda*. "Special patrolmen," who were law enforcement officers, were readily available but were not called until supervisory personnel had evaluated the results of the interrogation. The special patrolmen, held the court, were so readily available as to be functionally present and participating in the detention and questioning. See also, People v. Jones, 47 N.Y.2d 528, 419 N.Y.S.2d 447, 393 N.E.2d 443 (1979) (*Miranda* applied where police were alerted that suspect was under surveillance, later arrested the suspect and escorted him into store office, and remained outside office while store security personnel conducted interrogation).

§ 152

1. As the following notes make clear, the Court, in the course of the *Miranda* opinion, sometimes used different language. This failure to use uniform terminology, of course, confirms the conclusion, see text at n. 8 infra, that the Court did not intend any particular passage in the opinion to be a rigid framework for the warnings.

2. Miranda v. Arizona, 384 U.S. 436, 479 (1966).

3. Id. at 469. Compare id. at 479 ("anything [you say] can be used against [you] in a court of law").

4. Id. at 471. Compare id. at 479 ("[You] have the right to the presence of an attorney").

5. Id. at 479. Compare id. at 473 ("[You have] the right to consult with an attorney [and] if [you are] indigent a lawyer will be appointed to represent [you].").

ready aware of the substances of omitted warnings.[6] Omission of the fourth element, on the other hand, is apparently not fatal if the suspect was known to have an attorney already or to have ample funds to secure one. But if there is any doubt as to the justification for omitting it, this doubt will be resolved against the prosecution.[7]

The extent to which law enforcement officers have flexibility in administering the *Miranda* warnings was addressed in California v. Prysock.[8] The issue, as formulated by the majority, was whether there was compliance with the fourth element of the warning requirement, given that the officer had told the suspect that he had a right to talk to a lawyer before questioning and to have that lawyer present during all questioning and that he had the right to have a lawyer appointed to represent him at no cost to him. In an unreported opinion, an intermediate California appellate court had held the warning insufficient. According to the Supreme Court's majority, the state tribunal arrived at this conclusion on the basis that the officer had not informed the suspect, in the words of the *Miranda* opinion, that he had the right to have an attorney "appointed for him prior to any questioning." [9] Reversing, the Supreme Court held that "no talismanic incantation" is necessary to comply with *Miranda* [10] and that the question was whether the police fully conveyed to the suspect the substance of his *Miranda* rights.[11] The language used by the officer, the Court con-

cluded, conveyed to the suspect that his right to appointed counsel included the right to have one appointed before interrogation and to have that appointed lawyer be present during any interrogation that took place.

Perhaps the major issue posed by the formulation of the warning is related to the *Prysock* issue. Often, if not generally, law enforcement officials have no authority to "appoint" a lawyer for a suspect and no access to anyone with such authority, except during the regular subsequent processing of the defendant through the court system. Thus if a lawyer is to be appointed, this appointment will most likely take place when the defendant is presented before a judge for the initial appearance. May the warnings attempt to convey this to the suspect? Or, to put the issue differently, is it permissible for officers to add to the warnings, "We have no way of furnishing you with a lawyer but one will be appointed for you, if you wish, when you go to court?" [12]

The risk, of course, is that this will negate the effect of the remainder of the warnings. As modified, the warning may leave the suspect with the impression that he may be interrogated and that no right to counsel exists with regard to any such interrogation as is conducted prior to the court appearance. In *Prysock*, the majority strongly suggested that if, read as a whole, the warning suggested that appointed counsel would be available only after interrogation the warning would be inadequate.[13]

---

6. Id. at 471–472. The lower courts have generally held that there is no absolute necessity that officers give a further "fifth warning" to the effect that the defendant has a right to terminate the interview or questioning at any time. Crafton v. State, 545 S.W.2d 437, 439 (Tenn.Cr.App.1976). But such further warning has been described as the "better practice," Commonwealth v. Lewis, 374 Mass. 203, 371 N.E.2d 775 (1978), and the failure to include it has been identified as an important factor in determining the voluntariness of subsequent waivers. United States v. DiGiacomo, 579 F.2d 1211, 1214 (10th Cir. 1978).

7. 384 U.S. 436, at 473 n. 43.

8. 453 U.S. 355 (1981), on remand 127 Cal.App.3d 972, 180 Cal.Rptr. 15.

9. 453 U.S. at 359–360. As is discussed in n. 6 supra, the *Miranda* opinion did not use any consistent

terminology in regard to this element of the warning as well as in regard to others. This confirms the Court's conclusion that the *Miranda* opinion was not intended as a form to be used literally.

10. Id. at 359.

11. Id. at 361.

12. Lower courts have varied. Compare Commonwealth v. Johnson, 484 Pa. 349, 399 A.2d 111 (1979) (such a warning misleading and confusing at best and constitutes a subtle temptation to unsophisticated suspect to forego right to counsel) with Massimo v. United States, 463 F.2d 1171 (2d Cir. 1972), cert. denied 409 U.S. 1117 (1973) (such warning communicates to suspect the reality of the situation).

13. 453 U.S. at 360, citing with approval United States v. Garcia, 431 F.2d 134 (9th Cir. 1970). *Garcia*

Invoking the Right to Counsel. Given *Miranda's* rigid bar against interrogation of a suspect who invokes the right to counsel, whether a suspect has invoked this right is often an important question. Generally, this is best regarded as a waiver question; interrogation of an unrepresented suspect who is in custody cannot proceed in the absence of an effective waiver of the right to counsel.[14] But some situations may raise doubt as to whether the suspect's conduct has this effect. In Fare v. Michael C.,[15] the suspect, a sixteen year old youth, had asked to speak with his probation officer. The state courts had found that given the relationship between a juvenile and his probation officer, such action was sufficient to invoke *Miranda's per se* rule against interrogation until at least an opportunity for consultation with the probation officer was provided. Rejecting this, the Supreme Court reasoned that a probation officer is not capable of providing the legal advice or other services which *Miranda* contemplated would be rendered by a lawyer. To completely bar interrogation of one who indicated only a desire to consult with such a person, it concluded, would greatly expand the burden of *Miranda* without serving the interests that the decision was intended to protect.[16]

Provision of Counsel. Given the apparent intention of the *Miranda* Court to involve attorneys in the custodial interrogation process, it is at first surprising to find so little post-*Miranda* litigation concerning

the details of the requirement that counsel be provided and permitted to be present. This, however, can be explained quite readily. In the vast majority of cases defendants waive the right to appointed counsel and to the presence of counsel. If, therefore, there has been compliance with the warning requirements, the sole remaining issue in many cases is the effectiveness of the waivers. In the cases in which no waiver of the right to counsel is made, it seems quite likely that police simply forego interrogation. The task of obtaining counsel and the low likelihood that interrogation in the presence of counsel will be fruitful undoubtedly combine to discourage efforts to proceed when no waiver is forthcoming.

Insofar as the right to appointed counsel goes, it might be expected to raise questions such as the degree of indigency required for eligibility and the right to appointed counsel where a suspect's inability to obtain retained representation is due to other causes, such as unpopularity or the unavailability of lawyers willing to assume responsibility for the case. The right to counsel's assistance might be expected to raise other questions, such as the right to private consultation before and perhaps at intervals during the interrogation and perhaps counsel's right to prevent questioning at all. But since, for the reasons suggested above, few defendants appear to undergo custodial interrogation unless counsel has been waived, these issues seldom if ever arise.[17]

---

held inadequate a warning that the suspect could "have an attorney appointed to represent you when you first appear before the U. S. Commissioner or the Court."

14. See text at n. 18 infra.

15. 442 U.S. 707 (1979), rehearing denied 444 U.S. 887.

16. 442 U.S. at 722–723.

17. But see State v. Reed, 390 So.2d 1314 (La.1980) (Sixth Amendment right to counsel violated where retained counsel unable to consult with defendant because police failed for two days to produce jailed defendant for court appearances and falsely assured counsel that defendant was about to be produced); Fowler v. State, 6 Md.App. 651, 253 A.2d 409 (1969), affirmed 259 Md. 95, 267 A.2d 228 (officers' refusal to leave interrogation room so counsel could confer with client violated

right to counsel). It has been held that the right to counsel includes more than the right to an opportunity to contact counsel. See Lee v. State, 560 S.W.2d 82 (Tenn.Cr.App.1977) (error to continue interrogation where defendant permitted to call lawyer but lawyer was out of office at time). Where a suspect is represented by an attorney, law enforcement officers are not barred from accepting a waiver of counsel made without the lawyer's presence. See Porter v. State, 271 Ind. 180, 391 N.E.2d 801 (1979) (officers had no duty to arrange for attorney's presence during interrogation to which defendant consented without counsel's presence). See also Lamb v. Commonwealth, 217 Va. 307, 227 S.E.2d 737 (1976), in which the defendant consulted an attorney before surrendering. The attorney sought unsuccessfully to elicit a commitment from law enforcement officers that there would be no questioning and advised the defendant to make "no statement

Avoidance or Cessation of Interrogation. The *Miranda* opinion is somewhat ambiguous concerning the extent to which a suspect has the right to be free of any interrogation at all. At one point, the Court stated, "If the individual states that he wants an attorney, the interrogation must cease until an attorney is present." [18] Elsewhere, the Court appeared to speak more broadly: "If the individual indicates in any manner, at any time prior to or during questioning, that he wishes to remain silent, the interrogation must cease." [19] This broad statement was qualified, however, with the further comment that if an attorney is present and the suspect expresses a desire to remain silent, "there may be some circumstances in which further questioning would be permissible." [20] Self-incriminating responses made in response to interrogation conducted over such objections but in the presence of counsel, the Court indicated, *might* "in the absence of evidence of overbearing" be free of compulsion and thus a waiver of the right to remain silent. [21]

The issue is complicated by uncertainty as to whether there is or should be a distinction between further interrogation in the traditional sense, on the one hand, and, on the other, inquiries by law enforcement officers concerning a suspect's willingness to reconsider a previous decision to invoke a right that precludes interrogation. It is at least arguable that the second might be permitted in circumstances where the first is barred.

In Michigan v. Mosley,[22] the Court considered the effect of police action in reapproaching a defendant who, during a prior interrogation session, had apparently made an initial implied waiver of the right to counsel [23] but indicated a desire not to answer questions. *Miranda,* the Court concluded, could not reasonably be read as creating a *per se* prohibition of indeterminate duration against any further questioning of the suspect by any police officer about any subject, simply because the suspect had indicated a desire to remain silent. "[T]he admissibility of statements obtained after the person in custody has decided to remain silent depends under *Miranda* on whether his 'right to cut off questioning' was 'scrupulously honored.' " [24] On the facts before it, the Court concluded that the officer's action in reapproaching Mosley and soliciting a waiver of *Miranda* rights did not undercut Mosley's previous decision to remain silent. The Court emphasized that two hours had elapsed between Mosley's expression of a desire to remain silent and the officer's reapproach. The reapproach was by a different officer, who fully informed Mosley of his rights and gave him "a full and fair opportunity to exercise them." Finally, the offense for which the second officers sought to question Mosley was "unrelated" to the offenses in regard to which Mosley had previously expressed a desire to remain silent.[25]

The significance of *Mosley* was clouded, however, by Edwards v. Arizona.[26] During interrogation, discussion was addressed to a

whatsoever." When officers were reading him his *Miranda* rights, the defendant volunteered that whenever he made a statement, "it gets screwed around with a different meaning." The officer indicated a copy of any statement would go to his lawyer so "it couldn't get twisted around," and finished the warnings. The defendant's waiver made at this point was held valid and the confession given admissible.

18. 384 U.S. at 474.

19. Id. at 473–474.

20. Id. at 474 n. 44.

21. Id.

22. 423 U.S. 96 (1975), on remand 72 Mich.App. 289, 249 N.W.2d 393, appeal after remand 400 Mich. 181, 254 N.W.2d 29, cert. denied 434 U.S. 861.

23. The Court noted that Mosley at no time indicated a desire to consult with a lawyer and that no claim was made that the procedures followed in the beginning interrogation did not comply fully with *Miranda.* 423 U.S. at 97.

24. Id. at 104.

25. Whether the offenses were in fact unrelated is not clear. It can be argued that Mosley's initial refusal to answer questions was a response to efforts to question him about a series of robberies, including the one which the second officer sought to discuss with him. See id. at 120 (Brennan, J., dissenting).

26. 451 U.S. 477 (1981), rehearing denied 452 U.S. 973.

possible "deal" with law enforcement authorities. Edwards finally stated, "I want an attorney before making a deal," and was returned to jail. Next morning, two other detectives sent for him; the guard responded to Edwards' statement that he did not want to talk to any one by telling Edwards that he "had to" talk with the detectives. Edwards was then warned by the detectives and subsequently made an incriminating statement. Holding the statement inadmissible, the Court explained:

> [W]hen an accused has invoked his right to have counsel present during custodial interrogation, a valid waiver of that right cannot be established by showing only that he responded to further police-initiated custodial interrogation even if he has been advised of his rights. . . . [A]n accused . . ., having expressed his desire to deal with the police only through counsel, is not subject to further interrogation by the authorities unless counsel has been made available to him, unless the accused himself initiates further communication, exchanges or conversations with the police.[27]

If the accused initiates a meeting with police and during this meeting the officers engage in conduct amounting to interrogation,[28] the question becomes whether before that interrogation there was a valid waiver. In making this determination it is necessary to consider all of the circumstances, "including the necessary fact that the accused, not the police, reopened the dialogue with the authorities."[29] Turning to the facts before it, the Court concluded that Edwards had invoked his right to counsel and that he was thereafter subjected to custodial interrogation at the instance of police. His resulting statement was made without having had access to counsel and "did not amount to a valid waiver." Hence it was inadmissible.

The significance of *Mosley* and *Edwards* is not clear. Justice White, concurring in the *Mosley* result, predicted that voluntariness would become the standard by which to judge the waiver of the right to silence by a properly warned defendant.[30] *Mosley* does appear to reject a *per se* prohibition against reapproaching a defendant who has waived the right to counsel but invoked the right to silence. Whether there is a meaningful difference between the majority's standard—was the reapproach made in a way that "scrupulously honored" the suspect's continued right to cut off questioning—and the requirement that the ultimate waiver of the right to silence be "voluntary" is questionable. Perhaps the majority opinion is best read as imposing upon the prosecution an unusually heavy burden of establishing voluntariness where the facts show such a reapproach.

Edwards is more difficult to construe. It can, of course, be read as adopting a *per se* prohibition against reapproaching a defendant who has invoked *Miranda's* right to counsel, at least until counsel is present. Three justices concurred in the *Edwards* result on the ground that issue was whether the waiver was voluntary and that on the facts—including the reapproach by the officers—voluntariness had not been shown.[31] Justice Powell, joined by Justice Rehnquist, expressed concern regarding his inability to determine whether the majority was simply applying such a voluntariness standard or whether, in the alternative, it was adopting a

27. 451 U.S. at 484–485.

28. Id. at 486 n. 9.

29. Id. at 485. The scope of a waiver made after a defendant who has invoked the right to counsel initiates contact with law enforcement authorities is addressed in Wyrick v. Fields, 103 S.Ct. 394 (1982), discussed in § 153 infra.

30. Michigan v. Mosley, 423 U.S. 96, 108 (1975) (White, J., concurring), on remand 72 Mich.App. 289,

249 N.W.2d 393, appeal after remand 400 Mich. 181, 254 N.W.2d 29, cert. denied 434 U.S. 861.

31. Edwards v. Arizona, 451 U.S. 477, 488 (1981) (Burger, C. J., concurring in the judgment), rehearing denied 452 U.S. 973 (statement to suspect that he "had to" talk with officers rendered waiver involuntary); id. at 490 (Powell, J., joined by Rehnquist, J., concurring in the result).

rule that required exclusion upon a showing that the statement resulted from a police reapproach to the defendant.[32]

To the extent that *Miranda* should be developed in a way to provide brightline rules for determining the propriety of various law enforcement activities and the admissibility of confessions, *per se* rules of the sort *Edwards* may establish are desirable. On the other hand, as applied to some cases, such *per se* rules require the exclusion of apparently reliable confessions untainted by any substantive intrusion upon the suspect's Fifth Amendment interests. The issue is perhaps best put as whether the needs to discourage practices such as reapproaching defendants who have invoked their rights and to have brightline rules capable of easy application justifies an approach that results in loss of some valuable and untainted self-incriminating statements.

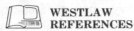
WESTLAW REFERENCES

synopsis,digest(miranda /p insufficien! confus! underst**d comprehend!)

Invoking Right to Counsel
invok! /s right /5 counsel attorney* lawyer* /p miranda

Accordance or Cessation of Interrogation
right /s silence /s violat! deny denied disregard! /p interrogat! reinterrogat! reapproach!
miranda /p reinterrogat! reapproach!

---

32. Id. (Powell, J., concurring in the result). The ambiguity of *Edwards* was emphasized by Oregon v. Bradshaw, 103 S.Ct. 2830 (1983), in which the suspect invoked the right to counsel. After he later asked, "What is going to happen to me?" a waiver of counsel was obtained and interrogation continued. No violation of *Miranda* was found, but there was no opinion of the Court. Eight justices apparently agreed that under *Edwards*, further discussion with a suspect who has invoked the right to counsel is permissible only if the suspect initates further discussion concerning the subject matter of the investigation. These justices split 4–4 on whether Bradshaw's question met this standard. Justice Powell, on the other hand, concluded that on a totality of the circumstances analysis, Bradshaw's waiver was valid and that should be determinative. But see Justice Marshall's comment that eight members of the Court "manifestly agree that *Edwards* did create a *per se* rule." Id., at 2840 n. 2 (Marshall, J., dissenting).

§ 153. Fifth Amendment Self-Incrimination: (d) Waiver of *Miranda* Rights

In most cases involving challenges to confessions given under circumstances rendering *Miranda* applicable, the disputed issues revolve around the sufficiency of the showing of waivers. At least three categories of issues arise: those concerning the adequacy of proof that the defendant actually made and manifested a decision to waive, those concerning the effectiveness of such a decision, and others concerning the scope of any such effective waiver as might have been shown.

Showing Waiver. In the *Miranda* opinion itself, the Court commented that an express statement to the effect that a suspect does not want an attorney and is willing to make a statement "could" constitute a waiver.[1] Arguably, *Miranda's* purpose of substituting objectively-applicable brightline standards for the vague, subjective voluntariness inquiries would be best served by a requirement of an express waiver. In North Carolina v. Butler,[2] however, the Court held that the North Carolina Court had erred in imposing a requirement that the suspect make an explicit written or oral statement of waiver. Finding no reason to require an explicit waiver, the Court held that the ulti

---

§ 153

1. Miranda v. Arizona, 384 U.S. 436, 475 (1966), rehearing denied 385 U.S. 890. There is some uncertainty as to the need for an affirmative showing of waiver. In contrast with the discussion in *Miranda* concerning the need to show waiver, there is other language suggesting that at least the right to counsel need not be respected unless affirmatively invoked. 384 U.S. at 474 ("If the individual states that he wants an attorney, the interrogation must cease until an attorney is present."). Conceptually and practically, it is quite important whether the right to counsel must be respected unless waiver is shown or whether, after proper warnings, interrogation can occur unless the suspect evidences a desire for counsel. Overall, the purpose of *Miranda* suggests a bar against interrogation unless a waiver occurred and can later be established. Best read, language such as that quoted earlier in this note probably refers to the possibility that an implied waiver can be shown where no request is made and the suspect's conduct permits the inference of waiver. See text at n. 3 infra.

2. 441 U.S. 369 (1979).

mate issue is whether the prosecution can prove that the suspect waived his rights. In some cases, the Court concluded, this can be done without showing expressly articulated words of waiver.[3]

But there are certain minimal requirements concerning the evidence necessary to prove the implied waiver that *Butler* permits. In *Miranda*, the Court commented that a waiver "will not be presumed simply from the silence of the accused after warnings are given or simply from the fact that a confession was in fact eventually obtained."[4] Nor will the fact that some questions have been answered previously constitute a waiver of the right to remain silent in regard to subsequent questions.[5] Apparently the prosecution's evidence of implied waiver is adequate only if there is sufficient conduct of the suspect shown, beyond the fact of confessing after the warnings, from which a reliable inference can be drawn that the suspect was aware of his rights and made a conscious choice not to exercise them.

Miranda and *Butler* both speak of a single "waiver," despite the fact that many situations involve both the right to the presence of counsel and the right to remain silent. But operative waivers of these two distinct rights may occur at significantly different times. In many situations, for example, it is necessary to inquire initially whether the suspect, before any interrogation

began, effectively waived his right to the presence of counsel. If such a waiver occurred and was effective, interrogation properly proceeded. But the important waiver of the right to remain silent may not have occurred until some time later. Even if submitting to interrogation and "agreeing" in some sense to respond to questions constitutes a waiver of the right to remain silent, the *Miranda* opinion itself makes clear that this does not preclude reassertion of the right to remain silent in regard to subsequent questions.[6] In many cases, then, it may be useful to consider separately whether there was adequate proof of waiver of both rights and, if so, whether both waivers were proved effective.

Effectiveness of Waiver. If the prosecution shows either an express waiver or sufficient facts from which the trial judge is willing to find an implied waiver, the prosecution must still meet the further requirement that the waiver be proved effective. This was reaffirmed in Tague v. Louisiana,[7] in which the State had rested upon a barebones showing that the suspect was given his warnings and confessed.[8] The Louisiana Court had upheld admission of the resulting confession on the basis of a presumption that since the suspect was given the warnings, he should— in the absence of contradictory evidence—be presumed to have understood them.[9] Because no evi-

---

3. In dissent, Justice Brennan urged that express waivers should be so easy to obtain where a defendant wishes to waive the rights and the task of inquiring as to an implied waiver is so difficult that *Miranda* should require an express waiver. 441 U.S. at 378–379 (Brennan, J., dissenting).

4. Miranda v. Arizona, 384 U.S. 436, 475 (1966), rehearing denied 385 U.S. 890.

5. Id. at 476.

6. See text at n. 5 supra.

In Fare v. Michael C., 442 U.S. 707 (1979), rehearing denied 444 U.S. 887, the Court held that the 16-year old suspect's request to speak with his probation officer did not constitute "a *per se* request to remain silent." 442 U.S. at 723. This arguably expressed the majority's view that this fact alone did not preclude a finding that his later incriminating admissions were made as a

result of an effective waiver of the right to remain silent. It also, however, may have meant that these words did not invoke any special limits imposed by *Miranda* upon continued questioning of a suspect who expresses a desire to remain silent or upon reapproaching such a suspect to solicit a reconsideration of the suspect's decision to preclude interrogation.

7. 444 U.S. 469 (1980), on remand 381 So.2d 507 (La.).

8. It is possible to read *Tague* as addressing the prosecution's need to show conduct and circumstances sufficient to show an implied waiver rather than the informed nature of a waiver that has adequately been shown. But this does not appear to be the general thrust of the discussion.

9. 372 So.2d 555 (La.1978).

dence was produced by the prosecution that the suspect "knowingly and intelligently waived his rights," the Supreme Court held, the trial court erred in admitting the statement.[10]

Although discussions such as those in the brief per curiam decision in *Tague* do not always draw the distinction, it appears that adequate analysis of purported *Miranda* waivers requires separate discussion of two requirements: the waiver must be shown to be voluntary and, in addition, to be "knowing" and "intelligent." As most usefully defined, the requirement that a waiver be knowing and intelligent addresses those matters of which the suspect must be aware in order for the waiver to be effective. The requirement of voluntariness, on the other hand, addresses the need for the decision to be free from certain improper influences. While *Tague* emphasizes the need for the prosecution to prove specifically that a waiver was "knowingly and intelligently" made, it seems clear that voluntariness must similarly be shown.

(1) *Voluntariness.* *Miranda* itself makes clear that the waiver must be "voluntary."[11] Perhaps the major issue is whether this means anything other than that the waiver must meet the same standard that under pre-*Miranda* case law was applied to the statement itself.[12] If so, it is arguable that *Miranda* has done little or nothing to simplify confession law as applied to most contexts. The decision, so read, would retain voluntariness law with all of its faults but require that it be applied in addition to a series of *per se* rules.[13]

The relevant policy considerations are arguably conflicting. Read as a whole, *Miranda* reflects greater sensitivity to the risk to Fifth Amendment interests posed by certain subtle influences that might be brought to bear upon a suspect's decisionmaking process; this suggests that the standard might reasonably be construed as tighter than that under pre-*Miranda* voluntariness law. On the other hand, *Miranda* also added significantly to a suspect's protection by the several *per se* requirements; arguably this justifies a relaxation of the voluntariness requirement as applied to waivers and a consequential reduction in the need to make the subjective and difficult inquiries required by the traditional standard.

Miranda itself is of little help. A showing of "lengthy interrogation or incommunicado incarceration" before a statement is made, the Court commented, will be "strong evidence" that any waiver was not effective.[14] Then, the Court continued by offering, "Moreover, any evidence that the accused was threatened, tricked, or cajoled into a waiver will, of course, show that the defendant did not voluntarily waive his privilege."[15]

Several rather focused questions are raised in this area. First, does *Miranda* change the traditional rule[16] that trickery or deception will not itself render a suspect's responding decision ineffective? The language from the *Miranda* opinion cited above suggests that a change was intended. But the lower courts have been reluctant to modify the longstanding approach that deception alone will not invalidate a suspect's decision.[17] Most lower courts, however, have failed to address the waiver issue as a sepa-

---

10. 444 U.S. at 471. The Court specifically noted that the officer had not testified to any efforts to establish Tague's general intellectual ability or whether he in fact understood the warnings. Id.

11. 384 U.S. at 476.

12. See § 147 supra.

13. On the other hand, perhaps the addition of the *per se* requirements mean that the task would have to be undertaken less frequently and, when undertaken, would be rendered easier of resolution by the courts'

ability to ascertain whether or not there had been compliance with these requirements.

14. 384 U.S. at 476.

15. Id.

16. See § 149 supra.

17. See cases cited in n. 18 infra. The Court itself has noted but avoided the issue several times. See Oregon v. Mathiason, 429 U.S. 492, 495 (1977) (officer's false statement to suspect that he had found suspect's fingerprints at scene, "whatever relevance this . . .

rate one. Rather, they have tended to regard evidence that deception was used during interrogation as raising instead the general "voluntariness" of the resulting confession and to regard this as appropriately resolved by applying the traditional voluntariness criterion.[18] This, of course, makes deception relevant but seldom if ever controlling. But occasionally courts have recognized that the effectiveness of a waiver of the *Miranda* rights as a new issue not necessarily tied to a pre-*Miranda* voluntariness law. In Edwards v. State,[19] for example, the Supreme Court of Indiana strongly condemned the use of deception to influence a suspect's decision to waive his *Miranda* rights. Apparently stopping short of adopting a blanket rule that any waiver influenced by deception would be ineffective, the court nevertheless stated that under the language of the *Miranda* opinion itself "deceptive practices of the police must weigh heavily against the State in determining the voluntariness of a waiver of rights." [20] On the facts of *Edwards*, the officers' false representation to Edwards that they had an eyewitness who would identify him as the perpetrator was held to render his subsequent waiver of counsel and silence ineffective.

A second focused question concerns the effect of a promise of benefit upon a defendant's waiver of the *Miranda* rights. While traditional voluntariness doctrine included a rigid prohibition against at least some promises, many courts have modified the doctrine so as to give it substantially more flexibility.[21] Whatever the current voluntariness doctrine is, should this be used to determine the effectiveness of a *Miranda*

waiver? Or have recent developments, including the recognition of the *Miranda* rights themselves, justified abandoning this approach for some other? The *Miranda* Court's statement that evidence indicating the accused was "cajoled into a waiver" will demonstrate the ineffectiveness of that waiver can, of course, be read literally. This would suggest application of earlier rigid standards.

Perhaps, however, the rationale for the special voluntariness promise rule suggests that it ought not to apply to determination of the effectiveness of *Miranda* waivers. The Supreme Court defended application of a promise rule to confessions but not guilty pleas on the ground that the latter are generally entered only with the assistance of counsel.[22] *Miranda*, of course, guarantees defendants undergoing custodial interrogation the right to representation in making the decision to confess. Does this suggest that since accused persons have a right to representation before making *Miranda* waivers as well as guilty pleas, neither decision should be rendered ineffective simply because it represents a response to a promise of a benefit? It can be argued, of course, that the *Miranda* waiver decision, despite the right to counsel, is quite often made without counsel and under circumstances in which the defendant is far more sensitive to inducement than will be the case later when the defendant must decide how to plead. Recognition of a right to counsel, then, may not justify treating the decision to confess in the same manner as the decision as to how to plead, especially when the decision to confess also embodies a decision not

---

may have to other issues in the case," is unrelated to whether there was "custody"); Michigan v. Mosley, 423 U.S. 96, 99 n. 5 (1975), on remand 72 Mich.App. 289, 249 N.W.2d 393, appeal after remand 400 Mich. 181, 254 N.W.2d 29, cert. denied 434 U.S. 861 (noting that Mosley had contended below that supression of his confession was required for, among other reasons, the use of "trickery" during the interrogation).

18. Sovalik v. State, 612 P.2d 1003 (Alaska 1980); State v. Pugh, 600 S.W.2d 114 (Mo.App.1980).

19. ____ Ind. ____, 412 N.E.2d 223 (1980).

20. 412 N.E.2d at 227. See also State v. Howard, 617 S.W.2d 656 (Tenn.Cr.App.1981) (waiver of counsel ineffective, in view of totality of factors including sheriff's efforts to lead defendant to believe that there was strong scientific evidence of his guilt). Cf. Matter of D.A.S., 391 A.2d 255 (D.C.App.1978) (if a voluntary and intelligent waiver is shown, it is then necessary to consider whether deception will nevertheless render statement inadmissible).

21. See § 148 supra.

22. Id. at note 6.

to invoke the right to counsel in deciding whether to confess.

As in the case of deception, the lower courts have generally failed to regard the criterion for determining the effectiveness of a *Miranda* waiver as a potentially different one than has traditionally been used to determine the ultimate admissibility of a confession under the voluntariness rule. As a result, the case discussions tend to be in terms of ultimate voluntariness and to reflect the general increasing distaste for a rigid requirement that a promise render a confession inadmissible.[23] Unfortunately, there has apparently been no effort to consider how, in light of *Miranda's* contribution to the law dealing with law enforcement interrogation as well as other relevant considerations, evidence that an accused waived the rights to counsel and silence in response to a promise of some future benefit should be evaluated.

The entire matter of waiver is complicated, of course, by the Court's apparent holding in Michigan v. Mosley [24] that in some situations at least the effectiveness of a waiver is determined not by voluntariness but rather by inquiry whether the suspect's continued right to cut off any questioning at all was "scrupulously honored." Whether law enforcement conduct or other circumstances that would not establish involuntariness might nevertheless preclude a showing of sufficient respect for the suspect's right to cut off questioning remains unclear.

Perhaps the most difficult aspect of voluntariness to address is the extent to which subtle influences upon defendants will invalidate waivers. An officer may, for example, before giving the warnings and soliciting a waiver (or perhaps in the course of doing this), engage the suspect in conversation. This in turn may, intentionally or not, reduce the suspect's emotional aversion to talking with the officer and to providing the officer with a self-incriminating admission. If, of course, this constitutes "interrogation," [25] to do it before an effective waiver of counsel is obtained constitutes a violation of one of *Miranda's per se* rules. If, however, it is determined not to constitute interrogation, will it render ineffective a waiver of the right to counsel? Even if it is interrogation, will it— if it is used after an effective waiver of counsel is obtained—invalidate a waiver of the right to remain silent, such waiver being made by the offer of the self-incriminating statement?

In general, lower courts appear to be reluctant to delve into the task of determining what law enforcement efforts to manipulate defendants' emotional tone will invalidate waivers.[26] In People v. Honeycutt,[27] however, the California Court confronted the effect of an officer's prewarning discussion with a murder suspect. The discussion followed a classic use of the "Mutt-and-Jeff" technique,[28] in which a hostile officer left and the interrogating officer, with a much more sympathetic approach, then addressed the suspect. The interrogating officer engaged in a half-hour conversation with the

23. Stobaugh v. State, 614 P.2d 767 (Alaska 1980); Davis v. State, 275 Ark. 264, 630 S.W.2d 1 (1982); State v. Alger, 100 Idaho 675, 603 P.2d 1009 (1979); State v. Edwards, 49 Ohio St.2d 31, 358 N.E.2d 1051 (1976), judgment affirming death penalty vacated 438 U.S. 911.

24. 423 U.S. 96 (1975), on remand 72 Mich.App. 289, 249 N.W.2d 393, appeal after remand 400 Mich. 181, 254 N.W.2d 29, cert. denied 434 U.S. 861, discussed in § 152 n. 22 supra.

25. See § 151 supra.

26. See State v. Miller, 76 N.J. 392, 388 A.2d 218 (1978):

> [W]e disagree . . . that the use of a psychologically-oriented technique in questioning a suspect is inherently coercive. Questioning of a suspect almost necessarily involves the use of psychological factors. . . . Use of a psychologically-oriented technique is not improper merely because it causes a suspect to change his mind and confess.

76 N.J. at 404, 388 A.2d at 224.

27. 20 Cal.2d 150, 141 Cal.Rptr. 698, 570 P.2d 1050 (1977).

28. See Miranda v. Arizona, 384 U.S. 436, 452 (1966), rehearing denied 385 U.S. 890.

suspect. This first involved past events and mutual acquaintances unrelated to the victim or the offense but then progressed to the victim himself; the suspect was told that the victim had been a suspect in a homicide case and was thought by the officer to be a homosexual. No discussion was addressed to the offense until the suspect indicated a willingness to discuss it. The *Miranda* warnings were then given, a waiver was obtained, and an incriminating statement taken. Finding the statement inadmissible, the California Court held that the spirit of *Miranda* prohibited use of a "conversation-warning-interrogation" sequence of events, where the prewarning conversation is designed to encourage the suspect to waive the rights of which he had not yet been informed.

Tactics such as those used in *Honeycutt* seem clearly contrary to the spirit of *Miranda*. *Miranda* is based upon the proposition that a suspect is entitled to be free of efforts to persuade him to make a self-incriminating statement or to do anything likely to lead to a self-incriminating statement unless a lawyer is present or the suspect has consented to such efforts in the absence of counsel. Where the law enforcement conduct conceals the fact that such efforts are being made, the suspect's ability to make the sort of choice required by *Miranda* is greatly impeded. On the other hand, the task of identifying what law enforcement conduct or circumstances constitutes such efforts is a difficult one. Arguably, *Miranda* was designed to eliminate the need for the sort of inquiry necessary to determine on a case-by-case basis whether such impermissible efforts have been used.

(2) *Requirement of "Knowing and Intelligent" Waiver.* While it is arguable that the Court's discussion in *Miranda* itself does not draw a clear distinction between the requirement that waivers be voluntary

and the need for a knowing and intelligent waiver, the inquiries were carefully separated in Edwards v. Arizona.[29] Edwards' confession had been admitted upon the state trial judge's determination that it was "voluntary." The Supreme Court found that the *Miranda* waiver issues had not been adequately addressed:

> [W]aivers of counsel must not only be voluntary, but constitute a knowing and intelligent relinquishment or abandonment of a known right or privilege . . . . [N]either the trial court nor the Arizona Supreme Court undertook to focus on whether Edwards understood his right to counsel and intelligently and knowingly relinquished it. It is thus apparent that the decision below misunderstood the requirement for finding a valid waiver of the right to counsel . . . .[30]

Merely recognizing the requirement, however, does not define it. Several issues are presented by this task. It would appear that at a minimum the requirement that a waiver be knowing and intelligent requires that the suspect have at least a barebones conscious understanding of the abstract rights involved, that is, those rights of which the suspect has been informed. This is confirmed by *Tague v. Louisiana*,[31] of course, in which the Court apparently held that the prosecution need do more than show the giving of the warnings and argue a presumption that one who is warned understands those warnings. Evidence that the suspect had normal intelligence or that the officer made further inquiries as to the suspect's actual understanding would appear, ordinarily at least, necessary and probably sufficient to meet the Court's requirement.

A more difficult problem is raised when it is claimed on behalf of a defendant that for some specific reason the defendant misunderstood or failed to assimilate the substance of the warning. Evidence of subnormal intelligence, for example, may be

29. 451 U.S. 477 (1981), rehearing denied 452 U.S. 973.

30. 451 U.S. at 482–483.

31. 444 U.S. 469 (1980), on remand 381 So.2d 507 (La.), discussed in the text at n. 7 supra.

offered, as may evidence of intoxication.[32] In some cases, defendants have offered evidence that at the time of the interrogation they refused to sign or write anything as proof that, despite the warning that anything one says can be used in court, the defendant did not in fact understand the admissibility of an oral admission.[33] Despite the logical implication from the requirement that evidence of actual misunderstanding will render a waiver invalid, lower courts have been quite hostile to such efforts.[34] In *Edwards*,[35] the defendant claimed that despite the detectives' effort to explain this, he did not understand the admissibility of an oral, unrecorded confession. Although the Supreme Court held only that the lower courts had not adequately resolved Edwards' claim that his waiver was invalid, this holding in the context presented arguably suggests that adequate proof of actual misunderstanding of the warnings renders a waiver invalid.

What sort of further information is necessary to render a waiver "intelligent" within the meaning of the requirement is unclear. It would be unrealistic to demand that a suspect have sufficient factual (and "legal") in-

formation necessary to make a reasoned decision concerning the tactical wisdom of providing the prosecution with a confession. But is it necessary that the defendant understand the basic nature of the offense to which he is confessing? The Pennsylvania Court has held that the suspect must be aware of "the general nature of the transaction giving rise to the investigation," although not necessarily the specific offense for which he might be charged.[36] Most courts, however, have rejected this approach.[37]

There is arguably a strong tension between *Miranda's* objective of providing brightline rules for interrogation and determining admissibility, on the one hand, and the need for an intelligent waiver, on the other. Among the objections to rigorous enforcement of a requirement that the suspect be "informed" is the difficulty of formulating rules precise enough so that officers will know when interrogation may proceed. A reasonable compromise might be to deal with problems of this sort not by broadening the requirements for a showing of an effective waiver but instead by imposing *per se* requirements that certain information be of-

32. United States v. Babb, 448 F.Supp. 794 (D.S.C. 1978); Gordon v. State, 387 A.2d 611 (Me.1978); Lowe v. State, 584 S.W.2d 239 (Tenn.Cr.App.1979).

33. Wantland v. State, 45 Md.App. 527, 413 A.2d 1376 (1980), vacated and remanded for reconsideration in light of Edwards v. Arizona, 451 U.S. 1014, on remand 49 Md.App. 636, 435 A.2d 102.

34. See Wantland v. State, 45 Md.App. 527, 413 A.2d 1376 (1980), vacated and remanded for reconsideration in light of Edwards v. Arizona, 451 U.S. 1014, on remand 49 Md.App. 636, 435 A.2d 102, rejecting the view that a suspect's misperception that an oral confession could not be used would invalidate a waiver. "We decline," the court reasoned, "to adopt the view that Miranda requires a waiver to be wisely made." 45 Md. App. at 538, 413 A.2d at 1383. Compare State v. Jones, 37 Ohio St.2d 21, 306 N.E.2d 409 (1974) (if suspect acts in such a way as to alert an interrogating officer that he does not understand the admissibility of oral self-incriminating statements, officer must, before further interrogation, insure that suspect fully and correctly understands this matter). There is some tendency to regard apparently even persuasive evidence of such misunderstanding as merely one factor to consider on the "totality of circumstances." See Forman v. Smith, 482 F.Supp. 941 (W.D.N.Y.1979), reversed on other grounds 633 F.2d 634 (2d Cir. 1980), cert. denied 450

U.S. 1001. This arguably confuses the inquiry into "voluntariness," where such a totality of the circumstances approach may be proper, with the different inquiry into whether the suspect had the specific awareness required to render the waiver a sufficiently "knowing" one.

35. See text at n. 29 supra.

36. See Commonwealth v. Dixon, 475 Pa. 17, 379 A.2d 553 (1977).

37. State v. Carter, 296 N.C. 344, 250 S.E.2d 263 (1979), cert. denied 441 U.S. 964 (ignorance of fact that victim had died was no more than factor to consider in determining whether waiver and confession were "voluntary"). The lower courts are even divided on whether the failure of interrogating officers to inform a defendant of the nature of the charge is a factor that may be considered in determining the effectiveness of a waiver. See State v. Goff, ___ W.Va. ___, 289 S.E.2d 473, 477 n. 8 (1982), collecting cases, concluding that "some information should be given to the defendant as to the nature of the charge in order that he can determine whether to intelligently and voluntarily exercise or waive his *Miranda* rights," and—presumably—holding that the failure to give such information to a suspect is at least relevant to the validity of a subsequently-made waiver.

fered to the suspect. If, for example, a requirement were to exist that before soliciting a waiver officers inform the suspect of their current perception of the events at issue, this might be an acceptable substitute for an inquiry, under waiver analysis, as to whether any subsequent waiver was made with adequate understanding of the underlying events.

Scope of a Waiver. If law enforcement officers obtain an effective waiver of the suspect's right to the presence of counsel (and perhaps of the right to be free from interrogation), what is the scope of that waiver? What, in other words, may the officers do without rewarning the suspect and obtaining a further waiver?

The issue was addressed in Wyrick v. Fields,[38] in which Fields, suspected of rape, had secured representation by retained counsel. He then requested a polygraph examination and executed a written "consent" form reciting his rights. After the conclusion of the examination, the examiner—without further advising Fields of his rights or situation and without securing any additional waiver—told Fields that there had been some deceit during the discussion and asked him whether he could explain why his answers were bothering him. Fields then acknowledged sexual activity with the victim. Protesting the admissibility of his statement to the examiner and certain "fruit" of it, Fields claimed that his waiver extended only to the administration of the polygraph test and not to any subsequent traditional interrogation; that since no effective waiver covering the post-test interrogation had been obtained and since he had earlier, by securing representation, invoked his right to counsel, that interrogation violated *Miranda.*

Summarily reversing the granting of habeas corpus relief to Fields, the Supreme Court held the interrogation permissible under *Miranda.* The Court apparently held that a waiver covers all law enforcement activity which the suspect should reasonably have foreseen would be included in the course of conduct in regard to which he waived counsel.[39] Since neither Fields nor his attorney could reasonably have failed to foresee that the polygraph test would be followed by questions concerning unfavorable results, the waiver encompassed such questioning. If, the Court suggested, a "significant change in the character of the interrogation" had occurred, it would be likely or perhaps certain that the initial waiver could not be construed as a waiver of the presence of counsel during the changed interrogation. But merely disconnecting the polygraph machine, the Court said, effected no such change in the interrogation. Where rewarning and further waiver are not necessary, the Court continued, it remains necessary that the suspect know of his continued right upon request to stop interrogation. Fields, however, had been informed of this before the test and the fact that the machine had been disconnected failed to show that he no longer was aware of this continuing right to stop interrogation.

Fields tends to confirm the approach that the lower courts have taken to other claims that developing circumstances required what is often called, "rewarning." To some extent, this is a misnomer; the real argument, of course, is not merely that the suspect must be rewarned but that additional waivers covering the further law enforcement activity be obtained. Lower courts have tended to hold that officers are precluded from relying upon a prior waiver only if there is such a change in circumstances that the earlier warnings and waiver are no longer reliable evidence of the suspect's current willingness to forego exercise of the rights.[40] Among the factors suggesting that a fur-

---

38.   103 S.Ct. 394 (1982).

39.   103 S.Ct. at 397.

40.   State v. Barfield, 298 N.C. 306, 340, 259 S.E.2d 510, 535–36 (1979), cert. denied 448 U.S. 907, rehearing denied 448 U.S. 918: "Repetition of *Miranda* warnings is not required where no inordinate time elapses between interrogations, the subject matter remains the same and there is no evidence that anything occurred which would serve to dilute the effect of the first warning." Where warnings were administered at the

ther waiver is necessary are the passage of time between the warnings and waiver, on the one hand, and the interrogation at issue, on the other. A change in interrogating officers suggests that rewarning may be necessary to assure that the defendant sufficiently understands that the officers now interrogating him are aware of his rights and prepared to respect any decision he might make to exercise them. If the location of interrogation is shifted or if other circumstances change, again rewarning and further waiver may be necessary to assure that continued interrogation does not run afoul of *Miranda*.

 WESTLAW REFERENCES

right /5 counsel attorney* lawyer* /s presen** /s violat! deny denied disregard! /p miranda)

Showing Waiver

synopsis,digest(miranda) & imply! implied! /s waive! waiving

miranda /p reinterrogat! reapproach! reassert!

Effectiveness of Waiver

synopsis,digest(miranda) & effective! /s waiv!

(1) Voluntariness

synopsis,digest(miranda & volunt! involunt! /p waiv!)

time and place of apprehension, no further warnings have been required at stationhouse interrogation taking place 45 minutes later, Burlison v. State, 369 So.2d 844 (Ala.Crim.App.1979), cert. denied 369 So.2d 854 (Ala.), or even several hours later, State v. Williams, 386 So.2d 27 (Fla.App.1980). See also, Johnson v. State, 56 Ala.App. 583, 324 So.2d 298 (1975), cert. denied 295 Ala. 407, 324 So.2d 305 (where defendant warned adequately several days earlier, officer's question, "Are you aware of your rights?", was sufficient compliance at later interrogation session).

§ 154

1. See generally Gandara, Admissibility of Confessions in Federal Prosecutions: Implementation of Section 3501 by Law Enforcement Officials and the Courts, 63 Geo.L.J. 305 (1974); Note, 42 Fordham L.Rev. 425 (1973). See also, Gangi, Confessions: Historical Perspective and a Proposal, 10 Houston L.Rev. 1087, 1095–1101 (1973); Schrock, Welch & Collins, Interrogational Rights: Reflections on Miranda v. Arizona, 52 So.Cal.L.Rev. 1, 4–15, 56 (1978).

2. 82 Stat. 197, Title II, § 701(a), codified as 18 U.S. C.A. § 3501. In relevant part, the statute provides:

§ 3501. Admissibility of Confessions

(a) In any criminal prosecution brought by the United States or by the District of Columbia, a confession . . . shall be admissible in evidence if it is voluntarily given. Before such confession is re-

synopsis,digest(miranda) & volunt! involunt! /p waiv! /p deception* deceiv! trick! misrepresent! coerc! threat! promis! lenien! help

synopsis,digest(miranda & volunt! involunt! /p waiv! /p deception* deceiv! trick! misrepresent! coerc! threat! promis! lenien! help)

miranda & mutt /3 jeff

Requirement of "Knowing & Intelligent" Waiver

synopsis,digest(miranda & kn*w! underst**d! /s intelligent! /s waiv!)

miranda & kn*w! underst**d! /s intelligent! /s waiv! /p intox! alcohol! dr*nk!

Scope of Waiver

synopsis,digest(miranda & waiv! /p reinterrogat! reapproach! resume! resuming continu! additional subsequent! later /s interrogat! question! reinterrogat! reapproach!)

§ 154. Fifth Amendment Self-Incrimination: (e) Legislative "Overruling" of *Miranda* [1]

In 1968, as part of the Omnibus Crime Control and Safe Streets Act of 1968, Congress passed legislation which, as passed and as presently codified, purports to overrule *Miranda* as that decision applies to the admissibility of confessions in federal criminal prosecutions.[2] Basically, the statute

ceived in evidence, the trial judge shall, out of the presence of the jury, determine any issue as to voluntariness. If the trial judge determines that the confession was voluntarily made it shall be admitted in evidence and the trial judge shall permit the jury to hear relevant evidence on the issue of voluntariness and shall instruct the jury to give such weight to the confession as the jury feels it deserves under all the circumstances.

(b) The trial judge in determining the issue of voluntariness shall take into consideration all the circumstances surrounding the giving of the confession, including (1) the time elapsing between arrest and arraignment of the defendant making the confession, if it was made after arrest and before arraignment, (2) whether such defendant knew the nature of the offense with which he was charged or of which he was suspected at the time of making the confession, (3) whether or not such defendant was advised or knew that he was not required to make any statement and that any such statement could be used against him, (4) whether or not such defendant had been advised prior to questioning of his right to the assistance of counsel; and (5) whether or not such defendant was without the assistance of counsel when questioned and when giving such confession.

The presence or absence of any of the above-mentioned factors to be taken into consideration by the

purports to make voluntariness the sole criterion for determining the admissibility of a confession. Among the factors to be considered in determining voluntariness are whether the defendant was advised or knew that he was not required to make a statement or that any such statement could be used against him, whether or not the defendant had been advised of his right to counsel, and whether or not the defendant had the assistance of counsel during interrogation. But the statute specifically provides that the presence or absence of any of the mentioned factors "need not be conclusive on the issue of voluntariness of the confession." At least one state legislature has enacted similar legislation applicable to state criminal prosecutions.[3]

To some extent, the statute clearly purports to change results required by *Miranda*. Under *Miranda*, a violation of the *per se* requirements is clearly intended to be conclusive in regard to the admissibility of the confession. The statute does not direct a complete abandonment of this approach. Instead, it provides that what are in effect violations of *Miranda's per se* requirements "need not" be conclusive in regard to admissibility. Arguably, then, a trial judge would remain free in a particular case to find the violation of *Miranda's* requirements conclusive. But insofar as the statute directs that in some cases a violation of these *per se* requirements need not require the exclusion of the resulting confession, it appears clearly inconsistent with what *Miranda* construed to be the requirements of the Fifth Amendment.

Perhaps the statute can be regarded as a response to the Court's encouragement offered in *Miranda* to legislatures to continue to search for increasingly effective ways of protecting the rights of suspects while also promoting efficient enforcement of the criminal law.[4] The "safeguards" established by *Miranda*—presumably including the *per se* requirements—were stated by the Court to be required "unless we are shown other procedures which are at least as effective in apprising accused persons of their right of silence and in assuring a continuous opportunity to exercise it . . . ."[5] But the statute is little more than a return to pre-*Miranda* voluntariness law and can scarcely be said to be the result of a search for new ways to assist law enforcement while protecting rights of accused persons.

The Senate report on the legislation suggests that it was stimulated by a view that *Miranda* required the costly suppression of confessions despite overwhelming evidence that the defendants had suffered no serious harm as a result of any violation of the case's requirements.[6] It does not appear that any actual effort was made to justify it as within the Court's invitation. Rather, there was a prevailing sentiment that the Court was simply wrong concerning the requirements of the Fifth Amendment and that the legislation was justified by the likelihood that by the time any issue under it rose to the Court, the Court's position would have changed.[7]

All in all, the legislation appears to be a largely symbolic expression of Congressional disagreement with the Court's basic conclusion in *Miranda* that the *per se* requirements were so important that they merited enforcement by excluding even voluntary confessions obtained in violation of them. Prosecutors faced with the task of defending convictions on appeal appear to have recognized the almost certain unconstitutionality of the statute, as virtually no appellate case law under it has arisen.

---

judge need not be conclusive on the issue of voluntariness of the confession. . . .

3.   Ariz.Rev.Stat. § 13–3988.

4.   Miranda v. Arizona, 384 U.S. 436, 467 (1966), rehearing denied 385 U.S. 890.

5.   Id.

6.   S.Rep. No. 1097, 90th Cong., 2nd Sess. (1968), [1966] U.S.Code Cong. & Ad.News 2112, 2127.

7.   Id. at 2138.

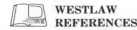 **WESTLAW REFERENCES**

18 /4 3501 & miranda

§ 155. Sixth Amendment Right to Counsel

In its pre-*Miranda* 1966 decision in Massiah v. United States,[1] the Supreme Court gave notice that the admissibility of self-incriminating statements would be affected by the Sixth Amendment right to counsel. Until 1977, however, this effect appeared limited largely if not entirely to statements elicited by or made in the presence of law enforcement undercover officers. Brewer v. Williams,[2] decided that year, made clear, however, that in some situations involving traditional law enforcement interrogation, the Sixth Amendment right to counsel as well as *Miranda's* Fifth Amendment right to such representation was a significant consideration. It is nevertheless useful to explore the Sixth Amendment right first in the context of undercover law enforcement investigations and then, separately, in other interrogation situations.[3]

Undercover Activities. Massiah itself involved a fairly typical law enforcement undercover investigation. Massiah and one Colson had been arrested and indicted for drug offenses. Colson, cooperating with federal law enforcement officers, permitted installation of a radio transmitter in his car. He then caused Massiah, while in the car, to engage in a conversation during which Massiah made self-incriminating admissions. The Court held that Massiah's Sixth Amendment rights had been violated "when there was used against him at his trial evidence of his own incriminating words, which federal agents had deliberately elicited from him after he had been indicted and in the absence of his counsel." [4] It is obvious that the law enforcement tactics used in *Massiah* could not have been used in a manner complying with the suspect's right to representation. Warning Massiah that he ought to consider securing legal advice is obviously incompatible with the nature of the investigation. In the undercover context, then, *Massiah*, when it applies, virtually prohibits elicitation of self-incriminating statements.

Determining when *Massiah* applies, however, is not easy. In *Massiah* itself, the suspect had been indicted. But other Sixth Amendment cases make clear that in general the Sixth Amendment right to counsel often applies before formal indictment or its equivalent. These decisions indicate that the right attaches when adversary judicial criminal proceedings have been begun.[5] In *Williams*—albeit in a nonundercover situation—the Court found that the right had attached when a judicial arrest warrant had been issued, Williams had been arrested on that warrant and presented before a magistrate, and the magistrate had "committed" him to custody.[6] While this is not perfectly clear, it appears that if a lawyer for the

§ 155

1. 377 U.S. 201 (1964).

2. 430 U.S. 387 (1977), rehearing denied 431 U.S. 925.

3. Justice Rehnquist has commented that the "doctrinal underpinnings" of *Massiah* "have been left largely unexplained" and, if the matter is carefully evaluated, the *Massiah* requirements are "difficult to reconcile with the traditional notions of the role of an attorney." As a result, he has urged the re-examination of the language, if not the actual holding, of *Massiah*. United States v. Henry, 447 U.S. 264, 290 (1980) (Rehnquist, J., dissenting). A majority of the Court, however, appears satisfied with the basic doctrine.

4. Massiah v. United States, 377 U.S. 201, 206 (1964).

5. The major cases deal with the Sixth Amendment's imposition of a right to counsel at pretrial confrontations between defendants and witnesses. See Moore v. Illinois, 434 U.S. 220 (1977), on remand 557 F.2d 411 (7th Cir.), cert. denied 440 U.S. 919 (right to counsel attached when complaint had been filed and defendant appeared in court pursuant to that complaint); Kirby v. Illinois, 406 U.S. 682 (1972).

6. Brewer v. Williams, 430 U.S. 387, 399 (1977), rehearing denied 431 U.S. 925 (no doubt can exist that judicial proceedings had begun and State does not contend otherwise). In Edwards v. Arizona, 451 U.S. 477 (1981), rehearing denied 452 U.S. 973, Edwards had been arrested on an arrest warrant issued pursuant to a complaint but apparently had not been presented before a magistrate. Somewhat belatedly, the State urged that under Arizona law the prosecution did not

State makes a court appearance in the proceedings, this is sufficient indication of the State's intention to pursue judicial proceedings to trigger the Sixth Amendment right to counsel.

Equally important is the requirement that the officer have "deliberately elicited" the self-incriminating statement. In United States v. Henry [7] the Court confirmed the requirement of "deliberate elicitation" but defined it quite broadly. The government agent in *Henry* had been specifically instructed not to question Henry or to initiate conversation concerning the pending charges. The record showed, however, that the agent was not a "passive listener;" apparently, at a minimum, the agent had engaged Henry in conversations and perhaps had steered those conversations in the direction of the events on which the charges were based. The government, "by intentionally creating a situation likely to induce Henry to make incriminating statements without the assistance of counsel," [8] had deliberately elicited the resulting statements within the meaning of *Massiah*. It appears to remain permissible, however, for a law enforcement agent to act as a mere passive observer. If the agent overhears self-incriminating admissions which the prosecution cannot be said to have induced, *Massiah* is no bar to the use of those statements.

There is lower court authority for the proposition that attachment of the right to counsel for one "offense" does not bring *Massiah* into play regarding other criminal activity. [9] Thus officers may continue an ongoing investigation concerning other offenses and, in the course of this investigation, may elicit self-incriminating statements

concerning that offense. Further, new investigations concerning offenses other than that for which adversary judicial proceedings have begun can apparently be initiated and similarly pursued. Determining when, however, the relationship between the "charged" offense and that which is the subject of continuing investigation is sufficiently close that *Massiah* bars the further investigation is a difficult inquiry. [10]

In the undercover context, at least, *Massiah* appears to be a subterfuge. To place the holding upon law enforcement's failure to respect the suspect's right to counsel when that right simply could not be implemented is at best misleading. It would be far preferable to face the issue directly: After the initiation of adversary proceedings (or at some other point), should law enforcement officials be absolutely barred from deliberately eliciting, by means of undercover activities, self-incriminating statements from a suspect? The answer may well be affirmative. But to frame the discussion in terms that suggest that such law enforcement activity might be permissible if certain procedural steps are taken is to invite distortion of the analysis.

Although the Supreme Court has not had occasion to address this, it appears clear from *Henry* that the Sixth Amendment right to counsel is violated only if the deliberate elicitation is by a person for whose conduct the prosecution is responsible. [11] Thus if a cofelon or cellmate, with no prearrangement with the prosecution, elicits self-incriminating statements from a defendant after the right has attached, no *Massiah* violation has occurred and the statements may be used. On the other hand, formal employment is

commence until the filing of a formal charge or the holding of a preliminary hearing. The Court did not address the matter. 451 U.S. at 480–481 n. 7.

7.   447 U.S. 264 (1980).

8.   447 U.S. at 274.

9.   See e.g., United States v. Capo, 693 F.2d 1330 (11th Cir. 1982); United States v. Moschiano, 695 F.2d 236 (7th Cir. 1982).

10.   See United States v. Capo, supra n. 9 (over dissent, arrest for possession of marijuana held not to bar

elicitation of statements regarding possession with intent to distribute and conspiracy).

11.   See United States v. Henry, 447 U.S. 264, 276 (1980) (Powell, J., concurring) ("the mere presence of a jailhouse informant who had been instructed to overhear conversations and to engage a criminal defendant in some conversations would not necessarily be unconstitutional").

not necessary to render the prosecution responsible for the actions of a private person within the meaning of this rule. When informal discussions and arrangements create prosecution responsibility is a difficult factual inquiry.

Police Interrogation Situations. Although *Massiah* issues were raised most frequently in regard to statements obtained during undercover investigations, there was no logical reason why the doctrine was restricted to these. In Brewer v. Williams,[12] the Court made clear that the Sixth Amendment right to counsel also applied to situations involving questioning by persons known to the suspect to be law enforcement officers and thus overlapped with the *Miranda* requirements to a considerable extent.

In *Williams*, the suspect, believed to have murdered a young girl, was transported from one location to another in a vehicle. He was accompanied by several officers; one of his lawyers was denied permission to make the trip with him. The trip required passing through the area in which Williams was believed to have hidden the victim's body. In an acknowledged effort to elicit from Williams the location of the victim's body, one officer expressed the view that location of the body would be difficult later and that they should locate it immediately so the victim could have a "Christian burial." Williams then led officers to the body. Finding no need to consider whether the officer's conduct violated *Miranda*, the Court concluded that Williams' Sixth Amendment right to counsel applied and was violated when the officer "deliberately and designedly" set out to elicit self-incriminating infor-

mation from Williams in the absence of Williams' attorneys.

At least in the context of nonundercover questioning, the Court assumed in *Williams* that the Sixth Amendment right to counsel could be waived.[13] But since the officer had made no effort, before making his "Christian burial" speech, to ascertain whether Williams wished to forego assistance of counsel, the case provided "no reasonable basis for finding that Williams waived his right to the assistance of counsel." [14]

While the Sixth Amendment right to counsel overlaps *Miranda's* similar Fifth Amendment right, it does address some situations not covered by *Miranda*. The Sixth Amendment, unlike *Miranda*, is not limited to situations in which the suspect is in custody.[15] However unlikely this may be, the Sixth Amendment can be violated by law enforcement efforts to elicit admissions after formal proceedings have commenced, even if the suspect is not in custody.

In regard to custodial interrogation, however, there is substantial overlap between the two rights. How do they differ? What, in other words, does a suspect gain by having the Sixth as well as the Fifth Amendment right to counsel? The Supreme Court has made no effort to establish subsidiary rules implementing the Sixth Amendment right equivalent to *Miranda's per se* rules. Presumably, however, at least those rights apply; it would be anomalous to conclude that the shift from the Fifth to the Sixth Amendment decreased the protections afforded the suspect. Thus a suspect must have at least the right to be warned, the right to prevent "deliberate elicitation" in the absence of counsel, and to have the pros-

---

12. 430 U.S. 387 (1977), rehearing denied 431 U.S. 925.

13. 430 U.S. at 401–406. The Court observed that it, like the lower court, was not holding that Williams could not, without notice to his retained lawyers, have waived the right to counsel. Rather, it was holding only that he did not. Id. at 405–406.

14. Id. See also, Estelle v. Smith, 451 U.S. 454 (1981) (defendant at psychiatric examination had Sixth

Amendment right to counsel and State made no claim of waiver; Court disclaims holding that defendant was "precluded" from making effective waiver).

15. See Rhode Island v. Innis, 446 U.S. 291, 300 n. 4 (1980), on remand ___ R.I. ___, 433 A.2d 646, cert. denied 456 U.S. 930 (custody in a Sixth Amendment case "is not controlling").

ecution prove waiver as a precondition to a finding of admissibility.

Perhaps the most likely difference lies in the standard for determining the effectiveness of a waiver of counsel. Given the uncertainties concerning the criteria for evaluating the effectiveness of the *Miranda* right to counsel,[16] comparative discussion is difficult. The most that can be said with confidence is that when the Sixth rather than the Fifth Amendment right to counsel is at issue, the prosecution's burden of proving waiver—probably the fact of waiver as well as its effectiveness—is heavier.[17]

There may also be a difference in the criterion for resolving the threshold question of whether law enforcement conduct intruded upon the protected interests. In Rhode Island v. Innis,[18] the Court observed that the definitions of "interrogation" under *Miranda's* right to counsel and "deliberate elicitation" under the Sixth Amendment "are not necessarily interchangeable, since the policies underlying the two constitutional protections are quite distinct."[19] To the extent that they differ, the definition of "deliberate elicitation" must be more restrictive. This seems clearly required by the increased need where the Sixth Amendment right applies to protect suspects from overbearing by the prosecution. The law enforcement conduct at issue in *Innis*,[20] although not "interroga-

tion" under *Miranda*, might well have constituted "deliberate elicitation" had the Sixth Amendment right applied to those facts.

 WESTLAW REFERENCES

Undercover Activities

miranda & digest("sixth amendment*" lawyer attorney counsel /p undercover informer* informant*)

miranda & undercover informer* informant* /p deliberate! purpose! intention! /s elicit! induc!

Police Interrogation Situations

miranda /p interrogat! /p sixth /p amendment* /p deliberate! purpose! intention! /s elicit! induc! interrogat!

miranda & tantamount deliberate! intention! /s elicit! induc! interrogat!

---

§ 156. Delay in Presenting Arrested Person Before Magistrate [1]

Local law in virtually every state as well as Rule 5(a) of the Federal Rules of Criminal Procedure requires that an arrested person be brought with some dispatch before a judicial officer for what, under the Federal Rules, is called the defendant's "initial appearance." Continuing controversy exists concerning the effect of a violation of these requirements upon the admissibility of a confession obtained during a period of confinement after the detaining officers failed to comply with the requirements.[2]

---

16. See § 153 supra.

17. See United States v. Mohabir, 624 F.2d 1140 (2d Cir. 1980). Other courts appear reluctant to draw such a distinction. United States v. Brown, 569 F.2d 236 (5th Cir. 1978) (en banc). There may also be a difference in the prosecution's burden concerning the fact of the making of the waiver decision. Thus waiver of the Sixth Amendment right may require a stronger showing of an "implied waiver" or perhaps—unlike *Miranda's* right to counsel—an express waiver. See generally, Notes, 82 Colum.L.Rev. 362, 60 B.U.L.Rev. 738 (1980).

18. 446 U.S. 291 (1980), on remand ___ R.I. ___, 433 A.2d 646, cert. denied 456 U.S. 930.

19. 446 U.S. at 300 n. 4.

20. See § 151 supra at n. 8.

§ 156

1. See generally, Hogan & Snee, The *McNabb-Mallory* Rule: Its Rise, Rationale and Rescue, 47 Geo.L.J.

1 (1958); Rothblatt & Rothblatt, Police Interrogation: The Right to Counsel and to Prompt Arraignment, 27 Brooklyn L.Rev. 24 (1960); Comment, 72 J.Crim.L. & C. 204 (1981); Note, 68 Yale L.J. 1003 (1959); Dec.Dig. Criminal Law ☜519(8).

2. Under the *McNabb-Mallory* rule, see text at n. 3 infra, the Supreme Court held that a confession obtained before a delay became violative of the requirement was admissible. United States v. Mitchell, 322 U.S. 65 (1944), rehearing denied 322 U.S. 770. It seems likely that under any version of the requirement, a similar approach would be taken. See Johnson v. State, 282 Md. 314, 329, 384 A.2d 709, 718 (1978), 8 U.Balt.L. Rev. 562 (1979). But compare Commonwealth v. Davenport, 471 Pa. 278, 370 A.2d 301 (1977), 23 Vill.L.Rev. 366 (1978) (if accused not presented within six hours after arrest, "any statement obtained after arrest but before arraignment shall not be admissible at trial").

McNabb-Mallory Rule. In McNabb v. United States,[3] the Supreme Court held that statements elicited from a defendant during a period in which federal officers had failed to comply with a statutory directive for prompt presentation of such persons before a magistrate were inadmissible at the defendant's subsequent federal criminal trial. This holding, the Court made clear, was not of constitutional dimensions. Rather, it was an exercise of the Court's supervisory power over lower federal courts. The substance of the statute so enforced in *McNabb* was incorporated into the Federal Rules of Criminal Procedure and after their effective date in 1946 the Court applied an identical exclusionary sanction to statements obtained in violation of the Rule 5(a) requirement of presentation before a magistrate without "unnecessary delay."[4] In Mallory v. United States,[5] the Court held that delay in presenting a defendant for purposes of permitting officers to interrogate him was "unnecessary" within the meaning of Rule 5(a). Thus the so-called *McNabb-Mallory* rule required the suppression in federal criminal prosecutions of confessions obtained by federal law enforcement officers during unnecessary periods of delay in presenting arrested persons before magistrates. If the only justification for the delay was to permit interrogation, the delay was impermissible and a resulting confession was inadmissible.

In 1968, the *McNabb-Mallory* rule was altered by Congressional action.[6] Under the statutory provision, a voluntary confession offered in a federal prosecution is not to be held inadmissible solely because of delay in bringing the person before a magistrate if the confession was given within six hours of the arrest or detention. A delay of over six hours is not itself to render a confession inadmissible if the delay is found to be reasonable, considering the distance to be traveled from the scene of the arrest to the nearest available magistrate and the means of transportation. In addition, the statute provides that if a confession offered by the government was made between arrest and "arraignment,"[7] the time elapsing between arrest and arraignment may be considered in determining the voluntariness of the confession but need not be conclusive on that issue. Delay, then, of six hours or less (or a longer period found to be reasonable) may not serve alone as the basis for excluding a confession. Delay of longer than six hours may—but need not—establish itself the inadmissibility of the confession.[8]

The *McNabb-Mallory* rule was clearly characterized by the Court as an exercise of its supervisory power[9] and thus is in no way binding in or even relevant to the admissibility of statements offered in state criminal prosecutions. Delay in presenting a defendant before a magistrate, however, has been identified by the Court as among those con-

---

3. 318 U.S. 332 (1943), rehearing denied 319 U.S. 784.

4. Upshaw v. United States, 335 U.S. 410 (1948).

5. 354 U.S. 449 (1957).

6. Pub.L. 90–351, Title II, § 701(a), 82 Stat. 210 (1968), codified as 18 U.S.C.A. § 3501.

7. "Arraignment" here is not being used in its technically correct sense, which means the appearance before the trial court at which the defendant is called upon to plead. See, e.g., Fed.R.Crim.P., Rule 10. Rather, it refers to the appearance made to comply with the requirement that an arrested person be presented before a magistrate. See Fed.R.Crim.P., Rule 5.

8. In United States v. Gaines, 555 F.2d 618 (7th Cir. 1977) the court held it error for a trial court automatically to exclude a statement because of a delay exceeding six hours. Discretion must be exercised in evaluat-

ing the admissibility of a statement under such circumstances:

> [T]he exercise of such judicial discretion depends upon a congeries of factors, including such elements as the deterrent purpose of the exclusionary rule, the importance of judicial integrity, and the likelihood that admission of the evidence would encourage violations of the Fourth Amendment.

555 F.2d at 623–624. Compare United States v. Sotoj-Lopez, 603 F.2d 789 (9th Cir. 1979) (delay of less than 18 hours, conceded by government to have been unnecessary, required suppression) with United States v. Shoemaker, 542 F.2d 561 (10th Cir. 1976), cert. denied 429 U.S. 1004 (delay of thirteen hours, on facts, did not render confession involuntary under statute).

9. McNabb v. United States, 318 U.S. 332, 340–347 (1943), rehearing denied 319 U.S. 784.

siderations relevant to the voluntariness of a confession.[10] But, at least in the absence of extremely aggravated circumstances, delay alone is almost certain to be insufficient to establish involuntariness.

State Exclusionary Sanctions for Violation of State Requirements. A majority of states have not adopted an exclusionary penalty for violation of their requirements of prompt presentation.[11] Following the Supreme Court's example, most hold that improper delay in presenting a defendant before a magistrate is no more than one of the many factors to be considered in determining voluntariness.[12] Some jurisdictions, however, have adopted more focused rules that in some situations require suppression of confessions solely because of delays in presentation.

The grounds for these exclusionary sanctions vary. A state judicial supervisory power, similar to the federal authority on which the *McNabb-Mallory* rule rested, was invoked by the Pennsylvania Court.[13] The North Carolina Court, on the other hand, relied upon a state statutory exclusionary rule [14] in adopting an exclusionary sanction for violation of the state statutory prompt presentation requirement.[15] The Supreme Court of West Virginia appears to have construed the prohibition against involuntariness as mandating exclusion of a confession without regard to other aspects of a situation where the primary purpose of the delay is to obtain a confession.[16] Defendants' right to a fair trial, presumably as protected by the state constitution, has been cited by the Kansas Court as potentially requiring, in some situations, that confessions be suppressed on these grounds.[17] The Wisconsin Court has read the state constitution's due process requirement as mandating the suppression of a confession related to an unreasonably long detention before presentation.[18]

Those jurisdictions adopting exclusionary sanctions also differ in the showing necessary to invoke the remedy. Some appear to utilize what might be called a *per se* approach, under which a defendant must show only that at the time the confession was given the defendant's custody had become violative of the prompt presentation requirement.[19] Several others, however, impose an apparently difficult-to-meet showing of causation.[20] The precise nature of the defendant's burden under this approach is unclear. It may be, however, that the defendant must show that the failure to present him before a magistrate and not merely the detention itself was a factual

---

10. Culombe v. Connecticut, 367 U.S. 568, 601–602 (1961).

11. State v. Richardson, 295 N.C. 309, 321–311, 245 S.E.2d 754, 762 (1978) (general rule stated as involving no constitutional duty to exclude confession because of delay in presentation).

12. Parker v. State, 351 So.2d 927, 933 (Ala.Crim. App.1977), writ quashed 351 So.2d 938 (Ala.); Sovalik v. State, 612 P.2d 1003, 1007 (Alaska 1980); People v. Harris, 28 Cal.3d 935, 171 Cal.Rptr. 679, 623 P.2d 240 (1981), cert. denied 454 U.S. 882; State v. Barry, 86 N.J. 80, 91, 429 A.2d 581, 586 (1981), cert. denied 454 U.S. 1017.

13. Commonwealth v. Davenport, 471 Pa. 278, 370 A.2d 301 (1977).

14. N.C.Gen.Stat. § 15A–974(2).

15. State v. Richardson, 295 N.C. 309, 245 S.E.2d 754 (1978).

16. State v. Mitter, ___ W.Va. ___, 289 S.E.2d 457 (1982).

17. State v. Crouch, 230 Kan. 783, 641 P.2d 394 (1982). Dismissal of the case might be required, the court indicated, if no other remedy would restore the opportunity to a fair trial. Suppression of physical evidence or a confession was clearly among those remedies less serious than dismissal that the court indicated would be considered if an improper delay was found.

18. Wagner v. State, 89 Wis.2d 70, 277 N.W.2d 849 (1979).

19. Commonwealth v. Davenport, 471 Pa. 278, 370 A.2d 301 (1977). See generally Comment, 72 J.Crim.L. & C. 204, 218–224 (1981).

20. State v. Richardson, 295 N.C. 309, 245 S.E.2d 754 (1978) (confession must be excluded if it would not have been obtained "but for" the delay); Schultz v. State, 510 S.W.2d 940 (Tex.Cr.App.1974). Compare Commonwealth v. Davenport, 471 Pa. 278, 370 A.2d 301 (1977) (defense need not show that unnecessary delay was "sole cause" of confession, but delay must be shown to have borne "some relationship" to confession) and State v. Hintz, 318 N.W.2d 915 (S.D.1982) (confession would be rendered inadmissible because of delay if "reasonable nexus" between delay and confession shown).

cause of the confession. Under such an approach, the defendant must apparently prove that if he had been promptly presented before a magistrate he would not have confessed.[21]

Several other variations exist. The West Virginia Court has focused upon the officers' intention. Only where the "primary purpose" of the delay is to obtain a confession must a resulting confession be excluded.[22] Under the approach of the Kansas Court, on the other hand, the inquiry must be, first, whether the delay in presentation has prejudiced the defendant's right to a "fair trial." If so, exclusion of a confession obtained during the delay is required only if this prejudice can be remedied by excluding the statement.[23]

Propriety of Delay. Insofar as prompt presentation requirements affect the admissibility of confessions—either under specific exclusionary rules or as part of the evaluation of voluntariness—it becomes important to identify the standard for determining when delay is improper. The requirements take several different approaches. Under one, the requirement is simply phrased in terms of a prohibition against "unnecessary" delay. Whether particular periods of delay are excessive is left to be litigated on a case-by-case basis.[24] A few jurisdictions impose rigid timeframes. In Commonwealth v. Davenport,[25] for example, the Pennsylvania Court—apparently disenchanted with the

difficulty of inquiring into the necessity of delay on the facts of each case—adopted a "six hour" rule. Under this approach, if—but only if—the defendant is not presented within six hours of arrest, a confession obtained during the period of custody must be excluded. A third approach combines the two just discussed. In Johnson v. State,[26] for example, the Court of Appeals of Maryland held that a confession is automatically excludable if it was obtained at a time when the delay had become in violation of the statutory requirement of presentation within 24 hours of arrest or at the first session of court following the arrest, whichever was first. If the delay did not violate these requirements but was in "the outer limits" established by the statute, a confession must be excluded if at the time it was made the delay had nevertheless become unnecessary.

Insofar as the necessity for delay is relevant, the definition of necessity is of obvious importance. There seems widespread agreement that delay necessary to accomplish the mechanics of processing a defendant—such as "booking"—is permissible without violating the requirements.[27] Further, it is widely accepted that delay may be permissible if it is to gather evidence other than self-incriminating statements of the arrestee. This is especially the case if that information—such as verification of an offered alibi—may result in release of the arrestee without presentation or other processing.[28]

21. The North Carolina Court has emphasized the extent to which a defendant was told by the officers of those rights which the magistrate would have told him about had a presentation taken place. State v. Hunter, 305 N.C. 106, 286 S.E.2d 535 (1982); State v. Richardson, 295 N.C. 309, 245 S.E.2d 754 (1978) (only right not told defendant by officers was right to communicate with friends and where no assertion made that this played a causal role in the making of the confession the confession is admissible).

22. State v. Mitter, ___ W.Va. ___, 289 S.E.2d 457 (1982). In *Mitter*, the court read the evidence as showing that the defendant had made a confession containing certain discrepancies with other information available to the officers. They retained the defendant without presenting him, in order to elicit a "more usable" confession. Thus the primary purpose of the delay was to secure a confession and the delay required

suppression. See also Raigosa v. State, 562 P.2d 1009 (Wyo.1977) (suppression required if delay was for purpose of obtaining a confession or if it was used to extract a confession).

23. State v. Crouch, 230 Kan. 783, 641 P.2d 394 (1982).

24. S.D. Codified Laws 23A–4–1.

25. 471 Pa. 278, 370 A.2d 301 (1977). A more flexible approach had been adopted previously in Commonwealth v. Futch, 447 Pa. 389, 290 A.2d 417 (1972).

26. 282 Md. 314, 384 A.2d 709 (1978).

27. See Johnson v. State, 282 Md. 314, 329, 384 A.2d 709, 717 (1978).

28. Id. See also Mallory v. United States, 354 U.S. 449, 454–455 (1957).

The major issue is whether or to what extent delay for purposes of interrogating the arrestee is permissible. Construing Rule 5(a), the Supreme Court has read the prompt presentation requirement as designed to minimize the opportunity for custodial interrogation of an arrestee. Thus it has held that any delay for purposes of conducting such interrogation is violative of the requirement.[29] In contrast, the Wisconsin Court has construed its state constitutional due process requirement as posing no bar to delay for determining whether to charge the defendant. This may include, the court reasoned, gathering of evidence and at least "proper and efficient" interrogation of the suspect. Presumably, delay for purposes of prolonged ("inefficient") or otherwise "improper" interrogation is prohibited.[30]

Analysis as Exclusionary Sanction Issue. The issue would be best approached as any other in which the ultimate question is whether an exclusionary sanction should be imposed for the violation of a legal requirement.[31] This, of course, requires identification of the legitimate interests served by the prompt presentation requirement, evaluation of their importance, and a determination as to whether those interests would be sufficiently furthered by an exclusionary sanction to justify the costs of such a sanction. The primary cost, of course, is the loss of reliable confessions that would otherwise be admissible.

The prompt presentation requirement potentially serves a number of functions related to confession law. It often assures that the arrestee will be informed of his rights to silence and representation. The appearance may also serve to inform the defendant of potential charges, thus providing him with information that may be useful in making an informed decision as to whether or not to exercise those rights. To some extent, of course, *Miranda* serves these same functions and thus may suggest that the prompt presentation requirement is less important for these purposes. On the other hand, the requirement that law enforcement personnel comply with *Miranda* may not duplicate the function of the initial appearance. Warnings or information provided by a judicial officer may be taken more seriously by a suspect than similar action taken by a police officer. Moreover, a judicial officer may lack the investigating officer's vested interest in having the underlying rights waived. Thus he might reasonably be regarded as likely to present a suspect with more effective warnings and a more effective opportunity to exercise a choice as to whether or not to exercise legal rights. Primary reliance, then, might reasonably be placed upon the magistrate's warnings; *Miranda* could thus be regarded as a stopgap measure designed to apply only before practicalities permit appearance before a judicial officer.

Presentation often results in arrangements being made for pretrial release. Thus it ends the opportunity for custodial interrogation. It is at least arguable that, despite *Miranda*, custodial interrogation still poses significant risks to important Fifth Amendment and related interests of arrestees. Just as *Miranda* found the rights to counsel and warnings so important to Fifth Amendment interests as to be required by that constitutional provision, the continued need to protect these interests may demand prompt presentation to minimize custody and thus the opportunity for custodial interrogation.

Presentation may also serve functions unrelated to confession interests. Insofar as presentation serves to implement arrestees' pretrial release, it may be significantly related to state and perhaps federal constitutional rights to bail or otherwise to avoid pretrial detention. Arrestees have a Fourth Amendment right to a judicial determination of probable cause before prolonged deten-

---

29. Mallory v. United States, 354 U.S. 449, 454–455 (1957) (delay must not be "of a nature to give opportunity for the extraction of a confession").

30. Wagner v. State, 89 Wis.2d 70, 277 N.W.2d 849 (1979).

31. See § 166 infra.

tion.[32] Prompt presentation may also be viewed as a means of implementing this right.[33]

It is important, then, to determine which interests—whether related to confessions and self-incrimination or not—are properly regarded as served by prompt presentation requirements.[34] Then, the nature and importance of those interests must be evaluated and other actual or potential means of furthering them considered. Finally, a judgment needs to be made as to whether any need for additional implementation of these interests is great enough to warrant adoption of an exclusionary sanction as a matter of federal or state constitutional requirement, state exclusionary rule law, or nonconstitutional judicial policy.

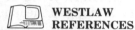 **WESTLAW
REFERENCES**

5(a)   /5   criminal fed.r.crim.p! crim.proc.

McNabb–Mallory Rule

5(a)   /5   criminal fed.r.crim.p! crim.proc.   &   18   /4
    3501
mcnabb—mallory

*State Exclusionary Sanctions for Violation
of State Requirement*

synopsis,digest(volunt! involuntar! "free will"   /p
    statement* admission* confess! selfincrimin!   &   delay!
    detain! detention   /p   present! arraign! magistrate*)

32. Gerstein v. Pugh, 420 U.S. 103 (1975), on remand 511 F.2d 528 (5th Cir.), on remand 422 F.Supp. 498 (D.Fla.).

33. In *Gerstein*, the Court impliedly rejected the proposition that the right of prompt presentation was of sufficient importance to arrestees' Fourth Amendment right to a probable cause determination to make such prompt presentation a Fourth Amendment requirement. While acknowledging that the initial presentation before the magistrate could be used to effectuate the Fourth Amendment right at issue, the Court also commented that the right might be implemented through a bail setting procedure or perhaps an accelerated preliminary hearing. 420 U.S. at 123–24.

34. Comment, 72 J.Crim.L. & C. 204, 232 (1981) argues that a rule excluding confessions for purposes of enforcing defendants' rights unrelated to confessions (such as access to bail, etc.) is irrational and would further those nonconfession objectives only at excessive costs.

§ 157

1. See generally Comment, 13 Houston L.Rev. 753 (1976); Note, 61 J.Crim.L.C. & P.S. 207 (1970); Su-

volunt! involuntar! "free will"   /p   statement* admission*
confess! selfincrimin!   &   delay! detain! detention   /p
present presented presentment arraign! magistrate*   &
intent! deliberate!   /s   elicit! induce!

Propriety of Delay

synopis,digest(present presented presentment arraign!
    magistrate*   /p   delay!   /p   interrogat! reinterrogat!
    /p   unnecessary excessive prolong! improper!)

Analysis as Exclusionary Action Issue

synopsis,digest(present presented presentment arraign!
    magistrate*   /p   delay! detention! detain!   /p   fifth 5th
    /2   amendment)

synopsis,digest(present presented presentment arraign!
    magistrate*   /p   delay! detention! detain!   /p   fourth
    4th   /2   amendment)

---

§ 157. Confessions Made During Custody Following Illegal Arrest or Other Detention [1]

In Wong Sun v. United States,[2] the Supreme Court made clear that oral or written self-incriminating admissions by a suspect could be the tainted "fruit" [3] of a detention of the suspect in violation of the suspect's Fourth Amendment rights and therefore subject to suppression on that ground. Subsequent decisions make clear that a claim based upon Fourth Amendment considerations can rest not only upon an arrest violative of the Fourth Amendment,[4] but also upon lesser detentions infringing upon Fourth

preme Court Review, Fourth Amendment—Admissibility of Statements Obtained During Illegal Detention, 70 J.Crim.L. & C. 446 (1979).

2. 371 U.S. 471 (1963).

3. For a general discussion of the "fruit of the poisonous tree" doctrine, see § 176 infra.

4. Taylor v. Alabama, 457 U.S. 687 (1982); Brown v. Illinois, 422 U.S. 590 (1975).

No reason appears why a confession following a detention invalid for reasons other than a Fourth Amendment violation could not be inadmissible on the same ground. See, for example, the discussion in § 156 supra, concerning the effect of a detention continued in violation of a prompt presentation requirement. It is necessary to consider, however, whether the legal requirement violated by the detention brings into play an exclusionary sanction, see § 166 infra, and, if so, whether that exclusionary sanction embodies the same attenuation of taint considerations as does the Fourth Amendment exclusionary rule.

Amendment reasonableness. These include stationhouse detentions for interrogation upon less than probable cause [5] and detentions pending the result of an application for a search warrant.[6]

Wong Sun also made clear, however, that consistent with traditional "fruit of the poisonous tree" analysis, the taint of the Fourth Amendment violation might become attenuated despite proof that "but for" the illegal detention, the admission would not have been made. Such "attenuation analysis" follows general Fourth Amendment exclusionary rule patterns,[7] but there are several special characteristics worth noting.

In Brown v. Illinois,[8] the Court rejected two proffered *per se* rules for finding attenuation. A determination that a confession is "voluntary," the Court held, is a threshold requirement; such a determination does not, however, establish that the taint of any preconfession illegal detention has been attenuated.[9] Further, compliance with the requirements of *Miranda* [10] will not automatically attenuate this taint.[11] If, on the other hand, the suspect decides to confess "as an act of free will unaffected by the initial illegality," this decision will attenuate the taint.[12] The burden of showing such attenuation is on the prosecution.[13] Whether the prosecution has met this burden must be addressed on the specific facts of each case:

> The *Miranda* warnings are an important factor . . . . But they are not the only factor to be considered. The temporal proximity of the arrest and the confession, the presence of intervening circumstances, . . . and, particularly, the purpose and flagrancy of the official misconduct are all relevant.[14]

A comparison of the facts of *Brown*, in which the taint of Brown's arrest was held

to render his confession invalid, with those of Rawlings v. Kentucky [15] illustrates the considerations. In *Rawlings*, officers properly on the premises observed marijuana seeds and smelled marijuana smoke. While several officers went to apply for a search warrant, the others detained those occupants of the premises who declined to submit to a body search before leaving. Rawlings, his female companion, Cox, and another individual remained on the premises. Forty-five minutes later, the officers returned with an apparently valid search warrant. The subjects were given *Miranda* warnings and Cox was then ordered to empty her purse. She poured the contents of her purse, including many controlled substances, on a table. She then turned to Rawlings and told him "to take what was his." Rawlings immediately acknowledged ownership of the substances; this acknowledgment was later challenged as the inadmissible product of the pre-warrant detention.

Brown, on the other hand, was arrested without probable cause by officers who held him at gunpoint and who had previously searched his apartment without a warrant. He was taken to the stationhouse, given *Miranda* warnings and within two hours of his arrest made the first of two incriminating statements. These were later challenged as the product of his unlawful arrest.

The Court held Brown's statements inadmissible but Rawling's properly used. In both cases, there was compliance with *Miranda* and apparently the statements were voluntary. Rawlings' statement followed the illegal detention of less than an hour while Brown's was preceded by a gap of on-

---

5. Dunaway v. New York, 442 U.S. 200 (1979).

6. Rawlings v. Kentucky, 448 U.S. 98 (1980).

7. See generally § 176 infra.

8. 422 U.S. 590 (1975).

9. 422 U.S. at 601–602, 604. See also, Taylor v. Alabama, 457 U.S. 687, 690 (1982); Dunaway v. New York, 442 U.S. 200, 217 (1979).

10. See §§ 150–53 supra.

11. 422 U.S. at 603. See also, Taylor v. Alabama, 457 U.S. 687 (1982) (giving of *Miranda* warnings three times did not attenuate taint).

12. 422 U.S. at 602–603.

13. Id. at 604.

14. Id. at 603–604.

15. 448 U.S. 98 (1980).

ly two hours.[16] Thus the cases were difficult if not impossible to differentiate on the
basis of the "temporal proximity of the arrest and the confession[s]."

But the circumstances of the delay were
held distinguishing. In *Brown*, the delay involved continuous questioning and processing of the suspect by the officers; in *Rawlings*, the atmosphere during the period was
described as "congenial" and this outweighed the relatively short duration.[17] No
significant intervening circumstances existed in *Brown* between the detention and
Brown's decision to confess. In *Rawlings*,
however, the otherwise proper discovery of
the drug in Cox's purse intervened. Accord-

ing to the evidence, Rawlings' decision to
make his statement was significantly influenced by his desire not to implicate Cox, a
consideration in no way attributable to the
illegal detention.[18]

Perhaps most important, however, was
the "purpose or flagrancy" of the primary illegality. Brown's detention was not merely
a brief stop but a full custodial arrest made
without the Fourth Amendment prerequisite
of probable cause. Further, it was accompanied by a possibly unnecessary display of
firearms, giving the appearance—according
to the Court—"of having been calculated to
cause surprise, fright and confusion." [19] Of
major importance was the officers' admis-

16. "[U]nder the strictest of custodial conditions,"
the Court commented in *Rawlings*, a gap of only 45
minutes "might not suffice to purge the initial taint."
448 U.S. at 107. See also Dunaway v. New York, 442
U.S. 200, 218 (1979) (no attenuation found where less
than two hours elapsed between improper detention
and first confession).

In Taylor v. Alabama, 457 U.S. 687 (1982) the delay
was six hours long. Finding the case a "virtual replica
of both *Brown* and *Dunaway*," the Court reasoned,
"[A] difference of a few hours is not significant where,
as here, petitioner was in police custody, unrepresented
by counsel, and he was questioned on several occasions, fingerprinted, and subjected to a line-up." 457
U.S. at 690.

17. 448 U.S. at 108. Apparently the Court regards
the time factor as significant in that the longer the
time period between the detention and the decision to
confess, the less likely it will be that the decision was
affected by the detention. On the other hand, it might
well be reasoned that the longer a suspect is deprived
of liberty pursuant to an illegal arrest or detention, the
more impact the detention is likely to have. In *Brown*,
the Court contrasted with the facts before it those of
Wong Sun. In *Wong Sun*, attenuation was found on a
showing that the challenged confession was made several days after the unlawful arrest and during that period the suspect had been presented before a magistrate and was released on his own recognizance. 422
U.S. at 604 n. 11, citing Wong Sun v. United States, 371
U.S. 471, 491 (1963).

18. Rawlings v. Kentucky, 448 U.S. 98, 108–109
(1980). See also Dunaway v. New York, 442 U.S. 200,
218–219 (1979) (in finding no attenuation, Court emphasizes that during one to two hour period no "intervening event of significance" occurred).

In Taylor v. Alabama, 457 U.S. 687 (1982) the prosecution urged that two intervening events attenuated
the taint. One was evidence that the defendant was

permitted to meet with his girlfriend and a male companion. The Court concluded:

> The state fails to explain how this five to ten minute
> visit, after which petitioner immediately recanted
> former statements that he knew nothing about the
> robbery and signed the confession, could possibly
> have contributed to his ability to consider carefully
> and objectively his options and to exercise his free
> will. This suggestion is particularly dubious in light
> of petitioner's uncontroverted testimony that his girl-
> friend was emotionally upset at the time of this visit.
> If any inference could be drawn, it would be that this
> visit had just the opposite effect.

457 U.S. at 691. After Taylor was arrested, fingerprints were taken from him and compared with those
on some items related to the offense. On the basis of
the match and other information, an arrest warrant
was "filed." Rejecting the argument that the filing of
this arrest warrant was an intervening circumstance
that attenuated the taint, the Court characterized it as
"irrelevant":

> The initial fingerprints, which were themselves the
> fruit of petitioner's illegal arrest, . . . and which
> were used to extract the confession from petitioner,
> cannot be deemed sufficient "attenuation" to break
> the connection between the illegal arrest and the con-
> fession merely because they also formed the basis
> for an arrest warrant that was filed while petitioner
> was being interrogated.

457 U.S. at 692. Four dissenters, on the other hand,
urged that attenuation should be found in light of the
combined effect of thrice-given *Miranda* warnings, the
absence of intimidating police conduct, the meeting between the defendant and his friends, and evidence that
the defendant spent most of the six hours between his
arrest and the challenged confession by himself rather
than being interrogated. 457 U.S. at 698–700
(O'Connor, J., dissenting).

19. 422 U.S. at 605. Compare Taylor v. Alabama,
457 U.S. 687 (1982) (fact that police did not physically
abuse suspect would not, given other considerations,
attenuate taint).

sion that the arrest was for "investigation" or "questioning." This, the Court concluded, suggested that the very purpose of the detention was to elicit self-incriminating statements.[20] In contrast, the propriety under Fourth Amendment standards of the detention in *Rawlings* was not clear; at worst, the detention could not be said to have been flagrantly improper. No use of firearms or even force occurred. The apparent purpose of the detention was not to secure incriminating admissions but instead to safeguard the premises so that a contemplated search would not be frustrated before it began. In *Rawlings*, the Court concluded, the prosecution had carried its burden of proving that the statement was an act of sufficiently free will to attenuate the taint of the detention; in *Brown* the prosecution had not.

In short, the taint of an improper detention is more likely to be found attenuated when a confession is challenged as the "fruit" of that detention upon the following showings:

(1) the purpose of the detention did not include a desire for an opportunity to elicit self-incriminating statements from the suspect, or even reason to believe that such self-incriminating statements would result;

(2) the initial detention involved a relatively small deviation from Fourth Amendment standards;

(3) the initial detention involved no or little use of force or firearms, or at least no more than was reasonably warranted by the situation;

(4) a considerable period of time elapsed between the initiation of the detention and the suspect's decision to make the challenged statement;

(5) the circumstances during the intervening period were such as might be expected to reduce any emotional excitement or concern generated by the detention;

(6) between the detention and the suspect's decision to confess, circumstances developed that provided a nontainted reason for the suspect's decision to confess, independent of any effect of the detention.

 WESTLAW REFERENCES

admission* statement* confess! /p custod! detention detain! delay! /p fourth 4th /2 amendment
synopsis,digest(admission* statement* confess! /p custod! detention detain! delay! /p fourth 4th amendment)
invalid! supress! exclu! /s admission* statement* confess! /p custod! detention detain! delay! /p fourth 4th /2 amendment)
admission* statement* confess! /p custod! detention detain! delay /s purpose intent! deliberate! flagran! /p fourth 4th /2 amendment

§ 158. "Fruits" of an Inadmissible Confession [1]

At early common law the inadmissibility of a confession did not affect the admissibility of other evidence obtained by use of that statement.[2] For example, if an accused were coerced into confessing to a murder and also into revealing the location of the fatal weapon, the weapon, if located, could be used in evidence although the confession itself would be inadmissible by virtue of the voluntariness requirement. The rationale for this position was that the confession was excluded because of its untrustworthiness. If the "fruits" of the confession were sufficiently probative of the defendant's guilt, however, the reason for excluding the confession did not extend to that evidence and hence it was admissible.

---

20. Id. ("The arrest, both in design and in execution, was investigatory. The detectives embarked upon this expedition for evidence in the hope that something might turn up.") See also Taylor v. Alabama, 457 U.S. 687 (no attenuation found, relying in part upon evidence that arrest and transportation to stationhouse were effected "in the hope that something would turn up"); Dunaway v. New York, 442 U.S. 200, 218 (1979) (in finding no attenuation, Court notes that defendant was "admittedly seized without probable cause in the hope that something might turn up").

§ 158

1. See generally 3 Wigmore, Evidence § 859 (Chadbourn rev. 1970); George, The Fruits of *Miranda*: Scope of the Exclusionary Rule, 39 U.Colo.L.Rev. 478 (1967); Notes, 41 Brooklyn L.Rev. 325 (1974), 6 Washburn L.J. 133 (1966); Dec.Dig. Criminal Law ⊚537. For a general discussion of the admissibility of evidence arguably tainted by earlier—or "primary"—illegality, see § 176 infra.

2. 3 Wigmore, Evidence § 859 (Chadbourn rev. 1970).

There now, however, appears to be virtually unanimous agreement that the prohibition against admission of "fruits of the poisonous tree," developed primarily in the context of the Fourth Amendment exclusionary rule,[3] applies fully when the poisonous tree is a confession rendered inadmissible by involuntariness.[4] The rationale for this position appears to be that the prohibition against evidentiary use of involuntary confessions rests as much upon a desire to prevent conduct rendering confessions involuntary as upon the need to preclude reliance upon unreliable confessions. Consequently, the increased deterrence accomplished by excluding "fruit" is as necessary in this context as it is in the Fourth Amendment area. Despite this agreement on the application of the fruits doctrine to involuntary confessions, several problems remain.

Fruit of Voluntary but Inadmissible Confession. Continued doubt exists as to whether the "fruits" doctrine applies, at least with the same vigor as in the Fourth Amendment area, when the "primary illegality" consists of a violation of *Miranda* or some other confession requirement arguably less important than that of voluntariness. In Michigan v. Tucker,[5] the Supreme Court specifically reserved decision on whether or not evidence derived from statements obtained in violation of *Miranda* must be excluded.[6] A number of lower courts have declined to exclude some evidence derived from *Miranda* violations;[7] this tendency has been especially pronounced when the challenged evidence consists of the testimony of witnesses located by information obtained in violation of *Miranda*.[8]

The rationale for such a distinction is not entirely clear. It cannot, of course, rest on the traditional assumption that such derivative evidence does not suffer from a reliability defect as does the confession itself. Violation of *Miranda* creates no such reliability defect. Most likely it rests upon a perception of the *Miranda* requirements as less important than other federal constitutional requirements relating to the gathering of evidence. Given this reduced significance of the *Miranda* rights, the Michigan Court seems to have reasoned, sufficient preventive effect is accomplished by excluding the confessions themselves and perhaps derivative evidence other than witnesses' testimony.[9]

Those courts applying at best a diluted fruits doctrine to some *Miranda* situations seem inclined to limit this approach to evidence derived from a violation of those requirements not part of the core demands of the Fifth Amendment. Thus the First Circuit has recently held[10] that the right to the presence of an attorney during custodial in-

---

3.   See generally § 176 infra.

4.   United States v. Downing, 665 F.2d 404 (1st Cir. 1981); Commonwealth v. Meehan, 377 Mass. 552, 387 N.E.2d 527 (1979), cert. dismissed 445 U.S. 39.

5.   417 U.S. 433 (1974).

6.   Id. at 447.

7.   United States ex rel. Hudson v. Cannon, 529 F.2d 890 (7th Cir. 1976); Wilson v. Zant, 249 Ga. 373, 290 S.E.2d 442 (1982); Bartram v. State, 33 Md.App. 115, 364 A.2d 1119 (1976), affirmed without consideration of this issue, 280 Md. 616, 374 A.2d 1119 (1977); People v. Kusowski, 403 Mich. 653, 272 N.W.2d 503 (1978); State v. Cook, 170 N.J.Super. 499, 406 A.2d 1340 (1979). Contra, United States v. Hensel, 509 F.Supp. 1376 (D.Me.1981); People v. Saiz, 620 P.2d 15, 20 (Colo. 1980); State v. Greene, 91 N.M. 207, 572 P.2d 935 (1977). Other courts regard the matter as open. See United States v. Massey, 437 F.Supp. 843 (D.Fla.1977), reversed 550 F.2d 300 (5th Cir.); Commonwealth v. Meehan, 377 Mass. 552, 387 N.E.2d 527 (1979), cert. dis-

missed 445 U.S. 39. In United States ex rel. Hudson v. Cannon, supra, the Seventh Circuit held that *Tucker* permits consideration, on a category-by-category basis, of whether the exclusion of particular categories of evidence derived from a failure to give *Miranda* warnings is justified by the deterrent effect of excluding such evidence.

8.   United States ex rel. Hudson v. Cannon, 529 F.2d 890 (7th Cir. 1976) (third party testimonial fruit of a failure to give *Miranda* warnings need not be excluded); Wilson v. Zant, 249 Ga. 373, 290 S.E.2d 442 (1982). Cf. United States v. Ceccolini, 435 U.S. 268 (1978) (Fourth Amendment exclusionary rule "should be invoked with much greater reluctance" where challenged evidence consists of testimony of witness discovered by exploiting illegality). See generally § 176 infra.

9.   People v. Kusowski, 403 Mich. 653, 662, 272 N.W.2d 503, 506 (1978).

10.   United States v. Downing, 665 F.2d 404, 407–409 (1st Cir. 1981).

terrogation is not a "prophylactic rule" created by *Miranda* but rather a Fifth Amendment requirement; a violation of this right, then, requires full application of traditional "fruit of the poisonous tree" analysis.

The same rationale used to justify a failure to apply standard "fruits" analysis to *Miranda* violations might, of course, also indicate that the "fruits" doctrine should not be applied fully to evidence derived from confessions obtained in other ways rendering the confessions themselves inadmissible. It is at least arguable, for example, that the requirement of prompt presentation before a magistrate [11] is no more important than the *Miranda per se* requirements, so the application of standard "fruits" analysis is no more appropriate whether improper delay rather than noncompliance with *Miranda's per se* requirements is established. On balance, such picking and choosing among primary illegalities seems inappropriate. The fruit of the poisonous tree doctrine should be applied uniformly to evidence derived from inadmissible self-incriminating statements, whatever the reason for the inadmissibility. It is likely that most courts would today take this approach.

Seriatim Confessions. Application of the "fruits" doctrine in the confession context has caused one especially important difficulty. This is created when a defendant has made several admissions or confessions and the first of these seriatim confessions is inadmissible. When are the subsequent confessions inadmissible "fruit" of the first? The problem was well put by Justice Jackson in United States v. Bayer: [12]

> Of course, after an accused has once let the cat out of the bag by confessing, no matter what the inducement, he is never thereafter free of the psychological and practical disadvantages of having confessed. He can never get the cat back in the bag. The secret is out for good. In such a sense, a later confession always may be looked upon as fruit of the first. [13]

In Lyons v. Oklahoma, [14] addressing the admissibility of a subsequent confession urged to be the fruit of an earlier involuntary one, the Court appeared to indicate that the result should turn upon whether the second confession can reasonably be regarded as having been stimulated by the continuing effect of the coercive practices that gave rise to the first. Some courts appear still to apply the *Lyons* approach to the seriatim confession situation, whether or not the primary illegality consisted of coercion. [15]

In *Lyons*, the Supreme Court found no occasion to consider the appropriateness of a presumption that confessions made after the giving of an involuntary confession are also involuntary. [16] Nevertheless, where the facts show seriatim confessions beginning with an inadmissible one, the lower courts have tended to place upon the prosecution

---

11. See § 156 supra.

12. 331 U.S. 532 (1947), rehearing denied 332 U.S. 785.

13. Id. at 540.

14. 322 U.S. 596 (1944). In *Lyons*, the Court upheld the admission of a second confession given twelve hours after the first where there had been a change in location and of the legal authorities holding the defendant in custody. None of the persons who had abused the defendant earlier was present when the second confession was given. See also, United States v. Bayer, 331 U.S. 532 (1947), rehearing denied 332 U.S. 785 (confession given six months after first confession, inadmissible for failure to present defendant before magistrate, was admissible); Leyra v. Denno, 347 U.S. 556 (1954), rehearing denied 348 U.S. 851 (second confession made within five hours of first inadmissible given showing that effect of first interrogation continued); Clewis v. Texas, 386 U.S. 707 (1967) (second confession

given eight days after first inadmissible, where there was continued custody and repeated interrogations and no break in the stream of events); Beecher v. Alabama, 389 U.S. 35 (1967) (first confession made under threat of death rendered second confession, given five days later, inadmissible, given continued custody and pain from first incident); Darwin v. Connecticut, 391 U.S. 346 (1968) (confession given day after involuntary confession inadmissible, where no break in stream of events shown).

15. State v. Derrico, 181 Conn. 151, 434 A.2d 356 (1980), cert. denied 449 U.S. 1064; State v. Allies, ___ Mont. ___, 621 P.2d 1080 (1980); State v. Paz, 31 Or. App. 851, 572 P.2d 1036 (1977). See also Matthews v. State, 261 Ark. 532, 549 S.W.2d 492, 494 (1977) (issue is "whether an inference as to the continuing effect of the coercive practices may fairly be drawn from the surrounding circumstances").

16. Lyons v. Oklahoma, 322 U.S. 596, 604 (1944).

the burden of establishing that an offered confession is free of the taint created by the earlier situation.[17] This, however, does not address the criterion to be used to determine whether the taint is still operative.

Some courts apply a diffuse analysis consistent with general attenuation of taint analysis.[18] Under this approach, among the factors tending to establish the admissibility of a confession given after the making of an inadmissible confession are (1) the lapse of a significant period of time between the making of the two statements; (2) a shift in locations between the two events; (3) the interjection of advice by counsel before the making of the challenged confession; and (4) the noncoercive manner of any interrogation that took place between the making of the two statements.[19] This approach, however, is merely a development of the *Lyons* analysis, under which the controlling issue is the risk that the second confession was stimulated by the same improper influence as the first.

Arguably the basic approach taken in *Lyons* is inappropriate, at least when the first confession is inadmissible for a reason other than involuntariness. When the only concern of the law was whether an offered confession had been influenced by considerations rendering confession involuntary, perhaps the admissibility of a subsequently-given confession was appropriately determined by inquiring whether that confession was influenced by the same considerations as rendered the first inadmissible. But the

admissibility of confessions is now affected significantly by legal requirements that do not necessarily focus upon influences bearing upon the defendant's decision to confess. Whether a confession is inadmissible because of a violation of *Miranda's per se* requirements, for example, is not affected by any inquiry into the impact upon the defendant's decisionmaking process. Even the inquiry into voluntariness has come to emphasize less the impact upon the defendant and more the need to discourage particular interrogation techniques and conditions.

Much of confession law, then, has become the application of an exclusionary remedy for violation of certain legal requirements related to elicitation or taking of confessions. This arguably renders the *Lyons* approach to evaluating the admissibility of seriatim confessions inappropriate. Exclusion is still appropriate, of course, where the primary illegality consists of an improper influence upon the accused and this influence continued to operate on the defendant when the decision was made to give the challenged confession. But taint analysis must encompass other considerations as well, including the need for exclusion of derivative evidence to further the preventive effect of the exclusionary sanction being applied and perhaps the need sufficiently to respect the demand for judicial integrity.

Given that much if not all of confession law now consists of application of exclusionary penalties for the violation of a variety of legal requirements, there is little reason for

---

17.   People v. Braeseke, 25 Cal.3d 691, 159 Cal.Rptr. 684, 602 P.2d 384 (1979), vacated and remanded 446 U.S. 932, on remand 28 Cal.3d 86, 168 Cal.Rptr. 603, 618 P.2d 149 (1980), cert. denied 451 U.S. 1021; People v. Founds, 621 P.2d 325, 327 (Colo.1981) (applied to confession obtained after first secured in violation of *Miranda*); Brewer v. State, 386 So.2d 232, 236 (Fla.1980) (coercion is presumed to continue); State ex rel. Williams v. Narick, ___ W.Va. ___, 264 S.E.2d 851 (1980) (rebuttable presumption that consecutive confessions are product of earlier confession).

This may apply, however, only where seriatim confessions involve subsequent confessions that are only an elaboration of the first or, perhaps, where they concern the same offense. See Bliss v. United States, 445 A.2d 625 (D.C.App.1982), modified 452 A.2d 172 (D.C.

App.), cert. denied 103 S.Ct. 756 (not applicable where second confession is to different crime from first).

18.   State v. Allies, ___ Mont. ___, 621 P.2d 1080, 1088 (1980); State v. Paz, 31 Or.App. 851, 572 P.2d 1036 (1977).

19.   In State v. Young, 344 So.2d 983 (La.1977), for example, the defendant confessed orally at the scene of the death of her spouse; this confession was held involuntary because of evidence that the defendant was under emotional stress at the time. A written confession given two hours later, however, was held admissible, given proof of considerable improvement in the defendant's emotional condition and evidence that she had been informed of her rights and had executed a written waiver of them.

fruits analysis in the confession area to differ from that used to apply other exclusionary sanctions.[20] When the primary illegality consists of a violation of a federal constitutional right of the confessing defendant, there seems little reason not to apply the fruits analysis developed in application of the Fourth Amendment exclusionary rule.

Under such an approach, the most appropriate focus is upon the accused's decision to give the subsequent confession and whether this decision was significantly influenced by awareness of his having made the inadmissible confession. If the defendant was unaware of the inadmissibility of the earlier confession, it will be quite likely that his decision to make the later one was influenced by his perception that he had little to lose. If, but only if, there is evidence that he was aware of the inadmissibility of his earlier admission and nevertheless chose to provide the prosecution with an admissible self-incriminating confirmation of his guilt should the subsequent confession be admissible. This would be consistent with taint analysis in the Fourth Amendment area, and no reason for applying a different standard in regard to confessions appears.

Such an approach was strongly suggested by Brown v. Illinois.[21] Two hours after his unlawful arrest, Brown made a statement implicating himself in a murder. This confession, the Court concluded, was fatally tainted by the unlawful arrest. During the next several hours, Brown assisted the officers in a successful search for another participant. After return to the station, he gave a second confession similar in content to the earlier one. In holding that the second statement "was clearly the result and the fruit of the first," the Court emphasized that Brown's incentive to avoid self-incrimination was vitiated, and the pressures on him to make the second, were bolstered, by "[t]he fact that [he] had made one statement, believed by him to be admissible," and by his successful efforts to secure additional evidence in the form of his co-felon, efforts that were the product of his decision to make the first confession.[22] The Court's emphasis was clearly upon the extent to which, at the time of his decision to make the second confession, Brown was influenced by his perception that the prosecution had available admissible evidence against him in the form of his previous confession and other information derived from it.

Other aspects of Fourth Amendment "fruits" analysis might also be appropriate here. Thus if the challenged evidence consists of the testimony of a witness located by exploiting information from an inadmissible confession, a greater readiness to find attenuation might well be appropriate. If the inevitable legitimate discovery exception is accepted for Fourth Amendment analysis,

---

20. See State v. Allies, ___ Mont. ___, 606 P.2d 1043, 1052 (1979), appeal after remand ___ Mont. ___, 621 P.2d 1080 ("fruit of the poisonous tree" doctrine applies to confessions in same manner as it does to search issues.).

21. 422 U.S. 590 (1975).

22. 422 U.S. at 605. This result is also suggested by Harrison v. United States, 392 U.S. 219 (1968). At issue in *Harrison* was not the admissibility of an out-of-court statement but rather testimony given at a prior trial after the prosecution had been improperly permitted to introduce an inadmissible out-of-court confession. Finding that the Government had failed to show that its illegal action in obtaining and using the confession did not "induce" the prior testimony at issue, the Court reasoned:

The question is not *whether* the petitioner made a knowing decision to testify, but *why*. If he did so in order to overcome the impact of confessions illegally obtained and hence improperly introduced, then his testimony was tainted by the same illegality that rendered the confessions themselves inadmissible.

392 U.S. at 223 (emphasis in original). It is possible, of course, that subsequent trial testimony might be more readily found to be a "fruit" of a confession than a subsequent out-of-court confession. Cf. 392 U.S. at 223, n. 9. But this seems unlikely. *Harrison* strongly suggests that where a reasonable likelihood appears that an inadmissible out-of-court confession stimulated another such admission, the subsequent confession is also inadmissible unless the prosecution shows that the defendant's decision to give the second confession was made for reasons unrelated to the first confession. See People v. Founds, 621 P.2d 325 (Colo.1981) (defendant's testimony that one reason he made second confession was that he had already confessed supported conclusion that second confession was inadmissible as the fruit of the first, obtained in violation of *Miranda*).

it quite likely should apply here as well. But in general there appears no reason to dilute the fruits doctrine when it is applied to situations in which the primary illegality and its direct results are interrogation techniques or similar matters and self-incriminating admissions.

 WESTLAW REFERENCES

Fruit of Voluntary but Inadmissible Confession

synopsis,digest(admission* statement* confess! /p fruit* /p volunt! ''free will'')

admission* statement* confess! /p fruit* /p volunt! ''free will'' /p miranda

admission* statement* confess! /p fruit* /p volunt! ''free will'' /p fourth 4th /2 amendment

Seriatum Confessions

synopsis,digest(admission* statement* confess! /p fruit* /p series seriatum subsequent! multiple additional another more different several /s confess! statement* admission*)

admission* statement* confess! /p fruit* /p series seriatum subsequent! multiple additional another more different several /p confess! statement* admission* /p factor* controlling determin!

admission* statement* confess! /p fruit* /p series seriatum subsequent! multiple additional another more different several /p confess! statement* admission* /p fourth 4th /p amendment

---

§ 159.   Judicial Confessions, Guilty Pleas, and Offers to Plea Bargain

Most confession law involves self-incriminating statements made by suspects to law enforcement personnel during the pre-judicial stages of a criminal case. But it not infrequently occurs that the prosecution seeks, at trial, to make use of a prior self-incriminating admission of the defendant made in a judicial context. These so-called ''judicial confessions'' may consist of a defendant's testimony in a different proceedings [1] or in a prior hearing during the criminal prosecution then being tried.[2] It may be a ''stipulation.'' [3] The offered admission might also consist of the defendant's entry of a plea of guilty, either in the same prosecution or in another prosecution involving factual issues that overlap with those in the present prosecution.[4] Or, the offer might consist of statements made by the defendant during the process of entry of such a guilty plea. The increasingly common requirement that a conviction following a guilty plea be based upon a record establishing that there is a ''factual basis'' for the plea or the finding that the defendant is guilty [5] means that trial judges often encourage or require that a defendant offering a plea make an in-court statement acknowledging guilt or at least establishing reason to believe the plea is accurate.[6]

In general, such judicial confessions are treated in the same manner as out-of-court confessions and are admissible if the same requirements are met. The requirement of

---

§ 159

1.   United States v. Wilson, 529 F.2d 913 (10th Cir. 1976) (admissions made during testimony at trial of another defendant).

2.   In re Johnson, 244 Cal.App.2d 274, 53 Cal.Rptr. 1 (1966) (statement at preliminary hearing); Brumit v. State, 220 So.2d 659 (Fla.App.1969), appeal dismissed 225 So.2d 908 (Fla.) (testimony during prior trial on same charge in which defendant admitted offense but claimed need for psychiatric help).

3.   People v. Aratico, 111 Misc.2d 1015, 445 N.Y.S.2d 951 (1981) (stipulation as to admissibility of certain bank records was a formal judicial admission and remained effective despite declaration of mistrial).

4.   United States v. Riley, 684 F.2d 542 (8th Cir. 1982) (defendant's plea of guilty to state misdemeanor pimping charge admissible as admission under Fed.R. Evid. 801(d)(2) in federal Mann Act prosecution). See United States v. Howze, 668 F.2d 322, 324 n. 3 (7th Cir. 1982) (general rule is that guilty plea in a collateral

criminal trial is admissible to prove an element of the crime charged). See generally § 265 infra.

A plea of nolo contendere is generally, for purposes of the criminal proceeding in which entered, substantially the same as a plea of guilty. It is not, however, admissible against the defendant in at least some later situations. Compare Fed.R.Evid. 410(2) (plea of nolo contendere not admissible ''in any civil or criminal proceeding'' against the defendant entering plea) with Vernon's Ann.Tex.Code Crim.Pro. art. 27.02(5) (''legal effect'' of plea of nolo contendere is that it may not be used against the defendant in any civil suit based on the same act upon which the criminal prosecution is based). See § 265 infra, text at n. 27.

5.   Fed.R.Crim.P. 11(f) (judgment should not be entered on plea of guilty ''without making such inquiry as shall satisfy [the court] that there is a factual basis for the plea'').

6.   People v. George, 69 Mich.App. 403, 245 N.W.2d 65 (1976), appeal denied 399 Mich. 857, 251 N.W.2d 258

corroboration, however, has been held inapplicable.[7] Among the most significant of the requirements applicable to judicial confessions is the right to counsel. A defendant's judicial confession given at a preliminary hearing in the case, then, is admissible only if the defendant's right to be represented by counsel at such proceedings, recognized in White v. Maryland,[8] was respected. A number of special considerations applicable exclusively or primarily to judicial confessions do exist, however.

Admissions Made During Testimony in Support of Constitutional Claims. In Simmons v. United States,[9] the Supreme Court held that a defendant testifying out of the presence of the trial jury and on the limited question of the admissibility of evidence challenged on Fourth Amendment exclusionary rule [10] grounds was entitled to be free of the use of that testimony to prove guilt at trial. It is widely assumed that other federal constitutional rights create a similar right to testify in support of a claim that these rights were violated, to make damaging admissions during such testimony, and to have such admissions excluded if offered to prove guilt at trial. In regard to rights other than those of federal constitutional dimensions, the states are free to determine whether a similar bar to the use of defendant testimony offered in support of the right should be excluded. It

appears to be generally assumed that exclusion is necessary to effective implementation of the underlying rights.[11] The general rule of admissibility of judicial confessions, then, is limited by the exception that renders inadmissible admissions made during testimony given out of the jury's presence for purposes of supporting a claim to some procedural right. It is widely assumed, however, that if a defendant takes the witness stand at trial and testifies in a manner inconsistent with these earlier admissions, the admissions may be used for the limited purpose of impeachment.[12]

Withdrawn Pleas and Related Admissions. The admissibility of guilty pleas and admissions made during the process of accepting those pleas presents a special problem when the plea has been withdrawn by leave of the court.[13] If the plea was withdrawn for reasons suggesting that it may have been inaccurate, of course, the fact of withdrawal suggests that the probative value of the plea is greatly reduced. On the other hand, trial judges may permit guilty pleas to be withdrawn for reasons that cast little or no doubt on the accuracy of the defendant's implied acknowledgment of guilt. In such cases, the argument for excluding that plea later is arguably weaker. In Kercheval v. United States,[14] however, the Supreme Court held—apparently as a matter

---

(admissions made in guilty plea proceeding used in later trial, but care taken not to disclose to jury that admissions were made in that particular context).

   7. See § 145 supra.

   8. 373 U.S. 59 (1963), conformed to 231 Md. 533, 191 A.2d 237 (finding preliminary hearing a critical stage of proceeding at which right to counsel applies, in part because any plea entered could be used against the defendant at later trial). See In re Johnson, 244 Cal.App. 2d 274, 53 Cal.Rptr. 1 (1966) (statement at examining trial inadmissible if right to counsel not respected).

   9. 390 U.S. 377 (1968), on remand 395 F.2d 769 (7th Cir.), appeal after remand 424 F.2d 1235.

  10. See § 165 infra.

  11. People v. D'Angelo, 401 Mich. 167, 178, 257 N.W.2d 655, 660 (1977) (if defendant testifies at pretrial hearing on entrapment, any testimony given—including possible admission of the crime charged or some aspect of it—will not be admissible against him to prove guilt).

  12. See People v. D'Angelo, n. 11 supra (testimony given at pretrial hearing on entrapment will be admissible to impeach defendant's trial testimony if that testimony contains material inconsistencies). See generally § 162 infra for a discussion of the use of otherwise inadmissible confessions to impeach a testifying defendant.

  13. The right to withdraw a plea is often discretionary with the trial judge but is sometimes broader. In federal practice, withdrawal is governed by Fed.R. Crim.P. 32(d), which is quite ambiguous. See, however, United States v. Brown, 617 F.2d 54, 55 (4th Cir. 1980), suggesting that under this rule withdrawal of a plea of guilty prior to sentencing "should normally be allowed" if the government has not been prejudiced by any reliance upon the plea. See also Wilson v. State, 515 S.W.2d 274 (Tex.Cr.App.1974) (in jury sentencing proceeding, defendant had absolute right to withdraw plea of guilty before evidence is closed and case sent to factfinder).

  14. 274 U.S. 220 (1927).

of federal evidence law—that the use of a withdrawn guilty plea in a federal criminal prosecution was impermissible, without regard to the reason for the withdrawal of the particular plea at issue. The Court's rationale was that the right to withdraw a plea is an important one and that to permit evidentiary use of a withdrawn plea would frustrate the policy objectives justifying the right of withdrawal.[15] It is arguable that when a plea is withdrawn for reasons of federal constitutional dimensions, effective implementation of those federal rights similarly demands that the plea not be used as an admission. But the Court has not addressed this.[16]

Both the Federal Rules of Evidence [17] and the Federal Rules of Criminal Procedure [18] now prohibit the evidentiary use of withdrawn pleas for all purposes. A growing number of state judicial decisions have

adopted the same position; many are based upon state statutes or court rules similar to the federal rules.[19] Similarly, the federal rules bar the use of "any statement made in the course of" a procedure regarding a plea of guilty which is later withdrawn.[20] Thus any admissions made by a defendant during a guilty plea hearing, for purposes of establishing a factual basis for the plea or the determination of guilt, are inadmissible if the plea itself is later withdrawn.[21] Some state provisions, however, permit use of withdrawn pleas and related statements for impeachment purposes if the defendant testifies at trial in an inconsistent manner.[22]

Admissions Related to "Plea Bargaining." A related exception that applies beyond judicial confessions has created significant controversy. In general, offers to compromise disputed claims are inadmissible.[23] Should some similar bar exist to use

---

15. 274 U.S. at 223–224.

16. In Hutto v. Ross, 429 U.S. 28 (1976) the Court considered the admissibility of a confession made under oath but not in court, after agreement on a plea bargain that did not call for such a confession. Subsequently, the plea bargain was withdrawn and the case went to trial; apparently no plea was ever entered pursuant to the bargain. At trial, the confession was offered and admitted. Upholding this action against constitutional challenge, the Court specifically noted that the case did not involve the admissibility of a withdrawn plea or of statements made during the plea negotiation process. 429 U.S. at 30 n. 3.

17. Fed.R.Evid. 410. See further § 265 infra, text at nn. 19–23.

18. Fed.R.Crim.P. 11(e)(6).

19. For statutory provisions, see Mich.R.Evid. 410; Nebraska Rev.Stat. § 27–410(1); S.D.Codified Laws 19–12–12. Probably the leading recent decision is People v. George, 69 Mich.App. 403, 245 N.W.2d 65 (1976), appeal denied 399 Mich. 857, 251 N.W.2d 258. See also Cambridge v. State, ___ Ind. ___, 428 N.E.2d 1252, 1254 (1981). Most recent cases involve efforts to use statements made by the defendant rather than the pleas themselves.

In State v. Alberti, 61 Hawaii 502, 605 P.2d 937 (1980), the defendant pleaded guilty in federal court to extortion. At his state trial on kidnapping charges arising out of the same incident, the prosecution offered his admissions at the federal guilty plea hearing. The defense unsuccessfully objected, urging that a defense motion to withdraw the plea and vacate the sentence had been filed. After the defendant's state conviction, the federal judge granted the motion to withdraw the plea. Citing *Kercheval*, the state appel-

late court upheld the admission of the defendant's statements, commenting that if the federal court motion had been granted before the offer in state court the result would have to be otherwise.

20. Fed.R.Evid. 410(3); Fed.R.Crim.P. 11(e)(6)(C). Both provisions recognize exceptions for situations in which the statement is offered either

(i) in any proceeding wherein another statement made in the course of the same plea or plea discussions has been introduced and the statement ought in fairness be considered contemporaneously with it, or (ii) in a criminal proceeding for perjury or false statement if the statement was made by the defendant under oath, on the record, and in the presence of counsel.

21. In People v. George, 69 Mich.App. 403, 245 N.W.2d 65 (1976), appeal denied 399 Mich. 857, 251 N.W.2d 258, the State urged that it should be permitted to use voluntary admissions under circumstances keeping from the trial jury the fact that these admissions were made in guilty plea proceedings. The court rejected this proposal, concluding that as a practical matter there was no way to separate the plea itself from admissions made during its acceptance; jurors must know, the court reasoned, that a defendant who made such admissions must have offered a plea of guilty. 69 Mich.App. at 406–407, 245 N.W.2d at 67. See also, State v. Melendez, 165 N.J.Super. 182, 397 A.2d 1117 (1979) (where defendant's guilty plea invalid because he was denied assistance of counsel, no admissions made during plea proceeding are admissible if he is retried).

22. See State v. Hansen, ___ Mont. ___, 633 P.2d 1202 (1981), discussing Mont.R.Evid. 410.

23. See § 274 infra.

of self-incriminating statements that are or might be part of the widely-followed practice of compromising criminal cases through plea bargaining? There is widespread perception that the desirability of encouraging plea bargaining, or at least of retaining it as a necessary evil, requires that defendants' offers to compromise by plea bargaining be given protection similar to that afforded other litigants' offers to compromise. Thus Fed.R. Evid. 410, as originally enacted, incorporated the then-effective provision of Fed.R.Crim.P. 11(e)(6). Both excluded "evidence of . . . an offer to plead guilty or nolo contendere to the crime charged or any other crime, [and] statements made in connection with, and relevant to, [such] offers." Insofar as this language bars the subsequent use of admissions made by defendants or their lawyers to prosecuting attorneys during the process of exploring whether plea bargaining should be pursued or during plea bargaining itself, it remains widely approved and probably reflects the result that most courts would reach even in the absence of controlling statutory or rule language.[24]

But this language was construed by an occasional case as rendering inadmissible admissions made by defendants to law enforcement officers in the hope of obtaining leniency.[25] To some extent, this may reflect reality in which "bargains" between defendants and police officers are entered into and subsequently respected if not formally enforced. On the other hand, such bargains ought to be discouraged for several reasons. Compromises of criminal cases are best made by prosecuting attorneys, whose perspective is broader and who are thus in a better position to take into account all relevant information and considerations. Further, the difficulty of establishing and enforcing defendant-law enforcement officer bargains makes them exceptionally risky, especially for inexperienced and naive defendants. In any case, both the Federal Rules of Evidence and the Federal Rules of Criminal Procedure were amended in 1980. Both now in specific terms bar the admission of any statement made in the course of plea discussions with "an attorney" for the prosecution which do not result in a plea of guilty.[26] Under the language of some state provisions, however, there remains the possibility that admissions made to law enforcement officers may be excludable as part of the plea negotiation process.[27]

 WESTLAW REFERENCES

"judicial confession*" /p admit! admiss!

Admissions Made During Testimony in Support of Constitutional Claims

sh 390 us 377

simmons /15 390 /5 377 & exclusionary /3 rule & date(after 1982)

Withdrawn Pleas and Related Admissions

headnote(rule* /10 410 11(e)(6)) & withdr*w! /p admission* plea* statement*

topic(157) /p withdr*w! /p statement* admission* plea*

157k208(6)

Admissions Related to "Plea Bargaining"

plea /10 bargain! /p incriminat! self-incriminat! /p admiss! inadmiss! bar

---

24. On the other hand, it seems equally true that a defendant is not entitled to introduce exculpatory statements made during plea negotiations. See State v. Davis, 70 Ohio App.2d 48, 434 N.E.2d 285 (1980) (defendant not entitled to introduce his rejection of an offered plea bargain, in large part because holding such evidence admissible would have a devastating effect on plea bargaining).

25. See 1980 Advisory Committee Note to the proposed amendment of Fed.R.Crim.P. 11(e)(6).

26. Fed.R.Evid. 410(4); Fed.R.Crim.P. 11(e)(6)(D). See § 274 infra.

27. See People v. Oliver, 111 Mich.App. 734, 314 N.W.2d 740 (1981) (statement of defendant to officer, "[I]f I said I did it, would it still be first degree murder?" where officer had said he always tries to help a guy who tells the truth is inadmissible, because defendant had an actual and reasonable expectation that statement was part of a plea discussion).

§ 160. "Tacit" or "Adoptive" Admissions and Confessions [1]

Pursuant to the general rules regarding admissions,[2] the prosecution is generally permitted in a criminal case to prove that an accusatory statement was made in the hearing of the defendant and that the defendant's response was such as to justify the inference that he agreed with or "adopted" the accusation. Such evidence is admissible as substantive proof of the defendant's guilt of the crime charged.[3] The adopting response may be simple silence under circumstances in which a reasonable person would challenge the accusation.[4] Or, it may be an equivocal response, i.e., one that does not clearly challenge the accuracy of the accusation.[5] It may also, of course, be an express affirmative agreement with the accusation [6] or conduct from which the defendant's belief in the truth of the accuracy of the assertion can be inferred.[7]

Underlying this theory of admission by failure to deny is the assumption that human nature is such that innocent persons will deny false accusations. Therefore, a failure of a person to deny a false accusation tends to prove his belief that the accusation is accurate. In both civil and criminal cases this assumption has been subjected to critical scrutiny, and accordingly safeguards designed to assure its proper use have been erected as an aspect of the law of evidence in both types of cases.[8] In addition, the tacit confession rule presents problems not raised by its counterpart in civil cases.

Constitutional Problems of Silence Generally. Griffin v. California,[9] decided in 1965, held that the Fifth Amendment prohibits drawing an inference of guilt from a criminal defendant's reliance upon the privilege against compelled self-incrimination.[10] The next year, in Miranda v. Arizona,[11] the Court held that custodial interrogation by law enforcement officers implicated the privilege and therefore a suspect in that situation had a right to silence protected by the Fifth Amendment. Since that time, there has been widespread recognition that a suspect's post-arrest silence is sufficiently likely to constitute reliance upon the right to avoid self-incrimination that *Griffin* bars use of that silence as proof of the defendant's guilt.[12]

The position that use of evidence to impeach a testifying defendant is less intrusive upon any interests violated by the obtaining of that evidence than is use of such evidence as direct proof of guilt, was reinforced by the Supreme Court's decision in Harris v. New York [13] that the Fifth Amendment did not bar the use of confessions obtained in violation of *Miranda* for such limited purposes. Whether a defendant's post-arrest silence in the face of accusations could constitutionally be used for impeachment if the defendant took the stand at trial was addressed in Doyle v. Ohio.[14]

§ 160

1. See generally, 3 Wigmore, Evidence § 821 n. 3 (Chadbourn rev. 1970); 4 id. §§ 1071, 1072 (Chadbourn rev. 1972); Gamble, The Tacit Admission Rule: Unreliable and Unconstitutional—A Doctrine Ripe for Abandonment, 14 Ga.L.Rev. 27 (1979); Comment, 123 U.Pa. L.Rev. 940 (1975); Notes, 25 Clev.St.L.Rev. 261 (1976), 112 U.Pa.L.Rev. 210 (1963); 29 Am.Jur.2d Evidence §§ 638–45; C.J.S. Criminal Law § 734(1); Annot., 77 A.L.R.2d 463, 115 A.L.R. 1510, 80 A.L.R. 1235; Dec. Dig. Constitutional Law ☞268(10), Criminal Law ☞407–408, Witnesses ☞347.

2. See § 262 infra as to the nature of admissions.

3. Id.

4. See § 271 infra.

5. § 271 n. 4 infra.

6. See § 269 infra.

7. Id.

8. See § 270 infra nn. 12–17.

9. 380 U.S. 609 (1965), rehearing denied 381 U.S. 957.

10. See generally § 131 supra.

11. 384 U.S. 436 (1966), rehearing denied 385 U.S. 890. See generally §§ 150–153, supra.

12. Comment, 123 U.Pa.L.Rev. 940, 945 (1975).

13. 401 U.S. 222 (1971). See generally, §§ 162, 178, supra.

14. 426 U.S. 610 (1976), 8 Loyola U. (Chi.) L.Rev. 438 (1977), 11 U.Rich.L.Rev. 667 (1977).

In *Doyle*, the defendants were charged with sale of marijuana to a police informer. At trial, they took the stand and testified that the transaction—which was not clearly observed by officers—was actually a sale by the informer to them. On cross-examination, the prosecution was permitted to elicit from each defendant that neither, after being arrested and given the *Miranda* warnings, told the arresting officer the version of the events offered at trial. The prosecution did not urge admission of the defendants' silence as proof of guilt but only as impeaching the defendants' credibility as witnesses. While the prosecution's theory was not made express, it appears that the defendants' silence in response to the accusation, inherent in the arrest was regarded as sufficient concession of its truth—or at least of the absence of any additional exculpatory facts—to justify putting the accusation and response before the jury. The Supreme Court held this constitutional error for two reasons. First, silence after arrest and *Miranda* warnings is "insolubly ambiguous." The person has been informed of the right to silence. If the silence is merely reliance upon that right, it is not, of course, evidence of consciousness of guilt. Permitting the jury to speculate on the inference under these circumstances, the Court apparently concluded,[15] would be constitutionally impermissible. Second, implicit in the *Miranda* warning of the right to silence is the assurance that silence will carry no penalty. To give an arrestee such an assurance and then permit use of that silence to impeach an explanation later offered at trial would be "fundamentally unfair and a deprivation of due process."[16] The evidentiary use of silence at the time of arrest and after administration of the *Miranda* warnings, the Court held, violates the Due Process Clause of the Fourteenth Amendment.[17]

Insofar as the result in *Doyle* turned upon the "insoluble ambiguity" of a suspect's silence, the same result might be expected in a variety of situations in which the suspect might have relied upon a perceived right to remain silent. In two post-*Doyle* cases, however, the Court appears to have abandoned this rationale for the *Doyle* result and thus also to have dramatically limited the potential effect of *Doyle*. In Jenkins v. Anderson,[18] defendant, at his state trial for murder, testified that his killing of the victim was in self-defense. On cross-examination, the prosecution elicited from him that he had not been apprehended for the offense until two weeks after the killing and during that time he had in no way raised any claim of self-defense. Finding no constitutional error, the Court characterized *Doyle* as resting upon the proposition that fundamental fairness prohibits inducing a suspect to remain silent by implicitly assuring him that silence cannot be used against him and then using that silence to impeach him. On the facts of *Jenkins*, the Court concluded, "no governmental action induced [Jenkins] to remain silent before arrest," and therefore "the fundamental unfairness present in *Doyle* is not present in this case."[19] It should be emphasized that *Jenkins* is not a decision in support of the wisdom of allowing prearrest silence to be used for impeachment; it goes no farther than to hold that a State may allow such impeachment without infringing upon federal constitutional rights. In Fletcher v. Weir,[20] the Court used the same rationale to find no constitutional error in impeaching a testifying defendant with silence after arrest but in the absence of *Miranda* warnings containing the implicit assurance that silence would not be used against the defendant.

---

15. 426 U.S. at 617. But see the Court's further comment that it found no necessity to express an opinion on the probative value of the silence at issue in the cases on the matter of credibility. Id. at 617 n. 8.

16. Id. at 618.

17. Id. at 619.

18. 447 U.S. 231 (1980), 94 Harv.L.Rev. 82 (1980), 49 U.Cinn.L.Rev. 857 (1980), 58 U.Det.J.Urban L. 307 (1981).

19. 447 U.S. at 240.

20. 455 U.S. 603 (1982) (per curiam).

Despite the early suggestion in *Doyle* to the contrary, then, the Court appears to have rejected the proposition that the ambiguity of a suspect's silence in the face of whatever accusation is inherent in an arrest unconstitutionally endangers a defendant's right to be convicted only upon reliable evidence proving guilt beyond a reasonable doubt. On the other hand, where—but only where—the government expressly or implicitly assures a defendant that there is a legal right to remain silent and that this right can be exercised without penalty, later evidentiary use of that silence, even for the limited purpose of impeachment, violates due process. It necessarily follows that where such assurances have been made, federal constitutional considerations preclude use of the silence as substantive evidence of guilt as well the use of the silence for impeachment.[21]

Doyle, Jenkins and *Weir* all concern only alleged concession of the truth of an accusation by failure to deny it. Are any federal constitutional concerns raised by other aspects of the tacit confession rule? In Anderson v. Charles,[22] Charles was charged with murder. The State's evidence included proof that the defendant had been found in possession of the victim's car. At trial, Charles testified that he had stolen the victim's car from a given location. The prosecution then elicited from him that after arrest and *Miranda* warnings, he had made a statement containing an acknowledgment that he took the car but from a different location. *Doyle* was found inapplicable:

Doyle does not apply to cross-examination that merely inquires into prior inconsistent statements. Such questioning makes no unfair use of silence because a defendant who voluntarily speaks after receiving *Miranda* warnings has not been induced to remain silent. As to the subject matter of his statements, the defendant has not remained silent at all.[23]

Further, the Court rejected the argument that Charles was actually cross-examined concerning his silence, that is, his failure to tell the officer the version of the events to which he testified at trial. It acknowledged that a statement which omits certain matters might, when attention is later focused upon those matters, be characterized as "silence." But it continued, "*Doyle* does not require any such formalistic understanding of 'silence,' and we find no reason to adopt such a view in this case."[24]

Silence in Judicial Proceedings. Failure to deny accusations presents special problems of both constitutional and nonconstitutional dimensions when the defendant's non-denial occurred in the course of judicial proceedings. Any federal constitutional problem appeared to have been laid to rest in Raffel v. United States.[25] Raffel was tried twice for conspiracy; his first trial ended in mistrial when the jury could not reach a verdict. At both trials, an officer testified that Raffel, after arrest, had made an incriminating admission. At his first trial, Raffel did not testify. At the second trial, he took the stand and denied having made the admission; on cross-examination, he was compelled to admit that he had not offered this testimony at his prior trial. After Raffel's conviction, the Circuit Court of Appeals

21. In South Dakota v. Neville, 103 S.Ct. 916 (1983) the State had used against the defendant at his trial his refusal to submit to a blood-alcohol test. Arresting officers had informed Neville that his refusal to take the test could lead to loss of his driver's license but had not told him that the refusal could be used in evidence against him. Neville contended that use of his refusal violated *Doyle* unless he was fully warned of the consequences of this action. Rejecting this, the Court explained:

> [W]e think it unrealistic to say that the warnings given here implicitly assure a suspect that no consequences other than those mentioned will occur. Im-

portantly, the warning that he could lose his driver's license made it clear that refusing the test was not a "safe harbor," free of adverse consequences.

103 S.Ct. at 924. It remains possible, of course, that a particular warning could so suggest that use of a refusal was prohibited as to bring *Doyle* into play.

22. 447 U.S. 404 (1980), rehearing denied 448 U.S. 912. See generally Note, 69 Va.L.Rev. 155 (1983).

23. 447 U.S. at 407.

24. Id. at 409.

25. 271 U.S. 494 (1926).

certified to the Supreme Court the question whether it constituted error to require Raffel to disclose that he had not testified at his first trial. Answering the certified question in the negative, the Court held that a defendant who takes the stand is subject to cross-examination as is any other witness and that a witness who denies making a relevant statement "may be cross-examined with respect to conduct on his part inconsistent with this denial." [26]

But the effect of *Raffel* was questioned in Grunewald v. United States.[27] Halperin, one of the defendants, took the stand and testified in his own defense. On cross-examination, he was asked a series of questions which he had previously been asked during a grand jury appearance. At trial, he answered them all in a manner consistent with innocence; the Government was then permitted to show that before the grand jury he had refused to answer the questions in reliance on his privilege against compelled self-incrimination. Finding error, the Court held that *Raffel* did not control. The abstract certified question answered in *Raffel*, the Court reasoned, concerned only whether such cross-examination is always constitutionally prohibited. *Raffel* did not address whether, on the facts of a particular case, the probative value of evidence that a defendant has previously remained silent in reliance on the privilege is outweighed by the risk of such evidence having an impermissible impact upon the jury.[28]

On the facts of *Grunewald*, the Court held, the trial judge should have refused to permit the inquiry because no sufficiently probative inference regarding Grunewald's credibility could be drawn from his action before the grand jury.[29] His assertions of the privilege had been accompanied by protestations of innocence. The hostile environment of the grand jury might well have convinced him that the grand jury would be an unwise forum in which to choose to assert specific factual matters tending to show innocence. Further, responding to the questions in the manner in which he responded at trial would in some ways have provided the Government with potentially incriminating information, although the answers would also, on a different theory, have been consistent with innocence. In short, the Government failed to show that given the accusation made and the circumstances, Grunewald's assertion of the privilege was a sufficiently reliable adoption of it to justify use for impeachment purposes at trial.

In *Hale*,[30] the Court specifically declined reaching whether *Raffel* had survived subsequent developments, especially *Griffin*.[31] But in Jenkins v. Anderson [32] the Court appeared to reaffirm *Raffel's* holding that the Fifth Amendment posed no absolute barrier to impeaching a testifying defendant with evidence of his failure to testify in an earlier judicial proceedings.[33] The absence of a total federal constitutional bar to the use of the evidence does not, of course, preclude its exclusion by rule of evidence; the sensitivity of the area and the difficulties inherent in making case-by-case evaluations strongly suggest the wisdom of such a rule.

 **WESTLAW REFERENCES**

tacit adoptive   /10   admission*   /p   silen** affirmation*

Constitutional Problems of Silence Generally
miranda   /15   384   /5   436   &   post-arrest   /s   silen**

---

26. 271 U.S. at 497–498.

27. 353 U.S. 391 (1957).

28. 353 U.S. at 420. But see the characterization of *Raffel* in United States v. Hale, 422 U.S. 171, 175 (1975) (*Raffel* rested upon a finding of sufficient inconsistency between prior silence and trial testimony on facts before Court).

29. Id. at 421–424.

30. United States v. Hale, 422 U.S. 171, 175 n. 4 (1975).

31. Griffin v. California, supra n. 9.

32. 447 U.S. 231 (1980); supra n. 18.

33. 447 U.S. at 237 n. 4 ("no Court opinion decided since *Raffel* has challenged its holding that the Fifth Amendment is not violated when a defendant is impeached on the basis of his prior silence"). See also Culhane v. Harris, 514 F.Supp. 746, 753–754 (S.D.N.Y. 1981) (*Raffel* remains good law and therefore comment on defendant's failure to testify at preliminary hearing not violative of federal constitution).

410k347 /p post-arrest impeach!

doyle /s ohio /15 426 /5 610 & date(after
    1/1/83)

"insolub** ambigu***"

doyle /p prior /5 inconsistent /5 statement*

Silence in Judicial Proceedings

110k656 110k393 & raffel /5 states

raffel & grunewald & probative /5 value inference*

5th fifth /2 amendment /p impeach! /p silen** /p
    testi! /p prior previous earlier

§ 161.   Determining Admissibility [1]

Considerations bearing upon procedures for determining the admissibility of a confession are closely related to those for raising and resolving exclusionary sanction issues.[2] Nevertheless, procedures for resolving confession issues require separate consideration, if for no other reason than the exceptional amount of federal constitutional case law bearing upon confession issues.

Role of Judge and Jury. Traditionally, procedures for determining the voluntariness of a confession offered by the prosecution in a trial to the jury have fallen into three categories. First is the pattern of the so-called New York procedure,[3] under which the trial judge makes a preliminary inquiry into voluntariness and excludes the confession only if its involuntariness is so clear as to present no issue. If, on the other hand, the evidence presents a fair question as to voluntariness or as to any factual matters relevant to the voluntariness issue, the confession is submitted to the jury with directions to determine voluntariness and to consider the confession on the issue of guilt or innocence only if it is determined to be vol-

untary. Procedures in a second category follow the "orthodox" rule,[4] under which the trial judge has sole responsibility for the matter. The trial judge, then, resolves any factual disputes and determines voluntariness; nothing is formally submitted to the jury. A third category consists of the Massachusetts procedure,[5] in which the trial judge makes a full determination of voluntariness and submits the confession to the jury only if the statement is determined to be voluntary. The jury, however, is instructed that it may also consider voluntariness and should not consider the confession in deciding guilt or innocence unless it finds the confession voluntary.

In Jackson v. Denno,[6] the New York procedure was held to violate the due process clause of the Fourteenth Amendment. It did not, the Court concluded, assure sufficiently reliable determinations of either the underlying factual issues upon which a claim of involuntariness is often based or of the final question of voluntariness itself. Three dangers were presented:[7] (1) The jury might consider the confession to be accurate and conclude from the confession that the defendant committed the act charged. This might seriously distort its judgment on any factual issues relating to the voluntariness of the confession. (2) The jury might find the confession involuntary and the evidence without the confession insufficient to establish guilt. In this situation, the jurors may fail to understand or accept the instruction directing them to give no consideration to an involuntary confession. (3) The jury might conclude that without the confession the evi-

---

§ 161

1. See generally, Meltzer, Involuntary Confessions: The Allocation of Responsibility Between Judge and Jury, 21 U.Chi.L.Rev. 317 (1954); 29 Am.Jur.2d Evidence §§ 582–90; C.J.S. Criminal Law Section 838 (1961); Annot., 1 A.L.R.3d 1252; Dec.Dig.Criminal Law ⊝531–532.

2. See § 180 infra.

3. See Stein v. New York, 346 U.S. 156 (1953), rehearing denied 346 U.S. 842, in which the constitutionality of the procedure was upheld.

4. See the cases listed in Appendix A to Opinion of Justice Black, Jackson v. Denno, 378 U.S. 368, 411–414 (1964).

5. See Commonwealth v. Preece, 140 Mass. 276, 277, 5 N.E. 494, 495 (1885). In many jurisdictions it is unclear from the appellate case law—or at least it was unclear prior to Jackson v. Denno, 378 U.S. 368 (1964), discussed in the text at n. 6, infra—which procedure is followed. In some jurisdictions, the approach combines the alternatives identified in the text. See Jackson v. Denno, 378 U.S. 368, 378 n. 9 (1964).

6. 378 U.S. 368 (1964).

7. See 378 U.S. at 382–384.

dence is insufficient to establish guilt but harbor doubts as to the voluntariness of the confession. This could create strong pressure to resolve either factual subissues or the ultimate voluntariness issue in favor of voluntariness, so as to avoid a verdict contrary to the "truth." The same fatal defects were found three years later [8] in an almost identical procedure whereby the prosecution was required to make only "a prima facie case that the alleged confession was voluntary" and the ultimate determination of voluntariness was left to the jury.

Jackson, then, establishes that a defendant who challenges the voluntariness of a confession offered by the prosecution is entitled, at a minimum, to an inquiry and determination by the trial judge that the confession was voluntary. Whether a similar right exists in regard to other federal constitutional issues affecting the admissibility of confessions is not clear. Arguably, voluntariness is a uniquely important federal constitutional demand. If so, the exceptional solicitude for determinations of voluntariness that gave rise to *Jackson* may not be appropriate or necessary when other objections—even those of federal constitutional dimensions—are raised to confessions. The general tendency, however, has been to regard this procedural right as applicable to other federal constitutional objections, including those based upon *Miranda*.[9]

Jackson is widely regarded as establishing a right to a hearing out of the presence of a trial jury. But this is an oversimplification. In Pinto v. Pierce,[10] the state trial judge had heard in the presence of the jury evidence establishing the voluntariness of the confession offered by the prosecution and held the confession voluntary. Reversing the lower courts' conclusion that this procedure was inconsistent with *Jackson*, the Supreme Court commented that it had "never ruled that all voluntariness hearing must be held outside the presence of the jury, regardless of the circumstances." [11] The defendant made no claim that the hearing was inadequate or in any other way unfair because it was held in the jury's presence. Nor did the procedure cause the jury to hear testimony it would not otherwise have heard. *Jackson*, therefore, was not violated.[12]

If the *Pierce* procedure was followed and the trial judge determined the confession to be involuntary, a mistrial clearly would have to be declared. An instruction to the jurors to disregard the testimony they had heard concerning the confession would be inadequate to assure the defendant that the guilt-innocence determination would be made without reference to the confession. Administrative pressures that might well bear upon a judge in such a situation to find a confession voluntary and thus avoid a timeconsuming and costly retrial suggest that such a procedure is unsound as posing too great a risk of compromising the trial judge's impartiality.

Burden of Proof. In Lego v. Twomey [13] the Court addressed the burden of proof on the issue of voluntariness. Rejecting the argument that voluntariness must be proved beyond a reasonable doubt, the Court stressed the absence of any indication that admissibility rulings under a lesser standard have been inaccurate or otherwise wanting in quality. Due process, the Court concluded, demands only that "the prosecution must

---

8. Sims v. Georgia, 385 U.S. 538 (1967), conformed to 223 Ga. 126, 153 S.E.2d 567, appeal after remand 223 Ga. 465, 156 S.E.2d 65, reversed 389 U.S. 404, conformed to 224 Ga. 36, 159 S.E.2d 290.

9. United States v. Danley, 564 F.2d 813, 815 (8th Cir. 1977) (hearing out of jury's presence required to resolve *Miranda* objection, citing *Jackson*); State v. Alston, 35 N.C.App. 691, 242 S.E.2d 523, 525 (1978), affirmed 295 N.C. 629, 247 S.E.2d 898 (hearing required on *Miranda* objection).

10. 389 U.S. 31 (1967). See generally the discussion of Watkins v. Sowders, 449 U.S. 341 (1981), in § 180 infra.

11. 389 U.S. at 32.

12. Id. Pierce also, however, had failed to object to having the voluntariness of his confession considered in the presence of the jury. This constituted an alternative ground for finding no violation of due process. Id. at 33.

13. 404 U.S. 477 (1972).

prove at least by a preponderance of the evidence that a confession was voluntary." [14] States clearly remain free to impose a higher standard,[15] and a number do demand that voluntariness be proved beyond a reasonable doubt.[16]

Need for Hearing. In Wainwright v. Sykes,[17] the Court made clear that *Jackson* does not mandate a hearing on voluntariness in the absence of a defense objection to the confession. Thus a state defendant who fails to comply with a state procedural requirement of a trial objection is not entitled to federal habeas corpus relief on the basis of the use of an involuntary confession unless he demonstrates cause for the noncompliance with the state requirement and prejudice from its application. Despite

Sykes, however, a number of lower courts have suggested or held that a *Jackson* hearing must be held before a confession is admitted whether requested or not [18] or that a trial judge must at least be alert to matters raising a voluntariness issue and to a need to order a *Jackson* hearing *sua sponte* where such issues exist whether an objection has been raised or not.[19]

A somewhat harder question is whether a trial judge is required to hold a hearing in the absence of a request for such a hearing. *Sykes* suggests not.[20] Perhaps, however, a defense objection, without more, is sufficient to bring into play the prosecution's constitutional duty to prove admissibility by at least a preponderance of the evidence. Thus a barebones objection on voluntariness

14. 404 U.S. at 489.

15. Id.

16. The leading case is probably People v. Jimenez, 21 Cal.3d 595, 147 Cal.Rptr. 172, 580 P.2d 672 (1978) which held that the higher burden was demanded by the importance of the right to be free from compelled self-incriminating, the minimal review on appeal of trial judge's decisions on voluntariness, and the need to avoid tainting the guilt-innocence determination with false confessions. See also, Magley v. State, 263 Ind. 618, 335 N.E.2d 811 (1975) (contrasting lesser standard required by *Twomey*); State v. Lovett, 345 So.2d 1139, 1142 (La.1977).

A number of procedural issues concerning the hearing itself have, of course, been raised. Given that the burden of proof is on the prosecution, it has been held that the prosecution should be required to call its witnesses before the defense is asked to produce evidence. State v. Smith, 409 So.2d 271, 171 (La.1982). Compare State v. Blakney, 185 Mont. 470, 605 P.2d 1093, 1099 (1979), vacated and remanded on other grounds, 451 U.S. 1013 (1981), on remand ___ Mont. ___, 641 P.2d 1045 (trial court may require defendant to "go forward with the evidence" to establish a prima facie case, but this is not recommended as standard procedure). If, however, the defense is required to present its evidence first there may be no prejudice and any error committed is unlikely to require reversal on appeal. See State v. Scott, 269 S.C. 438, 237 S.E.2d 886 (1977).

A few states have adopted a somewhat rigid rule that requires, if a defendant places voluntariness in issue, the prosecution to either produce all officers or other material witnesses to the defendant's interrogation or adequately to explain their nonproduction. The Illinois court has adhered to this position since People v. Rogers, 303 Ill. 578, 136 N.E. 470 (1922). See People v. Armstrong, 51 Ill.2d 471, 476, 282 N.E.2d 712, 715 (1972) (collecting cases). Mississippi has recently adopted this approach. Scott v. State, 382 So.2d 1091,

1093 (Miss.1980). See also, Kelly v. State, 414 So.2d 446 (Miss.1982) (showing that absent police officer was on vacation was not an adequate explanation of nonproduction).

The state courts have also split on the admissibility of mental health professional testimony to establish involuntariness. Error was found in the exclusion of such testimony in Commonwealth v. Johnston, 373 Mass. 21, 364 N.E.2d 1211 (1977). Contra, People v. Lewis, 103 Misc.2d 881, 427 N.Y.S.2d 177 (1980).

17. 433 U.S. 72 (1977), rehearing denied 434 U.S. 880.

18. State v. Persinger, ___ W.Va. ___, 286 S.E.2d 261, 266 (1982) (rule is simply that before admitting a confession trial court must hold hearing out of jury's presence and find voluntariness). See also, State v. McKeown, 23 Wn.App. 582, 596 P.2d 1100 (1979) (Wash.Cr.R. 3.5 mandates hearing, but failure to hold hearing is not reversible error if record shows there could not have been issue as to voluntariness).

19. United States v. Powe, 591 F.2d 833, 842–844 (D.C.Cir. 1978), appeal after remand 627 F.2d 1251 (although generally *Jackson* hearing need not be held *sua sponte*, if certain "alerting circumstances" arise judge may have duty to take more active role, to investigate need for a hearing, and perhaps to hold a hearing in the absence of any request). The Massachusetts court has held that a voir dire on voluntariness must be conducted even in the absence of a request if a "substantial claim" of involuntariness is raised. Commonwealth v. Harris, 371 Mass. 462, 358 N.E.2d 982 (1976). See also, Commonwealth v. Brady, 380 Mass. 44, 410 N.E.2d 695, 698 (1980).

20. Cf. United States v. Smith, 638 F.2d 131, 133 (9th Cir. 1981) (where defense objection made on voluntariness grounds but no "issue" raised and no hearing requested, trial court did not err in failing to hold hearing).

grounds may mandate a hearing at which the prosecution must present evidence meeting that burden.[21]

Judge's Finding on Admissibility. In Sims v. Georgia,[22] the Court held that a trial judge's conclusion that a challenged confession is voluntary "must appear from the record with unmistakable clarity."[23] It is not constitutionally necessary, however, that the trial judge make formal findings of fact, as on contested subissues, or write a formal opinion.[24] Nevertheless, sound policy and particularly the practicalities of effective appellate review strongly suggest specific findings concerning disputed subquestions of fact as well as a clear ultimate determination of voluntariness.[25]

Jackson, of course, focuses upon defendants' right to a determination of admissibility by the trial judge. The "Massachusetts procedure," the Court commented in *Jackson*, does not pose the same hazards as the condemned New York procedure.[26] Thus there is clearly no federal constitutional barrier to a state choosing, after the requisite determination by the judge has been made, to give the defendant a second opportunity to challenge voluntariness before the trial jury. In Lego v. Twomey,[27] the Court specifically rejected the argument that due process required the states to give defendants accorded their *Jackson* rights a "second forum" for their claim before the trial jury. *Jackson*, the Court reasoned, rejected the argument that a jury is better suited than a judge to determine voluntariness. Nor was the Court persuaded by the suggestion that trial judges' voluntariness determinations were sufficiently unreliable that fairness mandated a second inquiry into the same issue.[28]

Procedure in Bench Trials. A further issue concerns the application, if any, of *Jackson's* due process requirements where trial is to the bench rather than a jury. Several

---

21. See cases cited in nn. 17 and 18 supra. The duty to hold a hearing may, of course, arise because of state law. See Page v. State, 614 S.W.2d 819 (Tex.Cr App.1981) (Vernon's Ann.Tex.Code Crim.Pro. art. 38.22 requires hearing on voluntariness where objection is made even if no hearing is requested).

The failure to comply with *Jackson* does not automatically entitle a defendant to have the conviction invalidated. While the states remain free to grant such relief in all cases, see Greene v. State, 351 So.2d 941 (Fla.1977), federal constitutional concerns mandate only that, in the first instance, the state courts at some stage conduct an inquiry into the voluntariness of the confession. If this inquiry results in the confession being found voluntary, the defendant is entitled to no relief because he was not prejudiced by the violation of his due process rights during the trial. Jackson v. Denno, 378 U.S. 368, 394–95 (1964). See also, Wenson v. Stidham, 409 U.S. 224 (1972), modified 410 U.S. 904, on remand 506 F.2d 478 (8th Cir.), cert. denied 429 U.S. 941 (no federal habeas corpus relief granted to state defendant despite showing that state trial judge may have violated *Jackson* at trial, where on motion to vacate sentence state court conducted full inquiry into voluntariness of confession and found confession voluntary).

22. 385 U.S. 538 (1967), conformed to 223 Ga. 126, 153 S.E.2d 567, appeal after remand 223 Ga. 465, 156 S.E.2d 65, reversed 389 U.S. 400, conformed to 224 Ga. 36, 159 S.E.2d 290.

23. 385 U.S. at 544.

24. Id. See also LaVallee v. Delle Rose, 410 U.S. 690 (1973) (state trial judge's determination of volunta-

riness that did not specifically address whether particular factual issues were resolved against defendant was sufficient under 28 U.S.C.A. § 2254(d) to resolve those factual disputes so as to give the findings the statutory presumption of correctness); Wright v. State, 340 So. 2d 74, 77 (Ala.1977), on remand 340 So.2d 80 (Ala.Crim. App.) (expressly rejecting argument that trial court must make "some express factual or legal or factual-legal determination on the record . . . , that the defendant 'did knowingly and intelligently waive his right to remain silent' ").

25. In United States v. Medina, 552 F.2d 181 (7th Cir. 1977), cert. denied 434 U.S. 839, the court, after declining to find the procedure employed by the trial judge in violation of *Jackson*, continued:

> [I]t would have been the better practice for the trial judge to state that it [sic] found the statement to be voluntary by a preponderance of the evidence and to give reasons for so concluding.

552 F.2d at 186.

26. Jackson v. Denno, 378 U.S. 368, 378 n. 8 (1964). Where the matter is submitted to the jury, the "preferred practice"—at least under the Massachusetts rule—is for the trial judge to refrain from informing the jury of the judge's decisions on matters bearing upon voluntariness. See Commonwealth v. Chung, 378 Mass. 451, 392 N.E.2d 1015 (1979).

27. 404 U.S. 477 (1972).

28. 404 U.S. at 489–490.

early decisions held that the requirement of a separate hearing on voluntariness applied to bench trials as well as jury trials.[29] The overwhelming weight of lower court opinion, however, is to the contrary.[30] In United States ex rel. Placek v. Illinois,[31] the Seventh Circuit reasoned that a requirement of a separate hearing could be justified only on the assumption that a trial judge's decision on voluntariness will be compromised if the judge hears evidence bearing upon guilt or innocence before resolving the voluntariness issue. Such an assumption, however, would be contrary to widely accepted practice and theory, especially the presumption that a bench trial judge considers only relevant and admissible evidence in reaching his conclusions. The court consequently declined to condemn on due process grounds the practice of a trial judge carrying a motion to suppress along with the case and resolving it after also hearing the evidence bearing upon guilt or innocence. It wisely also declined to commend the procedure and commented, "Holding a pretrial hearing, or a separate hearing when the voluntariness issue is first raised at trial, seems preferable in order to minimize the possibility that . . . improper influences might arise."[32]

Appellate Review. If a trial judge has followed appropriate procedures in arriving at a determination of voluntariness, his conclusion will be given great deference on appeal. While the terminology used differs, appellate courts appear agreed that only in exceptional situations should trial judges' voluntariness determinations be overruled as contrary to the evidence introduced.[33]

---

29. United States ex rel. Spears v. Rundle, 268 F.Supp. 691, 695–96 (E.D.Pa.1967), affirmed 405 F.2d 1037 (3d Cir. 1969); United States ex rel. Owens v. Cavell, 254 F.Supp. 154 (M.D.Pa.1966).

30. United States v. Martinez, 555 F.2d 1269, 1272 (5th Cir. 1977); Matter of Appeal in Maricopa County Juvenile, 118 Ariz. 284, 287, 576 P.2d 143, 146 (App. 1978) (collecting cases); M. A. v. State, 384 So.2d 740 (Fla.App.1980); Beck v. State, 626 P.2d 327 (Okl.Cr. App.1981).

31. 546 F.2d 1298 (7th Cir. 1976).

32. 546 F.2d at 1306 n. 8.

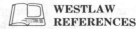

voluntar! involuntar! admiss! admit! /20 confession* & "new york" orthodox massachusetts /5 procedure rule

voluntar! involuntar! admiss! admit! /20 confession* /20 denno /5 hearing

voluntar! involuntar! admiss! admit! /20 confession* & denno /20 pinto pierce

Burden of Proof

digest(voluntar! involuntar! admiss! admit! /p confession* /p "burden of proof")

Need for Hearing

ic 433 us 72

sykes wainwright /15 433 /5 72 & need necessity request! /p hearing

110k532

Judge's Finding on Admissibility

synopsis,digest("judge" judicial /p finding* holding* /p admiss! admit! /p confession*)

Procedure in Bench Trials

110k260.11(2) & confession*

Appellate Review

appellate /s review /p voluntari! involuntari! /p confession*

---

§ 162. Use of Otherwise Inadmissible Confessions for Impeachment of Testifying Defendant [1]

The exception to many exclusionary sanctions for otherwise inadmissible evidence offered solely to impeach a testifying defendant is discussed in Chapter 15.[2] It is important in the present chapter, however, to note the special ramifications of this exception for those exclusionary sanctions that relate specifically or primarily to confessions.

Recent reinvigoration of impeachment exceptions to the federal constitutional exclu-

---

33. United States v. Wilkins, 659 F.2d 769, 775 (7th Cir. 1981), cert. denied 454 U.S. 1102; Moore v. State, 415 So.2d 1210, 1214–1215 (Ala.Crim.App.1982), cert. denied ___ U.S. ___; State v. Kalani, 3 Hawaii App. 334, 649 P.2d 1188, 1195 (1982); State v. Hunt, 212 Neb. 304, 322 N.W.2d 624 (1982).

§ 162

1. See generally the references cited in n. 1 to § 178 infra.

2. See § 178 infra.

sionary sanctions began with Harris v. New York,[3] in which the defendant Harris was charged with sale of heroin. Harris took the witness stand in own defense and acknowledged selling a package to a police undercover officer. He claimed, however, that the package contained only baking powder and that the entire transaction was an effort to defraud the purchaser. On cross-examination, the trial court permitted the prosecution to question Harris concerning an inconsistent statement he had given law enforcement officers during custodial interrogation following a *Miranda* warning that failed to include his right to appointed counsel. Finding no federal constitutional error, the Supreme Court characterized any speculative possibility that permitting impeachment use of such confessions would dilute the deterrent value of *Miranda's* exclusionary sanction as outweighed by the value of such statements in assessing the credibility of testifying defendants.[4]

Oregon v. Hass [5] presented a somewhat different situation. Hass had been adequately warned under *Miranda* and indicated a desire for representation. Interrogation nevertheless continued and the resulting statement was used to impeach Hass when, at trial, he testified in his own defense. Justice Brennan urged that the situation in *Hass* was distinguishable from *Harris*, in that permitting impeachment use of statements such as those at issue in *Hass* would greatly reduce the incentive provided by *Miranda's* exclusionary sanction for law enforcement officers to comply with *Miranda's* substantive requirements. Despite *Harris*, he suggested, law enforcement officers still had significant incentive to give full warnings so that any resulting state-

ment could be used to prove guilt. But permitting impeachment use of a confession resulting from continued questioning after the right to counsel is invoked removes the incentive to comply with the *Miranda* requirement at issue. If the officers cease questioning, it is virtually certain that no confession will be obtained. If, however, they continue questioning and a statement is obtained, it can at least be used for impeachment. In *Hass* situations, then, an impeachment exception may encourage officers to violate the right to counsel because they have nothing to lose and something potentially important—a confession usable for impeachment—to gain.[6] The majority, however, dismissed this possibility as "speculative" and held that the confession was properly used for impeachment.[7]

In both *Harris* [8] and *Hass*,[9] the Court noted that no claim had been made or evidence produced that the confessions were coerced or involuntary. But in Mincey v. Arizona [10] the Court was confronted with the use for impeachment of a confession obtained from the defendant under different circumstances. Mincey had been questioned while he lay severely injured in a hospital intensive care unit. He lost consciousness several times during the period of questioning. More than once, he communicated to the officer that he wished the questioning to cease until he had representation; it did not. At one point, a nurse suggested to Mincey that it would be "best" if he answered the officer's questions. On this record, the Supreme Court concluded, it was apparent that the statements were not the product of Mincey's "free and rationale choice," but rather were a consequence of an overbear-

3. 401 U.S. 222 (1971). For a critical analysis of the Court's treatment of the record in this case and the conclusions reached by the Court, see Dershowitz & Ely, Harris v. New York: Some Anxious Observations on the Candor and Logic of the Emerging Nixon Majority, 80 Yale L.J. 1198 (1971).

4. 401 U.S. at 225. Whether *Harris* abolished the apparent requirement of Walder v. United States, 347 U.S. 62 (1954) that a defendant testify to matters "collateral" to guilt or innocence of the crime charged be-

fore such impeachment is permissible is discussed in § 178 infra.

5. 420 U.S. 714 (1975).

6. 420 U.S. at 725 (Brennan, J., dissenting).

7. Id. at 723.

8. Harris v. New York, 401 U.S. 222, 224 (1971).

9. Oregon v. Hass, 420 U.S. 714, 722 (1975).

10. 437 U.S. 385 (1978).

ing of his will.[11] "*[A]ny* criminal trial use of against a defendant of his *involuntary* statement is a denial of due process of law",[12] the Court indicated, and consequently even the impeachment use of Mincey's confession was therefore impermissible.

Harris, Hass and *Mincey*, then, make clear that a confession inadmissible for reasons that do not cause the confession to fail to satisfy legal standards of trustworthiness for self-incriminating admissions may be used for impeachment. On the other hand, if the reason for a confession being inadmissible to prove guilt also establishes that the confession does not satisfy trustworthiness standards, the confession cannot be used for any criminal trial purpose, including impeachment of a defendant who testifies.

This distinction appears to be based upon two considerations. First, the "cost" of permitting impeachment use of an unreliable confession is higher. Despite limiting instructions, the jury may well consider it as tending to prove guilt; the risk that the guilt or innocence determination may be tainted by a false confession, of course, is an especially dangerous one. Second, the value of an unreliable confession for impeachment purposes is substantially less. Where a defendant's trial testimony and pretrial statements are inconsistent and there is reason to doubt the accuracy of the latter, there is less reason to fear that the defendant has committed perjury and to believe that admitting the confession would lead to a more accurate assessment of his credibility by the trial jury.

Probably the major issue in applying the *Harris-Hass-Mincey* rule to the federal constitutional doctrines affecting admissibility of confessions is whether the inquiry should focus directly upon the "trustworthiness" or accuracy of the confession or, instead, should address whether the confession fits within one of those categories of confessions that are regarded as a group to be unrelia-

ble. When the issue is the admissibility of a confession to prove guilt, the Court has made clear that the inquiry cannot be the accuracy of the particular confession. Rather, the trial judge must inquire exclusively whether the offered confession is "voluntary." [13] Perhaps the same approach is necessary here.

On the other hand, it can be argued that admitting confessions for impeachment purposes is quite unlikely to affect the conduct of law enforcement officers. Consequently, inquiry into the accuracy of a confession and permitting the impeachment use of "involuntary" but "trustworthy" confessions would not have the diluting effect upon the deterrent function of the voluntariness rule that the guilt-innocence rule is apparently designed to prevent. In any case, the Court's analysis in *Mincey* appears not to have considered directly the trustworthiness of the statement. Instead, the Court asked only whether the confession was involuntary within the meaning of that aspect of the voluntariness rule barring use of a confession obtained by an "overbearing of the will." Upon concluding that the confession was involuntary in this sense, the Court appears to have been willing to assume that it posed sufficient risk of untrustworthiness to bar its use for impeachment.

A further but related question concerns the significance in impeachment analysis of particular aspects of traditional voluntariness analysis. *Mincey* makes clear that a confession involuntary under that aspect of the involuntariness test addressing an "overbearing of the will" is thereby rendered unavailable for impeachment use. But what about confessions arguably coming within other voluntariness criteria? Will, for example, a promise of a benefit that has traditionally rendered a confession involuntary[14] now render that confession inadmissible for impeachment purposes? Is it permissible—or perhaps necessary—to inquire whether in

---

11. 437 U.S. at 401.

12. Id. at 398 (emphasis in original).

13. See § 147 supra.

14. See § 148 supra.

light of the promise the confession is sufficiently trustworthy to justify its use for this purpose? Or, as a possible compromise, might the inquiry be shifted away from the trustworthiness of this particular confession and instead be posed as whether the promise was of a sort likely, in general, to stimulate inaccurate confessions? [15] Similarly, is it necessary to consider whether such factors as deception [16] and intoxication [17] will be given the same effect in evaluating admissibility for impeachment under *Harris, Hass* and *Mincey* as they are given under traditional voluntariness analysis?

Harris and *Hass* leave little doubt that a confession inadmissible because of noncompliance with *Miranda's per se* requirements may nevertheless be admissible for impeachment. But what of confessions inadmissible for other federal constitutional reasons? If, for example, *Miranda's per se* requirements have been respected but the suspect's waiver of counsel is ineffective under *Miranda* standards,[18] will this necessarily render the confession inadmissible for impeachment? It may be necessary to consider further whether the confession is involuntary under pre-*Miranda* standards or, perhaps, whether it is ultimately trustworthy. It seems quite likely that a confession inadmissible to prove guilt because of a violation of the suspect's Sixth Amendment right to counsel [19] may be admissible for impeachment, subject to the issue analogous to that raised above regarding the effect of a determination that the waiver was ineffective.[20] Given the Court's holding that evidence obtained in violation of the Fourth Amendment right to be free from unreasonable searches is admissible for impeachment,[21] it seems necessarily to follow that a confession inadmissible for Fourth Amendment reasons [22] will, in the absence of more, be usable for impeachment.

An important procedural question raised by efforts to use otherwise inadmissible confessions for impeachment is the extent to which that use is permissible only upon the laying of a particular foundation. Specifically, is it necessary, before making impeachment use of such a confession, for the prosecution to show that, in the Court's *Harris* language, "the trustworthiness of the [confession] satisfied legal standards?" [23] Subject to the caveat required by the above discussion concerning the possible need directly to address the reliability of the statement, this generally can be posed as to whether a foundation showing of voluntariness is necessary for impeachment use.

Arguably a foundation requirement here would be more disruptive than where a confession is offered as part of the prosecution's case on guilt. The prosecution's right to use a statement for impeachment purposes may develop only during the course of cross-examination; to disrupt such cross-examination to address the adequacy of the prosecution's foundation may be more disruptive than compliance with *Jackson*. Further, the limited use made of the statement may mean that such preliminary requirements are less necessary than when the statement is offered for guilt purposes.

On the other hand, it seems unrealistic to regard such statements as actually being used only for credibility evaluation. Often prosecutors will know before beginning cross-examination of a testifying defendant that they will want to attempt such use of a confession. Even in other circumstances, in-

---

15. See the discussion of the approach of some courts to the promise issue, discussed in § 148 at n. 24 supra.

16. See § 149 supra.

17. See § 147, at note 29 supra.

18. See § 153 supra.

19. See § 155 supra.

20. See United States v. McManaman, 606 F.2d 919 (10th Cir. 1979), appeal after remand 653 F.2d 458 (vio-

lation of *Massiah* did not bar use of confession to impeach).

21. United States v. Havens, 446 U.S. 620 (1980), on remand 625 F.2d 1311 (5th Cir.), rehearing denied 448 U.S. 911, cert. denied 450 U.S. 995, discussed in § 178 at n. 12 infra.

22. See § 157 supra.

23. Harris v. New York, 401 U.S. 222, 224 (1971).

terruption of cross-examination to inquire as to the foundation for such use of a confession will be little more disruptive than interrupting the testimony of a police officer to hold a *Jackson* hearing concerning a confession as to which the officer is about to testify. In many if not most cases, the admissibility of a confession may be raised pretrial and at that time it would require little additional effort for the trial judge to rule on its admissibility to prove guilt and also for impeachment purposes. Lower courts are divided on the need for a foundation of this sort in all cases.[24] On balance, it would seem that such a foundation can be laid without undue burden on the prosecution or disruption of the trial and should be required.

States remain free, of course, to bar even impeachment use of confessions obtained in violation of federal constitutional standards and some have done so.[25]

WESTLAW REFERENCES

digest, synopsis(impeach! /p confess! /p illegal** unconstitutional** impermiss! inadmiss!

confess! /p impeach! /p untrustworth! trustworth!

harris & hass & mincey

mincey /15 437 & trustworth! untrustworth! unreliab! reliab! /s confession*

110k519(1)

---

24. Compare United States v. Scott, 592 F.2d 1139, 1142 (10th Cir. 1979) (foundation of voluntariness need not be laid, relying in part upon apparent absence of such a foundation in *Harris* and *Hass*) with Walker v. State, 369 So.2d 825 (Ala.1979), on remand 369 So.2d 826 (Ala.Crim.App.) (even if previously introduced evidence suggests lack of coercive influences, inculpatory statement can be used for impeachment only if state lays predicate consisting of proof that statement was free from coercive and involuntary influences).

25. People v. Disbrow, 16 Cal.3d 101, 127 Cal.Rptr. 360, 545 P.2d 272 (1976) (relying on Cal.Const. art. I, Sec. 15, providing protection against compelled self-incrimination, and finding no impeachment exception); Commonwealth v. Triplett, 462 Pa. 244, 341 A.2d 62 (1975) (rejecting use of confessions for impeachment on unclear grounds, but apparently on some state law basis).

§ 163

1. There is widespread perception that the Supreme Court has become increasingly disenchanted with *Miranda*. See Sonenshein, *Miranda* and the Burger

---

overbearing /10 will & confession*

foundation* /p voluntari! involuntari! reliab! unreliab! /p confess!

---

§ 163. Future of Confession Law

Predicting the course of a body of law with the convoluted history of American confession law is a risky task. It is possible, however, to identify issues that are likely to be of paramount importance in both federal constitutional law as well as in state law related to confessions. In addition, it may be useful to consider matters that *should* be addressed in confession law, whether or not it is possible to predict that they will in fact be considered with any frequency or care.

Federal Constitutional Doctrines. The immediate major question for Federal constitutional confession law is the continued vitality of *Miranda*.[1] This raises two subissues. The first is whether persons should continue to have a federal constitutional right to the presence of an attorney during custodial interrogation. How this is answered may well depend upon the importance given to the right to silence during such interrogation and the value of representation in implementing that right.

If it is important that suspects be protected against unwise confessions, confessions

---

Court: Trends and Counter trends, 13 Loyola U.L.J. 405 (1982); Stone, The *Miranda* Doctrine in the Burger Court, 1977 Sup.Ct.Rev. 99. Evidence can be found in Michigan v. Tucker, 417 U.S. 433 (1974), in which the Court distinguished between the Fifth Amendment privilege against self-incrimination itself and *Miranda's* "prophylactic rules" developed to protect that right. 417 U.S. at 450. *Tucker* appeared to hold that a more rigorous or rigid exclusionary sanction applied to the privilege itself than applied to the prophylactic rules. *Tucker* "appeared to deny *Miranda's* jurisprudential legitimacy," Sonenshein, supra, at 461, and was characterized by Stone, supra at 118, as "an outright rejection of the core premise of *Miranda.*" Sonenshein, however, reads more recent decisions—especially Rhode Island v. Innis, 446 U.S. 291 (1980), on remand ___ R.I. ___, 433 A.2d 646, cert. denied 456 U.S. 930, order amended by 456 U.S. 942, and Edwards v. Arizona, 451 U.S. 477 (1981), rehearing denied 452 U.S. 973, —as reflecting the Court's reconciliation with the proposition that *Miranda* survived *Tucker.* Sonenshein, supra, at 462.

made under misperceptions regarding facts and legal matter, and confessions influenced by officers' manipulation of the "emotional tone" of the exchange, the actual assistance of counsel might reasonably be regarded—in the abstract, at least—as a valuable if not essential means of implementing suspects' interests. On the other hand, suspects' interests may be adequately protected if safeguards against physical abuse are established. It may be, in other words, that the law ought not to attempt to protect suspects from being influenced in their decision whether to confess by such subtle and not overtly improper considerations as the apparent tactical wisdom of confessing and the emotional "tone" of the situation. If this protection is not desirable, the rationale for giving suspects the right to the presence of counsel becomes less persuasive.

In addition other and perhaps more "practical" considerations may be relevant. For example, widespread waiver of the right to counsel may establish that the *Miranda* right to counsel does not, in practice, mean actual representation. Rather, it may mean only the opportunity for such representation, an opportunity that is so often foregone that in most cases it merely adds to the mechanical complexity of documenting and evaluating a suspect's decision to submit and respond to interrogation. A right to representation that is seldom implemented might well be regarded as less important than a right that, in practice, meant that suspects often received the actual assistance of attorneys during the critical proceedings.

Even if the right to counsel is regarded as a useful method of protecting legitimate and important interests held by suspects, this protection may be accomplished at too great a cost.[2] There is clearly an important societal interest in having reasonable access to reliable evidence of suspects' guilt—including confessions. Insofar as the right to the presence of counsel denies law enforcement the opportunity to obtain that evidence, it may achieve its benefits at too great a cost. Yet it is arguable that the cost—effective exercise of the right to avoid self-incrimination—is an acceptable or perhaps just an inevitable one. But if instead the right to counsel functions by requiring trial courts to exclude confessions because of relatively minor—perhaps "technical"—defects in officers' implementation practices, the cost may be regarded as much different.

The second subquestion is the justification for characterizing all or some of *Miranda's* requirements as *per se* rules. Increasing doubt is developing concerning an inflexible exclusionary sanction that is brought into play upon the prosecution's inability to show compliance with the warning requirements, the failure to provide adequate representation, and the avoidance of any interrogation where such questioning is barred. A warning may inadvertently omit the information that anything said by the suspect could be used in court. Is exclusion of a resulting confession justified without inquiry into the state of mind of the suspect when he made the decision to confess, especially whether the decision was influenced by a misperception that an oral admission would not be usable at trial? Basically, the issue is whether the *Miranda* requirements are important enough to warrant excluding all confessions related to violations of them, without inquiry into whether the confessions were in fact

---

2. See Inbau, Over-reaction—The Mischief of Miranda v. Arizona, 73 J.Crim.L. & C. 797 (1982):

> The presence of counsel at an interrogation scene . . . is the most damaging feature of *Miranda's* mandate. Why? Because of the fact that when defense counsel appears, his first act is to advise his client to keep his mouth shut. . . .
>
> On the trial court level . . . it is considered fair and proper for defense counsel to keep the defendant off the witness stand and force the prosecu-

tion to prove its case without asking him to utter a single word. It is an entirely different matter, however, to require the police to invite the presence of counsel into an interrogation room, during the *investigation* of a criminal case. This signals . . . "the end of the interrogation."

Id. at 808 (emphasis in original), citing Miranda v. Arizona, 384 U.S. 436, 517 (1966), rehearing denied 385 U.S. 890 (Harlan, J., dissenting).

voluntary in some meaningful sense of that term.[3]

If *Miranda* and *Williams* are to be abandoned, the only feasible alternative appears to be that embodied in the federal statute[4] and suggested elsewhere.[5] This approach might retain formal requirements of the sort developed in *Miranda*, but violation would not automatically require exclusion of any resulting confessions. Rather, exclusion would be required only if after considering all circumstances—including the violation of these requirements—the challenged confession is determined to be "involuntary." This seems little more than a return to pre-*Miranda* voluntariness law. Conceivably, though not probably, after years of experience with *Miranda* the lower courts would apply the voluntariness requirement with greater sensitivity to the interests of suspects and the need of law enforcement personnel and trial courts for guidance than was the case before 1966.[6]

On balance, the *Miranda* requirements should be retained. It is, of course, impossible to defend them as an effective response to all of the problems created by law enforcement custodial interrogation. On the other hand, they represent the kind of precise and specific legal requirements that are necessary for effective administration of the criminal justice system.

Any evaluation of the right to the presence of counsel must take into account the frequency with which the right is waived. It is difficult to argue that *Miranda* has resulted in suspects being actually aided during custodial interrogation by the advice and supportive presence of counsel, but it is likely that in a significant number of cases suspects perceiving that they would benefit from assistance of counsel during interrogation do invoke it, with the result that law enforcement officers simply abandon interrogation. In this sense, the right to counsel may somewhat indirectly meet needs identified in the Court's 1966 opinion. Further, in those cases—almost certainly a small minority—in which counsel is made available and officers nevertheless seek to proceed with interrogation, the right to have counsel involved is arguably important enough to lend substantial support to the right as a whole.

In regard to the *per se* nature of the requirements, an absolute exclusionary sanction for noncompliance with these seems equally necessary. Case-by-case inquiries into whether a violation has had a sufficient impact upon a suspect's decision to confess are simply too timeconsuming to be practical, a return to the unrewarding inquiries into voluntariness. Further, they would inevitably dilute the preventive impact of such rules as exist. Finally, the flexibility of most alternative approaches creates too great a risk of serving as a basis for subtle sabotage of the legal requirements by trial courts hostile to the basic policy decisions underlying the requirements. Both the need for law enforcement guidelines and the value of relatively objective standards for determining admissibility of confessions militate in favor of continued efforts to develop *per se* rules.[7]

---

3. A similar issue, of course, is raised by the Sixth Amendment right to counsel. See § 155 supra. But the narrower applicability of the Sixth Amendment right arguably makes the importance of its *per se* rules an issue of less pervasive importance.

4. 18 U.S.C.A. § 3501, discussed and quoted in § 154 supra.

5. The major recent brief for "return" to a somewhat modified version of the voluntariness requirement is Grano, Voluntariness, Free Will and the Law of Confessions, 65 Va.L.Rev. 859 (1979).

6. See Grano, Voluntariness, Free Will and the Law of Confessions, 65 Va.L.Rev. 859 (1979).

7. In Fare v. Michael C., 442 U.S. 707 (1979), rehearing denied 444 U.S. 887, the Court defended *Miranda*:

> *Miranda's* holding has the virtue of informing police and prosecutors with specificity as to what they may do in conducting custodial interrogation, and of informing courts under what circumstances statements obtained during custodial interrogation are not admissible.

442 U.S. at 718. While this brief in defense of *Miranda's* continued vitality may somewhat overstate the certainty which it offers, the effort to develop *per se* rules seems clearly to hold promise of greater certainty than the major alternatives.

If *Miranda* is retained in approximately its present form, the future of federal constitutional confession law will involve primarily the issue of waiver. Most confessions obtained during custodial interrogation will continue to be elicited in the absence of counsel. Admissibility will therefore most often turn on whether there is sufficient proof of waiver and, if so, upon whether that waiver can be shown to meet applicable criteria for determining its effectiveness. The development of more precise criteria for resolving these waiver issues should be a major priority of federal constitutional law.

State Law Issues. The extent to which a confession must be excluded solely because of a failure to promptly present the arrested suspect before a judicial officer [8] is likely to remain almost entirely a matter of state law. More problematic is whether states will—or should—develop a series of *per se* state law requirements identical or similar to those imposed by *Miranda*. If the *Miranda per se* requirements are abandoned as a matter of federal constitutional law, the state law question will be of obvious and pervasive importance. The Supreme Court's narrow construction of at least some *Miranda* issues [9] suggests the desirability of considering state requirements that can be construed more broadly than the Supreme Court is inclined to construe the federal constitutional demands.

Further Issues. Despite the tremendous amount of litigation regarding confessions, there remain a number of very basic issues that have not been definitively resolved or—often—even addressed.[10] To a large degree, *Miranda* appears to have discouraged consideration of these issues by relying upon the involvement of lawyers in the interrogation process to prevent or resolve them, or at least to present them for judicial resolution. It is now beyond doubt, however, that the reliance in *Miranda* was misplaced. *Miranda* will not result in extensive involvement of attorneys in the custodial interrogation process. Any adequate development of American confession law will have affirmatively to seek out, formulate, and resolve these issues in order to develop a reasonably adequate approach to the regulation of interrogation practices and admissibility of resulting confessions.

First, it will be necessary to define when suspects should be subject to custodial interrogation. Almost all present case law deals with interrogation conducted during an opportunity presented by the suspect's fortuitous presence in law enforcement custody. Despite the development of other safeguards, it is unfair for arrestees who are unable to secure pretrial release to, for that reason, also be subject to interrogation risks. On the other hand, if custodial interrogation is an acceptable method of investigation, it should not be rendered unavailable by the fact that a suspect is properly determined not to be subject to pretrial detention. Any rational comprehensive approach to custodial interrogation law must address specifically (a) when and under what circumstances persons in custody for reasons other than interrogation may be approached for interrogation purposes; and (b) when and under what circumstances persons not in custody may be taken into custody for purposes of interrogation.[11]

8. See § 156 supra.

9. Among the most significant are recognition of an impeachment exception to *Miranda's* exclusionary sanction, see § 162 supra, the rejection of a requirement of an express waiver of the rights, see § 153 supra, and the Court's arguable reluctance to find the threshold requirements of "custody" and "interrogation," see § 151 supra.

10. See Frey, Modern Police Interrogation Law: The Wrong Road Taken, 42 U.Pitt.L.Rev. 731 (1981), arguing that *Miranda* fails to come to grips with what police practices should be condemned and "fails to af-

ford any consistent and practical protection of the suspect's legitimate interests, however these may be defined." Id., at 735.

11. Under present law enforcement practice, the only method of compelling a suspect to appear and submit to questioning is through the grand jury subpoena process. See Miller, Dawson, Dix & Parnas, Cases and Material on Criminal Justice Administration 476 (2nd ed. 1982). It has been proposed that this subpoena power might be given to prosecutors. Id., at 481. See also, Schaefer, The Suspect and Society (1967); Kauper, Judicial Examination of the Accused—A Remedy

Second, it will be necessary to address specifically the acceptability of various techniques used either to encourage waivers of the right to the presence of counsel or, after such waivers are obtained, to encourage self-incriminating statements.[12] Obviously, classification is difficult and some techniques may be so unique as to defy inclusion in any general class. But it is possible to identify some types of techniques the propriety of which ought at least to be subjected to searching re-examination. These include deception by the officers concerning factual material or legal rules relevant to the matter under investigation, representation by the officers concerning the actual or potential value to the suspect in confessing, and efforts by the officers to manipulate the suspect's emotional tone, as by reducing the suspect's emotional barriers to giving a self-incriminating statement.

Third has been the tendency of disputes to devolve into "swearing matches" between the officers and the defendant, disputes which have been regarded as disproportionately won by the officers.[13] *Miranda* was apparently based in part upon the anticipation that whether there had been compliance with at least the *per se* requirements would involve a sufficiently simple and direct inquiry, as contrasted with an issue of voluntariness, that the swearing match problem would be eliminated or at least greatly reduced. The emergence of waiver issues under *Miranda* has largely frustrated this expectation. Whether a waiver was made and, if so, whether the circumstances rendered it ineffective often turns on factual matters so similar to those controlling under pre-*Miran-*

da voluntariness issues that the swearing match problem remains little changed.

A requirement that interaction between officers and suspects related to interrogation or waiver of interrogation rights be recorded has been proposed.[14] If such recordings existed, disputes concerning the facts related to waivers and self-incriminating statements could often be resolved more expeditiously and reliably than is presently the case. There might, of course, be problems in assuring the completeness of such recordings.

Finally, it may be useful to reconsider the role of the courts in implementing limits upon custodial interrogation. Specifically, the role of the judicial officer at the initial appearance and, of course, the duty of officers to promptly present a detained suspect may have more potential that has been recognized for implementing the legal requirements applicable to these situations. Especially if the manner in which law enforcement officers administer the required warnings and pose the opportunity to waive rights is regarded as posing a significant risk of subtle discouragement to the exercise of those rights, the administration of such warnings by a judicial officer may take on more importance. But perhaps most important, the judicial officer might be given a more important role in determining whether and under what circumstances waivers may subsequently be sought and custodial interrogation may be undertaken.

If it is determined that the initial appearance may provide a vehicle for a desirable increase in judicial involvement in the custodial interrogation process, this would be quite relevant to the question whether an exclu-

for the Third Degree, 30 Mich.L.Rev. 1224 (1932) and Kamisar, Kauper's "Judicial Examination of the Accused" Forty Years Later—Some Comments on a Remarkable Article, 73 Mich.L.Rev. 15 (1974), suggesting interrogation by police or law enforcement officers in the presence of a judicial officer.

The application of *Miranda's* right to the presence of counsel during such interrogations is considered in Note, 57 Ind.L.J. 499 (1981–82).

12. See §§ 147–49, 153 supra.

13. See § 150 supra.

14. Kamisar, Introduction, in Police Interrogation and Confessions xvii (1980); Kamisar, Brewer v. Williams—A Hard Look at a Discomforting Record, 66 Geo.L.J. 209, 237–42 (1977); Model Code of Pre-arraignment Procedure Sec. 130.4 (Official Draft, 1975). See also, Frey, Modern Police Interrogation Law: The Wrong Road Taken, 42 U.Pitt.L.Rev. 731, 736 (1981); Williams, The Authentication of Statements to the Police, [1979] Crim.L.Rev. (Brit.) 1.

sionary sanction should attach to a failure of law enforcement officers to promptly present a detained suspect.[15] Prompt presentation might reasonably be regarded as at least as essential as law enforcement officer warnings to the effective implementation of suspects' rights in regard to custodial interrogation.

The early exception to the prohibition against out-of-court statements covering confessions and admissions by an accused person appears to have developed without full consideration of the wisdom of this action. Expansion of the voluntariness requirement from pleas to such out-of-court statements of the accused similarly appears to have been rather haphazard. The next major development in confession law—the Supreme Court's 1966 decision in Miranda v. Arizona—was more carefully thought out but now appears to have been somewhat naively based. Despite the Court's intentions and efforts, *Miranda* has not resulted in extensive involvement by lawyers on behalf of suspects in actual custodial interrogation situations. If—as appears to be the case—this involvement is not a realistic objective—confession law needs to confront

more directly the numerous substantive questions that became lost in the voluntariness rule's totality of the circumstances and that were left by *Miranda* for lawyers to resolve. The lesson of both the voluntariness rule and *Miranda* is that there is no realistic alternative to direct confrontation of the major questions concerning what persons under what circumstances should be subject to custodial interrogation and what techniques should be permitted during the interrogation. Addressing these questions should be the long-run objective of "the law of confessions."

 **WESTLAW REFERENCES**

Federal Constitutional Doctrines
sh 86 sct 1602
miranda /15 86 /5 1602 & date(after 6/1/83)
sh 97 sct 1232
brewer /15 97 /5 1232 & date(after 6/1/83)

State Law Issues
110k412.2(3) /p requisite* require!

Further Issues
"custodial interrogation" /10 start! begin! commenc!
encourag! coerc! threaten! induce! help! promise! /25
   self-incrimin! waive* /25 miranda

---

15. See Section 156, supra.

Chapter 15

THE PRIVILEGE CONCERNING IMPROPERLY OBTAINED EVIDENCE

Table of Sections

---

§ 164. Introduction

Probably the most important recent development in the law of evidence as applied to criminal litigation has been the increase in requirements that evidence be excluded because of the manner in which it was obtained. These requirements are appropriately characterized as rules of privilege rather than of incompetency.[1] Generally speaking,

---

§ 164

1. See the discussion in §§ 72 and 72.1 supra concerning the distinction between rules of privilege and those of incompetency. Exclusionary sanctions, however, like rules of competency, can only be invoked by one who is—or may be—the defendant in criminal litigation. When evidence obtained in a manner violating the rights of A is offered against B in a criminal prose-

cution in which only B is a defendant, A cannot raise objection. In this sense, the exclusionary sanctions resemble the rules of incompetency. Under the terms of the example just cited, A may lack the ability to invoke an exclusionary sanction because of the personal nature of the right violated by the manner in which the evidence was obtained; see § 179 infra.

444

their purpose is not to facilitate the accurate ascertainment of facts by safeguarding against unreliable or misleading evidence but rather to implement other interests embodied in the requirements violated by the manner in which the evidence was obtained.[2]

Discussion often focuses upon what purports to be "the exclusionary rule," by which is generally meant the Supreme Court's construction of the Fourth Amendment to the United States Constitution requiring the exclusion in both state and federal criminal prosecutions of evidence tainted by a violation of that provision.[3] This is unfortunate because it tends to lead discussion away from other contexts in which exclusion may be required because of the violation of other legal requirements.[4] Whether exclusion is or should be required in these contexts presents issues significantly different but no less important than those in the Fourth Amendment context.

For this reason, it is most useful to avoid discussion of any single exclusionary "rule." Instead, this area should be conceptualized as containing numerous possible exclusionary rules or sanctions. An exclusionary sanction may attach to almost any legal requirement. There are, then, potentially as many exclusionary sanctions as there are legal requirements that might be violated by the manner in which evidence is obtained. The Fourth Amendment exclusionary sanction may provide a useful framework for considering the desirability and scope of exclusionary sanctions for other legal requirements. But it is important not to accept uncritically the Fourth Amendment framework and to impose it upon other situations that may present significantly different considerations.

It is, of course, difficult to separate discussion of exclusionary sanctions from consideration of the underlying rules which these sanctions are imposed to enforce. On the other hand, practicality precludes any effort to consider here all the possible legal requirements that might be enforced by exclusionary sanctions. This chapter consequently presents detailed discussion primarily of the exclusionary sanctions which the Supreme Court has held applicable to certain federal constitutional rights and those federal constitutional rights themselves. It is important to keep in mind, however, that state legal requirements may be construed as imposing more stringent requirements than the federal provisions and these requirements may be enforced by exclusionary sanctions developed independent of the federal requirements.

§ 165. Development of the Federal Constitutional Exclusionary Sanctions [1]

The development of exclusionary sanctions to enforce various federal constitutional rights reveals a rather haphazard and confusing progression from the clear common law position that the legality of the source of evidence has no bearing on its admissibility [2] to the Court's eventual embracement of exclusionary sanctions as the constitutionally mandated enforcement devices for a varie-

---

2. The federal constitutional prohibition against the admissibility of certain testimony by witnesses who have been exposed to exceptionally suggestive procedures, see § 174, infra, is clearly an exception and is perhaps inappropriately classified with the other matters discussed in this chapter. The line between the right violated and the right to exclusion is also somewhat unclear in regard to the federal constitutional prohibition against use of evidence that "shocks the conscience." See § 175 infra.

Exclusion of evidence obtained in violation of a subject's privilege against compelled self-incrimination has been discussed in Chapter 13. Rules relating to the admissibility of confessions are discussed separately in Chapter 14. Categorizing the exclusionary require-

ments discussed in these two chapters as rules of privilege or incompetency may also present some similar problems.

3. See § 165 infra.

4. See generally the discussion in § 166 infra.

§ 165

1. See generally, 8 Wigmore, Evidence § 2184(a) (McNaughton rev. 1961); Note, Confusion Regarding Exclusion: The Evolution of the Fourth Amendment, 23 Ariz.L.Rev. 801 (1981); 29 Am.Jur.2d Evidence Sec. 411–12; C.J.S. Evidence Sec. 187.

2. See 8 Wigmore, Evidence § 2183 (McNaughton rev. 1961).

ty of federal constitutional requirements. None of the constitutional language from which these requirements arise, of course, specifies prohibitions against the admissibility of evidence obtained by violating those requirements. It was in regard to the Fourth Amendment and its prohibition against unreasonable searches and seizures that the Supreme Court developed these prohibitions.

Federal Constitutional exclusionary sanctions appear to have originated in confusion concerning the substance of Fourth and Fifth Amendment protection. In Boyd v. United States,[3] an unsuccessful claimant in a forfeiture action sought relief from the judgment of forfeiture on the ground that the trial court erred in receiving into evidence an invoice which the claimant had been compelled to produce by order of the trial court. Both the Fourth and Fifth Amendments were invoked. The Supreme Court held that the compulsory production of the document was subject to scrutiny under the Fourth Amendment[4] and to determine whether it was reasonable turned to the Fifth Amendment's prohibition against compelled self-incrimination. Finding an "intimate relationship" between the two provisions, the Court concluded that compelled production or other seizure of a person's private books or papers to be used in evidence against him was violative of the Fifth Amendment.[5] Ultimately, the Court held that the admission into evidence of the invoice, given the manner in which it was obtained, violated both the Fourth Amendment prohibition against unreasonable searches and seizures and the Fifth Amendment prohibition against compelled self-incrimination.[6]

But in Adams v. New York [7] the Court declined to apply this early exclusionary rule to a "pure" Fourth Amendment situation. Adams sought relief from a state conviction on the ground that the state had used in evidence over his objection certain papers obtained from him in an improper search. Finding no Fifth Amendment violation in the seizure of the papers, the Court distinguished Boyd as involving compelled production of items.[8] Apparently then treating the case as one involving a violation of the Fourth [9] but not the Fifth Amendment, the Court applied what it described as "the weight of authority as well as reason," embodied in the rule that courts will not pause to inquire as to the means by which competent evidence is obtained.[10] The reason for this position was not addressed, but almost certainly was regarded by the Court as the traditional one, which relied upon the cost of excluding reliable evidence and of making time-consuming collateral inquiries into potentially complex issues relating to the manner by which offered evidence was obtained by the proffering party.[11]

Ten years later, however, in Weeks v. United States [12] the Court held that as applied in federal criminal litigation the Fourth Amendment imposed an exclusionary sanction. Prior to Weeks' trial in federal court

---

3. 116 U.S. 616 (1885). *Boyd* has been recently described by the Court as containing the "roots" of the Fourth Amendment exclusionary rule adopted in Weeks v. United States, 232 U.S. 383 (1914). See Stone v. Powell, 429 U.S. 465, 483 n. 19 (1976), on remand 539 F.2d 693, rehearing denied 429 U.S. 874.

4. 116 U.S. at 622.

5. Id. at 633.

6. Id. at 634–35. While it is certainly arguable that no specific exclusionary sanction can be found in the language of the Fifth Amendment, that provision's prohibition against a person being "compelled . . . to be a witness against himself . . . ." does address some evidence admissibility matters. It appears that at least some members of the Court have regarded any such exclusionary sanctions as are created by the federal constitution as having their basis in this wording

of the Fifth Amendment. See Mapp v. Ohio, 367 U.S. 643, 666 (1961), rehearing denied 368 U.S. 871 (Black, J., concurring) (Fourth and Fifth Amendments together require exclusion of evidence obtained in violation of Fourth Amendment's prohibition against unreasonable searches and seizures).

7. 192 U.S. 585 (1904).

8. Id. at 598.

9. The Court assumed without deciding that the constitutional provisions at issue were binding upon the state. Id. at 594.

10. Id. at 594.

11. See 8 Wigmore, Evidence § 2183 (McNaughton rev. 1961).

12. 232 U.S. 383 (1914).

for use of the mails for gambling purposes, he moved in the trial court for the return of certain property obtained in what he alleged was an improper search. The trial court denied the motion insofar as it concerned items that were pertinent to Weeks' guilt of the pending charge. When these items were later offered by the Government at trial, Weeks objected and the trial court overruled his objection. Both actions of the trial court were assigned as error on appeal. Addressing only Weeks' claim that the trial court's actions violated the Fourth Amendment,[13] the Court emphasized that the case involved the refusal of the trial court to return improperly seized items to one from whom they had been taken, not "testimony offered at a trial where the court is asked to stop and consider the illegal means by which proofs, otherwise competent, were obtained . . . ."[14] Finding constitutional and reversible error, the Court distinguished *Adams* as not presenting a criminal defendant's right, upon proper motion, to return of papers illegally seized under the Fourth Amendment.[15] The Court's discussion as to why this should make a difference is not free of ambiguity, but suggests that refusing to return illegally seized property entailed more direct involvement by the trial court in the illegality than merely admitting testimony and thus, like the affirmative compelled production of items at issue in *Boyd*, was exceptionally offensive to the constitutional values.[16] The Court also stated, "If letters and private documents can thus be [improperly] seized and held and used in evidence against a citizen accused of an offense, the protection of the Fourth Amendment declaring his right to be secure against such searches and seizures is of no value, and, so far as those thus placed are concerned, might as well be stricken from the Constitution."[17] The significance of this language is unclear, however. Perhaps the Court meant that only by removing the evidentiary incentive for such conduct could unreasonable searches and seizures be prevented. This, of course, would suggest emphasis upon the preventive function of an exclusionary sanction. But the Court might also have meant that the use of evidence obtained by an unreasonable search or seizure so further infringed Fourth Amendment protected interests that—from the perspective of one subjected to an improper search or seizure—only an exclusionary remedy rendered the federal constitutional provision "of . . . value." If this was the Court's meaning, the Fourth Amendment exclusionary sanction would seem to have been embraced in part at least because of its ability to provide a meaningful remedy for those whose rights have been violated.

The manner in which *Adams* was distinguished in *Weeks* suggests that the Court's willingness to embrace the exclusionary sanction was in part at least because as presented the issue involved not only the admissibility of evidence but also the right to possession of items improperly taken from the defendant. Thus it is arguable that the right to have evidence excluded developed as an incident to a primary right to regain possession of illegally seized items. But any relationship between the right to have evidence excluded and the existence of another right to possession of a tangible item in the possession of the prosecution was destroyed by Silverthorne Lumber Co. v. United States,[18] in which the items obtained by the Government pursuant to an unreasonable search were returned to the defendants by order of the court. A subpoena was issued

---

13. Id. at 389. While it can be urged that the Court's language in *Weeks* made clear that the exclusionary rule embraced by the Court was based entirely upon the Fourth Amendment, this was not immediately accepted. See, e.g., Marron v. United States, 275 U.S. 192, 194 (1927) (it has "long been settled" that the Fifth Amendment protects against incrimination by the use of evidence obtained in violation of the Fourth Amendment).

14. 232 U.S. at 392.

15. Id. at 396.

16. Id. at 392.

17. Id. at 393.

18. 251 U.S. 385 (1920).

directing the defendants to produce the items and upon their noncompliance the defendants were found in contempt. The Court acknowledged that the Government was seeking to restrict *Weeks* to situations in which the Government was in wrongful physical possession of items. The Government urged, in the Court's words, "that the protection of the Constitution covers the physical possession but not any advantages that the Government can gain over the object of its pursuit by doing the forbidden act." To accept this view, the Court reasoned, would be to reduce the Fourth Amendment "to a form of words." It concluded that the essence of *Weeks* "is that not merely [that] evidence [improperly] acquired shall not be used before the Court but that it shall not be used at all." [19]

In Wolf v. Colorado,[20] the Court for the first time directly addressed the effect of the Fourth Amendment upon the States. Concluding that the core of the Fourth Amendment—the security of one's privacy against arbitrary intrusion by the police—was basic to a free society and therefore implicit in the concept of orderly liberty, the Court held that under Palko v. Connecticut [21] the Fourth Amendment prohibition against unreasonable searches and seizures was enforcible against the States through the Due Process clause of the Fourteenth Amendment. But it then distinguished this aspect of the Fourth Amendment from the exclusionary remedy and found the latter not binding on the States. A number of American jurisdictions and most of the English-speaking world had rejected the exclusionary sanction. Further, an exclusionary rule raises a number of questions that are not to be so dogmatically answered as to preclude the varying solutions which spring from an allowable range of judgment on issues not susceptible of quantitative solution.[22] While the States might well be barred from affirmatively sanctioning unreasonable searches and seizures,[23] the Court concluded, the Fourth and Fourteenth Amendments did not require them to exclude evidence obtained by such methods.

In 1952, however, the Court evidenced a willingness to impose at least a limited federal constitutional exclusionary requirement, albeit as a matter of general due process law. In Rochin v. California,[24] officers improperly broke into the defendant's bedroom, seized him, and caused him to vomit, thereby obtaining certain capsules of morphine. Without discussing any Fourth Amendment implications of the facts, the Court held that Rochin's conviction in state court of possession of the morphine violated his Fourteenth Amendment right to due process. "It has long since ceased to be true that due process of law is heedless of the means by which otherwise relevant and credible evidence is obtained," the Court commented.[25] Since the law enforcement activity by which the morphine was obtained was conduct that "shocks the conscience," the conviction resting upon that evidence violated due process.

By 1961, the Court was prepared to reconsider *Wolf's* conclusion that the Fourth Amendment exclusionary rule was not binding on the states. In Mapp v. Ohio,[26] this holding of *Wolf* was reversed. Since *Wolf*, the majority explained, more than half of those states considering whether to adopt the exclusionary sanction as a matter of state law had decided to do so. The weight of the relevant authority, then, could not be said to oppose the *Weeks* rule. More important, however, the Court read experience as contradicting the *Wolf* assumption that remedies other than the exclusionary rule could

19. 251 U.S. at 391.

20. 338 U.S. 25 (1949).

21. 302 U.S. 319 (1937).

22. 338 U.S. at 28.

23. Id. ("we have no hesitation in saying that were a State affirmatively to sanction such police incursion into privacy it would run counter to the guaranty of the Fourteenth Amendment").

24. 342 U.S. 165 (1952). See generally § 175 infra.

25. 342 U.S. at 172.

26. 367 U.S. 643 (1961), rehearing denied 368 U.S. 871.

be relied upon to enforce Fourth Amendment rights. The experience and decisions of the state courts as well as the Supreme Court's own decisions recognized the "obvious futility of relegating the Fourth Amendment to the protection of other remedies . . . ." [27] Consequently, the exclusionary rule was held an essential part of both the Fourth and Fourteenth Amendments and therefore binding on the states as well as the federal government.

Once it determined that an exclusionary sanction was an essential part of the Fourth Amendment right to be free from unreasonable searches and seizures, the Court proceeded to apply it uncritically to other federal constitutional rights. In contrast to the extensive consideration and discussion of the Fourth Amendment issue in *Weeks*, *Wolf* and *Mapp*, there has been virtually no discussion accompanying the Court's subsequent determinations that exclusionary sanctions are equally essential parts of the Fifth Amendment right to counsel during custodial law enforcement interrogation,[28] the Sixth Amendment right to counsel,[29] and the right to counsel during certain pretrial identification procedures.[30]

 WESTLAW REFERENCES

sh 232 us 383
weeks & 232 +s 383 & date(after 6/1/83)
mapp /s ohio & date(after 6/1/83)

§ 166. Exclusionary Sanctions Based on Federal Nonconstitutional and State Law [1]

Despite the high profile of the *Weeks-Mapp* Fourth Amendment exclusionary rule [2] in exclusionary sanction discussion, this remedy is not limited to Fourth Amendment or even federal constitutional contexts. It is useful to consider separately the application of nonconstitutional federal exclusionary sanctions by the Supreme Court and the existence of actual or potential exclusionary sanctions as matters of state law. Further, application of exclusionary sanctions beyond federal constitutional rights may create a need to define more carefully the scope of

---

27. 367 U.S. at 652.

28. Miranda v. Arizona, 384 U.S. 436 (1966), rehearing denied 385 U.S. 890. See generally § 150 supra.

29. Brewer v. Williams, 430 U.S. 387 (1977), rehearing denied 431 U.S. 925; Massiah v. United States, 377 U.S. 201 (1964). See generally § 155 supra.

30. Gilbert v. California, 388 U.S. 263 (1967); United States v. Wade, 388 U.S. 218 (1967). See generally § 173 infra. The Court's early decisions concerning the effect of an extraordinarily suggestive identification procedure indicated that here as well an exclusionary rule would be uncritically applied. See Foster v. California, 394 U.S. 440 (1968); Stovall v. Denno, 388 U.S. 293 (1967). But Watkins v. Sowders, 449 U.S. 341 (1981), discussed in § 180 infra, may indicate at least a partial rejection of the exclusionary sanction in this situation.

§ 166

1. An extensive literature has built up concerning rights under state law that may be enforcible by means of an exclusionary sanction. Brennan, State Constitutions and the Protection of Individual Rights, 90 Harv. L.Rev. 489 (1977); Howard, State Courts and Constitutional Rights in the Day of the Burger Court, 62 Va.L. Rev. 873 (1976); Developments in the Law: The Interpretation of State Constitutional Rights, 95 Harv.L. Rev. 1324 (1982); Comment, 33 Wash. & Lee L.Rev.

909 (1976); Notes, 1979 Hamline L.Rev. 83 (1979), 15 Am.Crim.L.Rev. 339 (1978). Some discussions have focused upon particular jurisdictions, Dawson, State-Created Exclusionary Rules in Search and Seizure: A Study of the Texas Experience, 59 Tex.L.Rev. 191 (1981), or particular issues, Hancock, State Court Activism and Searches Incident to Arrest, 68 Va.L.Rev. 1085 (1982). Most of this discussion, however, fails to distinguish between developments of rights under state law, on the one hand, and the development of an exclusionary sanction to remedy violation of those rights, on the other. See, e.g., Note, 62 Marq.L.Rev. 622 (1979), urging that depositors be regarded as having a privacy interest in bank records under Wis.Const. Art. I, Sec. 11, but ignoring whether an exclusionary sanction should attach to an intrusion. Project Report: Towards An Activist Role of State Bills of Rights, 8 Harv.Civ.Rts. & Civ.Lib.L.Rev. 271, 323–50 (1973) catalogues states' adoption of "the" exclusionary rule. It fails, however, to distinguish states' pre-*Mapp* adoption of an exclusionary remedy for violations of the Fourth Amendment and adoption of a state exclusionary sanction for violations of the state constitution, state statutes, or regulations promulgated by state administrative agencies.

2. This discussion again suggests the undesirability of regarding the current situation as involving only a single exclusionary rule; see § 164 supra.

the sanctions, a matter deserving specific discussion here.

Federal Nonconstitutional Exclusionary Rules. Weeks v. United States,[3] especially when read in light of Wolf v. Colorado,[4] represented the Supreme Court's embracement of the exclusionary rule as a matter of federal judicial policy for purposes of enforcing the Fourth Amendment's prohibition against unreasonable searches and seizures. Following *Weeks*, however, the Court appeared quite willing to apply the same sanction to violations of federal nonconstitutional requirements without critically considering the need or desirability of such action.

To some extent, this action might reflect an assumption on the part of the Court that for a search to be "reasonable" under the Fourth Amendment, it must not only meet requirements found in the Amendment itself but also others in applicable legislation. While this view appears to have been later rejected by the Court,[5] it may explain cases such as Grau v. United States.[6] In *Grau*, a search warrant was issued for the search of residential premises upon a showing of what the Court found was probable cause to believe the premises were used for manufacture and possession of illicit whiskey. Under the National Prohibition Act, no search warrant was permitted to issue for a private dwelling except upon a showing that the premises had been used for unlawful *sale* of illicit liquor. Finding that the affidavit was insufficient to support the finding required by statute that the premises had been used for sale, the Court concluded that the trial court erred in failing to exclude and return to Grau items seized during execution of the warrant. No consideration was given to the possibility that the warrant may have met Fourth Amendment requirements and that noncompliance with the Act should not have mandated exclusion of the evidence.

A similar approach is evident in the Supreme Court's willingness to exclude evidence obtained in violation of the federal statutory prohibition against so-called "no knock" entries.[7] In Miller v. United States,[8] the Court examined the background of the requirement of announcement prior to forcible entry and concluded that this "is deeply rooted in our heritage and should not be given grudging application."[9] An arrest made in a private dwelling after forcible entry without such notice, then, was "unlawful" and evidence seized in a search incident to that arrest "should have been suppressed."[10] While the Court explored the rationales for the prior announcement requirement, there was no explicit attention given to the need for an exclusionary sanction nor did the Court consider whether the value of an exclusionary rule in this context might be outweighed by the loss of reliable evidence.[11]

The Court's approach to wiretapping followed a similar willingness to apply uncritically an exclusionary sanction to violation of a federal—but not a state—statute. In Olmstead v. United States,[12] the Court held that intercepting a telephone conversation by means of a wiretap was neither a search nor a seizure within the meaning of the Fourth Amendment. Further, it invoked the common law rule rendering competent evidence admissible despite the manner in which it was obtained to reject the argument that the

---

3. 232 U.S. 383 (1914). See generally § 165 supra.

4. 338 U.S. 25 (1949). See generally § 165 supra.

5. Cady v. Dombrowski, 413 U.S. 433, 449 (1973) (failure to include seized item in inventory required by state law is "purely a question of state law").

6. 287 U.S. 124 (1932).

7. 18 U.S.C.A. § 3109. The Court's sympathy for the statutory requirement of advance notice prior to entry is evident in its willingness to construe the statute, applicable by its terms only to entry to execute a

search warrant, to entry to make an arrest. See Miller v. United States, 357 U.S. 301, 306 (1958).

8. 357 U.S. 301 (1958).

9. Id. at 313.

10. Id. at 314.

11. See also, Sabbath v. United States, 391 U.S. 585 (1968) (unannounced entry by opening closed but unlocked door violated statute and required suppression of resulting evidence).

12. 277 U.S. 438 (1928).

testimony should be rendered inadmissible because the wiretapping constituted a criminal offense in the state in which it occurred. But in Nardone v. United States,[13] the Court uncritically excluded the fruits of a wiretap violating the Communications Act of 1934, despite the absence of any explicit exclusionary remedy in the statute.[14]

Critical scrutiny of the need for or desirability of an exclusionary sanction for the violation of federal nonconstitutional "law" was avoided until 1979, when the Court was asked to apply such a sanction to a violation of an administrative regulation in United States v. Caceres.[15] Neither the United States Constitution nor federal legislation limits the ability of federal law enforcement officers to monitor or record, with the consent of one of the parties, a conversation between a Government agent and a third party.[16] Nevertheless, the Internal Revenue Service promulgated regulations requiring prior administrative authorization before such monitoring is undertaken. In *Caceres*, certain monitoring had taken place without adequate authorization but the trial judge, over defense objection, admitted evidence obtained by this monitoring. The Court affirmed, rejecting Caceres' argument that the regulations were of sufficient importance to privacy interests to justify "a rigid exclusionary rule." Without questioning the importance of the regulations or examining the

value that an exclusionary rule might have in stimulating compliance with them, the Court stressed the risk that judicial development of an exclusionary sanction might encourage administrative agencies to abandon or modify such rules:

> In the long run, it is far better to have rules like those contained in the IRS Manual, and to tolerate occasional erroneous administration of the kind displayed by this record, than either to have no rules except those mandated by statute, or to have them framed in a mere precatory form.[17]

The Court did not reject out-of-hand Caceres' alternative argument that violations of the regulations should be reviewed on a case-by-case basis to determine whether exclusion of the products was desirable. Apparently engaging in the requested review, the Court concluded that the facts presented a reasonable, good faith effort on the part of the officers to comply with the regulations in a situation where approval, if requested, would have been obtained. Given this, the Court found no reason to exercise whatever discretion might exist to exclude evidence obtained in violation of the regulations.[18]

Congressional action in this area is embodied in the federal electronic surveillance statute,[19] enacted in 1968. While this statute was clearly enacted in response to the Supreme Court's holding that the Fourth Amendment applied to certain surreptitious

---

13. 302 U.S. 379 (1937).

14. The statute prohibited, among other things, "divulg[ing] . . . of [the contents of an] intercepted communication to any person." "Taken at face value," the Court concluded, this language barred testimony based on an interception conducted in violation of the Act. But it seems equally clear that the Court could have concluded that this prohibition was intended to cover efforts at "blackmail" and other extrajudicial disclosures and that, in the absence of more specific language, Congress did not intend to change the traditional rule applied in *Olmstead*.

Similarly, the Court, pursuant to its supervisory power, adopted an exclusionary sanction mandating the suppression of a confession obtained during delay that violated a federal statute requiring that arrested defendants be promptly presented before a magistrate. McNabb v. United States, 318 U.S. 332 (1942), rehearing denied 319 U.S. 784. When this requirement was incor-

porated into the Federal Rules of Criminal Procedure, the exclusionary sanction was also brought along. See Upshaw v. United States, 335 U.S. 410 (1948); Mallory v. United States, 354 U.S. 449 (1957). See generally § 156 supra.

15. 440 U.S. 741 (1979).

16. See United States v. White, 401 U.S. 745 (1971), rehearing denied 402 U.S. 990, on remand 454 F.2d 435, cert. denied 406 U.S. 962.

17. 440 U.S. at 756.

18. The Court distinguished *Miller* on the ground that Caceres' surveillance violated no statute, 440 U.S. at 755 n. 21, and left open whether exclusion would have been necessary had the regulations been required by either statute or constitutional considerations. Id., at 749–50.

19. 18 U.S.C.A. § 2510 et seq.

surveillance of the spoken word,[20] it seems equally clear that in some aspects the statute goes beyond Fourth Amendment requirements and, as a matter of Congressional policy, imposes additional protections for the underlying privacy interests. The statute contains its own exclusionary sanction,[21] which provides that neither the contents of communications intercepted in violation of the statute nor evidence derived from those contents "may be received in evidence in any trial, hearing, or other proceeding in or before any court, grand jury, department, officer, agency, regulatory body, legislative committee or other authority of the United States, a State, or a political subdivision thereof . . . ."

Exclusionary Sanctions Based on State Law. As the Supreme Court noted in *Mapp*,[22] a number of state courts had, at that time, adopted as a matter of state judicial policy exclusionary sanctions for unlawful searches and seizures. It appears, however, that these decisions consisted primarily of adoption of state exclusionary sanctions applicable to evidence obtained in violation of the Fourth Amendment, which *Wolf* had made clear was binding on the states. State exclusionary remedies of this sort, of course, are subject to Supreme Court control in regard to their "substance." State courts were free, prior to *Mapp*, to adopt exclusionary rules of this sort and, following *Mapp*, appear entitled to exclude evidence on authority of such state remedies. But whether or not a violation of the Fourth Amendment occurred remains a matter of federal constitutional law, and a state court is not entitled

to substitute its own judgment on this matter for that of the Supreme Court.[23]

On the other hand, state courts also remain free to adopt, as a matter of state law, exclusionary sanctions for violations of requirements of state constitutional, statutory, and even administrative law. Where this is done, both the decision as to whether a violation of the underlying requirement has occurred and as to whether exclusion of resulting evidence is required are matters of state law, not subject to review by the United States Supreme Court. Almost all states have state constitutional provisions similar to the Fourth Amendment.[24] Therefore, the potential exists in most if not all states to develop as a matter of state law both prohibitions against certain law enforcement techniques not barred by the Fourth Amendment and to require the exclusion of evidence obtained in violation of these prohibitions.

This potential is likely to become of increasing importance. In the view of many, the United States Supreme Court is no longer pursuing the rigorous expansionist approach towards construction of the terms of the Fourth Amendment and other federal Constitutional provisions protecting those suspected of or charged with crimes that was evident in the decisions of the "Warren Court." [25] To the extent that the substance of the Fourth Amendment fails to keep pace with what some state tribunals regard as the desirable level of sensitivity to the rights of suspects and defendants, state courts are left with what may be the tempting option of developing a body of state search and seizure law with an exclusionary sanction

---

20. Katz v. United States, 389 U.S. 347 (1967), discussed in § 169 infra.

21. 18 U.S.C.A. § 2515.

22. See § 165 supra.

23. Texas v. White, 423 U.S. 67 (1975), rehearing denied 423 U.S. 1081.

24. See, e.g., Alaska Const., Art. I, Sec. 14; Cal. Const., Art. 1, Sec. 19; Ill.Const., Art. 1, Sec. 6; N.J. Const., Art. 1, Par. 7; N.Y.Const., Art. 1, Sec. 12; Pa. Const. Art. 1, Sec. 8; Tex.Const. Art. 1, Sec. 9. In those few states lacking a state equivalent of the

Fourth Amendment, other state constitutional language may provide a basis for finding state rights similar to those protected by the Fourth Amendment. E.g., Ariz.Const., Art. 2, Sec. 8 ("No person shall be disturbed in his private affairs, or his home invaded, without authority of law."). See generally, Hancock, State Court Activism and Searches Incident to Arrest, 68 Va.L.Rev. 1085, 1123 n. 124 (1982).

25. See Wilkes, The New Federalism in Criminal Procedure: State Court Evasion of the Burger Court, 62 Ky.L.J. 421 (1974).

more protective of suspects' rights or interests than the federal Constitution.[26]

The matter is not necessarily a judicial one, of course. Just as Congress developed a statutory exclusionary rule for violations of the federal electronic surveillance statute, state legislatures remain free to enact exclusionary remedies for violations of state law requirements. Some have done so. The Florida Constitution, for example, specifically prohibits the admission of evidence obtained in violation of the document's prohibition against unreasonable searches and seizures.[27] Texas, on the other hand, has long had a statutory exclusionary rule mandating exclusion of evidence obtained in violation of either the Constitution or laws of Texas.[28] Other provisions are more limited. Massachusetts, for example, bars by statute the admission into evidence in criminal proceedings of evidence seized in a search conducted incident to arrest that was made for purposes other than locating and removing weapons or evidence of crime on the person of the suspect.[29]

Exercising their option, of course, requires that states address as a matter of state policy the same matters that the Supreme Court addressed as matters of federal constitutional policy in *Mapp*. Thus state lawmaking authorities are entitled to decide anew whether the various bases that might be invoked for an exclusionary sanction are weighty enough to justify the time consumed in administering a broadened state exclusionary rule and any increase in the sacrifice of reliable evidence of accused persons' guilt.

The option need not be exercised on an "all-or-nothing" basis. That is, there is no need for exclusionary sanctions to be adopted, either legislatively or judicially, for all violations of state law requirements, for all violations of state constitutional requirements, or even for all violations of a particular state constitutional (or statutory) mandate. In general, however, state courts appear to be reluctant to consider carefully whether, if a blanket state exclusionary sanction is undesirable, the nature of particular state consti-

---

26. State v. Opperman, 247 N.W.2d 673 (S.D.1976), on remand from 428 U.S. 364 (1976). The Supreme Court reversed the South Dakota court's earlier holding that an extensive inventory search of a properly seized automobile violated the Fourth Amendment; the South Dakota court then concluded that the inventory inspection violated the state constitution and that this violation required suppression of the evidence regardless of the Fourth Amendment.

Whether it is appropriate for state courts to construe a state constitutional provision similar in terminology to a federal counterpart inconsistently with the construction given the federal provision by the Supreme Court is, of course, open to dispute. Van de Kamp & Gerry, Reforming the Exclusionary Rule: An Analysis of Two Proposed Amendments to the California Constitution, 33 Hastings L.J. 1109 (1982), for example, criticize the California Supreme Court's construction of that state's constitutional prohibition against unreasonable searches and seizures. They urge that a different construction is appropriate only where supported by a finding that "conditions" peculiar to the state support giving the words a meaning other than that given the same words in the Fourth Amendment. Id. at 1117, 1148. They do not address, however, why adoption of a state provision similar in terms to a federal provision should not be regarded as conferring upon state courts the legitimate power to consider independently the meaning those words should be given, in light of the available evidence concerning the intent of the framers of the federal language, such evidence relating to the

understanding of the state authors and voters, and other considerations relevant to construction of constitutional language. See also, Hale, Searches and Seizures in Violation of an Alabama Statute, 40 Ala.Law. 527 (1979) (Alabama courts should not apply exclusionary sanction for violation of state law, apparently because they are without authority to do so).

27. Fla.Const. Art. I, Sec. 12 ("Articles or information obtained in violation of this right shall not be admissible in evidence"). See Comment, 10 Fla.S.U. L.Rev. 369 (1982).

28. Vernon's Ann.Tex.Code Crim.P., art. 38.23. Dawson, State-Created Exclusionary Rules in Search and Seizure: A Study of the Texas Experience, 59 Tex. L.Rev. 191 (1981). See also, Alaska R.Crim.P. 26(g) (evidence illegally obtained may not be used for any purpose); R.I.Gen.L.1956, § 9–19–25 ("In the trial of any action in any court of this state, no evidence shall be admissible where the same shall have been procured by, through or in consequence of any illegal search and seizure as prohibited in section 6 of article 1 of the constitution of the state of Rhode Island.").

29. Mass.Gen.L.Ann. c. 276, § 1. This provision appears designed to change the result reached as a matter of Fourth Amendment law in United States v. Robinson, 414 U.S. 218 (1973) (search may be made incident to arrest even if on facts of case there is no reason to believe and in fact no belief that arrestee has weapon or destructible evidence).

tutional or statutory provisions is such that an exclusionary sanction would appropriately be made available for their violation.

An example of a more careful approach to these matters is Commonwealth v. Musi,[30] in which the defendant urged the exclusion of evidence obtained through a search pursuant to a warrant. No copy of the warrant and supporting affidavit, however, had been served on the persons present or the possessor of the item seized, although such service was required by state law. Addressing the question whether exclusion was required, the court explored several possible justifications that might require an exclusionary sanction and found none applicable. First, violation of the service requirement cast no doubt on the reliability of the evidence obtained. Second, there had been no showing that noncompliance with the service requirement constituted "intolerable government conduct which was widespread and cannot otherwise be controlled." Nor, third, was there any showing that the governmental conduct was particularly reprehensible so as to suggest that the need to preserve judicial integrity demanded application of the exclusionary sanction. Finally, the defendant had failed otherwise to show harm or prejudice to important interests that justified the extraordinary exclusionary sanction. In the absence of a showing that the case came within at least one of these categories, the court declined to adopt an exclusionary sanction for the state's requirement of service of a copy of a search warrant.[31]

Coverage of Nonconstitutional Exclusionary Sanctions. Exclusionary rules based on prohibitions other than federal constitutional rights present at least one major issue not raised by many or most federal constitutional exclusionary sanctions. It appears quite clear that the Fourth Amendment and similar federal constitutional provisions are designed to impose only outer limits within which state criminal justice systems are free to make numerous choices not dictated by federal constitutional law. Because of this aspect of the nature of the federal rights, *Mapp* and subsequent cases assume that if conduct violates the federal requirements, exclusion is appropriate.

But if exclusionary remedies are adopted for violation of statutory requirements or perhaps for state constitutional requirements more detailed in nature than their federal counterparts, this approach may be inappropriate. State law requirements related to criminal procedural matters reflect a wider variation in importance than do federal constitutional demands. While all federal constitutional requirements may be important enough to demand enforcement by exclusionary sanction, this may not be true of state requirements. Where the process by which search warrants are applied for, issued, executed, and returned is governed by detailed state statutory provisions, for example, some but not all of those requirements may be appropriate for enforcement by exclusionary sanction. The nature of many contexts to which the exclusionary sanction may be applied beyond federal constitutional law suggests a need for selectivity in determining what violations should invoke the exclusionary sanction.

---

30. 486 Pa. 102, 404 A.2d 378 (1979).

31. 486 Pa. at 114, 404 A.2d at 384. In contrast, consider the apparent position of the California Constitution barring judicially-created state exclusionary rules and limiting the state legislature's ability to create such sanctions. As a consequence of a 1982 initiative, the California Constitution now contains the following provision:

(d) Right to Truth-in-Evidence. Except as provided by statute hereafter enacted by a two-thirds vote of the membership in each house of the Legislature, relevant evidence shall not be excluded in any criminal proceeding. . . . Nothing in this section shall affect any existing statutory rule of evidence relating to privilege or hearsay, or Evidence Code, Sections 352, 782 or 1103. . . .

Cal.Const. Art. I, Sec. 28. Unlike other proposals for modification of California's state exclusionary rules, this provision makes no accommodation for exclusion required by the federal Constitution and severely limits legislative discretion concerning exclusionary sanctions. See Van de Kamp & Gerry, Reforming the Exclusionary Rule: An Analysis of Two Proposed Amendments to the California Constitution, 33 Hastings L.J. 1109, 1111–12 n. 9 (1982).

The matter is illustrated and a possible approach to it is reflected in the Supreme Court's treatment of the issue as raised by the federal statute regulating electronic surveillance of the spoken word.[32] The statute is quite detailed in its requirements, especially those governing the applications for and issuance, execution, and return of a court order authorizing interceptions of communications protected by the statute. Further, the statutory exclusionary rule on its face might be read as mandating exclusion of evidence which is the product of any violation of any of the statutory requirements. In United States v. Giordano,[33] the Supreme Court rejected such a construction of the statute. Instead, it held that Congress intended to mandate suppression only where:

> there is failure to satisfy any of those statutory requirements that directly and substantially implement the congressional intent to limit the use of intercept procedures to those situations clearly calling for the employment of this extraordinary investigative device.[34]

The inquiry required by the *Giordano* criterion is a somewhat subjective one. It is arguable that the Court, in applying it, has been insufficiently sensitive to the potential significance of some of the statutory requirement to the ultimate legislative purpose of limiting the use of surveillance techniques covered by the statute.[35] On the other hand, there seems no reasonable alternative to the basic approach of *Giordano*, which might reasonably serve as a model for administration of exclusionary sanctions that cover other detailed requirements.[36] The underlying legislative (or constitutional) purpose must be ascertained and an effort

must be made to determine how particular requirements relate to that purpose. Exclusion is appropriate only if the violated requirement appears to "directly and substantially implement" that purpose. To exclude evidence obtained following violation of any requirement, without an inquiry of this sort, would be a clear perversion of the purposes of the exclusionary sanction.

 WESTLAW REFERENCES

Federal Nonconstitutional Exclusionary Rules
electronic! telephone* conversation* communicat! /s
   surveillance tap tapped tapping bug bugged bugging
   wiretap! /s "exclusionary rule*"
110k394.3 /p "exclusionary rule*"
digest,synopsis(18 +s 2510 /p conversation
   communicat! wiretap! surveillance electronic! telephon!)

Coverage of Nonconstitutional Exclusionary Sanctions
suppress! exclude excluded exclusion excluding /p
   "court order*" /p intercept!

---

§ 167. Proceedings to Which Exclusionary Sanctions Are Applicable [1]

It is reasonably clear that the major federal constitutional exclusionary sanctions apply only to criminal-type litigation. Thus they create exceptions to, rather than change, the traditional rule that the manner in which relevant evidence is obtained does not affect its admissibility. But other exclusionary rules, by their terms, may be broader. Thus the statutory exclusionary rule in the federal electronic surveillance statute bars the use of evidence related to a violation of that statute "in any trial, hearing, or other proceeding in or before any court, grand jury, department, officer, agen-

32. 18 U.S.C.A. § 2510 et seq.

33. 416 U.S. 505 (1974).

34. Id. at 527.

35. See United States v. Donovan, 429 U.S. 413 (1977) (failure to name in application for intercept order a suspect whose conversations were to be intercepted did not require suppression of resulting evidence, because statutory requirement for identifying such persons in application does not play a substantive role in statutory scheme).

36. But consider proposals to limit exclusion of evidence to those situations where a "substantial" viola-

tion of the underlying rule has been established. See § 177 infra.

§ 167

1. See generally, De Reuil, Applicability of the Fourth Amendment in Civil Cases, 1963 Duke L.J. 472; Comment, 19 Baylor L.Rev. 263 (1967); Note, 55 Va.L. Rev. 1484 (1969); 29 Am.Jur.2d Evidence § 410; Annot., 5 A.L.R.3d 670; C.J.S. Evidence § 187; Dec.Digest Evidence ⇔154.

cy, regulatory body, legislative committee, or other authority of the United States, a State, or a political subdivision thereof . . . ." [2] Unquestionably, this is far broader than *Mapp's* Fourth Amendment exclusionary demand.

It is important to distinguish from the issue under discussion here the separate question of whether a violation of the underlying rule occurred. Efforts to apply exclusionary sanctions to noncriminal situations tend to confuse the two. For example, an objection that an offering party in divorce litigation obtained the evidence illegally involves two different questions. If reliance is placed on *Mapp's* Fourth Amendment exclusionary rule, the objecting party must first overcome the "substantive" problem posed by the limitation of the Fourth Amendment to governmental action.[3] No Fourth Amendment violation took place if the proffered evidence was obtained by private persons acting in their private capacities. Only if a Fourth Amendment violation is found—or if an exclusionary sanction is found applicable to some criminal, tort or property law rule the offering party violated—is it necessary to consider whether the exclusionary rule at issue applies to noncriminal litigation such as divorce proceedings.[4]

Most judicial concern has focused upon the application of the federal constitutional exclusionary rules and the Fourth Amendment sanction in particular. Insofar as these rules apply to "criminal" litigation, question has arisen as to their application to aspects of such litigation other than the determination of the defendant's guilt or innocence. Beyond technically "criminal" litigation, different considerations are raised by the rules' application to "quasi-criminal" litigation and "purely" civil proceedings.

Grand Jury Proceedings. Following its tradition of holding the rules of evidence inapplicable to grand jury proceedings,[5] the Supreme Court in United States v. Calandra [6] held the *Weeks-Mapp* Fourth Amendment exclusionary rule inapplicable as well. Thus a witness called before the grand jury was held to have no right to refuse to respond to questions on the ground that the questions were the product of a violation of the witness' Fourth Amendment rights. In reaching this result, the Court posed the controlling question as whether the potential injury to the role and function of the grand jury in applying the exclusionary rule would be outweighed by the benefits of the application of the rule in this context.[7] Applying the rule, it then reasoned, would greatly impede the valuable flexibility of the grand jury. Further, expanding the exclusionary rule to this extent would provide little incremental deterrent effect; few law enforcement officers would be encouraged to violate suspects' rights to obtain evidence to use in grand jury proceedings if that evidence could not be used at trial.

In Gelbard v. United States,[8] however, the Court held that the broad terms of the federal electronic surveillance statute required a different result. A grand jury witness, therefore, may not be penalized for refusing to respond to questions if those questions were based upon information obtained in violation of the witness' rights under the statute. This does not necessarily mean, however, that an indicted defendant is entitled to attack the indictment as based upon evidence or information obtained in violation of his rights under the statute, and the Court's discussion in *Gelbard* suggested that the statute was not intended to create this result.[9]

---

2. 18 U.S.C.A. § 2515.

3. See § 169 infra.

4. Sackler v. Sackler, 15 N.Y.2d 40, 255 N.Y.S.2d 83, 203 N.E.2d 481 (1964) (evidence obtained by husband and private detective admissible in divorce proceeding because Fourth Amendment does not apply to private searches).

5. See generally, Costello v. United States, 350 U.S. 359 (1956) (indictment cannot be attacked on basis that it was returned on hearsay).

6. 414 U.S. 338 (1974).

7. Id. at 348–52.

8. 408 U.S. 41 (1972).

9. Id. at 60.

Sentencing. The Supreme Court has not addressed the question whether the Fourth Amendment exclusionary rule bars the use of evidence at a post-conviction sentencing hearing, where the issue is not guilt or innocence but the severity of the penalty to be imposed. In Estelle v. Smith,[10] however, a unanimous Supreme Court held that evidence obtained in violation of a defendant's Sixth and Fourteenth Amendments right to counsel could not be used in a capital sentencing procedure. A majority further concluded that evidence obtained in violation of defendants' *Miranda*-type right to be warned of their right to silence before a psychiatric interview could not be used in this context. It may be, of course, that the unique importance of the life-death decision made in capital sentencing proceedings justifies application in those contexts of exclusionary rules that need not be applied in non-capital sentencing situations. But such a distinction is difficult to defend.

If a *Calandra*-type analysis [11] were undertaken here, a quite viable argument can be made that application of the federal constitutional exclusionary rules to sentencing would provide little incremental preventive effect but would significantly frustrate effective implementation of sentencing inquiries. Unfortunately, the *Smith* Court did not address the matter or even the applicability in this situation of the balancing approach used in *Calandra*. It may be, of course, that Fifth and Sixth Amendment rights are of greater importance to fair trial interests than Fourth Amendment rights and therefore that the *Calandra*-type of balancing analysis is appropriate only for considering the applicability of the Fourth Amendment exclusionary rule to situations such as grand jury appearances and criminal sentencing.

Quasi-Criminal Proceedings. It is clear that the Fourth Amendment exclusionary rule has some applicability to noncriminal litigation brought by a governmental entity against a person, at least where the litigation imposes what can be construed as a penalty and where this is imposed because of the person's commission of criminal activity. In One 1958 Plymouth Sedan v. Commonwealth of Pennsylvania,[12] the state had filed a forfeiture proceeding concerning an automobile owned by one McGonigle under a statute that gave the state a right to title to the vehicle upon proof that the vehicle had been used in the criminal transportation of illicit liquor. The forfeiture was clearly a penalty for the commission of a criminal act by McGonigle, the Court reasoned, and in light of the value of the vehicle could constitute a harsher penalty than could be imposed in a prosecution. Consequently, it would be incongruous to exclude the evi-

10. 451 U.S. 454 (1981). Dispute also exists as to the applicability of exclusionary sanctions in proceedings to revoke probation. Many courts—probably a majority—have held the major exclusionary sanctions inapplicable in this context. United States v. MacKenzie, 601 F.2d 221 (5th Cir. 1979), cert. denied 444 U.S. 1018; United States v. Frederickson, 581 F.2d 711, 713 (8th Cir. 1978) (all reported cases decline to apply Fourth Amendment exclusionary rule); Harris v. State, 270 Ark. 634, 606 S.W.2d 93 (1980); State v. Davis, 375 So.2d 69 (La.1979). See also, State v. Sears, 553 P.2d 907 (Alaska 1976) (state exclusionary rule not applicable) and State v. Spratt, 102 R.I. 192, 386 A.2d 1094 (1978) (neither Fourth Amendment nor state statutory exclusionary rule applicable). The rationale most often given is that under a *Calandra*-type analysis any increase in prevention accomplished by such an application of exclusionary sanctions would be outweighed by the harm done to the rehabilitative and protective functions of probation. See State v. Alfaro, 127 Ariz. 578, 623 P.2d 8 (1980). A substantial number of courts, however, have found exclusionary sanctions applicable in this context. United States v. Workman, 585 F.2d 1205 (4th Cir. 1978), appeal after remand 617 F.2d 48; Adams v. State, 153 Ga.App. 41, 264 S.E.2d 532 (1980); Grubbs v. State, 373 So.2d 905 (Fla.1979); Jones v. State, 567 S.W.2d 209 (Tex.Crim.App.1978). See generally, Annot., 77 A.L.R.3d 636; Dec.Digest Crim.L. ⊜982.9(5).

A similar but less frequently litigated issue is presented by parole revocation proceedings. Compare In re Martinez, 1 Cal.3d 641, 83 Cal.Rptr. 382, 463 P.2d 734 (1970), cert. denied 400 U.S. 851 (search and seizure and confession exclusionary rules not applicable) with People ex rel. Piccarillo v. State Board of Parole, 48 N.Y.2d 76, 421 N.Y.S.2d 842, 397 N.E.2d 354 (1979) (exclusionary sanctions in Fourth Amendment and state constitution for illegally seized evidence applicable in parole revocation proceedings). See generally, Dec.Digest, Pardon & Parole ⊜14.19.

11. See text at note 7 supra.

12. 380 U.S. 693 (1965), on remand 418 Pa. 457, 211 A.2d 536.

dence in the criminal proceeding but admit it in the forfeiture proceeding based upon the same criminal violation. "[T]he exclusionary rule," the Court concluded, "is applicable to forfeiture proceedings such as the one involved here."

But the matter was again addressed in United States v. Janis,[13] a civil proceeding for a tax refund in which the Government counterclaimed for the unpaid balance of the assessment. The assessment was based upon information concerning Janis' illegal bookmaking activities, obtained by state law enforcement officers pursuant to a defective search warrant but nevertheless in the "good faith" belief that the search was permissible. The lower federal courts held that the evidence from the unlawful search could not be utilized by the Government in the tax litigation. The Supreme Court reversed, concluding that "exclusion from federal civil proceedings of evidence unlawfully seized by a state criminal enforcement officer has not been shown to have a sufficient likelihood of deterring the conduct of the state police so that it outweighs the societal costs imposed by the exclusion."[14]

The significance of *Janis* is not clear. The case may, of course, rest heavily upon the intersovereign nature of the situation

and thus have no application where the evidence was improperly seized by agents of the sovereign bringing the noncriminal action.[15] Thus the Fourth Amendment exclusionary rule may remain applicable to even civil proceedings brought by the violating sovereign, at least where the objective of those proceedings is to impose what appears to be a penalty.[16] On the other hand, not all relief gained by a governmental entity may be a penalty; the exclusionary rule has been held inapplicable to a suit by the violating sovereign where the sovereign sought only compensation and not "punitive" damages.[17] Perhaps adequate deterrence is accomplished by prohibiting the sovereign from using illegally seized evidence to impose punitive sanctions and that exclusion is not required in what are essentially compensatory situations.

Where the evidence is not offered in support of a claim made by the violating sovereign but instead is offered in defense to a claim made by the wronged person, different considerations may apply. Permitting defensive use may not significantly blunt the preventive function of the rule. More important, a wronged person who seeks to benefit from the illegal conduct may be demanding the sort of remedial relief that the

13. 428 U.S. 433 (1976), on remand 540 F.2d 1022, rehearing denied 429 U.S. 874.

14. Id. at 454.

15. See Vander Linden v. United States, 502 F.Supp. 693 (S.D.Iowa 1980) (*Janis* limited to intersovereign violations and therefore evidence illegally obtained by federal officers excluded in civil action for refund of taxes and fraud penalty).

Of course, *Janis* may also be affected by the Court's apparent conclusion that the violation was a "good faith" one. See § 177 infra.

16. Lower courts have found the Fourth Amendment exclusionary rule applicable to proceedings brought by governmental units to enjoin conduct sought to be established by unlawfully seized evidence. Parish of Jefferson v. Bayou Landing Limited, Inc., 350 So.2d 158 (La.1977); State v. Spoke Committee, 270 N.W.2d 339 (N.D.1978). The rule has also been found applicable to proceedings before the Federal Trade Commission for an order requiring the respondent to cease and desist from certain activity, Knoll Associates, Inc. v. FTC, 397 F.2d 530 (7th Cir. 1968), and to a

treble damage action brought by a state under the federal antitrust laws. State of Iowa v. Union Asphalt & Roadoils, Inc., 281 F.Supp. 391 (S.D.Iowa 1968), affirmed sub nominee, Standard Oil Co. v. Iowa, 408 F.2d 1171 (8th Cir. 1969). In Board of Selectmen of Framingham v. Municipal Court, 373 Mass. 783, 369 N.E.2d 1145 (1977) illegally obtained evidence was held inadmissible in a proceeding to discharge a police officer. But compare, Ross v. Springfield School District No. 19, 56 Or.App. 197, 641 P.2d 600 (1982) (improperly obtained evidence of teacher's sexual misconduct held admissible in action for judicial review of teacher's dismissal citing *Janis*), and People v. Harfmann, 638 P.2d 745 (Colo.1981) (exclusionary rule not applicable to proceeding to discipline attorney). See generally Annot., 20 A.L.R.4th 546.

17. State Forester v. Umpqua River Navigation Co., 258 Or. 10, 478 P.2d 631 (1970), cert. denied 404 U.S. 826 (exclusionary rule inapplicable in suit by state subdivision created for firefighting purposes to recover actual costs for fighting fire caused by defendant's alleged negligence).

exclusionary rule is not intended to provide.[18]

"Purely" Civil Litigation. There is widespread, but not universal, agreement that the Fourth Amendment exclusionary sanction is inapplicable to litigation in which no governmental entity has a significant interest. Such litigation presents an important need for reliable evidence, of course, and there is reason to doubt that exclusion significantly serves to discourage official lawlessness. Thus in Honeycutt v. Aetna Insurance Co.,[19] the Fifth Circuit, relying heavily upon *Calandra,* held that defendant insurance company could use illegally seized evidence tending to show that the plaintiff insured intentionally started the fire at issue and thus was not entitled to benefits under the fire insurance policy at issue.[20]

A somewhat different situation is presented, however, when the objection to evidence in a civil proceeding is based upon wrongful conduct not of law enforcement officers but of the offering party. Since such conduct is generally private, no Fourth Amendment issue is raised. But the objection does require consideration of whether in civil litigation the policies that support the exclusionary sanctions applicable to criminal and quasi-

criminal litigation also support a rule applicable to purely civil litigation that renders evidence inadmissible upon a showing that it was obtained because of the wrongful conduct of the offering party. The leading case for exclusion, Williams v. Williams,[21] involved evidence offered by a husband in a divorce proceeding. The evidence had been obtained by the husband during an unauthorized entry into the wife's automobile. Holding the evidence inadmissible, the court reasoned that no individual should have greater rights than the government to invade the rights of others and that to admit the evidence would be to recognize such a greater right in the husband.

On balance, however, the *Williams* result is questionable. Adoption of such a rule as a preventive measure would be reasonable only upon a determination that the underlying problem of private lawlessness, perhaps of the sort at issue, is sufficiently widespread and immune from other solutions to justify an effort to deal with it by means of evidence law. It is unlikely that this determination can be made regarding private lawlessness in general or concerning most if not all subcategories of private lawlessness that might be developed. Whether a version of

---

18.   Jonas v. City of Atlanta, 647 F.2d 580 (5th Cir. 1981) (not error, on facts of case, to admit illegally seized evidence offered by defendant in § 1983 suit based on alleged wrongful arrest, mistreatment, and seizure of car). However, the court expressed "grave reservations" as to whether illegally seized evidence could be admitted to substantiate a "good faith" defense in such litigation. 647 F.2d at 588 n. 12. Compare Tanuvasa v. City and County of Honolulu, 2 Hawaii App. 102, 626 P.2d 1175 (1981), cert. granted (not error in damage action against police officers' employer to exclude illegally obtained evidence where, in addition, evidence was "remote" and "speculative").

19.   510 F.2d 340 (7th Cir. 1975), cert. denied 421 U.S. 1011.

20.   Most courts appear inclined to follow this view. See, e.g., Lamartiniere v. Department of Employment, 372 So.2d 690 (La.App.), writ denied, 375 So.2d 945 (La.) (defendant in civil action for employment claim not barred from using evidence seized in search under defective warrant to support defense that employee had been discharged for work-related misconduct). But see Tanuvasa v. City and County of Honolulu, 2 Hawaii App. 102, 626 P.2d 1175, 1181 (1981), cert.

granted ("The weight of authority favors the suppression of evidence obtained by the defendants by an unconstitutional search, even in civil cases.").

State courts have split on whether state statutes dealing with administration of chemical tests to determine drivers' intoxication affect admissibility of evidence in civil actions for damages based on the drivers' conduct. Compare McNitt v. Citco Drilling Co., 397 Mich. 384, 245 N.W.2d 18 (1976) (testimony based on blood tests taken in violation of statute not admissible in civil wrongful death action) with Tucker v. Pahkala, 268 N.W.2d 728 (Minn.1978) (similar evidence held admissible, citing *Janis*). The Georgia statute, Ga.Code § 68A–902.1, seems clearly to render results inadmissible in civil as well as criminal litigation, but has been held to permit the use of the evidence to impeach a testifying party. Ensley v. Jordan, 244 Ga. 435, 260 S.E.2d 480 (1979).

21.   8 Ohio Misc. 156, 221 N.E.2d 622 (1966). See also, Poor v. Di Mucci Home Builders, Inc., 103 Ill.App. 3d 543, 59 Ill.Dec. 581, 431 N.E.2d 1338 (1982) (in damage action, trial court did not abuse its discretion in excluding evidence derived from borings obtained by party's unlawful entry onto realty owned by other party).

the "judicial integrity" concern [22] justifies a purely civil exclusionary sanction is still more problematic. Even though this is so defined as to merge almost entirely into the preventive concern, it is doubtful that it can provide the support needed for such a dramatic departure from traditional evidence principles.

WESTLAW REFERENCES

Grand Jury Proceedings

"grand jury" "grand juries" /p "exclusionary rule*"

Sentencing

sentencing postconviction /p "exclusionary rule*" "fourth amendment"

quasicriminal /p "exclusionary rule*"

Purely Civil Litigation

civil private /p "exclusionary rule*" % topic(110) title(state people)

§ 168. Policy Bases for Exclusionary Sanctions [1]

The rationales for exclusionary sanctions, of course, are relevant to the basic question as to whether such sanctions are appropriate at all. In addition, however, they must also serve as the basis for a reasoned approach to resolving a number of subissues concerning the scope of exclusionary sanctions and the procedural manner of enforcing them.[2]

The policy considerations relevant to the wisdom of exclusionary sanctions have been treated in the preceding discussion almost exclusively in terms of the *Weeks-Mapp*

Fourth Amendment exclusionary rule.[3] While this is undoubtedly an important doctrine, it would be unfortunate for exclusionary sanction discussion to be limited to or even focused upon this context. Whether other constitutional, statutory, judicially-created, or administrative requirements should be enforced by exclusionary sanctions raises similar but distinguishable issues.[4] The debate concerning the Fourth Amendment exclusionary rule may offer a model for discussion of exclusionary sanctions in general or other particular exclusionary rules. But this model, as developed by the Supreme Court's decisions, may not be appropriate in other contexts. Moreover, some of the conclusions reached in the Fourth Amendment debate—assuming they are proper in that context—may not apply in other situations.

Discussion most appropriately begins with the assumption that relevant evidence should be admitted in the absence of important reasons for excluding it. Therefore, it is important to identify and consider the various rationales that might be invoked to defend an evidentiary sanction that renders relevant evidence inadmissible because it was obtained in a way that violated certain rules of conduct. In addition, similar attention must be paid to considerations that might outweigh or counterbalance those factors militating in favor of exclusionary sanctions or broad construction or application of those exclusionary sanctions as are appropriate. Finally, it is necessary to consider an

---

22. See § 168 infra.

§ 168

1. Cann & Egbert, The Exclusionary Rule: Its Necessity in Constitutional Democracy, 23 How.L.J. 299 (1980); Geller, Enforcing the Fourth Amendment: The Exclusionary Rule and Its Alternatives, 1975 Wash. U.L.Q. 621; Kaplan, The Limits of the Exclusionary Rule, 26 Stan.L.Rev. 1027 (1974); LaFave, Improving Police Performance Through the Exclusionary Rule, 30 Mo.L.Rev. 391 (1965); Miles, Decline of the Fourth Amendment: Time to Overrule Mapp v. Ohio? 27 Cath. U.L.Rev. 9 (1977); Paulsen, The Exclusionary Rule and Misconduct by the Police, 52 J.Crim.L., C. & P.S. 255 (1961); Sunderland, Liberals, Conservatives, and the Exclusionary Rule, 71 J.Crim.L. & C. 343 (1980); Sunderland, The Exclusionary Rule: A Requirement of Constitutional Principle, 69 J.Crim.L. & Crim. 141

(1978). For an interesting exchange, compare Kamisar, Is the Exclusionary Rule an "Illogical" or "Unnatural" Interpretation of the Fourth Amendment? 62 Judicature 66 (1978) with Wilkey, The Exclusionary Rule: Why Suppress Valid Evidence? 62 Judicature 214 (1978). See also, Kamisar, The Exclusionary Rule in Historical Perspective: The Struggle to Make the Fourth Amendment More than "An Empty Blessing," 62 Judicature 337 (1978); Wilkey, A Call for Alternatives to the Exclusionary Rule: Let Congress and the Trial Courts Speak, 62 Judicature 351 (1978).

2. See infra, for example, § 177 (good faith and other exceptions), § 178 (impeachment exception), § 179 (personal nature of rights), and § 181 (enforcement in collateral attacks upon convictions).

3. See § 165 supra.

4. See generally § 166 supra.

appropriate analysis for evaluation of the sometimes competing considerations.

Relevant Considerations. Proponents of exclusionary sanctions defend the rules on three basic grounds.

(1) Preventive Effect. A major function that might be served by exclusionary sanctions, of course, is the prevention of future violations of the rule being enforced by the exclusion of evidence. In the context of the Fourth Amendment exclusionary rule, the Supreme Court has indicated that prevention might be expected to occur in two distinct ways: deterrence and "education" or "assimilation."[5]

The extent to which conduct, especially law enforcement conduct, is and can be affected by the threat of excluding evidence in a criminal trial has been vigorously debated.[6] Detractors of the exclusionary sanctions argue that in many contexts law enforcement officers are subjected to influences that will often or invariably be more effective than the threat of excluding evidence. Officers' perception of personal safety considerations, for example, or the expectations of peers or immediate supervisors may suggest courses of action contrary to legal rules. If the consequence of violating the legal rules is at most the possible exclusion of evidence at some distant time, these other considerations are likely to be determinative. In other situations, the objective of gathering admissible evidence may not be a paramount consideration. It follows, of course, that excluding such evidence as is obtained is unlikely to affect officers' conduct.

Even if officers are inclined to comply with legal requirements of which they are aware and which they can understand, exclu-sionary rules may not result in their being provided with the information necessary for compliance. This may occur because courts and prosecutors fail to communicate legal requirements to field officers, at least in language that is both understandable and meaningful to these officers. It may also occur because the underlying rules, especially those developed in caselaw through the common law method, are insufficiently clear to permit statement in such terms. Further, circumstances may provide a fertile ground for the development of a disinclination to comply. Objections may be raised in so few cases that officers can realistically rely on the absence of challenge. Or, officers may find that they can frequently, by misrepresentation of the facts, prevail over any challenge that may be raised.

But prevention may occur by means other than such simple deterrence. In the Fourth Amendment context, the Court has referred to the "educative effect" as more important than immediate deterrence.[7] Emphasis upon the content and importance of the underlying legal requirements during enforcement of those requirements through the exclusionary sanction may encourage law enforcement authorities and others, consciously or otherwise, to incorporate those requirements into their own value systems. If the requirements become part of these value systems, it is assumed that they will often be followed as a matter of internal and perhaps unconscious preference, without regard to the threat of concrete sanctions for acting otherwise.

The success of exclusionary sanctions in general, and the Fourth Amendment rule in particular, in accomplishing prevention through either of these methods is difficult to evaluate. Empirical research has been

---

5. Stone v. Powell, 428 U.S. 465, 492 (1976) on remand 539 F.2d 693, rehearing denied 429 U.S. 874.

6. Empirical research has been minimal and troubled by methodological problems. The classic study is Oaks, Studying the Exclusionary Rule in Search and Seizure, 37 U.Chi.L.Rev. 665 (1970). See also, Canon, Is the Exclusionary Rule in Failing Health? 62 Ky.L.J. 681 (1974); Spiotto, Search and Seizure: An Empirical Study of the Exclusionary Rule and Its Alternatives, 2 J. Legal Studies 243 (1973). See generally, Kamisar, Does the Exclusionary Rule Affect Police Behavior? 62 Judicature 70 (1978).

7. Stone v. Powell, 428 U.S. 465, 492 on remand 539 F.2d 639, rehearing denied 429 U.S. 874 (1976) (referring to "over the long term").

undertaken concerning the effect of exclusionary sanctions for unreasonable searches and seizures, but in part because of severe methodological problems it is inconclusive.[8]

(2) "Judicial Integrity" Considerations. Proponents of exclusionary sanctions suggest [9] that exclusion can be justified in whole or in part on the basis of what the Supreme Court in Elkins v. United States [10] called "the imperative of judicial integrity." [11] But it is not always clear what is meant by this. The argument may, of course, be that it is wrong in itself, apart from any consequences that might flow therefrom, for courts to use evidence tainted by illegality committed in its obtainment.

On the other hand, some proponents of exclusionary sanctions appear to regard the judicial integrity argument as a utilitarian one, emphasizing the undesirable effects seen as flowing from the use by courts of improperly obtained evidence. Justice Brandeis' dissent in Olmstead v. United States,[12] for example, suggests that he regarded judicial rejection of evidence obtained by illegality as a valuable and perhaps necessary precondition to courts' ability to prevent further illegality. Unless courts preserve their status as law abiding by declining to utilize the fruits of others' illegal actions, they will lose their ability to encourage law abiding conduct by example and perhaps by threat.

Whether this latter view of the judicial integrity argument is consistent with reality is, at best, problematic. It is at least arguable that the public's perception of courts suffers greater harm when the courts are seen as releasing guilty persons for "technical" evidentiary reasons than when members of the public observe courts convicting guilty persons by using illegally obtained evidence.

In the context of the Fourth Amendment exclusionary rule, the Supreme Court has quite narrowly defined the considerations of judicial integrity that it regards as relevant to that sanction. In Janis v. United States [13] the Court commented, "The primary meaning of 'judicial integrity' in the context of evidentiary rules is that the courts must not commit or encourage violations of the Constitution." [14] Under this view, the imperative of judicial integrity has significance (as long as the courts themselves have not perpetrated the wrong) only if admission of the evidence would encourage further violations of the underlying rule. As the Court itself acknowledged in *Janis*, this conception of the judicial integrity consideration makes it virtually indistinguishable from the preventive function.[15] *Janis'* construction of the judicial integrity consideration, of course, need not be followed in other contexts, where it might well be appropriate to give effect to considerations related to judicial integrity other than any tendency that admission of the evidence might have to constitute judicial encouragement of future violations of the underlying rule.

(3) Exclusion as a Personal Remedy. Exclusionary rules could, of course, be defended as remedies for the underlying wrongs done criminal defendants.[16] Further, they might be defended as uniquely appropriate

---

8. See note 6, supra.

9. See, e.g., Kamisar, Is the Exclusionary Rule an "Illogical" or "Unnatural" Interpretation of the Fourth Amendment?, 62 Judicature 66 (1978).

10. 364 U.S. 206 (1960).

11. Id. at 222.

12. 277 U.S. 438 (1928). Justice Brandeis stated:

If the Government becomes a lawbreaker, it breeds contempt for law; it invites every man to become a law unto himself; it invites anarchy.

277 U.S. at 485 (Brandeis, J., dissenting).

13. 428 U.S. 433 (1976) on remand 540 F.2d 1022, rehearing denied 429 U.S. 874.

14. Id. at 458 n. 35.

15. Id. ("[T]his inquiry is essentially the same as the inquiry into whether exclusion would serve a deterrent purpose").

16. Perhaps the strongest support for the proposition that the Fourth Amendment exclusionary rule is in part at least designed to serve a remedial function is in the Supreme Court's discussion of what was previously regarded as the requirement of "standing." See Alderman v. United States, 394 U.S. 165, 174 (1969) appeal after remand 424 F.2d 20 ("We adhere . . . to the general rule that Fourth Amendment rights are personal rights which, like some other constitutional

remedies, given the nature of many of the rules to which they might be applied. It is undoubtedly impossible, for example, to "undo" the anxiety and other results of law enforcement intrusions into privacy and violations of other protected interests. If, however, the law's objective is as far as possible to place the person in the position he would have been in had no violation occurred, an exclusionary sanction furthers this in a unique fashion. Only an exclusionary sanction places the person in no greater risk of criminal conviction than he would have been in had the violation of protected interests not occurred. There is, however, widespread rejection of the personal remedial effect of exclusionary rules as a relevant policy consideration. This has been especially true of the Supreme Court's analysis of Fourth Amendment exclusionary rule concerns. In Elkins v. United States,[17] for example, the Court commented, "The [Fourth Amendment exclusionary rule] is calculated to prevent, not to repair."[18]

The rationale for this rejection of exclusionary rules as personal remedies appears to be based upon a perception that they provide a remedy to which defendants have no legitimate claim. No person has a legitimate claim to the ability to commit criminal offenses or to the ability to commit them and then to escape conviction. The fact that conviction may be possible only as the result of a violation of some right, then, creates no entitlement to either freedom from conviction or immunity from the use of reliable evidence of guilt.[19] While the provision of what amounts to a personal remedy of immunity from conviction may often be an effect of application of the exclusionary rules, the argument goes, this is an incidental and perhaps undesirable effect that is entitled to no weight in resolving exclusionary rule issues. The remedial effect is, under this approach, an undeserved but unavoidable windfall for criminal defendants.

Again, it is important to note that the Supreme Court's rejection of the Fourth Amendment exclusionary rule's remedial function as a legitimate consideration in Fourth Amendment exclusionary rule analysis does not compel the same result in other contexts. State courts, for example, might quite appropriately conclude that exclusionary sanctions are desirable for among other reasons that they relieve persons of disadvantages that would not have been visited upon them "but for" the violation of the persons' underlying rights.

Countervailing Considerations. In opposition to these considerations that support all or some exclusionary sanctions, there are a variety of factors that militate against adoption of such remedies.

(1) Loss of Reliable Evidence. The primary "cost" of exclusionary sanctions, of course, is the loss of evidence tending to show the guilt of particular criminal defendants. In many situations, the basis for excluding the evidence casts no doubt whatsoever upon the reliability of the evidence.[20] In these cases, the cost is especially high. On the other hand, violation of some rules enforced by exclusionary sanctions may cast at least some doubt as to the reliability of the challenged evidence.[21] In such situa-

---

rights, may not be vicariously asserted.") See generally § 179 infra.

17. 364 U.S. 206 (1960).

18. Id. at 217.

19. See Notes, 12 Am.Crim.L.Rev. 507, 508–10 (1975), 58 Yale L.J. 144, 153–54 (1948).

20. This is, for example, most obviously true concerning situations in which evidence is rendered inadmissible because of a violation of the Fourth Amendment or some other search or seizure requirement.

21. The due process prohibition against exceptionally suggestive procedures affecting witnesses, see

§ 174 infra, is clearly aimed directly at the reliability of the resulting evidence. The relationship between other rules and reliability is less direct. The Sixth Amendment right to counsel at certain pretrial confrontations between the defendant and a witness, see § 173 infra, was developed in large part to combat what were perceived by the Court as procedures and circumstances that sometimes cast doubt upon the reliability of the witnesses' incourt testimony. Similarly, the right to counsel during custodial police interrogation, see § 150 supra, was aimed in part at least at interrogation tactics that might affect the accuracy of the resulting confessions. But in neither situation does the violation of

tions, the strength of this consideration is arguably diminished.

(2) Cost of Implementation. Implementing exclusionary rules may exact significant operational costs. Resolving challenges to evidence may require substantial court time and resources; this may be especially true where prolonged inquiries must be conducted in the absence of trial juries, which may be required to sit idle for extended periods of time. The importance of these factors will vary, depending upon such matters as the frequency with which the exclusionary sanction is invoked, the nature of the issues raised, and the procedure applied for both raising and resolving of claims to the protection of the sanction.

(3) Loss of Public Support. There is ample reason to believe that broad segments of the public either fail to understand the bases for many exclusionary sanctions or disagree with the balance of considerations necessary to the conclusion that such sanctions are desirable. To the extent that this is the case, enforcement of the exclusionary sanctions may bring the judiciary into disrepute. This, in turn, may ultimately affect the ability of the judiciary to perform its functions, an ability which arguably depends upon the existence of widespread respect for and acceptance of the courts as forums.

(4) Federalism Considerations. Many of the considerations militating against exclusionary sanctions are arguably magnified when the exclusionary sanction at issue is one imposed upon the states as a matter of federal constitutional law. Operational costs, for example, may be increased. State prosecuting authorities may be required not only to defend against defendants' claims in state litigation, but may also be required to

defend against virtually the same claims in subsequent federal habeas corpus challenges to state convictions.[22] Probably more important, however, a federally-imposed exclusionary sanction deprives states of the ability to resolve as a matter of state policy the many difficult issues that must be addressed in making the decision as to whether an exclusionary sanction is appropriate in a given context. Depriving state legislatures and judiciaries of the ability to resolve these matters undoubtedly places a significant strain on the relationship between the states, and the federal government in general and the federal judiciary in particular.

Cost-benefit evaluations of exclusionary sanctions are difficult to consider in the abstract. It is therefore necessary to compare the results of such evaluations with alternatives to exclusionary sanctions, the effectiveness of these alternatives, and their costs. Imposition of civil liability upon law enforcement officers and the governmental entities that employ them has been the alternative traditionally offered.[23] Yet there are doubts that such civil remedies can reasonably be expected to have much impact. Persons who are wronged by law enforcement conduct are likely to make unattractive plaintiffs. Moreover, sufficient damages to make litigation attractive may be difficult to establish. These problems might be mitigated, however, by provisions for attorneys' fees and perhaps liquidated damages sufficient to provide an incentive for seeking redress through these means.

In addition, it is sometimes urged that realistic limits on law enforcement conduct must be largely self-imposed and consequently the law should seek to encourage internal rulemaking and enforcement by law

---

the right to the presence of counsel establish that the challenged evidence was also tainted by law enforcement conduct which might affect reliability. While as a general matter these rights are related to reliability, their violation in a particular case does not mandate legitimate doubts concerning the reliability of the resulting evidence.

22. The Supreme Court has addressed this concern by greatly limiting state defendants' ability to litigate

Fourth Amendment exclusionary rule issues in federal habeas corpus proceedings. See § 181 infra.

23. Foote, Tort Remedies for Police Violations of Individual Rights, 39 Minn.L.Rev. 493 (1955); Gilligan, The Federal Tort Claims Act—An Alternative to the Exclusionary Rule, 66 J.Crim.L. & C. 1 (1975).

enforcement agencies.[24] Whether self-regulation is realistic remains problematic, however, and it seems unlikely that major changes in law enforcement behavior will be effected by this method.[25]

Comparative Significance of the Considerations. Identification of the relevant considerations is only the first step. It is also necessary to evaluate these relevant and perhaps conflicting considerations.

In regard to the law of the Fourth Amendment exclusionary rule, the Supreme Court has developed a reasonably consistent approach for purposes of considering the variety of issues related to scope and procedural aspects. It has, of course, rejected any personal remedy function the exclusionary sanction might serve as a relevant consideration.[26] In addition to defining the "judicial integrity" consideration in a very narrow fashion,[27] it has—in Stone v. Powell,[28] for example—concluded that even this narrowly defined consideration is entitled to only a "limited role" in determining whether or how to apply the exclusionary rule in a particular context. The Court has rather focused upon the preventive function of the sanction and, more particularly, the incremental preventive effect that might reasonably be expected from any particular change. Thus the issue as frequently posed by the

Court is whether the increase in preventive function that might be expected from a given expansion of the rule justifies the increase in costs that might also be expected from the expansion at issue.[29] The incremental loss of reliable evidence of defendants' guilt has been a major consideration in determining the costs of proposed expansions.[30]

This approach to exclusionary rule issues, however, is certainly not binding in other contexts. State courts, for example, remain free to pursue different analyses in resolving the variety of subissues presented when defendants urge the adoption of exclusionary sanctions for violations of state constitutional and statutory requirements.[31] Further, it is at least arguable that the Supreme Court's Fourth Amendment approach is entitled to no special deference as a model for exclusionary sanction discussion in other contexts. It is quite clearly based upon a number of decisions—such as the rejection of personal remedy considerations and the narrow scope and limited weight given to judicial integrity considerations—that are inherently subjective in nature. Further, the absence of reliable empirical information about other matters that can be stated as objective fact questions means that the answers accepted by the Court's majority can

24. See Davis, An Approach to Legal Control of the Police, 52 Tex.L.Rev. 703 (1974). See also, Gilligan and Lederer, Replacing the Exclusionary Rule with Administrative Rulemaking, 28 Ala.L.Rev. 533 (1977); Quinn, The Effect of Police Rulemaking on the Scope of Fourth Amendment Rights, 52 J.Urban L. 25 (1974); Comment, 72 Nw.U.L.Rev. 595 (1977) (federal courts should, as a supplement to Fourth Amendment exclusionary rule, use supervisory power to require federal law enforcement agencies to formulate rules to minimize violations).

25. Other controls might also warrant consideration. See Comment, 72 J.Crim.L. & C. 993 (1981) (contempt of court), and Schwartz, Complaints Against the Police: Experience of the Community Rights Division of the Philadelphia District Attorney's Office, 118 U.Pa.L.Rev. 1023 (1970).

26. Text at note 17 supra.

27. Text at note 13 supra.

28. 428 U.S. 465, 485 (1976) on remand 539 F.2d 693, rehearing denied 429 U.S. 874.

29. See, for example, the Court's discussion of whether the Fourth Amendment exclusionary rule should be enforceable in federal habeas corpus proceedings. Stone v. Powell, 428 U.S. 465, 489–96 on remand 539 F.2d 693, rehearing denied 429 U.S. 874 (1976). See also Harris v. New York, 401 U.S. 222 (1971) (excluding evidence obtained in violation of Fourth Amendment when offered for impeachment of a testifying defendant would not provide sufficient incremental deterrence); Calandra v. United States, 414 U.S. 338 (1974) (uncertain increase in deterrence that would be accomplished by expanding Fourth Amendment exclusionary rule to grand jury proceedings does not justify costs). Cf. Rakas v. Illinois, 439 U.S. 128 (1978) rehearing denied 439 U.S. 1122.

30. Stone v. Powell, 428 U.S. 465, 490 (1976) on remand 539 F.2d 639, rehearing denied 429 U.S. 874 (evidence excluded under Fourth Amendment exclusionary rule "is typically reliable and often the most probative information bearing on the guilt or innocence of the defendant").

31. See § 166 supra.

scarcely be regarded as reliably established.[32] There is no reason why state tribunals and legislatures ought not to consider themselves as fully capable to make de novo inquiry into these concerns and to base state exclusionary sanction decisions upon independent judgments concerning the variety of issues related to those decisions.

 WESTLAW REFERENCES

topic(157) /p topic(exclu! inadmis! admit!) & "exclusionary rule*" "fourth amendment"

Relevant Considerations

"exclusionary rule*" /s deter deterr! prevent! educat! /p future foresee!

Countervailing Considerations

"exclusionary rule*" /s cost! expense! losses

Comparative Significance

state /s "exclusionary rule*" /s federal /s compar! contrast! conflict! difference differ* distinct! review!

---

§ 169. Evidence Obtained Pursuant to Unreasonable Searches and Seizures: (a) Definition of "Search" and "Seizure"

Defendants' efforts to invoke exclusionary sanctions in criminal litigation are most often based upon purported violation of the legal requirements related to searches and seizures. Thus "search and seizure" law has become the most widely discussed and litigated area of law related to exclusionary sanction enforcement. Because of the *Weeks-Mapp* Fourth Amendment exclusionary rule, discussion and litigation have, of course, often focused upon the requirements

of the Fourth Amendment's prohibition against unreasonable searches and seizures.[1] For that reason, the next four sections address the Supreme Court's resolution as a matter of Fourth Amendment law of a number of important search and seizure issues. Here, more than in any other area of exclusionary sanction enforcement, however, it is important to recognize that almost every Fourth Amendment issue has a distinguishable and independent state constitutional equivalent.[1a] Moreover, a number of matters that do not rise to the level of federal (or state) constitutional significance may nevertheless be affected by statutory or administrative law which may (or may not) be enforceable by an exclusionary sanction.

The threshold questions in Fourth Amendment exclusionary rule cases are first, whether a search or seizure within the meaning of the provision occurred, and, second, if so, how many of such distinguishable intrusions are involved. It is clear that these initial inquiries raise the basic question of the coverage of the protection extended by the Amendment.

Searches: Intrusions Upon Privacy Expectations. What constitutes a search that must be justified as reasonable must, for purposes of the Fourth Amendment, be answered by initial reference to Katz v. United States.[2] FBI agents had overheard Katz' end of a conversation over a public telephone; this was accomplished by placing an electronic listening and recording device on the outside of the telephone booth from

---

32. Justice Brennan, for example, has accused the majority of applying the balancing test in Fourth Amendment exclusionary rule cases "simply by declaring that so much exclusion is enough to deter police conduct," with the result that the "balancing effort is completely freewheeling." United States v. Havens, 446 U.S. 620, 633–34 (1980) on remand 625 F.2d 1131, rehearing denied 448 U.S. 911 (Brennan, J., dissenting).

§ 169

1. The Fourth Amendment reads:

The right of the people to be secure in their persons, houses, papers, and effects, against unreasonable searches and seizures, shall not be violated, and no Warrants shall issue, but upon probable cause, supported by Oath or affirmation, and particularly describ-

ing the place to be searched, and the persons or things to be seized.

1a. For an extensive discussion of state law developments in one area also covered by Fourth Amendment law, the right of arresting officers to search incident to an arrest, see Hancock, State Court Activism and Searches Incident to Arrest, 68 Va.L.Rev. 1085 (1982).

2. 389 U.S. 347 (1967). See generally, Ashdown, The Fourth Amendment and the "Legitimate Expectation of Privacy," 34 Vand.L.Rev. 1289 (1981); Note, 91 Yale L.J. 313 (1981); Annot., 57 A.L.R.Fed. 646 (use of "beeper"), 56 A.L.R.Fed. 772 (aerial surveillance), 48 A.L.R.3d 1178 (observations through binoculars).

which Katz placed the call. In response to the Government's argument that no search within the meaning of the Fourth Amendment took place, the Supreme Court attempted to articulate a general standard for determining whether Fourth Amendment protected activity was involved. First, the Court—speaking through Justice Stewart—rejected the argument that a search occurs only if there has been some physical intrusion into a protected area. "[T]he Fourth Amendment," Justice Stewart observed, "protects people, not places." [3] Second, it offered an alternative standard: "[W]hat [a person] seeks to preserve as private, even in an area accessible to the public, may be constitutionally protected." [4] Violating the privacy which a person justifiably—given the person's effort to preserve that privacy—relies upon constitutes a search within the meaning of the Amendment. [5] On the other hand, "[w]hat a person knowingly exposes to the public, even in his own home or office, is not a subject of Fourth Amendment protection," [6] and observing such exposed matter is no search.

Despite the apparent effort by the majority in *Katz* to articulate a useful standard for determining Fourth Amendment coverage, much subsequent discussion has instead had reference to Justice Harlan's concurring expression of his understanding of the criterion:

> [T]here is a twofold requirement, first that a person have exhibited an actual (subjective) expectation of privacy and, second, that the expectation be one that society is prepared to recognize as "reasonable." [7]

Discussions in subsequent cases, such as Smith v. Maryland, [8] suggest that the Court itself has found the language of Justice Harlan's concurrence a more accurate reflection of its view than the language of the *Katz* majority.

Intrusion into a protected expectation of privacy, then, constitutes a search. Both the majority and Justice Harlan agreed in *Katz* that on the facts Katz himself had a protected privacy interest in the contents of his conversation and the officers' action in overhearing the conversation intruded upon that expectation of privacy. The phone booth was glass and the fact of his presence in the booth was exposed to the general public; he had no reasonable expectation that he would be free from being observed in the booth. But he nevertheless reasonably believed that the contents of his conversation would not be accessible to members of the public, who could see him in the booth. The overhearing of the contents of his conversation was, therefore, a search.

Application of the *Katz* standard has not been easy. Often, courts have characterized observation by law enforcement officers that does not constitute a search under the *Katz* criterion as "plain view." [9] This is simply a statement that an officer, in a place where the officer has a right to be, who observes matters which the subject did not take care to protect from such observation, has not engaged in a search. This so-called "plain view observation" rule must be distinguished from the "plain view seizure" situation, discussed later. [10]

---

3. 389 U.S. at 351.

4. Id. at 351–52.

5. Interestingly, the Court also commented, "[T]he Fourth Amendment cannot be translated into a general constitutional 'right to privacy.'" Id. at 350.

6. Id. at 351.

7. Id. at 361 (Harlan, J., concurring).

8. 442 U.S. 735 (1979).

9. See Nicholas v. State, 502 S.W.2d 169 (Tex.Crim. App.1973) (while observation that negatives were lying on bar was exercise of plain view by officer properly in the room, officer's further action in picking up nega-

tives and holding them to the light to permit him to determine their contents was a "search" and thus not an exercise of "plain view").

10. § 170 infra.

The Court has held that use of a trained dog to "sniff" luggage in a public place does not amount to a search. United States v. Place, 103 S.Ct. 2637 (1983). While the process results in obtaining information concerning the content of the luggage, the Court reasoned, only limited information is obtained and the technique is relatively unintrusive. But other use of the "canine sniff" may invoke Fourth Amendment scrutiny. See Horton v. Goose Creek Independent

Applying *Katz*, the Supreme Court has held that persons do not have a reasonable expectation of privacy in their bank's records concerning accounts; therefore, obtaining those records by subpoena does not constitute a search.[11] Further, one who uses a telephone in a way evidencing a reasonable expectation of privacy in the contents of the conversation nevertheless does not have a similar expectation concerning the privacy of a number called; therefore, obtaining such a number by surreptitiously attaching a "pen register" to the phone does not constitute a search.[12] When the operator of an adult book store places magazines in clear wrappers on an open shelf, he has no expectation of privacy regarding the covers; the operator retains a reasonable expectation of privacy in the contents of the inside pages, however, because these have not been exposed to the public. Therefore, an officer who merely observes the covers through the wrapper does not search, but one who removes the wrapper and examines the inside pages does engage in a search within the meaning of the Fourth Amendment.[13]

Perhaps the major ambiguity in the *Katz* standard is the meaning of the requirement that the expectation of privacy be "reasonable." This seems clearly to mean that the expectation must be one that a reasonable person would entertain under the circumstances. In Smith v. Maryland,[14] presenting the pen register issue, the Court noted wide-

spread awareness that telephone companies use electronic equipment to record numbers dialed from phones for billing purposes and for detecting fraud and use of telephones for annoying or obscene calls. Even if Smith himself expected that the numbers dialed from his phone would not be available to others, therefore, this expectation would not be "reasonable" within the meaning of the *Katz* standard. The Court noted, however, that if widespread utilization of intrusive techniques caused citizens to abandon any expectation that they would be free from such intrusions, citizens' subjective expectations could play no meaningful role in ascertaining the scope of Fourth Amendment protection. "In determining whether a 'legitimate expectation of privacy' existed in such cases," it opined, "a normative inquiry would be proper."[15]

But the requirement of reasonableness may even further limit the scope of Fourth Amendment coverage than by imposing a requirement that the invaded expectation of privacy be reasonable in this statistical sense. It may also mean that there are certain expectations of privacy actually held by persons and which reasonable individuals would hold under the circumstances but which nevertheless, for significant reasons of Fourth Amendment policy, are not protected by the amendment. This construction of the requirement may help to explain several decisions regarding the scope of Fourth Amendment protection. In Hoffa v. United

---

School District, 690 F.2d 470 (5th Cir. 1982) (per curiam), rehearing en banc denied, 693 F.2d 524 (use of dogs to sniff school lockers and cars in school parking lot not search but use of animals to smell students at close range in classroom is search requiring individualized reasonable suspicion). See generally, Doe v. Renfrow, 451 U.S. 1022 (1981) (Brennan, J., dissenting from denial of certiorari).

11. United States v. Miller, 425 U.S. 435 (1976).

12. Smith v. Maryland, 442 U.S. 735 (1979).

13. Lo Ji Sales, Inc. v. New York, 442 U.S. 329 (1979).

In United States v. Knotts, 103 S.Ct. 1081 (1983), a unanimous Court found no "search" in the use of a radio-transmitting "beeper," concealed in chemicals sold

to the suspect, to follow the defendants and locate the beeper on certain private property. The information could have been obtained by visual surveillance, the Court noted, and "Nothing in the Fourth Amendment prohibited the police from augmenting the sensory faculties bestowed upon them at birth with such enhancement as science and technology afforded them in this case." 103 U.S. at 1086. Justice Stevens, however, declined to join in the Court's broad language, noting that use of electronic detection techniques may "implicate especially sensitive concerns." Id. at 1089 (Stevens, J., concurring in the judgment).

14. Supra n. 12.

15. Id. at 740 n. 5.

States,[16] for example, the Court held that no search was involved when law enforcement officials caused an associate of Hoffa's to feign continuing friendship and comaraderie, thereby causing Hoffa to permit the associate to overhear incriminating admissions by Hoffa that Hoffa would not otherwise have permitted him to overhear. It seems likely as well that Hoffa expected that his living place—and perhaps his life in general—would not involve surveillance by persons feigning friendship but functioning as undercover law enforcement officers. It is also likely that most persons in Hoffa's position would have entertained an expectation of the same sort. The Court's unwillingness to regard use of the undercover agent as a search and thus as subject to Fourth Amendment regulation (not prohibition) must be explained on other grounds. Arguably, the Court perceived the need for flexible availability of undercover techniques to be so great, and the task of formulating Fourth Amendment rules to regulate such techniques as so difficult, that on balance the privacy interest involved, although subjectively held and reasonable in a statistical sense, was not one which the Court was willing to recognize as reasonable in this broader sense of the term.

Private Party Intrusions Upon Privacy. A major limitation upon the scope of Fourth Amendment coverage that is apparently independent of the *Katz* standard is the "private party" rule. Since Burdeau v. McDowell [17] the Supreme Court has held that the Fourth Amendment does not protect against wrongful acts of private persons. The Amendment, the Court has reasoned, was intended by the framers as only a restraint on "the activities of sovereign authority." This position was reaffirmed in Walter v. United States,[18] decided in 1980.

Walter also made clear, however, that law enforcement activity subsequent to private wrongful conduct can become an intrusion upon Fourth Amendment protected privacy. In *Walter*, private persons to whom packages had been erroneously delivered wrongfully opened them and observed indications that they contained obscene films. But after the opened boxes were turned over to FBI agents, the agents, without first securing a warrant, viewed the films with a projector. The wrongful action of the private persons in opening the boxes was held not to affect the admissibility of the subsequently-discovered evidence of the films' obscene nature. But when the officers viewed the films, the Court further held, their action intruded upon Walter's privacy beyond the intrusion involved in the private persons' activity. Since the officers' activity was without a warrant, the search by them was unreasonable and its fruits were inadmissible.

Whose Privacy Was Violated? The definition of search—and to some extent seizure—is of special importance because of the personal nature of the rights at issue,[19] a matter formerly addressed as a requirement of "standing." The Supreme Court has

---

16. 385 U.S. 293 (1966) rehearing denied 386 U.S. 940. United States v. White, 401 U.S. 745 (1971) rehearing denied 402 U.S. 990, on remand 454 F.2d 435, cert. denied 406 U.S. 962 presented the question whether a search occurred when an undercover informer carried a transmitter and caused the subject's words to be simultaneously transmitted to officers hidden nearby. Four members of the Court concluded that this constituted a search. Justice Harlan attempted to reconcile this position with *Hoffa*, reasoning that the threat of electronic transmission of a conversation is more likely than mere surveillance to discourage discourse. Because of the impact of such action on privacy, he reasoned, it should be regarded as a search. 401 U.S. at 786–87 (Harlan, J., dissenting). The Court split 4–4 on the question of whether, under *Katz*, the conduct at issue constituted a search. It also split evenly on wheth-

er, given the ruling in Desist v. United States, 394 U.S. 244 (1969) rehearing denied 395 U.S. 931, *Katz* applied to the case. The controlling vote for upholding the admissibility of the challenged evidence was that of Justice Black, who took the position that *Katz* was wrongly decided, electronic surveillance cannot constitute a search, and therefore no Fourth Amendment issue was presented. 401 U.S. at 754 (Black, J., concurring in the result). A majority of the Court, however, appears to regard *White* as having settled the issue. See United States v. Caceres, 440 U.S. 741, 750–52 (1979). See also the discussion of grand jury appearances in the text at note 28, infra.

17. 256 U.S. 465 (1921).

18. 447 U.S. 649 (1980).

19. § 179 infra.

made clear that a defendant is entitled to suppression of evidence under the Fourth Amendment exclusionary rule only upon a showing that the evidence was fatally related to a search that intruded upon the defendant's personal privacy interests. Therefore, it is important not only to be able to determine whether law enforcement activity constituted a search but also to ascertain whose privacy interests were infringed by conduct that is unquestionably a search.

Traditionally, a search of a location was widely accepted as constituting an intrusion upon the privacy expectations of all persons legitimately present.[20] In Rakas v. Illinois,[21] however, the Supreme Court held that a search of an automobile did not violate any reasonable expectation of privacy held by persons who were mere passengers in the vehicle. Consequently, such persons were not entitled to exclusion of evidence found in a search of the automobile even upon a showing that the search violated Fourth Amendment standards.

Rakas raises two major questions relating to the task of identifying victims of a particular search. First, the Court suggested that in regard to an automobile a person who was more than merely legitimately present might experience a privacy intrusion as a result of a search of the car. But what is required? If the passenger has spent a prolonged period in the car, is that sufficient? If the passenger has also been permitted to store personal belongings in the car, is that sufficient? Rakas does not provide an answer. Second, will the same rule apply to searches of premises, especially residential premises? Arguably, Rakas turned in part upon the Court's position that privacy interests in automobiles are inherently less than

such interests in many other locations. Thus, the expectations one has in regard to residential premises, even those of another, may be sufficiently different that anyone legitimately on residential premises may have a privacy interest in those premises that is intruded upon by a search of them. But Rakas leaves this open.[22]

Seizures of Persons. It is clear that the Fourth Amendment contains a prohibition against unreasonable seizures, independent of its condemnation of unreasonable searches. Further, there can be no doubt that this prohibition addresses seizures of persons as well as seizures of physical items and less tangible "things." [23] It is important, therefore, to determine what constitutes a seizure of the person which, under the Fourth Amendment, may render inadmissible evidence obtained in relationship to it. Despite the obvious importance of the matter, the criterion for determining whether a seizure has occurred has been only minimally addressed in Supreme Court case law.

The matter arises most often in regard to field confrontations between citizens and law enforcement officers, where the citizen claims that a seizure occurred and the officer maintains that the situation never progressed beyond a purely voluntary confrontation. In Terry v. Ohio,[24] the Court assumed that no seizure took place in the field confrontation there at issue prior to the officer's action in grabbing the suspect to carry out a field frisk for weapons. The matter was not again raised until United States v. Mendenhall[25] and was not resolved in that case. No opinion attracted sufficient support to become the opinion of the Court. Justice Stewart, joined only by Justice Rehnquist, confronted the issue. He concluded

---

20. See Jones v. United States, 362 U.S. 257 (1960).

21. 439 U.S. 128 (1978) rehearing denied 439 U.S. 1122.

22. "It is unnecessary for us to decide here whether the same expectations of privacy are warranted in a car as would be justified in a dwelling place in analogous circumstances." 439 U.S. at 148.

23. See Terry v. Ohio, 392 U.S. 1 (1968), rejecting the argument that for Fourth Amendment purposes a

"seizure" of the person occurs only if officers make a "technical arrest." 392 U.S. at 16–20.

24. 392 U.S. 1 (1968). "We thus decide nothing today concerning the constitutional propriety of an investigative 'seizure' upon less than probable cause for purposes of 'detention' and/or interrogation." 392 U.S. 19 n. 16.

25. 446 U.S. 544 (1980) rehearing denied 448 U.S. 908.

that "a person has been 'seized' within the meaning of the Fourth Amendment only if, in view of all of the circumstances surrounding the incident, a reasonable person would have believed that he was not free to leave." [26] Under this view, an officer's subjective intent not to permit the citizen to break off the confrontation is irrelevant, except insofar as it may have been communicated to the citizen and thus have affected the citizen's perception. Applying this standard, Justice Stewart found no seizure of the defendant. Three other justices preferred to assume that a seizure occurred, but indicated that they did not necessarily disagree with Justice Stewart's articulation of the controlling criterion.[27]

This proposed standard is, of course, arguably consistent with *Katz'* articulation of the definition of search. Both focus upon the perception of the citizen and define Fourth Amendment terms so as to bring the provision into play when, but only when, the citizen perceives an intrusion upon the underlying privacy. Thus *Katz'* privacy standard can usefully be regarded as defining not just the term "search" but rather the scope of overall Fourth Amendment protection. The protection against seizures of the person as defined by Justice Stewart's *Mendenhall* criterion, can be construed as simply a specific application of the Amendment's general protection of reasonable expectations of personal privacy.

Insofar as Justice Stewart's *Mendenhall* opinion states what the Court is likely to accept as the standard, the Fourth Amendment coverage here may be subject to exception, as it is in regard to "searches," for situations where there are persuasive reasons for not protecting the privacy interest at issue. In United States v. Dionisio [28] and

United States v. Mara,[29] for example, the Court characterized it as "clear" that a compelled appearance before a grand jury pursuant to a subpoena was not a "seizure" in the Fourth Amendment sense. But if a reasonable person can harbor an expectation of freedom that is infringed by an arrest, it seems clear that compelled appearance pursuant to the court's contempt power infringes upon the same protected expectation. The result in *Dionisio* and *Mara* must rest on what the majority regarded as persuasive policy reasons for not subjecting grand jury seizures of witnesses to Fourth Amendment scrutiny. The seizure is relatively nonintrusive, the Court emphasized, because it is part of citizens' historical obligation to participate in grand jury investigations. It involves no stigma, the time can generally be arranged so as to reduce inconvenience, and abuse is minimized by subjecting the process to the control and supervision of the court which convened the grand jury. Further, to impose Fourth Amendment restrictions would significantly interfere with the grand jury's prized flexibility. The exclusion from Fourth Amendment coverage of appearances pursuant to grand jury subpoenas must be justified in terms of the Court's ability—as recognized in Justice Harlan's *Katz* concurrence—to refuse for important counterveiling reasons to protect subjectively held and statistically reasonable expectations of privacy.

Seizures of "Things." The terms of the Fourth Amendment leave no doubt that its protection extends to seizures of physical items as well as persons. Supreme Court case law has not addressed the question when a seizure of an item occurs, although this may be because there is almost never any doubt. It seems clear that when law en-

---

26. 446 U.S. at 554 (opinion of Stewart, J.).

27. 446 U.S. at 560 n. 1 (Powell, J., concurring in part and concurring in the judgment). Four members of the Court urged that the Court should assume a seizure took place because the Government did not contest this earlier in the case and further because this is a factual question best decided in the first instance by a trial court. Id. at 569 (White J., dissenting).

See also, Florida v. Royer, 103 S.Ct. 1319, 1326 (1983) (plurality opinion) (applying Justice Stewart's *Mendenhall* criterion).

28. 410 U.S. 1 (1973).

29. 410 U.S. 19 (1973).

forcement officers exercise dominion over an item so as to exclude the ability of others to do so, a seizure of that item has occurred and this must be justified as reasonable in Fourth Amendment terms.[30]

The question may become more complex when applied to "things" other than physical items. For example, *Katz* establishes that the Fourth Amendment protects the privacy of certain interpersonal communications. But intrusions into this privacy interest may involve both searches and seizures. On the facts of *Katz*, was the search completed by installing the electronic device on the exterior of the phone booth? Probably not, because most likely no actual intrusion upon protected privacy interests occurred until a conversation occurred and was "intercepted." Suppose, however, the equipment recorded the conversations, transmitted them to another device located some distance away, and permitted officers stationed at the location of the second device to listen to the conversations. If the device on the booth "searched," can it be said that the recording, the overhearing by the officers, and perhaps the transmission itself involved incremental intrusions into Katz' privacy that can usefully be conceptualized as "seizures" of the contents of the conversation?

Identification of Incremental Intrusions Into Privacy. Whatever the accuracy of the suggestion at the end of the preceding paragraph, it is clear from the Court's analyses that in many situations Fourth Amendment analysis of law enforcement conduct requires that such conduct be carefully broken down into units. The reasonableness under Fourth Amendment standards of each unit, then, must be separately considered.

The most reasonable approach to such a task is to seek to identify the points at which the law enforcement activity involved a sufficient incremental intrusion into protected privacy, in light of preceding intrusions. At each point where an incremental intrusion occurs, a separate search or seizure has taken place. Thus it becomes necessary to call the *Katz* standard into play to identify not only protected privacy interests but also to distinguish separate intrusions into a single privacy interest or perhaps into related privacy interests.

Law enforcement conduct concerning an apprehended suspect provides a useful example. The assumption of control over the suspect obviously constitutes a seizure of the person. An examination of the suspect's person and of the nature and contents of things found on the suspect's person is clearly an incremental intrusion into Fourth Amendment protected privacy that must be considered independently.[31] Further, Schmerber v. California [32] establishes that if and when the examination extends below the surface of the skin (as when a blood sample is taken), a separate intrusion occurs that must be examined for Fourth Amendment reasonableness. How finely the analysis must or may distinguish is far from clear. If, for example, the insertion of a needle into the suspect's body constitutes a privacy intrusion sufficiently beyond a search of the surface of the body as to constitute a "new" search, is the drawing of a sample of the suspect's blood a seizure that must be considered separately? Is subjecting the blood to intensive chemical analysis a further search? Whatever the answers, the question is best put in *Katz* terms: Did the aspect of the law enforcement conduct at issue constitute a sufficiently incremental intrusion into protected privacy interests to require that it be characterized as a separate search or seizure that must be independently justified as reasonable under Fourth Amendment standards? [33]

---

30. Cardwell v. Lewis, 417 U.S. 583 (1974); Warden v. Hayden, 387 U.S. 294 (1967).

31. United States v. Robinson, 414 U.S. 218 (1973); Chimel v. California, 395 U.S. 752 (1969) rehearing denied 396 U.S. 869.

32. 384 U.S. 757 (1966).

33. In United States v. Robinson, 414 U.S. 218 (1973), a search of Robinson's pocket resulted in discovery of a crumpled cigarette package. The officer took possession of this and examined its contents, which

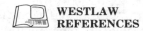

**WESTLAW
REFERENCES**

Searches: Intrusions Upon Privacy Expectations
digest,synopsis(privacy private personal /5 right* search!
    invad! invasion /p fourth /2 amendment)
title(hoffa) & cite(87 +s 1583)

Private Party Intrusions
349k3.3(4) /p privacy private

Whose Privacy Was Violated?
349k7(26) /p passenger* /p standing

Seizures of Persons
compel! subpoena! summon! /p "grand jury" /p
    seizure /p fourth 4 /2 amend!

Seizures of Things
seiz! /s voice* sound* conversation* communication*
    /p inanimate nonphysical tangible intangible /p fourth
    4 /2 amend!

Identification of Incremental Intrusions
blood urine urinalysis /p alcohol! intoxicated drunk!
    Inebriated drinking /p fourth 4 /2 amend!

---

§ 170. Evidence Obtained Pursuant to Unreasonable Searches and Seizures: (b) The Substantive Requirement of Adequate Information

The Supreme Court has construed the requirement of "reasonableness" imposed by the Fourth Amendment as involving two major considerations. One, the subject of this section, is what can usefully be regarded as the "substantive" requirement of sufficient information at the time the search or seizure is made to justify the intrusion into privacy. The other, which can be regarded as procedural, is the requirement that prior to the search (or perhaps seizure) the sufficiency of the information be submitted to a judicial of-

ficer for determination.[1] This is addressed in the next section.

"Probable Cause:" The Benchmark. The specific provision in the Fourth Amendment that "no Warrants shall issue, but upon probable cause . . . ." makes clear that intrusions upon Fourth Amendment privacy under warrants must be supported by information amounting to "probable cause." Probably for this reason, together with the central role the Court regards the warrant process as playing in search law, the Supreme Court has regarded probable cause as the benchmark standard for determining the sufficiency of information. Thus any search or seizure supported by less information that is necessary to constitute probable cause requires special consideration. On the other hand, more information than is necessary to meet this standard is not ordinarily required.

It is important to note that probable cause, like proof beyond a reasonable doubt or by a preponderance of the evidence, simply defines the measure of evidence and is meaningless without further specification as to what the evidence must tend to establish or prove. This requires that it be related to the intrusion at issue. Thus in situations involving a seizure of a suspect's person, the issue is frequently whether probable cause exists to believe the person guilty of an offense and thus subject to arrest. But when the intrusion is a search for physical items, the issue is generally whether there is probable cause to believe that the search will result in discovery of items which the officers

---

turned out to be contraband. Three members of the Court urged that the search of the cigarette package was a separate intrusion into Robinson's privacy that should be considered independently; they suggested a distinction between a search of the person and "a separate search of effects found on [one's] person." 414 U.S. at 255 (Marshall, J., dissenting). The majority, however, summarily commented, "Having in the course of a lawful search come upon the crumpled package of cigarettes, [the officer] was entitled to inspect it . . . ." Id. at 236. This is best read as not holding that once Robinson was properly subjected to a search of his person, he had no remaining privacy interests that were infringed by an examination of the contents of a container found on his person. Rather, as the

Court has subsequently made clear, the rationale for permitting a search incident to a custodial arrest justifies defining the scope of permissible search as extending to the contents of containers found on the arrestee's person, even if this involves an incremental intrusion into privacy; see § 171 infra.

§ 170

1. Whether the Fourth Amendment requirement of "reasonableness" imposes any limitations upon a search conducted in compliance with the warrant requirement and on the basis of sufficient information is problematic. See generally, Dix, Means of Executing Searches and Seizures as Fourth Amendment Issues, 67 Minn.L.Rev. 89 (1982).

will have a legal right to seize. Where a seizure of an item is at issue, the question is whether the officers have probable cause to believe that the item is one that, under the circumstances, they have the right to take into their possession as contraband, as fruits or instrumentalities of crime, or as evidence of the commission of or some person's guilt of a criminal offense.

General statements of the criterion are arguably of little value. In the leading case discussion, the Supreme Court commented that probable cause means more than "bare suspicion." It continued:

> Probable cause [concerning the commission of an offense] exists where "the facts and circumstances within their [the officers'] knowledge and of which they had reasonably trustworthy information [are] sufficient in themselves to warrant a man of reasonable caution in the belief that" an offense has been or is being committed.[2]

Perhaps more helpfully, the information establishing probable cause need not meet admissibility requirements imposed by evidentiary rules applicable at trial.[3] This is clearly justified by the impracticality of enforcing such rules during the investigation stage and further by the need to permit law enforcement officers to begin the initial steps of prosecution by arrest and search even if admissible evidence has not yet been developed. On the other hand, the Court has held that the fact that a person is, for unexplained reasons, "known" to law enforcement officers as being guilty of an offense is entitled to no weight at all in assessing the existence of probable cause.[4]

Informants' "Tips."[5] The difficulty of formulating a useful general standard for probable cause stimulated efforts by the Supreme Court to develop a more structured and objective analysis for testing information sufficiency in one limited situation, that presented when an officer or magistrate relies in part at least upon information from an informant. Effort was focused upon this area most likely because the Court perceived informants as themselves often heavily involved in criminal activity and thus as providing an especially suspect source of justification for invading Fourth Amendment interests.

Aguilar v. Texas[6] held that a conclusory claim that a reliable informant had stated that contraband was in certain premises did not constitute probable cause to believe this to be so. In order for the informant's tip to itself establish probable cause, the Court indicated, information of two additional types must be available. This additional information was defined by what are often called the two "prongs" of the *Aguilar* test. First, the available information would have to include the "underlying circumstances" relied upon by the informant in arriving at the conclusion that contraband items were there. Impliedly, of course, these circumstances would have to be such as to justify reliance on the informant's conclusion. Second, the available information would have to include specific information supporting a belief that the informant was, in a more general sense, "reliable." The first prong could be met by information that the informant claimed to have observed recently and personally the contraband at the location. If

---

2. Brinegar v. United States, 338 U.S. 160, 175–76 (1949). As was suggested in Bacigal, The Fourth Amendment in Flux: The Rise and Fall of Probable Cause, 1979 U.Ill.L.Forum 763, 771–76, the Court's case law does not provide clear criteria for making the two major decisions required by the probable cause question, i.e., whether there is a belief that the required certainty exists and, if so, whether that belief is based upon adequate information.

3. Jones v. United States, 362 U.S. 257, 271 (1960) (hearsay may serve as basis for warrant); Fed.R.Evid. 1101(d)(3).

4. Spinelli v. United States, 393 U.S. 410, 418–19 (1969). In United States v. Harris, 403 U.S. 573 (1971) three justices rejected *Spinelli's* holding that a police officer's knowledge of a suspect's reputation cannot be given weight. Id. at 583 (opinion of Burger, C.J.). This position did not attract a majority of the Court, however. For historical background of probable cause, see Weber, The Birth of Probable Cause, 11 Anglo–Am.L. Rev. 155 (1982).

5. Livermore, The Draper–Spinnelli Problem, 21 Ariz.L.Rev. 945 (1979).

6. 378 U.S. 108 (1964), on remand 382 S.W.2d 480.

there was information that the informant had provided information in the past and that law enforcement officials had, in reliable ways, found this previously-provided information to be correct, the second prong was met as well.

In Spinelli v. United States [7], the Court further suggested that a tip failing one or perhaps both prongs of the *Aguilar* test could nevertheless amount to probable cause if it was "saved" by either of two methods. First, if the tip included a substantial amount of detail in the information provided, this might have cured what would otherwise have been fatal defects. Second, if the officer corroborated in a reliable fashion a certain amount of the information provided by the informant, this might also, or alternatively, have cured the deficiency. While both *Aguilar* and *Spinelli* involved inquiries into whether a search warrant affidavit set out facts establishing probable cause, the Court's discussions made clear that it regarded the analysis as also applicable to whether information upon which an officer acted without a warrant rose to the level of probable cause.

But in Illinois v. Gates [8], the Court abandoned the structured analysis of *Aguilar* and *Spinelli*, and substituted a more flexible "totality of the circumstances" analysis. Under this approach, the inquiry is whether all of the information—including any bearing upon the informant's source and general reliability, the amount of detail provided, and any corroboration—justifies a "practical, common-sense" conclusion that there is a fair probability that the information is correct. Whether this will make a substantial difference in results is problematic. The Court itself indicated that under this approach probable cause would not be established, in the search warrant context, by conclusory statements that the officer simply believes and has reason to believe, or has

been told by a "credible person," that contraband is on certain premises.

The Court's abandonment of the *Aguilar-Spinelli* analysis was undoubtedly motivated in part by its conclusion that the analysis, if rigorously applied, was too stringent. It would, the Court commented, virtually always preclude reliance upon even corroborated information from anonymous informants, although such information would sometimes justify searches or arrests. In addition, however, the Court was influenced by its conclusion that the probable cause decision if correctly conceptualized is inherently a largely discretionary one that simply does not lend itself to the sort of structuring attempted in *Aguilar* and *Spinelli*.[9] Such structuring leads to complexities that are not meaningful to officers and magistrates making the initial probable cause decisions, the Court concluded. A totality of the circumstances approach, on the other hand, encourages the less rigorous judicial review that is appropriate in regard to such inherently discretionary and unstructurable decisions.

Gates, then, reflects in part the Supreme Court's disenchantment with its efforts to structure the probable cause standard as applied to one particular category of situations. If the Court is correct, any goal of judicial (or legislative) frameworks for making probable cause decisions may be illusory. Whether evidence amounting to probable cause exists may, perhaps, be a matter that must be left largely to the discretion of those applying the law. Review of determinations that probable cause existed, in exclusionary sanction litigation, might best be limited to demanding that the information available constituted a "substantial basis" for the decision.

Such an approach is required by *Gates* when the determination challenged on Fourth Amendment grounds was a decision

7.   393 U.S. 410 (1969).

8.   103 S.Ct. 2317 (1983), rehearing denied 104 S.Ct. 33.

9.   Id. at 2330–2331.

by a magistrate that a warrant affidavit contained sufficient information. Perhaps less deference needs to be given to a law enforcement officer's obviously "nonjudicial" determination that probable cause exists for warrantless action. But *Gates* implies that as a matter of Fourth Amendment law, even this determination is to be given greater deference than was the case under the structured *Aguilar-Spinelli* analysis.

Dilution or Abandonment of the Probable Cause Standard. While probable cause serves as the standard or assumed criterion for determining the sufficiency of information offered to justify a search or seizure, the Supreme Court has found sufficient flexibility in Fourth Amendment reasonableness to permit relaxation and sometimes abandonment of that requirement. It might seem that in regard to search or arrest warrants, little flexibility is permitted, given the specific command of the Fourth Amendment that "no Warrants shall issue, but upon probable cause . . . ." But the Court has not regarded itself as strictly bound by this language. Where governmental officials seek access to business or residential premises to determine whether there has been compliance with safety and health regulations, the Court has held that a search warrant is required,[10] although a warrant authorizing such an administrative inspection need not be based upon the same sort of information as would be necessary for a warrant authorizing a search for evidence of criminal activity. "Probable cause" for an administrative search need not depend upon specific information tending to indicate that a violation exists in any particular structure. Rather, " 'probable cause' to issue a warrant to inspect must exist if reasonable legislative or administrative standards for conducting an area inspection are satisfied with respect to a particular dwelling."[11] These standards may focus upon the passage of time, the nature of the structure, or the condition of the entire area. This dilution of the probable cause standard for administrative inspections was apparently based upon the Court's conclusions that such inspections are less intrusive upon privacy than traditional criminal investigation searches and that imposition of the traditional probable cause requirement would result in frustrating the only available method of enforcing important governmental regulations related to health and safety.[12]

In some other areas, these same considerations and related ones have resulted in abandonment of the probable cause standard. Perhaps the most significant has been the validation of certain detentions of the person on less than probable cause; these are discussed in Section 172, infra. In regard to some searches of premises licensed for certain exceptional uses,[13] the Court ap-

---

10. Camara v. Municipal Court, 387 U.S. 523 (1967) (residential premises); See v. City of Seattle, 387 U.S. 541 (1967) (business premises).

11. Camara v. Municipal Court, 387 U.S. 523, 538 (1967).

12. In Marshall v. Barlow's Inc., 436 U.S. 307 (1978), the Court held that work areas of facilities within the jurisdiction of the Occupational Safety and Health Act of 1970 could be "inspected" without consent only under the authority of a warrant. The warrant could issue, however, upon a "showing that a specific business has been chosen for OSHA search on the basis of a general administrative plan for the enforcement of the Act derived from neutral sources . . ." 436 U.S. at 321.

A similar but limited dilution of the probable cause requirement was recognized in Michigan v. Tyler, 436 U.S. 499 (1978). Once a fire is extinguished and an immediate investigation concluded, the Court held, fire officials need a warrant for further searches of the burned structure. But if the examination is merely a general one to determine the fire's origin, the warrant may issue upon a diluted administrative-type showing of probable cause. If probable cause to believe arson was committed is developed, however, further intrusions must be pursuant to a warrant issued under the traditional showing required for criminal investigatory search warrants.

13. What uses permit legislatively authorized inspections of this sort is not entirely clear. It appears that the sale of intoxicating liquor, Colonnade Catering Corp. v. United States, 397 U.S. 72 (1970), and dealing in firearms, United States v. Biswell, 406 U.S. 311 (1972) will qualify. But in Marshall v. Barlow's Inc., 436 U.S. 307 (1978), the Court rejected the proposition that engaging in any business subject to the jurisdiction of the Occupational Safety and Health Act of 1970 permitted such inspections. The "industries" at issue in *Colonnade Catering Corp.* and *Biswell*, unlike those involved in *Marshall*, have "a long tradition of

pears to have abandoned any informational requirement at all, at least where the searches or inspections are conducted pursuant to statutory schemes that impose reasonable limits upon them. Thus in Donovan v. Dewey,[14] the Court upheld the right of the Secretary of Labor to inspect mines subject to the Federal Mine Safety and Health Act of 1977, without a warrant and apparently without any information supporting the need for the particular inspection at issue. While the Court has not ruled directly on the matter, it appears virtually certain that searches of persons and items crossing the international border into the country and perhaps passing a point inside the country that is the "functional equivalent" of the border [15] require no informational basis at all.[16]

Again, the abandonment of the supporting information requirement is based upon the importance of the government interest involved, and the interference with enforcement of that interest that would be caused by imposing an informational requirement. In addition, these areas have a consent flavor that arguably reduces the intrusiveness

of the governmental intrusion. One need not leave the country or engage in highly regulated uses of one's premises; if one chooses either of these courses of action, one can reasonably anticipate governmental regulatory activity and consequently the "searches" or "inspections" should reasonably be experienced as less intrusive than other invasions of privacy.

Requirements Exceeding Probable Cause. The Supreme Court addressed the possibility that certain "plain view" seizures require more than probable cause in Texas v. Brown.[17] The lower court had held that an officer was entitled to seize a party balloon discovered during an automobile search only if he "knew" the balloon contained illicit drugs. Rejecting this apparent demand that more than probable cause exist to render the seizure reasonable, the Court commented that ordinarily probable cause is all that is necessary.

Lower court decisions suggest that in some search situations involving exceptionally severe intrusions upon privacy interest, traditional probable cause may not suffice.

---

close governmental supervision, of which any person who chooses to enter such a business must already be aware." 436 U.S. at 313.

14. 452 U.S. 594 (1981).

15. In United States v. Ramsey, 431 U.S. 606 (1977) the Court upheld the examination of mail entering the country. Under the applicable statute, inspection was permitted upon "reasonable cause to suspect" the mail contained improper material. But the Court stated, "Border searches . . . have been considered to be 'reasonable' by the single fact that the person or item in question had entered into our country from outside. There has never been any additional requirement that the reasonableness of a border search depended on the existence of probable cause." 431 U.S. at 619.

16. See Almeida–Sanchez v. United States, 413 U.S. 266, 272 (1973) (routine border searches "may in certain circumstances take place not only at the border itself but at its functional equivalents as well"). While the Supreme Court has not addressed the issue, lower federal courts have imposed an informational requirement upon extraordinarily intrusive border searches. While frisks or patdowns of persons crossing the border do not invoke this requirement, strip or body cavity searches do. See United States v. De Gutierrez, 667 F.2d 16, 19 (5th Cir. 1982). The standard for strip searches appears to be one of objective suspicion. See United States v. Asbury, 586 F.2d 973 (2d Cir. 1978) (rejecting 9th Circuit "real suspicion" requirement and

adopting 5th Circuit "reasonable suspicion" standard, because requirement that suspicion be "real" adds unnecessarily confusing factor). There appears agreement that body cavity searches, because of their greater intrusiveness, require more than strip searches. See United States v. De Gutierrez, supra. The Ninth Circuit requires for a body cavity search that the officers have a "clear indication" or a "plain suspicion" that the subject has contraband concealed in the body cavity. This requires more than "real suspicion" but less than probable cause. United States v. Aman, 624 F.2d 911, 912–13 (9th Cir. 1980); United States v. Shields, 453 F.2d 1235 (9th Cir. 1972), cert. denied 406 U.S. 910. Drawing the line between the types of search is not always easy. See United States v. Aman, supra, finding no need to decide whether an X-ray examination of the suspect to determine if objects were present in the body cavity was a "body cavity" search requiring a "clear indication" or "plain suggestion."

17. 103 S.Ct. 1535 (1983), on remand 657 S.W. 797 (Tex.Cr.App.). On the other hand, the Court has held that brief seizures of property for investigatory purposes—analogous to "field stops" of suspects—are permitted on *less than* probable cause. See United States v. Place, 103 S.Ct. 2637 (1983) (where officer has reasonable suspicion the luggage observed in airport contains contraband, brief seizure of that luggage to investigate the circumstances is permissible).

In People v. Scott, for example, law enforcement officers sought a court order compelling the defendant to submit to a medical procedure involving massaging of his prostate gland through his rectum in order to cause an ejaculation, which could be used for certain tests that might have confirmed his daughter's claim that sexual intercourse between the two had occurred. Where a warrant authorizing a bodily intrusion of this sourt is sought, the California Supreme Court held, the issuing judge must first determine if there is probable cause to believe the intrusion will result in obtaining evidence. If such probable cause is found, it continued, the judge

> must apply an additional balancing test to determine whether the character of the requested search is appropriate. Factors which must be considered include the reliability of the method to be employed, the seriousness of the underlying criminal offense and society's consequent interest in obtaining a conviction . . . , the strength of law enforcement suspicions that evidence of crime will be revealed, the importance of the evidence sought, and the possibility that the evidence may be recovered by alternative means less violative of Fourth Amendment freedoms.[18]

"Mere Evidence." Prior to Warden, Maryland Penitentiary v. Hayden,[19] Supreme Court case law could be read as establishing that a seizure of an item was unreasonable for purposes of the Fourth Amendment if the only basis for that seizure was reason to believe it constituted evidence of someone's guilt of a criminal offense.[20] The prohibition did not, then, apply to seizures of items on the basis of adequate reason to believe the items were contraband, fruits of a criminal

offense, or instrumentalities of the commission of a crime. The rule appeared to rest in part[21] upon the proposition that if society's interest in law enforcement possession of the item was based only upon reason to believe the item was of evidentiary value, the subject's interest in retaining possession was necessarily greater and therefore any interference with that continued possession was inherently unreasonable. The rule prohibiting seizure of items of "mere evidence," then, can be regarded as resting upon the proposition that no showing that an item was of evidentiary significance, even if that showing far exceeded the ordinary probable cause standard, could be sufficient under Fourth Amendment reasonableness analysis.

In *Hayden*, however, the Court abandoned the "mere evidence" rule. Recognizing that government has a legitimate interest in "proving crime," the Court held that upon a showing of probable cause to believe that items will aid in a particular apprehension or conviction, the items become subject to reasonable seizure under the Fourth Amendment. It remains open, however, whether persons may have so important a privacy interest in some items—such as a personal diary—that their seizure might have to be supported by a showing of more than traditional probable cause to believe them of evidentiary value to the prosecution.

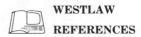

WESTLAW REFERENCES

"Probable Cause:" The Benchmark
topic(349) /p "probable cause" /p information /p officer*

---

18. 21 Cal.3d 284, at 293, 145 Cal.Rptr. 876, at 880, 578 P.2d 123, at 127 (1978). In addition, or perhaps as an alternative, a court order authorizing a "search" of such intrusiveness may require that greater procedural opportunities to challenge the search before it occurs be extended to the subject. United States v. Crowder, 543 F.2d 312 (D.C.Cir. 1976), cert. denied 429 U.S. 1062 (court order authorizing surgical removal of item from subject's body required full adversary hearing before trial judge and opportunity for appellate review before surgery was conducted).

19. 387 U.S. 294 (1967).

20. The leading case was Gouled v. United States, 255 U.S. 298 (1921).

21. In addition, the "mere evidence" rule appeared to rest in part on the supposition that use of evidence obtained from a defendant by search and seizure against that same defendant constituted compelled self-incrimination in violation of the Fifth Amendment. It is now clear that no compulsion to engage in testimonial activity is involved in such seizure and use of evidence, see § 126 supra, and that this concern is no longer significant. See Warden, Maryland Penitentiary v. Hayden, 387 U.S. 294, 302–03 (1967).

Informants' Tips

digest,synopsis(informant* tip* /s "probable cause") &
    total! /5 circumstances*

*Dilution or Abandonment of Probable Cause
Standard*

digest,synopsis(border* checkpoint* /s search! /s
    require! standard*)

Requirements Exceeding Probable Cause

extreme! excess! severe! /p intru! /p search! /p
    requir! standard*

Mere Evidence

hayden /s warden & date(after 6/1/83)

---

§ 171. Evidence Obtained Pursuant to Unreasonable Searches and Seizures: (c) The Procedural Requirement of a Search Warrant and Its Exceptions [1]

The language of the Fourth Amendment is ambiguous as to the methods to be employed to assure that the right of the people to be secure against unreasonable searches and seizures is not violated. Although the second clause specifies a warrant procedure, the relationship between the clauses is such that it is not clear whether the framers intended that a warrant be required for all or most searches, or whether and when a search made upon adequate information might be "reasonable" despite the absence of a search warrant.[2] Early Supreme Court cases vacillated,[3] but the Court has now committed itself to the position that the Fourth Amendment directs heavy reliance upon the search warrant process as a means of protecting the right to be free from unreasonable searches.[4] Searches, to be rea-

sonable, must be made under the authority of a valid search warrant unless the situation is brought within one of the exceptions to the warrant requirement. The rationale for this position was well stated by Mr. Justice Jackson:

> The point of the Fourth Amendment, which often is not grasped by zealous officers, is not that it denies law enforcement the support of the usual inferences which reasonable men draw from evidence. Its protection consists in requiring that those inferences be drawn by a neutral and detached magistrate instead of being judged by the officer engaged in the often competitive enterprise of ferreting out crime.[5]

Whether this emphasis upon the warrant process is justified is problematic. In theory, the warrant process prevents unjustifiable searches before they occur. The case law finds this possibility of such importance that as a general rule a search without a warrant is held invalid even if post-search scrutiny discloses that the officer had probable cause; thus maximum incentive is provided for officers to seek pre-search judicial evaluation of the adequacy of their information. But there is widespread suspicion that the underlying assumptions are incorrect. Magistrates may in fact exercise little independence in evaluating the sufficiency of information submitted with requests for warrants. If this is so, the Court's emphasis upon the warrant process has created a rather complex set of requirements for comparatively little return.[6] Further, it can be argued that the Court's emphasis upon the

---

§ 171

1. See generally, Bloom, Warrant Requirement—The Burger Court Approach, 53 U.Colo.L.Rev. 691 (1982).

The Fourth Amendment is set forth in § 169 n. 1 supra.

2. Landynski, Search and Seizure and the Supreme Court 42–44 (1966).

3. Compare Trupiano v. United States, 334 U.S. 699 (1948) (warrantless search unreasonable) with Harris v. United States, 331 U.S. 145 (1947) and United States v. Rabinowitz, 339 U.S. 56 (1950).

4. Chimel v. California, 395 U.S. 752, 762 (1969) rehearing denied 396 U.S. 869 ("general requirement that a search warrant be obtained").

5. Johnson v. United States, 333 U.S. 10, 13–14 (1948) (Jackson, J.).

6. Perhaps the most influential embodiment of a cynical approach to the warrant requirement appears in Model Code of Pre-Arraignment Procedure, Commentary on Article 220 (Official Draft 1975) (refers to "present perfunctory, routine character" of warrant procedure but nevertheless follows existing approach).

The most recent direct attack upon the warrant requirement was mounted by the Government in United States v. Chadwick, 433 U.S. 1 (1977), involving the search of a large footlocker seized in the defendants' possession. Officers had probable cause to believe it contained marijuana; the only issue was whether, after seizing it, they were obligated to delay a search until a warrant was obtained. The Government argued that

warrant process has deflected its attention from other matters that, if developed and emphasized, might prove more effective in controlling law enforcement activity. Whatever the merits of the matter, however, the role of the warrant requirement in Fourth Amendment reasonableness law is clear and therefore requires elaboration.

Warrants and "Plain View Seizures." The Court has apparently accepted the proposition that the general rule requiring a warrant applies only to searches and not to seizures. If, therefore, an officer is able to approach an item in a manner not constituting a search or pursuant to a search with some independent justification, there is no general requirement that the officer have a warrant authorizing the seizure of that item.[7] The officer's observation of an item in "plain view" is not a "search"; assumption of dominion over an item, while a "seizure" within the protection of the Fourth Amendment, is reasonable without regard to the existence or availability of a warrant. If an automobile which officers have probable cause to believe is subject to seizure is located on a public street, it may be seized. But if it is located on private property so that a search is necessary to ef-

fectuate the seizure, a search warrant (or other justification) is necessary to render the pre-seizure search reasonable in Fourth Amendment terms.[8] The position was recently defended by Justice Rehnquist:

> [W]hen a peace officer has observed an object in "plain view," the owner's remaining interests in the object are merely those of possession and ownership. . . . [R]equiring the police to obtain a warrant . . . generally would be a "needless inconvenience," that might involve danger to the police and public.[9]

Why a citizen's interest in "possession and ownership"—apparently as contrasted with the interest in secrecy concerning some aspects of the characteristics or contents of an object—are not entitled to the protection of the warrant requirement was not developed.

A strong suggestion appears in the opinions discussing plain view seizures that the right to make a warrantless seizure applies only where the officer comes upon the items "inadvertently."[10] Negatively put, no plain view seizure—under this approach—is permissible "where the discovery is anticipated, where the police know in advance the location of the evidence and intend to seize it . . . .", and reliance upon the plain view seizure doctrine is a pretext.[11] Whether a

---

the general requirement of a warrant be limited to searches of the home, and that other searches, especially those of movable personalty come upon in a public place, be evaluated under a more flexible standard of reasonableness. Rejecting this argument, the Court stressed the importance of the warrant requirement: "By placing personal effects inside a double-locked footlocker, respondents manifested an expectation that the contents would remain free from public examination. No less than one who locks the doors of his home against intruders, one who safeguards his personal possessions in this manner is due the protection of the Fourth Amendment Warrant Clause." 433 U.S. at 11. Even the dissenters rejected what they characterized as "an extreme view" of the warrant clause assumed by the Government's argument. Id. at 17 (Blackmun, J., dissenting).

7. See Harris v. United States, 390 U.S. 234 (1968) (warrantless seizure of automobile registration card plainly visible when door was lawfully opened, permissible). See generally, Lewis & Mannle, Warrantless Searches and the "Plain View" Doctrine: Current Perspective, 12 Crim.L.Bull. 5 (1976); Moylan, The Plain View Doctrine: Unexpected Child of the Great "Search Incident" Geography Battle, 26 Mercer L.Rev. 1047 (1975).

8. G.M. Leasing Corp. v. United States, 429 U.S. 338, 354 (1977) on remand 560 F.2d 1011, cert. denied 435 U.S. 923.

9. Texas v. Brown, 103 S.Ct. 1535, 1541 (1983), on remand 657 S.W.2d 797 (Tex.Cr.App.) (opinion of Rehnquist, J., announcing the judgment of the Court). See also, Coolidge v. New Hampshire, 403 U.S. 443, 467–468 (1971), rehearing denied 404 U.S. 874 (opinion of Stewart, J., announcing the judgment of the Court).

10. The suggestion originally appeared in Justice Stewart's plurality opinion in Coolidge v. New Hampshire, 403 U.S. 443, 469 (1971), rehearing denied 404 U.S. 874. In Texas v. Brown, 103 S.Ct. 1535, 1540 (1983), on remand 657 S.W.2d 797 (Tex.Cr.App.), Justice Rehnquist's plurality opinion described the *Coolidge* discussion of plain view as not binding precedent but as "the considered opinion of four Members of this Court" and therefore "obviously . . . the point of reference for further discussions of the issue."

11. The pretext aspect was added by Justice Rehnquist's *Brown* opinion; the remainder of the phraseology is from Justice Stewart's *Coolidge* opinion.

majority of the Supreme Court would impose such a limitation upon the right of plain view seizure is not clear. In any case, the meaning of "inadvertence" as used in any such requirement as exists is uncertain. Is a warrantless plain view seizure barred only if officers "knew" they would come upon the item and had this knowledge at a time when a warrant could have been obtained? Or are they to be faulted for not applying for a warrant in any case where their information was arguably sufficient to give them probable cause to believe the item would be come upon? If the plain view seizure rule is subject to a requirement of inadvertence, perhaps the rule is generally inaccurately stated. Correctly, the rule would apply only if, in addition to "plain view" and probable cause, the facts show inadvertent discovery. Perhaps, however, characterization of inadvertence as a limitation was intended to reflect the appropriate allocation of the burden of persuasion. Generally, the state probably bears the burden of justifying a warrantless search; if only a seizure is at issue, however, the burden may be upon a defendant attacking its validity to establish that the officers came upon the item "advertently."

Exceptions to Warrant Requirement. There is widespread agreement that most Fourth Amendment reasonable searches are warrantless searches that come within one of the exceptions to the general rule requiring a warrant. Those exceptions related to detentions of suspects are considered in Section 172. The others can only be briefly summarized here. It is important to note that the fact that a search comes within an exception to the warrant requirement does not mean that the requirement of probable cause is inapplicable.[12] Some searches are

exceptions to both the requirement of a warrant and the demand of probable cause; the two issues are, however, distinguishable.

Automobiles. Because of the high risk that delaying a search of a moving car until a warrant is obtained would frustrate the officer's ability to make the search, the Court has recognized an officer's right to stop and search a moving vehicle upon probable cause but without a warrant.[13] Further, this has been expanded to cover automobiles that were recently stopped but have been immobilized by the detention of the occupants.[14] Finally, if a right exists to search an automobile in the field, officers may—without any apparent need for Fourth Amendment justification—decide to delay the search until the vehicle is moved to a station house.[15] The basic exception, of course, is grounded upon the proposition that in most situations involving moving automobiles, delaying the search to secure a warrant will create too high a risk that the search will become impossible. But this is less seldom the case when the car has been stopped and especially when it has been moved to the station house. Whether the frequent existence of exigent circumstances supports the last two aspects of the exception is questionable. More likely, these must be justified on the basis that one's expectation of privacy in one's car is relatively low and therefore the warrant requirement may properly be more readily relaxed when only this reduced privacy interest is at risk.

Consent Searches.[16] A search or seizure pursuant to an effective consent is reasonable despite the absence of a warrant and the nonexistence of probable cause. The Supreme Court has recognized the effectiveness of certain so-called "third party" con-

---

12. § 170 supra.

13. Carroll v. United States, 267 U.S. 132 (1925); Brinegar v. United States, 338 U.S. 160 (1949).

14. Chambers v. Maroney, 399 U.S. 42 (1970) rehearing denied 400 U.S. 856. See Annot., 26 L.Ed.2d 893 (warrantless search of automobiles).

15. Chambers v. Maroney, 399 U.S. 42 (1970) rehearing denied 400 U.S. 856. While *Chambers* could have been construed as resting upon the demonstrated

need on the facts of that case to delay the search until the vehicle was moved to headquarters, the Court has since made clear that no such demonstration of need is required. Texas v. White, 423 U.S. 67 (1975) rehearing denied 423 U.S. 1081.

16. Gardner, Consent as a Bar to Fourth Amendment Scope—A Critique of a Common Theory, 71 J.Crim.L. & C. 443 (1980).

sents to searches of items [17] and premises.[18] Anyone with "joint access or control for most purposes" has authority to give an effective consent that will render the search reasonable even when challenged by others.[19] The rationale for this is not entirely clear. In United States v. Matlock,[20] however, the Court appeared to accept an assumption-of-risk rationale; by permitting others access to one's property, one assumes the risk that those persons will consent to a search of it.[21] Perhaps a more appropriate justification would address the subject's reasonable expectation of privacy and its scope. It is arguable that one who gives others sufficient access to property or premises so as to enable them to admit still others can have no reasonable expectation that his privacy will be "complete." At most, the reasonable expectation of privacy is conditioned upon the other person's willingness to withhold consent.

Whether the consent was articulated by the defendant challenging the search or by a third person, it must be "voluntary" to be effective. In Schneckloth v. Bustamonte,[22] the Supreme Court rejected the position that consent was a "waiver" to be tested under the standard criteria for an effective waiver of federal constitutional rights. Limiting the use of those criteria to purported waiver of rights guaranteed to a defendant to assure an accurate determination of guilt or innocence, the Court stressed that Fourth Amendment rights are accorded persons for other—and presumably less important—reasons.[23] Thus in order to establish an effective consent, the government need not prove that the consent was "knowingly" given in the sense that the person was aware of a right to refuse.[24] It follows, of course, that a consent need not be preceded by a warning that a right to refuse exists. Instead, the controlling question is whether, given the "totality of the circumstances," the consent was voluntary.[25] Among those factors relevant to the determination of this issue are the existence of detention (and the validity of any detention that existed),[26] the subject's awareness of the right to refuse,[27] a perception by the subject that the officers have legal authority to search without consent or that a search is inevitable whether consent is given or not,[28] any impairment of the subject that rendered the subject less able to resist,[29] any pressure placed on the subject,[30]

17. Frazier v. Cupp, 394 U.S. 731 (1969) (one of two joint users of duffel bag in whose house bag had been left could consent to search of entire bag).

18. United States v. Matlock, 415 U.S. 164 (1974) (woman with whom defendant shared bedroom could consent to search of bedroom).

19. United States v. Matlock, 415 U.S. 164, 171 n. 7 (1974).

20. 415 U.S. 164 (1974).

21. Id. at 171.

22. 412 U.S. 218 (1973) on remand 479 F.2d 1047.

23. Id. at 235–46. The Court described those rights as requiring a "knowing and intelligent" waiver as rights guaranteed to assure a "fair" trial. Id. at 241. But in the overall context, it is clear that by "fair" the Court meant "accurate."

24. Id. at 234.

25. Id. at 227.

26. In *Bustamonte*, the Court characterized the issue before it as the effectiveness of a consent given while not in custody. 412 U.S. at 248. Yet it appeared that the consent given in the case was given by a subject who, while not under formal arrest, was being detained. Id. at 220 (consent given after car "stopped"

and occupants, including person whose consent was at issue, had stepped out at the officer's "request"). In United States v. Watson, 423 U.S. 411 (1976), involving consent by a subject under formal arrest, this factor appears to have been given little weight by the Court in finding the consent voluntary.

27. Schneckloth v. Bustamonte, 412 U.S. 218, 249, on remand 479 F.2d 1047 (1973).

28. In Bumper v. North Carolina, 391 U.S. 543 (1968) appeal after remand 5 N.C.App. 528, affirmed 275 N.C. 670, 170 S.E.2d 457, the Court held ineffective an alleged consent given after officers represented that they had a search warrant for the premises. *Bumper* may be read as holding that words of consent articulated after officers assert a "claim of legal right" to search are, as a matter of law, ineffective. Or, it may be read that such a showing is entitled to especially great weight in applying the "totality of the circumstances" test.

29. See Schneckloth v. Bustamonte, 412 U.S. 218, 226 (1973) on remand 479 F.2d 1047 (need to consider youth of the subject, lack of education, low intelligence, and failure to inform him of his legal rights).

30. Id. (Need to consider length of detention, repeated and prolonged nature of questioning, and any

and perhaps the presence or absence of a "rational" motive for giving consent.[31] No single factor, however, is controlling.

Border Searches. Searches of persons and items crossing the international border into the country or passing a point that is the "functional equivalent" of the international border have been regarded as exceptions to the requirement of a warrant as well as to the requirement of supporting information.[32] This has also been extended to permit stops of automobiles and brief questioning of their occupants for purposes of determining national origin if this is done at a checkpoint located in reasonable proximity to the international border.[33] Obviously, a warrant requirement would be impractical for all such searches. But in addition, since these searches are subject to no requirement of adequate supporting information [34] it is arguable that the warrant process would be useless because there would be no determination for the issuing magistrate to make.

Inspections of Certain "Licensed Premises." While the Court has held that ordinary health or safety inspections without con-

sent must be conducted pursuant to warrants (albeit warrants issued under a diluted probable cause standard),[35] it has also identified certain statutory regulatory schemes that can validly permit inspections without prior warrant authority being obtained.[36] These appear to be schemes regulating uses of property for what can be characterized as uses with a tradition of close governmental regulation and perhaps that pose exceptionally high risks to important social interests. This exception can be justified on the need for inspectors to have flexibility in making inspections that would be reduced if a warrant requirement is imposed. In addition, the statutory schemes generally limit the inspections in ways that minimize their intrusiveness. But further, since no supporting information need exist for these inspections, again a warrant requirement would seem to serve little purpose.

Search for Person to be Arrested. Traditionally, courts have held that officers with grounds to arrest a suspect have quite broad power to make warrantless searches of premises to locate and arrest the suspect.[37]

---

use of "physical punishment" such as deprivation of food or sleep).

31. United States v. Mendenhall, 446 U.S. 544, 555–56 (1980) rehearing denied 448 U.S. 908 (opinion of Stewart, J.). Mendenhall allegedly consented to a search of her person; as it began, she took several packets of heroin from her undergarments and handed them to the officer. The defense claimed that her actions were so contrary to her obvious self-interest that the only permissible inference was that the consent was involuntary. Justice Stewart, speaking for a majority of the court on this issue, responded that "the question is not whether [Mendenhall] acted in her ultimate self-interest, but whether she acted voluntarily." He then continued to suggest that Mendenhall might have concluded that her self-interest would best be furthered by voluntarily cooperating with the officers in the hope of receiving lenient treatment later. Id. at 559 n. 7.

32. See Almeida-Sanchez v. United States, 413 U.S. 266, 272–73 (1973). See also, United States v. Ramsey, 431 U.S. 606 (1977).

33. United States v. Martinez-Fuerte, 428 U.S. 543 (1976) on remand 538 F.2d 858. A full search of a vehicle at such a checkpoint is not, however, permissible. See United States v. Ortiz, 422 U.S. 891 (1975). And roving patrols in the vicinity of the border are, despite the border considerations, subject to the Fourth

Amendment requirement of "objective suspicion" for an investigatory stop. United States v. Cortez, 449 U.S. 411 (1981) on remand 653 F.2d 1253, cert. denied 455 U.S. 923; United States v. Brignoni-Ponce, 422 U.S. 873 (1975).

34. § 170 supra.

35. § 170 supra.

36. Donovan v. Dewey, 452 U.S. 594 (1981) (warrantless inspection of mines as authorized by Federal Mine Safety and Health Act of 1977, 30 U.S.C.A. § 813(a)); United States v. Biswell, 406 U.S. 311 (1972) (inspection of premises used for carrying on business of firearms dealer licensed under Gun Control Act of 1968, 18 U.S.C.A. § 921 et seq.). In *Dewey*, the Court indicated that warrantless inspections were permitted by the Fourth Amendment only if a legislature had reasonably determined that such searches are necessary to a regulatory scheme and the "regulatory presence" is "sufficiently comprehensive and defined that the owner of commercial property cannot help but be aware that his property will be subject to periodic inspections undertaken for specific purposes." 452 U.S. at 600.

37. See, e.g., United States v. Latimer, 415 F.2d 1288 (6th Cir. 1969); People v. Sprovieri, 43 Ill.2d 223, 252 N.E.2d 531 (1969).

In Steagald v. United States,[38] however, the Court held that in the absence of consent or exigent circumstances, a search of third-party premises for a suspect was permissible only pursuant to a valid search warrant authorizing a search for that person. But in Payton v. New York,[39] the Court had held that the suspect's own premises could be searched for the suspect without a search warrant if the officers had a valid arrest warrant. The rationale for the *Payton* holding is not clear. Apparently the Court was willing to conclude that if the officers, by obtaining an arrest warrant, provided exceptional assurance that grounds for arrest existed, the intrusion into the suspect's privacy in his residence was insufficiently important to require protection by the warrant process.[40] The securing of an arrest warrant, of course, does not require the magistrate to address the likelihood of the subject being in his residence at any particular time. Yet the fact that premises are a suspect's living place may itself constitute probable cause to believe the suspect will be there at any particular time. It remains unclear whether an arrest warrant will be sufficient to protect the privacy interest of others who jointly occupy premises also occupied by the suspect sought in the search.

Exigent Circumstances. If a search fits within one of the categories described above, a warrantless search is permissible even if on the facts of a particular case an opportunity to secure a warrant existed. In addition, however, there is clearly a catchall category that permits a warrantless search where none of these exceptions applies if it is established that on the facts of the case the officers reasonably believed that delaying the search to seek a warrant would create an excessive risk that the search would be frustrated by the removal of the items or similar considerations.[41] It is unclear how great a risk of frustration the officers must reasonably perceive in order to justify a warrantless search. In Vale v. Louisiana,[42] however, the Court's action strongly suggested that where the search is of residential premises the perceived risk of destruction of the evidence must be quite high to justify a warrantless search. It remains unclear whether there is an intermediate quasi-exigent circumstance category of cases in which the officers lack the authority to search without a warrant but may "secure" the situation, as by preventing persons from entering or perhaps leaving, while a warrant is sought.[43]

Containers. A major subquestion presented by the warrant requirement concerns its applicability to containers found during otherwise appropriate law enforcement activity. May such containers be searched or must they be seized and searched only if a warrant specifically authorizing such a search is obtained? If a container, such as a large trunk locker, is located in the vicinity of an arrest but is not subject to search incident to that arrest, a search of it must be pursuant to a warrant unless other justification—such as exigent circumstances—exists.[44] In situations in which law enforcement officers have a right to conduct a full search, containers found during that search may be examined to determine their contents. During a search incident to arrest, for example, containers "immediately associated with the person of the arrestee" can be

---

38. 451 U.S. 204 (1981) on remand 656 F.2d 109, rehearing granted 664 F.2d 1241, on remand 664 F.2d 1242.

39. 445 U.S. 573 (1980) on remand 51 N.Y.2d 169, 433 N.Y.S.2d 61, 412 N.E.2d 1288.

40. Id. at 602–03 (1980).

41. Schmerber v. California, 384 U.S. 757 (1966) (warrantless extraction of blood without a warrant justified by reason to believe that delaying search to obtain a warrant would have resulted in absorption of blood alcohol and frustration of search).

42. 399 U.S. 30 (1970).

43. In Rawlings v. Kentucky, 448 U.S. 98 (1980), the Court assumed that the detention of the petitioner pursuant to the process of securing the residence while a warrant was sought was improper, but found that the challenged confession was not fatally tainted by the detention.

44. United States v. Chadwick, 433 U.S. 1 (1977).

examined pursuant to the officer's right to search the arrestee and items on the arrestee's person.[45] Officers with probable cause to believe contraband is located somewhere in an automobile may search the automobile and containers found inside.[46] But if the probable cause is "specific," in the sense that it justifies a conclusion that the contraband is only located within certain containers, a warrantless search of the car to locate those containers may be made and the containers may be seized. A search of the containers, however, requires a valid search warrant.[47]

Procedural Aspects of the Warrant Process. The Court's construction of the Fourth Amendment's warrant clause has included a number of what might be called "procedural" requirements relating to the issuance and execution of arrest and search warrants. On the other hand, it is clear that not all aspects of warrant law have been constitutionalized, and some remain matters of only state law.

The Court has held that a valid warrant may only be issued by a person with reasonable impartiality. A financial incentive to issue a warrant[48] or active participation in the execution of the warrant[49] will render the issuing person sufficiently "partial" to render the warrant invalid. Although arrest warrants for minor offenses may be issued by a clerk acting under the direction of a judicial

officer,[50] it is likely that search warrants and arrest warrants for serious offenses must be issued by a person holding a judicial office. It is doubtful, however, that the Fourth Amendment requires that the warrant be issued by a lawyer or law trained judge.[51]

The warrant must issue, under the terms of the Fourth Amendment, only "upon probable cause, supported by Oath or affirmation." But this probably permits the sworn showing of probable cause to be in oral as well as written form, at least if the oral showing is transcribed and made a formal part of the issuing court's records.[52] Most important, the information submitted must be sufficient to permit the issuing person to make an independent judgment as to whether probable cause exists. Thus the somewhat structured analysis for determining whether probable cause is shown by an informer's tip[53] applies here as well as in other probable cause contexts.

The language of the Amendment requires that the warrant issued be one "particularly describing the place to be searched, and the persons or things to be seized." Most concern has focused upon the adequacy of warrants' descriptions of the items which the officers are authorized to search for and seize if found. Specially rigorous requirements have been imposed where the items are of a kind possibly subject to First Amendment

45. United States v. Chadwick, 433 U.S. 1, 14–15 (1977) (dictum); United States v. Robinson, 414 U.S. 218 (1973) (search of crumpled cigarette package found on arrestee's person permissible during search incident to arrest).

46. United States v. Ross, 456 U.S. 798 (1982).

47. Arkansas v. Sanders, 442 U.S. 753 (1979) (where probable cause showing gave officers reason to believe contraband was contained in suitcase which Sanders had taken into taxi, officer lacking warrant could search taxi to locate and seize suitcase but could not search suitcase).

48. Connally v. Georgia, 429 U.S. 245 (1977) on remand 238 Ga. 403, 233 S.E.2d 381 (justice of the peace was paid $5 for each warrant issued and nothing for warrant application refused).

49. Lo-Ji Sales, Inc. v. New York, 442 U.S. 319 (1979) (magistrate accompanied officer to scene and

participated in examination of possibly obscene materials). See also, Coolidge v. New Hampshire, 403 U.S. 443 (1971) rehearing denied 404 U.S. 874 (search warrant in murder investigation invalid because issued by state Attorney General actively in charge of investigation and later chief prosecutor at trial).

50. Shadwick v. City of Tampa, 407 U.S. 345 (1972).

51. In Shadwick v. City of Tampa, supra n. 50, this argument was rejected in regard to arrest warrants for minor offenses. Cf. North v. Russell, 427 U.S. 328 (1976) (due process not denied by misdemeanor trial before nonlawyer judge, at least where defendant has right to trial *de novo* before law trained judge).

52. Fed.R.Crim.P. 41(c)(1) (oral testimony can supplement search warrant affidavit if it is taken down and "made part of the affidavit").

53. See the discussion as to the requirements for probable cause in § 170 supra.

"free speech" protection[54] or stolen items which are usually easily subject to precise description.[55] But in Andreson v. Maryland[56] the Court held that an authorization to search for and seize, among other things, "other fruits, instrumentalities and evidence of crime at this [time] unknown," when construed to refer to the land fraud offense for which the warrant had issued, was sufficiently precise.

Execution of search warrants also presents some matters of Fourth Amendment concern and others that may not rise to this level. The Supreme Court has, without significant discussion, enforced federal statutory requirements that officers announce their identity and purpose before breaking to enter to execute a search warrant.[57] It has not, however, determined whether the Fourth Amendment contains such a "prior announcement" requirement or, if so, what exceptions permitting so-called "no knock" entries exist.[58] While it has not specifically addressed the issue, the Court has strongly indicated that the timing of the execution of a search warrant is not of Fourth Amendment concern, so no special justification is needed—as a matter of federal constitutional law—for nighttime execution of such warrants.[59]

On the other hand, the scope of the search is clearly limited by the authorization in a search warrant. Persons on the premises at the time of the execution of a search warrant may be searched only if the warrant's authorization, fairly read, permits this and if the showing of probable cause on which the warrant was issued included probable cause to believe the items described might be on the person of such individuals.[60] Further, the Court's approach suggests a need to construe the language of warrants "against" the government: "[A] warrant to search a place cannot normally be construed to authorize a search of each individual in that place."[61] Within the premises described, the officers are limited by the warrant's description of the items they may look for and seize. Thus, while the majority in Stanley v. Georgia[62] did not reach the question, it seems clear that the warrant in issue in that case, which authorized a search for items related to bookmaking, did not authorize the officers executing the warrant to view films they came upon during the search. If, however, officers have not exceeded their authority to search under the warrant and come upon items in "plain view," they may generally seize those items despite the failure of the warrant to authorize this as long as they have probable cause

---

54. Stanford v. Texas, 379 U.S. 476 (1965) rehearing denied 380 U.S. 926.

55. See discussion in Gonzales v. State, 577 S.W.2d 226 (Tex.Crim.App.1979), cert. denied 444 U.S. 853.

56. 427 U.S. 463 (1976).

57. The Supreme Court case law involves situations in which the unannounced entry was for purposes of locating a suspect and arresting him. The Court was willing to regard the entry for this purpose as subject to the same requirements and to enforce those requirements with an exclusionary sanction. Sabbath v. United States, 391 U.S. 585 (1968); Miller v. United States, 357 U.S. 301 (1958).

58. Ker v. California, 374 U.S. 23 (1963) appeared to raise the issue of Fourth Amendment requirements for entry of residential premises by state officers to make an arrest. While the holding of the Court is difficult to discern, the case is best read as holding that the entry before the Court would come within an exception to any such Fourth Amendment requirement of prior announcement that might exist. Therefore, the Court did

not reach and decide whether a general Fourth Amendment requirement does apply.

59. See Gooding v. United States, 416 U.S. 430 (1974). No Fourth Amendment issue was before the Court, but the Court's analysis of the statutory issue presented indicates no tendency to regard the matter of nighttime execution as having Fourth Amendment implications.

60. Ybarra v. Illinois, 444 U.S. 85 (1979) rehearing denied 444 U.S. 1049.

61. Id. at 92 n. 4

62. 394 U.S. 557 (1969) on remand 225 Ga. 273, 167 S.E.2d 756. A majority of the Court decided the case on the ground that the First and Fourteenth Amendments bar the criminalization of possession of obscene material in the privacy of the home. Justice Stewart, however, concurred on the ground that the search involved in inspection of the films was beyond the scope of the warrant and not otherwise justifiable. Id. at 569–72 (Stewart, J., concurring in the result).

to believe the items are such as they have a right to seize.[63]

On the other hand, the Court has held that the requirements of a return on the warrant, often imposed by local law, are not of Fourth Amendment dimension. In Cady v. Dombrowski,[64] the officers failed to include two items in the inventory that was required as a part of the process of making a return of the warrant. Rejecting the assertion that this rendered the items inadmissible as a matter of Fourth Amendment law, the Court commented that "[t]he ramification of [this] 'defect,' if such it was, is purely a question of state law." [65]

Warrants and Non-Fourth Amendment Exclusionary Sanctions. Perhaps more than any other area of search law, the procedural aspects of the warrant process, and especially the search warrant process, provide often-unrecognized issues concerning the exclusionary sanction. A number of matters are apparently not of Fourth Amendment dimension; these include the execution of a warrant in the nighttime, compliance with return requirements, and perhaps the manner of gaining entry to premises to execute a warrant. Insofar as these remain matters of state law, the states remain free to consider the purposes of those requirements as exist in these areas, the importance of those purposes, and whether those purposes would be reasonably pursued at no more than acceptable expense by a state-imposed exclusionary sanction mandating the suppression of evidence obtained through searches conducted in violation of the requirements.

Further, there is a discernable trend in the Supreme Court's recent Fourth Amendment cases to contract application of the warrant

requirement.[66] To the extent that this is done, an opening is created for state courts to consider whether state requirements—constitutional or otherwise—may require resort to the warrant process where federal constitutional standards do not. While the Supreme Court's construction of the Fourth Amendment's reasonableness and warrant clauses provides an available model for construction of similarly phrased state provisions, state courts remain free to give their provisions independent construction and to reweigh for themselves the difficult policy considerations bearing upon the appropriate role of the warrant process in the investigation of crime.

 WESTLAW REFERENCES

Warrants and "Plain View Seizures"
topic(349) /p "plain view" /p necess! require! standard! /p warrant!

Automobiles
349k3.3(7) & date(1983)

Consent Searches
349k7(27) /p third another /2 party parties

Border Searches
digest,synopsis(border! checkpoint* /s search! /s auto* automobile* car cars truck* vehicle* van vans) & date(after 1976)

Licensed Premises
digest,synopsis(search! seiz! inspect! /p warrant* warrantless /p license* regulated controlled /10 industr! premises property)

Search for Person To Be Arrested
110k394.4(9) /p premise property dwelling house home residence apartment /s arrest! defendant

Exigent Circumstances
digest(requir! standard* /s warrant! /p exigen! "hot pursuit" destro! remov! conceal!) & date(after 1980)

Containers
topic(349) /p warrant! /s requir! standard! /s container* trunk* suitcase* briefcase* box! carton!

---

63. See the discussion of "plain view seizures" and the possible exception where the undescribed items are come upon "advertently" in the text at note 11, supra.

64. 413 U.S. 433 (1973).

65. Id. at 449.

66. See the decisions limiting the application of the search warrant requirement to "plain view" seizures, discussed in the text following note 7, supra, and to searches of "containers," discussed in the text following note 45, supra. Similarly, the Court has found the

warrant requirement inapplicable to searches of certain "stopped" automobiles, see text following note 14, supra, stopping of vehicles at fixed checkpoints related to the international border, see text following note 32 supra, and to the inspection of certain premises used for highly regulated commercial activities, see text following note 35, supra. In addition, the warrant requirement has been held inapplicable to arrests, see § 172 infra, and an arrest warrant has been held sufficient to render reasonable the entry of a suspect's own premises to search for him, see text following note 39 supra.

Procedural Aspects
349k3.4 /p specific! particular! precis!

Warrants and Non-Fourth
topic(349) /p warrant! /p high** strict! stringent /s
   standard* require! /s state federal

§ 172. Evidence Obtained Pursuant to Unreasonable Searches and Seizures: (d) Evidence Related to Seizures of the Person

Perhaps the most frequently-encountered exceptions to the general Fourth Amendment rule that warrants are required for searches are certain searches related to a confrontation between a citizen and a law enforcement officer. The right to make any such search at all and the scope of any such search as may be made depends upon two considerations. First is whether the confrontation involves a detention—or, in Fourth Amendment terms, a "seizure" of the citizen's person. The second is what sort of detention has been made. The Supreme Court has distinguished a number of different types of detentions for Fourth Amendment purposes, including detentions of persons on or near premises searched pursuant to a warrant,[1] detention of persons for brief questioning at fixed checkpoints located reasonably proximate to the border,[2] and detentions at the station house to implement certain investigational techniques such as fingerprinting.[3] But the major categories that require exploration are arrests and field detentions on less than probable cause.

Arrests and Incidental Searches. The broadest right to search that can be justified on the basis of an officer-citizen confronta-

tion arises when an officer has made an arrest. The arrest creates a need to locate weapons that the arrestee might use to resist or escape and any evidence that the arrestee might destroy. Obviously, the immediacy of this need precludes resort to the warrant requirement.[4] Moreover, the Court's conclusion that the arrest alone renders an incidental search reasonable [5] means that a warrant-issuing magistrate would serve no function, thus confirming the rationale for exempting these searches from the requirement of a warrant. Unfortunately, the Supreme Court has failed to define arrest for the purposes of this rule. The resulting confusion has been further complicated by its assumption that the right to conduct a search "incident to" an arrest requires that the arrest be a "custodial" one.[6] It appears most likely, however, that an arrest for purposes of the present rule is a detention of a person made for purposes of transporting that person to the station house with the intention of there pursuing formal criminal charges against that person.

Emphasizing the traditional acceptance of warrantless arrests, the Supreme Court has held that an arrest itself virtually never requires a warrant.[7] As a result, even if officers secure an arrest warrant and it is later held invalid, the arrest may be upheld as a valid warrantless arrest if other requirements are met.[8] The requirement of probable cause applies with full force in any situation, however, and a valid arrest may be made only on the basis of information amounting to probable cause to believe the

---

§ 172

1. Michigan v. Summers, 452 U.S. 692 (1981).

2. United States v. Brignoni-Ponce, 422 U.S. 873 (1975).

3. Davis v. Mississippi, 394 U.S. 721 (1969), appeal after remand 255 So.2d 916, cert. denied 409 U.S. 855 (dictum). In *Davis*, the Court suggested that such stationhouse detentions would require a warrant, albeit perhaps not a supporting showing of traditional probable cause. Id. at 728.

4. See discussion in Chimel v. California, 395 U.S. 752 (1969), rehearing denied 396 U.S. 869.

5. See text at note 10, infra.

6. United States v. Robinson, 414 U.S. 218, 235 (1973).

7. United States v. Watson, 423 U.S. 411 (1976), rehearing denied 424 U.S. 979. A warrant is required in certain circumstances to enter premises to search for a suspect and effect an arrest of that suspect. Further, if the entry is unreasonable, the resulting arrest will presumably fall as well. See § 170 supra.

8. The Court assumed this to be possible in Whiteley v. Warden, 401 U.S. 560 (1971) and Chimel v. California, 395 U.S. 752 (1969), rehearing denied 396 U.S. 869.

person guilty of an offense. It has been suggested, but the Court has not considered, that a custodial arrest for certain minor offenses may involve an intrusion into the suspect's privacy so disproportionate to the public interest involved that such an arrest is "unreasonable" in Fourth Amendment terms because of its custodial nature.[9]

If, however, a valid custodial arrest has been made, the officer may search the person of the arrestee and containers found on the arrestee's person. This may be done as an automatic consequence of the arrest; no reason to believe that the arrestee has destructable evidence or weapons need exist and, indeed, the officer need not even believe such items to be present.[10] In addition, the officer may search those areas which the arrestee might reasonably be expected to reach to secure access to evidence or weapons.[11] If the arrestee is moved, the right to search the arrestee's "area of reach" also may expand, although it is likely that the officer may not move the arrestee for the sole purpose of thereby expanding the right to search.[12]

The Court has held that the right to make an incidental search does not depend upon the officer having formally "made" or articulated words indicating an arrest before the search. If grounds for arrest existed and formal arrest was made soon after the search, the search can be regarded as "incidental" to the arrest.[13] Presumably, the ultimate question is whether immediately before the search the officer intended to subject the suspect to the rigors of an arrest, i.e., transportation to the station house and formal charging. Further, an incidental search can be delayed and conducted after the suspect has been jailed, at least if there is some reasonable basis for doing so.[14]

Field Confrontations and "Frisks". The Supreme Court has made clear that officers may detain a person in the field for purposes of inquiry and investigation upon less than probable cause. Apparently, the information on which such a seizure is based must be at least "reasonable suspicion" that the person has engaged or is engaged in criminal activity.[15] The Court has declined to decide whether or when such a stop may be

---

9. See Gustafson v. Florida, 414 U.S. 260, 266–67 (1973) (Stewart, J., concurring). See generally, Folk, The Case for Constitutional Constraints upon the Power to Make Full Custody Arrests, 48 U.Cinn.L.Rev. 321 (1979).

10. United States v. Robinson, 414 U.S. 218 (1973) (arrest for driving after revocation of driver's license by officer who entertained no fear for his safety nevertheless justified search of person and of crumpled cigarette package found in arrestee's pocket).

11. Chimel v. California, 395 U.S. 752 (1969), rehearing denied 396 U.S. 869. Automobiles present a special situation that has been handled separately. In New York v. Belton, 453 U.S. 454 (1981), on remand 55 N.Y.2d 49, 447 N.Y.S.2d 873, 432 N.E.2d 745, the Court, while purporting to do no more than determine the meaning of *Chimel's* principles in the automobile context, held that an officer who has made a lawful arrest of "the occupant" of an automobile may, incident to that arrest, search the passenger compartment of the automobile. This right applies even if, on the facts of a particular case, the occupant has been removed and will clearly be prevented from re-entering the automobile so as to be able to reach weapons or evidence contained therein. *Belton* must be viewed as promulgating a separate rule for searches of cars, rather than an application of *Chimel's* principles.

12. Washington v. Chrisman, 455 U.S. 1, 6 (1982) (officer who makes arrest may "remain literally at [the

arrestee's] elbow at all times" and could accompany arrestee into dormitory room).

13. Rawlings v. Kentucky, 448 U.S. 98 (1980). In Cupp v. Murphy, 412 U.S. 291 (1973), on remand 479 F.2d 1327, the Court held that where grounds to arrest existed, some search was permissible even if an arrest was not made. On the facts, officers who had probable cause to believe evidence was present under Murphy's fingernails were entitled to take scrapings from under his nails after he was alerted to their desire for such scrapings. Quite clearly, the Court wished to avoid creating an incentive for officers to effect an arrest, with its attendant restriction on liberty, where this was not regarded as necessary from a law enforcement perspective.

14. United States v. Edwards, 415 U.S. 800 (1974) (when arrestee was booked at 11:00 P.M., officers could require him the next morning to remove his trousers and exchange them for other clothing and those trousers could be examined; "normal processes incident to arrest and custody" were not completed until after clothing exchange had taken place).

15. United States v. Cortez, 449 U.S. 411 (1981), on remand 652 F.2d 1253, cert. denied 455 U.S. 923; Adams v. Williams, 407 U.S. 143 (1972). In Terry v. Ohio, 392 U.S. 1 (1968) the Court found that no pre-frisk detention had taken place, so that it did not need to address the right to detain a suspect for investigation, as

based upon an officer's reasonable suspicion that a person intends to commit an offense in the future and that the stop may deter such action.[16] Nor has it addressed whether a stop is permissible where the reasonable suspicion does not relate to the subject's own involvement in criminal activity but instead concerns the likelihood that the subject has information concerning someone's else involvement in crime. The Court has rejected without discussion the argument that such field stops should be limited to offenses more serious than certain "possession crimes," in view of the ease with which the detention power for such offenses might be abused.[17]

The justification for regarding such detentions on less than probable cause as reasonable rests in large part upon the assumption that limits upon the detentions render them

less intrusive upon privacy interests than arrests.[18] Despite this, however, the Court has not developed the limits on the field detention power that are imposed by the Fourth Amendment. It is not clear, for example, how long a detention on reasonable suspicion can last nor has the Court developed any limitations that might exist on movement of the subject from the area of the initial detention.[19]

A field confrontation between a law enforcement officer and a citizen can occur without giving rise to a detention demanding support by reasonable suspicion. The criterion for determining whether a detention has occurred is not well developed. In United States v. Mendenhall,[20] however, Justice Stewart suggested that contact between a member of the public and a police officer amounts to a detention only if "a reasonable

contrasted with seizing the suspect for the purposes of conducting the frisk. 392 U.S. at 19 n. 16.

The Court has found such reasonable suspicion lacking in several cases. In Reid v. Georgia, 448 U.S. 438 (1980), on remand 156 Ga.App. 78, 274 S.E.2d 164, reversed 247 Ga. 445, 276 S.E.2d 617 (per curiam), for example, the Court held that a showing that the defendant, upon arrival at the Atlanta airport, met a "drug courier profile" did not constitute justification for an investigatory stop. See also, Brown v. Texas, 443 U.S. 47 (1979) (observing defendant and another walking away from each other in an alley not reasonable suspicion concerning drug offense); United States v. Brignoni–Ponce, 422 U.S. 873 (1975) (apparent Mexican ancestry of car's occupants not reasonable suspicion that occupants were illegal aliens).

See generally, Preiser, Confrontations Initiated by the Police on Less than Probable Cause, 45 Albany L.Rev. 57 (1980); Note, 46 Albany L.Rev. 631 (1982).

16. In Terry v. Ohio, 392 U.S. 1 (1968) the officer believed that the suspects, confronted as they walked *away* from the area of suspicion, had been "casing" the premises for a robbery. If the confrontation had involved a detention, it would have been necessary to consider whether the detention was authorized by the New York "stop and frisk" statute which permitted a stop of a person reasonably suspected (among other things) of being "about to commit a felony or any of certain specified offenses . . . ." Further, it would have been necessary to consider whether and to what extent the Fourth Amendment permitted "preventive" stops of persons who, even if the officer's suspicions are confirmed, are not subject to arrest because they have not yet committed an offense. The Court's disposition of the case, of course, left the issue open. No further occasion has been presented for readdressing it.

17. In Adams v. Williams, 407 U.S. 143 (1972), Justice Brennan expressed hesitancy in extending the right to stop on less than probable cause to persons suspected of possession of narcotics. Id. at 151–52 (Brennan, J., dissenting). The majority, however, held the detention at issue in the case to be valid without reference to this argument.

18. Cf. Terry v. Ohio, 392 U.S. 1 (1968) (detention for frisk is "brief").

19. In Dunaway v. New York, 442 U.S. 200 (1979) officer with less than probable cause—but arguably reasonable suspicion—took Dunaway into custody, transported him to the station house, and questioned him. The Court held the detention invalid. It is unclear, however, whether the Fourth Amendment defect was the duration of the detention, the movement of Dunaway to the station house during the detention, the purpose of the detention (i.e., to conduct station house interrogation), or some combination of these factors.

Cf. United States v. Place, 103 S.Ct. 2637 (1983) (detention of luggage for 90 minutes on less than probable cause held improper and in dictum Court suggests that nonarrest detention of suspect for such a period would also be impermissible).

20. 446 U.S. 544 (1980), rehearing denied 448 U.S. 908. Justice Stewart's opinion was joined only by Justice Rehnquist. He found, applying his standard, that no seizure took place on the facts before the Court. Justice Powell, joined by the Chief Justice and Justice Blackmun, concurred on the basis that if a detention took place it was reasonable. Justice Powell indicated he did "not necessarily disagree" with Justice Stewart's analysis, apparently including the statement of the criterion. Id. at 560 n. 1 (Powell, J., concurring in part and concurring in the judgment).

person would have believed that he was not free to leave." Evidence that the citizen attempted to break off the confrontation but was either restrained or expressly told that restraint would be applied, of course, would be conclusive. But in other situations where no restraint had been used or expressly threatened a detention might still be found. Among the other factors that might suggest that a detention took place, Justice Stewart continued in *Mendenhall,* are the "threatening presence" of several officers, display of weapons, physical touching of the person, or "the use of language or tone of voice indicating that compliance with the officer's request might be compelled." [21] This standard appears likely to find favor with at least a majority of the Court.

In situations involving nonarrest confrontations between officers and citizens, the officers' right to search without consent is far less than in the arrest situation. In contrast to arrest situations, the fact that a confrontation or even a detention valid under the Fourth Amendment exists does not, in itself, justify any search. If—but only if—the officer also has reason to believe his safety is endangered he may conduct a search.[22] This search must generally at least be initially limited to a patdown of the outer garments of the citizen.[23] If that patdown discloses some confirmation that the citizen has a weapon on his person, the officer may conduct a more intrusive search—as by reaching into a pocket—to determine whether in fact a weapon is present. The Court has not specifically defined the "reason to believe" necessary for a frisk, but it seems clear that this is significantly less than probable cause to believe the citizen is in possession of a weapon. It probably reflects a standard similar or identical to the "reasonable suspicion" criterion used to determine the validity of a field detention for investigation.

Unlike the search incident to arrest situation, a valid field stop for investigation is not a necessary prerequisite for a reasonable frisk. In Terry v. Ohio,[24] the Court made clear that a nondetention confrontation between a citizen and a police officer could result in the development of reason to fear for safety and thus the right to frisk. Most frisks, however, will occur during a field stop. In such situations, it is likely that if the field stop is invalid because the officer lacked reasonable suspicion, the frisk will be regarded as a "fruit" of the detention and must fall with the stop itself.

 **WESTLAW REFERENCES**

Arrests and Incidental Searches
110k394.4(9) /p custod! detent! detain!

Field Confrontations and Frisks
sh 392 us 1
terry /15 392 /5 1 & date(after 6/1/83)

See also, Florida v. Royer, 103 S.Ct. 1319, 1326 (1983) (plurality opinion of Rehnquist, J., announcing the judgment of the Court) (applying same criterion).

21. Id. at 554.

22. Adams v. Williams, 407 U.S. 143, 146–48 (1972), considering separately the forcible stop of the defendant and the examination of the defendant for weapons.

23. In Sibron v. New York, 392 U.S. 40 (1968), a companion case to Terry v. Ohio, the officer had thrust his hand into Sibron's pocket and discovered heroin. Assuming a right to frisk, the Court held this impermissible, because "with no attempt at an initial limited exploration for arms, [the officer] thrust his hand into

Sibron's pocket . . . ." 392 U.S. at 65. But Adams v. Williams, 407 U.S. 143 (1972) makes clear that an initial frisk is not always necessary. In *Williams,* the officer reached into the car in which Williams was sitting and found and removed a gun from Williams' waistband. Although it upheld the officer's action, the Court did not explain the justification for failing to conduct an initial frisk. On the facts, this might have been justified by the officer's receipt of information that Williams did have a weapon and that it was "at his waist," or by the difficulty (or impossibility) of conducting a frisk of someone seated inside an automobile.

24. 392 U.S. 1 (1968).

§ 173. Right to Counsel at Lineups and Confrontations With Witnesses [1]

In two 1967 cases, United States v. Wade [2] and Gilbert v. California,[3] the Supreme Court held that under certain circumstances a criminal defendant compelled to participate in identification procedures has a Sixth and Fourteenth Amendment right to representation by counsel present at the procedure.[4] Violation of this right, the Court further held, invoked an exclusionary sanction.

Identification procedures such as lineups, the Court reasoned, contain a high potential for suggestiveness, with the resulting danger that the witness' identification testimony at trial will be the product of law enforcement suggestion rather than the witness' observation and memory. If an attorney representing the defendant is present at the identification procedure, the Court concluded, suggestive procedures will be effectively discouraged. Further, counsel will be alerted to any such suggestive aspects of the procedure as are not deterred and will be able, by effective cross-examination at trial, to recreate these for consideration by the trier of fact. The trier of fact, thus alerted to the witness' pretrial exposure, will give the witness' testimony only that weight to which it is objectively entitled. Violation of the right to counsel was held to be enforceable by an exclusionary sanction applicable to the trial testimony of the witness who observed the

defendant at an identification procedure conducted in violation of the right to counsel.

Both the right to counsel thus recognized and the exclusionary sanction applicable upon its violation are, however, subject to very significant limitations. In United States v. Ash,[5] the Court limited the right to representation to those identification procedures that involved a physical confrontation between the defendant and the witness. Thus there is no right to the presence of an attorney at a procedure during which the witness is merely shown photographs of suspects, including the defendant. Since the defendant is not personally involved in the process, the Court reasoned, the photo showing is not a "trial-like adversary confrontation," there is no danger that the defendant will be misled by his lack of familiarity with the law or overpowered by his adversary, and therefore there is no need for representation by counsel. But the right applies to even informal opportunities for personal confrontation. In Moore v. Illinois,[6] for example, the defendant's right was found violated when he was observed by the witness during a court appearance.

In addition, the right to counsel applies only to personal confrontations that occur after adversary judicial criminal proceedings have been begun.[7] In Moore v. Illinois,[8] however, the Court stressed that this did not mean that only after indictment or its equivalent must the right be respected. Rather,

§ 173

1. Decker, Moriarty & Albert, The Demise of Procedural Protections in Laywitness Identifications in Federal Court: Who is the Culprit? 9 Loyola U.L.J. 335 (1978); Levine & Tapp, The Psychology of Criminal Identification: The Gap from Wade to Kirby, 121 U.Pa.L.Rev. 1079 (1973); Salisbury, Eyewitness Identifications: A New Perspective on Old Law, 15 Tulsa L.J. 38 (1979): Comment, 77 Yale L.J. 390 (1967).

2. 388 U.S. 218 (1967).

3. 388 U.S. 263 (1967). A third case decided the same day, Stovall v. Denno, 388 U.S. 293 (1967) is considered in the following section.

4. The right includes the right to appointment of counsel for suspects unable to provide their own retained representation. Where, as in Wade and Gilbert, counsel have aready been appointed, the right includes

notification of counsel and counsel's presence, in the absence of an effective waiver. 388 U.S. at 237. The Court left open the possibility that counsel might not mean the defendant's own attorney, especially where location and notification of that attorney would result in substantial delay. In such situations, representation by substitute counsel might suffice. Id.

5. 413 U.S. 300 (1973).

6. 434 U.S. 220 (1977), on remand 577 F.2d 411, cert. denied 440 U.S. 919.

7. Kirby v. Illinois, 406 U.S. 682 (1972) held the right to counsel inapplicable to a confrontation between the defendant and a witness almost immediately upon the arrival of the defendant at the stationhouse.

8. 434 U.S. 220 (1977), on remand 577 F.2d 411, cert. denied 440 U.S. 919.

where a complaint had been signed and filed and the defendant appeared in court for a preliminary hearing to determine whether to bind him over for grand jury consideration, adversary proceedings had begun and the right to counsel applied.[9]

Finally, the right to counsel recognized in *Wade* and *Gilbert* is waivable.[10] Even a personal confrontation with a witness after adversary proceedings have commenced conducted in the absence of counsel is not a violation of the Sixth Amendment if the defendant has made an effective waiver of this right. The right to counsel is one of those rights extended to defendants to assure that trial results in an accurate determination of guilt or innocence; counsel's role is to safeguard against the trier of fact being influenced by unreliable identification testimony.[11] Therefore, the waiver must be a voluntary and intelligent relinquishment of a known and understood right.

In addition to these limitations upon the right itself, the exclusionary sanction brought into play by a showing of a violation of these rights contains a significant exception. In *Gilbert*, the Court applied a so-called *per se* exclusionary sanction to testimony by a witness concerning the witness' identification of the defendant at a lineup conducted in violation of the defendant's right to counsel.[12] Such testimony is never admissible. In *Wade* the Court held that generally a violation of the right to counsel would also require the suppression of a witness' in-court identification of the defendant if the witness had viewed the defendant at a lineup conducted in violation of the defen-

dant's right to counsel.[13] But applying the case law holding that the taint of illegal law enforcement activity may be "attenuated," [14] the Court held that such a witness may be permitted to make an in-court identification of the defendant if the prosecution shows, by clear and convincing evidence, that the in-court identification would have an "independent source," that is, would be based upon observations of the suspect other than those occurring at the time of the constitutionally deficient identification procedure. In regard to making the necessary determination, the Court stated:

> Application of [the] test . . . requires consideration of various factors; for example, the prior opportunity to observe the alleged criminal act, the existence of any discrepancy between any pre-lineup description and the defendant's actual description, any identification prior to lineup of another person, the identification by picture of the defendant prior to the lineup, failure to identify the defendant on a prior occasion, and the lapse of time between the alleged act and the lineup identification.[15]

Further, it is important to consider the suggestiveness of the identification procedure employed. The less suggestive the procedure, the stronger the prosecution's case is on the issue of independent source.[16]

There is significant question whether the right to counsel, especially as it has developed since *Wade* and *Gilbert*, is an effective means of dealing with the problem of suggestiveness in identification procedures. Whether triers of fact are sufficiently sensitive to the potential effects of suggestiveness upon eyewitness testimony is problematic. Thus even if the right was successful

---

9. Unfortunately, *Moore* did not address the question whether the filing of a complaint or a defendant's presentation before a magistrate alone are sufficient to constitute the initiation of criminal proceedings for purposes of the right.

10. United States v. Wade, 388 U.S. 218, 237 (1967) (notice to counsel and counsel's presence were a requisite to the lineup "absent an 'intelligent waiver' ").

11. See Schneckloth v. Bustamonte, 412 U.S. 218, 239–40 (1973), on remand 479 F.2d 1047.

12. Gilbert v. California, 388 U.S. 263, 272–72 (1967) (only a *per se* exclusionary rule applicable to such evi-

dence will assure that law enforcement authorities will respect the right to counsel).

13. United States v. Wade, 388 U.S. 218, 240–41 (1967) (limiting the exclusionary sanction to testimony concerning identifications made at the procedure itself "would render the right to counsel an empty one").

14. § 176 infra.

15. 388 U.S. at 241.

16. Id. at 242.

in enabling defense counsel to establish suggestiveness before the trier of fact, this might not lead to adequately critical assessment by the trier of fact of the witness' credibility. Of course, the mere possibility of such matters being developed during trial may encourage law enforcement agencies to avoid the suggestiveness in the first place. Perhaps more important, however, the limitations upon the right and its exclusionary sanction may greatly reduce the deterrent value. Waivers are probably easily obtained. Trial judges may quite readily find independent sources for offered in-court identifications and thus that testimony may be frequently admissible despite a violation of the right to counsel; whether the *per se* rule of exclusion applicable to testimony concerning identifications made at the procedure provides sufficient deterrence to suggestive procedures is doubtful. But most important, the inapplicability of the right to counsel to those identification procedures conducted before judicial proceedings are begun renders the right unavailable in what is quite likely a substantial number, and perhaps a significant majority, of pretrial identification procedures. The right may have no application to those situations in which it is most needed.

WESTLAW REFERENCES

digest(photo***** /s show*** /s represent*****
  counsel attorney /s right)

digest(indict! adversary /s identif! /s right /s
  counsel attorney represent!)

wade /15 388 /5 218 & date(after 6/1/83)

gilbert /15 388 /5 263 & date(after 6/1/83)

---

§ 174

1. See generally the sources cited in note 1, § 173 supra.

2. § 173 supra.

3. 388 U.S. 293 (1967).

4. Id. at 301–02.

§ 174. Due Process Prohibition Against Suggestive Lineups and Procedures With Witnesses [1]

At the same time as it decided the two seminal right-to-counsel-at-lineup cases, *Wade* and *Gilbert*,[2] the Supreme Court decided a third case that announced a separate and distinct doctrine relating to the admissibility of the testimony of witnesses who have been exposed to certain identification procedures. In Stovall v. Denno,[3] Stovall had been taken to the hospital room of the surviving victim of a murder-assault; he was handcuffed to one of the five accompanying police officers. The victim identified him at this showup and later at trial made an in-court identification. The Supreme Court held the right to counsel nonretroactive and thus no bar to admission of the victim's testimony. But it then turned to another claim made on behalf of Stovall, which it characterized as an argument that "the confrontation conducted in this case was so unnecessarily suggestive and conducive to irreparable mistaken identification that he was denied due process of law." This, it observed, "is a recognized ground of attack . . . independent of any right to counsel claim." Whether an identification procedure violates this due process requirement and mandates exclusion of resulting testimony, it continued, "depends on the totality of the circumstances surrounding it." Given the existence of doubt that the victim would survive her attack, the Court concluded, the presentation of Stovall to her in the manner chosen was "imperative" and no due process violation occurred.[4]

The nature of the due process requirement and the manner in which it should be applied was developed in Neil v. Biggers [5] and Manson v. Brathwaite.[6] In these cases, the

5. 409 U.S. 188 (1972). *Biggers* involved a lineup and trial conducted before the Court's decision in *Stovall*, see 409 U.S. at 200, and until *Brathwaite* there was some question whether the Court's emphasis upon reliability in *Biggers* might be limited to pre-*Stovall* factual situations.

6. 432 U.S. 98 (1977).

Court made clear that the rule was intended only to avoid certain risks of inaccurate in-court identifications and hence inaccurate determinations of guilt. It was not intended to serve the independent function of encouraging less suggestive identification procedures where this extremely high risk of error is not present. Consequently, despite the flavor of *Stovall*, any evidence that the suggestive nature of an identification procedure was unnecessary is irrelevant to whether the procedure and use of the results violated the defendant's due process rights.[7]

Biggers and *Brathwaite* made clear that in applying the due process rule, the sole concern is the reliability of the in-court testimony. If—but only if—the circumstances show "a very substantial likelihood of . . . misidentification" by the witness, due process requires exclusion of the testimony.[8] By "misidentifcation," the Court apparently means that the witness' testimony that he can identify the defendant as the perpetrator will not be based upon the witness' observations at the scene, his current recollection of those observations, and a comparison of those with the defendant's present appearance.[9] Rather, the testimony will be based upon the suggestion provided by the identification procedure.

In determining whether the required risk of misidentification exists, it is necessary, of course, to consider the amount and nature of suggestiveness resulting from the identification procedure.[10] Against this must be weighed any indications that the witness would nevertheless be able to make an accurate identification. In *Brathwaite*,[11] the Court enumerated several factors that might indicate the existence of such an ability: (1) the better the witness' opportunity to view the original events, the more likely it is that an accurate identification can be made; (2) the greater the witness' attention during that opportunity, the more likely it becomes that a permissible identification can be made; (3) the greater the consistency between the witness' description of the perpetrator given soon after the events and the appearance of the person identified at trial, the more likely it is that the identification will be permissible; (4) the greater the witness' certainty, i.e., expressed confidence in the accuracy of the identification, the more likely it is that the identification will be admissible; and (5) the shorter the time period between the original events and the identification procedure, the more likely it is that the witness will be able to make an accurate identification. Of course, the converse also applies. Defects in the witness' opportunity to observe or the witness' attention during those observations or a showing of significant inconsistencies between a description immediately after the event and the defendant's appearance will suggest an inability to make a sufficiently reliable identification.

The Supreme Court has decided only one case in which testimony was found to violate the due process standard. In Foster v. California,[12] the witness first viewed Foster in a three person lineup containing two persons

---

7. Manson v. Brathwaite, 432 U.S. 98, 114 (1977); Neil v. Biggers, 409 U.S. 188, 199–200 (1972).

8. Manson v. Brathwaite, 432 U.S. 98, 116 (1977); Neil v. Biggers, 409 U.S. 188, 198 (1972).

9. The language used by the Court suggests the possibility that reference might be had to the defendant's actual guilt or innocence. But this is unlikely. There is no rationale for limiting the rule to defendants who are shown by other evidence to be innocent. The comparison must be between what the witness would have said if the suggestive procedure had not been used and what the witness is prepared to say after being exposed to the suggestive procedure. If the prosecution claims that the use of the witness' testimony should not, given the other evidence showing guilt, in-

validate the conviction, the issue raised is one of application of the harmless error rule; see § 182 infra.

10. See Manson v. Brathwaite, 432 U.S. 98, 116 (1977) (although only single photograph showed to witness, photo was left for witness to view at his leisure and no officer was present imposing pressure upon witness to identify photo as that of perpetrator; there was "little pressure on the witness to acquiesce in the suggestion that a [single photograph] display entails").

11. See 432 U.S. at 114–16.

12. 394 U.S. 440 (1969). Due process claims were found without merit in Coleman v. Alabama, 399 U.S. 1 (1970), conformed to 46 Ala.App. 737, 239 So.2d 223; Simmons v. United States, 390 U.S. 377 (1968), on remand 395 F.2d 769, appeal after remand 424 F.2d 1235.

significantly shorter than Foster. When the witness tentatively identified Foster, a one-to-one confrontation was arranged. Again, the witness' identification was tentative. A second lineup was held; although it contained five persons, Foster was the only participant who had also taken part in the first lineup. After this procedure, the witness stated that he was convinced that Foster was the perpetrator. Finding a violation of due process the Court concluded that the police procedure rendered it "all but inevitable" that the witness would identify Foster whether or not he was the perpetrator and therefore so undermined the reliability of the witness' testimony as to violate due process.[13]

It remains unclear whether the due process prohibition is subject to the "independent source" exception developed in the right to counsel cases which sometimes permits in-court identification testimony despite the occurrence of a constitutionally defective identification procedure.[14] If the identification procedure is sufficiently suggestive to violate due process, is the prosecution nevertheless entitled to an opportunity to prove that the witness' in-court identification would have a source independent of the identification procedure? Lower courts have often assumed that such an opportunity is to be made available to the prosecution. But this seems inappropriate. The conclusion that the identification procedures were so suggestive as to create the required risk of misidentification seems to include a determination that the witness' testimony would be significantly affected by the observations at the scene of the events. To apply the independent source rule would seem to amount

to giving the prosecution two overlapping opportunities to stress the nature of the on-the-scene observations, one in the suggestiveness analysis and another in the independent source consideration. Under the better view, once the conclusion has been reached that an identification procedure was so suggestive as to violate due process, both in-court identification testimony and testimony concerning identifications made at the procedure should be excluded without the need for further consideration.[15]

The due process rule is obviously quite a broad one in that it applies whether or not adversarial prosecution had begun and regardless of whether a personal confrontation between the defendant and the witness occurs. Thus it applies to photograph showings and showups or lineups conducted immediately after the defendant has been taken into custody. On the other hand, the Court's reluctance to find the prohibition violated (except in *Foster*) makes equally clear that the rule is limited to exceptionally aggravated situations.

Conceptually, the due process rule is distinguishable from most other legal rules enforced by the exclusionary sanction. The other rules are designed to protect interests only indirectly if at all related to the accuracy of the challenged evidence and hence of the trial process. The due process rule, on the other hand, is designed to further *only* the interest in accuracy.[16] In any case, it is one of the few situations in which federal constitutional considerations bar submission of evidence to trial juries and reliance upon those juries to determine the appropriate credibility to give to the evidence. It makes clear that in at least very limited situations,

---

13. 394 U.S. at 443.

14. See Justice Black's concern in *Foster* regarding the failure of the majority to make clear whether on retrial the witness' in-court identification must be excluded. 394 U.S. at 445 (Black, J., dissenting).

15. If the prosecution's argument is that use of the testimony should not constitute reversible error in light of the overwhelming evidence of guilt, the applicable doctrine is harmless error; see § 182, infra. See also, Foster v. California, 394 U.S. 440, 444 (1969) (Court de-

clines to consider whether admission of testimony is harmless error because of a failure of lower courts to examine matter and remands for further proceedings).

16. See § 72 supra for extended comparison of rules of privilege and rules of exclusion generally. In Manson v. Brathwaite, 432 U.S. 98, 113 n. 13 (1977) the Court noted that unlike a warrantless search, a suggestive identification procedure does not in itself intrude upon a constitutionally protected interest.

the traditional methods of developing unreliability, such as cross-examination and impeachment, and the ability of jurors to make credibility evaluations cannot be relied upon to safeguard a criminal defendant's interest in being tried and convicted only upon reliable evidence of guilt.

 WESTLAW REFERENCES

topic(110 92) /p coerc! suggestiv! /s identif! lineup*
  procedure* action* activit! /p "due process" &
  date(after 1977)
digest,synopsis("independent source*" /p "due
  process" /p identif!)
110k339.10(6) & date(1983)
digest,synopsis("due process" /s reversible harmless
  /5 error /s identification*)

---

§ 175. Due Process Prohibition Against Conduct Which "Shocks the Conscience"

In Rochin v. California,[1] officers apparently lacking probable cause forcibly entered Rochin's bedroom, occupied by Rochin and his wife. Rochin seized two capsules from a nightstand and put them in his mouth. When the officers were unable to extract the capsules from his mouth, they transported him to a hospital where a physician forced an emetic solution into Rochin's stomach through a tube. This "stomach pumping" caused Rochin to vomit; in the vomited matter the two capsules were found. Rochin was charged with and convicted of possession of morphine found in the capsules; the capsules were the chief evidence used against him and were admitted over his objection.

The Supreme Court held that "the conviction of [Rochin] has been obtained by methods that offend the Due Process Clause" and must be invalidated. Relying on its decisions reversing convictions resting upon coerced confessions, the Court observed that "it has long since ceased to be true that due process of law is heedless of the means by which otherwise relevant and credible evidence is obtained."[2] Convictions obtained by methods that "shock the conscience," then, must fall as a matter of due process,[3] and this applies when the offensive methods are used to obtain evidence that is offered at trial. Turning to the application of these considerations to the case before it, the Court continued:

> Illegally breaking into the privacy of the petitioner, the struggle to open his mouth and remove what was there, the forcible extraction of his stomach's contents—this course of proceeding by agents of government to obtain evidence is bound to offend even hardened sensibilities. They are methods too close to the rack and the screw to permit of constitutional differentiation.[4]

It is not clear whether *Rochin* remains as viable authority for the proposition that due process requires the exclusion of evidence because of the methods by which it was obtained even if those methods did not violate other federal constitutional doctrines. It was decided during the period between *Wolf* and *Mapp* when the Court had held the Fourth Amendment applicable to the states but had not yet held the exclusionary remedy binding on the states.[5] There seems little doubt that tested under Fourth Amendment standards, the actions of the officers in *Rochin* constituted an unreasonable search and most likely as well an unreasonable detention. Perhaps *Rochin* reflected the Court's continued unwillingness to require the states to exclude all evidence obtained by conduct violating Fourth Amendment standards, but tempered with the caveat that extremely outrageous violation of that amendment required a remedy in a resulting prosecution. If so read, it is arguable that *Mapp* effectively superseded *Rochin*. Any conduct that would offend the *Rochin* standard, under this reading of the case, would also constitute a violation of the Fourth Amendment and exclusion would be re-

---

§ 175

1. 342 U.S. 165 (1952).
2. 342 U.S. at 172.

3. Id.
4. Id.
5. § 165 supra.

quired by *Mapp* without reference to *Rochin.*

On the other hand, *Rochin* may have continued vitality. It is very possible that law enforcement conduct may be offensive for reasons that do not give rise to violations of federal constitutional rights, at least as those are currently construed. In such cases, *Rochin* may well mean that evidence must be excluded if it was obtained in a manner that offends important values that are not embodied in specific constitutional doctrines, at least if the affront to those values was an extreme or outrageous one.

Excessive force may be a useful example. While the Supreme Court has not addressed the issue, there is substantial doubt that a search or detention will be rendered unreasonable for Fourth Amendment purposes by a showing that the officers used more force than reasonably appeared necessary to effect the search or detention.[6] But circumstances may arise in which the nature of the force used or the degree of excessiveness is so offensive to that aspect of privacy which relates to physical security that *Rochin* demands the exclusion of resulting evidence.[7]

 **WESTLAW REFERENCES**

"due process" /s shock! /5 conscience

rochin /p mapp

6. See generally, Dix, Means of Executing Searches and Seizures as Fourth Amendment Issues, 67 Minn.L. Rev. 89 (1982).

7. *Rochin* was distinguished in Breithaupt v. Abram, 352 U.S. 432 (1957), in which the Court found no due process violation in the use of evidence resulting from the drawing of a sample of blood from Breithaupt while he was unconscious. Emphasizing that blood tests have become routine in day-to-day life and that "the test as administered here would not be considered offensive by even the most delicate," the Court concluded that "a blood test taken by a skilled technician is not 'such conduct that shocks the conscience' . . . " within the meaning of *Rochin.* 352 U.S. at 437. See also, Schmerber v. California, 384 U.S. 757 (1966).

The Court has suggested that *Rochin* may, under some circumstances, not simply bar the admissibility of evidence but rather totally preclude prosecution. See United States v. Russell, 411 U.S. 423, 431–32 (1973)

excess! /s force /p search! seiz! arrest! /p "due process"

§ 176. The "Fruit of the Poisonous Tree" Doctrine and "Attenuation of the Taint"[1]

It would be possible to limit the effect of exclusionary rules to evidence obtained by law enforcement personnel contemporaneously with and as a direct result of the unlawful activity. This, however, has not been the construction given the sanctions. Again, the case law concerns almost exclusively the federal constitutional exclusionary rules and, in particular, the *Weeks-Mapp* Fourth Amendment sanction.

In Silverthorne Lumber Co. v. United States,[2] the trial court had suppressed certain documents and had ordered their return to the petitioners after determining that the documents had been obtained in an unreasonable search of an office. Nevertheless, the Government, relying upon information derived from the documents while they were in the Government's possession, sought to subpoena the documents from the petitioners, who resisted and were consequently held in contempt. The Supreme Court reversed the contempt citation. Characterizing the Government's position as "that the protection of the Constitution covers the physical possession [of the documents] but

(situation may exist in which conduct of law enforcement officers is "so outrageous" that "due process principles would absolutely bar the government from invoking judicial processes to obtain a conviction"). But compare, Hampton v. United States, 425 U.S. 484 (1976) (proof that government agent provided contraband which defendant is charged with selling would not create due process bar to conviction).

§ 176

1. See generally, R. Maguire, How to Unpoison the Fruit—The Fourth Amendment and the Exclusionary Rule, 55 J.Crim.L. C. & P.S. 307 (1964); Pitler, "The Fruit of the Poisonous Tree" Revisited and Shepardized, 56 Cal.L.Rev. 579 (1968); Annot., 43 A.L.R.3d 385; Dec. Digest Crim. Law ⬥ No. 394.1(3). The impact of an inadmissible confession upon other evidence is discussed in § 158 supra.

2. 251 U.S. 385 (1920).

not any advantages that the Government can gain over the object of its pursuit by doing the forbidden act," the Court rejected it: "The essence of a provision forbidding the acquisition of evidence in a certain way is that not merely evidence so acquired shall not be used before the Court but that it shall not be used at all." [3] In Nardone v. United States [4] Justice Frankfurter gave the doctrine applied in *Silverthorne Lumber Co.* its widely-used name by referring to a defendant's ability to obtain supression of evidence by establishing that it was "a fruit of the poisonous tree." [5]

A defendant has the right under the federal constitutional exclusionary sanctions, then, to have excluded any offered evidence that is the "fruit" of a demonstrated violation of the defendant's rights. In Wong Sun v. United States,[6] the Court referred to the evidence subject to exclusion as evidence "come at by exploitation of [the demonstrated] illegality . . . ." As this suggests, the initial question is one of "factual causation"—Was the challenged evidence rendered available to the prosecution as a factual result of the illegal activity? If this is not the case—if the challenged evidence had an actual source "independent" of the illegal activity—the "fruits" doctrine has no application. Where the required factual relationship between the illegal conduct and the challenged evidence exists, however, attention must then be turned to possible exceptions to the general rule that all fruit of the poisonous tree is inadmissible: the so-called "attenuation" doctrine and the inevitable legitimate discovery rule.

Independent Source. It follows from the statement of the doctrine above that it has no applicability to evidence obtained by the prosecution from sources factually unrelated to violations of a defendant's rights. This was recognized in *Silverthorne Lumber Co.,* in which the Court observed that "[i]f knowledge of [facts] is gained from an independent source they may be proved like any others . . . ." [7] This "independent source" aspect of the "fruits" rule has often been repeated [8] and was applied in United States v. Crews. [9] Crews had been improperly arrested and during the resulting detention a photograph was taken. This photo was shown to the victims of the offense, who identified Crews as the perpetrator. At trial, the trial judge ruled that the witnesses' pretrial identifications were inadmissible. He further concluded, however, that the witnesses' in-court identifications were based upon the witnesses' recollections of their observations at the time of the crimes; since these were untainted by the viewing of the illegally obtained photograph, therefore, they were admissible. The Supreme Court agreed, concluding that the challenged evidence was not the factual product of the illegal arrest and was therefore admissible.[10]

No Effect on Jurisdiction. Since Ker v. Illinois,[11] decided in 1886, the Supreme Court has consistently held that there is no federal constitutional bar to a court exercising jurisdiction over the person of a criminal defendant regardless of the manner in which the presence of the person was obtained.[12] In United States v. Blue,[13] the Court explained why this was not changed by the Court's commitment to the exclusionary remedy as the primary means of implementing many federal constitutional rights:

Our numerous precedents ordering the exclusion of . . . illegally obtained evidence assume implicitly that the remedy does not extend to barring the prosecution altogether. So drastic a step might advance marginally some

3. Id. at 392.

4. 308 U.S. 338 (1939).

5. Id. at 341.

6. 371 U.S. 471, 488 (1963).

7. 251 U.S. at 392.

8. E.g., Wong Sun v. United States, 371 U.S. 471, 487 (1963).

9. 445 U.S. 463 (1980).

10. Id. at 471–72.

11. 119 U.S. 436 (1886).

12. E.g., Frisbie v. Collins, 342 U.S. 519 (1952), rehearing denied 343 U.S. 937.

13. 384 U.S. 251 (1966).

of the ends served by exclusionary rules, but it would also increase to an intolerable degree interference with the public interest in having the guilty brought to book.[14]

The cost, of course, would be the complete and total loss of ability to convict the defendant, a cost not incurred in those cases where despite the suppression of some evidence pursuant to exclusionary sanctions other and admissible evidence sufficient for conviction nevertheless exists.[15]

Attenuation of Taint. As early as Nardone v. United States,[16] the Supreme Court suggested that challenged evidence might not be a suppressible "fruit" of demonstrated illegality even if there was a factual relationship between the illegality and the obtaining of the evidence. Despite a "causal connection" between illegality and the evidence, the Court commented, "[a]s a matter of good sense . . . such connection may have become so attenuated as to dissipate the taint." [17] This suggestion was repeated and applied in Wong Sun v. United States,[18] in which the Court contrasted evidence "come at by exploitation of . . . illegality" with evidence "come at . . . by means sufficiently distinguishable to be purged of the primary taint." [19]

Despite the simplicity with which the "attenuation" doctrine has been stated by the Court, determining whether attenuation has occurred is a difficult task. Several considerations seem to be relevant to whether attenuation has taken place in a given situation.

(1) Voluntary Choice. Perhaps the major thread running through the Court's attenuation cases is the significance the Court is willing to give to proof that the chain of events between an illegal action and the obtaining of the challenged evidence involved a voluntary decision by some person. In *Wong Sun*, for example, Wong Sun had been improperly arrested. He was released on his own recognizance, however, and several days later was present—under circumstances not described by the Court except for the observation that he had appeared "voluntarily"—at the Narcotics Bureau, where he was interrogated and made an incriminating statement. Without discussion, the Court concluded that the connection between his unlawful arrest and the making of the statement had become so attenuated as to dissipate the taint. Similarly, in United States v. Ceccolini [20] a witness had been located by following up information obtained during an unlawful search. In finding the taint attenuated, the Court emphasized the witness' voluntary (and in fact enthusiastic) decision to cooperate in the investigation upon being approached.[21]

(2) Time Sequence. It also seems clear that the longer the time period between the primary illegality and the obtaining of the challenged evidence, the more likely it is that attenuation has taken place. In *Wong Sun*, for example, the lapse of several days between the illegal arrest and the making of the statement was undoubtedly influential in the Court's decision. In contrast, another

---

14. Id. at 255.

15. In United States v. Crews, 445 U.S. 463 (1980), the defendant challenged an eyewitness' in-court identification testimony as the "fruit" of his unlawful arrest, reasoning that his presence in the courtroom was used by the witness in formulating the conclusion to which she testified. Five members of the Court regarded the matter as controlled by the *Ker* rule. Characterizing the argument as urging the suppression of the defendant's face because his presence in the courtroom resulted from an unlawful arrest, Justice White explained that to accept Crews' position "would be tantamount to holding that an illegal arrest effectively insulates one from conviction for any crime where an in-court identification is essential." 445 U.S. at 478 (White, J., concurring in the result).

16. 308 U.S. 338 (1939).

17. Id. at 341.

18. 371 U.S. 471 (1963).

19. Id. at 488.

20. 435 U.S. 268 (1978).

21. The witness was not specifically told of the illegally obtained information. Implicit in the Court's analysis is the suggestion that if the witness' decision to cooperate and testify had been influenced by awareness of the more direct fruits of the illegal search, the witness' decision would have been less "voluntary" and thus entitled to less weight as a factor suggesting attenuation.

confession by another defendant in that case, given moments after an unlawful detention began, was held to be the fruit of the detention.

(3) Magnitude of Misconduct. Several confession cases, beginning with Brown v. Illinois,[22] have indicated that the "purpose and flagrancy" of the primary illegality is relevant to attenuation of the taint. The rationale for this is not clear. It may be that the more flagrant the illegality, the more likely illegal conduct is to have a lasting impact upon those victimized by it. Or, it may be that the need to deter flagrant illegality or certain types of purposeful illegality is greater, and therefore attenuation of the taint and the accompanying exemption from the exclusionary sanction should be more sparingly found.

(4) Nature of Evidence at Issue. In at least one situation, the Supreme Court's case law makes clear that the nature of the challenged evidence should at least affect the attitude with which the search for attenuation should be undertaken. In *Ceccolini*, the Court rejected a *per se* rule that would have precluded the testimony of a witness from ever being the excludable fruit of prior illegality. But it made clear that lower courts should be more willing to find attenuation where the challenged evidence consists of such live-witness testimony. This position was apparently based upon the Court's perception that such testimony constitutes an unusually important and reliable type of evidence and consequently its exclusion involves a greater cost than is involved in enforcing the exclusionary sanction in other contexts. Witnesses often step forward voluntarily; they are not static, like papers hidden in a file. Where defendants challenge the admissibility of live witness testimony, "a closer, more direct link between the ille-

gality and that kind of testimony is required."[23]

A special attenuation issue is presented when one of the links in the chain between the primary illegality and the challenged evidence consists of action by a judicial officer. There is some indication in the case law that involvement of a judicial officer, if it does not automatically attenuate the taint, at least is a significant factor tending to show attenuation. In Johnson v. Louisiana,[24] for example, the defendant had been arrested under circumstances which he claimed rendered the arrest invalid. He was then presented before a magistrate who set bail; unable to make this bail, the defendant was committed to jail where he was viewed by the victim of a robbery. The victim identified the defendant as the perpetrator and later testified at Johnson's trial, over his objection that the testimony was the fruit of the illegal arrest. Finding that the taint of the arrest was attenuated, the Court emphasized the involvement of the magistrate: "At the time of the lineup, the detention of [Johnson] was under the authority of [the magistrate's] commitment."[25] Does this mean that if evidence is unlawfully obtained but is used to obtain a judicial authorization for further investigation the judicial nature of the authorization attenuates the taint? In Commonwealth v. White,[26] the Massachusetts court held that use of information obtained during improper interrogation of a suspect to obtain a search warrant did not attenuate the taint of the interrogation when the evidence obtained in the search was challenged. This was upheld by an equally divided Supreme Court without opinion.[27]

There seems no reason why involvement of a magistrate should have any special effect in attenuation analysis. Certainly there is no basis for believing that the magistrate's involvement somehow "cures" the il-

---

22. 422 U.S. 590 (1975). See also, Rawlings v. Kentucky, 448 U.S. 98 (1980).

23. United States v. Ceccolini, 435 U.S. 268, 278 (1978).

24. 406 U.S. 356 (1972).

25. Id. at 365.

26. 374 Mass. 132, 371 N.E.2d 777 (1977).

27. Massachusetts v. White, 439 U.S. 280 (1978) (per curiam).

legal nature of the earlier law enforcement activity. In *Johnson*, for example, it may be true that after his presentation before the magistrate, the technical basis for his continued detention was not the officer's authority to make a warrantless arrest but rather the magistrate's order of commitment. But there is no basis for concluding that in issuing this order of commitment the magistrate made any effort to evaluate the validity of the arrest or to mitigate the effect of any arrest that was determined to be invalid.

Inevitable Legitimate Discovery Exception.[28] Although the United States Supreme Court has not expressly ruled on the matter,[29] lower courts have almost uniformly recognized an exception to the Fourth Amendment and confession exclusionary rules for situations in which the prosecution establishes that the challenged evidence would have been properly obtained.[30]

This exception must be distinguished from other aspects of exclusionary rule law discussed above. Despite the tendency of some courts to confuse the two,[31] this exception is clearly distinguishable from the so-called "independent source" rule. Under the independent source doctrine, evidence is admissible because it was never tainted by illegal activity; the defendant has failed to show that "but for" the illegal activity, the evidence would not have been discovered as and when it was in fact discovered. The exception now under consideration, on the other hand, assumes the existence of a causal relationship between the illegal activity and the discovery of the challenged evidence but renders the evidence nevertheless admissible on the basis of proof of what would have happened had the illegal conduct been avoided or had it not led to discovery of the challenged evidence.

Similarly, this rule is distinguishable from attenuation of the taint. Under attenuation analysis, evidence is rendered admissible because of the length or nature of the chain of causal relationship between the illegal activity and discovery of the challenged evidence. The inevitable discovery doctrine, however, does not depend upon what in fact transpired between the improper conduct and discovery of the challenged evidence. Rather, it focuses upon proof of what would have occurred under certain hypothetical circumstances.

The rationale for the exception is, despite its widespread acceptance, somewhat unclear. Like the standing requirement, it might be justified in terms of an absence of "harm." Proof that the prosecution would have obtained evidence legitimately, of course, does not demonstrate that the ac-

28. See generally, 3 LaFave, Search and Seizure 620–28 (1978); LaCount & Girese, The "Inevitable Discovery" Rule, An Evolving Exception to the Constitutional Exclusionary Rule, 40 Alb.L.Rev. 483 (1976); R. Maguire, How to Unpoison the Fruit—The Fourth Amendment and the Exclusionary Rule, 55 J.Crim.L. C. & P.S. 307, 313–17 (1964) (referring to the rule as the "sine qua non" requirement); Notes, 74 Colum.L.Rev. 88 (1974), 5 Hofstra L.Rev. 137 (1976); Dec. Digest, Crim.L. ⊕394.1(1), 394.1(3).

29. In Brewer v. Williams, 430 U.S. 387 (1977), rehearing denied 431 U.S. 925, discussed in § 158 infra, the Court noted that despite the inadmissibility of the confession there at issue, evidence concerning the body of the deceased victim (which had been located through information contained in the confession) "might well be admissible on the theory that the body would have been discovered in any event, even had incriminating statements not been elicited . . . ." 430 U.S. at 406 n. 12. In fact, such evidence was admitted on retrial and the resulting conviction was affirmed on direct appeal. Reliance was placed on inevitable legitimate dis-

covery. State v. Williams, 285 N.W.2d 248 (Iowa 1979), cert. denied 446 U.S. 921. Federal habeas corpus relief was denied also in reliance upon the same doctrine. See Williams v. Nix, 528 F.Supp. 664 (S.D.Iowa 1981), reversed 700 F.2d 1164 (8th Cir. 1983), cert. granted 103 S.Ct. 2427.

30. E.g., United States v. Brookins, 614 F.2d 1037 (5th Cir. 1980); Fain v. State, 271 Ark. 874, 611 S.W.2d 508 (1981); Cook v. State, 374 A.2d 264, 267–68 (Del. 1977); State v. Williams, 285 N.W.2d 248 (Iowa 1979), cert. denied 446 U.S. 921; People v. Fitzpatrick, 32 N.Y.2d 499, 346 N.Y.S.2d 793, 300 N.E.2d 139 (1973), cert. denied 414 U.S. 1033; State v. Nagel, 308 N.W.2d 539 (N.D.1981); Commonwealth v. Brown, 470 Pa. 274, 368 A.2d 626 (1976).

31. E.g., Matter of Stedman, 305 N.C. 92, 286 S.E.2d 527, 533–34 (1982). Of course, the same policy considerations as support the independent source rule may well be relevant, and perhaps controlling, in this context.

cused suffered no intrusion upon privacy. Insofar as the availability of evidence resulting from that intrusion is a relevant consideration, however, it does demonstrate that— in this regard—the accused is not much worse off than he or she would have been had the intrusion not occurred. This justification relies upon the evidentiary results of the privacy intrusion rather than the intrusion itself. It is, therefore, arguably inconsistent with the Court's rejection of the remedial function of the exclusionary rule, a rejection which is based upon the assumption that the evidentiary effects of the exclusionary remedy upon litigants is at most an incidental side effect.[32]

Whether the exception can be justified in a manner consistent with the deterrent rationale for the exclusionary sanction is more problematic. An effort in this direction was made by the Fifth Circuit in United States v. Brookins:

> Deterrence is only marginally served by suppression of testimony derived from illegally obtained evidence if such testimony would have been discovered without the illegal actions, because the motivation for the illegal search or interrogation was not the quest for derivative evidence that the police were already pursuing and would probably have been discovered in any event.[33]

The meaning of this is not entirely clear. If the court means that officers cannot be motivated to expand their activities by a desire to obtain derivative evidence, this is simply not the case. A retrospective conclusion that evidence would have been obtained in a permissible fashion does not suggest the absence of a need to discourage officers from improper privacy intrusions of the sort actually made. If, of course, a prerequisite to application of the rule is a finding that the officers did not foresee and could not have foreseen the discovery of the challenged evi-

dence, this rationale would be more persuasive.

It seems most likely that the issue must be posed in the terms the Court has used to consider other aspects of exclusionary rule expansion:[34] what increased deterrence would be accomplished by excluding such evidence, and would this additional deterrence be accomplished without excessive costs in terms of loss of reliable evidence? So posed, the issue becomes quite difficult. Perhaps it can be said that few if any officers are likely to decide to engage in improper activity in reliance upon facts later developing that would render any resulting evidence admissible under the inevitable discovery doctrine. If so, the exception can be recognized without what appears to be a significant dilution of the deterrence to improper activity. This, however, is a negative justification and can suffice only if it is assumed that the exclusionary rule should be construed to admit improperly obtained evidence whenever subcategories can be defined in ways that to recognize them as exceptions would not affect the assumed general deterrent function of the sanction as a whole.

The major issue concerning the administration of the exception is the showing required to invoke it. Specifically, the lower courts have disagreed on the likelihood that must be shown concerning legitimate discovery of the evidence. Some courts appear to take the terminology used to describe the exception quite seriously, and hold that the prosecution must show, as a matter of certainty, that the evidence would have been discovered in a legitimate fashion.[35] Others, however, impose a more lenient standard. The Fifth Circuit has held that the prosecution need only prove a "reasonable probability" that the evidence would have been ob-

32. See § 168 supra.

33. United States v. Brookins, 614 F.2d 1037, 1047 (5th Cir.1980).

34. See § 168 supra.

35. Fain v. State, 271 Ark. 874, 611 S.W.2d 508 (1981) (state must prove by clear and convincing evidence that it would have obtained challenged evidence in a proper manner).

tained by proper methods.[36] Under the standard adopted by the New York Court of Appeals, "certitude" is not required, and "a very high degree of probability that the evidence in question would have been obtained independently of the tainted source" will suffice.[37]

Closely related is the burden of proof on the prosecution. Some courts, relying upon what appears to be the general requirement imposed by the Supreme Court in regard to issues affecting the admissibility of evidence under the Fourth Amendment exclusionary rule, require that the prosecution prove the required likelihood of legitimate discovery by only a preponderance of the evidence.[38] Others, apparently motivated by the perception that the exception poses extraordinarily high dangers of abuse, require clear and convincing evidence.[39]

In application, there seem to be at least two distinguishable areas in which the exception is invoked. One consists of cases in which the prosecution relies upon proof of specific conduct by investigators that, it is urged, would have led to legitimate discovery of the challenged evidence. In State v. Nagel,[40] for example, the state established that before the illegal entry at issue another officer, with information amounting to probable cause, had begun the process of apply-

ing for a search warrant for the premises. The warrant was in fact issued and executed after the illegal entry. Finding that the state had met its burden, the court emphasized that no information concerning the results of the illegal search, conducted before the warrant issued, was communicated either to the judge who issued the warrant or the officer who was applying for it.

In contrast with these cases are others in which the prosecution relies upon a general assumption that "routine police investigatory procedure" independent of the illegal conduct would have resulted in discovery of the challenged evidence. Undoubtedly the risks of improper application of the exception are greater in cases of this sort, and it should be applied sparingly if at all in these situations.[41]

Despite the widespread acceptance of this exception, its desirability remains uncertain. Justification must rest either upon the desirability of creating exceptions to the exclusionary rule where this can be done with little risk to the overall deterrent effect of the sanction or upon the lack of need for a remedy in those situations within its scope. Reliance upon the latter rationale is of dubious validity; if the value of exclusion as a personal remedy for accused persons cannot serve as a justification for the Fourth

---

36. United States v. Brookins, 614 F.2d 1037, 1048 (5th Cir.1980).

37. People v. Payton, 45 N.Y.2d 300, 408 N.Y.S.2d 395, 380 N.E.2d 224 (1978), reversed on other grounds, Payton v. New York, 445 U.S. 573 (1980). The New York court explained:

> The doctrine does not call for certitude as the literal meaning of the adjective "inevitable" would suggest. What is required is that there be a very high degree of probability that the evidence in question would have been obtained independently of the tainted source.

45 N.Y.2d at 313, 408 N.Y.S.2d at 401–02, 380 N.E.2d at 231. This approach was criticized by other members of the court:

> Now apparently the only thing inevitable about the inevitable discovery doctrine is that the police with the benefit of hindsight, will inevitably be able to show that they could have obtained the evidence lawfully by employing some other technique, no matter how hypothetical and no matter now involved or extraordinary resort to the procedure would have been.

45 N.Y.2d at 316, 408 N.Y.S.2d at 404, 380 N.E.2d at 233 (Wachtler, J., dissenting).

38. State v. Williams, 285 N.W.2d 248, 260 (Iowa 1979) cert. denied 446 U.S. 921.

39. Fain v. State, 271 Ark. 874, 611 S.W.2d 508 (1981).

40. 308 N.W.2d 539 (N.D.1981).

41. Crews v. United States, 389 A.2d 277, 291–95 (D.C.App.1978), reversed on other grounds, 445 U.S. 463 (1980), which appears to reject the doctrine in situations in which the prosecution relies upon "routine police investigatory procedure" as establishing the sufficient likelihood that the evidence would have been otherwise obtained. See United States v. Allen, 436 A.2d 1303, 1310–11 (D.C.App.1981).

The New York court has further limited the doctrine by holding it applicable only where the illegality of the conduct which gave rise to discovery of the challenged evidence was "of technical dimension." See People v. Sciacca, 45 N.Y.2d 122, 408 N.Y.S.2d 22, 379 N.E.2d 1153 (1978).

Amendment exclusionary rule, it seems to follow that lack of need for a personal remedy should not serve as the rationale for an exception to the rule.

If the exception is accepted, it appears clear that special caution must be exercised to avoid its abuse. Thus it would be desirable to require that the prosecution establish as a matter of fact that the challenged evidence would have been obtained properly, not merely that a significant likelihood of this occurring was present. Further, given the difficulties of establishing such hypothetical "facts," it would be appropriate to impose upon the prosecution the exceptionally high burden of proof by clear and convincing evidence.

Burdens of Proof and Proceeding. The allocation of the burdens of proof and proceeding in regard to the issues raised by the "fruits" doctrine are not entirely clear. In Nardone v. United States,[42] however, the Court commented that, in the wiretap context before it, the accused was entitled to an opportunity to "prove" that unlawful wiretapping was employed and that the evidence offered was a "fruit" of that activity. "This," the Court continued, "leaves ample opportunity to the Government to convince the trial court that its proof had an independent origin." [43] It seems likely—and reasonable—that a defendant challenging the admissibility of evidence bears the burden of persuasion with the regard to existence of a factual relationship between illegal conduct and the challenged evidence. Upon such proof, however, the prosecution is then quite likely to have the burden of persuasion concerning the existence of attenuation of the taint or the applicability of an exception to the general rule of exclusion.

Evaluation of "Fruits" Doctrine. The judicial involvement cases [44] illustrate especially well the failure of the "fruits" doctrine in general and of attenuation analysis

in particular to build upon any structured principle. It may be clear that excluding all evidence that would not have been discovered except for illegal action would be to pursue the deterrent objective of the exclusionary rule at too great a cost. It may be equally clear that limiting exclusion to items or evidence that were actually the subject of the illegality or its direct impact would also be unacceptable. Defining evidence which is the actual "subject" of illegal conduct may be impossible. Or, such a limited scope may blunt too significantly the preventive effect of the exclusionary sanction. On the other hand, the Court's current solution, embodied almost entirely in attenuation analysis, is no more satisfactory. It clearly mandates that a wide variety of factors be taken into account in determining when the taint of illegality ceases to have effect, thus avoiding any suggestion that it ignores relevant considerations. But the Court's approach provides little or no guidance in determining how to balance what are often conflicting considerations against each other or in how to reach a final, reasoned conclusion.

Justice White, dissenting in Harrison v. United States,[45] criticized the Court's approach to the attenuation issue as ignoring the functional relationship between attenuation and the deterrent purpose of the exclusionary rule.[46] Exclusion of "fruits" of law enforcement illegality is justified, he urged, only if to do so increases the deterrent value of the exclusionary sanction. Attenuation, then, might reasonably be found whenever the evidence is such that exclusion of the evidence would not increase the deterrent function of the rule or would provide insufficient deterrence to justify the loss of reliable evidence involved. More specifically, Justice White suggested, attenuation analysis might usefully focus upon whether at the time of the illegal conduct law enforcement officers foresaw—or might reasonably have foreseen—the discovery or development of the

---

42.   308 U.S. 338 (1939).

43.   Id. at 341.

44.   See text following note 23 supra.

45.   392 U.S. 219 (1968).

46.   Id. at 230–34 (White, J., dissenting).

challenged evidence. If discovery or development of this evidence was or could have been foreseen, the threat of its exclusion might be expected to provide an incentive for officers in similar situations to desist from activity of the sort at issue; no attenuation, therefore, should be found. But if this discovery or development could not have been foreseen, exclusion of evidence of the sort at issue could not be expected to affect law enforcement conduct. Its exclusion, therefore, would not serve the purposes of the rule. Regarding the taint of the illegality as having been attenuated would result in attenuation analysis producing results consistent with the underlying purpose being pursued.

Justice White's approach has at least theoretical attractiveness. There can be little doubt that it is desirable that exclusionary rule law ought, insofar as possible, to further the objectives of the exclusionary sanction, but also to avoid sacrificing reliable evidence where attainment of those objectives is not furthered by exclusion. On the other hand, requiring an inquiry into foreseeability whenever an attenuation issue is raised might prove burdensome and time consuming. Perhaps more important, however, even time consuming inquiries into foreseeability are unlikely to result in accurate resolution of particular cases. At worst, the inherent subjectivity of the foreseeability analysis might permit hostile trial judges consciously or otherwise to circumvent the basic exclusionary sanction by inaccurate findings of foreseeability that would be largely immune from appellate scrutiny. Foreseeability may be a conceptually satisfying standard for resolving attenuation cases. But it may not be an adequate criterion for

that purpose, given the need for structure in exclusionary rule law.

 **WESTLAW
REFERENCES**

"poisonous tree" /s   attenuat!

Independent Source
digest(source! /s independent /s witness! /p admiss! admit! inadmis! taint! untaint!)

Attenuation of Taint
digest(attenuat! /s taint! /p day* week* time* hour* minute* moment* seconds)

Inevitable Legitimate Discovery
crews   /15   445   /5   463

Burdens of Proof and Proceeding
digest(fruit* /s burden standard* /s proof prove*)

§ 177. "Good Faith" and Similar Exceptions

Recent disenchantment with exclusionary sanctions for rules relating to law enforcement conduct has given rise to demands for broader exceptions than are provided by the so-called "independent source" rule [1] and the "attenuation of taint" [2] doctrine. It is useful to distinguish the proposals for so-called "good faith" defenses from the flexible exclusionary sanction suggested by, among others, the American Law Institute.

"Good Faith" Exception.[3] There has been widespread support for an exception to the Fourth Amendment exclusionary sanction that would apply upon proof that the officers acted in a good faith—and reasonable—belief that their conduct was within legal requirements. In United States v. Williams,[4] thirteen of the twenty-four judges constituting the en banc Fifth Circuit Court of Appeals joined in an opinion that purport-

§ 177

1. See § 176 supra, at note 7.

2. See § 176 supra, at note 16.

3. See generally, Ball, Good Faith and the Fourth Amendment: The "Reasonable" Exception to the Exclusionary Rule, 69 J.Crim.L. & C. 635 (1978); Bernardi, The Exclusionary Rule: Is a Good Faith Standard

Needed to Preserve a Liberal Interpretation of the Fourth Amendment? 30 De Paul L.Rev. 51 (1980); Mertens & Wasserstrom, The Good Faith Exception to the Exclusionary Rule: Deregulating the Police and Derailing the Law, 70 Geo.L.J. 365 (1981).

4. 622 F.2d 830 (5th Cir. 1980) (en banc), cert. denied 449 U.S. 1127.

ed to find previous Supreme Court cases as supporting such an exception:

> Henceforth in this circuit, when evidence is sought to be excluded because of police conduct leading to its discovery, it will be open to the proponent of the evidence to urge that the conduct in question, if mistaken or unauthorized, was yet taken in a reasonable, good-faith belief that it was proper. If the court so finds, it shall not apply the exclusionary rule to the evidence.[5]

In Taylor v. Alabama,[6] however, the Court responded to the suggestion that it adopt a good faith exception by stating, "To date, we have not recognized such an exception, and we decline to do so here."[7]

The major argument in favor of such an exception to exclusionary sanctions is that it would permit the use of evidence in those situations in which no significant preventive function may be served by exclusion. Law enforcement officers who have exercised reasonable care in ascertaining the law and in attempting to apply it to the facts before them have arguably done all that the exclusionary sanctions can reasonably demand. Exclusion of evidence because the officers, despite their efforts, were incorrect in their conclusion that they were complying with the law would serve no function. Adequate incentive for law enforcement officers to exert their best efforts to comply with the law is created by excluding evidence in those cases where the officers have neither acted properly nor exercised reasonable care in determining whether their actions were within legal requirements.

On the other hand, it can be argued that excluding evidence obtained in what is ultimately determined to be an impermissible fashion will further the preventive function of the exclusionary sanctions, despite the officers' "good faith" belief that their actions were appropriate. Exclusion in such cases may create an incentive for officers to inform themselves more adequately concerning legal requirements and their application. Further, trial judges—especially those hostile to legal limitations on law enforcement conduct—may too readily and uncritically find that officers who acted improperly nevertheless had the "good faith" belief necessary to render the exclusionary sanction inapplicable. Law enforcement perception that the exception will be often and uncritically found applicable may blunt whatever deterrent impact the underlying exclusionary sanction can be expected to have.

A "good faith" exception may also be inconsistent with purposes of exclusionary sanctions other than that of deterrence. It may, for example, detract from the sanction's educative effect. Further, the need to assure judicial integrity may argue against such an exception. If use of evidence seized in violation of a litigant's rights is offensive to notions of the role of courts, this offensiveness arguably remains despite the perception of the officer who obtained the evidence that he was acting correctly. Administrative cost considerations may also argue against a good faith exception. Inquiries into officers' subjective states of mind and the reasonableness of these states

---

5. Id. at 846–47.

6. 457 U.S. 687 (1982).

7. Id. at 693. See also, Commonwealth v. Sheppard, 387 Mass. 488, 441 N.E.2d 725 (1982) (absence of Supreme Court authority precludes application of good faith exception to Fourth Amendment exclusionary rule). The Supreme Court has granted certiorari, 103 S.Ct. 3534 (1983), presumably to address the good faith exception issue.

In Illinois v. Gates, 103 S.Ct. 436 (1982) the Court restored the case to the calendar for reargument and ordered the parties "to address the question whether the rule requiring the exclusion of evidence at a criminal trial obtained in violation of the Fourth Amendment

. . . should to any extent be modified, so as, for example, not to require the exclusion of evidence obtained in the reasonable belief that the search and seizure at issue was consistent with the Fourth Amendment."

But when the decision was handed down, 103 S.Ct. 2317 (1983), rehearing denied 104 S.Ct. 33, the Court—"with apologies to all"—did not reach the issue. The state had not urged a good faith exception before the lower courts and those tribunals had not considered the matter; the prohibition against addressing claims neither pressed nor passed on below, reasoned the majority, precluded it from considering whether such an exception should be recognized.

of mind may be time consuming and difficult. Perhaps this means that accurate application of a good faith exception would be too difficult to accomplish at an acceptable cost. In any case, the risk of increasing the frequency and complexity of exclusionary sanction issues that need to be resolved by trial courts cannot be ignored in evaluating the desirability of a good faith exception.

"Nonsubstantial" Violations: The ALI "Exception." [8] A related but distinguishable approach is suggested by the exclusionary provisions of the American Law Institute's Model Code of Pre-Arraignment Procedure.[9] Under Section 290.2 of the Code, exclusion of evidence obtained as a result of a violation of the Code [10] is required only upon a determination that the violation was "substantial." In determining whether a violation was substantial, the trial court is told that in all cases a violation must be found substantial "if it was gross, willful and prejudicial to the accused." [11] In other cases, the trial court is to determine whether a violation was substantial on the basis of "all the circumstances," which are to include:

(a) the extent of deviation from lawful conduct;

(b) the extent to which the violation was wilful;

(c) the extent to which privacy was invaded;

(d) the extent to which exclusion will tend to prevent violations of this Code;

(e) whether, but for the violation, the things seized would have been discovered; and

(f) the extent to which the violation prejudiced the moving party's ability to support his motion, or to defend himself in the proceeding in which the things seized are sought to be offered in evidence against him.[12]

In addition, the trial court is directed to find a violation substantial regardless of the good faith of the individual officers involved if the violation "appears to be part of the practice of the law enforcement agency or was authorized by a high authority within it." [13]

While the proposal is structured in terms of an affirmative requirement for exclusion, that is, a finding that the violation is "substantial," it may be most realistic to consider it as proposing an exception to what should be assumed as the general rule of exclusion. Thus exclusion would not be appropriate, despite a showing that the underlying rule was violated, where the facts indicate that the violation was "nonsubstantial."

This approach has more flexibility than the "good faith" exception proposals. Apparently, it would permit a trial court to admit evidence upon a determination that the defendant was only minimally harmed by the violation of the underlying rule or that

---

8. See generally, Coe, The ALI Substantiality Test: A Flexible Approach to the Exclusionary Sanction, 10 Ga.L.Rev. 1 (1975).

9. ALI Model Code of Pre-Arraignment Procedure (Adopted Draft 1975). Another proposal is contained in Uniform Rules of Criminal Procedure, Rule 461(a). Clause (2) would require suppression of evidence obtained in violation of nonconstitutional legal requirements only if:

the violation significantly affected the discovery of the evidence or the defendant's substantial rights.

The "willful" nature of the violation would not be a consideration. Whether a violation significantly affected the defendant's substantial rights would depend upon the significance of the right violated and the degree of infringement of that right. Commentary to Rule 461, 199. But even if the violation did not meet this aspect of the criterion, supression would still be required if the violation "significantly affected the dis-

covery of the evidence." This would require a more "significant" relationship between the violation and the discovery of the evidence than is necessary to avoid attenuation under the "fruits" doctrine. Commentary, at 200.

10. ALI Model Code of Pre-Arraignment Procedure § 290.2 (Adopted Draft 1975). This section addresses only evidence obtained by a seizure. Another similar section addresses motions to suppress statements. Id. at 150.3 (statement to be suppressed for violation of the Code only if violation is "substantial"). Both sections carefully impose no requirement of a substantial violation where suppression is constitutionally required.

11. Id. § 290.2(3).

12. Id. § 290.2(4).

13. Id. § 290.2(3).

exclusion would not, because of the circumstances, discourage future violations. This, of course, offers the advantage of case-by-case consideration and the promise of assurance that exclusion will be directed only where to do so would further the underlying justifications for the exclusionary sanction.

This flexibility also serves as the basis for opposition to the exception. It may be attacked on the basis that it confuses what should be identified and addressed as separate and distinguishable issues. Whether, for example, challenged evidence should be admitted if the trial judge determines that it would have been discovered legitimately if the violation had not taken place [14] is arguably a specific issue that should be addressed. The proposal appears to permit a trial judge to consider a "chance" that this would occur as somehow offsetting the degree of intrusiveness of the violation. The flexibility of the proposed standard also suggests that conscientious implementation would require extensive inquiry into the circumstances of each case and thus add significantly to the administrative tasks of exclusionary sanctions.

Most significant, however, is the argument that the extreme flexibility of the standard would encourage unjustifiably broad application of it. This, in turn, would decrease the certainty of the exclusionary sanction for a violation of the underlying requirements and unacceptably blunt the preventive effect which can otherwise be expected from the rule.

**WESTLAW
REFERENCES**

"Good Faith" Exception
officer! /s "good faith" /p "fourth amendment"
exclusionary

14. See § 176, at note 28, supra.

§ 178

1. See generally, Bradley, *Havens*, *Jenkins* and *Salvucci*, and the Defendant's "Right" to Testify, 18 Am.Crim.L.Rev. 419 (1981); Comments, 20 Washburn L.J. 443 (1981), 73 Colum.L.Rev. 1476 (1973); Note, 8 Ind.L.Rev. 865 (1975). Cf. Annot., 80 A.L.R.2d 478.

"Nonsubstantial" Violations
digest,synopsis("substantial violation*" /p evidence)

§ 178. Use of Otherwise Inadmissible Evidence for Impeachment of a Testifying Defendant

When an exclusionary sanction is successfully invoked in criminal litigation, the effect is generally to preclude the prosecution from introducing the challenged evidence as proof of the defendant's guilt. If the defendant takes the witness stand and testifies in his own behalf, however, evidence improperly obtained may be relevant to his credibility. Whether exclusionary rules render tainted evidence inadmissible for this purpose presents what is often regarded as a separate issue. Again, most of the case law concerns the federal constitutional exclusionary sanctions. But there is some evidence that states are willing to consider independently the desirability and need for an impeachment exception to state law exclusionary rules.

Impeachment Exception to the Federal Constitutional Exclusionary Rules.[1] In Walder v. United States,[2] Walder was tried for four alleged sales of narcotics. He took the witness stand in his own defense and denied any dealings whatsoever with the purported purchasers. In response to further questions on direct examination, Walder denied ever having any narcotics in his possession, except pursuant to a physician's authorization. The government was then permitted to ask on cross-examination whether a police officer had taken narcotics from his home in 1950, and, when he denied that this had occurred, to prove that this event had taken place. In earlier litigation, the heroin obtained in the 1950 action had

Impeachment by contradiction is treated generally in § 47 supra; inadmissible evidence as "opening the door" is discussed in § 57 supra.

2. 347 U.S. 62 (1954).

been suppressed as having been obtained in an unlawful search. Nevertheless, the Supreme Court affirmed Walder's conviction. A defendant, Justice Frankfurter wrote for the Court, "must be free to deny all the elements of the case against him without thereby giving leave to the Government to introduce by way of rebuttal evidence illegally secured by it . . . ." [3] But this, he continued, "is hardly justification for letting the defendant affirmatively resort to perjurious testimony in reliance on the Government's disability to challenge his credibility." [4] The Court's decision was widely read as establishing an exception to the Fourth Amendment exclusionary rule and perhaps also to other federal constitutional exclusionary sanctions, permitting use of otherwise inadmissible evidence to impeach a testifying defendant but only when the defendant's testimony went beyond a simple denial of guilt and addressed "collateral matters."

The Supreme Court's increased enthusiasm for the exclusionary sanction and the rules enforced by this sanction during the years following the 1954 decision in Walder gave rise to speculation that the impeachment exception might be abandoned. This was fueled by language used in Miranda v. Arizona,[5] suggesting that incriminating statements obtained in violation of the guidelines established by that case would be inadmissible for impeachment as well as for purposes of proving guilt.

In Harris v. New York,[6] however, the Court reaffirmed the vitality of the Walder impeachment exception and made clear that it applied as well to the exclusionary sanction enforcing the Miranda requirements for custodial interrogation. In Harris, the Court held admissible for impeachment purposes a statement obtained from Harris during custodial interrogation conducted without warning Harris of his right to appointed counsel under Miranda. In addition to repeating the rationale for the exception articulated in Walder,[7] the majority also defended the exception in terms of what has come to be traditionary exclusionary rule analysis: any increase in deterrence accomplished by excluding testimony offered to impeach a testifying defendant would be outweighed by the loss of reliable evidence bearing upon accuseds' credibility.[8] To the argument that the possible use of evidence to impeach a defendant who testifies (or to deter a defendant from testifying in his own behalf) would encourage officers to violate the underlying legal requirements, the Court responded that this was no more than a "speculative possibility." [9]

It seems clear that in both Walder and Harris the Court was influenced by what it regarded as the exceptionally high cost of permitting possibly perjurious testimony to go uncontradicted. Apparently the Court perceived a higher cost to society when a defendant defeats conviction and punishment

---

3. 347 U.S. at 65. This was apparently the rationale of Agnello v. United States, 269 U.S. 20 (1925), in which the defendant was tried for participation in a drug sale. At trial, he took the witness stand and admitted participation in the activities but denied awareness that the substance involved was a drug. On cross-examination, he was asked whether he had ever seen narcotics and, when he responded negatively, whether he had ever seen a specific can of cocaine. On rebuttal, the prosecution was permitted to show that the cocaine had been obtained from Agnello's room in a search previously held invalid when the prosecution had offered the cocaine to prove Agnello's guilt. Rejecting the Government's argument that the cocaine was admissible "in rebuttal," the Court commented that Agnello "did nothing to waive his constitutional protection or to justify cross-examination in respect of [the cocaine]." 269 U.S. at 35. Thus the use of the cocaine at his trial was error. Id.

4. Id.

5. 384 U.S. 436 (1966), rehearing denied 385 U.S. 890. See generally, § 151 infra. In Miranda, the Court stated without qualification that statements which were in any manner incriminating "may not be used without the full warnings and effective waiver required . . . ." 384 U.S. at 477.

6. 401 U.S. 222 (1971).

7. See 401 U.S. at 225 (privilege to testify in one's own defense "cannot be construed to include the right to commit perjury").

8. Id. at 224. The language in Miranda suggesting inadmissibility for all purposes was characterized as "not at all necessary to the Court's holding" and therefore not controlling.

9. Id. at 225.

by successfully lying in court than when he achieves the same result by inducing the judge to suppress evidence against him.

Harris also appears to have eliminated the *Walder* requirement that the defendant go beyond a denial of guilt and testify as to collateral matters. While it is arguable that Harris' trial testimony went into matters that were collateral within the meaning of *Walder*,[10] the Court seems not to have relied upon that possibility. Rather, noting that *Walder* involved testimony as to "collateral matters," "whereas [Harris] was impeached as to testimony bearing more directly on the crimes charged," it found this distinction insufficient to warrant a result different from that reached in *Walder*.[11] The *Walder* "collateral matter" requirement appears to have been based on the assumption that defendants have an exceptionally important interest in being able to deny guilt in their own words before a trial jury. Their interest in being able to similarly put collateral matters before the jury is, on the other hand, substantially less. Consequently, only when the less important interest in putting collateral matters before the jury is at issue does the social interest in providing contradiction of possibly perjurious testimony prevail. *Harris* did not address this. Implicit in the Court's analysis, however, is the conclusion that under the cost-benefit analysis, the potential increase in deterrence that might be accomplished by extending the exclusionary rule to impeachment of a defendant's denial of guilt would not outweigh the cost of permitting potentially perjurious testimony, even of this sort, from going uncontradicted.

It was widely assumed that the *Walder-Harris* impeachment exception came into play only if the otherwise inadmissible evidence contradicted the defendant's testimony on direct examination. Since the defense controls the direct examination but not the cross-examination, only by affirmatively deciding on direct examination to offer a version of facts inconsistent with other reliable evidence did the defendant commit potential perjury in a sufficiently voluntary sense to justify rendering the exclusionary sanction partially inapplicable. But in United States v. Havens,[12] the Court held that otherwise inadmissible evidence admissible for impeachment under *Harris* and *Walder* could be used to contradict a defendant's testimony during cross-examination by the prosecution, as long as that testimony was in response to questions "plainly within the scope of the defendant's direct examination." Thus it appears that in order to retain full ability to invoke many exclusionary sanctions, a defendant must not only plan to avoid certain testimony on direct examination but must also consider whether response to proper cross-examination questions will require responses inconsistent with the otherwise inadmissible evidence available to the prosecution.

A major limitation upon the impeachment exception was foreshadowed in *Harris* by the Court's observation that the confession at issue there had not been challenged as co-

---

10. Harris had been charged with sale of heroin. In his trial testimony he admitted selling the contents of a glassine bag to the officer who was the alleged purchaser, but maintained that the scheme was really one to defraud the purchaser and that the bag contained only baking powder. 401 U.S. at 223.

11. Id. at 225. *Agnello,* discussed in n. 3 supra, was not discussed or mentioned in *Harris.*

Even after *Harris,* some courts regarded the "collateral matter" requirement of *Walder* as continuing to have vitality. See Volpicelli v. Salmack, 447 F.Supp. 652 (S.D.N.Y.1978), affirmed without opinion, 578 F.2d 1372 (2d Cir.) (general denial of guilt by testifying defendant will not permit impeachment by improperly obtained evidence). Any doubt, however, seems to have been dispelled by United States v. Havens, 446 U.S. 620 (1980), discussed in the text at n. 12, infra. In *Havens,* the Court took note of the *Agnello* holding and discussion and characterized *Agnello* as "limited" by *Walder, Harris,* and *Hass.* 446 U.S. at 624–25.

It is still probably true, however, that the prosecution cannot, on cross-examination, raise issues unrelated to the defendant's testimony on direct examination and then use illegally obtained evidence to contradict the answers given by the defendant. See United States v. Miller, 676 F.2d 359, 364 (9th Cir. 1982).

12. 446 U.S. 620 (1980), on remand 625 F.2d 1131, rehearing denied 448 U.S. 911, 30 De Paul L.Rev. 225 (1980), 30 Drake L.Rev. 192 (1980–81), 32 Syr.L.Rev. 637 (1981), 48 Tenn.L.Rev. 721 (1981).

erced or involuntary.[13] In Mincey v. Arizona,[14] the Court reaffirmed this suggestion that the *Walder-Harris* impeachment exception applies only to impeaching evidence whose "trustworthiness . . . satisfies legal standards." [15] Since the confession at issue in *Mincey* was obtained under circumstances rendering it involuntary, it could not be used to impeach *Mincey* at trial even though it was inconsistent with his trial testimony. The rationale for this limitation upon the impeachment exception seems to be that under the cost-benefit balancing process, the benefits from admitting testimony for impeachment outweigh the costs only where the impeaching testimony is highly reliable. Where the impeaching testimony is inadmissible for reasons that suggest unreliability, on the other hand, the balance tips in favor of exclusion.

This limitation on the impeachment exception raises several interesting questions. First, what violations of which federal constitutional requirements nevertheless permit the use of resulting evidence for impeachment? The Court's holdings establish that evidence obtained in violation of the Fourth Amendment's prohibition against unreasonable searches and seizures and that obtained in violation of at least *Miranda's per se* requirements can be used for impeachment. But what of violations of other federal constitutional rights, such as that to have counsel present at certain pretrial confrontations with witnesses and to be free from the use of the testimony of witnesses who have been subject to certain extraordinarily suggestive procedures?

A second issue is closely related. In considering whether evidence is admissible for impeachment, must or may the trial judge consider the apparent reliability or "trustworthiness" of the specific evidence offered?[16] Or, is it sufficient that the reason why the evidence is inadmissible to prove guilt a reason that does not, in general, create doubt as to the reliability of resulting evidence? In *Mincey*, it appears that the Court considered controlling its conclusion that the confession was involuntary because it was the result of an overbearing of the defendant's will, and the Court did not go on to consider whether in light of this the confession might nevertheless have been trustworthy. Such an approach, of course, has the advantage of relative ease of administration. Placing evidence offered for impeachment into already existing categories is probably less time-consuming or otherwise burdensome than a case-by-case inquiry into the reliability of each item of evidence offered for this purpose.

The Court has upheld the use for impeachment purposes of evidence obtained in violation of the Fourth Amendment's prohibition against unreasonable searches and seizures [17] and that obtained in violation of Miranda's *per se* requirements.[18] The nature of the legal basis for the inadmissibility of the evidence for purposes of proving guilt

---

13.   Harris v. New York, 401 U.S. 222, 224 (1971).

14.   437 U.S. 385 (1978).

15.   Id. at 398 quoting with approval from Harris v. New York, 401 U.S. 222, 224 (1971).

16.   In making the initial determination of admissibility of a confession, only "voluntariness" and not reliability can be considered. See § 147 infra.

17.   United States v. Havens, 446 U.S. 620 (1980), on remand 625 F.2d 1131, rehearing denied 448 U.S. 911.

18.   In Oregon v. Hass, 420 U.S. 714 (1975), the prosecution had offered a statement obtained as a result of interrogation continued after the suspect expressed a desire for the assistance of counsel. Justice Brennan urged that the situation was distinguishable from *Harris* because permitting the use of the Hass confession for impeachment would remove virtually all incentive for complying with Miranda in a situation involving a suspect who has expressed a desire to remain silent. *Harris* does not eliminate the incentive to give the warnings and seek waiver of counsel and submission to interrogation. But once a suspect has invoked the right to counsel and to halt interrogation until counsel is provided, compliance with *Miranda's* mandate that questioning cease will inevitably result in no evidence being obtained. If the law permits evidence obtained pursuant to a decision to nevertheless continue interrogation, officers faced with this situation have nothing to lose and something to gain, that is, the securing of a statement usable for impeachment. 420 U.S. at 725 (Brennan, J., dissenting). The majority regarded the issue as settled in *Harris* and announced, "we are not disposed to change it now." Id. at 723.

appeared to control, at least in the absence of a claim that on the facts of the particular case the violation cast doubt on the reliability of the evidence. More difficult questions will be presented by efforts to use for impeachment the testimony of witnesses who have identified a defendant at a pretrial confrontation conducted in violation of the defendant's right to counsel [19] or who have been submitted to extraordinarily suggestive procedures.[20] If case-by-case evaluations of reliability are neither necessary nor permitted, it may well be the case that a violation of the right to counsel does not create a sufficiently high risk of falsity to bar impeachment use but that a showing of an impermissibly suggestive procedure, given the substance of the standard for determining whether the constitutional requirement has been violated, does create a sufficiently high risk.

Finally, it seems reasonably clear that a defendant against whom otherwise inadmissible testimony is used for impeachment purposes is entitled to an instruction telling the jurors that they are to consider the testimony only as bearing upon the accused's credibility as a witness and not as tending to prove the accused's guilt of the crime charged.[21] As a practical matter, it seems unlikely that jurors would be either inclined or able to make this distinction. Consequently, in evaluating the desirability of the *Walder-Harris* exception to the exclusionary sanction, discussion should assume that where the exception applies the evidence will be in fact used to establish the defendant's guilt of the crime charged. Whatever the formal doctrine, it is unrealistic to conclude that the testimony will be considered only for purposes of credibility evaluation.

There may also be some question as to what constitutes only impeachment use of evidence permissible under this exception. It seems clear that questioning the defendant concerning the otherwise inadmissible matters and, if the defendant's answers in light of local impeachment rules permit this, proof of the matters for impeachment purposes is permitted. But the prosecution may go beyond this in a manner that constitutes explicit or implicit use of the evidence to prove guilt. In People v. Ricco,[22] for example, the defendant raised the defense of insanity. A certain statement made by the defendant to law enforcement officers was inadmissible to prove guilt because it had not been preceded by the requisite warnings. After the defendant himself testified on direct examination, he was asked if he remembered making the statement, which contained no references to the delusions which he had claimed on his direct examination to have been experiencing at the time of the offense. He responded that he did not recall. The state then proved by other testimony that the statements had in fact been made. On rebuttal, a psychiatrist testified for the State. He was given a hypothetical that included the subject making the statement that the State had been permitted to use for impeachment. When asked by the prosecutor whether the making of such a statement was consistent with the existence of delusions of the sort claimed by the defendant, the psychiatrist expressed a firm opinion that the defendant was intentionally simulating a mental disorder. The questions asked on cross-examination and the testimony that the defendant in fact made the statements which he claimed not to recall, the New York court held, was proper. But the further use of the statements as the basis for the psychiatrist's opinion, the court reasonably continued, went beyond impeachment. The statement was used to overcome a claim of insanity, a matter on which the State under New York law bore the burden of proof. Indirect use of the statement on guilt by presenting it through the psychiatrist's testi-

---

19. See § 173 supra.

20. See § 174 supra.

21. See Harris v. New York, 401 U.S. 222, 223 (1971) (trial judge instructed jury that statement could be considered only in passing on defendant's credibility and not as evidence of guilt).

22. People v. Ricco, 56 N.Y.2d 320, 452 N.Y.S.2d 340, 430 N.E.2d 1097 (1982).

mony, then, violated the defendant's right to have the statement used only for the purposes of impeachment.

Impeachment Exceptions to Other Exclusionary Sanctions. To the extent that Supreme Court case law creates exceptions to at least some of the federal constitutional exclusionary sanctions, the same approach need not, of course, be followed in other contexts. Some states have not followed it in developing exclusionary sanctions existing by virtue of state law. The Alaska Rules of Criminal Procedure, for example, specifically provide that, "Evidence illegally obtained shall not be used for any purpose including the impeachment of a witness."

Whether the Supreme Court's model should be followed presents an important question. The Court's approach focuses almost entirely upon the preventive function of the exclusionary sanction; if, as a matter of state policy, other functions of the sanction are determined to be of greater significance, the Supreme Court's model is likely to be inappropriate. Further, the critical issue posed by the Court's model is whether the possibility that evidence obtained would be relevant to and admissible for impeachment use would provide a significant incentive for law enforcement officers to violate requirements with which they would otherwise comply. The majority's response can only be characterized as based upon intuition. This can scarcely be regarded as precluding state tribunals or legislatures from legitimately substituting their own intuitive reactions or perhaps more empirically supported positions for that of the Court.

§ 179

1. Gutterman, Fourth Amendment Privacy and Standing: "Wherever the Twain Shall Meet," 60 N.C.L. Rev. 1 (1981); Kuhns, The Concept of Personal Aggrievement in Fourth Amendment Standing Cases, 65 Iowa L.Rev. 493 (1980); Mickenberg, Fourth Amendment Standing After Rakas v. Illinois: From Property to Privacy and Back, 16 N.Eng.L.Rev. 197 (1981); Slobogin, Capacity to Contest a Search and Seizure:" The Passing of Old Rules and Some Suggestions for New Ones, 18 Am.Crim.L.Rev. 387 (1981); Williamson,

Impeachment Exception to the Federal Constitutional Exclusionary Rules
110k338(6)
cross-examin! impeach! /p inadmissible /13 evidence walder /2 "united states" & harris /2 "New York"

Impeachment Exceptions to Other Exclusionary Sanctions
court(ak) & rule* /10 412 & exclusionary

§ 179. "Standing" and the Personal Nature of Rights Enforced by Exclusionary Sanctions [1]

A criminal defendant is entitled to have evidence excluded under the Fourth Amendment exclusionary rule and apparently under the other federal constitutional exclusionary sanctions only upon a showing that the evidence is fatally related to a violation of the defendant's own rights. Negatively put, this exclusionary rule gives a defendant no right to have evidence excluded upon a showing that it was obtained in violation of another person's rights.

Originally,[2] this was announced in terms that suggested a separate doctrine of "standing" to raise Fourth Amendment claims, distinct from the rules governing whether a violation of the underlying right had occurred. In Rakas v. Illinois,[3] however, the Supreme Court held that in the Fourth Amendment context no useful analytical purpose was served by retaining a notion of standing distinguishable from the merits of the Fourth Amendment claim. As a result of this dispensation of the "rubric of standing," the inquiry is simply one of substantive Fourth Amendment doctrine: Did the law enforcement conduct of which the

Fourth Amendment Standing and Expectations of Privacy: Rakas v. Illinois and New Directions for Some Old Concepts, 31 U.Fla.L.Rev. 831 (1979); 29 Am.Jur. 2d Evidence Sections 418–24; Annot., 86 A.L.R.2d 984, 992–93, 78 A.L.R.2d 246, 50 A.L.R.2d 531, 577–83, 4 L.Ed.2d 1999; Dec.Digest, Criminal Law ☜394.5(2), Search and Seizure ☜7(26).

2. See Jones v. United States, 362 U.S. 257 (1960).

3. 439 U.S. 128 (1978), rehearing denied 439 U.S. 1122.

defendant complains, assuming it occurred and was unlawful, intrude upon the defendant's privacy interests protected by the Fourth Amendment?[4]

The burden is upon the defendant to persuade the trial court that law enforcement conduct established to have occurred and to have violated the Fourth Amendment infringed the defendant's own Fourth Amendment rights.[5] Thus a trial judge considering a defense motion to suppress who concludes that the defendant has failed to meet this burden may resolve the case on this basis without ever reaching the legality of the conduct or, in some cases at least, whether the conduct ever occurred.

The justification offered by the Supreme Court for limiting the Fourth Amendment exclusionary rule to those who complain of a violation of their own rights has been curiously negative. Although the limitation was apparently applied as early as 1942[6] and was enunciated in "standing" terms in 1960,[7] the Court did not articulate a defense of it until Alderman v. United States[8] in 1969. Announcing that it would adhere to the position taken in earlier cases, the Court in *Alderman* explained that it was unconvinced that defining the Fourth Amendment exclusionary sanction so as to render it available to any defendant against whom illegally obtained evidence was offered would provide sufficient additional deterrence to justify the loss of reliable evidence involved. This rationale was repeated when the issue was again addressed in Rakas v. Illinois.[9] The California Supreme Court has suggested that the traditional Fourth Amendment

standing requirement must be based upon a perception of the exclusionary sanction as a remedy for personal wrongs.[10] This perception, of course, leads logically to the position that the rule should be defined so as to render it available only to those who have been wronged. To the extent that this is the rationale for the limitation, the limitation appears to be inconsistent with the Court's rejection of the potential remedial function of the Fourth Amendment exclusionary rule.[11]

Perhaps, however, an affirmative rationale can be offered that is consistent with the Court's perception of the Fourth Amendment's exclusionary sanction itself. A major purpose of the sanction is clearly to discourage improper law enforcement conduct. But this need not be regarded as the only purpose of the doctrine. The exclusionary rule may also be conceptualized as intended to strike a reasonable balance between the need for such discouragement and the need for reliable evidence of defendants' guilt. Thus the rule can be regarded as having dual purposes: deterrence and balance. Among the important subsidiary objectives, it follows, should be the prevention of useless loss of reliable evidence. The exclusionary remedy, therefore, should be structured insofar as possible so as to be available to defendants only when that availability will provide sufficient incremental deterrence to justify the loss of reliable evidence. Defining the rule so as to render it available only to defendants who can establish a violation of their own underlying rights, then, is consistent with the deterrence purpose and is affirmatively demanded by the coequal pur-

---

4. Id. at 133–40. Thus in Rawlings v. Kentucky, 448 U.S. 98 (1980), Rawlings sought to challenge the search of a companion's purse; the search resulted in discovery of certain drugs offered against Rawlings at his criminal trial. Prior to *Rakas*, the Court noted, the case would have presented two issues: first, did Rawlings have "standing" to challenge the search; and, second, whether he was a victim of the search. "After *Rakas*," the Court commented, "the two inquiries merge into one: whether governmental officials violated any legitimate expectation of privacy held by [Rawlings]." 448 U.S. at 106.

5. "The proponent of a motion to suppress has the burden of establishing that his own Fourth Amendment rights were violated by the challenged search or

seizure." Rakas v. Illinois, 439 U.S. 128, 131 n. 1 (1978), rehearing denied 439 U.S. 1122.

6. Goldstein v. United States, 316 U.S. 114 (1942). See also, Wong Sun v. United States, 371 U.S. 471 (1963).

7. Jones v. United States, 362 U.S. 257, 261 (1960).

8. 394 U.S. 165, 171–76 (1969), appeal after remand 424 F.2d 20.

9. 439 U.S. 128, 137 (1978).

10. People v. Martin, 45 Cal.2d 755, 759–60, 290 P.2d 855, 857 (1955).

11. Section 168 supra.

pose of striking a reasonable balance between deterrence and the need for evidence.

Supreme Court treatment of standing has involved only the exclusionary sanction attaching to the Fourth Amendment prohibition against unreasonable searches and seizures. There is no apparent reason, however, why the same analysis would not also be applied to the exclusionary remedies provided for other federal constitutional rights.

The states remain free, of course, to define state law exclusionary rules so as to render them available to defendants who can establish only a violation of another's underlying right. Most appear to have uncritically followed the Supreme Court's Fourth Amendment model and to have limited exclusionary sanctions to defendants asserting a violation of their own state rights. Several states, however, appear to have defined state exclusionary sanctions as not requiring that the demonstrated wrong have infringed upon the protected interests of the defendant challenging the admissibility of the evidence. The California Supreme Court, in People v. Martin,[12] held that a defendant was entitled to suppression of evidence obtained by improper search methods upon a showing that the search violated anyone's rights.[13] A 1974 revision of the Louisiana Constitution appears to create a right to exclusion upon proof that evidence was obtained in violation of that document's prohibition against unreasonable searches and seizures, without regard to whether the improper activity infringed protected interests of the objecting defendant.[14]

Compromise positions are, of course, available. The most attractive may be the suggestion that any person at whom a search or seizure was "directed" should be regarded as entitled to have the resulting evidence suppressed upon a showing that the search or seizure was unlawful.[15] This would have the merit of attaching the exclusionary sanction to law enforcement conduct designed to affect particular suspects, perhaps in reliance upon what is perceived to be the inability of those suspects to challenge the action. This "target" theory was rejected for purposes of the Fourth Amendment exclusionary sanction in Rakas v. Illinois.[16] The

---

12. 45 Cal.2d 755, 290 P.2d 855 (1955).

13. The *Martin* rule was reaffirmed in Kaplan v. Superior Court of Orange County, 6 Cal.3d 150, 98 Cal. Rptr. 649, 491 P.2d 1 (1971), appeal dismissed 407 U.S. 917. When confronted by a similar issue in the context of asserted violations of rights related to interrogation and confessions, however, the California court took a different approach. In People v. Varnum, 66 Cal.2d 808, 59 Cal.Rptr. 108, 427 P.2d 772 (1967), appeal dismissed 390 U.S. 529, the court conceptualized the right to counsel during interrogation (and the right to warnings related to such interrogation) as being violated only if the prosecution both conducted interrogation improperly *and* utilized the resulting admissions against the confessing person. Therefore, a defendant establishes no violation of anyone's rights unless he shows both improper interrogation and use of the evidence against the interrogated person. The end result, of course, is that only a confessing defendant can establish a violation of the underlying rights. On the other hand, when a defendant asserts that an offered confession was the "fruit" of an unlawful search, *Martin* rather than *Varnum* applies and the defendant is entitled to suppression of the confession upon a showing that the search was conducted in violation of someone else's privacy rights. See People v. Johnson, 70 Cal.2d 541, 75 Cal.Rptr. 401, 450 P.2d 865 (1969), cert. denied 395 U.S. 969.

14. La.Const., Art. I, Section 5, after setting out the right to be free from unreasonable searches and seizures, continues:

Any person adversely affected by a search or seizure conducted in violation of this Section shall have standing to raise its illegality in the appropriate court.

The Louisiana Supreme Court has taken the view that the purpose of this language was to increase the deterrent effect of the exclusionary sanction by rendering it available to even those defendants whose right of privacy was not violated by the law enforcement activity. State v. Cullotta, 343 So.2d 977 (La.1976).

15. If the exclusionary sanction is made available to more persons than those whose underlying rights were violated but fewer than all persons against whom resulting evidence might be offered, it may be appropriate and perhaps necessary to establish (or maintain) a body of "standing" doctrine separate and distinct from the law defining the underlying rights. See Rakas v. Illinois, 439 U.S. 128, 138 (1978), rehearing denied 439 U.S. 1122.

16. 439 U.S. 128, 133–38 (1978), rehearing denied 439 U.S. 1122. Language used in the federal electronic surveillance statute, 18 U.S.C.A. § 2510 et seq., suggests an intention to broaden the availability of the exclusionary sanction created by that statute. "Any aggrieved person" is authorized to move to suppress

Court stressed that determining what persons were targets within the meaning of the proposed rule would present substantial practical problems. Further, however, the Court relied upon the absence of convincing evidence that the increase in desirable deterrence accomplished by adoption of the target approach would be accomplished at a sufficiently low cost in terms of loss of reliable evidence.[17] Nevertheless, approaches such as this remain available for state law purposes.

The continued vitality of the requirement of a showing of a violation of one's own rights under the federal constitutional exclusionary sanctions increases the need to apply carefully those aspects of the underlying rights that define whose interests are intruded upon by various law enforcement activities. This has created greatest difficulty in regard to enforcement of the Fourth Amendment right to be free from unreasonable searches and seizures. Under *Rakas*, it is now necessary to call Fourth Amendment case law into service not only to determine whether a search or seizure occurred and, if so, whether it was reasonable, but also to inquire whether that search or seizure intruded upon the protected privacy interests of each particular defendant.[18]

The abandonment of any separate standing doctrine in Fourth Amendment law probably sealed the fate of the primary situation in which under pre-*Rakas* law standing was divorced from substantive Fourth Amendment doctrine. This was the so-called "automatic" standing rule. Under that rule, if a defendant was charged with possession of an item, and if that charge was based upon alleged possession at the time of a search or seizure which resulted in obtaining the item, the defendant had standing to challenge the search or seizure regardless of generally-applicable standing requirements.[19] In part, this rule rested on the Court's perception that to require such a defendant to establish standing in ordinary terms would, in many cases, compel the defendant to admit on the stand a sufficient connection with or interest in the item to provide the prosecution with a conclusive case on guilt should the case survive the challenge to the admissibility of the item.[20] This part of the rationale was destroyed by Simmons v. United States,[21] holding that testimony given at a hearing on a motion to suppress evidence is not admissible against the defendant at a subsequent trial. In United States v. Salvucci [22] the Court acknowledged this and abandoned the automatic standing doctrine, at least insofar as it was based upon the pre-*Simmons* assumption that to require of such defendants the same showing demanded of others would often result in a waiver of the privilege to remain silent on the issue of guilt or innocence.

But the automatic standing rule also rested in part upon what was perceived as the offensiveness of the prosecution taking inconsistent positions in a single proceeding.[23] Thus it was designed to eliminate the

---

evidence obtained in violation of the statute. 18 U.S.C.A. § 2518 (10)(a). "Aggrieved person" is defined as "a person who was a party to any intercepted wire or oral communication *or a person against whom the interception was directed.*" 18 U.S.C.A. § 2510(11) (emphasis supplied). But the Supreme Court has indicated that despite Congressional use of this terminology, Congress did not intend to extend the statutory exclusionary rule to persons only targets of the interception efforts. See Alderman v. United States, 394 U.S. 165, 175 n. 9 (1969), appeal after remand 424 F.2d 20. See also § 167 supra, at n. 8.

17. See 439 U.S. at 137–38.

18. § 169, at note 21, supra.

19. The rule was announced in Jones v. United States, 362 U.S. 257, 263 (1960). Brown v. United States, 411 U.S. 223 (1973) made clear that it was limited to those situations in which the possession on which the charge was based was possession at the time of the search which the defendant sought to challenge.

20. Jones v. United States, 362 U.S. 257, 263–64 (1960).

21. 390 U.S. 377 (1968), on remand 395 F.2d 769, appeal after remand 424 F.2d 1235, discussed in § 180, infra.

22. 448 U.S. 83 (1980).

23. Jones v. United States, 362 U.S. 257, 263–64 (1960) ("It is not consonant with the amenities, to put it mildly, of the administration of criminal justice to sanction such squarely contradictory assertions of power by the Government.").

need for the government, at the hearing on the motion to suppress, to deny that the defendant had a close relationship to the item and then later, at the trial on guilt or innocence, to attempt to prove such a relationship as part of its case on the possession charge. In *Salvucci*, however, the Court concluded that if there once was an inherent inconsistency between the positions that a defendant was "in possession" of an item, on the one hand, but did not experience an intrusion upon privacy by the search for and seizure of the item, on the other, current Fourth Amendment law makes clear that this is no longer the case. Thus, the Court abandoned the automatic standing rule and held that even a defendant charged with possession of the seized item must establish that his own Fourth Amendment rights were violated by the unreasonable search or seizure which led to the discovery of the item.

 WESTLAW REFERENCES

digest,synopsis(standing /s "fourth amendment" "exclusionary rule*")

439 +s 128 & rakas & date(after 6/1/83) "automatic standing"

§ 180. Enforcement of the Right to Exclusion: (a) Motions to Suppress and Appellate Review

Generally, of course, a challenge to the admissibility of evidence must be made at the time the evidence is offered but need not be made before that time. The objection will be resolved by the presiding judge when it is made.[1] Special characteristics of objections based on exclusionary rule grounds and the proceedings necessary to fairly resolve them, however, suggest that more specific and perhaps different provisions may be desirable and perhaps constitutionally necessary for resolution of exclusionary rule objections.

Exclusionary rule objections often raise complex factual questions that require extensive evidentiary hearings to resolve. Jurors' disinclination or perhaps inability to disregard apparently reliable evidence suggests that the resolution of these questions should, as a general rule, occur out of the presence of the trial jury. Further, the evidence question is often dispositive of the entire litigation. If the evidence is admissible, the defense has no desire for a contested trial on guilt or innocence; if it is inadmissible, the prosecution cannot hope to make an adequate case and therefore has no need for trial. To apply the traditional approach, then, may often result in a jury being empaneled only to be quickly shunted from the courtroom for a long period of time; upon return, the jurors are confronted with a situation that involves no real need for jury consideration. The administrative inefficiency of such proceedings is self-evident.

Providing reasonably for the raising and resolution of exclusionary rule issues raises a number of issues. Most are affected to some degree by the special characteristics of exclusionary sanction issues. Generally these are matters of trial procedure that can be, and with increasing frequency are, resolved as matters of statutory policy. Several, however, have significant federal (and perhaps state) constitutional implications, at least insofar as they apply to the raising and resolution of certain constitutional exclusionary sanction claims.

Judge's Determination of Admissibility. As a result of case law concerning the admissibility of confessions,[2] it has been widely assumed that a challenge to admissibility of

1. See § 52 supra.

2. See § 161 supra. While reliance may be placed upon general due process requirements, see United States v. Raddatz, 447 U.S. 667, 677–81 (1980), rehearing denied 448 U.S. 916, a more satisfying conceptual basis for constitutional requirements relating to the raising and resolution of such issues is the underlying right itself. Thus it can be urged that the Fourth Amendment right to be free from unreasonable searches and seizures and the exclusionary remedy for violations of that right also create a Fourth Amendment right to procedures that provide adequate assurance that particular defendants will be able to raise and ob-

evidence on all or most federal constitutional grounds entitles the challenging defendant, as a matter of federal constitutional law, to several things. First, the defendant is regarded as entitled to have the presiding judge determine admissibility and any subsidiary factual issues related to admissibility. If evidence is found admissible by the judge, a defendant may under state law have a right again to urge the objection to the trial jury but federal constitutional considerations do not require this.[3] Second, it has been assumed that a defendant has a right to present evidence related to the admissibility question. Third, a defendant's interests have been regarded as inadequately served if the judge permits the jury to hear the evidence, determines that the evidence is inadmissible, and instructs the jury to disregard the evidence. Thus the hearing at which evidence is taken is to be held out of the presence of the trial jury.

These assumptions were cast into doubt by the Supreme Court's decision in Watkins v. Sowders.[4] In *Watkins*, the state trial courts had admitted eyewitness identification testimony by witnesses who had been exposed to various pretrial identification procedures. The defendants had been permitted to develop before the jury the circumstances of those procedures but conviction resulted. In later litigation, the defendants asserted constitutional error in the failure of the trial judge to conduct a hearing out of the jury's presence on the admissibility of the witnesses' testimony, under Stovall v. Denno[5] and subsequent decisions barring the use of testimony upon a showing that the witness had been subjected to procedures creating a high likelihood of misidentification. The Supreme Court found no such defect in the procedure followed by the trial judge. It assumed that due process imposes a *per se* rule mandating a hearing outside the presence of the jury whenever the voluntariness of a confession is raised.[6] But any such *per se* rule as exists in the confession context, the Court continued, would not be applicable to challenges based upon *Stovall*.

The admissibility of evidence challenged under *Stovall* depends primarily upon its reliability, the Court reasoned, and juries can be trusted, if properly instructed, to assess such matters accurately. Consequently:

> A judicial determination outside the presence of the jury of the admissibility of identification evidence may often be advisable. In some circumstances, not presented here, such a determination may be constitutionally necessary. But it does not follow that the Constitution requires a *per se* rule compelling such a procedure in every case.[7]

The significance of *Watkins* is not clear. It may mean only that a hearing is not constitutionally mandated on a *Stovall* objection

tain accurate rulings on objections to the admissibility of evidence. Simmons v. United States, 390 U.S. 377 (1968), on remand 395 F.2d 769, appeal after remand 424 F.2d 1235, discussed in the text at n. 35 infra.

3. Vernon's Ann.Tex.Code Crim.Pro., art. 38.23 (where issue raised as to admissibility of evidence under state exclusionary rule, jury to be instructed to disregard evidence if it has reasonable doubt that evidence is admissible). Compare Lego v. Twomey, 404 U.S. 477, 489–90 (1972) (state defendant has no right to jury consideration of confession's voluntariness once judge has ruled on issue).

Further there is no federal constitutional requirement that the judge presiding over the guilt-innocence trial actually hear the testimony on which the determination of a Fourth Amendment claim is based. United States v. Raddatz, 447 U.S. 667 (1980) rehearing denied 448 U.S. 916 presented a challenge to a procedure in which motions to suppress evidence made in federal criminal litigation can be referred by the district judge

to a magistrate. If objections are filed to the magistrate's proposed findings and recommendations, the district judge is to make a *de novo* determination of findings or recommendations. This does not, however, require that the district judge himself rehear the evidence, although the judge has discretion to do so. The Supreme Court found no constitutional defect in this procedure. 447 U.S. at 677–81.

4. 449 U.S. 341 (1981).

5. 388 U.S. 293 (1967); see generally, § 174 supra.

6. The Court expressed some reservations as to whether any such *per se* rule existed in the confession area. This may mean only that the failure to hold a hearing out of the presence of the trial jury will not invalidate a conviction if it is later determined that the confession was nevertheless admissible. See 449 U.S. at 346 n. 3 (citing Pinto v. Pierce, 389 U.S. 31 (1967), rehearing denied 389 U.S. 997, so holding).

7. 449 U.S. at 349.

where no contested matter of fact is properly raised by the objection. It may mean that the failure to hold a hearing is not constitutionally fatal where the ultimate record makes clear that following such a hearing the challenged evidence would clearly have gone to the jury. Or, it may mean that in at least some cases a trial judge may hear evidence bearing on admissibility in the presence of the trial jury and if the challenged evidence is rendered inadmissible the defendant's rights are adequately protected if the trial jury is instructed to disregard the evidence. But it is also possible that *Watkins* has broader significance. It may mean that in some situations, at least, whether eyewitness testimony may, under *Stovall* and its progeny, be considered against the defendant is a decision that may constitutionally be entrusted, under proper instructions, to the trial jury.

If *Watkins* has this broader ramification, its apparent rationale may limit its application. The due process requirement of a hearing on and determination of a challenged confession's voluntariness, to the extent that it exists, is based upon doubt that a jury can be trusted, once it concludes that a confession is accurate, to disregard that confession on other grounds.[8] *Watkins* suggests this rationale does not apply where the only question submitted to the jury is the accuracy or reliability of the evidence. There is no risk that the jury will disregard other grounds for giving the evidence no weight, because no such other grounds are urged.

This, of course, suggests that *Watkins* is limited to exclusionary rules whose application depends upon the unreliability of the challenged evidence. The exclusionary sanction attached to testimony of witnesses subjected to extraordinarily suggestive identification procedures appears to be the only rule that meets this standard.

Despite *Watkins*, then, it seems likely that other exclusionary rules mandated by federal constitutional considerations must still be applied as an initial matter by the trial judge. Further, reasonably contested matters must be addressed at hearings held out of the presence of the trial juries. If a trial judge declines to follow this procedure and holds challenged evidence admissible on the basis of information developed before the jury, this may not constitute fatal constitutional error *if* the judge's determination that the evidence is admissible was sufficiently supported.[9] But if a trial judge pursues this route and concludes, after the matter has been developed before the jury, that the evidence is inadmissible, in all or most circumstances a mistrial must be declared. It will not be sufficient to sustain the defense objection and instruct the jury to disregard the evidence.

As should be obvious from this description of the options, a trial judge's decision to postpone ruling on a defense motion until relevant information has been developed before the jury is fraught with difficulties. Since a decision that the evidence is inadmissible will require aborting the trial, judges may be subject to strong administrative pressures to rule for the prosecution. Resolving exclusionary rule objections will often involve substantial exercises of discretion on the part of trial judges. Subjecting the exercise of discretion to one-sided pressures of this sort is extremely unwise. A reasonable argument can be made that a ruling made under such circumstances does not meet implied requirements of fairness that might be found in due process demands, the rights enforced by exclusionary sanctions, and in nonconstitutional requirements of fair trial procedure.

Whatever the constitutional demands, it seems quite clear that sound administrative

---

8. See § 161 supra.

9. See the discussion in n. 6 supra, concerning the Court's citation of Pinto v. Pierce, 389 U.S. 31 (1967), rehearing denied 389 U.S. 997.

The nonapplicability of the technical exclusionary rules of evidence, except those concerning privilege, to determinations by the court of preliminary questions of fact concerning admissibility of evidence is discussed in § 53 n. 8 supra.

policy dictates that proceedings to determine whether particular evidence is admissible in light of exclusionary rule objections be held out of the presence of the trial jury. The need to avoid tainting juries, the artificiality of relying on instructions to disregard, and defendants' interest in having such matters decided by a judge free of extraordinary administrative pressure to overrule such objections all militate in favor of proceedings out of the presence of the jury.

Pretrial Motions to Suppress.[10] To the extent that constitutional or other considerations dictate a determination of admissibility by the presiding judge based upon inquiry conducted out of the presence of the trial jury, this does not, of course, control when that inquiry or determination must be made. The concerns on which the requirement is based are as well met by a hearing held during trial while the jury is excluded from the courtroom as by a pretrial hearing held be-

10. Despite the frequent use of terms such as "motion to suppress" and "orders suppressing evidence" in statutes, court rules and judicial opinions, there is some uncertainty as to their meaning. This may be significant for several reasons. If only motions to suppress and not others are authorized pretrial, whether a motion is one "to suppress" may determine whether a trial court has authority to entertain it. Cf. Bosley v. State, 414 S.W.2d 468 (Tex.Crim.App.1967), cert. denied 389 U.S. 876. Where a motion to suppress but not other evidentiary motions must be made pretrial, infra, whether an objection is a suppression one may determine whether a defendant can raise it for the first time at trial. Perhaps most important, where an interlocutory appeal of an order suppressing evidence but not other evidentiary orders is authorized, see text at n. 37 infra, whether a trial court's action constitutes "suppression" of evidence may determine the appealability of the action.

Generally, those courts that have addressed the issue have defined a motion to suppress as a motion requesting that evidence be ruled inadmissible for what this Chapter has defined as exclusionary sanction reasons. Often, a pretrial motion to suppress is distinguished from a pretrial motion in limine. The latter is defined as a motion based on the ground that admission of the evidence would violate "some ordinary rule of evidence." See Department of Public Works and Buildings v. Roehrig, 45 Ill.App.3d 189, 3 Ill.Dec. 893, 359 N.E.2d 752 (1976). Unfortunately, discussion of these distinctions sometimes assumes that exclusionary sanctions are limited to violations of federal constitutional requirements. E.g., People v. Van De Rostyne, 63 Ill. 2d 364, 349 N.E.2d 16 (1976) (order excluding results of breathalyzer because officer had changed test ampoule between tests was not an appealable motion to suppress because it was not resolved by reference to the legality or perhaps constitutionality of the manner in which the evidence at issue was obtained). See also, State v. Boling, 5 Kan.App.2d 371, 617 P.2d 102, 107 (1980), holding that an "order . . . suppressing evidence" within the meaning of a statute authorizing state appeal is one which serves "either to vindicate constitutional rights or as a sanction for official conduct deemed prejudicial to the defendant, and in either case to deter such conduct in the future." Several cases have held that pretrial rulings that the prosecution may not use evidence of acts of misconduct other than the crime charged do not constitute rulings on motions to suppress evidence and thus are not appealable.

People v. Montgomery, 84 Ill.App.3d 695, 40 Ill.Dec. 183, 405 N.E.2d 1275 (1980); State v. Boling, supra.

Fed.R.Crim.P. 12(b)(3) requires that "motions to suppress evidence" be raised prior to trial, see text at note 11 infra, but does not define the term. Prior to the 1975 amendments to the rules, Fed.R.Crim.P. 41(e) provided that a motion to suppress could be made on grounds that evidence had been "illegally seized without warrant" or that although it had been seized during a search pursuant to a warrant, there were defects in the issuance, drafting, or execution of the warrant. The Advisory Committee notes to the 1975 amendments indicate that as a matter of practice motions to suppress under former Rule 41(e) were made on the basis of other forms of illegality, "such as the use of unconstitutional means to obtain a confession." The 1975 amendments to the rules deleted the detailed provision for motions to suppress in Rule 41(e) and inserted the much briefer reference to such motions in present Rule 12. The advisory notes strongly suggest that those motions present Rule 12(b)(3) is intended to require be made pretrial are limited to those based upon claims that the evidence at issue was illegally obtained. But insofar as Rule 12(b) permits (but does not require) pretrial raising of "any . . . objection, or request which is capable of determination without the trial of the general issue," it appears to authorize trial judges to entertain pretrial motions raising other evidentiary matters. See United States v. Cobb, 588 F.2d 607, 610 n. 2 (8th Cir. 1978), holding that Rule 12(b) authorized but did not require a pretrial defense motion in limine raising the admissibility of evidence of uncharged offenses.

The federal statute authorizing governmental appeal from pretrial rulings, 18 U.S.C.A. § 3731, is phrased in terms so broad that it appears to permit no argument that such appeals are limited to some form of "suppression" orders. The statute permits appeal from an "order . . . suppressing *or excluding* evidence" made before jeopardy attached (emphasis supplied). See United States v. Flores, 538 F.2d 939 (2d Cir. 1976), entertaining an appeal from a pretrial ruling that because of a Spanish court's extradition order the Government was barred from using at trial evidence of certain acts of the defendant's alleged coconspirators. The court's discussion indicates that it regarded the statute as authorizing appeal from any "evidentiary rulings that determine the manner in which [the charged] crime can be proven."

fore the jury is selected. On the other hand, administrative considerations, such as the need to minimize the waste of juror time awaiting the outcome of such inquiries, strongly suggests the value of holding such hearing pretrial. It is quite unlikely, however, that these or other reasons for preferring pretrial consideration of exclusionary rule objections rise to a constitutional level.

For reasons of this sort, statutes and court rules in many jurisdictions require that exclusionary rule issues ordinarily be raised by pretrial motion. Rule 12 of the Federal Rules of Criminal Procedure, for example, provides that motions to suppress evidence must be "raised" prior to trial and, further, within any shorter time period for the making of such motions established by the trial court.[11] Failure to raise objections to evidence within terms of this requirement results in a waiver of the right to exclusion, "but the court for cause shown may grant relief from the waiver." [12] Similar requirements exist in a number of states.[13]

In light of the tradition of limited discovery in criminal litigation, however, the defense may be unable, even by vigorous efforts, to determine before trial what potentially suppressible evidence is available to the prosecution. Where this is the case,

of course, the defense must be excused for noncompliance with any requirement as may exist concerning the filing of a pretrial motion to suppress. The end result, of course, is to frustrate the general need for pretrial identification and resolution of suppression issues. In response to this concern Federal Rule 12 authorizes the defendant to request notice of the government's intention to use at trial any evidence which the defendant may be entitled to discover.[14] The government is also authorized to give such notice, even in the absence of a defense request.[15] The purpose is to provide a vehicle for defense counsel to obtain pretrial the information necessary to render reasonable a demand that defense counsel raise by pretrial motion exclusionary rule issues likely to be raised by the government's case.[16]

Raising the matter by pretrial motion, of course, does not assure its pretrial resolution. Rule 12 provides that pretrial motions to suppress evidence (as well as other pretrial motions) shall be ruled upon before trial "unless the court, for good cause, orders that [the matter] be deferred for determination at the trial of the general issue or until after verdict . . . ." [17]

State provisions vary.[18] In general, however, orderly procedure strongly suggests

---

11. Fed.R.Crim.P. 12(b), (c).

12. Fed.R.Crim.P. 12(f).

13. E.g., West's Ann.Cal.Penal Code § 1538.5 (trial objection permitted only if "opportunity for [pretrial] motion did not exist or the defendant was not aware of the grounds for the motion"); Colo.R.Crim.P. 41(e)(g) (motion to suppress to be made before trial but court has discretion to hear objection during trial); Ohio Crim.R.P. 12(c) (motion to suppress must be made within 35 days of arraignment or 7 days before trial, whichever is earlier); N.Y.Crim.P.Law, Sec. 255.20(1); Pa.R. Crim.P. 307.

14. Fed.R.Crim.P. 12 (d)(2).

15. Fed.R.Crim.P. 12(d)(1). Some state statutes or court rules contain similar provisions. E.g., Ohio Crim. R.P. 12(D); N.Y.Crim.P.Law § 710.30 (state must give pretrial notice of intent to introduce confession or eyewitness identification by a witness who has previously identified the defendant).

16. The notice provisions are not limited to matters which might be the subject of a motion to suppress. Rule 12(d)(2) authorizes the defense to request notice of the government's intention to use at trial any evi-

dence which the defense would be entitled to discover under Rule 16. Perhaps this is intended to encourage the defense to utilize Rule 16's provisions for pretrial inspection of governmental evidence. But Rule 12(d) (2), despite this incorporation of Rule 16's discovery standards, provides that the defense request is authorized "in order to afford an opportunity to move to suppress evidence" under the provision in subdivision (b) (3).

17. Fed.R.Crim.P. 12(e). The rule does provide that determination of a motion shall not be deferred "if a party's right to appeal is adversely affected." Given the Government's right to interlocutory appeal, this appears to require—at least upon demand by the Government—that a defendant's motion to suppress be ruled on before trial. See United States v. Barletta, 492 F.Supp. 910, 912 n. 3 (D.Mass.1980), adhered to 500 F.Supp. 739, appeal dismissed 644 F.2d 50 (1st Cir.), on remand 512 F.Supp. 220, affirmed 652 F.2d 218.

18. Compare Ohio Crim.R.P. 12(E) (motion to suppress must be determined before trial) with Pa.R.Crim. P. 323(e) (motion may be heard before or at trial). There may, of course, be considerations that suggest that holding the hearing during or immediately before

the wisdom of pretrial resolution. The trial court's decision on the exclusionary rule issues may affect the parties' desire for trial on the merits. Timely determination of pretrial motions to suppress, then, may ease the task of reconciling plea bargaining and jury trial waivers with orderly control over dockets.

Burden of Proof.[19] In contrast to the situation presented by challenges to the admissibility of confessions on federal constitutional grounds, the Supreme Court has not definitively addressed the allocations of the various burdens in regard to resolution of challenges to evidence on Fourth Amendment and other federal constitutional bases. In Nardone v. United States,[20] the Court suggested in the wiretap context that a defendant challenging evidence on this ground had the burden of proving that unlawful wiretapping did in fact occur. This, of course, is most consistent with the traditional rule of motion practice that the moving party has the burden of proof.

Later, In Alderman v. United States,[21] the Court noted with apparent approval the acknowledgement by the petitioner that it had the burden of "going forward" with "specific evidence demonstrating taint" and the concession by the Government that it had the burden of persuasion on whether the challenged evidence was untainted. No occasion was found in United States v. Mat-

lock[22] to address whether the trial court had erred in requiring the Government to prove, by "the greater weight of the evidence," an effective consent to the search by which the challenged evidence had been obtained. The Court did, however, comment that "the controlling burden of proof at suppression hearings should impose no greater burden than proof by a preponderance of the evidence."[23] Finally, in Rawlings v. Kentucky,[24] the Court observed that the state defendant "of course" bore the burden of showing that the police action there at issue intruded upon his legitimate privacy interests and that it was illegal.

State provisions and decisions vary[25] and often leave the allocation of the matters somewhat in doubt. A fair reading of the Supreme Court's decisions, however, suggests that the Fourth Amendment will not bar placing upon a defendant even the burden of persuasion concerning whether conduct violating the federal constitutional requirements occurred, whether that conduct violated the particular defendant's protected rights, and whether the challenged evidence was discovered as the factual result of that conduct. Where, however, the prosecution seeks to escape the suppression penalty by means of attenuation, inevitable legitimate discovery, and similar methods the Fourth Amendment may well require that the burden of proof on such matters be placed upon the prosecution.

---

trial is wiser than hearing and resolving the matter earlier. If the case is quite certain to go to trial regardless of the outcome of the hearing on the motion, for example, holding the hearing at or immediately before trial may minimize inconvenience to witnesses. Or, if the judge anticipates potentially prejudicial publicity from the hearing on the motion to suppress, the risk may be reduced by postponing the hearing until the trial jury is selected and subject to restriction.

19. See generally, Dec. Digest Crim. Law ⊕394.5(4). § 53 n. 8 supra discusses the measure of persuasion required for preliminary questions.

20. 308 U.S. 338, 341 (1939).

21. 394 U.S. 165, 183 (1969), appeal after remand 424 F.2d 20.

22. 415 U.S. 164 (1974).

23. 415 U.S. at 177 n. 14. See generally, Saltzburg, Standards of Proof and Preliminary Questions of Fact,

27 Stan.L.Rev. 271 (1975), arguing that the Court too uncritically has accepted the preponderance standard without regard to whether particular categories of evidence present special needs demanding higher standards of admissibility. He concludes that the prosecution should have to prove voluntariness and compliance with *Miranda* beyond any reasonable doubt, id. at 294–95, but that the different considerations presented by search and seizure issues—especially the absence of any reliability concern—justifies the preponderance standard, id. at 296.

24. 448 U.S. 98, 104–05 (1980).

25. Compare Pa.R.Crim.Pro. 323(h) (prosecution has "the burden of going forward with the evidence and of establishing that the challenged evidence was not obtained in violation of the defendant's rights") with Ill. Rev.Stat. ch. 38. ¶ 114–12(b) ("the burden of proving that the search and seizure were unlawful shall be on the defendant").

The wide variation among issues that are raised by exclusionary sanction objections to evidence have persuaded some courts to develop subrules for more complex allocation of the burden of persuasion. For example, it is sometimes held that a showing by the prosecution that a search was made pursuant to a search warrant shifts to the defendant the burden of establishing some defect in the warrant or its execution.[26] On the other hand, a defendant who is regarded as having the burden of persuasion and who establishes that challenged evidence was obtained by means of a warrantless search may thereby shift to the prosecution the burden of establishing that the search was valid under one of the exceptions to the warrant requirement.[27] This may be done, for example, by showing that the search was incident to a lawful arrest.

The lack of uniformity is undoubtedly due in part to uncertainty as to the most efficient and fair allocations of the burdens. Requiring the prosecution to present affirmatively what is often a very complex case simply upon defense challenge may impose a significant and often useless burden on the prosecution. Yet in at least some cases the prosecution may have far greater access than the defense to information related to the means by which evidence was obtained. In regard to those matters on which it is appropriate for the defendant ultimately to

shoulder the burden of persuasion, then, it may nevertheless be appropriate to require the prosecution, upon defense challenge, to come forward with evidence establishing how the evidence was obtained. Such an approach might best serve the purpose of getting relevant evidence before the trial court without imposing an unduly harsh burden on the prosecution.[28]

Attacking Warrant Affidavits and Similar Matters. If evidence has been obtained through a search conducted under the authority of a search warrant issued on the basis of an affidavit which, on its face, establishes probable cause, the defense may seek an opportunity to prove that some or all of the information contained in the affidavit is false. In Franks v. Delaware [29] the Supreme Court held that a defendant is entitled as a matter of Fourth and Fourteenth Amendment law to a limited opportunity to mount such an attack upon a search warrant affidavit. A warrant must be held invalid, the Court made clear, only if a defendant establishes (a) that the affiant made a factual error in the warrant affidavit; (b) that the error was "material," that is, that if "the subject" of the falsity is set aside the remaining information is insufficient to establish probable cause; and (c) that the error was made with a certain intent, that is, that it was made deliberately or with reckless disregard for whether the assertion was cor-

---

26. State v. Jackson, 226 Kan. 302, 597 P.2d 255 (1979), cert. denied 445 U.S. 952.

27. State v. Pittman, 397 So.2d 1297 (La.1981).

28. This appears to have been the objective of the court in People v. Berrios, 28 N.Y.2d 361, 321 N.Y.S.2d 884, 270 N.E.2d 709 (1971):

> Since . . . a person [moving to suppress evidence] makes the claim because he contends that he is aggrieved and requests the court to give redress to an alleged wrong, it is most reasonable to require him to bear the burden of proof of that wrong. The People must, of course, always show that police conduct was reasonable. Thus, though a defendant who challenges the legality of a search and seizure has the burden of proving illegality, the People are nevertheless put to "the burden of *going forward* to show the legality of the police conduct in the first instance . . . ." [emphasis in original]. These

considerations require that the People show that the search was made pursuant to a valid warrant, consent, incident to a lawful arrest or . . . that no search at all occurred . . . .

28 N.Y.2d at 367–68, 321 N.Y.S.2d at 888–89, 270 N.E. 2d at 713. See also People v. Di Stefano, 38 N.Y.2d 640, 652, 382 N.Y.S.2d 5, 12, 345 N.E.2d 548, 555 (1976).

See also, Ariz.R.Crim.Pro. 16.2(b) (prosecution's burden of showing lawfulness of acquisition of evidence arises only after defense makes prima facie case, *if* evidence was obtained pursuant to valid search warrant or the defense is entitled to discover the circumstances surrounding the search or the making of the challenged confession).

29. 438 U.S. 154 (1978), on remand 398 A.2d 783 (Del.).

rect.[30] Unless defendants are able to make such attacks, the Court reasoned, the specific requirement of the Fourth Amendment that "no Warrants shall issue, but upon probable cause" would be reduced to a nullity.[31]

The *Franks* Fourth Amendment right, however, applies only to falsifications by the affiant. It appears to give a defendant no right to show that an informant misrepresented facts to the affiant, if the affiant accurately set out what the informant said and adequate factual bases for crediting the informant.[32] On the other hand, *Franks* is clearly no bar to states, as a matter of state law, providing defendants with broader opportunities to attack warrant affidavits. Such state rights might, for example, permit a defendant to prevail upon a showing that a source of information relied upon by the affiant made a material misrepresentation to the affiant. Or, the need to deter intentional misrepresentations by affiants might be regarded as requiring that a warrant be invalidated upon a showing of any intentional misrepresentation by the affiant, whether this concerned a "material" matter or not.

Franks also dealt with a defendant's Fourth and Fourteenth Amendment right to a factual hearing at which the defendant would be entitled to produce evidence in support of a claim that a warrant affidavit contained a falsification. This was clearly in response to the concern that the cost of permitting attacks would be unjustifiably increased by the need to hold time-consuming hearings to identify nonmeritorious claims.[33]

A hearing is required under *Franks* only if the defendant complies with two preliminary requirements. The first is essentially one of pleading. The defendant's "attack"—which will generally be by motion to suppress—must specifically identify the statements in the affidavit that the defense wishes to prove were false, it must contain a statement of reasons supporting the claim of falsity, and it must allege that the misstatements were material and made with the requisite intent. The second requirement is one of a preliminary offer of proof. The attack must be accompanied by affidavits or other "reliable" statements of potential defense witnesses or the absence of such statements must be "satisfactorily explained." [34] Obviously these are designed to enable trial judges to overrule motions to suppress or objections to evidence without the necessity of a factual hearing where the defense fails to demonstrate by its pleadings and offer of proof a high likelihood that if a hearing were to be held the defense would prevail on the merits. Again, of course, *Franks* is no barrier to the states permitting or requiring, as a matter of state law, the holding of factual hearings on lesser preliminary showings.

Franks deals specifically only with attempts to attack search warrant affidavits. But its rationale is applicable to other efforts to challenge the accuracy of the informational basis relied upon by the prosecution to support a search or seizure. It seems clear that similar attacks must be permitted upon arrest warrant affidavits and—where local requirements permit reliance upon such information—upon information sub-

30. 438 U.S. at 171–72.

31. Id. at 168. Prior to *Franks* however, a number of courts had held that defendants were completely barred from attacking the accuracy of search warrant affidavits. E.g., Phenix v. State, 488 S.W.2d 759 (Tex. Crim.App.1972). This position was also relied upon to justify refusing defendants' requests for disclosure of informants' names and other information that might have facilitated investigation of the accuracy of a search warrant affiant's assertions. Phenix v. State, supra. Whether the *Franks* right to attack the face of a warrant affidavit expands defendants' right to access to information that might facilitate such attack, such as the identity of informants, is uncertain. Cf. Hall v.

Illinois, 438 U.S. 912 (1978), remanding for reconsideration in light of *Franks* a state court's refusal to disclose the identity of a search warrant affiant.

32. Id. at 171 ("The deliberate falsity or reckless disregard whose impeachment is permitted today is only that of the affiant, not of any nongovernmental informant.").

33. Id. at 170 ("if a sensible threshold showing is required" no new large-scale commitment of judicial resources will be required to implement the Court's holding because "many claims will wash out at an early stage").

34. Id. at 171–72.

mitted to the warrant-issuing magistrate in a form other than a written affidavit. Whether *Franks* permits attack upon the accuracy of information relied upon to support a warrantless search or seizure is less clear. Its rationale, however, suggests that a defendant has a Fourth and Fourteenth Amendment right to challenge the accuracy of an officer's testimony as to matters purportedly within the officer's personal knowledge offered in support of warrantless action subject to scrutiny under the Amendments. Where, however, an officer testifies to having received information from a third party and to facts sufficient to render reliance upon that information reasonable, *Franks* would seem to create no right on the part of the defendant to attack the accuracy of the third party's information.

Use of Defendant's Testimony on Suppression Issues. When a defendant takes the stand and testifies at a hearing on a motion to suppress evidence made on Fourth Amendment grounds, the Fourth Amendment prohibits affirmative use by the prosecution of the defendant's testimony to prove his guilt at trial.[35] A defendant has a sufficiently important interest in an accurate resolution of Fourth Amendment claims, the Supreme Court has concluded, to require that he be free to testify in support of such claims without losing the right to avoid testifying at trial. It appears likely that most courts would generalize this approach, and prohibit the use at trial to prove guilt of defendants' testimony at any hearing held to resolve issues raised by efforts to invoke any of the exclusionary sanctions.

But a different issue is presented if a defendant who has testified in support of an exclusionary rule issue later at trial takes the witness stand and testifies in a manner inconsistent with his testimony of the suppression issue. In such situations, it is quite likely that the Fourth Amendment permits the use of the defendant's testimony at the suppression hearing for the purposes of impeachment at trial.[36] While a defendant has a legitimate interest in obtaining a full hearing on a Fourth Amendment claim, there is most likely no similar right to testify inconsistently, at least without having to defend such inconsistency before the factfinder on the issue of guilt or innocence.

Appellate Review. For several reasons, accommodating the unique characteristics of exclusionary rule issues in their criminal litigation context and the provision of appellate review that is both effective and efficient presents special problems that are addressed in several ways.

One problem is whether, and if so, how, appellate review should be available to the prosecution if a trial court suppresses evidence on motion of the defendant. If the case thereafter simply proceeds to verdict and judgment, with the result that the defendant is acquitted, it is clear that federal double jeopardy considerations bar prosecution appeal.[37] On the other hand, the Supreme Court has held that federal double jeopardy principles impose no barrier to interlocutory appeal taken by the prosecution before jeopardy attaches.[38] Interlocutory appeal by the prosecution from an order granting a pretrial motion to suppress, then, is constitutionally permissible.

---

35. Simmons v. United States, 390 U.S. 377 (1968), on remand 395 F.2d 769, appeal after remand 424 F.2d 1235.

36. See § 178 supra, considering the use of illegally obtained evidence for impeachment of a testifying defendant.

37. The Fifth Amendment prohibition against double jeopardy bars governmental appeal when a second trial of the defendant would be necessary in order to give the government relief. United States v. Wilson, 420 U.S. 332 (1975). This, as a general matter, bars

appeal from acquittals. See Fong Foo v. United States, 369 U.S. 141 (1962).

38. See Taylor v. United States, 207 U.S. 120, 127 (1907) (double jeopardy no bar to review by writ of error of trial court's action in quashing indictment, because jeopardy had not attached). See also United States v. Celestine, 215 U.S. 278 (1909) (review of decision or judgment sustaining a special plea in bar permitted when defendant had not, at the time of the motion, been put in jeopardy).

Arguably, the availability of such appellate review is also sound policy. To permit such appeals, of course, requires defendants to expend further effort and resources in defending a victory, which may infringe upon the same values protected by the prohibition against double jeopardy. The burden upon the defendant imposed by having to "defend" a win is arguably light, however, at least as compared to the burden of having to defend at the trial level against the prosecution's entire case. Further, the prosecution's interest in having recourse from an erroneous ruling by the trial judge is arguably significant, especially where that ruling jeopardizes the prosecution's ability to prove the accused's guilt. Against these considerations must be weighed the increased burden upon the appellate court system of such appeals and the danger that the appeal will prove to have been unnecessary by the defendant's acquittal at trial.

Statutory authority exists in a number of jurisdictions for interlocutory appeal in such cases by the prosecution.[39] Often, however, it is qualified by an effort to assure that such appeals are taken only when the trial court's ruling constitutes a serious impediment to the continuation of the prosecution. Under the federal statute, for example, the prosecutor must certify that the appeal is not being taken for purposes of delay and that the suppressed evidence is "a substantial proof of a fact material in the proceeding."[40] The New York statute requires a similar certification that the order leaves the proof available to the prosecution either insufficient "as a matter of law" or "so weak in its entirety that any reasonable possibility of prosecuting [the] charge to a conviction has been effectively destroyed."[41]

A second problem is reconciling appellate review of trial court decisions going against defendants with the realities of plea bargaining and the general rule that a plea of guilty results in a loss of the ability to challenge such matters as the admissibility of evidence which the prosecution would have offered had the case gone to trial.[42] Where the traditional rules apply, a defendant who has lost a motion to suppress can preserve his opportunity for appellate review only by going to trial and appealing from his conviction. This, of course, requires the defendant to forego whatever advantages might be available through plea bargaining and requires time-consuming trials that are demanded only to preserve issues already resolved for appellate review. A number of jurisdictions have resolved this by permitting a defendant to obtain judicial review of the trial court's ruling on a motion to suppress evidence even if, after that ruling, the defendant pleads guilty and is convicted on that plea.[43]

---

39. What sort of pretrial evidentiary rulings give rise to the right to appeal is addressed in n. 10, supra.

40. 18 U.S.C.A. § 3731. Because defendants can seek appellate relief from overruling of a defense motion to suppress if, and when, appeal is taken from any conviction that results, provisions are seldom made for interlocutory appeal by defendants from rulings on pretrial motions. The Supreme Court has construed 28 U.S.C.A. § 1291 as authorizing interlocutory appeal from pretrial rulings rejecting a claim of former jeopardy; the Court's discussion suggested a possible federal constitutional right to interlocutory appellate consideration. Abney v. United States, 431 U.S. 651 (1977). But it is quite unlikely that defendants have any federal constitutional right to an interlocutory appeal from rejection of an effort to invoke a federal constitutional exclusionary sanction. Cf. United States v. Hollywood Motor Car Co., Inc., 458 U.S. 263 (1982) (no interlocutory appeal from order refusing to dismiss indictment on grounds of alleged prosecutorial vindictive-

ness); United States v. MacDonald, 435 U.S. 850 (1978), on remand 585 F.2d 1211, cert. denied 440 U.S. 961 (no right to interlocutory appeal from rejection of federal constitutional speedy trial claim); United States v. North American Coal Exchange, 676 F.2d 99 (4th Cir. 1982) (denial of motion to suppress not appealable).

41. N.Y.Crim.P.Law § 450.20(8).

42. See generally Parker v. North Carolina, 397 U.S. 790 (1970); McMann v. Richardson, 397 U.S. 759 (1970), on remand 453 F.2d 745 (2d Cir.), on remand 340 F.Supp. 136 (D.C.N.Y.), affirmed 458 F.2d 1406 (loss of ability to challenge allegedly coerced confessions).

43. West's Ann.Cal.Penal Code § 1538.5(m); N.Y. Crim.P.Law § 710.70(2). When state law permits a defendant to appeal on exclusionary rule grounds despite a plea of guilty, that results in also "preserving" federal issues for consideration in federal habeas corpus litigation despite the plea of guilty. See Lefkowitz v. Newsome, 420 U.S. 283 (1975).

WESTLAW REFERENCES

Judge's Determination of Admissibility

title(watkins & sowders)

opinion(watkins /2 sowders) & date(after 1/13/81)

Pretrial Motions to Suppress

fed.r.crim.p. "criminal procedure" "federal rules" /2
12(b)(3)

digest(18 +s 3731) & "exclusionary rule*'" "fourth
amendment"

Burden of Proof

digest (burden* /2 proof proving persuasion "going
forward" /s motion hearing /2 suppress!)

Attacking Warrant Affidavits

digest,synopsis(affidavit affiant /s false /s information
/p warrant!)

*Use of Defendant's Testimony on Suppression
Issues*

digest,synopsis(motion hearing /2 suppress! /p
defendant /3 testimony testif! /p trial & fourth
/2 amendment

Appellate Review

digest,synopsis(appellate appeal /s suppress! /2
motion hearing /p "double jeopardy")

---

§ 181. Enforcement of the Right to Exclusion: (b) Enforcement in Collateral Attacks Upon Convictions [1]

Efforts to enforce the right to exclusion of improperly obtained evidence raise issues of special importance when those efforts consist of a collateral attack upon a criminal conviction that has been affirmed on direct appeal or from which no appeal was taken. All states provide for such collateral attack in state courts; the vehicle is often the writ of habeas corpus, although many jurisdictions have developed detailed collateral attack procedures by statute or court rule.[2]

§ 181

1. Boyte, Federal Habeas Corpus after *Stone v. Powell*: A Remedy Only for the Arguably Innocent?, 11 U.Rich.L.Rev. 291 (1977); Halpern, Federal Habeas Corpus and the *Mapp* Exclusionary Rule After Stone v. Powell, 82 Colum.L.Rev. 1 (1982); Robbins & Sanders, Judicial Integrity, the Appearance of Justice, and the Great Writ of Habeas Corpus: How to Kill Two Thirds (or More) With One *Stone*, 15 Am.Crim.L.Rev. 63 (1977).

2. See generally, Yackle, Postconviction Remedies, Ch. 1 (1981). The Supreme Court has never held that federal constitutional considerations demand that col-

Persons convicted of federal crimes in federal courts can seek relief under the federal statutory provision for collateral attack.[3] Perhaps most important, persons convicted in state courts can seek habeas corpus relief in federal court on the ground that their state-imposed penalty was inflicted upon them in violation of their federal rights.[4]

The major issues arise in the last context, when state defendants seek federal collateral relief from penalties imposed as a result of state convictions. Three major concerns arise in such litigation.

Bar to Collateral Relief. In Stone v. Powell,[5] decided in 1976, the Supreme Court held that a defendant convicted in state court is severely limited in seeking federal habeas corpus relief on Fourth Amendment exclusionary rule grounds. Specifically, the Court held that such a habeas corpus applicant is not to be granted relief upon a showing that evidence related to an unreasonable search and seizure was used to secure his conviction unless, in addition, he establishes that the state denied him an opportunity for full and fair litigation of his Fourth Amendment claim. A federal habeas corpus applicant who cannot make such a showing is not entitled to relief simply upon a showing that the state courts wrongfully resolved his claim that certain evidence should have been suppressed for Fourth Amendment reasons.

The *Powell* rule is not a holding that federal courts lack jurisdiction to entertain such claims.[6] Nor does it purport to be a construction of the federal statutes addressing the right of state defendants to federal re-

lateral attack be available. See Case v. Nebraska, 381 U.S. 336 (1965).

3. 28 U.S.C.A. § 2255 (collateral attack provided for by motion to vacate sentence). It is unclear whether this purports to supersede entirely provisions for habeas corpus. See United States v. Hayman, 342 U.S. 205 (1952).

4. 28 U.S.C.A. § 2254 (habeas corpus relief available for persons in state custody).

5. 428 U.S. 465 (1976), on remand 539 F.2d 693, rehearing denied 429 U.S. 874.

6. See 428 U.S. at 494 n. 37.

lief.[7] It appears best to be explained as a decision concerning the scope or substance of the exclusionary remedy which *Mapp* held the Fourth Amendment requires the states to extend to persons charged with crime in state courts. *Mapp* held that a state defendant who, at trial, establishes that certain evidence offered by the state is fatally related to a violation of the defendant's Fourth Amendment rights is entitled as a matter of Fourth Amendment law to have the evidence excluded; *Powell* held that this exclusionary remedy does not provide such a defendant with the right, after failing to prevail in a fair state court proceeding, to obtain a federal court's ruling on the merits of the Fourth Amendment claim.

In reaching its result in *Powell*, the Court reasoned that the primary justification for the Fourth Amendment exclusionary rule is deterrence of future violations of the Amendment's dictates.[8] Consequently, whether the rule embodies a right to raise issues in federal habeas corpus is to be determined by the balancing analysis used in other contexts to determine the appropriate scope of the exclusionary remedy: would the incremental prevention achieved by finding in the rule a right to habeas corpus relief outweigh the costs of making such relief available to state defendants with Fourth Amendment claims?[9]

Applying this analysis, the Court found reason to doubt that permitting Fourth Amendment claims to be raised in federal habeas corpus proceedings would increase the preventive value of the exclusionary rule as applied in trials and subsequent state procedures. Further, any such increment in prevention that might be expected would, the Court concluded, be outweighed by the increased loss of reliable evidence of state defendants' guilt.[10] In addition, the Court appeared to consider a variety of other "costs:" substantial federal judicial resources would be required to resolve the claims raised; availability of federal relief would reduce the finality of state convictions and thus blunt the deterrent value of criminal punishment; accurate resolution of the claims would often be difficult because the litigation would occur long after the events placed in issue.

In a footnote, the Court rejected the argument that state courts subject to federal judicial review only by the Supreme Court's certiorari authority could not be relied upon to resolve accurately defendants' Fourth Amendment claims and therefore access to federal habeas corpus relief was essential to accurate resolution of such claims:

> Despite differences in institutional environment and the unsympathetic attitude to federal constitutional claims of some state judges in years past, we are unwilling to assume that there now exists a general lack of appropriate sensitivity to constitutional rights in the trial and appellate courts of the several States.[11]

Powell raises several important further issues, but however these are resolved it is clear that the decision constitutes a major restriction on the Fourth Amendment exclusionary remedy.

The first problem raised by *Powell*, of course, is defining what constitutes an opportunity for full and fair litigation of a Fourth Amendment claim. The holding in *Powell* itself establishes that a showing that the state courts erroneously decided the merits of the Fourth Amendment claim does not in itself mean that the opportunity they provided the defendant was less than "full and fair." Post-*Powell* lower court decisions make reasonably clear that, if an opportunity for an apparently full and fair litigation of the issue existed, a showing that the defendant did not make use of that opportunity and thus did not obtain *any* deci-

---

7. Cf. 428 U.S. at 482 n. 17.

8. 428 U.S. at 486.

9. Id. at 489.

10. Id. at 489–90.
11. Id. at 493 n. 35.

sion on the merits of his claim will not entitle him to access to federal habeas courts.[12]

If the state tribunals blatantly refuse to entertain the claim or, if the case merits it, to consider evidence, on the other hand, it is likely that an insufficient opportunity to litigate existed.[13] But in situations less flagrant than this, the lower federal courts have been unwilling to permit federal habeas litigation. In Williams v. Brown,[14] for example, the defendant sought state habeas corpus relief on the ground that he was entitled to show certain factual errors in a search warrant affidavit. The state judge conducting the habeas proceeding had also presided over the trial and refused to reach the defendant's claim on the ground that it had been thoroughly gone into during trial. This was simply incorrect. As a result of this mistake, the defendant was given no consideration of the merits of his claim. Nevertheless, the Fifth Circuit affirmed denial of federal habeas relief on *Powell* grounds, reasoning that an error in determining whether a claim had already been resolved was indistinguishable from an error in deciding the merits of the claim.[15]

There is some indication in the post-*Powell* lower court cases that state courts may err so grievously in ascertaining the Fourth

Amendment standard or perhaps even in applying the standard that the opportunity to litigate an issue under what the state court perceives as the Fourth Amendment requirements is not full and fair within the meaning of *Powell*. In Gamble v. Oklahoma,[16] for example, the state courts refused to suppress evidence obtained by an illegal search reasoning that compliance with *Miranda* attenuated the taint; despite the defendant's reliance upon the Supreme Court's decision to the contrary in Brown v. Illinois,[17] the state courts apparently ignored that decision. Holding that federal habeas relief was available, the Tenth Circuit explained:

> [A] federal court is not precluded from considering Fourth Amendment claims in habeas corpus proceedings where the state court wilfully refuses to apply the correct and controlling constitutional standards. Deference to state court consideration of Fourth Amendment claims does not require federal blindness to a state court's wilful refusal to apply the appropriate constitutional standard.[18]

A second major issue presented by *Powell* is the extent to which it applies to exclusionary sanctions other than the Fourth Amendment exclusionary rule. The Court's emphasis in *Powell* upon the heavy cost it perceived in the loss of reliable evidence suggests that state defendants might not be

---

12. E.g., Caver v. Alabama, 577 F.2d 1188 (5th Cir. 1978), rehearing denied 592 F.2d 1190; Gates v. Henderson, 568 F.2d 830 (2d Cir. 1977), cert. denied 434 U.S. 1038.

13. See Doescher v. Estelle, 666 F.2d 285 (5th Cir. 1982), in which the defendant's pleadings were sufficient to entitle him to a factual hearing under Franks v. Delaware, 438 U.S. 154 (1978), on remand 398 A.2d 783 (Del.), at which he could offer evidence showing factual errors in the search warrant affidavit at issue in the case. Nevertheless, the state courts refused to hold such a factual hearing. The Fifth Circuit concluded that despite *Powell* Doescher was entitled to federal habeas relief.

14. 609 F.2d 216 (5th Cir. 1980).

15. The court suggested that *Powell* would not preclude federal relief if the defendant proved that "the processes provided by a state to fully and fairly litigate fourth amendment claims are routinely or systematically applied in such a way as to prevent the actual litigation of fourth amendment claims on their merits. . . ." 609 F.2d 216, 220. In Sneed v. Smith, 670 F.2d 1348, 1356 (4th Cir. 1982) the court noted but did

not address the possibility that a state procedure would not be adequate if the defendant showed deliberate condonation of perjury at the factual hearing or a flagrant disregard of a clear and dispositive legal principle.

See also, Palmigiano v. Houle, 618 F.2d 877 (1st Cir. 1980), cert. denied 449 U.S. 901, in which the appellate court acknowledged that the state courts had erroneously at the hearing on the defendant's motion to suppress placed on the defendant the burden of proving the absence of voluntary consent to the search at issue. Nevertheless, the court held that the state procedure provided the defendant with a full and fair opportunity under *Powell*. It reasoned that the determination hinged on the trial judge's assessment of the credibility of the person who gave the consent at issue, and that this could not have been affected by the allocation of the burden of proof. 618 F.2d at 882–83.

16. 583 F.2d 1161 (10th Cir. 1978).

17. 422 U.S. 590 (1975).

18. 583 F.2d at 1165.

barred from seeking federal habeas relief on the ground of federal claims which, if established, give rise to reason to question the reliability of the ultimately used evidence. To the extent that this is the standard, of course, it presents the further need to determine what federal constitutional objections are sufficiently related to reliability to bring them within the rule. Under such an approach, a state defendant would almost certainly be entitled to federal habeas corpus relief upon a showing that the state utilized a confession that was coerced under traditional standards. But whether the requirements of *Miranda* are sufficiently related to reliability to enable a state defendant to raise *Miranda* issues in federal habeas is less clear.[19]

The Court may, however, choose to limit *Powell* on other grounds. The decision may rest primarily upon what the Court perceived to be the exceptional costs of the Fourth Amendment exclusionary rule as enforced upon the states. Thus the need which the exclusionary sanction might create for states to defend against frequently raised and complex claims might be especially significant because it is not voluntarily undertaken by the states. To the extent that this is the basis for *Powell*, its applicability elsewhere might well turn upon whether other exclusionary sanctions impose a similarly offensive burden on the states to defend against similarly frequent and complex claims. Under this view, *Powell* may well be limited to the Fourth Amendment exclusionary rule which arguably creates unique tensions of this sort.[20]

Powell also raises interesting questions regarding state law exclusionary sanctions and state enforcement of federal law exclusionary sanctions. Should—or may—states decline to permit state defendants to raise Fourth Amendment issues in state post-conviction proceedings if the state's trial and direct appeal procedures provide a "full and fair" opportunity to litigate such matters? Should state defendants be able to raise state exclusionary sanction issues in state post-conviction proceedings, at least in the absence of a showing of a lack of an opportunity for "full and fair" litigation of them in the original prosecution? Some of the considerations relied upon in *Powell*, such as the value of finality in criminal litigation, militate in favor of limiting state defendants' access to state post-conviction proceedings. But to the extent that *Powell* is a response to the unique federalism tensions created by the Fourth Amendment and federal habeas relief, if may not provide an attractive model for situations where no such federalism tensions exist.

Exhaustion of State Remedies. The federal habeas corpus statute states explicitly that federal relief is to be denied an applicant who has been convicted in state court if the applicant has the ability to raise the matter asserted in state courts.[21] This, however, is limited to those state remedies that are available to the federal applicant at the time the application is filed; a previous failure to

---

19. The indication that *Powell* might be applicable only to matters not directly related to the accuracy of the state trial's outcome was confirmed by Jackson v. Virginia, 443 U.S. 307 (1979). In *Jackson*, the Court held that a state defendant was entitled to attack a state conviction on the ground of constitutional insufficiency of the evidence, despite the provision by the state courts of a "full and fair hearing" on that issue. This question, the Court explained, "is central to the basic question of guilt or innocence." 443 U.S. at 323. In Brewer v. Williams, 430 U.S. 387 (1977), rehearing denied 431 U.S. 925 the Supreme Court might have held *Powell* applicable to *Miranda* or *Miranda*-like objections, but did not. This may have little significance, as *Powell* was decided after the lower court decisions in *Williams* and was not argued to the Court in the

latter case. See 430 U.S. at 413–14 (Powell, J., concurring). Some lower courts have refused to expand *Powell* to bar federal habeas relief for *Miranda* violations. See Hinman v. McCarthy, 676 F.2d 343 (9th Cir. 1982) (rejecting proposed distinction between coerced and anti-*Miranda* confessions); Harryman v. Estelle, 616 F.2d 870, 872 n. 3 (5th Cir. 1980) (en banc), cert. denied 449 U.S. 860.

20. In Rose v. Mitchell, 443 U.S. 545 (1979), five members of the Court refused to rely upon *Powell* as barring a federal habeas applicant from claiming racial discrimination in the selection of the foreman of the grand jury that indicted him.

21. 28 U.S.C.A. § 2254(b), (c).

pursue a state remedy no longer available at the time of the filing of the application for federal relief does not bar the granting of federal relief.[22] An applicant has exhausted state remedies only if the specific claim sought to be raised in federal litigation has been raised in state court; having completed state proceedings without having raised the specific claim is not exhaustion within the meaning of the statute.[23]

Failure to Follow State Procedures. As was discussed in the preceding section, states are with increasing frequency imposing procedural requirements upon the manner in which state defendants must assert their exclusionary rule rights, including those rights that exist by virtue of the United States Constitution. If a state defendant fails to follow the procedures prescribed by the state for raising the right to exclusion and if under state law a loss of that right results, this constitutes a ground for denying federal habeas corpus relief, independent of the merits of the defendant's claim of a violation of federal constitutional rights. In exclusionary rule cases, of course, the major state requirement that bars federal relief is the frequently-imposed requirement that a defendant make a contemporaneous and specific objection to evidence on the same grounds he later relies upon for appellate or collateral attack relief.

Fay v. Noia [24] apparently held that a failure to follow state procedural requirements would result in loss of federal rights such as the right to have evidence obtained in violation of the Fourth Amendment excluded on-ly if that failure amounted to a knowing and deliberate waiver of the federal right. In Wainwright v. Sykes,[25] however, this standard was abandoned. Under *Sykes*, a state defendant seeking federal habeas corpus relief who has failed to comply with a state procedural requirement for raising the issue is entitled to have the federal habeas court reach the merits of his claim only if he establishes "cause" for the noncompliance and "some showing of actual prejudice resulting from the alleged constitutional violation." The "precise definition" of cause and prejudice were left for resolution in future decisions.[26]

If, however, despite a defendant's failure to follow a state procedure for raising a claim, the state courts nevertheless consider the merits of his claim, the *Sykes* requirement does not apply.[27] This is apparently based on the recognition that the bar to reaching the merits of the federal applicant's claim is a matter of state law that the state courts can determine is inapplicable. If the state courts make such a determination, no independent state ground for denying relief exists.

In conclusion, the matters discussed in this section have been presented primarily in the context of persons convicted in state courts applying for federal habeas corpus relief based upon alleged violations of federal rights for which federal law mandates an exclusionary sanction. But they may also arise in the same system in which the conviction occurred, whether that is the state or federal judiciary. The issues are, in those

---

22. See Fay v. Noia, 372 U.S. 391, 434–35 (1963).

23. See Picard v. Connor, 404 U.S. 270 (1971).

24. 372 U.S. 391 (1963).

25. 433 U.S. 72 (1977), rehearing denied 434 U.S. 880.

26. The "cause and prejudice" requirement was reaffirmed in Engle v. Isaac, 456 U.S. 107 (1982), in which the Court declined to replace it with a "plain error" standard. 456 U.S. at 134. The Court also provided some guidance as to the meaning of "cause" as used in *Sykes*. A defendant's perception that presentation of a claim to state courts would be futile cannot alone constitute "cause" for failing to present that claim pursuant to state requirements. Id. at 130.

Whether the novelty and unforeseeability of a constitutional claim might establish "cause" for failing to raise it was not addressed, see id. at 131, because the Court found that the "basis" for the claim at issue was available at the time of the trial in state court and other defense counsel had, at that time, perceived and litigated that claim. Id. at 131–32. Thus on the facts before the Court "cause" was not established. See also, United States v. Frady, 456 U.S. 152 (1982), rehearing denied 456 U.S. 1001.

27. See the discussion in Euell v. Wyrick, 675 F.2d 1007, 1008–9 (8th Cir. 1982), relying heavily upon County Court of Ulster v. Allen, 442 U.S. 140 (1979). See also, Engle v. Isaac, 456 U.S. 107, 135 n. 44 (1982).

contexts, quite similar. For example, a federal criminal defendant is not entitled to collateral relief in federal court on grounds that illegally obtained evidence was used at trial if he did not follow the federal requirements for raising the matter at trial. Nor is he entitled to relief in collateral attack proceedings if he still has available a remedy by appeal from the conviction.[28] Whether those rights to exclusion that exist by virtue of nonconstitutional federal law should be construed to create an exclusionary right enforceable only in trial and direct appeal proceedings raises an issue analogous to but distinguishable from that in *Powell.*

 WESTLAW REFERENCES

Bar to Collateral Relief

sh 428 us 465

stonc & 428 /3 465 & date(after 6/1/83)

diges(opportunit! /s litigat! & "fourth amendment"
/p collateral! "habeas corpus" review)

topic(197) /p full fully fair fairly /p opportunit! litigat!

Exhaustion of State Remedies

topic(197) /p exhaust! /s state /s remed! &
fourth 4 /2 amend! const.amend.

Failure to Follow State Procedures

digest,synopsis(cause /s prejudice & "habeas
corpus" relief collateral! & fourth 4 /2 amend!)

---

§ 182. Admission of Improperly Obtained Evidence as "Harmless Error"[1]

American courts quite early rejected the proposition that any trial error would require the granting of a new trial, thus giving rise to the doctrine of "harmless error" which identifies those errors not requiring such relief.[2] The rationale for regarding some errors as harmless, of course, rests largely upon considerations of economy and judicial efficiency. If it is sufficiently clear that another trial conducted without committing a particular error would lead to the same result, using judicial resources to conduct that retrial is obviously inefficient.[3]

The harmless error doctrine, especially as applied to errors of federal constitutional dimensions, has not been without its critics. Goldberg,[4] perhaps the most outspoken of the doctrine's opponents, describes it as "among the most insidious of legal doctrines."[5] More specifically, he urges that as applied the doctrine requires appellate courts to operate as "primary factfinders," a task that is excessively time consuming and which leads to unreliable results.[6] Further, he assails the doctrine as diminishing the protection afforded defendants by the rules whose violations are found harmless. The flexibility of the analysis required by the harmless error inquiry, he charges, permits courts hostile to the underlying rights at issue to dilute or destroy those rights by refusing to enforce them under the guise of finding errors in their implementation harmless.[7]

Whatever the merits of the harmless error rule as a general matter, its application to errors in the implementation of exclusionary sanctions creates special difficulties. This is

---

28. Adams v. United States ex rel. McCann, 317 U.S. 269 (1942) (subject to exception, general rule is that appeal rather than habeas corpus must be used if appeal is available).

§ 182

1. Goldberg, Harmless Error: Constitutional Sneak Thief, 71 J.C.L. & Crim. 421 (1980); Field, Assessing the Harmlessness of Federal Constitutional Error—A Process in Need of a Rationale, 125 U.Pa.L.Rev. 15 (1976); Mause, Harmless Constitutional Error: The Implications of Chapman v. California, 53 Minn.L.Rev. 519 (1969); Saltzburg, The Harm of Harmless Error, 59 Va.L.Rev. 988 (1973); Thompson, Unconstitutional Search and Seizure and the Myth of Harmless Error, 42 Notre Dame Law. 457 (1967); Notes, 64 Cornell L.Rev. 538 (1979), 83 Harv.L.Rev. 814 (1970); 5 Am. Jur.2d Appeal and Error §§ 776–819; Annot., 31 L.Ed.

2d 921; Annot., 30 A.L.R.3d 128; C.J.S. Criminal Law §§ 1887–1913; Dec. Digest Criminal Law ⚖1163(3). For a broad discussion of harmless error, see Traynor, The Riddle of Harmless Error (1970), dealing largely with rulings on evidence.

2. See generally, Saltzburg, supra note 1, at 998. The doctrine is applied principally during appellate review. But it may also be applied at the trial level by a judge who, after verdict, becomes convinced that evidence was improperly admitted and is faced with the question whether to grant a new trial.

3. See Note, 64 Cornell L.Rev. 538, 538 (1979).

4. Goldberg, supra n. 1.

5. Id. at 421.

6. Id. at 429–30.

7. Id. at 432, 436.

in large part because of the various and sometimes conflicting considerations bearing upon whether an unusually stringent criterion should be used for determining whether such errors are harmless.

First, as Saltzburg has pointed out, the applicability of the especially stringent burden of proof "beyond a reasonable doubt" in criminal litigation suggests a corresponding need for an especially stringent harmless error rule.[8] Second, the constitutional nature of many exclusionary sanctions and the assumption that the constitutional nature of the error is relevant to the choice of a harmless error standard or at least its application further suggests the need for an unusually stringent standard.[9] Finally, the highly controversial nature of the exclusionary sanctions and doubt as to their efficacy cannot help but affect the matter. This last consideration, of course, probably militates in favor of a more lenient approach, but this may not necessarily be so.

While standards for determining harmless error before Chapman v. California[10] differed,[11] there was widespread acceptance of the approach embodied in the federal statute which directs federal courts not to grant appellate relief for errors that do not "affect the substantial rights" of the appealing defendant.[12] In Chapman, however, the Supreme Court made clear that whether an error of federal constitutional dimensions was harmless so as to obviate the need for appellate relief was itself a federal constitutional

question. Where such an error could be harmless, the Court continued, the federal constitutional criterion to be applied requires that the party committing a federal constitutional error convince the court beyond a reasonable doubt that the error did not contribute to the jury verdict or conviction.[13]

In Chapman the Court suggested and in Holloway v. Arkansas[14] it held that some federal constitutional errors could not be harmless under the Chapman standard.[15] But it appears that violations of most, if not all, of the exclusionary sanctions mandated by the federal constitution might constitute harmless error under that criterion. Chapman's approving discussion of the Court's earlier decision in Fahy v. Connecticut[16] made clear that errors consisting of improper admission of evidence in violation of the Fourth Amendment exclusionary rules could be harmless error under the Chapman standard. In Gilbert v. California[17] the Court assumed that a failure to apply the exclusionary sanction applicable to a violation of a defendant's right to counsel at pretrial identification procedures[18] could be harmless under Chapman and Milton v. Wainwright[19] applied the Chapman standard to find admission of a confession obtained in violation of the Sixth Amendment right to counsel[20] harmless error.

Although there has been extensive discussion concerning some of the subtleties of the Chapman standard,[21] the basic contours of the inquiry it directs in situations where evi-

8. Saltzburg, supra n. 1, at 991.

9. Goldberg, supra n. 1, at 423.

10. 386 U.S. 18 (1967), rehearing denied 386 U.S. 987.

11. Saltzburg, supra n. 1, at 1010.

12. 28 U.S.C.A. § 2111 (judgment on hearing of appeal or writ of error is to be given "without regard to errors or defects which do not affect the substantial rights of the parties"). See also Fed.R.Civ.P. 61; Fed. R.Crim.P. 52(a); Fed.R.Evid. 103(a).

13. 386 U.S. at 24.

14. 435 U.S. 475 (1978).

15. Evidence improperly admitted over Fourth Amendment objections was held harmful after scrutiny under a harmless error standard in Whiteley v. War-

den, 401 U.S. 560, 569 n. 13 (1971) and Bumper v. North Carolina, 391 U.S. 543, 550 (1968), appeal after remand 5 N.C.App. 528, affirmed 275 N.C. 670, 170 S.E.2d 457.

16. 375 U.S. 85 (1963).

17. 388 U.S. 263, 274 (1967).

18. See § 173 supra.

19. 407 U.S. 371 (1972).

20. See § 155 supra.

21. A major concern has been whether emphasis should be placed upon the characteristics of the improperly admitted evidence or, in the alternative, upon the characteristics of the other evidence in the record tending to prove guilt. See, e.g., Field, supra note 1, at 16.

dence inadmissible under an exclusionary sanction was nevertheless admitted appear quite clear. The reviewing court must ask whether it is convinced beyond a reasonable doubt that without hearing the inadmissible evidence the trial jury would still have convicted the defendant.[22] In resolving this question, the court is to consider the weight which the jury is likely to have given the evidence. This, of course, will turn largely upon the court's perception of the persuasiveness with which the jury is likely to have regarded the evidence. In addition, the weight of other evidence introduced that tends to show guilt must be evaluated and weighed against the inadmissible evidence. In making this second inquiry, the reviewing court is to consider, among other things, the extent to which the other evidence was cumulative of the improperly admitted evidence and the extent to which the other evidence was contradicted by defense evidence. Ultimately, the decision must turn upon a comparison of the two categories of evidence. If the reviewing court entertains a reasonable doubt that a sufficient number of jurors to "hang" the jury would have voted for acquittal, the admission of the evidence cannot be regarded as harmless error under *Chapman*.[23]

Application of the *Chapman* standard is well illustrated by Milton v. Wainwright.[24] At Milton's trial for the murder of the woman with whom he had been living, evidence was introduced that before the crime Milton told an acquaintance that he disliked the vic-

tim and was interested only in getting some money out of her. Other evidence tended to show that Milton was financially pressed and had purchased and maintained insurance policies on the life of the victim. Further, the state's evidence showed that on the day of the crime Milton had purchased the car in which the victim drowned and that the doors would lock as they did, preventing the victim's escape, only as the result of careful manipulation of a safety device. Most damaging, two written confessions and a wire recording of a third, oral, confession were properly admitted. Improperly—the Supreme Court assumed—the trial court also admitted testimony by a police officer who had posed as a fellow prisoner and was thereby enabled to overhear further incriminating admissions by Milton during his pretrial incarceration. The presumably improperly admitted confession, the Court reasoned, was only cumulative of the other confessions, which appeared highly reliable. Given this, and the other evidence of Milton's guilt, the majority was left with "no reasonable doubt" that the trial jury would have reached the same verdict without hearing the officer's testimony.[25] If admission of that testimony was error, then, it was harmless and Milton was entitled to no relief from his conviction.

Some constitutional errors cannot constitute harmless error under *Chapman*, and it may be that some exclusionary rule issues come within that category. The most likely candidate for inclusion in this category is im-

---

22. This is most plainly articulated in Milton v. Wainwright, 407 U.S. 371, 377 (1972) ("Our review of the record . . . leaves us with no reasonable doubt that the jury . . . would have reached the same verdict without hearing [the improperly admitted testimony]").

23. In Harrington v. California, 395 U.S. 250 (1969), the Court noted the argument that a harmless error claim must be rejected if the court could imagine a single juror who without hearing the improperly admitted testimony would have remained unconvinced of guilt. Whether the Court accepted this is not clear. 395 U.S. at 254. This statement of the argument, however, oversimplifies it. If, of course, a unanimous jury is not required, a doubt that *all* jurors would have voted for conviction would not be sufficient. Moreover, the stan-

dard is most likely not whether the court could "imagine" a sufficiently large number of jurors remaining unconvinced but rather whether it was convinced beyond a *reasonable* doubt that in the absence of hearing the inadmissible testimony a sufficiently large number of jurors to prevent conviction would not have remained unconvinced of guilt. A creative judge could certainly imagine a scenario that would be so unlikely as not to raise a *reasonable* doubt.

24. 407 U.S. 371 (1972).

25. 407 U.S. at 377. The allegedly inadmissible confession was last in time, thus avoiding any question of possible impact on the voluntariness of the earlier confessions. See § 158 supra.

proper admission of involuntary confessions. In *Chapman* itself, the Court cited a prior coerced confession case as among those decisions which have "indicated that there are some constitutional rights so basic to a fair trial that their infraction can never be treated as harmless error . . . ." [26] Whether, in light of subsequent development of *Chapman's* harmless error doctrine, the Court would still adhere to this is uncertain.

Holloway v. Arkansas,[27] holding that the Court would not inquire whether improper joint representation was harmless error, suggests that the harmless error doctrine will be unavailable in those situations where the nature of the error makes inquiry into its effect so difficult that application of the *Chapman* standard would amount to "unguided speculation." [28] Under this approach, it is difficult to distinguish between the inquiry as to the effect of admission of an involuntary confession and inquiries into the effect of other confessions whose admission is clearly subject to the harmless error rule. Perhaps it can be argued that such confessions are so likely to be found persuasive by juries that any inquiry into the possibility that their admission made no difference would be "unguided speculation" within the meaning of *Holloway*. This does not appear tenable, however, in view of the likelihood that other confessions, subject to none of the concern regarding reliability that is created by involuntariness, are almost certain to be regarded by juries as equally persuasive. Despite the Court's reservations, even the admissibility of an involuntary confession is likely to be held to give rise to potentially no more than harmless error.

The *Chapman* standard, of course, is binding on the states only in regard to admission of evidence in violation of exclusionary sanctions mandated by the federal constitution. In regard to exclusionary rules that exist by virtue of state law, state courts (and legislatures) remain free to develop stricter or more lenient standards. Thus it would be permissible to abandon the harmless error approach and provide for defendants to obtain new trials whenever evidence was improperly admitted in violation of an exclusionary rule. Or, a new trial might be made available only if review resulted in a determination that the evidence introduced, excluding the improperly admitted evidence, was insufficient to support the conviction.

In evaluating the *Chapman* approach and the desirability of applying it in those situations not controlled by federal constitutional considerations, it would be useful to consider the extent to which the special characteristics of the exclusionary rules suggest an approach different from what might be appropriate in regard to other trial errors. Considerations of judicial economy, of course, apply to exclusionary rule cases as to others. Further, it can be urged that unnecessary reversals on exclusionary rule grounds would involve special costs not incurred elsewhere. Reversals of convictions on exclusionary rule grounds, especially where the error may not have affected the outcome of the proceeding, are exceptionally likely to erode public confidence in the proper administration of justice.

Whether the objections to inquiry into the harmfulness of an error apply with special force in exclusionary rule cases is problem-

---

26. 386 U.S. at 23, citing Payne v. Arkansas, 356 U.S. 560 (1958).

27. 435 U.S. 475 (1978).

28. The Court stressed the difficulty of assessing the reasons for an attorney's failure to take certain action and, turning to a particularly difficult specific example, explained:

> [T]o assess the impact of a conflict of interests on the attorney's options, tactics, and decisions in plea negotiations would be virtually impossible. Thus, an

inquiry into a claim of harmless error here would require, unlike most cases, unguided speculation.

435 U.S. at 491.

It would be possible, of course, to refuse to make the harmless error inquiry for reasons other than this difficulty of assessing the impact of the error on the outcome of the proceedings. Thus it might be urged that the need for maximum preventive impact to enforce a given rule requires a second trial in all cases where the rule was violated. But the Court has shown no inclination to formulate exceptions to the harmless error doctrine on this rationale.

atic. It is doubtful whether the inquiry into the effect of an exclusionary rule error is any more difficult than the inquiries demanded by the harmless error rule in other contexts. But it is less clear whether the harmless error rule might pose special risks in the exclusionary rule context of blunting the deterrent and other preventive effects of the underlying rules or of permitting circumvention of those rules by courts hostile to the substance of the rules themselves. Arguably, the primary preventive function of the exclusionary rules makes this consideration of much greater importance than it is properly given in the context of legal doctrines that are not designed primarily or exclusively to control conduct of law enforcement agencies.

The question can, of course, be put in the terms that the Supreme Court has frequently used in assessing possible expansions or contractions of the federal constitutional exclusionary rules themselves:[29] would the incremental prevention accomplished by invalidating all convictions following trials in which the trial court improperly admitted evidence over exclusionary rule objections outweigh the costs of retrials and perhaps of losing convictions in those cases where conviction on retrial may become impossible for fortuitous reasons? Whether law enforcement officers are affected, consciously or otherwise, by a rule applied primarily during appellate evaluation of the reversible nature of errors is, at best, doubtful. On the other hand, a *per se* rule mandating a new trial whenever evidence is improperly admitted over exclusionary rule objections might well increase public awareness and thus further the so-called educative effect of the rule.[30] Given the dearth of empirical evidence regarding these matters, however, little is available to help in addressing them.

29. See discussion in § 168 supra.

30. Id.

WESTLAW REFERENCES

digest,synopsis(harmless /2 error /p inadmiss! admissibility admissible admitted admit allow! exclud! exclusion! & fourth 4 /2 amend!)

chapman & 386 /3 18 & date(after 6/1/83)

digest,synopsis(harmless /5 error /p "beyond a reasonable doubt" & fourth 4 /2 amend!)

digest,synopsis(error /p harmless reversible /p confess! /p "habeas corpus" collateral! review! relief)

§ 183. The Future of the Exclusionary Sanctions

Widespread acceptance of exclusionary sanctions in criminal litigation developed almost exclusively as a result of the United States Supreme Court's enthusiasm for these sanctions as means of enforcing federal constitutional and statutory limits on law enforcement. During the past decade, however, the Court's enthusiasm has significantly diminished.

The Court has virtually abandoned all possible rationales for exclusionary sanctions other than the pragmatic preventive one. Moreover, the Court has become increasingly skeptical regarding the effectiveness of the evidentiary rules in preventing infringements upon the underlying protected interests in general and concerning the effectiveness of expansion of those rules in increasing whatever preventive effect the rules have. In addition, the Court has become increasingly sensitive to the cost of reliance upon exclusionary sanctions, especially the loss of reliable evidence of the guilt of those charged with serious criminal acts.

Nevertheless, the exclusionary remedies have become so widely accepted as a means of responding to violations of federal constitutional and statutory requirements applicable to the gathering of evidence that they are unlikely to be abandoned by the Court. But the Court will most likely continue to restrict the availability of the remedies where, in its view, this can be done without dramatically reducing the apparent preventive effect of the sanctions. Thus the future will see a continuation of the trend illustrated by the Court's resurrection and expansion of the impeachment exception,[1] its limitation upon state defendants' ability to enforce the Fourth Amendment exclusionary rule in federal habeas corpus litigation,[2] and its almost summary refusal to apply an exclusionary sanction to the violation of nonrequired regulation of federal administrative agencies.[3]

In large part because of the Supreme Court's previous enthusiasm for exclusionary sanctions, however, such evidentiary rules are likely to continue to play an important role in criminal litigation. Especially if the Supreme Court continues to contract the federal constitutional sanctions and the federal constitutional requirements which they enforce, state law exclusionary sanctions are likely to become of increasing importance. This increase in the importance of state law will result in the development—or recognition—of a number of arguably "new" issues for exclusionary rule law.

Much of the concern will, of course, focus upon the state rights and the extent to which they can or should be construed so as to provide suspects and other citizens greater protection from law enforcement actions than is provided by federal law. Further, substantial attention will have to be paid to which state rights are appropriately enforced by means of an evidentiary penalty attached to the prosecution at criminal trials. But in addition it will be necessary, insofar as state exclusionary sanctions are adopted, to address in the context of these sanctions the issues that have traditionally been discussed and to some extent resolved as matters of federal constitutional—and often simply Fourth Amendment—law. Thus such matters as the determination of attenuation of established taint, the need for litigants to establish a violation of their own rights, and the propriety of impeachment, "good faith"

and other exceptions must be considered in the state law context.

It is important that state courts and legislatures recognize that they have substantial flexibility in developing appropriate exclusionary sanctions for those state rights that are to be enforced in this manner. The Supreme Court's federal constitutional exclusionary rule case law is, of course, available as a model. It must not, however, be assumed uncritically to be untouchable. State judicial and legislative authorities must accept responsibility for addressing independently the important policy questions raised by possible state exclusionary sanctions. Whether to give significant weight to possible rationales for exclusionary sanctions other than the potential preventive effect of the sanctions, for example, is quite appropriate for *de novo* consideration by the states.

In addition, it is likely that increasing attention will be paid to greater structuring of the process for raising and resolving exclusionary rule matters. Pretrial resolution of exclusionary sanction issues will be encouraged by requirements of pretrial motions and disclosure obligations that make such requirements reasonable. Appellate review of trial court decisions on exclusionary rule issues will become increasingly available, both to the prosecution through interlocutory appeal procedures and to defendants who are willing to plead guilty if this can be done without loss of access to the appellate process. Litigation of exclusionary rule matters is further likely to be increasingly limited to the trial and direct appeal. Forums for presenting such issues as part of collateral attacks upon convictions are likely to become more difficult for convicted defendants to find.

Finally, it is likely that future development of exclusionary sanction law will result in increasing acceptance of the sanctions on grounds other than the pragmatic preventive

---

§ 183

1. See § 178 supra.

2. See § 181 supra.

3. See United States v. Caceres, 440 U.S. 741 (1979), discussed in § 166 at n. 15, supra.

rationale which the Supreme Court appears to regard as virtually the sole basis for the Fourth Amendment exclusionary rule. This is not to depreciate the importance of knowing the effect of exclusionary sanctions, and empirical research concerning this will be of continuing importance. But in large part because of post-*Mapp* experience with the Fourth Amendment exclusionary rule, the notion that the prosecution ought not to benefit from its own wrongdoing has become deeply ingrained in criminal litigation. It is quite unlikely that criminal evidence law will—or can—return to the common law notion that admissibility is, generally speaking, unaffected by the way in which proffered evidence was obtained.

 **WESTLAW REFERENCES**

trend* /s exclusion! /s sanction* rule*
caceres & 440 /3 741 & date(after 6/1/83)

Title 7
RELEVANCY AND ITS COUNTERWEIGHTS
Chapter 16
RELEVANCE [1]

Table of Sections

---

§ 184. Relevance as the Presupposition of Admissibility

The law of evidence presupposes that in judging the claims of litigants, it is important to discern the true state of affairs underlying the dispute. In pursuing this objective, it proceeds on the premise that the way to find the truth is to permit the parties to present to the court or jury all the evidence that bears on the issue to be decided. Of course, there are many rules that keep probative evidence from the finder of fact. The self-incrimination privilege is one.[2] But unless there is some distinct ground for refusing to hear such evidence, it should be received. Conversely, if the evidence lacks probative value, it should be excluded.[3]

Federal Rule of Evid. 402 and the corresponding Uniform Rule adopt these two "axioms" of the common law. The Federal Rule provides that

> All relevant evidence is admissible, except as otherwise provided by the Constitution of the United States, by Act of Congress, by these rules, or by other rules prescribed by the Supreme Court pursuant to statutory authority.

1. See generally M. Graham, Handbook of Federal Evidence 144–192 (1981); Lempert & Saltzburg, A Modern Approach to Evidence 148–157 (2d ed. 1983); 1 Louisell & Mueller, Federal Evidence §§ 91–114 (1978); 2 id. §§ 124–130; Rothstein, Federal Rules of Evidence §§ 401–403 (2d ed. 1982); Saltzburg & Redden, Federal Rules of Evidence Manual 86–123 (3d ed. 1982); 1 Weinstein & Berger, Evidence ¶¶ 401–403 (1982); 1 Wigmore, Evidence §§ 9–14 (3d ed. 1940); 22 Wright & Graham, Federal Practice and Procedure §§ 5161–5167, 5191–5224 (1978); 5 Am.Jur.2d Appeal and Error §§ 518, 799, 800, 802 (1967); 29 id. Evidence §§ 251–256, 260; 31A C.J.S. Evidence §§ 158–185 (1964); Dec.Dig. Evidence ⊕99–117 (1982).

§ 184

2. See Friendly, The Fifth Amendment Tomorrow: The Case for Constitutional Change, 37 U.Cin.L.Rev. 671 (1968); Ch. 13 supra.

3. See Thayer, Preliminary Treatise on Evidence 264–266 (1898); 1 Wigmore, Evidence §§ 9–10 (3d ed. 1940). Innumerable cases state this presupposition of admissibility. E.g., Schmeck v. City of Shawnee, 232 Kan. 11, 651 P.2d 585, 601 (1982); Trook v. Sagert, 171 Or. 680, 138 P.2d 900, 902 (1943). Where one party offers irrelevant evidence and the other party, having failed to object, seeks to counter this evidence, the additional irrelevant evidence may be admissible as a form of "fighting fire with fire." See § 57 supra.

Evidence which is not relevant is not admissible.[4]

WESTLAW REFERENCES

headnote(402 /p relevant /5 evidence)

§ 185. The Meaning of Relevancy and the Counterweights

To say that relevant evidence is generally admissible, while irrelevant evidence is not would be of little value without a suitable definition of relevance. This section therefore begins by clarifying the meaning of relevance. It then outlines the factors that can make even relevant evidence inadmissible.

There are two components to relevant evidence: materiality and probative value.[1] Materiality looks to the relation between the propositions for which the evidence is offered and the issues in the case. If the evidence is offered to help prove a proposition which is not a matter in issue, the evidence is immaterial. What is "in issue," that is, within the range of the litigated controversy, is determined mainly by the pleadings, read in the light of the rules of pleading and controlled by the substantive law. Thus, in

a suit for worker's compensation, evidence of contributory negligence would be immaterial, whether pleaded or not, since a worker's negligence does not affect his right to compensation.[2] But matters in the range of dispute may extend somewhat beyond the issues defined in the pleadings. Under flexible systems of procedure, issues not raised by the pleadings may be tried by express or implied consent of the parties.[3] In addition, the parties may draw in dispute the credibility of the witnesses and, within limits, produce evidence assailing and supporting their credibility.[4] Moreover, considerable leeway is allowed even on direct examination for proof of facts that do not bear directly on the purely legal issues, but merely fill in the background of the narrative and give it interest, color, and lifelikeness. Maps, diagrams and charts, for example, are material as aids to the understanding of other material evidence.[5]

The second aspect of relevance is probative value, the tendency of evidence to establish the proposition that it is offered to prove. Federal Rule and the Revised Uniform Evid. Rule 401, for instance, incorpo-

---

4. Fed.R.Evid. 402. See generally Weinstein & Berger, Basic Rules of Relevancy in the Proposed Federal Rules of Evidence, 4 Ga.L.Rev. 43 (1969); Wellborn, The Federal Rules of Evidence and the Application of State Laws in the Federal Courts, 45 Tex.L.Rev. 371, 371–96 (1977). Unif.R.Evid. (1974) 402 is similar. It reads:

All relevant evidence is admissible, except as otherwise provided by statute or by these rules or by other rules applicable in the courts of this state. Evidence which is not relevant is not admissible.

§ 185

1. See, e.g., James, Relevancy, Probability and the Law, 29 Calif.L.Rev. 689, 690–691 (1941).

2. For other applications of the materiality requirement, see, e.g., United States v. Cassidy, 616 F.2d 101 (4th Cir. 1979) (evidence that United States possession and use of nuclear weapons violates international law held immaterial in prosecution for desecrating the walls of the Pentagon); United States v. Johnson, 558 F.2d 744, 745–746 (5th Cir. 1977), cert. denied 434 U.S. 1065 (evidence of failure to claim certain deductions immaterial where defendant is charged with making false statements on tax return); United States v. Snow, 670

F.2d 749, 753–754 (7th Cir. 1982) (upholding the exclusion of testimony offered by a defendant charged with counterfeiting federal reserve notes intended to show that federal reserve notes are worthless, and hence that defendant lacked the necessary intent to defraud); People v. Wilkins, 408 Mich. 69, 288 N.W.2d 583 (1980), appeal after remand 115 Mich.App. 153, 320 N.W.2d 326 (police motivation for conducting surveillance of defendant immaterial in prosecution for possession of concealed weapon).

3. E.g., Fed.R.Civ.P. 15(b). See § 54 nn. 15–17 supra.

4. E.g., United States v. Robinson, 530 F.2d 1076, 1079 (D.C.Cir.1976). See generally Ch. 5 supra.

5. E.g., Brookhaven Landscape & Grading Co. v. J.F. Barton Contracting Co., 676 F.2d 516 (11th Cir. 1982), adhered to 681 F.2d 734 (chart contrasting anticipated and actual locations of boulders encountered in excavation admissible); Patton v. Archer, 590 F.2d 1319, 1323 (5th Cir. 1979) (chart of commodity price fluctuations admissible). Compare In re Air Crash Disaster, 635 F.2d 67, 73 (2d Cir. 1980) (proper to exclude chart of glide slope path that did not conform to stipulated facts). See generally §§ 213–214 infra.

rate these twin concepts of materiality and probative value. They read:

"Relevant evidence" means evidence having any tendency to make the existence of any fact that is of consequence to the determination of the action more probable or less probable than it would be without the evidence.

A fact that is "of consequence" is material,[6] and evidence that affects the probability that a fact is as a party claims it to be has probative force. Evidence that is probative often is said to have "logical relevance,"[7] while evidence lacking in probative value may be condemned as "remote"[8] or "speculative."[9]

Under our system, molded by the tradition of jury trial and predominantly oral proof, a party offers his evidence not *en masse*, but item by item. An item of evidence, being but a single link in the chain of proof,[10] need not prove conclusively the proposition for which it is offered.[11] It need not even make that proposition appear more probable then not.[12] Whether the entire body of one party's evidence is sufficient to go to the jury is one question. Whether a particular item of evidence is relevant to his case is quite another.[13] It is enough if the item could reasonably show that a fact is slightly more probable than it would appear without that evidence.[14] Even after the probative

6. United States v. Carriger, 592 F.2d 312, 315 (6th Cir. 1979). But see 22 Wright & Graham, supra § 184, note 1, § 5164, at 42. The Advisory Committee Note to Rule 401 criticizes the term "material" as "loosely used and ambiguous." At times, the term has been used somewhat differently than the way in which we have defined it. E.g., Morgan, Basic Problems of Evidence 183 (1962).

7. United States v. Eckmann, 656 F.2d 308, 312 (8th Cir. 1981). For a lucid probabilistic interpretation of what we call "probative value," see Lempert, Modeling Relevance, 75 Mich.L.Rev. 1021 (1977); Schum & Martin, Formal and Empirical Research on Cascaded Inference in Jurisprudence, 17 Law & Soc.Rev. 105 (1982); compare 22 Wright & Graham, supra § 184, note 1, § 5165, at 53–55 (insisting that the "word 'probable' in Rule 401 should not be confused with the concept that is employed in statistics," yet defining "probable" in terms of an "unstated folk epistemology" that a statistician would understand as assigning subjective probabilities).

8. Compare Sampson v. Missouri Pacific Railroad Co., 560 S.W.2d 573 (Mo.1978) (7 year old hospital records concerning alcoholism of plaintiff in negligence action too remote) with Hill v. Roleri, 615 F.2d 886, 891 (9th Cir. 1980) (speed of bus 10 minutes before accident not too remote) and State v. Green, 232 Kan. 116, 652 P.2d 697 (1982) (evidence that a husband charged with murdering his wife with an ax had thrown a hatchet at her nearly a year before not too remote). Remoteness relates not to the passage of time alone, but to the undermining of reasonable inferences due to the likelihood of supervening factors. Often, evidence excluded as being too "remote" has some probative value, but not enough in light of the countervailing concerns discussed in the remainder of this chapter. See, e.g., United States v. Beahm, 664 F.2d 414, 419 (4th Cir. 1981) (nine and one-half year old conviction for "unnatural and perverted sexual acts" erroneously used to impeach veracity of defendant, since it was too "remote in time," too "likely to inflame the jury," and was for "an offense that had minimal if any bearing on the likelihood that defendant would testify truthfully");

United States v. Ravich, 421 F.2d 1196, 1204 n. 10 (2d Cir. 1970), cert. denied 400 U.S. 834.

9. Speculativeness usually arises with regard to projections into the future or surmises about what might have happened had the facts been different than they were. Hoffman v. Sterling Drug Co., 485 F.2d 132 (3d Cir. 1973), on remand 374 F.Supp. 850 (error to admit expert calculations of future earnings that assumed a 6 percent annual salary increment); Annot., 26 A.L.R.3d 780 (admissibility of proposed subdivision on value of land in eminent domain proceeding). But see Croce v. Bromley Corp., 623 F.2d 1084, 1094 (5th Cir. 1980), cert. denied 450 U.S. 981 (in computing damages for wrongful death, the "speculative nature of the evidence" of the likely professional progress of the decedent "affects only the *weight* of the evidence"). Frequently, it is not the evidence but rather some surmise that is not supported by the evidence that is condemned as "speculative." Carlton v. H.C. Price Co., 640 F.2d 573, 579 (5th Cir. 1981) ("speculative for the jury to guess at a figure [for future medical expenses] in excess of those provided by the expert testimony").

10. See McCandless v. United States, 298 U.S. 342 (1936); Oseman v. State, 32 Wis.2d 523, 526, 145 N.W.2d 766, 768–769 (1966).

11. Doe v. New York City Department of Social Services, 649 F.2d 134, 147 (2d Cir. 1981), appeal after remand 709 F.2d 782 (1983); People v. Scott, 29 Ill.2d 97, 193 N.E.2d 814, 822–823 (1963).

12. Bush v. Jackson, 191 Colo. 249, 552 P.2d 509 (1976); McCormick, The Scope of Privilege in the Law of Evidence, 16 Tex.L.Rev. 447, 457–458 (1938). A few opinions do not perceive this. E.g., United States v. Hernandez-Miranda, 601 F.2d 1104 (9th Cir. 1974).

13. State v. Irebaria, 55 Hawaii 353, 519 P.2d 1246 (1974); State v. Giles, 253 La. 533, 218 So.2d 585 (1969).

14. Mutual Life Insurance Co. v. Hillmon, 145 U.S. 285 (1928) (discussing the admissibility of certain letters written by Walters and expressing an intention of going with Hillmon on a trip to Colorado, and reasoning that these "letters were competent, not as narratives of facts communicated to the writer by others,

force of the evidence is spent, the proposition for which it is offered still can seem quite improbable.[15] Thus, the common objection that the inference for which the fact is offered "does not necessarily follow" is untenable. It poses a standard of conclusiveness that very few single items of circumstantial evidence ever could meet.[16] A brick is not a wall.

But if even very weak material items of evidence are relevant, what sort of evidence is irrelevant for want of probative value? The long-standing distinction between "direct" and "circumstantial" evidence [17] helps answer this question. Direct evidence is evidence which, if believed, resolves a matter in issue. Circumstantial evidence may also be testimonial,[18] but even if the circumstances depicted are accepted as true, additional rea-

soning is required to reach the proposition to which it is directed. For example, a witness' testimony that he saw A stab B with a knife is direct evidence of whether A did indeed stab B. In contrast, testimony that A fled the scene of the stabbing would be circumstantial evidence of the stabbing (but direct evidence of the flight itself). Similarly, testimony of a witness that he saw A at the scene would be direct evidence of the facts asserted, but testimony that he saw someone who was disguised and masked, but had a voice and limp like A's, would be circumstantial evidence that the person seen was A.[19]

In terms of this dichotomy, direct evidence from a qualified witness offered to help establish a provable fact can never be irrelevant.[20] Circumstantial evidence, however,

nor yet as proof that he actually went away from Wichita, but as evidence that, shortly before the time when other evidence tended to show that he went away, he had the intention of going, and of going with Hillmon, which made it more probable both that he did go and that he went with Hillmon than if there had been no proof of such intention"); Insurance Co. v. Wilde, 78 U.S. (11 Wall.) 438, 440 (1870) ("It is well settled that if the evidence conduces to any reasonable degree to establish the probability or improbability of a fact in controversy, it should go to the jury"); United States v. Pugliese, 153 F.2d 497, 500 (2d Cir. 1945) (Learned Hand, Cir. J.) ("All that is necessary . . . is that each bit may have enough rational connection with the issue to be considered a factor contributing to an answer"); Schmeck v. City of Shawnee, 232 Kan. 11, 651 P.2d 585, 601 (1982) ("any evidence which has a tendency in reason to establish a material fact is relevant").

15. United States v. Curtis, 568 F.2d 643 (9th Cir. 1978).

16. Most circumstantial evidence commonly received could not pass so stringent a test. For instance, when a violent death is shown, evidence that the defendant accused of homicide was the beneficiary of a policy on the life of the deceased will be admitted. See generally 2 Wigmore, Evidence §§ 385, 390–391 (Chadbourn rev. 1979) (relevance of facts showing motive as evidence of doing an act). So too with evidence that the accused had an opportunity to commit the killing, 1 Wigmore, Evidence § 131, (3d ed. 1940), or that he expressed an intention to do so shortly before the death. Id. at §§ 102–103. Motive, opportunity and design, taken together, may make guilt more probable than not, but singly each falls far short of establishing so high a probability.

17. Perry's Administratrix v. Inter-Southern Life Insurance Co., 248 Ky. 491, 58 S.W.2d 906 (1933); Peo-

ple v. Bretagna, 298 N.Y. 323, 83 N.E.2d 537 (1949), cert. denied 336 U.S. 919; State v. Sanchez, 98 N.M. 428, 649 P.2d 496 (App.1982), cert. denied 98 N.M. 478, 649 P.2d 1391; Patterson, The Types of Evidence: An Analysis, 19 Vand.L.Rev. 1 (1965). The distinction is conceptually useful, but it has no direct importance in passing on the relevance of particular evidence. In this regard, it is worth noting that the fact that inferential value is an issue with respect to circumstantial but not direct evidence does not imply that the former is generally inferior. Both sorts of evidence are quite convincing on some occasions, but not nearly so telling in other instances. See, e.g., United States v. Andrino, 501 F.2d 1373, 1378 (9th Cir. 1974) ("circumstantial evidence is not less probative than direct evidence, and, in some instances, is even more reliable"); Hasson v. Ford Motor Co., 19 Cal.3d 530, 138 Cal.Rptr. 705, 564 P.2d 857 (1977). See also note 20 infra.

18. This characterization departs from that proposed at 1 Wigmore, Evidence § 25 (3d ed. 1940).

19. Privette v. Faulkner, 92 Nev. 353, 550 P.2d 404 (1976); cf. United States v. Eatherton, 519 F.2d 603 (1st Cir.), cert. denied 423 U.S. 987 (1975).

20. The rules governing the competency of witnesses to testify are discussed in Ch. 7 supra. If a disinterested witness is entirely disbelieved, what he says has no probative force. His testimony therefore could be characterized as "irrelevant," but the law usually has not regarded the evaluation of credibility as a facet of relevance. E.g., Brennan v. Braswell Motor Freight Lines, 396 F.Supp. 704 (N.D.Tex.1975) (admissible direct evidence found incredible). For a sophisticated, formal analysis of the effect of credibility on probative value, see Schum, Sorting out the Effects of Witness Sensitivity and Response-Criterion Placement upon the Inferential Value of Testimonial Evidence, 27 Organizational Behavior & Human Performance 153 (1981); Schum & Martin, supra n. 7.

can be offered to help prove a material fact, yet be so unrevealing as to be irrelevant to that fact. For instance, evidence that the government awarded a firm a lucrative contract is irrelevant on the issue of whether the firm damaged property leased to it because there is no reason to suppose that firms that handle large government contracts are more likely to damage such property than other lessees.[21] In short, to say that evidence is irrelevant in the sense that it lacks probative value is to say that knowing the circumstantial evidence does not justify any reasonable inference as to the fact in question.[22] Cases involving such evidence are few and far between.[23]

Yet, how can a judge know whether the evidence could reasonably affect an assessment of the probability of the fact to be inferred? In some instances, scientific research may show that the fact in issue is more likely to be true (or false) when such evidence is present than when it is not.[24] Ordinarily, however, the answer must lie in the judge's own experience, his general knowledge, and his understanding of human conduct and motivation. If one asks whether an attempted escape by a prisoner

charged with two serious but factually unconnected crimes is relevant to show consciousness of guilt of the first crime charged,[25] the answer will not be found in a statistical table of the attempts at escape by those conscious of guilt as opposed to those not conscious of their guilt. The judge can only ask himself, Could a reasonable juror believe that the fact that the accused tried to escape makes it more probable than it would otherwise be that the accused was conscious of guilt of the crime being tried? If the answer is yes, then the evidence is relevant. In other situations, the judge may need to consider explicitly not only whether the evidence reasonably could support the proposition for which it is offered, but also whether its absence might warrant negative inferences.[26]

In sum, relevant evidence is evidence that in some degree advances the inquiry. It is material and probative. As such, it is admissible, at least prima facie. But this relevance does not ensure admissibility. There remains the question of whether its value is worth what it costs. A great deal of evidence is excluded on the ground that the costs outweigh the benefits. Rule 403 of

---

21. City of Cleveland v. Peter Kiewit Sons' Co., 624 F.2d 749 (6th Cir. 1980). Evidence of wealth may, however, be admissible on the issue of punitive damages. Grant v. Arizona Public Service Co., 133 Ariz. 434, 652 P.2d 507, 522 (1982); Note, 44 Alb.L.Rev. 422 (1980).

22. United States v. Schipani, 289 F.Supp. 43, 56 (E.D.N.Y.1968), (denying motion to suppress), further proceedings reported as United States v. Schipani, 293 F.Supp. 156 (E.D.N.Y.1968), affirmed 414 F.2d 1262 (2d Cir. 1969), cert. denied 397 U.S. 922 (the test for relevancy is "whether a reasonable man might have his assessment of the probabilities of a material proposition changed by the piece of evidence"); Stewart v. People, 23 Mich. 63 (1871).

23. Most evidence seriously offered at trial has *some* probative value. Even when the courts dismiss evidence as devoid of probative value, one may well wonder whether the evidence is not more properly excludable on grounds of materiality or insufficient probative value given the countervailing considerations that can bar the use of relevant evidence. Jenkins v. Anderson, 447 U.S. 231, 247 (1980) (dissenting opinion arguing that the fact that defendant, who stabbed another allegedly in self-defense yet waited two weeks before going to the police is "so unlikely to be probative" of the falsity of his trial testimony that it is "simply irrelevant" as impeachment evidence); United

States v. Carter, 522 F.2d 666, 684 (D.C.Cir.1975) (error to admit photo of drawing found on desk pad and "doodles" found at scene of robbery where FBI agent testified that more experienced agents had told him that no valid comparisons could be made); Energy Transportation System v. Mackey, 650 P.2d 1152, 1156 (Wyo.1982) (owner's testimony on what land is worth to him "has no probative value in a condemnation case"). Note that *Mackey* does not bar an owner from testifying as to the fair market value of his property. Weathers v. State, 652 P.2d 970, 973 (Wyo.1982). For a discussion of the admissibility of evidence that is generally agreed to have no inferential value (on the issue of negligence), see § 201 infra (proof of liability insurance).

24. See Strong, Questions Affecting the Admissibility of Scientific Evidence, 1970 U.Ill.L.F. 1, 2–4.

25. E.g., People v. Yazum, 13 N.Y.2d 302, 246 N.Y.S.2d 626, 196 N.E.2d 263 (1963) (relevant); State v. Crawford, 59 Utah 39, 201 P. 1030 (1921) (irrelevant); State v. Piche, 71 Wn.2d 583, 430 P.2d 522, cert. denied 390 U.S. 912 (1967) (relevant). See § 271 infra.

26. Lindley & Eggleston, The Problem of Missing Evidence, 99 Law Q.Rev. 86 (1983); Saltzburg, A Special Aspect of Relevance: Countering Negative Inferences Associated with the Absence of Evidence, 66 Calif.L.Rev. 1011 (1978). See § 272 infra.

the Federal and Revised Uniform Evidence Rules categorize most of these costs. It codifies the common law power of the judge to exclude relevant evidence "if its probative value is substantially outweighed by the danger of unfair prejudice, confusion of the issues, or misleading the jury, or by considerations of undue delay, waste of time, or needless presentation of cumulative evidence."[27] Such factors often blend together in practice, but we shall elaborate on them briefly in the rough order of their importance. First, there is the danger of prejudice. In this context, prejudice does not simply mean damage to the opponent's cause.[28] Neither does it necessarily mean an appeal to emotion. Prejudice can arise, however, from facts that arouse the jury's hostility or sympathy for one side without regard to the probative value of the evidence.[29] Thus, evidence of convictions for prior, unrelated crimes may lead a juror to think that since the defendant already has a criminal record, an erroneous conviction would not be quite as serious as would otherwise be the case. A juror influenced in this fashion may be satisfied with a slightly less compelling demonstration of guilt than he should be.[30]

27. See generally Gold, Federal Rule of Evidence 403: Observations on the Nature of Unfairly Prejudicial Evidence, 58 Wash.L.Rev. 497 (1983). Prior to the 1974 revision, the Uniform Rules were slightly different. Original Uniform Rule 45 read:

Except as in these rules otherwise provided, the judge may in his discretion exclude evidence if he finds that its probative value is substantially outweighed by the risk that its admission will (a) necessitate undue consumption of time, or (b) create substantial danger of undue prejudice or of confusing the issues or of misleading the jury, or (c) unfairly and harmfully surprise a party who has not had reasonable opportunity to anticipate that such evidence would be offered.

Model Code of Evidence Rule 303(1) (1942) is nearly identical. Statutes in Kansas, Utah and Oklahoma, patterned on the old Uniform Rule, continue to make surprise a factor. See State v. Green, 232 Kan. 116, 652 P.2d 697, 702 (1982) (quoting Kan.Stat.Ann. 60–445); 12 Okla.Stat.Ann. § 2403 ("Relevant evidence may be excluded if its probative value is substantially outweighed by the danger of . . . unfair and harmful surprise); 9 Utah Code Ann., Utah Rule of Evidence, Rule 45. Whether surprise could justify exclusion of evidence at common law is doubtful, see Wigmore, Evidence §§ 1845, 1849 (Chadbourn rev. 1976), but some cases mention the unfair surprise arising when an opponent, having had no reasonable ground to anticipate the evidence, is unprepared to meet it, as grounds for exclusion. People v. Collins, 68 Cal.2d 319, 66 Cal.Rptr. 497, 438 P.2d 33 (1968); Stoelting v. Hauck, 32 N.J. 87, 159 A.2d 385 (1960); Thompson v. American Steel & Wire Co., 317 Pa. 7, 175 A. 541 (1934).

The factor of unfair surprise is not included in the Federal Rules and the revised Uniform Rules on the theory that the appropriate remedy is a continuance. See Advisory Committee Note to Fed.R.Evid. 403. Of course, a distinct issue occurs when the surprise results from the fact that the proponent breached a rule of pleading or discovery. Exclusion then may be used to enforce such rules. See, e.g., Fed.R.Civ.P. 37(b)(2)(B); 6 Wigmore, Evidence, § 1848 (Chadbourn rev. 1976).

In a unique departure from the common law approach, the state of California amended its constitution to provide that unprivileged, non-hearsay "relevant evidence shall not be excluded in any criminal proceeding." West's Ann.Cal.Const. Art. I, § 28(d). Whether this abrogation of the balancing requirement will endure is questionable. See Wall St.J., Nov. 26, 1982.

28. Green, Relevance and Its Limits, 1969 Ariz.St. L.J. (Law & Soc.Ord.) 533, 534. Other things being equal, the more probative the evidence is, the more damaging it will be. Evidence that the facts are contrary to one party's contentions always damages his case, but this cannot be ground for excluding the evidence. United States v. Monahan, 633 F.2d 984, 985 (1st Cir. 1980) (Rule 403 is not contravened by evidence that might show only that the defendant is guilty of the crime charged); Carter v. Hewitt, 617 F.2d 961, 972 (3d Cir. 1980) (Rule 403 "does not offer protection against evidence that is merely prejudicial in the sense of being detrimental to a party's case"); Ramos v. Liberty Mutual Insurance Co., 615 F.2d 334, 340 (5th Cir. 1980), clarified, rehearing denied 620 F.2d 464, cert. denied 449 U.S. 1112 (" 'unfair prejudice' as used in Rule 403 is not to be equated with testimony simply adverse to the opposing party"); State v. Rollo, 221 Or. 428, 438, 351 P.2d 422, 427 (1960) (remarking that advocate "is entitled to hit as hard as he can above, but not below, the belt").

29. State v. Flett, 234 Or. 124, 380 P.2d 634 (1963) ("tendency to prove the issue in dispute must be weighed against the tendency of the offered evidence to produce passion and prejudice out of proportion to its probative value"); Lease America Corp. v. Insurance Co. of North America, 88 Wis.2d 395, 276 N.W.2d 767 (1979) (evidence that causes the jury to base its decision on something other than the established propositions in the case is unfairly prejudicial). Prejudice may accrue to persons besides the parties to the litigation. United States v. Martorano, 557 F.2d 1, 10 (1st Cir. 1977). For a critical appraisal of the consistency of the opinions on prejudice, see Gold, supra note 27.

30. Lempert, supra note 7 (change in an ideal, hypothetical juror's "regret matrix" distorts his appreciation of the burden of persuasion). For a civil case in which this form of prejudice was found, see Harless v.

Second, whether or not "emotional" reactions are at work, relevant evidence can confuse,[31] or worse, mislead the trier of fact if he is not properly equipped to judge the probative worth of the evidence.[32] Third, certain proof and the answering evidence that it provokes might unduly distract the jury from the main issues.[33] Finally, the evidence offered and the counterproof may consume an inordinate amount of time.[34]

Analyzing and weighing the pertinent costs and benefits is no trivial task. Wise judges may come to differing conclusions in similar situations. Even the same item of evidence may fare differently from one case to the next, depending on its relationship to the other evidence in the cases and the importance of the issues on which it bears.[35] Accordingly, much leeway is given trial

---

Boyle-Midway Division, 594 F.2d 1051, 1058 (5th Cir. 1979) (proof that a 14-year-old boy had smoked marijuana on one occasion introduced for use in valuing the loss of his life held to be error, since the evidence was "highly prejudicial" yet "tenuous" and of "slight value" on the issue of damages). In evaluating prejudicial effect, courts may consider the likely efficacy of a curative instruction. United States v. Stevens, 595 F.2d 569, 571–572 (10th Cir. 1979).

31. Hamling v. United States, 418 U.S. 87 (1974) (criticized in Wright & Graham, supra § 184, note 1, § 5216 at 290, for misapplying this consideration); Shepard v. United States, 290 U.S. 96, 104 (1933) ("When the risk of confusion is so great as to upset the balance of advantage, the evidence goes out"); Renfro Hosiery Mills Co. v. National Cash Register Co., 552 F.2d 1061, 1069 (4th Cir. 1977) ("voluminous and complex" exhibits could have been excluded on the ground that they "had little if any probative value" and, among other defects, "might well have been confusing to a layman"). This concern has limited the use of scientific evidence. See Ch. 20 infra.

32. Lempert, supra note 7, calls this an "estimation problem" with regard to the "likelihood ratio" for this evidence. Psychological studies suggest some conditions under which jurors may systematically err in assessing the probative force of evidence. Most of this literature is described in Nisbett & Ross, Human Inference: Strategies and Shortcomings of Social Judgment (1980); Gold, supra note 27; Saks & Kidd, Human Inferential Processing and Adjudication: Trial by Heuristics, 15 Law & Soc.Rev. 124 (1980–81). Others have cautioned against over-enthusiastic reliance on the academic research. Loftus & Beach, Book Review, 34 Stan.L.Rev. 939, 950–956 (1982).

33. This condition could result from evidence that is so sensational and shocking that the jury would think of nothing else. Evidence of this nature is likely to be excluded as "prejudicial." A more common and subtle form of "distraction" can occur when the jury is tempted to rely on one type of evidence to the detriment of other important, but seemingly less revealing, evidence. See, e.g., People v. Golochowicz, 413 Mich. 298, 319 N.W.2d 518, 528 (1982) (speculating that "if evidence of the identity of the criminal actor is weak or tenuous, revelation that he has committed an unrelated similar crime may, by reason of its tendency to distract the jury from the identification issue, tempt it to compromise or ignore that central element of the case while focusing on the clearer proof of the defendant's other misconduct").

34. Renfro Hosiery Mills Co. v. National Cash Register Co., 552 F.2d 1061, 1069 (4th Cir. 1977) ("exhibits had little if any probative value but rather considerable potential for prolongation of the trial"); New Jersey v. Cavallo, 88 N.J. 508, 443 A.2d 1020, 1025 (1982) (preliminary showing of reliability required for expert testimony on psychological profile of rapists to prevent a "battle of experts" that "would consume substantial court time and cost both parties much time and expense"); cf. Reeve v. Dennett, 145 Mass. 23, 28, 11 N.E. 938, 943–944 (1887) (Holmes, J.) ("so far as the introduction of collateral issues goes, that objection is a purely practical one—a concession to the shortness of life").

In a sense, time-consumption is the fundamental reason to exclude relevant evidence. It might be thought, for example, that "estimation" problems (see note 32 supra) could be solved by supplying the jury with supplementary information or expert instruction in how to handle certain types of evidence that are prone to be misunderstood. Finkelstein & Fairley, A Bayesian Approach to Identification Evidence, 83 Harv.L.Rev. 489 (1970). Similarly, one could try to counter evidence condemned as prejudicial for the reason stated in note 30 supra by educating jurors more extensively in the meaning of the burden of persuasion. Nagel, Bringing the Values of Jurors in Line with the Law, 63 Judicature 189 (1979). Even if such strategies always had the desired effects, however, the probative value of the evidence rarely would justify the time and effort that would be consumed.

35. If other evidence, which does not carry the same dangers with it, could be used to establish the same fact, then the marginal probative value of the evidence in question is slight or non-existent. United States v. Spletzer, 535 F.2d 950, 955–956 (5th Cir. 1975) (error to admit certified copy of judgment of prior conviction when defendant offered to stipulate to fact of conviction); United States v. 88 Cases, More or Less, Containing Bireley's Orange Beverage, 187 F.2d 967, 975 (3d Cir. 1951) (error to introduce pictures of guinea pigs dying in agony from vitamin C deficiency after being put on diet of orange drink). Yet, there are cases that allow the prosecution to use gruesome photographs even when the cause of death is the subject of testimony and stipulation. United States v. Bowers, 660 F.2d 527, 529–530 (5th Cir. 1981) (color photographs of lacerated heart in prosecution for child abuse). See also United States v. Thevis, 665 F.2d 616, 635 (5th Cir. 1982), cert. denied 103 S.Ct. 57 (effect of stipulation); Annot., 73 A.L.R.2d 769 (1960). If other evidence of the same fact already has been introduced,

judges [36] who must fairly weigh probative value against probable dangers.[37] Nevertheless, discretion can be abused,[38] and some appellate courts have urged trial courts to articulate the reasoning behind their relevance rulings.[39] In certain areas, such as proof of character, comparable situations recur so often that relatively particularized rules channel the exercise of discretion.[40] In others, less structured discretion remains

---

the marginal value is also diminished, and the additional evidence might be excluded as "cumulative." People v. Cardenas, 31 Cal.3d 897, 904, 184 Cal.Rptr. 165, 168, 647 P.2d 569, 572 (1982) ("The fact that appellant and the witnesses were also members of [a Chicano youth gang] was cumulative and added little to further the prosecutor's objective of showing that the witnesses were biased because of their close association with appellant.") In this way, there can be a weighing of marginal costs and benefits even as to direct evidence. For cases on the power of the court to prevent excessive cumulation of witnesses, see United States v. Fernandez, 497 F.2d 730, 735–736 (9th Cir. 1974), cert. denied 420 U.S. 990, rehearing denied 421 U.S. 1017 (proper to exclude testimony of 17 witnesses to prove facts as to which five had already testified); Annot., 5 A.L.R.3d 169, 176–184. Conversely, if less troublesome evidence of comparable probative worth cannot be had, the marginal probative value of the evidence in question is enhanced. See, e.g., United States v. Frick, 588 F.2d 531, 538 (5th Cir. 1977), cert. denied 441 U.S. 913.

36. United States v. Hanson, 618 F.2d 1261, 1266 (8th Cir. 1980), cert. denied 449 U.S. 854 ("much leeway"). For discussions of the scope of discretion and the need for leeway, see James, supra note 1; Rosenberg, Judicial Discretion of the Trial Court, Viewed from Above, 22 Syracuse L.Rev. 635 (1971); Trautman, Logical or Legal Relevancy, 5 Vand.L.Rev. 385, 392–394 (1952).

37. For cases holding that it is error to fail to balance probative value against prejudicial effect, see Hrnjak v. Graymar, Inc., 4 Cal.3d 725, 94 Cal.Rptr. 623, 484 P.2d 599 (1971); State v. Dutremble, 392 A.2d 42, 46 (Me.1978). In weighing the value of the evidence against the dangers, courts should use their best estimates of the magnitudes of these factors. Some commentators have argued for other standards. Saltzburg & Redden, supra § 184, note 1, at 102, urge balancing "the maximum probative value of the evidence against the likely prejudicial effect." Dolan, Rule 403: The Prejudice Rule in Evidence, 49 S.Cal.L.Rev. 220, 233 (1976), recommends that courts "resolve all doubts concerning the balance [between probative value and prejudice] in favor of prejudice." Weinstein & Berger observe that trial courts lean toward giving the evidence its "maximum reasonable probative force and its minimum reasonable prejudicial value." 1 Weinstein & Berger, Evidence ¶ 403[03]. Nevertheless, using likely rather than extreme estimates of both the probative value and the counterweights to see whether the latter substantially outweigh the former seems the most reasonable course. If the competing factors, measured under this standard, are in equipoise, Rule 403 clearly requires admission, since it cannot then be said that the probative value "is substantially outweighed." Compare § 43 n. 9 (different allocation of burden as to evidence of conviction of crime for impeachment, covered by Federal Rule Evid. 609(a)(1)).

38. The standard for appellate review of the trial court's balancing has been stated in various, and sometimes conflicting, ways. United States v. Robinson, 560 F.2d 507 (2d Cir. 1977) (en banc), cert. denied 435 U.S. 905 (reversal requires showing that trial judge acted "arbitrarily or irrationally"); United States v. Johnson, 558 F.2d 744 (5th Cir. 1977), cert. denied 435 U.S. 1065 ("clearly erroneous" standard); United States v. Giese, 597 F.2d 1170, 1187 (9th Cir. 1979), cert. denied 444 U.S. 979 ("plain error" standard); State v. Williams, 133 Ariz. 220, 650 P.2d 1202, 1212 (1982) ("clear abuse" standard). The usual standard is simply abuse of discretion. Eichel v. New York Central Railroad Co., 375 U.S. 253, 256 (1963) (Harlan, J., concurring and dissenting); United States v. Snow, 670 F.2d 749, 752 (7th Cir. 1982). Some cases holding that trial courts abused their discretion are collected in Saltzburg & Redden, supra § 184, note 1, at 104–108, and others are included in the notes throughout this Title.

39. John McShain, Inc. v. Cessna Aircraft Co., 563 F.2d 632, 635 (3d Cir. 1977) ("the trial judge's familiarity with the tone and scope of the evidence presented to the jury puts him in an advantageous position to gauge the relative importance of potential prejudice and probative value. Nonetheless, the balance required is not a pro forma one. . . . The substantiality of the consideration given to competing interests can be best guaranteed by an explicit articulation of the trial court's reasoning"); United States v. Potter, 616 F.2d 384, 388 (9th Cir. 1979), cert. denied 449 U.S. 832 (it must appear "from the record as a whole that the trial judge adequately weighed the probative value and prejudicial effect of proffered evidence"); State v. Barringer, 32 Wn.App. 882, 650 P.2d 1129, 1132 (1982) ("The mere conclusion of a trial court that the probative value of the evidence outweighs the prejudice to the defendant is not enough to demonstrate a proper exercise of discretion. [I]t is helpful for appellate review if the trial court articulates on the record the factors considered"). See § 43 n. 9 supra.

40. See Ch. 17 infra (character and habit evidence); § 203 infra (scientific evidence). The "relevance rules" that have been extracted from repeated decisions about various types of evidence operate to exclude certain categories of evidence offered for particular purposes. When the evidence is introduced for some other purpose, however, admission is not required. Despite the "exception" to the "relevance rule," the trial judge has discretion to exclude the evidence if the usual counterweights warrant it. See § 186 note 3 infra.

prominent.[41] One way or another, however, admissible evidence must satisfy the cost-benefit calculus we have outlined.[42]

Some courts and textwriters have described this process of weighing marginal costs and benefits as a matter of "legal relevancy," [43] in that "legally relevant" evidence must have a "plus value" beyond a bare minimum of probative value.[44] This notion of "plus value" is at best an imprecise way to say that the probative value and the need for the evidence must outweigh the harm likely to result from admission, and most modern opinions do not rely on such potentially misleading terminology.[45]

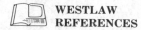

WESTLAW REFERENCES

digest(probative /5 value /p credibil! /10 witness**)

digest(probative /p "logical relevanc*" remote speculative)

digest(evidence /p circumstantial /p direct /p defin! dichotom! distinction*)

110k369.2(1) /p "judge" judicial /p inquir! determin!

topic(157) /p unfair /5 prejudic!

topic(157) /p abus! /5 discretion! /p "judge" judicial /p relevan** probative

---

41. See Ch. 18 infra (similar happenings and transactions); § 202 infra (pretrial experiments).

42. For more detailed applications of these principles, see § 12 (opinions on merits of the case); § 36 (self-contradiction on collateral matters); § 42 (extrinsic evidence of misconduct affecting credibility); § 43 (impeachment by evidence of conviction of crime); § 47 (impeachment by contradiction on collateral matters); ch. 17–20 (other "relevance rules"); § 274 (offers to compromise disputed claim); § 275 (safety measures after an accident).

43. Cotton v. United States, 361 F.2d 673, 676 (8th Cir. 1966); Hoag v. Wright, 34 App.Div. 260, 54 N.Y.S. 658, 662 (1898). The phrase also has been used to denote the more particularized rules that have crystallized from repeated precedents on the admissibility of certain types of evidence. E.g., State v. LaPage, 57 N.H. 245, 248 (1876); 1 Wigmore, Evidence § 12 (3d ed. 1940).

44. United States v. Johnson, 558 F.2d 744, 746 (5th Cir. 1977), cert. denied 434 U.S. 1065; Post v. United States, 407 F.2d 319, 323 (D.C.Cir. 1968), cert. denied 393 U.S. 1092, quoting Frank R. Jelleff, Inc. v. Braden, 233 F.2d 671, 679 (D.C.Cir. 1956), quoting 1 Wigmore, Evidence § 28 (3d ed. 1940).

45. The phrase "legal relevance" is misleading inasmuch as it blurs the distinction between evidence that is excluded because it lacks all probative force as to an issue that is of consequence to the outcome of the case and evidence that has probative worth but is excluded on other grounds. Similarly, "plus value" is not an intrinsic property of an item of evidence. Furthermore, these phrases may cause confusion between the distinct questions of whether the evidence is relevant and whether it is sufficient. See generally James, supra note 1; Trautman, supra note 36.

Chapter 17
CHARACTER AND HABIT

Table of Sections

---

§ 186. Character: In General [1]

Evidence of the general character of a party or witness[2] almost always has some probative value, but in many situations, the probative value is slight[3] and the potential for prejudice large. In other circumstances, the balance shifts the other way. Instead of engaging exclusively in the case-by-case balancing outlined in Chapter 16, however, the courts tend to pass on the admissibility of

§ 186

1. See generally M. Graham, Handbook of Federal Evidence §§ 404–405 (1981); Lempert & Saltzburg, A Modern Approach to Evidence 186–254 (2d ed. 1983); 2 Louisell & Mueller, Federal Evidence §§ 135–150 (1977); Rothstein, Federal Rules of Evidence §§ 404–405 (2d ed. 1982); Saltzburg & Redden, Federal Rules of Evidence Manual 124–76, 346–96 (3d ed. 1982); 2 Weinstein & Berger, Evidence ¶¶ 404–405 (1975); 1 Wigmore, Evidence §§ 55–58, 62–63, 192–218 (3d ed. 1940); 2 id. §§ 300–373 (Chadbourn rev. 1970); 3A id. §§ 977–988 (Chadbourn rev. 1970); 4 id. §§ 1104–1116 (Chadbourn rev. 1972); 5 id. §§ 1608–1621 (Chadbourn rev. 1974); 7 id. §§ 1980–1986 (Chadbourn rev. 1978); 22 Wright & Graham, Federal Practice and Procedure §§ 5231–5269 (1978); Uviller, Evidence of Character to Prove Conduct, 130 U.Pa.L.Rev. 845 (1982); Williams, The Problem of Similar Fact Evidence, 5 Dalhousie L.J. 281 (1979); 29 Am.Jur.2d Evidence §§ 336–343, 346, 363–364, 366; 22 C.J.S. Criminal Law §§ 676–691; 31 id. Evidence §§ 422–437; Dec.Dig. Criminal Law ⟨key⟩362–381 (1982); 16 id. Evidence ⟨key⟩106, 129–142.

2. On the meaning of the term "character," see supra § 195.

3. See M. Saks & R. Hastie, Social Psychology in Court 162–63 (1978). Lempert and Saltzburg emphasize that the marginal probative value of character evidence in proving individual actions generally is small. They argue that "however relevant character evidence is in the abstract, its incremental relevance in the context of a specific case is likely to be low. [Furthermore], evidence bearing on character is likely to be conflicting. Most individuals have engaged in actions sufficiently inconsistent to suggest diametrically opposed character traits and most people can point to individuals who hold very different evaluations of their character. Finally, there is a good deal of psychological evidence that attributes which we think of as character traits are dynamic rather than static aspects of personality. They differ over time as contexts change." Lempert & Saltzburg, A Modern Approach to Evidence 237 (2d ed. 1983) (footnotes omitted).

evidence of character and habit according to a number of rules with myriad exceptions that reflect the recurring patterns of such proof and its usefulness.[4]

Before turning to the details of the rules, it may be helpful to sketch two general considerations that are central to shaping and applying these rules. The first factor is the purpose for which the evidence of character is offered. If a person's character is itself an issue in the case, then character evidence is crucial. But if the evidence of character merely is introduced as circumstantial evidence of what a person did or thought, it is less critical. Other, and probably better, evidence of the acts or state of mind usually should be available. Exclusion is therefore much more likely when the character evidence is offered to help prove that a person acted in one way or another. Thus, Federal and Revised Uniform Evidence Rule (1974) 404(a), which basically codify common law doctrine, provide that subject to enumerated exceptions,[5]

Evidence of a person's character or a trait of his character is not admissible for the purpose of proving that he acted in conformity therewith on a particular occasion . . . .

The second consideration is the type of evidence offered to establish the character of an individual. Character is susceptible of proof by evidence of conduct that reflects some character trait, by a witness's testimony as to his own opinion based on personal observations, or by testimony as to reputation generally.[6] As one moves from the specific to the general in this fashion, the pungency and persuasiveness of the evidence declines, but so does its tendency to arouse undue prejudice, to confuse and distract, and to raise time-consuming side issues.[7] Traditionally, where character evidence could come in at all, the relatively neutral and unexciting reputation evidence was the preferred type.[8] Thus, prior to the adoption of the Federal Rules, the other methods of proving character could be employed only in narrowly defined situations.[9]

---

4. If a rule has evolved forbidding the use of character evidence for a particular purpose, then there is no need for ad hoc balancing of probative value as against prejudice, distraction, and the like. The exclusionary rule already reflects the judgment that the outcome of the balancing test should preclude admission. It does not follow, however that if character evidence falls under an exception to the general rule of exclusion, it is necessarily admissible. That the general rule mandating exclusion does not dictate the outcome merely means that the decision as to admission must be made in light of the general principle that relevant evidence is admissible unless its probative value is substantially outweighed by countervailing considerations. See supra Ch. 16. Hence, in these cases, individualized balancing is still essential. See, e.g., State v. Goebel, 36 Wn.2d 367, 218 P.2d 300, 306 (1950) ("this class of evidence . . . should not be admitted even though falling within the generally recognized exceptions to the rule of exclusion, when the trial court is convinced that its effect would be to generate heat instead of diffusing light, or . . . where the minute peg of relevancy will be completely obscured by the dirty linen hung upon it"); infra note 52, § 190.

5. There are three exceptions in Rule 404(a):

(1) *Character of Accused.* Evidence of a pertinent trait of his character offered by an accused, or by the prosecution to rebut the same;

(2) *Character of Victim.* Evidence of a pertinent trait or character of the victim of the crime offered by an accused, or by the prosecution to rebut the same, or evidence of a character trait of peaceful-

ness of the victim offered by the prosecution in a homicide case to rebut evidence that the victim was the first aggressor;

(3) *Character of Witness.* Evidence of the character of a witness, as provided in Rules 607, 608, and 609.

Rule 404(b) excludes evidence of other crimes, subject to many exceptions. See § 190 infra.

6. For subdivisions and qualifications, see 22 Wright & Graham, Federal Practice and Procedure § 5262 at 565.

7. Hale, Some Comments on Character Evidence and Related Topics, 22 So.Cal.L.Rev. 341, 342 (1949).

8. United States v. Polsinelli, 649 F.2d 793, 795 (10th Cir. 1981) ("Prior to the adoption of the present Federal Rules of Evidence, a character witness in a criminal proceeding was, in general, limited to testimony concerning defendant's community reputation. The witness was not allowed to express a personal opinion of defendant's character, no matter how close or long his association with the defendant."); Commonwealth v. United Food Corp., 374 Mass. 765, 374 N.E.2d 1331, 1336–1337 (1978) (reputation of lounge as a place for prostitution not provable by evidence of specific incidents).

9. Roughly stated, where character was being used as circumstantial evidence of conduct, it could be proved only by reputation evidence. Where character was in issue, it could be proved by specific instances or by reputation. There were, however, deviations from this pattern in various jurisdictions. See, e.g., 5 Wig-

Federal and Revised Uniform Evidence Rule (1974) 405(a), however, allow opinion testimony as well as reputation testimony to prove character whenever any form of character evidence is appropriate.[10] And, as at common law, when character is "in issue," as discussed in the next section, it also may be proved by testimony about specific acts.

 WESTLAW REFERENCES

eviden! /p character /p exclud! exclus! /p 404(a)
eviden! /p character /p 405 /p opinion* reputation*

---

more, Evidence §§ 1608–1621 (Chadbourn rev. 1974), 7 id. §§ 1981–1985 (Chadbourn rev. 1978).

10. Rule 405 reads as follows:

(a) *Reputation or opinion.* In all cases in which evidence of character or a trait of character of a person is admissible, proof may be made by testimony as to reputation or by testimony in the form of an opinion. On cross-examination, inquiry is allowable into relevant specific instances of conduct.

(b) *Specific instances of conduct.* In cases in which character or a trait of character of a person is an essential element of a charge, claim or defense, proof may also be made of specific instances of his conduct.

This liberalization of the rule for opinion evidence was controversial. The federal Advisory Committee noted that "In recognizing opinion as a means of proving character, the rule departs from usual contemporary practice in favor of that of an earlier day." Quoting Wigmore, it argued for "evidence based on personal knowledge and belief as contrasted with 'the second hand, irresponsible product of multiplied guesses and gossip which we term "reputation." '" The House Committee on the Judiciary, fearing that "wholesale allowance of opinion testimony might tend to turn a trial into a swearing contest between conflicting character witnesses," deleted this modification of the common law in its proposed draft. House Comm. on Judiciary, Fed. Rules of Evidence, H.R.Rep. No. 650, 93d Cong., 1st Sess., p. 7 (1973). During House debate, the language was reinstated. 120 Cong.Rec., Part 2, H 2370 (1974).

Although most commentators applaud this outcome, some have their doubts. Saltzburg and Redden express three concerns: (1) "that many people who harbor grudges against litigants may too freely express negative opinions as to character" and that cross-examination to show bias may not a sufficient safeguard against such testimony; (2) that "some influential citizens" may be able "to command 'popular' character witnesses to offer favorable opinions that will be influential with a jury"; and (3) that it may be unwise to permit psychiatric and other expert testimony as to an individual's character. Saltzburg & Redden, Federal Rules of Evidence Manual 166–67 (3d ed. 1982). The

§ 187. Character in Issue

A person's character may be a material fact that under the substantive law determines rights and liabilities of the parties. For example, in an action of defamation for a publication to the effect that plaintiff's character is bad, the publisher may raise the defense that the statement was true.[1] A complaint for negligence may allege that the defendant allowed an unfit person to use a motor vehicle or other dangerous object,[2] or that an employer was negligent in hiring or failing to supervise an employee with certain

---

first two concerns would seem to apply also to reputation evidence, and psychiatric testimony has not generally been thought to be equated with character.

§ 187

1. Weider v. Hoffman, 238 F.Supp. 437, 443 (M.D. Pa.1965) (testimony that libel plaintiff's magazines "were intended solely for a homosexual audience" was properly admitted to establish defense of truth); Pierson v. Robert Griffin Investigations, 92 Nev. 605, 555 P.2d 843, 844 (1976) (evidence of libel plaintiff's crimes committed more than ten years earlier was properly admitted to support defense of truth); Walkon Carpet Corp. v. Klapprodt, 89 S.D. 172, 231 N.W.2d 370, 374 (1975) (reputation for past misdeeds admissible in establishing truth (and mitigating damages) as to defendant's counterclaim of slander for plaintiff's statements concerning excessive drinking and sexual promiscuity); Moore v. Davis, 27 S.W.2d 153, 157 (Tex. Com.App.1930) (evidence of subsequent acts showing libel plaintiff to be an unfit judge properly admitted to show truth of statements made during election campaign); Talmadge v. Baker, 22 Wis. 65 (1868) (evidence of particular thefts wrongly excluded with respect to the alleged slander that "he is in the habit of picking up things"); 1 Wigmore, Evidence §§ 70–74 (3d ed. 1940); Louisell & Mueller, Federal Evidence § 138 at 158–162 (1977).

Reputation (not character) comes into issue when defendant seeks to mitigate damages by showing that plaintiff's reputation was bad. Meiners v. Moriarity, 563 F.2d 343, 351 (7th Cir. 1977); Proper v. Mowry, 90 N.M. 710, 568 P.2d 236, 243–244 (1977); Corabi v. Curtis Publishing Co., 441 Pa. 432, 273 A.2d 899, 920 (1971). Character traits may affect damages in other contexts. See infra § 188, n. 2.

2. Breeding v. Massey, 378 F.2d 171, 181 (8th Cir. 1967) (testimony as to four wrecks and five guilty pleas for driving while intoxicated properly elicited under Arkansas law); Allen v. Toledo, 109 Cal.App.3d 415, 167 Cal.Rptr. 270 (1980) (evidence of son's previous accidents admissible to prove father's knowledge that son was unfit to drive car); Curley v. General Valet Service, 270 Md. 248, 311 A.2d 231, 240–241 (1973) (testimony concerning driver's record of traffic offenses known to employer sufficient to permit finding of neg-

dangerous character traits.[3] When character has been put in issue by the pleadings in these and other such cases,[4] evidence of character must be brought forth.

In view of the crucial role of character in these situations, the courts usually hold that it may be proved by evidence of specific acts. The Federal and Revised Uniform Evidence Rule (1974) 405(b) follow this approach.[5] The hazards of prejudice, surprise

and time-consumption implicit in this manner of proof are more tolerable when character is itself in issue than when this evidence is offered as a mere indication that the defendant committed the acts that are the subject of the suit.

Yet, some courts do not simply permit evidence of specific acts to prove character when it is in issue. They insist on it[6] to the point of excluding opinion and reputation ev-

---

ligent entrustment); 1 Wigmore, Evidence § 80 (3d ed. 1940); 2 id. §§ 249–50 (Chadbourn rev. 1979); Louisell & Mueller, Federal Evidence § 143 at 162–64 (1977); Woods, Negligent Entrustment Revisited: Developments 1966–76, 30 Ark.L.Rev. 288 (1976); Notes, 30 Okla.L.Rev. 181, 182–83 (1977), 52 Or.L.Rev. 296, 301–03 (1973), 35 Tul.L.Rev. 244 (1960); Annot., 78 A.L.R.3d 1170 (negligent entrustment by rental agency), 19 A.L.R.3d 1175 (entrusting to excessive user of intoxicants), 120 A.L.R. 1311 (entrusting motor vehicle to unfit driver).

3. Hirst v. Gertzen, 676 F.2d 1252, 1263 (9th Cir. 1982) (previous brutal acts of sheriff toward Indian prisoners admissible in civil rights action arising from death of prisoner to show government negligence in supervising sheriff's activities as jailer); American Airlines v. United States, 418 F.2d 180, 197 (5th Cir. 1969) (prior inadequate performance in landing airplane under adverse conditions admissible to show employer's negligence in allowing this pilot to land aircraft); Morrow v. St. Paul City Railway Co., 74 Minn. 480, 77 N.W. 303 (1898) (liability to servant for negligent failure to select a competent fellow-servant); Annot., 78 A.L.R. 3d 359 (hiring independent contractor), 73 A.L.R.3d 1175 (hiring private investigator), 51 A.L.R.3d 981 (hospital selection of staff physician), 48 A.L.R.3d 359 (knowledge of employee's criminal record), 16 A.L.R.3d 564 (supplying physician for employees).

4. United States v. Masters, 622 F.2d 83, 88 (4th Cir. 1980) (evidence of other dealings in firearms admissible to prove defendant's status as a dealer subject to licensing requirement); United States v. Pauldino, 443 F.2d 1108, 1113 (10th Cir. 1971) (prosecution under statute that requires that defendant be shown to be in business of gambling, but court confused this point with exception for evidence of other crimes that shows common plan); Christy v. United States, 68 F.R.D. 375, 378 (N.D.Tex.1975) (rejecting government's contention that criminal record of inmate who allegedly raped visitor to prison was privileged from discovery in victim's suit claiming that government was negligent in assigning prisoner to minimum custody institution); Commonwealth v. United Food Corp., 374 Mass. 765, 374 N.E.2d 1331, 1337–1338 (1978) (evidence of specific instances of prostitution on premises as well as general reputation evidence properly relied on to show that lounge constituted a public nuisance).

Whether the defendant's propensity to commit a crime is in issue when the defendant raises the entrapment defense has generated some confusion. See, e.g.,

United States v. Burkley, 591 F.2d 903, 921 (D.C. Cir. 1978), cert. denied 440 U.S. 966 (defense of entrapment makes predisposition "in effect an essential element of the crimes charged," which makes Rule 404(b) applicable); United States v. Webster, 649 F.2d 346, 350 (5th Cir. 1981) (because predisposition is a state of mind, not a character trait, Rule 404(a)(1) does not permit government to prove predisposition to rebut entrapment defense); 22 Wright & Graham, Federal Practice and Procedure § 5235 at 379 ("the best method of reconciling the entrapment rule with Rule 404 is to consider it as a rule of substantive law beyond the reach of the Evidence Rules"). For further discussions of the nature of the defense and its evidentiary implications in federal cases, see, United States v. Russell, 411 U.S. 423 (1973), conformed to 479 F.2d 1046; United States v. Murzyn, 631 F.2d 525 (7th Cir. 1980), cert. denied 450 U.S. 923; United States v. Diggs, 649 F.2d 731, 737 (9th Cir. 1981), cert. denied 454 U.S. 970; Annot., 61 A.L.R.3d 293; Park, The Entrapment Controversy, 60 Minn.L.Rev. 163, 256–57 (1976). In states that use the objective test for entrapment the defense does not necessarily put defendant's character in issue. People v. Barraza, 23 Cal.3d 675, 153 Cal.Rptr. 237, 246, 591 P.2d 947, 956 (1979); State v. Nakamura, 65 Hawaii 74, 648 P.2d 183 (1982).

5. See supra § 186, n. 10. To implement the rule intelligently, most courts hold that the "essential element" requirement is met when a character trait is an "operative fact"—one that under the substantive law determines rights and liabilities of the parties. E.g., State v. Lehman, 126 Ariz. 388, 616 P.2d 63, 66 (1980); West v. State, 265 Ark. 52, 576 S.W.2d 718, 719 (1979). The Model Code permits all forms of character evidence "[a]s tending to prove a trait of a person's character when it is one of the facts necessary to establish a liability or defense or is a factor in the measure of damages . . . ." Model Code of Evidence Rule 305 (1942). For a case that seems to misapply these principles, see Crumpton v. Confederation Life Insurance Co., 672 F.2d 1248, 1252–1253 (5th Cir. 1982), rehearing denied 679 F.2d 250 (insurer's defense that death was not accidental within meaning of policy put deceased's character at issue).

6. McGowin v. Howard, 251 Ala. 204, 36 So.2d 323, 325 (1948) (entrusting automobile); Young v. Fresno Flume & Irrigation Co., 24 Cal.App. 286, 141 P. 29, 32 (1914) (liability to employee based on unfitness of fellow employee); Guedon v. Rooney, 160 Or. 621, 87 P.2d 209, 217 (1939) (entrusting automobile).

idence.[7] There seems little point to excluding reputation evidence, which ordinarily is the preferred mode of proof of character. Proof by means of opinion testimony is slightly more debatable, but most of the arguments against opinion evidence [8] do not apply when character is in issue. For example, the possibility that specific acts may be inquired into on cross-examination (which may prompt barring specific act evidence when character is not in issue) is hardly of concern, since the door to such evidence already is open. Because an opinion held by someone familiar with an individual and his conduct may rest on facts too detailed to be worth reciting yet still may be useful in evaluating character, many courts allow such opinion evidence when the character involved is for the so-called nonmoral traits of care, competence, skill or sanity.[9] On the other hand, as to the traits of moral character like peaceableness and honesty, courts that follow the tradition barring opinion evidence of the character of an accused as circumstantial evidence of conduct on a particular occasion presumably would frown on opinion evidence even when character is in issue.[10] In contrast, the Federal and the

Uniform Rules, as we have noted, allow opinion evidence as well as reputation and specific act evidence to prove character whenever it is in issue.[11]

 WESTLAW REFERENCES

405(b) /p specific /p act*
405(b) /p exclud! exclus! except! /p "opinion" reputation

§ 188. Character as Circumstantial Evidence: General Rule of Exclusion

Even when a person's character is not itself in issue in the sense we have described,[1] litigants may seek to introduce character-type evidence. In ascertaining whether such evidence is admissible, attention to the purpose for which the evidence is offered remains of the utmost importance. In some cases, even though a person's character is not itself in issue, evidence probative of his character may be relevant to proving a material fact that is distinct from whether the person acted in conformity with his character. Thus, where extortion is charged, the defendant's reputation for violence may be relevant to the victim's state of mind.[2] In

---

7. Reputation evidence may come in, however, to show that defendant knew that character was unfit. See cases cited supra note 6. For a forthright recognition that evidence of reputation as well as specific acts may prove the unfitness or incompetence of the servant alleged to have been negligently employed, see Winchester v. Padgett, 167 F.Supp. 444 (N.D.Ga.1952).

8. See supra § 186, note 10.

9. Marine Towing Co. v. Fairbanks, Morse & Co., 225 F.Supp. 467 (E.D.Pa.1963) (expert opinion as to skill of engine repair crew); Lewis v. Emery, 108 Mich. 641, 66 N.W. 569 (1896) (competency of fellow employee at sawmill); 7 Wigmore, Evidence § 1984 (Chadbourn rev. 1978).

10. In re Monaghan, 126 Vt. 53, 222 A.2d 665, 672–73 (1966) (opinions as to character of applicant for admission to bar inadmissible). But see Wilson v. Wilson, 128 Mont. 511, 278 P.2d 219, 222 (1954) (opinion as to fitness of parent admissible in custody proceeding), overruled on issue of award of attorneys fees in Trudgen v. Trudgen, 134 Mont. 174, 329 P.2d 225 (1958).

11. See supra, § 186, note 10.

§ 188

1. A party who brings in evidence of his good character sometimes may be said to have made character

an issue. See infra § 191. Unless the party's character is an element of an offense, claim or defense, however, his character is not "in issue" as described in § 187 supra.

2. United States v. DeVincent, 546 F.2d 452, 456–457 (1st Cir. 1976), cert. denied 431 U.S. 903 (within trial court's discretion to admit testimony concerning defendant's twenty-year-old conviction for armed robbery and ten year old murder indictment as relevant to borrower's state of mind); Carbo v. United States, 314 F.2d 718 (9th Cir. 1963) (proper to admit evidence of reputation of member of extortion conspiracy as strong-arm man to show impact on victims); cf. United States v. McClure, 546 F.2d 670, 672–673 (5th Cir. 1977), appeal after remand 577 F.2d 1021 (error to exclude testimony offered by defendant accused of selling heroin that the government's "contingent fee informant" had coerced other persons into making heroin sales to him after the defendant's sale).

The distinction between character in issue and character as circumstantial evidence of some other material fact is not always easily drawn. The courts usually state that various character traits of a decedent are in issue with regard to damages in an action for wrongful death. See, e.g., St. Clair v. Eastern Airlines, 279 F.2d 119, 121 (2d Cir. 1960) (observing that "Undoubtedly,

these cases the reputation itself, not the character that it tends to prove, is the significant fact; reputation is not used as evidence of how the person with the character traits behaved on a given occasion.[3]

In contrast, evidence that an individual is the kind of person who tends to behave in certain ways almost always has some value as circumstantial evidence as to how he acted (and perhaps with what state of mind) in the matter in question. By and large, persons reputed to be violent commit more assaults than persons known to be peaceable.[4] Yet, evidence of character in any form—reputation, opinion from observation, or specific acts—generally will not be received to prove that a person engaged in certain conduct or did so with a particular intent on a specific occasion,[5] so-called circumstantial use of character. The reason is the familiar one of prejudice outweighing probative value. Character evidence used for this purpose,

while typically being of relatively slight value, usually is laden with the dangerous baggage of prejudice, distraction, time consumption and surprise.[6]

At the same time, there are important exceptions to this general rule of exclusion.[7] The next six sections consider various applications of the rule and the exceptions.

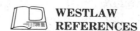 **WESTLAW
REFERENCES**

digest(reputation character /5 evidence /p admiss! admit!)

character reputation /5 evidence /p state /2 mind

§ 189. Character for Care in Civil Cases

The rule against using character evidence solely to prove conduct on a particular occasion has long been applied in civil cases.[1] The rule is invoked most uniformly when specific act evidence is proffered.[2] Negli-

---

personal habits and qualities are to some degree relevant considerations in determining an individual's earning ability and the support that his family would have received from him but for his death," but cautioning that "Except as they may show a propensity of the decedent to spend his money in ways which do not inure to the benefit of his family, the details of his personal life are not in issue"); Schmitt v. Jenkins Truck Lines, 170 N.W.2d 632, 655 (Iowa 1969) ("the trier of fact is entitled to consider on this issue of damages decedent's characteristics and habits including her . . . industriousness, disposition to earn, [and] frugality or lavishness"); Annot., 99 A.L.R.2d 972 (sobriety and morals of deceased in wrongful death action), 79 A.L.R.2d 819 (decedent's desertion or nonsupport of children). Arguably, the character traits here are but circumstantial evidence of what is truly in issue. See 22 Wright & Graham, Federal Practice and Procedure § 5235 at 370. But see supra § 187, note 5.

3. See supra § 185.

4. Studies of clinical and statistical predictions of violence reveal that the single best predictor of future violence is past violence. See Monahan, Predicting Violent Behavior: An Assessment of Clinical Techniques 92, 104 (1981).

5. See supra § 186.

6. Id.

7. See supra § 186, n. 5. Indeed, there are enough exceptions that some writers prefer to state the general rule as one of admissibility subject to exceptions for exclusion. E.g., Model Code of Evidence Rule 306 (1942) ("evidence of a trait of a person's character is admissible for the purpose of proving his conduct on a

specified occasion, except . . . ."). As we have noted, the Federal and Revised Uniform Evid. Rules state the general rule as one of exclusion. See supra § 186.

§ 189

1. Hirst v. Gertzen, 676 F.2d 1252, 1262 (9th Cir. 1982) (civil rights action); Slough, Relevancy Unraveled, 5 U.Kan.L.Rev. 404, 440–44 (1957); Annot., 91 A.L.R.3d 718 (other assaults), 67 A.L.R.2d 232 (other usurious transactions); infra § 192 and Ch. 18. The value of the rule in civil cases has been questioned. See Falknor, Extrinsic Factors Affecting Admissibility, 10 Rutgers L.Rev. 574, 581–84 (1956); cf. Uviller, Evidence of Character to Prove Conduct, 130 U.Pa.L.Rev. 845 (1982) (broader criticism). The Model Code and the Uniform Rules, prior to the 1974 revision, permitted the use of character evidence to prove conduct in civil cases, except on the issue of negligence. See Model Code Evidence Rule 306 (1942); original Unif.R.Evid. 47 & 48. Whether the rule should bar a civil defendant from proving his good character when the allegations against him state a criminal offense has also engendered debate, see infra § 192, as has its application to civil assault and battery cases in which the identity of the first attacker is in dispute. See infra § 193.

Notice that the rule does not apply to evidence used for another purpose than to prove conduct on a particular occasion. Section 190 catalogs most of these purposes. See also infra n. 2 and Ch. 18.

2. Hirst v. Gertzen, 676 F.2d 1252, 1262 (9th Cir. 1982) (sheriff's purportedly similar acts of taunting and brutalizing Indian prisoners, in a private civil rights action arising from the death of an Indian prisoner who hanged himself in his jail cell). Of course,

gence cases illustrate the point.[3] Evidence of negligent conduct of the defendant or his agent on other occasions may reflect a propensity for negligent acts, thus enhancing the probability of negligence on the occasion in question, but this probative force has been thought too slight to overcome the usual counterweights.[4] The same applies to evidence of other negligent acts of the plaintiff,[5] as well other instances of careful conduct.[6]

Most courts also reject proof of an actor's character for care by means of reputation evidence[7] or opinion testimony.[8] In the past, a minority of courts had admitted these types of evidence, often under the guise of evidence of "habit," when there were no eyewitnesses to the event.[9] A few even did so

---

we are speaking of specific acts other than those at bar. No doubt, evidence that someone acted negligently says something about that person's character, but we are concerned here with character as circumstantial evidence, that is, as evidence of a propensity to behave in a certain way which, in turn, makes it more likely that such behavior occurred on the occasion in question. A previous accident or negligent act that does something more than show character or predisposition may be admissible. Dallas Railway & Terminal Co. v. Farnsworth, 148 Tex. 584, 227 S.W.2d 1017, 1020 (1950) (in an action for an injury allegedly due to the abrupt starting of a street car, testimony that the driver had started abruptly once before on the same trip admissible to show motorman was nervous and in a hurry).

For an analysis of the problem of differentiating between acts offered to prove propensity and acts offered for another purpose, see Saltzburg & Redden, Federal Rules of Evidence Manual 126 n. 1 (3d ed. 1982); Kuhns, The Propensity to Misunderstand the Character of Specific Act Evidence, 66 Iowa L.Rev. 777 (1981).

3. For applications of the rule and its exceptions in other civil cases, see Miller v. Poretsky, 595 F.2d 780, 783–785 (D.C. Cir. 1978) (landlord's discrimination against other black tenants); Commonwealth v. Porter, 659 F.2d 306, 320 (3d Cir. 1981) (en banc), cert. denied 102 S.Ct. 3509 (pattern or practice of violating constitutional rights); Brown v. Miller, 631 F.2d 408 (5th Cir. 1980) (punitive damage award upset because independent bad act used in civil rights action); Cohn v. Papke, 655 F.2d 191, 193–194 (9th Cir. 1981) (improper to inquire into sexual preferences of plaintiff in civil rights action alleging brutality by police officers who arrested him for soliciting a homosexual act); infra Ch. 18.

4. Nelson v. Hartman, ___ Mont. ___, 648 P.2d 1176, 1178 (1982) (evidence that a truck driver was an unlicensed and habitual traffic offender "could not be used to prove any specific of negligence" in an automobile accident case); Alvin v. Toledo, 109 Cal.App.3d 415, 167 Cal.Rptr. 270, 273 (1980) (stating in dictum that evidence of involvement in other accidents inadmissible to prove negligence in accident in issue); Brownhill v. Kivlin, 317 Mass. 168, 57 N.E.2d 539, 540 (1944) (evidence that deceased had previously caused two fires by going to sleep while smoking properly excluded in action against estate for deceased's allegedly burning down a garage in which she perished); Thornburg v. Perleberg, 158 N.W.2d 188, 191 (N.D.1968) (improper for plaintiff in automobile accident case to ask defendant driver on cross-examination, "you have a constant record of accidents and traffic violations, do you not?"); Annot., 29 A.L.R.3d 791 (habit or reputation for care of deceased driver or passenger), 20 A.L.R.2d 1210 (non-involvement in other automobile accidents); 1 Wigmore, Evidence § 199 (3d ed. 1940).

5. Reyes v. Missouri Pacific Railroad Co., 589 F.2d 791 (5th Cir. 1979) (four prior misdemeanor convictions for public intoxication improperly admitted to show that plaintiff was intoxicated when run over by defendant's train); George v. Morgan Construction Co., 389 F.Supp. 253, 264–265 (E.D.Pa.1975) (plaintiff's safety record not admissible to show contributory negligence); Nesbitt v. Cumberland Contracting Co., 196 Md. 36, 75 A.2d 339, 342 (1950) (improper to cross-examine plaintiff, who drove car into pile of dirt and rocks that defendant left on highway, about convictions for reckless driving and driving without a license).

6. Ryan v. International Harvester Co., 204 Minn. 177, 283 N.W. 129, 131 (1938) (proper to prevent defendant's driver from testifying that he had never previously had a collision); Annot., 20 A.L.R.2d 1210.

7. Denbigh v. Oregon-Washington Railroad & Navigation Co., 23 Idaho 663, 132 P. 112 (1913) (testimony that engineer "was known as a prudent and careful engineer" properly excluded); Phinney v. Detroit United Railway Co., 232 Mich. 399, 205 N.W. 124 (1925) (testimony of conductor that motorman had a reputation for recklessness inadmissible); 1 Wigmore, Evidence § 65 (3d ed. 1940).

8. Harriman v. Pullman Palace-Car Co., 85 F. 353, 354 (8th Cir. 1898) (error to admit evidence that porter alleged to have injured plaintiff "was usually careful, competent, courteous and attentive"); Louisville & Nashville Railroad Co. v. Adams, 205 Ky. 203, 265 S.W. 623 (1924) (error to receive testimony that decedent killed at crossing was a careful driver); Greenwood v. Boston & Maine Railroad Co., 77 N.H. 101, 88 A. 217 (1913) (testimony of decedent's coworkers that decedent was careful in his work).

But a history of being careful about a particular danger may come in as habit rather than character. Hussey v. Boston & Maine Railroad Co., 82 N.H. 236, 133 A. 9 (1926) (evidence of lineman's "habitual care in the presence of charged wires" properly received in a case with no witnesses to accident); infra § 195.

9. Hawbaker v. Danner, 226 F.2d 843, 847 (7th Cir. 1956) ("habits of due care"); Pritchett v. Steinker Trucking Co., 108 Ill.App.2d 371, 247 N.E.2d 923, 926–927 (1958); Missouri-Kansas-Texas Railway v. McFerrin, 156 Tex. 69, 291 S.W.2d 931, 941–942 (1956).

if there were eyewitnesses with conflicting stories.[10] The Federal and Uniform Evidence Rules do not make such fine distinctions.[11] The prevailing pattern now is to exclude all forms of character evidence in civil cases when the evidence is employed merely to support an inference that conduct on a particular occasion was consistent with a person's character.[12]

This trend is apparent despite psychological studies of "accident proneness." It has been argued that scientific research establishing that drivers with inadequate training, defective vision, and certain attitudes and emotional traits are at risk for automobile accidents [13] should prompt a relaxation of the rule against evidence of character for negligence.[14] The argument seems to be that because a small number of drivers with identifiable characteristics account for the bulk of the accidents, they must drive improperly as a routine matter, and this provides a better than usual basis for inferring that the accident in issue resulted from such negligent driving. Presumably, the reform would be to admit evidence of previous accidents combined with proof that the particular driver fits the "accident proneness" profile.

A somewhat different proposal that also has yet to be implemented asks that aggregate and individual data concerning the actions of physicians should be admissible in malpractice cases.[15] For example, in deciding whether the removal of a patient's appendix was unnecessary surgery, the jury might be invited to consider whether the defendant physician performs appendectomies far more frequently than his colleagues. Although evidence of previous accidents or similar happenings should not be freely admitted, a suitable expert testifying about a departure from the customary standard of care should be permitted to rely on such information and to explain his analysis to the jury.[16] Moreover, where the statistically measured departure from the customary pattern is itself so great as to make it plain for all to see that the defendant is behaving differently from the norm, this statistic should be provable.[17]

10. Glatt v. Feist, 156 N.W.2d 819, 825 (N.D.1968) (habit evidence allowed in state that had applied the "no eyewitness" rule in a case in which the eyewitness testimony conflicted).

11. See Rules 404–405, supra § 186, nn. 5 and 10.

12. Reyes v. Missouri Pacific Railroad Co., 589 F.2d 791 (5th Cir. 1979); Barbieri v. Cadillac Construction Corp., 174 Conn. 445, 389 A.2d 1263 (1978); Feliciano v. City and County of Honolulu, 62 Hawaii 88, 611 P.2d 989, 991 (1980); infra § 200 n. 3.

13. See Maloney & Rish, The Accident-Prone Driver, 14 U.Fla.L.Rev. 364 (1962); James & Dickinson, Accident Proneness and Accident Law, 63 Harv.L.Rev. 769, 772–775 (1950); Trautman, Logical or Legal Relevancy—A Conflict in Theory, 5 Vand.L.Rev. 385, 399–400 (1952).

14. James & Dickinson, supra note 13, at 703; Trautman, supra n. 13, at 401; cf. Maloney & Rish, supra n. 13, at 378. But see Boodman, Safety and Systems Analysis, with Applications to Traffic Safety, 33 Law & Contemp.Prob. 488, 510 (1968) ("There are no reliable indicators of accident proneness"); Woody, Accident Proneness, 1981 Med. Trial Techniques Q. 74, 81 ("there is no clear-cut personality composite for the presumed accident prone personality").

15. Note, 7 U.C.D.L.Rev. 523 (1974); Annot., 33 A.L.R.3d 1056 (previous unnecessary surgeries); cf. United States v. Johnson, 634 F.2d 735, 736–737 (4th Cir. 1980), cert. denied 451 U.S. 907 (admitting testimony of government auditor that physician charged with tax evasion who had character witnesses attest to her honesty actually reported four times as many services per Medicaid patient as other Virginia physicians).

16. As Lempert & Saltzburg, A Modern Approach to Evidence 211 n. 41 (2d ed. 1983), caution, "There are at least two good reasons for [being reluctant to allow evidence of accident proneness]. First, accident proneness does not mean that one's negligence was responsible for a particular accident or series of accidents. Ordinary clumsiness or inattentiveness or a predeliction for risk may mean that one is likely to be in more than his share of accidents without engaging in behavior which ever rises to the level of negligence or contributory negligence. Second, involvement in a series of accidents may simply involve an unusual run of bad luck." The "bad luck" hypothesis is examined more fully infra § 196.

17. The statistical pattern can be proved without going into the prejudicial, distracting, or time-consuming details of other incidents. The value of the evidence is greatest in cases where each surgery or other event, viewed in isolation, could be a matter of reasonable professional judgment. In these situations, the need for such evidence justifies taking the risks associated with defendant's seeking to prove reasonable care in each of the other incidents. Notice also that whether or not one accepts the desirability of this limited in-

negligen! /p act* conduct /p propensit! /p
character reputation

§ 190. Bad Character as Evidence of Criminal Conduct: Other Crimes

If anything, the rule against using character evidence to prove conduct on a particular occasion applies even more strongly in criminal cases.[1] Unless and until the accused gives evidence of his good character,[2] the

prosecution may not introduce evidence of (or otherwise seek to establish)[3] his bad character.[4] The evidence of bad character would not be irrelevant, but in the setting of the jury trial particularly [5] the dangers of prejudice, confusion and time-consumption outweigh the probative value.[6]

This broad prohibition includes the specific and frequently invoked rule that the prosecution may not introduce evidence of other criminal acts of the accused unless the evidence is introduced for some purpose other [7]

---

road on the ban on character evidence, a consistent, narrow pattern of behavior may be admissible as a habit rather than a character trait. See infra § 195.

§ 190

1. There are intimations that the rule has constitutional overtones as applied to criminal defendants. United States v. Foskey, 636 F.2d 517, 523 (D.C.Cir. 1980) ("'a concomitant to the presumption of innocence,'" is that "It is fundamental to American jurisprudence that 'a defendant must be tried for what he did, not for who he is'"); Government of Virgin Islands v. Toto, 529 F.2d 278, 283 (3d Cir.1976) (prosecution's evidence of other crimes undermines presumption of innocence); State v. Manrique, 271 Or. 201, 531 P.2d 239, 241 (1975) ("constitutional right to be informed of the nature of the charge against him and to be held to answer only the crime named in the indictment").

2. See infra § 191.

3. The rule of exclusion encompasses questions which, though answered negatively, insinuate that the accused committed other crimes. United States v. Shelton, 628 F.2d 54, 56–57 (D.C.Cir.1980) (assault conviction reversed because government cross-examined defendant and defense witness so as to suggest that they "were members of the drug underworld involved in all sorts of skullduggery"). The rule may also bar other evidence carrying such insinuations. United States v. Fosher, 568 F.2d 207, 213 (1st Cir.1978), appeal after remand 590 F.2d 381 ("mug shots from a police department's 'rogues' gallery'"); State v. Kelly, 111 Ariz. 181, 526 P.2d 720, 729 (1974), cert. denied 420 U.S. 935 ("mug shots"); Miller v. State, ___ Ind. ___, 436 N.E.2d 1113, 1120 (1982) ("mug shot"); Annot., 30 A.L.R.3d 908 (admissibility of mug shots). Compare State v. Hicks, 133 Ariz. 64, 649 P.2d 267, 273 (1982) (testimony as to defendant's "known prints" did not come within rule).

4. Michelson v. United States, 335 U.S. 469, 475–476 (1948); United States v. Harris, 331 F.2d 185 (4th Cir. 1964) (reputation); Ex parte Thompson, 376 So.2d 766 (Ala.1979), on remand 376 So.2d 768 (reputation); People v. Madeson, 114 Colo. 120, 638 P.2d 18 (1981) (prior conviction); 1 Wigmore, Evidence §§ 55, 57 (3d ed. 1940). See Fed.R.Evid. 404(a); Rev.Unif.R.Evid. 404(a) (1974), reprinted supra § 186.

5. State v. Grogan, 628 P.2d 570 (Alaska 1981) (probative value of evidence in state's action under Consumer Protection Act that defendant had previously vandalized aircraft of customers who refused to pay their bills in full outweighed possible prejudice in civil nonjury trial).

6. United States v. Cook, 538 F.2d 1000, 1004 (3d Cir. 1976) ("long standing tradition that protects a criminal defendant from 'guilt by reputation' and from 'unnecessary prejudice'"); People v. Cardenas, 31 Cal. 3d 897, 184 Cal.Rptr. 165, 647 P.2d 569 (1982) (reversing due to cumulative prejudice from evidence that defendant charged with attempted murder and related offenses was addicted to narcotics and that defendant and defense witnesses all belonged to the same Chicano youth gang); Whitty v. State, 34 Wis.2d 278, 149 N.W.2d 557 (1967) cert. denied 390 U.S. 959 (1968) (describing "four bases" for the rules excluding proof of prior crimes); Kalven & Zeisel, The American Jury 160 (1966) (when a defendant's criminal record is known and the prosecution's case has contradictions the defendant's chances of acquittal are 38% compared to 68% otherwise); Doob, Evidence, Procedure, and Psychological Research, in Psychology and the Law 135 (G. Bermant, C. Nemeth & N. Vidmar ed. 1976) (jury simulation research). Cf. supra § 185 note 33. It is easy to argue that predisposition, if properly proved, is powerful, but not for that reason, prejudicial. See Uviller, Evidence of Character to Prove Conduct, 130 U.Pa.L.Rev. 845, 884–85 (1982). For a more perceptive analysis of the often slight probative value of other crimes evidence as against persons brought to trial for similar acts (as opposed to all persons with criminal convictions) and the ways in which the prior offense evidence can be prejudicial to them, see Lempert & Saltzburg, A Modern Approach to Evidence 216–19 (2d ed. 1983).

7. Evidence of other crimes brought forth as circumstantial proof of guilt for the offense charged is sometimes called "extrinsic offense evidence." United States v. Messersmith, 692 F.2d 1315 (11th Cir. 1982). The rule against such evidence is also called the "propensity rule" to emphasize the reasoning that the rule seeks to prevent. Lempert & Saltzburg, A Modern Approach to Evidence 215–16 (2d ed. 1983); 22 Wright & Graham, Federal Practice and Procedure § 5232 at 346.

than to suggest that because the defendant is a person of criminal character, it is more probable that he committed the crime for which he is on trial.[8] As Federal and revised Uniform Rule (1974) 404(b) put it:

> Evidence of other crimes, wrongs, or acts is not admissible to prove the character of a person in order to show that he acted in conformity therewith. It may, however, be admissible for other purposes, such as proof of motive, opportunity, intent, preparation, plan, knowledge, identity or absence of mistake or accident.

As the rule indicates, there are numerous other uses to which evidence of criminal acts

may be put, and those enumerated are neither mutually exclusive nor collectively exhaustive.[9] Subject to such caveats,[10] examination is in order of the principal purposes for which the prosecution may introduce evidence of a defendant's bad character. Following this listing, some general observations will be offered about the use of other crimes evidence for these purposes. The permissible purposes include:

(1) To complete the story of the crime on trial by placing it in the context of nearby and nearly contemporaneous happenings.[11]

---

8. 1 Wigmore, Evidence §§ 192–194 (3d ed. 1940); Slough & Knightly, Other Vices, Other Crimes, 41 Iowa L.Rev. 325 (1956); Lacy, Evidence of Crimes Not Charged, 31 Or.L.Rev. 267 (1952); Notes, 7 UCLA L.Rev. 463 (1966) 70 Yale L.J. 763 (1961). People v. Molineaux, 168 N.Y. 264, 61 N.E. 286, 294 (1901). Cases, as the sands of the sea, are collected in Dec.Dig. Criminal Law ⊨365, 369–374; 22A C.J.S., Criminal Law §§ 663–665, 682–691. Annot., 2 A.L.R.4th 1298 (drug addiction as motive for thefts), 2 A.L.R.4th 330 (other rapes), 92 A.L.R.3d 545 (subsequent offenses), 20 A.L.R.Fed. 125 (similar crimes in conspiracy prosecutions), 96 A.L.R.2d 768 (sentencing), 93 A.L.R.2d 1097 (narcotics sales), 87 A.L.R.2d 891 (other fires in arson prosecution), 86 A.L.R.2d 1132 (effect of acquittal on admissibility), 78 A.L.R.2d 1359 (similar false pretenses), 77 A.L.R.2d 841 (other sex offenses), 64 A.L.R.2d 823 (other gambling), 42 A.L.R.2d 854 (other robberies), 40 A.L.R.2d 817 (other illegal liquor sales), 34 A.L.R.2d 777 (other forgeries), 20 A.L.R.2d 1012 (other taking or giving of bribes), 105 A.L.R. 1288 (receiving stolen property), 63 A.L.R. 602 (identity).

9. United States v. Wesevich, 666 F.2d 984, 988–989 (5th Cir. 1982) (although evidence of "extraneous offenses [may] be admitted for purposes other than those expressly listed in Rule 404(b), evidence of another crime was erroneously admitted where its purpose was to show why a witness (not the defendant) acted as he did and where the evidence was highly prejudicial); United States v. Diggs, 649 F.2d 731, 737 (9th Cir. 1981), cert. denied 454 U.S. 970 ("Rule 404(b) is an inclusionary rule—i.e., evidence of other crimes is inadmissible under this rule only where it proves nothing but the defendant's criminal propensities"); Note, 71 Nw.U.L.Rev. 635 (1976).

10. The enumerated purposes are not all of the same type. Some are phrased in terms of the immediate inferences sought to be drawn (such as plan or motive) while others are phrased in terms of ultimate facts (such as knowledge, intent or identity) which the prosecution seeks to establish. See Stone, Exclusion of Similar Fact Evidence: America, 51 Harv.L.Rev. 988, 1026 (1938) ("Motive, intent, absence of mistake, plan and identity are not really all on the same plane. In-

tent, absence of mistake, and identity are facts in issue—*facta probanda*. Motive, plan, or scheme are *facta probantia*, and may tend to show any *facta probanda*").

11. United States v. Masters, 622 F.2d 83 (4th Cir. 1980) (upholding admission of taped conversations of the defendant with undercover agents despite reference to other sales and acts on grounds that the evidence was necessary to complete the story of the crime on trial as well as to prove that the defendant was "dealing"; on the latter point, see supra § 187); United States v. Ulland, 643 F.2d 537, 540–541 (8th Cir. 1981) (testimony as to financially troubled ventures admissible to show "immediate context" in prosecution for fraud in procuring checks that travelled in interstate commerce; State v. Villavicencio, 95 Ariz. 199, 388 P.2d 245 (1964) (upholding introduction of evidence of sale of narcotics to one person in prosecution for sale to another, where evidence showed that both sales took place at same time and place); State v. Klotter, 274 Minn. 58, 142 N.W.2d 568 (1966) (where guns taken in burglary of sporting goods store and burglary that same night of home of friend of defendant's family located five miles away were found in defendant's possession, the events were "connected closely enough in time, place and manner").

Of course, not every background fact is admissible under the "complete story" rationale. United States v. Childs, 598 F.2d 169 (D.C.Cir.1979) (emphasizing in dictum that other crimes evidence must not be more prejudicial than probative of the crime charged and cautioning that the court does not "subscribe to the broad proposition that evidence of other offenses may be introduced simply because it recounts events temporally related to the commission of a crime for which the accused is on trial"); United States v. Calhoun, 604 F.2d 1216 (9th Cir. 1979) (reversible error to admit evidence of bills taken in different bank robbery than the one charged); United States v. Dothard, 666 F.2d 498, 502 (11th Cir. 1982) ("Courts have admitted extrinsic act evidence to show a defendant's design or plan to commit the *specific* crime charged, but never to show a design or plan to commit '*crimes of the sort* with which he is charged' ").

The phrases "same transaction"[12] or, less happily, "res gestae"[13] often are used to denote evidence introduced for this purpose.

(2) To prove the existence of a larger plan,[14] scheme,[15] or conspiracy,[16] of which the crime on trial is a part. This will be relevant as showing motive, and hence the doing of the criminal act, the identity of the actor, or his intention.

(3) To prove other crimes by the accused so nearly identical in method as to earmark them as the handiwork of the accused.[17] Much more is demanded than the mere repeated commission of crimes of the same

12. United States v. Brooks, 670 F.2d 625, 628–629 (5th Cir. 1982) (evidence that marijuana as well as cocaine was found in defendant's car at border patrol checkpoint was properly admitted as proving "an uncharged offense arising out of the same transaction or series of transactions as the charged offense" of possession of cocaine with intent to distribute).

13. United States v. Masters, 622 F.2d 83, 86 (4th Cir. 1980); State v. Price, 123 Ariz. 166, 598 P.2d 985 (1979) ("This principle that the complete story of the crime may be shown even though it reveals other crimes has often been termed 'res gestae.' [W]e choose to refer to [it] as the 'complete story' principle").

14. Compare United States v. Lewis, 693 F.2d 189 (D.C.Cir.1982) (testimony concerning stolen money orders not charged in indictment admissible to show that defendant was "the mastermind of a common scheme"); United States v. Parnell, 581 F.2d 1374 (10th Cir. 1978), cert. denied 439 U.S. 1076 (previous fraudulent scheme admissible as "direct precursor" of conspiracy to purchase grain with forged cashiers checks); State v. Toshishige Yoshino, 45 Hawaii 206, 364 P.2d 638 (1961) (evidence of first robbery admissible in prosecution for second where defendant and others robbed first victim and obtained from him the name and address of their next victim); and State v. Long, 195 Or. 81, 244 P.2d 1033 (1952) (in prosecution for killing owner of truck, proper to prove as part of planned course of action that defendant used truck the next day for a robbery in which he shot an F.B.I. agent while fleeing) with United States v. Dothard, 666 F.2d 498, 504 (11th Cir. 1982) (because a false statement on a U.S. Army Reserve enlistment application, which was the basis of the charge against defendant, and a false statement made to a state driver's license examiner four years earlier were not "so intertwined . . . that they are separate components of a general plan," testimony of state official and prosecutor's comments on defendant's dishonest character constituted reversible error); State v. Manrique, 271 Or. 201, 531 P.2d 239, 242–243 (1975) (previous heroin sales not part of common scheme or plan); Note, 53 Ind.L.J. 805 (1978).

15. On the distinction, if there is one, between "plan" and "scheme," see 2 Louisell & Mueller, Federal Evidence § 140 at 140 (1977). The common plan exception includes crimes committed in preparation for the offense charged. United States v. Cepulonis, 530 F.2d 238 (1st Cir. 1976), cert. denied 426 U.S. 922 (testimony that bank robbers shot at a police officer and a passing motorist and evidence of a shotgun not used in the robbery properly admitted to show that defendants' plan was to distract police by firing and that they had assembled weapons for this purpose); United States v.

Carroll, 510 F.2d 507, 509 (2d Cir. 1975), cert. denied 426 U.S. 923 (other crimes done to determine if conspirators capable of handling mail truck robbery admissible in prosecution for attempted robbery of the mail truck); United States v. Leftwich, 461 F.2d 586 (3d Cir. 1972), cert. denied 409 U.S. 915 (theft of car admissible in prosecution for robbery accomplished with car) ; Annot., 47 A.L.R.Fed. 781.

16. United States v. Bermudez, 526 F.2d 89 (2d Cir. 1975), cert. denied 425 U.S. 970 (upholding admission of "traces of narcotics" and narcotics related equipment seized in home of conspirator six weeks after conspiracy to distribute cocaine ended); Annot., 20 A.L.R.Fed. 125.

If the "other crimes" evidence is part of the conspiracy charged, then it is direct rather than circumstantial evidence of the offense charged. Consequently, there is no reason to analyze the evidence in terms of the exceptions to the rule excluding "other crimes" evidence. United States v. Angelilli, 660 F.2d 23, 39 (2d Cir. 1981), cert. denied 455 U.S. 945, rehearing denied 456 U.S. 939. Some courts invoke the doctrine anyway. United States v. De La Torre, 639 F.2d 245, 250 (5th Cir. 1981) ("the guns were partial payment for the drugs and thus were an integral part of the conspiracy" and hence admissible "to show common plan or scheme"); United States v. Marino, 658 F.2d 1120, 1123 (6th Cir. 1981) (described infra § 189, n. 10).

17. People v. Peete, 28 Cal.2d 806, 169 P.2d 924, (1946), cert. denied 392 U.S. 790 (prior homicide by defendant accused of shooting the deceased from behind at close range in an attempt to sever the spinal cord admissible to identify defendant as murderer where previous homicide also involved a bullet from behind, severing the spinal cord at the neck); Whiteman v. State, 119 Ohio St. 285, 164 N.E. 51 (1928) (evidence of other robberies by defendants wearing uniforms, impersonating officers and stopping cars, thus "earmarking" them as the perpetrators of the offense charged); Rex v. Smith, 11 Cr.App.R. 229, 84 L.J.K.B. 2153 (1915), described in Marjoribanks, For the Defence: The Life of Edward Marshall Hall 321 (1937) (in this "brides of the bath" case it was shown that the man accused of drowning in the bathtub a woman whom he had bigamously "married" had later "married" several wives who left him their property and whom he then purportedly discovered drowned in the bath).

The phrase of which authors of detective fiction are fond, *modus operandi,* may be employed in this context. People v. Barbour, 106 Ill.App.3d 993, 62 Ill.Dec. 641, 646, 436 N.E.2d 667, 672 (1982) (distinguishing *modus operandi* from the common plan, scheme or conspiracy exception); Note, 1978 Utah L.Rev. 547.

class, such as repeated murders,[18] robberies[19] or rapes.[20] The pattern and characteristics of the crimes must be so unusual and distinctive as to be like a signature.[21]

18. United States v. Woods, 484 F.2d 127, 134 (4th Cir. 1973), cert. denied 415 U.S. 979 (evidence that defendant accused of suffocating her eight-month-old pre-adoptive foster son had custody of or access to nine children who suffered at least 20 cyanotic episodes resulting in the death of seven of them "admissible generally under the accident and signature exceptions"); People v. Golochowicz, 413 Mich. 298, 319 N.W.2d 518, 526 (1982) (although the question was too close to warrant reversal in itself, "there was not the requisite 'distinguishing, peculiar or special characteristics' " where "two unmarried male victims were both strangled, one bloodlessly and one after a beating, and their personal property of various kinds . . . stolen from their residences and later sold to friends of the defendant").

19. United States v. Myers, 550 F.2d 1036, 1046 (5th Cir. 1977), appeal after remand 572 F.2d 506, cert. denied 439 U.S. 847 ("An early afternoon robbery of an outlying bank situated on a highway, by revolver-armed robbers wearing gloves and stocking masks, and carrying a bag for the loot, is not such an unusual crime that it tends to prove that one of the two individuals involved must have been the single bandit in a similar prior robbery"); United States v. Phillips, 599 F.2d 134, 136–137 (6th Cir. 1979) ("Here there was only general testimony that defendant had committed other bank robberies—no common plan or distinctive pattern, no 'signature,' not even a similarity").

20. Compare State v. Sauter, 125 Mont. 109, 232 P.2d 731, 732 (1951) (in charge of forcible rape in automobile after picking up victim in barroom, other rapes following similar pickups were "too common . . . to have much evidentiary value in showing a systematic scheme or plan") with McGahee v. Massey, 667 F.2d 1357, 1360 (11th Cir. 1982), cert. denied 103 S.Ct. 255 (where man wearing a white, see-through bikini bathing suit approached a woman sunbathing at beach and raped her, it was within trial court's discretion to permit testimony that twice during the previous month the defendant, wearing a red see-through bathing suit, had exposed himself to other women at the same beach to demonstrate "the manner of operation, identity and type of clothing worn by the defendant"); Williams v. State, 110 So.2d 654, 663 (Fla.1959), cert. denied 361 U.S. 847 (that defendant hid in back seat of woman's car at shopping center and fled when woman screamed admissible to prove that six weeks later the defendant raped another woman outside the same shopping center after hiding in the back seat of her car); cf. United States v. Gano, 560 F.2d 990 (10th Cir. 1977) (permissible to show that defendant social worker charged with carnal knowledge of female under age of 16 had sexual relations with the girl's mother and had sold marijuana to mother and given marijuana to daughter).

As the facts in some of these cases may suggest, the courts tend to find distinctive similarities in sex cases

(4) To show a passion or propensity for unusual and abnormal sexual relations.[22] Initially, proof of other sex crimes always was confined to offenses involving the same parties,[23] but a number of jurisdictions now

more readily than in other situations. See infra note 24. In addition, if the rapist's method of operation is calculated to create the appearance of consent on the part of the victim, the similar acts evidence may be admitted to negate the defense of consent. Oliphant v. Koehler, 594 F.2d 547, 550–554 (6th Cir. 1979), cert. denied 444 U.S. 877. But see People v. Barbour, 106 Ill. App.3d 993, 62 Ill.Dec. 641, 436 N.E.2d 667 (1982) (error to introduce evidence of two prior incidents in which defendant had allegedly raped women whom he had known briefly socially since "identity was never in issue" and the fact that "two of defendant's former victims testified that they did not consent to defendant's sexual advances is wholly irrelevant to . . . *this* complainant's consent"). For more cases, see Annot., 2 A.L.R.4th 330.

21. Compare United States v. Pisari, 636 F.2d 855, 859 (1st Cir. 1981) (use of knife in prior robbery was not sufficient signature or trademark to warrant admission on charge of robbery of postal installation by knife) with United States v. Woods, 613 F.2d 629, 635 (6th Cir. 1980), cert. denied 446 U.S. 920 ("We find the circumstances of this case reveal a 'signature' on the crimes insofar as each was an armed robbery by robbers wearing ski masks, goggles and jumpsuits and using a stolen vehicle for a getaway car"). See generally People v. Haston, 69 Cal.2d 233, 70 Cal.Rptr. 419, 444 P.2d 91 (1968). A civil case considering this theory, but rejecting it as obviously inadequate for want of sufficient similarities, is Hirst v. Gertzen, 676 F.2d 1252, 1262 (9th Cir. 1982) (described supra § 189, n. 2).

22. Woods v. State, 250 Ind. 132, 235 N.E.2d 479 (1968) (other acts of rape and incest with same victim admissible to show "depraved sexual instinct"); State v. Schut, 71 Wn.2d 400, 429 P.2d 126 (1967) (prior acts of incest with victim admissible to show lustful inclination toward victim); Notes, 25 Tex.L.Rev. 421 (1947), 96 U.Pa.L.Rev. 872 (1948); Annot., 77 A.L.R.2d 841; cf. State v. Crossman, 229 Kan. 384, 387, 624 P.2d 461, 464 (1981) (where illicit sexual acts between an adult and a child are charged, similar, prior act evidence is admissible to establish the relationship of the parties, a continuing course of conduct between them, or to corroborate the testimony of the complaining witness as to the acts charged); Note, 25 UCLA L.Rev. 261 (1977); Annot., 2 A.L.R.4th 330. For criticism of this exception to the propensity rule, see Lempert & Saltzburg, A Modern Approach to Evidence 289–90 (2d ed. 1983). Admissibility under Fed. and Rev.Unif.R.Evid. (1974) 404 is highly doubtful.

23. State v. Searle, 125 Mont. 467, 239 P.2d 995 (1952) (sodomy); State v. Start, 65 Or. 178, 132 P. 512 (1913); State v. Pace, 187 Or. 498, 212 P.2d 755 (1949) (statutory rape); State v. Williams, 36 Utah 273, 103 P. 250 (1909) (statutory rape); authorities cited, supra n. 21. Naturally, if evidence of other sex crimes is admitted for another purpose, this limitation has no effect.

admit other sex offenses with other persons,[24] at least as to offenses involving sexual aberrations.[25]

(5) To show, by similar acts or incidents, that the act in question was not performed inadvertently, accidentally,[26] involuntarily,[27] or without guilty knowledge.[28] The similari-

---

See State v. Jensen, 153 Mont. 233, 455 P.2d 631, 634 (1969).

24. Lamar v. State, 245 Ind. 104, 195 N.E.2d 98 (1964); State v. Schlak, 253 Iowa 113, 116, 111 N.W.2d 289, 291 (1961) (evidence that defendant accused of sexually molesting a 15 year old girl had attacked others upheld as showing his motive—"to gratify his lustful desire by grabbing or fondling young girls"); State v. Bolden, 257 La. 60, 241 So.2d 490 (1970); State v. Edwards, 224 N.C. 527, 31 S.E.2d 516 (1944) (incest); Ordover, Admissibility of Patterns of Similar Sexual Conduct: The Unlamented Death of Character for Chastity, 63 Corn.L.Rev. 90 (1977); Notes, 40 Minn.L. Rev. 694 (1956), 46 Tul.L.Rev. 336 (1971), 13 Vand.L. Rev. 394 (1959); Annot., 2 A.L.R.4th 330.

Some courts do not admit evidence of sex crimes with other victims as revealing an incriminating propensity, but achieve a similar result by stretching to find other exceptions to the rule against extrinsic character evidence applicable. Findley v. State, 94 Nev. 212, 577 P.2d 867 (1978) (evidence that the defendant, charged with placing his hand on the "private parts" of a young girl, had behaved similarly with two women nine years earlier allowed to show intent or lack of mistake where defendant testified and denied the act); Gregg, Other Acts of Sexual Misconduct, 6 Ariz.L.Rev. 212 (1965); Trautman, Logical or Legal Relevancy, 5 Vand.L.Rev. 385, 406 (1951); Notes, 78 Harv.L.Rev. 426, 435 (1964), 70 Yale L.J. 763 (1961).

25. State v. McFarlin, 110 Ariz. 225, 517 P.2d 87 (1973) (overruling cases establishing an unqualified propensity rule). Defining aberrant sexual activity presents a considerable problem. At least one state has retreated further, entirely withdrawing its more lenient treatment of evidence of other sex crimes. Commonwealth v. Shively, 492 Pa. 411, 424 A.2d 1257, 1259–1260 (1981), overruling Commonwealth v. Kline, 361 Pa. 434, 65 A.2d 348 (1949).

26. United States v. DeLoach, 654 F.2d 763, 768–769 (D.C.Cir.1980), cert. denied 450 U.S. 1004 (in prosecution for submission of false information to procure a labor certificate for an alien where defendant disavowed knowledge of codefendant's false submissions, testimony of other aliens that defendant had swindled them by falsely promising to secure labor certificates was admissible to undercut "his defense of mistake"); United States v. Ross, 321 F.2d 61 (2d Cir. 1963), cert. denied 375 U.S. 894 (where defendant charged with securities fraud claimed he was an unwitting tool of his employer, it was proper to show on cross-examination that he had drifted among firms engaged in selling worthless securities by similar methods); United States v. Johnson, 634 F.2d 735 (4th Cir. 1980), cert. denied 451 U.S. 907 (evidence that physician accused of tax evasion submitted fraudulent medicaid billing properly admitted to rebut her claim that she was too devoted to patients to worry about finances); United States v. Woods, 484 F.2d 127 (4th Cir. 1973),

cert. denied 415 U.S. 979 (described supra, n. 18); United States v. Witschner, 624 F.2d 840, 843 (8th Cir. 1980), cert. denied 449 U.S. 994 (in prosecution for mail fraud based on submitting fraudulent medical insurance claims, evidence relating to patients not mentioned in the indictment admissible to show "that the submission of the false medical reports was not an accident"); United States v. Harris, 661 F.2d 138, 142 (10th Cir. 1981) (where father accused of murdering eight year old son claimed the fatal injuries occurred because he tripped while carrying the child on his shoulders, evidence of many bone fractures sustained by the infant months before were admissible, since "particularly in child abuse cases" the "admissibility of other crimes, wrongs or acts to establish intent and an absence of mistake or accident is well established"); People v. Williams, 6 Cal.2d 500, 58 P.2d 917 (1936) (where defendant accused of larceny by posing as a customer standing near owner of bag and taking purse from bag while owner was shopping, testimony of detectives that defendant took another purse from another woman's bag in the same manner admissible to refute defendant's claim that he picked the purse off the floor, thinking it lost); State v. Lapage, 57 N.H. 245, 294 (1876) (where there were repeated deaths of children in defendant's care, the court referred to a "class of cases . . . in which it becomes necessary to show that the act for which the prisoner was indicted was not accidental, e.g., where the prisoner had shot the same person twice within a short time, or where the same person had fired a rick of grain twice, or where several deaths by poison had taken place in the same family, or where the children of the same mother had mysteriously died"); Makin v. Attorney General of New South Wales, [1894] App.C. 57 (P.C. 1893) (in prosecution for murder of infant left with professional foster parent, evidence that twelve other babies entrusted to him without adequate payment for their support were found buried in the gardens of three houses he had formerly occupied was properly received on question of whether adoption was bona fide and death accidental); 2 Wigmore, Evidence § 312 (Chadbourn rev. 1979); Note, 63 Geo.L.J. 257 (1974).

27. United States v. Holman, 680 F.2d 1340, 1349 (11th Cir. 1982), rehearing denied 691 F.2d 512 (other smuggling incidents to rebut defense of coercion); United States v. Smith, 552 F.2d 257 (9th Cir. 1977) (intoxication); United States v. Hearst, 563 F.2d 1331 (9th Cir. 1977), rehearing denied 573 F.2d 579, cert. denied 435 U.S. 1000 (evidence of other crimes to negate anticipated defense of duress by publisher's daughter held for ransom by terrorist group and charged in bank robbery committed by group).

28. United States v. Rubio-Gonzalez, 674 F.2d 1067, 1075 (5th Cir. 1982) (record of illegal entries and deportations of defendant that revealed that defendant had migrated along the same path from the same part of Mexico as did the illegal aliens whom he was charged

ties between the act charged and the extrinsic acts need not be as extensive and striking as is required under purpose (3), and the various acts need not be manifestations of a unifying plan, as required for purpose (2).[29]

(6) To establish motive.[30]   The evidence of motive may be probative of the identity of the criminal[31] or of malice or specific intent.[32]   An application of this principle permits proof of criminal acts of the accused that constitute admissions by conduct designed to obstruct justice [33] or avoid punishment for a crime,[34] or of the crimes that

with concealing was admissible to show that he knew that these persons had entered the United States illegally); United States v. Wixom, 529 F.2d 217 (8th Cir. 1976) (evidence that defendant accused of distributing heroin had distributed an ounce of heroin on another occasion properly admitted to show that he knew he was distributing heroin); People v. Marino, 271 N.Y. 317, 3 N.E.2d 439 (1936) (evidence of previous sale of stolen car); 2 Wigmore, Evidence, §§ 301, 310, 324 (Chadbourn rev. 1979); McKusick, Other Crimes to Show Guilty Knowledge and Intent, 24 Iowa L.Rev. 471 (1939).

29. United States v. DeLoach, 654 F.2d 763, 769 (D.C.Cir.1980), cert. denied 450 U.S. 1004 (prior frauds that were admitted to negate defendant's claim of mistake or lack of knowledge "would not be admissible to show . . . identity from a pattern of operations so distinctive that only he could have submitted the fraudulent forms in this fashion").

30. United States v. Haldeman, 559 F.2d 31, 88 (D.C.Cir.1976), cert. denied 431 U.S. 933 (evidence of conspiracy of government officials to break into psychiatrist's office to obtain records of an opponent of government's war policy admissible to show motive for Watergate cover-up conspiracy); United States v. Wasler, 670 F.2d 539, 542 (5th Cir. 1982) (evidence of fraudulent loans admissible to show motive for allegedly fraudulent extension of loan by manager of federal credit union, since "[h]ad Wasler not managed to reduce his monthly payments, a default on the unauthorized loans might well have raised questions whose answers would have proved unpleasant"); United States v. Cyphers, 553 F.2d 1064 (7th Cir. 1977), cert. denied 434 U.S. 843 (testimony that shortly after a bank robbery a defendant asked a government informer to purchase $1000 worth of heroin for him admissible to show motive for robbery); United States v. Ulland, 643 F.2d 537, 541 (8th Cir. 1981) (described supra at § 187, n. 1); People v. Cardenas, 31 Cal.3d 897, 184 Cal.Rptr. 165, 169, 647 P.2d 569, 573 (1982) (evidence of narcotics addiction erroneously admitted to show financial motive for attempted robbery of food store, noting that "Prior cases have upheld the admission of [such evidence] where obtaining narcotics was the direct result of the crime committed" but not "where the object of the charged offense was to obtain money or an item other than narcotics"); State v. Green, 232 Kan. 116, 652 P.2d 697, 701 (1982) ("where a marital homicide is involved, evidence of a discordant marital relationship, and of defendant's previous ill treatment of his wife, including his prior threats to kill her, is competent as bearing on the defendant's motive and intent"); State v. Long, 195 Or. 81, 244 P.2d 1033 (1952) (testimony that defendant accused of murder used victim's truck to commit a robbery shortly afterward admissible);

Commonwealth v. Heller, 369 Pa. 457, 87 A.2d 287 (1952) (evidence of illicit relations with sister-in-law and of attempt to have her get divorce admissible against defendant accused of murdering his wife); State v. Gaines, 144 Wash. 446, 258 P. 508 (1927) (evidence that daughter was threatening to end incestuous relationship with defendant charged with murdering daughter); 2 Wigmore, Evidence § 390 (Chadbourn rev. 1979); Annot., 2 A.L.R.4th 1085 (drug addiction as motive).

It has been argued that where the evidence of motive sheds no light on why the defendant should be so motivated, it is nothing other than propensity evidence in disguise and should be excluded, at least from the prosecution case-in-chief. See Lempert & Saltzburg, A Modern Approach to Evidence 226 (2d ed. 1983).

31. State v. Green, 232 Kan. 116, 652 P.2d 697, 701 (1982) (where the "defendant claimed in essence that someone had broken into his wife's house to rob her and inflicted the fatal wounds prior to his arrival . . . evidence of the defendant's prior assaults on his wife was of great probative value on the issue of identity").

32. United States v. Benton, 637 F.2d 1052, 1056 (5th Cir. 1981), rehearing denied 645 F.2d 72 ("While motive is not an element of any offense charged . . . appellant's knowledge that Zambito might implicate him in the Florida homicides constituted a motive for appellant wanting to kill Zambito . . . . This evidence of motivation was relevant as tending to show the participation of appellant in the crime and to show malice or intent which are elements of the crimes charged"). In an assault or homicide case, evidence of the victim's violent history may be admissible to support a self-defense claim. See infra § 193 n. 3.

33. People v. Spaulding, 309 Ill. 292, 141 N.E. 196 (1923) (killing sole eyewitness to crime); State v. Shaw, ___ Mont. ___, 648 P.2d 287 (1982) (testimony that defendant threatened prosecution's key witness admissible to prove consciousness of guilt); State v. Trujillo, 95 N.M. 535, 624 P.2d 44 (1981) (flight and escape); Gibbs v. State, 201 Tenn. 491, 300 S.W.2d 890 (1957) (in prosecution for murder, evidence that defendant also killed daughter when she discovered body admissible (along with evidence that defendant had killed husband first, then the wife when she discovered this) to show motive and as "inseparable components of a completed crime"); see infra § 273.

34. People v. Gambino, 12 Ill.2d 29, 145 N.E.2d 42 (1957), cert. denied 356 U.S. 904 (escape and attempted escape while awaiting trial); State v. Brown, 231 Or. 297, 372 P.2d 779 (1962) (stealing cars to escape); see § 271 infra.

motivated the interference with the enforcement of the law.[35]

(7) To establish opportunity,[36] in the sense of access to or presence at the scene of the crime [37] or in the sense of possessing distinctive or unusual skills or abilities employed in the commission of the crime charged.[38]

(8) To show, without considering motive, that defendant acted with malice, deliberation, or the requisite specific intent.[39]

(9) To prove identity.[40] Although this is indisputably one of the ultimate purposes for which evidence of other criminal conduct will be received,[41] the need to prove identity should not be, in itself, a ticket to admission. Almost always, identity is the inference that flows from one or more of the theories just listed. The second (larger plan), third (distinctive device), and sixth (motive) seem to be most often relied upon to show identity.[42] In addition, the courts tend to apply stricter standards when the desired inference pertains to identity as opposed to state of mind.[43]

35. State v. Simborski, 120 Conn. 624, 182 A. 221 (1936) (evidence that defendant, who was accused of murdering police officer who was seeking to arrest him, had committed two burglaries a short while before was admissible to show motive and as res gestae); People v. Odum, 27 Ill.2d 237, 188 N.E.2d 720 (1963) (evidence in a murder prosecution that an earlier indictment for a different crime had named the deceased as a witness against defendant).

36. 1 Wigmore, Evidence § 131 (3d ed. 1940). But see 22 Wright & Graham, Federal Practice and Procedure, § 5241 at 484–486 (" 'opportunity' does not seem to have been accepted by courts as one of the permissible uses of other crimes").

37. United States v. DeJohn, 638 F.2d 1048, 1053 (7th Cir. 1981) (testimony of YMCA security guard and city police officer revealing that on other occasions defendant had obtained checks from a mailbox at YMCA was "highly probative of defendant's opportunity to gain access to the mailboxes and obtain the checks that he cashed" with forged endorsements).

38. United States v. Barrett, 539 F.2d 244 (1st Cir. 1976) (evidence admissible to show familiarity with sophisticated means of neutralizing burglar alarms).

39. Compare United States v. Beechum, 582 F.2d 898 (5th Cir. 1978) (en banc), cert. denied 440 U.S. 920 (evidence that defendant had possessed two stolen credit cards for 10 months admissible to prove that he intended to keep a planted silver dollar taken from the mails rather than to return it to postal authorities, as he claimed, on the theory that "because the defendant had unlawful intent in the extrinsic offense, it is less likely that he had lawful intent in the present offense") (1979) and United States v. Mitchell, 666 F.2d 1385, 1388 (11th Cir.), cert. denied 457 U.S. 1124 (testimony that defendant, who was charged with defrauding federal agency by selling part of mortgaged corn crop, was told upon delivering more corn to coop that payments would have to be issued jointly with the agency and that he responded by saying that he would take his corn elsewhere was admissible to prove intent to defraud with United States v. Foskey, 636 F.2d 517, 524 (D.C.Cir.1980) ("The mere fact that a person was [arrested] in the company of another who possesses drugs simply is not sufficient to justify a conclusion that he himself knowingly possessed drugs [when arrested together with the same person] two-and-one-half years

later," since "the linchpin element of intent in the prior incident" is missing) and United States v. Guerrero, 650 F.2d 728, 734 (5th Cir. 1981) (error to admit testimony of a patient who had obtained a prescription from defendant physician accused of illegally dispensing controlled substances to an undercover agent to the effect that defendant had a reputation for being free with pills and that she obtained and used the pills for non-medical purposes after giving a false medical history, since "absent some evidence that defendant acted with unlawful intent in prescribing to [the witness patient], it cannot be said that [her] testimony is in any way relevant to the question of his intent in prescribing to [the undercover agent]"). Also compare State v. Featherman, 133 Ariz. 340, 651 P.2d 868, 873 (App.1982) (to prove that defendant murdered his estranged wife, where decomposed body was found in garbage dump, testimony that defendant had hit her over the head with a baseball bat two months prior to her death was admissible as "directly relevant to his intent the night she was killed") with State v. Robtoy, 98 Wn.2d 30, 653 P.2d 284, 292 (1982) (evidence of unrelated murder ten months earlier erroneously admitted to prove premeditation since it only shows a propensity for premeditated murder). See United States v. Marino, 658 F.2d 1120, 1123 (6th Cir. 1981) (shotgun, pistols and ammunition seized in drug arrest admissible to show "intent to promote and protect" a conspiracy to import a $3.7 million shipment of cocaine); 2 Wigmore, Evidence §§ 363–65 (Chadbourn rev. 1979); Annot., 78 A.L.R.2d 1359 (other instances of false pretenses to show intent).

40. State v. King, 111 Kan. 140, 206 P. 883 (1922) (evidence that bodies of missing persons were on defendant's premises and that their effects were in his possession admissible to prove that he had killed an employee who had disappeared, whose effects were in defendant's possession, and whose burned body was found ten years later on defendant's premises).

41. See supra § 186 n. 10.

42. United States v. Bruner, 657 F.2d 1278 (D.C.Cir. 1981) (assaults of coconspirators and victims of "Fat Lady Conspiracy" admissible to show defendant's role as ringleader); cases cited, supra n. 14–25, 30–34.

43. United States v. Myers, 550 F.2d 1036, 1045 (5th Cir. 1977), cert. denied 439 U.S. 847 ("a much greater degree of similarity between the charged crime and the

(10) To impeach an accused who takes the witness stand by introducing past convictions.[44]

A number of procedural and other substantive considerations also affect the admissibility of other crimes evidence pursuant to these ten exceptions. To begin with, the fact that the defendant is guilty of another relevant crime need not be proved beyond a reasonable doubt. The measure of proof that the defendant is guilty of the other crime is variously described, including "substantial" [45] and "clear and convincing." [46] If

the quoted measures apply then the other crimes evidence should be potentially admissible even if the defendant was acquitted of the other charge.[47]

Second, the connection between the evidence and the permissible purpose should be clear,[48] and the issue on which the other crimes evidence is said to bear should be the subject of a genuine controversy.[49] For example, if the prosecution maintains that the other crime reveals defendant's guilty state of mind, then his intent must be disputed.[50] Likewise, if the accused does not deny per-

---

uncharged crime is required when the evidence of the other crime is introduced to prove identity than when it is introduced to prove a state of mind").

44. See Uviller, Evidence of Character to Prove Conduct, 130 U.Pa.L.Rev. 845, 860–77 (1982); supra § 43; cf. supra § 42 (provability for impeachment purposes of criminal conduct for which there has been no conviction).

45. People v. Albertson, 23 Cal.2d 550, 557–81, 596–99, 145 P.2d 7, 22 (1944); People v. Golochowicz, 413 Mich. 298, 319 N.W. 518, 521 (1982) (described supra at note 18). But see State v. Marahrens, 114 Ariz. 304, 307, 560 P.2d 1211, 1214 (1977) ("there must be evidence of that other crime substantial enough to take that case to a jury"); State v. Tharp, 96 Wn.2d 591, 593–94, 637 P.2d 961 (1981) (preponderance standard).

46. United States v. Dolliole, 597 F.2d 102 (7th Cir. 1979), cert. denied 442 U.S. 946; United States v. Cobb, 588 F.2d 607 (8th Cir. 1978), cert. denied 440 U.S. 947; United States v. Herrell, 588 F.2d 711 (9th Cir. 1978), cert. denied 440 U.S. 964; Tucker v. State, 82 Nev. 127, 412 P.2d 970 (1966). But see United States v. DeJohn, 638 F.2d 1048, 1052 n. 4 (7th Cir.1981) (clear and convincing standard only applicable to intent or motive exceptions). Contra United States v. Benedetto, 582 F.2d 898 (2d Cir.1978) (evidence sufficient to support a verdict); United States v. Beechum, 582 F.2d 898 (5th Cir. 1978) (en banc), cert. denied 440 U.S. 920. For an exchange of views on the desirability of the clear and convincing standard, see Lempert & Saltzburg, A Modern Approach to Evidence 222–24 (2d ed. 1983).

47. The cases are divided. Compare United States v. Mespoulede, 597 F.2d 329 (2d Cir.1979); United States v. Day, 591 F.2d 861 (D.C.Cir.1979); United States v. Keller, 624 F.2d 1154 (3d Cir.1980); State v. Perkins, 349 So.2d 161 (Fla.1977); and State v. Wakefield, 278 N.W.2d 307 (Minn.1979) (acquittal bars admission) with United States v. Etley, 574 F.2d 850 (5th Cir.1978), cert. denied 439 U.S. 967; Oliphant v. Koehler, 594 F.2d 547, 553–555 (6th Cir.1979), cert. denied 444 U.S. 877; United States v. Kills Plenty, 466 F.2d 240 (8th Cir.1972), cert. denied 410 U.S. 916; and United States v. Cleave, 599 F.2d 954 (10th Cir.1979) (acquittal does not bar admission). See also Annot., 86 A.L.R.2d 1132.

At least where the evidence of essentially identical crimes dispels the reasonable doubt that might be present when each crime is viewed in isolation, an acquittal should not preclude the proof of the earlier offense. See, e.g., Oliphant v. Koehler, supra (conviction following two previous acquittals and other complaints of rapes under similar circumstances that were arranged to suggest consent of the victims, the same defense being raised in the case at bar); United States v. Rocha, 553 F.2d 615 (9th Cir.1977) (conviction of defendant, who had been acquitted of transporting marijuana, was arrested a second time, a few months after his earlier arrest, while driving a van containing a large quantity of marijuana, and testified that this time he thought he was moving a load of furniture).

48. People v. Golochowicz, 413 Mich. 298, 319 N.W.2d 518, 523–524 (1982) ("the prosecutor's first duty is to identify, with specificity, the purpose for which the evidence is admissible," and trial judges should require "a showing by the prosecutor as to how such evidence is relevant" to this specified justification).

49. People v. Golochowicz, 413 Mich. 298, 319 N.W.2d 518, 524 (1982) ("evidence of other misconduct is not admissible in this state to negate mistake or accident, to prove motive, to show intent, to demonstrate the defendant's plan, scheme or system, or to prove his identity, unless one or more of these factors are genuinely in issue—not 'in issue' in the sense that criminal intent, identity, [etc.] are nearly always in issue to some greater or lesser degree in every case, but in issue or 'material' in the sense that they are genuinely controverted matters"); Thompson v. The King, [1918] App.C. 221, 232 ("The mere theory that a plea of not guilty puts everything material in issue is not enough . . . . The prosecution cannot credit the accused with fancy defences in order to rebut them at the outset with some damning piece of prejudice").

50. United States v. Figueroa, 618 F.2d 934, 941 (2d Cir.1980) (where codefendants suggested that they were selling coffee "grinds" rather than heroin as a "rip-off," the government could not use defendant's prior involvement on issue of intent because "no one . . . claimed that the trio was unwittingly selling . . . heroin, thinking it was some other substance"). Thus, some cases hold that the exceptions pertaining to intent are not available to the prosecution where the

forming the acts charged, the exceptions pertaining to identification are unavailing.[51]

Finally, even if one or more of the valid purposes for admitting other crimes evidence is appropriately invoked, there is still the need to balance[52] its probative value against the usual counterweights.[53] When the sole purpose of the other crimes evidence is to show some propensity to commit the crime at trial, there is no room for ad hoc balancing. The evidence is then unequivocally inadmissible—this is meaning of the rule against other crimes evidence.[54] But the fact that there is an accepted logical basis for the evidence other than the forbidden one of showing a proclivity for criminality may not preclude the jury from relying on a defendant's apparent propensity toward criminal behavior.[55] Accordingly, most recent authority recognizes that the problem is not merely one of pigeonholing, but of classifying and then balancing.[56] In deciding whether the danger of unfair prejudice and the like substantially outweighs the incremental probative value, a variety of matters must be considered, including the strength of the evidence as to the commission of the other crime, the similarities between the crimes, the interval of time that has elapsed between the crimes, the need for the evidence, the efficacy of alternative proof, and the degree to which the evidence probably will rouse the jury to overmastering hostility.[57] Certain procedures can aid in these determinations and in the presentation of evidence of other crimes.[58]

act charged unequivocally reveals the requisite intent. State v. Barker, 249 S.W. 75, 77 (Mo.1923) (auto theft); People v. Lonsdale, 122 Mich. 388, 81 N.W. 277 (1899) (abortion); 1 Wharton, Criminal Evidence § 245 (13th ed. 1972).

51. United States v. DeVaughn, 601 F.2d 42, 46 ("Since the concession that was offered would have established beyond question [defendant's] presence . . . and his identity as the recipient of the quinine, thus removing identity as an issue, the other-crime evidence was not admissible to prove identity"); Miller v. State, ___ Ind. ___, 436 N.E.2d 1113, 1120 (1982) (error in rape case to admit mug shot from prior charge where "there simply was no issue of identification"). Contra United States v. DeJohn, 638 F.2d 1048, 1052 n. 4 (7th Cir. 1981) (genuine controversy requirement applies only to intent or motive).

52. United States v. Lewis, 693 F.2d 189 (D.C.Cir. 1982); United States v. Cook, 538 F.2d 1000, 1003–04 (3d Cir. 1976); People v. Golochowicz, 413 Mich. 298, 319 N.W.2d 518, 527–29 (1982).

53. These are described supra at § 185.

54. Cf. supra § 186 n. 4.

55. See, e.g., Government of Virgin Islands v. Toto, 529 F.2d 278, 283 (3d Cir. 1976) ("A drop of ink cannot be removed from a glass of milk"); Doob supra § 190, n. 6 (jury simulation research suggesting that jurors do not completely adhere to limiting instruction); Note, 70 Yale L.J. 763 (1961) (inability of jurors to understand and obey limiting instructions). See also § 59 supra.

56. United States v. Fosher, 568 F.2d 207, 212–213 (1st Cir. 1978); People v. Cardenas, 31 Cal.3d 897, 184 Cal.Rptr. 165, 647 P.2d 569, 572 (1982); People v. Golochowicz, 413 Mich. 298, 319 N.W.2d 518, 521, 524 (1982).

57. Cases discussing these considerations are collected in M. Graham, Handbook of Federal Evidence § 404.5 (1981); Annot., 92 A.L.R.3d 545 (subsequent offenses). Another factor sometimes mentioned as entitled to consideration is surprise. People v. Kelley, 66 Cal.2d 232, 57 Cal.Rptr. 363, 424 P.2d 947 (1967). The remedy here would seem to be notice, State v. Spreigl, 272 Minn. 488, 139 N.W.2d 167 (1965), or a continuance. See § 185 supra.

58. To avoid prejudice, an offer of proof may be made outside the hearing of the jury. See United States v. Bailey, 505 F.2d 417, 420 (D.C.Cir.1974), cert. denied 420 U.S. 961; Grimaldi v. United States, 606 F.2d 332, 340 n. 9 (1st Cir.), cert. denied 444 U.S. 971. See Fed. and Rev.Unif.R.Evid. (1974) 103(c), and § 51 supra.

When the evidence of another crime is offered with regard to knowledge, intent or the like, it often will be wise to wait until the defendant has sharpened the issue by claiming accident, mistake, or involuntariness in his opening statement or presentation of evidence, or by raising special defenses in advance. See United States v. Benedetto, 571 F.2d 1246, 1249 (2d Cir.1978) ("should normally await the conclusion of the defendant's case, since the court will then be in the best position to balance the probative worth of, and the Government's need for, such testimony against the prejudice to the defendant"); supra § 190, note 3. Compare United States v. Webb, 625 F.2d 709, 710 (5th Cir.1980) (where " 'intent is not normally inferable from the nature of the act charged,' . . . and the defendant fails to give enforceable pre-trial assurances that he intends not to dispute criminal intent, the Government's case-in-chief may include such extrinsic offense evidence as would be admissible if intent were actively contested").

Where other crimes evidence is admitted, a limiting instruction may be given. United States v. Aims Back, 588 F.2d 1283 (9th Cir. 1979) (court may give cautionary instruction *sua sponte*). But judicial pronouncements to the contrary notwithstanding, e.g., United States v. Masters, 622 F.2d 83, 87–88 (4th Cir.1980),

topic(110) /p evidence /p bad /5 character
digest(404(b) /p exception*)
digest(evidence +3 crime* offense* /p exception*)
110k365
404(b) /p deprav! lewd! lascivious! illicit passion*
    propensit! abnormal! unusual uncommon deviant /25
    sex!
110k371(9)
digest(404(b) /p motive*)
digest(evidence +3 crime* offense* /p motive*)
digest(404(b) /p opportunit!)
digest(404(b) /p malic! deliberation)
digest(evidence +3 crime* offense* /p malic!
    deliberation)
110k369.15 & date(after 1980)
digest(evidence +3 crime* offense* /p impeach!)
digest(404(b) /p impeach!)

---

§ 191. Good Character as Evidence of Lawful Conduct: Proof by the Accused and Rebuttal by the Government

The prosecution, as we have seen in the preceding section, generally is forbidden to initiate evidence of the bad character of the defendant merely to imply that, being a bad person, he is more likely to commit a crime. This rule, in turn, is a corollary of the more general proscription on the use of character as circumstantial evidence of conduct. Yet, when the table is turned and the defendant in a criminal case seeks to offer evidence of his good character to imply that he is unlikely to have committed a crime, the general rule against propensity evidence is not applied.[1] In both situations, the character evidence is relevant circumstantial evidence, but when the accused chooses to rely on it to exonerate himself, the problem of prejudice is altogether different. Now, knowledge of the accused's character may prejudice the jury in his *favor*,[2] but the magnitude of the prejudice or its social cost is thought to be less.[3] Thus, the common law and the Federal and Revised Uniform Evid. Rules (1974) permit the defendant, but not the government, to open the door to character evidence.[4]

Not all aspects of the accused's character are open to scrutiny under this exception. The prevailing view [5] is that only pertinent

---

these instructions may be of limited value. See supra n. 55 and § 59 supra.

§ 191

1. See generally 1 Wigmore, Evidence §§ 55–60 (3d ed. 1940); 3A id. § 925 (Chadbourn rev. 1970); Dec. Dig. Criminal Law ⬅377–380. It is said that the practice of permitting evidence of good character began in the reign of Charles II with regard to capital cases. Reddick v. State, 25 Fla. 112, 5 So. 704 (1889). Later, the practice spread to cases in which the other testimony left guilt in doubt. See Daniels v. State, 18 Del. (2 Pen.) 586, 48 A. 196 (1901). Such limitations have long since been abandoned. Edgington v. United States, 164 U.S. 361 (1896).

2. See Lempert & Saltzburg, A Modern Approach to Evidence 237 (2d ed. 1983).

3. The difference in the rule as regards the prosecution and the defense has been characterized as an amelioration of the "brutal rigors" of the early criminal law. Maguire, Evidence—Common Sense and Common Law 204 (1947). But to say that the defendant deserves the benefit of all reasonable doubts and that good character may produce a reasonable doubt assumes what should be demonstrated—that the doubt is not the product of unfair prejudice as defined supra at § 185. Thus, one must consider whether a parade of character witnesses convinces most jurors that the defendant has led an exemplary life even when his past is not so unblemished and whether many defendants with checkered backgrounds will be in a position to produce such witnesses. Furthermore, to the extent that the ability to collect impressive character witnesses is concentrated among those accused of white collar rather than street crimes, one may question the fairness of an asymmetrical rule. See, e.g., United States v. Johnson, 634 F.2d 735, 736 (4th Cir. 1980), cert. denied 451 U.S. 907, in which the court drew the following sketch of the case: "Johnson is a medical doctor . . . who filed tax returns . . . which understated her income by approximately $120,000.00 . . . . Her defense at trial was inadvertence: she had nothing to do with preparing her tax returns because she cared nothing for money and chose, instead, to devote her time to the demanding personal needs of her patients. [S]he produced seven local witnesses—three physicians, a school board member, a public school teacher, a mortician, and a minister—who testified to her truthfulness, honesty, and compassion, and to the busy nature of her practice."

4. See, e.g., State v. Martin, 256 N.W.2d 85 (Minn. 1977); Fed.R.Evid. 404(a)(1); Rev.Unif.R.Evid. 404(a)(1) (1974) (for text see supra § 186 n. 5).

5. For deviations, see State v. Sentelle, 212 N.C. 386, 193 S.E. 405 (1937) (defendant charged with driving while intoxicated may not elicit testimony on reputation for sobriety, but must inquire as to general character; however, witness may volunteer information as to respect in which character good or bad).

traits—those involved in the offense charged [6]—are provable.[7] One charged with theft might offer evidence of honesty,[8] while someone accused of murder might show that he is peaceable, but not vice versa.[9] A few general traits, like being law-abiding, seem sufficiently relevant to almost any accusation.[10]

The common law has vacillated as regards the methods of establishing the good character of the accused. A rule of relatively recent origin limits proof to evidence of reputation for the pertinent traits.[11] This constraint supposedly prevents a witness from giving a personal opinion no matter how well grounded.[12] It also prohibits testimony concerning specific acts or their absence.[13]

The Federal and Revised Uniform Evidence Rules (1974) reinstate the earlier common law approach.[14] Rule 405(a) provides, in part, that:

> In all cases in which evidence of character or a trait of character of a person is admissible, proof may be made by testimony as to reputation or by testimony in the form of an opinion.

This liberalization was not achieved without debate.[15] It allows expert opinion testimony about an accused's character traits,[16] subject to the court's residual power to screen for

6. It might be thought that character traits tend to occur in clusters, so that evidence of a trait not involved in the crime charged has some probative value as to the trait in question. This argument overlooks the fact that if the general correlation between the traits actually holds for the defendant at bar, he should be able to provide more direct evidence of the pertinent trait.

7. A distinct situation, involving different rules, can arise if the accused takes the stand as a witness. If he does not testify that he has character traits that are inconsistent with the charges against him, the prosecution cannot introduce, by way of rebuttal, evidence that he lacks these traits. The rules under discussion here are simply inapplicable. On the other hand, regardless of the subject matter of his testimony, the prosecution may impeach his credibility by evidence of his bad character for veracity. As with any witness, his veracity at the time he testifies is in question. At common law, however, the accused could not support his veracity-character before the prosecution attacked it. E.g., State v. Howland, 157 Kan. 11, 138 P.2d 424 (1942) (defendant's evidence of veracity in statutory rape case properly excluded (1) as propensity evidence because not the trait involved in the crime, and (2) as supporting credibility because state had not attacked character for veracity). These matters, and the changes wrought by the Federal Rules, are addressed supra at §§ 41–44.

8. State v. Kramp, ___ Mont. ___, 651 P.2d 614, 618 (1982).

9. For other examples, see United States v. Jackson, 588 F.2d 1046 (5th Cir.1979), cert. denied 442 U.S. 941 (truthfulness not pertinent to narcotics charges); State v. Altamirano, 116 Ariz. 291, 569 P.2d 233 (1977) (brother's testimony as to defendant's part-time employment and fact that defendant was not a heroin addict not pertinent to traits involved in sale of heroin); State v. Howland, 157 Kan. 11, 138 P.2d 424 (1942) (veracity not pertinent to rape charge); State v. Hortman, 207 Neb. 393, 299 N.W.2d 187 (1980) (veracity not pertinent to charges of assault and abuse of an incompetent); Annot., 49 A.L.R.Fed. 478 (pertinent traits under

Rule 404(a)(1)). But see United States v. West, 670 F.2d 675, 682 (7th Cir.1982), cert. denied 457 U.S. 1124 (poorly reasoned opinion holding that "limited intelligence" is not a character trait at all, so that even though the characteristic may be pertinent to intent in accepting a bribe, the trial judge has discretion to exclude expert testimony on the point).

10. But see State v. Quinn, 344 Mo. 1072, 130 S.W.2d 511 (1939) (when offense is malum prohibitum rather than malum in se, it is proper to prove law-abiding character).

11. See 7 Wigmore, Evidence §§ 1981, 1986 (Chadbourn rev. 1978) (history and policy behind rule).

12. See supra § 186 n. 8.

13. Id. A witness who testifies that he lives in the defendant's community and has never heard of the defendant's character for the pertinent trait is qualified to testify that defendant's character for this trait is reputed to be good. People v. Van Gaasbeck, 189 N.Y. 408, 82 N.E. 718 (1907); Annot., 67 A.L.R. 1210 (negative proof of good character).

14. Model Code of Evidence Rule 306(2)(a) and the original version of the Uniform Rules, Rules 46 & 47, also permitted opinion testimony based on personal observation of conduct, and a few states had clung to the earlier tradition. Freeman v. States, 486 P.2d 967 (Alaska 1971); State v. Blake, 157 Conn. 99, 249 A.2d 232 (1968) (dictum); State v. Hartung, 239 Iowa 414, 30 N.W.2d 491 (1948); State v. Ferguson, 222 Iowa 1148, 270 N.W. 874 (1936).

15. See supra § 186 n. 10.

16. United States v. Hill, 655 F.2d 512 (3d Cir. 1981) (reversible error to exclude testimony of psychologist that defendant was unusually susceptible to government inducements offered to support entrapment defense); United States v. Staggs, 553 F.2d 1073 (7th Cir. 1977) (reversible error to exclude testimony of psychologist that defendant accused of assaulting a federal officer was more likely to hurt himself than to direct his aggressions toward others).

prejudice, distraction, and time-consumption.[17] Like the common law rules, it does not allow evidence of particular incidents.[18]

Where reputation evidence is employed, it may be confined to reputation at approximately the time of the alleged offense.[19] Furthermore, traditionally, only testimony as to the defendant's reputation in the community where the accused resided was allowed,[20] but increasing urbanization has prompted the acceptance of evidence as to reputation within other substantial groups of which the accused is a constantly interacting member, such as the locale where defendant works.[21]

When defendant does produce evidence of his good character as regards traits pertinent to the offense charged, whether by way of reputation or opinion testimony, he frequently is said to have placed his character "in issue."[22] The phrase is misleading. That a defendant relies on character witnesses to indicate that he is not predisposed to commit the type of crime in question does not transform his character into an operative fact upon which guilt or innocence may turn.[23] Defendant simply opens the door to proof of certain character traits as circumstantial evidence of whether he committed the act charged with the requisite state of mind.[24]

Ordinarily, if the defendant chooses to inject his character into the trial in this sense, he does so by producing witnesses who testify to his good character. By relating a personal history supportive of good character, however, the defendant may achieve the same result.[25] Whatever the method, once

---

17. See supra § 185.

18. United States v. Bendetto, 571 F.2d 1246 (2d Cir.1978) (honesty of meat inspector charged with taking bribes not provable by testimony of other packers that he did not solicit bribes from them); Government of Virgin Islands v. Petersen, 553 F.2d 324 (3d Cir. 1977) (evidence of membership in Rastafarians, who believe in non-violence, properly excluded); State v. Lehman, 126 Ariz. 388, 616 P.2d 63, 66 (1980) (proper to cross-examine defendant's character witness about specific instances when defendant behaved violently, but not to put on independent evidence of these incidents; see infra nn. 28–29 on the cross-examination issue).

19. Lomax v. United States, 37 App.D.C. 414 (D.C. Cir.1911); People v. Willy, 301 Ill. 307, 133 N.E. 859, 864 (1921); Commonwealth v. White, 271 Pa. 584, 115 A. 870 (1922) (remoteness within trial judge's discretion); Strader v. State, 208 Tenn. 192, 344 S.W.2d 546 (1961).

20. Baugh v. State, 218 Ala. 87, 117 So. 426 (1928).

21. United States v. Oliver, 492 F.2d 943 (8th Cir. 1974), appeal after remand 525 F.2d 731, cert. denied 424 U.S. 973 (college roommates of seven weeks acquaintance); United States v. White, 225 F.Supp. 514 (D.D.C.1963), cause remanded 349 F.2d 965 (4th Cir.) (dictum that community "is not necessarily a geographic unit, but is rather composed of the relationships with others which arise where a man works, worships, shops, relaxes and lives"); Hamilton v. State, 129 Fla. 219, 176 So. 89 (1937) (admitting reputation in locality where accused worked as hotel employee); State v. Jackson, 373 S.W.2d 4 (Mo.1963); Annot., 112 A.L.R. 1020; cf. supra § 44 (similar considerations with respect to a witness' character for veracity). See 5 Wigmore, Evidence §§ 1615–1616 (Chadbourn rev. 1974); Annot., 82 A.L.R.3d 525 (reputation at place of employment). See further § 324 infra.

22. E.g., Greer v. United States, 245 U.S. 559 (1918); West v. State, 265 Ark. 52, 576 S.W.2d 718 (1979).

23. On the proper meaning of character in issue, see supra § 187.

24. In State v. Stewart, 276 N.W.2d 51 (Minn.1979), for example, the court reasoned that the testimony of a girlfriend to the effect that the accused had a nonviolent character put his character at issue, which justified the state's introduction of evidence of bad character. Despite such language, it should be clear that the defendant's character for violence is merely circumstantial evidence of whether he committed the acts alleged.

25. Compare United States ex rel. Johnson v. Johnson, 531 F.2d 169 (3d Cir.1976), cert. denied 425 U.S. 997 with United States v. Lister, 608 F.2d 785, 790 (9th Cir.1979) (argument and testimony that defendant purchased property in Colorado to establish hydrophonics business and came from "a relatively privileged background" with no need to distribute cocaine did not open his characterization of "life style" to impeachment by reference to nine-year-old misdemeanor conviction for marijuana possession) and People v. Johnson, 409 Mich. 552, 297 N.W.2d 115 (1980) (defendant who testified that he did not like whites and would not have sold drugs to stranger at discount prices did not open his character to attack) and West v. State, 265 Ark. 52, 576 S.W.2d 178) (1979) (defense witnesses' testimony that manslaughter defendant attempted to avoid confrontations whenever the decedent threatened him did not put defendant's character for non-aggression in issue); cf. Government of Virgin Islands v. Roldan, 612 F.2d 775, 778 (3d Cir.1979), cert. denied 446 U.S. 920 (1980) (proper for government to ask on redirect whether witness who testified on cross that defendant "is a man who never bother anybody" knew of defendant's previous murder conviction); supra n. 7 and § 57.

the defendant gives evidence of pertinent character traits to show that he is not guilty, his claim of possession of these traits—but only these traits[26]—is open to rebuttal by cross-examination or direct testimony of prosecution witnesses. The prosecution may cross-examine a witness who has testified to the accused's reputation in order to probe the witness' knowledge of the community opinion, not only generally, but specifically as to whether the witness "has heard" that the defendant has committed particular prior [27] criminal acts that conflict with the reputation vouched for on direct examination.[28] Likewise, if a witness gives his opinion of defendant's character, then the prosecution can allude to pertinent bad acts by asking whether the witness knew of these matters in forming his opinion.[29] Indeed, eschewing the dubious distinction between questions of the form "Have you heard" as opposed to "Do you know," [30] the remainder

of Federal and Revised Uniform Rule (1974) 405(a) simply provides that

> On cross-examination, inquiry is allowed into relevant specific instances of conduct.

This power of the cross-examiner to reopen old wounds is replete with possibilities for prejudice.[31] Accordingly, certain limitations should be observed. The general responsibility of trial courts to weigh probative value against prejudice does not vanish because reference to other crimes or wrongs takes the form of insinuation or innuendo rather than concrete evidence.[32] The extent and nature of the cross-examination demands restraint and supervision.[33] Some questions that less experienced prosecutors could be tempted to ask may be improper under any circumstances.[34] As a precondition to cross-examination about other wrongs, the prosecutor should reveal, outside the hearing of the jury, what his basis is for believing in the rumors or incidents he proposes to ask about.[35] The court

---

26. United States v. Wooden, 420 F.2d 251 (D.C.Cir. 1969) (cross-examination as to drunkenness not proper for traits of honesty, peace, and quiet); State v. Kramp, 651 P.2d 614, 618 (Mont.1982) (cross-examination as to arrests for traffic and drunken driving offenses not proper for trait of honesty).

27. Inquiry into reputation as affected by the charges at bar is improper. United States v. Curtis, 644 F.2d 263, 268–69 (3d Cir.1981); United States v. Morgan, 554 F.2d 31 (2d Cir.1977), cert. denied 434 U.S. 965. See also n. 34 infra.

28. See 3A Wigmore, Evidence § 988 (Chadbourn rev. 1970); Dec. Dig., Witnesses ⟨key⟩294; Annot., 47 A.L.R.2d 1258, Annot., 71 A.L.R.2d 1504; supra n. 18. The logic of this form of impeachment is that since the crimes occurred, they caused community talk, but either (a) the witness has not heard it, which shows his ignorance of defendant's true reputation, or (b) the witness has heard of it but is dissembling or else applying a low standard of "goodness." See Michelson v. United States, 335 U.S. 469, 477–487 (1948).

29. See supra n. 18. There is an ungainly body of seemingly casuistric case law on the circumstances, if any, under which reputation-only witnesses can be asked what they know as distinguished from what they have heard. See Michelson v. United States, 335 U.S. 469, 488 ("grotesque structure," but worth preserving); Annot., 47 A.L.R.2d 1258, 1330.

30. According to the Advisory Committee's note to Federal Evid. Rule 405, "these distinctions are of slight if any practical significance, and the second sentence of subdivision (a) eliminates them as a factor in formulating questions."

31. Cf. supra § 190.

32. United States v. Lewis, 482 F.2d 632, 639 (D.C. Cir.1973); United States v. Bright, 588 F.2d 504 (5th Cir.1979), cert. denied 440 U.S. 972; Note, 9 U.C.D.L. Rev. 365 (1976); cf. supra § 190, n. 3.

33. Of course, cautionary instructions to the jury also may be employed. See Saltzburg & Redden, Federal Rules of Evidence Manual 160 (3d ed. 1982) (proposed instruction).

34. As previously observed, there are strictures concerning the pertinence and remoteness of the other wrongs. Questions about the effect of the charges being tried on reputation or opinion may be barred on the ground that it is unfairly prejudicial to ask the witness to indulge in a hypothetical assumption of the defendant's guilt. United States v. Polsinelli, 649 F.2d 793 (10th Cir.1981) (opinion witness); United States v. Hewitt, 663 F.2d 1381, 1391 (11th Cir.1981) (although the government could ask defendant's reputation witnesses whether they had heard of a pending indictment elsewhere, to ask whether hearing this fact would cause a witness to retract her testimony that defendant's reputation is good was "highly improper" because "the government had already shown that [she] knew little of [defendant's] reputation in the community by exposing her ignorance of his pending trial," and the witness was not an expert qualified to say how the community would react under hypothetical conditions). See also n. 27 supra.

35. It has been clear for some time that propounding a question in bad faith about a prior crime or wrong is ground for reversal. State v. Keul, 233 Iowa 852, 5 N.W.2d 849 (1942). But such reversals are rare.

should then determine whether there is a substantial basis for the cross-examination.[36]

The other prosecutorial counterthrust to the defendant's proof of good character is not so easily abused. The government may produce witnesses to swear to defendant's bad reputation [37] or, currently in most jurisdictions, their opinion of defendant's character.[38] As with defense character witnesses, the strictures concerning pertinent traits and remoteness apply. The courts had divided over the admissibility as rebuttal evidence of judgments of convictions for recent crimes displaying the same traits,[39] but with the adoption of the federal rules, few jurisdictions now allow such proof of specific instances of misconduct as rebuttal evidence.[40]

⌨ **WESTLAW REFERENCES**

110k376 /p "opinion" reputation

410k37(4) /p communit! area local!

digest(defendant* /p put* place* /p character reputation /5 issue)

110k378

410k274(2)

digest(405(a) /p hear*** kn*w!)

---

36. A number of cases recommend or require this type of procedure. United States v. Lewis, 482 F.2d 632, 639 (D.C.Cir.1973); United States v. Duke, 492 F.2d 693 (5th Cir.1974); United States v. Reese, 568 F.2d 1246 (6th Cir.1977); People v. Yoshimo Futamata, 140 Colo. 233, 343 P.2d 1058 (1959); State v. Hinton, 206 Kan. 500, 479 P.2d 910 (1971); People v. Dorrikas, 354 Mich. 303, 92 N.W.2d 305 (1958).

The use of arrest records for cross-examination has troubled many courts. The federal practice, upheld over a vigorous dissent in Michelson v. United States, 335 U.S. 469 (1948), allows it. Some jurisdictions have declined to follow *Michelson*. Commonwealth v. Scott, 496 Pa. 188, 436 A.2d 607 (1981); State v. Kramp, 651 P.2d 614, 618 (Mont.1982); cf. supra § 190, nn. 45–46 (necessary degree of proof of other crimes introduced to prove common plan, identity, absence of mistake, etc.). Even in federal courts, the fact of a previous arrest, by itself, no matter how well documented, should not constitute a sufficient basis for cross-examination. Compare United States v. McCollom, 664 F.2d 56, 58 (5th Cir.1981), cert. denied 456 U.S. 934 (cross-examination by reference to previous arrest for theft proper where lack of conviction resulted from a dismissal because defendant made restitution, so that a good faith factual basis for the alleged prior misconduct exists").

§ 192. Character in Civil Cases Where Crime Is in Issue

As explained above in § 191, in criminal cases the law relaxes its ban on evidence of character to show conduct to the extent of permitting a defendant to produce evidence of his good character. It is not unusual in civil litigation, however, for one party to accuse another of conduct that amounts to a criminal offense. For instance, much of the conduct that is the subject of civil antitrust, securities, and civil rights cases as well as a substantial proportion of more traditional civil actions, could also provide grist for the public prosecutor's mill.

Where the homologous crimes are largely regulatory or administrative, it may seem inappropriate to accord the civil party the same dispensation given criminal defendants whose lives or liberties are in jeopardy. But what of the party whose adversary's pleading or proof accuses him of what would be an offense involving moral turpitude, as in an action for conversion, a complaint arising from an alleged incident of police brutality, or a suit for a breach of a fire insurance policy in which the insurer refuses to pay because it believes that the insured set the

---

37. 3A Wigmore, Evidence § 988 (Chadbourn rev. 1970).

38. The rules concerning the mode of proof—reputation versus opinion—do not depend on which party introduces the evidence. See supra § 186.

39. The majority of the cases rejected the evidence. See, e.g., Eley v. United States, 117 F.2d 526 (6th Cir. 1941); State v. Myrick, 181 Kan. 1056, 317 P.2d 485 (1957); Zirkle v. Commonwealth, 189 Va. 862, 55 S.E.2d 24 (1949). The argument against the use of convictions for this purpose is much weaker than the one against the use of convictions to impeach the accused when he takes the stand as a witness. See supra § 43. If he stays off the stand, the jury may well infer that he is guilty despite instructions to the contrary, but no such inference is likely from the failure to open the door to reputation. In any event, the issue seems largely academic, since the prosecution can advert to the conviction on cross-examination.

40. United States v. Benedetto, 571 F.2d 1246, 1250 (2d Cir.1978) (dictum); State v. Lehman, 126 Ariz. 388, 616 P.2d 63, 66 (1980); supra § 186.

fire? Some courts have thought that the damage that may be done to the party's standing, reputation and relationships warrants according the civil defendant the same special dispensation.[1] These courts therefore permitted the party to introduce evidence of his good reputation for the traits involved.[2]

But this never has been the majority view. Since the consequences of civil judgments are less severe than those flowing from a criminal conviction, most courts have declined to pay the price that the concession would demand in terms of possible prejudice, consumption of time, and distraction from the issue.[3] Although the balance may be arguable,[4] the Federal and Revised Uniform

Evid. Rules (1974) adhere to the majority position. Rule 404 bars evidence of character in civil cases to show how a person probably acted on a particular occasion.[5]

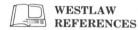 **WESTLAW REFERENCES**

digest(reputation character /p evidence /p civil)

§ 193. Character of Victim in Cases of Assault, Murder, and Rape

A well established exception to the rule forbidding character evidence to prove conduct applies to homicide and assault cases in which there is a dispute as to who was the first aggressor.[1] This exception permits the accused in such cases to introduce appropri-

§ 192

1. See, e.g., Hein v. Holdridge, 78 Minn. 468, 81 N.W. 522, 523 (1900) (emphasizing difficulty of meeting charges of "indecent assault, seduction and kindred cases" that affect "his fortune, his honor, his family").

2. Mourikas v. Vardianos, 169 F.2d 53, 59 (4th Cir. 1948) (conversion); People Loan & Investment Co. v. Travelers Insurance Co., 151 F.2d 437, 440–441 (8th Cir. 1945) (whether deceased was aggressor); United States v. Genovese, 133 F.Supp. 820 (D.N.J.1955) (dictum in naturalization case), affirmed 236 F.2d 757 (3d Cir.), cert. denied 352 U.S. 952 (1956); Mays v. Mays, 153 Ga. 835, 113 S.E. 154 (1922); Hein v. Holdridge, 78 Minn. 468, 81 N.W. 522 (1900), supra n. 1; Rogers v. Atlantic-Life Insurance Co., 135 S.C. 89, 133 S.E. 215 (1926) (fraud); Waggoman v. Ft. Worth Well Machine Supply Co., 124 Tex. 325, 76 S.W.2d 1005 (1934) (embezzlement counterclaim).

3. Bosworth v. Bosworth, 131 Conn. 389, 40 A.2d 186 (1944) (cruelty in divorce case); Northern Assurance Co. v. Griffin, 236 Ky. 296, 33 S.W.2d 7 (1930) (setting fire); Baker v. First National Bank of Santa Rosa, 176 Okl. 70, 54 P.2d 355 (1936) (replevin); Greenberg v. Aetna Insurance Co., 427 Pa. 494, 235 A.2d 582 (1967) (setting fire); Eisenberg v. Continental Casualty Co., 48 Wis.2d 637, 180 N.W.2d 726 (1970) (fraud). See generally 1 Wigmore, Evidence § 64 (3d ed. 1940); 13 Tex.L.Rev. 531 (1935); Adv.Comm.Note, Fed.R.Evid. 404(a).

4. See, e.g., Louisell & Mueller, Federal Evidence § 142 at 155 (1977) (approving of the minority position).

5. See supra § 188. Some complications arise in assault and battery cases. See generally Annot., 91 A.L.R.2d 708. When the issue is simply whether the defendant committed the act, the majority approach described above excludes defendant's evidence of his character for peacefulness. Feliciano v. City & County of Honolulu, 611 P.2d 989 (Hawaii 1980); Kornec v. Mike Horse Mining Co., 120 Mont. 1, 180 P.2d 252 (1947). But when the defendant pleads self-defense, he

usually may show plaintiff's reputation for turbulence if he proves it was known to him. Feliciano, supra; Annot., supra, at 728–729; cf. Commonwealth v. Stewart, 483 Pa. 176, 394 A.2d 968 (1978) (evidence of a single previous violent act of deceased's admissible to show homicide defendant's fear). The rationale is that the evidence then shows defendant's reasonable apprehension, and therefore is not used to prove that plaintiff acted in conformity with the character trait. Of course, this is also not an instance of the defendant's introducing evidence of his own good character. Likewise, since the exceptions described in § 190 supra apply in civil as well as criminal cases, evidence of defendant's bad character may be used to show malice to justify punitive damages. Finally, when there is a dispute as to who committed the first act of aggression, most courts, regardless of their alignment on the general question of defendant's use of good character evidence, seem to admit evidence of the good or bad character of both parties for peaceableness as shedding light on their probable acts. Cain v. Skillin, 219 Ala. 228, 121 So.2d 521 (1929); Feliciano, supra; Carrick v. McFadden, 216 Kan. 683, 533 P.2d 1249 (1975); Linkhart v. Savely, 190 Or. 484, 227 P.2d 187 (1951). But see Sims v. Sowle, 238 Or. 329, 395 P.2d 133 (1964). This result cannot be justified by saying that character here is "in issue." E.g., Bugg v. Brown, 251 Md. 99, 246 A.2d 235 (1968). The issue is clearly conduct on a particular occasion, and nothing more. The candid recognition that there is a special need beyond that in most cases of charges of crime in civil actions to know the dispositions of the parties seems called for.

§ 193

1. See generally 1 Wigmore, Evidence §§ 62, 63 (3d ed. 1940); Slough, Relevancy Unraveled, 5 Kan.L.Rev. 404 at 440 (1957); 40 Am.Jur.2d Homicide §§ 301–309; 40 C.J.S. Homicide § 272; Dec.Dig. Homicide ⟂188; Annot., 1 A.L.R.3d 571 (assault or homicide). It has been said that the common law (and Rule 404(a)(2)) permits one accused of any crime to prove that the vic-

ate evidence [2] of the victim's character for turbulence and violence.[3] In response, the prosecution may adduce evidence that the victim was a characteristically peaceful person.[4]

Federal and Revised Uniform Evidence Rule (1974) 404(a)(2) addresses such situations. It speaks to "pertinent" [5] character traits of the victims of crimes generally and specifically to the trait of nonviolence in homicide cases. It exempts from the usual rule of exclusion

> Evidence of a pertinent trait of character of the victim of the crime offered by the accused, or by the prosecution to rebut the same, or evidence of the character trait of peacefulness of the victim offered by the prosecution in homicide case to rebut evidence that the defendant was the first aggressor.

The fact that the character of the *victim* is being proved renders inapposite the usual concern over the untoward impact of evidence of the defendant's poor character on the jury's assessment of the case against him. There is, however, a risk of a different

form of prejudice. Learning of the victim's bad character could lead the jury to think that the victim merely "got what he deserved" and to acquit for that reason. Nevertheless, at least in murder and perhaps in battery cases as well, when the identity of the first aggressor is really in doubt, the probative value of the evidence ordinarily justifies taking this risk.

In some jurisdictions the fact that the defendant claims that he killed the victim to defend himself from attack may not trigger, in itself, the prosecution's power to introduce rebuttal evidence of the victim's non-violent nature. By one view, such counterproof is allowed only when the accused opens the door specifically by evidence of the victim's bad character for belligerence.[6] The federal rule quoted above clearly follows the contrary view in homicide cases. Since a dead victim cannot attest to his peaceable behavior during the fatal encounter, the last clause of Rule 404(a)(2) provides that whenever the accused claims self-defense and offers *any* type of evidence that

---

tim's character was such that acting in accordance with it would have diminished or cancelled the culpability of the defendant. Uviller, Evidence of Character to Prove Conduct, 130 U.Pa.L.Rev. 845, 856 (1982) ("Thus (theoretically, at least) a defendant accused of bribing a public official might show that the official in question had exhibited the trait of greed or abuse of power in order to advance a defense of extortion. Perhaps a person accused of 'joyriding' might be able to prove the owner's characteristic trait of generosity to support his claim that he was operating the car with the permission of the owner"). However, the restrictions of Rule 403 are not to be overlooked. See § 185 supra.

2. Evidence of past acts of violence is not a permissible mode of proof. Government of Virgin Islands v. Carino, 631 F.2d 226, 229 (3d Cir. 1980) (assault with intent to commit mayhem); supra § 186.

3. United States v. Greschner, 647 F.2d 740, 742 (7th Cir. 1981) (evidence of prior stabbing admissible under Fed.R.Evid. 404(a) as "evidence of pertinent character trait of a victim," but Rule 405 limitation on mode of proof of character ignored); State v. Wilson, 235 Iowa 538, 17 N.W.2d 138 (1945); Freeman v. State, 204 So.2d 842 (Miss.1967); Annot., A.L.R.3d 571, at 601. When the accused proves that he knew of the deceased's reputation for violence, he may give evidence of that reputation to show his reasonable apprehension of immediate danger. Smith v. United States, 161 U.S. 85, 88 (1896); 2 Wigmore, Evidence § 246 (Chadbourn rev. 1979); Annot., 1 A.L.R.3d 571, 576. Used for this

purpose, the evidence does not transgress the policy against employing character evidence to show conduct. Government of Virgin Islands v. Carino, 631 F.2d 226, 229 (3d Cir. 1980) (prior conviction for manslaughter admissible pursuant to Fed.R.Evid. 404(b) to "demonstrate the fear" of defendant); cf. supra § 192, n. 5. A minority view allows evidence of the victim's character only for this purpose, and not to show that the victim was the first aggressor. In these jurisdictions, the victim's reputation for aggression must be known to the defendant if the evidence is to be admissible. See 1 Wigmore, Evidence (3d ed. 1940), § 63; Uviller, Evidence of Character to Prove Conduct, 130 U.Pa.L.Rev. 845, 856 (1982).

4. State v. Brock, 56 N.M. 328, 244 P.2d 131 (1952). It is generally agreed that this evidence does not belong in the prosecution's main case. See, e.g., State v. Hicks, 133 Ariz. 64, 649 P.2d 267, 271 (1982); 40 Am. Jur.2d Homicide § 308.

5. See supra § 191.

6. People v. Hoffman, 195 Cal. 295, 311, 232 P. 974, 980 (1925); Annot., supra n. 1, at 473–479. This has the advantage to the accused of permitting him to give evidence of self-defense and still keep out altogether this "collateral" evidence of character, in keeping with the general tradition against using evidence of character to show conduct. It restricts the opportunity for the appeal to pity and vengeance implicit in the praise of the character of the deceased. See supra § 191.

the deceased was the first aggressor, the government may reply with evidence of the peaceable character of the deceased.[7]

A similar exception to the general rule against the use of character to prove conduct has pertained to the defense of consent in sexual assault cases. In the past, the courts generally admitted evidence of the victim's character for chastity,[8] although there were diverging lines of authority on whether the proof could be by specific instances [9] and on whether the prosecution could put evidence of chastity in its case in chief.[10]

Recently, however, nearly all jurisdictions have enacted "rape shield" laws.[11] The reforms range from barring all evidence of the victim's character for chastity to merely requiring a preliminary hearing to screen out inadmissible evidence on the issue. Federal Rule of Evidence 412 lies between these extremes.[12] Reversing the traditional preference for proof of character by reputation,[13] it bars reputation and opinion evidence of the victim's past sexual conduct, but permits evidence of specific incidents if certain substantive and procedural conditions are met.[14] These laws have withstood constitutional at-

---

7. 1 Wigmore, Evidence, § 63 n. 21 (3d ed. 1940) argued for this approach. It had substantial judicial support. E.g., Sweazy v. State, 210 Ind. 674, 5 N.E.2d 511 (1937); State v. Holbrook, 98 Or. 43, 192 P. 640 (1920). A few decisions achieved the same effect by more dubious reasoning. E.g., State v. Rutledge, 243 Iowa 179, 47 N.W.2d 251 (1951); State v. Brock, 56 N.M. 328, 338, 244 P.2d 131 (1952).

8. Gish v. Wisner, 288 F. 562 (5th Cir. 1923) (observing in civil case that "in a prosecution or suit for an assault with intent to commit rape, the rule is established by the great weight of authority that the general reputation for chastity of the complaining witness, who claims to be the victim, is material as bearing upon the vital question of her consent or nonconsent"); State v. Wood, 59 Ariz. 48, 122 P.2d 416 (1942), overruled, State ex rel. Pope v. Superior Court, 113 Ariz. 22, 545 P.2d 946 (1976); Annot., 94 A.L.R.3d 364 (complainant's prior sexual conduct in forcible rape cases), 90 A.L.R.3d 1300 (prior sexual conduct or general reputation for unchastity in statutory rape case); cf. 97 A.L.R. 3d 967 (incest victim's prior sexual acts with other persons); 59 A.L.R.3d 659 (rebutting mother's claim of chastity in paternity proceedings); cf. Kearse v. State, 88 S.W. 363, 364 (Tex.Cr.App.1905) (defense witness's testimony that he had kissed prosecutrix properly excluded because there was no showing that defendant "was cognizant of such improper conduct" and "[f]urthermore, the fact that prosecutrix may have kissed [the] witness . . . would be no argument that she would kiss appellant").

9. Compare State v. Wood, 59 Ariz. 48, 122 P.2d 416 (1942) (specific instance as well as reputation) with State v. Yowell, 513 S.W.2d 397 (Mo.1974) (reputation only).

10. Compare People v. Stephens, 18 Ill.App.3d 971, 310 N.E.2d 824 (1974) (allowed in state's case on theory that nonconsent is an element of that case) with Roper v. State, 375 S.W.2d 454 (Tex.Cr.App.1964) (issue of consent is not raised by not-guilty plea alone). See Annot., 35 A.L.R.3d 1452.

11. See generally, M. Graham, Handbook of Federal Evidence § 406 (1981); Saltzburg & Redden, Federal Rules of Evidence Manual 220–228 (3d ed. 1982) (identifying problems with Fed.R.Evid. 412); Berger, Man's

Trial, Woman's Tribulation, 77 Colum.L.Rev. 1 (1977); Letwin, "Unchaste Character," Ideology, and the California Rape Evidence Laws, 54 S.Cal.L.Rev. 35–89 (1980); Ordover, Admissibility of Patterns of Similar Sexual Conduct: The Unlamented Death of Character for Chastity, 63 Cornell L.Rev. 90 (1977); Tanford & Bocchino, Rape Victim Shield Laws and the Sixth Amendment, 128 U.Pa.L.Rev. 544 (1980); Annot., 95 A.L.R.3d 1181 (admissibility of complainant's reputation for unchastity).

12. Congress added Rule 412 by enacting the Privacy Protection for Rape Victims Act of 1978, Pub.L.No. 95–540, 92 Stat. 2046. The relatively sparse legislative history is set out in M. Graham, Handbook of Federal Evidence 279–283 (1981). For applications of the rule to bar defense evidence about the victim's prior sexual conduct, see Doe v. United States, 666 F.2d 43 (4th Cir. 1981) (upholding the Rule against a constitutional attack); Bell v. Harrison, 670 F.2d 656 (6th Cir. 1982); United States v. Holy Bear, 624 F.2d 853 (8th Cir. 1980); United States v. Nez, 661 F.2d 1203 (10th Cir. 1981). The Rule has also been invoked to limit pretrial inquiries along these lines. See Government of Virgin Islands v. Scuito, 623 F.2d 869 (3d Cir. 1980) (psychiatric examination denied); cf. Ghent, Victim Testimony in Sex Crimes Prosecutions: An Analysis of the Rape Shield Provision and the Use of Deposition Testimony under the Criminal Sexual Conduct Statute, 34 S.Car.L. Rev. 583 (1982).

13. See supra § 186.

14. The evidence may, of course, be admitted if the constitution mandates it. Rule 412(b)(1). In exceptional cases, the due process or confrontation clauses may require admission. But see Uviller, Evidence of Character to Prove Conduct, 130 U.Pa.L.Rev. 845, 859 n. 52 (1982). In any event, if the evidence pertains to past sexual behavior of the victim with an accused who claims consent, it may be admitted on that issue. Rule 412(b)(2)(B). Finally, if the evidence involves acts of the victim with other persons, the defendant may use it to prove that someone else was "the source of semen or injury." Rule 412(b)(2)(A). Special hearing procedures, with notice to the victim, designed to ensure, in addition, that "the evidence which the accused seeks to offer is relevant and that the probative value of such

tacks.[15] They reflect the judgment, evident also in the case law emerging during the period preceding their enactment,[16] that most evidence about chastity has far too little probative value on the issue of consent to justify extensive inquiry into the victim's sexual history.

 WESTLAW REFERENCES

topic(37 203) /p character reputation /5 evidence /p agress! violen! turbulen!

victim* /p character reputation /5 evidence /p agress! violen! turbulen!

synopsis,digest("rape shield")

headnote(412 /p sex! chas! unchas! promiscu!)

---

§ 194. Evidence of Character to Impeach a Witness

The familiar practice of impeaching a witness by producing evidence of his bad character for veracity amounts to using a character trait to prove that a witness is testifying falsely. As such, it constitutes a true exception to the policy against using evidence of character solely to show conduct. The chapter on impeachment discusses the scope of this exception.[1]

outweighs the danger of unfair prejudice" and that the questioning is appropriately limited. See Rule 412(c).

15. See Doe v. United States, 666 F.2d 43, 47–48 (4th Cir. 1981) (collecting state cases in note 9); Commonwealth v. Joyce, 382 Mass. 222, 415 N.E.2d 181 (1981); Annot., 1 A.L.R.4th 283 (constitutionality of rape shield laws).

16. United States v. Driver, 581 F.2d 80 (4th Cir. 1978), cert. denied 439 U.S. 987; United States v. Kasto, 584 F.2d 268, 271–272 (8th Cir. 1978), cert. denied 440 U.S. 930, overruling Packineau v. United States, 202 F.2d 681 (8th Cir. 1953) (involvement with persons other than the defendant); State ex rel. Pope v. Superior Court, 113 Ariz. 22, 545 P.2d 946 (1976), overruling State v. Wood, 59 Ariz. 48, 122 P.2d 416 (1942); McLean v. United States, 377 A.2d 74 (D.C.App.1977).

§ 194

1. See supra Ch. 5.

§ 195

1. See generally Green, Relevancy and Its Limits, 1969 Ariz.St.L.J. (Law & Soc.Ord.) 533, 549–51; Falknor, "Customary" Negligence, 12 Wash.L.Rev. 35 (1937); Lewan, Rationale of Habit Evidence, 16 Syracuse L.Rev. 39 (1964); 29 Am.Jur.2d Evidence §§ 303, 316–317; Notes, 25 B.U.L.Rev. 64 (1945), 33 B.U.L.Rev.

 WESTLAW REFERENCES

synopsis,digest(evidence /5 character reputation /p impeach! /p witness!)

---

§ 195. Habit and Custom as Evidence of Conduct on a Particular Occasion

Although the courts frown on evidence of a person's traits of character when introduced to prove how he acted on a given occasion, they are more receptive to evidence of his habits or of the customary behavior of organizations.[1] To understand this difference, one must appreciate the distinction between habit and character The two are easily confused. People sometimes speak of a habit for care, a habit for promptness, or a habit of forgetfulness. They may say that an individual has a bad habit of stealing or lying. Evidence of these "habits" would be identical to the kind of evidence that is the target of the general rule against character evidence.[2] Character is a generalized description of a person's disposition, or of the disposition in respect to a general trait, such as honesty, temperance or peacefulness.[3] Habit, in the present context, is more

205 (1953); Annot., 53 A.L.R.Fed. 703 (Rule 406), 10 A.L.R.4th 1243 (custom or habit of physician sued for malpractice), 100 A.L.R.3d 569 (sexual assault), 91 A.L.R.3d 718 (civil assault), 59 A.L.R.3d 1327 (habits of notary public), 29 A.L.R.3d 791 (auto accidents), 28 A.L.R.3d 1293 (pedestrian), 46 A.L.R.2d 103 (intemperance).

2. Sometimes the cases lose sight of this. E.g., United States v. Luttrell, 612 F.2d 396 (8th Cir.1980) ("habit" of not filing tax returns). The length of time separating each instance of a supposedly habitual practice is a factor in identifying a habit. This consideration also weighs against the result in *Luttrell*.

3. United States v. Sampol, 636 F.2d 621, 656 n. 21 (D.C.Cir.1980) (defense theory that cross-examination of government witness as to his role in other assassinations was under rule allowing evidence of habit "patently without merit"); Levin v. United States, 338 F.2d 265 (D.C.Cir.1964), cert. denied 379 U.S. 999 (1965) (acting in conformity with religious beliefs). The prohibition against "character" evidence arises in part because of the prejudicial nature of the traits that the parties commonly seek to expose. In deciding which personal characteristics qualify as traits of character, this consideration may be important. For more on the definition of character, see 22 Wright & Graham, Fed-

specific. It denotes one's regular response to a repeated situation.[4] If we speak of a character for care, we think of the person's tendency to act prudently in all the varying situations of life—in business, at home, in handling automobiles and in walking across the street. A habit, on the other hand, is the person's regular practice of responding to a particular kind of situation with a specific type of conduct.[5] Thus, a person may be in the habit of bounding down a certain stairway two or three steps at a time, of patronizing a particular pub after each day's work, or of driving his automobile without using a

seatbelt. The doing of the habitual act may become semi-automatic, as with a driver who invariably signals before changing lanes.[6]

Evidence of habits that come within this definition has greater probative value than does evidence of general traits of character.[7] Furthermore, the potential for prejudice is substantially less. By and large, the detailed patterns of situation-specific behavior that constitute habits are unlikely to provoke such sympathy or antipathy as would distort the process of evaluating the evidence.[8]

eral Practice and Procedure § 5233; Kuhns, supra § 189 n. 2.

4. United States v. Holman, 680 F.2d 1340 (11th Cir. 1982) (one previous attempt to convince skipper of fishing vessel to smuggle marijuana could not show a habit of coercing owners of boats into smuggling drugs); Meyer v. United States, 464 F.Supp. 317, 321 (D.Colo. 1979) ("regular response to a repeated situation"), affirmed 638 F.2d 155 (10th Cir.1980). Although it overstates the point (see n. 18 infra), at least one text has said that "the distinction is between Pavlov and Freud." 22 Wright & Graham, Federal Practice and Procedure § 5233 at 354. It has also been noted that "one could reasonably testify to having observed habitual behavior, but character is almost always a matter of opinion." Id.

5. Model Code of Evidence Rule 307(1) (1942) defined habit in this way: "Habit means a course of behavior of a person regularly repeated in like circumstances. Custom means a course of behavior of a group of persons regularly repeated in like circumstances."

6. For more examples, see Howard v. Capital Transit Co., 97 F.Supp. 578 (D.D.C.1951), affirmed 196 F.2d 593 (D.C.Cir.1952) (decedent's habit of using defendant's buses to return from work); Whittemore v. Lockheed Aircraft Corp., 65 Cal.App.2d 737, 151 P.2d 670 (1944) (practice of pilot to occupy left-hand seat when he would fly the plane); Fisette v. Boston & Maine Railroad, 98 N.H. 136, 96 A.2d 303 (1953) (looking and listening at railroad crossing); Halloran v. Virginia Chemicals, 41 N.Y.2d 386, 393 N.Y.S.2d 341, 361 N.E.2d 991 (1977) (using immersion coil in performing particular task); Glatt v. Feist, 156 N.W.2d 819 (N.D.1968) (crossing street outside crosswalk at particular place); Bown v. City of Tacoma, 175 Wash. 414, 27 P.2d 711 (1933) (riding on cars in alley where accident occurred); French v. Sorano, 74 Wis.2d 460, 247 N.W.2d 182 (1976) (hiding money in car).

7. Character may be thought of as the sum of one's habits, although doubtless it is more than this. Unquestionably, the uniformity of one's response to habit is far greater than the consistency with which one's conduct conforms to character or disposition. Even though character comes in only exceptionally as evi-

dence of an act, surely any sensible person in investigating whether a given individual did a particular act would be greatly helped in his inquiry by evidence as to whether that individual was in the habit of doing it.

8. Even if habit evidence, strictly defined, ordinarily is unlikely to be prejudicial in the sense of distorting the evaluative process, it may pose "estimation" problems. See Lempert & Saltzburg, A Modern Approach to Evidence 249–250 (2d ed. 1983) (concluding that these problems are not unduly severe). For example, "[a] murderer, in the habit of taking the six o'clock bus home from work, may kill someone at six-fifteen, counting on evidence of habit to establish an alibi." Id. at 249. Surely, this is a concern that underlies the refusal of the court in Levin v. United States, 338 F.2d 265 (D.C.Cir.1964), cert. denied 379 U.S. 999 (1966), to accept testimony as to the religious "habits" of the accused, offered to prove that he was at home observing the Sabbath rather than obtaining money through larceny by trick. However, religiously motivated practices, though volitional, can be undertaken with sufficient regularity to rise to the level of habits. Mere evidence of religious belief, however, would not show this; rather, it would indicate a disposition toward religious behavior—a character trait. But since a jury ordinarily can be trusted to appreciate the degree to which a criminal motive will lead one to deviate from habit, the suggestion in Levin that religious practices cannot be habits, id. at 272, seems unjustified. If regularly observed religious practices are not admissible as habit, it must be because the religious overtones of the habit would tempt the jury to misapply the law—a proposition whose truth is hardly obvious.

Intemperance seems one of the more potentially prejudicial habits. Partly, the problem stems from the fact that the term may denote a general disposition for excessive drinking (a trait) or a practice of drinking a certain number of glasses of whiskey every night at home (a habit). Thus, the probative force of what is loosely called the habit of intemperance to prove drunkenness on a particular occasion depends on the regularity and details of the characteristic behavior. This may help explain in part the conflicting results when evidence of "habitual intemperance" is brought forward. For various cases, see Louisell & Mueller, supra § 184, n. 1,

As a result, many jurisdictions accept the proposition that evidence of habit may be admissible to show an act.[9] These courts only reject the evidence if the putative habit is not sufficiently regular or uniform,[10] or the circumstances are not sufficiently similar to outweigh the dangers of prejudice, distraction and time-consumption.[11] The Federal,[12] Revised Uniform,[13] and Model [14] Rules all follow this pattern.

§ 157 at 217–18 n. 4; Annot., 46 A.L.R.2d 103 (motor vehicle accidents). In any event, because of the connotations of heavy drinking, the judge must be alert to the possibility of unfair prejudice that proof of a "habit of being drunk" may bring. See State v. Wadsworth, 210 So.2d 4 (Fla.1968) (imposing corroboration requirement); 1 Wigmore, Evidence § 96 (3d ed. 1940). Note, however, that the "habit" of sobriety may well point to unvarying abstention. It seems highly probative of sobriety on a particular occasion, and it has far less potential for prejudice. See Annot., 46 A.L.R.2d 103.

9. See Meyer v. United States, 638 F.2d 155 (10th Cir.1980) (dentist's testimony that it was his custom and habit to warn patients of risks of surgery to remove molars was adequate to support trial court's finding that dentist warned patient even though she denied being warned and the dentist had no specific recollection of warning her); cases cited supra n. 6.

10. This is tantamount to saying that there is not a sufficient indication of the existence of a habit. See, e.g. Reyes v. Missouri Pacific Railroad Co., 589 F.2d 791, 795 (5th Cir.1979) (four prior convictions for public intoxication over a 3.5 year period not sufficiently regular to rise to the level of habit evidence).

11. Levin v. United States, 338 F.2d 265 (D.C.Cir. 1965), cert. denied 379 U.S. 999 (1966).

12. Fed. and Rev.Unif.R.Evid. (1974) 406 provides:

Evidence of the habit of a person or of the routine practice of an organization, whether corroborated or not and regardless of the presence of eyewitnesses, is relevant to prove that the conduct was in conformity with the habit or routine practice.

13. Rev.Unif.R.Evid. (1974) 406 also includes a provision that Congress deleted from the proposed federal rules:

Habit or routine practice may be proved by testimony in the form of an opinion or by specific instances of conduct sufficient in number to warrant a finding that the habit existed or that the practice was routine.

The House Committee on the Judiciary deleted the subdivision, as stated in the Committee Report, "believing that the method of proof of habit and routine practice should be left to the courts to deal with on a case-by-case basis." House Comm. on Judiciary, Fed. Rules of Evidence, H.R.Rep. No. 650, 93d Cong., 1st Sess., p. 5 (1973).

A few state courts, however, exclude evidence of habit altogether.[15] Others admit it only if there are no eyewitnesses to testify about the events that are said to have triggered the habitual behavior.[16]

Even the jurisdictions that are reluctant to accept evidence of personal habits are willing to allow evidence of the "custom" of a business organization, if reasonably regular and uniform.[17] This may be because there is

14. Model Code of Evidence Rule 307(2) (1942):

Evidence of a habit of a person is admissible as tending to prove that his behavior on a specified occasion conformed to the habit. Evidence of a custom of a group of persons is admissible as tending to prove that their behavior on a specified occasion conformed to the custom.

15. See, e.g., Commonwealth v. Nagle, 157 Mass. 554, 32 N.E. 861 (1893); Fenton v. Aleshire, 238 Or. 24, 393 P.2d 217 (1964); Note, 33 B.U.L.Rev. 205 (1953); Annot., 28 A.L.R.3d 1293.

16. See, e.g., Missouri-Kansas-Texas Railroad Co. v. McFerrin, 156 Tex. 69, 291 S.W.2d 931, 941–942 (1956); Annot., 28 A.L.R.3d 1293; cf. supra § 189 (minority exception to rule excluding character evidence on issue of particular negligent conduct when there are no eyewitnesses).

The no-eyewitness rule seems unwise. The need for evidence of a true habit is no less because the eyewitnesses disagree or for some other reason (such as the very absence of eyewitnesses), the issue of fact is in doubt. Likewise, the prejudice of the evidence, if any, is no less when eyewitnesses are unavailable. Cereste v. New York, New Hampshire & H. R.R. Co., 231 F.2d 50, 53 (2d Cir.1956), cert. denied 351 U.S. 951.

17. Hazelwood School District v. United States, 433 U.S. 299, 316 n. 15 (1977) (pre-Title VII discrimination in hiring teachers might "support the inference that such discrimination continued" after law became effective); United States v. Oddo, 314 F.2d 115 (2d Cir.1963), cert. denied 375 U.S. 833 (customary practices of Immigration and Naturalization Service); Commonwealth v. Porter, 659 F.2d 306, 320 (3d Cir.1981), cert. denied 102 S.Ct. 3509 (incidents of a policeman's unlawful arrests, searches, assaults and harassments "admissible under Rule 406 to show a pattern or routine practice of a defendant or organization"); Spartan Grain & Mill Co. v. Ayers, 517 F.2d 214, 219 (5th Cir.1975) (evidence of how a firm handled eggs generally erroneously excluded where the firm was seeking damages for failure of eggs to hatch because of improper feed sold to it); United States v. Callahan, 551 F.2d 733 (6th Cir.1977) (error to exclude testimony that the routine of a construction company was to pay off local unions for the sake of expediency rather than out of fear of injury); Eaton v. Bass, 214 F.2d 896 (6th Cir.1954) (custom of inspecting trucks); Russell v. Pitts, 105 Ga.App. 147, 123 S.E.2d 708 (1961) (customary sterilization procedures in medical center); Commonwealth v. Torrealba, 316 Mass. 24, 54 N.E.2d 939 (1944) (custom of store to

no confusion between character traits and business practices, as there is between character and habit, or it may reflect the belief that the need for regularity in business and the organizational sanctions which may exist when employees deviate from the established procedures give extra guarantees that the questioned activity followed the usual custom.[18] Thus, evidence that a letter was written and signed in the course of business and put in the regular place for mailing usually will be admitted to prove that it was mailed.[19]

The existence of the personal habit or the business custom may be established by a knowledgeable witness's testimony that there was such a habit or practice.[20] Evidence of specific instances may also be used.[21] Naturally, there must be enough instances to permit the finding of a habit,[22] and there are other obvious limitations.[23]

WESTLAW REFERENCES

digest(evidence /3 habit*)
headnote(evidence /5 business! organization*
   corporation* /5 custom)

---

give sales slip with each purchase received as evidence that goods found in defendant's possession, with no record of sale, were stolen); Lundquist v. Jennison, 66 Mont. 516, 214 P. 67 (1923) (in action for breach of warranty of seed wheat when defendant denied selling seed wheat, evidence that defendant was engaged in business of selling seed wheat generally was admissible to show sale to plaintiff); Buxton v. Langan, 90 N.H. 13, 3 A.2d 647 (1939) (rule or practice of defendant's shop for employees to test brakes before renting out car); cases cited 1 Wigmore, Evidence § 93 (3d ed. 1940); Dec.Dig. Evidence ⟜139.

In a large number of cases, however, evidence of business routine standing alone has been held *insufficient* to prove the completion of an act. Corroboration that the routine was followed was required. Leasing Associates v. Slaughter & Son, 450 F.2d 174 (8th Cir. 1971) (stating that the majority rule required corroboration); United States v. Oddo, supra; and see infra n. 19. Following what appears to be the more reasonable view, see Mohr v. Universal C.I.T. Credit Corp., 216 Md. 197, 140 A.2d 49 (1958); Slough, Relevancy Unraveled, 5 Kan.L.Rev. 404, 409, 450–451 (1957), Federal and Revised Uniform Evid. Rule (1974) 406 expressly rejects the corroboration requirement. See supra nn. 11–12.

18.　Contrary to what the court may have implied in Levin v. United States, 338 F.2d 265 (D.C.Cir.1964), cert. denied 379 U.S. 999, the fact that an individual habit is not "semi-automatic," but involves an exercise of the will, should not preclude evidence of the habitual behavior. See, e.g., United States v. Seelig, 622 F.2d 207 (6th Cir.1980) cert. denied 449 U.S. 869; supra n. 7 (error to exclude expert testimony "as to the custom of pharmacists regarding the sales of over-the-counter exempt drugs").

19.　United States v. Scott, 668 F.2d 384, 388 (8th Cir.1981); United States v. Gomez, 636 F.2d 295, 297 (10th Cir.1981); United States v. Ziperstein, 601 F.2d 281, 295 (7th Cir.1979), cert. denied 444 U.S. 1031. Some cases say that the evidence, while admissible, is not sufficient, in that the employee who mailed the

item must testify (although he may rely on the custom) or that some other evidence that the custom was followed must be produced. See Note, 47 Mich.L.Rev. 420 (1948); Annot., 86 A.L.R. 541; 31A C.J.S. Evidence § 136(c). The requirement of corroboration is dying away. See United States v. Leathers, 135 F.2d 507, 510 (2d Cir.1943); United States v. Matzker, 473 F.2d 408, 411 (8th Cir.1973); supra n. 17.

20.　Typically, this is the method employed. See, e.g., 1 Wigmore, Evidence, § 93 (3d ed. 1940); 2 id. § 375 (Chadbourn rev. 1979); Rev.Unif.R.Evid. 406 (1974), supra n. 13.

21.　Petricevich v. Salmon River Canal Co., 92 Idaho 865, 452 P.2d 362 (1969) (dictum); Reagan v. Manchester Street Railway Co., 72 N.H. 298, 56 A. 314 (1903); 2 Wigmore, Evidence §§ 375–376 (Chadbourn rev. 1979); Rev. Uniform R.Evid. (1974) 406, supra nn. 12, 13. But there is a thin line between particular instances to prove habit or custom and particular instances to show character for care. See, e.g., Frase v. Henry, 444 F.2d 1228, 1232 (10th Cir.1971) (applying Kansas law); supra § 189.

22.　See, e.g., Strauss v. Douglas Aircraft Co., 404 F.2d 1152, 1158 (2d Cir.1969); Wilson v. Volkswagen of America, 561 F.2d 494, 511–512 (4th Cir.1977), cert. denied 434 U.S. 1020; Lewan, supra note 1; Model Code of Evidence Rule 307(3) ("many instances"); supra n. 9.

23.　The circumstances under which the habit or custom is followed must be present. Petricevich v. Salmon River Canal Co., 92 Idaho 865, 452 P.2d 362 (1969). As always, there are the limitations for cumulativeness, remoteness, unnecessary inflammatory quality, and so on. See supra § 185. Thus, citing illustrations to the Model Code of Evidence Rule 307, the Federal Advisory Committee mentions the possibility of admitting testimony by W that on numerous occasions he had been with X when X crossed a railroad track and that on each occasion X had first stopped and looked in both directions, but that offers of ten witnesses, each testifying to a different occasion, might be excluded in the discretion of the court. Note to Fed.R.Evid. 406(b).

Chapter 18
SIMILAR HAPPENINGS AND TRANSACTIONS

Table of Sections

§ 196. Other Claims, Suits or Defenses of a Party

To what extent should a party be permitted to demonstrate that his opponent has advanced similar claims or defenses against others in previous litigation?[1] Inescapably, two conflicting goals shape the rules of evidence in this area. Exposing fraudulent claims is important, but so is protecting innocent litigants from unfair prejudice. The easy cases are those in which one of these considerations clearly predominates. If the evidence reveals that a party has made previous, very similar claims and that these claims were fraudulent, then almost universally the evidence will be admissible[2] despite the dangers of distraction and time-consumption with regard to the quality of these other claims,[3] and despite the general prohibition on using evidence of bad character solely to show conduct on a given occasion.[4] At the other pole, if the evidence is merely that the plaintiff is a chronic litigant with re-

---

§ 196

1. See generally 1 Louisell & Mueller, Federal Evidence § 99 (1977); 3A J. Wigmore, Evidence §§ 963, 981 (Chadbourn rev. 1970); 22 Wright & Graham, Federal Procedure and Practice § 5170; Annot., 69 A.L.R.2d 593 (cross-examination of plaintiff in personal injury action); Fed.R.Evid. 401–405; Rev.Unif.R.Evid. 401–405 (1974); Dec.Dig. Evidence ⟐129–131, 141. This section examines evidence of other claims offered to cast doubt on the merits of the claim at bar. The same evidence, when offered to show that the claimant's injury existed prior to the conduct of which he now complains, raises other issues. See, e.g., Callihan v. Burlington Northern Inc., ___ Mont. ___, 654 P.2d 972 (1982) (proper to exclude prior settlements that would show a preexisting condition where the condition's preexistence was conceded). For a discussion of evidence of other claims offered to show prior accidents or injuries for still other purposes, see infra § 200.

2. Smith v. State Farm Fire & Casualty Co., 633 F.2d 401, 402–404 (5th Cir. 1980) (holding, however, that in an action on a fire insurance policy the trial court did not abuse its discretion in excluding evidence of four other fires destroying dwellings belonging to the decedent even though there was evidence that the decedent had burned three of these buildings to collect insurance); Sessmer v. Commonwealth, 268 Ky. 127, 103 S.W.2d 647 (1936) (evidence of other unfounded claims admissible to show system and plan in disbarment proceeding for conspiring to blackmail by asserting fictitious claims).

3. Lowenthal v. Mortimer, 125 Cal.App.2d 636, 643, 270 P.2d 942, 945–946 (1954) ("To negative any inference of unreasonable contentiousness, plaintiffs would be entitled to attempt an adequate explanation").

4. See supra Ch. 17. Although this result may seem little different from the use of evidence of other frauds in an action for deceit (see infra § 197), in those cases admission is justified to show knowledge, intent,

578

spect to all sorts of claims, the courts consider the slight probative value overborne by the countervailing factors. This evidence they usually exclude.[5]

In between lie the harder cases. Suppose the evidence is that the party suing for an alleged loss, such as fire damage to his property or personal injury in a collision, has made many previous claims of similar losses. The evidence surely is relevant. The probability of so many similar accidents happening to the same person by chance alone can be vanishingly small.[6] Yet, rare events do happen. There will always be some people who suffer the slings and arrows of outrageous fortune.[7] In itself, this fact gives no indication of prejudice. Presumably, a ju-

---

plan or scheme, etc., rather than to imply that the allegations at bar are more likely to be true because the defendant has a deceitful nature.

5. Lowenthal v. Mortimer, 125 Cal.App.2d 636, 270 P.2d 942 (1954) (error to allow defendant in an automobile accident case to cross-examine plaintiffs about 15 other suits not involving personal injuries); Palmeri v. Manhattan Railway Co., 133 N.Y. 261, 30 N.E. 1001, 1002 (1892) (evidence that plaintiff was an "habitual litigant" properly excluded in suit for slander and false imprisonment). Many courts disapprove of references to unconnected litigation even when it involves prior claims of the same genre. See, e.g., Nourse v. Welsh, 23 A.D.2d 618, 257 N.Y.S.2d 96 (1965); Middleton v. Palmer, 601 S.W.2d 759, 762 (Tex.Civ.App.1980) (stating general rule); Knight v. Hasler, 24 Wis.2d 128, 128 N.W.2d 407, 410 (1964) (error to permit cross-examination of plaintiff about two prior personal injury claims).

6. Mintz v. Premier Cab Association, 127 F.2d 744, 745 (D.C.Cir. 1942) ("Negligent injury is not unusual, but it is unusual for one person, not engaged in hazardous activities, to suffer it repeatedly within a short period and at the hands of different persons"); cf. San Antonio Traction Co. v. Cox, 184 S.W. 722, 724 (Tex. Civ.App.1916) (holding that proof that plaintiff's relatives had made at least 17 different claims for injuries allegedly incurred alighting from defendant's streetcars was properly excluded because there was no evidence of plaintiff's involvement in the other claims or his participation in a conspiracy, but opining that "[w]e think it so highly improbable that all these claims could be honest ones, that a jury would be justified in inferring that fraud had been practiced with regard to some of them").

This logic is not without its problems. The simplest probability model of the situation posits that each negligently caused accident has the same fixed probability (p) of happening. It follows that the probability (P) of an unbroken series of n accidents is given by p^n. In other words, the probability of all the accidents depends on how many accidents there are (n) and how likely each such accident is to occur (p). Unless p is one, the value of probability P for the series approaches zero as n becomes large. This model commonly is illustrated by the process of tossing a coin. For example, with an evenly balanced coin, the probability P of obtaining two heads in a row is $(1/2)^2 = 1/4$, but the probability of ten heads in a row is only $(1/2)^{10} = 1/1024$.

This probabilistic argument is easy to misunderstand or misapply. If the model holds, the low probability that a long series of similar, negligently caused acci-

dents will happen to the same person does not lower the probability that a particular one (including the one in question) occurred. After all, the fact that the probability of the series of ten heads is only 1/1024 does not change the probability (1/2) for a head on a particular toss, and the fact that nine heads in a row have appeared does not make it less probable that the coin will come up a head on the tenth toss.

However, a small P-value may well suggest that the probability model described above does not fit the reality. Thus, to support the claimant's position that the last accident was bona fide, one could reason that the only defect in the model is that the value of the probability p for each accident should be higher. Nevertheless, especially with large numbers of accidents, this reasoning will not be persuasive.

A less circular conclusion that could be drawn from the small P-value is that the form of the model is wrong—that something other than a series of independent accidents caused by someone's else negligence has befallen the claimant. There are two possibilities. The plaintiff could be honest but accident-prone. See Barnes v. Norfolk Southern Railway Co., 333 F.2d 192, 197 (4th Cir. 1964) (proper to exclude company correspondence about employee's previous accidents when purpose was to show that "because Barnes had a history of prior accidents with the railroad, the probabilities were high that he was contributorily negligent on the day of the accident"); Nourse v. Welsh, 23 A.D.2d 618, 257 N.Y.S.2d 96, 97 (1965) (cross-examination about prior accidents improperly "pursued for the obvious purpose of planting in the minds of the jurors that appellant was 'accident prone' "). The difficulty with this reasoning is that it runs squarely up against the bar to character evidence as proof of conduct on a particular occasion. Id. supra Ch. 17.

The remaining possibility is that plaintiff is fraudulently disposed or at least "claim-minded." But using this inference to conclude anything about the claim in issue also violates the character rule. Consequently, if an abnormal incidence of claims is an acceptable indication that the present one lacks merit, a forthright acknowledgement that this constitutes a true exception to the rule against using character to prove conduct seems called for.

7. Applying the probability model of note 6 to a large collection of identical individuals, it can be shown that the probability that at least one person will suffer *any* finite number of negligently caused accidents approaches one. If we keep tossing enough coins ten times each, sooner or later we will discover one that comes up heads all ten times.

ry can come to a reasonable judgment as to the relative likelihood of the alternatives.[8] Nevertheless, there is a form of prejudice inherent in this situation. The jury may disapprove of a person precisely because he is litigious.[9] It would seem that the judge, balancing probative value against prejudice, should admit the evidence only if the probability of coincidence seems negligible [10] or if the proponent has distinct evidence of fraud.[11]

So far, we have discussed evidence of a party's other claims introduced to raise a question about the instant claim or suit. Evidence of a witness' past accusations or de-

fenses introduced to attack the veracity of that witness presents comparable problems. In these situations, a litigant might seek to prove that the other accusations have been false as circumstantial evidence that the testimony just delivered is also false. Although this is a species of character evidence to show conduct, it usually will be admissible.[12] More problematically, the very fact that the witness repeatedly accuses many others of the same kind of behavior may seem too extraordinary to be explained as a mere coincidence.[13] The logic and issues here are perfectly analogous to those already addressed with regard to the filing

---

8. Mintz v. Premier Cab Association, 127 F.2d 744, 745 (D.C.Cir. 1942) ("It was for the jury to decide from all the evidence, and from its observation of appellant on the stand, whether she was merely unlucky or was 'claim-minded' ").

9. Lowenthal v. Mortimer, 125 Cal.App.2d 636, 643, 270 P.2d 942, 945–946 (1954) (commenting that "litigiousness, in the eyes of most people, reflects . . . upon character," and alluding to "the hostility ordinarily felt against one who constantly requires services of a court of law for the adjustment of life's problems"). Any other plausible inference seems also to raise a problem of prejudice. See supra n. 6.

10. The likelihood of repeated, substantially identical claims depends on the number of claims and the probability of each accident. See n. 6 supra. The degree of similarity among the claims is also important, inasmuch as a series of disparate but bona fide claims seems more likely than a string of very similar ones. Bunion v. Allstate Insurance Co., 502 F.Supp. 340, 342 (E.D.Pa.1980) (no showing of "any similarity among the accidents"); Testa v. Moore-McCormack Lines, 229 F.Supp. 154, 159 (S.D.N.Y.1964) (longshoreman's previous, very similar claim for slipping on grease inadmissible, since there was only one such prior claim).

A dictum in Hinkle v. Hampton, 388 F.2d 141, 144 (10th Cir. 1968), seems to go further. It would exclude all "evidence of other or collateral transactions." The courts in the District of Columbia go to the other extreme. They have said that whenever there have been other claims, it is up to the jury to decide whether the claimant is "unlucky or claim-minded." Mintz v. Premier Cab Association, 127 F.2d 744, 745 (D.C.Cir. 1942) (cross-examination of plaintiff about two prior personal injury claims); Manes v. Dowling, 375 A.2d 221, 223 (D.C.App.1977) (evidence of four subsequent personal injury claims admissible even though only one was of another parking lot accident); Evans v. Greyhound Corp., 200 A.2d 194, 196 (D.C.App.1964) (proper to cross-examine plaintiff suing for a fall while a passenger aboard a bus about two previous settled claims).

11. Hammann v. Hartford Accident & Indemnity Co., 620 F.2d 588, 589 (6th Cir. 1980) (upholding admis-

sion of evidence of four prior fires in insurance recovery action as bearing on motive and intent); Bunion v. Allstate Insurance Co., 502 F.Supp. 340, 342 (E.D.Pa. 1980). If the probability of coincidence is not negligible, so that extrinsic evidence of fault seems called for, that evidence should pertain to the prior claims. See Garcia v. Aetna Casualty & Surety Co., 657 F.2d 652, 654–655 (5th Cir. 1981) (error to allow cross-examination about previous fire that destroyed an insured building without any proof that the insured claimants' caused the earlier fire).

12. People v. Mascarenas, 21 Cal.App.3d 660, 98 Cal.Rptr. 728, 734 (1971) (error to exclude testimony about earlier fabricated charge of selling drugs offered to impeach 16 year old police informant who aspired to becoming a federal narcotics agent); Louisiana v. Cappo, 345 So.2d 443, 445 (La.1977) (error to bar defendant from cross-examining state's witness falsely accusing others of crimes); Fairfield Packing Co. v. Southern Mutual Fire Insurance Co., 193 Pa. 184, 44 A. 317 (1899) (evidence that employee of and witness for plaintiff made intentional false statement in another proof of loss for same fire).

Many courts see a special need for evidence of prior, similar false claims when the testimony of the complaining witness is crucial and when this witness is a minor or a woman alleging rape. See People v. Hurlburt, 166 Cal.App.2d 334, 342, 333 P.2d 82, 84–88 (1958) (rape prosecutrix); People v. Evans, 72 Mich. 367, 380, 40 N.W. 473, 478 (1888) (same); State v. Izzi, 115 R.I. 487, 348 A.2d 371 (1975) (error to exclude criminal assault defendant's proffered testimony of three other hospital attendants that 15 year old with a history of mental illness repeatedly accused attendants of causing injuries that were actually self-inflicted); Note, 32 Okla.L.Rev. 417 (1979); Annot., 75 A.L.R.2d 508 (1961) (similar false charges of complaining witness in sex offense cases). As to complainants in rape cases, see also § 45 at nn. 20–23 and § 193 at nn. 8–16.

13. Cf. supra notes 6–7 (analyzing this "it can't be a coincidence" argument).

of repeated, similar suits or claims.[14] However, in keeping with the customary relaxation of the standard of admissibility on cross-examination,[15] it is generally easier to elicit admissions about the other claims on cross-examination than it is to introduce the evidence by the testimony of the proponent's witnesses.[16]

 WESTLAW REFERENCES

synopsis,digest(same similar /5 act* claim* suit* injur*** loss** accident* defense* /p admissible inadmissible)

synopsis,digest(same similar /5 act* claim* suit* injur*** loss** accident* defense* /p probative)

§ 197. Other Misrepresentations and Frauds

In cases alleging fraud or misrepresentation, proof that the defendant perpetrated

---

14. When the witness is a party, the relevance of the other claims is two-fold. There is not only an indication that the party-witness is the sort of person who institutes false actions or raises false defenses, but also the suggestion that the party-witness is generally untruthful. Since both "claim-mindedness" and veracity come into play, courts that reject the "claim-mindedness" proof may allow the cross-examination of the party-witness. See Bunion v. Allstate Insurance Co., 502 F.Supp. 340, 342 (E.D.Pa.1980). The party-witness may also make specific statements on direct examination that open the door to cross-examination about other claims. Atkinson v. Atchison, Topeka & Santa Fe Railroad, 197 F.2d 244, 246 (10th Cir. 1952) (cross-examination tending to impeach plaintiff's testimony of particular careful driving habits); Hinkle v. Hampton, 388 F.2d 141, 144 (10th Cir. 1968) (impeaching plaintiff's testimony about extent of previous injuries).

15. See supra § 29.

16. Myrtle v. Checker Taxi Co., 279 F.2d 930, 934 (7th Cir. 1960) (cryptic observation about scope of cross-examination of plaintiff about prior injuries); Bunion v. Allstate Insurance Co., 502 F.Supp. 340, 342 (E.D.Pa.1980); cf. United States v. King, 505 F.2d 602, 610 (5th Cir. 1974) (evidence of repeated fraud "is viewed more favorably when it is introduced . . . on cross-examination").

§ 197

1. See generally Dec.Dig. Evidence ⊙135; 1 Louisell & Mueller, Federal Evidence § 101 (1977); 2 Wigmore, Evidence §§ 301–304, 321 (Chadbourn rev. 1979); Note, 2 UCLA L.Rev. 394 (1955); Fed.R.Evid. 401–405; Rev.Unif.R.Evid. 401–405 (1974); cf. supra § 190 (criminal cases).

2. The prejudicial impact of past frauds used solely to show fraudulent conduct on the occasion in question

---

similar deceptions frequently is received in evidence.[1] Such admission is not justified on the theory of "once a cheat, always a cheat."[2] Rather, at least one of three well entrenched[3] alternate theories that do not contravene the ban on using character traits solely as evidence of conduct typically is available.[4] To begin with, evidence of other frauds may help establish the element of knowledge—by suggesting that defendant knew that his alleged misrepresentation was false[5] or by indicating that defendant's participation in an alleged fraudulent scheme was not innocent or accidental.[6]

Second, the evidence may be admissible with respect to the closely related element of intent to deceive.[7] When other misrepresentations are used to show intent or knowledge, they need not be identical nor made

---

is thought to outweigh substantially the probative value. See supra Ch. 17.

3. E.g., Castle v. Bullard, 64 U.S. 172, 186 (1860) ("well recognised exceptions to the general rule").

4. The purposes for which the evidence may be admissible in civil cases have already been illustrated in the criminal context in § 190.

5. Penn Mutual Life Insurance Co. v. Mechanics' Savings Bank & Trust Co., 72 F. 413, 422 (6th Cir. 1896) ("It certainly diminishes the possibility that an innocent mistake was made in an untrue and misleading statement, to show similar but misleading statements of the same person about the same matter, because it is less probable that one would make innocent mistakes . . . in repeated instances than in one instance"), quoted in Morrison v. United States, 270 F.2d 1, 5 (4th Cir. 1967), cert. denied 361 U.S. 894; cf. United States v. Walls, 577 F.2d 690, 696–697 (9th Cir. 1978) (defaults on prior loans admissible to show lack of intent to repay), cert. denied 439 U.S. 893.

6. Weiss v. United States, 122 F.2d 675, 692–693 (5th Cir. 1941), cert. denied 314 U.S. 687, rehearing denied 314 U.S. 716 ("As to the other building frauds which Hart admittedly perpetrated on the state, and in which Weiss claims to have been an innocent actor, the evidence was admissible . . . . [A] man may be many times the dupe of another, but it is less likely that he should be so oftener than once"); In re Estate of Brandon, 55 N.Y.2d 206, 211–212, 448 N.Y.S.2d 436, 438–439 (1982) (prior judgments of undue influence admissible in an action alleging another instance of undue influence on an elderly woman by the owner of a nursing home, on the theory that "[w]here guilty

---

7. See note 7 on page 582.

under precisely the same circumstances as the one in issue.[8]

Finally, if the uttering of the misrepresentations or the performance of the fraudulent conduct is contested, then other misrepresentations or fraudulent acts that are evidently part of the same overall plan or scheme may be admissible to prove the conduct of the defendant.[9] The requirement of a common plan or scheme is well recognized, but it appears to be of questionable value in

civil cases. When there is conflicting testimony as to the making of the misrepresentation at issue, the value of evidence of other, very similar[10] misrepresentations—whether or not part of the same plan or scheme—in resolving the controversy should be sufficient to outweigh the danger of prejudice. As it is, the courts often manage to discern a larger plan when the various acts could well be described as separate transactions.[11]

---

knowledge or an unlawful intent is in issue, evidence of other similar acts is admissible to negate the existence of an innocent state of mind").

7. Edgar v. Fred Jones Lincoln-Mercury, 524 F.2d 162, 167 (10th Cir. 1975) (other instances of turning back automobile odometers admissible under Oklahoma law); Fulwider v. Woods, 249 Ark. 776, 461 S.W.2d 581 (1971) (action for recission for misrepresenting water supply on property); 2 Wigmore, Evidence §§ 302, 321 n. 1 (Chadbourn rev. 1979); cf. United States v. Marine, 413 F.2d 214, 216 (7th Cir. 1969), cert. denied 396 U.S. 1001 (criminal fraud); Annot., 78 A.L.R.2d 1359 (criminal taking by false pretenses), 34 A.L.R.2d 777 (other forgeries). An allegation of fraud is not in itself a ticket of admission. Dorcal, Inc. v. Xerox Corp., 398 So.2d 665 (Ala.1981) (general reference to Xerox's "intent, scheme or design" in leasing a copier to plaintiff did not require admission of testimony of another small business concerning the performance of its Xerox copier).

8. Some courts allow subsequent deceptive conduct to be considered on the issue of intent but not as to knowledge. See, e.g., Early v. Eley, 243 N.C. 695, 91 S.E.2d 919, 923 (1956) (evidence that defendants subsequently purchased stocks like those sold to plaintiffs and suffered loss admissible to show absence of fraudulent intent in sale to plaintiffs); 2 Wigmore, Evidence § 316 (Chadbourn rev. 1979); cf. Johnson v. State, 75 Ark. 427, 88 S.W. 905, 908 (1905) (subsequent conduct admissible to show criminal intent to defraud).

Whether before or after the events at bar, other deceptions cannot come in with respect to intent or knowledge if these matters are not prerequisites to liability and punitive damages are not sought. Johnson v. Gulick, 46 Neb. 817, 65 N.W. 883, 884 (1896) (deceit); Karsun v. Kelley, 258 Or. 155, 482 P.2d 533 (1971) (action under state Blue Sky Law for false statements inducing stock purchases); Standard Manufacturing Co. v. Slot, 121 Wis. 14, 98 N.W. 923, 924–925 (1904) (action on a contract).

9. Mudsill Mining Co. v. Watrous, 61 F. 163, 179 (6th Cir. 1894) (evidence that defendants had "salted" ore samples that other intended buyers took from mine is "competent and cogent evidence tending to establish their complicity in the like fraud now under consideration" since all the fraudulent acts were "in furtherance of same general design" to make a sale); Kindred v. State, 254 Ind. 127, 258 N.E.2d 411, 415 (1970) (repeated use of credit card in prosecution for forgery); Alt-

man v. Ozdoda, 237 N.Y. 218, 142 N.E. 591, 592–593 (1923) (other forgeries with respect to defense that promissory note forged); Karsun v. Kelley, 258 Or. 155, 482 P.2d 533 (1971) (substantially the same statements made to two other customers admissible as part of general plan to sell securities in violation of state Blue Sky Law); Shingleton Brothers v. Lasure, 122 W.Va. 1, 6 S.E.2d 252, 253–254 (1940) (misrepresentations inducing credit account); 2 Wigmore, Evidence § 304 (Chadbourn rev. 1979).

10. Of course, if the identity of the perpetrator of the fraud were in doubt, then other fraudulent acts of the party so like the conduct in suit and so distinctive as to earmark them as the work of the same person should be admissible to show that the party was the perpetrator. See supra § 190.

11. For example, in In re Estate of Brandon, 55 N.Y.2d 206, 448 N.Y.S.2d 436 (1982), the Appellate Division had upheld the trial court's allowing into evidence two prior judgments of undue influence "as tending to establish a common scheme or plan under which appellants inveigle into Murphy's place of residence aged and ailing residents of her nursing home for the purpose of stripping them of their life savings." Noting that the courts often are too ready to find a common plan, the Court of Appeals rejected this reasoning. It explained that "[u]nlike the intent exception, mere similarity between the acts is an insufficient predicate for admissibility under the common scheme or plan exception. . . . Indeed, there must be such a clear concurrence of common features—i.e., time, place and character—that 'the various acts are naturally to be explained as caused by a general plan of which they are the individual manifestations.'" Id. at 212, 448 N.Y.S.2d at 439. Here, it concluded, "there was no showing that the [prior] incidents had any direct connection, either in fact or in Mrs. Murphy's mind, with the fraud or undue influence visited upon Alice Brandon." Despite the striking similarities in the treatment of three elderly women, the Court of Appeals determined that the incidents could well be characterized as "separate and independant transactions entered into as the occasion arose." Id. at 213, 448 N.Y.S.2d at 440. With Brandon, compare, Baldwin v. Warwick, 213 F.2d 485, 486 (9th Cir. 1954) (testimony that defendants had drugged the drinks of other real estate agents and then won heavily from them at cards admissible to show an "overall scheme" that included drugging plaintiff's drinks at various bars at which plaintiff

§ 198. Other Contracts and Business Transactions

Evidence concerning other contracts or business dealings may be relevant to prove the terms of a contract, the meaning of these terms, a business habit or custom, and occasionally, the authority of an agent.[1] As to many of these uses, there is little controversy. Certainly, evidence of other transactions between the same parties readily is received when relevant to show the meaning they probably attached to the terms of a contract.[2] Likewise, when the existence of the terms is in doubt, evidence of similar contracts between the same parties is accepted as a vehicle for showing of a custom or continuing course of dealing between them, and as such, as evidence of the terms of the present bargain.[3] Also, when the authority of an agent is in question, other similar transactions that he has carried out on behalf of the principal are freely admitted.[4]

In the past, many courts had balked when contracts *with others* were offered to show the terms or the making of the contract in suit.[5] It is hard to understand why any hard and fast line should be drawn. As an historical matter, these decisions perhaps may be explained as manifestations of the perennial confusion between the concepts of sufficiency and relevancy,[6] or as products of the beguiling power of the mystical phrase *res inter alios acta*.[7] Yet, it seems clear that contracts of a party with third persons may

shook dice with defendants after having shown them certain real estate).

§ 198

1. See generally Dec.Dig. Evidence ⊜129(6); Louisell & Mueller, Federal Evidence § 100 (1977); 2 Wigmore, Evidence § 377 (Chadbourn rev. 1979); 22 Wright & Graham, Federal Practice and Procedure § 5170.

2. Hartford Steam Boiler Inspection & Insurance Co. v. Schwartzman Packing Co., 423 F.2d 1170, 1173–1174 (10th Cir. 1970) (prior contracts for insurance between same parties defining coverage broadly with specific exclusions of named items admissible to show meaning of later policy); Oskey Gasoline & Oil Co. v. OKC Refining, Inc., 364 F.Supp. 1137, 1142 (D.Minn.1973) ("with the contract not specifying which measurement standard was to be used, the most reasonable expectation is that it would be the method which both parties had previously used"); Aetna Insurance Co. v. Northwestern Iron Co., 21 Wis. 458 (1867) (testimony as to usual course of business of marine insurance companies admissible to "prove the understanding of the parties"); Bourne v. Gatliff, 11 C. & F. 45, 49, 70, 8 Eng.Rep. 1019 (H.L.1844) (to ascertain meaning of bill of lading provision on delivery of goods, previous transactions may be looked to); cf. U.C.C. §§ 1–205, 2–202 (course of dealing between parties).

3. Hyde v. Land-of-Sky Regional Council, 572 F.2d 988, 990 n. 4 (4th Cir. 1978) (prior written contract of employment admissible to prove terms of oral contract for continued employment); Burns v. Gould, 172 Conn. 210, 374 A.2d 193 (1977) (prior written contract between the parties to develop a nursing home that plaintiff said was "in line with" an alleged oral contract to develop a second nursing home properly admitted to prove the terms of the oral contract); Terminal Grain Corp. v. Rozell, 272 N.W.2d 800 (S.D.1978) (evidence of past dealings admissible to show that corn seller's silence did not constitute acceptance of grain terminal's offer to purchase corn); Karp v. Coolview of Wisconsin, 25 Wis.2d 299, 303, 130 N.W.2d 790, 792 (1964) (travel agent's prior extensions of credit to corporation admissible on issue of whether extension was to corporation or to individual). But an isolated previous instance, without an offer to prove more instances in a continued course of dealing, may not be admitted. Roney v. Clearfield County Grange Mutual Fire Insurance Co., 332 Pa. 447, 3 A.2d 365 (1939) (previous instance of insurance's agents filling in form without adequate information inadmissible).

4. Parker v. Jones, 221 Ark. 378, 253 S.W.2d 342, 344 (1952) (prior instances of treating as agent).

5. Johnson v. Gulick, 46 Neb. 817, 65 N.W. 883, 884 (1896) ("no reasonable presumption can be formed as to the making or executing of a contract by a party with one person, in consequence of the mode in which he has made or executed similar contracts with other persons. . . . [W]here the question between a landlord and his tenant is whether the rent was payable quarterly or half-yearly, it has been held irrelevant to consider what agreements subsisted between the landlord and other tenants, or of what time their rents would become due"); Turpin v. Branaman, 190 Va. 818, 58 S.E.2d 63, 65–66 (1950) (defendant's offer to show that his practice was to execute written contracts when buying apples for himself and oral ones when buying as broker rejected as irrelevant to issue of whether he bought apples from plaintiffs for himself or as broker).

6. See supra § 185.

7. The maxim "Res inter alios acta, aliis neque nocere neque prodesse potest" means "A thing done

show the party's customary practice and course of dealing and thus supply useful insights into the terms of his present agreement.[8] Indeed, even if there are but one or two such contracts, they may be useful evidence.[9] When, in a certain kind of transaction, a business has adopted a particular mode of handling a bargaining topic or standardized feature, such as warranty, discount or the like, it is often easier for it to cast a new contract in the same mold than it is to work out a new one. Moreover, some practices become so accepted in an industry that they may shape the meaning of most contracts in that field. As to these, evidence in the form of contracts or transactions involving neither of the parties may nevertheless be probative of the commercial relationship that exists between the parties.[10]

Inasmuch as there is no general danger of unfair prejudice inherent in evidence of other business transactions, strict rules or limits on admissibility seem inappropriate. The courts should admit such evidence in all cases where the testimony as to the terms of the present bargain is conflicting and where the judge finds that the risk of wasted time and confusion of issues does not substantially outweigh the probative value of the evidence of the other transactions. Many jurisdictions therefore leave evidence of other contracts or business dealings to the trial judge to evaluate on a case by case basis.[11]

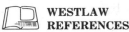 **WESTLAW REFERENCES**

157k129(6)

synopsis,digest(similar /p prior previous past earlier /p contract* transaction* business /p relevan! probative)

§ 199. Other Sales of Similar Property as Evidence of Value

When the market value of property needs to be determined, the price actually paid in a

---

between some can neither harm nor profit others." The maxim "Res inter alios acta alteri nocere non debet" states a key tenet of the principle of res judicata—that a person is not bound by litigation in which he does not participate. Although the shortened version of these maxims still appeals to some judges, invocation of the phrase serves more often than not to obscure any real analysis. See 1 Louisell & Mueller, Federal Evidence § 100 at 745 (1977); 2 Wigmore, Evidence § 458 (Chadbourn rev. 1979); 22 Wright & Graham, Federal Practice and Procedure § 5170 at 114. It has been said that the doctrine has been eroded. McLendon Pools v. Bush, 414 So.2d 92, 95 (Ala.Civ.App. 1982).

8. Joseph v. Krull Wholesale Drug Co., 147 F.Supp. 250, 258 (E.D.Pa.1956), affirmed 245 F.2d 231 (3d Cir.) (evidence of practice of making corporate officers' contracts terminable at will admissible to show whether the one in issue was for definite term); Moody v. Peirano, 4 Cal.App. 411, 88 P. 380, 382 (1906) (other sales of wheat from same shipment as "White Australian" properly admitted to show that defendant also warranted wheat sold to plaintiff to be "White Australian"); In re Isom's Estate, 193 Kan. 357, 394 P.2d 21, 29 (1964) (similar oral contracts to make will admissible to show existence of contract in suit); Krause v. Eugene Dodge, Inc., 265 Or. 486, 509 P.2d 1199, 1204 (1973) (fraud defendant's evidence about sales to others admitted to show the meaning of "new" car); Micke v. Jack Walters & Sons Corp., 70 Wis.2d 388, 234 N.W.2d 347, 349 (1975) (in ascertaining whether a term in an employment contract existed, the testimony of a former employee about what he had been told when hired was admissible with respect to the "corporate habit or routine practice" of the manager who claimed

that he told "all the men" he hired about the term in question); Super Tire Market v. Rollins, 18 Utah 2d 122, 417 P.2d 132, 135–136 (1966) (seller's evidence of policy not to give warranties admissible to show absence of warranty on tires); cf. supra § 195 (habit evidence).

9. Moody v. Peirano, 4 Cal.App. 411, 88 P. 380, 382 (1906) ("The number and frequency of the sales in which the warranty had been made, and their proximity in time to the sale made to the plaintiff, would be circumstances addressed to the discretion of the court"); cases cited, supra note 8.

10. The substantive law recognizes the pertinence of "usage of trade" in interpreting and supplementing the terms of a contract. Posttape Associates v. Eastman Kodak Co., 537 F.2d 751, 757–758 (3d Cir. 1976), appeal after remand 450 F.Supp. 407 (knowledge that film manufacturers typically limit their liability to replacing defective film could establish "agreement" so as to limit liability to producer of documentary films suing supplier for lost profits); U.C.C. § 1–205(2) to 1–205(6). In fields in which contracts are individualized and little in the way of standard practices have developed, evidence of unrelated contracts may not have enough bearing on the transaction in issue to be worth the distraction and time-consumption. See, e.g., Mass Appraisal Services v. Carmichael, 404 So.2d 666, 694 (Ala.1981).

11. Minnesota Farm Bureau Marketing Corp. v. North Dakota Agricultural Marketing Association, 563 F.2d 906, 911 (8th Cir. 1977) (no abuse of discretion to exclude prior grain contracts with two other farmers that were dissimilar to the contract at issue).

competitive market for comparable items is an obvious place to look.[1] The testimony of witnesses with first-hand knowledge of other sales,[2] or reliable price lists, market reports, or the like[3] may be received to show the market price.

The less homogeneous the product, the more difficulty there is in measuring market value in this way. Thus, cases involving land valuation, especially condemnation cases, frequently discuss the admissibility of evidence of other sales. A dying rule excludes the evidence entirely save in exceptional circumstances.[4] The dominant view gives the judge discretion to admit evidence of other sales.[5] The inquiry focuses on whether these sales have been sufficiently recent, and whether the other land is sufficiently nearby and alike as to character, situation, usability, and improvements, as to make it clear that the two tracts are comparable in value.[6] A weaker standard for similarity applies when the other sales are used as the basis for an expert judgment as to

§ 199

1. Indeed, when presented with the sometimes wildly disparate estimates of professional appraisers, courts have been known to remark that the sales prices of comparable properties are the best evidence of value. United States v. Bloom, 237 F.2d 158, 163 (2d Cir. 1956); United States v. 421.89 Acres of Land, 465 F.2d 336, 339 (8th Cir. 1972) (approving of jury instruction "where they are available, evidence of sales of comparable or similar lands is considered the best evidence of the value of the tract to which they are compared"); cf. Green v. United States, 460 F.2d 412 (5th Cir. 1972) (applying IRS regulations for valuing mineral interests). Cases and discussions can be found in 5 Nichols, Eminent Domain §§ 21.1–22.2 (3d ed. 1969); Sengstock & McAuliffe, What is the Price of Eminent Domain? 44 J.Urban L. 185 (1967); Notes, 43 Iowa L.Rev. 270 (1958), 12 Stan.L.Rev. 766 (1960); Annot., 12 A.L.R.3d 1064 (hearsay evidence of other sales as basis for expert opinion); 85 A.L.R.2d 110 (sales of other real property to show value); 79 A.L.R.2d 677, 746 (value of livestock); 55 A.L.R.2d 791 (prior sale of same property in eminent domain proceeding); 39 A.L.R.2d 209 (tax valuation as evidence of value); 7 A.L.R.2d 781 (offers to buy or sell real property as evidence of value); 155 A.L.R. 262 (sale of property taken or impaired by eminent domain); 118 A.L.R. 869 (sale of other real property); 29 Am.Jur.2d Evidence §§ 387–403; 31A C.J.S. Evidence §§ 182–183; 32 id. § 593; Dec.Dig. Evidence ⟂113(16), 142 and see generally Fed.R.Evid. 401–403; Rev.Unif.R.Evid. 401–403 (1974).

2. Harlan & Hollingsworth Corp. v. McBride, 45 Del. 85, 69 A.2d 9, 14 (1949) (machinery).

3. Although such reports would be hearsay if offered to show the actual sales recited, Doherty v. Harris, 230 Mass. 341, 119 N.E. 863 (1918), they should be admissible either under an exception to the hearsay rule or as evidence of what traders would have paid for such property. Friedman Iron & Supply Co. v. J.B. Beaird Co., 222 La. 627, 63 So.2d 144, 153 (1952) (trade journal); Curtis v. Schwartzman Packing Co., 61 N.M. 305, 299 P.2d 776, 778 (1956) (automobile dealers' "Blue Book"); 6 Wigmore, Evidence § 1702 (Chadbourn rev. 1976); Annot., 43 A.L.R. 1192 (newspapers and trade journals as evidence of market price); Fed.R.Evid. 803(17); U.C.C. § 2–723 (proof of market price of goods); § 321 infra.

4. This minority approach often is called the "Pennsylvania rule" (despite that state's abrogation of the rule by statute). See Sengstock & McAuliffe, supra note 1, at 194; Annot., 85 A.L.R.2d 110.

5. United States v. 429.59 Acres of Land, 612 F.2d 459, 462 (9th Cir. 1980); United States v. 320 Acres of Land, 605 F.2d 762, 801 (5th Cir. 1979) ("sound trial practice is to admit a liberal number of the 'most comparable' sales available, leaving it to the fact-finder to assess the ultimate probative worth of any and all sales admitted," and even some sales that reflect a noncompensable enhancement in value resulting from the government's operations may be admitted); Ex parte Graham, 380 So.2d 850, 852–53 (Ala.1979); Duke Power Co. v. Winebarger, 300 N.C. 57, 265 S.E.2d 227 (1980); City of Paducah v. Allen, 111 Ky. 361, 63 S.W. 981 (1901) ("here is where 'money talks' "); Annot., 85 A.L.R.2d 110.

6. United States v. 84.4 Acres of Land, 348 F.2d 117, 119 (3d Cir. 1965) (similarly sized and developed golf courses within 50 mile radius); United States v. 3727.91 Acres of Land, 563 F.2d 357, 361 (8th Cir. 1977) (average price for acreage that included agricultural land and timber not a reliable indicator of market value of levees and ditches on the land); Fairfield Gardens v. United States, 306 F.2d 167 (9th Cir. 1962) (properties too dissimilar); Department of Conservation v. Aspergren Financial Corp., 72 Ill.2d 302, 21 Ill.Dec. 153, 157, 381 N.E.2d 231, 235 (1978) (differences in water supply, sewage facilities and population densities too great for properties to be comparable); Tolman v. Carrick, 136 Vt. 188, 385 A.2d 1119 (1978) (error to exclude evidence of sale merely because property was in another town); Annot., 85 A.L.R.2d 110, 130. The proponent has the burden of showing similarity. United States ex rel. TVA v. Powelson, 319 U.S. 266, 273 (1943); Ashland Oil, Inc. v. Phillips Petroleum Co., 554 F.2d 381, 387 (10th Cir. 1975) (en banc), cert. denied 434 U.S. 821 ("Evidence of 'other sales' [of helium] falls far short of establishing a market without comparability being clearly established"); Arkansas State Highway Commission v. Witkowski, 236 Ark. 66, 364 S.W.2d 309, 311 (1963); Dawson v. Papio Natural Resources District, 206 Neb. 225, 292 N.W.2d 42 (1980), appeal after remand 210 Neb. 100, 313 N.W.2d 242.

value instead of being introduced as independent evidence of value.[7]

Since the value sought is what, on average, a willing buyer would have paid a willing seller, prices on other sales of a forced character, such as execution sales or condemnation awards for other tracts,[8] generally are inadmissible.[9] Many courts also exclude the condemnor's evidence of prices it paid to other owners on the theory that sales

made in contemplation of condemnation do not approximate the relevant market price.[10] Other courts, following what seems the better reasoned view, allow such evidence in the judge's discretion.[11]

Of course, any other sale must be genuine, and the price must be paid or substantially secured.[12] Likewise, actual sale prices rather than asking prices typically are required.[13]

---

7. United States v. 429.59 Acres of Land, 612 F.2d 459, 462 (9th Cir. 1980); Kamrowski v. State, 37 Wis.2d 195, 155 N.W.2d 125 (1967). Indeed, a qualified expert should be allowed to use sales of dissimilar properties in constructing a regression model that predicts the price at which any particular property will sell. Cf. State v. Dillingham Corp., 60 Hawaii 393, 591 P.2d 1049, 1060 (1979) (permissible for expert to testify about admittedly noncomparable "data properties").

8. Whewell v. Ives, 155 Conn. 602, 236 A.2d 92 (1967); Nantahala Power & Light Co. v. Sloan, 227 N.C. 151, 41 S.E.2d 361 (1947).

9. Knabe v. State, 285 Ala. 321, 231 So.2d 887 (1970); Waldenmaier v. State, 33 A.D.2d 75, 305 N.Y.S.2d 381 (1969); Annot., 85 A.L.R.2d 110, 157 (1962); 118 A.L.R. 870, 890 (1939).

10. Evans v. United States, 326 F.2d 827, 831 (8th Cir. 1964); Alaska Housing Authority v. Du Pont, 439 P.2d 427 (Alaska 1968); Socony Vacuum Oil Co. v. State, 170 N.W.2d 378, 382 (Iowa 1969); Kirkpatrick v. State, 53 Wis.2d 522, 192 N.W.2d 856, 857–58 (1972), cert. denied 409 U.S. 846; Annot., 85 A.L.R.2d 110, 163, 118 A.L.R. 870, 893; cf. Washington Metropolitan Area Transit Authority v. One Parcel of Land, 548 F.2d 1130 (3d Cir. 1977) (condemnor's offer to owner of tract in question not admissible). Most decisions exclude the evidence of prices paid by the condemnor even when the owner offers it as an admission by the condemnor. Alaska Housing Authority v. Du Pont, supra; Stewart v. Commonwealth, 337 S.W.2d 880 (Ky.1960). The reasoning is that the condemnor may be willing to pay a premium to acquire the land promptly and without litigation. See 5 Nichols, supra note 1, § 21.33.

11. The rationale is that the price paid would not be too far out of line, since neither party to the sale was compelled to agree on a price (as the seller is in an execution sale). While the owner knows that he may have his land taken by eminent domain, he also knows that then he will be entitled to a judicial appraisal of fair market value. While it is true that the owner may be willing to accept a lower price to avoid the costs of litigation, the condemnor may also tolerate paying a higher price to obtain the property promptly without having to make his case in court. Depending on the skills of the negotiators, the agreed upon prices may come close to the market value (or, more precisely, to the seller's and buyer's estimates of what a court would find this value to be). Thus, evidence of the prices that the condemnor has paid to other owners has been accepted as shedding sufficient light on the value

of the property. Transwestern Pipeline Co. v. O'Brien, 418 F.2d 15 (5th Cir. 1969); Commonwealth v. McGeorge, 369 S.W.2d 126 (Ky.1963); Annot., 85 A.L.R.2d 110, 163; cf. In re City of Bethlehem, 474 Pa. 75, 376 A.2d 641 (1977) (evenly divided on this point). In any event, it seems clear that when there is no threat to exercise the power of eminent domain, the simple fact that the purchaser has such power will not render the evidence of the sale inadmissible. Cain v. City of Topeka, 4 Kan.App.2d 192, 603 P.2d 1031, 1033–1034 (1979).

12. Macnaughtan v. Commonwealth, 220 Mass. 550, 108 N.E. 357 (1915) (option and sale admittedly made to influence legislation); Redfield v. Iowa State Highway Commission, 252 Iowa 1256, 110 N.W.2d 397, 401–402 (1961) (speculative term contract); Comment, 39 Yale L.J. 748 (1929). On the "cash or equivalent" rule, see, Surfside of Brevard v. United States, 414 F.2d 915 (5th Cir. 1969); *Redfield*, supra, 252 Iowa at 1262, 110 N.W.2d at 402; 5 Nichols, supra note 1, § 21.5.

13. E.g., State ex rel. Price v. Parcel No. 1, 243 A.2d 709, 711 (Del.1968); McAulton v. Goldstrin, ___ Hawaii ___, 656 P.2d 96, 97 (1982) (offers to buy car prior to accident); Perlmutter v. State Roads Commission, 259 Md. 253, 269 A.2d 586, 587 (1970); 31A C.J.S. Evidence § 182(3). This rule normally applies to options to buy or sell. United States v. Smith, 355 F.2d 807, 811–812 (5th Cir. 1966). It also covers offers concerning the land in question. See Department of Conservation, etc. v. Kyes, 57 Ill.App.3d 563, 15 Ill.Dec. 34, 37, 373 N.E.2d 304, 307 (1978); State v. Lincoln Memory Gardens 242 Ind. 206, 177 N.E.2d 655, 659 (1961); Annot., 7 A.L.R.2d 781. Asking prices are excluded, not because they have no probative value, but because efforts to determine their genuineness would be too costly. Missouri Baptist Hospital v. United States, 213 Ct.Cl. 505, 555 F.2d 290 (1977); State v. Morehouse Holding Co., 255 Or. 62, 357 P.2d 266, 267–278 (1960). However, if a party to the present action has offered to buy or sell the land in question or a similar neighboring parcel, evidence of his offer may constitute an admission, admissible against him as such. Springer v. City of Chicago, 135 Ill. 552, 26 N.E. 514 (1891); Durika v. School District, 415 Pa. 480, 203 A.2d 474 (1964); see Ch. 26 infra and n. 10 supra. When there have been no other sales, some courts admit evidence relating to offers. City of Chicago v. Lehmann, 262 Ill. 468, 104 N.E. 829 (1914). Others admit the evidence of asking prices more freely. Bingham v. Bridges, 613 F.2d 794 (8th Cir. 1980) (applying Oklahoma law).

WESTLAW REFERENCES

synopsis,digest(similar /p prior previous past earlier /p value price /s market* /p condemn! execution! "forced sale*" "tax sale*" auction*)

§ 200. Other Accidents and Injuries

The admissibility of evidence of other accidents and injuries is raised frequently in negligence and product liability cases.[1] In light of the prejudice that such evidence can carry with it, most judges will scrutinize it carefully.[2] The proponent therefore should be prepared to convince the judge of the need for the proof.

The purpose for the evidence is important in determining whether the proof will be admitted[3] and how strictly the requirement of similarity of conditions[4] will be applied. In practice, the various permissible purposes for proof of other accidents tend to blend together in that more than one purpose typically is available,[5] but for clarity of analysis we shall try to isolate each valid purpose.

To begin with, evidence of other accidents sometimes may be admissible to prove the existence of a particular physical condition, situation, or defect. For instance, the fact that several persons slipped and fell in the same location in a supermarket can help show that a slippery substance was on the floor.[6] At the same time, this proof is a bit sensational. Unless the defendant strenuously disputes the presence of the condition, the court may reject the evidence of the sim-

§ 200

1. See generally 63 Am.Jur.2d Products Liability §§ 16–17, 24; 29 id. Evidence §§ 305–314; 32 C.J.S. Negligence § 234; Dec.Dig. Evidence ⚷141; id. Negligence ⚷125; 1 Frumer & Friedman, Products Liability § 12.01 (1960); 1 Louisell & Mueller, Federal Evidence § 98; 2 Wigmore, Evidence §§ 252, 457–458 (Chadbourn rev. 1979); 22 Wright & Graham, Federal Practice and Procedure § 5170; Morris, Proof of Safety History in Negligence Cases, 61 Harv.L.Rev. 205 (1948); Annot., 42 A.L.R.3d 780 (other accidents to prove dangerous nature of product), 20 A.L.R.3d 1430 (discovery of defendant's knowledge of other injuries in product liability cases), 70 A.L.R.2d 167 (previous accidents at same place), 46 A.L.R.2d 935 (other failures of railroad crossing devices), 45 A.L.R.2d 1121 (explosion damage to other properties), 31 A.L.R.2d 190 (absence of other accidents), 26 A.L.R.2d 136, 195 (prior gas leaks); Fed.R.Evid. 401–405; Rev.Unif.R.Evid. 401–405 (1974).

2. At one time, a few courts, influenced by Collins v. Inhabitants of Dorchester, 60 Mass. (6 Cush.) 396 (1850), applied a rigid rule of exclusion. Hudson v. Chicago & Northwestern Railway Co., 59 Iowa 581, 13 N.W. 735 (1882); Bremner v. Inhabitants of Newcastle, 83 Me. 415, 22 A. 382 (1891). The modern cases commit the matter to the trial judge for a weighing of the advantages and disadvantages of admitting or excluding the evidence. Lindquist v. Des Moines Union Railway Co., 239 Iowa 356, 30 N.W.2d 120 (1947); Robitaille v. Netoco Community Theatres, 305 Mass. 265, 25 N.E.2d 749 (1949). Many cases stress the discretion so reposed in the trial judge. Jones & Laughlin Steel Corp. v. Matherne, 348 F.2d 394, 400 (5th Cir. 1965) (upholding admission); Nelson v. Brunswick Corp., 503 F.2d 376, 380 (9th Cir. 1974) (upholding exclusion of evidence of explosions and fires during resurfacing of other bowling alleys with the observation that "whether to admit such evidence is a matter generally for the trial court to decide, keeping in mind the collateral nature of the proof, the danger that it may afford a basis for improper inferences, the likelihood that it may cause confusion or operate to unfairly prejudice the party against whom it is directed and that it may be cumulative, etc."); Kopfinger v. Grand Central Public Market, 60 Cal.2d 852, 37 Cal.Rptr. 65, 70, 389 P.2d 529 (1964) (upholding admission of evidence of other falls in other locations in same store).

3. Many of the cases cited in this section make the point, discussed in § 189 supra, that evidence of other accidents or their absence is not admissible solely to show a character or propensity for careful or careless behavior.

4. For statements of the need for substantial similarity, see, McKinnon v. Skil Corp., 638 F.2d 270, 277 (1st Cir. 1981) (also emphasizing the trial judge's discretion to exclude evidence that meets this requirement if necessary to avoid "unfairness, confusion and undue expenditure of time"); Julander v. Ford Motor Co., 488 F.2d 839, 845–847 (10th Cir. 1973) (evidence of seven pending suits for alleged design defect in automobile steering mechanism improperly admitted in absence of showing that the other accidents occurred under similar circumstances). Of course, exactly identical circumstances cannot be realized and are not required. See Jones & Laughlin Steel Corp. v. Matherne, 348 F.2d 394, 400–401 (5th Cir. 1965) ("The differences between the circumstances of the accidents could have been developed to go to the weight to be given to such evidence"; defendant "had ample opportunity to explore these differences upon cross-examination or by its own witnesses").

5. Ramos v. Liberty Mutual Insurance Co., 615 F.2d 334, 339 (5th Cir. 1980) (collapse of similar mast on offshore oil rig two years earlier erroneously excluded, since the first accident was relevant to the manufactur-

6. See note 6 on page 588.

ilar accidents as unduly prejudicial and cumulative.

Second, the evidence of other accidents or injuries may be admissible to help show that the defect or dangerous situation caused the injury.[7] Thus, instances in which other patients placed on the same drug therapy contracted the same previously rare disease is circumstantial evidence that the drug caused

er's "notice of the defect, its ability to correct the defect, the mast's safety under foreseeable conditions, the strength of the mast, and, most especially, causation").

6. Bitsos v. Red Owl Stores, 459 F.2d 656, 659–660 (8th Cir. 1972) (that another person had fallen down steps in the same year and had complained of the need to clean the stairs was "circumstantial evidence that [a] foreign substance had been . . . on the steps" when plaintiff slipped and fell); Cameron v. Small, 182 S.W.2d 565, 570 (Mo.Sup.1944) (evidence that others had slipped on a ramp admissible as "tending to prove . . . that the surface of the ramp was unsafe, if the slipping of others occurred under the same conditions at that same place, and from the same cause, as the slipping of the plaintiff); Ringelheim v. Fidelity Trust Co., 330 Pa. 69, 198 A. 628, 629 (1938) ("proof that other persons had fallen at the same place on the same day" on a floor allegedly made slippery by an excess of polish "would show almost conclusively that the cause of such accidents was one common to all, namely, the condition of the floor, and not a mere coincidence of fault or ill luck of the individual victims"); Safeway Stores v. Bozeman, 394 S.W.2d 532, 538 (Tex.Civ.App. 1965) refused no reversible error (other falls on floor allegedly made slippery by "daily application of an oily sweeping compound").

Other cases of this kind include Gulf States Utility Co. v. Ecodyne Corp., 635 F.2d 517, 519 (5th Cir. 1981) (error in a bench trial to exclude evidence of structural failure of similar towers that defendant built for others); Bailey v. Kawasaki-Kisen, K.K., 455 F.2d 392, 397 (5th Cir. 1972), appeal after remand 478 F.2d 839 (reversible error to exclude evidence that boom fell a second time to show that the winch "was in some way defective"); Denison v. Weise, 251 Iowa 770, 102 N.W.2d 671 (1960) (loose seats on bar stools); Albers Mill Co. v. Carney, 341 S.W.2d 117 (Mo.1960) (testimony by other farmers as to moldy food from same lot admissible to show moldiness of food that plaintiff's turkeys ate); Parker v. Bamberger, 100 Utah 361, 116 P.2d 425 (1941) (defect in signal device).

7. Bailey v. Kawasaki-Kisen, K.K., 455 F.2d 392, 397 (5th Cir. 1972) appeal after remand 478 F.2d 839 (reversible error to exclude evidence that boom fell a second time to show that excess grease on the cables and drum of the winch was the cause of the injury a longshoreman sustained while dashing out of the way when boom fell a few minutes earlier); and see supra n. 5. Evidence of similar injuries under similar circumstances—but without the alleged actions or omissions

the disease in plaintiff's case.[8] However, since many unsuspected factors could contribute or cause the observed effects,[9] the conditions of the other injuries and the present one must be similar.[10] Although the use of evidence of other accidents to prove the existence of a condition (the first purpose listed above) can overlap the use of the evidence to prove that the condition caused plaintiff's injuries,[11] ordinarily, the need to

of the defendant—also may be admissible. Dick v. Lewis, 636 F.2d 1168, 1169 (8th Cir. 1981) (lay testimony about birth defects of other members of family admissible to refute claim that medical malpractice in handling the delivery caused cerebral palsy, spastic paraplegia, and mental retardation in 20 year old plaintiff).

8. Herbst, Ulfelder & Poskanzer, Association of Maternal Stilbesterol Therapy with Tumor Appearance in Young Women, 284 New Eng.J. Medicine 878 (1971) (first study linking a previously rare disease in young women with a drug prescribed to their mothers); cf. Gober v. Revlon, Inc., 317 F.2d 47, 49–50 (5th Cir. 1963) (allergic reactions to "Wonder Base" for nail polish); Carter v. Yardley & Co., 319 Mass. 92, 64 N.E.2d 693, 694–695 (1946) (reactions of other perfume users admissible to show that same perfume burned plaintiff's skin). As typically developed at trial, such evidence of other accidents is a crude version of a retrospective epidemiologic study. The evidence of other incidents that is implicit in more careful statistical studies of the association between a suspected causative agent and a disease or injury should be admissible as forming the basis for the expert's opinion. See supra § 15. For discussions of epidemiologic and statistical proof of causation, see Kaye, The Limits of the Preponderance of the Evidence Standard: Justifiably Naked Statistical Evidence and Multiple Causation, 1982 Am.B.Found. Research J. 487; infra § 210.

9. "Spurious correlations" are easily found in much observational data. Zeisel, Say It with Figures (5th rev. ed. 1968). Even experimental data can be all but useless when possible causes are "confounded." D. Moore, Statistics: Concepts and Controversies 60 (1979).

10. Rexall Drug Co. v. Nihill, 276 F.2d 637, 642 & 645 (9th Cir. 1960) (evidence of "strawy, dry and frizzy" hair from home permanent solution inadmissible to show that the treatment caused plaintiff's baldness); see supra n. 4.

11. In the slip-and-fall cases as well as some of the other cases cited supra n. 6, the finder of fact is invited to deduce from the presence of other accidents (1) that there were certain physical conditions (2) that caused all the injuries, including plaintiff's. But in other situations, only (2) justifies the evidence, since (1) is not in doubt. Johnson v. Yolo County, 274 Cal.App.2d 46, 79 Cal.Rptr. 33 (1969) (curve design of road as a cause of accidents); Poston v. Clarkson Construction Co., 401 S.W.2d 522 (Mo.App.1966) (blast damage to nearby

use the evidence for this second purpose is plainer. Causation is frequently in genuine dispute, and circumstantial evidence may be of great value in pursuing this elusive issue. Thus, receptivity to evidence of similar happenings to show causation is heightened when the defendant contends that the alleged conduct could not possibly have caused the plaintiff's injury.[12]

Third, and perhaps most commonly, evidence of other accidents or injuries may be used to show the risk that defendant's conduct created.[13] If the extent of the danger is material to the case, as it almost always is in personal injury litigation,[14] the fact that the same conditions produced harm on other occasions is a natural and convincing way of showing the hazard.[15] The requirement of substantial similarity is applied strictly here.[16]

Finally, the evidence of other accidents commonly is received to prove that the defendant knew, or should have known, of the danger.[17] Of course, if defendant's duty is

houses, not to prove blast, but to show cause of damage to plaintiff's house). Then there are cases in which (1) is the focal point of the controversy, and it is understood that if (1) holds, then so does (2). Gulf C. & Santa Fe Railway Co. v. Brooks, 73 S.W. 571 (Tex. Civ.App.1903), error refused (evidence of a later collapse of a gate and the ensuing replacement of a bolt in the hinge admissible to show that bolt was previously missing when the coal retained by the gate fell from tender and injured fireman).

12. Ringelheim v. Fidelity Trust Co., 330 Pa. 69, 198 A. 628 (1938) (evidence of other falls to refute testimony that polish hardens in five minutes); Texas & New Orleans Railroad Co. v. Glass, 107 S.W.2d 924, 926 (Tex.Civ.App.1931), error dismissed (testimony as to fires set by other oil burning locomotives admissible to refute testimony of railroad's experts that its oil burning locomotive would not emit sparks large enough to cause a fire). In food and drug cases the consumer often is rebutting a contention that he became ill from some other cause or that he is hypersensitive. See cases cited supra n. 8; Dec.Dig. Food ⊕25(i), Negligence ⊕125.

13. Mitchell v. Fruehauf Corp., 568 F.2d 1139, 1147 (5th Cir. 1978), rehearing denied 570 F.2d 1391 (applying Texas law to hold that other instances of meat swinging in refrigerated truck trailers and tipping them over admissible to show unreasonably dangerous design); Rimer v. Rockwell International Corp., 641 F.2d 450, 456 (6th Cir. 1981) (error to exclude evidence of 24 other aircraft accidents caused by alleged design defect in fuel intake system); Gulf Hills Dude Ranch v. Brinson, 191 So.2d 856, 861 (Miss.1966) (other accidents on same slippery floor); Turner v. City of Tacoma, 72 Wn.2d 1029, 435 P.2d 927, 931 (1967) (bumping into fire escape on sidewalk); cases cited supra nn. 4–12.

14. But see Vermont Food Industries v. Ralston Purina Co., 514 F.2d 456, 464–465 (2d Cir. 1975) (oversimplified suggestion that degree of danger not material in breach of warranty cases).

15. Of course, where the danger is obvious enough, evidence of other accidents would seem unnecessary and hence unduly prejudicial and time-consuming. City of Birmingham v. McKinnon, 200 Ala. 111, 75 So. 487 (1917) (stake and wire two feet above sidewalk).

16. For cases in which the requirement was held not satisfied, see Lolie v. Ohio Brass Co., 502 F.2d 741,

745 (7th Cir. 1974) (evidence that other metal cable clips used to hold power lines in coal mines released when line was pulled sharply inadmissible in absence of any showing that the clips were of the same quality and had the same characteristics as those defendant manufactured); Horn v. Chicago, Rock Island & Pacific Railway Co., 187 Kan. 423, 357 P.2d 815 (1960) (other accidents at railroad crossing too dissimilar); Royal Mink Ranch v. Ralston Purina Co., 18 Mich.App. 695, 172 N.W.2d 43 (1969) (other experiences with mix of feed from different supplier inadmissible to show effect of defendant's feed on mink); Perry v. Oklahoma City, 470 P.2d 974, 980 (Okl.1970) (inadequate detail about circumstances of accidents); see supra n. 4. Statistical analyses in which the differences are likely to be randomly distributed should be more readily admissible than testimony about particular accidents. Seese v. Volkswagenwerk, A.G., 648 F.2d 833, 846 (3d Cir. 1981) cert. denied 454 U.S. 867 (government statistics showing that on average VW vans were more likely to eject occupants in collisions were admissible despite the fact that there were many variables, such as speed and type of accident, that differ from case to case, see Ch. 20 infra (scientific evidence).

17. Hecht Co. v. Jocobson, 180 F.2d 13, 17 (D.C.Cir. 1950) (similar accident with escalator on different floor years earlier indicated need to replace with a safer model); Gober v. Revlon, Inc., 317 F.2d 47, 51 (4th Cir. 1963) (previous complaints of allergic reactions to "Wonder Base" for nail polish); Young v. Illinois Central Gulf Railway Co., 618 F.2d 332, 339 (5th Cir. 1980) (two recent prior accidents at grade crossing admissible to show that "a reasonably prudent railroad . . . would have taken precautions"); Bailey v. Southern Pacific Transp. Co., 613 F.2d 1385, 1389 (5th Cir. 1980), cert. denied 449 U.S. 836 (evidence of other accidents at different times of day and with cars approaching from opposite direction at crossing at which warning bell and signal light did not function admitted to show hazard and notice); Gardner v. Southern Railway Systems, 675 F.2d 949, 952 (7th Cir. 1982) (evidence of another fatal collision of truck and train at same crossing under similar conditions 15 months earlier should have been admitted "to show that the railroad had prior knowledge that a dangerous and hazardous condition existed"); 2 Wigmore, Evidence § 252 (Chadbourn rev. 1979); Annot., 70 A.L.R.2d 167, 179.

absolute, this theory is inapposite. In negligence cases, however, the duty is merely to use reasonable care to maintain safe conditions. Even in many strict product liability cases, demonstrating that the product is defective or unreasonably dangerous for its intended use requires an analysis of foreseeable risks.[18]

When the evidence of other accidents is introduced to show notice of the danger, subsequent accidents are not admissible under this rationale.[19] The proponent probably will want to show directly that the defendant had knowledge of the prior accidents, but the nature, frequency [20] or notoriety [21] of the incidents may well reveal that defendant knew of them or that he should have discovered the danger by due inspection. Since all that is required is that the previous injury or injuries be such as to call defendant's attention to the dangerous situation that resulted in the litigated accident, the similarity in the circumstances of the accidents can be considerably less than that which is demanded

when the same evidence is used for one of the other valid purposes.[22]

Having surveyed the utility of a history of accidents in establishing liability, we now consider the admissibility of a history of no accidents for exculpatory purposes.[23] One might think that if proof of similar accidents is admissible in the judge's discretion to show that a particular condition or defect exists, or that the injury sued for was caused in a certain way, or that a situation is dangerous, or that defendant knew or should have known of the danger, then evidence of the absence of accidents during a period of similar exposure and experience likewise would be receivable to show that these facts do not exist in the case at bar. Indeed, it would seem perverse to tell a jury that one or two persons besides the plaintiff tripped on defendant's stairwell while withholding from them the further information that another thousand persons descended the same stairs without incident.[24]

Customer complaints arising from similar experiences but not culminating in accidents may help establish that defendant had actual notice of the danger. Gardner v. Q.H.S., Inc., 448 F.2d 238, 244 (4th Cir. 1971); (complaints concerning flammability problems with hair curlers); New York Life Insurance Co. v. Seighman, 140 F.2d 930, 932 (6th Cir. 1944) (custodian received complaint about defective railing on third floor landing); Farley v. M.M. Cattle Co., 529 S.W.2d 751, 755 (Tex.1975), appeal after remand 549 S.W.2d 453, error refused no reversible error (previous incident in which horse named "Crowbar" had run toward another horse used to show cattle ranch's awareness that Crowbar was dangerous).

18. Rexrode v. American Laundry Press Co., 674 F.2d 826, 829 n. 9 (10th Cir. 1982) ("Under both federal and Kansas law, it is clear that evidence of the occurrence of other accidents involving substantially the same circumstances as the case at issue is admissible, pursuant to a strict liability theory, to establish notice, the existence of a defect, or to refute testimony by a defense witness that a given product was designed without safety hazards"), cert. denied 103 S.Ct. 137. But see supra note 14.

19. Julander v. Ford Motor Co., 488 F.2d 839, 846 (10th Cir. 1973); Ozark Air Lines v. Larimer, 352 F.2d 9 (8th Cir. 1965). In contrast, evidence admissible for one of the other valid purposes may relate to subsequent accidents. Kanelos v. Kettler, 406 F.2d 951, 956 n. 30 (D.C.Cir. 1968); Bailey v. Kawasaki-Kisen, K.K., 455 F.2d 392 (5th Cir. 1972), appeal after remand 478

F.2d 839; Taylor v. Northern States Power Co., 192 Minn. 415, 256 N.W. 674 (1934).

20. Moore v. Bloomington Decatur & Champaign Railroad Co., 295 Ill. 63, 67, 128 N.E. 721, 722 (1920).

21. Lombar v. East Tawas, 86 Mich. 14, 20, 48 N.W. 947, 948 (1891).

22. Gardner v. Southern Railway System, 675 F.2d 949, 952 (7th Cir. 1982); Young v. Illinois Central Gulf Railroad Co., 618 F.2d 332, 339 (5th Cir. 1980).

23. See generally 63 Am.Jur.2d Products Liability §§ 16, 24; 29 id. Evidence §§ 310–14; C.J.S. Negligence § 234(8); Dec.Dig. Negligence ⊚125; Annot., 31 A.L.R.2d 190.

24. Birmingham Union Railway Co. v. Alexander, 93 Ala. 133, 9 So. 525, 527 (1891) ("The negative proof in the one case, equally with the affirmative proof in the other, serves to furnish the means of applying to the matter the practical test of common experience"). On the other hand, there are special problems with proving the nonexistence of something. In particular, an absence of complaints does not necessarily mean that accidents have not been occurring. "Those who stumble without falling may be too busy to register a complaint, and complaints to one employee may not be passed on to the person who testifies that he has not heard of any trouble. Also, the condition of areas continually changes. The plaintiff may in fact be among the first to encounter a newly dangerous situation." Lempert & Saltzburg, A Modern Approach to Evidence 210 (2d ed. 1983). See Vermont Food Industries v. Ral-

Yet, many decisions lay down just such a general rule against proof of absence of other accidents.[25] In some cases, excluding such proof of safety may be justified on the ground that the persons passing in safety were not exposed to the same conditions as those that prevailed when the plaintiff's injury occurred.[26] The evidence of a thousand safe descents down the stairs would be far less convincing if it were revealed that all of these were made in daylight, while the two or three accidents occurred at night in poor lighting. However, the possibility that a very general safety record may obscure the influence of an important factor merely counsels for applying the traditional requirement of substantial similarity to evidence of the absence as well as the presence of other accidents.[27] When the experience sought to be proved is so extensive as to be sure to include an adequate number of similar situations, the similarity requirement should be considered satisfied.[28]

Neither can the broad proscription be justified by the other considerations that affect the admissibility of evidence. The problems of prejudice and distraction over "collateral issues" seem much more acute when it comes to proof of other accidents than when evidence of an accident-free history is proffered. Indeed, the defendant will seldom open this door if there is any practical likelihood that the plaintiff will dispute the safety record.

Consequently, few recent decisions can be found applying a general rule of exclusion.[29] A large number of cases recognize that lack of other accidents may be admissible to show (1) absence of the defect or condition alleged,[30] (2) the lack of a causal relationship

---

ston Purina Co., 514 F.2d 456, 464–465 (2d Cir. 1975) (complaints may not be passed from regional to national headquarters). While these factors should be considered in balancing probative value against the usual counterweights, they do not justify a flat rule of exclusion.

25. Hlavaty v. Song, 107 Ariz. 606, 491 P.2d 460, 463 (1971) (slipping off chair); Dill v. Dallas County Farmers' Exchange No. 177, 267 S.W.2d 677, 681 (Mo. 1954) ("testimony that no other invitee had ever fallen in defendant's store would tend to confuse issues"); Sanitary Grocery Co., Inc. v. Steinbrecher, 183 Va. 495, 32 S.E.2d 685, 687–688 (1945) (since "evidence must be confined to the point in issue," it was proper to exclude testimony that 1000 customers had entered store each day for 11 months without cutting themselves on sharp corner of shelf); Schiro v. Oriental Realty Co., 7 Wis.2d 556, 97 N.W.2d 385 (1959) (injury on part of lawn that plaintiff had used without mishap for 24 years).

26. Pittman v. Littlefield, 438 F.2d 659, 662 (1st Cir. 1971) (error to admit testimony that bags of plaster had never previously fallen from storage bin when plaintiff alleged that bin was secured improperly in this instance); Wray v. Fairfield Amusement Co., 126 Conn. 221, 10 A.2d 600 (1940) (absence of accidents on roller coaster should have been limited to passengers riding in seat where plaintiff alleged the strap was defective); Taylor v. Town of Monroe, 43 Conn. 36 (1875) (safety history of bridge did not include previous experience with runaway horses).

27. This is the approach followed in Walker v. Trico Manufacturing Co., 487 F.2d 595, 599 (7th Cir. 1973), cert. denied 415 U.S. 978 (failure to show that 45 other blow-mold machines and the circumstances of their use were sufficiently similar). A drastic application of the similarity requirement can be found in Vermont Food Industries, Inc. v. Ralston Purina Co., 514 F.2d 456,

464–465 (2d Cir. 1975) (absence of complaints at national headquarters about nutritional value of chicken feed "not probative" in part because nutritional value fluctuates with storage life and other variables).

28. Webb v. Thomas, 133 Colo. 458, 296 P.2d 1036, 1040 (1956) (over 12,000 persons using swimming pool up to time of trial with only plaintiff injured from diving in shallow end); Stein v. Trans World Airlines, 25 A.D.2d 732, 268 N.Y.S.2d 752 (1966) (error to exclude evidence that many thousands had walked through same area in air terminal without slipping); Erickson v. Walgreen Drug Co., 120 Utah 31, 232 P.2d 210, 214 (1951) (error to exclude evidence that no one had slipped on terrazzo entranceway, regardless of weather conditions, for the 15 years during which at least 4000 persons entered the store every day); Stark v. Allis Chalmers & Northwest Roads, 2 Wn.App. 399, 467 P.2d 854, 858 (1970) (no similar accident with 10,000 allegedly faultily designed tractors).

29. Most modern cases assume or quickly conclude that the safety record is admissible and focus on the similarity requirement. Darrough v. White Motor Co., 74 Ill.App.3d 560, 30 Ill.Dec. 467, 470, 393 N.E.2d 122, 125 (1979); 63 Am.Jur.2d Products Liability § 17; cases cited supra nn. 26 and 28, infra nn. 30–33.

30. Becker v. American Air Lines, 200 F.Supp. 243 (S.D.N.Y.1961) (safety history of altimeter); Birmingham Union Railway Co. v. Alexander, 93 Ala. 133, 9 So. 525, 527 (1890) ("the defendant should be allowed the benefit of proof that the track, as it was at the time, was constantly crossed by other persons, under similar condition, without inconvenience, hindrance, or peril, as evidence tending to show the absence of the alleged defect of that it was not the cause"); Menard v. Cashman, 93 N.H. 273, 41 A.2d 222 (1945) (absence of falls on stairway); Annot., 31 A.L.R.2d 190.

between the injury and the defect or condition charged,[31] (3) the nonexistence of an unduly dangerous situation,[32] or (4) want of knowledge (or of grounds to realize) the danger.[33]

 WESTLAW REFERENCES

digest(similar /p prior previous past earlier /10 accident* injur*** /p relevan! probative material

immaterial)

synopsis,digest(similar /p prior previous past earlier /10 accident* injur*** /p relevan! probative material immaterial /p danger! safe! unsafe)

slip! fall! /25 similar previous prior /25 condition* accident* circumstance* /25 evidence admissib! inadmissib!

synopsis,digest(similar /p prior previous past earlier /10 accident* injur*** disease* illness! /p relevan! probative material immaterial /p kn*w!)

---

31. Birmingham Union Railway Co. v. Alexander, 93 Ala. 133, 9 So. 525, 527 (1891) (described at n. 28 supra); Rayner v. Stauffer Chemical Co., 120 Ariz. 328, 585 P.2d 1240, 1243 (App.1978) (200 tests in which herbicide did not damage potatoes); Lawler v. Skelton, 241 Miss. 274, 130 So.2d 565 (1961) (effects of insecticide sprayed on various persons); Annot., 31 A.L.R.2d 190.

32. Zheutlin v. Sperry & Hutchinson Co., 149 Conn. 364, 179 A.2d 829 (1962) (50,000 others had used curb without falling); McCarty v. Village of Nashwauk, 282 Minn. 262, 164 N.W.2d 380, 382 (1969) (error to exclude evidence of absence of prior accidents on sidewalk); Wollaston v. Burlington Northern, Inc., 612 P.2d 1277, 1282 (Mont.1980) (no prior railroad crossing accidents); Wozniak v. 110 South Main St. Land & Development Improvement Corp., 61 A.D.2d 848, 402 N.Y.S.2d 69, 70 (1978) (no other falls in hotel parking lot); Rathbun v.

Humphrey Co., 94 Ohio App. 429, 113 N.E.2d 877 (1953) (amusement ride placed near trees used by thousands without complaint); Baker v. Lane County, 37 Or.App. 87, 586 P.2d 114, 117–118 (1978) (no other instances of children being injured at fairgrounds by reaching through outside fence to hold rope tethering horses); cases cited supra n. 26.

33. McCarty v. Village of Nashwauk, 282 Minn. 262, 164 N.W.2d 380, 382 (1969) (absence of falls on sidewalk); Wilk v. Georges, 267 Or. 19, 514 P.2d 877, 881 (1973) (absence of falls on planks in garden nursery); Annot., 31 A.L.R.2d 190. Of course, the purposes are overlapping, and not all opinions spell them out distinctly See, e.g., Borelli v. Top Value Enterprises, 356 Mass. 110, 248 N.E.2d 510 (1969) (absence of complaints of electric shock from carpet sweeper); Annot., 31 A.L.R.2d 190.

Chapter 19
INSURANCE AGAINST LIABILITY

Table of Sections

---

§ 201. Insurance Against Liability

A formidable body of cases holds that evidence that a party is or is not insured against liability is not admissible on the issue of negligence.[1] This doctrine rests on two premises. The first is the belief that whether one has insurance coverage reveals little about the likelihood that he will act carelessly. Subject to a few pathological exceptions, financial protection will not diminish the normal incentive to be careful, especially where life and limb are at stake.[2] Similarly, the argument that insured individuals or firms are more prudent and careful, as a group, than those who are self-insurers[3] seems tenuous,[4] and also serves to counteract any force that the first argument may have. Thus, the relevance of the evidence of coverage is doubtful. In addition, there is concern that the evidence would be prejudicial—that the mention of insurance invites higher awards than are justified,[5]

---

§ 201

1. See generally 21B Appleman, Insurance Law and Practice §§ 12812–12818 (1980); M. Graham, Handbook of Federal Evidence § 411.1 (1981); 2 Louisell & Mueller, Federal Evidence §§ 193–195 (1978); Saltzburg & Redden, Federal Rules of Evidence Manual § 411 (3d ed. 1982); 2 Weinstein & Berger, Federal Evidence ¶ 411; 2 Wigmore, Evidence § 282a (Chadbourn rev. 1979); 22 Wright & Graham, Federal Practice and Procedure §§ 5361–5369; Annot., 40 A.L.R.Fed. 541 (evidence of liability insurance in negligence actions), 77 A.L.R.2d 1154 (references to workers' compensation), 4 A.L.R.2d 761 (references to liability insurance in personal injury litigation); 58 Am.Jur.2d Negligence §§ 527–530; 29 id. Evidence §§ 404–407; 8 id. Automobiles and Highway Traffic §§ 963–964; 88 C.J.S. Trial §§ 53–54.

2. Brown v. Walter, 62 F.2d 798, 800 (2d Cir. 1933) (L. Hand, Cir. J. "There can be no rational excuse [for mentioning insurance] except the flimsy one that a man is more likely to be careless if insured. That is at most the merest guess, much more than outweighed by the probability that the real issues will be obscured"). Where one's accident history directly affects his premiums, the marginal effect on care should be especially slight. But see 22 Wright & Graham, supra note 1,

§ 5362 at 431 (coverage may alter behavior and is therefore relevant when the insured exposes others, but not himself, to danger).

3. Slough, Relevancy Unraveled, 5 U.Kan.L.Rev. 675, 710 (1957).

4. Moreover, it is but another way of saying that because an individual is usually prudent (as evidenced by the fact that he is thoughtful enough to buy insurance), he probably acted prudently in the circumstances of the accident. Such character evidence generally is disallowed. See supra § 189 (evidence of character for care).

5. Eichel v. New York Cent. Railroad Co., 375 U.S. 253, 255 (1963) ("It has long been recognized that evidence showing that defendant is insured creates a substantial likelihood of misuse"); Posttape Associates v. Eastman Kodak Co., 537 F.2d 751, 758 (3d Cir. 1976), appeal after remand 450 F.Supp. 407 ("Knowledge that a party is insured may also affect a verdict if the jury knows that some of the loss has been paid by insurance or that it would satisfy a judgment against a defendant"); Langley v. Turner's Express, 375 F.2d 296, 297 (4th Cir. 1967) (danger that "the jury may award damages without fault if aware that there is insurance coverage to pay the verdict"); Price v. Yellow Cab Co.,

---

and conversely, that the sympathy that a jury might feel for a defendant who must pay out of his own pocket could interfere with its evaluation of the evidence under the appropriate standard of proof.[6]

Despite these concerns and the general rule that evidence of the fact of insurance coverage is inadmissible to show negligence or reasonable care,[7] such evidence frequently is received. As with the exclusionary rules discussed in Chapters 17 (Character and Habit) and 18 (Similar Happenings and Transactions), the evidence may be admitted for some other purpose, providing of course that its probative value on this other issue is not substantially outweighed by its prejudicial impact.[8] The purposes for which such evidence may be offered are several.[9] Federal and Revised Uniform Rule (1974) 411 list most of them:

> Evidence that a person was or was not insured against liability is not admissible upon the issue whether he acted negligently or otherwise wrongfully. This rule does not require the exclusion of evidence of insurance against liability when offered for another purpose, such as proof of agency, ownership or control, or bias or prejudice of a witness.

The hypothesis that persons rarely purchase liability insurance to cover contingencies for which they are not responsible makes the evidence relevant to questions of agency,[10] ownership,[11] and control.[12] The fact of insurance can be relevant to the bias of a witness in a number of ways. For example, the witness may be an investigator or other individual employed by the insurance company.[13] Cross-examination affords the

---

443 Pa. 56, 278 A.2d 161, 166 (1971) (identifying this as "the chief reason" for the exclusionary rule).

6. See supra § 185 for a discussion of this form of prejudice. For descriptions and criticisms of empirical studies of the effect of disclosing whether a defendant is insured, see Broeder, The University of Chicago Jury Project, 38 Neb.L.Rev. 744, 753–54 (1959); Green, Blindfolding the Jury, 33 Tex.L.Rev. 157, 165 (1954); Kalven, The Jury, the Law, and the Personal Injury Damage Award, 19 Ohio St.L.J. 158, 171 (1958); Notes, 10 U.Fla.L.Rev. 68, 74 (1957), 29 Tex.L.Rev. 949, 955–56 (1951), 11 Ohio St.L.J. 370, 375 (1950).

7. Cases stating or applying the rule excluding evidence or mention of the fact that a party has liability insurance can be found in almost all jurisdictions. Many are cited throughout this section, and others are collected in Appleman, supra n. 1, at §§ 12831–12833; Annot., 40 A.L.R.Fed. 541, 4 A.L.R.2d 761 (1949). For cases dealing with references to the fact that a party has no coverage, see Courson v. Chandler, 258 Ark. 904, 529 S.W.2d 864, 865 (1975); Appleman, supra n. 1, at § 12838; Annots., supra n. 1.

8. For cases excluding evidence that fits into a permissible category, see Garfield v. Russell, 251 Cal.App. 275, 59 Cal.Rptr. 379, 382 (1967); Gerry v. Neugebauer, 83 N.H. 23, 136 A. 751, 753 (1927) (impeachment). For a discussion of the balancing process that is needed for all relevant evidence, see supra § 185.

9. See generally comment, 26 Corn.L.Q. 137 (1940).

10. Hunziker v. Schneidemantle, 543 F.2d 489, 495 n. 10 (3d Cir. 1976) (liability insurance may be admitted to show that pilot of light aircraft was acting as agent if adequate foundation is laid); McCoy v. Universal Carloading and Distributing Co., 82 F.2d 342, 344 (6th Cir. 1936) (whether driver of truck was agent or independent contractor); Eldridge v. McGeorge, 99 F.2d

835, 841 (8th Cir. 1938) (whether owner or driver of truck were an employee); Cook–O'Brien Construction Co. v. Crawford, 26 F.2d 574, 575 (9th Cir. 1928), cert. denied 278 U.S. 630 (whether worker injured by explosion was employee); Cherry v. Stockton, 75 N.M. 488, 406 P.2d 358, 360 (1965) (whether owner and driver of truck was employee); Biggins v. Wagner, 60 S.D. 581, 245 N.W. 385, 386–387 (1932) (same); cf. Ben M. Hogan Co. v. Nichols, 254 Ark. 771, 496 S.W.2d 404, 411–413 (1973) (policy inadmissible because it shed no light on issue of agency relationship between pertinent persons).

11. Newell v. Harold Shaffer Leasing Co., 489 F.2d 103, 110 (5th Cir. 1974) (check for repair bill from insurance company naming defendant as the insured properly received under Mississippi law "on the issue of ownership and agency"); Dubbins v. Crain Brothers, 432 F.Supp. 1060, 1069 (W.D.Pa.1976), modified on other grounds 567 F.2d 559 (3d Cir.) (ownership, possession, and custody of barge); Layton v. Cregan & Mallory Co., 263 Mich. 30, 248 N.W. 539 (1933) (ownership of automobile); Anderson v. Ohm, 258 N.W.2d 114, 118 (1977) (same); cf. Leavitt v. Glick Realty Corp., 362 Mass. 370, 285 N.E.2d 786, 787 (1972) (evidence of liability insurance to show ownership or control of building is not admissible when these matters are not disputed).

12. Pinckard v. Dunnavant, 281 Ala. 533, 206 So.2d 340, 342–343 (1968) (management and maintenance of premises); Appelhans v. Kirkwood, 148 Colo. 92, 365 P.2d 233, 239 (1961) (proof that father insured vehicle driven by son); Perkins v. Rice, 187 Mass. 28, 72 N.E. 323, 324 (1904) (defendant admitted ownership of premises but denied control of elevator).

13. Varlack v. SWC Caribbean, Inc., 550 F.2d 171, 176–177 (3d Cir. 1977) (defendant's witness, who testified that plaintiff's witness made an incriminating

usual means of revealing the relationship between the company and the witness.[14]

Plainly, these purposes do not exhaust the possibilities. Evidence of insurance may be admitted when it is an inseparable part of an admission of a party bearing on negligence or damages.[15] And, there are some less common uses.[16]

Furthermore, there are two other ways in which the fact of insurance can be brought home to the jury. Witnesses have been known to make unexpected and unresponsive references to insurance.[17] In these situ-

statement, employed as an investigator by defendant's liability carrier); Ingalls Shipbuilding Corp. v. Trehern, 155 F.2d 202, 203–204 (5th Cir. 1946) (cross-examination to show that defendant's witness was insurance adjuster); Vindicator Consolidated Gold Mining Co. v. Firstbrook, 36 Colo. 498, 86 P. 313, 314 (1906) (cross-examination to show witness acting as agent for insurance company); Pickett v. Kolb, 250 Ind. 449, 237 N.E.2d 105, 106 (1968) (error to sustain objection to question "who paid you to do this inspection? "); MacTyres, Inc. v. Virgil, 92 N.M. 446, 589 P.2d 1037, 1039 (1979) (abuse of discretion to exclude deposition of witness admitting to having lied to insurance representative); Rigelman v. Gilligan, 265 Or. 109, 506 P.2d 710, 714 (1973).

When plaintiff's witness is impeached by a prior inconsistent written statement prepared by an insurance adjuster and plaintiff disputes the correctness of the statement, the majority of courts allow the plaintiff to show the insurance company's employee prepared the statement for plaintiff's signature. Complete Auto Transit v. Wayne Broyles Engineering Corp., 351 F.2d 478, 481–482 (5th Cir. 1965); Roland v. Beckham, 408 S.W.2d 628, 633 (Ky.1966); Brave v. Blakely, 250 S.C. 353, 157 S.E.2d 726, 730 (1967). Contra Texas Co. v. Betterton, 126 Tex. 359, 88 S.W.2d 1039 (1936).

Some judges do not see any need for bringing the fact of insurance to light to demonstrate bias. See O'Donnell v. Bachelor, 429 Pa. 498, 240 A.2d 484, 486, 489 (1968) (error to limit cross-examination to show that defendant's insurer employed investigator-witness, for "Once a witness commits himself to the ocean of legal controversy, he must, under cross-examination, disclose the flag under which he sails." To which a dissent replied that disclosing the presence of the insurance company reveals "not only the flag, but the seamstress who sewed it" —a reference to the rule of some states that the impeachment be limited to showing that the witness was employed "on behalf of the defendant"). For a case holding that curtailing disclosure to this extent is within the trial court's discretion, see Matthews v. Jean's Pastry Shop, 113 N.H. 546, 311 A.2d 127 (1973).

14. Mideastern Contracting Corp. v. O'Toole, 55 F.2d 909, 912 (2d Cir. 1932) (L. Hand, Cir. J. "The defendant need not have put in the statement [that the plaintiff allegedly made] at all; when it chooses to do so, it laid open to inquiry its authenticity, and that inevitably involved the relation of the person who took it"); Eppinger & Russell Co. v. Sheely, 24 F.2d 153, 155 (5th Cir. 1928) (proper to ask physician testifying for defendant whether he was retained by employer's insurer); Charter v. Chleborad, 551 F.2d 246 (8th Cir. 1977), cert. denied 434 U.S. 856 (error to prohibit plaintiff in medi-

cal malpractice action from establishing on cross-examination that defendant's witness (an attorney who testified that plaintiff's expert witness had a bad reputation for truth and veracity) represents defendant's liability carrier from time to time); Dempsey v. Goldstein Brothers Amusement Co., 231 Mass. 461, 121 N.E. 429 (1919) (to show bias of physician who testified that plaintiff had no permanent injuries); Gibson v. Grey Motor Co., 147 Minn. 134, 179 N.W. 729, 730 (1920) (insurance investigator); cases cited n. 13 supra; cf. Ikerd v. Lapworth, 435 F.2d 197, 208 (7th Cir. 1970) (Indiana law permits asking expert who is paying him even when the answer would disclose the existence of insurance, but this exception does not apply when the expert does not testify); Averett v. Shircliff, 218 Va. 202, 237 S.E.2d 92, 96 (1977) (proper to prohibit impeachment of appraisers in this manner since they were not regular employees but independent appraisers who worked for many insurance companies); see supra n. 8.

15. If the reference to insurance can be severed without substantially lessening the probative value of the admission, this should be done. Cameron v. Columbia Builders, 212 Or. 388, 320 P.2d 251, 254 (1958); Connor v. McGill, 127 Vt. 19, 238 A.2d 777, 780 (1968). But where the reference to insurance is an "integral part" of the admission, the whole statement may be received. Herschensohn v. Weisman, 80 N.H. 557, 119 A. 705 (1923) (passenger warned driver to be more careful lest he have an accident and kill somebody, and defendant driver said "Don't worry, I carry insurance for that"); Reid v. Owens, 98 Utah 50, 93 P.2d 680, 685 (1939) (The reference to insurance in the statement "My boy is careless, and he drives too fast . . . . We have taken out insurance to protect him [and] if you won't prosecute . . . we will do all we can to help you get that $5,000 insurance" was "itself freighted with admission").

16. Posttape Associates v. Eastman Kodak Co., 537 F.2d 751, 758 (3d Cir. 1976), after remand 450 F.Supp. 407 (to show awareness of trade usage limiting liability for defective film to replacement value); Hannah v. Haskins, 612 F.2d 373, 375 (8th Cir. 1980) (cross-examination allowed where plaintiff adverted to insurance payments on direct examination and they may have been relevant to the nature and extent of plaintiff's injuries); Kubista v. Romaine, 87 Wn.2d 62, 549 P.2d 491, 496 (1976) (evidence that defendant's insurer had encouraged plaintiff to go to school to learn a new trade and had promised to take care of him admissible in rebuttal of defense that plaintiff could have mitigated damages by going back to work earlier).

17. Isler v. Burman, 305 Minn. 288, 232 N.W.2d 818, 822 (1975) (pastor twice referred to church's insurance

ations, the judge may declare a mistrial,[18] but it is a rare case in which he will do more than strike the reference and instruct the jury to ignore it.[19] Finally, in the examination of prospective jurors, most jurisdictions allow questions about employment by or interest in insurance companies.[20]

Despite its nearly universal acceptance, the wisdom of the general prohibition on injecting insurance into the trial, as it currently operates, is questionable. When the rule originated, insurance coverage of individuals was exceptional. In the absence of references to insurance at trial, a juror most probably would not have thought that a de-

fendant was insured. Today, compulsory insurance laws for motorists are ubiquitous, and liability insurance for homeowners and businesses has become the norm. Most jurors probably assume that defendants are insured.[21] Yet, few courts will allow a defendant to show that he is uninsured,[22] unless the plaintiff has opened the door to such evidence.[23] At a minimum, such a defendant, and indeed any party, should be entitled to an instruction that there has been no evidence as to whether or not any party is insured because the law is that the presence or absence of insurance should play no part in the case.[24]

---

even though church's counsel had told him not to); cases cited, infra nn. 18–19.

18. Garber v. Martin, 261 Or. 410, 494 P.2d 858 (1972). Reversal is nearly automatic where the disclosure is deliberate and stressed by counsel in questioning or argument. Pickwick Stage Lines v. Edwards, 64 F.2d 758, 762–63 (10th Cir. 1933); Jones Stewart & Co. v. Newby, 266 F. 287 (4th Cir. 1920).

19. Dindo v. Grand Union Co., 331 F.2d 138, 141 (2d Cir. 1964) ("the specific question asked required only a yes or no answer, and the witness voluntarily brought in the insurance company"); Lenz v. Southern Pacific Co., 493 F.2d 471, 472 (5th Cir. 1974) (counsel's "single inadvertent reference" to railroad investigator as "insurance investigator"); Hazeltine v. Johnson, 92 F.2d 866, 869–870 (9th Cir. 1937); Muehlebach v. Mercer Mortuary & Chapel, 93 Ariz. 60, 378 P.2d 741, 745 (1963); Evans v. Howard R. Green Co., 231 N.W.2d 907, 914–915 (Iowa 1975); Carver v. Lavigne, 160 Me. 414, 205 A.2d 159, 162 (1964) ("unpredictably elicited from an undoubtedly guileless witness"); De Spain v. Bohlke, 259 Or. 320, 486 P.2d 545, 546–47 (1971) (physician's reference to patients' nervousness as a result of being " 'hounded' by the insurance company"); Gumenick v. United States, 213 Va. 510, 193 S.E.2d 788, 796 (1973). But see Beherns v. Nelson, 86 S.D. 312, 195 N.W.2d 140, 141 (1972) (inadvertence rule not applicable where, contrary to his counsel's advice, plaintiff referred to insurance on direct examination).

20. In some jurisdictions the trial judge may allow or disallow the questioning, as he sees fit, and in general, many refinements and variations exist as to consultation with the court in advance and as to the questions that may be asked. It is usually said that the questions must be propounded in good faith. Such "good faith" involves establishing that the party is in fact insured, that prospective jurors may be associated with a liability carrier or otherwise unusually concerned with insurance policies or premiums. For cases and general discussions, see Drickersen v. Drickersen, 604 P.2d 1082, 1084–85 (Alaska 1979) (prospective juror's reference to rising insurance rates justified questioning entire panel on this point); King v. Westlake, 264 Ark. 555, 572 S.W.2d 841, 843–844 (1978) (questions

about effect of verdict on insurance premiums); Harvey v. Castleberry, 258 Ark. 722, 529 S.W.2d 324 (1975) ("Are any of you policyholders in any mutual insurance company writing automobile liability insurance policies? "); Robinson v. Faulkner, 163 Conn. 365, 306 A.2d 857, 863–864 (1972) (question about "interest or participation or connection with casualty companies"); Rosenthal v. Kolars, 231 N.W.2d 285, 287 (Minn.1975) (whether jurors or any of their close relatives had been employed as claims adjusters for company that writes medical malpractice insurance); Appleman, supra note 1, §§ 12813–12818; 2 Louisell & Mueller, supra note 1, § 195.

Some writers have proposed obtaining information about individual jurors with less prejudice by examining the venire before drawing panels for particular cases, Note, 52 Harv.L.Rev. 166 (1938), or by a questionnaire. Note, 43 Mich.L.Rev. 621 (1944).

21. This realization has not escaped the courts. B–Amused Co. v. Millrose Sporting Club, 168 F.Supp. 709, 710 (E.D.N.Y.1958) ("In this day and generation, nearly every juryman knows that the average negligence case is being defended by an insurance company. . . . The idea seems to die hard that what jurors know in their everyday business experience they close their minds to, when deliberating as jurors"); Young v. Carter, 121 Ga.App. 191, 173 S.E.2d 259, 261 (1970) (concurring opinion observing that "Any juror who doesn't know there is insurance in the case by this time [after voir dire] should probably be excused [as] an idiot"); Connelly v. Nolte, 237 Iowa 114, 21 N.W.2d 311, 320 (1946) (The juror "doesn't require a brick house to fall on him to give him an idea"). See also Broeder, Voir Dire, 38 S.Cal.L.Rev. 503, 525 (1965); n. 28 infra.

22. See Piechuck v. Magusiak, 82 N.H. 429, 135 A. 534 (1926) ("a form of the inadmissible plea of poverty"); cases cited supra n. 7.

23. Stehouwer v. Lewis, 249 Mich. 76, 227 N.W. 759, 761 (1929); Whitman v. Carver, 337 Mo. 1247, 88 S.W.2d 885, 887 (1935).

24. Cf. Saltzburg & Redden, supra n. 1, at 160 (analogous proposal for helping jury to understand why, in cross-examining character witnesses with ques-

More fundamentally, the underlying soundness of the general rule forbidding disclosure of the fact of insurance has been the object of scathing criticism.[25] Stripped to its essentials, the debate is not really over the application of the doctrines of relevancy and its counterweights. Hardly anyone questions the premise that the evidence is irrelevant to the exercise of reasonable care.[26] Neither does anyone contend that a party has a right to put irrelevant evidence into the record.[27] Rather, the arguments for the abandonment of the policy of secrecy are either pragmatic or idealistic. The pragmatic argument is straightforward. The conspiracy of silence is hard to maintain. Its costs include extensive and unnecessary arguments, reversals, and retrials stemming from elusive questions of prejudice and good faith. This state of affairs might be tolerable if the revelations of insurance were truly fraught with prejudice. But, as we have suggested, most jurors probably presuppose the existence of liability insurance anyway, and the heart of the policy of nondisclosure is surrendered when jurors are examined about their connection with insurance com-

panies. Consequently, the extent to which evidence of coverage or its absence is prejudicial is unclear.[28] Even the direction in which such prejudice might work is obscure.[29] In sum, the rule has become a hollow shell, expensive to maintain and of doubtful utility.

The other principal argument against the rule of secrecy is more difficult to evaluate, but standing alone, it is less persuasive. It arises from a certain conception of fairness—a conception that holds that the jury should know who the "real" parties in interest are. The insurance company, which under its policy has the exclusive right to employ counsel, defend the suit, and control the decision as to settling or contesting the action, is a party in all but name.[30] Unfortunately, this argument begs the question. If the substantive law is that the depth of the defendant's pocket has nothing to do with liability or damages, then why should the jury be apprised of this fact? To be sure, in many cases the relative wealth of the parties is manifest. A multinational corporation cannot disguise itself as a struggling member of the proletariat.[31] But where admit-

tions of the "have you heard" variety, counsel do not follow up negative responses).

25. See Morgan, Basic Problems of Evidence 212 (1961) (enforcement of rule produces "a lot of nonsense"); 2 Wigmore, Evidence § 282a at 134 (Chadbourn rev. 1979) (rule "impracticable"); Allen, Why Do Courts Coddle Insurance Indemnity Companies?, 61 Am.L.Rev. 77 (1927); Fannin, Disclosure of Insurance in Negligence Trials—The Arizona Rule, 5 Ariz.L.Rev. 83, 91–93 (1963); Green, supra n. 6, at 159 ("fantastic efforts . . . by the courts . . . to develop protection for indemnity carriers"); Slough, supra n. 3, at 711, 713 ("archaic legal principle" that has received an "avalanche of authoritative criticism").

26. But see 22 Wright & Graham, supra n. 1, § 5362 at 431, § 5363 at 443.

27. See supra § 184 (only relevant evidence is admissible). It might be said, however, that the identity of the insurer and the amount of coverage are relevant as "background facts." See 2 Louisell & Mueller, supra n. 1, § 193 at 365–66; Green, supra n. 6; supra § 185.

28. Muehlebach v. Mercer Mortuary & Chapel, 93 Ariz. 60, 378 P.2d 741, 744 (1963) ("the prejudicial content of a reference to liability insurance is largely a matter of the past. And, it has, in part, been made a thing of the past by the expenditures of vast sums of

money by insurance companies to educate prospective jurors of the claimed relation between large verdicts and insurance rates").

29. Shingleton v. Bussey, 223 So.2d 713, 718 (Fla. 1969) ("revelation of the interest of an insurer . . . should be more beneficial to insurers than the questionable 'ostrich head in the sand' approach which may mislead jurors to think that insurance coverage is greater than it is"); 2 Louisell & Mueller, supra n. 1, § 193 at 366–367 (footnotes omitted) ("In an age used to inflation, and to rising insurance premiums, jurors are likely at least to sense that over-generous awards unnecessarily augment costs which are passed on to the public in the form of higher premium rates"); Loftus, Insurance Advertising and Jury Awards, 65 A.B.A.J. 69 (1979) (jury simulation experiment indicating that "the subjects [mock jurors] exposed to the insurance had awarded less for pain and suffering than those who weren't").

30. In various jurisdictions, doctrines of joinder, subrogation or direct action may permit the insurance company to be named as a defendant. City Stores v. Lerner, 410 F.2d 1010 (D.C. Cir. 1969) (subrogation); 8 Appelman, supra n. 1, §§ 4831–4838; Note, 74 Harv.L.Rev. 357 (1960).

31. But cf. Wright & Graham, supra n. 1, § 5362 at 434–435 ("If the fear of juror prejudice is sufficient to

tedly irrelevant characteristics can be removed from the courtroom without great strain, it is hard to see why they should be retained. In the end, therefore, it is the more pragmatic analysis that should be decisive. The benefits of a half-hearted policy of secrecy are not worth the costs. If disclosure of the fact of insurance really is prejudicial, the corrective is not a futile effort at concealment, but the usual fulfillment by the court of its function of explaining to the jury its duty to decide according to the facts and the substantive law, rather than upon

sympathy, ability to pay, or concern about proliferating litigation and rising insurance premiums.

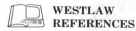

WESTLAW REFERENCES

synopsis,digest(411 /s evid! admit! admissible inadmissible)
388k127
157k113(13)
jur*** /p voirdire /p insurance
synopsis,digest(jur*** /5 instruction* /p insurance)
388k133.6(8)

---

allow an insurance company to masquerade as the Salvation Army, why should not a black litigant be permitted to hire a white to impersonate him at the counsel

table and from the witness stand in order to avoid the well known impact of racism on personal injury awards? ").

Chapter 20
EXPERIMENTAL AND SCIENTIFIC EVIDENCE

Table of Sections

§ 202. Pretrial Experiments

The dominant method of factual inquiry in the courts of law is observational. Witnesses relate what they have seen under naturally occurring conditions, and the judge or jury, observing the witnesses, accepts or rejects their stories with some degree of confidence. In many fields of science, naturalistic observations of people or things are also a principal means of gathering information (though the observations are made in a more structured fashion and are presented and analyzed in a different way). In other scientific disciplines, the major method for collecting data involves manipulating the environment. In its simplest and ideal form, a controlled experiment screens out or holds constant all extraneous variables so that the experimenter can measure the impact of the one factor of interest.[1]

The opportunities for applying the experimental method to factual controversies that arise in litigation are immense, but they generally go unrecognized and unused.[2] Some

---

§ 202

1. A grasp of the basic principles of experimentation in the natural and social sciences can be of great value to the attorney involved in the design and presentation of experiments conducted for litigation. The considerations that make a scientific experiment respected within the scientific community and those that should make an experiment convincing to a jury (and defensible as against expert attack) are largely the same. Acquaintance with this field is even more obviously relevant to the courtroom presentation of pre-existing scientific experiments. For elementary discussions of experimental design, see Kimble, How to Use (and Misuse) Statistics 62–82 (1978); Moore, Statis-

tics: Concepts and Controversies 56–82 (1979); Lind, Shapard & Cecil, Methods for Experimental Evaluation of Innovations in the Justice System, in Experimentation in the Law 80 (Federal Judicial Center 1981).

2. Courtroom experiments and demonstrations are considered infra at § 215. For more information on pretrial experiments, see, M. Graham, Handbook of Federal Evidence § 401.10 (1981); 1 Louisell & Mueller, Federal Evidence § 103 (1977); Scientific and Expert Testimony (2d ed. Imwinkelreid 1981); Moenssens & Inbau, Scientific Evidence in Criminal Cases (2d ed. 1978); Richardson, Modern Scientific Evidence §§ 4.1–4.33 (2d ed. 1974); Rothstein, Federal Rules of Evidence § 702 (2d ed. 1982); Saltzburg & Redden,

of the more frequently encountered types of experiments are tests of the composition [3] or physical properties [4] of substances or products, tests of the flammability or explosive properties of certain products,[5] tests of the effects of drugs and other products on human beings or other organisms,[6] tests of firearms to show characteristic, identifying features, or capabilities,[7] tests of the visibility of objects or persons under certain conditions,[8] tests of the speed of moving vehicles and of the effectiveness of brakes, headlights or other components.[9] Some of these experiments can be simple affairs, such as driving an automobile along a stretch of road to determine where a particular object on the road first becomes visible. Others are more complicated, requiring sophisticated machinery, statistical analysis of the results, or other specialized knowledge or procedures, and these are taken up in later sections.[10] Testimony describing the experiments may be received as substantive evidence, or it may form the basis for an expert opinion. The simplest experiments are often the most convincing, and expert testimony is not always cost-effective.[11]

Federal Rules of Evidence Manual 454 (3d ed. 1982); 2 Wigmore, Evidence §§ 445–460 (Chadbourn rev. 1979); 22 Wright & Graham, Federal Practice and Procedure § 5171 (1978); Fed.R.Evid. 401–403, 702; Unif.R.Evid. 401–403, 702 (1974); 29 Am.Jur.Evid. §§ 818–833; 32 C.J.S. Evidence ☞586–591; Dec.Dig. Evidence § 150.

3. State v. Spencer, 298 Minn. 456, 216 N.W.2d 131 (1974); infra n. 7, and § 203 n. 1 and §§ 205, 207 infra.

4. Alonzo v. State ex rel. Booth, 283 Ala. 607, 219 So.2d 858, 879 (1969), cert. denied 396 U.S. 931 (error to deny production of incriminating tape recordings for electronic testing of possible alterations); Patricia R. v. Sullivan, 631 P.2d 91 (Alaska 1981) (tests of temperatures attained by heater); Dritt v. Morris, 235 Ark. 40, 357 S.W.2d 13 (1962) (slipperiness of concrete floor due to sweeping compound); 65 Am.Jur.2d, Products Liability § 20; Annot., 76 A.L.R.2d 354; see infra § 207.

5. Gardner v. Q.H.S., Inc., 448 F.2d 238, 244 (4th Cir. 1971) (flammability tests on hair rollers); D'Hedouville v. Pioneer Hotel Co., 552 F.2d 886, 890–891 (9th Cir. 1977) (flammability tests on material from which hotel carpeting was made); Stumbaugh v. State, 599 P.2d 166, 169–172 (Alaska 1979) (experiment to show how arson defendant could have set fire with materials found in premises); Guinan v. Famous Players-Lasky Corp., 267 Mass. 501, 167 N.E. 235, 245 (1929) (tests of the flammability and explosive properties of scraps of motion picture film); Schmidt v. Plains Electric Co., 281 N.W.2d 794, 800–801 (N.D.1979) (flammability of drapes positioned near heater); Annot., 76 A.L.R.2d 354, 365–369, 76 id. at 204 (explosions); cf. Canada Life Assurance Co. v. Houston, 241 F.2d 523, 537 (9th Cir. 1957) (dropping rifle to see whether it would discharge on impact); Annot., 54 A.L.R.2d 922 (tests of electrical equipment or appliances).

6. Rayner v. Stauffer Chemical Co., 120 Ariz. 328, 585 P.2d 1240, 1244 (App.1978) (effect of herbicide on potato plants); Annot., 76 A.L.R.2d 354, 376–379.

7. Nicholson v. State, 570 P.2d 1058, 1064–1065 (Alaska 1977) (trajectory experiment); State v. Baublits, 324 Mo. 1199, 27 S.W.2d 16 (1930) (trajectory tests rejected); Annot., 86 A.L.R.2d 611 (tests to ascertain distance between gun and victim), 26 id. 892 (ballistics); cf. Annot., 1 A.L.R.4th 1072 (residue detection test to determine whether person handled or fired gun).

8. McDaniel v. Frye, 536 F.2d 625, 626, 628 (5th Cir. 1976) (visibility of truck); Stevens v. People, 97 Colo. 559, 51 P.2d 1022, 1024–1025 (1935) (whether headlight would illuminate oncoming car at particular place); Carpenter v. Kurn, 348 Mo. 1132, 157 S.W.2d 213, 215 (1941) (distance at which an observer could tell that a person sitting on railroad tracks is a human being); Norfolk & Western Railway Co. v. Henderson, 132 Va. 297, 111 S.E. 277, 281 (1922) (visibility of object the size of deceased two year old girl on railroad track); Annot., 78 A.L.R.2d 152.

9. Bauman v. Volkswagenwerk Aktiengesellschaft, 621 F.2d 230, 233–234 (6th Cir. 1980) (simulating sideswipe accident by banging on door handle with rubber mallet); Nanda v. Ford Motor Co., 509 F.2d 213, 223 (7th Cir. 1974) (striking car with a ram to see whether the force would dislodge fuel pipe); Ramseyer v. General Motors Corp., 417 F.2d 859, 864 (8th Cir. 1969) (simulation of 100,000 miles of driving wear on Corvair steering gear); Smith v. State Roads Commission, 240 Md. 525, 214 A.2d 792 (1965) (automobile swerve test); Christopher & Feder, Modeling of Vehicular Accidents, 26 J. Forensic Sci. 424, 430 (1981) (describing experiments with scale models said to "recreate what actually occurred at the scene of the accident" and to permit "reenactment of the actual collision . . . numerous times at nominal expense"); Annot., 78 A.L.R.2d 218 (speed and control experiments); cf. Annot., 29 A.L.R.3d 248 (deducing speed from skid marks), 9 id. at 976 (charts of braking distances, reactions times, etc. in negligence cases).

10. See infra §§ 203–211.

11. Johnson v. Young Mens Christian Association, ___ Mont. ___, 651 P.2d 1245, 1248–1249 (1982) (tossing diving ring into pool at location where drowning victim was found and timing how long it took two boys to retrieve it "supported the conclusion that it took one to one and one-half minutes to retrieve the victim from the pool," an elapsed time too short to have caused permanent brain damage); Larson v. Meyer, 161 N.W.2d 165 (N.D.1968) (whether tractor could pull milk truck out of rut without overturning).

Pretrial experiments will be admitted as evidence if their probative value is not substantially outweighed by the usual counterweights of prejudice, confusion of the issues, and time consumption.[12] The only form of prejudice that might operate in this context is that of giving experimental results more weight than they deserve. This should not be a serious barrier to admissibility unless the interpretation of the experiment would require expert testimony and specialized knowledge.[13] The extent to which the presentation will be distracting or time-consuming will vary from case to case. As for probative value, the courts often speak of the need for similarity between the conditions of the experiment and those that pertained to the litigated happening.[14]

In practice, however, this requirement of similarity is not applied to all pretrial experiments, or if it is nominally applied, the notion of "similarity" becomes almost infinitely flexible. The requirement is most meaningful and at its strictest when the experiment expressly seeks to replicate the event in question[15] to show that things could (or could not) have happened as alleged. But even in these case-specific experiments, differences between the experimental and actual conditions that only could make it harder for the experiment to be favorable to the proponent should be no obstacle to admission.[16] Furthermore, an event can never be perfectly reenacted or simulated. There are too many details to keep track of, and some defy precise re-creation. For example, the human agent in the happening to which the experiment pertains may be deceased, the vehicle may be destroyed, the surrounding circumstances may be known only vaguely, or the process of duplicating what actually happened may be too dangerous.[17] Consequently, although the similarity formula is sometimes overrigidly

12. Renfro Hosiery Mills Co. v. National Cash Register Co., 552 F.2d 1061, 1065 (4th Cir. 1977); supra § 185.

13. But see 22 Wright & Graham, supra note 2, § 5171 at 120 ("the word 'experiment' may create an aura of scientific certainty"). However, if the "experiment" is not designed, conducted, or described by a scientist and is not very scientific, the jury should not be so poisoned by the word "experiment" that a competent advocate would find it difficult to dispel the "aura." See infra n. 18.

14. Cases emphasizing the importance of similar conditions abound. Hall v. General Motors Corp., 647 F.2d 175, 180 (D.C.Cir. 1980) (experiments with automobile drive shaft taped rather than bolted at rear inadmissible); Renfro Hosiery Mills Co. v. National Cash Register Co., 552 F.2d 1061, 1066 n. 7 (4th Cir. 1977) (tests on mere prototype of computer under extreme conditions inadmissible to show that production model was unreliable under normal operating conditions); Barnes v. General Motors Corp., 547 F.2d 275, 277 (5th Cir. 1977) (error to admit experiment in which test automobile with engine largely disconnected from frame was driven with accelerator "mashed to the floor" when actual vehicle had engine mount with roll-stop feature); Jackson v. Fletcher, 647 F.2d 1020, 1023–1024, 1026–1028 (10th Cir. 1981) (acceleration experiment with a truck that weighed about half what the truck involved in the accident weighed "could have produced a result desired by defendants but not a true depiction"); Love v. State, 457 P.2d 622, 628 (Alaska 1969) (experiment to determine whether vessel would drift into restricted waters inadmissible for lack of similarity); State v. Smith Roads Commission, 240 Md. 525, 214 A.2d 792 (1965) (automobile swerve test per-

formed with sober driver, different vehicle, drier road conditions, and daylight illumination inadmissible as having nothing in common with accident except that both took place at the same curve); Spurlin v. Nardo, 145 W.Va. 408, 114 S.E.2d 913 (1960) (demonstrating that automobile mechanic with 35 years driving experience can stop a car descending a hill without using foot brakes not sufficiently similar); 29 Am.Jur.2d Evidence § 824; 32 C.J.S. Evidence § 590; Annot., 16 A.L.R.2d 354.

The burden of showing substantial similarity is on the proponent. Renfro Hosiery Mills Co. v. National Cash Register Co., supra, 552 F.2d at 1065–1066; Barnes v. General Motors Corp., supra, 547 F.2d at 277; Jackson v. Fletcher, supra, 647 F.2d at 1027; Robinson v. Morrison, 272 Ala. 552, 133 So.2d 230, 235 (1961) (visibility); Hightower v. Alley, 132 Mont. 349, 318 P.2d 243, 247 (1957) (experiment to measure time required to walk a given distance rejected where plaintiff's counsel, who was 11 years younger than plaintiff, did the walking); Enghlin v. Pittsburgh County Railway, 169 Okl. 106, 36 P.2d 32, 37 (1934) (experiment to find maximum speed of streetcar approaching intersection).

15. Jackson v. Fletcher, 647 F.2d 1020, 1027 (10th Cir. 1981), supra n. 14.

16. People v. Spencer, 58 Cal.App. 197, 208 P. 380, 393 (1922) (audibility test); Downing v. Metropolitan Life Insurance Co., 314 Ill.App. 222, 41 N.E.2d 297 (1941) (using larger men than deceased to see whether deceased could have reached gun and shot himself).

17. But see Louisville Gas & Electric Co. v. Duncan, 235 Ky. 613, 31 S.W.2d 915 (1930) (superintendent per-

applied,[18] most courts recognize that the requirement is a relative one.[19] If enough of the obviously important factors are duplicated in the experiment, and if the failure to control other possibly relevant variables is justified, the court may conclude that the experiment is sufficiently enlightening that it should come into evidence.[20] This determination typically is subject to review only for an abuse of discretion.[21]

On the other hand, the similarity requirement either is not applied or is highly diluted when the pretrial experiment does not purport to replicate the essential features of a

particular happening. There are many perfectly acceptable experiments of this nature. For example, if one party contends that certain acts or omissions could not produce—under any circumstances—the result in question, then the other party may conduct an experiment to falsify this hypothesis. Of course, the closer the experiment is to the conditions that actually pertained, the more useful the experiment will be, but merely refuting the opposing party's sweeping claim may be sufficiently valuable to make the evidence admissible.[22] Similarly, the proponent may offer to prove that something was not

suaded a miner to place himself in the same position as another miner who had been electrocuted).

18. Some courts evince a distinct distaste for experimental evidence. Navajo Freight Lines v. Mahaffy, 174 F.2d 305, 310 (10th Cir. 1949) ("Evidence of this kind should be received with caution, and only when it is obvious to the court, from the nature of the experiments, that the jury will be enlightened rather than confused. In many instances, a slight change in the conditions under which the experiment is made will so distort the result as to wholly destroy its value as evidence, and make it harmful rather than helpful"). This aversion would be appropriate if experiments were generally of little or no probative value and strongly prejudicial. Cf. supra §§ 186–194 (character evidence). More plausibly, the distrust of experimental evidence can be explained by the fact that many attorneys feel more comfortable with historical evidence based on personal recollections. However, there is no inherent reason that the average trial lawyer could not be equally skilled at discerning and elucidating for the jury any "slight changes" that would "wholly destroy" a defective proof by experiment. Rayner v. Stauffer Chemical Co., 120 Ariz. 328, 585 P.2d 1240, 1245 (App.1978) ("appellants were given ample opportunity to cross-examine the appellee's experts on these tests in order to illustrate any dissimilarities in conditions").

19. Ramseyer v. General Motors Corp., 417 F.2d 859, 864 (5th Cir. 1969) ("Perfect identity between experimental and actual conditions is neither attainable nor required. . . . Dissimilarities affect the weight of the evidence, not admissibility"); Lever Brothers v. Atlas Assurance Co., 131 F.2d 770, 777 (7th Cir. 1942) ("'Substantial similarity' . . . is a relative term . . . There are no hard and fast rules"); Jackson v. Fletcher, 647 F.2d 1020, 1027 (10th Cir. 1980) (conditions "need not be identical but they ought to be sufficiently similar so as to provide a fair comparison"); Hansen v. Howard O. Miller, Inc., 93 Idaho 314, 460 P.2d 739 (1969) (braking experiment admissible despite differences in automobile make, weight and tire size); Johnson v. Young Mens Christian Association, __ Mont. __, __, 651 P.2d 1245, 1246–1247 (1982) ("Although it is obvious that a diving ring has different dimensions than a small boy's body, this evidence was

probative [as] an indication of the time involved in effecting the rescue" of a drowning child in a swimming pool).

20. Patricia R. v. Sullivan, 631 P.2d 91, 101 (Alaska 1981) ("Of course, it can be argued that a 10-inch scrap of fiberglass wall insulation is not a fair substitute for a child in a blanket [who burned her face on a heater], but that goes more to the weight than the admissibility of the test"); Erickson's Dairy Products Co. v. Northwest Baker Ice Machine Co., 165 Or. 553, 109 P.2d 53, 55 (1941) (experiment to determine whether wallboard might have caught fire from welding operation using section of wallboard not involved in the fire); cases cited supra n. 16.

21. Hall v. General Motors Corp., 647 F.2d 175, 180 (D.C.Cir. 1980) ("The trial judge has broad leeway . . . her finding will not be upset unless it is clearly erroneous"); Barnes v. General Motors Corp., 547 F.2d 275 (5th Cir. 1977) (admission held to be an abuse of discretion); Wagner v. International Harvester Co., 611 F.2d 224, 232–233 (8th Cir. 1979); Derr v. Safeway Stores, 404 F.2d 634, 639 (10th Cir. 1968) ("The trial court is, of course, the first and best judge whether conditions of the experiment are sufficiently similar and enlightening to render the testimony based thereon admissible. And we must not disturb the court's ruling on these critical issues unless we are convinced it is clearly wrong"); State v. Lindsey, 284 N.W.2d 368, 374 (Minn.1979) ("clear showing of abuse" required); Schmidt v. Plains Electric Co., 281 N.W.2d 794, 800–801 (N.D.1979).

22. Chambers v. Silver, 103 Cal.App.2d 633, 230 P.2d 146 (1951) (where defendant claimed that he lost control because main leaf in spring at front wheel broke when wheel crossed a two inch deposit of soil on road, it was error to exclude experiment in which another vehicle with same suspension system was driven over 2 x 4 boards at 45–50 m.p.h.); State v. Don, 318 N.W.2d 801, 805 (Iowa 1982) (police experiment showing how long it took to drive from one place to another admissible to demonstrate that even if evidence in support of alibi defense were believed, defendant still would have had opportunity to commit crime).

the cause of the actionable result. To do so, he may use an experiment that shows that some other agent can bring about the same result.[23] Finally, the experiment may be introduced solely to illustrate or demonstrate a scientific principle [24] or empirical finding [25] that a jury, perhaps with the aid of an expert witness, can apply to the specifics of the case.[26] Thus, experiments showing general properties of materials are admitted

without confining the experiments to the conditions surrounding the litigated situation. Most of these analyses are referred to as tests rather than experiments. When this label is attached, the question becomes one, not of similarity,[27] but of authentication—making sure that the right material was tested and that it underwent no essential alterations before testing. With all these limited purpose experiments, the issue,

23. Lincoln v. Taunton Copper Manufacturing Co., 91 Mass. 181, 191 (1864) (detecting copper in grasses not exposed to contamination from defendant's mill); Coon v. Utah Construction Co., 119 Utah 446, 228 P.2d 997 (1951) (tests showing that defendant's trucks cause no greater vibrations in house than other traffic); 2 Wigmore, Evidence § 448 (Chadbourn rev. 1979).

24. Harkins v. Ford Motor Co., 437 F.2d 276, 278 (3d Cir. 1970) (no need to show similarity where demonstrations with other automobiles showed "general principles of physics universal in their application"); Brandt v. French, 638 F.2d 209, 212–213 (10th Cir. 1981) ("mechanical principals relative to . . . how a motorcycle leans when it turns"); Millers' National Insurance Co. v. Wichita Flour Milling Co., 257 F.2d 93, 99 (10th Cir. 1958) (physics principles applicable to dust explosions).

25. Ramseyer v. General Motors Corp., 417 F.2d 859 (8th Cir. 1959) (experiment to show normal wear and tear on automobile component); Patricia R. v. Sullivan, 631 P.2d 91, 98–101 (Alaska 1981) (tests to determine how hot the surfaces of a heater would get and whether safety device would operate); C.F. Church Division v. Golden, 429 P.2d 771, 775 (Okl.1967) (flammability of cellulose nitrate, a compound used in product); Horn v. Elgin Warehouse Co., 96 Or. 403, 190 P. 151 (1920) (in action for breach of warranty that wheat was Red Chaff, evidence that upon planting, the wheat germinated to produce Red Chaff was admissible without any showing of similarity in planting and growing conditions); Nordstrom v. White Metal Rolling & Stamping Co., 75 Wn.2d 629, 453 P.2d 619, 627 (1969) (testing ladder in various positions with various weights to see when it would tip over admissible not "to show how the accident happened, but to show how it could have happened"); supra note 5 (flammability cases). Cases in which an expert testifies to laboratory experiments designed to reveal the conditions under which eyewitness testimony is unreliable also fall in this category. See infra § 206. Consider also the cases collected in Annot., 9 A.L.R.3d 976 (charts of braking distances and reaction times).

26. Some cases recognize that similarity of conditions is unnecessary if the only purpose of the experiment is to explain an expert's testimony. Midwestern Wholesale Drug v. Gas Service Co., 442 F.2d 663, 665 (10th Cir. 1971) (experiments with another heater properly admitted "to render intelligible the expert testimony regarding the normal operation of such heaters"). Where the experimental results are not just graphic pedagogical devices, but substantive evidence that the

jury may use to analyze the occurence in question, the correct treatment of the similarity requirement is less obvious. One could say that when experiments reveal properties or traits that clearly apply under a wide range of conditions, the "substantial similarity" requirement is fulfilled because physical theory indicates that the gross differences are superficial and inconsequential. Although some opinions adopt such a view, others treat the substantial similarity requirement as stating a preference for duplicating conditions to the greatest extent feasible. The courts imposing this sometimes procrustean demand tend, however, to accept experiments elucidating "properties" as falling outside the rule. Palleson v. Jewell Co-op Elevator, 219 N.W.2d 8, 15–16 (Iowa 1974) (laboratory experiment to simulate events leading to explosion of gas burner admissible despite objections as to dissimilarities because it showed "general traits and capacities of materials" and "principles developed from certain demonstrated phenomena," namely, how a leaf fragment allegedly left in device during installation would cause gas to leak and how clearing the line in the manner purportedly done would have removed the leaf). Yet, as this illustration may suggest, these cases rarely provide an analysis of what it is that makes the experimental findings pertain to general properties or traits and why a more detailed simulation is unnecessary. For instance, in Council v. Duprel, 250 Miss. 269, 165 So.2d 134 (1964), the court held an experiment with herbicides admissible, because it "was not an effort to duplicate the conditions existing on appellant's farm" but merely an attempt "to establish the fact that 2,4–D is far more destructive to cotton than 2,4,5–T." Of course, the question for the jury was whether 2,4–D was more destructive on appellant's farm, and an experiment could have been designed to control for possible differences in soil conditions, humidity, and other variables. Assuming that these variables are inconsequential, as seems plausible, the court's result is clearly correct. It would therefore seem that either "substantial similarity" does not mean as similar as is practical, or the phrase should be abandoned in favor of a frank inquiry into whether bothering with the other variables would make the experiment so much more revealing as to be worth the additional effort and expense. Indeed, focusing directly on marginal costs and benefits gives some necessary definition to the substantial similarity test and, in reality, makes that language superfluous.

27. See Jackson v. Fletcher, 647 F.2d 1020, 1027 (10th Cir. 1981).

as always, is whether, on balance, the evidence will assist the jury.

Some courts distinguish between experiments commissioned for a specific lawsuit and those undertaken solely to obtain scientific knowledge of greater generality.[28] Although the latter have the advantage of being untainted by any interest in the litigation,[29] steps can be taken to improve case-specific experimentation as well. Consideration might be given to allowing the judge to exclude experiments unless the adversary has had reasonable notice, an opportunity to make suggestions, and to be present during the experiment.[30] Also worthy of consideration is appointment by the court of an impartial person to conduct or supervise an experiment.[31] Such procedures could lead to findings that would invite much less in the way of time-consuming or distracting attack and defense at trial.

28. Foster v. Agri-Chem, Inc., 235 Or. 570, 385 P.2d 184 (1963) (agricultural experiment station's tests of the effect of fertilizer on wheat yields).

29. Id. ("greater latitude should be shown in admitting" experiments conducted "for the sole purpose of obtaining scientific knowledge . . . because this type of evidence is free from the taint of interest or bias that might accompany the usual 'experiment'"). Of course, scientists rarely are devoid of self-interest or biases, but the process of exposing one's work to the scrutiny of the scientific community through publication acts as an important check.

30. See Fortunato v. Ford Motor Co., 464 F.2d 962, 966 (2d Cir. 1972), cert. denied 409 U.S. 1038 (dictum that "Test results should not even be admissible as evidence, unless made by a qualified, independent expert or unless the opposing party has the opportunity to participate in the test"). Under present practice, lack of notice and opportunity to be present are not grounds for rejection, but they may be argued on weight. United States v. Love, 482 F.2d 213, 218–219 (5th Cir. 1973), cert. denied 414 U.S. 1026 (no Sixth Amendment right to have defense expert present for chemical tests); Burg v. Chicago, Rock Island & Pacific Railway Co., 90 Iowa 106, 57 N.W. 680, 683 (1894) (visibility test); 32 C.J.S. Evidence § 587; 17 A.L.R.2d 1078. The recommendation offered here would allow rejection of experimental evidence on these grounds in appropriate circumstances to encourage better designed experiments and to obviate objections that could have been raised in advance. The proposal would not apply to routine laboratory tests, but would cover experiments initiated *post litem motam* for the purpose of litigation.

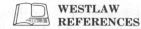

WESTLAW REFERENCES

pretrial /2 experiment* & court(ga)

§ 203. Scientific Tests in General: Admissibility and Weight

To deal effectively with scientific evidence, the attorney must know more than the rules of evidence. He must know something of the scientific principles as well. While he can rely on suitably chosen experts for advice about the more arcane points, he must have a sufficient grasp of the field to see what is essential and what is unnecessary detail and verbiage if he is to develop or counteract the evidence in the way that will have the most impact. In this chapter, we cannot explore in any depth the vast body of knowledge that comes into play in the forensic applications of science and medicine. Only a superficial sampling of a few areas will be attempted.[1] We shall focus on some of

31. Thus, in the course of the grand jury investigation of the White House's involvement in the Watergate break-in, a panel of six court-appointed experts agreeable to the Watergate Special Prosecutor and the White House conducted extensive tests to determine the cause of a notorious 18.5 minute gap on a subpoenaed tape recording of a conversation between President Nixon and an aide that took place shortly after the break-in. The experts' report made it plain that the gap consisted of intentional erasures made after the tape had been subpoenaed. The grand jury concluded that only a handful of people could have been responsible for these erasures, but it never secured sufficient evidence to prosecute any of these individuals. Watergate Special Prosecution Force, U.S. Dep't of Justice, Report 53 (1975).

§ 203

1. For example, we make no attempt even to survey the growing field of forensic economics. See generally Ballantine v. Central Railroad of New Jersey, 460 F.2d 540 (3d Cir. 1972), cert. denied 409 U.S. 879; Drayton v. Jiffee Chemical Corp., 591 F.2d 352, 364 (6th Cir. 1978); Schmitt v. Jenkins Truck Lines, 170 N.W.2d 632, 657–659 (Iowa 1969); Comments and Notes, 51 Neb.L. Rev. 663 (1972), 11 Ind.L.Rev. 647 (1978), 49 Temp.L.Q. 912 (1976), 63 Va.L.Rev. 105 (1977), 1976 Wash.U.L.Q. 135; Annot., 77 A.L.R.3d 1175, 1184–1192 (value of a housewife's services), 79 A.L.R.2d 259 (discounting to present value).

So too, we shall say little about the use of psychological and psychiatric testimony on mental health, competence, and sanity. See generally United States v. Lawson, 653 F.2d 299 (7th Cir. 1981), cert. denied 454 U.S.

the problems that can arise in making measurements and in interpreting the data so obtained. Sections 204 through 207 deal with laboratory or field tests (organized somewhat arbitrarily by scientific discipline) in which statistical analysis of the data does not play a major role. Sections 208 through 211 concern studies in which statistical analyses are prominent. In the remainder of this section, we discuss some general points concerning the admissibility of all such evidence and the weight that it should receive.

A. *Admissibility.* Most of the case law centers on the threshold question of admissibility. The principles of relevancy outlined in Chapter 16 are as applicable to scientific evidence as to any other kind, and the doctrines governing all expert testimony discussed in Chapter 3 operate here as well. Federal and Revised Uniform Rule of Evidence (1974) 702 specifically mentions scientific testimony, linking it with expert testimony generally:

> If scientific, technical, or other specialized knowledge will assist the trier of fact to understand the evidence or to determine a fact in issue, a witness qualified as an expert by knowledge, skill, experience, training or education, may testify thereto in the form of an opinion or otherwise.

However, many courts purport to apply special rules of admissibility when expert witnesses are called to testify about scientific tests or findings.[2] The most common special rule is that in addition to satisfying the traditional requirements of relevancy and

helpfulness to the trier of fact, the proponent must show general acceptance of the principle or technique in the scientific community.

This notion of a special rule for scientific evidence originated in 1923 in Frye v. United States.[3] *Frye* was a murder prosecution in which the trial court rebuffed defendant's effort to introduce results of a "systolic blood pressure test," a forerunner of the polygraph. On appeal, the defendant relied on the traditional rule governing expert testimony, but the Court of Appeals, without explanation or precedent, superimposed a new standard:

> Just when a scientific principle or discovery crosses the line between the experimental and demonstrable stages is difficult to define. Somewhere in this twilight zone the evidential force of the principle must be recognized, and while courts will go a long way in admitting expert testimony deduced from a well-recognized scientific principle or discovery, the thing from which the deduction is made must be sufficiently established to have gained general acceptance in the particular field in which it belongs.[4]

The opinion did not state clearly whether "the thing" that needed "to have gained general acceptance" was the link between conscious insincerity and changes in blood pressure or the ability of an expert to measure and interpret the changes, or both. The court concluded, however, that the deception test lacked the requisite "standing

---

1130; Allen, Foster & Rubin, Readings in Law and Psychiatry 69–73 (1968); Bromberg, The Uses of Psychiatry in the Law: A Clinical View of Forensic Psychiatry (1979); Bazelon, Psychiatrists and the Adversary Process, Sci.Am., June 1974, at 18; Bonnie & Slobogin, The Role of Mental Health Professionals in the Criminal Process, 66 Va.L.Rev. 427, 452–522 (1980); Diamond & Louisell, The Psychiatrist as an Expert Witness, 63 Mich.L.Rev. 1335 (1965); Annot., 55 A.L.R.3d 551 (expert opinion of sanity).

Medical jurisprudence in personal injury and malpractice cases is another field onto itself. See generally McQuade, Medical Practice for Lawyers (1980); Tennenhouse, Attorney's Medical Deskbook (1975).

2. See generally 1 Louisell & Mueller, supra n. 2 of § 202, at § 105; Moenssens & Inbau, supra n. 2 of

§ 202, at § 1.03; Richardson, supra n. 2 of § 202, at § 2.5; Weinstein & Berger, supra note 2 of § 202, at ¶ 702[03]; 22 Wright & Graham, supra n. 2 of § 202, at § 5168; Boyce, Judicial Recognition of Scientific Evidence in Criminal Cases, 8 Utah L.Rev. 313 (1963); Giannelli, The Admissibility of Novel Scientific Evidence, 80 Colum.L.Rev. 1197 (1980); McCormick, Scientific Evidence: Defining a New Approach to Admissibility, 67 Iowa L.Rev. 879 (1982); Strong, Questions Affecting the Admissibility of Scientific Evidence, 1970 U.Ill. L.F. 1; Note, Expert Testimony Based on Novel Scientific Techniques: Admissibility Under the Federal Rules of Evidence, 48 Geo.Wash.L.Rev. 774 (1980).

3. 293 F. 1013 (D.C. Cir. 1923).

4. Id. at 1014.

and scientific recognition among physiological and psychological authorities." [5]

The *Frye* standard was adopted by many courts in the ensuing years with scant discussion.[6] Polygraphy,[7] hypnotic and drug induced testimony,[8] voice stress analysis,[9] voice spectrograms,[10] ion microprobe mass spectroscopy,[11] infrared sensing of aircraft,[12] psychological profiles of battered women,[13] astronomical calculations,[14] and blood group typing,[15] all have fallen prey to its influence.

Especially in the last decade, however, the *Frye* standard has been subjected to critical analysis, limitation, modification, and finally, outright rejection.[16] Some courts have found the *Frye* standard satisfied in the teeth of expert testimony that the technique in question was too new and untried and the test results too inconclusive for court use.[17] While asserting the continuing vitality of the *Frye* standard, other courts have held that general acceptance goes to the weight rather than the admissibility of the evidence.[18] Still others have reasoned that the standard applies only to tests for truthfulness,[19] or to the underlying principles or methodology rather than the particular studies or results based on those principles or that methodology.[20] Many opinions have simply ignored

---

5. Id. Years after the conviction, another person confessed to the murder. Wicker, The Polygraphic Truth Test and the Law of Evidence, 22 Tenn.L.Rev. 711, 715 (1953).

6. Kaminski v. State, 63 So.2d 339, 340 (Fla.1952); Boeche v. State, 151 Neb. 368, 377, 37 N.W.2d 593, 597 (1949); Henderson v. State, 94 Okl.Cr. 45, 52–55, 230 P.2d 495, 502–505 (1951), cert. denied 342 U.S. 898. Once adopted, the standard was applied selectively. See Reed v. State, 283 Md. 374, 451–452, 391 A.2d 364, 403 (1978) (dissenting opinion) (*Frye* not applied in leading cases admitting expert testimony based on fingerprints, ballistics, intoxication tests, and X-rays); Giannelli, supra n. 2, at 1219–1221. It was applied consistently only in polygraph cases. See McCormick, supra n. 2, at 884.

7. See infra § 206(B).

8. See infra § 206(C).

9. See infra § 206(B).

10. See infra § 207.

11. United States v. Brown, 557 F.2d 541, 556–557 (6th Cir. 1977) (as applied to hair samples).

12. United States v. Kilgus, 571 F.2d 508, 510 (9th Cir. 1978) (customs officer tried to use military forward looking infrared tracking system to distinguish the aircraft he had previously followed from others of the same type).

13. See infra § 206(D).

14. United States v. Tranowski, 659 F.2d 750, 755–757 (7th Cir. 1981) (analysis of shadow length to determine time at which photograph taken).

15. See Huntington v. Crowley, 64 Cal.2d 647, 51 Cal.Rptr. 254, 414 P.2d 382 (1966) (Kell-Cellano test not generally accepted as giving accurate results); State v. Damm, 62 S.D. 123, 252 N.W. 7 (1933) (medical sciences not shown to be sufficiently agreed on "the transmissibility of blood characteristics"), on rehearing, 64 S.D. 309, 266 N.W. 667 (1936) (science found unanimously agreed).

16. McCormick, supra n. 2, details these developments. Although he concludes that the test reached its peak in a series of cases excluding voice spectrographic identifications, it has shown new vigor in subsequent cases excluding testimony of witnesses whose memories were stimulated by hypnosis. See infra § 206(C). The dearth of critical analysis in the previous 50 years has been attributed to the fact that most courts confronted with polygraph evidence thought it clear that the testimony should be suppressed and applied the standard with little comment. Other forms of scientific evidence tended to be accepted readily. In the past 15 years, however, the courts have witnessed a dramatic increase in the volume and complexity of scientific evidence. See McCormick, supra n. 2, at 884–85.

17. United States v. Stifel, 433 F.2d 431, 438 (6th Cir. 1970), cert. denied 401 U.S. 994 (neutron activation analysis of bomb fragments); Coppolino v. State, 223 So.2d 68 (Fla.App.1968), appeal dismissed memorandum 234 So.2d 120 (Fla.), cert. denied 399 U.S. 927 (test for presence of succinylcholine chloride specially developed to determine whether defendant had injected a lethal dose of this anesthetic into his wife); State v. Washington, 229 Kan. 47, 55, 622 P.2d 986, 992 (1981) (holding that despite a biochemist's testimony on the unreliability of enzyme analysis in identifying a blood sample, the "method is sufficiently accepted as reliable by the scientific community").

18. State v. Olivas, 77 Ariz. 118, 267 P.2d 893 (1954) (breathalyzer); People v. Marx, 54 Cal.App.3d 100, 126 Cal.Rptr. 350 (1975) (bitemark evidence); Jenkins v. State, 156 Ga.App. 387, 388, 274 S.E.2d 618, 619 (1980) (electrophoresis with blood samples). Despite the genuflection to *Frye*, this approach is equivalent to the outright repudiation of the general acceptance standard. In cases involving other types of scientific evidence, courts in these same jurisdictions revert to more conventional applications of the general acceptance standard. See infra § 206.

19. People v. Allweiss, 48 N.Y.2d 40, 421 N.Y.S.2d 341, 396 N.E.2d 735 (1979) (microscopic comparison of hair).

20. United States v. Williams, 583 F.2d 1194, 1198 (2d Cir. 1978) (spectrographic analysis of voice admissi-

the standard,[21] and many others have blithely equated it with a requirement of showing the accuracy and reliability of the scientific technique.[22] Finally, several jurisdictions expressly have rejected *Frye*, leaving the task of regulating the admission of scientific evidence to the normal doctrines of relevancy and helpfulness of expert testimony.[23] The adoption of the Federal Rules of Evidence has only intensified this process. These rules do not explicitly distinguish between scientific and other forms of expert testimony, and they permit experts to rely on facts or data not otherwise admissible into evidence as long as they are "reasonably relied upon by experts in [the] particular field."[24] Plainly, "reasonable reliance" is not synonymous with general acceptance.

A drumbeat of criticism of the *Frye* test provides the background music to the movement away from the general acceptance test. Proponents of the test argue that it assures uniformity in evidentiary rulings, that it shields juries from any tendency to treat novel scientific evidence as infallible, that it avoids complex, expensive, and time-consuming courtroom dramas, and that it insulates the adversary system from novel evidence until a pool of experts is available to evalu-

ble under traditional balancing test because "We deal here with the admissibility or non-admissibility of a particular type of scientific evidence, not with the truth or falsity of an alleged scientific 'fact' or 'truth'"), cert. denied 439 U.S. 1117; Ibn–Tamas v. United States, 407 A.2d 626, 638 (D.C.App.1979) (psychologist's study of characteristics of battered women need not be generally accepted if the methodology used to study the phenomenon has general scientific acceptance); cf. Ex parte Dolvin, 391 So.2d 677, 679–680 (Ala. 1980) (*Frye* standard not applicable to comparison of teeth in a skull with those in a photograph since the odontologist's testimony involved a "physical comparison" rather than a scientific experiment or test).

21. United States v. Baller, 519 F.2d 463 (4th Cir. 1975) (voice spectrograph), cert. denied 423 U.S. 1019; People v. LaSumba, 92 Ill.App.3d 621, 626, 47 Ill.Dec. 202, 205–206, 414 N.E.2d 1318, 1321–1322 (1980) (testing bloodstain for esterase D enzyme), cert. denied 454 U.S. 849; State v. Saterfield, 3 Kan.App.2d 212, 217, 592 P.2d 135, 140 (1979) (blood splattering); State v. Beachman, 37 Mont. 1558, 1560, 616 P.2d 337, 339 (1980) (rejecting polygraph evidence); supra n. 6.

22. United States v. Franks, 511 F.2d 25, 33 n. 12 (6th Cir. 1975) ("We deem general acceptance as being nearly synonymous with reliability. If a scientific process is reliable, or sufficiently accurate, courts may also deem it 'generally accepted'"), cert. denied 422 U.S. 1042, quoted in United States v. Distler, 671 F.2d 954, 961 (9th Cir. 1981), cert. denied 454 U.S. 827; State v. Hurd, 86 N.J. 525, 536, 432 A.2d 86, 91 (1981), quoting State v. Cary, 49 N.J. 343, 352, 230 A.2d 384, 389 (1967), on remand 99 N.J.Super. 323 ("According to our most recent formulation . . . ., the results of scientific tests are admissible only when they have 'sufficient scientific basis to produce uniform and reasonably reliable results and will contribute materially to the ascertainment of truth'"); cases cited, McCormick, supra n. 2, at 892 n. 83.

23. Whalen v. State, 434 A.2d 1346, 1354 (Del.1980) (field test for semen), cert. denied 455 U.S. 910; State v. Hall, 297 N.W.2d 80, 84–85 (Iowa 1980) (blood splatter analysis), cert. denied 450 U.S. 927; State v. Catanese, 368 So.2d 975, 980 (La.1979) (general acceptance

standard "is an unjustifiable obstacle to the admission of polygraph test results," but results inadmissible in criminal cases under balancing analysis); State v. Williams, 388 A.2d 500, 503–504 (Me.1978) (voice spectrograph); Barmeyer v. Montana Power Co., __ Mont. __, 657 P.2d 594, 598 (1983) ("corrosion analysis"); State v. Williams, 4 Ohio St.3d 53, 446 N.E.2d 444, 447–448 (1983) ("scientific nose-counting" not required for spectrogram to be admissible); State v. Kersting, 50 Or.App. 461, 623 P.2d 1095 (1981), affirmed 292 Or. 350, 638 P.2d 1145 ("reliability test" made microscopic hair analysis and comparisons admissible despite failure of the record to reveal general scientific acceptance), affirmed 292 Or. 350, 638 P.2d 1145 (1982); Phillips ex rel. Utah State Department of Social Services v. Jackson, 615 P.2d 1228, 1234–1235 (Utah 1980) ("sufficient proof of reliability and an adequate explanation of the pertinent variables and potential inaccuracies" of HLA test for paternity not established in the record); Watson v. State, 64 Wis.2d 264, 274, 219 N.W.2d 398, 403 (1974) (conflict in scientific opinion of hair identification method a matter of credibility for the jury); Cullin v. State, 565 P.2d 445, 453–454 (Wyo.1977).

24. Fed. and Rev.Unif.R.Evid. (1974) 703. For analyses of the viability of the *Frye* test under the new rules, see, 1 Louisell & Mueller, supra note 2 § 202, § 105 at 818 (test "probably" has survived); Saltzburg & Redden, supra n. 2 § 202, at 452 ("one can only guess"); Weinstein & Berger, supra n. 2 § 202, ¶702[3], at 702–16 (test eliminated); 22 Wright & Graham, supra n. 2 § 202, at § 5168 (test eliminated); Giannelli, supra n. 2 § 202, at 1229 (survival arguable); Note, supra n. 2 (survives with surgery). Conflicting cases are collected in McCormick, supra n. 2, at 885 n. 56. See also Barmeyer v. Montana Power Co., __ Mont. __, 657 P.2d 594, 598 (1983) ("the general acceptance rule is not in conformity with the spirit of the new rules of evidence"); State v. Williams, 40 Ohio St. 3d 53, 446 N.E.2d 444, 447 (1983) (rules 402, 403, and 702 establish "a more flexible standard . . . generally favoring *admissibility* of expert testimony whenever it is relevant and can be of assistance to the trier of fact").

ate it in court.[25] Most commentators agree, however, that these objectives can be attained satisfactorily with less drastic constraints on the admissibility of scientific evidence. In particular, it has been suggested that a substantial acceptance test be substituted for the general acceptance standard,[26] that a panel of scientists rather than the usual courts screen new developments for acceptance,[27] and that the traditional standards of relevancy and the need for expertise—and nothing more—should govern.[28]

The last mentioned method for evaluating the admissibility of scientific evidence is the most appealing. It avoids the difficult problems of defining how "general" the general acceptance must be, of discerning exactly what it is that must be accepted, and of determining the "particular field" to which the scientific evidence belongs and in which it must be accepted.[29] General scientific acceptance is a proper condition for taking judicial notice of scientific facts, but it is not a suitable criterion for the admissibility of scientific evidence. Any relevant conclusions supported by a qualified expert witness [30] should be received unless there are distinct reasons for exclusion. These reasons are the familiar ones of prejudicing or misleading the jury or consuming undue amounts of time.[31]

This traditional approach to the evidence does not make scientific testimony admissi-

25. United States v. Addison, 498 F.2d 741 (D.C. Cir. 1974) (voice spectrogram), questioned in United States v. McDaniel, 538 F.2d 408, 413 (D.C. Cir. 1976); United States v. Amaral, 488 F.2d 1148 (9th Cir. 1973) (psychology of eyewitness testimony); People v. Kelly, 17 Cal.3d 24, 31–32, 130 Cal.Rptr. 144, 148–149, 549 P.2d 1240, 1244–1245 (1976) (voice spectrogram); Reed v. State, 283 Md. 374, 385–389, 391 A.2d 364, 370–372 (1978) (voice spectrogram); State v. Cavallo, 88 N.J. 508, 443 A.2d 1020 (1982).

26. See United States v. Baller, 519 F.2d 463, 465 (4th Cir. 1975), cert. denied 423 U.S. 1019; Richardson, supra n. 2 § 202, § 2.5, at 24; cf. Latin, Tannehill & White, Remote Sensing Evidence and Environmental Law, 64 Calif.L.Rev. 1300, 1380 (1976) (reasonable acceptance standard); Note, supra n. 2, at 787 (preponderance of experts standard).

27. See, e.g., Kantrowitz, Controlling Technology Democratically, 63 Am.Sci. 505 (1975); Martin, The Proposed "Science Court," 75 Mich.L.Rev. 1058 (1977); Talbott, Science Court: A Possible Way to Obtain Scientific Certainty for Decisions Based on Scientific "Fact"? 8 Envtl.L. 827 (1978). For criticism of the idea, see Bazelon, Coping with Technology Through the Legal Process, 62 Corn.L.Rev. 817, 827–828 (1977); Sofaer, The Science Court: Unscientific and Unsound, 9 Envtl.L.Rev. 1 (1978). Inasmuch as a purely scientific tribunal should not be in the business of making value choice or policy decisions, see Martin, supra, a "science court" should only supply information to a legal decisionmaker about the technical merit of the techniques or principles. But if the science court is so structured, it does not resolve the question of what to do with the information—that is, whether general scientific acceptance or some other criterion should be the standard for admissibility. See McCormick, supra n. 2, at 906–08.

28. 1 Louisell & Mueller, supra n. 2 § 202, § 105; McCormick, supra n. 2; Strong, supra n. 2 (advocating some special rules for applying the general principles);

Trautman, Logical or Legal Relevancy, 5 Vand.L.Rev. 385, 395–396 (1952); cases cited, supra n. 16. 1 Louisell & Mueller, supra, § 107, also maintain that the general acceptance rule rarely has figured in civil cases. But see Starr v. Campos, 134 Ariz. 254, 655 P.2d 794, 796–797 (App.1982) (remanding for a finding on the acceptance of computer-assisted accident reconstruction); Giannelli, supra n. 2, at 1245–1250, proposes traditional balancing, except that in criminal cases, he would require the prosecution to persuade the court of the validity of the scientific technique beyond a reasonable doubt. McCormick, supra n. 2, at 908, argues convincingly against this proposal.

29. For discussions of these matters, Commonwealth v. Lykus, 367 Mass. 191, 203, 327 N.E.2d 671, 677 (1975) (general acceptance of voice spectrogram need only be shown among those who would be expected to be familiar with its use); Boyce, supra n. 2; Giannelli, supra n. 2, at 1208–1210, 1215–1219; Strong, supra n. 2; Note, supra n. 2, at 779.

30. With increasing specialization and overlapping of fields of expertise, the question of whether an expert is properly qualified can be difficult. A developing problem is the tendency of laboratory technicians or test equipment operators to testify to inferences or probability calculations based on their test results. See, e.g., People v. Kelly, 17 Cal.3d 24, 130 Cal.Rptr. 144, 549 P.2d 1240, 1250 (1976) ("Nash has an impressive list of credentials in the field of voice print analysis. However, these qualifications are those of *a technician and law enforcement officer, not a scientist*"). Even a scientist eminently qualified in one area may not be knowledgeable in another. For example, an immunogeneticist may have a detailed understanding of the chemistry of blood types and typing procedures, but only a superficial acquaintance with the serostatistical method for computing a probability of paternity. See infra § 211. Generally, cross-examination should expose such deficiencies.

31. See generally supra § 185.

ble on the say-so of a single expert.[32] Neither does it go to the other extreme and insist on a fully formed scientific concensus. It permits general scientific opinion of both underlying principles and particular applications to be considered in evaluating the worth of the testimony.[33] In so treating the yeas and nays of the members of a scientific discipline as but one indication of the validity, accuracy, and reliability of the technique, the traditional balancing method focuses the court's attention where it belongs—on the actual usefulness of the evidence in light of the full record developed on the power of the scientific test. Furthermore, unlike the general or the substantial acceptance standards, it is sensitive to the perceived degree of prejudice and unnecessary expense associated with the scientific technique in issue. Not every scrap of scientific evidence carries with it an aura of infallibility. Some methods, like bitemark identification and blood splatter analysis, are demonstrable in the courtroom. Where the methods involve principles and procedures that are comprehensible to a jury, the concerns over the evidence exerting undue influence and inducing a battle of the experts have little force.[34] On the other hand, when the nature of the technique is more esoteric, as with some types of statistical analyses and serologic tests, or when the inferences from the scientific evidence sweep broadly or cut deeply into sensitive areas, a stronger showing of probative value should be required.[35] This could result in the categorical exclusion of certain types of evidence, such as statements made while under the influence of "truth" serums. By attending to such considerations, the rigor of the requisite foundation can be adjusted to suit the nature of the evidence and the context in which it is offered.[36]

B. *Weight.* Whatever the standard for admissibility may be in a particular jurisdiction, arguments as to the weight that the jury should give to the evidence will be important. Indeed, skills in building cases with admissible scientific evidence and demolishing these same structures are becoming increasingly valuable as the forensic applications of science are becoming more

---

32. See State v. Catanese, 368 So.2d 975, 981 (La. 1979) (polygraph); State v. Philbrick, 436 A.2d 844, 861 (Me.1981) (error to allow detective to testify to reconstructing sequences of shootings from blood splatters in car when pathologist could not determine sequence, there was no literature on using splatterings to deduce a sequence, and detective's knowledge was limited to what he learned in a 3-week training course at "blood-splatter school"); State v. Boutilier, 426 A.2d 876, 879 (Me.1981) (state trooper's use of an inapposite formula (which he claimed to have checked by empirical testing) to calculate speed from skid marks should have been excluded, since there was no testimony that "the methodology [using the wrong formula] had sufficient scientific basis, or recognition to vouch for its reliability," but "We do not intimate that 'general scientific acceptance' is a *sine qua non* of a proposed method of determining facts; what we do regard as requisite . . . is a showing of *sufficient reliability*"); Phillips ex rel. Utah State Department of Social Services v. Jackson, 615 P.2d 1228, 1234–1237 (Utah 1980) (HLA tests for paternity).

33. See McCormick, supra n. 2.

34. Ex parte Dolvin, 391 So.2d 677 (Alabama 1980) ("physical comparisons" admitted); People v. Marx, 54 Cal.App.3d 100, 126 Cal.Rptr. 350 (1975) (bitemark analysis admitted); State v. Hall, 297 N.W.2d 80 (Iowa 1980), cert. denied 450 U.S. 927 (blood splatter analysis admitted).

35. See, e.g., People v. Collins, 68 Cal.2d 319, 66 Cal.Rptr. 497, 438 P.2d 33 (1968) (probability calculations); State v. Catanese, 368 So.2d 975, 981 (La.1979) (polygraph).

36. Building on various state and federal opinions, one state supreme court justice has outlined the factors for consideration in weighing probative value against possible prejudice:

(1) the potential error rate in using the technique, (2) the existence and maintenance of standards governing its use, (3) presence of safeguards in the characteristics of the technique, (4) analogy to other scientific techniques whose results are admissible, (5) the extent to which the technique has been accepted by scientists in the field involved, (6) the nature and breadth of the inference adduced, (7) the clarity and simplicity with which the technique can be described and its results explained, (8) the extent to which the basic data are verifiable by the court and jury, (9) the availability of other experts to test and evaluate the technique, (10) the probative significance of the evidence in the circumstances of the case, and (11) the care with which the technique was employed in the case.

McCormick, supra n. 2, at 911–912 (footnotes omitted). See also Trautman, supra n. 28.

commonplace.[37] Attention to possible infirmities in the collection and analysis of data can cut superficially impressive scientific evidence down to its proper size. To begin with, one might consider the process by which the forensic scientist makes his raw measurements.[38] Does subjective judgment play any role? If so, do different experts tend to find very different measured values, so that the measurement process can be described as unreliable?[39] Are the variations randomly distributed about some true mean, or are they biased in one direction or another, so that even if they are reliable, their accuracy is suspect? Then there are problems of interpretation. Is the quantity being measured the real item of interest, or at least a suitable proxy for that variable? In brief, considering the probable errors introduced at each stage of the scientific analysis, is the final result likely to be reliable, accurate, and meaningful?[40] The remainder of this chapter addresses these questions with regard to particular scientific tests and studies.

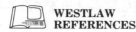
WESTLAW REFERENCES

Admissibility
frye /15 293 /5 1013
scientific /2 test* experiment* /p admissib!
   inadmissib!
frye /p polygraph!
frye /p hypno!

---

37. See Imwinkelreid, A New Era in the Evolution of Scientific Evidence, 23 Wm. & Mary L.Rev. 261 (1981).

38. "Measurement," in this context, includes qualitative observations of the presence or absence of some characteristic or property.

39. Here, the term "unreliable" is used in its technical sense, to refer to the reproducibility of results. Instruments (including human observers) that generate substantially different values each time a measurement of the same variable is made under the same conditions are said to be unreliable. In many situations, individually unreliable measurements can be combined to yield more reliable summary statistics, as when the scores of several judges are averaged in certain athletic competitions.

40. The term "validity" often is used to denote these last two qualities. That is, a valid technique or measuring device returns reasonably accurate values of the variables that the scientist purports to be mea-

§ 204. Particular Tests: Physics and Electronics: Speed Detection and Recording

Forensic applications of physics and electronics include motor vehicle accident reconstruction,[1] analysis of tape recordings,[2] and detecting and recording speed and other aspects of the movements of vehicles.[3] This section surveys the evidentiary features of speed detection and recording devices.

The branch of classical mechanics that deals with the motion of objects is called kinematics. The physicist defines average velocity as the distance travelled along a given direction in a specified time period divided by the length of this time period. Speed is the absolute value of velocity. The difference between speed and velocity is that the latter includes information as to the direction of travel, while the former merely states how fast the object moved. Acceleration is the change in velocity for a unit of time divided by the time elapsed. It states how quickly an object is speeding up or slowing down. Measuring such quantities without some mechanical aid is difficult to do accurately, although it can be easy enough to ascertain whether one vehicle is moving faster or slower than another.[4] A more elaborate application of these principles of kinematics to the detection and conviction of traffic offenders is recorded in an

---

suring. A valid method or measure is reliable, but not all reliable (consistent) measures are valid. When experts testify as to "reliability," it may be well to keep this distinction in mind. See United States v. Distler, 671 F.2d 954, 962 (6th Cir. 1981), cert. denied 454 U.S. 827 (apparently confusing expert estimates of reliability with assertions of validity).

§ 204

1. See supra n. 9, § 202.

2. Alonzo v. State ex rel. Booth, 283 Ala. 607, 219 So.2d 858, 879 (1969), cert. denied 396 U.S. 931; supra n. 31, § 202.

3. Here, as elsewhere in this chapter, the assignment of particular techniques to a scientific discipline such as physics, chemistry, biology, medicine, or psychology is inevitably somewhat arbitrary, since all of

---

4. See note 4 on page 611.

English case at the turn of the century in which a constable took readings from a watch with a second hand.[5] A progression of more sophisticated timing mechanisms followed,[6] culminating in the Visual Average Speed Computer and Record (VASCAR).[7] When a suspected violator's vehicle reaches a clearly marked point, such as an intersection, the operator activates the timer. When the police car reaches the same point, the operator activates a mechanism for recording the distance the police car travels as measured by its odometer. When the target vehicle reaches a second clearly marked point down the road, the police officer shuts off the timer, and when the police car arrives at this second point, he turns off the distance switch. The computer divides the measured distance by the measured time elapsed and displays this average speed.[8]

Initially, the courts required expert testimony concerning the principles and operation of the VASCAR.[9] However, the kinematic principles, which date back to the time of Galileo and Newton, are so well estab-

lished that they, like the ability of an electronic computer to divide two numbers, easily can be the subject of judicial notice.[10] The more serious issue, which goes to the weight and (in an extreme case, the admissibility) of the evidence, is the accuracy of the device under operational conditions. Errors can arise from a poorly calibrated odometer, from turning on and off the switches at the wrong times, and so on. A foundation indicating that the device is properly calibrated and the operator well trained in its use is usually required.[11]

A speed detector and recorder not so closely tied to police work is the tachograph. It consists of a tachometer and a recording mechanism that furnishes, over time, the speed and mileage of the vehicle to which it is attached.[12] It is used on trains, trucks and busses. Its readings have been admitted in civil and criminal cases, on a showing the particular device works accurately and an identification of which portion of the record generated pertains to the events in issue.[13]

these disciplines overlap. The "criminalistics" techniques mentioned infra § 207 are drawn from most of these fields.

4. Speedometer readings from the chase car or motorcycle have long been admitted. City of Spokane v. Knight, 96 Wash. 403, 165 P. 105 (1917).

5. Gorham v. Brice, 18 T.L.R. 424 (K.B. Div. 1902).

6. The simplest is the stopwatch, as employed by a stationary observer, see Fisher & Reeder, Vehicle Traffic Law 144 (1st ed.rev.1974), or by observers in aircraft. State v. Cook, 194 Kan. 495, 399 P.2d 835 (1965); Myren, Measurement of Motor Vehicle Ground Speed from Aircraft, 52 J.Crim.L.C. & P.S. 213 (1961); 14 Hastings L.J. 427 (1963); Annot., 27 A.L.R.3d 1442. The stopwatch method can be refined by laying sensitive tubes across the roadway at an appropriate distance apart and using the signals generated by passing cars to start and stop a timer. City of Webster Groves v. Quick, 323 S.W.2d 386 (Mo.App.1959); Office of Highway Planning, U.S. Dep't of Transp., Evaluation of Speed Monitoring Systems: Current State of the Art (1980); Annot., 47 A.L.R.3d 822, 872–75. Photographic methods, including stroboscopic analysis, also have been used to secure convictions. Commonwealth v. Buxton, 205 Mass. 49, 91 N.E. 128 (1910); People v. Pett, 13 Misc.2d 975, 178 N.Y.S.2d 550 (Police J.Ct., Nassau Cty. 1958). With regard to all these methods, see 7A Am.Jur.2d Automobile and Highway Traffic § 373.

7. Moenssens & Inbau, supra n. 2 § 202, at §§ 13.05–13.06; Richardson, Modern Scientific Evidence §§ 9.1–9.4 (2d ed.1974); Annot., 47 A.L.R.3d 822, 877.

8. Elementary calculus establishes that an average velocity cannot exceed the largest instantaneous velocity during the averaging period.

9. People v. Leatherbarrow, 69 Misc.2d 563, 330 N.Y.S.2d 676 (1972); People v. Persons, 60 Misc.2d 803, 303 N.Y.S.2d 728 (1969); Moenssens & Inbau, supra n. 2 § 202, at § 13.11.

10. State v. Finkle, 128 N.J.Super. 199, 319 A.2d 733, affirmed 66 N.J. 139, 329 A.2d 65 (1974), cert. denied 423 U.S. 836.

11. Compare Tiffin v. Whitmer, 32 Ohio Misc. 169, 61 O.O.2d 291, 290 N.E.2d 198 (Mun.Ct.1970) (evidence established accuracy of system and proper training and expertise of operator) with St. Louis v. Martin, 548 S.W.2d 622 (Mo.App.1970) (evidence insufficient to support conviction where police verified accuracy of VASCAR with a stopwatch but never verified accuracy of the stopwatch).

12. See generally Conrad, The Tachograph as Evidence of Speed, 8 Wayne L.Rev. 287 (1962); Annot., 73 A.L.R.2d 1025.

13. Compare Bell v. Kroger Co., 230 Ark. 384, 323 S.W.2d 424 (1959) (erroneously admitted where device had not been checked since its installation in truck

A more advanced kinematic recording instrument is the aircraft flight recorder.[14] It records time, airspeed, altitude, attitude (orientation of axes relative to some reference line or plane, such as the horizon), magnetic heading, vertical acceleration, and other instrument readings. These records can be extremely valuable in analyzing aircraft crashes. Admissibility turns on evidence of authenticity and expert testimony to explain how the machine operates and to interpret the marks on the chart.[15]

Radar equipment provides another means of measuring velocity.[16] Military or aircraft pulse-type radar involves more or less direct applications of the velocity-distance-time relationships previously discussed,[17] but police radar relies on a different theory.[18] In its simplest form, the radar speedmeter used by

police agencies transmits a continuous beam of microwaves of uniform frequency, detects the reflected signals, and measures the difference in frequency between the transmitted and reflected beams. It converts this frequency difference into a number for the speed of the object that has reflected the radiation. This conversion is based on a quantitative description of the phenomenon known as the Doppler effect. On both theoretical and experimental grounds, it is well established that electromagnetic radiation coming from an object moving relative to the observer is shifted to a higher frequency if the object is approaching, and to a lower frequency if the object is receding.[19] For the range of velocities of interest in traffic court, the extent of this Doppler shift is directly proportional to the relative speed.[20]

three years before accident and the graph conflicted sharply with the truck driver's testimony as to the number of stops he had made), and Texas & New Orleans Railroad Co. v. Lemke, 365 S.W.2d 148 (Tex.1963) (tape inadmissible without linking the indication of acceleration to any specific location); with Adkins v. Dirickson, 523 F.Supp. 1281 (E.D.Pa.1981) (device is sturdy and reliable and argument over accuracy only goes to weight of the evidence); Hall v. Dexter Gas Co., 277 Ala. 360, 170 So.2d 796 (1964) (admissible); Whitton v. Central of Georgia Railroad Co., 89 Ga.App. 304, 79 S.E.2d 331 (1953) (admissible in train-automobile collision case); Thompson v. Chicago & Eastern Illinois Railroad Co., 32 Ill.App.2d 397, 178 N.E.2d 151 (1961) (train speed tape admissible).

14. See generally DeLory, Flight Recording as Evidence in Civil Litigation, 9 Val.U.L.Rev. 321 (1974).

15. See 1 Kennelly, Litigation and Trial of Air Crash Cases 113–16 (1968); Speiser, Airplane Flight Recorders, 2 Forum 97 (1967); 13 N.Y.L.F. 677, 769 (1968).

16. See generally Fisher, Legal Aspects of Speed Measurement Devices (1967); Fisher & Reeder, supra n. 6; Richardson, supra n. 7, §§ 9.5–9.14; M. Skolnick, Radar Handbook (1970); 2 Wigmore, Evidence §§ 417b, 665a (Chadbourn rev.1979); Nat'l Highway Traffic Safety Ad., U.S. Dep't of Transp., Traffic Radar: Is it Reliable? (1980); Kopper, The Scientific Reliability of Radar Speedmeters, 33 N.C.L.Rev. 343 (1955); Carosell & Coombs, Radar Evidence in the Courts, 32 Dicta 323, 324 (1955); McCarter, Legal Aspects of Police Radar, 16 Clev.-Mar.L.Rev. 455 (1967); Trichter & Patterson, Police Radar 1980: Has the Black Box Lost its Magic? 11 St. Mary's L.J. 829 (1980); Comment, 48 Fordham L.Rev. 1138 (1980); 7A Am.Jur.2d Automobiles and Highway Traffic § 372 (1980).

17. The radar antenna transmits microwave radiation in pulses. The equipment measures the time it

takes for a pulse to reach the target and for its echo to return. Since the radiation travels at a known speed (the speed of light), this fixes the distance to the target. The changes in the distances as determined from the travel times of later pulses permit the target's velocity to be computed.

18. Some courts rely on the impressive precision of military and air traffic control radar in considering whether police radar meets the general acceptance test discussed supra, § 203. E.g., Commonwealth v. Whynaught, 377 Mass. 14, 384 N.E.2d 1212 (1979). Although the conclusion is correct, this reasoning overlooks the substantial differences in design, construction and theory of operation of Doppler effect radar and pulsed radar. Indeed, it has been remarked that inasmuch as police radar has no ranging capability, it is not, strictly speaking, a "radar" (Range Detection And Ranging) device. Carosell & Coombs, supra n. 15, at 325–26 (1955).

19. The Austrian physicist Christian Johann Doppler demonstrated and described the frequency shift of sound waves due to relative motion. A common illustration of the phenomenon is the heightened pitch of the whistle on an approaching train, followed by the lowered pitch as the train recedes. Perhaps this explains why the court in People v. Walker, 199 Colo. 475, 610 P.2d 496, 498 (1980), made the scientific blunder of suggesting that Doppler effect radar involves sound waves. Physicists now appreciate that all electromagnetic radiation and other forms of energy transmission exhibit the Doppler effect. Landsberg & Evans, Mathematical Cosmology 154–58 (1st ed. 2d printing 1979).

20. Hoyle, Astronomy and Cosmology: A Modern Course 237 (1975) (proportionality is a non-relativistic approximation); Greenwald, supra n. 16, at 58 n. 9; Kopper, supra n. 16, at 346–50.

When the radar set is at rest relative to the ground (earth's surface), it therefore gives the speed of the vehicle being tracked.

A more complicated version of the Doppler shift detector processes signals received at two distinct frequencies. This refinement allows the unit to be used conveniently in a moving vehicle. The shift in frequency of the beam as reflected off the road surface gives the speed of the police vehicle. The shift in frequency as reflected off the target vehicle gives its speed relative to the police car. In effect, circuitry in the radar unit adds the relative speed to the police car's speed to yield the ground speed of the target.

Most of the early cases admitting radar evidence of speeding involved testimony showing not only that the target car had been identified [21] and that a qualified operator had obtained the reading from a properly functioning device, but also explaining the Doppler effect, its application in the radar speedmeter, and the scientific acceptance of this method of measuring speed.[22] Within a few years, the courts began to take judicial notice of the underlying scientific principles and the capability (in theory) of the device to measure speed with tolerable accuracy.[23] Expert testimony on these subjects is no longer essential.[24]

The question of what must be proved to establish that the specific instrument was operating accurately has provoked more controversy. Decisions range from holdings that the evidence is inadmissible without independent verification of the accuracy of the system at the time and place of the measurement [25] to holdings that lack of evidence of testing goes to the weight but not the admissibility of the results.[26] Recent revelations that police radar units operating under field conditions may not be as reliable as had once been assumed may encourage adherence to the more stringent standards.[27]

Regardless of whether the jurisdiction has a particularized rule for the extent and type of testing needed for admissibility, evidence pertaining to the accuracy of the reading is admissible. There are many ways in which errors can creep into the system.[28] Stationary radar readings will be wrong if the transmission frequency changes, if the receiver misevaluates the frequency difference, if the radar is not held motionless, or if radiation from another source is attributed to the sus-

21. Honeycutt v. Commonwealth, 408 S.W.2d 421 (Ky.1966) (one vehicle adequately singled out of a group); Commonwealth v. Bartley, 411 Pa. 286, 191 A.2d 673 (1963) (one vehicle in a line of five adequately identified); 13 N.Y.L.F. 677, 774 (1966).

22. State v. Moffitt, 48 Del. 210, 100 A.2d 788 (1953); Hardaway v. State, 202 Tenn. 94, 302 S.W.2d 351 (1957) (dictum); cf. People v. Persons, 60 Misc.2d 803, 303 N.Y.S.2d 728 (1969) (VASCAR).

23. State v. Dantonio, 18 N.J. 570, 115 A.2d 35, (1955); Annot., 47 A.L.R.3d 822, 835–837.

24. Louisiana v. Spence, 418 So.2d 583, 587 (La. 1982); Commonwealth v. Whynaught, 377 Mass. 14, 384 N.E.2d 1212 (1979); Annot., 47 A.L.R.3d 822, 831–34. Some states enacted statutes to this effect. Sweeny v. Commonwealth, 211 Va. 668, 179 S.E.2d 509 (1971); Fisher, supra n. 16 at 69–75.

25. People v. Walker, 199 Colo. 475, 610 P.2d 496 (1980) (inadmissible when only one tuning fork used to check receiver and that fork not itself tested for accuracy within the last year); Commonwealth v. Whynaught, 377 Mass. 14, 384 N.E.2d 1212 (1979) (acceptability of testing left to discretion of trial court); State v. Doria, 135 Vt. 341, 376 A.2d 751 (1977); State v. Hanson, 85 Wis.2d 233, 270 N.W.2d 212 (1978); Lat-

in, Tannehill & White, Remote Sensing Evidence and Environmental Law, 64 Calif.L.Rev. 1300, 1413–14 (1976); Annot., 47 A.L.R.3d 822, 837–38; cf. State v. Gerdes, 291 Minn. 353, 191 N.W.2d 428 (1971) (conviction cannot rest entirely on radar measurement with device not externally tested). It is usually held that testing must be performed both before and after the measurement in question. See Moenssens & Inbau, supra n. 2, § 13.09 at 599.

26. State v. Dantonio, 18 N.J. 570, 115 A.2d 35 (1955) (dictum); People v. Dusing, 5 N.Y.2d 126, 181 N.Y.S.2d 493, 155 N.E.2d 393 (1959); Annot., 47 A.L.R.3d 822, 838–839. This seems to be the minority view. See Commonwealth v. Whynaught, 377 Mass. 14, 384 N.E.2d 1212 (1979).

27. See N.Y. Times, Nov. 27, 1979, sec. C p. 1 col. 6 ("Florida police clocked a . . . tree and a house moving at 28 miles an hour"); Trichter & Patterson, supra n. 16; Blackmore, Radar: Caught in Its Own Trap, Police Magazine, Sept. 1979, at 23; Comment, supra n. 16.

28. For more detailed analysis than is provided here, see Carosell & Coombs, supra n. 16; Trichter & Patterson, supra n. 16; Comment, supra n. 16.

pect's vehicle. Moving radar, being a more complex device, has more room for error. Acceleration of the patrol car, "cosine error," and "shadowing" can lead the instrument to underestimate the patrol car's speed, and hence to overstate the target vehicle's speed.[29]

Some of these potential sources of error can be minimized or excluded by careful operating procedures and on-site tests. These include the use of tuning forks vibrating at frequencies such that their linear motions will cause the speedmeter to register particular speeds if it is receiving properly, use of an internal, electronically activated tong for the same purpose, and simply checking that, when aimed at another police car, the radar reading corresponds with that car's speedometer reading. Of course, after a few years of use, tongs may not vibrate at the presumed frequency, an internal oscillator may need adjustment, and a car's speedometer may not be accurate. At least on the question of admissibility, however, most

courts recognize that independent errors are unlikely to be identical.[30] They tend to hold that some combination of these methods is sufficient to warrant admissibility.[31] Furthermore, a number of decisions, sometimes aided by statute, hold that tested radar readings can amount to proof beyond a reasonable doubt.[32]

 WESTLAW REFERENCES

car automobile vehicle /p accident crash /p
 reconstruct!
vascar "visual average speed"
tachograph

§ 205. Particular Tests: Biology and Medicine: Drunkenness, Blood and Tissue Typing

The forensic applications of the biological sciences and medicine are far too extensive and varied to be discussed fully here,[1] but we shall consider two groups of laboratory tests of biological samples that commonly

---

29. "Cosine error" can arise when the radar echo comes from a target that is not directly in front of the radar unit. It results from the fact that the Doppler shift is a function of the component of the relative velocity along the line of sight. See Comment, supra n. 16, at 1142–1143. "Shadowing" occurs when the reflection indicating the speed of the police car comes from slow-moving objects rather than stationary ones. Id. at 1143–1144. Tests of police radar units for these and other errors are described in the National Highway Traffic Safety Administration's report, supra n. 16.

30. State v. Shimon, 243 N.W.2d 571, 573 (Iowa 1976); State v. Hebert, 437 A.2d 185, 186 (Me.1971); State v. Graham, 322 S.W.2d 188, 197 (Mo.App.1959); State v. Kramer, 99 Wis.2d 700, 299 N.W.2d 882, 885–86 (1981).

31. State v. Newton, 421 A.2d 920, 922 (Del.Super. 1980) ("the proper foundation that must be laid . . . should include at least" evidence of operator qualifications and training, internal tests, external tests including "the use of a certified tuning fork and some verification that the speedometer of the patrol vehicle was checked for accuracy," and identification establishing that the suspect's vehicle was tracked rather than a more radio reflective object, such as a large truck); State v. Shimon, 243 N.W.2d 571, 573 (Iowa 1976) (admissible with testing by a single tuning fork and tracking of another police car whose speedmeter was independently calibrated); State v. Hebert, 437 A.2d 185 (Me.1981) (admissible with tests of receiver with two tuning forks to measure a range of speeds, internal os-

cillator, and tracking of another police car); State v. Kramer, 99 Wis.2d 700, 299 N.W.2d 882, 885 (1981) (two tuning forks); Comment, supra n. 16; Annot., 47 A.L.R.3d 822, 842–862; n. 25 supra. These rulings may seem odd since even when the detailed formulas for ensuring accuracy are not satisfied, the evidence almost always still meets the normal test for relevance. See supra § 185. The more exacting formulas may be justified, however, on the theory that the jury would overestimate the force of the evidence because of the aura of reliability and accuracy associated with the word "radar." Although a jury could be educated about the different types of radar and the weaknesses of police radar, the particularized rules of testing would be the more efficient way to proceed if the incidence of erroneously high readings is large. If this error rate is in fact high, then the stringent rules serve to lay to rest many residual doubts about the evidence in a cost-effective way.

32. See, e.g., Yolman v. State, 388 So.2d 1038 (Fla. 1980) (upholding as constitutional a statute creating a presumption on the basis of radar evidence if the operator is certified and the equipment tested every six months by a tuning fork test); People v. Stankovitch, 119 Ill.App.2d 187, 255 N.E.2d 461 (1970) (single tuning fork); Kansas City v. Hill, 442 S.W.2d 89 (Mo.App. 1969) (two tuning forks); Peterson v. State, 163 Neb. 669, 80 N.W.2d 688 (1957) (tracking another police car).

§ 205

1. See supra § 203 n. 1.

provide crucial evidence.[2] These are chemical tests for drunkenness [3] and serologic and related tests for blood and tissue types.[4]

A. *Drunkenness.* Physiologically, the amount of alcohol in the brain determines the degree of intoxication. Except in an autopsy, however, a direct measurement of the this quantity is not feasible. Nevertheless, samples of blood, urine, saliva, or breath can be taken, and the alcohol level in these samples can be measured. Using these measurements to determine whether a person is intoxicated raises two technical problems— the accuracy of the measurement itself, and the extent of the correlation between the concentration of alcohol in the sample and the degree of intoxication. There is room for concern on both these points.

Analysis of blood samples gives the most accurate and reliable results.[5] Various chemical techniques are available to measure the concentration of ethyl alcohol in the sample.[6] When proper laboratory procedures are followed and the sample is correctly obtained and preserved, these give reliable estimates.[7] Of course, there is always room for error in these measurements,[8] but the more fundamental problem lies in moving from an estimated value for the blood alcohol concentration (BAC) to a correct statement about the degree of intoxication during the crucial period. Even where the measured values are reliable and accurate, the substantial variability in tolerances for alcohol, absorption rates, and clearance rates, both among individuals and within the same individual from one situation to another, complicates efforts to deduce the true extent of intoxication at the time of an arrest or ac-

---

2. For references to some other laboratory tests on biological materials, see supra § 203 n. 1 & infra § 207.

3. See generally 1–3 Erwin, Defense of Drunk Driving Cases §§ 14.01–28.06 (3d ed.rev.1982); Moenssens & Inbau, Scientific Evidence in Criminal Cases §§ 2.01–2.11 (2d ed.1978); Richardson, Modern Scientific Evidence §§ 13.1–13.29 (2d ed.1974); Barnett, Blood and Urine Alcohol Test Procedures, 120 New L.J. 949 (1970); Bass, Gesser & Mount, Scientific Statistical Methodology, 5 Dalhousie L.J. 350, 354–363 (1979); Belloti, The Preparation and Trial of a Drunken Driving Case Involving a Breathalyzer, in Scientific and Expert Evidence 195 (2d ed. Imwinkelried 1981); Caplan, The Determination of Alcohol in Blood and Breath, in Forensic Science Handbook 592 (Saferstein ed.1982); Emerson, Hollyhead & Isaacs, The Measurement of Breath Alcohol, 70 J. Forensic Sci.Soc'y 3 (1980); Fitzgerald & Hume, The Single Chemical Test for Intoxication: A Challenge to Admissibility, 66 Mass.L.Rev. 23 (1981); Hutton, Cross-Examination of an Expert Criminalist in a Gas Chromatograph Case, in id. at 221; Mason & Dubowski, Breath-Alcohol Analysis: Uses, Methods and Some Forensic Problems, 21 J. Forensic Sci. 9 (1976) [hereinafter cited as Breath-Alcohol Analysis]; Mason & Dubowski, Alcohol, Traffic and Chemical Testing in the United States: A Resume and Some Remaining Problems, 20 Clinical Chemistry (1974); Watts, Tests for Intoxication, 45 N.C.L.Rev. 34 (1966); Comment, 5 N.Ky.L.Rev. 207 (1978); Annot., 96 A.L.R.3d 745 (proving tests done as statute or regulation require), 16 A.L.R.3d 748 (statutory presumption and inferences as to drunkenness); 7A Am.Jur.2d Automobiles and Highway Traffic §§ 305–307, 376–377, 380; Dec.Digest Criminal Law ⊸388. The present discussion confines itself to questions about the evidentiary value of the chemical tests by reason of their accuracy and validity. Chapters 13 and 15 address the search and seizure, self-incrimination and related due process issues. See also Note, Arrest Requirement for Administering Blood Tests, 1971 Duke L.J. 601; Annot., 72 A.L.R.3d 325 (1972) (taking blood from an unconscious driver). On the claim that the state's failure to preserve a test sample for independent testing by the defense amounts to a denial of due process, see Annot., 19 A.L.R.4th 509.

4. See infra text accompanying nn. 21–47.

5. See Fitzgerald & Hume, supra n. 3, at 23; Note, Arrest Requirements for Administering Blood Tests, supra note 3, at 602, citing Report of the Fourth International Conference on Alcohol and Traffic Safety, 1966 Crim.L.Rev. 69.

6. These range from classic separation and reaction techniques to gas liquid chromatography. For details, see 1 Erwin, supra n. 3, § 17; Caplan, supra n. 3, at 108–121.

7. Barnett, supra n. 3, at 950 (very small standard deviation in gas chromatograph readings on unclotted samples). A committee of the Toxicology Section of the American Academy of Forensic Sciences has recommended specific quality controls. See Caplan, supra n. 3, at 623.

8. 1 Erwin, supra n. 3, §§ 17.06–17.07; Moenssens & Inbau, supra § 202 n. 2, § 2.07; Barnett, supra n. 3, at 950 (noting that although "[a] clotted blood sample cannot be accurately analyzed by techniques currently in common use," 25% of samples prepared by the constabularies were clotted, and remarking that "[i]t is not clear . . . how the police analyze their clotted samples, but procedures such as banging the ampoule on a bench, mixing it with a paper clip and equally suspect methods have been referred to in courts by forensic analysts").

cident.[9] For these reasons, extrapolations based on direct measurements of BAC seem more perilous than is generally recognized.

Determinations resting exclusively on measurements of the alcohol contained in a sample of a person's breath are even more questionable.[10] Again, the problem is not the accuracy of the instrumentation as maintained and used in laboratory studies.[11] Although errors can arise from field operating conditions, individual variability, and extrapolation to the time in question, there is a further problem. A formula must be used to convert the figure for the concentration found in the breath to a BAC value. A single number presently is used as a multiplier in making this conversion, but the exact value of this parameter is debatable, and there are strong indications of substantial variability in the figure among individuals and within the same individual over time.[12]

These cautions concerning the scientific proof as applied in particular cases do not necessarily make the blood and breath test evidence inadmissible. On the contrary, when the tests are properly conducted and analyzed, the evidence of BAC can be of great value in deciding questions connected with intoxication. Since the link between high blood alcohol levels and intoxication as well as the accuracy of measurements made under ideal conditions is well established, under the usual principles governing scientific evidence,[13] the test results should be admissible if founded on a showing of authenticity and satisfactory care in the collection of the sample and its analysis.[14] Expert testimony ordinarily would be needed to establish that the party with the measured or inferred BAC was intoxicated during the period in question.[15]

---

9. 1 Erwin, supra n. 3, § 16.04[2]; Breath-Alcohol Analysis, supra n. 3, at 21 (Figure 3); Radlow & Hurst, Delayed Blood Alcohol Determinations in Forensic Applications, 2 Crim.Just.J. 281 (1979); Solomon, Jurimetrics, in Research Papers in Statistics 319, 326–329 (David ed. 1966). Fitzgerald & Hume, supra n. 3, cogently argue that since blood alcohol concentration (BAC) rises after drinking, then falls, a single measurement is not very revealing when one is interested in the BAC some time before the sample was taken. They urge that unless a second sample is analyzed to determine whether the level is rising or falling, the single test result should not even be admissible. Many courts and legislators have assumed, incorrectly, that a person's BAC inevitably is higher at the time of an accident than it is afterwards, at the time of testing (unless the person has consumed more alcohol after the accident). See, e.g., State v. Olivas, 77 Ariz. 118, 267 P.2d 893 (1954); Moenssens & Inbau, supra n. 3, § 2.03 at 75 (the "extrapolation theory . . . no longer possesses the full validity it was once thought to possess").

10. Urinalysis involving fluid that has accumulated in the bladder tends to give inaccurate BAC estimates, and the use of this technique is discouraged. See 2 Erwin, supra n. 3, § 25.01; Moenssens & Inbau, supra n. 3, § 2.04. Analysis of saliva is still more infrequent and problematical. Erwin, supra, § 25.04.

11. Alobaidi, Hill & Payne, Significance of Variations in Blood: Breath Partition Coefficient of Alcohol, 2 Brit.Med.J. 1479 (1976) (citing references); Breath-Alcohol Analysis, supra n. 3, at 21. For descriptions of various instruments, see 1 Erwin, supra n. 3, §§ 18.08, 19–21; 2 id. §§ 22–24A; Breath-Alcohol Analysis, supra, at 12–19; Caplan, supra n. 3, at 625–41. Statistical techniques could be used to give interval rather

than point estimates of BAC on the basis of breath alcohol measurements. See Bass, Gesser & Mount, supra n. 3, at 362–363; Lovell, Breath Tests for Determining Alcohol in the Blood, 178 Sci. 264 (1972).

12. 1 Erwin, supra n. 3, §§ 18.01–18.02; 3 id. § 33A; Alobaidi, Hill & Payne, supra n. 11; Bass, Gesser & Mount, supra n. 3, at 358–359; Breath-Alcohol Analysis, supra n. 3, at 20–29; Comment, supra n. 3, at 215–216. But see Caplan, supra n. 3, at 624 (studies showing that the usual multiplier understates BAC); Emerson, Hollyhead & Isaacs, supra n. 3 (concluding that the usual multiplier is reasonably accurate). At least one state statute making blood alcohol evidence admissible specifies that the usual multiplier is "prima facie" correct. Wisc.Stat.Ann. § 885.235(2a).

13. See supra § 203.

14. Ballou v. Henri Studios, 656 F.2d 1147 (5th Cir. 1981) (error to exclude expert testimony about intoxication based on finding that blood sample from deceased who drove into a truck parked on the shoulder of a highway contained .24% alcohol); McGough v. Slaugher, 395 So.2d 972, 977 (Ala.1981) (foundation insufficient for "admission under general evidence principles"); State v. Dille, 258 N.W.2d 565, 567–569 (Minn. 1977) (foundation sufficient for admission under statute providing that "the court may admit evidence of the amount of alcohol in the person's blood, breath, or urine as shown by a medical or chemical analysis"); 71 Am.Jur.2d, supra n. 3, § 377; Annot., 5 A.L.R.4th 1194 (admissibility of automobile passenger's BAC to show contributory negligence).

15. Mattingly v. Eisenberg, 79 Ariz. 135, 285 P.2d 174 (1955); Watts, supra n. 3. The sources of error outlined above may diminish the weight of this testimony. United States v. DuBois, 645 F.2d 642 (8th Cir.

In the context of traffic offenses, however, specialized statutes and regulations have largely supplanted the application of the common law principles and evidence codes in determining the admissibility of blood and breath test evidence.[16] The Uniform Vehicle Code illustrates some common provisions. In proceedings involving driving or control of a vehicle while under the influence of intoxicating liquor, it makes chemical test evidence of BAC admissible as long as it is obtained by certified persons following procedures that the state department of health has prescribed.[17] The results of this testing can trigger two rebuttable presumptions:[18] if BAC at the relevant time was .10% or more, that the individual was under the influence; and if BAC was .05% or less, that he was not. An intermediate reading is deemed "competent evidence" for consideration along with the other evidence in the case. In most jurisdictions, a party offering test results pursuant to such a statute must lay a foundation by producing witnesses to

explain the way the test is conducted, to identify it as duly approved under the statutory scheme, and to vouch for its correct administration in the particular case.[19] In recent years, some seventeen states have placed still more emphasis on chemical testing by enacting "per se" laws that make it a crime to drive while having a BAC of .10% or more.[20]

B. *Blood and Tissue Types.* Another group of chemical tests—those that identify blood and tissue types—are also often the subject of courtroom testimony. Elucidating the biochemical mechanisms by which a multicellular organism distinguishes between self and non-self—between its own cells and foreign substances—is a major research problem in biology.[21] The topic is fundamental to understanding the way in which the body responds to infections from microorganisms, to grafts of foreign tissues or materials, and to blood transfusions, and it is central to the study of allergies, tumors,

1981) (expert's attempt to extrapolate to BAC at time of accident when defendant had consumed more alcohol after the accident). When the time of testing is too remote or the manner of testing grossly erroneous, exclusion is proper. See cases cited, 7A Am.Jur.2d, supra n. 3, § 377.

16. See State v. Bender, 382 So.2d 697, 699 (Fla. 1980) (citing statutes); 2 Erwin, supra n. 3, § 26; 3 id. §§ 28.06, 33A; 8 Wigmore, Evidence § 2265 n. 6 (McNaughton rev. 1961); 7A Am.Jur.2d, supra n. 3, §§ 305, 380; Note, Arrest Requirement for Administering Blood Tests, supra n. 3, at 601–606; Annot., 16 A.L.R.3d 748. Although the Uniform Vehicle Code is written so as to apply to all incidents involving drunken driving, most of these statutes are restricted to prosecutions for driving while intoxicated. Moenssens & Inbau, supra n. 3, § 2.09 at 91. As a rule, attempts to invoke the statutorily prescribed presumptions and procedures in other prosecutions or civil actions have not been crowned with success. State v. Bender, supra, at 700; Mattingly v. Eisenberg, 79 Ariz. 135, 285 P.2d 174, 177 (1955); Annot., supra, at 751. But see 2 Erwin, supra, § 26.01. Even in the type of case to which the statute clearly applies, the more general evidentiary principles still can be critical. The state may rely on a test not yet approved pursuant to the statutory scheme. See State v. Mills, 133 Vt. 15, 328 A.2d 410 (1974) (gas chromatography admissible). Likewise, a party may call on "general evidence principles" in a civil action in which statutory procedures are available but not followed. See McGough v. Slaughter, 395 So. 2d 972, 977 (Ala.1981).

17. Previously, cases on the analysis of breath samples had divided, with a majority admitting the evidence. Compare People v. Bobczyk, 343 Ill.App. 504, 99 N.E.2d 567, 570 (1951) with People v. Morse, 325 Mich. 270, 38 N.W.2d 322 (1949) ("general scientific recognition that the breath test applied by the Hager Drunkometer will afford an accurate index of the alcoholic content of the blood" not established).

18. The Uniform Act refers to BAC "at the time alleged." Uniform Vehicle Code Ann. § 11–902(b). There are local variations as to whether BAC at the time of testing or at the extrapolated figure for an earlier time triggers the presumptions. See, e.g., Wis. Stat.Ann. § 885.235 (BAC of sample taken within 3 hours of "time in question" triggers statutory presumptions "without requiring any expert testimony as to its effect"); supra n. 9.

19. State v. Westbrook, 385 So.2d 13 (La.1980), on rehearing, 392 So.2d 1043, 1044–45; State v. Kolar, 206 Neb. 619, 294 N.W.2d 350, 353 (1980); State v. McClary, 59 Or.App. 553, 651 P.2d 145 (1982); City of West Allis v. Rainey, 36 Wis.2d 489, 153 N.W.2d 514 (1967) (expert testimony not required for test results to be admitted and for statutory presumptions to apply); Annot., 96 A.L.R.3d 745; 3 Erwin, supra n. 3, § 28.06.

20. Roberts v. State, 329 So.2d 296 (Fla.1976) (statute constitutional); Erwin, supra n. 3, § 33A.

21. See U.S. Dep't of Health, Educ. & Welfare, Report of the President's Biomedical Research Panel: Appendix A (1976); Leder, The Genetics of Antibody Diversity, Sci.Am., May 1982, at 108.

and autoimmune diseases.[22] Research in this field reveals that sticking out of the surface of cells are various molecules, called in this context, antigens.[23] For instance, a person with type A blood has the molecule known as an A antigen on his red blood cells.[24] Of course, red blood cells are not the only ones to possess antigens. Human Leucocyte Antigens (HLA) are found on the surface of most human cells, and there is an elaborate nomenclature for these. The full set of antigens that a cell possesses thus distinguishes it from the cells of other organisms. It is conceivable that each person is uniquely identifiable in this way. However, no one really knows exactly how many antigens there are. New ones continue to be discovered. In addition to the immunologically crucial antigens, cells and bodily fluids contain chemicals such as enzymes and other proteins that can differ from one person to another.[25]

Most enzymes and serum proteins are identified by a technique called electrophoresis, in which an electric field is applied to separate the molecules. A different type of test is used to detect antigens. The antigens react with other biologically produced molecules, called antibodies. Serologic tests consist of exposing a suspected antigen to its corresponding antibody and observing whether the expected reaction occurs. Errors involving misinterpretation, mislabeling, poor reagents, and the like are always possible, but workers in this field report that with stringent procedures and quality control standards, the risk of error can be made very small.[26]

The forensic use of these tests arises principally in two areas—identifying the perpetrators of violent crimes or sexual offenses

---

22. See Hyde & Patnode, Immunology (1978); Luciano, Vander & Sherman, Human Function and Structure 671–79 (1978).

23. The abbreviated explanation of the biomedical principles is drawn from such texts as Barrett, Textbook of Immunology (3d ed.1978); Bodmer & Cavalli-Sforza, Genetics, Evolution and Man (1976); Race & Sanger, Blood Groups in Man (6th ed.1975) (definitive reference on red blood cell types). For discussions in the context of paternity testing, see Am. Ass'n of Blood Banks, Inclusion Probabilities in Parentage Testing (Walker ed. 1983); Am. Ass'n of Blood Banks, Paternity Testing (1978); Paternity Testing by Blood Grouping (Sussman ed.1976); Ellman & Kaye, Probabilities and Proof: Can HLA and Blood Group Testing Prove Paternity? 54 N.Y.U.L.Rev. 1131 (1979); Joint AMA–ABA Guidelines: Present Status of Serologic Testing in Problems of Disputed Parentage, 10 Fam.L.Q. 247 (1976); Reisner & Bolk, A Layman's Guide to the Use of Blood Group Analysis in Paternity Testing, 20 J.Fam.L. 657 (1981–82); Wiener & Socha, Methods Available for Solving Medicolegal Problems of Disputed Parentage, 21 J. Forensic Sci. 42 (1976).

24. We are simplifying for ease of exposition. In fact, there are several distinct antigens that are included within type A blood. Consequently, the type A blood group can be divided into various subgroups corresponding to the presence or absence of the particular antigens. Ignoring subdivisions, type B blood corresponds to the B antigen, type AB to the combination of the A and B antigens, and type O blood lacks both the A and B antigens.

25. Blake & Sensabaugh, Genetic Markers in Human Semen: A Review, 21 J. Forensic Sci. 784 (1976); Nelson, Detection of the Rare PGM_1^3 Allele, 26

J. Forensic Sci. 75 (1981); Sensabaugh, Biochemical Markers of Individuality, in Forensic Science Handbook 338, 341–346 (Saferstein ed.1982).

26. Henningsen, Error Risks in Paternity Diagnosis by Bloodgrouping, in Inclusion Probabilities in Parentage Testing, supra n. 23; Schacter, Hsu & Bias, HLA and Other Genetic Markers in Disputed Paternity: A Report of 50 Cases, 9 Transplantation Proc. 233, 236–237 (1977). There are grounds to wonder whether all crime laboratories adhere to such standards. See Wiener, Foreword, Sussman, Blood Grouping Tests—Medicolegal Uses ix (1968) ($^1/_3$ of test reports on blood samples referred to independent expert for verification found to be in error); Imwinkelried, Foreword, in Scientific and Expert Evidence 4 (2d ed. Imwinkelried 1981) (six out of 158 crime laboratories responding to an LEAA survey provided "unacceptable" analyses of a blood sample). Dried bloodstains require special preparation and analysis. Brewer, Cropp & Sharman, A Low Ionic Strength, Hemagglutinating, AutoAnalyzer for Rhesus Typing of Dried Bloodstains, 21 J. Forensic Sci. 811 (1976); Kipps, Gm and Km Typing in Forensic Science, 19 J. Forensic Sci. Soc'y 27 (1979); Lee, Identification and Grouping of Bloodstains, in Forensic Sciences Handbook 267 (Saferstein ed.1982). For some enumerations of possible sources of error in serologic tests, see Anonymous v. Anonymous, 10 Ariz. 496, 500, 460 P.2d 32, 35 (App.1969); Jackson v. Jackson, 67 Cal.2d 245, 250 n. 1, 60 Cal. Rptr. 649, 652 n. 1, 430 P.2d 289, 292 (1967) (dissenting opinion); Marks, Paternity Case—Direct and Cross-Examination of a Plaintiff's Expert Immunohematologist, 1982 Med. Trial Technique Q. 335; Wraxall, Forensic Serology, in Scientific and Expert Evidence, supra, at 899.

from traces of blood or semen [27] and ascertaining parentage in child support cases or other litigation.[28] In general, the courts have moved from an initial position of mistrust of such evidence [29] to the present stage of taking judicial notice of the scientific acceptance or acceptability of serologic and related tests.[30] It is recognized that if the suspect's antigens do not match those in the sample found at the scene of a crime, then the incriminating trace does not consist of his blood. On the other hand, there is a difference of judicial opinion when it comes to

evidence showing that there is a match. Since some combinations of antigens are relatively common, a few courts have dismissed the positive test results for these antigens as irrelevant.[31] The better view—and the clear majority position [32]—is that positive findings are neither irrelevant nor so innately prejudicial as to justify a rule against their admission.[33]

Serologic tests have been used for the last half-century in paternity litigation. The underlying logic is based on a few principles of

27. See Jonakait, Will Blood Tell? 31 Emory L.J. 833 (1983); Annot., 2 A.L.R.4th 500. In these cases, other chemical tests also may be used to determine whether a stain is actually blood, whether it is human blood, and how long it has been exposed. Moenssens & Inbau, supra n. 3, §§ 6.08–6.10, 6.12; Dixon, Samudra, Stewart & Johari, A Scanning Electron Microscope Study of Dried Blood, 21 J. Forensic Sci. 797 (1976); Lee, supra n. 26; Lee & De Forest, A Precipitin-Inhibition Test on Denatured Bloodstains for the Determination of Human Origin, 21 J. Forensic Sci. 804 (1976).

28. In addition to the authorities cited, supra n. 23, see Krause, Child Support in America 213–278 (1981); Page-Bright, Proving Paternity—Human Leukocyte Antigen Test, 27 J. Forensic Sci. 135 (1982) (describing antigens and collecting cases); Note, 14 Ind.L.Rev. 831 (1981); Annot., 46 A.L.R.Fed. 176 (serologic tests to show parentage in immigration preference and derivative citizenship cases). The chair of the American Association of Blood Banks' Committee on Parentage Testing, referring to HLA and other tests and echoing the predictions of serologists in previous decades, stated that "This type of test will take us closer to the time when there need no longer be disputes concerning paternity, because test results will be so accurate that true fathers will be more likely to settle out of court than to fight a losing battle." 120 Sci. News 317 (1981) (quoting R. Walker). For an application of the analysis used in parentage testing to a case of kidnapping and extortion, see Kuo, Linking a Bloodstain to a Missing Person by Genetic Inheritance, 27 J. Forensic Sci. 438 (1982).

29. See cases cited supra § 203 n. 15. But see Krause, supra n. 28, at 214 (1974 survey found that 11% of judges never use serologic tests in paternity cases).

30. Houghton v. Houghton, 179 Neb. 275, 137 N.W. 2d 861, 869 (1965); Matter of Abe A., 56 N.Y.2d 288, 452 N.Y.S.2d 6, 12, 437 N.E.2d 265 (1982); State v. Meacham, 93 Wn.2d 738, 612 P.2d 795, 797 (1980); 29 Am.Jur.2d Evidence 104; Annot., supra n. 28. A notable exception is the Supreme Court of Utah, which declined to take judicial notice of the reliability and validity of HLA typing in evaluating claims of paternity. Phillips ex rel. Utah State Department of Social Service v. Jackson, 615 P.2d 1228 (Utah 1980).

31. State v. Peterson, 219 N.W.2d 665, 671 (Iowa 1974); People v. Macedonio, 42 N.Y.2d 944, 397 N.Y.S.2d 1002, 366 N.E.2d 1355 (1977); People v. Robinson, 27 N.Y.2d 864, 317 N.Y.S.2d 19, 265 N.E.2d 543 (1970). The Iowa Supreme Court has retreated from its dictum in *Peterson*. See State v. Mark, 286 N.W.2d 396, 412–413 (Iowa 1979). The New York Court of Appeals has acknowledged that "the relative rarity of the assailant's type of blood [goes] to weight rather than admissibility," but it has shown no disposition to overrule *Robinson* and *Macedonio*. See Matter of Abe A., 56 N.Y.2d 288, 452 N.Y.S.2d 6, 12, 12 n. 4, 437 N.E.2d 265 (1982).

32. See People v. Lindsey, 84 Cal.App.3d 851, 149 Cal.Rptr. 47, 54–55 (1978) (collecting cases); Annot., supra n. 27.

33. In one leading case, Shanks v. State, 185 Md. 437, 45 A.2d 85 (1945), the accused was charged with rape. The state proved that blood found on the coat of the accused, like that of his alleged victim, was type O. The defendant argued that since 45% of the population had type O blood, the evidence should have been excluded as too remote. The court reasoned that "The objection of remoteness goes to the weight of the evidence rather than its admissibility. To exclude evidence merely because it tends [only] to establish a possibility . . . would produce curious results not heretofore thought of. [T]hat the accused was somewhere near the scene of the crime would not, in itself, establish a probability [exceeding .5] that he was guilty, but only a possibility, yet such evidence is clearly admissible as a link in the chain." 45 A.2d at 87. Likewise, in Commonwealth v. Statti, 166 Pa.Super. 577, 73 A.2d 688, 692 (1950), the court held that "the admissibility of this evidence is not affected by the fact that Type O blood is common to perhaps 45% of the people of the world. It was still competent as some evidence, just as evidence of how an assailant was dressed, however conventionally, would be competent though by no means conclusive of identity." Some courts treat the positive findings as admissible solely to corroborate the other evidence pointing to the defendant. Commonwealth v. Mussoline, 429 Pa. 464, 240 A.2d 549 (1968).

human genetics.[34] Roughly speaking, portions of the DNA contained in the chromosomes of the nucleus of a cell—the genes—direct the synthesis of proteins. Different versions (or alleles) of these genes oversee the synthesis of the different antigens. Consequently, by ascertaining which antigens are present in an individual (the phenotype), one learns something about that individual's alleles (the genotype).[35] As such, the antigens can be thought of as genetic markers. Knowing the phenotypes of the child, mother, and putative father and applying the laws of inheritance, a geneticist can

say whether it would be possible for a child with the observed phenotype to have been born to the mother and the alleged father. That is, the medical expert can state that whoever the biological father was must have had certain genetic characteristics, which can be compared to those that the alleged father has. In this way, a man falsely accused—one who does not have the necessary characteristics—can be excluded.[36]

With an appropriate foundation, such negative test results are nearly always admissible,[37] although the weight accorded to an ex-

34. A more comprehensive and precise description of the mechanisms and terminology of inheritance can be found in any textbook on biology or genetics. See, e.g., Bodmer & Cavalli-Sforza, supra n. 23; Stern, Principles of Human Genetics (1978); Farnsworth, Genetics (1978). These texts and many of the references given supra at nn. 22–23 specifically describe the genetics of some simple blood group systems.

35. How much one learns depends on some details of the particular genetic system. With some exceptions that are irrelevant here, humans chromosomes come in pairs. One is inherited from the mother, the other from the father. (This ignores recombination, or crossing-over of segments of chromosomes. See Inclusion Probabilities in Parentage Testing, supra n. 23.) The cell nucleus thus contains two of each gene—one on each chromosome. If the two genes both act to express antigens, then the genotype giving rise to these antigens is known in its entirety. (Such a system is said to be codominant, because neither allele dominates the other. The genetic system underlying the HLA antigens is of this simple type. However, with HLA it is common to speak of "haplotype" rather than genotype. The haplotype is half of the genotype. It is the set of HLA alleles along one of the chromosomes. The other chromosome usually has a different haplotype. Because the same allele can appear in both haplotypes or a haplotype may have an allele that does not react with any of the known antisera, it is not always possible to specify uniquely a person's haplotypes on the basis of his HLA phenotypes). Instead of the genes being codominant, one "dominant" allele can function to the exclusion of its "recessive" partner. With these genetic systems, the phenotype does not always provide an unequivocal indication of the genotype. For example, the classic red blood cell types are thought to be the result of three alleles, designated A, B, and O. A person with type A blood could have the genotype AA or AO (since the O allele gives rise to neither A nor B antigens). Without testing other members of the family, there is no way to tell from serologic tests.

36. As with any empirical statement, absolute certainty is unattainable. In particular, an exclusion presupposes that simple Mendelian genetics is at work and that there has been no laboratory error. Furthermore, due to "silent" genes and weakly reacting reagents, not

all exclusions are unambiguous. Cf. Oi Lan Lee v. District Director, 573 F.2d 592, 595 n. 2 (9th Cir. 1978) (recognizing that certainty in blood test exclusions, as in all scientific determinations, is "a matter of degree").

37. See Little v. Streater, 452 U.S. 1 (1981) (holding that due process requires the state to finance blood tests for indigent paternity defendants and observing that "Unlike other evidence . . . blood test results, if obtained under proper conditions by qualified experts, are difficult to refute"); Beach v. Beach, 114 F.2d 479, 480–481 (D.C.Cir. 1940); Houghton v. Houghton, 179 Neb. 275, 137 N.W.2d 861, 868 (1965); Annot., 46 A.L.R.2d 1000; Office of Child Support Enforcement, U.S. Dep't of Health, Educ. & Welfare, Paternity Determination: Techniques and Procedures 25 (1977) (all trial judges in all jurisdictions surveyed admit findings of exclusion). Two doctrines may interfere with the admissibility or weight of exculpatory immunologic evidence. Most jurisdictions allow the defense of *exceptio plurium concubentium*, which permits the defendant in a paternity proceeding to escape liability by showing that the mother had sexual relations with some other man during the possible period of conception. See Ellman & Kaye, supra n. 23, at 1134 n. 12. Second, in a few jurisdictions the presumption of legitimacy accorded a child born of a married mother during wedlock is well-nigh conclusive. Jackson v. Jackson, 67 Cal.2d 245, 60 Cal.Rptr. 649, 430 P.2d 289 (1967) (biological parentage irrelevant if conception occurs during cohabitation, but in conjunction with other evidence blood tests may show that conception did not occur in this period), noted, 20 Stan.L.Rev. 754 (1968); Vincent B. v. Joan R., 126 Cal.App.3d 619, 179 Cal.Rptr. 9 (1981), appeal dismissed, 103 S.Ct. 31 (1982); 76 Nw. U.L.Rev. 669, 669 n. 1 (1981). The strength of this presumption, however, is waning. Ferguson v. Ferguson, 126 Cal.App.3d 744, 179 Cal.Rptr. 108, 109 (1981) (under an amendment to the California Evidence Code a husband can compel blood tests that can overcome the presumption); R.McG. v. J.W., 615 P.2d 666, 668 n. 4 (Colo.1980); Cortese v. Cortese, 10 N.J.Super. 152, 76 A.2d 717 (1950); Snapp, Krause & Haveman, The Use of Blood Typing in Cases of Disputed Parentage in England, in Krause, supra n. 23, at 635, 636; cases cited infra n. 39. See also § 67 supra as to spouse's competency to testify to non-access.

clusion varies. A few cases can be found upholding liability despite serologic proof of nonpaternity.[38] In other states, a properly conducted blood test that excludes the defendant is conclusive.[39]

Positive immunogenetic findings are another matter. Although European countries allow positive test results as tending to prove paternity,[40] the traditional rule in this country is that serologic tests are inadmissible for this purpose.[41] At one time, when only a few, widely shared antigens were known, this approach made some sense. For example, under the early ABO system, a positive test result merely meant that, on average, the accused was one of the 87% of the male population possessing the requisite genotypes.[42] Such evidence is not very probative, and the fear that the jury would give it

more weight than it deserved, cloaked as it was in the garb of medical expertise, prompted many courts to exclude it as unduly prejudicial.[43] For decades, however, this situation has been changing steadily. With the plethora of genetic markers now known, it is commonplace to determine that the biological father has genetic traits shared by one in several thousand men of the same race. Many laboratories are equipped to test reliably for enough antigens that such positive test results are simply too probative to be ignored.[44]

As a result, evidence that the accused has immunogenetic traits that are consistent with the claim that he is the biological father is received regularly in many trial courts. In the majority of states, this is a consequence of statutory innovation [45]—typically

38. The most notorious is Berry v. Chaplin, 74 Cal. App.2d 652, 664–665, 169 P.2d 442, 450–451 (1949) (sustaining jury verdict despite blood test evidence excluding the actor Charlie Chaplin). A more recent child support decision of this ilk, State v. Camp, 286 N.C. 148, 152–153, 209 S.E.2d 754, 756–757 (1974), provoked a statute, N.C.Gen.Stat. § 8–50.1(a)(1) (1981), making a definitive exclusion conclusive.

39. Jordan v. Mace, 144 Me. 351, 69 A.2d 670 (1949); Hanson v. Hanson, 311 Minn. 388, 390–391, 249 N.W.2d 452, 453 (1977) (reviewing the weight generally accorded exclusionary results); Houghton v. Houghton, 179 Neb. 275, 137 N.W.2d 861, 870 (1965); Krause, supra n. 28, at 218–219; cf. Oi Lan Lee v. District Director, 573 F.2d 592, 594–595 (9th Cir. 1978) (exclusions conclusive in Immigration and Naturalization Service proceedings); Annot., supra n. 28. The view that a negative test result is conclusive if the accuracy of the testing is not attacked directly is an application of the doctrine that where uncontroverted physical facts contradict the testimony of a witness, that testimony cannot be accepted and a verdict based on it cannot be sustained. Anonymous v. Anonymous, 10 Ariz. 496, 500, 460 P.2d 32, 35 (App.1969) ("To hold [that results which excluded the husband as the father of his wife's child were not conclusive] would be tantamount to this court, by judicial decree, declaring the laws of motion and gravity to be repealed").

40. But see Rigo, Le Code Napoléon et la Réalité Biologique en Matière de Filiation, in Biomathematical Evidence of Paternity 35 (Hummel & Gerchow ed. 1981).

41. Isaacson v. Obendorf, 99 Idaho 304, 581 P.2d 350, 354–55 (1978); J.B. v. A.F., 92 Wis.2d 696, 699–705, 285 N.W.2d 880, 881–884 (App.1979); cases and statutes cited, Krause, supra n. 28, at 220 n. 9; Krause, Illegitimacy: Law and Social Policy 127–31 (1971); 10 Am.Jur.2d Bastards § 118.

42. See Joint ABA–AMA Guidelines, supra n. 23, at 257–258.

43. See, e.g., State ex rel. Freeman v. Morris, 156 Ohio St. 333, 337, 102 N.E.2d 450, 452 (1951).

44. Ellman & Kaye, supra n. 23; Polesky & Krause, Blood Typing for Paternity, Current Capacities and Potential of American Laboratories—A Survey, 10 Fam. L.Q. 287 (1976) (collecting data on the capacity of blood banks and other laboratories to do serologic and related tests). An unexplained failure to test all the men whom a complainant indicates might have been the father or to perform a reasonably comprehensive battery of tests on each man may warrant exclusion of the evidence or a negative inference concerning it. See Ellman & Kaye, supra at 1158–61.

45. See, e.g., State ex rel. Beuchler Vinsand, 318 N.W.2d 208, 209 (Iowa 1982) (Iowa Code Ann. § 675.41 provides that "blood test results . . . are admissible"); Ariz.Rev.Stat. § 12–847(c) ("The results of the tests shall be received in evidence"); N.C.Gen.Stat. § 8–50.1(a) ("blood tests and comparisons . . . shall be admitted in evidence when offered by a duly qualified licensed practicing physician, duly qualified immunologist, duly qualified geneticist, or other qualified person"); Wis.Stat.Ann. § 885.23 ("The results of the tests shall be receivable as evidence in any case where exclusion from parentage is established or where a probability of paternity is shown to exist"); Uniform Parentage Act § 12 (1973) ("Evidence relating to paternity may include . . . blood test results" and "medical or anthropological evidence . . . based on tests performed by experts"); Kolko, Admissibility of HLA Test Results to Determine Paternity, 9 Fam.L.Rep. 4009, 4012 (1983) (state-by-state listing gives 30 states with "inclusionary" statutes).

poorly drafted or conceived.[46] In other instances, it is an example of the common law lugubriously digesting a technological advance.[47] The battle over the admissibility of serologic and related tests to prove paternity is ending. In its place, a fight over the efforts of many laboratories to give an exact statement of the "probability of paternity" is developing.[48]

 **WESTLAW REFERENCES**

Drunkenness

digest(alcohol! /p blood /p test! /p reliab! unreliab!)

Blood and Tissue Types

digest("human leu*ocyte" h.l.a.)

§ 206. Particular Tests: Psychology: Eyewitness Testimony, Lie Detection, Drugs, Hypnosis, and Profiles

The law and its procedures have long attracted the interest of psychologists.[1] Of late, that profession's courtroom-related activities have expanded dramatically, culminating in the creation of an American Board of Forensic Psychology to certify expertise in courtroom matters.[2] Although the preeminent contributions of psychologists and psychiatrists as expert witnesses have come in presenting clinical diagnoses or evaluations

in criminal and mental health cases,[3] at this point, we shall describe some other forensic applications. Specifically, this section surveys issues arising from expert testimony about the accuracy of eyewitness identifications, physiological indicators of deception, "truth" drugs and hypnosis, and "profiles" of certain types of offenders.[4]

A. *Eyewitness Testimony.* For many years, expert testimony has been received to show that mental disorders may have affected the testimony of eyewitnesses.[5] More recently, criminal defendants have called on psychologists to offer expert opinions on the factors that ordinarily influence the reliability of eyewitness identifications. Typically, the expert testifies to generalizations from experiments in which students or other subjects have witnessed a film or other enactment or description of the kind of events that are the subjects of courtroom testimony. In such studies, the accuracy of the recall of faces or facts is then tested under a variety of conditions. The overall findings indicate that such witnesses often make mistakes, that they tend to make more mistakes in cross-racial identifications as well as when the events involve violence, that errors are easily introduced by misleading questions asked shortly after the witness has viewed the simulated happening, and that the professed confidence of the subjects in their

---

46. For instance, the phrase "blood tests" can invite arguments. See Phillips ex rel. Utah State Department of Social Services v. Jackson, 615 P.2d 1228, 1233 (1980) (Uniform Paternity Act as enacted in Utah "was not intended to apply to HLA tests" as opposed to "blood test based on red blood cell groupings"); Simons v. Jorg, 375 So.2d 288, 289 (Fla.App.1979) (HLA typing "does not appear on its face to be a blood group test"); Ellman & Kaye, supra n. 23, at 1139 n. 4. More troublesome aspects of the statutes relate to the admission of calculations of the "probability of paternity." See infra § 211.

47. McQueen v. Stratton, 389 So.2d 1190 (Fla.App. 1980); Hennepin County Welfare Board v. Ayers, 304 N.W.2d 879, 882 (Minn.1981) ("where a proper foundation is laid, blood test results that confirm paternity are admissible"); Krause, supra n. 28, at 228; Ellman & Kaye, supra n. 23, at 1132 n. 7 (HLA tests); Kolko, supra n. 45, at 1413–83. Still more genetic probes, of a different sort, are on the way. See Ellman & Kaye, supra, at 1138 n. 37.

48. See infra § 211. For an analysis of the chain of custody, hearsay, and constitutional issues that arise in

blood testing cases as well as proposals for streamlining the procedures for admitting laboratory reports, see Broun, Producing Blood Tests in Court, in Krause, supra n. 23, at 246. On the power to compel blood tests, see Rose v. District Court, ___ Mont. ___, 628 P.2d 662 (1981); State v. Meacham, 93 Wn.2d 738, 612 P.2d 795 (1980); Broun, supra, at 248–259.

§ 206

1. See generally Loh, Psycholegal Research: Past and Present, 79 Mich.L.Rev. 659 (1981).

2. Monahan & Loftus, The Psychology of Law, 33 Ann.Rev. Psychology 441, 442 (1982).

3. See Loh, supra n. 1, at 672–677; supra § 203 n. 1.

4. Not all these items fall in the mainstream of modern academic psychology, but all involve attempts to probe the workings of the mind and human behavior.

5. See Annot., 20 A.L.R.3d 684.

identifications bears no consistent relation to the accuracy of these recognitions.[6]

Testimony about such research findings has been received in some cases and rejected in others.[7] Given the extreme deference usually accorded trial court decisions on the need for expert testimony, these decisions seem almost invariably to be upheld.[8] Many of the appellate opinions, however, display a distinct distaste for such testimony.[9] These opinions argue that since an appreciation of the limitations on eyewitnesses' perceptions and memory is within the ken of a lay jury, broad brush psychological testimony about these mechanisms would not appreciably assist the jury.[10] They point also to the standard concerns with scientific evidence—that lay jurors will overstate its importance and that its introduction will entail undue expense and confusion.[11] The more poorly reasoned opinions speak of invading the province of the jury.[12]

---

6. Bartol, Psychology and American Law 168–91 (1983); Clifford & Bull, The Psychology of Person Identification (1978); Cooke, The Role of the Forensic Psychologist (1979); Evaluating Eyewitness Evidence: Recent Psychological Research and New Perspectives (Lloyd-Bostock & Clifford ed. 1983); Loftus, Eyewitness Testimony (1979); Marshall, Law and Psychology in Conflict (2d ed. 1980); Saks & Hastie, Social Psychology in Court 167–191 (1978); Yarmey, The Psychology of Eyewitness Testimony (1979); Brigham & Barkowitz, Do "They All Look Alike?" The Effect of Race, Sex and Attitudes on the Ability to Recognize Faces, 8 J. Applied Soc. Psychology 306 (1978); Buckhout, Eyewitness Testimony, Sci.Am., Dec. 1974, at 23; Buckhout & Greenwald, Witness Psychology, in Scientific and Expert Evidence 1293 (2d ed. Imwinkelried 1981); Deffenbacher, Eyewitness Accuracy and Confidence, 4 Law & Human Behav. 243 (1980); Levine & Tapp, The Psychology of Criminal Identification: The Gap from *Wade* to *Kirby*, 121 U.Pa.L.Rev. 1079 (1973); Monahan & Loftus, supra n. 2, at 450; Penrod, Loftus & Winkler, The Reliability of Eyewitness Testimony: A Psychological Perspective, in The Psychology of the Courtroom 119 (Kerr & Bray ed. 1982); Wells, Lindsay & Ferguson, Accuracy, Confidence, and Juror Perceptions in Eyewitness Identification, 64 J. Applied Psychology 440 (1979); Note, 28 Stan.L.Rev. 969 (1977). The accuracy of "earwitnesses" also has been questioned, but systematic research into the factors that influence voice recognition is just beginning. See, e.g., Clifford, Rathborn & Bull, The Effects of Delay on Voice Recognition Accuracy, 5 Law & Human Behav. 201 (1981).

7. Since many trials in which expert testimony is admitted do not lead to published opinions, it is impossible to determine from reading cases the extent of the practice or even whether exclusion or admission is the more prevalent response of the trial judges. The psychologists report increasing use of their services. See authorities cited, Monaghan & Loftus, supra n. 2, at 450.

8. United States v. Watson, 587 F.2d 365, 369 (7th Cir. 1978) ("It is a matter in which the trial court has broad discretion"), cert. denied 439 U.S. 1132; State v. Helterbridle, 301 N.W.2d 545, 547 (Minn.1980); State v. Malmrose, 649 P.2d 56, 61 (Utah 1982); Hampton v. State, 92 Wis.2d 450, 285 N.W.2d 868, 872 (1979). However, in State v. Chapple, 660 P.2d 1208, 1224 (Ariz.1983), the court held that the trial court abused its discretion in excluding expert testimony where it "would have been of significant assistance."

9. State v. Chapple, 660 P.2d 1208, 1227 (Ariz.1983) (dissenting opinion) ("I have great reluctance to permit academia to take over the fact-finding function of the jury"); People v. Guzman, 47 Cal.App.3d 380, 386, 121 Cal.Rptr. 69, 72 (1975) ("How far should the courts go in allowing so-called scientific testimony, such as that of polygraph operators, hypnotists, 'truth drug' administrants, as well as purveyors of general psychological theories, to substitute for the common sense of the jury?"); State v. Goldsby, 59 Or.App. 66, 650 P.2d 952, 954 (1982) (Although "eyewitness identification evidence has a built-in potential for error," the law does not deal with that potential by allowing expert witnesses to debate the quality of the evidence for the jury"); State v. Malmrose, 649 P.2d 56, 61 (Utah 1982) ("such testimony would amount to a lecture to the jury about how they should perform their duties").

10. United States v. Fosher, 590 F.2d 381, 383 (1st Cir. 1979); United States v. Thevis, 665 F.2d 616, 641 (5th Cir. 1982), cert. denied 103 S.Ct. 57 ("the problems of perception and memory can be adequately addressed in cross-examination and . . . the jury can adequately weigh these problems through common sense evaluation"); Dyas v. United States, 376 A.2d 827, 832 (D.C.App.1977), cert. denied 434 U.S. 973; State v. Stucke, 419 So.2d 939, 944 (La.1982) ("the testimony . . . would not have been an aid to the jury"); State v. Ammons, 208 Neb. 812, 305 N.W.2d 812, 814 (1981) ("The accuracy or inaccuracy of eyewitness observation is a common experience of daily life").

11. United States v. Fosher, 590 F.2d 381, 383 (1st Cir. 1979); United States v. Thevis, 665 F.2d 616, 641 (5th Cir. 1982), cert. denied 103 S.Ct. 57 ("open the door to a barrage of marginally relevant psychological evidence"); United States v. Brown, 501 F.2d 146, 148–150 (9th Cir. 1974), reversed on other grounds sub nominee United States v. Nobles, 422 U.S. 225, on remand 522 F.2d 1274; Porter v. State, 94 Nev. 142, 576 P.2d 275, 278–79 (1978).

12. United States v. Brown, 540 F.2d 1048, 1054 (10th Cir. 1976), cert. denied, 429 U.S. 1100 ("opinion evidence cannot usurp the functions of the jury or be received if it touches the very issue before the jury"); Caldwell v. State, 267 Ark. 1053, 594 S.W.2d 24, 29 (App.1980) ("an invasion into the province of the trier of fact"); State v. Stucke, 419 So.2d 939, 945 (La.1982)

The matter cannot be disposed of this easily. Mounting concern over the reliability of eyewitness testimony lies at the heart of the Supreme Court's right to counsel and due process decisions in cases involving lineups and other pretrial identification procedures.[13] It may well be that without some counteracting influence, juries give too much weight to the witness's assertions of recognition.[14] To contend that juries know how to evaluate the reliability of the identifications without expert assistance, while simultaneously maintaining that the assistance would have too great an impact on the jury's deliberations, smacks of makeshift reasoning.[15] Admittedly, there are dangers—some obvious and some subtle—in translating laboratory and classroom demonstrations of witness fallibility into conclusions about the accuracy of a particular witness's identification in a real life setting.[16] Nevertheless, it would seem that the researchers have something to offer, and that where a case turns on uncorroborated eyewitness recognition, the courts should be receptive to expert testimony about the knowledge, gleaned from methodologically sound experimentation, concerning the factors that may have produced a faulty identification. Although the researcher must be circumspect in stating inferences about a particular witness's testimony,[17] the pertinent research findings should assist the jury in evaluating a crucial piece of evidence. While it seems that expert testimony on the psychology of eyewitness identifications may not be necessary or appropriate in many cases, in those instances where the case turns on the eyewitness testimony and

("invades the province of the jury and usurps its function"); State v. Ammons, 208 Neb. 812, 305 N.W.2d 812, 814 (1981). The best that can be said of such pronouncements is that they are unnecessary rhetoric, stating a conclusion but not giving a reason. If they were taken at face value and applied in other areas, the results would be intolerable. See, e.g., supra §§ 204 (radar evidence of speeding) & 205 (blood alcohol evidence of drunkenness and serologic evidence of paternity). See Fed. and Rev.Unif.R.Evid. (1974) 704 (opinions not objectionable because on ultimate issue); supra § 12. A few courts seem dubious of the scientific validity of the psychological research. Caldwell v. State, supra, 594 S.W.2d at 28 ("The field of perception and memory is alleged to be a science," but "the science of human perception testimony is new"); Porter v. State, 94 Nev. 142, 576 P.2d 275, 278 (1978) ("not a recognized field of expertise").

13. See supra § 176. There is no clear evidence of the prevalence of false identifications in court cases, and the incidence of erroneous convictions for this reason may be quite small. See Loh, supra n. 1, at 686. Nevertheless, miscarriages of justice do happen. See, e.g., Time Magazine, Jan. 12, 1981, at 51 (defendant, a 5 ft. 4 in. Polish emigré who insisted that he was interned in labor farms in Germany during the Second World War, but whom ten witnesses identified as a Gestapo agent who beat up and murdered Jews in two Polish towns from 1939 to 1943, showed on appeal that the Gestapo had a 5 ft. 7 in. height minimum and did not accept Poles).

14. See State v. Warren, 230 Kan. 385, 635 P.2d 1236, 1244 (1981) (requiring cautionary instruction in lieu of expert testimony); Note, supra n. 5.

15. The eyewitness researchers have responded to the judicial pronouncements that jurors know all they need to know without expert testimony. Applying the tools of their trade, these researchers have undertaken further studies to reveal what jurors know about the factors that seem to affect eyewitness performance, how closely this lay knowledge tracks the research findings, and what effect expert testimony has on jury deliberations. See Brigham & Bothwell, The Ability of Prospective Jurors to Estimate the Accuracy of Eyewitness Identifications, 7 Law & Human Behav. 19 (1983); Deffenbacher & Loftus, Do Jurors Share a Common Understanding Concerning Eyewitness Behavior? 6 Law & Human Behav. 15 (1982); Loftus, Impact of Expert Psychological Testimony on the Unreliability of Eyewitness Identification, 65 J. Applied Psychology 9 (1980).

16. Loh, supra n. 1, at 686–691 (psychological studies give information about average performance of all kinds of persons under conditions that may be structured to promote inaccuracies in the identifications); McCloskey & Egeth, Eyewitness Identification: What Can a Psychologist Tell a Jury? Am. Psychologist (in press).

17. Loftus, supra n. 6, at 200 ("Any psychologist who attempted to offer an exact probability for the likelihood that a witness was accurate would be going far beyond what is possible"). Although there is no longer any specific prohibition on allowing an expert to express an opinion on an "ultimate" fact, the need to avoid undue prejudice can justify curtailing an expert's testimony. Thus, it has been held that it is proper to allow a clinical psychologist to "testify regarding those factors which he believed could influence eyewitness identifications," but to prevent him "from stating to the jury his own opinion as to the reliability of [the particular] identification." Hampton v. State, 92 Wis.2d 450, 285 N.W.2d 868, 872 (1979). See also State v. Chapple, 660 P.2d 1208, 1219 (Ariz.1983) ("the 'generality' of the testimony is a factor which favors admission. Witnesses are permitted to express opinions on ultimate issues but are not required to testify to an opinion on the precise questions before the trier of fact").

the expert's assistance could make a difference, the scientific knowledge generally should be admitted.

B. *Detection of Deception.* Popular belief has it that lying and consciousness of guilt are accompanied by emotion or excitement that expresses itself in bodily changes—the blush, the gasp, the quickened heartbeat, the sweaty palm, the dry mouth. The skilled cross-examiner may face the witness with his lies and involve him in a knot of new ones, so that these characteristic signs of lying become visible to the jury. This is part of the demeanor of the witness that the jury is told it may observe and consider upon credibility.[18]

Internal stress also has been thought to accompany the process of lying. It is said that more than 4,000 years ago the Chinese would try the accused in the presence of a physician who, listening or feeling for a change in the heartbeat, would announce whether the accused was testifying truthfully.[19] The modern "lie detectors" operate on the same general principle.[20] While an interrogator puts questions to the suspect, the polygraph monitors and records several autonomic physiological functions, such as

18. See 3A Wigmore, Evidence § 946 (Chadbourn rev.1970); Dec.Dig. Witnesses ⊂⊃315. Summarizing the experimental research on behavioral lie detection, two psychologists conclude that skillful liars "manipulate the messages sent by their paralinguistic, face and body languages," that "vocal, non-content verbal cues, such as speech pitch or timbre and hesitations" are better indicators of lying, and that for most observers, detecting lies by any of these signs "is not especially accurate." Saks & Hastie, Social Psychology in Court 202 (1978).

19. N. Morland, An Outline of Scientific Criminology 59–60 (2d ed.1971). "Saliva tests" have also been used, the method of implementation varying according to the culture. The Chinese required the suspect to chew a mouthful of rice flour, then looked to see if it had remained dry. Bedouins required suspected liars to lick a hot iron. A burned tongue was a sign of lying. In Britain the test was to swallow a "trial slice" of bread and cheese. Inability to swallow was thought to reveal deception. Saks & Hastie, supra n. 18, at 192. See also Langley, The Polygraph Lie Detector, 16 Ala.Law. 209–10 (1955).

In earlier days, courts admitted evidence of the refusal of an accused to submit to a superstitious test of guilt on the theory that a jury could find that if he believed (however erroneously) in its efficacy, his refusal was an implied admission. State v. Wisdom, 119 Mo. 539, 24 S.W. 1047 (1894); 2 Wigmore, Evidence § 276(3) (Chadbourn rev.1979). For more modern cases involving the refusal of a witness to submit to a polygraph examination, see Aetna Insurance Co. v. Barnett Brothers, 289 F.2d 30 (8th Cir. 1961) (inadmissible since result of test would have been inadmissible); State v. Mottram, 158 Me. 325, 184 A.2d 225 (1962) (inadmissible in absence of showing as to reason for refusal).

20. The literature on the "lie detectors" is compendious, contentious, and of uneven quality. For a sampling of material on reliability, validity, or evidentiary status, see Bartol, Psychology and American Law 204–09 (1983); 1 Louisell & Mueller, Federal Evidence § 106(4) (1977); Lykken, A Tremor in the Blood: Uses and Abuses of the Lie-Detector (1981); Moenssens & Inbau, Scientific Evidence in Criminal Cases § 14 (2d ed.1978); Matte, The Art and Science of the Polygraph Technique (1980); Reid & Inbau, Truth and Deception: The Polygraph ("Lie Detection") Technique (2d ed. 1977); Richardson, Modern Scientific Evidence §§ 10.1–10.22 (2d ed.1974); Saks & Hastie, supra n. 18, at 192–200; Scientific and Expert Evidence 755–872 (2d ed. Imwinkelried 1981); 3A Wigmore, Evidence § 999 (Chadbourn rev.1970); 22 Wright & Graham, Federal Practice and Procedure § 5169 (1978); Yarmey, The Psychology of Eyewitness Testimony 171–74 (1979); Abbell, Polygraph Evidence: The Case Against Admissibility in Federal Criminal Trials, 15 Am.Crim.L.Rev. 29 (1977); Cavoukian & Heslegrave, The Admissibility of Polygraph Evidence in Court: Some Empirical Findings, 4 Law & Human Behav. 117 (1980); Gudjonsson, Lie Detection: Techniques and Countermeasures in Evaluating Witness' Evidence 137 (Lloyd-Bostock & Clifford eds.1983); Lykken, The Lie Detector and the Law, Crim. Defense, May-June 1981, at 19; Kleinmuntz & Szucko, On the Fallibility of Lie Detection, 17 Law & Soc.Rev. 85 (1981); Peters, A Survey of Polygraph Evidence in Criminal Trials, 68 A.B.A.J. 162 (1982); Podlesny & Raskin, Psychological Measures and the Detection of Deception, 84 Psychological Bull. 782 (1977); Raskin, Science, Competence, and Polygraph Techniques, Crim. Defense, May-June 1981, at 11; Raskin & Podlesny, Truth and Deception: A Reply to Lykken, 86 Psychological Bull. 54 (1979); Skolnick, Scientific Theory and Scientific Evidence, An Analysis of Lie Detection, 70 Yale L.J. 694 (1961); Tarlow, Admissibility of Polygraph Evidence in 1975: An Aid to Determining Credibility in a Perjury-Plagued System, 26 Hast.L.J. 917 (1975); Note, 73 Colum.L.Rev. 1120 (1973); 29 Am.Jur.2d Evidence § 831. Use of polygraph examinations in the military and civilian sectors of the government has been the target of congressional hearings. Use of Polygraphs as "Lie-Detectors" by the Federal Government: Hearings Before a Subcomm. of the House Comm. on Gov't Operations, 88th Cong., 2d Sess., Pts. 1–5 (1964). For a journalist's review of some of the testimony at these hearings, see Meisler, Trial by Gadget, The Nation, Sept. 28, 1964, at 169 (concluding that "The polygraph is a pernicious instrument that . . . should be relegated to a Smithsonian exhibit case as a monument to an American craze").

blood pressure, pulse rate, respiration rate and depth, and perspiration (by measuring skin conductance).[21]   In the most commonly used procedure, the "diagnosis" is made by comparing the responses to "control" questions with the reactions to "relevant" questions.[22]   If the autonomic disturbance associated with the relevant items seems greater or more persistent, then the subject is judged to be dissembling.[23]

The validity and reliability [24] of this procedure are hotly contested.   Polygraph exam-

iners claim that, properly administered, it is a highly effective means of detecting deception, and they cite figures such as 92%, 99%, and even 100% for its accuracy.[25]   Although some controlled experiments suggest that such accuracy is possible,[26] most psychologists reviewing the literature are not impressed with these bold assertions.   They see methodological flaws undermining the conclusions,[27] they suggest figures in the 63–72% range,[28] and they point out that the percentage figures of "accuracy" are inap-

There are more recent hearings that should be mentioned:

> Pressures in Today's Workplace: Hearing Before a Subcomm. of the House Comm. on Education and Labor, 96th Cong., 1st Sess., Pts. 1–3 (1979).

> Polygraph Control and Civil Liberties Protection Act: Hearings Before a Subcomm. of the Senate Comm. on the Judiciary, 95th Cong., 1st & 2d Sess. (1978).

> Privacy, Polygraphs and Employment: A Study Prepared by the Staff of a Subcomm. of the Senate Comm. on the Judiciary, 93d Cong., 2d Sess. (1974).

21.   For details of the devices, see Reid & Inbau, supra n. 20, at 5–6.   Some potential sources of instrumental error are identified in Laurendi, Opposition to the Admissibility of Lie Detector Tests in Criminal Cases, in Scientific and Experimental Evidence 805 (2d ed. Imwinkelried 1981).

22.   Moenssens & Inbau, supra n. 20, at 607–14; Kleinmuntz & Scuzco, supra n. 20, at 88–89.   Control questions attempt to force the subject to lie about some common transgression.   In an embezzlement case, a control question might be "Have you ever stolen anything?"   A relevant question is one that relates to the particular matter under investigation.   "Irrelevant" questions (for example, "Did you ever go to school?") are also asked.   At least three groups of interspersed questions of these types are recommended. Moenssens & Inbau, supra, at 608.   Contrivances such as the "card test" may be used to heighten the suspect's faith in the machine, and hence his anxiety over answering incriminating questions falsely.   Reid & Inbau, supra n. 20, at 42–43; Kleinmuntz & Szucko, supra n. 20, at 88–89.

23.   Numerical scoring to determine differences has been proposed.   Raskin, supra n. 20.   However, most analysts apply a less structured procedure. Kleinmuntz & Szucko, supra n. 20, at 89.   Numerous factors, including the apparent intelligence and educational background of the suspect, may be relied on in conjunction with the physiologic tracings.   Behavioral cues that are said to be symptomatic of deceptiveness or truthfulness include squirming, yawning, coughing, sniffling, gurgling, pausing, refusing to look the examiner in the eye, being late for the appointment, wanting to leave as soon as possible, becoming abusive and argumentative after the card test, being cooperative (but

not overly polite), and displaying confidence in the machine and its operator.   See Reid & Inbau, supra n. 20, at 17, 19, 23, 293–295.   But see id. at 296 ("sole or even major reliance should not be placed upon behavior symptoms: they should be considered only in the context of the entire Polygraph examination").

24.   As indicated supra in § 203, these terms have a specialized meaning.   Reliability refers to reproducibility of results (consistency), while validity relates to ability to measure whatever it is that one purports to measure (here, truthfulness).

25.   United States v. Oliver, 525 F.2d 731, 737 (8th Cir. 1975), cert. denied 424 U.S. 973 (The expert polygrapher "personally testified that he had conducted more than 50,000 examinations which were subjected to verification through supporting admissions, confessions, or additional evidence.   The accuracy of his diagnosis was estimated in excess of 90 percent"); Moenssens & Inbau, supra n. 20, § 14.09 at 616 ("it is reported that when the technique is properly applied by a trained, competent examiner, it is very accurate in its indications, with a *known* error percentage of less than one percent.   That conclusion is based on the examinations of over 100,000 persons suspected or accused of criminal offenses or involved in personnel investigations initiated by their employers, almost all of which examinations were conducted at the extensive facilities of John E. Reid and Associates.   It is also supported by validation studies reported in Journal articles"); Yarmey, supra n. 20, at 173 (citing to statements of polygraphers); cf. Lykken, supra n. 20, at 20, 23 (citing inflated claims concerning now discredited lie detection techniques).

26.   Raskin, supra n. 20, at 14; Podlesny & Raskin, supra n. 20.

27.   Meyer, Do Lie Detectors Lie? Science 82 (June, 1982) at 24, 26 ("virtually impossible to relate polygraph results with the truth in samples large enough to achieve genuine statistical validity"); Saks & Hastie, supra n. 18, at 199 (because the polygraph examiner relies on "other sources of information (the suspect's overt responses, gross body and facial reactions, and so forth)" it is difficult "to assess the reliability of polygraph evidence in a particular case or to character-

---

28.   See note 28 on page 627.

propriate measures of validity.[29] Attempts to determine the rate of false positives—of saying that someone is lying when he is actually telling the truth—have also been controversial. Some writers claim that these errors occur in only two to eight percent of the cases,[30] but there are also studies and analyses that put the expected rate of false positives in excess of 35%.[31] The skeptics also dispute the underlying theory. At best, the technique described above registers physiological correlates of anxiety, which is not quite the same thing as consciousness of guilt or lying. Questions can provoke inner turmoil even when they are answered truthfully.[32] As one critic has put it, "the polygraph pens do no special dance when we are lying."[33] In addition, there are numerous countermeasures that a suspect can use to mislead the analyst, some of which are said to be effective and difficult to detect.[34] It is feared that if the polygraph came into widespread use in court cases, these could cause the rate of false negatives—saying that the suspect is telling the truth when he is lying—to become intolerably high.

A variation on the polygraph examination procedure outlined above avoids some of these objections. This "conscious concealment" or "guilty knowledge" test [35] does not

ize the expertise of the examiner"); Yarmey, supra n. 20, at 173 ("That a court makes a particular decision does not in itself prove the accuracy of the polygraph examination"); Kleinmuntz & Szucko, supra n. 20, at 93 (pointing to possible bias in the selection of the sample polygraph recordings used in validity studies, weakness in the criteria by which accuracy is verified, and inadequate controls for variations in the analysts' skills); Lykken, supra n. 20, at 23–24 (criticizing laboratory and field studies).

28. See Lykken, supra n. 20, at 25; Lykken, The Detection of Deception, 86 Psychological Bull. 47 (1977). These estimates presume a group of examinees, half who tell the truth and half who lie, so that rolling dice or the like would produce, within the limits of statistical error, a 50% "accuracy" figure. For a rebuttal of these estimates, see Raskin, supra n. 20; Raskin & Podlesny, supra n. 20.

29. See Saks & Hastie, supra n. 21, at 198 ("A 90% 'hit rate,' identifying lies, would have quite different implications if we know that the 'false alarm rate,' classifying truthful answers as lies, was 80% as opposed to a case where the false alarm rate was 20%"); Abbell, supra note 20; cf. Kleinmuntz & Szucko, supra n. 20, at 86–87 (overall rate of agreement between two analysts is not a useful measure of inter-rater reliability). The overall accuracy, or hit rate, could be 100% even if the polygraph technique had no value at all. If a polygraph operator declares all suspects to be liars, and the rate of conviction in that jurisdiction is 100%, then he will be "proved" right in every case. If he picks 90% of the suspects—entirely at random—and declares that these are lying, and if the conviction rate is 90%, then the expected hit rate is (90%) (90%) = 81%. The hit rate statistic is even more misleading if the examination itself influences the disposition of the case.

30. Podlesny & Raskin, supra n. 20.

31. Lykken, supra n. 28 (estimating an average of 36–39% false positives); Kleinmuntz & Szucko, supra n. 20, at 96 (reporting their own study showing that correlation coefficients between diagnoses (of six examiners given polygraph records of 50 truthful and 50 untruthful subjects) and whether or not the examinees

were actually telling the truth ranged from .45 to .55, with false positives ranging from 18 to 50%, and citing other studies finding false positive rates of 49 and 55%). But see Raskin, supra n. 20; Raskin & Podlesny, supra n. 20.

32. Kleinmuntz & Szucko, supra n. 20, at 87 ("there is no reason to believe that lying produces distinctive physiological changes that characterize it and only it. . . . No doubt when we tell a lie many of us experience an inner turmoil, but we experience a similar turmoil when we are falsely accused of a crime, when we are anxious about having to defend ourselves against accusations, when we are questioned about sensitive topics—and, for that matter, when we are elated or otherwise emotionally stirred"). Those who support the technique, however, might counter that a skilled examiner takes time to put the subject at ease before taking any readings and that some of these sources of anxiety should affect responses to all questions and therefore not interfere with the differential analysis.

33. Lykken, as quoted in Kleinmuntz & Szucko, supra n. 20, at 88.

34. Saks & Hastie, supra n. 18, at 199; Yarmey, supra n. 20, at 173; Gudjonsson, supra n. 20, at 143–51. Advocates of polygraphy insist that the countermeasures that have been demonstrated to be effective in laboratory experiments would not work "in a real polygraph situation except on rather rare occasions." Abrams, Polygraphy, in Scientific and Expert Evidence 755, 800 (2d ed. Imwinkelried 1981). The critics remain skeptical. See, e.g., Abbell, supra n. 20, at 838–839. For a useful exchange on the ease and efficacy of countermeasures, "practice effects," and "friendly polygraphers," compare Raskin, supra n. 20, at 14–15, with Lykken, supra n. 20, at 19–20, 25–26.

35. See Lykken, supra n. 20. A variation of the guilty knowledge test, as elaborated by Lykken, is the peak of tension test in which the interrogator tries to determine the nature of a crime by suggesting a series of possibilities that gradually "narrow in" on the most likely candidate. Moenssens & Inbau, supra n. 20, § 14.07 at 614; Smith, The Polygraph, Sci.Am., Jan. 1967, at 25.

necessarily attempt to evaluate the truthfulness of any verbal response. It requires that the examiner know facts that a guilty subject, but not an innocent person, would know. The examiner presents multiple choice questions about these facts. Consistently high autonomic responses to the incriminating choices indicates some involvement in the offense.[36] Experimentation with this technique suggests that it can achieve false positive error rates of ten percent or less.[37]

Another group of devices that measure a physiological response to detect when a person is consciously concealing knowledge are the voice stress analyzers. They analyze the frequency spectrum of a speaker's voice to detect subaudible, involuntary tremors said to result from emotional stress. As of this writing, most of the scientific literature on these lie detection devices concludes that they have no validity.[38]

The courts have not greeted the modern methods of lie detection with enthusiasm.

Indeed, the case that announced the general-acceptance standard for the admissibility of scientific evidence involved a primitive version of the polygraph.[39] In the succeeding decades, many courts treated the early decision as if it established that polygraph results were inadmissible regardless of any improvements in the technology.[40] With the accelerating erosion of the general-acceptance requirement [41] and the growing acceptance of polygraphy in government and business,[42] however, a substantial number of courts have been willing to take a fresh look at the evidentiary value of the most commonly used polygraph tests.[43] Three principal positions on admissibility can now be seen, with some back and forth movement into and out of each category. First, there is the traditional rule that the test results are inadmissible when offered by either party, either as substantive evidence or as relating to the credibility of a witness.[44] Second, a substantial minority of jurisdictions have carved out an exception to the majority rule

36. Lykken offers this example: "If you did rob the loan company, you will recognize the woman you talked to, the one who gave you the money. I have some photographs here of women tellers in five different loan offices, just as they look to a customer. I will show these pictures to you one at a time. Just sit there quietly and look at each photograph." Lykken, Psychology and the Lie Detector Industry, 29 Am. Psychologist 725 (1974). If the number of such questions is reasonably large and the multiple choice alternatives equally plausible to an innocent person, the chance of a false positive can be kept quite small, although the chance of a false negative may be enhanced.

37. See Kleinmuntz & Szucko, supra n. 20, at 99–100 (reviewing studies).

38. Lykken, supra n. 20 (reviewing studies in Ch. 13); Saks & Hastie, supra n. 18, at 202 ("there is no scientific evidence to support the claim that they are accurate beyond chance levels"); Horvath, Detecting Deception: The Promise and the Reality of Voice Stress Analysis, 27 J. Forensic Sci. 340 (1982) ("the scientific evidence reported to date shows that voice stress analyzers are not effective in detecting deception: none of these devices has yet been shown to yield detection rates above chance levels in controlled situations"). Contra Kenety, The Psychological Stress Evaluator: The Theory, Validity and Legal Status of an Innovative 'Lie Detector,' 55 Ind.L.J. 349 (1980).

39. See supra § 203.

40. For two strenuous but futile efforts to lay the necessary foundation, see People v. Davis, 343 Mich.

348, 72 N.W.2d 269 (1955); People v. Leone, 25 N.Y.2d 511, 307 N.Y.S.2d 430, 255 N.E.2d 696 (1969).

41. See supra § 203.

42. See Lykken, supra n. 20.

43. Due process arguments have been marshalled in support of more generous admissibility rules. Compare McMorris v. Israel, 643 F.2d 458 (7th Cir. 1981), cert. denied 455 U.S. 967 (in circumstances of case and under state rule of evidence (subsequently repudiated), prosecutor's refusal to stipulate to admissibility deprived defendant of due process), with Conner v. Auger, 595 F.2d 407, 411 (8th Cir. 1979), cert. denied 444 U.S. 851 (exclusion in absence of stipulation consistent with due process and right to counsel). See generally Comment, 12 Conn.L.Rev. 324 (1980); Note, 55 Ind.L.J. 157 (1980). In this regard, it seems significant that no other country clearly countenances the use of polygraph evidence in court. Lykken, supra n. 20.

For cases on related legal matters, see Annot., 15 A.L.R. 4th 824 (references to fact that witness has taken polygraph), 11 A.L.R. 4th 733 (right of indigent to subsidized examination), 92 A.L.R. 3d 317 (admissibility on issue of voluntariness of confession), 89 A.L.R. 3d 230 (confessions induced by polygraph examination), 88 A.L.R. 3d 227 (references to fact that accused has taken polygraph test).

44. Pulakis v. State, 476 P.2d 474, 479 (Alaska 1970); State v. Mitchell, 402 A.2d 479, 482 (Me.1979); People v. Anderson, 637 P.2d 354, 358 (Colo.1981); People v. Baynes, 88 Ill.2d 225, 58 Ill.Dec. 819, 430 N.E.2d 1070 (1981); Kelley v. State, 288 Md. 298, 418 A.2d 217,

of unconditional exclusion. In these jurisdictions the trial court has the discretion to receive polygraph testimony if the parties stipulated to the admission of the results prior to the testing and if certain other conditions are met.[45] Third, in a handful of jurisdictions, admissibility even in the absence of a stipulation is said to be discretionary with the trial judge.[46]

The widespread and strongly rooted reluctance to permit the introduction of polygraph evidence is grounded in a variety of concerns.[47] The most frequently mentioned

is that the technique is "unreliable" due to inherent failings, a shortage of qualified operators, and the prospect that "coaching" and practicing would become commonplace if the evidence were generally admissible.[48] Yet, by themselves, such doubts are not sufficient to warrant a rigid exclusionary rule. A great deal of lay testimony routinely admitted is at least as unreliable and inaccurate, and other forms of scientific evidence involve risks of instrumental or judgmental error.[49]

---

219 (1980); State v. Biddle, 599 S.W.2d 182, 185 (Mo. 1980); State v. Beachman, ___ Mont. ___, 616 P.2d 337, 339 (1980); State v. Steinmark, 195 Neb. 545, 239 N.W. 2d 495, 497 (1976); Birdsong v. State, 649 P.2d 786, 788 (Okl.Cr.1982); State v. Frazier, ___ W.Va. ___, 252 S.E.2d 39, 49 (1979); State v. Dean, 103 Wis.2d 228, 307 N.W.2d 628 (1981); 27 Am.Jur.2d Evidence § 831; Annot., 43 A.L.R.Fed. 68.

The willingness or unwillingness of a witness or a party to submit to examination is also inadmissible in most of these jurisdictions. United States v. Fife, 573 F.2d 369, 373 (6th Cir. 1976) (willingness properly excluded), cert. denied 430 U.S. 933; United States v. Bursten, 560 F.2d 779, (7th Cir. 1977) (willingness properly excluded); Annot., 15 A.L.R.4th 824 (effect of informing jury that witness has taken polygraph test), 88 A.L.R.3d 227 (effect of informing jury that accused has taken polygraph test), infra note 71 (refusal to take test). Some courts do admit testimony concerning polygraph tests when it is not introduced to show the truth of the assertion or credibility, or when the evidence is introduced in post-trial proceedings. See, e.g., State v. Catanese, 368 So.2d 975, 982–983 (La.1979); People v. Barbara, 400 Mich. 352, 255 N.W.2d 171, 197–199 (1977); Annot., 92 A.L.R.3d 1317 (in connection with challenge to voluntariness of confession).

45. United States v. Alexander, 526 F.2d 161, 170 (8th Cir. 1975) (dictum); United States v. Oliver, 525 F.2d 731, 737 (8th Cir. 1975), cert. denied 424 U.S. 973; State v. Bullock, 262 Ark. 394, 557 S.W.2d 193 (1977); State v. Valdez, 91 Ariz. 274, 283–284, 371 P.2d 894, 900 (1962); People v. Trujillo, 67 Cal.App.3d 547, 136 Cal.Rptr. 672, 676 (1977); Codie v. State, 313 So.2d 754, 756 (Fla.1975); Pavone v. State, ___ Ind. ___, 402 N.E. 2d 976, 978–979 (1980); State v. Marti, 290 N.W.2d 570, 586–87 (Iowa 1980); State v. Roach, 223 Kan. 732, 576 P.2d 1082, 1086 (1978); State v. Milano, 297 N.C. 485, 256 S.E.2d 154, 162 (1979); State v. Souel, 53 Ohio St. 2d 123, 134, 372 N.E.2d 1318, 1323–1324 (1978); Cullin v. State, 565 P.2d 445, 457 (Wyo.1977); Annot., 53 A.L.R.3d 1005; cf. McMorris v. Israel, 643 F.2d 458 (7th Cir. 1981), cert. denied 455 U.S. 967 (due process required state prosecutor to stipulate to admissibility), said to have misread state law in State v. Dean, 103 Wis.2d 228, 307 N.W.2d 628 (1981). In many of these "stipulation" jurisdictions, the evidence is admissible for a limited purpose. See, e.g., State v. Valdez, supra.

46. United States v. Webster, 639 F.2d 174, 186 (4th Cir. 1981), cert. denied 456 U.S. 935, modified in other respects 669 F.2d 185 (upholding exclusion, but remarking that "The broad discretionary power of the district judge perhaps would have made admission of the polygraph evidence proper"); United States v. Glover, 596 F.2d 857, 867 (9th Cir. 1979), cert. denied 444 U.S. 860 (upholding exclusion); State v. Dorsey, 88 N.M. 184, 539 P.2d 204 (1975); cf. Commonwealth v. Vitello, 376 Mass. 426, 381 N.E.2d 582, 596–98 (1978) (inadmissible to prove guilt or innocence, but admissible to impeach credibility of a witness).

47. These are well outlined in People v. Baynes, 88 Ill.2d 225, 58 Ill.Dec. 819, 430 N.E.2d 1070 (1981); Commonwealth v. Vitello, 376 Mass. 426, 381 N.E.2d 582, 596–599 (1978); People v. Barbara, 400 Mich. 352, 255 N.W.2d 171 (1977); 22 Wright & Graham, supra n. 20; Abbell, supra n. 20.

48. Despite the statements of some courts that polygraphic lie detection has become more reliable, there is still doubt as to what the outcome should be under the general scientific acceptance test. Conner v. Auger, 595 F.2d 407, 411 (8th Cir. 1979), cert. denied, 444 U.S. 851 ("continued lack of agreement in the scientific community"); Saks & Hastie, supra n. 18, at 199–200 ("although polygraph techniques are sometimes referred to as 'scientific lie detection,' this label is undeserved in several respects," but "the future of the field is quite promising. The techniques already seem to have considerable validity, and additional competent research and higher standards of training and practice may bring them back into the courtroom"); Kleinmuntz & Szucko, supra n. 20, at 87 ("the reliability of the polygraph is difficult to gauge," and, as to validity, "polygraphic interrogation does poorly indeed"); Lykken, supra n. 20, at 26 ("The lie detector has no more business in the court room than a psychic or a deck of Tarot cards"). Voice stress analysis clearly flunks the general acceptance test. See supra n. 38. For cases excluding voice stress analyses, see State v. Ochalla, 285 N.W.2d 683 (Minn.1979); Kenety, supra n. 38.

49. Jackson v. Garrison, 495 F.Supp. 9, 11. (W.D. N.C.1979), reversed on other grounds 677 F.2d 371 (6th Cir.), cert. denied 454 U.S. 1036; cf. United States v. Oliver, 525 F.2d 731, 737 n. 11. (8th Cir. 1975), cert.

Rather, the argument against admissibility is, as usual, two-pronged. If the probative value of polygraph readings is slight (or would be if the barriers to admissibility were dropped), then their value easily is outweighed by the countervailing considerations. These counterweights are the danger that jurors would be unduly impressed with the "scientific" testimony [50] on a crucial and typically determinative matter,[51] that judicial and related resources would be squandered in producing and coping with the expert testimony, and that routine admissibility would put undesirable pressure on defendants to forfeit the right against self-incrimination.[52]

Some of these concerns may be overstated,[53] and the miscellaneous other reasons

that courts sometimes give for excluding polygraph tests may not withstand analysis.[54] Nonetheless, it would seem that opening up the matter to the discretion of the trial courts—without providing more detailed standards than the usual balancing prescription—could lead to untoward results.[55] Nor is the "stipulation only" approach very satisfactory.[56] Whether polygraph testimony should be admitted is doubtful, but if it is to be received, clear standards should be developed as to whether such testimony is admissible solely for impeachment purposes,[57] how important the testimony must be in the context of the other evidence in the case for admissibility to be warranted,[58] what type of examination should be administered,[59] what

denied 424 U.S. 973 (polygraph evidence meets the relevancy standard of the federal rules).

50. United States v. Alexander, 526 F.2d 161, 168 (8th Cir. 1975) ("polygraph evidence . . . is likely to be shrouded with an aura of near infallibility, akin to the ancient oracle of Delphi").

51. Id. at 169.

52. United States v. Bursten, 560 F.2d 779, 785 (7th Cir. 1977) ("trial by machine"). This may be part of a more generalized dignitary concern. Silving, Testing of the Unconscious in Criminal Cases, 69 Harv.L.Rev. 683 (1956).

53. Theorizing about the devastating impact of polygraph evidence is inevitably somewhat inconclusive. For expressions of opinion contrary to the received wisdom, see McMorris v. Israel, 643 F.2d 458, 462–463 (7th Cir. 1981), cert. denied 455 U.S. 967 ("Scientific evidence . . . has become more a part of the ordinary trial so that jurors may be more likely to use polygraph evidence with discretion"); 22 Wright & Graham, Federal Practice and Procedure § 5169, at 97–98; Peters, supra n. 20 (survey of 22 Wisconsin attorneys said to show that polygraph results introduced pursuant to stipulations were not overly credited and not disruptive of the trial); Tarlow, supra n. 20, at 968–969. One experimental study of the impact of such testimony did not find any dramatic effect. Cavoukian & Heslegrave, supra n. 20. See also Markwart & Lynch, The Effect of Polygraph Evidence on Mock Jury Decision-Making, 7 J. Police Sci. & Admin. 324 (1979); Carlson, Pasano & Jannuzzo, The Effect of Lie Detector Evidence on Jury Deliberations: An Empirical Study, 5 J. Police Sci. & Admin. 148 (1977). Of course, the real question is not whether this evidence has some impact. It is whether it has more of an effect than its actual probative value would warrant. See supra § 186.

54. As with expert psychological testimony on eyewitness identifications, it sometimes is said that polygraph results would not aid the jury because the credi-

bility of a witness is susceptible to resolution without expert testimony. United States v. Alexander, 526 F.2d 161, 169 n. 16 (8th Cir. 1975) ("polygraph evidence is not necessary since the jury is capable of performing the function served by the polygraph"). Talk of "prejudice to the jury process," People v. Anderson, 637 P.2d 354, 362 (Colo.1981), and affirmations that "the jury system is [not] yet outmoded," United States v. Stromberg, 179 F.Supp. 278, 280 (S.D.N.Y.1959), may reflect this cramped view of the scope of expert testimony in addition to the previously catalogued concerns.

55. State v. Dean, 103 Wis.2d 228, 307 N.W.2d 628, 653 (1981) ("The lack of such standards heightens our concern that the burden on the trial court to assess the reliability of stipulated polygraph evidence may outweigh any probative value the evidence may have"). However, this court doubted that satisfactory standards could evolve judicially. Id. ("adequate standards have not developed in the seven years since Stanislawski to guide the trial courts in exercising their discretion in the admission of polygraph evidence").

56. Recognizing that the presence of a stipulation does not enhance the validity or reliability of the examiner's conclusions, many courts have declined to relax their traditional exclusionary rule to recognize stipulations. Pulakis v. State, 476 P.2d 474, 479 (Alaska 1970); People v. Anderson, 637 P.2d 354, 361–362 (Colo. 1981); People v. Baynes, 88 Ill.2d 225, 58 Ill.Dec. 819, 430 N.E.2d 1070, 1077 (1981); State v. Frazier, ___ W.Va. ___, 252 S.E.2d 39, 49 (1979). Oklahoma and Wisconsin have defected from the ranks of "stipulation only" jurisdictions. Fulton v. State, 541 P.2d 871 (Okl. Cr.1975), noted, 12 Tulsa L.J. 682 (1977); State v. Dean, 103 Wis.2d 228, 307 N.W.2d 628 (1981), overruling State v. Stanislawski, 62 Wis.2d 730, 742–743, 216 N.W.2d 8, 14 (1974).

57. Commonwealth v. Vitello, 376 Mass. 426, 381 N.E.2d 582, 597 (1978).

58, 59. See notes 58 & 59 on page 631.

precautions should be taken against deceptive practices on the part of examinees,[60] and what procedures would be best to give an independent or opposing expert a meaningful opportunity to view or review the examination and analysis.[61]

C. *Drugs and Hypnosis.* Psychologists and psychiatrists have used hypnosis and hypnotic drugs for diagnosis and therapy. Resort to these techniques became prevalent in the treatment of traumatic war neuroses during World War II, and the methods have been applied to the treatment of hysterical amnesias, catatonic conditions, and psycho-

somatic disorders.[62] They have also been employed to test the truthfulness of a witness' testimony as well as to enhance his or her recall.[63]

Although the scientific study of hypnosis began over 200 years ago, a single, satisfactory explanation of the phenomenon has yet to emerge.[64] The scientific studies do make it clear, however, that people who are hypnotized or given so-called "truth serums" do not always tell the truth.[65] On the other hand, the most directly pertinent studies do suggest that in certain circumstances hypnosis can enhance memory.[66] The problem is

58. Id. at 596 n. 23; State v. Dean, 103 Wis.2d 228, 307 N.W.2d 628, 634 n. 7 (1981) (the argument for admissibility is most "compelling" when the finder of fact must choose between the conflicting stories of the complaining witness and the defendant with little or no corroborating evidence); Phannenstill, Usefulness of Polygraphic Results in Paternity Investigations, 21 J.Fam. L. 69 (1982–83).

59. The "guilty knowledge" or "conscious concealment" test seems more defensible than the "control question" test. See supra text accompanying nn. 35–37.

60. As with calibration checks of radar equipment (see supra § 204), this may be an instance in which those jurisdictions that are willing to admit such evidence should insist on "cost-effective" precautions to prevent errors even though the evidence would be at least minimally relevant without them.

61. See United States v. Alexander, 526 F.2d 161, 170 n. 17 (8th Cir. 1975); Abbell, supra note 20; cf. supra § 201 (suggesting cooperation in design and execution of pretrial experiments).

62. Hilgard, Hypnotic Susceptibility (1965); Erickson, Naturalistic Techniques of Hypnosis, 1 Am.J. Clinical Hypnosis 3 (1938); Packer, The Use of Hypnotic Techniques in the Evaluation of Criminal Defendants, 9 J. Psychiatry & L. 313 (1981). Highly controversial at first, hypnosis gradually gained acceptance within the scientific and medical communities and is now considered appropriate for use in experimental and clinical work. See Hilgard, supra, at 3–5.

63. See generally Bryan, Legal Aspects of Hypnosis (1962); 1 Louisell & Mueller, Federal Evidence § 202 note 2, § 106(5); Moenssens & Inbau, Scientific Evidence in Criminal Cases §§ 15.02–15.12 (1978); Richardson, Modern Scientific Evidence §§ 11.1–11.10 (2d ed. 1974); 3A Wigmore, Evidence § 998 (Chadbourn rev. 1970); Alderman & Barnette, Hypnosis on Trial, 18 Crim.L.Bull. 5 (1982); Scientific and Expert Evidence 1117–40 (2d ed. Imwinkelried 1981); Depres, Legal Aspects of Drug-Induced Statements, 14 U.Chi.L.Rev. 601 (1947); Dession, Freedman, Donnelly & Redlich, Drug Induced Revelation and Criminal Investigation, 62 Yale L.J. 315 (1953); Diamond, Inherent

Problems in the Use of Pretrial Hypnosis on a Prospective Witness, 68 Calif.L.Rev. 313 (1980); Falk, Posthypnotic Testimony—Witness Competency and the Fulcrum of Procedural Safeguards, 57 St. John's L.Rev. 30 (1982); Herman, The Use of Hypno-Induced Statements in Criminal Cases, 25 Ohio St.L.J. 1 (1964); Orne, The Use and Misuse of Hypnosis in Court, 27 Int'l J. Clinical & Experimental Hypnosis 311 (1979); Putnam, Hypnosis and Distortion in Eyewitness Testimony, 27 J. Clinical & Experimental Hypnosis 311 (1979); Sadoff, Psychiatric Involvement in the Search for Truth, 52 A.B.A.J. 251 (1966); Spiegel, Hypnosis and Evidence: Help or Hindrance? 347 Annals N.Y. Academy Sci. 73 (1979); Spector & Foster, Admissibility of Hypnotic Statements, 38 Ohio St.L.J. 567 (1977); Wagstaff, The Use of Hypnosis in Police Investigation, 21 J. Forensic Sci.Soc. 3 (1980); Warner, Hypnosis in Defense of Criminal Cases, 27 Int'l J. Clinical & Experimental Hypnosis 417 (1979); Notes, 57 Ind.L.J. 349 (1982), 67 Va.L.Rev. 1203 (1981), 60 Wash.U.L.Q. 1059 (1982), Annot., 92 A.L.R.3d 442, 1317; 29 Am.Jur.2d Evidence § 831.

64. See Note, 67 Va.L.Rev. 1203, at 1206–08 (1981) (reviewing scientific literature).

65. Bryan, supra n. 63, at 245–246 (hypnosis); Loftus, Eyewitness Testimony 107 (1979) ("even people who are mesmerized by hypnosis can fantasize, make mistakes, even lie"); Moenssens & Inbau, supra n. 63, § 15.02 (narcoanalysis); Yarmey, The Psychology of Eyewitness Testimony 175 (1979) ("Any attempt to discover truth through the so-called truth drugs such as sodium pentothal should be discouraged, since it does not produce the desired results"); id. at 177 ("Deeply hypnotized people who wish to hide information are able to fool even experienced hypnotists").

66. Saks & Hastie, Social Psychology in Court 190 (1978) ("there is substantial evidence that hypnotic suggestions can facilitate recall in an eyewitness situation. However, it is not clear whether the trance state is an essential component of the effect"); Yarmey, supra n. 65, at 177 (hypnosis); Note, The Admissibility of Testimony Influenced by Hypnosis, supra note 63, at 1208–1211.

that it also appears that it can *alter* memory.[67] Hypnotized persons are highly suggestible, and some authorities believe that when a hypnotist encourages a subject to relate everything he can possibly remember, the subject produces fragments and approximations of memory in an effort to be cooperative.[68] In addition, the subject may accept as his own recollections distortions inadvertently suggested by the hypnotist.[69] Finally, the hypnotic session may reinforce the witness' confidence in erroneous memories.[70]

Forensic applications of hypnosis can generate a variety of constitutional[71] and evidentiary issues. A party may seek admission of statements a witness made while under hypnosis or narcoanalysis to show directly the existence of certain facts, to impeach or buttress credibility, or to show the basis for a psychiatric or psychological opinion. Similarly, a party may offer the in-court testimony of a witness even though this testimony may be influenced or "tainted" by this person's prior exposure to such interrogation.

The courts have been most reluctant to admit such statements or testimony. In the first case to raise the issue, a California court stated in 1897 that "the law of the United States does not recognize hypnotism."[72] Since then the courts nearly always have excluded statements made under hypnosis[73] or narcoanalysis,[74] regardless of whether these statements are offered as

67. See Note, supra n. 64, at 1212–1214 (reviewing scientific literature).

68. Orne, supra n. 63, at 319; Spiegel, supra n. 16, at 78.

69. Putnam, supra n. 63 (experimental finding that hypnotized subjects made more errors in answering subtly misleading questions).

70. Orne, supra n. 63, at 332 (hypnosis "can bolster a witness whose credibility would easily have been destroyed by cross-examination but who now becomes quite impervious to such efforts, repeating one particular version of his story with great conviction"). For a case emphasizing the difficulty of cross-examining a previously hypnotized witness, see State v. Long, 32 Wn.App. 732, 649 P.2d 845, 847 (1982).

71. A confession resulting from an interrogation with drugs is a paradigm of an involuntary confession. See Townsend v. Sain, 372 U.S. 293, 307–308 (1963) (evidentiary hearing required on habeas corpus petition with respect to confession obtained 15 hours after narcotic addict undergoing withdrawal symptoms had been injected with phenobarbital and hyoscine). It has been said, however, that a person who will refrain from confessing to a competent investigator will also be able to withhold the truth under narcoanalysis, and conversely, that subjects who confess under narcoanalysis would have confessed under a competently conducted conventional interrogation. Moenssens & Inbau, supra n. 63, § 15.02 at 625. Perhaps a suspect could waive his constitutional protections, but his inability to exercise his normal judgment to request that the interrogation cease or that he consult with counsel complicates matters. See, e.g., Sparer, Some Problems Relating to the Admissibility of Drug Influenced Confessions, 24 Brooklyn L.Rev. 96 (1957); Stewart, Hypnosis, Truth Drugs, and the Polygraph, 21 U.Fla.L.Rev. 541 (1969). Commenting on a defendant's failure to undergo narcoanalysis is improper and can lead to reversal of a conviction. State v. Levitt, 36 N.J. 266, 176 A.2d 465, 469–470 (1961). But see People v. Draper, 304 N.Y.

799, 109 N.E.2d 342, 343 (1952), cert. denied 345 U.S. 944.

The use of hypnosis to enable a witness to remember details and hence to identify the defendant has been said to amount to an identification procedure to which the right to counsel attaches. Alderman & Barnette, supra n. 63, at 10–32. A few courts have found hypnotic methods so unnecessarily suggestive and conducive to irreparably mistaken identification that they deny the accused due process. Some have held that certain procedural safeguards are required if there is not to be such a due process violation. See Note, supra n. 64, at 1218–19.

72. People v. Ebanks, 117 Cal. 652, 665, 49 P. 1049, 1053 (1897) (excluding testimony about statements given under hypnosis), overruled on other grounds People v. Flannelly, 128 Cal. 83, 60 P.2d 670 (1900).

73. People v. Shirley, 31 Cal.3d 18, 181 Cal.Rptr. 243, 250–252, 641 P.2d 775, 782–784 (1982) (reviewing cases), cert. denied 103 S.Ct. 133; Strong v. State, ___ Ind. ___, 435 N.E.2d 969, 970 (1982) (composite drawing produced from witnesses' description given under hypnosis inadmissible because "evidence derived from a witness while he is in a hypnotic trance is inherently unreliable"); Commonwealth v. A Juvenile, 381 Mass. 727, 412 N.E.2d 339, 341 (1980) (citing cases for the proposition that "It is generally accepted that testimony while under hypnosis and evidence of what a subject said while under hypnosis are inadmissible"); cases cited, Note, supra n. 64, at 1205 n. 15; Annot., supra n. 63, § 5 (hypnotizing witness during trial), § 6 (recorded or transcribed pretrial statements made under hypnosis), § 7 (testimony describing pretrial statements given under hypnosis).

74. Lindsey v. United States, 16 Alaska 268, 237 F.2d 893, 896 (1956) (tape recording of sodium pentothal interrogation inadmissible to restore credibility after impeachment); State v. Hudson, 289 S.W. 920, 921 (Mo.1926) ("truth telling serum" is a "clap-trap" on a par with "the magic powers of philters, potions and

substantive evidence or as bearing on credibility. Posthypnotic testimony as to recollections enhanced or evoked under hypnosis has produced more divergent holdings. A few courts have said that such testimony is generally admissible, with objections as to its accuracy bearing on the weight that the finder of fact should give it.[75] But even in these jurisdictions there is a trend toward insisting that rigorous safeguards be observed before the hypnotically refreshed memories are admissible.[76] The more prevalent view is that testimony about the posthypnotic memories is inadmissible.[77] Typically, the courts adopting a strict exclusionary rule rely on the *Frye* test of general scientific ac-

ceptance,[78] although the same result probably could be reached by inquiring directly into the relative costs and benefits of the testimony. Indeed, the more modern cases support their invocation and application of the general acceptance standard by examining scientific testimony or literature on the value of hypnosis for recovering memories [79] and by referring to the usual concerns with scientific evidence—its suspected tendency to over-awe the jury and to consume time and resources—in a matter of particular sensitivity.[80]

When an expert uses narcoanalysis or hypnosis in his or her examination of a person to determine whether the individual is

---

cures by faith"); Cain v. State, 549 S.W.2d 707, 712 (Tex.Cr.App.1977) (citing cases to show that "[t]he great weight of authority in this country regards results of truth serum tests as inadmissible inasmuch as they have not yet attained scientific acceptance as reliable and accurate means of ascertaining truth or deception"), cert. denied 434 U.S. 845; cases cited, Moenssens & Inbau, supra n. 63, § 15.03 at 626 n. 6; Herman, supra n. 63, at 23–25.

75. Kline v. Ford Motor Co., 523 F.2d 1067, 1069–1070 (9th Cir. 1975); Pearson v. State, ___ Ind. ___, 441 N.E.2d 468, 472–73 (1983); State v. Jorgensen, 8 Or.App. 1, 9, 492 P.2d 312, 315 (1971) (hypnosis and sodium amytal); Chapman v. State, 638 P.2d 1280, 1282–1285 (Wyo.1982); Note, supra n. 64, at 353–360; Annot., supra note 63 at 461–464; cf. Sallee v. Ashblock, 438 S.W.2d 538 (Ky.1969) (testimony that sodium pentothal cured memory loss regarding an automobile accident was properly admitted to explain prior inconsistent statements).

76. United States v. Adams, 581 F.2d 193, 199 n. 12 (9th Cir. 1978), cert. denied 439 U.S. 1006; Pearson v. State, supra n. 75; State v. Hurd, 86 N.J. 525, 432 A.2d 86, 95–97 (1981) (elaborating strict procedural safeguards); State v. Long, 32 Wn.App. 732, 649 P.2d 845, 847 (1982) (reversing for failure to adhere to adequate procedural safeguards). The first case to admit hypnotically refreshed testimony, Harding v. State, 5 Md. App. 230, 236, 246 A.2d 302 (1968), cert. denied 395 U.S. 949, has been overruled. See Collins v. State, 52 Md.App. 186, 447 A.2d 1272, 1283 (1982); cf. Polk v. State, 48 Md.App. 382, 427 A.2d 1041 (1981) (remanding for determination of admissibility under general scientific acceptance test).

77. State ex rel. Collins v. Superior Court, 132 Ariz. 180, 644 P.2d 1266, 1294 (1982) (per se rule of exclusion); People v. Shirley, 31 Cal.3d 18, 181 Cal.Rptr. 243, 252–254, 641 P.2d 775, 784–786 (1982), cert. denied 103 S.Ct. 133; State v. Mack, 292 N.W.2d 764, 771 (Minn.1980) ("a witness whose memory has been 'revived' under hypnosis ordinarily may not be permitted to testify in a criminal proceeding to matters which he

or she 'remembered' under hypnosis"); Commonwealth v. Nazarovitch, 496 Pa. 97, 436 A.2d 170, 178 (1981) ("While we do not want to establish a *per se* rule of inadmissibility at this time, we will not permit the introduction of hypnotically-refreshed testimony until we are presented with more conclusive proof than has been offered to date of the reliability of the hypnotically-retrieved memory"). The recent commentary is divided. Compare Diamond, supra n. 63 (favoring per se rule of exclusion) with Notes, 57 Ind.L.J. 349 (1982) and 67 Va.L.Rev. 1203 (1981) (favoring admissibility under rigorous safeguards). Several jurisdictions following the per se rule of exclusion permit prehypnotic identifications or statements to be admitted if the proponent convincingly demonstrates that there is no possibility of any taint from the hypnotic interrogation. See State ex rel. Collins v. Superior Court, supra, 644 P.2d at 1296.

78. State ex rel. Collins v. Superior Court, 132 Ariz. 180, 644 P.2d 1266 (1982); People v. Shirley, 31 Cal.3d 18, 181 Cal.Rptr. 243, 641 P.2d 775 (1982), cert. denied 103 S.Ct. 133; People v. Gonzales, 415 Mich. 615, 329 N.W.2d 743 (1982). The general acceptance standard is discussed and criticized supra, § 203.

79. People v. Shirley, 31 Cal.3d 18, 181 Cal.Rptr. 243, 265, 641 P.2d 775, 797 (1982) ("for this limited purpose [of ascertaining general scientific acceptance] scientists have long been permitted to speak to the courts through their published writings in scholarly treatises and journals").

80. Id., 181 Cal.Rptr. at 264, 641 P.2d at 796 (hypnosis is invested with a "misleading aura of certainty which often envelops a new scientific process, obscuring its currently experimental nature"); State ex rel. Collins v. Superior Court, 132 Ariz. 180, 644 P.2d 1266, 1296–1297 (1982) (citing George Orwell's classic novel *1984* to underscore the proposition that "there are few dangers so great in the search for truth as man's propensity to tamper with the memory of others"); State v. Mack, 292 N.W.2d 764, 770 (Minn.1980) (adverting to "the difficulty and expense of calling experts qualified to testify to the uses of hypnosis").

insane, incompetent, or mentally incapacitated, the case for admissibility is much stronger.[81] A few courts have excluded expert opinions based on these techniques,[82] but this position seems difficult to defend even under the restrictive general acceptance standard. Most courts recognize that the opinions of the experts may be admitted and that the revelation of the details of what the subject said while under hypnosis or drugs is within the trial judge's discretion.[83] Thus, the trial court may permit the expert to give his opinion and an explanation of the information on which the expert relied, but curb the introduction of the statements made under hypnosis or narcoanalysis.[84]

D. *Profiles.* Psychological studies sometimes show a correlation between certain

traits or characteristics and certain forms of behavior. When this is the case, one can construct a diagnostic or predictive "profile" for such behavior.[85] For instance, retrospective analysis of individuals apprehended while smuggling drugs through airports shows that these persons tend to arrive from major points of distribution, to have little or no luggage with them, to look nervously about, to arrive in the early morning, and to have large amounts of cash in small bills.[86] Studies of "accident prone" persons indicate that such factors as having poor eyesight, being relatively young or old, and acting impulsively, aggressively or rebelliously are prevalent in this group.[87] Physicians regard certain patterns of physical injuries in children, which they designate the "battered child syndrome," as indicating repeated

81. See Packer, supra n. 62; Sadoff, supra n. 63.

82. People v. Ford, 304 N.Y. 697, 107 N.E.2d 595 (1952) (opinion on sanity based on sodium amytol interview inadmissible); cf. People v. Fournier, 86 Mich. App. 768, 273 N.W.2d 555, 561 (1978) (expert opinion as to intent based on sodium brevital interview); State v. Sinnott, 24 N.J. 408, 132 A.2d 298 (1957) (opinion of sexual propensities derived from sodium pentothal examination). Expert opinon testimony as to truthfulness derived from hypnotic techniques is almost invariably inadmissible. Cf. supra text accompanying notes 72–73. Mental health professionals do not seem to have any special ability to separate truth from falsehood in narcoanalytic and hypnotic sessions. Diamond, supra n. 63, at 337.

83. People v. Modesto, 59 Cal.2d 722, 732–33, 31 Cal.Rptr. 225, 231, 382 P.2d 33 (1963), appeal after remand 62 Cal.2d 436, 42 Cal.Rptr. 417, 398 P.2d 753, cert. denied 389 U.S. 1009 (error to exclude tape recording of hypnotic session pertinent to expert opinion on intent without balancing probative value against prejudicial effect); Lemmon v. Denver & Rio Grande Western Railroad Co., 9 Utah 2d 195, 341 P.2d 215, 219 (1959) (sodium amytol interview admissible with regard to diagnosis of amnesia); Moenssens & Inbau, supra n. 63, §§ 15.06, 15.11.

84. People v. Hiser, 267 Cal.App.2d 47, 72 Cal.Rptr. 906, 915–916 (1968) (tape recording of sodium pentothal and hypnotic interviews properly excluded); People v. Myers, 35 Ill.2d 311, 220 N.E.2d 297, 310 (1966), cert. denied 385 U.S. 1019 (testimony detailing defendant's response during sodium pentothal interview properly excluded); State v. Chase, 206 Kan. 352, 480 P.2d 62 (1971) (proper to exclude videotape of sodium amytal interview); State v. Harris, 241 Or. 224, 405 P.2d 492, 498–500 (1965) (tape recording of hypnotic interview); State v. White, 60 Wn.2d 551, 374 P.2d 942 (1962), cert. denied 375 U.S. 883, (tape recordings of sodium amytol and desoxyn interviews, properly excluded).

85. See generally Monahan, The Clinical Prediction of Violent Behavior (1981).

86. See Reid v. Georgia, 448 U.S. 438, 441 (1980) (per curiam) (the profile characteristics common to the suspect and the Drug Enforcement Administration's "informal" profile of drug couriers did not establish reasonable suspicion for a seizure of the person, since these characteristics merely "describe a very large category of presumably innocent travelers"); United States v. Mendenhall, 446 U.S. 544, 546 n. 1 (1980), rehearing denied 448 U.S. 908; United States v. Berry, 670 F.2d 583, 598–600 (5th Cir. 1982) (en banc) (more extensive description of DEA profiles and articulation of the standard for evaluating a claim that the profile establishes reasonable suspicion, namely, that "Although a match between defendant's characteristics and some of the characteristics on a drug courier profile does not automatically support a finding of reasonable suspicion, the fact that a characteristic of a defendant also happens to appear on the profile does not preclude its use as justification providing reasonable suspicion for a stop"). For other examples of the use of profiles in law enforcement or administrative actions, see United States v. Sanet, 666 F.2d 1370 (11th Cir. 1982) (Blue Shield's profiles of physicians' billings for Medicare beneficiaries); United States v. Lopez, 328 F.Supp. 1077 (E.D.N.Y.1971) (in camera hearing said to show that statistically validated profile used together with magnetometer to screen passengers boarding aircraft was "precisely designed to select only those who present a high probability of being dangerous"); Bohnstedt, Classification Instruments for Criminal Justice Decisions (1977); Rider, The Firesetter: A Psychological Profile, FBI Law Enforcement Bull. 1 (1980).

87. See supra § 189 n. 14.

physical abuse.[88] Indeed, we all evaluate information in the light of some such "profiles." Jurors, for example, can be said to bring to the courtroom their preconceived "profiles" which they then apply to decide who is lying and who is telling the truth, and who is likely to have committed an offense and who is innocent. Although there is no fundamental difference between the psychological and medical profiles and the more common, impressionistic ones, some of the former may have been derived in a more or less systematic and structured way, and some may have been tested by verifying that they give correct diagnoses or predictions when applied to new cases.[89] The correlations obtained in such prospective studies measure the validity of the profiles.[90]

In a growing number of cases, litigants have sought to introduce expert testimony as to the scientifically constructed or validated profiles. Women accused of murdering their husbands have pointed to the "battered wife syndrome" to support a plea of self-defense.[91] Prosecutors in sexual abuse cases have relied on the "rape trauma syndrome" to negate a claim of consent or to explain conflicting statements of the complainant.[92] In child abuse and homicide cases, prosecutors have called witnesses to establish that defendants exhibited the "battering parent syndrome."[93] And defendants accused of sexual offenses have offered testimony to the effect that they did not fit the profiles for sexual offenders.[94]

When the plaintiff or the government offers evidence that the defendant fits an incriminating profile, it may be excluded under the rule that prohibits evidence of character to show conduct on a particular occasion.[95] Yet, arguably the rule should not bar admission in all such cases.[96] After all,

---

88. United States v. Bowers, 660 F.2d 527, 529 (5th Cir. 1981). Many courts admit evidence of injuries sustained while in the parent's care to rebut the parent's claim that the death or damage was accidental. See supra § 190. In *Bowers*, the court also permitted for this purpose evidence of the general phenomenon and characteristics of battered children as well as the expert's opinion that the defendant's child suffered from the syndrome. See also In re M.S.H., 656 P.2d 1294, 1296 (Colo.1983); Lackey v. State, 246 Ga. 331, 271 S.E.2d 478 (1980); State v. Durfee, 322 N.W.2d 778, 782–785 (Minn.1982); State v. Wilkerson, 295 N.C. 559, 247 S.E.2d 905, 912 (1978); Annot., 98 A.L.R.3d 306.

89. Monahan, supra n. 85.

90. Cf. supra § 206(B) (validity studies of polygraphs as lie detectors).

91. Hawthorne v. State, 408 So.2d 801, 805–806 (Fla.App.1982) (remanding for findings on the qualifications of the expert and the reliability and validity of her methods); State v. Smith, 247 Ga. 612, 277 S.E.2d 678 (1981) (improperly excluded); Ibn-Tamas v. United States, 407 A.2d 626, 634 (D.C.App.1979) (erroneously excluded, but properly excluded after hearing on remand); Buhrle v. State, 627 P.2d 1374 (Wyo.1981) (inadmissible in absence of foundation showing validity and applicability to facts); Walter, Expert Testimony and Battered Women, 3 J. Legal Med. 267 (1982); Comment, 77 Nw.U.L.Rev. 348 (1982); Note, 35 Vand.L. Rev. 741 (1982); Annot., 18 A.L.R. 4th 1153; cf. State v. Baker, 120 N.H. 773, 424 A.2d 171 (1980) (admissible to rebut insanity defense).

92. State v. Marks, 231 Kan. 645, 647 P.2d 1292 (1982) (psychiatric testimony that complaining witness had been the victim of "a frightening assault, an attack" and was suffering from "the post-traumatic stress disorder known as rape trauma syndrome" admissible); State v. McGee, 324 N.W.2d 232, 233 (Minn. 1982) ("fundamental error" to admit physician's testimony that anxiety, nightmares, trouble sleeping and concentrating, and fear of being followed were symptoms consistent with rape trauma syndrome); State v. Middleton, 294 Or. 427, 657 P.2d 1215 (1983) (juvenile counselor's testimony that she found 14-year-old complainant's behavior during interview "very much in keeping with children who have complained of sex molestation at home" admissible; social worker's testimony that she found complainant's running away from foster homes and retracting statements made to police and grand jury "very typical for a teenage sex abuse victim" admissible).

93. State v. Loebach, 310 N.W.2d 58, 64 (Minn. 1981) ("until further evidence of the scientific accuracy and reliability of the syndrome can be established," the prosecution "will not be permitted to introduce evidence of 'battering parent' syndrome or to establish the character of the defendant as a 'battering parent' unless the defendant first raises that issue").

94. State v. Cavallo, 88 N.J. 508, 443 A.2d 1020 (1982) (testimony that defendant lacks the characteristics exhibited by rapists as encountered by psychiatrist in his practice properly excluded); People v. Jones, 42 Cal.2d 219, 266 P.2d 38 (1954) (psychiatric testimony that defendant was not a sexual deviate and was incapable of forming the intent to have sexual contact with his nine-year-old niece erroneously excluded).

95. See State v. Loebach, 310 N.W.2d 58, 63–64 (Minn.1981); supra § 190.

96. See United States v. Sanet, 666 F.2d 1370 (11th Cir. 1982); supra § 189 (profiles of physicians' billings and services).

the rule rests on the premise that the marginal probative value of character evidence generally is low while the potential for distraction, time-consumption and prejudice is high. If it were shown that the profile was both valid and revealing—that it distinguishes between offenders and non-offenders with great accuracy—then the balance might favor admissibility. It is far from clear, however, that any existing profile is this powerful.[97]

When the profile evidence is used defensively (to show good character, to restore credibility, or to prove apprehension in connection with a claim of self-defense), it falls under an exception to the rule against char-

acter evidence.[98] Admissibility then should turn on the extent to which the expert testimony would assist the jury viewed in the light of the usual counterweights.[99] The qualifications of the expert,[1] the reliability and validity of using the profile,[2] and the need for the evidence[3] thus affect the admissibility and of course the weight of the profile evidence.[4]

In some ways, profile evidence resembles expert testimony, considered at the outset of this section, describing the results of psychological research into eyewitness identifications. In both instances, the expert provides background information that may contradict lay impressions and that the jury can apply

97. Indeed, it is doubtful that all the "syndromes" or "profiles" listed above should be considered scientifically constructed or validated. They may, nevertheless, be accepted as working tools by clinicians. State v. Marks, 231 Kan. 645, 647 P.2d 1292, 1299 (1982) ("An examination of the literature clearly demonstrates that the so-called 'rape trauma syndrome' is generally accepted to be a common reaction to sexual assault"). To the extent that the testimony of research scientists or clinicians suggests that the evidence should be believed because it is scientific, the usual concerns relating to scientific evidence are present.

98. See supra §§ 191, 194.

99. In jurisdictions that adhere to the *Frye* standard, proof of general acceptance would also be required. See supra § 203. Cases discussing the degree of acceptance of certain profiles include Ibn-Tamas v. United States, 407 A.2d 626, 637–38, 655 (D.C.Ct.App. 1979) (methodology of clinical psychological research on battered women may be generally accepted, and specific findings based on 110 interviews need not be); State v. Marks, 231 Kan. 645, 647 P.2d 1292, 1299 (1982) (*Frye* test met by court's reading of scientific literature on rape trauma syndrome); State v. Cavallo, 88 N.J. 508, 443 A.2d 1020, 1025–1027 (1982) (defendant did not produce expert testimony, scientific or legal writings, or precedent to establish that psychiatrists can determine whether an individual possesses "particular mental characteristics peculiar to rapists"); State v. Thomas, 66 Ohio St.2d 518, 522, 423 N.E.2d 137, 140 (1981) ("the 'battered wife syndrome' is not sufficiently developed, as a matter of commonly accepted scientific knowledge, to warrant testimony under the guise of expertise"); Buhrle v. State, 627 P.2d 1374, 1377 (Wyo. 1981) ("research in the 'battered woman syndrome' is in its infancy," statistical analysis has not been completed, and acceptance is limited to the researchers and their funding institutions).

1. Comment, supra n. 91, at 365–367 (reviewing qualifications of expert witnesses in battered women cases).

2. Id. at 367–370 (reviewing cases); supra n. 99; cf. Dorsey v. State, 276 Md. 638, 350 A.2d 665 (1976) (police detective's testimony that 80% of persons arrested for armed robbery deny involvement in the crime). Where the profile establishes a base rate for truthful accusations or meritorious claims in cases like the one at bar, special problems arise. Ellman & Kaye, Probabilities and Proof: Can HLA and Blood Group Testing Prove Paternity, 54 N.Y.U.L.Rev. 1131, 1152 n. 98 (1979).

3. Comment, supra n. 91, at 348–365. Some courts assert that expert explanations of why battered women stay with the men who injure them is superfluous. State v. Thomas, 66 Ohio St.2d 518, 522, 423 N.E.2d 137, 140 (1981). The related objection that profile evidence invades the province of the jury also has been heard. Smith v. State, 247 Ga. 612, 277 S.E.2d 678, 680 (1981) (rejecting this argument).

4. It has been said that such evidence is prejudicial because it "would tend to stereotype defendant . . . ." State v. Thomas, 66 Ohio St.2d 518, 522, 423 N.E.2d 137, 140 (1981); cf. 1 Weinstein & Berger, Evidence ¶401[10] at 401–69 (profile testimony involves "the use of evidence of class characteristics to prove something about the behavior of the defendant"). The claim that there is something inherently prejudicial in this type of reasoning cannot withstand analysis. See infra § 208.

The objection that profile evidence invades the province of the jury, see supra n. 3, is too conclusory to be useful, but it may suggest the need to prevent any prejudice that would flow from an expert who would go beyond giving an opinion as to whether a person fits a profile. State v. Middleton, 294 Or. 427, 657 P.2d 1215 (1983) ("a witness, expert or otherwise, may not give an opinion whether he believes a witness is telling the truth"); Buhrle v. State, 627 P.2d 1374, 1377 (Wyo. 1981) (counsel represented that expert would testify that defendant "perceived herself to be acting in self-defense"); cf. supra n. 17 (undesirability of expert conclusion concerning eyewitness identification on basis of generalizations from experimental research).

to the case at hand, if persuaded to do so. Perhaps the greater receptivity of the appellate courts to psychological profile evidence stems from the fact that this type of testimony seems more like the clinical assessments routinely received from psychologists and physicians.[5] In addition, considering the subject matter of most of the psychological profiles that have come to the attention of the courts, it is possible that a growing sensitivity to women's issues has played some role.

 **WESTLAW REFERENCES**

Eyewitness Testimony
digest(eyewitness** /5 reliab! unreliab!)

5. State v. Middleton, 58 Or.App. 447, 648 P.2d 1296, 1300 (1982) (Since "admitted experts" were "explaining superficially bizarre behavior by identifying its emotional antecedents," their testimony "was as admissible as would be a doctor's testimony in a personal injury case that a party's physical behavior was consistent with a claimed soft tissue injury, although such an injury was not objectively verifiable"), affirmed 294 Or. 427, 657 P.2d 1215; Note, State v. Thomas: The Final Blow to Battered Women?, 43 Ohio St.L.J. 491, 508 (1982) (the expert "had offered an opinion based not on any methodology but rather on his extensive experience with battered women").

At the same time, one could make expert testimony on eyewitness identification sound like profile evidence. One could simply say that the "profile" or "syndrome" of an accurate (or inaccurate) eyewitness identification consists of the various factors studied in the experiments and that the identification in question "matches" this profile or is a "classic case" of this syndrome.

§ 207

1. "Criminalistics" refers to "the examination, evaluation, and interpretation of physical evidence." Dillon, Foreword, O'Hara & Osterburg, An Introduction to Criminalistics: The Application of the Physical Sciences to the Detection of Crime (1972). Despite the "criminal" root in the term, the topics surveyed in this section have obvious applications to many civil cases as well.

2. See generally Forensic Science Handbook (Saferstein ed. 1982); Moenssens & Inbau, Scientific Evidence in Criminal Cases (2d ed. 1978); O'Hara & Osterburg, supra n. 1; Scientific and Expert Evidence (2d ed. Imwinkelried 1981); Richardson, Modern Scientific Evidence (2d ed. 1974); 2–3 Wecht, Forensic Sciences (1981). Workers in this field may refer to the process of identifying or comparing samples as "individualization." For research suggesting an alarmingly high incidence of misidentifications by police laboratories of paint samples, blood samples, firearms, and the like, see Peterson, Fabricant & Field, Crime Laboratory

Detection of Deception
digest("lie detect!" polygraph /p reliab! unreliab!)

Drugs and Hypnosis
digest(hypno! narcoanaly! /p recollect!)

§ 207. Particular Tests: Criminalistics: Identifying Persons and Things

Many of the techniques of scientific criminal investigation, or criminalistics,[1] are aimed at identifying people or things.[2] Fingerprinting,[3] studying the trajectories and characteristics of bullets and firearms,[4] examining questioned documents,[5] detecting and identifying poisons and other drugs,[6] microscopically comparing hair samples and fi-

Proficiency Testing Program—Final Report (U.S. Dep't of Justice 1978).

3. People v. Jennings, 252 Ill. 534, 546–549, 96 N.E. 1077, 1081–1082 (1911); State v. Sanders, 224 Kan. 138, 578 P.2d 702 (1978); People v. Roach, 215 N.Y. 592, 604, 109 N.E. 618, 623 (1915); Castleton's Case, 3 Or. App. 74 (1909); Moenssens, Fingerprints and the Law (1969); Moenssens & Inbau, supra n. 2, §§ 7.01–7.18; Richardson, supra n. 2, §§ 18.1–18.14; Menzel, The Development of Fingerprints, in Scientific and Expert Testimony, supra n. 2, at 619; Annot., 28 A.L.R.2d 1115; cf. Annot., 35 A.L.R.2d 856 (shoe prints), 23 A.L.R.2d 112 (1952) (tire tracks).

4. Evans v. Commonwealth, 230 Ky. 411, 427–428, 19 S.W.2d 1091, 1098–99 (1929); Moenssens & Inbau, supra n. 59, §§ 4.01–4.28; Richardson, supra n. 2, §§ 17.1–17.19; 3 Wecht, supra n. 2, §§ 38.01–38.10; Cederbaum, The Ballistics Investigator, in Scientific and Expert Evidence, supra n. 2, at 657; Wilhelm, General Considerations of Firearms Identification and Ballistics, in id. at 675; supra § 202 n. 7.

5. United States v. Woodson, 526 F.2d 550 (9th Cir. 1975) (handwriting samples may go to the jury even when expert cannot determine whether they were written by the same person); Hilton, Scientific Examination of Questioned Documents (1981); Moenssens & Inbau, supra n. 2, §§ 10.01–10.22; Richardson, supra n. 2, §§ 19.1–19.14; 3 Wecht, Forensic Sciences §§ 39.01–39.06 (1981); Brunelle, Questioned Document Examination, in Forensic Science Handbook, supra n. 2, at 672; Brunelle & Pro, A Systematic Approach to Ink Identification, in Scientific and Expert Evidence, supra n. 2, at 709; Kelly, Questioned Document Examination, in id. at 695; Annot., 80 A.L.R.2d 272. Section 205 of the previous edition of this text is devoted to this topic. Authentication of documents by proof of handwriting is treated in § 221 infra.

6. United States v. Posey, 647 F.2d 1048 (10th Cir. 1981) (chemical spot tests, gas chromatography, mass spectroscopy, mixed infra-red spectroscopy, microcrystalline test, thin layer chromatography, ultraviolet

bers,[7] and matching blood stains [8] are among the better known examples. In addition, there is a vast array of less familiar techniques for detecting and analyzing what might be called "trace evidence" of criminal

or other activity.[9] These include other applications of microanalysis,[10] forensic odontology,[11] forensic anthropology,[12] and somewhat esoteric chemical and physical tests [13] used in connection with fingerprints,[14] firearms, [15]

spectroscopy and polarimeter test to prove that substance was L-cocaine, the optical isomer prohibited by statute); Roberts v. United States, 316 F.2d 489, 492 (3d Cir. 1963) (toxic effects of ethylene glycol); Coppolino v. State, 223 So.2d 68 (Fla.Dist.Ct.App.1968), appeal dismissed without opinion 234 So.2d 120 (Fla.), cert. denied 399 U.S. 927 (successful detection of previously undetectable poison in body of victim); State v. Lawson, 393 So.2d 1260 (La.1981) (drug identification); Cravey & Baselt, Introduction to Forensic Toxicology (1981); Lowry & Garriott, Forensic Toxicology—Controlled Substances and Dangerous Drugs (1979); Moenssens & Inbau, supra n. 2, §§ 6.01–6.05, 6.16–6.37; 2 Wecht, supra n. 2, §§ 31.01–31.10; Kurzman & Fullerton, Drug Identification, in Scientific and Expert Testimony, supra n. 2, at 521; Niyogi, Toxicology, in id. at 343; Stein, Laessig & Indriksons, An Evaluation of Drug Testing Procedures Used by Forensic Laboratories and the Qualifications of their Analysts, in id. at 433.

7. United States v. Hickey, 596 F.2d 1082, 1084 (1st Cir. 1979) (hairs found in getaway car "microscopically identical" to defendant's), cert. denied 444 U.S. 853, appeal after remand 265 F.2d 1030; United States v. Cyphers, 553 F.2d 1064 (7th Cir. 1977), cert. denied 434 U.S. 843 (defendants' hairs were "microscopically like" those recovered on articles used by robbers); State v. Hall, 297 N.W.2d 80, 87 (Iowa 1980), cert. denied 450 U.S. 927 (fibers from clothing); Pilcher v. State, 296 So.2d 682 (Miss.1974), cert. denied 420 U.S. 938 (fibers from sweater and "Negroid hair fragments"); People v. Allweiss, 48 N.Y.2d 40, 421 N.Y.S.2d 341, 396 N.E.2d 735 (1979) (hair); State v. Kersting, 50 Or.App. 461, 623 P.2d 1095 (1981) (hair), affirmed 292 Or. 350, 638 P.2d 1145 (1982); Moenssens & Inbau, supra n. 2, §§ 8.07–8.12, 8.23–8.24; Bisbing, The Forensic Identification and Association of Human Hair, in Forensic Science Handbook, supra n. 2, at 184; Annot., 23 A.L.R. 4th 1199.

8. See supra § 205(B).

9. The services of the FBI laboratories are enumerated in U.S. Dep't of Justice, Handbook of Forensic Science (1981).

10. Miller v. State, 240 Ark. 340, 399 S.W.2d 268 (1966) (soil samples); Sipera v. State, 286 Minn. 536, 175 N.W.2d 510 (1970) (microscopic and spectroscopic analysis of paint, plaster and tar to prove presence at burgled premises); Pilcher v. State, 296 So.2d 682 (Miss.1974), cert. denied 420 U.S. 938 (soil sample); Moenssens & Inbau, supra n. 59, §§ 8.13–8.22; De Forest, Foundations of Forensic Microscopy, in Forensic Science Handbook supra n. 2, at 416.

11. State v. Peoples, 227 Kan. 127, 605 P.2d 135 (1980) (bitemark evidence); People v. Middleton, 54 N.Y.2d 42, 444 N.Y.S.2d 581, 429 N.E.2d 100 (1981) (bitemark evidence scientifically accepted); State v. Jones, 273 S.C. 723, 731–732, 259 S.E.2d 120, 124–125

(1979) (bitemark evidence); Moenssens & Inbau, supra n. 2, §§ 16.01–16.10; Sperber, Forensic Odontology, in Scientific and Expert Testimony, supra n. 2, at 721; Note, 51 S.Cal.L.Rev. 309 (1978); Annot., 77 A.L.R.3d 1122 (bitemark evidence).

12. Ex parte Dolvin, 391 So.2d 677 (Ala.1980) (identification of skull); Moenssens & Inbau, supra n. 2, § 17.09; Annot., 18 A.L.R. 4th 1294 (identification of skeletal remains).

13. Readers interested in the many kinds of spectroscopy and chromatography should consult any organic chemistry text or laboratory coursebook. E.g., Roberts & Caserio, Basic Principles of Organic Chemistry 259–349, 1342–1366 (2d ed. 1977). For discussions with respect to forensic proof, see, State v. Sparks, 297 N.C. 314, 255 S.E.2d 373 (1979) (atomic absorption); Saferstein, Forensic Applications of Mass Spectrometry, in Forensic Science Handbook supra n. 2, at 92; Smith, Forensic Applications of High-Performance Liquid Chromatography, in id. at 28; supra § 205(A) (breath alcohol testing). On neutron activation analysis, see, 1 Louisell & Mueller, Federal Evidence § 106(6) (1977); Moenssens & Inbau, supra n. 2, §§ 9.01–9.10; Krishnan, Neutron Activation Analysis and Atomic Absorption Spectrometry, in Scientific and Expert Evidence, supra n. 2, at 279; Comment, 59 Calif.L.Rev. 997 (1973); Annot., 50 A.L.R.3d 117. For descriptions of still other techniques in the forensic scientist's arsenal, see United States v. Green, 525 F.2d 386, 392 (8th Cir. 1975) (expert testimony "on unique and specific similarities between the clothes worn by the men in the separate photographs"); State v. Hall, 297 N.W.2d 80 (Iowa 1980), cert. denied 450 U.S. 927 (blood splattering); Richardson, supra n. 2, § 22.16 (blood splattering); Judd, Scanning Electron Microscopy as Applied to Forensic Evidence Analysis, in Scientific and Expert Testimony, supra, at 873; Stevens & Messler, Trace Metal Detection Technique (TMDT), in id. at 1075.

14. Menzel, Laser Detection of Latent Fingerprints on Skin, 27 J.Forensic Sci. 918 (1982).

15. People ex rel. Gallagher v. District Court, 656 P.2d 1287, 1290–1292 (Colo.1983) (state's failure to permit trace metal test to show that victim had handled gun deprived defendant of due process even though test had only a 4% chance of giving a positive result even if victim had held the gun); Commonwealth v. Sero, 478 Pa. 440, 387 A.2d 63, 68 (1978) (neutron activation in experiment re-enacting features of the crime); Scientific and Expert Testimony, supra n. 2, at 289–342; Krishnan, Detection of Gunshot Residue: Present Status, in Forensic Science Handbook, supra n. 2, at 572; Ravreby, Analysis of Long-Range Bullet Entrance Holes by Atomic Absorption Spectrophotometry and Scanning Electron Microscopy, 27 J. Forensic Sci. 92 (1982); Annot., 1 A.L.R.4th 1072 (residue detection test to determine whether person fired gun).

glass fragments,[16] hair,[17] paints,[18] explosions and fires,[19] and questioned documents.[20]

While these methods are unquestionably of great value in many investigations, their use in the courtroom can pose problems. Perhaps to emphasize the scientific quality of the analysis, or merely in an effort to be as precise as possible, expert witnesses may state the results or implications of their tests in quantitative, probabilistic terms—a practice that causes difficulty for the courts.[21] Furthermore, a few of these analytic procedures or tests are themselves specially adapted or developed for forensic purposes and well known primarily in law enforcement circles. Consequently, the test of general scientific acceptance does not always work well in this context, and this incongruity can result in important opinions on the standards governing the admissibility of scientific evidence.[22]

The spectrographic analysis of human voices illustrates this last point.[23] Complex sound waves, such as those involved in speech, can be understood mathematically as sums of simple waveforms of various frequencies.[24] The frequency spectrum of such a sound wave is, in effect, a list of each such constituent frequency and its relative importance in describing the composite sound. For at least 40 years, electronic devices that analyze sound waves into these frequency components have been available. A spectrogram is a graphic representation of this information, that is, a picture of the frequency spectrum of a sound wave.[25] In the 1960's, it was proposed that the spectral characteristics of a speaker's voice could serve to identify that speaker. The theory behind this suggestion was that individuals have different but largely stable patterns in the way they manipulate their lips, teeth, and so on in speaking. From the outset, this hy-

16. Miller, Forensic Glass Comparisons, in Forensic Sciences Handbook, supra n. 2, at 139; Slater & Fong, Density, Refractive Index and Dispersion in the Examination of Glass, 27 J. Forensic Sci. 474 (1982); Stone & Thornton, Glass Evidence, in Scientific and Expert Testimony, supra n. 2, at 239.

17. United States v. Brown, 557 F.2d 541 (6th Cir. 1977) (ion microprobe mass spectroscopy not admissible as applied to hair samples); State v. Stevens, 467 S.W.2d 10 (Mo.1971), cert. denied 404 U.S. 994 (neutron activation analysis of hair samples admissible); Bisbing, supra n. 7.

18. Beech Aircraft Corp. v. Harvey, 558 P.2d 879 (Alaska 1976) (microscopic, spectrographic and chromatographic analysis of paint chips); State v. Hughey, 404 S.W.2d 725 (Mo.1966) (microscopic, spectrographic and chemical tests); Thornton, Forensic Paint Examination, in Forensic Science Handbook, supra n. 2, at 529.

19. United States v. Stifel, 433 F.2d 431 (6th Cir. 1970), cert. denied 401 U.S. 994 (neutron activation analysis results admissible); Jordan v. State, 481 P.2d 383 (Alaska 1971) (neutron activation analysis to show source of solder found in explosion debris); Yinon & Zitrin, The Analysis of Explosives (1981); Midkiff, Arson & Explosive Investigation, in Forensic Science Handbook, supra n. 2, at 222; Washington & Midkiff, Explosives, in Scientific and Expert Evidence, supra n. 2, at 587.

20. The examination can become quite complex, involving chemical, physical, psycholinguistic, and statistical techniques. United States v. Bruno, 333 F.Supp. 570 (E.D.Pa.1971) (chromatographic analysis of ink samples found unreliable and not generally accepted);

United States v. Hearst, 412 F.Supp. 893 (N.D.Cal. 1976), affirmed 563 F.2d 1331 (9th Cir.), cert. denied 435 U.S. 1000, criticized, Comment, Stylistics Evidence in the Trial of Patty Hearst, 1977 Ariz.St.L.J. 387; Niblett & Boreham, Cluster Analysis in Court, 1976 Crim.L.Rev. 175; Noblett, Use of a Scanning Monochromator as a Barrier Filter in Infrared Examinations of Documents, 27 J.Forensic Sci. 923 (1982); supra n. 5.

21. This complication is taken up infra at § 211.

22. See generally Giannelli, The Admissibility of Novel Scientific Evidence: Frye v. United States a Half Century Later, 80 Colum.L.Rev. 1197 (1980); McCormick, Scientific Evidence: Defining a New Approach to Admissibility, 67 Iowa L.Rev. 879 (1982); supra § 203.

23. See generally 1 Louisell & Mueller, supra note 13, § 106(7); Moenssens & Inbau, supra n. 2, §§ 12.01–12.09; National Research Council, On the Theory and Practice of Voice Identification (1979) [hereinafter NRC Report]; Richardson, supra n. 2, §§ 28.1–28.60; Tosi, Voice Identification: Theory and Legal Applications (1979); Thomas, Voiceprint—Myth or Miracle, in Scientific and Expert Testimony, supra n. 2, at 1015; Tosi, Voice Identification, in id. at 971; Tosi, New Developments in Voice Identification, in id. at 1005; Note, 21 Ariz.L.Rev. 349 (1980); Comment, 1980 Ariz.St.L.J. 217; Annot., 97 A.L.R.3d 294.

24. Marion, Classical Dynamics of Particles and Systems § 14.12 (1965).

25. For examples, see, Moenssens & Inbau, supra n. 2, § 12.05 at 571 (Figure 3); NRC Report, supra n. 23, at 4–5; Kersta, Speaker Recognition and Identification by Voiceprints, 40 Conn.B.J. 586 (1966).

pothesis has been controversial.[26] If it is false, then comparisons of spectrograms should not produce consistently correct identifications.[27] Despite a few early (and seemingly extravagant) claims of accurate identifications,[28] subsequent studies providing better approximations of realistic forensic conditions report misidentifications at rates ranging from 18% (12% false negatives and 6% false positives) to 70 and 80% (including 42% false positives).[29] Many scientists continue to express doubts about the reliability and validity of the current technique.[30]

Most courts applying the general scientific acceptance test to voice spectrographic evidence have held the evidence inadmissible.[31] In fact, this evidence has inspired some of the most spirited and thoughtful defenses of the general acceptance standard for scientific evidence.[32] On the other hand, faith in the method and a belief that jurors will not find it overly impressive has prompted some courts to bend the *Frye* test to the breaking point in order to conclude that the evidence should be admissible.[33] Whatever standard may be applied, however, it seems that until

26. See NRC Report supra n. 23, at 2 ("the assumption that intraspeaker variability is less than . . . interspeaker variability . . . is not adequately supported by scientific theory and data"); Bolt, Cooper, David, Denes, Pickett & Stevens, Speaker Identification by Speech Spectrograms: A Scientist's View of Its Reliability for Legal Purposes, 47 J. Acoustic Soc'y Am. 597 (1970); Thomas, supra n. 23, at 1026 ("controlled scientific experiments indicate that frequently the vocal equipment and its use by two different speakers produce results more similar than the results produced by the same speaker on two different occasions").

27. Since existing forensic methods for matching spectrograms entail considerable subjective judgment and probably can be made more reliable, the inverse does not hold. If it were shown that a careful and competent analyst could make accurate identifications, then the possible lack of reliability among analysts would not, in itself, justify an exclusionary rule, since individual qualifications and procedures can be examined in court. But see Moenssens & Inbau, supra n. 2, § 12.08 at 580, 582–583 (no responsible organization to certify competence, and leading experts disagree on whether particular findings are competently made).

28. Initial studies were conducted under artificial conditions that bore little resemblance to forensic applications. Moenssens & Inbau, supra n. 2, § 12.06; Thomas, supra n. 23, at 1035–1037. It has also been said that more recent studies have yet to examine some important variables. Moenssens & Inbau, supra, § 12.06 at 575; NRC Report, supra n. 23, at 58 ("What is in doubt is the degree of accuracy with which identifications can be made under all sorts of conditions, especially in forensic conditions . . . The presently available experimental evidence about error rates consists of results from a relatively small number of separate, uncoordinated experiments. These results alone cannot provide estimates of error rates that are valid over the range of conditions usually met in practice").

29. See Thomas, supra n. 2, at 1020, 1042–1043, 1046 (reviewing studies). See also Moenssens & Inbau, supra n. 2, § 12.06 at 574–575 (criticizing some of these studies); Bolt et al., Speaker Identification by Speech Spectrograms: Some Further Observations, 54 J. Acoustic Soc'y Am. 531, 534 (1973) ("laboratory evaluations of these methods show increasing errors as the

conditions for evaluation move toward real-life situations"). These statistics are useful, but, as with the accuracy figures for the polygraph studies mentioned supra at § 206(B), they should be supplemented by statistics that would take into account the error rates that would be expected if the scientific method did not work at all. Unfortunately, this is not easily accomplished, since "the scientific results reported to date do not provide quantitative information about the improvement in accuracy, if any, associated with the use of voicegrams." NRC Report, supra n. 23, at 25.

30. See NRC Report supra n. 23, at 58–70. But see Tosi, New Developments in Voice Identification, supra n. 23.

31. United States v. Addison, 498 F.2d 741 (D.C. Cir. 1974), questioned in United States v. McDaniel, 538 F.2d 408, 413 (D.C.Cir. 1976); People v. Kelly, 17 Cal.3d 24, 130 Cal.Rptr. 144, 549 P.2d 1240 (1976); Reed v. State, 283 Md. 374, 391 A.2d 364 (1978); Annot., supra n. 23.

32. See McCormick, supra n. 22, at 883–884. Defining the relevant scientific community has been something of a problem in these cases. Compare Reed v. State, 283 Md. 374, 391 A.2d 364 (1978) with Commonwealth v. Lykus, 367 Mass. 191, 327 N.E.2d 671 (1975). Ironically, in view of the indications of the unreliability of spectrographic voice identification, a court that perceives substantial risks of time-consumption, expense, and undue reliance on the expert testimony could adopt an exclusionary rule without recourse to the *Frye* test. See, e.g, State v. Andretta, 61 N.J. 544, 296 A.2d 644 (1972) (criticizing the study finding only 6% false positives). If one were to follow the approach to admitting scientific evidence suggested supra at § 203, one would balance marginal probative value against these counterweights. That is, one would ask whether what the technique adds to traditional forms of voice identification is worth what it costs. For information on the marginal improvement over mere listening, see Stevens, Williams, Carbonell & Woods, 44 J. Acoustical Soc'y Am. 1596 (1968) (ordinary listening more accurate); NRC Report, supra n. 23, at 25 (concluding that the experiments to date do not indicate how much improvement, if any, there is).

33. United States v. Williams, 583 F.2d 1194 (2d Cir. 1978), cert. denied 439 U.S. 1117; United States v. Ball-

further research makes the validity of the technique plainer, the courts will remain divided over the admissibility of voice spectrographic identification.[34]

 WESTLAW REFERENCES

bitemark /3 evidence indentif!
microscop! /5 hair
spectrograph! /s voice*
"frye test"

er, 519 F.2d 463 (4th Cir. 1975), cert. denied 423 U.S. 1019; McCormick, supra n. 22; Annot., supra n. 23. Many of these courts took the research of Dr. Oscar Tosi as establishing the accuracy of the technique. Some distinguished scientists drew the opposite conclusion. See Bolt et al. supra n. 29, at 533 ("we regard the 5% to 10% false identification rates seen [by Tosi] as artificial minima which are likely to increase when conditions depart from the laboratory situation;" "The Tosi experiments, in fact, show considerable disagreement among different panels of observers as to what constitutes a match").

34. For collections of cases coming to different conclusions, see Brown v. United States, 384 A.2d 647, 650 (D.C.App.1978) ("While the greater number of appellate opinions favor admissibility . . . the recent opinions . . . denying admission indicate the absence of a clear trend"); State v. Williams, 4 Ohio St.3d 53, 446 N.E.2d 444, 448 (1983) (admissible under Rules 402 and 702 on a foundation of "unrebutted evidence of reliability"); Annot., supra n. 23. For the conflicting views of the commentators, compare, e.g., Tosi, supra n. 23, and Comment, supra n. 23 (should be admissible) with Moenssens & Inbau, supra n. 2, §§ 12.07–12.08 (should be inadmissible); cf. Misner, Tape Recordings, Business Transactions via Telephone, and the Statute of Frauds, 61 Iowa L.Rev. 941, 956–963 (1976) (arguing for admissibility in civil cases). The NRC Report, supra n. 23, at 2, studiously avoids taking a position on the legal issues, except to say that "the technical uncertainties . . . are so great as to require that forensic applications be approached with great caution" and to recommend that "if it is used in testimony, then the limitations of the method should be clearly and thoroughly explained to the fact finder, whether judge or jury."

§ 208

1. As quoted in Moore, Statistics: Concepts and Controversies 3 (1979).

2. See, e.g., Spowls, The Admissibility of Sample Data into a Court of Law, 4 UCLA L.Rev. 222 (1957). In most large surveys, many persons are employed to do the interviewing or other forms of data collection.

§ 208. Statistical Studies: Surveys and Opinion Polls

Samuel Johnson once remarked that "You don't have to eat the whole ox to know the hide is tough."[1] In the past, courts required litigants to dismember and devour an ox or two in order to prove a point.[2] However, with the development and implementation of scientific survey methods,[3] the courts are much more receptive to proof based on sample data.[4] The Federal and Uniform Rules sweep aside traditional hearsay objections and allow the evidence to come in, if it is reasonably reliable, as the basis for an expert opinion.[5] Specially commissioned

Furthermore, when opinion polls are in issue, the individuals whose opinions were sampled are not testifying in court. Testimony as to the findings therefore is usually thought to involve hearsay, and historically this has been the major objection to survey evidence. Various arguments to circumvent or overcome the hearsay rule have been used by courts electing to receive the evidence. See, e.g., Texas Aeronautics Commission v. Braniff Airways, 454 S.W.2d 199, 203 (Tex. 1970), cert. denied 400 U.S. 943 ("admissible whether it is considered to be nonhearsay or within the state of mind exception to the hearsay rule"); Zeisel, The Uniqueness of Survey Evidence, 45 Cornell L.Q. 322 (1960); Note, 62 Va.L.Rev. 110 (1976); Annot., 76 A.L.R.2d 619; § 294 n. 4 infra.

3. For elementary discussions, see Freedman, Pisani & Purves, Statistics 301–19 (1978); Moore, supra n. 1, at 3–38, 100–120; Williams, A Sampler on Sampling (1978); Dean, Sampling to Produce Evidence on Which Courts Will Rely, Current Business Studies, Oct. 1953, at 5; Zeisel, supra n. 2. For more advanced works, see 1–2 Morris, Hurwitz & Madow, Sample Survey Methods and Theories (1953); Sudman, Applied Sampling (1976); Survey Sampling and Measurement (Namboodiri ed. 1978).

4. See generally 18 Am.Jur. Proof of Facts 2d 305 (admissibility of opinion surveys); Roper, Public Opinion Surveys in Legal Proceedings, 51 A.B.A.J. 44 (1965); Zeisel, supra n. 93; Note, 66 Harv.L.Rev. 498 (1953); Note, supra n. 2; Annot., supra n. 2.

5. Rule 703 departs from the common law in permitting an expert to testify to an opinion based on facts or data that are not admissible in evidence and to testify about this underlying information as long as it is "of the type reasonably relied on by experts in the particular field." The federal Advisory Committee's Note to this rule refers to survey evidence, observing that "The rule also offers a more satisfactory basis for ruling upon the admissibility of public opinion poll evidence. Attention is directed to the validity of the techniques employed rather than to relatively fruitless inquiries into whether hearsay is involved."

surveys, and especially opinion polls, have been used to support motions for a change of venue in criminal cases,[6] to show consumer perceptions in trademark and misleading advertising cases,[7] to unmask community standards in obscenity prosecutions,[8] and for numerous other purposes.[9] Advocates have also relied on pre-existing research involving

sample data in product liability, food and drug, environmental, and other cases.[10] The modern opinions have said that case-specific surveys are generally admissible if they are conducted according to the principles accepted by social scientists and statisticians for gathering and analyzing survey data.[11] This section therefore attempts to give an over-

6. See Barksdale, The Use of Survey Research Findings as Legal Evidence 47–123 (1957); Woodward, A Scientific Attempt to Provide Evidence for a Decision on Change of Venue, 17 Am.Sociology Rev. 447 (1952). In Irvin v. State, 66 So.2d 288, 291–92 (Fla. 1953), cert. denied 346 U.S. 927, rehearing denied 347 U.S. 914, the Florida Supreme Court upheld the trial judge's refusal to admit a public opinion survey in a pretrial hearing on the theory that the poll was "hearsay based upon hearsay" and that it was "useless" in revealing public attitudes toward the defendant, a black who had been convicted of rape but alleged that the verdict was the result of racial prejudice. The court disparaged the probative value of opinion polls by alluding to the errors of political pollsters in predicting the outcome of the 1948 presidential election. It regarded as much more informative the opinions given by witnesses who testified in court that the defendant could get a fair trial in the county, and it cited as an "illustration of the friendliness of the white people for the colored in the community . . . the recent construction of an elaborate memorial to a colored soldier who had been killed in World War II." Id. at 292. The more current view is that properly conducted polls can help reveal the extent of prejudice against a defendant in the district from which jurors would be drawn. A.B.A. Special Comm. on Minimum Standards for the Administration of Criminal Justice, Standards Relating to Fair Trial and Free Press § 3.2(c) (1968); Sherman, The Use of Opinion Polls in Continuance and Venue Hearings, 50 A.B.A.J. 357 (1964); Zeisel & Diamond, The Jury Selection in the Mitchell-Stans Conspiracy Trial, 1976 Am.B. Foundation Research J. 151. But see United States v. Mandel, 431 F.Supp. 90 (D.Md. 1977) (poll appeared to invade province of court and to be hearsay). Of course, the admissibility of a poll does not mean that it will succeed in demonstrating such widespread prejudice as would warrant a continuance or change in venue. United States v. Haldeman, 559 F.2d 31 (D.C.Cir.1976), cert. denied Ehrlichman v. United States, 431 U.S. 933 (voir dire examination may be given more weight than defendants' poll); United States v. Eagle, 586 F.2d 1193 (8th Cir. 1978).

7. American Footwear Corp. v. General Footwear Co., 609 F.2d 655, 663 (2d Cir. 1979), cert. denied 445 U.S. 951 (secondary meaning of "Bionic" not established by survey that showed consumers associated the word with certain television programs but not that they were confused as to who manufactured a "Bionic Boot"); United States v. 88 Cases, More or Less, Containing Bireley's Orange Beverage, 187 F.2d 967 (3d Cir. 1951), cert. denied 342 U.S. 861; Squirt Co. v. Seven-Up Co., 628 F.2d 1086 (8th Cir. 1980); Anti-Monopoly v. General Mills Fun Group, 684 F.2d 1316 (9th

Cir. 1982); Zippo Manufacturing Co. v. Roger's Imports, 216 F.Supp. 670 (S.D.N.Y.1963); cases cited, C.A. May Marine Supply Co. v. Brunswick Corp., 649 F.2d 1049 (5th Cir. 1981), cert. denied 454 U.S. 1125; Zeisel, supra n. 2; Annot., supra n. 2.

8. People v. Nelson, 88 Ill.App.3d 196, 43 Ill.Dec. 476, 410 N.E.2d 476 (1980) (survey showing that "a majority . . . of Illinois residents consider it acceptable for adults to view sexually explicit materials" was excluded erroneously, but testimony of the expert that these results showed no "consensus" was properly excluded as confusing, distracting, and unnecessary); Commonwealth v. Trainor, 374 Mass. 796, 374 N.E.2d 1216 (1978) ("A properly conducted public opinion survey, offered through an expert in conducting such surveys, is admissible in an obscenity case if it tends to show relevant standards," but the survey in question was properly excluded); Carlock v. State, 609 S.W.2d 787 (Tex.Cr.App.1981) (survey erroneously excluded); Bell, Determining Community Standards, 63 A.B.A.J. 1202 (1977); Lamont, Public Opinion Polls and Survey Evidence in Obscenity Cases, 15 Crim.L.Q. 135 (1973); McNamara & St. George, "Porno" Litigation, Community Standards, and the Phony Expert: A Case Study of Fraudulent Research in the Courtroom, 3 Sociological Practice 45 (1979); Annot., supra n. 2. Trying to use empirical methods to establish the existence of moral views may be fundamentally mistaken. Dworkin, Taking Rights Seriously (1977). As such, opinion polling may be better at demonstrating the lack of community standards than at establishing their existence or content.

9. Pittsburgh Press Club v. United States, 579 F.2d 751 (3d Cir. 1978) (tax-exempt club's mail survey of its members as to their sponsorship of income-producing uses of club facilities); C.A. May Marine Supply Co. v. Brunswick Corp., 649 F.2d 1049 (5th Cir. 1981), cert. denied 454 U.S. 1125 (survey of customers of dealer whose franchise was cancelled); Baumholser v. Amax Coal Co., 630 F.2d 550 (7th Cir. 1980) (survey of residents as to property damage from blasting operations); Rosado v. Wyman, 322 F.Supp. 1173, 1180 (E.D.N.Y. 1970) (determining welfare benefits), affirmed 437 F.2d 619 (2d Cir.), affirmed 402 U.S. 991; Boucher v. Bomhoff, 495 P.2d 77, 80–81, 83–86 (Alaska 1972) (survey as to effect of misleading language prefacing ballot measure); Wilcox v. Enstad, 122 Cal.App.3d 641, 176 Cal.Rptr. 560 (1981) (random sampling to verify signatures on recall petition).

10. See infra § 209.

11. Baumholser v. Amax Coal Co., 630 F.2d 550 (7th Cir. 1980) ("To qualify a study or opinion poll for admission into evidence, there must be a substantial

view of these principles—adherence to which affects the weight as well as the admissibility of survey evidence.[12] As the material collected in the notes will show, the courts have carefully examined whether the conclusions of the survey researchers rest on sample data collected in such a way as to permit fair inferences about the relevant factual questions.

Although many refinements are possible, the basic ideas behind scientific survey techniques are simple enough.[13] The researcher tries to collect information from a manageable portion (a sample) of a larger group (a population) in order to learn something about the population. Usually some number or numbers are used to characterize the population, and these are called parameters. For example, the proportion of all consumers who would mistake one product for another because of a similarity in the brand names is a population parameter. Sample data leads to statistics, such as the proportion of the persons in the sample who are confused by the similarity. These sample statistics are then used to estimate the population parameters. If 50% of the sample studied exhibited confusion between the products with the similar brand names, then one might conclude that 50% of the population would be confused. Under some circumstances, statistical methods enable the researcher not only to make an estimate, but to state the probability that this estimate differs from the unknown parameter by any given amount—that is, to quantify the error that may be lurking in the estimate.

Sampling underlies almost every pertinent research effort. Descriptive surveys, like those introduced in connection with change of venue motions, are almost always confined to a sample of the entire population. Surveys looking for causal explanations (such as a survey of homicide rates in states that do and states that do not have capital punishment) usually involve samples. Even experiments designed to investigate causation, such as a trial of a new drug, typically produce only sample data. Many such surveys are nonverbal. Since an employer's records can be inspected, no one needs to poll the current employees to obtain data on the distribution of wages paid to men as opposed to women. Other surveys are personal or verbal, as we know from experience with survey interviewers and written questionnaires.

What factors are likely to make such surveys produce accurate as opposed to misleading estimates? We can identify two major categories of errors: random errors and non-random errors.[14] There are many potential sources of non-random, or systematic errors. In personal surveys, these include the specification of the population to be sampled,[15] the technique for eliciting responses,[16]

---

showing of reliability. There must be some showing that the poll is conducted in accordance with generally accepted survey principles and that the results are used in a statistically correct manner"); C.A. May Marine Supply Co. v. Brunswick Corp., 649 F.2d 1049 (5th Cir. 1981), cert. denied 454 U.S. 1125 ("Surveys and customer questionnaires are admissible, if they are pertinent to the inquiry, upon a showing that the poll is reliable and was conducted in accordance with accepted survey methods"). But see Pittsburgh Press Club v. United States, 579 F.2d 751 (3d Cir. 1978) (for a survey itself to be admissible under Rule 803(24), it also must be "more probative on the issue than any other evidence"). Once a survey has been shown to conform to "conventional methodology," its arguable deficiencies usually are said to affect its weight rather than its admissibility. See, e.g., Squirt Co. v. Seven-Up Co., 628 F.2d 1086, 1091 (8th Cir. 1980).

12. See, e.g, C.A. May Marine Supply Co. v. Brunswick Corp., 649 F.2d 1049, n. 10 (5th Cir. 1981), cert.

denied 454 U.S. 1125; Otero v. Mesa County Valley School District, 408 F.Supp. 162, 167–168 (D.Colo.1975), vacated 568 F.2d 1312 (10th Cir.), on remand 470 F.Supp. 326, affirmed 628 F.2d 1271.

13. For introductions to sampling theory, see authorities cited, supra n. 3.

14. See generally, Gonzalez, Ogus, Shapiro & Tepping, Standards for Discussion and Presentation of Errors in Survey and Census Data, 70 J.Am. Statistical Ass'n 5 (1975).

15. Reddy Communications v. Environmental Action Foundation, 477 F.Supp. 936, 947 (D.D.C.1979) ("survey failed to account for the specific public exposed to . . . publications" that were available only by mail upon specific request and not "distributed or sold in the public marketplace where uninformed or easily gullible readers might be exposed to them").

16. For example, postcards mailed in response to a newspaper advertisement containing a questionnaire

the wording of the questions,[17] the method for choosing and finding respondents,[18] and the failure to pose questions that address the proper issues.[19] Unless those sources of non-random error cancel each other out, any estimates made on the basis of the sample data will be biased.[20] Making the sample size larger offers no protection against bias. It only produces a larger number of biased observations.

Random errors arise at two levels. The first is with respect to the observations on each unit sampled. In a nonverbal study, a measuring instrument (such as an instrument to determine breath alcohol content) might well give slightly different readings even on identical samples. A person seeking to get rid of an interviewer may say whatever pops into mind.[21] The process for making individual measurements or observations is rarely perfectly reliable. The second kind of random error results from variability from one sample to the next. One sample of air expelled from the lungs may be slightly dif-

ferent from the next in its concentration of alcohol. Even though great care may be taken to assure that the people selected for interviews are representative of the population, there can be no guarantee that another sample selected by the same procedure would give identical responses. As such, even if all the answers or measurements are individually free from error, sampling variability remains a source of statistical, or chance error.

If methods known as probability sampling are employed, however, the magnitude of the sampling error (but not of the non-random errors) can be estimated. Probability sampling also has been shown to be very effective in producing representative samples. The reason is that unlike human beings, blind chance is impartial. Probability sampling uses an objective chance process to pick the sample. It leaves no discretion to the interviewers. As a result, the researcher can compute the chance that any particular unit in the population will be selected for

about a product may introduce "nonresponse" bias, since disgruntled customers tend to respond in disproportionately large numbers; cf. Commonwealth v. Trainor, 374 Mass. 796, 374 N.E.2d 1216 (1978) ("There was no indication that the method of selection of the subjects to be interviewed assured a representative sample of the citizens of Boston. One might suspect that certain persons would decline to participate because of the method by which they were approached").

17. Pittsburgh Press Club v. United States, 579 F.2d 751 (3d Cir. 1978); Carlock v. State, 609 S.W.2d 787, 790 n. 3 (Tex.Cr.App.1981).

18. For example, the locations and time of day or night at which interviews are conducted can affect the characteristics of the sample. To avoid bias in selecting the units on which data is to be obtained, the sampling frame must be representative of the population, and the units in the sampling frame must have non-zero probabilities of being selected. In quota sampling, the sample is hand-picked by the interviewers to resemble the population in some key ways. The method seems logical, but it often gives bad results because of unintentional bias on the part of the interviewers. "Convenience samples" which, like the newspaper advertisement poll, make no effort to secure a representative sample, are especially likely to produce biased results.

19. This type of error seems to be uncomfortably prevalent in surveys intended for use in court. See, e.g., C.A. May Marine Supply Co. v. Brunswick Corp., 649 F.2d 1049 (5th Cir. 1981), cert. denied 454 U.S. 1125 (survey offered to prove lost profits from a franchise

termination was correctly excluded, since "Evidence tending to show business goodwill is not germane unless it demonstrates a 'going concern' value," and "general predisposition to purchase products at May Marine is not reflective of how many of a certain item would have been purchased"); Reddy Communications v. Environmental Action Foundation, 477 F.Supp. 936, 947 (D.D.C.1979) ("The interviewees . . . were shown two illustrations . . . in a context devoid of any background information and totally foreign from the usual manner in which the public would come in contact with either of the figures"); People v. Norwood, 37 Colo.App. 157, 547 P.2d 273 (1975) (survey showing that most city residents had heard of pending murder trial did not prove that they were prejudiced); Commonwealth v. Trainor, 374 Mass. 796, 374 N.E.2d 1216 (1978) ("The survey results apparently were offered as bearing on the question whether the films and magazines involved in this case displayed sexual conduct in a patently offensive way. The offer of proof made no attempt to connect an acceptance of, or an indifference to, the showing or sale of that material [which is all that the survey measured] with whether the particular sexual conduct involved in this case was depicted or described in a patently offensive way").

20. If the direction or magnitude of the bias can be determined, the results nonetheless may be useful.

21. The individual also may lie. If the persons being questioned have a motive to fabricate, the sample data may be biased. See, e.g., Pittsburgh Press Club v. United States, 579 F.2d 751 (3d Cir. 1979).

the sample. Stated another way, a probability sample is one in which each unit of the sampling frame has a known, non-zero probability of being selected. So-called "convenience" or "quota" samples do not have this property, and they are acceptable only in very special circumstances. A common type of probability sampling is simple random sampling, in which every unit has the same probability of being sampled. It amounts to drawing names at random without replacement.

The statistics derived from observations or measurements of random samples permit one to estimate the parameters of the population. In a consumer confusion survey for instance, some proportion of the sample of consumers who are interviewed will indicate confusion between the products. If the sample is a simple random sample, and if there are no non-random errors, then this sample proportion is an unbiased estimator of the proportion for all consumers. But it is only an estimate. After all, another random sample probably would not include precisely the same persons, and it probably would produce a slightly different proportion of responses indicating confusion. There is no single figure that expresses the extent of this statistical error. There are only probabilities. If one were to draw a second random sample, find the proportion of confused consumers in this group, then do the same for a third random sample, a fourth, and so on, one would obtain a distribution of sample proportions fluctuating about some central value.[22] Some would be far away from the mean, but most would be closer. Pursuing this logic in a rigorous way, the statistician computes a "confidence interval" and gives an "interval estimate" for the population proportion. He or she may report that at a 90% confidence level,

the population proportion is 50% plus or minus 10%. What this means is that if the same method for drawing samples and interviewing the customers were repeated a very large number of times, and if a 90% confidence interval were computed about each sample, 90% of these interval estimates would be correct. This many would include the population proportion, whatever that number happens to be.

Although testimony as to confidence intervals often is received in cases involving survey evidence, its meaning apparently remains obscure in many cases.[23] Note that a confidence of, say 90% does not necessarily mean that the interval estimate has a 90% probability of being correct. Strictly speaking, all that the classical statistical methodology reveals is that the particular interval was obtained by a method that gives intervals that would capture the true proportion in 90% of all possible samples. But each such interval estimate could be different. Thus, the "confidence" pertains to the process rather than to any particular result. Despite this difficulty in interpreting a confidence interval, the technique does give the finder of fact some idea of the risk of error in equating the sample proportion to the population figure. If the interval is small, even for a high level of "confidence," then the sample proportion is reasonably accurate, at least in the sense that taking more, or larger samples probably would give similar results.

The width of the confidence interval depends on three things. For a given sample, there is a trade-off between the level of confidence and the narrowness of the interval. One can be sure that the population proportion lies somewhere between zero and one. The confidence is 100% but the interval is so broad as to be useless. Lowering the confi-

---

22. The center of this distribution is characterized by the mean of all the sample proportions. The statistic known as the variance (or the square root of this quantity, the standard deviation) describes the width of the distribution of the sample proportions. For large samples, the sample proportions follow a bell shaped curve known as the normal distribution such that about

two-thirds of the sample proportions lie within one standard deviation on either side of the mean.

23. See, e.g., Johnson v. White, 353 F.Supp. 69, 75 (D.Conn.1972) ("The defendant adopted a pre-sample confidence interval of 95%, plus or minus 10%"), affirmed in part 528 F.2d 1228 (2d Cir.).

dence level narrows the range of the estimate; but there is more risk in concluding that the population value lies within the narrower interval. Second, for a given confidence and a fixed sample size, the width of the interval depends on how homogeneous the population is. If nearly every consumer would be confused (or nearly no one would be), then there will be minimal sampling variability, since almost all the possible samples can be expected to look alike. Hence, the confidence interval for any sample will be very narrow. On the other hand, if the population is highly variable, then there are more chances to draw aberrant samples, and the computed confidence interval for any sample will be larger. Third, whatever the makeup of the population, larger samples give more reliable results than smaller ones. However, the point of diminishing returns rapidly is reached in that adding the same amount to the sample size does little to narrow the confidence interval.[24] It is wrong to believe that one always needs to sample a substantial proportion of a large population to obtain an accurate estimate of a population parameter.

In assessing the statistical error of a survey, therefore, the courts should look to the

interval estimates rather than to untutored intuitions as to how large a sample is needed. Deciding what level of confidence is appropriate in a particular case, however, is a policy question and not a statistical issue.[25] Finally, in making use of surveys, it is important to remember that the statistical analysis does not address the non-random sources of error. A small confidence interval is not worth much if the data collection is badly flawed.[26]

**WESTLAW
REFERENCES**

opinion /2 poll /p evidence admissib! inadmissib!

§ 209. Statistical Studies: Correlations and Causes: Statistical Evidence of Discrimination

Survey evidence, as we described it in the previous section, involved sampling from some population, deriving statistics from the sample data, and offering some conclusion about the population in light of these sample statistics. In this section, we describe applications and extensions of this approach used to supply and interpret evidence on the issue of causation.[1] In environmental or drug litigation, for instance, a party may seek to

---

24. These properties follow from the remarks supra at n. 21. The width of the confidence interval is inversely proportional to the square root of the sample size. Thus, if the sample size is increased from, say, 50 to 200, the confidence interval is cut in half. To achieve another reduction of one-half, however, it is necessary to increase the sample size not by another 350, but by 600, to reach a size of 800. A third reduction of one-half would require a sample of 3200, and things only get worse as we continue. In sampling from very large populations, then, it is not the percentage of the population that is sampled that is important, but the absolute size of the sample. A sample of 100 is about as good for a population of 30,000 as it is for one of 3,000.

25. See Gonzales et al., supra n. 15, at 9; Kaye, Book Review, 80 Mich.L.Rev. 833, 840 (1980).

26. Fienberg, Comment, 77 J.Am.Stat.Ass'n 784, 785 (1982); Gonzales et al., supra n. 15. A distressing number of surveys completed by reputable survey organizations seem to be grossly deficient in complying with acceptable data collection techniques. See Bailor & Lauphier, Development of Survey Methods to Assess Survey Practices: A Report of the ASA Pilot Project on the Assessment of Survey Practices and Data Quali-

ty in Surveys of Human Populations (1978) (15 out of 26 federally sponsored surveys and 7 out of 10 others were so poorly planned and conducted that they "did not meet their objectives," and "pervasive" problems "of profound importance" went "unrecognized").

§ 209

1. In and of itself, statistical analysis can never prove that some factor A causes some outcome B. It can show that in a sample of observations, occurrences of B tend to be associated with those of A, and it can suggest that this statistical association probably would be observed for repeated samples. But the association, even though "statistically significant," need not be causal. For instance, a third factor C could be causing both A and B. Thus, over some time period, there may be a correlation between the number of people smoking cigarettes and the number of certain crimes committed, but if told that the population was growing rapidly during this time, no one would think that this proves that smoking causes crime. Experimental design and some forms of statistical analysis can help control for the effects of other variables, but even these merely help formulate, confirm or refute theories about causal relationships.

prove that a chemical is toxic or carcinogenic. Laboratory experiments, clinical tests, or epidemiologic studies may be relied on, but the conclusions of the scientific studies will involve statistical assessments.[2] In civil rights cases, a party may seek to prove that a class or an individual has been subjected to unlawful discrimination. Again, statistical evidence may be useful.[3] In antitrust litigation, a party may use statistical analysis to show that a merger has caused excessive concentration in the relevant market.[4] In business litigation generally, a party may apply statistical techniques to estimate lost profits or other damages resulting from illegal conduct.[5] In these and other sorts of cases,[6] the statistics, and inferences drawn from them, usually will be admissible via the testimony of a suitably qualified expert.[7]

The weight that may be given such testimony will depend, of course, on the skill of counsel and the ability and preparation of the witness. In addition, the methods that the expert uses to analyze and interpret that data, so as to assist the court or jury in understanding it, may be of great importance in determining the outcome. This section outlines one of the statistical concepts most frequently encountered in connection with sophisticated statistical proofs.[8] Because most cases addressing the usefulness of this concept currently arise in the context of discrimination issues, we shall draw on a few of the developments in this area to illustrate some general points about the presentation of statistical evidence.[9]

The courts have relied heavily on statistical evidence in cases in which a criminal defendant alleges that he was indicted by an unconstitutionally selected grand jury or an unconstitutionally empaneled petit jury.[10] There is no constitutionally permissible basis for systematically excluding, say, members of defendant's race from the population of citizens who are eligible for jury duty. Where direct evidence of discrimination is unavailable, or where additional proof is desired, statistical methods have been pressed into service. The usual procedure is to compare the proportion of the persons eligible for jury service who are in the class allegedly discriminated against [11] with the corresponding proportion appearing on jury venires or pools over some period of time.

2. See, cases cited, Delgado, Beyond Sindell: Relaxation of Cause-in-Fact Rules for Indeterminate Plaintiffs, 70 Calif.L.Rev. 881, 884 n. 15, 888 n. 34 (1982); Note, 35 Rutgers L.Rev. 163 (1982).

3. See generally Baldus & Cole, Statistical Proof of Discrimination (1980); Shafer & Ladd, Discrimination in Mortgage Lending (1981).

4. Lozowick, Steiner & Miller, Law and Quantitative Multivariate Analysis: An Encounter, 66 Mich.L. Rev. 1641 (1968).

5. Contemporary Mission v. Famous Music Corp., 557 F.2d 918, 927–928 (2d Cir. 1977); Spray-Rite Service Corp. v. Monsanto Co., 684 F.2d 1226, 1240–1241 (7th Cir. 1982).

6. See, e.g., Bishop v. Lomenzo, 350 F.Supp. 576, 583 n. 6 (E.D.N.Y.1972) (regression study showing relationship between voter turnout and the date on which voter registration closes); Downton, Legal Probability and Statistics, 145 J. Royal Statistical Soc.A. 395 (1982); Fienberg & Straf, Statistical Assessments as Evidence, id. 410; Gray, Statistics and the Law, 56 Mathematics Mag. 67 (1983).

7. Spray-Rite Service Corp. v. Monsanto Co., 684 F.2d 1226 (7th Cir. 1982); supra §§ 13, 208.

8. One elementary text that gives clear coverage of most important statistical techniques is Weiss & Has-

sell, Introductory Statistics (1982). Several introductory texts aimed at law students are in preparation, and one has been published. Barnes, Statistics as Proof: Fundamentals of Quantitative Evidence (1983). More specialized works on regression methods and linear models are cited infra at n. 26.

9. For more comprehensive or detailed coverage, see Baldus & Cole, supra n. 3; Connolly & Peterson, The Use of Statistics in Equal Employment Opportunity Litigation (1979); Kaye, Statistical Evidence of Discrimination, 77 J.Am. Statistical Ass'n 773 (1982).

10. Castaneda v. Partida, 430 U.S. 482 (1977); Finkelstein, Quantitative Methods in Law (1978); De Cani, Statistical Evidence in Jury Discrimination Cases, 65 J.Crim.L. & Criminology 234 (1974); Kairys, Kadane & Lehoczky, Jury Representativeness: Mandate for Multiple Source Lists, 65 Calif.L.Rev. 776 (1977); Kaye, supra n. 9; Zeisel, Dr. Spock and the Case of the Vanishing Women Jurors, 37 U.Chi.L.Rev. 1 (1969); Annot., 1 A.L.R.2d 1291.

11. This population proportion typically is obtained from census data. Inasmuch as the population changes over time and not every adult is eligible for jury service, some complications can arise. United States ex rel. Barksdale v. Blackburn, 610 F.2d 253, 262, 266 (5th Cir. 1980), cert. denied 454 U.S. 1056; Kaye, supra n. 9, at 780.

Substantial underrepresentation is taken as evidence of discrimination.[12] In early cases, the courts made purely intuitive assessments of the disparity in the proportions.[13]

Many recent cases use formal statistical reasoning to evaluate the quantitative evidence.[14] The logic begins from the assumption that selection of potential jurors is a random process, like blindly drawing differently colored marbles from an urn, in which the chance that a person in the protected class will be selected is the same in each instance. Under the "null" hypothesis, which is consistent with the defendant's position that there is no discrimination, the probability of picking a member of the protected class each time is simply the overall proportion of these individuals in the eligible population. The alternative to this hypothesis is not always specified clearly.[15] The statistical analyst calculates the probability that so few members of the protected class would be chosen for jury service if each selection were made by the random process described

above with the parameter stated in the null hypothesis. This probability is called a "P-value." It states the chance that the observed disparity resulted from bad luck, or coincidence. If it is very small, it is taken to indicate that the null hypothesis is implausible.[16] If the P-value, or probability of the data given the assumptions behind the null hypothesis, is large, it is taken to indicate that this hypothesis of no discrimination is consistent with the data. The P-value thus serves as an index of the statistical force of the quantitative evidence. The smaller the P-value, the more unlikely it is that the statistical disparity was the result of the chance process.

But it is not the only such index, and some statisticians do not think that it is the best.[17] One problem with its use in court is the tendency of some expert witnesses or judges to assume that because there is an arbitrary convention of insisting on P-values of .05 or less before labelling scientific findings "statistically significant," this same number

---

12. The courts usually measure the disparity by the difference between the population proportion (as deduced from census data) and the sample proportion (the actual rate of representation of jury venires). United States ex rel. Barksdale v. Blackburn, 610 F.2d 253, 256–257, 262–264 (5th Cir. 1980), cert. denied 454 U.S. 1056 (reviewing Supreme Court decisions). Kairys, Kadane & Lehoczky, supra n. 9, criticize the use of this "absolute disparity standard." There can be other statistical evidence of discrimination in a selection process. A particular pattern in the assignment of jurors can be suspicious. United States ex rel. Barksdale v. Blackburn, supra, at 268–69; Finkelstein, supra n. 9; Zeisel, Race Bias in the Administration of the Death Penalty: The Florida Experience, 95 Harv.L. Rev. 456 (1981).

13. Swain v. Alabama, 380 U.S. 202 (1965); Finkelstein, supra n. 10.

14. The rule in at least one federal circuit is that significance testing is mandatory for any statistical demonstration of racial discrimination. Moultrie v. Martin, 690 F.2d 1078, 1082–1083 (4th Cir. 1982).

15. Whether they are stated or not, only two such alternative hypotheses are ever considered in the mathematical analysis described here. A "one-sided" hypothesis states that the chance for selecting any member of the protected class for jury duty is less than the population proportion. In contrast, a "two-sided" hypothesis does not state on which side of the population proportion the true probability of selection falls. It only asserts that the individual selection probability dif-

fers from the population proportion. If the analyst uses a so-called "one-tailed" test, he or she is testing the null hypothesis against the one-sided alternative. A "two-tailed" test uses the two-sided alternative. Both these alternative hypotheses are stated within the context of the probability model that posits independent random selections of jurors with the same chance of selection for members of the protected class every time.

16. Procedurally, this will result in the statistics on underrepresentation being said to establish a prima facie case of discrimination, at least if there is some other evidence suggesting discrimination or the opportunity to discriminate. Most commentators agree that a gross disparity that cannot plausibly be explained by the null hypothesis should be enough, in itself, to establish the prima facie case. See Kaye, supra n. 9, at 776.

17. A.W.F. Edwards, Likelihood: An Account of the Statistical Concept of *Likelihood* and its Application to Scientific Inference (1972); Fienberg, Comment: The Increasing Sophistication of Statistical Assessments of Evidence in Discrimination Litigation, 77 J.Am. Statistical Ass'n 784 (1982); Natrella, The Relationship Between Confidence Intervals and Tests of Significance, 14 Am. Statistician 20 (1960). For a review of the alternatives, see Kaye, Book Review, 80 Mich.L.Rev. 833 (1982); Kaye, supra n. 9. Moore, Statistics: Concepts and Controversies 290–95 (1979), provides a simple and useful survey of some of the difficulties with using P-values routinely to test for significance.

should be required before the factfinder may rely on the quantitative results.[18] If the P-value is not to be misleading, its meaning must be clearly understood.[19] The factfinder must realize that the P-value is not itself evidence. It is not the statistic that directly states how large the observed underrepresentation is. It is merely one measure of the probative force of statistical evidence, and an incomplete measure at

that.[20] This is not to deny that it is a useful concept. Properly understood, it may assist the court (or, in appropriate cases, the jury) in assessing the statistical evidence.

This approach also is used in employment discrimination cases.[21] There is more difficulty in defining the relevant population from which employees are drawn,[22] there are more variables to consider,[23] the sample sizes tend to be smaller,[24] and the mechanics

18. See, e.g., Castaneda v. Partida, 430 U.S. 482, 496 n. 17 (1977); Moultrie v. Martin, 690 F.2d 1078, 1082–1083 (4th Cir. 1982). For an exchange of views on this issue, compare Kaye, supra n. 9, with Fienberg, supra n. 17. Many statisticians warn against the thoughtless use of the conventional significance levels. See, e.g., Moore, supra n. 17, at 290.

19. The writing and testimony of experts does not always provide a satisfactory explanation. Some presentations use technical terms like "significance" and "confidence' in ways that suggest that a statistician can tell a court or jury how certain it can be of one or another conclusion. Braun, Statistics and the Law: Hypothesis Testing and Its Application to Title VII Cases, 32 Hastings L.J. 59, 87 (1980) ("the techniques developed in this article, when properly applied, are irrefutable in what they demonstrate. When led to a rejection of the null hypothesis at a level of significance of .05, a court can be 95% confident that a disparity of treatment of the relevant groups exists"). But concepts of significance and confidence do not translate so easily into statements about beliefs. Shafer, A Theory of Evidence (1976); Kaye, supra n. 17; supra § 208 at 625–26 (explaining the meaning of a confidence interval); infra n. 20. It could be argued that to avoid misleading a jury, experts should not be permitted to speak of a "confidence" level. Cf. Brilmayer & Kornhauser, Review: Quantitative Methods and Legal Decisions, 46 U.Chi.L.Rev. 116 (1978) (certitude of legal decisionmakers need and perhaps should not correspond with computations of probabilities, especially Bayesian calculations).

20. It is incomplete because it speaks only to the risk of an erroneous finding for the plaintiff. Dawson, Are Statisticians Being Fair to Employment Discrimination Plaintiffs, 21 Jurimetrics J. 1 (1980); Henkel & McKeown, Unlawful Discrimination and Statistical Proof: An Analysis, 22 Jurimetrics J. 34 (1981); Kaye, supra n. 17, at 844 n. 41.

21. Hazelwood v. United States, 433 U.S. 299 (1977) (using z-statistics but not giving the corresponding P-values); Baldus & Cole, supra n. 9; Connolly & Peterson, supra n. 9; Sullivan, Zimmer & Richards, Federal Statutory Law of Employment Discrimination (1980); Braun, supra n. 19; Kaye, supra n. 17; Smith & Abram, Quantitative Analysis and Proof of Employment Discrimination, 1981 U.Ill.L.F. 33.

22. Haber & Gastwirth, Specifying the Labor Market for Individual Firms, Monthly Labor Rev., Aug. 1978, at 26; Shoben, Probing the Discriminatory Ef-

fects of Employee Selection Procedures with Disparate Impact Analysis Under Title VII, 56 Tex.L.Rev. (1977); authorities cited supra n. 21.

23. Ste. Marie v. Eastern Railroad Association, 650 F.2d 395, 400–401 (2d Cir. 1981) (failure to account for differences in qualifications of male and female employees made statistics with vanishingly small P-values "totally wanting in probative value"); Pouncy v. Prudential Insurance Co., 668 F.2d 795, 803 (5th Cir. 1982) ("appellant's statistical evidence is deficient because it 'fails to take into account the fact that a number of factors operate simultaneously to influence the amount of salary [an employee] receives.' . . . The discrepancies between the mean salary of black employees and the mean salary of white employees hired in specific years may be explained by . . . different job levels, different skill levels, previous training, and experience: all may account for unequal salaries in an environment free of discrimination"); Coble v. Hot Springs School District, 682 F.2d 721, 730–733 (8th Cir. 1982) (because "the probative value of appellant's statistical data is undermined by the small sample size for promotions and the failure to [use regression analysis to] consider the effect of education and experience together on salary," no prima facie case was established).

24. Contrary to what some courts may have implied, Equal Employment Opportunity Commission v. American National Bank, 652 F.2d 1176, 1193 n. 12 (4th Cir. 1981); Coble v. Hot Springs School District, 682 F.2d 721, 730 (8th Cir. 1982), a small sample size does not make a P-value or confidence interval any the less meaningful or applicable. See Schmid v. Frosch, 680 F.2d 248, 249 n. 4 (D.C.Cir. 1982). It merely affects the method of computing these quantities, and it reduces the ability of the statistical test to discriminate between the hypotheses. That is, with a smaller sample size, insisting on a particular P-value makes it more difficult to reject the null hypothesis and therefore increases the risk of falsely retaining this hypothesis. To put it more technically, the smaller sample size diminishes the power of the test—it has less of an a priori chance of detecting a true difference. Kaye, supra n. 17, at 844 n. 41. Since choosing to reject the null hypothesis if the P-value is less than some fixed number (the significance level) creates the same risk of a false positive (an incorrect decision that would favor the plaintiff) whatever the sample size may be, and because the smaller sample size increases the risk of a false negative (an incorrect decision for the defendant),

of computing P-values may differ, but the meaning of the P-value and of "statistical significance" is the same.[25] When complicated statistical models are used to account for the effects of many variables, however, many subtle errors are possible,[26] and an uncritical acceptance of the estimates derived from these models and their calculated P-values can be misleading.[27] In short, for this form of scientific testimony, the battle is not usually over the admissibility of the statistical evidence or the use of concepts like the P-value to assess the evidence. Rather, the battlelines are drawn when it comes to the weight that should be given the evidence.[28]

 WESTLAW REFERENCES

p-value* & court(ca)

---

to the extent it is appropriate to treat observational data as if it were derived from a random sampling process (which is a matter that affects small and large samples equally), a small P-value is as compelling for a small sample as it is for a large one.

25. When discriminatory intent is an element in the cause of action, and when it cannot be established solely by proof of disparate impact, the legal significance of the statistical data and, hence, of any P-value is attenuated.

26. Peterson, Pitfalls in the Use of Regression Analysis for the Measurement of Equal Employment Opportunity, 5 Int'l J. Policy Analysis & Information Systems 43 (1981). For detailed discussions of regression analysis, including some attention to the techniques of establishing its appropriateness in a given application, see Belsley, Kuh & Welsch, Regression, Diagnostics: Identifying Influential Data and Sources of Collinearity (1980); Neter & Wasserstrom, Applied Linear Statistical Models (1974); Wannacott & Wannacott, Regression: A Second Course in Statistics (1981); Weisberg, Applied Linear Regression (1980). For discussions focusing on legal applications but paying less attention to the many technical sources of error, see Barnes, supra n. 8; Finkelstein, The Judicial Reception of Multiple Regression Studies in Race and Discrimination Cases, 80 Colum.L.Rev. 737 (1980); Fisher, Multiple Regression in Legal Proceedings, 80 Colum.L.Rev. 702 (1980). Regression models are not the only techniques for multivariate analysis, and any P-value or confidence interval for an estimate derived from a regression model rests on a set of restrictive assumptions that may not hold in practice. Consequently, in some cases another approach may be superior.

27. Given enough latitude in the number of variables and the form of a statistical model, a statistician

§ 210. Probabilities as Evidence: Identification Evidence Generally

The previous two sections discussed the use of probability calculations in connection with statistical studies. When the statistical analyst takes properly collected sample data, computes some statistics such as a proportion, a difference between two means, or a regression coefficient, and calculates a P-value or a confidence interval for each such statistic, the courts are willing to rely on the probabilities in assessing the force of the statistical evidence. Especially in criminal cases, however, the courts are substantially more reluctant to admit probability calculations intended to show the identity of a wrongdoer.[1] This section examines the admissibility of probability calculations relating to the myriad forms of identification evidence—eyewitness testimony, blood tests,

---

eventually can construct a particular model that will fit the data remarkably well and have low P-values for the quantities of interest. This same model easily can be worthless in the sense that it probably would not work well with any other data. Yet, models with as many as 128 variables have been relied on in court. See Fienberg, supra n. 17. Another problem is the tendency of some courts to misuse the descriptive statistic R-squared when, as is almost always the case, there are statistics or P-values that are much more to the point. See, e.g., Valentino v. Postal Service, 511 F.Supp. 917, 944 (D.D.C.1981), affirmed 674 F.2d 56 (D.C.Cir) (defendant's model said to give a better estimate of a regression coefficient merely because it "measured many more variables" and yielded a larger R-squared).

28. An emerging issue is whether P-values (or the test statistics that underlie them) should be used to formulate a rigid rule as to what is needed to establish or rebut a prima facie case involving statistical proof of disparate treatment or impact. See, e.g., Equal Employment Opportunity Commission v. American National Bank, 652 F.2d 1176, 1191 (4th Cir. 1981) (rejecting a mechanical rule for rebutting a prima facie case by means of a high P-value); Gay v. Waiters' and Dairy Lunchmen's Union, 694 F.2d 531, 551–553 (9th Cir. 1982) ("It would be improper to posit a quantitative threshold above which statistical evidence of disparate racial impact is sufficient as a matter of law to infer discriminatory intent, and below which it is insufficient as a matter of law").

§ 210

1. See generally Eggleston, Evidence, Proof and Probability (2d ed.1983); Finkelstein, Quantitative Methods in Law (1978); Ball, The Moment of Truth: Probability Theory and Standards of Proof, 14 Vand.L. Rev. 807 (1961); Birmingham, Remarks on 'Probability'

fingerprints, bitemarks, questioned document examinations, microanalysis, and so on.[2] The next section focuses on the role of probability calculations in paternity litigation.

In one important sense, all evidence is statistical. Admittedly, courts sometimes suggest that evidence about a class of objects cannot be used to support a conclusion about a particular member of the class.[3] But we rely on such evidence all the time. Law schools admit students with high grades and test scores because they have had favorable experiences with other such students,[4] sur-

geons perform drastic operations on patients because they have had beneficial effects in some proportion of cases in the past, legislatures enact statutes making it an offense to drive with a blood alcohol concentration exceeding an amount seen to impair the functioning of a sample of persons, and juries tend to convict or acquit defendants because of hunches or beliefs about how certain classes of people behave, and they award damages in wrongful death cases with the assistance of mortality tables that reflect the experiences of many other men or women.

in Law, 12 Ga.L.Rev. 535 (1978); Brilmayer & Kornhauser, Review: Quantitative Methods and Legal Decisions, 46 U.Chi.L.Rev. 116 (1978); Braun, Probability Theory as a Tool of Evidence in Criminal Cases, 1982 Utah L.Rev. 41; Broun & Kelly, Playing the Percentages and the Law of Evidence, 1970 U.Ill.L.F. 23 (1970); Cullison, Identification by Probabilities and Trial by Arithmetic, 6 Hous.L.Rev. 471 (1969); Ellman & Kaye, Probabilities and Proof: Can HLA and Blood Group Testing Prove Paternity, 54 N.Y.U.L.Rev. 1131 (1979); Fairley & Mosteller, A Conversation About Collins, 41 U.Chi.L.Rev. 242 (1974); Finkelstein & Fairley, A Bayesian Approach to Identification Evidence, 83 Harv.L.Rev. 489 (1970); Finney, Probabilities Based on Circumstantial Evidence, 72 J.Am. Statistical Ass'n 316 (1977); Gerjuoy, The Relevance of Probability Theory to Problems of Relevance, 18 Jurimetrics J. 1 (1977); Liddle, Mathematical and Statistical Probability as a Test of Circumstantial Evidence, 19 Case W.Res.L.Rev. 254 (1968); Kaye, The Laws of Probability and the Law of the Land, 47 U.Chi.L.Rev. 34 (1979); Osterburg, The Evaluation of Physical Evidence in Criminalistics, 60 J.Crim.L., Crimin., & Police Sci. 97 (1969); Saks & Kidd, Human Information Processing and Adjudication: Trial by Heuristics, 15 Law & Society 123 (1980–81); Stripinis, Probability Theory and Circumstantial Evidence, 22 Jurimetrics J. 59 (1981); Tribe, Trial by Mathematics: Precision and Ritual in the Legal Process, 84 Harv.L.Rev. 1329 (1971); Annot., 36 A.L.R.3d 1194.

2. For descriptions of or references to the techniques of scientific criminology, see supra § 207. Probability calculations also are offered from time to time in civil cases. Mapes Casino v. Maryland Casualty Co., 290 F.Supp. 186 (D.Nev.1968) (to show loss at crap tables due to employee defalcation); Gastwirth, A Probability Model of a Pyramid Scheme, Am. Statistician, May 1977, at 79; Meier & Zabell, Benjamin Pierce and the Howland Will, 75 J.Am. Statistical Ass'n 497 (1980); supra § 209.

3. United States v. Rangel-Gonzales, 617 F.2d 529, 532 (9th Cir. 1980) (that very few aliens, when advised of right to consult with Consulate, do so, "would not appear to have any bearing on what this particular individual would have done"). When it comes to inani-

mate objects, however, the courts are much quicker to recognize the usefulness of generalizations derived from the experience of others. Seese v. Volkswagenwerk A.G., 648 F.2d 833, 846 (3d Cir. 1981), cert. denied 454 U.S. 867 (government statistical reports showing that Volkswagen vans were more likely to eject occupants in an accident than other vans were admissible). A statistician might try to reconcile these results by reasoning that the inference in the first case is weaker because there is more variability among human beings or the circumstances they confront than there is among Volkswagen vans. Cf. United States v. Rangel-Gonzales, supra, at 532 n. 3 ("the party offering the evidence must at least show that the conduct of others . . . occurred in comparable circumstances"); Dorsey v. State, 276 Md. 638, 350 A.2d 665, 669 (1976) (manifest error to permit a detective to testify that 75–80% of his robbery arrests led to convictions, in part because of "the absence of any showing of similarity between the appellant's arrest and those other investigations"). Even so, it seems hard to deny that the statistical evidence as to people is not "relevant" under Rule 402. See Kaye, Paradoxes, Gedanken Experiments and the Burden of Proof, 1981 Ariz.L.J. 635, 639–640; supra § 185; cf. Saks & Kidd, supra n. 1, at 151–154 (decrying "the myth of particularized proof"). Thus, a more convincing distinction might be that where the statistical indicators pertain to volitional conduct, the courts are cautious because they place great weight on a conception of human autonomy and dignity that the coldly statistical analysis would undermine. To put it another way, shying away from the statistical predictions reflects a belief that everyone should have the opportunity to depart from the statistical norm. Cf. Underwood, Law and the Crystal Ball: Predicting Behavior with Statistical Inference and Individualized Judgment, 88 Yale L.J. 1408 (1979) (analyzing the policies and values that may lead decisionmakers to avoid using formal statistical methods of predicting individual behavior).

4. Of course, educational institutions (or employers) also may admit (or hire) such individuals to achieve a certain status or because those doing the admitting (or hiring) themselves have similar backgrounds and feel more comfortable in dealing with these persons.

So, too, any expert giving any opinion on whether the scientific test identifies the defendant as being the person who left the incriminating trace, such as a fingerprint, bullet, or bloodstain, necessarily bases this conclusion on an understanding or impression of how similar the items being compared are and how common it is to find items with these similarities.[5] If these beliefs have any basis in fact, it is to be found in the general experience of the criminalists or more exacting statistical studies [6] of these matters. In brief, the reluctance to allow testimony or argument about probabilities must be justified, if at all, on the basis of something other than an undifferentiated claim about the logical weakness of relying on probabilities derived from statistics about other persons or things. In fact, a variety

of more conventional concerns about "probability evidence"—a term that is something of a misnomer [7]—surface in the decisions in this area. These relate to the probative value of the explicit quantification and the tendency of the seemingly impressive numbers to mislead or confuse the jury.[8]

To begin with, for more than a hundred years there have been attempts to compute the probability of observing a conjunction of certain incriminating characteristics by assuming that each characteristic is statistically independent and that the probabilities of these presumably independent characteristics could be obtained by introspection.[9] In what may be the most notorious of these cases, police apprehended a man and a woman fitting descriptions supplied by eyewitnesses near the scene of a robbery. The

---

5. See Commonwealth v. Drayton, 386 Mass. 39, 434 N.E.2d 997, 1005 (1982).

6. Aitken & MacDonald, An Application of Discrete Kernel Methods to Forensic Odontology, 28 Applied Statistics 55, 58–59 (1979); Ryland, Kopec & Somerville, The Evidential Value of Automobile Paint. Part II: Frequency of Occurrence of Topcoat Colors, 26 J. Forensic Sci. 64 (1981).

7. The phrase "probability evidence" is used as a convenient shorthand for testimony or argument involving probability calculations. The probabilities are not themselves evidence. They are numbers ranging from zero to one that may be used in drawing conclusions from the statistical or other evidence. When counsel uses such numbers as rhetorical flourishes to emphasize the strength of the evidence, no question of the admissibility of evidence is raised. Hicks, Famous Jury Speeches 216–229 (1925) (in arguing that a document was not authentic, counsel told the jury to "Take up your table of logarithms and figure away until you are blind, and such an accident could not happen in as many thousand, billion, trillion, quintillion years as you can express by figures").

8. The leading expositor of these concerns is Tribe, supra 1. See also Broun & Kelly, supra n. 1. For commentary arguing that these dangers are overstated, see Saks & Kidd, supra n. 1; Stripinis, supra n. 1; Wagner, Book Review, 1979 Duke L.J. 1071. A related argument is that if the probability evidence is all there is to go on, it may force a quantification, and thence a degradation, of the burden of persuasion or the presumption of innocence. See Nesson, Reasonable Doubt and Permissive Inferences, 92 Harv.L.Rev. 1187 (1978); Tribe, supra. For conflicting views on the corresponding problem of "naked statistical evidence" in civil cases, see Brook, Inevitable Errors: The Preponderance of the Evidence Standard in Civil Litigation, 18 U. Tulsa L.J. 79 (1982) (reviewing the literature); Callen,

Notes on a Grand Illusion: Some Limits on the Use of Bayesian Theory in Evidence Law, 57 Ind.L.J. 1 (1982); Kaye, The Limits of the Preponderance of the Evidence Standard, 1982 Am.B.Foundation J. 487; Tyree, Proof and Probability in the Anglo-American Legal System, 23 Jurimetics J. 89 (1982).

9. Miller v. State, 240 Ark. 340, 399 S.W.2d 268, 270 (1966) (taking the probability that two randomly selected soil samples would have the same color to be $1/10$, that they would have the texture to be $1/100$, and the same density, $1/1000$, the expert testified that "On random basis when you get two samples to match all these, it would be one in one million"); People v. Collins, 68 Cal.2d 319, 66 Cal.Rptr. 497, 438 P.2d 33 (1968); People v. Risley, 214 N.Y. 75, 86–87, 108 N.E. 200, 203 (1915) (expert calculated that the probability of defendant's typewriter producing letters with peculiarities that matched those on an allegedly forged document was "one in four thousand million"); Meier & Zabell, supra n. 2 (testimony in 1867 that 30 matches in the strokes of a contested signature on a will revealed that it had been traced, since the probability of so many matches arising by chance was "once in 2,666 millions of millions of millions"); cf. Commonwealth v. Drayton, 386 Mass. 39, 434 N.E.2d 997, 1005 (1982) (fingerprint examiner stated on re-direct examination that the probability that prints with 12 points of similarity could be made by two different people was "one out of 387 trillion"); State v. Sneed, 76 N.M. 349, 414 P.2d 858 (1966), after remand 78 N.M. 615, 435 P.2d 768 (expert's calculation of 240 billion to one odds for a combination of characteristics, including the use of the alias "Robert Crosset," was improperly admitted even though there was some empirical basis (including an examination of the frequencies of names in a telephone directory) for the probabilities that were multiplied together, because "the validity of the estimates [had] not been demonstrated").

prosecutor proposed figures for the frequencies of such things as an interracial couple in a car, a girl with a pony tail, a partly yellow automobile, a man with a mustache, and so on. A mathematics professor testified to the rule that the joint probability of a series of independent events is the product of the probabilities of each event. Applying this rule to the "conservative estimates" that he had propounded, the prosecutor concluded that there was but one chance in 12 million that any couple possessed the distinctive characteristics of the defendants, and he argued that "the chances of anyone else besides these defendants being there, . . . having every similarity, . . . is something like one in a billion." [10]

In these cases, the appellate courts hold that it is error to admit such testimony on the ground that the hypothesized values used in computing the probability of the joint event are sheer speculation.[11] Because such computations therefore have little basis in fact and are presented in the guise of expert analysis, they are excluded under the principle that their prejudicial impact clearly outweighs their probative value.

In another group of cases, there is some data that can be employed in calculating the joint probability. While many forensic experts are content to describe the points of similarity between the incriminating traces and material taken from the defendant or his belongings and to leave it to jury to decide how unlikely it would be to find all these similarities by mere coincidence,[12] from time to time, the experts testify to vanishingly small probabilities.[13] The appellate

10. People v. Collins, 68 Cal.2d 319, 66 Cal.Rptr. 497, 438 P.2d 33 (1968).

11. Miller v. State, 240 Ark. 340, 399 S.W.2d 268, 270 (1966), supra n. 9 ("Dr. Mathews had made no tests on which he could reasonably base his probabilities . . . nor did he base his testimony on studies of such tests made by others;" hence "Admission of the unsubstantiated, speculative testimony on probabilities was clearly erroneous"); People v. Risley, 214 N.Y. 75, 108 N.E. 200 (1915), supra n. 9 ("The statement of the witness was not based upon actual observed data, but was simply speculative"); cf. Commonwealth v. Drayton, 386 Mass. 39, 434 N.E.2d 997 (1982), supra n. 9 ("if admissible at all [a probability of coincidence] should at least be accompanied by an expert explanation of the calculations on which it is based"). People v. Collins also relied on two other defects in the testimony. The court criticized the expert's use of the multiplication rule for the probabilities of independent events because there had been no showing that the events were independent and there was reason to believe that many were in fact dependent. This criticism is not as powerful as it first might appear to be. The more general formula for computing the probability of a joint event when the conjoined events are dependent also involves multiplying a series of probabilities. Since the values for the probabilities that are multiplied together are contrived anyway, one could apply the appropriate formula to suitably manufactured probabilities to reach the same result. See Fairley & Mosteller, supra n. 1. Second the *Collins* court reasoned that the jury would misuse even a correctly calculated probability. This argument is discussed below.

12. United States v. Hickey, 596 F.2d 1082, 1084, 1089 (1st Cir. 1979), cert. denied 444 U.S. 853 (inspection of hairs revealed that the samples were "microscopically identical," and hence that the incriminating hairs "could have" been the defendant's); United States v. Cyphers, 553 F.2d 1064, 1071–1072 (7th Cir.

1977), cert. denied 434 U.S. 843 ("the expert's opinion that the hairs found on the items used in the robbery 'could have come' from the defendants was entitled to be admitted for whatever value the jury might give it"); State v. Washington, 229 Kan. 47, 622 P.2d 986, 988 (1981) (although foreign pubic hairs left on murder victim showed 21 microscopic similarities and no differences when compared to defendant's, expert was unable to say that the foreign hairs "came from [defendant] beyond any scientific doubt").

13. United States v. Massey, 594 F.2d 676, 679 (8th Cir. 1979) (expert testified that "the Canadians have done a study where they have come up with a chance of one in 4,500 these hairs could have come from another individual"); State v. Garrison, 120 Ariz. 255, 258–259, 585 P.2d 563, 566–567 (1978) (expert testified that "the probability factor of two sets of teeth being identical in a case similar to this is, approximately, eight in one million"); State v. Smiley, 27 Ariz.App. 314, 317, 554 P.2d 910, 914 (1976) ("one out of a thousand probability" that three different girls had the same uncommon type of hair); People v. Woodward, No. 108551 (Cal.Super.Ct., San Mateo County, July 7, 1964) (expert presenting the results of neutron activation analysis of paint samples testified that the chance of a coincidental match for the seven elements detected was one in 100,000 and that it was therefore 99.98% certain that the tool used in a burglary was the defendant's), criticized in Comment, 59 Calif.L.Rev. 997 (1971); People v. DiGiacomo, 71 Ill.App.3d 56, 27 Ill. Dec. 232, 233–234, 388 N.E.2d 1281, 1282–1283 (1979) ("the chances of the [hair] sample . . . belonging to another person would be 1 in 4500"); Commonwealth v. Drayton, 386 Mass. 39, 434 N.E.2d 997, 1005 (1982) (chance of two people leaving fingerprints that have 12 points of similarities is "one out of 387 trillion"); State v. Carlson, 267 N.W.2d 170, 173 (Minn. 1978) ("a 1-in-800 chance that the pubic hairs stuck to the victim were not [defendant's] and a 1-in-4,500

responses to estimates that have some empirical basis are more divided.[14] Although very few cases can be found excluding computations that the court considered well founded,[15] the reasons given for excluding some of the calculations are that the jury would misconstrue the meaning of the probability or overemphasize the number, or

that it would be too difficult to explain its true meaning.[16]

In evaluating these decisions, it is important to distinguish between explicit calculations of the probability of guilt or coincidence and the presentation of relevant background statistics.[17] If the offender, whoever he or she may have been, left a

chance [for] the head hairs found on the victim''); State v. Scarlett, 121 N.H. 37, 426 A.2d 25, 28 (1981) (FBI agent testified, incorrectly, that a study showed that "when hair specimens are found to be consistent with respect to all these different microscopic characteristics . . . , the chances of them having come from anyone else are forty-five to one", rather than $1/4500$); State v. Coolidge, 109 N.H. 403, 260 A.2d 547, 559 (1969) (expert testified that matches among particles of clothing would occur coincidentally with a probability of $1/10^{27}$), reversed on other grounds 403 U.S. 443, rehearing denied 404 U.S. 874, computation criticized, Broun & Kelly, supra § 209 n. 24, at 47, and Tribe, supra n. 24, § 209 at 1342 n. 40; State v. Sneed, 76 N.M. 349, 414 P.2d 858 (1966), after remand 78 N.M. 615, 435 P.2d 768 (described supra n. 9); Kuo, Linking a Bloodstain to a Missing Person by Genetic Inheritance, 27 J. Forensic Sci. 438, 442 (1982) (reporting that testimony that "eight in a thousand randomly selected couples would possess the necessary traits by those six genetic markers to qualify as parents of the person whose blood was found on the boat" contributed to a conviction in a kidnapping and extortion case); cf. People v. Trujillo, 32 Cal.2d 105, 194 P.2d 681, 684 (1948) ("the chances were one in a hundred billion that this number of matches [among fibers from clothing] would be a coincidence," but the opinion does not indicate how this number was calculated), cert. denied 335 U.S. 887; People v. Middleton, 54 N.Y.2d 42, 444 N.Y.S.2d 581, 585, 429 N.E.2d 100 ("the odds against the [dental] characteristics . . . being duplicated in any other person's mouth were 'astronomical' ''); State v. Clayton, 646 P.2d 723 (Utah 1982) ("probability testimony" about hair samples, but opinion does not give numbers).

14. Compare United States v. Massey, 594 F.2d 676, 679–681 (8th Cir. 1979) (where an expert referred to a study indicating that the probability of matching hair samples by coincidence was 1/4500 but could not explain this study, it was plain error for the prosecutor to argue that the evidence was "better than 99.44 percent . . . better than Ivory soap, if you remember the commercial" because "By using such misleading mathematical odds the prosecutor 'confuse[d] the probability of concurrence of the identifying marks with the probability of mistaken identification' ''); State v. Carlson, 267 N.W.2d 170 (Minn.1978) (hair); State v. Sneed, 76 N.M. 349, 414 P.2d 858 (1966) (described supra n. 9) with United States ex rel. DiGiacomo v. Franzen, 680 F.2d 515 (7th Cir. 1982) (hair); State v. Garrison, 120 Ariz. 255, 258–259, 585 P.2d 563, 566–567 (1978); People v. Trujillo, 32 Cal.2d 105, 112–13, 194 P.2d 681, 685–86 (1948), cert. denied 335 U.S. 887; People v. DiGiacomo, 7 Ill.App.3d 56, 388 N.E.2d 1281, 1283

(1979) (hair); State v. Coolidge, 109 N.H. 403, 417–423, 260 A.2d 547, 558–561 (1969) (particles of clothing), reversed on other grounds 403 U.S. 443; State v. Clayton, 646 P.2d 723, 727 (Utah 1982) (probability testimony about hair admissible); cf. Commonwealth v. Drayton, 386 Mass. 39, 434 N.E.2d 997, 1006 (1982) (avoiding deciding whether a quantitative statement of the probability of coincidence is admissible, but noting that although such testimony "raises special problems," "probability figures that are offered only to show the basis of an expert's opinion, and are presented in a way that minimizes the chance of misleading the jury, might stand on different footing").

When the probabilities are derived from studies that the expert is not prepared to defend, a hearsay objection may be effective. See State v. Scarlett, 121 N.H. 37, 426 A.2d 25, 28 (1981); supra § 15; infra § 324.2. But see State v. Garrison, supra; State v. Clayton, supra, 646 P.2d at 725–727.

15. State v. Carlson, 267 N.W.2d 170, 176 (Minn. 1978), may be the only reported case where a court squarely held that it was error to admit a probability "based on empirical scientific data of unquestioned validity." Ironically, the study on which the probability estimates in that case were founded has since been questioned. See Barnette & Ogle, Probabilities and Human Hair Comparison, 27 J. Forensic Sci. 272 (1982). The Massachusetts Supreme Judicial Court has intimated that it may not follow *Carlson* and the Utah Supreme Court has declined to do so. See supra n. 14.

16. See People v. Collins, 68 Cal.2d 319, 320, 66 Cal. Rptr. 497, 438 P.2d 33 (1968) ("Mathematics, a veritable sorcerer in our computerized society, while assisting the trier of fact in the search for truth, must not cast a spell over him"); State v. Carlson, 267 N.W.2d 170, 176 (Minn.1978) ("psychological impact of the suggestion of mathematical precision" cannot be dispelled, and "Testimony expressing opinions or conclusions in terms of . . . probability can make the uncertain seem all but proven, and suggest, by quantification, satisfaction of the requirement that guilt be established 'beyond a reasonable doubt' ''). For a different view, see State v. Clayton, 646 P.2d 723, 727 n. 1 (Utah 1982) ("We do not share that philosophy having a higher opinion of the jury's ability to weigh the credibility of such figures when properly presented and challenged").

17. State v. Washington, 229 Kan. 47, 622 P.2d 986, 994–995 (1981) (citing cases to support the proposition that in contrast to probabilities not based on adequate data, "population percentages on the percentage of certain combinations of blood characteristics, based on established facts, are admissible as relevant to identification"); infra n. 20. Even in State v. Carlson, 267

bloodstain at the scene of the crime that matches the defendant's blood types, the scientific evidence cannot be interpreted intelligently without some knowledge of how frequently these blood types occur in the relevant population.[18] We have already remarked that if the expert offers any conclusion as to whether the defendant left the incriminating trace, he or she is relying, either explicitly or *sub rosa*, on estimates of these quantities. Without being informed of such background statistics, the jury is left to its own speculations. Where reasonable estimates of the population frequencies are available, they should not be kept from the jury. To be sure, there are risks in this policy. A juror who hears that only one out of every five, or for that matter, one out of every 10,000 persons, possesses the traits that characterize the true offender may be tempted to subtract this statistic from one to

arrive at the incorrect conclusion that the remainder is the probability that the defendant is guilty.[19] Nevertheless, it should not be so difficult for defense counsel to correct any such misapprehension by pointing out that the frequency estimate merely establishes that the defendant is one member of a class of persons who have the incriminating characteristics.[20] The distribution of these characteristics in the population at large simply determines whether this class of persons whom the scientific evidence would identify as a possible offender is large or small.[21]

In principle, a statistician could do more than state the frequency at which the scientific tests would implicate persons. First, in those cases in which the identifying characteristics were not the very basis on which the defendant was picked from the general population, the expert could be explicit about the P-value for the findings.[22] Second, val-

---

N.W.2d 170, 175 (Minn.1978), the court held that it was error to allow an explicit estimate of the probability of misidentification based on hair samples, but it did not suggest that there was any error in expert testimony that "only .85 percent of the population would have blood with the same combination of . . . characteristics as the victim's blood and the matching stains found on [defendant's] jacket".

18. Sensabaugh, Biochemical Markers of Individuality, in Forensic Science Handbook 338, 403 (Saferstein ed. 1982) ("the interpretation of individualization typing results is intimately tied to population frequency statistics; without being provided the appropriate statistical information the triers of fact have no rational basis for deciding the significance of a type-for-type match"). This observation applies to more than blood typing. Even fingerprint evidence, which the courts often assert uniquely identifies individuals, merely establishes a probability. Aitken & MacDonald, supra n. 2, at 58; Osterburg, Parthasarathy, Raghavan & Solove, Development of a Mathematical Formula for the Calculation of Fingerprint Probabilities Based on Individual Characteristics, 72 J.Am.Statistical Ass'n 772 (1977). On the other hand, obtaining reliable estimates of the population frequencies can be difficult. Barnette & Ogle, supra, n. 15; Osterburg, An Inquiry into the Nature of Proof, 9 J.Forensic Sci. 413, 420–426 (1964) (survey indicating that fingerprint experts vary in their estimates of the frequency of particular print characteristics); Comment, supra n. 13. All too often, the sample statistics are treated as if they permit an exact statement of the population parameters.

19. If there are only two possibilities—that the trace evidence comes from defendant or that the match is coincidental—and if the probability of the latter event is very small, this intuitive but fallacious interpretation may be approximately correct. See Meier & Zabell, supra n. 2, at 502.

20. Ellman & Kaye, supra n. 1, at 1146; Comment, supra n. 13, at 1016–1017. Contra Jonakait, When Blood Is Their Argument, 1983 u. Ill.L.F. 369.

21. People v. Lindsey, 84 Cal.App.3d 851, 149 Cal. Rptr. 47 (1978) ("The chemist stated that approximately 36 percent of the population would secrete type 'O' blood antigenes [sic] into bodily fluids such as semen"); Shanks v. State, 185 Md. 437, 45 A.2d 85, 90 (1945) ("if the jury or judge is told that 45% of the population have 'O' blood, we cannot assume that this statement would be disregarded and not given its proper weight"); State v. Carlson, 267 N.W.2d 170, 175 (Minn. 1978) (incriminating genetic markers would be found in .85% of population). See generally Tribe, supra n. 1; Comment, supra n. 13, at 1028, 1039–1071.

22. Roughly speaking, the P-value is the probability of the evidence given the null hypothesis. See supra § 209 (discussing P-values in discrimination cases). If the null hypothesis in this context is that the trace evidence did not come from the defendant, then the P-value is the probability that the scientific test or identification procedure would give a positive result for a person selected at random from the relevant population. Thus, if the test is perfectly accurate, it is simply the proportion of people in the relevant population with the incriminating traits. As indicated in the text, this method of obtaining the P-value presupposes that the suspect has been selected for testing on the basis of traits that are statistically independent of those that the test detects. Obviously, this assumption does not hold in a case like People v. Collins, where the selection of the suspects is highly correlated with the characteristics in question. On the other hand, in cases of individualization by immunogenic markers, the police do

iant efforts have been made to calculate conditional probabilities pertaining to the number of people in some population who have the incriminating characteristics.[23] One could imagine admitting testimony about these probabilities.[24] Finally, and perhaps most satisfying from the mathematical standpoint, it has been proposed that the expert apply Bayes' rule to show jurors how the frequency data would increase a previously established probability that the person tested is the one who left the incriminating traces.[25] This proposal has been attacked on both philosophical [26] and practical [27] grounds. It has been said in reply that the pragmatic objections are the more persuasive.[28] Certainly, having an expert testify to the "probability of guilt" given the evidence

would be inadvisable.[29] But whether the benefits of using this method of statistical inference solely to educate the jury by displaying the probative force of the evidentiary findings would be worth the costs in terms of time-consumption and possible confusion is a closer question.[30] Outside of the parentage testing area, however, Bayesian calculations rarely are seen in court.[31]

In general, it appears that the explicit use of the theories of probability and statistical inference, either as a basis for the opinions of the experts themselves or as a course of education for jurors in how to think about scientific identification evidence, remains controversial. As long as counsel and the experts do not try to place a scientific seal

---

not normally identify suspects on the basis of any knowledge of these traits.

Although there are dangers in having criminalists whose expertise does not extend to the theory of statistical inference testify about probabilities (or for attorneys to try to describe them), see, e.g., State v. Garrison, 120 Ariz. 255, 585 P.2d 563 (1978) (dissenting opinion); Kirk & Kingston, Evidence Evaluation and Problems of General Criminalistics, 9 J.Forensic Sci. 434 (1964), it also should be kept in mind that jurors acting on their own initiative may well interpret a population frequency estimate as a probability.

23. The opinion in People v. Collins sported a mathematical appendix purporting to show that the conditional probability of there being more couples with the characteristics of the Collins's given that there was at least one such couple was .41. 68 Cal.2d at 333–335, 438 P.2d at 42–43, 66 Cal.Rptr. at 506–507. This calculation involves an approximation to the binomial distribution with the population size taken to be the reciprocal of the hypothesized frequency of the identifying characteristics. This assumption about the population size is contrived. See Fairley & Mosteller, supra n. 1. For proposed refinements and improvements, see Charrow & Smith, A Conversation About "A Conversation About Collins," 64 Geo.L.J. 669 (1976); Finney, supra n. 1; Smith & Charrow, Upper and Lower Bounds for Probability of Guilt Based on Circumstantial Evidence, 70 J.Am.Statistical Ass'n 555 (1975); Stripinis, supra n. 1.

24. Presumably, the defense might offer them to defuse the impact of numbers like the one out of twelve million figure in Collins.

25. See Good, Probability and the Weighing of Evidence 66–67 (1950); Finkelstein, supra n. 1, at 85–104; Cullison, supra n. 1, at 484–502; Ellman & Kaye, supra n. 1; Finkelstein & Fairley, supra n. 1; Fairley, Probabilistic Analysis of Identification Evidence, 2 J.Legal Stud. 493 (1973). The mechanics of this approach are briefly stated in the next section. The usual sugges-

tion is that the expert present an illustrative chart showing how, in view of the frequency with which the incriminating traits are to be found in the relevant population, the identification evidence would affect a broad spectrum of prior probabilities. The expert need not ask the jurors to choose any particular prior probability to express their estimate of the strength of the nontest evidence.

26. See Callen, supra n. 8; Brilmayer & Kornhauser, supra n. 1. Both these articles use the term "Bayesian" carelessly. They appear to object to the subjective or personal interpretation of probability as well as to Bayesian statistical inference (which treats a population parameter as a random variable). Bayesian inference requires one to accept the subjective interpretation, but the converse is not true. For a defense of the personal or subjective interpretation of probability, see Kaye, see n. 3.

27. See Tribe, supra note 1 (Bayesian calculations "dwarf soft variables," threaten the presumption of innocence and encourage jurors to err by misestimating and misusing the prior probability of guilt).

28. Ellman & Kaye, supra n. 1; Kaye, supra n. 1.

29. Nor does this seem to be what the proponents of Bayesian presentations have recommended. See Ellman & Kaye, supra n. 1; Finkelstein & Fairley, A Comment on "Trial by Mathematics," 84 Harv.L.Rev. 1801 (1971); supra n. 25.

30. Compare Finkelstein & Fairley, supra n. 25, and authorities cited, supra n. 8, with Tribe, A Further Critique of Mathematical Proof, 84 Harv.L.Rev. 1810 (1971).

31. But see Fienberg, Comment: The Increasing Sophistication of Statistical Assessments of Evidence in Discrimination Litigation, 77 J.Am.Statistical Ass'n 784 (1982) (advocating Bayesian analyses of data in discrimination cases); Fienberg & Kadane, The Presentation of Bayesian Statistical Analyses in Legal Proceedings, 32 The Statistician (in press).

of approval on results not shown to be scientifically based, however, it would seem that there is room for some judicious use of these theories to put the identification evidence in reasonable perspective.

 **WESTLAW REFERENCES**

"bayes' theorem" & court(ks)

§ 211. Probabilities as Evidence: Paternity Testing

Problems of questioned or disputed parentage have plagued mankind, perhaps ever since the origin of the species. The Talmud tells of a case in which a widow married her brother-in-law before the required three month waiting period after the death of her husband. She gave birth to a child scarcely six months later. The rabbis reasoned that either the child was a full term baby fathered by the deceased husband or a premature child of the second husband. Since the mother had shown no visible signs of pregnancy three months after her first husband's death, the matter was not easy to settle. As one rabbi said, "it is a doubt."[1]

Many legislators, courts, and commentators now think that newly discovered serologic and statistical methods permit such doubts to be dispelled in the vast majority of cases.[2] In section 205(B) we described the methods of detecting immunogenetic markers and the principles of human genetics that allow this information to be applied to resolve cases of disputed parentage. We saw that a majority of states now admit the results of blood and tissue typing tests not merely to exclude the alleged father as the biological father, but, when he is not excluded, to help prove that he is the biological father. In most, if not all of these jurisdictions, an expert may go beyond reporting the positive test findings. To assist the trier of fact in interpreting these positive results, he or she, under generally applicable evidentiary principles,[3] may give reliable estimates of the frequencies that characterize the distribution of the incriminating genetic markers in the population of males of the pertinent race. That is, if the population data warrant it, the expert may testify to the proportion of the relevant male population that the test would exclude—a parameter that is sometimes converted into the "probability of exclusion."[4] To this extent, the procedures

§ 211

1. For a Bayesian interpretation of the rabbinical arguments, see Rabinovitch, Probability and Statistical Inference in Ancient and Medieval Jewish Literature 58–60 (1973). As to the presumption of the husband's paternity, see § 343 n. 66 infra.

2. In essence, they are right, but most of the commentary and opinions are riddled with misconceptions and meaningless or obscure phrases. For instance, in holding that a state may not constitutionally require that an action to establish paternity be brought before the child is one year old, the Supreme Court noted that "Traditional blood tests do not prove paternity. They prove nonpaternity, excluding from the class of potential fathers a high percentage of the general male population. . . . More recent developments . . . have sought not only to 'prove nonpaternity' but also to predict paternity with a high degree of probability." Mills v. Habluetzel, 456 U.S. 91 n. 4 (1982). The only "more recent development" cited is HLA typing, which does exactly what the "traditional blood tests" do—it "excludes from the class of possible fathers a high percentage of the general male population." HLA typing, like other serologic tests, detects cell surface antigens. None of the tests "predicts paternity." None can "prove nonpaternity" except in the same sense that it

can prove paternity—by establishing the probabilities of these events. For an unambiguous exclusion, the probability of paternity is close to zero (for most realistic prior probabilities of paternity). For an inclusion that involves a respectable number of genetic systems, the probability of paternity is near one (for most realistic prior probabilities). A careful reading of the remainder of this section should clarify these remarks.

3. See supra § 210.

4. In practice, "probability of exclusion" may be used to denote two distinct concepts. Some experts use it to refer to the proportion of the male population that a single test or the battery of tests would exclude as the biological father without regard to the phenotypes of the mother and child tested in any given case. See, e.g., State ex rel. Hausner v. Blackman, 7 Kan. App.2d 693, 648 P.2d 249, 253 (1982) ("The HLA test alone has a probability of exclusion of 78 percent to 80 percent and when it is used in addition to the six other tests, the probability of exclusion rises to at least 91 percent to 95 percent"); Joint AMA–ABA Guidelines: Present Status of Serologic Testing in Problems of Disputed Parentage, 10 Fam.L.Q. 247, 253–258 (1976). This figure is a measure of the ability of the serologic tests to exclude falsely accused males across a spectrum of cases. It is sometimes called a "mean" or a

are essentially the same as those that apply to scientific identification evidence generally.[5]

Yet, many experts believe that testimony limited to the test results and the probability of exclusion is incomplete and sometimes misleading.[6] They would prefer to testify to "the probability of paternity,"[7] and some jurisdictions allow such testimony.[8] Although many states have statutes that permit positive test results to be received into evidence,[9] very few of these statutes say whether the probabilities derived from these test results also are admissible.[10] In the ab-

---

"cumulative" probability of exclusion. See AMA–ABA Guidelines, supra. It also has been called a prior probability of exclusion, although it is clearly not the prior probability used in the Bayesian computations described infra. See Reisner & Bolk, A Layman's Guide to the Use of Blood Group Analysis in Paternity Testing, 20 J.Family L. 657, 670–671 (1981–82). It is useful to the laboratory in deciding which tests to include in its standard battery, but it is not well suited to measuring the power of the tests employed in a particular case where the phenotypes of the mother and child are known. In this situation, the "probability of exclusion" that should be testified to is, in effect, the proportion of males in the relevant population who have the incriminating phenotypes—those that the biological father, whoever he was, could have had, given the types of the mother and child.

5. See supra § 210. But in State ex rel. Hausner v. Blackman, 7 Kan.App.2d 693, 648 P.2d 249, 253 (1982), the court held that it was error for an expert to testify that "his tests had an approximate 70 percent probability of exclusion and he was unable to exclude the defendant" without also testifying to "the likelihood of the defendant's paternity." Although the opinion made the patently fallacious assertions that "evidence of the failure of a man to be excluded . . . has no tendency in reason to prove paternity [and] does not render an inference of paternity more probable than it would be without that evidence," id., the court's true concern seemed to be that the jury would incorrectly assume that because the probability of exclusion was .7, the probability of paternity was .3. See id., 648 P.2d at 251–252. It implied that if this latter probability had been calculated via Bayes' Theorem, the evidence would have been admissible. Id. at 252.

6. See, e.g., Peterson, A Few Things You Should Know About Paternity Tests (But Were Afraid to Ask), 22 Santa Clara L.Rev. 667, 677–681 (1982). The scientists and physicians do not all agree on which approach is scientifically the soundest. See, Am.Ass'n of Blood Banks, Inclusion Probabilities in Parentage Testing (Walker ed. 1983).

7. County of Ventura v. Marcus, 139 Cal.App.3d 612, 189 Cal.Rptr. 8, 9 (1983) (there "was an 85.95% probability that Peter Marcus was the father"); Alinda V. v. Alfredo V., 125 Cal.App.3d 98, 101, 177 Cal.Rptr. 839, 840 (1981) (98.95% "probability of paternity"); Ellman & Kaye, Probabilities and Proof: Can HLA and Blood Group Testing Prove Paternity, 54 N.Y.U.L.Rev. 1154 (1979); Walker, Probability in the Analysis of Paternity Test Results, in Am.Ass'n of Blood Banks, Paternity Testing 69 (Silver ed. 1978). Other terms are used in lieu of "probability." See, e.g., Carlyon v. Weeks, 387 So.2d 465, 466 (Fla.App.1980) ("the plausi-

bility of paternity . . . is 99.9%"); State ex rel. Buechler v. Vinsand, 318 N.W.2d 208, 211 (Iowa 1982) (98.06% "plausibility"); Tice v. Richardson, 7 Kan.App. 2d 509, 644 P.2d 490, 494 (1982) ("a plausibility of paternity in defendant of 99.96%"); State ex rel. Williams v. Williams, 609 S.W.2d 456, 457 (Mo.App.1980) ("there was an 81.15% possibility that Ronald was the father"). These "plausibilities" and "possibilities" are computed in the same way as the probability of paternity. Sometimes the symbol W or the phrase "likelihood of paternity" (which should not be confused with the likelihood ratio discussed infra this section) are employed. E.g., Joint AMA–ABA Guidelines, supra n. 4, at 262.

8. See Ellman & Kaye, supra n. 7; Kolko, Admissibility of HLA Test Results to Determine Paternity, 9 Fam.L.Rep. 4009 (1983); supra n. 7.

9. See Kolko, supra n. 8; supra § 205(B).

10. A few of these statutes speak to the use of probability calculations, but usually in garbled terms. The Uniform Parentage Act, adopted at least in part in 10 states, specifies in section 12 that "Evidence relating to paternity may include . . . blood test results, weighted in accordance with evidence, if available, of the statistical probability of the alleged father's paternity." It is surprisingly hard to say what these words mean. In mathematics, there are statistics and there are probabilities, but there are not "statistical probabilities" as opposed to any other kind. Perhaps, the intent behind the choice of this phrase is to emphasize that there must be sufficient sample data to permit accurate estimate of population frequencies for the pertinent genotypes. If so, computations that use HLA typing results may not always qualify for admissibility. See Selvin, Some Statistical Properties of the Paternity Ratio, in Inclusion Probabilities in Parentage Testing, supra n. 6 (large bias and variance of population estimates). Furthermore, it is not clear what the "evidence of the statistical probability of . . . paternity" is. Presumably, the word "evidence" here is intended to connote an expert's calculation of the probability. The Iowa statute, which the National Conference of State Legislatures praised as "exemplary," Kolko, supra n. 8, provides that "Blood test results which show a statistical probability of paternity are admissible and shall be weighed along with other evidence of the alleged father's paternity." Iowa Code Ann. § 675.41. Since all blood test results show some probability of paternity, it is hard to know which probability calculations, if any, this provision was intended to make admissible as an accompaniment to testimony that the test results were positive. A 1982 amendment to Md.Code 1957, Art. 16, § 66G is the oddest of these disappointing legislative efforts. It provides that "The test results may be received in evi-

sence of a statute explicitly authorizing the expert to give the "probability of paternity," admissibility should turn on whether probability testimony is sufficiently likely to aid the jury in properly assessing the probative value of the positive findings.[11] To answer this question, one must first understand what the "probability of paternity" is. For this reason, this section indicates how this probability is computed.[12] It then argues that this approach is not suited for courtroom use and suggests some alternative methods of assisting the jury or court to weigh the positive test results along with the other evidence in the case to reach a decision as to paternity.[13]

The probability of paternity, as conventionally computed, is a deceptively simple application of an elementary result in probability theory discovered by the Reverend Thomas Bayes in the nineteenth century. Bayes' formula can be interpreted as showing the effect of a new item of evidence on a previously established probability.[14] Suppose, to save space, we let B stand for the event that the alleged father is the biological father, we let Odds(B) designate the odds [15]

in favor of this event (before we learn the outcome of the laboratory tests), and we use the letter T to denote the test evidence (the phenotypes of the mother, child and father). Most testifying experts who realize how the probability of paternity is calculated take the prior odds to be 1 (i.e., 50–50) on the theory that doing so shows that they are neutral as between plaintiff and defendant.[16] Adopting these odds amounts to assuming that the accusation of paternity is as likely to be true as to be false. Bayes' rule tells us how to update these Odds(B) to account for the test results T. In particular, it says to multiply the prior odds by a quantity called the likelihood ratio to produce the new odds that the alleged father is the biological father, which we write as Odds(B/T), for the odds of B given the test results T. In symbols, $Odds(B/T) = LR \times Odds(B)$, where LR is an abbreviation for likelihood ratio. For the standard assumption that the prior odds are 1, the posterior odds of paternity are just $Odds(B/T) = LR$.

This likelihood ratio can be computed as the ratio of two probabilities.[17] The numerator is the probability that the phenotypes T

dence . . . if testing was sufficiently extensive to exclude 97.3% of putative fathers who are not biological fathers, and the statistical probability of the alleged father's paternity is at least 97.3 percent." Most of the statutes follow this pattern of making properly obtained "test results" admissible without indicating whether the "probability of paternity" deduced from these test results and the population data is also to be admissible. However, a few statutes explicitly authorize the court to allow the probability figure into evidence. Mich.C.L.A. § 722.716 ("a calculation of the probability of paternity . . . based on the result of a blood or tissue typing test shall be admissible in evidence in the trial of the case"); N.C.Gen.Stat. § 8–50.1(a) ("the statistical likelihood of the alleged parent's parentage, if available, shall be admitted in evidence").

11. The arguments that might allow testimony as to probabilities to be admitted in the absence of a definitive statute are outlined supra in § 210.

12. Other references on this point include Am. Ass'n of Blood Banks, Paternity Testing (Silver ed. 1978); Inclusion Probabilities in Parentage Testing, supra n. 6; Biomathematical Evidence of Paternity (Hummel & Gerchow ed. 1982); Paternity Testing by Blood Grouping (2d ed. Sussman 1976). Much of the notation and terminology in this field bears little resemblance to standard statistical nomenclature and abbreviations,

but a table collecting and defining most of the important mathematical abbreviations can be found in Aickin & Kaye, Some Mathematical and Legal Considerations in Using Serologic Tests to Prove Paternity, in Inclusion Probabilities in Parentage Testing, supra n. 6.

13. The argument sketched here relies heavily on Aickin & Kaye, supra n. 12, and Ellman & Kaye, supra n. 7.

14. References in the law journals to the elementary version of Bayes' formula are given supra in § 210. See also Kaplan, Decision Theory and the Factfinding Process, 20 Stan.L.Rev. 1065 (1968); Lempert, Modeling Relevance, 75 Mich.L.Rev. 1021 (1977).

15. A probability P for some outcome corresponds to odds of P/(1–P) to 1 in favor of that outcome. For example, if the probability of paternity is 1/2, the odds are 1/2 divided by 1/2, or 1 to 1.

16. Reisner & Bolle, supra n. 4, at 674 ("Traditionally, laboratories use a neutral figure of 50% in their calculations"); Terasaki, Resolution by HLA Testing of 1000 Paternity Cases not Excluded by ABO Testing, 16 J.Fam.L. 543 (1978).

17. Being a ratio of two conditional probabilities, the likelihood ratio is not itself a probability. Unlike probabilities, which are bounded by 0 and 1, the likelihood ratio can exceed one. This point has escaped more than one expert. See, e.g., State ex rel. Buechler

would be found if the alleged father really were the biological father. The denominator is the probability that the phenotypes T would be found if the alleged father were not the biological father. In other words, the likelihood ratio states how many times more likely it is that the tests would show the phenotypes T if the alleged father were the biological father than if he were not.[18] It often is referred as the "paternity index." The computation of the numerator is relatively simple. It is just the probability that a man with the phenotypes of the alleged father and a woman with the mother's phenotypes would produce an offspring with the child's phenotypes. The computation of the denominator is trickier. The denominator is the probability that a man other than the alleged father would produce an offspring with the child's phenotypes. But which man? Some "alternative men" could not produce this type of child. They are the ones whom the tests would exclude. Others would have the same probability of producing this type of child as does the alleged father. These are the ones who have the same phenotypes that he does. Still others would produce this type of child with other probabilities. Their phenotypes differ from the alleged father's but are still consistent with the genotypes of the biological father. The conventional solution is to invent a "random man"—a hypothetical entity whose genotypes (and hence phenotypes) are a kind of

average across all these men. Assuming that the estimates of the population gene frequencies are completely free from error, the computation can proceed.

Suppose, for example, that given the estimated gene frequencies, it is 50 times more likely to obtain a child with the observed phenotypes from a man with the alleged father's phenotypes than from the imaginary "random man." Bayes' formula then states that Odds(B/T) = 50 x Odds(B). For prior odds of 1, this means that the odds that the alleged father is the biological father are 50 to 1. The corresponding probability of paternity is 50/51 = .98, or 98%. These are the kind of numbers of which the experts testifying to the "probability of paternity" speak.[19]

Should the results of these calculations ever be admissible? Resorting to the "random man" to form the likelihood ratio and postulating prior odds of 1 create grave problems for any courtroom presentation. It is tempting to dismiss the choice of the prior odds as contrived, speculative, and lacking any scientific basis.[20] It sounds like some of the classic cases in which an expert multiplied together probabilities that had no basis in fact.[21] Here, however, there is some hard data suggesting that these prior odds understate the incidence of truthful accusations of paternity and therefore favor the alleged father, who would be the objecting party.[22]

v. Vinsand, 318 N.W.2d 208, 211 (Iowa 1982). Some experts call the likelihood ratio the "likelihood of paternity." Reisner & Bolk, supra n. 4, at 671–672. This language invites the trier of fact to confuse it with the probability of paternity. What is worse, some experts further distort the fact that the "paternity index" is not a probability by presenting it as "a percent." Id. at 672. In this way, some leaders in the field of parentage testing have been known to fool themselves into thinking that a likelihood ratio is a probability. E.g., State ex rel. Buechler v. Vinsand, 318 N.W.2d 208, 211 (1982).

18. One can define another likelihood ratio—one that gives the relative likelihood of positive test results (an inclusion) as opposed to negative ones (an exclusion). This likelihood differs from the one defined in the text because, for some of the genetic systems involved, more than one set of male phenotypes are consistent with the obligatory genotypes—those that the

biological father must have had to produce an offspring with the child's phenotypes in a mating with the mother. It has been said that there is a serious question as to which of these two likelihood ratios should be used in Bayes' formula. See Aickin & Kaye, supra n. 12.

19. See supra n. 7.

20. See Alinda V. v. Alfredo V., 125 Cal.App.3d 98, 101, 177 Cal.Rptr. 839, 840 (1981); Sensabaugh, Biochemical Markers of Individuality, in Forensic Science Handbook 339, 403 (Saferstein ed. 1982) ("There is, of course, no objective basis for the estimation of this prior probability by the serologic expert").

21. See supra § 210.

22. Ellman & Kaye, supra n. 7, at 1150–1151; Heise, Keever & McMahan, A Critical Analysis of Paternity Determination Using HLA and Five Erythrocyte Antigen Systems, 4 Am.J.Forensic Medicine & Pa-

Nonetheless, to serve up any single number computed in this fashion as "the" probability of paternity connotes more than the mathematical logic possibly can deliver. Most persons hearing that the probability of paternity is 98% would think that the alleged father's role in the affair is conclusively confirmed. Indeed, the experts have developed standardized phrases, which they call "verbal predicates," to characterize the numbers.[23] Yet, in view of the way in which the "probability of paternity" is calculated, many men—all those who share the alleged father's phenotypes—would have "probabilities of paternity" of 98%. Some non-excluded men might have even higher "probabilities of paternity." In at least one unreported case, a man later shown to be sterile had a "probability of paternity" of this magnitude as determined from HLA typing. Unless an expert can somehow explain that the calculated "probability of paternity" is not the chance that the alleged father, as distinguished from all other possible fathers, is the biological father, the expert should not be allowed to put this "probability" before the jury. Furthermore,

it would appear that any accurate explanation of why the "probability of paternity" does not mean the probability that the alleged father, rather than any other man, is the biological father, and then of what it does mean, would be hopelessly confusing. Consequently, testimony as to the "probability of paternity," as it typically is calculated, should not be allowed. Such testimony seems unable to fulfill its only legitimate function—assisting the jury in weighing the positive test results along with the other evidence in the case.[24] The same rule of exclusion should apply to the "verbal predicates" that some experts attach to probabilities of paternity computed in this way.[25]

This rule would not prohibit the introduction of the serologic evidence and an explanation of its significance. The fact that competently performed serologic tests prove the alleged father's phenotypes to be consistent with the claim of paternity is always relevant and useful evidence. The strength of this evidence, like other forms of identification evidence, can be shown to some ex-

thology 15 (1983); Hummel, Conradt & Kundinger, The Realistic Prior Probability from Blood Group Findings for Cases Involving One or More Men, in Biomathematical Evidence of Paternity, supra n. 12, at 73–87; Peterson, supra n. 6, at 704–707; Silver, An Introduction to Paternity Testing, in Am. Ass'n of Blood Banks, supra n. 12, at xi–xii. This empirical justification raises the issue of using an average figure for the veracity of claimants to judge the merits of an individual claim. Ellman & Kaye, supra; Reisner & Bolk, supra n. 4, at 673; supra § 210.

23. Carlyon v. Weeks, 387 So.2d 465, 466 (Fla.App. 1980) ("the plausibility of paternity for Miles is 99.9%, making paternity 'practically proved' in the terminology of Hummel"). In their orthodox version, the "predicates" range from "not useful" (less than 80%) to "practically proved" (99.80–99.90%). What should be said if the probability of paternity were still higher is not specified. Joint AMA–ABA Guidelines, supra n. 4, at 262.

24. The probability would not be unduly misleading and would be of distinct value if the entire trial were conducted as an exercise in Bayesian inference with the serologic evidence being the first datum. The probability that serologists now calculate could become the next prior probability, to be modified according to the likelihood ratio for the next piece of evidence, and

so on. When all the evidence was in and counted, the final probability of paternity would determine the outcome. But it seems pointless and potentially misleading and confusing to process only one type of evidence in this way.

25. The "verbal predicates" convey less information than the numbers to which they are attached. In some cases they are even more misleading than a statement of the "probability of paternity." County of Ventura v. Marcus, 139 Cal.App.3d 612, 189 Cal.Rptr. 8, 12 (1983) (because the "verbal predicate" of "undecided" is attached to probabilities in the .80–.90 range, the court reached the patently false conclusion that "It is therefore equally valid to infer therefrom that he is not the father as to infer that he is the father"); State ex rel. Williams v. Williams, 609 S.W.2d 456, 457 (Mo.App. 1980) ("the expert testified that a possibility or probability of paternity of less than 80% is no help at all in determining paternity. He stated that he preferred a probability of more than 90%"). The expert's testimony should be complete enough to permit the jury to decide for itself how much is enough. There are means of explaining the significance of the positive test findings that allow this, but the translation of dubious probability calculations into conclusions that do not draw on the qualifications and specialized knowledge of the expert is hardly the way to proceed.

tent by testimony about the probability of exclusion or related concepts.[26]

There is also a strong argument for using a Bayesian approach (though not the one previously described) to help the jury evaluate the evidence. Instead of viewing the evidence from the position of a laboratory, which, having nothing else to go on, is driven to such artifacts as using prior odds of one, one can adjust the focus to the trial, where other evidence is available to the decisionmaker. As noted in section 210, the expert could show the jury how the test results would affect not merely a prior probability of one-half, but a whole spectrum of prior probabilities. It could be made clear to the jurors that the purpose of this exposition is not to compel them to assign a prior

probability to the other evidence in the case, but to permit them to gauge the strength of the positive test findings and to weigh these findings, along with the other evidence, in the manner that they think best. By using variable instead of fixed prior odds, the expert can display the statistical force of the evidence without attempting to quantify—on the basis of incomplete information—the one thing that the jury must decide with the benefit of all the evidence in the case: the probability of paternity.[27]

 **WESTLAW REFERENCES**

paternity blood h.l.a. "human leu*ocyte" serologic! /2 test* /p probabilit! /p evidence admissib! inadmissib!

---

26. See supra text accompanying nn. 3–5.

27. This quantity, however, it may be computed, should not be confused with a confidence level, a sig-

nificance level, or a P-value. These very different probabilities are defined supra at §§ 209–210.

Title 8

DEMONSTRATIVE EVIDENCE

Chapter 21

DEMONSTRATIVE EVIDENCE

Table of Sections

§ 212. Demonstrative Evidence in General [1]

There is a type of evidence which consists of things, e.g., weapons, whiskey bottles, writings,[2] and wearing apparel, as distinguished from the assertions of witnesses (or hearsay declarants) about things. Most broadly viewed, this type of evidence includes all phenomena which can convey a relevant firsthand sense impression to the trier of fact,[3] as opposed to those which serve merely to report the secondhand sense impressions of others. Thus, for example, demeanor evidence, i.e. the bearing, expres-

---

§ 212

1. See 4 Wigmore, Evidence §§ 1150–1169 (Chadbourn rev. 1972); C.J.S. Evidence §§ 601–622; Dec.Dig. Evidence ⊕188–195, Criminal Law ⊕404 (1–4), Trial ⊕28 and 375.

Demonstrative evidence, as a generic class, is not singled out for specific treatment by the Federal or Revised Uniform Rules of Evidence. As is stressed in the text infra at nn. 22, 23 demonstrative evidence is particularly likely to raise issues to which Rules 402–403 are applicable. The Federal Rules provide:

Rule 402. Relevant Evidence Generally Admissible; Irrelevant Evidence Inadmissible.

All relevant evidence is admissible, except as otherwise provided by the Constitution of the United States, by Act of Congress, by these rules, or by other rules prescribed by the Supreme Court pursuant to statutory authority. Evidence which is not relevant is not admissible.

Rule 403. Exclusion of Relevant Evidence on Grounds of Prejudice, Confusion, or Waste of Time.

Although relevant, evidence may be excluded if its probative value is substantially outweighed by the danger of unfair prejudice, confusion of the issues, or misleading the jury, or by considerations of undue delay, waste of time, or needless presentation of cumulative evidence.

The revised Uniform Rules are identical except for adaptation of Rule 402 to state use.

2. Writings, except insofar as they contain statements which the writing is offered to prove, are examples of the present subject. They have, however, developed rules of their own which are treated independently. See Ch. 22 (authentication) and Ch. 23 (documentary originals).

3. Schertzinger v. Williams, 198 Cal.App.2d 242, 17 Cal.Rptr. 719 (1961).

sion, and manner of a witness while testifying,[4] is an instance of the type of evidence here considered, but the statements which he utters are not.

Evidence from which the trier of fact may derive a relevant firsthand sense impression is almost unlimited in its variety. As a result, the problem of satisfactorily labeling and classifying has proved a difficult one,[5] and it will be seen variously referred to as real, autoptic, demonstrative, tangible, and objective. For present purposes, the term "demonstrative" will be used to refer to the generic class, though it should be noted that some courts employ this term in a more limited sense.[6]

Since "seeing is believing," and demonstrative evidence appeals directly to the senses of the trier of fact,[7] it is today universally felt that this kind of evidence possesses an immediacy and reality which endow it with particularly persuasive effect.[8] Largely as a result of this potential, the use of demonstrative evidence of all types has increased dramatically during recent years, and the trend seems certain to continue in the immediate future. At the same time, demonstrative evidence remains the exception rather than the rule, and its use raises certain problems for a juridical system the

mechanics of which are essentially geared to the reception of *viva voce* testimony by witnesses. Some of these problems are so commonly raised by the offer of demonstrative evidence, and are so frequently made the bases of objections to its admission, that they deserve preliminary note.[9]

It has already been noted that evidence from which the trier of fact may derive his own perceptions, rather than evidence consisting of the reported perceptions of others, possesses unusual force. Largely for this reason, demonstrative evidence is frequently objected to as "prejudicial," by which is usually meant that the capacity of the evidence to inspire emotions such as, e.g., sympathy or repugnance, outweighs its probative value for the issues in litigation.[10] Again, even if no essentially emotional response is likely to result, demonstrative evidence may convey an impression of objective reality to the trier. Thus, the courts are frequently sensitive to the objection that the evidence is "misleading," and zealous to insure that there is no misleading differential between objective things offered at trial and the same or different objective things as they existed at the time of the events or occurrences in litigation.[11]

4. While demeanor evidence is analytically a type of demonstrative evidence, it is inseparably related to oral testimony and is thus treated elsewhere. See § 245, text at notes 8–13 infra.

5. See, Michael & Adler, Real Proof, 5 Vand.L.Rev. 344 (1952); Nokes, Real Evidence, 65 L.Q.Rev. 57 (1949); Patterson, Types of Evidence, 19 Vand.L.Rev. 1 (1965); 4 Wigmore, Evidence § 1150 (Chadbourn rev. 1972).

6. I.e., as contrasted with "real" evidence. See discussion at n. 25 infra.

7. While the great bulk of demonstrative evidence is directed to the sense of sight, each of the other senses may on occasion be appealed to. See, e.g., Ragusa v. American Metal Works, Inc., 97 So.2d 683 (La. App.1957) (hearing); People v. Kinney, 124 Mich. 486, 83 N.W. 147 (1900) (taste); McAndrews v. Leonard, 99 Vt. 512, 134 A. 710 (1926) (touch); Rust v. Guinn, ___ Ind.App. ___, 429 N.E.2d 299 (1981) (smell).

8. Of the many articles emphasizing the point, the following may be cited: Belli, Demonstrative Evidence and the Adequate Award, 22 Miss.L.J. 284 (1951); Dombroff, Innovative Developments in Demonstrative

Evidence Techniques and Associated Problems of Admissibility, 45 J.Air L. 139 (1980); Dooley, Demonstrative Evidence—Nothing New, 42 Ill.B.J. 136 (1953); Gamble, Using Demonstrative Evidence, 26 La.B.J. 215 (1979); Hinshaw, Use and Abuse of Demonstrative Evidence: The Art of Jury Persuasion, 40 A.B.A.J. 479 (1954); Hare, Demonstrative Evidence, 27 Ala.Law. 193 (1966); Kilroy, Seeing Is Believing, 8 Kan.L.Rev. 445 (1960); Knepper, Exhibits and Demonstrative Evidence, 30 Ins.L.J. 133 (1963); Lay, Use of Real Evidence, 37 Neb.L.Rev. 501 (1958); Perlman, Demonstrative Evidence, 33 Ky.S.B.J. 5 (1969); Spangenburg, The Use of Demonstrative Evidence, 21 Ohio St.L.J. 178 (1960).

9. For an extended treatment of the objections commonly raised to demonstrative evidence, see Cady, Objections to Demonstrative Evidence, 32 Mo.L.Rev. 333 (1967).

10. For types of demonstrative evidence to which this objection is frequently raised, see n. 22 and § 215 infra.

11. See discussion at n. 26 infra.

Further, and apart from its bearing on the issues of the case, demonstrative evidence as a class presents certain essentially logistical difficulties for the courts. Since the courts are basically structured, architecturally and otherwise, to receive the testimony of witnesses, the presentation of demonstrative evidence may require that the court physically move to receive it, or that unwieldy objects or paraphernalia be introduced into the courtroom, actions which may occasion delay and confusion.[12] Finally, while oral testimony is easily incorporated into a paper record for purposes of appellate review, demonstrative evidence will sometimes be insusceptible to similar preservation and transmission.[13]

The cogency and force of the foregoing objections to the introduction of demonstrative evidence will obviously vary greatly with the nature of the particular item offered, and the purpose and need for its introduction in the particular case. Since the types of demonstrative evidence and the purposes for which it is sought to be introduced are extremely varied, it is generally viewed as appropriate to accord the trial judge broad discretion in ruling upon the admissibility of many types of demonstrative evidence.[14]

Despite its great variety, certain classifications of demonstrative evidence appear both valid and useful. First, like other evidence, it may be either direct or circumstantial. If a material issue in the case is whether an object does or does not possess a perceptible feature, characteristic, or quality, the most satisfactory method of demonstrating the truth of the matter will ordinarily be to produce the object so that the trier of fact may perceive the quality, or its absence, for himself. Thus, where a party seeks damages for the loss of a limb or for an injury leaving a disfiguring scar, exhibition of the person will constitute direct evidence of a material fact.[15] Similarly, exhibition of the chattel purchased in an action for breach of warranty will, at least if the quality or characteristic warranted is a perceivable one, constitute direct evidence on the issue of condition.[16] In these cases no process of inference, at least in the ordinary sense, is required.[17] Similarly, exhibition of a person to establish such facts as race [18] and age [19] may perhaps also be considered examples of demonstrative evidence of a direct sort, though the immediate perceptibility of these qualities may on occasion be subject to more doubt.

Demonstrative evidence may also be offered for its circumstantial value, i.e., as the

---

12. See, e.g., § 214 (motion pictures) and § 216 (views) infra.

13. E.g., Indiana Appellate Rules, Rule 7.2(A)(3)(b) provides as follows:

Exhibits—Physical Objects. Physical objects (except papers, maps, pictures and like materials) which, because of their nature cannot be incorporated in a transcript, shall not be sent to this Court on appeal, but shall remain in the custody of the trial court below until the appeal is terminated. However, such objects shall be briefly named and identified in the transcript following the exhibit number therein. A photograph of such exhibits may be included in the transcript.

14. E.g., the types of demonstrative evidence discussed in §§ 213–216 infra.

15. See Calumet Paving Co. v. Butkus, 113 Ind.App. 232, 47 N.E.2d 829 (1943) (exhibition of plaintiff's shoulder most satisfactory evidence of injury); Hendricks v. Sanford, 216 Or. 149, 337 P.2d 974 (1959) (exhibition "completely relevant" to show declivity in plaintiff's back). See § 215 nn. 1–6 infra.

16. See, e.g., Woodward & Lothrop v. Heed, 44 A.2d 369 (D.C.Mun.App.1945) (breach of implied warranty on fur coat; "When the issue of fact is the condition of . . . an article, the introduction in evidence of the thing itself, to enable a jury to observe its condition, is competent and persuasive evidence.")

17. 4 Wigmore, Evidence § 1150 (Chadbourn rev. 1972).

18. See, e.g., White v. Holderby, 192 F.2d 722 (5th Cir. 1951).

19. See, e.g., United States ex rel. Fong On v. Day, 54 F.2d 990, 991 (2d Cir. 1932) ("it can hardly be doubted that [the jury] are at liberty to use their senses and draw an inference as to the person's age from his physical appearance"); State v. Dorathy, 132 Me. 291, 170 A.2d 506 (1934). But see Watson v. State, 236 Ind. 329, 140 N.E.2d 109 (1957) (appearance of defendant not alone sufficient to support finding as to age), noted in 15 Wash. & L.L.Rev. 290 (1958).

basis for an inference beyond those facts which are perceivable. Such is the case when the exhibition of a person is made for the purpose of demonstrating his relationship to another, as in a filiation proceeding.[20] The use of demonstrative evidence is even more clearly circumstantial when articles of clothing worn at the time of his arrest by the defendant in a robbery prosecution are exhibited to the jury to demonstrate their conformity with the descriptions of the robber given by witnesses.[21]

The practical significance of the foregoing distinction lies in the fact that direct evi-

dence, because of its eminently satisfactory character, will always be admitted unless the situation involves some overriding contrary consideration of prejudice or physical difficulty.[22] When circumstantial evidence is involved, however, in the present context as elsewhere, the trial judge will generally be viewed as possessing a broader discretionary power to weigh the probative value of the evidence against whatever prejudice, confusion, surprise and waste of time are entailed, and to determine admissibility accordingly.[23]

---

20. Many states hold that the trial court may, in its discretion, permit a child to be exhibited in a filiation proceeding for the purpose of showing a resemblance to the putative father. See, e.g., Judway v. Kovacs, 4 Conn.Cir. 713, 239 A.2d 556 (1967) (dictum); Glascock v. Anderson, 83 N.M. 725, 497 P.2d 727 (1972), 1973 Wash.U.L.Rev. 245. The practice is by no means universally accepted. See 1 Wigmore, Evidence § 166 (3d ed. 1940); Annot., 40 A.L.R. 111, 95 A.L.R. 314; Dec. Dig. Bastards ⬤63.

21. See, e.g., Caldwell v. United States, 338 F.2d 385 (8th Cir. 1964); Vanleeward v. State, 220 Ga. 135, 137 S.E.2d 452 (1964).

22. Rich v. Ellerman & Bucknall Steamship Co., 278 F.2d 704, 708 (2d Cir. 1960) ("Autoptic proference is always proper, unless reasons of policy apply to exclude it;" error to exclude photos of plaintiff's injuries). Thus, though it is commonly recognized that gruesome and shocking demonstrative evidence may prejudice and inflame the jury, the gruesome nature of an item of direct evidence is today seldom viewed as warranting exclusion. 4 Wigmore, Evidence §§ 1157, 1158 (Chadbourn rev. 1972); Dec.Dig. Crim.Law ⬤404, Evidence ⬤188.

Gruesome photographs or other tangible evidence have been held properly admitted in innumerable criminal cases. In some instances this result is said to be justified on the ground that potential prejudice does not support the exclusion of material evidence. State v. Murphy, 610 S.W.2d 382, 385 (Mo.App.1980) ("The only discretion a trial court has to deny admission of demonstrative evidence is if the evidence is both irrelevant to a material issue and also inflammatory or prejudicial"); State v. Bucanis, 26 N.J. 45, 138 A.2d 739 (1958) (conviction upheld though pictures were "more harmful than illuminating"); Wilson v. State, 247 Ind. 680, 221 N.E.2d 347 (1966) (gruesomeness not considered where evidence relevant); Martin v. State, 475 S.W.2d 265 (Tex.Cr.App.1972) (photos not excludable solely for gruesomeness). Even where a balancing of probative value against prejudice is approved in theory, see § 185 supra, admission is usually upheld. United States v. McRae, 593 F.2d 700, (5th Cir. 1979), cert. denied 444 U.S. 862 (photos of "exploded head" of victim wife, alleged improperly admitted under Fed.R.Evid.

403; Rule 403 held not meant to "even out" evidence or unrealistically to "sanitize" trial); State v. Kelly, 122 Ariz. 495, 595 P.2d 1040 (App.1979) (balancing required, but no error to permit victim to display scars from wounds); State v. Bott, 310 Minn. 331, 246 N.W.2d 48 (1976) (semble). There is, however, a small but growing body of authority to the effect that a serious imbalance of prejudice over probative value requires exclusion. People v. Gibson, 56 Cal.App.3d 119, 128 Cal.Rptr. 302 (1976) (photographs' potential for prejudice "substantially outweighed" probative value; error to admit); Commonwealth v. Chacko, 480 Pa. 485, 391 A.2d 999 (1978) (error to admit gruesome photos where not "of essential evidentiary value"); State v. Banks, 564 S.W.2d 947 (Tenn.1978) (error to admit photographs where prejudicial effect substantially outweighed probative value).

Cases are collected in Annot., 159 A.L.R. 1413, 73 A.L.R.2d 769.

Where materiality is entirely lacking, of course, the admission of prejudicial demonstrative evidence is improper. See, e.g., State v. Bischert, 131 Mont. 152, 308 P.2d 969 (1957). But attempts to remove materiality by admitting or stipulating to the fact to be proved are rarely successful. See, e.g., United States v. Brady, 595 F.2d 359 (6th Cir. 1979), cert. denied 444 U.S. 862 (stipulation that victims died by gunshot did not eliminate materiality of photos of victims lying in pools of blood in bank; photos relevant to show killings occurred in course of robbery); People v. Mireles, 79 Ill. App.3d 173, 34 Ill.Dec. 475, 398 N.E.2d 150 (1979) (admission of photos of victim and wires with which she was strangled upheld where defendant admitted killing and pleaded insanity).

Many older decisions hold preservation of decency in the courtroom to be a policy warranting exclusion of some autoptic evidence. See, e.g., Garvick v. Burlington, Cedar Rapids & Northern Railway Co., 124 Iowa 691, 100 N.W. 498 (1904); Guhl v. Whitcomb, 109 Wis. 69, 85 N.W. 142 (1901). Most modern authority, however, reverses the priorities. See, e.g., Jensen v. South Adams County Water and Sanitation District, 149 Colo.

---

23. See note 23 on page 667.

As with other circumstantial evidence, of course, demonstrative evidence offered for its circumstantial value may give rise to more than one inference. Thus introduction of a firearm taken from the defendant on his arrest and shown to be similar to that used in the commission of the offense charged may imply both that the defendant was the robber and that the defendant is a dangerous individual given to carrying firearms. If a permissible inference is present, admission will generally be upheld, a limiting instruction being deemed sufficient to prevent any untoward damage.[24]

Again, demonstrative evidence may be classified as to whether the item offered did or did not play an actual and direct part in the incident or transaction giving rise to the trial. Objects offered as having played such a direct role, e.g., the alleged weapon in a murder prosecution, are commonly called "real" or "original" evidence and are to be distinguished from evidence which played no such part but is offered for illustrative or other purposes.[25] It will be readily apparent that when real evidence is offered an adequate foundation for admission will require testimony first that the object offered is *the* object which was involved in the incident, and further that the condition of the object is substantially unchanged.[26] If the offered item possesses characteristics which are fairly unique and readily identifiable, and if the substance of which the item is composed is relatively impervious to change, the trial court is viewed as having broad discretion to admit merely on the basis of testimony that the item is the one in question and is in a substantially unchanged condition.[27] On the other hand, if the offered evidence is of such a nature as not to be readily identifiable, or

---

102, 368 P.2d 209 (1962); Sullivan v. Minneapolis, St. Paul & Sault Ste. Marie Railway Co., 55 N.D. 353, 213 N.W. 841 (1927).

23. See, e.g., Bertram v. Harris, 423 P.2d 909 (Alaska 1967) (whiskey bottle found in defendant's car after accident; within trial court's discretion to exclude when fact testified to). See also, E. C. Heddin v. Delhi Gas Pipeline Co., 522 S.W.2d 886 (Tex.1975) (photos of dead animals killed in pipe leakage accident had "no relevance" in eminent domain case).

Fed. and Rev.Unif.R.Evid. (1974) 403 provide exclusion for prejudice only if "probative value is substantially outweighed by the danger of unfair prejudice . . . ."

24. United States v. Cunningham, 423 F.2d 1269 (4th Cir. 1970). See also United States v. Robinson, 560 F.2d 507 (2d Cir. 1977), cert. denied 435 U.S. 905 (a careful balancing of relevance versus prejudice; not error to admit; judge minimized impact by denying admission of the weapon itself, but opinion cites with apparent approval cases admitting the weapons). Absent proof of similarity, no permissible inference is raised. Compare Little v. United States, 490 F.2d 686 (8th Cir. 1974). In Moore v. Illinois, 408 U.S. 786 (1972), the Court refused to set aside on due process grounds a murder conviction involving admission of a shotgun admittedly of a different gauge from that used in the killing, on the grounds that the due process claim had not been raised in the State courts and in any event no due process denial was shown.

An exception is generally made to the rule stated in the case of "mug shots" relevant to prove identification of a criminal defendant by a victim. In the event the photograph bears any indication suggestive of previous incarceration of the defendant, its admission will frequently be held to constitute error. Blue v. State,

250 Ind. 249, 235 N.E.2d 471 (1968); Annot., 30 A.L.R.3d 908.

25. Smith v. Ohio Oil Co., 10 Ill.App.2d 67, 134 N.E.2d 526 (1956), n. 34, infra.

26. See, e.g., Witt Ice & Gas Co. v. Bedway, 72 Ariz. 152, 231 P.2d 952 (1951); Gutman v. Industrial Commission, 71 Ohio App. 383, 50 N.E.2d 187 (1942) (no testimony that steering wheel offered was from car in question); Semet v. Andorra Nurseries, Inc., 421 Pa. 484, 219 A.2d 357 (1966) (no testimony that photo offered was of the same ladder from which plaintiff fell). See also 7 Wigmore, Evidence § 2129 (Chadbourn rev. 1978).

27. See, e.g., Walker v. Firestone Tire & Rubber Co., 412 F.2d 60 (2d Cir. 1969) (tire rim and tire; admission discretionary where exhibit not easily alterable); Toole v. State, 146 Ga.App. 305, 246 S.E.2d 338 (1978) (distinguishing fungible items from distinct physical objects which can be identified by "mere observation"); State v. Sugimoto, 62 Hawaii 259, 614 P.2d 386 (1980) (trial court has discretion to admit items, here a check, without complete chain of custody when item is identifiable and relatively impervious to change; American Reciprocal Insurers v. Bessonette, 241 Or. 500, 405 P.2d 529 (1965) (water pipe, admission discretionary where nature and environment of exhibit did not raise substantial doubts of authenticity or unchanged condition). But cf. Cheek v. Avco Lycoming Division, 56 Ill. App.3d 217, 13 Ill.Dec. 902, 371 N.E.2d 994 (1977) (airplane engine which had been in hands of several mechanics who had worked on it and replaced parts not admissible). If the object offered is not claimed to possess any unique trait material to the suit, strict proof of identity is sometimes foregone. See, e.g., Isaacs v. National Bank of Commerce, 50 Wn.2d 548, 313 P.2d

to be susceptible to alteration by tampering or contamination, sound exercise of the trial court's discretion may require a substantially more elaborate foundation.[28] A foundation of the latter sort will commonly entail testimonially tracing the "chain of custody" of the item with sufficient completeness to render it improbable that the original item has either been exchanged with another or been contaminated or tampered with.[29] It should, however, always be borne in mind that foundational requirements are essentially requirements of logic, and not rules of art. Thus, e.g., even a radically altered item of real evidence may be admissible if its pertinent features remain unaltered.[30]

Real evidence consisting of samples drawn from a larger mass are also generally held admissible, subject to the foregoing requirements pertaining to real evidence generally, and subject to the further requirement that the sample be established to be accurately representative of the mass.[31]

Demonstrative evidence, however, is by no means limited to items which may properly be classed as "real" or "original" evidence. It is today increasingly common to encounter the offer of tangible items which are not themselves contended to have played any part in the history of the case, but which are instead tendered for the purpose of rendering other evidence more comprehensible to the trier of fact.[32] Examples of types of items frequently offered for purposes of illustration and clarification include models, maps, photographs, charts, and drawings.[33] If an article is offered for these purposes, rather than as real or original evidence, its specific identity or source is generally of no significance whatever.[34] Instead, the theory justifying admission of these exhibits requires only that the item be sufficiently explanatory or illustrative of relevant testimony in the case to be of potential help to the trier of fact.[35] Whether the admission of a particular exhibit will in fact be helpful, or

684 (1957); see also Comment, 61 Nw.U.L.Rev. 472 (1966).

For a clear statement of the relativity of foundation requirements, see Loza v. State, 263 Ind. 124, 325 N.E.2d 173 (1975).

28. See State v. Myers, 351 Mo. 332, 172 S.W.2d 946 (1943); State v. Boehme, 71 Wn.2d 621, 430 P.2d 527 (1967); Comment, 61 Nw.U.L.Rev. 472 (1966). Chemical specimens are frequently recognized as raising possibilities of mistaken exchange, tampering and contamination. See, e.g., Novak v. District of Columbia, 82 U.S.App.D.C. 95, 160 F.2d 588 (1947); Annot., 21 A.L.R.2d 1216. The various business records statutes, however, have proved of great utility in securing admission of regularly marked and labeled specimens. See, e.g., Gass v. United States, 135 U.S.App.D.C. 11, 416 F.2d 767 (1969).

29. See Erickson v. North Dakota Workmen's Compensation Bureau, 123 N.W.2d 292 (N.D.1963); see also, Gallego v. United States, 276 F.2d 914 (9th Cir. 1960) (narcotics, tracing sufficient to justify exercise of trial court's discretion in admitting); People v. Malone, 4 N.Y.2d 8, 197 N.E.2d 189 (1964) (tracing sufficient). It has sometimes been suggested that stringent tracing requirements, arguably appropriate in criminal prosecutions, should be relaxed in civil cases. See Woolley v. Hafner's Wagon Wheel, Inc., 22 Ill.2d 413, 176 N.E.2d 757 (1961) reversing 27 Ill.App.2d 1, 169 N.E.2d 119 (1960), 110 U.Pa.L.Rev. 895 (1962).

30. See United States v. Skelley, 501 F.2d 447 (7th Cir. 1974) (unlawful possession of counterfeit; admission of counterfeit bills all bearing identical serial numbers held proper to prove knowledge of counterfeit

against general objection based upon change in color from green to blue).

31. Kunzman v. Cherokee Silo Co., 253 Iowa 885, 114 N.W.2d 534 (1962); Annot., 95 A.L.R.2d 681. See also People v. Porpora, 91 Cal.App.Supp.3d 13, 154 Cal. Rptr. 400 (1979) (admission of sample data to show percentage of Pacific Mackerel in defendant's catch proper where predicated on statistical showing that sample was representative).

32. Smith v. Ohio Oil Co., 10 Ill.App.2d 67, 134 N.E.2d 526 (1956) (holding skeleton properly admitted to illustrate medical testimony and distinguishing between "real" and "demonstrative" evidence).

33. 3 Wigmore, Evidence § 790 (Chadbourn rev. 1970). But a map or photograph can easily figure in the history of a case and thus constitute real evidence. Goldner & Mrovka, Demonstrative Evidence and Audio-Visual Aids at Trial, 8 U.Fla.L.Rev. 185, 187 (1955).

34. See, e.g., Cohen v. Kindlon, 366 F.2d 762 (2d Cir. 1966) (failure to establish authorship of sketch used for illustration held "of no consequence"); Intermill v. Heumesser, 154 Colo. 496, 391 P.2d 684 (1964) (admission of X rays of unidentified person testified to be "normal" upheld and "encouraged"). But an occasional trial judge will be found confusing illustrative exhibits with real evidence and rejecting the former. See, e.g., Hernke v. Northern Insurance Co., 20 Wis.2d 352, 122 N.W.2d 395 (1963).

35. See, e.g., Slow Development Co. v. Coulter, 88 Ariz. 122, 353 P.2d 890 (1960) (charts, etc., admissible to illustrate anything witness allowed to describe); McKee v. Chase, 73 Idaho 491, 253 P.2d 787 (1953) (excel-

will instead tend to confuse or mislead the trier, is a matter commonly viewed to be within the sound discretion of the trial court.[36]

 WESTLAW REFERENCES

digest(demonstrative /2 evidence /p photo! picture* /p prejudic!)

digest(demonstrative /2 evidence /p firearm* gun* rifle* pistol*)

synopsis,digest(x-ray* /5 evidence)

---

§ 213. Maps, Models, and Duplicates [1]

Among the most frequently utilized types of illustrative evidence are maps, sketches, diagrams,[2] models and duplicates.[3] Unlike real evidence, the availability of which will frequently depend upon circumstances beyond counsel's control, opportunities for the use of the types of demonstrative evidence here considered are limited only by counsel's ability to recognize them. The potential of these aids for giving clarity and interest to

spoken statements seems sure to guarantee their continued and expanded use in the future.[4]

While all jurisdictions allow the use of demonstrative items to illustrate and explain oral testimony, there is considerable diversity of judicial opinion concerning the precise evidentiary status of articles used for this purpose.[5] Even in the majority of jurisdictions where there is no apparent bar to, or restriction upon, their full admission, it is not uncommon for maps, models, etc., to be displayed and referred to without being formally offered or admitted into evidence.[6] While no absolute prohibition would appear to be justified concerning such informal use of illustrative items, numerous appellate courts have commented upon the difficulties created on appeal when crucial testimony has been given in the form of indecipherable references to an object not available to the reviewing court.[7] By the more common, and clearly preferable practice, illustrative objects will be identified by the witness as sub-

---

lent statement of theory of admission); Kroeger v. Safranek, 161 Neb. 182, 72 N.W.2d 831 (1955). See also Dec.Dig. Witnesses ⟐252. A number of courts, while allowing illustrative exhibits, assert they are not "substantive" evidence. See, e.g., State v. Gardner, 228 N.C. 567, 46 S.E.2d 824 (1948). The practical consequences of the latter view are discussed in §§ 213, 216, infra.

36. See, e.g., Smith v. Ohio Oil Co., 10 Ill.App.2d 67, 134 N.E.2d 526 (1956), supra n. 34; Commonwealth, Department of Highways v. Garland, 394 S.W.2d 450 (Ky.1965) (exclusion of photos held abuse of discretion); Workman v. McIntyre Construction Co., ___ Mont. ___, 617 P.2d 1281 (1980) (abuse of discretion to reject sample traffic sign; demonstrative evidence inadmissible only where irrelevant or prejudicial); State v. Ray, 43 N.J. 19, 202 A.2d 425 (1964) (sound discretion would permit helpful charts; dictum).

§ 213

1. 3 Wigmore, Evidence §§ 790, 791 (Chadbourn rev. 1970); Dec.Dig. Evidence ⟐194 (duplicates, models and casts), 358 (maps, plats and diagrams), Criminal Law ⟐404(1)–(2), Trial ⟐39, Witnesses ⟐252.

2. Cases involving maps, sketches and diagrams are collected in Annot., 9 A.L.R.2d 1044.

3. Cases involving models and duplicates in various contexts are collected in Annot., 69 A.L.R.2d 424 (models of sites in civil actions), 23 A.L.R.3d 825 (models of property taken by eminent domain), 58 A.L.R.2d 689 (models and charts of human anatomy in civil cases), 93 A.L.R.2d 1097 (similar, criminal cases).

4. See authorities cited § 212 n. 8 supra.

5. A majority of jurisdictions appear to view maps, models, etc., used to illustrate testimony as fully admissible. See Annots., 9 A.L.R.2d 1044, 69 A.L.R.2d 424. However, the following variegated positions are to be noted: Crocker v. Lee, 261 Ala. 439, 74 So.2d 429 (1954) ("The use of a map . . . for illustration must be distinguished from its admission in evidence"); State v. Peters, 44 Hawaii 1, 352 P.2d 329 (1959) ("irregular" to admit sketch used for illustration); Baker v. Zimmerman, 179 Iowa 272, 161 N.W. 479 (1917) (whether illustrative item formally admitted "insignificant," but it should not be taken to jury room); McCormick v. Smith, 246 N.C. 425, 98 S.E.2d 448 (1957) (map not "substantive evidence" but properly used to aid description); Chambers v. Robert, 160 N.E.2d 673 (Ohio App.1959) (stating illustrative sketch should not be admitted and opponent is entitled, on demand, to an instruction that item is illustrative).

6. See, e.g., Maxwell v. State, 236 Ark. 694, 370 S.W.2d 113 (1963); Grantham v. Herod, 320 S.W.2d 536 (Mo.1959); Traders & General Insurance Co. v. Stone, 258 S.W.2d 409 (Tex.Civ.App.1953) (model spine and nerve charts used but not offered; no error). But compare Handford v. Cole, 402 P.2d 209 (Wyo.1965) (error to allow reference to drawings before formally identified and introduced).

7. See, e.g., Radetsky v. Leonard, 145 Colo. 358, 358 P.2d 1014 (1961); Meglemry v. Bruner, 344 S.W.2d 808 (Ky.1961); State ex rel. State Highway Commission v. Hill, 373 S.W.2d 666 (Mo.1963) (remanding for new trial because of obscurity of record).

stantially correct representations and will be formally introduced as part of the witness' testimony, in which they are incorporated by reference.[8]

Illustrative exhibits may often properly and satisfactorily be used in lieu of real evidence. As previously noted, articles actually involved in a transaction or occurrence may have become lost or be unavailable, or witnesses may be unable to testify that the article present in court is the identical one they have previously observed. Where only the generic characteristics of the item are significant no objection would appear to exist to the introduction of a substantially similar "duplicate."[9] While the matter is generally viewed as within the discretion of the trial court,[10] it has been suggested that it would constitute reversible error to exclude a duplicate testified to be identical to the object involved in the occurrence.[11] On the other hand, if there is an absence of testimony that the object to be illustrated ever existed the introduction of a "duplicate" may

foster a mistaken impression of certainty and thus merit exclusion.[12]

Models, maps, sketches, and diagrams (as distinguished from duplicates) are by their nature generally not confusable with real evidence, and are admissible simply on the basis of testimony that they are substantially accurate representations of what the witness is endeavoring to describe.[13] Some discretionary control in the trial court is generally deemed appropriate, however, since exhibits of this kind, due to inaccuracies, variations of scale, etc., may on occasion be more misleading than helpful.[14] Nevertheless, when the trial court has exercised its discretion to admit, it will only rarely be found in error, at least if potentially misleading inaccuracies have been pointed out by witnesses for the proponent, or could have been exposed upon cross-examination.[15]

 **WESTLAW REFERENCES**

digest(illustrative demonstrative /2 evidence /p map*)

---

8. See Handford v. Cole, 402 P.2d 209 (Wyo.1965).

Correspondingly, the blackboard as a device for illustrating testimony and argument has been replaced by an easel with a large pad of paper on which drawings may be made and the sheets included in the record on review when appropriate.

9. See, e.g., People v. Jordan, 188 Cal.App.2d 456, 10 Cal.Rptr. 495 (1961) (where real evidence unavailable, similar object may be admitted); Sherman v. City of Springfield, 77 Ill.App.2d 195, 222 N.E.2d 62 (1966) (error to exclude accurate duplicate where original unobtainable); Warren v. Allgood, 344 So.2d 151 (Miss. 1977) (lime established as similar to that drifting across highway from defendant's field held properly admitted). Similar results have been reached by admitting objects as real evidence on the basis of equivocal "identifications." See, e.g., Crosby v. State, 2 Md.App. 578, 236 A.2d 33 (1967) (unique gun "looking like" that used admitted); Isaacs v. National Bank of Commerce, 50 Wn.2d 548, 313 P.2d 684 (1957) (hose "believed" to be the hose in question admitted). But compare Alston v. Shiver, 105 So.2d 785 (Fla.1958) (error to admit axe handle 3 feet long to illustrate one 2 feet long).

10. See, e.g., State v. McClain, 404 S.W.2d 186 (Mo. 1966). An even more permissive view is suggested by Finch v. W. R. Roach Co., 295 Mich. 589, 295 N.W. 324 (1940) (duplicate admissible if proponent introduces testimony from which similarity might be found).

11. Cincinnati, New Orleans & Texas Pacific Railway Co. v. Duvall, 263 Ky. 387, 92 S.W.2d 363 (1936)

(error to exclude model of car step proved to be exact duplicate); Rich v. Cooper, 234 Or. 300, 380 P.2d 613 (1963) (error to exclude exact duplicates; dictum).

12. See Young v. Price, 50 Hawaii 430, 442 P.2d 67 (1968) (comprehensive discussion of problem).

13. See, e.g., Grayson v. Williams, 256 F.2d 61 (10th Cir. 1958) (plat admissible where substantially accurate but not exact); United States v. D'Antonio, 324 F.2d 667 (3d Cir. 1963) (blackboard sketch not to scale admissible), cert. denied 376 U.S. 909; City of Tucson v. LaForge, 8 Ariz.App. 413, 446 P.2d 692 (1968) (model; semble). But cf. Swiney v. State Highway Department, 116 Ga.App. 667, 158 S.E.2d 321 (1967) (no error to exclude map not established as accurate).

14. San Mateo County v. Christen, 22 Cal.App.2d 375, 71 P.2d 88 (1937) (engineer's model excluded; "while models may frequently be of great assistance . . . even when constructed to scale they may frequently, because of the great disparity in size . . . also be very misleading, and trial courts must be allowed wide discretion . . . ").

15. See, e.g., Grandquest v. Williams, 273 Ala. 140, 135 So.2d 391 (1961) (not error to admit sketch and toy autos not to scale where witness pointed out inaccuracies and could have been further cross-examined); Arkansas State Highway Commission v. Rhodes, 240 Ark. 565, 401 S.W.2d 558 (1966) (inaccuracies not misleading where explained); Mississippi Road Supply Co. v. Baker, 199 So.2d 820 (Miss.1967) (cross-examination as to inaccuracies allowed, no chance of misleading).

digest(illustrative demonstrative /2 evidence /p drawing* sketch** diagram*)

§ 214. Photographs,[1] Movies,[2] and Sound Recordings [3]

The principle upon which photographs are most commonly admitted into evidence is the same as that underlying the admission of illustrative drawings, maps and diagrams. Under this theory, a photograph is viewed merely as a graphic portrayal of oral testimony, and becomes admissible only when a witness has testified that it is a correct and accurate representation of relevant facts personally observed by the witness.[4] Accordingly, under this theory, the witness who lays the foundation need not be the photographer nor need he know anything of the time, conditions, or mechanisms of the taking.[5] Instead he need only know about the facts represented or the scene or objects photographed, and once this knowledge is shown he can say whether the photograph correctly and accurately portrays these facts. Once the photograph is thus verified it is admissible as a graphic portrayal of the verifying witness' testimony into which it is incorporated by reference.[6]

The foregoing doctrine concerning the basis on which photographs are admitted is clearly a viable one and has undoubtedly served to facilitate the introduction of the general run of photographs. Unfortunately, however, some courts have tended to carry the implications of the theory to unwonted lengths, admitting photographs as "illustrative" evidence but denying them "substantive" effect.[7] It is believed that this distinction is essentially groundless,[8] and fails to

§ 214

1. 3 Wigmore, Evidence §§ 790–798 (Chadbourn rev. 1970) Scott, Photographic Evidence (2d ed. 1967); C.J.S. Evidence §§ 709–716; Dec.Dig. Evidence ⚫359(1), 380.

2. 3 Wigmore, Evidence § 798(a) (Chadbourn rev. 1970) Dec.Dig. Evidence ⚫359(6); Paradis, The Celluloid Witness, 37 U.Colo.L.Rev. 235 (1965).

3. Dec.Dig. Evidence ⚫359(5), 380.

4. 3 Wigmore, Evidence § 790, at 218 (Chadbourn rev. 1970): ". . . the mere picture . . . cannot be received except as a non-verbal expression of the *testimony of some witness* competent to speak to the facts represented." State v. Smith, 27 N.J. 433, 142 A.2d 890, 899 (1958) ("Fundamentally, photographs are deemed to be pictorial communications of a qualified witness.") In the effort to establish photographs as accurately illustrative of the data observed by the witness, it is sometimes forgotten that the data itself must be relevant. Knihal v. State, 150 Neb. 771, 36 N.W.2d 109, 9 A.L.R.2d 891 (1949) (holding photos improperly received where foundation established only that photo correctly portrayed objects photographed but did not establish what objects were.); Beattie v. Traynor, 114 Vt. 495, 49 A.2d 200, 204 (1946) ("A photograph . . . is merely a witness' pictured expression of the data observed by him . . . and its admission, when properly verified, rests on the relevancy of the fact pictured."). Kleveland v. United States, 345 F.2d 134 (2d Cir. 1965) (improper to exclude photo not seen taken by witness); Kortz v. Guardian Life Insurance Co., 144 F.2d 676 (9th Cir. 1944) (proper foundation may be laid either by photographer or another qualified person.); Adams v. City of San Jose, 164 Cal.App. 2d 665, 330 P.2d 840 (1958).

5. Kooyumjian v. Stevens, 10 Ill.App.2d 378, 135 N.E.2d 146, 151 (1956) ("The witness need not be the photographer, nor need he know anything of the time or condition of the taking, but he must have personal knowledge of the scene or object in question and testify that is correctly portrayed by the photograph.") Even if the photograph is defective, or is taken after the scene or object in question has undergone changes, it may still come in if substantially correct and potentially helpful to the jury. Driver v. Worth Construction Co., 264 S.W.2d 174 (Tex.Civ.App.1954), reversed on other grounds, 154 Tex. 66, 273 S.W.2d 603 (subsequent photo of scene admissible despite changed conditions); Owens v. Anderson, 58 Wn.2d 448, 364 P.2d 14 (1961) (slight changes in scene went to weight). But seriously defective photography or radically altered conditions may work exclusion. Stormont v. New York Central Railroad Co., 1 Ohio App.2d 414, 205 N.E.2d 74, n. 1 (1964) (improper to admit photos so poor as to distort conditions); Jones v. Talbot, 87 Idaho 498, 394 P.2d 316 (1964) (drastically altered conditions; photos properly excluded).

6. Finch v. W. R. Roach Co., 295 Mich. 589, 295 N.W. 324, 326 (1940).

7. See, e.g., Foster v. Bilbruck, 20 Ill.App.2d 173, 155 N.E.2d 366 (1959) (stating that photos stand on same footing as maps and models, and are not themselves evidence); State v. Bass, 249 N.C. 209, 105 S.E.2d 645 (1958) (citing many North Carolina precedents drawing the distinction.)

8. See Gardner, The Camera Goes to Court, 24 N.C.L.Rev. 233, 245 (1956) (cogent criticism of the distinction). Some courts explicitly reject the distinction, State v. Goyet, 120 Vt. 12, 132 A.2d 623, 631 (1957) (". . . a photograph is admissible in evidence, not merely as a map or diagram representing things to

warrant the practical consequences which are sometimes seen to flow from it.[9]

The products of certain applications of the photographic process do not readily lend themselves to admission in evidence on the foregoing theory.[10] X-ray photographs are a common example, and are of course constantly admitted, despite the fact that no witness has actually viewed the objects portrayed.[11] The foundation typically required for X-rays is calculated to demonstrate that a reliable scientific process was correctly utilized to obtain the product offered in evidence. Earlier recognized only sporadically,[12] this same approach has in recent years found greatly increased acceptance as applied to various products of the photographic process.[13] Under this doctrine, commonly referred to as the "silent witness" theory of admission, photographic evidence may draw its verification, not from any witness who

has actually viewed the scene portrayed on film, but from the reliability of the process by which the representation was produced. The foundation required will thus resemble that required for the admission of the products of other scientific processes, i.e., that the application in the present instance was a valid one. Such a foundation, of course, is relatively more elaborate than the simple one required under the traditional theory; however, the "silent witness" doctrine will today afford an alternative route to the introduction of photographic evidence in circumstances which preclude resort to the older theory.

The interest and vividness of photographs may be heightened by utilization of various techniques of photography, such as having the photographs taken in color, or having them enlarged so that pertinent facts may be more readily observed. While the use of

---

which a witness testifies, but as direct evidence of things which have not been directly described by a witness as having come from his observation."); a majority of courts simply seems to ignore it. See cases cited 3 Wigmore, Evidence § 792, note 1 (Chadbourn rev. 1970); Dec.Dig. Evidence ⟨key⟩359.

9. In those jurisdictions in which a photograph is considered merely illustrative, the adverse party may be entitled to an instruction that the photo is not substantive evidence. See Honeycutt v. Cherokee Brick Co., 196 N.C. 556, 146 S.E. 227 (1929); Hunt v. Wooten, 238 N.C. 42, 76 S.E.2d 326 (1953). Or, like other "illustrative" evidence, the jury may not be permitted to take the photo to the jury room. See cases cited supra § 213 n. 5; and see generally § 217 infra.

10. Comment, Photographic Evidence—Is There a Recognized Basis for Admissibility? 8 Hast.L.J. 310 (1957) (noting that scenes photographed by infrared flash or by electronically triggered surveillance cameras are not seen by any potential witness.) For additional illustrations of photographic evidence presenting difficulties under ordinary theory, see People v. Bowley, 59 Cal.2d 855, 31 Cal.Rptr. 471, 382 P.2d 591 (1963). And see 3 Wigmore, Evidence (Chadbourn rev.) § 790, p. 219.

11. See 3 Wigmore, Evidence § 795 (Chadbourn rev. 1970) Dec.Dig. Evidence ⟨key⟩380.

12. People v. Bowley, 59 Cal.2d 855, 31 Cal.Rptr. 471, 382 P.2d 591, 595 (1963) ("We hold . . . that a photograph may, in a proper case, be admitted into evidence not merely as illustrated testimony of a human witness but as probative evidence in itself of what it shows."); People v. Doggett, 83 Cal.App.2d 405, 188 P.2d 792 (1948) (photos of defendants committing crime against nature; no other witnesses but photos admit-

ted on basis of testimony by expert photographer that they were not composites or otherwise altered); State v. Matheson, 130 Iowa 440, 103 N.W. 137, 138 (1905) (" . . . the court takes judicial notice of the fact that by the ordinary photographic process a representation can be secured, sufficiently truthful and reliable to be considered as evidence with reference to objects which are in a condition to be thus photographed without regard to whether they have been actually observed by any witness or not.").

13. Among the substantial number of decisions relying expressly on the theory, the following may be cited: United States v. Bynum, 567 F.2d 1167 (1st Cir. 1978); State v. Kasold, 110 Ariz. 558, 521 P.2d 990 (1974); Bergner v. State, 397 N.E.2d 1012 (1979) ("The 'silent witness theory' for the admission of photographic evidence permits the use of photographs at trial as *substantive* evidence, as opposed to merely demonstrative evidence. Thus, under the silent witness theory there is no need for a witness to testify a photograph accurately represents what he or she observed; the photograph 'speaks for itself' "); Ferguson v. Commonwealth, 212 Va. 745, 187 S.E.2d 189 (1972), cert. denied 409 U.S. 861.

The two different theories of admissibility of photographs are reflected in these illustrations of authentication techniques in Fed.R.Evid. 901(b):

(1) *Testimony of witness with knowledge.* Testimony that a matter is what it is claimed to be.

. . .

(9) *Process or system.* Evidence describing a process or system used to produce a result and showing that the process or system produces an accurate result.

these techniques clearly increases the number of factors subject to distortion, the basic standard governing admission of photos generally remains applicable.[14] Thus color and enlarged photographs have generally been viewed as admissible provided the photo represents the scene depicted with substantial accuracy.[15]

A somewhat more troublesome problem is presented by posed or artificially reconstructed scenes, in which people, automobiles, and other objects are placed so as to conform to the descriptions of the original crime or collision given by the witnesses.[16] When the posed photographs go no further than to portray the positions of persons and objects as reflected in the undisputed testimony, their admission has long been generally approved.[17] Frequently, however, a posed photograph will portray only the version of the facts supported by the testimony of the proponent's witness. The dangers inherent in this situation, i.e., the tendency of the photographs unduly to emphasize certain testimony and the possibility that the jury may confuse one party's reconstruction with objective fact, have led many courts to

exclude photographs of this type.[18] The orthodox theory of photos as merely illustrated testimony, however, can be viewed to support the admission of any photo reflecting a state of facts testified to by a witness and the current trend would appear to be to permit even photos of disputed reconstructions in some instances.[19]

Motion pictures, when they were first sought to be introduced in evidence, were frequently objected to and sometimes excluded on the theory that they afforded manifold opportunities for fabrication and distortion.[20] Even those older decisions which upheld the admission of motion pictures appear to have done so on the basis of elaborate foundation testimony detailing the methods of taking, processing, and projecting the film.[21] More recently, however, it appears to have become generally recognized that, as with the still photograph, the reliability and accuracy of the motion picture need not necessarily rest upon the validity of the process used in its creation, but rather may be established by testimony that the motion picture accurately reproduces phe-

14. See, e.g., Johnson v. Clement F. Sculley Construction Co., 255 Minn. 41, 95 N.W.2d 409 (1959) (color photos of personal injury admissible if accurate); Commonwealth Department of Highways v. Williams, 317 S.W.2d 482 (Ky.1958) (semble); State v. Clark, 99 Or. 629, 196 P. 360 (1921) (enlargements held admissible if not misleading). Nor does the presence of both factors together necessitate exclusion. See Commonwealth v. Makarewicz, 333 Mass. 575, 132 N.E.2d 294 (1955) (enlarged color photos held properly admitted).

15. See Annot., 53 A.L.R.2d 1102 (collecting cases on color photos); 72 A.L.R.2d 308 (enlargements). The following cases suggest that some failure to achieve exact reproduction is permissible: Green v. City and County of Denver, 111 Colo. 390, 142 P.2d 277 (1943) (color photos held admissible to show condition of putrid meat despite underexposure which made meat appear darker than it was.); State v. Smith, 27 N.J. 433, 142 A.2d 890 (1958) (color transparencies showing "bloody areas" admissible in trial court's discretion though witness testified pictures might "exaggerate on the red side").

16. Cases involving posed photos are collected in Annots., 27 A.L.R. 913, 19 A.L.R.2d 877. See also, Dec.Dig. Criminal Law ⟨⟩438(k).

17. Langley v. State, 90 Okl.Cr. 310, 213 P.2d 886 (1950) (photos found illustrative of factual circumstances rather than party theory held properly admit-

ted); Pollack v. State, 215 Wis. 200, 253 N.W. 560 (1934) (murder; photos of defendants in positions which they indicated they occupied at time of shooting). See also Note, 7 W. & M.L.Rev. 137 (1966) (collecting cases involving posed photos).

18. Martin v. State, 217 Miss. 506, 64 So.2d 629 (1953) (photos inadmissible where positions of persons shown was in dispute); Lynch v. Missouri-K.-T. Ry. Co., 333 Mo. 89, 61 S.W.2d 918 (1933).

19. Tumey v. Richardson, 437 S.W.2d 201 (Ky.1969) (photos of posed accident scene admissible despite conflict in testimony as to material particulars). A number of courts have adopted the intermediate position that photos of partisan reconstruction are admissible if a pressing necessity is shown. State v. Oldham, 92 Idaho 124, 438 P.2d 275 (1968); State v. Ray, 43 N.J. 19, 202 A.2d 425 (1964). See also, Note, 47 Ky.L.J. 117 (1958) (arguing for freer admission of posed photos).

20. Gibson v. Gunn, 206 App.Div. 464, 202 N.Y.S. 19 (1923); Massachusetts Bonding & Insurance Co. v. Worthy, 9 S.W.2d 388 (Tex.Civ.App.1928) ("It is common knowledge that pictures showing a person in action may be made very deceptive . . . ;" not error to exclude).

21. McGoorty v. Benhart, 305 Ill.App. 458, 27 N.E.2d 289 (1940) (motion pictures of malingerer admitted after laying of elaborate foundation).

nomena actually perceived by the witness.[22] Under this theory, though the requisite foundation may, and usually will, be laid by the photographer, it may also be provided by any witness who perceived the events filmed.[23] Of course, if the foundation testimony reveals the film to be distorted in some material particular, exclusion is the proper result.[24]

Judicial discretion in the admission or exclusion of motion pictures is constantly emphasized in the decisions,[25] and is perhaps largely attributable to the fact that the presentation of this kind of evidence will involve considerable expenditure of time and inconvenience. At the same time, however, when motion pictures are offered which reproduce the actual facts or original events in controversy, such as films of an allegedly incapacitated plaintiff shoveling snow or playing baseball,[26] or post-arrest films of an allegedly intoxicated driver,[27] the cogency of the evidence is such that the taking of considerable time and trouble to view the evidence would appear amply warranted.[28]

Somewhat more difficult questions are posed by moving pictures taken of an injured party pursuing ordinary day-to-day activities, offered for the purpose of bringing home to the trier of fact the implications and significance of the injury for which damages are sought.[29] With respect both to their relevance and to the possible objections which may legitimately be raised against them, these films are closely akin to bodily demonstrations of injuries in court.[30] Both species of evidence therefore ought to be governed by the same rule, to wit, both should be admissible only in the sound discretion, and under the strict control, of the trial court.[31]

The extreme vividness and persuasiveness of motion pictures, however, is a two-edged sword. If the film does not portray original facts in controversy, but rather represents a staged reproduction of one party's version of those facts, the danger that the jury may confuse art with reality is particularly great.[32] Further, the vivid impressions on the trier of fact created by the viewing of motion pictures will be particularly difficult to limit or, if the film is subsequently

22. Long v. General Electric Co., 213 Ga. 809, 102 S.E.2d 9 (1958) (motion picture held admissible on basis of foundation testimony by witness-photographer that it portrayed what he saw); Haley v. Hockey, 199 Misc. 512, 103 N.Y.S.2d 717 (Sup.Ct.1950) (movie admissible upon identification of persons and actions filmed). See also, International Union v. Russell, 264 Ala. 456, 88 So.2d 175 (1956), affirmed 356 U.S. 634 (1958); Annot., 62 A.L.R.2d 686, 9 A.L.R.2d 921.

23. The witness through whom the foundation for introduction of motion pictures, as distinguished from stills, is laid must have been present when the pictures were taken. See Hare, Demonstrative Evidence, 27 Ala.Law. 193 (1966).

24. Powell v. Industrial Commission, 4 Ariz.App. 172, 418 P.2d 602 (1966) (films misrepresenting speed of actions portrayed inadmissible), vacated on other grounds 102 Ariz. 11, 423 P.2d 348 (1967); Utley v. Heckinger, 235 Ark. 780, 362 S.W.2d 13 (1962) (preferable not to have shown portion of film which accelerated portrayed action).

25. Luther v. Maple, 250 F.2d 916 (8th Cir. 1958) (no abuse of discretion despite appellate court's belief that admission had been unwise); International Union v. Russell, 264 Ala. 456, 88 So.2d 175 (1956), affirmed 356 U.S. 634 (question within discretion of trial court, reviewable only for gross abuse).

26. Heiman v. Market Street Railway Co., 21 Cal. App.2d 311, 69 P.2d 178 (1937); McGoorty v. Benhart,

305 Ill.App. 458, 27 N.E.2d 289 (1940); Lamburt v. Wolf's, Inc., 132 So.2d 522 (La.App.1961).

27. Lanford v. People, 159 Colo. 136, 409 P.2d 829 (1966) (motion picture of alleged drunk driver admissible though film disclosed defendant's declination to take sobriety test; extensive review of pertinent authorities). See also, Commonwealth v. Roller, 100 Pa. Super. 125 (1930) (sound motion picture of defendant's confession).

28. Barham v. Nowell, 243 Miss. 441, 138 So.2d 493 (1962) (error to exclude motion pictures which in trial court's opinion were not "clear"); Wren v. St. Louis Public Service Co., 333 S.W.2d 92 (Mo.1960) (containing suggestion that if cogent motion pictures could not be satisfactorily viewed in courtroom, court should move to see them).

29. See Comment, 49 U.M.K.C.L.Rev. 179 (1981).

30. See § 215 infra.

31. For a case in which such discretion was seemingly soundly applied, see Grimes v. Employers Mutual Insurance Co., 73 F.R.D. 607 (D.Alaska 1977) (trial court reviewed film prior to admission and ordered exclusion of certain segments).

32. See Sanchez v. Denver & Rio Grande Western Railroad Co., 538 F.2d 304 (10th Cir. 1976), cert. denied 429 U.S. 1042 (1977) (stressing special scrutiny to be accorded motion picture showing reenactment of human conduct but holding motion picture admissible);

deemed to be inadmissible, to expunge by judicial instruction.

The latter difficulty may be largely eliminated by a preliminary viewing of the film by the trial court in chambers, and the decided cases suggest that this expedient is widely employed.[33] The former difficulty, while not so easily met, may be of less significance today than formerly, due to a higher level of jury sophistication concerning motion pictures.[34]

In recent years the more flexible technology of the videotape has begun substantially to replace the motion picture as the medium for bringing representations involving movement to the trier of fact.[35] Despite the fact that the videotape operates on principles quite different from those underlying the motion picture, both theories on which the latter have been admitted are equally applicable to the new technology. Thus, while the admissibility of videotape evidence has sometimes been specifically provided for by rule or statute,[36] such treatment is not a necessary precondition to reception of this type of evidence.

Sound recordings will sometimes be offered as an integral part of a motion picture, but a recording alone may of course also be probative of relevant facts. When a sound recording consists of spoken words, questions concerning the "best evidence" rule and the rule of completeness may be raised.[37] But sound recordings may also be offered as reproducing relevant nonverbal sounds, and when this is the purpose the considerations potentially affecting admissibility are substantially similar to those relating to motion pictures. Thus, the recording will generally be admitted if a witness testifies that the recording as played is an accurate reproduction of relevant sounds previously audited by the witness.[38] On occasion, too, sound recordings may be admitted upon a foundation analogous to that sometimes recognized for films taken by surveillance cameras.[39] This will consist of a showing of the accuracy and completeness of the recording by scientific and corroborative evidence.[40]

French v. City of Springfield, 65 Ill.2d 74, 2 Ill.Dec. 271, 357 N.E.2d 438 (1976) (viewpoint of film may condition jury to accept party's theory; film inadmissible).

33. Wren v. St. Louis Public Service Co., supra note 28. Additional cases are collected in Paradis, The Celluloid Witness, 37 U.Colo.L.Rev. 235, 246 at n. 52 (1965).

34. Greeneich v. Southern Pacific Co., 189 Cal.App. 2d 100, 11 Cal.Rptr. 235 (1961), criticized in 47 Iowa L.Rev. 1138 (1963); Streit v. Kestel, 108 Ohio App. 241, 161 N.E.2d 409 (1949) (films of staged reenactment admissible in discretion of trial court where substantial similarity of conditions shown); Paradis, op. cit. n. 33, supra, at p. 267.

But some cases seem to strain jury capacities beyond reasonable limits. See Randall v. Warnaco, Inc., 677 F.2d 1226 (8th Cir. 1982) (videotapes of five young women in turn pouring gasoline on logs, and spilling some, admissible to show absorptive properties of logs, but not as reenactment of events leading up to fire in tent).

35. See, e.g., People v. Heading, 39 Mich.App. 126, 197 N.W.2d 325 (1972) (videotape admissible on same type of foundation as motion picture). See also, Annot., 60 A.L.R.3d 333.

See Cunningham, Videotape Evidence: Technological Innovation in the Trial Process, 36 Ala.Law. 228 (1975);

Stewart, Videotape: Use in Demonstrative Evidence, 21 Def.L.J. 253 (1972). For an interesting suggestion as to the use of videotaping to insure availability of evidence in certain types of cases, see Peters & Wilkes, Videotaping of Surgery for Use as Demonstrative Evidence in Medical Malpractice Litigation, 16 Duq.L.Rev. 360 (1977).

36. See, e.g., Ohio R.Civ.Pro., Rule 40.

37. See Ch. 23 infra; § 56 supra.

38. Wilms v. Hand, 101 Cal.App.2d 811, 226 P.2d 728 (1951) (recordings of dog noises emanating from veterinary establishment and alleged to be a nuisance); Ragusa v. American Metal Works, 97 So.2d 683 (La. App.1957) (recordings of factory noises; semble). Cases dealing with the admissibility of sound recordings are collected in Annots., 58 A.L.R.2d 1024, 57 A.L.R.3d 746; Dec.Dig., Evidence ⟺358(5).

39. See n. 15 supra.

40. In the unusual case of State v. Smith, 85 Wn.2d 840, 540 P.2d 424 (1975) the murder victim took the precaution of carrying a tape recorder with him while keeping an appointment with his murderer. The resulting tape of the event, found during the autopsy, was held admissible on the basis of scientific testimony and other evidence corroborating its accuracy and completeness.

 **WESTLAW REFERENCES**

"motion picture*" movie* film* /p demonstrative illustrative /p evidence

videotape* /5 evidence

sound* /2 record! /s evidence

tape /2 record! /s evidence /s reliab! unreliab!

---

§ 215. Bodily Demonstrations: Experiments in Court

The exhibition of a wound or physical injury, e.g., the injury sustained by a plaintiff in a personal injury action, will frequently be the best and most direct evidence of a material fact.[1] Not surprisingly, therefore, exhibitions of physical injuries to the jury are commonly allowed.[2] In most jurisdictions the matter is viewed as subject to the discretion of the trial court,[3] but has sometimes been said to be a matter of right on the part of the injured party.[4] Further, in those ju-

risdictions which hold the matter to be discretionary, a trial court is rarely reversed for permitting a bodily exhibition. Thus, when the exhibition is permitted no abuse of discretion is generally found present even though the injury displayed was particularly shocking,[5] or even where the injury's nature or existence need not have been proved because admitted.[6]

Judicial opinion has been somewhat more divided concerning the propriety of going beyond the mere exhibition of an injury or physical condition by having the injured person perform actions or submit to manipulation by a physician.[7] The dangers inherent in demonstrations of this latter type include undue emotional response on the part of the jury and the fact that manifestations of pain and impairment of function are easily feigned and difficult to test by cross-examination.[8] Nevertheless, this matter too is

---

§ 215

1. Calumet Paving Co. v. Butkus, 113 Ind.App. 232, 47 N.E.2d 829 (1943) ("There is no other class of evidence more satisfactory or convincing . . . than the production and inspection of the very object or person whose condition is being investigated . . . ."); Chicago, Rock Island & Gulf Railway Co. v. DeBord, 62 Tex.Civ.App. 302, 132 S.W. 845 (1910) (exhibition of injuries proper; "evidence of a very high degree.") The significance of the exhibition, however, will vary with the issue to be proved. See Radosh v. Shipstad, 17 A.D.2d 660, 230 N.Y.S.2d 295 (1962) (exhibition of professional ice-skater in costume improper in breach of contract suit where issue was whether skater's weight at a prior time justified suspension.)

2. See Annot., 66 A.L.R.2d 1334; Dec.Dig. Evidence ⟨key⟩192, Trial ⟨key⟩27. See n. 15, § 212, supra.

3. See, e.g., Spaak v. Chicago & Northwestern Railway Co., 231 F.2d 279 (7th Cir. 1956) (exhibition of injured foot; discretion of trial court not abused); Darling v. Charleston Community Memorial Hospital, 50 Ill.App.2d 253, 200 N.E.2d 149, 185 (1964), affirmed 33 Ill.2d 326, 211 N.E.2d 253 (1965), cert. denied 383 U.S. 946 ("Permitting the plaintiff to exhibit the stump of his amputated leg is within the discretion of the court, and only if there be an abuse of discretion . . . would such be reversible error"; no abuse found).

4. Olson v. Tyner, 219 Iowa 251, 257 N.W. 538 (1934) (plaintiff stripped to the waist to display shriveled left arm dangling "as though suspended by a string;" ". . . appellee had the right to exhibit to the jury his arm to show the condition he was in"); Missouri, Kansas & Texas Railway Co. v. O'Hare, 39 S.W.2d 939, 941 (Tex.Civ.App.1931) (". . . we think appellee had the right if he desired, to exhibit his in-

jured arm to the jury;" but propriety of repeated exhibitions questioned.).

5. Slattery v. Marra Brothers, 186 F.2d 134, 138 (2d Cir. 1951) (" . . . ordinarily it would seem that the very hideousness of the deformity was a part of the suffering of the victim, and could not rationally be excluded in assessment of his damages."); Beal v. Southern Union Gas Co., 66 N.M. 424, 349 P.2d 337 (1960) (not abuse of discretion in allowing plaintiff whose eyes, nose and ears were burned out to display injuries); Shell Petroleum v. Perrin, 179 Okl. 142, 64 P.2d 309 (1936) (not error to permit mother of little girl suing for injury to eye to remove girl's glass eye before the jury).

6. Stegall v. Carlson, 6 Ill.App.2d 388, 128 N.E.2d 352 (1955) (exhibition proper even where fact and nature of injury not disputed); Chicago, Burlington & Quincy Railway Co. v. Krayenbuhl, 70 Neb. 766, 98 N.W. 44 (1904) (rejecting contention that injury may not be displayed where admitted.) But compare Harper v. Bolton, 239 S.C. 541, 124 S.E.2d 54 (1962) (finding abuse in admission of plaintiff's removed and preserved eye where loss of eye was admitted). But compare Curry v. American Enka, Inc., 452 F.Supp. 178 (E.D.Tenn.1977) (suggesting such demonstrations proper only where shedding light on a controverted fact; court refuses under any circumstances to compel unwilling jurors to feel plaintiff's "flesh," in this case his hands).

7. Annot., 66 A.L.R.2d 1382; Dec.Dig. Evidence ⟨key⟩192.

8. The possible objections to the practice are enumerated in Clark v. Brooklyn Heights Railway Co., 177 N.Y. 359, 69 N.E. 647 (1904) (criticizing demonstration, but holding matter discretionary).

commonly left to the discretion of the trial courts, and that discretion is frequently exercised in favor of permitting the demonstration.[9] Occasional cases have, however, held the allowance of a particular demonstration to be an abuse of trial court discretion, a fact which may suggest that the tactic is a somewhat hazardous one for the party utilizing it.[10]

In addition to active demonstrations of physical injuries, in-court reenactment of material events by witnesses has been held permissible to illustrate testimony.[11]

Whether demonstrations in the form of experiments in court are to be permitted is also largely subject to the discretion of the trial judge.[12] Unlike experiments performed out

of court, the results of which are generally communicated testimonially, in-court experimentation may involve considerable confusion and delay, and the trial judge is viewed as in the best position to judge whether the game is worth the candle.[13] Simple demonstrations by a witness are usually permitted, and may be strikingly effective in adding vividness to the spoken word.[14]

In addition to the limitations arising from the desirability of orderly and expeditious proceedings, in-court experiments are held to the same basic requirement of similarity of conditions which is applicable to experimental evidence generally.[15] This requirement may be particularly difficult to meet under courtroom conditions, and many proposed courtroom experiments have been

9. Happy v. Walz, 224 S.W.2d 380 (Mo.App.1951) (manipulation of feet and legs by doctor); Wilson & Co. v. Campbell, 195 Okl. 323, 157 P.2d 465 (1945) (going beyond mere exhibition requires discretionary control by trial court; no abuse to allow cross-plaintiff to demonstrate numbness of injured leg by use of pins); Green v. Boney, 233 S.C. 49, 103 S.E.2d 732 (1958) (no abuse of discretion to permit plaintiff, once sworn, to demonstrate limp to jury.) But discretion may equally be exercised in the opposite direction. Hehir v. Bowers, 85 Ill.App.3d 625, 40 Ill.Dec. 918, 921, 407 N.E.2d 149, 152 (1980) (no abuse of discretion to deny plaintiff opportunity to demonstrate limited range of motion in injured shoulder; "The allowance of such demonstrations by an injured party is generally frowned upon"). It may be noted that testimony as to pain and impairment of use is also subject to fabrication.

10. Willis v. Browning, 161 Mo.App. 461, 143 S.W. 516 (1912) (permitting plaintiff to show how she could walk without crutches held reversible error; court distinguishes mere exhibition of injury); Peters v. Hockley, 152 Or. 434, 53 P.2d 1059 (1936) (abuse of discretion to permit demonstration calculated to make plaintiff cry out in pain.) It would appear that screaming by the party being manipulated, though sometimes viewed as not prejudicial, is a factor likely to lead to reversal. See cases cited Annot., 66 A.L.R.2d 1382.

11. See State v. Anderson, 171 Mont. 188, 557 P.2d 795 (1976) (DWI prosecution; patrolman witness allowed to demonstrate manner in which defendant walked following arrest); State v. Page, 31 N.C.App. 740, 230 S.E.2d 433 (1976) (demonstration of events testified to by rape victim staged by victim and police officer "playing" defendant's role).

12. Lynch v. Missouri K.–T. Ry. Co., 333 Mo. 89, 61 S.W.2d 918 (1933) (admission of experimental evidence, whether experiment performed in or out of court, said to be "peculiarly within the discretion of the trial judge.") See also, Rex v. Duncan, [1944] 1 K.B. 713, Ct.Crim.App. (spiritualist medium, prosecuted under

witchcraft statute, refused permission to summon departed spirits to courtroom); Coca Cola Co. v. Langston, 198 Ark. 59, 127 S.W.2d 263 (1939) (witness offered to swallow teaspoon of ground glass; refusal to permit discretionary); Raymond v. J. R. Watkins Co., 88 F.Supp. 932 (D.Minn.1950), reversed on other grounds 184 F.2d 925 (breach of implied warranty on shampoo; discretion whether to allow defendant to shampoo another person in court exercised against experiment); Otte v. Taylor, 180 Neb. 795, 146 N.W.2d 78 (1966) (physician allowed to swallow nembutal tablets at beginning of testimony and to testify an hour later he was not drowsy; discretion to permit upheld). Compare Schleunes v. American Casualty Co., 528 F.2d 634 (5th Cir. 1976) (action on accidental death policy, with defendant claiming suicide; in view of sharp conflict in expert testimony, abuse of discretion to refuse to allow defendant's expert to demonstrate that rifle with which insured shot himself could not be fired without taking additional steps inconsistent with accidental firing).

13. See Otte v. Taylor, op. cit. supra n. 12; Hassebroek v. Norman, 236 Or. 209, 387 P.2d 824 (1963) (trial court refused to permit demonstration of child's toy which had injured plaintiff; "A request for a courtroom demonstration creates a problem peculiarly directed to the trial judge.")

14. Hamilton v. Pepsi Cola Bottling Co., 132 A.2d 500 (Mun.Ct.App.D.C., 1957) (no abuse in permitting demonstration that pop bottles could be unsealed and resealed without detection); Backstrom v. New York Life Insurance Co., 194 Minn. 67, 259 N.W. 681 (1935) (issue as to suicide or accidental shooting; witness who discovered body allowed to demonstrate its position by lying on the floor.); Geisel v. Mantl, 427 S.W.2d 525 (Mo.1968) (suit for personal injuries allegedly due to wobbly handrail; jurors held properly allowed to pull on scale previously used in out-of-court experiment to "see how much 25 pounds is.")

15. See § 202 supra.

held properly excluded on this ground.[16] Nevertheless, the well-planned courtroom experiment may provide extremely striking and persuasive evidence, and the opportunities for utilizing such experiments should not be overlooked.

 WESTLAW REFERENCES

exhibit! /5 wound* injur*** /p evidence
157k192

§ 216. Views [1]

The courts, like the prophet, have sensibly recognized that if a thing cannot be brought to the observer, the observer must go to the thing. Venturing forth to observe places or objects which are material to litigation but which cannot feasibly be brought, or satisfactorily reproduced, within the courtroom,

is termed a "view." While statutes or court rules concerning views are in effect in nearly all states,[2] it is frequently said that even without express statutory authorization there is an inherent power in the trial judge to order a view by the jury [3] or, in a judge-tried case, to take a view himself.[4] This power extends to views of personalty [5] realty, and to criminal [6] as well as civil cases.

Since a view is often time-consuming and disruptive of the ordinary course of a trial, the trial judge is in most instances vested with a wide leeway of discretion to grant or refuse a view.[7] It is to be noted, however, that in a number of state statutes provide that in certain types of cases, notably eminent domain, either party is entitled to a view upon request as a matter of right.[8] Where the grant of a view is discretionary with the trial court, as is usually the case,

---

16. Burriss v. Texaco, Inc., 361 F.2d 169 (4th Cir. 1966) (within trial court's discretion to refuse to permit re-enactment of fire on model of railroad yard where model was not to scale); Whitehurst v. Revlon, Inc., 307 F.Supp. 918 (E.D.Va.1969) (experiment to show inflammability of nail polish disallowed; conditions in court dissimilar to those of plaintiff's home); Pond v. Anderson, 241 Iowa 1038, 44 N.W.2d 372 (1952) (witness testified she overheard other end of a telephone call taken by her husband; not abuse of discretion to disallow experiment whether witness could overhear remote end of call to phone on judge's desk since conditions dissimilar); Beasley v. Ford Motor Co., 237 S.C. 506, 117 S.E.2d 863 (1961) (proper to refuse experiment to show gasoline in contact with hot metal surface will not ignite; "A hot plate in the hands of the witness would hardly be comparable to the hot automobile motor . . . "). But experiments may sometimes illustrate a material fact even where similarity of conditions is lacking. See Davis v. Walter, 259 Iowa 837, 146 N.W.2d 247 (1966) (demonstration of operation of hazard lights proper in discretion of trial court simply to show mode of operation).

§ 216

1. 4 Wigmore, Evidence §§ 1162–1169 (Chadbourn rev. 1972); Dec.Dig. Trial ⊜28, Criminal Law ⊜641.

2. See the rules and statutes collected in 4 Wigmore, Evidence § 1163, notes 7, 8 (Chadbourn rev. 1972).

3. Basham v. Owensboro City Railroad Co., 169 Ky. 155, 183 S.W. 492 (1916); State v. Black, 193 Or. 295, 236 P.2d 326 (1951) (inherent power of trial court to order view of stolen cattle unaffected by statute expressly sanctioning only views of realty); State v. Coburn, 82 Idaho 437, 354 P.2d 751 (1960) (view of automobiles, semble). Compare Steward v. State, 75 Nev. 498, 346

P.2d 1083 (1959) (holding a truck to be a "place" within meaning of statute authorizing views of places).

4. Bobrick v. Taylor, 171 Colo. 375, 467 P.2d 822 (1970); In re Digbie's Estate, 79 N.E.2d 159 (Ohio App. 1948).

5. See, e.g., cases cited note 3 supra. Even views of persons have sometimes been allowed. Nizer v. Phelps, 252 Md. 185, 249 A.2d 112 (1969) (view of personal injury victim in nursing home held permissible). Compare, however, Knight v. Landis, 11 Ga.App. 536, 75 S.E. 834 (1912) (holding views of personalty impermissible as a matter of "adopted common law," though stating that "no valid distinction" exists between views of realty and personalty). Compare Arnold v. Laird, 94 Wn.2d 867, 621 P.2d 138 (1980) (mistakenly assuming that views must be of realty, but upholding propriety of jury's viewing of defendant's dog "Blanket" on courthouse lawn as an "observation.")

6. Schonfeld v. United States, 277 F. 934 (2d Cir. 1921); State v. O'Day, 188 La. 169, 175 So. 838 (1937) (trial court had power to order view in criminal case despite absence of statutory authorization).

7. Nearly every opinion stresses the discretion of the trial court. See, e.g., Hodge v. United States, 75 U.S.App.D.C. 332, 126 F.2d 849 (1942) (denial upheld as discretionary); Zipp v Gasen's Drug Stores, Inc., 449 S.W.2d 612 (Mo.1970) (denial of view discretionary even where view would have been "helpful"); Bizich v. Sears, Roebuck & Co., 391 Pa. 640, 139 A.2d 663 (1958) (grant upheld); Dec.Dig. Trial ⊜28(2). The trial judge's discretion extends to denying a view even though requested by both parties. Illinois Basin Oil Association v. Lynn, 425 S.W.2d 555 (Ky.1968); Floyd v. Williams, 198 Miss. 350, 22 So.2d 365 (1945).

8. E.g., Fla.Stat.Ann. § 75.071; Ill.Rev.Stat.1982, Ch. 47, ¶ 9.

factors which are commonly stated to be appropriate for consideration by the court in determining whether to a grant a view include the importance to the issue of the information to be gained by the view,[9] the extent to which this information has or could have been secured from maps, photographs, or diagrams [10] and the extent to which the place or object to be viewed has changed in appearance since the controversy arose.[11]

The appropriate procedures to be followed in connection with views are widely regulated by statute. At common law, and generally in civil cases today, the presence of the trial judge at a view is not required,[12] the more common practice being for the jury to be conducted to the scene by "showers," expressly commissioned for the purpose.[13] At-

tendance at the view by the parties and their counsel is generally permitted though subject to the discretion of the trial judge.[14] In criminal cases, the rights of the defendant to have the judge present at the view, and to be present himself, are frequently provided for by statute.[15] Moreover, when testimony is taken at the view, or the view itself is deemed to constitute evidence, the right of the defendant to be present in all probability possesses a constitutional underpinning.[16]

Statutory and constitutional considerations aside, the advisability of trial court attendance at views is strongly suggested by the numerous cases in which unauthorized comments, obviously hearsay,[17] have been made to the jury, or other improper events have occurred during the course of the

---

9. Eizerman v. Behn, 9 Ill.App.2d 263, 132 N.E.2d 788 (1956) (denial of view of washing machine upheld; present condition of washer of little significance where issue was condition at earlier time).

10. Peake v. Omaha Cold Storage Co., 158 Neb. 676, 64 N.W.2d 470 (1954) (numerous maps and pictures in evidence; denial of view upheld as discretionary); State v. Holden, 75 Wn.2d 413, 451 P.2d 666 (1969) (semble). See also Zipp v. Gasen's Drug Store, Inc., 449 S.W.2d 612 (Mo.1970) (other evidence, including photographs, precluded "right" to have view).

11. Wimberly v. City of Paterson, 75 N.J.Super. 584, 183 A.2d 691 (1962) (denial of view not abuse of discretion where conditions changed and scene fully described by witnesses); Burke v. Thomas, 313 P.2d 1082 (Okl.1957) (denial proper within trial court's discretion where seasonal change of foliage had drastically altered scene.) Annot., 85 A.L.R.2d 512, collecting cases concerning effect of changed conditions upon propriety of granting view.

12. Sims Motor Transportation Lines, Inc. v. Foster, 293 S.W.2d 226 (Ky.1956) (attendance of trial judge at view in civil case discretionary); Yeary v. Holbrook, 171 Va. 266, 198 S.E. 441 (1938) (similar holding; review of earlier authorities concerning views).

13. On occasion, the trial judge will act as shower, Yeary v. Holbrook, 171 Va. 266, 198 S.W. 441 (1938), or appoint counsel for the parties to act as showers, Snyder v. Commonwealth of Massachusetts, 291 U.S. 97 (1934).

14. Sims Motor Transportation Lines, Inc. v. Foster, supra n. 12.

15. As to the trial judge's obligation to attend a view in criminal cases, see, McCollum v. State, 74 So.2d 74 (Fla.1954) (holding local statute made trial judge's attendance mandatory; extensive review of authorities); State v. Rohrich, 135 N.W.2d 175 (N.D.1965) (semble). Annot., 47 A.L.R.2d 1227 (necessity for presence of trial judge at view by jury in criminal case.)

Many states accord the defendant the right to be present at a view in a criminal case. State v. MacDonald, 229 A.2d 321 (Me.1967); Noell v. Commonwealth, 135 Va. 600, 115 S.E. 679 (1923). Others hold the matter to be discretionary. Commonwealth v. Belenski, 276 Mass. 35, 176 N.E. 501 (1931).

16. In Snyder v. Commonwealth of Massachusetts, 291 U.S. 97 (1934) the Supreme Court held, four justices dissenting, that due process had not been denied a defendant who was refused the opportunity to be present at a view, even if it were assumed that the right of confrontation guaranteed by the Sixth Amendment is "reinforced" by the Fourteenth. Thus, even though the confrontation clause has now been held operative against the states by virtue of the Fourteenth Amendment, Pointer v. Texas, 380 U.S. 400 (1965), the defendant appears to have no federally guaranteed right to attend a view in every instance. The Court, however, carefully limited its holding in Snyder to the facts of that case. These included the fact that a view is not deemed evidence in Massachusetts, that no oral testimony was taken at the view, and that the judge, court reporter, and also defendant's counsel were present. Compare State v. Garden, 267 Minn. 97, 125 N.W.2d 591 (1963) (holding defendant's constitutional rights violated by a view by jury in custody of sheriff, at which neither judge, court reporter nor defendant was present; "the substance of defendant's right is to know what transpired during the viewing.") See also Annot., 30 A.L.R. 1358; 90 id. 597.

In United States v. Walls, 443 F.2d 1220 (6th Cir. 1971) the court, without reaching the constitutional issue of Snyder, and predicating its decision upon its supervisory authority, found reversible error in denying the defendant and his counsel the opportunity to attend a view.

17. 4 Wigmore, Evidence § 1167 (Chadbourn rev. 1972).

view.[18] Presence of the trial judge would seem to afford the best guarantee available against the occurrence of events of this nature. On the other hand, where the trial judge is present to rule on admissibility, and provision for preparation of a proper record is made, there would appear no inherent vice in receiving testimony or allowing demonstrations or experiments during a view.[19] These practices, however, have often been looked upon with disfavor by appellate courts,[20] and some jurisdictions appear to hold reception of testimony or experiments during a view improper under any circumstances.[21]

Closely related to the above questions is the troublesome problem of what evidentiary status a view possesses. A large number of jurisdictions, probably a majority, holds that a view is not itself evidence, but is only to assist the trier of fact in understanding and evaluating the evidence.[22] This doctrine undoubtedly rests in large part upon the consideration that facts garnered by the jury from a view are difficult or impossible to embody in the written record, thus rendering review of questions concerning weight or sufficiency of the evidence impracticable.[23] At the same time, however, this doctrine ignores the fact that many other varieties of demonstrative evidence are to some extent subject to the same difficulty, and further that it is unreasonable to assume that jurors, however they may be instructed, will apply the metaphysical distinction suggested and ignore the evidence of their own senses when it conflicts with the testimony of the witnesses. Commentators have uniformly condemned the downgrading of views to non-evidentiary status,[24] and a substantial number of courts holds a view to be evidence like any other.[25] The latter position appears to be the preferable one, at least when modified by the caveat that where the question is one of sufficiency, a view alone cannot logically be considered to constitute sufficient evidence of a fact the establishment of which ordinarily requires the introduction of expert testimony.

---

18. Scott v. Tubbs, 43 Colo. 221, 95 P. 540 (1908) (new trial required where petitioner entertained jury in saloon following view); Juett v. Calhoun, 405 S.W.2d 946 (Ky.1966) (error to allow jurors and party to ride together to view unaccompanied by officer.) Annot., 45 A.L.R.2d 1128.

19. State v. O'Day, 188 La. 169, 175 So. 838, 841 (1937) ("It would seem that it would be better to explain the locus by testimony on the scene . . . ."); Tarr v. Keller Lumber & Construction Co., 106 W.Va. 99, 144 S.E. 881 (1928). For discussion of the question, generally favoring allowance of testimony and experiments at views, see Wendorf, Some Views on Jury Views, 15 Baylor L.Rev. 379, 394 (1963).

20. Yeary v. Holbrook, 171 Va. 266, 198 S.E. 441 (1938) (stating, "We do not approve the use of witnesses on a view . . . ," but finding no reversible error under circumstances.)

21. State v. Delaney, 15 Utah 2d 338, 393 P.2d 379 (1964) (statute authorizing views held not to authorize taking of testimony thereon); Brooks v. Gilbert, 250 Iowa 1164, 98 N.W.2d 309 (1960) ("recreation" of accident on view "never" permissible). A number of courts have found experiments during views involving the participation of jurors particularly offensive. See Cole v. McGhie, 59 Wn.2d 436, 367 P.2d 844 (1962) (citing numerous cases.)

22. Ernst v. Broughton, 213 Or. 253, 324 P.2d 241 (1959); Doherty v. Providence Journal Co., 94 R.I. 392,

181 A.2d 105 (1962); Kearns v. Hall, 197 Va. 736, 91 S.E.2d 648 (1956).

23. As to the ability of the trial judge to direct a verdict or grant a new trial for insufficiency of evidence where a view has been had, see Keeney v. Ciborowski, 304 Mass. 371, 24 N.E.2d 17 (1940). Compare Beatty v. Depue, 78 S.D. 395, 103 N.W.2d 187 (1960) (holding view does not constitute evidence, but that reviewing court should consider fact view was taken in ruling upon sufficiency of evidence).

24. Hardman, The Evidentiary Effect of a View: Stare Decisis or Stare Dictis, 53 U.W.Va.L.Rev. 103 (1951); Hardman, The Evidentiary Effect of a View— Another Word, 58 U.W.Va.L.Rev. 69 (1956); Wendorf, Some Views on Jury Views, 15 Baylor L.Rev. 379 (1963).

25. Neel v. Mannings, Inc., 19 Cal.2d 647, 122 P.2d 576 (1942) (view was "independent" evidence); Chouinard v. Shaw, 99 N.H. 26, 104 A.2d 522 (1954) (jury, as "sensible" persons, expected to consider view along with other evidence); Moore, Kelly & Reddish, Inc. v. Shannondale, Inc., 152 W.Va. 549, 165 S.E.2d 113 (1968).

Some courts have finessed the problems of sufficiency-evaluation attendant upon holding a view evidence by holding also that a verdict or finding must be supported by evidence apart from the view. See In re State Highway Running Through Section 2, Township 12, Cass County, 129 Neb. 822, 263 N.W. 148 (1935).

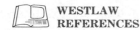

§ 217. Exhibits in the Jury Room [1]

Under modern American practice it is common to allow many types of tangible exhibits to be taken by the jury for consideration during the deliberations,[2] provided that the exhibits have been formally admitted into evidence.[3] The question whether a particular exhibit may be taken by the jury is widely viewed as subject to discretionary control by the trial judge,[4] but in some jurisdictions jury access to at least certain types of exhibits is apparently made mandatory either by judicial holding or legislative enactment.[5]

The current practice extends, unlike that at common law,[6] to written exhibits generally except for those which are testimonial in nature, such as depositions, dying declarations in writing, etc.[7] The reason underlying this latter exception is that writings which are merely testimony in a different form should not, by being allowed to the jury, be unduly emphasized over other purely oral testimony in the case.[8] As an exception to the exception, however, written or recorded confessions in criminal cases, despite their obvious testimonial character, are in many jurisdictions allowed to be taken by the jury,[9] apparently on the theory that their centrality in the case warrants whatever emphasis may result.

The practice of allowing nontestimonial written evidence generally to be taken by the jury would appear to be supported by many of the same considerations which underlie the so-called "Best Evidence Rule."[10] Legal rights and liabilities are frequently a

---

§ 217

1. 6 Wigmore, Evidence § 1913 (Chadbourn rev. 1976); Dec.Dig. Trial ⟨⟩307, Criminal Law ⟨⟩858.

2. See Dec.Dig. Trial ⟨⟩307, Criminal Law ⟨⟩858.

3. It is uniformly viewed as improper to permit the jury to take with it items not admitted.
Osborne v. United States, 351 F.2d 111 (8th Cir. 1965); People v. Holcomb, 370 Ill. 299, 18 N.E.2d 878 (1938). However, it would appear that most courts hold that the unadmitted exhibit must have been of a potentially prejudicial nature to warrant reversal. Lyon v. Bush, 49 Hawaii 116, 412 P.2d 662 (1966) (jury use of unadmitted charts and tables showing damages not shown prejudicial); Dallago v. United States, 138 U.S.App.D.C. 276, 427 F.2d 546 (1969) (unexplained presence of prejudicial record in jury room held reversible error).

4. People v. Allen, 17 Ill.2d 55, 160 N.E.2d 818 (1959) (matter largely discretionary); Pakul v. Montgomery Ward Co., 282 Minn. 360, 166 N.W.2d 65 (1969) (within trial court's discretion to withhold exhibits from jury); Durdella v. Trenton-Philadelphia Coach Co., 349 Pa. 482, 37 A.2d 481 (1944) (sending documentary exhibits with jury largely discretionary).

5. Texas Employers Insurance Association v. Applegate, 205 S.W.2d 412 (Tex.Civ.App.1947) (statute held to require trial judge, upon written motion of one party, to send written exhibits to jury room). See also McCaffrey v. Glendale Acres, Inc., 250 Or. 140, 440 P.2d 219 (1968) (exhibits are part of evidence and "should" go to jury room; dictim). But in some jurisdictions, statutes apparently mandatory in terms have been construed not to preempt exercise of trial judge discretion. See Mongar v. Barnard, 248 Iowa 899, 82 N.W.2d 765 (1957).

6. For explanation of the now obsolete common law practice limiting writings which could be taken to those under seal, see People v. Bartone, 12 Misc.2d 926, 172 N.Y.S.2d 976 (1958).

7. Whitehead v. Seymour, 120 Ga.App. 25, 169 S.E.2d 369 (1969) (improper to allow depositions and answers to interrogatories to go to jury room, but rule does not apply to writings within Best Evidence rule); State v. Solomon, 96 Utah 500, 87 P.2d 807 (1939) (transcript of testimony at prior trial should not be sent to jury room; "The law does not permit depositions or witnesses to go to the jury room. Why should a witness be allowed to go there in the form of written testimony?").

8. Thus exhibits which, though tangible, are merely embodiments of oral testimony are said properly kept from the jury. See, e.g., Gallagher v. Viking Supply Corp., 3 Ariz.App. 55, 411 P.2d 814 (1966) (proper to refuse to send chart which illustrated testimony to jury room); Dibert v. Ross Pattern & Foundry Development Co., 105 Ohio App. 264, 152 N.E.2d 369 (1958) (practice of sending exhibit marked by witness to jury room not approved). It may also be noted that the same principle underlies the frequently encountered prohibition against note-taking by jurors. See Annot., 14 A.L.R.3d 831.

9. People v. Caldwell, 39 Ill.2d 346, 236 N.E.2d 706 (1968) (citing numerous authorities favoring practice.) But compare State v. Lord, 42 N.M. 638, 84 P.2d 80 (1938) (holding confession not authorized to be sent to jury room under local statute).

10. Whitehead v. Seymour, 120 Ga.App. 25, 169 S.E.2d 369 (1969) (indicating writings subject to the Best Evidence rule are appropriate for jury examination).

function of particular words and figures, and may be drastically affected by seemingly minor variations in phraseology.[11] Thus crucial documents, such as deeds, contracts, or ledger sheets may frequently be of vital help to the jury.[12] On the other hand, where a writing is of only minor relevance, despatch to the jury may induce an emphasis upon it out of proportion to its intrinsic worth.[13]

The case for allowing the jury to take with it tangibles other than writings is somewhat weaker, at least if in-court examination of the tangible by the jury has been had. As noted in an earlier section, demonstrative evidence has peculiar force which arguably does not stand in need of yet additional augmentation.[14] Further, the relevant characteristics of many tangible exhibits are sufficiently gross as not to require the close perusal appropriate to writings, while at the other end of the spectrum there appears some anomaly in allowing independent jury inspection of tangibles the relevant features of which are so fine as to require expert exposition and interpretation.[15] Nevertheless,

the sending of tangible exhibits to the jury room is today probably so well established as to be practically irreversible.

A major problem stemming from relatively free jury access to tangible exhibits other than writings is that of controlling jury use of them for purposes of experimentation. The general limitations upon the introduction of evidence of experiments obviously become largely meaningless if the jury is allowed to conduct experiments of its own devising in the jury room. In attempting to distinguish between proper and improper jury use of tangible exhibits, the most commonly drawn distinction is between experiments which constitute merely a closer scrutiny of the exhibit and experiments which go "beyond the lines of the evidence" introduced in court and thus constitute the introduction of new evidence in the jury room.[16] The decisions reached under the aegis of this rubric are perhaps not totally reconcilable.[17] Most courts, however, emphasize the immunity of jury-conducted experiments from adversary scrutiny as

See generally Chapter 23 infra.

11. See Morgan, Basic Problems of Evidence 385 (1962).

12. See State of New Jersey v. Clawans, 38 N.J. 162, 183 A.2d 77 (1962) (subornation of perjury; sworn statement in conflict with later testimony properly allowed in jury room).

13. The problem seems one best left to trial judge discretion as is done in many jurisdictions. See Durdella v. Trenton-Philadelphia Coach Co., 349 Pa. 482, 37 A.2d 481 (1944) (contradictory statement containing only minor discrepancies properly withheld in trial judge's discretion); Wilson v. Pennsylvania Railroad Co., 421 Pa. 419, 219 A.2d 666 (1966) (sending impeaching writing to jury room within trial court's discretion).

14. Some courts, however, have viewed the persuasive character of demonstrative evidence as *supporting* jury access to it! See People v. Williams, 187 Cal. App.2d 355, 9 Cal.Rptr. 722 (1960) (not error to permit gruesome photos of victim to go to jury room where photos showed "more persuasively" than testimony what happened).

15. The view here suggested appears to find support in scattered decisions. See, e.g., People v. McElroy, 63 Ill.App.2d 403, 211 N.E.2d 444 (1965) (proper exercise of discretion to refuse to allow handwriting

exemplars introduced and passed among jury to go to jury room; comparison properly to be made during reception of evidence).

16. Imperial Meat Co. v. United States, 316 F.2d 435 (10th Cir. 1963); Higgins v. Los Angeles Gas & Electric Co., 159 Cal. 651, 115 P. 313 (1911).

17. Compare, e.g., the following holdings: Wilson v. United States, 116 F. 484 (9th Cir. 1902) (prosecution for smuggling of opium "prepared for smoking;" whether opium so prepared was required to be proved by prosecution and could not be left to be ascertained by jury experiment in which opium was burned); United States v. Beach, 296 F.2d 153 (4th Cir. 1961) (improper for jury to experiment with adding machines to determine noise level, that fact bearing upon credibility of witness in case); Ingram v. State, 363 S.W.2d 284 (Tex.Cr.App.1963) (not error for jury to open and mix Copenhagen snuff with water to ascertain whether it smelled like rum as testified by witness); Taylor v. Commonwealth, 90 Va. 109, 17 S.E. 812 (1893) (holding that where defendant introduced evidence that the firing pin of his rifle did not make marks on cartridge cases similar to those of murder weapon, jury properly disassembled defendant's rifle to detect tampering with firing pin). Cases involving experimentation by the jury outside the courtroom are collected in Annot., 95 A.L.R.2d 351.

their preeminently objectionable feature.[18] Thus it would seem correct to say that jury experimentation is improper if reasonable grounds existed for an adversary attack on the experiment by the complaining party and, in addition, if nothing transpiring during the in-court proceedings rendered such an attack inappropriate. Specifically, experiments which are merely reruns of in-court experiments, or which use techniques of examination not markedly different from those employed during trial are not generally held to fall within the proscribed class.[19] On the other hand, jury experiments utilizing techniques or equipment substantially different from any employed in court tend to be held error, at least where counsel has not specifically acquiesced in the experiment, such as by arguing that the jury should be allowed certain tools.[20]

 WESTLAW REFERENCES

100k858
digest(exhibit! /p jury /2 room /p discretion!)

---

18. United States v. Beach, 296 F.2d 153 (4th Cir. 1961); Higgins v. Los Angeles Gas & Electric Co., 159 Cal. 651, 115 P. 313 (1911).

19. Taylor v. Reo Motors, Inc., 275 F.2d 699 (10th Cir. 1960) (not improper for jury to dismantle and reassemble heat exchanger in jury room where essentially similar operation had been performed by experts in court); Geo. C. Christopher & Son, Inc. v. Kansas Paint & Color Co., Inc., 215 Kan. 185, 523 P.2d 709 (1974) (jury scraped paint samples with pocket knife; "An experiment or demonstration is proper when conducted by the jury with the use of exhibits properly submitted to it for the purpose of testing the truth of statements made by witnesses or duplicating tests made by witnesses in open court"). People v. Thorngate, 10 Mich. App. 317, 159 N.W.2d 373 (1968) (proper for jury to examine exhibits with magnifying glass); Layton v. Palmer, 309 S.W.2d 561 (Mo.1958) (semble); State v. Zobel, 81 S.D. 260, 134 N.W.2d 101 (1965) (within trial court's discretion to allow jury to have viewer with which to look at colored slides projected in court). And

clearly no error will be found where the complaining party invited the experiment, United States v. Hawkins, 595 F.2d 751 (D.C.Cir. 1978), cert. denied 441 U.S. 910 (use of binoculars to test credibility of police witnesses suggested by defense counsel).

20. United States v. Beach, 296 F.2d 153 (4th Cir. 1961) (experiment with adding machine to ascertain level of noise produced held improper; court notes possible objections relating to accuracy to which experiment was subject); Jensen v. Dikel, 244 Minn. 71, 69 N.W.2d 108 (1955) (error for court to furnish tools for jury experiment in absence of express consent of parties); King v. Railway Express Agency, Inc., 94 N.W.2d 657 (N.D.1959) (introduction of ruler and string into jury room for purpose of experiment without consent of parties constituted error.)

For a suggestion of the possible problems involved in establishing that an improper jury experiment has in fact been performed, see State v. James, 70 Wn.2d 624, 424 P.2d 1005 (1967). See § 68 supra.

Title 9

WRITINGS

Chapter 22

AUTHENTICATION [1]

Table of Sections

---

§ 218. General Theory: No Assumption of Authenticity

The concept of authentication, although continually used by the courts without ap-

parent difficulty, seems almost to defy precise definition. Some writers have construed the term very broadly, as does Wigmore when he states that "when a claim

---

1. 7 Wigmore, Evidence §§ 2128–2169 (Chadbourn rev. 1978); Tracy, The Introduction of Documentary Evidence, 24 Iowa L.Rev. 436 (1939); Dec.Dig. Evidence ☞369–382,

The subject of authentication is covered by Article IX of the Federal Rules of Evidence, which provides as follows:

Rule 901. Requirement of Authentication or Identification.

(a) **General Provision.**—The requirement of authentication or identification as a condition precedent to admissibility is satisfied by evidence sufficient to support a finding that the matter in question is what its proponent claims.

(b) **Illustrations.**—By way of illustration only, and not by way of limitation, the following are exam-

ples of authentication or identification conforming with the requirements of this rule:

(1) *Testimony of Witness With Knowledge.*—Testimony that a matter is what it is claimed to be.

(2) *Nonexpert Opinion on Handwriting.*—Nonexpert opinion as to the genuineness of handwriting, based upon familiarity not acquired for purposes of the litigation.

(3) *Comparison by Trier or Expert Witness.*—Comparison by the trier of fact or by expert witnesses with specimens which have been authenticated.

(4) *Distinctive Characteristics and the Like.*—Appearance, contents, substance, internal patterns, or other distinctive characteristics, taken in conjunction with circumstances.

684

or offer involves impliedly or expressly any element of *personal connection with a cor-*

(5) *Voice Identification.*—Identification of a voice, whether heard firsthand or through mechanical or electronic transmission or recording, by opinion based upon hearing the voice at any time under circumstances connecting it with the alleged speaker.

(6) *Telephone Conversations.*—Telephone conversations, by evidence that a call was made to the number assigned at the time by the telephone company to a particular person or business, if (A) in the case of a person, circumstances, including self-identification, show the person answering to be the one called, or (B) in the case of a business, the call was made to a place of business and the conversation related to business reasonably transacted over the telephone.

(7) *Public Records or Reports.*—Evidence that a writing authorized by law to be recorded or filed and in fact recorded or filed in a public office, or a purported public record, report, statement, or data compilation, in any form, is from the public office where items of this nature are kept.

(8) *Ancient Documents or Data Compilation.*—Evidence that a document or data compilation, in any form, (A) is in such condition as to create no suspicion concerning its authenticity, (B) was in a place where it, if authentic, would likely be, and (C) has been in existence 20 years or more at the time it is offered.

(9) *Process or System.*—Evidence describing a process or system used to produce a result and showing that the process or system produces an accurate result.

(10) *Methods Provided by Statute or Rule.*—Any method of authentication or identification provided by Act of Congress or by other rules prescribed by the Supreme Court pursuant to statutory authority.

Rule 902. Self-Authentication

Extrinsic evidence of authenticity as a condition precedent to admissibility is not required with respect to the following:

(1) *Domestic Public Documents Under Seal.*—A document bearing a seal purporting to be that of the United States, or of any State, district, Commonwealth, territory, or insular possession thereof, or the Panama Canal Zone, or the Trust Territory of the Pacific Islands, or of a political subdivision, department, officer, or agency thereof, and a signature purporting to be an attestation or execution.

(2) *Domestic Public Documents Not Under Seal.*—A document purporting to bear the signature in his official capacity of an officer or employee of any entity included in paragraph (1) hereof, having no seal, if a public officer having a seal and having official duties in the district or political subdivision of the officer or employee certifies under

McCormick et al. on Evid. 3rd Ed. H.B.—16

poreal object, that connection must be made to appear . . . ."[2] So defined, "authenti-

seal that the signer has the official capacity and that the signature is genuine.

(3) *Foreign Public Documents.*—A document purporting to be executed or attested in his official capacity by a person authorized by the laws of a foreign country to make the execution or attestation, and accompanied by a final certification as to the genuineness of the signature and official position (A) of the executing or attesting person, or (B) of any foreign official whose certificate of genuineness of signature and official position relates to the execution or attestation or is in a chain of certificates of genuineness of signature and official position relating to the execution or attestation. A final certification may be made by a secretary of embassy or legation, consul general, consul, vice consul, or consular agent of the United States, or a diplomatic or consular official of the foreign country assigned or accredited to the United States. If reasonable opportunity has been given to all parties to investigate the authenticity and accuracy of official documents, the court may, for good cause shown, order that they be treated as presumptively authentic without final certification or permit them to be evidenced by an attested summary with or without final certification.

(4) *Certified Copies of Public Records.*—A copy of an official record or report or entry therein, or of a document authorized by law to be recorded or filed and actually recorded or filed in a public office, including data compilations in any form, certified as correct by the custodian or other person authorized to make the certification, by certificate complying with paragraph (1), (2), or (3) of this rule or complying with any Act of Congress or rule prescribed by the Supreme Court pursuant to statutory authority.

(5) *Official Publications.*—Books, pamphlets, or other publications purporting to be issued by public authority.

(6) *Newspapers and Periodicals.*—Printed materials purporting to be newspapers or periodicals.

(7) *Trade Inscriptions and the Like.*—Inscriptions, signs, tags, or labels purporting to have been affixed in the course of business and indicating ownership, control, or origin.

(8) *Acknowledged Documents.*—Documents accompanied by a certificate of acknowledgment executed in the manner provided by law by a notary public or other officer authorized by law to take acknowledgments.

(9) *Commercial Paper and Related Documents.*—Commercial paper, signatures thereon, and documents relating thereto to the extent provided by general commercial law.

---

2. See note 2 on page 686.

cation" is not only a necessary preliminary to the introduction of most writings in evidence, but also to the introduction of various other sorts of tangibles. For example, an article of clothing found at the scene of a crime can hardly constitute relevant evidence against the defendant unless his ownership or previous possession of the article is shown. Since authentication of tangibles other than writings,[3] has been treated elsewhere, however, the term authentication will here be used in the limited sense of proof of authorship of, or other connection with, writings.[4]

It is clear that the relevancy of a writing to a particular issue raised in litigation will frequently be logically dependent upon the existence of some connection between that writing and a particular individual.[5] If Y sues X for libel and attempts to introduce into evidence a writing containing libelous statements concerning Y, it will readily appear that the writing is relevant only if some connection between the writing and X exists, as where X authored or published it. The real question, however, is not whether such a connection is logically necessary for relevancy, but rather what standards are to be applied in determining whether the connection has been made to appear.

In the everyday affairs of business and social life, it is the custom to look merely at the writing itself for evidence as to its source. Thus, if the writing bears a signature purporting to be that of X, or recites that it was made by him, we assume, nothing to the contrary appearing, that it is exactly what it purports to be, the work of X. At this point, however, the law of evidence has long differed from the commonsense assumption upon which each of us conducts his own affairs, adopting instead the position that the purported signature or recital of authorship on the face of a writing will *not* be accepted as sufficient preliminary proof of authenticity to secure the admission of the writing in evidence.[6] The same attitude has traditionally extended as well to the authority of agents, with the result that if an instrument recites that it is signed by A as agent for P, not only must additional proof be given that A actually did the signing, but also of the fact that he was P's agent and authorized to sign.[7]

---

(10) *Presumptions Under Acts of Congress.*— Any signature, document, or other matter declared by Act of Congress to be presumptively or prima facie genuine or authentic.

Rule 903. Subscribing Witness' Testimony Unnecessary

The testimony of a subscribing witness is not necessary to authenticate a writing unless required by the laws of the jurisdiction whose laws govern the validity of the writing.

The corresponding provisions of the revised Uniform Rules are for all practical purposes identical.

§ 218

2. 7 Wigmore, Evidence § 2129 at 564 (Chadbourn rev. 1978).

3. See § 212 supra.

4. Though the connection necessary to establish relevancy will most frequently be authorship, it may in a given case consist of a variety of other relationships. In Bodrey v. Bodrey, 246 Ga. 122, 269 S.E.2d 14 (1980) the offered item was a love letter found by a wife in her husband's desk drawer. The court held that for purposes of the litigation the authorship of the letter was immaterial, and that the necessary connection was the wife's finding.

5. See, e.g., Palfy v. Rice, 473 P.2d 606 (Alaska 1970) (authentication necessary to establish relevancy of document); Fed.R.Evid. 901, Adv.Com.Note. See also the discussion of conditional relevancy, §§ 53 and 58 supra.

6. McGowan v. Armour, 248 F. 676 (8th Cir. 1918) (letter bearing purported writer's signature, found in addressee's pocket, excluded); Continental Baking Co. v. Katz, 68 Cal.2d 512, 67 Cal.Rptr. 761, 897, 439 P.2d 889 (1968) ("We understand that in some legal systems it is assumed that documents are what they purport to be unless shown to be otherwise. With us it is the other way around. Generally speaking, documents must be authenticated in some fashion before they are admissible . . . ."); Idaho First National Bank v. Wells, 100 Idaho 256, 596 P.2d 429 (1979) (error to admit promissory notes without authentication); City of Randleman v. Hinshaw, 2 N.C.App. 381, 163 S.E.2d 95 (1968) (authentication of writing necessary to admission); Beltran v. State, 144 Tex.Cr.R. 338, 163 S.W.2d 211 (1942) (written confession purporting to be signed by accused); 7 Wigmore, Evidence § 2130, note 1 (Chadbourn rev. 1978); Dec.Dig. Evidence ⊛370(1).

7. Grey v. First National Bank, 393 F.2d 371 (5th Cir. 1968); Lee v. Melvin, 40 So.2d 837 (Fla.1949); Cliff Compton, Inc. v. Leon, 355 Mass. 153, 243 N.E.2d 182 (1969); Dec.Dig. Evidence ⊛370(5).

The principal justification urged for this judicial agnosticism toward the authorship of documents is that it constitutes a necessary check on the perpetration of fraud. Thus it is quite conceivable that the libelous writing previously adduced by way of example is not the work of X but of some third person who, for reasons of his own, wishes to embroil X in difficulties,[8] or to libel Y without suffering any adverse consequences. It is also possible that Y has himself fabricated the writing to provide himself with a cause of action.

Another possibility against which traditional authentication is sometimes suggested to guard is that of mistaken attribution of a writing to one who fortuitously happens to possess the same name, etc., as the author.

On the other side of the coin, requiring proof of what may correctly be assumed true in 99 out of 100 cases is at best time-consuming and expensive. At the worst, the requirement will occasionally be seen to produce results which are virtually indefensible.[9]

Thus, while traditional requirements of authentication admittedly furnish some slight obstacles to the perpetration of fraud or occurrence of mistake in the presentation of writings, it has frequently been questioned whether these benefits are not outweighed by the time, expense, and occasional untoward results entailed by the traditional negative attitude toward authenticity of writings.[10]

WESTLAW REFERENCES

evid! fed.r.evid!   /10   901   /p   authentic!

---

§ 219. Authentication by Direct Proof: (a) In General

The simplest form of direct testimony authenticating a writing as that of X, is the production of a witness who swears that he saw X sign the offered writing.[1] Other examples would be the testimony of X himself, the signer, acknowledging execution, or the admission of authenticity by an adverse party in the present action, either made out of court and reported by another witness or shown by the party's own letter or other writing, or in the form of the party's testi-

---

Some of the difficulties of proof raised by this rule are in some jurisdictions resolved by statutes providing for the admissibility of instruments bearing what purports to be a corporate seal and further creating a presumption that any person whose name appears on such a sealed writing had authority to execute the instrument for the corporation. E.g., N.C.Gen.Stat. § 55–36(c). Without benefit of statutes, some courts have been willing to accept the former proposition but not the latter. Robertson v. Burstein, 105 N.J.L. 375, 146 A. 355 (1929).

8. See Hughes v. Samuels Brothers, 179 Iowa 1077, 159 N.W. 589 (1917) (undertaker mailed business card of competitor to man whose wife was seriously ill).

9. Mancari v. Frank P. Smith, Inc., 72 U.S.App.D.C. 398, 114 F.2d 834 (1940), 26 Iowa L.Rev. 134, 15 So. Calif.L.Rev. 115 (plaintiff sued as a result of mention of his name in a widely distributed circular which purported to be issued by a manufacturer and a local retailer of shoes. Held, Judge Rutledge dissenting, that the trial court properly directed a verdict for defendant on the ground that the terms of the circular did not make a prima facie case of defendant's authorship); Keegan v. Green Giant Co., 150 Me. 283, 110 A.2d 599 (1954), 103 U.Pa.L.Rev. 1095, 29 Temp.L.Q. 109 (plaintiff sued for personal injuries resulting from eating peas from a can labeled with the name of the defen-

dant. Held, over a strong dissenting opinion, that the trial court properly refused to admit the label as evidence of defendant's connection with the peas, and properly directed a verdict for defendant.)

By adopting Federal Rule Evid. 902(7), Maine has overturned *Keegan.*

10. See the quotation from Jeremy Bentham in 7 Wigmore, Evidence § 2148, p. 606 (Chadbourn rev. 1978); Alexander & Alexander, The Authentication of Documents Requirement: Barrier to Falsehood or to Truth? 10 S.D.L.Rev. 266 (1973); Broun, Authentication and Content of Writings, 1969 L. & Soc.O. 611; Erich, Unnecessary Difficulties of Proof, 32 Yale L.J. 436 (1923); Strong, Liberalizing the Authentication of Private Writings, 52 Cornell L.Q. 284 (1967).

§ 219

1. Manifestly this is a sufficient authentication. Cottingham v. Doyle, 122 Mont. 301, 202 P.2d 533 (1949); Zodiac Corp. v. General Electric Credit Corp., 566 S.W.2d 341 (Tex.Civ.App.1979); Durham v. State, 422 P.2d 691 (Wyo.1967). Connections other than by signing may be similarly established. See United States v. Rizzo, 418 F.2d 71 (7th Cir. 1969) (cards mailed to promote business of house of ill fame admissible where witness testified she had helped prepare "similar" cards for defendants).

mony on the stand.[2] It is generally held that business records may be authenticated[3] by the evidence of one familiar with the books of the concern, such as a custodian or supervisor, who has not made the record or seen it made, that the offered writing is actually part of the records of the business.[4]

WESTLAW REFERENCES

business /3 record* /p authentic! /p custod! familiar!

---

§ 220. Authentication by Direct Proof: (b) Requirement of Production of Attesting Witnesses.[1]

Our rules about the production of subscribing witnesses are survivals of archaic law. They have their origins in Germanic practice earlier than jury trial, when pre-appointed transaction-witnesses were the only kind of witnesses that could be summoned or heard in court. When jury trial came in, the attesting witnesses at first were summoned along with the jurors themselves, and this practice seems to have lingered until the middle fifteen hundreds.[2] The rule in its modern common law form requires, when a document signed by subscribing witnesses is sought to be authenticated by witnesses, that an attesting witness must first be called,[3] or all attesters must be shown to be unavailable,[4] before other witnesses can be called to authenticate it.[5]

The requirement has no application where the foundation for introducing the document is the opponent's judicial admission[6] of its genuineness,[7] either by stipulation of the parties in writing or in open court, or under modern rules and statutes by the opponent's failure to deny the genuineness of the writing.[8] Though it has been suggested that extra-judicial admissions also, if in writing, might properly be held to dispense with the

---

2. See Ch. 26 infra.

3. Merely supplying the requirement that the books be identified as such, though other foundation proof may be required before the records will be accepted as evidence of the facts recorded under the hearsay exception for Business Records. See §§ 307–311 infra.

4. Rosenberg v. Collins, 624 F.2d 659, 665 (5th Cir. 1980) ("Any person in a position to attest to the authenticity of certain records is competent to lay the foundation for the admissibility of the records . . . ."); Rice v. United States, 411 F.2d 485 (8th Cir. 1969) (prosecution for theft of articles in interstate commerce, baggage tags showing destination properly admitted as business record on foundation testimony of company official who had not prepared tags); Miller v. State, 224 A.2d 592 (Del.1966) (church records; current pastor not preparing entries in question); Hood v. Commonwealth Trust & Savings Bank, 376 Ill. 413, 34 N.E.2d 414 (1941) (cashier could "identify" bank's books though some entries made before he was employed); State v. Smith, 55 Wn.2d 482, 348 P.2d 417 (1960) (records identified, and mode of preparation established, by one not the custodian or keeper). See § 312 infra.

§ 220

1. 4 Wigmore, Evidence §§ 1287–1321 (Chadbourn rev. 1972); Dec.Dig. Evidence ⟨key⟩374; C.J.S. Evidence § 739.

2. Thayer, Preliminary Treatise on Evidence 502 (1898).

3. If there are several attesters only one must be called. Sowell v. Bank of Brewton, 119 Ala. 92, 24 So. 585 (1898) (note); Allgood v. Allgood, 230 Ga. 312, 196

S.E.2d 888 (1973) (deed properly admitted though only one of two attesting witnesses testified; attestation said only to affect recordability); Shirley v. Fearne, 33 Miss. 653, 69 Am.Dec. 375 (1857) (deed with two attesters, though only one required by law.) But the Chancery rule in England required the calling or accounting for all attesters, and a few American jurisdictions continued to impose the requirement in will cases. In re Coons' Estate, 154 Neb. 690, 48 N.W.2d 778 (1951); Swindoll v. Jones, 41 Tenn.App. 89, 292 S.W.2d 531 (Tenn.App.1955). Cases concerning the requirement in will cases are collected in Dec.Dig. Wills ⟨key⟩303(4). For a collection of statutes affecting the question, see 4 Wigmore, Evidence § 1304 (Chadbourn rev. 1972).

4. Howard v. Russell, 104 Ga. 230, 30 S.E. 802 (1898) (semble: deed). But seemingly if there are more attesters than the law requires only the number required must be accounted for. Snider v. Burks, 84 Ala. 57, 4 So. 225, 226 (1888) (three witnesses to a will, only two accounted for, sufficient). And if the attesting witnesses' identities cannot be ascertained, even proof of unavailability may be held unnecessary. Skaling v. Remick, 97 N.H. 106, 82 A.2d 81 (1951). Statutes defining "unavailability" are collected in 4 Wigmore, Evidence § 1310 (Chadbourn rev. 1972).

5. For a summary statement of the rule, see 4 Wigmore, Evidence § 1289 (Chadbourn rev. 1972).

6. As to meaning, see § 265 infra.

7. Jones v. Henry, 84 N.C. 320, 323 (1881) (stipulation of record, "defendants admit execution of bond" dispenses with producing attester); 4 Wigmore, Evidence § 1296 (Chadbourn rev. 1972).

8. See § 228 infra.

production of attesters, such American authority as exists seems to deny that extrajudicial admissions of any sort have this effect.[9]

The requirement is that the attesting witnesses be called before other authenticating witnesses are heard, but it is not required that the attesters give favorable testimony establishing the writing. So even if they profess want of memory [10] or even deny that they attested,[11] the writing may be established by other proof, and conversely if they support the writing, other proof may establish that it is not authentic.[12] Moreover, since the party calling the attester is required by law to do so, the prohibition upon impeaching one's own witness is held inapplicable.[13]

This requirement of calling particular persons, or accounting for them, to authenticate the writing is often inconvenient, and of doubtful expediency, and various exceptions have been carved out by the courts, as for ancient documents,[14] writings only "collaterally" involved in the suit,[15] and for certified copies of recorded conveyances, where the

original is not required to be produced.[16] A more sweeping reform, generally effected by statute but on occasion by judicial decision, has been to dispense with the requirement of calling attesting witnesses except when the writing to be offered is one required by law to be attested.[17]

WESTLAW REFERENCES

authenticat! /p produc! /p attest! /p witness** & court(ks)

§ 221. Authentication by Direct Proof: (c) Proof of Handwriting [1]

A witness is placed on the stand. "Will you state whether you are acquainted with the handwriting of X?" "I am." "Will you look at this letter (or this signature) and tell me whether it is in the handwriting of X?" "It is." These or similar questions and answers are part of the familiar routine of authenticating writings, a routine which might be supposed to possess a rationale until note is taken of the qualifications typically required to be shown as part of his testimony

---

9. 4 Wigmore, Evidence § 1300 (Chadbourn rev. 1972).

10. Abbott v. Abbott, 41 Mich. 540, 2 N.W. 810 (1879); In Matter of Katz' Will, 277 N.Y. 470, 14 N.E. 2d 797 (1938) (will may be established in direct opposition to testimony of subscribing witnesses); In re Ellis' Will, 235 N.C. 27, 69 S.E.2d 25 (1952); In re Estate of Farnsworth, 176 N.W.2d 247 (S.D.1970) (failure of attesting witnesses to recall execution does not preclude valid testamentary disposition).

11. Wheat v. Wheat, 156 Conn. 575, 244 A.2d 359 (1968); In re Lyons' Estate, 166 Ohio St. 207, 141 N.E.2d 151 (1957).

12. In re O'Connor's Estate, 105 Neb. 88, 179 N.W. 401, 12 A.L.R. 199 (1920). In re Estate of Silvestri, 44 N.Y.2d 260, 405 N.Y.S.2d 424, 376 N.E.2d 897 (1978).

13. Amerine v. Amerine, 177 Kan. 481, 280 P.2d 601 (1955); In re Warren's Estate, 138 Or. 283, 4 P.2d 635, 79 A.L.R. 389 (1931).

14. Smythe v. Inhabitants of New Providence Township, 263 F. 481, 484 (3d Cir. 1920) ("the subscribing witnesses are presumed to be dead").

15. Steiner v. Tranum, 98 Ala. 315, 13 So. 365 (1893) (trover for horse: note given by plaintiff as evidence of his purchase, held "collateral"); Lugosch v. Public Service Railway Co., 96 N.J.Eq. 472, 126 A. 170 (Ch.1924) (writing offered to impeach, "collateral"). Compare Snead v. Stephens, 242 Ala. 76, 5 So.2d 740 (1941)

where it was held that in a suit for destruction of plaintiff's mortgage lien on cotton by defendant's resale of the cotton, the mortgage itself was not collateral. The reversal of the judgment for plaintiff because of his failure to produce the subscribing witness to a writing the genuineness of which was not actually in doubt, illustrates the profitless aridity of the requirement.

16. Powers v. Russell, 13 Pick. (Mass.) 69, 75 (1832); 4 Wigmore, Evidence § 1318 (Chadbourn rev. 1972). Seemingly some courts would admit the original recorded deed, without calling subscribers under statutes providing that they "prove themselves." See Foxworth v. Brown, 120 Ala. 59, 24 So. 1, 4 (1898) and § 228 infra.

17. See, e.g., McKinney's N.Y. CPLR 4537. Various statutes of similar import are collected in 4 Wigmore, Evidence § 1290 (Chadbourn rev. 1972). The same rule appears in some jurisdictions to have been adopted by judicial decision. See Auto Owners Finance Co., Inc. v. Rock, 121 Vt. 194, 151 A.2d 292 (1959). (And see Fed. and Rev.Unif.R.Evid. (1974) 903, supra § 218, n. 1.

§ 221

1. See Berman, A Connecticut Commentary on Authenticating Private Documents, 28 Conn.B.J. 173 (1954); Tracy, Documentary Evidence, 24 Iowa L.Rev. 436 (1939); Dec.Dig. Evidence ⊕378(4). See also 20 Am.Jur. Proof of Facts 335 (bibliography).

by the witness through whom such a foundation is laid. These qualifications are minimal to say the least. Thus it is generally held that anyone familiar with the handwriting of a given person may supply authenticating testimony in the form of his opinion that a writing or signature is in the handwriting of that person.[2] Adequate familiarity may be present if the witness has seen the person write,[3] or if he has seen writings *purporting* to be those of the person in question under circumstances indicating their genuineness. Examples of the latter situation include instances where the witness has had an exchange of correspondence with the person,[4] or has seen writings which

the person has asserted are his own,[5] or has been present in an office or other place where genuine writings of a particular person in the ordinary course of business would naturally be seen.[6]

The same assumptions which underlie lay witness authentication based upon familiarity with individual handwriting may be seen to justify another well-established doctrine, that of authentication by handwriting specimens or "exemplars." The common law limited the use of exemplars for comparison purposes to writings otherwise admissible in the case,[7] but this rule has generally been modified by rule or statute[8] to allow handwriting samples to be admitted solely for the

2.   See, e.g., Clark v. Grimsley, 270 So.2d 53 (Fla. App.1972) (family friend and frequent visitor familiar with decedent's handwriting competent); Apple v. Commonwealth, 296 S.W.2d 717 (Ky.1956) (lay witness' testimony of familiarity and identity warranted admission); Noyes v. Noyes, 224 Mass. 125, 112 N.E. 850 (1916) ("anybody familiar with a person's handwriting" may authenticate).

3.   Auto Owners Finance Co. Inc. v. Rock, 121 Vt. 194, 151 A.2d 292 (1959). A single observation is frequently held sufficient. See United States v. Standing Soldier, 538 F.2d 196 (8th Cir. 1976); cert. denied 429 U.S. 1025; State v. Bond, 12 Idaho 424, 86 P. 43 (1906); State v. Freshwater, 30 Utah 442, 85 P. 447 (1906). Further, the observation need not have been recent. See In re Diggins' Estate, 68 Vt. 198, 34 A. 696 (1896) (one observation, 20 years previously, apparently held sufficient.) But a few states apply more rigorous standards. Compare Storm v. Hansen, 41 N.J.Super. 249, 124 A.2d 601 (1956) (lay identification "weak and unsatisfactory" at best; substantial familiarity required).

4.   Paccon, Inc. v. United States, 185 Ct.Cl. 24, 399 F.2d 62 (1968) (witness qualified to authenticate where he had seen 100 other documents purportedly signed by person over course of contract); Phoenix State Bank & Trust Co. v. Whitcomb, 121 Conn. 32, 183 A. 5 (1935) (witness shown to have had business dealings with purported author); Mack Financial Corp. v. Harnett Transfer, Inc., 42 N.C.App. 116, 256 S.E.2d 491 (1979) (familiarity through ordinary course of business).

5.   Hershberger v. Hershberger, 345 Pa. 439, 29 A.2d 95 (1942) (witnesses had charged account of person with checks purporting to have been drawn by him, and he had not questioned them).

6.   United States v. American Radiator & Standard Sanitary Corp., 433 F.2d 174 (3d Cir. 1970), cert. denied 401 U.S. 948 (secretary who had "at times" been familiar with handwriting of purported author allowed to authenticate); Hamilton v. Smith, 74 Conn. 374, 50 A. 884 (1902) (engineer who had frequently worked with maps signed by former town surveyor could authenti-

cate latter's signature); Kinney v. Youngblood, 216 Ga. 354, 116 S.E.2d 608 (1960) (witness who had lived in apartment in defendant's home for three years and testified she knew his signature); Priest v. Poleshuck, 29 N.J.Super. 401, 102 A.2d 636 (1954) (bookkeeper competent to authenticate signature of employee); In re McDowell's Will, 230 N.C. 259, 52 S.E.2d 807 (1949) (granddaughter's identification of signature as that of grandfather with whom she lived held sufficient without testimony that witness "knew" handwriting of grandfather).

7.   Doe v. Newton, 5 A. & E. 514 (1836); 7 Wigmore, Evidence § 2001 (Chadbourn rev. 1978). The earlier rule, while somewhat arbitrarily restrictive, had the advantage of eliminating certain troublesome questions concerning the creation and selection of exemplars. Under the rule here discussed these questions tend to recur. See United States v. Lam Muk Chiu, 522 F.2d 330 (2d Cir. 1975) (exemplars prepared by defendant for litigation and not under court supervision, offered to show defendant had not authored incriminating letters; "objectionable as self-serving"); contra, United States v. Pastore, 537 F.2d 675, 35 A.L.R. Fed. 616 (2d Cir. 1976) (exemplars prepared by witnesses for trial but not under court supervision held admissible to show witnesses had not endorsed checks as contended by defendant; self-interest of witnesses held not to bar admission). See also, Elliot v. United States, 385 A.2d 183 (D.C.App.1978) (defendant sent twin brother to furnish handwriting exemplars ordered by court).

A distinguishable type of problem is raised, unrelated to the reliability of the exemplar, when the exemplar would be inadmissible for some other reason. See United States v. Turquitt, 557 F.2d 464 (5th Cir. 1977) (document introduced as exemplar suggested commission of earlier crime by defendant; held: admission improper where exemplar was cumulative and unnecessary as well as prejudicial).

8.   State statutes and rules on the subject are collected in 7 Wigmore, Evidence § 2016 (Chadbourn rev. 1978). And see Fed.R.Evid. 901(b)(3) supra § 218, n. 1.

purpose of comparison. Some conflict of authority exists concerning the standard by which the authenticity of such specimens is to be determined.[9] Once admitted,[10] however, an apparent majority of jurisdictions hold that the genuineness of other offered writings alleged to be the work of the same author becomes a question for the trier of fact who may, but need not, be assisted in this task by expert comparisons.[11]

Demonstration is available, if demonstration is thought to be needed, that evidence of the foregoing varieties is essentially meaningless in cases where the authenticity is actually disputed.[12] If a writing is in fact questioned no person not trained in the science and art of document examination is truly competent to distinguish a skilled forgery from a genuine writing. Certainly it is incredible that an unskilled layman who saw the person write once a decade before could make such a differentiation. In the event of an actual controversy over genuineness, both logic and good advocacy demand a more scientific approach and resolution of the issue mainly upon the testimony of bona fide handwriting experts.[13]

The minimal qualifications required of the ordinary witness authenticating a writing by identification of handwriting are defensible only on the basis that no more than one in a hundred writings is questioned. The current permissive standards allow the admission of the general run of authentic documents with a minimum of time, trouble, and expense. The latter argument, however, may prove too much since even greater savings in these commodities might safely be achieved by simply presuming the authenticity of writings for purposes of admissibility in the absence of proof raising a question as to genuineness.[14]

 WESTLAW REFERENCES

authenticat! /p prove* proof /p handwriting signature*

§ 222. Authentication by Circumstantial Evidence: (a) Generally

As has been seen there are various ways in which writings may be authenticated by direct evidence. Nevertheless, it will frequently occur that no direct evidence of authenticity of any type exists or can be found. Resort must then be had to circumstantial proof and it is clear that authentication by circumstantial evidence is uniformly recognized as permissible.[1] Certain configurations of circumstantial evidence have in fact been so frequently held to authenticate particular types of writings that they have come to be recognized as distinct rules, e.g., the ancient documents rule, the reply doc-

9. Compare, e.g., State v. Fortier, ___ R.I. ___, 427 A.2d 1317 (1981) (stating genuineness of exemplars required to be proved to trial court beyond a reasonable doubt in criminal case); United States v. Mangan, 575 F.2d 32 (2d Cir. 1978), cert. denied 439 U.S. 931 (exemplars held sufficiently authenticated by circumstantial evidence of production from proper custody).

10. See n. 8 supra. Where the stated rule is followed the disputed document is sufficiently authenticated by being tendered for admission along with the authenticated exemplar. See United States Industries, Inc. v. Borr, 157 N.W.2d 708 (N.D.1968).

11. See, e.g., United States v. Woodson, 526 F.2d 550 (9th Cir. 1975) (disputed documents properly admissible for comparison with exemplars by jury despite fact that expert witness for proponent testified to inability to draw conclusion as to common authorship). See, also, Forte v. Schiebe, 145 Cal.App.2d 296, 302 P.2d 336 (1963) (similar procedure followed with respect to typewritten instrument).

12. Inbau, Lay Witness Identification of Handwriting (An Experiment), 34 Ill.L.Rev. 433 (1939); Hilton, The Detection of Forgery, 30 J.Crim.L. & Criminology 568 (1939).

13. See § 207 nn. 5, 20 supra.

14. Broun, Authentication and Contents of Writings, 1969 Law & Soc.Ord. 611; Levin, Authentication and Content of Writings, 10 Rut.L.Rev. 632 (1956); Strong, Liberalizing the Authentication of Private Writings, 52 Cornell L.Q. 284 (1967).

§ 222

1. See, e.g., Champion v. Champion, 368 Mich. 84, 117 N.W.2d 107 (1962) (authentication on basis of circumstantial evidence upheld); Harlow v. Commonwealth, 204 Va. 385, 131 S.E.2d 293 (1963) (acknowledging permissibility of circumstantial evidence to authenticate, but holding specific evidence offered insufficient).

trine, etc. These more or less formalized rules are treated in succeeding sections.[2]

It is important to bear in mind, however, that authentication by circumstantial evidence is not limited to situations which fall within one of these recurrent patterns. Rather, proof of any circumstances which will support a finding that the writing is genuine will suffice to authenticate the writing.[3]

WESTLAW REFERENCES

circumstantial** /2 prove* proof evidence /15 authentic! genuine!

§ 223. Authentication by Circumstantial Evidence: (b) Ancient Documents [1]

A writing which has been in existence for a number of years will frequently be difficult to authenticate by direct evidence. Where the maker of an instrument, those who witnessed the making, and even those familiar with the maker's handwriting have over the course of years died or become unavailable, the need to resort to authentication by circumstantial evidence is apparent.[2]

---

2. See §§ 223–226 infra.

3. See, e.g., United States v. Gordon, 634 F.2d 639 (1st Cir. 1980); United States v. Natale, 526 F.2d 1160 (2d Cir. 1975), cert. denied 425 U.S. 950 (1976); United States v. Sutton, 426 F.2d 1202 (D.C.Cir. 1969); Cotton States Mutual Insurance Co. v. Clark, 114 Ga.App. 439, 151 S.E.2d 780 (1966); People v. Lynes, 64 A.D.2d 543, 406 N.Y.S.2d 816 (1978), affirmed 49 N.Y.2d 286, 425 N.Y.S.2d 295, 401 N.E.2d 405; McFarland v. McFarland, 176 Pa.Super. 342, 107 A.2d 615 (1954).

§ 223

1. 7 Wigmore, Evidence, §§ 2137–2146 (Chadbourn rev. 1978); Dec.Dig. Evidence ⊙372; C.J.S. Evidence §§ 743–752.

2. Louden v. Apollo Gas Co., 273 Pa.Super. 549, 417 A.2d 1185 (1980) (rule prevents difficulty or impossibility of authenticating ancient writings by ordinary means). When possible, of course, the authenticity of ancient documents may be proved by direct evidence. Kanimaya v. Choctaw Lumber Co., 147 Okl. 90, 294 P. 817 (1930).

3. See Gaskins v. Guthrie, 162 Ga. 103, 132 S.E. 764 (1926) (showing of particular fact not essential, if totality of circumstances afford finding of genuineness.)

4. Wynne v. Tyrwhitt, [1821] 4 Barn. & Ald. 376, 106 Eng.Rep. 975 (rule founded on great difficulty of

---

The circumstances which may, in a given case, raise an inference of the genuineness of an aged writing are of course quite varied, and any combination of circumstances sufficient to support a finding of genuineness will be appropriate authentication.[3] Facts which may be suggested as indicative of genuineness include unsuspicious appearance, emergence from natural custody, prompt recording, and, in the case of a deed or will, possession taken under the instrument. Age itself may be viewed as giving rise to some inference of genuineness in that an instrument is unlikely to be forged for fruition at a time in the distant future.

The frequent necessity of authenticating ancient writings by circumstantial evidence [4] plus the consideration that certain of the above facts probative of authenticity are commonly found associated with genuine older writings have led the courts to develop a rule of thumb for dealing with the question.[5] Under this rule a writing is sufficiently authenticated as an ancient document if the party who offers it satisfies the judge that the writing is thirty years old,[6] that it is

---

proving handwriting after lapse of time.) See also 7 Wigmore, Evidence § 2137 (Chadbourn rev. 1978).

5. See, e.g., Steele v. Fowler, 111 Ind.App. 364, 41 N.E.2d 678 (1942) ("When a document appears to be at least 30 years old and is found in proper custody, and is unblemished by alterations and otherwise free from suspicion, it is admissible without proof of execution."); Boucher v. Wallis, 236 S.W.2d 519 (Tex.Civ.App.1951) (semble).

6. The selection of 30 years is justified by Wigmore as being the normal period beyond which direct evidence of authenticity becomes practically unavailable. This justification however, would appear to support 30 years as a rough standard only and to fall short of warranting such quibbles as whether the period should be measured from execution to filing of action or introduction of evidence. See Reuter v. Stuckart, 181 Ill. 529, 54 N.E. 1014 (1899) (execution to introduction proper measure). Viewing the rule positively, existence for a substantial period of time less than 30 years might be viewed as raising an inference of genuineness, and to warrant flexible application of the rule. See Lee Pong Tai v. Acheson, 104 F.Supp. 503 (E.D.Pa. 1952) (26-year-old document admitted); Neustadt v. Coline Oil Co., 141 Okl. 113, 284 P. 52 (1929) cert. denied 282 U.S. 799 (19 year-old document admitted under circumstances.)

unsuspicious in appearance,[7] and further proves that the writing is produced from a place of custody natural for such a document.[8] In addition to the foregoing requirements, some jurisdictions, if the writing is a dispositive one such as a deed or a will, impose the additional condition that possession must have been taken under the instrument.[9] The documents which may be authenticated under the rule here described, however, are not limited to dispositive instruments, and the rule has been applied to allow authentication of a wide variety of writings.[10]

In the case of a writing which purports to be executed by an agent, executor, or other person acting under power or authority from another, proof of the facts which authenticate the writing as an ancient document gives rise to a presumption that the person signing was duly authorized.[11]

It should be borne in mind that, despite the utility of the rule here discussed, it is merely a rule of authentication, the satisfaction of which does not necessarily guarantee the admission of the writing authenticated. Thus, it is sometimes forgotten that a writing may be proved perfectly genuine and yet remain inadmissible as being, e.g., hearsay or secondary evidence.[12] This source of confusion is compounded by a partial overlap between the requirements of the present

---

Age of a writing may be proved circumstantially by appearance and contents. Louden v. Apollo Gas Co., 273 Pa.Super. 549, 417 A.2d 1185 (1980) (age of document attested by date of cancellation of revenue stamp and spelling of "Pittsburg"). The purported date of the document, while providing some evidence of age, is obviously not conclusive. In re McGary's Estate, 127 Colo. 495, 258 P.2d 770 (1953).

The required age is reduced to 20 years in Or.Rev. Stat. 41.360(34); Fed.R.Evid. 901(b)(8) supra § 218, n. 1.

7. Stewart Oil Co. v. Sohio Petroleum Co., 202 F.Supp. 952 (D.C.Ill.1962) affirmed 315 F.2d 759 (alleged ancient document rejected as smacking of fraud); Apo v. Dillingham Investment Corp., 50 Hawaii 369, 440 P.2d 965 (1968) (misspelling of grantor's name and other irregularities; deeds excluded as suspicious; Muehrcke v. Behrens, 43 Wis.2d 1, 169 N.W.2d 86 (1969) ("When the instrument shows an alteration on its face it is the obligation of the party offering it to explain the alteration".); Roberts v. Waddell, 94 S.W.2d 211 (Tex.Civ.App.1936) (purported deed rejected because of mutilation and other reasons).

8. Sage v. Dayton Coal & Iron Co., 148 Tenn. 1, 251 S.W. 780 (1922) (careful preservation of instrument by one interested in subject matter raises inference of genuineness.) Proper custody would appear to extend to cover possession by any person so connected with the document that he might reasonably be found in possession of it without fraud. Ward v. Cameron, 76 S.W. 240 (Tex.Civ.App.1903).

9. The concept underlying the possession requirement has more recently been reflected in statutory enactments creating *presumptions* of authenticity of aged documents which, in addition to the usual requirements for authentication, have been "acted upon" as genuine by persons having an interest in the matter. West's Ann.Cal.Evid.Code, § 643; Or.Rev.Stat. 41.360(34). The strengthened inference of genuineness arising from the added circumstance of action on the instrument probably warrants treatment as a presumption. But such statutes need not be construed as rendering the raising of a presumption essential to admission, since the mere inference of authenticity should suffice for this purpose. See Devereau v. Frazier Mountain Park & Fisheries Co., 248 Cal.App.2d 323, 56 Cal.Rptr. 345 (1967) (suggesting the conclusion here recommended on the basis of an arguably unnecessary flexible reading of the statute).

Conversely, failure to act may create suspicion sufficient to exclude. Hulihee v. Heirs of Hueu (K), 57 Hawaii 312, 555 P.2d 495 (1976), rehearing denied 57 Hawaii 387, 556 P.2d 920 (not error to exclude ancient documents in bench trial where conduct of grantor and grantee contradicted import of document).

10. See, e.g., Kirkpatrick v. Tapo Oil Co., 144 Cal. App.2d 404, 301 P.2d 274 (1956) (ledger entries); Steele v. Fowler, 111 Ind.App. 364, 41 N.E.2d 678 (1942) (plat of town); Sinkora v. Wlach, 239 Iowa 1392, 35 N.W.2d 40 (1948) (foreign passports admitted; foreign church records of birth excluded); Trustees v. Farmers & Citizens Savings Bank Co., 66 Abs. 332, 113 N.E.2d 409 (Ohio App.1953) (old newspaper).

11. Wilson v. Snow, 228 U.S. 217 (1913) (deed of executrix; ". . . the ancient deed proves itself, whether it purports to have been signed by the grantor in his own right, as agent under power of attorney or—the original records having been lost—by an administrator under a power of sale given by order of court, not produced but recited in the deed itself"); Baumgarten v. Frost, 143 Tex. 533, 186 S.W.2d 982, 159 A.L.R. 428 (1945) (presumption recognized, but here receiver's assignment could not be presumed authorized where court's records intact and failed to show confirmation).

12. Town of Ninety-Six v. Southern Railway Co., 267 F.2d 579 (4th Cir. 1959) ("The fact that an instrument is an ancient document does not affect its admissibility in evidence further than to dispense with proof of its genuineness"; ancient letter excluded as inadmissible hearsay); King v. Schultz, 141 Mont. 94, 375 P.2d 108 (1962) (". . . ancient document rule does not change the basis for admission of evidence other than as to genuineness . . . ").

rule and those of the distinct doctrine which holds that recitals in certain types of ancient instruments may be received as evidence of the facts recited.[13] The latter doctrine, however, constitutes an exception to the rule against hearsay and is quite distinct from the present rule concerning authentication. It is discussed in another place.[14]

The preferable and majority view is that satisfaction of the ancient document requirements will serve to authenticate an ancient copy of an original writing.[15] And a fresh certified copy of an instrument of record for thirty years will prove the ancient writing,[16] though perhaps with the additional qualification that before the copy can come in, the original documents rule must be satisfied by showing the unavailability of the original.[17] Admission of a writing as an ancient document does, however, dispense with the production of attesting witnesses.[18]

WESTLAW REFERENCES

"ancient document*"

---

13. The two doctrines are contrasted in Town of Ninety-Six v. Southern Railway Co., supra n. 12. Numerous cases noting the distinction in connection with old maps and plats are found in Annot., 46 A.L.R.2d 1318 (admissibility of ancient maps and the like under the ancient document rule).

14. See § 323 infra.

15. Schell v. City of Jefferson, 357 Mo. 1020, 212 S.W.2d 430 (1948) (ancient copy of city plat, original not available, held improperly excluded, one judge dissenting); and see 7 Wigmore, Evidence § 2143 (Chadbourn rev. 1978) (supporting majority position and collecting older authorities). But some jurisdictions hold that the rule does not apply to copies. See Anderson v. Anderson, 150 Neb. 879, 36 N.W.2d 287 (1949) ("the rule applies only to original instruments . . ."); Solomon v. Beck, 387 S.W.2d 911 (Tex.Civ.App.1965) (examined copy of ancient instrument not admissible under rule).

16. See Hodge v. Palms, 117 F. 396 (6th Cir. 1902); Solomon v. Beck, supra n. 15. The certified copy of the long-recorded writing obviously has a stronger claim to admissibility than the ancient unrecorded copy. See 7 Wigmore, Evidence § 2143 (Chadbourn rev. 1978).

17. Sudduth v. Central of Georgia Railway Co., 201 Ala. 560, 77 So. 350 (1917); Woods v. Bonner, 89 Tenn. 411, 18 S.W. 67 (1890); Emory v. Bailey, 111 Tex. 337, 234 S.W. 660, 662 (1921) ("on filing proper affidavit of loss," under statute). See § 240 infra.

18. See § 220 supra.

§ 224. Authentication by Circumstantial Evidence: (c) Custody [1]

If a writing purports to be an official report or record and is proved to have come from the proper public office where such official papers are kept, it is generally agreed that this authenticates the offered document as genuine.[2] This result is founded on the probability that the officers in custody of such records will carry out their public duty to receive or record only genuine official papers and reports. Similarly, where a public office is the depository for private papers, such as wills, conveyances, or income tax returns, the proof that such a purporting deed, bill of sale, tax return or the like has come from the proper custody is usually accepted as sufficient authentication.[3] This again can be sustained on the same principle if it appears that the official custodian had a public duty to verify the genuineness of the papers offered for record or deposit and to accept only the genuine.

As is true with ancient documents, the question of the authenticity of official

---

§ 224

1. 7 Wigmore, Evidence §§ 2158–2160 (Chadbourn rev. 1978); Dec.Dig. Evidence ⊕366, Criminal Law ⊕444.

2. United States v. Ward, 173 F.2d 628 (2d Cir. 1949) (records from files of Selective Service, identified by custodian); Tameling v. Commissioner, 43 F.2d 814 (2d Cir. 1930) (official assessment role shown to emanate from official custody admissible without further authentication); State v. Miller, 79 N.M. 117, 440 P.2d 792 (1968) (fingerprint record from F.B.I. file; stating rule in terms of above text).

3. United States v. Olson, 576 F.2d 1267 (8th Cir. 1978), cert. denied 439 U.S. 896 (W–4E forms and tax returns purportedly filed by defendant; court dismisses suggestion forms filed by another D.D. Olson). Brooks v. Texas General Indemnity Co., 251 F.2d 15 (5th Cir. 1958) (application for benefits produced from files of Veteran's Administration); Sternberg Dredging Co. v. Moran Towing & Transportation Co., Inc., 196 F.2d 1002 (2d Cir. 1952) (letter report filed in compliance with statutory requirement and produced from official custody held improperly excluded; opinion by L. Hand, J.); Wausau Sulphate Fibre Co. v. Commissioner, 61 F.2d 879 (7th Cir. 1932) (waiver bearing purported signature of taxpayer, from Bureau's files); Halko v. State, 209 A.2d 895 (Del.1965) (application for driver's license produced from official files admissible under local statutes).

records should not be confused with the ultimate admissibility of such records. It is quite possible for a public record to be perfectly genuine, and yet remain inadmissible for some distinguishable reason, e.g., that it is excludable hearsay.[4]

Some question exists whether the rule which accepts, as prima facie genuine, documents which are shown to emerge from official custody should be extended beyond the field of public duty and recognized as to writings found in private custody. Since the circumstances of private custody are infinitely more varied than those of public custody, a new rule in an already rule-ridden area seems inadvisable. No such rule, in fact, is needed, provided that, in their discretion, courts recognize that proof of private custody, together with other circumstances, is frequently strong circumstantial evidence of authenticity.[5]

 WESTLAW REFERENCES

custod! /p authentic! /p official public /2 record* document*

§ 225. Authentication by Circumstantial Evidence: (d) Knowledge: Reply Letters and Telegrams [1]

When a letter, signed with the purported signature of X, is received "out of the blue," with no previous correspondence, the traditional "show me" skepticism of the common law trial practice [2] prevails, and the purported signature is not accepted as authentication,[3] unless authenticity is confirmed by additional facts.[4]

One circumstance recognized as sufficient is the fact that the letter discloses knowledge that only the purported signer would be likely to have.[5] Moreover, a convenient

---

4. See, e.g., Matthews v. United States, 217 F.2d 409 (5th Cir. 1954) (statutorily required reports of sugar sales produced from government files properly identified but held inadmissible as hearsay).

5. Proof of private custody has frequently been so viewed. Reeves v. Warden, Maryland Penitentiary, 346 F.2d 915, 926, n. 29 (3d Cir. 1965) (incriminating note, discovered under petitioner's underclothing in bureau used exclusively by petitioner in petitioner's bedroom, which detailed activities of petitioner would have been admissible as against relevancy objection; dictum); United States v. Imperial Chem. Ind., 100 F.Supp. 504 (S.D.N.Y.1951), supplemented 105 F.Supp. 215 (unsigned documents from corporate defendant's files admissible against corporation as authentic declarations of corporate agents; possibility of spurious or forged documents in files rejected as highly improbable); State v. Smith, 246 Ga. 129, 269 S.E.2d 21 (1980), on remand 156 Ga.App. 250, 274 S.E.2d 646 (possession of letter plus additional facts held sufficient to authenticate). Cf. People v. Manganaro, 218 N.Y. 9, 112 N.E. 436 (1916).

§ 225

1. 7 Wigmore, Evidence §§ 2148, 2153–2154 (Chadbourn rev. 1978); C.J.S. Evidence § 706b; Dec. Dig. Evidence ⊜378, Criminal Law ⊜444.

2. See § 218 supra.

3. Early v. State, 42 Ala.App. 200, 158 So.2d 495 (1963); Continental Baking Co. v. Katz, 68 Cal.2d 512, 67 Cal.Rptr. 761, 439 P.2d 889 (1968); Westland Distributing, Inc. v. Rio Grande Motorway, Inc., 38 Colo. App. 292, 555 P.2d 990 (1976) (stating rule as in text but admitting letter on basis of facts known to writer); State v. Golden, 67 Idaho 497, 186 P.2d 485 (1947). See also Harlow v. Commonwealth, 204 Va. 385, 131 S.E.2d

293 (1963) (unsigned telegram inadmissible without proof of authorship).

4. Greenbaum v. United States, 80 F.2d 113 (9th Cir. 1935) (letter purporting to be signed for corporation by agent held authenticated by proof that person signing was agent of corporation and city of posting was the place of business of company); Fuller v. State, 437 P.2d 772 (Alas.1968) (telegram admissible where proved to have been paid for by occupant of room, and defendant was shown to have been occupant); Cotton States Mutual Insurance Co. v. Clark, 114 Ga.App. 439, 151 S.E.2d 780 (1966) (surrounding circumstances, including facts that letter was on defendant's letterhead and contract was on defendant's form, sufficient for authentication).

5. United States v. Lam Muk Chiu, 522 F.2d 330 (2d Cir. 1975) (letters referring to prior agreement of defendant with narcotics informer); United States v. Sutton, 138 U.S.App.D.C. 208, 426 F.2d 1202 (1969) (notes suggesting defendant's plan for murder-suicide held authenticated where subsequent events observed by eyewitnesses followed note's predictions); Westland Distributing, Inc. v. Rio Grande Motorway, Inc., 38 Colo.App. 292, 555 P.2d 990 (1976) (letter disclosing knowledge unique to purported author and sent in response to phone conversation between adressee and purported author); People v. Munoz, 70 Ill.App.3d 76, 26 Ill.Dec. 509, 388 N.E.2d 133 (1979) (letter from jail bearing defendant's nickname and cell number and referring to facts known to only four people held sufficient to authenticate; not necessary to disprove possible authorship by all others); State v. Milum, 202 Kan. 196, 447 P.2d 801, 803 (1968) ("Proof of the genuineness of a letter may be established when the contents themselves reveal knowledge peculiarly referable to a certain person . . . "); Champion v. Champion,

practice recognizes that if a letter has been written to X, and the letter now offered in evidence purports to be written by X and purports to be a reply to the first letter (that is either refers to it, or is responsive to its terms) and has been received without unusual delay, these facts authenticate it as a reply letter.[6] This result may be rested upon the knowledge-principle, mentioned above. In view of the regularity of the mails the first letter would almost invariably come exclusively into the hands of X, or those authorized to act for him, who would alone know of the terms of the letter. It is supported also by the fact that in common experience we know that reply letters do come from the person addressed in the first letter.

These same arguments apply to reply telegrams, but with a reduced degree of certainty. Some of the employees of the telegraph company, as well as the addressee, know the contents of the first telegram. Moreover, the instances of misdelivery of telegrams

may be more numerous relatively than misdeliveries of letters. These considerations have led some courts to reject for reply telegrams this theory of authentication.[7] The contrary view, that the inference of authenticity of the reply telegram is substantial and sufficient,[8] seems more reasonable and expedient.

When the reply letter purports to be signed by an agent or other representative of X, the addressee of the first letter, the authority of the signing representative is presumed.[9]

The first step in authentication of the reply letter is to prove that the first letter was dated and was duly mailed at a given time and place addressed to X.[10] Seemingly oral testimony to these facts should suffice as to the first letter if the reply letter refers to it by date.[11] If, however, the reply letter only refers to it by reciting or responding to its terms, then since the terms of the first letter

368 Mich. 84, 117 N.W.2d 107 (1962) (knowledge of recipient's itinerary on European tour and of letters received at other points held circumstances indicating authenticity); State ex rel. Kunz v. Woodmansee, 156 Or. 607, 69 P.2d 298 (1937) (series of letters showing intimate knowledge of details of life of alleged writer); Casto v. Martin, ___ W.Va. ___, 230 S.E.2d 722 (1976) (typewritten memo relating details of complex business transaction known only to defendant; authentication sufficient where defendant did not deny authorship); Annot., 9 A.L.R. 984. After a letter is written a statement about its contents may identify the declarant as the writer. See Deaderick v. Deaderick, 182 Ga. 96, 185 S.E. 89 (1936). See Fed.R.Evid. 901(b)(4) supra § 218, n. 1.

6. Winel v. United States, 365 F.2d 646, 648 (8th Cir. 1966) (". . . one of the principal situations where the authenticity of a letter is provable by circumstantial evidence arising out of the letter's context . . . is where it can be shown that the letter was sent in reply to a previous communication."); Purer & Co. v. Aktiebolaget Addo, 410 F.2d 871 (9th Cir. 1969), cert. denied 396 U.S. 834; Namerdy v. Generalcar, 217 A.2d 109 (D.C.App.1966); Wheton v. Daly, 93 N.H. 150, 37 A.2d 1 (1944) (Page, J.: "It is a fair inference, considering the habitual accuracy of the mails, that the letter addressed to B reached the real B, and that an answer referring to the contents of A's letter and coming back in due course of mail, leaves only a negligible chance that any other than B has become acquainted with the contents of A's letter so as to forge a reply.");

Conner v. Zanuzoski, 36 Wn.2d 458, 218 P.2d 879 (1950).

7. Smith v. Easton, 54 Md. 138, 146, 39 Am.St.Rep. 355 (1880); Howley v. Whipple, 48 N.H. 487, 488 (1869).

8. House Grain Co. v. Finerman & Sons, 116 Cal. App.2d 485, 253 P.2d 1034 (1953) (reply telegram held "self-authenticating"); Peterman v. Vermont Savings Bank, 181 La. 403, 159 So. 598 (1935); Annot. 5 A.L.R.3d 1018. The same principle, of course, should serve to authenticate telegrams in response to letters and vice versa. See Menefee v. Bering Manufacturing Co., 166 S.W. 365 (Tex.Civ.App.1914) (telegram received in response to letter admitted).

9. Reliance Life Insurance Co. v. Russell, 208 Ala. 559, 94 So. 748 (1922) (to rebut presumption of genuineness of reply letter not sufficient to show that purported sender did not sign it but must show that he did not authorize another to sign for him); Capitol City Supply Co. v. Beury, 69 W.Va. 612, 72 S.E. 657 (1911) (similar to last); Anstine v. McWilliams, 24 Wn.2d 230, 163 P.2d 816 (1945) (authority of purported agent, signing for principal presumed; full discussion and citations); Dec. Dig. Evidence ∞378(3).

10. Consolidated Grocery Co. v. Hammond, 99 C.C.A. 195, 175 F. 641 (5th Cir.1910) (statement in purported reply letter referring to previous letter does not suffice); Kvale v. Keane, 39 N.D. 560, 168 N.W. 74 (1918) (must make preliminary proof that first letter was duly addressed, stamped and posted).

11. See § 233 infra.

become important,[12] probably it would be necessary to satisfy the Best Evidence Rule. If X, as usually would be the case, is the party-opponent, and has the first letter in his hands, it would be necessary to give him notice to produce it, before a copy could be used to prove its terms.[13]

 WESTLAW
REFERENCES

157k378(2)

§ 226. Authentication by Circumstantial Evidence: (e) Telephone Messages and Other Oral Communications [1]

Modern technology makes commonplace the receipt of oral communications from persons who are heard but not seen. The problems of authentication raised by these communications are substantively analogous to the problems of authenticating writings. Thus, if the witness has received, e.g., a telephone call out of the blue from one who identified himself as "X", this is not sufficient authentication of the call as in fact coming from X.[2] The requisite additional proof may take the form of testimony by the witness that he is familiar with X's voice and that the caller was X.[3] Or authentication may be accomplished by circumstantial evidence pointing to X's identity as the caller,[4] such as if the communication received reveals that the speaker had knowledge of facts that only X would be likely to know.[5] These same modes of authentication are also recognized where communications have been received or recorded by modern devices other than the telephone.[6]

12. See § 233 infra.

13. See § 239 supra.

§ 226

1. 7 Wigmore, Evidence § 2155 (Chadbourn rev. 1978); Notes, 11 N.C.L.Rev. 344 (1933), 26 Wash.U.L. Q. 433 (1941); Annot., 71 A.L.R. 5, 105 A.L.R. 326; Dec.Dig. Evidence ☞148; 29 Am.Jur.2d Evidence §§ 380–386; C.J.S. Evidence § 188.

2. Price v. State, 208 Ga. 695, 69 S.E.2d 253 (1952) (identity of communicator not established); Texas Candy & Nut Co. v. Horton, 235 S.W.2d 518, 521 (Civ.App. Tex.1950) ("When the party called over a telephone depends entirely upon the word of the party calling as to his identity, the conversation is . . . inadmissible.").

3. People v. Ostrand, 35 Ill.2d 520, 221 N.E.2d 499 (1966) (identification of caller's voice held sufficient authentication); Chartrand v. Registrar of Motor Vehicles, 345 Mass. 321, 187 N.E.2d 135 (1963) (exclusion of phone conversation held error where witness not a party to call identified voice). The familiarity with a voice necessary to authenticate by voice identification may be acquired subsequent to the call. United States v. Watson, 594 F.2d 1330 (10th Cir.1979), cert. denied, 444 U.S. 840 (1979); State v. Porter, 251 S.C. 393, 162 S.E.2d 843 (1968); Massey v. State, 160 Tex.Cr.R. 49, 266 S.W.2d 880 (1954) (identification of voice sufficient where witness met caller for first time one year after call). But see Hires v. Price, 75 Ill.App.2d 202, 220 N.E.2d 327 (1966) (familiarity acquired by listening to alleged caller during trial recess insufficient.) Note, 33 J.Crim.L. 487 (1943). See Fed.R.Evid. 901(b)(5), supra § 218, n. 1.

4. Carbo v. United States, 314 F.2d 718 (9th Cir. 1963) (call held authenticated by circumstantial evidence where testimony showed one conspirator had stated that call would be made and another had inquired when recipient could be reached by phone); Robinson v. Branch Brook Manor Apartments, 101 N.J. Super. 117, 243 A.2d 284 (1968) ("preferred rule" today allows authentication by circumstantial evidence, including events occurring both before and after call).

5. United States v. LoBue, 180 F.Supp. 955 (S.D. N.Y.1960) (call held authenticated by caller's knowledge of facts subsequently confirmed); People v. Lynes, 64 A.D.2d 543, 406 N.Y.S.2d 816 (1978), affirmed 49 N.Y. 286, 425 N.Y.S.2d 295, 401 N.E.2d 405 (detective called defendant and left message he wished defendant to call back; return call held sufficiently authenticated); Gutowsky v. Halliburton Oil Well Cementing Co., 287 P.2d 204 (Okla.1955) (identity of caller held sufficiently established by apparent knowledge of subject matter of conversation). But compare Smithers v. Light, 305 Pa. 141, 157 A. 489 (1931) (caller purporting to be customer X of brokerage house orders sale of designated stocks held by broker; authentication held insufficient without adverting to knowledge factor). See Fed.R.Evid. 901(b)(4), supra § 218, n. 1.

6. Radio: LeRoy v. Sabena Belgian World Airlines, 344 F.2d 266 (2d Cir.1965) (radio transmission from airliner prior to crash held authenticated by equivocal voice identification plus circumstantial evidence); United States v. Sansone, 231 F.2d 887 (2d Cir.1956) (incriminating comments of defendant transmitted over concealed transmitter held authenticated by voice identification plus long range visual identification). Recordings: United States v. Madda, 345 F.2d 400 (7th Cir.1965) (tape recording of bribe attempt upon party to conversation's testimony identifying voices and asserting recording to be accurate reflection of conversation); In re Roth's Estate, 15 O.O.2d 234, 170 N.E.2d 313 (1960) (recording of bedside conversation with decedent; semble); Annot., 58 A.L.R.2d 1008.

A somewhat easier problem is presented when the witness testifies that he himself placed a telephone call to a number listed to X, and that the person answering identified himself as X. In such a situation the accuracy of the telephone system, the probable absence of motive to falsify and the lack of opportunity for premeditated fraud all tend to support the conclusion that the self-identification of the speaker is reliable. Thus most courts today view proof of proper placing of a call plus self-identification of the speaker as sufficient proof of authenticity to admit the substance of the call.[7] Moreover, it is likewise held that where it is shown that the witness has called the listed number of a business establishment and spoken with someone purporting to speak for the concern, with respect to matters within its ordinary course of business, it is presumed that the speaker was authorized to speak for the employer.[8]

WESTLAW REFERENCES

telephone phone   /3   message* call* conversation*   /p authentic!

§ 227. Functions of Judge and Jury in Authentication [1]

If direct testimony of the authorship of a writing or of an oral statement is given, this is sufficient authentication and the judge has no problem on that score.[2] The writing or statement comes in,[3] if not otherwise objectionable. When the authenticating evidence is circumstantial, however, the question whether reasonable men could find its authorship as claimed by the proponent, may be a delicate and balanced one, as to which the judge must be accorded some latitude of judgment.[4] Accordingly, it is often said to be a matter of discretion.[5] It must be noticed, however, that authenticity is not to be classed as one of those preliminary questions of fact conditioning admissibility under technical evidentiary rules of competency or

---

7. Palos v. United States, 416 F.2d 438 (5th Cir. 1969) (government informer shown to have dialed listed number, asked for defendant and received answer, "This is he"; sufficient to authenticate); United States v. Benjamin, 328 F.2d 854 (2d Cir. 1964) (applying rule that proper dialing plus self-identification of party call constitute prima facie authentication); United States v. Scolly, 546 F.2d 255 (9th Cir. 1976), cert. denied 430 U.S. 970 (semble); Everette v. D.O. Briggs Lumber Co., 250 N.C. 688, 110 S.E.2d 288 (1959) (semble, and holding in addition that voice familiarity acquired through such calls may be relied upon to authenticate subsequent calls). See, however, the dictum to the contrary in Colbert v. Dallas Joint Stock Land Bank, 136 Tex. 268, 150 S.W.2d 771 (1941). See Fed.R.Evid. 901 (b)(6), supra § 218, n. 1.

8. Crist v. Pennsylvania Railroad Co., 96 F.Supp. 243, 245 (W.D.Pa.1951) (". . . one who answers a telephone call from the place of business of the person called for, and undertakes to respond as his agent, is presumed to have authority to speak for him in respect to the general business there carried on and conducted."); Thruway Service City, Inc. v. Townsend, 116 Ga. App. 379, 157 S.E.2d 564 (1967) (admissions of fault by persons answering at defendant's phone admissible); Ratliff v. City of Great Falls, 132 Mont. 89, 314 P.2d 880 (1957) (presumption of authority in absence of affirmative proof of wrong connection or officious intermeddler). Fielding Home for Funerals v. Public Savings Life Insurance Co., 271 S.C. 117, 245 S.E.2d 238, 240 (1978) ("[A] business by installing a telephone and impliedly inviting its use for business communications,

creates a prima facie presumption that the person who answers and responds in regard to its ordinary business is authorized to speak in such matters"). The rule applies even lacking any indication of the identity of the answerer. Lynn v. Farm Bureau Mutual Auto Insurance Co., 264 F.2d 921 (4th Cir. 1959). While the probabilities of the situation alone adequately support the rule, it is sometimes said to rest upon the agency principle of apparent authority. Sauber v. Northland Insurance Co., 251 Minn. 237, 87 N.W.2d 591 (1958). This latter justification, however, may possibly generate unfortunate limitations on the rule.

§ 227

1. Dec.Dig. Evidence ⊜382; C.J.S. Evidence §§ 624, 625.

2. See §§ 219–221 supra.

3. See Epperson v. State, 600 P.2d 1051 (Wyo.1979) (receipt for sale of property defendant charged with converting admitted authentic by complaining witness; error to exclude on ground witness claimed to have been drunk when he signed).

4. See §§ 222–226 supra.

5. United States v. Sutton, 138 U.S.App.D.C. 208, 426 F.2d 1202 (1969) (determination of admissibility by trial court held largely discretionary); State v. Milum, 202 Kan. 196, 447 P.2d 801 (1968) (semble); Lundgren v. Union Indemnity Co., 171 Minn. 122, 213 N.W. 553 (1927) (exclusion of telegrams, where more convincing evidence of authenticity available, not abuse of discretion).

privilege. As to these latter, the trial judge will permit the adversary to introduce controverting proof on the preliminary issue in support of his objection, and the judge will decide this issue, without submission to the jury, as a basis for his ruling on admissibility.[6] On the other hand, the authenticity of a writing or statement is not a question of the application of a technical rule of evidence. It goes to genuineness and conditional relevance, as the jury can readily understand. Thus, if a prima facie showing is made, the writing or statement comes in, and the ultimate question of authenticity is left to the jury.[7]

WESTLAW REFERENCES

digest("judge" /p discretion! authentic! /p evidence)

§ 228. Escapes from the Requirement of Producing Evidence of Authenticity: Modern Theory and Practice

As the foregoing sections clearly imply, the authentication of writings and other communications by formal proof may prove troublesome, time consuming, and expensive even in cases where no legitimate doubt concerning genuineness would appear to exist. The ultimate explanation for the continuing insistence upon the furnishing of such proof, justifiable only upon assumptions which accord very little with common sense, is of course obscure. It may be speculated, however that in part the explanation is to be found in various procedural devices which afford escape from authentication requirements. Use of these devices will avert some of the impatience which might otherwise be engendered by formal authentication requirements. The legislatures, too, have frequently nibbled at the problem by enacting statutes relieving the rigors of authentication in what would otherwise be particularly

troublesome contexts. Among these "escapes from authentication," the following are particularly noteworthy.

Requests for Admission.[1] Under the practice in the Federal courts as provided by Rules 36 and 37(c) of the Federal Rules of Civil Procedure, and under analogous rules or statutes in many states, a party may serve upon an adversary a written request for admission of the genuineness of any relevant document described in the request. If the adversary unreasonably fails within a specified time to serve an answer or objection, genuineness is admitted. If genuineness is denied and the requesting party thereafter proves the genuineness of the document at trial, the latter may apply for an order of court requiring the adversary to pay him the reasonable costs of making the authenticating proof.

Securing Admission at Pretrial Conference.[2] Under Rule 16 in the Federal courts and under analogous rules and statutes in many states, it is provided that a pretrial conference of the attorneys may be called by the court to consider among other things, "the possibility of obtaining admissions of fact and of documents which will avoid unnecessary proof." Of course, similar stipulations often are secured in informal negotiation between counsel, but a skilful judge may create at a pretrial conference an atmosphere of mutual concession unusually favorable for such admissions. This function of the pretrial practice has been considered one of its most successful features.

Statutes and Rules Requiring Special or Sworn Denial of Genuineness of Writing. A provision of practice acts and rules of procedure may require that when an action is brought upon a written instrument, such as a note or contract, copied in the complaint, the genuineness of the writing will be

---

6. See § 53 supra.

7. Adv.Com. Notes, Fed.R.Evid. 104(a) and (b) and 901(a).

§ 228

1. Wright, The Law of Federal Courts 592 (4th ed. 1983).

2. Id. at 601.

deemed admitted unless a sworn denial be included in the answer.[3]

Writings Which "Prove Themselves:" Acknowledged Documents, Certified Copies, and Law Books Which Purport to be Printed by Authority. There are certain kinds of writings which are said to "prove themselves" or to be "self-identifying." In consequence one of these may be tendered to the court and, even without the shepherding angel of an authenticating witness, will be accepted in evidence for what it purports to be. This convenient result is reached in two stages. First, by statutes which often provide that certain classes of writings, usually in some manner purporting to be vouched for by an official, shall be received in evidence "without further proof." This helpful attribute is most commonly given by these statutes to (1) deeds, conveyances or other instruments, which have been acknowledged by the signers before a notary public,[4] (2) certified copies of public records,[5] and (3) books of statutes which purport to be printed by public authority.[6]

But in the first two of these classes of writings, which can qualify only when the acknowledgment is certified by a notary or the copy certified by the official who has custody of the record, how is the court to know without proof that the signature or seal appearing on the writing is actually that of the official whose name and title are recited? This second step is supplied by the traditional doctrines which recognize the seal or signature of certain types of officers, including the keeper of the seal of state, judicial officers, and notaries public, as being of themselves sufficient evidence of the genuineness of the certificate.[7] Moreover in many state codes particular provisions supplement or clarify tradition by specifying that the seals or signatures of certain classes of officialdom shall have this self-authenticating effect.[8]

Federal Rules of Evidence. The concept of self-authentication, previously recognized by statute in the case of the certain relatively limited classes of writings noted above, is given an expanded ambit of operation by the Federal Rules of Evidence. Rule 902 accords prima facie authenticity not only to those types of writings such as acknowledged writings and public records which have commonly enjoyed such treatment by statute but also to various other types of writings not previously so favored. Among these new classes of self-authenticating writings are included books, pamphlets and other publications issued by public authority, newspapers and periodicals, and trade inscriptions and labels indicating ownership, control or origin.[9] Presumptive authenticity, as provided for by the rule, does not pre-

3. See, e.g., Ariz.R.Civ.Pro., Rule 9(i)6.

4. West's Ann.Cal.Evid.Code, § 1451 ("A certificate of the acknowledgment of a writing other than a will, or a certificate of the proof of such a writing, is prima facie evidence of the facts recited in the certificate and the genuineness of the signature of each person by whom the writing purports to have been signed, if the certificate meets [designated statutory requirements]."); Ky.Rev.Stat. 422.100 (1982) ("All instruments of writing required by law to be notarized, that are notarized, shall be received as evidence without further authentication."). Statutes of this general variety are collected in 5 Wigmore, Evidence § 1676 (Chadbourn rev. 1974) and are discussed in Tracy, Introduction of Documentary Evidence, 24 Iowa L.Rev. 436, 439 (1939). See Fed.R.Evid. 902(8), supra § 218, n. 1.

5. The doctrine and statutes are discussed in 5 Wigmore, Evidence § 1677 (Chadbourn rev. 1974). Dec. Dig. Evidence ⚖338–349 collects cases. See Fed.R. Evid. 902(4), supra § 218, n. 1.

6. Statutes are compiled in 5 Wigmore, Evidence § 1684 (Chadbourn rev. 1974). Their most frequent and useful employment is in the proof of statutes of sister states and of foreign countries, see § 335 infra.

7. The history and theory of the subject are reviewed and the decisions and statutes collected in 7 Wigmore, Evidence §§ 2161–2168 (Chadbourn rev. 1978).

8. See, e.g., the Uniform Acknowledgment Act, which attributes self-authenticating effect to acknowledgments taken by officers of the state in which the document is offered, and officers of the United States acting outside the country. Other statutes are collected in 7 Wigmore, Evidence §§ 2162, 2167 (Chadbourn rev. 1978).

9. Fed.R.Evid. 902, supra § 218 n. 1. In State v. Rines, 269 A.2d 9 (Me.1970) the court relied upon the proposed version of the rule in holding that the manufacturer's certificate made a sufficient prima facie case of the contents of swab and tubes in a kit designed to

clude evidentiary challenge of the genuineness of the offered writing, but simply serves to obviate the necessity of preliminary authentication by the proponent to secure admission. This commonsense approach was long overdue and might well be extended to apply to all writings purporting to have a connection with the party against whom offered.[10] The suggestion rests not only upon the proposition that the overwhelming majority of such writings will be genuine, but in addition on the superior position of the adversary to demonstrate through evidence that the purported connection of a writing with him is attributable to fraud or mistake.[11]

 WESTLAW REFERENCES

synopsis,digest(request* /3 admission* /p genuine!)

Securing Admission to Pretrial Conference

pretrial /2 conference* /p admission* /p civ.proc. rule* /5 16

Statutes and Rules Requiring Special or Sworn Denial of Genuineness of Writing

civ.pro! /5 93(h) & court(tx)

Writings Which "Prove Themselves"

topic(157 /1 k338 k339 k340 k341 k342 k343 k344 k345 k346 k347 k348 k349)

Federal Rules of Evidence

selfauthenticat! /p rule* /5 902

---

draw and preserve blood for a blood-alcohol test. Compare Keegan v. Green Giant Co., supra, § 218 n. 8.

10. Broun, Authentication and Contents of Writings, 1969 Law & Soc. Order 611; Strong, Liberalizing

the Authentication of Private Writings, 52 Cornell L.Q. 284 (1967).

11. Strong, Liberalizing the Authentication of Private Writings, supra, note 10.

Chapter 23

THE REQUIREMENT OF THE PRODUCTION OF THE ORIGINAL WRITING AS THE "BEST EVIDENCE"

Table of Sections

§ 229. The "Best Evidence" Rule

Thayer[1] tells us that the first appearance of the "best evidence" phrase, is a statement in 1700 by Holt, C.J. (in a case in which he admitted evidence questioned as secondary) to the effect that "the best proof that the nature of the thing will afford is only required."[2] This statement given as a reason for receiving evidence, that it is the best which can be had—a highly liberalizing principle—not surprisingly gives birth to a con-verse and narrowing doctrine that a man must produce the best evidence that is available—second-best will not do. And so before 1726 we find Baron Gilbert in one of the earliest treatises on Evidence saying, "the first and most signal rule in relation to evidence is this, that a man must have the utmost evidence the nature of the fact is capable of . . . "[3] Blackstone continues the same broad generalizing and combines both the positive and negative aspects of the "best evidence" idea when he says, ". . .

---

§ 229

1. Thayer, Preliminary Treatise on Evidence at the Common Law 489 (1898).

2. Ford v. Hopkins, 1 Salk. 283, 91 Eng.Rep. 250 (1700).

3. Gilbert, Evidence (2d ed.) 4, 15–17, quoted Thayer, op.cit. 490.

the best evidence the nature of the case will admit of shall always be required, if possible to be had; but if not possible then the best evidence that can be had shall be allowed." [4] Greenleaf in this country in 1842 was still repeating these wide abstractions.[5]

Thayer, however, writing in 1898, points out that these broad principles, though they had some influence in shaping specific evidence rules in the 1700s, were never received as adequate or accurate statements of governing rules, and that actually "the chief illustration of the Best Evidence principle, the doctrine that if you would prove the contents of a writing, you must produce the writing itself" is an ancient rule far older than any notion about the "best" evidence.[6] While some modern opinions still refer to the "best evidence" notion as if it were today a general governing legal principle [7] most would adopt the view of modern textwriters [8] that there is no such general rule.[9] The only actual rule that the "best evidence" phrase denotes today is the rule requiring the production of the original writing.[10]

WESTLAW REFERENCES

best +1 evidence /s available permissible require! unavailable
157k157(1)

§ 230. Original Document Rule [1]

The specific context in which it is generally agreed that the best evidence principle is applicable today should be definitely stated

---

4. Blackstone, Commentaries 368, quoted Thayer op.cit. 491.

5. 1 Greenleaf, Evidence Part 2, ch. 4, §§ 82–97 (1842), quoted and analyzed in Thayer, op.cit., 484–487.

6. Arnett v. Helvie, 148 Ind.App. 476, 267 N.E.2d 864 (1971) (principle relied upon to uphold exclusion of expert testimony as to yield of farm; court states testimony of tenant farmers would have been best evidence); Matter of Fortney's Estate, 5 Kan.App.2d 14, 611 P.2d 599 (1980) (no abuse of discretion to exclude evidence on ground other more reliable evidence existed); Thayer, op.cit. 497–506.

7. Padgett v. Brezner, 359 S.W.2d 416, 422 (Mo. App.1962) (". . . the best evidence of which the case in its nature is susceptible and which is in the power of the party to produce, or is capable of being produced must always be produced in proof of every disputed fact;" rule applied to writing but said also to control operation of hearsay rule).

8. See 4 Wigmore, Evidence § 1174 (Chadbourn rev. 1972). See also Maguire, Evidence: Common Sense and Common Law 32 (1947); 2 Morgan, Basic Problems of Evidence 332 (1954); Comment, 14 Ark.L.Rev. 153 (1959) (pointing out a consistent broader application essentially impracticable).

9. See, e.g., Chandler v. United States, 318 F.2d 356 (10th Cir.1963) (rule held not to require production of whiskey bottles alleged not to have carried federal revenue stamps); Meyer v. State, 218 Ark. 440, 236 S.W.2d 996 (1951) ("The best evidence rule deals with writings alone . . . ;" rule held not to require production of piece of bologna); State v. Dow, 392 A.2d 532 (Me.1978) (rule did not apply to require production of lobsters alleged to be less than 3³/₁₆ inches); State ex rel. Alderson v. Halbert, 137 W.Va. 883, 74 S.E.2d 772 (1953) (semble).

10. Buffalo Insurance Co. v. United Parking Stations, Inc., 277 Minn. 134, 152 N.W.2d 81 (1967) (the rule applies only to writings and is not a broad general principle applicable throughout the law of evidence).

As a moral argument, however, which may be marshaled on many evidence questions, the idea still has appeal. ". . . The fact that any given way of proof is all that a man has must be a strong argument for receiving it if it be in a fair degree probative; and the fact that a man does not produce the best evidence in his power must always afford strong ground of suspicion." Thayer, op.cit. 507. The "best evidence" notion has sometimes been given as a reason for admitting hearsay evidence when it is the most reliable which can be procured. See, e.g., Edwards v. Swilley, 196 Ark. 633, 118 S.W.2d 584 (1938). Contra: Fordson Coal Co. v. Vanover, 291 Ky. 447, 164 S.W.2d 966 (1942).

The effect of failure to call witnesses or to produce evidence is discussed in § 272, infra.

§ 230

1. 4 Wigmore, Evidence §§ 1177–1282 (Chadbourn rev. 1972); Dec.Dig. Crim.Law ⚓398–403, Evidence ⚓157–187; 32A C.J.S. Evidence, §§ 776–850; 29 Am. Jur.2d Evidence §§ 448–492. See also Model Code of Evidence Rule 602, and the comments thereon in Rogers, The Best Evidence Rule, 1945 Wis.L.Rev. 278.

Fed.R.Evid. 1002 states the basic rule as follows:

To prove the content of a writing, recording, or photograph, the original writing, recording, or photograph is required, except as otherwise provided in these rules or by Act of Congress.

Rule 1001(3) defines the term "original:"

An "original" of a writing or recording is the writing or recording itself or any counterpart intended to have the same effect by a person executing or issuing it. An "original" of a photograph includes the negative or any print therefrom. If data are stored in a computer or similar device, any printout or other

and its limits clearly defined. The rule is this: in proving the terms of a writing, where the terms are material, the original writing must be produced unless it is shown to be unavailable for some reason other than the serious fault of the proponent. The discussion in the following sections is directed to adding content to this basic framework.

 WESTLAW REFERENCES

headnote("best evidence" & writing*)
di best evidence rule
di original document rule

§ 231. The Reasons for the Rule

Since its inception in the early 18th century, various rationales have been asserted to underlie the "best evidence rule." Many older writers have asserted that the rule is essentially directed to the prevention of fraud.[1] Wigmore, however, vigorously attacked this thesis on the analytical ground that it does not square with certain recognized applications and non-applications of the rule.[2] Most modern commentators follow his lead in asserting that the basic premise justifying the rule is the central position which the written word occupies in the law.[3] Because of this centrality, presenting to a court the exact words of a writing is of

more than average importance, particularly in the case of operative or dispositive instruments such as deeds, wills or contracts, where a slight variation of words may mean a great difference in rights. In addition, it is to be considered (1) that there has been substantial hazard of inaccuracy in some of the commonly utilized methods of making copies of writings, and (2) oral testimony purporting to give from memory the terms of a writing is probably subject to a greater risk of error than oral testimony concerning other situations generally. The danger of mistransmitting critical facts which accompanies the use of written copies or recollection, but which is largely avoided when an original writing is presented to prove its terms, justifies preference for original documents.

At the same time, however, it would appear a mistake totally to disregard all other justifications for the rule. It has long been observed that the opportunity to inspect original writings may be of substantial importance in the detection of fraud.[4] At least a few modern courts and commentators appear to regard the prevention of fraud as an ancillary justification of the rule.[5] Unless this view is accepted it is difficult to explain the rule's frequent application to copies produced by modern techniques which virtually

output readable by sight, shown to reflect the data accurately, is an "original".

The corresponding provisions of the revised Uniform Rules are identical, except that Rule 1002 has changes appropriate for state use.

§ 231

1. 1 Greenleaf, Evidence 93 (1842); 1 Starkie, Evidence 387 (5th Am.ed.1834); 1 Taylor, Evidence § 391 (1887).

2. 4 Wigmore, Evidence § 1180 (Chadbourn rev. 1972).

The inconsistencies noted by Wigmore are three: (1) that the rule is properly applicable even where the court may be satisfied that the proponent of secondary evidence is in utmost good faith; (2) that the rule is similarly applicable where possession by a third party should logically remove any suspicion of fraudulent suppression by the proponent, and (3) that were inference of fraud the foundation of the rule it should also apply to objects as well as writings, which it is at least generally agreed it does not.

3. See, e.g., Morgan, Basic Problems of Evidence 385 (1962).

4. Thus Quintilian, writing circa A.D. 88, is quoted by Osborn as stating:

It is therefore necessary to examine all the writings related to a case; it is not sufficient to inspect them; they must be read through; for very frequently they are either not at all such as they were asserted to be, or they contain less than was stated, or they are mixed with matters that may injure the client's cause, or they say too much and lose all credit from appearing to be exaggerated. We may often, too, find a thread broken, or wax disturbed, or signatures without attestation . . . .

Osborn, Questioned Documents, XVI (2d ed. 1929).

5. United States v. Manton, 107 F.2d 834 (2d Cir. 1939); Rogers, The Best Evidence Rule, 20 Wis.L.Rev. 278 (1945).

eliminate the possibility of unintentional mis-transmission.

Finally, one leading opinion [6] intimates that the rule should be viewed to protect not only against mistaken or fraudulent mis-transmissions but also against intentional or unintentional misleading through introduction of selected portions of a comprehensive set of writings to which the opponent has no access. This seems to engraft upon the best evidence rule an aspect of completeness not heretofore observed.

Whatever rationale is viewed to support the rule, it will be observed that the advent of modern discovery and related procedures under which original documents may be examined before trial rather than at it, have substantially reduced the need for the rule. Nevertheless, it has been pointed out that at present limitations on the availability of these alternatives leaves the original documents rule a continuing and important sphere of operations.[7]

 WESTLAW REFERENCES

"best evidence" /p complete! fraud! incomplete! mislead*** mistake* mistransmission

---

§ 232. What Are Writings? Application to Objects Inscribed and Uninscribed [1]

A rule which permitted the judge to insist that all evidence must pass his scrutiny as being the "best" or most reliable means of proving the fact would be a sore incumbrance upon the parties, who in our system have the responsibility of proof. In fact, as we have seen, no such general scrutiny is sanctioned, but only as to "writings" is a demand for the "best," the original, made.[2] This limitation on the ambit of the rule rests largely on the practical realization that writings exhibit a fineness of detail, lacking in chattels generally, which will often be of critical importance. Prevention of loss of this fine detail through mistransmission is a basic objective of the rule requiring production of documentary originals.

But while writings may be generally distinguished from other chattels with respect to the amount and importance of the detail they exhibit, chattels bearing more or less detailed inscriptions are far from uncommon. Thus, when an object such as a policeman's badge, a flag, or a tombstone bears a number or legend the terms of which are relevant the problem is raised as to whether the object shall be treated as a chattel or a writing. It is here clearly unwise to adapt a purely semantic approach and to classify the object according to whether its written component predominates sufficiently to alter the label attached to it in common parlance.[3] At the same time, however, it would seem also unnecessary to classify as writings, as apparently do the Federal and Revised Uniform Rules (1974),[4] any object which carries

6. Toho Bussan Kaisha, Limited v. American President Lines, Limited, 265 F.2d 418, 76 A.L.R.2d 1344 (2d Cir.1959).

7. Cleary & Strong, The Best Evidence Rule: An Evaluation in Context, 51 Iowa L.Rev. 825 (1966).

Fed.R.Evid. and Rev.Unif.R.Evid. (1974) 1003 implicitly recognize these justifications of the original documents rule by allowing admission of "duplicates" produced by modern copying methods where only exactitude is at stake, but withholding admissibility if a genuine question of authenticity of the original is raised or it would be unfair to allow use of the duplicate rather than the original. For text of the Rule and further discussion, see § 236 infra.

§ 232

1. 4 Wigmore, Evidence § 1182 (Chadbourn rev. 1972); Dec.Dig. Evidence ⊕170, Criminal Law ⊕400(1)

2. See § 229 supra.

3. Comment, 21 Rut.L.Rev. 526, 538 (1967).

4. Fed.R.Evid. 1001(1) and (2) contain the following definitions:

"Writings" and "recordings" consist of letters, words, or numbers, or their equivalent, set down by handwriting, typewriting, printing, photostating, photographing, magnetic impulse, mechanical or electronic recording, or other form of data compilation.

"Photographs" include still photographs, X-ray films, video tapes, and motion pictures.

The Advisory Committee's Note to Federal Rule Evid. 1001(1), however, observes, "Traditionally the rule requiring the original centered upon accumulations of data and expressions affecting legal relations set forth in words and figures."

an inscription of any sort whatsoever. In the final analysis, it is perhaps impossible to improve upon Wigmore's suggestion,[5] followed by a number of courts,[6] that the judge shall have discretion to apply the present rule to inscribed chattels or not in light of such factors as the need for precise information as to the exact inscription, the ease or difficulty of production, and the simplicity or complexity of the inscription.

Within this general framework, certain types of chattels warrant specific mention. Thus, sound recordings, where their content is sought to be proved,[7] so clearly involve the identical considerations applicable to writings as to warrant inclusion within the present rule.[8] Somewhat more questionable are the provisions of the Federal and Revised Uniform Rules of Evidence (1974)

which bring photographs within the rule in those relatively rare instances in which their contents are sought to be proved.[9] However, while it is difficult to accept that photographs of objects exhibit more intricacy of detail than do the objects photographed, concentrating attention upon content does provide rationale for bringing photographs within it where their contents are sought to be proved. Certainly, the original of a photograph may afford indices of chicanery which secondary evidence of its contents would not betray,[10] and this is likely to be of unusual importance where photographic products are offered "to speak for themselves." Further, it should be noted that X rays were frequently held to be within the rule even before the advent of the recent codifications.[11]

The corresponding provisions of the Revised Uniform Rules differ only in inserting "sounds" after "words" in paragraph (1).

Under Rule 1002, supra n. 11, the original documents rule applies to writings, recordings, and photographs as thus defined.

Application of the rule has not, traditionally, been so broad. See, e.g., Streeter v. State, 60 Ga.App. 190, 3 S.E.2d 235 (1939) (witness allowed to testify that numbers of stolen automobile tires were on list found in defendant's possession); Quillen v. Commonwealth, 284 Ky. 792, 145 S.W.2d 1048 (1940) (testimony as to license number without production of plate).

Note, Article X: Contents of Writings, Recordings, and Photographs, 12 Land & W.L.Rev. 716 (1977) observes that "[b]ecause Rule 1002 by itself is susceptible to the possibility of an excessively technical application by the courts, the remainder of the Rules in Article X include built-in exceptions to prevent this possibility." None of the exceptions contained in Fed.R. Evid. 1003–1007, however, appears to speak directly to the problem here noted.

5. 4 Wigmore, Evidence § 1182 (Chadbourn rev. 1972).

6. United States v. Duffy, 454 F.2d 809 (5th Cir. 1972) (testimony that shirt inscribed "D–U–F" was found in stolen car; admission did not violate rule where inscription was simple and evidence not critical); State v. Lewark, 106 Kan. 184, 186 P. 1002 (1920) (receiving stolen automobile: judge in discretion properly permitted testimony that engine number appeared to be altered, without requiring production of automobile); Quillen v. Commonwealth, 284 Ky. 792, 145 S.W.2d 1048 (1940) (theft of automobile, testimony as to license number properly allowed without producing plate, where number not disputed); Mattson v. Minnesota & North Wisconsin Railroad Co., 98 Minn. 296, 108 N.W. 517 (1906) (wrappers on dynamite, not shown to

be detachable; proper exercise of discretion to allow description without production).

7. For a discussion of those instances in which content is sought to be proved, see § 233 infra.

8. See Forrester v. State, 224 Md. 337, 167 A.2d 878 (1961) (rule applied to exclude testimony concerning conversation which had been recorded, but which witness had not overheard; recording in such case treated like writing). But, under the currently prevailing theory described in § 233 infra, the rule does not apply to recordings the "contents" of which are not sought to be shown. See, e.g., People v. Swayze, 220 Cal.App.2d 476, 34 Cal.Rptr. 5 (1963) (rule not applicable to require recording of conversation actually overheard by officer offering to testify). The application of the rule to tapes is the subject of Annot., 58 A.L.R.3d 598.

9. The usual theory on which photographs and representations are admitted does not require proof of the "contents" of the picture. See § 214 supra. But contents will be seen to be involved in copyright and defamation cases where the picture is the allegedly offending article, or where a photograph is tendered as having evidentiary value apart from merely "illustrating" the testimony of a witness.

The Federal Rule would not appear to reverse the traditional non-application of the rule to other representations. See, e.g., Lucas v. Williams [1892] 2 Q.B. 113 (C.A.) (original of painting not required in action for infringing copyright by selling photos of it).

10. See, e.g., United States v. Tranowski, 659 F.2d 750 (7th Cir. 1981) (to support alibi, defendant introduced photo allegedly taken at time of alleged crime; government unsuccessfully sought to introduce testimony of astronomer to the effect that shadows in photo were inconsistent with position of sun on that date).

11. Cellamare v. Third Avenue Transit Corp., 273 App.Div. 260, 77 N.Y.S.2d 91 (1948) (rule applicable to

**WESTLAW
REFERENCES**

"best evidence" /p engrav*** inscription* label*
   legend* mark* "serial number*"

"best evidence" /p photograph* picture* recording*
   x-ray*

§ 233. What Constitutes Proving the Terms

It is apparent that this danger of mis-transmission of the contents of the writing, which is the principal reason for the rule, is only important when evidence other than the writing itself is offered for the purpose of proving its terms. Consequently, evidence that a certain document is in existence [1] or as to its execution [2] or delivery [3] is not within the rule and may be given without producing the document.[4]

In what instances, then, can it be said that the terms of a writing are sought to be proved, rather than merely its identity, or existence? First, there are certain writings

which the substantive law, e.g., the Statute of Frauds, the parol evidence rule, endow with a degree of either indispensability or primacy.[5] Transactions to which substantive rules of this character apply tend naturally to be viewed as written transactions, and writings embodying such transactions, e.g., deeds, contracts, judgments, etc., are universally considered to be within the present rule when actually involved in the litigation. Contrasted with the above described types of writings are those, essentially unlimited in variety, which the substantive law does not regard as essential or primary repositories of the facts recorded. Writings of this latter sort may be said merely to happen to record the facts of essentially nonwritten transactions.[6] Testimony descriptive of nonwritten transactions is not generally considered to be within the scope of the present rule and may be given without producing or explaining the absence of a writing recording the facts.[7] Thus, evidence of a payment may be given without

---

X ray); Simon v. Hendricks, 330 P.2d 186 (Okl.1958) (expert not permitted to testify to contents of X ray).

Decisions considering the question of the application of the present rule to motion pictures are collected in Annot., 62 A.L.R.2d 658.

§ 233

1. Fish v. Fleishman, 87 Idaho 126, 391 P.2d 344 (1964) (check stub to show existence of check); Mickle v. Blackmon, 252 S.C. 202, 166 S.E.2d 173 (1969) (existence of scientific writings properly established through testimony).

2. Redwine v. King, 366 P.2d 921 (Okl.1961) (proof that lease had been executed not requiring production of lease); Villiers v. Republic Financial Services, Inc., 602 S.W.2d 566 (Tex.Civ.App.1980) refused n.r.e. (oral testimony as to fact of assignment does not violate rule).

3. Higgins v. Arizona Savings & Loan Association, 90 Ariz. 55, 365 P.2d 476 (1961) (oral testimony receivable to show handwritten notes had been sent, rather than their contents).

4. See Dec.Dig. Evidence ☞159, 161(1). This sort of evidence will usually entail a more or less general discription of a writing not considered to be proof of its terms. See, e.g., Hardy v. Hardy, 221 Ga. 176, 144 S.E.2d 172 (1965) (description of notes including testimony of dates and amounts held not proof of terms); Chambless v. State, 94 Okl.Cr. 140, 231 P.2d 711 (1951) (officers could testify that there was a federal liquor

license on defendant's premises, but could not give "contents"). The problem will be seen to be very similar to that described above, § 232 supra.

5. See 4 Wigmore, Evidence § 1242 (Chadbourn rev. 1972). See also Marson Coal Co. v. Insurance Co., ___ W.Va. ___, 210 S.E.2d 747 (1975) (insurance policy covering only flights piloted by person with 1900 "logged" flying hours; held, "logged" hours not synonymous with actual flying hours, thus rule required production of logs).

6. Lund v. Starz, 355 Mich. 497, 94 N.W.2d 912 (1959) ("where the matter to be proved is a substantive fact which exists independently of any writing, although evidenced thereby, and which can be as fully and satisfactorily established by parol as by written evidence, then both classes of evidence are primary . . . .").

7. Sayen v. Rydzewski, 387 F.2d 815 (7th Cir.1967) (amount of income allowed to be proved without records); Allen v. W.H.O. Alfalfa Mill Co., 272 F.2d 98 (10th Cir.1959) (costs of production); Herzig v. Swift & Co., 146 F.2d 444 (2d Cir.1945) (earnings provable without records); Lin Manufacturing Co. v. Courson, 246 Ark. 5, 436 S.W.2d 472 (1969) (company policy provable without production of written statement thereof); People v. Kulwin, 102 Cal.App.2d 104, 226 P.2d 672 (1951) (policeman who overheard conversation between defendants can testify thereto without producing sound-recording); Mars v. Meadville Telephone Co., 344 Pa. 29, 23 A.2d 856 (1942) (earnings).

production of the receipt,[8] or evidence of a marriage without production of the marriage certificate.[9]

While, however, many facts may be proved without resort to writings which record them, the party attempting to prove a fact may choose to show the contents of a writing for the purpose. Thus, for example, a writing may contain a recital of fact which is admissible under an exception to the hearsay rule. Here the recited fact might possibly be established without the writing, but if the contents are relied upon for the purpose the present rule applies and oral testimony as to its contents will be rejected unless the original writing is shown to be unavailable.[10]

Distinguishable from the situation in which the witness undertakes to state the fact based upon what he has seen in a writing, is the situation in which the witness testifies that the fact did not occur because relevant records contain no mention of it. This negative type of testimony is usually held not to constitute proof of contents and thus not to require production of records.[11] But it will be seen that care in the application of

this exception is required, since testimony as to what does not appear may easily involve a questionable description by the witness of the details which do appear. Perhaps a better approach would be to treat such "non-entry" testimony as a form of summary, which in fact it is, and to subject it to the safeguards employed in that context.[12]

It has long been held that records too voluminous to be conveniently produced and examined in court may be summarized and their import testified to by a witness, usually an expert, who has reviewed the entirety.[13] The Federal and Revised Uniform Rules of Evidence (1974) recognize and clarify this helpful practice, and also provide appropriate safeguards by requiring that the originals be made available for examination and copying by other parties.[14] These requirements, of course, tacitly assume that reasonable notice be given of the intent to offer summaries.[15] And, since the summaries admitted under this rule are being introduced substantively in place of the matters summarized, it has reasonably been held that a foundation is required for such evi-

---

8. Kendall v. Hargrave, 142 Colo. 120, 349 P.2d 993 (1960); Gonzalez v. Hoffman, 9 Mich.App. 522, 157 N.W.2d 475 (1968).

9. Lopez v. Missouri Kansas & Texas Railway Co. of Texas, 222 S.W. 695 (Tex.Civ.App.1920) (foreign marriage).

10. Mitchell v. Emblade, 80 Ariz. 398, 298 P.2d 1034 (1956) (error to allow witness with no knowledge of independent fact to testify as to what records showed); People v. Poindexter, 18 Ill.App.3d 436, 305 N.E.2d 400 (1973) (semble); Mel-Mar Co. v. Chemical Products Co., 273 S.W.2d 126 (Tex.Ct.App.1954), refused n.r.e. (semble).

11. State v. Nano, 273 Or. 366, 543 P.2d 660 (1975). See also Fed.R.Evid. and Rev.Unif.R.Evid. (1974) 803(7) and 803(10), discussed infra respectively in § 307 and § 320.

12. See text infra at n. 16.

13. Harris v. United States, 356 F.2d 582 (5th Cir. 1966) (summarization by expert of records available for inspection held proper); State v. Schrader, 64 N.M. 100, 324 P.2d 1025 (1958) (summary testimony admissible where records available for inspection but not introduced); Aldridge v. Burchfiel, 421 P.2d 655 (Okl.1966). But compare Bolling Co. v. Barrington Co., 398 S.W.2d 28 (Mo.App.1965) (summaries inadmissible where records not introduced and unavailable through absence from jurisdiction).

A distinction must be made between the situation treated here, in which the matters summarized are themselves being offered into evidence, and the situation discussed elsewhere, § 212 at nn. 32–36, in which the summary is merely illustrative. In the latter situation, juries are commonly instructed that the summary or chart is not itself evidence but should be used only as an aid in understanding the evidence. See Holland v. United States, 348 U.S. 121 (1954); United States v. Conlin, 551 F.2d 534 (2d Cir.1977), cert. denied 434 U.S. 831.

14. Fed.R.Evid. and Rev.Unif.R.Evid. (1974) 1006 provide:

The contents of voluminious writings, recordings, or photographs which cannot conveniently be examined in court may be presented in the form of a chart, summary, or calculation. The originals, or duplicates, shall be made available for examination or copying, or both, by other parties at a reasonable time and place. The court may order that they be produced in court.

And see United States v. Kim, 595 F.2d 755 (D.C.Cir. 1978) (summary of Korean bank records inadmissible where underlying records not made available at trial).

15. Annot., 80 A.L.R.3d 405.

dence which establishes both the admissibility of the underlying data and the accuracy of the summary.[16]

Certain criticisms may be leveled at the commonly applied distinction between facts the legal efficacy of which is affected by recordation, and facts which are legally effective whether or not contained in a writing. Thus it has been suggested that in modern law there are few if any instances in which a writing is anything more than a recordation of some nonwritten fact. For example, a written contract, it may be contended, merely records the operative legal fact, which is the agreement of the parties.[17] Moreover, the distinction has proved a difficult one to apply, and does not adequately serve to reconcile various common applications and non-applications of the rule. Thus it is commonly held that oral evidence of a witness's prior testimony is receivable even though that testimony is embodied in a transcript.[18] But when a confession has been both orally made and reduced to writing, numerous courts require the writing.[19] Dying declarations both spoken and reduced to writing have produced a similar contrariety of opinion.[20]

Perhaps the most satisfactory solution to the problem would be to abandon the distinction between transactions essentially written and nonwritten and allow the application of the rule to turn upon the trial judge's determination of such factors as the centrality of the writing to the litigation, the importance of bringing the precise words of the writing before the trier, and the danger of mistransmission or imposition in the absence of the original. The result would simply be to merge the present confusing and confused doctrine with the collateral documents exception discussed below,[21] or at least to enlarge the scope of the latter.

 WESTLAW REFERENCES

"best evidence" /s content* essence provision* term* /s contract* deed* document* writing*

"best evidence" /p content* essence provision* term* /p confession* "dying declaration" "marriage certificate" nonexistence receipt*

"best evidence" /p summar! "synopsis"

§ 234. Writings Involved Only Collaterally [1]

At nearly every turn in human affairs some writing—a letter, a bill of sale, a newspaper, a deed—plays a part. Consequently any narration by a witness is likely to include many references to transactions consisting partly of written communications or other writings. A witness to a confession, for example, identifies the date as being the day after the crime because he read of the crime in the newspaper that day, or a witness may state that he was unable to procure a certain article because it was patented. It is apparent that it is impracticable to forbid such references except upon condition that the writings (e.g., the newspaper, and the patent) be produced in court. Recognition of an exception exempting "collateral writings" from the operation of the basic rule has followed as a necessary concession to expedition of trials and clearness of narration, interests which outweigh, in the case of merely incidental references to documents, the need for perfect exactitude in the presentation of these documents' contents.

16. Needham v. White Laboratories, Inc., 639 F.2d 394 (7th Cir.1981), cert. denied 454 U.S. 927.

17. See the dissenting opinion of Prettyman, J., in Meyers v. United States, 84 U.S.App.D.C. 101, 171 F.2d 800 (1948), cert. denied 336 U.S. 912.

18. See, e.g., Meyers v. United States, supra, note 17; State v. Bixby, 27 Wn.2d 144, 177 P.2d 689 (1947). But compare, Benge v. Commonwealth, 298 Ky. 562, 183 S.W.2d 631 (1944). Annot., 11 A.L.R.2d 30.

19. See 4 Wigmore, Evidence § 1332 (Chadbourn rev. 1972).

20. See Annot., 112 A.L.R. 43.

21. See § 234 infra. Such a merger has been previously suggested. Comment, 41 Or.L.Rev. 138 (1962). See also Comment, 14 Ark.L.Rev. 153 (1960) (noting that the two rules are inseparably commingled).

§ 234

1. 4 Wigmore, Evidence § 1254 (Chadbourn rev. 1972); Dec.Dig. Evidence ⊕171, Criminal Law ⊕401; C.J.S. Evidence § 781; Annot., 1 A.L.R. 1143. See also Note, 11 N.C.L.Rev. 342 (1933).

While writings are frequently held to be collateral within the meaning of the present exception,[2] the purposes for which references to documents may be made by witnesses are so variegated that the concept of collateralness defies precise definition. Three principal factors, however, should, and generally do, play a role in making the determination of collateralness. These are: the centrality of the writing to the principal issues of the litigation;[3] the complexity of the relevant features of the writing;[4] and the existence of genuine dispute as to the contents of the writing.[5] Evaluation and weighting of these factors in the particular instance may perhaps best be left to the discretion of the trial judge, and as elsewhere in the application of this essentially adminis-

trative rule, exercise of that discretion should be reviewed only for grave abuse.[6]

WESTLAW REFERENCES

"best evidence"   /p   collateral**
157k171

§ 235. Which Is the "Writing Itself" That Must Be Produced?[1] Telegrams,[2] Counterparts[3]

What should be the application of the basic rule where two documents, X and Y, exist, X having been created first and Y being some variety of reproduction of X? Copies, of course, are frequent and in most cases the document first prepared will be the one whose initial production is required by the

---

2. Lin Manufacturing Co. v. Courson, 246 Ark. 5, 436 S.W.2d 472 (1969) (evidence of local companies' policies against hiring persons with back trouble allowed on damage without production of written policy statements; result also justified on ground that policy not a written fact, see § 233 supra); Farr v. Zoning Board of Appeals, 139 Conn. 577, 95 A.2d 792 (1953) (parties allowed to establish standing as aggrieved property owners without producing documents of title); Wilkins v. Hester, 119 Ga.App. 389, 167 S.E.2d 167 (1969) (witness testifying to value of car allowed to establish status as used car dealer without production of license, even though license was "best evidence"); Wilson Trans. Co. v. Owens-Illinois Glass Co., 125 N.J.L. 636, 17 A.2d 581 (1941) (plaintiff seeking to show damages due to defendant's breach of contract by proving sale of trucks acquired to haul defendant's goods not required to produce documentary proof of ownership); State v. Vaughan, 243 Ind. 221, 184 N.E.2d 143 (1962) (testimonial reference to ownership of properties surrounding tract condemned permissible as collateral fact); Sundberg v. Hurley, 89 N.M. 511, 554 P.2d 673 (1976), cert. denied 90 N.M. 9, 558 P.2d 621 (in medical malpractice action, testimony as to how many patients with similar injury had been treated in hospitals in last five years did not require hospital records); Prudential Insurance Co. of America v. Black, 572 S.W.2d 379 (Tex.Civ.App. 1978) (in suit to recover unpaid rent, plaintiff's status as successor in interest to original lessor should have been allowed to be proved by parol).

See also, Annot., 1 A.L.R. 1143 (admissibility of parol evidence to prove title involved only collaterally).

3. A few courts have gone so far as to classify as collateral all writings which do not form the foundation of the cause of action or defense. Freeman v. Commercial Union Assurance Co., 317 S.W.2d 563 (Tex.Civ. App.1958); Doman v. Baltimore & Ohio Railroad Co., 125 W.Va. 8, 22 S.E.2d 703 (1942); C.J.S. Evidence § 781. This rule would appear unduly embracive as excluding from the operation of the general rule all

nonwritten facts and even many written facts which, though not the basis of the action, possess substantial evidentiary significance. See, e.g., State v. Anderson, 5 N.C.App. 614, 169 S.E.2d 38 (1969) (production of threatening note handed prosecuting witness during perpetration of alleged attempted rape held not excused as collateral fact).

Cf. Fed.R.Evid. and Rev.Unif.R.Evid. (1974) 1004 provide:

> The original is not required, and other evidence of the contents of a writing, recording, or photograph is admissible if—
>
> . . .
>
> (4) **Collateral Matters.** The writing, recording, or photograph is not closely related to a controlling issue.

4. Testimony as to the nature of inscribed chattels is thus sometimes admitted as evidence of collateral facts. See § 232 supra.

5. Farr v. Zoning Board of Appeals, 139 Conn. 577, 95 A.2d 792 (1953) (citing absence of evidentiary challenge of status of plaintiffs as property owners as one basis for failing to require documentary evidence of title).

6. Compare 4 Wigmore, Evidence § 1253 (Chadbourn rev. 1972).

§ 235

1. 4 Wigmore, Evidence § 1232 (Chadbourn rev. 1972).

2. 4 Wigmore, Evidence § 1236 (Chadbourn rev. 1972); Dec.Dig. Evidence ⚖168, 183(14); C.J.S. Evidence §§ 792, 814.

3. 4 Wigmore, Evidence § 1233 (Chadbourn rev. 1972); Dec.Dig. Evidence ⚖186(6); C.J.S. Evidence § 821.

rule. But the problem is not always so simple. For example, X may be a telegram written by the sender and handed to the company for transmission; or X may be a libelous handwritten letter given to a stenographer for copying and sending, and Y the letter actually received by the addressee; or X may be a ledger sheet in the creditor's books and Y the account rendered made up therefrom and sent to the debtor.

In any of the above cases, if a party in court offers document Y in evidence, what determines whether the document is "the writing itself" offered to prove its own terms, or merely a "copy" offered to establish the terms of X? The answer here clearly does not depend upon the chronology of creation or the ordinary semantic usage which would denominate Y as a "copy."[4] Instead it will depend upon the substantive law of contracts, defamation, property, and the like. The question to be asked, then, is whether, under the substantive law, the creation, publication, or other use of Y may be viewed as affecting the rights of the parties in a way material to the litigation. If the answer to this question is affirmative, the fact that Y happens to be a copy of another writing is completely immaterial.[5] Decisions illustrative of instances in which the terms of "copies" are the facts sought to be proved are cited below.[6]

It will also frequently occur that a written transaction, such as a contract or deed, will be evidenced by several counterparts or identical copies, each of which is signed by the parties or, at any rate, intended to be equally effective as embodying the transaction.[7] Such multiple counterparts are frequently termed "duplicate (or triplicate, etc.) originals". Each of these counterparts is admissible as an "original" without producing or accounting for the others,[8] but before secondary evidence may be resorted to, all

4. 4 Wigmore, Evidence §§ 1232, 1235(2) and (3) (Chadbourn rev. 1972); Comment, 14 Ark.L.Rev. 153, 160 (1960).

5. McDonald v. Hanks, 52 Tex.Civ.App. 140, 113 S.W. 604, 607 (1908), where the court said: "If a writer desiring to preserve a copy of a letter, writes at the same time two copies exactly alike, one of which he proposes to send and the other to keep, it is a matter of indifference which copy he sends, but the one sent becomes the original and the other a copy, no matter by what force of evidence it is shown to be an absolutely accurate copy." See also Illinois Tuberculosis Association v. Springfield Marine Bank, 282 Ill.App. 14 (1935) (bank mailed carbon of statement to customer; held, original).

6. United States v. Rangel, 585 F.2d 344 (8th Cir. 1978) (altered photocopies of charge card receipts submitted in support of fraudulent claim for reimbursement were best evidence rather than "original" altered charge slips); United States v. Gerhart, 538 F.2d 807 (8th Cir.1976) (photocopies of original checks, submitted in support of loan application, were "originals" required by rule, but secondary evidence admissible under circumstances); Carpenter v. Dressler, 76 Ark. 400, 89 S.W. 89 (1905) (executed deed rather than public transcript of grant held the original under then existing state substantive law); Fuchs & Lang Manufacturing Co. v. Kittredge & Co., 242 Ill. 88, 89 N.E. 723 (1909) (blueprint from which machine had been assembled, rather than drawing of which blueprint was a copy, held original when offered to show operation of machine); Prussing v. Jackson, 208 Ill. 85, 69 N.E. 771 (1904) (libel action against writer of letter printed in newspaper; letter rather than printed matter held original); State v. Calongne, 111 Kan. 332, 206 P. 1112

(1922) (prosecution for fraud defended on ground facts represented were believed by defendant to be true; telegrams received by defendant purporting to detail financial status of corporation held originals); In re Stringer's Estate, 80 Wyo. 389, 343 P.2d 508 (1959) (where testator actually executed only a "copy" of will, copy held the original dispositive instrument).

7. Courts have differed considerably with respect to what may constitute a duplicate original. Compare Tampa Shipbuilding & Eng. Co. v. General Const. Co., 43 F.2d 309 (5th Cir.1930) ("Duplicates exist only when the two instruments have both been recognized and established by the parties concerned as evidence of their act, as where the parties to the sale sign a memorandum with carbon copy and each keeps one") with Parr Construction Co. v. Pomer, 217 Md. 539, 144 A.2d 69 (1958) (holding an ordinary unsigned retained copy is a duplicate), commented upon in Note, 20 Md.L.Rev. 50 (1960). See also American Fire & Casualty Insurance Co., Inc. v. Bryan, 379 So.2d 605 (Ala.Civ.App.1979) (critical fact to be shown is intent of parties to create two or more copies equal to one another). Compare Fed.R.Evid. 1001 which avoids the internally contradictory phrase "duplicate originals." See also § 236 infra.

8. Fistere, Inc. v. Helz, 226 A.2d 578, 579 (D.C.App. 1967) ("When a document is executed in duplicate or multiplicate form, each of the parts is deemed an original and may be used without accounting for any other part"); In re King's Estate, 572 S.W.2d 200 (Mo.App. 1978) (duplicate deposit slip stamped and delivered to depositor held admissible as duplicate original); Cross v. Everybodys, 357 S.W.2d 156 (Tex.Civ.App.1962) (production of one duplicate original satisfies best evidence rule).

of the counterparts must be shown to be unavailable.[9]

 WESTLAW REFERENCES

"best evidence" /p counterpart* "duplicate original*'' telegram*

§ 236. Reproductions: Carbons: Printed and Multigraph Copies: Photo and Xerographic Copies [1]

The treatment of copies under the rule requiring the production of the original document can only properly be understood when viewed in light of the technological history of copying itself. In its earliest stages, the rule appears to have developed against a background of copying performed by individuals of the Bob Cratchit sort, transcribing manually not always under the best of conditions. Errors under such circumstances were routinely to be expected. Only marginally greater reliability was to be found in the so-called letter-press. Here the original was written or typed in copying ink or with copying pencil. Presumably influenced by the infirmities present in such modes of copying, the courts generally declined to accept subsequently created copies as equivalent to originals.[2]

The advent of carbon paper, however, made possible the creation of copies of substantially greater reliability and legibility. Here, since the copy is made by the same stroke as the original, there was an apparent factual distinction between these copies and copies produced subsequent to the original by the older methods.[3] It moreover became common, as it is today, to create multiple counterparts of a contract or transaction through the use of carbon paper, with each copy duly signed either through the same medium or individually. What makes such writings counterparts, of course, is the signing with intent to render each co-equal with the others, and the doctrine of counterparts can therefore hardly apply to a retained carbon copy which is not intended as a communication at all.[4] However, the fact that many true counterparts are made by the use of carbons coupled with the notion that writings generated simultaneously by the same stroke are in some way superior, has caused a great number of courts to treat all carbons as if they were duplicate originals, i.e., as admissible without accounting for the original.[5]

More comprehensibly, there is warrant for believing that the courts will accept as primary evidence of the contents of a given book or a given issue of a newspaper any

9. Norris v. Billingsley, 48 Fla. 102, 37 So. 564 (1904); Raceland Stockyards, Inc. v. Giaise, 352 So.2d 392 (La.App.1977), writ denied 354 So.2d 206 (subsequent copy held inadmissible where offeror failed to account for multiple originals); American Empire Life Insurance Co. v. Long, 344 S.W.2d 513 (Tex.Civ.App. 1961) (photostatic copy of newspaper admissible; showing that no original copy of newspaper available).

§ 236

1. 4 Wigmore, Evidence § 1234 (Chadbourn rev. 1972); Dec.Dig. Evidence ⟨key⟩174(1), 186(6); C.J.S. Evidence §§ 815, 816, 821; Annot., 65 A.L.R.2d 342 (carbons), 76 A.L.R.2d 1356 (photographic copies).

2. See Philipson v. Chase, 2 Camp. 110, 170 Eng. Rep. 1097 (K.B.1809) (book entry on attorney's bill not admissible); Nodin v. Murray, 3 Camp. 228, 170 Eng. Rep. 1363 (1812) (deficiencies of letter-press copy noted by Lord Ellenborough); Federal Union Surety Co. v. Indiana Lumber & Manufacturing Co., 176 Ind. 328, 95 N.E. 1104 (1911).

3. Many of the early cases dealing with carbons emphasize the simultaneous nature of the duplicate's crea-

tion. See, e.g., International Harvester Co. v. Elfstrom, 101 Minn. 263, 112 N.W. 252 (1907).

4. Lockwood v. L. & L. Freight Lines, 126 Fla. 474, 171 So. 236 (1936).

5. Carmichael Tile Co. v. McClelland, 213 Ga. 656, 100 S.E.2d 902 (1957) (retained carbon copy of letter admissible though unsigned); Eastover Co. v. All Metal Fabricators, Inc., 221 Md. 428, 158 A.2d 89 (1960) (fact that offered bills were carbons "of no importance"); State v. Stockton, 38 Tenn.App. 90, 270 S.W.2d 586 (1954) (carbon copies of records or reports created simultaneously admissible as duplicate originals, no indication of signing or other manifestation of intent). Contra: Lockwood v. L. & L. Freight Lines, 126 Fla. 474, 171 So. 236 (1936) (carbon is duplicate only when intended to stand equal); Shirer v. O.W.S. & Associates, 253 S.C. 232, 169 S.E.2d 621 (1969) (semble; general rule of carbons as duplicates distinguished and rejected). See also, Annot., 65 A.L.R.2d 342; Notes, 20 Md.L.Rev. 50 (1960), 19 Ohio St.L.J. 520 (1958), 3 Vill.L. Rev. 217 (1958).

other book or newspaper printed from the same sets of fixed type, or the same plates or mats. A like result should be reached as to all copies run off from the same mat by the multigraph, lithoprint or other duplicating process.[6]

In the present day, copying by various photographic and other processes has become commonplace, replacing the carbon for many purposes. Various types of photographic copying, of course, produce facsimiles of an extremely high degree of verisimilitude, and thus might have been expected, as have carbons, to win recognition as duplicate originals. In fact, an early judicial step in this direction was taken in a celebrated federal court of appeals decision[7] which held that "recordak" photographs of checks which had been paid, preserved by a bank as part of its regular records were admissible under the Federal Business Records Act. Subsequently, a uniform act was prepared under which photographic copies, regularly kept, of business and public records are admissible without accounting for the original.[8] This act has been widely adopted.[9] In the cases, however, in which photographs of writings have been offered to show the terms of the original, without the aid of specific statutes, they have been almost uniformly treated as secondary evidence, inadmissible unless the original is accounted for.[10]

The resulting state of authority, favorable to carbons but unfavorable to at least equally reliable photographic and xerographic reproductions, appears inexplicable on any basis other than that the courts, having fixed upon simultaneous creation as the characteristic distinguishing of carbons from copies produced by earlier methods have on the whole been insufficiently flexible to modify that concept in the face of newer technological methods which fortuitously do not exhibit that characteristic. Insofar as the primary purpose of the original documents requirement is directed at securing accurate information from the contents of material writings, free of the infirmities of memory and the mistakes of hand-copying, we may well conclude that each of these forms of mechanical copying is sufficient to fulfill the policy. Insistence upon the original, or accounting for it, places costs, burdens of planning, and hazards of mistake upon the litigants. These may be worth imposing where the alternative is accepting memory or hand-copies. They are probably not worth imposing when risks of inaccuracy are reduced to a minimum by the offer of a mechanically produced copy.

At the same time, however, if the original documents requirement is conceded to be supported by the ancillary purpose of fraud prevention, it will be seen that even copies produced by photographic or xerographic processes are not totally as desirable as the original writing. Many indicia of putative fraud such as watermarks, types of paper and inks, etc., will not be discernable on the copy. The most reasonable accommodation of the purposes of the basic rule to modern copying to date would appear to be that of the Federal Rules of Evidence.[11] Under

6. See Rex v. Watson, 2 Stark. 116, 171 Eng.Rep. 591 (N.P.1817) (to prove contents of printed placard which had been posted, other placards from same printing admitted); Redding v. Snyder, 352 Mich. 241, 89 N.W.2d 471 (1958) (copy of printed instruction pamphlet admitted).

7. United States v. Manton, 107 F.2d 834 (2d Cir. 1938).

8. Uniform Photographic Copies of Business and Public Records as Evidence Act, 9A U.L.A. 584.

9. 14 U.L.A. (1980). Following preparation of the uniform act, its substance was expressly incorporated into the Federal Business Records Act, now 28 U.S.C.A. § 1732.

10. Cox v. State, 93 Ga.App. 533, 92 S.E.2d 260 (1956) (photostatic copy secondary evidence); Benefield v. State, 355 P.2d 874 (Okl.Cr.1960) (photostat held admissible under the uniform act; court noting by way of dictum that common law rule was contrary). See also, Annot. 76 A.L.R.2d 1356, 142 A.L.R. 1270, and Note, 34 Iowa L.Rev. 83 (1948).

11. Fed.R.Evid. and Rev.Unif.R.Evid. (1974) 1001(4) define "duplicate":

A "duplicate" is a counterpart produced by the same impression as the original, or from the same matrix, or by means of photography, including enlargements and miniatures, or by mechanical or electronic re-recording, or by chemical reproduction, or

Federal Rule 1001(4) copies produced by photography or chemical reproduction or equivalent techniques are classed as "duplicates," and, under Rule 1003 are declared admissible as originals unless a genuine question is raised as to the authenticity of the original or it appears under the circumstances that it would be unfair to admit the duplicate in lieu of the original.[12]

An even more recent challenge to the flexibility of the rule requiring documentary originals has appeared in the form of machine readable records stored on punch cards or magnetic tape. Obviously, where records are originally deposited in such media nothing akin to a conventional documentary original will be created. To the credit of the courts, records there stored have gen-

by other equivalent techniques which accurately reproduces [sic] the original.

Fed.R.Evid. and Rev.Unif.R.Evid. (1974) 1003 provide:

A duplicate is admissible to the same extent as an original unless (1) a genuine question is raised as to the authenticity of the original or (2) in the circumstances it would be unfair to admit the duplicate in lieu of the original.

See discussions in Weinstein & Berger, Evidence ¶1003 (1978); Broun, Authentication and Content of Writings, 1969 Law & Soc.Ord. 611, 613.

12. Under the Federal Rule, if there is neither a challenge to authenticity nor potential unfairness the duplicate will be admissible; there is no need to establish one of the excuses for non-production of original provided for by Fed.R.Evid. 1004. United States v. Benedict, 647 F.2d 928 (9th Cir.1981), cert. denied 454 U.S. 1087.

Decided cases suggest that the requisite challenge to genuineness must be relatively specific. See United States v. Georgalis, 631 F.2d 1199 (5th Cir.1980), rehearing denied 636 F.2d 315 (exclusive government possession of duplicates for five year period raised no issue of genuineness); CTS Corp. v. Piher International Corp., 527 F.2d 95 (7th Cir.1975), cert. denied 424 U.S. 978 (1976) (error to exclude duplicate where record reflected no basis for questioning genuineness). The requirement that introduction of the duplicate entail no "unfairness" to other parties continues the doctrine that the duplicate must be a full rendition of the relevant material. See Toho Bussan Kaisha, Limited v. American President Lines, Inc., 265 F.2d 418 (2d Cir. 1959) (photostats of portions of records in Japan prepared for litigation excluded); Adv.Com.Notes, Fed.R. Evid. 1003.

13. United States v. De Georgia, 420 F.2d 889 (9th Cir.1969) (negative information obtained from computer of business corporation admitted on basis of founda-

erally fared well in the face of objection predicated on the original document rule, and machine printouts of such records have been admitted.[13]

 WESTLAW REFERENCES

"best evidence" /p carbon* "magnetic tape" newspaper* print***

"best evidence" /p photocop*** photographic photostat** xerox

uniform +s photographic +s copies +s act

fed.r.evid! evid! /4 1003

§ 237. Excuses for Nonproduction of the Original Writing: (a) Loss or Destruction [1]

The production-of-documents rule is principally aimed, not at securing a writing at all

tion testimony establishing mode of recordation and company's reliance thereon); King v. State ex rel. Murdock Acceptance Corp., 222 So.2d 393 (Miss.1969) (computer printouts admissible as "shop books" in absence of modern business records statute); Transport Indemnity Co. v. Seib, 178 Neb. 253, 132 N.W.2d 871 (1965) (business entries made into computer in ordinary course of business held admissible in form of computer printout). See also, Note, 55 Cornell L.J. 1033 (1970); Annot., 11 A.L.R.3d 1377; § 314 infra.

Fed.R.Evid. and Rev.Unif.R.Evid. (1974) 1001(3) provide in part:

If data are stored in a computer or similar device, any printout or other output readable by sight, shown to reflect the data accurately, is an "original."

§ 237

1. 4 Wigmore, Evidence §§ 1193–1198 (Chadbourn rev. 1972); Dec.Dig. Evidence ⇔178; C.J.S. Evidence §§ 823, 824.

Fed.R.Evid. and Rev.Unif.R.Evid. (1974) 1004 provide:

The original is not required, and other evidence of the contents of a writing, recording, or photograph is admissible if—

(1) *Originals Lost or Destroyed.* All originals are lost or have been destroyed, unless the proponent lost or destroyed them in bad faith; . . . .

Since the original writing rule is classed as a technical rule of evidence, preliminary questions of fact arising in connection with its application are resolved by the judge in most instances. See § 53 supra. Fed.R. Evid. 1008 provides:

When the admissibility of other evidence of contents of writings, recordings, or photographs under these rules depends upon the fulfillment of a condition of fact, the question whether the condition has

hazards and in every instance, but at securing the best *obtainable* evidence of its contents.[2] Thus, if as a practical matter the document cannot be produced because it has been lost or destroyed, the production of the original is excused and other evidence of its contents becomes admissible.[3] Failure to recognize this qualification of the basic rule would in many instances mean a return to the bygone and unlamented days in which to lose one's paper was to lose one's right. Recognition of the same qualification also squares with the ancillary purpose of the basic rule to protect against the perpetration of fraud, since proof that failure to produce the original is due to inability to do so tends logically to dispel the otherwise possible inference that the failure stems from design.

Loss or destruction may sometimes be provable by direct evidence but more often the only available evidence will be circumstantial, usually taking the form that appropriate search for the document has been made without discovering it. It would appear that where loss or destruction is sought to be proved by circumstantial evidence of unavailing search, the declarations of a former custodian as to loss or destruction may

be admitted to show the nature and results of the search,[4] though if offered as direct evidence of loss or destruction itself such declarations would be incompetent as hearsay.[5]

Where loss or destruction is sought to be shown circumstantially by proof of unsuccessful search, it is obvious that the adequacy of the showing will be largely dependent upon the thoroughness and appropriateness of the search. It was laid down in certain early decisions that when the writing is last known to have been in a particular place or in the hands of a particular person, then that place must be searched or the person produced,[6] and statements to the same effect are to be found in modern decisions.[7] It is believed, however, that these statements are best considered as general guides or cautions, rather than strict and unvarying rules. Virtually all jurisdictions view the trial judge as possessing some degree of discretion in determining the preliminary question as to whether it is feasible to produce the original document.[8] Such discretion is particularly appropriate since the character of the search required to show probability of loss or destruction will, as a practical matter, depend on the circumstances of each

---

been fulfilled is ordinarily for the court to determine in accordance with the provisions of rule 104. However, when an issue is raised (a) whether the asserted writing ever existed, or (b) whether another writing, recording, or photograph produced at the trial is the original, or (c) whether other evidence of contents correctly reflects the contents, the issue is for the trier of fact to determine as in the case of other issues of fact.

The revised Uniform Rule is identical except for slight, and meaningless, changes in style.

2. Fauci v. Mulready, 337 Mass. 532, 150 N.E.2d 286 (1958) (common law "best evidence" rule preferential rather than exclusionary); Vreeland v. Essex Lock & Manufacturing Co., Inc., 135 Vt. 1, 370 A.2d 1294 (1976) (semble).

3. See Sellmayer Packing Co. v. Commissioner, 146 F.2d 707 (4th Cir.1944); Stipe v. First National Bank, 208 Or. 251, 301 P.2d 175 (1956); Hayes v. Bouligny, 420 S.W.2d 800 (Tex.Civ.App.1967).

4. Massie v. Hutcheson, 296 S.W. 939 (Tex.Civ. App.1927), error refused (testimony that deceased grantee said: "Ashes tell no story" when questioned concerning deed, held admissible over objection that it was hearsay). See Interstate Investment Co. v. Bailey (Ky.1906) 93 S.W. 578, 580 ("What Elijah Davis learned

that Stidham said about the loss of the paper may not have been evidence of its loss . . . yet it was evidence of his good faith in not prosecuting the inquiry further.") 4 Wigmore, Evidence § 1196(3) (Chadbourn Rev.1972).

5. Moore v. State, 179 Miss. 268, 175 So. 183 (1937) (testimony that addressee of letter said she had destroyed it properly excluded as hearsay, but error to admit secondary evidence of letter's contents).

6. Cook v. Hunt, 24 Ill. 535 (1860); Vandergriff v. Piercy, 59 Tex. 371 (1883).

7. Ragen v. Bennigsen, 10 Ill.App.2d 356, 135 N.E.2d 128 (1956).

8. See, e.g., American Fire & Casualty Insurance Co., Inc. v. Bryan, 379 So.2d 605 (Ala.App.1979) (sufficiency of foundation laid for introduction of secondary evidence largely discretionary with trial court; proof of destruction properly held sufficient); Pennsylvania National Mutual Casualty Insurance Co. v. Burns, 375 So. 2d 302 (Fla.App.1979) (semble; proof of loss); Stipe v. First National Bank, 208 Or. 251, 301 P.2d 175 (1956) (no absolute rule governing sufficiency of search; matter absolutely within discretion of trial judge); Vaught v. Nationwide Mutual Insurance Co., 250 S.C. 65, 156 S.E.2d 627 (1967) (trial court has discretion, though not absolute, to determine sufficiency of search).

case. Factors such as the relative importance of the document and the lapse of time since it was last seen have been seen to bear upon the extent of search required before loss or destruction may be inferred.[9] The only general requirement, however, should be that all reasonable avenues of search should be explored to the extent that reasonable diligence under the circumstances would dictate.[10]

If the original document has been destroyed by the person who offers evidence of its contents, the evidence is not admissible unless, by showing that the destruction was accidental or was done in good faith, without intention to prevent its use as evi-

dence, he rebuts to the satisfaction of the trial judge, any inference of fraud.[11]

 WESTLAW REFERENCES

"best evidence"   /p   destroy** destruction los* misplace* missing
157k161(1)

§ 238. Excuses for Nonproduction of the Original Writing: (b) Possession by a Third Person [1]

When the writing is in the hands of a third person who is within the geographical limits of the trial court's subpoena power, the safest course is to have a writ of subpoena duces tecum served on the possessor summon-

---

9. Gathercole v. Miall, 15 M. & W. 319, 153 Eng. Rep. 872 (Exch.1846); United States v. Ross, 321 F.2d 61 (2d Cir.1963) cert. denied 375 U.S. 894 (insignificant paper prepared three years before trial; much less search required where subject is a useless paper which may reasonably be supposed lost); Agee v. Messer-Moore Insurance & Real Estate Co., 165 Ala. 291, 51 So. 829 (1910) (search required varies with value and importance of document). Compare United States v. Marcantoni, 590 F.2d 1324 (5th Cir.1979), cert denied 441 U.S. 937 (failure to discover stolen bills on execution of search warrant raised sufficient inference of destruction to allow testimony concerning serial numbers by detective who had seen bills earlier).

10. Rash v. Peoples Deposit Bank & Trust Co., 91 F.Supp. 825 (E.D.Ky.1950) (no fixed degree of diligence required in search, but rather such search as nature of the case suggests); Pendley v. Murphy, 112 Ga.App. 33, 143 S.E.2d 674 (1965) (proponent must exhaust those sources which are suggested by facts of case); Chagnon Lumber Co. v. Patenaude, 103 N.H. 448, 174 A.2d 415 (1961) (every case of loss must be determined on its own facts). Of course, testimony by the last custodian, or lack of it, is properly viewed as a significant circumstance. Sylvania Electric Products Inc. v. Flanagan, 352 F.2d 1005 (1st Cir.1956) (each case of loss to be determined on its own circumstances; however, foundation insufficient where proponent never denied records were in existence and in fact testified he had some at home); Wray Williams Display Co. v. Finley, 391 So.2d 1253 (La.App.1980), writ refused 396 So. 2d 930 (testimony that originals were in plaintiff's files insufficient, but error held harmless); In re 716 Third Avenue Holding Corp., 255 F.Supp. 268 (S.D.N.Y.1964) rev'd on other grounds, 340 F.2d 42 (2d Cir.) (testimony by president of corporation that corporation records had disappeared held insufficient proof of loss without showing of search); Wiggins v. Stapleton Baptist Church, 282 Ala. 255, 210 So.2d 814 (1968).

11. Reynolds v. Denver & Rio Grande Western Railway Co., 174 F.2d 673 (10th Cir.1949) (secondary evi-

dence admissible if no "fraud or bad faith" in destruction); McDonald v. United States, 89 F.2d 128 (8th Cir. 1937) (government not precluded in kidnapping case from giving evidence of numbers on ransom bills by fact that subordinate official had improvidently had bills destroyed); In re Rasnick, 77 N.J.Super. 380, 186 A.2d 527 (1962) (secondary evidence allowed where proponent had voluntarily destroyed original in a fit of rage where trial court found destruction free from suspicion under circumstances); Schroedl v. McTague, 256 Iowa 772, 129 N.W.2d 19 (1964) (semble; discussion and criticism of strict prohibition against offer of secondary evidence by destroyer of original). For an example of the stricter view, see Booher v. Brown, 173 Or. 464, 146 P.2d 71 (1944) (offering party must be "without neglect or fault").

Fed. and Rev.Unif.R.Evid. (1974) 1004 provide:

> The original is not required, and other evidence of the contents of a writing, recording, or photograph is admissible if—
>
> (1) *Originals lost or destroyed*. All originals are lost or have been destroyed, unless the proponent lost or destroyed them in bad faith; or

.   .   .

§ 238

1. 4 Wigmore, Evidence §§ 1211–1213 (Chadbourn rev.1972); Dec.Dig. Evidence ⚷179(3); C.J.S. Evidence §§ 830, 831.

Fed. and Rev.Unif.R.Evid. (1974) 1004 provide:

> The original is not required, and other evidence of the contents of a writing, recording, or photograph is admissible if—

.   .   .

> (2) *Original Not Obtainable*. No original can be obtained by any available judicial process or procedure; or

.   .   .

ing him to bring the writing to court at the trial,[2] though some decisions will excuse resort to subpoena if the possessor is privileged not to produce it,[3] and others suggest that proof of a hostile or unwilling attitude on his part will be a sufficient excuse.[4]

If the writing is in the possession of a third person out of the state or out of the reach of the court's process, a showing of this fact alone will suffice, in the view of many courts, to excuse production of the writing.[5] This practice has the merit of being an easy rule of thumb to apply, but the basic policy of the original document requirement would tend to support the view of a substantially equal number of courts that a further showing must be made. These latter courts require that, before secondary evidence is used, the proponent must show ei-

ther that he has made reasonable but unavailing efforts to secure the original from its possessor,[6] or circumstances which persuade the court that such efforts, had they been made, would have been fruitless.[7]

WESTLAW REFERENCES

"best evidence" /p jurisdiction retriev*** subpoena 157k179(3)

---

§ 239. Excuses for Nonproduction of the Original Writing: (c) Failure of Adversary Having Possession to Produce After Notice[1]

A frequently used method of showing that it is impracticable for the proponent to produce the original writing is to prove, first, that the original is in the hands of his adver-

---

2. Many decisions require this. See, e.g., Security Trust Co. v. Robb, 142 F. 78 (3d Cir.1906); Pendley v. Murphy, 112 Ga.App. 33, 143 S.E.2d 674 (1965) (error to admit secondary evidence where no subpoena duces tecum issued to last known custodian); Schall v. Northland Motor Car Co., 123 Minn. 214, 143 N.W. 357 (1913) (in possession of trustee in bankruptcy; "he is subject to subpena the same as other citizens"). If the possessor disobeys the summons, the party's production of the original should, of course, be excused.

3. See, e.g., People v. Powell, 71 Cal.App. 500, 236 P. 311 (1925) (letters tending to incriminate possessors).

4. Mahanay v. Lynde, 48 Cal.App.2d 79, 119 P.2d 430 (1941) (adversary's mother got possession of paper and refused to give it back); Ragley-McWilliams Lumber Co. v. Hare, 130 S.W. 864, 868 (Tex.Civ.App.1910) (family Bible of third person, which plaintiffs tried to and were unable to obtain).

5. United States v. Ratliff, 623 F.2d 1293 (8th Cir. 1980), cert. denied 449 U.S. 876; Waters v. Mines, 260 Ala. 652, 72 So.2d 69 (1954); Moss v. State, 208 Ark. 137, 185 S.W.2d 92 (1945); Silvey v. Wynn, 102 Ga.App. 283, 115 S.E.2d 774 (1960); Flaharty v. Reed, 170 Kan. 215, 225 P.2d 98 (1950); Thurman v. St. Louis Public Service Co., 308 S.W.2d 680 (Mo.1957); Haire v. State, 118 Tex.Cr.R. 16, 39 S.W.2d 70 (1931).

6. E.g., Londoner v. Stewart, 3 Colo. 47, 50 (1876); McDonald v. Erbes, 231 Ill. 295, 83 N.E. 162 (1907); Sherman v. Sherman, 290 Ky. 237, 160 S.W.2d 637 (1942); Summons v. State, 156 Md. 390, 144 A. 501 (1929); Gasser v. Great Northern Insurance Co., 145 Minn. 205, 176 N.W. 484 (1920) (sufficiency of efforts a matter for judge's discretion); Mahoney-Jones Co. v. Osborne, 189 N.C. 445, 127 S.E. 533 (1925); Pringey v. Guss, 16 Okl. 82, 83, 86 P. 292, 8 Ann.Cas. 412 (1906); Bruger v. Princeton & S. etc. Ins. Co., 129 Wis. 281, 109 N.W. 95 (1906).

In *McDonald, Sherman, Summons* and *Bruger*, it is suggested that in some circumstances due diligence may require the proponent to take the deposition of the out-of-state possessor of the writing. Deposing the out-of-state holder, however, in addition to being inconvenient and expensive, will often be ineffective to obtain documents in the holder's possession. See Orton v. Poe, 19 Conn.Supp. 145, 110 A.2d 623 (Super.Ct.1954) (statute authorizing issuance of state subpenas to procure depositions needed in out-of-state litigation construed not to authorize subpenas duces tecum). The problems incident to obtaining documents held by third persons outside the jurisdiction are reviewed in Cleary & Strong, The Best Evidence Rule: An Evaluation in Context, 51 Iowa L.Rev. 825 (1966). The uncertainties of the available techniques are such that resort to them should seemingly not ordinarily be required.

7. Viereck v. United States, 139 F.2d 847, 850 (D.C. Cir.1944), cert. denied 321 U.S. 794 ("It is hard for even a fertile imagination to conjure up so futile a gesture under the circumstances, as a demand by the United States upon Germany for the production of these letters."); Missouri, Kansas & Texas Railway Co. v. Dilworth, 95 Tex. 327, 67 S.W. 88, 89 (1902) (waybill in hands of carrier outside the state, which they probably would not part with); Bruger v. Princeton & S., etc., Ins. Co., 129 Wis. 281, 109 N.W. 95, 97 (1906) ("unless it is clear that they would have been fruitless").

On this ground, efforts to secure public records in another state or country, which are not allowed to be removed under their law or practice, would not be required to be shown before using a copy. Sansoni v. Selvaggi, 121 N.J.L. 274, 2 A.2d 355 (1938) (postal savings passbook impounded by post-office in Italy); De la Garza v. McManus, 44 S.W. 704 (Tex.Civ.App.1898) (deed in archives in Mexico, presumably not removable,

---

1. See note 1 on page 718.

WRITINGS

sary or under his control,[2] and second, that the proponent has notified him to produce it at the trial and he has failed to do so. Observe that the notice is without compulsive force,[3] and is designed merely to account for nonproduction of the writing by the proponent, and thus to enable him to use secondary evidence of the writing's terms. If the proponent actually needs the production of the original itself he will resort to subpoena duces tecum or under modern rules the motion for an order to produce. But when the notice is offered as an excuse for resorting to secondary evidence the adversary cannot fairly complain that he was only given opportunity, not compelled, to make the writing available.

An oral notice may be sufficient,[4] but the safest and almost universal practice is to give written notice beforehand to the party or his attorney, describing the particular documents, and then to call upon the adversary orally at the trial for the writings requested.[5] It is held that the nature of the complaint or of the defense may constitute a sufficient implied notice that the pleader is charging the adversary with possession of the original and that he considers its production essential.[6] As to the time of serving notice it is sufficient if it allows the adversary a fair opportunity under the existing circumstances to produce the writing at the trial.[7] Accordingly, if it appears at the trial itself that the adversary has the original paper in

provable by examined copy). As to domestic public records, see § 240 infra.

§ 239

1. 4 Wigmore, Evidence §§ 1202–1210 (Chadbourn rev. 1972); Dec.Dig. Evidence ☜179(2), 184, 185(1–12), Criminal Law ☜402(2); C.J.S. Evidence §§ 832–834, 843–848; 29 Am.Jur.2d Evidence §§ 467–469.

Fed.R.Evid. and Rev.Unif.R.Evid. (1974) 1004 provide:

> The original is not required, and other evidence of the contents of a writing, recording, or photograph is admissible if—
>
> . . .
>
> (3) *Original in Possession of Opponent*. At a time when an original was under the control of the party against whom offered, he was put on notice, by the pleadings or otherwise, that the contents would be a subject of proof at the hearing, and he does not produce the original at the hearing;
>
> . . . .

2. American Fire & Casualty Co. v. Kaplan, 183 A.2d 914 (D.C.Mun.App.1962); Jones v. Texas Department of Public Safety, 392 S.W.2d 176 (Tex.Civ.App. 1965); Threatt v. Threatt, 212 Miss. 555, 54 So.2d 907 (1951) (notice to defendant provided sufficient foundation where original shown to be in possession of defendant's father).

Proof of possession by the opponent without proof of notice is generally insufficient. Padgett v. Brezner, 359 S.W.2d 416 (Mo.App.1962) (mere possession by adversary did not afford basis for admitting secondary evidence); In re Estate of Reuss, 422 Pa. 58, 220 A.2d 822 (1966) (copy of letter excluded where no demand made for original in hands of opponent). But compare Transamerica Insurance Co. v. Bloomfield, 401 F.2d 357 (6th Cir. 1968) (not error to admit copies of corporate records, apparently without notice, where oppo-

nent "was familiar with . . . books and could produce them himself if he so desired"); Gardner v. Bernard, 401 S.W.2d 415 (Mo.1966) (semble).

3. Bova v. Roanoke Oil Co., 180 Va. 332, 23 S.E.2d 347, 144 A.L.R. 364 (1942). The failure to produce, however, might have another tactical consequence, namely, that of giving rise to an inference adverse to the party so failing. Missouri-K.-T. Railroad Co. v. Elliott, 102 F. 96, 102 (8th Cir. 1900). See § 272 infra.

By contrast, production following notice may in some states lead to the tactical advantage of procuring admission of otherwise inadmissible material. See § 55 supra.

4. Especially when given in open court during the trial. Kerr v. McGuire, 28 N.Y. 446, 453 (1863). But see note 7 infra.

5. For details of the practice, see 4 Wigmore, Evidence § 1208 (Chadbourn rev. 1972).

6. How v. Hall, 14 East 274, 104 Eng.Rep. 606 (K.B.1811) (trover for bond); 612 North Michigan Avenue Building Corp. v. Factsystem, Inc., 54 Ill.App.3d 749, 12 Ill.Dec. 613, 370 N.E.2d 236 (1977); Stipe v. First National Bank, 208 Or. 251, 301 P.2d 175 (1956) (copy of document attached to pleading is sufficient notice to other party to produce); Harris v. State, 150 Tex.Cr.R. 137, 199 S.W.2d 522 (1947) (notice held afforded by content of indictment for forgery). Similarly, a defensive pleading charging plaintiff with possession of a document necessary to the defense may serve as notice. J. L. Owens v. Bemis, 22 N.D. 159, 133 N.W. 59 (1911).

7. Beard v. Southern Railway Co., 143 N.C. 136, 55 S.E. 505 (1906) (notice during trial not timely when adversary would have to go to his home in another town to get the writing). See also Waddell v. Trowbridge, 94 W.Va. 482, 119 S.E. 290 (1923) (notice to produce given at the trial timely as to one document, not as to another).

the courtroom, an immediate notice then and there is timely.[8]

Some exceptions, under which notice is unnecessary before using secondary evidence of a writing in the adversary's possession, have been recognized. The first is well sustained in reason. It dispenses with the need for notice when the adversary has wrongfully obtained or fraudulently suppressed the writing.[9] The others seem more questionable. There is a traditional exception that no notice is required to produce a writing which is itself a notice.[10] This is understandable in respect to giving notice to produce a notice to produce, which would lead to an endless succession of notices, but there seems little justification for extending the exception, as the cases do, to notices generally. Finally an exception is made by the majority view for writings in the hands of the accused in a criminal prosecution. Under this view, secondary evidence may be received without notice to the accused to produce.[11] The logic of deriving this position, as seems to have been done, from the privilege against self-incrimination is dubious. For while a demand upon the accused to produce which is delivered before the jury clearly has a tendency to coerce the defendant and thus cheapen the privilege,[12] there is no logical necessity that the demand be so delivered.[13] Since the object of notice is to protect against imposition upon the opponent, and since this object may be achieved in the case of the criminal defendant by notice before trial, the minority view under which the prosecution must give notice as a necessary precondition to the use of secondary evidence [14] seems the fairer and more reasonable stand.[15]

 WESTLAW REFERENCES

best secondary /1 evidence /p notice notification /p adversar*** defendant* opponent* "opposing part***" plaintiff* /p contract* deed* document* writing* 157k179(2)

---

§ 240. Excuses for Nonproduction of the Original Writing: (d) Public Records[1]

If the contents of the judgment of a court or of an executive proclamation are to be proved, shall the proponent be required to produce the original writing? The accepted view is that, in general, public and judicial

---

8. Brownlee v. Hot Shoppes, Inc., 23 App.Div.2d 848, 259 N.Y.S.2d 271 (1965) (held error to refuse secondary evidence where plaintiff during trial demanded the original which he asserted was in the courtroom in defendant's possession and defendant did not deny the allegation); Williams v. Metropolitan Life Insurance Co., 202 S.C. 384, 25 S.E.2d 243 (1943) (no previous notice required where paper called for is in court).

9. Cheatham v. Riddle, 8 Tex. 162 (1852) (party's principal "had gotten possession of the instrument and fled the country with it"); Meyer v. General American Corp., 569 P.2d 1094 (Utah 1977) (semble); 4 Wigmore, Evidence § 1207 (Chadbourn rev. 1972).

10. Colling v. Treweek, 6 B. & C. 394, 108 Eng.Rep. 497 (1827); Eisenhart v. Slaymaker, 14 Serg. & R. 153 (Pa.1826) ("otherwise . . . a fresh necessity would be constantly arising, *ad infinitum*, to prove notice of the preceding notice; so that the party would at every step be receding instead of advancing.")

11. Lisansky v. United States, 31 F.2d 846 (4th Cir. 1929); Dean v. State, 240 Ala. 8, 197 So. 53 (1940); State v. Pascarelli, 2 Conn.Cir. 305, 198 A.2d 239 (1963); Annot., 67 A.L.R. 77.

12. Notice delivered before the jury has frequently been held a violation of the privilege. See, e.g., McKnight v. United States, 115 F. 972 (6th Cir. 1902); Commonwealth v. Valeroso, 273 Pa. 213, 116 A. 828

(1922); Powell v. Commonwealth, 167 Va. 558, 189 S.E. 433 (1937); and cases collected in 110 A.L.R. 101.

As to compelling production generally by an accused, see § 126 supra.

13. Thus courts following the minority view discussed below commonly require that the notice be outside the jury's presence. State v. Hollingsworth, 191 N.C. 595, 132 S.E. 667 (1926) (accused should be given notice outside jury's presence). More questionable is the position that demand before the jury is improper but may be cured by jury instruction. State v. Haye, 72 Wn.2d 461, 433 P.2d 884 (1968).

14. "The object of the notice is not to compel the party to produce the paper, for no such power is assumed, either directly or indirectly, by placing him under a disadvantage if he does not produce it. Its object is to enable the prisoner to protect himself against the falsity of the secondary evidence." State v. Kimbrough, 13 N.C. (2 Dev.L.) 431 (1830).

15. Rex v. Ellicombe, 5 Car. & P. 522, 172 Eng.Rep. 1681 (1933); Kirk v. State, 227 So.2d 40 (Fla.App.1969); Annot., 67 A.L.R. 77.

§ 240

1. 4 Wigmore, Evidence §§ 1215–1222 (Chadbourn rev. 1972); Dec.Dig. Evidence ☞177, Criminal Law ☞444.

records and public documents are required by law to be retained by the official custodian in the public office designated for their custody, and courts will not require them to be removed.[2] To require removal would be inconvenient for the public who might desire to consult the records and would entail a risk of loss of or damage to the official documents. Accordingly, statutes and rules have provided for the issuance of certified copies and for their admission in evidence in lieu of the original.[3] In addition, examined copies, authenticated by a witness who has compared it with the original record, are usually receivable.[4]

 **WESTLAW REFERENCES**

"best evidence" /p judicial public +3 document* record*
157k175

§ 241. Preferences Among Copies and Between Copies and Oral Testimony[1]

The basic policy of the original document requirement is that of specially safeguard-

ing the accuracy of the presentation in court of the terms of a writing. If the original is unavailable does the same policy require a preference among the secondary methods of proving the terms? Some means of proof are clearly more reliable than others. In order of reliability the list might go something like this: (1) a mechanically produced copy, such as a photograph or xerograph, a carbon, a letter-press copy, etc.,[2] (2) a firsthand copy by one who was looking at the original while he copied (immediate copy, sworn copy), (3) a copy, however made, which has been compared by a witness with the original and found correct (examined copy), (4) a secondhand or mediate copy, i.e., a copy of a firsthand copy, (5) oral testimony as to the terms of the writing, with memory aided by a previously made memorandum, and (6) oral testimony from unaided memory. There are many additional variations.

There is one rule of preference that is reasonable and is generally agreed on by the courts, namely, that for judicial and other public records, a certified, sworn or examined copy is preferred,[3] and other evi-

---

2. Doe v. Roberts, 13 M. & W. 520, 530, 153 Eng. Rep. 217 (Exch.1844) ("When directed to be kept in any particular custody, and so deposited they are provable by examined copies . . . on the ground of the great inconvenience of removing them"); State v. Black, 31 N.J.Super. 418, 422, 107 A.2d 33, 35 (1954) ("It is firmly established in this State that a public document may be proved by producing the original . . . and on grounds of public convenience a well-known rule of the common law allows proof of such document by duly authenticated copies whenever the original would be admissible, a public document being for this purpose, a document, either judicial or non-judicial, which is public in its nature and which the public had the right to inspect.").

If, however, the original record of which proof is to be made is a record of the very court which is trying the present case, then it seems, since the original writing can be produced without violating the rule and policy against removal, production should be required, if formal proof is to be made. Roby v. Title Guarantee & Trust Co., 166 Ill. 336, 46 N.E. 1110 (1896); 4 Wigmore, Evidence § 1215(b) (Chadbourn rev. 1972). But judicial notice would be simpler, see § 330 infra.

3. Fed.R.Evid. 1005 provides:

The contents of an official record, or of a document authorized to be recorded or filed and actually recorded or filed, including data compilations in any form, if otherwise admissible, may be proved by

copy, certified as correct in accordance with rule 902 or testified to be correct by a witness who has compared it with the original. If a copy which complies with the foregoing cannot be obtained by the exercise of reasonable diligence, then other evidence of the contents may be given.

The Revised Uniform Rule is identical except for a slight, and meaningless, difference in style. As to computerized records, see Annot., 71 A.L.R.3d 232.

4. See Doe v. Roberts, quoted supra note 2 and Fed. R.Evid. 1005 quoted supra note 3. Nor have certified copies traditionally been preferred to examined copies. See Smithers v. Lowrance, 100 Tex. 77, 93 S.W. 1064 (1906); 4 Wigmore, Evidence § 1273(1) (Chadbourn rev. 1972).

§ 241

1. 4 Wigmore, Evidence §§ 1265–1280 (Chadbourn rev. 1972); Byrdseye, Degrees of Secondary Evidence, 6 Wash.L.Rev. 21 (1931); Notes, 30 So.Cal.L.Rev. 355 (1957), 38 Mich.L.Rev. 864 (1940); Dec.Dig. Evidence ⟐186; C.J.S. Evidence § 784.

2. See § 236 supra.

3. Jones v. Melindy, 62 Ark. 203, 36 S.W. 22 (1881) (proof of record of mortgage through testimony of custodian disallowed; use of examined or certified copy required); Whittier v. Leifert, 72 N.D. 528, 9 N.W.2d 402

dence of the terms of the record cannot be resorted to unless the proponent has no such copy available, and the original record has been lost or destroyed so that a copy cannot now be made.[4]

As to writings other than public records, there are two general approaches to the problem. First there is the view, fathered by some of the English decisions and espoused by a minority of the American cases, that "there are no degrees of substantive evidence."[5] This position has the virtues of simplicity and easiness of application. In addition, it may be observed that failure to apply the basic rule as between varieties of secondary evidence leaves unimpaired a substantial practical motivation to produce more satisfactory secondary evidence where it appears to exist. This practical motivation, of

course, stems from apprehension of the adverse inference which may be drawn from failure to produce more satisfactory secondary evidence indicated to exist and not shown to be unavailable. These considerations have led the draftsmen of most modern codes of evidence to adopt the so-called "English" view.[6]

The second view is followed by a majority of the courts which have passed on the question. Here a distinction is recognized between types of secondary evidence, with a written copy being preferred to oral testimony,[7] and, under circumstances varying from state to state, and an immediate copy being preferred to a more remote one.[8] This view is justifiable chiefly on the ground that there is some incongruity in pursuing the policy of obtaining the terms of writings with fullest

---

(1943) (rule stated; dictum); 4 Wigmore, Evidence § 1269 (Chadbourn rev. 1972).

The requirement is relaxed in most jurisdictions, by statute or decision, to allow a witness to be asked upon cross-examination as to his conviction of crime. Bosarge v. State, 273 Ala. 329, 139 So.2d 302 (1962) (best evidence rule did not require certified copy of records where accused had already testified to convictions); Gaskill v. Gahman, 255 Iowa 891, 124 N.W.2d 533 (1963) (proof of witness' prior conviction may, under statute, be made by his own testimony or proof of record); Clemens v. Conrad, 19 Mich. 170, 175 (1869) ("The danger that he will falsely testify to a conviction that never took place or that he may be mistaken about it, is so slight, that it may almost be looked upon as imaginary"). But compare Rolland v. State, 235 Ga. 808, 221 S.E.2d 582 (1976) (witness cannot be discredited even by own testimony of conviction; record required); People v. Moses, 11 Ill.2d 84, 143 N.E.2d 1 (1957) (where witness is accused, conviction must be proved by introduction of record). See Dec.Dig. Witnesses ☜350, 359. Impeachment by proof of conviction is treated generally in § 43 supra.

4. People v. Cotton, 250 Ill. 338, 95 N.E. 283 (1911).

5. Doe d. Gilbert v. Ross, 7 M. & W. 102, 151 Eng. Rep. 696 (Exch.1840) (shorthand notes of counsel's statement at former trial of contents of settlement allowed, although attested copy requiring but not bearing a stamp was in existence); Beaty v. Southern Railway Co., 80 S.C. 527, 61 S.E. 1006 (1908) ("there is no division of degrees of proof in case of the loss of an instrument"); Rick Furniture Co. v. Smith, 202 S.W. 99 (Tex.Civ.App.1918). Cases subscribing to the English view are collected in Byrdseye, Degrees of Secondary Evidence, 6 Wash.L.Rev. 21 (1931); Note, 38 Mich.L. Rev. 864 (1940).

6. The Federal and Revised Uniform Rules contain no provision for "degrees" of secondary evidence.

Fed.R.Evid. 1004, Advisory Committee's Note; United States v. Gerhart, 538 F.2d 807 (8th Cir. 1976). But compare, Report of New Jersey Supreme Court Committee on Evidence 232 (1963); West's Ann.Cal.Evid. Code § 1505.

7. Riggs v. Tayloe, 22 U.S. (9 Wheat.) 483, 486, 6 L.Ed. 140 (1824) (original contract destroyed, oral testimony permitted; "the party [after accounting for original] may read a counterpart or if there is no counterpart an examined copy, or if there should not be an examined copy, he may give parole evidence of its contents."); Murphy v. Nielsen, 132 Cal.App.2d 396, 282 P.2d 126 (1955) (held error to receive parol where copies shown to exist; holding now codified by West's Ann.Cal.Evid.Code § 1505); Cummings v. Pennsylvania Fire Insurance Co., 153 Iowa 579, 134 N.W. 79 (1911); Baroda State Bank v. Peck, 235 Mich. 542, 209 N.W. 827 (1926) (application of American rule affirmed by equally divided appellate court; full discussion). See also Note, 38 Mo.L.Rev. 475 (1973).

8. When the original is a public record and hence not producible, a certified or examined copy may be obtained at any time, and a copy of a copy would everywhere be excluded. Lasater v. Van Hook, 77 Tex. 650, 655, 14 S.W. 270 (1890) (deed record; examined copy of a certified copy excluded). When the original is unavailable and there is no copy of record, then under the majority view the proponent would be required to produce an immediate copy, if available, before using a copy of a copy. Schley v. Lyon, 6 Ga. 530, 538 (1849); State v. Cohen, 108 Iowa 208, 78 N.W. 857 (1899). Contra, under the minority, "no degrees" doctrine: Goodrich v. Weston, 102 Mass. 362 (1869).

The various situations are distinguished and the decisions collected in 4 Wigmore, Evidence § 1275 (Chadbourn rev. 1972).

accuracy, by structuring a highly technical rule to that end, only to abandon it upon the unavailability of the original. In formulating this general approach of discrimination among types of secondary evidence, the courts following the American rule have sought to avoid a position which would require the proponent to produce or account for all possible copies that may have existed. A reasonable standard is suggested by an early New York judge, who said:

"I do not mean to contend that there are any arbitrary or inflexible degrees of secondary evidence, rendering it necessary for a party, who is driven to that description of proof, to show affirmatively, in every instance that there is no higher degree within his power, than the one he offers; but I think it may be safely said, that where it appears in the very offer, or from the nature of the case itself, or from the circumstances attending the offer, that the party has better and more reliable evidence at hand, and equally within his power, he shall not be permitted to resort to the inferior degree first".[9]

WESTLAW
REFERENCES

157k186

---

§ 242. Adversary's Admission as to the Terms of a Writing [1]

Many American courts have followed the lead of Baron Parke's decision in Slatterie v. Pooley [2] and have held admissions by a party opponent admissible to prove the terms of a writing.[3] Upon reflection, however, it will be seen that Baron Parke's decision squares rather poorly with the primary modern day policy in favor of obtaining the contents of writings with accuracy.[4] The evidence determined admissible in Slatterie v. Pooley was actually at two removes from the writing itself, being witness' report of the defendant's comment. Perhaps the policy of holding admissible any admission which a party-opponent chooses to make will suffice to justify the first step, but the second frequently raises the possibility of erroneous transmission without corresponding justification. Accordingly, some American decisions have rejected testimony relating oral admissions concerning contents of writings.[5]

It will be observed, however, that the second possibility of mistransmission noted above is effectively eliminated where no testimonial report of the admission is required. Thus, the desirable solution, towards which it is believed the decisions may be drifting, is to receive admissions to evidence a document's terms (1) when the admission itself is in writing and is produced in evidence,[6] or (2) when the party himself, on the stand in this

---

9. Slossen, J. in Healy v. Gilman, 1 Bosw. (14 N.Y. Super.) 235 at 242 (1857), quoted in note, 38 Mich.L. Rev. 864, 874 (1940).

§ 242

1. 4 Wigmore, Evidence §§ 1255–1257 (Chadbourn rev. 1972); Dec.Dig. Evidence ⟵172; C.J.S. Evidence § 788; Notes, 20 Md.L.Rev. 50 (1960), 17 Tex.L.Rev. 371 (1939).

2. 6 M. & W. 665, 151 Eng.Rep. 579 (Exch.1840).

3. In the following cases testimony of a third person as to a party's oral admission was received: Dunbar v. United States, 156 U.S. 185 (1895) (oral admission that telegram received was identical to one sent by party); Metropolitan Life Insurance Co. v. Hogan, 63 F.2d 654 (7th Cir. 1933) (oral admission by agent of nature of paper received from beneficiary); Morey v. Hoyt, 62 Conn. 542, 26 A. 127 (1893) (reviewing older authorities and approving Slatterie v. Pooley).

4. See 1 Jones, Evidence § 261 (5th ed. 1958); Fed. R.Evid. 1007, Advisory Committee's Note.

5. Grimes v. Fall, 15 Cal. 63 (1860) (oral testimony that party admitted that he was assignee under what court assumed to be written assignment, held inadmissible); Prussing v. Jackson, 208 Ill. 85, 69 N.E. 771 (1904) (stating that verbal admissions as to content of writings would, if admitted, abrogate basic rule).

6. Written admissions were held receivable in Clarke v. Warwick C. M. Co., 174 Mass. 434, 54 N.E. 887 (1899); Swing v. Cloquet Lumber Co., 121 Minn. 221, 141 N.W. 117 (1913) ("The rule is sound in principle, at least where the admissions are in writing"); Taylor v. Peck, 21 Grat., (62 Va.) 11 (1871). Even more clearly should a written pleading containing the admission be sufficient. Coca-Cola Bottling Co. v. International Filter Co., 62 Ind.App. 421, 113 N.E. 17 (1916).

or some other trial or hearing, makes the admission about the contents of the writing or concedes that he made such an admission on a former occasion.[7] Oral testimony by a witness that he heard the party's admission as to the terms of the writing, despite the authority of Slatterie v. Pooley, should be excluded.[8]

 WESTLAW REFERENCES

best secondary +1 evidence & adversar***
   opponent* parties party /s admissi*** admit* /s
   document* writing*

§ 243. Review of Rulings Admitting Secondary Evidence

It will be seen from the earlier sections of this chapter that the requirement of the production of original writings, with the several excuses for nonproduction and the exceptions to the requirement itself, make up a fairly complex set of regulations for administration by the trial judge. Mistakes in the application of these rules are, understandably, not infrequent. The purpose of this system of rules, on the other hand, is simple and practical. That purpose is to secure the most reliable information as to the contents of documents, when those terms are disputed. A mystical ideal of seeking "the best evidence" or the "original document," as an end in itself is no longer the goal. Consequently when an attack is made, on motion for new trial or on appeal, upon the judge's admission of secondary evidence, it seems that the reviewing tribunal, should ordinarily make inquiry of the complaining counsel, "Does the party whom you represent actually dispute the accuracy of the evidence received as to the material terms of the writing?" If the counsel cannot assure the court that such a good faith dispute exists, it seems clear that any departure from the regulations in respect to secondary evidence must be classed as harmless error.[1]

 WESTLAW REFERENCES

synopsis("best evidence" /s decision discretion*** error
   violat***)

---

7. Admissions on the witness stand have frequently been viewed as sufficient though the distinction between in and out-of-court admissions is not generally made: Johnson v. U-Haul of Southern Alabama, 357 So.2d 665 (Ala.Civ.App.1978) (admission by party in open court); Parr Construction Co. v. Pomer, 217 Md. 539, 144 A.2d 69 (1958); Gardner v. City of Columbia Police Department, 216 S.C. 219, 57 S.E.2d 308 (1950). Contra, Prussing v. Jackson, supra, note 5.

8. Fed. and Rev.Unif.R.Evid. (1974) 1007 provide:

Contents of writings, recordings, or photographs may be proved by the testimony or deposition of the party against whom offered or by his written admission, without accounting for the nonproduction of the original.

§ 243

1. Myrick v. United States, 332 F.2d 279 (5th Cir. 1964) (not error to admit photostatic copies of checks in absence of suggestion to trial judge that they were in-

correct); Johns v. United States, 323 F.2d 421 (5th Cir. 1963) (not error to admit admittedly accurate copy of wire recording); Sauget v. Johnston, 315 F.2d 816 (9th Cir. 1963) (not error to admit copy when opponent had original agreement and on appeal made no claim of any discrepancy).

Compare, National Fire Insurance Co. v. Evertson, 153 Neb. 854, 46 N.W.2d 489 (1951) where the possibility of this approach was overlooked. There a judgment was reversed, partly on the ground that a material written settlement was proved only by a carbon copy. On the motion for new trial the winning plaintiff produced the original writing which corresponded with the carbon, but the court on appeal said that the judgment could not be "propped up" in that way.

As stated in the Advisory Committee's Note, the prevailing attitude toward harmless error in part furnishes the basis for Federal Rule 1003, dealing with admissibility of duplicates. See § 236 supra.

Title 10
THE HEARSAY RULE AND ITS EXCEPTIONS
Chapter 24
THE HEARSAY RULE

Table of Sections

§ 244. The History of the Rule Against Hearsay[1]

In an oft-quoted passage, Wigmore calls the rule against hearsay "that most characteristic rule of the Anglo-American Law of Evidence—a rule which may be esteemed, next to jury trial, the greatest contribution of that eminently practical legal system to the world's methods of procedure."[2] How did this rule come about?

The development of the jury was, no doubt, an important factor.[3] It will be remembered that the jury in its earlier forms was in the nature of a committee or special commission of qualified persons in the neighborhood to report on facts or issues in dispute. So far as necessary its members conducted its investigations informally among those who had special knowledge of the facts. Attesting witnesses to writings were summoned with the jurors and apparently participated in their deliberations,[4] but the practice of calling witnesses to appear in court and testify publicly about the facts to the jury is a late development in jury trial.

---

§ 244

1. The brief discussion here is based upon 5 Wigmore, Evidence § 1364 (Chadbourn rev. 1974). See also 9 Holdsworth's History of English Law 214–219 (1926). The story of the development of jury trial and of the emergence of the practice of producing witnesses in court to testify before the jury is recounted in Thayer, Preliminary Treatise on Evidence, chs. 2–4, esp.

ch. 3 (1898). See also Plucknett, A Concise History of the Common Law 120–130 (5th ed. 1956).

2. 5 Wigmore, supra n. 1, at p. 28.

3. Professor Morgan chose rather to view the rule as a development of the adversary system. See n. 19, infra.

---

4. See note 4 on page 725.

Though something like the jury existed at least as early as the 1100's,[5] this practice of hearing witnesses in court does not become frequent until the later 1400's. The change-over to the present conception that the normal source of proof is not the private knowledge or investigation of the jurors, but the testimony of witnesses in open court, is a matter of gradual evolution thereafter. Finally, in the 1500's it has become, though not yet the exclusive source of proof, the normal and principal one.[6]

It is not until this period of the gradual emergence of the witness testifying publicly in court that the consciousness of need for exclusionary rules of evidence begins to appear. It had indeed been required even of the early witnesses to writings that they could speak only of "what they saw and heard"[7] and this requirement would naturally be applied to the new class of testifying witnesses. But when the witness has heard at firsthand the statement of X out of court that he has seen and heard a blow with a sword, or witnessed a trespass on land, as evidence of the blow or the trespass, a new question is presented. Certainly it would seem that the earlier requirement of knowledge must have predisposed the judges to skepticism about the value of hearsay.[8]

Accordingly, it is the value of hearsay, its sufficiency as proof, that is the subject of discussion in this gestation period. And so through the reigns of the Tudors and the Stuarts there is a gradually increasing drumfire of criticism and objections by parties and counsel against evidence of oral hearsay declarations. While the evidence was constantly admitted, the confidence in its reliability was increasingly undermined.[9] It was derided as "a tale of a tale"[10] or "a story out of another man's mouth."[11] Parallel with this increasingly discredited use of casual oral hearsay was a similar development in respect to transcribed statements made under oath before a judge or judicial officer, not subject to cross-examination by the party against whom it is offered.[12] In criminal cases in the 1500's and down to the middle 1600's the main reliance of the prosecution was the use of such "depositions" to make out its case.[13] As oral hearsay was becoming discredited, uneasiness about the use of "depositions" began to take shape, first in the form of a limitation that they could only be used when the witness could not be produced at the trial.[14] It will be noted that the want of oath and the unreliability of the report of the oral statement cannot be urged against such evidence but only the want of cross-examination and observation of demeanor.

It was in the first decade after the Restoration that the century or so of criticism of hearsay had its final effect in decisions rejecting its use, first as to oral hearsay and then as to depositions. Wigmore finds that the period between 1675 and 1690 is the time of crystallization of the rule against hearsay.[15] For a time the rule was qualified by the notion that hearsay, while not independently admissible, could come in as confirmatory of other evidence,[16] and this qualification survived down to the end of the 1700's in the limited form of admitting a wit-

4. Thayer, Preliminary Treatise on Evidence 97 (1898).

5. Thayer, supra n. 1, at pp. 53–65.

6. 5 Wigmore, supra n. 1, at p. 15.

7. Thayer, supra n. 1, at pp. 101, 519; 9 Holdsworth, History of English Law 211 (1926).

8. See Thayer, supra n. 1, at pp. 518, 519; 9 Holdsworth, History of English Law 215 (1926).

9. 5 Wigmore, supra n. 1, at p. 18.

10. Colledge's Trial, 8 How.St.Tr. 549, 663 (1681) (counsel for prosecution warning his own witness), cited in 5 Wigmore, supra n. 1, at n. 32.

11. Gascoigne's Trial, 7 How.St.Tr. 959, 1019 (1680) (warning by judge, but evidence finally admitted) cited in 5 Wigmore, supra n. 1, at n. 32.

12. 5 Wigmore, Evidence supra n. 1, at pp. 20–25.

13. 9 Holdsworth, History of English Law 218 (1926).

14. 5 Wigmore, supra n. 1, at p. 23.

15. 5 Wigmore, supra, n. 1, at p. 18.

16. 5 Wigmore, supra n. 1, at p. 19.

ness's prior consistent statements out of court to corroborate his testimony.[17]

Whether the rule against hearsay was, with the rest of the English law of evidence, in fact "the child of the jury"[18] or the product of the adversary system[19] may be of no great contemporary significance. The important thing is that the rule against hearsay taking form at the end of the seventeenth century was neither a matter of "immemorial usage" nor an inheritance from Magna Charta but, in the long view of English legal history, was a late development of the common law.

Holdsworth thinks that the immediate influences leading to the crystallization of the rule against hearsay, at the particular time in the late 1600's when this occurred, were first, a strong dictum by Coke in his Third Institute denouncing "the strange conceit that one may be an accuser by hearsay,"[20] and second, the rejection of the attempt to naturalize in English law the canon and civil law requirement of "two witnesses"[21] and the consequent urge to provide some compensating safeguard.[22] As we have seen in the next preceding section, a century of increasing protests against the use of hearsay had preceded the establishment of the rule, but most of the specific weaknesses of hearsay, which were the underlying reasons for the adoption of the rule, and which have explained its survival, were not clearly pointed out until after the beginning of the 1700's when the newly established rule came to be rationalized by the judges and the text writers.

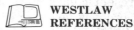 **WESTLAW REFERENCES**

histor! /5 hearsay

§ 245. The Reasons for the Rule Against Hearsay:[1] Exceptions to the Rule

The factors upon which the credibility of testimony depends are the perception, memory, and narration of the witness. (1) *Perception.* Did the witness perceive what he describes, and did he perceive it accurately? (2) *Memory.* Has the witness retained an accurate impression of his perception? (3) *Narration.* Does his language convey that impression accurately?[2] Some writers subdivide inaccuracy of narration into ambiguity and insincerity, resulting in four rather than three factors.[3] However, it seems apparent that ambiguity and insincerity, as well as honest mistake, all manifest themselves as inaccuracy of narration.

In order to encourage witnesses to put forth their best efforts and to expose inaccuracies which might be present with respect to any of the foregoing factors, the Anglo-American tradition evolved three conditions under which witnesses ordinarily will be required to testify: oath, personal presence at

17. 5 Wigmore, supra n. 1, at p. 20.

18. Thayer, Preliminary Treatise on Evidence 47, also 2–4, 180 (1898).

19. Morgan, The Jury and the Exclusionary Rules of Evidence, 4 U.Chi.L.Rev. 247, 258 (1937), Hearsay Dangers and the Application of the Hearsay Concept, 62 Harv.L.Rev. 177 (1948), also in Selected Writings on Evidence and Trial 764, 766–768 (Fryer ed. 1957).

20. Coke thus condemned the holding in Thomas's case, Dyer 99b (1553) to the effect that under a statute of Edward VI requiring two witnesses in treason if one accuser speaks from his own knowledge, "and he relate it to another, the other may well be an accuser." Coke Third Inst. 25 (1641).

21. An elaborate system attaching numerical values to various kinds of evidence.

22. 9 Holdsworth, History of English Law 217, 218 (1926).

§ 245

1. See 5 Wigmore, Evidence § 1362 (Chadbourn rev. 1974); Weinstein & Berger, Evidence ¶ 800[01]; Maguire, The Hearsay System: Around and Through the Thicket, 14 Vand.L.Rev. 741, 743–749 (1961); Morgan, Hearsay Dangers and the Application of the Hearsay Concept, 62 Harv.L.Rev. 177 (1948); Introductory Note: The Hearsay Problem, Fed.R.Evid., 28 U.S.C.A. p. 522.

2. 2 Wigmore, Evidence § 478 (Chadbourn rev. 1979); Strahorn, A Reconsideration of the Hearsay Rule and Admissions, 85 U.Pa.L.Rev. 484 (1937). In United States v. Byrnes, 644 F.2d 107 (2d Cir. 1981), some considerable confusion resulted when both judge and court reporter understood that witness was describing unlawfully imported foreign parrots as "citizen" birds, when in fact "psittacine" was intended.

3. Morgan, supra n. 1; Tribe, Triangulating Hearsay, 87 Harv.L.Rev. 957 (1974).

the trial, and cross-examination.[4] The rule against hearsay is designed to insure compliance with these ideal conditions, and when one of them is absent the hearsay objection becomes pertinent.

In the hearsay situation, two "witnesses" are involved. The first complies with all three of the ideal conditions for the giving of testimony, but his testimony consists of reporting what the second "witness" said. The second "witness" is the out-of-court declarant; his statement was not given in compliance with the ideal conditions, yet it contains the information that is of concern in the case.

Oath. Among the earliest of the criticisms of hearsay, and one often repeated in judicial opinions down to the present, is the objection that the out-of-court declarant who made the hearsay statement commonly speaks or writes without the solemnity of the oath administered to witnesses in a court of law.[5] The oath may be important in two aspects. As a ceremonial and religious symbol it may induce in the witness a feeling of special obligation to speak the truth, and also it may impress upon the witness the danger of criminal punishment for perjury, to which the judicial oath or an equivalent solemn affirmation would be a prerequisite condition. Wigmore considers that the objection for want of an oath is incidental and not essential, and suggests that this is demonstrated by the fact that a hearsay statement, even if under oath, is still rejected.[6] But the fact that the oath is not the only requirement of the rule against hearsay does not prove that it is not an important one. Nor

does the fact that the oath may have diminished in significance with the passage of time mean that today it is without significance; no disposition to abolish it (other than to allow affirmation as a substitute) is apparent.[7]

Personal presence at trial. Another objection early asserted and repeated of late is the want of opportunity, in respect to the out-of-court declarant, for observation of his demeanor, with the light that this may shed on his credibility, that would be afforded if he were a witness on the stand.[8]

The solemnity of the occasion and possibility of public disgrace can scarcely fail to impress the witness,[9] and falsehood no doubt becomes more difficult if the person against whom directed is present.

Moreover, personal presence eliminates the danger that in the oral reporting of an out-of-court statement the witness reporting the statement may do so inaccurately. It seems probable that the reporting of words spoken is subject to special dangers of inaccuracy beyond the fallibility common to all reproduction from memory of matters of observation,[10] and this seems a substantial danger in the admission of hearsay. It is true as Wigmore points out [11] that not all hearsay is subject to this danger. Written statements can be produced in court and can be tested with reasonable accuracy for genuineness and freedom from alteration. Moreover, as Morgan has suggested, the reporting in court of spoken words for nonhearsay purposes, as in proving the making of an

---

4. California v. Green, 399 U.S. 149, 155 (1970); Strahorn, supra n. 2.

5. Bridges v. Wixon, 326 U.S. 135, 153 (1945); Chapman v. Chapman, 2 Conn. 347, 7 Am.Dec. 277 (1817); State v. Saporen, 205 Minn. 358, 285 N.W. 898 (1939); Hawkins, Pleas of the Crown, b. II, c. 46, § 44 (1716), in 5 Wigmore, Evidence, p. 7 (Chadbourn rev. 1974); Gilbert, Evidence, p. 4 (1760 ed.).

6. 5 Wigmore, supra n. 5, at p. 10.

7. See, e.g., Fed.R.Evid. 603:

Before testifying, every witness shall be required to declare that he will testify truthfully, by oath or

affirmation administered in a form calculated to awaken his conscience and impress his mind with his duty to do so.

8. Mattox v. United States, 156 U.S. 237, 242 (1895), quoted with approval, Ohio v. Roberts, 448 U.S. 56 (1980); Sahm, Demeanor Evidence: Elusive and Intangible Imponderables, 47 A.B.A.J. 580 (1961).

9. Strahorn, supra n. 2.

10. Stewart, Perception, Memory, and Hearsay, 1970 Utah L.Rev. 1, 13, 19.

11. 5 Wigmore, supra n. 6, at § 1363(1).

oral contract or the utterance of a slander,[12] is subject to this same risk of misreporting. Neither argument seems conclusive. In any event, no distinction is in general made between written and spoken hearsay.[13]

Cross-examination. It would be generally agreed today that noncompliance with the third condition is the main justification for the exclusion of hearsay. This is the lack of any opportunity for the adversary to cross-examine the absent declarant whose out-of-court statement is reported by the witness. Thus as early as 1668 we find a court rejecting hearsay because "the other party could not cross-examine the party sworn."[14] Judicial expressions stress this as a principal reason for the hearsay rule.[15] Cross-examination, as Bentham pointed out,[16] was a distinctive feature of the English trial system, and the one which most contributed to the prestige of the institution of jury trial. He called it "a security for the correctness and completeness of testimony." The nature of this safeguard which hearsay lacks is indicated by Chancellor Kent: "Hearsay testimony is from the very nature of it attended with . . . doubts and difficulties and it cannot clear them up. 'A person who relates a hearsay is not obliged to enter into any particulars, to answer any questions, to solve any difficulties, to reconcile any contradictions, to explain any obscurities, to remove any ambiguities; he entrenches himself in the simple assertion that he was told so, and leaves the burden entirely on his dead or absent author.' . . ." [17] In perhaps his most famous remark, Wigmore described cross-examination as "beyond any doubt the greatest legal engine ever invented for the discovery of truth."[18]

Hearsay that is admitted. It is easy, however, to overplay the unreliability of hearsay. Eminent judges have spoken of its "intrinsic weakness."[19] If this were meant to imply that all hearsay of its very nature is unworthy of reliance in a court of law, of course the implication is quite insupportable. The contrary is proved by the fact that courts are constantly receiving, as we shall see, hearsay evidence of various kinds under the numerous exceptions to the hearsay rule,[20] and by the doctrine established in most jurisdictions that when hearsay evidence, which would have been excluded if objected to, is let in without objection, it may be taken into consideration if it appears to be reliable in the particular case, as sufficient to sustain a verdict or finding of the fact thus proved.[21] The truth, of course, is that hearsay evidence, ranging as it does from mere thirdhand rumors to sworn affidavits of credible observers, has as wide a scale of reliability, from the highest to the lowest, as we find in testimonial or circumstantial evidence generally, depending as they all do upon the frailties of perception, memory, narration, and veracity of men and women. Indeed, it is the failure to adjust the rules of admissibility more flexibly and realistically to these variations in the relia-

---

12. Where the utterance of the words is an "operative fact," see Morgan, A Suggested Classification of Utterances Admissible as Res Gestae, 31 Yale L.J. 229 (1922). See § 249, infra.

13. The English Evidence Act 1938, 1 & 2 Geo. VI, c. 28, accorded a greater admissibility to hearsay evidence in documentary form. The distinction was virtually abandoned when the Civil Evidence Act 1968, c. 64, Pt. I, § 2, greatly broadened the admissibility of hearsay without regard to its form. Compare Stewart, Perception, Memory, and Hearsay, 1970 Utah L.Rev. 1.

14. 2 Rolle's Abr. 679, pl. 9 (1668), cited by Morgan, Jury Trials and the Exclusionary Rules of Evidence, 4 U.Chi.L.Rev. 247, 253 (1937).

15. Pointer v. Texas, 380 U.S. 400, 404 (1965); California v. Green, 399 U.S. 149, 158 (1970).

16. Rationale of Judicial Evidence, b. II, ch. IX, and b. III, ch. XX (1827) quoted 5 Wigmore, Evidence § 1367 (Chadbourn rev. 1974).

17. Coleman v. Southwick, 9 John. 50 (N.Y.1812), in 5 Wigmore, supra n. 16, § 1364 at p. 6.

18. 5 Wigmore, supra n. 16, at p. 32. Quoted with approval, California v. Green, 399 U.S. 149, 158 (1970).

19. Marshall, C. J. in Mima Queen v. Hepburn, 7 Cranch 295 (1813) and Story, J. in Ellicott v. Pearl, 10 Pet. 412, 436, 9 L.Ed. 475 (1836), both cited 5 Wigmore, supra n. 16, § 1363 at p. 11.

20. Chs. 25–33 infra; Ladd, The Hearsay We Admit, 5 Okla.L.Rev. 271 (1952). Most of the cases dealing with hearsay involve the exceptions.

21. See Annot., 104 A.L.R. 1130, 79 A.L.R.2d 890, and § 54, supra, where the matter is developed.

bility of hearsay that as we shall see has constituted one of the pressing needs for liberalization of evidence law.[22]

Few persons question the desirability of a general policy of requiring that testimony be given by witnesses in open court, under oath, and subject to cross-examination, which is the objective of the rule against hearsay. The problem area is found in the operation of the rule in excluding evidence as a means of effectuating that policy.

WESTLAW
REFERENCES

hearsay /p oath swear*** sworn /p perjur*** religious solemn!

hearsay /p purpose* reason* rationale* /s demeanor

opinion(hearsay /s absence inability lack*** not /5 cross-examin!)

digest(hearsay /s lack no* +3 challenge* except! object! protest!)

30k1050.1(10)

---

§ 246. A Definition of Hearsay[1]

A definition cannot, in a sentence or two, furnish ready answers to all the complex problems of an extensive field, such as hearsay. It can, however, furnish a helpful general focus and point of beginning, as well as a memory aid in arranging some of the solutions.

The following definition is from the Federal Rules of Evidence, in effect in about half the states as well as in the federal courts.[2]

It has, in addition, been quoted with approval or adopted outright on a case-by-case basis in states where the Federal Rules have not been adopted in their entirety,[3] and is generally consistent with the views now expressed in common law jurisdictions.[4] Federal Rule of Evidence 801 provides:

> **(a) Statement**. A "statement" is (1) an oral or written assertion or (2) nonverbal conduct of a person, if it is intended by him as an assertion.

> **(b) Declarant**. A "declarant" is a person who makes a statement.

> **(c) Hearsay**. "Hearsay" is a statement, other than one made by the declarant while testifying at the trial or hearing, offered in evidence to prove the truth of the matter asserted.

Before going into the sections of text that follow, dealing with various aspects of what is and is not hearsay, certain preliminary observations should be made.

The word "assert" appears prominently in the quoted rule but is nowhere defined. What does it mean? The contemporary dictionary meaning is to state positively or strongly, and accordingly a person may be described as being assertive. However, in the world of evidence, the word "assert" carries no connotation of being positive or strong. A favorite of writers in the field for at least a century and a half, the word simply means *to say that something is so*, e.g.

---

22. See § 325 infra. Loevinger, Facts, Evidence and Legal Proof, 9 W.Res.L.Rev. 154, 165 (1958), suggests "that there can be little utility in a class which is so broad as to include the prattling of a child and the mouthings of a drunk, the encyclical of a pope, a learned treatise, an encyclopedia article, a newspaper report, an unverified rumor from anonymous sources, an affidavit by a responsible citizen, a street corner remark, the judgment of a court . . . ."

§ 246

1. For discussions, see 5 Wigmore, Evidence § 1361 (Chadbourn rev. 1974), 6 id. § 1766 (Chadbourn rev. 1976); Maguire, The Hearsay System: Around and Through the Thicket, 14 Vand.L.Rev. 741 (1961); Morgan, Hearsay Dangers and the Application of the Hearsay Concept, 62 Harv.L.Rev. 177 (1948); Strahorn, A Reconsideration of the Hearsay Rule and Admissions, 85 U.Pa.L.Rev. 484 (1937); Tribe, Triangulating Hearsay, 87 Harv.L.Rev. 957 (1974); Weinstein, Probative

Force of Hearsay, 46 Iowa L.Rev. 331 (1961); Federal Rules of Evidence, Introductory Note: The Hearsay Problem, 28 U.S.C.A. p. 522.

Formulating definitions of hearsay has proved to be a great challenge to the writers, less so to the courts.

2. For a review of the state provisions, see Weinstein & Berger, Evidence ¶ 801(a)–(c)[02]. None varies significantly from the federal version.

3. State v. Miller, 204 N.W.2d 834 (Iowa 1973); Long v. Asphalt Paving Co., 47 N.C.App. 564, 268 S.E.2d 1 (1980).

4. Isaacson v. Obendorf, 99 Idaho 304, 581 P.2d 350 (1978); People v. Carpenter, 28 Ill.2d 116, 190 N.E.2d 738 (1963); McClain v. State, ___ Ind. ___, 410 N.E.2d 1297 (1980); People v. Edwards, 47 N.Y.2d 493, 419 N.Y.S.2d 45, 392 N.E.2d 1229 (1979); State v. Santos, ___ R.I. ___, 413 A.2d 58 (1980).

that an event happened or that a condition existed.[5]

The definition of hearsay contained in Federal Rule of Evidence 801(a)–(c), quoted above, is affirmative in form; it says that an out-of-court assertion, offered to prove the truth of the matter asserted, is hearsay. For example, witness W reports on the stand that declarant D has stated that X was driving a car at a given time and place. Proponent is trying with this evidence to prove that X did so act. The out-of-court assertion is being offered to prove the truth of the matter asserted, and by definition it is hearsay. Alternatively, if the out-of-court statement is measured against the policy underlying the hearsay rule, its evidentiary value depends upon the credibility of the declarant without the assurances of oath, presence, or cross-examination, and again the result is classification as hearsay.

The definition in the rule does not in terms say that everything not included within the definition is not hearsay. However, exclusion from the definition of everything not included within its terms, was the intended effect of the rule, according to the Advisory Committee's Notes which accompanied the rules during their submission to the public, submission to the Supreme Court, transmission to the Congress, consideration by the Congress, and eventual adoption. No challenge to this reading of the rule was offered.[6] The rule's definition must, therefore, be taken as meaning that out-of-court conduct that is not an assertion, or that,

even though assertive, is not offered to prove the truth of the matter asserted, is not hearsay. What is, or is not, an assertion thus becomes an important inquiry in some situations. Moreover, if the policy underlying the hearsay rule is stretched to include all situations where the evidentiary value of a statement depends on the credibility of an out-of-court declarant, in however slight a degree or without regard to offsetting factors, there exists the possibility of conflict between the rule's underlying policy and the definition. These matters will be considered in the sections which follow.

Not in presence of party against whom offered. A remarkably persistent bit of courthouse folklore is the practice of objecting to out-of-court statements because not made in the presence of the party against whom offered. From the foregoing discussion, the lack of relationship between this objection and the concept of hearsay is apparent.[7] The presence or absence of the party against whom an out-of-court statement is offered has significance only in a few particular situations, e.g., when a statement spoken in his presence is relied upon to charge him with notice,[8] or when failure to deny a statement spoken in his presence is the basis for claiming that he acquiesced in or adopted the statement.[9]

 **WESTLAW REFERENCES**

headnote(hearsay /s assertion* remark* statement* /s establish proof prove support % exception*)
di hearsay

---

5. This meaning appears in the Oxford Dictionary but is labeled obsolete. The meaning ascribed in the text is clear, however, from the context of the writers. Bentham, Rationale of Judicial Evidence, b. 6, c. 4 (1827); Cross on Evidence 4, 380 (3d ed. 1967, 469 (5th ed. 1979); Wigmore, supra n. 1; American Law Institute Model Code of Evidence, Rule 501. The frequency of usage of the term makes the absence of definition more noteworthy; apparently the writers have all understood what was meant. Professor Morgan did attempt a definition, Hearsay Dangers and the Application of the Hearsay Concept, 62 Harv.L.Rev. 177, 216 (1948), but the result is less helpful than his other writings.

6. This construction finds obvious reinforcement in the provision of Rule 802 that "Hearsay is not admissi-

ble . . . ." It could scarcely be contemplated that, with hearsay just having been defined in Rule 801, some different concept of hearsay is intended in Rule 802.

7. Adkins v. Brett, 184 Cal. 252, 193 P. 251 (1920); People v. Carpenter, 28 Ill.2d 116, 190 N.E.2d 738 (1963); Mason & Hengen, The Hearsay Rule in Mississippi: "Out of the Presence of the Adverse Party—In the Presence of the Adverse Party," 47 Miss.L.J. 423 (1976).

8. See § 249, infra.

9. See § 250, infra.

fed.r.evid! evid.　/3　801(c)

§ 247. Distinction Between Hearsay Rule and Rule Requiring Firsthand Knowledge

There is a rule, more ancient than the hearsay rule, and having some kinship in policy, which is to be distinguished from it. This is the rule that a witness is qualified to testify to a fact susceptible of observation, only if it appears that he had a reasonable opportunity to observe the fact.[1] Thus, if a witness testifies that on a certain day flight 450 arrived at the airport at X on time, and from his other evidence it appears that he was not in X at the time in question, and hence could only have spoken from conjecture or report of other persons, the proper objection is not hearsay but want of personal knowledge. Conversely, if the witness testifies that his brother *told* him that he came in on the flight and it arrived on time, the objection for want of knowledge of when the plane arrived is inappropriate, because the witness purports to speak from his own knowledge only of what his brother said, and as to this he presumably had knowledge. If the testimony in this latter case was offered to show the time of the plane's arrival, the appropriate objection is hearsay.[2] The distinction is one of the form of the testimony, whether the witness purports to give the facts directly upon his own credit (though it may appear later that he was speaking only

on the faith of reports from others) or whether he purports to give an account of what another has told him and this is offered to evidence the truth of the other's report. However, when it appears, either from the phrasing of his testimony or from other sources, that the witness is testifying on the basis of reports from others, though he does not in terms testify to their statements, the distinction loses much of its significance, and courts may simply apply the label "hearsay."[3]

 WESTLAW REFERENCES

absen** lack*** no*　/12　direct firsthand personal　/3 awareness kn*w* knowledge　/s　assert! statement* testif! testimony　/p　hearsay

§ 248. Instances of the Application of the Hearsay Rule

A few examples of the rejection of evidence under the general hearsay rule excluding extra-judicial assertions offered to prove the facts asserted will indicate the scope of its operation. Evidence of the following oral statements has been excluded: on the issue whether deceased had transferred his insurance to his new automobile, testimony that he said he had made the transfer;[1] to prove that veniremen had read newspaper articles, testimony of deputy sheriff that attorney said that one venireman said that other venireman had read the articles;[2] to prove that driver was driving with consent of in-

---

§ 247

1. See § 10 supra.

2. For discussion of the distinction, see 2 Wigmore, Evidence § 657 (Chadbourn rev. 1979), 5 id. §§ 1361, 1363(3) (Chadbourn rev. 1974).

3. See, e.g., United States v. Brown, 548 F.2d 1194 (5th Cir. 1977) (prosecution for preparing fraudulent income tax returns; IRS auditor testified, on basis of interviews with taxpayers, that high percentage of returns prepared by defendant overstated deductions); State v. Conway, 351 Mo. 126, 171 S.W.2d 677 (1943) (testimony of officer as to money in possession of accused when arrested, apparently based on reports of others); Capan v. Divine Providence Hospital, 270 Pa. Super. 127, 410 A.2d 1282 (1979), reversed on other grounds 287 Pa.Super. 364, 430 A.2d 647 (wife, who was not present at the time, attempted to testify that

hospital supplied physician for late husband); Robertson v. Coca Cola Bottling Co. of Walla Walla, Wash., 195 Or. 668, 247 P.2d 217 (1952) (testimony of bottling plant manager as to strength and thickness of glass in bottle based upon measurements made by third parties). When a hearsay statement is offered as coming within an exception to the hearsay rule, it is usually required that the declarant must meet the knowledge-qualification, see § 10 supra. This is sometimes confused with the hearsay objection.

§ 248

1. Carantzas v. Iowa Mutual Insurance Co., 235 F.2d 193 (5th Cir. 1956).

2. Lowell v. Daly, 148 Conn. 266, 169 A.2d 888 (1961).

sured owner, testimony that owner said after the accident that the driver had his permission;[3] in rebuttal of defense of entrapment, criminal reputation of defendant to show predisposition;[4] to show defendant's control of premises where marijuana was found, testimony of police officer that neighbors said person of same name occupied the premises.[5]

Instances of exclusion of written statements as hearsay when offered in court as evidence of their truth are likewise frequent. Thus, the following have been determined to be hearsay: written estimates of damages or cost of repairs, made by an estimator who does not appear as a witness;[6] written appraisal of stolen trailer by appraiser who did not testify;[7] invoices, bills, and receipts as independent evidence of the making of repairs, payment, and reasonableness of charges;[8] the written statement of an absent witness to an accident;[9] newspaper accounts as proof of matters of fact reported therein;[10] statements in will that testator's second wife had agreed to devise property to

his children, as proof of that agreement;[11] medical report, by a physician who did not testify, to prove that plaintiff had sustained injuries in a subsequent accident;[12] manufacturer's advertising claims as proof of reliability of "Intoximeter."[13]

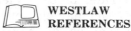

WESTLAW REFERENCES

hearsay nonhearsay /p assert! /s not /s establish
  proof prove support /s matter

§ 249. Some Out-of-Court Utterances Which Are Not Hearsay[1]

The hearsay rule forbids evidence of out-of-court assertions to prove the facts asserted in them. If the statement is not an assertion or is not offered to prove the facts asserted, it is not hearsay. A few of the more common types of nonhearsay utterances are discussed in the present section.

Verbal acts.[2] When a suit is brought for breach of a written contract, it would not occur to anyone, when a writing is offered as

---

3. Coureas v. Allstate Insurance Co., 198 Va. 77, 92 S.E.2d 378 (1956). Distinguish the speaking of words of permitting as a verbal act under § 249 infra.

4. United States v. McClain, 531 F.2d 431 (9th Cir. 1976), cert. denied 429 U.S. 835.

5. State v. Klutts, 204 Neb. 616, 284 N.W.2d 415 (1979).

6. Home Mutual Fire Insurance Co. v. Hagar, 242 Ark. 693, 415 S.W.2d 65 (1967); Alliance Mutual Casualty Co. v. Atkins, 316 S.W.2d 783 (Tex.Civ.App.1958); Miles v. New Orleans Public Service Co., 393 So.2d 877 (La.App.1981).

7. United States v. Williams, 661 F.2d 528 (5th Cir. 1981).

8. Pacific Gas & Electric Co. v. G. W. Thomas Drayage & Rigging Co., 69 Cal.2d 33, 69 Cal.Rptr. 561, 442 P.2d 641 (1968). The courts have indicated, however, that the items would be admissible to corroborate testimony. And see People v. Davis, 269 Ill. 256, 110 N.E. 9 (1915); Byalos v. Matheson, 328 Ill. 269, 159 N.E. 242 (1927), as to receipted bills.

9. Izzo v. Crowley, 157 Conn. 561, 254 A.2d 904 (1969).

10. Hickock v. Hand, 190 Kan. 224, 373 P.2d 206 (1962); Marley v. Providence Journal Co., 86 R.I. 229, 134 A.2d 180 (1957); Deramus v. Thornton, 160 Tex. 494, 333 S.W.2d 824 (1960); Annot., 55 A.L.R.3d 663.

11. Colgrove v. Goodyear, 325 Mich. 127, 37 N.W.2d 779, 10 A.L.R.2d 1029 (1949).

12. Potts v. Howser, 274 N.C. 49, 161 S.E.2d 737 (1968).

13. City of Sioux Falls v. Kohler, 80 S.D. 34, 118 N.W.2d 14 (1962).

§ 249

1. Morgan, Basic Problems of Evidence 248–253 (1962); Weinstein & Berger, Evidence ¶¶ 801(a)[01]–801(c)[01]; 6 Wigmore, Evidence § 1766 (Chadbourn rev. 1976).

2. A distinction must be drawn between objectively manifested intent or other state of mind and actual intent or other state of mind. Professor Morgan was severely critical of the terms "verbal act" and "verbal part of an act" when used to describe out-of-court statements offered as proof of the *actual* intent or other state of mind of the declarant. However, he conceded the propriety and convenience of the terms when "confined to utterances entirely without the scope of the [hearsay] rule, because not offered to prove the matter asserted in them." Morgan, A Suggested Classification of Utterances Admissible as Res Gestae, 31 Yale L.J. 229, 235 (1922). He described the verbal conduct here being considered as "Utterance[s] which are] operative fact[s]." Id. at 231. Wigmore, Evidence § 1770 (Chadbourn rev. 1976) uses the phrase "utterances forming a part of the issue." Weinstein & Berger ¶ 801(c)[01] employ the terminology here used, describing it as generally used by courts and commentators.

evidence of the contract sued on, to suggest that it is hearsay. Similarly proof of oral utterances by the parties in a contract suit constituting the offer and acceptance which brought the contract into being, are not evidence of assertions offered testimonially but rather of utterances—verbal conduct—to which the law attaches duties and liabilities.[3] Other obvious instances are evidence of the utterance by the defendant of words relied on as constituting a slander or deceit for which damages are sought. Additional cases illustrating the principle are described in the note.[4]

Verbal parts of acts.[5] The legal significance of acts taken alone and isolated from surrounding circumstances may be unclear. Thus the bare physical act of handing over money to another person is susceptible of

many interpretations. The possibilities include loan, payment of a debt, bribe, bet, gift, and no doubt many other kinds of transactions. Explanatory words which accompany and give character to the transaction are not hearsay when under the substantive law the pertinent inquiry is directed only to objective manifestations rather than to the actual intent or other state of mind of the actor.[6] Similar considerations are commonly said to prevail when the character of an establishment is sought to be proved by evidence of statements made in connection with activities taking place on the premises.[7]

Utterances and writings offered to show effect on hearer or reader.[8] When it is proved that D made a statement to X, with the purpose of showing the probable state of mind thereby induced in X, such as being

3. NLRB v. H. Koch & Sons, 578 F.2d 1287 (9th Cir. 1978); Gyro Brass Manufacturing Corp. v. United Auto Aircraft and Agricultural Implement Workers, 147 Conn. 76, 157 A.2d 241 (1959).

4. United States v. Bruner, 657 F.2d 1278 (D.C.Cir. 1981) (properly authenticated prescriptions about 5,000 in number, issued by nontestifying physician in prosecution for controlled substance conspiracy); United States v. Jones, 663 F.2d 567 (5th Cir.1981) (in prosecution for threatening court officers, threatening words were "paradigmatic nonhearsay"; United States v. Gibson, 675 F.2d 825 (6th Cir.1982) app. pndg. (a command); United States v. Gibson, 690 F.2d 697 (9th Cir. 1982), cert. denied 103 S.Ct. 1446 (fraudulent representations by defendant's salesmen); Digman v. Johnson, 18 Ill.2d 424, 164 N.E.2d 34 (1960) (agent's testimony as to principal's statement granting him authority to act as agent); Hanson v. Johnson, 161 Minn. 229, 201 N.W. 322 (1924) (spoken words constituting a partition of corn crop between landlord and tenant); Patterson-Stocking, Inc. v. Dunn Brothers Storage Warehouses, Inc., 201 Minn. 308, 276 N.W. 737 (1937) (evidence of instructions given by owner to driver, to show whether driver was acting with consent of owner at time of accident).

5. Weinstein & Berger, Evidence ¶801(c)[01]; 6 Wigmore, Evidence §§ 1772–1786 (Chadbourn rev. 1976).

6. National Bank of the Metropolis v. Kennedy, 84 U.S. (17 Wall.) 19 (1873) (conversation between parties on issue whether cashier made loan for bank or for himself); Rush v. Collins, 366 Ill. 307, 8 N.E.2d 659 (1937) (statements by party claiming prescriptive easement in alley, showing his use was adverse); In re Cronholm's Estate, 38 Ill.App.2d 141, 186 N.E.2d 534 (1962) (statement of depositor indicating lack of dona-

tive intent in establishing joint bank account); Butler v. Butler, 253 Iowa 1084, 114 N.W.2d 595 (1962) (statements showing that conveyance was in trust). See also the discussion in connection with the nebulous concept *res gestae,* infra § 288.

7. Numerous cases involve prosecutions for conducting a gambling establishment, often those accepting bets on horse races. If a person, while handing over money, says, "Here's $100. on Thunderer to show in the fourth," the words would qualify as the verbal part of an act, i.e. the act of betting. In some of the cases, police who were on the premises during a raid, answered incoming telephone calls by persons saying they wished to place specified bets. These phone calls have been classed as verbal acts. State v. Tolisano, 136 Conn. 210, 70 A.2d 118, 13 A.L.R.2d 1405 (1949); State v. Romero, 165 Conn. 239, 332 A.2d 64 (1973); Annot., 13 A.L.R.2d 1409. Morgan suggested that the "dangers of misinterpretation of this non-narrative language seems frequently not to be perceived," it being "quite possible, though perhaps highly improbable" that the caller intended something other than a bet and was using a secret code. He admitted that "it would be an extremely rare case where either counsel or court would even notice, much less discuss, such a problem." Morgan, Hearsay Dangers and the Application of the Hearsay Concept, 62 Harv.L.Rev. 177, 198 (1948). In fact, the hearsay question has been raised rather often but apparently never with success. Annot., 13 A.L.R.2d 1405.

For an alternative analytical route to classification as nonhearsay in the gambling cases, see United States v. Zenni, 492 F.Supp. 464 (E.D.Ky.1980), infra § 250, n. 19.

8. Weinstein & Berger, Evidence ¶ 801(c)[01]; 6 Wigmore, Evidence § 1789 (Chadbourn rev. 1976).

put on notice or having knowledge,[9] or motive,[10] or to show the information which X had as bearing on the reasonableness [11] or good faith or voluntariness [12] of the subsequent conduct of X, or anxiety,[13] the evidence is not subject to attack as hearsay. The same rationale applies to proof by the defendant, in cases of assault or homicide, of communicated threats made to him by the person whom he is alleged to have killed or assaulted. If offered to show his reasonable apprehension of danger it is not offered for a hearsay purpose; [14] its value for this purpose does not depend on the truth of the statement.

In the situations discussed above, as will appear from the illustrative cases cited in the notes, the out-of-court statement will frequently have an impermissible hearsay aspect as well as the permissible nonhearsay aspect. For example, the inspector's statement that the tires were defective is susceptible of being used improperly by the trier of fact as proof that the tires were in fact defective, rather than only as notice of defective condition, with other proof being required of the fact of defective condition. Or

the evidence that the man who lit the match said he was from the gas company might improperly be taken as proof of agency, rather than as a circumstance bearing on the reasonableness of plaintiff's conduct. Generally the disposition has been to admit the evidence with a limiting instruction, unless the need for the evidence for the proper purpose is substantially outweighed by the danger of improper use.[15] However, one area of apparently widespread abuse should be noted. In criminal cases, an arresting or investigating officer should not be put in the false position of seeming just to have happened upon the scene; he should be allowed some explanation of his presence and conduct. His testimony that he acted "upon information received," or words to that effect, should be sufficient.[16] Nevertheless, cases abound in which the officer is allowed to relate historical aspects of the case, replete with hearsay statements in the form of complaints and reports, on the ground that he was entitled to give the information upon which he acted.[17] The need for the evidence is slight, the likelihood of misuse great.

9. Player v. Thompson, 259 S.C. 600, 193 S.E.2d 531 (1972) (testimony that inspector said in presence of defendants that tires were defective, to prove notice of that condition).

10. Emich Motors Corp. v. General Motors Corp., 181 F.2d 70 (7th Cir.1950), reversed on other grounds 340 U.S. 558 (complaining letters from customers offered to show that cancellation of dealer's franchise was not motivated by dealer's refusal to finance car sales through defendant's finance affiliate); United States v. Cline, 570 F.2d 731 (8th Cir.1978) (threat by victim that he would turn defendant in to the U.S. marshal, to show motive for murder).

11. McAfee v. Travis Gas Corp., 137 Tex. 314, 153 S.W.2d 442 (1941) (injuries due to gas explosion which occurred when man to whom plaintiff was pointing out leaks in pipeline struck match; on issue of contributory negligence, plaintiff's testimony that man said he was from pipeline company); Johnson v. Misericordia Community Hospital, 97 Wis.2d 521, 294 N.W.2d 501 (1980) (negligent investigation of qualifications of physician granted surgical privileges; records and committee reports of other hospital not hearsay to show information available to defendant hospital). As to probable cause, see § 180 n. 8 supra.

12. United States v. Rubin, 591 F.2d 278 (5th Cir. 1979), cert. denied 444 U.S. 864 (prosecution of labor organizer for embezzling union funds by taking unau-

thorized salary increases; error to exclude testimony of defendant that union presidents told him union constitutions were flexible, offered on issue of intent); Gray v. Maxwell, 206 Neb. 385, 293 N.W.2d 90 (1980) (proper to admit evidence of telephone conversation as bearing on listener-party's voluntariness in relinquishing child).

13. Ferrara v. Galluchio, 5 N.Y.2d 16, 176 N.Y.S.2d 996, 152 N.E.2d 249 (1958) (statement to plaintiff by dermatologist that condition might become cancerous, in medical malpractice action for causing X-ray burns).

14. See § 295 infra.

15. See § 59 supra.

16. United States v. Hilliard, 569 F.2d 143 (D.C.Cir. 1977); State v. Turner, 392 So.2d 436 (La.1981); People v. Eady, 409 Mich. 356, 294 N.W.2d 202 (1980).

17. Illustrative cases are Cobb v. State, 244 Ga. 344, 260 S.E.2d 60 (1979) (officer testified to "victim's statements as to the details of the crimes and partial identification of his assailant and the getaway car"); Walters v. State, 271 Ind. 598, 394 N.E.2d 154 (1979) (murder; officer testified that victim's father said accused had a "vendetta" against the victim); State v. Thomas, 61 Ohio St.2d 223, 400 N.E.2d 401 (1980) (officer testified that he had information about a bookmaking operation in Roseville). Contra, United States v. Escobar, 674 F.2d 469 (5th Cir.1982) (error to allow

Indirect versions of hearsay statements; group statements. If the purpose of offered testimony is to use an out-of-court statement to evidence the truth of facts stated therein, the hearsay objection cannot be obviated by eliciting the purport of the statement in indirect form.[18] Thus evidence as to the purport of "information received" by the witness,[19] or testimony of the results of investigations made by other persons,[20] offered as proof of the facts asserted out of court, are properly classed as hearsay.

Whether this approach should be applied to collective or group decisions presented by the testimony of one of the group is a matter of some uncertainty. The situation most likely to arise is probably a decision reached after consultation by a group of doctors. Authority on the hearsay question is scattering.[21] In any event, the problem seems largely academic in view of the liberalization of the expert opinion rule to allow opinions to be based on reports of others [22] and of the regular entry rule to include opinions and diagnoses.[23]

Reputation. In the earlier stages of jury trial, when the jurors were expected to seek out the facts by neighborhood inquiries (instead of having the witnesses bring the facts through their testimony in court) community reputation was a frequent source of information for the jurors. When in the late 1600's the general doctrine excluding hearsay began to take form [24] the use of reputation either directly by the jurors or through the testimony of the witnesses, in certain areas of proof, was so well established that exceptions to the hearsay rule for reputation in these ancient uses soon came to be recognized.[25]

Reputation is a composite description of what the people in a community have said and are saying about a matter. A witness who testifies to reputation testifies to his generalized memory of a series of out-of-court statements. Whether reputation is hearsay depends on the same tests we have applied to evidence of other particular out-of-court statements.[26] Accordingly proof of reputation will often not be hearsay at all. Thus, in an action for defamation, where an element of damages is injury to the plaintiff's reputation, and the defendant offers on the issue of damages, evidence that the plaintiff's reputation was bad before the slander,[27] the evidence is not hearsay. Another example is proof of reputation in the community offered as evidence that some person in the community had knowledge of the reputed facts.[28]

---

officer to testify that he ran name of one defendant through computer and obtained print-out that he was "a known narcotics smuggler").

18. Falknor, "Indirect" Hearsay, 31 Tul.L.Rev. 3 (1956).

19. Hobart v. Hobart Estate Co., 26 Cal.2d 412, 159 P.2d 958 (1945) (dictum); Dougherty v. City of New York, 267 App.Div. 828, 45 N.Y.S.2d 808 (1944), and see the cases in § 248, notes 62, 65 and 66.

20. Greenland Development Corp. v. Allied Heating Products Co., 184 Va. 588, 35 S.E.2d 801, 164 A.L.R. 1312 (1945) (trial court excluded on grounds of want of knowledge and of hearsay and ruling held correct; as to which rule was applicable, the form of the testimony, not clearly disclosed, would in principle determine, see § 247, supra).

21. Bauman v. People, 130 Colo. 248, 274 P.2d 591 (1954) (staff report inadmissible hearsay); Village of Ponca v. Crawford, 18 Neb. 551, 26 N.W. 365 (1886) (consultation among independent practitioners inadmissible hearsay; Clark v. Hudson, 265 Ala. 630, 93 So.2d 138 (1957) (inadmissible hearsay, whether consultation of independent practitioners or staff, resolving conflict

in earlier decisions); Nail v. State, 231 Ark. 70, 328 S.W.2d 836 (1959), and Rodgers v. State, 261 Ark. 293, 547 S.W.2d 419 (1977) (staff report not hearsay or in violation of confrontation rights).

22. See § 15 supra.

23. See § 307 infra.

24. See § 244 supra.

25. 5 Wigmore, Evidence § 1580 (Chadbourn rev. 1974).

26. See § 246 supra.

27. As to the restrictions upon, and the allowability of the evidence under varying circumstances, see 1 Wigmore, Evidence §§ 70–76 (3d ed. 1940).

28. Lubbock Feed Lots v. Iowa Beef Processors, 630 F.2d 250 (5th Cir.1980), rehearing denied 634 F.2d 1355 (apparent agency); Otis Elevator Co. v. McLaney, 406 P.2d 7 (Alaska 1965) (knowledge of condition of elevator door); Brennan v. Mayo, Sheriff, 105 Mont. 276, 72 P.2d 463 (1937) (sheriff's knowledge of plaintiff's ownership in action for conversion by him). In these cases, an inference is required from the existence of reputation to the fact of knowledge.

Applying again the general definition we may conclude that evidence of reputation is hearsay only when offered to prove the truth of the fact reputed and hence depending for its value on the veracity of the collective asserters.[29] There are moreover, exceptions to the rule against hearsay, for reputation of particular facts, often restricted to certain uses and issues.[30]

Evidence of reputation, not falling within the established exceptions, when offered to prove the fact reputed, is constantly being excluded as hearsay,[31] as for example, when reputation is offered to prove ownership,[32] sanity,[33] the existence of a partnership,[34] or a predisposition to commit crime, to rebut a defense of entrapment.[35]

Prior statements of witnesses; admissions of party-opponents. The status of prior statements of witnesses[36] and of admissions by party-opponents[37] as hearsay is discussed in later sections.

WESTLAW REFERENCES

nonhearsay "not hearsay" /p acceptance defam! deceit offer "oral contract*" slander term*

nonhearsay "not hearsay" /p amplif! clarif! explain*** explan! verbal!

hearsay nonhearsay /p reputation

110k421(1)

Other cases inject reputation as an element of negligent failure to inquire as to matters which inquiry would have disclosed. Western Stone Co. v. Whalen, 151 Ill. 472, 38 N.E. 241 (1894) (negligence in employing incompetent servant). The reputation of a third person may be a circumstance bearing upon the reasonableness of conduct in other ways. E.g. Lopez v. Heezen, 69 N.M. 206, 365 P.2d 448 (1961) (on issue whether defendant negligently sold firearm with improperly designed safety device, good reputation of manufacturer of device properly admitted).

In general, see 2 Wigmore, Evidence §§ 249, 251–259 (Chadbourn rev. 1979).

29. Brown v. Brown, 242 Ala. 630, 7 So.2d 557 (1942); Otis Elevator Co. v. McLaney, supra n. 3; 5 Wigmore, Evidence §§ 1580, 1609 (Chadbourn rev. 1974); and see § 324 infra.

30. See § 324 infra.

31. See cases collected in Dec.Dig. Evidence ⟨322, 324.

32. Brown v. Brown, 242 Ala. 630, 7 So.2d 557 (1942); Louisville & Nashville Terminal Co. v. Jacobs, 109 Tenn. 727, 72 S.W. 954 (1903).

§ 250. Conduct as Hearsay: "Implied Assertions"

Nonverbal conduct. Thus far our examination into what is and is not hearsay has been confined to out-of-court words, either spoken or written. Under the definition in § 246, if they constitute an assertion and are offered as proof that the matter asserted happened or existed, they are hearsay.

Additional inquiry readily shows that nonverbal conduct may unmistakably be just as assertive in nature as though expressed in words. No one would contend, if, in response to a question "Who did it?," one of the auditors held up his hand, that this gesture could be treated as different from an oral or written statement. Other illustrations are the act of pointing to a particular person in a lineup as the equivalent of saying "That's the man,"[1] or the sign language used by persons with impaired speech or hearing. These are clear instances of "nonverbal conduct of a person, if it is intended by him as an assertion," which under our hearsay definition receives the same treatment as oral or written assertions. The only difference is that an oral or written asser-

33. In re Nelson's Will, 210 N.C. 398, 186 S.E. 480, 105 A.L.R. 1443 (1936) with annotation on this point.

34. Greep v. Bruns, 160 Kan. 48, 159 P.2d 803, 811 (1945); 5 Wigmore, Evidence § 1624 (Chadbourn rev. 1974).

35. United States v. McClain, 531 F.2d 431 (9th Cir. 1976), cert. denied 429 U.S. 835.

36. § 251 infra.

37. § 262 infra.

§ 250

1. United States v. Caro, 569 F.2d 411 (5th Cir.1978) (conspiracy to possess heroin; government agent testified that one defendant "pointed out" the house of his source; held hearsay).

In the most frequently encountered instance, testimony as to the making of a prior out-of-court identification by pointing or similar act, the identifier usually also testifies as a witness, thus raising the question whether prior statements by witnesses are hearsay. See § 251 infra.

tion is assumed, without further ado, to have been intended as such by virtue of being assertive in form, while in the case of the nonverbal conduct an intent to assert must be found by the judge as a precondition to classification as hearsay.

In contrast to the examples of clearly assertive nonverbal conduct given in the preceding paragraph, other situations may arise in which the conduct is just as clearly nonassertive. Thus an uncontrollable action or reaction by its very nature precludes any intent to make an assertion. Two cases will illustrate the difference. In the first, People v. Clark,[2] a murder suspect was described by witnesses as wearing a jacket with a fur-lined collar. The officer who arrested defendant at his home testified that he asked defendant if he had a jacket with a fur-lined collar, and that defendant turned to his wife and said, "I don't have one like that, do I dear?" The wife fainted. In the second case, Stevenson v. Commonwealth,[3] also a prosecution for murder, an officer testified he went to defendant's home and asked the wife for the shirt defendant was wearing when he arrived home after the time the murder was committed, and that she handed him a shirt. (Blood stains were found on the shirt.) In the first case, the conduct was

held to have been nonassertive and hence not subject to the hearsay rule, while in the second it was held that the wife intended to assert that the shirt was the one in question, and her conduct was within the hearsay rule.

The disputed area lies between these extremes.

So-called "implied assertions." In the early part of the 19th century, the celebrated case of Wright v. Tatham [4] wound its way through the English courts. John Marsden, a country gentleman, had by will left his estate to one Wright, who had risen from a menial station to the position of steward and general man of business for Marsden. The legal heir, Admiral Tatham, brought proceedings to recover the manors of the estate, alleging that Marsden was not competent to make a will. Defendant Wright, supporting the will, offered in evidence several letters that had been written to the deceased by third persons no longer living.[5] The theory of the offer was that the letters indicated a belief on the part of the writers that Marsden was mentally competent, from which it might be inferred that he was in fact competent. The letters were admitted and the will sustained. However, upon retrial after reversal, the letters were excluded, and the verdict was against the will. The

2. 6 Cal.App.3d 658, 86 Cal.Rptr. 106 (1970). It is, of course, possible that the wife feigned the fainting, or that it was genuine but caused by the general stress of the situation rather than by the reference to the jacket. These aspects are discussed at a later point in the text. Stronger instances of involuntary conduct may be Cole v. United States, 327 F.2d 360 (9th Cir. 1964) (to establish that robbery was by intimidation, testimony that bank teller was pale and shaking not hearsay); Bagwell & Stewart, Inc. v. Bennett, 214 Ga. 780, 107 S.E.2d 824 (1959) (testimony that members of family became sick and vomited because of odors of defendant's plant not hearsay).

See also People v. Gwinn, 111 Mich.App. 223, 314 N.W.2d 562 (1981) (rape victim cried upon viewing defendant's photograph).

Compare State v. Posten, 302 N.W.2d 638 (Minn. 1981) (sexual assault; proper to admit evidence that 6-year old victim had nightmares and in her sleep exclaimed, "Stop it, Ray";) and Plummer v. Ricker, 71 Vt. 114, 41 A. 1045 (1898) (damages for dog bite of child; evidence that child in sleep said, "Take him off," not admissible, though offered only to show effect on victim's nerves).

3. 218 Va. 462, 237 S.E.2d 779 (1977).

4. 7 Adolph. & E. 313, 112 Eng.Rep. 488 (Exch.Ch. 1837), and 5 Cl. & F. 136 (H.L.1838). For further details of the litigation occasioned by "Silly" Marsden's will, see the entertaining and perceptive article, Maguire, The Hearsay System: Around and Through the Thicket, 14 Vand.L.Rev. 741 (1961).

5. The letters are set out in full in 112 Eng.Rep. Repr. 490–494 (1837). One of the letters, from the Vicar of the Parish, strongly urges the testator to have his attorney meet with the attorney of the Parish, for the purpose of agreeing upon a statement of facts about some dispute between the testator and the Parish to be laid before counsel to whose opinions both sides should submit. Another is from a curate appointed by the testator, written on his resignation and expressing his gratitude and respect. Two others invite the testator to come, in company with the steward, to certain meetings to be held apparently for purposes connected with local public business or politics. A letter from a cousin describes conditions that he found on a voyage to America.

House of Lords ended eight years of litigation by upholding the ruling that the letters were inadmissible as being equivalent to hearsay evidence of the opinions of the writers. The holding was perhaps most pithily put by Baron Parke in these words:

> The conclusion at which I have arrived is, that proof of a particular fact which is not of itself a matter in issue, but which is relevant only as implying a statement or opinion of a third person on the matter in issue, is inadmissible in all cases where such a statement or opinion not on oath would be of itself inadmissible; and, therefore, in this case the letters which are offered only to prove the competence of the testator, that is the truth of the implied statements therein contained, were properly rejected, as the mere statement or opinion of the writer would certainly have been inadmissible.[6]

To describe the evidence in Wright v. Tatham as "implied statements," i.e. implied assertions, as suggested by Baron Parke is, of course, to prejudge the issue, for it is to extrajudicial assertions that the hearsay rule applies.

During the progress of the case hundreds of pages of opinions were written by the judges and numerous examples posed, including these:

(1) proof that the underwriters have paid the amount of the policy, as evidence of the loss of a ship; (2) proof of payment of a wager, as evidence of the happening of the event which was the subject of the bet; (3) precautions of the family, to show the person involved was a lunatic; (4) as evidence of sanity the election of the person in question to high office; (5) "the conduct of a physician who permitted a will to be executed by a sick testator;" (6) "the conduct of a deceased captain on a question of seaworthiness, who, after examining every part of the vessel embarked in it with his family."

Taking example (6) as an illustration, the line of reasoning suggested is (a) that the captain's conduct tends to prove that he believed the ship to be seaworthy, and (b) that from this belief the conclusion might be drawn that the ship was in fact seaworthy. This, the judges said, was the equivalent of an out-of-court statement by the captain that the ship was seaworthy and hence inadmissible hearsay. Functional equivalence can, however, be misleading. The vital element of intent to assert is missing from each of the examples.

In many of the cases after Wright v. Tatham the presence of an arguable hearsay issue went unrecognized.[7] The earlier cases tended to favor the objection,[8] but the current trend is much in the opposite direction. The Federal Rule,[9] for example, as well as numerous decisions,[10] requires that nonver-

---

6. 7 Adolph. & E. at 388, 112 Eng.Rep. at 516.

7. Falknor, The "Hear-Say" Rule as a "See-Do" Rule: Evidence of Conduct, 33 Rocky Mt.L.Rev. 133, 135 (1961).

8. Hanson v. State, 160 Ark. 329, 254 S.W. 691 (1923) (to show failing condition of bank, evidence that other banks demanded payment of collections in cash); People v. Bush, 300 Ill. 532, 133 N.E. 201 (1921) (on issue whether prosecuting witness had venereal disease, evidence that institution in which she was placed did not segregate her, as was done with venereal cases); Powell v. State, 88 Tex.Cr.R. 367, 227 S.W. 188 (1921) (to rebut claim of accused that his grandmother had authorized him to sell her cow, evidence that on her return she demanded back the cow from the purchaser).

Similarly, flight of a third person has been held to be the equivalent of a confession by him and hence inadmissible as hearsay. People v. Mendez, 193 Cal. 39, 223 P. 65 (1924); State v. Menilla, 177 Iowa 283, 158 N.W. 645 (1916). However, note should be taken of the trend to admit third-person confessions under the

hearsay exception for declarations against interest. See § 278, infra.

9. See § 246 supra.

10. State v. Izzo, 94 Ariz. 226, 383 P.2d 116 (1963) (evidence that wife did not return home night before her murder as proof of her fear of accused husband); Taylor v. Centennial Bowl, Inc., 65 Cal.2d 114, 52 Cal. Rptr. 561, 416 P.2d 793 (1966) (evidence of requests for police assistance as proof of prior disturbances on premises); Belvidere Land Co. v. Owen Park Plaza, Inc., 362 Mich. 107, 106 N.W.2d 380 (1960) (evidence of receipt of telephone calls and visitors asking for Owen Park Plaza to show confusion with Owen Park Apartments); Puget Sound Rendering, Inc. v. Puget Sound By-Products, 26 Wn.App. 724, 615 P.2d 504 (1980) (semble); Long v. Asphalt Paving Co., 47 N.C.App. 564, 268 S.E.2d 1 (1980) (issue whether North Carolina residents killed in plane crash on trip to Florida were in course of employment; evidence that they were seen walking around Florida job site).

bal conduct must be intended to be an assertion if it is to be classed as hearsay.

Is this trend consistent with the policies that underlie the hearsay rule? A satisfactory resolution can be had only by making an evaluation in terms of the dangers which the hearsay rule is designed to guard against, i.e., imperfections of perception, memory, and narration. It is believed that such an analysis can result only in rejecting the view that evidence of conduct, from which may be inferred a belief, from which in turn may be inferred the happening of the event which produced the belief, is the equivalent of an assertion that the event happened and hence hearsay. People do not, prior to raising their umbrellas, say to themselves in soliloquy form, "It is raining," nor does the motorist go forward on the green light only after making an inward assertion, "The light is green."[11] The conduct offered in the one instance to prove it was raining and in the other that the light was green, involves no intent to communicate the fact sought to be proved, and it was recognized long ago that purposeful deception is less likely in the absence of intent to communicate.[12] True, the threshold question whether communication was in fact intended may on occasion present difficulty,[13] yet the probabilities against intent are so great as to justify imposing the burden of establishing it upon the party urging the hearsay objection.[14]

Even though the risks arising from purposeful deception may be slight or nonexistent in the absence of intent to communicate, the objection remains that the actor's perception and memory are untested by cross-examination for the possibility of honest mistake. However, in contrast to the risks from purposeful deception those arising from the chance of honest mistake seem more sensibly to be factors useful in evaluating weight and credibility rather than grounds for exclusion. Moreover, the kind of situation involved is ordinarily such as either to minimize the likelihood of flaws of perception and memory or to present circumstances lending themselves to their evaluation. While the suggestion has been advanced that conduct evidence ought to be admitted only when the actor's behavior has an element of significant reliance as an assurance of trustworthiness,[15] a sufficient response here too is that the factor is one of evaluation, not a ground for exclusion.[16] Undue complication ought to be avoided in the interest of ease of application. The same can be said with respect to the possibility that the conduct may be ambiguous so that the trier of fact will draw a wrong inference.[17] Finally, a rule attaching the hearsay tag to the kind of conduct under consid-

See also the discussion of conduct as evidence of marriage, legitimacy, family history, etc., in 2 Wigmore, Evidence §§ 268–272 (Chadbourn rev. 1979).

11. The examples are from Falknor, The "Hear-Say" Rule as a "See-Do" Rule: Evidence of Conduct, 33 Rocky Mt.L.Rev. 133 (1960).

12. Seligman, An Exception to the Hearsay Rule, 26 Harv.L.Rev. 146, 148 (1912): "only conduct apparently intended to convey thought can come under the ban of the hearsay rule."

13. Finman, Implied Assertions as Hearsay: Some Criticism of the Uniform Rules of Evidence, 14 Stan.L. Rev. 682, 695 (1962). See, e.g., Norris v. Detroit United Railway, 185 Mich. 264, 151 N.W. 747 (1915) (testimony of physician that plaintiff flinched when pressure was applied to allegedly injured ankle, held hearsay).

14. Falknor, supra n. 11 at 136; Maguire, The Hearsay System: Around and Through the Thicket, 14 Vand.L.Rev. 741, 765 (1961); Advisory Committee Note, Fed.R.Evid. 801(a).

15. Varying versions are found in McCormick, The Borderland of Hearsay, 39 Yale L.J. 489, 504 (1930); Morgan, Hearsay and Non-Hearsay, 48 Harv.L.Rev. 1138, 1159 (1935); Falknor, Silence as Hearsay, 89 U.Pa.L.Rev. 192, 217 (1940). The position was essentially a transitional one, with the element of reliance being advanced as a justification for breaking away from the existing pattern of exclusion, rather than as a requirement. See n. 23 infra.

16. Morgan, Hearsay, 25 Miss.L.J. 1, 8 (1953); Falknor, The "Hear-Say" Rule as a "See-Do" Rule: Evidence of Conduct, 33 Rocky Mt.L.Rev. 133, 137 (1961).

17. Maguire, The Hearsay System: Around and Through the Thicket, 14 Vand.L.Rev. 741, 760 (1961). Compare Finman, Implied Assertions as Hearsay: Some Criticism of the Uniform Rules of Evidence, 14 Stan.L.Rev. 682, 688 (1962).

eration is bound to operate unevenly, since the possibility of a hearsay objection will more often than not simply be overlooked.[18]

Out-of-court assertions not offered to prove the truth of the matter asserted. The preceding discussion relates to hearsay aspects of nonassertive conduct. Wright v. Tatham, on which the discussion is largely based, did not, however, involve nonassertive conduct; it involved conduct that was, in a measure at least, assertive. The hearsay status of assertive conduct must now be considered. If one of the letters had said, "Marsden, you are competent to make a will," it would clearly fall within the definition of hearsay, an out-of-court assertion offered to prove the truth of the matter asserted. But that was not the case: the letters, though assertive in form, were not offered to prove the truth of what was asserted. The letter from the cousin describing conditions found on his voyage to America for example was not offered as evidence of conditions in America but as evidence that the writer believed Marsden to be of reasonable intelligence, from which belief competency might be inferred. Under these conditions, should the evidence be treated as hearsay?

The pattern of the current decisions [19] and the Federal Rules and their counterparts [20] is to answer the question in the negative: the out-of-court assertion is not hearsay if offered as proof of something other than the matter asserted. The supporting arguments, however, are somewhat less compelling than is so with respect to nonassertive conduct, since the presence of an assertion reintroduces intent as an element of risk to be considered. This risk is believed not to be of such dimension as to mandate treatment as hearsay: the intent does not embrace the inference suggested, and the likelihood of purposeful deception is accordingly lessened.

At this point it is apparent from the treatment of what is and what is not hearsay that the definition of hearsay previously advanced is less inclusive than the logical and analytical possibilities would allow. At a fairly early stage of his career, Professor Morgan, whose bright mind contributed much to the law of evidence, suggested:

> A comprehensive definition of hearsay . . . would include (1) all conduct of a person, verbal or nonverbal, intended by him to operate as an assertion when offered either to prove the truth of the matter asserted or to prove that the asserter believed the matter asserted to be true, and (2) all conduct of a person, verbal or nonverbal, not intended by him to operate as an assertion, when offered either to prove both his state of mind and the external event or condition which caused him to have that state of mind, or to prove that his state of mind was truly reflected by that conduct.[21]

Further thought and observation, however, apparently convinced him that a definition of hearsay expanded to the outer limits sug-

---

18. Falknor supra n. 16, at 137.

19. United States v. Mejias, 552 F.2d 435 (2d Cir. 1977), cert. denied 434 U.S. 847 (receipted hotel bill found in defendant's possession not hearsay for purpose of establishing connection between him and hotel); United States v. Marino, 658 F.2d 1120 (6th Cir.1981) (semble); United States v. Mazyak, 650 F.2d 788 (5th Cir.1981), cert. denied 455 U.S. 922 (letter found on vessel addressed to all four defendants and vessel, not hearsay for purpose of linking defendants with vessel and one another); United States v. Hensel, 699 F.2d 18 (1st Cir.1983), cert. denied 103 S.Ct. 2431 (drinking glass bearing defendant's nickname not hearsay for purpose of connecting him with occupants of premises where found); Wilkinson v. Service, 249 Ill. 146, 94 N.E. 50 (1911) (statements by testator that children lacked affection for him, not hearsay for purpose of showing his state of mind); Loetsch v. New York City

Omnibus Corp., 291 N.Y. 308, 52 N.E.2d 448 (1943) (action by husband for wrongful death; on issue of damages, statements in wife's will castigating husband and bequeathing him one dollar, not hearsay for purpose of showing unlikelihood of contribution by wife to support of husband; error to exclude); Long v. Asphalt Paving Co., 47 N.C.App. 564, 268 S.E.2d 1 (1980) (evidence that one employee while driving past asphalt plant near job site in Florida said to other, "That is where you can get the asphalt," not hearsay to prove they were in course of employment on plane trip from North Carolina to Florida during which both were killed).

20. See § 246 supra. The history of the development is traced in 5 Wigmore § 1362 n. 1 (Chadbourn rev. 1974).

21. Morgan, Hearsay and Non-Hearsay, 48 Harv.L. Rev. 1138, 1144 (1935).

gested by logic and analysis was undesirable, with needless complication of the hearsay rule that outweighed any supposed advantage. He first advocated removing nonassertive conduct from the hearsay definition.[22] Then he took the final step of removing from the definition assertive conduct not offered to prove the matter asserted.

The adoption of Uniform Rule 62(1) and Rule 63 defining hearsay evidence would be a boon to lawyers and judges. Rule 62(1) reads " 'Statement' means not only an oral or written expression but also non-verbal conduct of a person intended by him as a substitute for words in expressing the matter stated." And Rule 63 states: "Evidence of a statement which is made other than by a witness while testifying at the hearing offered to prove the truth of the matter asserted is hearsay." These provisions would avoid all the conflicts in the decisions where the evidence describes conduct from which a relevant inference may be drawn and where very careful analysis is required to determine whether the process of reasoning requires the trier to treat the party exhibiting the conduct as if he were testifying.[23]

One further word should be added. The decision that a given item of evidence is not hearsay, or that it is hearsay but falls within an exception to the hearsay rule, may not in every case be conclusive when the evidence is attacked as contrary to the values sought to be protected by the hearsay rule. One class of litigants, namely accused persons in criminal cases, are the objects of special solicitude. Among the rights conferred upon them by the Sixth Amendment is the right of confrontation, and though evidence may not be classed as hearsay the possibility that it may violate the right of confrontation may require further examination.[24]

Knowledge. On an issue whether a given person was alive at a particular time, evidence that he said something at the time would be proof that he was alive. Whether he said, "I am alive," or "Hi, Joe," would be immaterial; the inference of life is drawn from the fact that he spoke, not from what was said. No problem of veracity is involved. In terms of the definition of hearsay, the first statement is not offered to prove what is asserted, since that is merely coincidence; the second statement is not even an assertion. Neither is hearsay.[25]

An extension of this analysis is applicable to declarations evincing knowledge, notice, or awareness of some fact. Proof that one talks about a matter demonstrates on its face that he was conscious or aware of it, and veracity does not enter into the situation. Caution is, however, indicated, since the self-proving aspect is limited strictly to what is said. Thus, the statement, "I know geometry," establishes no more than that the speaker is aware of the term "geometry", not that he has command of that subject. On the other hand, if the statement is itself a proposition of geometry, it is self-evident that the speaker does know geometry pro tanto; whether he prefaces his statement with "I know," is immaterial.[26]

---

22. "It would be a boon to lawyers and litigants if hearsay were limited by the court to assertions, whether by words or substitutes for words, made otherwise than by a witness in the process of testifying in the instant trial or hearing. . . . It would exclude [from the definition of hearsay] evidence of a declarant's conduct offered to prove his state of mind and the facts creating that state of mind if the conduct did not consist of assertive words or symbols." Morgan, Hearsay, 25 Miss.L.J. 1, 8 (1953).

23. Morgan, Basic Problems of Evidence 253 (1962). Compare the transition apparent in Blakey, You Can Say That if You Want—The Redefinition of Hearsay in Rule 801 of the Proposed Federal Rules of Evidence, 35 Ohio St.L.J. 601 (1974), both "nonassertive acts and implied assertions" should be treated as hearsay, and Blakey, An Introduction to the Oklahoma Evidence

Code: Hearsay, 14 Tulsa L.J. 635, 681 (1979), "implied assertions" based on assertive conduct should be classed and treated as hearsay.

24. See § 252 infra.

25. State v. Peeler, 126 Ariz. 254, 614 P.2d 335 (1980) (officer's testimony that elderly victim was mentally competent following sexual assault, based on what she said, not hearsay).

26. United States v. Parry, 649 F.2d 292 (5th Cir. 1981) (defendant in narcotics prosecution claimed good faith belief that he was helping agents locate dealers; error to exclude mother's testimony that, when she asked defendant about incoming phone calls, he said they were from S., a narcotics agent with whom he was working; admissible to show knowledge of identity of caller); Borderland Coal Co. v. Kerns, 165 Ky.

When the existence of knowledge is sought to be used as the basis for a further inference, the possibility of infringing upon the hearsay rule is apparent. That possibility becomes a reality when the purpose of the evidence of knowledge is to prove the existence of the fact known. Statements of memory or belief are not generally allowed as proof of the happening of the event remembered or believed, since allowing the evidence would destroy the hearsay rule.[27] For this purpose, knowledge seems to be indistinguishable from memory and belief. There remains, however, the possibility of drawing from evidence of knowledge an inference other than the existence of the fact known.

Cases of establishing the identity of a person offer the possibility of an inference of this kind. Thus evidence that a person made statements indicating knowledge of matters likely to have been known only to X is receivable as tending to prove that he was in fact X.[28] In somewhat different vein, the often discussed case of Bridges v. State,[29] a prosecution for taking indecent liberties with a female child, involved the admissibility of evidence that the victim, in reporting the incident, gave a description of the house and its surroundings and of the room and its furnishings, where the alleged offense occurred. Other evidence showed that the description fitted the house and room where the defendant lived. While it has been suggested that the evidence depended for its value upon the observation, memory, and veracity of the child, and thus shared the hazards of hearsay,[30] the testimony nevertheless had value independently of these factors. Other witnesses had described the physical characteristics of the locale, and her testimony was not relied upon for that purpose. Once other possible sources of her knowledge were eliminated, which the court was satisfied was the case, the only remaining inference was that she had acquired that knowledge through a visit to the premises. The evidence was not within the ban of the hearsay rule.

Silence as hearsay. One aspect of the conduct-as-hearsay problem is presented by cases where a failure to speak or act is offered to support an inference that conditions were such as would not evoke speech or action in a reasonable person.[31] The cases are likely to fall into two classes: (1) evidence of absence of complaints from other customers as disproof of claimed defects of goods or food or from other persons who would have been affected as disproof of a claimed injurious event or condition,[32] and (2) evidence from members of a family that a particular

---

487, 177 S.W. 266 (1915) (declarations by foreman before accident as to incompetence of fellow servant to show knowledge by foreman and company); Annot., 141 A.L.R. 704, 713; 2 Wigmore, Evidence §§ 265, 266 (Chadbourn rev. 1979).

27. See § 296 infra.

28. Nehring v. McMurrian, 94 Tex. 45, 57 S.W. 943 (1900); Moxley's Will, 103 Vt. 100, 152 A. 713 (1931). In the famous Tichborne heirship litigation a reverse application, i.e. lack of knowledge of things that would have been known to the missing son, was used to discredit the claimant to the estate. 2 Wigmore, Evidence § 270 (Chadbourn rev. 1979); Jaffee, Son and Heir— The Story of the Tichborne Case, 21 A.B.A.J. 107 (1935).

29. 247 Wis. 350, 19 N.W.2d 529 (1945), rehearing denied 247 Wis. 350, 19 N.W.2d 862. Compare State v. Galvan, 297 N.W.2d 344 (Iowa 1980) (defendant charged with aiding and abetting murder in which victim was bound, then stabbed and bludgeoned; evidence indicated defendant's two-year old daughter was in his company during the time when the murder was committed; the disputed evidence was that two days later the child bound her own hands with a belt from her mother's robe and made gestures as though beating herself on the chest; held hearsay but admissible as part of the *res gestae*. The end result is certainly defensible but scarcely on the grounds advanced. Comment, 66 Iowa L.Rev. 985 (1981). See n. 4, § 250, supra.

30. Morgan, Evidence 1941–1945, 59 Harv.L.Rev. 481, 544 (1946).

31. Falknor, Silence as Hearsay, 89 U.Pa.L.Rev. 192 (1940), The "Hear-Say" Rule as a "See-Do" Rule, 33 Rocky Mt.L.Rev. 133, 134 (1961).

32. Cases favoring a nonhearsay classification include Cain v. George, 411 F.2d 572 (5th Cir.1969); Silver v. New York Central Railroad, 329 Mass. 14, 105 N.E.2d 923 (1952); St. Louis Southwestern Railway of Texas v. Arkansas & Texas Grain Co., 42 Tex.Civ.App. 125, 95 S.W. 656 (1906), error dismissed. Contrary, Payson v. Bombardier, Limited, 435 A.2d 411 (Me.1981) (hearsay but admissible under exception for absence of regular entry); Menard v. Cashman, 94 N.H. 428, 55

member never mentioned an event, or claim to or disposition of property, to prove nonoccurrence or nonexistence.[33] Often the presence of an arguable hearsay question is neither noted nor discussed.[34]

While the cases at common law were divided as to the hearsay status of this kind of evidence, it appears under the definition of hearsay in Section 246 supra that the evidence, not being intended as an assertion, is not hearsay.[35] It should be noted, however, that the support for admissibility, aside from any question of hearsay, may be stronger in the cases of absence of complaints than in other cases of silence. The other cases present a variety of situations which in some instances suggest motivations for silence other than nonoccurrence of the disputed event, calling for evaluation in terms of the so-called "prejudice" rule.[36]

Negative results of inquiries. Somewhat related questions arise in respect to testimony by a witness that he has made inquiries among the residents of a given place where a certain person is claimed to live, and that he has been unable to find anyone who knows him or has any information about him. When offered upon an issue as to whether due diligence has been exercised in attempting to locate a missing witness or other person, it is clear that testimony as to

the results of the inquiries is not hearsay but is merely a narration of acts and efforts showing due diligence.[37] However, the evidence of inquiries and inability to secure information may be offered as proof of the nonexistence of the person sought to be located, or of the fact that no such person lives at the place in question. Then it may be argued that this is merely an indirect way of placing in evidence the statements of those of whom inquiry was made for the purpose of proving the truth of what they asserted.[38] It is true that the residents of whom inquiry was made could be brought in to testify as to their want of knowledge but only at the price of substantial inconvenience and loss of time.[39] However, application of the hearsay definition [40] yields a satisfactory avoidance of the hearsay argument. The question asked would in essence have been, "Do you know, or have you ever heard of, a person named Tom Jones in this community?", with the answer, "No." The assertion in the answer is that the declarant has not heard of the person, but the inference suggested from the aggregate of the answers is not that the declarants had not heard of such a person, but rather that such a person does not exist. Almost all the cases have in any event ruled in favor of admitting the evidence, influenced no doubt by

A.2d 156 (1947); Leech v. Hudson & Manhattan Railroad Co., 113 N.J.Law 366, 174 A. 537 (1934), affirmed 115 N.J.Law 114, 178 A. 754; George W. Saunders Live Stock Commission Co. v. Kincaid, 168 S.W. 977 (Tex.Civ.App.1914), error dismissed. Comment, 84 Dick.L.Rev. 605 (1980); Annot., 31 A.L.R.2d 190, 230.

33. Favoring nonhearsay are Latham v. Houston Land & Trust Co., 62 S.W.2d 519 (Tex.Civ.App.1933), error dismissed; State v. Childers, 196 La. 554, 199 So. 640 (1940). Contrary Sherling v. Continental Trust Co., 175 Ga. 672, 165 S.E. 560 (1932); Lake Drainage Commissioners v. Spencer, 174 N.C. 36, 93 S.E. 435 (1917).

34. E.g., Landfield v. Albiani Lunch Co., 268 Mass. 528, 168 N.E. 160 (1929).

35. Federal Rule Evid. 803(7) treats the absence of a regular entry when one would ordinarily have been made, offered to prove the nonoccurrence of the event that would have been recorded, as an exception to the hearsay rule. The Advisory Committee's Note, however, observes that it probably is not hearsay under the Federal Rules but is included as an exception to lay at rest any question raised by cases that have held not

only that such evidence is hearsay but also that it does not fall within any exception to the hearsay rule. See § 307 infra.

36. Fed.R.Evid. 403. See § 185 supra.

37. Britton v. State, 2 Md.App. 285, 234 A.2d 274 (1967) (efforts to locate witness); Kraynick v. Nationwide Insurance Co., 72 N.J.Super. 34, 178 A.2d 50 (1962), on remand 80 N.J.Super. 296, 193 A.2d 419 (efforts to locate insured under liability policy, in support of defense of failure to cooperate); 5 Wigmore, Evidence § 1414(2) (Chadbourn rev. 1974).

Absence of tidings and inability to locate a missing person are elements of the presumption of death after absence of a person for seven years. See § 343 infra.

38. The argument was upheld in State v. Rosenthal, 123 Wis. 442, 102 N.W. 49 (1905).

39. As was done in People v. Kosearas, 410 Ill. 456, 102 N.E.2d 534 (1951), and Dunn v. State, 15 Okl.Cr. 245, 176 P. 86 (1918).

40. See § 246 supra.

considerations of convenience, probable accuracy, and the difficulties that often attend the proving of a negative, often without reference to a possible hearsay problem [41] but classifying as nonhearsay when the question is raised.[42]

Silence as an admission by a party-opponent is treated elsewhere.[43]

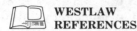

**WESTLAW
REFERENCES**

fed.r.evid! evid! /3 801(a)

hearsay /p gesture* nonverbal sign-language unspoken /p assert!

nonhearsay "not hearsay" /p inform! statement* utterance* writing* /s anxiety conduct kn*w* knowledge motiv! notice notif! reasonable!

hearsay nonhearsay /p diligence "fail*** to speak" nonexistence silence /p assert!

§ 251. Prior Statements of Witnesses as Substantive Evidence [1]

As previously observed,[2] the traditional view had been that a prior statement of a witness is hearsay if offered to prove the happening of matters asserted therein. This categorization has not, of course, precluded using the prior statement for other purposes, e.g., to impeach the witness by showing a self-contradiction if the statement is inconsistent with his testimony [3] or to support his credibility under certain circumstances when the statement was consistent with his testimony.[4] But the prior statement has been admissible as proof of matter asserted therein, i.e. as "substantive" evidence, only when falling within one of the exceptions to the hearsay rule. This position has increasingly come under attack in recent years on both logical and practical grounds.

The logic of the orthodox view is that the previous statement of the witness is hearsay since its value rests on the credit of the declarant, who, when the statement was made, was not (1) under oath, (2) in the presence of the trier, or (3) subject to cross-examination.[5]

The counter-argument goes as follows: (1) The oath is no longer a principal safeguard of the trustworthiness of testimony.[6] Affidavits, though under oath, are not exempted from the hearsay rule. Moreover, of the nu-

41. E.g., People v. Sharp, 53 Mich. 523, 19 N.W. 168 (1884).

42. State v. Wentworth, 37 N.H. 196, 200, 217 (1858) (nonexistence of person in whose company accused claimed to have been at time of crime); Thomas v. State, 54 Okl.Cr. 97, 14 P.2d 953 (1932) (nonexistence of purported drawer of check); Annot., 49 A.L.R.2d 877. In Warrick v. Giron, 290 N.W.2d 166 (Minn.1980), a medical malpractice action, defense witnesses testified that a search of textbooks and recent articles showed no evidence that the surgical procedures employed were improper; held not hearsay, not offered to prove the truth of the matter asserted in the literature.

The analogy to public opinion polls and surveys will be apparent. See § 294 infra. Compare Reputation, supra this section.

43. See the general coverage in § 270 infra, and the discussion of the particular problems of treating the silence of a criminal defendant as an admission or confession in § 161 supra.

§ 251

1. 3A Wigmore, Evidence § 1018 (Chadbourn rev. 1970), 4 id. § 1132 (1972); Weinstein & Berger, Evidence ¶¶ 801(d)(1)[01]–801(d)(1)(C)[02]; Annot., 133 A.L.R. 1454; Dec.Dig. Witnesses ⊕397.

2. See § 34 supra with respect to prior inconsistent statements, and § 49 supra as to prior consistent statements.

3. The opposite party has, of course, been entitled to a jury instruction as to the limited use of the evidence. Ritter v. People, 130 Ill. 255, 22 N.E. 605 (1889); Medlin v. County Board of Education, 167 N.C. 239, 83 S.E. 483 (1914). Failure to give the instruction, though not requested, has been held plain error. United States v. Lipscomb, 425 F.2d 226 (6th Cir.1970). Contra, State v. Ray, 259 La. 105, 249 So.2d 540 (1971).

4. See § 49 supra.

5. State v. Saporen, 205 Minn. 358, 285 N.W. 898 (1939); Ruhala v. Roby, 379 Mich. 102, 150 N.W.2d 146 (1967); Beaver and Biggs, Attending Witnesses' Prior Declarations as Evidence: Theory vs. Reality, 3 Ind. Leg.Forum 309 (1970). The Supreme Court of California used the same logic to conclude that a departure from traditional doctrine violated the Sixth Amendment right of confrontation. People v. Johnson, 68 Cal.2d 646, 68 Cal.Rptr. 599, 441 P.2d 111 (1968), cert. denied, 393 U.S. 1051, and People v. Green, 70 Cal.2d 654, 75 Cal.Rptr. 782, 451 P.2d 422 (1969). This conclusion was rejected and *Green* reversed in California v. Green, 399 U.S. 149 (1970). See also on remand, People v. Green, 3 Cal.3d 981, 92 Cal.Rptr. 494, 479 P.2d 998 (1971).

6. Morgan, Hearsay Dangers and the Application of the Hearsay Concept, 62 Harv.L.Rev. 177 (1948). See 6 Wigmore, Evidence § 1827 (Chadbourn rev. 1976) for discussions of value of oath and id. § 1831 for similar references on the efficacy of penalties for perjury.

merous exceptions where evidence is admitted despite its being hearsay, in only one instance is the out-of-court statement required to have been under oath. And that instance, namely prior testimony, may arguably be regarded as a case of nonhearsay rather than as a hearsay exception.[7]

(2) With respect to affording the trier of fact the advantage of observing the demeanor of the witness while making the statement, Judge Learned Hand's classic statement puts it:

> If, from all that the jury see of the witness, they conclude that what he says now is not the truth, but what he said before, they are none the less deciding from what they see and hear of that person and in court.[8]

(3) The principal reliance for achieving credibility is no doubt cross-examination,[9] and this condition is thought to be satisfied. As Wigmore, who originally adhered to the traditional view, expressed it:

> Here, however, by hypothesis the witness is present and subject to cross-examination. There is ample opportunity to test him as to the basis for his former statement. The whole purpose of the hearsay rule has been already satisfied.[10]

The question remains whether cross-examination in order to be effective must take place at the time when the statement is made. The opinion where the orthodox view finds its most vigorous support urges:

> The chief merit of cross-examination is not that at some future time it gives the party op-

ponent the right to dissect adverse testimony. Its principal virtue is the immediate application of the testing process. Its strokes fall while the iron is hot. False testimony is apt to harden and become unyielding to the blows of truth in proportion as the witness has opportunity for reconsideration and influence by the suggestions of others . . . .[11]

Yet the fact in the case was that the witness did change his story very substantially; rather than hardening, his testimony yielded to something between the giving of the statement and the time of testifying.[12] This appears to be so in a very high proportion of the cases, and the circumstances most frequently suggest that the "something" which caused the change was an improper influence.

An additional persuasive factor against the orthodox rule is the superior trustworthiness of earlier statements, on the basis that memory hinges on recency. The prior statement is always nearer and usually very much nearer to the event than is the testimony. The fresher the memory, the fuller and more accurate it is.[13] The requirement of the hearsay exception for memoranda of past recollection, that the matter have been recorded while fresh in memory,[14] is based precisely on this principle.

These various considerations led to a substantial movement to abandon the orthodox view completely. Thus the Model Code of Evidence provided:

---

7. See § 254 infra.

8. Di Carlo v. United States, 6 F.2d 364 (2d Cir. 1925).

9. Morgan, supra n. 6; 5 Wigmore, Evidence § 1367 (Chadbourn rev. 1974).

10. 3A Wigmore, Evidence § 1018, p. 996 (Chadbourn rev. 1970). See also Model Code of Evidence, Comment to Rule 503(b), p. 234.

11. State v. Saporen, 205 Minn. 358, 362, 285 N.W. 898, 901 (1939).

12. Both *Saporen*, supra n. 11 and Ruhala v. Roby, 379 Mich. 102, 150 N.W.2d 146 (1967), a more recent vociferous defense of the orthodox view, reveal a searching disclosure of the inconsistencies between earlier statement and testimony and of the witness' explanation of his change of position. The orthodox position was effectively demolished in California v. Green, 399 U.S. 149 (1970).

13. Stewart, Perception, Memory, and Hearsay: A Criticism of Present Law and the Proposed Federal Rules of Evidence, 1970 Utah L.Rev. 1, 8–22, discussing the characteristics of memory, with citations of numerous psychological authorities. A counter-argument which carried considerable weight when the Federal Rules were under review in the Congress, particularly in the House of Representatives, was that law enforcement officials and claim adjusters often improperly influence the making and content of statements.

14. See § 301 infra. Note also that the regularly kept records exception requires that the entry be made at or near the time of the transaction recorded. Infra § 306.

Evidence of a hearsay declaration is admissible if the judge finds that the declarant . . . is present and subject to cross-examination.[15]

Substantial support for this position began to appear in the decisions.[16]

Under the Model Code-Wigmore position, all prior statements of witnesses, regardless of their nature, were exempted from the ban of the hearsay rule. This complete rejection of the orthodox rule resulted in uneasiness that a practice might develop among lawyers whereby a carefully prepared statement would be offered in lieu of testimony, merely tendering the witness for cross-examination on the statement.[17] The practice seems not in fact to have materialized in the jurisdictions where the orthodox rule was rejected,[18] but the potential for abuse nevertheless remained. As a consequence, the Advisory Committee on Federal Rules of Evidence adopted an intermediate position, neither admitting nor rejecting prior statements of witnesses *in toto*, but exempting from classification as hearsay certain prior statements thought by circumstances to be free of the danger of abuse. The exempt statements are (A) inconsistent statements, (B) consistent statements when admissible to rebut certain attacks upon the credibility of the witness, and (C) statements of identification. Federal Rule of Evidence 801(d)(1) provides:

(d) **Statements which are not hearsay.** A statement is not hearsay if—

(1) **Prior statement by witness.** The declarant testifies at the trial or hearing and is subject to cross-examination concerning the statement, and the statement is (A) inconsistent with his testimony, and was given under oath subject to the penalty of perjury at a trial, hearing, or other proceeding, or in a deposition, or (B) consistent with his testimony and is offered to rebut an express or implied charge against him of recent fabrication or improper influence or motive, or (C) one of identification of a person made after perceiving him; . . .

(A) Prior inconsistent statements. Any abuse arising from planned use of statement in place of witness is unlikely when the statement is an inconsistent one. Moreover, the witness who has told one story aforetime and another today has opened the gates to all the vistas of truth which the common law practice of cross-examination and re-examination was invented to explore. The reasons for the change of face, whether forgetfulness, carelessness, pity, terror, or greed, may be explored by the two questioners in the presence of the trier of fact, under oath, casting light on which is the true story and which the false. It is hard to escape the view that evidence of a prior inconsistent statement, when declarant is on the stand to explain it if he can, has in high degree the safeguards of examined testimony.[19] In addition, allowing it as substantive evidence pays a further dividend in avoiding a limiting instruction quite unlikely to be heeded by a jury.

When is a prior statement inconsistent?[20] On the face of it, a prior statement describing an event would not be inconsistent with testimony by the witness that he no longer

---

15. Model Code of Evidence Rule 503(b). To the same effect was the original Uniform Rule 63(1) (1953).

16. Hobbs v. State, 359 P.2d 956 (Alaska 1961), cert. denied 367 U.S. 909; Jett v. Commonwealth, 436 S.W.2d 788 (Ky.1969); Thomas v. State, 186 Md. 446, 47 A.2d 43 (1946); Letendre v. Hartford Accident & Indemnity Co., 21 N.Y.2d 518, 289 N.Y.S.2d 183, 236 N.E.2d 467 (1968); Vance v. State, 190 Tenn. 521, 230 S.W.2d 987 (1950), cert. denied 339 U.S. 988; Gelhaar v. State, 41 Wis.2d 230, 163 N.W.2d 609 (1969). See also the discussion in United States v. De Sisto, 329 F.2d 929 (2d Cir.1964).

17. E.g. Dow, KLM v. Tuller: A New Approach to Admissibility of Prior Statements of a Witness, 41 Neb. L.Rev. 598 (1962).

18. Probably for the commonsensical reason that testimony of a live witness in the vast majority of cases will carry greater conviction than his previously prepared statement. And see Maguire, Evidence: Common Sense and Common Law 63 (1947).

19. Almost all the cases cited in n. 16 supra involved prior inconsistent statements, as did California v. Green, 399 U.S. 149 (1970), overruling the claim that admission of such evidence violated Sixth Amendment confrontation rights. For recent decisions adopting the allowance of prior inconsistent statements as substantive evidence, see Gibbons v. State, 248 Ga. 858, 286 S.E.2d 717 (1982), and State v. Copeland, ___ S.C.

20. See note 20 on page 747.

remembers the event.[21] Yet the tendency of unwilling or untruthful witnesses to seek refuge in forgetfulness is well recognized.[22] Hence the judge may be warranted in concluding under the circumstances the claimed lack of memory of the event is untrue and in effect an implied denial of the prior statement, thus qualifying it as inconsistent and nonhearsay.[23] In the absence of such a finding, the presence of inconsistency is difficult to maintain.

As originally drafted by the Advisory Committee and transmitted to the Congress by the Supreme Court, the Federal Rule contained no requirement as to the conditions under which the prior inconsistent statement must be made. The Congress, however, imposed strict limitations, adding the language "given under oath subject to the penalty of perjury [24] at a trial, hearing, or other proceeding, or in a deposition . . . ." [25] The result of the limitation is to confine substantive use of prior inconsistent statements virtually to those made in the course of judicial proceedings, including grand jury testimony,[26] although allowing use for impeachment without regard to the Congressional limitation. Where both are present in the same case, the likelihood of jury confusion is evident.

(B) Prior consistent statements. While prior consistent statements are hearsay by the traditional view and inadmissible as substantive evidence,[27] they have nevertheless been allowed a limited admissibility for the purpose of supporting the credibility of a witness, particularly to show that a witness whose testimony has allegedly been influenced told the same story before the influence was brought to bear.[28] No sound reason is apparent for denying substantive effect when the statement is otherwise admissible. The witness can be cross-examined fully. No abuse of prepared statements is evident. The attack upon the witness has opened the door. The giving of a limiting instruction is needless and useless.

(C) Statements of identification. When A testifies that on a prior occasion B pointed to the accused and said, "That's the man who robbed me," the testimony is clearly hearsay. If, however, B is present in court, testifies on the subject of identity, and is available for cross-examination, a case within the present section is presented. Similarly if B has himself testified to the prior identification. Admissibility of the prior identification in all these situations has the support of substantial authority in the cases, often without recognition of the presence of

---

__, 300 S.E.2d 63 (1982), cert. denied 103 S.Ct. 1802, reh. denied 103 S.Ct. 3099.

20. See § 34 supra, as to the requirement of inconsistency in prior statements used for impeachment.

21. E.g., People v. Sam, 71 Cal.2d 194, 77 Cal.Rptr. 804, 454 P.2d 700 (1969) (two years between event and trial).

22. 3A Wigmore, Evidence § 1043 (Chadbourn rev. 1970).

23. United States v. Insana, 423 F.2d 1165 (2d Cir. 1970), cert. denied 400 U.S. 841; California v. Green, 399 U.S. 149 (1970), on remand in People v. Green, 3 Cal.3d 981, 92 Cal.Rptr. 494, 479 P.2d 998 (1971), petition dismissed 404 U.S. 801; Vogel v. Percy, 691 F.2d 843 (7th Cir.1982); State v. Lenarchik, 74 Wis.2d 245, 247 N.W.2d 80, 99 A.L.R.3d 906 (1976); Annot., 99 A.L.R.3d 934.

24. The contention that a statement under oath was constitutionally mandated by Bridges v. Wixon, 326 U.S. 135 (1945) was laid at rest in California v. Green, 399 U.S. 149, 163 n. 15 (1970).

25. A proposal to include also a requirement that the prior statement have been subject to cross-exami-

nation was rejected. The effect was to allow use of grand jury testimony.

26. E.g., United States v. Mosley, 555 F.2d 191 (8th Cir.1977), cert. denied 434 U.S. 851, and United States v. Morgan, 555 F.2d 238 (9th Cir.1977), both allowing grand jury testimony. In United States v. Castro-Ayon, 537 F.2d 1055, 37 A.L.R.Fed. 848 (9th Cir.1976), cert. denied 429 U.S. 983, testimony given before an immigration officer during an interrogation authorized by statute was allowed as given in an "other proceeding," perhaps opening up a wide area of administrative proceedings. However, statements given to law enforcement officers generally, even under oath, do not qualify. United States v. Livingston, 661 F.2d 239 (D.C.Cir.1981); Martin v. United States, 528 F.2d 1157 (4th Cir.1975).

27. United States v. Smith, 490 F.2d 789 (D.C.Cir. 1974). See generally Travers, Prior Inconsistent Statements, 57 Neb.L.Rev. 974 (1978).

28. United States v. Shulman, 624 F.2d 384 (2d Cir. 1980). Compare United States v. Hamilton, 689 F.2d 1262 (6th Cir.1982), cert. denied 103 S.Ct. 753, 754. See generally § 49 supra.

a hearsay problem.[29] Justification is found in the unsatisfactory nature of courtroom identification [30] and the safeguards which now surround staged out-of-court identifications.[31]

The requirement of cross-examination. With respect to each of the categories of prior statements discussed above, the Federal Rule requires that declarant testify at the trial or hearing and that he be "subject to cross-examination concerning the statement . . . ." [32] The requirement that he testify appears to offer no problem, but the requirement that he be subject to cross-examination concerning the statement calls for exploration. The problem area will generally be prior inconsistent statements. As has been observed, if the witness testifies that he does not remember the event and the judge finds the asserted lack of memory to be genuine, the prior statement is not inconsistent with the testimony and does not fall within the exemption, and the question of cross-examination upon the statement is not reached.[33] If the asserted lack of memory is found to

be false under the circumstances, and the witness does not deny making the statement but offers explanation of his change of position, he may be cross-examined as to the circumstances and as to his explanation, and the cross-examination requirement is satisfied.[34] If he denies making the statement,[35] and also denies the event, it has been held that the result is more favorable to the cross-examiner than could be produced by eliciting an admission that the statement was made and an explanation of change of position, and that cross-examination requirements are satisfied.[36]

WESTLAW REFERENCES

hearsay /s witness /s previous prior +3 declaration* statement* testimony utterance*

"model code" +2 evidence /s rule +3 503

fed.r.evid! evid! /s 801(d)(1)

hearsay /p witness /s previous prior /6 conflicting contradictory differ*** inconsistent /s declaration* statement* testimony utterance*

hearsay /p witness /s previous prior /6 compatible consistent /s declaration* statement* testimony utterance*

---

29. Annot., 71 A.L.R.2d 449.

United States v. De Sisto, supra n. 21, was actually a case involving the admissibility of extrajudicial statements of identification by a witness, with the added factors that some of the statements were made before the grand jury and some at a former trial of the case.

30. 4 Wigmore, Evidence § 1130 (Chadbourn rev. 1972).

31. United States v. Wade, 388 U.S. 218 (1967); Gilbert v. California, 388 U.S. 263 (1967); Stovall v. Denno, 388 U.S. 293 (1967); §§ 124, 176 supra. Although the California Court generally condemned prior statements of witnesses as violating the right of confrontation, n. 5 supra, admissibility of a prior statement of identification was upheld in People v. Gould, 54 Cal.2d 621, 7 Cal.Rptr. 273, 354 P.2d 865 (1960). See generally Mauet, Prior Identification in Criminal Cases: Hearsay and Confrontation Issues, 24 Ariz.L.Rev. 29 (1982).

32. Fed.R.Evid. 801(d)(1). Constitutional aspects of cross-examination generally are discussed in § 252 infra.

33. Text supra at notes 20–23.

34. This was the situation in California v. Green, 399 U.S. 149 (1970), as developed on remand in People v. Green, 3 Cal.3d 981, 92 Cal.Rptr. 494, 479 P.2d 998 (1971), petition dismissed 404 U.S. 801. See also cases cited in n. 23 supra.

35. An issue as to the making of the statement is unlikely to arise under the limitations incorporated in

the Federal Rule by the Congress, elimination of such issues being the purpose of the limitations. See text supra at n. 25. Issues of this nature can arise, however, in states which have adopted the Federal Rule without the Congressional limitations, e.g. State v. Cruz, 128 Ariz. 538, 627 P.2d 689 (1981), and may require decision under Rule 403, the so-called "prejudice" rule or in terms of the sufficiency of the evidence. It has been suggested that the objective of the Congressional limitations can be achieved with a less strictly drawn provision, extending to statements in writing, or admitted by declarant to have been made, or electronically recorded. Graham, Employing Inconsistent Statements for Impeachment and as Substantive Evidence: A Critical Review and Proposed Amendments of Federal Rules of Evidence 801(d)(1)(A), 613, and 607, 75 Mich.L. Rev. 1565 (1977).

36. Nelson v. O'Neil, 402 U.S. 622 (1971). While the cross-examination question was presented as a claimed denial of confrontation rights, the result seems no less valid as a construction of the Federal Rule requirement.

For discussion of various possible situations raising the cross-examination requirement, see Weinstein & Berger, Evidence ¶ 801(d)(1)(A)[02]–[09]. Compare Bein, Prior Inconsistent Statements: The Hearsay Rule, 801(d)(1)(A) and 803(24), 26 UCLA L.Rev. 967 (1979).

hearsay /p witness /s previous prior /6 identi! /s declaration* statement* testimony utterance*

digest(hearsay /p cross-exam! /p witness /s previous prior +3 declaration* statement* testimony utterance*)

157K317(17)

---

§ 252. Constitutional Problems of Hearsay: Confrontation and Due Process [1]

A discussion of constitutional limitations upon the use of hearsay might well commence with the observation that their outline is somewhat less than clear.[2] This unclarity may be the result of choosing the Sixth Amendment to the Constitution of the United States, adopted in 1787, as the principal vehicle. The confrontation clause of the Sixth Amendment requires "that in all criminal prosecutions, the accused shall enjoy the right . . . to be confronted with the witnesses against him." Nearly every state constitution has a like provision.[3] Prior to 1965, the federal provision was not applied to the States,[4] but in that year the Supreme

Court ruled that the Fourteenth Amendment made the federal confrontation clause obligatory upon the States.[5] Consequently the emphasis in this discussion is upon the decisions of the Supreme Court of the United States.

The confrontation clause in terms is applicable only to criminal prosecutions [6] and may be invoked only by the accused. Thus it is unavailable to the prosecution in a criminal proceeding or to either party in civil litigation.[7] So basic, however, are the values thought to be served by confrontation that confrontation requirements on occasion are found constitutionally extended to persons other than the accused in a criminal case as an aspect of due process.[8]

Certain facets of the right of confrontation and the right to due process, while relevant to the values sought to be protected by the hearsay rule, do not bear directly upon it. Of these facets, one is the right of an accused to be present at every stage of his trial as an aspect of confrontation.[9] Anoth-

---

§ 252

1. See generally 5 Wigmore, Evidence §§ 1365, 1395–1400 (Chadbourn rev. 1974); Weinstein & Berger, Evidence ¶ 800[04]; Davenport, The Confrontation Clause and the Co-conspirator Exception in Criminal Prosecutions: A Functional Analysis, 85 Harv.L.Rev. 1378 (1972); Griswold, The Due Process Revolution and Confrontation, 119 U.Pa.L.Rev. 711 (1971); Mauet, Prior Identification in Criminal Cases: Hearsay and Confrontation Issues, 24 Ariz.L.Rev. 29 (1982); Natali, Green, Dutton and Chambers: Three Cases in Search of a Theory, 7 Rutgers Cam.L.J. 43 (1975); Read, The New Confrontation—Hearsay Dilemma, 45 So.Cal.L. Rev. 1 (1971); Seidelson, Hearsay Exceptions and the Sixth Amendment, 40 Geo.Wash.L.Rev. 76 (1971); Westen, The Future of Confrontation, 77 Mich.L.Rev. 1185 (1979); The Supreme Court 1970 Term, 85 Harv.L.Rev. 3, 188–199 (1971); Note, Confrontation and the Hearsay Rule, 75 Yale L.J. 1434 (1966); Dec.Dig. Criminal Law ⬳662; C.J.S. Criminal Law §§ 999–1009; Annot., 23 L.Ed.2d 853.

2. The point is illustrated by the judicial history of West's Ann.Cal.Evid.Code § 1235, exempting prior inconsistent statements of a witness from the ban of the hearsay rule. All seven members of the Supreme Court of California united in the conclusion that the admission of such testimony was in violation of the right of confrontation guaranteed by the Constitution of the United States. People v. Johnson, 68 Cal.2d 646, 68 Cal.Rptr. 599, 441 P.2d 111 (1968), cert. denied 393 U.S. 1051; People v. Green, 70 Cal.2d 654, 75 Cal.Rptr. 782, 451 P.2d 422 (1969), vacated and remanded 399 U.S.

149. In California v. Green, 399 U.S. 149 (1970), all but one of the justices of the Supreme Court of the United States agreed that the California Court was in error. See also Ohio v. Roberts, 448 U.S. 56 (1980).

3. They are collected and quoted in 5 Wigmore, Evidence § 1397 (Chadbourn rev. 1974).

4. West v. Louisiana, 194 U.S. 258 (1904). Of course, a State's interpretation of its own confrontation requirements could, and still may, result in exclusion. See, e.g., State v. Storm, 127 Mont. 414, 265 P.2d 971 (1954).

5. Pointer v. Texas, 380 U.S. 400 (1965). The decision resulted in a substantial increase in confrontation cases, which previously had been relatively infrequent.

6. An investigative proceeding may be so essentially criminal in nature as to make the clause applicable. Jenkins v. McKeithen, 395 U.S. 411 (1969) (Louisiana Labor-Management Commission charged with exposing violators of criminal laws).

7. The hearsay rule is, of course, not subject to these limitations.

8. Greene v. McElroy, 360 U.S. 474 (1959) (security clearance proceeding; alternative basis for holding); Willner v. Committee on Character and Fitness, 373 U.S. 96 (1963) (denial of admission to bar after passing examination); Rauh, Nonconfrontation in Security Cases: The Greene Decision, 45 Va.L.Rev. 1175 (1959).

9. The earlier view that a trial could never proceed in the absence of the defendant, Lewis v. United States, 146 U.S. 370 (1892), now stands substantially

er is the defense right to disclosure by the prosecution of material exculpatory evidence as an element of due process.[10] In the same vein, though ostensibly not constitutionally based, is the disclosure of prior statements of government witnesses mandated by the *Jencks* decision and the statute that it sired.[11] The right to counsel is a thread running through much of this constitutional fabric. Procedural aspects of sentencing appear to be in a state of some flux, probably long overdue in view of the great impact of sentencing upon one convicted of crime.[12]

Turning to examination of the relationship between the hearsay rule and the constitutional right of confrontation, the similarity of their underpinnings is evident.[13]

In the late 1700's when confrontation provisions were first included in American bills of rights, the general rule against hearsay had been accepted in England for a hundred years,[14] but it was equally well established that hearsay under certain circumstances might be admitted.[15] A fair appraisal may be that the purpose of the American provision was to guarantee the maintenance in criminal cases of the hard-won principle of the hearsay rule, without abandoning the accepted exceptions which had not been questioned as to fairness, but forbidding especially the practice of using depositions taken in the absence of the accused. This last was later abandoned by the English judges[16] and forbidden by statute.[17] While the Clause, as

---

modified. An accused may, whether on a theory of waiver or of forfeiture, lose the right to be present by voluntarily absenting himself after the trial has begun, Diaz v. United States, 223 U.S. 442 (1912), or by conducting himself in so disruptive a manner that the trial cannot proceed with him in the courtroom, Illinois v. Allen, 397 U.S. 337 (1970).

Whether the right of confrontation entitles an accused to be present at a view is discussed in § 216 supra.

10. Arguably at least, this right of disclosure might be based on the confrontation clause. The prototype case of Brady v. Maryland, 373 U.S. 83 (1963), was, however, decided before *Pointer*, supra n. 5, ruled that the confrontation clause applies to the States. The scope of the right is delineated in United States v. Agurs, 427 U.S. 97 (1976).

11. See § 97 supra. Semerjian, The Right of Confrontation, 55 A.B.A.J. 152 (1969), maintains that the *Jencks* disclosure is constitutionally mandated.

12. In Williams v. New York, 337 U.S. 241 (1949), overriding a jury recommendation of life imprisonment, the judge imposed the death penalty on the basis of a presentence report, disclosed only in part at the sentencing hearing. This procedure, it was held, did not violate due process and was consistent with the modern penological philosophy of fitting the punishment to the offender, not readily accomplished through open-court testimony with cross-examination. Some breaking away from this virtually total absence of procedural safeguards is apparent. In Specht v. Patterson, 386 U.S. 605 (1967), *Williams* was held inapplicable to imposing an indeterminate life sentence under the Colorado Sex Offenders Act, following a conviction of indecent liberties carrying a maximum of 10 years. The Court pointed out that sentencing under the act required new findings, bringing confrontation into play. In 1975 Federal Rule of Criminal Procedure 32(c) was amended to provide for disclosure of the presentence report, subject to certain limitations. The overwhelming importance of the sentence in capital cases has fo-

cused attention upon record showings of the bases for imposing the penalty. Gardner v. Florida, 430 U.S. 349 (1977). Limitations upon judicial discretion imposed by so-called determinate sentencing may have their procedural impact. See Crump, Determinate Sentencing: The Promises and Perils of Sentence Guidelines, 68 Ky. L.J. 1 (1979–80).

13. As to hearsay, see § 245 supra.

In Mattox v. United States, 156 U.S. 237, 242 (1895) the Court pointed out that the primary purpose of the Confrontation Clause "was to prevent depositions or *ex parte* affidavits . . . in lieu of a personal examination and cross-examination of the witness in which the accused has an opportunity, not only of testing the recollection and sifting the conscience of the witness, but of compelling him to stand face to face with the jury in order that they may look at him, and judge by his demeanor on the stand and the manner in which he gives his testimony whether he is worthy of belief."

14. See § 244, supra.

15. E.g., former testimony, Rex v. Vipont, 2 Burr. 1163, 97 Eng.Repr. 767 (1761); Rex v. Radbourne, 1 Leach C.L. 457 (1787); Rex v. Jolliffe, 4 Term R. 285, 100 Eng.Repr. 1022 (1791), all cited 15 A.L.R. 498, 500; and dying declarations, 5 Wigmore, Evidence § 1430 (Chadbourn rev. 1974); § 281, supra.

"We are bound to interpret the Constitution in the light of the law as it existed at the time it was adopted. . . . Many of its provisions in the nature of a Bill of Rights are subject to exceptions, recognized long before its adoption, and not interfering at all with its spirit. Such exceptions were obviously intended to be respected." Mattox v. United States, 156 U.S. 237, 243 (1895).

16. 5 Wigmore, Evidence § 1364(8) (Chadbourn rev. 1974); 9 Holdsworth, Hist.Eng.Law 219 (1926).

17. 11 and 12 Vict. ch. 42 (1848), known as Sir John Jervis's Act; see 1 Stephen, Hist.Crim.Law of England 220 (1883).

it appears in the Sixth Amendment, in terms makes no provision for exceptions, in fact it has not been so construed.

Unfortunately perhaps, a large portion of the confrontation cases in the Supreme Court have involved the admissibility of former testimony.[18] Emphasis in these cases has been placed upon the importance of (1) cross-examination and (2) personal presence of the witness at the trial.

(1) The right of cross-examination as evolved at common law has generally been thought to be fulfilled by affording an opportunity to cross-examine; cross-examination need not in fact take place.[19] Under the confrontation clause, the matter has been further refined. If the former testimony was given at an earlier full trial of the same case and is now offered at a retrial in place of the live testimony of the witness, who has become unavailable, mere opportunity without actual cross-examination probably suffices.[20] However, if the former testimony was given on an occasion other than a full trial, commonly a preliminary hearing, concern focuses on whether cross-examination did in fact take place and whether it was the

"equivalent of significant cross-examination." [21]

(2) Under the confrontation clause, as under the hearsay rule,[22] unavailability of the witness is a condition precedent to the admissibility of former testimony.[23] Since the fact that the witness is unavailable at the time of trial lends no added weight or credibility to his former testimony, it is apparent the requirement of unavailability is a means of effecting a policy of preferring the testimony of the witness in person at the trial over a presentation of his testimony as given on the former occasion. However, if the cross-examination requirement discussed above has been satisfied, use of the former testimony will not violate the confrontation clause if the witness is shown to be unavailable. Hence the confrontation cases have devoted considerable attention to what constitutes unavailability. In the leading case, Barber v. Page,[24] the witness, at the time of trial, was incarcerated in a federal penitentiary in an adjoining state; the prosecution made no effort to induce federal authorities to produce him. Admission of a transcript of his testimony given at the preliminary hearing was ruled error, since a good faith

---

18. Pointer v. Texas, 380 U.S. 400 (1965); Barber v. Page, 390 U.S. 719 (1968); California v. Green, 399 U.S. 149 (1970); and Ohio v. Roberts, 448 U.S. 56 (1980), all involved testimony given at the preliminary hearing of the case. Mancusi v. Stubbs, 408 U.S. 204 (1972), involved usability of a Tennessee conviction as a predicate for stiffer punishment on a New York conviction; the original Tennessee conviction had been set aside for ineffective assistance of counsel because appointed only four days before trial; retrial, with use of former testimony, resulted also in the conviction in question. United States v. Mattox, 156 U.S. 237 (1895), was a retrial of the same case, using testimony given at the original trial.

19. Supra § 19; infra § 255.

20. In *Mattox*, supra n. 18, the now deceased witnesses had in fact been "fully examined and cross-examined" at the original trial. In Ohio v. Roberts, supra n. 18, at p. 70, the Court points out that *Green*, supra n. 10, though suggesting that opportunity to cross-examine at preliminary hearing might satisfy confrontation requirements, did not in fact present the question, and the question remains open. Nevertheless, in cases where the original testimony was given at full trial and an election not to cross-examine was made under trial conditions, to hold that opportunity suffices is not unfair. See § 255 infra.

21. Ohio v. Roberts, 448 U.S. 56, 70–71 (1980). The Court amplified the quoted phrase by pointing out that counsel had at the preliminary hearing inquired into the witness's sincerity, and accuracy of perception, memory, and narration, all of which "comported" with the principal purpose of cross-examination. In *Pointer*, supra n. 18, defendant was unrepresented by counsel and made no effort himself to cross-examine at the preliminary hearing. Later use of this testimony at trial was held a violation of the right of confrontation. In *Green*, supra n. 18 at p. 165, the Court scrutinized the cross-examination at the preliminary hearing and found it sufficient. In *Mancusi*, supra n. 18, cross-examination was also found in fact to have been sufficient.

The argument that cross-examination at a preliminary hearing can never satisfy the confrontation requirement because of the limited scope and purpose of the proceeding has been rejected. Ohio v. Roberts, supra, at p. 72.

22. See § 255 infra.

23. In the *Mattox* retrial supra n. 18, as in the early former testimony cases generally, the witnesses in question had died in the interim between the two trials.

24. 390 U.S. 719 (1968).

effort to produce the witness was required but was not shown.[25]

The emphasis which cross-examination and presence of the witness have received in the former testimony cases should not be allowed to obscure the fact that in a variety of situations it has been held that out-of-court statements falling within recognized hearsay exceptions, and dispensing with cross-examination or presence or both, have been ruled not to deny confrontation rights. Included are dying declarations,[26] declarations of a coconspirator,[27] public records[28] and certificates that no such record exists,[29] recorded past recollection,[30] entries in the regular course of business,[31] excited utterances,[32] and declarations of the state of mind of the declarant.[33] On occasion State rules allowing hearsay evidence that would have been excluded under more traditional views have been held not to offend against the confrontation clause.[34] Decisions excluding evidence that qualifies under a hearsay exception are rare.[35]

Though recognizing that the hearsay rule and the confrontation clause are designed to protect similar values,[36] the Supreme Court from time to time reaffirms its position that the confrontation clause is not a mere codification of the hearsay rule.[37] Since the confrontation clause controls in not only the federal system but also those of the States, a different position would scarcely be tenable. What then are the guidelines? Eschewing generalizations, and indicating an intention to proceed on a case-by-case basis,[38] the Court has nevertheless committed itself to some broad standards, notably "indicia of reliability which have been widely viewed as determinative of whether a statement may be placed before the jury though there is no confrontation of the declarant,"[39] and to "afford the trier of fact a satisfactory basis for evaluating the truth of the prior statement".[40] The former seems to contemplate the generally accepted hearsay exceptions,[41] while the latter points to consideration of the circumstances of the particular case. In addition, the Court has recognized

---

25. More recently, the Court after detailed examination of the prosecution's efforts to secure attendance of the missing witness pronounced them adequate. Ohio v. Roberts, 448 U.S. 56 (1980). As to unavailability generally, see § 253 infra.

26. In the original appeal in Mattox v. United States, 146 U.S. 140 (1892), exclusion of a dying declaration offered by defendant was held error. In the second appeal, supra n. 18, dying declarations were used to demonstrate that both cross-examination and presence might be foregone without offending confrontation rights.

27. Delaney v. United States, 263 U.S. 586 (1924); Dutton v. Evans, 400 U.S. 74 (1970).

28. Reed v. Beto, 343 F.2d 723 (5th Cir.1965).

29. United States v. Lee, 589 F.2d 980 (9th Cir. 1979), cert. denied 444 U.S. 969.

30. United States v. Kelly, 349 F.2d 720 (2d Cir. 1965), cert. denied 384 U.S. 947.

31. United States v. Lipscomb, 435 F.2d 795 (5th Cir.1971), cert. denied 401 U.S. 980.

32. United States v. Nick, 604 F.2d 1199 (9th Cir. 1979).

33. Lenza v. Wyrick, 665 F.2d 804 (8th Cir.1981).

34. California v. Green, 399 U.S. 149 (1970) (prior inconsistent statement of witness); Dutton v. Evans, 400 U.S. 74 (1970) (greatly enlarged scope of declaration of coconspirator). In addition, the right of confrontation has been held waived and uncross-examined grand jury

testimony properly admitted against him, when defendant was responsible for the intervening death of the witness, United States v. Thevis, 665 F.2d 616 (5th Cir. 1982), cert. denied 456 U.S. 1008 or intimidated him into silence, United States v. Carlson, 547 F.2d 1346 (8th Cir.1976), cert. denied 431 U.S. 914. The government's burden of proof is by a preponderance. United States v. Mastrangelo, 693 F.2d 269 (2d Cir.1982), on remand 561 F.Supp. 1114; Steele v. Taylor, 684 F.2d 1193 (6th Cir.1982), cert. denied 103 S.Ct. 1501, rehearing denied 103 S.Ct. 2113.

35. Possible examples are Kirby v. United States, 174 U.S. 47 (1899) (error to convict of possessing stolen postage stamps when only evidence of theft was record of conviction of thieves, with which compare Federal Rule of Evidence 803(22)), and Barber v. Page, 390 U.S. 719 (1968) (requirement of unavailability in former testimony case beyond what had previously been rather widely thought to be necessary).

36. California v. Green, 399 U.S. 149, 155 (1970).

37. Stein v. New York, 346 U.S. 156, 196 (1953); California v. Green, supra n. 36, at 155.

38. Ohio v. Roberts, 448 U.S. 56, 66 n. 9 (1980).

39. Dutton v. Evans, 400 U.S. 74, 89 (1970).

40. California v. Green, supra n. 36, at 161.

41. Ohio v. Roberts, supra n. 38, at 66. "Reliability can be inferred without more in a case where the evidence falls within a firmly rooted hearsay exception."

that confrontation exceptions are not static but may be enlarged if there is no departure from the reason for the general rule.[42]

 WESTLAW REFERENCES

confront! "sixth amendment" /p hearsay nonhearsay

"sixth amendment" /p confront! cross-exam! /p equivalen** opportunity unavailability

confront! "sixth amendment" /p "business record*" coconspirator* "dying declaration*" "excited utterance*" "past recollection*" "public record*"

---

§ 253. The Hearsay Exceptions: Unavailability of the Declarant [1]

In the concluding portion of the earlier section discussing the reasons for the rule against hearsay,[2] the point was made that the difficulty with the rule lies in the procedure of excluding evidence as a means of effectuating the policy of requiring that testimony be given in open court, under oath, and subject to cross-examination. The problem arises from the wide variation in the reliability of evidence which by definition is classed as hearsay. The traditional solution has been found in recognition of numerous exceptions where it has been thought that "circumstantial guarantees of trustworthiness" [3] justified departure from the general rule excluding hearsay. These exceptions are the subjects of several of the chapters which follow.

The pattern of the exceptions as evolved by the decisional process of the common law

and generally in effect today divides the hearsay exceptions into two groups.[4] In the first, the availability or unavailability of the declarant is not a relevant factor: the exception is applied without regard to it. In the second group, a showing of unavailability is a condition precedent to applying the exception. The theory of the first group is that the out-of-court statement is at least as reliable as would be his testimony in person, so that producing him would involve pointless delay and inconvenience. The theory of the second group is that, while it would be preferable to have live testimony, if the declarant is unavailable, the out-of-court statement will be accepted.[5] The pattern to a large extent is the product of history and experience, and, as might be expected of a body of law created by deciding cases as they arose in necessarily random fashion, it is not in all respects consistent. Nevertheless, it has stood the test of time and use, and offers a substantial measure of predictability. While the number of the exceptions may at first glance appear extraordinarily complex,[6] many are encountered only rarely; the actual working collection probably numbers no more than 10 or a dozen.

The importance accorded unavailability in the scheme of hearsay exceptions requires that it be considered in some detail.

Preliminarily it may be observed that while the rather general practice is to speak loosely of unavailability of the witness, the

---

42. Snyder v. Massachusetts, 291 U.S. 97, 107 (1934).

§ 253

1. 5 Wigmore, Evidence §§ 1401–1414, 1420–1422 (Chadbourn rev. 1974); Dec.Dig. Evidence ⊙284, 576, 577, Criminal Law ⊙542, 543.

2. § 245 supra.

3. 5 Wigmore, Evidence § 1422 (Chadbourn rev. 1974).

4. See, e.g. Fed.R.Evid. 803 and 804. The requirement that a declarant have firsthand knowledge, applicable to most but not all hearsay exceptions, is discussed in § 10 supra.

5. The usual exceptions requiring a showing of unavailability are former testimony, § 255 infra; dying declarations, § 282 infra; declarations against interest,

§ 280 infra; and statements of pedigree and family history, § 322. See Fed.R.Evid. 804. After an uneasy history, unavailability has virtually disappeared as a requirement for entries in the regular course of business.

While most of the earlier cases on what constitutes unavailability involved former testimony, the increased scope of the exception for declarations against interest has shifted the flow of decisions in that direction.

For advocacy of extending the unavailability requirement to additional hearsay exceptions where not now applicable, see Stewart, Perception, Memory, and Hearsay: A Criticism of Present Law and the Proposed Federal Rules of Evidence, 1970 Utah L.Rev. 1, 25–36.

6. For example, Federal Rules Evid. 803 and 804 together include 27 specifically defined exceptions and two "residual" exceptions.

critical factor is actually the unavailability of his testimony.[7] As will be seen, the witness may be physically present in court but his testimony nevertheless unavailable. Of course if the unavailability is by procurement of the party offering the hearsay statement, the requirement ought not to be regarded as satisfied.[8]

In principle probably anything which constitutes unavailability in fact ought to be considered adequate. However, the rules have grown up around certain recurring fact situations, and the problem is therefore approached in that pattern. Depositions receive special treatment at the end of the section.

Federal Rule of Evidence 804(a) provides a convenient list of the generally recognized unavailability situations. It provides as follows: [9]

(a) Definition of Unavailability. "Unavailability as a witness" includes situations in which the declarant—

(1) is exempted by ruling of the court on the ground of privilege from testifying concerning the subject matter of his statement; or

(2) persists in refusing to testify concerning the subject matter of his statement despite an order of the court to do so; or

(3) testifies to a lack of memory of the subject matter of his statement; or

(4) is unable to be present or to testify at the hearing because of death or then existing physical or mental illness or infirmity; or

(5) is absent from the hearing and the proponent of his statement has been unable to procure his attendance (or in the case of a hearsay exception under subdivision (b)(2), (3), or (4), his attendance or testimony) by process or other reasonable means.

A declarant is not unavailable as a witness if his exemption, refusal, claim of lack of memory, inability, or absence is due to the procurement or wrongdoing of the proponent of his statement for the purpose of preventing the witness from attending or testifying.

(1) Exercise of privilege. The exercise of a privilege not to testify renders the witness unavailable to the extent of the scope of the privilege.[10]

(2) Refusal to testify. If a witness simply refuses to testify, despite the bringing to bear upon him of all appropriate judicial pressures, the conclusion that as a practical matter he is unavailable can scarcely be avoided, and that is the holding of the great weight of authority.[11]

(3) Claimed lack of memory. A claim of lack of memory made by the witness on the stand should satisfy the requirement of un-

---

7. Phillips v. Wyrick, 558 F.2d 489, 494 (8th Cir. 1977), cert. denied 434 U.S. 1088; Johnson v. People, 152 Colo. 586, 384 P.2d 454 (1963), cert. denied 376 U.S. 922; State v. Stewart, 85 Kan. 404, 116 P. 489 (1911).

8. Motes v. United States, 178 U.S. 458 (1900) (chief witness for government disappeared from custody because of extraordinary conduct of officer in charge of case, which Court charitably described as "negligent"). This is the effect of the final paragraph of Fed.R.Evid. 804(a), text infra at n. 9. The provision was held inapplicable in United States v. Seijo, 595 F.2d 116 (2d Cir. 1979) (depositions of illegal aliens who had been deported before trial used at trial), and United States v. Mathis, 550 F.2d 180 (4th Cir.1976) (witness mistakenly released from federal prison because of confusion with another prisoner of same name).

In United States v. Evans, 635 F.2d 1124 (4th Cir. 1980), cert. denied 452 U.S. 943, defendant offered his own out-of-court admission of another crime, asserting his claim of the privilege against self-incrimination as grounds of unavailability. The court found that the

statement under the circumstances did not qualify as a declaration against interest, noting but not deciding that the defendant by claiming the privilege might be procuring his own unavailability.

9. The corresponding revised Uniform Rule (1974) is to the same effect.

10. United States v. Zurosky, 614 F.2d 779 (1st Cir. 1979), cert. denied 446 U.S. 967; Phillips v. Wyrick, 558 F.2d 489 (8th Cir.1977), cert. denied 434 U.S. 1088; People v. Settles, 46 N.Y.2d 154, 412 N.Y.S.2d 874, 385 N.E.2d 612 (1978); Fed.R.Evid. 804(a)(1), text supra at n. 9; Annot., 45 A.L.R.2d 1354. As the Advisory Committee's Note points out, the requirement of a ruling by the court clearly implies that an actual claim of privilege must be made. See United States v. Pelton, 578 F.2d 701 (8th Cir.1978), cert. denied 439 U.S. 964. Compare United States v. Thomas, 571 F.2d 285 (5th Cir.1978), where declarant was a codefendant being jointly tried, who elected not to take the stand.

---

11. See note 11 on page 755.

availability.[12] If the claim is genuine, the testimony is simply unavailable by any realistic standard. The earlier cases, however, indicated concern that the claimed lack might not be genuine, particularly in former testimony cases, where the witness who learns that the adversary has discovered new fuel for cross-examination or for other reasons seeks refuge in forgetfulness.[13] This concern appears not to be well grounded, especially when the parallel to the witness who simply refuses to testify, discussed above, is noted. The witness who falsely asserts loss of memory is simply refusing to testify in a way that he hopes will avoid a collision with the judge. He is present in court, by definition, and subject to cross-examination. If his claim is false, he is in principle at least liable to contempt proceedings, though perhaps less effectively than in cases of simple refusal. The trend is to recognize asserted loss of memory as sufficient.[14] If the forgetfulness is only partial, the appropriate solution would appear to be resort to present testimony to the extent of

recollection, implementing with the hearsay testimony to the extent required.[15]

(4) Death; physical or mental illness.
Death was the form which unavailability originally assumed with most of the relevant exceptions.[16] Physical disability to attend the trial or testify is a recognized ground.[17] The relative scarcity of decisions passing upon the degree of permanency required supports the conclusion that most of the cases are handled by continuance. Some authority accepts a relatively temporary disability as sufficient.[18] The matter would appear to be appropriate generally for the exercise of discretion by the judge, with due regard for the prospects for recovery, the importance of the testimony, and the prompt administration of justice. As in criminal cases where absence is relied upon to establish unavailability of a witness against the accused,[19] a higher standard may also be required with respect to disability. Mental incapacity,[20] including failure of faculties due to disease,

---

Though no formal claim of privilege was made, the court ruled that the existence of the privilege, his right to assert it, and his unavailability were "patent."

Most of the cases involve claims of self-incrimination.

11. Annot., 92 A.L.R.3d 1138; Fed.R.Evid. 804(a)(2), text supra at n. 9. An actual order is required, United States v. Oliver, 626 F.2d 254 (2d Cir.1980), pointing out that a recalcitrant witness bent on helping a defendant by not testifying may point to the court's order as forcing him to do so.

12. Fed.R.Evid. 804(a)(3), text supra at n. 9, so provides. See McDonnell v. United States, 472 F.2d 1153 (8th Cir.1973), cert. denied 412 U.S. 942.

13. Annot., 129 A.L.R. 843.

The Report of the House Committee on the Judiciary said with respect to Federal Rule Evid. 804(a)(3) that "the Committee intends no change in existing federal law under which the court may choose to disbelieve the declarant's testimony as to his lack of memory." House Comm. on Judiciary, Fed. Rules of Evidence, H.R.Rep. 650, 93d Cong., 1st Sess., p. 15 (1973). The consequences of such belief are not explained. If the result was thought to be exclusion, it is simply contrary to the wording of the rule which operates whether the claim is true or false.

14. United States v. Garris, 616 F.2d 626 (2d Cir. 1980), cert. denied 447 U.S. 926; United States v. Palumbo, 639 F.2d 123 (3d Cir.1981), cert. denied 454 U.S. 819; United States v. Amaya, 533 F.2d 188 (5th

Cir.1976), cert. denied 429 U.S. 1101, all decided under the Federal Rule; Anderson v. Gaither, 120 Fla. 263, 162 So. 877 (1935); Commonwealth v. Graves, 484 Pa. 29, 398 A.2d 644 (1979).

15. Anderson v. Gaither, 120 Fla. 263, 162 So. 877 (1935); Commonwealth v. Graves, 484 Pa. 29, 398 A.2d 644 (1979).

16. Mattox v. United States, 156 U.S. 237 (1895). The grounds discussed in this subsection are all recognized in Fed.R.Evid. 804(a)(4), text supra at n. 9.

17. Vigoda v. Barton, 348 Mass. 478, 204 N.E.2d 441, 26 A.L.R.3d 482 (1965) (illness such as to render witness unable to travel); Norburn v. Mackie, 264 N.C. 479, 141 S.E.2d 877 (1965) (detrimental to health to appear as witness).

18. Chase v. Springvale Mills Co., 75 Me. 156 (1883); People v. Droste, 160 Mich. 66, 125 N.W. 87 (1910); Harris v. Reeves, 421 S.W.2d 689 (Tex.Civ.App.1967). Compare United States v. Faison, 679 F.2d 292 (3d Cir. 1982) (court admitted former testimony of witness in hospital following heart attack; remanded with directions to grant new trial if he would be available to testify). Contra, Peterson v. U.S., 344 F.2d 419 (5th Cir. 1965) (pregnancy not sufficient).

19. See discussion of Barber v. Page, text infra at nn. 26, 29.

20. As to mental capacity of witnesses generally, see § 62 supra. Marler v. State, 67 Ala. 55 (1880); George v. Moorhead, 399 Ill. 497, 78 N.E.2d 216 (1948).

senility, or accident,[21] is also a good ground of unavailability. Here again a substantial measure of discretion seemingly must be reposed in the trial judge.

(5) Absence. Mere absence of the declarant from the hearing, standing alone, does not establish unavailability. Under the Federal Rule,[22] the proponent of the hearsay statement must in addition show that he is unable to procure declarant's attendance (1) by process or (2) by other reasonable means. State requirements vary, especially with respect to (2). Furthermore, the requirements of the confrontation clause must be observed. (1) The relevant process is subpoena, or, in appropriate situations, writ of habeas corpus ad testificandum. If a witness is beyond the reach of process, obviously process cannot procure his attendance. Substantial differences in the reach of process exist between civil and criminal cases. For example, in the federal system service of a civil subpoena is limited to the district or any place outside the district within 100 miles of the place of hearing,[23] while a criminal subpoena may be served anywhere in the country and under some circumstances even abroad.[24] And, while in State courts process in civil cases will usually not be effective beyond State boundaries, most States have enacted the Uniform Act To Secure the Attendance of Witnesses from Without a State in Criminal Proceedings,[25] which in effect permits extradition of witnesses from another State in criminal cases. If a witness against the accused in a criminal case is within the reach of process, the prosecution must resort to process in both State and federal cases.[26] If a witness cannot be found, it is evident that resort to process cannot be effective. The proponent of the hearsay statement must, however, show that the witness cannot be found. In criminal cases, the showing required of the prosecution with regard to witnesses against the accused is strict, described as a "good-faith effort,"[27] applicable in both State and federal prosecutions. A lesser showing may be adequate as to defense witnesses in criminal cases and witnesses generally in civil cases, where confrontation requirements do not apply.[28] (2) In addition to inability to procure attendance by process, the confrontation clause requires the prosecution, before introducing a hearsay statement of the type where unavailability is required, also to show that declarant's attendance cannot be procured through good-faith efforts by other means. Here, too, the standard is strict. In Barber v. Page,[29] the confrontation clause was held to

---

21. Walden v. Sears, Roebuck & Co., 654 F.2d 443 (5th Cir.1981) (proper to admit earlier deposition of child victim who suffered memory impairment as result of bicycle accident). In United States v. Amaya, 533 F.2d 188, 191 (5th Cir.1976), cert. denied 429 U.S. 1101, the court said that impairment of memory from supervening accident need not be permanent but "only be in probability long enough so that, with proper regard to the importance of the testimony, the trial cannot be postponed."

22. Fed.R.Evid. 804(a)(5), text supra at n. 9.

23. Fed.R.Civ.P. 45(e)(1).

24. Fed.R.Crim.P. 45(e); 28 U.S.C.A. § 1783.

25. 11 U.L.A. 1.

26. Barber v. Page, 390 U.S. 719 (1968).

27. Ohio v. Roberts, 448 U.S. 56, 74 (1980). The witness, soon after testifying at the preliminary hearing, had left her Ohio apartment about a year before the trial. The prosecution issued five subpoenas to her at her parents' home, also in Ohio, without service. Her parents had talked by telephone with her through contact established via a social worker in San Francisco, about a year before trial. She called her parents by telephone and said she was traveling outside Ohio, but did not say where she was traveling or the place from which she was calling. No member of the family knew where she was. The prosecution did not attempt to telephone the social worker. On these facts, the Court held that the prosecution had satisfied the good-faith effort requirement, saying that "the great improbability" that attempting to locate the social worker would have resulted in locating the witness "neutralizes any intimation that a concept of reasonableness" required that it be done. 448 U.S. at p. 76.

28. Many cases are cited in 5 Wigmore § 1405 (Chadbourn rev. 1974), but most are criminal cases decided prior to Barber v. Page, supra n. 27. In Perricone v. Kansas City Southern Railway Co., 630 F.2d 317 (5th Cir.1980), appeal after remand 704 F.2d 1376, no subpoena was issued; a telephone call to the directory listing of the witness would have reached a recording with his new number; and after verdict, within two hours defendant's investigator found the witness working about a mile from the courthouse. Admission of the former testimony of the witness was held without sufficient predicate.

29. Supra n. 26.

require a State prosecutor, before using at trial the preliminary hearing testimony of a witness presently incarcerated in a federal penitentiary in an adjoining State, to take appropriate steps to induce the federal authorities to produce him at the trial. When the witness is beyond the reach of process for reasons other than imprisonment, the least that would seem to satisfy confrontation requirements would be a request to appear, with reimbursement for travel and subsistence expenses.[30] When the confrontation clause does not apply, i.e. civil cases and defense witnesses in criminal cases, the authorities are divided as to whether attempts must be made to induce the witness to attend voluntarily. Some authorities, including the Federal Rule, require an effort

through reasonable means.[31] Others require no more than a showing that the witness is beyond the reach of process.[32]

When absence is relied upon as grounds of unavailability, some jurisdictions impose a further requirement that inability to take the deposition of the missing witness also be shown.[33]

Depositions.[34] Unavailability may appear as a requirement at two different stages in connection with depositions: (1) the right to take a deposition at all may be subject to certain conditions, of which the most common is unavailability to testify at the trial,[35] or (2) the right to use a deposition at the trial in place of the personal appearance of the deponent is usually conditioned upon his unavailability.[36] The matter is largely gov-

---

30. Nevertheless, in Mancusi v. Stubbs, 408 U.S. 204 (1972), the Court ruled that permanent residence in a foreign country was a sufficient showing that the witness was beyond the reach of process and that efforts to induce him to return voluntarily to testify in a State trial need not be shown. The result may well have been influenced by the fact that the disputed former testimony had been used in a Tennessee trial resulting in a murder conviction which New York sought to use as the predicate for stiffer punishment for a New York conviction; it was not used in New York on the issue of guilt.

31. Ibanez v. Wilson, 222 Mass. 129, 109 N.E. 814 (1915); see Ben Realty Co. v. Gothberg, 56 Wyo. 294, 109 P.2d 455 (1941); Fed.R.Evid. 804(a)(5), text supra at n. 9.

32. Wolski v. National Life & Acc. Ins. Co., 135 Neb. 643, 283 N.W. 381 (1939) (decided before local adoption of Federal Rules); Healy v. Rennert, 9 N.Y.2d 202, 213 N.Y.S.2d 44, 173 N.E.2d 777 (1961).

If the witness was legally competent at the time his former testimony was given, but becomes incompetent before trial, as by death of the adverse party under a Dead Man statute, the unavailability requirement has been held satisfied. Habig v. Bastian, 117 Fla. 864, 158 So. 508 (1935). See 5 Wigmore, Evidence § 1409 (Chadbourn rev. 1974). Since the Federal Rules as promulgated by the Supreme Court contained no provision on legal incompetency of this kind, no provision was made for supervening disqualification, nor is any now included. The question may arise in diversity cases under Rule 601 as revised by the Congress. Recognition of supervening disqualification as unavailability would be in accord with the spirit of the Federal Rules.

33. Fed.R.Evid. 804(a)(5) imposes the requirement except as to former testimony. Despite the similarity of former testimony and depositions, some jurisdictions have imposed the deposition requirement without ex-

cepting former testimony. Brownlie v. Brownlie, 351 Ill. 72, 183 N.E. 613 (1932). The Federal Rules as promulgated by the Supreme Court had no deposition requirement. It was added at the insistence of the House of Representatives over the objection of the Senate Committee on the Judiciary that it was needless, impractical, highly restrictive, expensive, and time-consuming. Senate Comm. on Judiciary, Fed. Rules of Evidence, S.Rep. No. 1277, 93d Cong., 2d Sess., p. 20 (1974); H.R.Fed.Rules of Evidence, Conf. Rep. No. 1597, 93d Cong., 2d Sess., p. 12 (1974).

34. 5 Wigmore, Evidence §§ 1411, 1415, 1416 (Chadbourn rev. 1974); 23 Am.Jur.2d Depositions §§ 7, 11, 112–120, 311; C.J.S. Depositions §§ 9–16, 92(2).

35. For state statutes and rules containing such restrictions in both civil and criminal cases, see 5 Wigmore, Evidence § 1411 (Chadbourn rev. 1974).

Restrictions on the right to take a deposition lose their significance and tend to disappear as emphasis on depositions shifts away from use at trial as a substitute for testimony by the deponent in person to such other uses as discovery and obtaining statements with a view to impeachment or introduction as an admission of a party-opponent. Thus no general restrictions upon the right to take depositions are imposed by the Federal Rules of Civil Procedure and State rules patterned upon them, although judicial restraints may be imposed in exceptional situations. See F.R.Civ.P. 26(c), 30(d).

36. E.g., F.R.Civ.P. 32(a)(3):

The deposition of a witness, whether or not a party, may be used by any party for any purpose if the court finds: (A) that the witness is dead; or (B) that the witness is at a greater distance than 100 miles from the place of trial or hearing, or is out of the United States, unless it appears that the absence of the witness was procured by the party offering the deposition; or (C) that the witness is unable to attend

erned by statute or rule, and those in force locally should be consulted.[37]

The use of depositions in criminal cases requires particular consideration in view of the higher standards of confrontation applicable to evidence presented against an accused. Legislation providing for depositions in criminal cases, sometimes by express constitutional sanction, is in effect in a number of jurisdictions.[38] No constitutional problems are apparent when the deposition is to be taken and used by the accused.[39] When, however, the deposition is to be used *against* the accused, it seems evident that the unavailability standards of Barber v. Page,[40] previously discussed in this section,

or testify because of age, sickness, infirmity, or imprisonment; or (D) that the party offering the deposition has been unable to procure the attendance of the witness by subpoena; or (E) upon application and notice, that such exceptional circumstances exist as to make it desirable, in the interest of justice and with due regard to the importance of presenting the testimony of witnesses orally in open court, to allow the deposition to be used.

The high degree of similarity between the foregoing specifications of what satisfies unavailability and those for hearsay discussed earlier in this section is of course, evident.

37. See statutes and rules collected in 5 Wigmore, Evidence § 1411 (Chadbourn rev. 1974).

38. See 5 Wigmore, Evidence §§ 1398, n. 6, 1411 (Chadbourn rev. 1974).

39. Under Fed.R.Crim.P. 15(a) the taking of depositions by either side remains limited:

(a) **When taken.** Whenever due to exceptional circumstances of the case it is in the interest of justice that the testimony of a prospective witness of a party be taken and preserved for use at trial . . . .

Their use at trial, under Fed.R.Crim.P. 15(e), is also more restricted than in civil cases:

(e) **Use.** At the trial or upon any hearing, a part or all of a deposition, so far as otherwise admissible under the rules of evidence, may be used as substantive evidence if the witness is unavailable, as unavailability is defined in Rule 804(a) of the Federal Rules of Evidence, or the witness gives testimony at the trial or hearing inconsistent with his deposition. Any deposition may also be used by any party for the purpose of contradicting or impeaching the testimony of the deponent as a witness. . . .

Compare n. 36 supra.

are applicable.[41] If these standards are met, there must, of course, be meaningful opportunity to confront and cross-examine, with its concomitant right to counsel, when the deposition is taken.[42]

 WESTLAW REFERENCES

declarant* witness** /p unavailab! "not available" /p memory privilege refus*** self-incriminat***

declarant* witness** /s unavailab! "not available" /s death disabilit*** disease* illness** incapacit! insan***

declarant* witness** /s unavailab! "not available" /s effort "good faith" locat*** process subpoena

declarant* witness** /s unavailab! "not available" /s deposition*

fed.r.evid! evid! /3 804(a)

40. Supra nn. 26, 29.

41. Fed.R.Crim.P. 15(c) provides:

(c) **Payment of expenses.** Whenever a deposition is taken at the instance of the government, or whenever a deposition is taken at the instance of a defendant who is unable to bear the expenses of the taking of the deposition, the court may direct that the expense of travel and subsistence of the defendant and his attorney for attendance at the examination and the cost of the transcript of the deposition shall be paid by the government.

In United States v. King, 552 F.2d 833, 41 A.L.R.Fed. 735 (9th Cir.1976), cert. denied 430 U.S. 966, the Government took the depositions of two witnesses who were incarcerated in a Japanese prison. Defendants, on bail, and their attorneys attended at government expense. In the course of the depositions, defendants and counsel withdrew, complaining of the strict security measures imposed by the Japanese government, and the taking proceeded without them. The court found no infringement of constitutional rights.

42. In United States v. Benfield, 593 F.2d 815 (8th Cir.1979), on testimony by a psychiatrist that the victim of a kidnapping should not be subjected to stress, the judge ordered a motion of the Government that her deposition be taken. The deposition was videotaped, with accused observing on a monitor in another room, unknown to the witness, and a buzzer for accused to sound when he wished to consult with counsel. The court ruled that the confrontation rights of accused had been violated, pointing out that his role was essentially that of accessory after the fact and that he had neither threatened nor harmed the witness. Compare Kansas City v. McCoy, 525 S.W.2d 336, 80 A.L.R.3d 1203 (Mo.1975), permitting an expert for the city to give his testimony via closed circuit television in ordinance violation prosecution. Annot., 80 A.L.R.3d 1212.

Chapter 25

TESTIMONY TAKEN AT A FORMER HEARING OR IN ANOTHER ACTION [1]

Table of Sections

---

§ 254. Introductory: Is It Hearsay? Scope of Statutes and Rules

Upon compliance with requirements which are designed to guarantee an adequate opportunity of cross-examination, plus showing that the witness is unavailable, evidence may be received in the pending case, in the form of a written transcript or an oral report, of a witness's previous testimony. This testimony may have been given by deposition or at a trial, either in a separate case or proceeding, or in a former hearing of the present pending case.[2] Usually called "former testimony", this evidence may be classified, depending upon the precise formulation of the rule against hearsay, as an exception to the hearsay prohibition on the one hand, or as a class of evidence where the requirements of the hearsay rule are complied with, on the other. The former view is accepted generally by the courts,[3] rules,[4] and textwriters,[5] the latter was espoused by Wig-

---

1. See 5 Wigmore, Evidence §§ 1370, 1371, 1386–1389 (requirements of adequate opportunity to cross-examine); §§ 1402–1415 (unavailability of witness); §§ 1660–1669 (Chadbourn rev. 1974) (proof by official notes, records, reports, etc.); Weinstein & Berger, Evidence ¶ 804(b)(1)[01]–[06]; Falknor, Former Testimony and the Uniform Rules: A Comment, 38 N.Y.U.L.Rev. 651 (1963); Hinton, Changes in Hearsay Exceptions, 29 Ill.L.Rev. 422, 427 (1934); Martin, The Former—Testimony Exception in the Proposed Federal Rules of Evidence, 57 Iowa L.Rev. 547 (1972).

See also Dec.Dig. Evidence ⊚⟞575–583, Criminal Law ⊚⟞540–548; C.J.S. Evidence §§ 384–402; Annots., 15

A.L.R. 495, 79 id. 1392, 122 id. 425, 159 id. 1240, 159 id. 119.

§ 254

2. For opinions stating the common law rule, see, e.g., Gaines v. Thomas, 241 S.C. 412, 128 S.E.2d 692 (1962); State v. Carr, 67 S.D. 481, 294 N.W. 174 (1940); State v. Ortego, 22 Wn.2d 552, 157 P.2d 320 (1945).

3. George v. Davie, 201 Ark. 470, 145 S.W.2d 729 (1941); Walker v. Walker, 14 Ga. 242, 249 (1853);

4, 5. See notes 4 & 5 on page 760.

more.[6] The present work adheres to the former classification by adopting a definition of hearsay which would include all testimony given by deposition or at a previous trial or hearing, in the present or another litigation, provided it is now offered as evidence of the facts testified to.[7] Cross-examination, oath, the solemnity of the occasion, and in the case of transcribed testimony the accuracy of reproduction of the words spoken, all combine to give former testimony a high degree of credibility. To allow its use, then, only upon a showing of unavailability may seem to relegate it to an undeserved second class status. The result is, however, explainable in terms of the great significance traditionally attached to having the witness present in open court.

Many of the exceptions to the hearsay rule have been developed almost solely through the judicial process; others have been widely regulated by statute, and the present exception is of the latter class. It will be impossible in this brief work to describe the variations in the statutes of the different states. The usual approach, however, has been that these statutes on former testimony are "declaratory" of the common law, so far as they go, and not the exclusive test of admissibility. Accordingly, if the evidence meets the common law requirements, it will usually come in even though the permissive provisions of the statute do not mention the particular common law doctrine which the evidence satisfies,[8] and correspondingly when the common law imposes a restriction not mentioned in the statute, the restriction has been said to govern, unless the circumstances show a legislative intention to abrogate it.[9]

In some instances these statutes have been replaced by Federal and Revised Uniform Evidence Rule (1974) 804(b)(1), which is in effect in many jurisdictions and provides:

(b) **Hearsay exceptions.** The following are not excluded by the hearsay rule if the declarant is unavailable as a witness:

(1) **Former testimony.** Testimony given as a witness at another hearing of the same or a different proceeding, or in a deposition taken in compliance with law in the course of the same or another proceeding, if the party against whom the testimony is now offered, or, in a civil action or proceeding, a predecessor in interest, had an opportunity and similar motive to develop the testimony by direct, cross, or redirect examination.

It is important to notice at the outset that former testimony may often be given in evidence without meeting the requirements discussed in this chapter such as identity of parties and issues and unavailability of the witness. These requirements are applicable only when admission of the evidence is

Gaines v. Thomas, 241 S.C. 412, 128 S.E.2d 692 (1962); Lone Star Gas Co. v. State, 137 Tex. 279, 153 S.W.2d 681 (1941).

4. See, e.g., Fed.R.Evid. and Rev. Uniform R.Evid. (1974) 804(b)(1), infra text at n. 9.

5. See, e.g., Cross, Evidence 568 (5th ed. 1979); 1 Greenleaf, Evidence § 163 (3d ed. 1846); 3 Jones, Evidence § 308 (5th ed. 1958); Morgan, Basic Problems of Evidence 255 (1962).

6. 5 Wigmore, Evidence § 1370 (Chadbourn rev. 1974). This view has occasionally been approved by the courts, see, e.g., Habig v. Bastian, 117 Fla. 864, 158 So. 508, 510 (1935); Garner v. Pennsylvania Public Utilities Com'n, 177 Pa.Super. 439, 110 A.2d 907 (1955), and has been adopted by other textwriters, e.g. Chamberlayne, Trial Evidence § 729 (2d ed. by Tompkins, 1936).

7. See § 246 supra.

8. In re White's Will, 2 N.Y.2d 309, 141 N.E.2d 416, 160 N.Y.S.2d 841 (1957), (testimony given in lunacy

proceeding held admissible in proceeding to contest lunatic's will, under statute declaring former testimony admissible if subject matter and parties are the same); State v. Ham, 224 N.C. 128, 29 S.E.2d 449 (1944) (statute making testimony on preliminary hearing admissible when subscribed and certified does not limit admission under common law practice where stenographer swears report accurate, though not subscribed or certified). Contra, Tom Reed Gold Mining Co. v. Moore, 40 Ariz. 174, 11 P.2d 347 (1932).

9. Illinois Steel Co. v. Muza, 164 Wis. 247, 159 N.W. 908 (1916) (Wis.St.Ann. 325.31 providing for admission of former testimony "where the party against whom it is offered shall have had an opportunity to cross-examine" is declaratory of common law and hence is qualified by condition that the opportunity to cross-examine must be on substantially the same issues). Federal Rules are now in effect in Wisconsin.

sought under this particular exception. When the former testimony is offered for some nonhearsay purpose,[10] as to show the commission of the act of perjury,[11] or to show that the witness by testifying adversely to the accused furnished the motive for the murder of the witness,[12] or to refresh recollection, or impeach a witness at the present trial by proving that he testified differently on a former occasion,[13] the restrictions of the hearsay exception do not apply. Likewise, if offered for a hearsay purpose but under some other exception, e.g., as the admission of a party-opponent,[14] or past recollection recorded,[15] only the requirements of the exception under which it is offered, and not those of the present exception need be satisfied.

 **WESTLAW REFERENCES**

deposition* testif! testimony /10 former previous prior /10 case* hearing* proceeding* /s hearsay

10. See 5 Wigmore, Evidence § 1387, notes 5–7 (Chadbourn rev. 1974).

11. See State v. Wykert, 198 Iowa 1219, 199 N.W. 331 (1924) where admissibility for this purpose is assumed, and where proof of former testimony of other witnesses to show the materiality of the perjured testimony is also sanctioned.

12. Suggested by the facts in Nordan v. State, 143 Ala. 13, 39 So. 406 (1905) though the opinion does not quite reach this point.

13. People v. Ferraro, 293 N.Y. 51, 55 N.E.2d 861 (1944). See also People v. Hawley, 111 Calif. 78, 43 P. 404 (1896) (testimony of accused at preliminary hearing admissible to impeach: it seems that it would have been as readily receivable as an admission).

Use of depositions to impeach or contradict the deponent's testimony as a witness is provided under F.R. Civ.P. 32(a)(1) and F.R.Crim.P. 15(e).

14. Bogie v. Nolan, 96 Mo. 85, 9 S.W. 14 (1888); Tuttle v. Wyman, 146 Neb. 146, 18 N.W.2d 744 (1945). See 5 Wigmore, Evidence, § 1416(1) (Chadbourn rev. 1974). As to depositions, see F.R.Civ.P. 32(a)(2).

15. State v. Hacker, 177 N.J.Super. 533, 427 A.2d 109 (1981).

§ 255

1. While it has been held that predicate for admission of former testimony is not laid without an affirmative showing that the witness was sworn, Monahan v. Clemons, 212 Ky. 504, 508, 279 S.W. 974 (1926); Jolly v. State, 269 So.2d 650 (Miss.1972), the preferable view is that evidence that the witness testified justifies an inference that he was sworn. Poe v. State, 95 Ark.

fed.r.evid! evid! /3 804(b)(1)

§ 255. The Requirement of Oath and Opportunity for Cross-Examination: Confrontation and Unavailability.

The former testimony, to be admitted under this exception to the hearsay rule, must have been given under the sanction of the oath [1] or such form of affirmation as is accepted as legally sufficient. More important, and more often drawn in question, is the requirement that the party against whom the former testimony is now offered, or a party in like interest, must have had a reasonable opportunity to cross-examine.[2] Actual cross-examination, of course, is not essential, if the opportunity was afforded and waived.[3] The opportunity must have been such as to render the conduct of the cross-examination or the decision not to cross-examine meaningful in the light of the

172, 129 S.W. 292 (1910); Meyers v. State, 112 Neb. 149, 198 N.W. 871 (1924); Keith v. State, 53 Ohio App. 58, 4 N.E.2d 220 (1936).

2. United States v. Jones, 402 F.2d 851 (2d Cir. 1968), and Young v. United States, 132 U.S.App.D.C. 142, 406 F.2d 960 (1968) (testimony given by witnesses before grand jury not admissible against accused); Fender v. Ramsey, 131 Ga. 440, 62 S.E. 527 (1908) (ex parte affidavit used in former trial inadmissible); Edgerley v. Appleyard, 110 Me. 337, 86 A. 244, Ann.Cas 1914D, 474 (testimony taken at coroner's inquest inadmissible for want of opportunity to cross-examine); Citizens' Bank and Trust Co. v. Reid Motor Co., 216 N.C. 432, 5 S.E.2d 318 (1939) (direct examination taken before Workmen's Compensation Commissioner where witness refused to submit to cross-examination not receivable in evidence in judicial proceeding for compensation); and cases cited C.J.S. Evidence § 390; Dec. Dig. Evidence ⇒578, Criminal Law ⇒544. See Stearsman v. State, 237 Ind. 149, 143 N.E.2d 81 (1957) (witness died of a heart attack during cross-examination; that part of his testimony as to which he had been cross-examined admitted).

If the former testimony was given at other than a full trial, the confrontation cases tend to scrutinize the adequacy of the actual cross-examination. See 252 at nn. 19–21 supra.

What constitutes a party "in like interest" is considered in § 256 infra.

3. State v. Logan, 344 Mo. 351, 126 S.W.2d 256, 122 A.L.R. 417 (1939) (murder: witness at former trial not cross-examined by counsel for accused); State v. Roe-

circumstances which prevail when the former testimony is offered. A difference of circumstances may be such as to bar compliance with this requirement.[4] In many of the cases the former testimony was given at a preliminary hearing, and an argument can be made that strategy often dictates little or no cross-examination at that stage, since ample opportunity will be afforded at trial. However, the argument has not been received favorably by the courts.[5] If a right to counsel exists when the former testimony is offered, a denial of counsel when the testimony was taken renders it inadmissible.[6] However, a general finding of ineffective representation, e.g. for lack of preparation, at the prior hearing does not per se require rejection of the testimony; the adequacy of the cross-examination under the facts will be determined.[7] An improper curtailment of the right to cross-examine has been held to be a denial of an adequate opportunity to cross-examine,[8] but restrictions upon cross-

examination are not such a denial unless such as to render the testimony inherently unreliable.[9]

Is the opportunity for direct and redirect examination the equivalent of the opportunity for cross-examination? If party A (or his predecessor in interest) calls and examines a witness in the first hearing, and this testimony is offered against A in a second trial, may it come in against the objection of want of opportunity to cross-examine? The decisions sensibly hold that it may.[10]

If former testimony is offered under the former testimony exception to the hearsay rule, then it is offered as a substitute for testimony given in person in open court, and the strong policy favoring personal presence requires that unavailability of the witness be shown, before the substitute is acceptable. This requirement of unavailability and problems of confrontation, common to certain other hearsay exceptions, are discussed elsewhere.[11] If the witness is present in court

buck, 75 Wn.2d 67, 448 P.2d 934 (1968); 5 Wigmore, Evidence § 1371 (Chadbourn rev. 1974).

4.   United States v. Atkins, 618 F.2d 366 (5th Cir. 1980), rehearing denied 629 F.2d 1350 (proper to exclude testimony on preliminary matter, now offered to exculpate D, in which he did not participate and government had no motive to cross-examine). See further at §§ 256, 257 infra.

5.   State v. Parker, 161 Conn. 500, 289 A.2d 894 (1971) (test is opportunity for cross-examination, not use made of it); Commonwealth v. Mustone, 353 Mass. 490, 233 N.E.2d 1 (1968) (risk of unavailability of witness at trial and consequent loss of cross-examination is assumed); State v. Crawley, 242 Ore. 601, 410 P.2d 1012 (1966). Cf. Government of Virgin Islands v. Aquino, 378 F.2d 540 (3d Cir.1967) (rule of admissibility followed with reluctance). In California v. Green, 399 U.S. 149 (1970) and Ohio v. Roberts, 448 U.S. 56, 72 (1980), the argument was rejected as a ground of constitutional attack. Similarly, many depositions are taken merely for discovery, with slight incentive to cross-examine, but F.R.Civ.P. 32(a) attaches no significance to this fact when the witness becomes unavailable and the deposition is offered in his stead. Wright Root Beer Co. v. Dr. Pepper Co., 414 F.2d 887 (5th Cir.1969). Compare Ill.Sup.Ct.R. 202, 212.

6.   Pointer v. Texas, 380 U.S. 400 (1965) (error to admit at trial testimony given at preliminary hearing where accuseds were not represented by counsel; Sixth Amendment right of confrontation includes opportunity to cross-examine by counsel in this situation and applies to proceedings in state as well as federal courts).

7.   Mancusi v. Stubbs, 408 U.S. 204 (1972); State v. West, 363 So.2d 513 (La.1978).

8.   State v. Halsey, 34 N.M. 223, 279 P. 945 (1929); Gill v. State, 148 Tex.Cr.R. 513, 188 S.W.2d 584 (1945) and see the original opinion in the same case, 147 Tex. Cr.R. 392, 181 S.W.2d 276 (1944).

9.   United States ex rel. Haywood v. Wolff, 658 F.2d 455 (7th Cir.1981), cert. denied 454 U.S. 1088 (denial of inquiry as to address and prior statements did not render testimony inherently unreliable); Commonwealth v. Scarborough, 491 Pa. 300, 421 A.2d 147 (1980) (not unfair to limit cross to scope of direct).

10.   Louisville & Nashville Railroad Co. v. Scott, 232 Ala. 284, 167 So. 572 (1936); People v. Bird, 132 Cal. 261, 64 P. 259 (1901); Dwyer v. State, 154 Me. 179, 145 A.2d 100 (1958); Pratt v. State, 53 Tex.Cr.R. 281, 109 S.W. 138 (1908); Also Fed.R.Evid. 804(b)(1). However, if motivation to explore a particular aspect was absent, the effect is the same as with cross-examination, Commonwealth v. Meech, 380 Mass. 490, 403 N.E.2d 1174 (1980). See n. 4, supra.

In view of the close parallel between depositions and former testimony, it is noteworthy that F.R.Civ.P. 32(a) makes depositions admissible against any party present at, represented at, or with due notice of the taking. See also 5 Wigmore, Evidence § 1389 (Chadbourn rev. 1974).

Whether testimony previously offered by a party may be treated as an adoptive admission is discussed in § 269 infra.

11.   See §§ 252, 253, supra.

and testifies, then cognizance should be taken of the possibility that his former testimony may be receivable as a prior statement of a witness.[12] Thus in a jurisdiction allowing the latter, exclusion for reasons having to do with availability will be required only when the witness is absent from court but not unavailable in the necessary degree.[13]

If the former testimony is used as a prior inconsistent statement for impeachment or as an admission of a party-opponent, unavailability is not a prerequisite.[14]

WESTLAW REFERENCES

former** previous** prior /5 testimony /s circumstance* (lack** ineffective present /5 attorney counsel lawyer) limitation* restriction* waive* /s cross-exam!

former** previous** prior /5 testimony /s opportunit*** possibilit*** /s cross-exam!

demonstrat! show*** /3 unavailab! /p former** previous** prior /5 testimony

307ak76

110k662(6)

§ 256. Adequacy of Cross-Examination: "Identity of Parties" [1]

The haste and pressure of trials causes lawyers and judges to speak in catchwords or shorthand phrases in talking about evi-

dence rules. Thus "identity of parties" is often spoken of as a requirement for the admission of former testimony.[2] It is a convenient phrase to indicate a situation where the underlying requirement of adequacy of the present opponent's opportunity of cross-examination would usually be satisfied. But a *requirement* of identity of parties—and so we shall see of "identity of issues" [3]—is hardly a useful generalization, because it obscures the end in view, and because it must be hedged with qualifications too many and too wide for the rule to be helpful. Some of these follow.

It is clear, for example, that if the two present adversary parties, proponent of the evidence and his opponent, were parties in the former proceedings in which the testimony was taken, it is immaterial that there are additional parties in either or both proceedings not common to the two suits.[4]

Again, whether we have regard to the present party offering the former testimony, or only to the present party against whom it is offered (which we shall see is the better view) it is sufficient that the present party, though not the same, is a successor in interest to the corresponding party in the former suit. This notion, to which the courtroom attaches the slogan "privity" [5] is again some-

---

12. See § 251, supra.

13. See California v. Green, 399 U.S. 149 (1970), pointing out, with respect to constitutional requirements of confrontation, that former testimony may be admitted if the witness is unavailable to the requisite degree and that no different result should follow where the witness is actually produced.

14. See § 37 supra (prior inconsistent statements), § 262 (admissions).

§ 256

1. See generally 5 Wigmore, Evidence § 1386 (Chadbourn rev. 1974); Falknor, Former Testimony and the Uniform Rules: A Comment, 38 N.Y.U.L.Rev. 651, 652–655 (1963); 20 Am.Jur., Evidence § 690; C.J.S. Evidence §§ 387, 388; Dec.Dig. Evidence ⬥580, Criminal Law ⬥546; Annot., 142 A.L.R. 673.

2. Unfortunately some statutes and rules are phrased in this way, see e.g., McKinney's New York CPLR 4517. But see Fleury v. Edwards, 14 N.Y.2d 334, 251 N.Y.S.2d 647, 200 N.E.2d 550 (1964).

3. See § 257 infra.

4. Philadelphia, Wilmington, & Baltimore Railroad Co. v. Howard, 54 U.S. (13 How.) 307, 14 L.Ed. 157 (1851) (additional coplaintiff in former suit); Allen v. Chouteau, 102 Mo. 309, 14 S.W. 869, 871 (1890) (additional parties in former suit); Annot., 142 A.L.R. 689.

Likewise if parties have been dropped. Freeby v. Incorporated Town of Sibley, 195 Iowa 200, 186 N.W. 685, 195 Iowa 200, 191 N.W. 867 (1922).

5. See Bryan v. Malloy, 90 N.C. 508, 511 (1883) where the court said "Privity in the sense here used is a privity to the former action. To make one a privy to an action, he must be one who has acquired an interest in the subject-matter of the action, either by inheritance, succession, or purchase from a party to the action subsequent to its institution."

Illustrations of privity in the strict sense are grantor-grantee, Stephens v. Hoffman, 263 Ill. 197, 104 N.E. 1090 (1914), and in ordinary litigation a now deceased party and his administrator, Gibson v. Gagnon, 82 Colo. 108, 257 P. 348 (1927). In wrongful death cases the decisions are divided, some ruling in favor of privity between deceased and his administrator, Kentucky Traction & Terminal Co. v. Downing's Administrator,

times spoken of as a requirement, rather than merely as a situation which satisfies the aim of adequate protection of the party-opponent. As a requirement it is indefensibly strict.[6]

Even more important is another inroad upon "identity." This is the recognition, under Wigmore's guidance,[7] by modern judges who place substance before form, that it is only the party *against* whom the former testimony is now offered, whose presence as a party in the previous suit is significant.[8] The older decisions which insisted on "reciprocity" or "mutuality," that is, that the party *offering* the former testimony in the present suit must also have been a party in the prior proceeding,[9] seem without any supporting

basis. It is said by the sponsors of the older view that if the party against whom the testimony is offered were seeking to use the same testimony against the offering party he could not do so, because the present proponent was not a party to the former suit. This is true, if identity or privity is insisted on, but the result in that imaginary situation seems to have little bearing on the question of what is fair in respect to the actual situation where former testimony is offered against a party who did have adequate opportunity to cross-examine. The "reciprocity" doctrine can best be explained as proceeding from a mere uneasiness over the extension of the admission of former testi-

159 Ky. 502, 167 S.W. 683 (1914), and others holding to the contrary on the dubious ground that the wrongful death cause of action is a new one created by statute rather than one which survives, Arsnow v. Red Top Cab Co., 159 Wash. 137, 292 P. 436 (1930). Privity between the State which prosecuted D for assault and battery and police officer who sued him civilly for the same conduct has been denied, Bolden v. Carter, 269 Ark. 391, 602 S.W.2d 640 (1980), and held not to exist between husband and wife, Lord v. Boschert, 47 Ohio App. 54, 189 N.E. 863 (1934), or between passenger and driver, Osburn v.Stickel, 187 So.2d 89 (Fla.App.1966).

6. There is no magic for this purpose in the fact of succession. The question is whether the former party had substantially the same motive to cross-examine about the same matters as the present party would have. So the better later cases look to "identity of interest" rather than to technical succession. See note 12 infra.

7. 5 Wigmore, Evidence § 1388, p. 111 (Chadbourn rev. 1974).

8. Insul-Wool Insulation Corp. v. Home Insulation, 176 F.2d 502 (10th Cir.1949) (depositions taken in prior action for infringement admissible against plaintiff in subsequent action against other defendants for infringement of same patent); North River Insurance Co. v. Walker, 161 Ky. 368, 170 S.W. 983 (1914) (suit on fire insurance policy; defense, arson by plaintiff and her deceased husband; held testimony of deceased witness taken at examining trial of plaintiff and husband admissible against plaintiff); Harrell v. Quincy, Omaha & Kansas City Railroad Co., 186 S.W. 677 (Mo.1916) (deposition taken in widow's action for wrongful death admissible against same defendant in similar action by children); School District of City of Pontiac v. Sachse, 274 Mich. 345, 264 N.W. 396 (1936) (evidence taken in criminal trial for fraud admitted against same defendant when sued civilly for restitution); Gaines v. Thomas, 241 S.C. 412, 128 S.E.2d 692 (1962) (testimony of deceased witness given at instance of defendant in

action by administrator of driver of other car against owner of truck involved in collision properly admitted in action by injured bystander against administrator. Federal and Revised Uniform Rule Evid. (1974) 804(b) (1) is to the same effect. See text following n. 9 supra. Bailey v. Southern Pacific Transportation Co., 613 F.2d 1385 (5th Cir.1980), cert. denied 449 U.S. 836.

9. See, e.g., Morgan v. Nicholl, L.R. 2 C.P. 117 (1866) (action in ejectment by father; plaintiff seeks to use testimony of deceased witness taken in former action for the same land brought by son who supposed that his father was dead; excluded on ground that testimony could not have been used by defendants against present plaintiff for want of privity or identity of parties); Metropolitan St. Railway Co. v. Gumby, 99 F. 192, 198 (2d Cir.1900) (suit by infant's mother claiming damages for loss of services due to injury, held, testimony of deceased witness taken in former suit brought in infant's behalf against the same defendant for the same injury could not be used by plaintiff, no privity or reciprocity); McInturff v. Insurance Co. of North America, 248 Ill. 92, 93 N.E. 369, 140 Am.St.Rep. 153, 21 Ann.Cas. 176 (1910) (M. was tried on criminal charge for arson; after trial he kills T., witness for state; M. then sues on fire insurance policy; held, insurance company cannot use testimony of T. given at the criminal trial; surely this is a flagrant sacrifice of justice on the altar of technicalism); Concordia Fire Insurance Co. v. Wise, 114 Okl. 254, 246 P. 595, 46 A.L.R. 456 (1926) (suit on fire policy; former testimony in trial of present plaintiff for arson, not admissible against him in present action); Annot., 142 A.L.R. 687, citing additional cases. Referring to some of these cases, the North Carolina court said: "These authorities, in our opinion, sacrifice substance to form, and exclude material evidence which has been subjected to the tests of truth, and in favor of a party who has had an opportunity to cross-examine." Hartis v. Charlotte Electric Railway Co., 162 N.C. 236, 237, 78 S.E. 164 (1913).

mony to the entire area in which the justifying grounds are applicable.[10]

Moreover, under what seems the practical and expedient view, if the party against whom the former testimony is now offered though not a party to the former suit, or in "privity" as a successor in interest of any party therein, yet actually cross-examined the witness (personally or by counsel) about the matters which he would now want to cross-examine about, or was actually accorded a fair opportunity for such cross-examination and had a like motive for such examination, then the former testimony may be received.[11] Finally, the natural next step is to recognize, as progressive courts have done, that neither identity of parties nor privity between parties is essential. These are merely means to an end. Consequently, if it appears that in the former suit a party having a like motive to cross-examine about the same matters as the present party would have, was accorded an adequate opportunity for such examination, the testimony may be received against the present party.[12] Identity of interest in the sense of motive, rather than technical identity of cause of action or title, is the test. The argument that it is unfair to force upon a party another's cross-examination or decision not to cross-examine a witness loses its validity with the realization that other hearsay exceptions involve no cross-examination whatever, and further that the choice is not between perfect and

---

10. See the court's remarks in the *McInturff* case in the next preceding note: "If the rule contended for by plaintiff in error were good law, then in an action against a carrier by a passenger for a personal injury the testimony of a witness since deceased would be admissible against the same carrier for an injury sustained in the same accident by another passenger, an employé, a licensee, or a trespasser, simply because the carrier against whom the testimony was offered had on the former trial an opportunity to cross-examine the witness. This rule would carry us too far afield for proof, and we cannot sanction it." (93 N.E. at p. 371). Cf. Wade v. King, 19 Ill. 301 (1857).

11. Tug Raven v. Trexler, 419 F.2d 536 (4th Cir. 1969), cert. denied 398 U.S. 936 (testimony given at Coast Guard inquiry into cause of disaster admissible in wrongful death proceeding against respondent who was represented and allowed to cross-examine; also admissible against others similarly situated who had not appeared); In re Durant, 80 Conn. 140, 67 A. 497, 10 Ann.Cas. 539 (1907) (disbarment proceedings charging that defendant conspired to procure perjured testimony of Mrs. D in a divorce suit; testimony of Mrs. D in that divorce suit now offered against defendant, who had cross-examined as attorney for the wife: held admissible. "The requirement of an identity of parties is only a means to an end. This end was attained when the defendant availed himself of the unrestricted opportunity to cross-examine Mrs. Delkescamp."); Brownlee v. Bunnell, 31 Ky.L. 669, 103 S.W. 284 (1907) (former testimony received against defendants in present suit on ground that though not parties to former suit they employed lawyers who defended the action at their instance); Charlesworth v. Tinker, 18 Wis. 633, 635 (1864) (civil action for assault; testimony given in prior criminal assault prosecution admissible, relying on statute giving power to complainant to control prosecution for assault; ". . . the true test . . . is, did the party who is to be affected by it have the power of cross-examining the witness, or at least have an opportunity of doing so?"); Fleury v. Edwards, 14 N.Y.2d 334, 251 N.Y.S.2d 647, 200 N.E.2d 550 (1964) (testimo-

ny of one driver, given at license revocation hearing of both drivers, held admissible in death action by his administrator against other driver, who was present and cross-examined; outstanding opinions). Compare Rumford Chemical Works v. Hygienic Chemical Co., 215 U.S. 156 (1909) (testimony in a former suit inadmissible against one who contributed to expense of defending former suit, but had no "right to intermeddle").

Cases disclosing relaxation of strict requirements in disbarment proceedings are collected in Annot., 161 A.L.R. 898.

12. This view finds support in a growing number of decisions. Tug Raven v. Trexler, supra n. 40; Cox v. Selover, 171 Minn. 216, 213 N.W. 902 (1927), (testimony taken in former trial against guarantor, who was officer, stockholder, and attorney for corporate principal maker, which intervened after first trial, admissible against intervenor in later trial); Bartlett v. Kansas City Public Service Co., 349 Mo. 13, 160 S.W.2d 740, 142 A.L.R. 666 (1942) (testimony given for defendant in prior suit by husband for loss of services of injured wife, admissible for defendant in wife's separate action for same injury); Travelers Fire Ins. Co. v. Wright, 322 P.2d 417 (Okl.1958) (action on fire policy by two partners, with defense of arson by one partner; testimony given against one partner in criminal trial for arson admissible); Proulx v. Parrow, 115 Vt. 232, 56 A.2d 623 (1948) (testimony given in previous action against husband for removal of boundary fence admissible against wife in later action for declaration of location of boundary). In cases where privity in the strict sense does not exist between a person suing for injuries and his administrator suing for death caused thereby, identity of interest is advanced as a basis for admitting in the later case testimony given in the former. Hartis v. Charlotte Electric Railway Co., 162 N.C. 236, 78 S.E. 164, Ann.Cas.1915A, 811 (1913); St. Louis Southwestern Railway v. Hengst, 36 Tex.Civ.App. 217, 81 S.W. 832 (1904).

The case law has not as yet explored the validity of this theory with respect to criminal defendants.

imperfect conditions for the giving of testimony but between imperfect conditions and no testimony at all.[13]

Conformably with the views expressed in the foregoing paragraph, the Supreme Court promulgated Federal Rule 804(b)(1), recognizing a hearsay exception for former testimony if the party against whom now offered, or a party "with similar motive and interest," had had opportunity to examine the witness.[14] The House Committee on the Judiciary objected on the ground that "it is generally unfair to impose upon the party against whom the hearsay evidence is being offered responsibility for the manner in which the witness was previously handled by another party."[15] Accordingly the House substituted a requirement that "the party against whom the testimony is now offered, or in a civil action or proceeding a predecessor in interest, had an opportunity and similar motive" to examine the witness. Concluding that "the difference between the two versions is not great,"[16] the Senate acceded to the House version, which was enacted.[17] The matter may not be as simple as the Senate thought.

Unlike the Court's version, Rule 804(b)(1) as enacted draws a distinction between criminal and civil cases. In criminal cases, the party against whom the former testimony is now offered must have been a party to the former proceeding; there is no substitution. If the former testimony is offered against the accused, the rule as enacted eliminates doubts under the confrontation clause raised by the Court's version which accepted examination by a substitute. However, in terms the rule as enacted insists on identity of prosecution also, which seemingly would bar a defendant in a federal prosecution from introducing exculpatory testimony from a re-

lated State case given by a since deceased witness. Exclusion of such evidence implicates due process considerations,[18] and quite likely was not intended by the Congress.

In civil cases the rule as enacted requires that there have been opportunity to examine the witness by the party against whom now offered or by a "predecessor in interest" with similar motive. The explanation offered by the Report of the House Committee is cryptic. After asserting the general unfairness of requiring a party to accept another's examination of a witness, quoted above,[19] the Report adds, "The sole exception to this, in the Committee's view, is when a party's predecessor in interest in a civil action or proceeding had an opportunity and similar motive to examine the witness. The Committee amended the Rule to reflect these policy determinations."[20] Quite clearly the House Committee intended to reject the approach of the Court's rule in criminal cases and to substitute a more restricted version. It is by no means clear, however, that the Congressional intent was also to that effect in civil cases. In fact, a sensible reading virtually compels the conclusion that the intent was to leave the Court's rule intact in civil cases. The contrary view as to the effect of the Congressional amendment in this regard expressed in the 1978 Pocket Part to this work is now believed to be in error and should be disregarded. Had it been intended to reinstate the outmoded concept of privity as developed at the common law, a statement to that effect could easily have been included, with unmistakeable meaning, but no such statement was made. The draftsmen at this point seemingly were searching for a suitable phrase to describe an acceptable substitute examiner, and they settled upon "predecessor in interest." In

---

13. Morgan, The Law of Evidence, 1941–1945, 59 Harv.L.Rev. 481, 551 (1946). And see Falknor, Former Testimony and the Uniform Rules: A Comment, 38 N.Y.U.L.Rev. 651, 655 (1963).

14. 46 F.R.D. 377.

15. House Committee on the Judiciary, Fed.Rules of Evidence, H.R.Rep. No. 650, 93d Cong., 1st Sess., p. 15 (1973).

16. Senate Committee on the Judiciary, S.Rep. No. 1277, 93d Cong., 2d Sess., p. 28 (1974).

17. Set forth in text following § 254, n. 9 supra.

18. Chambers v. Mississippi, 410 U.S. 284 (1973). See discussions in §§ 19 supra and 278 infra.

19. Supra at n. 15.

20. Supra n. 15.

reality, of course, the key is that the prior examiner, however described, had "similar motive." As the court said in the leading, and virtually only, case construing the rule, "[T]he previous party having like motive to develop the same testimony about the same material facts, is, in the final analysis, a predecessor in interest to the present party."[21]

WESTLAW REFERENCES

former** previous** prior /5 testif! testimony /s (identi*** /5 parties party) privity

parties party +1 "against whom" /s former** previous** prior /5 testif! testimony

former** previous** prior /5 testif! testimony /s mutuality reciproc***

identical identity same similar /s interest* motiv! /s cross-exam! /p former** previous** prior /5 testif! testimony

fed.r.evid! evid! /3 804(b)(1)

former** previous** prior /5 testif! testimony /p predecessor successor +3 interest /s motiv! % topic(110)

157k5771/2

---

21. Lloyd v. American Export Lines, Inc., 580 F.2d 1179, 1187 (3d Cir.1978), cert. denied 439 U.S. 969. As the result of a fight between crew members Lloyd and Alvarez, Lloyd sued the shipowner, which joined Alvarez as third-party defendant. Alvarez then counterclaimed against the shipowner. Both Lloyd and Alvarez claimed negligence by the shipowner in employing a known dangerous person. Prior to trial, a Coast Guard hearing was held to determine whether Lloyd's mariner's document should be suspended or revoked because of the incident. Both Lloyd and Alvarez were represented by counsel and testified at the hearing. At the trial Lloyd did not appear and was found to be unavailable. His former testimony was offered by the shipowner but excluded. This ruling was overturned on appeal. The majority opinion held that the phrase "predecessor in interest" was not a return to requiring privity or a common property interest and that there was a sufficient community of interest between the Coast Guard officer conducting the hearing and Alvarez to satisfy the rule. Both were inquiring into the same facts with a view to determining whether a penalty should be imposed. A concurring opinion took the position that some meaning (not specified) should be attached to "predecessor in interest" and that there was not the kind of "common motive" that would satisfy the rule. However, admissibility was proper under the residual exception of Rule 804(b)(5). 580 F.2d 1190.

§ 257. Adequacy of Cross-Examination: Identity of Issues [1]

Questions as to identity of the issues, or of the facts, involved in the former and present proceedings often arise in association with questions about identity or privity of parties. This is to be expected because any supposed requirement of identity of issues, is, like the rule about parties,[2] merely a means of fulfilling the policy of securing an adequate opportunity of cross-examination by the party against whom testimony is now offered or by someone in like interest. It is often said that the issue in the two suits must be the same.[3] But certainly the policy mentioned does not require that all the issues (any more than all the parties) in the two proceedings must be the same, but at most that the issue on which the testimony was offered in the first suit must be the same as the issue upon which it is offered in the second. Additional issues or differences in regard to issues upon which the former testimony is not offered are of no consequence.[4] Moreover, insistence upon precise identity of issues, which might have some appropriateness if the question were one of

---

See also Rule v. International Association of Bridge Workers, 568 F.2d 558 (8th Cir.1977) (error to exclude deposition taken in prior action where interest of party against whom there offered was calculated to induce as thorough cross-examination as interest of party against whom now offered, citing Fed.R.Evid. 801(b)(1)).

§ 257

1. See 5 Wigmore, Evidence §§ 1386, 1387 (Chadbourn rev. 1974); C.J.S. Evidence § 389; Dec. Dig. Evidence ⊂⊃579, Criminal Law ⊂⊃545; Annot., 70 A.L.R.2d 494.

2. See § 256 supra.

3. Statutes occasionally so provide, e.g., 42 Pa.C.S. A. § 5917 ("of the same criminal issue").

4. Bartlett of Kansas City Public Service Co., 349 Mo. 13, 160 S.W.2d 740, 142 A.L.R. 666 (1942) (immaterial that husband's prior action involved issue of loss of wife's services not present in wife's later personal injury action, since witnesses did not testify on issue of damages); Hartis v. Charlotte Electric Railway Co., 162 N.C. 236, 78 S.E. 164, 1915A, 811 (1913) (similarly as to different measures of damages between personal injury action and later wrongful death action).

res judicata or estoppel by judgment, are out of place with respect to former testimony where the question is not of binding anyone, but merely of the salvaging, for what it may be worth, of the testimony of a witness not now available in person. Accordingly, modern opinions qualify the requirement by demanding only "substantial" identity of issues.[5]

It follows that neither the form of the proceeding, the theory of the case, nor the nature of the relief sought needs be the same. Though there have been occasional holdings imposing such requirements,[6] it is manifest that they hve no pertinence to the policy of adequacy of opportunity for cross-examination, and the more convincing opinions reject them.[7] Thus, in criminal cases where the first indictment charges one offense, e.g., robbery, and the second, another distinct offense, such as murder of the person robbed,

it is usually considered sufficient that the two indictments arise from the same transaction.[8] Other patterns recur in the cases. One involves introducing at the trial of a criminal case testimony given at the preliminary hearing. In another, testimony given against the accused in an earlier criminal trial is offered against him in a civil case to which he is a party. In both situations admissibility is favored.[9] It seems, then, that the requirement should be restated, not as a mechanical one of identity or even of substantial identity of issues, but rather as a requirement that the issues in the first proceeding and hence the purpose for which the testimony was there offered, must have been such that the present opponent (or some person in like interest) had an adequate motive for testing on cross-examination the credibility of the testimony now offered.[10]

---

5. State v. Brinkley, 354 Mo. 337, 189 S.W.2d 314 (1945) (testimony for defendants in prosecution against police officers for fatally assaulting M admissible for accused in prosecution for perjured testimony before grand jury that police had beaten him and M); In re White's Will, 2 N.Y.2d 309, 160 N.Y.S.2d 841, 141 N.E.2d 416 (1957) (testimony given in lunacy proceeding where issue was capacity to manage affairs admissible in will contest on issue of competency to make a will). Many cases state the rule in terms of "substantial" identity of issues, e.g. School District of City of Pontiac v. Sachse, 274 Mich. 345, 264 N.W. 396 (1936); Proulx v. Parrow, 115 Vt. 232, 56 A.2d 623 (1948). Some statutes likewise specify "substantial" identity of issues as the test. Ga.Code, § 38–314 (1981).

For examples of failure to meet the test of substantial identity of issues, see State v. Augustine, 252 La. 983, 215 So.2d 634 (1968) (testimony given at hearing on competency to stand trial not admissible on issue of insanity at time of offense); Monahan v. Monahan, 29 App.Div.2d 1246, 289 N.Y.S.2d 812 (1968) (impeachment testimony by female witness for prosecution in unrelated felony trial of D that she had stayed at hotels with D, not admissible to prove adultery in divorce action against D).

6. Tom Reed Gold Mines Co. v. Moore, 40 Ariz. 174, 11 P.2d 347 (1932) (under superseded statute limiting use to "the same action" testimony taken in personal injury action cannot be used in later death action); Hooper v. Southern Railway Co., 112 Ga. 96, 37 S.E. 165, 168 (1900) (testimony taken in suit for personal injuries to minor brought by father as next friend not admissible in suit by father for his own loss of the child's services, there being different defenses available in the two suits—not substantially the same issue).

7. See cases cited in nn. 4 and 5 supra.

8. Fox v. State, 102 Ark. 393, 144 S.W. 516 (1912) (first trial of defendant for being accessory to murder, second, for being accessory to robbery, on same occasion); State v. Boyd, 140 Kan. 623, 38 P.2d 665 (1934) (embezzlement, misappropriation by custodian of public funds); State v. Brown, 331 Mo. 556, 56 S.W.2d 405 (1932); State v. Brinkley, 354 Mo. 337, 189 S.W.2d 314 (1945) (first trial manslaughter prosecution against officers who arrested present defendant and his companion, who died after the arrest; second trial, prosecution of defendant for perjury in testifying before grand jury that he and his companion were beaten by officers at time of first arrest); State v. Swiden, 62 S.D. 208, 252 N.W. 628 (1934) (robbery, murder); State v. Dawson, 129 W.Va. 279, 40 S.E.2d 306 (1946) (robbery, murder); cases are collected in Annot., 122 A.L.R. 430.

9. Admissibility of testimony given at the preliminary hearing is provided by statutes in fair number. 5 Wigmore, Evidence § 1375 (Chadbourn rev. 1974). Ample support also exists in the cases. Id.; California v. Green, 399 U.S. 149 (1970); Ohio v. Roberts, 448 U.S. 56 (1980). Annots., 15 A.L.R. 495, 79 id. 1392, 122 id. 425, 159 id. 1240; see also § 252, n. 21, and § 255 supra.

The modern decisions likewise support admissibility in the criminal-civil situation. North River Insurance Co. v. Walker, 161 Ky. 368, 170 S.W. 983 (1914) (arson); School District of City of Pontiac v. Sachse, 274 Mich. 345, 264 N.W. 396 (1936) (embezzlement); Bryant v. Trinity Universal Insurance Co., 411 S.W.2d 945 (Tex. Civ.App.1967) (arson).

10. State v. Von Klein, 71 Or. 159, 142 P. 549 (1914) (testimony as to polygamous marriage given on trial for larceny of jewels of supposed wife, as evidence of scheme, admissible on later trial for polygamy). Federal and Revised Uniform Rule Evid. (1974) 804(b)(1),

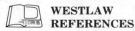

former** previous** prior /5 testif! testimony /p
   most** substantial** /5 identical identity same similar
   /s issue* matter* point* question* relief theor***
157k579
former** preliminary previous** prior /3 civil criminal
   hearing* indict! proceeding* suit* /45 testif! testimony
   /p chance* opportunit*** /s cross-exam! question
   /p admissib!

§ 258. The Character of the Tribunal and of the Proceedings in Which the Former Testimony Was Taken

If the accepted requirements of the administration of the oath, adequate opportunity to cross-examine on substantially the same issue, and present unavailability of the witness, are satisfied then the character of the tribunal and the form of the proceedings are immaterial, and the former testimony should be received.[1] Accordingly, when these con

ditions are met, testimony taken before arbitrators,[2] or before a committing magistrate at a preliminary hearing,[3] or in a sworn examination before the Comptroller by the Corporation Counsel of a person asserting a claim against a city,[4] or at a driver's license revocation hearing,[5] or at a broker's license revocation hearing,[6] or at a Coast Guard hearing,[7] or hearing on motion to suppress,[8] has been held admissible. For lack in the particular proceeding of some of these requisites, testimony given in the course of a coroner's inquest,[9] of a legislative committee hearing,[10] and of a general examination before the referee under the Bankruptcy Act,[11] has been excluded. Or a statute may call for exclusion.[12]

It has been held that if the court in the former proceeding lacked jurisdiction of the subject matter, the former testimony is inadmissible,[13] but it was determined in a Colora-

---

text supra fol. § 254, n. 9. Bailey v. Southern Pacific Transportation Co., 613 F.2d 1385 (5th Cir.1980), cert. denied 449 U.S. 836 (proper to admit testimony given for plaintiff in another case at same crossing also based on claim lights not working).

§ 258

1. See 6 Wigmore, Evidence §§ 1373–1376 (Chadbourn rev. 1974); C.J.S. Evidence §§ 385, 386; Dec.Dig. Evidence ☞557½, Criminal Law ☞539(1).

2. Bailey v. Woods, 17 N.H. 365, 372 (1845) ("It does not seem to be an objection to the competency of the evidence of the deceased witness, that it was given at a hearing before arbitrators. We do not understand that the admissibility of such evidence depends so much upon the particular character of the tribunal, as upon other matters. If the testimony be given under oath in a judicial proceeding, in which the adverse litigant was a party, and where he had the power to cross-examine, and was legally called upon to do so, the great and ordinary tests of truth being no longer wanting, the testimony so given is admitted in any subsequent suit between the parties. Greenl.Ev. 1. It seems to depend rather upon the right to cross-examine, than upon the precise nominal identity of the parties. Id. An arbitration is a judicial proceeding, and the principle of the rule seems to apply as well to cases of this character as to technical suits at law.").

3. See § 255, n. 5 and § 257, n. 9, supra; Dec.Dig., Criminal Law ☞539–545.

4. Boschi v. City of New York, 187 Misc. 875, 65 N.Y.S.2d 425 (1946); Rothman v. City of New York, 273 App.Div. 780, 75 N.Y.S.2d 151 (1947).

5. Fleury v. Edwards, 14 N.Y.2d 334, 251 N.Y.S.2d 647, 200 N.E.2d 550 (1964).

6. Wellden v. Roberts, 37 Ala.App. 1, 67 So.2d 69 (1952), affirmed 259 Ala. 517, 67 So.2d 75.

7. Lloyd v. American Export Lines, supra § 256, n. 21.

8. United States v. Zurosky, 614 F.2d 779 (1st Cir. 1979), cert. denied 446 U.S. 967; United States v. Poland, 659 F.2d 884 (9th Cir.1981), cert. denied 454 U.S. 1059.

9. Edgerley v. Appleyard, 110 Me. 337, 86 A. 244 (1913) (for want of opportunity of cross-examination); Wilson v. Marshall Enterprises, 361 F.2d 887 (4th Cir. 1966); 6 Wigmore, Evidence § 1374 (Chadbourn rev. 1976). Occasionally it is made competent by statute. Los Angeles County v. Industrial Accident Commission, 123 Cal.App. 12, 11 P.2d 434 (1932) (in workmen's compensation proceedings).

10. Newman v. United States ex rel. Frizzel, 43 App.D.C. 53 (1914) (here said to be incompetent and irrelevant) reversed on other grounds, 238 U.S. 537 (1915); State ex rel. Blankenship v. Freeman, 440 P.2d 744, 759 (Okl.1968).

11. In re National Boat and Engine Co., 216 F. 208 (D.Me.1914) (for want of a defined issue); Todd v. Bradley, 99 Conn. 307, 122 A. 68 (1923) (here the testimony of third person; use of bankrupt's testimony as admission distinguished).

12. State Road Department v. Levato, 199 So.2d 714 (Fla.1967) (provision requiring exclusion at trial of testimony of appraisers at pretrial hearing under "quick take" eminent domain statute).

13. In re Colbert's Estate, 51 Mont. 455, 153 P. 1022 (1915); Deering v. Schreyer, 88 App.Div. 457, 85 N.Y.S. 275 (1903), noted 17 Harv.L.Rev. 422. The court in Mc-

do case,[14] that the fact that it may ultimately be held that the court is without power to grant the relief sought, does not deprive the court of power to compel attendance of witnesses and to administer oaths, and accordingly the former testimony was held admissible.[15] The question it seems is not one of regularity but of reliability. A glaring usurpation of judicial power would call for a different ruling, but where the first court has substantial grounds for believing that it has authority to entertain the proceeding, and the party called upon to cross-examine should consider that the existence of jurisdiction is reasonably arguable, it seems that the guaranties of reliability are present. The question should be viewed, not as one of limits of jurisdiction, but of whether the sworn statements of a witness, now dead or unavailable, about the facts of which he had knowledge, were made under such circumstances of opportunity and motive for cross-examination as to make them sufficiently trustworthy to be used in the effort to ascertain the truth. In like vein, no significance attaches to the circumstance that the earlier trial resulted in a mistrial [16] or a hung jury.[17]

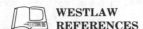

WESTLAW REFERENCES

character form nature type   /4   "court" hearing*
proceeding* tribunal   /s   former** previous** prior   /5

Adams' Executors v. Stilwell, 13 Pa.St. 90 (1850) assumes that jurisdiction is essential.

14. Jerome v. Bohn, 21 Colo. 322, 40 P. 570 (1895).

15. The result is consistent with United States v. United Mine Workers, 330 U.S. 258 (1947).

16. People v. Schwarz, 78 Cal.App. 561, 248 P. 990 (1926).

17. People v. Hines, 284 N.Y. 93, 29 N.E.2d 483 (1940).

§ 259

1. C.J.S. Criminal Law § 892; C.J.S. Evidence § 384, p. 948; Annot., 159 A.L.R. 119.

2. Wellden v. Roberts, 37 Ala.App. 1, 67 So.2d 69 (1962), affirmed 259 Ala. 517, 67 So.2d 75; Calley v. Boston & Maine Railroad, 93 N.H. 359, 42 A.2d 329, 159 A.L.R. 115 (1945).

3. Leach v. Nelson, 50 N.D. 538, 196 N.W. 755 (1924), critically noted 8 Minn.L.Rev. 629.

testif! testimony

§ 259. Objections and Their Determination [1]

May objections to the former testimony, or parts thereof, which could have been asserted when it was first given in evidence, be made for the first time when offered at the present trial? There are sweeping statements in some opinions that this may always be done,[2] and in others that it is never allowable.[3] The more widely approved view, however, is that objections which go merely to the form of the testimony, as on the ground of leading questions, unresponsiveness, or opinion, must be made at the original hearing, when they can be corrected,[4] but objections which go to the relevancy or the competency of the evidence may be asserted for the first time when the former testimony is offered at the present trial.[5]

Whether the former testimony meets the requirements of the present exception to the hearsay rule may depend on a question of fact. For example, is the witness unavailable? This and other preliminary questions of fact are treated elsewhere.[6]

Impeachment of witnesses whose former testimony is introduced is considered under

4. Kemp v. Government of Canal Zone, 167 F.2d 938 (5th Cir.1948); People v. Britt, 62 Cal.App. 674, 217 P. 767 (1923); Sherman Gas & Electric Co. v. Belden, 103 Tex. 59, 123 S.W. 119, 27 L.R.A.,N.S., 237 (1909); Note, 8 Minn.L.Rev. 629; Annot., 159 A.L.R. 119.

5. Aetna Insurance Co. v. Koonce, 233 Ala. 265, 171 So. 269 (1936) (dictum).

A similar rule with respect to depositions is found in F.R.Civ.P. 32(d)(3). The similarities between depositions and former testimony are persuasive.

With respect to objections to the competency of the witness, compare State v. Pierson, 337 Mo. 475, 85 S.W.2d 48 (1935) (error to refuse to allow accused to go into possible incompetency at time of giving original testimony by witness whose insanity supervened), and Habig v. Bastian, 117 Fla. 864, 158 So. 508 (1935) (testimony given by party at former trial not rendered inadmissible by supervening death of opposite party which rendered witness incompetent).

6. See § 53 supra.

the topic of impeaching hearsay declarants generally.[7]

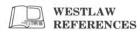

WESTLAW REFERENCES

objection* /s former** previous** prior /5 testif! testimony /s later second subsequent /3 proceeding* trial*

§ 260. Methods and Scope of Proof [1]

When only a portion of the former testimony of a witness is introduced by the proponent, the result may be a distorted and inaccurate impression. Hence the adversary is entitled to the introduction of such other parts as fairness requires, and to have them introduced at that time, rather than waiting until the presentation of his own case.[2] He may, however, wait if he chooses.[3]

In proving the former testimony at least four theories of admissibility may be employed.

(1) Any *firsthand* observer of the giving of the former testimony may testify to its purport from his unaided memory.[4] This and the next method were formerly used much more frequently than in the present era of court stenographers. The witness, to qualify, need not profess to be able to give the exact words of the former witness,[5] but he must, if the evidence is to come in under the present exception, satisfy the court that he is able to give the substance of all that the witness has said, both on direct and cross-examination,[6] about the subject matter relevant to the present suit.[7] By the more convenient practice the proponent need not prove all of the former testimony relevant to the present case, but only such as he desires to use, leaving to the adversary to call for such of the remaining part as he wishes.[8]

(2) A firsthand observer may testify to the purport of the former testimony by using a memorandum, such as the judge's, counsel's, or the stenographer's notes, or the stenographer's transcript, to *refresh the present memory* of the witness.[9]

---

7. See § 37 supra.

§ 260

1. See 4 Wigmore, Evidence § 1330 (Chadbourn rev. 1972), 5 id. §§ 1666–1669 (Chadbourn rev. 1974), 7 id. §§ 2098, 2099, 2103 (Chadbourn rev. 1978); Dec.Dig. Criminal Law ☞547, Evidence ☞582; C.J.S. Criminal Law § 898; C.J.S. Evidence §§ 397–401; Annot., 11 A.L.R.2d 30.

2. The additional portions will usually, though not necessarily, consist of the original cross-examination. Waller v. State, 102 Ga. 684, 28 S.E. 284 (1897); City of Boulder v. Stewardson, 67 Colo. 582, 189 P. 1 (1920); Randall v. Peerless Motor Car Co., 212 Mass. 352, 99 N.E. 221, 231 (1912).

3. Fed. and Rev.Unif.R.Evid. (1974) 106 provides:

When a writing or recorded statement or part thereof is introduced by a party, an adverse party may require him at that time to introduce any other part or any other writing or recorded statement which ought in fairness to be considered contemporaneously with it.

The language virtually restates Fed.R.Civ.P. 32(a)(4).

4. Meyers v. United States, 84 U.S.App.D.C. 101, 171 F.2d 800 (1948), cert. denied 336 U.S. 912; Phillips v. Wyrick, 558 F.2d 489 (8th Cir.1977), cert. denied 434 U.S. 1088. Vander Veen v. Yellow Cab Co., 89 Ill.App. 2d 91, 233 N.E.2d 68 (1967); State ex rel. Blankenship v. Freeman, 440 P.2d 744, 760 (Okl.1968); State v. Crawley, 242 Or. 601, 410 P.2d 1012 (1966); State v. Roebuck, 75 Wn.2d 67, 448 P.2d 934 (1968).

5. Ruch v. Rock Island, 97 U.S. 693 (1878) (precise language not necessary; "if a witness from mere memory, professes to give the exact language, it is a reason for doubting his good faith and veracity"); Vander Veen v. Yellow Cab Co., 89 Ill.App. 2d 91, 233 N.E.2d 68 (1967); 7 Wigmore, Evidence § 2098, note 4 (Chadbourn rev. 1978).

6. Tibbets v. Flanders, 18 N.H. 284, 292 (1846); Monahan v. Clemons, 212 Ky. 504, 276 S.W. 924 (1926).

7. Bennett v. State, 32 Tex.Cr.R. 216, 22 S.W. 684 (1893) ("If a witness can testify to the substance of all that is said on direct and cross examination upon one subject, it will be admissible, though there may be other portions of said testimony, as to other matters, not remembered by the witness."); Foley v. State, 11 Wyo. 464, 72 P. 627 (1903) (must state "the whole of what was said on the particular subject which he is called to prove"); 7 Wigmore, Evidence, §§ 2098, note 4, 2099(4) (Chadbourn rev. 1978). But the sensible qualification, that it suffices if the proponent is able to fill the gaps by the testimony of other witnesses has been made in a case where the former testimony was proved, not under the present exception, but to support a charge of perjury. Commonwealth v. Shooshanian, 210 Mass. 123, 96 N.E. 70 (1911).

8. Waller v. State, 102 Ga. 684, 28 S.E. 284 (1897); City of Boulder v. Stewardson, 67 Colo. 582, 189 P. 1 (1920); Randall v. Peerless Motor Car Co., 212 Mass. 352, 99 N.E. 221 (1912).

9. Ruch v. Rock Island, 97 U.S. 693 (1878); Armstrong Furniture Co. v. Nickle, 110 Ga.App. 686, 140

(3) In most states the magistrate's report of the testimony at a preliminary criminal hearing,[10] and the official stenographer's transcribed notes of the testimony [11] at the trial of a case, civil or criminal, are admitted, when properly authenticated, as evidence of the fact and purport of the former testimony either by statute or under the hearsay exception for *official written statements*.[12] There is generally no rule of preference for these reports, however, and any observer, including the stenographer himself, may be called to prove the former testimony without producing the official report or transcript.[13]

(4) A witness who has made written notes or memoranda of the testimony at the time of the former trial, or while the facts were fresh in his recollection, and who will testify that he knows that they are correct may use the notes as memoranda of *past recollection recorded*.[14]

WESTLAW REFERENCES

"judge" magistrate observer reporter stenographer /6   purport record! report* transcript! /s former**

S.E.2d 72 (1964); Commonwealth v. Mustone, 353 Mass. 490, 233 N.E.2d 1 (1968); Travelers Fire Insurance Co. v. Wright, 322 P.2d 417 (Okla.1958). As to refreshing recollection generally, see § 9 supra.

10. Haines v. State, 109 Ga. 526, 35 S.E. 141 (1900); 5 Wigmore, Evidence, § 1667 (Chadbourn rev. 1974) (citing cases pro and con).

11. See, e.g., Snyder v. Cearfoss, 190 Md. 151, 57 A.2d 786 (1948); Blalock v. Whisnant, 216 N.C. 417, 5 S.E.2d 130 (1939) (transcript contained in case on appeal); Proulx v. Parrow, 115 Vt. 232, 56 A.2d 623 (1948) (certified copy of transcript). Statutes to this effect and Fed.R.Civ.P. 80 are cited in 5 Wigmore, Evidence § 1669, note 2 (Chadbourn rev. 1974). See also cases (and statutes cited therein) in Dec.Dig. Evidence ⊶582(3).

Objections to the use of the common law bill of exceptions based on the manner of its preparation are no longer pertinent in view of modern methods of reporting testimony. See Roth v. Smith, 54 Ill. 431 (1870); 5 Wigmore, Evidence § 1668 (Chadbourn rev. 1974).

12. For the requirements of this exception see Ch. 32 infra.

13. Napier v. Commonwealth, 306 Ky. 75, 206 S.W. 2d 53 (1947) (county attorney's evidence as to testimony before grand jury); Terry v. State, 132 Tex.Cr. 283, 103 S.W.2d 766 (1937) (stenographer can testify from recollection); 4 Wigmore, Evidence § 1330(2) (Chadbourn rev. 1972).

previous** prior /5   testif! testimony
157k582

§ 261. Possibilities of Improving Existing Practice

The discussion in the preceding sections of this chapter leads to the conclusion that the treatment of former testimony should, as a minimum, be brought into conformity with Federal Rule Evid. 804(b)(1), construed as indicated in § 256 supra, in jurisdictions which have not already done so by rule or decision. This is not to suggest, however, that reexamination of this hearsay exception, as with others, should not be a continuing process.

The basic factors entering into the former testimony exception have been considered to be (1) unavailability of the witness, (2) opportunity for examination, and (3) reasonable equivalency of examination. Each should be subjected to further scrutiny.

(1) Few, if any, other hearsay exceptions measure up in reliability to former testimony. Yet former testimony is one of a very

Since the matter sought to be proved is the former testimony and not the contents of the transcript, literally the so-called Best Evidence Rule does not apply. § 233 supra. However, the importance of accuracy and the superiority of the transcript in this respect make a powerful argument for the opposite result. Cowart v. State, 44 Ala.App. 201, 205 So.2d 250 (1967); Walker v.Walker, 14 Ga. 242 (1853); State v. Luttrell, 366 S.W.2d 453 (Mo.1963); and see Prettyman, J., dissenting in Meyers v. United States, 84 U.S.App.D.C. 101, 115, 171 F.2d 800, 814 (D.C.Cir.1948), 23 So.Cal.L. Rev. 113.

14. Commonwealth v. Mustone, 353 Mass. 490, 233 N.E.2d 1 (1968) (any witness may qualify his notes as a reliable record of past recollection); State v. Maynard, 184 N.C. 653, 113 S.E. 682 (1922) (proper for stenographer to read his notes of preliminary examination, where he testifies to their correctness, though not subscribed or certified as required for official record); Newton v. State, 150 Tex.Cr. 500, 202 S.W.2d 921 (1947) (stenographer may read from notes, if he swears correct); 3 Wigmore, Evidence (Chadbourn rev. 1970) § 737(1).

For the requirements of this theory of admissibility, see §§ 299–303 herein.

Whether the witness testifies on the basis of present recollection refreshed or past recollection recorded seems to be of little practical importance in proving former testimony, and the cases usually make no point of the matter.

small group upon which the requirement of unavailability is imposed. The incongruity of according this second-class status to former testimony is apparent when it is compared with such exceptions as declarations of present bodily or mental state, or excited or spontaneous utterances, where no showing of unavailability is required. Some improvement might be gained from a procedure of giving the opposing party notice of intent to offer former testimony, thus affording him the opportunity to produce the witness in person if he so desires and if the witness is available. An offer of former testimony against the accused in a criminal case under this kind of procedure may be of doubtful validity under the confrontation clause but need not necessarily be dismissed without serious consideration.[1] However, in civil cases, or when the former testimony is offered in a criminal case by the accused, no constitutional impediment is apparent under such a notice procedure.[2] In fact, in civil cases the matter might well be left to the ordinary processes of discovery, with no formal notice procedure at all.

(2) The suggestion has been made that opportunity for cross-examination should be eliminated as a requirement. Other hearsay

exceptions, it is pointed out, involve no cross-examination at all, and the exception for former testimony should not be singled out for special attention.[3] It should be noted, however, that without cross-examination, former testimony becomes virtually indistinguishable from an affidavit, essentially ex parte in nature. While affidavits are widely accepted as a means of establishing relevant factual foundations for procedures at various stages of litigation,[4] they have failed to gain acceptance as a means of resolving disputed issues in the trial process itself. A hearing at which no cross-examination is permitted lacks not only the reliability-insuring factor of cross-examination itself, but in addition is unlikely to entail any degree of the solemnity thought to be conducive to truthfulness.

(3) In achieving a reasonable equivalency of the former examination to what might be accomplished in a present examination, as to both facts and credibility, the concept of a prior party with opportunity and similar motive probably goes as far is practicable. Anything less savors of return to concepts of privity. Going beyond raises questions of fairness and perhaps of due process.

§ 261

1. The interrelationship between the Sixth Amendment rights of an accused to be confronted by the witnesses against him and to have compulsory process for witnesses in his favor, and their corresponding burdens, is discussed in Westen, Confrontation and Compulsory Process: A Unified Theory of Evidence for Criminal Cases, 91 Harv.L.Rev. 567 (1978).

2. A notice procedure is provided by the English Evidence Act of 1968. Civil Evidence Act 1968, c. 64, Part I, §§ 2(1) and 8.

Professor McCormick believed that the unavailability requirement should be abandoned, at least in civil cases. McCormick, Evidence 500. In any event, in civil cases the standard of unavailability for former testimony should be no more exacting than for depositions, in view of the strong similarity between these two forms of evidence. Fed.R.Civ.P. 32(a).

3. The Model Code of Evidence virtually abandoned unavailability as a requirement.

See Rule 503: Evidence of a hearsay declaration is admissible if the judge finds that the declarant

(a) is unavailable as a witness, or

(b) is present and subject to cross-examination.

Rule 511: Evidence of a hearsay statement which consists of testimony given by the declarant as a witness in an action or in a deposition taken according to law for use in an action is admissible for any purpose for which the testimony was admissible in the action in which the testimony was given or for use in which the deposition was taken, unless the judge finds that the declarant is available as a witness and in his discretion rejects the evidence.

See also the Comment appended to Rule 511 explaining the effect of the two rules.

The failure of existing rules admitting these other types of hearsay declarations to furnish guaranties of trustworthiness comparable to the test of cross-examination is demonstrated in detail in Morgan, Foreword, Model Code of Evidence, pp. 36–49 (1942).

4. E.g., Fed.R.Civ.P. 4(g) (proof of service); id. 6(d) (affidavits in support of motions); id. 43(e) (same).

Chapter 26

ADMISSIONS OF A PARTY–OPPONENT [1]

Table of Sections

---

§ 262. Nature and Effect

"Anything that you say may be used against you," according to the familiar phrase. It offers a convenient point of beginning for the examination of the use of admissions in evidence.

Admissions are the words or acts of a party-opponent, or of his predecessor or representative, offered as evidence against him. As indicated, they may be classified as *express* admissions, which are statements of the opposing party, or of some person such as an agent or a predecessor in interest, whose words may fairly be used against him, and admissions by *conduct* of the party-opponent or of those representing him. Among the theories on which the probativeness and admissibility of admissions have been explained and supported, the following seem most helpful.

Morgan's view [2] is that admissions come in as an exception to the hearsay rule, if hearsay is given the usual definition of declara-

---

1. 4 Wigmore, Evidence §§ 1048–1087 (Chadbourn rev. 1972); Weinstein & Berger, Evidence ¶ 801(d)(2)[01]–801(d)(2)(E)[02]; Falknor, Vicarious Admissions and the Uniform Rules, 14 Vand.L.Rev. 855 (1961), Hearsay, 1969 Law & Soc. Order 591, 600–605; Hetland, Admissions in the Uniform Rules: Are They Necessary? 46 Iowa L.Rev. 307 (1961); Morgan, Admissions, 12 Wash.L.Rev. 181 (1937); Strahorn, A Reconsideration of the Hearsay Rule and Admissions, 85 U.Pa.L.Rev. 484 (1937); Dec. Dig. Evidence ⟠200–265, Criminal Law ⟠405–415; C.J.S. Evidence §§ 270–383; Adv.Com. Note to Fed.R.Evid. 801(d)(2); West's Ann.Cal.Evid.Code §§ 1220–1227.

§ 262
2. Morgan, Basic Problems of Evidence 265 (1962).

tions made out of court, not subject to cross-examination, and received as evidence of the truth of the matter declared. Exceptions to the hearsay rule usually are justified on the ground that evidence meeting the requirements of the exception possesses special reliability, plus perhaps special need because of the unavailability of the declarant. Yet no objective guaranty of trustworthiness is furnished by the admissions rule. The party is not even required to have had firsthand knowledge of the matter declared; the declaration may have been self-serving when it was made; and the declarant is probably sitting in the courtroom. As Morgan himself admits, "The admissibility of an admission made by the party himself rests not upon any notion that the circumstances in which it was made furnish the trier means of evaluating it fairly, but upon the adversary theory of litigation. A party can hardly object that he had no opportunity to cross-examine himself or that he is unworthy of credence save when speaking under sanction of an oath." [3]

Wigmore, after pointing out that the party's declaration has generally the probative value of any other person's assertion, says that it has in addition a special value when offered *against* him, in that he is discredited (like a witness impeached by contradictory statements) by his statements inconsistent with his present claim asserted in his pleadings and in the testimony on which he relies. And it passes the gauntlet of the hearsay rule, which requires that extra-judicial assertions be excluded if there was no opportunity for the opponent to cross-examine, because it is the opponent's own declaration and "he does not need to cross-examine himself." He then adds that "the Hearsay Rule

is satisfied" since the party "now as opponent has the full opportunity to put himself on the stand and explain his former assertion." [4]

Strahorn suggests an alternative theory which classes all admissions of a party offered against him, whether words or acts, as being *conduct* offered as circumstantial evidence rather than for its assertive, testimonial value. Its circumstantial value is that which Wigmore pointed out, namely, the quality of inconsistency with the party's present claim. "The hearsay rule applies to those statements for which the only justification is their narrative content. It is inapplicable to those which are conduct, i.e., for which the trustworthiness of the utterance is a matter of indifference. So it is with admissions. The writer feels that inasmuch as all admissions, express and otherwise, can be rationalized as the relevant conduct of the speaker, it is unnecessary to predicate their admissibility on the basis of a possible narrative effect not possessed by all of them." [5]

On balance, the most satisfactory justification of the admissibility of admissions is that they are the product of the adversary system, sharing, though on a lower and nonconclusive level, the characteristics of admissions in pleadings or stipulations. This view has the added advantage of avoiding the need to find with respect to admissions the circumstantial guarantees of trustworthiness which traditionally characterize hearsay exceptions; admissions are simply classed as nonhearsay. This is the position taken in the Federal and Revised Uniform Rules (1974), which provide: [6]

3. Id. at 266.

4. 4 Wigmore, Evidence § 1048 (Chadbourn rev. 1972).

5. Strahorn, The Hearsay Rule and Admissions, 85 U.Pa.L.Rev. 484, 564, at 573, 576 (1937). See also Schloss v. Traunstine, 135 N.J.L. 11, 49 A.2d 677 (1946).

6. The decision to classify admissions as nonhearsay in the Federal Rules, rather than as a hearsay ex-

ception, was not based on purely theoretical grounds. Believing that no catalog of hearsay exceptions could possibly include all trustworthy hearsay evidence that might evolve, the Advisory Committee included provisions in general terms for hearsay not within one of the enumerated exceptions but having comparable guarantees of trustworthiness. See § 324.1 infra. The inclusion of admissions, which possess no objective guarantee of trustworthiness, as an exception would not have been consistent with this pattern.

Rule 801

DEFINITIONS

The following definitions apply under this article:

. . .

(d) Statements which are not hearsay. A statement is not hearsay if—

. . .

(2) Admission by party-opponent. The statement is offered against a party and is (A) his own statement, in either his individual or a representative capacity or (B) a statement of which he has manifested his adoption or belief in its truth, or (C) a statement by a person authorized by him to make a statement concerning the subject, or (D) a statement by his agent or servant concerning a matter within the scope of his agency or employment, made during the existence of the relationship, or (E) a statement by a coconspirator of a party during the course and in furtherance of the conspiracy.

As a matter of convenience, in recognition of the tradition of treating admissions as an exception to the hearsay rule, the discussion of them is taken up at this point in this textbook.[7]

Regardless of the precise theory of admissibility, it is clear that admissions of a party come in as substantive evidence of the facts admitted,[8] and that no foundation or predicate by first examining the party himself, as distinguished from the usual procedure for impeaching a witness by proof of his prior inconsistent statement,[9] is a prerequisite for proof of admissions.[10]

When we speak of admissions, without qualifying adjective, we customarily mean evidential admissions, that is, words oral or written, or conduct of a party or his representative offered in evidence against him. These *evidential* admissions are to be distinguished from *judicial* admissions. Judicial admissions are not evidence at all, but are formal admissions in the pleadings in the case, or stipulations, oral or written, by a party or his counsel which have the effect of withdrawing a fact from issue and dispensing wholly with the need for proof of the fact.[11] Thus the judicial admission, unless it should be allowed by the court to be withdrawn, is conclusive in the case, whereas the evidential admission is not conclusive but is always subject to be contradicted or explained.[12]

Confessions of crime are a particular kind of admission, governed by special rules discussed in the chapter on Confessions.[13]

A type of evidence with which admissions may be confused is evidence of declarations against interest. The latter, coming in under a separate exception to the hearsay rule, to be admissible must have been against the declarant's interest when made.[14] No such requirement applies to admissions. If a person making the statement, may deprive the admission of substantial weight.

As to treating admissions as nonhearsay, see also Cox v. Esso Shipping Co., 247 F.2d 629, 632 (5th Cir. 1957); United States v. United Shoe Machinery Corp., 89 F.Supp. 349, 351 (D.C.Mass.1950).

7. This treatment also conforms to earlier editions of this work.

8. United States v. Cline, 570 F.2d 731 (8th Cir. 1978); Olson v. Hodges, 236 Iowa 612, 19 N.W.2d 676 (1945) and Silvey & Co., Inc. v. Engel, 204 Neb. 633, 284 N.W.2d 560 (1979) (error to instruct jury that an admission could be considered merely as discrediting the party's testimony); Lambros v. Coolahan, 185 Md. 463, 45 A.2d 96 (1945) (witness' report of party's oral admission, though denied by party, sufficient to take the issue to the jury); Greenwood v. Harris, 362 P.2d 85 (Okl.1961) (admission sufficient to supply need for expert testimony in medical malpractice action); Dec. Dig. Evidence ☞200, 217, 222(1), 265(1); 4 Wigmore, Evidence §§ 1055, 1056 (Chadbourn rev. 1972). Additional circumstances, e.g., want of knowledge by per-

9. See § 37 supra.

10. Cox v. Esso Shipping Co., 247 F.2d 629 (5th Cir. 1957); Brown v. Calumet River Railway Co., 125 Ill. 600, 18 N.E. 283 (1888); 4 Wigmore, Evidence § 1051(1) (Chadbourn rev. 1972).

11. See § 265 infra. In the same category are admissions in response to a request to admit under Fed. R.Civ.P. 36. Finman, The Request for Admissions in Federal Civil Procedure, 71 Yale L.J. 371 (1962).

12. Aide v. Taylor, 214 Minn. 212, 7 N.W.2d 757 (1943); 4 Wigmore, Evidence §§ 1058, 1059 (Chadbourn rev. 1972). As to admissions in pleadings other than the effective pleadings in the case, see § 265 infra.

13. Ch. 14 supra.

14. See § 276 infra.

son states that a note is forged, and then later acquires the note and sues upon it, the previous statement will come in against him as an admission, though he had no interest when he made the statement. Of course, most admissions are actually against interest when made, but there is no such requirement.[15] Hence the common phrase in judicial opinions, "admissions against interest," [16] is an invitation to confuse two separate exceptions to the hearsay rule and to engraft upon admissions an against-interest requirement without basis in reason or authority. Other distinctions are that admissions must be the statements of a party to the lawsuit (or his predecessor or representative) and must be offered, not for, but against him, whereas the declaration against interest need not be and usually is not made by a party or his predecessor or representative, but by some third person.[17] Finally, the declaration against interest exception admits the declaration only when the declarant has become unavailable as a witness, whereas no such requirement is applied to admissions of a party.[18]

If there are several parties on one side of the litigation, whether plaintiffs or defendants, the admission of one of these co-parties is admissible only against himself. It is not admissible merely by virtue of the co-party relationship against the other parties with whom he is aligned.[19]

WESTLAW REFERENCES

digest,synopsis(admission* /p party parties opponent* /p exception /p hearsay)

admission* /p party parties opponent* /p nonhearsay (not +2 hearsay)

topic(157) & digest (admission* /s party parties opponent* & declaration* statement* /s interest*)

§ 263. Testimonial Qualifications: Mental Competency: Personal Knowledge [1]

The nature of admissions as a general proposition denies any significance to the question whether the party making the admission must meet standards of competency established for witnesses.[2] Thus disqualifications, if still recognized, arising from the marital relationship or "Dead Man's" acts lack relevancy in the case of admissions. No reason exists to exclude an otherwise receivable admission because the party making it was married or is now dead. The single exception calling for consideration is lack of mental capacity. Some cases involve statements by badly injured persons, possibly al-

---

15. One of the clearest expressions to this effect is in State v. Anderson, 10 Or. 448, 452 (1882). On a charge of murdering his brother, the state gave in evidence defendant's admissions that he had no means before his brother's death. In holding these admissible over the objection that they were not against interest, the court said: "But the admissibility of a party's own previous statements or declarations in respect to the subject in controversy, as evidence against him, does not in any manner depend upon the question whether they were for or against his interest at the time they were made, or afterwards. The opposite party has a right to introduce them if relevant and voluntarily made, no matter how they may stand or have stood in relation to the interest of the party making them." The statement retains its validity. United States v. Rios Ruiz, 579 F.2d 670, 676 (5th Cir.1978). See 4 Wigmore, Evidence § 1048 (Chadbourn rev. 1972).

16. The phrase continues to appear with embarrassing frequency. See Kekua v. Kaiser Foundation Hospital, 601 P.2d 364 (Hawaii 1979), and Hofer v. Bituminous Casualty Co., 260 Iowa 816, 148 N.W.2d 485 (1967), both characterizing the phrase as misleading and deploring the usage.

17. See § 276 infra.

18. See 4 Wigmore, Evidence §§ 1048, 1049 (Chadbourn rev. 1972); Fed.R.Evid. 801(d)(2), 804(b)(4).

19. There may, of course, be an additional relationship, over and above that of being co-parties, which will render the evidence admissible. See §§ 267, 268 infra.

See O'Neal v. Morgan, 637 F.2d 846 (2d Cir.1980), cert. denied 451 U.S. 972 (civil rights action against four police officers for beating plaintiff's intestate; trial judge excluded telephone call admitting that defendants did the beating; evidence established that caller was a defendant but not which one; remanded with directions to allow the evidence and instruct jury to consider it against each defendant who failed to persuade jury he was not the caller, by analogy to tort cases where proved that one member of group inflicted harm but not which one).

§ 263

1. See 4 Wigmore, Evidence § 1053 (Chadbourn rev. 1972).

2. See Ch. 7 supra.

so under sedation.[3] While the older decisions tended to mount an inquiry into the capacity of the declarant and to exclude if it was found not to exist,[4] the more modern ones view the question as going to weight rather than admissibility.[5] The latter position represents a preferable allocation of the functions of judge and jury and is consistent with current thinking concerning mental competency as a qualification of witnesses.[6] The adversary roots of admissions by parties make caution appropriate in applying this reasoning to statements by children.[7] Substantive rules of liability for torts may suggest acceptable standards of responsibility for such admissions.[8] Hearsay exceptions such as that for excited utterances should be explored as possibly offering a more satisfactory avenue to admissibility in evidence in a particular case.[9]

The requirement that a witness speak from firsthand knowledge would seem to be applicable to hearsay declarations generally [10] and it has sometimes been applied to admissions,[11] but the traditional view and the greater number of decisions hold that it is not.[12] These latter argue that when a man speaks against his own interest it is to be supposed that he has made an adequate investigation.[13] While this self-disserving feature might attach to most admissions, we have seen that admissions are competent evidence though not against interest when made. As to these the argument does not apply, and it seems sufficient to justify the

---

3. In some States legislation restricts the admissibility of statements obtained from injured persons within a specified time after the injury was sustained. Mass.Gen.Laws Ann., c. 233, § 23A; Wis.Stats.Ann. 904.12; Annot., 22 A.L.R.2d 1269.

4. Jacobson v. Carlson, 302 Mich. 448, 4 N.W.2d 721 (1942); Ammundson v. Tinholt, 228 Minn. 115, 36 N.W.2d 521 (1949). Oddly, both cases speak of utterances of a party incapable of narrating.

5. Currier v. Grossman's of New Hampshire, Inc., 107 N.H. 159, 219 A.2d 273 (1966); Finnerty v. Darby, 391 Pa. 300, 138 A.2d 117 (1958).

Attention is directed to statutes restricting the admissibility of statements obtained from injured persons within specified periods after the injury was sustained. Mass.G.L.A., c. 233, § 23A; Minn.Stats.Ann. § 602.01; Wis.Stats.Ann. § 904.12.

6. See § 62 supra.

7. Occasional broad statements that an infant cannot make an admission, Knights Templar & Masons' Life Indemnity Co. v. Crayton, 209 Ill. 550, 70 N.E. 1066 (1904), generally have not been followed.

8. See, e.g., Howard v. Hall, 112 Ga.App. 247, 145 S.E.2d 70 (1965); Reed v. Kabureck, 229 Ill.App. 36 (1923), suggesting substantive tort liability as a measure for admissions. See Prosser, Torts 154–157, 996–1000 (4th ed. 1971). Contract law, in view of its tenderness toward even very mature infants, is unhelpful.

An admission by a child under 9 years of age was upheld in Hardman v. Helene Curtis Industries, Inc., 48 Ill.App.2d 42, 198 N.E.2d 681 (1964); under 7 in Atchison, Topeka & Santa Fe Railroad Co. v. Potter, 60 Kan. 808, 58 P. 471 (1899); and 6 years old in Rolfe v. Olson, 87 N.J.Super. 242, 208 A.2d 817 (1965). In Fontaine v. Devonis, 114 R.I. 541, 336 A.2d 847 (1975), exclusion of the statement of a 3½ year old child that he just ran out in the street and got hit by a car was upheld. Cases are collected in Annot., 12 A.L.R.3d 1051.

The view here expressed is at some variance from earlier editions of this work.

9. See § 297 infra.

10. See e.g., §§ 285, 300, 310 infra.

11. Coca-Cola Bottling Co. v. Munn, 99 F.2d 190, 197 (4th Cir.1938) (previous admission by plaintiff, now suing for injury due to lye in bottled drink, that it would be impossible for a bottle to have any lye in it after going through defendant's plant, held properly excluded); Paschall v. Gulf, Colorado & Santa Fe Railway Co., 100 S.W.2d 183, 192, 193 (Tex.Civ.App.1936) (action for death of husband in collision, letter of wife, who was not present, that family was not holding defendant, a friend of deceased, responsible, written before investigating facts, held improperly admitted).

12. Mahlandt v. Wild Canid Survival and Research Center, Inc., 588 F.2d 626 (8th Cir.1978) (agent's statement without firsthand knowledge admissible against both agent and principal; see n. 15 infra); Janus v. Akstin, 91 N.H. 373, 20 A.2d 552 (1941) (action for attack by defendant's dog, defendant's statement that dog jumped on the decedent held admissible though defendant not present); Reed v. McCord, 160 N.Y. 330, 341, 54 N.E. 737 (1899) (statement by defendant, employer, as to how injury happened, though he was not present); Salvitti v. Throp, 343 Pa. 642, 23 A.2d 445 (1942) (automobile collision; evidence that owner of truck acknowledged that his driver was at fault admitted, though owner not present). Additional cases are collected in Annot., 54 A.L.R.2d 1069. See 4 Wigmore, Evidence § 1053 (Chadbourn rev. 1972).

This question is often joined with the problem whether repetition of another's statement is an adoptive admission. See Reed v. McCord supra, and § 269 infra.

13. On occasion it may appear affirmatively that an investigation was in fact conducted. Pekelis v. Transcontinental & Western Air, Inc., 187 F.2d 122 (2d Cir. 1951); Mahlandt v. Wild Canid Survival and Research Center, Inc., infra n. 15.

general dispensing with the knowledge qualification to say that admissions which become relevant in litigation usually concern some matter of substantial importance to the declarant upon which he would probably have informed himself so that they possess, even when not based on firsthand observation, greater reliability than the general run of hearsay. Moreover, the possibility is substantial that the declarant may have come into possession of significant information not known to his opponent.

The validity of dispensing with firsthand knowledge in the case of admissions by agents has been questioned vigorously by a leading text on the Federal Rules of Evidence, advocating the insertion of such a requirement by construction.[14] The proposal has not met with judicial acceptance.[15]

---

14. Weinstein & Berger, Evidence ¶ 801(d)(2) (C)[01]–(D)[01] at pp. 801–157, 164. It is argued that the desired result could be reached by applying the rationale of Rule 805 (hearsay within hearsay), although admissions are not hearsay, or by applying Rule 403 (exclusion for prejudice or confusion). The fact that admissions are subject to explanation to avoid or lessen their force is believed, however, to afford adequate safeguards, without sacrificing the evidential usefulness of admissions.

15. Mahlandt v. Wild Canid Survival and Research Center, Inc., 588 F.2d 626 (8th Cir.1978) (report of alleged biting of child by wolf, made by employee of research center in whose backyard wolf was confined, after investigation but without personal knowledge, admissible against research center under Federal Rule 801(d)(2)(D)). See also Russell v. United Parcel Service, Inc., 666 F.2d 1188 (8th Cir.1981).

In approaching admissions generally, the Advisory Committee's Note to Federal Rule 801(d)(2) observed:

The freedom which admissions have enjoyed from technical demands of searching for an assurance of trustworthiness in some against-interest circumstance, and from the restrictive influences of the opinion rule and the rule requiring firsthand knowledge, when taken with the apparently prevalent satisfaction with the results, calls for generous treatment of this avenue to admissibility.

§ 264. Admissions in Opinion Form: Conclusions of Law

If the want of knowledge of the party does not exclude his admissions, as indicated in the preceding section, it would seem clear that the opinion rule should not. As we have seen, that rule has as its object the regulation of the interrogation of a witness on the stand, so as to elicit his answers in the more concrete form rather than in terms of inference. In its modern form it is a rule of preference for the more concrete answers, if the witness can give them, rather than a rule of exclusion.[1] In any view, this rule, designed to promote the concreteness of answers on the stand, is grotesquely misapplied to out-of-court statements, such as admissions, where the declarant's statements are made without thought of the form of courtroom testimony and where it can only be applied by excluding the statement, whereas in the courtroom if the opinion objection is sustained, counsel may reframe his question in the preferred form. Accordingly, the prevailing view is that admissions in the form of opinions are competent.[2] Most

§ 264

1. See § 18 supra.

2. Russell v. United Parcel Service, Inc., 666 F.2d 1188 (8th Cir.1981) (discrimination action by employee; proper to admit statements by supervisors that plaintiff was being treated in manner complained of because manager was out to cause her trouble for filing lawsuits and claims against the company); Cox v. Esso Shipping Co., 247 F.2d 629 (5th Cir.1957) (master's report that seaman's injury was due in part to own neglect); Pekelis v. Transcontinental & Western Air, Inc., 187 F.2d 122 (2d Cir.1951) (report by airline investigating board as to cause of accident); Strickland v. Davis, 221 Ala. 247, 128 So. 233 (1930) (defendant after accident said it was his fault; held admissible, rejecting the application to admissions of requirements for testimony on the stand, and the objection that the statement expressed a conclusion of law); Swain v. Oregon Motor Stages, 160 Or. 1, 82 P.2d 1084, 118 A.L.R. 1225 (1938) (plaintiff, bus passenger suing for injury in collision with automobile, stated in accident report that driver of automobile to blame, admissible; extensive discussion); Wells v. Burton Lines, 228 N.C. 422, 45 S.E.2d 569 (1947) (plaintiff after collision said it was his fault); Woods v. Townsend, 144 Tex. 594, 192 S.W.2d 884 (1946) (will contest for undue influence; admission of proponent, "we got the papers fixed . . . but the old man didn't know what he was doing"); Southern Passenger Motor Lines v. Burke, 187 Va. 53, 46

often the question arises in connection with statements of a participant in an accident that it was his fault, or not the fault of the other participant. Against these and like statements, the additional objection is often urged that they are conclusions of law. But this should be no objection either. While conceivably a party might give an opinion on an abstract question of law, such are not the statements actually offered in evidence. These always include in them an application of a standard to the facts; thus they suggest what the declarant thinks the facts are to which he is applying the standard of "fault," or other legal or moral standard involved in his statement. The factual bearing is not to be ignored merely because the statement may also indicate the party's assumptions as to the law.[3] It is, of course, conceivable that the legal principle may be so technical as to deprive an admission of significance.

In addition, it should be remembered that evidential admissions are subject to explanation.

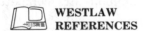

WESTLAW REFERENCES

157k201 /p conclusion! opinion*

---

§ 265. Admissions in Pleadings:[1] Pleas of Guilty

The final pleadings upon which the case is tried state the contentions of each party as to the facts, and by admitting or denying the opponent's pleading, they define the fact issues which are to be tried by the process of proof. Thus, the court must look to the pleadings as part of the record in passing on the relevancy of evidence, and in ascertaining the issues to be submitted to the jury. For these purposes it is not necessary to offer the pleadings in evidence.[2] They are used as judicial and not as evidential admissions, and for these purposes, until withdrawn or amended, are conclusive.[3] But suppose a party desires to use an averment or admission in his adversary's final pleading, as a basis in his argument for the existence of some subordinate fact or as the foundation for some adverse inference. The greater number of states permit the party to do this by quoting or reading the pleading as part of the record,[4] but a substantial minority require that the party, in order to make this use of it, must first have introduced the relevant passage from the opponent's pleading as part of his own evidence during the course of the trial.[5] This requirement affords an opportunity to the pleader to give explanatory evidence, such as that the allegation was made through inadvertence or mistake,[6] so far as this may be allowable, and avoids the possibility of a surprise inference from the pleading in closing argument. It may be that these considerations justify the departure from consistency.

An important exception to the use of the pleadings in the case as admissions must be noted. A basic problem which attends the use of written pleadings is uncertainty

---

S.E.2d 26 (1948) (plaintiff's statement that collision not due to fault or negligence of defendant's driver); 4 Wigmore, Evidence § 1053(3) (Chadbourn rev. 1972); Annot., 118 A.L.R. 1230. See Adv. Comm. Note supra n. 15.

3. See decisions cited in n. 2 supra.

§ 265

1. 4 Wigmore, Evidence §§ 1064–1067 (Chadbourn rev. 1972); Dec.Dig. Evidence ⟐208, 265(8)(11); C.J.S. Evidence §§ 300–306; Annot., 52 A.L.R.2d 516.

2. Wright v. Lincoln City Lines, Inc., 160 Neb. 714, 71 N.W.2d 182 (1955).

3. Roth v. Roth, 45 Ill.2d 19, 258 N.E.2d 838 (1970) (pleadings); Hake v. George Weideman Brewing Co., 23 Ohio St.2d 65, 52 O.O.2d 366, 262 N.E.2d 703 (1970)

(admission in opening statement); Note, 64 Colum.L. Rev. 1121 (1964).

4. Grand Trunk Western Railway Co. v. Lovejoy, 304 Mich. 35, 7 N.W.2d 212 (1942); Hildreth v. Hudloe, 282 S.W. 747 (Mo.App.1926); Gibson v. Koutsky-Brennan-Vana Co., 143 Neb. 326, 9 N.W.2d 298 (1943); and cases cited in 4 Wigmore Evidence § 1064, note 1 (Chadbourn rev. 1972).

5. Louisville & Nashville Railroad Co. v. Hull, 113 Ky. 561, 68 S.W. 433 (1902); Gossler v. Wood, 120 N.C. 69, 27 S.E. 33 (1897); Mullen v. Union Central Life Insurance Co., 182 Pa. 150, 37 A. 988 (1897) (affidavit of defense).

6. This reason is found in Smith v. Nimocks, 94 N.C. 243 (1886).

whether the evidence as it actually unfolds at trial will prove the case described in the pleadings. Traditionally a failure in this respect, i.e. a variance between pleading and proof, could bring disaster to the pleader's case. As a safeguard against developments of this kind, the common law evolved the use of counts, each a complete separate statement of a different version of the same basic claim, combined in the same declaration, to take care of variance possibilities.[7] The same was done with defenses. Inconsistency between counts or between defenses was not prohibited; in fact it was essential to the successful use of the system.[8] Also essential to the success of the system was a prohibition against using allegations in one count or defense as admissions to prove or disprove allegations in another.[9] For a time, under the influence of the Field Code of 1848, the view prevailed that in a given case there could exist only one set of facts and that inconsistent statements and defenses were therefore not allowable.[10] Nevertheless, uncertainty has persisted as to how a case will in fact develop at trial, and some procedure is needed for dealing with problems of variance. The modern equivalent of the common law system is the use of alternative and hypothetical forms of statement

of claims and defenses, regardless of consistency.[11] It can readily be appreciated that pleadings of this nature are directed primarily to giving notice and lack the essential character of an admission. To allow them to operate as admissions would render their use ineffective and frustrate their underlying purpose. Hence the decisions with seeming unanimity deny them status as judicial admissions,[12] and generally disallow them as evidential admissions.[13]

The trend is to expand the application of the exception described above to the general rule of admissibility to include, not only the common law practice and modern hypothetical and alternative allegations, but in addition situations in which a more skillful pleader would have avoided the pitfalls of admissions by resorting to one of those techniques. For example, in Frank R. Jelleff, Inc. v. Braden,[14] an action against a retailer for burns suffered from a flammable garment, counsel for the retailer, fearing the running of the statute of limitations against its indemnity claim against the manufacturer, sued the latter in another jurisdiction, alleging that the original plaintiff had been burned by the flammable product. This allegation was introduced by plaintiff in the

7. Thus in Hart v. Longfield, 7 Mod. 148, 87 Eng. Rep. 1156 (1703), where plaintiff wished to proceed in both indebitatus assumpsit and quantum meruit for nourishing Edward Longfield, Holt, C.J., observed that Edward Longfield should be stated as a different child in each count, multiplying him as many times as there were counts.

"Records containing from ten to fifteen special counts or pleas are by no means rare. . . . Of these, the greater proportion and frequently the whole relate to the same substantial cause of action or defence. They are merely different expositions of the same case, and expositions of it often inconsistent with each other." Report of Common Law Procedure Commission, Parlt. Papers 1830, quoted in 9 Holdsworth, Hist.Eng.Law 305, 306 (3d ed. 1944).

The counterpart in equity practice was to allege in the alternative.

8. Gould v. Oliver, 2 Man. & G. 208 (C.P.1840); Note, 17 Tex.L.Rev. 191 (1939), quoted in Garman v. Griffin, 666 F.2d 1156 (8th Cir.1981).

9. Harington v. Macmorris, 5 Taunt. 228, 128 Eng. Rep. 675 (1813); Herman v. Fine, 314 Mass. 67, 49 N.E.2d 597 (1943). See also n. 8 supra.

McCormick et al. on Evid. 3rd Ed. H.B.—18

10. Clark, Code Pleading 460 (2d ed. 1947).

11. Fed.R.Civ.P. 8(e)(2); James & Hazard, Civil Procedure 89 (1977); Green, Basic Civil Procedure 114–118 (2d ed. 1979).

12. Schneider v. Lockheed Aircraft Corp., 658 F.2d 835 (D.C.Cir.1981), cert. denied 455 U.S. 994 (error to allow use as evidentiary admission concession of correctness of allegations in pleading made only for purposes of arguing motion directed against sufficiency of pleading); McCormick v. Kopmann, 23 Ill.App.2d 189, 161 N.E.2d 720 (1959) (allegation of decedent's freedom from contributory negligence in count 1 not negated by allegation that his intoxication caused accident in count 4); Aetna Insurance Co. v. Klein, 318 S.W.2d 464 (Tex. Civ.App.1958), reversed on other grounds 160 Tex. 61, 325 S.W.2d 376 (general denial not negated by contrary statements in special pleas).

13. Macheca v. Fowler, 412 S.W.2d 462 (Mo.1967); Van Sickell v. Margolis, 109 N.J.Super. 14, 262 A.2d 209 (1969), affirmed 55 N.J. 355, 262 A.2d 203; Furlong v. Donhals, Inc., 81 R.I. 46, 137 A.2d 734 (1958). Contra, Tway v. Hartman, 181 Okl. 608, 75 P.2d 893 (1938).

14. 98 U.S.App.D.C. 180, 233 F.2d 671 (1956).

original action over objection, and the ruling was sustained.[15] The penalty is a severe one for an inartful failure to plead hypothetically, and cases reaching an opposite result appear to be on the increase.[16] The same trend is evident in cases involving separate actions against different defendants to recover for the same injury.[17] The trend is consistent with the prevailing view that the primary purpose of pleadings is to give notice and that alternative or hypothetical allegations are not usable as admissions, but the extent to which it will prevail is difficult to estimate.

A further possible exception, not widely recognized, is denial of status as an admission to amended, withdrawn, or superseded pleadings on the theory that to admit them into evidence contravenes the policy of liberality in amendment.[18]

The question whether a plea of guilty, formally tendered, in a criminal case shall come in evidence as an admission where the accused is later allowed to plead not guilty and is tried on the charge, presents competing considerations of policy. On the one hand, it may be argued, a plea of guilty if freely and understandingly made is so likely to be true that to withhold it from the jury seems to ask them to do justice without knowledge of one of the most significant of the relevant facts. Similar admissions have been received in civil cases, leaving it to the adversary to rebut or explain.[19] But here, liberty or life is at stake, and a decision can scarcely be reached without taking into account the circumstances surrounding the withdrawal. If the leave to withdraw is granted because of denial of assistance of counsel, lack of ratification by the accused, involuntariness, or similar reason,[20] it is evident that a manifest injustice is sought to be corrected. If the withdrawn plea is nevertheless allowed into evidence, the effectiveness of the corrective measure is greatly impaired. Additionally, allowing the evidence virtually compels the accused to explain why he pleaded guilty, with resultant encroachment upon the privilege against self-incrimination and intrusion into sensitive areas of the attorney-client relationship. Under these circum-

15. In the indemnity action, the manufacturer then took the position that counsel for the original defendant was grossly negligent in filing the complaint against it and that recovery should be barred. Frank R. Jelleff, Inc. v. Pollak Brothers, Inc., 171 F.Supp. 467 (N.D.Ind.1957).

16. Garman v. Griffin, 666 F.2d 1156 (8th Cir.1981) (action for death of child run over by school bus from which he had alighted, against driver and alleged bus manufacturer; latter was dismissed; error to admit for defendant driver plaintiffs' allegation that bus was defectively constructed so as to preclude complete view by driver). Several of the cases involve third-party complaints or cross-claims for indemnity with concessions in the original pleadings being offered to offset the indemnity claims. Douglas Equipment, Inc. v. Mack Trucks, Inc., 471 F.2d 222 (7th Cir.1972); Continental Insurance Co. of New York v. Sherman, 439 F.2d 1294 (5th Cir.1971); Malauskas v. Tishman Construction Corp., 81 Ill.App.3d 759, 36 Ill.Dec. 875, 401 N.E.2d 1013 (1980). Contra, Schenck v. Pelkey, 176 Conn. 245, 405 A.2d 665 (1978) (guest sued homeowners for swimming pool accident alleging negligence; manufacturer and seller added as defendants, with allegation of failure to give warnings or directions; settled and dismissed as to homeowners; held, original complaint admissible for remaining defendants on issue of proximate cause).

17. Estate of Spinosa, 621 F.2d 1154 (1st Cir.1980) (product liability action against truck manufacturer for death of driver and injury to passenger; proper to exclude complaint in earlier action against owner, alleging that accident was result of his negligent failure to maintain); Meador v. City of Salem, 51 Ill.2d 572, 284 N.E.2d 266 (1972) (proper to exclude workman's compensation claim, offered in statutory action against city for same injury, on issue of employment); Schuster v. Fletcher, 74 Ill.App.2d 249, 219 N.E.2d 588 (1966) (separate actions by plaintiff, each alleging different cause for injuries; exclusion upheld).

18. Fed.R.Civ.P. 15(a) provides "leave [to amend] shall be freely given when justice so requires." Cases on the use of withdrawn or superseded pleadings as evidential admissions are collected in Annot., 52 A.L.R.2d 516 and predominate in favor of admissibility.

19. Cases cited in n. 28 infra. Fed.R.Evid. 410 bars withdrawn pleas of guilty from subsequent use in both criminal and civil cases. See n. 21 infra. Compare Morrissey v. Powell, 304 Mass. 268, 23 N.E.2d 411, 124 A.L.R. 1522 (1939), upholding admissibility of plea of guilty, although it was later withdrawn and defendant acquitted.

20. These are set forth as grounds for withdrawal in A.B.A. Standards for Criminal Justice, Standard 14–2.1.

See also Fed.R.Crim.P. 11(c) and (d) setting forth the requirements for accepting pleas of guilty and nolo contendere.

stances the withdrawn plea should be excluded.[21] If, on the contrary, withdrawal may be made without a showing of the kind described above,[22] exclusion would not in principle follow automatically but would depend upon standards governing the admissibility of confessions.[23]

A recurring question is whether a plea of guilty to a criminal charge should be allowed in evidence in a related civil action. Generally the evidence is admitted.[24] While a plea of guilty to a traffic offense is in theory no different from a plea of guilty to other offenses,[25] recognition that people plead guilty to traffic charges for reasons of convenience

and without much regard to guilt and collateral consequences has led to some tendency to exclude them from evidence.[26] Pleas of *nolo contendere* or *non vult*, in jurisdictions where allowed,[27] are generally regarded as inadmissible,[28] and in fact that attribute is a principal reason for their employment.[29]

Subject to the qualifications noted in the preceding discussion, pleadings are generally usable against the pleader. If they are the effective pleadings in the case, they have the standing of judicial admissions.[30] Amended, withdrawn, or superseded pleadings in the case are no longer judicial admissions,[31] but may be used as evidentiary ad-

---

21. Kercheval v. United States, 274 U.S. 220 (1927); People v. Spitaleri, 9 N.Y.2d 168, 212 N.Y.S.2d 53, 173 N.E.2d 35 (1961); A.B.A. Standards for Criminal Justice Standard 14–2.2. Cases pro and con are collected in Annot., 86 A.L.R.2d 326.

Fed.R.Evid. 410 provides:

Except as otherwise provided in this rule, evidence of the following is not, in any civil or criminal proceeding, admissible against the defendant who made the plea or was a participant in the plea discussions:

    (1) a plea of guilty which was later withdrawn;

    (2) a plea of nolo contendere;

    (3) any statement made in the course of any proceedings under rule 11 of the Federal Rules of Criminal Procedure or comparable state procedure regarding either of the foregoing pleas; or

    (4) any statement made in the course of plea discussions with an attorney for the prosecuting authority which do not result in a plea of guilty or which result in a plea of guilty later withdrawn.

However, such a statement is admissible (i) in any proceeding wherein another statement made in the course of the same plea or plea discussions has been introduced and the statement ought in fairness be considered contemporaneously with it, or (ii) in a criminal proceeding for perjury or false statement if the statement was made by the defendant under oath, on the record and in the presence of counsel.

To the same effect is Fed.R.Crim.P. 11(e)(6). See also West's Ann.Cal.Evid.Code § 1153.

The admissibility of offers and statements made in the course of plea bargaining is discussed in § 274 infra.

22. See n. 20 supra.

23. The same would seem to be true with respect to "pleas of guilty" made, often without formal authorization of law, before committing magistrates. See cases in Annot., 141 A.L.R. 1335.

24. Teitelbaum Furs, Inc. v. Dominion Insurance Co., 58 Cal.2d 601, 25 Cal.Rptr. 559, 375 P.2d 439

(1962), cert. denied 372 U.S. 966; Jacobs v. Goodspeed, 180 Conn. 415, 429 A.2d 915 (1980); Scogin v. Nugen, 204 Kan. 568, 464 P.2d 166 (1970); Brohawn v. Transamerica Insurance Co., 276 Md. 396, 347 A.2d 842 (1975); Annot., 18 A.L.R.2d 1287, 1307. The authorities agree that evidence is admissible to explain the guilty plea.

25. Ando v. Woodberry, 8 N.Y.2d 165, 203 N.Y.S.2d 74, 168 N.E.2d 520 (1960), Notes, 9 Buffalo L.Rev. 373, 74 Harv.L.Rev. 1452.

26. Hannah v. Ike Topper Structural Steel Co., 120 Ohio App. 44, 201 N.E.2d 63 (1963). Statutory prohibitions against introducing traffic convictions have been construed as applying also to guilty pleas. Jones v. Talbot, 87 Idaho 498, 394 P.2d 316 (1964). See also § 318 infra.

Graham, Admissibility in Illinois of Convictions and Pleas of Guilty to Traffic Offenses in Related Civil Litigation, 1979 So.Ill.U.L.J. 209, 222, suggests that Federal Rule 803(22), excluding offenses punishable by imprisonment for less than one year from a hearsay exception for judgments of guilty of crime, affords an analogy for also excluding pleas of guilty to minor offenses.

27. E.g., Fed.R.Crim.P. 11.

28. Federal Deposit Insurance Corp. v. Cloonan, 165 Kan. 68, 193 P.2d 656 (1948); State v. La Rose, 71 N.H. 435, 52 A. 943 (1902); Fed.R.Evid. 410, supra n. 21. It may be assumed that this is a factor considered by the judge in exercising his discretion to allow or deny the plea.

29. For the use of the plea in antitrust actions, see City of Burbank v. General Electric Co., 329 F.2d 825 (9th Cir.1964); Seamans et al., Use of Criminal Pleas in Aid of Private Antitrust Actions, 10 Antitrust Bull. 795 (1965); 10 A.L.R. Fed. 328.

30. Supra n. 3.

31. Taliaferro v. Reirdon, 197 Okl. 55, 168 P.2d 292 (1946); Kirk v. Head, 137 Tex. 44, 152 S.W.2d 726 (1941).

missions.[32]   A party's pleading in one case may be used as an evidentiary admission in other litigation.[33]

How far is it necessary to connect the pleading with the party against whom it is sought to be used in evidence as an admission?   Certainly if it be shown to have been sworn to,[34] or signed by the party himself that would be sufficient.[35]   More often, however, the pleading is prepared and signed by counsel, and the older view holds that it is not sufficient to show that the pleading was filed or signed by the party's attorney of record, and the statements therein will be presumed to be merely "suggestions of counsel" unless other evidence is produced that they were actually sanctioned by the client.[36]   The trend today, however, is to the sensible view that pleadings shown to have been prepared or filed by counsel employed by the party, are prima facie regarded as authorized by him and are entitled to be received as his admissions.[37]   It is open to the party to give evidence that the pleading was filed upon incorrect information and without his actual knowledge but such a showing goes only to the weight, not the admissibility of the pleading.[38]

 WESTLAW REFERENCES

157k208(1)

32.   Annot., 52 A.L.R.2d 516.

33.   Missouri Pacific Railway Co. v. Zolliecoffer, 209 Ark. 559, 191 S.W.2d 587 (1946); Bartolatta v. Calvo, 112 Conn. 385, 152 A. 306 (1930); Korelski v. Needham, 77 Ill.App.2d 328, 222 N.E.2d 334 (1966); Himelson v. Galusz, 309 Mich. 512, 15 N.W.2d 727 (1944); Dec.Dig. Evidence ⟺208(2); C.J.S. Evidence § 303.

34.   Hall v. Guthrie, 10 Mo. 621 (1847) (sworn bill in chancery); Johnson v. Vutte, 41 Mont. 158, 108 P. 1057 (1910) (admission in sworn answer); Dec.Dig. Evidence ⟺208(4).

35.   Radclyffe v. Barton, 161 Mass. 327, 37 N.E. 373 (1894); Annot., 14 A.L.R. 22, 26.

36.   Fidelity & Deposit Co. v. Redfield, 7 F.2d 800 (9th Cir. 1925); Reichert v. Jerome H. Sheip, Inc., 206 Ala. 648, 91 So. 618 (1921).   Cases pro and con are collected in Annots. 14 A.L.R. 22, 23, 90 A.L.R. 1393, 1394, 63 A.L.R.2d 412, 428, 444.

37.   Frank R. Jelleff, Inc. v. Braden, 98 U.S.App. D.C. 180, 233 F.2d 671 (1956), supra n. 14; Fibreboard

110k274(10)

§ 266.   Testimony by the Party Against Himself [1]

It happens not infrequently that a party while testifying on the stand or on pretrial examination may admit some fact which if true is fatal, or at least adverse, to his cause of action or defense.   If at the end of the trial the party's admission stands unimpeached and uncontradicted, then like unimpeached and uncontradicted testimony generally it is conclusive against him.   Frequently this situation is what the courts are referring to when they say somewhat misleadingly that a party is "bound" by his own testimony.   The controversial question is whether he is bound by his own testimony in the sense that he will not be allowed to contradict it by other testimony, or if contradictory testimony has been received the judge and jury are required to disregard it and to accept as true the party's self-disserving testimony, as a judicial admission.

Three main approaches are reflected in the decisions.   They tend to some extent to merge together and do not necessarily lead to different results in particular situations.   First, the view that a party's testimony in this respect is like the testimony of any other witness called by the party, that is, the

Paper Products Corp. v. East Bay Union, 227 C.A.2d 675, 39 Cal.Rptr. 64, 83 (1964); Collens v. New Canaan Water Co., 155 Conn. 477, 234 A.2d 825 (1967); Allen v. United States F. & G. Co., 269 Ill. 234, 109 N.E. 1035 (1915); Carlson v. Fredsall, 228 Minn. 461, 37 N.W.2d 744 (1949).

38.   Kucza v. Stone, 155 Conn. 194, 230 A.2d 559 (1967) (personal injury: after P testified he had recovered from injuries received in earlier accident, D introduced complaint from that case, alleging "almost any imaginable" injury, some permanent; error to exclude P's testimony as to whether he had discussed allegations with attorney in earlier case).   See also cases cited in n. 37 supra.

§ 266

1.   See 9 Wigmore, Evidence § 2594a (Chadbourn rev. 1981); Annot., 169 A.L.R. 798; Notes, 22 Va.L. Rev. 365, 36 Mich.L.Rev. 688, 9 Vand.L.Rev. 879; Dec. Dig. Evidence ⟺265(10); C.J.S. Evidence § 1040(3).

party is free (as far as any rule of law is concerned) to elicit contradictory testimony from the witness himself or to call other witnesses to contradict him.[2] Obviously, however, the problem of persuasion may be a difficult one when the party seeks to explain or contradict his own words, and equally obviously the trial judge would often be justified in saying, on motion for directed verdict, that reasonable minds in the particular state of the proof could only believe that the party's testimony against his interest was true.

Second, the view that the party's testimony is not conclusive against contradiction except when he testifies unequivocally to matters "in his peculiar knowledge." These matters may consist of subjective facts, such as his own knowledge or motivation,[3] or they may consist of objective facts observed by him.[4]

Third, the doctrine that a party's testimony adverse to himself is in general to be treated as a judicial admission, conclusive against him,[5] so that he may not bring other witnesses to contradict it, and if he or his adversary does elicit such conflicting testimony it will be disregarded. Obviously, this general rule demands many qualifications and exceptions. Among these are the following: (1) The party is free to contradict, and thus correct, his own testimony; only when his own testimony taken as a whole unequivocally affirms the statement does the rule of conclusiveness apply.[6] The rule is inapplicable, moreover, when the party's testimony (2) may be attributable to inadvertence[7] or to a foreigner's mistake as to meaning,[8] or (3) is merely negative in effect,[9] or (4) is avowedly uncertain, or is an estimate or opinion[10] rather than an assertion of concrete fact, or (5) relates to a matter as to which the party could easily have been

2. Alamo v. Del Rosario, 69 App.D.C. 47, 98 F.2d 328 (1938) (personal injury from automobile collision; plaintiff testified that defendant, his host, the driver, stopped the car, whereas negligence alleged was that he made an untimely left turn; held, jury entitled to believe other witnesses; masterly exposition of the policy of the doctrine, by Edgerton, J.); Guenther v. Armstrong Rubber Co., 406 F.2d 1315 (3d Cir. 1969) (variance in describing tire which caused injury); Kanopka v. Kanopka, 113 Conn. 30, 154 A. 144, 80 A.L.R. 619 (1931) (collision; plaintiff, foreigner speaking through interpreter, excited at time of accident and trial, not concluded by her testimony; general rule that party's testimony, unless intended as unequivocal concession, not conclusive); Cox v. Jones, 138 Or. 327, 5 P.2d 102 (1931) (automobile collision at intersection, plaintiff's testimony as to her own speed and as to seeing approaching truck not conclusive); Wiley v. Rutland Railway Co., 86 Vt. 504, 86 A. 808 (1913) (injury to pedestrian run over by backing train; plaintiff's testimony as to when she looked at track, not a judicial admission); Gale v. Kay, 390 P.2d 596 (Wyo.1964).

3. Monsanto Chemical Co. v. Payne, 354 F.2d 965 (5th Cir. 1966); Findlay v. Rubin Glass and Mirror Co., 350 Mass. 169, 213 N.E.2d 858 (1966); Peterson v. American Family Mutual Insurance Co., 280 Minn. 482, 160 N.W.2d 541 (1968); Bockman v. Mitchell Bros. Truck Lines, 213 Or. 88, 320 P.2d 266 (1958).

4. Bell v. Harmon, 284 S.W.2d 812 (Ky.1955) (plaintiff's version of automobile collision in which he was involved); Verry v. Murphy, 163 N.W.2d 721, 735 (N.D.1969) (plaintiff's version of business transaction).

5. Stearns v. Chicago, Rock Island & Pacific Railway Co., 166 Iowa 566, 578, 148 N.W. 128 (1914) (plain-

tiff's testimony that he did not stop his train as he should have, though contradicted, conclusive on contributory negligence); Taylor v. Williams, 190 So.2d 872 (Miss.1966) (plaintiff passenger's testimony that defendant was not driving, conclusive despite admission in his answer and testimony. "Swore herself out of court"); Massie v. Firmstone, 134 Va. 450, 114 S.E. 652 (1922) (plaintiff real estate broker suing for commission testified that his commission was conditional on sale going through and that it had not; despite contradictory testimony, plaintiff bound by his own evidence).

See also cases in note 4 supra.

6. Chaplain v. Dugas, 323 Mass. 91, 80 N.E.2d 9 (1948); Virginia Electric & Power Co. v. Mabin, 203 Va. 490, 125 S.E.2d 145 (1962).

7. Martin v. Kansas City, 340 S.W.2d 645 (Mo.1960) (statement immediately corrected); Security National Bank v. Johnson, 195 Okl. 107, 155 P.2d 249, 169 A.L.R. 790 (1944) (where doubtful whether statement of party was a slip of the tongue, and was inconsistent with other parts of his testimony, question is for jury).

8. Krikorian v. Dailey, 171 Va. 16, 197 S.E. 442 (1938).

9. Waller v. Waller, 187 Va. 25, 46 S.E.2d 42, 45 (1948).

10. Taylor v. Williams, 190 So.2d 872 (Miss.1966); Van Buskirk v. Missouri-Kansas-Texas Railway Co., 349 S.W.2d 68 (Mo.1961); Petit v. Klinke, 152 Tex. 142, 254 S.W.2d 769 (1953); Mendoza v. Fidelity & Guaranty Insurance Underwriters, Inc., 606 S.W.2d 692 (Tex. 1980).

mistaken, such as the swiftly moving events just preceding a collision in which the party was injured.[11]

Of these three approaches the first, which rejects any restrictive rule and leaves to the judgment of the jurors, the judge, and the appellate court, to evaluate the party's testimony and the conflicting evidence, in the circumstances of the particular case, with only the standard of reason to guide them, seems preferable in policy and most in accord with the tradition of jury trial.

The second theory, binding the party as to facts within his "peculiar knowledge," is based on the assumption that as to such facts the possibility that he may be mistaken substantially disappears. If the facts are subjective ones (knowledge, motivation), the likelihood of successful contradiction is slight, but even then the assumption may be questioned. "If he is human it does not disappear. Knowledge may be 'special' without being correct. Often we little note nor long remember our 'motives, purposes, or knowledge.' There are few if any subjects on which plaintiffs are infallible."[12]

The third theory is also of doubtful validity. In the first place the party's testimony, uttered by a layman in the stress of examination, cannot with justice be given the conclusiveness of the traditional judicial admission in a pleading or stipulation,[13] deliberately drafted by counsel for the express purpose of limiting and defining the facts in issue.[14] Again, a general rule of conclusiveness necessitates an elaboration of qualifications and exceptions which represent a transfer to the appellate court of some of the traditional control of the jury by the trial judge, or in a nonjury case of the judge's factfinding function. These duties call for an exercise of judgment by the judge who has heard and seen the witnesses. The supervision by appellate judges of this trial process can best be exercised under a flexible standard, rather than a rule of conclusiveness.

Moreover, this rule leads to mechanical solutions, unrelated to the needs of justice and calculated to proliferate appeals, in certain special situations. One is the situation where the opponent by adroit cross-examination has maneuvered the party into an improvident concession.[15] Another is the case of the defendant who is protected by liability insurance and who testifies to facts which will help the plaintiff to win.[16] Yet another is the situation where both parties testify against their respective interests.[17] Here

---

11. McCormack v. Haan, 20 Ill.2d 75, 169 N.E.2d 239 (1960); Crew v. Nelson, 188 Va. 108, 49 S.E.2d 326 (1948).

12. Edgerton, J., in Alamo v. Del Rosario, 69 App. D.C. 47, 98 F.2d 328, 332 (1938).

13. As to judicial admissions see § 262 at n. 11 supra, and 9 Wigmore, Evidence §§ 2588–2594 (Chadbourn rev. 1981).

14. This much, however, should be conceded, even under the liberal view contended for that a party is not generally concluded by his testimony. That is, if a party testifies deliberately to a fact fatal to his case, the judge if his counsel, on inquiry, indicates no intention to seek to elicit contradictory testimony, may give a nonsuit or directed verdict. Under these circumstances, the party and his counsel advisedly manifest an intention to be bound. See Kanopka v. Kanopka, 113 Conn. 30, 154 A. 144, 147 (1931), and the annotator's discussion, 169 A.L.R. 801. Compare Oscanyan v. Arms Co., 103 U.S. 261, 263 (1880) holding it proper to direct a verdict on counsel's opening statements, which disclosed that the purpose of the action was to collect a bribe.

15. Driscoll v. Virginia Electric & Power Co., 166 Va. 538, 181 S.E. 402 (1935).

16. Vondrashek v. Dignan, 200 Minn. 530, 274 N.W. 609 (1937) (on question of contributory negligence of plaintiff passenger, defense concluded by defendant's testimony that nobody could tell that he was under the influence). See Note, 36 Mich.L.Rev. 688. Preferable results are to deny conclusiveness to the testimony of defendant-insured, Christie v. Eager, 129 Conn. 62, 26 A.2d 352 (1942), or to allow the introduction of contradicting evidence by the defense. King v. Spencer, 115 Conn. 201, 161 A. 103 (1932), 32 Colum.L.Rev. 1243; contra, Spadaro v. Palmisano, 109 So.2d 418 (Fla.App. 1959). In Horneman v. Brown, 286 Mass. 65, 190 N.E. 735 (1935), in a compulsory liability insurance jurisdiction the defense was allowed to impeach the defendant-insured by a prior inconsistent statement.

17. Sutherland v. Davis, 286 Ky. 743, 151 S.W.2d 1021 (1941) (suit by woman, guest, who had been picked up by defendant, driver of car; plaintiff testified that she knew that defendant was too drunk to drive and that she could have alighted after she knew this; defendant testified that though he had had some drinks, he was sober; held, the admissions by plaintiff

the rule of conclusiveness may be thought to decide the issue against the party who has the burden of proof.[18]

Finally, the moral emphasis is wrong. Early cases where the rule of conclusiveness was first used may have been cases where the judges were outraged by seeming attempts by parties to play fast and loose with the court. But examination of numerous decisions demonstrates that this is far from being the typical situation of the party testifying to self-disserving facts. Instead of the unscrupulous party, it is the one who can be pushed into an admission by the ingenuity or persistence of adverse counsel,[19] or it is the unusually candid or conscientious party willing to speak the truth to his own hurt, who is penalized by the rule of conclusiveness.[20] It is to be hoped that the courts may revert to the older, simpler, and more flexible practice.

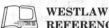

WESTLAW REFERENCES

157k265(10)

---

precluded recovery, and she was barred from producing any evidence to the contrary).

   18. See Chakales v. Djiovanides, 161 Va. 48, 170 S.E. 848 (1933) and Annot., 169 A.L.R. at 815.

   19. Gilbert v. Bostona Mines Co., 121 Mont. 397, 195 P.2d 376 (1948); Kipf v. Bitner, 150 Neb. 155, 33 N.W.2d 518 (1948) (admission extracted from plaintiff on taking of deposition, not conclusive).

   20. "Since his testimony was adverse to his interests, he is more likely to have been mistaken than lying. The proposed rule actually punishes him for two things, his honesty and his error." Edgerton, J. in Alamo v. Del Rosario, 69 App.D.C. 47, 98 F.2d 328, 331 (1938), and see Burruss v. Suddith, 187 Va. 473, 47 S.E. 546 (1948).

§ 267

   1. Fed.R.Evid. 801(d)(2) includes in its definition of admissions of a party: "(C) a statement by a person authorized by him to make a statement concerning the subject, or (D) a statement by his agent or servant concerning a matter within the scope of his agency or employment, made during the existence of the relationship, or (E) a statement by a coconspirator of a party during the course and in furtherance of the conspiracy."

The Revised Uniform Rule (1974) is to the same effect.

   2. Nuttall v. Holman, 110 Utah 375, 173 P.2d 1015 (1946).

§ 267. Representative Admissions [1]

When a party to the suit has expressly authorized another person to speak on his behalf, it is an obvious and accepted extension of the admission rule, to admit against the party the statements of such person.[2] In the absence of express authority, how far will the statements of an agent be received as the principal's admission by virtue of the employment relationship? The early texts and cases used as analogies the doctrine of the master's substantive responsibility for the acts of the agent and the notion then prevalent in evidence law that words accompanying a relevant act are admissible as part of the *res gestae*. Thus they formulated the inadequate theory that the agent's statements could be received against the principal only when made at the time of, and in relation to, some act then being performed in the scope of the agent's duty.[3] A later theory that gained currency in the writings [4] and opinions,[5] is that the admissibility of the agent's statements into evidence as admis-

---

Under Fed.R.Civ.P. 30(b)(6) a party which is a corporation, partnership, association, or governmental agency may be required to designate a person who will testify on its behalf by deposition. Fed.R.Civ.P. 32(a)(2) makes the deposition usable by an adverse party for any purpose against the party.

   3. Fairlie v. Hastings, 10 Ves.Jr. 123, 127, 32 Eng. Rep. 792 (Ch., 1804); Vicksburg & Meridian Railroad v. O'Brien, 119 U.S. 99 (1886).

   4. See 4 Wigmore, Evidence § 1078 (Chadbourn rev. 1972); Morgan, Admissions, 12 Wash.L.Rev. 181, 193 (1937); Restatement Second, Agency, §§ 284–291, especially § 286:

In an action between the principal and a third person, statements of an agent to a third person are admissible in evidence against the principal to prove the truth of facts asserted in them as though made by the principal, if the agent was authorized to make the statement or was authorized to make, on the principal's behalf, any statements concerning the subject matter.

   § 288: . . .

(2) Authority to do an act or to conduct a transaction does not of itself include authority to make statements concerning the act or transaction.

---

   5. See note 5 on page 788.

sions of the principal is measured by precisely the same tests as the principal's substantive responsibility for the conduct of the agent, that is, the words of the agent will be received in evidence as the admissions of the principal if they were spoken within the scope of the authority of the agent to speak for the employer. This formula makes it plain that the statements of an agent employed to give information (a so-called "speaking agent") may be received as the employer's admissions, regardless of want of authority to act otherwise, and conversely that authority to act, e.g., the authority of a chauffeur to drive a car, would not carry with it automatically the authority to make statements to others describing what he was doing or had done. Examples of cases applying the test are given below.[6]

Probably the most frequent employment of this test is in the exclusion of statements made by employees after an accident, to the injured party, to a police officer, or to some bystander, about the accident not made in furtherance of the employer's interest, but as a "mere narrative." [7] This is the logical application of these tests, but the assumption that the test for the master's responsibility for the agent's *acts* should be the test for using the agent's statements as *evidence* against the master is a shaky one. The rejection of such post-accident statements coupled with the admission of the employee's testimony on the stand is to prefer the weaker to the stronger evidence. The agent is well informed about acts in the course of the business, his statements offered against the employer are normally against the employer's interest, and while the employment continues, the employee is not likely to make the statements unless they are true. Moreover, if the admissibility of admissions is viewed as arising from the adversary system, responsibility for statements of one's employee is a consistent aspect. According-

(3) Authority to make statements of fact does not of itself include authority to make statements admitting liability because of such facts.

5.   Griffiths v. Big Bear Stores, Inc., 55 Wash.2d 243, 347 P.2d 532, 535 (1959) (". . . [D]eclarations and admissions against interest by an agent may not be shown except when they are within the scope of the agency, as established by the evidence in the case;"); Rudzinski v. Warner Theatres, Inc., 16 Wis.2d 241, 114 N.W.2d 466, 468 (1962) ("In order for an agent's statement to be admissible against his principal, it must have been spoken within the scope of the authority of the agent to speak for the principal."). Compare Fed. R.Evid. 801(d)(2)(C) and (D), text infra fol. n. 8. For (D), Washington substitutes "(iv) a statement by his agent or servant acting within the scope of his authority to make the statement for the party . . ." West's Rev.Wash.Code Ann. 801(d)(2)(iv). Wis.Stat. Ann. 908.01(4)(b)(3) and (4) is the same as the Federal Rule.

6.   Statements of agent received against principal: Pan-American Petroleum & Transport Co. v. United States, 273 U.S. 456 (1927) (statements by president of corporations before Senate Committee investigating Teapot Dome oil leases admissible in suit by government against corporations to cancel leases); Cox v. Esso Shipping Co., 247 F.2d 629 (5th Cir. 1957) (shipmaster's report of accident); Partin v. Great Atlantic & Pacific Tea Co., 102 N.H. 62, 149 A.2d 860 (1959) (store manager's statement indicating plaintiff's fall due to negligence of employees); Spett v. President Monroe Building & Manufacturing Corp., 19 N.Y.2d 203, 278 N.Y.S.2d 826, 225 N.E.2d 527 (1967) (statement by manager of business indicating that skid causing plain-

tiff's injury was put in place by employees); McDonnell v. Montgomery Ward & Co., 121 Vt. 221, 154 A.2d 469 (1959) (statement by service representative as to condition of appliance).

Statements of agent excluded: Bristol Wholesale Grocery Co. v. Municipal Lighting Plant Commission, 347 Mass. 668, 200 N.E.2d 260 (1964) (statement of plant manager that explosion was defendant's fault); Roush v. Alkire Truck Lines, Inc., 299 S.W.2d 518 (Mo. 1957) (truck driver's statement that brakes were defective); Lakeside Hospital v. Kovar, 131 Ohio St. 333, 2 N.E.2d 857 (1936) (statement of managing director of hospital of circumstances of injection of wrong solution into patient); Preston v. Lamb, 20 Utah 2d 260, 436 P.2d 1021 (1968) (statement of waitress that floor on which plaintiff slipped had been waxed excessively); Rudzinski v. Warner Theatres, Inc., 16 Wis.2d 241, 114 N.W.2d 466 (1962) (usher's admonition of janitor for not having mopped wet spots). Some of these jurisdictions have since adopted rules that would change the result.

It is important to distinguish situations where the declaration of the agent comes in on other theories. Thus, if the agent and the principal are both parties to the suit, the agent's statement is of course received against him, though it may not be admissible against the principal. Annot., 27 A.L.R.3d 966. Again, the agent's declaration often comes in against both as a spontaneous exclamation made under stress of excitement, sometimes unhappily referred to as *res gestae* (see § 297 infra).

7.   See cases of exclusion, in n. 6 supra.

ly, the predominant view now favors broader admissibility of admissions by agents if the statement concerned a matter within the scope of the declarant's employment and was made before that relationship was terminated.[8] Of course, admissibility of the traditional authorized statement continues.

Federal Rule of Evidence 801(d)(2)(C) and (D) and the corresponding Revised Uniform Rule (1974) are in conformity with the preceding paragraph. They provide:

> A statement is not hearsay if—
>
> . . .
>
> The statement is offered against a party and is . . . (C) a statement by a person authorized by him to make a statement concerning the subject,[9] or (D) a statement by his agent or servant concerning a matter within the scope of his agency or employment, made during the existence of the relationship [10] . . . .

Under any of these views, the party offering evidence of the alleged agent's admission must first prove the fact and scope of the agency of the declarant for the adverse party.[11] This he may of course do by the testimony of the asserted agent himself, or by anyone who knows, or by circumstantial evidence. Evidence of the purported agent's past declarations asserting the agency, are inadmissible hearsay when offered to show the relation.[12] If this preliminary fact of the declarant's agency is disputed, the question is one of "conditional relevancy." [13]

The question also arises whether a statement by an agent, in order to qualify as an admission, must be made to an outsider rather than to the principal or to another agent. Typical instances are the railway conductor's report of a wreck or accident, or a letter to the home office from a manager of a branch office of a bank. If the agent's statement thus offered against the principal as an admission, though plainly made in the scope of authority, was a statement made to the principal himself, some courts have re-

8.   See Model Code of Evidence Rule 508(a).

Grayson v. Williams, 256 F.2d 61 (10th Cir. 1958); KLM Royal Dutch Airlines v. Tuller, 110 U.S.App.D.C. 282, 292 F.2d 775 (1961), cert. denied 368 U.S. 921; Joseph T. Ryerson & Sons, Inc. v. H.A. Crane & Brothers, Inc., 417 F.2d 1263 (3d Cir. 1969); Martin v. Savage Truck Line, 121 F.Supp. 417 (D.D.C.1954); state court cases are collected in 4 Wigmore, Evidence § 1078 (Chadbourn rev. 1972).

Dow, KLM v. Tuller: A New Approach to Admissibility of Prior Statements of a Witness, 41 Neb.L.Rev. 598 (1962); Falknor, Vicarious Admissions and the Uniform Rules, 14 Vand.L.Rev. 855 (1961), Hearsay, 1969 Law & Soc.Order 591, 600; Morgan, The Rationale of Vicarious Admissions, 42 Harv.L.Rev. 461 (1929). Compare Note, 54 Wash.L.Rev. 97 (1978).

9.   Illustrative of statements by persons authorized to speak on the subject are Baughman v. Cooper-Jarrett, Inc., 530 F.2d 529 (3d Cir. 1976), cert. denied 429 U.S. 825 (action for conspiring to prevent obtaining employment in trucking industry; statement of reason for denying plaintiff employment, viz. blacklisting, made by employee charged with duty of screening applications and telling applicants reason for rejection); Kingsley v. Baker/Beech-Nut Corp., 546 F.2d 1136 (5th Cir. 1977) (action for severance pay; overheard telephone conversation in which plaintiff's superior said he would make him quit); see also Reid Brothers Logging Co. v. Ketchikan Pulp Co., 699 F.2d 1292 (9th Cir. 1983).

10.   As to statements relating to matters within scope of employment or agency, see Scofi v. McKeon

Construction Co., 666 F.2d 170 (5th Cir. 1982) (statement by subcontractor's superintendent indicating that he understood that his employer was responsible for safety precautions on the job). The difficulty of drawing a clear line between authorized statements and those relating to scope is apparent. Often a statement will fall into both categories, e.g., statements by agent authorized to investigate and report. Collins v. Wayne Corp., 621 F.2d 777 (5th Cir. 1980) (motor vehicle collision expert); Rutherford v. State, 605 P.2d 16 (Alaska 1979) (state trooper's report of motor vehicle accident involving another trooper).

11.   Labor Hall Association v. Danielsen, 24 Wn.2d 75, 163 P.2d 167, 161 A.L.R. 1079 (1945); 4 Wigmore, Evidence § 1078 (Chadbourn rev. 1972); Dec.Dig. Evidence ⊂⊃258(1).

12.   Neither the fact nor the extent of the agency can be so proved. 4 Wigmore, Evidence § 1078, p. 176 (Chadbourn rev. 1972). But the purported agent's declarations if offered to show that the other party dealt with him as an agent would not be hearsay, and would be admitted. Friend Lumber Co. v. Armstrong Building Finish Co., 276 Mass. 361, 177 N.E. 794, 80 A.L.R. 599 (1931), with note on this point. And the asserted agent's declarations may come in to show his intention to act for the principal rather than for himself. See § 268 infra. The possibility of using the spontaneous declaration of the agent should also be considered. See § 297 infra.

13.   See § 53 supra.

fused to admit it,[14] unless the principal has himself adopted it.[15] Others have let such a statement come in.[16] The issue is usually assumed to be this: are such reports competent as admissions? Under the former view the question, does the agent speak for the principal in such a report, is answered: the doctrine of *respondeat superior* does not apply to transactions between the agent and the principal.[17] This statement is doubtless intended to suggest that some analogies, not specified, in the rules of substantive liability of principals should be controlling. But why other analogies, such as instances of statements made by a party himself not intended for the outside world, as where he is overheard talking to himself, or where he makes entries in a secret diary, should not be equally available, is not apparent. It seems clear that these latter statements and entries

would be received against him as admissions.[18]

The analogies are helpful, and reliability also favors admissibility. While slightly less reliable as a class than the agent's authorized statements to outsiders, intra-organization reports are generally made as a basis for some action, and when this is so, they share the reliability of business records.[19] They will only be offered against the principal when they admit some fact disadvantageous to the principal, and this kind of statement by an agent is likely to be true. No special danger of surprise, confusion, or prejudice from the use of the evidence is apparent. There seems little basis, then, for shaping our rule of competency of admissions to exclude this type of statement, and the Federal and Revised Uniform Rules (1974) admit them.[20]

14. Swan v. Miller [1919], 1 Ir.R. 151 (C.A.) (reviewing English authorities); Lever Brothers Co. v. Atlas Assur. Co., 131 F.2d 770, 776 (7th Cir. 1942) (report of investigating engineers on explosion); Standard Oil Co. of California v. Moore, 251 F.2d 188, 218 (9th Cir. 1958) (reports of employees), noted 44 Va.L.Rev. 619; United States v. United Shoe Machinery Corp., 89 F.Supp. 349 (D.Mass.1950) (intracorporate letters and reports); Carroll v. East Tennessee, V. & G. Railway, 82 Ga. 452, 10 S.E. 163, 6 L.R.A. 214 (1889) (written report of accident, made after investigation, by conductor to superintendent); Atchison, Topeka & Santa Fe Railway v. Burks, 78 Kan. 515, 96 P. 950, 18 L.R.A.,N.S. 231 (1908) (reports of car inspectors as to defective coupler); Warner v. Maine Central Railroad, 111 Me. 149, 88 A. 403, 47 L.R.A.,N.S. 830 (1913) (station agent's report to general manager about fire); Bell v. Milwaukee Electric Railway & Light Co., 169 Wis. 408, 172 N.W. 791 (1919) (written report of accident made by street-car conductor, at end of his run); Restatement Second, Agency § 287:

> Statements by an agent to the principal or to another agent of the principal are not admissible against the principal as admissions; such statements may be admissible in evidence under other rules of evidence.

15. United States v. United Shoe Machinery Corp., supra, n. 14; Pekelis v. Transcontinental and Western Air, Inc., 187 F.2d 122, 23 A.L.R.2d 1349 (2d Cir. 1951) (reports of investigating boards, appointed by airline, admitted as adoptive admissions).

16. The Solway, 10 P.D. 137 (1885) (letter by master of ship to owners); Chicago, St. Paul, Minneapolis & Omaha Railway Co. v. Kulp, 102 F.2d 352, 133 A.L.R. 1445 (8th Cir. 1939) (conductor's report to employer as to cause of injury to brakeman); Hilbert v. Spokane In-

ternational Railway, 20 Idaho 54, 116 P. 1116 (1911) (section foreman's written report to company about a fire); Lemen v. Kansas City Southern Railway, 151 Mo.App. 511, 515, 132 S.W. 13 (1910) (oral report by conductor to station-agent, "Better send your section gang up the road. I think we set something on fire there."); Metropolitan Life Insurance Co. v. Moss, 109 S.W.2d 1035 (Tex.Civ.App.1937) (medical examiner's report to insurance company of state of health of applicant); Supreme Lodge, Knights of Honor v. Rampy, 45 S.W. 422 (Tex.Civ.App.1898, writ of error refused) (report by officers of local lodge to supreme lodge concerning good standing of member).

17. Morgan, The Rationale of Vicarious Admissions, 42 Harv.L.Rev. 461, 463 (1929).

18. While it may be argued that the agent authorized to make statements to his principal does not speak for him, Morgan, Basic Problems of Evidence 273 (1962), communication to an outsider has not generally been thought to be an essential characteristic of an admission. Thus a party's books or records are usable against him, without regard to any intent to disclose to third persons. 5 Wigmore § 1557; Adv.Comm.Note, Fed.R.Evid. 801(d)(2)(C). See Reid Brothers Logging Co. v. Ketchikan Pulp Co., 699 F.2d 1292, 1307 n. 25 (9th Cir. 1983).

19. This special trustworthiness is pointed out by Professor Morgan in the article referred to in the next preceding note (42 Harv.L.Rev. at 463, n. 4), although he contends that this furnishes no reason for using the representation formula in this situation as a theory of admissibility.

20. "The rule is phrased broadly so as to encompass both [statements to principals and to third persons]." Adv.Comm.Note, Fed.R.Evid. 801(d)(2)(C).

Attorneys.[21] If an attorney is employed to manage a party's conduct of a lawsuit he has *prima facie* authority to make relevant judicial admissions by pleadings, by oral or written stipulations, or by formal opening statement, which unless allowed to be withdrawn are conclusive in the case.[22] Such formal and conclusive admissions should be, and are, framed with care and circumspection, and in a leading English case, these admissions are contrasted with an attorney's oral out-of-court statement, and the latter characterized as "merely a loose conversation," [23] and it is often said that the client is not "bound" by the "casual" statements of his attorney out of court.[24] The use of the word "bound" is obviously misleading. The issue is not whether the client is "bound," as he is by a judicial admission, but whether the attorney's extrajudicial statement is admissible against the client as a mere evidential admission made by an agent. A natural if unconscious tendency to protect the client, and perhaps the attorney, against the hazard of evidence of statements by his attorney more strictly than in respect to statements by other types of agents is more manifest in the older cases.[25] The later cases, properly it seems, measure the authority of the attorney to make out-of-court admissions by the same tests of express or implied authority as would be applied to other agents,[26] and when they meet these tests admit as evidentiary admissions the statements of attorneys in letters or oral conversations made in the course of efforts for the collection or resistance of claims, or negotiations for the settlement of suits or controversies, or the management of any other business in behalf of the client.[27]

Partners.[28] A partner is an agent of the partnership for the conduct of the firm busi-

---

21. 4 Wigmore, Evidence § 1063 (Chadbourn rev. 1972); Morgan, Admissions, 12 Wash.L.Rev. 181, 188 (1937); Dec.Dig. Evidence ⊙246. The continued relative scarcity of authorities bespeaks the ongoing discreetness of the legal profession.

22. See the discussion of judicial admissions supra § 265.

23. Petch v. Lyon, 9 Q.B. 147, 153, 115 Eng.Rep. 1231, 1233 (1846).

24. E.g., Jackson v. Schine Lexington Corp., 305 Ky. 823, 205 S.W.2d 1013, 1014 (1947) (copy of intended pleading, never filed, sent to plaintiff's attorney by defendant's, containing admission, held inadmissible. "The general rule is that an attorney has no power to prejudice his client by admissions of fact made out of court. Though he may be the agent of his client, such agency does not carry the implication of authority to make binding admissions other than in the actual management of the litigation."); Hogenson v. Service Armament Co., 77 Wn.2d 209, 461 P.2d 311, 314 (1969) (letter from plaintiff's attorney to defendant giving notice of breach of warranty and inaccurate version of circumstances of injury. "The sentence . . . was gratuitous information . . . tentative and casual . . . . It is neither distinct nor formal nor intended to dispense with the formal proof of a fact at trial.").

25. Wagstaff v. Wilson, 4 Barn. & Ad. 339, 110 Eng.Rep. 483 (1832) (trespass for taking a horse: letter offered from defendant's attorney of record stating that defendant had distrained the horse, written in reply to letter from plaintiff's attorney to defendant, excluded for want of proof that it was written with defendant's sanction); Saunders v. McCarthy, 90 Mass. 42, 45 (1864) (oral statements by attorney of relevant facts during conversation with adverse party before

suit for the purpose of settling the controversy, held, "mere matters of conversation").

26. "If the admission is clearly within the scope of his agency, express or implied, he has the same authority to bind his client as any other agent." Offutt, J. in Brown v. Hebb, 167 Md. 535, 175 A. 602, 607, 97 A.L.R. 366 (1934). See also Carroll v. Pratt, 247 Minn. 198, 76 N.W.2d 693 (1956) (same as other agents; mere attorney-client relation not sufficient).

27. Gerhart v. Henry Disston & Sons, Inc., 290 F.2d 778, 789 (3d Cir. 1961) (statement by lawyer handling business negotiation); Suntken v. Suntken, 223 Iowa 347, 272 N.W. 132 (1937) (admissions of fact in attorney's letter written in course of negotiations for compromise); Graber v. Griffin, 210 Kan. 142, 500 P.2d 35 (1972) (tenant's attorney wrote landlord that tenant considered he had lease for stated term); Brown v. Hebb, 167 Md. 535, 175 A. 602, 97 A.L.R. 366 (1937) (doctor sent bill for $1500, patient's lawyer replied by letter offering $300 "for the services rendered" held admissible as an acknowledgment of a debt for services, tolling limitations); Noel v. Roberts, 449 S.W.2d 572 (Mo.1970) (letter from plaintiff's attorney stating that employee rather than defendant assaulted plaintiff, on question of punitive damages).

Possible application of the privilege for offers of compromise should not be overlooked. See § 274, infra.

28. 4 Wigmore, Evidence § 1078, p. 180 (Chadbourn rev. 1972); Crane & Bromberg, Partnership 320, 459 (3d ed. 1968); Rowley, Partnership § 51.9 (2d ed. 1960); Reuschlein & Gregory, Agency and Partnership § 199 (1979); Dec.Dig. Evidence ⊙249; Annot., 73 A.L.R. 447.

ness.[29] Accordingly, when the existence and scope of the partnership have been proved,[30] the statement of a partner made in the conduct of the business of the firm comes in evidence as the admission of the partnership.[31] What of statements of a former partner made after dissolution? The cases are divided,[32] but it seems that since a continuing power is recognized in each former partner to do such acts as are reasonably necessary to wind up and settle the affairs of the firm,[33] he should likewise be regarded as having authority to speak for the former partners in making such statements of fact as are reasonably incident to collecting the claims and property and paying the debts of the firm.[34] Beyond this, it seems that his admissions should be competent only against himself.

Co-conspirators.[35] Analogous to partnerships are conspiracies to commit a crime or an unlawful or tortious act. If A and B are engaged in a conspiracy the acts and declarations of B occurring while the conspiracy is actually in progress and in furtherance of the design are provable against A, because they are acts for which he is criminally or civilly responsible, as a matter of substantive law.[36] But B's declarations may also be proved against A as representative admissions, to prove the truth of the matter declared, and only then are they within our present topic. The courts have seldom discriminated between declarations offered as conduct constituting part of the conspiracy and declarations offered as vicarious admission of the facts declared,[37] and even when offered for the latter purpose, generally have imposed the same test, namely that the declaration must have been made while the conspiracy was continuing, and must have constituted a step in furtherance of the venture.[38]

---

29. As to the scope of the partner's agency, see Crane & Bromberg, Partnership § 49, p. 275 (3d ed. 1968).

30. This, of course, must be established by evidence other than the out-of-court declarations of the purported partner. Humboldt Livestock Auction, Inc. v. B & H Cattle Co., 155 N.W.2d 478 (Iowa 1967). See notes 11 and 12 supra, for like holdings as to agents.

31. Uniform Partnership Act, § 11: "An admission made by any partner concerning partnership affairs within the scope of his authority as conferred by this act is evidence against the partnership." Wieder v. Lorenz, 164 Or. 10, 99 P.2d 38 (1940) (failure by one member of firm to answer letter to him on firm business, admitted against partnership); King v. Wesner, 198 S.C. 289, 16 S.E.2d 289 (1941) statement of partner about accident of employee, made to representative of Industrial Commission who was investigating accident was in course of firm business and admissible against firm).

The relevance of Federal Rule Evid. 801(d)(2)(C) and (D), text supra at n. 9, to partnerships seems apparent, and earlier cases to the contrary should be considered overruled.

32. They are collected in Annot., 73 A.L.R. 447, 459–473.

33. Crane & Bromberg, Partnership § 80, p. 454 (3d ed. 1968).

34. Crane & Bromberg, Partnership § 80, p. 459 (3d ed. 1968); Rowley, Partnership § 51.9, p. 447 (2d ed. 1960).

35. 4 Wigmore, Evidence § 1079 (Chadbourn rev. 1972); Davenport, The Confrontation Clause and the Co-conspirator Exception in Criminal Cases: A Functional Analysis, 85 Harv.L.Rev. 1378 (1972); Klein, Conspiracy—The Prosecutor's Darling, 24 Brooklyn L.Rev. 1 (1957); Levie, Hearsay and Conspiracy, 52 Mich.L.Rev. 1159 (1954); Morgan, Admissions, 12 Wash.L.Rev. 181, 194 (1937), Rationale of Vicarious Admissions, 42 Harv.L.Rev. 461, 464 (1929); Note, 25 U.Chi.L.Rev. 530 (1958); Dec.Dig. Criminal Law ⬅423–427, Evidence ⬅253.

36. 4 Wigmore, Evidence § 1079 (Chadbourn rev. 1972).

Judge Learned Hand in Van Riper v. United States, 13 F.2d 961, 967 (2d Cir. 1926):

Such declarations are admitted upon no doctrine of the law of evidence, but of the substantive law of crime. When men enter into an agreement for an unlawful end, they become ad hoc agents for one another, and have made "a partnership in crime." What one does pursuant to their common purpose, all do, and, as declarations may be such acts, they are competent against all.

37. Many, if not most, conspirator statements qualify as nonhearsay verbal acts, as is occasionally recognized. United States v. Hassell, 547 F.2d 1048 (8th Cir. 1977). A conspiracy mounted and carried on without words is difficult to imagine.

38. Krulewitch v. United States, 336 U.S. 440 (1949); Wong Sun v. United States, 371 U.S. 471, 490 (1963); Marjason v. State, 225 Ind. 652, 75 N.E.2d 904 (1947); People v. Davis, 56 N.Y. 95, 102 (1874). The procedure for determining preliminary questions of fact with regard to declarations of co-conspirators is discussed in § 53 supra.

The Federal and Revised Uniform Rules (1974) are consistent with the foregoing statement. Rule 801(d)(2)(E) is as follows:

A statement is not hearsay if—

The statement is offered against a party and is . . . (E) a statement by a co-conspirator of a party during the course and in furtherance of the conspiracy.

Literally applied, the "in furtherance" requirement calls for general exclusion of statements possessing evidential value solely as admissions,[39] yet in fact more emphasis seems to be placed upon the "during continuation" aspect and any statement so qualifying in point of time may be admitted in evidence without much regard to whether it in fact furthered the conspiracy.[40] These latter decisions may represent a parallel to the cases allowing in evidence against the principal declarations of an agent which relate to the subject of the agency, even though the agent was not authorized to make a statement.[41] Both the "in furtherance" and the "during continuation" requirement call for exclusion of admissions and confessions made after the termination of the conspiracy.[42] Questions arise, of course, as to when termination occurs. Under some circumstances, extending the duration of the conspiracy beyond the commission of the principal crime to include concomitant and closely connected disposition of its fruits [43] or concealment of its traces appears justifiable, as in the case of police officers engaged in writing up a false report to conceal police participation in a burglary [44] or disposal of the body after a murder.[45] However, attempts to expand the so-called "concealment phase" to include all efforts to avoid detection have generally failed, as in Krulewitch v. United States,[46] a Mann Act prosecution, where the Court held it error to admit evidence of a co-conspirator's statement that it would be better for the girls to take the blame than the defendant, because "he couldn't stand it." The statement was made after the round

39. For examples of statements held not to have been in furtherance, see United States v. Green, 600 F.2d 154 (8th Cir. 1979) (conspiracy to possess checks stolen from the mail; statement by one conspirator to unindicted coconspirator, while waiting in car for other two conspirators to cash check in store, that one of the other two had taken the checks from mailbox); United States v. Eubanks, 591 F.2d 513 (9th Cir. 1979) (statement by member of conspiracy to nonmember that he was going to Tucson to obtain narcotics from another member); State v. Podor, 154 Iowa 686, 135 N.W. 421 (1912) (statement of one co-conspirator to outsider that he and another were going to cause girls to become prostitutes not admissible against other). The line between pure history or description and statements in furtherance is obviously difficult to draw. See United States v. Haldeman, 181 U.S.App.D.C. 254, 559 F.2d 31, 110 (1976) discussing the tangled skeins of past, present, and future in the Watergate cover-up.

When the Federal Rules were pending in the Congress, strenuous but unsuccessful efforts were made to delete the in furtherance requirement. United States v. Harris, 546 F.2d 234 (8th Cir. 1976). Similar, and also unsuccessful, efforts had been directed against the Advisory Committee. Model Code of Evidence Rule 508(b) had no in furtherance requirement.

40. See, e.g., United States v. Annunziato, 293 F.2d 373 (2d Cir. 1961), cert. denied 368 U.S. 919 (prosecution of business agent of union for accepting money from employer; statement of employer's president that he had received telephoned request from defendant asking for money, held admissible); United States v.

Patton, 594 F.2d 444 (5th Cir. 1979) (marijuana conspiracy; testimony by member of conspiracy that two other members each told him marijuana was being purchased for appellant; held, admissible); United States v. Piccolo, 696 F.2d 1162 (6th Cir. 1983) (statement as to source of cocaine intended to give confidence to those involved, held admissible). See also United States v. Harris, 546 F.2d 234 (8th Cir. 1976) (conspiracy to use mails to defraud insurance companies by faking accidents; statements by conspirator who was "victim" while in hospital, exchanging information with another individual there under the same circumstances under an unrelated scheme, held "a close case," but harmless if any error).

Judge Learned Hand described the conspiracy charge as "that darling of the modern prosecutor's nursery." Harrison v. United States, 7 F.2d 259, 263 (2d Cir. 1925).

41. See text supra at nn. 7–10.

42. See the many cases in Annot., 4 A.L.R.3d 671.

43. United States v. Kahan, 572 F.2d 923 (2d Cir. 1978), cert. denied 439 U.S. 832 (sale of hijacked property).

44. Reed v. People, 156 Colo. 450, 402 P.2d 68 (1965).

45. Dailey v. State, 233 Ala. 384, 171 So. 729 (1937).

46. 336 U.S. 440 (1949). In United States v. Floyd, 555 F.2d 45 (1977), burning the getaway car was ruled not a part of conspiracy to rob a bank. See also Annot., 4 A.L.R.3d 671.

trip travel was finished and the various participants had been arrested.[47]

While statements made after the termination of the conspiracy are inadmissible, subsequent acts which shed light upon the nature of the conspiratorial agreement have been held admissible.[48]

The existence of a conspiracy in fact is sufficient to support admissibility, and a conspiracy count in the indictment is not required nor need declarant be indicted.[49] The evidence is similarly admissible in civil cases, where the conspiracy rule applies to tortfeasors acting in concert.[50]

Joint obligors; declarations of principal offered against surety. It is asserted that when two parties are jointly liable as obligors, the declarations of one are receivable as an admission against the other.[51] The element of authorization to speak in furtherance of the common enterprise, as in the case of agency, partnership or conspiracy, however, can hardly be spelled out from the mere relation of joint obligors, and admissibility of declarations on this basis has been criticised.[52] In fact, almost all the modern cases adduced in support are cases involving the special situation of declarations of a principal offered as admissions against a surety, guarantor, indemnitor or other person secondarily liable.[53] The declarations have been usually held admissible.[54] Although Model Code Rule 508(c) and the original Uniform Rule sanctioned the practice, it was not included in the Federal or Revised Uniform Rules (1974) on the theory that declarations against interest would take care of worthy cases.

Statements of government agents in criminal cases. In a criminal prosecution, statements by the agent of an accused may be admitted against the accused, but statements by agents of the government have been held not admissible against the government.[55] "This apparent discrimination is explained by the peculiar posture of the parties in a criminal prosecution—the only party on

47. Compare Evans v. State, 222 Ga. 392, 150 S.E.2d 240 (1960), in which the "concealment phase" was extended to the extraordinary limit of allowing a co-conspirator's statement implicating the accused, made more than a year after the commission of the crime, and wholly unrelated to any effort at concealment, immediate or otherwise. The conviction was sustained against constitutional attack in Dutton v. Evans, 400 U.S. 74 (1970). See § 252 supra.

See also State v. Roberts, 95 Kan. 280, 147 P. 828 (1915), for an expanded application of the "concealment phase."

48. Lutwak v. United States, 344 U.S. 604 (1953) (subsequent acts of parties admissible to show phony nature of marriages in prosecution for conspiracy to evade immigration laws).

49. United States v. Nixon, 418 U.S. 683, 701 (1974); United States v. Dawson, 576 F.2d 656 (5th Cir. 1978); United States v. Kendricks, 623 F.2d 1165 (6th Cir. 1980). Moreover, acquittal of declarant on the conspiracy charge does not preclude use of his statement, in view of the different burdens of proof for guilt and admissibility. United States v. Cravero, 545 F.2d 406 (5th Cir. 1976), cert. denied 430 U.S. 983; United States v. Gil, 604 F.2d 546 (7th Cir. 1979).

50. Nathan v. St. Paul Mutual Insurance Co., 251 Minn. 74, 86 N.W.2d 503 (1957); Greer v. Skyway Broadcasting Co., 256 N.C. 382, 124 S.E.2d 98 (1962).

51. 4 Wigmore, Evidence § 1077 (Chadbourn rev. 1972); Lowe v. Huckins, 356 Ill. 360, 190 N.E. 683 (1934) (joint makers of note).

52. Morgan, Admissions, 12 Wash.L.Rev. 181, 195 (1937).

53. See 4 Wigmore, Evidence § 1077 (Chadbourn rev. 1972).

54. See, e.g., Scovill Manufacturing Co. v. Cassidy, 275 Ill. 462, 114 N.E. 181, 185 (1916) (statement of president of corporation, whose account was guaranteed by defendant, made to plaintiff, to whom guaranty was made, admissible since made as part of the operations of the business which was the subject of the guaranty); Linnell v. London & Lancashire Indemnity Co., 74 N.D. 379, 22 N.W.2d 203 (1946) (suit on fidelity bond of manager of business; books kept by manager or under his supervision with respect to business covered by bond, admissible against surety); United American Fire Insurance Co. v. American Bonding Co., 146 Wis. 573, 131 N.W. 994 (1911) (suit on surety bond of agent of insurance company; agent's statement to secretary of insurance company as to amount collected, made after he had resigned but while he was under duty to account, admissible as "res gestae"). Contra: Atlas Shoes Co. v. Bloom, 209 Mass. 563, 95 N.E. 952 (1911) (admissions of one, whose account was guaranteed by defendant, that he had received goods described in account presented to him, inadmissible against defendant). Stearns, Suretyship 343 (5th ed. 1951). Annots., 60 A.L.R. 1500, 65 A.L.R.2d 631.

55. United States v. Santos, 372 F.2d 177 (2d Cir. 1967); United States v. Pandilidis, 524 F.2d 644 (6th Cir. 1975), cert. denied 424 U.S. 933; United States v. Kampiles, 609 F.2d 1233 (7th Cir. 1979), cert. denied 446 U.S. 954.

the government side being the Government itself whose many agents and actors are supposedly uninterested personally in the outcome of the trial and are historically unable to bind the sovereign." [56] A more plausible explanation is the desirability of affording the Government a measure of protection against errors and indiscretions on the part of at least some of its many agents. The cases ruling against admissibility involve statements by agents at the investigative level,[57] with statements by government attorneys after the initiation of proceedings having been held admissible.[58] A dividing line in terms of the relative position of the agent in question may well serve to balance the conflicting interests involved.[59] The Federal and Revised Uniform Rules (1974) do not specifically address the question but do not contain anything inconsistent with these views.[60]

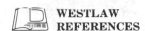

WESTLAW REFERENCES

157k246

157k249

110k424

157k250

---

§ 268. Declarations by "Privies in Estate": Joint Tenants and Predecessors in Interest [1]

The notion that "privity," or identity of interest, as between the declarant and the party against whom the declaration is offered, justifies its introduction against the party as an admission has been generally accepted by the courts. Thus the declaration of one joint tenant or joint owner against another may be received,[2] but not that of a tenant in common,[3] a co-legatee or co-devisee,[4] or a co-trustee,[5]—so strictly is the distinction derived from the law of property applied in this context. The more frequent and important application of this property analogy is the use of declarations of a predecessor in title to land or personalty or choses in action, against his successor. The successor has been thought of as acquiring his interest burdened with the same liability of having the declarations used against him that his predecessor was subject to.[6] The declarations presumably must relate to the declarant's interest in the property or to his transactions and intentions in reference thereto, and they must have been made while he was the owner of the interest now claimed by the successor party, not before the declarant ac-

---

56. United States v. Santos, supra n. 55, at p. 180.

57. Cases cited supra n. 55.

58. United States v. Morgan, 581 F.2d 933 (D.C.Cir. 1978) (defendant offered affidavit of government detective containing statement by informant, approved by Assistant United States Attorney and presented to magistrate in support of application for search warrant; error to exclude. The court emphasized the authority of the attorney to represent the government, and also suggested as an alternative ground for admissibility the view that the Government had adopted the statement under Rule 801(d)(2)(B)).

59. See Note, 59 B.U.L.Rev. 400 (1979).

60. United States v. Kampiles, supra n. 55, at p. 1246.

§ 268

1. 4 Wigmore, Evidence §§ 1080–1087 (Chadbourn rev. 1972); Morgan, Rationale of Vicarious Admissions, 42 Harv.L.Rev. 462, 470 (1929), Admissions, 12 Wash.L. Rev. 181, 197 (1937); Falknor, Hearsay, 1969 Law & Soc. Order 591, 603; Model Code of Evidence, Com-

ment on Rule 508; Dec.Dig. Evidence ☜226, 229–236; C.J.S. Evidence §§ 322–341.

2. 4 Wigmore, Evidence § 1081 (Chadbourn rev. 1972); La Furia v. New Jersey Insurance Co., 131 Pa. Super. 413, 200 A. 167 (1938) (in suit against fire insurance company by husband and wife, where property held by entireties, husband's admission receivable against wife).

3. Dan v. Brown, 4 Cow. (N.Y.) 483, 492 (1825).

4. Shailer v. Bumstead, 99 Mass. 112, 127 (1868). And in will contests most courts go to the extreme of saying that since it is not admissible against the others, it is not even admissible against the co-legatee himself who made the declaration, since there can only be a judgment for or against the will as a whole. Belfield v. Coop, 8 Ill.2d 293, 134 N.E.2d 249, 58 A.L.R.2d 1008 (1956).

5. Davies v. Ridge, 3 Esp. 101, 170 Eng.R.R. 553 (N.P.1800).

6. 4 Wigmore, Evidence § 1080 (Chadbourn rev. 1972).

quired or after he parted with such interest.[7] Under this theory have been received the declarations of grantors, transferors, donors, and mortgagors of land and personalty against the transferees and mortgagees;[8] of decedents against their representatives, heirs and next of kin;[9] by a prior possessor against one who claims prescriptive title relying on such prior possession;[10] and of former holders of notes and other choses in action against their assignees.[11] It should be borne in mind that such substantive concepts as bona fide purchase and holder in due course may make the evidence immaterial and hence inadmissible for that reason.[12]

The importation into the evidence field of the niceties of property doctrines of identity of interest and privity of estate has been criticized by Morgan. "The dogma," he says, "of vicarious admissions, as soon as it passes beyond recognized principles of representation, baffles the understanding. Joint ownership, joint obligation, privity of title, each and all furnish no criterion of credibility, no aid in the evaluation of testimony."[13] While Wigmore counters that "the Hearsay rule stands in dire need, not of stopping its violation, but of a vast deal of (let us say) elastic relaxation. And this is one of the places where that relaxation can

7. Austin v. Austin, 237 Ark. 127, 372 S.W.2d 231 (1963) (grantor's statement made after delivery of deed not admissible against grantee); Charles R. Allen, Inc. v. Island Cooperative Association, 234 S.C. 537, 109 S.E.2d 446 (1959) (assignor's statement made after assignment of draft not admissible against assignee); Dec.Dig. Evidence ⊜230(3); C.J.S. Evidence § 323.

8. Kennedy v. Oleson, 251 Iowa 418, 100 N.W.2d 894 (1960) (admission of predecessor that building encroached); Liberty National Bank & Trust Co. v. Merchants' and Manufacturers' Paint Co., 307 Ky. 184, 209 S.W.2d 828 (1948) (statement of predecessor about party wall); 4 Wigmore, Evidence § 1082 (Chadbourn rev. 1972); Dec.Dig. Evidence ⊜231-233.

9. Webb v. Martin, 364 F.2d 229 (3d Cir. 1966) (testimony given by decedent in criminal case receivable as admission in action against his administrator); Estate of Fushanis v. Poulos, 85 Ill.App.2d 114, 229 N.E.2d 306 (1967) (writing in files of decedent admissible to establish trust against his estate); Mannix v. Baumgardner, 184 Md. 600, 42 A.2d 124 (1945) (statement in subsequently revoked will admissible on issue of existence of contract to devise); Dec.Dig. Evidence ⊜236.

In wrongful death actions by administrators or other representatives, some courts by a hypertechnical concept of privity have said that, since the statute gives a new cause of action at death, the administrator's death claim is not derivative, and statements of the deceased are not receivable against the administrator as admissions. They may, of course, qualify under other hearsay exceptions but with stricter requirements for admissibility. In other aspects of the same case, however, privity undeniably exists, e.g., when liability is asserted *against* the estate or when the administrator joins a claim for conscious suffering, if it survives. The result is a hodgepodge of inconsistencies. See Shamgochian v. Drigotas, 343 Mass. 139, 177 N.E.2d 588 (1961) (decedent's statement of not blaming driver who struck him admissible as admission on count for conscious suffering, but barely gets in on wrongful death count under statute allowing statements of decedents made on personal knowledge); Carpenter v. Davis, 435 S.W.2d 382 (Mo.1968) (statement by decedent of no fault of defendant barred as admission in wrong-

ful death case by lack of privity, and not qualified as declaration against interest because in opinion form, though opinion aspect would not require exclusion of an admission). · The results are indefensible.

10. Barnes v. Young, 238 Ark. 484, 382 S.W.2d 580 (1964); Atlantic Coast Line Railway Co. v. Gunn, 185 Ga. 108, 194 S.E. 365 (1938).

11. Taylor-Reed Corp. v. Mennen Food Products, Inc., 324 F.2d 108 (7th Cir. 1963) (statement by assignor of patent admissible against assignee); Baptist v. Bankers Indemnity Co., 377 F.2d 211 (2d Cir. 1967) (statement by insured admissible against his judgment creditor in latter's action against liability insurer, on theory that judgment creditor was in effect assignee of insured); Johnson v. Riecken, 185 Neb. 78, 173 N.W.2d 511 (1970) (statement by assignor of claim for medical expenses); Trudeau v. Lussier, 123 Vt. 358, 189 A.2d 529 (1963) (statement by assignor of past due note).

In a suit on a life insurance policy by the beneficiary may the declarations of the insured in his lifetime be offered by the defendant insurance company against the beneficiary, as the admissions of a predecessor in interest? The answer has been made in some cases to turn upon the technical distinction between policies wherein the insured reserves the power to change the beneficiary and those where no such power is reserved. Bernard v. Metropolitan Life Insurance Co., 316 Ill. App. 655, 45 N.E.2d 518 (1942); Rosman v. Travelers' Insurance Co., 127 Md. 689, 96 A. 875, Ann.Cas.1918C, 1047 (1916); 4 Wigmore, Evidence § 1081 (Chadbourn rev. 1972); Annot., 86 A.L.R. 146, 161. The distinction is tenuous.

12. Bradstreet v. Bradstreet, 158 Me. 140, 180 A.2d 459, 463 (1962); 4 Wigmore, Evidence § 1084 (Chadbourn rev. 1972).

13. Morgan, Admissions, 12 Wash.L.Rev. 181, 202 (1937). If the admissibility of admissions is regarded as the product of the adversary system, rather than as arising from circumstantial guarantees of trustworthiness justifying a hearsay exception, the conclusion is nevertheless the same, since the privity concept goes beyond reasonable standards of party responsibility.

best be granted, in view of the commonly useful service of this class of evidence. After the heat of a controversy has brought it into court, testimony on the stand is often much less trustworthy than the original statements of the same persons made before controversy." [14] His argument is actually one for expanding the admissibility of contemporaneous statements, with privity a more or less fortuitous aspect. Following Morgan's view, the Model Code omitted any provision for admitting these declarations, and the Federal and Revised Uniform Rules (1974) follow the same pattern.[15] The meritorious cases will in general qualify as declarations against interest or other hearsay exception more soundly based than admissions founded on privity.

 **WESTLAW REFERENCES**

topic(157) & privy privies privit! & declaration* statement* /s predecessor* successor* /s land propert! interest*

___

§ 269. Admissions by Conduct: (a) Adoptive Admissions [1]

One may expressly adopt another's statement as his own. That is an explicit admission like any other, is to be classed as an express admission, and calls for no further discussion. In this text the term adoptive admission is applied to evidence of other conduct of a party which manifests circumstantially the party's assent to the truth of a statement made by another person.[2]

Federal and Revised Uniform Rule (1974) 801(d)(2) provide:

> A statement is not hearsay if—
>
> The statement is offered against a party and is . . . (B) a statement of which he has manifested his adoption or belief in its truth . . . .

The mere fact that the party declares that he has heard that another person has made a given statement is not standing alone sufficient to justify a finding that the party has adopted the third person's statement.[3] The circumstances surrounding the party's declaration must be looked to in order to determine whether the repetition did indicate an approval of the statement.[4]

The question of adoption often arises in life and accident insurance cases when the defendant insurance company offers statements which the plaintiff beneficiary attached to the proof of death or disability,

___

14. 4 Wigmore, Evidence § 1080a, p. 144 (Chadbourn rev. 1972).

15. Huff v. White Motor Corp., 609 F.2d 286, 290–291 (7th Cir. 1979).

§ 269

1. 4 Wigmore, Evidence §§ 1069–1075 (Chadbourn rev. 1972).

2. In this text, admissions by silence are treated separately. See § 270 infra.

3. Cedeck v. Hamiltonian Savings & Loan Association, 551 F.2d 1136 (8th Cir. 1977) (sex discrimination action; proper to exclude testimony that since-deceased branch manager said to plaintiff concerning her request for promotion, "I was told [by unidentified person] that 'Yes, we know she's qualified but unless she's flat-chested and wears pants, there's no way.'"; not an adoption); Stephens v. Vroman, 16 N.Y. 381 (1857) (stresses the hearsay nature of the statements, without discussing whether repetition is adoption); Reed v. McCord, 160 N.Y. 330, 54 N.E. 737, 740 (1899) (employer's statement as to facts of accident, though he was without personal knowledge, admissible, but distinguishing a statement that "he had heard" that such was the fact, which would be inadmissible).

4. Adoption shown: United States v. Morgan, 581 F.2d 933 (D.C.Cir. 1978) (Assistant United States Attorney approved affidavit, characterizing informant as reliable, containing informant's statements, for presentation to magistrate for purpose of obtaining issuance of warrant; held adoption of statements); United States v. Marino, 658 F.2d 1120 (6th Cir. 1981) (defendant's possession of airline tickets, receipted hotel bills, and other documents offered by prosecution to prove interstate travel, characterized as adoption); Pekelis v. Transcontinental & Western Air, Inc., 187 F.2d 122 (2d Cir. 1951) (report of accident investigating board used by defendant as a basis for remedial measures and also filed with CAB); In re Gaines' Estate, 15 Cal.2d 255, 100 P.2d 1055 (1940) (statement by nephew to bank officers, as to what uncle said was his purpose in placing deposit box and bank account in joint tenancy with nephew); Oxley v. Linnton Plywood Association, 205 Or. 78, 284 P.2d 766 (1955) (timber cruiser's report filed by defendant in support of SEC registration statement) contra. United States v. Felix-Jerez, 667 F.2d 1297 (9th Cir. 1982) (answers of nonEnglish-speaking prisoner, through guard acting as interpreter, to questions put by assistant marshal, typed by latter); Cowan v. Allamakee County Benevolent Society, 232 Iowa 1387, 8 N.W.2d 433 (1943) (insurance beneficiary's statement

such as the certificate of the attending physician, or the coroner's report. The fact that the beneficiary has thus tendered it as an exhibit accompanying a formal statement or "proof" presented for the purpose of having the company act upon it by paying the claim, should certainly be enough, standing alone, to secure the admission of the accompanying statements.[5] In actual life, however, the surrounding circumstances often show that an inference of adoption would be most unrealistic. This is clear when the beneficiary expressly disavows the accompanying statement,[6] and it seems that exclusion of the attached statement should likewise follow when the statements of the beneficiary in the proofs are clearly contrary to those in the exhibits.[7] Moreover, when the company's agent prepared the proof for signature and procured the accompanying documents, as he frequently does as a helpful service to the beneficiary, it seems reasonable to hold that the inference of adoption of statements in the exhibits should not be drawn, if the agent has failed to call the beneficiary's attention to inconsistencies between the proof and the exhibits.[8] Again the argument seems strong that if accompanying statements, such as the certificate of the attending physician as to particular facts called for, are required to be furnished under the terms of the policy, the statements are not then attached by the choice or will of the beneficiary, and the sponsorship inferable from a voluntary tendering of another's statement cannot here be inferred.[9]

Does the introduction of evidence by a party constitute an adoption of the statements therein, so that they may be used against him as admissions [10] in a subsequent lawsuit? The answer ought to depend upon whether the particular circumstances warrant the conclusion that adoption in fact occurred, and not upon the discredited notion that a party vouches for his own witnesses. When a party offers in evidence a deposition or an affidavit to prove the matters stated therein, he knows or should know the contents of the writing so offered, and presumably he desires that all of the contents be considered on his behalf, since he is at liberty to offer only part, if he desires. Accordingly, it is reasonable to conclude that the writing so introduced may in another suit be used against him as an adoptive admission.[11] In respect to oral testimony, however, the in-

that the doctors told him that insured had died of cancer). See also cases in n. 3 supra.

5. Cases admitting the statements on this theory are numerous, Russo v. Metropolitan Life Insurance Co., 125 Conn. 132, 3 A.2d 844 (1939) (but court stressed there was no contractual obligation here to furnish the doctor's certificate filed with the proof); Rudolph v. John Hancock Mutual Life Insurance Co., 251 N.Y. 208, 167 N.E. 223 (1929) (statement in doctor's certificate an adoptive admission, though contrary to beneficiary's own statement in the proof of death, and though attending doctor's statement was required by policy; three judges dissenting); Thornell v. Missouri State Life Insurance Co., 249 S.W. 203 (Tex.Com.App. 1923) (rule applied though proofs prepared by agents of company). Contra, Liberty National Life Insurance Co. v. Reid, 276 Ala. 25, 158 So.2d 667 (1963) (claimant not "bound" unless "made at his request or ratified by him"). Decisions are collected in 4 Wigmore, Evidence § 1073, note 10 (Chadbourn rev. 1972); Dec.Dig. Evidence ⌐215(1); Annot., 1 A.L.R.2d 365.

6. Krantz v. John Hancock Mutual Life Insurance Co., 335 Mass. 703, 141 N.E.2d 719 (1957); Goldschmidt v. Mutual Life Insurance Co., 102 N.Y. 486, 7 N.E. 408 (1886). In the absence of disavowal, it is arguable that the case is one of admission by failure to deny. See § 270 infra.

7. See the dissenting opinion in *Rudolph* supra n. 5.

8. New York Life Insurance Co. v. Taylor, 79 U.S. App.D.C. 66, 147 F.2d 297 (1945).

9. This view is supported by the decision in Bebbington v. California Western Life Insurance Co., 15 Cal.2d 255, 100 P.2d 1055 (1947), 61 Harv.L.Rev. 535; Carson v. Metropolitan Life Insurance Co., 156 Ohio St. 104, 100 N.E.2d 197, 28 A.L.R.2d 344 (1951). The *Rudolph* case, note 5 supra, is opposed.

10. Thus escaping the requirements which would be imposed if it were offered under the hearsay exception for Former Testimony (see Ch. 25, supra) such as identity of parties and issues, and unavailability of the witness.

Whether offering the testimony on direct satisfies the former testimony requirement of cross-examination is discussed in § 255, at note 8, supra.

11. Richards v. Morgan, 10 Jurist N.S. 559, 122 Eng.Rep. 600 (Q.B.1864) (depositions); Hallett v. O'Brien, 1 Ala. 585, 589 (1840) (affidavit or deposition said to be adopted if used in evidence, but not where merely filed); 4 Wigmore, Evidence § 1075, note 2 (Chadbourn rev. 1972).

ference of sponsorship of the statements is not always so clear, but here too, circumstances may justify the conclusion that when the proponent placed the witness on the stand to prove a particular fact, and the witness so testified, this was an adoptive admission of the fact in a later suit. But how is the party offering the testimony in the later suit to show that a given statement of the witness at the former trial was intended to be elicited by the proponent who put him on the stand, or was contrary to or outside that intention? The form and context of the proponent's question would usually, but not always, give the clue. In view of the prevailing custom of interviewing one's witness before putting him on the stand, it would seem that a practical working rule would admit against the proponent the direct testimony of his own witness as presumptively elicited to prove the facts stated, in the absence of counter proof that the testimony came as a surprise to the interrogator, or was repudiated in the course of argument.[12] Testimony elicited on cross-examination may be drawn out to reveal the witness's mendacity and should not be assumed to have been relied on by the examiner as evidence of the facts stated,[13] but reliance must affirmatively appear

In conformity with the views expressed in the general discussion herein of the respective functions of judge and jury in determin-

ing preliminary questions of fact, it is believed that the statement should be admitted upon the introduction of evidence sufficient to support a finding of adoption.[14]

Similar to adoptive admissions are the instances where the party has referred an inquirer to another person whose anticipated statements he approves in advance.[15] These admissions by reference to a third person are perhaps more properly classifiable as representative or vicarious admissions, rather than adoptive.

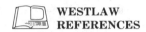 **WESTLAW REFERENCES**

headnote("adoptive admission*")

§ 270. Admissions by Conduct: (b) Silence [1]

If a statement is made by another person in the presence of a party to the action, containing assertions of facts which, if untrue, the party would under all the circumstances naturally be expected to deny, his failure to speak has traditionally been receivable against him as an admission.[2] Whether the justification for receiving the evidence is the assumption that the party has intended to express his assent and thus has adopted the statement as his own, or the probable state of belief to be inferred from his conduct is

---

12. Bageard v. Consolidated Traction Co., 64 N.J.L. 316, 45 A. 620 (1900) (testimony of witness at former trial which corroborated plaintiff's testimony which is now inconsistent with his present version); Keyser Canning Co. v. Klots Throwing Co., 98 W.Va. 487, 128 S.E. 280 (1925) (testimony as to cause of fire). Contra, British Thomson-Houston Co. v. British, etc., Cables, Limited [1924] 2 Ch. 160, 38 Harv.L.Rev. 262 (involving expert testimony, a most unlikely situation for finding nonadoption).

13. In O'Connor v. Bonney, 57 S.D. 134, 231 N.W. 521 (1930) (questions and answers on cross-examination by the present defendant of expert witnesses at a previous trial of the present malpractice action, held inadmissible against the defendant).

14. The situation is one of conditional relevancy, treated in §§ 53, 58 supra.

15. See, e.g., General Finance Co. v. Stratford, 71 App.D.C. 343, 109 F.2d 843 (1940) (plaintiff in garnish-

ment directed by garnishee's agent to go over records with bookkeeper; bookkeeper's statements admissible against garnishee); 4 Wigmore, Evidence § 1070 (Chadbourn rev. 1972).

§ 270

1. See 4 Wigmore, Evidence §§ 1071–1073 (Chadbourn rev. 1972); Heller, Admissions by Acquiescence, 15 U. of Miami L.Rev. 161 (1960); Morgan, Admissions, 12 Wash.L.Rev. 181, 187 (1937); Note, 112 U.Pa.L.Rev. 210 (1960); Annot., 70 A.L.R.2d 1099; Dec.Dig. Evidence ⊙=220, Criminal Law ⊙=407; C.J.S. Evidence §§ 294–298.

The general question whether silence is hearsay is treated in § 250, text at notes 31–36, supra, and particular aspects of silence as an admission in criminal cases are discussed in § 160 supra.

2. 4 Wigmore, Evidence § 1071 (Chadbourn rev. 1972).

probably unimportant.[3] Since it is the failure to deny that is significant, an equivocal or evasive response may similarly be used against him on either theory,[4] but if his total response adds up to a clear-cut denial, this theory of implied admission is not properly available.[5]

Despite the offhand appeal of this kind of evidence, the courts have often suggested that it be received with caution, an admonition that is especially appropriate in criminal cases.[6] Several characteristics of the evidence should be noted. First, its nature and the circumstances under which it arises often amount to an open invitation to manufacture evidence.[7] Second, ambiguity of inference is often present. Silence may be motivated by many factors other than a sense of guilt or lack of an exculpatory story.[8] As indicated at the opening of this chapter, everyone knows that anything you say may be used against you: silence is golden. Third, the constitutional limitations

of *Miranda* apply to the use of this type of evidence in criminal cases, but only where there is custodial interrogation.[9] Fourth, while in theory the statement is not offered as proof of its contents but rather to show what the party acquiesced in,[10] the distinction is indeed a subtle one; the statement is ordinarily highly damaging and of a nature likely to draw attention away from the basic inquiry whether acquiescence in fact did occur.

Despite the array of circumstances raising doubts as to the reliability of this kind of evidence, the Supreme Court has not found any absolute federal constitutional barriers against its use, other than those imposed by *Miranda*.[11] Nevertheless, the courts have evolved a variety of safeguarding requirements against misuse, of which the following are illustrative. (1) The statement must have been heard by the party claimed to have acquiesced.[12] (2) It must have been understood by him.[13] (3) The subject matter

3. The language of the Federal and Revised Uniform Rules (1974) includes both "adoption" and "belief in its truth." See text supra fol. n. 2, § 269.

4. Examples of responses held to be equivocal: People v. Tolbert, 70 Cal.2d 790, 76 Cal.Rptr. 445, 452 P.2d 661 (1969) ("Forget about it," in reply to landlady's statement that police had found gun in bathroom and question whether he had put it there); Commonwealth v. Jefferson, 430 Pa. 532, 243 A.2d 412 (1968) ("Glad it was all over," when confronted with a statement implicating him). Not infrequently the equivocal response is the result of trying to outsmart a skilled interrogator who knows the ground rules. E.g., Commonwealth v. McGrath, 351 Mass. 534, 222 N.E.2d 774 (1967). Examples of responses held not to be equivocal: People v. Hanley, 317 Ill. 39, 147 N.E. 400 (1925) ("It will take twelve men to try me."); Boulton v. State, 214 Tenn. 94, 377 S.W.2d 936 (1964) ("Why did you do this to me?," in response to accusation in presence of alleged victim). The lack of a satisfactory dividing line deprives the "equivocal response" theory of much of its validity.

5. United States v. Lilley, 581 F.2d 182 (8th Cir. 1978) (after hearing without comment husband's statement implicating her, defendant made contradictory statement; held, no adoption); Commonwealth v. Locke, 335 Mass. 106, 138 N.E.2d 359 (1956); Commonwealth of Pennsylvania ex rel. Smith v. Rundle, 423 Pa. 93, 223 A.2d 88 (1966).

6. People v. Aughinbaugh, 36 Ill.2d 320, 223 N.E.2d 117 (1967); Boulton v. State, 214 Tenn. 94, 377 S.W.2d 936 (1964); Gamble, The Tacit Admission Rule: Unreli-

able and Unconstitutional, 14 Ga.L.Rev. 27 (1979); Note, 112 U.Pa.L.Rev. 210, 213–14 (1963).

7. Particularly in criminal cases when the accused is conveniently at hand to be confronted with a detailed accusatory statement. People v. Bennett, 413 Ill. 601, 110 N.E.2d 175 (1953) (error to admit). Many of the cases cited would now, of course, be decided on *Miranda* grounds.

8. In Doyle v. Ohio, 426 U.S. 610 (1976), the Court spoke of silence following receipt of *Miranda* warnings as "insolubly ambiguous," id. at 617, and on that and other grounds overturned a state conviction in which it was admitted. The year before, the Court had overturned a federal conviction on nonconstitutional grounds, simply on account of the inadequacy of the inference from silence. United States v. Hale, 422 U.S. 171 (1975). However, in Jenkins v. Anderson, 447 U.S. 231 (1980), allowing failure to deny as an admission in a pre-arrest non *Miranda* situation in a state prosecution was held to violate neither Fifth nor Fourteenth Amendment. See § 160 supra.

9. See § 160 supra.

10. Greenberg v. Stanley, 30 N.J. 485, 153 A.2d 833 (1959).

11. See n. 8 supra.

12. United States v. Sears, 663 F.2d 896 (9th Cir. 1981) (whether defendant with impaired hearing heard, for jury).

13. People v. Aughinbaugh, 36 Ill.2d 320, 223 N.E.2d 117 (1967) (error to admit evidence of defendant's failure to respond to identification in lineup in

must have been within his knowledge. At first glance, this requirement may appear inconsistent with the general dispensation with firsthand knowledge with respect to admissions, yet the unreasonableness of expecting a person to deny a matter of which he is not aware seems evident;[14] he simply does not have the incentive or the wherewithal to embark upon a dispute. (4) Physical or emotional impediments to responding must not be present.[15] (5) The personal makeup of the speaker, e.g., young child, or his relationship to the party or the event, e.g., bystander,[16] may be such as to make it unreasonable to expect a denial. (6) Probably most important of all, the statement itself must be such as would, if untrue, call for a denial under the circumstances.[17] The list is not an exclusive one, and other factors will suggest themselves. The essential inquiry in each case is whether a reasonable person would have denied under the circumstances, with answers not lending themselves readily to mechanical formulations.

Preliminary questions of admissibility in connection with admissions by acquiescence appear to fall within the category of condi-

tional relevancy. The judge should admit the evidence upon the introduction of foundation proof sufficient to support a finding that the requirements for admissibility have been satisfied.[18]

Failure to reply to a letter or other written communication.[19] If a written statement is handed to a party and read by him, in the presence of others, his failure to deny assertions contained therein, when under the circumstances it would be natural for him to deny them if he did not acquiesce, may be received as an admission, as in case of similar failure to deny an oral statement.[20] Moreover, if a party receives a letter containing several statements, which he would naturally deny if untrue, and he states his position as to some of the statements, but fails to comment on the others, this failure will usually be received as evidence of an admission.[21] More debatable is the question whether the failure to reply at all to a letter or other written communication shall come in as an admission by silence. Certainly such a failure to reply will often be less convincing than silence in the face of an oral charge.[22] And it is often announced as a

---

absence of showing that he knew what crime he was charged with).

14. Dierks Lumber & Coal Co. v. Horne, 216 Ark. 155, 224 S.W.2d 540 (1949); People v. Aughinbaugh, supra n. 13; Refrigeration Discount Corp. v. Catino, 330 Mass. 230, 112 N.E.2d 790 (1953). But see 4 Wigmore, Evidence § 1072 (Chadbourn rev. 1972). The general absence of a firsthand knowledge requirement for admissions is discussed in § 263 supra.

15. E.g., physical injury of the party or confusion attending an accident. Klever v. Elliott, 212 Or. 490, 320 P.2d 263, 70 A.L.R.2d 1094 (1958); Beck v. Dye, 200 Wash. 1, 92 P.2d 1113, 127 A.L.R. 1022 (1939). But see Doherty v. Edwards, 227 Iowa 1264, 290 N.W. 672 (1940) (proper to admit evidence of defendant driver's failure to deny fatally injured passenger's statement, "We were going too fast.").

16. Robinson v. State, 235 Miss. 100, 108 So.2d 583 (1959) (error to admit evidence of failure to deny statement of two and one-half year old child, "Daddy shot mother dear."); Beck v. Dye, supra n. 15.

17. United States v. Flecha, 539 F.2d 874 (2d Cir. 1976) (upon arrest, statement by one arrestee, "Why so much excitement? If we are caught, we are caught." was not such as to call for response from fellow arrestee against whom offered). Though not a requirement, incriminating content of the statement is to be consid-

ered in determining whether an ordinary person would deny. United States v. Shulman, 624 F.2d 384 (2d Cir. 1980).

18. See the general treatment of preliminary questions in §§ 53, 58, supra.

19. See 4 Wigmore, Evidence § 1073, nn. 3 and 4 (Chadbourn rev. 1972); Note, 4 Vand.L.Rev. 364 (1951); Dec.Dig. Evidence ⬩220(8); C.J.S. Evidence § 297(b); Annots., 8 A.L.R. 1163, 34 id. 560, 55 id. 460.

20. See Grier v. Deputy, 15 Del. 152, 40 A. 716 (1894) (item in newspaper read to party).

21. Hellenic Lines, Limited v. Gulf Oil Corp., 340 F.2d 398 (2d Cir. 1965); Wieder v. Lorenz, 164 Ore. 10, 99 P.2d 38 (1940).

22. "Men use the tongue much more readily than the pen. Almost all men will reply to and deny or correct a false statement verbally made to them. It is done on the spot and from the first impulse. But when a letter is received making the same statement, the feeling which readily prompts the verbal denial not unfrequently cools before the time and opportunity arrive for writing a letter. Other matters intervene. A want of facility in writing, or an aversion to correspondence, or habits of dilatoriness may be the real causes of the silence. As the omission to reply to letters may be explained by so many causes not applicable to silence

"general rule," subject to exceptions, that failure to answer a letter is not receivable as an admission.[23] This negative form of statement seems undesirable as tending toward over-strict rulings excluding evidence of material value.[24] It is believed that the more acceptable view is that the failure to reply to a letter, containing statements which it would be natural under all the circumstances for the addressee to deny if he believed them untrue, is receivable as evidence of an admission by silence.[25] Two factors particularly tend to show that a denial would be naturally forthcoming, first, where the letter was written as part of a mutual correspondence between the parties,[26] and second,

where the proof shows that the parties were engaged together in some business or other relationship or transaction which would make it improbable that an untrue communication from one to the other about the transaction or relationship would be ignored.[27] The most common instance of this latter situation is the transmission by one party to such a business relationship to the other of a statement of account or bill rendered. A failure to question such a bill or statement is uniformly received as evidence of an admission of its correctness.[28] On the other hand, if the negotiations have been broken off by one party's taking a final stand, thus indicating his view that further communication

---

when the parties are in personal conversation, we do not think the same weight should be attached to it as evidence." Aldis, J. in Fenno v. Watson, 31 Vt. 345, 352 (1858).

23. See, e.g., Fidelity & Casualty Co. v. Beeland Brothers Mercantile Co., 242 Ala. 591, 7 So.2d 265, 267 (1942); Levin v. Van Horn, 412 Pa. 322, 194 A.2d 419 (1963); Annot., 8 A.L.R. 1163.

24. See cases described in the second paragraph of n. 27 infra.

25. Megarry Brothers, Inc. v. United States, 404 F.2d 479 (8th Cir. 1968); Boerner v. United States, 117 F.2d 387, 390, 391 (2d Cir. 1941); Mahoney v. Kennedy, 188 Wis. 30, 205 N.W. 407, 411 (1925).

26. The significance of this is always conceded, see, e.g., Boerner v. United States, 117 F.2d 387, 391 (2d Cir. 1941); Wieder v. Lorenz, 164 Ore. 10, 99 P.2d 38, 44, 45 (1940); Annot., 8 A.L.R. 1163.

27. Willard Helburn, Inc. v. Spiewak, 180 F.2d 480, 482 (2d Cir. 1950) (letter stating terms of previous oral transaction between caller and callee, held, circumstances such as to make an answer natural); E.P. Hinkel & Co. v. Washington Carpet Corp., 212 A.2d 328 (D.C.App.1965) (correspondence arising from six-year course of mutual dealings); Commonwealth Life Insurance Co. v. Elliott, 423 S.W.2d 898 (Ky.1968) (rule applied to retention of premium receipt book by beneficiary who could not read!); Ross v. Reynolds, 112 Me. 223, 91 A. 952 (1914) (failure of seller to reply to letter from buyer, complaining that automobile sold had been misrepresented by seller); Keeling-Easter Co. v. R.B. Dunning, 113 Me. 34, 92 A. 929 (1915) (similar to last); Trainer v. Fort, 310 Pa. 570, 578, 165 A. 232 (1933) (action by real estate broker for commission under oral contract made over the telephone with defendant; letter written by defendant to plaintiff immediately after conversation reciting terms of agreement differently, and unanswered by plaintiff, admissible).

But this factor is often disregarded, and a letter from one with whom the addressee is engaged in business transactions is treated as if it no more called for a

reply than would a letter from a stranger, "a bolt from the blue." See, e.g., A.B. Leach & Co. v. Peirson, 275 U.S. 120, 55 A.L.R. 457 (1927) (suit by one who had purchased bonds from defendant investment concern upon alleged oral agreement by defendant's agent that defendant would repurchase bonds at same price on demand. Held, defendant's failure to answer plaintiff's letter asserting such contract, inadmissible. Holmes, J.: "A man cannot make evidence for himself by writing a letter containing the statements that he wishes to prove. He does not make the letter evidence by sending it to the party against whom he wishes to prove the facts. He no more can impose a duty to answer a charge than he can impose a duty to pay by selling goods." But is it not "natural" to answer such a letter from a customer who has bought bonds? Of course, it is the silence, not the letter alone, that is significant, and the question is one not of duty but of probability); Fidelity & Casualty Co. v. Beeland Brothers Mercantile Co., 242 Ala. 591, 7 So.2d 265 (1942) (claim by assisting attorneys in suit defended by liability insurance company for attorney's fees against insurance company, which defended on ground plaintiffs were employed by insured; letter written by plaintiffs to defendants, after original suit concluded, setting out their version of the arrangement for their services, and unanswered, excluded.) See also Southern Stone Co., Inc. v. Singer, 665 F.2d 698 (5th Cir. 1982) (error to admit failure to answer letter from other party's lawyer though apparently extensive course of dealings; perhaps court influenced by possible reluctance to answer letter from opposing lawyer).

This restrictive attitude is especially marked in the seduction, breach of promise, and bastardy cases, where the defendant fails to answer an accusatory letter from the alleged victim. See e.g., Snead v. Commonwealth, 138 Va. 787, 121 S.E. 82, 34 A.L.R. 550 (1924).

28. Megarry Brothers, Inc. v. United States, 404 F.2d 479 (8th Cir. 1968); Milliken v. Warwick, 306 Mass. 192, 28 N.E.2d 224 (1940); Bradley v. McDonald, 218 N.Y. 351, 113 N.E. 340 (1916).

would be fruitless,[29] or if the letter was written after litigation was instituted, these circumstances tend to show that failure to answer is not to be received as an admission.[30]

 WESTLAW REFERENCES

headnote(admission* /s silence)
157k220(8)

---

§ 271. Admissions by Conduct: (c) Flight and Similar Acts [1]

"The wicked flee when no man pursueth." Many acts of a defendant after the crime seeking to escape the toils of the law are uncritically received as admissions by conduct, constituting circumstantial evidence of consciousness of guilt and hence of the fact of guilt itself. In this class are flight from the scene [2] or from one's usual haunts [3] after the crime, assuming a false name,[4] shaving off a beard,[5] resisting arrest,[6] attempting to bribe arresting officers,[7] forfeiture of bond by failure to appear,[8] escapes or attempted escapes from confinement,[9] and attempts of the accused to take his own life.[10]

If the flight is from the scene of the crime, evidence of it seems to be wholly acceptable as a means of locating the accused at the critical time and place. However, in many situations, the inference of consciousness of guilt of the particular crime is so uncertain and ambiguous and the evidence so prejudicial [11] that one is forced to wonder whether the evidence is not directed to punishing the "wicked" generally rather than resolving the issue of guilt of the offense charged.[12] Particularly troublesome are the

29. Kitzke v. Turnidge, 209 Or. 563, 307 P.2d 522 (1957) (to defendant's letter suggesting settlement the "Bible way" plaintiff responded by filing suit).

30. Canadian Bank of Commerce v. Coumbe, 47 Mich. 358, 11 N.W. 196, 199 (1882).

§ 271

1. See, for general statements, United States v. Jackson, 572 F.2d 636 (7th Cir. 1978); State v. Torphy, 217 Ind. 383, 28 N.E.2d 70, 72 (1940); State v. Barry, 93 N.H. 10, 34 A.2d 661 (1943); State v. Henderson, 182 Or. 147, 184 P.2d 392, 413 (1947). See also Hutchins and Slesinger, Consciousness of Guilt, 77 U.Pa.L. Rev. 725 (1929); 2 Wigmore, Evidence § 276; Note, 65 Va.L.Rev. 597 (1979); Dec.Dig. Criminal Law ☞351.

2. State v. Townsend, 201 Kan. 122, 439 P.2d 70 (1968); Davis v. State, 171 Neb. 333, 106 N.W.2d 490 (1960). If a "flight" instruction is given, it must be reasonable to infer flight. United States v. Myers, 550 F.2d 1036 (5th Cir. 1977). Compare State v. Bruton, 66 Wash.2d 111, 401 P.2d 340 (1965) (error to instruct that flight might be considered as evidence of guilt when defendants merely walked away from scene of alleged shoplifting), and State v. Owen, 94 Ariz. 404, 385 P.2d 700 (1963), vacated on other grounds 378 U.S. 574, on remand 96 Ariz. 274, 394 P.2d 206 (flight instruction not erroneous when defendants left rape victim in desert and returned to town).

3. Pierce v. State, 256 N.E.2d 557 (Ind.1970). Testimony which merely describes a search of certain areas, without establishing them as customary resorts of the accused, does not qualify. Commonwealth v. Carita, 356 Mass. 132, 249 N.E.2d 5 (1969).

4. United States v. Boyle, 675 F.2d 430 (1st Cir. 1982); People v. Waller, 14 Cal.2d 693, 96 P.2d 344 (1939).

5. People v. Slutts, 259 Cal.App.2d 886, 66 Cal.Rptr. 862 (1968), or conversely, growing one. United States v. Jackson, 476 F.2d 249 (7th Cir. 1973).

6. People v. Sustak, 15 Ill.2d 115, 153 N.E.2d 849 (1958) (details admissible as going to weight; fact that resisting arrest is a separate offense does not require exclusion). Nor is resistance essential in order to admit the circumstances of arrest. Lenzi v. State, 456 S.W.2d 99 (Tex.Cr.App.1970) (possession of pistol at time of arrest).

7. Cortes v. State, 135 Fla. 589, 185 So. 323, 327 (1938); State v. Nelson, 65 N.M. 403, 338 P.2d 301 (1959).

8. Affronti v. United States, 145 F.2d 3 (8th Cir. 1944) (government could show defendant by failing to appear forfeited bonds in other cases pending against him, as well as this one); Williams v. State, 148 Tex.Cr. R. 427, 187 S.W.2d 667 (1945).

9. State v. Ford, 259 Iowa 744, 145 N.W.2d 638 (1966); State v. Thomas, 63 Wn.2d 59, 385 P.2d 532 (1963).

10. People v. Duncan, 261 Ill. 339, 103 N.E. 1043 (1914); Commonwealth v. Goldenberg, 315 Mass. 26, 51 N.E.2d 762 (1943); State v. Painter, 329 Mo. 314, 44 S.W.2d 79 (1931); State v. Lawrence, 196 N.C. 562, 146 S.E. 395 (1929) (but Brogden, J. dissented on this point); Commonwealth v. Giacobbe, 341 Pa. 187, 19 A.2d 71 (1941); Annot., 22 A.L.R.3d 840.

11. "Flight evidence tends to be highly prejudicial but only marginally probative . . . ." Note, 65 Va. L.Rev. 597, 612 (1979).

12. See, e.g., Wong Sun v. United States, 371 U.S. 471, 483, n. 10 (1963): "[W]e have consistently doubted the probative value in criminal trials of evidence that the accused fled the scene of an actual or supposed crime." Earlier the Court had denied that the biblical quotation opening this section was "an accepted axiom

cases where defendant flees when sought to be arrested for another crime,[13] or is wanted for another crime,[14] or is not shown to know that he is suspected of the particular crime.[15] Is a general sense of guilt to be accepted? [16] Perhaps the chief offenders are the cases of attempted suicide.[17]

A leading case suggests with respect to evidence of flight:

> Its probative value as circumstantial evidence of guilt depends upon the degree of confidence with which four inferences can be drawn: (1) from the defendant's behavior to flight; (2) from flight to consciousness of guilt; (3) from consciousness of guilt to consciousness of guilt concerning the crime charged; and (4) from consciousness of guilt concerning the crime charged to actual guilt of the crime charged.[18]

In addition, the potential for prejudice of flight evidence should be weighed against its probative value. Critical scrutiny is called for in each particular case.[19]

While the great bulk of the decisions involve criminal prosecutions, flight also finds recognition in civil actions.[20]

 WESTLAW REFERENCES

headnote(admission*   /s   flight flee!)

§ 272. Admissions by Conduct: (d) Failure to Call Witnesses or Produce Evidence:[1] Refusal to Submit to a Physical Examination[2]

When it would be natural under the circumstances for a party to call a particular witness,[3] or to take the stand himself as a witness in a civil case,[4] or voluntarily to produce documents or other objects in his possession as evidence,[5] and he fails to do so,

---

of criminal law." Alberty v. United States, 162 U.S. 499, 511 (1896).

13. State v. Nelson, 65 N.M. 403, 338 P.2d 301 (1959) (murder; proper to admit evidence of attempt to bribe officer and flight when arrested for reckless driving).

14. People v. Yazum, 13 N.Y.2d 302, 196 N.E.2d 263, 246 N.Y.S.2d 626 (1963) (evidence of flight not excluded in New York trial because accused was also wanted in Ohio). United States v. Boyle, supra, n. 4, suggests that defendant using an alias may be trying to evade detection for *all* his crimes.

15. Shorter v. United States, 412 F.2d 428 (9th Cir. 1969) (showing of knowledge is not required). In general the cases simply overlook the problem. However an occasional case specifies knowledge as a requirement. People v. Harris, 23 Ill.2d 270, 178 N.E.2d 291 (1961), and see Embree v. United States, 320 F.2d 666 (9th Cir. 1963), sought to be distinguished in *Shorter,* supra. Circumstantial proof of knowledge may, of course, suffice. Commonwealth v. Osborne, 433 Pa. 297, 249 A.2d 330 (1969).

Compare 2 Wigmore, Evidence § 276 (Chadbourn rev. 1979).

16. Martin v. State, 236 Ind. 524, 141 N.E.2d 107, 109 (1957) (resistance to arrest is evidence of guilt, "though not necessarily guilt of the crime charged.").

17. Note 10, supra; Note, 7 N.C.L.Rev. 290 (1929).

18. United States v. Myers, 550 F.2d 1036, 1049 (5th Cir. 1977). But compare United States v. Kalish, 690 F.2d 1144, 1155 (5th Cir. 1982), cert. denied 103 S.Ct. 735, suggesting that the four-inference test of *Myers* applies only to the propriety of giving a flight instruction and not to the admissibility of flight evidence generally.

19. See Federal and Revised Uniform Rule 403 and § 185 supra.

20. Gaul v. Noiva, 155 Conn. 218, 230 A.2d 591 (1967) (attempt to flee from scene of automobile accident); Jones v. Strelecki, 49 N.J. 513, 231 A.2d 558 (1967) (failure to stop after striking pedestrian, in violation of Motor Vehicle Act).

§ 272

1. See 2 Wigmore, Evidence §§ 285–291 (Chadbourn rev. 1979); Comment, 61 Calif.L.Rev. 1422 (1973); Dec. Dig. Evidence ⬥77, Criminal Law ⬥317; C.J.S. Evidence § 156.

Saltzburg, A Special Aspect of Relevance: Countering Negative Inferences Associated with the Absence of Evidence, 66 Calif.L.Rev. 1011 (1978), deals with the related but distinct problem where the absence of evidence is occasioned by judicial ruling.

2. 8 Wigmore, Evidence § 2220, note 19 (McNaughton rev. 1961); Dec.Dig. Damages ⬥206(8).

3. Secondino v. New Haven Gas Co., 147 Conn. 672, 165 A.2d 598 (1960).

4. Kelsey v. Connecticut State Employees Association, 179 Conn. 606, 427 A.2d 420 (1980); Williams v. Ricklemann, 292 S.W.2d 276 (Mo.1956).

See § 132, supra, as to extent to which an accused waives privilege against self-incrimination by testifying.

5. Gray v. Callahan, 143 Fla. 673, 197 So. 396, 400 (1940); Martin v. T.L. James & Co., 237 La. 633, 112 So.2d 86 (1959); Welsh v. Gibbons, 211 S.C. 516, 46 S.E.2d 147 (1948).

tradition has allowed his adversary to use this failure as the basis for invoking an adverse inference. An analogous inference may be drawn if a party unreasonably declines to submit, upon request, to a physical examination,[6] or refuses to furnish handwriting examplars.[7]

Most of the controversy arises in respect to failure to call a witness. The classic statement was,

> [I]f a party has it peculiarly within his power to produce witnesses whose testimony would elucidate the transaction, the fact that he does not do it creates the presumption that the testimony, if produced, would be unfavorable.[8]

The cases actually fall into two groups.[9] In the first, an adverse inference may be drawn against a party for failure to produce a witness reasonably assumed to be favorably disposed to the party.[10] In the second, the inference may be drawn against a party who has exclusive control over a material witness but fails to produce him, without regard to any possible favorable disposition of the witness toward the party.[11] Cases in the second group are increasingly less frequent, due in part, no doubt, to the growth of discovery and other disclosure requirements. In either group, if the testimony of the witness would be merely cumulative, the inference is unavailable.[12]

Despite the plenitude of cases recognizing the inference, refusal to allow comment or to instruct does not often serve as a ground for reversal. This counsel of caution is reinforced by several factors. Possible conjecture or ambiguity of inference is often present.[13] The possibility that the inference may be drawn invites waste of time in calling un-

---

6. Texas & New Orleans Railway Co. v. Rooks, 292 S.W. 536 (Tex.Com.App.1927) (but request addressed to attorneys insufficient); 8 Wigmore, Evidence § 2220, n. 19 (McNaughton rev. 1961). The significance of the inference in respect to physical examination is greatly diminished by prevailing rules providing for compulsory physical examination and penalties for noncompliance. F.R.Civ.P. 35, 37(b). See § 3 supra. As to blood-alcohol tests, see Annot., 87 A.L.R.2d 370.

7. United States v. Nix, 465 F.2d 90 (5th Cir. 1972), cert. denied 409 U.S. 1013; State v. Haze, 218 Kan. 60, 542 P.2d 720 (1975).

8. Graves v. United States, 150 U.S. 118, 121 (1893).

9. United States v. Ariza-Ibarra, 651 F.2d 2 (1st Cir. 1981), cert. denied 454 U.S. 895.

10. United States v. Mahone, 537 F.2d 922 (7th Cir. 1976), cert. denied 429 U.S. 1025 (government failed to call state police officer who was present at scene of arrest and might have testified on disputed matters); Secondino v. New Haven Gas Co., 147 Conn. 672, 165 A.2d 598 (1960) (personal injury plaintiff failed to call treating physician); Feldstein v. Harrington, 4 Wis.2d 380, 90 N.W.2d 566 (1958) (defendant failed to call physician who examined plaintiff at defendant's request). In the foregoing cases the inference was allowed. In the following cases the relationship and circumstances were held not to warrant the inference: United States v. Ariza-Ibarra, supra n. 9 (no effort by defense to produce informer on basis of information furnished by government; no showing that testimony would have benefited defendant); Labit v. Santa Fe Marine, Inc., 526 F.2d 961 (5th Cir. 1976), cert. denied 429 U.S. 827 (judge allowed argument but denied instruction; plaintiff in suit against employer did not call fellow employee, of relatively subordinate status, with deposition available); United States v. Bramble, 680 F.2d 590 (9th

Cir. 1982) (defense counsel interviewed informer and said she did not want him to stay around to testify). Cases dealing with the effect of particular relationships between party and witness are collected in Annot., 5 A.L.R.2d 893.

Note should be taken of the requirement that the State produce or account for all material witnesses in hearings on the issue whether a confession was voluntary. People v. Sims, 21 Ill.2d 425, 173 N.E.2d 494 (1961), cert. denied 369 U.S. 861.

11. Stuart v. Doyle, 95 Conn. 732, 112 A. 653 (1921) (defendant failed to produce two licensed drivers in his employ, identity unknown to plaintiff, to testify whether third employee driving defendant's car was in scope of employment); Haas v. Kasnot, 371 Pa. 580, 92 A.2d 171 (1952) (defendant failed to produce third motorist claimed by him to have been responsible for collision, whose identity was unknown to plaintiff).

12. Gafford v. Trans-Texas Airways, 299 F.2d 60 (6th Cir. 1962) (co-pilot testified; no inference from failure to call command pilot); State v. Brown, 169 Conn. 692, 364 A.2d 186 (1975) (chief toxicologist testified; no inference from failure to call two subordinates who analyzed substance under his direction). Testimony that would aid in resolving a conflict in testimony is not regarded as cumulative. Geiger v. Schneyer, 398 Pa. 69, 157 A.2d 56 (1960).

13. Oliphant v. Snyder, 206 Va. 932, 147 S.E.2d 122, 126 (1966) ("Any presumption that he [10-year old passenger-son of defendant driver] would have testified adversely to his father is pure speculation."). United States v. Busic, 587 F.2d 577 (3d Cir. 1978) lists numerous reasons other than unfavorable testimony for not calling a witness. In Griffin v. California, 380 U.S. 609 (1965), rehearing denied 381 U.S. 957, possible reasons for the accused's not testifying are explored.

necessary witnesses [14] or in presenting evidence to explain why they were not called.[15] Failure to anticipate that the inference may be invoked entails substantial possibilities of surprise.[16] And finally, the availability of modern discovery and other disclosure procedures serves to diminish both the justification [17] and the need [18] for the inference.

It is often said that if the witness is "equally available" to both parties, no inference springs from the failure of either to call him.[19] This can hardly be accurate, as the inference may be allowed when the witness could easily be called or subpoenaed by either party. What is in fact meant is that when so far as appears the witness would be as likely to be favorable to one party as the other, there will be no inference.[20] But even here, it seems that equality of favor is nearly always debatable, and that though the judge thinks the witness would be as likely to favor one party as the other, he should permit either party to argue the inference against the adversary.[21]

A party may be at liberty to call a witness, but may have a privilege against the witness's being called by the adversary, as when under the local statute an accused in a criminal case may call his wife, but the state may not. Or it may be clear that all the information that a witness has is subject to a privilege which the party may exert, as in the case where by statute the party is privileged against disclosure by his physician of information learned in consultation or examination. In these situations probably the majority of courts would forbid an adverse inference from a failure to call.[22] Of course, an inference from the failure of the accused himself in a criminal case to take the stand is constitutionally forbidden.[23] The policy considerations in respect to the allowability of comment upon the exercise of evidential privileges are discussed elsewhere.[24]

The specific procedural effect of the inference from failure to call a witness is seldom discussed. Some courts have said that the party's failure to call the witness or produce

14. See, e.g., Ballard v. Lumbermens Mutual Casualty Co., 33 Wis.2d 601, 148 N.W.2d 65, 73 (1967) ("A party to a lawsuit does not have the burden, at his peril, of calling every possible witness to a fact, lest his failure to do so will result in an inference against him.").

15. The party is, of course, entitled to explain the nonproduction. United States v. McCaskill, 481 F.2d 438 (2d Cir. 1976); Case v. New York Central Railway Co., 329 F.2d 936 (2d Cir. 1964). Explanation must be based on what appears in the record. United States v. Latimer, 511 F.2d 498 (10th Cir. 1975), appeal after remand 548 F.2d 311 (government testimony in bank robbery prosecution showed surveillance camera was activated, but no pictures were offered or explanation of absence; defense argued that film was not produced because it did not identify defendant; error to allow government in reply argument to state that camera malfunctioned and in fact photographed FBI agent who arrived some time later).

16. State v. Clawans, 38 N.J. 162, 183 A.2d 77 (1962) (suggesting that proper practice is to require party proposing to invoke the inference give notice at the close of the opponent's case).

17. If discovery is available but not employed, the party ought not to be allowed to resort to the necessarily somewhat speculative inference when discovery would substitute certainty. Jenkins v. Bierschenk, 333 F.2d 421 (8th Cir. 1964). The argument against allowing the inference is even stronger when a deposi-

tion has in fact been taken. Labit v. Santa Fe Marine, Inc., supra n. 10; Atlantic Coast Line Railroad Co. v. Larisey, 269 Ala. 203, 112 So.2d 203 (1959); Critzer v. Shegogue, 236 Md. 411, 204 A.2d 180 (1964); Bean v. Riddle, 423 S.W.2d 709 (Mo.1968).

18. Discovery procedures offer a more direct means of compelling the production of evidence. A parallel to the diminished importance of the so-called best evidence rule is evident. Cleary & Strong, The Best Evidence Rule: An Evaluation in Context, 51 Iowa L.Rev. 825 (1966).

19. Atlantic Coast Line Railroad Co. v. Larisey, 269 Ala. 203, 112 So.2d 203 (1959); Ellerman v. Skelly Oil Co., 227 Minn. 65, 34 N.W.2d 251 (1948); Bean v. Riddle, 423 S.W.2d 709 (Mo.1968).

20. United States v. Mahone, 537 F.2d 922 (7th Cir. 1976). The unusual stretching of the meaning of "availability" apparently is the result of the need to fit the two previously mentioned groups of cases into the language of Graves, supra n. 8.

21. United States v. Erb, 543 F.2d 438 (2d Cir. 1976), cert. denied 429 U.S. 981; Dawson v. Davis, 125 Conn. 330, 5 A.2d 703 (1939); Commonwealth v. Niziolek, 380 Mass. 513, 404 N.E.2d 643 (1980); Baker v. Salvation Army, Inc., 91 N.H. 1, 12 A.2d 514 (1940).

22. See § 80 supra.

23. See § 131 supra.

24. See § 80 supra.

the evidence creates a "presumption" [25] that the testimony would have been unfavorable. It is usually phrased in terms, however, of "may" rather than "must" and seemingly could at most be only a "permissive," not a mandatory presumption, i.e. an inference described as a presumption in order to avoid local prohibitions against judges commenting on the evidence.[26] Moreover, unlike the usual presumption, it is not directed to any specific presumed fact or facts which are required or permitted to be found. One who has the burden of producing evidence of a fact in issue, cannot supply the lack of proof by relying on this "presumption." [27] "The extent of a party's right to invoke his opponent's failure to call an available witness, when such right exists, is to impair the value of the latter's proofs, and to give greater credence to the positive evidence of the former, upon any issue upon which it is shown that such witness might have knowledge." [28]

A possible practical effect of calling it a presumption is that it might incline some courts adopting this usage to regard its inclusion in the instructions as a matter of right. Most courts customarily speak of the party's conduct as creating an "inference." [29] Doubtless some of these courts would consider that the party has a right to have such inference explained in the instructions, on proper request. Others no doubt would say that the instruction is proper but not required.[30] Still others would condemn it as a comment on the evidence.[31]

Of course, all courts permit counsel to argue the inference where the inference is an allowable one.

In jurisdictions where the judge retains his common law power to comment on the evidence, certainly a fair comment on failure to produce witnesses or evidence is traditionally allowable. In other jurisdictions, there is no harm if local practice sanctions a discretion in the judge to include an instruction. It is submitted, however, that a practice which gives a party a right to such instruction is undesirable.[32] If made a matter of right it is hard to escape the development of elaborate rules of law defining the circumstances when the right exists. To make it a matter of right has the advantage, it is true, of focussing past experience on the problem presented at the trial, but the cost here of complex rules far outweighs the gain.

A similar effect, of spinning a web of rules, flows from the practice of tight control of the argument on the inference. It is wiser to hold that if an argument on failure to produce proof is fallacious, the remedy is the usual one, namely the answering argu-

25. Tepper v. Campo, 398 Ill. 496, 76 N.E.2d 490 (1948); Stephenson v. Golden, 279 Mich. 710, 276 N.W. 849 (1938); Robinson v. Haydel, 177 Miss. 233, 171 So. 7 (1937); Wolfe v. Wolfe, 120 W.Va. 389, 198 S.E. 209 (1938).

26. See discussion of these terms in Ch. 36 infra.

27. Maszczenski v. Myers, 212 Md. 346, 129 A.2d 109 (1957); Stimpson v. Hunter, 234 Mass. 61, 125 N.E. 155 (1919); Pacific Finance Corp. v. Rucker, 392 S.W.2d 554 (Tex.Civ.App.1965); 2 Wigmore, Evidence § 290 (Chadbourn rev. 1979). Compare Morrow v. United States, 408 F.2d 1390 (8th Cir. 1969) (in prosecution for placing life in jeopardy, jury could infer that gun was loaded in absence of introduction of contrary evidence by accused); City of Omaha v. American Theatre Corp., 189 Neb. 441, 203 N.W.2d 155 (1973) (defendant's failure to produce film in response to subpoena established violation of obscenity law).

28. Snow, J. in Stocker v. Boston & Maine Railroad Co., 84 N.H. 377, 151 A. 457, 70 A.L.R. 1320, 1323, (1930). See Annot., 70 A.L.R. 1326.

29. See, e.g., Gross v. Williams, 149 F.2d 84 (8th Cir. 1945); National Life Co. v. Brennecke, 195 Ark. 1088, 115 S.W.2d 855 (1938); Dawson v. Davis, 125 Conn. 330, 5 A.2d 703 (1939).

30. See Knott v. Hawley, 163 Minn. 239, 203 N.W. 785 (1925).

For illustrative instructions, see Cromling v. Pittsburgh & L.E.R. Co., 327 F.2d 142 (3d Cir. 1964); Schemenauer v. Travelers Indemnity Co., 34 Wis.2d 299, 149 N.W.2d 644 (1967).

31. Hartman v. Hartman, 314 Mo. 305, 284 S.W. 488 (1926).

32. "If it commends itself to reason, born of common judgment and experience, the jury will apply it without hint or argument from the Court. . . . Those cases are sound which deny to the inference any quality other than mere argument. Here again a safe and logical test is: if counsel is free to argue it, the Court is not." Alexander, Presumptions: Their Use and Abuse, 17 Miss.L.J. 1, 14 (1945).

ment and the jury's good sense.[33] Thus the judge would be called on to intervene only when the argument can be said, under the general standard, to be not merely weak or unfounded, but unfair and prejudicial.[34]

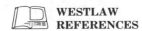

WESTLAW REFERENCES

157k77
110k317

§ 273. Admissions by Conduct: (e) Misconduct Constituting Obstruction of Justice [1]

We have seen in the preceding section that a party's failure to produce evidence when he is free to produce or withhold may be treated as an admission. As might be expected, wrongdoing by the party in connection with his case amounting to an obstruction of justice is also commonly regarded as an admission by conduct. By resorting to wrongful devices he is said to give ground for believing that he thinks his case is weak and not to be won by fair means, or in criminal cases that the accused is conscious of guilt. Accordingly, a party's false statement about the matter in litigation, whether before suit [2] or on the stand,[3] his fabrication of false documents,[4] his undue pressure, by bribery [5] or intimidation [6] or other means, to influence a witness to testify for him or to avoid testifying, his destruction or concealment of relevant documents or objects,[7] his

---

33. In United States v. Cotter, 60 F.2d 689, 692 (2d Cir. 1932) the court (L. Hand, J.) in rejecting defendant's complaint of the judge's refusal to instruct the jury to disregard the prosecution's argument based on defendant's failure to call witnesses, said, "A judge is not required to intervene here any more than in any other issue of fact. He must indeed, as he always must, keep the prosecution in a criminal case within bounds; . . . just as he must keep passion out of the debate and hold the parties to the issues. But he is not charged with correcting their non sequiturs; the jury are to find these for themselves. So the judge in the case at bar was not required to correct the argument, that the failure of the defendants to call the four witnesses was a ground for supposing that they would swear against them. He might have done so, but he need not; so far as we know, Sears v. Duling, 79 Vt. 334, 65 A. 990, is the only decision to the contrary and it does not persuade us." See also Alabama Power Co. v. Goodwin, 210 Ala. 657, 99 So. 158 (1924) (trial judge must not pass upon the logical propriety of arguments).

34. In passing on this the trial judge has a substantial measure of discretion. Lebas v. Patriotic Assurance Co., 106 Conn. 119, 137 A. 241 (1927).

§ 273

1. 2 Wigmore, Evidence §§ 278, 291 (Chadbourn rev. 1979); Maguire & Vincent, Admissions Implied from Spoliation, 45 Yale L.J. 226 (1935); Dec.Dig. Criminal Law ☞351(8), 351(10), Evidence ☞78, 79, 110, 219(2); C.J.S. Evidence §§ 151–155, 293.

2. Wilson v. United States, 162 U.S. 613 (1896) (false explanations of incriminating circumstances in murder case); United States v. Boekelman, 594 F.2d 1238 (9th Cir. 1979) (false exculpatory statements); People v. Showers, 68 Cal.2d 639, 68 Cal.Rptr. 459, 440 P.2d 939 (1968) (false explanation by accused as to why he was searching in patch of ivy where heroin was found); State v. De Matteo, 186 Conn. 696, 443 A.2d

915 (1982) (false statement to police as to whereabouts at time of crime); Commonwealth v. Lettrich, 346 Pa. 497, 31 A.2d 155 (1943) (child-murder by custodian, false statements as to child's whereabouts to avert inquiry and suspicion).

3. Sheehan v. Goriansky, 317 Mass. 10, 56 N.E.2d 883 (1944) (defendant's testimony which from other evidence jury could find to be false); Hall v. Merrimack Mutual Fire Insurance Co., 91 N.H. 6, 13 A.2d 157 (1940) (deliberately false testimony at first trial acknowledged to be false at the second).

4. United States v. Wilkins, 385 F.2d 465 (4th Cir. 1967) (letter fabricated to explain failure to report income for tax purposes); Western States Grocery Co. v. Mirt, 190 Okl. 299, 123 P.2d 266 (1942) (falsified witness-statement placed in evidence).

5. State v. Rolfe, 92 Idaho 467, 444 P.2d 428 (1968) (attempt to bribe witness). People v. Gambony, 402 Ill. 74, 83 N.E.2d 321 (1949) (indecent liberties with a child: attempts to "buy off" the prosecuting witnesses); Davis v. Commonwealth, 204 Ky. 601, 265 S.W. 10 (1924) (letter offering bribe for favorable testimony); Commonwealth v. Leo, 379 Mass. 34, 393 N.E.2d 410 (1979) (semble Gambony, supra).

6. State v. Adair, 106 Ariz. 4, 469 P.2d 823 (1970); State v. Belkner, 117 N.H. 462, 374 A.2d 938 (1977) (plan to kill witness); State v. Hill, 47 N.J. 490, 221 A.2d 725 (1966); Price v. State, 37 Wis.2d 117, 154 N.W.2d 222 (1967).

7. Jones v. State, 223 Ga. 157, 154 S.E.2d 228 (1967), reversed on other grounds 389 U.S. 24 (murder; accused buried body); Hubbard v. State, 187 So.2d 885 (Miss.1966) (accused pushed his automobile into 40-foot deep lake after fatal accident); Welborn v. Rigdon, 231 S.W.2d 127 (Mo.1950) (suit by plaintiff for money advanced to improve defendant's property; defendant's conduct in wilfully destroying plaintiff's receipts held "an admission of plaintiff's claim").

attempt to corrupt the jury,[8] his hiding [9] or transferring [10] property in anticipation of judgment—all these are instances of this type of admission by conduct. Of course, it is not enough to show that a third person did the acts, such as bribing a witness, charged as obstructive. They must be connected to the party himself, or in the case of a corporation to one of its superior officers, by showing that he did the act or authorized it by words or other conduct.[11] Moreover, the circumstances of the act must manifest bad faith. Mere negligence is not enough,[12] for it does not sustain the inference of consciousness of a weak case.

A question may well be raised whether the relatively modest probative value of this species of evidence is not often outweighed by its prejudicial aspects.[13] The litigant who

would not like to have a stronger case must indeed be a rarity. It may well be that the real underpinning of the rule of admissibility is a desire to impose swift punishment, with a certain poetic justice, rather than concern over niceties of proof.[14] In any event, the evidence is generally admitted, despite incidental disclosure of another crime.[15]

What is the probative reach of these various kinds of "spoliation" admissions, beyond their great tactical value in darkening the atmosphere of the party's case? [16] They should, it seems, entitle the proponent at least to an instruction that the adversary's conduct may be considered as tending to corroborate the proponent's case generally, and as tending to discredit the adversary's case generally.[17] This is worthwhile in itself and as carrying with it the corresponding right

8. People v. Marion, 29 Mich. 31, 39 (1874); McHugh v. McHugh, 186 Pa. 197, 40 A. 410 (1898).

9. State v. Bruce, 24 Me. 71 (1844) (procuring property by threats; evidence of concealment).

10. Burdett v. Hipp, 252 Ala. 37, 39 So.2d 389 (1949) (defendant's conveyance of his property to kin after suit filed); Johnson v. O'Brien, 258 Minn. 502, 105 N.W.2d 244, 88 A.L.R.2d 577 (1960) (same); Annot., 80 A.L.R. 1139.

11. State v. Sorbo, 174 Conn. 253, 382 A.2d 221 (1978) (unconnected threats); Morgan v. Commonwealth, 283 Ky. 588, 142 S.W.2d 123 (1940) (attempted bribery of witness, error to admit because no showing of defendant's connection with the act); Annot., 79 A.L.R.3d 1156. Family relationship is not a sufficient connection. Roby v. State, 587 P.2d 641 (Wyo.1978).

The suggestion in the text as to corporations is taken from Maguire & Vincent, Admissions Implied from Spoliation, 45 Yale L.J. 226, 251 (1935). City of Austin v. Howard, 158 S.W.2d 556 (Tex.Civ.App.1942) (attempts by Mayor and City Manager to prevent witness from testifying in suit against City, held admissible though assent of Council not shown. "Manifestly they were actively interested and participating on behalf of the City in the conduct of the trial as they had a right to do, and their conduct should be deemed, under such circumstances, to be within the general scope of their authority."). Compare Nowack v. Metropolitan Street Railway Co., 166 N.Y. 433, 439, 60 N.E. 32, 34 (1901) (evidence of attempted bribery by defendant's claim agent was held receivable, not only as the representative admission of defendant corporation, but because it cast doubt upon the other witnesses secured by him).

12. Berthold-Jennings Lumber Co., St. Louis, Iron Mountain & Southern Railway Co., 80 F.2d 32 (8th Cir. 1935) (action for overcharge; waybills covering shipments had been destroyed by defendant, held, doctrine of spoliation inapplicable; only applies to conduct indi-

cating fraud, whereas destruction here was routine, with no desire to suppress evidence); Gallup v. St. Louis, Iron Mountain & Southern Railway Co., 140 Ark. 347, 215 S.W. 586 (1919) (similar).

13. Occasional exclusion is found where the conduct is particularly macabre or inflammatory. United States v. Weir, 575 F.2d 668 (8th Cir. 1978) (three assassination threats plus attempted killing, error); United States v. McManaman, 606 F.2d 919 (10th Cir. 1979), appeal after remand 653 F.2d 458 ("inflammatory talk of the plan of murders must have predominated in impact over the discussion of drug dealing;" error).

See generally § 185 supra.

14. Few opinion writers have been as frank as in Pomeroy v. Benton, 77 Mo. 64, 86 (1882): "It is because of the very fact that the evidence of the plaintiff, the proofs of his claim or the muniments of his title, have been destroyed [by defendant], that the law, in hatred of the spoiler, baffles the destroyer, and thwarts his iniquitous purpose, by indulging a presumption which supplies the lost proof, and thus defeats the wrongdoer by the very means he had so confidently employed to perpetrate the wrong."

15. Sireci v. State, 399 So.2d 964 (Fla.1981) (attempt to have prosecution witness killed); State v. Armstrong, 170 Mont. 256, 552 P.2d 616 (1976) (shoplifting to obtain coat to replace bloodstained similar coat worn during homicide).

16. For an illuminating discussion, see Maguire & Vincent, Admissions Implied from Spoliation, 45 Yale L.J. 226, 235–249 (1935).

17. See Maguire & Vincent, supra n. 16, at 243–249; Prudential Insurance Co. v. Lawnsdail, 235 Iowa 125, 15 N.W.2d 880 (1944) (destruction of record "authorizes an inference which tends to corroborate the evidence" on the other side); Hay v. Peterson, 6 Wyo. 419, 45 P. 1073, 1076–9 (1896) (destruction of records of deceased

of the proponent's counsel to argue these inferences. But a crucial and perplexing question remains, namely, does the adverse inference from the party's obstructive conduct supply the want of any evidence of a fact essential to the other party's case? Certainly the primitive impulse is strong, and an analogy has been suggested to the practice under statutes and rules permitting the court to enter a default against a party who refuses to make discovery.[18] Certainly also when the conduct points toward an inference about a particular specific fact, as in the case of bribery of an attesting witness to absent himself from the probate hearing, or the destruction of a particular deed or letter,

there is likely to be a greater willingness to allow an inference as to the fact,[19] though the only other information available is the proponent's claim about it in his pleading. Where the conduct is not directed toward suppression of any particular fact, as in attempts to "buy off" the prosecution, to suborn the jury, or to defeat recovery by conveyance of property, an inference as to the existence of a particular fact not proved is more strained. Without adverting to this distinction many decisions have supported the general doctrine that the inference from obstructive conduct by the adversary will not supply a want of proof of a particular fact essential to the proponent's case.[20]

by plaintiff, defendant entitled to instruction on presumption but one requested by him not properly qualified).

The courts often speak of a "presumption" against the spoliator. Long v. Earle, 277 Mich. 505, 269 N.W. 577 (1936); Dec.Dig. Evidence ⇔78, 79. Most presumptions may stand in lieu of proof of specific facts, see Ch. 36 infra, but this "presumption" against the spoliator is usually given only a general persuasive effect, rather than a probative one. Walker v. Herke, 20 Wn.2d 239, 147 P.2d 255 (1944).

18. Maguire & Vincent, supra n. 16, at 235. Fed.R. Civ.P. 37(b)(2) authorizes orders that facts be taken as established or precluding the offender from introducing evidence; also judgment by default.

19. See 2 Wigmore, Evidence § 291 (Chadbourn rev. 1979), wherein the author contends that the failure or refusal to produce, or the destruction of a document, sufficiently identified by the proof, is evidence from which alone its contents can be inferred to be unfavorable to the one chargeable with the obstructive conduct. For support of this view see McCleery v. Mc-Cleery, 200 Ala. 4, 75 So. 316 (1917).

In the famous case of Armory v. Delamirie, 1 Stra. 505, 93 Eng.Rep. 664 (K.B.1722) the chimney sweeper's boy found a mounted jewel and took it to a goldsmith's shop to be valued. But the goldsmith's apprentice kept the stone, and gave back only the socket. The boy sued the goldsmith for the conversion of the jewel. After evidence had been given of what a jewel of the finest water that would fit the socket would be worth, the Chief Justice instructed the jury, "that unless the defendant did produce the jewel, and shew it not to be of the finest water, they should presume the strongest against him, and make the value of the best jewels the measure of their damages." It will be noted that in this picturesque landmark case, the limits of the inference were marked out by the evidence of the size of the socket, and of the value of the finest jewel that would fit it.

20. Gage v. Parmelee, 87 Ill. 329, 343 (1877) (bill to set aside for fraud a partnership settlement agree-

ment; proof showed that on being shown a copy of the bill, defendant burned all the bills and papers of the firm. "This culpable act of the destruction of the books justly prejudices the case of the appellee, and we have the inclination to give to it the full legitimate effect against him that may be warranted. But we do not see how, under the proofs in the case, it can be made avail of here, to the advantage of appellant, unless there be allowed to it the effect of supplying proof. This, we do not think, can rightly be done. Proof must be made of the allegations of the bill. The destruction of the books does not make such proof. The presumption of law does not go to that extent. In the weighing of conflicting testimony, there might be scope for the operation of this presumption against the appellee; or, in the denial to him of any benefit of secondary evidence."). See also, Larsen v. Romeo, 254 Md. 220, 255 A.2d 387 (1969); Parsons v. Ryan, 340 Mass. 245, 163 N.E.2d 293 (1960); Login v. Waisman, 82 N.H. 500, 136 A. 134 (1927); Patch Manufacturing Co. v. Protection Lodge, 77 Vt. 294, 329, 60 A. 74 (1905); Walker v. Herke, 20 Wn.2d 239, 147 P.2d 255 (1944).

Supporting the contrary view, that evidence of spoliation does supply proof of facts alleged by the proponent, are statements in the following opinions, though the holdings may not reach so far: Middleton v. Middleton, 188 Ark. 1022, 68 S.W.2d 1003, 1006 (1934); Pomeroy v. Benton, 77 Mo. 64, 85 (1882); In re Lambie's Estate, 97 Mich. 49, 56 N.W. 223, 225 (1893). A sprinkling of decisions has even gone further and has ascribed to spoliation the effect of a conclusive presumption, that the despoiler cannot dispute. Middleton v. Middleton, supra ("where the instrument destroyed is of such nature as to destroy all evidence, there follows a conclusive presumption that if produced it would have established the claim of the adversary"). Or hold that the despoiler cannot dispute the presumption by his own unsupported testimony. Downing v. Plate, 90 Ill. 268, 273 (1878). But later cases reject the conclusive presumption theory. Hall v. Merrimack Mutual Fire Insurance Co., 91 N.H. 6, 13 A.2d 157, 159

§ 274. Admissions by Conduct: (f) Offers to Compromise Disputed Claim [1]

In general. It may be argued an offer by the claimant to accept a sum in compromise of a disputed claim may be used against him as an admission of the weakness of his claim. Or, conversely, it may be argued that an offer by his adversary to pay a sum in compromise may be used against the adversary as an admission of the weakness of his position. In either case there is general agreement that the offer of compromise is not admissible on the issue of liability, although the reason for exclusion is not always clear.

Two grounds for the rule of inadmissibility may be advanced: lack of relevancy and policy considerations.[2] (1) The relevancy of the offer will vary according to circumstances, with a very small offer of payment to settle a very large claim being much more readily construed as a desire for peace rather than an admission of weakness of position. Relevancy would increase, however, as the amount of the offer approached the amount claimed. (2) The policy aspect is to promote the settling of disputes, which would be discouraged if offers of compromise were admitted in evidence. Resting the rule on this basis has the advantage of avoiding difficult questions of relevancy. On this basis, the rule would be available as an objection to one who made the offer in question and is a party to the suit in which the evidence is offered.

To call into play the exclusionary rule, there must be an actual dispute,[3] or at least an apparent difference of view between the parties as to the validity or amount of the claim.[4] An offer to pay an admitted claim is not privileged.[5] There is no policy of encouraging compromises of undisputed claims. They should be paid in full. If the validity of the claim and the amount due are undisputed, an offer to pay a lesser sum in settlement [6] or to pay in installments [7] would accordingly be admissible.

What is excluded? The offer of course,[8] and any suggestions or overtures of settlement.[9] How far do any accompanying statements of fact made by either party during oral negotiations or correspondence looking to settlement share the privilege? The generally accepted doctrine has been that an admission of fact in the course of negotiations

---

(1940); Walker v. Herke, 20 Wn.2d 239, 147 P.2d 255, 261 (1944).

§ 274

1. 4 Wigmore, Evidence §§ 1061, 1062 (Chadbourn rev. 1972); Dec.Dig. Evidence ⌐213, 214, 219(3), Criminal Law ⌐408; C.J.S. Evidence §§ 285–290.

2. See the discussion of theory in Morgan, Basic Problems of Evidence 209 (1962). The cases in general do not display much concern as to the basis of the rule.

3. Ogden v. George F. Alger Co., 353 Mich. 402, 91 N.W.2d 288 (1958) (substantial offer to plaintiff for surrender of his contract, made before controversy arose, not excludable under rule).

4. Tindal v. Mills, 265 N.C. 716, 144 S.E.2d 902 (1965).

5. Hunter v. Hyder, 236 S.C. 378, 114 S.E.2d 493 (1960) (defendant admitted cutting timber from plaintiff's land and said he wanted to straighten it out).

6. Person v. Bowe, 79 Minn. 238, 82 N.W. 480 (1900) (plaintiff sued for wages claimed to be due him as a farm laborer, and offered evidence that when he de-

manded his pay the defendant said that he could not pay then, but would let the plaintiff have $20, and would pay the rest about the middle of November, and if the plaintiff "would throw off five dollars" he would at once pay the claim).

7. Tindal v. Mills, 265 N.C. 716, 144 S.E.2d 902 (1965) (offer to give a series of notes for undisputed claim).

8. Outlook Hotel Co. v. St. John, 287 F. 115 (3d Cir. 1923) (letter offering settlement privileged though not expressly without prejudice).

9. Armstrong v. Kline, 64 Cal.App.2d 704, 149 P.2d 445 (1944) ("she asked me what I thought about settling"); North River Insurance Co. v. Walker, 161 Ky. 368, 170 S.W. 983 (1914) ("if you will come to Paducah we will try to make a compromise settlement."); Coulter, Inc. v. Allen, 624 P.2d 1199 (Wyo.1981) (letter from party that it would like to "settle this out of court"). Contra Shaeffer v. Burton, 151 W.Va. 761, 155 S.E.2d 884 (1967) ("I am sure that if we get together . . . we can settle this problem amicably," admissible).

is not privileged [10] unless it is hypothetical [11]—"we admit for the sake of the discussion only"—or unless it is expressly stated to be "without prejudice," [12] or unless it is inseparably connected with the offer,[13] so that it cannot be correctly understood without reading the two together.[14]

This traditional doctrine of denying the protection of the exclusionary rule to statements of fact has had serious drawbacks, however. It has tended to discourage freedom of communication in attempting compromise, and, taken with its exceptions, it has involved difficulties of application. As a result the trend is to extend the protection to all statements made in compromise negotiations, either by decision [15] or by rule.

Federal Rule of Evidence 408, set forth below, is consistent with the foregoing observations, including an extension of its protection to all statements made in compromise negotiations.

> Evidence of (1) furnishing or offering or promising to furnish, or (2) accepting or offering or promising to accept, a valuable consideration in compromising or attempting to compromise a claim which was disputed as to either validity or amount, is not admissible to prove liability for or invalidity of the claim or its amount. Evidence of conduct or statements made in compromise negotiations is likewise not admissible. This rule does not require the exclusion of any evidence otherwise discoverable merely because it is presented in the course of compromise negotiations.[16] This rule also does not require exclusion when the evidence is offered for another purpose, such as proving bias or prejudice of a witness, negativing a contention of undue delay, or proving an effort to obstruct a criminal investigation or prosecution.[17]

The exclusionary rule is designed to exclude the offer of compromise only when it is tendered as an admission of the weakness of the offering party's claim or defense, not when the purpose is otherwise. Thus, for example, the rule does not call for exclusion when the compromise negotiations are sought to be proved as an explanation of delay in taking action [18] or to explain prior statements [19] or to show the extent of legal services rendered in conducting them,[20] or failure to seek employment to mitigate damages.[21] As in other situations where evidence is admissible for one purpose but not for another, an evaluation is required in terms of weighing probative value and need

10. State v. Stevens, 248 Minn. 309, 80 N.W.2d 22 (1956) (admission of paternity in effort to compromise paternity claim); Cole v. Harvey, 200 Okl. 564, 198 P.2d 199 (1948) (suit for work done; no error in receiving evidence of statements of amount due, during negotiations for compromise); Dunning v. Northwestern Electric Co., 186 Or. 379, 199 P.2d 648 (1948) rev'd on other grounds 186 Or. 379, 206 P.2d 1177 (reference in letter to injuries sustained "when you ran into fallen pole"). Cases are collected in Annot., 15 A.L.R.3d 13.

11. Jones v. Jernigan, 29 N.M. 399, 223 P. 100 (1924).

12. White v. Old Dominion Steamship Co., 102 N.Y. 660, 6 N.E. 289 (1886) and cases cited, Annot., 15 A.L.R.3d 13, 33.

13. See cases on "independent" statements, Annot., 15 A.L.R.3d 13, 27.

14. Home Insurance Co. v. Baltimore Warehouse Co., 93 U.S. 527, 548 (1876); Sanford v. John Finnegan Co., 169 S.W. 624 (Tex.Civ.App.1914).

15. Hatfield v. Max Rouse & Sons, Northwest, 100 Idaho 840, 606 P.2d 944 (1980).

16. Perhaps out of a superabundance of caution, to allay fears that the rule might be used as a device for immunizing all kinds of evidence simply by mentioning it during the course of negotiations, the Congress added the third sentence to the rule as adopted by the Supreme Court. Senate Comm. on Judiciary, Fed.Rules of Evidence, S.Rep. No. 1277, 93d Cong., 2d Sess. p. 10 (1974).

17. The Revised Uniform Rules (1974) differs in two respects. (1) It adds "or any other claim" at the end of the first sentence. (2) It does not include the third sentence.

18. Waiver of failure to give notice or make proof of loss within required time; Federal Mutual Insurance Co. v. Lewis, 231 Md. 587, 191 A.2d 437 (1963); Travelers Insurance Co. v. Barrett, 366 S.W.2d 692 (Tex. Civ.App.1963); Graham v. San Antonio Machine & Supply Corp., 418 S.W.2d 303 (Tex.Civ.App.1967); Annot., 49 A.L.R.2d 87.

19. Central Soya Co. v. Epstein Fisheries, Inc., 676 F.2d 939 (7th Cir. 1982); Fieve v. Emmeck, 248 Minn. 122, 78 N.W.2d 343 (1956); Malatt v. United Transit Co., 99 R.I. 263, 207 A.2d 39 (1965).

20. Wolf v. Mutual Benefit Health & Accident Association, 188 Kan. 694, 366 P.2d 219 (1961).

21. Kubista v. Romaine, 87 Wash.2d 62, 549 P.2d 491 (1976) (insurance adjuster told plaintiff he would be taken care of if he went to school to learn new trade).

against likelihood of prejudice, with due regard to the probable efficacy of a limiting instruction.[22]

Evidence of present party's compromise with third persons. In an action between P and D a compromise offer or a completed compromise by D with T, a third person, having a claim similar to P's arising from the same transaction may be relevant as showing D's belief in the weakness of his defense in P's present action. Nevertheless, the same consideration of policy which actuates the courts to exclude an offer of compromise made by D to P, namely the danger of discouraging compromises, also applies here. Accordingly the prevailing view is that the compromise offer or payment made by the present defendant is privileged when offered as an implied admission of liability.[23] But, though inadmissible for this purpose, it may well come in for another purpose. A defendant for example places on the stand in a personal injury case a witness who was injured in the same collision. Here it seems clear that if the witness has made a claim on his own account against the defendant, inconsistent with his present favorable testimony, this may be proved to impeach the witness. And it further seems reasonable that if the witness has been paid or promised money in compromise of his claim, this may likewise be shown in impeachment, as evidence of bias.[24] The need for evaluating the credibility of the witness may be as insistent as the policy of encouraging compromise. If, however, the witness sought to be impeached by showing the compromise with a third person, is one of the present parties, the question is more debatable. The danger that the evidence will be used substantively as an admission is greater, and as the party's interest is apparent the need for additional evidence on credibility is less. This impeachment of party-witnesses, however, has occasionally been sanctioned.[25]

Compromise-evidence in criminal cases.[26] The policy of protecting offers of compromise in civil cases does not extend to efforts to stifle criminal prosecution by "buying off" the prosecuting witness or victim.[27] Indeed, we have seen that it is classed as an implied admission and received in evidence as such.[28] The public policy against compounding crimes is said to pre-

---

22. See § 59 supra.

23. Hawthorne v. Eckerson Co., 77 F.2d 844 (2d Cir. 1935); Lewis v. Dixie-Portland Flour Mills, Inc., 356 F.2d 54 (6th Cir. 1966); McCallum v. Harris, 379 S.W.2d 438 (Ky.1964); Tregellas v. American Oil Co., 231 Md. 95, 188 A.2d 691 (1963); Annot., 20 A.L.R.2d 304; Fed.R.Evid. 408, text at n. 17 supra.

A settlement which is offered as proof of the liability of a third party, arising out of the transaction in suit, is not within the privilege since the evidence will not harm the parties to the compromise. But it may be attacked as conduct-as-hearsay. See, e.g., Daly v. Publix Cabs, 128 Neb. 403, 259 N.W. 163 (1935) (suit by passenger against operator of taxicab for injury incurred when another automobile collided with taxicab; evidence offered by taxicab operator that driver of other automobile paid damages to taxicab, excluded as hearsay as to passenger; decided before Nebraska adopted Federal Rules). See § 250 supra.

A compromise may take the form of a consent judgment. Hentschel v. Smith, 278 Minn. 86, 153 N.W.2d 199 (1967).

24. Dornberg v. St. Paul City Railway Co., 253 Minn. 52, 91 N.W.2d 178 (1958); Joice v. Missouri-Kansas-Texas Railway Co., 354 Mo. 439, 189 S.W.2d 568, 161 A.L.R. 383 (1945); Rynar v. Lincoln Transit Co., 129 N.J.L. 525, 30 A.2d 406 (1945) (Case, J., discusses

balance of need for impeachment and danger of improper use; here admissible in judge's discretion); Fed. R.Evid. 408, text at n. 17 supra; Annot., 161 A.L.R. 395. Of course, the opponent would be entitled to an instruction limiting the use of the evidence to the question of credibility. Contra, Fenberg v. Rosenthal, 348 Ill.App. 510, 109 N.E.2d 402 (1952). See § 40 supra.

25. Luis v. Cavin, 88 Cal.App.2d 107, 198 P.2d 563 (1948); Burke v. Commercial Standard Insurance Co., 38 So.2d 644 (La.App.1949).

When a payment made by another tortfeasor is relied upon to reduce the liability of the defendant, the preferable practice is for the judge, rather than the jury, to perform the arithmetic, Brooks v. Daley, 242 Md. 185, 218 A.2d 184 (1966); Sheets v. Davenport, 181 Neb. 621, 150 N.W.2d 224 (1967); 9 U.L.A. 242.

26. See Dec.Dig. Criminal Law ☞408.

27. State v. Burt, 249 N.W.2d 651 (Iowa 1977) (shoplifting; two days later defendant returned to store and offered to pay for coat, denying having stolen it; held proper to admit to support inference he stole coat); Carter v. State, 161 Tenn. 698, 34 S.W.2d 208 (1931) (offer by accused to settle with complaining witness admissible).

28. § 273 at n. 5 supra.

vail.[29]   On the other hand, in recent years the legitimacy of settling criminal cases by negotiations between prosecuting attorney and accused, whereby the latter pleads guilty in return for leniency, has been generally recognized.[30]   Effective criminal law administration in many localities would hardly be possible if a large proportion of the charges were not disposed of by compromise.   Here, then, policy encourages compromise, and, as in civil cases, that policy is furthered by protecting from disclosure at trial not only the offer but also statements made during negotiations.[31]   Federal Rule of Evidence 410, as amended in 1980, provides:

> Except as otherwise provided in this rule, evidence of the following is not, in any civil or criminal proceeding, admissible against the defendant who made the plea or was a participant in the plea discussions:
>
> (1) a plea of guilty which was later withdrawn;
>
> (2) a plea of nolo contendere:
>
> (3) any statement made in the course of any proceedings under rule 11 of the Federal Rules of Criminal Procedure or comparable state procedure regarding either of the foregoing pleas; or
>
> (4) any statement made in the course of plea discussions with an attorney for the prosecuting authority which do not result in a plea of guilty or which result in a plea of guilty later withdrawn.
>
> However, such a statement is admissible (i) in any proceeding wherein another statement

made in the course of the same plea or plea discussions has been introduced and the statement ought in fairness be considered contemporaneously with it, or (ii) in a criminal proceeding for perjury or false statement if the statement was made by the defendant under oath, on the record and in the presence of counsel.[32]

Although it seems clear that the original version of the Federal Rule was intended to extend its protection only to offers and statements made in the course of negotiations between the accused and the United States attorney or his representative, since no one else has authority to conduct such negotiations for the government,[33] the rule did not in terms so state.   As a consequence some decisions held that efforts to make deals with a considerable variety of federal law enforcement officers were within the rule.[34]   The rule accordingly was amended as stated above to make crystal clear that only negotiations "with an attorney for the prosecuting authority" fall within the rule's protection.

If the transaction on which the prosecution is based gives rise also to a civil right of action, a compromise or offer of compromise of the civil claim if no agreement to stifle the criminal prosecution is involved should seemingly be privileged when offered at the criminal trial.[35]

Effect of acceptance of offer of compromise.   If an offer of compromise is accepted and a contract is thus created, the party ag-

---

29.   State v. Burt, supra n. 27.

30.   Santobello v. New York, 404 U.S. 257 (1971), on remand 39 A.D.2d 654, 331 N.Y.S.2d 776.

31.   As to offers, Bennett v. Commonwealth, 234 Ky. 333, 28 S.W.2d 24 (1930);   State v. Abel, 320 Mo. 445, 8 S.W.2d 55 (1928).   As to statements, State v. Byrd, 203 Kan. 45, 453 P.2d 22 (1969);   Shriver v. State, 632 P.2d 420 (Okl.Cr.1980), cert. denied 449 U.S. 983 (no rule or statute needed).

32.   Fed.R.Crim.P. 11(e)(6) is to the same effect. See A.B.A. Standards for Criminal Justice, Standards Relating to Pleas of Guilty, 3.1;   Annot., 59 A.L.R.3d 441.

33.   United States v. Stirling, 571 F.2d 708 (2d Cir. 1978), cert. denied 439 U.S. 824;   United States v. Arroyo-Angulo, 580 F.2d 1137 (2d Cir. 1978), cert. denied 439 U.S. 913.

34.   The cases are collected in United States v. Grant, 622 F.2d 308 (8th Cir. 1980).

Revised Uniform Rule (1974) 410 consists of only the first sentence of the original Federal Rule and reads as follows:

> Evidence of a plea later withdrawn, of guilty, or admission of the charge, or nolo contendere, or of an offer so to plead to the crime charged or any other crime, or of statements made in connection with any of the foregoing withdrawn pleas or offers, is not admissible in any civil or criminal action, case, or proceeding against the person who made the plea or offer.

35.   Ecklund v. United States, 159 F.2d 81 (6th Cir. 1947);   Carter v. State, supra n. 27.

grieved may sue on the contract and obviously may prove the offer and acceptance.[36] Moreover, if after such a contract is made and the offering party repudiates it, the other may elect to sue on the original cause of action and here again it seems the repudiating party may not claim privilege against proof of the compromise.[37] The shield of the privilege does not extend to the protection of those who repudiate the agreements the making of which the privilege is designed to encourage.

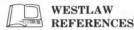 **WESTLAW REFERENCES**

headnote(admission* /s offer* /s compromise settle!)
157k219(3) /p third +2 party parties
topic(110) /p headnote(offer* /s compromise settle!)
89k21

---

§ 275. Admissions by Conduct: (g) Safety Measures After an Accident: [1] Payment of Medical Expenses

After an accident causing injury, the owner of the premises or of the enterprise will often take remedial measures by repairing a defect, installing a safety device, changing safety rules, or discharging the employee apparently at fault. Are these new safety measures, which might have prevented the injury, admissible to prove negligence as an implied acknowledgment by conduct that due care required that these measures should have been taken before the injury? In many instances the evidence, particularly when the remedial measures follow immediately the happening of the injury, may be very persuasive of the actor's belief as to the precautions required by due care before the accident. Nevertheless, the courts on occasion broadly assert that the evidence when offered for this purpose is irrelevant.[2] While, like much circumstantial evidence, it admits of varying explanations,[3] some of them consistent with due care, for this purpose it would often meet the usual standards of relevancy.[4] The predominant reason for excluding such evidence, however, is not lack of probative significance but a policy against discouraging the taking of safety measures.[5] At all events the courts do exclude, when offered as admissions of negligence or fault, evidence of remedial safety measures taken after an injury,[6] such as repairs,[7] changes in construction,[8] installation of new safety devices [9] such as lights, gates,

---

36. Union Trust Co. v. Resisto Manufacturing Co., 169 Md. 381, 181 A. 726 (1935); C.J.S. Evidence § 290.

37. Reese v. McVittie, 119 Colo. 29, 200 P.2d 390 (1948).

§ 275

1. 2 Wigmore, Evidence § 283 (Chadbourn rev. 1979); Weinstein & Berger, Evidence ¶¶ 407[01]–[07]; Fincham, Federal Rule of Evidence 407 and Its State Variations, 49 UMKC L.Rev. 338 (1981); Dec.Dig. Negligence ☞131; Annot., 170 A.L.R. 7, 64 A.L.R.2d 1296, 50 A.L.R.Fed. 935.

2. See, e.g., Columbia and P.S.R. Co. v. Hawthorne, 144 U.S. 202 (1892); Terre Haute & I.R. Co. v. Clem, 123 Ind. 15, 23 N.E. 965, 966 (1890); Morse v. Minneapolis & St. Louis Railroad Co., 30 Minn. 465, 16 N.W. 358, 359 (1883).

Also see Bramwell, B., in Hart v. Lancashire & Yorkshire Railway Co., 21 L.T.R.N.S. 261, 263 (1869), denying that "because the world gets wiser as it gets older, therefore it was foolish before."

3. See § 185 supra.

4. See § 185 supra.

5. See § 74. Compare the court's statement in Ashland Supply Co. v. Webb, 206 Ky. 184, 266 S.W. 1086

(1925): "There are two reasons why evidence of subsequent repair should not be admitted. One is that, while it may be necessary to subsequently repair the appliance, it does not follow from that that the appliance was defective at the time of the accident. The other reason is that, if such evidence were admitted, it would have a tendency to cause employers to omit making needed repairs for fear that the precaution thus taken by them could be used as evidence against them."

The policy basis of the rule is attacked vigorously in Schwartz, The Exclusionary Rule on Subsequent Repairs—A Rule in Need of Repair, 7 Forum 1 (1971). Maine Evidence Rule 407(a) allows the evidence.

6. Annot., 64 A.L.R.2d 896.

7. Kentucky & West Virginia Power Co. v. Stacy, 291 Ky. 325, 164 S.W.2d 537, 170 A.L.R. 1 (1942); Potter v. Dr. W.H. Groves etc. Hospital, 99 Utah 71, 103 P.2d 280 (1940).

8. Limbeck v. Interstate Power Co., 69 F.2d 249 (8th Cir. 1934); Livingston v. Fuel, 245 Ark. 618, 433 S.W.2d 380 (1968).

9. Erickson's Dairy Products Co. v. Northwest etc. Co., 165 Or. 553, 109 P.2d 53 (1941) (use of asbestos to protect wall against fire).

or guards, changes in rules and regulations,[10] changes in the practice of the business,[11] or the discharge of an employee charged with causing the injury.[12]

When the repairs or changes are effected by a third person, the policy ground for exclusion is no longer present, and the tendency is to admit the evidence.[13]

The ingenuity of counsel in suggesting other purposes has made substantial inroads upon the general rule of exclusion.[14] Thus evidence of subsequent repairs or changes has been admitted as evidence of the defendant's ownership or control[15] of the premises or his duty to repair[16] where these are disputed; as evidence of the possibility or feasibility of preventive measures, when properly in issue;[17] as evidence, where the jury has taken a view, or where the defendant has introduced a photograph of the scene, to explain that the situation at the time of the accident was different;[18] as evidence of what was done later to show that the earlier condition as of the time of the accident was as plaintiff claims, if the defendant disputes this:[19] as evidence that the faulty condition later remedied, was the cause of the injury

10. S.E.C. v. Geon Industries, Inc., 531 F.2d 39, 52 (2d Cir. 1976) (under Fed.R.Evid. 407); Ware v. Boston & Maine Railroad, 92 N.H. 373, 31 A.2d 58 (1943). Distinguish rules in effect at the time of the occurrence, which are generally held admissible, though somewhat similar policy considerations are present. Young v. Illinois Central Gulf R. Co., 618 F.2d 332 (5th Cir. 1980); Winters, The Evidentiary Value of Defendant's Safety Rules in a Negligence Action, 38 Neb.L.Rev. 906 (1959); Annot., 50 A.L.R.2d 16.

11. Hatfield v. Levy Brothers, 18 Cal.App.2d 798, 112 P.2d 277 (1941) (evidence that defendant company stopped waxing floor after accident), reversed on other grounds, 18 Cal.2d 798, 117 P.2d 841 (1941).

12. Armour & Co. v. Skene, 153 F. 241 (1st Cir. 1907) (discharge of driver one year after accident erroneously admitted but not prejudicial); Turner v. Hearst, 115 Cal. 394, 47 P. 129 (1896) (libel; error to permit plaintiff to prove discharge of reporter, "similar to proof of precaution taken after an accident"). See also Rynar v. Lincoln Transit Co., 129 N.J.L. 525, 30 A.2d 406 (1943); Engel v. United Traction Co., 203 N.Y. 321, 96 N.E. 731 (1911).

13. Farner v. Paccar, Inc., 562 F.2d 518 (8th Cir. 1977) (under Fed.R.Evid. 407); Davis v. Fox River Tractor Co., 518 F.2d 481 (10th Cir. 1975); Wallner v. Kitchens of Sara Lee, Inc., 419 F.2d 1028 (7th Cir. 1970) (guards installed on machine by owner after accident, properly admitted against manufacturer); Brown v. Quick Mix Co., 75 Wash.2d 833, 454 P.2d 205 (1969) (same). The relevancy problem of course, becomes more acute since the theory of an admission is not available. Moreover, a hearsay problem arises if conduct is regarded as hearsay. See § 250 supra.

14. Norwood Clinic Inc. v. Spann, 240 Ala. 427, 199 So. 840, 843 (1941) ("if such evidence has a tendency to prove some other disputed issue," admissible); Annot., 64 A.L.R.2d 1296, 1305.

15. Powers v. J.B. Michael & Co., 329 F.2d 674 (6th Cir. 1964) (defendant contractor subsequently put out warning signs, to show control of that section of highway); Kuhn v. General Parking Corp., 98 Ill.App.3d 570, 54 Ill.Dec. 191, 424 N.E.2d 941 (1981) (defective floor); Dubonowski v. Howard Savings Institution, 124 N.J.L. 368, 12 A.2d 384 (1941) (control by landlord of

stairs); Scudero v. Campbell, 288 N.Y. 328, 43 N.E.2d 66 (1942) (similar).

16. Wallner v. Kitchens of Sara Lee, Inc., supra n. 17; Kuhn v. General Parking Corp., supra n. 15 (repair of floor); Carleton v. Rockland, 110 Me. 397, 86 A. 334, Ann.C.1915A 1209 (repairs by street railway of steps leading from platform).

17. Determining when feasibility is properly an issue has proved troublesome. If defendant claims the precaution was not feasible, the evidence is clearly admissible. See note 21 infra. The nature of the accident as proven by plaintiff may raise a doubt whether preventive measures were practicable. Indianapolis, etc., Railroad Co. v. Horst, 93 U.S. 291, 295, 296 (1876); Boeing Airplane Co. v. Brown, 291 F.2d 310 (9th Cir. 1961); Brown v. Quick Mix Co., 75 Wash.2d 833, 454 P.2d 205 (1969). Or plaintiff may rely on a statute which is construed to make proof of feasibility a part of plaintiff's case. Rich v. Tite-Knot Pine Mill, 245 Or. 185, 421 P.2d 370 (1966). But even in these later cases, the plaintiff might well be limited to other types of evidence, such as opinion or customary practices of such businesses, where these are available and sufficient. See Miniea v. St. Louis Cooperage Co., 175 Mo.App. 91, 157 S.W. 1006, 1012 (1913); Blais v. Flanders Hardware Co., 93 N.H. 370, 42 A.2d 332, 335 (1945) ("descriptive testimony could readily be given"). Unrestricted use of feasibility evidence would obviously eliminate the exclusionary rule in its entirety. See further at n. 49 below.

18. Lunde v. National Citizens' Bank, 213 Minn. 278, 6 N.W.2d 809 (1942) (view); Achey v. Marion, 126 Iowa 47, 101 N.W. 435 (1904) (to explain photograph introduced by defendant). But the plaintiff may not introduce a photograph of the altered scene merely for the purpose of showing the repairs in the guise of explanation. Gignoux v. St. Louis Public Service Co., 180 S.W.2d 784 (Mo.App.1944); Hadges v. New York Rapid Transit Corp., 259 App.Div. 154, 18 N.Y.S.2d 304 (1940).

19. Chicago v. Dalle, 115 Ill. 386, 5 N.E. 578 (1885) (injury due to alleged loose plank in sidewalk, evidence that sidewalk repaired at this place to show previous condition); Chicago Burlington & Quincy Railroad Co. v. Krayenbuhl, 65 Neb. 889, 91 N.W. 880, 885, 59

by showing that after the change the injurious effect disappeared;[20] and as evidence contradicting facts testified to by the adversary's witness.[21]

Federal and Revised Uniform Rule (1974) 407 are in conformity with the foregoing discussion and provide as follows:

> When, after an event, measures are taken which, if taken previously, would have made the event less likely to occur, evidence of the subsequent measures is not admissible to prove negligence or culpable conduct in connection with the event. This rule does not require the exclusion of evidence of subsequent measures when offered for another purpose, such as proving ownership, control, or feasibility of precautionary measures, if controverted, or impeachment.

The encouragement of remedial measures, as has already been indicated, is the principal reason for the rule excluding evidence that such measures were taken. Liberal admission of remedial measure evidence for purposes other than as an admission of negligence seriously undercuts the basic policy of the rule. Hence Rule 407, set forth above, specifically requires that when the evidence is offered for another purpose that purpose must be controverted.[22] Ownership, control, and feasibility of precautionary measures are mentioned as illustrations of other purposes. If the other purpose is not controverted, the evidence is inadmissible.[23] The fact that the other purpose is controverted should not be taken as a guarantee of admissibility, however; the possibility of misuse of the evidence as an admission of fault still requires a balancing of probative value and need against potential prejudice under Rule 403. The availability of other means of proof is an important factor in this balancing process.[24]

In product liability cases a trend away from the basic rule of exclusion of evidence of subsequent remedial measures was initiated by Ault v. International Harvester Company.[25] It has been suggested that the difference in result is warranted by the fact

L.R.A. 920 (1902) (agent's locking of turntable to show it was unlocked at time of injury to child); Fargle v. Sumpter Lighting Co., 110 S.C. 560, 96 S.E. 909 (1918) (defect in electrical appliances provable, where necessary, by evidence of later repairs). This doctrine, unless limited to cases where the condition is disputed and the proof by repairs is essential, can serve to rob the principal rule of practical effect. See e.g., City of Montgomery v. Quinn, 246 Ala. 154, 19 So.2d 529 (1944) (action for death caused by falling of rotten limb of tree; act of city in immediately removing other dead limbs admitted to show condition); Williams v. Milner Hotels Co., 130 Conn. 507, 36 A.2d 20 (1944) (suit by guest for injury by being bitten by rat while in bed in his room; apparently existence of rat holes was formally denied in pleadings but not actually in dispute; plaintiff allowed to introduce photographs showing holes covered with tin, as evidence of previous condition).

20. Kentucky Utilities Co. v. White Star Coal Co., 244 Ky. 759, 52 S.W.2d 705 (1932) (proof that everything went well following a second fire, when a defective transformer was removed, admissible to show cause); Texas & New Orleans Railroad Co. v. Anderson, 61 S.W. 424 (Tex.Civ.App.1901) (evidence of removal of obstruction in ditch and that thereafter flood water ran off plaintiff's land, admitted to show obstruction cause of flooding).

21. American Airlines, Inc. v. United States, 418 F.2d 180 (5th Cir. 1969) (evidence of change in instrument and in flight practices after accident to rebut claims of adequacy and nonfeasibility); Daggett v. Atchison, Topeka & Santa Fe Railway Co., 48 Cal.2d

655, 313 P.2d 557, 64 A.L.R.2d 1283 (1957) (evidence that flashing light was installed in place of wigwag signal after crossing accident to impeach testimony that wigwag was safest type); Runkle v. Burlington Northern Railroad Co., ___ Mont. ___, 613 P.2d 982 (1980) (error to exclude evidence of installation of flasher to impeach testimony that crossing was not extra-hazardous).

22. For an example of controverting feasibility, see Anderson v. Malloy, 700 F.2d 1208 (8th Cir. 1983) (action against motel owners for rape of guest; error to exclude evidence that defendants installed peepholes and chain locks on doors after event, when defendants testified that to have done so would have been "false security").

Nonrule cases have not insisted on a requirement that the other purpose be controverted. Boeing Airplane Co. v. Brown, 291 F.2d 310 (9th Cir. 1961) (subsequent design change admissible though feasibility stipulated; nonjury case); doCanto v. Ametek, Inc., 367 Mass. 776, 328 N.E.2d 873 (1975) (general concession of practicability did not require exclusion of evidence of subsequent design changes to show feasibility).

23. Werner v. Upjohn Co., 628 F.2d 848 (4th Cir. 1980) cert. denied 449 U.S. 1080; Foster v. Ford Motor Co., 621 F.2d 715 (5th Cir. 1980); Bauman v. Volkswagenwerk Aktiengesellschaft, 621 F.2d 230 (6th Cir. 1980).

24. See § 185 supra.

25. 13 Cal.3d 113, 117 Cal.Rtpr. 812, 528 P.2d 1148 (1974).

that negligence cases focus on the conduct of the defendant while product liability cases focus on the nature of the product.[26] However, the true bases of the departure are probably rejection of the assumption that admitting the evidence discourages people from taking of remedial steps when the "people" in question are large manufacturers,[27] and a desire to spread losses.[28] Some courts have followed the lead of *Ault*, either as a matter of construing Rule 407 or as common law,[29] while others have rejected both its reasoning and its result.[30]

The admissibility of recall letters has been approached in somewhat similar vein, as the first step in the taking of remedial steps. The courts have divided on the question.[31]

Payment of medical expenses. Similar considerations of doubtful relevancy and of public policy underlie the generally accepted exclusion of evidence of payment or offers to pay medical and like expenses of an injured person. Federal and Revised Uniform Rule (1974) 409 accordingly provide:

> Evidence of furnishing or offering or promising to pay medical, hospital, or similar expenses occasioned by an injury is not admissible to prove liability for the injury.

The rule is in conformity with the run of common law decisions.[32] Unlike compromise, where negotiation is an essential part of the process and requires protection against disclosure, communications are incidental and hence unprotected.[33]

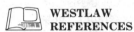 **WESTLAW REFERENCES**

272k131

offer* promise* /s pay /s medical hospital* /s admission*

---

26. Shaffer v. Honeywell, Inc., 249 N.W.2d 251, 257, n. 7 (S.D.1976).

27. Ault v. International Harvester Co., supra n. 25, 13 Cal.3d at 120, 117 Cal.Rptr., at 815, 528 P.2d at 1151.

28. Caprara v. Chrysler Corp., 52 N.Y.2d 114, 436 N.Y.S.2d 251, 417 N.E.2d 545 (1981).

29. Robbins v. Farmers Union Grain Terminal Association, 552 F.2d 788 (8th Cir. 1977); Farner v. Paccar, Inc., 562 F.2d 518 (8th Cir. 1977); Caterpillar Tractor Co. v. Beck, 624 P.2d 790 (Alaska 1981); Caprara v. Chrysler Corp., supra n. 28; Shaffer v. Honeywell, Inc., supra n. 26; Chart v. General Motors Corp., 80 Wis.2d 91, 258 N.W.2d 680 (1978); Annot., 50 A.L.R. Fed. 1001.

30. Cann v. Ford Motor Co., 658 F.2d 54 (2d Cir. 1981), cert. denied 456 U.S. 960; Knight v. Otis Elevator Co., 596 F.2d 84 (3d Cir. 1979); Werner v. Upjohn Co., 628 F.2d 848 (4th Cir. 1980), cert. denied 449 U.S.

1080; Grenada Steel Industries, Inc. v. Alabama Oxygen Co., 695 F.2d 883 (5th Cir. 1983).

31. Supporting admissibility, Farner v. Paccar, Inc., supra n. 56; Manieri v. Volkswagenwerk A.G., 151 N.J. Super. 422, 376 A.2d 1317 (1977); Barry v. Manglass, 55 A.D.2d 1, 389 N.Y.S.2d 870 (1976); Fields v. Volkswagen of America, Inc., 555 P.2d 48 (Okl.1976). See also Dollar v. Long Manufacturing, North Carolina, Inc., 561 F.2d 613 (5th Cir. 1977), cert. denied 435 U.S. 996 (properly used for impeachment under Rule 407). Contra, Vockie v. General Motors Corp., 66 F.R.D. 57 (E.D.Pa.1975), affirmed without opinion 523 F.2d 1052 (3d Cir.); Landry v. Adam, 282 So.2d 590 (La.App. 1973). See Annot., 84 A.L.R.3d 1220.

32. Hughes v. Anchor Enterprises, 245 N.C. 131, 95 S.E.2d 577 (1956); Annot., 20 A.L.R.2d 291, 65 A.L.R.3d 932.

33. Hughes v. Anchor Enterprises, supra n. 59; Advisory Comm.Note, Fed.R.Evid. 409.

Chapter 27

DECLARATIONS AGAINST INTEREST

Table of Sections

---

§ 276. General Requirements: Distinction Between Declarations Against Interest and Parties' Admissions [1]

To satisfy the instant exception to the hearsay rule in its traditional form, two main requirements have been imposed: first, the declaration must state facts which are against the pecuniary or proprietary interest of the declarant, or the making of the declaration itself must create evidence which would endanger his pocketbook if the statement were not true; [2] second, the declarant must be unavailable at the time of trial. [3] The first requirement has been believed to furnish the safeguard of special trustworthiness justifying most of the exceptions to the hearsay rule. The second is largely an historical development but operates usefully as a limiting factor. Minor qualifications may be added. The interest involved must not be too indirect or remote. [4] The declarant, as in the case of hearsay exceptions generally, [5] must, so far as appears, have had the oppor-

---

§ 276

1. See generally, 5 Wigmore, Evidence §§ 1455–1477 (Chadbourn rev. 1974); Jefferson, Declarations Against Interest: An Exception to the Hearsay Rule, 58 Harv.L.Rev. 1 (1944); Morgan, Declarations Against Interest, 5 Vand.L.Rev. 451 (1952); Note, 64 B.U.L. Rev. 148 (1976); Annot., 105 A.L.R. 398 (subsequent statement by donor on issue of gift), 65 A.L.R.2d 631 (employee's statement in action on fidelity bond), 73 A.L.R.2d 1180 (statement by another defendant in accident case), and 34 A.L.R.Fed. 412 (application of Fed.R. Evid. 804(b)(3)); Dec.Dig. Evidence ⚖272–284, Criminal Law ⚖417(15); C.J.S. Evidence §§ 217–224.

2. See §§ 277–279 infra.

3. See § 280 infra.

4. Smith v. Blakey, L.R. [1916] 2 Q.B. 326 (letter of clerk advising employer of arrival of "three huge cases" in his charge and stating terms of contract with consignor, held not admissible, "the possibility that this statement might make him liable in case of their being lost is an interest of too remote a nature"); Giberson v. Wilson, 322 S.W.2d 466 (Ky.1959) ("the act of an insured in changing the beneficiary of an insurance policy is not against his pecuniary or proprietary interest" although he gives up the right to have proceeds paid to his estate); In re Estate of Simms, 442 S.W.2d 426 (Tex.Civ.App.1969) (statement of declarant that she had destroyed will and codicil of another, at a time when declarant had no interest in the estate of the maker of the will, was not a declaration against interest). But compare § 277, nn. 2, 3 infra.

5. See, e.g., §§ 285, 300, 310 infra.

tunity to observe the facts,[6] as witnesses must have.[7]

Although occasional judicial opinions and texts fail to distinguish this exception from the one for parties' admissions,[8] the traditional distinctions, adopted by Wigmore,[9] drawing the line clearly between the two exceptions, is generally observed. Thus the admissions of a party-opponent come in without satisfying any of the requirements for declarations against interest. An admission need not have been against interest when made,[10] though it will usually happen that it was. The party making the admission need not be, and seldom is, unavailable.[11] Nor does the party making the admission need to have had personal knowledge of the fact admitted.[12] Accordingly, when the admission of a party is sought to be introduced, it should be offered as and tested by the requirements for parties' admissions, not those for declarations against interest. On the other hand, when the statements were those of a nonparty declarant, now dead or unavailable and the position of the declarant is found not to meet the requirements of "privity" necessary to class him as a party's predecessor, where recognized, then the theory of declarations against interest may be a case-saving ticket of admission.[13]

The Federal Rules preserve the hearsay exception as broadly developed at common law with respect to statements against pecuniary or proprietary interest and in addition expand into the area of statements against penal interest. Rule 804(b)(3) reads:

> The following are not excluded by the hearsay rule if the declarant is unavailable as a witness:
>
> **(3) Statement against interest.** A statement which was at the time of its making so far contrary to the declarant's pecuniary or proprietary interest, or so far tended to subject him to civil or criminal liability, or to render invalid a claim by him against another, that a reasonable man in his position would not have made the statement unless he believed it to be true. A statement tending to expose the declarant to criminal liability and offered to exculpate the accused is not admissible unless corroborating circumstances clearly indicate the trustworthiness of the statement.

The Revised Uniform Rule (1974) in addition includes statements incurring social disapproval and excludes statements implicating both declarant and the accused.[14]

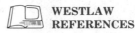 **WESTLAW REFERENCES**

fed.r.evid! evid!   /3   804(b)(3)
157k272

---

6. The requirement is sometimes more stringently stated by demanding that the facts must have been "within the declarant's peculiar knowledge." See, e.g., Gleadow v. Atkins, 1 C. and M. 410, 149 Eng.Rep. 459 (Exch.1833); Price v. Humble Oil & Refining Co., 152 S.W.2d 804, 813 (Tex.Civ.App.1941). But doubtless nothing more than the usual knowledge qualification is intended to, or can reasonably, be required. See Aetna Life Insurance Co. v. Strauch, 179 Okl. 617, 67 P.2d 452, 454 (1937) ("must have concerned a fact personally cognizable by declarant"); Windorski v. Doyle, 219 Minn. 402, 18 N.W.2d 142, 146 (1945) ("a matter of which he was personally cognizant"); 5 Wigmore, Evidence § 1471(a) (Chadbourn rev. 1974); C.J.S. Evidence § 220. While neither the Federal nor the Revised Uniform Rules specifically mention this requirement, Rule 602 requires firsthand knowledge of witnesses generally, and in hearsay situations the declarant is in reality the witness. See Advisory Committee's Note, Fed.R. Evid. 803.

7. See § 10 supra.

8. See Ch. 26 supra.

9. 5 Wigmore, Evidence § 1475 (Chadbourn rev. 1974); C.J.S. Evidence § 217b.

10. See § 262 supra; § 277 infra.

11. See § 262 supra.

12. See § 263 supra.

13. Kwiatowski v. John Lowry, Inc., 276 N.Y. 126, 11 N.E.2d 563, 114 A.L.R. 916 (1937) annotated (in death action, statements against interest by decedent come in as declarations against interest); Aetna Life Insurance Co. v. Strauch, 179 Okl. 617, 67 P.2d 452 (1937) (suit by administrator of wife against insurance company on policy on her life; confession of husband, since electrocuted, of plot to secure policy and kill her, admitted as declaration against interest); and see C.J.S. Evidence § 219d. For discussion of privity, see § 268 supra.

14. The differences between the Federal and Revised Uniform Rule are discussed under various topics below. Cases under the Federal Rule are collected in 34 A.L.R.Fed. 412.

§ 277. Declarations Against Pecuniary or Proprietary Interest: Declarations Affecting Claim or Liability for Damages

The traditional field for this exception has been that of declarations against proprietary or pecuniary interest. Common instances of the former are acknowledgments that the declarant does not own certain land or personal property, or that he has conveyed or transferred it.[1] Moreover, a statement by one in possession that he holds an interest less than complete ownership has traditionally been regarded as a declaration against interest,[2] though it is obviously ambiguous, and in England has even been received when offered to establish the existence of the interest claimed by the declarant.[3]

The clearest example of a declaration against pecuniary interest is an acknowledgment that the declarant is indebted.[4] Here

the declaration, standing alone, is against interest on the theory that to owe a debt is against one's financial interests. This theory is routinely followed even though it may not be applicable in particular circumstances. Less obviously an acknowledgment of receipt of money in payment of a debt owing to the declarant is also traditionally classed as against interest.[5] Here the fact of payment itself is probably advantageous to the receiver, but the acknowledgment of it is regarded as against interest because it is evidence of the reduction or extinguishment of the debt.[6] Of course, a receipt for money which the receiver is to hold for another is an acknowledgment of a debt.[7] Similarly, a statement that one holds money in trust is against interest.[8]

We have seen that an acknowledgment of indebtedness by the declarant is recognized

§ 277

1. Dean v. Wilkerson, 126 Ind. 338, 26 N.E. 55 (1890) (declarations of father, offered by the son after father's death, that he had given notes to son); Smith v. Moore, 142 N.C. 277, 55 S.E. 275 (1906) (declaration by deceased life tenant that she had made a deed to her son-in-law and the reason for making the deed); Mehus v. Thompson, 266 N.W.2d 920 (N.D.1978) (grantor's statements after delivery in support of deed); First National Bank v. Holland, 99 Va. 495, 39 S.E. 126, 128 (1890) (husband's declaration of gift to wife).

2. McLeod v. Swain, 87 Ga. 156, 13 S.E. 315 (1891) (plaintiff in ejectment offers her former tenant's declarations that they held land as her tenants); Lamar v. Pearre, 90 Ga. 377, 17 S.E. 92 (1892) (possessor's declarations that land had been bought with trust funds); Dooley v. Baynes, 86 Va. 644, 10 S.E. 974 (1890) (possessor's declarations that he held only a life estate).

3. In Regina v. Overseers of Birmingham, 1 B. & S. 763, 121 Eng.Rep. 897 (K.B.1861) and in Regina v. Governors and Guardians of Exeter, L.R. 4 Q.B. 341 (1869) declarant's assertions of tenancy were admitted, not to prove that he did not have a fee simple, but that he had a tenancy at the stated rental. This use is disapproved in 5 Wigmore, Evidence § 1458 (Chadbourn rev. 1974).

4. German Insurance Co. v. Bartlett, 188 Ill. 165, 58 N.E. 1075 (1900) (in suit of deceased husband's creditors against wife to whom he had conveyed property, she was allowed to prove his declarations that he was indebted to her); Truelsch v. Northwestern Mutual Life Insurance Co., 186 Wis. 239, 202 N.W. 352 (1925) (suit by wife on life policy on husband; husband's employer claims lien on policy for money embezzled and used to pay premiums; husband's letter to wife before his suicide acknowledging defalcations admitted as declaration against interest).

5. Palter Cap Co. v. Great Western Life Assurance Co., [1936] 2 D.L.R. 304 (physician's entry in cash book of money received from patient, to show date of consultation); Mentzer v. Burlingame, 85 Kan. 641, 118 P. 698 (1911) (declaration of holder that notes were paid).

6. Coffin v. Bucknam, 12 Me. 471, 473 (1835) (entry of part payment on note by deceased former holder admitted for administrator suing on note, to avoid statute of limitations; "the indorsement was then clearly against his interest, furnishing proof that he had received part of the contents of the note;" Chenango Bridge Co. v. Paige, 83 N.Y. 178 (1880) (treasurer's books showing amount of tolls received admitted "as they charged him with the amount of such tolls"). Cases supporting this theory are cited and analyzed in Jefferson, op. cit., § 276, n. 1, 58 Harv.L.Rev. at 8–17, and Morgan, op. cit. § 276, n. 1, 5 Vand.L.Rev. 454–456. Wigmore, however, without adequate discussion, rejects it. 5 Wigmore, Evidence § 1462 (Chadbourn rev. 1974).

7. Manning v. Lechmere, 1 Atk. 453, 26 Eng.Rep. 288 (Ch.1737) (L.Ch. Hardwicke: "Where there are old rentals, and bailiffs have admitted money received by them, these rentals are evidence of the payment because no other can be had"); Barry v. Bebbington, 4 Term R. 514, 100 Eng.Rep. 1149 (1792) (steward's receipts); Keesling v. Powell, 149 Ind. 372, 49 N.E. 265 (1898) (statement by tax officer that taxes had been paid in).

8. Gleadow v. Atkin, 1 Cr. & M. 410, 149 Eng.Rep. 459 (Ex., 1833). See also Wilkins v. Enterprise TV, Inc., 231 Ark. 958, 333 S.W.2d 718 (1960) (declarant, ostensibly the president and principal stockholder of the corporation, stated he was only salaried employee).

as against interest. The English cases seem to have been narrowly channeled in the areas of debt and property, but the American cases have extended the field of declarations against interest to include acknowledgment of facts which would give rise to a liability for unliquidated damages for tort[9] or seemingly for breach of contract.[10] A corresponding extension to embrace statements of facts which would constitute a defense to a claim for damages which the declarant would otherwise have, has been recognized in this country.[11]

The Federal and Revised Uniform Rules (1974), texts of which appear at the end of section 276 supra, are broadly drawn to include statements against pecuniary or proprietary interest in general, and more specifically those tending to subject declarant to civil liability, without being limited to tort or contract, and those tending to invalidate a claim by him against another.[12] This aspect of the rule thus occupies the entire area developed by the common law except for some of the more fanciful English decisions in tenancy cases.[13]

WESTLAW REFERENCES

declaration* statement* /s pecuniary proprietary /2 interest* nature

§ 278. Penal Interest:[1] Interest of Prestige or Self-Esteem

In 1844 in the Sussex Peerage Case[2] the House of Lords, ignoring precedents, determined that a declaration confessing a crime committed by declarant is not receivable as a

9. Weber v. Chicago, Rock Island & Pacific Railway Co., 175 Iowa 358, 151 N.W. 852, 864 (1915) (action by passenger for injury in derailment: declaration of K., who later became insane, that he had unbolted the rails, admitted as against interest as constituting "basis of an action against him for damages"); Halvorsen v. Moon & Kerr Lumber Co., 87 Minn. 18, 91 N.W. 28 (1902) (plaintiff sues defendant for destruction of his shop from fire on defendant's premises; held, defendant entitled to prove declarations of S., plaintiff's employee, since deceased, that plaintiff's fire due to boiling over of lard kettle, of which S. was in charge, while S. had gone out of the room; the facts furnish the basis of a "pecuniary claim" for negligence); Windorski v. Doyle, 219 Minn. 402, 18 N.W.2d 142 (1945) (action against tavern owner for death of patron struck by another patron; declarations of bartender, since dead, that assault was unprovoked, and that he had warned offending patron against threats, held receivable for plaintiff as declaration against interest; the facts "may reasonably furnish a basis of a pecuniary claim against him as he was in sole charge of the bar-room;" in this case, consciousness of speaking against interest seems unlikely); Duncan v. Smith, 393 S.W.2d 798 (Tex.1965) (statement of a driver that he passed illegally on the right side of a vehicle and ran into a bridge).

Some cases have applied a more liberal rule. Gichner v. Antonio Triano Tile and Marble Co., 133 U.S.App.D.C. 250, 410 F.2d 238 (1968) (it is enough if the statement could reasonably provide an important link in a chain of evidence that is the basis for civil liability; statement that declarant smoked in a building later found burned held sufficiently against interest).

Compare Merritt v. Chonowski, 58 Ill.App.3d 192, 15 Ill.Dec. 588, 373 N.E.2d 1060 (1978) (dram shop action; proper to exclude statement by customer on leaving bar that he had had six drinks; not against interest because before accident).

10. Jefferson, op. cit., supra § 276, n. 1 at 30, n. 62, but the cases cited are explainable under the theory of admissions of a party's predecessor.

11. Walker v. Brautner, 59 Kan. 117, 121, 124, 52 P. 80 (1898) (action for death of engineer; his declarations after the collision that he had not kept a lookout received as against interest); Kwiatowski v. John Lowry Inc., 276 N.Y. 126, 11 N.E.2d 563, 114 A.L.R. 916 (1937) (death action; statements by deceased showing no liability admissible both as admissions and as declarations against interest); Jewell v. El Paso Electric Co., 47 S.W.2d 328 (Tex.Civ.App.1932) (death action; statement of deceased that it was his own fault, admitted as against interest); Annot., 114 A.L.R. 921. But compare Tucker v. Oldbury Urban District Council, [1921] 2 K.B. 317 (Ct.App.) where in death action for alleged injury causing blood poison, declarations of deceased after time of alleged injury that he left work because of a "whitlow," were held properly rejected because he then had made no claim and was not conscious that the statement was against interest.

See also Home Insurance v. Allied Telephone Co., 246 Ark. 1065, 442 S.W.2d 211 (1969) (statement of nonparty driver of automobile, that "it looks like something that could not be helped," held against interest since declarant was potentially liable and declaration absolved another driver in accident of fault).

12. For text of rules, see § 276 supra at n. 14.

13. Cases cited n. 3 supra.

§ 278

1. 5 Wigmore, Evidence §§ 1476, 1477 (Chadbourn rev. 1974); Note, 56 B.U.L.Rev. 148 (1976); Annot., 162 A.L.R. 446, 92 A.L.R.3d 1164, 34 A.L.R.Fed. 412; C.J.S. Criminal Law § 749; Dec.Dig. Criminal Law ⚷417(15).

2. 11 Cl. & F. 85, 8 Eng.Rep. 1034 (1844).

declaration against interest. This decision, perhaps more than any other, was influential in confining the development of this exception to the hearsay rule within narrow materialistic limits. It was generally followed in this country in criminal cases for many years.[3] In civil cases, courts, while not repudiating the limitation, have sometimes been able to justify the admission of the third person's confession of crime upon the theory that the particular crime was also a tort and thus the fact declared was against material interest in subjecting the declarant to liability for damages.[4]

Was the practice of excluding third-person confessions in criminal cases justified? It certainly could not be justified on the ground that an acknowledgment of facts rendering one liable to criminal punishment was less trustworthy than an acknowledgment of a debt. The motivation for the exclusion has no doubt been a different one, namely, the fear of opening a door to a flood of witnesses testifying falsely to confessions that were never made or testifying truthfully to confessions that were false. This fear was based on the likely criminal character of witness and declarant, reinforced by the requirement that declarant be unavailable. Wigmore rejects the argument of the danger of perjury since the danger is one that attends all human testimony, and concludes that "any rule which hampers an honest man in exonerating himself is a bad rule, even if it also hampers a villain in falsely passing for an innocent."[5] Under this banner, saluted also by Holmes, J.,[6] in a famous dissent, courts began to relax the rule of exclusion of declarations against penal interest in particular situations[7] or generally.[8]

The inclusion of declarations against penal interest in the Federal and Revised Uniform Rules (1974) has given great impetus to this exception to the hearsay rule, and most of the recent case law and literature dealing with declarations against interest has centered on this aspect and its concomitant problems.[9]

---

3. State v. Stallings, 154 Conn. 272, 224 A.2d 718 (1966) (confession of declarant other than defendant, but the court judicially noticed that the declarant had been tried and acquitted on the same charge); Bryant v. State, 197 Ga. 641, 30 S.E.2d 259 (1944); Rushing v. State, 88 Okl.Cr. 82, 199 P.2d 614 (1948); Commonwealth v. Antonini, 165 Pa.Super. 501, 69 A.2d 436 (1949) (offered against the accused), and numerous cases cited in sources in note 1 supra.

4. Weber v. Chicago, Rock Island & Pacific Railway Co., 175 Iowa 358, 151 N.W. 852, 864 (1915) (confession that declarant had unbolted rail, causing derailment of train).

5. 5 Wigmore, Evidence § 1477, p. 359 (Chadbourn rev. 1974).

6. "The confession of Joe Dick, since deceased, that he committed the murder for which the plaintiff in error was tried, coupled with circumstances pointing to its truth, would have a very strong tendency to make anyone outside of a court of justice believe that Donnelly did not commit the crime. I say this, of course, on the supposition that it should be proved that the confession really was made, and that there was no ground for connecting Donnelly with Dick. The rules of evidence in the main are based on experience, logic, and common sense, less hampered by history than some parts of the substantive law. There is no decision by this court against the admissibility of such a confession; the English cases since the separation of the two countries do not bind us; the exception to the hearsay rule in the case of declarations against interest is well known; no other statement is so much against interest as a confession of murder; it is far more calculated to convince than dying declarations, which would be let in to hang a man (Mattox v. United States, 146 U.S. 140); and when we surround the accused with so many safeguards, some of which seem to me excessive, I think we ought to give him the benefit of a fact that, if proved, commonly would have such weight. The history of the law and the arguments against the English doctrine are so well and fully stated by Mr. Wigmore that there is no need to set them forth at greater length. 2 Wigmore, Ev. §§ 1476, 1477." Holmes, J., dissenting in Donnelly v. United States, 228 U.S. 243 (1913).

7. People v. Lettrich, 413 Ill. 172, 108 N.E.2d 488 (1952); Brady v. State, 226 Md. 422, 174 A.2d 167 (1961) (discussion of previous Maryland cases); Hines v. Commonwealth, 136 Va. 728, 117 S.E. 843, 35 A.L.R. 431 (1923) (murder, with circumstantial evidence pointing both to accused and to third person, since deceased; held, accused entitled to prove third person's confession); Newberry v. Commonwealth, 191 Va. 445, 61 S.E.2d 318 (1950) (defendant charged with murder of his wife; circumstances indicated his brother as possible killer; brother refused to testify on ground of immunity as joint indictee; held, "under facts and circumstances of this case," accused was entitled to introduce brother's confession).

8. People v. Spriggs, 60 Cal.2d 868, 36 Cal.Rptr. 841, 389 P.2d 377 (1964); People v. Brown, 26 N.Y.2d 88, 308 N.Y.S.2d 825, 257 N.E.2d 16 (1970).

9. See supra at § 276, n. 14 for text of rules.

During the course of the expansion of the hearsay exception to include declarations against penal interest, the situation principally in contemplation and raised in the cases was a confession or other statement by a third person offered by the defense to *exculpate* the accused. The traditional distrust of declarations against penal interest had evolved in that setting, and as a result the Federal and Revised Uniform Rules (1974) included a prohibition against admitting an exculpatory statement in evidence "unless corroborating circumstances clearly indicate the trustworthiness of the statement." [10] While the possibility was recognized that statements against penal interest might *inculpate* an accused person, as for example the defendant Joe in the statement "Joe and I robbed the bank," offered by the prosecution, the question of their admissibility was raised infrequently in cases or the literature.[11] As will be seen in the section that follows, the two kinds of statements, exculpatory and inculpatory, raise some different as well as some similar questions.

The effect was evident not only through adoption of the rules as a whole, but also piecemeal by decision. See e.g. State v. Gold, 180 Conn. 619, 431 A.2d 501 (1980), cert. denied 449 U.S. 920. A source of impetus was also no doubt Chambers v. Mississippi, 410 U.S. 284 (1973), ruling that exclusion of several confessions of a third party exculpating the accused, given "under circumstances that provided considerable assurances of their reliability," coupled with inability of accused to cross-examine the confessing party, who testified as a witness, because of the local "voucher rule", was a denial of due process. The against-interest aspect was emphasized as an assurance that the confessions were trustworthy. The decision was carefully limited to the situation presented and is of uncertain constitutional dimension. The thrust of the opinion is in the direction of establishing criteria *requiring* admission in evidence, and it should not be read as setting forth minimum standards for admission.

10. It is the hearsay statement that must be corroborated, United States v. Atkins, 558 F.2d 133 (3d Cir. 1977), cert. denied 434 U.S. 972, not the testimony of the witness testifying to it on the stand, since his credibility can be tested by the usual procedures. United States v. Goodlow, 500 F.2d 954 (8th Cir. 1974). Whether the corroboration requirement is satisfied is for the judge. United States v. Guillette, 547 F.2d 743 (2d Cir. 1976), cert. denied 434 U.S. 839; United States v. Bagley, 537 F.2d 162, 34 A.L.R.Fed. 403 (5th Cir. 1976), cert. denied 429 U.S. 1075. See Weinstein & Berger, Evidence ¶ 804(b)(3)[03].

Whether the hearsay exception for declarations against interest should be enlarged to include declarations against "social" interests has been the occasion of differences of opinion. Traditionally interests of this nature were not regarded as of sufficient moment to insure reliability. Following in the pattern of the original Uniform Rule, the Federal Rule as promulgated by the Supreme Court included statements tending to make the declarant "an object of hatred, ridicule, or disgrace," but the provision was deleted from the rule as enacted by the Congress. It was reinstated in the Revised Uniform Rule (1974).[12]

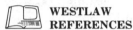 **WESTLAW REFERENCES**

110k417(15)

§ 279. Determining What Is Against Interest: Confrontation Problems

(a) The time aspect. As observed at the beginning of this chapter, the theory underlying the hearsay exception for declarations

11. Douglas v. Alabama, 380 U.S. 415 (1965), and Bruton v. United States, 389 U.S. 818 (1968), involved confessions by a codefendant inculpating the accused. *Douglas* did not consider or discuss the possibility of admissibility as a declaration against interest, merely remarking in § 276, n. 3 that no recognized exception to the hearsay rule was involved. *Bruton* assumed inadmissibility and focused on the ineffectiveness of instructing the jury to apply the confession only to the confessing codefendant. A dissent pointed to the Court's traditional distrust of codefendant confessions. Against this uncertain background, the Federal Advisory Committee first proposed a rule excluding all inculpatory statements, Preliminary Draft, Rule 8–04(b)(4) (March, 1969) 46 F.R.D. 378. Eventually, however, the committee deleted the provision, believing that, although statements made while in custody might well be motivated by a desire to curry favor with the authorities and hence fail to qualify as against interest, other circumstances might lead to the opposite conclusion and the matter should be decided on a case-by-case basis. In that form the Federal Rule was approved by the Supreme Court and enacted by the Congress. The deleted provision was reinstated in the Revised Uniform Rules (1974). See § 276, n. 14 supra.

12. For text of rules, see supra at § 276, n. 14. See Timber Access Industries Co. v. United States Plywood-Champion Papers, Inc., 263 Or. 509, 503 P.2d 482 (1972) (statement by defendant's former plant manager that he had made an improvident contract).

against interest is that people do not make statements that are disadvantageous to themselves without substantial reason to believe that the statements are true.[1] Reason indicates that the disadvantage must exist at the time the statement is made; otherwise it can exert no influence on declarant to speak the truth. That the statement may at another time prove to be disadvantageous, or for that matter advantageous, is without significance. This characteristic of contemporaneity is implicit in the cases, though seldom discussed, but is thought to have been departed from in some measure when the admissibility of contextual statements, discussed below, is involved.

(b) The nature of the statement. The statement must be such "that a reasonable man in his position would not have made the statement unless he believed it to be true,"[2] in view of the statement's contrariety to declarant's interest. As indicated earlier,[3] the traditional declaration against interest was a statement that could be used in evidence in a manner adverse to declarant's pecuniary or proprietary interest. A declaration against penal interest is one that would be admissible against declarant in a criminal prosecution; it need not be a confession[4] but must involve substantial exposure to criminal liability.[5]

A controversial area has been the so-called "contextual" or related statements. In the seminal case of Higham v. Ridgway,[6] in order to prove the date of birth of an individual, an entry in the record book of a male midwife was introduced, showing a charge for attendance upon the mother for birth of a son, together with an entry six months later showing payment of the charge. The entry of payment, said the court, "was in prejudice of the party making it." But, though the entry of payment may have been against interest, the issue in the case was not payment but the birth six months earlier. To this objection, the court replied, "By the reference to the ledger, the entry there [of the birth] is virtually incorporated in the other entry [of payment], of which it is explanatory." In civil cases, as in Higham v. Ridgway, to admit the critical related statement or part of the statement is acceptable, even though not itself against interest, if it is closely enough connected and neutral as to interest.[7]

Judicial scrutiny in criminal cases has been more exacting. When the statement is offered by way of exculpating the accused, complete rejection of related or contextual statements is not insisted upon,[8] although a rather tight integration appears to be contemplated.[9] However, when the statement is offered by the prosecution to inculpate the

---

§ 279

1. See also Advisory Committee's Note, Fed.R.Evid. 804(b)(3).

2. Federal and Revised Uniform Rule (1974) 804(b)(3) supra at § 276 n. 14.

3. Cases cited in § 277 supra.

4. United States v. Barrett, 539 F.2d 244 (1st Cir. 1976); United States v. Bagley, 537 F.2d 162, 34 A.L.R.Fed. 403 (5th Cir. 1976), cert. denied 429 U.S. 1075; United States v. Thomas, 571 F.2d 285 (5th Cir. 1978).

5. United States v. Hoyos, 573 F.2d 1111 (9th Cir. 1978).

6. 10 East 109, 103 Eng.Rep. 717 (K.B.1808). One senses that this feat of judicial imagination might not have been achieved if the hearsay exception for entries in the regular course of business had then been sufficiently developed to cover the situation.

7. Taylor v. Witham, 3 Ch.Div. 605 (1875) (Taylor paid Witham £ 2000; after Taylor's death his executor contended this was a loan, Witham that it was a gift;

entry in Taylor's books of three months' interest, £ 20, paid by Witham admitted for the executor to show a loan "since the natural meaning of the entry standing alone" was against interest; Knapp v. St. Louis Trust Co., 199 Mo. 640, 98 S.W. 70 (1906), and Palter Cap. Co. v. Great Western Life Assurance Co., [1936] 2 D.L.R. 304 are virtually identical with Higham v. Ridgway, supra n. 6. For additional cases see 5 Wigmore, Evidence § 1465 (Chadbourn rev. 1974). Model Code of Evidence Rule 509(2) allowed "a declaration against interest and such additional parts thereof, including matter incorporated by reference, as the judge finds to be so closely connected with the declaration against interest as to be equally trustworthy."

8. United States v. Barrett and United States v. Thomas supra n. 4. In both opinions the court buttressed its finding of sufficient integration by pointing out that the statement in any event disclosed guilty knowledge by the declarant. See also United States v. Brainard, 690 F.2d 1117, 1124 (4th Cir. 1982).

9. United States v. Hoyos supra n. 5.

accused, an even stricter approach is sometimes found: the requirements of the Confrontation Clause of the Sixth Amendment are said in some judicial opinions to require rejection of any part or related statement not in itself against interest.[10]

(c) The factual setting. Whether a statement was against interest will often depend on outside facts that existed at the time the statement was made but were not disclosed in the statement. Admissibility then would hinge on these external facts. For example, whether a statement that declarant is a member of a certain partnership is against his pecuniary interest would depend upon whether the firm is clearly solvent, or is on the other hand of doubtful solvency or insolvent.[11] And a statement that one has a contract to purchase a given amount of wheat at a certain price is against, or for interest, depending upon the price of wheat in the market at the time the statement was made.

If the factual setting suggests that declarant anticipated no damaging disclosure, is the circumstantial guarantee of trustworthiness present? A relation of trust and confidence between speaker and listener would militate, arguably, against awareness that the making of the statement might be against declarant's interest. The question was raised in the Sussex Peerage Case,[12] where the statement was to declarant's son, and answered in the negative. The case has not, however, been followed, and the fact that the statement was made to declarant's

daughter,[13] or to a friend and cellmate,[14] or "in the course of a conversation with friends over cards,[15] has not ruled out admissibility. The always-existent possibility of disclosure appears to be enough. In fact, the existence of a friendly relationship is on occasion mentioned as a factor favoring admissibility.[16]

The factual setting in which the statement is made is given particular importance in cases of statements against penal interest inculpating the accused, since admissibility must be measured against standards fixed by the Confrontation Clause of the Sixth Amendment as well as by the rule of evidence. Particular significance is attached to the fact that the declarant was at the time in the custody of law enforcement authorities, if such was the case. It has been held that the fact of custody alone, with its attendant likelihood of motivation by a desire to curry favor with the authorities, bars a finding that the statement was against interest and requires exclusion.[17] While courts generally do not accord such conclusive effect to the fact of custody, agreement is general that great weight be given to it.[18] Some courts have imposed an additional factual safeguard upon the use of statements inculpating an accused person by requiring that they be corroborated, thus in effect reading into Federal Evid. Rule 804(b)(3) with regard to inculpatory statements the same provision there expressly stated with regard to exculpatory statements.[19]

---

10. People v. Leach, 15 Cal.3d 419, 124 Cal.Rptr. 752, 541 P.2d 296 (1975), cert. denied 424 U.S. 926. See also United States v. Love, 592 F.2d 1022 (8th Cir. 1979); Tague, Perils of the Rulemaking Process: The Development, Application, and Unconstitutionality of Rule 804(b)(3)'s Penal Interest Exception, 69 Geo.L.J. 851 (1981); Comment, 66 Calif.L.Rev. 1189 (1978).

11. See Humes v. O'Bryan, 74 Ala. 64, 78 (1883) (suit against Humes on alleged partnership debt contracted by Glover; held, declaration by Glover, made when business was insolvent, that Hume was not a partner, was a declaration against interest, though otherwise if business had not been insolvent).

12. 11 Cl. & F. 85, 8 Eng.Rep. 1034 (1844).

13. United States v. Goins, 593 F.2d 88 (8th Cir. 1979, cert. denied 444 U.S. 827.

14. United States v. Bagley, 537 F.2d 162, 34 A.L.R. Fed. 403 (5th Cir. 1976), cert. denied 429 U.S. 1075.

15. United States v. Barrett, 539 F.2d 244 (1st Cir. 1976).

16. Chambers v. Mississippi, supra § 278, n. 9.

17. United States v. Sarmiento-Perez, 633 F.2d 1092 (5th Cir. 1980), cert. denied 103 S.Ct. 77.

18. United States v. Garris, 616 F.2d 626 (2d Cir. 1980), cert. denied 447 U.S. 926; United States v. Palumbo, 639 F.2d 123 (3d Cir. 1981), cert. denied 454 U.S. 819; United States v. Riley, 657 F.2d 1377 (8th Cir. 1981).

19. United States v. Alvarez, 584 F.2d 694 (5th Cir. 1978); United States v. Riley, 657 F.2d 1377 (8th Cir. 1981); Tague, supra n. 10, at p. 996; Comment, 66 Cal. L.Rev. 1189, supra n. 10, at p. 1216.

(d) Motive: Actual state of mind of declarant. In strictest logic, attention in cases of declarations against interest, as with other hearsay exceptions, should focus on the actual state of mind produced in the declarant by the supposed truth-inducing circumstances and a reasonable-man standard would be irrelevant. That, of course, is not the case: the usual standard is that found in Federal Evidence Rule 804(b)(3), "that a reasonable man would not have made the statement unless he believed it to be true." Difficulties of proof, probabilities, and the unavailability of the declarant all favor the accepted standard. It can scarcely be doubted, however, that statements of declarant disclosing his ostensible actual mental state would be received and in an appropriate case control.

The exception has often been stated as requiring that there have been no motive to falsify.[20] This is too sweeping, and the limitation can probably best be understood merely as a qualification that even though a statement be against interest in one respect, if it appears that declarant had some motive, whether of self-interest or otherwise, which was likely to lead to misrepresentation of the facts, the statement should be excluded.[21]

WESTLAW REFERENCES

declaration* statement* /s against /s interest /p confrontation

digest,synopsis(declaration* statement* /s against /s interest /p time contemporane!)

headnote(804(b)(3) /p confrontation)

"united states" /5 barrett /15 539 /3 244

804(b)(3) /p motiv! intent! "state of mind"

§ 280.   Unavailability of the Declarant

While the requirement of unavailability followed its own course of development at common law with respect to declarations against interest, as was the case with other hearsay exceptions requiring unavailability of the declarant, the pattern is now largely standardized. See section 253 supra for discussion in detail of what satisfies the requirement.

WESTLAW REFERENCES

headnote(unavailab! /p 804(b)(3))

declaration* statement* /s against /s interest /p unavail!

---

20. German Insurance Co. v. Bartlett, 188 Ill. 165, 58 N.E. 1075, 1077 (1900); Halvorsen v. Moon & Kerr Lumber Co., 87 Minn. 18, 91 N.W. 28, 29 (1902); Hill v. Robinson, 592 S.W.2d 376 (Tex.Civ.App.1980).

21. Demasi v. Whitney Trust & Savings Bank, 176 So. 703 (La.App.1937) affidavit of depositor that previous withdrawals had been with her consent, excluded because it appeared that affidavit was presented by bank for her signature as prerequisite for withdrawing balance of account; Roe v. Journegan, 175 N.C. 261, 95 S.E. 495 (1918) (issue as to delivery from father to son of deed of 1881; son's statement thereafter that he had no land, that his father had offered him some but he would not accept it, excluded because son apparently believed he would get the land in fee by deed or inheritance, and the deed of 1881 conveyed only a life estate).

Chapter 28
DYING DECLARATIONS

Table of Sections

---

§ 281. Introductory [1]

Of the doctrines which authorize the admission of special classes of out-of-court statements as exceptions to the hearsay rule, the doctrine relating to dying declarations is the most mystical in its theory and traditionally the most arbitrary in its limitations. The notion of the special likelihood of truthfulness of deathbed statements was widespread, of course, long before the recognition of a general rule against hearsay in the early seventeen hundreds. It is natural enough, then, that about as soon as we find a hearsay rule we also find a recognized exception for dying declarations.[2]

 WESTLAW REFERENCES

203k200
digest,synopsis("dying declaration*")

---

§ 281

1. See 5 Wigmore, Evidence §§ 1430–1452 (Chadbourn rev. 1974); Weinstein & Berger, Evidence ¶ 804(b)(2)[01]; Dec.Dig. Homicide ☞200–221, Evidence ☞275½; C.J.S. Homicide §§ 286–306; 40 Am. Jur.2d Homicide §§ 347–394; Quick, Some Reflections on Dying Declarations, 6 How.L.Rev. 109 (1960); Jaffee, The Constitution and Proof by Dead or Unavailable Declarants, 33 Ark.L.Rev. 228 (1979); Note, 46 Iowa L.Rev. 375 (1961).

2. See the early cases listed in 5 Wigmore, Evidence § 1430, note 1 (Chadbourn rev. 1974).

The classic statement of the basis of the rule is that of Chief Baron Eyre in Rex v. Woodcock, 1 Leach 500, 168 Eng.Rep. 352 (K.B.1789):

Now the general principle on which this species of evidence is admitted is, that they are declarations made in extremity, when the party is at the point of death, and when every hope of this world is gone; when every motive to falsehood is silenced, and the mind is induced by the most powerful considerations to speak the truth; a situation so solemn, and so awful, is considered by the law as creating an obligation equal to that which is imposed by a positive oath administered in a Court of Justice.

The present state of religious belief, naturally, affords ample grounds for differences as to the underpinnings of the rule. However, the courts in general have declined to allow exploration of declarant's religious views. Annot., 16 A.L.R. 411. Religious beliefs of witnesses generally is the subject of § 48 supra.

§ 282. Requirements That Declarant Must Have Been Conscious of Impending Death and That Death Actually Ensue

The central notions of the popular reverence for deathbed statements are embodied in two important limitations upon the dying declaration exception as evolved at common law. Unlike the more recent limitations, which will be mentioned later, these two are arguably rational, though possibly they have drawn too sharply the lines of restriction.

The first of these two limitations is that the declarant must at the time he made his statement have been conscious that death was near and certain.[1] He must have lost all hope of recovery.[2] It is arguable that a belief in the mere probability of impending death would make most men strongly disposed to tell the truth and hence guarantee the needed special reliability. But belief in the certainty of impending death, not its mere likelihood or probability, is the formula that was insisted on and rigorously applied. Perhaps this limitation reflects some lack of confidence in the reliability of "deathbed" statements generally. Usually this belief in the certainty of impending death is proved by evidence of the declarant's own statements of belief at the time, his expression of his "settled hopeless expectation."[3] That the deceased should have made such a statement is not required,[4] however; and his belief may be shown circumstantially by the apparent fatal quality of the wound,[5] by the statements made to the declarant by the doctor or by others that his condition is hopeless,[6] and by other circumstances.[7]

The description of declarant's mental state in the Federal and Revised Uniform Rules (1974) is less emphatic than in the common law cases, merely saying "while believing that his death was imminent." Evidence that would satisfy the common law would satisfy the rule, and perhaps a lesser showing would suffice. Lack of a requirement in the rule that declarant actually die supports this conclusion.[8]

§ 282

1. For statements of the formula, see People v. Tilley, 406 Ill. 398, 94 N.E.2d 328, 331 (1950); State v. Dunlap, 268 N.C. 301, 150 S.E.2d 436 (1966) ("full apprehension of danger of death" is necessary); Thomas v. Commonwealth, 183 Va. 501, 32 S.E.2d 711 (1945).

2. Shepard v. United States, 290 U.S. 96 (1933) (leading opinion by Cardozo, J.); Tillman v. State, 44 So.2d 644 (Fla.1950); People v. Allen, 300 N.Y. 222, 90 N.E.2d 48 (1949). If made under consciousness of doom a later revival of hope will not be ground of exclusion. State v. Reed, 53 Kan. 767, 37 P. 174 (1894); Goff v. Commonwealth, 433 S.W.2d 350 (Ky.1968). A request for an ambulance, United States v. Etheridge, 424 F.2d 951 (6th Cir. 1970), cert. denied 400 U.S. 993, or for a physician, State v. Evans, 124 Mo. 397, 28 S.W. 8 (1894), does not negate loss of hope. Contra where future plans are announced, State v. Elias, 205 Minn. 156, 285 N.W. 475 (1939) (decedent told defendant wife who had shot him that he was going to divorce her).

3. Long v. Commonwealth, 262 Ky. 619, 90 S.W.2d 1007 (1936); State v. Eubanks, 277 Minn. 257, 152 N.W.2d 453 (1967); Hawkins v. State, 220 Tenn. 383, 417 S.W.2d 774 (1967). As to the sufficiency of such statements, see Annot., 53 A.L.R.3d 785.

4. State v. Mitchell, 209 N.C. 1, 182 S.E. 695 (1935); Commonwealth v. Knable, 369 Pa. 171, 85 A.2d 114 (1952), and see Shepard v. United States, 290 U.S. 96, 100 (1933) ("There is no unyielding ritual of words to be spoken by the dying").

McCormick et al. on Evid. 3rd Ed. H.B.—19

5. Bland v. State, 210 Ga. 100, 78 S.E.2d 51 (1953); Rouse v. State of Mississippi, 222 So.2d 145 (Miss. 1969); Commonwealth v. Smith, 424 Pa. 9, 225 A.2d 691 (1967). But the mere fact that the wound was mortal will not alone show consciousness of doom unless its nature were such as to reveal to the declarant its fatal character. Fulton v. State, 209 Miss. 565, 47 So.2d 883 (1950); State v. McDaniel, 272 N.C. 556, 158 S.E.2d 874 (1968) vacated on other grounds 392 U.S. 665 (showing that declarant was actually at the point of death and in great agony held insufficient).

6. Sisk v. State, 182 Ga. 448, 185 S.E. 777 (1936) (doctor); State v. Peters, 90 N.H. 438, 10 A.2d 242 (1939) (nurse); Chandler v. State, 7 Md.App. 646, 256 A.2d 695 (1969) (police officer).

7. See cases collected in 5 Wigmore, Evidence § 1442 (Chadbourn rev. 1974); Dec.Dig. Homicide ⊜203–205; Annot., 53 A.L.R.3d 1196.

8. The complete text of Fed.R.Evid. 804(b)(2) is:

   The following are not excluded by the hearsay rule if the declarant is unavailable as a witness: . . . (2) In a prosecution for homicide or in a civil action or proceeding, a statement made by a declarant while believing that his death was imminent, concerning the cause or circumstances of what he believed to be his impending death.

The Uniform Rule omits the language preceding the first comma.

The method of dealing with the preliminary fact question of consciousness of impending death is discussed in a previous chapter.[9]

The second limitation related to the popular reverence for deathbed statements is that the declarant must be dead when the evidence is offered.[10] It is not required that the death must have followed at any very short interval after the declaration. Periods even extending into months have been held not too long. The test is the declarant's belief in the nearness of death when he made the statement, not the actual swiftness with which death ensued.[11]

Neither the Federal nor the Revised Uniform Evidence Rules contain any requirement that declarant be dead.[12] They do require that declarant be unavailable, which of course, includes death as well as other situations.[13]

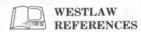

WESTLAW REFERENCES

203k203

"dying declaration*" /p impending imminent /p death

§ 283. Limitation to Use in Criminal Homicide Cases, and Other Arbitrary Limitations

If the courts in their creation of rules about dying declarations had stopped here, we would have had a narrow, perhaps, but rational and understandable practice. The requirement of consciousness of impending death arguably tends to guarantee a sufficient degree of special reliability, and the requirement that declarant be dead and thus unavailable as a witness is an ample showing of the necessity for the use of hearsay,

if necessity be required. This simple rationale of dying declarations sufficed the courts up to the beginning of the eighteen hundreds, and these declarations were admitted in civil and criminal cases without distinction[1] and seemingly without untoward results. The subsequent history of the rule is an object lesson in the use of precedents to preserve and fossilize the judicial mistakes of an earlier generation.

A mistake this development seems to have been. Sergeant East in 1803 in his widely used treatise, Pleas of the Crown, wrote: "Besides the usual evidence of guilt in general cases of felony, there is one kind of evidence more peculiar to the case of homicide, which is the declaration of the deceased, after the mortal blow, as to the fact itself, and the party by whom it is committed. Evidence of this sort is admissible in this case on the fullest necessity; for it often happens that there is no third person present to be an eye-witness to the fact; and the usual witness on occasion of other felonies, namely, the party injured himself, is gotten rid of."[2] This was seized upon for what it was obviously not intended to be, namely, an announcement that the sole justification of the admission of dying declarations is the necessity of punishing murderers, who might otherwise escape for lack of the testimony of the victim. This need may exist, but the proposition that the use of dying declarations should be limited to instances where it exists surely does not follow. Nevertheless this proposition was elaborated into a series of what may well be classed as arbitrary limiting rules, as contrasted with the two more rational limitations already mentioned.

---

9. See § 53, supra.

10. State v. Carden, 209 N.C. 404, 183 S.E. 898 (1936); 5 Wigmore, Evidence § 1431 (Chadbourn rev. 1974).

11. See, e.g., Emmett v. State, 195 Ga. 517, 25 S.E.2d 9 (1943) (survived 3½ months, admitted); People v. Denton, 312 Mich. 32, 19 N.W.2d 476 (1945) (survived 11 days); 5 Wigmore, Evidence § 1441 (Chadbourn rev. 1974); Dec.Dig. Homicide ⟺204.

12. For text of applicable rules, see n. 8 supra.

13. Unavailability is discussed in § 253 supra.

§ 283

1. See Wright v. Littler, 3 Burr. 1244, 1247, 1255, 97 Eng.Rep. 812 (K.B.1761) (in ejectment, death-bed statement that declarant had forged a will, received) and other cases cited 5 Wigmore, Evidence § 1431, note 1 (Chadbourn rev. 1974).

2. East, 1 Pleas of the Crown, 353, 1803, quoted 5 Wigmore, Evidence § 1431 (Chadbourn rev. 1974).

The first of these is the rule that the use of dying declarations is limited to cases of criminal homicide.[3] Although the English courts in the seventeen hundreds had not done so,[4] nearly all courts, building upon the later theory of necessity, refused to admit dying declarations in civil cases,[5] whether death actions or other civil cases, or in criminal cases other than those charging homicide as an essential part of the offense. Thus in prosecutions for abortion [6] and rape,[7] though death of the woman may have ensued, the declarations are held inadmissible. Probably this restriction proceeds from a feeling on the part of the judges that dying declarations, despite their supposed guaranty of trustworthiness, are a dangerous kind of testimony, which a jury is likely to handle too emotionally. But is their emotion likely to be less in a murder prosecution than in a civil action for death or in a prosecution for abortion?

As promulgated by the Supreme Court, the Federal Rule contained no limitation as to type of case in which dying declarations were admissible, and the Revised Uniform Evidence Rule (1974) continues in that form. While the Federal Rule was before the Congress, however, at the instance of the House Committee on the Judiciary an amendment limiting use of dying declarations to prosecutions for homicide and civil actions or proceedings was adopted, and the rule was enacted as amended.[8] Thus under the Federal Rule, dying declarations are admissible in all cases except non-homicide criminal cases.

The concept of necessity limited to protection of the state against the slayer who might go free because of the death of his victim, spun out another consequence. This is the further limitation that not only must the charge be homicide, but also, the defendant in the present trial must be charged with the death of the declarant.[9] In a case,[10] in which a marauder shot a man and his wife at the same time, and the defendant was put on trial for the murder of the husband only, the dying declaration of the wife identifying the defendant as the assailant was offered by the State. It was excluded under this doctrine. Wigmore's comment is, "Could one's imagination devise a more senseless rule of exclusion, if he had not found it in our law?" [11] No such limitation appears in either Federal or Revised Uniform Rules (1974).

Less arbitrary, but a source of controversy, is the third of these corollary limitations, i.e., that the declarations are admissible only insofar as they relate to the circumstances of the killing and to the events more or less nearly preceding it in time and leading up to

---

3. United States v. Sacasas, 381 F.2d 451 (2d Cir. 1967) (bank robbery, etc., excluded); People v. Stison, 140 Mich. 216, 103 N.W. 542 (1905) (incest, excluded); Taylor v. Commonwealth, 122 Va. 886, 94 S.E. 795, 797 (1918) (assault excluded); Dec.Dig. Homicide ☞211.

4. See n. 1 supra.

5. Prudential Ins. Co. v. Keeling's Adm'x, 271 Ky. 558, 112 S.W.2d 994 (1938) (claim for double indemnity for fatal accident, in suit on life policy); Ross v. Cooper, 38 N.D. 173, 164 N.W. 679 (1917) (death injury); Blair v. Rogers, 185 Okl. 63, 89 P.2d 928 (1939) (death injury); Dec.Dig. Evidence ☞275½.

6. Winfrey v. State, 174 Ark. 729, 296 S.W. 82 (1927); State v. Meyer, 64 N.J.L. 382 (1900) (death not an essential element of the crime, but only affected the punishment). But where the crime charged is homicide by abortion, the declaration is admissible. State v. Yochelman, 107 Conn. 148, 139 A. 632 (1927) (manslaughter); Piercy v. State, 138 Neb. 301, 293 N.W. 99 (1940).

7. Frogge v. Commonwealth, 296 Ky. 726, 178 S.W. 2d 405 (1944).

8. For text of the rules see § 282, n. 8 supra.

By way of justification, the Committee Report stated:

> The Committee did not consider dying declarations as among the most reliable forms of hearsay. Consequently, it amended the provision to limit their admissibility in criminal cases to homicide prosecutions, where exceptional need for the evidence is present.

House Comm. on Judiciary, Fed.Rules of Evidence, H.R.Rep. No. 650, 93d Cong., 1st Sess., p. 15 (1973).

9. People v. Cox, 340 Ill. 111, 172 N.E. 64, 69 A.L.R. 1215 (1930) (annotated); State v. Puett, 210 N.C. 633, 188 S.E. 75 (1936); Dec.Dig. Homicide ☞211.

10. Westberry v. State, 175 Ga. 115, 164 S.E. 905 (1932); see also People v. Cox, supra n. 9.

11. 5 Wigmore, Evidence § 1433, note 1 (Chadbourn rev. 1974).

it.[12] Under this version declarations about previous quarrels between the accused and his victim would be excluded, while transactions between them leading up to and shortly before the present attack would be received.[13] Some limitation as to time and circumstances seems unavoidable, but precise phrasing is not possible. The Federal and Revised Uniform Evidence Rules (1974) require that the statement be "concerning the cause or circumstances of what he believed to be his impending death."[14] Within this more liberal framework decisions may be made in terms of remoteness and prejudice under Rule 403.[15]

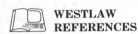

WESTLAW REFERENCES

203k214

digest("dying declaration*" /p criminal /p civil) & court(nc)

"dying declaration*" /p cause circumstances* /p killing murder death

§ 284. Admissible on Behalf of Accused as Well as for Prosecution

One might have anticipated that the strict application of the above mentioned concept of necessity would have led the courts to restrict the use of dying declarations to intro-

duction by the prosecution, but the unfairness of such a result was too apparent, and it is well settled that they will be received on behalf of the defendant.[1]

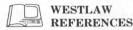

WESTLAW REFERENCES

"dying declaration*" /p mattox

§ 285. Application of Other Evidentiary Rules: Personal Knowledge: Opinion: Rules About Writings

Other principles of evidence law present recurrent problems in their application to dying declarations. If it appears that the declarant did not have adequate opportunity to observe the facts recounted, the declaration will be rejected for want of the knowledge qualification.[1] This knowledge requirement has sometimes been confused with the opinion rule, and in some instances this confusion may have led courts to make the statement that opinions in dying declarations will be excluded.[2] Of course the traditional opinion rule, designed as a regulation of the manner of questioning of witnesses in court, is entirely inappropriate as a restriction upon out-of-court declarations.[3] Accordingly, most courts including some that have pro-

---

12. Lucas v. Commonwealth, 153 Ky. 424, 155 S.W. 721 (1913); Connor v. State, 225 Md. 543, 171 A.2d 699 (1961) (proper for court to exclude reference to residence of defendant, etc., when remaining statement of deceased was complete); Walthall v. State, 144 Tex.Cr. R. 585, 165 S.W.2d 184 (1942); 5 Wigmore, Evidence § 1344 (Chadbourn rev. 1974); Dec.Dig. Homicide ⊜214(2).

13. Smith v. Commonwealth, 236 Ky. 736, 33 S.W. 2d 688 (1930) (that defendant had fired on deceased at previous times); Jones v. State, 236 P.2d 102 (Okl.Cr. 1951) (that defendant had threatened to kill deceased the day before the killing); Webb v. State, 133 Tex.Cr. R. 32, 106 S.W.2d 683 (1937) (describing previous quarrel, on same afternoon, which had subsided, excluded).

14. For text of rules, see supra at § 282, n. 8.

15. See § 185 supra.

§ 284

1. Mattox v. United States, 146 U.S. 140, 151 (1892); State v. Puett, 210 N.C. 633, 188 S.E. 75 (1936). Neither Federal nor Revised Uniform Evid. Rules (1974) limits use to the prosecution.

§ 285

1. Jones v. State, 52 Ark. 347, 12 S.W. 704 (1889) (where declarant could not see who shot him, declaration that H. shot him properly excluded); Strickland v. State, 167 Ga. 452, 145 S.E. 879, 881 (1928) (requirement satisfied); 5 Wigmore, Evidence § 1445(2) (Chadbourn rev. 1974). When there is room for doubt as to whether the statement is based on knowledge, the question is for the jury. Bland v. State, 210 Ga. 100, 78 S.E.2d 51 (1953). Expressions of suspicion or conjecture are to be kept out. Shepard v. United States, 290 U.S. 96 (1933).

2. Roberts v. Commonwealth, 301 Ky. 294, 191 S.W.2d 242 (1946) (but declarations here held admissible); State v. Wilks, 278 Mo. 481, 213 S.W. 118 (1919); Hollywood v. State, 19 Wyo. 493, 120 P. 471 (1912). See also, Miller v. Goodwin, 246 Ark. 552, 439 S.W.2d 308 (1969) (if both matter of fact and of opinion are involved, the judge has discretion to admit subject to request for instruction that matter of opinion not be considered).

3. See Commonwealth v. Plubell, 367 Pa. 452, 80 A.2d 825 (1951), and Pendleton v. Commonwealth, 131 Va. 676, 109 S.E. 201, 209 (1921) following 5 Wigmore,

fessed to apply the opinion rule here, have admitted declarations such as "He shot me down like a dog," [4] "He shot me without cause," [5] and "He done it a-purpose" [6] and the like,[7] which would traditionally have been excluded as opinions, if spoken by a witness on the stand.

Another problem is the application of the so-called best evidence rule.[8] Often the dying victim, perhaps as different people visit him, will make several oral statements about the facts of the crime; and in addition, he may make a written statement by his own hand; or the person hearing the statement may write it down and procure the declarant to sign it. When is the writing required to be produced or its absence accounted for? As to the separate oral statement, it is clear that this is provable without producing a later writing.[9] It is equally clear, of course, that the terms of a written dying statement cannot be proved as such without producing or accounting for the writing.[10] What if the witness who heard the oral statement, which was taken down and signed, offers to testify to what he heard? Wigmore argues that the execution of the writing does not call into play the parol evidence rule, since that rule is limited to contracts and other "legal

acts;" [11] but to a limited extent the courts have held otherwise. They have not excluded evidence of other oral statements on the same occasion, not embraced in the writing,[12] but as to oral declarations taken down and embodied in a writing signed or adopted by the deceased, these have been held not provable by one who heard them, but only by producing the written statement itself if available.[13] Even though it represents a departure from the usual practice of freedom in proving oral statements, and an extension of the doctrine of integration into a new field, the result may be justified by the need here for accuracy in transmitting to the tribunal the exact terms of the declarant's statement.

 WESTLAW REFERENCES

"dying declaration*" /p opinion* /p fact* & court(mi)

powell +2 state & "dying declaration*" & court(ms)

§ 286. Instructions as to the Weight to Be Given to Dying Declarations [1]

There has been much theorizing in texts and opinions as to the weight to be given to dying declarations, abstractly or in compari-

---

Evidence § 1447 (Chadbourn rev. 1974). See § 18 supra.

The Advisory Committee's Note to Fed.R.Evid. 804(b)(2) indicates that statements may be in the form of an opinion, as permitted for testimony under Rule 701. Federal and Revised Uniform Evid. Rules (1974) 701 and 704 should resolve most doubts in favor of admissibility.

4. State v. Saunders, 14 Or. 305, 12 P. 441 (1886). See Finley v. State, 92 Tex.Cr. 543, 244 S.W. 527 (1922) ("He shot me in cold blood.").

5. State v. Williams, 168 N.C. 191, 83 S.E. 714 (1914).

6. Pippin v. Commonwealth, 117 Va. 919, 86 S.E. 152 (1915).

7. Powell v. State, 238 Miss. 283, 118 So.2d 304 (1960). Decisions are collected in 5 Wigmore, Evidence § 1447 (Chadbourn rev. 1974); Annots., 25 A.L.R. 1370, 63 A.L.R. 567, 86 A.L.R.2d 905; C.J.S. Homicide § 299; Dec.Dig. Homicide ☞215(4).

8. See Ch. 23 supra.

9. Gray v. State, 185 Ark. 515, 48 S.W.2d 224 (1932); Dunn v. People, 172 Ill. 582, 50 N.E. 137 (1898); State v. Sweeney, 203 Iowa 1305, 214 N.W. 735 (1927).

10. See § 233 supra.

11. 5 Wigmore, Evidence § 1450(b) (Chadbourn rev. 1974).

12. Commonwealth v. Haney, 127 Mass. 455 (1879) (oral declarations of consciousness of impending death on same occasion as the written statement, allowed to be proved).

13. Rex v. Gay, 7 C. & P. 230, 173 Eng.Rep. 101 (N.P.1835); Williams v. State, 26 Ala.App. 531, 163 So. 333 (1935) (rule stated but here not shown to be signed); People v. Glenn, 10 Cal. 32, 37 (1858) (prosecution bound to produce writing but having done so can prove similar oral declarations made at other times); Couch v. State, 93 Tex.Cr. 27, 245 S.W. 692 (1922) (similar to Williams v. State, above). Contra: State v. Whitson, 111 N.C. 695, 16 S.E. 332 (1892) (dictum).

§ 286

1. Cases are collected in Notes, 32 Neb.L.Rev. 461 (1953), 41 Iowa L.Rev. 375 (1961); Annot., 167 A.L.R. 147; C.J.S. Homicide § 304.

son with the testimony of a witness. In consequence the practice has grown up in some states of requiring [2] or permitting [3] the judge to instruct the jury that these declarations are to be received with caution. In other states such instructions have been held to be improper.[4] Again one court has required that the jury be told that a dying declaration is not to be regarded as having the same value and weight as sworn testimony.[5] Others have considered it proper to direct the jury that they should give the dying declaration the same weight as the testimony of a witness.[6] While there may be merit in a standardized practice of giving cautionary instructions, the direction to give the declaration a predetermined fixed weight seems of questionable wisdom. The weight of particular dying declarations depends upon so many factors varying from case to case that no standardized instruction will fit all situations. Certainly in jurisdictions where the judge retains his common law power to comment on the weight of the evidence, the dying declaration is a most appropriate subject for individualized comment. But where he is shorn of this power as in most States, it seems wiser to leave the weight of the declaration to the arguments of counsel, the arbitrament of the jury, and the consideration of the judge on motion for new trial.

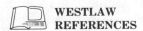

WESTLAW REFERENCES

203k218
203k221
"dying declaration*" /p weight instruct!

§ 287. Decisional and Statutory Extensions of Common Law Admissibility

In a landmark decision,[1] the Kansas court had before it an action by the executor of the seller to recover on a land sale contract. Should the dying statement of the seller of "the truth about the sale" be admitted? An affirmative answer required departure from traditional common law limitations in two respects: (1) the case was civil, not a criminal homicide prosecution, and (2) the statement was unrelated to the cause or circumstances of death. "We are confronted," the court said, "with a restrictive rule of evidence commendable only for its age, its respectability resting solely upon a habit of judicial recognition, formed without reason, and continued without justification," and ruled in favor of admissibility. As observed in earlier sections of this chapter, willingness to expand admissibility with respect to the type of case, witnessed by the Federal and Revised Uniform Rules (1974), has prevailed. Departure from the limitation that the statement relate to the circumstances of death, however, is found only in occasional rules and statutes. The limitation was not in the original Uniform Rules,[2] but it is found in the Federal and Revised Uniform Evid. Rules (1974).[3] The umbrella of trustworthiness has generally not been felt to extend so far.

WESTLAW REFERENCES

headnote("dying declaration*" /p relat*** concern*** caus*** circumstance*)
63(5) /s evidence & court(nj)

---

2. Humphreys v. State, 166 Tenn. 523, 64 S.W.2d 5 (1933); State v. Mayo, 42 Wash. 540, 85 P. 251 (1906).

3. Dowdell v. State, 194 Ga. 578, 22 S.E.2d 310 (1942); Commonwealth v. Meleskie, 278 Pa. 383, 123 A. 310 (1924).

4. Shenkenberger v. State, 154 Ind. 630, 57 N.E. 519 (1900).

5. People v. Mleczko, 298 N.Y. 153, 81 N.E.2d 65 (1948); People v. Bartelini, 285 N.Y. 433, 35 N.E.2d 29 (1941). See also approving such a charge Mitchell v. Commonwealth, 178 Va. 407, 17 S.E.2d 370 (1941).

6. State v. Johns, 152 Iowa 383, 132 N.W. 832 (1911). See also Hubbard v. State, 208 Ga. 472, 67

S.E.2d 562 (1951) (holding it not erroneous to instruct that dying declarations "stand upon the same plane of solemnity as statements made under oath"); Commonwealth v. Brown, 388 Pa. 613, 131 A.2d 367 (1957) (court approved instruction that declaration can be given "the same effect as though it were made under oath", but added it would seem advisable for judge to omit any comparison).

§ 287

1. Thurston v. Fritz, 91 Kan. 468, 138 P. 625 (1914).

2. Original Uniform Rule 63(5).

3. Supra § 283, n. 14.

Chapter 29

SPONTANEOUS STATEMENTS

Table of Sections

§ 288. Res Gestae and the Hearsay Rule [1]

The term *res gestae* seems to have come into common usage in discussions of admissibility of statements accompanying material acts or situations in the early 1800's.[2] At this time the theory of hearsay was not well developed, and the various exceptions to the hearsay rule were not clearly defined. In this context, the phrase *res gestae* served as a convenient vehicle for escape from the hearsay rule in two primary situations. In the first, it was used to explain the admissibility of statements that were not hearsay at all.[3] In the second, it was used to justify the admissibility of statements which today come within the four exceptions discussed in this chapter: (1) statements of present bodily condition, (2) statements of present mental states and emotions, (3) excited utterances, and (4) statements of present sense impressions. Despite the increased sophistication of the hearsay rule and its exceptions today, however, courts still occasionally speak in terms of *res gestae* [4] rather than in terms of more precise hearsay doctrine.

Initially, the term *res gestae* was employed to denote words which accompanied the principal litigated fact, such as the murder, collision, or trespass, which was the subject of the action. Usage developed,

---

§ 288

1. See generally, 6 Wigmore, Evidence §§ 1745, 1767 (Chadbourn rev. 1976); Comment, 20 Baylor L.Rev. 229 (1968); 29 Am.Jur.2d Evidence §§ 708–737; C.J.S. Evidence §§ 403–421.

2. 6 Wigmore, Evidence § 1767 (Chadbourn rev. 1976).

3. See § 289 infra.

4. E.g., State v. Galvan, 297 N.W.2d 344 (Iowa 1980), supra § 250, n. 28.

however, to the point where the phrase seemed to embody the notion that evidence of any concededly relevant act or condition might bring in likewise the words which accompanied it. Two main policies or motives are discernable in this recognition of *res gestae* as a password for the admission of otherwise inadmissible evidence. One is a desire to permit each witness to tell his story in a natural way by telling all that happened at the time of the narrated incident, including those details which give life and color to the story. Truth is a seamless web, and the naturalness with which the details fit each other gives confirmation to the witness' entire account.[5] The other policy, emphasized by Wigmore and those following his leadership, is the recognition of spontaneity as the source of special trustworthiness. This quality of spontaneity characterizes to some degree nearly all the types of statements which have been labeled *res gestae.*

Commentators [6] and, less frequently, courts,[7] have criticized use of the phrase *res gestae*. Its vagueness and imprecision are, of course, apparent. Moreover, traditional limitations on the doctrine, such as the requirement that it be used only in regard to the principal litigated fact and the frequent insistence of concurrence (or at least a close relationship in time) between the words and the act or situation, have restricted its usefulness as a tool for avoiding unjustified application of the hearsay rule. Historically, however, the phrase served its purpose. Its very vagueness made it easier for courts to broaden its coverage and thus provide for the admissibility of certain statements in

new situations. But the law has now reached a stage at which widening admissibility will be best served by other means. The ancient phrase can well be jettisoned, with due acknowledgment that it served its era in the evolution of evidence law.

 **WESTLAW
REFERENCES**

"res gestae" /p useless harmful shibboleth /p
    wigmore
"res gestae" /p principal primary central ultimate main
    /4 issue* fact*

---

§ 289. Spontaneous Statements as Nonhearsay: Circumstantial Proof of a Fact in Issue [1]

The types of spontaneous statements discussed in this chapter are often treated by courts as hearsay, and in that event it is considered that in order to be admissible they must come within an exception to the general rule excluding hearsay. In many cases, however, this maneuver is unnecessary because the statements are not hearsay in the first place. As suggested in an earlier section,[2] hearsay is most appropriately defined as assertive statements or conduct offered to prove what is asserted. But many so-called spontaneous statements are in fact not assertive statements or, if assertive, are not offered to prove the truth of the assertions made. For example, it is clear that the statements, "I plan to spend the rest of my life here in New York" or "I have lost my affection for my husband" are hearsay, when offered to prove the plan to remain in New York or the loss of affection. On the

---

5. "[T]he admissibility of the proofs as res gestae has as its justifying principle that truth, like the Master's robe, is of one piece, without seam, woven from the top throughout, that each fact has its inseparable attributes and its kindred facts materially affecting its character, and that the reproduction of a scene with its multiple incidents, each created naturally and without artificiality and not too distant in point of time, will by very quality and texture tend to disclose the truth." Robertson v. Hackensack Trust Co., 1 N.J. 304, 63 A.2d 515, 519 (1949) (Case, J.).

6. "The marvelous capacity of a Latin phrase to serve as a substitute for reasoning, and the confusion of thought inevitably accompanying the use of inaccu-

rate terminology, are nowhere better illustrated than in the decisions dealing with the admissibility of evidence as 'res gestae'." Morgan, A Suggested Classification of Utterances Admissible as Res Gestae, 31 Yale L.J. 229 (1922). See also 6 Wigmore, Evidence § 1767 (Chadbourn rev. 1976).

7. See, e.g., Cox v. State, 64 Ga. 374, 410 (1897) (Bleckley, C. J.).

§ 289

1. See generally 6 Wigmore, Evidence §§ 1715, 1766–1790 (Chadbourn rev. 1976).

2. See § 246 supra.

other hand, statements such as "I have been happier in New York than in any other place," when offered to show the speaker's intent to remain in New York, or "My husband is a detestable wretch," offered to show lack of affection for the husband, will or will not be classed as hearsay, depending upon the position taken with respect to the question whether "implied assertions" are to be classed as hearsay. That question is discussed elsewhere.[3]

If the statement which is offered in evidence is not classed as hearsay, then no further consideration of the matters developed in this chapter is required. But if it is classed as hearsay, then these matters may become pertinent to the question of admissibility.

 WESTLAW REFERENCES

digest(declaration* statement* assert! /s immediate! spontaneous! /s exception "not hearsay" nonhearsay)

§ 290. "Self-Serving" Aspects of Spontaneous Statements [1]

The notion that a party's out-of-court statements could not be evidence in his favor because of their "self-serving" nature seems to have originated as an accompaniment of the now universally discarded rule forbidding parties to testify.[2] When this rule of disqualification for interest was abrogated by statute, any sweeping rule of inadmissibility regarding "self-serving" statements should have been regarded as abolished by

implication. This, however, has not been the case.

The hearsay rule excludes all hearsay statements unless within some exception to the rule. Thus no specific rule is necessary to cover so-called self-serving out-of-court statements.[3] If a statement with a self-serving aspect falls within an exception to the hearsay rule, the judgment underlying the exception, that as to those declarations the assurances of trustworthiness outweigh the dangers inherent in hearsay, should be taken as controlling and the declaration admitted despite its self-serving aspects. Most courts would agree that this is the proper approach when the self-serving statement falls within one of the well-established exceptions, such as the business records exception, excited utterances, and spontaneous statements of present bodily feelings or symptoms. But in regard to less settled exceptions, such as that for statements of present state of mind or emotion, there has been less agreement. Some courts have applied a purported general rule of exclusion of self-serving statements in this area.[4] Others have rejected any blanket rule of exclusion, although the self-serving aspects of the declaration have been taken into account in applying a requirement that the statements have been made under circumstances of apparent sincerity.[5]

The Federal and Revised Uniform Evid. Rules (1974) covering hearsay exceptions for spontaneous statements, discussed in the remaining sections of this chapter, make no

3. See § 250 supra.

§ 290

1. See generally, 6 Wigmore, Evidence § 1732 (Chadbourn rev.1976); Comment, Admissibility of Self-Serving Declarations, 14 Ark.L.Rev. 105 (1959); Comment, 61 Mich.L.Rev. 1306 (1963); 29 Am.Jur.2nd Evidence §§ 621–622; C.J.S. Evidence § 216; Dec.Dig. Evidence ⊙271, Criminal Law ⊙413.

2. See Phipson, Evidence par. 1582, 1583 (12th ed., Buzzard, 1976). The rule forbidding parties to testify is discussed at § 65 supra.

3. Caplan v. Caplan, 83 N.H. 318, 142 A. 121, 127 (1928); State v. Price, 272 S.E.2d 103 (N.C.1980); Commonwealth v. Murphy, 493 Pa. 35, 425 A.2d 352 (1981).

Some courts, however, continue to treat the matter in terms of a rule excluding self-serving statements. Dickey v. State, 240 Ga. 634, 242 S.E.2d 55 (1978); Marts v. State, ___ Ind. ___, 432 N.E.2d 18 (1982).

4. People v. Smith, 8 Cal.2d 502, 104 P.2d 510 (1940) (letters of defendant to his wife not admissible in his prosecution for her murder to prove affection); State v. Barnett, 156 Kan. 746, 137 P.2d 133 (1943) (statement of defendant tending to show fear not admissible).

5. E.g., Lee v. Mitcham, 69 App.D.C. 17, 98 F.2d 298 (1938); United States v. Matot, 146 F.2d 197 (2d Cir.1944); Kelly v. Bank of America, 112 Cal.App.2d 388, 246 P.2d 92 (1952); Caplan v. Caplan, 83 N.H. 318, 142 A. 121 (1928).

special provision for self-serving statements. However, when spontaneity is the only, or perhaps the principal, guarantee of trustworthiness, its absence may be indicated by the self-serving character of the statement, and exclusion may be the result. In addition, the discretion of the judge to exclude evidence when he finds that danger of misleading the jury outweighs its probative value should be noted.[6] The concept of self-serving may also surface in the form of motive to falsify, a ground for exclusion of some kinds of otherwise admissible hearsay.[7]

 WESTLAW REFERENCES

spontaneous! immediate! excited /s declaration* statement* utterance* /p selfserving

§ 291. Statements of Bodily Feelings, Symptoms, and Condition: (a) In General [1]

Statements of the declarant's present bodily condition and symptoms, including pain and other feelings, to prove the truth of the statements have been generally recognized as an exception to the hearsay rule.[2] Special reliability is considered to be furnished by the spontaneous quality of the declarations, assured by the requirement that the declaration purport to describe a condition presently existing at the time of the statement.[3] This assurance of reliability is almost certainly not always effective, however, since some statements describing present symptoms or the like are probably not spontaneous but rather calculated misstatements. Nevertheless, a sufficiently large percentage are undoubtedly spontaneous to justify the exception. The strong likelihood of spontaneity is also the basis for dispensing with any showing of unavailability of the declarant. Being spontaneous, the hearsay statements are considered of greater probative value than the present testimony of the declarant.[4]

Despite occasional indications to the contrary,[5] declarations of present bodily condition generally have not been required to be made to a physician in order to qualify for the present exception. Any person who had the opportunity to hear the statement may testify to it.[6] The exception is, however, limited to descriptions of present condition, and therefore excludes description of past pain or symptoms [7] as well as accounts of the

---

6. See § 185 supra. The risk of unwarranted judicial excursions into credibility should not be overlooked.

7. E.g., accident reports, § 308 infra, and police reports, § 317 infra.

§ 291

1. See generally, 6 Wigmore, Evidence §§ 1718–1723 (Chadbourn rev.1976); Annot., 64 A.L.R. 557; 29 Am.Jur.2nd Evidence §§ 655–656; C.J.S. Evidence §§ 242–246; Dec.Dig. Evidence ⊙127, 128, 268.

2. E.g., Fidelity Service Insurance Co. v. Jones, 280 Ala. 195, 191 So.2d 20 (1966) (declarant complained of sickness or blackouts); Shover v. Iowa Lutheran Hospital, 252 Iowa 706, 107 N.W.2d 85 (1961) (witness testified, concerning plaintiff, that "She said she hurt."); Indian Oil Tool Co. v. Thompson, 405 P.2d 104 (Okl. 1965) (deceased stated that he had a tight feeling in his chest); Claspermeyer v. Florsheim Shoe Store Co., 313 S.W.2d 198 (Mo.App.1958) (wife complained to husband that she had a pain in her chest); Fagan v. Newark, 78 N.J. 294, 188 A.2d 427 (1963) (deceased said he felt dizzy and ill).

3. See 6 Wigmore, Evidence § 1714 (Chadbourn rev. 1976).

4. See 6 Wigmore, Evidence § 1718 (Chadbourn rev. 1976).

5. West Chicago Street Railway Co. v. Kennelly, 170 Ill. 508, 48 N.E. 996 (1897); Kennedy v. Rochester City and Brighton Railroad Co., 130 N.Y. 654, 29 N.E. 141 (1891).

6. Shover v. Iowa Lutheran Hospital, 252 Iowa 706, 107 N.W.2d 85 (1961) (hospital patient's roommate); Caspermeyer v. Florsheim Shoe Store Co., 313 S.W.2d 198 (Mo.App.1958) (wife); Fagan v. Newark, 78 N.J. Super. 294, 188 A.2d 427 (1963) (wife); Plank v. Heirigs, 83 S.D. 173, 156 N.W.2d 193 (1968) (nurse).

7. Lowery v. Jones, 219 Ala. 201, 121 So. 704 (1929); Martin v. P. H. Hanes Knitting Co., 189 N.C. 644, 127 S.E. 688 (1925). See generally, 6 Wigmore, Evidence § 1722(b) (Chadbourn rev.1976). Courts have sometimes been relatively lax in classifying symptoms, as "present" symptoms, however. See Hartford Accident & Indemnity Co. v. Baugh, 87 F.2d 240 (5th Cir.1937), noted in 36 Mich.L.Rev. 142 (1937) ("He came to the office and told me that his sputum was stained with blood" admissible); Bloomberg v. Laventhal, 179 Cal. 616, 178 P. 496 (1919) (testimony that plaintiff complained that he had pains in the head and could not sleep admissible).

events furnishing the cause of the condition.[8]

Judicial opinions have frequently said that, in order to qualify under this hearsay exception, the statement must be a "natural and spontaneous" expression of present bodily condition.[9] In practice this seems to have meant that the only foundation ordinarily required is a showing of a statement describing a then existing bodily condition of the declarant, reserving to the judge, however, discretion to exclude if circumstances disclose clearly that the statement was made with a view to manufacturing evidence.[10]

The Federal and Revised Uniform Evidence Rules (1974) contain a hearsay exception, without regard to the unavailability of the declarant, for

> A statement of the declarant's then existing . . . physical condition (such as . . . pain and bodily health) . . . .[11]

This provision in general incorporates the considerations set forth in the preceding discussion. While the rule in terms contains no requirement that the statement be spontaneous, it is clear from the Advisory Committee's Note to the Federal Rule that the rule is a specialized application of the broader rule recognizing a hearsay exception for statements describing a present sense impression,[12] the cornerstone of which is spontaneity. If circumstances clearly indicate a lack of spontaneity, e.g. an intention to manufacture evidence, exclusion should follow.[13]

WESTLAW REFERENCES

statement* stated say said tell told /s physical body bodily /s sensation* feeling* symptom* condition pain! hurt! /p hearsay
157k268

§ 292. Statements of Bodily Feelings, Symptoms, and Condition: (b) Statements to Physicians Consulted for Treatment [1]

Statements of a presently existing bodily condition made by a patient to a doctor consulted for treatment [2] have almost universally been admitted as evidence of the facts stated,[3] and even courts greatly limiting the admissibility of declarations of bodily condition generally have admitted statements made under these circumstances.[4] Although statements to physicians are not likely to be entirely spontaneous, since they are usually made in response to questions, their reliability is assured by the likelihood that the patient believes that the effectiveness of the treatment he receives may depend largely upon the accuracy of the information he provides the physician.[5] Because of this strong assurance of reliability courts tend to expand the exception to include statements

---

8. See 6 Wigmore, Evidence § 1722(a) (Chadbourn rev. 1976).

9. Rogers v. Detroit, 289 Mich. 86, 286 N.W. 167 (1939) ("The controlling test of the admissibility of exclamations of pain is 'spontaneity.'"); Caspermeyer v. Florsheim Shoe Store Co., 313 S.W.2d 198 (Mo.App. 1958); Fagan v. Newark, 78 N.J.Super. 294, 188 A.2d 427 (1963).

10. Appellate courts, affirming trial court decisions to admit such declarations, have often emphasized those circumstances of the declarations which suggest reliability. E.g., Fagan v. Newark, 78 N.J.Super. 294, 188 A.2d 427 (1963) (deceased's declaration that he felt dizzy and ill was made naturally and without apparent premeditation); Indian Oil Tool Co. v. Thompson, 405 P.2d 104 (Okl.1965) (emphasis on fact that deceased's declaration that he had a pain in his chest made while "under shock").

11. Fed.R.Evid. and Rev.Unif.R.Evid. (1974) 803(3).

12. Advisory Committees Notes, Fed.R.Evid. 803(1), (3).

13. The judge's discretion to exclude misleading evidence should also be considered. See § 185 supra.

§ 292

1. See generally, 6 Wigmore, Evidence §§ 1719–1720 (Chadbourn rev.1976), 29 Am.Jur.2nd Evidence §§ 683–686; C.J.S. Evidence § 246(b); Annot., 37 A.L.R.3d 778, 783–816, 55 A.L.R.Fed. 689; Dec.Dig. Evidence ⊂=128.

2. Statements made to non-treating physicians are discussed in § 293 infra.

3. Kometani v. Heath, 50 Hawaii 89, 431 P.2d 931 (1967); 6 Wigmore, Evidence § 1719 (Chadbourn rev. 1976).

4. Greinke v. Chicago City Railway Co., 234 Ill. 564, 85 N.E. 327 (1908).

5. "All . . . statements made by the patient to the examining physician as to his present or past symptoms are known by the patient who is seeking medical assistance to be required for proper diagnosis and treatment and by reason thereof, are viewed as highly

made by a patient to a physician concerning *past* symptoms.[6] This seems appropriate, as patients are likely to recognize the importance to their treatment of accurate statements as to past as well as present symptoms.[7] Some courts may, however, continue to admit the testimony only for the limited purpose of "explaining the basis for the physician's conclusion" rather than to prove the fact of the prior symptoms.[8]

The exception may be taken one step further to encompass statements made to a physician concerning the cause or the external source of the condition to be treated. In some cases the special assurance of reliability—the patient's belief that accuracy is essential to effective treatment—also applies to statements concerning the cause, and a physician who views this as related to diagnosis and treatment might reasonably be expected to communicate this to the patient and perhaps take other steps to assure a reliable response.[9] However, when statements as to causation enter the realm of fixing fault it is unlikely that the patient or the physician regarded them as related to diag-

nosis or treatment. In such cases, the statements lack any assurance of reliability and would properly be excluded. "Thus a patient's statement that he was struck by an automobile would qualify, but not his statement that the car was driven through a red light."[10] Some courts may nevertheless still adhere to a position requiring the exclusion of any statements related to cause.[11]

Federal and Revised Uniform Evidence Rule (1974) 803(4) provide a hearsay exception, regardless of availability of declarant, for

> Statements made for purposes of medical diagnosis or treatment and describing medical history, or past or present symptoms, pain, or sensations, or the inception or general character of the cause or external source thereof insofar as reasonably pertinent to diagnosis or treatment.

The statement need not have been made to a physician; one made to a hospital attendant, ambulance driver, or member of the family may qualify.[12] Nor does the rule require that the statement be made by the patient.[13] The rule is broadly drawn as to sub-

---

reliable and apt to state true facts." Goldstein v. Sklar, 216 A.2d 298, 305 (Me.1966).

6. Meaney v. United States, 112 F.2d 538 (2d Cir. 1940) (discussion by L. Hand, J.); Roosa v. Boston Loan Co., 132 Mass. 439 (1882); Peterson v. Richfield Plaza, 252 Minn. 215, 89 N.W.2d 712, 712–22 (1958) (physician permitted to testify as to plaintiff's statements concerning symptoms experienced prior to examination); Kennedy v. Upshaw, 66 Tex. 442, 1 S.W. 308 (1886); Missouri, Kansas & Texas Railway Co. v. Dalton, 56 Tex.Civ.App. 82, 120 S.W. 240 (1909).

7. See the discussions in Meaney v. United States, 112 F.2d 538 (2d Cir.1940) and Peterson v. Richfield Plaza, 252 Minn. 215, 89 N.W.2d 712, 719–722 (1958).

8. Bases for expert opinions are discussed in § 15 supra.

With regard to statements to psychiatrists, the reasoning that supports the hearsay exception for statements to physicians generally may be questioned, since the credibility of the statement may be skewed by the very condition under inquiry, as well as by the breadth of the psychiatric interview. The practice of admitting psychiatric interviews with instructions limiting their use to showing the basis of the psychiatrist's opinion has greater validity than similar limitation upon medical history generally. See State v. Griffin, 99 Ariz. 43, 406 P.2d 397 (1965); State v. Wade, 296 N.C. 454, 251 S.E.2d 407 (1979); State v. Myers, 222 S.E.2d 300 (W.Va.1976). The wide variation of possible situations

suggests resort to the judge's discretion to exclude under Federal Rule 403 if appropriate. See § 185 supra; Annot., 55 A.L.R.Fed. 689, 699.

9. Shell Oil Co. v. Industrial Commission, 2 Ill.2d 590, 119 N.E.2d 224 (1954) (patient's statement that he slipped while pulling pipe and injured back).

10. Advisory Committee's Note, Fed.R.Evid. 803(4). See also Hassell v. State, 607 S.W.2d 529 (Tex.Cr.App. 1981) (criminal assault; error to admit child victim's statement to physician that defendant mother hit her with a broom).

11. Brewer v. Henson, 96 Ga.App. 501, 100 S.E.2d 661 (1957) (physician's testimony as to what plaintiff said concerning circumstances of automobile collision not admissible); Bauer v. Independent Stave Co., 417 S.W.2d 693 (Mo.App.1967) (surgeon's testimony that plaintiff reported that he did considerable tugging and pulling on a small cart properly disregarded in determining how injury occurred); Mott v. Clark, 88 R.I. 257, 146 A.2d 924 (1958) (statement to physician at time of admission to hospital that injuries were sustained when plaintiff was knocked down by someone opening restaurant door not admissible).

12. Advisory Committee's Note, Fed.R.Evid. 803(4).

13. See Welter v. Bowman Dairy Co., 318 Ill.App. 305, 47 N.E.2d 739 (1943) (statement by mother of sick baby admitted).

ject matter, including medical history and descriptions of past and present symptoms, pain, and sensations. Descriptions of cause are allowed if they reasonably pertain to diagnosis or treatment,[14] but statements of fault are unlikely to qualify.[15]

 WESTLAW REFERENCES

157k128 /p hearsay

---

§ 293. Statements of Bodily Feelings, Symptoms, and Condition: (c) Statements Made to Physicians Employed Only to Testify [1]

Many courts have drawn a sharp line between statements made to physicians consulted by the declarant for purposes of treatment and those made to physicians consulted solely with the anticipation that the physician will testify in court on the declarant's behalf. The limitations placed on the latter have differed among jurisdictions.

1. Numerous courts have held that descriptive statements of present pain or symptoms made to a physician consulted solely for purposes of preparing him to testify in the declarant's behalf are not admissible as substantive evidence of the pain or symptom under the general exception to the hearsay rule for statements of bodily condition.[2] This restriction is based on the con-

clusion that where the declarant does not anticipate that his treatment's effectiveness will depend upon the accuracy of his statements, the underlying rationale for the exception does not exist. Moreover, if the declarant anticipates that enhancement of his symptoms will inure to his benefit in the subsequent litigation, there is also an affirmative motive to falsify or at least exaggerate. For these reasons, the general exception has been held inapplicable.

2. If a physician has been consulted for purposes of treatment, courts that would refuse to admit the physician's testimony of the "history" related by the patient as evidence of the truth of the matters asserted may admit it for the limited purpose of "explaining the basis of the physician's opinion".[3] A few courts, however, have held or indicated that physicians consulted solely for purposes of testimony may not recount what was told them, even for the purpose of explaining their opinions or conclusions.[4]

3. A few courts, emphasizing the self-serving nature of representations made to physicians consulted for purposes of subsequent testimony, have adopted the extreme position that those physicians are confined to giving opinions based solely upon objective facts personally observed by them or upon hypothetical questions. Any opinion or conclusion based even in part upon "subjec-

---

14. United States v. Iron Shell, 633 F.2d 77 (8th Cir. 1980), cert. denied 450 U.S. 1001 (child victim's description of rape to medical examiner admitted); State v. Red Feather, 205 Neb. 734, 289 N.W.2d 768 (1980) (same).

15. Roberts v. Hollocher, 664 F.2d 200 (8th Cir. 1981) (proper to exclude physician's diagnosis, in suit claiming police brutality, that plaintiff's condition was "consistent with excessive force" as probably based on plaintiff's account); Garcia v. Watkins, 604 F.2d 1297 (10th Cir.1979) (statement by one of plaintiffs to driver that defendant had forced their vehicle off the road).

§ 293

1. See generally, Annot., 37 A.L.R.3d 778; 29 Am. Jur.2nd Evidence § 684; C.J.S. Evidence § 246(b); Annot., 37 A.L.R.3d 778, 816–26.

2. Gentry v. Watkins-Carolina Trucking Co., 249 S.C. 316, 154 S.E.2d 112 (1967), adopting the "majority" view that a physician consulted as a prospective witness may testify to the plaintiff's statements of pres-

ent condition and past symptoms; that the testimony is not admissible as proof of the facts stated but, in the absence of fraud or bad faith, as information relied upon by the physician to support his opinion. See also Wilkinson v. Grover, 181 So.2d 591 (Fla.App.1965); Wolfson v. Rumble, 121 Ga.App. 549, 174 S.E.2d 469 (1970) (subjective complaints of pain made to "examining physician" not admissible to prove pain but admissible to explain diagnosis).

3. See § 292 n. 8 supra. See also Commonwealth Division of Forestry v. Farler, 391 S.W.2d 371 (Ky.App. 1965); Uberto v. Kaufman, 348 Mass. 171, 202 N.E.2d 822 (1964). See generally Dec.Dig. Evidence ⟨key⟩555(j).

4. Korleski v. Needham, 77 Ill.App.2d 328, 222 N.E.2d 334 (1966); Mary Helen Coal Corp. v. Bigelow, 265 S.W.2d 69 (Ky.App.1954); Cruce v. Gulf, Mobil, & Ohio Railroad Co., 361 Mo. 1138, 238 S.W.2d 674 (1951) (may relate declarations of present symptoms only); Brotherhood of Locomotive Firemen and Enginemen v. Raney, 101 S.W.2d 863 (Tex.Civ.App.1937).

tive" facts, i.e., what the subject has said about the history of his condition or his symptoms, is therefore inadmissible.[5] This, of course, is inconsistent with general medical practice which involves use of this information in forming opinions acted upon in the course of treatment and with the modern rule that medical opinions based in part upon factors not within the personal knowledge of the testifying physician are admissible.[6]

The dubious propriety of these restrictions was probably at least partially responsible for the limited view taken by the courts as to what constitutes consultation solely for purposes of obtaining testimony from the physician consulted. The basic question was whether there was any significant treatment motive; if this existed, any additional motive of obtaining testimony was to be ignored.[7] For example, a physician's testimony should not be governed by these restrictions despite the fact that he was consulted after the declarant retained an attorney [8] or even at the attorney's recommendation.[9] The fact that no treatment was actually given is not controlling,[10] but subsequent reliance upon advice of a treatment nature given by the physician is strong evidence of a treatment motive for the initial consultation.[11]

These restrictions have not stood the test of analysis or of the realities of practice. The nonsense of saying, particularly to juries, that patients' statements may be considered as explaining the physician's opinion but not as proof of the matter stated is now widely recognized. Also, contrived evidence has been avoided at too great cost in departure from the realities of medical practice. Accordingly, the trend is strongly in the direction of eliminating any differences in the admissibility of patients' statements to testifying as contrasted with treating physicians. The Federal and Revised Uniform Evidence Rules (1974) treat both alike.[12] The general reliance upon "subjective" facts by the medical profession and the ability of its members to evaluate the accuracy of statements made to them is considered sufficient protection against contrived symptoms.[13]

 WESTLAW REFERENCES

physician* doctor* /s purpose* prepar! /4 testify! testimony trial litigat! /p inadmissible hearsay

---

§ 294. Statements of Mental State: (a) Statements of Present Mental or Emotion-

---

5. For an extreme example see Shaughnessy v. Holt, 236 Ill. 485, 86 N.E. 256 (1908) (error to admit error of physicians that plaintiff's responses when touched with test tubes of hot and cold water indicated nervous deterioration, although she herself testified that her answers were true. Compare Dickeson v. Baltimore & Ohio Chicago Terminal Railroad Co., 42 Ill.2d 103, 245 N.E.2d 762 (1969) (I.Q. test results not subjective). Illinois has since by decision adopted Fed.R. Evid. 703, which no doubt overrules *Shaughnessy*. See § 15 supra.

6. See § 15 supra.

7. Jensen v. Elgin, Joliet and Eastern Railway Co., 24 Ill.2d 383, 182 N.E.2d 211 (1962); Erdman v. Frazin, 39 Wis.2d 1, 158 N.W.2d 281 (1968).

8. Yellow Cab Co. v. Hicks, 224 Md. 563, 168 A.2d 501 (1961); General Motors Corp. v. Altson, 252 Md. 51, 249 A.2d 130 (1969); Plesko v. Milwaukee, 19 Wis.2d 210, 120 N.W.2d 130 (1963).

9. Yellow Cab Co. v. Hicks, 224 Md. 563, 168 A.2d 501 (1961).

10. Fisher Body Division, General Motors Corp. v. Altson, 252 Md. 51, 249 A.2d 130 (1969).

11. Padgett v. Southern Railway Co., 396 F.2d 303, 308 (6th Cir. 1968) (actual reliance by plaintiff upon physician's advice "is sufficient to eliminate the danger of self-serving declarations made to physician merely to qualify him as an expert for trial."); Conway v. Tamborini, 68 Ill.App.2d 190, 215 N.E.2d 303 (1966) (daily performance of exercises prescribed by physician relied upon in sustaining trial court's finding that consultation was not solely for purposes of obtaining testimony). But see Jensen v. Elgin, Joliet and Eastern Railway Co., 24 Ill.2d 383, 182 N.E.2d 211 (1962) (where plaintiff consulted physician at attorney's request and without knowledge of his regular doctor there was nothing to indicate that plaintiff thought his statements would be used as a basis for treatment and the physician was treated as one consulted solely in anticipation of testimony).

12. Rule 803(4) provides a hearsay exception for statements "made for purposes of diagnosis *or* treatment." (Emphasis supplied).

13. The bases of expert opinion are discussed in § 15 supra. A hearsay exception for data relied upon is treated in § 324.1 infra.

al State to Show a State of Mind or Emotion in Issue[1]

The substantive law often makes legal rights and liabilities hinge upon the existence of a particular state of mind or feeling in a person involved in the transaction at issue. Thus such matters as the intent to steal or kill, or the intent to have a certain paper take effect as a deed or will, or the maintenance or transfer of the affections of a spouse may come into issue in litigation. When this is so the mental or emotional state of the person becomes an ultimate object of search. It is not sought to be proved as evidence from which the person's earlier or later conduct may be inferred but as an operative fact upon which a cause of action or defense depends. While such a state may be proved by the person's actions, the statements of the person are often a primary source of evidence on this matter.[2] In most cases, the statements are not assertive of the declarant's present state of mind and are therefore not hearsay.[3] Courts, however, have tended to lump together statements asserting the declarant's state of mind, hence arguably hearsay, with those tending to prove the state of mind circumstantially, arguably nonhearsay, applying a general exception to the hearsay rule without regard to the possibility that many could be treated simply as nonhearsay.[4]

§ 294

1. See generally, 6 Wigmore, Evidence §§ 1714, 1725 1740 (Chadbourn rev.1976); Hinton, States of Mind and the Hearsay Rule, 1 U.Chi.L.Rev. 394 (1934); Morgan, Evidence 1941–1945, 59 Harv.L.Rev. 481 (1946); 29 Am.Jur.2nd Evidence §§ 650–652, 654; C.J.S. Evidence §§ 255–258; Dec.Dig. Evidence ⬥268, 269, 271(6), Criminal Law ⬥415(1), (3), (5).

2. The person in question may, of course, testify as to his own mental or emotional state. United States v. Dozier, 672 F.2d 531 (5th Cir.1982), rehearing denied 677 F.2d 113, cert. denied 103 S.Ct. 256.

3. See § 246 supra.

In Loetsch v. New York City Omnibus Corp., 291 N.Y. 308, 52 N.E.2d 448 (1943), a suit by a husband for the death of his wife, on the issue of damages, measured by the pecuniary value to the husband of his wife's continuance of life, the defendant offered in evidence the will of the wife, containing this statement: "Whereas I have been a faithful, dutiful, and loving wife to my husband, Dean Yankovich, and whereas he has reciprocated my tender affections for him with acts of cruelty and indifference, and whereas he has failed to support and maintain me in that station of life which would have been possible and proper for him, I hereby limit my bequest to him to one dollar." On appeal, the exclusion of this statement was held erroneous, and the court (Thacher, J.) said, "Such statements are evidence of the decedent's state of mind and are probative of a disposition on the part of the declarant which has a very vital bearing upon the reasonable expectancy, or lack of it, of future assistance or support if life continues. . . . No testimonial effect need be given to the statement, but the fact that such a statement was made by the decedent, whether true or false, is compelling evidence of her feelings toward, and relations to, her husband. As such it is not excluded under the hearsay rule but is admissible as a verbal act."

Compare United States v. Taglione, 546 F.2d 194 (5th Cir.1977), holding it error, in prosecution for extortion, to exclude evidence that accused asked his lawyer if it would be all right to negotiate for a reward, as relevant to intent. While the evidence seems not to be hearsay, the court treated it as falling within the hearsay exception for declarations of state of mind. The result is, of course, the same either way. See, also United States v. Green, 680 F.2d 520 (7th Cir.1982), cert. denied 103 S.Ct. 493 (proper to admit contemporaneous statements of victim indicating lack of consent in kidnap prosecution).

4. E.g., Rosenbloom v. Metromedia, Inc., 289 F.Supp. 737, 748 (E.D.Pa.1968) reversed on other grounds 415 F.2d 892 (3d Cir.1969) (plaintiff's testimony that former customers stated, "You are a racketeer. We won't have anything to do with you." admissible to establish customer's motive for refusing to deal with plaintiff); Beliveau v. Goodrich, 185 Neb. 98, 173 N.W.2d 877 (1970) (agent's declaration after loss of suit that a new petition would be filed was admissible to prove the bona fides of the defense of the first suit); Doern v. Crawford, 36 Wis.2d 470, 153 N.W.2d 581 (1967) (statement of plaintiff that he did not like being away from his wife was admissible to prove his intent that his absence be only temporary where plaintiff's status as an insured under an insurance policy depended upon whether his absence was intended to be permanent).

Similar hearsay questions arise with respect to public opinion and other polls. See the thoughtful opinion of Feinberg, J., in Zippo Manufacturing Co. v. Rogers Imports, Inc., 216 F.Supp. 670 (S.D.N.Y.1963). Since the question whether responses given by those polled are hearsay does not affect admissibility, the critical issues tend to hinge upon the acceptability of techniques employed, the propriety of the questions used, the selection of the universe to be studied, choice of samples, and so on, all of which lie in the realm of relevancy. Literature on the subject includes: Blum et al., The Art of Opinion Research: A Lawyer's Appraisal of an Emerging Service, 24 U.Chi.L.Rev. 1 (1956); Bonynge, Trademark Surveys and Techniques and Their Use in Litigation, 48 A.B.A.J. 329 (1962); Sprowls, The Admissibility of Sample Data into a Court of Law: A Case

The special assurance of reliability for statements of present state of mind rests, as in the case with statements of bodily condition, upon their spontaneity and probable sincerity.[5] This has been assured by the requirements that the statements must purport to relate to a condition of mind or emotion existing at the time of the statement and, as sometimes stated, must have been made under circumstances indicating apparent sincerity.[6] As was said in a famous case, if the declarant were called to testify "his own memory of his state of mind at a former time is no more likely to be clear and true than a bystander's recollection of what he then said."[7] Unavailability of declarant is not required.[8]

Common examples of statements used to prove mental state at the time of the statement include statements of intent to make a certain place the declarant's home offered to establish domicile,[9] statements expressive of mental suffering to prove that element of

damages,[10] a statement of willingness to allow one the use of the declarant's automobile offered to prove that the car was used with the owner's consent under the terms of an insurance policy,[11] statements accompanying a transfer of property showing intent, or lack of intent, to defraud creditors,[12] statements of ill will to show malice or the required state of mind in criminal cases,[13] and statements showing fear.[14]

Although it is required that the statement describe a state of mind or feeling existing at the time of the statement, the evidentiary effect of the statement is broadened by the notion of the continuity in time of states of mind. For example, if a declarant tells on Tuesday of his then-existing intention to go on a business trip for his employer the next day, this will be evidence not only of his intention at the time of the statement but also of the same purpose the next day when he is on the road.[15] Continuity may also look backwards. Thus, when there is evidence

History, 4 U.C.L.A.L.Rev. 222 (1957); Zeisel, The Uniqueness of Survey Evidence, 45 Cornell L.Q. 322 (1960); Annot., 76 A.L.R.2d 619. See also Advisory Committee's Note, Fed.R.Evid. 703.

5. See 6 Wigmore, Evidence § 1714 (Chadbourn rev. 1976); see § 291 supra.

6. Elmer v. Fessenden, 151 Mass. 359, 24 N.E. 208 (1889) (must be "made with no apparent motive for misstatement"); Hall v. American Friends Service Committee, Inc., 74 Wn.2d 467, 445 P.2d 616 (1968) (must be "circumstantial probability" of trustworthiness). But see Smith v. Smith, 364 Pa. 1, 70 A.2d 530 (1950) (self-serving nature of declaration goes only to weight). See § 290 supra.

7. Mutual Life Insurance Co. v. Hillmon, 145 U.S. 285, 295 (1892).

8. See § 253 supra as to unavailability.

9. Matter of Newcomb, 192 N.Y. 238, 84 N.E. 950 (1908) (evidence that testatrix wrote to friends indicating her intention to make New Orleans her permanent home admissible); Smith v. Smith, 364 Pa. 1, 70 A.2d 630 (1950) (statement of intent to live in Florida admissible). See generally, 6 Wigmore, Evidence §§ 1727, 1984 (Chadbourn rev.1976); Restatement Second, Conflict of Laws 81 (1971).

10. Missouri, Kansas & Texas Railway Co. v. Linton, 141 S.W. 129 (Tex.Civ.App.1911) (plaintiff's statement that "She felt like her heart would burst and that she could not live" admissible to prove damages for mental anguish).

11. American Employers Insurance Co. v. Wentworth, 90 N.H. 112, 5 A.2d 265 (1939). Perhaps

more properly classed as a verbal act. See § 249 supra.

12. Sanger Brothers v. Colbert, 84 Tex. 668, 19 S.W. 863 (1892) (transferor's statement when receiving price that he intended to pay his debts admissible).

13. E.g., Hall v. State, 31 Tex.Cr.R. 565, 21 S.W. 368 (1893) (threats against victim admissible in murder case in which accused introduced evidence of intoxication to disprove malice). See generally, 6 Wigmore, Evidence § 1732 (Chadbourn rev.1976).

14. United States v. Adcock, 558 F.2d 397, 43 A.L.R. Fed. 851 (8th Cir.1977), cert. denied 434 U.S. 921 (statements by extortion victim); L.K.M. v. Department for Human Resources, 621 S.W.2d 38 (Ky.App. 1981) (statements by children in proceeding to terminate parental rights).

15. Lewis v. Lowe & Campbell Athletic Goods Co., 247 S.W.2d 800 (Mo.1952). See also Ickes v. Ickes, 237 Pa. 582, 85 A. 885 (1912) (husband's statements on day before leaving wife admissible to prove his motive on that day and the next when he did leave); In re Goldsberry's Estate, 95 Utah 379, 81 P.2d 1106 (1938) (statements of testator on day before will executed admissible to show undue influence on that day and on next when will was executed).

Some of the cases of statements of intent have insisted that the statement closely accompany in time some step in furtherance of the act. Common examples are purpose or destination of a journey, domicile, and suicide. Gassaway v. Gassaway & Owen, 220 N.C. 694, 18 S.E.2d 120 (1942) (error in compensation case to admit statement of decedent showing intent to be on job

that a will has been mutilated by the maker, his subsequent statements of a purpose inconsistent with the will are received to show his intent to revoke it at the time he mutilated it.[16] Similarly, whether payment of money or a conveyance was intended by the donor as a gift may be shown by his statement made before, at the time of, or after the act or transfer.[17] Since, however, the duration of states of mind or emotion varies with the particular attitudes or feelings at issue and with the cause, it is reasonable to require as a condition of invoking the continuity notion that the statement mirror a state of mind which, in light of all the circumstances including proxity in time, has some probability of being the same condition existing at the material time. Where there is room for doubt, the matter should be left to the discretion of the trial judge.

Declarations such as those involved here frequently include assertions other than as to state of mind, as, for example, assertions that the defendant's acts caused the state of mind. The truth of those assertions may coincide with other issues in the case, such as

whether the defendant's acts did in fact cause the state of mind. When this is so, the normal practice is to admit the statement and direct the jury to consider it only in proof of the state of mind and to disregard it as evidence of the other issues.[18] Compliance with these instructions is probably beyond the jury's ability and almost certainly beyond their willingness. Where there is adequate evidence on the other issues, this probably does little harm. But in a case where the mental state is provable by other available evidence and the danger of harm from improper use by the jury of the offered declarations is substantial, the judge's discretion to exclude the statements has been recognized.[19]

Federal and Revised Uniform Evidence Rule (1974) 803(3) provide a hearsay exception, without regard to unavailability of declarant, for

A statement of the declarant's then existing state of mind, emotion, sensation . . . (such as intent, plan, motive, design, mental feeling . . . .

when killed in automobile collision, since not connected with act of departure or preparation to depart); Viles v. Waltham, 157 Mass. 542, 32 N.E. 901 (1892) (proper to admit statement of intent to change residence since close in time to departure for new residence); Greenacre v. Filbey, 276 Ill. 294, 114 N.E. 536 (1916) (dram shop action for death of deceased killed by train while lying on track; proper to exclude statements showing preoccupation with suicide over two year period, since none was made for previous two weeks). No such requirement is found in Federal or Revised Uniform Evid. Rules (1974) 803(3), nor is one founded in reason. Any problem of remoteness in time should be approached from the point of view of relevancy. See § 185 supra.

16. Crampton v. Osborn, 356 Mo. 125, 201 S.W.2d 336 (1947).

17. Casey v. Casey, 97 Cal.App.2d 875, 218 P.2d 842 (1950) (statements of decedent after conveyance admissible to show whether it was intended as gift or in trust); O'Neal v. O'Neal, 9 N.J.Super. 36, 74 A.2d 614 (1950) (oral statements of transferor of land admissible to rebut resulting trust). It has been held that if the donor's words at the time of transfer unequivocally indicate an intent to make a gift, his subsequent statements to the contrary will not be received. Shaver v. Canfield, 21 Cal.App.2d 734, 70 P.2d 507 (1937); Wilbur v. Grover, 140 Mich. 187, 103 N.W. 583 (1905). But this has been held inapplicable where the issue is

whether there was, at the time of the transfer, the intent required for delivery and thus for a gift. Williams v. Kidd, 170 Cal. 631, 151 P. 1 (1915). See generally, Annot., 105 A.L.R. 398, 402, 410.

18. Greater New York Live Poultry Chamber of Commerce v. United States, 47 F.2d 156 (2d Cir.1931) (in prosecution for conspiracy to restrain interstate trade in poultry, statements of receivers as to why they refused to sell to recalcitrant market men admissible to show state of mind of declarants but not to show external facts asserted as the basis for this state of mind, and defendant would have been entitled to such an instruction had he requested it); Adkins v. Brett, 194 Cal. 252, 193 P. 251 (1920) (in alienation of affection case, wife's statements concerning relations with defendant admissible to show feelings of wife but not to prove acts and conduct of defendant described in the statements); Johnson v. Richards, 50 Idaho 150, 294 P. 507 (1930) (husband's statements concerning wife, when admissible in suit for alienation of affections, competent only to prove husband's state of mind); Elmer v. Fessenden, 151 Mass. 359, 24 N.E. 208 (1889); Schoot v. Townsend, 106 Tex. 322, 166 S.W. 1138 (1914). The legitimacy of inferring from state of mind the happening of the act claimed to have caused the state of mind is discussed in § 296 infra.

19. See the discussion by Olney, J. in Adkins v. Brett, 184 Cal. 252, 193 P. 251, 254 (1920).

The rule is entirely consistent with the hearsay exception as developed by the courts at common law and discussed above in this section of text.

Insanity. A main source of proof of mental competency or incompetency is the conduct of the person in question, showing his normal or abnormal response to the circumstances of his environment. By this test, every act of the subject's life, within reasonable limits of time, would be relevant to the inquiry.[20] Whether the conduct is verbal or nonverbal is immaterial, and the same is true as to whether it is assertive or nonassertive in form. It is offered as a response to environment, not to prove anything that may be asserted, and is not hearsay.[21] Thus it makes no difference whether declarant says, "I am King Henry the Eighth," or "I believe that I am King Henry the Eighth." Both are offered as evidence of irrationality, and niceties of form should not determine admissibility. If, nevertheless, it is argued that abnormal conduct can be simulated, thereby becoming assertive and therefore hearsay, a short answer is that in that event the evidence would be admissible under the hearsay exception that is the subject of this section.[22] Such inquiries are needless, however, and there is obvious common sense in the judicial disposition to treat alike all irrational manifestations, regardless of form, offered to show mental incompetence, and to admit them under the simpler formula of nonhearsay.[23]

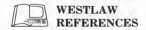

WESTLAW REFERENCES

statement* /40 mental emotional mind /2 state /6 issue

statement* /p "state* of mind" feeling* /4 time /p hearsay

digest(statement* declaration* /s intend! intent**** /s hearsay)

803(3)

§ 295. Statements of Mental State: (b) Statements of Intention Offered to Show Subsequent Acts of Declarant[1]

In the previous section, it was made clear that statements of mental state are generally admissible to prove the declarant's state of mind when that state of mind is at issue. But the probative value of a state of mind obviously may go beyond the state of mind itself. Where a state of mind would tend to prove subsequent conduct, can the two inferential processes be linked together and the statements of state of mind be admitted as proof of the conduct?[2] Can, in other words, X's statements indicating an intent to kill Y be admitted to prove that intent and also that X did in fact subsequently kill Y? The problem at the latter point becomes one of relevancy.

This presents a somewhat more difficult question than the matter of admissibility of statements to show only the state of mind.

---

20. State v. Rodriguez, 126 Ariz. 28, 612 P.2d 684 (1980); Lock v. State, ___ Ind. ___, 403 N.E.2d 1360 (1980); 2 Wigmore, Evidence §§ 228, 229 (Chadbourn rev.1979); Green, Proof of Mental Incompetency and the Unexpressed Major Premise, 53 Yale L.J. 271, 276 (1944); Dec.Dig. Criminal Law ⊃354, Mental Health ⊃8.

21. See §§ 246, 250 supra.

22. People v. Wolfe, 61 Cal.2d 795, 40 Cal.Rptr. 271, 394 P.2d 959 (1964); Ross v. State, 217 Ga. 569, 124 S.E.2d 280 (1962); McGarrh v. State, 249 Miss. 247, 148 So.2d 494, 506 (1963).

23. See Green, op. cit., supra n. 20, at pp. 272, 273. People v. Wolfe, supra n. 22; Young v. Colorado Nat. Bank, 148 Colo. 104, 365 P.2d 701, 710 (1961); Ross v. State, supra n. 22; Sollers v. State, 73 Nev. 248, 316 P.2d 917 (1957).

§ 295

1. See generally, 6 Wigmore, Evidence §§ 1725–26 (Chadbourn rev.1976); Hinton, States of Mind and the Hearsay Rule, 1 U.Chi.L.Rev. 394 (1934); Hutchins & Slesinger, Some Observations on the Law of Evidence—State of Mind to Prove an Act, 38 Yale L.J. 283 (1929); J. Maguire, The Hillmon Case—Thirty-three Years After, 38 Harv.L.Rev. 709 (1925); Seligman, An Exception to the Hearsay Rule, 26 Harv.L.Rev. 146 (1912); Saltzburg, A Special Aspect of Relevance: Countering Negative Inferences Associated with the Absence of Evidence, 66 Calif.L.Rev. 1011, 1046–1054 (1978); Note, 35 Vand.L.Rev. 659 (1982); 29 Am.Jur. 2nd Evidence § 653; C.J.S. Evidence § 256, p. 675. For an historical account of *Hillmon*, see MacCracken, The Case of the Anonymous Corpse, 19 American Heritage 51 (1968).

2. See 1 Wigmore, Evidence § 102 (3d ed.1940).

The special reliability of the statements is less in the present situation, since it is significantly less likely that a declared intention will be carried out than it is that a declared state of mind is actually held. X's declaration that he intends to kill Y is much stronger proof that at the time of the statement (or subsequently) X bore Y malice than it is proof that X in fact later killed Y. Nevertheless, undeniably a person who intended to kill another person is more likely to have done so than a person not shown to have had that intent. The accepted standard of relevancy, i.e. more probable than without the evidence,[3] is easily met.

Despite the failure until fairly recently to recognize the potential value of statements of state of mind to prove subsequent conduct, it is now clear that out-of-court statements which tend to prove a plan, design, or intention of the declarant are admissible, subject to the usual limitations as to remoteness in time and perhaps apparent sincerity [4] common to all statements of mental state, to prove that the plan, design, or intention of the declarant was carried out by the declarant.[5] The leading case is Mutual Life Ins. Co. v. Hillmon,[6] arising out of a suit on life insurance policies by the wife of the insured, Hillmon. The principal issue was whether Hillmon had in fact died; a body had been found at Crooked Creek, Kansas, and the parties disputed whether the body was that of Hillmon. Plaintiff's theory was that Hillmon had left Wichita, Kansas, about March 5, 1879, with one Brown and that on the night of March 18, 1879, while Hillmon

and Brown were camped at Crooked Creek, Hillmon was killed by the accidental discharge of a gun. The defendants, on the other hand, maintained that one Walters had accompanied Hillmon and that the body found at Crooked Creek was Walters'. Defendants offered testimony that Walters had, on or about March 5, 1879, written to his sister that "I expect to leave Wichita on or about March 5, with a certain Mr. Hillmon." An objection to this and similar evidence was sustained. The United States Supreme Court reversed on the ground that the evidence of the letters should have been admitted:

> "The letters . . . were competent not as narratives of facts communicated to the writer by others, nor yet as proof that he actually went away from Wichita, but as evidence that, shortly before the time when other evidence tended to show that he went away, he had the intention of going, and of going with Hillmon, which made it more probable both that he did go and that he went with Hillmon than if there had been no proof of such intention." [7]

Both the Federal Rules and the Revised Uniform Rules (1974) provide a hearsay exception for statements of intent, without regard to the availability of the declarant.[8] While neither in terms addresses the question of admitting intent for the purpose of proving the doing of the intended act, there can be no doubt that the *Hillmon* rule continues. In fact, the Federal Advisory Committee's Note states, "The rule of Mutual Life Ins. Co. v. Hillmon, 145 U.S. 285 (1892), allowing evidence of intention as tending to prove the doing of the act intended, is, of

3. § 185 supra.

4. See § 294, n. 6.

5. United States v. Jenkins, 579 F.2d 840 (4th Cir. 1978), cert. denied 439 U.S. 967 (1971) (statement of W that she was going to L's house admissible in perjury case to show falsity of D's testimony that she did not); United States v. Annunziato, 293 F.2d 373 (2d Cir.1961) (testimony that H. Terker said that he had received a phone call from defendant requesting some money and that he had agreed to deliver it admissible to prove delivery); Nuttall v. Reading Co., 235 F.2d 546, 551–552 (3d Cir.1956) (testimony that deceased asked his employer over the phone, "Why are you forcing me to come to work the way I feel?" and then said, "I guess

I will have to come, then," admissible in FELA case to prove that deceased did go to work under compulsion); Maryland Paper Products Co. v. Judson, 215 Md. 557, 139 A.2d 219 (1958) (wife's testimony that deceased told her that it would be necessary to go to work because he had to stop off on the way to pick up a gear wheel admissible to prove that deceased had in fact picked up the gear wheel).

6. 145 U.S. 285 (1892). The case is discussed in the sources cited in n. 1 supra.

7. 145 U.S. at 295–96.

8. Rule 803(3). See § 294, text following n. 19.

course, left undisturbed." [9]   A number of subsidiary problems remain to be considered, however, both under the Federal and Uniform Rules and under the common law decisions.

The suggestion has been made that unavailability of the declarant should be a requirement.[10]   In fact, in virtually all the cases admitting the statements of intent as proof of the doing of the intended act the declarant was unavailable, and it may well be that the resulting need for the evidence influenced the courts in the direction of admissibility.   However, the decisions do not indicate unavailability as a requirement, nor do the Federal and Uniform Rule.

In somewhat similar vein, in virtually all the cases admitting the evidence the intent stated was quite concrete, i.e. to do a specific act at a specific time and so on.   Again, this quality of specificity is not stated as a requirement, but undeniably probative value is enhanced by its presence.   Its absence not only detracts from probative value but, in its vague generality, may tend to stray into areas of character evidence closed to prosecutors.[11]

The danger of unreliability is greatly increased when the action sought to be proved is not one that the declarant could have per-

formed alone but rather is one that required the cooperation of another person.   If completion of a plan or design requires not only the continued inclination and ability of the declarant to complete it but also the inclination and ability of someone else, arguably the likelihood that the design or plan was completed is substantially less.   Despite some objection,[12] however, courts have not imposed the limitation.   In *Hillmon* itself, in fact, Walters' successful completion of his plan to leave Wichita depended upon the continued willingness of Hillmon to have Walters as a companion and upon Hillmon's willingness and ability to leave at the time planned.   However, it was common ground to all parties that Hillmon did in fact go to Crooked Creek, and the Supreme Court had no occasion to consider this aspect of the case.[13]

A further related problem is raised by the tendency of declarant's statement to prove cooperative action on the part of another person.   If those cooperative actions themselves are at issue, there is a significant danger that the jury will use the declarant's statements as proof not only of the declarant's actions but also of the cooperative actions by the third person.   In effect, the declarant's statement will be taken as proof of

---

9.   Adv.Comm.Note, Fed.R.Evid. 803(3).

10.   Hunter v. State, 40 New Jersey 495 (1878); Hutchins & Slesinger, Some Observations on the Law of Evidence—State of Mind to Prove an Act, 38 Yale L.J. 283, 289 (1929).   Contra, Hinton, States of Mind and the Hearsay Rule, 1 U.Chi.L.Rev. 394, 416 (1934).

11.   E.g., United States v. Curtis, 568 F.2d 643 (9th Cir.1978) (murder-rape; not error to admit statement by defendant one month before event, "[H]e said if he ever took a lady out and she didn't give him what he wanted, he'd kick their [expletive deleted] and take it."

12.   E.g., the dissenting opinion by Mr. Justice Traynor in People v. Alcalde, 24 Cal.2d 177, 148 P.2d 627, 633 (1944):

"It is my opinion that the trial court erred in admitting the testimony that the deceased said . . . that she was going out with 'Frank' [the evening of her murder] . . . .   A statement of intention is admissible to show that the declarant did the intended act. . . .   A statement as to what one person intended to do, however, cannot safely be accepted as evidence of what another probably did. . . . The statement of the deceased in this case that she

was going out with Frank is also a statement that he was going out with her, and it could not be admitted for the limited purpose of showing that she went out with him at the time in question without necessarily showing that he went with her."

The concern of Mr. Justice Traynor is with the use of the statement to prove an act on the part of one other than the declarant when that act is itself an important issue in the case.   Much the same objection, however, can be raised to using the statement to prove only the act of the declarant when that act must necessarily have involved cooperative acts by others, even cooperative acts not directly at issue or material.

13.   In addition to People v. Alcalde, 24 Cal.2d 177, 148 P.2d 627 (1944), discussed in note 12 supra, see United States v. Pheaster, 544 F.2d 353 (9th Cir.1976), cert. denied 429 U.S. 1099 (pre-rules case admitting statement by alleged kidnap victim of intent to meet accused at specified time and place); Hunter v. State, 40 N.J.L. 495 (1878) (statement of murder victim that he was going on a business trip with the accused properly admitted); State v. Vestal, 278 N.C. 561, 180 S.E.2d 755 (1971) (same).

the other person's intent and as proof that this intent was carried out. For example, in the homicide prosecution of Frank, a witness testifies that on the morning of the killing the victim said, "I am going out with Frank tonight." While this tends to prove the victim's acts, it also tends to prove that Frank, the accused, went out with the victim, a fact very much in issue. Despite the danger that juries will be neither willing nor able to make the distinction, courts have tended to admit the statements in these cases with limiting instructions, of questionable effectiveness, directing the jury to consider them only on the issue of the declarant's actions.[14]

Acceptance of the use of statements of state of mind to prove subsequent conduct and recognition of occasions for its application by the courts have differed among types of situations. In will cases, for example, it is now generally established that

when the acts of the decedent are at issue, his previous declarations of intention are received as evidence of his later conduct.[15] Such statements may come in on issues of forgery,[16] alteration,[17] contents of a will,[18] and whether acts of revocation were done by the testator.[19] Despite early decisions to the contrary, or decisions greatly restricting their use,[20] statements of intent to commit suicide have been admitted when offered by the accused in homicide cases to prove that the victim took his own life and in insurance cases to show that the insured took his own life.[21] There has been greater resistance, however, to accepting in criminal cases threats of a third person to commit the act with which the accused is charged as evidence that the act was committed by the third person and therefore not by the accused. Although some opinions suggest an

---

14. See the cases cited in n. 13 supra. See also, State v. Farnam, 82 Or. 211, 161 P. 417 (1916) involving a homicide prosecution. Testimony was received that on the day of the killing the victim, when invited to a friend's house, replied that she could not come because she thought the accused was coming. This was affirmed, although the appellate court indicated that the defendant would have been entitled to a limiting instruction had he requested one. An even more difficult feat by the jury may be called for by an instruction limiting the purpose of the evidence to proving opportunity. State v. Phillips, 68 N.D. 113, 277 N.W. 609 (1938), 86 U.Pa.L.Rev. 904. The Federal Advisory Committee's Note to Rule 803(3) is silent as to this aspect of the *Hillmon* rule. The Report of the House Committee on the Judiciary states, "[T]he Committee intends that the Rule be construed to limit the doctrine of [*Hillmon*], . . . so as to render statements of intent by a declarant admissible only to prove his future conduct, not the future conduct of another person." House Comm. on Judiciary, Fed. Rules of Evidence, H.R.Rep. No. 650, 93d Cong., 1st Sess., p. 13 (1973). The effect on this practice is not wholly clear.

On occasion the problem appears to go unrecognized. Commonwealth v. Lowenberg, 481 Pa. 244, 392 A.2d 1274 (1978) (statement of murder victim that she wanted to see accused held admissible without discussion of relevancy problem). If the action of the other person is proved by evidence other than the hearsay statement, the problem has been said not to arise. United States v. Cicale, 691 F.2d 95, 103 (2d Cir.1982), cert. denied 103 S.Ct. 1771.

15. See 6 Wigmore, Evidence § 1735 (Chadbourn rev.1976).

16. Atherton v. Gaslin, 194 Ky. 460, 239 S.W. 771 (1922); State v. Ready, 78 N.J.L. 599, 75 A. 564 (Ct. of

Errors and Appeals, 1909); Johnson v. Brown, 51 Tex. 65, (1879). Contra, Throckmorton v. Holt, 180 U.S. 552 (1901). Such evidence, however, weighs lightly when contradicted by the testimony of expert document examiners. See In re Creger's Estate, 135 Okl. 77, 274 P. 30 (1929). See generally, Annot., 62 A.L.R.2d 855.

17. Doe d.Schallcross v. Palmer, 16 Q.B. 747, 117 Eng.Rep. 1067 (1851).

18. Sugden v. Lord St. Leonards, 1 Prob.Div. 154 (Ct.App.1876).

19. Stuart v. McWhorter, 238 Ky. 82, 36 S.W.2d 842 (1931). See generally, Annot., 24 A.L.R.2d 514.

20. Commonwealth v. Felch, 132 Mass. 22 (1882); State v. Punshon, 124 Mo. 448, 27 S.W. 1111 (1894), both overruled by decisions cited in n. 21 infra. See generally, 6 Wigmore, Evidence § 1726 n. 4 (Chadbourn rev.1976).

21. Probably the leading homicide case is Commonwealth v. Trefethen, 157 Mass. 180, 31 N.E. 961 (1892), overruling previous case law. See also People v. Salcido, 246 Cal.App.2d 450, 54 Cal.Rptr. 820 (1966); People v. Parriera, 237 Cal.App.2d 275, 46 Cal.Rptr. 835 (1965); Bowie v. State, 185 Ark. 834, 49 S.W.2d 1049 (1932); State v. Ilgenfritz, 215 Mo. 615, 173 S.W. 1041 (1915); Commonwealth v. Santos, 275 Pa. 515, 119 A. 596 (1932). In regard to insurance cases, see Browner v. Royal Indemnity Co., 246 F. 637 (5th Cir. 1917); Smith v. National Beneficial Society, 123 N.Y. 85, 25 N.E. 197 (1890); Klein v. Knights and Ladies of Security, 87 Wash. 179, 151 P. 241 (1915). See generally, Annot., 86 A.L.R. 146, 157; Dec.Dig. Homicide ⟾177. Compare Annot., 93 A.L.R. 413, 426 (admissibility of declarations of insured to negative defense of suicide).

absolute exclusionary rule,[22] others recognize a discretionary power in the trial judge to admit them if he finds sufficient accompanying evidence of motive, overt acts, opportunity, or other circumstances giving substantial significance to the threats.[23]

Homicide and assault cases present another special problem. If the accused claims self-defense, and threats of the victim were known to the accused, these threats are admissible to prove the accused's apprehension of danger and its reasonableness.[24] When used for this purpose, of course, the statements of the victim are not hearsay. But uncommunicated threats pose a more serious problem. They are admissible, if at all, to show the victim's intention to attack the accused and further that he carried out his intention, thus committing the first act of aggression in the fatal altercation.[25] Fear that juries will abuse the evidence has led some courts [26] to admit proof of uncommunicated threats only under qualification. Some of them require only that there be some additional evidence that the victim was the aggressor; testimony by the accused will ordinarily be sufficient.[27] Others require that proof other than the accused's own testimony must admit of some doubt that the accused was the aggressor.[28] Still others hold that the other evidence must itself be sufficient to present a jury question on the issue of which participant was the initial agressor.[29] No qualification appears in the Federal Rules.

The matter of the admissibility of statements of state of mind to prove subsequent conduct is a far different question from that

22. People v. King, 276 Ill. 138, 114 N.E. 601 (1916); Buel v. State, 104 Wis. 132, 80 N.W. 78 (1899). See generally, 1 Wigmore, Evidence § 140 (3d ed. 1940).

23. Alexander v. United States, 138 U.S. 353 (1891); Marrone v. State, 359 P.2d 969, 984–85 (Alas.1961); People v. Perkins, 59 P.2d 1069, 1074–75 (Cal.App.) affirmed 8 Cal.2d 502, 66 P.2d 631 (1937); Dubose v. State, 10 Tex.App. 230 (1881). The restricted admissibility of the evidence has been justified as follows:

"[T]his rule . . . rests fundamentally upon the same considerations which led to the early adoption of the elementary rules that evidence to be admissible must be both relevant and material. It rests upon the necessity that trials of cases must be both orderly and expeditious . . . . To this end it is necessary that the scope of inquiry into collateral and unimportant issues must be severely limited. It is quite apparent that if evidence of motive alone upon the part of other persons were admissible, that in a case involving the killing of a man who had led an active and aggressive life it might be possible for the defendant to produce evidence tending to show that hundreds of other persons had some motive or animus against the deceased; that a great many trial days might be consumed in the pursuit of inquiries which could not be expected to lead to any satisfactory conclusion." People v. Mendez, 193 Cal. 39, 223 P. 65, 70 (1924).

Compare Fed.R.Evid. 403, supra § 185.

24. State v. Jackson, 94 Ariz. 117, 383 P.2d 229 (1963); Morrison v. Lowe, 267 Ark. 361, 590 S.W.2d 299 (1979), appeal after remand 270 Ark. 668, 606 S.W.2d 569; State v. Mitchell, 144 Me. 320, 68 A.2d 387 (1949). See generally, 2 Wigmore, Evidence § 247 (Chadbourn rev.1979); Dec.Dig. Homicide ⊂⇒190(8).

25. See the discussion in Commonwealth v. Rubin, 318 Mass. 587, 63 N.E.2d 344 (1945). Communicated threats are also admissible for this purpose, of course, but this use is usually ignored because of their stronger significance as proof of reasonable apprehension by the accused. See generally 18 U.Chi.L.Rev. 337 (1951); Annot., 98 A.L.R.2d 9 (homicide cases), 98 A.L.R.2d 195 (assault cases); Dec.Dig. Homicide ⊂⇒190(7).

26. Some courts have held the evidence admissible without mention of qualification. Carnes v. Commonwealth, 453 S.W.2d 595 (Ky.App.1970). Others have held it inadmissible without mention of any circumstances in which it might be properly admitted. Burgess v. State, 226 Ga. 529, 175 S.E.2d 829 (1970).

27. Harris v. State, 400 P.2d 64 (Okl.Cr.1965) (some other evidence to support a plea of self-defense); State v. Griffin, 277 S.C. 193, 285 S.E.2d 631 (1981) (semble).

28. Sanders v. State, 245 Ark. 321, 432 S.W.2d 467 (1968) (must be doubt as to who was aggressor); Decker v. State, 234 Ark. 518, 353 S.W.2d 168 (1962); Bowyer v. State, 2 Md.App. 454, 235 A.2d 317 (1967) (must be some evidence of self-defense and some question as to who was aggressor); State v. Debo, 8 Ohio App.2d 325, 222 N.E.2d 656 (1966) (evidence must leave it doubtful who was aggressor).

29. State v. Murdle, 5 N.C.App. 610, 169 S.E.2d 17 (1969) (requiring "testimony *ultra* sufficient to carry the case to the jury tending to show that the killing may have been done from a principle of self preservation"). Some courts would apparently require that the proof amount to a showing of some specific overt act on the part of the victim. State v. Mitchell, 144 Me. 320, 68 A.2d 387 (1949) (must be evidence of some act on the part of the victim that might constitute an attack justifying self-defense); Shinall v. State, 199 So.2d 251 (Miss.1967) cert. denied 389 U.S. 1014 (other proof must show some overt act at the time of the homicide that would cause the slayer to believe that his life was in imminent danger).

of the sufficiency of these statements, standing alone, to support a finding that the conduct occurred.[30] It has reasonably been said that the declarations are themselves insufficient to support the finding and therefore that statements of intention are admitted in corroboration of other evidence to show the acts.[31]

**WESTLAW
REFERENCES**

hillmon & 145 /5 285
statement* declaration* /4 inten! /p hearsay
threat! /s selfdefense /s admissible hearsay

_____

§ 296. Statements of Mental State: (c) Statements of State of Mind to Show Memory or Belief as Proof of Previous Happenings [1]

As was seen in the preceding section, under the *Hillmon*[2] doctrine, statements of intent to perform an act are admissible as proof that the act was in fact done. In contrast, however, a statement by declarant that he had in fact done the act would be excluded by the hearsay rule. Thus Walters' statement that he intended to go to Crooked Creek was admissible, but a later statement by him that he had been to Crooked Creek would have been excluded. Yet it may be argued plausibly that the first statement, which was admitted, is inferior as evidence to the second, which would have been excluded. This is because both statements, it is said, involve the truthfulness of the declarant, but the second statement involves the further risk that supervening events may frustrate the carrying out of the stated

intent. Minds are changed, tickets are lost; popular sayings, literature, and experience are filled with plans that went awry. Accordingly, the argument goes, if the inferior evidence of intent is admitted as proof that the act was done, the superior statement that the act was in fact done should certainly be admitted. In other words, hearsay statements of memory or belief should be admitted as proof that the matter remembered or believed did happen.[3] The result would, of course, be the demise of the hearsay rule, and the courts have not accepted it.

Forty years after *Hillmon*, in Shepard v. United States,[4] a murder prosecution, the trial court had admitted testimony that the victim, the wife of the physician-defendant, had stated to a nurse, "Dr. Shepard has poisoned me." Reversing, the Supreme Court rejected the argument that the statement was admissible as a statement of state of mind:

"[Mutual Life Ins. Co. v. Hillmon] marks the high water line beyond which courts have been unwilling to go. It has developed a substantial body of criticism and commentary. Statements of intention, casting light upon the future, have been sharply distinguished from statements of memory, pointing backwards to the past. There would be an end, or nearly that, to the rule against hearsay if the distinction were ignored.

"The testimony now questioned faced backwards and not forward. This at least it did in its most obvious implications. What is even more important, it spoke of a past act by someone not the speaker.[5]"

After the decision in *Shepard*, the blanket exclusion of statements of memory or belief to prove past events was the subject of sub-

_____

30. See Atherton v. Gaslin, 194 Ky. 460, 239 S.W. 771 (1922).

31. E.g., United States v. Moore, 571 F.2d 76, 49 A.L.R.Fed. 915 (2d Cir.1978) (statements of intent insufficient under circumstances to prove interstate transportation in federal kidnap case); Prichard v. Harvey, 272 Ky. 58, 113 S.W.2d 865 (1938) (declarations alone insufficient to rebut presumption of revocation of lost will).

§ 296

1. See generally, Hinton, States of Mind and the Hearsay Rule, 1 U.Chi.L.Rev. 394, 403–23 (1934);

Hutchins and Slesinger, Some Observations on the Law of Evidence—State of Mind to Prove an Act, 38 Yale L.J. 283, 289–98 (1929); J. Maguire, The Hillmon Case—Thirty-three Years After, 38 Harv.L.Rev. 709, 719–31 (1925); Seligman, An Exception to the Hearsay Rule, 26 Harv.L.Rev. 146 (1912).

2. 145 U.S. 285 (1891). See text supra at § 295, n. 6.

3. Seligman, An Exception to the Hearsay Rule, 26 Harv.L.Rev. 146, 157 (1912).

4. 290 U.S. 96 (1933).

5. Id. at 105–106.

stantial reexamination. Occasional statutes allowed receipt of statements by deceased persons made in good faith and upon personal knowledge before the commencement of the action.[6] The Model Code of Evidence went much farther by allowing any hearsay statement by an unavailable declarant.[7] The original Uniform Rules represented a substantial retreat: they broadly excluded statements "of memory or belief to prove the fact remembered or believed,"[8] but opened up a small area by allowing statements by an unavailable declarant describing an event or condition recently perceived while his recollection was clear, made in good faith prior to the commencement of the action.[9] The Federal Rule, as presented to and adopted by the Supreme Court, incorporated this base, with the added limitation that the statement not be in response to the

instigation of a person engaged in investigating, litigating, or settling a claim.[10] In the Federal Rules as finally enacted by the Congress the prohibition against introducing statements of memory or belief to prove the fact remembered or believed, except as to wills, was retained,[11] but the liberalizing provision for statements of unavailable declarants was omitted and is not in the Federal Rules. It is, however, included for civil cases in the revised Uniform Rules (1974).[12] Courts generally have shown unwillingness to move to the liberal treatment in the absence of rule or statute.[13]

From the blanket exclusion of statements of memory or belief to prove past events, the courts have carved out an area of admissibility for statements by testators made after the execution of an alleged will. Thus testator's statements that he has or has not

---

6. Mass.Gen.Laws Ann. c. 233, § 65; R.I.Gen.Laws 1956, § 9–19–11. The Massachussetts statute was enacted before *Shepard*, that of Rhode Island after. The Massachussetts statute in terms applies in civil cases only. The Rhode Island statute is not thus limited, but in practice appears to be used only in civil cases.

7. Model Code of Evidence Rule 503(a).

8. Uniform Rules Evid. (1953) 63 (12).

9. Id. 63(4)(c).

10. Fed.R.Evid. (Rev.Draft 1971) 804(b)(2); 51 F.R.D. 315.

11. The pertinent Federal Rule in this area, then, is Fed.R.Evid. 803(3):

> The following are not excluded by the hearsay rule, even though the declarant is available as a witness:
>
> . . .
>
> *(3) Then existing mental, emotional, or physical condition.* A statement of the declarant's then existing state of mind . . . but not including a statement of memory or belief to prove the fact remembered or believed unless it relates to the execution, revocation, identification, or terms of declarant's will.

See Marshall v. Commonwealth Aquarium, 611 F.2d 1 (1st Cir.1979) (proper to exclude party's earlier statement as to terms of contract, offered by him to prove terms); Prather v. Prather, 650 F.2d 88 (5th Cir.1981) (similar testimony; error to admit).

12. Rev.U.R.Evid. (1974) 804(b)(5);

> *(b) Hearsay exceptions.* The following are not excluded by the hearsay rule if the declarant is unavailable as a witness:
>
> . . .

> *(5) Statement of recent perception.* In a civil action or proceeding, a statement, not in response to the instigation of a person engaged in investigating, litigating, or settling a claim, which narrates, describes, or explains an event or condition recently perceived by the declarant, made in good faith, not in contemplation of pending or anticipated litigation in which he was interested, and while his recollection was clear.

The Revised Uniform Rules also include the prohibition against memory or belief to prove the fact remembered or believed. R. 803(3).

13. See United States v. Murray, 297 F.2d 812, 816 (2d Cir.1962) cert. denied 369 U.S. 828 (objection properly sustained to question as to whether given individual ever indicated that he had lent Ed Murray money because this would tend primarily to show whether or not such a loan had been made); Stone v. Union Fire Ins. Co., 106 Colo. 522, 107 P.2d 241 (1940) (statement by insurance agent that he had never been notified of chattel mortgage on insured property, erroneously admitted); People v. Steiner, 30 N.Y.2d 762, 333 N.Y.S.2d 423, 284 N.E.2d 577 (1972) (error to admit entries in deceased wife's diary that accused husband was having extramarital affair as motive for murdering her); State v. Vestal, 278 N.C. 561, 180 S.E.2d 755 (1971) (error to admit note written by homicide victim which would tend to prove victim's assertion that facts existed which would give defendant motive to kill victim, although victim's statements of intent to go on trip with victim were admissible). Where, however, strong need exists and indications of reliability are present, some courts have admitted it. Lee v. Mitcham, 69 App.D.C. 17, 98 F.2d 298 (1938); Yarborough v. Prudential Insurance Co., 99 F.2d 874, on rehearing, 100 F.2d 547 (5th Cir.1939); Quayle v. Mackert, 92 Idaho 563, 447 P.2d 679 (1968).

made a will, or that he has made a will of a particular purport, or that he has or has not revoked a will, all are excepted from the ban of the hearsay rule by a preponderance of the recent decisions.[14] Some courts reach this result by a special exception to the hearsay rule for retrospective declarations in will cases.[15] Impetus to recognize such an exception is furnished by the unavailability of the person who best knew the facts and often was the only person with that knowledge, viz. the testator. Special reliability is suggested by the undeniable firsthand knowledge and lack of motive to deceive,[16] though the possibility may exist that testator wished to deceive his relatives.[17] Other courts have simply regarded these statements as statements of memory or belief raising an inference that the belief must have been prompted by facts and acceptable as proof of those facts.[18] The suggestion has also been made, with no small measure of obscurity, that these statements may be regarded not as offered to prove the truth of assertions contained therein but as conduct circumstantially evincing a belief and thus not falling within the hearsay prohibition.[19] The Federal and Revised Uniform Rule

(1974), after creating a hearsay exception for statements of declarant's then existing state of mind, in general terms denies the benefit of the exception to statements of state of mind offered to prove the happening of the event causing the state of mind but from the denial exempts a statement that "relates to the execution, revocation, identification, or terms of declarant's will."[20] This is in accord with the case developments discussed above.

A recurring problem arises in connection with the admissibility of accusatory statements made before the act by the victims of homicide.[21] If the statement is merely an expression of fear, i.e. "I am afraid of D," no hearsay problem is involved since the statement falls within the hearsay exception for statements of mental or emotional condition. This does not, however, resolve the question of admissibility. Since nothing indicates that the victim's emotional state is in issue in the case, the purpose of the offer of the statement must be to suggest the additional step of inferring some further fact from the existence of the emotional state. The obvious inference from the existence of fear is that some conduct of D, probably

---

14. Burton v. Wylde, 261 Ill. 397, 103 N.E. 976 (1914) (later statements of testator admissible on issue of intent to revoke by mutilation); Loy v. Loy, 246 S.W.2d 578 (Ky.App.1952) (statements of testator competent to corroborate other evidence of execution); Lewis v. Lewis, 241 Miss. 83, 129 So.2d 353 (1961) (testimony that deceased had said, "I have got [my will] right here in my pocket" admissible to show existence of will when authorship of offered holographic will in doubt); In re Roeder's Estate, 44 N.M. 429, 103 P.2d 631 (1940) (statements admissible to corroborate other evidence of changes in will); In re Karras' Estate, 109 Ohio App. 403, 166 N.E.2d 781 (1959) (statements of deceased in regard to execution of will admissible where execution was at issue). Contra, Barger v. Barger, 221 Ind. 530, 48 N.E.2d 813 (1943) (post-testamentary declarations inadmissible as evidence of contents of will); Hursh v. Crook, 292 S.W.2d 305 (Mo.1956) (where genuineness of signature at issue, deceased's statement that "Katie wrote my name and I saw her do it" inadmissible). Such statements, if admissible, are probably not enough to sustain a finding. Loy v. Loy, 246 S.W.2d 578 (Ky.App.1952) (statements of deceased alone not enough to sustain a finding of execution of a lost will). See generally 6 Wigmore, Evidence § 1736 (Chadbourn rev.1976); Annots., 28 A.L.R.3d 994, 5 A.L.R.3d 360, 68 A.L.R.2d 855, 41 A.L.R.2d 393,

399–400, 148 A.L.R. 1225, 79 A.L.R. 1447; Dec.Dig. Wills ⟂297.

15. Loy v. Loy, 246 S.W.2d 578 (Ky.App.1952); In re Roeder's Estate, 44 N.M. 429, 103 P.2d 631 (1940).

16. See the argument of Jessell, M.R. in Sugden v. Lord St. Leonards, L.R. [1876] 1 Prob.Div. 154, 241 (Ct.App.).

17. Boylan v. Meeker, 28 N.J.L. 274, 283 (1860):

"A devisor . . . may, to secure his own peace and comfort during life, to relieve himself from unpleasant importunities of expectant heirs, conceal the nature of his testamentary dispositions, and make statements calculated and intended to deceive those with whom he is conversing."

18. Keen v. Keen, L.R. 1873, 3 P. & D. 105; 6 Wigmore, Evidence § 1736, p. 173 (Chadbourn rev.1976).

19. Sugden v. Lord St. Leonards, L.R. [1876] 1 Prob.Div. 154, 202.

20. In Howard Hughes Medical Institute v. Gavin, 96 Nev. 905, 621 P.2d 489 (1980), the court held that the rule does not permit declarations of the testator to be used to supply one of the two credible witnesses required by statute to prove a lost will.

21. Annot., 74 A.L.R.3d 963.

mistreatment or threats, occurred to cause the fear.[22] The possibility of overpersuasion, the prejudicial character of the evidence, and the relative weakness and speculative nature of the inference, all argue against admissibility as a matter of relevance.[23] Even if one is willing to allow the evidence of fear standing alone, however, the fact is that such cases seem to occur but rarely. In life, the situation assumes the form either of a statement by the victim that D has threatened him, from which fear may be inferred, or perhaps more likely a statement of fear because D has threatened him.[24] In either event, the cases have generally excluded the evidence.[25] Not only does the evidence possess the weaknesses suggested above for expressions of fear standing alone, but in addition it seems unlikely that juries can resist using the evidence for forbidden purposes in the presence of specific disclosure of misconduct of D.[26] A strong case for exclusion under *Shepard* [27] is made. While the same pressing need for the evidence may be present as that which led to the invention of the hearsay exception for dying declarations,[28] constructing a case for

trustworthiness is vastly more difficult, and need alone has never been thought sufficient to support a hearsay exception.[29] However, the possibility of saving the day for admissibility in the worthier cases by resort to the hearsay exceptions for startled utterances or dying declarations should not be overlooked.[30]

 WESTLAW REFERENCES

citation(290 +s 96) & judge(cardozo)
statement* declaration* testimony testif! remark** /s
   decedent* /5 fear! afraid

---

§ 297. Excited Utterances [1]

Although sometimes still discussed under the terminology of *res gestae*,[2] an exception to the hearsay rule for certain statements made under the influence of a startling event is universally recognized. Formulations of the exception differ, but all agree on two basic requirements. First, there must be an occurrence or event sufficiently startling to render inoperative the normal reflective thought processes of an observer. Sec-

22. See State v. Bauers, 25 Wn.2d 825, 172 P.2d 279 (1946).

23. Supra § 185. But see State v. Shirley, 7 Or. App. 166, 488 P.2d 1401 (1971); State v. Bauers, supra n. 22.

24. United States v. Brown, 490 F.2d 758 (D.C.Cir. 1974).

25. United States v. Brown, supra n. 24; United States v. Day, 591 F.2d 861, 881 (D.C.Cir.1979); Commonwealth v. DelValle, 351 Mass. 489, 221 N.E.2d 922 (1966); State v. Wauneka, 560 P.2d 1377 (Utah 1977). Contra, State v. Gause, 107 Ariz. 491, 489 P.2d 830 vacated and remanded (on other grounds) in light of Stewart v. Massachusetts, 408 U.S. 845 (1971), commented upon 14 Ariz.L.Rev. 550 (1972); Commonwealth v. Wright, 455 Pa. 480, 317 A.2d 271 (1974). See Seidelson, The State of Mind Exception to the Hearsay Rule, 13 Duquesne L.Rev. 251 (1974); Rice, The State of Mind Exception to the Hearsay Rule: A Response to "Secondary Relevance," 14 Duquesne L.Rev. 219 (1976); Note, 1977 Utah L.Rev. 85.

26. United States v. Day, 591 F.2d 861, 883 (D.C. Cir.1979).

27. Supra, n. 4.

28. See State v. Gause, supra n. 25.

29. Note, 1977 Utah L.Rev. 85, 101, "[A] person gains no credibility by dying."

30. See §§ 297, 298 infra. As a matter of application of the Federal and revised Uniform Rules, equating fear with "memory or belief" under 803(3) seems acceptable in the nonexcited utterance situation, leaving the credible excited utterance situation to be treated under 803(2). Similarly as to 803(1), for present sense impressions.

§ 297

1. See generally, 6 Wigmore, Evidence §§ 1745–64 (Chadbourn rev.1976); Hutchins & Slesinger, Spontaneous Exclamations, 28 Colum.L.Rev. 432 (1928); Slough, Spontaneous Statements and State of Mind, 46 Iowa L.Rev. 224 (1961); Notes, 45 Cornell L.Q. 810 (1960), 29 La.L.Rev. 661 (1969), 54 Mich.L.Rev. 133 (1955); Annot., 13 A.L.R.3d 1114 (statements relating to cause of fires); Annots., 4 A.L.R.3d 149, 74 A.L.R.3d 963 (accusatory statements by homicide victims); Annot., 78 A.L.R.2d 300 (statements by bystanders at time of arrest); Annot., 53 A.L.R.2d 1245 (statements relating to cause of motor vehicle accidents); Annot., 163 A.L.R. 15 (in actions founded on accidents); 29 Am.Jur.2d Evidence §§ 708–737; C.J.S. Evidence §§ 403–421; Dec. Dig. Evidence ⚖︎118–128½, Criminal Law ⚖︎363, 366, 368.

2. E.g., Carroll v. Guffey, 20 Ill.App.2d 470, 156 N.E.2d 267 (1959); Comment, 63 Ky.L.J. 168 (1975).

ond, the statement of the declarant must have been a spontaneous reaction to the occurrence or event and not the result of reflective thought. Although additional requirements are found and will be discussed subsequently, these two elements are undeniably the essence of the exception.

The rationale for the exception lies in the special reliability which is regarded as furnished by the excitement suspending the declarant's powers of reflection and fabrication.[3] This factor also serves to justify dispensing with any requirement that the declarant be unavailable, because it suggests that his testimony on the stand, given at a time when his powers of reflection and fabrication are operative, is at least no more reliable than his out-of-court statement.[4] The entire basis for the exception is, of course, subject to question. While psychologists would probably concede that excitement minimizes the possibility of reflective self-interest influencing the declarant's statements, they have questioned whether this might be outweighed by the distorting effect of shock and excitement upon the de-

clarant's observation and judgment.[5] Despite this doubt concerning its justification, however, the exception is well established.

The sufficiency of the event or occurrence itself to qualify under this exception is seldom questioned. Physical violence, though often present, is not required. An automobile accident,[6] pain or an injury,[7] an attack by a dog,[8] a fight,[9] or even seeing a photograph in a newspaper[10] all may qualify. The courts look primarily to the effect upon the declarant and, if satisfied that the event was such as to cause adequate excitement, the inquiry is ended. A somewhat more serious issue is raised by the occasional requirement of proving the exciting event by some proof other than the statement itself. Under generally prevailing practice, the statement itself is taken as sufficient proof of the exciting event and therefore the statement is admissible despite absence of other proof that an exciting event occurred.[11] Some courts, however, have taken the position that an excited utterance is admissible only if other proof is presented which sup-

---

3. See generally, 6 Wigmore, Evidence § 1747 (Chadbourn rev.1976). The hearsay exception entails no denial of confrontation rights, even though the declarant is unavailable. McLaughlin v. Vinzant, 522 F.2d 448 (1st Cir. 1975), cert. denied 423 U.S. 1037.

4. See Mobile & Montgomery Railroad Co. v. Ashcraft, 48 Ala. 15, 31 (1872): "We regard these declarations as . . . more convincing . . . than the testimony to that effect of the persons themselves some time after the occurrence."

5. "One need not be a psychologist to distrust an observation made under emotional stress; everybody accepts such statements with mental reservation. . . . Fiore tells of an emotionally upset man who testified that hundreds were killed in an accident; that he had seen their heads rolling from their bodies. In reality only one man was killed, and five others injured. Another excited gentlemen took a pipe for a pistol. Besides these stories from real life, there are psychological experiments which point to the same conclusion. After a battle in a classroom, prearranged by the experimenter but a surprise to the students, each one was asked to write an account of the incident. The testimony of the most upset students was practically worthless, while those who were only slightly stimulated emotionally scored better than those left cold by the accident." Hutchins & Slesinger, Spontaneous Exclamations, 28 Colum.L.Rev. 432, 437 (1928) (footnote references omitted).

See also, Stewart, Perception, Memory, and Hearsay: A Criticism of Present Law and the Proposed Federal Rules of Evidence, 1970 Utah L.Rev. 1, 27.

6. McCurdy v. Greyhound Corp., 346 F.2d 224 (3d Cir.1965).

7. Arkansas Louisiana Gas Co. v. Evans, 397 P.2d 505 (Okl.1964) (pain in chest running into arms).

8. Johnston v. Ohls, 76 Wn.2d 398, 457 P.2d 194 (1969).

9. Martin v. Estrella, 107 R.I. 247, 266 A.2d 41 (1970).

10. United States v. Napier, 518 F.2d 316 (9th Cir. 1975), cert. denied 423 U.S. 895 (exclamation by victim of kidnaping and violence, with resulting impairment of communication abilities, with "great distress and horror" on seeing newspaper photograph of defendant, "He killed me.")

11. See, e.g, Stewart v. Baltimore & Ohio Railroad Co., 137 F.2d 527 (2d Cir.1943); Industrial Commission v. Diveley, 88 Colo. 190, 294 P. 532 (1930); Johnston v. W.S. Nott Co., 183 Minn. 309, 236 N.W. 466 (1931); Collins v. Equitable Life Insurance Co., 122 W.Va. 171, 8 S.E.2d 825 (1940). See § 53 supra, pointing out that the rules of evidence do not generally apply to preliminary fact questions of admissibility.

ports a finding of fact that the exciting event did occur.[12]

The question most frequently raised when a purported excited utterance is offered involves the second requirement. In all cases the ultimate question is whether the statement was the result of reflective thought or whether it was rather a spontaneous reaction to the exciting event. Initially, of course, it is necessary that the declarant be affected by the exciting event. It is generally not required that he be actually involved in the event; an excited utterance by a bystander is admissible.[13] However, if the identity of the bystander-declarant is undisclosed, the courts have been reluctant to admit.[14]

Probably the most important of the many factors entering into this determination is the time factor.[15] If the statement occurs while the exciting event is still in progress, courts have little difficulty finding that the excitement prompted the statement.[16] But as the time between the event and the state-

ment increases, so does the reluctance to find the statement an excited utterance. Although one court has held a statement made fourteen hours after a physical beating to be the product of the excitement caused by the beating,[17] other courts have held statements made within minutes of the event not admissible.[18] Perhaps an accurate rule of thumb might be that where the time interval between the event and the statement is long enough to permit reflective thought, the statement will be excluded in the absence of some proof that the declarant did not in fact engage in a reflective thought process.[19] Testimony that the declarant still appeared "nervous" or "distraught" and that there was a reasonable basis for continuing emotional upset will often suffice.[20] The nature of the exciting event and the declarant's concern with it are relevant, of course. Thus a statement made by the victim's wife one hour after a traffic accident was held admissible where the husband was still in the emergency room and she was obviously still

---

12. Truck Insurance Exchange v. Michling, 364 S.W.2d 172 (Tex.1963), reversing 358 S.W.2d 697 (Tex. Civ.App.1962), a workmen's compensation case. The deceased had returned home, pale, batting his eyes, and stumbling. He reported to his wife that he had struck his head when the bulldozer he had been driving had slipped off a hill. This statement was held inadmissible as there was no evidence of the exciting event other than the assertion in the statement itself. See also Hartford Accident and Indemnity Co. v. Hale, 400 S.W.2d 310 (Tex.1966).

13. People v. Caviness, 38 N.Y.2d 227, 379 N.Y.S.2d 695, 342 N.E.2d 496 (1975); El Rancho Restaurants, Inc. v. Garfield, 440 S.W.2d 873 (Tex.Civ.App.1969), ref. n.r.e.; Annot., 53 A.L.R.2d 1253.

14. Potter v. Baker, 162 Ohio St. 488, 124 N.E.2d 140 (1955); Garrett v. Howden, 73 N.M. 307, 387 P.2d 874 (1963).

15. See Annot., 56 A.L.R.2d 372 (spontaneity as question for court or jury).

16. Schwam v. Reece, 213 Ark. 431, 210 S.W.2d 903 (1948) (bus driver's exclamation, "I have no brakes" just before collision admissible); New York, Chicago & St. Louis Railroad Co. v. Kovatch, 120 Ohio St. 532, 166 N.E. 682 (1929) (exclamation that train had run over child made while train was still passing crossing held admissible).

17. State v. Stafford, 237 Iowa 780, 23 N.W.2d 832 (1946).

18. Alabama Power Co. v. Ray, 249 Ala. 568, 32 So. 2d 219 (1947) (five minutes); Swearinger v. Klinger, 91 Ill.App.2d 251, 234 N.E.2d 60 (1968) (five to 15 minutes).

19. Taft v. Western World Insurance Co., 220 So.2d 226 (La.App.1969) (error to admit statements concerning accident by another patient in nursing home made 30 minutes after patient had fallen); Fontenot v. Pan American Fire & Casualty Co., 209 So.2d 105 (La.App. 1968) (statement by driver made 40 minutes after accident inadmissible); Marshall v. Thomason, 241 S.C. 84, 127 S.E.2d 177 (1962) (statements to police officer 30 minutes after accident inadmissible).

20. McCurdy v. Greyhound Corp., 346 F.2d 224 (3d Cir.1965) (statement to police officer 15 minutes after accident admissible; testimony that declarant was still "nervous" and "shooken up" when police arrived); Hilyer v. Howat Concrete Co., Inc., 578 F.2d 422 (D.C.Cir.1978) (statement made by worker between 15 and 45 minutes after fellow worker was fatally run over by truck, with evidence indicating continuing excitement); United States v. Golden, 671 F.2d 369 (10th Cir.1982) cert. denied 456 U.S. 919 (statement 15 minutes after assault by officer, with 120 m.p.h. chase in interval). May v. Wright, 62 Wn.2d 69, 381 P.2d 601 (1963) (statement by witness to accident involving an automobile running over a child made 20 minutes after accident admissible; officer testified declarant "seemed upset").

concerned about his condition.[21] Other factors may indicate the opposite conclusion. Evidence that the statement was self-serving [22] or made in response to an inquiry,[23] while not justification for automatic exclusion, is an indication that the statement was the result of reflective thought, and where the time interval permitted such thought these factors might swing the balance in favor of exclusion. Proof that between the event and the statement the declarant performed tasks requiring relatively careful thought, of course, is strong evidence that the effect of the exciting event had subsided.[24] Because of the wide variety of factual situations, appellate courts have recognized wide discretion in trial courts to determine whether in fact a declarant was at the time of an offered statement still under the influence of an exciting event.[25]

Whether the excited utterance should be required to relate to the exciting event has occasioned a difference of opinion. Some cases have excluded statements for failing to meet this test.[26] The question often arises when an excited utterance following

an accident is relied upon to prove that declarant was an agent and acting in the scope of his employment. Wigmore suggests that a requirement that the declaration elucidate the event seems to have been taken from the verbal act doctrine without adequate analysis.[27] However, it seems undeniable that the probabilities are substantially greater that a statement related to an exciting event is a spontaneous reaction than a statement related to something else. In a leading case the United States Court of Appeals for the District of Columbia concluded that the requirement was a "spurious element" of the exception, but that failure to describe the exciting event was a factor to consider in evaluating the spontaneity of the statement.[28] In any event, the court sustained admission of a driver's statement following an accident, on the issue of agency, that he had to call on a customer and was in a hurry to get home.[29] Federal and Revised Uniform Rule (1974) 803(2) provide a hearsay exception, regardless of availability of declarant, for

> a statement relating to a startling event or condition made while the declarant was under the

---

21. Gibbs v. Wilmeth, 261 Iowa 1015, 157 N.W.2d 93 (1968).

22. Micheli v. Toye Brothers Yellow Cab Co., 174 So.2d 168 (La.App.1965) (self-serving statement made to employer's investigator 15 minutes after automobile accident properly excluded).

23. Gibbs v. Wilmeth, 261 Iowa 1015, 157 N.W.2d 93 (1968): ("[A] statement in answer to a question does not necessarily violate the res gestae rule. The important consideration is the spontaneity of the statement, however elicited."); Bosin v. Oak Lodge Sanitary District No. 1, 251 Or. 554, 447 P.2d 285 (1968) (fact that statement was in response to question is "not conclusive against admissibility" but a factor for consideration).

Compare Bowman v. Barnes, ___ W.Va. ___, 282 S.E. 2d 613 (1981) (grade crossing death; error to admit statement by since deceased engineer 44 minutes after accident to investigating police officer, taken down in writing).

24. Compare Hamilton v. Missouri Petroleum Products Co., 438 S.W.2d 197 (Mo.1969) (where evidence showed that after accident declarant put out flares to warn traffic, went to the aid of an injured party, and advised injured party not to move, statements made 25 minutes after accident inadmissible) with McCurdy v. Greyhound Corp., 346 F.2d 224 (3d Cir.1965) (where proof showed that after accident declarant first muttered incomprehensibly and then walked around aim-

lessly and was still nervous when police arrived, statement made 15 minutes after accident admissible).

25. Swearinger v. Klinger, 91 Ill.App.2d 251, 234 N.E.2d 60 (1968); Johnston v. Ohls, 76 Wn.2d 398, 457 P.2d 194 (1969).

26. Cook v. Hall, 308 Ky. 500, 214 S.W.2d 1017 (1948) (statement by son of automobile's owners after accident that he had permission to drive the car inadmissible); Bagwell v. McLellan Stores Co., 216 S.C. 207, 57 S.E.2d 257 (1949) (bystander's statement, after observing fall, that the floor had just been oiled inadmissible). The foregoing cases take an unduly narrow view of what is related. Compare Keefe v. State, 50 Ariz. 293, 72 P.2d 425 (1937) (when mother discovered children in "immoral conduct," little girl said D did such things to her several days earlier; error to admit); State v. Walton, 432 A.2d 1275 (Me.1981) (semble).

27. 6 Wigmore, Evidence § 1752 (Chadbourn rev. 1976).

28. Murphy Auto Parts Co. v. Ball, 102 U.S.App. D.C. 416, 249 F.2d 508, 511 (1957), cert. denied 355 U.S. 932 (1958). *Murphy* was applied in Felder v. Pinckney, 244 A.2d 481 (D.C.App.1968) (statement of one who observed co-employee fall that Mr. Pinckney hired him admissible); Sawyer v. Miseli, 156 A.2d 141 (D.C.App. 1959) (statement of driver after accident that owner had given him permission to drive car admissible).

29. Murphy Auto Parts Co. v. Ball, supra n. 28.

stress of excitement caused by the event or condition.

While the outcome of a few cases might be different, depending on whether relation to the exciting event is considered as a requirement or as a factor bearing on spontaneity, the former seems to be a simpler route to substantially the same destination.[30] It is also justified as a clarification of the difference in theory between excited utterances and statements of present sense impressions discussed in section 298 which follows.

Must the declarant meet the tests of competency for a witness? In a modified manner the requirement that a witness have had an opportunity to observe that to which he testifies[31] is applied. Direct proof is not necessary; if the circumstances appear consistent with opportunity by the declarant, this is sufficient.[32] If there is doubt the question is for the jury.[33] Especially in cases where the declaration is of low probative value, however, it is usually held inadmissible if there is no reasonable suggestion that the declarant had an opportunity to observe.[34]

On the theory that there is a countervailing assurance of reliability—the requirement of excitement—the other aspects of competency are not applied. Thus an excited utterance is admissible despite the fact that the declarant was a child and would have been incompetent as a witness for that reason,[35] or the declarant was incompetent by virtue of mental illness[36] or the declarant was a spouse of the defendant in the criminal case in which the statement was offered.[37]

It has sometimes been stated that an excited utterance must not be an opinion.[38] Such a blanket limitation is unjustified, in view of the nature and present standing of the opinion rule.[39] Where the declarant is an in-court witness, it is probably appropriate to require him to testify in concrete terms rather than conclusory generalizations. But in everyday life people often talk in conclusory terms and when these statements are later offered in court there is no opportunity to require the declarant to substitute more specific language. Here, as elsewhere, the opinion rule should be applied sparingly, if at all, to out-of-court speech. Nevertheless, courts have sometimes excluded excited utterances on the grounds that they violate the opinion rule, especially in

---

30. Compare Maynard v. Hall, 61 Ariz. 32, 143 P.2d 884 (1943) (under similar facts, statement of agency held admissible as related).

31. See § 10 supra.

32. See § 10 supra; McLaughlin v. Vinzant, 522 F.2d 448 (1st Cir.1975), cert. denied 423 U.S. 1037.

33. See §§ 53, 58 supra.

34. Warfield v. Shell Oil Co., 106 Ariz. 181, 472 P.2d 50 (1970) (offer of statement of bystander failed to show that speaker had witnessed event); Ungefug v. D'Ambrosa, 250 Cal.App.2d 61, 58 Cal.Rptr. 223 (1967) (where ambulance driver merely reported that someone had said the victim had been hit by a car that had not stopped, there was insufficient proof of an opportunity to observe; although direct proof that declarant witnessed the event is not necessary, "the fact that the declarant was a percipient witness should not be purely a matter of speculation or conjecture"); Clements v. Peyton, 398 S.W.2d 477 (Ky.App.1965) (testimony that "some guys sitting in the bar" said there had been another wreck at the corner inadmissible because there was no showing of their reasonable opportunity to observe facts on which to base this conclusion). Compare Annot., 7 A.L.R.2d 1324 (inability of declarant to recollect and narrate facts as to which statement relates as affecting admissibility of excited utterance).

35. New York, Chicago & St. Louis Railway Co. v. Kovatch, 120 Ohio St. 532, 166 N.E. 682 (1929) (five year old girl); Houston v. Quinones, 142 Tex. 282, 177 S.W.2d 259 (1944) (three year old girl); Marcum v. Bellomy, 157 W.Va. 636, 203 S.E.2d 367 (1974) (dog bite; boy under six screamed "Prince bite me.") Johnston v. Ohls, 76 Wn.2d 398, 457 P.2d 194 (1969) (four year old girl "presumably not competent to testify directly" told officer that dog which had attacked her had jumped out at motorcycle on which she had been riding with her father). See Annot., 83 A.L.R.2d 1368 (declarant's age as affecting admissibility of excited utterance).

36. Wilson v. State, 49 Tex.Cr.R. 50, 90 S.W. 312 (1905). But cf. Gough v. General Box Co., 302 S.W.2d 884 (Mo.1957) (excited utterance inadmissible because of declarant was unconscious at the time of the statement).

37. Robbins v. State, 73 Tex.Cr.R. 367, 166 S.W. 528 (1914) (declaration of murder defendant's wife, "Poor man! He lost his life trying to protect me." admissible).

38. Johnston v. Ohls, 76 Wn.2d 398, 457 P.2d 194 (1969).

39. See § 18 supra.

situations in which the declarant's statement places blame upon himself or another.[40] Despite possible danger that these opinions may be given exaggerated weight by a jury, the need for knowledge of the facts usually outweighs this danger and the better view admits excited statements of opinion.[41]

Sex cases. In rape cases traditionally,[42] and increasingly in cases of sex offenses generally,[43] evidence has been held admissible that the victim made complaint. The only time requirement is that the complaint have been made without a delay which is unexplained or is inconsistent with the occurrence of the offense, in general a less demanding time aspect than with the typical excited utterance situation.[44] In its origin, the theory of admissibility was to repel any inference that because the victim did not complain no outrage had in fact transpired. Accordingly, if the victim did not testify, evidence of complaint was not admissible.[45] While admissible evidence under traditional doctrine included only the fact that complaint was made,[46] the trend is to allow details of the offense and the identity of the

offender, a result which appears wholly justifiable.[47]

Complaints by victims of rape and other sex offenses are treated as excited utterances by the Federal and Revised Uniform Rules (1974), there being no provisions in the rules directed specifically to sex cases. It seems unlikely that a separate approach to rape would have developed historically if the doctrine admitting excited utterances as a hearsay exception had evolved at an earlier time. Considerably broader admissibility results under the excited utterance exception: any traditional limitation to merely the fact that complaint was made gives way to the admission of all related details and the identity of the offender; coverage expands to all sex offenses, rather than being confined to rape only; the victim-declarant need not testify. Any charge of recent fabrication may be met as in other cases, including use of prior consistent statements to rebut.[48] While arguably some diminution of the permissible time lapse may be entailed, all legitimate needs appear to be satisfied by the excited utterance exception.[49]

---

40. Whitney v. Sioux City, 172 Iowa 336, 154 N.W. 497 (1915) (statement by passenger in automobile, "We were going too fast" inadmissible); Gray v. Boston Elevated Railway Co., 215 Mass. 143, 102 N.E. 71 (1913) (statement by spectator to sudden start of train "It was his own fault," inadmissible); Bowers v. Kugler, 140 Neb. 684, 1 N.W.2d 299 (1941) (statement by driver of one vehicle in accident, "Oh, my God! It might have been my fault." inadmissible); Neisner Brothers v. Schaefer, 124 Ohio St. 311, 178 N.E. 269 (1931) (store clerk's declaration, "I am sorry I caused it; I should not have dropped the paper on the floor," inadmissible).

41. Cross Lake Logging Co. v. Joyce, 83 F. 989 (8th Cir.1897) (statement "I wouldn't have lost my leg if you had done as you agreed to and put another man in his place," admissible); Atlantic Coast Line Railroad Co. v. Crosby, 53 Fla. 400, 43 So. 318 (1907) (statement of mother of injured child, "It was all my fault," admissible); State v. Sloan, 47 Mo. 604 (1871) (statement of shooting victim to the effect that defendant had not been at fault because victim had drawn on the difficulty by attacking the defendant, admissible).

42. 4 Wigmore, Evidence §§ 1134–1140 (Chadbourn rev.1972), 6 id. §§ 1760, 1761 (Chadbourn rev.1976).

43. People v. Burton, 55 Cal.2d 328, 11 Cal.Rptr. 65, 359 P.2d 433 (1961) (indecent liberties with child); People v. Bonneau, 323 Mich. 237, 35 N.W.2d 161 (1948) (same). Contra, People v. Romano, 306 Ill. 502, 138

N.E. 169 (1923); Leybourne v. Commonwealth, 22 Va. 374, 282 S.E.2d 12 (1981).

44. See the careful explication of the distinctions between excited utterances and complaint of rape by Underwood, J., in People v. Damen, 28 Ill.2d 464, 193 N.E.2d 25 (1963). See also State v. Stevens, 289 N.W.2d 592 (Iowa 1980).

45. People v. Lewis, 252 Ill. 281, 96 N.E. 1005 (1911) (victim died before trial); 4 Wigmore, Evidence § 1136 (Chadbourn rev.1972).

46. 6 Wigmore, Evidence § 1760 (Chadbourn rev. 1976).

47. Cases cited in 6 Wigmore, Evidence § 1761, n. 2 (Chadbourn rev.1976).

48. State v. Roy, 140 Vt. 219, 436 A.2d 1090 (1981). See §§ 49, 251 supra.

49. A tendency is apparent in cases of sex offenses against children of tender years to be less strict with regard to permissible time lapse and to the fact that the statement was in response to inquiry. State v. Duncan, 53 Ohio St. 215, 373 N.E.2d 1234 (1978); State v. Bouchard, 31 Wn.App. 381, 639 P.2d 761 (1982). This so-called "tender years" exception has been held not to have been eliminated by the adoption of Federal Rule 803(2). People v. Turner, 112 Mich.App. 381, 316 N.W.2d 426 (1982), judgment vacated 417 Mich. 947, 332 N.W.2d 150.

di excited utterance

"excited utterance*'' /s spontan! /s reflect!

excited spontaneous +2 utterance* declaration* /s nervous! distraught upset

803(2) /p excit! spontaneous startl! /s statement* utterance*

excited spontaneous /s statement* utterance* declaration* /p witness** testify testimony /5 incompeten!

victim* /s complain** /s rape* /s delay!

§ 298. Unexcited Statements of Present Sense Impressions [1]

Although Dean Wigmore's creative work did much to clarify the murky concept of *res gestae*, his analysis of spontaneous declarations may have led to one unfortunate restricting development of this exception. Professor Thayer, reviewing the *res gestae* cases in 1881,[2] had concluded that this was an exception based on the contemporaneousness of statements. He read the law as creating an exception for "statements . . . made by those present when a thing took place, made about it and importing what is present at the very time . . . ."[3] Wigmore, however, saw as the basis for the spontaneous exclamation exception to the hearsay rule not the contemporaneousness of the exclamation but rather the nervous excitement produced by the exposure of the declarant to an exciting event.[4] As a result, the American law of spontaneous statements shifted emphasis from what Thayer

had observed to a requirement of an exciting event and a resulting stilling of the declarant's reflective faculties.[5] This, as Professor Morgan pointed out, was unfortunate.[6] Given the danger of unreliability caused by the very emotional excitement required for excited utterances, it makes little sense to admit them while excluding other out-of-court statements which may have equal assurances of reliability and lack the inherent defects of excited utterances.[7]

Under Morgan's leadership arguments were made for restoring Thayer's view of the law by recognizing another exception to the hearsay rule for statements concerning nonexciting events which the declarant is observing at the time he makes the declarations. Although these statements lack whatever assurance of reliability there is in the effect of an exciting event, other factors offer safeguards. First, since the report concerns observations being made at the time of the statement it is safe from any error caused by a defect of the declarant's memory. Second, a requirement that the statement be made contemporaneously with the observation means that there will be little or no time for calculated misstatement. Third, the statement will usually have been made to a third person (the witness who subsequently testifies to it) who, being present at the time and scene of the observation, will probably have an opportunity to observe the situation himself and thus provide a check on the accuracy of the declarant's statement, i.e. furnish corroboration.[8] Moreover,

Cases on time lapse for excited utterances in sex cases are collected in Annot., 89 A.L.R.3d 102.

§ 298

1. See generally, Hutchins & Slesinger, Some Observation on the Law of Evidence, 28 Colum.L.Rev. 432, 439–40 (1928); Morgan, Res Gestae, 12 Wash.L. Rev. 91 (1937); Morgan, A Suggested Classification of Utterances Admissible as Res Gestae, 31 Yale L.J. 229, 236–38 (1922); Waltz, The Present Sense Impression Exception to the Rule Against Hearsay: Origins and Attributes, 66 Iowa L.Rev. 689 (1981); Note, Spontaneous Exclamations in the Absence of a Startling Event, 46 Colum.L.Rev. 430 (1946). Compare Annot., 140 A.L.R. 874 (admissibility of statements regarding conduct of driver of car subsequently involved in a collision).

2. Thayer, Bedingfield's Case—Declarations as a Part of the Res Gestae, 15 Am.L.Rev. 1 (1881).

3. Id. at 83.

4. 6 Wigmore, Evidence § 1747 (Chadbourn rev. 1976). Compare Morgan, Res Gestae, 12 Wash.L.Rev. 91, 98 (1937).

5. Morgan, supra n. 4 at 96.

6. Id.

7. Morgan, A Suggested Classification of Utterances Admissible as Res Gestae, 31 Yale L.J. 229, 236 (1922).

8. Corroboration as a suggested requirement for admission in evidence is discussed infra in the text at n. 20.

since the declarant himself will often be available for cross-examination, his credibility will be subject to substantial verification before the trier of fact.

The courts generally did not rush to the support of the proposed exception for unexcited statements of present sense impressions. A considerable number continued to admit contemporaneous statements under *res gestae* language without emphasis on the presence or absence of an exciting event.[9] In a large proportion of these decisions an event at least arguably exciting was present. However, cases recognizing the exception for unexcited statements of present sense impressions began to emerge. The case most commonly cited to illustrate judicial recognition of the exception is *Hous-*

ton Oxygen.[10] Although an exciting event was arguably present, the opinion disclaimed reliance upon it and expressly based its decision upon the exception for unexcited declarations of present sense impressions. A more compelling case on its facts, decided in the same year 1942, is Tampa Electric Co. v. Getrost.[11] Judicial acceptance gradually gained momentum.[12] The relative infrequence of cases in point no doubt arises from the fact that unexciting events as a practical matter do not often give rise to statements that later become relevant in litigated situations.

The principal impetus for recognition of the hearsay exception for unexcited statements of present sense impressions came through the rulemaking process. The Model

---

9. Kelly v. Hanwick, 228 Ala. 336, 153 S. 269 (1934) (bystander's statement when he saw automobile coming that at the speed at which it was traveling it could not make the curve held admissible); Moreno v. Hawbaker, 157 Cal.App.2d 627, 321 P.2d 538 (1958) (testimony of witness that when he saw two motorcycles proceeding at a high rate of speed and without lights he said, "Look at those fools go" admissible as a spontaneous utterance); McCaskill v. State, 227 So.2d 847 (Miss.1969) (testimony that victim had called witness and said she was at the doctor's getting something done about her pregnancy admissible, but suggestion that rule is limited to abortion prosecutions); Sellers v. Montana-Dakota Power Co., 99 Mont. 39, 41 P.2d 44 (1935) (statements by persons in burning building that the smell of the smoke indicated that the fire came from gas held admissible); Hornschurch v. Southern Pacific Co., 101 Or. 280, 203 P. 886 (1921) (testimony that bystander called to those in automobile to stop held admissible); Marks v. I.M. Pearlstine & Sons, 203 S.C. 318, 26 S.E.2d 835 (1943) (statement by one watching trucks racing by that the "trucks are going to kill someone" held admissible). Contra, Wrange v. King, 114 Kan. 539, 220 P. 259 (1923); Ideal Cement Co. v. Killingsworth, 198 So.2d 248 (Miss.1967); Shadowski v. Pittsburg Railways Co., 226 Pa. 537, 75 A. 730 (1910); Barnett v. Bull, 141 Wash. 139, 250 P. 955 (1926). See generally Note, 46 Colum.L.Rev. 430 (1946).

10. Houston Oxygen Co., Inc. v. Davis, 139 Tex. 1, 161 S.W.2d 474 (1942). Defendant had offered the testimony of a Mrs. Cooper that when the plaintiff's car passed her about four miles before the accident at issue she had said that "they must have been drunk, that we would find them, somewhere on the road wrecked if they kept that rate of speed up." Objection to the testimony concerning the remark was sustained, and the Texas Supreme Court reversed. "[The statement] is sufficiently spontaneous to save it from the suspicion of being manufactured evidence. There was no time

for a calculated statement." 161 S.W.2d at 476. See also Anderson v. State, 454 S.W.2d 740 (Tex.Cr.App. 1970) (witness' testimony that a neighbor had said, "Seems like there is a car being stripped down the street there" admissible); Claybrook v. Acreman, 373 S.W.2d 287 (Tex.Civ.App.1963) (statements of bystanders such as "They won't last long at that rate of speed" improperly excluded). It is, of course, arguable that an exciting event was in fact present in each of these cases.

11. 151 Fla. 558, 10 So.2d 83 (1942) (action for wrongful death of lineman by electrocution; statement of fellow lineman that deceased had returned from nearby house and said he had telephoned central station to deactivate line that they were going to work on).

12. State v. Flesher, 286 N.W.2d 215 (Iowa 1979) (murder; husband of victim properly permitted to testify that he had a telephone conversation with her shortly before her death; that he heard a knock; that she left the phone, returned, and said, "It's Joan [the accused]."); State v. Cawthorne, 290 N.C. 639, 227 S.W.2d 528 (1976) (murder of cab driver; proper to admit testimony of dispatcher that victim radioed that he had two fares for particular address); Hall v. DeSaussure, 41 Tenn.App. 572, 297 S.W.2d 81 (1956), cert. denied 201 Tenn. 164, 297 S.W.2d 90 (medical malpractice; error to exclude testimony offered by plaintiff that another doctor on examining X ray taken nine months after the operation said, "He certainly did take a big chunk out of your spine." See also Commonwealth v. Coleman, 458 Pa. 112, 326 A.2d 387, 74 A.L.R.3d 954 (1974) (testimony of witness that prospective murder victim said over telephone that defendant would not let her leave apartment, that he would hang up phone, and that he was going to kill her, admissible as present sense impression). Concurring judge believed better classed as excited utterance.

Code of Evidence [13] and the original Uniform Rules [14] provided for such an exception. The Federal Rules and the Revised Uniform Rules (1974) provide a hearsay exception, without regard to the availability of the declarant, for

> a statement describing or explaining an event or condition made while the declarant was perceiving the event or condition, or immediately thereafter.[15]

In addition to the absence of any requirement of an exciting event, the hearsay exception for statements of present sense impressions differs from the exception for excited utterances in two other significant respects. First, while excited utterances need only "relate" [16] to the startling event or condition, present sense impressions are confined to "describing or explaining" [17] the event or condition perceived. This limitation is consistent with the theory underlying the present sense impression exception, that fabrication and forgetfulness are precluded by the absence of time lapse between perception and utterance. Second, while the time within which an excited utterance may be made is measured by the duration of the stress caused by the exciting event,[18] the present sense impression statement may be made only while declarant was actually "perceiving" the event or "immediately thereafter." [19] This shortened period is also consis-

tent with the theory of the present sense impression exception. While principle might seem to call for a limitation to exact contemporaneity, some allowance must be made for the time needed for translating observation into speech. The appropriate inquiry is whether sufficient time elapsed to have permitted reflective thought.

The suggestion has been made that corroboration by an "equally percipient" witness should be recognized as a further requirement for admitting statements of present sense impression into evidence.[20] The proposal represents a radical departure from the general pattern of exceptions to the hearsay rule. The only instance in which a requirement of corroboration is found is where a statement against penal interest by a third person, e.g. a third party confession, is offered by way of exculpation of an accused person. There the common law had set its face strictly against admission in evidence. In order to increase the acceptability of a reversal of this position, the Advisory Committee incorporated in Federal Rule 804(b)(3) a requirement that the hearsay statement be corroborated.[21] The present sense impression exception offers no such need; its underlying rationale offers sufficient assurances of reliability without the superaddition of a further requirement of corroboration. The decisions have not re-

---

13. Model Code of Evidence Rule 512(a).

14. Uniform Rules Evid. 63(4)(a), (b) (1953).

15. Fed.R.Evid. 803(1); Uniform Rules Evid. 803(1) (1974).

16. Section 297, text at notes 26–30 supra.

17. Text at note 15 supra.

18. Section 297, text at notes 15–25 supra.

19. Text at note 15 supra, for Fed.R.Evid. and Uniform Rules Evid. (1974) 803(1). In the following cases the time requirement for present sense impressions was held to have been satisfied: United States v. Peacock, 654 F.2d 339 (5th Cir.1981) (comments made by deceased husband of witness as to contents of telephone conversation with defendant immediately following conversation); United States v. Blakey, 607 F.2d 779, 60 A.L.R. Fed. 509 (7th Cir.1979) (statement by decedent to witnesses indicating payment of bribe to police officer defendants in adjoining room, spoken between several and 23 minutes after officers departed); United States v. Earley, 657 F.2d 195 (8th Cir.1981)

(statement by murder victim immediately after hanging up telephone, expressing concern and saying voice sounded like defendant). Contra, Hilyer v. Howat Concrete Co., 578 F.2d 422 (D.C.Cir.1978) (lapse of not less than 15 minutes between accidental death of coworker and statement held to bar present sense impression, but statement admissible as excited utterance); United States v. Cain, 587 F.2d 678 (5th Cir.1979), cert. denied 440 U.S. 975, appeal after remand 615 F.2d 380 (CB transmission received by state trooper, reporting seeing men answering description of defendants leaving stolen truck, made when they were some five miles from the truck, apparently by foot travel).

20. Waltz, The Present Sense Impression Exception to the Rule Against Hearsay: Origins and Attributes, 66 Iowa L.Rev. 689, 883 (1981); Foster, Present Sense Impressions: An Analysis and a Proposal, 10 Loy.Chi. L.J. 299 (1977). Compare Note, 56 Tex.L.Rev. 1053 (1978).

21. See § 278 supra.

quired it,[22] and the Federal and Revised Uniform Rules (1974) do not require it.[23] It is true, of course, that the limits of the exception in terms of time and subject matter in and of themselves almost automatically insure that the witness who reports the making of the statement must have himself perceived the actual event or at least have perceived circumstances strongly suggesting the event. This aspect has been mentioned by the writers as an added assurance of accuracy, but a justification for ad-

mission is not the same as a requirement for admission.[24] The matter had better be left for consideration as an aspect of weight and sufficiency of the evidence rather than becoming an added needlessly complicating requirement for admissibility.

 WESTLAW REFERENCES

"present sense impression*"
803(1)

---

22. Waltz, supra n. 20, at p. 889.

23. When the Advisory Committee on Federal Rules of Evidence intended to abolish a common law requirement of corroboration, it said so. See Fed.R.Evid. 406 (evidence of habit relevant for certain purposes "whether corroborated or not.")

24. The legal mind is on occasion seemingly unable to resist the temptation to drive in one more nail, albeit it be a crooked one. The mischief that may result is illustrated by the cases insisting that statements of intent closely accompany in time some step in furtherance of the intent. See § 294 note 15 supra.

Chapter 30
RECORDS OF PAST RECOLLECTION

Table of Sections

§ 299. History and Theory of the Exception [1]

By the middle 1600s it had become customary to permit a witness to refresh his memory by looking at a written memorandum and to testify from his then-revived memory.[2] It often happened, however, that, although examining the writing did not bring the facts recorded back to the witness' memory, he was able to recognize the writing as one prepared by him and was willing to testify on the basis of the writing that the facts recited in it were true. By the 1700s this also was accepted as proper,[3] although the theoretical difficulty of justifying the result was often swept under the rug by referring to it by the old term of "refreshing recollection," which clearly did not fit it.[4]

Beginning with the early 1800s, the courts came to distinguish between the two situations, and to recognize that the use of past recollection recorded was a far different matter from permitting the witness to testify from a memory refreshed by examining a writing.[5]

As the rule permitting the introduction of past recollection recorded developed, it required that four elements be met: (1) the witness must have had firsthand knowledge of the event, (2) the written statement must be an original memorandum made at or near the time of the event and while the witness had a clear and accurate memory of it, (3) the witness must lack a present recollection of the event, and (4) the witness must vouch for the accuracy of the written memorandum.[6]

§ 299

1. See generally 3 Wigmore, Evidence §§ 734–755 (Chadbourn rev.1970). Blakely, Past Recollection Recorded: Restrictions on Use as Exhibit and Proposals for Change, 17 Hous.L.Rev. 411 (1980); Morgan, The Relation Between Hearsay and Preserved Memory, 40 Harv.L.Rev. 712 (1927); Annot., 82 A.L.R.2d 473, § 105(b), 125 A.L.R. 19, 80–187, 35 A.L.R.Fed. 605; 29 Am.Jur.2d Evidence § 877; C.J.S. Evidence § 696; Dec.Dig. Evidence ⊗355, 356, 377, Criminal Law ⊗435, Witnesses ⊗253–260.

2. 3 Wigmore, Evidence § 735 (Chadbourn rev. 1970). See § 9 supra.

3. Id.

4. Id.

5. Acklen's Executor v. Hickman, 63 Ala. 494 (1879); State v. Easter, 185 Iowa 476, 170 N.W. 748 (1919); State v. Legg, 59 W.Va. 315, 53 S.E. 545 (1906).

6. Vicksburg & Meridian Railroad Co. v. O'Brien, 119 U.S. 99 (1886); Kinsey v. State, 49 Ariz. 201, 65

With the passage of time, these requirements have been the subject of modifications and refinements, discussed in the sections that follow. The rule appears as Rule 803(5) of the Federal and Revised Uniform Rules (1974) as a hearsay exception, with no unavailability of the declarant specified except such as may be required in order to comply with the provisions of the rule, as follows:

> A memorandum or record concerning a matter about which a witness once had knowledge but now has insufficient recollection to enable him to testify fully and accurately, shown to have been made or adopted by the witness when the matter was fresh in his memory and to reflect that knowledge correctly. If admitted, the memorandum or record may be read into evidence but may not itself be received as an exhibit unless offered by an adverse party.

The usefulness of the hearsay exception is apparent from the variety of items the courts have admitted into evidence under its sponsorship: hospital records,[7] reporter's transcripts of testimony,[8] police reports,[9] statements of witnesses,[10] and safe deposit box inventories.[11]

Whether recorded recollection should in fact be classed as a hearsay exception, or as not hearsay at all, may be arguable since the reliability of the assertions rests upon the veracity of a witness who is present and testifying.[12] Which way the argument is decided seems not to have affected the require-

ments for admissibility, however, and it is convenient to treat recorded recollection as a hearsay exception since some lack of memory is required, though less than total.[13]

Should the writing be admitted into evidence and be allowed to be taken to the jury room? Some difference of opinion is apparent.[14] However, the testimonial nature likely to characterize the writing makes a strong argument against the practice, just as depositions are generally not given to the jury.[15] The Federal and Revised Uniform Rule (1974), quoted above, solve the problem by resort to the ancient practice of reading the writing into evidence, but not admitting it as an exhibit unless offered by the adverse party.

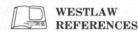

WESTLAW REFERENCES

refresh! /4 memory /s record! /4 "past recollection*"
803(5)

§ 300. Firsthand Knowledge

The usual requirement for witnesses [1] and also for hearsay declarants since they in reality are witnesses, that they must have had firsthand knowledge of the facts is also enforced in regard to past recollection recorded. Thus, where an inventory was offered and the witness produced to lay the necessary foundation testified that it had been

---

P.2d 1141 (1937); Mathis v. Stricklind, 201 Kan. 655, 443 P.2d 673 (1968).

7. Minor v. City of Chicago, 101 Ill.App.3d 823, 57 Ill.Dec. 410, 428 N.E.2d 1090 (1981).

8. United States v. Arias, 575 F.2d 253 (9th Cir. 1978), cert. denied 439 U.S. 868; United States v. Patterson, 678 F.2d 774 (9th Cir.1982).

9. United States v. Sawyer, 607 F.2d 1190 (7th Cir. 1979), cert. denied 445 U.S. 943. Compare United States v. Oates, 560 F.2d 45 (2d Cir.1977), on remand 445 F.Supp. 351 (E.D.N.Y.), affirmed 591 F.2d 1332, and see § 317 infra. Dennis v. Scarborough, 360 So.2d 278 (Ala.1978).

10. United States v. Williams, 571 F.2d 344 (6th Cir. 1978), cert. denied 439 U.S. 841; United States v. Senak, 527 F.2d 129 (7th Cir.1975), cert. denied 425 U.S. 907.

11. Mathis v. Stricklind, 201 Kan. 655, 443 P.2d 673 (1968).

12. See Kinsey v. State, 49 Ariz. 201, 65 P.2d 1141 (1937); Curtis v. Bradley, 65 Conn. 99, 31 A. 591, 595 (1894); Morgan, The Relation Between Hearsay and Preserved Memory, 40 Harv.L.Rev. 717, 719 (1927). Compare the treatment of prior inconsistent statements of a witness, § 251 supra. As to possible constitutional problems of confrontation, see § 252 supra.

13. Adv.Comm. Note, Fed.R.Evid. 803(5).

14. Fisher v. Swartz, 333 Mass. 265, 130 N.E.2d 575 (1955), overruling Bendett v. Bendett, 315 Mass. 59, 52 N.E.2d 2 (1943).

15. Section 217 supra. United States v. Judon, 567 F.2d 1289 (5th Cir.1978), appeal after remand 581 F.2d 553. For a contrary view, see Blakely, supra n. 1.

§ 300

1. See § 10 supra.

made only partly from his own inspection and partly from information provided by his assistant, the inventory was inadmissible.[2]

WESTLAW REFERENCES

record! /4 "past recollection" /s firsthand /4 knowledge

---

§ 301. Written Statement Made While the Witness' Memory Was Clear

Despite some cases suggesting the contrary,[1] the exception as generally stated requires that there be a written formulation of the memory.[2] The Federal and Revised Uniform Rule (1974)[3] use the somewhat broader terms "memorandum or record," which a tape recording, for example, should satisfy. Moreover, the original memorandum must be produced or accounted for as is generally required when the contents of documents are sought to be proved.[4]

This writing need not, however, have been prepared by the witness himself if the witness read and adopted it. Multiple-participant situations are considered further in section 303, below.

The writing must have been prepared or recognized as correct at a time close enough to the event to insure accuracy.[5] Some opinions use the older strict formulation that requires the writing to have been made or recognized as correct "at or near the time" of the events recorded.[6] This finds some support in psychological research suggesting that a rapid rate of forgetting occurs within the first two or three days following the observation of the event.[7] But the tendency seems to be towards acceptance of the formulation favored by Wigmore[8] which would require only that the writing be made or recognized at a time when the events were fairly fresh in the mind of the witness. The formula of Federal and Revised Uniform Rule (1974) 803(5) is "when the matter was fresh in his [the witness'] memory."[9] The cases vary as to the length of time lapse allowable.[10]

WESTLAW REFERENCES

record! memorand! writing* /s witness! /s true correct! accurat! clear! /s memory remember** /s time

---

2. Town of Norwalk ex rel. Fawcett v. Ireland, 68 Conn. 1, 35 A. 804 (1896). See also Mercurio v. Frascitelli, 116 R.I. 237, 354 A.2d 736 (1976) (proper to exclude officer's accident report based in part on what he observed and in part on what parties told him); People v. Zalimas, 319 Ill. 186, 149 N.E. 759 (1925) (druggist's memorandum of sale of arsenic to a given person not admissible to prove sale to that person because druggist did not have firsthand knowledge of purchaser's identity).

§ 301

1. Shear v. Van Dyke, 17 N.Y.S.Ct.Rep. 528, 10 Hun. 528 (1877) (to prove amount of hay loaded, plaintiff offered R's testimony to the effect that he could not now recall but that he had known and had told the plaintiff, who then testified that he had been told by R that fourteen loads had been loaded); Hart v. Atlantic Coast Line Railroad Co., 144 N.C. 91, 56 S.E. 559 (1907).

2. See 3 Wigmore, Evidence § 744 (Chadbourn rev. 1970).

3. Text supra § 299 following n. 6.

4. See Ch. 23 supra.

5. Maxwell's Executors v. Wilkinson, 113 U.S. 656 (1885); 3 Wigmore, Evidence § 745 (Chadbourn rev. 1970).

6. E.g., Gigliotti v. United Illuminating Co., 151 Conn. 114, 193 A.2d 718, 723 (1963) (written statement must be excluded if it was not made "at or about the time of the events recorded in it").

7. Hutchins and Slesinger, Some Observations on the Law of Evidence—Memory, 41 Harv.L.Rev. 860 (1928); Gardner, The Perception and Memory of Witnesses, 18 Corn.L.Q. 391, 393 (1933); Stewart, Perception, Memory, and Hearsay: A Criticism of Present Law and the Proposed Federal Rules of Evidence, 1970 Utah L.Rev. 1.

8. 3 Wigmore, Evidence § 745 (Chadbourn rev. 1970).

9. Text following § 299, n. 6 supra.

10. Nonrules cases: Gigliotti v. United Illuminating Co., 151 Conn. 114, 193 A.2d 718 (1963) (six weeks, proper to exclude); Calandra v. Norwood, 81 A.D.2d 650, 438 N.Y.S.2d 381 (1981) (four and one-half months, error to admit). Rules cases: United States v. Senak, 527 F.2d 129 (7th Cir.1975), cert. denied 425 U.S. 907, (three years, not error to admit); United States v. Williams, 571 F.2d 344 (6th Cir.1978), cert. denied 439 U.S. 841 (six months, not error to admit).

§ 302. Impairment of Recollection [1]

The traditional formulation of the rule, still adhered to by some courts, requires that before a past recollection recorded could be received in evidence the witness who made or recognized it as correct must testify that he lacks any present memory of the events and therefore is unable to testify concerning them.[2]

Some courts have rejected this requirement in circumstances suggesting that although the witness may have sufficient present recollection to cause the offer not to meet the traditional requirement nevertheless the circumstances of the case suggest that the prior recorded statement would be more complete and more reliable than testimony based upon the present memory of the witness.[3] An occasional case has supported complete abandonment of the requirement, arguing that failure of memory adds nothing to the credibility of the statement.[4] In many cases, perhaps most, it is undoubtedly true that present recollection, clouded by the passage of time, is less accurate than a statement made at a time when recollection was fresh and clear. But complete abandonment of this requirement would probably encourage the use of statements prepared for purposes of the litigation under the supervision of claims adjusters or attorneys or under other circumstances casting significant doubt upon the reliability of the statement.[5] An accommodation of these various aspects may be found in phrasing the requirement as a lack of sufficient present recollection to enable the witness to testify fully and accurately, a standard which is gaining increasing judicial adherents,[6] as well as appearing in the Federal and Revised Uniform Rules (1974).[7]

 WESTLAW REFERENCES

require! necess! must /s no not lack! impair! unable /4 memory remember recall /p "past recollection*"

§ 303. Proving the Accuracy of the Written Statement [1]: Multi-Party Situations

As a final assurance of reliability, it has traditionally been required that witnesses laying the foundation for the written statement not only establish firsthand knowledge, preparation of the statement at a time sufficiently close to the event, and at least some inability presently to recall the event,

---

§ 302

1. See generally, 3 Wigmore, Evidence § 738 (Chadbourn rev.1970).

2. Bennefield v. State, 281 Ala. 283, 202 So.2d 55 (1967); Minor v. City of Chicago, 101 Ill.App.3d 823, 57 Ill.Dec. 410, 428 N.E.2d 1090 (1981); State v. Contreras, 105 R.I. 523, 253 A.2d 612 (1969) (written statement not admissible despite witness' testimony that events were fresher in his mind when statement was prepared than during testimony).

If it is apparent from the face of the statement that a reasonable person could not presently recall the facts, failure to establish lack of present knowledge by direct testimony will not cause the admission of the statement to become error. Cohen v. Berry, 188 A.2d 302 (D.C.App.1963) (despite lack of record on present knowledge, admission of record of exact days and hours worked over an eight month period not error because it is "inconceivable" that witness could have recalled figures).

3. State v. Bindhammer, 44 N.J. 372, 209 A.2d 124, 132 (1965) ("Since the judicial search is for truth and accuracy it would indeed be self-defeating for a court to compel a reporter to testify from memory rather than from his notes or transcription; and this would be

so regardless of the extent of the reporter's present recollection."); State v. Sutton, 253 Or. 24, 450 P.2d 748 (1969) (checklist used by police officer in administering breath analysis machine admissible despite officer's apparently refreshed recollection, because it was likely to be more trustworthy).

4. Jordan v. People, 151 Colo. 133, 376 P.2d 699 (1962), cert. denied 373 U.S. 944; State v. Sutton, 253 Or. 24, 450 P.2d 748 (1969). See also Wigmore, Evidence § 738 (Chadbourn rev.1970).

5. See Fed.R.Evid. 803(5), Advisory Committee's Note.

6. E.g., Commonwealth v. Shaw, 494 Pa. 364, 431 A.2d 897 (1981). In Elam v. Soares, 282 Or. 93, 577 P.2d 1336 (1978), under the reasoning of the Federal Advisory Committee supra n. 5, the court abandoned its advocacy of no requirement of impaired memory in favor of the Federal Rule.

7. Text following § 299, n. 6 supra; United States v. Felix-Jerez, 667 F.2d 1297 (9th Cir. 1982).

§ 303

1. 3 Wigmore, Evidence § 747 (Chadbourn rev. 1970).

but in addition that either the person who prepared the writing or one who read it at a time close to the event testify to its accuracy.[2] This may be accomplished by a statement that he presently remembers that he correctly recorded the fact or that he recognized the writing as accurate at the time he read it.[3] But if his present memory is less effective, it is sufficient if he testifies that he knows it is correct because it was his habit or practice to record such matters accurately or to check them for accuracy.[4] At the extreme, it is even sufficient if he testifies that he recognizes the signature on the statement as his and he believes it correct because he would not have signed it if he had not believed it true at the time.[5]

No particular method of proving the accuracy of the memorandum is prescribed by Federal and Revised Uniform Rule (1974) 803(5), which merely requires that it be "shown . . . to reflect that knowledge correctly." [6] If an adequate foundation has been laid, it is not grounds for exclusion that the witness' testimony as to the accuracy of the statement is contradicted by other testimony.[7]

The traditional past recollection recorded was a one-person affair. The verifying witness was also the person who made the original observation and the person who recorded it. When the verifying witness has not prepared the report but merely examined it and found it accurate, the matter involves what might be called a cooperative report. But in this situation, only the person who read and verified the report need be called. A somewhat different type of cooperative report exists when a person (R) reports orally facts known to him to another person (W), who writes them down. A salesman or timekeeper, for example, may report sales or time to a bookkeeper. In this type of situation, courts have held the written statement admissible if R swears to the correctness of his oral report (although he may not remember the detailed facts) and W testifies that he faithfully transcribed R's oral report.[8]

Federal and Revised Uniform Rule (1974) 803(5) are in terms unclear with respect to multi-person situations. As prescribed by the Supreme Court the rule simply stated "made when the matter was fresh in his memory," leaving unrestricted the persons who might contribute to making the memorandum. This was consistent with multiple person involvement in the process of observing and recording, as the Advisory Committee pointed out.[9] The Congress unfortunately amended the quoted phrase to read "made or adopted by the witness when the matter was fresh in his memory." If "by the witness" is read as modifying "made," the result is to restrict the scope of the rule by raising doubt as to whether multiple party

---

2. Williams v. Stroh Plumbing & Electric, Inc., 250 Iowa 599, 94 N.W.2d 750 (1959).

3. Stanton v. Pennsylvania Railroad Co., 32 Ill.App. 2d 406, 178 N.E.2d 121 (1961) (patient-slips from doctor's office admissible where nurse testified that she had made entries and that they were accurate when made); Mathis v. Stricklind, 201 Kan. 655, 443 P.2d 673 (1968) (inventory of safe deposit boxes admissible when those making examination testified that notes were correct when taken). Compare Bennefield v. State, 281 Ala. 283, 202 So.2d 55 (1967) (only stenographer who took down confession could authenticate it; detective's affirmance of its correctness "merely confounded its hearsay character").

4. Hancock v. Kelly, 81 Ala. 368, 2 So. 281, 286 (1887); Newton v. Higdon, 226 Ga. 649, 177 S.E.2d 57 (1970) (lawyer testifies to practice in witnessing wills).

5. Walker v. Larson, 284 Minn. 99, 169 N.W.2d 737 (1969) (it is adequate if one with knowledge recognizes the signature as his and testifies that he would not

have signed it without reading it and determining it to be accurate, and suggestions in Hodas v. Davis, 203 App.Div. 297, 196 N.Y.S. 801 (1922) to the contrary disapproved); Dennis v. Scarborough, 360 So.2d (Ala. 1978) (semble).

6. Text following § 299, n. 6 supra.

7. Asaro v. Parisi, 297 F.2d 859, 863 (1st Cir.1962), cert. denied 370 U.S. 904.

8. Rathbun v. Brancatella, 93 N.J.Law 222, 107 A. 279 (1919) (A saw the license number of the car that struck plaintiff and called it out; B wrote it on an envelope, since destroyed, and gave it to the investigating officer, who copied it into his report, produced in court; each testified; held, admissible). See also United States v. Booz, 451 F.2d 719 (3d Cir.1971); Curtis v. Bradley, 65 Conn. 99, 31 A. 591 (1894); State v. Kreuser, 91 Wis.2d 242, 280 N.W.2d 270 (1979).

9. Advisory Committee's Note, Fed.R.Evid. 803(5).

participation is allowed. However, legislative history indicates that it was not the purpose of the Congress to narrow the scope of the rule or to preclude the various multi-person situations.[10] Hence the words "by the witness" should be read as modifying only the word "adopted," and not as requiring that the memorandum be the product of a single witness. This construction conforms with the traditional pattern, permitting multiple participants as long as each is called and in its total their testimony establishes compliance with the requirements of the rule.

WESTLAW REFERENCES

require! necess! must /8 testif! vouch! /8 true truth! accura! /s "past recollection*"

---

10. Senate Committee on the Judiciary, Fed. Rules of Evidence, S.Rep. No. 1277, 93d Cong., 2d Sess., p. 27 (1974).

Chapter 31

REGULARLY KEPT RECORDS

Table of Sections

§ 304. Admissibility of Regularly Kept Records

Regularly kept records may be offered in evidence in many different situations, although in almost all the record is offered as evidence of the truth of its terms. In such cases the evidence is clearly hearsay and some exception to the hearsay rule must be invoked if the record is to be admitted. Often no special exception is needed, however, as the record comes within the terms of another exception. For example, if the record was made by a party to the suit it is admissible against him as an admission.[1] If the entrant is produced as a witness, the record may be used to refresh his memory[2] or may come in as a record of past recollection.[3] Sometimes the record may be admissible as a declaration against interest.[4] The present chapter is concerned only with those situa-

§ 304

1. Stein v. Commissioner of Internal Revenue, 322 F.2d 78, 82 (5th Cir.1963) ("It was not error for the Tax Court to accept the entries in Stein's notebooks that showed daily net gambling winnings and fail to give credence to the entries in said notebooks that showed daily net losses. The entries showing daily net gambling winnings were in the nature of declarations against interest while the entries showing daily net losses were in the nature of self serving declarations."); Vickers v. Ripley, 226 Ark. 802, 295 S.W.2d 309 (1956); Parker v. Priestley, 39 So.2d 210, 215 (Fla. 1949) (party's account books admitted against him as admission despite statute providing such books shall be admissible in his favor); Wentz v. Guaranteed Sand &

Gravel Co., 205 Minn. 611, 287 N.W. 113 (1939); Utilities Insurance Co. v. Stuart, 134 Neb. 413, 278 N.W. 827 (1938). See generally § 262 supra; Dec.Dig. Evidence ⟺354(18).

2. E.g., Cohen v. Berry, 188 A.2d 302 (D.C.Ct.App. 1963). See generally § 9, supra; Dec.Dig. Witnesses ⟺255(7)–(8).

3. Ettelson v. Metropolitan Life Insurance Co., 164 F.2d 660 (2d Cir.1947); Note, 9 U.Calif. Davis L.Rev. 147 (1976). See generally, Ch. 30 supra; Dec.Dig. Evidence ⟺355(5)–(6).

4. See generally, Ch. 27 supra; Dec.Dig. Evidence ⟺354(24).

tions in which none of these alternative theories of admissibility is available, or if available is not resorted to, and a specific exception to the hearsay rule for regularly kept records must be invoked.

 WESTLAW REFERENCES

"regularly kept record*"

§ 305. The Origin of the Regularly Kept Records Exception and the Shopbook Vestige[1]

By the 1600's in England a custom emerged in the common law courts of receiving the "shop books" of tradesmen and craftsmen as evidence of debts for goods sold or services rendered on open accounts. Since most tradesmen were their own book-keepers, the rule permitted a reasonable means of avoiding the harsh common law rule preventing a party from appearing as a witness in his own behalf. Nevertheless, theoretical objections to the self-serving nature of this evidence, apparently coupled with abuse of it in practice, led to a statutory curb in 1609,[2] limiting the use of a party's shopbooks to a period of one year after the debt was created except where a bill of debt was given or where the transaction was between merchants and tradesmen. The higher courts refused to recognize the books at all after the year had elapsed, although in practice such evidence was received in the lower courts with small claims jurisdiction.

During the 1700's a broader doctrine began to develop in the English common law courts. At first, this permitted only the use of regular entries in the books of a party by a deceased clerk, but this was expanded to cover books regularly kept by third persons who had since died. By 1832 the doctrine

was firmly grounded and its scope was held to include all entries made by a person, since deceased, in the ordinary course of his business.

The development of the doctrine in America was less satisfactory, however. In the colonies limited exceptions for the books of a party based on the English statute of 1609 and Dutch practice were in force. In addition to requiring that the entries be regularly made at or about the time of the transaction and as a part of the routine of the business, other common restrictions were that (1) the party using the book not have had a clerk, (2) the party file a "supplemental oath" to the justness of the account, (3) the books bear an honest appearance, (4) each transaction not exceed a certain limited value, (5) witnesses testify from their experience in dealing with the party that the books are honest, (6) the books be used only to prove open accounts for goods and services furnished the defendant (thus making them unavailable for proof of loans, and goods and services furnished under special contract or furnished to third persons on defendant's credit), and (7) other proof be made of the actual delivery of some of the goods.[3]

Not until the early 1800's did the American equivalent of the English general exception for regular business entries by deceased persons emerge. As the doctrine gained acceptance, however, often no provision was made for the "shop books" of a party, whose admissibility continued to be controlled by the restrictive statutes. This made little sense, especially in view of the fact that abolition of the party's disqualification as a witness[4] removed the justification for treating the books of a party as a special problem. Most courts today take the reasonable position that if shop book statutes remain, they

§ 305

1. See generally, 5 Wigmore, Evidence § 1518 (Chadbourn rev.1974); Radtke v. Taylor, 105 Or. 559, 210 P. 863 (1922) (Harris, J.); 30 Am.Jur.2d Evidence §§ 918–926.

2. 7 Jac. I, ch. 12 (1609).

3. See sources cited in n. 1 supra.

4. See § 65 supra. The retention of a vestige of the old common law disqualification of a party in the "dead man's statutes" adopted by many jurisdictions created a special problem. These statutes prohibited a party from testifying in an action brought by or against a decedent's estate regarding transactions with the deceased; see § 65 supra. It has generally been held, however, that use of the shop books (and the sup-

are to be regarded as an alternative ground of admissibility. A party's books offered in his own behalf, then, may be admissible even if they do not meet the shop book act requirements if they meet the tests for regularly kept records generally.

WESTLAW REFERENCES

shopbook*

§ 306. The Regularly Kept Records Exception in General [1]

The hearsay exception for regularly kept records is justified on grounds analogous to those underlying other exceptions to the hearsay rule. Unusual reliability is regarded as furnished by the fact that in practice regularly kept records have a high degree of accuracy (as compared to other memoranda). The very regularity and continuity of the records are calculated to train the recordkeeper in habits of precision; if of a financial nature, the records are periodically checked by balance-striking and audits; and in actual experience the entire business of the nation and many other activities function in reliance upon records of this kind. The impetus for resort to these hearsay statements at common law arose when the person or persons who made the entry and upon whose knowledge it was based were unavailable as witnesses because of death, insanity, disappearance or other reason.

The common law exception had four elements: (a) the entries must be original entries made in the routine of a business, (b) the entries must have been made upon the personal knowledge of the recorder or of someone reporting to him, (c) the entries must have been made at or near the time of the transaction recorded, and (d) the recorder and his informant must be shown to be unavailable.[2] If these conditions were met, the business entry was admissible to prove the facts recited in it.

The regularly kept records exception had evolved within the context of simple business organizations, with the typical records of a double-entry system of journal and ledger. In this setting the common law requirements were not unduly burdensome. Control and management of complex organizations require correspondingly complicated records, however, and the organizations of business, government, and institutions in general were becoming increasingly intricate. While the theory of the exception was sound, some of the common law requirements were incompatible with modern conditions. The limitation to "business" records was unduly restrictive. The requirement of an "original" record was inconsistent with modern developments in record keeping. The need to account for nonproduction of all participants in the process of assembling and recording information was a needless and disruptive burden in view of the unlikelihood that any of the persons involved would remember a particular transaction or its details. And there were uncertainties as to what witnesses were required to be called to lay the necessary foundation for the records. Since the courts seemed unable to resolve these difficulties, relief was sought in legislation, and the exception is now governed by statute or rule virtually everywhere.

plemental oath necessary for their use) was not "testimony" within the meaning of the dead man's statutes, Roth v. Headlee, 238 Iowa 1340, 29 N.W.2d 923 (1947), or that the use of shop books of a party was an exception to the dead man's statute. House v. Beak, 141 Ill. 290, 30 N.E. 1065 (1892). See generally, 5 Wigmore, Evidence § 1554 (Chadbourn rev.1974); Annot., 6 A.L.R. 756.

§ 306

1. See generally, 5 Wigmore, Evidence §§ 1517–1561 (Chadbourn rev.1974); Morgan, et al.,

The Law of Evidence, Some Proposals for Its Reform, ch. 5 (1927); Laughlin, Business Entries and the Like, 46 Iowa L.Rev. 276 (1961); Note, Revised Business Entry Statutes: Theory and Practice, 48 Colum.L.Rev. 920 (1948); Annot., 13 A.L.R.3d 284 (admissibility of party's books to prove loans or payment by that party); Annot., 77 A.L.R.3d 115 and 31 A.L.R.Fed. 457 (police reports); 30 Am.Jur.2d Evidence §§ 927–961; C.J.S. Evidence §§ 682–695; Dec.Dig. Evidence ⟨key⟩350, 354, 361, 376, 383(8), Criminal Law ⟨key⟩434.

2. Laughlin, supra n. 1, at p. 282.

The principal statutes were the Commonwealth Fund Act and the Uniform Business Records as Evidence Act.[3] Their essential features are now incorporated in Federal and Revised Uniform Rule (1974) 803(6) which provides a hearsay exception, without regard to unavailability of declarant, as follows:

A memorandum, report, record, or data compilation, in any form, of acts, events, conditions, opinions, or diagnoses, made at or near the time by, or from information transmitted by, a person with knowledge, if kept in the course of a regularly conducted business activity, and if it was the regular practice of that business activity to make the memorandum, report, record, or data compilation, all as shown by the testimony of the custodian or other qualified witness, unless the source of information or the method or circumstances of preparation indicate lack of trustworthiness. The term "business" as used in this paragraph in-

3. The Commonwealth Fund Act provided:

Any writing or record, whether in the form of an entry in a book or otherwise, made as a memorandum or record of any act, transaction, occurrence or event shall be admissible in evidence in proof of said act, transaction, occurrence or event, if the trial judge shall find that it was made in the regular course of any business, and that it was the regular course of such business to make such memorandum or record at the time of such act, transaction, occurrence or event or within a reasonable time thereafter. All other circumstances of the making of such writing or record, including lack of personal knowledge by the entrant or maker, may be shown to affect its weight, but they shall not affect its admissibility. The term business shall include business, profession, occupation and calling of every kind.

Morgan et al., The Law of Evidence, Some Proposals for Its Reform 63 (1927).

Several states and the Congress adopted this act. For federal courts it has been superseded by Federal Rule 803(6).

The Uniform Act provided:

§ 1. Definition. The term "business" shall include every kind of business, profession, occupation, calling or operation of institutions, whether carried on for profit or not.

§ 2. Business Record. A record of an act, condition or event, shall, in so far as relevant, be competent evidence if the custodian or other qualified witness testifies to its identity and the mode of its preparation, and if it was made in the regular course of business, at or near the time of the act, condition or event, and if, in the opinion of the court, the

cludes business, institution, association, profession, occupation, and calling of every kind, whether or not conducted for profit.[4]

 WESTLAW REFERENCES

803(6) /p rule* record* hearsay

§ 307. Types of Records [1]: Opinions: Absence of Entry

The usual statements of the rule suggest that oral reports are not within it, even if the other requirements for admissibility are met. The common law cases tended to speak in terms of entries in account books, the subject usually under consideration.[2] The Commonwealth Fund Act [3] used the terms "writing or record", and the Uniform Act [4] spoke of "record." The Federal and Revised Uniform Rules (1974) [5] include a "memorandum, report, record, or data com-

sources of information, method and time of preparation were such as to justify its admission.

9A U.L.A. 506 (1965).

After wide adoption, the Uniform Act was superseded by Original Uniform Rule 63(13), which in turn has been superseded by Revised Uniform Rule (1974) 803(6). The Federal Rule and the Revised Uniform Rule are identical.

4. The language "if kept in the course of a regularly conducted business activity, and if it was the regular practice of that business activity to make the memorandum, report, record, or data compilation, all" was substituted by the Congress for the Supreme Court's provision, "all in the course of a regularly conducted activity". The Congress also added the definition of "business" in the second sentence and made a few other changes of no significance. House Comm. on Judiciary, Fed. Rules of Evidence, H.R.Rep. No. 650, 93d Cong., 1st Sess., p. 14 (1973); Senate Comm. on Judiciary, Fed. Rules of Evidence, S.Rep. No. 1277, 93d Cong., 2d Sess., p. 16 (1974); H.R., Fed. Rules of Evidence, Conf.Rep. No. 1597, 93d Cong., 2d Sess., p. 11 (1974).

§ 307

1. See generally, 5 Wigmore, Evidence § 1528 (Chadbourn rev.1974). See also Annot., 83 A.L.R. 806 (admissibility of loose leaf systems of account).

2. See § 305 supra. In Baltimore & Ohio Southwestern Railroad Co. v. Tripp, 175 Ill. 251, 51 N.E. 831 (1898), a record of engine inspections was held properly excluded because not a book of account.

3. Section 306, n. 2 supra.

4. Section 306, n. 3 supra.

5. Text fol. § 306, n. 3 supra.

pilation". Of these, only the term "report" in the Federal and Revised Uniform Rule (1974) is arguably broad enough to include an oral report, and there the provision that the report be "kept" negates the idea that oral reports are within the rule.[6] Nevertheless the English position is that oral reports may qualify under the exception [7] and some American courts have admitted oral reports on the basis of a partial analogy to business records.[8]

Under the common law exception, the entries were required to be "original" entries and not mere transcribed records or copies.[9] This was based on the assumption that the original entries were more likely to be accurate than subsequent copies or transcriptions. In business practice, however, it is customary for daily transactions such as sales or services rendered to be noted upon slips, memorandum books or the like by the person most directly concerned, and for someone else to collect these memoranda and from them make entries into a perma-

nent book such as a journal or ledger. In these cases, the entries in the permanent record sufficiently comply with the requirement of originality.[10] They would certainly be admissible if the slips or memoranda disappeared, and should, it seems, be admissible as the original permanent entry without proof as to the unavailability of the tentative memoranda. This also serves the interest of convenience, since it is much easier to use a ledger or similar source than slips or temporary memoranda when the inquiry is into the whole state of an account. Of course, the slips or memoranda would also be admissible if they should be offered.[11] The Federal and Revised Uniform Rules (1974) do not require that the entry be original but allow "any form." [12]

It has been suggested that entries in the form of opinions are not admissible if the declarant was not an expert making a statement concerning a matter within his expertise and as to which he would be competent to express an opinion if testifying in per-

---

6. Id.

7. 5 Wigmore, Evidence § 1528 (Chadbourn rev. 1974); citing Sussex Peerage Case, 11 Cl. & F. 113 (1844). See also Cross, Evidence 560 (5th ed. 1979). Wigmore suggests that the English requirement that the person making the report have a duty to do so (see § 308 infra) provides a sufficient additional assurance of reliability to justify expanding the exception to include oral reports.

8. Williams v. Walton & Whann Co., 9 Houst. (Del.) 322, 32 A. 726 (1892) (oral reports admissible if made regularly); Geralds v. Champlin, 93 N.H. 157, 37 A.2d 155 (1944) (oral reports of deceased foreman to superintendent regarding employee's complaints of trouble with his leg, made as part of checkup system admissible).

The possibility of achieving admissibility of otherwise conforming oral reports by resort to the "residual" hearsay exception should not be overlooked. See § 324.2 infra.

9. See generally, 5 Wigmore, Evidence §§ 1532, 1558 (Chadbourn rev.1974); Annot., 17 A.L.R.2d 235; 30 Am.Jur.2d Evidence §§ 941–945. In a typical double-entry bookkeeping system, the journal or daybook in which transactions are entered in chronological order is the first permanent record. A strict literal interpretation of "book of original entry" under this system would be limited to the journal. The ledger, to which items are transferred according to classification and

which furnishes the "controls" of the business, however, obviously serves up information in far more usable form, and its accuracy is equally assured by its being a part of the entire system. Accordingly, while insistence is sometimes found that the journal be used, the case has generally been otherwise. Statutes containing the expression "book of original entry" offer occasional difficulty.

10. Grand Strand Construction Co., Inc. v. Graves, 269 S.C. 594, 239 S.E.2d 81 (1977) (secretary made entries in ledger from man-hours tabulated by job foreman on scraps of paper handed to her or left under office door, sometimes telephoned; scraps not kept); Vickers v. Ripley, 226 Ark. 802, 295 S.W.2d 309 (1956) (ledger account made up from sales tickets or invoices); Tull v. Turek, 38 Del.Ch. 182, 147 A.2d 658 (1958) (ledger in which entries were made once each year from data supplied by plaintiffs); Cascade Lumber Terminal, Inc. v. Cvitanovich, 215 Or. 111, 332 P.2d 1061 (1958) (looseleaf subsidiary ledger in which bookkeeper made entries from log scalers' sheets on which number of logs delivered was initially entered); Tri-Motor Sales, Inc. v. Travelers Indemnity, 19 Wis.2d 99, 119 N.W.2d 327 (1963) (account books made from purchase invoices and hard copies of sales slips, and not the invoices and slips themselves, were "original entries").

11. Annot., 21 A.L.R.2d 773.

12. Text § 306 supra at n. 4.

son.[13] In general, the opinion rule should be restricted to governing the manner of presenting courtroom testimony and should have little application to the admissibility of out-of-court statements as a matter of form.[14] The Federal and Revised Uniform Rule (1974)[15] specifically provide that an admissible regularly kept record may include opinions. These will, of course, ordinarily be expert opinions, and they will be subject to requirements governing proper subjects for expert opinions and qualifications of experts. For further discussion in connection with hospital records, see section 313 infra.

Sometimes the absence of an entry relating to a particular transaction is offered as proof that no such transaction took place.[16] For example, proof is offered that a car rental agency's records show no lease or rental activity in regard to a certain vehicle, as tending to show that the defendant in whose possession it was found had stolen it.[17] The majority of courts have admitted the evidence for this purpose,[18] and Federal and Revised Uniform Rule (1974) 803(7) specifically so provides:

> Evidence that a matter is not included in the memoranda reports, records, or data compilations, in any form, kept in accordance with the provisions of paragraph (6),[19] to prove the nonoccurrence or nonexistence of the matter, if

the matter was of a kind of which a memorandum, report, record, or data compilation was regularly made and preserved, unless the sources of information or other circumstances indicate lack of trustworthiness.[20]

 WESTLAW REFERENCES

"oral report*" "original entr***" /s admissib! hearsay 803(7)

---

§ 308. Made in the Routine of a "Business"[1]: Accident Reports

The early cases construed the requirement of a "business" literally, and accordingly excluded, as not concerned with "business," records of temperature kept daily as an avocation[2] and private records kept in connection with an individual's financial affairs.[3] The Commonwealth Fund Act[4] defined "business" to "include business, profession, occupation and calling of every kind." The Uniform Act[5] added "operation of institutions, whether carried on for profit or not." In the Federal and Revised Uniform Rule (1974) "business" includes "business, institution, association, profession, occupation, and calling of every kind, whether or not conducted for profit."[6] This rule, applying to a "memorandum, report, record, or data compilation, in any form", of a "business" thus

---

13. Standard Oil Co. v. Moore, 251 F.2d 188, 214 (9th Cir.1957):

> "A good many of the exhibits . . . contain expressions of opinion, or conclusions, concerning the reason why another oil company or a noncustomer service station operator took, or failed to take, certain action, or concerning the probable course such companies would follow in the future. Expressions of opinion or conclusions on such matters do not call for professional or scientific knowledge or skill. It follows that exhibits containing such recitals were not admissible [under the former federal statute]."

14. See § 18 supra.

15. Text fol. § 306, n. 3 supra.

16. See generally, 5 Wigmore, Evidence § 1531 (Chadbourn rev.1974); 30 Am.Jur.2d Evidence § 959; C.J.S. Evidence § 687.

17. United States v. De Georgia, 420 F.2d 889 (9th Cir. 1969).

18. United States v. De Georgia, 420 F.2d 889, 891–894 (9th Cir.1969).

19. For paragraph (6), see text fol. § 306, n. 3 supra.

20. The Federal Advisory Committee's Note suggests the evidence is not hearsay.

§ 308

1. See generally, 30 Am.Jur.2d Evidence §§ 937, 939; C.J.S. Evidence § 685(1).

2. Arnold v. Hussey, 111 Me. 224, 88 A. 724 (1913).

3. In re Cummings' Estate, 226 Iowa 1207, 286 N.W. 409 (1939) (plaintiff's memorandum book of loans made by him inadmissible because he was not in the loan business). See Annot., 68 A.L.R. 692 (check stubs).

4. Section 306, n. 2 supra.

5. Section 306, n. 3 supra.

6. Text fol. § 306, n. 3 supra. The definition alternates between emphasizing the kind of entity that carries on an activity and the kind of activity that is carried on.

broadly defined, is of great scope. It has been held to encompass such diverse items as a catalog,[7] attaching envelopes to bids upon opening,[8] a hospital's scrapbook of newspaper articles showing visiting hours,[9] prison counselor's report to staff psychiatrist of incident involving prisoner,[10] invoices from suppliers,[11] an automobile lease by dealer,[12] and an appraisal of a painting for purposes of insurance,[13] all in addition, of course, to account books and their counterparts which might more readily fall within the usual concept of business records.[14] Hospital records are specially treated in section 313 infra, and computer-stored records are the subject of section 314 infra. Diaries, if of a purely personal nature or for purposes of litigation, do not fall within the rule,[15] but if kept for business purposes are within the rule,[16] and likewise as to memoranda of telephone conversations.[17] Church records, admissible at common law, are the subject of Federal and Revised Uniform Rule (1974) 803(11).[18]

Under the English rules, both the matter or event recorded and the recording of it must have been performed pursuant to a duty to a third person.[19] This is not the case under the American law.[20]

Problems are raised by the purpose of the report and the circumstances of its preparation, particularly reports of accidents. The leading case is Palmer v. Hoffman,[21] a suit against railroad trustees arising out of an accident at a railroad crossing. The engineer of the train involved was interviewed two days after the accident by a representative of the railroad and a representative of the state Public Utilities Commission. He signed a statement giving his version of the incident. The engineer died before trial, and the statement was offered by the defendants who offered to prove that the railroad obtained such statements in the regular course of its business. Affirming the trial court's exclusion of the report, the Supreme Court of the United States stated:

"[The report] is not a record made for the systematic conduct of the business as a business. An accident report may affect that business in the sense that it affords information on which the management may act. It is not, however, typical of entries made systematically or as a matter of routine to record events or occurrences, to reflect transactions with others, or to provide internal controls. . . . Unlike payrolls, accounts receivable, accounts payable, bills of lading and the like, these reports are

---

7. United States v. Grossman, 614 F.2d 295 (1st Cir. 1980).

8. United States v. Patterson, 644 F.2d 890 (1st Cir.1981).

9. United States v. Reese, 568 F.2d 1246 (6th Cir. 1977).

10. Stone v. Morris, 546 F.2d 730 (7th Cir.1976).

11. In re King Enterprises, Inc., 678 F.2d 73 (8th Cir.1982).

12. United States v. Page, 544 F.2d 982 (8th Cir. 1976).

13. United States v. Licavoli, 604 F.2d 613 (9th Cir. 1979), cert. denied 446 U.S. 935.

14. Nonrule cases include: United States v. Keane, 522 F.2d 534 (7th Cir.1975), cert. denied 424 U.S. 976; Thompson v. State, 270 Ind. 442, 386 N.E.2d 682 (1979) (autopsy report); State v. Spray, 221 Kan. 67, 558 P.2d 129 (1976) (retail price tags on merchandise); Porter v. State, 623 S.W.2d 374 (Tex.Cr.App.1981), cert. denied 456 U.S. 965 (tape of police radio messages); Hill v. Joseph T. Ryerson & Son, Inc., ___ W.Va. ___, 268 S.E.2d 296 (1980) (paint stick markings on shipment of pipe).

15. Clark v. City of Los Angeles, 650 F.2d 1033 (9th Cir. 1981), cert denied 456 U.S. 927.

16. United States v. McPartlin, 595 F.2d 1321 (7th Cir.1979), cert. denied 444 U.S. 833; United States v. Hedman, 630 F.2d 1184 (7th Cir.1980), cert. denied 450 U.S. 965.

17. Annot., 94 A.L.R.3d 975.

18. Fed. and Rev.Unif.R.Evid. (1974) 803 (11):

Statements of births, marriages, divorces, deaths, legitimacy, ancestry, relationship by blood or marriage, or other similar facts of personal or family history, contained in a regularly kept record of a religious organization.

19. Cross, Evidence 560 (5th ed. 1979).

20. Hutchins v. Berry, 75 N.H. 416, 75 Atl. 650 (1910); Lebrun v. Boston & M.R. Co., 83 N.H. 293, 142 Atl. 128 (1928) (dictum). See generally, 5 Wigmore, Evidence, § 1524 (Chadbourn rev. 1974). No requirement in terms of duty is found in the Federal or Revised Uniform Rules (1974), but the equivalent results from requiring that all participants be in this course of the business. See § 310 infra.

21. 318 U.S. 109 (1943).

calculated for use essentially in the court, not in the business. Their primary use is in litigating, not in railroading."[22]

Consequently, the report was held not to have been made "in the regular course" of the business within the meaning of the federal statute then providing for the admissibility of business records.[23]

It has been urged that *Palmer* violated the letter of the statute,[24] and the lower courts did not deal with it uniformly. The most reasonable reading of it, however, is that it did not create a blanket rule of exclusion for accident reports or similar records kept by businesses. Rather, it recognized a discretionary power in the trial court to exclude evidence which meets the letter of the business records exception but which, under the circumstances, appears to lack the reliability which business records are assumed ordinarily to have.[25] The existence of a motive and opportunity to falsify the record, especially in the absence of any countervailing

factors weighing against such action, should be primary factors considered.[26] The Federal and Revised Uniform Rules (1974) incorporate this reading of *Palmer* by allowing admission in evidence if the report otherwise complies with the requirements of the rule "unless the source of information or the method or circumstances of preparation indicate lack of trustworthiness."[27]

Police reports and records can, of course, meet the requirements for the regularly kept records exception to the hearsay rule. They can also qualify under the hearsay exception for public records and reports.[28] Federal and Revised Uniform Rule (1974) 803(8) contains certain restrictions upon the use of police reports in criminal cases. In jurisdictions where the Federal and Revised Uniform Rules (1974) are in effect the question has arisen whether the limitation expressed in Rule 803(8) can be avoided by offering police reports under the regularly kept records exception which contains no

---

22. Id. at 113–114.

23. For text of the former federal statute see § 306, n. 2 supra.

24. Laughlin, Business Entries and the Like, 46 Iowa L.Rev. 276, 289 (1961). Contra, Comment, 43 Colum.L.Rev. 392 (1943).

25. Among the cases under the former federal statute holding reports of this kind inadmissible in reliance upon *Palmer*, see Colorificio Italiano Max Meyer S.P.A. v. S/S Hellenic Wave, 419 F.2d 223 (5th Cir. 1969) (survey report inadmissible in admiralty case because intended use is in litigation); Picker X-Ray Corp. v. Freker, 405 F.2d 916 (8th Cir.1969) (hospital "incident report" concerning accident, written by business manager shown to have been aware at the time of the possibility of litigation, inadmissible); Hussein v. Isthmian Lines, Inc., 405 F.2d 946 (5th Cir.1968) (forms used by ship's officers to cause agents in foreign ports to obtain medical attention for crew members inadmissible, because they were essentially reports by physicians to an employer regarding employees' physical condition); United States v. Kim, 595 F.2d 755 (D.C.Cir. 1979) (telex from foreign bank describing activity in bank account of accused, sent for use in litigation, inadmissible). In favor of admissibility, Mitchell v. American Export Isbrandtsen Lines, Inc., 430 F.2d 1023 (2d Cir.1970) (report of illness by ship's physician admissible, because it was not made for purposes of litigation and the maker was available for examination at trial); Caldecott v. Long Island Lighting Co., 417 F.2d 994 (2d Cir.1969) (medical examiner's report properly admitted, because there was no incentive to falsify); Gaussen v. United Fruit Co., 412 F.2d 72 (2d Cir.1969)

(suggestion that letter from ship's captain to employer regarding accident investigation on ship revealing that injured employee was intoxicated would be admissible); Vaccaro v. Alcoa Steamship Co., 405 F.2d 1133 (2d Cir. 1968) (report made by army employee should have been admitted since he had no motive to falsify). Where the party offering the report was not the party with the opportunity to falsify it, the report has been held admissible on the ground that no prejudice to the complaining party is possible, Lewis v. Baker, 526 F.2d 470 (2d Cir.1975) (railroad accident report made pursuant to railroad and I.C.C. rules); Korte v. New York, New Haven & Hartford Railroad Co., 191 F.2d 86 (2d Cir. 1951), cert. denied 342 U.S. 868, noted 37 Corn.L.Q. 290, 5 Vand.L.Rev. 651 (plaintiff offers report of physical examination made by physician employed by defendant). See also Leon v. Penn Central Co., 428 F.2d 528 (7th Cir.1970) (plaintiff offers accident report made by defendant's employee).

26. Thus where the only function that the report serves is to assist in litigation or its preparation, many of the normal checks upon the accuracy of business records are not operative. Reliance upon the report's accuracy in the day-to-day operation of the business is significant. Lewis v. Baker, supra n. 25.

27. Text supra § 306 at n. 4. See Stone v. Morris, 546 F.2d 730 (7th Cir.1976) (memo by prison counselor to staff psychiatrist recounting events leading up to injury of prisoner admissible); Abdel v. United States, 670 F.2d 73 (7th Cir.1982) (investigators' reports admissible in proceedings to disqualify supermarket for food stamp violations).

28. See generally Ch. 32 infra.

such limitation. The answer under the Federal Rules has been in the negative, and the same result would seem to follow under the Revised Uniform Rules (1974). The matter is discussed in greater detail in section 317 infra.

WESTLAW REFERENCES

any every /4 institution association profession
    occupation calling /p "business record*"

accident* /3 report* /p "business record*"

palmer +s hoffman & 318 +s 109

803(8) /p police! "law enforcement"

---

§ 309. Made at or Near the Time of the Transaction Recorded [1]

A substantial factor in the reliability of any system of records is the promptness with which transactions are recorded.

The formula of Federal and Revised Uniform Rule (1974) 803(6) is "at or near the time".[2] Whether an entry made subsequent to the transaction has been made within a sufficient time to render it within the exception depends upon whether the time span between the transaction and the entry was so great as to suggest a danger of inaccuracy by lapse of memory.[3]

§ 309

1. See generally, 5 Wigmore, Evidence §§ 1526, 1550 (Chadbourn rev.1974); 30 Am.Jur.2d Evidence § 938; C.J.S. Evidence § 690; Dec.Dig.Evidence ☞354(12).

2. Text § 306, at n. 4 supra. Compare the hearsay exception for recorded past recollection where insurance against lapse of memory is phrased "when the matter was fresh in his memory." § 301 supra. This appearance of inconsistency is resolved by the fact that recorded recollection entails an inquiry into the actual recollection of the witness on the stand, while regularly kept records involve an objective standard for persons participating in the process but not called as witnesses.

3. The circumstances must be taken into consideration in each case. Missouri Pacific Railway Co. v. Austin, 292 F.2d 415 (5th Cir.1961). Periods of varying length have been ruled too long under the facts: Hiram Ricker & Sons v. Students International Medita-

WESTLAW REFERENCES

803(6) /p "near the time"

---

§ 310. Personal Knowledge: All Participants in Regular Course [1]

The common law exception for regularly kept records required that the entries have been made by one with personal knowledge of the matter entered or upon reports to him by one with personal knowledge.[2] The entrant was required to be acting in the regular course of business, and if the information was supplied by another, that person also was required to be acting in the regular course of business.[3] If the information was transmitted through intermediaries, they, too, were subject to the same requirement.[4] The application of the regular course requirement to all participants in the process of acquiring, transmitting, and recording information was consistent with, indeed mandated by, the theory of the hearsay exception.[5]

Reform legislation in general has not dealt clearly with the questions whether the information must initially be acquired by a person with firsthand knowledge and whether he and all other persons involved in the process must be acting in the regular course of the business. The Commonwealth Fund Act [6] required that the record be "made in

tion Society, 501 F.2d 550 (1st Cir.1974) (one week); Missouri Pacific Railway Co. v. Austin, supra (two months); United States v. Kim, 595 F.2d 755 (D.C.Cir. 1979) (two years).

§ 310

1. See generally, Wigmore, Evidence §§ 1530, 1530a, 1555 (Chadbourn rev. 1974); 30 Am.Jur.2d Evidence §§ 951–953; C.J.S. Evidence §§ 692–693; Dec. Dig.Evidence ☞354(11).

2. Lord v. Moore, 37 Me. 208, 220 (1854).

3. 5 Wigmore, Evidence § 1530 (Chadbourn rev. 1974).

4. Rathborne v. Hatch, 80 App.Div. 115, 80 N.Y.S. 347 (1903) (floor member of stock brokerage firm reported his sales to boys who telephoned the information to office).

5. § 306 supra.

6. § 306, n. 2 supra.

the regular course of . . . business" and provided that "other circumstances . . . , including lack of personal knowledge by the entrant or maker, may be shown to affect its weight, but they shall not affect its admissibility." The Uniform Act [7] also required that the record be "made in the regular course of business," and in addition required that "in the opinion of the court, the sources of information, method and time of preparation were such as to justify its admission." Federal and Revised Uniform Rule (1974) 803(6) [8] requires that the record be "made . . . by, or from information transmitted by, a person with knowledge, if kept in the course of a regularly conducted business activity . . . ." Assuming, as is reasonable, that "knowledge" means firsthand knowledge, then Rule 803(6) answers the first part of the question above in the affirmative, to the effect that the person who originally feeds the information into the process must have firsthand knowledge. The two Acts, however, are vague in terms on this point. As to whether the person making the record must be in the regular course of business, both the Acts and Rule 803(6), the first two saying "made" and the latter "kept", in the regular course of business, answer in the affirmative. Stretching "made" and "kept", however, respectively to include both the original acquisition of the information and its transmission to the recorder is troublesome.

These doubts have largely been resolved by referring to the underlying theory of the exception, namely, a practice and environment encouraging the making of accurate records. If any person in the process is not acting in the regular course of the business, then an essential link in the trustworthiness chain fails, just as it does when the person feeding in the information does not have firsthand knowledge. The leading case is Johnson v. Lutz,[9] decided under the New York version of the Commonwealth Fund Act, holding inadmissible a police officer's report insofar as it was not based upon his personal knowledge but on information supplied by a bystander. Wigmore was bitterly critical of the decision,[10] but the courts generally have followed its lead,[11] whatever the statute or rule.

When the matter recorded itself satisfies the conditions of some other hearsay exception, the requirement that the person initially acquiring the information be in the regular course of the business is not insisted upon. For example, if a police officer in his report of an automobile accident includes a statement by one of the drivers who later becomes a party to litigation, the statement qualifies as an admission, and the report may be used to prove it; it is immaterial that the officer has no firsthand knowledge of the correctness of the statement. The

---

7. § 306, n. 3 supra.

8. Text § 306 at n. 4 supra.

9. 253 N.Y. 124, 170 N.E. 517 (1930).

10. 5 Wigmore, Evidence § 1561a, p. 490, § 1561b, p. 507 (Chadbourn rev. 1974). But compare § 1530, p. 451:

> (4) the conclusion is, then, that *where an entry is made by one person in the regular course of business, recording an oral or written report, made to him by other persons in the regular course of business, of a transaction lying in the personal knowledge of the latter persons, there is no objection to receiving that entry under the present exception, verified by the testimony of the former person only, or of a superior who testifies to the regular course of business, provided the practical inconvenience of producing on the stand the numerous other persons thus concerned would in the partic-*

ular case outweigh the probable utility of doing so. (Italics in original.)

11. Under the various acts: United States v. Grayson, 166 F.2d 863 (2d Cir.1948); Colvin v. United States, 479 F.2d 998 (9th Cir.1973); United States v. Smith, 172 U.S.App.D.C. 297, 521 F.2d 957, 31 A.L.R. Fed. 437 (1975); Fagan v. City of Newark, 78 N.J. Super. 294, 188 A.2d 427 (1963); Haas v. Kasnot, 371 Pa. 580, 92 A.2d 171 (1952); Hutchinson v. Plante, 175 Conn. 1, 392 A.2d 488 (1978). Under Federal Rule 803(6): United States v. Baker, 693 F.2d 183 (D.C.Cir. 1982) (prosecution for selling stolen government checks; error, though harmless, to admit Treasury form executed by payee to prove nonpayment and non-negotiation, since payee not in regular course); United States v. Lieberman, 637 F.2d 95 (2d Cir.1980) (hotel guest registration card filled out with name of defendant by person registering not admissible as business record to prove that defendant did register).

matter is discussed further in connection with multiple hearsay.[12]

Direct proof of actual knowledge may be difficult, and it may even be impossible to prove specifically the identity of the informant with actual knowledge. Evidence that it was someone's business duty in the organization's routine to observe the matter will be prima facie sufficient to establish actual knowledge. This does not dispense with the need for personal knowledge, but permits it to be proved by evidence of practice and a reasonable assumption that general practice was followed in regard to a particular matter, or by other appropriate circumstances.[13]

 WESTLAW REFERENCES

personal! /2 know! /s record** entry entries enter /p regular! /4 business**
johnson +s lutz /p admissib! inadmissib! hearsay

§ 311. Unavailability [1]

If the person who made a business record were present as a witness, the record could be used to refresh his recollection, or if he were even then unable to recall the facts, his testimony might be such as to qualify the record as past recollection recorded.[2] This was true at common law as it is under rules and statutes today. If, however, the witness for some reason could not be produced in court, i.e. was unavailable, then these avenues to admissibility for the business record could not be used. A need for a special hearsay exception for business records in such cases was apparent. And, as sometimes happens, the reason why the rule came into existence was incorporated in the rule as a requirement, in this instance a requirement of unavailability.

The process of calling a series of participants, only to have each testify that referring to the business record did not refresh his recollection, or at best to give rote testimony that it was his practice to be accurate, was a manifest waste of the court's time and disruptive of the business organization in question with no corresponding benefit. Yet no other result could be expected from participants in the keeping of records under modern conditions.[3] The reliability of the record could be shown by evidence other than the testimony of participants, as had been done when a participant was unavailable. Accordingly, unavailability as a requirement virtually [4] disappeared.

---

12. See § 324.3 infra.

Observe that the requirement of firsthand knowledge by a person in the regular course of business may be satisfied by other proof of the correctness of the record. United States v. Smith, 609 F.2d 1294 (9th Cir. 1979) (hotel guest registration card filled out with name of defendant by person registering properly admitted as proof that defendant did register when circumstantial evidence connected defendant with the registration). Compare United States v. Lieberman, supra n. 11, where connecting evidence was not produced.

Observe also that the record may be usable for a nonhearsay purpose without satisfying the requirement. United States v. Smith, 172 U.S.App.D.C. 297, 521 F.2d 957, 31 A.L.R.Fed. 437 (1975) (entry in police record of what complaining witness said not competent to prove truth of what was said, since he was not acting in the course of business, but usable for impeachment).

13. United States v. Lieberman, 637 F.2d 95 (2d Cir. 1980); United States v. McGrath, 613 F.2d 361 (2d Cir. 1979), cert. denied 446 U.S. 967, Senate Comm. on the Judiciary, Fed. Rules of Evidence, S.Rep. No. 1277, 93d Cong., 2d Sess., p. 17 (1974).

§ 311

1. See generally 5 Wigmore, Evidence § 1521 (Chadbourn rev. 1974); Dec.Dig. Evidence ⊆354(22)– (22½).

2. 5 Wigmore, Evidence § 1521 (Chadbourn rev. 1974); § 306 supra.

3. See L. Hand, J., in Massachusetts Bonding & Insurance Co. v. Norwich Pharmacal Co., 18 F.2d 934, 938 (2d Cir.1927): "It ought to appear that . . . the missing entrants, if called, would in the nature of things have no recollection of the events recorded and could do no more than corroborate the existing testimony as to the course of business in which they had a part . . . ."

4. Massachusetts Bonding & Insurance Co. v. Norwich Pharmacal Co., supra n. 3; Jennings v. United States, 73 F.2d 470 (5th Cir.1934) (work record vouched for by employment manager in charge of records admissible—"It was not necessary to produce or account for the person or persons who had made the notations in the absence of some proof throwing suspicion upon the genuineness of the record itself."); Continental National Bank v. First National Bank, 108 Tenn. 374, 68 S.W. 497 (1912); Heid Brothers, Inc. v. Commercial National Bank, 240 S.W. 908, 24 A.L.R. 904 (Tex.Com.

The Commonwealth Fund Act [5] and the Uniform Act [6] did not in terms address the unavailability requirement, but their silence was clearly meant to do away with it.[7] Federal and revised Uniform Rule (1974) 803(6) specifically eliminated the unavailability requirement by including the regularly kept records exception in a rule dealing with a group of exceptions where the hearsay rule does not operate to exclude the evidence "even though the declarant is available as a witness."

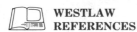 **WESTLAW REFERENCES**

"business record*" 803(6) /p unavailab! availab! /s declarant* witness**

§ 312. Proof: Who Must Be Called to Establish Admissibility [1]

The demise of the requirement of unavailability, discussed in the preceding section, had its impact upon the method of proving business records, as was intended. No longer was it necessary to call each available participant and exhaust the possibility of refreshing his memory or establishing the record as past recollection recorded; [2] compliance with the requirements for regularly kept records was provable by other means. Thus any witness with the necessary knowl-

edge about the particular record-keeping process could testify that it was the regular practice of the business to make such records, that the record was made in the regular course of business upon the personal knowledge of the recorder or of someone reporting to him, in the regular course of business, and that the entries were made at or near the time of the transaction. The Commonwealth Fund Act [3] did not deal with the matter of proof expressly, although a principal purpose of the Act was to alleviate the burdensome requirements of proof imposed by the common law. The Uniform Act,[4] however, provided that the foundation might be laid by "the custodian or other qualified witness," and this language is incorporated in Federal and revised Uniform Rule 803(6). Numerous decisions have analyzed its effect.

Perhaps the most commonly encountered witness is a person in authority in the record-keeping department of the business. Whether or not such a person falls within the term "custodian" may be questioned, but certainly he is "a qualified witness." [5] In fact, anyone with the necessary knowledge is qualified.[6] Problems may arise when one business organization seeks to introduce records in its possession but actually prepared by another. It seems evident that

App.1922); French v. Virginia Railway Co., 121 Va. 383, 93 S.E. 585 (1917); Willett v. Davis, 30 Wn.2d 622, 193 P.2d 321 (1948); State v. Larue, 98 W.Va. 677, 128 S.E. 116 (1925).

5. Supra § 306, n. 2.

6. Supra § 306, n. 3.

7. See Rossemanno v. Laclede Cab Co., 328 S.W.2d 677 (Mo.1959), holding that a medical report was admissible under the Uniform Act although the doctor who made the report was in the city and apparently available. After suggesting that there was no requirement of unavailability, the court added, "Moreover, it is inconceivable that a busy medical practitioner would have an independent recollection of each entry made in his business records and be able to testify from personal recollection as to when and by whom all entries were made." Id. at 681–82.

§ 312

1. See generally 5 Wigmore, Evidence § 1530 (Chadbourn rev. 1974); Green, The Model and Uniform Statutes Relating to Business Entries as Evidence, 31

Tulane L.Rev. 49, 55 (1956); Laughlin, Business Entries and the Like, 46 Iowa L.Rev. 276, 294–296 (1961); 30 Am.Jur.2d Evidence §§ 947–953; C.J.S. Evidence §§ 682(3), 693; Annot., 21 A.L.R.2d 773.

2. See § 311, n. 4 supra.

3. Supra § 306, n. 2.

4. Supra § 306, n. 3.

5. Rosario v. Amalgamated Ladies' Garment Cutters' Union, 605 F.2d 1228 (2d Cir.1979), cert. denied 446 U.S. 919 (police report prepared under supervision of testifying officer and containing substance of complaint, offered against complaining witness in false arrest action).

6. American International Pictures, Inc. v. Price Enterprises, Inc., 636 F.2d 933 (4th Cir.1980), cert. denied 451 U.S. 1010 (reports of theatre attendance checkers to show understatement of receipts in action by movie distributors to recover agreed percentage as rentals, with testimony by officers of checking companies authenticating reports and detailing procedures for selection, training, and supervision of checkers).

mere possession or "custody" of records under these circumstances does not qualify employees of the possessing party to lay the requisite foundation,[7] and that the transmittal of information by the custodian as to the contents of records in his possession does not qualify the transmittee to lay the foundation.[8] However, when the business offering the records of another has made an independent check of the records,[9] or can establish accuracy by other means,[10] the necessary foundation may be established.

 WESTLAW REFERENCES

establish*** lay*** /4 foundation* admissib! /s business regular! /4 record*

§ 313. Special Situations: (a) Hospital Records [1]

In some jurisdictions, specific statutory authority for the admission of hospital records exists.[2] Although some courts hesitated to expand the business record exception by decision to noncommercial establishments such as hospitals, all would concede today that hospital records are admissible upon the same basis as other regularly kept records.[3] This result is appropriate, for the safeguards of trustworthiness of the records of the modern hospital are at least as substantial as the guarantees of reliability of the records of business establishments.[4] Progress in medical skills has been accompanied by improvements and standardization of the practice of recording facts concerning the patient, and these recorded facts are routinely used to make decisions upon which the health and life of the patient depend.

Preliminary proof. As in the case of commercial records, a foundation for hospital records must be established by proof of a practice to make such records accurately and promptly and of the making of the specific record in the course of this hospital routine.[5] Although the common law requirement that each entrant and informant be produced has been enforced,[6] courts have modified this requirement in its application

---

7. NLRB v. First Termite Control Co., Inc., 646 F.2d 424 (9th Cir.1981) (to prove interstate transportation of lumber, bookkeeper of respondent testified she had received and paid freight bill showing origin outside state; she had no knowledge of circumstances of preparation; held, witness not qualified and freight bill inadmissible).

8. United States v. Davis, 571 F.2d 1354 (5th Cir. 1978).

9. United States v. Ullrich, 580 F.2d 765 (5th Cir. 1978), rehearing denied 589 F.2d 1114 (documents originating with Ford Motor Company retained by dealer and integrated into its records); United States v. Carranco, 551 F.2d 1197 (10th Cir.1977) (freight bill prepared by one carrier for transshipment by another carrier, whose representative testified to procedure of checking and use).

10. United States v. Veytia-Bravo, 603 F.2d 1187 (5th Cir.1979), cert. denied 444 U.S. 1024 (records of former firearms dealer kept pursuant to ATF regulations and sent to ATF for permanent storage). See also United States v. Flom, 558 F.2d 1179 (5th Cir.1977); Mississippi River Grain Elevator, Inc. v. Bartlett & Co., 659 F.2d 1314 (5th Cir.1981).

§ 313

1. See generally, 6 Wigmore, Evidence § 1707 (Chadbourn rev. 1976); Hale, Hospital Records as Evidence, 14 So.Cal.L.Rev. 99 (1941); Braham, Case

Records of Hospitals and Doctors Under Business Records Act, 21 Temple L.Q. 113 (1948); Laughlin, Business Entries and the Like, 46 Iowa L.Rev. 276, 299–305 (1961); Annot., 75 A.L.R. 378; Annot., 120 A.L.R. 1124; Annot., 69 A.L.R.3d 22.

2. See 6 Wigmore, Evidence § 1707, n. 1 (Chadbourn rev. 1976).

Some statutes allow certified copies. Ohio R.C. 2317.422.

3. United States v. Sackett, 598 F.2d 739 (2d Cir. 1979) (under Federal Rule); Buckler v. Commonwealth, 541 S.W.2d 935 (Ky.1976) (under "shopbook" hearsay exception); Graham v. State, 547 S.W.2d 531 (Tenn. 1977) (under Uniform Act).

4. See Globe Indemnity Co. v. Reinhart, 152 Md. 439, 446, 137 A. 43, 46 (1927); Schmidt v. Reimenschneider, 196 Minn. 612, 265 N.W. 816, 817 (1936).

5. State v. Guaraneri, 59 R.I. 173, 194 A. 589 (1937); State v. Weeks, 70 Wn.2d 951, 425 P.2d 885 (1967).

6. Wright v. Upson, 303 Ill. 120, 135 N.E. 209 (1922) (hospital record inadmissible because one of two nurses who participated in entries was not accounted for); but compare Wilson v. Clark, 84 Ill.2d 186, 49 Ill.Dec. 308, 417 N.E.2d 1322 (1981), cert. denied 454 U.S. 836 (allowing physician's opinion relying on hospital records without calling all persons making entries).

to hospital records as well as with other business records.[7]

History. Under standard practice, a trained attendant at hospitals enters upon the record a "personal history," [8] including an identification of the patient and an account of the present injury or illness and the events and symptoms leading up to it. This information, which may be obtained from the patient himself or someone accompanying him, is sought for its bearing upon diagnosis and treatment of the patient's injury or disease. Is this history admissible to prove assertions of facts it may contain? This is a matter of application of the regularly kept records rule, and the primary issue is whether or not the specific entry involved was an entry made in the regular course of the hospital's business. If the subject matter falls within those things which under hospital practice are regarded as relevant to diagnosis or treatment, it is within the regular course of business.[9] If, on the other hand, the subject matter does not relate to diagnosis or treatment, the making of the entry was not within the regular course of the hospital's business and thus it is not admissible even for the limited purpose of proving that the statement was made.[10]

Assuming that the hospital record is admissible to prove that the statement contained in the history was made, is this statement admissible to prove the truth of assertions made in it? In accordance with the general rule, it seems clear that the business record exception cannot support use of the history because the declarant's action in relating the history was not part of a business routine of which he was a regular participant. Here as elsewhere, however, if the history comes within one of the other exceptions to the hearsay rule it is admissible.[11] The statements may, for example constitute admissions of a party opponent when offered against the patient,[12] dying declarations,[13] declarations against interest,[14] and excited utterances.[15]

Diagnostic statements. Professional standards for hospital records contemplate that entries will be made of diagnostic findings at various stages.[16] These entries are clearly in the regular course of the operations of the hospital. The problem which they pose is one of the admissibility of "opinions." [17] In the hospital records area, the opinion is usually one of an expert who

7. Harris v. Smith, 372 F.2d 806, 816–17 (8th Cir. 1967) (adequate foundation was laid under federal statute when attending physician identified hospital record as photostatic copy of hospital record concerning patient; not fatal that no witness specifically stated that in the hospital doctors routinely made reports, since court can rely upon "ordinary habits and customs"); State v. Anderson, 384 S.W.2d 591 (Mo.1964) (testimony by custodian that record was from hospital medical records library which was kept in the usual and ordinary course of the business of the hospital was adequate foundation under the Uniform Act). See § 312, supra.

8. See Hale, Hospital Records as Evidence, 14 So. Cal.L.Rev. 90, 113–14 (1941).

9. See §§ 292, 293 supra.

10. See Green v. Cleveland, 150 Ohio St. 441, 83 N.E.2d 63 (1948) (statement of patient that she fell off a street car and caught her heel not incident to treatment); Commonwealth v. Harris, 351 Pa. 325, 41 A.2d 688 (1945) (patient's statement that he had been shot by a white man not related to treatment, since race of man who shot him not material to treatment). See §§ 292, 293 supra.

11. See § 324.3, infra.

12. Watts v. Delaware Coach Co., 5 Del.Super. 283, 58 A.2d 689 (1948).

13. See Ch. 28, supra.

14. See Ch. 27, supra.

15. See § 297, supra. If no hearsay exception can be successfully invoked, the record is not admissible.

Petrocelli v. Gallison, 679 F.2d 286 (1st Cir.1982) (surgical malpractice; proper to exclude statement that nerve was severed during operation, in hospital record for later surgery, apparently on information from patient's wife); A.H. Angerstein, Inc. v. Jankowski, 55 Del. 304, 187 A.2d 81 (1962) (statement in medical record by unidentified person who called physician at hospital could not be used to prove that patient had received electrical shock); Bouchie v. Murray, 376 Mass. 524, 381 N.E.2d 1295 (1978) (automobile collision; error to admit evidence that wife, who was not a passenger, told plaintiff's psychiatrist that plaintiff was "enraged and out of control" just before and at time of accident).

16. See Hale, Hospital Records as Evidence, 14 So. Cal.L.Rev. 90, 113–14 (1941).

17. See § 307, supra.

would unquestionably be permitted to give it if personally testifying. While the requirement of qualification does not disappear, if it is shown that the record is from a reputable institution, in the absence of any indication to the contrary it may be inferred that regular entries were made by qualified personnel.[18]

When an expert opinion is offered by a witness personally testifying, the expert is available for cross-examination on that opinion. If the opinion is offered by means of a hospital record, no cross-examination is possible. Consequently, there is a tendency somewhat to limit those opinions which can be introduced by this method. The admissibility of ordinary diagnostic findings customarily based on objective data and not usually presenting more than average difficulty of interpretation is usually conceded.[19] On the other end of the continuum, diagnostic opinions which on their face are speculative are reasonably excluded.[20] In the absence of the availability of the declarant for explanation and cross-examination, the probative value of this evidence is outweighed by the danger that it will be abused or mislead the jury. If the opinion is in connection with a central dispute in the case, such as causation, a court may well be reluctant to permit a decision to be made upon the basis of an uncross-examined opinion, and require that the witness be produced.[21]

Privilege. In most states, patients have been afforded a privilege against disclosure by physicians of information acquired in attending the patient and necessary for diagnosis and treatment.[22] It is possible to interpret the privilege broadly as including any information obtained by hospital personnel related to treatment. While it seems fairly clear that hospital records are privileged to the extent that they incorporate statements made by the patient to the physician and the physician's diagnostic findings,[23] application of the privilege to information obtained by nurses or attendants presents a greater problem. On one hand, it is arguable that privilege statutes should be strictly construed and most do not mention nurses or attendants.[24] On the other hand, information is usually gathered and recorded by them as agents for the physician and for the purpose of aiding the physician in treatment and diagnosis.[25] The problem is one of interpreting the underlying privilege. If it would

18. Allen v. St. Louis Public Service Co., 365 Mo. 677, 285 S.W.2d 663 (1956) (qualifications of physician will be "presumed" from testimony that he was a resident at a hospital); Webber v. McCormick, 63 N.J. Super. 409, 164 A.2d 813 (1960) (X-ray report prepared by hospital technician and entered in hospital record admissible without proof of technician's qualifications, since it would be presumed from making of report in course of hospital business). Contra, Martin v. Baldwin, 215 Ga. 243, 110 S.E.2d 344 (1951).

19. Federal and revised Uniform Rule (1974) 803(6) specifically includes "opinions, or diagnoses". This does not however, insure admissibility of all such entries, as the rule only removes the bar of hearsay. An opinion or diagnosis may still be excluded on grounds of misleading the jury, etc., under Rule 403. See § 185, supra.

20. Boland v. Jundo, 395 S.W.2d 206 (Mo.1965) (interpretation of X ray as, it "could be a small chip fracture" could have been excluded as based upon speculation); La Mantia v. Bobmeyer, 382 S.W.2d 455 (Mo. App.1964) (statement in record by physician that "I have a hunch [the patient] will have further difficulty from time to time . . . ." not admissible because it was based on speculation and conjecture).

21. Skogen v. Dow Chemical Co., 375 F.2d 692 (8th Cir.1967) (not error to exclude entry that plaintiffs' condition was caused by inhalation of insecticide).

22. See Ch. 11, supra.

23. The language in most cases suggests that hospital records are privileged only to the extent that they contain communications from physicians that would be privileged were the physician testifying in person. Ferguson v. Quaker City Life Insurance Co., 129 A.2d 189 (D.C.App.1957); Newman v. Blom, 249 Iowa 836, 89 N.W.2d 349 (1958); State ex rel. Benoit v. Randall, 431 S.W.2d 107 (Mo.1968); Unick v. Kessler Memorial Hospital, 107 N.J.Super. 121, 257 A.2d 134 (1969); Sims v. Charlotte Liberty Mutual Insurance Co., 256 N.C. 32, 125 S.E.2d 326 (1962).

24. A few statutes do specifically mention nurses. See 8 Wigmore, Evidence § 2380 n. 5 (McNaughton rev. 1961).

25. The general approach seems to be that a nurse or other member of a hospital staff comes within the privilege only if acting under the direction of a specific physician. See Sims v. Charlotte Liberty Mutual Insurance Co., 256 N.C. 32, 125 S.E.2d 326 (1962) (dictum) (entries by nurses, technicians or others in hospital records not privileged unless assisting or acting under the direction of a physician). See also Collins v. How-

bar the direct testimony of the nurses or attendants, it should also bar use of their hearsay statements under this exception; if it would not, the statements in the hospital records should not be held privileged.

 WESTLAW REFERENCES

requir! necess! need must /s hospital /4 record* /s foundation* admissib!

admissib! admit! inadmissib! hearsay /s hospital /4 record* /s history histories diagnos!

hospital /4 record* /s privileg!

---

§ 314. Special Situations: (b) Computer Printouts [1]

Even though the scrivener's quill pens in original entry books have been replaced by magnetic tapes, microfiche files and computer printouts, the theory behind the reliability of regularly kept business records remains the same and computer-generated evidence is no less reliable than original entry books provided a proper foundation is laid.[2]

With the explosive development of electronic data processing, most business and business-type records are generated by so-called computers. Courts have agreed that their admissibility in evidence is governed by the hearsay exception for regularly kept records, whether at common law or in the form of a statute or rule.[3] Federal and revised Uniform Rule (1974) 803(6) specifically applies to a "data compilation, in any form".[4]

The usual conditions for the exception are applicable.[5] The differences between quill pens and sophisticated electronic equipment, however, require some further exploration of foundation requirements. While the product of the quill pen can be inspected visually, electronically processed data is not a visual counterpart of the machine record and for the most part is not subject to visual inspection until it takes the final form of a printout. Thus with the computer the process by which data moves from input to printout assumes a position of importance. Implicit in the requirements of the regularly kept record exception is a trustworthy process of collecting and recording data, expressed in negative terms in the escape clause, "unless the source of information or the method or circumstances of preparation indicate lack of trustworthiness."[6] Hence it

---

ard, 156 F.Supp. 322 (S.D.Ga.1957) (dictum) (nurse taking blood test was agent of hospital rather than physician and therefore privilege would not include her); State v. Burchett, 302 S.W.2d 9 (Mo.1957) (nurse who was on duty as hospital employee and helped patient into hospital before physician arrived was not acting as agent of physician and therefore not within privilege). The privilege has been held applicable to an intern. Franklin Life Insurance Co. v. William J. Champion and Co., 353 F.2d 919 (6th Cir.1965).

§ 314

1. Bender, Computer Law: Evidence and Procedure (1982); Manual for Complex Litigation (5th ed. 1982); Freed, Computer Print-Outs, 16 Am.Jur. Proof of Facts 273; Johnston, A Guide for the Proponent and Opponent of Computer-Based Evidence, 1 Computer L.J. 667 (1979); Singer, Proposed Changes to the Federal Rules of Evidence as Applied to Computer-Generated Evidence, 7 Rut.J. Computers, Tech. & Law 157 (1979); Sprowl, Evaluating the Credibility of Computer-Generated Evidence, 52 Chi.-Kent L.Rev. 547 (1976); Annot., 11 A.L.R.3d 1377, 7 A.L.R.4th 8.

2. Brandon v. State, 272 Ind. 92, 396 N.E.2d 365, 370 (1979).

3. Monarch Federal Savings & Loan Association v. Genser, 156 N.J.Super. 107, 383 A.2d 475, 482–483 (1977), citing many cases.

4. Fed.R.Evid. 803(6), Advisory Committee's Note: "[The term] includes, but is by no means limited to, electronic computer storage." See also Report of Senate Committee on the Judiciary.

The same or similar terminology also appears in varying contexts in Rules 803(7), (8), (9), and (10), and in 1001(1) and (3).

5. See §§ 306–311 supra.

6. The aspects of trustworthiness peculiar to computer-generated evidence are occasionally treated as problems of authentication. Weinstein & Berger, Evidence ¶ 901(b)(9)[02]; Singer, supra n. 20 at p. 167. Accordingly Fed.R. 901(b)(9) is called into play: "[T]he following are examples of authentication . . . conforming with the requirements of this rule: . . . (9) Evidence describing a process or system used to produce a result and showing that the process or system produces an accurate result." It is true that the quoted language aptly describes trustworthiness aspects peculiar to computers. In this respect, however, it merely duplicates Rule 803(6). The emphasis of Rule 901 is upon showing that the offered item of evidence is what it is claimed to be, i.e. that it is genuine, and the rule as applied to computer evidence seems directed more to the point that the printout is a correct reflection of what is in the machine, rather than that what is in the machine is correct. In any event, the courts generally have found Rule 803(6) adequate to

is appropriate to inquire as to the stages where inaccuracy may enter into the computer process, and for this purpose a division may be made between (1) the purely mechanical and (2) the human element.

(1) The universality of the use of computerized equipment bespeaks its accuracy; few mistakes result from defects of equipment.[7] Hence testimony describing equipment should ordinarily be limited to the function that each unit performs in the process, and that each is adequate for the purpose.[8] Excursions into theory are not required or ordinarily appropriate.[9]

(2) Stages at which human error may enter in will vary according to the particular system and equipment employed. The following may, however, be expected: (a) Programming and the nature of checks upon its correctness. (b) The data entry process (input). This may be mechanical as in the case of automatic recording of telephone calls. (c) Controls at various stages to insure accuracy. (d) Security, including such things as access by unauthorized persons and the manner of keeping files. A well laid foundation will touch upon these aspects with em-

phasis depending upon circumstances. If the record is that of a disinterested nonparty, as where telephone calls are sought to be proved in a case where the telephone company is not a party, relaxation of the requirements is appropriate and recognized.[10]

While it has been suggested that the Federal Rules should be amended by adding a rule specifically dealing with computer-generated evidence,[11] the courts appear in general to have dealt competently with the admissibility of such evidence by applying Rule 803(6) or its common law or statutory counterparts, construed as outlined above. Any attempt at more specific treatment ought to be undertaken only with awareness of the English experience,[12] and the adverse comment that it has evoked.[13]

As noted in an earlier section, in order to qualify under the hearsay exception for regularly kept records, a record must have been made in the regular course of business, and documents made for use in particular litigation do not meet that requirement. Also, because of the motivation factor, they probably lack the trustworthiness contemplated by the exception.[14] Furthermore, the regu-

---

cover all aspects and seldom, if ever, refer to an authentication approach. Johnston, supra n. 1, at p. 669; Manual for Complex Litigation § 2.716 (5th ed. 1982); United States v. Vela, 673 F.2d 86 (5th Cir.1982), rehearing denied 677 F.2d 113.

7. "[N]o court could fail to notice the extent to which businesses today depend on computers for a myriad of functions." United States v. Russo, 480 F.2d 1228, 1239 (6th Cir.1973), cert. denied 414 U.S. 1157. "[T]he scientific reliability of such machines can scarcely be questioned." People v. Gauer, 7 Ill.App.3d 512, 514, 288 N.E.2d 24, 25 (1972). As to accuracy of equipment, see also Singer, supra n. 1, at p. 163.

8. Apparently drawing upon the practice of witnesses in describing equipment as "standard," some courts have mandated such testimony, King v. State ex rel. Murdock Acceptance Corp., 222 So.2d 393 (Miss.1969); Brandon v. State, 272 Ind. 92, 396 N.E.2d 365 (1979). As an approach to adequacy, the requirement is unduly restrictive. Compare United States v. Vela, 673 F.2d 86 (5th Cir. 1982), rehearing denied 677 F.2d 113.

9. Foundation proof occupied 141 pages of the record in the seminal case of Transport Indemnity Co. v. Seib, 178 Neb. 253, 132 N.W.2d 871 (1965). History shows, however, that as new technologies develop and win acceptance, courts move in the direction of taking judicial notice of the validity of the underlying scientif-

ic principle. Radar is a case in point, §§ 210 supra and 330 infra, and it is reasonable to conclude that the principles of electronic data processing are now a proper subject of judicial notice and do not require proof. In a somewhat different setting, the Advisory Committee's Note to Federal Rule 901(b)(9) suggests the taking of judicial notice of the accuracy of a process or system.

10. Manual for Complex Litigation § 2.716, p. 122 (5th ed. 1982).

11. Singer, supra n. 1, at p. 174.

12. St.1968, ch. 64, Part I, § 5. Cross on Evidence ch. XVIII, § 3(B) (5th ed. 1979).

13. "[T]he section is a morass of drafting. The problem with computer evidence is not the accuracy of the calculation but the reliability of the data fed in and the transcription and interpretation of the 'print-out' data produced." Newark & Samuels, Civil Evidence Act 1968, 31 Mod.L.Rev. 668, 670 (1968). "It is suggested that the whole turgid repetition could be abridged by making the sole condition of admissibility that the computer should have been operating properly at all material times." Tapper, Computers and the Law 29 (1973), quoted in Cross, supra n. 12.

14. § 308 supra. The documents may, however, come in under some other ticket of admission, e.g. a summary under § 233 supra.

larly kept records exception requires that entries be made at or near the time of the event recorded.[15] Questions thus may arise whether a computer printout made long after the data were entered into the system conform with these requirements of the exception. The question as to the time aspect is answered by observing that the time requirement refers to the time when the entry into the data bank was originally made, not the time of making the printout.[16] The question with respect to documents prepared for use in litigation is answered as follows:

"Nor should a printout produced for trial (provided again that it satisfies foundational requirements) pose special admissibility problems. A printout is a compilation of stored data. If the data and the retrieval process are themselves reliable, the arrangement of the data in a form designed to aid the litigation should not necessarily present a barrier to its admission greater than that of, for example, a manual collation of related business records. Furthermore, advances in computer technology

may render unrealistic a requirement that a given printout, rather than its underlying data, has been used in the regular course of business. Sometimes, for example, data are randomly recorded in the computer in the sequence in which events occur or in which information is received, rather than as organized bundles relating to specific customers or transactions. When directed to do so, the machine will collect and print out all the data relating to a particular transaction or customer. Such a printout is not a visual counterpart of the machine record but, rather, a compilation of scattered, related information. . . . This evidence should not be rejected merely because it is not a visual counterpart of the machine record; but the court must carefully consider whether the reliability of this evidence has been compromised in any way." [17]

 WESTLAW REFERENCES

business! regular! /4 record* /s computer! "data compilation in any form"

---

15. § 309 supra.

16. Westinghouse Electric Supply Co. v. B.L. Allen, Inc., 138 Vt. 84, 413 A.2d 122 (1980).

17. Manual for Complex Litigation § 2.716, p. 123, footnotes omitted. See also Westinghouse Electric Supply Co. v. B.L. Allen, Inc., supra n. 16; Johnson, supra n. 1, at p. 674.

Chapter 32

PUBLIC RECORDS, REPORTS, AND CERTIFICATES

Table of Sections

§ 315. The Exception for Public Records and Reports: (a) In General[1]

The common law evolved an exception to the hearsay rule for written records and reports of public officials under a duty [2] to make them, made upon firsthand knowledge of the facts.[3] These statements are admissible as evidence of the facts recited in them. While statutes upon the subject have been enacted in great number and should be consulted, they have not been viewed as supplanting the common law rule. The common law has been relaxed and broadened by decisions, statutes, and rules, discussed in the sections that follow. Federal Rule of Evidence 803(8) provides, without regard to the unavailability of the declarant, a hearsay exception for:

Records, reports, statements, or data compilations, in any form, of public offices or agencies, setting forth (A) the activities of the office of agency, or (B) matters observed pursuant to duty imposed by law as to which matters there was a duty to report, excluding, however, in criminal cases matters observed by police officers and other law enforcement personnel, or (C) in civil actions and proceedings and against the Government in criminal cases, factual findings resulting from an investigation made pursuant to authority granted by law, unless the sources of information or other circumstances indicate lack of trustworthiness.[4]

---

§ 315

1. See generally, 5 Wigmore, Evidence §§ 1630–1684, p. 735 (Chadbourn rev. 1974); Wallace, Official Written Statements, 46 Iowa L.Rev. 256 (1961); Dutton, The Official Records Exception to the Hearsay Rule in California, 6 Santa Clara Law. 1 (1965); Note, 30 Mont.L.Rev. 227 (1969); Dec.Dig. Evidence ⊛318(4), 333–349, 383(3), (4), Criminal Law ⊛429, 430.

2. While there has been some insistence that the duty be imposed by statute, the view has generally prevailed that the duty requirement is satisfied if the record is reasonably necessary for the efficient administration of the office. Annot., 80 A.L.R.3d 414.

3. Firsthand knowledge by a subordinate is sufficient. See Olender v. United States, 210 F.2d 795 (9th Cir.1954), cert. denied 352 U.S. 982.

4. Revised Uniform Rule Evid. (1974) 803(8) differs in important respects:

To the extent not otherwise provided in this paragraph, records, reports, statements, or data compilations in any form of a public office or agency setting forth its regularly conducted and regularly recorded

The special trustworthiness of official written statements is found in the declarant's official duty and the high probability that the duty to make an accurate report has been performed.[5] The possibility that public inspection of some official records will reveal any inaccuracies and cause them to be corrected (or will deter the official from making them in the first place) has been emphasized by the English courts, which have imposed a corresponding requirement that the official statement be one kept for the use and information of the public.[6] This limitation has been criticised and the American courts reasonably have not adopted it.[7] Although public inspection may provide some additional assurance of reliability, requiring public access to the record would mean that some statements would be rendered inadmissible although sufficiently reliable to justify admission.[8]

The impetus for this category of hearsay exception is found in the inconvenience of requiring public officials to appear in court and testify concerning the subject matter of their records and reports.[9] Not only would this disrupt the administration of public affairs, but it almost certainly would create a class of official witnesses. Moreover, given the volume of business in public offices, the official written statement will usually be more reliable than the official's present

memory. For these same reasons, there is no requirement that the declarant be shown to be unavailable as a witness.

The convenience of proving by certified copy [10] and the simplicity of foundation requirements in most cases [11] make the official records exception an attractive choice over business records when an option is afforded.

WESTLAW REFERENCES

public + 1 record* report* /s hearsay 803(8)

---

§ 316. The Exception for Public Records and Reports: (b) Activities of the Office: Matters Observed: Investigative Reports

Under Federal Rule Evid. 803(8) [1] matters falling within the hearsay exception for public records and reports are divided into three groups. This grouping offers a convenient approach also to the common law and statutory background.

(A) Activities of the office. The first group includes probably the oldest and still most commonly encountered kind of public records, records of the activities of the office itself. An example is the record of receipts and disbursements of the Department of the

---

activities, or matters observed pursuant to duty imposed by law and as to which there was a duty to report, or factual findings resulting from an investigation made pursuant to authority granted by law. The following are not within this exception to the hearsay rule: (i) investigative reports by police and other law enforcement personnel; (ii) investigative reports prepared by or for a government, a public office, or an agency when offered by it in a case in which it is a party; (iii) factual findings offered by the government in criminal cases; (iv) factual findings resulting from special investigation of a particular complaint, case, or incident; and (v) any matter as to which the sources of information or other circumstances indicate lack of trustworthiness.

5. Chesapeake & Delaware Canal Co. v. United States, 250 U.S. 123 (1919).

Compare United States v. Lange, 466 F.2d 1021 (9th Cir.1972) (not error to admit householders' forms and letters informing post office that second mailings had been received after post office order to dealers in erotic

literature to cease mailing). See also § 310 supra, concerning regular entries.

6. See Lilley v. Pettit, [1946] K.B. 401, [1946] 1 All. E.R. 593, holding the regimental records of a soldier inadmissible because they were not kept for the use and information of the public. See generally, Cross, Evidence 517 (5th ed. 1979).

7. Jones v. State, 267 Ind. 405, 369 N.E.2d 418 (1977); 5 Wigmore, Evidence § 1632 (Chadbourn rev. 1974). See also Cross, supra n. 6.

8. 5 Wigmore, Evidence § 1632, p. 620 (Chadbourn rev. 1974).

9. 5 Wigmore, Evidence § 1631 (Chadbourn rev. 1974).

10. See § 240 supra.

11. See § 224 supra.

§ 316

1. For text of rule, see text at § 315, n. 4 supra.

Treasury.[2] In addition to the assurances of reliability common to public records and reports generally, this group also has the assurances of accuracy that characterize business records. Accordingly in most instances they are admitted in evidence routinely.

(B) Matters observed pursuant to duty. The second group consists of matters observed and reported, both pursuant to duty imposed by law. Rainfall records of the Weather Bureau are illustrative.[3] These records too are of a relatively noncontroversial nature, except where the matter is observed by a police officer or other law enforcement personnel, which limitation is discussed in the concluding portion of (C) below.

(C) Investigative reports. Investigative reports, the third group, as the name indicates embody the results of some kind of investigation and accordingly almost by definition are not the product of firsthand knowledge on the part of the declarant, which is characteristic of most hearsay exceptions. Also, investigations vary with respect to the timeliness and nature of the inquiry, the procedures followed, possible motivational factors, and the skill of the official or agency.[4] It is not surprising that considerable differences of view developed among courts regarding the wisdom of admitting investigative reports as an exception to the rule against hearsay.[5] The trend, however, has been to recognize that much useful evidence is to be found in investigative reports, with impetus from the many statutory enactments providing for admissibility.[6] Rule 803(8) provides a hearsay exception, but in order to allow the variables enumerated above to be given appropriate weight according to circumstances attaches a condition, "unless the sources of information or other circumstances indicate lack of trustworthiness." Other restrictions are found in the rule's requirement that the investigation be "made pursuant to authority granted by law" and in the limitation to "factual findings."[7]

2. Chesapeake & Delaware Canal Co. v. United States, supra § 315, n. 5.

3. United States v. Meyer, 113 F.2d 387 (7th Cir. 1940), cert. denied 311 U.S. 706. See also United States v. Arias, 575 F.2d 253 (9th Cir.1978), cert. denied 439 U.S. 868 (official court reporter's transcript of trial).

4. Adv.Comm. Note, Fed.R.Evid. 803(8).

5. Favoring admissibility, see United States v. Dumas, 149 U.S. 278 (1893), affirmed 149 U.S. 287 (statement of account certified by Postmaster General in action against postmaster); McCarty v. United States, 185 F.2d 520 (5th Cir.1950), rehearing denied 187 F.2d 234 (Certificate of Settlement of General Accounting Office showing indebtedness and letter from Army Official stating that Government had performed in action on contract to purchase and remove waste food from Army camp; Moran v. Pittsburgh-Des Moines Steel Co., 183 F.2d 467 (3d Cir.1950) (report of Bureau of Mines as to cause of gas tank explosion); Smith v. Universal Services, Inc., 454 F.2d 154 (5th Cir.1972), on remand 360 F.Supp. 441 (D.Ala.) (in action for employment discrimination, error to exclude Equal Employment Opportunity Commission's investigation report and finding of probable cause). Contra, Franklin v. Skelly Oil Co., 141 F.2d 568 (10th Cir.1944); (State Fire Marshal's report of cause of gas explosion); Lomax Transportation Co. v. United States, 183 F.2d 331 (9th Cir.1950) (Certificate of Settlement from General Accounting Office in action for naval supplies lost in warehouse fire).

Cases in which investigative police reports have been offered as business records have generally ruled against admissibility on the ground that persons furnishing information were not acting in the course of the business, § 310 at n. 9 supra; Annot., 69 A.L.R.2d 1148, without considering admission as a public report.

6. See Adv.Comm. Note, Fed.R.Evid. 803(8)(C) and the numerous federal statutes there collected. See also the statutes concerning records of vital statistics, § 317 infra.

7. For text of rule, see text supra at § 315, n. 4. The meaning of the term "factual findings" is left unclear by the legislative history. The Advisory Committee's Note, after referring to the federal statutes conferring admissibility upon various kinds of investigative reports, concluded "the willingness of Congress to recognize a substantial measure of admissibility for evaluative reports is a helpful guide." The Report of the House Committee on the Judiciary took an opposing stand: "The Committee intends that the phrase 'factual findings' be strictly construed and that evaluations or opinions contained in public reports shall not be admissible under this Rule." House Comm. on Judiciary, Fed. Rules of Evidence, H.R.Rep. No. 650, 93d Cong., 1st Sess., p. 14 (1973). The Report of the Senate Committee on the Judiciary rejected this view: "The committee takes strong exception to this limited understanding of the application of the rule. . . . The committee concludes that the language of the rule together with the explanation provided by the Advisory Committee furnish sufficient guidance on the admissibility of evaluative reports." Senate Comm. on Judici-

Restrictions on use by prosecution in criminal cases. As submitted by the Supreme Court and enacted by the Congress, clause (C) prohibits the use of investigative reports as evidence against the accused in a criminal case. The limitation was included because of "the almost certain collision with confrontation rights which would result" from using investigative reports against accused.[8] Clause (B) as transmitted by the Supreme Court to the Congress simply provided for including in the public records and reports exception "(B) matters observed pursuant to duty imposed by law." In the course of debate on the floor of the House concern was expressed lest the provision might allow the introduction against the accused of a police officer's report without producing the officer as a witness subject to cross-examination. Accordingly the provision was amended by adding the italicized words to read "(B) matters observed pursuant to duty imposed by law *as to which matters there was a duty to report, excluding, however, in criminal cases matters observed by police officers and other law en-*

forcement personnel", and as amended was enacted.[9] The amendment raises a number of questions of varying importance. (1) Can the accused in a criminal case use a report falling under (B)? Clearly he can use an investigative report which falls under (C), but the language of (B) simply prohibits use in criminal cases, which literally includes use by either prosecution or defense. This meaning is quite evidently not what the Congress had in mind, and the construction is that the defendant may use a group (B) report of a police officer.[10] (2) Who are "other law enforcement personnel"? Defining them to include "any officer or employee of a governmental agency which has law enforcement responsibilities" [11] may with further experience prove to be needlessly broad, but the inclusion of a Customs Service chemist analyzing the seized substance in a narcotics case [12] and a border Customs Inspector [13] within the term can scarcely be questioned. (3) Does the limitation of clause (B) apply to routine records? When the question has been squarely presented, substantial authority has answered, No, the

ary, Fed. Rules of Evidence, S.Rep. No. 1277, 93d Cong., 2d Sess., p. 18 (1974).

The case for liberal construction is strong. Favoring admissibility:

Robbins v. Whelan, 653 F.2d 47 (1st Cir.1981) (error to exclude National Highway Safety Bureau report on performance of various models of automobiles); Lloyd v. American Export Lines, Inc., 580 F.2d 1179 (3d Cir. 1978), cert. denied 439 U.S. 969 (action involving altercation between crew members; proper to admit decision and order of Coast Guard hearing examiner that charges of assault and intoxication of crew member were not proved); Mac Towing Inc. v. American Commercial Lines, 670 F.2d 543 (5th Cir.1982) (action arising out of collision; proper to admit accident report by Coast Guard); Local Union No. 59 v. Namco Electric, Inc., 653 F.2d 143 (5th Cir.1981) (proper to admit letter stating NLRB findings in union's action against corporation for breach of contract); Baker v. Elcona Homes Corp., 588 F.2d 551 (6th Cir.1978), cert. denied 441 U.S. 933 (proper to admit state police accident report made after investigation, stating that car entered intersection against red light; but see Miller v. Caterpillar Tractor Co., 697 F.2d 141 (6th Cir.1983)); Plummer v. Western International Hotels Co., 656 F.2d 502 (9th Cir.1981) (error to exclude EEOC findings in racial discrimination action). Contra, Angelo v. Bacharach Instrument Co., 555 F.2d 1164 (3d Cir.1977) (in employment discrimination action, proper to exclude EEOC

determination letter issued following ex parte investigation without formal proceedings, as possibly misleading jury); Meder v. Everest & Jennings, Inc., 637 F.2d 1182 (8th Cir.1981) (proper to exclude police report of wheelchair accident as untrustworthy since officer could not recall source of information); Denny v. Hutchinson Sales Corp., 649 F.2d 816 (10th Cir.1981) (in action for housing discrimination, not error to exclude as untrustworthy report of state civil rights commission made after ex parte investigation without formal procedures or opportunity to cross-examine). See Annot., 47 A.L.R.Fed. 321.

8.   Adv.Comm. Note, Fed.R.Evid. 803(8)(C).

9.   120 Cong.Rec., Pt. 2, 86–88 (1974).

10.   United States v. Smith, 521 F.2d 957, 31 A.L.R. Fed. 437 (D.C.Cir.1975).

11.   United States v. Oates, 560 F.2d 45, 68 (2d Cir. 1977), on remand 445 F.Supp. 351 (D.N.Y.) affirmed 591 F.2d 1332. Compare United States v. Hansen, 583 F.2d 325, 333 (7th Cir.1978), cert. denied 439 U.S. 912 ("other law enforcement personnel" does not include city building inspector).

12.   United States v. Oates, supra n. 11. Compare United States v. Coleman, 203 U.S.App.D.C. 326, 631 F.2d 908 (1980) (a "difficult question," not decided).

13.   United States v. Orozco, 590 F.2d 789 (9th Cir. 1979), cert. denied 442 U.S. 920.

Congress did not intend to exclude routine, essentially nonadversarial observations,[14] although incorporated in police records. (4) Can the limitation of (B), and also that of (C), be avoided by resorting to some other hearsay exception? This is the most important of the questions, and it arises when the evidence in question complies with the requirements of some other hearsay exception which contains no restriction as to the use of police records and reports or investigative reports against an accused person. For example, police reports can often qualify as recorded past recollection, and laboratory tests of materials have often been admitted as business records. Neither of these hearsay exceptions contains any limitation like those of Rule 803(8)(B) and (C). The case first considering the question answered with an unequivocal and uncompromising No; the Congress meant to exclude law enforcement and investigative reports against defendants in criminal cases whatever route around the hearsay rule was chosen.[15] Further consideration by other courts, however, has led to a most substantial modification: the limitations of (B) and (C) will not be extended to other hearsay exceptions if the maker is pro-

duced in court as a witness, subject to cross-examination, since the essential purpose of the Congress was simply to avoid uncross-examined evidence.[16]

 WESTLAW REFERENCES

activit! observ! investig! /s public office* agenc!
  department! bureau* /p "public record*" /p
  admissib! hearsay
prosecut! /s report* observation* investigation* /10
  police! "law enforcement" /10 admissib! inadmissib!
  hearsay

§ 317. The Exception for Public Records and Reports: (c) Vital Statistics

If the requirement that the out-of-court declarant have an official duty to make the report were strictly enforced, such matters as a clergyman's return upon a marriage license indicating his performance of the ceremony and the report of an attending physician as to the fact and date of birth or death would be inadmissible. Consequently this requirement has been relaxed in regard to matters involving various general statistics. Where the report was made to a public agency by one with a professional—although not

---

14. United States v. Grady, 544 F.2d 598 (2d Cir. 1976) (unlawful export of firearms; not error to admit records of Ulster Constabulary of serial numbers and receipt of weapons in Northern Ireland; congressional purpose was to prevent proof of government's case by police reports of observations of crime, routine recording not within prohibition); United States v. Hernandez-Rojas, 617 F.2d 533 (9th Cir.1980), cert. denied 449 U.S. 864 (illegal reentry by alien; warrant of deportation with notation "deported to Mexico" properly admitted; Congress did not intend to exclude routine nonadversarial matters); United States v. Orozco, 590 F.2d 789 (9th Cir.1979), cert. denied 442 U.S. 920 (narcotics case; not error to admit Customs Service computer cards with license numbers of cars crossing border; no adversarial confrontation of nature which might cloud perception). As to laboratory analyses reports, see n. 12 supra. Numerous state court decisions have ruled in favor of routine laboratory or similar reports. Hing Wan Wong v. Liquor Control Commission, 160 Conn. 1, 273 A.2d 709 (1970), cert. denied 401 U.S. 938 (analysis of contents of seized glass by state toxicologists); People v. Black, 84 Ill.App.3d 1050, 40 Ill. Dec. 322, 406 N.E.2d 23 (1980) (decal affixed to breathalyzer by Department of Public Health certifying tested and found accurate); State v. Walker, 53 Ohio St.2d 192, 374 N.E.2d 132, 7 O.O.3d 368 (1978) (police log book showing calibration of breath testing de-

vice); Law v. Kemp, 276 Or. 581, 556 P.2d 109 (1976) (report of blood-alcohol test by technician in office of State Medical Examiner); Robertson v. Commonwealth, 211 Va. 62, 175 S.E.2d 260 (1970) (positive report of test for seminal fluid by State Medical Examiner in rape case).

15. United States v. Oates, 560 F.2d 45, 78 (2d Cir. 1977). But compare United States v. Grady, supra n. 14.

16. United States v. Sawyer, 607 F.2d 1190 (7th Cir. 1979), cert. denied 445 U.S. 943 (restrictions of Rule 803(8) not intended to apply to recorded recollection of testifying officer); United States v. King, 613 F.2d 670 (7th Cir.1980) (restrictions of Rule 803(8) not applicable to Social Security investigative reports admitted as business records under Rule 803(6) where investigators testified). See also United States v. Coleman, 203 U.S. App.D.C. 326, 631 F.2d 908 (1980) (narcotics case; not error to admit envelopes with notations identifying substance inside and note cards with descriptions and driver license data where all officers making notations testified). In United States v. Cain, 615 F.2d 380 (5th Cir.1980), an escape report from correctional institution offered to show accused could have been in vincinity of crime was ruled inadmissible though offered under Rule 803(6) as a business record, but there is no showing what foundation was laid or who testified.

necessarily "official"—duty to make the report, such as a minister or a physician, the law has generally admitted the record to prove the truth of the reporter's statement. An alternative approach is simply to regard the maker of the report as acting as an official for that purpose.[1] The mere fact that a report is required by law, e.g. a motorist's accident report, is not sufficient,[2] since the person making the report can scarcely be regarded as acting in a temporary official capacity or under a professional duty.

The law concerning records of vital statistics is largely statutory, and states generally have legislation on the subject. Federal and Revised Uniform Rule Evid. (1974) 803(9) provides a hearsay exception for:

> Records or data compilations, in any form, of births, fetal deaths, deaths, or marriages, if the report thereof was made to a public office pursuant to requirements of law.

While the rule looks largely to local law to determine the duty to make the report and for its content, in federal courts it should not be regarded as borrowing and incorporating the local law as to admissibility. The federal rule governs as to admissibility.

As to routine matters, such as place and date of birth or death and "immediate" cause of death, e.g. drowning or gunshot wound, admissibility is seldom questioned.

However, entries in death certificates as to the "remote" cause of death, e.g. suicide, accident, or homicide, usually are made on the basis of information obtained from other persons and predictably involve the questions that have been raised with regard to investigative reports generally,[3] and courts have divided on admissibility.[4] The restrictions on using police and investigative reports against accused persons contained in Federal Rule Evid. 803(8)(B) and (C) are no doubt applicable to this aspect of records of vital statistics.[5] Otherwise the liberality envisioned for investigative reports under Federal Rule Evid. 803(8)(C) should prevail.[6]

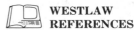

WESTLAW REFERENCES

marriage birth death /4 certif! /p "public record*" /p admissib! inadmissib! hearsay

§ 318. The Exception for Public Records and Reports: (d) Judgments in Previous Cases, Especially Criminal Convictions Offered in Subsequent Civil Cases [1]

Insofar as reports of official investigations are admissible under the official written statement exception, it would seem that the judgment of a court, made after the full investigation of a trial, would also be admissible in subsequent litigation to prove the

§ 317

1. See 5 Wigmore, Evidence § 1633a (Chadbourn rev. 1974).

2. Ezzo v. Geremiah, 107 Conn. 670, 142 A. 461 (1928). Statutes requiring such reports commonly provide that they are not admissible in evidence. Leebove v. Rovin, 363 Mich. 569, 111 N.W.2d 104 (1961).

3. § 316 at nn. 5–8 supra.

4. Annot., 21 A.L.R.3d 418. See also Morgan, The Law of Evidence 1941–1945, 59 Harv.L.Rev. 481, 560–561 (1946); Comment, 25 Rutgers L.Rev. 507 (1971). Statutes commonly provide that a death certificate is prima facie evidence of the "facts" stated therein. Courts desiring to exclude the evidence have often justified the result on the grounds that investigative type entries are opinions or conclusions rather than facts. Annot., 21 A.L.R.3d 418.

5. § 316 at nn. 8–16 supra.

Compare California State Life Ins. Co. v. Fuqua, 40 Ariz. 148, 10 P.2d 958 (1932) (in action of life policy,

error to exclude death certificate describing cause of death as "gunshot wounds inflicted by officers . . . in the performance of their duties") and State v. Barker, 94 Ariz. 383, 385 P.2d 516 (1963) (proper in murder prosecution to exclude death certificate stating "justifiable homicide"; civil rule not applicable in criminal cases.)

6. § 316, n. 7 supra.

§ 318

1. See generally, 4 Wigmore, Evidence § 1346a (Chadbourn rev. 1972); 5 id. § 1671a (Chadbourn rev. 1974); Cowen, The Admissibility of Criminal Convictions in Subsequent Civil Proceedings, 40 Calif.L.Rev. 225 (1952); Hinton, Judgment of Conviction—Effect on a Civil Case as Res Judicata or as Evidence, 27 Ill.L. Rev. 195 (1932); Note, Admissibility and Weight of a Criminal Conviction in a Subsequent Civil Action, 39 Va.L.Rev. 995 (1953); Annot., 18 A.L.R.2d 1287; Annot., 31 A.L.R. 261; Dec.Dig. Judgments ☞648.

truth of those things necessarily determined in the first action. Guilty pleas and statements made in the course of litigation may constitute declarations against interest [2] or admissions of a party-opponent [3] and under those exceptions avoid the bar of the hearsay rule. Where the doctrines of res judicata or collateral estoppel, or in modern terminology claim preclusion or issue preclusion, make the determinations in the first case binding in the second, of course, the judgment in the first case is not only admissible in the second, but it is as a matter of substantive law conclusive against the party. If neither res judicata nor collateral estoppel applies, however, the courts have traditionally been unwilling to admit judgments in previous cases.[4] The judgments have been regarded as hearsay and not within any exception to the hearsay rule.

A variety of reasons have been advanced for this rule. Civil cases often involve numerous issues, and it may be difficult to determine what issues a judgment in fact determined. This, however, argues only for a requirement that one offering a judgment establish as a prerequisite for its admissibility that it did in fact determine an issue relevant to the instant litigation. It is also argued that the party against whom the judgment is offered may not have had an opportunity to be present and to participate in the first action. This misses the point, however as the appropriate question in deciding whether the hearsay objection should be sustained in this context is not the party's opportunity to have been present at the official investigation but rather whether that investigation provided adequate assurance of reliability. In many cases the party will in fact have been present and have had not only an opportunity but a strong motive to defend. This argument against admissibility does, nevertheless, have merit in regard to judg-

ments of any sort against anyone other than the defendant and perhaps even judgments in civil cases against the defendant, offered against him in subsequent criminal litigation. Admitting the former judgments in a criminal case would certainly violate the defendant's constitutional right of confrontation,[5] and perhaps the latter. Other arguments against admissibility of prior judgments relate to the danger of undue prejudice, and orderly administration. It is sometimes asserted that juries are unlikely to grasp the distinction between a prior judgment offered as mere evidence and one offered under circumstances making the judgment conclusive; thus even if there is no substantive law making the judgment conclusive, juries are likely to give it that effect. In addition, it is argued that there is a danger that if such judgments are admissible parties offering them will tend to rely heavily upon them and not introduce significant amounts of other evidence, with the result that the evidence available in the second case will not be adequate upon which to reach a reliable decision.

These arguments have caused many courts to exclude a prior civil judgment offered in a subsequent civil case. There is, however, a growing tendency to admit a prior conviction for a serious criminal offense in a subsequent civil action. In these situations, the party against whom the judgment is offered was generally the defendant in the criminal case and therefore had not only the opportunity but also the motive to defend fully. In addition, because of the heavy burden of proof in criminal cases, a judgment in such a situation represents significantly more reliable evidence than a judgment in a civil case. The tendency is most noticeable when the judgment is offered in a subsequent civil case in which the convicted defendant seeks affirmatively to

---

2. See Ch. 27 supra.

3. See Ch. 26 supra. As to guilty pleas, see especially § 265.

4. 5 Wigmore, Evidence § 1671a (Chadbourn rev. 1974).

5. Kirby v. United States, 174 U.S. 47 (1899) (error to convict for possession of stolen postage stamps where only evidence that stamps were stolen was the record of thieves' conviction). Distinguish situations where conviction is an element of an offense, e.g., selling firearms to a convicted felon.

benefit from his criminal offense, for example, a convicted arsonist sues to recover upon his fire insurance policy. The strong desire to prevent this result undoubtedly has influenced courts to permit the introduction of the judgment of conviction,[6] and some courts also hold that the judgment is conclusive proof that the party committed the relevant acts with the state of mind required for criminal liability.[7] It is a short step, and one which a number of courts have taken, from this position to the admissibility of a prior criminal conviction generally in a civil action against the criminal defendant.[8] A number of courts have limited this rule to convictions for serious offenses, reasoning that convictions for misdemeanors do not represent sufficiently reliable determinations to justify dispensing with the hearsay objections.[9] Judgments of acquittal, however, are still inadmissible in large part, of course, because they may not present a determination of innocence but rather only a decision that the prosecution has not met its heavy burden of proof beyond a reasonable doubt.[10]

The trend toward broader admissibility is apparent in Federal Rule Evid. 803(22), which provides a hearsay exception for:

> Evidence of a final judgment, entered after a trial or upon a plea of guilty (but not upon a plea of nolo contendere), adjudging a person guilty of a crime punishable by death or imprisonment in excess of one year, to prove any fact essential to sustain the judgment, but not including, when offered by the Government in a criminal prosecution for purposes other than impeachment, judgments against persons other than the accused. The pendency of an appeal may be shown but does not affect admissibility.[11]

---

6. The leading case is Schindler v. Royal Insurance Co., 258 N.Y. 310, 179 N.E. 711 (1932) (in suit by plaintiff on insurance policy, defended by insurer on ground that plaintiff's fraudulent claim voided policy, insurer could introduce plaintiff's conviction for presenting false and fraudulent proof of loss, although this would only be prima facie proof of facts). For additional cases see Annot., 18 A.L.R.2d 1287.

7. The leading case is Eagle, Star and British Dominions Insurance Co. v. Heller, 149 Va. 82, 140 S.E. 314 (1927) (in suit by plaintiff on insurance policy, defended by insurer on theory that loss was not accidental but rather fraudulently caused by insured, plaintiff's conviction for willfully burning goods with intent to injure insurer was not only admissible but also determinative and could only be attacked upon grounds of fraud, perjury, collusion or some similar theory). The Virginia court has denied any intention to repudiate the requirement of mutuality in preclusion situations generally and has confined the reach of the *Eagle* case to the convict seeking to profit from his own wrong. Norfolk & Western Railway Co. v. Bailey Lumber Co., 221 Va. 638, 272 S.E.2d 217 (1980). For additional cases, see Annot., 18 A.L.R.2d 1287.

8. E.g., Asato v. Furtado, 52 Hawaii 284, 474 P.2d 288, 293 (1970):

> "While there is a divergence of authority on this point, we think the better reasoned rule is that . . . the prior judgment should be admissible as evidence where the following factors are present. (1) It must be shown that the issue on which the judgment is offered was necessarily decided in the prior trial. (2) A judgment on the merits must have been rendered. (3) It must appear that the party against whom the judgment is offered had a full and fair opportunity to litigate the claim, and especially to contest the specific issue on which the judgment is

offered. In other words, it must appear that the party against whom the judgment is offered had a full and complete 'day in court' on that issue, with the opportunity to call and cross examine witnesses and to be presented by counsel."

The majority of courts admitting the conviction do not hold it conclusive.

A number of courts apparently still adhere to the traditional position that these judgments are not admissible, at least if the convicted criminal is not affirmatively attempting to take financial advantage of his crime. See Annot., 18 A.L.R.2d 1287.

9. Haynes v. Rollins, 434 P.2d 234 (Okl.1967); Kirkendall v. Korseberg, 247 Or. 75, 427 P.2d 418 (1967); Loughner v. Schmelzer, 421 Pa. 283, 218 A.2d 768 (1966) (evidence of defendant's conviction for failure to drive on the right side of the highway not admissible in personal injury action, although felony conviction would be); Graham, Admissibility in Illinois of Convictions and Pleas of Guilty to Traffic Offenses in Related Civil Litigation, 1979 So.Ill.U.L.J. 209; Annot., 18 A.L.R.2d 1287, 1295; Notes, 50 Colum.L.Rev. 529, 35 Cornell L.Q. 872.

10. Mew Sun Leong v. Honolulu Rapid Transit Co., 52 Hawaii 138, 472 P.2d 505 (1970) (acquittal of driver on criminal charges arising out of accident not admissible in civil action, "nor should it be mentioned by counsel to the jury); Massey v. Meurer, 25 A.D.2d 729, 268 N.Y.S.2d 735 (1966) (error to admit defendant's acquittal for driving while intoxicated in personal injury action).

11. The Revised Uniform Rule (1974) is identical with two exceptions. It omits, without change of meaning, the somewhat redundant language in parentheses. It also places in brackets, as an optional deletion, "entered after a trial or upon a plea of guilty,"

The following characteristics of the exception should be noted: (1) Only criminal judgments of conviction are included. Judgments in civil cases are not included, their effect being left to the law of res judicata or preclusion.[12] (2) Only crimes of felony grade, i.e. punishable by death or imprisonment for more than one year,[13] are included thus eliminating problems associated with convictions of lesser crimes.[14] (3) The rule does not apply to judgments of acquittal.[15] (4) When offered by the government in criminal prosecutions, judgments of conviction of persons other than the accused are admissible only for purposes of impeachment.[16] When the judgment of conviction is offered in a civil case, however, it is treated as are investigative reports generally, and there is no limit as to parties against whom admissible. (5) Judgments entered on pleas of nolo contendere are not included within the exception.[17] (6) The provision merely excludes a qualifying judgment from the bar of the hearsay rule. It does not purport to dictate the use to be made of the judgment once it is admitted in evidence. Applicable rules of res judicata or preclusion will be given effect. Otherwise the evidence may be used "substantively" or for impeachment, as may be appropriate.[18]

WESTLAW
REFERENCES

conviction* /s subsequent! later follow! /s civil /4 action* case cases proceeding*

"res judicata" "collateral! estop!" preclusion /s subsequent! later follow! /4 civil

convict! judgment* /s "nolo contendere" /s admissib! inadmissib!

§ 319. The Exception for Official Certificates: (a) In General

A certificate, for purposes of the law of evidence, is a statement in writing by an official that certain matters of fact are so or have happened, issued to someone who applies. It is not a part of the public records of the issuing office, although a common form of certificate is a statement that a document to which it is attached is a correct copy of such a record.[1] The common law was strict about admitting certificates as hearsay exceptions, requiring statutory authority for the most part.[2]

The relation between certification and a public record may be illustrated by proof of marriage. If the celebrant of a marriage issues a certificate that he has performed the marriage and gives it to the parties, this document is not a public record, and admission in evidence must be under some other hear-

---

thus making the rule applicable also to judgments rendered on pleas of nolo contendere. See n. 17 infra.

The problem of ascertaining what facts are "essential to sustain the judgment" where a general verdict is rendered, is considered in Columbia Plaza Corp. v. Security National Bank, 676 F.2d 780, 789 (D.C.Cir.1982).

12. In Lloyd v. American Export Lines, Inc., 580 F.2d 1179 (3d Cir.1978), cert. denied 439 U.S. 969, a shipping line appealed from a judgment in favor of a crew member for failure to protect him from another crew member. The court ruled that it was error to exclude a Japanese criminal conviction of the claimant for the assault. The proceedings, said the court, met the standards of civilized jurisprudence.

13. See § 43 as to convictions under the law of another jurisdiction.

14. See n. 9 supra.

15. United States v. Viserto, 596 F.2d 531 (2d Cir. 1979), cert. denied 444 U.S. 841. The effect of the omission is merely to leave the bar of the hearsay rule in place with respect to such judgments. Their status in other settings is not affected by the rule.

16. United States v. Vandetti, 623 F.2d 1144 (6th Cir.1980) (in prosecution for conducting a gambling enterprise by five or more persons, error in D's separate trial to admit earlier convictions of codefendants). See also n. 9 supra.

17. To admit the judgment would effectively nullify the most important characteristic of nolo pleas. See § 265, at nn. 27–28 supra. Whether the rule, with its exclusion of judgments based on nolo pleas, applies to convictions used for impeachment is discussed in § 84 supra.

18. Eastern Renovating Corp. v. Roman Catholic Bishop of Springfield, 554 F.2d 4 (1st Cir.1977) (in action on construction contracts, not error to admit convictions of plaintiff based on fraudulent alterations of contracts sued upon; jury could use substantively rather than just for impeachment).

§ 319

1. Certification of copies of public records receives further treatment in § 320 infra.

2. 5 Wigmore, Evidence § 1674 (Chadbourn rev. 1974).

say exception. If, however, the celebrant makes a "return" of the license, i.e. a redelivery to the issuing official with an endorsement of the manner in which the authority was exercised, then the return becomes a part of the public record, admissible under that hearsay exception.

Federal and Revised Uniform Rule Evid. (1974) 803(12) provides a certification procedure with respect to marriage and similar ceremonies:

> Statements of fact contained in a certificate that the maker performed a marriage or other ceremony or administered a sacrament, made by a clergyman, public official, or other person authorized by the rules or practices of a religious organization or by law to perform the act certified, and purporting to have been issued at the time of the act or within a reasonable time thereafter.[3]

Certification is also provided for a large variety of matters by statutes, with corresponding provisions for admissibility in evidence.[4] These statutes are continued in effect under Federal Rule of Evidence 402[5] and the corresponding Revised Uniform Rule (1974).[6]

WESTLAW REFERENCES

certificate* /4 hearsay

---

§ 320. The Exception for Official Certificates: (b) Certified Copies or Summa-

ries of Official Records: Absence of Record

When a purported copy of a public record is presented in court accompanied by a certificate that the purported copy is correct, a two-layered hearsay problem is presented. First, is the public record within the hearsay exception for that kind of record? And second, is the certificate within the hearsay exception for official certificates? The first question has been considered in the earlier sections of this chapter. The second question involves a specialized application of the certification procedure discussed generally in the immediately preceding section.

The early common law generally required a statutory duty to certify.[1] The Supreme Court of the United States, however, long ago rejected this position with respect to certification of copies of public records,[2] and American common law has been and is that a custodian has by virtue of his office the implied duty and authority to certify to the accuracy of a copy of a public record in his official possession.[3] Present day usual practice is to prove public records by copy certified correct by the custodian, and many statutes so provide.[4] Federal Rule Evid. 1005 allows proof of public records by copy, without producing or accounting for the original,[5] and Rule 902(4) provides for authentication by certificate as follows:

> A copy of an official record or report or entry therein, or of a document authorized by law to be recorded or filed and actually recorded or

---

3. Compare the wider range of matters provable by records of religious organizations under Federal and Revised Uniform Rule Evid. (1974) 803(11):

> Statements of births, marriages, divorces, deaths, legitimacy, ancestry, relationship by blood or marriage, or other similar facts of personal or family history, contained in a regularly kept record of a religious organization.

4. 5 Wigmore, Evidence § 1674, n. 7 (Chadbourn rev. 1974) collects numerous federal and state statutes.

5. Fed.R.Evid. 802:

> Hearsay is not admissible except as provided by these rules or by other rules prescribed by the Supreme Court pursuant to statutory authority or by Act of Congress.

6. Rev.Unif.R.Evid. 802:

> Hearsay is not admissible except as provided by law or by these rules.

§ 320

1. 5 Wigmore, Evidence § 1677 (Chadbourn rev. 1974).

2. Church v. Hubbart, 6 U.S. (2 Cranch) 187 (1804); United States v. Percheman, 32 U.S. (7 Pet.) 51 (1883).

3. Stevison v. Earnest, 80 Ill. 513 (1875); Adv. Comm. Note, Fed.R.Evid. 902(4).

4. 5 Wigmore, Evidence § 1680 (Chadbourn rev. 1974).

5. The corresponding Revised Uniform Rule (1974) differs only in minor detail. See § 230 supra.

filed in a public office, including data compilations in any form, certified as correct by the custodian or other person authorized to make the certification, by certificate complying with paragraph (1), (2), or (3) of this rule or complying with any Act of Congress or rule prescribed by the Supreme Court pursuant to statutory authority.[6]

In the absence of a statute to the contrary, the usual view has been that authority to certify copies of public records is construed literally as requiring a copy and does not include paraphrases or summaries. Thus a certificate saying "our records show X" is not admissible to prove X.[7]

By analogy to the rule that nonoccurrence of an event may be proved by a business record containing no entry of the event in question where the practice was to record such events,[8] proof of nonoccurrence may be made by absence of an entry in a public record where such matters are recorded.[9] However, absence of the entry or record could at common law be proved only by tes-

timony of the custodian.[10] This limitation has been modified by many statutes,[11] and Federal and Revised Uniform Rule Evid. (1974) 803(10) provide:

> To prove the absence of a record, report, statement, or data compilation, in any form, or the nonoccurrence or nonexistence of a matter of which a record, report, statement, or data compilation, in any form, was regularly made and preserved by a public office or agency, evidence in the form of a certification in accordance with rule 902, or testimony, that diligent search failed to disclose the record, report, statement, or data compilation, or entry.[12]

The rule is phrased to include not only proving nonoccurrence of an event of which a record would have been made, but also the nonfiling of a document allowed or required by law to be filed.[13]

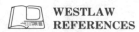 **WESTLAW REFERENCES**

certif! /4 record* copy copies /s hearsay

---

6. The corresponding Revised Uniform Rule (1974) differs only in minor detail.

7. Golder v. Bressler, 105 Ill. 419 (1883) (error to admit certificate of Secretary of State that records showed appointment of named persons as trustees of Bank of Illinois, instead of actual copy of record); In re Kostohris' Estate, 96 Mont. 226, 29 P.2d 829 (1934) (custodian's certificate that records showed listed payments to veteran inadmissible to prove payments). Wigmore criticizes the requirement and collects statutes allowing certification of effect or substance of records. 5 Wigmore, § 1678(6) (Chadbourn rev. 1974). See Department of Public Aid v. Estate of Wall, 81 Ill. App.3d 394, 36 Ill.Dec. 798, 401 N.E.2d 639 (1980) (proper to admit list of payments made on behalf of decedent certified by director of department; need not be a literal copy of record).

8. § 307 supra.

9. 5 Wigmore, § 1633(6) (Chadbourn rev. 1974).

10. 5 Wigmore § 1678(7) (Chadbourn rev. 1974).

11. Id. at n. 4.

12. United States v. Lee, 589 F.2d 980 (9th Cir. 1979), cert. denied 444 U.S. 969 (affidavit that records showed no employment of accused by CIA, contrary to his contention).

13. United States v. Neff, 615 F.2d 1235 (9th Cir. 1980), cert. denied 447 U.S. 925 (willful failure to file income tax returns; proper to admit IRS certificate of nonfiling during years in question).

Chapter 33

VARIOUS OTHER EXCEPTIONS TO THE HEARSAY RULE

Table of Sections

§ 321. Learned Writings, Industry Standards, and Commercial Publications [1]

Learned writings, such as treatises, books, and articles regarding specialized areas of knowledge or skills are, when offered to prove the truth of matters asserted in them, clearly hearsay. Nevertheless, Wigmore has argued strongly for an exception for such material.[2] In practice, he asserts, much of the testimony of experts testifying in person consists of information they have obtained from such sources. Permitting the sources to be proved directly would not be as great a change as might at first be supposed and would greatly improve the quality of information presented to trial courts in litigated cases. Moreover, he suggests there are sufficient assurances of trustworthiness to justify equating a learned treatise with a personally-testifying expert. Not only does the author of the treatise have no bias in any particular case,[3] but it is also likely that he was motivated in writing the treatise by a strong desire to state accurately the full truth. The authors are also aware that their material will be read and evaluated by others in their field, and there is therefore additional strong pressure to be accurate.

§ 321

1. See generally 6 Wigmore, Evidence §§ 1690–1708 (Chadbourn rev. 1976); Goldman, The Use of Learned Treatises in Canadian and United States Litigation, 24 U. Toronto L.J. 423 (1974); Hoffman & Hoffman, Use of Standards in Products Liability Litigation, 30 Drake L.Rev. 283 (1980–81); Notes, 29 U.Cinn.L.Rev. 255 (1960), 46 Iowa L.Rev. 463 (1961), 56 Iowa L.Rev. 1028 (1971), 66 Mich.L.Rev. 183 (1967), 71 Nw.U.L.Rev. 678 (1976), 27 S.Car.L.Rev. 766 (1976); 29 Am.Jur.2d Evidence §§ 888–893; C.J.S. Evidence §§ 717–722; Annot., 17 A.L.R.3d 993 and 84 A.L.R.2d 1338 (medical trea-

tises), 58 A.L.R.3d 148 (safety codes); Dec.Dig. Evidence ⚖360–365, 381.

2. 6 Wigmore, Evidence §§ 690–692 (Chadbourn rev. 1976).

3. But see O'Brien v. Angley, 63 Ohio St.2d 159, 407 N.E.2d 490, 17 O.O.3d 98 (1980) (editorial in medical journal attacking practice of "defensive medicine" by following manufacturer's recommendations, offered in medical malpractice action claiming negligence in failing to follow recommendations of manufacturer of drug; error to admit).

Virtually all courts have, to some extent, permitted the use of learned materials in the cross-examination of an expert witness.[4] Most courts have permitted this use where the expert has relied upon the specific material in forming the opinion to which he testified on direct,[5] some of these courts have extended the rule to situations in which the witness admits to having relied upon some general authorities although not that particular material sought to be used to impeach him.[6] Other courts have required only that the witness himself acknowledge that the material sought to be used to impeach him is a recognized authority in his field; if he does so, the material may be used although the witness himself may not have relied upon it.[7] Finally, some courts have permitted this use without regard to the witness' having relied upon or acknowledged the authority of the source if the cross-examiner establishes the general authority of the material by any proof or by judicial notice.[8] Traditionally, however, the material may be considered only as going to the witness' competency or the accuracy of his conclusions; most courts have been unwilling to adopt a broad exception to the hearsay rule for treatises and other professional literature.[9] Wigmore suggests a number of arguments in support of this position, none of which he feels justifies the refusal to recognize the exception: (a) professional skills and knowledge shift rapidly, so printed material is likely to be out of date; (b) a trier of fact is likely to be confused by being exposed to material designed for the professionally-trained reader; (c) the opportunity to take sections of material out of context creates a danger of unfair use; (d) most matters of expertise are really matters of skill rather than academic knowledge of the sort that can or is put on written pages, and therefore personally-appearing witnesses are likely to be better sources of evidence than written material. The only meritorious objection, Wigmore concludes, is the basic hearsay objection that the author is not available for cross-examination. This, he feels, is outweighed by the need for the evidence and the other assurances of its accuracy.[10]

Only two courts have judicially adopted a broad exception of this nature,[11] although statutes in a number of jurisdictions have to some extent permitted use of the material.[12] Other courts in increasing number have made inroads upon the traditional position by allowing the use of published government agency, professional, and industry standards and manuals in tort cases as tending to prove the standard of care.[13]

Federal and Revised Uniform Rule Evid. (1974) 803(18) provide a hearsay exception for:

> To the extent called to the attention of an expert witness upon cross-examination or relied upon by him in direct examination, statements contained in published treatises, periodicals, or pamphlets on a subject of history, medicine, or other science or art, established as a reliable authority by the testimony or admission of the witness or by other expert testimony or by judicial notice. If admitted, the statements may be read into evidence but may not be received as exhibits.

4. Annot., 60 A.L.R.2d 77.

5. Id. at 81–87.

6. Id. at 87–93.

7. Id. at 94–98.

8. Darling v. Charleston Community Memorial Hospital, 33 Ill.2d 326, 211 N.E.2d 253 (1965), cert. denied 383 U.S. 946; Annot., 60 A.L.R.2d 77, 98–104.

9. Annot., 17 A.L.R.3d 993, 84 A.L.R.2d 1338.

10. 6 Wigmore, Evidence § 1690 (Chadbourn rev. 1976).

11. City of Dothan v. Hardy, 237 Ala. 603, 188 So. 264 (1939); Lewandowski v. Preferred Risk Mutual Insurance Co., 33 Wis.2d 69, 146 N.W.2d 505 (1966). Wisconsin adheres to the same position by rule. Wis. Stat.Ann. § 908.03(18).

12. Statutes are collected in 6 Wigmore, Evidence § 1693, n. 2 (Chadbourn rev. 1976).

13. Mississippi Power & Light Co. v. Johnson, 374 So.2d 772 (Miss.1979) (National Electrical Safety Code in electric shock case); Nordstrom v. White Metal Rolling & Stamping Corp., 75 Wn.2d 629, 453 P.2d 619 (1969) (American Standard Safety Code for Portable Metal Ladders); Annot., 58 A.L.R.3d 148.

The rule is broadly worded as to subjects: "history, medicine, or other science or art," sufficient to include standards and manuals published by government agencies and industry and professional organizations.[14] The reliability of the publication must be established as provided in the rule. A significant limitation is that the publication must be called to the attention of an expert on cross-examination or relied upon by him in direct examination, a provision designed to ensure that the materials are used only under the chaperonage of an expert to assist and explain in applying them. This policy is furthered by the prohibition against admission as exhibits, to prevent the taking of the materials to the jury room.[15]

A related hearsay exception in process of evolving by the courts presents some difficulty in definition but is fairly easy to recognize. It includes publications such as reports of market prices,[16] professional directories,[17] city directories,[18] telephone directories,[19] and mortality and annuity tables[20] used by life insurance companies. The motivation for accuracy is high, and public acceptance depends upon reliability. Accordingly Federal and Revised Uniform

Rule Evid. (1974) 803(17) provide a hearsay exception for:

> Market quotations, tabulations, lists, directories, or other published compilations, generally used and relied upon by the public or by persons in particular occupations.

 WESTLAW REFERENCES

synopsis,digest(treatise* text! publication* periodical* "learned writing*" /s hearsay)

treatise* text! publication* periodical* "learned writing*" /s examin! crossexamin! /s expert*

"market quotation*" "market price*" tabulation* table tables directory directories compilation* /s public occupation* profession! /s admissib! inadmissib! hearsay

§ 322. Statements and Reputation as to Pedigree and Family History [1]

One of the oldest exceptions to the hearsay rule encompasses statements concerning family history, such as the date and place of births and deaths of members of the family and facts about marriage, descent, and relationship.[2] Under the traditional rule, declarations of the person whose family situation is at issue are admissible,[3] as are declarations by other members of the family[4] and

14. McKinnon v. Skil Corp., 638 F.2d 270 (1st Cir. 1981) (injury from circular power saw; Underwriter's Laboratory standards); Dawson v. Chrysler Corp., 630 F.2d 950 (3d Cir.1980), cert. denied 450 U.S. 959 (automobile crashworthiness report prepared for federal Department of Transportation); Johnson v. William C. Ellis & Sons Iron Works, 609 F.2d 820 (5th Cir.1980) (American Standard Safety Code for Power Presses).

15. Advisory Committee's Note, Fed.R.Evid. 803(18); Tart v. McGann, 697 F.2d 75 (2d Cir.1982).

16. Virginia v. West Virginia, 238 U.S. 202 (1915); Uniform Commercial Code § 2–724; 6 Wigmore, Evidence § 1704 (Chadbourn rev. 1976).

17. Louisville & Nashville Railroad Co. v. Kice, 109 Ky. 786, 60 S.W. 705 (1901); Annot., 7 A.L.R.4th 639.

18. State ex rel. Keefe v. McInerney, 63 Wyo. 280, 182 P.2d 28 (1947).

19. Id.

20. Henderson v. Harness, 184 Ill. 520, 56 N.E. 786 (1900) (to show expectancy in valuing life estate); Levar v. Elkins, 604 P.2d 602 (Alaska 1980) (lack of normal health does not require exclusion).

§ 322

1. See generally, 5 Wigmore, Evidence §§ 1480–1503, 1601–1606 (Chadbourn rev. 1974); Hale, Proof of Facts of Family History, 2 Hastings L.J. 1 (1950); Notes, 5 Ark.L.Rev. 58 (1951), 32 Iowa L.Rev. 779 (1947); 29 Am.Jur.2d Evidence §§ 508–522; C.J.S. Evidence §§ 225–231; Annot., 15 A.L.R.2d 1412 (declarations of persons other than family member as to pedigree); Annot., 29 A.L.R. 372 (entries in family Bible as evidence); Dec.Dig. Evidence ⚫285–297.

2. "Family history" is narrowly construed to include only such matters as are enumerated in the text. Sargent v. Coolidge, 399 A.2d 1333, 1345 (Me.1979), appeal after remand 433 A.2d 748 (what property mother intended to convey by deed not family history). The travels admitted in Strickland v. Humble Oil & Refining Co., 140 F.2d 83 (5th Cir.1944), cert. denied 323 U.S. 712, rehearing denied 323 U.S. 812, were for the purpose of identifying the traveler and establishing kinship.

3. Balazinski v. Lebid, 65 N.J.Super. 483, 168 A.2d 209 (1961); In re Estate of McClain, 481 Pa. 435, 392 A.2d 1371 (1978).

4. E.g., Minor Child v. Michigan State Health Commissioner, 16 Mich.App. 128, 167 N.W.2d 880 (1969) (mother's statement as to identity of son's father;

even, under a liberal view adopted by some courts, declarations by nonfamily members with a close relationship to the family.[5] These statements are admissible, however, only upon a showing that the declarant is unavailable,[6] that the statement was made before the origin of the controversy giving rise to the litigation in which the statement is offered (i.e., *ante litem motam*)[7] and that there was no apparent motive for the declarant to misrepresent the facts.[8] Under the strict traditional view the relationship of declarant to the family has to be proved by independent evidence, but this requirement does not apply where declarant's own family relationships are the subject of the hearsay statement.[9] Firsthand knowledge by declarant of the facts of birth, death, kinship, or the like is not required.[10] The general difficulty of obtaining other evidence of family matters, reflected in the unavailability requirement, furnishes impetus for the hearsay exception. Assurances of reliability are found in the probability that in the absence of any motive for lying, the discussions of relatives (and others intimately related to

them) as to family members will be accurate.[11]

Federal Rule of Evidence 804(b)(4), continuing the requirement of unavailability of declarant,[12] provides a hearsay exception for statements of personal or family history:

(A) A statement concerning the declarant's own birth, adoption, marriage, divorce, legitimacy, relationship by blood, adoption, or marriage, ancestry, or other similar fact of personal or family history, even though declarant had no means of acquiring personal knowledge of the matter stated; or (B) a statement concerning the foregoing matters, and death also, of another person, if the declarant was related to the other by blood, adoption, or marriage or was so intimately associated with the other's family as to be likely to have accurate information concerning the matter declared.[13]

The rule follows the liberal view in allowing statements by intimate associates of the family. It eliminates the traditional requirements that the statement have been made *ante litem motam*[14] and without motive to misrepresent,[15] leaving these aspects to be treated as questions of weight or possibly excluded under Rule 403 in extreme cases.[16]

Brown v. Conway, 598 S.W.2d 549 (Mo.App.1980) (same).

5. For the "liberal" (and minority) view, see Minor Child v. Michigan State Health Commissioner, 16 Mich. App. 128, 167 N.W.2d 880 (1969) (statements of "family and close acquaintances" regarding child's paternity admissible); In re Lewis' Estate, 121 Utah 385, 242 P.2d 565 (1952) (declaration as to paternity of child by woman who had made arrangements for birth and who was present at birth admissible, although she was not related to family whose pedigree was questioned; "the likelihood of her declarations being true are very great").

See 5 Wigmore, Evidence § 1487 (Chadbourn rev. 1974) (criticizing the requirement of family membership); Annot., 15 A.L.R.2d 1412. Because a nonfamily member often offers to testify not simply as to the conclusory fact but rather to the community or neighborhood reputation as to that fact, the issue may be intertwined with the admissibility of reputation.

6. In re Stone's Estate, 78 Idaho 632, 308 P.2d 597 (1957); Lopez v. Texas Department of Human Resources, 631 S.W.2d 251 (Tex.App.1982).

7. This requirement means that the statement must have been made not only prior to the litigation but also prior to the development of the controversy that subse-

quently ended in litigation. Hartford National Bank & Trust v. Prince, 28 Conn.Super. 348, 261 A.2d 287 (1968); In re Estate of Cunha, 49 Hawaii 273, 414 P.2d 925 (1966) 5 Wigmore, Evidence § 1483.

8. Hartford National Bank & Trust v. Prince, 28 Conn.Super. 348, 261 A.2d 287 (1968) (denials of paternity inadmissible because they were made at a time when the declarant was interested in another woman and therefore had some motive to misrepresent his relationship to his estranged wife by denying sexual relationships with her).

9. In re Estate of McClain, 481 Pa. 435, 392 A.2d 1371 (1978) (as the court observes, declarant is certainly a member of his own family).

10. See generally, 5 Wigmore, Evidence § 1486 (Chadbourn rev. 1974).

11. 5 Wigmore, Evidence § 1482 (Chadbourn rev. 1974).

12. As to unavailability, see § 253 supra.

13. The corresponding revised Uniform Rule (1974) differs insignificantly.

14. N. 7 supra.

15. N. 8 supra.

16. § 185 supra.

The narrow view of what is included in family history is continued.[17]

The traditional hearsay exception went beyond the statements described above and has allowed the use of contemporary records of family history, such as entries in a family Bible [18] or on a tombstone,[19] even though the author may not be identifiable. Federal and Revised Uniform Rule of Evid. (1974) 803(13) follow this pattern in providing a hearsay exception, without regard to availability of the declarant, for:

> Statements of fact concerning personal or family history contained in family Bibles, genealogies, charts, engravings on rings, inscriptions on family portraits, engravings on urns, crypts, or tombstones, or the like.

Matters of family history traditionally have also been provable by reputation in the family,[20] or, under some decisions, in the community.[21] The tradition is continued in Federal and Revised Uniform Rule of Evidence (1974) 803(19), by a hearsay exception for:

> Reputation among members of his family by blood, adoption, or marriage, or among his associates, or in the community, concerning a person's birth, adoption, marriage, divorce, death, legitimacy, relationship by blood, adoption, or marriage, ancestry, or other similar fact of his personal or family history.

Also continuing a traditional exception is the usability of judgments as proof of family history under Federal and Revised Uniform Rule of Evidence (1974) 803(23):

> Judgments as proof of matters of personal, family or general history, or boundaries, essential to the judgment, if the same would be provable by evidence of reputation.[22]

 **WESTLAW REFERENCES**

family personal /4 history background /s admit! admissib! inadmissib! hearsay

§ 323. Recitals in Ancient Writings and Documents Affecting an Interest in Property [1]

As observed in a preceding section,[2] a writing has usually been regarded as sufficiently authenticated if the offering party proves that it is at least 30 years old,[3] the trial judge finds that it is unsuspicious in appearance, and the party proves that it was produced from a place of custody natural for such a writing. This "ancient documents" rule, however, traditionally has related only to authentication. American courts have nevertheless sometimes recognized a hearsay exception for statements in a writing which meets these requirements.[4] Thus what originated as an aspect of authentica-

---

17. N. 2 supra.

18. Annot., 29 A.L.R. 372. For use of family Bibles, as well as other methods, to prove family or personal history in Social Security matters, see 20 C.F.R. §§ 404.715–404.728 (1982).

19. Conn v. Boylan, 224 N.Y.S.2d 823 (Sup.Ct.1962).

20. Kelly's Heirs v. McGuire, 15 Ark. 555 (1885); Geisler v. Geisler, 160 Minn. 463, 200 N.W. 742 (1924).

21. In re Wulf's Estate, 242 Iowa 1012, 48 N.W.2d 890 (1951) ("common talk or general report" that X was Y's father, admissible). Wigmore states that community reputation is always admissible to prove that persons living together were married. 5 Wigmore, Evidence § 1602 (Chadbourn rev. 1974). See also Daniels v. Johnson, 216 Ark. 374, 226 S.W.2d 571 (1950).

22. See Advisory Committee's Note, Fed.R.Evid. 803(23) for background.

§ 323

1. See generally, Wickes, Ancient Documents and Hearsay, 8 Tex.L.Rev. 451 (1930); Notes, 26 Harv.L.

Rev. 544 (1913), 83 U.Pa.L.Rev. 247 (1934), 33 Yale L.J. 412 (1924); 29 Am.Jur.2d Evidence §§ 856, 861–865; C.J.S. Evidence §§ 743–752; Annot., 46 A.L.R.2d 1318 (admissibility of maps, plats, field notes, surveys and tracings under the ancient documents rule); Annot., 6 A.L.R. 1437 (admissibility of recital in ancient deed as evidence of the facts recited); Annot., 29 A.L.R. 630 (dispensing with proof of proper custody as a condition of invoking the ancient documents rule); Dec.Dig. Evidence ⬤372.

2. § 223 supra.

3. Federal and Revised Uniform Rule Evid. (1974) 901(b)(8) reduces the period to 20 years.

4. Kirkpatrick v. Tapo Oil Co., 144 Cal.App.2d 404, 301 P.2d 274 (1956); State of Nebraska, Department of Public Roads v. Parks, 185 Neb. 794, 178 N.W.2d 788 (1970); Tillman v. Lincoln Warehouse Corp., 72 A.D.2d 40, 423 N.Y.S.2d 151 (1979); Muehrcke v. Behrens, 43 Wis.2d 1, 169 N.W.2d 86 (1969); Wickes, Ancient Documents and Hearsay, 8 Tex.L.Rev. 451 (1930).

tion has become in some jurisdictions also an exception to the hearsay rule.

The stimulus for such a hearsay exception is found in the same reasons which gave rise to the special authentication rule: after passage of such a period of time, witnesses are unlikely to be available or, if available, to recall reliably the events at issue. As to assurances of trustworthiness, the mere age of the writing it may be contended, offers little assurance of truth; it is unlikely that lying was less common 30, or 20 years ago. Advocates of the exception [5] argue, however, that sufficient assurances of reliability exist. First, the dangers of mistransmission are minimized since the rule applies only to written statements. Second, the age requirement virtually assures that the assertion will have been made long before the beginning of the present controversy. Consequently, it is unlikely that the declarant had a motive to falsify, and, in any case, the statements are almost certainly uninfluenced by partisanship. Finally, some additional assurance of reliability is provided by insistence, insofar as practicable, that the usual qualifications for witnesses and out-of-court declarants be met. Thus the writing would be inadmissible if the declarant lacked the opportunity to know firsthand the facts asserted.[6]

Nearly all courts will apply the hearsay exception to recitals in an ancient deed. Thus recitals of the contents and execution of an earlier instrument, of heirship, and of consideration are nearly everywhere received to prove those facts.[7] It is arguable that, especially where possession has been taken under the deed, these cases involve unusual assurances of reliability and the rule should be limited to them.[8] A number of courts, however, have applied the exception to other types of documents.[9]

Federal and Revised Uniform Rule (1974) 803(16) contain a broadly worded hearsay exception for statements in ancient documents:

> Statements in a document in existence twenty years or more the authenticity of which is established.

While the rule itself contains no limitation as to the kind of document that may qualify, as long as it is at least 20 years old and properly authenticated,[10] evidence offered under the rule is subject to the requirements applicable to hearsay exceptions generally, such as firsthand knowledge by declarant,[11] and

---

5. Wickes, Ancient Documents and Hearsay, 8 Tex. L.Rev. 451 (1930).

6. See §§ 10, 247 supra.

Russell v. Emerson, 108 N.H. 518, 240 A.2d 52 (1968) (map dated 1888 not admissible under ancient documents rule because there was no evidence as to who prepared it); Budlong v. Budlong, 48 R.I. 144, 136 A. 308 (1927) (book found in desk of office of poor farm not admissible to prove truth of entry suggesting birth of child to specific individual, because there was not proof of the qualifications of the writer to testify to this, and in fact no proof of writer's identity at all).

As to the requirement that the writing not be suspicious on its face see Muehrcke v. Behrens, 43 Wis.2d 1, 169 N.W.2d 86 (1969).

7. See 5 Wigmore, Evidence §§ 1573–1574 (Chadbourn rev. 1974); Annot., 6 A.L.R. 630. The age requirement is insisted upon. Caranta v. Pioneer Home Improvements, Inc., 81 N.M. 393, 467 P.2d 719 (1970) (recital in deed that grantor was sole heir of X not admissible to prove heirship because deed was only 12 years old).

8. See Town of Ninety Six v. Southern Railway Co., 267 F.2d 579 (4th Cir.1959). See also Robinson v. Peterson, 200 Va. 186, 104 S.E.2d 788 (1958).

9. State for Use of Common Schools v. Taylor, 135 Ark. 232, 205 S.W. 104 (1918) (recital of sale of land in "plat book" of state land office); Kirkpatrick v. Tapo Oil Co., 144 Cal.App.2d 404, 301 P.2d 274 (1956) (account book); Whitman v. Shaw, 166 Mass. 451, 44 N.E. 333 (1896) (map to show boundaries); Department of Public Roads v. Parks, 185 Neb. 794, 178 N.W.2d 788 (1970) (consent petition, filed to make land a public road); Tillman v. Lincoln Warehouse Corp., 72 A.D.2d 40, 423 N.Y.S.2d 151 (1979) (action for failure to redeliver china; error to exclude ancient inventory certified by professional appraiser reciting that inspection took place at warehouse, offered to prove original delivery there). Wiener v. Zweib, 128 S.W. 699 (Tex.Civ.App. 1910), affirmed 105 Tex. 262, 141 S.W. 771 (1911), 147 S.W. 867 (1912) (entries in minutes of lodge to show fact and time of member's death); Muehrcke v. Behrens, 43 Wis.2d 1, 169 N.W.2d 86 (1969) (town record book).

10. Authentication requirements are set forth in Federal and Revised Uniform Rule Evid. (1974) 901(b)(8). See § 223 supra.

11. See § 323, n. 6 supra. Firsthand knowledge may appear from the statement or be inferable from circumstances. Adv.Comm. Note, Fed.R.Evid. 803. In Dallas County v. Commercial Union Assurance Co., 286

to possible exclusion under Rule 403, the "prejudice" rule.[12]

A related hearsay exception is recognized by Federal and Revised Uniform Rule of Evidence (1974) 803(15):

> A statement contained in a document purporting to establish or affect an interest in property if the matter stated was relevant to the purpose of the document, unless dealings with the property since the document was made have been inconsistent with the truth of the statement or the purport of the document.

This exception has no requirement of age of the document, but it is limited to title documents, such as deeds, and to statements relevant to the purpose of the document. The circumstances under which documents of this nature are executed, the character of the statements that will qualify, and the nonapplicability of the exception if subsequent dealings have been inconsistent with the truth of the statement or the purport of the document, are considered sufficient guarantees of trustworthiness.[13] A compan-ion rule deals with the evidentiary status of recording such documents.[14]

 WESTLAW REFERENCES

ancient +1 document* writing*

§ 324. Reputation: Land Boundaries: General History: Miscellaneous [1]

An earlier section pointed out that reputation is hearsay when offered to prove the truth of the reputed fact, but not otherwise, and that even when hearsay is subject to certain exceptions.[2] Some of the exceptions have been discussed elsewhere: proof of character,[3] such as that of a witness for veracity[4] or that of an accused person insofar as relevant to the crime charged,[5] and matters of family history.[6] Other exceptions are discussed below.

When the location of boundaries of land is at issue, reputation is admitted to prove that location.[7] Traditionally, the reputation had not only to antedate the beginning of the

---

F.2d 388 (5th Cir.1961), the court admitted a 58-year-old newspaper story of a fire at the courthouse, then under construction, pointing out the general public interest in such an occurrence; the probability that a reporter would have written the story without a visit to the scene is indeed slight. Newspaper reports have also been held admissible as proof of reputation with regard to matters provable by reputation. See § 324 infra. However, firsthand knowledge by news reporters may well generally be the exception rather than the rule, and the admissibility of stories in ancient newspapers except as suggested above may be in doubt under the rule. See, e.g., Sherrill v. Estate of Plumley, 514 S.W.2d 286 (Tex.Civ.App.1974), refused n.r.e. (obituary notice in ancient newspaper not admissible to prove heirship; no showing of identity of reporter or of his source of information; *Dallas County* distinguished on basis of firsthand knowledge and matter of local interest).

12. See § 185 supra.

13. Adv.Comm. Note, Fed.R.Evid. 803(15).

14. Federal and Revised Uniform Rule Evid. (1974) 803(14) provide a hearsay exception for:

> The record of a document purporting to establish or affect an interest in property, as proof of the content of the original recorded document and its execution and delivery by each person by whom it purports to have been executed, if the record is a record of a public office and an applicable statute authorizes the recording of documents of that kind in that office.

§ 324

1. See generally 5 Wigmore, Evidence §§ 1580–1626 (Chadbourn rev. 1974); 29 Am.Jur.2d Evidence §§ 503–507; C.J.S. Evidence §§ 422–453; Dec.Dig. Evidence ⚖︎322–324.

2. § 249 at nn. 24–35 supra.

3. § 186 supra.

4. § 44 supra.

5. § 191 supra.

6. § 322 supra.

7. Eagan v. Colwell, 86 Idaho 525, 388 P.2d 999 (1964); Burrow v. Brown, 190 So.2d 855 (Miss.1966); Kardell v. Crouch, 326 S.W.2d 869, 879 (Tex.Civ. App.1959). See generally, 5 Wigmore, Evidence §§ 1582–1595 (Chadbourn rev. 1974); 12 Am.Jur.2d Boundaries §§ 106–110; C.J.S. Evidence § 234(b); Dec. Dig. Boundaries ⚖︎35(2). In England the use of the evidence is limited to public boundaries or other public rights. Nichols v. Parker, 14 East. 331n., 104 Eng. Rep. 629 (N.P.1805). But in this country (except in a few states) it extends also to private boundaries. Hail v. Haynes, 312 Ky. 357, 227 S.W.2d 918 (1950); Hemphill v. Hemphill, 138 N.C. 504, 51 S.E. 42 (1905). See 5 Wigmore, Evidence § 1587 (Chadbourn rev. 1974). Some cases have expanded the exception beyond evidence of reputation and admitted hearsay statements of specific individuals. Kay Corp. v. Anderson, 72 Wn. 2d 879, 436 P.2d 459 (1967) (statement of out-of-court declarant as to location of boundary admitted under rule).

present controversy but also be "ancient," i.e., go back to a past generation.[8] Some recent cases suggest that the requirement is only that the monuments or markers of the original survey must have disappeared.[9] Federal and Revised Uniform Rule Evid. (1974) 803(20), set forth below, dispense completely with a requirement that the reputation be ancient or that the passage of time have rendered other evidence of the boundaries unavailable.

Reputation is also admissible to prove a variety of facts which can best be described as matters of general history.[10] Wigmore suggests that the matter must be an ancient one "or one as to which it would be unlikely that living witnesses could be obtained."[11] Federal and Revised Uniform Rule of Evidence (1974) 803(20) do not require this, although by use of the term "history" some requirement of age is no doubt imposed. In addition, the matter must be one of general interest, so that it can accurately be said that there is a high probability that the matter underwent general scrutiny as the community reputation was formed.[12] Thus

when the navigable nature of a certain river was at issue, newspaper accounts and histories describing the use made of it during the nineteenth century were admissible to prove its general reputation for navigability at that time.[13]

Federal and Revised Uniform Rule of Evidence (1974) 803(20) provide a hearsay exception consistent with the foregoing observations for proof of boundaries and matters of general history by reputation evidence:

> Reputation in a community, arising before the controversy, as to boundaries of or customs affecting lands in the community, and reputation as to events of general history important to the community or State or nation in which located.[14]

In addition to these well-developed exceptions, reputation evidence is sometimes admitted under statute or local law to prove a variety of other miscellaneous matters,[15] such as ownership of property,[16] financial standing,[17] and maintenance of a house as an establishment for liquor-selling or prostitution.[18]

---

8. 5 Wigmore, Evidence § 1582 (Chadbourn rev. 1974).

9. Johnstone v. Nause, 233 Miss. 584, 102 So.2d 889 (1958) (where monuments of a survey have disappeared, evidence of common reputation is admissible as to location of boundaries and corners); Kardell v. Crouch, 326 S.W.2d 869, 879 (Tex.Civ.App.1959) (admissible after destruction of markers and a "long lapse of time"); Blain v. Woods, 145 W.Va. 297, 115 S.E.2d 88 (1960) (where monuments of survey not lost, proper to exclude testimony of grantor's children as to boundary).

10. See generally, 5 Wigmore, Evidence §§ 1597–1599 (Chadbourn rev. 1974); 29 Am.Jur.2d Evidence §§ 506–507, 887; C.J.S. Evidence §§ 233–237; Annot., 58 A.L.R.2d 615. Se also, Morris v. Harmer's Heirs' Lessee, 32 U.S. (7 Pet.) 554, 558 (1833): "Historical facts of general and public notoriety may indeed be proved by reputation, and that reputation may be established by historical works of known character and accuracy."

The kinship to judicial notice is apparent. See § 330 infra.

11. 5 Wigmore, Evidence § 1597 (Chadbourn rev. 1974).

12. 5 Wigmore, Evidence § 1598 (Chadbourn rev. 1974); Annot., 58 A.L.R.2d 615, 619–626.

13. Montana Power Co. v. FPC, 87 U.S.App.D.C. 316, 185 F.2d 491, 497–498 (1950), cert. denied 340 U.S. 947; County of Darlington v. Perkins, 269 S.C. 572, 239 S.E.2d 69 (1977) (action to establish existence of public r.o.w.; proper to admit old diaries and newspapers to show reputation for use).

14. As to proof by judgments, see § 322, n. 22 supra.

15. See 5 Wigmore, Evidence §§ 1620–1626 (Chadbourn rev. 1974).

16. Chicago & Eastern Illinois Railroad Co. v. Schmitz, 211 Ill. 446, 71 N.E. 1050 (1904) (reputation that particular railway owned tracks sufficient evidence of ownership in personal injury action). See 5 Wigmore, Evidence § 1626(4) (Chadbourn rev. 1974).

17. Lucas v. Swan, 67 F.2d 106, 110 (4th Cir.1933) (reputation of endorsers for insolvency). Contra, Coleman v. Lewis, 183 Mass. 485, 67 N.E. 603 (1903). See generally, 5 Wigmore, Evidence § 1623 (Chadbourn rev. 1974).

18. Elder v. Stark, 200 Ga. 452, 37 S.E.2d 598 (1946) (reputation as "blind tiger"); State v. Mauch, 236 Iowa 217, 17 N.W.2d 536 (1945) (reputation of premises and defendant as to keeping house of ill fame); Commonwealth v. United Food Corp., 374 Mass. 765, 374 N.E.2d 1331 (1978). See 5 Wigmore, Evidence § 1620

**WESTLAW
REFERENCES**

"general history" boundar! borderline* property line* /s
hearsay

§ 324.1 The Residual Hearsay Exceptions [1]

Despite the extensive array of specific hearsay exceptions in the Federal Rules, the Advisory Committee felt that "It would . . . be presumptuous to assume that all possible desirable exceptions to the hearsay rule have been catalogued and to pass the hearsay rule to oncoming generations as a closed system." [2] Therefore both of the comprehensive rules adopted by the Supreme Court dealing with hearsay exceptions, the one rule for situations where availability of the declarant does not matter and the other where unavailability is required, concluded with a residual exception: "A statement not specifically covered by any of the foregoing exceptions but having comparable circumstantial guarantees of trustworthiness." [3] As a precaution against excessive resort to the provision in the two rules as a means of effectively destroying the hearsay rule, the Advisory Committee observed, "They do not contemplate an unfettered exercise of judicial discretion, but they do provide for treating new and presently unanticipated situations which demonstrate a trustworthiness within the spirit of the specifically stated exceptions." [4]

While the Rules were under consideration in the Congress, the House Committee on the Judiciary struck the provisions in their entirety: too much uncertainty was injected into the law of evidence; any additional hearsay exceptions should be created by amending the Rules. The Senate Committe did not agree with this extreme position but suggested further restrictions to be incorporated. The differences were compromised and as enacted the clause now provides hearsay exceptions for:

A statement not specifically covered by any of the foregoing exceptions but having equivalent circumstantial guarantees of trustworthiness, if the court determines that (A) the statement is offered as evidence of a material fact; (B) the statement is more probative on the point for which it is offered than any other evidence which the proponent can procure through reasonable efforts; and (C) the general purposes of these rules and the interests of justice will best be served by admission of the statement into evidence. However, a statement may not be admitted under this exception unless the proponent of it makes known to the adverse party sufficiently in advance of the trial or hearing to provide the adverse party with a fair opportunity to prepare to meet it, his intention to offer the statement and the particulars of it, including the name and address of the declarant.[5]

The Revised Uniform Rules contain the same language.[6]

Whether the residual exception should be applied liberally or restrictively has been a matter of some difference of opinion. The argument has been made that the legislative history is ambiguous: though the House deleted the provision entirely and the Senate Committee Report stated that it should be used "very rarely and only in exceptional circumstances," liberal decisions were used as illustrations; moreover, the enacted text makes no mention of limiting use to excep-

---

(Chadbourn rev. 1974); Dec.Dig. Disorderly House ⊛16.

In the latter situation, common usage has absorbed the rule of evidence into the terms "house of ill fame" and "house of ill repute."

§ 324.1

1. Imwinkelreid, The Scope of the Residual Hearsay Exception in the Federal Rules of Evidence, 15 San Diego L.Rev. 239 (1978); Notes, 31 Rutgers L.Rev. 687

(1978), 61 Neb.L.Rev. 187 (1982); Annot., 36 A.L.R.Fed. 742.

2. Advisory Committee's Note, Fed.R.Evid. 803(24).

3. Fed.R.Evid. 803(24) and 804(b)(6), as adopted by the Supreme Court. 56 F.R.D. 303, 322.

4. Advisory Committee's Note, Fed.R.Evid. 803(24).

5. Fed.R.Evid. 803(24) and 804(b)(5).

6. Rev.Unif.R.Evid. (1974) 803(24) and 804(b)(6).

tional circumstances.[7] Nevertheless, the attitude of the Advisory Committee and of both Houses of the Congress was clearly one of conservatism toward resorting to the exception, and the courts generally have announced respect for that position.[8]

Equivalent circumstantial guarantees of trustworthiness. In applying the residual exception, the central focus is upon the question whether the situation before the court offers "equivalent circumstantial guarantees of trustworthiness," i.e. equivalent to those offered by the various specific hearsay exceptions enumerated in the two rules. Since the range in degree of trustworthiness among the specific exceptions is admittedly considerable, should the standard be that of the lowest, the highest, or some sort of estimated average? When the question has been asked, the answer seems to have been, "Not necessarily the highest." [9] Generally, however, the question has not been raised in terms, and a sort of concensus average seems to be assumed.

The courts do not appear to be developing further class-type hearsay exceptions readily susceptible of being catalogued. However, as the volume of decided cases increases, certain recurring factors are acquiring recognition as significant in deciding whether to apply the residual exception. Among them are: whether the statement was under oath,[10] the duration of the time lapse between event and statement,[11] motivation to speak truthfully or otherwise,[12] and whether declarant had firsthand knowledge.[13] These are factors that bear upon the declarant at the time of making the statement, as is characteristic of the specific hearsay exceptions generally, and fairly fall within the description "equivalent circumstantial gaurantees of trustworthiness." In addition, the courts have recognized further factors which did not bear upon declarant at the time he was speaking but which, viewed in retrospect, tend to support the truthfulness of his statement. These include: corroboration,[14] whether the declarant has recanted or reaffirmed the statement,[15] and whether the de-

7. A liberal construction is espoused by Imwinkelreid, supra n. 1. To the contrary are Notes, 31 Rutgers L.Rev. 687 (1978) and 61 Neb.L.Rev. 187 (1982). All three review the history of the exception. For briefer histories see United States v. Kim, 595 F.2d 755 (D.C.Cir.1979), and United States v. Bailey, 581 F.2d 341 (3d Cir.1978).

8. E.g., United States v. Kim and United States v. Bailey, supra n. 7. Note also 28 U.S.C.A. § 2076, enacted at the same time as the Rules and imposing strict congressional controls over the making of amendments.

9. United States v. West, 574 F.2d 1131, 50 A.L.R. Fed. 833 (4th Cir.1978).

10. United States v. Bailey, 581 F.2d 341 (3d Cir. 1978); United States v. White, 611 F.2d 531 (5th Cir. 1980), cert. denied 446 U.S. 992; United States v. Carlson, 547 F.2d 1346 (8th Cir.1976), cert. denied 431 U.S. 914; United States v. Barlow, 693 F.2d 954 (6th Cir. 1982).

11. Robinson v. Shapiro, 646 F.2d 734 (2d Cir.1981) (account of conversation with building superintendent by repair crew foreman upon return to roof); United States v. Medico, 557 F.2d 309 (2d Cir.1977), cert. denied 434 U.S. 986 (lapse of five minutes); United States v. Iaconetti, 406 F.Supp. 554 (E.D.N.Y.1976), affirmed 540 F.2d 574 (2d Cir.) (same day), cert. denied 429 U.S. 1041, rehearing denied 430 U.S. 911; United States v. White, 611 F.2d 531 (5th Cir.1980), cert. denied 446 U.S. 992 (three months).

12. Robinson v. Shapiro, 646 F.2d 734 (2d Cir.1981); United States v. Bailey, 581 F.2d 341 (3d Cir.1978); United States v. White, 611 F.2d 531 (5th Cir.1980), cert. denied 446 U.S. 992; Huff v. White Motor Corp., 609 F.2d 286 (7th Cir.1979); United States v. Barlow, 693 F.2d 954 (6th Cir.1982).

13. Huff v. White Motor Corp., 609 F.2d 286 (7th Cir.1979); United States v. Carlson, 547 F.2d 1346 (8th Cir.1976), cert. denied 431 U.S. 914; United States v. Barlow, 693 F.2d 954 (6th Cir.1982).

14. United States v. West, 574 F.2d 1131 (4th Cir. 1978); United States v. Garner, 574 F.2d 1141 (4th Cir. 1978), cert. denied 439 U.S. 936; United States v. Ward, 552 F.2d 1080 (5th Cir.1977), cert. denied 434 U.S. 850; United States v. Barlow, 693 F.2d 954 (6th Cir.1982); State v. Beam, 206 Neb. 248, 292 N.W.2d 302 (1980). Taking the contrary view that corroboration is not relevant for purposes of the residual exceptions is Huff v. White Motor Corp., 609 F.2d 286, 293 (7th Cir.1979). United States v. Boulahanis, 677 F.2d 586 (7th Cir. 1982), cert. denied 103 S.Ct. 375 suggests that corroboration may tend to undermine a claim that the hearsay is the most probative available evidence. See n. 22 infra.

15. United States v. Leslie, 542 F.2d 285 (5th Cir. 1976), rehearing denied 545 U.S. 168 (prosecution witnesses admitted making statements against accused but testified in his favor, asserting forgetfulness or untruth of statements); United States v. Carlson, 547 F.2d 1346 (8th Cir.1976), cert. denied 431 U.S. 914 (witness reaffirmed truth of grand jury testimony but re-

clarant is now subject to cross-examination.[16] Strictly speaking, these may not be "equivalent circumstantial guarantees of trustworthiness" in the language of the residual exception, but it would be unrealistic to ignore their bearing on the question of the truthfulness of the hearsay statement. Each situation still depends largely upon its own particular circumstances, and the force of precedent is developing rather slowly. The present status may well be a replay of the early stages of the evolution of the currently accepted specific exceptions.

Notice. The most significant addition engrafted by the congressional process upon the Supreme Court's version of the residual exception is the requirement that notice be given sufficiently in advance of trial to enable the adverse party to prepare to meet the hearsay evidence.[17] Although on occasion a policy of rigid enforcement has been announced,[18] the courts generally have been willing to dispense with notice if the need for the hearsay arises on the eve of trial or in the course of trial when possible injustice is avoided by the offer of a continuance or other circumstances.[19]

Other requirements. The remaining requirements added by the Congress, lettered (A), (B), and (C), have had no appreciable impact upon the application of the residual exception.[20] Item (A), requiring that the statement be offered as evidence of a material fact, is a restatement of the general requirement that evidence be relevant.[21] Requirement (B), that the evidence be more probative than any other evidence that proponent can obtain on the point through reasonable efforts, receives occasional application.[22] Requirement (C), that the general purposes of the rules and the interests of justice will be served by admitting the evidence, in effect restates Rule 102.[23]

 **WESTLAW REFERENCES**

"circumstantial guarantee*" /s trustworthiness
sh 581 f2d 341

---

§ 324.2   Basis for Expert Opinion as a Hearsay Exception

An expert witness may, under Federal and Revised Uniform Rule (1974) 703,[1] base an opinion on facts or data that are not "admissible in evidence" if of a type reasonably re-

---

fused to testify for prosecution at trial); United States v. Barlow, 693 F.2d 954 (6th Cir.1982).

16. United States v. Bailey, 581 F.2d 341 (3d Cir. 1978); United States v. Leslie, 542 F.2d 285 (5th Cir. 1976), rehearing denied 545 U.S. 168; United States v. Iaconetti, 406 F.Supp. 554 (E.D.N.Y.1976), affirmed 540 F.2d 574 (2d Cir.), 36 A.L.R.Fed. 734, cert. denied 429 U.S. 104, rehearing denied 430 U.S. 911.

17. See final sentence of the exception, text supra at n. 5.

18. United States v. Oates, 560 F.2d 45, 72 n. 30 (2d Cir.1977), on remand 445 F.Supp. 351 (D.N.Y.) affirmed 591 F.2d 1332. The question of notice was not in fact raised on appeal.

19. United States v. Iaconetti, supra n. 16 (notice given at beginning of weekend recess; no continuance requested); United States v. Bailey, supra n. 16 (prosecution witness refused to testify during trial; continuance offered in connection with prior statement); United States v. Carlson, supra n. 15 (grand jury witness announced on eve of trial that he would not testify for prosecution because of threats by accused; notice not required).

20. For the text of the residual exception, see text supra at n. 5.

21. Fed.R.Evid. 401, 402. See Huff v. White Motor Corp., 609 F.2d 286, 294 (7th Cir.1979).

22. Huff v. White Motor Corp., supra n. 21 (statement of deceased truck driver as to origin of truck fire more probative than other available evidence). In United States v. Mathis, 559 F.2d 294 (5th Cir.1977), the requirement was invoked to exclude the prior statement of a prosecution witness who was available to testify.

See United States v. Boulahanis, 677 F.2d 586 (7th Cir.1982), cert. denied 103 S.Ct. 375 (evidence need not be essential; sufficient if it is the most probative reasonably available on a material issue).

23. Huff v. White Motor Corp., supra n. 21 (interests of justice served by increasing likelihood that jury will ascertain the truth).

§ 324.2

1. See § 15 supra. The rule has been adopted piecemeal in jurisdictions that have not adopted the rules as a whole. E.g., Wilson v. Clark, 84 Ill.2d 186, 49 Ill.Dec. 308, 417 N.E.2d 1322 (1981), cert. denied 454 U.S. 836.

lied upon by experts in the field. An expert must, of course, be allowed to disclose to the trier of fact the basis facts for his opinion, as otherwise the opinion is left unsupported in midair with little if any means for evaluating its correctness.[2] This raises the apparent anomaly that the expert may testify to evidence even though it is inadmissible. The anomaly disappears, however, when the language of the rule is given its proper meaning that the expert himself may give the necessary foundation testimony for the introduction of basis testimony that traditionally would have been inadmissible without producing numerous other witnesses.[3] It does not mean that the expert becomes the sole judge of the admissibility of the basis facts: they must still be of a type reasonably relied upon by experts in the field, and they are subject to such general evidentiary principles as exclusion for prejudice or irrelevancy.[4] Subject to the foregoing comments, the basis facts may be testified to by the expert, and accordingly they are in evidence. The effect of Rule 703 has been to create a hearsay exception, or perhaps dispense with the requirement of firsthand knowledge, as the case may be. What, however, is the status of the evidence thus admitted? Is it admitted fully as substantive evidence or only for the limited purpose of "explaining the opinion"? Standing alone is it sufficient to make a prima facie case? How may it be argued to the jury? Should a limited instruction be given?

Some authority has taken the position that evidence of the kind here under discussion is admissible only for the limited purpose of "explaining" the opinion.[5] In general, however, the rules have rejected limited use hearsay exceptions, particularly the kind here involved.[6] Moreover, it is pointed out that, if the expert's testimony is the only proof of an essential basis fact, the result of a limited use is effectively to bar the expert from presenting his opinion and to nullify Rule 703.[7]

The above analysis may, however, be needlessly complex and in some degree contrived. In the formulating of Rule 703, the attention of the draftsmen was directed to eliminating or at least reducing needless and artificial obstacles in the way of presenting expert opinion testimony. The solution adopted was to permit the substitution of the professional judgment of the expert as to the reliability of the basis facts as a substitute for the traditional process of producing a series of witnesses to establish them. The Advisory Committee explained:

"Thus a physician in his own practice bases his diagnosis on information from numerous

---

2. Blakey, An Introduction to the Oklahoma Evidence Code: The Thirty-Fourth Hearsay Exception, 16 Tulsa L.J. 1, 14 (1980); Saltzburg & Redden, Federal Rules of Evidence Manual 426–27 (2d ed. 1977); Bryan v. John Bean Division, 566 F.2d 541 (5th Cir.1978); United States v. Sims, 514 F.2d 147 (9th Cir.1975), cert. denied 423 U.S. 845. Compare Rothstein, Understanding the New Federal Rules of Evidence 81–84 (1973).

3. Fed.R.Evid. 705, Adv.Comm. Note: "The rule allows counsel to make disclosure of the underlying facts or data as a preliminary to the giving of an expert opinion, if he chooses . . . ."

4. See § 185 supra.

5. Saltzburg & Redden, Federal Rules of Evidence Manual 427 (2d ed. 1977); McElhaney, Expert Witnesses and the Federal Rules of Evidence, 28 Mercer L.Rev. 463, 482 n. 83 (1977).

6. Rule 803(4) rejects the traditional distinction between statements to a nontreating physician by a patient and those to a treating physician for hearsay purposes. The Advisory Committee commented in its note to Rule 803(4):

"Conventional doctrine has excluded from the hearsay exception, as not within its guarantee of truthfulness, statements to a physician consulted only for the purpose of enabling him to testify. While these statements were not admissible as substantive evidence, the expert was allowed to state the basis of his opinion, including statements of this kind. The distinction thus called for was one most unlikely to be made by juries. The rule accordingly rejects the limitation. This position is consistent with the provision of Rule 703 that the facts on which expert testimony is based need not be admissible in evidence if of a kind ordinarily relied upon by experts in the field."

Observe also the treatment of prior consistent and inconsistent statements of witnesses under Rule 801(d)(1) (A) and (B).

Blakey, supra n. 2, at pp. 35–37; §§ 292 and 293 supra.

7. Blakey, supra n. 2, at p. 37.

sources and of considerable variety, including statements by patients and relatives, reports and opinions from nurses, technicians, and other doctors, hospital records, and X rays. Most of them are admissible in evidence, but only with the expenditure of substantial time in producing and examining various authenticating witnesses. The physician makes life-and-death decisions in reliance upon them. His validation, expertly performed and subject to cross-examination, ought to suffice for judicial purposes." [8]

While not thinking specifically in terms of a hearsay exception, the draftsmen nevertheless by a different route reached the same standard of reliability as is embodied in the residual hearsay exception of Rules 803(24) and 804(b)(5), that is, "equivalent circumstantial guarantees of trustworthiness." This approach goes to the heart of the problem and offers the appropriate standard for determining the admissibility as substantive evidence of the expert's basis facts. [9]

WESTLAW REFERENCES

expert* /s inadmissible "not admissible" hearsay /6 data datum fact facts information
157k555 /p hearsay /p expert*

---

§ 324.3 Hearsay Within Hearsay: Multiple Hearsay

"On principle it scarcely seems open to doubt that the hearsay rule should not call for exclusion of a hearsay statement which includes a further hearsay statement when both conform to the requirements of a hearsay exception." [1] The common law followed this reasoning,[2] and it is incorporated in Federal and Revised Uniform Rule of Evidence (1974) 805:

> Hearsay included within hearsay is not excluded under the hearsay rule if each part of the combined statements conforms with an exception to the hearsay rule provided in these rules.

In the usual situation, two stages of inquiry are involved.[3] First, does the primary statement qualify under a hearsay exception? If so, the hearsay rule allows its use to prove that the included statement was made, if that is the end of the inquiry.[4] Ordinarily, however, the included statement will be offered to prove the truth of what it asserts, and in that event the second stage of inquiry is required, namely does the included statement also qualify under a hearsay exception? If the answer again is in the affirmative, there is compliance with the rule.

As an example of compliance, to show product confusion the supervisor of a consumer survey as witness lays the foundation for reports made by interviewers of replies made by interviewees; the primary hearsay, namely the report, qualifies as a business record, and the included hearsay, namely the answers of interviewees, qualifies under the state of mind exception.[5] As an example of noncompliance, in a murder trial a police officer testifies that A told him that B confessed to A that B committed the crime. Although B's confession to A, the included statement, is against penal interest, A's

---

8. Adv.Comm.Note, Fed.R.Evid. 703.

9. Rennick v. Fruehauf Corp., 82 Wis.2d 793, 264 N.W.2d 264, 269 (1978) (medical opinions and diagnoses in report of consulting neurologist, used by testifying physician in support of his diagnosis "has sufficient trustworthiness to permit admission in direct proof.") Supporting limited admissibility are Bryan v. John Bean Division and United States v. Sims, supra n. 2, in neither case being necessary to the decision.

§ 324.3

1. Adv.Comm.Note, Fed.R.Evid. 805.

2. United States v. Maddox, 444 F.2d 148 (2d Cir. 1971); Minor v. City of Chicago, 101 Ill.App.3d 823, 57 Ill.Dec. 410, 428 N.E.2d 1090 (1981).

3. No limit on the number of layers of hearsay that may be involved is found at common law or under the rules. However, attenuation of probative value has been suggested as layers increase. Comment, 15 Wayne L.Rev. 1077, 1231 (1969).

4. Out-of-court utterances that are not hearsay are discussed in § 249 supra.

5. Zippo Manufacturing Co. v. Rogers Imports, Inc., 216 F.Supp. 670 (S.D.N.Y.1963); Bradley v. Booz, Allen & Hamilton, Inc., 67 Ill.App.3d 156, 23 Ill.Dec. 839, 384 N.E.2d 746 (1978).

statement to the police officer, the primary statement falls under no hearsay exception.[6]

An oft recurring version of multiple hearsay involves a primary hearsay exception in the form of a regularly kept business record [7] which includes a further hearsay statement. If the included statement is by a person acting in the routine of the business, the regularly kept records exception takes care of the matter and no further exception need be invoked. However, if the person whose statement is included is not in the routine of the business, resort must be had to a further exception.[8] In that event it might be argued that the primary statement did not qualify under a hearsay exception since the regularly kept records exception requires that the informant be in the routine of the business. The courts, however, have not so held, but have taken the view that the regularly kept records exception actually involves in itself multiple hearsay, namely a primary stage consisting of the record and an included stage consisting of what was reported to the recorder.[9]

At common law, one of the hearsay statements might consist of an admission,[10] which was regarded as a hearsay exception. Since admissions are not classed as hearsay under the Federal and Revised Uniform Rules (1974), the question may arise whether an admission may qualify as a hearsay exception for purposes of the multiple hearsay rule. One answer has been that admissions are within the spirit and purpose of the rule.[11] An easier answer may be that only one hearsay problem arises; if it is satisfied by an exception, no further hearsay difficulty remains.[12]

 WESTLAW REFERENCES

"business record*"   /p   multiple double triple level** tier** "totem pole"   /4   hearsay

---

6. People v. Hawkins, 114 Mich.App. 714, 319 N.W.2d 644 (1982); Boyer v. State, 91 Wis.2d 647, 284 N.W.2d 30 (1979).

7. See generally Ch. 31 supra.

8. See § 308 supra.

9. United States v. Baker, 693 F.2d 183 (D.C. Cir. 1982).

10. United States v. Maddox, supra n. 2.

11. United States v. Lang, 589 F.2d 92, 99 n. 2 (2d Cir.1978).

12. United States v. Basey, 613 F.2d 198, 201 n. 1 (9th Cir.1979), cert. denied 446 U.S. 919.

Similar arguments may be made concerning other out of court statements declared not to be hearsay by Federal and Revised Uniform Rule Evid. (1974) 801(d) (1).

Chapter 34

THE PRESENT AND FUTURE OF RULES ABOUT HEARSAY

Table of Sections

---

§ 325. Evaluation of the Present Rules

Before laying down his pen as he concluded his work on evidence in 1842, Professor Greenleaf wrote:

> "The student will not fail to observe the symmetry and beauty of this branch of the law . . . and will rise from the study of its principles convinced, with Lord Erskine, that 'they are founded in the charities of religion,—in the philosophy of nature,—in the truths of history,—and in the experience of common life.' " [1]

Not many persons today would apply this evaluation to the development of the rule against hearsay in the common law tradition. Did the common law go overboard in its insistence on the best? Certainly, picking a quarrel with insistence upon high quality in judicial factfinding would be difficult to justify, and yet more than a suspicion is raised that the rules have not always yielded the quality sought and have exacted too high a price. Criticism centers upon the complexity of the pattern of the rules and upon doubts whether in reality they achieve their purpose of screening the good from the bad.

First, with respect to the complexity of the rule against hearsay and its exceptions, the number of exceptions naturally depends upon the minuteness of the classification. The Federal Rules contain 31 exceptions and exclusions, and the Revised Uniform Rules (1974) top that number by one.[2] Wigmore requires over a thousand pages to cover hearsay, and its treatment preempted 25% of the original edition of the present work. Most of the complication of course arises in connection with the exceptions, leading readily to the conclusion that a general rule so riddled with exceptions is "farcical." [3] The conclusion may be too facile. Probably less than 10, and possibly no more than a half dozen, of the exceptions are encountered with any frequency in the trial of cases, and to require mastery of them, plus an awareness of the others and a working knowledge of what is and is not hearsay, should not un-

---

§ 325

1. Greenleaf, Evidence § 584 (1st ed. 1842).

2. Included in the count are two "residual" exceptions and two exclusions by definition.

3. Nokes, The English Jury and the Law of Evidence, 31 Tulane L.Rev. 153, 167 (1956). Cross describes the list of exceptions as "most unwieldy", Evidence 509 (5th ed. 1979), and "massive." Comment, 56 Canadian Bar Rev. 306, 308 (1978).

duly tax the intellectual resources of a learned profession.

The second complaint, that the rule against hearsay and its exceptions fail to screen reliable from unreliable hearsay on a realistic basis, is of more serious proportion. The trustworthiness of hearsay ranges from the highest reliability to utter worthlessness. Illustrative of the kinds of hearsay, i.e., uncross-examined statements offered to prove the facts stated in them, are the following: history books, newspapers, business records, official records and certificates, affidavits, letters and other written statements, simple oral hearsay, multiple hearsay (A reports that B said that C said, and so on), reputation, and gossip or rumors.[4] Whether these infinitely varying, plastic situations can ever be completely and satisfactorily captured in a set of rules may well be doubted. Yet similar doubts pervade most other areas of the law and are not generally regarded as cause for despair. If the heart of the problem is that the exceptions are unacceptable in detail, a perusal of the preceding chapters dealing with hearsay indicates that much has been done in recent years to rationalize the rules and to improve their practical workability, more along evolutionary lines than revolutionary. But if the basic difficulty is simply that no hearsay system based on classes of exceptions can truly succeed, a totally different approach would be required.

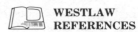

WESTLAW REFERENCES

di hearsay
digest(rule* +s 803 804 805)

§ 326. Basic Shifts in the Contemporary Pattern [1]

Frontal attacks upon the traditional common law hearsay pattern have been for the most part legislative in nature rather than judicial.

Pursuant to a suggestion from James Bradley Thayer, the Massachusetts Hearsay Statute of 1898 was enacted as follows: "A declaration of a deceased person shall not be inadmissible in evidence as hearsay if the Court finds that it was made in good faith before the commencement of the action and upon the personal knowledge of the declarant." [2] After a quarter century of experience under the act a questionnaire was addressed to the lawyers and judges of the state to ascertain their views as to the merits of the act. Of those having experience with the operation of the act, 71 percent thought that its effects were wholesome and only 19 percent were of the opposite opinion.[3] The American Bar Association in 1938 recommended a liberalized version of the act for adoption by the states.[4]

The English Evidence Act of 1938 [5] allowed the introduction of written statements, made on the personal knowledge of

---

4. McCormick, Tomorrow's Law of Evidence, 24 A.B.A.J. 507, 512 (1938); Morgan, Foreword, Model Code of Evidence 46 (1942). See § 245, n. 22 supra.

§ 326

1. For a comprehensive review of evidence law reform in the English-speaking world, see Neil Brooks, The Law Reform Commission of Canada's Evidence Code, 16 Osgoode Hall L.J. 240 (1978).

2. Mass. Acts 1898, ch. 535.

The present version of the Act is: "In any action or other civil judicial proceeding, a declaration of a deceased person shall not be inadmissible in evidence as hearsay or as private conversation between husband and wife, as the case may be, if the court finds that it was made in good faith and upon the personal knowledge of the declarant." Mass.G.L.Ann. c. 233, § 65, as amended 1941 and 1943.

3. Morgan et al. (constituting the Commonwealth Fund Committee), The Law of Evidence: Some Proposals for Its Reform 39–49 (1927).

4. "That declarations of a deceased or insane person should be received in evidence if the trial judge shall find (1) that the person is dead or insane, (2) that the declaration was made and (3) that it was made in good faith before the commencement of the action and upon the personal knowledge of the declarant." Vanderbilt, Minimum Standards of Judicial Administration 321, 338 (1949).

5. St.1938, c. 28, Evidence. See Maugham, Observations on the Law of Evidence, 17 Can. Bar Rev. 469 (1939); Cowen and Carter, The Interpretation of the Evidence Act, 1938, 12 Mod.L.Rev. 145 (1949); Comment, 34 Ill.L.Rev. 974 (1940).

the maker or in the regular course of business, if the maker was called as a witness or was unavailable. Even though the maker was neither called nor unavailable, the judge might admit the statement if satisfied that undue delay or expense would otherwise be involved. Statements made by interested persons when proceedings were pending or instituted were excluded from the act. It applied only in civil cases.

These limitations were loosened and new ones added in 1968.[6] Hearsay statements, whether written or oral, are made admissible to the extent that testimony of the declarant would be admissible, regardless of whether he is called as a witness,[7] though it is contemplated that ordinarily prior statements would not be admitted at the behest of the proponent if the declarant is called.[8] Notice is required of intent to offer a hearsay statement under the act, and the opposite party is given the right to require production of declarant as a witness, if available.[9] The act is far more complex than the foregoing résumé would indicate. Like its predecessor of 1938 and the Massachusetts statute, it applies only in civil cases. Efforts to revise the English law of evidence in criminal cases have not succeeded.

The drafters of the Model Code of Evidence of the American Law Institute took a bold course about hearsay. They drafted a sweeping new exception to the hearsay rule as follows:

"Evidence of a hearsay declaration is admissible if the judge finds that the declarant

(a) is unavailable as a witness, or

(b) is present and subject to cross-examination." [10]

This rule, however, was qualified and safeguarded by other rules which (1) limited its application to declarations by persons with personal knowledge and excluded hearsay upon hearsay,[11] and (2) empowered the trial judge to exclude such hearsay whenever its probative value was outweighed by the likelihood of waste of time, prejudice, confusion or unfair surprise.[12] The traditional exceptions, in addition to the new sweeping one, were retained in general.[13]

The liberalizing of the use of hearsay was a chief ground of opposition to the Model Code in professional discussion and no doubt substantially accounted for the failure of the Code to be adopted in any jurisdiction.[14]

Nevertheless, the controversy over the Model Code awakened a new interest in the improvement of evidence law. Accordingly, the Commissioners on Uniform State Laws, in cooperation with the American Law Institute and building on the foundation of the Model Code, drafted and adopted a more modestly reformative code, styled the Uniform Rules of Evidence. The American Bar Association approved this action.[15]

Instead of admitting, as does the Model Code rule quoted above, virtually all firsthand hearsay of an unavailable declarant, the original Uniform Rules substituted a hearsay exception for statements by unavailable declarants describing a matter recently perceived and made in good faith prior to the commencement of the action. A similar provision is found in Rule 804(b)(5) of the Revised Uniform Rules (1974), but its counterpart was dropped from the Federal Rules by the Congress. As to prior statements by witnesses present at the hearing, the original Uniform Rules adopted substantially the broad provisions of the Model Code rule quoted above, but the revised Uniform Rules (1974) follow the much narrower congres-

---

6. St.1968, c. 64, Civil Evidence. Comment, Newark & Samuels, 31 Mod.L.Rev. 668 (1968).

7. Id., Part I, § 2(1).

8. Id., Part II, § 2(2).

9. Id., Part I, § 8(2).

10. Model Code of Evidence Rule 503.

11. Id., Rule 501(3).

12. Id., Rule 303.

13. Id., Rules 504–529.

14. Despite its failure to achieve adoption, the influence of the Code upon decisions and writings in the field of evidence has been enormous.

15. 39 A.B.A.J. 1029 (1953).

sional version of Federal Rule of Evidence 801(d)(1).[16] As in the Model Code, the other traditional exceptions were retained and liberalized.

The Advisory Committee on Federal Rules of Evidence approached its task with awareness of the criticisms that had been leveled against the common law system of class exceptions to the hearsay rule. It also was aware that the Model Code's lack of acceptance was to a large extent the result of having outrun the profession's willingness to abide by a basically altered approach to hearsay in the shape of free admissibility of prior statements of unavailable declarants.[17] In its first draft circulated for comment,[18] the committee endeavored to rationalize the hearsay exceptions in general terms, while at the same time maintaining continuity with the past. For these ends, two rules were included, one covering situations where it made no difference whether declarant was available [19] and the other applying only when declarant was unavailable.[20] The first of these rules opened with the general provision:

> A statement is not excluded by the hearsay rule if its nature and the special circumstances under which it was made offer assurances of accuracy not likely to be enhanced by calling the declarant as a witness, even though he is available.

This general provision was followed by 23 illustrative applications derived from common law exceptions, not to be considered an exclusive listing. The second of the rules again opened with a general provision:

> A statement is not excluded by the hearsay rule if its nature and the special circumstances under which it was made offer strong assur-

ances of accuracy and the declarant is unavailable as a witness.

It, too, was followed by a list of illustrative applications derived from the common law, although a shorter one, with again a caution that the enumeration not be considered exclusive. While the response of the profession indicated that it was prepared to accept a substantial revision in the area of hearsay, the profession opted for a larger measure of predictability than the proposal was thought to offer. As a result, the two general provisions quoted above were withdrawn, and the two rules were revised by converting the illustrations into exceptions in the common law tradition, with the addition of two residual exceptions to take care of unforeseen situations that might arise. Many of the exceptions were clarified and revised to take advantage of the common law experience and to conform with present day thinking. In this form, the rules with some alterations were enacted into law by the Congress as Rules 803 and 804. They are now in effect in about half the States, which have adopted the Federal Rules, with local changes of varying significance.

From the foregoing discussion, it will be seen that the pattern of a general rule of exclusion of hearsay, subject to numerous exceptions ticketed in advance by class, has persisted. Even the civil English Act of 1968 specifically preserved some of the old landmark exceptions (admissions, published works dealing with matters of a public nature, public documents, records, and reputation) as proof of various matters and exempted them from the notice provisions of the act.[21] Presumably, as in the American enumerations of exceptions where unavailability is not a factor, the hearsay evidence is

16. See § 251 supra.

17. §§ 28 and 29 of the proposed Evidence Code of the Law Reform Commission of Canada contain provisions similar to those of Model Code Rule 503, supra n. 9. Report on Evidence, Law Reform Commission of Canada (1975). The proposal has encountered similar resistance and has not been adopted.

18. Preliminary Draft of Proposed Rules of Evidence for the United States District Courts and Magis-

trates, Committee on Rules of Practice and Procedure of the Judicial Conference of the United States (March, 1969), 46 F.R.D. 161.

19. Id., Rule 8–03, 46 F.R.D. 345.

20. Id., Rule 8–04, 46 F.R.D. 377.

21. St.1968, c. 64, Part I, § 9.

considered as good as or better than testimony by the declarant on the witness stand. The English have not yet succeeded in updating the law of criminal evidence. A 1972 proposal [22] raised "such a storm of protest, informed and ill informed, as to prevent the enactment of any of its recommendations, controversial or uncontroversial." [23] Efforts are continuing.

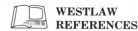

WESTLAW REFERENCES

modif! liberaliz! loosen! broaden! widen! /s hearsay /2 rule*

---

§ 327. The Future of Hearsay

This book, and all others on the subject, is testimony that the law of evidence can and does change. In the general field of protecting triers against false testimony, there has been a virtually complete shift from treating interest as a ground for exclusion to regarding it as bearing on weight and credibility.[1] Is a similar shift in store for hearsay?

Regardless of whether the hearsay rule was, as a matter of history, the child of the jury system,[2] there is little doubt that the felt need for controlling the use of hearsay is more pronounced in jury cases than in nonjury cases. In part this attitude may be a product of the close association between the right to a jury and the right of confrontation in criminal cases. The English developments in the direction of relaxing limitations on hearsay in civil cases,[3] seem obviously to have been inspired by the virtu-

al disappearance in that country of jury trial in such cases. Corresponding changes have not transpired with respect to criminal cases, where the jury remains.

In the United States, the rights of confrontation and jury trial, both constitutionally based, combine to make unlikely any unprecedented wholesale opening of the gates to hearsay in criminal cases. One may, however, speculate that the civil jury is entering upon a period of attrition, commencing with a trend to reduce its size following the decision of the Supreme Court of the United States that the jury contemplated in the right to jury trial may consist of less than 12 members.[4] Cognizance has been taken in an earlier section [5] of the generally more relaxed attitude in administering the exclusionary rules of evidence in nonjury cases. This attitude of course encompasses the rule against hearsay. An even more relaxed attitude prevails in administrative proceedings.[6] Perhaps no more than an acceleration of this process is involved in the vigorous advocacy of eliminating the hearsay rule entirely in nonjury civil cases which is encountered in some quarters.[7]

In somewhat different vein is the suggestion that admissibility of hearsay in civil cases, jury or nonjury, be based upon the judge's *ad hoc* evaluation of its probative force, with certain procedural safeguards.[8] Obviously a substantially greater measure of discretion in the judge is contemplated, with a corresponding decrease in the impact of precedent and predictability.[9] Moreover,

---

22. Criminal Law Revision Commission, Eleventh Report, Evidence (General), Cmd. 4991 (1972).

23. Cross, Comment, 56 Canadian Bar Rev. 306, 307 (1978).

§ 327

1. See § 65 supra.

2. See § 244 supra.

3. See § 326, notes 5–9, supra.

4. Williams v. Florida, 399 U.S. 78 (1970).

5. § 60 supra.

6. See §§ 352 and 353 infra.

7. E.g., Davis, Hearsay in Nonjury Cases, 83 Harv. L.Rev. 1362 (1970) (hearsay should be admitted in nonjury civil cases without ruling on its admissibility).

8. See Weinstein, Probative Force of Hearsay, 46 Iowa L.Rev. 331 (1961), collecting the literature and making an impressive case in its own right.

9. "It is tempting to meet such variability by giving trial judges some range of discretion as to admissibility. But it is uncomfortable to go to trial without knowing whether important evidence will be let in or excluded." Maguire, The Hearsay System: Around and Through the Thicket, 14 Vand.L.Rev. 741, 776 (1961).

"The suitor must feel that success is dependent upon the truth of his contentions and not upon the personali-

the judge is thrust squarely into the area of credibility, traditionally reserved to juries. Suggested procedural safeguards are notice, judge's comment on evidence, greater control by judges over juries, and greater control by appellate courts over trial courts. However, a notice requirement has the disadvantage of adding a further complication to an already overcrowded array of pretrial procedures and is contrary to modern theories of general pleading implemented by discovery.[10] And the controls envisioned, as with admissibility in the first instance, find their roots in discretionary judicial evaluation of the evidence. These objections are, however, by no means conclusive and may be thought less objectionable than the deficiencies of the existing system.

More than 50 years age, Professor McCormick wrote, much in the Benthamic tradition:

> Eventually, perhaps, Anglo-American court procedure may find itself gradually but increasingly freed from emphasis on jury trial with its contentious theory of proof. With responsibility for the ascertainment of facts vested in professional judges, the stress will be shifted from the crude technique of admitting or rejecting evidence to the more realistic problem of appraising its credibility. Psychologists meantime will have built upon their knowledge of the statistical reliability of witnesses in groups a technique of testing the veracity of individual witnesses and assessing the reliability of particular items of testimony. Judges and advocates will then become students and practitioners of an applied science of judicial proof.[11]

Appealing as this prospect may be, it becomes increasingly evident that it represents a long view indeed.

There are those who take a completely opposed view, advocating instead a sort of hyperextension of Professor Morgan's fine-tuned analysis and definition of hearsay, with the result of complicating rather than simplifying the management of hearsay.[12] Somewhat in between are those who, though not maintaining that traditional hearsay principles are carved in granite, point to certain obstacles in the way of radical change. These include the likelihood that oral statements may be misreported, enhancing the balance of advantage that already exists on the part of the prosecution and wealthy organizations in litigation due to superior facilities for generating evidence, distrust of the ability and impartiality of trial judges, and the fact that the hearsay rule presently is applied more liberally than it is written.[13]

The divergence of these points of view offers assurances that the law of hearsay will in the future be no more static than in the past, that it will continue to challenge its observers, and that proposals for its change will receive the most searching scrutiny. Other than to say that liberalization will probably continue as a general rule to dominate the course of development, prediction is hazardous.

 **WESTLAW REFERENCES**

hearsay /s nonjury jury-waived "administrative hearing*"

---

ty of the judge . . . who determines what evidence he will receive or submit to the consideration of the jury." Lehman, Technical Rules of Evidence, 26 Colum. L.Rev. 509, 512 (1926).

10. The emphasis on notice in the English statute probably derives at least in part from the virtual nonexistence of discovery in the English practice. See § 326, n. 9 supra.

11. McCormick, Evidence, Encyclopedia of the Social Sciences, v. 3, pp. 637, 646 (1931, reissue of 1937).

12. E.g., Park, McCormick on Evidence and the Concept of Hearsay, 65 Minn.L.Rev. 423 (1981). See § 250 nn. 21–23, supra.

13. Lempert & Saltzburg, A Modern Approach to Evidence 519 (2d ed. 1982).

Title 11

JUDICIAL NOTICE

Chapter 35

JUDICIAL NOTICE

Table of Sections

---

§ 328. The Need for and the Effect of Judicial Notice [1]

The traditional notion that trials are bifurcated proceedings involving both a judge and a panel of twelve jurors has obviously had a profound impact on the overall development of common law doctrine pertaining to evidence. The very existence of the jury, after all, helped create the demand for the rigorous guarantees of accuracy which typify the law of evidence, witness the insistence upon proof by witnesses having first-hand knowledge, the mistrust of hearsay, and the insistence upon original documents and their authentication by witnesses. Thus it is that the facts in dispute are commonly established by the jury after the carefully controlled introduction of formal evidence, which ordinarily consists of the testimony of witnesses. In light of the role of the jury, therefore, it is easy enough to conclude that, whereas questions concerning the tenor of the law to be applied to a case fall within the province of the judge, the determination of questions pertaining to propositions of fact is uniquely the function of the jury. The life of the law has never been quite so elementa-

---

§ 328

1. See generally, 9 Wigmore, Evidence §§ 2565–2583 (Chadbourn rev. 1981); Thayer, Preliminary Treatise on the Law of Evidence, c. 7 (1898); J. Maguire, Evidence—Common Sense and Common Law 166–175 (1947); Davis, Official Notice, 62 Harv.L.Rev. 537 (1949), Judicial Notice, 55 Colum.L.Rev. 945 (1955); Keeffe, Landis & Shaad, Sense and Nonsense about Judicial Notice, 2 Stan.L.Rev. 664 (1950); McNaughton,

Judicial Notice—Excerpts Relating to the Morgan-Wigmore Controversy, 14 Vand.L.Rev. 779 (1961); Morgan, Judicial Notice, 57 Harv.L.Rev. 269 (1944); Roberts, Preliminary Notes Toward a Study of Judicial Notice, 52 Cornell L.Q. 210 (1967); Roberts, Judicial Notice: An Exercise in Exorcism, 19 N.Y.L.F. 745 (1974); Comment, 13 Vill.L.Rev. 528 (1968); Dec.Dig. Evidence ⊕1–52; C.J.S. Evidence §§ 6–102; 29 Am.Jur.2d Evidence §§ 14–122.

ry, however, because judges on numerous occasions take charge of questions of fact and excuse the party having the burden of establishing a fact from the necessity of producing formal proof. These hybrid questions of fact, dealt with by judges as if they were questions pertaining to law, are the raw materials out of which the doctrine of judicial notice has been constructed.[2]

With what manner of questions pertaining to facts do judges concern themselves?[3] Whether a well known street was in fact within a local business district as alleged by a litigant, in which case a certain speed limit obtained, may be dealt with by the judge during the trial of a negligence case.[4] That is to say, the judge may instruct the jury that the street in question was within a business district, dispensing thereby with the need to introduce evidence to this effect.[5] Then again, questions of fact arise about which reasonably intelligent people might not have in mind the information in question, but where they would agree that the facts are verifiable with certainty by consulting

authoritative reference sources. At a time when Sunday contracts were taboo, for example, the question arose during the trial of a warranty action whether the relevant sales instrument, dated June 3, 1906, had been executed on a Sunday. In this instance the trial judge was reversed for leaving the question to the jury to deliberate upon as a question of fact.[6] Experience reveals, therefore, that two categories of facts clearly fall within the perimeters of judicial notice, these being facts generally known with certainty by all the reasonably intelligent people in the community and facts capable of accurate and ready determination by resort to sources of indisputable accuracy.

In both of the examples enumerated thus far it should be carefully noted that the facts of which judicial notice was taken were "adjudicative" facts. They were facts about the particular event which gave rise to the lawsuit and, like all adjudicative facts, they helped explain who did what, when, where, how, and with what motive and intent.[7] Further, either because they were facts so

---

2. Harper v. Killion, 345 S.W.2d 309, 311 (Tex.Civ. App.1961) ("The doctrine of judicial notice is one of common sense. The theory is that, where a fact is well-known by all reasonably intelligent people in the community, or its existence is so easily determinable with certainty from unimpeachable sources, it would not be good sense to require formal proof."). See also Porter v. Sunshine Packing Corp., 81 F.Supp. 566, 575 (W.D.Pa.1948), reversed in part 181 F.2d 348 (3d Cir.); Williams v. Commonwealth, 190 Va. 280, 291–292, 56 S.E.2d 537, 542–543 (1949).

3. Compare with the classification in the text: Fed.R.Evid. 201:

   (a) Scope of Rule. This rule governs only judicial notice of adjudicative facts.

   (b) Kinds of Facts. A judicially noticed fact must be one not subject to reasonable dispute in that it is either (1) generally known within the territorial jurisdiction of the trial court or (2) capable of accurate and ready determination by resort to sources whose accuracy cannot reasonably be questioned.

   (c) When Discretionary. A court may take judicial notice, whether requested or not.

   (d) When Mandatory. A court shall take judicial notice if requested by a party and supplied with the necessary information.

   (e) Opportunity to Be Heard. A party is entitled upon timely request to an opportunity to be heard as to the propriety of taking judicial notice and the ten-

or of the matter noticed. In the absence of prior notification, the request may be made after judicial notice has been taken.

   (f) Time of Taking Notice. Judicial notice may be taken at any stage of the proceeding.

   (g) Instructing Jury. In a civil action or proceeding, the court shall instruct the jury to accept as conclusive any fact judicially noticed. In a criminal case, the court shall instruct the jury that it may, but is not required to, accept as conclusive any fact judicially noticed.

Uniform Rule of Evidence 201 (1974) is identical except for the last subsection which reads:

   (g) Instructing Jury. The court shall instruct the jury to accept as conclusive any fact judicially noticed.

4. Varcoe v. Lee, 180 Cal. 338, 181 P. 223 (1919).

5. Id. at 344, 181 P. at 226 ("Judicial notice is a judicial short cut, a doing away . . . with the formal necessity of evidence because there is no real necessity for it.").

6. Beardsley v. Irving, 81 Conn. 489, 71 A. 580 (1909).

7. United States v. Gould, 536 F.2d 216, 219–20 (8th Cir.1976), n. 10 infra; Mainline Investment Corp. v. Gaines, 407 F.Supp. 423 (N.D.Tex.1976) (in contract case where issue was one of impossibility, the economic events surrounding the oil embargo were adjudicative

commonly known in the jurisdiction or so manifestly capable of accurate verification, they were facts reasonably informed people in the community would regard as propositions not reasonably subject to dispute.

Another species of facts figures prominently in discussions of judicial notice which, to continue to employ the terminology coined by Professor K.C. Davis,[8] are denominated "legislative" facts. Judicial notice of these facts occurs when a judge is faced with the task of creating law, by deciding upon the constitutional validity of a statute,[9] or the interpretation of a statute,[10] or the extension or restriction of a common law rule,[11] upon grounds of policy, and the policy is thought to hinge upon social, economic, political or scientific facts. Illustrative of this phenomenon was Hawkins v. United States [12] in which the Court refused to discard the common law rule that one spouse could not testify against the other, saying, "Adverse testimony given in criminal proceedings would, we think, be likely to destroy almost any marriage." This conclusion rests upon a certain view of the facts about marriage but, needless to say, the facts taken to be true in this instance were hardly indisputable. Observe, moreover, that these facts were not part and parcel of the disputed event being litigated but bore instead upon the court's own thinking about the tenor of the law to be invoked in deciding that dispute.

It is axiomatic, of course, that the judge decides whether a given set of facts constitutes an actionable wrong or a certain line of cross-examination is relevant. A judge, unless he is to be reversed on appeal, is bound to know the common and statutory law of his own jurisdiction. Commonly enough even this truism has been incorporated into the law of evidence by saying that judges must judicially notice the law of their own forum.[13] This manner of speaking has served to interpolate into the field of judicial notice the procedural mechanisms by which the applicable law is fed into the judicial process.[14] Foreign law, of course, was once more germane to the topic of judicial notice because that body of law was (for convenience) treated as fact, so much so that the law of a jurisdiction other than the forum had to be pleaded and proved just like any other question of fact, but a peculiar one which only the judge came to decide, and hence its inclusion within the topic of judicial notice.[15] Indeed, lumped along with foreign law as a proper subject for treatment under the caption of judicial notice has been the forum's own administrative law and local municipal ordinances, together with a hotchpot of internal judicial administrative details concerning the courts themselves, such as their own personnel, records, organization and jurisdictional boundaries.[16] The recognition appears to be growing, however, that the manner in which the law is insinuated in-

facts subject to judicial notice under Rule 201(b) both because they were generally known locally and capable of ready verification); Gilbertson v. State, 69 Wis.2d 587, 230 N.W.2d 874 (1975) (judicial notice cannot be taken of the potential damage which might be caused by placing a shovel in a generator because this was neither a matter of common knowledge nor one capable of ready verification from sources of indisputable accuracy); Davis, Judicial Notice, 55 Colum.L.Rev. 945, 952 (1955).

8. Davis, An Approach to Problems of Evidence in the Administrative Process, 55 Harv.L.Rev. 364 (1942).

9. Perez v. Lippold, 32 Cal.2d 711, 198 P.2d 17 (1948).

10. United States v. Gould, 536 F.2d 216 (8th Cir. 1976) (proper for judge to instruct jury as a matter of statutory interpretation that cocaine hydrochloride is a derivative of the coca leaf and hence a controlled sub-

stance; Fed.R.Evid. 201(g) not applicable, since not an adjudicative fact).

11. Southern Cotton Oil Co. v. Anderson, 80 Fla. 441, 86 So. 629 (1920). Although the term judicial notice is not actually invoked, an excellent illustration of this phenomenon is inherent in Gillespie v. Dew, 1 Stew. 229, 230 (Ala.1827).

12. 358 U.S. 74, 78 (1958). See § 331 n. 15 infra.

13. Hoyt v. Russell, 117 U.S. 401 (1886).

14. Cross, Evidence 155 (5th ed. 1979) ("It is sometimes said that the judges take judicial notice of the Common Law, but there is no need to deal separately with this aspect of the subject.").

15. Keeffe, Landis & Shaad, Sense and Nonsense About Judicial Notice, 2 Stan.L.Rev. 664, 673–675 (1950).

16. See § 335 infra.

to the judicial process is not so much a problem of evidence as it is a concern better handled within the context of the rules pertaining to procedure.[17]

 WESTLAW REFERENCES

"judicial notice" /s "common! know!" /s community
   jurisdiction
"judicial notice" /s foreign /s legislat! statut! rule
   rules law*
di judicial notice

---

§ 329. Matters of Common Knowledge

The oldest and plainest ground for judicial notice is that the fact is so commonly known in the community as to make it unprofitable to require proof, and so certainly known as to make it indisputable among reasonable

men.[1] Though this basis for notice is sometimes loosely described as universal knowledge, manifestly this could not be taken literally[2] and the more reflective opinions speak in terms of the knowledge of "most men,"[3] or of "what well-informed persons generally know,"[4] or "the knowledge that every intelligent person has."[5] Observe that these phrases tend progressively to widen the circle of facts within "common knowledge." Moreover, though usually facts of "common knowledge" will be generally known throughout the country, it is sufficient as a basis for judicial notice that they be known in the local community where the trial court sits.[6]

What a judge knows and what facts a judge may judicially notice are not identical data banks. A famous colloquy in the Year

17. Compare, e.g., Fed.R.Evid. 201, supra n. 3; Fed. R.Civ.P. 44.1, 28 U.S.C.A. (determination of foreign law). See § 335 infra.

§ 329

1. Varcoe v. Lee, 180 Cal. 338, 346–347, 181 P. 223, 227 (1919). ("The test, therefore in any particular case where it is sought to avoid or excuse the production of evidence because the fact to be proven is one of general knowledge and notoriety, is: (1) Is the fact one of common, everyday knowledge in that jurisdiction, which everyone of average intelligence and knowledge of things about him can be presumed to know? and (2) is it certain and indisputable? If it is, it is a proper case for dispensing with evidence, for its production cannot add or aid."); Indoor Recreation Enterprises v. Douglas, 194 Neb. 715, 719, 235 N.W.2d 398, 401–402 (1975) ("For a fact to be judicially noticed [under Rule 201], it is not enough that it rests upon conjecture or suspicion, on gossip or rumor, or that it be commonly asserted, if that be true. The general rule is that in order that a fact may properly be the subject of judicial notice, if must be '*known*'—that is, well *established* and *authoritatively settled*, without qualification or contention.")

2. The late Dean F. McDermott of Suffolk Law School aptly exposed the absurdity of this approach by succinctly translating it into the rule that "Judicial notice may only be taken of those facts every damn fool knows." See, however, Layne v. Tribune Co., 108 Fla. 177, 183, 146 So. 234, 237 (1933) ("What everybody knows the courts are assumed to know, and of such matters may take judicial cognizance."); In re Buszta's Estate, 18 Misc.2d 716, 717, 186 N.Y.S.2d 192, 193 (Surr.Ct.1959) ("Generally speaking, a court may take judicial notice of facts which are universally known and recognized.")

3. Rives v. Atlanta Newspapers, Inc., 110 Ga.App. 184, 190, 138 S.E.2d 100, 104 (1964), rev'd on other

grounds 220 Ga. 485, 139 S.E.2d 395 ("Consequently, courts will take judicial notice of that which is within the knowledge of most men").

4. Brandon v. Lozier-Broderick & Gordon, 160 Kan. 506, 511, 163 P.2d 384, 387 (1945).

5. Strain v. Isaacs, 59 Ohio App. 495, 514, 18 N.E.2d 816, 825 (1938).

6. Varcoe v. Lee, 180 Cal. 338, 346, 181 P. 223, 226 (1919) ("It would be wholly unreasonable to require proof, if the fact became material, as to the general location in the city of San Franciso of its city hall before a judge and jury made up of residents of that city and actually sitting in the building. But before a judge and jury in another county, proof should be made. The difference lies in the fact being one of common knowledge in one jurisdiction and not in the other."); Morgan, Judicial Notice, 57 Harv.L.Rev. 269, 277 (1944) ("Even in the federal court sitting in San Francisco the trial judge and jury might be ignorant of the fact, and the judge might well without a further showing . . . let the jury determine the fact according to the weight of the evidence.")

But "night club gossip and stories appearing in newspapers" . . . . while their content may be common knowledge, are not a source indisputable facts pertaining to "wealth or . . . any other necessary fact." Berry v. Chaplin, 74 Cal.App.2d 669, 675–676, 169 P.2d 453, 458 (1946) (Los Angeles trial court could not take judicial notice of extent of wealth of Charles Chaplin based upon his public image as presented in the press).

There are intimations that local customs may not be noticed. See, e.g., First National Bank v. Commercial Bank & Trust Co., 137 Wash. 335, 242 P. 356 (1926). But, under the present principle, if generally and certainly known in the community, they should be.

Books shows that a clear difference has long been taken between what judges may notice judicially and the facts that the particular judge happens personally to know.[7] It is not a distinction easy for a judge to follow in application, but the doctrine is accepted that actual private knowledge by the judge is no sufficient ground for taking judicial notice of a fact as a basis for a finding or a final judgment,[8] though it may still be a ground, it is believed, for exercising certain discretionary powers, such as granting a motion for new trial to avoid an injustice,[9] or in sentencing.[10]

Similarly, what a jury member knows in common with every other human being and what facts are appropriately circumscribed by the doctrine of judicial notice are not the same thing. Traditionally those facts so generally known within the community as not to be reasonably subject to dispute have been included within the perimeters of judicial notice under the caption of common knowledge. At the same time, however, it is often loosely said that the jury may consider, as if proven, facts within the common knowledge of the community.[11] Thus it is very easy to confound into one common denominator facts to which the evidentiary discipline of judicial notice applies and the residual data the jury members bring along with them as rational human beings.

7. Anon., Y.B. 7 Hen. IV, f. 41, pl. 5 (1406), from which the following is an excerpt: "Tirwhit: Sir, let us put the case that a man kills another in your presence and sight, and another who is not guilty is indicted before you and is found guilty of the same death, you ought to respite the judgment against him, for you know the contrary, and report the matter to the King to pardon him. No more ought you to give judgment in this case . . . Gascoigne, C.J. One time the King himself asked me about this very case which you have put, and asked me what was the law, and I told him just as you say, and he was well pleased that the law was so."

8. Gibson v. Von Glahn Hotel Co., 185 N.Y.S. 154, 155 (Sup.Ct.1920) (where the issue of absolute liability as an innkeeper turned on the question whether defendant's establishment was a hotel, the trial judge volunteered: "I know the Von Glahn Hotel as well as the witness does himself; I will give you a ruling now it is a hotel." Held, reversed). Accord: Darnell v. Barker, 179 Va. 86, 18 S.E.2d 271 (1942); Shafer v. Eau Claire, 105 Wis. 239, 81 N.W. 409 (1900).

It is believed that only rarely today would one encounter a trial judge who felt free to use his personal knowledge of facts. Morgan, Judicial Notice, 57 Harv. L.Rev. 269, 274 n. 7 (1944). But see: Beychok v. St. Paul Mercury Indemnity Co., 119 F.Supp. 52 (W.D.La. 1954) (trial judge took judicial notice that the luncheonette stool from which plaintiff fell "had been in the same condition for at least fifteen years before plaintiff's unfortunate accident occurred, without any incidents having taken place, so far as we know, to have indicated that it was a source of danger." The judge, however, treated this datum as a matter of "common knowledge.").

But see United States v. Alvarado, 519 F.2d 1133 (5th Cir.1975) (trial judge could judicially notice location of border checkpoint because he had previously tried another case involving the facility and the same facts appeared in a previous appellate report).

9. It is clear that trial judges have a great deal of discretion in ruling upon motions for new trials. Os-

borne v. United States, 351 F.2d 111 (8th Cir.1965); Commonwealth v. Brown, 192 Pa.Super. 498, 162 A.2d 13 (1960). Given this wide discretion it has been suggested that not only can courts use judicial notice quite freely, but that "perhaps" they should. Comment, The Presently Expanding Concept of Judicial Notice, 13 Vill.L.Rev. 528, 540 (1968).

But see Government of Virgin Islands v. Gereau, 523 F.2d 140 (3d Cir.1975), cert. denied 424 U.S. 917 (in passing on motion for new trial, judge erred in determining credibility as between juror and jury matron on the basis of his own knowledge about the matron's need for extra income; in basing his fact finding on personal knowledge he was taking judicial notice of an adjudicative fact which did not possess the necessary cachet of either Fed.R.Evid. 201(b)(1) or (2)).

10. Williams v. New York, 337 U.S. 241 (1949).

11. Marshall v. State, 54 Fla. 66, 44 So. 742, 743 (1907) (Instruction, "You will bring to bear in consideration of the evidence . . . in addition, all that common knowledge of men and affairs, which you as reasonable men have and exercise in the everyday affairs of life," approved). In principle of course the knowledge of a juror about the facts of the particular case should not be considered. He should testify. See, e.g., Edelstein v. Roskin, 356 So.2d 38 (Fla.App.1978). Perhaps, in strictness, expertness of particular jurors about values, skills, or occupational knowledge should not be used by the jury, not being common to the jurors and shared by the community. Some courts have held that instructions on jury-knowledge which fail to make this clear are ground for reversal. Downing v. Farmers' Mutual Fire Insurance Co., 158 Iowa 1, 138 N.W. 917 (1912). But there is much force to the contrary view that this restriction sacrifices one of the chief values of jury trial, and is a restriction which jurors cannot and will not obey. Solberg v. Robbins Lumber Co., 147 Wis. 259, 133 N.W. 28 (1911) (instruction permitting jurors to pool their individual knowledge, approved).

Whereas in the typical vehicular accident case the well-known character of a street can be dealt with informally as background information which helps everyone visualize the scene, the question becomes a formal one to be dealt with as part of the doctrine of judicial notice if the precise character of the street becomes an adjudicative fact in the case being tried.[12]   Again, while the meaning of words is normally left to the informal common sense of the jury, the precise meaning of a word in a contract case which may be outcome determinative should be dealt with formally as a problem of judicial notice.[13]

The cases in which judicial notice is taken of indisputable facts commonly known in the community where the facts noticed are actually adjudicative ones appear to be relatively rare.   In most instances, notwithstanding the invocation of the language of judicial notice, the facts either involve background information helpful in assaying the evidence relevant to the adjudicative facts[14] or involve facts relevant to the process of formulating the tenor of the law to be applied to the resolution of the controversy.[15]   Indeed, there is a growing recognition that the common knowledge variety of fact plays only a very minor role on the judicial notice scene.[16]

 **WESTLAW REFERENCES**

"judicial notice"   /s   "personal! know!"

§ 330.   Facts Capable of Certain Verification

The earlier and probably still the most familiar basis for judicial notice is "common knowledge," but a second and distinct principle has come to be recognized as an even more significant ground for the invocation of the doctrine.   This extension of judicial notice was first disguised by a polite fiction so that when asked to notice a fact not generally known, but which obviously could easily be ascertained by consulting materials in common use, such as the day of the week on which January 1 fell ten years ago, the judges resorted to calendars but purported to be "refreshing memory" as to a matter of common knowledge.[1]   Eventually it was recognized that involved here was an important extension of judicial notice to the new field of facts "capable of accurate and ready demonstration,"[2] "capable of such instant and unquestionable demonstration, if desired, that no party would think of imposing a falsity on the tribunal in the face of an intelligent adversary,"[3] or "capable of immediate and accurate demonstration by resort to easily accessible sources of indisputable accuracy."[4]   It is under this caption, for example,

12.   Davis, A System of Judicial Notice Based on Fairness and Convenience, in Perspectives on Law 69, 73–74 (Pound ed. 1964).

13.   Palestroni v. Jacobs, 8 N.J. 438, 73 A.2d 89, reversed 10 N.J.Super. 266, 77 A.2d 183 (1953).   Compare Tennessee Gas Transmission Co. v. Hall, 277 S.W.2d 733 (Tex.Civ.App.1955) (jurors took into account the chance that a deep "chisel" plow could cut into an underground pipe).   Technical words, having been compiled in dictionaries, may differ from facts known only to farmers familiar with their own technology.

14.   Pacific Gas & Electric Co. v. W.H. Hunt Estate Co., 49 Cal.2d 565, 319 P.2d 1044 (1957) (water pipes sometimes break from accidental causes); Portee v. Kronzek, 194 Pa.Super. 193, 166 A.2d 328 (1960) (people visit taverns to meet friends).   Compare: Hughes v. Vestal, 264 N.C. 500, 142 S.E.2d 361 (1965); Ennis v. Dupree, 262 N.C. 224, 136 S.E.2d 702 (1964).

15.   Hawkins v. United States, 358 U.S. 74 (1958); Perez v. Lippold, 32 Cal.2d 711, 198 P.2d 17 (1948).

16.   Comment, 13 Vill.L.Rev. 528, 532 (1968) ("[T]he traditional test [is] whether the fact to be noticed is within the common knowledge of the community.   However, there has been a modern trend away from this test and towards one which provides that a fact may be noticed if it is verifiably certain by reference to competent, authoritative sources.").

§ 330

1.   Friend v. Burnham & Morrill Co., 55 F.2d 150, 151 (1st Cir.1932) ("The District Court in this case was warranted, therefore, in taking judicial notice of any common or general knowledge relating to canning cooked foods, and to refresh his recollection by reference to standard publications.").

2.   Note, 47 Colum.L.Rev. 151 (1947).

3.   9 Wigmore, Evidence § 2571, p. 732 (Chadbourn rev. 1981).

4.   See Fed.R.Evid. 201(b)(2) supra § 328, n. 3.

that courts have taken judicial notice of the scientific principles which, while verifiable but not likely commonly known, justify the evidentiary use of radar,[5] blood tests for intoxication [6] and nonpaternity,[7] handwriting [8] and typewriter identification,[9] and ballistics.[10]

Attempts to formulate inventories of verifiable facts of which courts will take judicial notice have begun to fall into disrepute because the principle involved can better be illustrated by way of example.[11] Thus in State v. Damm [12] defendant was on trial for rape after one of his stepdaughters gave birth to a child. The defense sought a court order authorizing blood tests by which it was hoped to prove his innocence by way of negative results. Even if the tests produced a negative result, however, the testimony recounting the tests would be relevant to the question of guilt or innocence only if it was true that properly administered blood tests evidencing a negative result excluded the possibility of paternity. To leave this preliminary question pertaining to the then present state of scientific knowledge to the jury to decide as best they could on the basis of possibly conflicting testimony would appear absurd.[13] There being only one right answer to the question whether the principle was accepted in the appropriate scientific circles, the question fell within the province of judicial notice. Even so, the trial judge in this particular case was held not to have erred in refusing the request because, given the time and place, the defense was not able to produce the data necessary to illustrate to him that the principle was an accepted one within the scientific community. Presumably, of course, an opposite result would obtain today.[14]

Thus it is that while the various propositions of science are a suitable topic of judicial notice, the content of what will actually be noticed is subject to change as the tenets of science evolve.[15] It is manifest, more-

---

5. State v. Graham, 322 S.W.2d 188 (Mo.1959). For a discussion of the limits to which counsel may go in arguing scientific facts before a jury, see Levin & Levy, Persuading the Jury with Facts Not in Evidence: The Fiction-Science Spectrum, 105 U.Pa.L.Rev. 139 (1956).

6. State v. Miller, 64 N.J.Super. 262, 165 A.2d 829 (1960). There has recently developed a tendency to make scientific evidence admissible by legislative enactment, e.g., Uniform Act on Paternity, 9A U.L.A. 626.

7. Jordan v. Mace, 144 Me. 351, 69 A.2d 670 (1949); Houghton v. Houghton, 179 Neb. 275, 137 N.W.2d 861 (1965). See also, Uniform Act on Paternity, 9A U.L.A. 626.

8. Adams v. Ristine, 138 Va. 273, 122 S.E. 126 (1924); Fenelon v. State, 195· Wis. 416, 217 N.W. 711 (1928). See generally, Note, 13 N.Y.L.F. 677 (1968).

9. United States v. Hiss, 107 F.Supp. 128 (S.D.N.Y. 1952); People v. Risley, 214 N.Y. 75, 108 N.E. 200 (1915).

10. People v. Fisher, 340 Ill. 216, 172 N.E. 743 (1930).

11. See, e.g., Keeffe, Landis & Shaad, Sense and Nonsense About Judicial Notice, 2 Stan.L.Rev. 664, 667 (1950) ("General rules describing particular facts that can be judicially noticed are worthless.").

12. 64 S.D. 309, 266 N.W. 667 (1936).

13. Keeffe, Landis & Shaad, op. cit. n. 11 supra, at 670. ("It brings discredit upon the legal profession and it makes a mockery of a court of justice to permit a jury to accept or reject in accordance with their prejudices a fact capable of exact scientific determination.").

14. See n. 7, supra.

15. State v. Damm, 64 S.D. 309, 266 N.W. 667 (1936) was decided five years after the trial, by which time the principle behind blood tests to determine paternity had become well established. While conceding as much, the appellate court did not reverse the trial judge's earlier decision to exclude the test results because when made, that decision had not been an erroneous one.

As consensus develops in the scientific community that the principle underlying a new technology is valid and that reliable hardware has become available, judicial notice enables judges to incorporate these advances into trials as a matter of law. Standards for admissibility of scientific evidence are discussed in § 203 supra. Whether the person employing the hardware was qualified to do so, the hardware was properly maintained and it was correctly used remain questions of fact. People v. Flaxman, 74 Cal.App.3d Supp. 16, 141 Cal.Rptr. 799 (1977) (radar); State v. Finkle, 128 N.J.Super. 199, 319 A.2d 733 (1974), affirmed 66 N.J. 139, 329 A.2d 65, cert. denied 423 U.S. 836 (speed gun).

Thus far the results of lie detector tests have not been judicially noticed as reliable because the results depend more upon the expertise of the operator than upon the inherent reliability of the mechanism itself. See, e.g., United States v. Masri, 547 F.2d 932, 43 A.L.R.Fed. 60 (5th Cir.1977), rehearing denied 550 F.2d

over, that the principle involved need not be commonly known in order to be judicially noticed; it suffices if the principle is accepted as a valid one in the appropriate scientific community. In determining the intellectual viability of the proposition, of course, the judge is free to consult any sources that he thinks are reliable,[16] but the extent to which judges are willing to take the initiative in looking up the authoritative sources will usually be limited. By and large, therefore, it is the task of counsel to find and to present in argument and briefs such references, excerpts and explanations as will convince the judge that the fact is certain and demonstrable. Puzzling enough in this regard, it has been noted that "nowhere can there be found a definition of what constitutes competent or authoritative sources for purposes of verifying judicially noticed facts." [17]

Illustrative as they are, scientific principles hardly exhaust the verifiable facts of which courts take judicial notice. Historical facts fall within the doctrine, such as the dates upon which wars began and terminated.[18] Geographical facts [19] are involved, particularly with reference to the boundaries of the state in which the court is sitting [20] and of the counties,[21] districts [22] and townships [23] thereof, as well as the location of the capital of the state and the location and identity of the county seats.[24] Whether common knowledge or not, courts notice the identity of the principal officers of the national government [25] and the incumbents of principal state offices.[26] Similarly, while obviously not necessarily a matter of common knowledge, judges take notice of the identity of the officers of their courts, such as the other judges,[27] the sheriffs,[28] clerks,[29] and attorneys; [30]

42, cert. denied 431 U.S. 932. Lie detection techniques are discussed in § 206 supra.

16. Brown v. Piper, 91 U.S. 37, 42 (1875) ("any means . . . which he may deem safe and proper"); People v. Mayes, 113 Cal. 618, 626, 45 P. 860, 862 (1896) ("any source of information which he may deem authentic, either by inquiry of others, or by the examination of books, or by receiving the testimony of witnesses"); Fringer v. Venema, 26 Wis.2d 366, 372–73, 132 N.W.2d 565, 569 (1965) ("can be verified to a certainty by reference to competent authoritative sources"); 9 Wigmore, Evidence § 2568a, at 720 (Chadbourn rev. 1981).

17. Comment, The Presently Expanding Concept of Judicial Notice, 13 Vill.L.Rev. 528, 545 (1968).

18. Unity Co. v. Gulf Oil Corp., 141 Me. 148, 40 A.2d 4, 156 A.L.R. 297 (1944) (dates of declaration of World War II and beginning of rationing); Miller v. Fowler, 200 Miss. 776, 28 So.2d 837 (1947) (that acts of warfare between Japan and the United States had not entirely ceased on Aug. 14, 1945); 29 Am.Jur.2d Evidence §§ 73–76.

19. See, e.g., Swarzwald v. Cooley, 39 Cal.App.2d 306, 103 P.2d 580 (1940) (meaning of phrase, "ordinary hightide," in the vicinity of Laguna Beach).

20. Watson v. Western Union Telegraph Co., 178 N.C. 471, 101 S.E. 81 (1919); 29 Am.Jur.2d Evidence § 63.

21. State ex Inf. Gentry v. Armstrong, 315 Mo. 298, 286 S.W. 705 (1926) (location of city and county of St. Louis); Elmore County v. Tallapoosa County, 221 Ala. 182, 128 So. 158 (1930) (area and boundaries); 29 Am. Jur.2d Evidence § 64.

22. Board of Education v. State, 222 Ala. 70, 131 So. 239 (1930) (school district).

23. Nelson v. Thomas, 103 Cal.App. 108, 283 P. 982 (1930).

24. Bunten v. Rock Springs Grazing Association, 29 Wyo. 461, 215 P. 244 (1923).

25. United States ex rel. Petach v. Phelps, 40 F.2d 500 (2d Cir.1930) (assistants to the Secretary of Labor); Lyman Flood Prevention Association v. City of Topeka, 152 Kan. 484, 106 P.2d 117 (1940) (time of retirement of Woodring as Secretary of War).

26. Picking v. Pennsylvania Railroad Co., 151 F.2d 240 (3d Cir.1945) (that named defendants were officials of Pennsylvania and New York); Patten v. Miller, 190 Ga. 123, 8 S.E.2d 757 (1940) (chairman, State Highway Board).

27. Payne v. Williams, 47 Ariz. 396, 56 P.2d 186 (1936) (Supreme Court notices names of superior court judges, their counties and terms); Alexander v. Gladden, 205 Or. 375, 288 P.2d 219 (1955) (Supreme Court notices the organization of its own court and lower courts under its supervision).

28. Sowers-Taylor Co. v. Collins, 14 S.W.2d 692 (Mo. App.1929) (names of officers authorized to serve process).

29. Favre v. Louisville & Nashville Railroad Co., 180 Miss. 843, 178 So. 327 (1938).

30. Squire v. Bates, 132 Ohio St. 161, 5 N.E.2d 690 (1936) (persons who have been admitted and dates of their admission).

of the duration of terms and sessions,[31] and of the rules of court.[32]

It would seem obvious that the judge of a court would take notice of all of the records of the institution over which he presides, but the courts have been slow to give the principle of judicial notice its full reach of logic and expediency. It is settled, of course, that the courts, trial and appellate, take notice of their own respective records in the present litigation, both as to matters occurring in the immediate trial,[33] and in previous trials or hearings.[34] The principle seemingly is equally applicable to matters of record in the proceedings in other cases in the same court, and some decisions have recognized this,[35] but many courts still adhere to the needless requirement of formal proof, rather than informal presentation, of recorded proceedings in other suits in the same court.[36] Matters of record in other courts are usually denied notice even though it would appear manifest that these public documents are logically subject to judicial notice as readily verifiable facts.[37]

In the increasingly important practice of judicial notice of scientific and technological facts, some of the possibilities of error are, first, that the courts may fail to employ the doctrine of judicial notice in this field to the full measure of its usefulness; second, that they may mistakenly accept as authoritative scientific theories that are outmoded or are not yet received by the specialists as completely verified; and third, that in taking judicial notice of accepted scientific facts, the courts, in particular cases may misconceive the conclusions or applications which are supposed to flow from them. Of these, it seems that the first has thus far been the most frequent shortcoming.

 WESTLAW REFERENCES

"judicial notice" /s accurate! accuracy definit! certain! unquestion! precis! immediat! instant! ready readily /4 demonstrat! ascertain! verif! shown support**

"judicial notice" /s science* scientific

---

31. Vance v. Harkey, 186 Ark. 730, 55 S.W.2d 785 (1933) (Supreme Court knows that term at which decree entered has elapsed).

32. A trial court, of course, knows its own rules without formal proof. Wallace v. Martin, 166 So. 874 (La.App.1936). And on general principles an appellate court knows judicially what the trial court judicially knew. See § 333 n. 12 infra. Nevertheless, many appellate courts have refused to notice trial court rules, unless embodied in the bill of exceptions. See, e.g., Scovill Manufacturing Co. v. Cassidy, 275 Ill. 462, 114 N.E. 181 (1916) (where municipal court rules not in bill of exceptions, appellate court erred in ordering the rules certified to them and considering them when certified); and cases cited C.J.S. Evidence § 49. This inconvenient formalism has been repudiated by statute in Illinois, see Boettcher v. Howard Engraving Co., 389 Ill. 75, 58 N.E.2d 866 (1945) (applying S.H.A. ch. 51, § 48b now ch. 110, ¶ 8–1002). And elsewhere by decision, see e.g., Hudson v. Hoster, 47 N.E.2d 637 (Ct. App.Ohio, 1942) (Court of Appeals will notice rules and customary practices of the Common Pleas Court).

33. Nichols v. Nichols, 126 Conn. 614, 13 A.2d 591 (1940) (superseded pleading, claimed to constitute admission, will be noticed but must be called to trial court's attention); 29 Am.Jur.2d Evidence § 57.

34. Collins v. Leahy, 347 Mo. 133, 146 S.W.2d 609 (1940) (where city map was part of record of prior appeal to Supreme Court, court would take notice of it on subsequent appeal though not introduced in evidence at later trial); 29 Am.Jur.2d Evidence § 57.

35. Green v. Warden, United States Penitentiary, 699 F.2d 364 (7th Cir.1983) (plaintiff's extensive record of litigation in both federal and other courts); Willson v. Security-First National Bank, 21 Cal.2d 705, 134 P.2d 800 (1943); South Shore Land Co. v. Petersen, 226 Cal. App.2d 725, 38 Cal.Rptr. 392 (1964); Johnson v. Marsh, 146 Neb. 257, 19 N.W.2d 366 (1945); Meck v. Allen Properties, Inc., 206 Misc. 251, 132 N.Y.S.2d 674 (1954).

36. Guam Investment Co. v. Central Building, Inc., 288 F.2d 19 (9th Cir.1961); Murphy v. Citizens' Bank, 82 Ark. 131, 100 S.W. 894 (1907); Fleming v. Anderson, 187 Va. 788, 48 S.E.2d 269 (1948); 29 Am.Jur.2d Evidence § 58.

37. But see Zahn v. Transamerica Corp., 162 F.2d 36, 48 n. 20 (3d Cir.1947). See also Funk v. Commissioner, 163 F.2d 796 (3d Cir.1947). It has been suggested, moreover, that in practice trial judges do look at related court files. Weinstein, Mansfield, Abrams & Berger, Cases and Materials on Evidence 1249–50 (7th ed. 1983).

§ 331. Social and Economic Data Used in Judicial Law-Making: "Legislative" Facts [1]

It is conventional wisdom today to observe that judges not only are charged to find what the law is, but must regularly make new law when deciding upon the constitutional validity of a statute,[2] interpreting a statute,[3] or extending or restricting a common law rule.[4] The very nature of the judicial process necessitates that judges be guided, as legislators are, by considerations of expediency and public policy.[5] They must, in the nature of things, act either upon knowledge already possessed or upon assumptions,[6] or upon investigation of the pertinent general facts, social,[7] economic,[8] political,[9] or scientific.[10] An older tradition once prescribed that judges should rationalize their result solely in terms of analogy to old doctrines leaving the considerations of expediency unstated. Contemporary practice indicates that judges in their opinions should render explicit their policy-judgments and the factual grounds therefor. These latter have been helpfully classed as "legislative facts," as contrasted with the "adjudicative facts" which are historical facts pertaining to the incidents which give rise to lawsuits.[11]

Constitutional cases argued in terms of due process typically involve reliance upon legislative facts for their proper resolution. Whether a statute enacted pursuant to the police power is valid, after all, involves a twofold analysis. First, it must be determined that the enactment is designed to achieve an appropriate objective of the police power; that is, it must be designed to protect the public health, morals, safety, or general welfare.[12] The second question is whether, in light of the data on hand, a leg-

---

§ 331

1. See Davis, Administrative Law Treatise, Ch. 15 (1958, supp. 1965), an unusually original and enlightening discussion; Davis, An Approach to Problems of Evidence in the Administrative Process, 55 Harv.L.Rev. 364, 402 (1942); Davis, Judicial Notice, 55 Colum.L. Rev. 945, 952 (1955); Note, 61 Harv.L.Rev. 692 (1948).

2. Perez v. Lippold, 32 Cal.2d 711, 198 P.2d 17 (1948) (statute outlawing interracial marriage); Stanton v. Stanton, 421 U.S. 7, 15 (1975) ("The presence of women in business, in the professions, in government and, indeed, in all walks of life where education is a desirable, if not always a necessary, antecedent is apparent and a proper subject of judicial notice." This data bore on the question whether it was any longer permissible constitutionally to vary the duty of child support between males and females on the basis of a different age of attaining adulthood.)

3. Roe v. Wade, 410 U.S. 113 (1973) (history of abortion statutes).

4. Scurti v. City of New York, 40 N.Y.2d 433, 387 N.Y.S.2d 55, 354 N.E.2d 794 (1976) (ancient distinctions between licensees, trespassers and invitees seen not to reflect modern day needs).

5. Cardozo, The Nature of the Judicial Process, 113–125 (1921); Frank, Law and the Modern Mind, ch. 4 (1930).

6. Village of Euclid v. Ambler Realty Co., 272 U.S. 365 (1926) (proper exercise of police power to exclude apartment houses from residential districts because they tend to be mere parasites and come near to being nuisances); Potts v. Coe, 78 U.S.App.D.C. 297, 140 F.2d 470 (1944) (incentive to invent supplied by patent law will not work in organized research because it destroys teamwork).

7. Brown v. Board of Education, 347 U.S. 483 (1954), supplemented 349 U.S. 294, (racially segregated schools can never be equal notwithstanding their equality of teachers or equipment because the very act of segregation brands the segregated minority with a feeling of inferiority); Roe v. Wade, 410 U.S. 113 (1973) (canvass of historical, social and medical data in opinion articulating constitutional norms governing regulation of abortions).

8. SEC v. Capital Gains Research Bureau, Inc., 300 F.2d 745 (2d Cir.1961), reversed 375 U.S. 180, (judicial notice taken that advice tendered by small advisory service could not influence stock market generally); same case, 375 U.S. 180 (1963) (judicial notice taken that the advice tendered could influence the market price).

9. Baker v. Carr, 369 U.S. 186 (1962) (contemporary notions of justice require that equal apportionment of voting districts be made a legal and perforce largely mathematical question rather than a purely political one).

10. Durham v. United States, 94 U.S.App.D.C. 228, 214 F.2d 862 (1954) (psychiatric learning pertinent to the scientific soundness of the right-and-wrong test of criminal insanity).

See particularly Ballew v. Georgia, 435 U.S. 223 (1978) (critical evaluation of studies themselves to determine whether empirical data suggested that progressively smaller juries were less likely to engage in group deliberation).

11. Davis, Administrative Law Treatise § 15.03 (1958).

12. Bilbar Construction Co. v. Board of Adjustment, 393 Pa. 62, 141 A.2d 851 (1958).

islature still beholden to reason could have adopted the means they did to achieve the aim of their exercise of the police power.[13] In Burns Baking Co. v. Bryan,[14] for example, the question was whether, concerned about consumers being misled by confusing sizes of bread, the Nebraska legislature could decree not only that the bakers bake bread according to distinctively different weights but that they wrap their product in wax paper lest any post-oven expansion of some loaves undo these distinctions. A majority of the court held the enactment unconstitutional because, in their opinion, the wrapping requirement was unreasonable. Mr. Justice Brandeis, correctly anticipating the decline of substantive due process, dissented, pointing out that the only question was whether the measure was a reasonable legislative response in light of the facts available to the legislators themselves.[15] Then, in a marvelous illustration of the Brandeis-brief technique, he recited page after page of data illustrating how widespread was the problem of shortweight and how, in light of nationwide experience, the statute appeared to be a reasonable response to the environmental situation.[16]

Given the bent to test due process according to the information available to the legislature, the truth-content of these data are not directly relevant. The question is whether sufficient data exist which could influence a reasonable legislature to act, not whether ultimately these data are true.[17] This is not the same case as when a court proceeds to interpret a constitutional norm and, while they still rely upon data, the judges *qua* legislators themselves proceed to act as if the data were true. In Brown v. Board of Education,[18] for example, the Court faced the issue whether segregated schools, equal facility and teacher-wise, could any longer be tolerated under the equal protection clause. The question was not any longer whether a reasonable legislator could believe these schools could never be equal, but whether the *judges* believed that the very act of segregating branded certain children with a feeling of inferiority so deleterious that it would be impossible for them to obtain an equal education no matter how equal the facilities and teachers. Thus the intellectual legitimacy of this kind of decision turns upon the actual truth-content of the legislative facts taken into account by the judges who propound the decision. While not necessarily indisputably true, it would appear that these legislative facts must at least appear to be more likely than not true if the opinion is going to have the requisite intellectual legitimacy upon which the authority of judge-made rules is ultimately founded.[19]

13. See the discussion running throughout the several opinions in Griswold v. Connecticut, 381 U.S. 479 (1965). See also Johnson v. Opelousas, 488 F.Supp. 433 (W.D.La.1980), reversed 658 F.2d 1065 (5th Cir.) (curfew reasonable in light of judicially noticed increasing after-dark crime rates).

14. 264 U.S. 504 (1924).

15. Accord: West Coast Hotel Co. v. Parrish, 300 U.S. 379 (1937); Olsen v. Nebraska ex rel. Western Reference & Bond Association, 313 U.S. 236, 133 A.L.R. 1500 (1941). See also Lochner v. New York, 198 U.S. 45 (1905) (Holmes, J. dissenting.)

16. The opponents of a statute can resort to extra-record legislative facts to support their argument that it is invalid. In Burns Baking Co. v. Bryan, 264 U.S. 504 (1924), the statute regulating bread sizes was struck down because it was "contrary to common experience and unreasonable to assume there could be any danger of . . . deception." See also Defiance Milk Products Co. v. DuMond, 309 N.Y. 537, 132 N.E.2d 829 (1956) (statute requiring inordinately large size cans

for retail sale of evaporated skimmed milk held invalid because judicial notice was taken that it would be incredible to believe consumers needed protection against deception practiced with regard to the nature of this product).

17. Note that Fed.R.Evid. 201 deals only with adjudicative facts. See n. 3 § 328 supra.

18. 347 U.S. 483 (1954), supplemented 349 U.S. 294.

19. See. e.g., the reaction to Durham v. United States, 94 U.S.App.D.C. 228, 214 F.2d 862 (1954), wherein on the basis of psychiatric data the court formulated a new test for criminal insanity. Some psychiatrists accepted the result: Roche, Criminality and Mental Illness—Two Faces of the Same Coin, 22 U.Chi. L.Rev. 320 (1955). The American Law Institute rejected it. Model Penal Code, Tentative Draft No. 4, 159–60 (1955). See also Brown v. Board of Education, 347 U.S. 483 (1954), supplemented 349 U.S. 294, wherein for the psychological impact of segregation the court relied upon, inter alia, the work of Dr. Kenneth B. Clark. Dr. Clark felt compelled thereafter publicly to

When making new common law, judges must, like legislators, do the best they can assaying the data available to them and make the best decision they can of which course wisdom dictates they follow. Should they, for example, continue to invoke the common law rule of *caveat emptor* in the field of real property, or should they invoke a notion of implied warranty in the instance of the sale of new houses? [20] Should they require landlords of residential units to warrant their habitability and fitness for the use intended? [21] While sociological, economic, political and moral doctrine may abound about questions like this, none of these data are likely indisputable.[22]

Thus it is that, in practice, the legislative facts upon which judges rely when performing their lawmaking function are not indisputable. At the same time, cognizant of the fact that his decision as lawmaker can affect the public at large, in contradistinction to most rulings at trials which affect only the parties themselves, a judge is not likely to rely for his data only upon what opposing counsel tender him. Obviously enough, therefore, legislative facts tend to be the most elusive facts when it comes to propounding a codified system of judicial notice.[23]

 WESTLAW REFERENCES

legislative /s "judicial notice"
di brandeis brief

---

§ 332. The Uses of Judicial Notice [1]

Judges have been prone to emphasize the need for caution in applying the doctrine of judicial notice.[2] The great writers of evidence, on the other hand, having perhaps a wider view of the needs of judicial administration, advocate a more extensive use of the doctrine. Thus Thayer suggests: "Courts may judicially notice much that they cannot

---

respond to critics of his work. Clark, The Desegregation Cases: Criticism of the Social Scientists Role, 5 Vill.L.Rev. 224, 236–40 (1960). But see Van den Haag, Social Science Testimony in the Desegregation Cases—A Reply to Professor Kenneth Clark, 6 Vill.L.Rev. 69 (1960).

20. Schipper v. Levitt & Sons, Inc., 44 N.J. 70, 207 A.2d 314 (1965) (mass developer of homes who assembled final product out of component parts treated as a manufacturer and implied warranty imposed).

21. Lemle v. Breeden, 51 Hawaii 426, 462 P.2d 470 (1969) (application of implied warranty recognizes changes in history of leasing transactions and takes into account contemporary housing realities).

22. Recall the notion in Hawkins v. United States, 358 U.S. 74 (1958), discussed supra at § 328, n. 12, that admitting the testimony of one spouse against another would destroy their marriage. Justice Stewart suggested at the time that the proposition might well be nothing more than an unsound assumption in cases where the spouse's testimony was actually voluntary. Id. at 81–82 (concurring opinion). In 1980, the rule was modified to allow voluntary testimony. Trammel v. United States, 445 U.S. 40 (1980). Justice Stewart insisted that nothing had changed since 1958 except the Court's willingness to adhere to assumptions rooted in hoary sentiments. Id. at 53–54 (concurring opinion). For further discussion of *Trammel*, see § 66 supra.

See particularly Davis, A System of Judicial Notice Based on Fairness and Convenience, in Perspectives of Law, 69, 82 (Pound ed. 1964) ("judge-made law would stop growing if judges, in thinking about questions of law and policy, were forbidden to take into account the

facts they believe, as distinguished from facts which are 'clearly . . . within the domain of the indisputable.' ") If the data available on appeal are conflicting, however, a court can remand the case to trial so these data can be more effectively explored by introducing them there in the form of evidence subject to cross-examination. See, e.g., Borden's Farm Products Co. v. Baldwin, 293 U.S. 194 (1934).

23. Note that Fed.R.Evid. 201, reproduced at § 328 n. 3 supra, does not purport to regulate the notice of legislative facts. See particularly Chief Justice Burger's concurring opinion in Roe v. Wade, 410 U.S. 113, 207 (1973), rehearing denied 410 U.S. 959 ("I am somewhat troubled that the Court has taken notice of various scientific and medical data in reaching its conclusion; however, I do not believe that the Court has exceeded the scope of judicial notice accepted in other contexts.").

§ 332

1. Thayer, Preliminary Treatise on the Law of Evidence 308–309 (1898); 9 Wigmore, Evidence § 2567 (Chadbourn rev. 1981); Davis, A System of Judicial Notice Based on Fairness and Convenience, in Perspectives of Law 69 (Pound ed. 1964); Morgan, Judicial Notice, 57 Harv.L.Rev. 269 (1941); McNaughton, Judicial Notice—Excerpts Relating to the Morgan-Wigmore Controversy, 14 Vand.L.Rev. 779 (1961); Roberts, Preliminary Notes Toward a Study of Judicial Notice, 52 Cornell L.Q. 210 (1967).

2. See, e.g., Varcoe v. Lee, 180 Cal. 338, 345, 181 P. 223, 226 (1919); State v. Clousing, 205 Minn. 296, 285 N.W. 711, 123 A.L.R. 465, 470 (1939).

be required to notice. That is well worth emphasizing; for it points to a great possible usefulness in this doctrine, in helping to shorten and simplify trials. . . . The failure to exercise it tends daily to smother trials with technicality and monstrously lengthens them out." [3] And Wigmore says, "The principle is an instrument of usefulness hitherto unimagined by judges." [4]

The simple litany that judicial notice encapsulates facts commonly known and facts readily verifiable is useful as a rule-of-thumb but not as a precise litmus test. The courts' willingness to resort to judicial notice is apparently influenced by a number of less specifically definable circumstances. A court is more willing to notice a general than a specific fact, as for example, the approximate time of the normal period of human gestation, but not the precise maximum and minimum limits.[5] A court may be more willing to notice a fact if it is not an ultimate fact, that is, a fact which would be determinative of a case.[6] Suppose, for example, that a plaintiff in a vehicular negligence action specifically alleged that the defendant was driving too fast in a business district and the testimony, if believed, would indicate that the automobile in question caused a long skid mark on the highway surface. The trial judge might be less willing to no-

tice that the street in question was within the business district than he would to notice that any properly equipped automobile travelling at the maximum speed appropriate in such a district could be stopped within x feet of the braking point. In the first example, the trial judge would appear to be invading the province of the jury to determine the facts pertinent to what had happened, whereas in the second he would be merely establishing rather quickly a piece of data which would aid the jury during their deliberations on the ultimate issue of negligence.[7]

Agreement is not to be had whether the perimeters of the doctrine of judicial notice enclose only facts which are indisputably true or encompass also facts more than likely true.[8] If, on the one hand, the function of the jury is to resolve disputed questions of fact, an argument can be made that judges should not purport to make decisions about facts unless they are indisputable facts. If this argument is accepted, it follows that once a fact has been judicially noticed, evidence contradicting the truth of the fact is inadmissible because by its very nature, a fact capable of being judicially noticed is an indisputable fact which the jury must be instructed to accept as true.[9] If, on the other hand, the function of judicial notice is to expedite the trial of cases, an argument can be

---

3. Thayer, Preliminary Treatise on Evidence 309 (1898).

4. 9 Wigmore, Evidence § 2583, p. 819 (Chadbourn rev. 1981).

5. Compare Equitable Trust Co. v. McComb, 19 Del. Ch. 387, 168 A. 203 (1933), with Commonwealth v. Kitchen, 299 Mass. 7, 11 N.E.2d 482 (1937).

6. This idea was suggested in Thayer, Preliminary Treatise on the Law of Evidence 306 (1898) and was repeated in McCormick, Evidence § 323 (1954), and Comment, 13 Vill.L.Rev. 528, 533–534 (1968). Illustrative of a case involving the judicial notice of an ultimate fact is State v. Lawrence, 120 Utah 323, 234 P.2d 600 (1951), where the lower court took judicial notice of the fact that the value of the car allegedly stolen by the defendant was worth in excess of $50.00, the amount required for a larceny conviction, but on appeal was reversed.

7. However, in Varcoe v. Lee, supra § 328 n. 4, judicial notice was taken that the street was in a business district, and in Hughes v. Vestal, 264 N.C. 500, 142 S.E.2d 361 (1965) the trial judge was reversed for

instructing the jury from a table of stopping distances. See n. 21 infra.

8. See e.g. McNaughton, Judicial Notice—Excerpts Relating to the Morgan-Wigmore Controversy, 14 Vand.L.Rev. 779 (1961).

9. Most convincingly expounded by Morgan, Judicial Notice, 57 Harv.L.Rev. 269 (1944), and by the same author in The Law of Evidence 1941–1945, 59 Harv.L. Rev. 481, 482–487 (1946). In agreement are Maguire, Evidence—Common Sense and Common Law, 174 (1947) ("the judge's decision to take judicial notice should be final"); Keeffe, Landis & Shaad, Sense and Nonsense About Judicial Notice, 2 Stan.L.Rev. 664, 668 (1950) ("The better view would seem to be that a fact, once judicially noticed, is not open to evidence disputing it"); McCormick, Judicial Notice, 5 Vand.L.Rev. 296, 321–322 (1952) ("the weight of reason and the prevailing authority support the view that a ruling that a fact will be judicially noticed precludes contradictory evidence and requires that the judge instruct the jury that they must accept the fact as true"); McNaughton, Judicial Notice—Excerpts Relating to the Morgan-Wigmore Controversy, 14 Vand.L.Rev. 779, 780 (1961) ("the

made that judges should dispense with the need for time-consuming formal evidence when the fact in question is likely true. If this argument is accepted, it follows that evidence contradicting the judicially noticed fact is admissible and that the jury are ultimately free to accept or reject the truth of the fact posited by judicial notice.[10]

A facile resolution of this conflict suggests itself readily enough. That is, the controversy might be exposed as a misunderstanding caused by a failure to take into account the distinction between "adjudicative" and "legislative" facts.[11] This would be true if the instances where judicial notice was restricted to indisputable facts involved only adjudicative facts whereas potentially disputable facts were only noticed within a legislative context. Whether the decided cases sustain this symmetry is itself a matter of dispute because authority exists which illustrates that some courts are not loathe judicially to notice a potentially disputable

fact within what is at least arguably an adjudicative context.[12]

The most recent efforts to deal with judicial notice have exhibited a trend away from extrapolating an all-inclusive definition of a doctrine in favor of promulgating modest guidelines which would regularize what are perceived to be the essential applications of judicial notice. One approach would restrict formalized judicial notice regulation to those situations in which only adjudicative facts are involved.[13] Limiting judicial notice to adjudicative facts and then only to indisputable ones leaves unresolved the question whether a jury in a criminal case should be instructed that they must accept the inexorable truth of the noticed fact. In terms of logic and pure reason it would appear that a jury as a rational deliberative body must accept properly judicially noticed facts.[14] Viewed through the lens of democratic tradition as a protection against an overbearing sovereign, a criminal trial jury may be a body which ought to be free to return a result which as

impregnability of Morgan's position"). In accord also is Fed.R.Evid. 201 supra § 328 n. 3.

Judicial authority includes Phelps Dodge Corp. v. Ford, 68 Ariz. 190, 196, 203 P.2d 633, 638 (1949) ("A fact of which a court may take judicial notice must be indisputable. This being true it follows that evidence may not be received to dispute it"); Nicketta v. National Tea Co., 338 Ill.App. 159, 87 N.E.2d 30 (1949) (trial court properly took notice on pleadings that trichinosis cannot be contracted from eating properly cooked pork, and dismissed complaint; evidence thereon unnecessary); Commonwealth v. Marzynski, 149 Mass. 68, 21 N.E. 228 (1889) (court will take notice that tobacco and cigars are not medicine and exclude testimony to the contrary); Soyland v. Farmers Mutual Fire Insurance Co., 71 S.D. 522, 528, 26 N.W.2d 696, 699 (1947) ("it is not permissible for a court to take judicial knowledge of a fact that may be disputed by competent evidence.").

10. Most convincingly expounded by Wigmore in 9 Wigmore, Evidence § 2567a (Chadbourn rev. 1981) ("That a matter is judicially noticed means merely that it is taken as true without the offering of evidence by the party who should ordinarily have done so. This is because the Court assumes that the matter is so notorious that it will not be disputed. But the opponent is not prevented from disputing the matter by evidence if he believes it disputable"). In agreement are Thayer, A Preliminary Treatise on Evidence at the Common Law 308 (1898) ("taking judicial notice does not import that the matter is indisputable"); Davis, A System of Judicial Notice Based on Fairness and Convenience, in

Perspectives of Law 69, 94 (Pound ed. 1964) ("the ultimate principle is that extra-record facts should be assumed whenever it is convenient to assume them"); Davis, Judicial Notice, 1969 L. & Soc. Order 513, 515–516 ("the practical course is to take notice and allow challenge later whenever the court believes that challenge is unlikely").

Makos v. Prince, 64 So.2d 670, 673 (Fla.1953) (judicial notice "does not prevent an opponent's disputing the matter"); Macht v. Hecht Co., 191 Md. 98, 102, 59 A.2d 754, 756 (1948) ("judicial notice . . . does not . . . prevent the presentation of contrary evidence"); Timson v. Manufacturers Coal & Coke Co., 220 Mo. 580, 598, 119 S.W. 565, 569 (1909) ("Judicial notice . . . does not preclude the opposite party from rebutting such prima facie case"). See also, State v. Duranleau, 99 N.H. 30, 104 A.2d 519 (1954); State v. Kincaid, 133 Or. 95, 285 P. 1105 (1930).

11. See §§ 328, 330, supra.

12. See, e.g., Securities and Exchange Commission v. Capital Gains Research Bureau, Inc., 375 U.S. 180 (1963); Daniel v. Paul, 395 U.S. 298 (1969). Compare Davis, Judicial Notice, 1969 L. & Soc. Order 515, 521–523, and Cleary, Foreword to Symposium on Federal Rules of Evidence, 1969 L. & Soc. Order 509, 510.

13. Fed.R.Evid. 201, Advisory Committee's Note, Subdivision (a). "This is the only evidence rule on the subject of judicial notice. It deals only with judicial notice of 'adjudicative' facts."

14. Compare Rev.Uniform Rule of Evidence (1974) 201(g) with Fed.R.Evid. 201(g). See § 328 n. 3 supra.

an exercise in logic flies in the face of reason.[15]

Another approach would narrow the range of judicial notice by de-escalating the significance of the conflict between questions peculiarly the province of juries and questions of fact handled by judges.[16] Judges have, for example, always dealt with preliminary questions of fact even in jury trials.[17] Thus, while the admissibility of the results of blood tests raises a question of fact pertaining to the reliability of such tests, the judges deal with this question as a preliminary step in ruling on relevancy, a function that is itself peculiarly a judicial one.[18] Indeed, if trials are examined functionally, it can be demonstrated that judges have always had to decide questions pertaining to facts without any apparent infringement of the jury's domain, whether this be in ruling on demurrers,[19] during pretrial hearings,[20] on motions for nonsuit or to set aside verdicts,[21] or at sentencing.[22] This may indicate, after all,

that the scope of judicial notice varies according to the function the judge is performing when judicial notice is taken.

It may be the case that there is no easy rule-of-thumb technique adequate unto the day to serve as an easy capsulation of the judicial notice phenomenon. Protagonists of the indisputable-only definition of judicial notice concede that in criminal cases the jury must be left free in the ultimate analysis to determine the truth or falsity of any adjudicative fact.[23] Protagonists of the disputability thesis might be expected to resolve the controversy by suggesting that, whereas in jury cases there is some merit in the notion that judicial notice should be restricted to indisputable facts in order not to infringe on the role of the jury,[24] the disputable theory works quite efficiently within the context of the jury-waived cases, which probably means that it applies in most cases which come to trial.[25] The fact of the matter is

15. United States v. Jones, 580 F.2d 219 (6th Cir. 1978). See Fed.R.Evid. 201(g), supra § 328 n. 3; United States v. Anderson, 528 F.2d 590, 592 (5th Cir.1976), cert. denied 429 U.S. 837 (judicial notice taken that the Federal Correctional Institution at Tallahassee, Florida, was within federal jurisdiction. "The trial judge instructed the jury '. . . you may and are allowed to accept that as fact proven before you just as though there had been evidence to that effect before you.' The court did not tell the jury in the words of the rule that the jury 'may, but is not required to accept as conclusive any fact judicially noticed.' Such variance from the rule is not reversible error.")

Thus it is crucial to know whether a judicially noticed fact is actually an adjudicative or a legislative one. See, e.g., United States v. Gould, 536 F.2d 216 (8th Cir. 1976) (proper for judge to instruct jury that cocaine hydrochloride is a derivative of the coca leaf and hence a controlled substance legislators intend to include within a broad prohibition); National Organization for Reform of Marijuana Laws v. Bell, 488 F.Supp. 123 (D.D.C.1980).

16. See particularly Comment, 13 Vill.L.Rev. 528 (1968).

17. Maguire & Epstein, Preliminary Questions of Fact in Determining the Admissibility of Evidence, 40 Harv.L.Rev. 392 (1927). See § 53 supra.

18. Gorton v. Hadsell, 63 Mass. (9 Cush.) 508, 511 (1852) ("But it is the province of the judge, who presides at trial, to decide all questions on the admissibility of evidence.").

19. Nicketta v. National Tea Co., 338 Ill.App. 159, 87 N.E.2d 30 (1949).

20. Stafford v. Ware, 187 Cal.App.2d 227, 9 Cal. Rptr. 706 (1960).

21. Clayton v. Rimmer, 262 N.C. 302, 136 S.E.2d 562 (1964) (reviewing court took judicial notice of table of stopping distances of automobiles in reversing denial of motion for nonsuit). Compare Hughes v. Vestal, 264 N.C. 500, 142 S.E.2d 361 (1965) (error to instruct jury as to stopping distance at given speed, taken from same table).

22. Williams v. New York, 337 U.S. 241 (1949).

23. State v. Main, 94 R.I. 338, 180 A.2d 814 (1962); State v. Lawrence, 120 Utah 323, 234 P.2d 600 (1951).

24. In large measure the Morgan rationale limiting judicial notice to indisputable facts assumes a jury trial context, see particularly Morgan, Judicial Notice, 57 Harv.L.Rev. 269, particularly 269 (1944). Nonjury tried cases may be more analogous to administrative practice in which case it is suggested that judges "should assume facts freely, stating them whenever a party may possibly want to challenge them." Davis, A System of Judicial Notice Based on Fairness and Convenience, in Perspectives of Law 69, 80 (Pound ed. 1964).

25. See particularly, Davis, A System of Judicial Notice Based on Fairness and Convenience, in Perspectives of Law 69, 69–73 (Pound ed. 1964).

Note should be taken that the indisputable theory does not foreclose consideration of countervailing data

that this solution has not received as much notoriety as might be expected.[26]

The very fact that the trend of these recent investigations has been calculated to resolve the problems associated with judicial notice by narrowing the dimensions of that concept has, however, raised a new problem which must be dealt with in the future. If judicial notice is restricted to instances where judges deal with facts in an adjudicative context, the instances where judges deal with legislative facts is left unregulated insofar as procedural guide-lines are concerned. The significance of this problem can be best illustrated within the context of the next section.

 **WESTLAW REFERENCES**

"judicial notice" /4 scope restict! limit! includ! cover! exten!

---

§ 333. Procedural Incidents

An elementary sense of fairness might indicate that a judge before making a final rul-

ing that judicial notice will be taken should notify the parties of his intention to do so and afford them an opportunity to present information which might bear upon the propriety of noticing the fact, or upon the truth of the matter to be noticed.[1] Although the original version of the Uniform Rules of Evidence required it,[2] only a rare case insists that a judge must notify the parties before taking judicial notice of a fact on his own motion,[3] and some authorities suggest that such a requirement is needless.[4] It may very well be the case that a trial judge need only consider notifying the parties if on his own motion he intends to take judicial notice of a less than obviously true fact.[5] In every other instance, after all, the request by one party asking the judge to take judicial notice will serve to apprise the opposing party of the question at hand. While there may, nevertheless, exist in practice a rough consensus with regard to procedural niceties when trial judges take judicial notice of adjudicative facts, this is not the end of the matter. The cases universally assume the nonexis-

---

but merely fixes the time of consideration at the preliminary determination whether judicial notice should be taken. In nonjury cases the difference may be without practical significance. See § 333 infra.

26. A possible explanation may be found in the close, if not complete, coincidence between a disputable judicially noticed fact and a rebuttable presumption. This relationship has largely passed undetected and without comment. One of the few cases sensing the relationship is Fringer v. Venema, 26 Wis.2d 366, 132 N.W.2d 565, rehearing denied 26 Wis.2d 366, 133 N.W.2d 809 (1965) (action under statute imposing absolute liability on owner of bull over six months old; absent proof of age of defendant's bull which escaped and serviced plaintiff's heifers, court refused to take judicial notice that bull with such capacity was six months old but raised a rebuttable presumption to that effect). See § 334 n. 5 infra; § 343, infra.

§ 333

1. Model Code of Evidence Rule 804 (1942).

2. Original Uniform Rule 10(1) (1953) provided: "The judge shall afford each party reasonable opportunity to present to him information relevant to the propriety of taking judicial notice of a matter or the tenor of the matter to be noticed." Compare Fed.R.Evid. and Unif.R.Evid. 201(e), quoted at § 328 n. 3 supra, providing for a hearing on request.

3. Compare Fringer v. Venema, 26 Wis.2d 366, 373, 132 N.W.2d 565, 570 (1965) rehearing denied 26 Wis.2d

366, 133 N.W.2d 809 ("However, before judicial notice of such fact can be taken, adequate notice must be given to the parties to enable them to be heard on the question of verifiable certainty.") with Varcoe v. Lee, 180 Cal. 338, 343, 181 P. 223, (1919) ("It would have been much better if counsel for the plaintiff or the trial judge himself had inquired of defendants' counsel . . . whether there was any dispute").

4. Davis, A System of Judicial Notice Based on Fairness and Convenience, in Perspectives of Law 69, 75 (Pound ed. 1964) ("In ninety-nine instances of judicial notice out of a hundred, a notification of the parties of intent to take judicial notice is inconvenient and serves no good purpose.") The fact probably is that most instances of judicial notice pass without detection, and that most of those which are detected are not questioned. Hence an inclusive requirement of advance notice would result only in confusion and controversy where none existed before. See § 334 n. 10 infra.

5. Comment, 13 Vill.L.Rev. 528, 543–44 (1968) (suggesting that it would be a waste of time to notify the parties when the fact to be noticed is "a truly indisputable" one but warning that, should a trial judge notice a debatable adjudicative fact without notice to the parties, there might occur a denial of the right to trial by jury). See also Bulova Watch Co., Inc. v. K. Hattori & Co., Limited, 508 F.Supp. 1322 (E.D.N.Y.1981), at n. 11 infra.

tence of any need for a structured adversary-style ancillary hearing with regard to legislative facts.[6] Indeed, even with regard to adjudicative facts, the practices of appellate courts tend to support the argument that there exists no real felt need to formalize the practice of taking judicial notice.[7]

Legislative facts, of course, have not fitted easily into any effort to propound a formalized set of rules applicable to judicial notice. These facts, after all, tend to be less than indisputable ones and hence beyond the pale of judicial notice. What then of the requirement that, before judicial notice is taken, the parties be afforded a reasonable opportunity to present information relative to the propriety of taking judicial notice and the tenor of the matter to be noticed? By and large the parties have this opportunity during arguments over motions as to the appropriate law to be applied to the controversy, by exchanging briefs, and by employing the technique exemplified by the Brandeis brief. It appears, therefore, that there exists no felt need to formalize the procedures pertaining to the opportunity to be heard with reference to legislative facts.[8] Even

so, there are cases where the legislative facts which form the basis of an appellate opinion first appear in the decision itself and counsel never have the opportunity to respond to them.[9] Presumably current practice relies upon the sound discretion of judges to maintain discipline in this regard by presupposing a peer-group style general insistence among the judges on a fundamental notion of elementary fairness.[10] However ill-defined because rooted in a sense of due process rather than bottomed on a precise calculus of rules, this notion of fairness may prove to be the common denominator which will continue to link together judicial notice of legislative and adjudicative facts.[11]

With regard to the treatment of adjudicative facts by appellate courts, the common starting point is the axiom that these tribunals can take judicial notice to the same extent as can trial courts.[12] At the very least, this rule suggests the obvious fact that appellate courts can review the propriety of the judicial notice taken by the court below [13] and can even take judicial notice on their own initiative of facts not noticed below.[14] Nonetheless the recitation of these princi-

---

6. See, e.g., Judge Jerome Frank's concurring opinion in United States v. Roth, 237 F.2d 796, 814 (2d Cir. 1956) (in case involving allegedly obscene publications, appellate judge relied in part upon letter written to him by a sociologist in response to his own inquiry); G. Currie, Appellate Courts Use of Facts Outside the Record by Resort to Judicial Notice and Independent Investigation, 1960 Wis.L.Rev. 39.

7. See, e.g., Mills v. Denver Tramway Corp., 155 F.2d 808 (10th Cir.1946).

8. See, e.g., Fed.R.Evid. 201 Advisory Committee Note (denying need for "any formal requirements of notice other than those already inherent in affording opportunity to hear and be heard and exchanging briefs.") But see Davis, Judicial Notice, 1969 Law & Soc. Order 513, 526 (suggesting that procedural rules are needed to assure adequate opportunity to be heard when legislative facts are noticed).

9. United States v. Roth, 237 F.2d 796, 814 (2d Cir. 1956) (see note 6 above). When the same case was on appeal to the Supreme Court, the Solicitor General sent that court a carton of "hard-core pornography" for their perusal. Lockhart & McClure, Censorship of Obscenity: The Developing Constitutional Standards, 45 Minn.L.Rev. 5, 26 (1960).

10. See also Durham v. United States, 94 U.S.App. D.C. 228, 214 F.2d 862 (1954) (court relied upon the ar-

ticles by many medico-legal writers in establishing a new test for criminal responsibility, all of which may not have been debated by counsel as to their respective merits); People v. Finkelstein, 11 N.Y.2d 300, 229 N.Y.S.2d 367, 183 N.E.2d 661 (1961), cert. denied 371 U.S. 863.

11. Bulova Watch Co., Inc. v. K. Hattori & Co., Limited, 508 F.Supp. 1322 (E.D.N.Y.1981) (parties invited to respond to propriety of taking judicial notice and to tenor of what was noticed with regard to facts about operations of foreign multinational corporations bearing on jurisdiction in the forum, the purpose being both to avoid egregious errors and to reinforce confidence in the court's fairness); Davis, Facts in Lawmaking, 80 Col.L.Rev. 931 (1980) (need to create system of notice and comment when Supreme Court makes major policy decisions bottomed on judicially noticed legislative facts).

12. Varcoe v. Lee, 180 Cal. 338, 181 P. 223 (1919). Note, 42 Mich.L.Rev. 509 (1943) (collection of cases.)

13. In re Bowling Green Milling Co., 132 F.2d 279 (6th Cir.1942); Verner v. Redman, 77 Ariz. 310, 271 P.2d 468 (1954); Fringer v. Venema, 26 Wis.2d 366, 132 N.W.2d 565 (1965).

14. Hunter v. New York, Ontario & Western Railway, 116 N.Y. 615, 23 N.E. 9 (1889) (took judicial notice of height of typical man to reverse judgment based up-

ples fails to portray the full flavor of the actual practice of appellate courts in taking judicial notice on their own initiative of what would appear to be adjudicative facts.

In this regard the case of Mills v. Denver Tramway Corp.,[15] may be instructive. Plaintiff had alighted from a trolley car, walked behind it and crossed the parallel set of tracks, where he was struck by a car going in the opposite direction. Plaintiff appeared to be manifestly guilty of contributory negligence, a sound enough conclusion plaintiff next attempted to overcome by invoking the doctrine of the last-clear-chance. That is, at the penultimate moment of the trial, plaintiff requested a jury instruction to the effect that, if the motorman had had a chance to sound the trolley bell, the harm might still have been avoided, in which case plaintiff was entitled to prevail. The trial judge refused the instruction because no evidence was ever introduced to indicate that the trolley had a bell.[16] The appellate tribunal reversed, giving plaintiff a new trial, reciting the fact that "streetcars have bells." If all trolley cars had bells, a fact the trial court could have taken judicial notice of had it ever been requested to do so, it would be quite appropriate for the appellate court to take notice of the very same fact. But was it an indisputable fact that *all* streetcars had bells? Arguably most did, in which case the appellate court was taking judicial notice, not of an indisputable fact, but only of a more-than-likely-true fact. More plausibly, the court reasoned that, in all likelihood, the trolley had a bell, in which instance plaintiff should have, as part of his case, proceeded to introduce evidence to substantiate a plau-

sible claim on the last-clear-chance theory. Alternatively, had no bell existed, plaintiff should have made that omission the basis of his claim. In either event, a sense of justice cried out for a trial of the case with all the facts fully developed. If, however, this was the sense of justice which moved the appellate tribunal, their invocation of the statement that "all streetcars have bells," a disputable proposition, sheds no real light either on the question whether judicial notice extends to disputable adjudicative facts or whether the parties must be afforded a hearing before judicial notice is taken. Given the need for appellate courts on occasion to reverse results below on a factual basis, judicial notice serves as a convenient device by which to give the practice the appearance of legal propriety. This being true, it would appear that the chances of adequately formalizing judicial notice even of adjudicative facts at the appellate level may be a slim one indeed.[17]

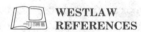

WESTLAW REFERENCES

title(mills & denver & tramway) & court(ca10)

---

§ 334. Trends in the Development of Judicial Notice of Facts

It appears that, by and large, agreement has been reached on a rough outline of the perimeters of judicial notice as applied to adjudicative facts at the trial level.[1] A workable procedural schemata which would appear to guarantee fairness already exists in the event that judicial notice is restricted to indisputable facts.[2] The only question remaining is whether, in order to expedite the trial

---

on notion that claimant was seated when box car entered railway tunnel). Fed.R.Evid. 201(f) allows judicial notice to be taken at any stage of the proceeding. § 328 n. 3 supra.

15. 155 F.2d 808 (10th Cir.1946).

16. Interestingly enough, Professor Davis might suggest in this instance that the trial judge would have been right not to take judicial notice. Davis, A System of Judicial Notice Based on Fairness and Convenience in Perspectives of Law 94 (Pound ed. 1964), ("Nothing short of bringing facts into the record, so that an opportunity is allowed for cross-examination and for pre-

sentation of rebuttal evidence and argument, will suffice for disputed adjudicative facts at the center of the controversy.")

17. See *seriatim* the decisions in Securities and Exchange Commission v. Capital Gains Research Bureau, Inc., 191 F.Supp. 897 (S.D.N.Y.1961), affirmed 300 F.2d 745 (2d Cir.), reversed 375 U.S. 180 (1963).

§ 334

1. See Fed.R.Evid. and Unif.R.Evid. 201, quoted at § 328 n. 3 supra.

2. See § 333 supra.

of cases, judges should be allowed to excuse the proponent of a fact likely true of the necessity of producing formal evidence thereof, leaving it to the jury to accept or reject the judicially noticed fact, and of course, allowing the opponent to introduce evidence contradicting it.[3]   Indeed, the present controversy might be put in a new light by limiting judicial notice to indisputable facts [4] and then raising the question, whether, as part of the law associated with the burden of proof and presumptions, a judge can properly expedite trials by himself ruling that very likely true facts are presumptively true unless the jury care to find otherwise.[5]

Whatever the ultimate doctrinal synthesis of judicial notice of adjudicative facts comes to be, a viable formulation of rules laying down a similarly rigid procedural etiquette with regard to legislative facts has not proved feasible.[6]   Given the current recognition that nonadjudicative facts are inextricably part and parcel of the law formulation process in a policy-oriented jurisprudence, there may be no need to formulate a distinctly judicial notice-captioned procedure with regard to nonadjudicative facts.   These data are fed into the judicial process now whenever rules of law are brought to the attention of judges in motions, memoranda and briefs. Thus, whatever rules govern the submission

of law in the litigation process have already preempted the nonadjudicative field and made unnecessary separate treatment thereof within the context of judicial notice.[7]

There has been an increasing awareness, moreover, that quite apart from judicial notice, the trial process assumes that the participants therein bring with them a vast amount of everyday knowledge of facts in general.[8]   To think, after all, presupposes some data about which to think.   In an automobile accident case, for example, both the judge and the jury constantly draw on their own experiences as drivers, as observers of traffic, and as live human beings, and these experiences are reduced in their minds to propositions of fact which, since they have survived themselves, are probably fairly accurate.   This substratum of data the participants bring into the courthouse has, however, tended to confuse the judicial notice scene.   On the one hand, this subliminal-like data is sometimes confused with the "common knowledge"-style of adjudicative facts with which formal judicial notice is concerned.   On the other hand, judges constantly invoke references to these same everyday facts when they write opinions because, when formally articulated, it is impossible "to think" without reference to them.[9]   It may very well be the case that judges have

3. See § 332 supra.

4. See e.g., Fed.R.Evid. 201, reproduced at § 328 n. 3 supra.

5. This obviously is a compromise. Some authorities limit judicial notice to indisputable facts in every instance, whether the facts be either adjudicative or legislative ones. Morgan, Judicial Notice, 57 Harv.L. Rev. 269 (1944). Others seem to suggest that all judicially noticed facts are assumptions capable of being rebutted by proof. Thayer, A Preliminary Treatise on Evidence at the Common Law 309 (1898); 9 Wigmore, Evidence § 2567 (Chadbourn rev. 1981). It has been the peculiar genius of Professor K.C. Davis to perceive the difference between adjudicative and legislative facts. Davis, Official Notice, 62 Harv.L.Rev. 537 (1949). Even so, recent efforts to codify judicial notice have insisted upon the indisputability concept with respect to adjudicative facts only. Fed.R.Evid. 201. Professor Davis remains adamant that adjudicative facts can be disputable ones. Davis, Judicial Notice, 1969 Law & Soc. Order 513. The Thayer-Wigmore-Davis argument is that efficiency cries out for a mechanism by which formal evidence can be dispensed with when a

fact appears to be fairly incontestable. Thayer appears to have perceived that this kind of fact was a variant of the law of procedure. See, e.g., Morgan, Judicial Notice, 57 Harv.L.Rev. 269, 285–286 (1944) ("Both [Wigmore's] and Mr. Thayer's statements of the proper effect of taking judicial notice are startlingly like their statements of the effect of presumptions.") See also Fringer v. Venema, 26 Wis.2d 366, 132 N.W.2d 565 (1965); § 332 n. 6 supra; § 343, infra.

It will be observed that the Federal Rules of Evidence make no effort to set forth a catalog of presumptions. Fed.R.Evid. 301. Compare West's Ann.Cal. Evid.Code, §§ 630–668.

6. See § 333 supra.

7. See, e.g., Fed.R.Evid. 201, reproduced at § 328 n. 3 supra.

8. See § 329 supra.

9. See, e.g., People v. Enders, 38 Misc.2d 746, 237 N.Y.S.2d 879 (N.Y.C.Crim.Ct.1963) (in deciding which, if either, between an absentee store proprietor and his butcher to whom he gave orders, was liable under a statute making it a crime to doctor meat, judge con-

tended, when extrapolating the obvious, to invoke the words, "I take judicial notice of" to explain the presence of these facts in their minds, thereby unnecessarily glutting the encyclopedias with trivia which are, when formally collected, highly misleading indices of the true scope of judicial notice as such.[10]

All of which would appear to indicate that the doctrine of judicial notice may ultimately be reduced to a workable consensus. Current trends would indicate that this consensus will, if it comes to fruition, involve reducing judicial notice to narrow confines within an adjudicative context. Controversy and intellectual excitement will not end there, however, because the phenomena excluded from the domain of judicial notice will then have to be collected and rationalized within the perimeters of a new concept, perhaps oriented around the study of thinking-about-facts techniques involved within the judicial process.[11]

 WESTLAW REFERENCES

"judicial notice" /s experience* belief* observation* & court(ma)

---

§ 335. The Judge's Task as Law-Finder: Judicial Notice of Law

It would appear to be self-evident that it is peculiarly the function of the judge to find and interpret the law applicable to the issues in a trial, and in a jury case, to announce his findings of law to the jury for their guid-

ance. The heavy-footed common law system of proof by witnesses and authenticated documents is too slow and cumbrous for the judge's task of finding what the applicable law is. Usually this law is familiar lore and if not he relies on the respective counsel to bring before him the statutes, reports, and source books, and these everyday companions of judge and counsel are read from informally in discussion or cited and quoted in trial and appellate briefs. Occasionally the judge will go beyond the cited authorities to make his own investigation. In the ordinary process of finding the applicable law, the normal method then is by informal investigation of any sources satisfactory to the judge. Thus this process has been traditionally described in terms of the judge taking judicial notice of the law applicable to the case at hand. Indeed, when the source-material was not easily accessible to the judge, as in the case of "foreign law" or city ordinances, law has been treated as a peculiar species of fact, requiring formal proof. We shall see, however, that as these materials become more accessible, the tendency is toward permitting the judges to do what perhaps they should have done in the beginning, that is, to rely on the diligence of counsel to provide the necessary materials, and accordingly to take judicial notice of *all* law. This seems to be the goal toward which the practice is marching.

Domestic law. As to domestic law generally, the judge is not merely permitted to take judicial notice but required to do so,[1] at

---

cluded they both were because "the hamburger has become one of the most popular menu items in the United States.")

10. Often enough these propositions of generalized knowledge are not picked up as illustrations of judicial notice, which after all proves the point. See, e.g., Village of Euclid v. Ambler Realty Co., 272 U.S. 365 (1926) (apartment houses come near to being nuisances in single-family residential areas); Escola v. Coca Cola Bottling Co., 24 Cal.2d 453, 150 P.2d 436 (1944) (concurring opinion) (manufacturers are best situated to underwrite losses attributable to defective products); Webster v. Blue Ship Tea Room, Inc., 347 Mass. 421, 198 N.E.2d 309 (1964) (in considering whether restaurant impliedly warranted fish chowder to be free of all miniscule bones court reflected that "Chowder is an an-

cient dish preëxisting even 'the appetites of our seamen and fishermen' ").

11. This would, in fact, represent a return to Thayer. See, Preliminary Treatise on Evidence at the Common Law 278–279 (1898) ("Whereabout in the law does the doctrine of judicial notice belong? Wherever the process of reasoning has a place, and that is everywhere. Not peculiarly in the law of evidence. . . . The subject of judicial notice, then, belongs to the general topic of legal or judicial reasoning.")

§ 335

1. Strain v. Isaacs, 59 Ohio App. 495, 514, 18 N.E.2d 816, 825 (Ohio App.1938) (dictum); Randall v. Commonwealth, 183 Va. 182, 186, 31 S.E.2d 571, 572 (1944) (dictum); 29 Am.Jur.2d Evidence § 27. Some states pro-

least if requested, although in a particular case a party may be precluded on appeal from complaining of the judge's failure to notice a statute where his counsel has failed to call it to the judge's attention.[2] This general rule that judicial notice will be taken of domestic law means that state trial courts will notice Federal law,[3] which is controlling in every state, and has been held to mean that in a Federal trial court the laws of the states, not merely of the state where it is sitting, are domestic and will be noticed.[4] Similarly all statewide or nationwide executive orders and proclamations, which are legally effective, will be noticed.[5] Under this same principle, even the laws of antecedent governments will be noticed.[6]

State and national administrative regulations having the force of law will also be noticed, at least if they are published so as to be readily available.[7] When such documents are published in the Federal Register it is provided that their contents shall be judicially noticed.[8] Private laws [9] and municipal ordinances,[10] however, are not commonly included within the doctrine of judicial notice

---

vide by statute for judicial notice of local public statutes; e.g., West's Ann.Cal.Evid.Code § 451; McKinney's N.Y. CPLR 4511(a).

2. Great American Insurance Co. v. Glenwood Irrigation Co., 265 F. 594 (10th Cir.1920) (in action for damage from fire trial court's failure to charge that, under Colorado statute, leaving fire unextinguished would impose liability regardless of negligence, could not be complained of because plaintiff failed to call statute to judge's attention). See, however, an illuminating comment, Overlooking Statutes, 30 Yale L.J. 855 (1921), which suggests that errors arising from ignorance of a statute should be corrected on appeal except in cases where the public interest is not involved and counsel's failure to cite the statute can be construed as a waiver.

A judge, of course, may undertake an independent investigation of the applicable law, but ordinarily judges rely on opposing counsel to bring to their attention the appropriate sources of law. Matthews v. McVay, 241 Mo.App. 998, 1006, 234 S.W.2d 983, 988–989 (1950).

3. Peters v. Double Cola Bottling Co., 224 S.C. 437, 79 S.E.2d 710 (1954). Some states by statute provide for judicial notice of the Federal Constitution and statutes, e.g., West's Ann.Cal.Evid. Code § 451; McKinney's N.Y. CPLR 4511(a).

4. In a federal court exercising original jurisdiction, its local law is the law of all the states. Hanley v. Donoghue, 116 U.S. 1 (1885); Lane v. Sargent, 217 F. 237 (1st Cir.1914); Gediman v. Anheuser Busch, 299 F.2d 537 (2d Cir.1962); Gallup v. Caldwell, 120 F.2d 90 (3d Cir.1941). This rule of judicial notice being a matter of procedure rather than substantive law, it seems that the controlling force of state substantive law, under Erie Railroad Co. v. Tompkins, 304 U.S. 64 (1938), is inapplicable. But see Keeffe, Landis & Shaad, Sense and Nonsense about Judicial Notice, 2 Stan.L.Rev. 664, 686 (1950).

On appeal, however, from a state court, the federal Supreme Court will not notice the law of another state unless the state court below would have done so. Hanley v. Donoghue, 116 U.S. 1 (1885).

5. Dennis v. United States, 339 U.S. 162 (1949) (executive order of the President providing standards for discharge of government employees on loyalty

grounds); Heyward v. Long, 178 S.C. 351, 183 S.E. 145, 114 A.L.R. 1130 (1936) (Governor's proclamation declaring highway department in state of insurrection); 29 Am.Jur.2d Evidence § 40; Dec.Dig. Evidence ⏀46.

6. Ponce v. Roman Catholic Church, 210 U.S. 296 (1908) (Spanish laws in Puerto Rico); South Shore Land Co. v. Petersen, 226 Cal.App.2d 725, 38 Cal.Rptr. 392 (1964) (Mexican laws in California).

7. Case authority illustrates that some courts will take judicial notice of administrative regulations. Southwestern Bell Telephone Co. v. Bateman, 223 Ark. 432, 266 S.W.2d 289 (1954); Groendyke Transport Inc. v. State, 208 Okl. 602, 258 P.2d 670 (1953); Smith v. Highway Board, 117 Vt. 343, 91 A.2d 805 (1952). Contra: Atlanta Gas Light Co. v. Newman, 88 Ga.App. 252, 76 S.E.2d 536 (1953); Finlay v. Eastern Racing Association Inc., 308 Mass. 20, 30 N.E.2d 859 (1941). Several states provide by statute for judicial notice of administrative regulations, e.g., West's Ann.Cal.Evid. Code § 451; McKinney's N.Y. CPLR 4511. Other states provide by statute for judicial notice of published compilations of administrative regulations, e.g., Alas.R.Civ.Proc. 43; Wis.Stats.1975, § 902.03.

8. 44 U.S.C.A. § 1507. While some state courts take judicial notice of federal administrative regulations, Hough v. Rapidair, Inc., 298 S.W.2d 378 (Mo. 1957); Dallas General Drivers v. Jax Beer Co., 276 S.W.2d 384 (Tex.Civ.App.1955), others will not. Gladieux v. Parney, 93 Ohio App. 117, 106 N.E.2d 317 (1951); Buice v. Scruggs Equipment Co., 37 Tenn.App. 556, 267 S.W.2d 119 (1953). It would appear that the Federal Register Act should bind state courts. But see Mastrullo v. Ryan, 328 Mass. 621, 622, 105 N.E.2d 469, 470 (1952).

9. Chambers v. Atchison, Topeka & Santa Fe Railway Co., 32 Ariz. 102, 255 P. 1092 (1927); Bolick v. City of Charlotte, 191 N.C. 677, 132 S.E. 660 (1926).

10. Ramacciotti v. Zinn, 550 S.W.2d 217 (Mo.App. 1977); Kamarath v. Bennett, 549 S.W.2d 784 (Tex.Civ. App.1977), reversed on other grounds 568 S.W.2d 658. A municipal court may be required to take judicial notice of the local municipal ordinances. Tipp v. District of Columbia, 69 App.D.C. 400, 102 F.2d 264 (1939); Wis.Stats. § 902.03.

and these must be pleaded and proved. To the extent that these items become readily available in compilations, it may be expected that they will become subject to judicial notice; [11] whereas, in the meantime, it would appear appropriate for judges to take judicial notice of both private laws and municipal ordinances if counsel furnish a certified copy thereof.

The law of sister states. It is easy to see how the difference of languages and inaccessibility of source books should have led the English courts to develop the common law rule that the laws of foreign nations would not be noticed but must be pleaded and proved as facts.[12] The assumption in the earlier cases in this country [13] that the courts of one state must treat the laws of another state as foreign for this purpose is less understandable and to the afterview seems a deplorable instance of mechanical jurisprudence. Yet it remains today, in nearly every one of the increasingly few states which have not yet adopted a reformatory statute, the common law rule that notice will not be given to the laws of sister states.[14] This is probably the most inconvenient of all the limitations upon the practice of judicial notice. Notice here could certainly be justified on the principle of certainty

and verifiability,[15] and the burden on the judge could be minimized by casting the responsibility upon counsel either to agree upon a stipulation as to the law or to produce on each side for the benefit of the court all materials necessary for ascertaining the law in question.

Under this hoary practice when a required pleading and proof of the foreign law has been overlooked, or has been unsuccessfully attempted, the resulting danger of injustice is somewhat mitigated by the presumption that the law of the sister state is the same as that of the forum,[16] or more simply the practice of applying local law if the law of the other state is not invoked and proven.[17] But this presumption-tool is too rough for the job in hand, particularly when the materials for ascertaining the laws of sister states are today almost as readily accessible as those for local law, and in any event counsel as officers of the court are available to find and present those materials to the judge in just the same informal and convenient fashion as if they were arguing a question of local law.[18]

In 1936 the Conference of Commissioners on Uniform Laws drafted the Uniform Judicial Notice of Foreign Law Act [19] which was adopted in substance by more than half the

11. 29 Am.Jur.2d Evidence § 35. Judicial notice of municipal ordinances is sometimes provided for by statute, e.g., Alas.R.Civ.Proc. 43; McKinney's N.Y. CPLR 4511.

12. See, e.g., Fremoult v. Dedire, 1 P.Wms. 429, 24 Eng.Rep. 458 (1718); Mostyn v. Fabrigas, 1 Cowp. 161, 98 Eng.Rep. 1021 (1774). For the history of this rule see Sass, Foreign Law in Civil Litigation: A Comparative Survey, 16 Am.J.Comp.L. 332, 335–339 (1968).

13. See, e.g., Brackett v. Norton, 4 Conn. 517, 520 (1823).

14. Southern Express Co. v. Owens, 146 Ala. 412, 41 So. 752 (1906); Gapsch v. Gapsch, 76 Idaho 44, 277 P.2d 278, 54 A.L.R.2d 416 (1954); Brown v. Perry, 104 Vt. 66, 156 A. 910 (1931). But see Prudential Insurance Co. of America v. O'Grady, 97 Ariz. 9, 12–13, 396 P.2d 246, 248 (1964).

15. See § 330 supra.

16. Scott v. Scott, 153 Neb. 906, 46 N.W.2d 627, 23 A.L.R.2d 1431 (1951).

17. Haggard v. First National Bank, 72 N.D. 434, 8 N.W.2d 5 (1942).

18. Prudential Insurance Co. of America v. O'Grady, 97 Ariz. 9, 12, 396 P.2d 246, 248 (1964) ("In this modern day with easy access to many law libraries with copies of the state statutes and the state and national reporter systems, and the obvious fact that the states are not 'foreign' to each other, the reason for the common law rule no longer exists.").

19. Its substantive provisions follow:

"Section 1. (Judicial Notice.) Every court of this state shall take judicial notice of the common law and statutes of every state, territory and other jurisdiction of the United States. Section 2. (Information of the Court.) The court may inform itself of such laws in such manner as it may deem proper, and the court may call upon counsel to aid it in obtaining such information. Section 3. (Ruling Reviewable.) The determination of such laws shall be made by the court and not by the jury, and shall be reviewable. Section 4. (Evidence as to Laws of other Jurisdiction.) Any party may also present to the trial court any admissible evidence of such laws, but, to enable a party to offer evidence of the law in another jurisdiction or to ask that judicial notice be taken thereof, reasonable notice shall be given to the ad-

states.[20] This legislation provides that every court within the adopting state shall take judicial notice of the common law and statutes of every other state. While the Act removes the necessity to prove the law of another state, most courts do not feel obliged by it to notice the law of another state on their own initiative.[21] Indeed, in order to invoke the benefits of the Foreign Law Act a litigant must give reasonable notice in the pleadings or otherwise to the adverse party of his intention to do so,[22] failing which the courts are apt to refuse to take judicial notice or admit evidence as to the sister-state law relied on, invoking once again the presumption that it is the same as the law of the forum.[23]

The Uniform Judicial Notice of Foreign Law Act pertained to the law of sister states and did not address the issue of the law of other nations.[24] It was supplanted in 1962 when the National Conference of Commissioners on Uniform Laws approved Article IV of the Uniform Interstate and International Procedure Act.[25] Calculated to address judicial notice of true foreign law, the new Act implicates the law of sister states as well because it imposes the same discipline when the law of *any* extraforum jurisdiction is invoked.[26] Thus a party who intends to raise an issue of the law of a sister state should give notice of an intention to do so, either in the pleadings or by any other reasonable method of written notice.[27] It is the court which determines the tenor of what actually will be noticed about the law of a sister state,[28] and the court may go beyond the materials furnished it by the parties in arriving at its own determination.[29] Article IV, however, has yet to win widespread adoption.[30]

---

verse parties either in the pleadings or otherwise. Section 5. (Foreign Country.) The law of a jurisdiction other than those referred to in Section 1 shall be an issue for the court, but shall not be subject to the foregoing provisions concerning judicial notice." 1936 Handbook Nat'l. Conference of Commissioners on Unif. State Laws 355–359; 1945 id. 124; 9A Uniform Laws Ann. 553 (1965).

20. 9A Uniform Laws Ann. 550 (1965). Listed as having adopted this legislation are about half the states. See 13 Uniform Laws Annot. 496 (1980).

Some states have enacted their own legislation providing for judicial notice of law of sister states, e.g. Ark.Stat. § 28–109; West's Ann.Cal.Evid.Code § 452; Mass.Gen.Laws Ann. c. 233, § 70; McKinney's N.Y. CPLR 4511.

21. Kingston v. Quimby, 80 So.2d 455 (Fla.1955) ("a party invoking . . . the Act is required to have the record reveal that fact and to have the record show the authorities which will be relied upon with reference to the foreign law."); Strout v. Burgess, 144 Me. 263, 68 A.2d 241, 12 A.L.R.2d 939 (1949).

22. Boswell v. Rio De Oro Uranium Mines, Inc., 68 N.M. 457, 362 P.2d 991 (1961) (cases construing Act generally hold that the judicial notice requirement merely relieves party of formal proof but was not designed to remove necessity of at least informing court of the content of foreign law to be noticed).

23. Scott v. Scott, 153 Neb. 906, 46 N.W.2d 627, 23 A.L.R.2d 1431 (1951).

24. See the text of that act produced at note 19, supra.

25. 13 U.L.A. 459 (1980).

Determination of Foreign Law

§ 4.01. [Notice]

A party who intends to raise an issue concerning the law of any jurisdiction or governmental unit thereof outside this state shall give notice in his pleadings or other reasonable written notice.

§ 4.02 [Materials to be Considered]

In determining the law of any jurisdiction or governmental unit thereof outside this state, the court may consider any relevant material or source, including testimony, whether or not submitted by a party or admissible under the rules of evidence.

§ 4.03. [Court Decision and Review]

The court, not jury, shall determine the law of any governmental unit outside this state. Its determination is subject to review on appeal as a ruling on a question of law.

§ 4.04. [Other Provisions of Law Unaffected]

This Article does not repeal or modify any other law of this state permitting another procedure for the determination of foreign law.

26. See § 4.01 reproduced above at n. 25.

27. Id.

28. See § 4.03 reproduced above at n. 25.

29. See § 4.02 reproduced above at n. 25.

30. The Uniform Interstate and International Procedure Act has been adopted in Arkansas, Massachusetts, Michigan, Oklahoma and Pennsylvania. 13 U.L.A. 459 (1980). One has, however, always to see whether Article IV thereof has been altered or deleted. The Oklahoma version speaks to "the United States"

The law of foreign countries. At common law, foreign law was treated as a matter of fact: pleading and proof were required, and the jury decided what the foreign law was.[31] As early as 1936 the Uniform Judicial Notice of Foreign Law Act reflected the idea that the tenor of the law of a foreign country was a question for the court and not for the jury.[32] What is significant is the fact that this selfsame 1936 Act, adverted to in the preceding section, contained no provision for the judicial notice of the law of other nations.[33] The parties were left not only to pleading but proving, albeit to a judge and not a jury, the law of other nations.[34]

The longevity of the ancient notion that a party had "to prove" the law of another nation was likely rooted in the fact that the sources of extranational law were not easily accessible even in urban centers.[35] A healthy pragmatism seems to have ameliorated the harshness of any rule demanding strict proof. Sworn to or certified copies of extranational statutes or decisions gave way to the use of copies thereof in a book printed by the authority of the foreign state or proved to be commonly recognized in its courts.[36]

Even so, the very idea that a party was engaged in "proving" a point of extranational law fairly invited complications. The written text of any law suggests that its "black letter" be interpreted in light of any germane decisions, treatises or commentaries. This under common law proof must be accomplished by taking the testimony in person or by deposition of an expert in the foreign law.[37] The adversary of course is free to take the testimony of other experts if he can find them on his side, and the cross-examination of conflicting experts is likely to accentuate the disagreements.[38] This method of proof seems to maximize expense and delay[39] and hardly seems best calculated to ensure a correct decision by our judges on questions of foreign law. It could be vastly improved by pre-trial conferences in which agreements as to undisputed aspects of the foreign law could be secured, and by the appointment by the court of one or more experts on foreign law as referees or as court-chosen experts to report their findings to the court.[40]

instead of "this state" so that the new Act applies only to the law of foreign nations. Massachusetts omits Article IV entirely. See: 13 U.L.A. at 496. Massachusetts has a statute regulating the judicial notice of the law of sister states and another governing the judicial notice of both true foreign nations and sister states. Mass.Gen.Laws Ann. c. 233, § 70; Mass.R.Civ.Proc. Rule 44.1.

31. See generally, 9 Wigmore, Evidence § 2573 (Chadbourn rev. 1981).

32. See § 5, reproduced at n. 19 supra.

33. See the text of that act reproduced at n. 19 supra.

34. That this can still be a problem, witness Schlesinger, A Recurrent Problem in Transnational Litigation: The Effect of Failure to Invoke or Prove the Applicable Foreign Law, 59 Cornell L.Rev. 1 (1973).

35. See, e.g., Report of the Committee on Foreign and Comparative Law of the Assoc. of the Bar of the City of New York, 22 The Record (Supplement—Committee Reports 1966–67) 31 (1967).

36. See, e.g., Uniform Proof of Statutes Act, 9B U.L.A. 628 (1966).

37. A case illustrating this practice is In re Nielsen's Estate, 118 Mont. 304, 165 P.2d 792 (1946) (deposition of legal counselor of Danish Legation discussing legal treatises and giving opinion as to inheritance rights of aliens under Danish law). See also, Application of Chase Manhattan Bank, 191 F.Supp. 206 (D.C.N.Y.1961) (a mere translation of foreign statute without the background, context, or area of internal application is insufficient to establish the precise tenor of what foreign law is).

38. "It is the writer's impression that under the present practice of the courts, skillful advocates may succeed in developing confusing divergencies between experts on purely verbal matters in situations where coherent and well-substantiated written opinions would eliminate all difficulties." Nussbaum, The Problem of Proving Foreign Law, 50 Yale L.J. 1018, 1029 (1941).

39. Professor Nussbaum cites an example where a court would not be satisfied unless plaintiffs brought an Argentine lawyer to New York City. Nussbaum, Proving the Law of Foreign Countries, 3 Am.J.Comp.L. 60, 63–64 (1954).

40. The parties can stipulate the tenor of the foreign law. Harris v. American International Fuel & Petroleum Co., 124 F.Supp. 878 (W.D.Pa.1954).

Following the lead of several states which by statute have provided that the court must take judicial notice [41] or permit the court to do so in its discretion,[42] the practice obtaining in the federal courts has been codified to make the tenor of foreign law a question of law for the court.[43] Thus it is that a party who intends to raise an issue of foreign-nation law must give notice of his intention to do so, either in his pleadings or by any other reasonable method of written notice.[44] Once the issue of foreign law is raised, the court need not, in its effort to determine the tenor of that law, rely upon the testimony and other materials proffered by the litigant, but may engage in its own research and consider any relevant material thus found.

In turn the new Uniform Interstate and International Procedure Act's Article IV will, if generally enacted, unify state practice along the lines of the federal model.[45] Thus again the invocation of extranational law would necessitate written notice, by way of the pleadings or any reasonable alternative, and the court, licensed to engage in its own researches, would ultimately fix the actual tenor of whatever was noticed.[46] Concomitantly, recourse to the law of a sister state is included within the same process so that a single procedure will obtain whenever the law of a jurisdiction outside the forum becomes an issue.[47]

The unwillingness of the courts to notice the laws of other countries creates difficulties where the party whose case or defense depends, under conflicts rules, upon foreign law and he fails to prove that law as a fact. There are several solutions. First, the court may decide the issue against him for failure of proof.[48] This is often a harsh and arbitrary result. Second, the court may simply apply the law of the forum on the ground that no other law is before it,[49] especially if the parties have tried the case as if local law were applicable.[50] Third, the court may presume that the law of the other country is the same as that of the forum,[51] thus reaching the same result as under the second theory but raising intellectual difficulties because the presumption is so frequently contrary to fact. When the doctrine involved is one of common law, but the other nation is not a common law country, some courts will de-

---

41. See, e.g., Mass.Gen.Laws Ann. c. 233, § 70 ("The court shall take judicial notice of the law . . . of any state . . . or of a foreign country whenever the same shall be material.") The attention of the court must be drawn to the foreign law before this statute becomes mandatory. Commercial Credit Corp. v. Stan Cross Buick, Inc., 343 Mass. 622, 180 N.E.2d 88 (1962).

42. See, e.g., McKinney's N.Y. CPLR 4511(b).

43. Fed.R.Civ.P. 44.1:

A party who intends to raise an issue concerning the law of a foreign country shall give notice in his pleadings or other reasonable written notice. The court, in determining foreign law, may consider any relevant material or source, including testimony, whether or not submitted by a party or admissible under the Federal Rules of Evidence. The court's determination shall be treated as a ruling on a question of law.

Rule 26.1 of the Federal Rules of Criminal Procedure is substantially the same.

44. Ruff v. St. Paul Mercury Insurance Co., 393 F.2d 500 (2d Cir.1968) (court would not take judicial notice of Liberian law when plaintiff never gave written notice of intent to rely upon foreign law).

45. 13 U.L.A. 459 (1980). See the text of this act reproduced at note 25 supra.

46. See §§ 4.01–4.03, reproduced at note 25 supra.

47. See particularly § 4.01, reproduced at note 25 supra.

48. Walton v. Arabian American Oil Co., 233 F.2d 541 (2d Cir.1956), cert. denied 352 U.S. 872 (Arkansas plaintiff sued Delaware corporation in federal court in New York for injuries sustained in Saudi Arabia, did not allege or offer to prove foreign law; case dismissed because plaintiff failed to introduce evidence of foreign law upon which issue burden of proof was his). See also Cuba Railroad Co. v. Crosby, 222 U.S. 473 (1912).

49. Leary v. Gledhill, 8 N.J. 260, 84 A.2d 725 (1951) (in suit arising out of transaction executed in France wherein plaintiff did not prove foreign law, court applied domestic law); Note, 37 Cornell L.Q. 748 (1952).

50. Watford v. Alabama & Florida Lumber Co., 152 Ala. 178, 44 So. 567 (1907).

51. See generally, the illuminating discussion in Nussbaum, op. cit. supra at n. 26, 50 Yale L.J. 1018, 1035 et seq. (1941); Medina Fernandez v. Hartman, 260 F.2d 569 (9th Cir.1958) (absent a showing to the contrary it is a familiar principle that foreign law is presumed same as domestic); Leary v. Gledhill, 8 N.J. 260, 84 A.2d 725 (1951).

cline to apply the presumption.[52] On the other hand, when the common law rule invoked is a part of the common fund of all civilized systems, such as the binding force of ordinary commercial agreements, the presumption is applied though the foreign country is not a common law country.[53] Moreover, by what is probably the prevailing and more convenient view, if the question would be governed locally by a statute, a like statute in the foreign country may be presumed.[54]

International and Maritime Law. The rules, principles and traditions of "international law," or "the law of nations," will be noticed in Federal and state courts.[55] Maritime law is similary subject to judicial notice but only insofar as these rules have become part of the general maritime law.[56] Less widely recognized maritime rules of foreign countries are treated like foreign law generally and are required to be proved,[57] unless they have been published here by government authority as the authentic foreign law,[58] or they have been embodied in a widely adopted international convention.[59] Peculiarly enough, the presumption of identity of foreign law with the local law, which would seem to be unusually convenient and realis-

tic in the maritime field, has been narrowly restricted.[60]

The future of judicial notice of law. When a judge presiding in the presence of a jury decides a question of fact, a sufficiently unique event occurs to merit special treatment because the jury is thought to perform the factfinding role in common law countries. This appears to explain why judicial notice of facts has been a topic of evidence law ever since Thayer authored his pioneering treatise. There is nothing very remarkable about a judge ruling on the tenor of the law to be applied to the resolution of the controversy, however, because by definition this is the very function judges are supposed to perform. When the sources of law were dubious at best, the job of sorting out the applicable law was shifted to the jury, witness how foreign law and municipal ordinances were treated as questions of fact. When next judges began to rule on the tenor of this law, even though it was still "fact" to be developed by the parties, there may have been some justification for describing this process as judicial notice. As all law has become increasingly accessible and judges have tended to assume the duty to rule on the tenor of all law, the notion that this pro-

52. Cuba Railroad Co. v. Crosby, 222 U.S. 473 (1912) (law of Cuba as to responsibility of employer for injury to employee); Philp v. Macri, 261 F.2d 945 (9th Cir.1958) (law of defamation of Peru cannot be presumed same as that of State of Washington). But see Louknitsky v. Louknitsky, 123 Cal.App.2d 406, 266 P.2d 910 (1954) (law of China presumed to be identical with community property law of California).

53. Cuba Railroad Co. v. Crosby, 222 U.S. 473 (1912) (dictum); Parrot v. Mexican Central Railway Co., Limited, 207 Mass. 184, 93 N.E. 590 (1941) (presumption that defendant would be liable in Mexico on agreement made there by its general passenger agent, under "universally recognized fundamental principles of right and wrong").

54. Wickersham v. Johnson, 104 Cal. 407, 38 P. 89 (1894) (sale of note by English executors, powers of executors presumed to be limited as under California statute); Murphy v. Murphy, 145 Cal. 482, 78 P. 1053 (1904) (California statutory rate of interest presumed to prevail as to amount due on English judgment). Contra: Parrot v. Mexican Central Railway Co., 207 Mass. 184, 93 N.E. 590 (1911) (dictum).

55. The Paquete Habana, 175 U.S. 677, 700 (1899) ("International law is part of our law and must be as-

certained and administered by the courts of justice. . . . "); Skiriotes v. Florida, 313 U.S. 69, 73 (1941) (international law is "a part of our law and as such is the law of all States of the Union").

56. The New York, 175 U.S. 187 (1899); Boyd v. Conklin, 54 Mich. 583, 20 N.W. 595 (1884).

57. Black Diamond Steamship Corp. v. Robert Stewart & Sons, Limited, 336 U.S. 386 (1949).

58. The New York, 175 U.S. 187 (1899).

59. Black Diamond Steamship Corp. v. Robert Stewart & Sons, Limited, 336 U.S. 386 (1949).

60. Ozanic v. United States, 165 F.2d 738 (2d Cir. 1948) (in libel for damage to Yugoslavian vessel on high seas libellant has burden to prove Yugoslav law as fact. "However it might be in respect to British maritime law, we cannot assume that the law of Yugoslavia, a civil law country and not even a great maritime power, is the same in respect to the measure of damages as that of the United States."); Sonnesen v. Panama Transport Co., 298 N.Y. 262, 82 N.E.2d 569 (1948) (court would not notice Panamanian law as to seaman's right of maintenance and cure, nor would it assume Panamanian maritime law same as ours).

cess is part of judicial notice has become increasingly an anachronism. Evidence, after all, involves the proof of facts. How the law is fed into the judicial machine is more appropriately an aspect of the law pertaining to procedure.[61] Thus it is that the electronic bleeps sounded by today's data processing equipment are actually tolling the intellectual death knell of this discrete subject-matter

hitherto dealt with as a subdivision of the law of evidence.

 WESTLAW REFERENCES

synopsis,digest(judicial! /s notice /8 ordinance*)
157k35 /p judicial! /2 notice
judicial! /2 notice /s foreign /2 countr! nation*

---

61. Note on Judicial Notice of Law, Adv.Com.Note, Fed.R.Evid. 201.

Title 12
BURDEN OF PROOF AND PRESUMPTIONS
Chapter 36
THE BURDENS OF PROOF AND PRESUMPTIONS [1]

Table of Sections

1. See 9 Wigmore, Evidence §§ 2483–2498 (Chadbourn rev. 1981) (general theory), id. 2499–2550 (burdens and presumptions in specific instances); Morgan, Basic Problems of Evidence, chs. 2, 3, (1962); Morgan, Some Problems of Proof under the Anglo-American System of Litigation 70–86 (1956); James & Hazard, Civil Procedure §§ 7.5–7.11 (2d ed. 1977); Weinstein & Berger, Evidence, ¶¶ 300[01]–303[08]; 21 Wright & Graham, Federal Practice and Procedure §§ 5121–5148; Allen, Presumptions, Inferences and Burden of Proof in Federal Civil Actions—An Anatomy of Unnecessary Ambiguity and a Proposal for Reform, 76 Nw.U.L.Rev. 892 (1982); Allen, Structuring Jury Decisionmaking in Criminal Cases: A Unified Constitutional Approach to Evidentiary Devices, 94 Harv.L.Rev. 321 (1980); Allen, More on Constitutional Process-of-Proof Problems in Criminal Cases, 94 Harv. L.Rev. 1795 (1981); Ball, The Moment of Truth: Probability Theory and Standards of Proof, 14 Vand.L. Rev. 807 (1961); Cleary, Presuming and Pleading: An Essay on Juristic Immaturity, 12 Stan.L.Rev. 5 (1959); Gausewitz, Presumptions in a One-Rule World, 5 Vand. L.Rev. 324 (1952); Jeffries & Stephan, Defenses, Presumptions and Burden of Proof in the Criminal Law, 88 Yale L.J. 1325 (1979); Ladd, Presumptions in Civil Actions, 1977 Ariz.St.L.J. 275; Laughlin, In Support of the Thayer Theory of Presumptions, 52 Mich.L.Rev. 195 (1953); McCormick, Charges on Presumptions, 5 N.C.L.Rev. 291 (1927); McCormick, What Shall the Trial Judge Tell the Jury About Presumptions? 13 Wash.L.Rev. 185 (1938); McNaughton, Burden of Production of Evidence: A Function of a Burden of Persuasion, 68 Harv.L.Rev. 1382 (1955). Nesson, Rationality, Presumption and Judicial Comment: A Response to Professor Allen, 94 Harv.L.Rev. 1574 (1981); Nesson, Reasonable Doubt and Permissive Inferences: The Value of Complexity, 92 Harv.L.Rev. 1187 (1979); Underwood, The Thumb on the Scales of Justice: Burdens of Persuasion in Criminal Cases, 86 Yale L.J. 1299 (1977); Fed.R.Evid. 301, 302; C.J.S. Evidence §§ 103–157; 29 Am.Jur.2d Evidence §§ 159–248, 1163–1178; Dec.Dig. Evidence ⚖53–98, Trial ⚖205, 234(7), 237, Criminal Law ⚖305–336, 778, 789.

§ 336. The Burdens of Proof: The Burden of Producing Evidence and the Burden of Persuasion

"Proof" is an ambiguous word. We sometimes use it to mean evidence, such as testimony or documents. Sometimes, when we say a thing is "proved" we mean that we are convinced by the data submitted that the alleged fact is true. Thus, "proof" is the end result of conviction or persuasion produced by the evidence. Naturally, the term "burden of proof" shares this ambivalence. The term encompasses two separate burdens of proof.[2] One burden is that of producing evidence, satisfactory to the judge, of a particular fact in issue.[3] The second is the burden of persuading the trier of fact that the alleged fact is true.[4]

The burden of producing evidence on an issue means the liability to an adverse ruling (generally a finding or directed verdict) if evidence on the issue has not been produced. It is usually cast first upon the party who has pleaded the existence of the fact, but as we shall see, the burden may shift to the adversary when the pleader has discharged his initial duty.[5] The burden of producing evidence is a critical mechanism in a jury trial, as it empowers the judge to decide the case without jury consideration when a party fails to sustain the burden.

The burden of persuasion becomes a crucial factor only if the parties have sustained their burdens of producing evidence and only when all of the evidence has been introduced. It does not shift from party to party during the course of the trial simply because it need not be allocated until it is time for a decision. When the time for a decision comes, the jury, if there is one, must be instructed how to decide the issue if their minds are left in doubt. The jury must be told that if the party having the burden of persuasion has failed to satisfy that burden, the issue is to be decided against him. If there is no jury and the judge finds himself in doubt, he too must decide the issue against the party having the burden of persuasion.

What is the significance of the burden of persuasion? Clearly, the principal significance of the burden of persuasion is limited to those cases in which the trier of fact is actually in doubt. Possibly, even in those cases, juries disregard their instructions on this question and judges, trying cases without juries, pay only lip service to it, trusting that the appellate courts will not disturb their findings of fact.[6] Yet, even if an empirical study were conclusively to demonstrate both a regular disregard for jury instructions and a propensity on the part of judges to decide issues of fact without regard to their express statements concerning

§ 336

2. The two meanings of "burden of proof" were pointed out by certain nineteenth century judges, e.g., Shaw, C.J. in Powers v. Russell, 30 Mass. (13 Pick.) 69, 76 (1832), and Brett, M.R., in Abrath v. N.E. Ry. Co., 11 Q.B.D. 440, 452 (1883), but the distinction and its consequences were first emphasized and elaborated by James Bradley Thayer in his Preliminary Treatise on Evidence ch. 9 (1898). Modern cases making the distinction are collected in Dec.Dig. Evidence ☞90.

3. The burden of producing evidence is sometimes termed the "burden of evidence" (C.J.S. Evidence § 103) or "the duty of going forward." Thayer, supra n. 2, at 355.

4. Wigmore terms this "the risk of nonpersuasion." 9 Evidence § 2485 (Chadbourn rev. 1981). Thayer, supra, n. 2 at 353, noting one meaning of "burden of proof," said: ". . . It marks . . . [t]he peculiar duty of him who has the risk of any given proposition on which parties are at issue,—who will lose the case if

he does not make this proposition out, when all has been said and done." Se-Ling Hosiery v. Margulies, 364 Pa. 45, 70 A.2d 854, 856 (1950).

The discussion of burdens of proof in this chapter is directed to the burdens as they are applicable to an entire proceeding. Questions of burden of proof also occur in connection with rulings on the admissibility of individual items of evidence. See § 53 supra.

5. See § 338 infra.

6. In the first edition of this text, Dean McCormick stated:

"In the writer's view [the burden of producing evidence] has far more influence upon the final outcome of cases than does the burden of persuasion, which has become very largely a matter of the technique of the wording of instructions to juries. This wording may be chosen in the particular case as a handle for reversal, but will seldom have been a factor in the jury's decision." § 307, at 634 n. 2.

the allocation of the burden of persuasion, rules allocating and describing that burden could not be discarded by a rational legal system. A risk of nonpersuasion naturally exists any time one person attempts to persuade another to act or not to act. If the other does not change his course of action or nonaction, the person desiring change has, of course, failed.[7] If no burden of persuasion were acknowledged by the law, one possible result would be that the trier of fact would purport to reach no decision at all. The impact of nondecision would then fall by its own weight upon the party, usually the plaintiff, who sought a change in the status quo. Although this is generally where the law would place the burden anyhow, important policy considerations may dictate that the risk should fall on the opposing party.[8]

Another possibility would be that the trier of fact would itself assign a burden of persuasion, describing that burden as it saw fit by substituting its own notions of policy for those now made available to it as a matter of law. Such a result would be most undesirable. Considerations of policy that are sufficient to suggest that in some instances the burden of persuasion be assigned to the party desiring a maintenance of the status quo are strong enough to dictate the need for a consistent rather than a case by case determination of the question. Other policy considerations, such as those that have led the law to require that the prosecution in a criminal case prove the defendant guilty beyond a reasonable doubt,[9] are sufficient to require that the jury be explicitly and clearly instructed as to the measure of the burden as well as its allocation. Although judges

and juries may act contrary to the law despite the best attempts to persuade them to do otherwise, we can at least give them the benefit of thoughtful guidance on the questions of who should bear the burden of persuasion and what the nature of that burden should be. In jury trials, perhaps the problem has not been in the concept of a burden of persuasion, but rather in the confusing jury instructions that abound on this point of law. In nonjury trials, if judges are not in fact following rules of law allocating the burden, the fault may lie not in the concept but with thoughtless judicial and legislative allocations and descriptions of the burden.

 WESTLAW REFERENCES

di burden of proof
di burden of producing evidence
di burden of persuasion

§ 337. Allocating the Burdens of Proof [1]

In most cases, the party who has the burden of pleading a fact will have the burdens of producing evidence and of persuading the jury of its existence as well.[2] The pleadings therefore provide the common guide for apportioning the burdens of proof. For example, in a typical negligence case the plaintiff will have the burdens of (1) pleading the defendant's negligence (2) producing evidence of that negligence and (3) persuading the trier of fact of its existence. The defendant will usually have the same three burdens with regard to the contributory negligence of the plaintiff.[3]

---

7. For a comparison of the burden of persuasion in litigated and in nonlitigated situations see 9 Wigmore, Evidence § 2485 (Chadbourn rev. 1981).

8. See § 337 infra.

9. See § 341 infra.

§ 337

1. James & Hazard, Civil Procedure § 7.8 (2d ed. 1977); 9 Wigmore, Evidence § 2486 (Chadbourn rev. 1981); Cleary, Presuming and Pleading: An Essay on Juristic Immaturity, 12 Stan.L.Rev. 5 (1959); Epstein, Pleading and Presumptions, 40 U.Chi.L.Rev. 556 (1973);

C.J.S. Evidence §§ 103–110, 112–113; Dec.Dig. Evidence ⊜90–97.

2. Reliance Life Insurance Co. v. Burgess, 112 F.2d 234 (8th Cir.1940), cert. denied 311 U.S. 699; Buda v. Fulton, 261 Iowa 981, 157 N.W.2d 336 (1968); In re Ewing's Estate, 234 Iowa 950, 14 N.W.2d 633 (1944); Dec. Dig. Evidence ⊜91.

3. The relationship of the burden of pleading to the burdens of proof raises the question of the consequences of a party mistakenly pleading a fact upon an issue which his adversary had the burden of raising by an affirmative pleading. In the relatively few cases

However, looking for the burden of pleading is not a foolproof guide to the allocation of the burdens of proof. The latter burdens do not invariably follow the pleadings. In a federal court, for example, a defendant may be required to plead contributory negligence as an affirmative defense and yet, where jurisdiction is based upon diversity of citizenship, the applicable substantive law may place the burdens of producing evidence and persuasion with regard to that issue on the plaintiff.[4] More significantly, reference to which party has pleaded a fact is no help at all when the rationale behind the allocation is questioned or in a case of first impression where there are no established pleading rules.

The burdens of pleading and proof with regard to most facts have been and should be assigned to the plaintiff who generally seeks to change the present state of affairs and who therefore naturally should be expected to bear the risk of failure of proof or persuasion. The rules which assign certain facts material to the enforcibility of a claim to the defendant owe their development partly to traditional happen-so and partly to considerations of policy.[5]

The determination of appropriate guidelines for the allocation of the burdens has been somewhat hindered by the judicial repetition of two doctrines, one erroneous and the other meaningless. Statements are found primarily in older cases to the effect that even though a party is required to plead a fact, he is not required to prove that fact if his averment is negative rather than affirmative in form.[6] Such a rule would place an entirely undue emphasis on what is ordinarily purely a matter of choice of forms.[7] Moreover, these statements were probably to be understood as properly applying only to the denial by a party of an opponent's previous pleading, and now one who has the burden of pleading a negative fact as part of his cause of action generally has the accompanying burdens of producing evidence and persuasion.[8] The second misleading doc-

---

dealing with the question, the prevailing view is that a mistake in pleading will not generally affect the allocation of the burdens of proof. For example, the courts have held that plaintiff's unnecessary allegation that he was in the exercise of due care, does not affect the defendant's burdens with regard to contributory negligence. Fitchburg Railway Co. v. Nichols, 85 F. 945 (1st Cir.1898); Bevis v. Vanceburg Telephone Co., 132 Ky. 385, 113 S.W. 811 (1908); Wintrobe v. Hart, 178 Md. 289, 13 A.2d 365 (1940). However, if a trial judge erroneously assigns the burdens of proof to a party who has mistakenly pleaded an issue, a few courts have held that this party has invited the error and has no ground of complaint. Vycas v. St. George Guard Society, 97 Conn. 509, 117 A. 692, 693 (1922) ("A defendant who unnecessarily elaborates a general denial by alleging facts inconsistent with the allegations denied is in no position to complain, in case the court takes him at his word and erroneously instructs the jury as to the burden of proof."); Hatch v. Merigold, 119 Conn. 339, 176 A. 266, 96 A.L.R. 1114, 1116 (1935) (plaintiff by pleading lack of contributory negligence waived benefit of statute placing burden of persuasion on defendant on this issue); Boswell v. Pannell, 107 Tex. 433, 180 S.W. 593, 596 (1915) (defendant by pleading affirmatively voluntarily assumed burden of persuasion and cannot complain when assigned to him). Probably the greater number of cases would reject this qualification. See e.g., Schmitz v. Mathews, 133 Wash. 335, 336, 233 P. 660, 661 (1925) ("not an invitation . . . . to commit error . . . merely an opportunity"). See Comment, 39 Yale L.J. 117 (1929).

4. See Palmer v. Hoffman, 318 U.S. 109 (1943); Sampson v. Channell, 110 F.2d 754 (1st Cir.1940), cert. denied 310 U.S. 650; James & Hazard, supra n. 1, § 3.6 at 104–105, 2A Moore, Federal Practice ¶ 8.27[2] at 1849 (2d Ed.1982).

5. Although the following discussion generally relates to all cases, civil and criminal, there are additional problems in criminal cases, particularly with regard to the allocation of the burden of persuasion. See §§ 341, 346, infra.

6. Walker v. Carpenter, 144 N.C. 674, 676, 57 S.E. 461 (1907) ("The first rule laid down in the books on evidence is to the effect that the issue must be proved by the party who states an affirmative, not by the party who states a negative.") Similar statements can be found in more recent cases. Levine v. Pascal, 94 Ill. App.2d 43, 236 N.E.2d 425 (1968).

7. But see Epstein, Pleading and Presumptions, supra n. 1 at 571–582.

8. Chase Manhattan Bank v. O'Connor, 82 N.J. Super. 382, 197 A.2d 706, 709 (1964) (party alleging nondelivery of stock certificates had the burden of proving that issue); Saari v. George C. Dates and Associates, 311 Mich. 624, 19 N.W.2d 121 (1945) (wrongful discharge: defendant pleaded plaintiff's failure to perform, burden on defendant); Johnson v. Johnson, 229 N.C. 541, 50 S.E.2d 569 (1948) (plaintiff alleging in reply that deed was forged had burden of establishing nonexecution by purported grantor). It is sometimes said that the party pleading a negative need not prove it when the facts are peculiarly within the knowledge

trine is that the party to whose case the element is essential has the burdens of proof. Such a rule simply restates the question.[9]

The actual reasons for the allocation of the burdens may be no more complex than the misleading statements just discussed. The policy of handicapping a disfavored contention [10] probably accounts for the requirement that the defendant generally has all three burdens with regard to such matters as contributory negligence, statute of limitations, and truth in defamation. Convenience in following the natural order of storytelling may account for calling on the defendant to plead and prove those matters which arise after a cause of action has matured, such as payment, release, and accord and satisfaction.

A doctrine often repeated by the courts is that where the facts with regard to an issue lie peculiarly in the knowledge of a party, that party has the burden of proving the issue. Examples are the burdens commonly placed upon the defendant to prove payment, discharge in bankruptcy, and license.[11] This consideration should not be overemphasized. Very often one must plead and prove matters as to which his adversary has superior access to the proof. Nearly all required allegations of the plaintiff in actions for tort or breach of contract relating to the defendant's acts or omissions describe matters peculiarly in the defendant's knowledge. Correspondingly, when the defendant is required to plead contributory negligence, he pleads facts specially known to the plaintiff.

Perhaps a more frequently significant consideration in the fixing of the burdens of proof is the judicial estimate of the probabilities of the situation. The risk of failure of proof may be placed upon the party who contends that the more unusual event has occurred.[12] For example, where a business re-

---

of the other party. Allstate Finance Corp. v. Zimmerman, 330 F.2d 740, 744 (5th Cir.1964). Or more mildly that as to the party pleading a negative the law will be satisfied with a lesser quantum of proof, particularly when the facts are within the knowledge of the adverse party. In re Chicago Railways Co., 175 F.2d 282, 290 (7th Cir.1949), cert. denied 338 U.S. 850. The important consideration in these cases, however, is not which party has the negative, but which party has the knowledge of the facts. Fitzgerald v. Wright, 155 N.J. Super. 494, 382 A.2d 1162 (1978) (decision to allocate to plaintiff burden of proving extent of injury so as to reach no-fault threshold based on superior knowledge of injured party, not statutory terminology). See also Wiles v. Mullinax, 275 N.C. 473, 168 S.E.2d 366 (1969) (plaintiff had the burden of proving the defendant's failure to procure insurance coverage, notwithstanding negative form of the issue; Sharp, J. arguing in dissent that the burden should be placed upon the defendant, not only because of its negative form but also because the defendant had "peculiar knowledge of the fact in issue and therefore the better means of proving it.") See text accompanying n. 11 infra. See also C.J.S. Evidence §§ 105, 112; Dec.Dig. Evidence ⊕92, 93.

9. See Cleary, supra n. 1, at 11.

10. The phrase is borrowed from Clark, Code Pleading § 96 at 610 (2d ed. 1947) where these considerations and the relation of the pleading rules to the burden of proof are lucidly discussed.

For a discussion of a disfavored contention, see In re Regional Rail Reorganization Proceedings, 421 F.Supp. 1061, 1073 (Special Court 1976) (railroad's position with regard to pension plan).

11. See, e.g., Fed.R.Civ.P. 8(c); Cleary, supra n. 1 at 12; cases cited, n. 8, supra. Expanded pretrial discovery would seem to have diminished greatly whatever importance this factor had in allocating the burdens. However, there has been no rush by the courts to reassess allocations between the parties in the light of expanded discovery, perhaps attesting to the fact that exclusive knowledge in one party has seldom been the controlling reason for assigning the burdens of proof.

12. See Cleary, supra n. 1 at 12–13, observing that in assigning the burdens the courts will occasionally consider the probabilities of the situation generally and sometimes will consider the probabilities with reference to litigated cases. "No reason for the shift is apparent, and it may be unconscious. The litigated cases would seem to furnish the more appropriate basis for estimating probabilities."

In Ball, The Moment of Truth: Probability Theory and Standards of Proof, 14 Vand.L.Rev. 807, 817–818 (1961) the author questions the use of probabilities to allocate the burden of persuasion. He suggests that if the burden is assigned to the party whose case depends upon the happening of the least likely event the probabilities are really counted against him twice—once in the jury's own initial assessment of the probabilities which is likely to be similar to that made by the courts and once in the assignment of the burden of persuasion. A similar point is made with regard to the use of presumptions having their basis in probability in Laughlin, In Support of the Thayer Theory of Presumptions, 52 Mich.L.Rev. 195, 212 (1953).

See also General Motors Corp. v. Toyota Motor Co., 467 F.Supp. 1142, 1173 (S.D.Ohio 1979), reversed in

lationship exists, it is unlikely that services will be performed gratuitously. The burden of proving a gift is therefore placed upon the one who claims it. Where services are performed for a member of the family, a gift is much more likely and the burden of proof is placed on the party claiming the right to be paid.[13]

In allocating the burdens, courts consistently attempt to distinguish between the constituent elements of a promise or of a statutory command, which must be proved by the party who relies on the contract or statute, and matters of exception, which must be proved by his adversary.[14] Often the result of this approach is an arbitrary allocation of the burdens, as the statutory language may be due to a mere casual choice of form by the draftsman. However, the distinction may be a valid one in some instances, particularly when the exceptions to

a statute or promise are numerous. If that is the case, fairness usually requires that the adversary give notice of the particular exception upon which he relies and therefore that he bear the burden of pleading. The burdens of proof will not always follow the burden of pleading in these cases.[15] However, exceptions generally point to exceptional situations. If proof of the facts is inaccessible or not persuasive, it is usually fairer to act as if the exceptional situation did not exist and therefore to place the burden of proof and persuasion on the party claiming its existence.[16]

As has been stated, the burdens of producing evidence and of persuasion with regard to any given issue are both generally allocated to the same party. Usually each is assigned but once in the course of the litigation and a safe prediction of that assignment can be made at the pleading stage. Howev-

part on other grounds 667 F.2d 504 (6th Cir.1981), cert. denied 102 S.Ct. 1994.

13. See James & Hazard, supra n. 1 at 252.

14. With regard to contracts, see Corbin, Contracts § 751 (1960); 5 Williston, Contracts § 674 (1961). With regard to statutes, see Annot. 130 A.L.R. 440. On the question generally see, Cleary, supra note 1 at 8–10; Stone, Burden of Proof and the Judicial Process, 60 L.Q.Rev. 262 (1944).

The operation of the distinction in insurance contracts may be illustrated as follows: In an action on a life insurance policy with an exception for death by suicide the defendant has all of the burdens on the issue of suicide. But in a suit on an accident policy, or on the double indemnity provision of a life policy, since suicide is not an accident, the plaintiff must plead accident and, at least tentatively, will have both burdens of proof on the issue.

Schleunes v. American Casualty Co., 528 F.2d 634 (5th Cir.1976) (accidental death benefits); Blythe v. Kanawha Insurance Co., 279 F.Supp. 8 (W.D.N.C.1968) (double indemnity provision). See also, Note, 46 Colum.L.Rev. 802, 810 (1946). The allocation of the burdens of proof to the plaintiff in an accident policy or double indemnity provision case may be only tentative due to the operation of a presumption against suicide. See §§ 343, 344, infra.

15. An illustration of a divergence between the burdens of pleading and proof in an analogous situation is the treatment of conditions precedent in contracts, particularly in insurance contracts, by most courts. For example, in a federal court the defendant will be required to plead the nonoccurrence of a particular condition precedent [Fed.R.Civ.P. 9(c)] but he may not have the burdens of proof with regard to that issue. See 2A

Moore, Federal Practice ¶ 9.04 at 9–42 (2d ed. 1982); 5 Williston, Contracts, § 674 at 181 (1961).

16. This consideration, of course, is simply a specific application of the use of an estimate of the probabilities to fix the burdens. In Stone, supra, n. 14 the learned writer examines the opinions in Joseph Constantine Steamship Ltd. v. Imperial Smelting Corp., Ltd., [1942] A.C. 154 (H.L.) which determined the novel question whether upon the plea of frustration in an action on a contract, the defendant or the plaintiff has the burdens of producing evidence and of persuasion on the issue whether the frustration was contributed to by the fault of the defendant. The opinions in placing the burdens upon the plaintiff stress the formal distinction between an essential element of the defense and an exception to its operation, and purport to reach their conclusions mainly upon definitions, logic, and analogy. The author urges that as to this new question, the judges might more fruitfully have grounded their decision upon considerations of justice and policy, such as the following: "Let it be assumed then that in the great majority of frustration cases no fault of the parties was operative; and let it be assumed that in these cases the impossibility of proof mentioned by the lords is present. A rule requiring the defendant pleading frustration to negative fault will then *ex hypothesi* do injustice to the great majority of defendants. While on the other hand, a rule requiring the plaintiff to prove fault will *ex hypothesi* do injustice to only a small minority of plaintiffs." (p. 278).

See Northwestern Mutual Life Insurance Co. v. Linard, 498 F.2d 556 (2d Cir.1974), for discussion of allocation of burdens in actions on insurance policies and, in particular, exploration of difference between arson under fire policy and scuttling of ship under marine policy.

er, the initial allocation of the burden of producing evidence may not always be final.
The shifting nature of that burden may
cause both parties to have the burden with
regard to the same issue at different points
in the trial.[17] Similarly, although the burden
of persuasion is assigned only once—when it
is time for a decision—a prediction of the allocation of that burden, based upon the
pleadings, may have to be revised when evidence is introduced at trial.[18] Policy considerations similar to those that govern the initial allocation of the burden of producing
evidence and tentatively fix the burden of
persuasion govern the ultimate assignment
of those burdens as well.[19]

In summary, there is no key principle governing the apportionment of the burdens of
proof. Their allocation, either initially or ultimately, will depend upon the weight that is
given to any one or more of several factors,
including: (1) the natural tendency to place
the burdens on the party desiring change, (2)
special policy considerations such as those

disfavoring certain defenses, (3) convenience, (4) fairness, and (5) the judicial estimate of the probabilities.[20]

**WESTLAW
REFERENCES**

synopsis,digest(burden /10 gift)
synopsis(shift! /s burden* /4 prov*** proof produc!
 persua!)

§ 338. Satisfying the Burden of Pro-
ducing Evidence

Let us suppose that the plaintiff, claiming
an estate in land for John Smith's life, had
the burden of pleading, and has pleaded,
that John Smith was alive at the time the action was brought. He seeks to fulfill the
burden of producing evidence of this fact.

To do this he may offer *direct* evidence,
e.g., of witness Jones, who saw Smith alive
in the clerk's office when the complaint in
the action was filed. From this the inference of the truth of the fact to be proved de-

---

17. See § 338 infra.

18. See § 344 infra.

19. See § 343 infra.

20. Declaratory judgment actions provide an excellent example of the problems of allocating the burdens
of proof. Where the plaintiff seeks a declaratory judgment as a basis for some further affirmative claim
against the defendant, there is no special problem; the
burdens will be allocated as usual, with the major
share going to the plaintiff. Jerry Vogel Music Co. v.
Forster Music Publisher, 147 F.2d 614 (2d Cir.1945),
cert. denied 325 U.S. 880 (suit for declaration that
plaintiff was owner of copyrighted song; plaintiff had
burden to establish ownership and defendant to establish defense of joint ownership); McNally v. Moser, 210
Md.App. 127, 122 A.2d 555, 60 A.L.R.2d 388 (1956) (defendant landlord claiming illegal use of leased premises
had both the burden of producing evidence and the burden of persuasion on the question). But when the
traditional positions of plaintiff and defendant are
transposed, the courts have had considerable difficulty
in determining the allocation of the burdens. In these
cases, the competing policies discussed in this section
clearly emerge. For example, some courts have held
that when an insurance company sues for a declaration
of nonliability the defendant insured should have the
burden on the issues on which he would bear the burden had he sued to establish his rights under the policy. The leading case is Travelers Insurance Co. v.
Greenough, 88 N.H. 391, 190 A. 129 (1937), where the
court stated that a contrary conclusion "would place
the plaintiff in a position of undue disadvantage." See

also Preferred Accident Insurance Co. v. Grasso, 186
F.2d 987 (2d Cir.1951) (opinion by Clark, J.) Accord,
Utah Farm Business Insurance Co. v. Dairyland Insurance Co., 634 F.2d 1326 (10th Cir.1980); Fireman's
Fund Insurance Co. v. Videfreeze Corp., 540 F.2d 1171
(3d Cir.1976), cert. denied 429 U.S. 1053. Other courts
have seen no such disadvantage and hold that the burdens should rest on the party bringing the suit. Reliance Life Insurance Co. v. Burgess, 112 F.2d 234
(1940), cert. denied 311 U.S. 699 (Sanborn, J. dissenting
on this question); First National Bank of Or. v. Mala-
dy, 242 Or. 353, 408 P.2d 724 (1965) (strong dissent on
this question by Perry, J.). The competing policies are
also reflected in Professor Moore's discussion of this
problem, 6A Moore, Federal Practice ¶ 57.31[2] at
57–266 (2d ed. 1982). He argues that the doctrine of
the *Greenough* case is "unwise in its own context," in
that it is "reasonable and fair" for the plaintiff insurer
to bear the burdens in such a case. He takes a different view, however, of the burdens in an action by an
alleged infringer for a declaration of noninfringement
or invalidity of defendant's patent, copyright, or trademark. Professor Moore bases his argument on the relevant considerations that it may be difficult for the accused infringer to prove that his activities have in no
way infringed the defendant's rights and that in the
vast majority of such cases, the basis for the declaratory action is an extrajudicial charge of infringement
"which the defendant has made and nobody knows better than he what lies behind his charge." Id. at
57–269. See generally on these questions, Annot., 23
A.L.R.2d 1243; Dec.Dig. Declaratory Judgment
⟐341–343.

pends only upon the truthfulness of Jones. Or, he may offer *circumstantial* evidence, which requires a weighing of probabilities as to matters other than merely the truthfulness of the witness. For example, he may secure the testimony of Jones that Jones received a letter in the mail which was signed "John Smith" one month before the action was brought and that he recognized the signature as Smith's. Patently in this latter case, the tribunal may be satisfied that Jones is speaking the truth, and yet the tribunal may decline to infer the fact of Smith's being alive when the action began.

How strongly persuasive must the offered evidence be to satisfy the burden? A "scintilla" of evidence will not suffice.[1] The evidence must be such that a reasonable man could draw from it the inference of the existence of the particular fact to be proved or, as put conversely by one federal court, "if there is substantial evidence opposed to the [motion for directed verdict], that is evidence of such quality and weight that reasonable and fair-minded men in the exercise of impartial judgment might reach different conclusions, the [motion] should be denied."[2]

One problem that has troubled the courts is whether the test for the granting of a di-

rected verdict should vary, depending upon the required measure of persuasion if the case goes to the jury. For example in a criminal case where the prosecution must persuade the jury beyond a reasonable doubt,[3] should the test for a directed verdict be whether the evidence could satisfy reasonable men beyond a reasonable doubt? Some courts have said no, perhaps believing with Judge Learned Hand that, although the gravity of the consequences often makes judges more exacting in criminal cases, the line between proof that should satisfy reasonable men and the evidence that should satisfy reasonable men beyond a reasonable doubt is, in the long run, "too thin for day to day use."[4]

However, most courts applied the stricter test.[5] A clear trend toward universal adoption of the stricter test[6] may have been effectively solidified into a constitutional dictate by the United States Supreme Court in 1979. In Jackson v. Virginia,[7] the Court held that a federal court reviewing a state court conviction on a *habeas corpus* petition must determine whether a rational factfinder could have found the petitioners guilty beyond a reasonable doubt. Argua-

§ 338

1. See James & Hazard, Civil Procedure § 7.11 at 272 (2d ed. 1977) where the authors refer to the "judicial legend" that there once was a "scintilla rule" under which an adverse verdict could be directed only when there was literally no evidence and state that "if there ever was such a notion all that remains of it today is its well nigh universal repudiation." See also Dec.Dig. Trial ☞139(1). The above cited section of the James & Hazard text contains a full discussion of the question of the sufficiency of evidence to withstand a motion for directed verdict. See also 9 Wigmore, Evidence § 2494 (Chadbourn rev. 1981).

2. Boeing Co. v. Shipman, 411 F.2d 365, 374 (5th Cir.1969). The above quoted statement refers also to motions for judgment notwithstanding the verdict. The tests are usually the same. See 5A Moore, Federal Practice ¶ 50.07(2) (2d ed. 1982).

Because the ruling that a party has not satisfied his burden of producing evidence precludes a jury determination of the merits of the case, some courts, particularly federal courts, have been plagued by constitutional worries in formulating tests for the granting of directed verdicts. For an excellent discussion of the directed verdict in the federal courts, see Cooper, Direc-

tions for Directed Verdicts: A Compass for Federal Courts, 55 Minn.L.Rev. 903 (1971).

3. See § 341 infra.

4. United States v. Feinberg, 140 F.2d 592, 594 (2d Cir.1944), cert. denied 322 U.S. 726. See also Hays v. United States, 231 F. 106 (8th Cir.1916), affirmed sub nom. Caminetti v. United States, 242 U.S. 470 (1916); State v. Nutley, 24 Wis.2d 527, 129 N.W.2d 155, 163 (1964), cert. denied 380 U.S. 918. This approach, of course, leaves the beyond-a-reasonable-doubt standard as a test to be applied by the jury.

5. Riggs v. United States, 280 F.2d 949 (5th Cir. 1960); Curley v. United States, 160 F.2d 229 (D.C.Cir. 1947), cert. denied 331 U.S. 837; State v. Rocker, 52 Hawaii 336, 475 P.2d 684 (1970).

6. Even in Judge Hand's own circuit, his "single test" rule was replaced by a test requiring that the evidence be such as could satisfy reasonable men beyond a reasonable doubt. United States v. Taylor, 464 F.2d 240 (2d Cir.1972). See also State v. Stevens, 26 Wis.2d 451, 132 N.W.2d 502 (1965).

7. 443 U.S. 307 (1979), rehearing denied 444 U.S. 890.

bly no trial judge should apply a lesser standard on a motion for a directed verdict.[8]

Generally no difficulty occurs where the evidence is direct. Except in rare cases,[9] it is sufficient, though given by one witness only, however negligible a human being he may be. But if the evidence is circumstantial, forensic disputes often arise as to its sufficiency to warrant a jury to draw the desired inference. In fact, in few areas of the law have so many words been spoken by the courts with so little conviction. One test frequently expounded in criminal cases is that where the prosecution relies upon circumstantial evidence, the evidence must be so conclusive as to exclude any other reasonable inference inconsistent therewith.[10] The test is accurate enough in criminal cases, but adds little at least to the stricter test for criminal cases discussed above. A similar formula is sometimes expounded in civil cases [11] but seems misplaced in civil litigation. It leaves little for the jury and far exceeds what is needed to prevent verdicts based upon speculation and conjecture. Courts rejecting the formula in civil cases have stated that the burden of producing evidence is satisfied, even by circumstantial evidence, if "there be sufficient facts for the jury to say reasonably that the preponderance favors liability." [12]

Other tests and other phrasings of the tests discussed here are myriad,[13] but irrespective of the test articulated, in the last analysis the judge's ruling must necessarily rest on his individual opinion, formed in the light of his own common sense and experience, as to the limits of reasonable inference from the facts proven. However, certain situations recur and give rise repeatedly to litigation, and a given judge, in his desire for consistency and the consequent saving of time and mental travail, will rule alike whenever the same situation is proved and its sufficiency to warrant a certain inference is questioned. Other judges follow suit and a standardized practice ripening into a rule of law results. Most of these rules are positive rather than negative. They announce that certain types of fact-groups are sufficient to enable the person who has the first duty to go forward with evidence to fulfill that burden, i.e., they enable him to rest after proving them without being subject to the penalty of an adverse ruling.

Suppose the one who had the initial burden of offering evidence in support of the alleged fact, on pain of an adverse ruling, does

---

8. For examples of state courts reaching this conclusion, see People v. Hampton, 407 Mich. 354, 285 N.W.2d 284 (1979), cert. denied 449 U.S. 885; State v. Hudson, 277 S.C. 200, 284 S.E.2d 773 (1981). But see Norris v. State, ___ Ind. ___, 419 N.E.2d 129 (1981) (court rejects "rational trier of fact" standard enunciated in *Jackson*). See also discussion in Brandis, North Carolina Evidence (2d Ed.1982) § 210 at 154.

9. In extreme circumstances, such as where a witness's testimony is flatly contradicted by indisputable physical facts or laws of nature, his testimony may be disregarded. Scott v. Hansen, 228 Iowa 37, 289 N.W. 710 (1940). In a few other instances, such as where a defendant is charged with perjury, the law imposes an artificial requirement of corroboration. See James & Hazard, supra n. 1 at 270–271.

10. State v. Love, 106 Ariz. 215, 474 P.2d 806 (1970); People v. Branion, 47 Ill.2d 70, 265 N.E.2d 1 (1970), cert. denied 403 U.S. 907; Dec.Dig. Criminal Law ⬤552(3). In Holland v. United States, 348 U.S. 121 (1954), the Court held that the trial court did not err in refusing to instruct the jury in these terms. Although this holding would not seem to compel the rejection of this language as a directed verdict test, most federal circuits have so held. E.g., United States v. Thomas,

303 F.2d 561 (6th Cir.1962); United States v. Hamrick, 293 F.2d 468 (4th Cir.1961). Contra, Battles v. United States, 388 F.2d 799 (5th Cir.1968).

11. Bowers v. Maire, 179 Neb. 239, 137 N.W.2d 796 (1965); Schmidt v. Pioneer United Dairies, 60 Wn.2d 271, 373 P.2d 764 (1962). See also Burns, Weighing Circumstantial Evidence, 2 S.Dak.L.Rev. 36 (1957).

12. Smith v. Bell Telephone Co., 397 Pa. 134, 153 A.2d 477 (1959). See also Rumsey v. Great Atlantic & Pacific Tea Co., 408 F.2d 89 (3d Cir.1969); Comment, 12 Vill.L.Rev. 326 (1967).

13. A frequently stated corollary to the rules concerning the sufficiency of circumstantial evidence is that one circumstantial inference may not be based upon another. See cases collected in Annot., 5 A.L.R.3d 100. Despite its frequent repetition by some courts, such a rule can actually amount to nothing more than a makeweight argument to be used when a court believes that the inferences sought to be drawn are too remote or speculative. See Shutt v. State, 233 Ind. 169, 117 N.E.2d 892 (1954). Any other interpretation of the rule would severely impede the ordinary and valid uses of circumstantial evidence. See generally 1 Wigmore, Evidence § 41 (3d ed. 1940).

produce evidence barely sufficient to satisfy that burden, so that the judge can just say, "A reasonable jury *could* infer that the fact is as alleged, from the circumstances proved." If the proponent then rests, what is the situation? Has the duty of going forward shifted to the adversary? Not if we define that duty as the liability to a peremptory adverse ruling on failing to give evidence, for if at this juncture the original proponent rests and the adversary offers no proof, the proponent will not be entitled to the direction of a verdict in his favor on the issue, but rather the court will leave the issue to the decision of the jury. But it is frequently said that in this situation the duty of going forward has shifted to the adversary,[14] and this is unobjectionable [15] if we bear in mind that the penalty for silence is very different here from that which was applied to the original proponent. If he had remained silent at the outset he would irrevocably have lost the case on this issue, but the only penalty now applied to his adversary is the risk, if he remains silent, of the jury's finding against him, though it may find for him. Theoretically he may have this risk still, even after he has offered evidence in rebuttal. It is simpler to limit "duty of going forward" to the liability, on resting, to an adverse ruling, and to regard the stage just discussed (where the situation is that if both parties rest, the issue will be left to the jury) as one in which neither party has any duty of going forward.[16]

In the situation just discussed, the party who first had the duty, i.e., the necessity, of giving proof, has produced evidence which requires the judge to permit the jury to infer, as it chooses, that the fact alleged is or is not true. It is a permitted, but not a compulsory, inference. Is it possible for the original proponent of evidence to carry his

proof to the stage where if he rests, he will be entitled to a directed verdict, or its equivalent, on the issue? Undoubtedly, with a qualification to be noted, this is possible, and when it occurs there is a shifting to the adversary of the duty of going forward with the evidence, in the strictest sense. Such a ruling means that in the judge's view the proponent has not merely offered evidence from which reasonable men could draw the inference of the truth of the fact alleged, but evidence from which (in the absence of evidence from the adversary) reasonable men could not help but draw this inference. Thus, as long ago as 1770, Lord Mansfield told the jury that upon the issue of whether defendant had published a libel, proof of a sale of the book in defendant's shop was, being unrebutted, "conclusive." [17]

In the case first supposed at the beginning of this section, if the plaintiff brought forward the *direct* evidence of Jones that Smith was alive when the complaint was filed, and there is no contrary evidence at all, or if he brings forward circumstantial evidence (that is, evidence that Smith was seen alive in perfect health 10 minutes before the complaint was filed) which is, in the absence of contrary circumstances, irresistibly convincing, the jury should not be left to refuse to draw the only rational inference.

If we do not permit the jury to draw an inference from insufficient data, as where the proponent has failed to sustain his initial duty of producing evidence, we should not permit the jury to act irrationally by rejecting compelling evidence. Here again the ruling, from repeated occurrence of similar facts, may become a standardized one. However, the statement that one who has the duty of going forward can go forward far enough not merely to escape an adverse peremptory ruling himself, but to subject his

14.   Speas v. Merchants Bank & Trust Co., 188 N.C. 524, 530, 125 S.E. 398, 401 (1924); C.J.S. Evidence § 110 at 187.

15.   But see Stansbury, North Carolina Evidence § 203 (1963) at 526 n. 27 where the author refers to such a characterization as "misleading at least." See also Brandis, supra n. 8, § 203 at 137 n. 27.

16.   For a judicial discussion of the example given in this paragraph, see Pennsylvania v. United States, 361 F.Supp. 208 (M.D.Pa.1973), affirmed 414 U.S. 1017.

17.   Rex v. Almon, 5 Burr. 2686, 98 Eng.Rep. 411 (K.B.1770).

opponent to one if the latter declines to take up the gage by producing evidence, has the following qualification. Obviously if the testimony were conflicting as to the truth of the facts from which the inference of the fact in issue is desired to be drawn, and the judge believes the inference (conceding the truth of the premise) is irresistible to rational minds, he can only make a conditional peremptory ruling. He directs the jury, if you believe the evidence that fact A is so then you must find fact B, the fact in issue. In some jurisdictions, if the party seeking the ruling has the burden of persuasion on the issue, as assigned on the basis of the pleadings, he can only get a conditional ruling, though his witnesses are undisputed and unimpeached.[18] But, in either event, if the inference is overwhelming, the jury is instructed not to cogitate over that, but only over the truthfulness of those who testify to the basic data.

We have seen something of the mechanics of the process of "proceeding" or "going forward" with evidence, viewed from the point of view of the *first* party who is stimulated to produce proof under threat of a ruling foreclosing a finding in his favor. He may in respect to a particular issue pass through three states of judicial hospitality: (a) where if he stops he will be thrown out of court; (b) where if he stops and his adversary does nothing, his reception will be left to the jury; and (c) where if he stops and his adversary does nothing, his victory (so far as it depends on having the inference he desires drawn) is at once proclaimed. When-

ever the first producer has presented evidence sufficient to get him to the third stage and the burden of producing evidence can truly be said to have shifted, his adversary may in turn pass through the same three stages. His evidence again may be (a) insufficient to warrant a finding in his favor, (b) sufficient to warrant a finding, or (c) irresistible, if unrebutted.

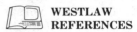 **WESTLAW REFERENCES**

di scintilla

scintilla /s suffic! insufficient

di burden of going forward

di directed verdict

§ 339. Satisfying the Burden of Persuasion: (a) The Measure of Persuasion in Civil Cases Generally [1]

According to the customary formulas a party who has the burden of persuasion of a fact must prove it in criminal prosecutions "beyond a reasonable doubt," [2] in certain exceptional controversies in civil cases, "by clear, strong and convincing evidence," [3] but on the general run of issues in civil cases "by a preponderance of evidence." [4] The "reasonable doubt" formula points to what we are really concerned with, the state of the jury's mind, whereas the other two divert attention to the evidence, which is a step removed, being the instrument by which the jury's mind is influenced.[5] These latter phrases, consequently, are awkward

---

18. E.g., Alexander v. Tingle, 181 Md. 464, 30 A.2d 737 (1943); Hoerath v. Sloan's Moving & Storage Co., 305 S.W.2d 418 (Mo.1957). Contra, Colthurst v. Lake View State Bank of Chicago, 18 F.2d 875 (C.C.A.Iowa 1927). See generally cases cited in Annot., 62 A.L.R.2d 1191.

§ 339

1. 9 Wigmore, Evidence § 2498 (Chadbourn rev. 1981); Morgan, Basic Problems of Evidence 21–26 (1962); Morgan, Some Problems of Proof 81–86 (1956); Ball, The Moment of Truth: Probability Theory and Standards of Proof, 14 Vand.L.Rev. 807 (1961); McBaine, Burden of Proof: Degrees of Belief, 32 Calif. L.Rev. 242 (1944); Winter, The Jury and the Risk of

Nonpersuasion, 5 Law & Society Rev. 335 (1971); Annot., 93 A.L.R. 155; C.J.S. Evidence §§ 1020–1022; Dec. Dig. Evidence ☜598, Trial ☜237.

2. See § 341 infra.

3. See § 340 infra.

4. In McBaine, supra n. 1 at 246, Prof. McBaine cogently suggests that these formulas are equivalent to statements that the trier must find that the fact is (a) almost certainly true, (b) highly probably true, and (c) probably true.

5. See Morgan, Basic Problems of Evidence, supra n. 1 at 23.

vehicles for expressing the degree of the jury's belief.[6]

What is the most acceptable meaning of the phrase, proof by a preponderance, or greater weight, of the evidence? Certainly the phrase does not mean simple volume of evidence or number of witnesses.[7] One definition is that evidence preponderates when it is more convincing to the trier than the opposing evidence. This is a simple common-sense explanation which will be understood by jurors and could hardly be misleading in the ordinary case. It may be objected, however, that it is misleading in a situation where, though one side's evidence is more convincing than the other's, the jury is still left in doubt as to the truth of the matter.[8] Compelling a decision in favor of a party who has introduced evidence that is simply better than that of his adversary would not be objectionable if we hypothesize jurors who bring none of their own experience to the trial and who thus view the evidence in a vacuum. Of course, no such case could exist.[9] We expect and encourage jurors to use their own experience to help them reach a decision, particularly in judging the credibility of witnesses.[10] That experience may tell them, for example, that although the plaintiff has introduced evidence and the defendant has offered nothing in opposition, it is still unlikely that the events occurred as contended by the plaintiff. Thus, it is entirely consistent for a court to hold that a party's evidence is sufficient to withstand a motion for directed verdict and yet to uphold a verdict for his adversary.[11]

The most acceptable meaning to be given to the expression, proof by a preponderance, seems to be proof which leads the jury to find that the existence of the contested fact is more probable than its nonexistence.[12] Thus the preponderance of evidence becomes the trier's belief in the preponderance of probability. Some courts have boldly accepted this view.[13]

---

6. This may be evidenced by a study which showed that the jurors responding to a questionnaire asking them to express their beliefs in terms of numerical probabilities had a significantly different understanding of the phrase "by a preponderance of evidence" than did judges responding to the same questionnaire. The jurors thought the requirement called for a far greater showing of probability than did the judges. Simon, Quantifying Burdens of Proof, 5 Law & Society Rev. 319, 325 (1971). Similarly, in 1937, 843 jurors responded to a questionnaire asking the question, "What propositions of law were most difficult to understand?" Highest on the list was "preponderance of the evidence," named by 232 jurors. "Proximate cause" was second with 203. Trial by Jury (report of a conference), 11 U.Cin.L.Rev. 119, 192 n. 18 (1937).

7. Courts often specifically inform the jury that the number of witnesses is not conclusive. Illinois Pattern Jury Instruction (Civil) 2.07 (1971); South Dakota Pattern Jury Instruction (Civil) 2.07 (1968); Livingston v. Schreckengost, 255 Iowa 1102, 125 N.W.2d 126, 131 (1963).

8. See discussion by Wolfe, J., in McDonald v. Union Pacific Railroad Co., 109 Utah 493, 167 P.2d 685, 689 (1946) (". . . I can conceive of a case where the jury might be more convinced that the evidence of one side is nearer the truth than that of the other side and yet not feel that the evidence satisfied them as to the right to recover.") See also McBaine, supra n. 1 at 248; Trickett, Preponderance of Evidence and Reasonable Doubt, 10 The Forum, Dickinson School of Law 75, 77 (1906) quoted 9 Wigmore, Evidence § 2498 at 326.

9. See Winter, supra n. 1 at 339.

10. See, e.g., Illinois Pattern Jury Instructions (Civil) 1.04, 2.01 (1971). See also Ball, supra n. 1 at 829, where the author suggests that "instructions which tell the jury that they shall use what they know in common as men, should be juxtaposed with the direction to find 'from the evidence.'"

11. See Morgan, Basic Problems of Evidence, supra n. 1 at 22.

12. See Model Code of Evidence Rule 1(3): "'Burden of persuasion of a fact' means the burden which is discharged when the tribunal which is to determine the existence or non-existence of the fact is persuaded by sufficient evidence to find that the fact exists;" 1(5): "'Finding a fact' means determining that its existence is more probable than its non-existence . . ." See also Morgan, Some Problems of Proof, supra n. 1 at 84–85.

13. E.g., Murphy v. Waterhouse, 113 Cal. 467, 45 P. 866 (1896) (error to charge that jury must be "convinced"; "preponderance of probability" is sufficient); Norton v. Futrell, 149 Cal.App.2d 586, 308 P.2d 887, 891 (1957) ("The term 'probability' denotes an element of doubt or uncertainty and recognizes that where there are two choices, it is not necessary that the jury be absolutely certain or doubtless, but that it is sufficient if the choice selected is more probable than the choice rejected."); Beckwith v. Town of Stratford, 129 Conn. 506, 29 A.2d 775 (1942) (standard in civil cases is proof which produces a reasonable belief of probability of the existence of the material facts); Moffie v. Slawsby, 77 N.H. 555, 94 A. 193 (1915) (a finding that the

Other courts have been shocked at the suggestion that a verdict, a truth-finding, should be based on nothing stonger than an estimate of probabilities. They require that the trier must have an "actual belief" in, or be "convinced of" the truth of the fact by this "preponderance of evidence." [14] Does this mean that they must believe that it is certainly true? Hardly, since it is apparent that an investigation by fallible men based upon the testimony of other men, with all their defects of veracity, memory, and communication, cannot yield certainty. Does it mean a kind of mystical "hunch" that the fact must be true? This would hardly be a rational requirement. What it would most naturally be understood to mean by the jury (in the unlikely event that it should carry analysis so far) is that it must be persuaded that the truth of the fact is not merely more probable than not, but highly probable. This is more stringent than our tradition or the needs of justice warrant, and seems equivalent to the standard of "clear, strong and convincing proof," hitherto thought to be appropriate only in exceptional cases.[15]

Much of the time spent in the appellate courts over the metaphysics of "preponderance" has been wasted because of the courts' insistence upon the cabalistic word. This bemusement with word-magic is particularly apparent in the decisions dealing with the use of the word "satisfaction" or its derivatives in referring to the effect of the evidence on the jury's mind.[16] Some courts, with more logic than realism, have condemned its use as equivalent to proof beyond a reasonable doubt unless qualified by the word "reasonable." [17] Other courts have

transferee probably knew that the note was usurious is a finding that the party having the burden had satisfied the trier of fact); Livanovitch v. Livanovitch, 99 Vt. 327, 328, 131 A. 799 (1926) ("If . . . you are more inclined to believe from the evidence that he did so deliver the bonds . . . even though your belief is only the slightest degree greater than that he did not, your verdict should be for the plaintiff," approved; "a bare preponderance is sufficient though the scales drop but a feather's weight"); Washington Pattern Jury Instructions (Civil) 21.01 (1967) ("When it is said that a party has the burden of proof on any proposition . . . it means that you must be persuaded, considering all the evidence in the case, that the proposition on which he has the burden of proof is more probably true than not true.") See also discussion by Judge Maris in Burch v. Reading Co., 240 F.2d 574 (3d Cir.1957), cert. denied 353 U.S. 965; C.J.S. Evidence § 1021 at 652, n. 99.

Despite the mathematical tone of the words used to describe this standard, any attempt to translate the standard into mathematical terminology (such as through the use of percentages) presents special problems which seem beyond the ken of most lawyers and the needs of the courts. See the interesting discussion in Kaye, The Paradox of the Gatecrasher and Other Stories, 1979 Ariz.St.L.J. 101.

14. Lummus, J. in Sargent v. Massachusetts Accident Co., 307 Mass. 246, 29 N.E.2d 825, 827 (1940) ("It has been held not enough that mathematically the chances somewhat favor a proposition to be proved; for example, the fact that colored automobiles made in the current year outnumbered black ones would not warrant a finding that an undescribed automobile of the current year is colored and not black, nor would the fact that only a minority of men die of cancer warrant a finding that a particular man did not die of cancer. . . . After the evidence has been weighed, that

proposition is proved by a preponderance of the evidence if it is made to appear more likely or probable in the sense that actual belief in its truth, derived from the evidence, exists in the mind or minds of the tribunal notwithstanding any doubts that may still linger there.") See also Lampe v. Franklin American, 339 Mo. 361, 96 S.W.2d 710, 723, 107 A.L.R. 465 (1936) (no error to refuse charge, "If you find and believe that it is more probable," etc., since a verdict must be based on "what the jury finds to be facts rather than what they find to be 'more probable' "); Anderson v. Chicago Brass Co., 127 Wis. 273, 106 N.W. 1077, 1079 (1906) (not only must charge require that party with burden produce evidence of greater convincing power but that "it must be such as to satisfy or convince . . . the jury of the truth of his contention.")

See also Bazemore v. Davis, 394 A.2d 1377 (D.C.App. 1978), where the court perceived a need for more certainty in child custody cases than would result in a correct determination "more often than not." However, the court referred to the value of evidence available in the case as opposed to the applicability of presumptions or standardized inferences.

15. See § 340 infra.

16. See the unbelievable number of decisions on this question in Annot., 147 A.L.R. 380. The volume of cases dealing with the issue has, however, decreased considerably in more recent years. See Dec.Dig. Trial ⟊237(6).

17. Torrey v. Burney, 113 Ala. 496, 21 So. 348, 351 (1897) ("Before it can be said that the mind is 'satisfied' of the truth of a proposition, it must be relieved of all doubt or uncertainty, and this degree of conviction is not required even in criminal cases."); Nelson v. Belcher Lumber Co., 232 Ala. 116, 166 So. 808 (1936) (usual statement, "reasonably satisfies the jury by the evi-

pragmatically, although perhaps reluctantly permitted its use, even without the qualification.[18] Although certainly juries should be clearly and accurately instructed with regard to the question of the measure of persuasion in civil cases, it is hard to believe that variations in language such as those involved in the courts' difficulties with the use of the word "satisfaction" lead to any differences in jurors' attitudes.[19] Thoughtfully drafted pattern jury instructions should prove helpful in reducing unnecessarily spent appellate court time on these questions.[20] Where no pattern instruction is available, however, trial judges would be wise to search for the locally accepted phraseology and to adhere to it religiously.

 WESTLAW REFERENCES

synopsis,digest(preponderance /4 evidence /s likel! probab! believe belief) % topic(110)

---

dence"); Rasp v. Baumbach, 223 S.W.2d 472 (Mo.1949) (the word "reasonable" essential).

18. Netzer v. Northern Pacific Railway Co., 238 Minn. 416, 57 N.W.2d 247 (1953), cert. denied 346 U.S. 831 (not misleading when use is in conjunction with a detailed and correct instruction of fair preponderance of the evidence); McDonald v. Union Pacific Railroad Co., 109 Utah 493, 167 P.2d 685 (1946) (use permitted); Burks v. Webb, 199 Va. 296, 99 S.E.2d 629, 639 (1957) (use was harmless error but phrase "preponderance of the evidence" preferable).

19. Difficulties of language have led some courts to hold that the phrase "preponderance of evidence" is one of common knowledge and that it is not necessary to define it. Brunton v. Stapleton, 65 Colo. 576, 179 P. 815 (1919); Hardee v. York, 262 N.C. 237, 136 S.E.2d 582 (1964) (in the absence of a prayer for special instructions); Annot., 93 A.L.R. 155, 156.

20. See, e.g., Illinois Pattern Jury Instruction (Civil) 21.01 (2d ed. 1971); North Carolina Pattern Instruction 101.10 (1980); Washington Pattern Jury Instruction (Civil) 21.01 (1967). Not all pattern jury instructions on this question are helpful to the jury even though they may withstand appeal. See, e.g., Florida Standard Jury Instruction 3.9 (1967): " 'Greater weight of the evidence' means the more persuasive and convincing force and effect of the entire evidence in the case."

§ 340. Satisfying the Burden of Persuasion: (b) Requirement of Clear and Convincing Proof[1]

While we have seen that the traditional measure of persuasion in civil cases is by a preponderance of evidence,[2] there is a limited range of claims and contentions which the party is required to establish by a more exacting measure of persuasion. The formula varies from state to state, but among the phrases used are the following: "by clear and convincing evidence,"[3] "clear, convincing and satisfactory,"[4] "clear, cogent and convincing,"[5] and "clear, unequivocal, satisfactory and convincing."[6] The phrasing within most jurisdictions has not become as standardized as is the "preponderance" formula, but even here the courts sometimes are surprisingly intolerant of slight variations from the approved expression.[7] No high degree of precision can be attained by these groups of adjectives. It has been persuasively suggested that they could be more simply and intelligibly translated to the jury if they were instructed that they must be

§ 340

1. 9 Wigmore, Evidence § 2498, pp. 329–334 (Chadbourn rev. 1981); C.J.S. Evidence § 1023; 30 Am. Jur.2d Evidence §§ 1166, 1167; Dec.Dig. Trial ☞237(3).

2. See § 339 supra.

3. Murillo v. Hernandez, 79 Ariz. 1, 281 P.2d 786, 791 (1955) (oral trust).

4. In re Williams' Will, 256 Wis. 338, 41 N.W.2d 191 (1950) (mental incapacity and undue influence).

5. Frazier v. Loftin, 200 Ark. 4, 137 S.W.2d 750, 752 (1940) (claim of fraud inducing signing of contract, leases and deed).

6. Capps v. Capps, 110 Utah 468, 175 P.2d 470, 473 (1946) (oral trust).

7. Molyneux v. Twin Falls Canal Co., 54 Idaho 619, 35 P.2d 651, 94 A.L.R. 1264 (1934) ("clear, positive, and unequivocal" imposes too heavy a burden as opposed to "clear and satisfactory" or "clear and convincing"). See also Williams v. Blue Ridge Building & Loan Association, 207 N.C. 362, 177 S.E. 176 (1934), where the court, with perhaps more justification, held that the trial judge had erred in telling the jury that the words "clear, strong and convincing" proof meant that the plaintiffs "must . . . satisfy you to a moral certainty."

persuaded that the truth of the contention is "highly probable." [8]

The requirement of proof more than usually convincing for certain types of contentions seems to have had its origins in the standards prescribed for themselves by the chancellors in determining questions of fact in equity cases.[9] However, it has now been extended to certain types of actions tried before juries, and the chancellors' cautionary maxims are now conveyed to the jury in the form of instructions on the burden of persuasion.[10]

Among the classes of cases to which this special standard of persuasion has been applied are the following: (1) charges of fraud [11] and undue influence,[12] (2) suits on oral contracts to make a will,[13] and suits to establish the terms of a lost will,[14] (3) suits for the specific performance of an oral contract,[15] (4) proceedings to set aside, reform or modify written transactions [16] or official

8. McBaine, Burden of Proof: Degrees of Belief, 32 Calif.L.Rev. 242, 246, 253–254 (1944).

9. See Henkle v. Royal Exchange Assurance Co., 1 Ves.Sen. 317, 319, 27 Eng.Rep. 1055, 1056 (Ch. 1749) (suit to reform insurance policy: relief denied for insufficiency of proofs; Lord Ch. Hardwicke: "There ought to be the strongest proof possible"); Marquis Townshend v. Stangroom, 6 Ves.Jun. 328, 333, 31 Eng.Rep. 1076 (Ch. 1801) (similar); Carpenter v. Providence Washington Insurance Co., 45 U.S. (4 How.) 185, 224 (1846) (suit in equity to require the defendant insurance company to endorse an acknowledgment of notice on the policy; held, claim of fraud fails because such a charge should be strengthened "by very satisfactory auxiliaries though not perhaps by so strong evidence as is necessary in reforming contracts"). American equity cases on the degree of proof necessary in reforming contracts are collected in 3 Pomeroy Equity Jurisprudence § 859a (5th ed., Symons, 1941). In Iowa the requirement of "clear, satisfactory and convincing" proof is limited to cases in equity. Davis v. Davis, 261 Iowa 992, 156 N.W.2d 870 (1968); Jamison v. Jamison, 113 Iowa 720, 84 N.W. 705 (1900).

10. Minton v. Farmville-Woodward Lumber Co., 210 N.C. 422, 187 S.E. 568 (1936) (suit to establish oral trust; facts tried to jury in North Carolina); Kisting v. Westchester Fire Insurance Co., 290 F.Supp. 141 (W.D. Wis.1968), affirmed 416 F.2d 967 (7th Cir.1969) (defense of arson in action on fire insurance policy). Washington Pattern Jury Instructions (Civil) 160.02, 160.03 (1967); Dec.Dig. Trial ⬉237(3). In Texas, however, where, as in North Carolina, the facts in equity as well as law issues are tried to a jury, the "clear and convincing" standard may not be prescribed in the instructions. The trial judge, moreover, may not direct a verdict if he considers the evidence not "clear and convincing," but he may use the test, in appropriate cases, to set aside a verdict. Sanders v. Harder, 148 Tex. 593, 227 S.W.2d 206 (1950), critically noted, 28 Tex.L.Rev. 988 (1950). See also Boenker v. Boenker, 405 S.W.2d 843 (Tex.Civ.App.1966).

11. Holley Coal Co. v. Globe Industrial Co., 186 F.2d 291 (4th Cir.1950) (suit on employees' fidelity bond, defense that plaintiff's officers colluded with embezzlers); Buzard v. Griffin, 89 Ariz. 42, 358 P.2d 155 (1961) (election fraud); Dec.Dig. Fraud ⬉58(1). In some instances the policy of placing such a special burden on one who claims to be the victim of fraud is debatable. See Rice-Stix Dry Goods Co. v. Montgomery,

164 Ark. 161, 261 S.W. 325, 329 (1924), where the court said: "While fraud at law, as well as in equity, is never to be presumed and must be proved, yet in actions at law one who has the burden of proof to establish fraud meets the requirements of the rule when he proves the fraud only by a preponderance of the evidence. The same rule likewise prevails in equity, except in those cases where the rescission, cancellation, or reformation of a writing for fraud of one party and mistake of the other, or mutual mistake, is the relief sought, in which latter case, as we have stated, the proof of fraud or mistake must be clear, unequivocal, and decisive." See also Household Finance Corp. v. Altenberg, 5 Ohio St. 2d 190, 214 N.E.2d 667 (1966) (no special standard in action to recover money, even where fraud is alleged).

12. In re Mazanec's Estate, 204 Minn. 406, 283 N.W. 745, 748 (1939).

13. Lindley v. Lindley, 67 N.M. 439, 356 P.2d 455 (1960). And so of an oral gift asserted after the donor's death. Wyatt v. Moran, 81 R.I. 399, 103 A.2d 801 (1954). Apparently even stronger proof is needed of such claims in Missouri. See St. Louis Union Trust Co. v. Busch, 346 Mo. 1237, 145 S.W.2d 426 (1940) (claim of oral gift; forceful, clear and conclusive testimony which convinces the court beyond a reasonable doubt of its truthfulness).

14. In re Ainscow's Will, 42 Del. 3, 27 A.2d 363, 365 (1942). See also 7 Wigmore, Evidence § 2106 (Chadbourn rev. 1978).

15. Hyder v. Newcomb, 236 Ark. 231, 365 S.W.2d 271, 274 (1963) (evidence of parol contract to convey land must be clear, satisfactory and convincing); Steketee v. Steketee, 317 Mich. 100, 26 N.W.2d 724, 726 (1947) (terms of agreement must be established by convincing proof).

16. Philippine Sugar Estates Development Co. v. Government of Philippine Islands, 247 U.S. 385 (1918) (reformation of written contract for mutual mistake); Newmister v. Carmichael, 29 Wis.2d 573, 139 N.W.2d 572 (1966) (same); Carlisle v. Carlisle, 225 N.C. 462, 35 S.E.2d 418, 421 (1945) (to establish an oral trust in land taken by deed absolute); Gillock v. Holdaway, 379 Ill. 467, 41 N.E.2d 504 (1942) (to show that deed was intended as mortgage); Dec.Dig. Mortgages ⬉38(2). But see, Ward v. Lyman, 108 Vt. 464, 188 A. 892, 893 (1937) ("The jurisdiction of a court of equity to reform a written instrument will be exercised only when the

acts [17] on grounds of fraud, mistake or incompleteness, and (5) miscellaneous types of claims and defenses,[18] varying from state to state, where there is thought to be special danger of deception, or where the court considers that the particular type of claim should be disfavored on policy grounds.[19]

The appellate court, under the classical equity practice, tried the facts *de novo*, upon the deposition testimony in the record, and thus it was called on to apply anew the standard of clear and convincing proof in its study of the evidence. But in the modern system there are usually restrictions upon appellate review of a judge's findings of fact, even in equity issues. Thus, in the federal courts under Rule 52(a) his findings will only be reversed when "clearly erroneous." And in jury-tried cases the verdict will be reviewed only to the extent of determining whether there was evidence from which reasonable men could have found the verdict. Will the appellate court, then, today, if there was substantial evidence from which the judge or jury could have made the findings it did, consider the question whether the evidence met the "clear and convincing" standard, in a case where it applies? On the one side is the argument that the judge or jury, seeing the witnesses, had superior opportunities to assess their convincingness,[20] and on the other the view that rules should be so shaped as to free the courts of last resort to employ most effectively their wisdom and sense of justice.[21]

WESTLAW REFERENCES

di clear and convincing proof

case* action* proceeding* /10 requir! necess! must /4 clear /4 convincing

---

mistake is established by evidence so strong and conclusive as to place it beyond reasonable doubt.")

17. Bernstein v. Bernstein, 398 Ill. 52, 74 N.E.2d 785 (1947) (proof to impeach the correctness of a notary's certificate of acknowledgment of a deed); Nichols v. Sauls' Estate, 250 Miss. 307, 165 So.2d 352 (1964) (same as to acknowledgment of power of attorney).

18. Krisher v. Duff, 331 Mich. 699, 50 N.W.2d 332 (1951) (statutory presumption that member of owner's family was driving it with his consent can be overcome only by testimony that is clear, positive and credible and plaintiff entitled to have jury instructed to that effect: see discussion § 344 n. 39 infra); In re Berge's Estate, 234 Minn. 31, 47 N.W.2d 428 (1951) (to establish oral contract to adopt); Vaux v. Hamilton, 103 N.W.2d 291 (N.D.1960) (negligence action; where agency is denied must be proved by clear, convincing and satisfactory evidence); Marcum v. Zaring, 406 P.2d 970 (Okl. 1965) (invalidity of marriage); Stevenson v. Stein, 412 Pa. 478, 195 A.2d 268 (1963) (to prove adverse possession; "credible, clear and definitive proof"); Wilson v. Wilson, 145 Tex. 607, 201 S.W.2d 226 (1947) (presumption that property acquired during marriage is community property can only be overcome by clear and satisfactory evidence); King v. Prudential Insurance Co., 13 Wn.2d 414, 125 P.2d 282 (1942) (services by daughter in father's shop presumed gratuitous and presumption could not be overcome except by clear and convincing evidence).

19. A few courts have stated that the requirement of a burden of proof greater than a preponderance of the evidence may depend upon the probability of proving the claim and, therefore, if it is unlikely that an allegation can be supported, clear and convincing evidence will be required to prove it. General Motors Corp. v. Toyota Motor Co., 467 F.Supp. 1142, 1173 (S.D.

Ohio 1979), reversed in part on other grounds 667 F.2d 504 (6th Cir.1981), cert. denied 456 U.S. 937. See also Ziegler v. Hustisford Farmer's Mutual Insurance Co., 238 Wis. 238, 298 N.W. 610 (1941) (citing Jones, Commentaries on Evidence (2d Ed.) Vol. 2, p. 1036 § 563). Such a rationale, if carried very far logically, would make it virtually impossible to prove a difficult claim. See also Ball, supra § 339, n. 1.

20. Beeler v. American Trust Co., 24 Cal.2d 1, 147 P.2d 583 (1944) (review of judge's findings); Davis v. Pursel, 55 Colo. 287, 134 P. 107 (1913) (review of findings of judge and jury). In both these cases the lower court found that deeds were intended as mortgages and on appeal it was held that, there being substantial evidence, it was for the trial court alone to decide whether the evidence was clear and convincing. More recent examples are Buck v. Jewett, 170 Cal.App.2d 115, 338 P.2d 507 (1959); Gem-Valley Ranches, Inc. v. Small, 90 Idaho 354, 411 P.2d 943 (1966). See also Dec. Dig. Appeal and Error ⊜1009(1)–(4).

21. See dissenting opinion of Judge Traynor in Beeler v. American Trust Co., supra n. 20; Note, 60 Harv. L.Rev. 111, 118 (1946). Examples of cases where the appellate courts have imposed their own measure of "clear and convincing proof" to reverse the finding below include: Equitable Life Assurance Society v. Aaron, 108 F.2d 777 (6th Cir.1940) (reformation of policy); Langford v. Sigmon, 292 Ky. 650, 167 S.W.2d 820 (1943) (oral trust in land conveyed); Hurst v. Stowers, 399 P.2d 477 (Okl.1965) (adverse possession). The problem discussed in the text is quite similar to the question of the relationship of the measure of proof to the burden of producing evidence, discussed above, § 338, text accompanying nn. 9–12. See also, Morgan, Basic Problems of Evidence 24–26 (1962).

§ 341. Satisfying the Burden of Persuasion: (c) Proof Beyond a Reasonable Doubt [1]

As we have seen with reference to civil cases, a lawsuit is essentially a search for probabilities. A margin of error must be anticipated in any such search. Mistakes will be made and in a civil case a mistaken judgment for the plaintiff is no worse than a mistaken judgment for the defendant. However, this is not the case in a criminal action. Society has judged that it is significantly worse for an innocent man to be found guilty of a crime than for a guilty man to go free. The consequences to the life, liberty, and good name of the accused from an erroneous conviction of a crime are usually more serious than the effects of an erroneous judgment in a civil case. Therefore, as stated by the Supreme Court in recognizing the inevitability of error even in criminal cases, "[w]here one party has at stake an interest of transcending value—as a criminal defendant his liberty—this margin of error is re-

duced as to him by the process of placing on the other party the burden . . . of persuading the factfinder at the conclusion of the trial of his guilt beyond a reasonable doubt." [2] In so doing, the courts may have increased the total number of mistaken decisions in criminal cases, but with the worthy goal of decreasing the number of one kind of mistake—conviction of the innocent. [3]

The demand for a higher degree of persuasion in criminal cases was recurrently expressed from ancient times, [4] but its crystallization into the formula "beyond a reasonable doubt" seems to have occurred as late as 1798. [5] It is now accepted in common law jurisdictions as the measure of persuasion by which the prosecution must convince the trier of all the essential elements of guilt. In 1970, the Supreme Court explicitly held that the due process clause "protects the accused against conviction except upon proof beyond a reasonable doubt of every fact necessary to constitute the crime with which he is charged." [6]

§ 341

1. 9 Wigmore, Evidence § 2497 (Chadbourn rev. 1981); Morgan, Some Problems of Proof 85 (1956); McBaine, Burden of Proof: Degrees of Belief, 32 Calif. L.Rev. 242, 255 (1944); Nesson, Reasonable Doubt and Permissive Inferences: The Value of Complexity, 92 Harv.L.Rev. 1187 (1979); C.J.S. Criminal Law §§ 566–578, 1267–1284; Dec.Dig. Criminal Law ⟜326–336, 789.

2. Speiser v. Randall, 357 U.S. 513, 525–526 (1958). See also In re Winship, 397 U.S. 358, 369–372 (1970) (concurring opinion by Harlan, J.).

3. Ball, The Moment of Truth: Probability Theory and Standards of Proof, 14 Vand.L.Rev. 807, 816 (1961). See also Kaplan, Decision Theory and the Factfinding Process, 20 Stan.L.Rev. 1065, 1073–1077 (1968); Winter, The Jury and the Risk of Nonpersuasion, 5 Law & Society Rev. 335, 339–343 (1971).

4. Thayer, Preliminary Treatise on Evidence 558, 559 (1898) quotes passages in Corpus Juris, dating from the fourth century, and from Coke's 3d Institute, to this effect.

5. "Its first appearance, so far as we have been able to determine, was in the high-treason cases tried in Dublin in 1798, as reported by MacNally [Rules of Evidence on Pleas of the Crown; Dublin, 1802], who was himself counsel for the defense. 'It may also,' he says, 'at this day, be considered a rule of law, that, if the jury entertain a reasonable doubt upon the truth of the testimony of witnesses given upon the issue they are sworn well and truly to try, they are bound' to ac-

quit." May, Reasonable Doubt in Civil and Criminal Cases, 10 Am.L.Rev. 642, 656 (1876) quoted in Note, 69 U.S.L.Rev. 169, 172 (1935).

6. In re Winship, supra n. 2 at 364. In that case, the Court held that proof beyond a reasonable doubt is among the essentials of due process and fair treatment required during the adjudicatory stage when a juvenile is charged with an act which would constitute a crime if committed by an adult.

The jury is not required to believe each fact in an aggregate of circumstantial evidence beyond a reasonable doubt. People v. Klinkenberg, 90 Cal.App.2d 608, 204 P.2d 47, 62 (1949); State v. Raine, 93 Idaho 862, 477 P.2d 104 (1970); State v. Barry, 93 N.H. 10, 34 A.2d 661, 663 (1943) (not essential that each fact bearing on identity be established beyond reasonable doubt). Or facts unrelated to guilt, such as venue. Barragan v. State, 141 Tex.Cr.R. 12, 147 S.W.2d 254, 256 (1941).

The *Winship* case has also had an impact on instructions concerning the jury's consideration of the testimony of certain witnesses. In Cool v. United States, 409 U.S. 100 (1972), the Court held that an instruction, that the jury must believe an accomplice's testimony on behalf of the defendant beyond a reasonable doubt before giving it the same effect as other testimony, violated *Winship*. But see Cupp v. Naughten, 414 U.S. 141 (1973), where the Court held that an instruction stating that every witness is presumed to speak the truth did not violate *Winship*, despite the fact that the

A simple instruction that the jury will acquit if they have a reasonable doubt of the defendant's guilt of the crime charged in the indictment is ordinarily sufficient.[7] Courts, however, frequently paint the lily by giving the jury a definition of "reasonable doubt." A famous early instance was the oft-echoed statement of Chief Justice Shaw in the trial of Prof. Webster for the murder of Dr. Parkman: "It is that state of the case, which, after the entire comparison and consideration of all the evidence, leaves the minds of jurors in that condition that they cannot say they feel an abiding conviction, to a moral certainty, of the truth of the charge."[8] It is an ancient maxim that all definitions are dangerous and this one has been caustically criticized as raising more questions than it answers.[9] Other defini-

tions, often more carefully balanced to warn against the overstressing of merely possible or imaginary doubts, have become customary in some jurisdictions.[10] Reasonable doubt is a term in common use almost as familiar to jurors as to lawyers. As one judge has said it needs a skillful definer to make it plainer by multiplication of words,[11] and as another has expressed it, the explanations themselves often need more explanation than the term explained.[12] A definition in terms locally approved is proper, but if not requested by accused is not required.[13] Whether if so requested it is the judge's duty to define the term, is a matter of dispute,[14] but the wiser view seems to be that it lies in his discretion,[15] which should ordinarily be exercised by declining to define, unless the jury itself asks for a fuller explanation.[16]

defendant had neither taken the witness stand nor presented any witnesses on his behalf.

7. See, e.g., State v. Lafferty, 416 S.W.2d 157 (Mo. 1967); Illinois Pattern Jury Instructions (Criminal) 2.03 (1981).

8. Commonwealth v. Webster, 59 Mass. (5 Cush.) 295, 320 (1850).

9. Trickett, Preponderance and Reasonable Doubt, 10 The Forum, Dickinson School of Law, 76 (1906) quoted, 9 Wigmore, Evidence § 2497 at 322 (Chadbourn rev. 1981).

10. They are set out by the hundreds in Dec.Dig. Criminal Law ☞789 and in 36 Words and Phrases 483–544 (Perm.Ed.1962).

11. Newman, J. in Hoffman v. State, 97 Wis. 571, 73 N.W. 51, 52 (1897).

12. Mitchell, J. in State v. Sauer, 38 Minn. 438, 38 N.W. 355 (1888), referring to the definition, "a doubt for which you can give a reason," said, "Like many other definitions of the term which have been given, it does not define, but itself requires definition. The most serious objection to it is that it is liable to be understood as meaning a doubt for which a juror could express or state a reason in words. A juror may, after a consideration and comparison of all the evidence, feel a reasonable doubt as to the guilt of a defendant, and yet find it difficult to state the reason for the doubt. The term 'reasonable doubt' is almost incapable of any definition which will add much to what the words themselves imply. In fact it is easier to state what it is not than what it is; and it may be doubted whether any attempt to define it will not be more likely to confuse than to enlighten a jury. A man is the best judge of his own feelings, and he knows for himself whether he doubts better than any one else can tell him. Where any explanation of what is meant by a reasonable doubt is required, it is safer to adopt some definition

which has already received the general approval of the authorities, especially those in our own state."

See also Bartels, Punishment and the Burden of Proof in Criminal Cases: A Modest Proposal, 66 Iowa L.Rev. 869 (1981) and the discussion in Nesson, supra n. 89 at 1196, where the author argues that reasonable doubt is a concept intended to be complex. "As long as the concept is left ambiguous, members of the observing public may assume that they share with jury members common notions of the kinds and degrees of doubt that are unacceptable."

13. State v. Hall, 267 N.C. 90, 147 S.E.2d 548 (1966), and cases cited C.J.S. Criminal Law § 1268 at 658, n. 63. See also People v. Cagle, 41 Ill.2d 528, 244 N.E.2d 200, 204 (1969) ("This court has repeatedly held that the legal concept of 'reasonable doubt' needs no definition, and that where an involved instruction on that concept is given it may be deemed prejudicial error [citing cases].").

14. Recognizing a duty are Mundy v. United States, 85 U.S.App.D.C. 120, 176 F.2d 32 (1949) (here waived by failure to request); Blatt v. United States, 60 F.2d 481 (3d Cir.1932) (reversal for refusal to define); Friedman v. United States, 381 F.2d 155 (8th Cir.1967) (duty recognized; given charge approved).

No duty: United States v. Lawson, 507 F.2d 433 (7th Cir.1974), cert. denied 420 U.S. 1004. Jackson v. State, 225 Ga. 553, 170 S.E.2d 281 (1969); State v. Velsir, 61 Wyo. 476, 159 P.2d 371 (1945). For cases pro and con, see Dec.Dig. Criminal Law ☞789(3).

15. State v. Broome, 268 N.C. 298, 150 S.E.2d 416 (1966).

16. Pattern jury instructions defining reasonable doubt include California Jury Instruction (Criminal) 2.90 (1979) North Carolina Pattern Instructions (Criminal) 101.10 (1974).

There are certain excuses or justifications allowed to the defendant, which although provable for the most part under the plea of not guilty, are spoken of for some purposes as "affirmative defenses." [17] Among these are self-defense,[18] duress,[19] insanity,[20] intoxication [21] and claims that the accused is within an exception or proviso in the statute defining the crime.[22] Sometimes only the burden of producing evidence will be assigned to the defendant.[23] Under certain circumstances the burden of persuasion with regard to some of these defenses may be allocated to the defendant and correspondingly, the prosecution may be relieved of proving the absence of the defense. The allocation and operation of the burdens of proof with regard to these defenses present difficult policy, as well as constitutional, problems. These problems will be discussed together with the special problems related to presumptions in criminal cases.[24]

Despite occasional statements to the contrary,[25] the reasonable doubt standard generally has been held inapplicable in civil cases, regardless of the nature of the issue involved.[26] For example, when a charge of crime is at issue in a civil action, the threatened consequences of sustaining the accusation, though often uncommonly harmful to purse or prestige, are not generally as serious as in a prosecution for the crime. Accordingly the modern American cases have come around to the view that in the interest of justice and simplicity a reasonable doubt measure of persuasion will not be imposed.[27] Most courts have said that a preponderance of the evidence is sufficient,[28] although some have increased the standard to "clear and convincing." [29]

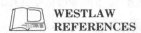

**WESTLAW
REFERENCES**

di beyond a reasonable doubt
winship /p 397 +s 358 /p "due process" /s
"reasonable doubt"

17. 9 Wigmore, Evidence §§ 2501, 2512, 2514 (Chadbourn rev. 1981); 22A C.J.S. Criminal Law §§ 572–577; Dec.Dig. Criminal Law ⊕329–333.

18. Brown v. State, 48 Del. 427, 105 A.2d 646 (1954); see also cases collected C.J.S. Homicide § 195.

19. State v. Sappienza, 84 Ohio St. 63, 95 N.E. 381 (1911).

20. State v. Finn, 257 Minn. 138, 100 N.W.2d 508 (1960).

21. State v. Church, 169 N.W.2d 889 (Iowa 1969).

22. State v. Tonnisen, 92 N.J.Super. 452, 224 A.2d 21 (1966), cert. denied 48 N.J. 443, 226 A.2d 431 (separate proviso clause).

23. See, e.g., United States v. Bailey, 444 U.S. 394 (1980), on remand 675 F.2d 1292 (defenses of duress and necessity).

24. §§ 346–348 infra.

25. St. Louis Union Trust Co. v. Busch, 346 Mo. 1237, 145 S.W.2d 426, 430 (1940) ("It is a general rule that a gift, inter vivos, sought to be established after the alleged donor's death, must be proven by forceful, clear and conclusive testimony which convinces the court beyond a reasonable doubt of its truthfulness.")

26. See 9 Wigmore, Evidence § 2498 (Chadbourn rev. 1981).

However, note that, particularly in light of *Winship*, proceedings which are nominally civil but which may result in "the drastic impairment of the liberty and reputation of an individual" may be governed by the reasonable doubt standard. People v. Pembrock, 62 Ill.2d

317, 342 N.E.2d 28, 29 (1976) ("sexually dangerous person"). Accord: United States ex rel. Stachulak v. Coughlin, 520 F.2d 931 (7th Cir.1975), cert. denied 424 U.S. 947, (Illinois "sexually dangerous person" proceeding); People v. Burnick, 14 Cal.3d 306, 121 Cal. Rptr. 488, 535 P.2d 352 (1975) ("mentally disturbed sex offender").

27. Sundquist v. Hardware Mutual Fire Insurance Co., 371 Ill. 360, 21 N.E.2d 297, 124 A.L.R. 1375 (1939) (suit on fire policy, defense of false statement by assured; abandons earlier rule in Illinois, and reviews similar shift of decisions elsewhere); Sivley v. American National Insurance Co., 454 S.W.2d 799 (Tex.Civ. App.1970) (drunk driving). See also cases cited in Annot., 124 A.L.R. 1378; Dec.Dig. Evidence ⊕596(2).

28. See cases cited n. 27 supra.

29. Ziegler v. Hustisford Farmers' Mutual Insurance Co., 238 Wis. 238, 298 N.W. 610 (1941) (suit on fire policy, defense, arson by insured; trial court correctly placed burden on defendant by "clear and satisfactory evidence.")

There are varying views on the necessary measure of persuasion in civil actions with criminal overtones, such as disbarment proceedings. In disbarment proceedings, most courts seem to reject the reasonable doubt standard as the measure of proof, but are divided upon whether "preponderance" or "clear and convincing" is the measure. Compare, In re Trask, 46 Hawaii 404, 380 P.2d 751 (1963) (preponderance) with In re Farris, 229 Or. 209, 367 P.2d 387 (1961) (clear and convincing). See also cases cited at C.J.S. Attorney and Client § 103.

§ 342. Presumptions: In General [1]

One ventures the assertion that "presumption" is the slipperiest member of the family of legal terms, except its first cousin, "burden of proof." One author has listed no less than eight senses in which the term has been used by the courts.[2] Agreement can probably be secured to this extent, however: a presumption is a standardized practice, under which certain facts are held to call for uniform treatment with respect to their effect as proof of other facts.

Returning for a moment to the discussion of satisfying the burden of producing evidence,[3] assume that a party having the burden of producing evidence of fact A, introduces proof of fact B. The judge, using ordinary reasoning, may determine that fact A might reasonably be inferred from fact B, and therefore that the party has satisfied his burden, or as sometimes put by the courts, has made out a "prima facie" case.[4] The judge has not used a presumption in the sense of a standardized practice, but rather has simply relied upon a rational inference. However, in ruling on a motion for directed verdict the judge may go beyond his own mental processes and experience and find that prior decisions or existing statutes have

established that proof of fact B is sufficient to permit the jury to infer the existence of fact A. He has thus used a standardized practice but has he necessarily used a presumption? Although some courts have described such a standardized inference as a presumption,[5] most legal scholars have disagreed.[6] They have saved the term to describe a significantly different sort of a rule, one that dictates not only that the establishment of fact B is sufficient to satisfy a party's burden of producing evidence with regard to fact A, but also at least compels the shifting of the burden of producing evidence on the question to his adversary. Under this view, if proof of fact B is introduced and a presumption exists to the effect that fact A can be inferred from fact B, the party denying the existence of fact A must then introduce proof of its nonexistence or risk having a verdict directed or a finding made against him. Further some authorities state that a true presumption should not only shift the burden of producing evidence, but also require that the party denying the existence of the presumed fact assume the burden of persuasion on the issue as well.[7]

Certainly the description of a presumption as a rule that, at a minimum, shifts the burden of producing evidence is to be preferred, at least in civil cases.[8] Inferences that a trial judge decides may reasonably be drawn

---

§ 342

1. 9 Wigmore, Evidence §§ 2490–2492 (Chadbourn rev. 1981); Morgan, Basic Problems of Evidence 31–32 (1962); Thayer, Preliminary Treatise on Evidence, ch. 8 (1898); Allen, Presumptions in Civil Actions Reconsidered, 66 Iowa L.Rev. 843 (1981); Gausewitz, Presumptions in a One-Rule World, 5 Vand.L.Rev. 324 (1952); Ladd, Presumptions in Civil Actions, 1977 Arizona St. L.J. 275; C.J.S. Evidence §§ 114–118; Dec.Dig. Evidence ⇔53–89.

2. Laughlin, In Support of the Thayer Theory of Presumptions, 52 Mich.L.Rev. 195, 196–207 (1953). The term may be used in a sense totally unrelated to this discussion. Thus, when the Illinois court said, "Courts are presumed to be no more ignorant than the public generally . . . ," it was not dealing with any concern of procedure but was positing a point of beginning for thinking about the scope of judicial notice. Chicago v. Murphy, 313 Ill. 98, 104, 144 N.E. 802, 803 (1924).

3. See § 338 supra.

4. The term "prima facie case" is often used in two senses and is therefore an ambiguous and often misleading term. It may mean evidence that is simply sufficient to get to the jury, or it may mean evidence that is sufficient to shift the burden of producing evidence. See 9 Wigmore, Evidence § 2494. The term is used here in its former sense—evidence that is simply sufficient to withstand a motion for directed verdict.

5. Hunt v. Eure, 189 N.C. 482, 127 S.E. 593, 597 (1925): "A presumption of negligence, when establishing a prima facie case, is still only evidence of negligence for the consideration of the jury, and the burden of the issue remains on the plaintiff."

6. Thayer, supra n. 1, at 317, 321, 326; 9 Wigmore, Evidence § 2490 (Chadbourn rev. 1981). See also Morgan, supra n. 1, at 32.

7. See § 344 infra.

8. See, e.g., Original Uniform Rule 13 (1953): "A presumption is an assumption of fact resulting from a rule of law which requires such fact to be assumed from another fact or group of facts found or otherwise

from the evidence need no other description, even though the judge relies upon precedent or a statute rather than his own experience in reaching his decision. In most instances, the application of any other label to an inference will only cause confusion.[9] In criminal cases, however, there are rules that traditionally have been labeled presumptions, even though they do not operate to shift even the burden of producing evidence. The jury is permitted but not required to accept the existence of the presumed fact even in the absence of contrary evidence.[10]

Recently, the Supreme Court resurrected the term "permissive presumption" to describe these rules.[11] The term presumption will be used in this text in the preferred sense discussed above in referring to civil cases, but with the qualification suggested in referring to criminal cases.

There are rules of law that are often incorrectly called presumptions that should be specifically distinguished from presumptions at this point:

Conclusive presumptions. The term presumption as used above always denotes a rebuttable presumption, i.e., the party against whom the presumption operates can always

introduce proof in contradiction. In the case of what is commonly called a conclusive or irrebuttable presumption, when fact B is proven, fact A must be taken as true, and the adversary is not allowed to dispute this at all. For example, if it is proven that a child is under seven years of age, the courts have stated that it is conclusively presumed that he could not have committed a felony. In so doing, the courts are not stating a presumption at all, but simply expressing the rule of law that someone under seven years old cannot legally be convicted of a felony.[12]

Res ipsa loquitur. Briefly and perhaps oversimply stated, res ipsa loquitur is a rule that provides that a plaintiff may satisfy his burden of producing evidence of a defendant's negligence by proving that he has been injured by a casualty of a sort that normally would not have occurred in the absence of the defendant's negligence.[13] Although a few jurisdictions have given the doctrine the effect of a true presumption even to the extent of using it to assign the burden of persuasion,[14] most courts agree that it simply describes an inference of negligence.[15] Prosser calls it a "simple matter

---

established in the action." See, also Fed.R.Evid. 301; West's Ann.Cal.Evid. Code § 600(a).

9. In the first edition of this text, Dean McCormick used the term "permissive presumption" to describe a rule of law that held that a fact was sufficient to warrant, but not require, a desired inference. Some cases use the term "presumption of fact" to describe the same sort of rule. Bradley v. S. L. Savidge, Inc., 13 Wn.2d 28, 123 P.2d 780 (1942). For the reasons set forth in the text, both of these labels are here rejected. Certainly, standardized inferences are valuable to the law and there are times when courts will specifically want to bring their existence to the attention of the jury. However, their value will remain intact and the jury may still be informed of their existence when it is beneficial to do so, without the need to refer to them by a label that implies that they have a greater procedural effect than the one with which they are naturally endowed. See discussion with regard to res ipsa loquitur, this section, below.

10. See § 346 infra.

11. Allen v. County Court of Ulster County, 442 U.S. 140 (1979).

12. See Morgan, supra n. 1, at 31; 9 Wigmore, Evidence § 2492 (Chadbourn rev. 1981).

13. See Prosser, Torts §§ 39, 40 (4th ed. 1971); 2 Harper & James, Law of Torts §§ 19.5–19.12 (1956); James, Proof of the Breach in Negligence Cases, 37 Va.L.Rev. 179, 194–228 (1951); Prosser, Res Ipsa Loquitur in California, 37 Calif.L.Rev. 183 (1949); 9 Wigmore, Evidence § 2509 (Chadbourn rev. 1981).

14. Weiss v. Axler, 137 Colo. 544, 328 P.2d 88 (1958); Prosser, Torts, supra n. 13, at 230–231. Prosser states that the burden of persuasion may properly be shifted to the defendant for reasons of policy in certain res ipsa loquitur cases such as those in which the defendant (e.g., a carrier) owed a special responsibility to plaintiff. He adds, however, that for these same policy reasons, the burden of persuasion "should rest upon [the defendant] even when the plaintiff offers the direct testimony of eyewitnesses; and such a policy does not seem properly to be connected with res ipsa loquitur at all."

15. Sweeney v. Erving, 228 U.S. 233, 240 (1913) (injury to patient from X-ray machine; held, no error to refuse charge that placed burden of persuasion on defendant; "res ipsa loquitur means that the facts of the occurrence warrant the inference, not that they compel such an inference.") See also Gardner v. Coca Cola Bottling Co., 267 Minn. 505, 127 N.W.2d 557 (1964). Mobil Chemical Co. v. Bell, 517 S.W.2d 245 (Tex.1974).

of circumstantial evidence."[16] Most frequently, the inference called for by the doctrine is one that a court would properly have held to be reasonable even in the absence of a special rule. Where this is so, res ipsa loquitur certainly need be viewed no differently from any other inference.[17] Moreover, even where the doctrine is artificial—where it is imposed for reasons of policy rather than logic[18]—it nevertheless remains only an inference, permitting but not requiring, the jury to find negligence. The only difference is that where res ipsa loquitur is artificially imposed, there is better reason for informing the jury of the permissibility of the inference than there is in the case where the doctrine simply describes a rational inference. Although theoretically a jury instruction of this kind might be viewed as violating a state rule prohibiting comment on the evidence, the courts have had little difficulty with the problem and have consistently approved and required, where requested, instructions that tell the jury that a finding of

negligence is permissible.[19] Obviously these instructions can and should be given without the use of the misnomer "presumption."

The presumption of innocence. Assignments of the burdens of proof prior to trial are not based on presumptions. Before trial no evidence has been introduced from which other facts are to be inferred. The assignment is made on the basis of a rule of substantive law providing that one party or the other ought to have one or both of the burdens with regard to an issue.[20] In some instances, however, these substantive rules are incorrectly referred to as presumptions. The most glaring example of this mislabeling is the "presumption of innocence" as the phrase is used in criminal cases.[21] The phrase is probably better called the "assumption of innocence" in that it describes our assumption that, in the absence of contrary facts, it is to be assumed that any person's conduct upon a given occasion was lawful.[22] In criminal cases, the "presumption of innocence" has been adopted by judg-

16. Prosser, Torts, supra n. 13 at 231.

17. As in the case of any inference, on occasion res ipsa loquitur may have such rational force as to compel a shifting of the burden of producing evidence and a directed verdict for the plaintiff if defendant does not satisfy the shifted burden. See, e.g., Alabama & Vicksburg Railway Co. v. Groome, 97 Miss. 201, 52 So. 703 (1910); Whitley v. Hix, 207 Tenn. 683, 343 S.W.2d 851 (1961). Such a shift is not artificial in the sense that it is imposed for policy reasons. It occurs simply as a result of the logical strength of plaintiff's case. See discussion § 338, supra.

18. See, e.g., Ybarra v. Spangard, 25 Cal.2d 486, 154 P.2d 687 (1944) (unconscious patient permitted to have benefit of res ipsa loquitur against all the doctors and hospital employees involved despite fact that not all could reasonably have been held responsible). Accord: Kolakowski v. Voris, 83 Ill.2d 388, 47 Ill.Dec. 392, 415 N.E.2d 397 (1981).

19. Powell v. Moore, 228 Or. 255, 364 P.2d 1094 (1961) (instruction on res ipsa loquitur permissible). See also Centennial Mills, Inc. v. Benson, 234 Or. 512, 383 P.2d 103 (1963), where the court recognized the rule of the *Powell* case as an exception to the general rule prohibiting instructions on inferences. For other cases permitting or requiring an instruction that an inference of negligence is warranted in a res ipsa loquitur case see Annot., 173 A.L.R. 880. For an example of the form of such an instruction see Illinois Pattern Jury Instructions (Civil) 22.01 (1971).

20. See § 337 supra.

21. The above discussion refers only to the common use of the term in reference to the accused in criminal cases. Although there may be a true presumption of innocence with regard to charges of misconduct or crime in civil cases or in criminal cases with regard to alleged crimes collaterally involved, most courts using the phrase in these cases are probably only talking about an inference of innocence. The language is usually ambiguous; e.g., TRW, Inc. v. N.L.R.B., 393 F.2d 771, 774 (6th Cir.1968) (". . . it must be presumed in the absence of evidence, that one who chooses to exercise a right conferred by law intends to exercise that right in a legal manner."); Moroni v. Brawders, 317 Mass. 48, 57 N.E.2d 14, 18 (1944) ("[The presumption of innocence] is not only a technical presumption, one 'of law, but is also . . . . a presumption 'of fact,' which means that an inference that conduct is of that sort is warranted even when not required."); Immerman v. Ostertag, 83 N.J.Super. 364, 199 A.2d 869, 874 (1964) ("Ordinarily there is a reasonable presumption that individuals would not commit a crime as serious as perjury or false swearing. However, that presumption loses its force where, as here, the evidence shows that the persons in question lack respect for the truth.")

22. "In the first place, the so-called presumption of innocence is not, strictly speaking, a presumption in the sense of an inference deduced from a given premise. It is more accurately an assumption which has for its purpose the placing of the burden of proof upon anyone who asserts any deviation from the socially desirable ideal of good moral conduct." Alexander, J., in Carr v. State, 192 Miss. 152, 4 So.2d 887, 888 (1941).

es as a convenient introduction to the statement of the burdens upon the prosecution, first of producing evidence of the guilt of the accused and, second, of finally persuading the jury or judge of his guilt beyond a reasonable doubt. Most courts insist on the inclusion of the phrase in the charge to the jury,[23] despite the fact that at that point it consists of nothing more than an amplification of the prosecution's burden of persuasion. Although the phrase is technically inaccurate and perhaps even misleading in the sense that it suggests that there is some inherent probability that the defendant is innocent, it is a basic component of a fair trial.[24] Like the requirement of proof beyond a reasonable doubt, it at least indicates to the jury that if a mistake is to be made it should be made in favor of the accused, or as Wigmore stated, "the term does convey a special and perhaps useful hint . . . in that it cautions the jury to put away from their minds all the suspicion that arises from the arrest, the indictment, and the arraignment, and to reach their conclusion solely from the legal evidence adduced."[25]

 **WESTLAW REFERENCES**

di presumption
presumption* /s shift! /s burden /2 persua!
"permissive presumption*"

See also Ashford & Risinger, Presumptions, Assumptions and Due Process in Criminal Cases, A Theoretical Overview, 79 Yale L.J. 165, 173 (1969).

23. A leading case is Commonwealth v. Madeiros, 255 Mass. 304, 151 N.E. 297 (1926) (refusal to instruct on presumption reversible error though judge instructed that indictment and custody were not to be taken against him and that they should not decide on suspicion). See also McDonald v. United States, 109 U.S. App.D.C. 98, 284 F.2d 232 (1960), and cases collected in C.J.S. Criminal Law § 1221; Dec.Dig. Criminal Law ⊛778(3).

24. In Taylor v. Kentucky, 436 U.S. 478 (1978), the Court stated that, although the presumption of innocence is not articulated in the Constitution, it is a basic component of a fair trial under our system. Therefore, under the circumstances of the case, the trial court's refusal to give a requested instruction on the presumption resulted in a violation of the defendant's right to a fair trial as guaranteed by the Fourteenth Amendment.

25. 9 Wigmore, Evidence § 2511 at 407 (Chadbourn rev. 1981).

"res ipsa" /s presumption* /s inference*
di presumption of innocence

§ 343. Reasons for the Creation of Presumptions: Illustrative Presumptions [1]

A presumption shifts the burden of producing evidence, and may assign the burden of persuasion as well. Therefore naturally, the reasons for creating particular presumptions are similar to the considerations which have already been discussed,[2] that bear upon the initial or tentative assignment of those burdens.[3] Thus, just as the burdens of proof are sometimes allocated for reasons of fairness, some presumptions are created to correct an imbalance resulting from one party's superior access to the proof. An example of such a presumption is the rule that as between connecting carriers, the damage occurred on the line of the last carrier.[4] Similarly, notions, usually implicit rather than expressed, of social and economic policy incline the courts to favor one contention by giving it the benefit of a presumption, and correspondingly to handicap the disfavored adversary. A classic instance is the presumption of ownership from possession, which tends to favor the prior possessor and to make for the stability of estates.[5] A presumption may also be created to avoid an im-

§ 343

1. Particular presumptions are listed in 9 Wigmore, Evidence §§ 2499–2540 (Chadbourn rev. 1981); C.J.S. Evidence §§ 120–157; Dec.Dig. Evidence ⊛55–83.

2. See § 337 supra.

3. For other discussions of the bases of presumptions see Watkins v. Prudential Insurance Co., 315 Pa. 497, 173 A. 644, 648 (1934); Morgan, Basic Problems of Evidence 32–34 (1962); Cleary, Presuming and Pleading: An Essay on Juristic Immaturity, 12 Stan.L.Rev. 5 (1959); Ladd, Presumptions in Civil Actions, 1977 Ariz. St.L.J. 275.

4. When the shipper proves that he delivered the goods to the first carrier in good condition and received them from the last in bad condition, the damage is presumed to have occurred on the line of the last carrier. Chicago & North Western Railway Co. v. C. C. Whitnack Products Co., 258 U.S. 369 (1922) (the rule is not changed by the Carmack Amendment making initial carrier liable); C.J.S. Carriers § 440 n. 35.

5. Oklahoma Central Railway Co. v. Guthrie, 175 Okl. 40, 52 P.2d 18, 23 (1935) (railway premises); Guyer

passe, to reach some result, even though it is an arbitrary one. For example, presumptions dealing with the survivorship of persons who died in a common disaster are necessary in order that other rules of law may operate, even though there is actually no factual basis upon which to believe that one party or the other was likely to have died first. [6] Generally, however, the most important consideration in the creation of presumptions is probability. Most presumptions have come into existence primarily because the judges have believed that proof of fact B renders the inference of the existence of fact A so probable that it is sensible and timesaving to assume the truth of fact A until the adversary disproves it. [7]

Obviously, most presumptions are based not on any one of these grounds alone, but have been created for a combination of reasons. Usually, for example, a presumption is based not only upon the judicial estimate of the probabilities but also upon the difficulties inherent in proving that the more probable event in fact occurred. [8] Moreover, as is the case with initial allocations of the burdens, the reasons for creation of presumptions are often tied closely to the perti-

nent substantive law. This is particularly true with regard to those presumptions which are created, at least in part, to further some social policy. [9]

Although it would be inappropriate to attempt to list the hundreds of recognized presumptions, [10] following is a brief discussion of a few illustrative presumptions and the reasons for their creation:

Official actions by public officers, including judicial proceedings, are presumed to have been regularly and legally performed. [11] Reason: probability and the difficulty of proving that the officer conducted himself in a manner that was in all ways regular and legal.

A letter properly addressed, stamped and mailed is presumed to have been duly delivered to the addressee. [12] Reason: probability and the difficulty of proving delivery in any other way.

When the plaintiff has been injured by the negligent operation of a vehicle, then upon proof of further facts he may have the benefit of presumptions in moving against the nondriving defendant. If the plaintiff seeks to prove agency, he may secure the advantage of the presumption that the person

---

v. Snyder, 133 Md. 19, 104 A. 116 (1918) (personal property); 9 Wigmore, Evidence § 2515 (Chadbourn rev. 1981).

6. See Morgan, supra n. 3 at 33.

7. In the first edition of this text, Dean McCormick stated that another ground for the creation of presumptions is "procedural convenience" and cited the example of the presumption of sanity as it operates in criminal cases to save "the state the fruitless trouble of proving sanity in the great number of cases where the question will not be raised." Undoubtedly, procedural convenience is a reason for this rule. However, the so-called presumption of sanity is simply a description of the initial assignment of the burden of producing evidence to the defendant and is not actually a presumption. See § 346 infra.

8. See § 337.

9. The presumptions in employment discrimination cases are a good example. See e.g. Texas Department of Community Affairs v. Burdine, 450 U.S. 248 (1981), on remand 647 F.2d 513.

10. For a list of some traditional common law presumptions, see West's Ann.Cal.Evid.Code, §§ 600 et seq. No corresponding catalog appears in the Federal or Revised Uniform Rules (1974).

11. Thompson v. Consolidated Gas Utilities Corp., 300 U.S. 55 (1937) (regulations of administrative board, purporting to be made under delegated authority, presumed to be supported by justifying facts); S. S. Kresge Co. v. Davis, 277 N.C. 654, 178 S.E.2d 382 (1971) (good faith administration of the law by law enforcement officers and city officials is presumed); State ex rel. Lawrence v. Burke, 253 Wis. 240, 33 N.W.2d 242 (1948) (habeas corpus after judgment of conviction; judge presumed to have informed accused of right to counsel); West's Ann.Cal.Evid.Code, § 664; 9 Wigmore, Evidence § 2534 (Chadbourn rev. 1981); Dec. Dig. Evidence ☞82, 83. See also Hammond v. Brown, 323 F.Supp. 326, 355 (N.D.Ohio 1971), affirmed 450 F.2d 480 (6th Cir.) where, in an action to enjoin criminal prosecutions arising out of the Kent State rioting, the court presumed that the petit jurors who would hear the case would act impartially.

12. Franklin Life Insurance Co. v. Brantley, 231 Ala. 554, 165 So. 834 (1936); Employer's National Life Insurance Co. v. Willits, 436 S.W.2d 918 (Tex.Civ.App. 1968); 9 Wigmore, Evidence § 2519 (Chadbourn rev. 1981); Dec.Dig. Evidence ☞71.

driving the vehicle was doing so in the scope of his employment and in the course of the business of the defendant, merely by proving that the defendant was the owner. [13] In a number of states the plaintiff must not only prove ownership to gain the benefit of the presumption of agency, but also that the driver is regularly employed by the defendant. [14] If the plaintiff seeks to prove liability in a state having a statute making the owner liable for acts of one driving with the owner's consent, the plaintiff may secure the advantage of the presumption that the person driving was doing so with the owner's consent merely by showing ownership. [15] In some states the plaintiff must not only

prove ownership to gain the benefit of the presumption but also that a special relationship existed between the driver and the defendant. [16] Reasons behind these presumptions: probability, fairness in the light of defendant's superior access to the evidence, and the social policy of promoting safety by widening the responsibility in borderline cases of owners for injuries caused by their vehicles.

When a bailor proves delivery of property to a bailee in good condition and return in a damaged state, or a failure to return after due demand, a presumption arises that the damage or loss was due to the negligence or fault of the bailee. [17] Reason: fairness in

---

13. 9 Wigmore, Evidence § 2510a (Chadbourn rev. 1981). Malone v. Hanna, 275 Ala. 534, 156 So.2d 626 (1963); Van Court v. Lodge Cab Co., 198 Wash. 530, 89 P.2d 206, 211 (1939); Hollen v. Reynolds, 123 W.Va. 360, 15 S.E.2d 163 (1941); and see decisions collected Dec.Dig. Automobiles ⊂242(5), 242(6); Annots., 42 A.L.R. 898, 900, 74 A.L.R. 951, 96 A.L.R. 634; Note, 1953 U.Ill.L.F. 121. Proof, in turn, that a business vehicle bore defendant's name raises a "presumption" of ownership, and hence of agency and scope of employment, under this view. Brill v. Davajon, 51 Ill.App.2d 445, 201 N.E.2d 253 (1964); Cappello v. Aero Mayflower Transit Co., 116 Vt. 64, 68 A.2d 913 (1949). So also as to proof that the car bore a license number issued to defendant.

Compare Frew v. Barto, 345 Pa. 217, 26 A.2d 905 (1942), with Lanteigne v. Smith, 365 Pa. 132, 74 A.2d 116 (1950).

In some states, there is an inference of agency from ownership rather than a presumption. Chappell v. Dean, 258 N.C. 412, 128 S.E.2d 830 (1963) (interpreting North Carolina statute); Breeding v. Johnson, 208 Va. 652, 159 S.E.2d 836 (1968). See also Walker v. Johnston, 236 S.W.2d 534 (Tex.Civ.App.1951) ("inference" of ownership from identification on vehicle); Rodgers v. Jackson Brewing Co., 289 S.W.2d 307 (Tex.Civ.App. 1956) ("rebuttable presumption" of ownership from identification on vehicle): Kimbell Milling Co. v. Marcet, 449 S.W.2d 100 (Tex.Civ.App.1969) (citing both the *Walker* and the *Rodgers* case but finding it unnecessary to determine whether the rule describes an inference or a presumption).

14. Manion v. Waybright, 59 Idaho 643, 86 P.2d 181 (1938) ("operated by one in the general employ of defendant"); Galloway Motor Co. v. Huffman's Administrator, 281 Ky. 841, 137 S.W.2d 379 (1940); Collins v. Leahy, 347 Mo. 133, 146 S.W.2d 609 (1941); Howell v. Olson, 452 P.2d 768 (Okl.1969); Dec.Dig. Automobiles ⊂242(6); Annot., 42 A.L.R. 915, 74 A.L.R. 962, 96 A.L.R. 641.

15. Young v. Masci, 289 U.S. 253 (1933); McKirchy v. Ness, 256 Iowa 744, 128 N.W.2d 910 (1964); West's

Ann.Cal.Vehicle Code § 17150; Iowa Code Ann. § 321.493; McKinney's N.Y. Vehicle and Traffic Law § 388(1).

16. O'Dea v. Amodeo, 118 Conn. 58, 170 A. 486 (1934); Christiansen v. Hilber, 282 Mich. 403, 276 N.W. 495 (1937); Conn.Gen.St.Ann. § 52–182 (making presumption of consent applicable to the family car or boat); Mich.Comp.Laws Ann. § 9.2101. See also § 344, infra, nn. 18–23 and accompanying text.

17. See, e.g., Compton v. Daniels, 98 Idaho 915, 575 P.2d 1303 (1978); Bowman v. Vandiver, 243 Ky. 139, 47 S.W.2d 947, 948 (1932); Gray v. E.J. Longyear Co., 78 N.M. 161, 429 P.2d 359 (1967); Trammell v. Whitlock, 150 Tex. 500, 242 S.W.2d 157 (1951); 9 Wigmore, Evidence § 2508 (Chadbourn rev. 1981); Comment, 4 Baylor L.Rev. 327 (1952); C.J.S. Bailments § 50; Dec.Dig. Bailments ⊂31(1). The presumption casts the burden on the bailee of proceeding with evidence of the cause of the loss, e.g., fire, theft, damage from collision. Some cases hold that, if the facts thus disclosed are consistent with due care, e.g., a fire of unknown origin, the bailee has satisfied the burden. Exporters' & Traders Compress & Warehouse Co. v. Schulze, 265 S.W. 133 (Tex.Com.App.1924) (fire); Chaloupka v. Cyr, 63 Wn.2d 463, 387 P.2d 740 (1963) (fire). But other cases, more soundly it seems, require the bailee to go further and give evidence of facts from which the jury could reasonably find that the loss was not caused by the bailee's negligence. Downey v. Martin Aircraft Service, Inc., 96 Cal.App.2d 94, 214 P.2d 581 (1950) (fire); General Exchange Insurance Corp. v. Service Parking Grounds, Inc., 254 Mich. 1, 235 N.W. 898 (1931) (damage to car while stolen).

Section 7–403(1)(b) of the Uniform Commercial Code provides that a bailee may excuse his failure to deliver goods to the party holding a document of title by establishing "damage to or delay, loss or destruction of the goods for which the bailee is not liable [, but the burden of establishing negligence in such cases is on the person entitled under the document]." The bracketed language is optional. Most jurisdictions have omitted it (37 out of 51 adopting the code). See Uniform Com-

the light of the superior access of the bailee to the evidence of the facts surrounding the loss; probability.

Proof that a person has disappeared from his home and has absented himself therefrom for at least seven years and that during this time those who would be expected to hear from him have received no tidings from him and after diligent inquiry have been unable to find his whereabouts, raises a presumption that he died at some time during the seven year period.[18] The rule, though not very ancient,[19] is already antiquated in that the seven year period is undoubtedly too long considering modern communications and transportation.[20] Reasons: probability and the social policy of enforcing family security provisions such as life insurance, and of settling estates.[21]

---

mercial Code Reporting Service, Current Materials (1971). In most jurisdictions in which the section has been adopted without the optional language the question is still open as to whether the bailee has the burden of persuasion as well as the burden of producing evidence on the question of negligence. See Bigham, Presumptions, Burden of Proof and the Uniform Commercial Code, 21 Vand.L.Rev. 177, 191 (1968).

See also Reserve Insurance Co. v. Gulf Florida Terminal Co., 386 So.2d 550 (Fla.1980), upholding as constitutional an amendment to § 7–403(1) placing burden of proving negligence on bailor only in the event of losses exceeding $10,000.

18. Green v. Royal Neighbors of America, 146 Kan. 571, 73 P.2d 1 (1937); Magers v. Western & Southern Life Insurance Co., 335 S.W.2d 355 (Mo.App.1960); Donea v. Massachusetts Mutual Life Insurance Co., 220 Minn. 204, 19 N.W.2d 377 (1945). See the exhaustive treatment of this presumption in Jalet, Mysterious Disappearance: The Presumption of Death and the Administration of the Estates of Missing Persons or Absentees, 54 Iowa L.Rev. 177 (1968). See also 9 Wigmore, Evidence § 2531a (Chadbourn rev. 1981); C.J.S. Death § 6; Dec.Dig. Death ⟋2. The presumption has been enacted into statute in somewhat more than half the states. See Jalet, supra at 198.

A few jurisdictions dispense with the requirement of search and inquiry. See, e.g., Banks v. Metropolitan Life Insurance Co., 142 Neb. 823, 8 N.W.2d 185 (1943). See also cases collected in Annot., 99 A.L.R.2d 307.

It is often stated that it is one of the required facts of the presumption that the absence be "unexplained." Butler v. Mutual Life Insurance Co., 225 N.Y. 197, 121 N.E. 758 (1919). See cases collected in C.J.S. Death § 6 n. 39. It is believed, however, that this is misleading. The more reasonable view, it seems, is not that the proponent of the presumption must show that the absence is "unexplained," but that explanatory circumstances (e.g., that the person was a fugitive from justice), whether brought out by the proponent or the opponent, are to be considered by the jury in rebuttal of the presumption. Shaw v. Prudential Insurance Co. of America, 158 Wash. 43, 290 P. 694 (1930); see also Ewing v. Metropolitan Life Insurance Co., 191 Wis. 299, 210 N.W. 819 (1926).

Under the majority view, there is no presumption as to the time of death within the seven years. Peak v. United States, 353 U.S. 43 (1957) (construing federal statute); Ferril v. Kansas City Life Insurance Co., 345 Mo. 777, 137 S.W.2d 577 (1940). But a minority, in aid of the settlement of controversies over succession, recognize a presumption that the death occurred at the end of the seven years. In re Chicago & North Western Railway Co., 138 F.2d 753 (7th Cir. 1943), cert. denied 321 U.S. 789 (Illinois law) (presumption of continuance of life controls for period up to the end of seven years, when person is first accounted dead); Edwards v. Equitable Life Assurance Society of United States, 296 Ky. 448, 177 S.W.2d 574 (1944). But under either view the circumstances of the disappearance may be sufficient evidence that the death occurred at or about the time of disappearance. See Edwards v. Equitable Life Assurance Society, supra; Ferril v. Kansas City Life Insurance Co., supra. See also Hefford v. Metropolitan Life Insurance Co., 173 Or. 353, 363, 144 P.2d 695 (1944).

19. Thayer traces it to an English case of 1804. Doe d. George v. Jesson, 6 East 80, 102 Eng.Rep. 1217. But the period of seven years seems to derive from the Bigamy Act of 1604 and from a statute of 1667 which provided "in the case of estates and leases depending upon the life of a person who should go beyond the seas, or otherwise absent himself within the kingdom for seven years, that where the lessor or reversioner should bring an action to recover the estate, the person thus absenting himself should 'be accounted as naturally dead,' if there should be no 'sufficient and evident proof of the life,' and that the judge should 'direct the jury to give their verdict as if the person . . . were dead.' " Preliminary Treatise on Evidence 319–324 (1898).

20. See 9 Wigmore, Evidence § 2531b (Chadbourn rev. 1981). Wigmore advocated the adoption of the Uniform Absence as Evidence of Death and Absentees' Property Act which provides no set period for a presumption of death but left the matter of death to be determined in each case as a question of fact. 8 U.L.A. § 1 (1972). The act was adopted in three states, Maryland, Tennessee and Wisconsin in 1941, but has not been adopted since. Maryland repealed its act in 1973. 1st Sp.Sess. ch. 2 § 1.

Several states provide for a length of absence less than seven years. See e.g. New Jersey Stat.Ann. 3A:40–1 (5 years); McKinney's N.Y. EPTL 2–1.7 (5 years); Ark.Stat. § 62–1601 (5 years).

21. See Robb v. Horsey, 169 Md. 227, 181 A. 348, 351 (1935). See also Jalet, supra, n. 18 at 181–182.

In the tracing of titles to land there is a useful presumption of identity of person from identity of name. Thus, when the same name appears in the chain of title first as grantee or heir and then as grantor, it will be presumed that it was the same person in each case.[22] Reasons: the convenience of enabling the court and the parties to rely upon the regularity of the apparent chain of title, until this is challenged by evidence contesting identity; the social policy of quieting claims based on the face of the record; and probability.

Proof that a child was born to a woman during the time when she was married creates the presumption that the offspring is the legitimate child of the husband.[23] Despite the controversy over whether presumptions generally shift the burden of persuasion upon the opponent,[24] it is universally agreed that in the case of this presumption, the adversary contending for illegitimacy does have the burden.[25] This burden, moreover, is usually measured not by the normal standard for civil cases of preponderance of the evidence, but rather by the requirement of clear, convincing, and satisfactory proof, as most courts say,[26] or even by the criminal formula, beyond a reasonable doubt.[27] In addition, as pointed out elsewhere in this work, the contender for illegitimacy is further handicapped by a rule rendering incompetent the testimony or declarations of the spouses offered to show nonaccess, when the purpose is to bastardize the child.[28] Reasons: social policy, to avoid the visitation upon the child of the sins of the parents caused by the social stigma of bastardy and the common law rules (now generally alleviated by statutes) as to the incapacities of the *filius nullius*, the child of no one; probability.

When violent death is shown to have occurred and the evidence is not controlling as

22. E.g., Edelstein v. Pon, 183 Cal.App.2d 795, 7 Cal.Rptr. 65 (1960); Huston v. Graves, 213 S.W. 77 (Mo.1919). See also Breznik v. Braun, 11 Ill.2d 564, 144 N.E.2d 586 (1957). See general discussion of inferences or presumptions from identical names in 9 Wigmore, Evidence § 2529 (Chadbourn rev. 1981) and cases collected in Dec.Dig. Evidence ⊗55, Names ⊗14.

23. In re Findlay, 253 N.Y. 1, 170 N.E. 471, 473 (1930) (opinion by Cardozo, C.J., tracing the history and limits of the presumption); Bernheimer v. First National Bank, 359 Mo. 1119, 225 S.W.2d 745 (1949) ("presumption of legitimacy is the strongest known to law"); 9 Wigmore, Evidence § 2527 (Chadbourn rev. 1981); Notes, 33 Harv.L.Rev. 306 (1920), 35 Mo.L.Rev. 449 (1970); C.J.S. Bastards § 3; 10 Am.Jur.2d Bastards §§ 10–44; Dec.Dig. Illegitimate Children ⊗2–4. The presumption applies even when the child was conceived before, and born after, marriage. State v. E. A. H., 246 Minn. 299, 75 N.W.2d 195 (1956). See cases collected Annot., 57 A.L.R.2d 729. Interesting problems of presumptions arise when a child is conceived while the wife is married to husband number one and is born after she married number two. See cases collected in Annot., 57 A.L.R.2d 729, 778 and 46 A.L.R.3d 158. Presumptions have often developed into rules of substantive law. Here, however, the course of evolution has been from a rule of substantive law into a rebuttable presumption. But the strictness of an older day when if the husband was not beyond the four seas, the child was conclusively assumed to be his, lingers in modified form. Thus, for example, West's Ann.Cal. Evid.Code, § 621 provides that "the issue of a wife cohabiting with her husband, who is not impotent, is conclusively presumed to be legitimate." Somewhat more moderately, the court in Haugen v. Swanson, 219 Minn.

123, 16 N.W.2d 900, 902 (1944), held that a husband's paternity could be excluded "by proof of miscegenation, or of his impotency, or of the negative results of reliable blood tests by impartial physicians."

The Minnesota Supreme Court subsequently softened its approach to the nature of the rebuttal proof required. Golden v. Golden, 282 N.W.2d 887, 889 (Minn.1979) (facts which would, if accepted, tend to exclude all reasonable probability of his parenthood of the child upon the ground of nonaccessibility). For blood tests to prove or disprove paternity, see § 211 supra.

24. See § 344, infra.

25. See the opinion of Sturdevant, J., in In re Jones' Estate, 110 Vt. 438, 8 A.2d 631, 128 A.L.R. 704 (1939) recognizing this allocation of the burden of persuasion, but characterizing this apportionment of the burden as a "rule of substantive law"—an analysis that may be questioned, see § 344 infra. Cases are collected in Annot., 128 A.L.R. 713.

26. The variations in phraseology are wide. In re Davis' Estate, 169 Okl. 133, 36 P.2d 471 (1934) ("strong, satisfactory and conclusive"); State ex rel. Walker v. Clark, 144 Ohio St. 305, 58 N.E.2d 773 (1945) ("clear and convincing"); In re Thorn's Estate, 353 Pa. 603, 606, 46 A.2d 258, 260 (1946) ("clear, direct, satisfactory and irrefragable"); Annot., 128 A.L.R. supra n. 25 at 718–722.

27. In re Jones' Estate, 110 Vt. 438, 8 A.2d 631, 128 A.L.R. 704 (1939); Annot., 128 A.L.R. supra n. 69 at 717.

28. See § 67 supra.

to whether it was due to suicide or accident, there is a presumption against suicide.[29] Reasons: the general probability in case of a death unexplained, which flows from the human revulsion against suicide, and, probably, a social policy which inclines in case of doubt toward the fruition rather than the frustration of plans for family protection through insurance.

WESTLAW REFERENCES

official judicial /2 action* proceeding* /s presum! /4 regular! legal!

presumption* /s letter* /s send* sent mail** post**

presumption* /s child! /s husband legitima!

---

29. Dick v. New York Life Insurance Co., 359 U.S. 437 (1959) (North Dakota law); Life & Casualty Insurance Co. v. Daniel, 209 Va. 332, 163 S.E.2d 577 (1968); C.J.S. Evidence § 135(b); Dec.Dig. Evidence ⊕59. See also cases collected Annot., 85 A.L.R.2d 722. In some states an inference rather than a presumption against suicide is recognized. Watkins v. Prudential Insurance Co. of America, 315 Pa. 497, 173 A. 644 (1934); C.J.S. § 135(b) nn. 29, 30.

§ 344

1. Morgan, Basic Problems of Evidence 34–44 (1962), Some Problems of Proof 74–81 (1956); 9 Wigmore, Evidence §§ 2490-2493 (Chadbourn rev. 1981); James & Hazard, Civil Procedure § 7.9 (2d ed 1977); Allen, Presumptions in Civil Actions Reconsidered, 66 Iowa L.Rev. 843 (1981); Allen, Presumptions, Inferences and Burden of Proof in Federal Civil Actions— An Anatomy of Unnecessary Ambiguity and a Proposal for Reform, 76 Nw.U.L.Rev. 892 (1982); Bohlen, The Effect of Rebuttable Presumptions of Law upon the Burden of Proof, 68 U.Pa.L.Rev. 307 (1920); Cleary, Presuming and Pleading: An Essay on Juristic Immaturity, 12 Stan.L.Rev. 5 (1959); Gausewitz, Presumptions in a One-Rule World, 5 Vand.L.Rev. 324 (1952); Hecht & Pinzler, Rebutting Presumptions: Order Out of Chaos, 58 B.U.L.Rev. 527 (1978); Ladd, Presumptions in Civil Actions, 1977 Ariz.St.L.J. 275; Laughlin, In Support of the Thayer Theory of Presumptions, 52 Mich.L.Rev. 195 (1953); Louisell, Construing Rule 301: Instructing the Jury on Presumptions in Civil Actions and Proceedings, 63 Va.L.Rev. 281 (1977); Mueller, Instructing the Jury Upon Presumptions in Civil Cases: Comparing Federal Rule Evid. 301 with Uniform Rule 301, 12 Land & Water L.Rev. 219 (1977); Annot., 5 A.L.R.3d 19; C.J.S. Evidence §§ 116, 117, 119; Dec.Dig. Evidence ⊕85–89, Trial ⊕205.

2. A presumption may be similarly significant in a case tried without a jury. In such a case, the judge must consider what effect, if any, the presumption has, both when he decides whether a party having the bur-

§ 344. The Effect of Presumptions in Civil Cases [1]

The trial judge must consider the effect of a presumption in a civil jury trial at two stages: (1) when one party or the other moves for a directed verdict and (2) when the time comes to instruct the jury.[2]

Sometimes the effect of a presumption, at either stage, is easy to discern; it follows naturally from the definition of the term. Thus, where a party proves the basic facts giving rise to a presumption,[3] he will have satisfied his burden of producing evidence with regard to the presumed fact and therefore his adversary's motion for directed verdict will be denied. If his adversary fails to

---

den of producing evidence has satisfied that burden and when he decides the case based upon all of the evidence. However, many of the problems concerning the effect to be given presumptions have centered around the question of what, if anything, a jury is to be told about them. This section is therefore primarily directed to the jury trial. Nevertheless, it should be remembered throughout the discussion that many of the problems raised, particularly with regard to the effect of a presumption upon the burden of persuasion, exist whether or not the case is tried to a jury.

3. The test for whether evidence is sufficient to support a finding of the existence of the basic facts of a presumption should be the same as that used to assess the sufficiency of any proof introduced for the purpose of satisfying a party's burden of producing evidence. The problem in general is discussed in § 338, supra. Theoretically, there is no reason why the basic facts of a presumption cannot be proved by circumstantial rather than direct evidence, or even by the use of another presumption, the basic facts of which are established by sufficient evidence. See, e.g., Savarese v. State Farm Mutual Automobile Insurance Co., 150 Cal.App.2d 518, 310 P.2d 142 (1957) (proof of a regular business practice of mailing a cancellation notice held to be sufficient to give rise to a presumption of receipt of that notice). A problem may arise, however, from the fact that a presumption is, by definition, a standardized inference. Therefore, a party seeking to establish the basic facts of a presumption through the use of circumstantial evidence may run head-on into the dogma that an inference may not be based upon another inference. See cases collected at 5 A.L.R.3d 100 (1966). The answer to the dilemma is that the "rule" against basing an inference on an inference or a presumption on a presumption should not be viewed as a rule at all but rather only as a warning against the use of inferences that are too remote or speculative. See § 338, n. 13. Such a warning ought to be heeded in the case of the basic facts of presumptions but should not be elevated to the status of an inflexible rule.

offer any evidence or offers evidence going only to the existence of the basic facts giving rise to the presumption and not to the presumed fact, the jury will be instructed that if they find the existence of the basic facts, they must also find the presumed fact.[4] To illustrate, suppose plaintiff proves that a letter was mailed, that it was properly addressed, that it bore a return address, and that it was never returned. Such evidence is generally held to raise a presumption that the addressee received the letter.[5] Defendant's motion for a directed verdict, based upon nonreceipt of the letter, will be denied. Furthermore, if the defendant offers no proof on this question (or if he attempts only to show that the letter was not mailed and offers no proof that the letter was not in fact received) the jury will be instructed that if they find the existence of the facts as contended by plaintiff, they must find that the letter was received.

But the problem is far more difficult where the defendant does not rest and does not confine his proof to contradiction of the basic facts, but instead introduces proof tending to show the nonexistence of the presumed fact itself. For example, what is the effect of the presumption in the illustration given above, if the defendant takes the stand and testifies that he did not in fact receive the letter? If the plaintiff offers no

additional proof, is the defendant now entitled to the directed verdict he was denied at the close of the plaintiff's case? If not, what effect, if any should the presumption have upon the judge's charge to the jury? The problem of the effect of a presumption when met by proof rebutting the presumed fact has literally plagued the courts and legal scholars. The balance of this section is devoted to that problem.

(A) The "Bursting Bubble" Theory and Deviations from It

The theory. The most widely followed theory of presumptions in American law has been that they are "like bats of the law flitting in the twilight, but disappearing in the sunshine of actual facts."[6] Put less poetically, under what has become known as the Thayer or "bursting bubble" theory, the only effect of a presumption is to shift the burden of producing evidence with regard to the presumed fact. If that evidence is produced by the adversary, the presumption is spent and disappears. In practical terms, the theory means that, although a presumption is available to permit the party relying upon it to survive a motion for directed verdict at the close of his own case, it has no other value in the trial. The view is derived from Thayer,[7] sanctioned by Wigmore,[8] adopted in the Model Code of Evidence,[9] and seem-

---

4. Whether a party who has relied on a presumption and who has introduced undisputed and unimpeached evidence with regard to the basic facts of that presumption may have a verdict directed in his favor on the issue, instead of the conditional peremptory ruling suggested in the text, will depend upon whether there is a prohibition in the jurisdiction against directing a verdict in favor of the party to whom the burden of persuasion is tentatively assigned on the basis of the pleadings. See § 338, n. 18 and accompanying text, supra.

5. See § 343 n. 12 and accompanying text supra.

6. Lamm J. in Mockowik v. Kansas City, St. Josephs & Council Bluffs Railroad Co., 196 Mo. 550, 571, 94 S.W. 256, 262 (1906), quoted in 9 Wigmore, Evidence § 2491 (Chadbourn rev. 1981). See also Bohlen, supra n. 1 at 314, where presumptions are described: "Like Maeterlinck's male bee, having functioned they disappear."

7. Thayer, Preliminary Treatise on Evidence, ch. 8, *passim*, and especially at 314, 336 (1898). Thayer,

however, seems not to have had in mind a rule of law as inflexible as the doctrine that bears his name. He at least recognized the possibility of different rules for different presumptions. See Gausewitz, Presumptions, 40 Minn.L.Rev. 391, 406–408 (1956) where the "Thayer" doctrine, but not Thayer's scholarship, is criticized.

8. 9 Wigmore, Evidence § 2491(2) (Chadbourn rev. 1981). See, however, the apparent modification of his views as expressed later in the same volume, § 2498a, sub-sec. 21.

9. Model Code of Evidence Rule 704(2) (1942): ". . . when the basic fact . . . has been established . . . and evidence has been introduced which would support a finding of the nonexistence of the presumed fact . . . the existence or non-existence of the presumed fact is to be determined exactly as if no presumption had ever been applicable . . .," and Comment, "A presumption, to be an efficient legal tool must . . . (2) be so administered that the jury never hear the word presumption used since it carries unpredictable connotations to different minds. . . ."

ingly been made a part of the Federal Rules of Evidence.[10] It has been adopted, at least verbally, in countless modern decisions.[11]

The theory is simple to state, and if religiously followed, not at all difficult to apply. The trial judge need only determine that the evidence introduced in rebuttal is sufficient to support a finding contrary to the presumed fact.[12] If that determination is made, certainly there is no need to instruct the jury with regard to the presumption.[13] The opponent of the presumption may still not be entitled to a directed verdict, but if his motion is denied, the ruling will have nothing to do with the existence of a presumption. As has been discussed, presumptions are frequently created in instances in which the basic facts raise a natural inference of the presumed fact. This natural inference may be sufficient to take the case to the jury, despite the existence of contrary evidence and despite the resultant destruction of the presumption. For example, in the case of the presumption of receipt of a letter, referred to above, the defendant may destroy the presumption by denying receipt. Nevertheless, a jury question is presented, not because of the presumption, but because of the natural inference flowing from the plaintiff's showing that he had mailed a properly addressed letter that was not returned.[14] On the other hand, the basic facts may not present a natural inference of sufficient strength or breadth to take the case to the jury. In such an instance, the court may grant a directed verdict against the party who originally had the benefit of the presumption.[15]

Deviations from the theory—in general. The "bursting bubble" theory has been criticized as giving to presumptions an effect that is too "slight and evanescent" when viewed in the light of the reasons for the creation of the rules.[16] Presumptions, as we have seen, have been created for policy reasons that are similar to and may be just as strong as those that govern the allocation of the burdens of proof prior to the introduction of evidence.[17] These policy considerations may persist despite the existence of proof rebutting the presumed fact. They may be completely frustrated by the Thayer rule when the basic facts of the presumption do not give rise to an inference that is naturally sufficient to take the case to the jury.

10. Fed.R.Evid. 301.

11. See cases collected at Annot., 5 A.L.R.3d 19; Dec.Dig. Evidence ⊕85–86, 89.

12. The evidence must be "credible." See Hildebrand v. Chicago, Burlington & Quincy Railroad Co., 45 Wyo. 175, 17 P.2d 651 (1933); Cleary, supra n. 1 at 18. See also Gausewitz, supra n. 1 at 327–328.

13. See, e.g., Orient Insurance Co. v. Cox, 218 Ark. 804, 238 S.W.2d 757 (1951); Ammundson v. Tinholt, 228 Minn. 115, 36 N.W.2d 521 (1949).

14. Rosenthal v. Walker, 111 U.S. 185 (1884); American Surety Co. v. Blake, 54 Idaho 1, 27 P.2d 972, 91 A.L.R. 153 (1933); Winkfield v. American Continental Insurance Co., 110 Ill.App.2d 156, 249 N.E.2d 174, 176 (1969) ("If the addressee denies the receipt of the letter then the presumption is rebutted and receipt becomes a question to be resolved by the trier of fact."); Stacey v. Sankovich, 19 Mich.App. 688, 173 N.W.2d 225 (1969) ("[The] presumption may be rebutted by evidence, but whether it was is a question for the trier of fact."); Southland Life Insurance Co. v. Greenwade, 138 Tex. 450, 159 S.W.2d 854, 857 (1942) ("We agree . . . that a presumption as such is not evidence and that it vanished as such in view of the opposing evidence; but we do not agree that the evidentiary facts upon which it was established, could no longer be considered by the trier of facts."). Cf. Grade v. Mariposa

County, 182 Cal. 75, 64 P. 117 (1901); Tremayne v. American SMW Corp., 125 Cal.App.2d 852, 271 P.2d 229 (1954) (nonjury cases in which court affirmed finding of nonreceipt based upon simple denial despite evidence that the correspondence was duly mailed).

15. E.g., Lovelace v. Sherwin-Williams Co., 681 F.2d 230 (4th Cir.1982) (presumption in employment discrimination case rebutted; judgment notwithstanding the verdict entered against plaintiff); O'Brien v. Equitable Life Assurance Society, 212 F.2d 383 (8th Cir.1954), cert. denied 348 U.S. 835 (presumption of accidental death, rebutted by opponent).

16. Morgan & Maguire, Looking Backward and Forward at Evidence, 50 Harv.L.Rev. 909, 913 (1937). See also, Morgan, Some Problems of Proof 74–81 (1956). Other writers are in accord, see, e.g., Cleary, supra n. 1 at 18; Gausewitz, supra n. 1 at 342. Contra, Laughlin, supra n. 1.

The strict operation of the bursting bubble theory may give a presumption less force than an inference such as res ipsa loquitur, which may not disappear with the introduction of evidence by the defendant explaining the situation. See, e.g., Mitchell v. Saunders, 219 N.C. 178, 13 S.E.2d 242 (1941), and discussion in Brandis, North Carolina Evidence, § 227 at 215 (2d Rev.Ed.1982).

17. See § 343 supra.

Similarly, even if the natural inference is sufficient to present a jury question, it may be so weak that the jury is unlikely to consider it in its decision unless specifically told to do so. If the policy behind certain presumptions is not to be thwarted, some instruction to the jury may be needed despite any theoretical prohibition against a charge of this kind.

These considerations have not gone unrecognized by the courts. Thus, courts, even though unwilling to reject the dogma entirely, often find ways to deviate from it in their treatment of at least some presumptions, generally those which are based upon particularly strong and visible policies. Perhaps the best example is the presumption of legitimacy arising from proof that a child was born during the course of a marriage. The strong policies behind the presumption are so apparent that the courts have universally agreed that the party contending that the child is illegitimate not only has the burden of producing evidence in support of his contention, but also has a heavy burden of persuasion on the issue as well.[18]

Another example of special treatment for certain presumptions is the effect given by some courts to the presumption of agency or of consent arising from ownership of an automobile.[19] The classic theory would dictate that the presumption is destroyed once the defendant or the driver testifies to facts sufficient to support a finding of nonagency or an absence of consent. Some courts have so held.[20] However, other courts have recognized that the policies behind the presumption, i.e., the defendant's superior access to the evidence and the social policy of widening the responsibility for owners of motor vehicles, may persist despite the introduction of evidence on the question from the defendant, particularly when that evidence comes in the form of his own or his servant's testimony. These courts have been unwilling to rely solely upon the natural inferences that might arise from plaintiff's proof,[21] and instead require more from the defendant in rebuttal, such as, that his evidence be "uncontradicted, clear, convincing and unimpeached." [22] Moreover, many courts also hold that the special policies behind the presumption require that the jury be informed of its existence.[23]

Deviations from the theory—conflicting presumptions. Frequent deviations from the rigid dictates of the "bursting bubble" theory occur in the treatment of conflicting presumptions. A conflict between presumptions may arise as follows: W, asserting that she is the widow of H, claims her share of his property, and proves that on a certain day she and H were married. The adversary then proves that three or four years before W's marriage to H, W married another man. W's proof gives her the benefit of the presumption of the validity of a marriage. The adversary's proof gives rise to the gen-

---

18. See § 343 nn. 23–28 and accompanying text supra.

19. See § 343 nn. 13–16 and accompanying text supra.

20. Peoples v. Seamon, 249 Ala. 284, 31 So.2d 88 (1947); McIver v. Schwartz, 50 R.I. 68, 145 A. 101 (1929). See additional cases collected at Annot., 5 A.L.R.3d 19, 66–69.

21. Where the presumption is held to be destroyed, the natural inference arising from plaintiff's proof of ownership may or may not be sufficient to send the case to the jury, depending both upon the court's view of the inference and the nature of the rebutting proof. Compare Peoples v. Seamon, supra n. 20 (question for the jury), with Kavanaugh v. Wheeling, 175 Va. 105, 7 S.E.2d 125 (1940) (inference insufficient to prove car used in owner's business; verdict for plaintiff set aside).

22. Bradley v. S. L. Savidge, Inc., 13 Wn.2d 28, 123 P.2d 780, 791 (1942) (defendant's evidence held to meet test). See also Standard Coffee Co. v. Trippet, 108 F.2d 161 (5th Cir.1939) (Texas law); Krisher v. Duff, 331 Mich. 699, 50 N.W.2d 332, 337 (1951) ("Generally speaking, the evidence to make this presumption disappear should be positive, unequivocal, strong and credible. The presumption is given more weight because of the dangerous instrumentality involved and the danger of permitting incompetent driving on the highway; and because the proof or disproof of consent or permission usually rests almost entirely with the defendants.").

23. Grier v. Rosenberg, 213 Md. 248, 131 A.2d 737 (1957); Kirsher v. Duff, supra n. 22 (no need to mention statute, but jury should be told that defendant must come forward with evidence of a clear, positive and credible nature to refute the presumptions of knowledge or consent).

eral presumption of the continuance of a status or condition once proved to exist, and a specific presumption of the continuance of a marriage relationship. The presumed facts of the claimant's presumption and those of the adversary's are contradictory.[24] How resolve the conflict? Thayer's solution would be to consider that the presumptions in this situation have disappeared and the facts upon which the respective presumptions were based shall simply be weighed as circumstances with all the other facts that may be relevant, giving no effect to the presumptions.[25] Perhaps when the conflicting presumptions involved are based upon probability or upon procedural convenience, the solution is a fairly practical one.[26]

The particular presumptions involved in the case given as an example, however, were not of that description. On the one hand, the presumption of the validity of a marriage is founded not only in probability, but in the strongest social policy favoring legitimacy and the stability of family inheritances and expectations.[27] On the other hand, the presumptions of continuance of lives and marriage relationships are based chiefly on probability and trial convenience, and the probability, of course, varies in accordance

with the length of time for which the continuance is to be presumed in the particular case. This special situation of the questioned validity of a second marriage has been the principal area in which the problem of conflicting presumptions has arisen. Here, courts have not been willing to follow Thayer's suggestion of disregarding both rival presumptions and leaving the issue to the indifferent arbitrament of a weighing of circumstantial inferences. They have often preferred to formulate the issue in terms of a conflict of presumptions and to hold that the presumption of the validity of marriage is "stronger" and should prevail.[28] The doctrine that the weightier presumption prevails should probably be available in any situation which involves conflicting presumptions, and where one of the presumptions is grounded in a predominant social policy.

Another and perhaps even better approach to the problem is to sidestep the conflict entirely and create a new presumption. Such a presumption has evolved in cases involving conflicting marriages. Under this rule, where a person has been shown to have been married successively to different spouses, there is a presumption that the earlier mar-

24. For an exhaustive collection of cases discussing these presumptions and the conflict between them see Annot., 14 A.L.R.2d 7. See Yarbrough v. United States, 169 Ct.Cl. 589, 341 F.2d 621 (1965); Ventura v. Ventura, 53 Misc.2d 881, 280 N.Y.S.2d 5 (1967); DeRyder v. Metropolitan Life Insurance Co., 206 Va. 602, 145 S.E.2d 177 (1965).

25. See Thayer, Preliminary Treatise on Evidence 346 (1898) followed in 9 Wigmore, Evidence § 2493 (Chadbourn rev. 1981); Model Code of Evidence Rules 701(3), 704(2). For a convincing exposition of the contrary view that as between conflicting presumptions the one founded on the stronger policy should prevail, see Morgan, Some Observations Concerning Presumptions, 44 Harv.L.Rev. 906, 932 n. 41 (1931).

26. City of Montpelier v. Town of Calais, 114 Vt. 5, 39 A.2d 350 (1944) (each side invoked the presumption of official regularity in respect to the acts of its own officers, and the court held that the case would be determined without regard to the presumptions).

See also Legille v. Dann, 544 F.2d 1 (D.C.Cir. 1976) (presumption of regularity of the mails rebutted by evidence of the regularity of Patent Office practice).

27. State v. Rocker, 130 Iowa 239, 106 N.W. 645, 649 (1906) ("where necessary to sustain the legitimacy

of children or in making disposition of property interests. . . ."). See Nixon v. Wichita Land & Cattle Co., 84 Tex. 408, 19 S.W. 560, 561 (1892), where Gaines, J. quotes the following from 1 Bishop, Marriage and Divorce § 457 (6th Ed. 1881): "It being for the highest good of the parties, of the children, and of the community that all intercourse between the sexes in form matrimonial should be such in fact, the law, when administered by enlightened judges, seizes upon all probabilities, and presses into its service all things else, which can help it in each particular case to sustain the marriage, and repel the conclusion of unlawful commerce."

28. Smiley v. Smiley, 247 Ark. 933, 448 S.W.2d 642 (1970); Apelbaum v. Apelbaum, 7 A.D.2d 911, 183 N.Y.S.2d 54 (1959); Meade v. State Compensation Commissioner, 147 W.Va. 72, 125 S.E.2d 771 (1962); Greensborough v. Underhill, 12 Vt. 604, 607 (1839); cases collected in Annot., 14 A.L.R.2d, supra, n. 24, at 37–44; Dec.Dig. Marriage ⇔40(9). See also Rev. Uniform Rule Evid. (1974) 301(b) "If presumptions are inconsistent, the presumption applies that is founded upon weightier considerations of policy. If considerations of policy are of equal weight neither presumption applies."

riage was dissolved by death or divorce before the later one was contracted.[29] While of course the presumption is rebuttable, as in the case of the presumption of legitimacy, many courts place a special burden of persuasion upon the party attacking the validity of the second marriage by declaring that the presumption can only be overcome by clear, cogent, and convincing evidence.[30]

Deviations from the theory—instructions to the jury. Because of the strength of the natural inferences that generally arise from the basic facts of a presumption, judges are seldom faced with the prospect of directing a verdict against the party relying upon a presumption. Similarly, conflicting presumptions are relatively rare. However, far more frequently courts have justifiably held that the policies behind presumptions necessitate an instruction that in some way calls the existence of the rule to the attention of the jury despite the Thayerian proscription against the practice. The digests give abundant evidence of the widespread and unquestioning acceptance of the practice

of informing the jury of the rule despite the fact that countervailing evidence has been adduced upon the disputed inference.[31]

Given the frequency of the deviation, however, the manner in which the jury is to be informed has been a matter of considerable dispute and confusion. The baffling nature of the presumption as a tool for the art of thinking bewilders one who searches for a form of phrasing with which to present the notion to a jury. Most of the forms have been predictably bewildering. For example, judges have occasionally contented themselves with a statement in the instructions of the terms of the presumption, without more. This leaves the jury in the air, or implies too much.[32] The jury, unless a further explanation is made, may suppose that the presumption is a conclusive one, especially if the judge uses the expression, "the law presumes."

Another solution, formerly more popular than now, is to instruct the jury that the presumption is "evidence," to be weighed and considered with the testimony in the case.[33]

29. J. J. Cater Furniture Co. v. Banks, 152 Fla. 377, 11 So.2d 776 (1943); Nicholas v. Idaho Power Co., 63 Idaho 675, 125 P.2d 321 (1942); Brown v. Brown, 51 Misc.2d 839, 274 N.Y.S.2d 484 (1966); cases collected in 9 Wigmore, Evidence § 2506 (Chadbourn rev. 1981); Annot., 14 A.L.R.2d at 20–29, 55 C.J.S. Marriage § 43(3) (1948); Dec.Dig. Marriage ⟨key⟩40(5, 6). Since the policy reasons are absent, the presumption is held inapplicable in prosecutions for bigamy. Fletcher v. State, 169 Ind. 77, 81 N.E. 1083 (1907); Wright v. State, 198 Md. 163, 81 A.2d 602 (1951).

30. Kolombatovich v. Magma Copper Co., 43 Ariz. 314, 30 P.2d 832 (1934); Marcum v. Zaring, 406 P.2d 970 (Okl.1965); Annot., 14 A.L.R.2d at 45–47; Dec.Dig. Marriage ⟨key⟩40(10, 11).

See also Panzer v. Panzer, 87 N.M. 29, 528 P.2d 888 (1974) (presumption of validity of latest marriage can be overcome by "clear and convincing" evidence).

31. Dec.Dig. Trial ⟨key⟩205, 234(7). Nevada Pattern Civil Jury Instructions 2.41; Washington Pattern Jury Instructions (Civil) 24.00 (1967).

32. See the criticism of such a charge in Garrettson v. Pegg, 64 Ill. 111 (1872). See also Kettlewell v. Prudential Insurance Co. of America, 6 Ill.App.2d 434, 128 N.E.2d 652 (1955). But an instruction merely directing the jury to consider the presumption against suicide without explaining its effect was thought sufficient in Radius v. Travelers Insurance Co., 87 F.2d 412 (9th Cir. 1937).

33. For example, prior to 1965, the California courts held that a presumption is evidence to be weighed along with all other evidence in the case and that the jury should be so instructed. Smellie v. Southern Pacific Co., 212 Cal. 540, 299 P. 529 (1931) (setting forth the doctrine); Gigliotti v. Nunes, 45 Cal.2d 85, 286 P.2d 809, 815 (1955) (setting forth a typical instruction). In 1965, however, the state adopted a new evidence code which classified the procedural effect of presumptions according to the policies behind their creation and which specifically rejected the notion that a presumption is evidence. West's Ann.Cal.Evid.Code, § 600. See thorough discussion of this shift in Note, 53 Calif. L.Rev. 1439, 1480–87 (1965). See also notes 55–57 and accompanying text infra.

During congressional consideration of the Federal Rules, the Senate and Conference Committees rejected as "ill-advised" a House of Representatives version of Rule 301 which in effect treated presumption as evidence. See Senate Comm. on Judiciary, Fed. Rules of Evidence, S.Rep. No. 1277, 93d Cong., 2d Sess., p. 9 (1974); H.R. Fed.Rules of Evidence, Conf.Rep. No. 1597, 93d Cong., 2d Sess., p. 5 (1974). With this legislative history, it seems highly unlikely that an instruction to the jury referring to a presumption as evidence would be proper under the Federal Rule. See Mueller, supra n. 1 at 285.

For cases holding that a presumption is evidence see Annot., 5 A.L.R.3d 19, 35–39. For criticisms of the "presumption is evidence" rule see McBaine, Presump-

This avoids the danger that the jury may infer that the presumption is conclusive, but it probably means little to the jury, and certainly runs counter to accepted theories of the nature of evidence.

More attractive theoretically, is the suggestion that the judge instruct the jury that the presumption is to stand accepted, unless they find that the facts upon which the presumed inference rests are met by evidence of equal weight, or in other words, unless the contrary evidence leaves their minds in equipoise, in which event they should decide against the party having the burden of persuasion upon the issue.[34] It is hard to phrase such an instruction without conveying the impression that the presumption itself is "evidence" which must be "met" or "balanced." The overriding objection, however, is the impression of futility that it conveys. It prescribes a difficult metaphysical task for the jury, and, in actual use, may mystify rather than help the average juror.[35]

One possible solution, perhaps better than those already mentioned, would be for the trial judge simply to mention the basic facts of the presumption and to point out the general probability of the circumstantial inference as one of the factors to be considerd by the jury.[36] By this technique, however, a true presumption would be converted into nothing more than a permissible inference. Moreover, the solution is simply not a feasible one in many jurisdictions without at least a new interpretation of another aspect of the law. The trial judge in most states must tread warily to avoid an expression of opinion on the facts. Although instructions on certain standardized inferences such as *res ipsa loquitur* are permitted,[37] the practice, wisely or not, may frown on any explanation of the allowable circumstantial inferences from particular facts as "invading the province of the jury."[38]

Where the "bursting bubble" rule is discarded in favor of a rule which operates to fix the burden of persuasion,[39] the problem

---

tions; Are They Evidence? 26 Calif.L.Rev. 519 (1938); Gausewitz, Presumptions in a One-Rule World, 5 Vand. L.Rev. 324, 333–34 (1952).

34. See, e.g., Klunk v. Hocking Valley Railroad Co., 74 Ohio St. 125, 77 N.E. 752 (1906); Tresise v. Ashdown, 118 Ohio St. 307, 160 N.E. 898 (1928). Although the general rule in Ohio now seems to be that a presumption disappears when met by contrary proof, see, e.g., Ayers v. Woodward, 166 Ohio St. 138, 140 N.E.2d 401 (1957), 1 Ohio Jury Instructions § 5.13 (1968), a standard instruction has been issued in that state in substantially the form suggested in the text with regard to an inference of contributory negligence arising from the plaintiff's own proof, 1 Ohio Jury Instructions § 9.11 (1968) and in somewhat similar form with regard to the presumption of agency arising from the owner's presence in an automobile. 1 Id. § 15.31 (1968).

Two authors have recently argued in favor of instructing the jury, at least with regard to certain presumptions, that it should find the presumed fact "unless it finds on the basis of all the evidence in the case that the nonexistence of that fact is at least as probable as its existence." Louisell, supra n. 1 at 305 et seq.; Mueller, supra n. 1 at 285 et seq.

35. Similar problems exist with regard to instructions that inform the jury that they should find for the proponent of the instruction unless they believe evidence which reasonably tends to rebut the presumed fact in which case the presumption should be disregarded and the case decided from all of the evidence.

See, e.g., Washington Pattern Jury Instructions 24.03 (1967).

36. A suggestion of the propriety of such a charge was made in Jefferson Standard Life Insurance Co. v. Clemmer, 79 F.2d 724 (4th Cir.1935). In federal court, however, the trial judge retains his common law powers to explain allowable inferences from circumstantial evidence.

37. See § 342 n. 19 and accompanying text supra.

38. See, e.g., Pridmore v. Chicago, Rock Island & Pacific Railway Co., 275 Ill. 386, 114 N.E. 176 (1916); Kennedy v. Phillips, 319 Mo. 573, 5 S.W.2d 33 (1928); Lappin v. Lucurell, 13 Wn.App. 277, 534 P.2d 1038, 1043 (1975).

39. Examples of such a rule or variations on it include Dick v. New York Life Insurance Co., 359 U.S. 437 (1959) (North Dakota rule re presumption of accidental death); Lewis v. New York Life Insurance Co., 113 Mont. 151, 124 P.2d 579 (1942) (presumption of accidental death); In re Swan's Estate, 4 Utah 2d 277, 293 P.2d 682 (1956) (presumption of fraud and undue influence in will contest). See also O'Dea v. Amodeo, 118 Conn. 58, 170 A. 486, 488 (1934) (statutory presumption that car driven by member of owner's family was being operated as a family car; ". . . the presumption shall avail the plaintiff until such time as the trier finds proven the circumstances of the situation with reference to the use made of the car and the authority of the person operating it to drive it, leaving the burden then upon the plaintiff to establish, in view of the facts so found, that the car was being operated

of alerting the jury to the presumption should not exist. Under this theory, a presumption may ordinarily be given a significant effect without the necessity of mentioning the word "presumption" to the jury at all. There is no more need to tell the jury why one party or the other has the burden of persuasion where that burden is fixed by a presumption than there is where the burden is fixed on the basis of policies apparent from the pleadings. The jury may be told simply that, if it finds the existence of the basic facts, the opponent must prove the non-existence of the presumed fact by a preponderance of evidence, or, in some instances, by a greater standard. Even in those instances in which the presumption places the burden of persuasion on the same party who initially had the burden, there would seem to be no reason to mention the term.[40] If the courts feel that the operation of the presumption warrants a higher standard of proof, the measure of persuasion can be increased as is now done in the case of the presumption of legitimacy. However,

unless we are willing to increase the measure of persuasion,[41] nothing can be gained by informing the jury of the coincidence. The word "presumption" would only tend to confuse the issue.[42]

(B) Attempts to Provide a Single Rule Governing the Effect of Presumptions

Perhaps, the greatest difficulty with the "bursting bubble" approach is that, in spite of its apparent simplicity, the conflicting desires of the courts to adopt it in theory and yet to avoid its overly-rigid dictates have turned it into a judicial nightmare of confusion and inconsistency.[43] This state of affairs has caused legal scholars not only to search for a better rule, but for a single rule that would cover all presumptions.

Many writers came to the view that the better rule for all presumptions would provide that anything worthy of the name "presumption" has the effect of fixing the burden of persuasion on the party contesting the existence of the presumed fact.[44] A principal technical objection to such a rule

---

at the time as a family car."); Krisher v. Duff, 331 Mich. 699, 50 N.W.2d 332, 339 (1951) (under statutory presumption that member of family using car is doing so with owner's consent, error to refuse to charge the jury that the adversary must come forward with evidence of a "clear, positive and credible nature" to refute the presumption). See also Rev. Uniform Rule Evid. (1974) 301.

40. See discussion in Levin, Pennsylvania and the Uniform Rules of Evidence: Presumptions and Dead Man Statutes, 103 U.Pa.L.Rev. 1, 27 (1954). The problem of instructing the jury with regard to a presumption operating against the party having the burden of persuasion is most likely to occur in the case of the presumption of due care. See State of Maryland for the Use of Geils v. Baltimore Transit Co., 329 F.2d 738 (4th Cir. 1964), cert. denied 379 U.S. 842, rehearing denied 379 U.S. 917, on remand 37 F.R.D. 34 (D.C.Md.), particularly the thoughtful dissent by Haynsworth, J., 329 F.2d at 742–748.

41. Rev. Uniform Rule Evid. (1974) 301, which adopts this rule for all presumptions, contains no provision for an increased measure of persuasion.

42. See also, James & Hazard, Civil Procedure 261 (2d ed. 1977). Dean McCormick in the first edition of this text disagreed with this position, stating (p. 672): "As I have indicated earlier in this paper, I am inclined to think that it is a more natural practice, especially under the American tied-judge system, to mention the presumption, so that the jury may appreciate the legal

recognition of a slant of policy or probability as the reason for placing on the party this particular burden. If this is true when the presumption operates (as it usually would) in favor of the plaintiff, who has the general burden of proof, so that the presumption would result in an issue being singled out and the burden thereon placed on the defendant, much more is it true when the presumption operates in favor of the defendant. In such case under the orthodox view the presumption would be swallowed up in the larger instruction that the plaintiff has the burden on everything that he has pleaded. This smothers any hint of the recognized policy or probabilities behind the particular presumption."

43. The confused situation in two states is described in Graham, Presumptions in Civil Cases in Illinois: Do They Exist? 1977 S.Ill.L.J. 1 (1977), and Comment, Presumptions in Texas: A Study in Irrational Jury Control, 52 Tex.L.Rev. 1329 (1974).

44. See Morgan, Some Problems of Proof 74–81 (1956): Cleary, supra n. 1 at 20; Gausewitz, supra n. 1 at 342; Supreme Court Draft of the Federal Rules of Evidence, 56 F.R.D. 183, 208 (1972). The rule that a presumption operates to fix the burden of persuasion has been called the Pennsylvania rule. However, if the rule ever had general application in that state, it certainly no longer does. See, e.g., Allison v. Snelling & Snelling, Inc., 425 Pa. 519, 229 A.2d 861 (1967); Waters v. New Amsterdam Casualty Co., 393 Pa. 247, 144 A.2d 354 (1958).

has been that it requires a "shift" in the burden of persuasion something that is, by definition of the burden, impossible.[45] The argument seems misplaced, in that it assumes that the burden of persuasion is fixed at the commencement of the action. However, as we have seen,[46] the burden of persuasion need not finally be assigned until the case is ready to go to the jury. Thus, using a presumption to fix that burden would not cause it to shift, but merely cause it to be assigned on the basis of policy considerations arising from the evidence introduced at the trial rather than those thought to exist on the basis of the pleadings.[47] Certainly there is no reason why policy factors thought to be controlling at the pleading stage should outweigh factors bearing upon the same policies that arise from the evidence. Just the reverse should be true.

Certainly, some presumptions have been interpreted consistently as affecting the burden of persuasion without a great deal of discussion of a "shifting" burden of proof.[48] The real question is more fundamental: should this rule which is applicable to some presumptions be applicable universally? The answer to that query depends, not on theoretical distinctions between shifting as opposed to reassigning the burden of persuasion, but upon whether the policy behind the creation of all presumptions is always strong enough to affect the allocation of the burden of persuasion as well as the burden of producing evidence.

One of the leading proponents of the rule allocating the burden of persuasion as a universal rule was Professor Morgan.[49] Although Professor Morgan served as a reporter for the Model Code of Evidence, he was unable to persuade the draftsmen of that code to incorporate into it a provision embracing this view of the effect of presumptions.[50] The Model Code instead takes a rigid Thayerian position.[51] However, Morgan also was active in the drafting of the original Uniform Rules of Evidence where he had considerably more success in inducing an adoption of his theory. The original Uniform Rules provided that where the facts upon which the presumption is based have "probative value" the burden of persuasion is assigned to the adversary; where there is no such probative value, the presumption has only a Thayerian effect and dies when met by contrary proof.[52]

The Uniform Rules, although having much to commend them, presented problems.[53] Obviously, they did not provide for a single rule. Different courts could give different answers to the question whether a particular presumption has probative value. The possibilities of inconsistency and confusion, although reduced by the rules, were still present. Further, the distinction made was a thin one that disregarded the existence of strong social policies behind some presumptions that lack probative value. Certainly if a presumption is not based on probability but rather is based solely upon social policy, there may be more, and not less, reason to

45. Laughlin, supra n. 1 at 211.

46. See § 336 supra.

47. The policies behind the allocation of the burden of persuasion are discussed generally in § 337 supra. The policies behind the creation of presumptions are discussed in § 343 supra.

48. See § 343, text accompanying nn. 23–27, supra, concerning the presumption of legitimacy. See also cases cited n. 39 supra and Brandis, North Carolina Evidence, § 235 at 234–36 (2d rev. ed., 1982) for a discussion of the effect of a presumption of regularity.

49. Morgan, Some Problems of Proof, supra n. 44 at 81.

"Just as the courts have come to recognize that there is no a priori formula for fixing the burden of

persuasion, so they should recognize that if there is a good reason for putting on one party or the other the burden of going forward with evidence—if it might not as well have been determined by chance—it ought to be good enough to control a finding when the mind of the trier is in equilibrium."

50. See Morgan, Foreword to Model Code of Evidence at 54–65 (1942).

51. Model Code of Evidence Rule 704. For text see n. 9 supra.

52. Original Unif.R.Evid. 14 (1953).

53. See the criticism in Cleary, supra n. 1 at 28; Gausewitz, Presumptions, 40 Minn.L.Rev. 391, 401–410 (1956).

preserve it in the face of contrary proof. A presumption based on a natural inference can stand on its own weight either when met by a motion for a directed verdict or in the jury's deliberations. A presumption based on social policy may need an extra boost in order to insure that the policy is not overlooked. Morgan apparently recognized the weakness of the distinction made by the rule and seemed to have agreed to it only to allay fears that a provision giving to all presumptions the effect of fixing the burden of persuasion might be unconstitutional.[54]

An approach almost directly opposite to the one taken in the Uniform Rules is taken in California's Code of Evidence, adopted in 1965. Under the California Code, presumptions based upon "public policy" operate to fix the burden of persuasion;[55] presumptions that are established "to implement no public policy other than to facilitate the determination of a particular action" are given a Thayerian effect.[56] The California approach is an improvement over the Uniform Rules but is still not completely satisfactory. The line between presumptions based on public policy and those which are not may not be easy to draw.[57] Furthermore, although the California distinction is sounder than that made in the Uniform Rules, it is not completely convincing. The fact that the policy giving rise to a presumption is one that is concerned with the resolution of a particular dispute rather than the implementation of broader social goals, does not necessarily mean that the policy is satisfied by the shifting of the burden of producing evidence and that it should disappear when contrary proof is introduced. California asks

the wrong question about the policies behind presumptions. The inquiry should not be directed to the breadth of the policy but rather to the question whether the policy considerations behind a certain presumption are sufficient to override the policies that tentatively fix the burdens of proof at the pleading stage.

The Federal Rules of Evidence, as adopted by the Supreme Court and submitted to the Congress, took the approach advocated by Morgan. The proposed Rule 301 provided that "a presumption imposes on the party against whom it is directed, the burden of proving that the non-existence of the presumed fact is more probable than its existence."[58] However, the draft did not survive congressional scrutiny and Rule 301, as enacted, has a distinct Thayerian flavor:

> In all civil actions and proceedings not otherwise provided for by Act of Congress or by these rules, a presumption imposes on the party against whom it is directed, the burden of going forward with evidence to rebut or meet the presumption but does not shift to such party the burden of proof in the sense of the risk of non-persuasion, which remains throughout the trial upon the party of whom it was originally cast.[59]

Some legal scholars have argued that Federal Rule 301 does not preclude instructions which at least alert the jury to the strength of logic and policy underlying a presumption, even though evidence contrary to the existence of the presumed fact has been introduced.[60] Furthermore, there has been willingness on the part of the federal courts to find that certain acts of Congress create presumptions of greater vitality than that

---

54. Morgan, Presumptions, 10 Rutgers L.Rev. 512, 513, (1956).

55. West's Ann.Cal.Evid.Code §§ 605–606.

56. Id. §§ 603–604.

57. See note, 53 Calif.L.Rev. 1439, 1445–1450 (1965).

58. 56 F.R.D. 183, 208.

59. Fed.R.Evid. 301.

60. Louisell, Construing Rule 301: Instructing the Jury on Presumptions in Civil Actions and Proceedings, 63 Va.L.Rev. 281 (1977); Mueller, Instructing the Jury Upon Presumptions in Civil Cases: Comparing Federal

Rule 301 and Uniform Rule 301, 12 Land and Water L.Rev. 219 (1977). Certainly, given the federal judge's authority to comment on the evidence, the jury may be instructed that it may infer the existence of the presumed fact from the basic facts. Louisell and Mueller go further and argue that, depending upon the nature of the presumption, the jury may be instructed either (1) that upon finding of the basic facts it should also find the presumed fact unless upon all the evidence in the case it finds that the nonexistence of the presumed fact is at least as probable as its existence; or (2) that the basic facts are strong evidence of the presumed fact. Louisell, id. at 314; Mueller, id. at 285–286.

provided by Rule 301 [61] or even that certain presumptions in existence at the time of the adoption of Rule 301 are not subject to the procedure set forth in that rule.[62] On the other hand, the rule has also served as a guideline for courts wishing to give a "bursting bubble" effect to a presumption, even where the court may not necessarily believe itself bound by the dictates of Rule 301.[63]

The matter is further complicated by the fact that many of the states thus far adopting new evidence rules based upon the federal rules, have taken the approach of original Rule 301 and allocate the burden of persuasion based upon the presumption.[64] Likewise, the Revised Uniform Rules of Evidence (1974), reject the "bursting bubble" and contain a Rule 301 almost identical to the rule submitted by the Supreme Court to the Congress.[65]

(C) The Search for the Grail

Despite the best efforts of legal scholars, instead of having one rule to govern all presumptions in all proceedings, we are left in some ways in a more confusing state than that which existed prior to the adoption of the Federal Rules.[66] Neither Morgan's view that all presumptions operate to assign the burden of persuasion nor the Thayerian concept of a disappearing presumption has yet to win the day.

The problem may be inherent in the nature of the concept of a "presumption." At least one author has argued that the concept is an artificial one, an attempt to do through a legal fiction what courts should be doing directly; [67] that the term "presumption" should be eliminated from legal usage and the functions which it serves replaced by direct allocations of the burdens of proof and by judicial comment accurately describing the logical implication of certain facts.[68] In one sense, the suggestion is attractive. The courts should indeed be discussing the propriety of allocating the burdens of proof, rather than the conceptual technical application of a presumption. Yet, both the term and concept of a presumption, however misunderstood, are so engrained in the law that it is difficult to imagine their early demise. Furthermore, as the author recognizes, there are instances in which the evidence introduced at the trial may be such as to give rise to a rule of law which shifts or reassigns the burdens of proof. He calls this a

---

61. Plough, Inc. v. Mason and Dixon Lines, 630 F.2d 468 (6th Cir. 1980); Solder Removal Co. v. United States International Trade Commission, 582 F.2d 628 (C.C.P.A.1978); N.L.R.B. v. Tahoe Nugget, Inc., 584 F.2d 293 (9th Cir. 1978), cert. denied 442 U.S. 921, rehearing denied 444 U.S. 887.

62. James v. River Parishes Co., Inc., 686 F.2d 1129 (5th Cir. 1982).

63. Lovelace v. Sherwin-Williams Co., 681 F.2d 230 (4th Cir. 1982); Reeves v. General Foods Corp., 682 F.2d 515 (5th Cir. 1982). See also Texas Department of Community Affairs v. Burdine, 450 U.S. 248 (1981), on remand 647 F.2d 513 (5th Cir.) (analysis of a presumption in a manner consistent with Rule 301, but without reference to that rule).

64. See compilation of state adaptations of Federal Rule 301 in Weinstein & Berger, Evidence at T–22 (1982).

65. Rev. Uniform Rule Evid. (1974) 301(a) provides:

In all actions and proceedings not otherwise provided for by statute or by these rules, a presumption imposes on the party against whom it is directed the burden of proving that the nonexistence of the presumed fact is more probable than its existence.

Several of the states adopting the Federal Rules have taken the Uniform Rule approach, see, e.g., Ark. Evid.Rule 301; Maine Evid.Rule 301; Wyoming Evid. Rule 301.

66. The problem is made even more complex by Fed.R.Evid. 302 which provides:

In civil actions and proceedings, the effect of a presumption respecting a fact which is an element of a claim or defense as to which state law supplies the rule of decision is determined in accordance with state law.

67. Allen, Presumptions, Inferences and Burden of Proof in Federal Civil Actions—An Anatomy of Unnecessary Ambiguities and a Proposal for Reform, 76 Nw. U.L.Rev. 892 (1982); Allen, Presumptions in Civil Actions Reconsidered, 66 Iowa L.Rev. 843 (1981). Allen proposes a revision of Rule 301 which would reflect his analysis. 72 Nw.U.L.Rev. at 907–08.

68. The present editor also suggested the elimination of the concept of a presumption, at least with regard to presumptions which transfer one of the burdens of proof with regard to an element of a case. Cleary, Presuming and Pleading: An Essay on Juristic Immaturity, 12 Stan.L.Rev. 5 (1959).

"conditional imperative" [69] and recognizes that in such a case the allocation of the burdens of proof cannot be made prior to trial. While the term "conditional imperative" may be just as good as "presumption," it is no better and the same set of problems which exist with regard to presumptions are just as likely to occur regardless of the label employed.

The answer may be that there is no single solution to the problem. The resistance of the courts and legislatures to a universal rule of presumptions is reflective of the fact that there are policies of varying strength behind different presumptions and therefore a hierarchy of desired results. In one instance, the policy may be such as only to give rise to a standardized inference, a rule of law which gets the plaintiff to the jury but does not compel a directed verdict in his favor. In another instance, the policy may be strong enough to compel a directed verdict in his favor, thus shifting the burden of producing evidence to the opposing party, but not strong enough to reassign the burden of persuasion.[70] In still another instance, the policy may be strong enough to reassign the burden of persuasion.

Attempts to categorize presumptions according to policy considerations have been thoughtful and well-meaning.[71] Unfortunately, they have fallen short of the mark, largely because of the inherent difficulty of the task. Each presumption is created for its own reasons—reasons which are inextricably intertwined with the pertinent substantive law. These substantive considerations have a considerable impact on the procedural effect desirable for a particular

presumption. The diversity of the considerations simply defies usable categorization. The law and lawyers are accustomed to considering the dictates of the substantive law in determining the initial allocation of the burdens of proof. The task should not be thought too onerous in connection with the operation of presumptions which, after all, simply operate to reallocate those burdens during the course of the trial.

Rather than attempting to provide a single rule for all presumptions, a task which has thus far proved futile, the draftsmen of evidence codes might instead provide guidelines for the appropriate but various effects which a presumption may have on the burdens of proof. The courts and legislatures would then have the opportunity to select the appropriate effect to be given to a particular presumption. The term presumption seems likely to be with us forever; it also seems likely that different presumptions will continue to be viewed as having different procedural effects; we can only hope to insure that the concept which the term "presumption" represents is applied constructively and rationally.

WESTLAW
REFERENCES

bubble /4 burst!

157k89

presumption* /s "public policy"

presumption* /s agen** consen! /s automobile*
    vehicle* car cars /s rebut!

conflict! opposite /2 presumption*

word! language /s instruct! /3 jury /s
    presumption*

title(james +s "river parishes") & court(ca5)

---

69. See Allen, supra n. 67, 66 Iowa L.Rev. at 850–51. Allen, however, would attempt to solve the problem of the conditional imperative by having the trial judge decide all questions of fact upon which the allocation of a burden of production or persuasion is conditioned. See Allen's proposed Rule 301, supra, n. 67, 72 Nw.U.L.Rev. at 907.

70. There are, various problems which remain even when a presumption clearly falls into this category. For example: If sufficient evidence contrary to the

presumed facts is introduced, should the proponent of the presumption survive a renewed motion for directed verdict? What, if anything, should the jury be told about either the existence of the presumption or the strength of the basic facts? The answers to these questions may also vary among various presumptions and with regard to evidence introduced in each case.

71. See the discussion of the original Uniform Rules of Evidence and the California Evidence Code, text accompanying nn. 52–57, supra.

§ 345. Constitutional Questions in Civil Cases

Serious questions under the United States Constitution are raised by the creation and use of presumptions in criminal cases. Those questions are discussed in subsequent sections.[1] Although there are constitutional considerations involved in the use of presumptions in civil cases, the problems are simply not of the same magnitude. In a criminal case, the scales are deliberately overbalanced in favor of the defendant through the requirement that the prosecution prove each element of the offense beyond a reasonable doubt.[2] Any rule that has even the appearance of lightening that burden is viewed with the most extreme caution. However, there is no need for this special protection for any one party to a civil action. The burdens of proof are fixed at the pleading stage, not for constitutional reasons, but for reasons of probability, social policy, and convenience.[3] There is no reason why the same policy considerations, as reflected in the operation of a presumption, should not be permitted further to effect an allocation of the burdens of proof during the course of the trial.

Nevertheless, the courts articulate a "rational connection" test in civil cases, which requires that such a connection exist between the basic facts and the presumed facts in order for the presumption to pass constitutional muster. Recent cases have applied the test, but upheld the presumption.[4] Obviously, under certain circumstances a presumption could operate in such an arbitrary manner as to violate fundamental due process considerations, even in a civil case.[5] But to impose a strictly applied "rational connection" limitation upon the creation of presumptions in civil cases would mean that only presumptions based on probability would be permissible. Such a limitation would ignore other, equally valid, reasons for the creation of the rules. Considerations which have been either explicitly rejected or severely limited in criminal cases, such as the comparative knowledge of the parties with regard to the facts [6] and the power of the legislature to do away with a claim or a defense entirely,[7] should remain significant in determining the validity of a civil presumption.[8]

Perhaps the most difficult question with regard to civil presumptions is whether a

§ 345

1. Sections 347–349 infra.

2. See § 341 supra with regard to the nature of the prosecution's burden; see § 347 infra with regard to the constitutional limits on the effect that a presumption may have upon that burden.

3. See § 337 supra.

4. Usery v. Turner Elkhorn Mining Co., 428 U.S. 1, 28 (1976), where the Court stated that presumptions arising under the civil statute involving "matters of economic regulation" were to be tested by a rational connection test. See also United States Steel Corp. v. Oravetz, 686 F.2d 197 (3d Cir. 1982).

5. See Benham v. Edwards, 501 F.Supp. 1050 (N.D. Ga.1980) where the court held that a statutory presumption of continued insanity of persons acquitted in a criminal case on insanity grounds was invalid as a denial of equal protection and due process. On appeal, the Court of Appeals modified the trial court's decision, but upheld the decision with regard to the invalidity of the presumption. In so holding, it relied exclusively on an equal protection argument. 678 F.2d 511 (5th Cir. 1982).

6. See Morrison v. California, 291 U.S. 82, 91 (1934), discussed in § 347 n. 27 infra.

7. See Ferry v. Ramsey, 277 U.S. 88 (1928), a civil action in which the Court, through Holmes, J., upheld a Kansas statute imposing liability upon bank directors who, knowing of their bank's insolvency, assented to the reception of deposits, and further providing that proof of the bank's insolvency should be prima facie evidence of the directors' knowledge and assent. Mr. Justice Holmes noted: "It is said that the liability is founded by the statute upon the directors' assent to the deposit and that when this is the ground the assent cannot be proved by artificial presumptions that have no warrant from experience. But the short answer is that the statute might have made the directors personally liable to depositors in every case, if it had been so minded, and that if it had purported to do so, whoever accepted the office would assume the risk. The statute in short imposed a liability that was less than might have been imposed, and that being so, the thing to be considered is the result reached, not the possibly inartificial [i.e. inartistic] or clumsy way of reaching it."

8. See Weinstein & Berger, Evidence ¶ 301[01]; Note, 55 Colum.L.Rev. 527, 538–39 (1955).

presumption may operate to assign the burden of persuasion. The question arises from the contrast between two Supreme Court cases considering the validity of presumptions of negligence operating against railroads. In the first, Mobile, J. & K. C. R. R. v. Turnipseed,[9] decided in 1910, the Court considered a Mississippi statutory presumption of negligence operating against a railroad in an action for death of an employee in a derailment. The statute provided that proof of injury inflicted by the running of railroad cars would be "prima facie evidence of the want of reasonable skill and care" on the part of the railroad. Noting that the only effect of the statute was to impose on the railroad the duty of producing some evidence to the contrary, the court held that the rational connection between the fact proved and the fact presumed was sufficient to sustain the presumption.

However, in 1929, in Western & Atlantic R. R. v. Henderson,[10] the Court struck down a Georgia statute making railroads liable for damage done by trains, unless the railroad made it appear that reasonable care had been used, "the presumption in all cases being against the company." In Henderson the plaintiff alleged that her husband had been killed in a grade crossing collision. The jury was instructed that negligence was presumed from the fact of injury and that the burden was therefore on the railroad to show that it exercised ordinary care. The Court held that the mere fact of a collision between a train and a vehicle at a crossing furnished no basis for any inference as to negligence and that therefore the presumption was invalid. Turnipseed was distinguished on the ground that the Mississippi

presumption raised "merely a temporary inference of fact" while the Georgia statute created "an inference that is given effect of evidence to be weighed against opposing testimony and is to prevail unless such testimony is found by the jury to preponderate."[11]

Although perhaps a grade crossing collision differs from a derailment and therefore Turnipseed and Henderson can be distinguished on their facts, it is nevertheless fair to read Henderson as imposing constitutional limitations on the effect of at least some presumptions. However, as has been cogently pointed out,[12] Henderson may simply no longer be valid law. The case assumed the necessity of a showing of negligence. But the concept of negligence has lost most of its sanctity since 1929.[13] Although there is considerable doubt as to what the Court would have done in that year, there is little doubt today that a legislature would be permitted at least to relegate lack of negligence to the status of an affirmative defense. If negligence could be so reduced, a presumption which assigned the burden of persuasion could logically be treated no differently.

Since Henderson, the Court has, on at least one occasion, approved a state presumption that operated to fix the burden of persuasion on the party controverting the presumed fact. In that case, Dick v. New York Life Insurance Co.[14] the Court approved a North Dakota common law rule that imposed on the defendant insurance company, defending against the operation of an accidental death clause, the burden of persuading the jury that the death of the insured was due to suicide.[15]

The questionable status of Henderson in light of recent developments in tort law, the

9. 219 U.S. 35 (1910).

10. 279 U.S. 639 (1929).

11. Id. at 643–644.

12. See Advisory Committee's Note to Federal Rule 301 as adopted by the Supreme Court, 56 F.R.D. 208; Fornoff, Presumptions—The Proposed Federal Rules of Evidence, 24 Ark.L.Rev. 401, 412–413 (1971).

13. See Prosser, Torts 494–496 (4th ed. 1971).

14. 359 U.S. 437 (1959).

15. See also Lavine v. Milne, 424 U.S. 577 (1976), where the Court upheld a New York statutory "rebuttable presumption" which provided that a person applying for a certain type of welfare assistance within 75 days after voluntary cessation of employment would be deemed to have quit his employment for purposes of affecting his welfare rights. The Court noted that the applicant bore the burden of persuasion with regard to all issues under the application and that therefore the "presumption" did no more than make that burden absolutely clear with regard to this issue. In the course

holding of the Court in *Dick*, and the illogic of treating presumptions differently from other rules of law allocating the burden of persuasion, all make it extremely unlikely that there are now serious constitutional limits on the effect that may be given to presumptions in civil cases.[16]

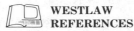

WESTLAW REFERENCES

title(dick +s "new york life") & judge(warren)

§ 346. Affirmative Defenses and Presumptions in Criminal Cases: (a) Terminology

As has been earlier pointed out, the courts and legislatures do not always use the term presumption in the sense either that the term is used in this text or by the same courts and legislatures on other occasions.[1] The use of loose terminology is perhaps even more prevalent in dealing with presumptions operating in criminal cases than in civil cases. The best example is one that has already been given. The "presumption of innocence" is not a presumption at all, but simply another way of stating the rule that the prosecution has the burden of proving the guilt of the accused beyond a reasonable doubt.[2]

Similarly, the courts and writers have struggled to define and distinguish presumptions and affirmative defenses.[3] Certainly, these procedural devices have factors in common. Yet, as the devices are traditionally defined, there are some significant variations between them that have caused the courts to treat them differently.

1. Affirmative defenses. The term affirmative defense is traditionally used to describe the allocation of a burden, either of production or of persuasion, or both, to the defendant in a criminal case.[4] The burden is fixed by statute or case law at the beginning of the case and does not depend upon the introduction of any evidence by the prosecution. For example, a crime may be statutorily defined as consisting of elements A and B. However, the accused may be exonerated or the offense reduced in degree upon proof of C. C is an affirmative defense. In some instances, the defendant may simply

---

of its decision the Court states: ". . . it is not for us to resolve the question of where the burden ought to lie on this issue. Outside the criminal law area, where special concerns attend, the locus of the burden of persuasion is normally not an issue of federal constitutional moment." Id. at 585.

16. The possibility of constitutional limitations on the effect of presumptions in civil cases caused the draftsman of the original Uniform Rules of Evidence (1953) to distinguish between presumptions having probative value, as to which the burden of persuasion is upon the party against whom the presumption operates, and presumptions without probative value, which disappear where contrary proof is introduced. Unif.R. Evid. (1953) 14. See Morgan, Presumptions, 10 Rutgers L.Rev. 512, 513 (1956). This distinction now seems completely unnecessary. See the excellent discussion of this question in Note, 53 Calif.L.Rev. 1439, 1967–71 (1965).

See also the discussion in § 344, text accompanying notes 50–54, supra. The Revised Uniform Rules (1974) provide that all presumptions operate to assign the burden of persuasion. Uniform Rule 301. See § 344, text accompanying n. 65, supra.

This discussion applies only to rebuttable presumptions. Conclusive presumptions are really statements of substantive law (see § 342 supra) and, if not necessarily or universally true in part, may be fundamentally unfair and therefore unconstitutional. E.g., Cleveland Board of Education v. LaFleur, 414 U.S. 632 (1974) (conclusive presumption that teacher who is 4 or 5 months pregnant is physically incapable of continuing her duties held unconstitutional).

§ 346

1. See § 342, text accompanying n. 2. The converse of the proposition stated in the text is also true: rules that are treated as presumptions are not always called by that name. For an illustration of the use and misuse of terminology in this area of the law see the list of statutes "that provide that proof of specified facts has a procedural effect" contained in the Working Papers of the National Commission on Reform of Federal Criminal Laws, Volume 1, at 27–31 (1970).

2. See § 342 supra.

3. See Allen, Structuring Jury Decision-Making in Criminal Cases: A Unified Constitutional Approach to Evidentiary Devices, 94 Harv.L.Rev. 321 (1980); Ashford & Rissinger, Presumptions, Assumptions, and Due Process in Criminal Cases: A Theoretical Overview, 79 Yale L.J. 165 (1969); Jeffries & Stephan, Defenses, Presumptions and Burden of Proof in the Criminal Law, 88 Yale L.J. 1325 (1979).

4. 9 Wigmore, Evidence §§ 2501, 2512, 2514 (Chadbourn rev. 1981); 22A C.J.S. Criminal Law §§ 572–577; Dec.Dig. Criminal Law ⟐329–333.

have the burden of production of evidence with regard to C; in the event that burden is satisfied, the prosecution will then have the burden of persuading the jury of elements A, B, *and* C beyond a reasonable doubt. In other instances, the defendant will have both the burden of production and the burden of persuasion.[5] Thus, the prosecution will have no burden with regard to C; the defendant must both introduce proof of C and persuade the jury of its existence. Usually, the measure of persuasion imposed on the defendant with regard to an affirmative defense is a preponderance of the evidence.[6]

2. Presumptions. Presumptions have already been defined as a standardized practice under which certain facts are held to call for uniform treatment with respect to their effect as proof of other facts.[7] In civil cases, the term presumption is properly reserved for a rule that provides that upon proof of certain basic facts, at least the burden of producing evidence with regard to certain presumed facts shifts. As has been discussed, a presumption may in some instances operate to allocate the burden of persuasion as well.[8]

A somewhat different terminology has been used more or less consistently in criminal cases. The tendency in criminal cases has been to describe any standardized rule which permits the inference of one fact from another as a presumption, regardless of whether the rule operates to shift the burden of production. Thus, assume a crime with three elements, A, B and C. A rule of ·law provides that fact C may be inferred from proof of A and B. Such a rule is usually described as a presumption, whether or

not any burden is actually shifted to the defendant. In most instances, no burden shifts; the presumption operates only to permit the prosecution to make out a prima facie case by proof of A and B alone. The jury will be instructed that it may, but is not required to, infer the existence of fact C from proof of facts A and B.

The United States Supreme Court has resurrected terminology used in the first edition of this text[9] to describe the different effects of presumptions in criminal cases. In County Court of Ulster County v. Allen,[10] the court distinguished between mandatory and permissive presumptions. A mandatory presumption is one which operates to shift at least the burden of production. It tells the trier of fact that it must find the presumed fact upon proof of the basic fact, "at least unless the defendant has come forward with some evidence to rebut the presumed connection between the two facts."[11] The Court further sub-divided mandatory presumptions into two parts: presumptions that merely shift the burden of production to the defendant and presumptions that shift the burden of persuasion. A permissive presumption is one which allows, but does not require, the trier of fact to infer the presumed fact from proof of the basic facts. Under the *Allen* decision, these various kinds of presumptions differ not only procedurally, but also with regard to the tests for their constitutional permissibility as well.

**WESTLAW
REFERENCES**

di affirmative defense

"burden of persuasion"   /s   "affirmative defense*"

---

5. A New Federal Criminal Code, proposed in 1971 but not as yet enacted by the Congress, divides what have been referred to generally as affirmative defenses into (1) defenses, which need not be negated by the prosecution unless "the issue is in the case as a result of evidence sufficient to raise a reasonable doubt on the issue," and (2) affirmative defenses, which must be proved by the defendant by a preponderance of the evidence. Proposed Federal Criminal Code § 103. Final Report of the National Commission on Reform of Federal Criminal Cases 3 (1971).

6. Patterson v. New York, 432 U.S. 197 (1977); State v. McCauley, 130 W.Va. 401, 43 S.E.2d 454 (1947).

7. Section 342 supra.

8. Section 344 supra.

9. Section 308.

10. 442 U.S. 140 (1979).

11. Id. at 157.

§ 347. Affirmative Defenses and Presumptions in Criminal Cases: (b) Constitutionality

The past decade has brought some noteable developments with regard to the constitutionality of both affirmative defenses and presumptions.

1. Affirmative defenses. Historically, many states placed both the burden of production and the burden of persuasion on the accused with regard to several classical affirmative defenses, including insanity [1] and self-defense.[2] The allocation to the defendant of the burdens of proof with regard to insanity survived constitutional challenge in 1952. In Leland v. Oregon,[3] the Supreme Court held that the defendant could be required to prove his insanity at the time of the alleged crime beyond a reasonable doubt. On the other hand, some limitations were imposed on the creation or effect of affirmative defenses. For example, one United States Court of Appeals held unconstitutional a state's allocation of the burden of persuasion to the accused with regard to alibi.[4] The court reasoned that an alibi was a mere form of denial of participation in the criminal act, not a true affirmative defense.

Although perhaps foreshadowed by the treatment given the defense of alibi, the real revolution in thought with regard to affirmative defenses occurred in the mid-1970's with two pivotal Supreme Court decisions.

In Mullaney v. Wilbur,[5] the Court reversed a Maine murder conviction where the jury had been instructed, in accordance with longstanding state practice, that if the prosecution proved "that the homicide was both intentional and unlawful, malice aforethought was to be conclusively implied unless the defendant proved by a fair preponderance of the evidence that he acted in the heat of passion on sudden provocation," in which event the defendant would be guilty only of manslaughter. The placing of this burden on the defendant was said to violate the dictates of In re Winship [6] that the due process clause requires the prosecution to prove beyond a reasonable doubt every fact necessary to constitute the crime charged. Although recognizing that under Maine law murder and manslaughter were but degrees of the same crime, the Court noted that *Winship* applied to instances in which the issue is degree of criminal culpability as well as to cases of guilt or innocence.[7]

The *Mullaney* case was surprising in view of the long history in some jurisdictions of placing the burden of reducing the degree of a homicide on the defendant.[8] However, given the holding and rationale of *Winship*, it was not totally unexpected. It was certainly possible, and perhaps fair, to read the *Mullaney* case broadly so as to require the imposition of the burden of persuasion on the prosecution with regard to many, if not all, of the traditional affirmative defenses.[9]

§ 347

1. Leland v. Oregon, 343 U.S. 790 (1952), rehearing denied 344 U.S. 848; State v. Finn, 257 Minn. 138, 100 N.W.2d 508 (1960). See also, cases in C.J.S. Homicide § 194.

2. Brown v. State, 9 Terry (48 Del.) 427, 105 A.2d 646 (1954); see also C.J.S. Homicide § 195.

3. Supra n. 1.

4. Stump v. Bennett, 398 F.2d 111 (8th Cir.1968), cert. denied 393 U.S. 1001, striking down an Iowa practice, which Iowa discontinued. State v. Galloway, 167 N.W.2d 89 (Iowa 1969), appeal after remand 187 N.W.2d 725. See also, Commonwealth v. McLeod, 367 Mass. 500, 326 N.E.2d 905 (1975).

5. 421 U.S. 684, 686 (1975).

6. 397 U.S. 358 (1970), conformed to 27 N.Y.2d 728, 314 N.Y.S.2d 536, 262 N.E.2d 675. See discussion in text accompanying n. 6, § 341 *supra.*

7. In *Winship*, the Court referred to the immensely important interests of the accused in a criminal case arising from both the possibility of loss of personal liberty and the stigma attached to conviction. In re Winship supra n. 6, at 363–64. In *Mullaney*, the Court noted that the consequences of a verdict of murder differed significantly from that of manslaughter, both in terms of loss of liberty and in the stigma attached to the conviction. Mullaney v. Wilbur, supra n. 5 at 697–98.

8. See, e.g., State v. Boyd, 278 N.C. 682, 180 S.E.2d 794 (1971). See also, LaFave & Scott, Handbook of Criminal Law 534–540 (1972).

9. Comments, 36 Ohio St.L.J. 828 (1975), 11 Harv. C.R.–C.L.L.Rev. 390 (1976).

Indeed, the opinion was read by several state courts as constitutionally compelling the prosecution to bear the burden of persuasion with regard to various affirmative defenses.[10] Only the existence of the *Leland*[11] opinion, not expressly overruled in *Mullaney*, prevented one federal court from applying *Mullaney* to impose upon a state the burden of persuasion with regard to an insanity defense.[12]

The first real indication that the holding in *Mullaney* had far more narrow limits came when the Court, in Rivera v. Delaware,[13] dismissed, as not presenting a substantial federal question, an appeal from a conviction in which the defendant had borne the burden of proving his insanity. The indication became a certainty when the Court decided Patterson v. New York.[14] In *Patterson*, the Court upheld a New York procedure under which an accused is guilty of murder in the second degree if he is found, beyond a reasonable doubt, to have intentionally killed another person. The crime may be reduced to manslaughter if the defendant proves by a preponderance of the evidence that he had acted under the influence of "extreme emotional disturbance." The Court held that the New York procedure did not violate due process noting, in the language of *Winship*, " 'every fact necessary to constitute the crime with which [Patterson was] charged had to be proved beyond a reasonable doubt.' "[15] *Mullaney* was distinguished as dealing with a situation in which the defendant was asked to disprove an essential element of the prosecution's case—malice aforethought.[16] New York, unlike Maine, did not include malice aforethought in its definition of murder. By this omission, New York had avoided the defect found fatal in *Mullaney*, even though the defense involved in the *Patterson* case was but an expanded version of the "heat of passion on sudden provocation" involved in *Mullaney*.

Although the Court's approach in *Patterson* has been much criticized as overly formalistic,[17] the case when read in conjunction with *Mullaney* suggests a procedural analysis which, at least for the time being, provides some guidelines for the courts. Only a true affirmative defense, as defined above, may operate to allocate the burden of persuasion to the accused. Such a defense would consist of facts which exonerate the defendant or reduce the degree of the offense and do not simply disprove an element of the crime. Under this analysis, the lower courts have universally upheld the allocation of the burden of persuasion to the accused with regard to insanity.[18] The allocation of the burden with regard to self-defense[19] and other designated affirmative defenses[20] has

---

10. Commonwealth v. Rodriguez, 370 Mass. 684, 352 N.E.2d 203 (1976) (self-defense); State v. Matheson, 363 A.2d 716 (Me.1976) (entrapment). The broadest interpretation of *Mullaney* was in Evans v. State, 28 Md.App. 640, 349 A.2d 300, 307 (1975), affirmed 278 Md. 197, 362 A.2d 629, where the court stated that *Mullaney* applied to prohibit the placing of the burden of persuasion on the defendant with regard to "a. Any theory of justification . . . b. Any theory of excuse . . . . c. Any theory of mitigation . . . . d. Intoxication, e. Entrapment, f. Duress or Coercion, g. Necessity."

11. Supra, nn. 1 and 3.

12. Buzynski v. Oliver, 538 F.2d 6 (1st Cir.1976), cert. denied 429 U.S. 984.

13. 429 U.S. 877 (1976).

14. 432 U.S. 197 (1977). In *Patterson*, the Court indicated that, in dismissing *Rivera* it meant to confirm the continuing validity of *Leland*. Id. at 204.

15. Id. at 206.

16. Id. at 215.

17. Allen, supra § 346 n. 3; Jeffries & Stephan, supra § 346 n. 3; See also Cole v. Stevenson, 620 F.2d 1055, 1063–1066 (4th Cir.1980), cert. denied 449 U.S. 1004, (dissent by Murnaghan, J.).

18. Walker v. Butterworth, 599 F.2d 1074 (1st Cir. 1979), cert. denied 444 U.S. 937; Kuzeminski v. Perini, 614 F.2d 121 (6th Cir.1980), cert. denied 449 U.S. 866; Duisen v. Wyrick, 566 F.2d 616 (8th Cir.1977); People v. Drew, 22 Cal.3d 333, 149 Cal.Rptr. 275, 583 P.2d 1318 (en banc 1978).

19. Berrier v. Egeler, 583 F.2d 515 (6th Cir.1978), cert. denied 439 U.S. 955 (absence of self-defense an element of murder); Williams v. Mohn, 462 F.Supp. 756 (N.D.W.Va.1978), modified 605 F.2d 1208 (4th Cir.) (absence of self-defense not an element of murder).

20. Farrell v. Czarnetsky, 566 F.2d 381 (2d Cir. 1977), cert. denied 434 U.S. 1077 (defendant required to prove that weapon not loaded in first-degree robbery case); United States ex rel. Goddard v. Vaughn, 614

had mixed treatment, usually based upon the language of the particular statutes.

Note that this analysis mentions only the allocation of the burden of persuasion. Based on the *Patterson* case the courts have had no trouble with an affirmative defense which simply requires the defendant to bear a burden of production.[21] Thus, even though absence of self-defense is considered an element of a crime as defined in a particular state, so as to prohibit the allocation of the burden of persuasion to the accused, the accused may be required to introduce at least some evidence of self-defense in order for the issue to be placed before the jury.[22]

2. Presumptions. The Supreme Court has substantially defined the constitutional limitations on the use of presumptions in criminal cases in a relatively recent series of opinions, culminating in the 1979 decisions in County Court of Ulster County v. Allen[23] and Sandstrom v. Montana.[24]

The first of these cases was Tot v. United States,[25] decided in 1943. In *Tot* defendants were convicted under a provision of the Federal Firearms Act making it "unlawful for any person who has been convicted of a crime of violence to receive any firearm . . . which has been shipped . . . in interstate . . . commerce" and further providing that "the possession of a firearm . . . by any such person shall be presumptive evidence that such firearm was . . . received by such person in violation of this Act." In holding that the presump-

tion violated due process, the Court stated that "a statutory presumption cannot be sustained if there be no rational connection between the fact proved and the ultimate fact presumed, if the inference of the one from proof of the other is arbitrary because of lack of connection between the two in common experience."[26] The court noted that although state laws might make acquisition difficult, it did not follow from proof of mere possession that the firearms must have been received by the defendants in interstate commerce subsequent to the adoption of the federal act. The firearm might have been acquired intrastate in violation of state law, or, since manufactured years earlier, acquired prior to the adoption of either the state regulation or the federal statute in question.

Perhaps as significant as the Court's adoption of a "rational connection" test for presumptions in criminal cases, was its treatment of two other tests suggested by the government. In addition to advancing rationality as a test, the government had argued that the validity of the presumption could alternatively be tested by the "comparative convenience of producing evidence of the ultimate fact." The Court answered that argument by stating that "comparative convenience" was simply a "corollary" to the controlling rational connection test and that "[t]he argument from convenience is admissible only where the inference is a permissible one . . . ."[27]

The government had also argued that Congress' *greater power* to enact a statute to

---

F.2d 929 (3d Cir.1980), cert. denied 449 U.S. 844 (defendant could have burden of proving voluntary intoxication). See also United States v. Calfon, 607 F.2d 29 (2d Cir.1979), cert. denied 444 U.S. 1085 (no burden on defendant to prove duress in federal court, but no constitutional prohibition against allocation of the burden of persuasion to defendant).

21. Supra n. 14 at 230. See discussion in Jeffries & Stephan, supra § 346 n. 3 at 1334. The placing of a burden of production on the defendant with regard to duress and necessity was specifically recognized by the Supreme Court in United States v. Bailey, 444 U.S. 394 (1980).

22. State v. Patterson, 297 N.C. 247, 254 S.E.2d 604 (1979), appeal after remand 50 N.C.App. 280, 272 S.E.2d 924.

23. 442 U.S. 140 (1979).

24. 442 U.S. 510 (1979), on remand 184 Mont. 391, 603 P.2d 244.

25. 319 U.S. 463 (1943).

26. Id. at 467.

27. The government's argument was apparently based upon a statement by Cardozo, J., in Morrison v. California, 291 U.S. 82, 91 (1934), to the effect that, even if there is no "sinister significance" in the evidence presented there "must be in any event a manifest disparity in convenience of proof and opportunity for knowledge."

prohibit the possession of all firearms by persons convicted of violent crimes, necessarily *included the lesser power* to create the presumption in question.[28] The court rejected the argument, stating first that the government's contention could not sustain the presumption of acquisition after the effective date of the act, and second that "it is plain that Congress, for whatever reason, did not seek to pronounce general prohibition of possession . . . in order to protect interstate commerce, but dealt only with their future acquisition in interstate commerce." [29]

Additional enlightenment with regard to constitutional limits on the creation of presumptions came in two 1965 cases dealing with presumptions enacted to aid the government in prosecuting liquor cases. In United States v. Gainey,[30] the Court considered the validity of a statute which provided that presence at the site is sufficient to convict a defendant of the offense of carrying on the business of distilling without giving bond, "unless the defendant explains such presence to the satisfaction of the jury." The Court applied the rational connection test of *Tot*, but this time sustained the validity of the presumption. However, in United States v. Romano,[31] the court struck down as violative of the principle of *Tot*, an identical presumption with regard to the companion offense of possession of an illegal still.

The Court's reasoning in distinguishing the two presumptions is not difficult to follow. The crime of *carrying on* an illegal distilling business, involved in the *Gainey* case, was an extremely broad one, which, viewed in the light of the aiding and abetting statute, covered almost every conceivable act connected with the operation of a still. A person's unexplained presence at the still made it highly likely that he had something to do with the operation. Yet, as the Court noted, prior to the enactment of

the statutory presumption, the courts had differed in assessing the natural inference that might be derived from such facts. The Court in *Gainey* concluded:

"Congress was undoubtedly aware that manufacturers of illegal liquors are notorious for the deftness with which they locate arcane spots for plying their trade. Legislative recognition of the implications of seclusion only confirms what the folklore teaches—that strangers to the illegal business rarely penetrate the curtain of secrecy. . . . . " [32]

It is fair to interpret *Gainey* as simply sustaining Congress' power to standardize a natural inference. However, no such natural inference existed with regard to the presumption of *possession* from unexplained presence in the statute involved in *Romano*. As to that presumption, the Court stated:

"Presence tells us only that the defendant was there and very likely played a part in the illicit scheme. But presence tells us nothing about what the defendant's specific function was and carries no legitimate, rational or reasonable inference that he was engaged in one of the specialized functions connected with possession, rather than in one of the supply, delivery or operational activities having nothing to do with possession. Presence is relevant and admissible evidence in a trial on a possession charge; but absent some showing of the defendant's function at the still, its connection with possession is too tenuous to permit a reasonable inference of guilt—'the inference of the one from proof of the other is arbitrary . . . .' " [33]

In *Romano*, the court also rejected the "greater includes the lesser argument" urged in the *Tot* case, this time somewhat more clearly:

". . . It may be, of course, that Congress has the power to make presence at an illegal still a punishable crime, but we find no clear indication that it intended to so ex-

28. 319 U.S. at 467–470.

29. 319 U.S. at 472.

30. 380 U.S. 63 (1965).

31. 382 U.S. 136 (1965).

32. 380 U.S. at 67.

33. 382 U.S. at 141.

ercise this power. The crime remains possession, not presence, and, with all due deference to the judgment of Congress, the former may not constitutionally be inferred from the latter." [34]

Tot, Gainey and *Romano* left important questions unanswered. First, the "rational connection" test was vague. Was it a test of relevancy or a test of probative sufficiency? If it was a test of relevancy, a presumption would be valid if the proved fact tended to prove the presumed fact. If it was a test of sufficiency, the existence of the presumed fact would have to be shown to be more likely than not to exist or perhaps even have to be shown to exist beyond a reasonable doubt. Second, the presumption approved in *Gainey* enacted into statute an inference that might fairly have been drawn even without the statute. Would the Court sustain a presumption not based upon a natural inference but upon Congressional review of empirical data which was not to be submitted to the jury in each individual case? [35] Third, would Justice Black's dissent in *Gainey* eventually attract a majority of the Court? In that dissent,[36] joined in part by Justice Douglas,[37] Justice Black stated that the use of the presumption in question unconstitutionally impaired the defendant's "right to have a jury weigh the facts of his case without any congressional interference through predetermination of what evidence would be sufficient to prove the facts necessary to convict in a particular case." [38] He further condemned the presumption as depriving the defendant of his right to remain silent by forcing him to rebut the presumed facts.[39] An adoption of the Black view

would necessarily mean the abrogation of all statutory presumptions operating against the defendant in a criminal case.

In 1969, the Court partially answered the first of these questions and at least suggested answers to the other two. In Leary v. United States [40] it considered a presumption providing that possession of marihuana was sufficient evidence to authorize conviction of transporting and concealing the drug *with knowledge of its illegal importation* unless the defendant explained his possession to the satisfaction of the jury. In reviewing the prior holdings on the question, the court stated:

"The upshot of *Tot, Gainey* and *Romano* is, we think, that a criminal statutory presumption must be regarded as 'irrational' or 'arbitrary,' and hence unconstitutional, unless it can at least be said with substantial assurance that the presumed fact is more likely than not to flow from the proved fact on which it is made to depend. And in the judicial assessment the congressional determination favoring the particular presumption must, of course weigh heavily." [41]

The Court then went on to hold that the presumption, insofar as it dealt with the defendant's knowledge that the drug was illegally imported, was unconstitutional under this standard. It did not purport to consider the validity of the other presumed fact under the statute—the actual illegal importation. To support its conclusion, the Court conducted an extensive examination of both the legislative history of the statute, which it found to be inadequate standing alone to support the presumption, and other, govern-

---

34. Id. at 144.

35. The Court in *Gainey* perhaps suggested the answer to this question, stating: "The process of making the determination of rationality is, by its nature, highly empirical, and in matters not within specialized judicial competence or completely commonplace, significant weight should be accorded the capacity of Congress to amass the stuff of actual experience and cull conclusions from it. . . ." 380 U.S. at 67.

36. Id. at 74–88.

37. Justice Douglas approved the statute as providing a mere "rule of evidence" that the jury was free to

accept or reject as it saw fit. Id. at 72. He believed, however, that the judge's charge to the jury that the inference could be drawn "unless the defendant by the evidence in the case and by proven facts and circumstances explains such presence to the satisfaction of the jury" was an improper comment on the defendant's silence. Id. at 74.

38. Id. at 81.

39. Id. at 87–88.

40. 395 U.S. 6 (1969) (opinion by Harlan, J.).

41. Id. at 36.

mental and nongovernmental, reports and books, published before and after the enactment of the statute in 1956. From this examination, the Court concluded that, although most domestically consumed marihuana comes from abroad, "it would be no more than speculation were we to say that even as much as a majority of possessors 'knew' the source of their marihuana." [42] This conclusion was, the Court found, sufficient to render the "knowledge" portion of the presumption invalid.

The Court in *Leary* did not merely hold that the proved fact must rationally tend to prove the presumed fact. It held, as its careful examination of the available literature clearly indicates, that the presumed fact must actually be more likely than not to exist if the proved fact exists.[43] In a footnote to its above quoted statement of the "more likely than not" rule, the Court added that because of its finding that the presumption was unconstitutional under this standard, it would not reach the question "whether a criminal presumption which passes muster when so judged must also satisfy the criminal 'reasonable doubt' standard if proof of the crime charged or an essential element thereof depends upon its use." [44]

Moreover, the Court's extensive reference to data outside the record as well as failure to incorporate into its opinion the objections raised by Mr. Justice Black in his dissent in *Gainey*,[45] suggested that the other two questions raised above would be answered in favor of the statutory presumption. This suggestion was borne out in 1970 in Turner v. United States.[46]

In *Turner*, the Court dealt with two presumptions. One was identical with the presumption struck down in *Leary*, except that the drugs involved in *Turner* were heroin and cocaine rather than marihuana. The other provided that the absence of appropriate tax paid stamps from narcotic drugs found in the defendant's possession would be "prima facie evidence" that he purchased or distributed the drugs from other than the original stamped package. Again the Court conducted an extensive review both of the legislative records with regard to these statutes and of other pertinent literature in the field. In addition, it surveyed the records of other narcotics cases for evidence to support or rebut the inferences called for by the statutes. It concluded that the "overwhelming evidence" was that the heroin consumed in the United States is illegally imported and that Turner therefore must have known this fact.[47] Based upon this conclusion, the presumption as to illegal importation of heroin was upheld. In contrast, the Court struck down the same presumption with regard to the illegal importation of cocaine, finding that it could not be "sufficiently sure either that the cocaine that Turner possessed came from abroad or that Turner must have known that it did." [48] Similarly, the Court sustained the "stamped package" presumption as to heroin and struck it down as to cocaine, finding that "there can be no reasonable doubt" that one who possessed heroin did not purchase it from a stamped package [49] but that because of the availability of cocaine from legal channels there was "a reasonable possibility" that Turner had in fact obtained the cocaine from a legally stamped package.[50]

---

42. Id. at 53.

43. See the analysis of this aspect of the *Leary* case in Note, The Unconstitutionality of Statutory Criminal Presumptions, 22 Stan.L.Rev. 341, 346 (1970).

44. 395 U.S. at 36 n. 64.

45. Mr. Justice Black wrote a concurring opinion in *Leary* holding the presumption invalid essentially for the reasons stated in his *Gainey* dissent. Id. at 55–56.

46. 396 U.S. 398 (1970). For discussions of the *Turner* case see Christie & Pye, Presumptions and As-

sumptions in the Criminal Law: Another View, 1970 Duke L.J. 919; Notes, 2 St. Mary's L.J. 115 (1970), 24 Sw.L.J. 551 (1970), 22 Stan.L.Rev. 341 (1970).

47. Id. at 415–416.

48. Id. at 419.

49. Id. at 422.

50. Id. at 423–424.

In *Turner*, the Court again found it unnecessary specifically to adopt a test that would require that the presumed fact be shown to exist beyond a reasonable doubt. However, the Court's frequent reference to that standard in *Turner*,[51] coupled with its decision in In re Winship [52] recognizing that such a measure of proof is constitutionally required in criminal cases, seemed to make it likely that the reasonable doubt standard would be applied to test the validity of presumptions.[53]

Not long after *Turner*, the Court applied the rationale of the cases involving statutory presumptions to a common law presumption. In Barnes v. United States,[54] the Court upheld a conviction for possession of stolen treasury checks in which the jury had been instructed in accordance with the traditional common law inference that the knowledge necessary for conviction may be drawn from the unexplained possession of recently stolen goods. The Court still refrained from adopting either a more-likely-than-not or a reasonable doubt standard in its review of the presumption, but held rather that the presumption in question satisfied both. In addition to the predictable extension of the statutory presumption reasoning to a common law presumption, the *Barnes* opinion is further enlightening in its statement of the reasonable doubt standard. In *Turner*, the Court seemed to be looking for a virtually inevitable connection between presumed and basic facts.[55] The Court in *Barnes* states an easier test: whether "the evidence necessary to invoke the inference is sufficient for a rational juror to find the inferred fact beyond a reasonable doubt."[56]

A break in this more or less tidy progression of cases came in 1979 with the decision in County Court of Ulster County v. Allen.[57] The New York prosecution in *Allen* was for illegal possession of, inter alia, handguns.[58] Four persons, three adult males and a 16-year-old girl, were tried jointly. The evidence showed that two large-caliber handguns were seen in the front of the car in an open handbag belonging to the 16-year-old. A New York statute provided that, with certain exceptions, the presence of a firearm in an automobile was presumptive evidence of its illegal possession by all persons then occupying the vehicle. The jury was instructed with regard to the presumption but told that the presumption "need not be rebutted by affirmative proof or affirmative evidence but may be rebutted by any evidence or lack of evidence in the case."[59]

The federal Court of Appeals affirmed the District Court's grant of habeas corpus, holding that the New York statute was unconstitutional on its face because it swept within its compass many individuals who would in fact have no connection with a

---

51. For example, the Court stated:

". . . To possess heroin *is* to possess imported heroin. Whether judged by the more-likely-than-not standard applied in Leary v. United States, supra, or by the more exacting reasonable-doubt standard normally applicable in criminal cases, § 174 is valid insofar as it permits a jury to infer that heroin possessed in this country is a smuggled drug. . . ." Id. at 416.

52. 397 U.S. 358 (1970). See § 341 supra at n. 6.

53. See Christie & Pye, supra n. 46 at 923 n. 24. In its apparent adoption of the reasonable doubt standard, the Court did not recognize the argument put forth by some writers that in order for a presumption to be valid, not only must there be a high probability of correlation between the fact proved and the fact presumed, but there must also be a high probability that the accused can rebut the presumption. See Ashford & Risinger, Presumptions, Assumptions and Due Process in Criminal Cases: A Theoretical Overview, 79 Yale L.J. 165 (1969); Note, 53 Va.L.Rev. 702, 735 (1967). For a criticism of this approach see Christie & Pye, supra, at 926–933. See also Abrams, Statutory Presumptions and the Federal Criminal Law: A Suggested Analysis, 22 Vand.L.Rev. 1135, 1145–46 (1969).

54. 412 U.S. 837 (1973).

55. See the Court's statement in *Turner* that "to possess heroin *is* to possess imported heroin," (emphasis by the Court) supra n. 51, at 416.

56. Barnes v. United States supra n. 54 at 843.

57. 442 U.S. 140 (1979).

58. The defendants were also charged with the possession of a machinegun and heroin found in the trunk of the car. The jury acquitted all four defendants on these charges. Id. at 144.

59. Id. at 161 n. 20.

weapon even though they were present in a vehicle in which the weapon was found.[60]

The Supreme Court reversed, stating that the Court of Appeals had improperly viewed the statute on its face. The Court stated that the ultimate test of any device's constitutional validity is that it not undermine the factfinder's responsibility at trial, based on evidence adduced by the state, to find the ultimate facts beyond a reasonable doubt. Therefore, mandatory and permissive presumptions[61] must be analyzed differently. It is appropriate to analyze mandatory presumptions on their face. Where a mandatory presumption is used, the defendant may be convicted based upon the presumption alone as the result of the failure of the accused to introduce proof to the contrary. The Court reasoned that in such an instance the presumption would be unconstitutional unless the basic facts, standing alone, are sufficient to support the inference of guilt beyond a reasonable doubt.[62] In the case of a permissive presumption the jury is told only that it may, but need not, find the defendant guilty based upon the basic facts. Thus, the validity of the presumption must be tested, not in the abstract, but rather in connection with all of the evidence in the case. The Court stated:

> "Because this permissive presumption leaves the trier of fact free to credit or reject the inference and does not shift the burden of proof, it affects the application of the 'beyond a reasonable doubt' standard only if, under the facts of the case, there is no rational way the trier could make the connection permitted by the inference. For only in that situation is there any risk that an explanation of the permissible inference to a jury, or its use by a jury, has

caused the presumptively rational factfinder to make an erroneous factual determination."[63]

The Court found that the instruction in *Allen* created a permissive, not a mandatory, presumption. The Court considered all of the evidence in the case and found a rational basis for a finding of guilty beyond a reasonable doubt, noting that the jury could have reasonably rejected the suggestion advanced on appeal by the adult defendants that the handguns were solely in the possession of the 16-year-old.[64]

In the same term, the Court decided Sandstrom v. Montana.[65] In *Sandstrom*, the defendant was charged with deliberate homicide, which under Montana law would consist of purposely and knowingly causing the death of another. Defendant claimed that the degree of the offense should be reduced in that he suffered from a personality disorder aggravated by alcohol consumption. The jury was instructed in accordance with Montana law that the "law presumes that a person intends the ordinary consequences of his voluntary acts."[66] Defendant was convicted and his conviction was upheld by the Montana Supreme Court. The United States Supreme Court reversed, holding that the jury could have interpreted the instruction with regard to the presumption of intention of the ordinary consequences of voluntary acts as creating either a conclusive presumption or shifting the burden of persuasion with regard to the question of intent to the defendant. Citing *Mullaney* and *Patterson* as well as *Ulster*, the Court found that such a shift of the burden would be constitutionally impermissible. The fact that the jury could have interpreted the instruction either

---

60. Allen v. County Court, 568 F.2d 998 (2d Cir. 1978).

61. See § 346, text accompanying nn. 10–11 supra.

62. County Court of Ulster County v. Allen, supra, n. 57 at 167. The Court's language with regard to mandatory presumption is similar to that used in Barnes v. United States, supra n. 54. See text accompanying n. 56 supra.

63. County Court of Ulster County v. Allen, supra n. 57 at 157. The dissenting opinion, written by Justice Powell and joined by Justices Brennan, Marshall and

Stewart rejected the majority's heavy reliance on the distinction between mandatory and permissive presumptions, noting that presumptions, even if permissive, pose dangers. ". . . [T]o be constitutional a presumption must be at least more likely than not true." 442 U.S. at 172.

64. Id. at 164.

65. 442 U.S. 510 (1979), on remand 184 Mont. 391, 603 P.2d 244.

66. Id. at 513.

as permissive or as shifting only the burden of production did not matter so long as the instruction could also have been interpreted as imposing heavier burdens on the defendant.

After *Allen* and *Sandstrom*, presumptions in criminal cases are likely to be tested as follows: Mandatory presumptions, at least those which operate to place a burden of persuasion on the defendant, will be rigidly scrutinized in accordance with a test which requires that a rational juror could find the presumed fact beyond a reasonable doubt from the basic facts.[67] In making this assessment, the Court will not consider the other evidence in the case. However, consistent with cases such as *Leary* and *Turner*, the Court should be able to use its power to notice legislative facts which might support the inference to be drawn. On the other hand, permissive presumptions will be constitutionally acceptable if there is a rational way, considering all of the evidence in the case, that the jury could draw the inference suggested by the presumption. Whether a presumption is mandatory or permissive is to be gleaned from an analysis of the instructions to the jury.[68]

 WESTLAW REFERENCES

leland & 343 +s 790
432 +s 197 /p patterson /p mullaney /p 421 +s 684
"comparative convenience"
"rational connection" /s presumption*

title(timothy +s leary) & judge(harlan) & date(1969) sh 396 us 398
reasonable rational /2 juror* jury /p sandstrom
92k266(7)

---

§ 348. Affirmative Defenses and Presumptions in Criminal Cases: (c) Special Problems

Not surprisingly, several questions remain from the active constitutional development in this area of the law over the past decade.

1. The creation of affirmative defenses. The *Patterson* case tied the question of the constitutionality of affirmative defenses directly to the formalistic notion that a true affirmative defense is one that does not simply go to negative an element of the offense. The question remains as to when something is an element of an offense. Many cases have looked only to the language of the statute [1] although some have considered how the statute has been interpreted by the state courts.[2]

Can the state create an affirmative defense simply by carefully excluding it from the elements of the offense? The answer to this question would seem to be a qualified yes. In *Patterson*, the Court suggested that there were constitutional limitations on the creation of affirmative defenses.[3] Those limits may depend upon whether the state may, under the U.S. Constitution, punish the activity without reference to the affirmative defense. For example, assume an offense

---

67. Some writers have argued, based upon *Patterson*, *Allen* and *Sandstrom*, that a presumption may not be used to assign a burden of persuasion at all. Allen, Proof Beyond Reasonable Doubt, Chaos in the Lower Courts, 20 Amer.Crim.L.Rev. 1, 12 (1982); Graham, Presumptions—More Than You Wanted to Know and Yet Were Too Disinterested to Ask, 17 Crim.L. Bull. 431, n. 439 (1981).

68. The Court in *Allen* carefully analyzed the instructions given in earlier Supreme Court cases concerning presumptions. Using this analysis, the Court classified the presumptions in *Barnes* and *Gainey*, as well as one of the presumptions in *Turner*, as permissive. The other presumption in *Turner*, as well as the presumptions involved in *Leary*, *Romano* and *Tot*, were classified as mandatory. County Court of Ulster County v. Allen, supra, n. 57 at 157–159, nn. 44–45. The opinions in these earlier cases did not contain an

analysis similar to that of the *Allen* case nor did any of these cases appear to turn on the question whether the presumption involved was "mandatory" or "permissive."

§ 348

1. Fawell v. Czarnetsky, 566 F.2d 381 (2d Cir. 1977). cert. denied 434 U.S. 1077.

2. Berrier v. Egeler, 583 F.2d 515 (6th Cir. 1978), cert. denied 439 U.S. 955; Holloway v. McElroy, 632 F.2d 605 (5th Cir. 1980), cert. denied 451 U.S. 1028. In dissent from the denial of certiorari in *Holloway*, Justice Rehnquist stated that, in his view, the state should be permitted to label as an affirmative defense that which could otherwise be considered an element of a crime. 451 U.S. at 1028.

3. 432 U.S. at 210 (1977).

which has consisted of the elements A, B, C, all of which had to be proved by the prosecution beyond a reasonable doubt. The legislature carefully amends the statute covering the offense so as to make the elements of the offense A and B only, but provides that the accused may be exonerated if he proves C by a preponderance of the evidence. Such a new statute would be constitutional if the state may, consistent with the Eighth Amendment and substantive due process, punish the individual to the extent provided by the statute based upon proof of A and B only.

Such an analysis suggests another, less formalistic, approach to the treatment of affirmative defenses. Under this approach, if the state can constitutionally exclude an element from an offense, it can require the defendant to bear the burden of persuasion with regard to that element.[4] In other words, in the above example, if the state could exclude C from the definition of the crime, it could make the accused prove C, whether or not C is formally removed as an element of the offense. This theory has yet to be adopted by a court.

2. Affirmative defenses or presumptions? Despite the differences between affirmative defenses and presumptions, as the terms are used by the courts and legal scholars, the impact of these procedural devices is often identical. Thus, in one jurisdiction, the accused may have the burden of producing evidence that he acted in self-defense—an affirmative defense.[5] As indicated earlier, such an allocation would be clearly constitutional.[6] However, in another jurisdiction, the law may provide that once the state has proved that the defendant intentionally killed the deceased, there is a presumption of unlawfulness.[7] The presumption is mandatory in the sense that it requires the defendant to introduce evidence with regard to self-defense although the ultimate burden of persuasion may remain with the state. The effect of this presumption is identical to that of the affirmative defense. Should it be tested by the rules governing affirmative defenses, or should the rigid tests of *Allen* and *Sandstrom* with regard to mandatory presumptions be applied? [8]

A rational answer would be that devices having the same procedural impact should be treated identically, regardless of their label. If a device which places the burden of production on the defendant initially is constitutionally acceptable, another device which simply delays that allocation should also pass muster.[9] Such an analysis would require that the courts consider defenses and presumptions individually to determine whether in each case, the burden placed upon the accused is unconstitutional. The problem is, of course, that the courts have not provided a meaningful framework for such an analysis. One possibility, as suggested above,[10] is to view the question in terms of substantive constitutional analysis.

---

4. See the excellent articulations of essentially this theory in Allen, Structuring Jury Decisionmaking in Criminal Cases: A Unified Constitutional Approach to Evidentiary Devices, 94 Harv.L.Rev. 321 (1980); Allen, More on Constitutional Process-of-Proof Problems in Criminal Cases, 94 Harv.L.Rev. 1795 (1981); Jeffries & Stephan, Defenses, Presumptions and Burden of Proof in the Criminal Law, 88 Yale L.J. 1325 (1979). Others have dissented from the analysis. Nesson, Rationality, Presumptions and Judicial Comment: A Response to Professor Allen, 94 Harv.L.Rev. 1574 (1981). See also, Underwood, The Thumb on the Scales of Justice: Burdens of Persuasion in Criminal Cases, 86 Yale L.J. 1299 (1977) where the author takes issue with similar approaches advocated by Professor Allen in earlier articles.

5. Berrier v. Egeler, 583 F.2d 515 (6th Cir. 1978), cert. denied 439 U.S. 955 (Michigan procedure).

6. See text accompanying § 347, nn. 21–22 supra.

7. State v. Patterson, 297 N.C. 247, 254 S.E.2d 604 (1979). See discussion in Brandis, North Carolina Evidence § 218 (2d Rev. Ed. 1982).

8. The Court in *Sandstrom* did hint that presumptions which operated only to shift the burden of production might be treated differently from other mandatory presumptions. Sandstrom v. Montana, 442 U.S. 510, 519 (1979), on remand 184 Mont. 391, 603 P.2d 244.

9. Similar arguments have been convincingly made comparing the allocation of the burden of persuasion by a presumption and by an affirmative defense. Allen, supra n. 44, 94 Harv.L.Rev. at 357; Weinstein & Berger, Evidence ¶ 303[6] at 303–41.

10. See text accompanying n. 4 supra.

If the state may constitutionally punish an individual based upon proof of elements A and B only, it may shift to the accused either the burden of persuasion or the burden of production or both by whatever means it sees fit—affirmative defense or presumption. One problem with this analysis is that the courts have thus far been unwilling to undertake it, but have relied instead on the safer, formalistic notions of *Patterson*. Furthermore, the Eighth Amendment and related concepts of substantive due process have not yet proved to be an effective check on legislative decisions with regard to punishment.[11] Another approach, perhaps more likely to be palatable to the courts, would build upon a suggestion made by Justice Powell in his dissent in *Patterson*. He suggested that the prosecution be required to prove beyond a reasonable doubt at least those factors which "in the Anglo-American legal tradition" had made a difference in punishment or stigma.[12] Although troublesome if taken to its logical extent,[13] the notion that we should consider historical factors is not without merit.

Perhaps the only real answer is to recognize that, as in the case of presumptions in civil cases, there is no single approach to the problem. As in civil cases, each device which allocates the burdens of proof in criminal cases is created for different reasons and presents different kinds of problems for the state, for the defendant, and for the judge and jury. Each device needs to be tested on its own merits. The different treatment received by insanity and self-defense after the *Patterson* case lends support to this analysis.[14]

In testing either an affirmative defense or a presumption, the courts need to take into account many factors. The fact that the device in question is either an affirmative defense or a presumption is perhaps relevant to the question of notice to potential violators, but should not be controlling in most cases. Included in the analysis should be considerations such as the kind of burden placed on the defendant (production or persuasion), whether the state could have punished the defendant based solely upon the proof of elements as to which the prosecution retains the burdens of proof, and considerations such as the nature of the burden the state has had historically with regard to the element in question. Based upon such an analysis, as in civil cases, there will be different results for different presumptions or affirmative defenses. However, such results are more likely to be consistent with the policies behind the criminal law, as well as with constitutional considerations, than if a single test was applied.

3. When is it Proper to Submit an Issue Involving A Presumed Fact to the Jury? In deciding the question whether a case involving a presumed fact should be submitted to the jury, the trial judge must necessarily be guided by the dictates of Jackson v. Virginia:[15] a jury verdict will be upheld, even against collateral attack, only if the evidence was sufficient for a reasonable man to find the defendant guilty beyond a reasonable doubt. In the rare instance in which a mandatory presumption is involved, the problem is not difficult. The presumption will be tested by the constitutional test of whether the presumed fact flows beyond a reasonable doubt from the basic facts. If the presumption meets that test, it is by definition sufficient to get to the jury, provided the other elements of the crime are supported by sufficient evidence. However, because of the rigid requirements for the validity of mandatory presumptions, almost all presumptions will be permissive. Therefore, under the *Allen* case, the trial judge must look to the rational effect of the presump-

---

11. Rummel v. Estelle, 445 U.S. 263 (1980), and discussion in Nesson, supra, n. 4 at 1580–1581.

12. Patterson v. New York, 432 U.S. 197, 226–227 (1977).

13. See Jeffries & Stephan, supra n. 4 at 1362–1363.

14. See § 347 nn. 18–19 and accompanying text.

15. 443 U.S. 307 (1979), rehearing denied 444 U.S. 890; see § 338 supra, text accompanying nn. 6–7.

tion in connection with all of the other evidence in the case. Perhaps the best statement of a test for the sufficiency of the evidence under these circumstances is contained in Revised Uniform Rule (1974) 303(b):

> *(b) Submission to the jury.* The court is not authorized to direct the jury to find a presumed fact against the accused. If a presumed fact establishes guilt or is an element of the offense or negatives a defense, the court may submit the question of guilt or of the existence of the presumed fact to the jury, but only if a reasonable juror on the evidence as a whole, including the evidence of the basic facts, could find guilt or the presumed fact beyond a reasonable doubt. If the presumed fact has a lesser effect, the question of its existence may be submitted to the jury provided the basic facts are supported by substantial evidence or are otherwise established, unless the court determines that a reasonable juror on the evidence as a whole could not find the existence of the presumed fact.[16]

Given the dictates of Jackson v. Virginia and County Court of Ulster County v. Allen, no other proposed formulation of the rule seems acceptable.[17]

4. Instructing the Jury on Presumptions. The distinction made in the *Allen* case between permissive and mandatory presumptions, makes the exact language of instructions on presumptions critical. Unless a presumption is strong enough to meet the stringent test for mandatory presumptions, the trial judge must use caution in charging the jury so as to place no burden whatsoever on the defendant.

Again, the Revised Uniform Rules provide a suggested pattern for such an instruction. Uniform Rule 303(c) provides:

Instructing the Jury. Whenever the existence of a presumed fact is submitted to the jury, the court shall instruct the jury that it may regard the basic facts as sufficient evidence of the presumed fact but is not required to do so. In addition, if the presumed fact establishes guilt or is an element of the offense or negatives a defense, the court shall instruct the jury that its existence, on all the evidence, must be proved beyond a reasonable doubt.[18]

This instruction seems to meet most of the problems raised in the *Allen* case, as well as those suggested by Sandstrom v. Montana. One additional problem has been suggested.[19] In *Allen*, the court stated that the prosecution could not rest its case entirely on a presumption unless the facts proved were sufficient to support the inference of guilt beyond a reasonable doubt.[20] Therefore, where the prosecution relies solely upon a presumption and not any other evidence, as in *Allen*, not only must the presumed fact flow beyond a reasonable doubt from the basic facts, but the jury must be able to find the basic facts beyond a reasonable doubt. At least two states have adopted the essence of the Revised Uniform Rule, but, in order to cover this situation, have added language which requires that the basic facts be proved beyond a reasonable doubt.[21]

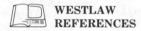

WESTLAW REFERENCES

ic 583 f2d 515
instruct! charg! submi! /4 jury juror* /p mandatory
  permissive /p ulster
"rule 309" & court(oregon)

---

§ 349. Choice of Law [1]

The significance of the burdens of proof and of the effect of presumptions upon

---

16. The Revised Uniform Rule (1974) is almost identical to Proposed Federal Rule 303(b) sent by the Supreme Court to Congress but not enacted.

17. See Model Penal Code § 112(5)(a); Proposed Federal Rule of Criminal Procedure 25.1, S. 1437, 95th Cong., 1st Session (1977) (not adopted).

18. Again, the Revised Uniform Rule (1974) is almost identical to Proposed Federal Rule 303(c) sent by the Supreme Court to Congress but not enacted.

19. Weinstein & Berger, supra n. 8 at 303–37.

20. County Court of Ulster County v. Allen, supra § 347 n. 57, at 167.

21. Hawaii Evidence Rule 306; Oregon Evidence Rule 309.

§ 349

1. Morgan, Choice of Law Governing Proof, 58 Harv.L.Rev. 153, 180–194 (1944); Sedler, The Erie Out-

those burdens has already been discussed. Certainly the outcome of litigation may be altered depending upon which party has the burden of persuasion.[2] Where there is little evidence available on an issue, the burden of producing evidence may also control the outcome.[3] Recognizing the impact of these rules upon outcome, the federal courts, applying the doctrine of Erie Railroad Co. v. Tompkins,[4] have consistently held that where an issue is to be decided under state law, that law controls both the burdens of proof and presumptions with regard to that issue.[5] Federal Rule of Evidence 302 limits the operation of this rule with respect to presumptions to cases in which the presumption operates "respecting a fact which is an element of a claim or defense as to which state law supplies the rule of decision."[6] "Tactical presumptions," those that operate as to a lesser aspect of the case, will be governed by the federal rule.[7] While no court has specifically made the distinction contemplated in the rule, the reasoning is sound. Although tactical presumptions may in some instances influence the outcome of a case,

their effect is no greater than that of a rule governing the admission or exclusion of a single item of evidence. As in the case of those rules, the desirability of providing a uniform procedure for federal trials through a fixed rule governing tactical presumptions outweighs any preference for increased certainty of identity of result in state and federal courts.

Of course Erie problems are not the only choice of law problems. The question remains, even for federal courts having resolved to apply state rather than federal law:[8] what state's law is applicable? Unlike the federal courts applying the Erie rule, the state courts generally have not considered the impact of the burdens of proof and presumptions on the outcome of the lawsuit to be controlling. The general rule expressed is that both the burdens of proof and presumptions are "procedural" in the sense that the law of the forum governs rather than the law of the state whose substantive rules are otherwise applicable.[9] However, as in the case of most general rules with regard to the subject matter of

---

come Test as a Guide to Substance and Procedure in the Conflicts of Laws, 37 N.Y.U.L.Rev. 813, 855–865 (1962); Restatement, Second, Conflict of Laws §§ 133, 134 (1971); Annot., 35 A.L.R.3d 289; C.J.S. Conflict of Laws § 22(9); Dec.Dig. Actions ⚖➙66.

2. See § 336 supra.

3. See § 338 supra. See also §§ 342 and 344 supra as to the operation of presumptions with regard to both the burden of producing evidence and the burden of persuasion.

4. 304 U.S. 64 (1938).

5. Dick v. New York Life Insurance Co., 359 U.S. 437 (1959); Palmer v. Hoffman, 318 U.S. 109 (1943); Cities Service Oil Co. v. Dunlap, 308 U.S. 208 (1939); Federal Insurance Co. v. Areias, 680 F.2d 962 (3d Cir. 1982). See also, 10 Moore Federal Practice ¶ 3.02 (2d ed. 1982).

6. See Hewitt v. Firestone Tire & Rubber Co., 490 F.Supp. 1358 (E.D.Va.1980) and Ritter v. Prudential Insurance Co., 538 F.Supp. 398 (N.D.Ga.1982), for applications of this rule. Conversely, Revised Uniform Rule of Evidence (1974) 802 provides:

In civil actions and proceedings, the effect of a presumption respecting a fact which is an element of a claim or defense as to which federal law supplies the rule of decision is determined in accordance with federal law.

7. Fed.R.Evid. 302, Advisory Committee's Note. The following example of a tactical presumption is taken from Cleary, Presuming and Pleading: An Essay on Juristic Immaturity, 12 Stan.L.Rev. 5, 26 (1959): "In an action upon an account, plaintiff, desiring to prove defendant's failure to deny as an admission of liability, may prove the mailing of a statement of account to defendant and rely upon the presumption that it was received by him in due course of the mails. The presumed fact of delivery is much smaller than an element in the case. . . ."

8. In determining which state law to apply, the federal courts are bound by the conflict of laws rule of the state in which they are sitting. Klaxon v. Stentor Electric Manufacturing Co., 313 U.S. 487 (1941). See generally cases collected in Annot., 21 A.L.R.2d 247, 257. For examples of the approach taken by a federal court in a situation where a choice between the laws of two states with regard to presumptions had to be made, see Maryland Casualty Co. v. Williams, 377 F.2d 389 (5th Cir. 1967); Melville v. American Home Assurance Co., 584 F.2d 1306 (3d Cir. 1978).

9. Broderick v. McGuire, 119 Conn. 83, 174 A. 314 (1934) (New York presumption arising from certificate of superintendent of banks not applicable); Davis Cabs, Inc. v. Evans, 42 Ohio App. 493, 182 N.E. 327 (1932) (Kentucky presumption of negligence where speed limit exceeded not applicable). See cases in Annot., 35 A.L.R.3d 289, 299.

this chapter, instances in which an exception to this general rule has been held applicable are perhaps as numerous as instances in which the rule has been applied. The principal exception to the basic dogma has been variously phrased but its gist is that the forum will apply the rule of a foreign jurisdiction with respect to the burdens of proof or presumptions where that rule is inseparably connected to the substantive right created by the foreign state.[10]

The general rule and its principal exception[11] have proved difficult to apply. The plethora of conflicting decisions under the test amply illustrates the problems inherent in attempting to distinguish between rules that are inseparably connected with substantive law and those that are not.[12] The distinction is indeed a hollow one. Regardless of the nature of the claim or defense, rules with respect to the burdens of proof always have the same potential effect upon the decision in the case. If insufficient evidence is available, the party having the burden of producing evidence will lose the decision. If the jury is in doubt, the party having the burden of persuasion will lose. As has been observed, cases in which the burden of proof is so closely interwoven with the substantive

right as to make a separation of the two impossible constitute either all or none of the litigated cases.[13]

A somewhat better approach to the problem is taken by the Second Restatement of Conflict of Laws which states that the forum will apply its own local law in determining which party has the burdens of proof "unless the primary purpose of the relevant rule of the otherwise applicable law is to affect decision of the issue rather than to regulate the conduct of the trial."[14] The rule sounds very much like the test applied in *Erie* cases. However, the comments and illustrations to the applicable sections of the Restatement indicate that the Restatement is to be interpreted in much the same way as the more traditional statements just discussed; the assumption is that the rule is one concerned with "trial administration," not the decision of the issue.[15] The assumption seems wrong. The burdens of proof are almost always allocated for the primary purpose of affecting the decision in the case where there is no evidence or where the jury is in doubt. To say that these rules merely govern the conduct of the trial, as in the case of rules concerning the admission and

---

10. Pilot Life Insurance Co. v. Boone, 236 F.2d 457, 462 (5th Cir. 1956) ("The effect of this presumption against suicide is so inseparably connected with the substantive right to defend under the applicable policy exception, that we think that the law of South Carolina [which was held to govern the substantive issues] should be given effect in preference to the contrary rule prevailing in Alabama [the state in which the district court was sitting].") ; Buhler v. Maddison, 109 Utah 267, 176 P.2d 118, 123 (1947); Precourt v. Driscoll, 85 N.H. 280, 157 A. 525, 527 (1931). For a more recent application of these same principles see Melville v. American Home Assurance Co., supra n. 8.

11. Another frequently stated exception is that the law of the foreign jurisdiction governs "conclusive presumptions." See, e.g., Maryland Casualty Co. v. Williams, supra n. 8 at 394–95. However, as discussed earlier in this chapter, § 342, n. 12 and accompanying text, these "presumptions" are better viewed as rules of substantive law and are therefore clearly not within the purview of the general rule.

12. See generally cases collected in Annot., supra n. 9, at 303 et seq. The courts are perhaps most divided on this issue where the forum's rule with regard to the burden of proving contributory negligence differs from

that of the foreign state whose law is otherwise applicable. Compare Foley v. Pittsburgh-Des Moines Co., 363 Pa. 1, 68 A.2d 517 (1949), and Weir v. New York, New Haven & Hartford Railroad Co., 340 Mass. 66, 162 N.E.2d 793 (1959) (law of the forum controls) with Gordon's Transports, Inc. v. Bailey, 41 Tenn.App. 365, 294 S.W.2d 313 (1956); Valleroy v. Southern Railway Co., 403 S.W.2d 553 (Mo.1966) (foreign law controls.) See Restatement, Second, Conflict of Laws § 133, Reporter's Note at 369 (1971). See also cases collected at Annot., supra n. 9 at 318–327.

13. Morgan, supra n. 1, at 185.

14. §§ 133, 134 (1971). Section 595 of the first Restatement stated that the law of the forum governs both "proof" and "presumptions." The comment to that section (p. 710) noted that the foreign law might be applied if "the remedial and substantive portions of the foreign law are so bound together that the application of the usual procedural rule of the forum would seriously alter the effect of the operative facts under the law of the appropriate foreign state."

15. Id., § 133, Comment at 366–68, § 134, Comment at 370–72.

exclusion of evidence, gives far too much emphasis to form over substance.[16]

A better approach to the choice of law problem would be to adopt the federal rule used in *Erie* cases as a rule of general application. Such a rule would provide that the law of the state or states supplying the substantive rules of law should govern questions concerning the burdens of proof as

well as presumptions operating with regard to a fact constituting an element of a claim or defense.[17]

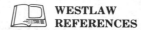 **WESTLAW REFERENCES**

forum /s govern! control! appl! /s "burden* of proof" presumption*

---

16. Where the evidence is plentiful, of course, the allocation of the burden of producing evidence cannot have a significant effect upon the decision in the case. In such a case, the rule assigning the burden is simply a rule affecting the order of proof—a matter that logically should be governed by the law of the forum. However, providing different rules to be applied where there is sufficient evidence to satisfy the burden of producing evidence and where there is not, would require a full review of the evidence before a decision as to choice of law could be made, a procedure at best wasteful of precious judicial time.

As long as the allocation of the burden of producing evidence has a potentially significant impact on the decision in the case, as it must have in every situation, a single rule, calling for the allocation of the burden of producing evidence as part of the substantive law to be

applied in the case, should be followed. For a discussion suggesting the possibility of a different rule where there is plentiful evidence see Sedler, supra n. 1, at 865.

17. For a similar view, see Sedler, supra n. 1.

In the first edition of this text, Dean McCormick took the position that the burden of persuasion has a relatively insignificant effect upon the outcome of the litigation (see discussion of this question in § 336 supra) and that the allocation of that burden should therefore be viewed as a matter of "procedure." (p. 686). Professor Morgan took an opposite approach, recognizing the impact of the burden of persuasion upon the outcome, but relegating the burden of producing evidence to the status of procedure. Morgan, supra n. 1, at 191–194.

Title 13

ADMINISTRATIVE EVIDENCE

Chapter 37

ADMINISTRATIVE EVIDENCE

Table of Sections

§ 350. Introduction to Administrative Adjudication [1]

As the problems facing federal and state governments have multiplied in number and complexity, these governments have created administrative agencies to devise and enforce new policies. This growth has been uneven and with few exceptions relatively slow. Even as late as 1960 the federal government exercised major regulatory responsibility in only five fields: antitrust, communications, financial markets and institutions, food and drugs, and transportation. Beginning in the mid-1960's, however, the number of federal regulatory agencies and the scope of regulatory activity greatly expanded. For example, between 1960 and 1976 the number of federal agencies substantially regulating some aspect of private activity grew from 34 to 83; whereas in 1930 there were but 18 federal regulatory bodies.[2] This expansion is also reflected in other measures of agency activity. During the 1970's the pages of federal regulations in the Federal Register tripled, federal regulatory budgets increased sixfold, agency personnel grew from under 30,000 to over 80,000, and the amount of the gross national product produced by industries regulated by state or federal governments jumped from under 10 to around 25 percent.[3]

---

§ 350

1. See generally 1 Davis, Administrative Law Treatise, ch. 1 (2d ed. 1978, 1982 Supp.) (hereinafter "Davis").

2. See Schultze, The Public Use of Private Interest 7–8 (1977).

3. See Breyer, Regulation and Its Reform 1 (1982).

Much, perhaps most, of this growth has focused on the use of agency rulemaking to write new regulations. At the same time administrative trials—denominated "adjudications" by the federal Administrative Procedure Act (APA)[4]—have continued to grow and the federal government now employs approximately 1,200 administrative law judges.[5] (By contrast, there are approximately 500 federal district judges hearing all federal civil and criminal cases.[6]) The number of administrative trials annually dwarfs the number of cases heard each year in federal court. Yet the range of administrative trials is as great as those heard by federal judges. That is, administrative adjudications extend from relatively insubstantial workers' compensation claims to precedent-setting antitrust merger rulings involving millions of dollars and affecting thousands of employees.

At first glance many, and perhaps most, administrative adjudications appear to be merely carbon copies of judicial trials. Their administrative hearing is usually public, and in most cases the hearing is conducted in an orderly and dignified manner, although not necessarily with the formality of a judicial trial. Evidence is admissible only if reliable and material; cross-examination is frequently relied upon to challenge witness credibility; and the administrative judge's decision must be supported by substantial evidence.[7]

Closer analysis, however, reveals many differences.[8] Agency hearings tend to produce evidence of general conditions as distinguished from facts relating solely to the respondent. Administrative agencies more consciously formulate policy by adjudicating (and rulemaking) than do courts. Consequently, administrative adjudications may require that the administrative law judge consider more consciously the impact of his decision upon the public interest as well as upon the particular respondent.[9] In addition, testimonial evidence and cross-examination often play less important roles in administrative hearings.[10]

Even more important is the fact that an administrative hearing is tried to an *administrative law judge* and never to a *jury*. Since many of the rules governing the admission of proof in judicial trials are designed to protect the jury from unreliable and possibly confusing evidence,[11] the rules need not be applied with the same vigor in proceedings solely before an administrative law judge.[12] The administrative judge decides both the facts and the law to be applied. Usually a lawyer, he is generally experienced on the very question he must decide. Consequently, the technical common law rules governing the *admissibility* of evi-

4. 5 U.S.C.A. §§ 551(7), 554.

5. See generally Administrative Conference of the United States, Federal Administrative Law Judge Hearings: A Statistical Report for Fiscal Year 1975 (1978); Comptroller General of the United States, Administrative Law Process: Better Management is Needed (May 15, 1978).

6. See Annual Report of the Director of the Administrative Office of the United States Courts 1981, in Reports of the Proceedings of the Judicial Conference of the United States 125–30 (1982).

7. See Gellhorn, Rules of Evidence and Official Notice in Formal Administrative Hearings, 1971 Duke L.J. 1, 12–26.

8. See 3 Davis ch. 16 (1980).

9. But see Chayes, The Role of the Judge in Public Law Litigation, 89 Harv.L.Rev. 1281 (1976).

10. For particularly penetrating insights on whether such evidence can be dispensed with in deciding

questions of policy, see Robinson, The Making of Administrative Policy: Another Look at Rulemaking and Adjudication and Administrative Procedure Reform, 118 U.Pa.L.Rev. 485, 521–522 (1970). See also Pierce, The Choice Between Adjudicating and Rulemaking for Formulating and Implementing Energy Policy, 31 Hast.L.J. 1 (1979).

11. "[The law of evidence is] a piece of illogical, but by no means irrational, patchwork; not at all to be admired, nor easily to be found intelligible, except as a product of the jury system. . . . where ordinary untrained citizens are acting as judges of fact." Thayer, Preliminary Treatise on Evidence at the Common Law 509 (1898).

12. Regardless of whether the hearsay and best evidence rules are products of the jury system, in fact neither rule is applied with the same strictness in cases tried to a judge and not the jury. See § 60 and Ch. 34 supra.

dence have generally been abandoned by administrative agencies.[13]

Courts accept whatever cases the parties present; their familiarity with the subject matter is accidental. Agencies, on the other hand, have only limited jurisdictions and handle selected cases; administrative law judges and agency members who review the adjudicative decisions of administrative law judges are either experts or have at least a substantial familiarity with the subject matter. The administrative agency may therefore be allowed greater leeway and deference (on appellate review) in deciding questions of fact and law. In addition, an agency usually is staffed by experts whose reports, commonly relating to matters adjudicated before the agency, are made available to administrative judges and commissioners alike.

While this development of agency experience and expertness is commonly offered as a justification for administrative agencies,[14] it also creates a basic conflict between assuring fairness to the private respondent on the one hand and promoting efficient use of reliable information on the other. The respondent, for example, wants an opportunity to rebut or explain all the "evidence" which the administrative judge or agency relies upon in making its decision. Yet the agency wishes to avoid the burden of having to prove once again previously established "facts." This conflict has led to the development of the concept of official notice, specifically recognized in the APA (Administrative Procedure Act), which regularizes the procedure for agency reliance on proven facts.[15]

§ 351. Law Governing Administrative Evidence

The legal framework governing the conduct of formal administrative adjudication is not complex and can be best understood by first examining the law which determines the kind of proof an agency can receive into evidence.

(a) *Federal Law.* Until the passage of the Administrative Procedure Act of 1946,[1] the receipt of evidence in federal administrative proceedings was limited only by general constitutional requirements of fairness and privilege together with the vague directions implicit in the standard for judicial review developed by appellate courts or written into agency enabling acts.

The requirement of fairness generally means only that the respondent

> shall have an opportunity to be heard and cross-examine the witnesses against him and shall have time and opportunity at a convenient place, after the evidence against him is produced and known to him, to produce evidence and witnesses to refute the charges. . . .[2]

The test for judicial review typically provides that "[t]he finding of the Commission

---

13. See generally Richardson v. Perales, 402 U.S. 389 (1971). See also §§ 352 and 353 infra.

14. The significance of this experience and expertness has, however, been authoritatively questioned. See Jaffe, Judicial Control of Administrative Action 25 (1965); Schwartz, Legal Restriction of Competition in the Regulated Industries: An Abdication of Judicial Responsibility, 67 Harv.L.Rev. 436, 471–75 (1954). For other theories on the justification for administrative agencies, see Stigler, The Theory of Economic Regulation, 2 Bell J. of Econ. & Mgmt.Sci. 3 (1971); Posner, Theories of Economic Regulation, 5 Bell J. of Econ. & Mgmt.Sci. 335 (1974); Breyer, Analyzing Regulatory

Failure: Mismatches, Less Restrictive Alternatives, and Reform, 92 Harv.L.Rev. 547 (1979).

15. 5 U.S.C.A. § 556(e). See § 359 infra.

§ 351

1. 5 U.S.C.A. §§ 551–59, 701–06, 3105, 3344, 5362, 7521.

2. N.L.R.B. v. Prettyman, 117 F.2d 786, 790 (6th Cir. 1941). See also Morgan v. United States, 304 U.S. 1, 18–19 (1938); Hornsby v. Allen, 326 F.2d 605, 608 (5th Cir. 1964).

as to the facts, if supported by substantial evidence, shall be conclusive." [3]

Either standard could be read as a command that administrative agencies must rely upon common law rules of evidence barring hearsay and other secondary evidence, since the private respondent could neither confront nor cross-examine upon the evidence, or since the evidence was not competent and therefore not substantial. Neither the agencies nor the courts have accepted these contentions.[4] The exclusionary rules of evidence were designed, at least initially, to assure that evidence admitted would be relevant and reliable. But the opportunity for confrontation is not the sole measure of reliability.

As early as the turn of this century, the Supreme Court ruled that the Interstate Commerce Commission—the first regulatory agency to conduct formal adjudicatory hearings—was not bound by the exclusionary rules:

> The [ICC's] inquiry should not be too narrowly constrained by technical rules as to the admissibility of proof. Its function is largely one of investigation, and it should not be hampered in

making inquiry pertaining to interstate commerce by those narrow rules which prevail in trials at common law . . . .[5]

Occasionally federal authority has held that the admission of legally incompetent evidence is reversible error. But these decisions are exceptional and erroneous unless other grounds can be established for rejecting the evidence.[6] Indeed, by 1941 the Supreme Court had confidently noted that "it has long been settled that the technical rules for the exclusion of evidence applicable in jury trials do not apply to proceedings before federal administrative agencies in the absence of a statutory requirement that such rules are to be observed." [7]

With the adoption of the federal Administrative Procedure Act, Congress appeared to be codifying this case law by providing that "[a]ny oral or documentary evidence may be received" in an administrative adjudication.[8] Specific statutes may, however, override the application of the APA to agency hearings. In a few instances Congress has either exempted an agency's hearings from the APA or has specified that other procedures shall govern certain administrative hearings.[9]

---

3. 15 U.S.C.A. § 45(c) (Federal Trade Commission Act). See also Developments in the Law—Remedies Against the United States and its Officials, 70 Harv.L. Rev. 827, 904–05 (1957).

4. See 3 Davis § 16:4.

5. I.C.C. v. Baird, 194 U.S. 25, 44 (1904). In response to a challenge to an ICC order based partly on hearsay, the Court observed that "[e]ven in a court of law, if evidence of this kind is admitted without objection, it is to be considered, and accorded its natural probative effect . . . ." Spiller v. Atchison, Topeka & Santa Fe Railway, 253 U.S. 117, 130 (1920).

6. Compare Tri-State Broadcasting Co. v. FTC, 96 F.2d 564 (D.C.Cir. 1938), with FTC v. Cement Institution, 333 U.S. 683, 705–06 (1948), rehearing denied 334 U.S. 839. In response to the *Tri-State* ruling that the admission of all hearsay is improper since it deprives the respondent of its right to cross-examine, Dean Wigmore commented acidly: "No wonder the administrative agencies chafe under such unpractical control." 1 Wigmore, Evidence § 4b, p. 34 (3d ed. 1940).

7. Opp Cotton Mills, Inc. v. Administrator, Department of Labor, 312 U.S. 126, 155 (1941).

8. 5 U.S.C.A. § 556(d).

9. See S.Doc. 248, 79th Cong.2d Sess. 216 (1946); cf. 8 U.S.C.A. § 1252(b) applied in Marcello v. Bonds, 349 U.S. 302 (1955), rehearing denied 350 U.S. 856.

For example, the Taft-Hartley Act amended the National Labor Relations Act to provide that the Board's adjudications, "shall, so far as practicable, be conducted in accordance with the rules of evidence applicable in the district courts of the United States under the rules of civil procedure for the district courts of the United States. . . . " Labor-Management Relations Act § 10(b), 61 Stat. 146 (1947), 29 U.S.C.A. § 160(b). Section 10(b) of the 1935 Act, which Taft-Hartley modified, provided that "rules of evidence prevailing in courts of law or equity shall not be controlling." 49 Stat. 454 (1935). Although it seems doubtful that this amendment was intended to impose jury trial rules on Board hearings, at least one court has held that "hearsay evidence must [now] be excluded from consideration by the Board and by [the reviewing court]." N.L.R.B. v. Amalgamated Meat Cutters, 202 F.2d 671, 673 (9th Cir. 1953); accord, 1 Cooper, State Administrative Law 384 (1965) (hereinafter cited "Cooper"). But see N.L.R.B. v. International Union of Operating Engineers, Local 12, 413 F.2d 705, 707 (9th Cir. 1969). In general, however, reviewing courts have concluded that the mere admission of hearsay is not within the purview of the Taft-Hartley amendment. E.g., N.L.R.B. v. Philadelphia Iron Works, Inc., 211

Moreover, Congress' adoption of the "substantial evidence" standard for judicial review of formal adjudications [10]—partly in response to a perceived lack of rigor in the proof required in agency trials [11]—fostered the notion that the rule against hearsay or other restrictions might still be mandated in particular circumstances (e.g., where specific facts were in issue and witness credibility was key). This view seemed at least plausible where the congressional objective was not made clear.

In 1971, in Richardson v. Perales,[12] the Supreme Court gave strong evidence that narrow interpretation of agency authority to admit and rely on reliable hearsay and other evidence was not favored. There the Court sustained the Social Security Administration's denial of a claim for disability benefits even though the only testimony presented at the administrative hearing was by Perales, his doctor, and a fellow employee—and all supported Perales' claim. The agency, in denying the claim, relied on hospital records and the written reports of four examining physicians. Its decision had been overturned by the Court of Appeals which had ruled that hearsay uncorroborated by oral testimony could not constitute substantial evidence when the hearsay was directly contradicted by the testimony of live medical witnesses and by the claimant in person. The Supreme Court, however, upheld the Social Security Administration. It emphasized that the reports were impartial, consistent, and based on personal examinations by com-

petent physicians. Moreover, Perales had not exercised his right to subpoena the examining physicians in order to cross-examine them. It argued that the "sheer magnitude" of the administrative burden and desirability of informal procedures supported this approach. In the circumstances, the procedure satisfied both the congressional design as well as requirements of "fundamental fairness." [13]

(b) *State Law.* The constitutional limitations applied to federal agencies also impose restraints upon state hearings. The states in turn have freed their administrative agencies from the "rules of evidence," but not always for the same reasons. Most state agencies were created as political-administrative bodies rather than as quasi-judicial commissions. Thus, writing in 1965, Professor Cooper observed

> Fifty years ago, the typical state agencies would include, perhaps, rural township supervisors who as members of local boards of assessors would estimate the value of their neighbors' farms, and statehouse politicians who as a railroad commission would bargain with railroad attorneys concerning the granting of franchises and the fixing of rates, and insurance commissioners who would watch with a wary eye the premiums charged by fire insurance companies . . . , and—in the more progressive states—"committees of arbitration" who would informally arbitrate compensation claims of workers injured in industrial accidents under the newfangled workmen's compensation laws.[14]

F.2d 937, 942–43 (3d Cir. 1954); N.L.R.B. v. Carpet, Linoleum and Resilient Tile Layers Local Union No. 419, 213 F.2d 49, 53 (10th Cir. 1954). See generally Archer, Query: Should Administrative Agencies Tailor Exclusionary Evidence Rules Specifically for Their Own Proceedings? An Illustrative Study of the NLRB, 3 Ind. Leg.F. 339 (1970).

10. 5 U.S.C.A. § 706(2)(E) (Administrative Procedure Act).

11. See Universal Camera Corp. v. N.L.R.B., 340 U.S. 474 (1951); Jaffe, Judicial Review: Substantial Evidence on the Whole Record, 64 Harv.L.Rev. 1233 (1951).

12. 402 U.S. 389 (1971). The particular ruling was that physicians' reports adduced by the agency were

admissible and satisfied the requirement of "substantial evidence," though opposed by live expert testimony on behalf of claimant.

13. It should also be noted that three Justices dissented. They would have reversed the agency decision on the grounds that evidence which had not been tested by cross-examination "is of no value," that uncorroborated hearsay does not constitute "substantial evidence" under the APA, and that the agency's reliance on written reports was therefore an impermissible "cutting of corners."

14. 1 Cooper 379 (footnotes omitted).

Neither these state agencies nor the parties appearing before them could have followed judicial rules of evidence. As the agencies became more sophisticated, and their hearings more formal, the presentation of evidence was formalized. Now, as with federal agencies, their hearings are often indistinguishable from nonjury civil trials. Nevertheless, the original approach that state agencies are not restricted by common law rules in the admission of evidence has continued.[15] Professor Cooper contended that this liberal approach had long ago outrun its reasons.[16] Attributing its continuance to legislative lethargy, to arbitrary agency desire to operate with a free hand, and to the judicial trend toward relaxation of exclusionary rules in court cases, he decried this laxity concerning the application of common law rules and suggested that state agencies be "required to follow the rules of evidence to about the same extent and in about the same way as judges do when trying cases without juries." [17]

This argument failed to recognize, however, that the "nonjury evidence" standard was more indefinite than might be thought.[18] Thus it is not surprising that the 1961 Model State Administrative Procedure Act's provision,[19] that the rules of evidence applicable in nonjury civil cases be followed in state agency adjudication, was adopted in only six states. The Model Act was revised once again in 1981, this time adhering more closely to the federal model. Section 4–212 provides that the hearing officer shall exclude evidence on proper objection only if it is "irrelevant, immaterial, unduly repetitious" or because it is privileged.[20] It further specifically provides that "[e]vidence may not be excluded solely because it is hearsay."

The trend in state agencies, both by statute and court rule, continues to be away from—rather than toward—the technical rules of admissibility.

 WESTLAW REFERENCES

rule* /2 evidence /s administrative /2 adjudication* hearing* proceeding*
15ak313
5 +s 556 /p evidence

§ 352. Admissibility of Evidence

Administrative agencies generally are not restricted in the kind of evidence they can admit. The mere admission of proof that would be excluded as irrelevant, immaterial, incompetent, or redundant under the rules of evidence adopted in a jury trial will not restrict enforcement of an agency's decision.[1] The APA confirms this practice in

---

15. Many state statutes explicitly provide that the common law rules of evidence applicable to jury trials shall not govern agency hearings. E.g., Mass.Gen. Laws Ann. c. 30A, § 11(2); West's Ann.Cal. Labor Code §§ 5708, 5709. Several practical reasons have been offered for not following rigid common law rules of evidence in state hearings; agency hearings are often held at one or a few central locations distant from the scene of events, making it difficult for eyewitness participants to testify; hearings may be held shortly after the complaint is filed, making the advance preparation and the marshalling of the best witnesses and documentary evidence difficult; and the heavy caseload volume, much of which is routine and involves only matters of small consequence, renders formal requirements of proof inappropriate. See Benjamin, Administrative Adjudication in the State of New York 175–76 (1942) (hereinafter "Benjamin").

16. 1 Cooper 380–81.

17. Id.

18. 3 Davis §§ 16:3–16:4. But see § 60 supra, for discussion of the application of the exclusionary rules in nonjury trials.

19. Revised Model State Administrative Procedure Act § 10(1) (1961).

20. Revised Model State Administrative Procedure Act § 4–212 (1981):

(a) Upon proper objection, the presiding officer shall exclude evidence that is irrelevant, immaterial, unduly repetitious, or excludable on constitutional or statutory grounds or on the basis of evidentiary privilege recognized in the courts of this state. In the absence of proper objection, the presiding officer may exclude objectionable evidence. Evidence may not be excluded solely because it is hearsay.

§ 352

1. Opp Cotton Mills, Inc. v. Administrator, Department of Labor, 312 U.S. 126, 155 (1941). On the other hand, several states have followed the lead of the Revised Model Act that "[i]rrelevant, immaterial, or unduly repetitious evidence *shall* be excluded." Alaska

section 556(d) by providing that "[a]ny oral documentary evidence may be received, but the agency as a matter of policy shall provide for the exclusion of irrelevant, immaterial, or unduly repetitious evidence." [2]

Note that the APA opens the door to *any* evidence which the administrative law judge admits and only *suggests* that insignificant and redundant evidence should be rejected, giving the agencies broad discretion. Moreover, the APA pointedly omits hearsay or other "incompetent" evidence from the list of evidence which should not be received.[3] Thus, the exclusion of otherwise legally inadmissible evidence from an administrative hearing may be error.[4] Furthermore, it is clear that the exclusion of relevant, material, and competent evidence by the administrative law judge will be grounds for reversal if that refusal is prejudicial.[5]

The courts have pressed the agencies to abide by the spirit of these rules. The leading example of such pressure—which in fact antedates the APA—is found in Samuel H.

Moss, Inc. v. FTC,[6] where a distinguished panel of the Second Circuit admonished a hearing examiner for rigidly following the rules of evidence:

> [I]f the case was to be tried with strictness, the examiner was right . . . . Why either he or the [Federal Trade] Commission's attorney should have thought it desirable to be so formal about the admission of evidence, we cannot understand. Even in criminal trials to a jury it is better, nine times out of ten, to admit, than to exclude, evidence and in such proceedings as these the only conceivable interest that can suffer by admitting any evidence is the time lost, which is seldom as much as that inevitably lost by idle bickering about irrelevancy or incompetence. In the case at bar it chances that no injustice was done, but we take this occasion to point out the danger always involved in conducting such a proceeding in such a spirit, and the absence of any advantage in depriving either the Commission or ourselves of *all evidence which can conceivably throw any light upon the controversy.*[7]

More recent cases have repeated their admonition.[8]

Stat. § 44.62.460(d) (1980); West's Ann.Cal.Gov. Code § 11513; Ga. Code § 3A–116(a); Vernon's Ann.Mo. Stat. § 536.070(8); R.I.Gen. Laws § 42–35–10(a); W.Va. Code, 29A–5–2(a); Wis.Stat.Ann. 227.08. There is, however, a paucity of case authority interpreting and applying these statutes, although courts have occasionally expressed their disapproval of the admission of such evidence. See Bunting Bristol Transfer, Inc. v. Pennsylvania Public Utility Commission, 418 Pa. 286, 292, 210 A.2d 281, 284 (1965); D.F. Bast, Inc. v. Pennsylvania Public Utility Commission, 397 Pa. 246, 251, 154 A.2d 505, 508 (1959). Several cases suggest that state courts have been critical of agency receipt of hearsay evidence, essentially on grounds that the particular evidence lacked probative force. E.g., Gomez v. Industrial Commission, 72 Ariz. 265, 233 P.2d 827 (1951); Zawisza v. Quality Name Plate, Inc., 149 Conn. 115, 176 A.2d 578 (1961). But only occasional—and usually earlier—state decisions have reversed agency rulings merely on the grounds of the receipt of hearsay evidence. See, e.g., In re Trustees of Village of Westminster, 108 Vt. 352, 187 A. 519 (1936).

2. 5 U.S.C.A. § 556(d). Not only the Act's words but also the legislative history make clear that the exclusionary rules do not govern the admissibility of evidence in administrative hearings and that the provision for exclusion applied only to "irrelevant, immaterial, or unduly repetitious evidence" and not to legally incompetent evidence. United States ex rel. Dong Wing Ott v. Shaughnessy, 116 F.Supp. 745, 750 (S.D.N.Y.1953), affirmed on other grounds 220 F.2d 537 (2d Cir.), cert. denied 350 U.S. 847; see 2 Davis § 16:4. See also Richardson v. Perales, 402 U.S. 389 (1971); Klinestiver v. Drug Enforcement Administration, 606 F.2d 1128 (D.C. Cir. 1979) ("competent" evidence standard of DEA act is coextensive with APA § 556(d)).

3. See the authorities cited in n. 2 supra. In this context, the definition of hearsay is secondhand information which would not come within any of the exceptions to the hearsay rule.

4. See e.g., Catholic Medical Center of Brooklyn and Queens, Inc. v. N.L.R.B., 589 F.2d 1166 (2d Cir. 1978), appeal after remand 620 F.2d 20 (error under APA § 556(d) for NLRB to exclude evidence of alleged union misconduct that was relevant and not protected by privilege or countervailing policy).

5. N.L.R.B. v. Burns, 207 F.2d 434 (8th Cir. 1953); Prince v. Industrial Commission, 89 Ariz. 314, 361 P.2d 929 (1961); People ex rel. Hirschberg v. Board of Supervisors, 251 N.Y. 156, 167 N.E. 204 (1929); see 1 Cooper 367–71 (collecting authorities). But see n. 4, § 351 supra.

6. 148 F.2d 378 (2d Cir. 1945), cert. denied 326 U.S. 734, rehearing denied 326 U.S. 809, motion denied 155 F.2d 1016 (2d Cir.) (per curiam, decision by Clark, A. Hand and L. Hand, JJ.).

7. Id. at 380 (emphasis added).

8. Multi-Medical Convalescent and Nursing Center v. N.L.R.B., 550 F.2d 974 (4th Cir. 1977), cert. denied 434 U.S. 835; Resort Car Rental System, Inc. v. FTC, 518 F.2d 962 (9th Cir. 1975), cert. denied 423 U.S. 827.

Many reasons support the open admission of hearsay and other legally incompetent evidence in administrative hearings.[9] Foremost among them is the fact that the exclusionary rules do not determine the probative value of the proffered evidence. Professor Davis, the leading proponent that hearing officers should make no distinction between hearsay and nonhearsay evidence, makes the point this way:

> [T]he reliability of hearsay ranges from the least to the most reliable. The reliability of non-hearsay also ranges from the least to the most reliable. Therefore the guide should be a judgment about the reliability of particular evidence in a particular record in particular circumstances, not the technical hearsay rule with all its complex exceptions.[10]

Most hearsay in administrative hearings is documentary. The standard of admissibility thus applied by both reviewing courts and administrative law judges is that "an administrative tribunal is not required to exclude hearsay evidence in the form of a document if its authenticity is sufficiently convincing to a reasonable mind and if it carries sufficient assurance as to its truthfulness."[11]

To require that an administrative law judge refuse to admit hearsay makes no sense where there is no jury to protect and the trier of fact is equally exposed to the evidence whether he admits or excludes it.[12] Admission without a ruling—as long as the evidence has some element of reliability—does no harm and can prove more efficient than requiring a ruling which may later be held erroneous. Discarding the exclusionary rules of admission eliminates the need for the parties to interpose protective objections—the objections being preserved by their briefs to the law judge or agency—and relieves the law judge of making difficult rulings before all the evidence is available. It assures a complete, yet not necessarily unduly long, record and might well avoid the need to reopen the record. Hearsay, of course, is not subject to current, in-court cross-examination, but that limitation affects the weight the evidence carries, not its admissibility.[13]

The fact that administrative hearings need not follow the exclusionary rules and the fact that the admission of remote or repetitious evidence is not reversible error does not suggest that "anything goes" or that all proffered evidence, whatever its relevance or trustworthiness, should be admitted. Wholesale admission would only add to delay and further expand records which are already often very long. Nor can an efficient adjudicatory system decide anew each time the question is presented whether some particular evidence should be admitted. However, most agencies have not fully developed regulations governing the extent to which the exclusionary rules should not be applied.[14] Nonetheless, the admissibility of evidence in administrative hearings depends more upon the *importance* of the evidence in relation to the ultimate issues rather than upon the legal standards of relevance and materiality.[15]

9. Patterson, Hearsay and the Substantial Evidence Rule in the Federal Administrative Process, 13 Mercer L.Rev. 294, 304–06 (1962); cf. Builders Steel Co. v. Commissioner, 179 F.2d 377, 379 (8th Cir. 1950); Davis, Hearsay in Nonjury Cases, 83 Harv.L.Rev. 1362, 1366 (1970).

10. Davis, Hearsay in Administrative Hearings, 2 Geo.Wash.L.Rev. 689 (1964). One commentator has asserted that nine-tenths of the problems involved in applying the exclusionary rules in administrative hearings—or, at least, those that come to reviewing courts—involve hearsay. Note, 46 Ill.L.Rev. 915, 919 n. 23 (1952).

11. Fairfield Scientific Corp. v. United States, 222 Ct.Cl. 167, 611 F.2d 854, 859 (1979), appeal after remand 655 F.2d 1062.

12. Donnelly Garment Co. v. N.L.R.B., 123 F.2d 215, 224 (8th Cir. 1942); see 3 Davis § 16:11. But see Note, Improper Evidence in Nonjury Trials: Basis for Reversal? 79 Harv.L.Rev. 407, 409–11 (1965).

13. See Calhoun v. Bailor, 626 F.2d 145 (9th Cir. 1980), cert. denied 452 U.S. 906; Reil v. United States, 197 Ct.Cl. 542, 456 F.2d 777 (1972); Peters v. United States, 187 Ct.Cl. 63, 408 F.2d 719, 724 (1969); W. Gellhorn & Byse, Administrative Law 713–14, 772 (5th ed. 1970).

14. 3 Davis § 16:5.

15. The basic point made earlier should not be ignored—namely, that administrative hearings generally follow the time-tested judicial pattern of receiving evidence. Cf. W. Gellhorn, Federal Administrative Proceedings 75–82 (1941). It is also clear that agencies

Several significant and useful deviations from the judicial pattern appear in administrative hearings. The first, already noted, involves the relatively free receipt of hearsay evidence. Equally important is the manner in which oral testimony is received. Witnesses in agency hearings are frequently permitted freedom to testify in a simple, natural and direct fashion, without unnecessary interruptions from either the attorney who is directing the questioning or his adversary.[16] Only when the witness strays far afield, or the question is remote will an objection be sustained. A third departure permitted from judicial practice occurs when the administrative law judge is uncertain whether to exclude the evidence on the grounds of incompetency, irrelevancy, or immateriality. In administrative hearings the tendency is to admit the evidence. Other techniques, principally the use of written presentations and shortened hearings, are discussed below.[17]

Since the administrative hearings differ so widely in scope and significance, it is impossible to suggest a single standard to govern the admission of all evidence. It is probably still true, however, as one keen observer noted over 40 years ago, that the more closely administrative proceedings approach judicial proceedings in formality and in the nature of the issues to be tried, the greater the degree to which the exclusionary rules will be applied.[18] Nor has improvement been made to the standard suggested by the Attorney General's Committee on Administrative Procedure in 1941: "The ultimate test of admissibility must be whether the proffered evidence is reliable, probative and relevant.

The question in each case must be whether the probability of error justifies the burden of stricter methods of proof."[19]

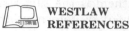

§ 353. Evaluation of Evidence

In contrast to the effect of a trial court's decision to receive hearsay evidence in a jury trial, an administrative law judge's decision to receive hearsay in an administrative adjudication is only the first step in determining its impact upon the tribunal's decision. The admission of evidence in a jury trial is often considered the last effective legal control over the use (or abuse) of such evidence because of the assumption that the jury will rely upon or be swayed by it regardless of whether its reliability has been established. In an administrative hearing, on the other hand, as in the case of nonjury trials, it is assumed that the law judge will not rely upon untrustworthy evidence in reaching his decision. Thus if there is "competent" or trustworthy evidence to support the decision, the reviewing court presumes that the administrative law or trial judge relied on that evidence in reaching his decision.[1]

Nevertheless, the more difficult—and often crucial—question for the hearing officer is the determination of whether he should

have not adequately explored methods to streamline the process of obtaining reliable evidence. See Selected Reports of the Administrative Conference of the United States 1961–1962, S.Doc. No. 24, 88th Cong., 1st Sess. 90–91 (1963).

16. See W. Gellhorn & Lauer, Administration of the New York Workmen's Compensation Law II, 37 N.Y. U.L.Rev. 204, 209 (1962).

17. See § 358 infra.

18. Benjamin 178; see Davis, An Approach to Problems of Evidence in the Administrative Process, 55 Harv.L.Rev. 364, 386–90 (1942).

19. Final Report of Attorney General's Committee on Administrative Procedure, S.Doc. No. 8, 77th Cong., 1st Sess. 71 (1941).

§ 353

1. See Fishing Fleet, Inc. v. Trident Insurance Co., 598 F.2d 925, 929 (5th Cir.1979); Northwestern National Casualty Co. v. Global Moving & Storage, Inc., 533 F.2d 320, 324 (6th Cir.1976); Goodman v. Highlands Insurance Co., 607 F.2d 665, 668 (5th Cir.1979). See generally Note, 79 Harv.L.Rev. 407 (1965); § 60 supra.

rely upon hearsay evidence in reaching his decision. The administrative law judge's concern is with the reliability or probative worth of the evidence.[2] Jury trial rules of evidence exclude hearsay on the theory that it is untrustworthy unless within an exception.[3] More specifically, the risk that hearsay evidence is untrustworthy and that it might be relied upon by the decision maker is, in general, so great that it must be excluded unless some other reason justifies its admission. The party against whom the evidence is admitted can neither confront nor cross-examine the out-of-court declarant to test its probative worth.

But on the other side of the ledger is the fact that each of us constantly relies upon hearsay evidence in making important decisions. Without hearsay, commerce would stop, government would cease to function, and education would be reduced to each teacher's personal experience (and even the latter would often be based upon hearsay). It is not surprising, then, that no legal system outside the Anglo-American realm has adopted so restrictive a rule of evidence. Scholars have rejected its across-the-board application and the courts are increasingly rejecting its application, even in jury cases.[4]

Nonetheless, the fact that some hearsay may prove reliable is no guarantee that all hearsay is reliable. Nor is it responsive to observe that the rules of evidence already admit much that is worthless. Why, it could be asked, should more that is worthless be admitted in order to find some that is trustworthy, particularly when there is no assurance that the factfinder will rely on the latter and disregard the former? It could also be contended that unless probative evidence could be distilled or some alternative protection devised, the admission of hearsay would not promote justice. The administrative regulations governing the receipt and evaluation of evidence indicate that the agencies themselves have not adequately wrestled with this issue.[5]

The courts have provided only scant guidance in upholding administrative reliance on some hearsay evidence. Judge Learned Hand has offered the classic formulation:

> [The examiner] did indeed admit much that would have been excluded at common law, but the act specifically so provides . . . [N]o doubt, that does not mean mere rumor will serve to "support" a finding, but hearsay may do so, at least if more is not conveniently available, and if in the end the finding is supported by *the kind of evidence on which responsible persons are accustomed to rely in serious affairs.*[6]

Administrative law judges and agencies have adhered to this commonsense standard instinctively.[7] At the same time, several criteria applied in evaluating the reliability of hearsay can be discerned.[8]

The following are the most significant:

(a) What is the "nature" of the hearsay evidence? If the hearsay is likely to be reliable, it usually becomes an exception to the

---

2. The same weighing process is often involved in the examiner's decision whether to receive the evidence. If it is unlikely to be probative, he will not receive it regardless of the inapplicability of the hearsay rule. See § 352 supra.

3. See § 245 supra.

4. See, e.g., Weinstein, Probative Force of Hearsay, 46 Iowa L.Rev. 331 (1961). See also Fed.R.Evid. 803(24), 804(b)(5); § 324.1 supra.

5. See 3 Davis § 16:5.

6. N.L.R.B. v. Remington Rand, 94 F.2d 862, 873 (2d Cir.1938), cert. denied 304 U.S. 576 (emphasis added), reversed on other grounds 110 F.2d 148 (2d Cir.). See also International Association of Machinists, etc. v. N.L.R.B., 110 F.2d 29, 35 (1939), affirmed 311 U.S. 72; Bene & Sons, Inc. v. FTC, 299 F. 468, 471 (2d Cir.1924).

Several states—both by judicial decree and by statute—have adopted this test to permit agency departures from the exclusionary rules where compliance is impracticable and where the evidence is "of a type commonly relied upon by reasonably prudent men in the conduct of their affairs." See, e.g., Ring v. Smith, 5 Cal.App.3d 197, 204, 85 Cal.Rptr. 227, 232 (1970); Ga. Code § 3A–116(a); Mich.Comp.Laws Ann. § 3.560(175); R.I.Gen.Laws § 42–35–10; W.Va. Code 29A–5–2(a).

7. See Multi-Medical Convalescent and Nursing Center of Towson v. N.L.R.B., 550 F.2d 974, 976–78 (4th Cir.1972), cert. denied 434 U.S. 835; Sigmon, Rules of Evidence Before the I.C.C., 31 Geo.Wash.L.Rev. 258 (1962); Note, 55 Harv.L.Rev. 820, 827–33 (1942).

8. 3 Davis § 16:6, pp. 243–45.

hearsay rule. Moreover, if the evidence is intrinsically trustworthy, agencies have taken the next logical step and relied, if necessary, upon this evidence in deciding cases, even though it technically constitutes hearsay and does not fall within any of the recognized exceptions. One example of intrinsically reliable hearsay, intra- and intercorporate documents not shown to be within the business records exception, was the subject of a celebrated opinion by Judge Wyzanski in a nonjury trial not dissimilar from an administrative hearing. [9] An even clearer example of the reliability criteria is newspaper reports. [10] Stories of significant news events are likely to be reliable. Newspapers normally do not report accidents which did not occur. On the other hand, newspaper summaries of public comments are commonly inaccurate—at least if one may believe those who claim to be misquoted—because of the difficulty of hearing and then summarizing another's views. Even so-called verbatim transcripts commonly suffer from significant errors as a result of the pressure of time deadlines. Note that the hearsay quality of each report is identical. Yet the accident report will be treated as solid support for an administrative decision and the speech summary, unless corroborated, will not. [11]

(b) Is better evidence available? The necessary substantiation for the reliability of hearsay evidence may arise from the failure of respondent to controvert the hearsay when the necessary proof is readily available to him, even though there is no testimonial or documentary exhibit of such available "support." A leading example of this position is United States ex rel. Vajtauer v. Commissioner, [12] where the Supreme Court upheld a deportation order based on a finding that the alien had advocated the overthrow of the government by force. The alien gave his name as Emanuel Vajtauer, a "Doctor of Psychology" and editor of the "Spravedlvost." In making his finding the director relied upon two items of hearsay: a pamphlet bearing the name of Dr. E.M. Vajtauer as author; and a newspaper report of a speech by a Dr. Vajtauer, editor of the "Spravedlvost," supporting revolution. Both items became convincing evidence when "the appellant, confronted by this record, stood mute. . . . His silence without explanation other than that he would not testify until the entire evidence was presented, was in itself evidence that he was the author." [13]

---

9. United States v. United Shoe Machinery Corp., 89 F.Supp. 349, 355, 356 (D.Mass.1950), 60 Yale L.J. 363 (1951). More recently such questions have focused on computers and reliance on "computer evidence" in contested hearings. See Note, 126 U.Pa.L.Rev. 425 (1977). In general see Fed.R.Evid. 803(24), 804(b)(5); § 324.1 supra.

10. See Davis, An Approach to Problems of Evidence in the Administrative Process, 55 Harv.L.Rev. 364, 390 (1942); cf. Dallas County v. Commercial Union Assurance Co., 286 F.2d 388 (5th Cir.1961); Wathen v. United States, 208 Ct.Cl. 342, 527 F.2d 1191, 1199 (1975), cert. denied 429 U.S. 821.

11. See Montana Power Co. v. FPC, 185 F.2d 491, 498 (D.C.Cir.1950), cert. denied 340 U.S. 947, rehearing denied 341 U.S. 912; United States ex rel. Vajtauer v. Commissioner, 273 U.S. 103 (1927).

12. Id. n. 11 supra.

13. Id. at 111. But see Griffin v. California, 380 U.S. 609 (1965), rehearing denied 381 U.S. 957; §§ 131, 270 supra. Workers' compensation cases furnish a further illustration. In one typical case, the testimony revealed that the workman went home, told his wife that he was hurt while at work, repeated the same story to a doctor, and then died. No one saw the accident. No better evidence was available. Placing special reliance on the statute's remedial purpose, the agency relied upon this hearsay evidence even though it fell outside the spontaneous exclamation exception. Greenfarb v. Arre, 62 N.J.Super. 420, 163 A.2d 173 (1960); see John W. McGrath Corp. v. Hughes, 264 F.2d 314 (2d Cir. 1959), cert. denied 360 U.S. 931; Associated General Contractors of America v. Cardillo, 106 F.2d 327, 329 (D.C.Cir.1939); cf. G. & C. Merriam Co. v. Syndicate Publishing Co., 207 F. 515, 518 (2d Cir.1913) (quoting trial court opinion by L. Hand, J.). See generally, Larson, The Law of Workmen's Compensation § 79 (1952) and 2 id. (Supp.1970). On the other hand, if credible firsthand witnesses were to have told another story— for example, that the accident happened elsewhere— the hearing officer would likely have rejected the hearsay testimony, especially if the eyewitness testimony is corroborated by convincing circumstantial evidence. Jacobowitz v. United States, 191 Ct.Cl. 444, 424 F.2d 555 (1970); In re Rath Packing Co., 14 N.L.R.B. 805, 817 (1939); see Glaros v. Immigration and Naturalization Service, 416 F.2d 441 (5th Cir.1969) (hearsay cor-

(c) How important or unimportant is the subject matter in relation to the cost of acquiring "better" evidence? Many examples are available. If the out-of-hearing declarant is readily available and the question involves the respondent's livelihood or security—as is often the case in security and deportation matters—hearsay by itself carries little weight. [14] If, however, the matter is but one of thousands of compensation claims—as in social security and workers' compensation cases—and the declarant's appearance would be relatively costly or time-consuming, hearsay alternatives such as letters or other written evidence might prove decisive. [15] It has likewise been held that in the granting of a license an agency may rely upon evidence which would not be adequate in revoking the same license. [16]

(d) How precise does the agency's factfinding need to be? The Interstate Commerce Commission's reliance on "typical evidence" and the Federal Trade Commission's use of survey evidence are examples of agency dependence on statistical averages to determine facts in particular cases where legal or policy decisions are not dependent upon exact determinations. For instance, survey evidence of consumer understanding

indicating that a substantial proportion of the public were misled by respondent's advertising will support a finding that it constitutes an unfair or deceptive act. [17] Still another example is the fixing of a rate for commodities transported by one carrier on the basis of costs incurred by similarly situated carriers. [18]

(e) What is the administrative policy behind the statute being enforced? The range of necessary reliability is affected by the type of policy which the administrative hearing is designed to promote. For example, the social security and workers' compensation programs are intended to provide benefits quickly at low cost. The refusal to rely upon reports in such hearings would run counter to the purposes for which the statutes are designed. [19]

When focusing on these criteria, it is essential to consider the central point that evaluation of hearsay and other technically incompetent evidence cannot be accomplished in the abstract; the evidence must be examined in the light of the particular record. This includes, at a minimum, an examination of the quality and quantity of the evi-

roborated by other evidence); N.L.R.B. v. Operating Engineers, Local 12, 25 Ad.L.2d 832 (9th Cir.1969) (no objection raised to admission of hearsay). See § 297 supra.

14. E.g., Young v. Board of Pharmacy, 81 N.M. 5, 462 P.2d 139 (1969); Outagamie County v. Town of Brooklyn, 18 Wis.2d 303, 118 N.W.2d 201 (1962); see Reilly v. Pinkus, 338 U.S. 269 (1949). Contra, Peters v. United States, 187 Ct.Cl. 63, 408 F.2d 719 (1969), criticized in Note, Hearsay and Confrontation in Administrative Hearings, 48 N.C.L.Rev. 608 (1970).

15. Richardson v. Perales, 402 U.S. 389 (1971), supra § 351, n. 6; Marmon v. Railroad Retirement Board, 218 F.2d 716 (3d Cir.1955); Ellers v. Railroad Retirement Board, 132 F.2d 636 (2d Cir.1943). For a reverse application of this principle, see Staskel v. Gardner, 274 F.Supp. 861, 863 (E.D.Pa.1967) (hearsay not sufficient evidence to deny claim); Rios v. Hackney, 294 F.Supp. 885 (N.D.Tex.1967).

16. Davis, Hearsay in Administrative Hearings, 32 Geo.Wash.L.Rev. 689, 699 (1964); see FTC v. Cement Institute, 333 U.S. 683, 705–06 (1948), rehearing denied 334 U.S. 839.

17. E.g. Arrow Metal Products Corp., 53 F.T.C. 721, 727, 733–34 (1957), affirmed per curiam, 249 F.2d 83

(3d Cir.); Rhodes Pharmacal Co., 49 F.T.C. 263 (1952), affirmed 208 F.2d 382, 386–87 (7th Cir.), reversed on other grounds 348 U.S. 940. See generally Bernacchi, Trademark Meaning and Non-Partisan Survey Research, 30 Ad.L.Rev. 447 (1978).

18. Atchison, Topeka & Santa Fe Railway v. United States, 225 F.Supp. 584 (D.Colo.1964); New England Division Case, 261 U.S. 184, 197–198 (1923); see 2 Sharfman, The Interstate Commerce Com'n 376–80 (1931). See also Skelly Oil Co. v. FPC, 375 F.2d 6 (10th Cir. 1967), modified sub nom. Permian Basin Area Rate Cases, 390 U.S. 747 (1968), rehearing denied 392 U.S. 917.

19. Richardson v. Perales, 402 U.S. 389 (1971), supra § 351, n. 6. Several states have also adopted specific statutes governing the use of copies of documentary evidence. See Ga.Code, § 3A–116(b); Hawaii Rev. Stat. § 91–10(2); Md.Code 1957, Art. 41, § 252(b); Mass.Gen.Laws Ann. c. 30A, § 11(4); Mich.Comp.Laws Ann. § 3.560(176); Minn.Stat.Ann. § 14.60; Neb.Rev. Stat. § 84–914(3); 75 Okl.Stat.Ann. § 310(2); Or.Rev. Stat. 183.450(2); R.I.Gen.Laws 1956, § 42–35–10(b); West's RCWA § 34.04.100(2). See also Fed.R.Evid. 1003.

dence on each side, as well as the circumstantial setting of the case. [20]

WESTLAW REFERENCES

"administrative law judge*'" (hearing* +2 examiner* officer*) /s hearsay

"business record*'" newspaper* /p administrative /2 adjudication* hearing* proceeding*

averag! statistic! survey** /s admissib! evidence /p administrative agenc*** board* bureau commission* department* panel* /2 adjudication* hearing* proceeding* % title(commonwealth people state)

§ 354. The Substantial Evidence Rule

Once the agency has determined that legally incompetent evidence can be admitted and relied upon in making an administrative decision, it might appear that the subject of hearsay evidence in administrative hearings has been exhausted. While the agency's admission and use of legally incompetent evidence is subject to judicial review, this review of administrative determinations of fact should be confined to determining whether the decision is supported by the evidence in the record. Judicial review of administrative evidence has not been so limited, however. As a substitute for rules of admissibility, courts apply the so-called "substantial evidence" rule to judicial review of agency action in seeking to assure fairness to the parties.

As applied to administrative findings, the substantial evidence rule possesses two branches, one of which is sound, and the oth-

er unsound. The first consists of an overall standard of review of the findings of fact. Except for the distinctive features of judicial review of administrative action, it does not differ conceptually from the "sufficiency" standard applied in judicial review of jury verdicts.[1] In this sense, substantial evidence is evidence

> affording a substantial basis of fact from which the fact in issue can be reasonably inferred. . . . [I]t must be enough to justify, if the trial were to a jury, a refusal to direct a verdict when the conclusion sought to be drawn from it is one of fact for the jury.[2]

This standard measures both the quantitative and qualitative sufficiency of the evidence.[3] Its proper application takes into account the rationale of the exclusionary rules of evidence, the reliability of the hearsay evidence—including the opportunity for cross-examination, the availability of better evidence, and the appearance of corroborating evidence—and the needs of administrative economy. According to the still leading opinion of Universal Camera Corp. v. NLRB,[4] this judicially evolved standard of review of administrative factfinding is incorporated into the Administrative Procedure Act, except that the Act broadens judicial review to assure that the reviewing court takes "into account whatever in the record fairly detracts from its weight." [5] In other words, the reviewing court should review the whole record to determine whether there is a rational basis in it for the findings of fact supporting the agency's decision.[6]

---

20. For a review of the cases, see Jacobowitz v. United States, 191 Ct.Cl. 444, 424 F.2d 555 (1970).

§ 354

1. E.g. Wilkerson v. McCarthy, 336 U.S. 53, 57 (1949), rehearing denied 336 U.S. 940; § 339 supra.

2. N.L.R.B. v. Columbian Enameling & Stamping Co., 306 U.S. 292, 299–300 (1939). See also Consolo v. FMC, 383 U.S. 607, 618–21 (1966), on remand 373 F.2d 674 (D.C.Cir.); Richardson v. Perales, 402 U.S. 389 (1971), supra § 351 n. 12. The substantial evidence test applied to jury verdicts and administrative findings is in contrast to appellate review of a court's fact determinations in a nonjury case where findings are measured by the "clearly erroneous" test. See United States v. United States Gypsum Co., 333 U.S. 364, 395 (1948), rehearing denied 333 U.S. 869; Ethyl Corp. v.

EPA, 451 F.2d 1, 34–35 n. 74 (D.C.Cir. 1976), cert. denied 426 U.S. 941; N.L.R.B. v. Southland Manufacturing Co., 201 F.2d 244, 246 (4th Cir. 1952); Wright, Law of Federal Courts 647–50 (4th ed. 1983).

3. See Benjamin 192; 1 Cooper 404–05.

4. 340 U.S. 474 (1951).

5. Id. at 488.

6. The intricacies and problems which arise in applying this standard are not within our concern here. See generally Greater Boston Television Corp. v. FCC, 444 F.2d 841, 850–52 (D.C.Cir. 1970), cert. denied 403 U.S. 923; Robinson, Gellhorn & Bruff, The Administrative Process 132–41 (2d ed. 1980). For a review of state authority, see Cooper 722–55, which is extremely critical of the substantial evidence standard.

In reviewing administrative decisions, some appellate courts—primarily state—added a second branch to the substantial evidence test, warping the test into a rigid rule for denying credibility to uncorroborated hearsay evidence. Known as the "legal residuum rule" because it required that an administrative finding be supported by some evidence admissible in a jury trial—that is, by a residuum of "legal" evidence—it has been severely criticized by scholars, and its application has strained judicial reasoning.[7]

The residuum rule is both logically unsound and administratively impractical. In a trial before a lay jury hearsay evidence admitted without objection is given its natural, probative effect and may be the sole support for a verdict. But under the residuum rule hearsay cannot support a decision by an experienced or expert administrator. The rule ignores the reliability of technically incompetent evidence, rendering all such evidence ineffective unless corroborated. However, if corroborated, regardless of how slight the legal evidence, the same hearsay evidence will provide the substantial evidence needed to support the administrative finding.

This rule may also become a trap for the unwary, particularly where the administrative law judge is not expert in the rules of evidence or where the parties are not represented by counsel. In fact it encourages law judges to apply the hearsay rule and exclude probative evidence in order to avoid possible error. In its instinctive protection of fairness in administrative hearings, through assuring that the decision is supported by evidence subject to confrontation and cross-examination, the residuum rule seems unassailable. What it fails to consider, however, is that much "legal" evidence within the hearsay exceptions is equally untested. Yet the latter is accepted even in jury trials because of its probable reliability. Consequently the residuum rule's mechanical prohibition against uncorroborated hearsay is unsound. Its sound objectives can be secured through the sensitivity of the hearing officers and the wise application of the substantial evidence test which measures the quantity and quality of the supporting evidence regardless of its category or label.

As others have recounted at substantial length, the residuum rule generally lacks acceptance in federal courts.[8] Increasingly the states refuse to apply it.[9]

---

7. 3 Davis § 16:16; Benjamin 189–92; 1 Wigmore, Evidence § 4B, p. 39 (3d ed. 1940). But see 1 Cooper 410–12.

The earliest case applying this rule illustrates its weakness. In Carroll v. Knickerbocker Ice Co., 218 N.Y. 435, 113 N.E. 507 (1916), the New York Court of Appeals reversed a worker's compensation award in a death case where the commission's finding of accidental injury was based wholly on hearsay testimony of statements by the deceased workman. The workman, who developed delirium tremens and died within six days, had told his wife, a neighbor, and his family and hospital physician that a 300-pound cake of ice had fallen upon his abdomen. Each party related this story to the commission. However, the case record also contained substantial contradictory evidence. The workman's helper on the ice truck, along with two cooks working in the saloon where the ice was delivered also testified that they were present at the same time and place where the accident presumably occurred but they neither saw nor heard the incident. In addition, the hospital physicians found no bruises, discolorations, or abrasions on the workman's body. In light of the lack of testimonial or physical corroboration of the workman's story which probably would have been available if the hearsay statement had been trustworthy, the ob-

vious self-interest in the deceased's statement, and the possibility of the workman's being inebriated when he made his statement, the court reasonably could have ruled that credence could not be placed in the supporting hearsay evidence and that it did not, therefore, constitute substantial evidence. Instead, after noting that the commission could "accept any evidence that is offered" under the New York Workman's Compensation Act, the court laid down the rule that "still in the end there must be a residuum of legal evidence to support the claim before an award can be made." Id. at 441, 113 N.E. at 509. It therefore held that when substantial evidence is required, "hearsay testimony is no evidence." Id.

8. 3 Davis § 16:6, and see Richardson v. Perales, 402 U.S. 389 (1971), supra § 351 n. 12; Johnson v. United States, 628 F.2d 187 (D.C.Cir. 1980).

9. See Tauber v. County Board of Appeals, 257 Md. 202, 262 A.2d 513, 518 (1970); Neuman v. City of Baltimore, 251 Md. 92, 246 A.2d 583 (1968); 1 Cooper 406–10. The 1981 Revised Model State Administrative Procedure Act provides in part:

4-215(d) . . . Findings must be based upon the kind of evidence on which reasonably prudent persons are accustomed to rely in the conduct of their

**WESTLAW
REFERENCES**

di substantial evidence
universal +2 camera /p "substantial evidence"
15ak791
residuum /7 rule

---

§ 355. Opinion Evidence and Expert Testimony [1]

The presentation of expert and nonexpert opinions is increasingly common in administrative hearings. Medical issues arising in workers' compensation claims are often complex, technical and beyond the knowledge of either the hearing officer or the agency. An administrative decision to license a hydroelectric plant, to locate a public housing project, to discontinue a bus line, or to grant a liquor license invariably evokes strong community concern. [2] The public views advanced are likely to be expressed in terms of opinions and to include reference to the views of others. To deny the public an opportunity to testify is to invite public rejec-

tion of the agency decision or judicial reversal because public participation is required under the agency's enabling legislation.

The general admissibility of expert and nonexpert testimony in administrative hearings is no longer open to question, but doubt still exists regarding the weight an expert's views should be given. [3] For a time agencies and reviewing courts followed early judicial reasoning and refused to hear expert testimony on the very question that the agency was created to decide. [4] Other courts took the position that it would be unfair for an agency to rely on its own expertness or the expert testimony of its staff when their opinions were contradicted by outside experts. [5] In rejecting these contradictory appeals to ignorance, courts now recognize legislative intention to establish expert agencies. Therefore, agency decisions which rely on the agency's own expertness are upheld when the respondent offers no contrary expert testimony or when expert testimony offered by staff members and outside experts conflicts. [6] Some courts

serious affairs and may be based upon such evidence even if it would be inadmissible in a civil trial.

The Commissioners' Comment further dispels any doubts when it states: "this Act rejects the 'residuum rule,' under which findings can be made only if supported, in the record, by at least a 'residuum' of legally admissible evidence."

§ 355

1. See generally Gellhorn, Proof of Consumer Deception Before the Federal Trade Commission, 17 U.Kan.L.Rev. 559 (1969).

2. Cf. Vermont Yankee Nuclear Power Corp. v. Natural Resources Defense Council, Inc., 435 U.S. 519 (1978); Sierra Club v. Costle, 657 F.2d 298 (D.C.Cir. 1981); Scenic Hudson Preservation Conference v. FPC, 354 F.2d 608 (2d Cir. 1965), cert. denied 384 U.S. 941, appeal after remand 453 F.2d 463 (2d Cir.), cert. denied 407 U.S. 926; Citizens for Allegan County, Inc. v. FPC, 414 F.2d 1125 (D.C.Cir.1969); Office of Communication of United Church of Christ v. FCC, 359 F.2d 994 (D.C. Cir.1966); Norwalk CORE v. Norwalk Redevelopment Agency, 395 F.2d 920 (2d Cir.1968).

3. Office of Communication of United Church of Christ v. FCC, supra n. 2; see Gellhorn, Public Participation in Administrative Proceedings, 81 Yale L.J. 359 (1972).

4. Cf. § 12 supra; Corn v. State Bar, 68 Cal.2d 461, 67 Cal.Rptr. 401, 439 P.2d 313 (1968). The courts have generally discarded the earlier view that agency opin-

ions need supporting expert testimony, and agencies are now free to use their own judgment. Compare Boggs & Buhl v. Commissioner, 34 F.2d 859 (3d Cir. 1929), with Kline v. Commissioner, 130 F.2d 742 (3d Cir.1942), cert. denied 317 U.S. 697.

5. Brennan v. State Board of Medical Examiners, 101 Cal.App.2d 193, 225 P.2d 11 (1950). See § 12 supra.

6. E.g., Pacific Power & Light Co. v. FPC, 141 F.2d 602 (9th Cir.1944); Contractors v. Pillsbury, 150 F.2d 310, 313 (9th Cir.1945); see McCarthy v. Sawyer-Goodman Co., 194 Wis. 198, 215 N.W. 824 (1927).

This is an exceedingly brief summary of what can be a complex issue. For an excellent analysis and attempt to balance the right of respondent to a decision based on "record" evidence with the administrative need to avoid unproductive hearings, see Davis & Randall, Inc. v. United States, 219 F.Supp. 673 (W.D.N.Y. 1963), where Judge Friendly applied the following test:

Without wishing to be held to the letter, we suggest that a rejection of unopposed testimony by a qualified and disinterested expert on a matter susceptible of reasonably precise measurement, without the agency's developing its objections at a hearing, ought to be upheld only when the agency's uncommunicated criticisms appear to the reviewing court to be both so compelling and so deeply held that the court can be fairly sure the agency would not have been affected by anything the witness could have said had he known of them, *and* the court would

have gone even further and given excessive deference to the knowledge of the administrative agency by upholding its decision in the face of uncontradicted expert testimony to the contrary.[7] However, the demands of fairness are now generally accepted, and an agency seeking to rely on its expertise must present expert testimony subject to cross-examination on the record or give the respondent fair notification that official notice will be taken of such "facts."[8]

WESTLAW REFERENCES

expert personal   /2   opinion testif! testimony   /p
   administrative agenc***   /2   adjudication* decision*
   hearing* proceeding*

§ 356. Privilege in Administrative Proceedings

Witnesses in administrative hearings have the same general duty incumbent on all citizens in judicial trials to give testimony; "the public has a right to every man's testimony."[1] Because the demand comes from the community as a whole, rather than from the parties, and because the obligation is essential to any search for justice, "all privileges

of exemption from this duty are exceptional."[2] Read literally, the APA's provision in section 556(d) that "[a]ny oral or documentary evidence may be received,"[3] authorizes the receipt of privileged evidence in administrative hearings.[4]

Nevertheless, administrative hearings have generally followed the judicial lead in recognizing numerous exceptions to the obligation to testify. The exceptions are of two kinds. A few, such as the exclusion of illegally obtained evidence and the assertion of the right against self-incrimination, are constitutional commands. Others, such as the privileges protecting attorney-client and the attorney's work product, are founded upon the need to protect interests without constitutional dimension yet having sufficient social importance to warrant the sacrifice of full factual disclosure.[5]

Even though administrative agencies do not as a rule impose criminal penalties, their adjudicative procedures are not exempt from constitutional limitations, and the chapters of this text which deal with the various constitutional privileges should be consulted.

§ 356

1. 12 Cobbett's Parliamentary History 675, 693 (1812), quoted in 4 Wigmore, Evidence 2965–66 (1st ed. 1905).

2. 8 Wigmore, Evidence § 2192, p. 73 (McNaughton rev. 1961).

3. 5 U.S.C.A. § 556(d).

4. Professor Davis once made the provocative suggestion that § 7(c) authorizes agency rejection of unsound or questionable privileges. 2 Davis § 14.08, at 287 (1958, 1965 Supp.). It seems doubtful, however, that this provision can reasonably be interpreted as addressing itself to the question of testimonial privilege; rather, the legislative history suggests that its purpose is to avoid binding administrative agencies to technical rules of evidence. 92 Cong.Rec. 2157, 5653 (1946); see Attorney General's Manual on Administrative Procedure Act 76 (1947). In any case, it is now clear that the agencies generally "respect rules of privilege" and thus litigation seldom results. See 3 Davis § 16:10.

Privileges under state law are generally governed by statutes sufficiently broad in terms to apply to administrative proceedings. The same generalization cannot be made in the federal area. See § 76 supra.

5. See Chapter 8 supra.

have been bound to affirm, despite the expert's hypothetical rebuttal out of deference for the agency's judgment on so technical a matter.
Id. at 679.

7. See, e.g., Arcadia Realty Co. v. Commissioner, 295 F.2d 98, 103 (8th Cir.1961); Gaddy v. State Board of Registration for Healing Arts, 397 S.W.2d 347, 355 (Mo.1965). But see Jaffe, Judicial Control of Administrative Action 607–10 (1965). Judicial approval of agency reliance upon its own expertise is inappropriate, of course, where the expert opinion is patently fallacious or "intrinsically nonpersuasive." See Davis & Randall, Inc. v. United States, supra n. 6 at 678; Sternberger v. United States, 185 Ct.Cl. 528, 401 F.2d 1012, 1016 (1968). Approval is equally inappropriate where the opinion is based on inferences from facts in the record. Interstate Power Co. v. Federal Power Commission, 236 F.2d 372, 385 (8th Cir.1956), cert. denied 352 U.S. 967; see Market St. Railway Co. v. Railroad Commission, 324 U.S. 548, 559–560 (1945).

8. Moschogianis v. Concrete Material & Manufacturing Co., 179 Minn. 177, 228 N.W. 607 (1930); see § 359 infra.

In Camara v. Municipal Court,[6] and See v. Seattle,[7] the Supreme Court applied the Fourth Amendment's strictures against unreasonable searches and seizure of property to administrative health and fire inspections,[8] albeit in somewhat qualified form. These decisions left open the possibility that warrants would not be required for administrative searches where a license was required to conduct the business in question and the grant of a license was effectively conditioned on the applicant's consent to warrantless searches. Later cases confirmed that warrantless searches were permissible in industries subject to a licensing system which involved intensive regulation.[9] Expansion of this exception was halted in Marshall v. Barlow's, Inc.,[10] when the Supreme Court ruled that businesses subject to oversight by the Occupational Safety and Health Administration were not "pervasively regulated" and thus could assert the Fourth Amendment privilege against surprise inspections of the workplace. The privilege

against unreasonable search is also limited to that which is truly private. Thus a warrant is not necessary if the evidence gathered by the inspector is in "plain view."[11]

While these cases involved direct challenges to administrative inspections, it is also clear that the constitutional objection is available at the hearing even though no objection is asserted at the time the inspection is made.[12] And, in Knoll Associates, Inc. v. FTC,[13] the Court of Appeals of the Seventh Circuit set aside an FTC order on the ground that the Commission's acceptance and use of corporate documents, known to be stolen on behalf of the government, violated the Fourth Amendment.

Many cases uphold the Fifth Amendment privilege against self-incrimination in administrative proceedings.[14] However, the self-incrimination privilege has been limited. First, the threatened penalty must be criminal rather than civil in nature.[15] In many regulatory areas, the sanction which the wit-

---

6. 387 U.S. 523 (1967).

7. 387 U.S. 541 (1967).

8. See generally Notes, 78 Harv.L.Rev. 801 (1965), 77 Yale L.J. 521 (1968).

Compare Wyman v. James, 400 U.S. 309 (1971), declining to apply the Fourth Amendment's proscription to visit by caseworker to welfare recipient's home under compulsion of loss of benefits. Search and seizure is treated in Ch. 15 supra.

9. Colonnade Catering Corp. v. United States, 397 U.S. 72 (1970) (licensed retail liquor establishment); United States v. Biswell, 406 U.S. 311 (1972) (firearms dealer). See generally McManis & McManis, Structuring Administrative Inspections: Is There Any Warrant for a Search Warrant? 26 Am.U.L.Rev. 942 (1977); § 170, text at nn. 10–12 supra. See also Donovan v. Dewey, 452 U.S. 594 (1981) (pervasive regulatory exception applicable to mining industry where statute required inspection of all mines and specified the frequency of inspection).

10. 436 U.S. 307 (1978). See discussion of administrative searches in § 170, text at nn. 10–16 supra.

11. Id. See also Air Pollution Variance Board of Colorado v. Western Alfalfa Corp., 416 U.S. 861 (1974) (emission from smokestack visible from public areas of factory grounds). "Plain view" is discussed further in § 171, text at nn. 7–11 supra.

12. See Finn's Liquor Shop, Inc. v. State Liquor Authority, 24 N.Y.2d 647, 301 N.Y.S.2d 584, 249 N.E.2d 440 (1969), cert. denied 396 U.S. 840; Leogrande v. State Liquor Authority, 25 A.D.2d 225, 268 N.Y.S.2d

433 (1966), reversed on other grounds 19 N.Y.2d 418, 227 N.E.2d 302, 280 N.Y.2d 381 (1967); Pennsylvania Liquor Control Board v. Leonardziak, 210 Pa.Super. 511, 233 A.2d 606 (1967); cf. Parrish v. Civil Service Commission, 66 Cal.2d 260, 57 Cal.Rptr. 623, 425 P.2d 223 (1967). Compare Elder v. Board of Medical Examiners, 241 Cal.App.2d 246, 50 Cal.Rptr. 304 (1966) (dictum), with Pierce v. Board of Nursing Education & Nurse Registration, 255 Cal.App.2d 463, 63 Cal.Rptr. 107 (dictum). Contra, National Labor Relations Board v. South Bay Daily Breeze, 415 F.2d 360, 364 (9th Cir. 1969) (alternative holding), cert. denied 397 U.S. 915; Solomon v. Liquor Control Commission, 4 Ohio St.2d 31, 212 N.E.2d 595 (1966), cert. denied 384 U.S. 928.

13. 397 F.2d 530 (7th Cir.1968). Where the documents are obtained independently of any purpose to help the government, they have been held to be admissible. United States v. Marzano, 537 F.2d 257 (7th Cir. 1976) cert. denied 429 U.S. 1038; United States v. Newton, 510 F.2d 1147 (7th Cir.1975).

14. E.g., Murphy v. Waterfront Commission, 378 U.S. 52 (1964); Smith v. United States, 337 U.S. 137 (1949). In this situation, the respondent fears the potential administrative order less than the subsequent use of his testimony in a criminal proceeding.

See generally Ch. 13 supra.

15. United States v. Ward, 448 U.S. 242 (1980) (requirement that persons responsible for oil spills in navigable waters must report the spills to appropriate government agencies not a violation of Fifth Amendment despite civil penalties of $5,000 for each spill); Kennedy v. Mendoza-Martinez, 372 U.S. 144, 168–169

ness fears may be labeled a "civil penalty," a "forfeiture" or a similar term rather than a crime. When this occurs, the court must determine whether the statutory penalty is sufficiently punitive in purpose or effect to be considered criminal. Second, the privilege is available only to natural persons and therefore does not protect corporations and other legal entities. [16] The purpose of the self-incrimination provision is to protect individuals from the government's use of the "third degree" and similar coercive tactics to extract confessions of personal wrong-doing. Thus it does not exempt the officers of corporations and other business associations from testifying about the records of their organizations. [17] Because the privilege is personal to the witness, an individual cannot refuse to testify on the ground that his testimony might incriminate some other person. [18] Third, the privilege attaches only to compelled testimonial utterances and not to other communications. [19] Numerous cases have dealt with the question of whether a particular statement has been coerced or whether it is testimonial in nature. Recent cases have, in general, taken a restrictive view of the privilege. [20] Thus, even if the documents being sought are personal records, are in his possession, and contain handwritten notations, the agency may still be able to obtain them through use of a search warrant. [21] On the other hand, the Fifth Amendment analysis may be different

if the agency seeks to compel an individual to report information rather than trying to get access to existing documents. [22] That is, where the government requires an individual or business to keep business records and make them available to government on demand, such "required records" are not immune from disclosure so long as the underlying regulatory program was a proper exercise of governmental power and the recordkeeping requirement was not designed to make otherwise lawful conduct illegal. [23] Finally, the privilege can be defeated by the grant of immunity from criminal prosecution. [24] Federal agencies commonly have been authorized to grant immunity and compel a witness to testify even if the evidence implicates him. [25] The agency must find that the testimony is "necessary to the public interest," and it must obtain the approval of the Attorney General before immunizing the witness. [26]

On the federal level, neither the Congress nor the agencies have focused on whether administrative agencies must recognize testimonial privileges not constitutionally required. In a leading case concerning the enforcement of an SEC subpoena, Judge Learned Hand expressly assumed that agency proceedings are "subject to the same testimonial privileges as judicial proceedings." [27] Other federal courts have either made the same assumption or considered the matter a question of federal law. [28] At any

(1963). See generally Flemming v. Nestor, 363 U.S. 603, 613–21 (1960); § 121 supra.

16. See § 128 supra.

17. See Bellis v. United States, 417 U.S. 85 (1974); § 129 supra.

18. Couch v. United States, 409 U.S. 322 (1973); § 120 supra.

19. Couch v. United States, supra n. 18; Fisher v. United States, 425 U.S. 391 (1976). See §§ 124, 125 supra.

20. Id. See 1 Davis § 4:24.

21. Andresen v. Maryland, 427 U.S. 463 (1976). See § 127 supra.

22. See Shapiro v. United States, 335 U.S. 1, 6 (1948), rehearing denied 335 U.S. 836.

23. See discussion of required reports in § 142 supra.

24. See § 143 supra.

25. 18 U.S.C.A. §§ 6001–6005.

26. 18 U.S.C.A. § 6004.

27. McMann v. Securities & Exchange Commission, 87 F.2d 377, 378 (2d Cir.1937), cert. denied 301 U.S. 684.

28. E.g. Colton v. United States, 306 F.2d 633 (2d Cir.1962), cert. denied 371 U.S. 951; Falsone v. United States, 205 F.2d 734 (5th Cir.1953), cert. denied 346 U.S. 864; United States v. Threlkeld, 241 F.Supp. 324 (W.D.Tenn.1965); In re Kearney, 227 F.Supp. 174 (S.D. N.Y.1964). Contra, Baird v. Koerner, 279 F.2d 623 (9th Cir.1960); In re Bretto, 231 F.Supp. 529 (D.Minn.1964) (*Baird* applied pursuant to stipulation of the parties). For a perceptive student comment questioning accuracy of this assessment of the choice of law problem, see Comment, Privileged Communications Before Federal Administrative Agencies: The Law Applied in the Dis-

rate, agencies have generally accorded privileged treatment to communications between attorney and client, physician and patient and husband and wife. [29] But they have not been anxious to extend such privileges. For example, the accountant-client privileges recognized by a few states has not been accepted by federal agencies. [30] Business secrets have been protected grudgingly, although agencies have become more sophisticated in recent years in protecting both the witness and the adjudicative process by *in camera* receipt of sensitive data. [31]

Claims of privilege for government secrets are particularly important in administrative hearings. Any attempt to probe the government's case by discovery, subpoena of agency witnesses, or cross-examination is quickly met by claims that the information sought is privileged. Actually, government secrets privilege is asserted as an umbrella for three types of information: state secrets involving military or diplomatic information; requests that executive officers testify; and official government information which may range from the identity of informers and internal management materials to staff studies unrelated to any litiga-

tion. [32] Only the third, omnibus exception has special significance for administrative adjudications; the judicial rules applicable to state secrets and executive officer testimony are followed in agency hearings. An exploration of all the twists and turns given agency applications of the omnibus exception is beyond the scope of this chapter. [33] In any event, exculpatory information in an agency's possession or file data which may aid respondent's preparation or presentation of his case must be disclosed by the agency. [34] The alternative is to drop the prosecution against the respondent. [35] Anything less would violate the commands of procedural due process which every adjudication must observe. [36]

Almost half the states provide that rules of privilege applicable in court proceedings must apply in administrative hearings. [37] Courts and agencies in other states have reached the same position as a matter of policy. [38] The scope of the statutory recognition of privileged communications in the states tends to exceed the testimonial exception recognized by federal courts. [39] On the other hand, where agency proceedings are excepted or where no statutory mandate ex-

trict Courts, 31 U.Chi.L.Rev. 395 (1964). For more about Baird v. Koerner, supra, see § 90 supra.

29. In re Federal Trade Commission Line of Business Report Litigation, 595 F.2d 685 (D.C.Cir.1977), cert. denied 439 U.S. 958.

30. See, e.g., Federal Trade Commission v. St. Regis Paper Co., 304 F.2d 731 (7th Cir.1962); Falsone v. United States, n. 28 supra.

31. Federal Trade Commission v. Lonning, 539 F.2d 202 (D.C.Cir.1976); Federal Trade Commission v. Texaco, Inc., 517 F.2d 137 (D.C.Cir.1975) cert. denied 431 U.S. 974; Wearly v. Federal Trade Commission, 462 F.Supp. 589 (D.N.J.1978); vacated 616 F.2d 662, cert. denied 449 U.S. 822, 16 C.F.R. § 3.45.

32. See Ch. 12 supra.

33. For an explanation of one agency's approach, see Gellhorn, The Treatment of Confidential Information by the Federal Trade Commission: The Hearing, 116 U.Pa.L.Rev. 401, 423–27 (1968); Gellhorn, The Treatment of Confidential Information by the Federal Trade Commission: Pretrial Practices, 36 U.Chi.L.Rev. 113, 157–77 (1968); cf. Moore-McCormack Lines, Inc. v. United States, 188 Ct.Cl. 644, 413 F.2d 568 (1969). The Freedom of Information Act, 5 U.S.C.A. § 552 has eased access to some agency files for the public, but it

has had little effect on agency application. Exxon Corp. v. FTC, 589 F.2d 582 (3d Cir.1978) cert. denied 441 U.S. 943; Federal Trade Commission v. Anderson, 442 F.Supp. 1118 (D.D.C.1977); see § 108 supra.

34. E.g., Sperandeo v. Dairy Employees Local 537, 334 F.2d 381 (10th Cir.1964); National Labor Relations Board v. Capitol Fish Co., 294 F.2d 868 (5th Cir.1961); Union Bag-Camp Paper Corp. v. Federal Trade Commission, 233 F.Supp. 660, 666 (S.D.N.Y.1964); Sperry & Hutchinson Co. v. Federal Trade Commission, 256 F.Supp. 136 (S.D.N.Y. 1966); cf. Miller v. Pate, 386 U.S. 1 (1967); Giles v. Maryland, 386 U.S. 941 (1967); Brady v. Maryland, 373 U.S. 83, 87–88 (1963); United States v. Bryant, 439 F.2d 642 (D.C.Cir.1971).

35. See Sperandeo v. Dairy Employees Local 537, n. 34 supra; cf. United States v. Andolschek, 142 F.2d 503 (2d Cir.1944); Berger & Krash, Government Immunity from Discovery, 59 Yale L.J. 1451, 1453 (1950).

36. E.g., FCC v. Pottsville Broadcasting Co., 309 U.S. 134, 143–144 (1940).

37. 1 Cooper 396–97 (collecting authorities).

38. E.g., New York City Council v. Goldwater, 284 N.Y. 296, 31 N.E.2d 31 (1940); Benjamin 171.

39. E.g., Okl.Stat.Ann. § 75–310(1).

ists, state agencies have relaxed or avoided testimonial privileges where the rationale for the privilege is weak or not particularly appropriate. For example, several states have held that the physician-patient privilege cannot bar a worker's compensation commission's search for the truth. [40]

In summary, the trend appears to be toward narrowing testimonial privileges in administrative hearings and, where practical, toward resort to alternative protections against unnecessary public disclosure.

 WESTLAW REFERENCES

self-incriminat! /s administrative agenc*** /2
   adjudication* hearing* proceeding*
attorney clergy! doctor lawyer physician psychiatrist /p
   privilege* /p administrative agenc*** /2
   adjudication* decision* hearing* proceeding*
administrative /s inspect! unwarranted warranted /p
   marshall +s barlow

§ 357. Presentation of Case: Burden of Proof and Presumptions

The customary common law rule that the moving party has the burden of proof—including not only the burden of going forward but also the burden of persuasion—is generally observed in administrative hearings. Section 556(d) of the APA, for example, provides: "Except as otherwise provided by statute, the proponent of a rule or order has the burden of proof." [1] State courts have reached the same result in connection with state administrative proceedings. [2]

In most hearings the burden of persuasion is met by the usual civil case standard of "a preponderance of evidence." The rule appli-

cable to federal administrative adjudications was not settled, however, until 1981. In Steadman v. SEC, [3] a broker-dealer being prosecuted by the commission for fraudulent activities had challenged the proceeding, arguing that violation of the antifraud provisions of the securities laws must be proved by the equity standard of clear and convincing evidence. He contended that the potentially severe sanctions (revocation of his license) as well as the circumstantial and inferential nature of the evidence used to prove intent to defraud, required the higher standard of proof. A divided Court rejected his argument. The Court held that the language of Section 556(d) of the APA and the legislative history both show Congress intended that administrative adjudications be measured by the usual standard.

On the other hand, where Congress has not spoken and grave issues of personal security are at stake in an administrative hearing, as in a deportation proceeding, the courts are free to exercise their traditional oversight powers and fashion appropriate standards. Thus in Woodby v. INS, [4] the Supreme Court ruled that in deportation proceedings where liberty is at stake, the government must establish its allegations by "clear, unequivocal, and convincing evidence."

It is also not uncommon for courts to employ the substantial evidence standard to impose a special burden of proof on administrative agencies. This is particularly true in compensation benefits cases where the legislative design is read as favoring awards despite inadequate evidentiary support. A series of cases involving social security and

---

40. See, e.g., Cooper's Inc. v. Long, 224 So.2d 866 (Miss.1969); Danussi v. Easy Wash, Inc., 270 Minn. 465, 134 N.W.2d 138 (1965).

§ 357

1. 5 U.S.C.A. § 556(d).

2. E.g., State ex rel. Utilities Commission v. Carolina Power & Light Co., 250 N.C. 421, 109 S.E.2d 253 (1959); Pennsylvania Labor Relations Board v. Sansom House Enterprises, Inc., 378 Pa. 385, 106 A.2d 404 (1954); Crossroads Recreation, Inc. v. Broz, 4 N.Y.2d 39, 172 N.Y.S.2d 129, 149 N.E.2d 65 (1958); Interna-

tional Minerals & Chemical Corp. v. New Mexico Public Service Commission, 81 N.M. 280, 466 P.2d 557 (1970).

3. 450 U.S. 91 (1981).

4. 385 U.S. 276 (1966); Jaffe, Administrative Law: Burden of Proof and Scope of Review, 79 Harv.L.Rev. 914 (1966). A fact cannot be proved by less than a preponderance of the evidence. Charlton v. Federal Trade Commission, 543 F.2d 903, 907 (D.C.Cir.1976) ("in American law a preponderance of the evidence is rock bottom at the factfinding level of civil litigation.")

other compensation proceedings has required that the agency accept the claimant's uncontroverted evidence even though the claimant has the burden of proof. [5] Nor can these cases be explained away on the grounds of judicial acceptance of uncontradicted medical testimony in support of the claim, since the agencies are also dealing with malingering and false claims. On the other hand, reviewing courts are more concerned with the remedial, risk-spreading purposes of the statutes and the comparative inability of the claimant to present additional proof. [6] Similar tendencies occasionally appear in such diverse areas as police suspension matters [7] and draft exemption cases [8] where the courts have given increasing scrutiny to the overall fairness of administrative adjudications.

These cases can also be viewed as establishing a presumption in certain administrative adjudications since they affect the burden of proof. The history of workers' compensation illustrates this alternative analysis. Although many state acts have created a presumption in favor of the claimant, several state courts formerly gave these provisions no effect. [9] In interpreting a federal compensation act in Del Vecchio v. Bowers, [10] the Supreme Court held that this "benefit" presumption was sufficient to carry claimant's burden of persuasion in the absence of opposing evidence. However, once rebuttal evidence is introduced, the statutory presumption is overcome and the agency must decide the case solely on the evidence in the record. [11] Similar analysis supports the presumption of the correctness of official administrative action. [12]

On the other hand, the opposite approach is often taken in administrative adjudications where the activities of business respondents are tested. For example, an advertiser may have the burden of establishing any advertising claim, and if it is the type of claim whose truth can be determined only by scientific tests—for example, a claim that respondent's tires will stop a car 25 percent more quickly than other tires—the advertiser's fully-documented proof must *antedate* the representation; the prosecuting agency need only show that the claim was made. [13] That is to say, substantive law interpretations can affect the burden of proof as much as procedural requirements.

 **WESTLAW REFERENCES**

burden* /2 "going forward" persuasion proof /10 administrative agenc*** /2 adjudication* hearing* proceeding*
burden* /s "administrative procedure act" a.p.a.
clear convincing unequivocal /6 evidence /p "individual interest*" deportation denaturalization expatriation /s adjudication* hearing* proceeding*

5. Kerner v. Flemming, 283 F.2d 916 (2d Cir.1960); Young & Co. v. Shea, 397 F.2d 185 (5th Cir.1968), rehearing en banc denied 404 F.2d 1059, cert. denied 395 U.S. 920; Stark v. Weinberger, 497 F.2d 1092 (7th Cir. 1972); Newport News Shipbuilding Co. v. Director, 592 F.2d 762 (4th Cir.1979). See generally, Jaffe, Judicial Control of Administrative Action 608 (1965).

6. However, where the evidence is likely to be available only to respondent, the burden of persuasion or of going forward may be imposed on him. See, e.g., Day v. National Transportation Safety Board, 414 F.2d 950 (5th Cir.1969); Smyth v. United States Civil Service Commission, 291 F.Supp. 568, 573 (E.D.Wis.1968).

7. Kelly v. Murphy, 20 N.Y.2d 205, 282 N.Y.S.2d 254, 229 N.E.2d 40 (1967).

8. Dickinson v. United States, 346 U.S. 389, 396 (1953); cf. Mulloy v. United States, 398 U.S. 410 (1970). But see Dickinson v. United States, supra, at 399 (dissenting opinion).

9. E.g., Joseph v. United Kimono Co., 194 App.Div. 568, 185 N.Y.S. 700 (1921).

10. 296 U.S. 280 (1935).

11. Id. at 286. This view now prevails in some state courts. E.g., Cellurale's Case, 333 Mass. 37, 127 N.E.2d 787 (1955); 2 Larson, The Law of Workmen's Compensation Sec. 80.33 (1952). This also illustrates that problems of burden of proof are, in essence, often questions of substantive law. See Republic Aviation Corp. v. National Labor Relations Board, 324 U.S. 793 (1945).

12. E.g., Cupples Hesse Corp. v. State Tax Commission, 329 S.W.2d 696 (Mo.1959); Goldfarb v. Department of Revenue, 411 Ill. 573, 104 N.E.2d 606 (1952).

13. Firestone Tire & Rubber Co., 81 F.T.C. 398 (1972), 481 F.2d 246 (6th Cir.), cert. denied 414 U.S. 1112; Pfizer, Inc., 81 F.T.C. 23 (1972); cf. 16 C.F.R. § 3.40.

§ 358. Presentation of Case: Written Evidence and Cross-Examination

Perhaps the most distinctive feature of many administrative hearings, particularly in contrast to nonjury trials, is the substitution of written evidence for oral testimony. This written evidence takes several forms. In its simplest and least productive aspect, some witnesses appear, if at all, simply for cross-examination, with the written questions and answers read into the record in lieu of the usual oral question-answer format. This "canned dialogue" has been criticized as leading to the withholding of the true facts from the administrative law judge and assuring that the case will be decided on grounds other than the evidence in the record. [1] But if applied more sensitively, written evidence can expedite and simplify formal administrative proceedings through reducing the controversy to verified written statements which are then exchanged by the parties for the purpose of rebuttal. [2] Federal administrative agencies have frequently relied upon this technique, the Interstate Commerce Commission for almost half a century. [3] With the cooperation of the parties, this procedure can result in greater precision than where the facts are presented orally.

The ICC's written procedures are probably the most sophisticated of all agencies. In time, the Commission's "modified" procedure has been streamlined into an administrative version of summary judgment. [4] Under the ICC's rules of procedure, any party may request use of the modified procedure by filing a verified statement setting forth the facts, argument, and exhibits on which he relies. [5] The opposing party must either admit or deny each material allegation, explaining each exception he takes to the facts and argument of his adversary. Unless there are material facts in dispute or the objecting party explains why he cannot properly present his case by affidavits, a decision will then be rendered on the written case. This rule exceeds the concept of summary

§ 358

1. As one leading administrative practitioner describes the impact of canned testimony:

> I don't believe that I am wholly unique in being put immediately to sleep when it is read. That tedium is eliminated when the written testimony is used, without reading, as direct examination subject to oral cross. I have not, however, yet seen an examiner who has really mastered the unspoken direct testimony. The 25% that is really strong won't be touched in cross-examination and cannot easily be brought out in redirect, so in most cases the examiner proceeds until briefing time, at the best, and forever at the worst, in amiable ignorance of the heart of the testimony. The few hours of direct examination that are saved by written direct testimony come at too high a price.

Gardner, Shrinking the Big Case, 16 Ad.L.Rev. 5, 12–13 (1963).

2. See W. Gellhorn, Federal Administrative Proceedings 100–15 (1941); Selected Reports of the Administrative Conference of the United States 1961–1962, S.Doc. No. 24, 88th Cong. 1st Sess. 92 (1963); Woll, Administrative Law 37–48 (1963); Final Report of Attorney General's Committee on Administrative Procedure, S.Doc. No. 8, 77th Cong., 1st Sess. 69–70 (1941); Brown, Public Service Commission Procedure—A Problem and a Suggestion, 87 U.Pa.L.Rev. 139 (1938).

3. See American Public Gas Association v. Federal Power Commission, 498 F.2d 718 (D.C.Cir.1974) (example of effective use of written material in lieu of oral presentations). State agencies have also made extensive use of written evidence. See letter from member of State Corporation Commission of Virginia, 38 J.Am.Jud.Soc. 61 (1954).

4. Early in the 1920's, the ICC abbreviated the usual oral hearing before a commissioner or examiner through the use of a "shortened" procedure. Upon consent of the parties, oral testimony was dispensed with, and a decision was rendered upon stipulated, sworn statements of fact. Despite encomiums from administrative law experts, this procedure did not prove particularly successful, since the parties could avoid the shortened procedure at any time by requesting a formal hearing. Consequently, in 1942 the ICC substituted what it called a "modified" procedure whereby each party submitted his case in writing for the purpose of obtaining agreement on as many facts as possible. The parties then confined their oral testimony to the remaining points in dispute. While more successful than the "shortened" procedure, this modified procedure did not eliminate a formal hearing when the parties could not agree on the facts. See Woll, The Development of Shortened Procedure in American Administrative Law, 45 Cornell L.Q. 56, 62–66 (1959); Hosmer, Some Notes on a Perennial Procedural Problem, 5 I.C.C. Prac.J. 275 (1938); Mohundro, Improvements in Procedure Before the Commission, 20 I.C.C. Prac.J. 75, 79–81 (1952); Three Letters on Procedure Before the I.C.C., id. 196.

5. 49 C.F.R. § 1100.45; see id. § 1100.49, 1100.50, 1100.53.

judgment currently applied under the Federal Rules of Civil Procedure by placing the burden on the parties to prove that an oral hearing is necesasary. [6] An oral hearing is not presumed to be the proper method for hearing a case.

Written evidence has been relied upon most successfully in rate or price control proceedings, where economic and expert analysis rather than sensorily-perceived phenomena provide the bulk of the evidence. [7] Credibility based upon conflicting stories relating what each witness observed is seldom involved. Often the advance preparation of written evidence is limited to the contentions of the party having the burden of proof; in others the opposing party's evidence is included. The elimination of surprise cannot be objected to since surprise has no proper place in the hearing when credibility is not in issue. Cross-examination is not used to establish a party's case. Its major purpose here is "not to reduce . . . [the expert] witness to a shattered hulk by the admission of error, but to explore all of the considerations entering into what must remain a matter of judgment." [8]

As explained by the Second Interim Administrative Conference, the benefits of written evidence are manifold:

(1) [The] exchange of written evidence facilitates settlement techniques in situations in which there is staff participation; (2) the hearing examiner, after studying the direct evidence of the parties prior to hearing, can participate in the case in an intelligent fashion, leading to more effective use of conference techniques and more informed rulings at the

hearing; (3) in a substantial number of cases, particularly those of less moment, the parties may be satisfied with their written presentations, and an oral hearing becomes unnecessary; and (4) the efforts of the parties at the oral hearing, if one is necessary, are confined to clarifying the major issues through informed cross-examination. Properly handled, written procedures should result in a more adequate record being produced in a shorter space of time. [9]

Section 556(d) of the APA recognizes the propriety of written presentations with only limited cross-examination: "In rule making or determining claims for money or benefits or applications for initial licenses any agency may, when a party will not be prejudiced thereby, adopt procedures for the submission of all or part of the evidence in written form." [10] Existing case law supports the use of written presentations by any agency in a type of proceeding where the interest of any party is not prejudiced. [11]

Where cross-examination is necessary for protection against untrustworthy evidence, it cannot be avoided. Section 556(d) of the APA specifically preserves the right of cross-examination in agency adjudications: "A party is entitled . . . to conduct such cross-examination as may be required for a full and true disclosure of the facts." [12] State law is identical. [13] Through this provision the APA recognizes one of the fundamentals of a fair hearing—namely a reasonable opportunity to test and controvert adverse evidence whether or not such evidence is a statement of opinion, observation, or consideration of the witness. Cross-examination has several potential uses: to

---

6. See E. Gellhorn & Robinson, Summary Judgment in Administrative Adjudication, 84 Harv.L.Rev. 612 (1970); Fed.R.Civ.P. 56. The ICC's procedure has withstood attacks upon due process grounds. E.g., Allied Van Lines Co. v. United States, 303 F.Supp. 742 (C.D.Cal.1969).

7. See Selected Reports of the Administrative Conference of the United States 1961–1962, S.Doc. No. 24, 88th Cong., 1st Sess. 92 (1963).

8. Id.

9. Id. at 93.

10. 5 U.S.C.A. § 556(d).

11. See Yakus v. United States, 321 U.S. 414 (1944). The 1981 Revised Model State Administrative Act tracks this case law by providing in § 4–212(d) that "Any part of the evidence may be received in written form if doing so will expedite the hearing without substantial prejudice to the interests of any party."

12. 5 U.S.C.A. § 556(d).

13. See Hyson v. Montgomery County Council, 242 Md. 55, 67–68 n. 1, 217 A.2d 578, 585–86 n. 1 (1966); 1 Cooper 371–79 (collecting cases). The 1981 model state act makes similar provision for cross-examination. Revised Model State Administrative Procedure Act § 4–211(2) (1981).

bring out matters left untouched by direct examination; to test the accuracy of a witness' perception as well as his ability to observe; to probe his truthfulness; to question his memory and narration; and to expose the basis of any opinions he has expressed. In other words, "cross-examination is a means of getting at the truth; it is not truth itself." [14] Yet unless credibility is directly in issue—and then only on occasion—cross-examination usually does no more than demonstrate forensic talent or score trial points irrelevant to the final decision. [15] As an experienced agency practitioner, who later became an eminent federal judge, observed: "Only rarely . . . can you accomplish something devastating on cross-examining an expert . . . . [M]ore often it is love's labor lost." [16]

Perception of this point is the key to a reconciliation of the right of cross-examination with the seemingly inconsistent administrative practice of relying on hearsay testimony and written evidence whether or not the declarant is unavailable. The legislative history of the APA makes clear that Congress was seeking to draw a line between an unlimited right of unnecessary cross-examination and a reasonable opportunity to test opposing evidence. [17] The test, stated abstractly, is that cross-examination must be allowed when it is required for determining the truth. If witness veracity and demeanor are not critical, there is no requirement for cross-examination so long as sufficient opportunity for rebuttal exists; if credibility is a key factor, and the objecting party can show that the absence of cross-examination of the witness may have prejudiced his case, the denial of cross-examination could be fatal to an agency decision. [18] Statistical compilations and surveys are admissible only if the person responsible for—and having full knowledge of the preparation of—the exhibit is available. In addition, the raw data upon which the exhibit is based should be available to the opposing party. [19] It has been proposed that the right to cross-examine in at least some administrative proceedings be reduced to a privilege "to be granted only in the virtually unlimited discretion of the hearing officer." This proposal is only part of a recommended restructuring of the administrative hearing into a conference proceeding where almost all the evidence would be submitted in written form. [20]

Finally, administrative agencies are required to apply the "*Jencks* rule"—namely, that after a government witness has testified, the prosecution must disclose prior statements by the witness relating to his testimony. [21] Application of this rule in agency

---

14. W. Gellhorn & Byse, Administrative Law 713 (5th ed. 1970).

15. See § 30 supra.

16. Leventhal, Cues and Compasses for Administrative Lawyers, 20 Ad.L.Rev. 237, 246 (1968); accord, Prettyman, Trying an Administrative Dispute, 45 Va.L. Rev. 179, 190–91 (1959).

17. Sen.Doc. No. 248, 79th Cong., 2d Sess. 208–09, 271 (1946); Attorney General's Manual on the Administrative Procedure Act 77–78 (1947).

18. E.g., In re Chapman Radio & Television Co., 6 F.C.C.2d 768 (1967); see Peters v. United States, 187 Ct.Cl. 63, 408 F.2d 719 (1969); Brown v. Macy, 222 F.Supp. 639 (E.D.La.1963), affirmed 340 F.2d 115 (5th Cir.1965).

19. Wirtz v. Baldor Electric Co., 119 U.S.App.D.C. 122, 337 F.2d 518 (1964); see Carter-Wallace, Inc. v. Gardner, 417 F.2d 1086, 1095–96 (4th Cir.1969), cert. denied 398 U.S. 938 (party not entitled to cross-examination if alternative method of investigating accuracy available); Zeisel, The Uniqueness of Survey Evidence, 45 Cornell L.Q. 322, 345–46 (1960). See generally § 251 supra.

20. Westwood, Administrative Proceedings; Techniques of Presiding, 50 A.B.A.J. 659, 660 (1964). See also Recommendation No. 19, Selected Reports of the Administrative Conference of the United States 1961–61, S.Doc. No. 24, 88th Cong. 1st Sess. 51, 96–97 (1963); Cramton, Some Modest Suggestions for Improving Public Utility Rate Proceedings, 51 Iowa L.Rev. 267, 276–78 (1966).

21. Jencks v. United States, 353 U.S. 657 (1957). The "*Jencks* Rule" was initially applied to administrative agencies in Communist Party of the United States v. Subversive Activities Control Board, 102 U.S.App. D.C. 395, 254 F.2d 314 (1958) and National Labor Relations Board v. Adhesive Products Corp., 258 F.2d 403 (2d Cir.1958); see Selected Reports of the Administrative Conference of the United States 1961–1962, S.Doc. No. 24, 88th Cong., 1st Sess. 132 (1963). See generally § 97 supra for discussion of the rule in its present form.

hearings has been the subject of controversy. [22] The Administrative Conference has suggested that prior statements be made available to the respondent at the prehearing conference. [23] If this view were adopted the question would no longer be one of evidence but rather one of discovery.

 WESTLAW REFERENCES

15ak463 /p cross-exam!

"administrative procedure act" a.p.a. /p right /s cross-exam! (present +3 evidence)

jencks /6 doctrine principle rule /p administrative agenc*** /2 adjudication* hearing* proceeding*

"interstate commerce commission" i.c.c. /p "modified procedure"

§ 359. Official Notice [1]

Official notice, like its judicial notice counterpart, involves reliance by the presiding officer—in this case the administrative law judge—on extra-record information. That is, the law judge in making a decision bypasses the normal process of proof and relies upon facts and opinions not supported by evidence "on the record." Several characteristics of official notice should be observed. First, a specific procedure similar to

that for judicial notice has been established to receive extra-record facts, with the parties receiving notice and an opportunity to rebut the "noticed" facts. [2] Second, extra-record facts usually have first been developed by the agency's expert staff or accumulated from previous agency decisions. But official notice is not limited to information in agency files. In fact, it may be taken at the initiation of one of the parties. Third, agency recognition of extra-record facts is clearly not limited to "indisputable" facts. Rather, official notice may extend to almost any information useful in deciding the adjudication as long as elemental fairness is observed. [3]

On the other hand, in administrative adjudication, official notice is frequently confused with the process of decisionmaking. In reaching a conclusion, the administrative law judge or agency may rely on its special skills, whether they include particular expertness in engineering, economics, medicine, or electricity, just as a federal or state judge may freely use his legal skills in reading statutes and applying decided cases in the preparation of his opinion. But such evaluations are not within the concept of of-

22. FTC: Papercraft Corp., 25 Ad.L.2d 1122 (FTC 1969); Star Office Supply Co., 24 Ad.L.2d 472 (FTC 1968); enforced by order [1967–1970 Transfer Binder] Trade Reg.Rep. Para. 19,228 (FTC 1970); Inter-State Builders, Inc., 19 Ad.L.2d 7 (FTC 1966), 21 Ad.L.2d 1078 (FTC 1967); L.G. Balfour Co., 19 Ad.L.2d 35 (FTC 1966); Viviano Macaroni Co., 19 Ad.L.2d 69 (FTC 1966); see E. Gellhorn, The Treatment of Confidential Information by the Federal Trade Commission: The Hearing, 116 U.Pa.L.Rev. 401, 428–33 (1968). NLRB: National Labor Relations Board v. Borden Co., 392 F.2d 412 (5th Cir.1968); see Alleyne, The "Jencks Rule" in NLRB Proceedings, 9 B.C.Ind. & Comm.L.Rev. 891 (1968). Department of Labor: Wirtz v. Rosenthal, 388 F.2d 290 (9th Cir.1967); Wirtz v. B.A.C. Steel Products, Inc., 312 F.2d 14 (4th Cir.1962); Mitchell v. Roma, 265 F.2d 633 (3d Cir.1959). Selective Service: Rogers v. United States, 263 F.2d 283 (9th Cir.1959), cert. denied 359 U.S. 967; Bouziden v. United States, 251 F.2d 728 (10th Cir.1958), cert. denied 356 U.S. 927.

23. ACUS Recommendation No. 70–4, 1 C.F.R. § 305.70–4; see Tomlinson, Discovery in Agency Adjudication, 1971 Duke L.J. 89.

§ 359

1. See generally 3 Davis, ch. 15; 1 Cooper 412–20; Final Report of the Attorney General's Committee on

Administrative Procedure, S.Doc. No. 8, 77th Cong., 1st Sess. 71–73 (1941); Benjamin 206–21; W. Gellhorn, Federal Administrative Proceedings 82–99 (1941); W. Gellhorn, Official Notice in Administrative Adjudication, 20 Tex.L.Rev. 131 (1941); Jaffe, Administrative Procedure Re-Examined: The Benjamin Report, 56 Harv.L.Rev. 704, 717–719 (1943).

The term "official notice" is probably unfortunate in suggesting too much of a parallel to judicial notice. Much that is done and advocated to be done in the name of official notice might with less violence to the language be catalogued under presumptions. The latter affinity is noted elsewhere. See § 333 supra.

2. 5 U.S.C.A. § 556(d). See Fed.R.Evid. 201(e) and § 333 supra.

3. At least one observer has suggested that agencies should apply the doctrine of judicial notice to broad, general facts of common knowledge which are of an undisputed nature, thus avoiding the notice and rebuttal requirements of official notice, and limit official notice—with its procedural requirements—to disputable facts. Muir, The Utilization of Both Judicial and Official Notice by Administrative Agencies, 16 Ad. L.Rev. 333 (1964).

The kinds of facts noticeable in judicial proceedings are discussed in Chapter 35 supra.

ficial notice. Official notice is concerned with the *process of proof*, not with the *evaluation of evidence*. The difference between an administrative tribunal's use of non-record information included in its expert knowledge, as a substitute for evidence or notice, and its application of its background in evaluating and drawing conclusions from the evidence that is in the record, is, however, primarily a difference of degree rather than of kind. In principle, reliance upon the administrative law judge's knowledge in the process of proof is permissible only within the confines of official notice, whereas the administrative judge's use of his experience in the evaluating "*proof* is not only unavoidable but, indeed, desirable." [4]

The troublesome problem, as with most questions of law, is that a fine line cannot be drawn with precision. Benjamin illustrates the point:

> When the State Liquor Authority concludes, from evidence in the record as to the size of food bills and gas bills paid (in relation to the volume of liquor business), that the holder of a restaurant liquor license is not conducting a *bona fide* restaurant, is the Authority using its experience and knowledge to evaluate and draw conclusions from the evidence, or is it using its experience and knowledge as a substitute for further evidence as to the normal relation of the size of food and gas bills to the volume of food business? . . . My own view is that . . . the procedure described is permissible [evaluation]; but until the courts have decided specific questions of this character, it is impossible to anticipate with any certainty what their decision would be. [5]

Beyond this or other examples, little guidance can be offered.

The primary thrust behind official notice is to simplify or ease the process of proof. Where facts are known or can be safely assumed, the process of proving what is al-ready known is both time consuming and unduly formal. When facts have been proven before, further proof becomes tiresome, redundant, and lacking in common sense. At times even the obvious could be difficult or time-consuming to prove, without affecting the final result, which was never in doubt. Moreover, administrative agencies were often created to become repositories of knowledge and experience. It would defeat their existence to require adherence to traditional methods of proof when alternative and equally fair methods are readily available. On the other hand, in developing an alternative method, it is necessary to safeguard the elements of a fair trial preserved by the traditional forms of proof. The 1941 Attorney General's Committee accurately summarized the need:

> The parties, then, are entitled to be apprised of the data upon which the agency is acting. They are entitled not only to refute but, what in this situation is usually more important, to supplement, explain, and give different perspective to the facts upon which the agency relies. In addition, upon judicial review, the court must be informed of what facts the agency has utilized in order that the existence of supporting evidence may be ascertained. [6]

The Congress sought to recognize and reconcile these concerns by a single sentence in section 556(e) of the APA: "When an agency decision rests on official notice of a material fact not appearing in the evidence in the record, a party is entitled, on timely request, to an opportunity to show the contrary." [7] The procedure is simple. Official notice is a means by which an agency can avoid hearing further evidence on a material fact in the case if it notifies the parties that unless they prove to the contrary the agency's findings will include that particular fact and allows the parties an opportunity to present contrary evidence.

---

4. See, e.g., Interstate Commerce Commission v. Louisville & Nashville Railroad, 227 U.S. 88, 98 (1913); Feinstein v. New York Central Railroad, 159 F.Supp. 460, 464 (S.D.N.Y.1958) (L. Hand, J.). See the discussion of "legislative" facts in § 331 supra.

5. Benjamin 212.

6. Final Report of the Attorney General's Committee on Administrative Procedure, supra n. 8, at 72; see Ohio Bell Telephone Co. v. Public Utilities Commission, 301 U.S. 292, 303–04 (1937).

7. 5 U.S.C.A. § 556(e).

Federal Trade Commission cases illustrate the practice. After hearing dozens of cases indicating that consumers preferred American to foreign-made goods—and holding, therefore, that a failure to disclose the foreign origin of these goods was a false and deceptive act [8]—the commission advised respondents in Manco Watch Strap Co. [9] that it would not hear evidence on this issue in the future. Then, in subsequent cases where the FTC took official notice and the respondents could not prove that American consumers preferred their foreign goods or that the consumers had no particular preference, the Commission upheld orders barring sales of goods not bearing the requisite disclosures. [10] On the other hand, if respondents could show that consumers preferred French over American perfumes, for example, the "noticed finding" would not apply. [11]

Practically, then, the primary effect of taking official notice is to transfer the burden of proof on that material fact—usually from the agency to the respondent. The significance of this tactic varies in proportion to the difficulty of the proponent in establishing that fact originally, and of the cost and effort of the opponent in disproving it. In most instances where agencies have taken official notice, the costs have been slight since the result has seemed obvious. Where the fact is less obvious, however, that cost could prove substantial. [12]

The academic controversy over official notice has centered upon the limitation of judicial notice to undisputed facts and attempts to categorize the types of facts which can be officially noticed. The former is examined elsewhere in this text. [13] On the other hand, the APA's guidance of what facts can be noticed is essentially nonexistent; it merely sets forth the procedure which must be followed for taking notice of "material facts." By omission it appears to suggest that facts which are not material can be noticed in the manner of a judge at a judicial trial, but it does not tell how to determine which facts are material and can therefore be noticed. In any event, the term "material" seems not to be used in its classic sense.

The Attorney General's Committee on Administrative Procedure suggested a distinction between "litigation" and "non-litigation" facts:

> If information has come to an agency's attention in the course of investigation of the pending case, it should be adduced only by the ordinary process. . . . But if the information has been developed in the usual course of business of the agency, if it has emerged from nu-

---

8. American Merchandise Co., 28 F.T.C. 1465 (1939) (gloves and thumbtacks); Vulcan Lamp Works, Inc., 32 F.T.C. 7 (1940) (flashlight bulbs); The Bolta Co., 44 F.T.C. 17 (1947) (sunglass lenses); L. Heller & Son, Inc., 47 F.T.C. 34 (1950), affirmed 191 F.2d 954 (7th Cir. 1951) (imitation pearls); Atomic Prods., Inc., 48 F.T.C. 289 (1951) (mechanical pencils); Rene D. Lyon Co., 48 F.T.C. 313, 787 (1951) (watch bands); Royal Sewing Mach. Corp., 49 F.T.C. 1351 (1953) (sewing machine parts); William Adams, Inc., 53 F.T.C. 1164 (1957) (cutlery handles); Utica Cutlery Co., 56 F.T.C. 1186 (1960) (stainless steel hardware); Oxwall Tool Co., 59 F.T.C. 1408 (1961) (hand tools). This listing is also further testimony to the FTC's historic concentration on trivia.

9. 60 F.T.C. 495 (1962).

10. Savoy Watch Co., 63 F.T.C. 473 (1963) (watch cases); Baldwin Bracelet Corp., 61 F.T.C. 1345 (1962), affirmed 117 U.S.App.D.C. 85, 325 F.2d 1012 (1963) (watch cases); Brite Manufacturing Co., 65 F.T.C. 1067 (1964), affirmed 120 U.S.App.D.C. 383, 347 F.2d 477 (1965) (watch bands).

11. In its pursuit of the Grail, the FTC has in fact held that consumers prefer French perfumes and that it therefore is deceptive not to disclose the domestic origin of perfume. See, e.g., Fioret Sales Co., 26 F.T.C. 806, affirmed 100 F.2d 358 (2d Cir.1938); Etablissements Rigaud, Inc., 29 F.T.C. 1032 (1939) modified 125 F.2d 590 (2d Cir.1942); Harsam Distributors, Inc., 54 F.T.C. 1212 (1958), affirmed 263 F.2d 396 (2d Cir.1959).

12. In the unusual event that the evidence is split with the moving party having the burden of establishing that material fact by a preponderance of the evidence, official notice may be the difference between winning and losing the case. In assessing the place of official notice, one should also take into account (a) the cost of establishing a general negative—which is, in part, the reason for assigning the burden of proof to the moving party, see § 337 nn. 6–8 supra; (b) the desirability of cross-examination; and (c) the impact of denying confrontation—all of which are intimately connected with the decision as to whether official notice is appropriate. The relevance of presumption theory is evident. See §§ 342, 343, supra.

13. Ch. 35 supra.

merous cases, if it has become part of the factual equipment of the administrators, it seems undesirable for the agencies to remain oblivious of their own experience [and, they should take notice of such facts]. [14]

Professor Davis, on the other hand, rejects the notion that significance could be attached to the time when the factual data was collected. His criticism of the Committee's distinction stems from his conclusion that it would "encourage guesswork" and "discourage extra-record research of the kind that is especially needed for creation of law or policy. It would mean [for example, that] an agency could notice only those statutes that it has previously encountered!" [15] This criticism seems somewhat unfair since the Committee's basic point defining reliable facts—those previously established by the agency—is sound. Davis is right, however, when he points out that the Committee rule is too narrow. As an alternative, he offers a different standard for deciding whether an administrator may use extra-record facts:

> When a court or an agency finds facts concerning the immediate parties—who did what, where, when, how, and with what motive or intent—[it] is performing an adjudicative function, and the facts are conveniently called adjudicative facts. When a court or an agency develops law or policy, it is acting legislatively; the courts have created the common law through judicial legislation, and the facts which inform the tribunal's legislative judgment are called legislative facts. . . . Legislative facts are ordinarily general and do not concern the immediate parties. [16]

On this basis, Davis asserts that legislative facts usually need not be brought into the record by official notice; where critical, a party should be able to challenge them by brief and argument. He contends that adjudicative facts, on the other hand, must be brought into the record—unless they are indisputable—either through direct proof or by official notice. Nothing less will meet the cardinal principles of a fair hearing—notice and an opportunity to test and rebut opposing evidence. Whether adjudicative facts can be officially noticed or must be established by direct proof depends, he says, on three variables: how close the facts are to the center of the controversy; the extent to which the facts are adjudicative or legislative; and the degree to which the facts are certain. As the adjudicative facts move closer to the basic issues of the hearing, relate to the parties, and are disputed, the usual methods of proof must be observed; as they move in the opposite direction, official notice is permissible. [17]

Professor Jaffe has suggested an attractive alternative approach:

> [W]here the facts bear closely and crucially on the issue, and are prima facie debatable, they should be developed in evidentiary fashion—by which is meant simply that they should be referred to in such a manner as to enable the opponent to offer rebuttal. Such facts will not necessarily be "adjudicative". . . . [18]

Thus, as Davis himself concedes, the categories he defines do not in themselves resolve which facts can be noticed in particular cases. He is certainly correct when he points out that the central problem is to reconcile procedural fairness with convenience and the use of agency knowledge. The difficulty with his analysis lies not in his categories which are original and helpful, but rather that many cases fall outside his definitions. A sampling of cases illustrates this point. The existence of the Great Depression is a "legislative" fact which an agency can include in its findings without notice to the parties, but a specific price

14.　Final Report of the Attorney General's Committee on Administrative Procedure, supra n. 1 at 72.

15.　2 Davis § 15.03, at 363–64 n. 43 (1958).

16.　Id. § 15.03, at 353.

17.　Id. § 15.10.

18.　Jaffe, Administrative Procedure Re-Examined: The Benjamin Report, 56 Harv.L.Rev. 704, 719 (1943);

cf. Wyzanski, A Trial Judge's Freedom and Responsibility, 65 Harv.L.Rev. 1281, 1295–1296 (1952). The Davis labels of "adjudicative" and "legislative" facts are commonly recited by agencies and courts to justify official notice decisions.

trend, also a general legislative fact, cannot be used to update the figures in the record without notice to the parties. [19] Since a specific price trend can be readily verified, taking notice is appropriate; the burden of proving any substantial error is not likely to be significant. Similarly, the courts have upheld agencies' official notice of scientific data, technical facts, and articles in academic journals, [20] although many courts contend that this places too great a burden on the opponent to refute the "noticed evidence." [21]

Of greater consequence is the fact that reliance upon Davis' categories distracts from the central question of fairness—that is, is it fair in the particular hearing to take official notice and *transfer the burden of proof* to the opposing party? Two cases involving the use of the record of a related hearing, each of which reaches an opposite result, are perhaps the clearest examples of this suggested "fairness of the transfer of the burden of proof" analysis. In United States v. Pierce Auto Freight Lines, Inc., [22] the ICC held two separate hearings on competing applications for truck service between San Francisco and Portland. Each applicant intervened in the other hearing, but the cases were not consolidated. In reaching its decision, the Commission relied on evidence appearing in only one record. The procedure was upheld because both applicants were parties to both proceedings and both had ample opportunity to present evidence, to cross-examine witnesses, and otherwise to protect their interests.

In the second case, Dayco Corp. v. FTC, [23] the FTC sought to take official notice of the distribution system and practices used by the respondent, a manufacturer of auto replacement parts, since the system had been the subject of a prior proceeding. That prior proceeding, in which respondent was only a witness, was brought against his customers. The court ruled that the FTC's attempt to take official notice of these "adjudicative facts" from the first proceeding was improper because the manufacturer was not a party, but only a witness to the prior proceeding. To allow official notice in this circumstance, the court reasoned, would have eliminated the commission's entire burden of proof. The agency had asserted that its reliance on prior knowledge merely shifted the burden of going forward to respondent and this burden (of correcting any FTC errors in describing respondent's distribution system) was minimal when compared with the cost of proving these same facts again. The FTC's argument is not persuasive. If the agency merely sought to shift the burden of going forward, it could have introduced the prior record as reliable hearsay evidence subject to rebuttal or as written evidence with an offer to make the witnesses available for cross-examination. If handled in this manner—rather than under the official notice rubric—the fact-trier would still have to determine whether the prior record accurately portrayed respondent's distribution system. The court may also have perceived that there was no compelling need to approve the commisssion's

---

19. Ohio Bell Telephone Co. v. Public Utilities Commission, 301 U.S. 292 (1937); West Ohio Gas Co. v. Public Utilities Commission, 294 U.S. 63, 68 (1935); cf. United States v. Baltimore & Ohio South Western Railroad, 226 U.S. 14, 20 (1912).

20. E.g., McDaniel v. Celebrezze, 331 F.2d 426 (4th Cir.1964); Alabama-Tennessee Natural Gas Co. v. Federal Power Commission, 359 F.2d 318 (5th Cir.1966), cert. denied 385 U.S. 847; see 46 C.F.R. § 502.226 (FMC 1970). The CAB's rules note 43 separate reports and other resource materials of which it automatically takes official notice in economic proceedings. 14 C.F.R. § 302.24(m)(1).

21. See, e.g., Sayers v. Gardner, 380 F.2d 940 (6th Cir.1967); Sosna v. Celebrezze, 234 F.Supp. 289 (E.D.

Pa.1964); Cook v. Celebrezze, 217 F.Supp. 366 (W.D. Mo.1963).

22. 327 U.S. 515 (1946); see Safeway Stores, Inc. v. Federal Trade Commission, 366 F.2d 795, 803 (9th Cir. 1966), cert. denied 386 U.S. 932. Cf. Zimmerman v. Board of Regents, 31 A.D.2d 560, 294 N.Y.S.2d 435 (1968).

23. 362 F.2d 180 (6th Cir.1966). The judicial reception is more hospitable where the fact being noticed is of a less personal (i.e. adjudicative) nature. See, e.g., Dombrovskis v. Esperdy, 321 F.2d 463, 467 (2d Cir. 1963).

proposal since the FTC could (and should) have avoided the burden of re-proof by joining the respondent as a party in the first proceeding. Official notice, in other words, is not properly a procedural device to avoid the requirement of section 556(e) of the APA that the moving party has the burden of proof. If that burden is to be placed on respondent as a condition of doing business, it should be accomplished openly through a shift in substantive policy rather than covertly by manipulation of procedural devices.

When the issue of official notice is viewed in this manner, the Davis criteria and the Attorney General's Committee's distinctions are helpful, but not dispositive. On the other hand, judging from the small number of reported cases, the doctrine of official notice has apparently not been used extensively or creatively by many agencies. This reluctance may be partly the result of uncertainties in the applicable legal standards. Without clear tests indicating when official notice is proper, agencies may be unwilling to risk reversal by taking notice of nonrecord facts. Nonetheless, it remains a potentially useful device for simplifying and expediting hearings.

WESTLAW REFERENCES

critical crucial main material /4 fact* /p "official notice"

"official notice" /p contradict*** contrary rebut!

adjudicative judicial legislative /2 fact* /p "official notice"

Appendix A
WESTLAW REFERENCES

Analysis

The WESTLAW System

WESTLAW is a computer-assisted legal research service of West Publishing Company. WESTLAW is accessible through several alternative public communications networks. The materials available from WESTLAW are contained in databases stored at a central computer in St. Paul, Minnesota.

The WESTLAW user sends a query, or message, to the computer where it is processed and documents are identified that satisfy the search request. The text of the retrieved documents is then stored on magnetic disks and transmitted to the user. The data moves through a telecommunication network. The user sees the documents on a video display terminal. When the documents appear on the terminal the user can decide whether or not further research is desired. If another search is necessary, the query may be recalled for editing, or an entirely new query may be sent to the computer. Documents displayed on the terminal may be printed out or, on some terminals, the text may be stored in its own magnetic disks.

In addition to the extensive state and federal case law library to which the preformulated queries in this hornbook are addressed, WESTLAW provides access to many specialized libraries. For example, WESTLAW contains separate topical databases for areas of the law such as federal tax, patents and copyrights, bankruptcy, communications, labor, securities, antitrust and business regulation, military justice, admiralty, and government contracts. WESTLAW also contains the text of the U.S. Code and the Code of Federal Regulations, West's IN-STA–CITE™, Shepard's[R] Citations, *Black's Law Dictionary*, and many other legal sources.

Improving Legal Research with WESTLAW

Traditional legal research begins with the examination of texts, treatises, case digests, encyclopedias, citators, annotated law reports, looseleaf services, and periodicals. These secondary sources of the law provide compilations and summaries of authoritative material contained in primary legal sources. The goal of legal research is to analyze and interpret the primary sources.

In their familiar printed form, such primary sources appear in the state and regional reporters, federal reporters, and in statutory codes and administrative materials. In WESTLAW, these documents are extensively represented in electronic databases, or libraries.

WESTLAW permits access to the many court decisions and other legal documents that do not get indexed or digested into manual systems of secondary legal sources. With WESTLAW it is possible to index any significant term or combination of terms in an almost unlimited variety of grammatical relationships with other terms by formulating a query composed of those terms.

WESTLAW queries may be made as broad or as specific as desired, depending upon the context of the legal issue to be researched.

WESTLAW queries add a dynamic aspect to the text of this hornbook. Since new cases are continuously being added to the WESTLAW databases as they are decided by the courts, the addition of queries provides a type of self-contained updating service to the publication. Since a query may be addressed to the entire range of cases contained in the database designated for a search—from the earliest decisions to the most recent—the search results obtained from WESTLAW reflect the most current law available on any given issue.

In addition, WESTLAW queries augment the customary role of footnotes to the hornbook text by directing the user to a wider range of supporting authorities. Readers may use the preformulated queries supplied in this edition "as is" or formulate their own queries in order to retrieve cases relevant to the points of law discussed in the text.

Query Formulation: (a) What a WESTLAW Query Is

The query is a message to WESTLAW. It instructs the computer to retrieve documents containing terms in the grammatical relationships specified by the query. The terms in a query are made up of words and/or numbers that pinpoint the legal issue to be researched.

An example of the kind of preformulated queries that appear in this publication is reproduced below. The queries corresponding to each section of the text are listed at the end of the section.

judicial /2 notice

This query illustrates what a standard request to WESTLAW looks like—words or numbers describing an issue, tied together by connectors. These connectors tell WESTLAW in what relationships the terms must appear. WESTLAW will retrieve all documents from the database that contain the terms appearing in those relationships.

The material that follows explains the methods by which WESTLAW queries are formulated, and shows how users of *McCormick on Evidence* can employ the preformulated queries in this publication in their research of evidence law. In addition, there are instructions that will enable readers to modify these queries to fit the particular needs of their research.

Query Formulation: (b) The TRAC Method

The acronym "TRAC" is a convenient mnemonic device for a systematic approach to query formulation on WESTLAW. "TRAC" stands for Terms, Roots, Alternatives, and Connectors. This step-by-step method is explained below.

T *Terms.* After determining the legal issue that is to be researched, the first step in query formulation is to select the key terms from the issue that will be used as search terms in the query. Words, numbers, and various other symbols may be used as search terms.

The goal in choosing search terms is to select the most unique terms for the issue. In selecting such terms it is frequently helpful to imagine how the terms might appear in the language of the documents that will be searched by the query. Moreover, it is necessary to consider the grammatical and editorial structure of the document. This involves a consideration of how the writer of the document (i.e., judge or headnote and synopsis writer) has worded both the factual and legal components of the issues involved in the case.

Although traditional book research generally starts with a consideration of the general legal concepts under which particular problems are subsumed, WESTLAW research starts with a consideration of specific terms that are likely to appear in documents that have addressed those problems. This is so because documents are retrieved from WESTLAW on the basis of the terms they contain. Accordingly, the more precisely terms can be identified that will single out the desired documents, the more relevant the search results will be.

R *Root Expansion (!) and Universal Character (*).* When constructing queries it is necessary to consider various forms of the search terms that are selected. Plurals, possessives, and derivative forms of words should be anticipated due to the variety of ways in which the language in a document

may be worded. Various tenses of verbs should also be considered. There are two devices available on WESTLAW for automatically generating alternative forms of search terms in a query.

One device is an unlimited root expansion. Placement of the ! symbol at the end of the root term generates other word forms from the root. For example, attaching the ! symbol to the root term CONFESS in the following query:

confess! /p miranda

instructs the computer to generate the words CONFESS, CONFESSES, CONFESSING, CONFESSION, and CONFESSIONS as search terms for the query. This saves time and space that would otherwise be consumed in typing each of the alternative words in the query.

The other device permits the generation of all possible characters from a designated part of a term. This is done by placing the * symbol at the location in the term where universal character generation is desired. For example, placing the * at the end of the term FORCE in the following query:

force* /s confession

instructs the computer to generate all words containing FORCE plus one letter. (In this example, the words FORCE and FORCED would both be generated.) Additional * symbols may be placed on the term to function as multiple placeholders when needed. For example, placing three * symbols on the term INTERROGAT in the following query:

interrogat*** /3 juvenile minor

instructs the computer to generate all forms of the root term INTERROGAT with up to three additional characters. Thus, the words INTERROGATE, INTERROGATES, and INTERROGATION would be generated by this query. The * symbol may also be embedded inside of a term as in the following query:

withdr*w /p plea /2 "no contest" "nolo contendere"

This will generate the alternative terms WITHDRAW and WITHDREW.

A *Alternative Terms.* Once the initial search terms have been selected for a query, it is important to consider alternative terms, synonyms, and antonyms for those terms. The nature of the legal issue will determine which terms are desirable.

As an illustration, in formulating a query to research the issue of whether a confession given during an illegal detention is admissible evidence, the researcher might first choose as search terms (with their appropriate root expansions) the following:

confess! detention illegal**

Clearly, the term ADMISSION* would be a good alternative for CONFESS!. Similarly, the terms DETAIN! and CUSTODY would be added as synonyms for DETENTION. In addition, the term UNLAWFUL** would be an appropriate synonym for ILLEGAL** in this context. Adding these alternatives to the initial search terms produces the following terms:

confess! admission*   detention detain!
    custody   illegal** unlawful**

Note that a space, which means "or", should be left between search terms and their alternatives.

C *Connectors.* The next step in query formulation is to consider the appropriate grammatical context in which the search terms will appear. Using the example provided in the preceding section, proximity connectors will now be placed between the three groups of alternative search terms to obtain the following query:

confess! admission* /p detention detain! custody /p
    illegal** unlawful**

This query would instruct the computer to retrieve documents in which CONFESS! or ADMISSION* appear in the same paragraph as DETENTION or DETAIN! or CUSTODY and also within the same paragraph as ILLEGAL** or UNLAWFUL**.

Query Formulation: (c) Proximity Connectors

Proximity connectors allow search terms to be ordered so that relevant documents will be retrieved from WESTLAW. The connectors and their meanings appear below.

Space (or). A space between search terms means "or." Leaving a space between the query terms CONFESSION and ADMISSION

confession admission

instructs the computer to retrieve documents that contain either the word CONFESSION or the word ADMISSION (or both).

& (and) or (ampersand). The & symbol means "and." Placing the & between two terms instructs the computer to retrieve documents that contain both of the terms. The terms on either side may be in reverse order. For example, if the & is inserted between the terms WAIVER and PRIVILEGE

waiver & privilege

the computer will retrieve documents containing both the word WAIVER and the word PRIVILEGE in the same document. In any such retrieved document, the word WAIVER may either precede or follow the word PRIVILEGE. The & may be placed between groups of alternative terms. For example, placing the & between WAIVER or ABANDONMENT and PRIVILEGE or RIGHT

waiver abandonment & privilege right

instructs the computer to retrieve documents in which the terms WAIVER or ABANDONMENT (or both) and PRIVILEGE or RIGHT (or both) appear in the same document.

/p (same paragraph). The /p symbol means "within the same paragraph." It requires that terms to the left of the /p appear within the same paragraph as terms to the right of the connector. For example, placing a /p between the terms WAIVER and PRIVILEGE

waiver /p privilege

will instruct the computer to retrieve documents in which WAIVER and PRIVILEGE occur in the same paragraph. The terms on each side of the /p may appear in the document in any order within the paragraph. As with &, the /p connector may be placed between groups of alternative terms. Thus, the query

waiver abandonment /p privilege right

will command the retrieval of all documents in which the words WAIVER or ABANDONMENT (or both) occur in the same paragraph as the words PRIVILEGE or RIGHT (or both).

/s (same sentence). The /s symbol requires that one or more search terms on each side of the /s appear in the same sentence. If a /s is placed between the words WAIVER and PRIVILEGE

waiver /s privilege

the computer is instructed to retrieve documents that have the word WAIVER and the word PRIVILEGE in the same sentence, without regard to which of these words occurs first in the sentence.

The /s may be placed between groups of alternative terms. Inserting a /s between the terms WAIVER or ABANDONMENT and PRIVILEGE or RIGHT

waiver abandonment /s privilege right

instructs the computer to retrieve documents with either the words WAIVER or ABANDONMENT (or both) within the same sentence as the words PRIVILEGE or RIGHT (or both), regardless of which terms appear first.

+s (precedes within sentence). The +s symbol requires that one or more terms to the left of the +s precede one or more terms to the right of the +s within the same sentence. The query

waiver +s privilege

instructs the computer to retrieve all documents in which the word WAIVER precedes the word PRIVILEGE in the same sentence. The +s connector, like the other connectors, may be used between groups of alternative terms. Thus, the query

waiver abandonment +s privilege right

instructs the computer to retrieve all documents in which the words WAIVER or ABANDONMENT (or both) precede the

words PRIVILEGE or RIGHT (or both) in the same sentence.

/n (numerical proximity-within n words). The /n symbol means "within n words," where n represents any whole number between 1 and 255, inclusive. It requires terms to appear within the designated number of words of each other. For example, placing a /5 between the terms WAIVER and PRIVILEGE

waiver /5 privilege

instructs the computer to retrieve all documents in which the term WAIVER occurs within five words of the term PRIVILEGE. Numerical proximities may also be used between groups of alternative search terms. In addition, the + symbol may be used to require that terms to the left of the numerical proximity symbol precede the terms to the right of the symbol. Thus, placing the +5 symbol between the words WAIVER or ABANDONMENT and PRIVILEGE or RIGHT

waiver abandonment +5 privilege right

instructs the computer to retrieve cases in which either the word WAIVER or the word ABANDONMENT (or both) occurs within five words preceding the word PRIVILEGE or the word RIGHT (or both).

"_____" (quotation marks/phrase). Quotation marks can be thought of as the most restrictive grammatical connector. Placing terms within quotation marks instructs the computer to retrieve all documents in which the terms appear in the precise proximity (i.e., contiguousness) and order that they have within the quotation marks. For example, placing the following terms within quotation marks

"res gestae"

instructs the computer to retrieve all documents in which the term RES appears adjacent to, and precedes, the term GESTAE. Phrases that are constructed with quotation marks may be used as alternatives by leaving a space between them.

"res gestae" "excited utterance"

instructs the computer to retrieve all documents in which either the phrase RES GESTAE or EXCITED UTTERANCE (or both) occurs.

This technique of query formulation is effective when used to search legal terms of art, legal concepts, or legal entities that occur together as multiple terms. Some examples are: "corpus delicti", "dying declaration" and "work product."

Phrase searching should be limited to those instances in which it is certain that the terms will always appear adjacent to each other and in the same order. For example, it would not be advisable to to use the terms BUSINESS, RECORD*, and EXCEPTION* as a phrase in the following query:

"business record* exception*" /p hearsay

Despite the entrenchment into legal jargon of the phrase "business record exception", these terms may occur in a different order and not be adjacent to each other. For example, they might appear in the language of relevant case law as ". . . the exception for business records . . .."

Therefore, a better query to use in searching for these terms would be:

business /5 record* /5 exception* /p hearsay

% (exclusion). The % symbol means "but not." It instructs the computer to exclude documents that contain terms appearing after the % symbol. For example, to retrieve documents containing the terms WITNESS** and TESTIMONY within the same sentence, but not the term EXPERT within the same sentence as TESTIMONY, the following query would be used:

witness** /s testimony % expert /s testimony

Query Formulation: (d) General Principles of Query Formulation

The art of query formulation is the heart of WESTLAW research. Although the researcher can gain technical skills by using the terminal, there is no strictly mechanical procedure for formulating queries. One must first comprehend the meaning of the legal issue to be researched before beginning a search on WESTLAW. Then the user will need to supply imagination, insight, and legal knowledge with awareness of the capabilities of WESTLAW to formulate a useful query. Effective query formulation requires an alternative way of thinking about the legal research process.

Using WESTLAW is a constant balancing between generating too many documents and missing important documents. In general, it is better to look through a reasonable number of irrelevant documents than it is to be too restrictive and miss important material. The researcher should take into consideration at the initial query formulation stage what he or she will do if too many, or not enough documents are retrieved. Thought should be given as to how the query might be narrowed or the search broadened, and what can be done if the initial search retrieves zero documents.

Some issues by nature require more lengthy queries than others; however, it is best to strive for efficiency in structuring the query. Look for unique search terms that will eliminate the need for a lengthy query. Keep in mind that WESTLAW is literal. Consider all possible alternative terms. Remember that searching is done by syntactic structure and often not by legal concepts.

Always keep in mind the parameters of the system as to date and database content. Especially consider inherent limitations of the computer. It doesn't think, create, or make analogies. The researcher must do that for the computer. The computer looks for terms in the documents in relationships specified in the query. The researcher should know what he or she is looking for, at least to the extent of knowing how the terms are likely to show up in relevant documents.

The *WESTLAW Reference Manual* should be consulted for more information on query formulation and WESTLAW commands. The *Reference Manual* is updated periodically to reflect new enhancements of

WESTLAW. It provides detailed and comprehensive instructions on all aspects of the WESTLAW service and offers numerous illustrative examples on the proper format for various types of queries. Material contained in the *Reference Manual* enables the user to benefit from all of WESTLAW's capabilities in an effective and efficient manner.

Search Techniques: (a) Field Searching

Documents in WESTLAW are divided into separate sections called fields. The computer can be instructed to search for terms within designated fields. This technique is known as field searching. Moreover, in reviewing the documents that have been retrieved in a search, the user may instruct the computer to display specified fields. The fields available for WESTLAW case law databases are described below.

Title Field. The title field contains the title of the case (e.g., Mapp v. Ohio).

Citation Field. The citation field contains the citation of the case (e.g., 562 F.2d 1153).

Court Field. The court field contains abbreviations that allow searches for case law to be restricted to particular states, districts, or courts.

Judge Field. The judge field contains the name of the judge or justice who wrote the majority opinion.

Synopsis Field. The synopsis field contains the synopsis of the case, prepared by West editors.

Topic Field. The topic field contains the Digest Topic name and number, the Key Number, and the text of the Key line for each digest paragraph.

Digest Field. The digest field contains digest paragraphs prepared by West editors. It includes headnotes, corresponding Digest Topics and Key Numbers, the title and citation of the case, court, and year of decision.

Headnote Field. The headnote field contains the language of the headnotes, exclu-

sive of the Digest Topic and Key Number lines and case identification information.

Opinion Field. The opinion field contains the text of the case, court and docket numbers, names of attorneys appearing in the case, and judges participating in the decision.

The format for a query that will instruct the computer to search for terms only within specified fields consists of the field name followed by a set of parentheses containing the search terms and grammatical connectors, if any. For example, to retrieve the case appearing at 562 F.2d 1153, the citation field restriction, followed by a set of parentheses containing the volume and page numbers of the citation separated by the $+3$ connector may be used:

```
citation(562  +3  1153)
```

or

```
cite(562  +3  1153)
```

This query specifies that the volume number must precede the page number within three words in the citation field of the case.

Correspondingly, to retrieve the case entitled *Mapp v. Ohio*, the title field, followed by a set of parentheses containing the names of the parties separated by the & connector may be used:

```
title(mapp  &  ohio)
```

Combination Field Searching

Fields may be combined in a query. For example, terms may be searched for in the digest field and, at the same time, the query may limit the search to the courts of a particular state. The following query illustrates this technique:

```
digest(best  +1  evidence  /p  original)  &  court(il)
```

This query instructs the computer to retrieve documents containing the words BEST, EVIDENCE, and ORIGINAL within the designated proximities in the digest field, and that were issued from Illinois courts, as designated with the court field restriction. Any number of different fields may be combined with this method.

Moreover, terms may be searched in clusters of fields by joining any number of field names by commas. One application of this technique is to search for terms in the combined synopsis and digest fields. This technique is illustrated below:

```
synopsis,digest(polygraph*  "lie detector*"
    /p  impeach!)
```

In this example the terms POLYGRAPH*, "LIE DETECTOR*"', and IMPEACH! are searched in the synopsis and digest fields simultaneously.

The *WESTLAW Reference Manual* should be consulted for further instruction on how to perform searches using the field restrictions.

Search Techniques: (b) Date Restriction

Queries may be restricted to retrieve documents appearing before, after, or on a specified date, or within a range of dates. The date restriction format consists of the word DATE followed by the appropriate restriction(s) within parentheses. The words BEFORE and AFTER may be used to designate the desired date relationships. Alternatively, the symbols < and > may be used. Moreover, the month and day and year may be spelled out (e.g., January 1, 1984) or they may be abbreviated as follows: 1–1–84, or 1/1/84. The date restriction is joined to the rest of the query by the & symbol. For example, to retrieve documents decided or issued after December 31, 1982 that discuss the spousal privilege for marital communications, any of the following formats could be used:

```
spous** marital husband* wi*e*  /
   3  privilege  &  date(after 12/31/82)

spous** marital husband* wi*e*  /
   3  privilege  &  date(> december 31, 1982)

spous** marital husband* wi*e*  /
   3  privilege  &  date(> 12–31–82)
```

To retrieve documents decided after December 31, 1980 and before March 31, 1983, the following format could be used:

```
spous** marital husband wi*e*  /3  privilege
   &  date(after 12/31/80 and before 3/15/83)
```

The date restriction may be placed only at the beginning or the end of the query.

Search Techniques: (c) Digest Topic and Key Number Searching

Searches may be performed using West Digest Topic and Key Numbers as search terms. When this stategy is used, the search term consists of a West Digest Topic Number followed by the letter k, followed by a Key Number classified as a subheading under the Digest Topic. The computer will retrieve all cases that contain a headnote classified with the designated Digest Topic and Key Number. For example, to retrieve cases that contain the Digest Topic classification for Witnesses (Digest Topic Number 410) and the Key Number for Order, Course and Extent of Examination (Key Number 224), the following query would be used:

```
410k224
```

A related search technique employs Digest Topic classification numbers in conjunction with other search terms. Since the Digest Topic Numbers appear in the topic and digest fields of the cases, the numbers should be searched for only in these fields. For example, to retrieve cases classified under the Digest Topic for Evidence (Digest Topic Number 157) that deal with the notion of "unfair prejudice", the following queries would be appropriate:

```
topic(157)  /p  unfair! undu**  /2  prejudic!
digest(157  /p  unfair! undu**  /2  prejudic!)
```

A complete list of Digest Topics and their numerical equivalents appears in the *WESTLAW Reference Manual.*

Using WESTLAW as a Citator

Research in evidence law frequently entails finding decisions that apply to specific sections of state evidence codes, to the Federal Rules of Evidence, or to other court decisions. WESTLAW can be used to retrieve documents that contain citations or references to such authority. Because citation styles are not always uniform, special care must be taken to identify variant forms of citations.

Retrieving Cases that Cite State Evidence Codes and Statute Sections

Court decisions that cite to sections of state evidence codes or to sections of state statutes are retrievable by including the section number in the query. For example, to retrieve cases that cite section 90.103 of the Florida Evidence Code, the following query could be used:

90.103 & court(fl)

Since the section number is a unique term, it is not necessary to use additional search terms in the query. The appearance of 90.103 in Florida case law is not likely to be anything other than a citation to that particular section. Using the number 90.103 as in the above query will also automatically retrieve all cases citing to subsections of section 90.103.

Cases which cite to specific subsections of statutes and codes are retrievable by including the subsection number in the query as follows:

90.103(2)

Retrieving Cases that Cite the Federal Rules of Evidence

Cases in WESTLAW are derived from West Reporters which routinely include citations to the Federal Rules of Evidence in their headnotes. An illustration of a headnote containing a citation to Federal Rules of Evidence, Rule 612, appears below.

R 1 OF 11   P 11 OF 31   FED   T

701 F.2d 1340

(9)

410k255(1)

WITNESS

k. Memoranda in general.

C.A.Ala. 1983.

Court has obligation to prevent witnesses from putting into record contents of otherwise inadmissible writing under guise of refreshing recollection, but where there is careful supervision by court, testimony elicited through refreshing recollection may be proper even though document used to refresh witness memory is inadmissible, and no abuse of discretion was shown in admission of such testimony by trial court in case at bar. Fed.Rules Evid. Rule 612, 28 U.S.C.A.: Fed Rules Cr.Proc. Rule 16, 18 U.S.C.A.

U.S. v. Scott

Accordingly, to retrieve cases that contain citations to the Federal Rules of Evidence, the following format is recommended:

headnote(evid. evidence /10 rule* /10 612)

A similar strategy can be used when searching without the headnote field restriction. To perform such a search, use the following format:

rule* fed.r.evid! /3 612 & refresh! /3 recollection

In this example, the descriptive terms RE-FRESH! and RECOLLECTION are added since the number 612, even when appearing within the designated proximity of three words from the term RULE* or FED.R.EVID!, could stand for many things other than the rule of evidence desired. It could stand for a reporter volume or page number, for instance. The added descriptive terms help to ensure more relevant results.

Retrieving Cases that Cite Other Court Decisions

WESTLAW can be used as a citator of other court decisions if the title of the decision, its citation, or both, are known. When only the title of the case is known, use the following format:

mapp /5 ohio

This query instructs the computer to retrieve all documents that have cited the case of *Mapp v. Ohio*. The /5 grammatical connector requires that the word MAPP occur within the five words of OHIO.

If the citation of the case is known, a query may be constructed that will retrieve documents that have cited the case. This is done by using the numbers of the citation as search terms in the query. For example, to retrieve cases that have cited to *Mapp* by its citation, 81 S.Ct. 1684, use the following format:

81 /3 1684

If both the citation and the case title are known, the following formats may be used:

```
mapp  /5  ohio  /15  81  /3  1684
mapp  /15  81  /3  1684
```

In the first example above the computer is instructed to retrieve all documents that contain the terms MAPP, OHIO, 81, and 1684 within the number of words designated by the numerical proximity connectors separating each term. This query would retrieve all documents that contain the full citation: Mapp v. Ohio, 81 S.Ct. 1684. The query in the second example above could be used if the name of only one party was known.

The date restriction may be utilized to retrieve documents that cite cases within a given year, range of years, or before or after a given date. For example, to retrieve all documents that have cited *Mapp v. Ohio* after the year 1982, this query could be used:

```
mapp  /5  ohio  &  date(after 12/31/82)
```

Retrieving the Federal Rules of Evidence

The text of the Federal Rules of Evidence may be retrieved on WESTLAW. The Rules appear in the USC (United States Code) database.

To retrieve a specific rule, include the letters FREV, followed by the & symbol and the number of the rule to be retrieved, within the citation field restriction. Thus, to retrieve Rule 804, you would use the following format:

```
citation(frev  &  804)
```

Rules of evidence may also be retrieved by a descriptive word search. For example, if you did not know the specific number of a Federal Rule of Evidence, but knew that it concerned the hearsay exceptions applicable when the declarant is unavailable, you could use the following query to retrieve the text of the rule:

```
citation(frev)  &  hearsay  &  exception*  &  unavailab!
```

The letters FREV are included in the citation field restriction to insure that a rule of evidence, rather than a portion of the United States Code, is retrieved. This is followed by terms that are descriptive of the content of the particular rule desired.

Shepard's [R] Citations on WESTLAW

From any point in WESTLAW, case citations may be entered to retrieve Shepard's listings for those citations. To enter a citation to be Shepardized, the following formats are appropriate:

```
sh 161 u.s. 483
```

or

```
sh 161 us 483
```

or

```
sh161us483
```

When the citation is entered, Shepard's listings for the citation will be displayed. To shepardize a citation it is not necessary to be in the same database as that of the citation. For example, a Supreme Court citation may be entered from the Pacific Reporter database.

West's INSTA–CITE ™

INSTA–CITE, West Publishing Company's case history system, allows users to quickly verify the accuracy of case citations and the validity of decisions. It contains prior and subsequent case histories in chronological listings, parallel citations and precedential treatment.

Some examples of the kind of direct case history provided by INSTA–CITE are: "affirmed", "certiorari denied", "decision reversed and remanded", and "judgment vacated." A complete list of INSTA–CITE direct case history and precedential treatment notations appears in the *WESTLAW Reference Manual.*

The format for entering a case citation consists of the letters IC followed by the citation, with or without spaces and periods:

```
ic 433 u.s. 72
```

or

```
ic 433 us 72
```

or

```
ic 433us72
```

Black's Law Dictionary

WESTLAW contains an on-line version of *Black's Law Dictionary.* The dictionary incorporates definitions of terms and phrases of English and American law.

Along with the preformulated queries in this publication appear references to *Black's Law Dictionary* for many important terms in evidence law. The format of such commands is as follows:

di hearsay

The command consists of letters DI followed by the term to be defined. To see the definition of a phrase, enter the letters DI followed by the phrase (without quotation marks):

di excited utterance

If the precise spelling of a term to be defined is not known, or a list of dictionary terms is desired, a truncated form of the word may be entered with the root expansion symbol (!) attached to it:

di res!

or

di res gest!

The first example will produce a list of all dictionary terms that begin with RES. The second example will produce a list of dictionary terms, the first of which is RES GESTAE. From the list of terms a number corresponding to the desired terms can be entered to obtain the appropriate definitions.

WESTLAW Case Law Databases

This section discusses the WESTLAW case law databases, in which the preformulated queries in this publication have been designed to be used. The case law databases consist of cases from the National Reporter System.

Cases in WESTLAW are in "full text plus." That is, they include the court's decision enhanced by a synopsis of the decision and headnotes stating the legal propositions for which the decision stands. The headnotes are classified to West's Key Number classification system.

WESTLAW contains many databases not discussed here. For example, there are databases that contain the entire United States Code, Code of Federal Regulations, and federal topical databases covering such areas as bankruptcy, patents and copyrights, federal tax, government contracts, communications, securities, labor, antitrust, admiralty, and military justice.

The case law databases are divided into two kinds: state databases and federal databases. The state databases contain state appellate cases compiled from reporters for geographical regions. These regional reporters (with their corresponding database identifiers indicated in parentheses) are: Atlantic (ATL), Northeastern (NE), Northwestern (NW), Pacific (PAC), Southeastern (SE), Southern (SO), Southwestern (SW).

In addition, WESTLAW has individual state databases containing decisions from specific states. The database identifier for an individual state database consists of the state's postal abbreviation followed by a hyphen followed by the letters CS (e.g., MN–CS for Minnesota cases).

The federal databases in which the queries in this publication will provide the most useful searches are: Supreme Court (SCT), U.S. Courts of Appeals (CTA) and U.S. District Courts (DCT).

WESTLAW also contains individual U.S. Court of Appeals databases. The database identifier for an individual court of appeals database consists of the letters CTA followed by the number of the federal circuit (e.g., CTA8 for the Eighth Circuit Court of Appeals.)

It is not recommended that the preformulated queries be used in the federal topical databases, since the issues in evidence law are of more general import.

Some of the preformulated queries retrieve relevant cases predominantly from state databases. Other queries are more appropriate for use in the federal databases. However, most issues to which the queries relate are sufficiently broad or have been so widely litigated that cases may be retrieved from either state or federal databases. Finally, some issues may have been litigated only in particular jurisdictions, so that a given query may retrieve cases in one state but not in another.

In some instances, the query itself indicates which database it is to be used in. If a query contains a court restriction to a particular state or to a particular federal circuit, then that query should only be used in the database that contains that state or district. For example, the following query contains a court restriction for Kansas cases:

60–437 & court(ks)

and therefore should be used in the Pacific Reporter (PAC) database, since that is the database in which Kansas cases appear. Alternatively, the query could be used in the KS–CS database, without the court field restriction. Similarly, the following query contains a court restriction for cases from the Federal Courts of Appeals for the ninth and tenth circuits:

incrimin! /p foreign! /s countr!
    sovereign & court(ca9 ca10)

Accordingly, the query should be used in the CTA database, since that is the only database which contains all of the cases from the Federal Circuit Courts of Appeals. Alternatively, the query could be used in either the CTA9 database or the CTA10 database.

WESTLAW Hornbook References: (a) Query Format

The queries that appear in this publication are intended to be illustrative. They are approximately as general as the material in the hornbook text to which they correspond.

Although all of the queries in this publication reflect proper format for use with WESTLAW, there is seldom only one "correct" way to formulate a query for a particular problem. This is so, even though some techniques are clearly better than others. Therefore, the queries reflect a wide range of alternative ways that queries may be structured for effective research. Such variances in query style reflect the great flexibility that the WESTLAW system affords its users in formulating search strategies.

For some research problems, it may be necessary to make a series of refinements to the queries, such as the addition of search terms or the substitution of different grammatical connectors, to adequately fit the particular needs of the individual researcher's problem. The responsibility remains with the researcher to "fine tune" the WESTLAW queries in accordance with his or her own research requirements. The primary usefulness of the preformulated queries in this hornbook is in providing users with a foundation upon which further query construction can be built.

Individual queries in this hornbook may retrieve from one to over a hundred cases, depending on which database they are addressed to. If a query does not retrieve any cases in a given database, it is because there are no decisions in that reporter which satisfy the requirements of the query. In this situation, to search another database with the same query, enter the letter S followed by the initials DB, followed by the new database identifier. Thus, if a query was initially addressed to the NE (Northeastern Reporter) database, but retrieved no documents, the user could then search the PAC (Pacific Reporter) database with same query by entering the following command:

s db pac

This command instructs WESTLAW to search the Pacific Reporter database with the same query that was previously used in the Northeastern Reporter database.

The maximum number of cases retrieved by a query in any given database will vary, depending on a variety of factors, including the relative generality of the search terms and connectors, the frequency of litigation or discussion of the issue in the courts, and the number of documents comprising the database.

WESTLAW Hornbook References: (b) Textual Illustrations

This section explains how the WESTLAW references provided in this hornbook may be used in researching actual evidence problems that the student or practitioner will encounter. Examples from the text of this edition have been selected to illustrate how the queries can be expanded, restricted, or altered to meet the specific needs of the reader's research.

A segment of the text from Chapter 22, section 222, of *McCormick on Evidence* appears below:

§ 222. Authentication by Circumstantial Evidence:

(a) Generally

As has been seen there are various ways in which writings may be authenticated by direct evidence. Nevertheless, it will frequently occur that no direct evidence of authenticity of any type exists or can be found. Resort must then be had to circumstantial proof and it is clear that authentication by circumstantial evidence is uniformly recognized as permissible.[1] Certain configurations of circumstantial evidence have in fact been so frequently held to authenticate particular types of writings that they have come to be recognized as distinct rules, e.g., the ancient documents rule, the reply doctrine, etc. These more or less formalized rules are treated in succeeding sections.[2]

It is important to bear in mind, however, that authentication by circumstantial evidence is not limited to situations which fall within one of these recurrent patterns. Rather proof of any circumstances which will support a finding that the writing is genuine will suffice to authenticate the writing.[3]

The text of section 222 discusses authentication of writings by circumstantial evidence. The query corresponding to the text contains the search terms CIRCUMSTANTIAL**, PROVE*, PROOF, EVIDENCE, AUTHENTIC!, and GENUINE!. Note that these terms are generally descriptive of the commentary that appears in this section of the hornbook. The term CIRCUMSTANTIAL** is connected to the alternative terms PROVE*, PROOF, and EVIDENCE by the / 2 grammatical connector, which requires that the term CIRCUMSTANTIAL** and the word PROVE* (and its derivatives), or the word PROOF, or the word EVIDENCE, appear within two words of each other. The /15 grammatical connector requires that the term(s) to the right of the /15 symbol appear within fifteen words of the (grammatically connected) group of words to the left of the /15 symbol.

In order to retrieve cases discussing the authentication of writings by circumstantial evidence, the following query:

circumstantial** indirect** /2 prove* proof evidence / 15 authentic! genuine!

is given as a suggested search strategy on WESTLAW.

A headnote of a case that was retrieved by this query from the ATL (Atlantic Reporter) database appears below:

R 1 OF 8 P 5 OF 25 ATL T

217 A.2d 109

(4)

157k370(1)

EVIDENCE

k. In general.

D.C.App. 1966

Documentary evidence must be **authenticated** before it will be admitted, but **authentication** need not be by direct **proof**, and **circumstantial** evidence will suffice under proper conditions.

NAMERDY v. GENERALCAR

An illustration of the relevant portion of the text of a case (State v. Adamson, 665 P.2d 972, Ariz, 1983) that was retrieved by this query from the PAC (Pacific Reporter) database appears below:

R 7 OF 12 P 49 OF 92 PAC T

665 P.2d 972

As for the typewritten note, Wynn testified as the motion to suppress hearing as follows: it was the victim's habit to leave such notes; the note was typed on newspaper copy paper; the note was placed in Wynn's typewriter after 5:30 the afternoon before the bombing and before 10:30 the morning of the bombing; and the note ended with the victim's typewritten signature. We believe that typewritten notes, like telegrams, may be **authenticated** by **circumstantial evidence**. People v. Thompson, 111 Mich.App. 324, 314 N.W.2d 606 (1982); Harlow v. Commonwealth,

204 Va. 385, 131 S.E.2d 293 (1963). Proof of circumstances which will support a finding that the writing is genuine will suffice to authenticate the writing. Champion v. Champion, 368 Mich. 84, 117 N.W.2d 107 (1962); Bain v. Commonwealth, 215 Va. 89, 205 S.E.2d 641 (1974); McCormick on Evidence s 222 (2d ed. 1972). We believe the facts in this case provide the necessary circumstantial evidence to indicate that the victim authored the note.

The query can be altered to meet the needs of individual researchers. For example, a student or practitioner may wish to find authority on the issue of whether the authenticity or genuineness of a specific type of writing—a letter—may be established by use of circumstantial evidence. In this situation, the preformulated query shown above can be modified to retrieve documents relevant to the new issue as follows:

circumstantial** indirect** /2 prove* proof evidence
    /15 authentic! genuine! /p letter*

The search term LETTER* is added to the original query because it is a more specific term corresponding to the more specific nature of the new issue. It is joined to the original query with a /p connector since any relevant cases on this issue will most likely use the word LETTER (or LETTERS) within the same paragraph as the rest of the terms.

A headnote of a case that was retrieved by this query from the PAC (Pacific Reporter) database appears below:

R 1 OF 2   P 6 OF 9   PAC   T

495 P.2d 313

110k444

CRIMINAL LAW

k. **Authentication** of documents.

Utah 1972.

Genuineness of **letter** may be established by **circumstantial** evidence.

State v. Abram

Ranking Documents Retrieved on WESTLAW: Age and Term Options

Documents retrieved by a query can be ordered in either of two ways. One way is to order retrieved documents by their dates,

with the most recent documents displayed first. This is ranking by AGE. Using the AGE option is suggested when the user's highest priority is to retrieve the most recent decisions from a search.

Alternatively documents can be ranked by the frequency of appearance of query terms. This is ranking by TERMS. When a search is performed with the TERMS option, the cases containing the greatest number of different search terms will be displayed first.

When a database is accessed by entering a database identifier, WESTLAW displays a message indicating the ranking options available. Once the user selects which type of ranking, AGE or TERMS, is desired, WESTLAW responds with a screen requesting that the query be entered.

The queries offered in this hornbook were formulated and tested for relevancy with use of the TERMS option. Accordingly, in certain instances use of the AGE option with the preformulated queries may display less relevant, yet more recent cases, first.

Conclusion

This appendix has reviewed methods that can be used to obtain the most effective legal research in evidence law possible. *McCormick on Evidence* combines the familiar hornbook publication with a powerful and easily accessed computerized law library. The WESTLAW references at the end of each section of the hornbook text provide a basic framework upon which the law student or lawyer can structure additional research on WESTLAW. The preformulated queries may be used as provided or they may be tailored to meet the needs of specific researchers' problems. The power and flexibility of WESTLAW affords users of this publication a unique opportunity to greatly enhance their access to and understanding of the law of evidence.

Table of Cases

A

L

S

U

Uberto v. Kaufman, 841

Uhlman v. Farm Stock & Homes Co., 112

Ulland, United States v., 558, 562

Ullmann v. United States, 290

Ullrich, United States v., 882

Ulrich v. Chicago, Burlington & Quincy Railroad Co., 103

Ungefug v. D'Ambrosa, 858

Unick v. Kessler Memorial Hospital, 255, 884

Union Bag-Camp Paper Corp. v. Federal Trade Commission, 1022

Union Planters National Bank v. ABC Records, Inc., 183

Union Trust Co. v. Resisto Manufacturing Co., 815

United American Fire Insurance Co. v. American Bonding Co., 794

United Food Corp., Commonwealth v., 550, 552, 906

United Mine Workers, United States v., 770

United Services Automobile Association v. Werley, 230

United Shoe Machinery Corp., United States v., 208, 209, 210, 212, 776, 790, 1014

United States v. _____ (see opposing party)

United States ex rel. (see name of party)

United States Fidelity & Guaranty Co. v. Continental Baking Co., 141

United States Gypsum Co., United States v., 1016

United States Hoffman Can Corp., In re, 343

United States Industries, Inc. v. Borr, 691

United States Steel Corp. v. Oravetz, 985

Unity Co. v. Gulf Oil Corp., 926

Universal Camera Corp. v. NLRB, 1008, 1016

Upshaw v. United States, 410, 451

Upjohn Co. v. United States, 208, 232, 233, 236, 237

Urioste, State v., 300

Usery v. Turner Elkhorn Mining Co., 985

Utah Farm Business Insurance Co. v. Dairyland Insurance Co., 952

Utica Cutlery Co., 1030

Utilities Commission, State ex rel. v. Carolina Power & Light Co., 1023

Utilities Insurance Co. v. Stuart, 870

Utley v. Heckinger, 674

Utley, People v., 362

V

V., Alinda v. Alfredo V., 658, 660

Vaccaro v. Alcoa Steamship Co., 877

Vail v. Vail, 301

Vaise v. Delaval, 165

Vajtauer, United States ex rel. v. Commissioner, 1014

Valdez, State v., 629

Vale v. Louisiana, 484

Valentino v. Postal Service, 650

Valeroso, Commonwealth v., 719

Valleroy v. Southern Railway Co., 1002

Van Alstine's, In re, 192

Van Buskirk v. Missouri-Kansas-Texas Railway Co., 785

Van Court v. Lodge Cab Co., 970

Van Dam, State v., 303

Van De Rostyne, People v., 521

Van Dyke, People v., 84

Van Gaasbeck, People v., 101, 567

Van Horn v. Commonwealth, 218

Van Riper v. United States, 792

Van Sickell v. Margolis, 781

Vance v. Harkey, 927

Vance v. State, 219, 253, 746

Vander Linden v. United States, 458

Vander Veen v. Yellow Cab Co., 771

Vanderbilt v. State, 378

Vandergriff v. Piercy, 715

Vandetti, United States v., 297, 896

Vanleeward v. State, 666

Vann v. State, 220

Varcoe v. Lee, 920, 922, 930, 931, 934, 935

Vargas, People v., 173

Varlack v. SWC Carribbean, Inc., 594

Varnum, People v., 516

Vaughan v. Martin, 246

Vaughan, State v., 710

Vaught v. Nationwide Mutual Insurance Co., 715

Vaux v. Hamilton, 961

Vedin v. McConnell, 96

Veen, Vander v. Yellow Cab Co., 771

Vega v. Bloomsburgh, 3

Vega-Limon, United States v., 370

Vehicular Parking, United States v., 209

Vela, United States v., 886

Velarde-Villarreal v. United States, 273

Velsir, State v., 95, 963

Ventresco v. Bushey, 163

Ventromile v. Malden Electric Co., 140

Ventura v. Ventura, 977

Ventura, County of v. Marcus, 658, 661

Verdugo, State v., 290, 291

Vermont Food Industries, Inc. v. Ralston Purina Co., 38, 589, 590, 591

Vermont Yankee Nuclear Power Corp. v. Natural Resources Defense Council, Inc., 1018

Verner v. Redman, 935

Verry v. Murphy, 785

Vestal, State v., 848, 852

Veytia-Bravo, United States v., 882

Vick v. Cochran, 39

Vickers v. Ripley, 870, 874

Vickers, United States v., 303

Vicksburg & Meridian Railroad v. O'Brien, 787, 864

Viereck v. United States, 717

Viglia, United States v., 34

Vigoda v. Barton, 755

Viens v. Lanctot, 57

Vigliano, State v., 104

Viles v. Waltham, 845

Village of (see name of village)

Villavicencio, State v., 558

Villeneuve v. Manchester Street Railway Co., 70

Villiers v. Republic Financial Services, Inc., 707

*

Table of Statutes and Rules

CALIFORNIA

West's Annotated Evidence Code

Sec.	This Work Page
771	21
785	84
787	91
788	93
	96
801(b)	35
	40
802	35
804	42
	35
	40
805	31
912(a)	198
913	178
916	144
917	193
918	174
954	176
	222
956	222
	231
972	199
980	197
	198
981	192
993	253
994	253
995	253
996	256
998	257
1000	258
1001	258
1003	258
1004	258
1010	246
1040	263
1153	783
1202	81
1220–1227	774
1235	749
1451	700
1505	721

West's Annotated Government Code

Sec.	This Work Page
11513	1010

West's Annotated Labor Code

Sec.	This Work Page
5708	1009
5709	1009

West's Annotated Penal Code

Sec.	This Work Page
631(c)	176

CALIFORNIA

West's Annotated Penal Code

Sec.	This Work Page
632(d)	176
866.5	316
938.1	277
1112	107
1324	354
	357
1324.1	354
1538.5	522
1538.5(m)	527

West's Annotated Vehicle Code

Sec.	This Work Page
17150	970

COLORADO

Revised Statutes

Sec.	This Work Page
16–5–204(4)(d)	339

Rules of Criminal Procedure

Rule	This Work Page
41(e)	522
41(g)	522

CONNECTICUT

General Statutes Annotated

Sec.	This Work Page
52–145	93
52–182	970
52–208	151
	154

DISTRICT OF COLUMBIA

Code

Tit.	This Work Page
14–101	158
14–104	83
14–305	99

FLORIDA

Constitution

Const. Art.	This Work Page
1, § 12	453

KANSAS

Statutes Annotated

KENTUCKY

Revised Statutes

Rules of Civil Procedure

Rules of Criminal Procedure

LOUISIANA

Constitution

Revised Statutes

MAINE

Rules of Evidence

MARYLAND

Code 1957

MARYLAND

Code 1957

Code, Courts and Judicial Proceedings

MASSACHUSETTS

General Laws Annotated

Acts and Resolves

Rules of Civil Procedure

MICHIGAN

Compiled Laws Annotated

Rules of Evidence

MICHIGAN

Rules of Evidence

Rule	This Work Page
611(b)	51

MINNESOTA

Statutes Annotated

Sec.	This Work Page
14.60	1015
169.09, subd. 13	273
602.01	778

Rules of Criminal Procedure

Rule	This Work Page
18.05	277

MISSOURI

Vernon's Annotated Statutes

Sec.	This Work Page
491.070	52
536.070(8)	1010
546.260	52
	59

MONTANA

Rules of Evidence

Rule	This Work Page
410	424

NEBRASKA

Revised Statutes

Sec.	This Work Page
27–410(1)	424
84–914(3)	1015

NEVADA

Revised Statutes

Sec.	This Work Page
50.095	93

NEW HAMPSHIRE

Revised Statutes Annotated

Sec.	This Work Page
516:24	84

NEW JERSEY

Constitution

Art.	This Work Page
1, par. 7	452
I, § 5	158

Statutes Annotated

Sec.	This Work Page
2A:84A–22.2	252
3A:40–1	971

Rules of Evidence

Rule	This Work Page
8(2)	138
20	84
22	91
	102
22(b)	82
39	178
47	102
57	35
	42
58	35
	42

NEW MEXICO

Statutes Annotated

Sec.	This Work Page
20–1–12	198
31–6–4(B)	339
31–6–4(C)	339

Rules of Evidence

Rule	This Work Page
611(b)	51

NEW YORK

Constitution

Art.	This Work Page
I, § 3	157
1, § 12	452

McKinney's Civil Practice Law and Rules

Sec.	This Work Page
4504	250
	254
4511	939
	940
	941
4511(a)	939
4511(b)	943
4514	83

NEW YORK

McKinney's Civil Practice Law and Rules

Sec.	This Work Page
4515	35
	42
4537	689

McKinney's Criminal Procedure Law

Sec.	This Work Page
50.10	354
50.20	354
60.35	83
60.50	366
255.20(1)	522
450.20(8)	527
710.30	522
710.70(2)	527

McKinney's Estates, Powers and Trusts Law

Sec.	This Work Page
2–1.7	971

McKinney's Vehicle and Traffic Law

Sec.	This Work Page
388(1)	970

NORTH CAROLINA

General Statutes

Sec.	This Work Page
8–50.1(a)	621
	659
8–50.1(a)(1)	621
8–53	260
15A–974(2)	411
55–36(c)	687

OHIO

Revised Code

Sec.	This Work Page
2317.02	191
	224
2317.422	882
2945.40	43

Rules of Civil Procedure

Rule	This Work Page
40	675

OHIO

Rules of Criminal Procedure

Rule	This Work Page
12(D)	522
12(E)	522

Rules of Evidence

Rule	This Work Page
601	157
607	83

OKLAHOMA

Statutes Annotated

Tit.	This Work Page
12, § 2403	545
22, § 340	277
75, § 310(1)	1022
75, § 310(2)	1015

OREGON

Revised Statutes

Sec.	This Work Page
41.360(34)	693
44.040	224
136.425(1)	366
183.450(2)	1015

Rules of Evidence

Rule	This Work Page
309	1000
608(1)(b)	91

PENNSYLVANIA

Constitution

Const. Art.	This Work Page
1, § 8	452

Statutes

Tit.	This Work Page
28, § 312	157
42, § 5919	100

Rules of Criminal Procedure

Rule	This Work Page
307	522
323(e)	522
323(h)	523

Index

References are to pages

EXPERT WITNESSES—Cont'd
Grounds for expert opinion, 35–38, 41, 42.
Hearsay,
    Basis of testimony, 909–911.
    Inadmissible evidence, 38–41.
Hypothetical questions, 35–38, 41, 42.
Improvement of practice, 42–45.
Inadmissible facts, 38–41.
Interviews, 2.
Judges, calling witnesses, 17, 43.
Publications, hearsay exception, 899, 901.
Qualifications, 33, 34.
Regularly kept records, 874, 875.
    Hospitals, 883, 884.
Reports, 38–40.
Supporting evidence, 37–41.
Ultimate fact, 30, 31.

EXPERTS
Attorney-client privilege, trial preparation, 236, 237.

FAMILY HISTORY
Hearsay exception, 901–903.

FATHER
Competency of witnesses, 163, 164.

FETAL DEATH
Reporting, physician-patient privilege, 251.

FIFTH AMENDMENT
See Self-Incrimination Privilege.

FINANCIAL STANDING
Reputation, hearsay exception, 906.

FINGERPRINTING
Probabilities, 650–657.
Scientific evidence, 637, 639.

FIRSTHAND KNOWLEDGE
    See, also, Expert Witnesses.
Admission of party-opponent, 778, 779.
Competency of witnesses, 167, 168.
Conjecture, 25.
Dying declarations, 832.
Hearsay distinguished, 731.
Observation, 23–25.
Recorded past recollection, 865, 866.
Regularly kept records, 878–880.
Requirement of, 23–25.

FLIGHT
Admission of party, 803, 804.

FOREIGN LAW
Judicial notice, 921, 942–944.
Opinions, 31.

FORENSIC MEDICINE
See Scientific Techniques.

FORM OF QUESTIONS
    See, also, Expert Witnesses.
    Generally, 9 et seq.
Argumentative questions, 14.

FORM OF QUESTIONS—Cont'd
Completeness, rule of, 70, 71.
Judges, 14–17.
Leading questions, 11–13.
Misleading questions, 14.
Narrative, 9, 10.
Refreshing recollection, 17–22.
Specific, 9, 10.

FORMER TESTIMONY
    Generally, 759 et seq.
Cross-examination, 761, 762.
    Adequacy, 763–768.
        Identity of issues, 767, 768.
        Identity of parties, 763–767.
    Improvements, 773.
Hearsay aspects, 759.
Identity of issues, cross-examination, 767, 768.
Identity of parties, cross-examination, 763–767.
Impeachment of witness, 763.
Improvement of, 772, 773.
Jurisdiction, 769, 770.
Methods of proving, 771, 772.
Oath, 761.
Objections, 770.
Predecessor in interest, cross-examination, 766, 767.
Proceedings, nature of, 769, 770.
Proof of, 771, 772.
Privity, 763, 764.
Reciprocity, 764, 765.
Statutory provisions, 760.
Tribunal, nature of, 769, 770.
Unavailability of witness, 762, 763.
    Improvements, 773.

FOUNDATION
See Preliminary Questions of Fact; particular topics.

FOURTH AMENDMENT
See Improperly Obtained Evidence.

FRAUD
Similar happenings, 581, 582.

FRISK
Search and seizure, 491.

"FRUIT OF POISONOUS TREE"
    See, also, Confessions; Improperly Obtained Evidence.
    Generally, 498–506.
Attenuation of taint, 500–502.
Burden of proof and proceeding, 505.
Discovery of evidence, legitimate, 502–505.
Evaluation of doctrine, 505, 506.
Independent source, 499.
Inevitable legitimate discovery, 502–505.
Jurisdiction, 498, 499.

GEOGRAPHY
Judicial notice, 926.

GOOD FAITH
Improperly obtained evidence, exclusion, 506–508.
Production of witnesses, appeals, 126.

WILLS
Attorney-client privilege, 227–229.
Physician-patient privilege, 258.

WIRETAPPING
See Electronic Surveillance.

WITHDRAWAL OF EVIDENCE
Objection, 133, 134.

WIVES
See, also Marital Communications Privilege.
Competency of witnesses, 161–164, 168.

WORDS AND PHRASES
Accused, self-incrimination privilege, 315–317.
Adjudicative facts, judicial notice, 920.
Admissions, 362, 774, 776.
Affirmative defense, 987, 988.
Authentication, 684–686.
Best evidence rule, 702, 703.
Burden of persuasion, 947.
Burden of producing evidence, 947.
Business, regularly kept records, 875.
Character, 574.
Circumstantial evidence, 543.
Common knowledge, judicial notice, 922.
Confession, 361–363.
Exculpatory statement, 362.
Habit, 574, 575.
Hearsay, 729, 730.
Identity of parties, 763.
Incriminatory response, self-incrimination, witness, 340, 341.
Legislative facts, judicial notice, 921.
Necessity, confessions, delay, 412.
Permissive presumption, 966.
Plain view, search and seizure, 467.
Preponderance of evidence, proof by, 957–959.
Presumption, 965.
    Criminal cases, 988.

WORDS AND PHRASES—Cont'd
Permissive, 966.
Probability of paternity, 659, 660.
Probable cause, 473, 474.
Reasonable doubt, proof beyond, 963.
Relevancy, 541, 542.
Res gestae, spontaneous declarations, 835, 836.
Search and seizure, 466–469.
    Plain view, 467.
    Probable cause, 473, 474.
    Reasonableness, 468, 469.
    Searches, 466–470.
    Seizure,
        Person, 470, 471.
        Things, 471, 472.
Seizure, see Search and seizure this topic.
Unavailability, witness, hearsay, 754.

WORK PRODUCT
Attorney-client privilege, 234–237.
    Criminal cases, 238–242.
Discovery, attorney-client privilege, 234–242.

WORKERS' COMPENSATION
Physician-patient privilege, 257.

WRITINGS
See, also, Authentication; Original Writing Rule.
Administrative adjudications, 1025–1028.
Partial, introduction, 145, 146.
Cross-examination, inconsistent writings, 61–63.
Dead man statutes, 159, 160.
Exhibits in jury room, 681, 682.

WRONGFUL DEATH
Physician-patient privilege, waiver, 256.

X–RAYS
Best evidence rule, 706.
Demonstrative evidence, 672.

†